ST/ESA/STAT/SER.R/46

Department of Economic and Social Affairs
Département des affaires économiques et sociales

2016
Demographic Yearbook
Annuaire démographique

Sixty-seventh issue/Soixante-septième édition

United Nations
New York, 2017

The Department of Economic and Social Affairs of the United Nations Secretariat is a vital interface between global policies in the economic, social and environmental spheres and national action. The Department works in three main interlinked areas: (i) it compiles, generates and analyses a wide range of economic, social and environmental data and information on which Member States of the United Nations draw to review common problems and to take stock of policy options; (ii) it facilitates the negotiations of Member States in many intergovernmental bodies on joint courses of action to address ongoing or emerging global challenges; and (iii) it advises interested Governments on the ways and means of translating policy frameworks developed in United Nations conferences and summits into programmes at the country level and, through technical assistance, helps build national capacities.

Le Département des affaires économiques et sociales du Secrétariat de l'Organisation des Nations Unies sert de relais entre les orientations arrêtées au niveau international dans les domaines économiques, sociaux et environnementaux et les politiques exécutées à l'échelon national. Il intervient dans trois grands domaines liés les uns aux autres : i) il compile, produit et analyse une vaste gamme de données et d'éléments d'information sur des questions économiques, sociales et environnementales dont les États Membres de l'Organisation se servent pour examiner des problèmes communs et évaluer les options qui s'offrent à eux; ii) il facilite les négociations entre les États Membres dans de nombreux organes intergouvernementaux sur les orientations à suivre de façon collective afin de faire face aux problèmes mondiaux existants ou en voie d'apparition; iii) il conseille les gouvernements intéressés sur la façon de transposer les orientations politiques arrêtées à l'occasion des conférences et sommets des Nations Unies en programmes exécutables au niveau national et aide à renforcer les capacités nationales au moyen de programmes d'assistance technique.

NOTE

Symbols of United Nations documents are composed of capital letters combined with figures. Mention of such a symbol indicates reference to a United Nations document.

The designations employed and the presentation of material in this publication do not imply the expression of any opinion whatsoever on the part of the Secretariat of the United Nations concerning the legal status of any country, territory, city or area, or of its authorities, or concerning the delimitation of its frontiers or boundaries.

Where the designation "country or area" appears in the headings of tables, it covers countries, territories, or areas.

NOTE

Les cotes des documents de l'Organisation des Nations Unies se composent de lettres majuscules et de chiffres. La simple mention d'une cote dans un texte signifie qu'il s'agit d'un document de l'Organisation.

Les appellations employées dans cette publication et la présentation des données qui y figurent n'impliquent de la part du Secrétariat de l'Organisation des Nations Unies aucune prise de position quant au statut juridique des pays, territoires, villes ou zones, ou de leurs autorités, ni quant au tracé de leurs frontières ou limites.

L'appellation "pays ou zone" figurant dans les titres des rubriques des tableaux désigne des pays, des territoires, ou des zones.

ST/ESA/STAT/SER.R/46

UNITED NATIONS PUBLICATION
Sales number: B.18.XIII.1 H

PUBLICATION DES NATIONS UNIES
Numéro de vente: B.18.XIII.1 H

ISBN 978-92-1-051110-0
eISBN 978-92-1-362711-2
Print ISSN: 0082-8041
Online ISSN: 2412-0006

Topics of the Demographic Yearbook series: 1948 - 2016

Sujets des diverses éditions de l'Annuaire démographique : 1948 - 2016

Year Année	Sales No. - Numéro de vente	Issue - Edition	Special topic - Sujet spécial
1948	49.XIII.1	First-Première	General demography-Démographie générale
1949-50	51.XIII.1	Second-Deuxième	Natality statistics-Statistiques de la natalité
1951	52.XIII.1	Third-Trosième	Mortality statistics-Statistiques de la mortalité
1952	53.XIII.1	Fourth-Quatrième	Population distribution-Répartition de la population
1953	54.XIII.1	Fifth-Cinquième	General demography-Démographie générale
1954	55.XIII.1	Sixth-Sixième	Natality statistics -Statistiques de la natalité
1955	56.XIII.1	Seventh-Septième	Population censuses-Recensement de population
1956	57.XIII.1	Eighth-Huitième	Ethnic and economic characteristics of population-Caractéristiques ethniques et économiques de la population
1957	58.XIII.1	Ninth-Neuvième	Mortality statistics- Statistiques de la mortalité
1958	59.XIII.1	Tenth-Dixième	Marriage and divorce statistics- Statistiques de la nuptialité et de la divortialité
1959	60.XIII.1	Eleventh-Onzième	Natality statistics- Statistiques de la natalité
1960	61.XIII.1	Twelfth-Douzième	Population trends- l' évolution de la population
1961	62.XIII.1	Thirteenth-Treizième	Mortality Statistics- Statistiques de la mortalité
1962	63.XIII.1	Fourteenth-Quatorzième	Population census statistics I- Statistiques des recensements de population I
1963	64.XIII.1	Fifteenth-Quinzième	Population census statistics II- Statistiques des recensements de population II
1964	65.XIII.1	Sixteenth-Seizième	Population census statistics III- Statistiques des recensements de population III
1965	66.XIII.1	Seventeenth-Dix-septième	Natality statistics- Statistiques de la natalité
1966	67.XIII.1	Eighteenth-Dix-huitième	Mortality statistics I- Statistiques de la mortalité I
1967	E/F.68.XIII.1	Nineteenth-Dix-neuvième	Mortality statistics II - Statistiques de la mortalité II
1968	E/F.69.XIII.1	Twentieth-Vingtième	Marriage and divorce statistics-Statistiques de la nuptialité et de la divortialité
1969	E/F.70.XIII.1	Twenty-first-Vingt et unième	Natality statistics-Statistiques de la natalité
1970	E/F.71.XIII.1	Twenty-second-Vingt-deuxième	Population trends-l' évolution de la population
1971	E/F.72.XIII.1	Twenty-third-Vingt-troisième	Population census statistics I- Statistiques de recensements de population I
1972	E/F.73.XIII.1	Twenty-fourth-Vingt-quatrième	Population census statistics II- Statistiques des recensements de population II
1973	E/F.74.XIII.1	Twenty-fifth-Vingt-cinquième	Population census statistics III- Statistiques des recensements de population III
1974	E/F.75.XIII.1	Twenty-sixth-Vingt-sixième	Mortality statistics - Statistiques de la mortalité
1975	E/F.76.XIII.1	Twenty-seventh-Vingt-septième	Natality statistics- Statistiques de la natalité
1976	E/F.77.XIII.1	Twenty-eighth-Vingt-huitième	Marriage and divorce statistics- Statistiques de la nuptialité et de la divortialité
1977	E/F.78.XIII.1	Twenty-ninth-Vingt-neuvième	International Migration Statistics- internationales
1978	E/F.79.XIII.1	Thirtieth-Trentième	General tables- Tableaux de caractère général
1978	E/F.79.XIII.8	Special issue-Edition spéciale	Historical supplement-Supplément rétrospectif
1979	E/F.80.XIII.1	Thirty-first-Trente et unième	Population census statistics-Statistiques des recensements de population
1980	E/F.81.XIII.1	Thirty-second-Trente-deuxième	Mortality statistics- Statistiques de la mortalité
1981	E/F.82.XIII.1	Thirty-third-Trente-troisième	Natality statistics-Statistiques de la natalité
1982	E/F.83.XIII.1	Thirty-fourth-Trente-quatrième	Marriage and divorce statistics-Statistiques de la nuptialité et de la divortialité
1983	E/F.84.XIII.1	Thirty fifth-Trente-cinquième	Population census statistics I-Statistiques des recensements de population I

Topics of the Demographic Yearbook series: 1948 - 2016

Sujets des diverses éditions de l'Annuaire démographique : 1948 - 2016

Year Année	Sales No. - Numéro de vente	Issue - Edition	Special topic - Sujet spécial
1984	E/F.85.XIII.1	Thirty-sixth- Trente-sixième	Population census statistics II- Statistiques des recensements de population II
1985	E/F.86.XIII.1	Thirty-seventh- Trente-septième	Mortality statistics- Statistiques de la mortalité
1986	E/F.87.XIII.1	Thirty-eighth- Trente-huitième	Natality statistics- Statistiques de la natalité
1987	E/F.88.XIII.1	Thirty-ninth- Trente-neuvième	Household composition- Les éléments du ménage
1988	E/F.89.XIII.1	Fortieth- Quarantième	Population census statistics- Statistiques des recensements de population
1989	E/F.90.XIII.1	Forty-first- Quarante-et-unième	International Migration Statistics- Statistiques des migration internationales
1990	E/F.91.XIII.1	Forty-second- Quarante-deuxième	Marriage and divorce statistics- Statistiques de la nuptialité et de la divortialité
1991	E/F.92.XIII.1	Forty-third- Quarante-troisième	General tables- Tableaux de caractère général
1991	E/F.92.XIII.9	Special Issue	Population Ageing and the Situation of Elderly Persons Vieillissement de la population et situation des personnes âgées
1992	E/F.94.XIII.1	Forty-fourth- Quarante-quatrième	Fertility and mortality statistics- Statistiques de la fecondité et de la mortalité
1993	E/F.95.XIII.1	Forty-fifth- Quarante-cinquième	Population census statistics I- Statistiques des recensements de population I
1994	E/F.96.XIII.1	Forty-sixth- Quarante-sixième	Population census statistics II- Statistiques des recensements de population II
1995	E/F.97.XIII.1	Forty-seventh- Quarante-septième	Household composition-Les éléments du ménage
1996	E/F.98.XIII.1	Forty-eighth- Quarante-huitième	Mortality statistics- Statistiques de la mortalité
1997	E/F.99.XIII.1	Forty-ninth- Quarante-neuvième	General tables- Tableaux de caractère général
1997	E/F.99.XIII.12	Special issue- Edition spéciale (CD)	Historical supplement- Supplément rétrospectif
1998	E/F.00.XIII.1	Fiftieth- Cinquantième	General tables- Tableaux de caractère général
1999	E/F.01.XIII.1	Fifty-first- Cinquante-et-unième	General tables- Tableaux de caractère général
1999	E/F.02.XIII.6	Special issue- Edition spéciale (CD)	Natality Statistics- Statistiques de la natalité
2000	E/F.02.XIII.1	Fifty-second- Cinquante-deuxième	General tables- Tableaux de caractère général
2001	E/F.03.XIII.1	Fifty-third- Cinquante- troisième	General tables- Tableaux de caractère général
2002	E/F.05.XIII.1	Fifty-fourth- Cinquante-quatrième	General tables- Tableaux de caractère général
2003	E/F.06.XIII.1	Fifty-fifth- Cinquante-cinquième	General tables- Tableaux de caractère général
2004	E/F.07.XIII.1	Fifty-sixth- Cinquante-sixième	General tables- Tableaux de caractère général
2005	E/F.08.XIII.1	Fifty-seventh- Cinquante-septième	General tables- Tableaux de caractère général
2006	E/F.09.XIII.1	Fifty-eighth- Cinquante-huitième	General tables- Tableaux de caractère général
2007	E/F.10.XIII.1	Fifty-ninth- Cinquante-neuvième	General tables- Tableaux de caractère général
2008	E/F.11.XIII.1	Sixtieth- Soixantième	General tables- Tableaux de caractère général
2009 - 2010	B.12.XIII.1 H	Sixty-first- Soixante-et-unième	General tables- Tableaux de caractère général
2011	B.13.XIII.1 H	Sixty-second Soixante- deuxième	General tables- Tableaux de caractère général

Topics of the Demographic Yearbook series: 1948 - 2016

Sujets des diverses éditions de l'Annuaire démographique : 1948 - 2016

Year Année	Sales No. - Numéro de vente	Issue - Edition	Special topic - Sujet spécial
2012	B.14.XIII.1 H	Sixty-third Soixante- troisième	General tables- Tableaux de caractère général
2013	B.15.XIII.1 H	Sixty-fourth Soixante- quatrième	General tables- Tableaux de caractère général
2014	B.16.XIII.1 H	Sixty-fifth Soixante- cinquième	General tables and Whipple's Index, censuses,1985-2014 - Tableaux de caractère général et l'indice de Whipple, recensements, 1985-2014
2015	B.17.XIII.1 H	Sixty-sixth Soixante- sixième	General tables and Whipple's Index, censuses,1985-2015 - Tableaux de caractère général et l'indice de Whipple, recensements, 1985-2015
2016	B.18.XIII.1 H	Sixty-seventh Soixante- septième	General tables and Whipple's Index, censuses,1985-2016 - Tableaux de caractère général et l'indice de Whipple, recensements, 1985-2016

CONTENTS - TABLE DES MATIERES

FERTILITY

FOETAL MORTALITY

INFANT AND MATERNAL MORTALITY

GENERAL MORTALITY

NATALITÉ

MORTALITÉ FŒTALES

MORTALITÉ INFANTILE ET MORTALITÉ LIÉE À LA MATERNITÉ

MORTALITÉ GÉNÉRALE

EXPLANATIONS OF SYMBOLS

Category not applicable	..
Data not available...	...
Magnitude zero or less than half of unit employed	-
Provisional	*
Data tabulated by year of registration rather than occurrence	+
Based on less than specified minimum	◆
Relatively reliable data	Roman type
Data of lesser reliability	*Italics*

EXPLICATION DES SIGNES

Sans objet	..
Données non disponibles	...
Néant ou chiffre inférieur à la moitié de l'unité employée	-
Données provisoires	*
Donnée exploitées selon l'année de l'enregistrement et non l'année de l'événement	+
Rapport fondé sur un nombre inférieur à celui spécifié...	◆
Données relativement sûres...	Caractères romains
Données dont l'exactitude est moindre	*Italiques*

INTRODUCTION

The *Demographic Yearbook* is an international compendium of national demographic statistics provided by national statistical authorities to the Statistics Division of the United Nations Department of Economic and Social Affairs. The *Demographic Yearbook* is part of the set of coordinated and interrelated publications issued by the United Nations and its specialized agencies, designed to supply statistical data for such users as demographers, economists, public-health workers and sociologists. Through the co-operation of national statistical services, available official demographic statistics are compiled in the *Demographic Yearbook* for more than 230 countries or areas throughout the world.

The *Demographic Yearbook 2016* is the sixty-seventh issue in a series published by the United Nations since 1948. It contains tables on a wide range of demographic statistics, including a world summary of selected demographic statistics, statistics on the size, distribution and trends in national populations, fertility, foetal mortality, infant and maternal mortality, general mortality, nuptiality and divorce. Data are shown by urban/rural residence, as available. The volume provides Technical Notes, a synoptic table, a historical index and a listing of the issues of the *Demographic Yearbook* published to date. This issue of *Demographic Yearbook* contains data as available including reference year 2016.

This edition of the *Demographic Yearbook* features also table 3a with Whipple's index by sex and urban/rural residence for the population censuses conducted worldwide since 1985. Whipple's index is an index of age preference in age reporting and can therefore serve to highlight some of the problems related to age distribution.

The Technical Notes on the Statistical Tables are provided to assist the reader in using the tables. Table A, the synoptic table, provides an overview of the completeness of data coverage of the current *Demographic Yearbook*. The cumulative historical index is a guide on content and coverage of all sixty-seven issues, and indicates, for each of the topics that have been published, the issues in which they are presented and the years covered. It also contains a list of tables published online through UNdata[1] (http://data.un.org/Explorer.aspx?d=POP). A list of the *Demographic Yearbook* issues, with their corresponding sales numbers and the special topics featured in each issue are shown on pages iii and iv. Additionally, all issues of the *Demographic Yearbook* are available online at the Statistics Division's website: https://unstats.un.org/unsd/demographic/products/dyb/dyb2.htm.

Until the 48th issue (1996), each issue consisted of two parts, the general tables and special topic tables, published in the same volume[2]. Beginning with the 49th issue (1997), the special topic tables were being disseminated in digital format as supplements to the regular issues. Two CD-ROMs have been issued: the *Demographic Yearbook Historical Supplement*, which presents a wide panorama of basic demographic statistics for the period 1948 to 1997, and the *Demographic Yearbook: Natality Statistics*, which contains a series of detailed tables dedicated to natality and covering the period from 1980 to 1998. Later on, three volumes of *Demographic Yearbook* Special Census Topics for the 2000 round of censuses, covering the period from 1995 to 2004, were published on-line at http://unstats.un.org/unsd/demographic/products/dyb/dybcens.htm. Current *Demographic Yearbook* population and housing censuses data for the 2000, 2010 and 2020 rounds (1995 to the present) are presented at http://unstats.un.org/unsd/demographic/products/dyb/dybcensusdata.htm. These datasets cover basic population characteristics, educational, household, ethnocultural and economic characteristics, and also foreign-born and foreign population. Special tabulations on household and economic characteristics with data based on population censuses since 1995 are available respectively at http://unstats.un.org/unsd/demographic/products/dyb/dyb_Household/dyb_household.htm and http://unstats.un.org/unsd/demographic/products/dyb/dyb_Eco/dyb_eco.htm.

Population statistics are not available for all countries or areas, for a variety of reasons. In an effort to provide estimates of mid-year population and of selected vital statistics for all countries and areas, two annexes are presented. Annex I presents United Nations population estimates for the period 2007-2016 and Annex II presents the medium variant estimates of crude birth and death rates, infant mortality and total fertility rates, as well as life expectancy at birth over the period 2015-2020. These data were produced by the United Nations Population Division and are published in the *2017 Revision of World Population Prospects*[3].

Demographic statistics shown in this issue of the *Demographic Yearbook* are available online at the *Demographic Yearbook* website http://unstats.un.org/unsd/demographic/products/dyb/dyb2016.htm. Information about the Statistics Division's data collection and dissemination programme is also available on the same website. Additional information can be made available by contacting the Statistics Division of the United Nations Department of Economic and Social Affairs at demostat@un.org.

TECHNICAL NOTES ON THE STATISTICAL TABLES

1. GENERAL REMARKS

1.1 Arrangement of Technical Notes

These Technical Notes are designed to provide the reader with relevant information related to the statistical tables. Information pertaining to the *Demographic Yearbook* in general is presented in the sections dealing with geographical aspects, population and vital statistics. In addition, preceding each table are notes describing the variables, remarks on the reliability and limitation of the data, countries and areas covered, and information on the presentation of earlier data. When appropriate, details on computation of rates, ratios or percentages are presented.

1.2 Arrangement of tables

The numbering of tables from one issue of *Demographic Yearbook* to the next is preserved to the extent possible. However, since for some of the tables the numbering may not correspond exactly to those in previous issues, the reader is advised to use the historical index that appears at the end of this book to find the reference to data in earlier issues.

1.3 Source of data

The statistics presented in the *Demographic Yearbook* are national data provided by official statistical authorities unless otherwise indicated. The primary source of data for the *Demographic Yearbook* is a set of questionnaires sent annually by the United Nations Statistics Division to over 230 national statistical services. Data reported on these questionnaires are supplemented, to the extent possible, with data taken from official national publications, official websites and through correspondence with national statistical services. In the interest of comparability, rates, ratios and percentages have been calculated by the Statistics Division of the United Nations, except for the life table functions, the total fertility rate, and also crude birth rate and crude death rate for some countries or areas as appropriately noted. The methods used by the Statistics Division to calculate these rates and ratios are described in the Technical Notes for each table. The population figures used for these computations are those pertaining to the corresponding years published in this or previous issues of the *Demographic Yearbook*.

In cases when data in this issue of the *Demographic Yearbook* differ from those published in earlier issues or related publications, statistics in this issue may be assumed to reflect revisions to the data received by June 2017.

2. GEOGRAPHICAL ASPECTS

2.1 Coverage

Data are shown for all individual countries or areas that provided information. Table 3 is the most comprehensive in geographical coverage, presenting data on population and surface area for all countries or areas with a population of at least 50 persons. Not all of these countries or areas appear in subsequent tables. In many cases the data required for a particular table are not available. In general, the more detailed the data required for a table, the fewer the number of countries or areas that can provide them.

In addition, rates and ratios are presented only for countries or areas reporting at least a minimum number of relevant events. The minimums are stated in the Technical Notes to individual tables.

Except for summary data shown for the world and by major areas and regions in tables 1 and 2 and data shown for capital cities and cities with a population of 100 000 or more in table 8, all data are presented

2

at the national level. The number of countries or areas shown in each table is provided in table A, the synoptic table.

2.2 Territorial composition

To the extent possible, all data, including time series data, relate to the territory within 2016 boundaries. Exceptions are footnoted in individual tables. Relevant clarifications are specified below.

Data relating to **Denmark** exclude Faeroe Islands and Greenland, which are shown separately.

Data relating to **Finland** include Åland Islands, unless otherwise indicated by a footnote.

Data relating to **France** exclude Overseas Departments, namely, French Guiana, Guadeloupe, Martinique and Réunion, which are shown separately, unless otherwise indicated by a footnote.

Data relating to **United Kingdom of Great Britain and Northern Ireland** exclude Guernsey, Isle of Man and Jersey which are shown separately.

Data relating to **Western Sahara** comprise the Northern Region (former Saguia el Hamra) and Southern Region (former Rio de Oro).

2.3 Nomenclature

Because of space limitations, the country or area names listed in the tables are generally the commonly employed short titles currently in use[4] in the United Nations, the full titles being used only when a short form is not available. The latest version of the *Standard Country or Area Codes for Statistics Use* can be accessed at https://unstats.un.org/unsd/methodology/m49/.

2.3.1 Order of presentation

Countries or areas are listed in English alphabetical order within the following continents: Africa, North America, South America, Asia, Europe and Oceania.

The designations and presentation of the material in this publication were adopted solely for the purpose of providing a convenient geographical basis for the accompanying statistical series. The same qualification applies to all notes and explanations concerning the geographical units for which data are presented.

2.4 Surface area data

Surface area data shown in table 1 represent the land area, whereas in table 3 the total surface area unless otherwise indicated. The total surface area comprises land area and inland waters (assumed to consist of major rivers and lakes) and excluding only Polar Regions and uninhabited islands. The surface area given is the most recent estimate available. They are presented in square kilometres; a conversion factor of 2.589988 having been applied to surface areas originally reported in square miles.

2.4.1 Comparability over time

Comparability over time in surface area estimates for any given country or area may be affected by changes in the surface area estimation procedures, increases in actual land surface by reclamation, boundary changes, changes in the concept of "land surface area" used or a change in the unit of measurement used. In most cases it was possible to ascertain the reason for a revision; otherwise, the latest figures have generally been accepted as correct.

2.4.2 International comparability

Lack of international comparability between surface area estimates arises primarily from differences in definition. In particular, there is considerable variation in the treatment of coastal bays, inlets and gulfs, rivers and lakes. International comparability is also impaired by the variation in methods employed to estimate surface area. These range from surveys based on modern scientific methods to conjectures based on diverse types of information. Some estimates are recent while others may not be. Since neither the exact method of determining the surface area nor the precise definition of its composition and time reference is known for all countries or areas, the estimates in table 3 should not be considered strictly comparable from one country or area to another.

3. POPULATION

Population statistics, that is, those pertaining to the size, geographical distribution and demographic characteristics of the population, are presented in a number of tables of the *Demographic Yearbook*.

Summary estimates of the mid-year population of the world, major areas and regions for selected years and of its age and sex distribution in 2016 are set forth in tables 1 and 2, respectively.

Data for countries or areas include population census figures, estimates based on results of sample surveys (in the absence of a census), postcensal or intercensal estimates and those derived from continuous population registers. In the present issue of the *Demographic Yearbook*, the latest available census figure of the total population of each country or area and mid-year estimates for 2010 and 2016 are presented in table 3. Mid-year estimates of total population for ten years (2007-2016) are shown in table 5 and mid-year estimates of urban and total population by sex for ten years (2007-2016) are shown in table 6. The latest available data on population by age, sex and urban/rural residence are given in table 7. The latest available figures on the population of capital cities and of cities or urban agglomerations of 100 000 or more inhabitants are presented in table 8.

The statistics on total population, population by age, sex, or urban/rural distribution are used for the calculation of rates in the *Demographic Yearbook*. Vital rates by residence (urban/rural), age or sex were calculated using data presented in tables 6 or 7 in this issue or the corresponding tables of previous issues of the *Demographic Yearbook*.

3.1 Sources of variation of data

The comparability of data is affected by several factors, including (1) the definition of total population; (2) the definition used to classify the population into its urban/rural components; (3) the accuracy of age reporting; (4) the extent of over-enumeration or under-enumeration in the most recent census or other source of benchmark population statistics; and (5) the quality of population estimates. These five factors will be discussed in some detail in sections 3.1.1 to 3.2 below. Other relevant problems are discussed in the technical notes to the individual tables. Readers interested in more detail, relating in particular to the basic concepts of population size, distribution and characteristics as elaborated by the United Nations, should consult the *Principles and Recommendations for Population and Housing Censuses, Revision 3*[5].

3.1.1 Total population

The most important impediment to comparability of total populations is the difference between the concept of a *de facto* and *de jure* population. A *de facto* population includes all persons physically present in the country or area at the reference date. The *de jure* population, by contrast, includes all usual residents of the given country or area, whether or not they were physically present in the area at the reference date. By definition, therefore, a *de facto* total and a *de jure* total are not entirely comparable.

Comparability of even two *de facto* or *de jure* totals is often affected by the fact that strict conformity to either of these concepts is rare. For example, some so-called *de facto* counts do not include foreign military, naval and diplomatic personnel present in the country or area on official duty, and their accompanying family and household members; some do not include foreign visitors in transit through the country or area or transients on ships in harbours. On the other hand, they may include such persons as merchant seamen and fishermen who are temporarily out of the country or area working at their trade.

The *de jure* population figure presents even greater variations in comparability, in part because it depends in the first place on the concept of "usual residence", which varies from one country or area to another and is difficult to apply consistently in a census or survey enumeration. For example, non-national civilians temporarily in a country or area as short-term workers may officially be considered residents after a stay of a specified period of time or they may be considered as non-residents throughout the duration of their stay; at the same time, these individuals may be officially considered as residents or non-residents of the country or area from which they came, depending on the duration and/or purpose of their absence. Furthermore, regardless of the official treatment, individual respondents may apply their own interpretation of residence in responding to the inquiry. In addition, there may be considerable differences in the accuracy with which countries or areas are informed about the number of their residents temporarily out of the country or area.

The population statistics presented in the tables of the *Demographic Yearbook* refer to the *de facto* population or to the *de jure* population. In an effort to overcome, to the extent possible, the effect of the lack of strict conformity to either the *de facto* or the *de jure* concept given above, significant exceptions with respect to inclusions and exclusions of specific population groups, are footnoted when they are known.

A possible source of variation within the statistics of a single country or area may arise from the fact that some countries or areas collect information on both the *de facto* and the *de jure* population in, for example, a census, but prepare detailed tabulations for only the *de jure* population. Hence, even though the total population shown in table 3 is de facto, the figures shown in the tables presenting various characteristics of the population, for example, urban/rural distribution, age and sex distribution, may be on the *de jure* concept.

3.1.2 Urban/rural classification

International comparability of urban/rural distributions is seriously impaired by the wide variation among national definitions of the concept of "urban". The definitions used by individual countries or areas and their implications are shown at the end of technical notes for table 6.

3.1.3 Age distribution

The classification of population by age is a core element of most analyses, estimation and projection of population statistics. Unfortunately, age data are subject to a number of sources of error and non-comparability. Accordingly, the reliability of age data should be of concern to users of these statistics.

3.1.3.1 Collection and compilation of age data

Age is the estimated or calculated interval of time between the date of birth and the date of the census or survey, expressed in completed solar years[6]. There are two methods of collecting information on age. The first is to obtain the date of birth for each member of the population in a census or survey and then to calculate the completed age of the individual by subtracting the date of birth from the date of enumeration[7]. The second method is to record the individual's completed age at the time of the census or survey, that is to say, age at last birthday.

The recommended method is to calculate age at last birthday by subtracting the exact date of birth from the date of the census. Some practices, however, do not use this method but instead calculate the difference between the year of birth and the year of the census. Classifications of this type are footnoted whenever possible. They can be identified to a certain extent by a smaller than expected population under one year of age. However, an irregular number of births from one year to the next or age selective omission of infants may also obscure the expected population under one year of age.

3.1.3.2 Errors in age data

Errors in age data may be due to a variety of causes, including ignorance of the correct age; reporting years of age in terms of a calendar concept other than completed solar years since birth[8]; carelessness in reporting and recording age; a general tendency to state age in figures ending in certain digits (such as zero, two, five and eight); a tendency to exaggerate length of life at advanced ages; a subconscious aversion to certain numbers; and wilful misrepresentations.

These reasons for errors in reported age data are common to most investigations of age and to most countries or areas, and they may significantly impair comparability of the data.

As a result of the above-mentioned difficulties, the age-sex distribution of population in many countries or areas shows irregularities which may be summarized as follows: (1) a deficiency in the number of infants and young children; (2) a concentration at ages ending with zero and five (that is, 5, 10, 15, 20, ...); (3) heaping at even ages (for example, 10, 12, 14, ...) relative to odd ages (for example, 11, 13, 15, ...); (4) unexpectedly large differences between the frequency of males and females at certain ages; and (5) unaccountably large differences between the frequencies in adjacent age groups. Comparing of identical age-sex cohorts from successive censuses, as well as studying the age-sex composition of each census, may reveal these and other inconsistencies, some of which in varying degree are characteristic of even the most modern censuses.

This edition of the *Demographic Yearbook* features a tabulation (table 3a) with Whipple's index by sex and urban/ rural residence for the population censuses conducted worldwide since 1985. Whipple's index is an index of age preference in age reporting and can therefore serve to highlight some of the problems related to age distribution.

4. VITAL STATISTICS

For purposes of the *Demographic Yearbook*, vital statistics of concern are those of live birth, death, foetal death, marriage and divorce.

This volume of the *Demographic Yearbook* presents tables on fertility, nuptiality and divorce as well as tables on mortality referring to foetal mortality, infant and maternal mortality and general mortality.

4.1 Sources of variation of data

Most of the vital statistics data published in this *Demographic Yearbook* are sourced from national civil registration systems. The completeness and the accuracy of the data that these systems produce vary from one country or area to another.

The provision for a national civil registration system is not universal, and in some cases, the registration system covers only certain vital events. For example, in some countries or areas only births and deaths are registered. There are also differences in the effectiveness with which national laws pertaining to civil registration operate in the various countries or areas. The manner in which the law is implemented and the degree to which the public complies with the legislation determine the reliability of vital statistics obtained from the civil registers.

It should be noted that some statistics on marriage and divorce are obtained from sources other than civil registers. For example, in some countries or areas, the only source for data on marriages is church registers. Divorce statistics, on the other hand, are obtained from court records and/or civil registers according to national practice. The actual compilation of these statistics may be the responsibility of the civil registrar, the national statistical office or other government offices.

Other factors affecting international comparability of vital statistics are much the same as those that must be considered in evaluating the variations in other population statistics. Differences in statistical definitions of vital events, differences in geographical and ethnic coverage of the data and diverse tabulation procedures may also influence comparability.

In addition to vital statistics from civil registers, some vital statistics published in the *Demographic Yearbook* are official estimates. These estimates are frequently from population censuses and sample surveys. As such, their comparability may be affected by the national completeness of reporting in population censuses and household surveys, whether a *de facto* or *de jure* based census, non-sampling and sampling errors and other sources of bias.

Readers interested in more detailed information on standards for vital statistics should consult the *Principles and Recommendations for a Vital Statistics System Revision 3*[9]; *Handbook on Civil Registration and Vital Statistics Systems: Preparation of a Legal Framework*[10]; *Handbook on Civil Registration and Vital Statistics Systems: Management, Operation and Maintenance*[11]; *Handbook on Civil Registration and Vital Statistics Systems: Developing Information, Education and Communication*[12]; *Handbook on Civil Registration and Vital Statistics Systems: Policies and Protocols for the Release and Archiving of Individual Records*[13]; and *Handbook on Civil Registration and Vital Statistics Systems: Computerization*[14]. The *Handbook on the Collection of Fertility and Mortality Data*[15] provides information in collection and evaluation of data on fertility and mortality collected in population censuses and household surveys. These publications are also available on the website at https://unstats.un.org/unsd/demographic/standmeth/principles/default.htm and http://unstats.un.org/unsd/demographic/standmeth/handbooks/default.htm.

4.1.1 Statistical definition of events

An important source of variation lies in the statistical definition of each vital event. The *Demographic Yearbook* attempts to collect data on vital events, using the standard definitions put forth in Chapter I of *Principles and Recommendations for a Vital Statistics System Revision 3*. These definitions are as follows:

LIVE BIRTH *is the complete expulsion or extraction from its mother of a product of conception, irrespective of the duration of pregnancy, which after such separation breathes or shows any other evidence of life such as beating of the heart, pulsation of the umbilical cord, or definite movement of voluntary muscles, whether or not the umbilical cord has been cut or the placenta is attached; each product of such a birth is considered live-born.*

DEATH *is the permanent disappearance of all evidence of life at any time after the occurrence of live birth, i.e., the postnatal cessation of vital functions without capability of resuscitation. This definition excludes foetal deaths.*

FOETAL DEATH *is death prior to the complete expulsion or extraction from its mother of a product of conception, irrespective of the duration of the period of gestation. Death is indicated by the fact that after such separation, the foetus does not breathe or show any other evidence of life, such as beating of the heart, pulsation of the umbilical cord, or definite movement of voluntary muscles.*

MARRIAGE *is an act, ceremony or process by which the legal relationship of spouses is constituted. The legality of the union may be established by civil, religious or other means as recognized by the laws of each country. Countries may wish to expand the definition to cover civil unions if they are registered. In that case, registered partnership usually refers to a legal construct, entailing registration with the public authorities according to the laws of each country, that becomes the basis for legal conjugal obligations between two persons.*

DIVORCE *is a final legal dissolution of a marriage, that is, the separation of spouses that confers on the parties the right to remarriage under civil, religious and/or other provisions, according to the laws of each country. In the case where a country recognizes registered partnerships, a legal dissolution of a registered partnership constitutes the legal final dissolution of such a partnership, according to national laws, which confers on the parties the right to enter into another partnership or marriage.*

In addition to these internationally recommended definitions, the *Demographic Yearbook* collects and presents data on abortions, defined as:

ABORTION *is defined, with reference to the woman, as any interruption of pregnancy before 28 weeks of gestation with a dead foetus. There are two major categories of abortion: spontaneous and induced. Induced abortions are those initiated by deliberate action undertaken with the intention of terminating pregnancy; all other abortions are considered spontaneous.*

4.1.2 Problems relating to standard definitions

A basic problem affecting international comparability of vital statistics is deviations from the standard definitions of vital events. An example of this can be seen in the cases of live births and foetal deaths. In some countries or areas, an infant must survive for at least 24 hours, to be inscribed in the live-birth register. Infants who die before the expiration of the 24-hour period are classified as late foetal deaths and, barring special tabulation procedures, they would not be counted either as live births or as deaths. Similarly, in several other countries or areas, those infants who are born alive but die before registration of their birth, are also considered late foetal deaths.

Unless special tabulation procedures are adopted in such cases, the live-birth and death statistics will both be deficient by the number of these infants, while the incidence of late foetal deaths will be increased by the same amount. Hence the infant mortality rate is underestimated. Although both components (infant deaths and live births) are deficient by the same absolute amount, the deficiency is proportionately greater in relation to the infant deaths, causing greater errors in the infant mortality rate than in the birth rate.

Moreover, the practice exaggerates the late foetal death ratios. Some countries or areas make provision for correcting this deficiency (at least in the total frequencies) at the tabulation stage. Data for which the correction has not been made are indicated by a footnote whenever possible.

The definitions used for marriage and divorce also present problems for international comparability. Unlike birth and death, which are biological events, marriage and divorce are defined only in terms of law and custom and as such are less amenable to universally applicable statistical definitions. They have therefore been defined for statistical purposes in general terms referring to the laws of individual countries or areas. Laws pertaining to marriage and particularly to divorce, vary from one country or area to another. With respect to marriage, the most widespread requirement relates to the minimum age at which persons may marry but frequently other requirements are specified.

When known the minimum legal age of men and women at which marriage can occur with or without parental consent is presented in table 24-1. Laws and regulations relating to the dissolution of marriage by divorce range from total prohibition, through a wide range of grounds upon which divorces may be granted, to the granting of divorce in response to a simple statement of desire or intention by spouses.

4.1.3 Fragmentary geographical or ethnic coverage

Ideally, vital statistics for any given country or area should cover the entire geographical area and include all ethnic groups. Fragmentary coverage is, however, not uncommon. In some countries or areas, registration is compulsory for only a small part of the population, limited to certain ethnic groups, for example. In other places there is no national provision for compulsory registration, but only municipal or state ordinances that do not cover the entire geographical area. Still others have developed a registration area that comprises only a part of the country or area, the remainder being excluded because of inaccessibility or for economic and cultural considerations that make regular registration practically impossible.

4.1.4 Tabulation procedures

4.1.4.1 By place of occurrence

Vital statistics presented at the national level relate to the de facto, that is, the present-in-area population. Thus, unless otherwise noted, vital statistics for a given country or area cover all the events that occur within its present boundaries and among all segments of the population therein. They may be presumed to include events among nomadic tribes and indigenous peoples, and among nationals and foreigners. When known, deviations from the de facto concept are footnoted.

Urban/rural differentials in vital rates for some countries may vary considerably depending on whether the relevant vital events were tabulated on the basis of place of occurrence or place of usual residence. For example, if a substantial number of women residing in rural areas near major urban centres travel to hospitals or maternity homes located in a city to give birth, urban fertility and neo-natal and infant mortality rates will usually be higher (and the corresponding rural rates will usually be lower) if the events are tabulated on the basis of place of occurrence rather than on the basis of place of usual residence. A similar process will affect general mortality differentials if substantial numbers of persons residing in rural areas use urban health facilities when seriously ill.

4.1.4.2 By date of occurrence versus by date of registration

To the extent possible, the vital statistics presented in the *Demographic Yearbook* refer to events that occurred during the specified year, rather than to those that were registered during that period. However, a considerable number of countries or areas tabulate their vital statistics not by date of occurrence, but by date of registration. Because such statistics can be misleading, the countries or areas known to tabulate vital statistics by date of registration are identified in the tables by a plus sign "+". Since information on the method of tabulating vital statistics is not available for all countries and areas, tabulation by date of registration may be more prevalent than the symbols on the vital statistics tables would indicate.

Because quality of data is inextricably related to the timeliness of registration, this must always be considered in conjunction with the quality code description in section 4.2.1 below. If registration of births is complete and timely (code "C"), the ill effects of tabulating by date of registration, are, for all practical purposes, nullified. Similarly, with respect to death statistics, the effect of tabulating events by date of registration may be minimized in many countries or areas in which the sanitary code requires that a death must be registered before a burial permit can be issued, and this regulation tends to make registration prompt. With respect to foetal death, registration is usually done right away or not at all. Therefore, if registration is prompt, the difference between statistics tabulated by date of occurrence and those tabulated by date of registration may be negligible. In many cases, the length of the statutory time period allowed for registering various vital events plays an important part in determining the effects of tabulation by date of registration on the comparability of data.

With respect to marriage and divorce, the practice of tabulating data by date of registration does not generally pose serious problems. In many countries or areas marriage is a civil legal contract which, to establish its legality, must be celebrated before a civil officer. It follows that for these countries or areas registration would tend to be almost automatic at the time of, or immediately following, the marriage ceremony. Because the registration of a divorce in many countries or areas is the responsibility solely of the court or the authority which granted it, and since the registration record in such cases is part of the records of the court proceedings, it follows that divorces are likely to be registered soon after the decree is granted.

On the other hand, if registration is not prompt, vital statistics by date of registration will not produce internationally comparable data. Under the best circumstances, statistics by date of registration will include primarily events that occurred in the immediately preceding year; in countries or areas with less developed systems, tabulations will include some events that occurred many years in the past. Examination of available information reveals that delays of many years are not uncommon for birth registration, though the majority is recorded between two to four years after birth.

As long as registration is not prompt, statistics by date of registration will not be internationally comparable either among themselves or with statistics by date of occurrence.

It should also be mentioned that lack of international comparability is not the only limitation introduced by date-of-registration tabulation. Even within the same country or area, comparability over time may be lost by the practice of counting registrations rather than occurrences. If the number of events registered from year to year fluctuates because of *ad hoc* incentives to stimulate registration, or to the sudden need, for example, for proof of (unregistered) birth or death to meet certain requirements, vital statistics tabulated by date of registration are not useful in measuring and analyzing demographic levels and trends. All they can give is an indication of the fluctuations in the need for a birth, death or marriage certificate and the work-load of the registrars. Therefore, statistics tabulated by date of registration may be of very limited use for either national or international studies.

4.2 Quality of published vital statistics

The quality of vital statistics can be assessed in terms of a number of factors. Most fundamental is the completeness of the civil registration system on which these statistics are based.

4.2.1 Quality code for vital statistics from registers.

In the *Demographic Yearbook* annual "Questionnaire on Vital Statistics" national statistical offices are asked to provide their own estimates of the completeness of the births, deaths, late foetal deaths, marriages and divorces recorded in their civil registers.

On the basis of information from the questionnaires, from direct correspondence and from relevant official publications, it has been possible to classify current national statistics from civil registers of birth, death, infant death, late foetal death, marriage and divorce into three broad quality categories, as follows:

C: Data estimated to be virtually complete, that is, representing at least 90 per cent of the events occurring each year.

U: Data estimated to be incomplete, that is representing less than 90 per cent of the events occurring each year.

|: Data not derived from civil registration systems but considered reliable, such as estimates derived from population and housing censuses.

...: Data for which no specific information is available regarding completeness.

These quality codes appear in the first column of the tables which show total frequencies and crude rates (or ratios) over a period of years for all tables on live births, late foetal deaths, infant deaths, deaths, marriages, and divorces. Reliability of maternal mortality statistics is provided by the World Health Organisation.

The classification of countries and areas in terms of these quality codes may not be uniform. Nevertheless, it was felt that national statistical offices were in the best position to judge the quality of their data. It was considered that even the very broad categories that could be established on the basis of the available information would provide useful indicators of the quality of the vital statistics presented in the *Demographic Yearbook*.

Among the countries or areas indicating that the registration of live births was estimated to be 90 per cent or more complete (and hence classified as "C" or "+C" in table 9), the following countries or areas provided information on the method used to evaluate the completeness estimate:

(a) Demographic analysis – Argentina, Australia, Austria, Brazil, Bulgaria, Chile, China - Hong Kong SAR, Croatia, Egypt, Estonia, Italy, Latvia, Lithuania, Malaysia, Malta, Mauritius, New Zealand, Panama, Republic of Moldova, Saudi Arabia, Seychelles, South Africa, Sweden and Venezuela (Bolivarian Republic of).

(b) Dual record check – Australia, Austria, Bahrain, Belgium, Brazil, Cuba, Cyprus, Estonia, Faeroe Islands, Greenland, Hungary, Israel, Italy, Latvia, Malaysia, Mongolia, Montserrat, New Zealand, Norway, Qatar, Republic of Korea, Saint Vincent and the Grenadines, Uruguay and Venezuela (Bolivarian Republic of).

(c) Other specified methods -- Aruba, Australia, Bolivia (Plurinational State of), Brazil, Curaçao, Denmark, France, Georgia, Germany, Guatemala, Ireland, Jordan, Kyrgyzstan, Liechtenstein, Luxembourg, Malaysia, Panama, Philippines, Poland, Puerto Rico, Romania, Singapore, Slovenia, Spain, State of Palestine, Sweden, Uzbekistan and Venezuela (Bolivarian Republic of).

Among the countries or areas indicating that the registration of late foetal-deaths was estimated to be 90 per cent or more complete (and hence classified as "C" or "+C" in table 12), the following countries or areas provided information on the method used to evaluate the completeness estimate:

(a) Demographic analysis -- Argentina, Austria, Bulgaria, Croatia, Egypt, Estonia, Italy, Latvia, Lithuania, Malta, Mauritius, Republic of Korea, Saudi Arabia, Sweden and Venezuela (Bolivarian Republic of).

(b) Dual record check -- Austria, Cuba, Estonia, Greenland, Hungary, Israel, Italy, Latvia, Lithuania, Montserrat, New Zealand and Norway.

(c) Other specified methods – Denmark, Germany, Kyrgyzstan, Luxembourg, Poland, Puerto Rico, Romania, Slovenia, Spain, Sweden and Uzbekistan.

Among the countries or areas indicating that the registration of infant deaths was estimated to be 90 per cent or more complete (and hence classified as "C" or "+C" in table 15), the following countries or areas provided information on the method used to evaluate the completeness estimate:

(a) Demographic analysis -- Argentina, Australia, Austria, Brazil, Bulgaria, Chile, China - Hong Kong SAR, Croatia, Egypt, Estonia, Israel, Italy, Latvia, Lithuania, Malta, Mauritius, New Zealand, Panama, Republic of Korea, Republic of Moldova, Saudi Arabia, Seychelles and Sweden.

(b) Dual record check -- Austria, Bahrain, Belgium, Brazil, Cuba, Cyprus, Estonia, Faeroe Islands, Greenland, Hungary, Ireland, Israel, Italy, Latvia, Lithuania, Montserrat, New Zealand, Norway and Qatar.

(c) Other specified methods -- Aruba, Brazil, Curaçao, Cayman Islands, Denmark, Germany, Kyrgyzstan, Liechtenstein, Luxembourg, Poland, Puerto Rico, Romania, Singapore, Slovenia, Spain, Sweden and Uzbekistan.

Among the countries or areas indicating that the registration of deaths was estimated to be 90 per cent or more complete (and hence classified as "C" or "+C" in table 18), the following countries or areas provided information on the method used to evaluate the completeness estimate:

(a) Demographic analysis -- Argentina, Australia, Austria, Brazil, Bulgaria, Chile, China - Hong Kong SAR, Croatia, Egypt, Estonia, Israel, Italy, Latvia, Lithuania, Malta, Mauritius, New Zealand, Panama, Republic of Korea, Republic of Moldova, Saudi Arabia, Seychelles, South Africa, Sweden, United States of America and Venezuela (Bolivarian Republic of).

(b) Dual record check -- Austria, Bahrain, Belgium, Brazil, Cuba, Cyprus, Estonia, Faeroe Islands, Greenland, Hungary, Israel, Italy, Latvia, Lithuania, Mongolia, Montserrat, New Zealand, Norway, Qatar and Venezuela (Bolivarian Republic of).

(c) Other specified methods -- Aruba, Brazil, Curaçao, Denmark, France, Germany, Kyrgyzstan, Liechtenstein, Luxembourg, Malaysia, Poland, Puerto Rico, Romania, Saint Vincent and the Grenadines, Singapore, Slovenia, Spain, Sweden, United States of America and Uzbekistan.

Among the countries or areas indicating that the registration of marriages was estimated to be 90 per cent or more complete (and hence classified as "C" or "+C" in table 23), the following countries or areas provided information on the method used to evaluate the completeness estimate:

(a) Demographic analysis -- Argentina, Australia, Austria, Bulgaria, Chile, China - Hong Kong SAR, Croatia, Egypt, Estonia, Italy, Latvia, Lithuania, Malta, Mauritius, Republic of Moldova, Saudi Arabia, Seychelles, Sweden and Venezuela (Bolivarian Republic of).

(b) Dual record check – Austria, Belgium, Cuba, Estonia, Faeroe Islands, Hungary, Israel, Italy, Latvia, New Zealand, Norway, Qatar, Republic of Korea and State of Palestine.

(c) Other specified methods -- Aruba, Curaçao, Denmark, Dominican Republic, France, Germany, Jordan, Kyrgyzstan, Liechtenstein, Luxembourg, Poland, Puerto Rico, Romania, Slovenia, Spain, Sweden, Tajikistan and Uzbekistan.

Among the countries or areas indicating that the registration of divorces was estimated to be 90 per cent or more complete (and hence classified as "C" or "+C" in table 24), the following countries or areas provided information on the method used to evaluate the completeness estimate:

(a) Demographic analysis – Austria, Bulgaria, Croatia, Dominican Republic, Egypt, Estonia, Italy, Latvia, Lithuania, Republic of Moldova, Saudi Arabia, Seychelles, Sweden and Venezuela (Bolivarian Republic of).

(b) Dual record check -- Belgium, Cuba, Estonia, Faeroe Islands, Hungary, Israel, Italy, Latvia, New Zealand, Norway, Qatar, Republic of Korea and State of Palestine.

(c) Other specified methods -- Aruba, Australia, Curaçao, Cyprus, Denmark, Jordan, Kyrgyzstan, Liechtenstein, Luxembourg, Mauritius, Poland, Puerto Rico, Romania, Slovenia, Sweden, Tajikistan and Uzbekistan.

4.2.2 Treatment of vital statistics from registers

On the basis of the quality code described above, the vital statistics shown in all tables of the *Demographic Yearbook* are treated as either reliable or unreliable. Data coded "C" are considered reliable and appear in roman type. Data coded "U" or "..." are considered unreliable and appear in *italics*.

It should be noted that the indications of reliability used for infant mortality rates, maternal mortality ratios and late foetal death ratios (all of which are calculated using the number of live births in the denominator) are determined on the basis of the quality codes for infant deaths, deaths and late foetal deaths respectively. To evaluate these rates and ratios more precisely, one would have to take into account the quality of the live-birth data used in the denominator of these rates and ratios. The quality codes for live births are shown in table 9 and described more fully in the text of the technical notes for that table.

4.2.3 Treatment of estimated vital statistics

In addition to data from vital registration systems, estimated frequencies and rates of the events, usually *ad hoc* official estimates that have been derived either from the results of a population census or sample survey or by demographic analyses, also appear in the *Demographic Yearbook*. Estimated frequencies and rates have been included in the tables because it is assumed that they provide information that is more accurate than that from existing civil registration systems. By implication, they are assumed to be reliable and as such they are set in roman type.

Estimated data are denoted by the symbol "|".

4.3 Cause of death

World Health Organization (WHO) Member States are bound by the International Nomenclature Regulations to provide the Organization with cause of death data coded in accordance with the current revision of the International Statistical Classification of Diseases and Related Health Problems (ICD). In order to promote international comparability of cause of death statistics, the World Health Organization organizes and conducts an international conference for the revision of the ICD on a regular basis in order to ensure that the Classification is kept current with the most recent clinical and statistical concepts. The data are now usually submitted to WHO at the full four-character level of detail provided by the ICD and are compiled and stored in the WHO Mortality Database at the level of detail as provided by the country. Data from the WHO Mortality Database are available in electronic format at http://www3.who.int/whosis/menu.cfm.

Although revisions provide an up-to-date version of the ICD, such revisions create several problems related to the comparability of cause of death statistics. The first is the lack of comparability over time that inevitably accompanies the use of a new classification. The second problem affects comparability between countries and areas because they may adopt a new classification at different times. The more refined the classification becomes the greater is the need for expert clinical diagnosis of cause of death. In many countries or areas, few of the deaths occur in the presence of an attendant who is medically trained, i.e., most deaths are certified by a non-medically trained attendant. Because the ICD contains many diagnoses that cannot be identified by a non-medically trained person, the ICD is not always accurately or precisely used, which affects international comparability particularly between countries and areas where the level of medical services differs widely.

The chapters of the tenth revision[16], consist of an alphanumeric coding scheme of one letter followed by three numbers at the four-character level. Chapter one contains infectious and parasitic diseases, chapter two refers to all neoplasms, chapter three to disorders of the immune mechanism including diseases of the blood and blood-forming organs; and chapter four to endocrine, nutritional and metabolic diseases. The remaining chapters group diseases according to the anatomical site affected, except for chapters that refer to mental disorders; complications of pregnancy, childbirth and the puerperium; congenital malformations; and conditions originating in the perinatal period. Finally, an entire chapter is devoted to symptoms, signs, and abnormal findings.

4.3.1 Maternal mortality

According to the tenth revision of the ICD, "Maternal death" is defined as the death of a woman while pregnant or within 42 days of termination of pregnancy, irrespective of the duration and the site of the pregnancy, from any cause related to or aggravated by the pregnancy or its management but not from accidental or incidental causes.

"Maternal deaths" should be subdivided into direct and indirect obstetric deaths. Direct obstetric deaths are those resulting from obstetric complications of the pregnant state (pregnancy, labour and puerperium), from interventions, omissions, incorrect treatment, or from a chain of events resulting from any of the above. Indirect obstetric deaths are those resulting from previous existing disease or disease that developed during pregnancy and which was not due to direct obstetric causes, but which was aggravated by physiologic effects of pregnancy.

While the denominator for the maternal mortality ratio theoretically should be the number of pregnant women, it is impossible to determine the number of pregnant women. A further recommendation by the tenth revision is therefore that maternal mortality ratios be expressed per 100,000 live births or per 100,000 total births (live births and foetal deaths). The maternal mortality ratio calculated here is expressed per 100,000 live births. Although live births do not represent an unbiased estimate of pregnant women, this figure is more reliable than other estimates. In particular, live births are more accurately registered than live births plus foetal deaths.

---

1   UNdata is an internet based data service maintained by the Statistics Division of the United Nations Department of Economic and Social Affairs.

2   There are two exceptions – the 1978 and 1991 issues, which were disseminated in separate volumes from the respective regular issues.

3   United Nations, Department of Economic and Social Affairs, Population Division (2017). *2017 Revision of World Population Prospects* (http://esa.un.org/unpd/wpp/).

4   ST/ESA/STAT/SER.M/49/Rev.4/WWW ; https://unstats.un.org/unsd/methodology/m49/; see also Standard Country or Area Codes for Statistical Use, Sales No. M.98.XVII.9, United Nations, New York, 1999.

5   Sales No. E.15.XVII.10, United Nations, New York, 2015.

6   Ibid, para. 4.151.

7   Alternatively, if a population register is used, completed ages are calculated by subtracting the date of birth of individuals listed in the register from a reference date to which the age data pertain.

8   A source of non-comparability may result from differences in the method of reckoning age, for example, the Western versus the Eastern or, as it is usually known, the English versus the Chinese system. By the latter, a child is considered one year old at birth and advances an additional year at each Chinese New Year. The effect of this system is most obvious at the beginning of the age span, where the frequencies in the under-one-year category are markedly understated. The effect on higher age groups is not so apparent. Distributions constructed on this basis are often adjusted before publication, but the possibility of such aberrations should not be excluded when census data by age are compared.

9   Sales No. E.13.XVII.10, United Nations, New York, 2014.

10 Sales No. E.98.XVII.7, United Nations, New York, 1998.

11 Sales No. E.98.XVII.11, United Nations, New York, 1998.

12 Sales No. E.98.XVII.4, United Nations, New York, 1998.

13 Sales No. E.98.XVII.6, United Nations, New York, 1998.

14 Sales No. E.98.XVII.10, United Nations, New York, 1998.

15 Sales No. E.03.XVII.11, United Nations, New York, 2004.

16 *International Statistical Classification of Diseases and Related Health Problems*, Tenth Revision, Volume 2, World Health Organization, Geneva, 1992.

INTRODUCTION

L'Annuaire démographique est un recueil de statistiques démographiques internationales qui est établi par la Division de statistique du Département des affaires économiques et sociales de l'Organisation des Nations Unies. Il fait partie d'un ensemble de publications complémentaires publiées par l'Organisation des Nations Unies et les institutions spécialisées, qui ont pour objet de fournir des statistiques aux démographes, aux économistes, aux spécialistes de la santé publique et aux sociologues. Grâce à la coopération des services nationaux de statistique, il a été possible de faire figurer dans la présente édition de *l'Annuaire démographique* les statistiques officielles disponibles pour plus de 230 pays ou zones du monde entier.

L'Annuaire démographique 2016 est la soixante-septième édition d'une série que publie l'ONU depuis 1948. Le présent volume comprend un aperçu mondial des statistiques démographiques de base et des tableaux qui regroupent des statistiques sur la dimension, la répartition et les tendances de la population, la natalité, la mortalité fœtale, la mortalité infantile et la mortalité liée à la maternité, la mortalité générale, la nuptialité et la divortialité. Des données classées selon le lieu de résidence (zone urbaine ou rurale) sont présentées dans un grand nombre de tableaux. L'*Annuaire démographique* contient des notes techniques, un tableau synoptique, un index historique et une liste des éditions de *l'Annuaire démographique* publiées jusqu'à présent. Cette édition de l'*Annuaire démographique* contient les données disponibles couvrant les années de référence jusqu'à 2016.

La présente édition de l'*Annuaire démographique* comprend aussi le tableau 3a avec l'indice de Whipple selon le sexe et la résidence urbaine/rurale pour les recensements de la population effectués dans le monde entier depuis 1985. L'indice de Whipple est un indice de préférence pour certains âges dans la déclaration de l'âge et peut donc servir à mettre en évidence certaines des difficultés liées à la répartition par âge.

Les notes techniques sur les tableaux statistiques sont destinées à aider le lecteur. Le tableau A, qui correspond au tableau synoptique, donne un aperçu de l''exhaustivité des données publiées dans la présente édition de l'*Annuaire démographique*. Un index cumulatif donne des renseignements sur les matières traitées dans chacune des 67 éditions et sur les années sur lesquelles portent les données. L'index contient aussi une liste des tableaux publiés en ligne à travers le portail UNdata[1] (http://data.un.org/Explorer.aspx?d=POP). Les numéros de vente des éditions antérieures et une liste des sujets spéciaux traités dans les différentes éditions sont indiqués aux pages iii et iv. En plus, toutes les éditions de l'*Annuaire démographique* sont disponibles en ligne sur le site web de la Division des Statistiques : https://unstats.un.org/unsd/demographic/products/dyb/dyb2.htm

Jusqu'à la 48ᵉ édition (1996), chaque édition se composait de deux parties : les tableaux de caractère général et ceux sur des sujets spéciaux, publiés dans le même volume[2]. À partir de 49ᵉ édition (1997), les tableaux sur les sujets spéciaux ont été publiés dans un format numérique en tant que suppléments à l'*Annuaire démographique*. Deux CD-ROM ont été produits : l'*Annuaire démographique : Supplément historique*, qui présente un grand nombre de statistiques démographiques pour la période allant de 1948 à 1997, et l'*Annuaire démographique : Statistiques de la natalité*, qui contient des tableaux détaillés sur la natalité pour la période allant de 1980 à 1998. Par la suite, trois volumes concernant l'*Annuaire démographique* consacrés à des thèmes de recensement spéciaux pour le cycle de recensements de 2000 ont été publiés en ligne à l'adresse suivante : http://unstats.un.org/unsd/demographic/products/dyb/dybcens.htm. Les données actuelles sur les thèmes du recensement de l'*Annuaire démographique* pour les années de référence entre 1995 et aujourd'hui, lorsqu'elles sont disponibles, sont présentées sur http://unstats.un.org/unsd/demographic/products/dyb/dybcensusdata.htm. Ils comprennent des données sur la population selon les principales caractéristiques démographiques, scolaires, ethnoculturelles et économiques, les caractéristiques des ménages ainsi que des données sur les étrangers dans le pays ou les personnes nées à l'étranger. Particulièrement, on a présenté sous forme de table aux adresses suivantes, les données des recensements pour les années de référence entre 1995 et aujourd'hui, qui portent sur les thèmes des caractéristiques des ménages et des caractéristiques économiques : http://unstats.un.org/unsd/demographic/products/dyb/dyb_Household/dyb_household.htm et http://unstats.un.org/unsd/demographic/products/dyb/dyb_Eco/dyb_eco.htm

Les statistiques sur la population ne sont pas disponibles pour tous les pays et zones pour plusieurs raisons. Deux annexes sont présentées afin d'offrir des estimations sur la population en milieu d'année et un aperçu des statistiques de l'état civil pour chaque pays ou zone. La première porte sur des estimations concernant la population pour la période 2007-2016. La seconde présente les estimations des variantes moyennes concernant les taux bruts de natalité et de mortalité, la mortalité infantile, les indicateurs synthétiques de fécondité et l'espérance de vie à la naissance pour la période 2015-2020. Ces données ont été établies par la Division de la population de l'ONU et publiées dans les *Perspectives de la population mondiale : La révision de 2017*[3].

Les statistiques démographiques figurant dans la présente édition de l'*Annuaire démographique* sont disponibles en ligne sur les pages Web consacrées à l'*Annuaire démographique* : http://unstats.un.org/unsd/demographic/products/dyb/dyb2016.htm. On trouvera également des renseignements sur le programme de collecte et de diffusion des données de la Division de statistique sur le même site. Il est possible de se procurer d'autres données en contactant la Division de statistique du Département des affaires économiques et sociales de l'Organisation des Nations Unies à l'adresse suivante : demostat@un.org.

NOTES TECHNIQUES SUR LES TABLEAUX STATISTIQUES

1. REMARQUES D'ORDRE GÉNÉRAL

1.1 Notes techniques

Les notes techniques ont pour but de donner au lecteur des informations pertinentes en lien avec les tableaux statistiques. Les renseignements qui concernent l'*Annuaire démographique* en général sont présentés dans des sections portant sur diverses considérations géographiques, sur la population et sur les statistiques de natalité et de mortalité. Les tableaux sont ensuite commentés séparément et l'on trouvera pour chacun une description des variables et des observations sur la fiabilité et les lacunes des données ainsi que sur les pays et zones visés et sur les données publiées antérieurement. Des détails sont également donnés, le cas échéant, sur le mode de calcul des taux, quotients et pourcentages.

1.2 Tableaux

Dans la mesure du possible, la numérotation des tableaux dans les éditions successives de l'*Annuaire démographique* est préservée. Comme la numérotation des tableaux ne correspond pas exactement à celle des éditions précédentes, il est recommandé de se reporter à l'index qui figure à la fin du présent ouvrage pour trouver les données publiées dans les précédentes éditions.

1.3 Origine des données

Sauf indication contraire, les statistiques présentées dans l'*Annuaire démographique* sont des données nationales fournies par les organismes de statistique officiels. Elles sont recueillies essentiellement au moyen de questionnaires qui sont envoyés tous les ans à plus de 230 services nationaux de statistique. Les données communiquées en réponse à ces questionnaires sont complétées, dans toute la mesure possible, par des données tirées de publications nationales officielles et des sites web d'organismes officiels et des renseignements communiqués par les services nationaux de statistique à la demande de l'ONU. Pour que les données soient comparables, les taux, rapports et pourcentages ont été calculés par la Division de statistique de l'ONU, à l'exception des paramètres des tables de mortalité et des indicateurs synthétiques de fécondité ainsi que des taux bruts de natalité et de mortalité pour certains pays et zones, qui ont été dûment signalés en note. Les méthodes suivies par la Division pour le calcul des taux et rapports sont décrites dans les notes techniques relatives à chaque tableau. Les chiffres de population utilisés pour ces calculs sont ceux qui figurent dans la présente édition de l'*Annuaire démographique* ou qui ont paru dans des éditions antérieures.

Chaque fois que l'on constatera des différences entre les données du présent volume et celles des éditions antérieures de l'*Annuaire démographique*, ou de certaines publications apparentées, on pourra en conclure que les statistiques publiées cette année sont des chiffres révisés communiqués à la Division de statistique avant juin 2017.

2. CONSIDÉRATIONS GÉOGRAPHIQUES

2.1 Portée

Des données sont présentées sur tous les pays ou zones qui en ont communiquées. Le tableau 3, le plus complet, contient des données sur la population et la superficie de chaque pays ou zone ayant une population d'au moins 50 habitants. Ces pays ou zones ne figurent pas tous dans les tableaux qui suivent. Dans bien des cas, les données requises pour un tableau particulier n'étaient pas disponibles. En général, les pays ou zones qui peuvent fournir des données sont d'autant moins nombreux que les données demandées sont plus détaillées.

De plus les taux et rapports ne sont présentés que pour les pays ou zones ayant communiqué des chiffres correspondant à un nombre minimal de faits considérés. Les minimums sont indiqués dans les notes techniques relatives à chacun des tableaux.

À l'exception des données récapitulatives présentées dans les tableaux 1 et 2 pour l'ensemble du monde et les grandes zones et régions et des données relatives aux capitales et aux villes de 100 000 habitants ou plus dans le tableau 8, toutes les données se rapportent aux pays. Le nombre de pays sur lequel porte chacun des tableaux est indiqué dans le tableau A.

2.2 Composition territoriale

Autant que possible, toutes les données, y compris les séries chronologiques, se rapportent au territoire de 2016. Les exceptions à cette règle sont signalées en note à la fin des tableaux. Des clarifications importantes sont présentées ci-dessous.

Les données relatives au **Danemark** ne comprennent pas les Iles Féroé et le Groenland, qui font l'objet de rubriques distinctes.

Les données relatives à la **Finlande** comprennent les Îles d'Åland, sauf indication contraire en note de bas de page.

Les données relatives à la **France** ne comprennent pas les départements d'outre-mer, à savoir, la Guyane française, Guadeloupe, la Martinique et La Réunion, qui font l'objet de rubriques distinctes, sauf indication contraire en note de bas de page.

Les données relatives au **Royaume-Uni de Grande-Bretagne et d'Irlande du Nord** ne comprennent pas la Guernesey, l'île de Man et Jersey, qui font l'objet de rubriques distinctes.

Les données relatives au **Sahara Occidental** comprennent la région septentrionale (ancien Saguia-el-Hamra) et la région méridionale (ancien Rio de Oro).

2.3 Nomenclature

En règle générale, pour gagner de la place, on a jugé commode de désigner dans les tableaux les pays ou zones par les noms abrégés couramment utilisés par l'Organisation des Nations Unies[4], les désignations complètes n'étant utilisées que lorsqu'il n'existait pas de forme abrégée. La liste des désignations des pays ou zones est disponible à l'adresse suivante : https://unstats.un.org/unsd/methodology/m49/.

2.3.1 Ordre de présentation

Les pays ou zones sont classés dans l'ordre alphabétique anglais et regroupés par continent comme ci-après : Afrique, Amérique du Nord, Amérique du Sud, Asie, Europe et Océanie.

Les appellations employées dans la présente édition et la présentation des données qui y figurent n'ont d'autre objet que de donner un cadre géographique commode aux séries statistiques. La même observation vaut pour toutes les notes et précisions concernant les unités géographiques pour lesquelles des données sont présentées.

2.4 Superficie

Les données relatives à la superficie qui figurent dans le tableaux 1 représentent la superficie des terres alors que les données relatives à la superficie qui figurent dans le tableaux 3 représentent la superficie totale, sauf indication contraire par une note. La superficie totale englobe les terres émergées (la superficie des terres) et les eaux intérieures qui sont censées comprendre les principaux lacs et cours d'eau, mais excluent les régions polaires et les îles inhabitées. Les données relatives à la superficie correspondent aux chiffres estimatifs les plus récents. Les superficies sont toutes exprimées en kilomètres carrés ; les chiffres qui avaient été communiqués en miles carrés ont été convertis au moyen d'un coefficient de 2,589988.

2.4.1 Comparabilité dans le temps

La révision des estimations antérieures de la superficie, des augmentations effectives de la superficie terrestre due par exemple à des travaux d'assèchement, à des rectifications de frontières, à des changements d'interprétation du concept de « terres émergées » ou à l'utilisation de nouvelles unités de mesure peut avoir des incidences sur la comparabilité dans le temps des estimations relatives à la superficie d'un pays ou d'une zone donnés. Dans la plupart des cas, il a été possible de déterminer la raison de ces révisions ; toutefois, même lorsque la raison n'était pas connue, on a généralement admis que ces derniers sont exacts.

2.4.2 Comparabilité internationale

Le manque de comparabilité internationale entre les données relatives à la superficie est dû principalement à des différences de définition. En particulier, la définition des golfes, baies et criques, lacs et cours d'eau varie sensiblement d'un pays à l'autre. La diversité des méthodes employées pour estimer les superficies nuit elle aussi à la comparabilité internationale. Certaines données proviennent de levés effectués selon des méthodes scientifiques modernes ; d'autres ne représentent que des conjectures reposant sur diverses catégories de renseignements. Certains chiffres sont récents, d'autres pas. Étant donné que ni la méthode de calcul de la superficie ni la composition du territoire et la date à laquelle se rapportent les données ne sont connues avec précision pour tous les pays ou zones, les estimations figurant dans le tableau 3 ne doivent pas être considérées comme rigoureusement comparables d'un pays ou d'une zone à une autre.

3. POPULATION

Les statistiques de la population, c'est-à-dire celles qui se rapportent à la dimension, à la répartition géographique et aux caractéristiques démographiques de la population, sont présentées dans un certain nombre de tableaux de *l'Annuaire démographique*.

Les tableaux 1 et 2 présentent respectivement des estimations récapitulatives de milieu d'année de la population du monde, des grandes zones et régions, pour certaines années présélectionnées, ainsi que de sa répartition selon l'âge et le sexe pour l'année 2016.

Les données concernant les pays ou les zones représentent les résultats de recensements de population, des estimations fondées sur les résultats d'enquêtes par sondage (s'il n'y a pas eu recensement), des estimations postcensitaires ou intercensitaires, ou des estimations établies à partir de données provenant des registres permanents de population. Dans la présente édition, le tableau 3 indique pour chaque pays ou zone le chiffre le plus récent de la population totale issu du dernier recensement et des estimations établies au milieu de l'année 2010 et de l'année 2016. Le tableau 5 contient des estimations de la population totale au milieu de chaque année pendant 10 ans (2007-2016), et le tableau 6 des estimations de la population urbaine et de la population totale, par sexe, au milieu de chaque année pendant 10 ans (2007-2016). Les dernières données disponibles sur la répartition de la population selon l'âge, le sexe et le lieu de résidence (zone urbaine ou rurale) sont présentées dans le tableau 7. Les derniers chiffres disponibles sur la population des capitales et des villes de 100 000 habitants ou plus sont regroupés dans le tableau 8.

On a utilisé pour le calcul des taux les statistiques de la population totale et de la population répartie selon l'âge, le sexe ou le lieu de résidence (zone urbaine ou rurale). Les taux démographiques selon la résidence (urbaine/rurale), l'âge ou le sexe ont été calculés à partir des données présentées dans les tableaux 6 ou 7 de la présente édition ou dans les tableaux correspondants d'éditions précédentes de *l'Annuaire démographique*.

3.1 Sources de variation des données

Plusieurs facteurs influent sur la comparabilité des données : 1) la définition de la population totale ; 2) les définitions utilisées pour faire la distinction entre population urbaine et population rurale ; 3) les difficultés liées aux déclarations d'âge ; 4) l'étendue du surdénombrement ou du sous-dénombrement dans le recensement le plus récent ou dans une autre source de statistiques de référence sur la population ; 5) la qualité des estimations relatives à la population. Ces cinq facteurs sont analysés en détail aux sections 3.1.1 à 3.2 ci-après. D'autres questions seront traitées dans les notes techniques relatives à chaque tableau. Pour plus de précisions concernant, notamment, les notions fondamentales de dimension, de répartition et de caractéristiques de la population qui ont été élaborées par l'Organisation des Nations Unies, le lecteur est invité à se reporter aux *Principes et recommandations concernant les recensements de la population et de l'habitat, Révision 3*[5].

3.1.1 Population totale

Le principal obstacle à la comparabilité des données relatives à la population totale est la différence qui existe entre population de fait et population de droit. La population de fait comprend toutes les personnes présentes dans le pays ou la zone à la date de référence, tandis que la population de droit comprend toutes celles qui résident habituellement dans le pays ou la zone, qu'elles y aient été ou non présentes à la date de référence. Par définition, la population totale de fait et la population totale de droit ne sont donc pas rigoureusement comparables entre elles.

Même lorsque l'on veut comparer deux totaux qui se rapportent à des populations de fait ou deux totaux qui se rapportent à des populations de droit, on risque souvent de faire des erreurs pour cette raison qu'il est rare que l'une et l'autre notions soient appliquées strictement. Pour citer quelques exemples, certains chiffres qui sont censés porter sur la population de fait ne tiennent pas compte du personnel militaire, naval et diplomatique étranger en fonction dans le pays ou la zone, ni des membres de leurs familles et de leurs ménages ; d'autres ne comprennent pas les visiteurs étrangers de passage dans le pays ou la zone ni les personnes à bord de navires ancrés dans des ports. En revanche, il arrive que l'on compte des personnes, inscrits maritimes et marins pêcheurs par exemple, qui, en raison de leur activité professionnelle, se trouvent hors du pays ou de la zone de recensement.

Les risques de disparités sont encore plus grands quand il s'agit de comparer des populations de droit, car les comparaisons dépendent au premier chef de la définition que l'on donne à l'expression « lieu de résidence habituel », qui varie d'un pays ou d'une zone à l'autre et qu'il est, de toute façon, difficile d'appliquer uniformément pour le dénombrement lors d'un recensement ou d'une enquête. Par exemple, les civils étrangers qui se trouvent temporairement dans un pays ou une zone comme travailleurs à court terme peuvent officiellement être considérés comme résidents après un séjour d'une durée déterminée, mais ils peuvent aussi être considérés comme non-résidents pendant toute la durée de leur séjour ; ailleurs, ces mêmes personnes peuvent être considérées officiellement comme résidents ou comme non-résidents du pays ou de la zone d'où elles viennent, selon la durée et, éventuellement, la raison de leur absence. Qui plus est, quel que soit son statut officiel, chacun des recensés peut, au moment de l'enquête, interpréter à sa façon la notion de résidence. De plus, les autorités nationales ou les entités responsables des zones ne savent pas toutes avec la même précision combien de leurs résidents se trouvent temporairement à l'étranger.

Les chiffres de population présentés dans les tableaux de l'*Annuaire démographique* représentent la population de fait ou la population de droit. Lorsque l'on savait que les données avaient été recueillies selon une définition de la population de fait ou de la population de droit qui s'écartait sensiblement de celle exposée plus haut, on l'a signalé en note, de manière à compenser dans toute la mesure possible les conséquences des divergences.

Il peut y avoir hétérogénéité dans les statistiques d'un même pays ou d'une même zone dans le cas des pays ou zones qui ne font une exploitation statistique détaillée des données que pour la population de droit alors qu'ils recueillent des données sur la population de droit et sur la population de fait à l'occasion d'un recensement, par exemple. Ainsi, tandis que les chiffres relatifs à la population totale qui figurent au tableau 3 se rapportent à la population de fait, ceux des tableaux qui présentent des données sur diverses caractéristiques de la population, par exemple le lieu de résidence (zone urbaine ou rurale), l'âge et le sexe, peuvent être basés sur le concept de la population de droit.

3.1.2 Lieu de résidence (zone urbaine ou rurale)

L'hétérogénéité des définitions nationales du terme « urbain » nuit considérablement à la comparabilité internationale des données concernant la répartition selon le lieu de résidence. Les définitions utilisées par les différents pays ou zones et leurs implications sont exposées à la fin des notes techniques correspondant au tableau 6.

3.1.3 Répartition par âge

La répartition de la population selon l'âge est un paramètre fondamental de la plupart des analyses, estimations et projections relatives aux statistiques de la population. Malheureusement, ces données sont sujettes à un certain nombre d'erreurs et difficilement comparables. C'est pourquoi pratiquement tous les utilisateurs de ces statistiques doivent considérer ces répartitions avec la plus grande circonspection.

3.1.3.1 Collecte et exploitation des données sur l'âge

L'âge est l'intervalle de temps déterminé par calcul ou par estimation qui sépare la date de naissance de la date du recensement et qui est exprimé en années solaires révolues[6]. Les données sur l'âge peuvent être recueillies selon deux méthodes : la première consiste à obtenir la date de naissance de chaque personne à l'occasion d'un recensement ou d'un sondage, puis à calculer l'âge en années révolues en soustrayant la date de naissance de celle du dénombrement[7]. La seconde consiste à enregistrer l'âge en années révolues au moment du recensement, c'est-à-dire l'âge au dernier anniversaire.

La méthode recommandée consiste à calculer l'âge au dernier anniversaire en soustrayant la date exacte de la naissance de la date du recensement. Toutefois, on n'a pas toujours recours à cette méthode ; certains pays ou zones calculent l'âge en faisant la différence entre l'année du recensement et l'année de la naissance. Lorsque les données sur l'âge ont été établies de cette façon, on l'a signalé chaque fois que possible par une note. On peut d'ailleurs s'en rendre compte dans une certaine mesure, car les chiffres dans la catégorie des moins d'un an sont plus faibles qu'ils ne devraient l'être. Cependant, un nombre irrégulier de naissances d'une année à l'autre ou l'omission de certains âges parmi les moins d'un an peut aussi fausser les chiffres de la population de moins d'un an.

3.1.3.2 Erreurs dans les données sur l'âge

Les causes d'erreurs dans les données sur l'âge sont diverses : on peut citer notamment l'ignorance de l'âge exact, la déclaration d'années d'âge correspondant à un calendrier différent de celui des années solaires révolues depuis la naissance[8], la négligence dans les déclarations et dans la façon dont elles sont consignées, la tendance générale à déclarer des âges se terminant par certains chiffres tels que 0, 2, 5 ou 8, la tendance pour les personnes âgées à exagérer leur âge, une aversion subconsciente pour certains nombres, et les fausses déclarations faites délibérément.

Les causes d'erreurs mentionnées ci-dessus, communes à la plupart des enquêtes sur l'âge et à la plupart des pays ou zones, peuvent nuire sensiblement à la comparabilité.

À cause des difficultés indiquées ci-dessus, les répartitions par âge et par sexe de la population d'un grand nombre de pays ou de zones font apparaître les irrégularités suivantes : 1) sous-estimation des groupes d'âge correspondant aux enfants de moins d'un an et aux jeunes enfants ; 2) polarisation des déclarations sur les âges se terminant par les chiffres 0 ou 5 (c'est-à-dire 5, 10,15, 20...) ; 3) prépondérance des âges pairs (par exemple 10, 12, 14...) au détriment des âges impairs (par exemple 11, 13, 15...) ; 4) écart considérable et surprenant entre le rapport masculin/féminin à certains âges ; 5) différences importantes et difficilement explicables entre les données concernant des groupes d'âge voisins. En comparant les statistiques provenant de recensements successifs pour des cohortes identiques sur le plan de l'âge et de la répartition par sexe et en étudiant la répartition par âge et par sexe de la population à chaque recensement, on peut déceler l'existence de ces incohérences et de quelques autres, un certain nombre d'entre elles se retrouvant à des degrés divers même dans les recensements les plus modernes.

La présente édition de l'*Annuaire démographique* comprend le tableau 3a avec l'indice de Whipple selon le sexe et la résidence urbaine/rurale pour les recensements de la population effectués dans le monde entier depuis 1985. L'indice de Whipple est un indice de préférence pour certains âges dans la déclaration de l'âge et peut donc servir à mettre en évidence certaines des difficultés liées à la répartition par âge.

4. STATISTIQUES DE L'ÉTAT CIVIL

Aux fins de l'*Annuaire démographique*, on entend par statistiques de l'état civil les statistiques des naissances vivantes, des décès, des morts fœtales, des mariages et des divorces.

Dans le présent volume de l'*Annuaire démographique*, on a présenté des tableaux sur la natalité, la mortalité, la nuptialité et la divortialité. Les tableaux consacrés à la mortalité sont groupés sous les rubriques suivantes : mortalité fœtale, mortalité infantile, mortalité liée à la maternité et mortalité générale.

4.1 Sources de variations des données

La plupart des statistiques de l'état civil publiées dans le présent volume de l'*Annuaire démographique* émanent des systèmes nationaux d'enregistrement des faits d'état civil. Le degré d'exhaustivité et d'exactitude de ces données varie d'un pays ou d'une zone à l'autre.

Il n'existe pas partout de système national d'enregistrement des faits d'état civil et, dans quelques cas, seuls certains faits sont enregistrés. Par exemple, dans certains pays ou zones, seuls les naissances et les décès sont enregistrés. Il existe également des différences quant au degré d'efficacité avec lequel les lois relatives à l'enregistrement des faits d'état civil sont appliquées dans les divers pays ou zones. La fiabilité des statistiques provenant des registres d'état civil dépend des modalités d'application de la loi et de la mesure dans laquelle le public s'y soumet.

Il est à signaler que dans certains cas les statistiques de la nuptialité et de la divortialité sont tirées d'autres sources que les registres d'état civil. Dans certains pays ou zones, par exemple, les seules données disponibles sur la nuptialité proviennent des registres des églises. Selon la pratique suivie par chaque pays, les statistiques de la divortialité sont tirées des actes des tribunaux et/ou des registres d'état civil. L'officier de l'état civil, le service national de statistique ou d'autres services administratifs peuvent être chargés d'établir ces statistiques.

Les autres facteurs qui influent sur la comparabilité internationale des statistiques de l'état civil sont à peu près les mêmes que ceux qu'il convient de prendre en considération pour interpréter les variations observées dans les statistiques de la population. La définition des faits d'état civil aux fins de statistique, la portée des données du point de vue géographique et ethnique ainsi que les méthodes d'exploitation des données sont autant d'éléments qui peuvent influer sur la comparabilité.

En plus des statistiques tirées des registres d'état civil, l'*Annuaire démographique* présente des statistiques de l'état civil qui sont des estimations officielles nationales, fondées souvent sur les résultats de sondages ou des recensements de la population. Aussi leur comparabilité varie-t-elle en fonction du degré d'exhaustivité des déclarations recueillies lors des recensements de la population ou d'enquêtes sur les ménages, des erreurs d'échantillonnage ou autres, et des distorsions d'origines diverses.

Pour plus de détails sur les normes d'établissement des statistiques d'état civil, le lecteur pourra se reporter aux : *Principes et recommandations pour un système de statistiques de l'état civil, troisième révision*[9] ; *Manuel des systèmes d'enregistrement des faits d'état civil et de statistiques de l'état civil : Élaboration d'un cadre juridique*[10] ; *Manuel des systèmes d'enregistrement des faits d'état civil et de statistiques de l'état civil : Gestion, fonctionnement et tenue*[11]; *Manuel des systèmes d'enregistrement des faits d'état civil et de statistiques de l'état civil : Élaboration de programmes d'information, d'éducation et de communication*[12] ; *Manuel des systèmes d'enregistrement des faits d'état civil et de statistiques de l'état civil : Principes et protocoles concernant la communication et l'archivage des documents individuels*[13]; *Manuel des systèmes d'enregistrement des faits d'état civil et de statistiques de l'état civil : Informatisation*[14]. Le *Manuel de collecte de données sur la fécondité et la mortalité*[15] fournit des informations ayant trait à la collecte et à l'évaluation des données sur la fécondité, sur la mortalité et sur d'autres faits d'état civil, qui ont été recueillies au cours des enquêtes sur les ménages. Ces publications sont également disponibles sur le Web à partir des adresses suivantes : https://unstats.un.org/unsd/demographic/standmeth/principles/default.htm et http://unstats.un.org/unsd/demographic/standmeth/handbooks/default.htm.

4.1.1 Définition des faits d'état civil aux fins de la statistique

Une cause importante d'hétérogénéité dans les données est le manque d'uniformité des définitions des différents faits d'état civil. Aux fins de *l'Annuaire démographique*, il est recommandé de recueillir les données relatives aux faits d'état civil en utilisant les définitions établies au Chapitre I des *Principes et recommandations pour un système de statistiques de l'état civil, troisième révision*. Ces définitions sont les suivantes :

La *NAISSANCE VIVANTE* est *l'expulsion ou l'extraction complète du corps de la mère, indépendamment de la durée de la gestation, d'un produit de la conception qui, après cette séparation, respire ou manifeste tout autre signe de vie, tel que battement de cœur, pulsation du cordon ombilical ou contraction effective d'un muscle soumis à l'action de la volonté, que le cordon ombilical ait été coupé ou non et que le placenta soit ou non demeuré attaché ; tout produit d'une telle naissance est considéré comme « enfant né vivant ».*

Le *DÉCÈS* est *la disparition permanente de tout signe de vie à un moment quelconque postérieur à la naissance vivante (cessation des fonctions vitales après la naissance sans possibilité de réanimation). Cette définition ne comprend pas les morts fœtales.*

La *MORT FŒTALE* est *le décès d'un produit de la conception lorsque ce décès est survenu avant l'expulsion ou l'extraction complète du corps de la mère, indépendamment de la durée de la gestation. Le décès est indiqué par le fait qu'après cette séparation le fœtus ne respire ni ne manifeste aucun signe de vie, tel que battement de cœur, pulsation du cordon ombilical ou contraction effective d'un muscle soumis à l'action de la volonté.*

Le *MARIAGE* est *l'acte, la cérémonie ou la procédure qui établit un rapport légal entre les époux. L'union peut être rendue légale par une procédure civile ou religieuse, ou par toute autre procédure, conformément à la législation du pays.*

Le *DIVORCE* est *la dissolution légale et définitive des liens du mariage, c'est-à-dire la séparation des époux qui confère aux parties le droit de se remarier civilement ou religieusement, ou selon toute autre procédure, conformément à la législation du pays.*

En plus de ces notions définies internationalement, *l'Annuaire démographique* recueille et met à disposition ces données sur les avortements :

Par référence à la femme, *l'AVORTEMENT se définit comme toute interruption de grossesse qui est survenue avant 28 semaines de gestation et dont le produit est un fœtus mort. Il existe deux grandes catégories d'avortement : l'avortement spontané et l'avortement provoqué. L'avortement provoqué a pour origine une action délibérée entreprise en vue d'interrompre une grossesse. Tout autre avortement est considéré comme spontané.*

4.1.2 Problèmes posés par les définitions établies

Les variations par rapport aux définitions établies des faits d'état civil sont le principal obstacle à la comparabilité internationale des statistiques de l'état civil. Un exemple en est fourni par le cas des naissances vivantes et celui des morts fœtales. Dans certains pays ou zones, il faut que le nouveau-né ait vécu 24 heures pour pouvoir être inscrit sur le registre des naissances vivantes. Les décès d'enfants qui surviennent avant l'expiration du délai de 24 heures sont classés parmi les morts fœtales tardives et, en l'absence de méthodes spéciales d'exploitation des données, ne sont comptés ni dans les naissances vivantes ni dans les décès. De même, dans plusieurs autres pays ou zones, les décès d'enfants nés vivants et décédés avant l'enregistrement de leur naissance sont également comptés parmi les morts fœtales tardives.

À moins que des méthodes spéciales n'aient été adoptées pour l'exploitation de ces données, les statistiques des naissances vivantes et des décès ne tiendront pas compte de ces cas, qui viendront en revanche accroître d'autant le nombre des morts fœtales tardives. Le taux de mortalité infantile sera donc sous-estimé. Bien que les éléments constitutifs du taux (décès d'enfants de moins d'un an et naissances vivantes) accusent exactement la même insuffisance en valeur absolue, les lacunes sont proportionnellement plus fortes pour les décès de moins d'un an, ce qui cause des erreurs plus importantes dans les taux de mortalité infantile.

De plus, cette pratique augmente les rapports de mortinatalité. Quelques pays ou zones effectuent les ajustements nécessaires pour corriger cette anomalie (du moins dans les fréquences totales) au moment de l'établissement des tableaux. Si aucun ajustement n'a été effectué, cela est indiqué dans les notes chaque fois que possible.

Les définitions du mariage et du divorce posent aussi un problème du point de vue de la comparabilité internationale. Contrairement à la naissance et au décès, qui sont des faits biologiques, le mariage et le divorce sont uniquement déterminés par la législation et la coutume et, de ce fait, il est moins facile d'en donner une définition statistique qui ait une application universelle. À des fins statistiques, ces notions ont donc été définies de manière générale par référence à la législation de chaque pays ou zone. La législation relative au mariage et plus particulièrement au divorce varie d'un pays ou d'une zone à l'autre. En ce qui concerne le mariage, l'âge de nubilité est la condition la plus fréquemment requise, mais il arrive souvent que d'autres conditions soient exigées.

Lorsqu'il est connu, l'âge minimum auquel le mariage peut avoir lieu avec le consentement des parents (et dans certains cas sans le consentement des parents) est indiqué au tableau 24-1. Les lois et règlements relatifs à la dissolution du mariage par le divorce vont de l'interdiction absolue, en passant par diverses conditions requises pour l'obtention du divorce, jusqu'à la simple déclaration, par l'épouse, de son désir ou de son intention de divorcer.

4.1.3 Couverture géographique ou ethnique fragmentaire

En principe, les statistiques de l'état civil devraient s'étendre à l'ensemble du pays ou de la zone auxquels elles se rapportent et englober tous les groupes ethniques. En fait, il n'est pas rare que les données soient fragmentaires. Dans certains pays ou zones, l'enregistrement n'est obligatoire que pour une petite partie de la population, par exemple pour certains groupes ethniques. Dans d'autres, il n'existe pas de disposition qui prescrive l'enregistrement obligatoire sur le plan national, mais seulement des règlements ou décrets des municipalités ou des États, qui ne s'appliquent pas à l'ensemble du territoire. Il en est encore autrement dans d'autres pays ou zones où les autorités ont institué une zone d'enregistrement comprenant seulement une partie du territoire, le reste étant exclu en raison des difficultés d'accès ou parce qu'il est pratiquement impossible, pour des raisons d'ordre économique ou culturel, d'y procéder à un enregistrement régulier.

4.1.4 Méthodes de présentation des données

4.1.4.1 Selon le lieu de l'événement

Les statistiques de l'état civil qui sont présentées pour l'ensemble du territoire national se rapportent à la population de fait ou la population présente. En conséquence, sauf indication contraire, les statistiques de l'état civil relatives à une zone ou à un pays donné portent sur tous les faits survenus dans l'ensemble de la population, à l'intérieur des frontières actuelles de la zone ou du pays considéré. On peut donc estimer qu'elles englobent les faits d'état civil survenus dans les tribus nomades et parmi les populations autochtones ainsi que parmi les ressortissants du pays et les étrangers. Des notes signalent les exceptions lorsque celles-ci sont connues.

Pour certains pays, les écarts entre les taux démographiques pour les zones urbaines et pour les zones rurales peuvent varier notablement selon que les faits d'état civil ont été exploités sur la base du lieu de l'événement ou du lieu de résidence habituel. Par exemple, si un nombre appréciable de femmes résidant dans des zones rurales proches de grands centres urbains accouchent dans les hôpitaux ou maternités d'une ville, les taux de fécondité ainsi que les taux de mortalité néo-natale et infantile seront généralement plus élevés dans les zones urbaines (et par conséquent plus faibles dans les zones rurales) si les faits sont exploités en se fondant sur le lieu de l'événement et non sur le lieu de résidence habituel. Le phénomène sera le même dans le cas de la mortalité générale si un bon nombre de personnes résidant dans des zones rurales font appel aux services de santé des villes lorsqu'elles sont gravement malades.

4.1.4.2 Selon la date de l'événement ou la date de l'enregistrement

Autant que possible, les statistiques de l'état civil figurant dans l'Annuaire démographique se rapportent aux faits survenus pendant l'année considérée et non aux faits enregistrés au cours de ladite année. Bon nombre de pays ou zones, toutefois, exploitent leurs statistiques de l'état civil selon la date de l'enregistrement et non selon la date de l'événement. Comme ces statistiques risquent d'induire en erreur, les pays ou zones dont on sait qu'ils établissent leurs statistiques d'après la date de l'enregistrement sont signalés dans les tableaux par un signe plus « + ». On ne dispose toutefois pas pour tous les pays ou zones de renseignements complets sur la méthode d'exploitation des statistiques de l'état civil et les données sont peut-être exploitées selon la date de l'enregistrement plus souvent que ne le laisserait supposer l'emploi des signes.

Étant donné que la qualité des données est inextricablement liée aux retards dans l'enregistrement, il faudra toujours considérer en même temps le code de qualité qui est décrit à la section 4.2.1 ci-après. Évidemment, si l'enregistrement des naissances est complet et effectué en temps voulu (code « C »), les effets perturbateurs de la méthode consistant à exploiter les données selon la date de l'enregistrement seront pratiquement annulés. De même, s'agissant des statistiques des décès, les effets pourront bien souvent être réduits au minimum dans les pays ou zones où le code sanitaire subordonne la délivrance du permis d'inhumer à l'enregistrement du décès, ce qui tend à hâter l'enregistrement. Quant aux morts fœtales, elles sont généralement déclarées immédiatement ou ne sont pas déclarées du tout. En conséquence, si l'enregistrement se fait dans un délai très court, la différence entre les statistiques établies selon la date de l'événement et celles qui sont établies selon la date de l'enregistrement peut être négligeable. Dans bien des cas, la durée des délais légaux accordés pour l'enregistrement des faits d'état civil est un facteur dont dépend dans une large mesure l'incidence sur la comparabilité de l'exploitation des données selon la date de l'enregistrement.

En ce qui concerne le mariage et le divorce, la pratique consistant à exploiter les statistiques selon la date de l'enregistrement ne pose généralement pas de graves problèmes. Le mariage étant, dans de nombreux pays ou zones, un contrat juridique civil qui, pour être légal, doit être conclu devant un officier de l'état civil, il s'ensuit que dans ces pays ou zones l'enregistrement a lieu presque systématiquement au moment de la cérémonie ou immédiatement après. De même, dans de nombreux pays ou zones, le tribunal ou l'autorité qui a prononcé le divorce est seul habilité à enregistrer cet acte, et comme l'acte d'enregistrement figure alors sur les registres du tribunal l'enregistrement suit généralement de peu le jugement.

En revanche, si l'enregistrement n'a lieu qu'avec un certain retard, les statistiques de l'état civil établies selon la date de l'enregistrement ne sont pas comparables sur le plan international. Au mieux, les statistiques par date de l'enregistrement prendront surtout en considération des faits survenus au cours de l'année précédente ; dans les pays ou zones où le système d'enregistrement n'est pas très développé, il y entrera des faits datant de plusieurs années. Il ressort des documents dont on dispose que des retards de plusieurs années dans l'enregistrement des naissances ne sont pas rares, encore que, dans la majorité des cas, les retards ne dépassent pas deux à quatre ans.

Tant que l'enregistrement se fera avec retard, les statistiques fondées sur la date d'enregistrement ne seront comparables sur le plan international ni entre elles ni avec les statistiques établies selon la date de fait d'état civil.

Il convient également de noter que l'exploitation des données selon la date de l'enregistrement ne nuit pas seulement à la comparabilité internationale des statistiques. Même à l'intérieur d'un pays ou d'une zone, le procédé qui consiste à compter les enregistrements et non les faits peut compromettre la comparabilité des chiffres sur une longue période. Si le nombre des faits d'état civil enregistrés varie d'une année à l'autre (par suite de l'application de mesures visant tout particulièrement à encourager l'enregistrement ou parce qu'il est subitement devenu nécessaire de produire le certificat d'une naissance ou d'un décès non enregistré pour l'accomplissement de certaines formalités), les statistiques de l'état civil établies d'après la date de l'enregistrement ne permettent pas de quantifier ni d'analyser l'état et l'évolution de la population. Tout au plus peuvent-elles révéler l'évolution des conditions d'exigibilité de l'acte de naissance, de décès ou de mariage et les fluctuations du volume de travail des bureaux d'état civil. Les statistiques établies selon la date de l'enregistrement peuvent donc ne présenter qu'une utilité très réduite pour des études nationales ou internationales.

4.2 La qualité des statistiques de l'état civil qui sont publiées

La qualité des statistiques de l'état civil peut être évaluée en se fondant sur plusieurs facteurs. Le facteur essentiel est la complétude du système d'enregistrement des faits d'état civil d'après lequel ces statistiques sont établies.

4.2.1 Codage qualitatif des statistiques provenant des registres de l'état civil

Dans le questionnaire relatif au mouvement de la population qui leur est envoyé chaque année dans le cadre de l'établissement de *l'Annuaire démographique*, les services nationaux de statistique sont invités à donner leur propre évaluation du degré de complétude des données sur les naissances, les décès, les décès d'enfants de moins d'un an, les morts fœtales tardives, les mariages et les divorces figurant dans leurs registres d'état civil.

D'après les renseignements directement communiqués par les gouvernements ou extraits des questionnaires ou de publications officielles pertinentes, il a été possible de classer les statistiques de l'enregistrement des faits d'état civil (naissances, décès, décès d'enfants de moins d'un an, morts fœtales tardives, mariages et divorces) en trois grandes catégories, selon leur qualité :

C : Données jugées pratiquement complètes, c'est-à-dire représentant au moins 90 % des faits d'état civil survenant chaque année.

U : Données jugées incomplètes, c'est-à-dire représentant moins de 90 % des faits survenant chaque année.

| : Données ne provenant pas des systèmes nationaux d'enregistrement des faits d'état civil, mais jugées fiables, telles que les estimations dérivées des recensements de population ou du logement.

... : Données dont le degré de complétude ne fait pas l'objet de renseignements précis.

Ces codes de qualité figurent dans la première colonne des tableaux qui présentent, pour un nombre d'années déterminé les chiffres absolus et les taux (ou rapports) bruts concernant les naissances vivantes, les morts fœtales tardives, les décès d'enfants de moins d'un an, les décès, les mariages et les divorces. Les niveaux de fiabilité des statistiques de mortalité maternelle sont transmis par l'Organisation mondiale de la santé.

La classification des pays ou zones selon ces codes de qualité peut ne pas être uniforme. On a estimé néanmoins que les services nationaux de statistique étaient les mieux placés pour juger de la qualité de leurs données. On a pensé que les catégories que l'on pouvait distinguer sur la base des renseignements disponibles, bien que très larges, permettaient cependant de se faire une idée de la qualité des statistiques de l'état civil publiées dans *l'Annuaire démographique*.

Sur les pays ou zones qui ont estimé à 90 % ou plus le degré d'exhaustivité de leur enregistrement des naissances vivantes (classé « C » ou « +C » dans le tableau 9), les pays ou zones suivants ont communiqué des renseignements concernant les bases sur lesquelles leur estimation reposait :

a) Analyse démographique : Afrique du Sud, Arabie saoudite, Argentine, Australie, Autriche, Brésil, Bulgarie, Chili, Chine - Hong Kong RAS, Croatie, Égypte, Estonie, Italie, Lettonie, Lituanie, Malaisie, Malte, Maurice, Nouvelle-Zélande, Panama, République de Moldova, Seychelles, Suède et Venezuela (République bolivarienne du).

b) Double contrôle des registres : Australie, Autriche, Bahreïn, Belgique, Brésil, Chypre, Cuba, Estonie, Groenland, Hongrie, Îles Féroé, Israël, Italie, Lettonie, Malaisie, Mongolie, Montserrat, Norvège, Nouvelle-Zélande, Qatar, République de Corée, Roumanie, Saint Vincent et les Grenadines, Uruguay et Venezuela (République bolivarienne du).

c) Autre méthode : Allemagne, Aruba, Australie, Bolivie (État plurinational de), Brésil, Curaçao, Danemark, Espagne, État de Palestine, France, Géorgie, Guatemala, Irlande, Jordanie, Kirghizstan, Liechtenstein, Luxembourg, Malaisie, Mexique, Ouzbékistan, Panama, Philippines, Pologne, Porto Rico, Roumanie, Singapour, Slovénie, Suède et Venezuela (République bolivarienne du).

Sur les pays ou zones qui ont estimé à 90 % ou plus le degré d'exhaustivité de leur enregistrement des morts fœtales tardives (classé « C » ou « +C » dans le tableau 12), les pays ou zones suivants ont communiqué des renseignements concernant les bases sur lesquelles leur estimation reposait :

a) Analyse démographique : Arabie saoudite, Argentine, Autriche, Bulgarie, Croatie, Égypte, Estonie, Italie, Lettonie, Lituanie, Malte, MauriceMexique, République de Corée, Suède et Venezuela (République bolivarienne du).

b) Double contrôle des registres : Autriche, Cuba, Estonie, Groenland, Hongrie, Israël, Italie, Leetonie,

Lituanie, Montserrat, Norvège et Nouvelle-Zélande.

c) Autre méthode : Allemagne, Danemark, Espagne, Kirghizstan, Luxembourg, Ouzbékistan, Pologne, Porto Rico, Roumanie, Slovénie et Suède.

Sur les pays ou zones qui ont estimé à 90 % ou plus le degré d'exhaustivité de leur enregistrement des décès à moins d'un an (classé « C » ou « +C » dans le tableau 15), les pays ou zones suivants ont donné des indications touchant la base de cette estimation :

a) Analyse démographique : Arabie saoudite, Argentine, Australie, Autriche, Brésil, Bulgarie, Chili, Chine - Hong Kong RAS, Croatie, Égypte, Estonie, Israël, Italie, Lettonie, Lituanie, Malte, Maurice, Nouvelle-Zélande, Panama, République de Corée, République de Moldova, Seychelles et Suède.

b) Double contrôle des registres : Autriche, Bahreïn, Belgique, Brésil, Cuba, Chypre, Estonie, Groenland, Hongrie, Îles Féroé, Irlande, Israël, Italie, Lettonie, Lituanie, Montserrat, Norvège, Nouvelle-Zélande et Qatar.

c) Autre méthode : Allemagne, Aruba, Brésil, Curaçao, Danemark, Espagne, Îles Caïmans, Kirghizstan, Liechtenstein, Luxembourg, Ouzbékistan, Pologne, Porto Rico, Roumanie, Singapour, Slovénie et Suède.

Sur les pays ou zones qui ont estimé à 90 % ou plus le degré d'exhaustivité de leur enregistrement des décès (classé « C » ou « +C » dans le tableau 18), les pays ou zones suivants ont donné des indications touchant la base de cette estimation :

a) Analyse démographique : Arabie saoudite, Afrique du Sud, Argentine, Australie, Autriche, Brésil, Bulgarie, Chili, Chine - Hong Kong RAS, Croatie, Égypte, Estonie, États-Unis d'Amérique, Israël, Italie, Lettonie, Lituanie, Malte, Maurice, Nouvelle-Zélande, Panama, République de Corée, République de Moldova, Seychelles, Suède et Venezuela (République bolivarienne du).

b) Double contrôle des registres : Autriche, Bahreïn, Belgique, Brésil, Cuba, Chypre, Estonie, Groenland, Hongrie, Îles Féroé, Israël, Italie, Lettonie, Lituanie, Mongolie, Montserrat, Norvège, Nouvelle-Zélande, Qatar et Venezuela (République bolivarienne du).

c) Autre méthode : Allemagne, Aruba, Brésil, Curaçao, Danemark, Espagne, États-Unis d'Amérique, France, Kirghizstan, Liechtenstein, Luxembourg, Malaisie, Ouzbékistan, Pologne, Porto Rico, Roumanie, Saint Vincent et les Grenadines, Singapour, Slovénie et Suède.

Sur les pays ou zones qui ont estimé à 90 % ou plus le degré d'exhaustivité de leur enregistrement des mariages (classé « C » ou « +C «» dans le tableau 23), les pays ou zones suivants ont communiqué des renseignements concernant les bases sur lesquelles leur estimation reposait :

a) Analyse démographique : Arabie saoudite, Argentine, Australie, Autriche, Bulgarie, Chili, Chine - Hong Kong RAS, Croatie, Égypte, Estonie, Italie, Lettonie, Lituanie, Malte, Maurice, République de Moldova, Seychelles, Suède et Venezuela (République bolivarienne du).

b) Double contrôle des registres : Autriche, Belgique, Cuba, Estonie, État de Palestine, Hongrie, Îles Féroé, Israël, Italie, Lettonie, Norvège, Nouvelle-Zélande, Qatar et République de Corée.

c) Autre méthode : Allemagne, Aruba, Curaçao, Danemark, Espagne, France, Kirghizstan, Jordanie, Liechtenstein, Luxembourg, Ouzbékistan, Pologne, Porto Rico, République dominicaine, Roumanie, Slovénie, Suède et Tadjikistan.

Sur les pays ou zones qui ont estimé à 90 % ou plus le degré d'exhaustivité de leur enregistrement des divorces (classé « C » ou « +C » dans le tableau 24), les pays ou zones suivants ont communiqué des renseignements concernant les bases sur lesquelles leur estimation reposait :

a) Analyse démographique : Arabie saoudite, Autriche, Bulgarie, Croatie, Égypte, Estonie, Italie, Lettonie, Lituanie, République de Moldova, République dominicaine, Seychelles, Suède et Venezuela (République bolivarienne du).

b) Double contrôle des registres : Belgique, Cuba, Estonie, État de Palestine, Hongrie, Îles Féroé,

Israël, Italie, Lettonie, Norvège, Nouvelle-Zélande, Qatar et République de Corée.

c) Autre méthode : Aruba, Australie, Chypre, Curaçao, Danemark, Jordanie, Kirghizstan, Liechtenstein, Luxembourg, Maurice, Ouzbékistan, Pologne, Porto Rico, Roumanie, Slovénie, Suède et Tadjikistan.

4.2.2 Traitement des statistiques tirées des registres d'état civil

Dans tous les tableaux de l'*Annuaire démographique*, on a indiqué le degré de fiabilité des statistiques de l'état civil en se fondant sur le codage qualitatif décrit ci-dessus. Les statistiques codées « C », jugées sûres, sont imprimées en caractères romains. Celles qui sont codées « U » ou « ... », jugées douteuses, sont reproduites en *italique*.

Il convient de noter que, pour les taux de mortalité infantile, les taux de mortalité maternelle et les rapports de morts fœtales tardives (calculées en utilisant au dénominateur le nombre de naissances vivantes), les indications relatives à la fiabilité sont déterminées sur la base des codes de qualité utilisés pour les décès d'enfants de moins d'un an, les décès totaux et les morts fœtales tardives, respectivement. Pour évaluer ces taux et rapports de façon plus précise, il faudrait tenir compte de la qualité des données relatives aux naissances vivantes, utilisées au dénominateur dans leur calcul. Les codes de qualité pour les naissances vivantes figurent au tableau 9 et sont décrits plus en détail dans les notes techniques se rapportant à ce tableau.

4.2.3 Traitement des estimations fondées sur les statistiques de l'état civil

En plus des données provenant des systèmes d'enregistrement des faits d'état civil, l'*Annuaire démographique* contient aussi des estimations relatives aux fréquences et aux taux. Il s'agit d'estimations officielles, généralement calculées à partir des résultats d'un recensement de la population ou d'un sondage ou par analyse démographique. Si des estimations concernant les fréquences et les taux figurent dans les tableaux, c'est parce que l'on considère qu'elles fournissent des renseignements plus exacts que les systèmes existants d'enregistrement des faits d'état civil. En conséquence, elles sont également jugées sûres et sont donc imprimées en caractères romains.

Les données estimatives sont dénotées par le «|».

4.3 Causes de décès

Les États membres de l'Organisation mondiale de la santé (OMS) sont tenus de communiquer à celle-ci les données sur les causes de décès codifiées selon la révision en vigueur de la Classification internationale des maladies et des problèmes de santé connexes (CIM). Pour assurer la comparabilité internationale des statistiques des causes de décès, l'OMS organise régulièrement des conférences internationales de révision de la Classification internationale des maladies afin de suivre, au fur et à mesure, les progrès les plus récents de la médecine clinique et de la statistique. Les données sont généralement présentées à l'OMS selon le degré de détail à tous les quatre caractères requis par la CIM et sont compilées et archivées dans la Base de données sur la mortalité de l'OMS au degré de détail présenté par le pays. Les données de la Base de données sur la mortalité de l'OMS sont disponibles sur le site Internet suivant : http://www3.who.int/whosis/menu.cfm.

Les révisions de la CIM permettent certes de disposer d'une version actualisée, mais elles posent plusieurs problèmes de comparabilité des statistiques des causes de décès. Le premier tient au manque de comparabilité dans le temps, qui accompagne inévitablement la mise en œuvre d'une classification nouvelle. Le deuxième est celui de la comparabilité entre pays ou zones, car les différents pays peuvent adopter la nouvelle classification à des époques différentes. Établir la cause des décès exige des compétences de plus en plus poussées à mesure que la classification devient plus précise. Or, dans beaucoup de pays ou zones, il est rare que les décès se produisent en présence d'un témoin possédant une formation médicale et le certificat de décès est le plus souvent établi par quelqu'un qui n'est pas qualifié sur le plan médical. Étant donné que la CIM répertorie de nombreux diagnostics qu'il est impossible d'établir si l'on n'a pas de formation en médecine, la CIM n'est pas toujours exactement ou précisément utilisée ce qui affecte la comparabilité internationale, notamment entre pays ou zones où la qualité des services médicaux est très disparate.

Les chapitres de la dixième révision[16] se fondent sur un système de codification alphanumérique à une lettre suivie de trois chiffres pour les catégories à quatre caractères. Le chapitre 1 concerne les maladies infectieuses et parasitaires et le chapitre 2 l'ensemble des néoplasmes. Le chapitre 3 a trait aux troubles du système immunitaire, aux maladies du sang et aux organes hématopoïétiques. Le chapitre 4 porte sur les maladies du système endocrinien, de la nutrition et du métabolisme. Les autres chapitres groupent les maladies selon leur site anatomique, à l'exception de ceux qui concernent les affections mentales, les complications de la grossesse, de l'accouchement et des suites de couches, les malformations congénitales et les affections de la période périnatale. Enfin, un chapitre entier est consacré aux symptômes, manifestations et résultats anormaux.

4.3.1 Mortalité liée à la maternité

D'après la dixième révision de la CIM, la « mortalité liée à la maternité » est définie comme le décès d'une femme survenu au cours de la grossesse ou dans un délai de 42 jours après sa terminaison, quelle qu'en soit la durée et la localisation, pour une cause quelconque déterminée ou aggravée par la grossesse ou les soins qu'elle a motivés, mais ni accidentelle ni fortuite.

Les « décès liés à la maternité » doivent se répartir en décès par cause obstétricale directe et indirecte. Les décès par cause obstétricale directe sont ceux qui résultent de complications obstétricales de l'état de grossesse (grossesse, travail et suites de couches), d'interventions, d'omissions, d'un traitement incorrect ou d'un enchaînement d'événements de l'un quelconque des facteurs ci-dessus. Les décès par cause obstétricale indirecte sont ceux qui résultent d'une maladie préexistante ou d'une affection apparue au cours de la grossesse, sans qu'elle soit due à des causes obstétricales directes, mais qui a été aggravée par les effets physiologiques de la grossesse.

En théorie, le nombre de femmes enceintes aurait dû être pris comme dénominateur pour le taux de mortalité maternelle, mais il est impossible de déterminer ce nombre. En conséquence, il est en outre recommandé dans la dixième révision d'exprimer les taux de mortalité maternelle sur la base de 100 000 naissances vivantes ou 100 000 naissances totales (naissances vivantes et morts fœtales). Le taux de mortalité maternelle est ici calculé par 100 000 naissances vivantes. Bien que les naissances vivantes ne permettent pas d'évaluer sans distorsion le nombre des femmes enceintes, leur nombre est plus fiable que d'autres estimations car le nombre des naissances vivantes est plus exactement enregistré que celui des naissances vivantes et des morts fœtales.

---

[1] UNdata est un service de données en ligne géré par la Division de statistique du Département des affaires économiques et sociales de l'Organisation des Nations Unies.

[2] Les éditions de 1978 et de 1991 font exception à la règle, puisque les tableaux sur des sujets spéciaux ont été publiés séparément.

[3] Organisation des Nations Unies, Département des affaires économiques et sociales, Division de la population (2017). Perspectives de la population mondiale : La révision de 2017 (http://esa.un.org/unpd/wpp/).

[4] ST/ESA/STAT/SER.M/49/Rev.4/WWW ; https://unstats.un.org/unsd/methodology/m49/ ; voir également Code standard des pays et des zones à usage statistique, numéro de vente : M.98.XVII.9, Nations Unies, New York, 1999.

[5] Numéro de vente : E.15.XVII.10, Nations Unies, New York, 2015.

[6] Ibid., par. 4.151.

[7] Lorsque l'on utilise un registre de la population, on peut également calculer l'âge en années révolues en soustrayant la date de naissance de chaque personne inscrite sur le registre de la date de référence à laquelle se rapportent les données sur l'âge.

[8] L'emploi de méthodes différentes de calcul de l'âge, par exemple la méthode occidentale et la méthode orientale, ou, comme on les désigne plus communément, la méthode anglaise et la méthode chinoise, représente une cause de non-comparabilité. Selon la méthode chinoise, on considère que l'enfant est âgé d'un an à sa naissance et qu'il avance d'un an à chaque nouvelle année chinoise. Les répercussions de cette méthode sont particulièrement apparentes dans les données pour le premier âge : les données concernant les enfants de moins d'un an sont nettement inférieures à la réalité. Les effets sur les chiffres relatifs aux groupes d'âge suivants sont moins visibles. Les séries ainsi établies sont souvent ajustées avant d'être publiées, mais il ne faut pas exclure la possibilité d'aberrations de ce genre lorsque l'on compare des données censitaires sur l'âge.

[9] Numéro de vente : E.13.XVII.10, publication des Nations Unies, New York, 2014.

[10] Numéro de vente : F. 98.XVII.7, publication des Nations Unies, New York, 1998.

[11] Numéro de vente : F.98.XVII.11, publication des Nations Unies, New York, 1998.

[12] Numéro de vente : F.98.XVII.4, publication des Nations Unies, New York, 1998.

[13] Numéro de vente : F.98.XVII.6, publication des Nations Unies, New York, 1998.

[14] Numéro de vente : F.98.XVII.10, publication des Nations Unies, New York, 1998.

[15] Numéro de vente : F.03.XVII.11, United Nations, New York, 2004.

[16] Organisation mondiale de la santé, Classification statistique internationale des maladies et problèmes de santé connexes, dixième révision, vol. 2, Genève, 1992.

Table A. Demographic Yearbook 2016 synoptic table: Availability of data by country/area, table and sex, where applicable
Tableau A. Tableau synoptique de l'Annuaire démographique 2016 : Disponibilité des données par pays ou zone, tableau et le sexe, si disponible

		General topic and table number - Sujet général et numéro de tableau															
Continent and country or area / Continent et pays ou zone	Table totals	Summary - Apercu			Population							Fertility - Natalité			Foetal mortality - Mortalité foetale		
		3		4	5	6		7		8		9	10		11	12	13	14
		Total	M/F			Total¹	M/F	Total	M/F	Total	M/F		Total	M/F				
Total number of countries or areas - Total des pays ou zones	..	240	226	181	224	228	228	218	214	208	165	172	153	130	87	89	62	49

AFRICA - AFRIQUE

Continent and country or area	Table totals	3 Total	3 M/F	4	5	6 Total¹	6 M/F	7 Total	7 M/F	8 Total	8 M/F	9	10 Total	10 M/F	11	12	13	14
Algeria - Algérie	17	•	•	•	•	•	•	•	•	•	...	•	...	...	•	•	...	...
Angola	7	•	•	...	•	•	•	•	...	•	...	•	...	...	...	...	...	...
Benin - Bénin	13	•	•	•	•	•	•	•	...	•	•	•	...	...	•	...	...	...
Botswana	19	•	•	•	•	•	•	•	•	•	...	•	•	•	•	...	...	...
Burkina Faso	10	•	•	...	•	•	•	•	•	•	...	...	...	...	•	...	...	...
Burundi	14	•	•	•	•	•	•	•	•	•	•	...	...	...	•	•	•	...
Cabo Verde	11	•	•	...	•	•	•	•	•	•	•	•	...	...	...	...	...	...
Cameroon - Cameroun	9	•	•	...	•	•	•	•	•	•	•	...	...	...	...	...	...	...
Central African Republic - République centrafricaine	2	•	•	...	...	...	...	...	...	...	...	...	...	...	...	...	...	...
Chad - Tchad	4	•	•	...	...	•	•	•	...	•	...	...	...	...	...	...	...	...
Comoros - Comores	2	•	•	...	...	...	...	...	...	...	...	...	...	...	...	...	...	...
Congo	8	•	•	...	•	•	•	•	•	•	...	...	...	...	...	...	...	...
Côte d'Ivoire	18	•	•	•	•	•	•	•	•	•	•	•	•	•	•	...	...	...
Democratic Republic of the Congo - République démocratique du Congo	2	•	•	...	...	...	...	...	...	...	...	...	...	...	...	...	...	...
Djibouti	7	•	•	...	•	•	•	•	•	•	...	...	...	...	...	...	...	...
Egypt - Égypte	27	•	•	•	•	•	•	•	•	•	•	•	•	•	•	•	...	...
Equatorial Guinea - Guinée équatoriale	8	•	•	...	•	•	•	•	•	•	...	...	...	...	...	...	...	...
Eritrea - Érythrée	2	•	•	...	...	...	...	...	...	...	...	...	...	...	...	...	...	...
Ethiopia - Éthiopie	9	•	•	...	•	•	•	•	•	•	•	...	...	...	...	...	...	...
Gabon	6	•	•	...	•	•	•	•	•	•	•	...	...	...	...	...	...	...
Gambia - Gambie	4	•	•	...	...	•	•	•	...	•	...	...	...	...	...	...	...	...
Ghana	17	•	•	•	•	•	•	•	•	•	•	•	•	•	•	...	...	...
Guinea - Guinée	18	•	•	•	•	•	•	•	•	•	•	•	•	•	•	...	...	...
Guinea-Bissau - Guinée-Bissau	10	•	•	•	•	•	•	•	•	•	•	...	...	...	...	...	...	...
Kenya	18	•	•	•	•	•	•	•	•	•	•	•	•	•	•	...	...	...
Lesotho	19	•	•	•	•	•	•	•	•	•	•	•	•	•	•	...	...	...
Liberia - Libéria	12	•	•	•	•	•	•	•	•	•	•	...	...	...	•	...	...	...
Libya - Libye	8	•	•	•	•	•	•	•	•	•	...	...	...	...	...	...	...	...
Madagascar	5	•	•	...	•	...	...	•	•	•	•	...	...	...	...	...	...	...
Malawi	14	•	•	...	•	•	•	•	•	•	•	•	...	...	•	...	...	...
Mali	13	•	•	•	•	•	•	•	•	•	•	•	...	...	•	...	...	...
Mauritania - Mauritanie	11	•	...	•	•	•	•	•	•	•	•	•	...	...	•	...	...	...
Mauritius - Maurice	27	•	•	•	•	•	•	•	•	•	•	•	•	•	•	•	•	•
Mayotte	14	•	•	•	•	•	•	•	•	•	...	•	...	...	•	...	...	...
Morocco - Maroc	12	•	...	•	•	•	•	•	•	•	•	•	...	...	•	...	...	...
Mozambique	12	•	•	•	•	•	•	•	•	•	•	•	...	...	•	...	...	...
Namibia - Namibie	14	•	•	...	•	•	•	•	•	•	•	•	•	•	•	...	...	...
Niger	12	•	•	...	•	•	•	•	•	•	•	...	...	...	•	...	...	...
Nigeria - Nigéria	7	•	•	...	•	•	•	•	...	•	...	•	...	...	•	...	...	...
Republic of South Sudan - République de Soudan du Sud	13	•	•	...	•	•	•	•	•	•	•	...	...	...	...	...	...	...
Reunion - Réunion	25	•	•	•	•	•	•	•	•	•	•	•	•	•	•	•	...	...
Rwanda	13	•	•	•	•	•	•	•	•	•	•	•	...	...	•	...	...	...
Saint Helena ex. dep. - Sainte-Hélène sans dép.	21	•	...	•	•	•	•	•	•	•	•	•	•	•	•	...	...	...
Saint Helena: Ascension - Sainte-Hélène: Ascension	6	•	...	...	•	•	•	•	•	...	...	...	...	...	...	...	...	...
Saint Helena: Tristan da Cunha - Sainte-Hélène: Tristan da Cunha	4	•	...	...	•	•	•	•	•	...	...	...	...	...	...	...	...	...
Sao Tome and Principe - Sao Tomé-et-Principe	15	•	•	•	•	•	•	•	•	•	•	•	•	•	•	...	...	...
Senegal - Sénégal	13	•	•	•	•	•	•	•	•	•	•	•	...	...	•	...	...	...
Seychelles	23	•	•	•	•	•	•	•	•	•	...	•	•	•	•	...	•	...
Sierra Leone	17	•	•	•	•	•	•	•	•	•	•	•	...	...	•	...	...	...
Somalia - Somalie	3	•	•	...	...	...	...	•	...	•	...	...	...	...	...	...	...	...
South Africa - Afrique du Sud	23	•	•	•	•	•	•	•	•	•	•	•	•	•	•	...	...	...
Sudan - Soudan	9	•	•	...	•	•	•	•	•	...	...	•	...	...	•	...	...	...
Swaziland	13	•	•	•	•	•	•	•	•	...	...	•	...	...	•	...	...	...
Togo	8	•	•	...	•	•	•	•	•	•	...	...	...	...	...	...	...	...
Tunisia - Tunisie	17	•	•	•	•	•	•	•	•	...	...	•	•	...	...	...	...	...

Table A. Demographic Yearbook 2016 synoptic table: Availability of data by country/area, table and sex, where applicable
Tableau A. Tableau synoptique de l'Annuaire démographique 2016 : Disponibilité des données par pays ou zone, tableau et le sexe, si disponible

Continent and country or area / Continent et pays ou zone	General topic and table number - Sujet général et numéro de tableau												
	Infant and maternal mortality - Mortalité infantile et mortalité liée à la maternité			General mortality - Mortalité générale					Nuptiality and divorces - Nuptialité et divortialité			
	15	16 Total	16 M/F	17	18	19 Total	19 M/F	20	21	22	23	24	25
Total number of countries or areas - Total des pays ou zones	127	110	108	127	166	152	150	73	184	134	110	116	85

AFRICA - AFRIQUE

Continent and country or area	15	16 Total	16 M/F	17	18	19 Total	19 M/F	20	21	22	23	24	25
Algeria - Algérie	•	...	...	...	•	•	•	...	•	•	...	...	...
Angola	...	...	...	...	...	...	...	...	...	...	...	...	...
Benin - Bénin	...	...	...	...	•	...	...	...	•	...	...	...	...
Botswana	•	...	...	...	•	•	•	...	•	•	•	...	...
Burkina Faso	...	...	...	...	...	...	...	...	•	...	...	...	...
Burundi	...	...	...	...	...	...	...	...	•	...	...	...	...
Cabo Verde	...	•	...	•	...	...	...	...	...	...	...	...	...
Cameroon - Cameroun	...	...	...	...	...	...	...	...	...	...	...	...	...
Central African Republic - République centrafricaine	...	...	...	...	...	...	...	...	...	...	...	...	...
Chad - Tchad	...	...	...	...	...	...	...	...	...	...	...	...	...
Comoros - Comores	...	...	...	...	...	...	...	...	...	...	...	...	...
Congo	...	...	...	...	...	•	...	...	...	...	...	...	...
Côte d'Ivoire	•	...	...	...	•	...	...	...	•	•	...	•	...
Democratic Republic of the Congo - République démocratique du Congo	...	...	...	...	...	...	...	...	...	...	...	...	...
Djibouti	...	...	...	...	...	...	...	...	•	...	...	...	...
Egypt - Égypte	•	•	•	•	•	•	•	...	•	•	•	•	•
Equatorial Guinea - Guinée équatoriale	...	...	...	...	...	...	...	...	...	...	...	...	...
Eritrea - Érythrée	...	...	...	...	...	...	...	...	...	...	...	...	...
Ethiopia - Éthiopie	...	...	...	...	...	...	...	...	...	...	...	...	...
Gabon	...	...	...	...	...	...	...	...	...	...	...	...	...
Gambia - Gambie	...	...	...	...	...	...	...	...	...	...	...	...	...
Ghana	...	...	...	...	•	•	•	...	•	...	...	...	...
Guinea - Guinée	•	...	...	...	•	•	•	...	•	...	...	...	...
Guinea-Bissau - Guinée-Bissau	...	...	...	...	...	...	...	...	•	...	...	...	...
Kenya	•	...	...	...	•	•	•	...	•	...	...	...	...
Lesotho	...	...	...	...	•	•	•	...	•	...	•	•	•
Liberia - Libéria	...	...	...	...	...	...	...	...	•	...	...	...	...
Libya - Libye	...	...	...	•	...	...	...	...	•	...	...	...	...
Madagascar	...	...	...	...	...	...	...	...	...	...	...	...	...
Malawi	...	...	...	...	•	...	...	...	•	...	...	...	...
Mali	...	...	...	...	...	...	...	•	...	...	...	...	...
Mauritania - Mauritanie	...	...	...	...	...	...	...	•	...	...	...	...	...
Mauritius - Maurice	•	•	•	•	•	•	•	...	•	•	•	•	•
Mayotte	...	...	...	•	•	...	...	...	•	...	...	•	...
Morocco - Maroc	...	...	...	•	...	•	...	...	...	...	...	...	...
Mozambique	...	...	...	...	...	•	...	...	...	...	...	...	...
Namibia - Namibie	...	...	...	...	...	•	...	...	...	...	...	...	...
Niger	...	...	...	...	...	...	...	...	...	...	...	•	...
Nigeria - Nigéria	...	...	...	...	...	...	...	...	...	...	...	...	...
Republic of South Sudan - République de Soudan du Sud	...	...	...	...	•	...	...	•	•	...	...	...	...
Reunion - Réunion	...	•	•	•	•	•	•	...	•	•	...	...	...
Rwanda	...	...	...	...	...	...	...	...	•	...	...	...	...
Saint Helena ex. dep. - Sainte-Hélène sans dép.	•	•	•	...	•	•	•	...	•	•	•	•	...
Saint Helena: Ascension - Sainte-Hélène: Ascension	...	...	...	...	...	...	...	...	...	...	...	...	...
Saint Helena: Tristan da Cunha - Sainte-Hélène: Tristan da Cunha	...	...	...	...	...	...	...	...	...	...	...	...	...
Sao Tome and Principe - Sao Tomé-et-Principe	...	...	...	...	•	•	•	...	•	...	...	...	...
Senegal - Sénégal	...	...	...	...	•	...	...	...	...	...	...	...	...
Seychelles	•	...	...	•	•	•	•	...	•	•	•	•	•
Sierra Leone	•	...	...	•	•	•	•	...	...	...	...	...	...
Somalia - Somalie	...	...	...	...	...	...	...	...	...	...	...	...	...
South Africa - Afrique du Sud	•	...	...	•	•	•	•	•	•	•	•	•	•
Sudan - Soudan	...	...	...	...	•	...	...	...	•	...	...	•	...
Swaziland	...	...	...	...	...	...	...	•	...	...	...	...	...
Togo	...	...	...	...	...	...	...	...	...	...	...	...	...
Tunisia - Tunisie	...	...	...	•	...	...	...	...	•	...	...	•	...

Table A. Demographic Yearbook 2016 synoptic table: Availability of data by country/area, table and sex, where applicable
Tableau A. Tableau synoptique de l'Annuaire démographique 2016 : Disponibilité des données par pays ou zone, tableau et le sexe, si disponible (continued - suite)

Continent and country or area / Continent et pays ou zone	Table totals	Summary - Apercu 3 Total	3 M/F	4	5	Population 6 Total¹	6 M/F	7 Total	7 M/F	8 Total	8 M/F	Fertility - Natalité 9	10 Total	10 M/F	11	Foetal mortality - Mortalité foetale 12	13	14
AFRICA - AFRIQUE																		
Uganda - Ouganda	10	•	•	•	•	•	•	•			...	...	...	...	...	...		...
United Republic of Tanzania - République Unie de Tanzanie	12	•	•	•	•	•	•	•	•	•	•	•	...	...	...	...	...	...
Western Sahara - Sahara occidental	3	•	•	...	...	...	...	...	...	•	•	•	...	...	...	...	...	...
Zambia - Zambie	13	•	•	...	•	•	•	•	•	•	•	...	...	•	...	•	...	...
Zimbabwe	11	•	•	...	•	•	•	•	•	•	•	...	...	...	...	...	...	...
AMERICA, NORTH - AMÉRIQUE DU NORD																		
Anguilla	16	•	•	•	•	•	...	...	•	...	•	...	•	...	...	...	...	...
Antigua and Barbuda - Antigua-et-Barbuda	11	•	...	•	•	•	•	...	...	•	...	•	...	...	...	...	...	...
Aruba	25	•	•	•	•	•	•	•	•	•	•	•	•	•	•	•	•	...
Bahamas	25	•	•	•	•	•	•	•	...	•	•	•	•	•	•	•	•	...
Barbados - Barbade	20	•	•	•	•	•	•	•	...	•	•	•	•	•	•	•	•	...
Belize	21	•	•	•	•	•	•	•	...	•	•	•	•	•	•	•	•	...
Bermuda - Bermudes	28	•	•	•	•	•	•	•	•	•	•	•	•	•	...	•	•	...
British Virgin Islands - Îles Vierges britanniques	13	•	•	•	•	•	•	...	...	•	•	•	...	•	...	•	...	...
Canada	22	•	•	•	•	•	•	•	•	•	•	•	•	•	•	•	•	•
Cayman Islands - Îles Caïmanes	19	•	•	•	•	•	•	•	...	•	•	•	...	•	•	•	...	...
Costa Rica	29	•	•	•	•	•	•	•	•	•	•	•	•	•	•	•	•	•
Cuba	29	•	•	•	•	•	•	•	•	•	...	•	•	•	•	•	•	•
Curaçao	23	•	•	•	•	•	•	...	...	•	•	•	•	•	...	•	...	...
Dominica - Dominique	13	•	•	•	•	•	•	...	...	•	...	•	...	•	...	•	...	...
Dominican Republic - République dominicaine	29	•	•	•	•	•	•	•	•	•	•	•	•	•	•	•	•	...
El Salvador	26	•	•	•	•	•	•	•	•	•	•	•	•	•	•	•	•	...
Greenland - Groenland	21	•	•	•	•	•	•	•	•	•	•	•	•	•	•	...	...	...
Grenada - Grenade	14	•	•	•	•	•	•	•	•	•	...	...	•	•	...	...	...	...
Guadeloupe	17	•	•	•	•	•	•	•	•	•	...	...	•	•	...	...	...	...
Guatemala	25	•	•	•	•	•	•	•	•	•	•	•	•	•	...	•	...	...
Haiti - Haïti	9	•	...	•	•	•	•	•	•	...	...	•	...	...	...	...	...	...
Honduras	13	•	•	•	•	•	•	•	•	•	...	•	...	•	...	...	...	...
Jamaica - Jamaïque	22	•	•	•	•	•	•	•	•	•	•	•	•	•	•	•	...	...
Martinique	25	•	•	•	•	•	•	•	•	•	•	•	•	•	•	•	•	...
Mexico - Mexique	30	•	•	•	•	•	•	•	•	•	•	•	•	•	•	•	•	•
Montserrat	21	•	•	•	•	•	•	•	...	•	•	•	•	•	...	•	•	•
Nicaragua	16	•	•	...	•	•	•	•	•	...	•	...	•	•	...	...	...	...
Panama	28	•	•	•	•	•	•	•	•	•	•	•	•	•	•	•	...	...
Puerto Rico - Porto Rico	27	•	•	•	•	•	•	•	•	•	•	•	•	•	•	•	...	...
Saint Kitts and Nevis - Saint-Kitts-et-Nevis	10	•	•	•	•	•	•	...	...	...	•	•	...	•	...	...	...	...
Saint Lucia - Sainte-Lucie	16	•	•	•	•	•	•	•	•	•	•	•	...	•	...	...	...	...
Saint Pierre and Miquelon - Saint Pierre-et-Miquelon	4	•	...	...	•	...	...	...	...	•	...	...	...	...	...	...	...	...
Saint Vincent and the Grenadines - Saint-Vincent-et-les Grenadines	23	•	•	•	•	•	•	•	•	•	•	9	•	•	...	•	...	...
Saint-Barthélemy	1	•	...	...	...	...	...	...	...	...	...	...	...	...	...	...	...	...
Saint-Martin (French part) - Saint-Martin (partie française)	1	•	...	...	...	...	...	...	...	...	...	...	...	...	...	...	...	...
Sint Maarten (Dutch part) - Saint-Martin (partie néerlandaise)	13	•	•	•	•	•	•	•	•	•	•	•	•	•	...	...	...	...
Trinidad and Tobago - Trinité-et-Tobago	23	•	...	•	•	•	•	•	•	•	•	•	•	•	...	...	...	...
Turks and Caicos Islands - Îles Turques et Caïques	20	•	•	•	•	•	•	•	•	•	•	•	•	...	•	•	•	•
United States of America - États-Unis d'Amérique	26	•	•	•	•	•	•	•	•	•	•	•	...	•	•	•	•	...
United States Virgin Islands - Îles Vierges américaines	16	•	•	•	•	•	•	•	•	•	•	•	•	...	•	...	...	...

Table A. Demographic Yearbook 2016 synoptic table: Availability of data by country/area, table and sex, where applicable
Tableau A. Tableau synoptique de l'Annuaire démographique 2016 : Disponibilité des données par pays ou zone, tableau et le sexe, si disponible (continued - suite)

Continent and country or area / Continent et pays ou zone	General topic and table number - Sujet général et numéro de tableau												
	Infant and maternal mortality - Mortalité infantile et mortalité liée à la maternité				General mortality - Mortalité générale					Nuptiality and divorces - Nuptialité et divortialité		
	15	16 Total	16 M/F	17	18	19 Total	19 M/F	20	21	22	23	24	25
AFRICA - AFRIQUE													
Uganda - Ouganda	...	...	...	...	...	...	...	...	•	...	...	...	...
United Republic of Tanzania - République Unie de Tanzanie	...	...	...	...	•	...	...	...	...	...	...	...	...
Western Sahara - Sahara occidental	...	...	...	...	...	...	...	...	...	...	...	...	...
Zambia - Zambie	...	...	...	...	...	•	•	...	...	...	...	...	...
Zimbabwe	...	...	...	...	...	...	•	•	...	...	...	...	...
AMERICA, NORTH - AMÉRIQUE DU NORD													
Anguilla	•	...	...	•	•	•	•	...	•	•	•	...	...
Antigua and Barbuda - Antigua-et-Barbuda	...	...	...	•	•	•	•	...	•	•	•	...	...
Aruba	•	•	•	•	•	•	•	...	•	•	•	•	•
Bahamas	•	•	•	•	•	•	•	...	•	•	•	...	...
Barbados - Barbade	...	•	•	•	•	•	•	...	•	•	•	...	...
Belize	•	•	•	•	•	•	•	...	•	•	•	...	...
Bermuda - Bermudes	•	•	•	•	•	•	•	...	•	•	•	•	•
British Virgin Islands - Îles Vierges britanniques	...	...	...	•	•	•	•	...	•	•	•	...	...
Canada	•	•	•	•	•	•	•	•	•	•	•	•	•
Cayman Islands - Îles Caïmanes	...	•	•	•	•	•	•	...	•	•	•	...	...
Costa Rica	•	•	•	•	•	•	•	•	•	•	•	•	•
Cuba	•	•	•	•	•	•	•	•	•	•	•	•	•
Curaçao	•	•	•	...	•	•	•	•	•	•	•	•	•
Dominica - Dominique	...	...	•	•	•	•	•	...	•	•	•	•	•
Dominican Republic - République dominicaine	•	•	•	•	•	•	•	...	•	•	•	•	•
El Salvador	•	•	•	•	•	•	•	...	•	•	•	•	•
Greenland - Groenland	•	...	...	...	•	•	•	...	...	...	...	...	...
Grenada - Grenade	...	...	...	•	•	...	...	...	...	...	...	...	...
Guadeloupe	...	...	...	•	•	...	...	...	•	•	...	...	...
Guatemala	•	•	•	•	•	•	•	...	•	•	•	•	•
Haiti - Haïti	...	...	...	...	...	...	...	...	...	...	...	...	...
Honduras	...	...	...	•	...	...	...	...	...	...	...	...	...
Jamaica - Jamaïque	...	•	•	•	•	•	•	...	•	•	•	•	•
Martinique	...	•	•	•	•	•	•	...	•	•	•	•	•
Mexico - Mexique	•	•	•	•	•	•	•	...	•	•	•	•	•
Montserrat	•	•	•	•	•	•	•	...	...	•	•	...	...
Nicaragua	...	•	•	•	•	...	...	...	•	•	•	•	•
Panama	•	•	•	•	•	•	•	...	•	•	•	•	•
Puerto Rico - Porto Rico	•	•	•	•	•	•	•	•	•	•	•	...	...
Saint Kitts and Nevis - Saint-Kitts-et-Nevis	...	...	...	•	•	...	...	...	•	•	...	...	...
Saint Lucia - Sainte-Lucie	...	...	...	•	...	...	...	...	...	...	...	•	...
Saint Pierre and Miquelon - Saint Pierre-et-Miquelon	...	...	...	•	...	...	...	...	...	...	...	...	...
Saint Vincent and the Grenadines - Saint-Vincent-et-les Grenadines	•	•	•	•	•	•	•	...	•	•	•	•	...
Saint-Barthélemy	...	...	...	...	...	...	...	...	...	...	...	...	...
Saint-Martin (French part) - Saint-Martin (partie française)	...	...	...	...	...	...	...	...	...	...	...	...	...
Sint Maarten (Dutch part) - Saint-Martin (partie néerlandaise)	...	...	...	...	•	...	...	...	•	...	...	•	...
Trinidad and Tobago - Trinité-et-Tobago	•	•	•	•	•	•	•	...	•	•	...	...	•
Turks and Caicos Islands - Îles Turques et Caïques	•	...	...	•	•	...	...	...	•	•	•	...	...
United States of America - États-Unis d'Amérique	•	•	•	•	•	•	•	•	•	•	•	...	...
United States Virgin Islands - Îles Vierges américaines	•	...	...	•	•	•	...	...	...	...	...	...	...

Table A. Demographic Yearbook 2016 synoptic table: Availability of data by country/area, table and sex, where applicable
Tableau A. Tableau synoptique de l'Annuaire démographique 2016 : Disponibilité des données par pays ou zone, tableau et le sexe, si disponible (continued - suite)

General topic and table number - Sujet général et numéro de tableau

Continent and country or area / Continent et pays ou zone	Table totals	Summary - Apercu 3 Total	M/F	4	5	Population 6 Total[1]	M/F	7 Total	M/F	8 Total	M/F	9	Fertility - Natalité 10 Total	M/F	11	Foetal mortality - Mortalité foetale 12	13	14
AMERICA, SOUTH - AMÉRIQUE DU SUD																		
Argentina - Argentine	21	•	•	•	•	•	•	•	•	•	•	•	...	...		•	...	...
Bolivia (Plurinational State of) - Bolivie (État plurinational de)	18	•	•	•	•	•	•	•	•	•	•	•	...	...	•	...	...	...
Brazil - Brésil	26	•	•	•	•	•	•	•	•	•	•	•	...	...	•	•	...	...
Chile - Chili	27	•	•	•	•	•	•	•	•	...	•	•	•	...	•	•	•	...
Colombia - Colombie	25	•	•	•	•	•	•	•	•	•	•	•	•	...	•	•	...	...
Ecuador - Équateur	29	•	•	•	•	•	•	•	•	...	•	•	•	•	•	•	•	•
Falkland Islands (Malvinas) - Îles Falkland (Malvinas)	8	•	•	...	...	•	•	•	•	•	•	•	...	...	...	...	...	...
French Guiana - Guyane française	21	•	•	•	•	•	•	•	•	•	•	•	...	...	•	...	...	...
Guyana	10	•	•	...	•	•	•	•	•	•	•	•	...	...	...	...	...	...
Paraguay	22	•	•	•	•	•	•	•	•	...	•	•	...	...	•	•	•	...
Peru - Pérou	24	•	•	•	•	•	•	•	•	•	•	•	•	...	•	•	...	...
Suriname	22	•	•	•	•	•	•	•	•	•	•	•	•	...	•	•	...	...
Uruguay	25	•	•	•	•	•	•	•	•	•	•	•	•	•	•	•	...	...
Venezuela (Bolivarian Republic of) - Venezuela (République bolivarienne du)	26	•	•	•	•	•	•	•	•	...	•	•	•	•	•	•	...	...
ASIA - ASIE																		
Afghanistan	10	•	•	...	•	•	•	•	•	•	•	...	...	...	...	...	...	...
Armenia - Arménie	29	•	•	•	•	•	•	•	•	•	•	•	•	...	•	•	...	•
Azerbaijan - Azerbaïdjan	30	•	•	•	•	•	•	•	•	•	•	•	•	•	•	•	•	•
Bahrain - Bahreïn	28	•	•	•	•	•	•	•	•	•	•	•	•	•	•	•	•	...
Bangladesh	20	•	•	•	•	•	•	•	•	•	•	•	•	•	•	•	•	...
Bhutan - Bhoutan	10	•	•	...	•	•	•	•	•	•	•	...	...	...	...	...	...	...
Brunei Darussalam - Brunéi Darussalam	25	•	•	•	•	•	•	•	•	•	•	•	•	...	•	•	...	...
Cambodia - Cambodge	9	•	•	...	•	•	•	•	•	•	•	...	...	...	...	...	...	...
China - Chine[2]	17	•	•	•	•	•	•	•	•	•	•	•	...	...	...	...	...	...
China, Hong Kong SAR - Chine, Hong Kong RAS	29	•	•	•	•	•	•	•	•	•	•	•	•	...	•	•	...	...
China, Macao SAR - Chine, Macao RAS	27	•	•	•	•	•	•	•	•	•	•	•	•	...	•	•	...	...
Cyprus - Chypre	25	•	•	•	•	•	•	•	•	...	•	•	•	•	•	•	...	...
Democratic People's Republic of Korea - République populaire démocratique de Corée	13	•	•	...	...	•	•	•	•	•	•	•	...	...	...	...	...	...
Georgia - Géorgie	27	•	•	•	•	•	•	•	•	•	•	•	•	•	•	•	•	...
India - Inde[3]	14	•	•	•	•	•	•	•	•	•	•	•	...	...	•	•	...	...
Indonesia - Indonésie	16	•	•	•	•	•	•	•	•	...	•	•	...	...	•	•	...	...
Iran (Islamic Republic of) - Iran (République islamique d')	22	•	•	•	•	•	•	•	•	•	•	•	•	...	•	•	...	...
Iraq	14	•	•	•	•	•	•	•	•	•	•	•	...	...	•	...	...	...
Israel - Israël[4]	30	•	•	•	•	•	•	•	•	•	•	•	•	•	•	•	•	•
Japan - Japon	30	•	•	•	•	•	•	•	•	•	•	•	•	•	•	•	•	•
Jordan - Jordanie	17	•	•	•	•	•	•	•	•	•	•	•	...	...	•	•	...	...
Kazakhstan	28	•	•	•	•	•	•	•	•	•	•	•	•	...	•	•	•	...
Kuwait - Koweït	26	•	•	•	•	•	•	•	•	•	•	•	•	...	•	•	...	...
Kyrgyzstan - Kirghizstan	30	•	•	•	•	•	•	•	•	•	•	•	•	•	•	•	•	•
Lao People's Democratic Republic - République démocratique populaire lao	11	•	•	•	•	•	•	•	•	•	•	...	...	...	•	...	...	...
Lebanon - Liban	13	•	•	•	...	•	•	•	•	•	•	•	...	...	•	...	...	...
Malaysia - Malaisie	20	•	•	•	•	•	•	•	•	•	•	•	...	•	•	•	•	...
Maldives	23	•	•	•	•	•	•	•	•	...	•	•	•	•	•	•	•	...
Mongolia - Mongolie	27	•	•	•	•	•	•	•	•	•	•	•	•	•	•	•	•	...
Myanmar	21	•	•	•	•	•	•	•	•	•	•	•	•	•	•	...	...	...
Nepal - Népal	10	•	•	...	•	•	•	•	•	•	•	•	...	...	...	...	...	...
Oman	25	•	•	•	•	•	•	•	•	•	•	•	•	...	•	•	...	...
Pakistan[5]	14	•	•	...	•	•	•	•	•	•	•	•	...	...	•	...	...	...
Philippines	22	•	...	•	•	•	•	•	•	•	•	•	...	...	•	•	...	...
Qatar	27	•	•	•	•	•	•	•	•	•	•	•	•	...	•	•	...	...
Republic of Korea - République de Corée	28	•	•	•	•	•	•	•	•	•	•	•	•	•	•	•	•	...
Saudi Arabia - Arabie saoudite	19	•	•	•	•	•	•	•	•	•	•	•	•	...	•	•	...	...
Singapore - Singapour	29	•	•	•	•	•	•	•	•	•	•	•	...	•	•	•	•	•

34

Table A. Demographic Yearbook 2016 synoptic table: Availability of data by country/area, table and sex, where applicable
Tableau A. Tableau synoptique de l'Annuaire démographique 2016 : Disponibilité des données par pays ou zone, tableau et le sexe, si disponible (continued - suite)

Continent and country or area / Continent et pays ou zone	General topic and table number - Sujet général et numéro de tableau												
	Infant and maternal mortality - Mortalité infantile et mortalité liée à la maternité			General mortality - Mortalité générale					Nuptiality and divorces - Nuptialité et divortialité			
	15	16 Total	16 M/F	17	18	19 Total	19 M/F	20	21	22	23	24	25

AMERICA, SOUTH - AMÉRIQUE DU SUD

	15	16 T	16 M/F	17	18	19 T	19 M/F	20	21	22	23	24	25
Argentina - Argentine	•	...	...	•	•	•	•	•	•	•	...	...	•
Bolivia (Plurinational State of) - Bolivie (État plurinational de)	...	•	...	...	•	•	•	•	•	•	•	•	•
Brazil - Brésil	•	•	•	•	•	•	•	•	•	•	•	•	•
Chile - Chili	•	•	•	•	•	•	•	•	•	•	•	•	•
Colombia - Colombie	•	•	•	•	•	•	•	•	...	•	•	•	•
Ecuador - Équateur	•	•	•	•	•	•	•	•	•	•	•	•	•
Falkland Islands (Malvinas) - Îles Falkland (Malvinas)	...	...	...	...	...	...	...	•	...	...	...	...	...
French Guiana - Guyane française	...	•	•	•	•	...	...	•	...	•	•	...	...
Guyana	...	...	...	•	•	...	...	•	•	•	...	...	...
Paraguay	•	•	...	•	•	•	•	•	•	•	...	...	...
Peru - Pérou	•	•	•	•	•	•	•	•	•	•	•	...	•
Suriname	•	•	•	•	•	•	•	•	•	•	...	•	•
Uruguay	•	•	•	•	•	•	•	•	•	•	...	•	•
Venezuela (Bolivarian Republic of) - Venezuela (République bolivarienne du)	•	•	•	•	•	•	•	...					

ASIA - ASIE

	15	16 T	16 M/F	17	18	19 T	19 M/F	20	21	22	23	24	25
Afghanistan	...	...	...	...	...	...	...	•	...	...	...	...	
Armenia - Arménie	•	•	•	•	•	•	•	•	•	•	•	•	•
Azerbaijan - Azerbaïdjan	•	•	•	•	•	•	•	•	•	•	•	•	•
Bahrain - Bahreïn	•	•	•	•	•	•	•	•	•	•	•	•	•
Bangladesh	•	•	•	•	•	...	•	•	•	...	...	...	
Bhutan - Bhoutan	...	...	...	...	...	...	...	•	...	...	...	...	
Brunei Darussalam - Brunéi Darussalam	•	...	...	•	•	•	•	•	•	•	•	•	
Cambodia - Cambodge	...	...	...	...	•	...	...	•	...	...	...	...	
China - Chine[2]	...	...	...	...	•	•	•	•	•	...	•	...	
China, Hong Kong SAR - Chine, Hong Kong RAS	•	•	•	•	•	•	•	•	•	•	•	...	
China, Macao SAR - Chine, Macao RAS	•	•	•	...	•	•	•	•	•	•	•	•	
Cyprus - Chypre	•	•	•	•	•	•	•	•	•	•	•	•	
Democratic People's Republic of Korea - République populaire démocratique de Corée	...	•	•	•	•	•	•	•	...	...	...	•	
Georgia - Géorgie	•	•	•	•	•	•	•	•	•	•	•	•	
India - Inde[3]	•			•	•			•	...				
Indonesia - Indonésie	...		...		•		•	•	•		•	...	
Iran (Islamic Republic of) - Iran (République islamique d')	•			•	•			•	•	•	•	...	
Iraq	•			•	...	...	•	•	•	•	...		
Israel - Israël[4]	•	•	•	•	•	•	•	•	•	•	•	•	
Japan - Japon	•	•	•	•	•	•	•	•	•	•	•	•	
Jordan - Jordanie	...			•	...	...	•	•	•	...	...		
Kazakhstan	•	•	•	•	•	•	•	•	•	•	•	•	
Kuwait - Koweït	•	•	•	•	•	•	•	•	•	•	•	•	
Kyrgyzstan - Kirghizstan	•	•	•	•	•	•	•	•	•	•	•	•	
Lao People's Democratic Republic - République démocratique populaire lao	...			...	...			•	...	...	•	...	
Lebanon - Liban	•			•	•	•	...	•	•	...	•	...	
Malaysia - Malaisie	•	•	•	•	•	•	•	•	•	•	•	•	
Maldives	•			•	•	•	•	•	•	•	•	...	
Mongolia - Mongolie	•	•	•	...	•	•	•	•	•	•	•	•	
Myanmar	•	•	•	•	•	•	•	•	•	•	•	•	
Nepal - Népal	...			...	...		...	•	•		•	...	
Oman	•			•	•	•	•	•	•	•	•	•	
Pakistan[5]	...		...	•	...		•	•	...		•	...	
Philippines	•	•	•	•	•	•	•	•	•	•	•	•	
Qatar	•			•	•	•	•	•	•	•	•	•	
Republic of Korea - République de Corée	•	•	•	•	•	•	•	•	•	•	•	•	
Saudi Arabia - Arabie saoudite	•	...	...	•	•	•	•	•	•	...	...		
Singapore - Singapour	•	•	•	•	•	•	•	•	•	•	•	•	

Table A. Demographic Yearbook 2016 synoptic table: Availability of data by country/area, table and sex, where applicable
Tableau A. Tableau synoptique de l'Annuaire démographique 2016 : Disponibilité des données par pays ou zone, tableau et le sexe, si disponible (continued - suite)

General topic and table number - Sujet général et numéro de tableau

Continent and country or area / Continent et pays ou zone	Table totals	Summary - Apercu				Population						Fertility - Natalité				Foetal mortality - Mortalité foetale		
		3 Total	3 M/F	4	5	6 Total[1]	6 M/F	7 Total	7 M/F	8 Total	8 M/F	9	10 Total	10 M/F	11	12	13	14

ASIA - ASIE

Sri Lanka	20	•	•	•	•	•	•	•	•	•	•	•	...	...	•	...	...
State of Palestine - État de Palestine	23	•	•	•	•	•	•	•	•	...	•	•	...	...	•	...	...
Syrian Arab Republic - République arabe syrienne	10	•	•	...	•	•	•	•	•	...	...	...	...	...	...	...	...
Tajikistan - Tadjikistan	26	•	•	•	•	•	•	•	•	•	•	...	...	•	•	•	•
Thailand - Thaïlande	22	•	•	•	•	•	•	•	•	•	•	•	...	...	•	•	...
Timor-Leste	12	•	•	•	•	•	•	•	•	•	•	•	...	...	...	...	...
Turkey - Turquie	27	•	•	•	•	•	•	•	•	•	•	•	•	•	•	•	•
Turkmenistan - Turkménistan	3	•	...	...	...	•	...	...	...	...	...	...	...	...	...	...	...
United Arab Emirates - Émirats arabes unis	14	•	•	•	•	•	...	•	•	...	...	...	...	...	...	...	...
Uzbekistan - Ouzbékistan	29	•	•	•	•	•	•	•	•	•	•	•	•	•	•	•	•
Viet Nam	9	•	•	•	•	•	•	...	...	...	...	...	...	...	...	...	...
Yemen - Yémen	12	•	•	•	•	•	•	...	•	...	...	...	...	...	...	...	...

EUROPE

Åland Islands - Îles d'Åland	27	•	•	•	•	•	•	•	•	•	•	•	•	•	•	•	•
Albania - Albanie	25	•	•	•	•	•	•	•	•	•	•	•	•	•	...	•	...
Andorra - Andorre	23	•	•	•	•	•	•	•	•	•	•	•	•	•	•	...	•
Austria - Autriche	28	•	•	•	•	•	•	•	•	•	•	•	•	•	•	...	•
Belarus - Bélarus	29	•	•	•	•	•	•	•	•	•	•	•	...	•	•	•	•
Belgium - Belgique	30	•	•	•	•	•	•	•	•	•	•	•	•	•	•	•	•
Bosnia and Herzegovina - Bosnie-Herzégovine	23	•	...	•	•	•	•	...	...	•	•	•	•	•	...	•	...
Bulgaria - Bulgarie	30	•	•	•	•	•	•	•	•	•	•	•	•	•	•	•	•
Croatia - Croatie	29	•	•	•	•	•	•	•	•	•	•	•	•	•	•	•	•
Czechia - Tchéquie	30	•	•	•	•	•	•	•	•	•	•	•	•	•	•	•	•
Denmark - Danemark	30	•	•	•	•	•	•	•	•	•	•	•	•	•	•	•	•
Estonia - Estonie	30	•	•	•	•	•	•	•	•	•	•	•	•	•	•	•	•
Faeroe Islands - Îles Féroé	29	•	•	•	•	•	•	•	•	•	•	•	•	•	•	•	•
Finland - Finlande	30	•	•	•	•	•	•	•	•	•	•	•	•	•	•	•	•
France	29	•	•	•	•	•	•	•	•	•	•	•	•	•	...	•	•
Germany - Allemagne	30	•	•	•	•	•	•	•	•	•	•	•	•	•	•	•	•
Gibraltar	18	•	•	•	•	•	•	•	•	•	•	•	•	•	...	•	...
Greece - Grèce	28	•	•	•	•	•	•	•	•	•	•	•	•	•	•	•	•
Guernsey - Guernesey	12	•	•	•	•	•	•	...	•	...	...	...	...	...	...	...	...
Holy See - Saint-Siège	6	•	...	•	•	...	...	...	...	...	...	...	...	...	...	...	...
Hungary - Hongrie	30	•	•	•	•	•	•	•	•	•	•	•	•	•	•	•	•
Iceland - Islande	28	•	•	•	•	•	•	•	•	•	•	•	•	•	•	•	•
Ireland - Irlande	26	•	•	•	•	•	•	•	•	•	•	•	•	•	...	•	•
Isle of Man - Île de Man	15	•	•	•	•	•	•	•	•	•	•	•	•	...	•	•	•
Italy - Italie	30	•	•	•	•	•	•	•	•	•	•	•	•	•	•	•	•
Jersey	15	•	•	•	•	•	•	•	•	•	•	•	•	•	...	•	•
Latvia - Lettonie	30	•	•	•	•	•	•	•	•	•	•	•	•	•	•	•	•
Liechtenstein	23	•	•	•	•	•	•	•	•	•	•	•	•	•	...	•	•
Lithuania - Lituanie	30	•	•	•	•	•	•	•	•	•	•	•	•	•	•	•	•
Luxembourg	28	•	•	•	•	•	•	•	•	•	•	•	•	•	•	...	•
Malta - Malte	28	•	•	•	•	•	•	•	•	•	•	•	•	•	•	...	•
Monaco	12	•	•	•	•	•	•	•	•	•	•	•	...	•	•	•	•
Montenegro - Monténégro	26	•	•	•	•	•	•	•	•	•	•	•	•	•	•	...	•
Netherlands - Pays-Bas	28	•	•	•	•	•	•	•	•	•	•	•	•	•	•	•	•
Norway - Norvège	29	•	•	•	•	•	•	•	•	•	•	•	•	•	•	•	•
Poland - Pologne	30	•	•	•	•	•	•	•	•	•	•	•	•	•	•	•	•
Portugal	30	•	•	•	•	•	•	•	•	•	•	•	•	•	•	•	•
Republic of Moldova - République de Moldova	29	•	•	•	•	•	•	•	•	•	•	•	•	•	•	...	•
Romania - Roumanie	30	•	•	•	•	•	•	•	•	•	•	•	•	•	•	•	•
Russian Federation - Fédération de Russie	30	•	•	•	•	•	•	•	•	•	•	•	•	•	•	•	•
San Marino - Saint-Marin	27	•	•	•	•	•	•	•	•	•	•	•	•	•	•	...	•
Serbia - Serbie	30	•	•	•	•	•	•	•	•	•	•	•	•	•	•	•	•
Slovakia - Slovaquie	30	•	•	•	•	•	•	•	•	•	•	•	•	•	•	•	•
Slovenia - Slovénie	30	•	•	•	•	•	•	•	•	•	•	•	•	•	•	•	•
Spain - Espagne	30	•	•	•	•	•	•	•	•	•	•	•	•	•	•	•	•

Table A. Demographic Yearbook 2016 synoptic table: Availability of data by country/area, table and sex, where applicable
Tableau A. Tableau synoptique de l'Annuaire démographique 2016 : Disponibilité des données par pays ou zone, tableau et le sexe, si disponible (continued - suite)

Continent and country or area / Continent et pays ou zone	Infant and maternal mortality - Mortalité infantile et mortalité liée à la maternité				General mortality - Mortalité générale					Nuptiality and divorces - Nuptialité et divortialité			
	15	16 Total	16 M/F	17	18	19 Total	19 M/F	20	21	22	23	24	25
ASIA - ASIE													
Sri Lanka	...	...	...	•	•	•	•	...	•	•	•	...	...
State of Palestine - État de Palestine	•	•	•	...	•	•	•	•	...	•	•	•	•
Syrian Arab Republic - République arabe syrienne	...	...	...	•	•	...	...	...	...	•	•	•	•
Tajikistan - Tadjikistan	...	...	...	•	•	•	•	•	...	•	•	•	•
Thailand - Thaïlande	•	•	•	•	•	•	•	•	...	•	•	•	•
Timor-Leste	...	...	...	•	•	...	...	...	...	•	...	...	...
Turkey - Turquie	•	•	•	•	•	•	•	•	•	•	•	•	•
Turkmenistan - Turkménistan	...	...	...	•	•	•	•	•	...	•	•	•	•
United Arab Emirates - Émirats arabes unis	...	...	...	•	•	•	•	...	...	•	•	•	•
Uzbekistan - Ouzbékistan	•	•	•	•	•	•	•	...	...	•	•	•	•
Viet Nam	...	...	...	...	...	...	...	•	...	...	...	...	...
Yemen - Yémen	...	...	...	...	•	...	...	...	...	...	...	...	...
EUROPE													
Åland Islands - Îles d'Åland	•	•	•	...	•	•	•	•	•	•	•	•	...
Albania - Albanie	•	•	•	...	•	•	•	•	•	•	•	•	...
Andorra - Andorre	•	•	•	...	•	•	•	...	•	•	•	...	•
Austria - Autriche	•	•	•	•	•	•	•	•	•	•	•	•	•
Belarus - Bélarus	•	•	•	•	•	•	•	•	•	•	•	•	•
Belgium - Belgique	•	•	•	•	•	•	•	•	•	•	•	•	•
Bosnia and Herzegovina - Bosnie-Herzégovine	•	•	•	•	•	•	•	...	•	•	•	•	•
Bulgaria - Bulgarie	•	•	•	•	•	•	•	•	•	•	•	•	•
Croatia - Croatie	•	•	•	•	•	•	•	•	•	•	•	•	•
Czechia - Tchéquie	•	•	•	•	•	•	•	•	•	•	•	•	•
Denmark - Danemark	•	•	•	•	•	•	•	•	•	•	•	•	•
Estonia - Estonie	•	•	•	•	•	•	•	•	•	•	•	•	•
Faeroe Islands - Îles Féroé	•	•	•	...	•	•	•	•	•	•	•	•	•
Finland - Finlande	•	•	•	•	•	•	•	•	•	•	•	•	•
France	•	•	•	•	•	•	•	•	•	•	•	•	•
Germany - Allemagne	•	...	...	...	•	•	•	•	•	•	•	•	...
Gibraltar	•	•	•	•	•	•	•	•	•	•	•	•	•
Greece - Grèce	•	•	•	•	•	•	•	•	•	•	•	•	•
Guernsey - Guernesey	...	...	...	...	•	•	•	•	•	...	...	...	...
Holy See - Saint-Siège	...	...	...	...	...	...	...	...	...	...	...	...	...
Hungary - Hongrie	•	•	•	•	•	•	•	•	•	•	•	•	•
Iceland - Islande	•	•	•	•	•	•	•	•	...	•	...	•	•
Ireland - Irlande	•	•	•	•	•	•	•	•	•	•	•	•	...
Isle of Man - Île de Man	•	•	•	•	•	•	•	•	•	...	•	•	•
Italy - Italie	•	•	•	•	•	•	•	•	•	•	•	•	•
Jersey	...	...	...	...	•	•	•	•	•	•	...	•	•
Latvia - Lettonie	•	•	•	•	•	•	•	•	•	•	•	•	•
Liechtenstein	•	•	•	...	•	•	•	•	•	•	•	•	•
Lithuania - Lituanie	•	•	•	•	•	•	•	•	•	•	•	•	•
Luxembourg	•	•	•	•	•	•	•	•	•	•	•	•	•
Malta - Malte	•	•	•	•	•	•	•	•	•	•	•	•	•
Monaco	...	...	...	•	•	•	•	...	•	...	...	...	...
Montenegro - Monténégro	•	•	•	•	•	•	•	•	•	•	•	•	•
Netherlands - Pays-Bas	•	•	•	•	•	•	•	•	•	•	•	•	•
Norway - Norvège	•	•	•	•	•	•	•	•	•	•	•	•	•
Poland - Pologne	•	•	•	•	•	•	•	•	•	•	•	•	•
Portugal	•	•	•	•	•	•	•	•	•	•	•	•	•
Republic of Moldova - République de Moldova	•	•	•	•	•	•	•	•	•	•	•	•	•
Romania - Roumanie	•	•	•	•	•	•	•	•	•	•	•	•	•
Russian Federation - Fédération de Russie	•	•	•	•	•	•	•	•	•	•	•	•	•
San Marino - Saint-Marin	•	•	•	•	•	•	•	•	•	•	•	•	•
Serbia - Serbie	•	•	•	•	•	•	•	•	•	•	•	•	•
Slovakia - Slovaquie	•	•	•	•	•	•	•	•	•	•	•	•	•
Slovenia - Slovénie	•	•	•	•	•	•	•	•	•	•	•	•	•
Spain - Espagne	•	•	•	•	•	•	•	•	•	•	•	•	•

General topic and table number - Sujet général et numéro de tableau

Continent and country or area / Continent et pays ou zone	Table totals	Summary - Apercu 3 Total	3 M/F	4	5	Population 6 Total¹	6 M/F	7 Total	7 M/F	8 Total	8 M/F	Fertility - Natalité 9	10 Total	10 M/F	11	Foetal mortality - Mortalité foetale 12	13	14

EUROPE

Svalbard and Jan Mayen Islands - Îles Svalbard et Jan Mayen	3	•	•	...	•	...	•	...	•	...	•	...	•	...	•	...	...	...
Sweden - Suède	30	•	•	•	•	•	•	•	•	•	•	•	•	•	•	•	•	•
Switzerland - Suisse	30	•	•	•	•	•	•	•	•	•	•	•	•	•	•	•	•	•
TFYR of Macedonia - L'ex-R. y. de Macédoine	29	•	•	•	•	•	•	•	•	•	•	•	•	•	•	•	•	...
Ukraine	29	•	•	•	•	•	•	•	•	•	•	•	...	•	•	•	•	•
United Kingdom of Great Britain and Northern Ireland - Royaume-Uni de Grande-Bretagne et d'Irlande du Nord	29	•	•	•	•	•	•	•	•	•	•	•	•	•	•	•	•	•

OCEANIA - OCÉANIE

American Samoa - Samoas américaines	18	•	•	•	•	•	•	•	...	•	•	...	•	...	...	...
Australia - Australie	28	•	•	•	•	•	•	•	•	•	•	•	•	•	•	•
Cook Islands - Îles Cook	17	•	•	•	•	•	•	•	...	•	•	...	...	...	...
Fiji - Fidji	18	•	•	•	•	•	•	•	•	•	•	...	•	...	...	...
French Polynesia - Polynésie française	17	•	•	•	•	•	•	•	•	•	•	...	•	...	...	...
Guam	23	•	•	•	•	•	•	•	•	•	•	•	•	•	•	•
Kiribati	11	•	•	...	•	•	•	•	•	...	...	•	...	...	...
Marshall Islands - Îles Marshall	9	•	•	...	•	•	•	•	•	...	...	•	...	...	...
Micronesia (Federated States of) - Micronésie (États fédérés de)	9	•	•	...	•	•	•	•	•	...	•	...	...	...
Nauru	14	•	•	•	•	•	•	•	•	...	•	•	•	...	...
New Caledonia - Nouvelle-Calédonie	22	•	•	•	•	•	•	•	•	•	•	•	...	...	...
New Zealand - Nouvelle-Zélande	29	•	...	•	•	•	•	•	•	•	•	•	•	•	•	•
Niue - Nioué	14	•	•	...	•	•	•	•	•	•	...	•	...	...	...
Norfolk Island - Île Norfolk	11	•	•	•	...	•	•	•	...	•	...	•	...	...	...
Northern Mariana Islands - Îles Mariannes septentrionales	15	•	•	•	•	•	•	•	•	•	...	...	...
Palau - Palaos	14	•	•	•	•	•	•	•	•	...	•	•	•	...	...
Papua New Guinea - Papouasie-Nouvelle-Guinée	9	•	•	...	•	•	...	•	...	•	...	...	...
Pitcairn	12	•	•	•	•	•	•	•	•	...	•	...	...	...
Samoa	19	•	•	•	•	•	•	•	•	•	...	•	•	...	...
Solomon Islands - Îles Salomon	9	•	•	...	•	•	•	•	•	...	•	...	...	...
Tokelau - Tokélaou	8	•	•	...	•	•	•	...	•	•	...	...	...
Tonga	10	•	•	...	•	•	•	•	•	...	•	...	...	...
Tuvalu	8	•	...	...	•	•	•	...	•	...	...	...	...
Vanuatu	9	•	•	...	•	•	•	•	•	...	...	...	...
Wallis and Futuna Islands - Îles Wallis et Futuna	13	•	•	...	•	•	•	•	•	...	...	•	...	...	...

38

Table A. Demographic Yearbook 2016 synoptic table: Availability of data by country/area, table and sex, where applicable
Tableau A. Tableau synoptique de l'Annuaire démographique 2016 : Disponibilité des données par pays ou zone, tableau et le sexe, si disponible (continued - suite)

Continent and country or area / Continent et pays ou zone	General topic and table number - Sujet général et numéro de tableau												
	Infant and maternal mortality - Mortalité infantile et mortalité liée à la maternité				General mortality - Mortalité générale					Nuptiality and divorces - Nuptialité et divortialité		
	15	16 Total	16 M/F	17	18	19 Total	19 M/F	20	21	22	23	24	25
EUROPE													
Svalbard and Jan Mayen Islands - Îles Svalbard et Jan Mayen	...	...	...	...	...	...	...	...	...	...	...	...	...
Sweden - Suède	•	•	•	•	•	•	•	•	•	•	•	•	•
Switzerland - Suisse	•	•	•	•	•	•	•	•	•	•	•	•	•
TFYR of Macedonia - L'ex-R. y. de Macédoine	•	•	•	•	•	•	•	•	•	•	•	•	...
Ukraine	•	...	•	•	•	•	•	•	•	•	•	•	...
United Kingdom of Great Britain and Northern Ireland - Royaume-Uni de Grande-Bretagne et d'Irlande du Nord	•	•	•	...	...	...	...	...	...	...	•	•	...
OCEANIA - OCÉANIE													
American Samoa - Samoas américaines	•	...	...	...	...	...	...	...	•	...	...	•	...
Australia - Australie	•	•	•	...	...	...	...	...	•	...	•	•	•
Cook Islands - Îles Cook	•	...	...	...	...	...	...	•	...	...	...	...	...
Fiji - Fidji	...	...	...	...	•	...	...	•	...	...	...	...	...
French Polynesia - Polynésie française	•	•	...	...	•	...	...	•	...	...	...	•	...
Guam	•	•	...	...	•	...	•	...	...	...	...	...	...
Kiribati	...	...	...	...	•	...	•	...	...	...	...	...	...
Marshall Islands - Îles Marshall	...	...	...	...	•	...	...	...	...	...	...	...	...
Micronesia (Federated States of) - Micronésie (États fédérés de)	...	...	...	...	...	...	...	•	...	...	...	...	...
Nauru	...	...	...	...	...	...	...	...	•	...	...	...	...
New Caledonia - Nouvelle-Calédonie	•	•	•	...	•	...	...	•	...	•	...	...	...
New Zealand - Nouvelle-Zélande	•	•	•	•	•	...	•	•	...	•	•	•	•
Niue - Nioué	...	...	...	...	•	...	...	...	...	•	...	...	...
Norfolk Island - Île Norfolk	...	...	...	...	•	...	...	...	...	...	...	...	...
Northern Mariana Islands - Îles Mariannes septentrionales	•	...	...	...	•	...	...	•	...	...	...	...	•
Palau - Palaos	•	...	...	...	•	...	...	•	...	...	...	...	...
Papua New Guinea - Papouasie-Nouvelle-Guinée	...	...	...	...	...	...	...	...	...	...	...	...	...
Pitcairn	...	...	...	...	...	...	...	...	...	...	...	...	•
Samoa	...	...	...	...	...	...	...	•	...	...	...	...	...
Solomon Islands - Îles Salomon	...	...	...	...	...	...	...	•	...	...	...	...	...
Tokelau - Tokélaou	...	...	...	...	...	...	...	...	...	...	...	...	...
Tonga	...	...	...	...	...	...	...	•	...	...	...	...	...
Tuvalu	...	...	...	...	...	...	...	•	...	...	...	...	...
Vanuatu	...	...	...	...	...	...	...	•	...	...	...	...	...
Wallis and Futuna Islands - Îles Wallis et Futuna	...	...	...	...	•	...	•	...	...	...	•	...	...

FOOTNOTES - NOTES

* Data presented in the table. - Les données présentées dans le tableau.

... Data not available. - Données non disponibles.

1 Including countries with data on total population by sex but without data on urban population. - Y compris les pays avec des données sur la population totale selon le sexe mais pas sur la population urbaine.

2 For statistical purposes, the data for China do not include those for the Hong Kong Special Administrative Region (Hong Kong SAR), Macao special Administrative Region (Macao SAR) and Taiwan province of China. - Pour la présentation des statistiques, les données pour Chine ne comprennent pas la Région Administrative Spéciale de Hong Kong (Hong Kong RAS), la Région Administrative Spéciale de Macao (Macao RAS) et Taïwan province de Chine.

3 Including data for the Indian-held part of Jammu and Kashmir, the final status of which has not yet been determined. - Y compris les données pour la partie du Jammu et du Cachemire occupée par l'Inde dont le statut définitif n'a pas encore été déterminé.

4 Including data for East Jerusalem and Israeli residents in certain other territories under occupation by Israeli military forces since June 1967. - Y compris les données pour Jérusalem-Est et les résidents israéliens dans certains autres territoires occupés depuis 1967 par les forces armées israéliennes.

5 Excluding data for the Pakistan-held part of Jammu and Kashmir, the final status of which has not yet been determined. - Non compris les données concernant la partie du Jammu et Cachemire occupée par le Pakistan dont le statut définitif n'a pas été déterminé.

Table 1 – Demographic Yearbook 2016

Table 1 presents for the world and major areas and regions estimates of the order of magnitude of population size, rates of population increase, crude birth and death rates, land area as well as population density.

Description of variables: Estimates of world population by major areas and by regions are presented for 1960, 1970, 1980, 1990, 2000, 2010 and 2016. Average annual percentage rates of population growth, crude birth and crude death rates are shown for the period from 2015 to 2020. Land area in square kilometers and population density estimates relate to 2016.

All population estimates and rates presented in this table were prepared by the Population Division of the United Nations Department of Economic and Social Affairs, and have been published in the *2017 Revision of World Population Prospects*[1].

The scheme of regionalization used for these estimates is described below. Although some continental totals are given, this table presents six major areas that are so drawn as to obtain greater homogeneity in sizes of population, types of demographic circumstances and accuracy of demographic statistics. Five of the major areas are subdivided into a total of 20 regions, which are arranged within the major areas; these regions together with Northern America, which is not subdivided, make a total of 21 regions.

The major areas of Northern America and Latin America and the Caribbean are distinguished, rather than the conventional continents of North America and South America, because population trends in the middle American mainland and the Caribbean region more closely resemble those of South America than those of America north of Mexico. Data for the traditional continents of North and South America can be obtained by adding Central America and Caribbean region to Northern America and deducting from Latin America. Latin America, as defined here, has somewhat wider limits than it would be if defined only to include the Spanish-speaking, French-speaking and Portuguese-speaking countries.

The average annual percentage rates of population growth are calculated by the Population Division of the United Nations using an exponential rate of increase.

Crude birth and crude death rates are expressed in terms of the average annual number of births and deaths, respectively, per 1 000 mid-year population. These rates are estimated.

The land areas of regions are estimated by the Population Division of the United Nations.

Computation: Density, calculated by the Statistics Division of the United Nations, is the number of persons in the total population of 2016 per square kilometer of the respective land area.

Reliability of data: With the exception of land area, all data are set in *italic* type to indicate their conjectural quality.

Limitations: The estimated orders of magnitude of population and land area are subject to all the basic limitations set forth in connection with table 3, and to the same qualifications set forth for population and surface area statistics in sections 3 and 2.4 of the Technical Notes, respectively.

Likewise, rates of population increase and population density are affected by the limitations of the original figures. However, it may be noted that, in compiling data for regional and major areas totals, errors in the components may tend to compensate each other and the resulting aggregates may be more reliable than the quality of the individual components would imply.

Because of their estimated character, many of the birth and death rates shown should also be considered only as orders of magnitude, and not as measures of the true level of fertility or mortality.

In interpreting the population densities, one should consider that some of the regions include large segments of land that are uninhabitable or barely habitable, and density values calculated as described make no allowance for this, nor for differences in patterns of land settlement.

Composition of major areas and regions

AFRICA

Eastern Africa
Burundi
Comoros
Djibouti
Eritrea
Ethiopia
Kenya
Madagascar
Malawi
Mauritius
Mayotte
Mozambique
Réunion
Rwanda
Seychelles
Somalia
South Sudan
Uganda
United Republic of Tanzania
Zambia
Zimbabwe

Middle Africa
Angola
Cameroon
Central African Republic
Chad
Congo
Democratic Republic of the
  Congo
Equatorial Guinea
Gabon
Sao Tome and Principe

Northern Africa
Algeria
Egypt
Libyan Arab Jamahiriya
Morocco
Sudan
Tunisia
Western Sahara

Southern Africa
Botswana
Lesotho
Namibia
South Africa
Swaziland

Western Africa
Benin
Burkina Faso
Cabo Verde
Côte d'Ivoire
Gambia
Ghana
Guinea
Guinea-Bissau
Liberia
Mali
Mauritania
Niger
Nigeria
Saint Helena
Senegal
Sierra Leone
Togo

ASIA

Eastern Asia
China
China, Hong Kong SAR
China, Macao SAR
Democratic People's
  Republic of Korea
Japan
Mongolia
Republic of Korea

South-Central Asia
Afghanistan
Bangladesh
Bhutan
India
Iran (Islamic Republic of)
Kazakhstan
Kyrgyzstan
Maldives
Nepal
Pakistan
Sri Lanka
Tajikistan
Turkmenistan
Uzbekistan

South-Eastern Asia
Brunei Darussalam
Cambodia
Indonesia
Lao People's Democratic
  Republic
Malaysia
Myanmar
Philippines
Singapore
Thailand
Timor Leste
Viet Nam

Western Asia
Armenia
Azerbaijan
Bahrain
Cyprus
Georgia
Iraq
Israel
Jordan
Kuwait
Lebanon
Oman
Qatar
Saudi Arabia
State of Palestine
Syrian Arab Republic
Turkey
United Arab Emirates
Yemen

EUROPE

Eastern Europe
Belarus
Bulgaria
Czech Republic
Hungary
Poland
Republic of Moldova
Romania
Russian Federation
Slovakia
Ukraine

Northern Europe
Åland Islands
Denmark
Estonia
Faeroe Islands
Finland
Guernsey
Iceland
Ireland
Isle of Man
Jersey
Latvia
Lithuania
Norway
Sweden
United Kingdom of Great Britain
  and Northern Ireland

Southern Europe
Albania
Andorra
Bosnia and Herzegovina

Croatia
Gibraltar
Greece
Holy See
Italy
Malta
Montenegro
Portugal
San Marino
Serbia
Slovenia
Spain
TFYR of Macedonia

Western Europe
Austria
Belgium
France
Germany
Liechtenstein
Luxembourg
Monaco
Netherlands
Switzerland

LATIN AMERICA and the CARIBBEAN

Caribbean
Anguilla
Antigua and Barbuda
Aruba
Bahamas
Barbados
Bonaire, Saba and Sint Eustatius
British Virgin Islands
Cayman Islands
Cuba
Curaçao
Dominica
Dominican Republic
Grenada
Guadaloupe

Haiti
Jamaica
Martinique
Montserrat
Puerto Rico
Saint Kitts and Nevis
Saint Lucia
Saint Vincent and the
  Grenadines
Sint Maarten (Dutch part)
Trinidad and Tobago
Turks and Caicos Islands
United States Virgin
  Islands

Central America
Belize
Costa Rica
El Salvador
Guatemala
Honduras
Mexico
Nicaragua
Panama

South America
Argentina
Bolivia (Plurinational State of)
Brazil
Chile
Colombia
Ecuador
Falkland Islands (Malvinas)
French Guiana
Guyana
Paraguay
Peru
Suriname
Uruguay
Venezuela (Bolivarian Republic of)

NORTHERN AMERICA
Bermuda
Canada
Greenland
Saint Pierre and Miquelon
United States of America

OCEANIA

Australia and New Zealand
Australia
New Zealand
Norfolk Island

Melanesia
Fiji
New Caledonia
Papua New Guinea
Solomon Islands
Vanuatu

Micronesia
Guam
Kiribati
Marshall Islands
Micronesia (Federated States of)
Nauru
Northern Mariana Islands
Palau

Polynesia
American Samoa
Cook Islands
French Polynesia
Niue
Pitcairn
Samoa
Tokelau
Tonga
Tuvalu
Wallis and Futuna Islands

---

[1] *United Nations, Department of Economic and Social Affairs, Population Division (2017). World Population Prospects: The 2017 Revision* (http://esa.un.org/unpd/wpp/)

Tableau 1 – *Annuaire démographique 2016*

Le tableau 1 présente, pour l'ensemble du monde et les grandes zones et régions, des estimations concernant l'ordre de grandeur de la population, les taux d'accroissement démographique, les taux bruts de natalité et de mortalité, la superficie des terres et la densité de peuplement.

Description des variables : des estimations de la population mondiale par grandes zones et régions sont présentées pour 1960, 1970, 1980, 1990, 2000 et 2010 ainsi que pour 2016. Les taux annuels moyens d'accroissement de la population et les taux bruts de natalité et de mortalité portent sur la période allant de 2015 à 2020. Les indications concernant la superficie des terres exprimée en kilomètres carrés et les estimations de la densité de population se rapportent à 2016.

Toutes les estimations de population et les taux de natalité, taux de mortalité et taux annuels d'accroissement de la population qui sont présentés dans le tableau 1 ont été établis par la Division de la population du Département des affaires économiques et sociales de l'Organisation des Nations Unies, et ont été publiés dans les *Perspectives de la population mondiale : La révision de 2017* [1].

Bien que l'on ait donné certains totaux pour les continents (tous les autres pouvant être calculés), on a réparti le monde en six grandes zones qui ont été découpées de manière à obtenir une plus grande homogénéité du point de vue des dimensions de population, des types de situations démographiques et de l'exactitude des statistiques démographiques. Cinq de ces six grandes zones ont été subdivisées en 20 régions. Avec l'Amérique septentrionale, qui n'est pas subdivisée, on arrive à un total de 21 régions.

Au lieu de faire la distinction classique entre l'Amérique du Nord et l'Amérique du Sud, on a choisi d'opérer une comparaison entre l'Amérique septentrionale et l'Amérique latine et Caraïbes, parce que les tendances démographiques dans la partie continentale de l'Amérique centrale et dans la région des Caraïbes se rapprochent davantage de celles de l'Amérique du Sud que de celles de l'Amérique au nord du Mexique. On obtient les données pour les continents traditionnels de l'Amérique du Nord et de l'Amérique du Sud en extrayant les données concernant l'Amérique centrale et les Caraïbes de celles relatives à l'Amérique latine et en les regroupant avec celles relatives à l'Amérique septentrionale. L'Amérique latine ainsi définie a par conséquent des limites plus larges que celles des pays ou zones de langues espagnole, portugaise et française qui constituent l'Amérique latine au sens le plus strict du terme.

Les taux annuels moyens d'accroissement de la population sont calculés par la Division de la population de l'Organisation des Nations Unies en appliquant un taux d'accroissement exponentiel.

Les taux bruts de natalité et de mortalité représentent respectivement le nombre annuel moyen de naissances et de décès par millier d'habitants en milieu d'année. Ces taux sont estimatifs.

La superficie des terres pour les régions a été estimée par la Division de la population de l'Organisation des Nations Unies.

Calculs : la densité, calculée par la Division de statistique de l'Organisation des Nations Unies, est égale au rapport entre l'effectif total de la population en 2016 et la superficie des terres exprimée en kilomètres carrés.

Fiabilité des données : á l'exception des données concernant la superficie des terres, toutes les données sont reproduites en *italique* pour en faire ressortir le caractère conjectural.

Insuffisance des données : les estimations concernant l'ordre de grandeur de la population et la superficie des terres reposent en partie sur les données du tableau 3 ; elles appellent donc toutes les réserves fondamentales formulées à propos de ce tableau, et celles qui ont été respectivement formulées aux sections 3 et 2.4 des Notes techniques en ce qui concerne les statistiques relatives à la population et à la superficie.

Les taux d'accroissement et les indices de densité de la population se ressentent eux aussi des insuffisances inhérentes aux données de base. Toutefois, il est à noter que, lorsque l'on additionne des données par territoire pour obtenir des totaux régionaux et par grandes zones, les erreurs qu'elles comportent arrivent parfois à s'équilibrer, de sorte que les agrégats obtenus peuvent être un peu plus exacts que chacun des éléments dont on est parti.

Vu leur caractère estimatif, nombre des taux de natalité et de mortalité du tableau 1 doivent être considérés uniquement comme des ordres de grandeur et ne sont pas censés mesurer exactement le niveau de la natalité ou de la mortalité.

Pour interpréter les valeurs de la densité de population, on se souviendra qu'il existe dans certaines des régions de vastes étendues de terres inhabitables ou à peine habitables et que les chiffres calculés selon la méthode indiquée ne tiennent compte ni de ce fait ni des différences de dispersion de la population selon le mode d'habitat.

Composition des grandes zones et régions

AFRIQUE

Afrique orientale
Burundi
Comores
Djibouti
Érythrée
Éthiopie
Kenya
Madagascar
Malawi
Maurice
Mayotte
Mozambique
Ouganda
République-Unie de Tanzanie
Réunion
Rwanda
Seychelles
Somalie
Soudan du Sud
Zambie
Zimbabwe

Afrique centrale
Angola
Cameroun
Congo
Gabon
Guinée équatoriale
République centrafricaine
République démocratique du Congo
Sao Tomé-et-Principe
Tchad

Afrique septentrionale
Algérie
Égypte
Jamahiriya arabe libyenne
Maroc
Sahara occidental
Soudan
Tunisie

Afrique australe
Afrique du Sud
Botswana
Lesotho
Namibie
Swaziland

Afrique occidentale
Bénin
Burkina Faso
Cabo Verde

Côte d'Ivoire
Gambie
Ghana
Guinée
Guinée-Bissau
Libéria
Mali
Mauritanie
Niger
Nigéria
Sainte-Hélène
Sénégal
Sierra Leone
Togo

AMÉRIQUE LATINE ET CARAÏBES

Caraïbes
Anguilla
Antigua-et-Barbuda
Aruba
Bahamas
Barbade
Bonaire, Saint-Eustache et Saba
Cuba
Curaçao
Dominique
Grenade
Guadeloupe
Haïti
Îles Caïmanes
Îles Turques et Caïques
Îles Vierges américaines
Îles Vierges britanniques
Jamaïque
Martinique
Montserrat
Porto Rico
République dominicaine
Saint-Kitts-et-Nevis
Sainte-Lucie
Saint-Martin
(partie néerlandaise)
Saint-Vincent-et-les
Grenadines
Trinité-et-Tobago

Amérique centrale
Belize
Costa Rica
El Salvador
Guatemala
Honduras

Mexique
Nicaragua
Panama

Amérique du Sud
Argentine
Bolivie (État plurinational de)
Brésil
Chili
Colombie
Équateur
Guyana
Guyane française
Îles Falkland (Malvinas)
Paraguay
Pérou
Suriname
Uruguay
Venezuela (République bolivarienne du)

AMÉRIQUE SEPTENTRIONALE

Bermudes
Canada
États-Unis d'Amérique
Groenland
Saint-Pierre-et-Miquelon

ASIE

Asie orientale
Chine
Chine, Région administrative spéciale de Hong Kong
Chine, Région administrative spéciale de Macao
Japon
Mongolie
République de Corée
République populaire démocratique de Corée

Asie centrale et Asie du Sud
Afghanistan
Bangladesh
Bhoutan
Inde
Iran (République Islamique d')
Kazakhstan
Kirghizistan
Maldives
Népal
Ouzbékistan

Pakistan
Sri Lanka
Tadjikistan
Turkménistan

Asie du Sud-Est
Brunéi Darussalam
Cambodge
Indonésie
Malaisie
Myanmar
Philippines
République démocratique populaire lao
Singapour
Thaïlande
Timor-Leste
Viet Nam

Asie occidentale
Arabie saoudite
Arménie
Azerbaïdjan
Bahreïn
Chypre
Émirats arabes unis
État de Palestine
Géorgie
Iraq
Israël
Jordanie
Koweït
Liban
Oman
Qatar
République arabe syrienne
Turquie
Yémen

EUROPE

Europe orientale
Bélarus
Bulgarie
Fédération de Russie
Hongrie

Pologne
République de Moldova
République tchèque
Roumanie
Slovaquie
Ukraine

Europe septentrionale
Danemark
Estonie
Finlande
Guernesey
Île de Man
Îles d'Åland
Îles Féroé
Îles Svalbard et Jan Mayen
Irlande
Islande
Jersey
Lettonie
Lituanie
Norvège
Royaume-Uni de Grande-Bretagne et d'Irlande du Nord
Suède

Europe méridionale
Albanie
Andorre
Bosnie-Herzégovine
Croatie
Espagne
Gibraltar
Grèce
Italie
L'ex-R. y. de Macédoine
Malte
Monténégro
Portugal
Saint-Marin
Saint-Siège
Serbie
Slovénie

Europe occidentale
Allemagne
Autriche
Belgique
France
Liechtenstein
Luxembourg
Monaco
Pays-Bas
Suisse

OCÉANIE

Australie et Nouvelle-Zélande
Australie
Île Norfolk
Nouvelle-Zélande

Mélanésie
Fidji
Îles Salomon
Nouvelle-Calédonie
Papouasie-Nouvelle-Guinée
Vanuatu

Micronésie
Guam
Îles Mariannes septentrionales
Îles Marshall
Kiribati
Micronésie (États fédérés de)
Nauru
Palaos

Polynésie
Îles Cook
Îles Wallis et Futuna
Nioué
Pitcairn
Polynésie française
Samoa
Samoa américaines
Tokélaou
Tonga
Tuvalu

---

[1] *Organisation des Nations Unies, Département des affaires économiques et sociales, Division de la population (2017). Perspectives de la population mondiale : La révision de 2017* (http://esa.un.org/unpd/wpp/)

1. Population, rate of increase, birth and death rates, land area and density for the world, major areas and regions: selected years
Population, taux d'accroissement, taux de natalité et taux de mortalité, superficie des terres et densité pour l'ensemble du monde, les régions macro géographiques et les composantes géographiques : diverses années

Major areas and regions / Régions macro géographiques et composantes	Mid-year population estimates - Estimations de population au milieu de l'année (millions)							Annual rate of increase - Taux d'accroissement annuel (%)	Crude birth rate - Taux bruts de natalité	Crude death rate - Taux bruts de mortalité	Land area (km2) - Superficie des terres (km2) (000s)	Density - Densité[1]
	1960	1970	1980	1990	2000	2010	2016	2015-2020			2016	
WORLD TOTAL - ENSEMBLE DU MONDE	3 033.2	3 700.6	4 458.4	5 330.9	6 145.0	6 958.2	7 467.0	1.1	19	8	130 094	57
AFRICA - AFRIQUE	285.1	366.5	480.0	634.6	817.6	1 049.4	1 225.1	2.5	34	8	29 648	41
Eastern Africa - Afrique orientale	84.2	110.3	147.5	198.6	261.1	347.0	410.6	2.7	35	7	6 667	62
Middle Africa - Afrique centrale	32.4	41.1	53.6	71.3	96.1	131.4	158.6	3.0	40	10	6 497	24
Northern Africa - Afrique septentrionale	63.7	83.1	107.7	141.2	172.6	204.3	229.4	1.8	24	6	7 769	30
Southern Africa - Afrique méridionale	19.8	25.8	33.7	42.8	52.3	59.0	64.3	1.3	21	9	2 651	24
Western Africa - Afrique occidentale	85.1	106.1	137.5	180.5	235.5	307.8	362.2	2.7	38	11	6 064	60
LATIN AMERICA AND CARIBBEAN - AMÉRIQUE LATIN ET CARAÏBES	221.1	288.1	364.3	445.9	525.8	597.6	639.0	1.0	16	6	20 139	32
Caribbean - Caraïbes	20.7	25.3	29.8	34.2	38.4	41.7	43.6	0.6	17	8	226	193
Central America - Amérique centrale	51.5	69.9	92.7	114.7	138.0	160.6	175.0	1.3	19	5	2 452	71
South America - Amérique méridionale	148.8	192.8	241.8	297.0	349.4	395.3	420.5	0.9	16	6	17 461	24
NORTHERN AMERICA - AMÉRIQUE SEPTENTRIONALE	204.8	231.1	254.4	280.3	312.8	342.9	358.6	0.7	12	8	18 652	19
ASIA - ASIE	1 700.5	2 137.8	2 642.5	3 221.3	3 730.4	4 194.4	4 462.7	0.9	16	7	31 033	144
Eastern Asia - Asie orientale	803.0	996.4	1 191.8	1 388.8	1 512.4	1 595.8	1 641.9	0.3	11	8	11 560	142
South Central Asia - Asie centrale méridionale	618.1	774.6	980.0	1 239.7	1 508.3	1 768.5	1 916.1	1.2	20	7	10 327	186
South Eastern Asia - Asie méridionale orientale	213.3	280.6	357.0	444.1	524.7	597.3	641.8	1.1	18	7	4 341	148
Western Asia - Asie occidentale	66.0	86.2	113.8	148.8	185.0	232.7	262.9	1.7	21	5	4 805	55
EUROPE	605.9	657.4	694.2	721.7	727.2	737.2	741.4	0.1	10	11	22 135	33
Eastern Europe - Europe orientale	253.6	276.2	294.8	309.9	304.0	294.5	292.9	-0.2	11	13	18 053	16
Northern Europe - Europe septentrionale	81.8	87.4	89.9	92.1	94.5	100.3	103.6	0.5	12	9	1 702	61
Southern Europe - Europe méridionale	117.9	127.7	138.8	143.8	145.7	153.9	152.2	-0.1	9	10	1 295	118
Western Europe - Europe occidentale	152.6	166.1	170.7	175.9	183.0	188.4	192.7	0.3	10	10	1 085	178
OCEANIA - OCÉANIA	15.8	19.7	23.0	27.1	31.2	36.6	40.1	1.4	16	7	8 486	5
Australia and New Zealand - Australie et Nouvelle Zélande	12.7	15.7	17.8	20.4	22.9	26.5	28.8	1.2	13	7	7 946	4
Melanesia - Melanésie	2.7	3.4	4.4	5.7	7.2	9.0	10.1	1.9	26	7	530	19
Micronesia	0.2	0.2	0.3	0.4	0.5	0.5	0.5	0.8	20	6	3	165
Polynesia - Polynésie	0.3	0.4	0.5	0.5	0.6	0.7	0.7	0.7	20	6	8	84

FOOTNOTES - NOTES

[1] Population per square kilometre of land area. Figures are estimates of population divided by land area and are not to be considered as either reflecting density in the urban sense or as indicating the supporting power of a territory's land and resources. - Habitants par kilomètre carré. Il s'agit simplement du quotient calculé en divisant la population par la superficie des terres et n'est par considéré comme indiquant la densité au sens urbain du terme ni l'effectif de population que les terres et les ressources du territoire sont capables de nourrir.

Table 2 - *Demographic Yearbook 2016*

Table 2 presents estimates of population and the percentage distribution by age group and sex as well as the sex ratio for all ages; data are presented for the world, the six major areas and the twenty regions for 2016.

Description of variables: All population estimates presented in this table are prepared by the Population Division of the United Nations Department of Economic and Social Affairs. These estimates are published (using more detailed age groups) in the *2017 Revision of World Population Prospects*[1].

The scheme of regionalization used for these estimates is discussed in detail in the technical notes for table 1. Age groups presented in this table are: 0-14 years, 15-64 years, and 65 years or over. Sex ratio refers to the number of males per 100 females of all ages.

The percentage distributions and the sex ratios that appear in this table were calculated by the Statistics Division of the United Nations Department of Economic and Social Affairs using the estimates prepared by the Population Division of the United Nations Department of Economic and Social Affairs.

Reliability of data: All data are set in *italic* type to indicate their conjectural quality.

Limitations: The data presented in this table are from the same series of estimates, prepared by the Population Division of the United Nations, presented in table 1. The estimated orders of magnitude of population are subject to all the basic limitations set forth for population statistics in section 3 of the Technical Notes. In brief, because they are estimates, these distributions by broad age groups and sex should be considered only as orders of magnitude. However, in compiling data for regional and major areas' totals, errors in the components tend to compensate each other and the resulting aggregates may be somewhat more reliable than the quality of the individual components would imply.

In addition, data in this table are limited by factors affecting data by age. These factors are described in the technical notes for table 7. Because the age groups presented in this table are broad, these problems are minimized.

---

[1] *United Nations, Department of Economic and Social Affairs, Population Division (2017). World Population Prospects: The 2017 Revision* (http://esa.un.org/unpd/wpp/)

Tableau 2 – Annuaire démographique 2016

Le tableau 2 présente, pour l'ensemble du monde, les six grandes zones et les vingt régions, des estimations concernant la population en 2016 ainsi que sa répartition en pourcentage selon des tranches d'âge et le sexe, et le rapport de masculinité pour tous les âges.

Description des variables : toutes les données figurant dans le tableau 2 ont été établies par la Division de la population du Département des affaires économiques et sociales de l'Organisation des Nations Unies, et ont été publiés dans les *Perspectives de la population mondiale : La révision de 2017*[1].

La classification géographique utilisée pour établir ces estimations est exposée en détail dans les notes techniques relatives au tableau 1. Les groupes d'âge présentés dans ce tableau sont définis comme suit : de 0 à 14 ans, de 15 à 64 ans et 65 ans ou plus. Le rapport de masculinité correspond au nombre d'individus de sexe masculin pour 100 individus de sexe féminin sans considération d'âge.

Les pourcentages et les rapports de masculinité qui sont présentés dans le tableau 2 ont été calculés par la Division de statistique du Département des affaires économiques et sociales de l'Organisation des Nations Unies à partir des estimations établies par la Division de la population de l'Organisation des Nations Unies.

Fiabilité des données : toutes les données figurant dans ce tableau sont reproduites en *italique* pour en faire ressortir le caractère conjectural.

Insuffisance des données : les données de ce tableau appartiennent à la même série d'estimations, établie par la Division de la population de l'Organisation des Nations Unies, que celles qui figurent au tableau 1. Les estimations concernant l'ordre de grandeur de la population appellent donc toutes les réserves fondamentales qui ont été formulées à la section 3 des Notes techniques à propos des statistiques relatives à la population. Sans entrer dans le détail, il convient de préciser que les données relatives à la répartition par grand groupe d'âge et par sexe doivent être considérées uniquement comme des ordres de grandeur en raison de leur caractère estimatif. Toutefois, il est à noter que, lorsque l'on additionne des données par territoire pour obtenir des totaux régionaux et par grandes zones, les erreurs qu'elles comportent arrivent parfois à s'équilibrer, de sorte que les agrégats obtenus peuvent être un peu plus exacts que chacun des éléments dont on est parti.

En outre, les donnés figurant dans le tableau 2 comportent certaines imprécisions en raison des facteurs influant sur les données par âge (voir à ce propos les notes techniques relatives au tableau 7). Ces imprécisions sont cependant atténuées du fait de l'étendue des groupes d'âge présentés dans le tableau 2.

---

[1] *Organisation des Nations Unies, Département des affaires économiques et sociales, Division de la population (2017). Perspectives de la population mondiale : La révision de 2017 (http://esa.un.org/unpd/wpp/)*

2. Estimates of population and its percentage distribution by age group and sex, and sex ratio, for the world, major areas and regions: 2016
Estimations de la population et pourcentage de répartition selon les tranches d'âge et le sexe, et le rapport de masculinité, pour l'ensemble du monde, les grandes régions et les régions géographiques : 2016

Major areas and regions / Grandes régions et régions	Population (millions)												Sex ratio - Rapport de masculinité[1]
	Both sexes - Les deux sexes				Male - Masculin				Female - Féminin				
	All ages - Tous âges	0-14	15-64	65+	All ages - Tous âges	0-14	15-64	65+	All ages - Tous âges	0-14	15-64	65+	
WORLD TOTAL - ENSEMBLE DU MONDE													
Number - Nombre	7 467	1 944	4 889	634	3 767	1 005	2 477	285	3 700	939	2 413	349	
Percent - Pourcentage	100.0	26.0	65.5	8.5	100.0	26.7	65.7	7.6	100.0	25.4	65.2	9.4	101.8
AFRICA - AFRIQUE													
Number - Nombre	1 225	502	681	43	612	254	338	19	613	248	342	23	
Percent - Pourcentage	100.0	41.0	55.6	3.5	100.0	41.6	55.3	3.1	100.0	40.4	55.8	3.8	99.7
Eastern Africa - Afrique orientale													
Number - Nombre	411	177	221	12	204	89	109	6	207	88	112	7	
Percent - Pourcentage	100.0	43.1	53.9	3.0	100.0	43.8	53.5	2.7	100.0	42.4	54.3	3.3	98.4
Middle Africa - Afrique centrale													
Number - Nombre	159	72	82	5	79	36	41	2	80	36	41	3	
Percent - Pourcentage	100.0	45.6	51.5	2.9	100.0	46.1	51.3	2.6	100.0	45.2	51.6	3.2	99.2
Northern Africa - Afrique septentrionale													
Number - Nombre	229	74	143	12	115	38	71	6	114	36	71	7	
Percent - Pourcentage	100.0	32.5	62.2	5.3	100.0	33.1	62.0	4.8	100.0	31.8	62.4	5.8	100.9
Southern Africa - Afrique méridionale													
Number - Nombre	64	19	42	3	32	10	21	1	33	10	21	2	
Percent - Pourcentage	100.0	30.0	65.0	5.0	100.0	30.8	65.3	3.9	100.0	29.2	64.8	6.1	96.3
Western Africa - Afrique occidentale													
Number - Nombre	362	159	193	10	182	81	97	5	180	78	97	5	
Percent - Pourcentage	100.0	43.9	53.3	2.8	100.0	44.4	53.0	2.6	100.0	43.3	53.6	3.0	101.3
LATIN AMERICA AND CARIBBEAN - AMÉRIQUE LATIN ET CARAÏBES													
Number - Nombre	639	161	428	50	316	82	212	22	323	79	216	28	
Percent - Pourcentage	100.0	25.2	66.9	7.8	100.0	26.1	67.0	6.9	100.0	24.4	66.9	8.7	97.8
Caribbean - Caraïbes													
Number - Nombre	44	11	29	4	22	6	14	2	22	5	14	2	
Percent - Pourcentage	100.0	24.7	65.7	9.6	100.0	25.5	65.7	8.8	100.0	24.0	65.7	10.3	98.0
Central America - Amérique centrale													
Number - Nombre	175	49	114	11	87	25	57	5	88	24	58	6	
Percent - Pourcentage	100.0	28.2	65.4	6.4	100.0	29.0	65.1	5.9	100.0	27.3	65.7	6.9	98.5
South America - Amérique méridionale													
Number - Nombre	420	101	285	35	207	52	141	15	213	50	144	20	
Percent - Pourcentage	100.0	24.1	67.7	8.2	100.0	24.9	67.9	7.2	100.0	23.3	67.5	9.3	97.4
NORTHERN AMERICA - AMÉRIQUE SEPTENTRIONALE													
Number - Nombre	359	67	237	54	177	34	119	24	181	33	118	30	
Percent - Pourcentage	100.0	18.7	66.1	15.2	100.0	19.3	67.0	13.7	100.0	18.1	65.2	16.7	98.0
ASIA - ASIE													
Number - Nombre	4 463	1 087	3 027	349	2 283	569	1 551	163	2 179	518	1 475	186	
Percent - Pourcentage	100.0	24.4	67.8	7.8	100.0	24.9	67.9	7.1	100.0	23.8	67.7	8.5	104.8
Eastern Asia - Asie orientale													
Number - Nombre	1 642	282	1 170	190	840	151	600	89	802	131	570	101	
Percent - Pourcentage	100.0	17.2	71.3	11.5	100.0	17.9	71.5	10.6	100.0	16.4	71.1	12.5	104.8
South Central Asia - Asie centrale méridionale													
Number - Nombre	1 916	557	1 253	106	985	291	643	51	931	266	610	55	
Percent - Pourcentage	100.0	29.1	65.4	5.5	100.0	29.6	65.3	5.2	100.0	28.6	65.5	5.9	105.8
South Eastern Asia - Asie méridionale orientale													
Number - Nombre	642	170	433	39	321	87	217	17	321	83	216	22	
Percent - Pourcentage	100.0	26.5	67.4	6.1	100.0	27.2	67.5	5.2	100.0	25.8	67.3	6.9	99.8
Western Asia - Asie occidentale													
Number - Nombre	263	78	171	14	137	40	91	6	126	38	80	8	
Percent - Pourcentage	100.0	29.6	65.0	5.3	100.0	29.1	66.4	4.5	100.0	30.3	63.5	6.2	109.3
EUROPE													
Number - Nombre	741	117	491	133	358	60	243	54	383	57	248	78	
Percent - Pourcentage	100.0	15.8	66.3	17.9	100.0	16.8	68.0	15.2	100.0	14.9	64.6	20.5	93.4
Eastern Europe - Europe orientale													
Number - Nombre	293	47	201	44	138	24	98	16	155	23	103	29	
Percent - Pourcentage	100.0	16.2	68.6	15.2	100.0	17.7	70.9	11.4	100.0	14.9	66.6	18.5	88.9
Northern Europe - Europe septentrionale													
Number - Nombre	104	18	66	19	51	9	33	9	53	9	33	11	
Percent - Pourcentage	100.0	17.5	64.1	18.4	100.0	18.2	65.1	16.7	100.0	16.9	63.1	20.0	97.2
Southern Europe - Europe méridionale													
Number - Nombre	152	22	99	31	74	11	50	13	78	11	50	18	
Percent - Pourcentage	100.0	14.4	65.3	20.3	100.0	15.2	66.9	17.9	100.0	13.7	63.7	22.6	95.4

2. Estimates of population and its percentage distribution by age group and sex, and sex ratio, for the world, major areas and regions: 2016
Estimations de la population et pourcentage de répartition selon les tranches d'âge et le sexe, et le rapport de masculinité, pour l'ensemble du monde, les grandes régions et les régions géographiques : 2016 (continued - suite)

Major areas and regions	Population (millions)												Sex ratio - Rapport de masculinité[1]
	Both sexes - Les deux sexes				Male - Masculin				Female - Féminin				
Grandes régions et régions	All ages - Tous âges	0-14	15-64	65+	All ages - Tous âges	0-14	15-64	65+	All ages - Tous âges	0-14	15-64	65+	
Western Europe - Europe occidentale													
Number - Nombre	193	30	124	38	95	15	63	17	98	15	62	22	
Percent - Pourcentage	100.0	15.5	64.6	19.9	100.0	16.1	66.1	17.8	100.0	14.9	63.1	22.0	97.0
OCEANIA - OCÉANIA													
Number - Nombre	40.12	9.43	25.82	4.87	20.07	4.85	12.95	2.27	20.05	4.58	12.87	2.60	
Percent - Pourcentage	100.0	23.5	64.4	12.1	100.0	24.2	64.5	11.3	100.0	22.8	64.2	13.0	100.1
Australia and New Zealand - Australie et Nouvelle Zélande													
Number - Nombre	28.79	5.48	18.92	4.38	14.31	2.81	9.45	2.05	14.47	2.67	9.48	2.33	
Percent - Pourcentage	100.0	19.0	65.7	15.2	100.0	19.7	66.0	14.3	100.0	18.4	65.5	16.1	98.9
Melanesia - Melanésie													
Number - Nombre	10.13	3.58	6.13	0.41	5.15	1.85	3.11	0.18	4.98	1.73	3.01	0.23	
Percent - Pourcentage	100.0	35.4	60.5	4.1	100.0	35.9	60.5	3.6	100.0	34.8	60.5	4.7	103.4
Micronesia													
Number - Nombre	0.52	0.15	0.34	0.03	0.26	0.08	0.17	0.02	0.26	0.08	0.17	0.02	
Percent - Pourcentage	100.0	29.6	64.2	6.3	100.0	30.2	64.1	5.8	100.0	28.9	64.3	6.8	101.6
Polynesia - Polynésie													
Number - Nombre	0.68	0.21	0.43	0.04	0.35	0.11	0.22	0.02	0.33	0.10	0.21	0.02	
Percent - Pourcentage	100.0	30.2	63.3	6.5	100.0	30.6	63.5	5.9	100.0	29.8	63.0	7.2	103.5

FOOTNOTES - NOTES

[1] Males per 100 females of all ages - Hommes pour 100 femmes de tous âges

Table 3 - *Demographic Yearbook 2016*

Table 3 presents for each country or area of the world the total, male and female population enumerated at the latest population census, estimates of the mid-year total population for 2010 and 2016, the average annual exponential rate of population increase (or decrease) for the period 2010 to 2016, the surface area and the population density for 2016.

Description of variables: The total, male and female population is the population enumerated at the most recent census for which data are available. The date of this census is given. Population census data are usually the results of a nation-wide gathering of individual information through full field enumeration. Alternatively, other approaches for generating reliable statistics on population and housing can be used by countries, such as the use of population registers. Data that are the result of such an alternative approach are also coded as census and are footnoted accordingly. Also, the results of sample surveys, essentially national in character, may be presented showing the appropriate code.

Mid-year population estimates refer to the population on 1 July. Otherwise, a footnote is appended. Mid-year estimates of the total population are those provided by national statistical offices.

Surface area, expressed in square kilometres, refers to the total surface area, comprising land area and inland waters (assumed to consist of major rivers and lakes) and excluding polar regions as well as uninhabited islands. Exceptions to this are noted. Surface areas, originally reported in square miles by the country or area, have been converted to square kilometres using a conversion factor of 2.589988.

Computation: The annual rate of population increase is the average annual exponential rate of population growth between 2010 and 2016, computed by the Statistics Division of the United Nations Department of Economic and Social Affairs using the unrounded mid-year estimates of 2010 and 2016. This rate is expressed as percentage.

Density is the number of persons in the 2016 total population per square kilometre of total surface area.

Reliability of data: Reliable mid-year population estimates are those that are based on a complete census (or a sample survey) and have been adjusted by a continuous population register or on the basis of the calculated balance of births, deaths and migration. Mid-year estimates of this type are considered reliable and appear in roman type. Mid-year estimates not calculated on this basis are considered less reliable and are shown in italics.

Census data and sample survey results are considered reliable and, therefore, appear in roman type.

Rates of population increase that were calculated using population estimates considered less reliable, as described above, are set in italics rather than roman type.

All surface area data are assumed to be reliable and therefore appear in roman type.

Population density data, however, are considered reliable or less reliable on the basis of the reliability of the 2016 population estimates used as the numerator.

Limitations: Statistics on the total population enumerated at the time of the census, surface area data and estimates of the mid-year total population are subject to the same qualifications as have been set forth for surface area and population data in sections 2.4 and 3 of the Technical Notes, respectively.

Regarding the limitations of census data, it should be noted that although census data are considered reliable, and therefore appear in roman type, the actual quality of census data varies widely from one country or area to another. When known, an estimate of the extent of over-enumeration or under-enumeration is given in footnotes.

Rates of population increase are subject to all the qualifications of the population estimates mentioned above. In some cases, they simply reflect the rate calculated or assumed in constructing the estimates themselves when adequate measures of natural increase and net migration were not available. Despite their shortcomings, these rates provide a useful index for studying population change and can be also useful in evaluating the accuracy of vital and migration statistics.

Population density data as shown in this table give only an indication of actual population density as they do not take account of the dispersion or concentration of population within countries or areas nor the proportion of habitable land. They should not be interpreted as reflecting density in the urban sense or as indicating the supporting power of a territory's land and resources.

Tableau 3 – *Annuaire démographique 2016*

Le tableau 3 indique pour chaque pays ou zone du monde la population totale selon le sexe d'après les derniers recensements effectués, les estimations concernant la population totale au milieu de l'année 2010 et de l'année 2016, le taux moyen d'accroissement annuel exponentiel positif ou négatif de la population pour la période allant de 2010 à 2016, ainsi que la superficie et la densité de population en 2016.

Description des variables : la population masculine et féminine totale est, la population enregistrée lors du recensement le plus récent sur lequel on dispose de données. La date de ce recensement est indiquée. Les données des recensements de la population sont habituellement le résultat d'un collecte à l'échelle nationale des données individuelles obtenues au moyen d'un dénombrement complet. Les pays peuvent recourir à d'autres moyens pour établir des statistiques fiables sur la population et le logement, tels que des registres de la population. Les données obtenues par ce moyen sont présentées comme celles d'un recensement et sont annotées en conséquence. Par ailleurs, les résultats des enquêtes par sondage, réalisées habituellement à l'échelle nationale, peuvent être présentés à l'aide du code correspondant. Les estimations de la population en milieu d'année sont celles de la population au 1ᵉʳ juillet. Lorsque la date est différente, cela est signalé par une note. Les estimations de la population totale en milieu d'année sont celles qui ont été communiquées par les services nationaux de statistique.

La superficie - exprimée en kilomètres carrés - représente la superficie totale, c'est-à-dire qu'elle englobe les terres émergées et les eaux intérieures (qui sont censées comprendre les principaux lacs et cours d'eau) mais exclut les régions polaires et certaines îles inhabitées. Les exceptions à cette règle sont signalées en note. Les superficies initialement exprimées en miles carrés par les pays ou les zones ont été transformées en kilomètres carrés au moyen d'un coefficient de conversion de 2,589988.

Calculs : le taux d'accroissement annuel est le taux exponentiel annuel moyen de variation (en pourcentage) de la population entre 2010 et 2016, calculé par la Division de statistique du Département des affaires économiques et sociales de l'Organisation des Nations Unies à partir des estimations en milieu d'année non arrondies pour les années 2010 et 2016.

La densité est égale au rapport de l'effectif total de la population en 2016 à la superficie totale, exprimée en kilomètres carrés.

Fiabilité des données : les estimations en milieu d'année qui sont considérées sûres sont fondées sur un recensement complet (ou sur une enquête par sondage) et ont été ajustées en fonction des données provenant d'un registre permanent de population ou en fonction de la balance établie par le calcul des naissances, des décès et des migrations. Les estimations de ce type sont considérées comme sûres et apparaissent en caractères romains. Les estimations en milieu d'année dont le calcul n'a pas été effectué sur cette base sont considérées comme moins sûres et apparaissent en italique.

Les données de recensements ou les résultats d'enquêtes par sondage sont considérés comme sûrs et apparaissent par conséquent en caractères romains.

Les taux d'accroissement de la population, calculés à partir d'estimations jugées moins sûres d'après les normes décrites ci-dessus, sont indiqués en italique plutôt qu'en caractères romains.

Toutes les données de superficie sont présumées sûres et apparaissent par conséquent en caractères romains. En revanche, les données relatives à la densité de la population sont considérées plus ou moins sûres en fonction de la fiabilité des estimations de la population en 2016 ayant servi de numérateur.

Insuffisance des données : les statistiques portant sur la population totale dénombrée lors d'un recensement, les données de superficie et les estimations de la population totale en milieu d'année appellent les mêmes réserves que celles formulées aux sections 2.4 et 3 des Notes techniques à propos des statistiques relatives à la superficie et à la population.

S'agissant de l'insuffisance des données obtenues par recensement, il convient d'indiquer que, bien que ces données soient considérées comme sûres et apparaissent par conséquent en caractères romains, leur qualité réelle varie considérablement d'un pays ou d'une région à l'autre. Lorsque l'on possédait les renseignements voulus, on a donné une estimation du degré de sur-dénombrement ou de sous-dénombrement.

Les taux d'accroissement appellent toutes les réserves formulées plus haut à propos des estimations concernant la population. Dans certains cas, ils représentent seulement le taux calculé ou que l'on a pris pour base pour établir les estimations elles-mêmes lorsque l'on ne disposait pas de mesures appropriées de l'accroissement naturel et des migrations nettes. Malgré leurs imperfections, ces taux fournissent des indications intéressantes pour l'étude du mouvement de la population et, utilisés avec les précautions nécessaires, ils peuvent également servir à évaluer l'exactitude des statistiques de l'état civil et des migrations.

Les données relatives à la densité de population figurant dans le tableau 3 n'ont qu'une valeur indicative en ce qui concerne la densité de population effective, car elles ne tiennent compte ni de la dispersion ou de la concentration de la population à l'intérieur des pays ou zones, ni de la proportion du territoire qui est habitable. Il ne faut donc y voir d'indication ni de la densité au sens urbain du terme ni du nombre d'habitants qui pourraient vivre sur les terres et avec les ressources naturelles du territoire considéré.

3. Population by sex, annual rate of population increase, surface area and density
Population selon le sexe, taux d'accroissement annuel de la population, superficie et densité

Continent, country or area and census date / Continent, pays ou zone et date du recensement	Census type[a]	Population at the latest available census / Population d'après le dernier recensement disponible (in units — en unités)			Estimate type[a]	Mid-year estimates / Estimations au milieu de l'année (in thousands — en milliers)		Annual rate of increase / Taux d' accrois sement annuel 2010-16	Surface area / Superficie (km²) 2016	Density / Densité 2016[b]
		Both sexes / Les deux sexes	Male / Masculin	Female / Feminin		2010	2016			
AFRICA - AFRIQUE										
Algeria - Algérie										
16 IV 2008 .... DF		34 452 759[1]	17 428 500[1]	17 024 259[1]	DJ	35 978	40 836	2.1	2 381 741	17
Angola										
16 V 2014 .... DF		25 789 024	12 499 041	13 289 983	DF	17 430[2]	...	...	1 246 700	...
Benin - Bénin										
11 V 2013 .... DJ		10 008 749	4 887 820	5 120 929	DF	8 779[3]	10 883[4]	3.6	114 763	95
Botswana										
9 VIII 2011 .... DF		2 024 904	988 957	1 035 947	DJ	1 823	2 231[5]	3.4	582 000	4
Burkina Faso										
9 XII 2006 .... DF		14 196 259	6 842 560	7 353 699	DJ	15 731[3]	...	...	272 967	...
Burundi										
16 VIII 2008 .... DF		7 877 728	3 838 045	4 039 683	DF	9 461	11 215	2.8	27 874	402
Cabo Verde										
16 VI 2010 .... DJ		491 683	243 403	248 280	DF	494[3]	531[3]	1.2	4 033	132
Cameroon - Cameroun										
11 XI 2005 .... DF		17 052 134	8 408 495	8 643 639	DF	19 648[3]	22 710[3]	2.4	475 650	48
Central African Republic - République centrafricaine										
8 XII 2003 .... DF		3 151 072	1 569 446	1 581 626		...	...	...	622 984	...
Chad - Tchad										
20 V 2009 .... DJ		11 175 915	5 509 522	5 666 393		...	...	...	1 284 000	...
Comoros - Comores										
1 IX 2003 .... DF		575 660[6]	285 590[6]	290 070[6]		...	...	...	2 235	...
Congo										
28 IV 2007 .... DF		3 697 490	1 821 357	1 876 133		...	...	...	342 000	...
Côte d'Ivoire										
15 V 2014 .... DF		22 224 509	11 441 896	10 782 613	DF	20 845[7]	23 950[8]	2.3	322 462	74
Democratic Republic of the Congo - République démocratique du Congo										
1 VII 1984 .... DF		29 916 800	14 543 800	15 373 000		...	...	...	2 344 858	...
Djibouti										
29 V 2009 .... DF		818 159	440 067	378 092	DF	841[9]	...	...	23 200	...
Egypt - Égypte										
21 XI 2006 .... DF		72 798 031	37 219 056	35 578 975	DF	78 685	91 023	2.4	1 002 000	91
Equatorial Guinea - Guinée équatoriale										
20 VI 2015 .... DF		1 222 442	651 820	570 622	DF	1 622[10]	...		28 051	...
Eritrea - Érythrée										
9 V 1984 .... DF		2 748 304	1 374 452	1 373 852		...	...	...	117 600	...
Ethiopia - Éthiopie										
29 V 2007 .... DF		73 750 932	37 217 130	36 533 802	DF	79 634[11]	92 205[11]	2.4	1 104 300	83
Gabon										
22 V 2013 .... DF		1 811 079	934 072	877 007		...	...	...	267 668	...
Gambia - Gambie										
15 IV 2013 .... DF		*1 882 450	*930 699	*951 751		...	...	...	11 295	...
Ghana										
26 IX 2010 .... DF		24 658 823	12 024 845	12 633 978	DF	...	28 308[12]		238 537	119
Guinea - Guinée										
15 III 2014 .... DF		10 523 261	5 084 306	5 438 955	...	10 537[3]	*11 319	...	245 836	46
Guinea-Bissau - Guinée-Bissau										
15 III 2009 .... DF		1 497 859	725 956	771 903	DF	1 460[3]	1 548[3]	1.0	36 125	43
Kenya										
24 VIII 2009 .... DF		38 610 097	19 192 458	19 417 639	DF	38 474[13]	45 389[13]	2.8	591 958	77
Lesotho										
13 IV 2006 .... DF		1 741 406	818 379	923 027	DF	1 892[3]	1 933[3]	0.4	30 355	64
Liberia - Libéria										
21 III 2008 .... DF		3 476 608	1 739 945	1 736 663	DF	3 627	...	...	111 369	...
Libya - Libye										
15 IV 2006 .... DF		*5 298 152[14]	*2 687 513[14]	*2 610 639[14]	DF	5 689[14]	...	...	1 676 198	...
Madagascar										
1 VIII 1993 .... DF		12 238 914	6 088 116	6 150 798	DF	20 142[3]	...	...	587 295	...

Continent, country or area and census date — Continent, pays ou zone et date du recensement	Census type[a]	Population at the latest available census — Population d'après le dernier recensement disponible (in units — en unités)			Estimate type[a]	Mid-year estimates — Estimations au milieu de l'année (in thousands — en milliers)		Annual rate of increase — Taux d' accrois sement annuel 2010-16	Surface area — Superficie (km²) 2016	Density — Densité 2016[b]
		Both sexes — Les deux sexes	Male — Masculin	Female — Feminin		2010	2016			
AFRICA - AFRIQUE										
Malawi										
8 VI 2008 .... DF	DF	13 077 160	6 358 933	6 718 227	DF	13 948[3]	16 833[3]	3.1	117 726	143
Mali										
1 IV 2009 .... DF	DF	14 528 662	7 204 990	7 323 672	DF	15 370[15]	...	...	1 240 192	...
Mauritania - Mauritanie										
24 III 2013 .... DF	DF	3 460 388[16]	...	...	DF	3 341[3]	3 783[3]	2.1	1 030 700	4
Mauritius - Maurice[17]										
4 VII 2011 .... DF	DF	1 237 000	611 053	625 947	DJ	1 281[18]	1 263[19]	-0.2	1 979	638
Mayotte										
21 VIII 2012 .... DJ	DJ	212 645	103 173	109 471	DJ	...	*235[20]	...	374	629
Morocco - Maroc										
1 IX 2014 .... DJ	DJ	33 848 242	...	...	DF	31 894[21]	34 487[22]	1.3	446 550	77
Mozambique										
1 VIII 2007 .... DF	DF	20 252 223	9 746 690	10 505 533	DF	22 417[3]	26 424[3]	2.7	799 380	33
Namibia - Namibie										
28 VIII 2011 .... DF	DF	2 113 077	1 021 912	1 091 165	DF	2 143[3]	2 324[23]	1.4	824 116	3
Niger										
10 XII 2012 .... DF	DF	16 734 935	8 183 513	8 551 422	DJ	15 204[3]	19 865[24]	4.5	1 267 000	16
Nigeria - Nigéria										
21 III 2006 .... DF	DF	140 431 790	71 345 488	69 086 302	DF	159 608[25]	193 393[25]	3.2	923 768	209
Republic of South Sudan - République de Soudan du Sud										
21 IV 2008 .... DF	DF	8 260 490	4 287 300	3 973 190	DF	9 497[26]	...	...	658 841	...
Reunion - Réunion										
1 I 2010 .... DJ	DJ	821 136	398 006	423 130	DJ	821[20]	*851[20]	0.6	2 513	339
Rwanda										
15 VIII 2012 .... DF	DF	10 393 542	4 981 197	5 412 345	DF	10 413[3]	11 533[24]	1.7	26 338	438
Saint Helena ex. dep. - Sainte-Hélène sans dép.										
7 II 2016 .... DF	DF	4 802	...	...	DF	4	5	1.5	122	38
Saint Helena: Ascension - Sainte-Hélène: Ascension										
7 II 2016 .... DJ	DJ	556[27]	...	...	...	...	...	...	88	...
Saint Helena: Tristan da Cunha - Sainte-Hélène: Tristan da Cunha										
9 II 2016 .... DJ	DJ	271[27]	...	...	...	...	...	...	98	...
Sao Tome and Principe - Sao Tomé-et-Principe										
13 V 2012 .... DJ	DJ	178 739	88 867	89 872	DF	164	...	...	964	...
Senegal - Sénégal										
19 XI 2013 .... DF	DF	13 357 492	6 658 089	6 699 403	DJ	12 509[28]	14 800[3]	2.8	196 712[29]	75
Seychelles										
26 VIII 2010 .... DF	DF	90 945	46 912	44 033	DF	90	...	...	457	...
Sierra Leone										
5 XII 2015 .... DF	DF	7 092 113	3 490 978	3 601 135	DF	5 747	...	...	72 300	...
Somalia - Somalie										
15 II 1987 .... DF	DF	7 114 431	3 741 664	3 372 767		...	...	...	637 657	...
South Africa - Afrique du Sud										
10 X 2011 .... DF	DF	51 770 560	25 188 791	26 581 769	DF	50 979	55 909	1.5	1 221 037	46
Sudan - Soudan										
21 IV 2008 .... DF	DF	30 894 000	15 786 677	15 107 323	DF	32 962	39 648	3.1	...	...
Swaziland										
11 III 2007 .... DF	DF	844 223	405 868	438 355	DF	1 056	1 133[20]	1.2	17 363	65
Togo										
6 XI 2010 .... DJ	DJ	6 191 155	3 009 095	3 182 060	DF	6 191[3]	7 143[3]	2.4	56 785	126
Tunisia - Tunisie										
23 IV 2014 .... DF	DF	10 982 754	5 472 338	5 510 416	DF	10 547	11 299	1.1	163 610	69
Uganda - Ouganda										
27 VIII 2014 .... DF	DF	34 634 650	16 897 849	17 736 801	DF	31 785	36 561[8]	2.3	241 550	151

Continent, country or area and census date / Continent, pays ou zone et date du recensement	Census type[a]	Population at the latest available census / Population d'après le dernier recensement disponible (in units — en unités)			Estimate type[a]	Mid-year estimates Estimations au milieu de l'année (in thousands — en milliers)		Annual rate of increase Taux d' accrois sement annuel 2010-16	Surface area Superficie (km²) 2016	Density Densité 2016[b]
		Both sexes Les deux sexes	Male Masculin	Female Feminin		2010	2016			
AFRICA - AFRIQUE										
United Republic of Tanzania - République Unie de Tanzanie										
26 VIII 2012 .... DF	DF	44 928 923[30]	21 869 990[30]	23 058 933[30]	DF	43 188[31]	50 143[24]	2.5	947 303	53
Western Sahara - Sahara occidental[32]										
31 XII 1970 .... DF	DF	76 425	43 981	32 444		...	...	...	266 000	...
Zambia - Zambie										
16 X 2010 .... DF	DF	12 526 314	6 117 253	6 409 061	DF	...	15 934[3]	...	752 612	21
Zimbabwe										
17 VIII 2012 .... DF	DF	13 061 239	6 280 539	6 780 700	DF	...	14 240[33]	...	390 757	36
AMERICA, NORTH - AMÉRIQUE DU NORD										
Anguilla										
11 V 2011..................... DF	DF	13 572	6 707	6 865	DF	16	...		91	...
Antigua and Barbuda - Antigua-et-Barbuda										
27 V 2011 .... DF	DF	88 566	...	...	DF	91	...	...	442	...
Aruba										
29 IX 2010 .... DJ	DJ	101 484	48 241	53 243	DJ	102	110	1.3	180	613
Bahamas										
3 V 2010 .... DJ	DJ	351 461	170 257	181 204	DF	335[3]	*373[3]	1.8	13 940	27
Barbados - Barbade										
1 V 2010 .... DJ	DJ	277 821[34]	133 018[34]	144 803[34]	DF	278	...	...	431	...
Belize										
12 V 2010 .... DJ	DJ	322 453	161 227	161 226	DF	324	378	2.6	22 966	16
Bermuda - Bermudes										
20 V 2010 .... DJ	DJ	64 237[35]	30 858[35]	33 379[35]	DJ	64[12]	62[12]	-0.6	53	1 164
British Virgin Islands - Îles Vierges britanniques										
12 VII 2010 .... DF	DF	28 054	13 820	14 234	DF	28	...		151	...
Canada										
2 V 2011 .... DJ	DJ	33 476 690	16 414 225	17 062 455	DJ	34 005[36]	*36 286[37]	1.1	9 093 507[38]	4
Cayman Islands - Îles Caïmanes										
10 X 2010 .... DJ	DJ	55 036[39]	27 218[39]	27 818[39]	DJ	56	...	...	264	...
Costa Rica										
30 V 2011 .... DJ	DJ	4 301 712	2 106 063	2 195 649	DJ	4 538[40]	4 890[41]	1.2	51 100	96
Cuba										
14 IX 2012 .... DF	DF	11 167 325	5 570 825	5 596 500	DJ	11 171	11 239	0.1	109 884	102
Curaçao										
26 III 2011..................... DF	DF	150 563	68 848	81 715	DJ	149[42]	160[43]	1.2	444	360
Dominica - Dominique										
14 V 2011 .... DF	DF	68 913	34 973	33 940	DF	71	...	...	750	...
Dominican Republic - République dominicaine										
1 XII 2010 .... DJ	DJ	9 445 281	4 739 038	4 706 243	DF	9 479[3]	10 075[3]	1.0	48 671	207
El Salvador										
12 V 2007 .... DJ	DJ	5 744 113	2 719 371	3 024 742	DF	6 183[44]	6 521[44]	0.9	21 041	310
Greenland - Groenland										
1 I 2008 .... DJ	DJ	56 462[45]	29 885[45]	26 577[45]	DJ	57[45]	56[45]	-0.1	2 166 086	0
Grenada - Grenade										
12 V 2011 .... DF	DF	106 667	53 898	52 769	DF	105	...	...	345	...
Guadeloupe										
1 I 2010 .... DJ	DJ	403 355[46]	187 932[46]	215 423[46]	DJ	403[47]	*396[47]	-0.3	1 705	232
Guatemala										
24 XI 2002 .... DJ	DJ	11 237 196	5 496 839	5 740 357	DF	14 362[31]	...		108 889	
Haiti - Haïti										
11 I 2003 .... DJ	DJ	8 373 750	4 039 272	4 334 478	DJ	10 085[48]	...		27 750	
Honduras										
10 VIII 2013 .... DF	DF	8 303 771	4 052 316	4 251 456	DF	8 046[49]	...	...	112 492	...

3. Population by sex, annual rate of population increase, surface area and density
Population selon le sexe, taux d'accroissement annuel de la population, superficie et densité (continued - suite)

Continent, country or area and census date — Continent, pays ou zone et date du recensement	Census type[a]	Population at the latest available census — Population d'après le dernier recensement disponible (in units — en unités)			Estimate type[a]	Mid-year estimates Estimations au milieu de l'année (in thousands — en milliers)		Annual rate of increase Taux d'accroissement annuel 2010-16	Surface area Superficie (km²) 2016	Density Densité 2016[b]
		Both sexes Les deux sexes	Male Masculin	Female Feminin		2010	2016			
AMERICA, NORTH - AMÉRIQUE DU NORD										
Jamaica - Jamaïque										
4 IV 2011 .... DJ	DJ	2 697 983[50]	1 334 533[50]	1 363 450[50]	DJ	2 702	2 729	0.2	10 991	248
Martinique										
1 I 2010 .... DJ	DJ	394 173	182 073	212 100	DJ	394[20]	*377[20]	-0.7	1 128	334
Mexico - Mexique										
12 VI 2010 .... DF	DF	112 336 538[51]	54 855 231[51]	57 481 307[51]	DJ	114 256[3]	122 273[3]	1.1	1 964 375	62
Montserrat										
12 V 2011 .... DJ	DJ	4 922	2 546	2 376	DF	5	5	0.1	103	49
Nicaragua										
4 VI 2005 .... DJ	DJ	5 142 098	2 534 491	2 607 607	DJ	5 816	...	...	130 373	...
Panama										
16 V 2010 .... DF	DF	3 405 813	1 712 584	1 693 229	DF	3 662[12]	4 037[12]	1.6	75 320	54
Puerto Rico - Porto Rico										
1 IV 2010 .... DJ	DJ	3 725 789[52]	1 785 171[52]	1 940 618[52]	DJ	3 721[53]	3 411[54]	-1.4	8 868	385
Saint Kitts and Nevis - Saint-Kitts-et-Nevis										
15 V 2011 .... DF	DF	*46 398	*22 846	*23 552	DF	*53	...	...	261	
Saint Lucia - Sainte-Lucie										
10 V 2010 .... DJ	DJ	165 770	83 502	82 268		...	...	...	539[55]	...
Saint Pierre and Miquelon - Saint Pierre-et-Miquelon										
1 I 2013 .... DJ	DJ	6 286	...	...		...	...	...	242	
Saint Vincent and the Grenadines - Saint-Vincent-et-les Grenadines										
12 VI 2012 .... DF	DF	109 188[56]	55 551[56]	53 637[56]	DJ	110	...	...	389	
Saint-Barthélemy										
1 I 2013 .... DJ	DJ	9 417	...	...		...	...	...	22	...
Saint-Martin (French part) - Saint-Martin (partie française)										
1 I 2013 .... DJ	DJ	36 457	...	...		...	...	...	53	...
Sint Maarten (Dutch part) - Saint-Martin (partie néerlandaise)										
9 IV 2011 .... DF	DF	33 609	15 868	17 741	DJ	36	...	...	34	...
Trinidad and Tobago - Trinité-et-Tobago										
9 I 2011 .... DF	DF	1 332 901	...	...	DF	1 318[18]	1 354[19]	0.5	5 127	264
Turks and Caicos Islands - Îles Turques et Caïques										
25 I 2012 .... DF	DF	*31 458[57]	*16 037[57]	*15 421[57]	DJ	35	38	1.6	948[58]	40
United States of America - États-Unis d'Amérique										
1 IV 2010 .... DJ	DJ	308 745 538	151 781 326	156 964 212	DJ	309 348[59]	323 128[59]	0.7	9 833 517	33
United States Virgin Islands - Îles Vierges américaines										
1 IV 2010 .... DJ	DJ	106 405[52]	50 854[52]	55 551[52]	DJ	106[60]	...	...	347	...
AMERICA, SOUTH - AMÉRIQUE DU SUD										
Argentina - Argentine										
27 X 2010 .... DF	DF	40 117 096	19 523 766	20 593 330	DF	40 788[61]	43 590[61]	1.1	2 780 400	16
Bolivia (Plurinational State of) - Bolivie (État plurinational de)										
21 XI 2012 .... DF	DF	10 059 856	5 019 447	5 040 409	DF	10 031	10 985	1.5	1 098 581[62]	10
Brazil - Brésil										
31 VII 2010 .... DJ	DJ	190 755 799	93 406 990	97 348 809	DJ	195 498[63]	206 081[63]	0.9	8 515 767	24

3. Population by sex, annual rate of population increase, surface area and density
Population selon le sexe, taux d'accroissement annuel de la population, superficie et densité (continued - suite)

Continent, country or area and census date / Continent, pays ou zone et date du recensement	Census type[a]	Population at the latest available census / Population d'après le dernier recensement disponible (in units — en unités)			Estimate type[a]	Mid-year estimates / Estimations au milieu de l'année (in thousands — en milliers)		Annual rate of increase / Taux d' accrois sement annuel 2010-16	Surface area / Superficie (km²) 2016	Density / Densité 2016[b]
		Both sexes / Les deux sexes	Male / Masculin	Female / Feminin		2010	2016			
AMERICA, SOUTH - AMÉRIQUE DU SUD										
Chile - Chili										
24 IV 2002 .... DF		15 116 435	7 447 695	7 668 740	DF	17 094	18 192	1.0	756 102	24
Colombia - Colombie										
22 V 2005 .... DF		41 468 384	20 336 117	21 132 267	DJ	45 510[64]	48 748[64]	1.1	1 141 748	43
Ecuador - Équateur										
28 XI 2010 .... DF		14 483 499	7 177 683	7 305 816	DF	15 012[65]	16 529[65]	1.6	257 217[66]	64
Falkland Islands (Malvinas) - Îles Falkland (Malvinas)[67]										
15 IV 2012 .... DF		2 840[68]	1 491[68]	1 349[68]		...	...	...	12 173	...
French Guiana - Guyane française										
1 I 2013 .... DJ		244 118	121 653	122 465	DJ	229[20]	*263[20]	2.3	83 534	3
Guyana										
15 IX 2012 .... DF		*747 884	*372 547	*375 337	DF	752	...	...	214 969	...
Paraguay										
28 VIII 2002 .... DF		5 163 198	2 603 242	2 559 956	DF	6 266[69]	6 855[69]	1.5	406 752	17
Peru - Pérou										
21 X 2007 .... DF		27 412 157	13 622 640	13 789 517	DF	29 462[70]	31 489[70]	1.1	1 285 216	25
Suriname										
13 VIII 2012 .... DJ		541 638	270 629	271 009	DJ	531	...	...	163 820	...
Uruguay										
4 X 2011 .... DJ		3 286 314	1 577 725[71]	1 708 481[71]	DJ	3 397	3 480[3]	0.4	173 626	20
Venezuela (Bolivarian Republic of) - Venezuela (République bolivarienne du)										
1 IX 2011 .... DJ		27 227 930	13 549 752	13 678 178	DF	28 524	31 029	1.4	912 050	34
ASIA - ASIE										
Afghanistan										
23 VI 1979 .... DF		13 051 358[72]	6 712 377[72]	6 338 981[72]	DF	24 486[73]	27 657[73]	2.0	652 864	42
Armenia - Arménie										
12 X 2011 .... DF		2 871 771	1 346 729	1 525 042	DJ	3 256	2 993	-1.4	29 743	101
Azerbaijan - Azerbaïdjan										
13 IV 2009 .... DJ		8 922 447	4 414 398	4 508 049	DF	9 054	9 756	1.2	86 600	113
Bahrain - Bahreïn										
27 IV 2010 .... DJ		1 234 571	768 414	466 157	DJ	1 229	1 424	2.5	778	1 829
Bangladesh										
15 III 2011 .... DF		144 043 697	72 109 796	71 933 901	DF	148 620	160 800	1.3	147 570	1 090
Bhutan - Bhoutan										
30 V 2005 .... DF		634 982	333 595	301 387	DF	696[74]	769[74]	1.7	38 394	20
Brunei Darussalam - Brunéi Darussalam										
20 VI 2011 .... DJ		393 372	203 144	190 228	DF	387[42]	...	...	5 765	...
Cambodia - Cambodge										
3 III 2008 .... DF		13 395 682[75]	6 516 054[75]	6 879 628[75]	DF	14 303[76]	...	...	181 035	...
China - Chine										
1 XI 2010 .... DJ		1 339 724 852[77]	686 852 572[77]	652 872 280[77]	DF	1 337 700[78]	...	...	9 600 000	...
China, Hong Kong SAR - Chine, Hong Kong RAS										
30 VI 2011 .... DJ		7 071 576[79]	3 303 015[79]	3 768 561[79]	DJ	7 024	7 337	0.7	1 106	6 633
China, Macao SAR - Chine, Macao RAS										
12 VIII 2011 .... DF		625 674	305 398	320 276	DJ	537	...	...	30[80]	...
Cyprus - Chypre										
1 X 2011 .... DJ		840 407[81]	408 780[81]	431 627[81]	DJ	829[82]	848[83]	0.4	9 251	92
Democratic People's Republic of Korea - République populaire démocratique de Corée										
1 X 2008 .... DJ		24 052 231	11 721 838	12 330 393		...	...	...	120 538	...

3. Population by sex, annual rate of population increase, surface area and density
Population selon le sexe, taux d'accroissement annuel de la population, superficie et densité (continued - suite)

Continent, country or area and census date / Continent, pays ou zone et date du recensement	Census type[a]	Population at the latest available census / Population d'après le dernier recensement disponible (in units — en unités)			Estimate type[a]	Mid-year estimates / Estimations au milieu de l'année (in thousands — en milliers)		Annual rate of increase Taux d'accrois sement annuel 2010-16	Surface area Superficie (km²) 2016	Density Densité 2016[b]
		Both sexes Les deux sexes	Male Masculin	Female Feminin		2010	2016			
ASIA - ASIE										
Georgia - Géorgie										
5 XI 2014 .... DJ		3 713 804	1 772 864	1 940 940	...	4 453	3 719[84]	...	69 700	53
India - Inde										
9 II 2011............................ DF		1 210 854 977[85]	623 270 258[85]	587 584 719[85]	DF	1 182 105[86]	...	...	3 287 263	...
Indonesia - Indonésie										
1 V 2010 .... DJ		237 641 326	119 630 913	118 010 413	DJ	238 519[87]	258 705[87]	1.4	1 910 931	135
Iran (Islamic Republic of) - Iran (République islamique d')										
24 X 2011 .... DJ		75 149 669	37 905 669	37 244 000	DJ	74 340[88]	79 686[88]	1.2	1 628 750[38]	49
Iraq										
16 X 1997 .... DF		19 184 543[89]	9 536 570[89]	9 647 973[89]	DF	32 211	...	...	435 052	...
Israel - Israël										
27 XII 2008 .... DF		7 412 180[90]	3 663 910[90]	3 748 270[90]	DJ	7 624[91]	...	...	22 072	...
Japan - Japon										
1 X 2015 .... DJ		*127 110 047	*61 829 237	*65 280 810	DJ	128 070[92]	126 995[93]	-0.1	377 930[94]	336
Jordan - Jordanie										
30 X 2015 .... DF		9 531 712[95]	5 046 822[95]	4 484 890[95]	DF	6 699[96]	9 798[96]	6.3	89 318	110
Kazakhstan										
25 II 2009 .... DF		16 009 597	7 712 224	8 297 373	DF	16 322	...	...	2 724 902	...
Kuwait - Koweït										
21 IV 2011 .... DF		3 065 850	1 738 372	1 327 478	DF	2 933	3 925[20]	4.9	17 818	220
Kyrgyzstan - Kirghizstan										
24 III 2009 .... DJ		5 362 793	2 645 921	2 716 872	DJ	5 448[97]	6 080[97]	1.8	199 949	30
Lao People's Democratic Republic - République démocratique populaire lao										
1 III 2015 .... DJ		6 492 400	3 254 800	3 237 600	DJ	6 230[98]	6 906[98]	1.7	236 800	29
Lebanon - Liban										
1 X 2011 .... SDF		3 779 859[99]	1 840 940[99]	1 938 919[99]		...	...	...	10 452	...
Malaysia - Malaisie										
6 VII 2010 .... DJ		28 334 135[100]	14 562 638[100]	13 771 497[100]	DJ	28 589[101]	31 661[101]	1.7	330 345	96
Maldives										
20 IX 2014 .... DF		402 071[102]	227 749[102]	174 322[102]	DF	320	350[103]	1.5	300	1 167
Mongolia - Mongolie										
11 XI 2010 .... DF		2 647 199	1 314 246	1 332 953	DF	2 739	3 089	2.0	1 564 116	2
Myanmar										
29 III 2014 .... DF		51 486 253[104]	24 824 586[104]	26 661 667[104]	DF	59 780[105]	52 917[106]	-2.0	676 553	78
Nepal - Népal										
22 VI 2011 .... DJ		26 494 504	12 849 041	13 645 463	DJ	28 044	28 431[23]	0.2	147 181	193
Oman										
12 XII 2010 .... DF		2 773 479	1 612 408	1 161 071	DF	...	4 414[107]	...	309 500	14
Pakistan										
2 III 1998 .... DF		130 579 571[108]	67 840 137[108]	62 739 434[108]	DF	173 510[108]	...	...	796 095	...
Philippines										
1 VIII 2015 .... DJ		100 979 303[109]	...	...	DJ	93 135[12]	103 243[12]	1.7	300 000	344
Qatar										
20 IV 2015 .... DF		2 404 776	1 816 981	587 795	DF	1 715	2 618	7.0	11 607	226
Republic of Korea - République de Corée										
1 XI 2015 .... DJ		51 069 375	25 608 502	25 460 873	DJ	49 554	51 246	0.6	100 339	511
Saudi Arabia - Arabie saoudite										
27 IV 2010 .... DF		27 236 156	15 531 471	11 704 685	DF	*27 563[110]	31 742	2.4	2 206 714	14
Singapore - Singapour										
30 VI 2010 .... DJ		3 771 721[111]	1 861 133[111]	1 910 588[111]	DJ	5 077[112]	5 607[112]	1.7	719[113]	7 799
Sri Lanka										
20 III 2012 .... DJ		20 359 439	9 856 634	10 502 805	...	20 675	*21 203	...	65 610	323
State of Palestine - État de Palestine										
1 XII 2007 .... DF		3 669 244[114]	1 862 027[114]	1 807 217[114]	DF	4 048	4 817	2.9	6 020	800
Syrian Arab Republic - République arabe syrienne										
22 IX 2004 .... DF		*17 921 000[115]	*9 161 000[115]	*8 760 000[115]	DF	20 619[115]	...	...	185 180	...

3. Population by sex, annual rate of population increase, surface area and density
Population selon le sexe, taux d'accroissement annuel de la population, superficie et densité (continued - suite)

Continent, country or area and census date / Continent, pays ou zone et date du recensement	Census type[a]	Population at the latest available census / Population d'après le dernier recensement disponible (in units — en unités)			Estimate type[a]	Mid-year estimates / Estimations au milieu de l'année (in thousands — en milliers)		Annual rate of increase Taux d'accrois sement annuel 2010-16	Surface area Superficie (km²) 2016	Density Densité 2016[b]
		Both sexes Les deux sexes	Male Masculin	Female Feminin		2010	2016			
ASIA - ASIE										
Tajikistan - Tadjikistan										
21 IX 2010 .... DF		7 564 502	3 817 004	3 747 498	DF	7 519	*8 641	2.3	142 600	61
Thailand - Thaïlande										
1 IX 2010 .... DJ		65 981 659	32 355 032	33 626 627	DJ	63 878	65 932	0.5	513 120	128
Timor-Leste										
11 VII 2015 .... DF		*1 167 242	*588 561	*578 681		...	...	...	14 919	...
Turkey - Turquie										
3 X 2011 .... DJ		74 526 000[116]	37 431 000[116]	37 095 000[116]	DJ	73 723[117]	...	...	780 004	...
Turkmenistan - Turkménistan										
10 I 1995 .... DF		4 483 251	2 225 331	2 257 920		...	...	...	488 100	...
United Arab Emirates - Émirats arabes unis										
5 XII 2005 .... DF		4 106 427[118]	2 806 141[118]	1 300 286[118]	DF	8 264[118]	9 121[119]	1.6	71 024[38]	128
Uzbekistan - Ouzbékistan										
12 I 1989 .... DJ		19 810 077	9 784 156	10 025 921	DJ	28 562[120]	...	...	448 969	...
Viet Nam										
1 IV 2009 .... DJ		85 846 997	42 413 143	43 433 854	DF	86 947[121]	*92 695[121]	1.1	330 967	280
Yemen - Yémen										
16 XII 2004 .... DF		19 685 161	10 036 953	9 648 208	DJ	23 154[3]	...		527 968	
EUROPE										
Åland Islands - Îles d'Åland										
31 XII 2000 .... DJ		25 776[122]	12 700[122]	13 076[122]	DJ	28[45]	29[45]	0.7	1 583	18
Albania - Albanie										
1 X 2011 .... DJ		2 800 138	1 403 059	1 397 079	DF	2 913	2 886[20]	-0.2	28 748	100
Andorra - Andorre										
31 XII 2011 .... DJ		78 115[45]	39 863[45]	38 252[45]	DJ	70[123]	72[45]	0.5	468	155
Austria - Autriche										
31 X 2011 .... DJ		8 401 940	4 093 938	4 308 002	DJ	8 361	8 690[20]	0.6	83 882	104
Belarus - Bélarus										
14 X 2009 .... DJ		9 503 807	4 420 039	5 083 768	DJ	9 491	9 498[20]	0.0	207 600	46
Belgium - Belgique										
1 I 2011 .... DJ		11 000 638	5 401 718	5 598 920	DJ	10 896	11 311[20]	0.6	30 528	371
Bosnia and Herzegovina - Bosnie-Herzégovine										
30 IX 2013 .... DJ		*3 791 622	...	...	DF	3 843	*3 513	-1.5	51 209	69
Bulgaria - Bulgarie										
1 II 2011 .... DJ		7 364 570	3 586 571	3 777 999	DJ	7 534	7 154[20]	-0.9	110 372	65
Croatia - Croatie										
1 IV 2011 .... DJ		4 284 889	2 066 335	2 218 554	DJ	4 295	4 191[20]	-0.4	56 594	74
Czechia - Tchéquie										
25 III 2011 .... DJ		10 436 560	5 109 766	5 326 794	DJ	10 474	10 554[20]	0.1	78 870	134
Denmark - Danemark[124]										
1 I 2011 .... DJ		5 560 628[45]	2 756 582[45]	2 804 046[45]	DJ	5 545[45]	5 724[45]	0.5	42 921	133
Estonia - Estonie										
31 XII 2011 .... DJ		1 294 455	600 526	693 929	DJ	1 331	1 316[20]	-0.2	45 227	29
Faeroe Islands - Îles Féroé										
11 XI 2011 .... DJ		48 346	25 125	23 221	DJ	49	50	0.3	1 393	36
Finland - Finlande										
31 XII 2010 .... DJ		5 375 276	2 638 416	2 736 860	DJ	5 335[125]	5 507[125]	0.5	336 861[126]	16
France										
1 I 2006 .... DJ		61 399 541[127]	29 714 539[127]	31 685 002[127]	DJ	62 918[127]	*64 732[127]	0.5	551 500	117
Germany - Allemagne										
9 V 2011 .... DJ		80 219 695	39 145 941	41 073 754	DJ	81 757	82 176[128]	0.1	357 386	230
Gibraltar										
12 XI 2012 .... DJ		32 194[129]	16 061[129]	16 133[129]	DF	31[130]	...	...	6	...
Greece - Grèce										
9 V 2011 .... DF		10 816 286	5 303 223	5 513 063	DF	11 121	10 784[20]	-0.5	131 957	82
Guernsey - Guernesey										
31 III 2015 .... DJ		62 612	31 028	31 584	DF	62[131]	63[131]	0.1	64	980

3. Population by sex, annual rate of population increase, surface area and density
Population selon le sexe, taux d'accroissement annuel de la population, superficie et densité (continued - suite)

Continent, country or area and census date — Continent, pays ou zone et date du recensement	Census type[a]	Population at the latest available census — Population d'après le dernier recensement disponible (in units — en unités)			Estimate type[a]	Mid-year estimates — Estimations au milieu de l'année (in thousands — en milliers)		Annual rate of increase — Taux d'accroissement annuel 2010-16	Surface area — Superficie (km²) 2016	Density — Densité 2016[b]
		Both sexes — Les deux sexes	Male — Masculin	Female — Feminin		2010	2016			
EUROPE										
Holy See - Saint-Siège[132]										
1 VII 2009 .... DF	DF	466[133]	320	146	DF	0[134]	...	...	0[135]	...
Hungary - Hongrie										
1 X 2011 .... DF	DF	9 937 628	4 718 479	5 219 149	DJ	10 000	9 830[136]	-0.3	93 022	106
Iceland - Islande										
31 XII 2011 .... DJ	DJ	315 556[137]	158 151[137]	157 405[137]	DJ	318[137]	333[138]	0.7	103 000	3
Ireland - Irlande										
24 IV 2016 .... DJ	DJ	4 761 865	2 354 428	2 407 437	DF	4 560	4 725[136]	0.6	69 825	68
Isle of Man - Île de Man										
24 IV 2016 .... DJ	DJ	83 314	41 269	42 045	DJ	83[139]	86[139]	0.6	572	150
Italy - Italie										
9 X 2011 .... DJ	DJ	59 433 744	28 745 507	30 688 237	DJ	59 277	60 666[20]	0.4	302 073	201
Jersey										
27 III 2011 .... DF	DF	97 857	48 296	49 561	DJ	97	104	1.2	116	898
Latvia - Lettonie										
1 III 2011 .... DJ	DJ	2 070 371	946 102	1 124 269	DJ	2 098	1 969[20]	-1.1	64 573	30
Liechtenstein										
31 XII 2010 .... DF	DF	36 149	17 886	18 263	DJ	36	38[20]	0.7	160	235
Lithuania - Lituanie										
1 III 2011 .... DJ	DJ	3 043 429	1 402 604	1 640 825	DJ	3 097	2 889[136]	-1.2	65 286	44
Luxembourg										
1 II 2011 .... DJ	DJ	512 353	254 967	257 386	DJ	507	576[20]	2.1	2 586	223
Malta - Malte										
20 XI 2011 .... DF	DF	417 432	207 625	209 807	DJ	415[140]	434[141]	0.8	315	1 378
Monaco										
7 VI 2016 .... DJ	DJ	37 308[142]	18 240[142]	19 068[142]	DJ	36[142]	38[143]	1.1	2	19 100
Montenegro - Monténégro										
1 IV 2011 .... DJ	DJ	620 029	306 236	313 793	DJ	617	622[136]	0.1	13 812	45
Netherlands - Pays-Bas										
1 I 2011 .... DJ	DJ	16 655 799	8 243 482	8 412 317	DJ	16 615	16 979[20]	0.4	41 542	409
Norway - Norvège										
19 XI 2011 .... DJ	DJ	4 979 955[144]	2 495 777[144]	2 484 178[144]	DJ	4 889[145]	5 237[145]	1.1	323 772	16
Poland - Pologne										
31 III 2011 .... DJ	DJ	38 044 565	18 420 389	19 624 176	DJ	38 042[145]	37 967[136]	0.0	312 679	121
Portugal										
21 III 2011 .... DF	DF	10 282 306	4 868 755	5 413 551	DJ	10 573	10 341[20]	-0.4	92 226	112
Republic of Moldova - République de Moldova										
5 X 2004 .... DF	DF	3 386 673[146]	1 629 689[146]	1 756 984[146]	DJ	3 562[146]	3 553[147]	0.0	33 846	105
Romania - Roumanie										
20 X 2011 .... DF	DF	20 039 141	9 736 342	10 302 799	DJ	20 247[145]	19 760[136]	-0.4	238 391	83
Russian Federation - Fédération de Russie										
14 X 2010 .... DF	DF	143 436 145	66 457 074	76 979 071	DJ	142 849	...	...	17 098 246	...
San Marino - Saint-Marin										
7 XI 2010 .... DF	DF	*30 652	*14 791[148]	*15 818[148]	DF	33[45]	34[149]	0.4	61	557
Serbia - Serbie										
1 X 2011 .... DJ	DJ	7 186 862[150]	3 499 176[150]	3 687 686[150]	DJ	7 291[150]	7 058[151]	-0.5	88 499	80
Slovakia - Slovaquie										
21 V 2011 .... DJ	DJ	5 397 036	2 627 772	2 769 264	DJ	5 391	5 431	0.1	49 035[152]	111
Slovenia - Slovénie										
1 I 2015 .... DJ	DJ	2 062 874	1 022 229	1 040 645	DJ	2 049	2 064[20]	0.1	20 273	102
Spain - Espagne										
1 XI 2011 .... DJ	DJ	46 815 915	23 104 350	23 711 560	DJ	46 562	46 446[138]	0.0	505 944	92
Svalbard and Jan Mayen Islands - Îles Svalbard et Jan Mayen										
1 XI 1960 .... DF	DF	3 431[153]	2 545[153]	886[153]		...	...	...	62 422	...
Sweden - Suède										
31 XII 2011 .... DJ	DJ	9 482 855[45]	4 726 834[45]	4 756 021[45]	DJ	9 378[45]	9 851[154]	0.8	438 574	22
Switzerland - Suisse										
31 XII 2011 .... DF	DF	8 035 391	3 973 280	4 062 111	DJ	7 825	8 327[155]	1.0	41 291	202

3. Population by sex, annual rate of population increase, surface area and density
Population selon le sexe, taux d'accroissement annuel de la population, superficie et densité (continued - suite)

Continent, country or area and census date — Continent, pays ou zone et date du recensement	Census type[a]	Population at the latest available census — Population d'après le dernier recensement disponible (in units — en unités)			Estimate type[a]	Mid-year estimates Estimations au milieu de l'année (in thousands — en milliers)		Annual rate of increase Taux d' accrois sement annuel 2010-16	Surface area Superficie (km²) 2016	Density Densité 2016[b]
		Both sexes Les deux sexes	Male Masculin	Female Feminin		2010	2016			
EUROPE										
TFYR of Macedonia - L'ex-R. y. de Macédoine										
31 X 2002 .... DJ		2 022 547	1 015 377	1 007 170	DF	2 055	2 072	0.1	25 713	81
Ukraine										
5 XII 2001 .... DF		48 240 902	22 316 317	25 924 585	DF	45 871	42 591[156]	-1.2	603 500	71
United Kingdom of Great Britain and Northern Ireland - Royaume-Uni de Grande-Bretagne et d'Irlande du Nord[157]										
27 III 2011 .... DF		63 379 787	31 126 054	32 253 733	DJ	62 759	65 383[136]	0.7	242 495	270
OCEANIA - OCÉANIE										
American Samoa - Samoas américaines										
1 IV 2010 .... DJ		55 519[52]	28 164[52]	27 355[52]	DJ	67[52]	...	...	199	...
Australia - Australie										
9 VIII 2011 .... DF		21 727 158[158]	10 737 148[158]	10 990 010[158]	DJ	22 032[42]	24 129[19]	1.5	7 692 024	3
Cook Islands - Îles Cook[159]										
1 XII 2016 .... DF		*17 459	*8 597	*8 862	DF	24	...	...	236	...
Fiji - Fidji										
16 IX 2007 .... DF		837 271	427 176	410 095	DF	857	...	...	18 272	...
French Polynesia - Polynésie française										
22 VIII 2012 .... DJ		268 207	136 996	131 211	DF	265	...	...	4 000	...
Guam										
1 IV 2010 .... DJ		159 358	81 552	77 806	DJ	...	163[52]	...	549	296
Kiribati										
10 X 2010 .... DF		103 058	50 796	52 262		...	...	...	726[160]	...
Marshall Islands - Îles Marshall										
3 IV 2011 .... DF		53 158	27 243	25 915	DF	54[161]	...	...	181	...
Micronesia (Federated States of) - Micronésie (États fédérés de)										
1 IV 2010 .... DJ		102 843	52 193	50 650	DJ	108[3]	...	...	702	...
Nauru										
31 X 2011 .... DF		10 084	5 105	4 979		...	...	...	21	...
New Caledonia - Nouvelle-Calédonie										
26 VIII 2014 .... DF		268 767	135 542	133 225	DF	250	275[20]	1.6	19 100	14
New Zealand - Nouvelle-Zélande										
5 III 2013 .... DJ		4 242 048	...	...	DJ	4 351[162]	4 693[162]	1.3	268 107	18
Niue - Nioué										
11 IX 2011 .... DF		1 611	802	809	DJ	1	...	...	260	...
Norfolk Island - Île Norfolk										
9 VIII 2011 .... DF		2 302	1 082	1 220		...	...	...	36	...
Northern Mariana Islands - Îles Mariannes septentrionales										
1 IV 2010 .... DF		53 883	27 746	26 137	DF	48	...	...	457	...
Palau - Palaos										
13 IV 2015 .... DJ		17 661	9 433	8 228	DF	21	...	...	459	...
Papua New Guinea - Papouasie-Nouvelle-Guinée										
10 VII 2011 .... DF		*7 059 653	*3 663 249	*3 396 404	DF	...	8 151[163]	...	462 840	18
Pitcairn										
31 XII 2013 .... DJ		49	23	26		...	...	...	5	...
Samoa										
7 XI 2016 .... DF		*192 126	*98 663	*93 463	DF	184	195	1.0	2 842	69

3. Population by sex, annual rate of population increase, surface area and density
Population selon le sexe, taux d'accroissement annuel de la population, superficie et densité (continued - suite)

Continent, country or area and census date / Continent, pays ou zone et date du recensement	Census type[a]	Population at the latest available census / Population d'après le dernier recensement disponible (in units — en unités)			Estimate type[a]	Mid-year estimates / Estimations au milieu de l'année (in thousands — en milliers)		Annual rate of increase / Taux d' accrois sement annuel 2010-16	Surface area / Superficie (km²) 2016	Density / Densité 2016[b]
		Both sexes / Les deux sexes	Male / Masculin	Female / Feminin		2010	2016			
OCEANIA - OCÉANIE										
Solomon Islands - Îles Salomon										
22 XI 2009 .... DF	DF	515 870	264 455	251 415	DF	*555*[3]	*639*[3]	*2.3*	28 896	*22*
Tokelau - Tokélaou										
18 X 2016 .... DF	DF	1 285	652	633		...	...	...	12	...
Tonga										
30 XI 2016 .... DJ	DJ	*100 745	*50 312	*50 433		...	...	...	747	...
Tuvalu										
4 XI 2012 .... DF	DF	10 782	...	...	DF	...	*10*[163]	...	26	*388*
Vanuatu										
7 XI 2016 .... DF	DF	272 459	138 265	134 194	DF	*239*	...	...	12 189	...
Wallis and Futuna Islands - Îles Wallis et Futuna										
22 VII 2013 .... DF	DF	12 197	5 927	6 270	DF	...	*12*[163]	...	142	*83*

FOOTNOTES - NOTES

Italics: estimates which are less reliable. - Italiques : estimations moins sûres.

* Provisional. - Données provisoires.

a 'Code' indicates the source of data, as follows:
DF - De facto
DJ - De jure
SDF - Sample survey, de facto
SDJ - Sample survey, de jure

Le 'Code' indique la source des données, comme suit :
DF - Population de fait
DJ - Population de droit
SDF - Enquête par sondage, population de fait
SDJ - Enquête par sondage, Population de droit

b Population per square kilometre of surface area. Figures are estimates of population divided by surface area and are not to be considered either as reflecting density in the urban sense or as indicating the supporting power of a territory's land and resources. - Nombre d'habitants au kilomètre carré. Il s'agit simplement d'éstimations de la population divisé par celui de la superficie: il ne faut pas y voir d'indication de la densité au sens urbain du terme ni de l'effectif de population que les terres et les ressources du territoire sont capables de nourrir.

1 Total resident population including common and collective households of nomadic population, and population counted separately. - Population résidente totale y compris les ménages ordinaires et collectifs de la population nomade, et la population comptée à part.
2 Unrevised data that do not take into account the results of the 2014 population census. - Ces données n'ont pas été revisées et elles ne prennent pas en compte les résultats du recensement de la population de 2014.
3 Data refer to national projections. - Les données se réfèrent aux projections nationales.
4 Projections based on the 2013 Population Census. - Projections fondées sur le recensement de la population de 2013.
5 Data based on the 2011 Census. - Données fondées sur le recensement de 2011.
6 Excluding Mayotte. - Non compris Mayotte.
7 Estimates based on the 2014 Population Census. - Estimations fondées sur le recensement de la population de 2014.
8 Projections based on the 2014 Population Census. - Projections fondées sur le recensement de la population de 2014.
9 Data are calculated from the results of the Population and Housing Census of 2009. - Les données sont calculées à partir des résultats du recensement de la population et de l'habitat de 2009.

10 Data refer to projections based on the 1983 Population Census. - Les données se réfèrent aux projections basées sur le recensement de la population de 1983.
11 Estimates considering also the results of the 2007 Population Census. - Estimations en prennant en considération les résultats du recensement de la population de 2007.
12 Data based on the 2010 Population Census. - Les données sont fondées sur le recensement de la population de 2010.
13 Post-censal estimates based on the 2009 Population Census. - Les estimations post-censitaire fondées sur le recensement de la population de 2009.
14 Data refer to Libyan nationals only. - Les données se raportent aux nationaux libyens seulement.
15 Projections considering also the results of the 2009 Population Census results. - Projections en prennant en considération les résultats du recensement de la population de 2009.
16 Including nomadic population. - Y compris la population nomade.
17 Excludes the islands of St. Brandon and Agalega. - Non compris les îles St. Brandon et Agalega.
18 Based on the results of the 2000 Population Census. - Basé sur les résultats du recencement de la population de 2000.
19 Based on the results of the 2011 Population Census. - Basé sur les résultats du recencement de la population de 2011.
20 Data refer to 1 January. - Données se raportent au 1 janvier.
21 Based on the results of the 2004 Population Census. - D'après des résultats du recencement de la population de 2004.
22 Projections based on the results of national survey on population and health conducted between 2010 and 2011, and especially population and housing census 2014. - Des projections de la population fondées sur les résultats de l'enquête nationale de la population et de la santé réalisée entre 2010 et 2011 et, surtout, du recensement général de la population et de l'habitat de 2014.
23 Data refer to projections based on the 2011 Population Census. - Les données se réfèrent aux projections basées sur le recensement de la population de 2011.
24 Projections based on the 2012 Population and Housing Census. - Projections fondées sur le recensement 2012 de la population et des logements.
25 Data are projections based on the 2006 Population Census. - Projections fondées sur le recensement de la population de 2006.
26 Data are projections based on the 2008 Population and Housing Census. - Projection basée sur le recensement 2008 de la population et des logements.
27 Data refer to Saint Helenian resident population. - Pour la population résidante de Sainte-Hélène.
28 Data refer to 31 December. - Données se raportent au 31 décembre.
29 Surface area is based on the 2002 population and housing census. - La superficie est fondée sur les données provenant du recensement de la population et du logement de 2002.
30 Data have not been adjusted for underenumeration, estimated at 7 per cent. - Les données n'ont pas été ajustées pour compenser les lacunes du dénombrement, estimées à 7 p. 100.

³¹ Projections based on the 2002 Population Census. - Projections fondées sur le recensement de la population de 2002.

³² Comprising the Northern Region (former Saguia el Hamra) and Southern Region (former Rio de Oro). - Comprend la région septentrionale (ancien Saguia-el-Hamra) et la région méridionale (ancien Rio de Oro).

³³ Projections based on the 2012 Population Census. - Projections fondées sur le recensement de la population de 2012.

³⁴ Data refers to resident population adjusted for the undercount of 18 per cent and including the institutional population. - Les données concernent la population résidente, y compris la population des institutions, et ont été ajustées pour tenir compte du sous-dénombrement estimé à 18 p. 100.

³⁵ Bermuda is 100 per cent urban. - 100 pour cent de la population des Bermudes est urbaine.

³⁶ Final intercensal estimates. - Estimations inter-censitaires definitives.

³⁷ Preliminary postcensal estimates. - Estimations post censitaires préliminaires.

³⁸ Land area only. - La superficie des terres seulement.

³⁹ Excluding the institutional population. - Non compris la population dans les institutions.

⁴⁰ Based on the national household surveys 2010-2014 and the 2011 population census. - D'après les données de l'enquête nationale des ménages 2010-2014 et les résultats du recensement de la population de 2011.

⁴¹ Based on the national household survey of 2016. - D'après l'enquête nationale auprès des ménages de 2016.

⁴² Intercensal estimates. - Estimations inter-censitaires.

⁴³ Postcensal estimates. - Estimations post censitaires.

⁴⁴ Estimates or projections based on the 2007 Population Census. - Estimations ou projections fondées sur le recensement de la population de 2007.

⁴⁵ Population statistics are compiled from registers. - Les statistiques de la population sont compilées à partir des registres.

⁴⁶ Excluding data for Saint Barthélémy and Saint Martin. - Non compris les données pour Saint Barthélémy et Saint Martin.

⁴⁷ Excluding data for Saint Barthélémy and Saint Martin. Data refer to 1 January. - Non compris les données pour Saint Barthélémy et Saint Martin. Données se raportent au 1 janvier.

⁴⁸ Projections produced by l'Institut Haïtien de Statistique et d'Informatique (IHSI) and the Latin American and Caribbean Demographic Centre (CELADE) - Population Division of ECLAC. - Les données sont projections produits par l'Institut Haïtien de Statistique et d'Informatique (IHSI) et le centre démographique de l'Amérique latine et les Caraïbes - Division de la population de la CEPALC.

⁴⁹ Data refer to projections based on the 2001 Population Census. - Les données se réfèrent aux projections basées sur le recensement de la population de 2001.

⁵⁰ The figures represent the census counts adjusted for under-coverage. Adjustments are done by applying weights calculated (to 4 decimal places) for each sex and age group to the enumerated population when the tabulations are produced. Minor discrepancies between totals and the sum of the component parts of a table and minor discrepancies between the totals across tables are due to rounding after weights are applied. - Les chiffres représentent le dénombrement résultant du recensement ajusté pour tenir compte du sous-dénombrement. Les ajustements sont effectués en appliquant un coefficient de pondération calculé (à la quatrième décimale) pour chaque sexe et groupe d'âges de la population dénombrée lors de l'établissement des tableaux. Les écarts mineurs entre les totaux et la somme des éléments constitutifs d'un tableau ainsi qu'entre les totaux figurant dans différents tableaux sont dus au fait que les chiffres sont arrondis après la pondération.

⁵¹ Including an estimation of 1 334 585 persons corresponding to 448 195 housing units without information of the occupants. - Y compris une estimation de 1 334 585 personnes correspondant aux 448 195 unités d'habitation sans information sur les occupants.

⁵² Including armed forces stationed in the area. - Y compris les militaires en garnison sur le territoire.

⁵³ Including armed forces stationed in the area. Based on the results of the 2010 Population Census. - Y compris les militaires en garnison sur le territoire. D'après le résultats du recensement de la population de 2010.

⁵⁴ Including armed forces stationed in the area. Postcensal estimates. - Y compris les militaires en garnison sur le territoire. Estimations post censitaires.

⁵⁵ Refers to habitable area. Excludes St. Lucia's Forest Reserve. - S'applique à la zone habitable. Exclut la réserve forestière de Sainte-Lucie.

⁵⁶ Population in households only. - Population dans les ménages seulement.

⁵⁷ Excluding residents of institutions. - À l'exclusion de personnes en établissements de soins.

⁵⁸ Including low water level for all islands (area to shoreline). - Incluent le niveau de basses eaux pour toutes les îles.

⁵⁹ Excluding U.S. Armed Forces overseas and civilian U.S. citizens whose usual place of residence is outside the United States. Postcensal estimates. - Non compris les militaires américains à l'étranger et les civils américains dont le lieu de résidence habituel est en dehors des États-Unis. Estimations post censitaires.

⁶⁰ Including armed forces stationed in the area. Source: U.S. National Center for Health Statistics, National Vital Statistics Reports (NVSR). - Y compris les militaires en garnison sur le territoire. Source : US National Center for Health Statistics, National Vital Statistics Reports (NVSR).

⁶¹ Projections based on the 2010 Population and Housing Census. - Projections fondées sur le recensement 2010 de la population et des logements.

⁶² Data updated according to "Superintendencia Agraria". Interior waters correspond to natural or artificial bodies of water or snow. - Données actualisées d'après la « Superintendencia Agraria ». Les eaux intérieures correspondent aux étendues d'eau naturelles ou artificielles et aux étendues neigeuses.

⁶³ Data include persons in remote areas, military personnel outside the country, merchant seamen at sea, civilian seasonal workers outside the country, and other civilians outside the country, and exclude nomads, foreign military, civilian aliens temporarily in the country, transients on ships and Indian jungle population. Data refer to national projections. - Y compris les personnes vivant dans des régions éloignées, le personel militaire en dehors du pays, les marins marchands, les ouvriers saisonniers en dehors du pays, et autres civils en dehors du pays, et non compris les nomades, les militaires étrangers, les étrangers civils temporairement dans le pays, les transiteurs sur des bateaux et les Indiens de la jungle. Les données se réfèrent aux projections nationales.

⁶⁴ Data are revised projections taking into consideration also the results of the 2005 census. - Les données sont des projections révisées tenant compte également des résultats du recensement de 2005.

⁶⁵ Data based on the 2010 Population Census. Excludes nomadic Indian tribes. - Les données sont fondées sur le recensement de la population de 2010. Non compris les tribus d'Indiens nomades.

⁶⁶ Excludes nomadic Indian tribes. - Non compris les tribus d'Indiens nomades.

⁶⁷ A dispute exists between the governments of Argentina and the United Kingdom of Great Britain and Northern Ireland concerning sovereignty over the Falkland Islands (Malvinas). - La souveraineté sur les îles Falkland (Malvinas) fait l'objet d'un différend entre le Gouvernement argentin et le Gouvernement du Royaume-Uni de Grande-Bretagne et d'Irlande du Nord.

⁶⁸ Excluding military personnel and their families, visitors and transients. - Non compris les militaires et leur familles, ni les visiteurs et transients.

⁶⁹ Estimates or projections considering also the results of the 2012 Population Census. - Estimations ou projections en prennant en considération les résultats du recensement de la population de 2012.

⁷⁰ Data refer to 30 June. Estimates or projections based on the 2007 Population Census. - Données se raportent au 30 juin. Estimations ou projections fondées sur le recensement de la population de 2007.

⁷¹ Figures for male and female population do not add up to the figure for total population, because they exclude 108 homeless people of unknown sex. - Les chiffres relatifs à la population masculine et féminine ne correspondent pas au chiffre de la population totale, parce que l'on en a exclu 108 personnes sans toit dont le sexe n'est pas connu.

⁷² Data refer to the settled population based on the 1979 Population Census and the latest household prelisting. The refugees of Afghanistan in Iran, Pakistan, and an estimated 1.5 million nomads, are not included. Excluding nomad population. - Les données se rapportent à la population stationnaire sur la base du recensement de 1979 et du recensement préliminaire des logements le plus récent. Sont exclus les réfugiés d'Afghanistan en Iran et au Pakistan et les nomades estimés à 1,5 million. Non compris les nomades.

⁷³ Data refer to the settled population based on the 1979 Population Census and the latest household prelisting. The refugees of Afghanistan in Iran, Pakistan, and an estimated 1.5 million nomads, are not included. - Les données se rapportent à la population stationnaire sur la base du recensement de 1979 et du recensement préliminaire des logements le plus récent. Sont exclus les réfugiés d'Afghanistan en Iran et au Pakistan et les nomades estimés à 1,5 million.

⁷⁴ Data refer to projected figures based on the Population and Housing Census 2005 (district projection). - Les données se réfèrent aux projections basées sur le recensement de la population et de l'habitat de 2005 (projections locales).

⁷⁵ Excluding foreign diplomatic personnel and their dependants. - Non compris le personnel diplomatique étranger et les membres de leur famille les accompagnant.

⁷⁶ Excluding foreign diplomatic personnel and their dependants. Data based on the 2008 Population Census. - Non compris le personnel diplomatique étranger et les membres de leur famille les accompagnant. Données fondées sur le recensement de population de 2008.

⁷⁷ Data are from Communique of the National Bureau of Statistics of the People's Republic of China on Major Figures of the 2010 Population Census (No.1). For statistical purposes, the data for China do not include those for the Hong Kong Special Administrative Region (Hong Kong SAR), Macao Special

Administrative Region (Macao SAR) and Taiwan province of China. - Données issues du communiqué du Bureau national de la statistique de la République populaire de Chine sur les chiffres importants du recensement de 2010 (n° 1). Pour la présentation des statistiques, les données pour la Chine ne comprennent pas la Région Administrative Spéciale de Hong Kong (Hong Kong RAS), la Région Administrative Spéciale de Macao (Macao RAS) et Taïwan province de Chine.

[78] For statistical purposes, the data for China do not include those for the Hong Kong Special Administrative Region (Hong Kong SAR), Macao Special Administrative Region (Macao SAR) and Taiwan province of China. Data have been estimated on the basis of the annual National Sample Survey on Population Changes. - Pour la présentation des statistiques, les données pour la Chine ne comprennent pas la Région Administrative Spéciale de Hong Kong (Hong Kong RAS), la Région Administrative Spéciale de Macao (Macao RAS) et Taïwan province de Chine. Les données ont été estimées sur la base de l'enquête annuelle "National Sample Survey on Population Changes".

[79] Data refer to Hong Kong resident population at the census moment, which covers usual residents and mobile residents. Usual residents refer to two categories of people: (1) Hong Kong permanent residents who had stayed in Hong Kong for at least three months during the six months before or for at least three months during the six months after the census moment, regardless of whether they were in Hong Kong or not at the census moment; and (2) Hong Kong non-permanent residents who were in Hong Kong at the census moment. Mobile Residents, they are Hong Kong permanent residents who had stayed in Hong Kong for at least one month but less than three months during the six months before or for at least one month but less than three months during the six months after the census moment, regardless of whether they were in Hong Kong or not at the census moment. - Les données se rapportent à la population résidente à Hong Kong au moment du recensement. Cette population est composée des résidents habituels et des résidents mobiles. La population résidente est partagée en deux catégories: (1) les résidents permanents qui ont habité à Hong Kong au moins trois mois pendant les six mois précédents ou les six mois suivants le recensement; (2) les habitants non-permanents de Hong Kong qui étaient à Hong Kong au moment du recensement. La population mobile se rapporte aux résidents permanents de Hong Kong qui ont habité à Hong Kong pendant les six mois après le recensement pour une période comprise entre un mois et trois mois, indépendamment du fait qu'ils étaient à Hong Kong au moment du recensement au pays.

[80] Inland waters include the reservoirs. - Les eaux intérieures comprennent les réservoirs.

[81] Data refer to government controlled areas. - Les données se rapportent aux zones contrôlées par le Gouvernement.

[82] Data refer to government controlled areas. Data refer to annual average population. - Les données se rapportent aux zones contrôlées par le Gouvernement. Les données correspondent à la population annuelle moyenne.

[83] Data refer to government controlled areas. Data refer to 1 January. - Les données se rapportent aux zones contrôlées par le Gouvernement. Données se raportent au 1 janvier.

[84] Based on the results of the 2014 Population Census. - D'après les résultats du recensement de la population de 2014.

[85] Includes data for the Indian-held part of Jammu and Kashmir, the final status of which has not yet been determined. - Y compris les données pour la partie du Jammu et du Cachemire occupée par l'Inde dont le statut définitif n'a pas encore été déterminé.

[86] Includes data for the Indian-held part of Jammu and Kashmir, the final status of which has not yet been determined. Data refer to projections based on the 2001 Population Census. - Y compris les données pour la partie du Jammu et du Cachemire occupée par l'Inde dont le statut définitif n'a pas encore été déterminé. Les données se réfèrent aux projections basées sur le recensement de la population de 2001.

[87] Data are based on the publication: "Indonesia Population Projection 2010-2035" - Les données sont basées sur la publication : << Indonesia Population Projection 2010-2035 >>

[88] Data refer to the Iranian Year which begins on 21 March and ends on 20 March of the following year. - Les données concernent l'année iranienne, qui commence le 21 mars et se termine le 20 mars de l'année suivante.

[89] Excluding the population in three autonomous provinces in the north of the country. - La population des trois provinces autonomes dans le nord du pays est exclue.

[90] Data are rounded for confidentiality reasons. Includes data for East Jerusalem and Israeli residents in certain other territories under occupation by Israeli military forces since June 1967. - Chiffres arrondis pour des raisons de confidentialité. Y compris les données pour Jérusalem-Est et les résidents israéliens dans certains autres territoires occupés depuis 1967 par les forces armées israéliennes.

[91] Includes data for East Jerusalem and Israeli residents in certain other territories under occupation by Israeli military forces since June 1967. - Y compris les données pour Jérusalem-Est et les résidents israéliens dans certains autres territoires occupés depuis 1967 par les forces armées israéliennes.

[92] Excluding diplomatic personnel outside the country and foreign military and civilian personnel and their dependants stationed in the area. - Non compris le personnel diplomatique hors du pays ni les militaires et agents civils étrangers en poste sur le territoire et les membres de leur famille les accompagnant.

[93] Excluding diplomatic personnel outside the country and foreign military and civilian personnel and their dependants stationed in the area. Because of rounding, totals are not in all cases the sum of the respective components. Estimates based on the complete counts of the 2015 Population Census - Non compris le personnel diplomatique hors du pays ni les militaires et agents civils étrangers en poste sur le territoire et les membres de leur famille les accompagnant. Les chiffres étant arrondis, les totaux ne correspondent pas toujours rigoureusement à la somme des composants respectifs. Estimations basées sur le dénombrement complet du recensement de la population de 2015.

[94] Data refer to 1 October 2007. - Les données se réfèrent au 1er octobre 2007.

[95] Excluding data for Jordanian territory under occupation since June 1967 by Israeli military forces. - Non compris les données pour le territoire jordanien occupé depuis juin 1967 par les forces armées israéliennes.

[96] Excluding data for Jordanian territory under occupation since June 1967 by Israeli military forces. Data refer to 31 December. - Non compris les données pour le territoire jordanien occupé depuis juin 1967 par les forces armées israéliennes. Données se raportent au 31 décembre.

[97] Data refer to annual average population. - Les données correspondent à la population annuelle moyenne.

[98] Estimates based on the results of 2015 population census. - Estimations fondées sur les résultats du recensement de la population de 2015.

[99] Source: Living conditions of household survey, October 2011 to September 2012. - Source: Enquête sur les conditions de vie des ménages, octobre 2011 à septembre 2012.

[100] Data have been adjusted for underenumeration. - Les données ont été ajustées pour compenser les lacunes du dénombrement.

[101] Estimates based on the adjusted results of the Population and Housing Census of 2010. - Les estimations sont fondée sur les résultats ajustées du recensement de la population et de l'habitat de 2010.

[102] Data refer to resident population that includes Maldivians and foreigners. - Les données concernent la population résidente, qui comprend des Maldiviens et des étrangers.

[103] Data refer to resident Maldivian population. - Les données concernent la population maldivienne résidente.

[104] The total for the whole country includes 1,206,353 persons estimated not to have been counted in parts of States of Rakhine, Kachin and Kayin. - Le total pour l'ensemble du pays s'élève à 1 206 353 personnes qui ne vivaient pas dans les États rakhine, kachin et kayin.

[105] Data refer to 1 October. - Données se raportent au 1 octobre.

[106] Data refer to 1 October. Based on the results of the 2014 Population Census. - Données se raportent au 1 octobre. D'après les résultats du recensement de la population de 2014.

[107] Data refer to registered population data from Royal Oman Police. - Les données portent sur la population enregistrée par la police royale de l'Oman.

[108] Excluding data for the Pakistan-held part of Jammu and Kashmir, the final status of which has not yet been determined. - Non compris les données concernant la partie du Jammu et Cachemire occupée par le Pakistan dont le statut définitif n'a pas été déterminé.

[109] Excluding 2134 Filipinos in Philippine Embassies, Consulates and Missions Abroad. - Excepté 2134 Philippins travaillant dans les ambassades, les consulats et les missions des Philippines à l'étranger.

[110] Data based on the preliminary results of the 2010 Population and Housing Census. - D'après les résultats préliminaires du recensement de la population et des logements de 2010.

[111] Data are based on the latest register-based population estimates for 2010. Data refer to resident population which comprises Singapore citizens and permanent residents. Urban and rural breakdown not applicable as Singapore is a city-state. - Données basées sur les estimations démographiques les plus récentes fondées sur les registres de 2010. Les données se rapportent à la population résidente composé des citoyens de Singapour et des résidents permanents. La ventilation entre zones urbaines et zones rurales ne s'applique pas à Singapour, puisqu'il s'agit d'une ville État.

[112] Data refer to total population, which comprises Singapore residents and non-residents. Data refer to 30 June. Data exclude residents who have been away from Singapore for a continuous period of 12 months or longer as at the reference date. - Les données se rapportent à la population totale composé des résidents de Singapour et les non résidents. Données se raportent au 30 juin. Non compris les résidents hors de Singapour pour une période ininterrompue de 12 mois ou plus avant de la date de référence.

113 The land area of Singapore comprises the mainland and other islands. - La superficie terrestre de Singapour comprend l'île principale et les autres îles.

114 Data have not been adjusted for underenumeration. - Les données n'ont pas été ajustées pour compenser les lacunes du dénombrement.

115 Including Palestinian refugees. - Y compris les réfugiés de Palestine.

116 Based on a sample taken at the time of census. Because of rounding, totals are not in all cases the sum of the respective components. - D'après un échantillon obtenu au moment du recensement. Les chiffres étant arrondis, les totaux ne correspondent pas toujours rigoureusement à la somme des composants respectifs.

117 Data refer to 31 December. Data based on Address Based Population Registration System. - Données se rapportent au 31 décembre. Les données sont basées sur le registre national de la population basé sur l'adresse.

118 Data include non-national population. - Les données comprennent les non-nationaux.

119 Data include non-national population. Data refer to 31 December. - Les données comprennent les non-nationaux. Données se raportent au 31 décembre.

120 Data refer to resident population. - Les données concernent la population résidente.

121 Data are adjusted according to the results of the 2009 census and 2014 intercensus. - Les données ont été ajustées à partir des résultats du recensement de la population de 2009 et des données intercensitaires de 2014.

122 Statistics are compiled from registers. - Les statistiques sont compilées à partir des registres.

123 Decrease in population due to revision in administrative registers. Population statistics are compiled from registers. Data refer to 1 January. - Diminution de la population due à la révision des registres administratifs. Les statistiques de la population sont compilées à partir des registres. Données se raportent au 1 janvier.

124 Excluding Faeroe Islands and Greenland shown separately, if available. - Non compris les Iles Féroé et le Groenland, qui font l'objet de rubriques distinctes, si disponible.

125 Population statistics are compiled from registers. Excluding Åland Islands. - Les statistiques de la population sont compilées à partir des registres. Non compris les Îles d'Åland.

126 Excluding Åland Islands. - Non compris les Îles d'Åland.

127 Excluding diplomatic personnel outside the country and including members of alien armed forces not living in military camps and foreign diplomatic personnel not living in embassies or consulates. - Non compris le personnel diplomatique hors du pays et y compris les militaires étrangers ne vivant pas dans des camps militaires et le personnel diplomatique étranger ne vivant pas dans les ambassades ou les consulats.

128 Data refer to 1 January. Data based on the 2011 Census. - Données se raportent au 1 janvier. Données fondées sur le recensement de 2011.

129 Excluding military personnel, visitors and transients. - Non compris les militaires, ni les visiteurs et transients.

130 Excluding military personnel, visitors and transients. Data refer to 31 December. - Non compris les militaires, ni les visiteurs et transients. Données se raportent au 31 décembre.

131 Data refer to 31 March. - Données se raportent au 31 mars.

132 Data refer to the Vatican City State. - Les données se rapportent à l'Etat de la Cité du Vatican.

133 The population figure is 466 persons. - La population est égale à 466 personnes.

134 The population figure is 466 persons. Data refer to 6 December. - La population est égale à 466 personnes. Données se raportent au 6 décembre.

135 Surface area is 0.44 km². - Superficie: 0,44 km².

136 Data refer to 1 January. Data refer to usually resident population. - Données se rapportent au 1 janvier. Les données concernent la population habituellement résidente.

137 Data refer to registered resident population. - Les données concernent la population enregistrée résidente.

138 Data refer to registered resident population. Data refer to 1 January. - Les données concernent la population enregistrée résidente. Données se raportent au 1 janvier.

139 Data refer to 30 April. - Données se raportent au 30 avril.

140 Including civilian nationals temporarily outside the country. - Y compris les civils nationaux temporairement hors du pays.

141 Including civilian nationals temporarily outside the country. Data refer to 1 January. - Y compris les civils nationaux temporairement hors du pays. Données se raportent au 1 janvier.

142 Data refer to resident population only. - Pour la population résidante seulement.

143 Data refer to resident population only. Data refer to 1 January. - Pour la population résidante seulement. Données se raportent au 1 janvier.

144 Including residents temporarily outside the country. Population statistics are compiled from registers. - Y compris les résidents se trouvant temporairement hors du pays. Les statistiques de la population sont compilées à partir des registres.

145 Data refer to usually resident population. - Les données concernent la population habituellement résidente.

146 Excluding Transnistria and the municipality of Bender. - Les données ne tiennent pas compte de l'information sur la Transnistria et la municipalité de Bender.

147 Excluding Transnistria and the municipality of Bender. Data refer to 1 January. - Les données ne tiennent pas compte de l'information sur la Transnistria et la municipalité de Bender. Données se raportent au 1 janvier.

148 Figures for male and female may not add up to the total, since they do not include the category "Unknown". - La somme des chiffres indiqués pour les sexes masculin et féminin peut n'être pas égale au total parce qu'elle n'inclut pas la catégorie " inconnue ".

149 Population statistics are compiled from registers. Data refer to 1 January. - Les statistiques de la population sont compilées à partir des registres. Données se raportent au 1 janvier.

150 Excludes data for Kosovo and Metohia. - Sans les données pour le Kosovo et Metohie.

151 Excludes data for Kosovo and Metohia. Based on the results of the 2011 Population Census. - Sans les données pour le Kosovo et Metohie. Basé sur les résultats du recencement de la population de 2011.

152 Excluding inland water. - Exception faite des eaux intérieures.

153 Inhabited only during the winter season. The Norwegian population of these islands is included also in the de jure population of Norway. - N'est habitée que pendant la saison d'hiver. La population norvégienne de ces îles est comprise également dans la population de droit de la Norvège.

154 Data refer to 1 January. Population statistics are compiled from registers. Data refer to registered resident population. - Données se raportent au 1 janvier. Les statistiques de la population sont compilées à partir des registres. Les données concernent la population enregistrée résidente.

155 Data refer to legal resident population. Data refer to 1 January. - Les données concernent la population légalement résidente. Données se raportent au 1 janvier.

156 Data refer to 1 January. The Government of Ukraine has informed the United Nations that it is not in a position to provide statistical data concerning the Autonomous Republic of Crimea and the city of Sevastopol. - Données se raportent au 1 janvier. Le gouvernement Ukrainien a informé l'ONU qu'il n'est pas en mesure de fournir des données statistiques concernant la République autonome de Crimée et la ville de Sébastopol.

157 Excluding Channel Islands (Guernsey and Jersey) and Isle of Man, shown separately, if available. - Non compris les îles Anglo-Normandes (Guernesey et Jersey) et l'île de Man, qui font l'objet de rubriques distinctes, si disponible.

158 This data has been randomly rounded to protect confidentiality. Individual figures may not add up to totals, and values for the same data may vary in different tables. Including population in off-shore, migratory and shipping. - Ces données ont été arrondies de façon aléatoire afin d'en préserver la confidentialité. La somme de certains chiffres peut ne pas correspondre aux totaux indiqués et les valeurs des mêmes données peuvent varier d'un tableau à un autre. Y compris les populations extraterritoriales, les populations nomades et les populations maritimes.

159 Excluding Niue, shown separately, which is part of Cook Islands, but because of remoteness is administered separately. - Non compris Nioué, qui fait l'objet d'une rubrique distincte et qui fait partie des îles Cook, mais qui, en raison de son éloignement, est administrée séparément.

160 Land area only. Excluding 84 square km of uninhabited islands. - La superficie des terres seulement. Exclut des îles inhabitées d'une superficie de 84 kilomètres carrés.

161 Projections are prepared by the Secretariat of the Pacific Community based on the 1999 census of population and housing. - Les projections sont préparées par le Secrétariat de la Communauté du Pacifique à partir des résultats du recensement et de l'habitat de 1999.

162 Because of rounding, totals are not in all cases the sum of the respective components. - Les chiffres étant arrondis, les totaux ne correspondent pas toujours rigoureusement à la somme des composants respectifs.

163 Estimates are prepared by the Secretariat of the Pacific Community based on the last population and housing census. - Les estimations sont préparées par le Secrétariat de la Communauté du Pacifique à partir des résultats du dernier recensement de la population et de l'habitat.

Table 3a – *Demographic Yearbook 2016*

Table 3a presents the values of the Whipple's index by sex, urban or rural residence, for total area and both sexes combined, according to the availability of the underlying data in the *Demographic Yearbook* database.

The data used to compile these indices are the datasets of population by single years of age, sex, and urban or rural residence, of the population censuses conducted worldwide since 1985. These datasets have been reported by the National Statistical Offices to the United Nations Statistics Division via the *Demographic Yearbook* questionnaires.

The footnotes that appear at the end of this table are notes that refer to the respective dataset of population by single years of age, sex, and urban or rural residence.

Whipple's index is an index of age preference in age reporting. The way it is calculated for this table, it is meant to indicate preference or avoidance of ages ending in digits "0" (zero) or "5" (five) during age reporting for a population census.

The formula used to calculate the values of the Whipple's index for this table is:

$$\frac{P25+P30+P35+P40+P45+P50+P55+P60}{\frac{1}{5}(P23+P24+P25+\cdots+P58+P59+P60+P61+P62)}*100$$

where Px refers to the number of persons of age x in completed years. The sum in brackets in the denominator is the sum of the number of persons of every single age from 23 to 62.

The values of the Whipple's index generally vary between 100, indicating no preference for "0" or "5" (in other words no heaping in ages ending in "0" or "5"), and 500, indicating that age reporting was entirely concentrated in ages ending in digits "0" or "5". The higher than 100 the value of the index, the higher is the heaping of age reporting in ages ending in "0" or "5".

For more information about the measurement of age and digit preference, please refer to *The Methods and Materials of Demography, Second Edition* (2004), Edited by Jacob S. Siegel and David A. Swanson.

Le tableau 3a présente les valeurs de l'indice de Whipple par sexe, résidence urbaine ou rurale, pour la superficie totale et les sexes combinés, selon la disponibilité des données sous-jacentes dans la base de données de l'*Annuaire démographique*.

Les données utilisées pour établir ces indices sont les séries de données de la population par âge simple, sexe et résidence urbaine ou rurale, pour les recensements de la population effectués dans le monde entier depuis 1985. Ces séries de données sont communiquées par les services nationaux de statistique à la Division de statistique de l'Organisation des Nations Unies par le biais des questionnaires de l'*Annuaire démographique*.

Les notes qui figurent à la fin de ce tableau sont des notes renvoyant aux différentes séries de données de la population par âge simple, sexe et résidence urbaine ou rurale.

L'indice de Whipple est un indice de préférence de certains âges dans les déclarations de l'âge. La manière dont il est calculé pour ce tableau permet d'indiquer l'attraction ou la répulsion pour des âges se terminant par les chiffres « 0 » (zéro) ou « 5 » (cinq) lors de la déclaration de l'âge effectuée dans le cadre d'un recensement de population.

La formule utilisée pour calculer les valeurs de l'indice de Whipple pour ce tableau est la suivante:

$$\frac{P25+P30+P35+P40+P45+P50+P55+P60}{\frac{1}{5}(P23+P24+P25+\cdots+P58+P59+P60+P61+P62)} *100$$

Px étant le nombre de personnes d'âge x en années révolues. La somme entre parenthèses en dénominateur est la somme du nombre de personnes selon l'âge simple de 23 à 62 ans.

Les valeurs de l'indice de Whipple varient généralement entre 100, indication d'absence de préférence pour « 0 » ou « 5 »(en d'autres termes pas de prépondérance des âges se terminant par « 0 » ou « 5 »), et 500, indiquant que les déclarations de l'âge étaient entièrement polarisées sur les âges se terminant par les chiffres « 0 » ou « 5 ». Plus la valeur de l'indice est supérieure à 100, plus les déclarations de l'âge sont polarisées sur les âges se terminant par « 0 » ou « 5 ».

Pour en savoir plus sur la mesure de l'âge et la préférence pour les chiffres, prière de consulter l'ouvrage intitulé *The Methods and Materials of Demography, Second Edition (2004),* publié sous la direction de Jacob S. Siegel et David A. Swanson.

Continent, country or area, date and code[a] Continent, pays ou zone, date et code[a]	Total			Urban - Urbaine			Rural - Rurale		
	Both sexes Les deux sexes	Male Masculin	Female Féminin	Both sexes Les deux sexes	Male Masculin	Female Féminin	Both sexes Les deux sexes	Male Masculin	Female Féminin
AFRICA - AFRIQUE									
Algeria - Algérie[1]									
16 IV 2008 (CDJC)	100.7	100.5	100.9	100.7	100.5	100.9	100.7	100.6	100.8
Angola									
16 V 2014 (CDFC)	106.1	105.3	106.8	104.9	104.5	105.4	108.2	107.1	109.1
Benin - Bénin									
15 II 1992 (CDFC)	216.1	205.6	224.6	185.4	171.6	197.9	234.6	228	239.6
11 II 2002 (CDJC)	229.1	218.9	237.8	190.4	180.1	200	257.5	250	263.5
Botswana									
21 VIII 1991 (CDFC)	104.8	106.6	103.3	102.4	103.6	101.4	107.7	110.8	105.3
17 VIII 2001 (CDFC)	100.9	101.8	100.2	...	...	...	...	...	...
9 VIII 2011 (CDFC)	100.8	101.3	100.3	101.7	101.8	101.6	99	100.5	97.5
Burkina Faso									
10 XII 1985 (CDJC)	193	173.8	208.4	153.1	140.9	166.7	198.6	179.4	213.2
10 XII 1996 (CDJC)	162.6[2]	144[2]	177.5[2]	99.5[3]	99.6[3]	99.5[3]	99.6[3]	99.7[3]	99.5[3]
9 XII 2006 (CDJC)	145.1	133.8	154.5	131.1	130.5	131.8	150.2	135.3	161.5
Burundi									
16 VIII 1990 (CDJC)	152.9	141.7	163	...	...	...	...	...	...
16 VIII 2008 (CDJC)	156.8	149.4	164.4	137.2	136.5	138.3	159.4	151.5	167.1
Cabo Verde									
23 VI 1990 (CDFC)	111.9	110.7	112.8	108	107.7	108.3	115.3	113.7	116.4
16 VI 2010 (CDJC)	105.8	105.7	105.9	105.3	105.1	105.6	106.7	106.8	106.5
Cameroon - Cameroun									
11 XI 2005 (CDJC)	173.5	165.1	181.4	...	...	...	...	...	...
Central African Republic - République centrafricaine									
8 XII 1988 (CDFC)	139.4	132	146.1	129.9	125.2	134.3	144.5	135.8	152.3
Congo									
1 I 1985 (CDJC)	107.3	107.5	107.1	...	...	...	...	...	...
28 IV 2007 (CDFC)	103.5	103.1	103.8	...	...	...	...	...	...
Côte d'Ivoire									
1 III 1988 (CDFC)	126.3	117.3	136.2	116.4	112.7	121	132.7	120.5	145
15 V 2014 (CDJC)	116.5	114.3	118.9	112.3	111.8	112.9	121.2	117.1	125.6
Egypt - Égypte									
21 XI 2006 (CDFC)	196.5	175.3	218.2	177.1	162.7	191.9	213.5	186.4	241.4
Ethiopia - Éthiopie									
11 X 1994 (CDFC)	272.3	258.9	285	248.7	232.6	264	276.5	263.7	288.7
29 V 2007 (CDFC)	252.1	241	262.9	232.3	222.5	242.4	256.7	245.4	267.5
Gabon									
31 VII 1993 (CDFC)	116.6	115.9	117.4	...	...	...	...	...	...
Gambia - Gambie									
15 IV 1993 (CDFC)	229.8	215.2	244.5	191.2	183.2	201.2	256.2	241.6	268.9
Ghana									
26 III 2000 (CDFC)	184	175.8	191.6	159.7	154.7	164.5	205.6	195.2	215.3
26 IX 2010 (CDFC)	159.1	155.2	162.5	138.3	136.6	139.8	184.7	178.2	190.6
Guinea - Guinée									
15 III 2014 (CDFC)	200.7	185	214	166.2	160.8	171.9	221.1	202.1	235.4
Guinea-Bissau - Guinée-Bissau[4]									
15 III 2009 (CDJC)	137.8	128.9	145.7	...	...	...	...	...	...
Kenya									
24 VIII 1989 (CDJC)	147.8	142.6	152.8	144.1	140.8	149.4	148.9	143.3	153.5
24 VIII 1999 (CDFC)	148.3	143.2	153.2	...	...	...	...	...	...
24 VIII 2009 (CDFC)	146.4	144.6	148.2	141.1	141.1	141.2	149.8	147.1	152.2
Lesotho									
13 IV 2006 (CDJC)	105.3	105.8	104.9	...	...	...	...	...	...
Liberia - Libéria									
21 III 2008 (CDFC)	142.2	136.3	148.1	...	...	...	...	...	...
Malawi									
1 IX 1987 (CDFC)	138.5	137.9	139.1	...	...	...	...	...	...
1 IX 1998 (CDFC)	147.7	149.2	146.4	142.6	146.5	137.3	148.7	149.7	147.7
8 VI 2008 (CDFC)	120.6	121	120.2	113	114.7	111	122.2	122.5	121.9
Mali									
1 IV 1987 (CDJC)	184.5	171.4	195.9	163.7	154.1	173	190.4	176.7	202
1 IV 1998 (CDJC)	180.1	166.8	192.3	166.5	158	175.2	185.6	170.7	198.6
1 IV 2009 (CDFC)	156.5	145.7	166.6	142.7	139.1	146.8	161.1	148.2	172.5
Mauritius - Maurice[5]									
1 VII 1990 (CDFC)	103.4	102.4	104.3	...	...	...	...	...	...
2 VII 2000 (CDJC)	102.4	102.1	102.7	102.3	102	102.7	102.5	102.2	102.7

Continent, country or area, date and code[a] Continent, pays ou zone, date et code[a]	Total			Urban - Urbaine			Rural - Rurale		
	Both sexes Les deux sexes	Male Masculin	Female Féminin	Both sexes Les deux sexes	Male Masculin	Female Féminin	Both sexes Les deux sexes	Male Masculin	Female Féminin
AFRICA - AFRIQUE									
4 VII 2011 (CDJC)	100.6	101	100.3	100.8	101.2	100.3	100.5	100.9	100.2
Mayotte									
31 VII 2007 (CDJC)	124.4	126.9	122.3	...	...	...	...	...	...
21 VIII 2012 (CDJC)	101.1	102.9	99.6	...	...	...	...	...	...
Morocco - Maroc									
1 IX 2004 (CDFC)	113.4	108.4	118	110.1	107.5	112.5	118.2	109.8	126.2
Mozambique									
1 VIII 1997 (CDJC)	118.6	117.9	119.3	111.7	110.9	112.4	121.5	121	121.9
1 VIII 2007 (CDFC)	126	126.2	125.9	...	...	...	...	...	...
Namibia - Namibie									
21 X 1991 (CDFC)	105.8	104.9	106.5	103.5	102.9	104.2	107.1	106.4	107.6
27 VIII 2001 (CDFC)	103.9	103.2	104.5	103.6	102.9	104.4	104.1	103.5	104.6
28 VIII 2011 (CDFC)	103.9	103.8	104	104.3	103.6	105	103.4	104.1	102.9
Niger									
20 V 2001 (CDJC)	270.1	254.7	285.2	...	...	...	...	...	...
10 XII 2012 (CDJC)	105.1	104.7	105.4	...	...	...	...	...	...
Nigeria - Nigéria									
26 XI 1991 (CDFC)	293.5	279.8	307.1	...	...	...	...	...	...
Republic of South Sudan - République de Soudan du Sud									
21 IV 2008 (CDFC)	183.1	178.4	187.9	...	...	...	...	...	...
Reunion - Réunion									
15 III 1990 (CDFC)	99.9	99.8	100.1	...	...	...	...	...	...
8 III 1999 (CDJC)	100	100.3	99.7	...	...	...	...	...	...
Rwanda									
16 VIII 2002 (CDJC)	106.3	106.6	106.1	107.4	108.3	106.2	106	106	106.1
15 VIII 2012 (CDJC)	110.2	110.4	109.9	108.3	109.3	107.1	110.6	110.7	110.5
Saint Helena ex. dep. - Sainte-Hélène sans dép.									
8 III 1998 (CDJC)	101	98.8	103.3	...	...	...	...	...	...
10 II 2008 (CDJC)[6]	98.8	99.9	97.8	...	...	...	...	...	...
Saint Helena: Ascension - Sainte-Hélène: Ascension									
8 III 1998 (CDJC)	117.5	111	130.7	...	...	...	...	...	...
Sao Tome and Principe - Sao Tomé-et-Principe									
4 VIII 1991 (CDFC)	102.7	101.5	103.8	...	...	...	...	...	...
25 VIII 2001 (CDJC)	105.7	106.2	105.3	...	...	...	...	...	...
13 V 2012 (CDJC)	104.1	103.2	105	...	...	...	...	...	...
Seychelles									
17 VIII 1987 (CDFC)	100.9	102.8	99	...	...	...	...	...	...
26 VIII 1994 (CDFC)	100.9	99.9	102	...	...	...	...	...	...
29 VIII 1997 (CDFC)	101.6	100.8	102.5	...	...	...	...	...	...
26 VIII 2002 (CDJC)	100.8	99.2	102.5	...	...	...	...	...	...
26 VIII 2010 (CDFC)	101.3	101.7	101	...	...	...	...	...	...
South Africa - Afrique du Sud									
5 III 1985 (CDFC)	124.3	120.9	127.7	...	...	...	...	...	...
7 III 1991 (CDFC)	113.1	111.5	114.7	...	...	...	...	...	...
10 X 1996 (CDFC)[7]	100.5	100.3	100.7	99.3	99.5	99.1	102.5	101.7	103.1
Swaziland									
25 VIII 1986 (CDFC)	125.9	125.4	126.3	118.3	118.2	118.5	129.3	130.1	128.8
11 V 1997 (CDFC)	120.6	121.5	119.7	116.9	117.9	115.8	122.3	123.7	121.2
11 V 2007 (CDJC)	99.8	101.2	98.6	99	100.7	97.4	100.1	101.5	99.1
Tunisia - Tunisie									
20 IV 1994 (CDFC)	102.4	102.4	102.4	102.4	102.4	102.4	102.4	102.3	102.4
Uganda - Ouganda									
12 I 1991 (CDFC)	168	154.8	180.5	158.6	150.8	167.3	169.4	155.5	182.2
12 IX 2002 (CDFC)	134.2	129.6	138.4	128.2	128.5	128	135.2	129.7	140
27 VIII 2014 (CDFC)	131.5	129	133.7	130.6	132.2	129	131.8	127.7	135.4
United Republic of Tanzania - République Unie de Tanzanie									
28 VIII 1988 (CDFC)	189.2	175.1	201.8	173.7	167.3	180.7	193.3	177.4	206.7
26 VIII 2012 (CDFC)	154.4	152.6	156.1	139.5	141.5	137.7	162.3	158.8	165.5
Zambia - Zambie									
20 VIII 1990 (CDFC)	120.7	121.9	119.6	117.2	119.8	114.2	123.1	123.5	122.7
25 X 2000 (CDFC)	127.6	128.9	126.3	123.9	125.3	122.4	129.9	131.4	128.5
16 X 2010 (CDJC)	123.8	126.8	120.7	122.3	125.2	119.3	124.9	128.2	121.8

3a. Whipple's Index by sex and urban/rural residence, 1985 - 2016
L'indice de Whipple par le sexe et la résidence urbaine/rurale, 1985 - 2016 (continued - suite)

Continent, country or area, date and code[a] Continent, pays ou zone, date et code[a]	Total			Urban - Urbaine			Rural - Rurale		
	Both sexes Les deux sexes	Male Masculin	Female Féminin	Both sexes Les deux sexes	Male Masculin	Female Féminin	Both sexes Les deux sexes	Male Masculin	Female Féminin
AFRICA - AFRIQUE									
Zimbabwe									
18 VIII 1992 (CDFC)............	120.6	122.2	119.2	115.9	119.5	111.4	123.7	124.6	123
17 VIII 2002 (CDFC)............	115.1	115.2	115	109.7	110.9	108.4	119	119	119.1
17 VIII 2012 (CDFC)............	110.8	110.8	110.8	...	...	...	...	...	...
AMERICA, NORTH - AMÉRIQUE DU NORD									
Anguilla									
13 IV 1992 (CDFC)............	104.8	109	100.4	...	...	...	...	...	...
9 V 2001 (CDFC)............	104.4	105.8	103.1	...	...	...	...	...	...
Antigua and Barbuda - Antigua-et-Barbuda									
28 V 2001 (CDFC)............	104.3	103.1	105.4	...	...	...	...	...	...
Aruba									
6 X 1991 (CDJC)............	99.3	99.4	99.3	...	...	...	...	...	...
14 X 2000 (CDJC)............	103.9[8]	103.3	104.5	...	...	...	...	...	...
29 IX 2010 (CDJC)[8]............	103.4	103.6	103.3	...	...	...	...	...	...
Bahamas									
1 V 1990 (CDFC)............	103.4	102.3	104.5	...	...	...	...	...	...
1 V 2000 (CDFC)............	101.5	100.4	102.5	...	...	...	...	...	...
3 V 2010 (CDJC)............	101.3	101.6	101.1	...	...	...	...	...	...
Barbados - Barbade									
1 V 2000 (CDFC)............	103.8	104.4	103.3	...	...	...	...	...	...
Belize									
12 V 1991 (CDFC)............	103.5	103.2	103.8	...	...	...	...	...	...
12 V 2010 (CDJC)............	104.2	103.9	104.5	...	...	...	...	...	...
Bermuda - Bermudes									
20 V 1991 (CDJC)............	99	97.9	100	...	...	...	...	...	...
20 V 2000 (CDJC)[9]............	100.2	100	100.3	...	...	...	...	...	...
20 V 2010 (CDJC)[10]............	100.9	101.1	100.8	100.9	101.1	100.8	...	...	...
British Virgin Islands - Îles Vierges britanniques									
12 V 1991 (CDJC)............	102.6	104.5	100.5	...	...	...	...	...	...
Canada									
4 VI 1991 (CDJC)............	99.6	99.6	99.6	99.6	99.6	99.7	99.6	99.6	99.5
14 V 1996 (CDJC)............	99.7	99.7	99.7	...	...	...	...	...	...
15 V 2001 (CDJC)............	99.7	99.7	99.8	99.8	99.8	99.8	99.6	99.5	99.8
16 V 2006 (CDJC)[8]............	99.9	100	99.9	100	100	100	99.6	99.6	99.7
2 V 2011 (CDJC)............	100.8	101	100.7	100.9	101.1	100.8	100.4	100.6	100.3
Cayman Islands - Îles Caïmanes									
15 X 1989 (CDFC)............	104.1	102.7	105.5	...	...	...	...	...	...
10 X 2010 (CDJC)[9]............	102.3	102.8	101.8	102.3	102.8	101.8	...	...	...
Costa Rica									
26 VI 2000 (CDJC)............	109.1	109.8	108.4	108.6	108.9	108.3	109.9	111.1	108.6
30 V 2011 (CDJC)............	104	104.2	103.9	103.8	103.8	103.9	104.6	105.2	103.9
Cuba									
7 IX 2002 (CDJC)............	102.2	102.5	101.9	102.5	102.7	102.2	101.5	102	100.9
14 IX 2012 (CDFC)............	101.5	101.6	101.3	...	...	...	...	...	...
Dominican Republic - République dominicaine									
24 IX 1993 (CDJC)............	116.5	114.9	118	111.5	109.9	113	123.5	121.4	125.5
18 X 2002 (CDJC)............	108	108.9	107.1	105.8	106.3	105.4	112.1	113.5	110.7
1 XII 2010 (CDJC)............	111.5	113.8	109.2	109.9	111.9	108.1	116.5	119.3	113.1
El Salvador									
27 IX 1992 (CDFC)............	126	127.5	124.6	119.9	119.7	120	133.5	136.6	130.7
12 V 2007 (CDJC)............	105.9	107.1	105	105.3	106.3	104.5	107.3	108.7	106.2
Guadeloupe									
8 III 1999 (CDJC)............	100.5	100.5	100.4	...	...	...	...	...	...
Honduras									
11 V 1988 (CDFC)............	104.1	104.5	103.6	102.4	102.5	102.3	105.3	105.9	104.8
28 VII 2001 (CDJC)............	121.8	123.3	120.4	118.5	118.8	118.3	125.1	127.5	122.7
10 VIII 2013 (CDFC)............	119.7	121.6	118.1	120	120.9	119.1	119.4	122.4	116.6
Jamaica - Jamaïque									
7 IV 1991 (CDJC)............	107.6	108.8	106.5	...	...	...	...	...	...
10 IX 2001 (CDJC)[11]............	107.4	108.7	106.1	106.9	107.5	106.4	107.9	110	105.7

3a. Whipple's Index by sex and urban/rural residence, 1985 - 2016
L'indice de Whipple par le sexe et la résidence urbaine/rurale, 1985 - 2016 (continued - suite)

Continent, country or area, date and code[a] Continent, pays ou zone, date et code[a]	Total			Urban - Urbaine			Rural - Rurale		
	Both sexes Les deux sexes	Male Masculin	Female Féminin	Both sexes Les deux sexes	Male Masculin	Female Féminin	Both sexes Les deux sexes	Male Masculin	Female Féminin
AMERICA, NORTH - AMÉRIQUE DU NORD									
4 IV 2011 (CDJC)	103.3	103.4	103.1	103.6	103.6	103.6	102.8	103.2	102.5
Martinique									
15 III 1990 (CDJC)	104.4	104.1	104.6	...	...	...	...	...	...
Mexico - Mexique									
12 III 1990 (CDJC)	125.2	123.5	126.8	...	...	...	...	...	...
14 II 2000 (CDJC)	116.7	116.5	116.9	114.8	114.3	115.3	123.4	124.3	122.7
17 X 2005 (CDJC)	118.8	118.7	118.9	117.5	117	117.9	123.8	124.8	122.8
12 VI 2010 (CDFC)[12]	114	114.1	113.9	113.7	113.6	113.9	115.1	116.2	114.1
Montserrat									
12 V 2011 (CDJC)	101.9	95.9	108.4	...	...	...	...	...	...
Nicaragua									
4 VI 2005 (CDJC)	111.6	112.8	110.5	108.5	109.2	107.8	116.4	117.8	115.1
Panama									
13 V 1990 (CDFC)	109.3	109.2	109.3	104.6	104.5	104.8	115.6	115	116.3
14 V 2000 (CDFC)	103.2	103.3	103.2	...	...	...	...	...	...
Puerto Rico - Porto Rico									
1 IV 1990 (CDJC)	105.6	106.1	105.1	...	...	...	...	...	...
1 IV 2000 (CDJC)	101.7	102	101.6	...	...	...	...	...	...
1 IV 2010 (CDJC)[13]	102	102	102	...	...	...	...	...	...
Saint Lucia - Sainte-Lucie									
12 V 1991 (CDFC)	110.5	110.5	110.4	...	...	...	...	...	...
22 V 2001 (CDFC)	105.5	105.8	105.2	104	100.5	107.3	106.2	108	104.4
Saint Pierre and Miquelon - Saint Pierre-et-Miquelon									
8 III 1999 (CDFC)	100.5	104.6	96.1	...	...	...	...	...	...
Saint Vincent and the Grenadines - Saint-Vincent-et-les Grenadines									
12 V 1991 (CDFC)	106.6	105.2	107.9	...	...	...	...	...	...
12 VI 2001 (CDFC)	105.3	105.3	105.3	105.6	106.8	104.4	105.1	104.1	106.1
Sint Maarten (Dutch part) - Saint-Martin (partie néerlandaise)									
9 IV 2011 (CDFC)	100.7	100.2	101.2	...	...	...	...	...	...
Trinidad and Tobago - Trinité-et-Tobago									
9 I 2011 (CDJC)	106.6	107.2	105.9	...	...	...	...	...	...
Turks and Caicos Islands - Îles Turques et Caïques									
10 IX 2001 (CDFC)	104.2	100.1	108.6	...	...	...	...	...	...
United States of America - États-Unis d'Amérique									
1 IV 1990 (CDJC)	104.5	104.8	104.2	...	...	...	...	...	...
1 IV 2000 (CDJC)[14]	101.8	102.1	101.5	102.1	102.4	101.7	100.8	101	100.5
1 IV 2010 (CDJC)	102.2	102.5	102	102.4	102.7	102.2	101.5	101.7	101.2
AMERICA, SOUTH - AMÉRIQUE DU SUD									
Argentina - Argentine									
15 V 1991 (CDFC)	104.2	103.3	105.2	...	...	...	...	...	...
18 XI 2001 (CDFC)	102.4	101.8	103	...	...	...	...	...	...
27 X 2010 (CDFC)	102.6	102.5	102.7	102.6	102.5	102.7	102.5	102.9	102
Bolivia (Plurinational State of) - Bolivie (État plurinational de)									
3 VI 1992 (CDFC)	125.4	121.1	129.5	111.4	108	114.4	146.1	139.4	152.7
5 IX 2001 (CDFC)	114.6	113.1	116	109.1	108	110.2	124.6	121.9	127.6
21 XI 2012 (CDFC)	110.4	110.5	110.3	108	108.1	108	115.7	115.4	116.1
Brazil - Brésil									
1 IX 1991 (CDJC)	103.3	103.3	103.3	102.3	102.3	102.2	107.2	106.9	107.4
1 VIII 2000 (CDJC)[15]	104.2	104.3	104	103.6	103.7	103.5	107.1	107.3	107
31 VII 2010 (CDJC)	104.8	105.6	104.1	104.7	105.4	104	105.6	106.6	104.4
Chile - Chili									
22 IV 1992 (CDFC)	100.3	98.9	101.7	100.2	98.6	101.7	101	100.2	101.9
24 IV 2002 (CDFC)	99.5	98.5	100.5	99.4	98.2	100.5	100.2	100	100.4
Colombia - Colombie									
15 X 1985 (CDFC)	147.9	146.5	149.2	139.8	136.8	142.4	166.9	166.5	167.3

Continent, country or area, date and code[a] / Continent, pays ou zone, date et code[a]	Total			Urban - Urbaine			Rural - Rurale		
	Both sexes Les deux sexes	Male Masculin	Female Féminin	Both sexes Les deux sexes	Male Masculin	Female Féminin	Both sexes Les deux sexes	Male Masculin	Female Féminin
AMERICA, SOUTH - AMÉRIQUE DU SUD									
24 X 1993 (CDFC).........................	118.9	117.7	120	111.7	108.9	114.1	139.6	139.9	139.4
22 V 2005 (CDFC).........................	103.5	104.2	102.9	102.1	102.4	101.8	108.6	109.8	107.3
22 V 2005 (CDJC).........................	103.5	104.2	102.9	102.1	102.4	101.8	108.7	109.9	107.3
Ecuador - Équateur									
25 XI 1990 (CDFC)[16]	132.5	131.2	133.8	122.9	121	124.7	146.6	145.4	147.9
25 XI 2001 (CDFC)[16]	112.1	111.8	112.4	107.9	107	108.7	119.9	120.4	119.4
28 XI 2010 (CDFC).........................	103.7	104.1	103.3	103	103.4	102.7	104.9	105.4	104.4
French Guiana - Guyane française									
15 III 1990 (CDJC)	106.2	105.7	106.7	...	...	...	...	...	...
8 III 1999 (CDJC)	101.1	100.9	101.3	...	...	...	...	...	...
Paraguay									
26 VIII 1992 (CDFC).....................	108.6	107.9	109.3	105.7	104.3	107	112	111.8	112.3
28 VIII 2002 (CDFC).....................	104.8	104.3	105.2	103.2	102.6	103.7	107.1	106.5	107.8
Peru - Pérou									
21 X 2007 (CDFC).........................	109.4	109.1	109.6	106.9	106.5	107.3	118.8	118.5	119.1
Suriname									
2 VIII 2004 (CDJC)......................	101.1	100.4	102	102.4[17]	101.4[17]	103.5[17]	98.3[17]	98.2[17]	98.4[17]
13 VIII 2012 (CDJC).....................	101.7	101.8	101.7	...	...	...	...	...	...
Uruguay									
23 X 1985 (CDFC).........................	106.2	104.9	107.4	106.2	104.7	107.5	106.3	106.1	106.5
22 V 1996 (CDFC).........................	103.3	102.8	103.8	103.2	102.5	103.8	104	104.5	103.3
1 VI 2004 (CDFC)[18]	106	105.9	106.2	106.1	105.9	106.3	105.4	105.7	105
4 X 2011 (CDJC)	101.8	101.9	101.7	101.8	101.9	101.7	101.8	101.6	102
Venezuela (Bolivarian Republic of) - Venezuela (République bolivarienne du)									
20 X 1990 (CDFC)[19]	106.4	106.5	106.3	105	104.8	105.3	114.9	116.1	113.4
1 IX 2011 (CDJC)	101.3	101.6	101	101.3[20]	101.6[20]	101[20]	101.4[20]	102[20]	100.7[20]
ASIA - ASIE									
Armenia - Arménie									
10 X 2001 (CDJC)	103	102.8	103.3	103.7	103.7	103.8	101.6	101.1	102.1
12 X 2011 (CDJC)	101.8	101.5	102	102.4	102.3	102.6	100.6	100.2	101
Azerbaijan - Azerbaïdjan									
27 I 1999 (CDJC)	100.4	99.8	101	100.3	99.8	100.8	100.5	99.7	101.2
13 IV 2009 (CDJC)	100.4	100.1	100.7	100.8	100.3	101.3	99.9	99.7	100.1
Bahrain - Bahreïn									
16 XI 1991 (CDFC).......................	96.6	98.3	93.6	...	...	...	...	...	...
7 IV 2001 (CDJC)	100.2	99.9	100.9	...	...	...	...	...	...
27 IV 2010 (CDJC)	100.2	99.3	101.9	...	...	...	...	...	...
Bangladesh[21]									
22 I 2001 (CDFC)	299.5	295.8	303.4	283.1	277.9	289.8	305	302.6	307.4
Bhutan - Bhoutan									
30 V 2005 (CDFC)........................	116.4	117.7	114.9	118.7	119.6	117.4	115.4	116.8	113.9
Brunei Darussalam - Brunéi Darussalam									
7 VIII 1991 (CDFC)......................	98.8	98.7	98.8	...	...	...	...	...	...
20 VI 2011 (CDJC)	100.9	101.6	100.2	100.6	101.3	99.8	102	102.3	101.6
Cambodia - Cambodge									
3 III 1998 (CDFC).......................	118.1	116.2	119.6	119.8	117.6	121.8	117.6	115.9	119.1
3 III 2008 (CDFC)[22]	109.9	108.2	111.3	109.7	108.5	110.8	109.9	108.1	111.5
China - Chine									
1 VII 1990 (CDFC).......................	101	101.1	100.9	101.9	102	101.8	100.6	100.7	100.5
1 XI 2000 (CDJC)	101.7	101.7	101.6	101.6	101.8	101.4	101.7	101.7	101.7
1 XI 2010 (CDJC)[23]	98.8	98.9	98.8	98.7	98.9	98.6	98.9	98.9	99
China, Hong Kong SAR - Chine, Hong Kong RAS									
11 III 1986 (CDFC)	101.7	101.4	102.1	101.7	101.3	102.1	102.1	102.5	101.7
15 III 1996 (CDFC)......................	99.7	99.8	99.7	...	...	...	...	...	...
14 III 2001 (CDJC)[24]	100.2	100.3	100.1	...	...	...	...	...	...
14 VII 2006 (CDJC)[25]	98.3	98.4	98.3	...	...	...	...	...	...
30 VI 2011 (CDJC)[24]	99.4	100	98.9	...	...	...	...	...	...

Continent, country or area, date and code[a] Continent, pays ou zone, date et code[a]	Total			Urban - Urbaine			Rural - Rurale		
	Both sexes Les deux sexes	Male Masculin	Female Féminin	Both sexes Les deux sexes	Male Masculin	Female Féminin	Both sexes Les deux sexes	Male Masculin	Female Féminin
ASIA - ASIE									
China, Macao SAR - Chine, Macao RAS									
30 VIII 1991 (CDJC)	100.8	101.4	100.3	...	...	...	...	...	...
23 VIII 2001 (CDJC)	95.5	94.7	96.2	...	...	...	...	...	...
12 VIII 2011 (CDJC)	98.9	97.6	100	...	...	...	...	...	...
Cyprus - Chypre									
1 X 1992 (CDJC)........................	98.7	98.3	99	98.8	98.4	99.3	98.4	98.3	98.5
1 X 2001 (CDJC)[26]	100.7	100.7	100.6	100.9	101.4	100.4	100.1	99.1	101.1
1 X 2011 (CDJC)[26]	105.4	106.6	104.4	...	...	...	...	...	...
Democratic People's Republic of Korea - République populaire démocratique de Corée									
31 XII 1993 (CDJC)	105	105.2	104.7	104.4	104.6	104.2	105.8	106.2	105.5
1 X 2008 (CDJC)	101	100.6	101.3	...	...	...	...	...	...
Georgia - Géorgie									
17 I 2002 (CDJC)	101.4	101.7	101.1	101.6	102	101.3	101.1	101.4	100.8
5 XI 2014 (CDJC)	99.9	99.9	99.8	99.8	99.6	99.9	100	100.4	99.7
India - Inde									
1 III 1991 (CDFC)[27]	290.3	292.6	287.9	258.7	253.8	264.3	302.1	307.7	296.2
1 III 2001 (CDFC)[28]	230	241	218.4	217.2	216.8	217.8	235.5	252	218.7
9 II 2011 (CDFC)[29]	171	174.6	167.4	152.9	151	154.9	180.5	187.1	173.8
Indonesia - Indonésie									
31 X 1990 (CDFC)	163.3	160.2	166.3	139.7	135.8	143.7	174.2	171.7	176.5
30 VI 2000 (CDJC)[30]	152.2	151.3	153.1	136.8	136.4	137.2	164.2	163.1	165.2
1 V 2010 (CDJC)	114.5	114.2	114.9	110.2	110.2	110.2	119	118.4	119.7
Iran (Islamic Republic of) - Iran (République islamique d')									
22 IX 1986 (CDFC)........................	122.6	121.1	124.1	114.4	113.4	115.5	133.1	131.3	134.8
11 IX 1991 (CDJC)	128.7	127	130.4	122.5	121.3	123.9	138.5	136.4	140.6
11 IX 1994 (CDJC)	107.4	106.8	108.1	107.1	108	106.2	107.8	104.5	111.2
23 X 1996 (CDJC)	108.8	108.6	109	105.7	105.6	105.8	114.1	114	114.3
28 X 2006 (CDJC)[31]	111.6	110.4	112.8	109.3	108.5	110.1	117.2	115.2	119.2
24 X 2011 (CDJC)	103.7	103.8	103.5	103.6	103.8	103.5	103.7[32]	103.8[32]	103.6[32]
Iraq									
16 X 1997 (CDFC)........................	106.2	105.6	106.8	105.5	104.9	106.1	108	107.6	108.5
Israel - Israël									
4 XI 1995 (CDFC)[33]	101.4	101.8	101	101.3	101.8	100.9	101.9	101.5	102.3
4 XI 1995 (CDJC)	101.1	101.1	101.1	101	101	101	101.5	101.6	101.4
27 XII 2008 (CDFC)[34]	98.9	99	98.9	99	99.1	98.9	98.6	98.3	99
Japan - Japon									
1 X 1985 (CDFC)........................	98.4	98.4	98.3	98.3	98.4	98.2	98.7	98.5	98.8
1 X 1990 (CDFC)	98.9	98.9	98.9	98.9	99	98.8	98.8	98.6	99
1 X 1995 (CDFC)........................	99	99	99	99	99.1	99	98.8	98.6	98.9
1 X 2000 (CDJC)	99.1	99.1	99	99.1	99.2	99	99	98.8	99.2
1 X 2005 (CDJC)[35]	99.1	99.2	99.1	99.2	99.2	99.1	99	98.8	99.1
1 X 2010 (CDJC)[35]	100.9	100.9	100.9	100.9	100.9	100.8	101	100.9	101.1
Jordan - Jordanie									
1 X 2004 (CDFC)[36]	100.8	100.4	101.3	...	...	...	...	...	...
30 X 2015 (CDFC)[37]	111.4	112.3	110.3	...	...	...	...	...	...
Kazakhstan									
12 I 1989 (CDFC)	98.9	98.8	99	98.7	98.6	98.8	99.2	99	99.4
26 II 1999 (CDJC)[38]	99.9	99.8	99.9	100.1	100	100.2	99.5	99.5	99.4
Kuwait - Koweït									
20 IV 1985 (CDFC)........................	139.5	142.6	133.9	...	...	...	...	...	...
21 IV 2011 (CDFC)........................	102.2	102.6	101.7	102.2	102.6	101.7	...	...	...
Kyrgyzstan - Kirghizstan									
12 I 1989 (CDJC)	99.3	99.1	99.5	98.4	98	98.8	99.9	99.8	100.1
24 III 1999 (CDJC)	99.4	99.2	99.6	99.2	98.9	99.5	99.5	99.3	99.7
24 III 2009 (CDJC)	100.6	100.5	100.8	...	...	...	...	...	...
Lao People's Democratic Republic - République démocratique populaire lao									
1 III 2005 (CDJC)	138.3	136.4	140.2	120.8[39]	120.9[39]	120.6[39]	146[39]	143.3[39]	148.5[39]
1 III 2015 (CDJC)	129.3	128.4	130.2	...	...	...	...	...	...
Malaysia - Malaisie									
14 VIII 1991 (CDFC)........................	114.2	113.8	114.6	110.3	110.2	110.3	118.8	117.9	119.7
6 VII 2010 (CDJC)	120.4	120.7	120	120.6	120.7	120.5	119.7	120.6	118.7

Continent, country or area, date and code[a] Continent, pays ou zone, date et code[a]	Total			Urban - Urbaine			Rural - Rurale		
	Both sexes Les deux sexes	Male Masculin	Female Féminin	Both sexes Les deux sexes	Male Masculin	Female Féminin	Both sexes Les deux sexes	Male Masculin	Female Féminin
ASIA - ASIE									
6 VII 2010 (CDJC)[40]	120.7	121.1	120.3	...	...	...	...	...	...
Maldives									
25 III 1985 (CDFC)	176.7	175.3	178.4	166.3	170.9	159.4	180.7	177.2	184.2
8 III 1990 (CDFC)	156.4	159.9	152.7	149.3	154.5	142.6	159.2	162.4	156.1
25 III 1995 (CDFC)	143.1	144.5	141.7	137.3	137.9	136.7	145.5	147.5	143.5
31 III 2000 (CDFC)	106.9	109.5	104.3	...	...	...	...	...	...
21 III 2006 (CDFC)[41]	103.8	104.9	102.8	104	105.5	102.5	103.7	104.5	102.9
20 IX 2014 (CDFC)[42]	105.4	109.8	99.1	106.1	110.5	100.1	105	109.4	98.3
Mongolia - Mongolie									
5 I 2000 (CDFC)	99.9	99.6	100.2	99.9	99.7	100.1	99.9	99.5	100.2
11 XI 2010 (CDJC)	101.6	101.3	101.9	101.7	101.4	102	101.5	101.3	101.7
Myanmar[43]									
29 III 2014 (CDFC)	123.3	124	122.6	115.8	116	115.6	126.7	127.6	125.8
Nepal - Népal									
22 VI 1991 (CDJC)	202.4	195.6	209	186.2	179.2	193.9	204.2	197.6	210.5
22 VI 2001 (CDJC)	206.1	205.7	206.6	...	...	...	...	...	...
22 VI 2011 (CDJC)	188.6	191.3	186.2	169.9	167.8	172	193.1	197.5	189.3
Oman									
7 XII 2003 (CDFC)	158.5	165.6	146.9	154.9	163.1	141.1	170.2	174.1	164.4
Philippines									
1 IX 1995 (CDJC)	115.7	116.5	114.9	...	...	...	...	...	...
1 V 2000 (CDJC)	110.8	111.6	110	...	...	...	...	...	...
1 VIII 2007 (CDJC)	104.8	104.9	104.7	...	...	...	...	...	...
1 V 2010 (CDJC)[44]	108.5	109.1	107.9	...	...	...	...	...	...
Qatar									
16 III 1986 (CDFC)	149.1	151.9	140.2	...	...	...	...	...	...
Republic of Korea - République de Corée									
1 XI 1985 (CDFC)	99.4	98.9	99.8	99.6	99.4	99.8	98.8	97.9	99.6
1 XI 1990 (CDFC)	99.5	99.2	99.8	99.6	99.4	99.8	99.1	98.5	99.7
1 XI 1995 (CDJC)	99.9	99.7	100.1	100	99.8	100.2	99.4	99.2	99.6
1 XI 2000 (CDJC)[45]	100	99.8	100.2	100.2	100	100.4	99.2	98.9	99.4
1 XI 2005 (CDJC)[45]	100.4	100.2	100.6	100.6	100.4	100.8	99.4	99.2	99.7
1 XI 2015 (CDJC)	101.8	101.3	102.3	...	...	...	...	...	...
Singapore - Singapour									
30 VI 2000 (CDJC)	98.2	98.1	98.3	...	...	...	...	...	...
30 VI 2010 (CDJC)[46]	99.7	99.7	99.7	...	...	...	...	...	...
Sri Lanka									
17 VII 2001 (CDFC)[47]	97	97.5	96.4	98.2	98.5	97.8	96.8[48]	97.3[48]	96.2[48]
20 III 2012 (CDJC)	100.2	100.3	100	100.3	100.7	100	100.1	100.2	100.1
State of Palestine - État de Palestine									
9 XII 1997 (CDFC)[49]	109.1	103	115.3	...	...	...	...	...	...
1 XII 2007 (CDFC)[30]	103.8	102.6	104.9	104.4[50]	103.2[50]	105.7[50]	100.8	100	101.6
Syrian Arab Republic - République arabe syrienne[51]									
3 IX 1994 (CDFC)	111.8	109.9	113.8	111.9	110.4	113.5	111.7	109.2	114.1
Tajikistan - Tadjikistan									
12 I 1989 (CDJC)	99	98.9	99.1	97.6	97.1	98	99.9	100	99.9
20 I 2000 (CDFC)	99.3	99.2	99.4	100.1	100	100.1	99	98.9	99.1
21 IX 2010 (CDFC)	103.6	103.9	103.4	105.8	106.6	105	102.8	102.9	102.7
Thailand - Thaïlande									
1 IV 2000 (CDJC)[52]	104.7	104.7	104.8	108.1	108.1	108.1	103	103	103
1 IX 2010 (CDJC)	110.6	111.1	110.1	115.6	116.2	115	106.3	106.8	105.8
Timor-Leste									
11 VII 2010 (CDFC)	130.3	128.9	131.7	126	125.6	126.5	132.3	130.6	134
Turkey - Turquie									
20 X 1985 (CDFC)	149.4	133.8	165.3	...	...	...	...	...	...
21 X 1990 (CDFC)	139.7	128.9	150.8	...	...	...	...	...	...
22 X 2000 (CDFC)	125.7	123.2	128.3	122.7	121.3	124.2	131.7	127.2	136.4
3 X 2011 (CDJC)[53]	101.2	101.7	100.8	101.4	101.7	101.1	100.8	101.5	99.9
Viet Nam									
1 IV 1989 (CDJC)	98.5	98.1	98.8	98.3	97.8	98.8	98.4	98	98.7
1 IV 1999 (CDJC)	99.2	98.8	99.6	99.1	98.6	99.6	99.3	98.8	99.7
1 IV 2009 (CDJC)	100.4	99.8	100.9	100.6	100	101.1	100.3	99.8	100.8
Yemen - Yémen									
16 XII 1994 (CDFC)	293.9	282.6	304.9	245	229.6	265	311.7	305.8	316.8

3a. Whipple's Index by sex and urban/rural residence, 1985 - 2016
L'indice de Whipple par le sexe et la résidence urbaine/rurale, 1985 - 2016 (continued - suite)

Continent, country or area, date and code[a] Continent, pays ou zone, date et code[a]	Total			Urban - Urbaine			Rural - Rurale		
	Both sexes Les deux sexes	Male Masculin	Female Féminin	Both sexes Les deux sexes	Male Masculin	Female Féminin	Both sexes Les deux sexes	Male Masculin	Female Féminin
EUROPE									
Åland Islands - Îles d'Åland[54]									
31 XII 2000 (CDJC)	100.7	101.5	99.8	102.9	101.9	103.8	99	101.2	96.7
Austria - Autriche									
15 V 1991 (CDJC)	97.9	97.9	97.9	97.8	97.9	97.7	98.2	98.1	98.2
15 V 2001 (CDJC)	97.4	97.5	97.3	97.3	97.5	97.2	97.5	97.3	97.6
31 X 2011 (CDJC)	100	100.1	100	100.2	100.2	100.2	99.7	99.8	99.7
Belarus - Bélarus									
12 I 1989 (CDJC)	99.4	99.3	99.5	98.9	98.8	99.1	100.3	100.3	100.2
16 II 1999 (CDJC)	99.6	99.4	99.8	99.7	99.6	99.9	99.2	98.9	99.5
14 X 2009 (CDJC)	101.5	101.6	101.5	101.7	101.6	101.7	101	101.3	100.7
Belgium - Belgique									
1 X 2001 (CDJC)	99.5	99.4	99.7	99.5	99.4	99.7	99.2	98.9	99.4
1 I 2011 (CDJC)	100	99.9	100.1	100	99.9	100.1	100.3	99.1	101.6
Bosnia and Herzegovina - Bosnie-Herzégovine									
31 III 1991 (CDJC)	100.4	100.5	100.2	...	...	...	...	...	...
Bulgaria - Bulgarie									
1 II 2011 (CDJC)	101.2	101	101.4	101.1	100.9	101.3	101.4	101.4	101.4
Croatia - Croatie									
31 III 1991 (CDFC)	99.1	99.2	99.1	99	99.3	98.8	99.2	99.1	99.4
31 III 2001 (CDJC)	98.2	98.4	98.1	98.3	98.6	98.1	98.1	98.1	98.2
1 IV 2011 (CDJC)	100.3	100.5	100.2	100.3	100.4	100.2	100.4	100.5	100.2
Czechia - Tchéquie									
3 III 1991 (CDJC)	99	98.8	99.1	...	...	...	...	...	...
1 III 2001 (CDJC)	99.2	99.1	99.3	99	98.9	99.1	99.8	99.8	99.9
25 III 2011 (CDJC)	99.6	99.6	99.7	99.5	99.4	99.6	99.9	100.1	99.8
Denmark - Danemark[55]									
1 I 1991 (CDJC)	100.5	100.6	100.5	...	...	...	...	...	...
Estonia - Estonie									
31 III 2000 (CDJC)	100	99.7	100.3	100.2	100	100.4	99.7	99.1	100.2
31 XII 2011 (CDJC)	100	100	100.1	100.1	100	100.1	100	99.9	100.2
Finland - Finlande									
17 XI 1985 (CDJC)	99.8	99.9	99.6	...	...	...	...	...	...
31 XII 1990 (CDJC)	99.5	99.6	99.5	...	...	...	...	...	...
31 XII 2000 (CDJC)	99.5	99.6	99.4	99.9	100.1	99.7	98.9	98.9	98.8
31 XII 2010 (CDJC)	100.1	100.1	100	100	100.1	99.8	100.3	100	100.5
France									
5 III 1990 (CDJC)	99.2	99	99.3	99.5	99.4	99.6	98.2	98.1	98.4
8 III 1999 (CDJC)[56]	100.5	100.5	100.5	100.5	100.5	100.5	100.8	100.7	100.8
Germany - Allemagne									
9 V 2011 (CDJC)	100	100	100.1	100	100	100.1	100.1	100.1	100.1
Gibraltar									
14 X 1991 (CDFC)	105.7	104.9	106.6	...	...	...	...	...	...
12 XI 2001 (CDFC)[57]	98	98.6	97.5	...	...	...	...	...	...
12 XI 2012 (CDJC)[58]	99.5	100.3	98.7	...	...	...	...	...	...
Greece - Grèce									
17 III 1991 (CDFC)	108.8	107.4	110.1	108.5	107.3	109.7	109.1	107.6	110.7
18 III 2001 (CDJC)[59]	105	104.9	105.1	104.8	104.6	104.9	105.8	105.7	106
9 V 2011 (CDFC)	101.4	101.8	101.1	101.3	101.6	101.1	101.8	102.3	101.2
Guernsey - Guernesey									
23 III 1986 (CDJC)	96.1	96.1	96	...	...	...	...	...	...
13 III 1996 (CDJC)	97.5	98.5	96.6	...	...	...	...	...	...
29 IV 2001 (CDJC)	97.2	97.4	96.9	...	...	...	...	...	...
Hungary - Hongrie									
1 I 1990 (CDFC)	102.1	102.5	101.8	102.4	102.8	102	101.7	101.9	101.5
1 II 2001 (CDFC)	101.6	101.8	101.5	101.9	102.2	101.6	101.2	101.2	101.2
1 X 2011 (CDFC)	100.2	100.2	100.2	100.1	100.2	100.1	100.4	100.3	100.5
Ireland - Irlande									
21 IV 1991 (CDFC)	100.5	100.5	100.4	...	...	...	...	...	...
28 IV 1996 (CDFC)	100.2	100.2	100.1	100.3	100.5	100.2	99.9	99.7	100
28 IV 2002 (CDFC)	99.5	99.8	99.2	99.7	99.9	99.4	99.3	99.5	99
23 IV 2006 (CDFC)	100.9	101	100.8	101	101.2	100.8	100.8	100.7	100.8
10 IV 2011 (CDFC)[60]	100.7	101	100.5	100.9	101.2	100.5	100.5	100.5	100.4
Isle of Man - Île de Man									
6 IV 1986 (CDJC)	99.2	98.6	99.8	...	...	...	...	...	...
14 IV 1991 (CDJC)	97.7	98.1	97.3	...	...	...	...	...	...
14 IV 1996 (CDJC)	97.9	98.9	97	...	...	...	...	...	...

3a. Whipple's Index by sex and urban/rural residence, 1985 - 2016
L'indice de Whipple par le sexe et la résidence urbaine/rurale, 1985 - 2016 (continued - suite)

Continent, country or area, date and code[a] Continent, pays ou zone, date et code[a]	Total			Urban - Urbaine			Rural - Rurale		
	Both sexes Les deux sexes	Male Masculin	Female Féminin	Both sexes Les deux sexes	Male Masculin	Female Féminin	Both sexes Les deux sexes	Male Masculin	Female Féminin
EUROPE									
29 IV 2001 (CDJC)	97.8	98	97.5	...	...	...	...	...	...
23 IV 2006 (CDJC)	98.3	98.4	98.3	...	...	...	...	...	...
27 III 2011 (CDJC)........................	99.3	100.4	98.2	...	...	...	...	...	...
24 IV 2016 (CDJC)	99	99.3	98.7	...	...	...	...	...	...
Italy - Italie									
21 X 2001 (CDJC)	101.1	101	101.1	...	...	...	...	...	...
9 X 2011 (CDJC)	99.8	99.8	99.8	...	...	...	...	...	...
Jersey									
23 III 1986 (CDFC)	98	98	98	...	...	...	...	...	...
10 III 1991 (CDJC)	99.2	100.6	97.8	...	...	...	...	...	...
10 III 1996 (CDJC)	99.4	100.7	98.1	...	...	...	...	...	...
11 III 2001 (CDJC)	98.9	99.6	98.3	...	...	...	...	...	...
27 III 2011 (CDFC)	100	100.7	99.3	...	...	...	...	...	...
Latvia - Lettonie									
31 III 2000 (CDJC)[61]	100.5	100.2	100.7	100.4	100.4	100.4	100.6	99.8	101.5
1 III 2011 (CDJC)........................	99.4	99.6	99.3	99.5	99.7	99.3	99.3	99.3	99.4
Liechtenstein									
31 XII 2010 (CDFC)	100.5	102.1	99	...	...	...	...	...	...
Lithuania - Lituanie									
12 I 1989 (CDJC)	100.6	100.5	100.7	100.7	100.6	100.8	100.3	100.2	100.4
6 IV 2001 (CDJC)	99.8	99.7	99.9	99.4	99	99.7	100.8	101.1	100.5
1 III 2011 (CDJC)........................	100	100.1	99.9	100	100.2	99.8	100	99.9	100
Luxembourg									
15 II 2001 (CDJC)	99.2	98.9	99.6	...	...	...	...	...	...
1 II 2011 (CDJC)........................	99.7	99	100.4	...	...	...	...	...	...
Malta - Malte									
26 XI 1995 (CDJC)	101.2	101.2	101.2	101.2	101.2	101.2	125.7	107.6	138.4
27 XI 2005 (CDJC)	101.3	101.9	100.6	101.2	102	100.5	114.3	100	127.3
20 XI 2011 (CDFC)	99.4	100	98.9	99.4	99.9	98.9	100.3	102.3	98.1
Monaco									
21 VI 2000 (CDJC)	100.9	99.9	101.9	...	...	...	...	...	...
Montenegro - Monténégro									
31 X 2003 (CDJC)	100.2	99.9	100.5	100.2	99.6	100.8	100.2	100.3	100
1 IV 2011 (CDJC)	100	99.7	100.3	99.9	99.3	100.5	100.1	100.2	99.9
Netherlands - Pays-Bas									
1 I 2002 (CDJC)	101.2	101.3	101	101.3	101.5	101.1	101	101.1	101
1 I 2011 (CDJC)........................	100.2	100.2	100.2	...	...	...	...	...	...
Norway - Norvège									
3 XI 1990 (CDJC)........................	99.9	99.9	99.9	99.9	99.9	100	99.9	100	99.8
3 XI 2001 (CDJC)[62]	100.1	100.1	100.1	100.1	100.1	100.2	99.7	99.9	99.6
19 XI 2011 (CDJC)[62]	99.8	99.8	99.7	99.7[63]	99.6[63]	99.7[63]	100.1[63]	100.4[63]	99.8[63]
Poland - Pologne									
6 XII 1988 (CDFC)........................	100.5	100.6	100.4	100.5	100.6	100.4	100.5	100.6	100.5
20 V 2002 (CDJC)[64]	100.7	100.7	100.7	100.9	100.8	100.9	100.4	100.5	100.2
31 III 2011 (CDJC)........................	100.1	100.1	100.1	100.1	100.1	100.1	100.1	100.1	100
Portugal									
15 IV 1991 (CDFC)........................	101.4	101.7	101.1	101.4	101.7	101.2	101.3	101.6	101.1
21 III 2011 (CDJC)	100.7	100.8	100.5	100.8	101	100.7	100.4	100.4	100.3
Republic of Moldova - République de Moldova									
12 I 1989 (CDJC)	100.5	100.4	100.5	100.2	99.9	100.4	100.7	100.8	100.6
5 X 2004 (CDFC)[65]	103.2	103.3	103.2	102.9	102.9	102.9	103.5	103.5	103.5
Romania - Roumanie									
7 I 1992 (CDJC)	96.2	96.2	96.2	95.6	95.8	95.4	97.1	96.8	97.4
18 III 2002 (CDJC)	95.8	95.9	95.8	95.3	95.5	95.2	96.5	96.3	96.7
20 X 2011 (CDJC)	96.6	96.6	96.6	96.4	96.5	96.3	96.8	96.7	96.9
Russian Federation - Fédération de Russie									
12 I 1989 (CDJC)	97.8	97.7	97.9	97.7	97.6	97.7	98.3	98.2	98.4
14 X 2010 (CDJC)	103	103	103	103.5	103.5	103.5	101.7	101.6	101.7
Serbia - Serbie[66]									
31 III 2002 (CDJC)	99.9	99.9	100	100.4	100.4	100.5	99.2	99.3	99.2
1 X 2011 (CDJC)	99.4	99.2	99.5	99.7	99.3	100	98.9	99.1	98.7
Slovakia - Slovaquie									
3 III 1991 (CDJC)	100	99.8	100.2	...	...	...	...	...	...
25 V 2001 (CDJC)	99.5	99.5	99.6	99.7	99.6	99.8	99.3	99.3	99.3
21 V 2011 (CDJC)	100.2	100.2	100.3	100.3	100.2	100.4	100.2	100.2	100.1

3a. Whipple's Index by sex and urban/rural residence, 1985 - 2016
L'indice de Whipple par le sexe et la résidence urbaine/rurale, 1985 - 2016 (continued - suite)

Continent, country or area, date and code[a] Continent, pays ou zone, date et code[a]	Total			Urban - Urbaine			Rural - Rurale		
	Both sexes Les deux sexes	Male Masculin	Female Féminin	Both sexes Les deux sexes	Male Masculin	Female Féminin	Both sexes Les deux sexes	Male Masculin	Female Féminin
EUROPE									
Slovenia - Slovénie									
31 III 1991 (CDJC)	99	99.1	98.9	99.7	99.7	99.6	98.4	98.6	98.1
31 III 2002 (CDJC)	101.9	102.1	101.8	102.2	102.3	102.2	101.6	101.9	101.3
1 I 2011 (CDJC)...............................	100.6	100.1	101.3	100.7	100.1	101.3	100.6	100	101.3
Spain - Espagne									
1 III 1991 (CDJC)	102.4	102.4	102.3	...	...	...	...	...	...
1 XI 2001 (CDFC)[67].......................	99	99	99	99	99	98.9	99.1	99	99.1
1 XI 2011 (CDJC)	98.3	98.6	98.1	...	...	...	...	...	...
Sweden - Suède									
1 XI 1990 (CDJC)	99.7	99.8	99.6	...	...	...	...	...	...
31 XII 2003 (CDJC)	100	100	100.1	...	...	...	...	...	...
31 XII 2011 (CDJC)	99.7	99.8	99.6	...	...	...	...	...	...
Switzerland - Suisse									
4 XII 1990 (CDJC)	100.6	100.9	100.2	100.7	100.9	100.5	100.2	100.7	99.7
5 XII 2000 (CDFC)..........................	99.7	99.9	99.5	99.7	99.9	99.6	99.5	99.9	99.1
31 XII 2011 (CDJC)	99.9	99.9	99.9	99.9	99.9	99.8	100	99.9	100.1
TFYR of Macedonia - L'ex-R. y. de Macédoine									
20 VI 1994 (CDJC)	100.2	100.2	100.2	100	100.1	99.8	100.6	100.5	100.8
31 X 2002 (CDJC)	100.3	100.3	100.3	...	...	...	...	...	...
Ukraine									
5 XII 2001 (CDFC)...........................	102.7	102.7	102.7	103.1	103.1	103.2	101.7	101.8	101.5
United Kingdom of Great Britain and Northern Ireland - Royaume-Uni de Grande-Bretagne et d'Irlande du Nord[68]									
21 IV 1991 (CDFC)[69].....................	98	98	98	...	...	...	...	...	...
29 IV 2001 (CDFC)[70].....................	98.1	98	98.1	98.2	98.2	98.2	97.6	97.5	97.7
27 III 2011 (CDJC)...........................	100.2	100.3	100.2	100.3	100.3	100.3	99.8	99.8	99.8
OCEANIA - OCÉANIE									
Australia - Australie									
30 VI 1986 (CDFC)...........................	101.6	101.7	101.5	101.6	101.6	101.5	101.8	102	101.6
6 VIII 1991 (CDFC)...........................	101.7	101.4	102.1	...	...	...	...	...	...
9 VIII 1996 (CDFC)...........................	101.6	101.5	101.7	...	...	...	...	...	...
7 VIII 2001 (CDJC)...........................	101.4	101.3	101.5	101.4	101.3	101.5	101.3	101.4	101.3
8 VIII 2006 (CDJC)[71]	100.2[72]	100.3[72]	100.2[72]	100.2	100.2	100.1	100.4	100.5	100.3
9 VIII 2011 (CDJC)[71]	100.8[72]	100.8[72]	100.7[72]	100.7	100.7	100.7	101.3	101.3	101.3
Cook Islands - Îles Cook[73]									
1 XII 1996 (CDJC)............................	99.1	97.2	101.1	...	...	...	...	...	...
Fiji - Fidji									
31 VIII 1986 (CDFC).........................	105.4	105	105.7	...	...	...	...	...	...
25 VIII 1996 (CDFC).........................	100.2	100.6	99.8	99.8	99.9	99.7	100.6	101.3	99.9
French Polynesia - Polynésie française									
3 IX 1996 (CDFC).............................	98.6	97.8	99.5	...	...	...	...	...	...
20 VIII 2007 (CDJC)	102.8	103.2	102.4	...	...	...	...	...	...
Guam									
1 IV 1990 (CDJC)	107.1	106.2	108.2	107	105.5	108.7	107.2	106.6	107.8
1 IV 2000 (CDJC)[13]	100.3	100.4	100.3	...	...	...	...	...	...
Kiribati									
10 X 2010 (CDFC)............................	104.7	103.3	105.9	106	106	106.1	103.3	100.7	105.7
Marshall Islands - Îles Marshall									
13 XI 1988 (CDFC)...........................	101.2	103.3	98.9	...	...	...	...	...	...
1 VI 1999 (CDFC)............................	104	106.2	101.7	...	...	...	...	...	...
New Caledonia - Nouvelle-Calédonie									
4 IV 1989 (CDFC)............................	99.5	99.4	99.6	...	...	...	...	...	...
New Zealand - Nouvelle-Zélande									
4 III 1986 (CDJC)	100.7	100.6	100.7	100.7	100.7	100.8	100.2	99.9	100.6
5 III 1991 (CDFC)	100.3	100.4	100.3	100.5	100.6	100.4	99.7	99.3	100
5 III 1996 (CDJC)	100	100	100	100.1	100.1	100.1	99.5	99.5	99.5
6 III 2001 (CDJC)[71]	100	99.9	100	100.2	100.1	100.2	99	99	99.1
7 III 2006 (CDFC)[71]	99.7	...	...	...	...	...	...	...	...
7 III 2006 (CDJC)[71]........................	99.6	99.7	99.6	99.7	99.8	99.7	99.1	99.3	98.9

Continent, country or area, date and code[a] Continent, pays ou zone, date et code[a]	Total			Urban - Urbaine			Rural - Rurale		
	Both sexes Les deux sexes	Male Masculin	Female Féminin	Both sexes Les deux sexes	Male Masculin	Female Féminin	Both sexes Les deux sexes	Male Masculin	Female Féminin
OCEANIA - OCÉANIE									
Niue - Nioué									
29 IX 1986 (CDFC)..........	105.8	106	105.6	...	...	...	...	...	...
7 IX 2001 (CDFC)..........	98.5	93.8	103.4	...	...	...	...	...	...
Northern Mariana Islands - Îles Mariannes septentrionales									
1 IV 1990 (CDFC)..........	108	108.4	107.4	111.7	111.2	112.1	106.6	107.5	105.3
Palau - Palaos									
15 IV 2000 (CDFC)..........	103.4	105.5	100.5	...	...	...	...	...	...
Papua New Guinea - Papouasie-Nouvelle-Guinée									
11 VII 1990 (CDFC)..........	139	140.1	137.7	...	...	...	...	...	...
9 VII 2000 (CDFC)..........	134	134.2	133.8	131	133.4	128	134.5	134.4	134.7
Pitcairn									
31 XII 1991 (CDFC)..........	96.2	90.9	100	...	...	...	...	...	...
Samoa									
5 XI 2001 (CDFC)..........	96.4	95.9	97	...	...	...	...	...	...
Tokelau - Tokélaou									
18 X 2011 (CDFC)..........	102.7	104.3	101.2	...	...	...	...	...	...
18 X 2011 (CDJC)[74]..........	105.7	109.6	102	...	...	...	...	...	...
Tonga									
28 XI 1986 (CDJC)..........	98.2	99	97.4	...	...	...	...	...	...
30 XI 1996 (CDFC)[75]..........	100.7	101.7	99.6	...	...	...	...	...	...
30 XI 2006 (CDJC)..........	98.6	97.8	99.4	95.2	93.3	97.2	99.7	99.3	100.1
Tuvalu									
1 XI 2002 (CDFC)..........	98.5	100.8	96.4	...	...	...	...	...	...
Vanuatu									
16 V 1989 (CDJC)..........	106.9	104.8	109	102.4	98.1	107.8	108.1	106.8	109.3
16 XI 2009 (CDJC)..........	110.5	111.3	109.7	...	...	...	...	...	...
7 XI 2016 (CDFC)..........	112.2	112.9	111.6	...	...	...	...	...	...
Wallis and Futuna Islands - Îles Wallis et Futuna									
3 X 1996 (CDFC)..........	96	97.8	94.3	...	...	...	...	...	...

FOOTNOTES - NOTES

Italics: estimates which are less reliable. - Italiques : estimations moins sûres.

* Provisional. - Données provisoires.

[a] 'Code' indicates the source of data, as follows:
CDFC - Census, de facto, complete tabulation
CDJC - Census, de jure, complete tabulation

Le 'Code' indique la source des données, comme suit :
CDFC - Recensement, population de fait, tabulation complète
CDJC - Recensement, population de droit, tabulation complète

[1] Data refer to population in housing units and collective living quarters only. - Correspond aux personnes qui vivent dans des unités d'habitation et dans des logements collectifs seulement.
[2] Data for urban and rural do not add up to the total; reason for discrepancy not ascertained. - La somme des données pour la résidence urbaine et rurale n'est pas égale au total; on ne sait pas comment s'explique la divergence.
[3] Urban and rural data were reported in different years and do not add up to the total. - Les données concernant la population urbaine et la population rurale portent sur des années différentes et leur somme ne correspond pas au total cité.
[4] Excludes collective living quarters. - Exclut les logements collectifs.
[5] Excludes the islands of St. Brandon and Agalega. - Non compris les îles St. Brandon et Agalega.
[6] Data refer to Saint Helenian resident population. - Pour la population résidante de Sainte-Hélène.
[7] Data have been adjusted for underenumeration, estimated at 6.8 per cent. - Les données ont été ajustées pour compenser les lacunes du dénombrement estimées à 6,8 p. 100.

[8] Because of rounding, totals are not in all cases the sum of the respective components. - Les chiffres étant arrondis, les totaux ne correspondent pas toujours rigoureusement à la somme des composants respectifs.
[9] Excluding the institutional population. - Non compris la population dans les institutions.
[10] Bermuda is 100 per cent urban. - 100 pour cent de la population des Bermudes est urbaine.
[11] Total represents population in private dwellings, the non-institutional population and persons found on the streets between the hours of 5am and 7am on September 26, 2001; the figures represent the census counts adjusted for under-coverage. - Le total représente la population vivant dans des logements privés et les personnes trouvées dans la rue entre 5 et 7 heures du matin le 26 septembre 2001, mais ne tient pas compte des personnes vivant dans des établissements; les chiffres sont ceux du recensement corrigés pour tenir compte du sous-dénombrement.
[12] Including an estimation of 1 334 585 persons corresponding to 448 195 housing units without information of the occupants. - Y compris une estimation de 1 334 585 personnes correspondant aux 448 195 unités d'habitation sans information sur les occupants.
[13] Including armed forces stationed in the area. - Y compris les militaires en garnison sur le territoire.
[14] Excluding U.S. Armed Forces overseas and civilian U.S. citizens whose usual place of residence is outside the United States. - Non compris les militaires américains à l'étranger et les civils américains dont le lieu de résidence habituel est en dehors des États-Unis.
[15] Data include persons in remote areas, military personnel outside the country, merchant seamen at sea, civilian seasonal workers outside the country, and other civilians outside the country, and exclude nomads, foreign military, civilian aliens temporarily in the country, transients on ships and Indian jungle population. - Y compris les personnes vivant dans des régions éloignées, le personel militaire en dehors du pays, les marins marchands, les ouvriers saisonniers en dehors du pays, et autres civils en dehors du pays, et non compris les nomades, les

militaires étrangers, les étrangers civils temporairement dans le pays, les transiteurs sur des bateaux et les Indiens de la jungle.

[16] Excludes nomadic Indian tribes. - Non compris les tribus d'Indiens nomades.

[17] The districts of Paramaribo and Wanica are considered urban areas, whereas all other districts are considered more or less rural areas. - Les districts de Paramaribo et de Wanica sont considérés comme des zones urbaines, les autres districts étant considérés comme des zones rurales à divers degrés.

[18] Unrevised data. Data refer to resident population in Uruguay according to Census Phase 1, carried out between the months of June and July 2004. - Les données n'ont pas été révisées. Les données se rapportent à la population résidente en Uruguay d'après la phase 1 du recensement, qui a eu lieu entre juin et juillet 2004.

[19] Excluding Indian jungle population. - Non compris les Indiens de la jungle.

[20] For operational purposes, population centers with 2,500 and more inhabitants are considered as urban area and less than 2,500 are considered as rural area. - À des fins opérationnelles, les centres de population comptant 2 500 habitants ou plus sont considérés comme zones urbaines, ceux qui en comptent moins de 2 500 comme zones rurales.

[21] Data have not been adjusted for underenumeration, estimated at 4.96 per cent. - Les données n'ont pas été ajustées pour compenser les lacunes du dénombrement, estimées à 4,96 p.100.

[22] Excluding foreign diplomatic personnel and their dependants. - Non compris le personnel diplomatique étranger et les membres de leur famille les accompagnant.

[23] For statistical purposes, the data for China do not include those for the Hong Kong Special Administrative Region (Hong Kong SAR), Macao Special Administrative Region (Macao SAR) and Taiwan province of China. Data exclude 2.3 million servicemen, 4.65 million persons with permanent resident status difficult to define, and 0.12 per cent undercount based on the post enumeration survey. - Pour la présentation des statistiques, les données pour la Chine ne comprennent pas la Région Administrative Spéciale de Hong Kong (Hong Kong RAS), la Région Administrative Spéciale de Macao (Macao RAS) et Taïwan province de Chine. Les données ne comprennent pas 2,3 millions de militaires, 4,65 millions de personnes ayant le statut de résident permanent mais difficiles à définir, et des lacunes estimées à 0,12 pour cent sur la base de l'enquête de vérification du recensement.

[24] Data refer to Hong Kong resident population at the census moment, which covers usual residents and mobile residents. Usual residents refer to two categories of people: (1) Hong Kong permanent residents who had stayed in Hong Kong for at least three months during the six months before or for at least three months during the six months after the census moment, regardless of whether they were in Hong Kong or not at the census moment; and (2) Hong Kong non-permanent residents who were in Hong Kong at the census moment. Mobile Residents, they are Hong Kong permanent residents who had stayed in Hong Kong for at least one month but less than three months during the six months before or for at least one month but less than three months during the six months after the census moment, regardless of whether they were in Hong Kong or not at the census moment. - Les données se rapportent à la population résidente à Hong Kong au moment du recensement. Cette population est composée des résidants habituels et des résidants mobiles. La population résidente est partagée en deux catégories: (1) les résidents permanents qui ont habité à Hong Kong au moins trois mois pendant les six mois précédents ou les six mois suivants le recensement; (2) les habitants non-permanents de Hong Kong qui étaient à Hong Kong au moment du recensement. La population mobile se rapporte aux résidents permanents de Hong Kong qui ont habité à Hong Kong pendant les six mois après le recensement pour une période comprise entre un mois et trois mois, indépendamment du fait qu'ils étaient à Hong Kong au moment du recensement au pays.

[25] Data refer to Hong Kong resident population at the census moment, which covers usual residents and mobile residents. Usual residents refer to two categories of people: (1) Hong Kong permanent residents who had stayed in Hong Kong for at least three months during the six months before or for at least three months during the six months after the census moment, regardless of whether they were in Hong Kong or not at the census moment; and (2) Hong Kong non-permanent residents who were in Hong Kong at the census moment. Mobile Residents, they are Hong Kong permanent residents who had stayed in Hong Kong for at least one month but less than three months during the six months before or for at least one month but less than three months during the six months after the census moment, regardless of whether they were in Hong Kong or not at the census moment. Data are estimates from sample enquiry. - Les données se rapportent à la population résidente à Hong Kong au moment du recensement. Cette population est composée des résidants habituels et des résidants mobiles. La population résidente est partagée en deux catégories: (1) les résidents permanents qui ont habité à Hong Kong au moins trois mois pendant les six mois précédents ou les six mois suivants le recensement; (2) les habitants non-permanents de Hong Kong qui étaient à Hong Kong au moment du recensement. La population mobile se rapporte aux résidents permanents de

Hong Kong qui ont habité à Hong Kong pendant les six mois après le recensement pour une période comprise entre un mois et trois mois, indépendamment du fait qu'ils étaient à Hong Kong au moment du recensement au pays. Les données sont des chiffres estimatifs dérivés d'une enquête par sondage.

[26] Data refer to government controlled areas. - Les données se rapportent aux zones contrôlées par le Gouvernement.

[27] Excluding data for Jammu and Kashmir. - Non compris les données concernant la partie du Jammu et Cachemire.

[28] Includes data for the Indian-held part of Jammu and Kashmir, the final status of which has not yet been determined. Excluding Mao-Maram, Paomata and Purul sub-divisions of Senapati district of Manipur. The population of Manipur including the estimated population of the three sub-divisions of Senapati district is 2,291,125 (Males 1,161,173 and females 1,129,952). - Y compris les données pour la partie du Jammu et du Cachemire occupée par l'Inde dont le statut définitif n'a pas encore été déterminé. Non compris les subdivisions Mao-Maram Paomata et Purul du district de Senapati dans l'État du Manipur. Cet État compte 2 291 125 habitants (1 161 173 hommes et 1 129 952 femmes), y compris la population estimative des trois subdivisions du district de Senapati.

[29] Includes data for the Indian-held part of Jammu and Kashmir, the final status of which has not yet been determined. - Y compris les données pour la partie du Jammu et du Cachemire occupée par l'Inde dont le statut définitif n'a pas encore été déterminé.

[30] Data have not been adjusted for underenumeration. - Les données n'ont pas été ajustées pour compenser les lacunes du dénombrement.

[31] Differences between the total country figures and sum of urban and rural areas are due to the inclusion of unsettled population. - Les différences entre les chiffres pour l'ensemble du pays et la somme des zones urbaines et rurales s'expliquent par l'inclusion de la population non sédentaire.

[32] Including unsettled population. - Y compris la population non sédentaire.

[33] The data is from the census sample. - Données extraites de l'échantillon de recensement.

[34] Because of rounding, totals are not in all cases the sum of the respective components. Includes data for East Jerusalem and Israeli residents in certain other territories under occupation by Israeli military forces since June 1967. Data are rounded for confidentiality reasons. - Les chiffres étant arrondis, les totaux ne correspondent pas toujours rigoureusement à la somme des composants respectifs. Y compris les données pour Jérusalem-Est et les résidents israéliens dans certains autres territoires occupés depuis 1967 par les forces armées israéliennes. Chiffres arrondis pour des raisons de confidentialité.

[35] Excluding diplomatic personnel outside the country and foreign military and civilian personnel and their dependants stationed in the area. - Non compris le personnel diplomatique hors du pays ni les militaires et agents civils étrangers en poste sur le territoire et les membres de leur famille les accompagnant.

[36] Excluding data for Jordanian territory under occupation since June 1967 by Israeli military forces. Including registered Palestinian refugees and Jordanians abroad. - Non compris les données pour le territoire jordanien occupé depuis juin 1967 par les forces armées israéliennes. Y compris les réfugiés palestiniens enregistrés et les Jordaniens à l'étranger.

[37] Excluding data for Jordanian territory under occupation since June 1967 by Israeli military forces. - Non compris les données pour le territoire jordanien occupé depuis juin 1967 par les forces armées israéliennes.

[38] Unrevised data. - Les données n'ont pas été révisées.

[39] Excluding usual residents not in the country at the time of census. - À l'exclusion des résidents habituels qui ne sont pas dans le pays au moment du recensement.

[40] Data have been adjusted for underenumeration. - Les données ont été ajustées pour compenser les lacunes du dénombrement.

[41] Total population is taken as de facto and de jure together. - Population totale considérée comme de fait et de droit.

[42] Data refer to resident population that includes Maldivians and foreigners. - Les données concernent la population résidente, qui comprend des Maldiviens et des étrangers.

[43] Data refer to enumerated population. The total for the whole country excludes 1,206,353 persons estimated not to have been counted in parts of States of Rakhine, Kachin and Kayin. - Les données se rapportent à la population dénombrée. L' effectif de la population pour le pays ne comprend pas les personnes qui ne sont pas dénombrées dans certaines régions des États de Rakhine, Kachin et Kayin estimées à un chiffre de 1 206 353 personnes.

[44] Excluding 2739 Filipinos in Philippine Embassies, Consulates and Missions Abroad. - Excepté 2739 Philippins travaillant dans les ambassades, les consulats et les missions des Philippines à l'étranger.

[45] Excluding foreigners. - Non compris les étrangers.

[46] Data are based on the latest register-based population estimates for 2010. Data refer to resident population which comprises Singapore citizens and permanent residents. - Données basées sur les estimations démographiques les plus récentes fondées sur les registres de 2010. Les données se rapportent à la

population résidente composé des citoyens de Singapour et des résidents permanents.

[47] The Population and Housing Census 2001 did not cover the whole area of the country due to the security problems; data refer to the 18 districts for which the census was completed only (in three districts it was not possible to conduct the census at all and in four districts it was partially conducted). Unrevised data. - Le recensement de la population et du logement de 2001 n'a pas été réalisé sur la superficie totale du pays à cause de problèmes de sécurité; les données ne concernent que les 18 districts entièrement recensés (3 districts n'ont pas été recensés du tout, et 4 ont été recensés en partie). Les données n'ont pas été révisées.

[48] Data for rural areas include data of estate sectors consist of all plantations which are 20 acres or more in extent and with ten or more resident labourers. - Les données pour les zones rurales comprennent celles pour les domaines, dont l'ensemble des plantations de plus de 10 hectares comptant au moins 10 travailleurs résidents.

[49] Total population does not include Palestinian population living in those parts of Jerusalem governorate which were annexed by Israel in 1967, amounting to 210 209 persons. Likewise, the results does not include the estimates of not enumerated population based on the findings of the post enumeration study, i.e 83 805 persons. - Les données relatives à la population totale ne comprennent pas la population palestinienne -équivalent à 210 209 personnes - habitant dans les territoires du gouvernorat de Jérusalem qui ont été annexés par Israël en 1967. Egalement, les données ne tiennent pas compte des estimations de la population calculée sur la base des résultats de l'enquête postcensitaire, équivalent à 83 805 personnes.

[50] Data for urban include population in refugee camps - Les données pour la population urbaine comprennent la population dans les camps réfugiés.

[51] Including Palestinian refugees. - Y compris les réfugiés de Palestine.

[52] All persons falling within the scope of the census were enumerated on a de jure basis, except students who were enumerated on a de facto basis. - Toutes les personnes englobées dans le recensement ont été dénombrées comme population de droit, à l'exception des étudiants qui ont été dénombrés comme population de fait.

[53] Based on a sample taken at the time of census. Because of rounding, totals are not in all cases the sum of the respective components. The figures were calculated by dividing and rounding to thousand. Therefore, "0" may indicate value of less than 500. - D'après un échantillon obtenu au moment du recensement. Les chiffres étant arrondis, les totaux ne correspondent pas toujours rigoureusement à la somme des composants respectifs. Les chiffres ont été calculés en divisant et en arrondissant au millier. Par conséquent, "0" peut indiquer une valeur inférieure à 500.

[54] Statistics are compiled from registers. - Les statistiques sont compilées à partir des registres.

[55] Excluding Faeroe Islands and Greenland shown separately, if available. - Non compris les Iles Féroé et le Groenland, qui font l'objet de rubriques distinctes, si disponible.

[56] Data include Overseas Departments. - Y compris les données des départements d'outre-mer.

[57] Excluding families of military personnel, visitors and transients. - Non compris les familles des militaires, ni les visiteurs et transients.

[58] Excluding military personnel, visitors and transients. - Non compris les militaires, ni les visiteurs et transients.

[59] Including armed forces stationed outside the country and alien armed forces in the area. - Y compris les militaires nationaux hors du pays et les militaires étrangers en garnison sur le territoire.

[60] The figures refer to usual residents in private households and persons present in communal establishments during the 2011 census. - Données se rapportant aux résidents habituels membres de ménages privés et aux personnes recensées dans des établissements collectifs au recensement de 2011.

[61] Age classification is based on the difference between the year of birth and the year of the census, rather than on completed years of age. - La classification par âge est fondée sur la différence entre l'année de naissance et l'année de recensement,et non sur l'âge en années révolues.

[62] Including residents temporarily outside the country. Population statistics are compiled from registers. - Y compris les résidents se trouvant temporairement hors du pays. Les statistiques de la population sont compilées à partir des registres.

[63] The total number may include 'Unknown residence', but the categories urban and rural do not. - Le nombre total peut inclure les personnes dont la résidence n'est pas connue, à l'inverse des catégories de population urbaine et rurale.

[64] Excluding civilian aliens within the country, but including civilian nationals temporarily outside the country. - Non compris les civils étrangers dans le pays, mais y compris les civils nationaux temporairement hors du pays.

[65] Excluding Transnistria and the municipality of Bender. Excluding non-residents present in country at time of census. - Les données ne tiennent pas compte de l'information sur la Transnistria et la municipalité de Bender. Non compris les non-résidents présents dans le pays au moment du recensement.

[66] Excludes data for Kosovo and Metohia. - Sans les données pour le Kosovo et Metohia.

[67] Excluding transients visitors. - Non compris les visiteurs en transit.

[68] Excluding Channel Islands (Guernsey and Jersey) and Isle of Man, shown separately, if available. - Non compris les îles Anglo-Normandes (Guernesey et Jersey) et l'île de Man, qui font l'objet de rubriques distinctes, si disponible.

[69] Counts for the 1991 Census are taken from 'Key Statistics for Urban and Rural Areas: Great Britain 1991' published volume basen on the usually resident population. - Les chiffres du recensement de 1991 sont extraits de l'ouvrage « Key Statistics for Urban Areas: Great Britain 1991 » et sont fondés sur la notion de résidence habituelle.

[70] Counts for the 2001 Census are taken from 'Key Statistics table 1 for the Urban/Rural classification: England and Wales' available on CD based on the usually resident population. - Les chiffres du recensement de 2001 proviennent du tableau intitulé « Key Statistics table 1 for the Urban/Rural classification: England and Wales » disponible sur CD-ROM et sont fondés sur la notion de résidence habituelle.

[71] This data has been randomly rounded to protect confidentiality. Individual figures may not add up to totals, and values for the same data may vary in different tables. - Ces données ont été arrondies de façon aléatoire afin d'en préserver la confidentialité. La somme de certains chiffres peut ne pas correspondre aux totaux indiqués et les valeurs des mêmes données peuvent varier d'un tableau à un autre.

[72] Including population in off-shore, migratory and shipping. - Y compris les populations extraterritoriales, les populations nomades et les populations maritimes.

[73] Excluding Niue, shown separately, which is part of Cook Islands, but because of remoteness is administered separately. - Non compris Nioué, qui fait l'objet d'une rubrique distincte et qui fait partie des îles Cook, mais qui, en raison de son éloignement, est administrée séparément.

[74] Data includes Tokelaun Public Service employees and their immediate families based in Apia but excludes non-residents present at the time of the census. - Les données comprennent les agents de la fonction publique des Tokélaou et leur famille directe basés à Apia mais excluent les non-résidents présents au moment du recensement.

[75] Data refer to Tongans and part-Tongans only. - Les données ne concernent que la population tongane et partie-Tongans seulement.

Table 4 - *Demographic Yearbook 2016*

Table 4 presents, for each country or area of the world, basic vital statistics for the period 2012 - 2016: live births, crude birth rate, deaths, crude death rate, rate of natural increase, infant deaths, infant death rate, life expectancy at birth by sex and total fertility rate.

Description of variables: The vital events and rates shown in this table are defined as follows[1]:

Live birth is the complete expulsion or extraction from its mother of a product of conception, irrespective of the duration of pregnancy, which after such separation breathes or shows any other evidence of life such as beating of the heart, pulsation of the umbilical cord, definite movement of voluntary muscles, whether or not the umbilical cord has been cut or the placenta is attached; each product of such a birth is considered live born.

Death is the permanent disappearance of all evidence of life at any time after live birth has taken place (post-natal cessation of vital functions without capability of resuscitation).

Infant deaths are deaths of live born infants under one year of age.

Life expectancy at birth is defined as the average number of years of life for males and females if they continued to be subject to the same mortality experienced in the year(s) to which these life expectancies refer.

The total fertility rate is the average number of children that would be born alive to a hypothetical cohort of women if, throughout their reproductive years, the age-specific fertility rates remained unchanged. The standard method of calculating the total fertility rate is the sum of the age-specific fertility rates.

Crude birth rates and crude death rates presented in this table are calculated using the number of live births and the number of deaths obtained from civil registers. These civil registration data are used only if they are considered reliable (estimated completeness of 90 per cent or more).

Similarly, infant mortality rates presented in this table are calculated using the number of live births and the number of infant deaths obtained from civil registers. If, however, the registration of births or infant deaths for any given country or area is estimated to be less than 90 per cent complete, the rates are not calculated.

For some countries, the data and rates presented in this table are based on vital statistics data sourced from censuses or demographic surveys.

Rate computation: The crude birth and death rates are the annual number of each of these vital events per 1 000 mid-year population. Infant mortality rate is the annual number of deaths of infants under one year of age per 1 000 live births in the same year.

Rates of natural increase are the difference between the crude birth rate and the crude death rate. It should be noted that the rates of natural increase presented here may differ from the population growth rates presented in table 3 as rates of natural increase do not take net international migration into account while the population growth rates do.

Crude birth rates, crude death rates and infant mortality rates that appear in this table have been calculated by the United Nations Statistics Division, unless otherwise noted. Exceptions include official estimated rates for India, which were based on the sample registration system. Rates calculated by the United Nations Statistics Division presented in this table have been limited to those countries or areas having a minimum number of 30 events (for live births, deaths or infant deaths) in a given year.

Reliability of data: Rates calculated on the basis of registered vital statistics which are considered unreliable (estimated to be less than 90 per cent complete) are not calculated. Estimated rates, prepared by individual countries or areas, are presented whenever applicable.

The designation of vital statistics as being either reliable or unreliable is discussed in general in section 4.2 of the Technical Notes. The technical notes for tables 9, 15 and 18 provide specific information on reliability of statistics on live births, infant deaths and deaths, respectively.

The values shown for life expectancy in this table come from official life tables. It is assumed that, if necessary, the basic data (population and deaths classified by age and sex) have been adjusted for deficiencies before their use in constructing the life tables.

Limitations: Statistics on births, deaths and infant deaths are subject to the same qualifications as have been set forth for vital statistics, in general, in section 4 of the Technical Notes and in the technical notes for individual tables presenting detailed data on these events (table 9, live births; table 15, infant deaths; table 18, deaths).

In assessing comparability it is important to take into account the reliability of the data used to calculate the rates, as discussed above.

The problem of obtaining precise correspondence between numerator (births and deaths) and denominator (population for crude birth and death rates) as regards the inclusion or exclusion of armed forces, refugees, displaced persons and other special groups is particularly difficult where vital rates are concerned.

It should also be noted that crude rates are particularly affected by the age-sex structure of the population. Infant mortality rates, and to a much lesser extent crude birth rates and crude death rates, are affected by the variation in the definition of a live birth and tabulation procedures.

NOTES

[1] *Principles and Recommendations for a Vital Statistics System Revision 3,* Sales No. E.13.XVII.10, United Nations, New York, 2014.

Tableau 4 – *Annuaire démographique 2016*

Le tableau 4 présente, pour chaque pays ou zone du monde, des statistiques de base de l'état civil pour les années 2012 – 2016 : les naissances vivantes, le taux brut de natalité, les décès, le taux brut de mortalité et le taux d'accroissement naturel de la population, les décès d'enfants de moins d'un an et le taux de mortalité infantile, l'espérance de vie à la naissance par sexe et l'indice synthétique de fécondité.

Description des variables : les faits d'état civil utilisés aux fins du calcul des taux présentés dans le tableau 4 sont définis comme suit[1] :

La naissance vivante est l'expulsion ou l'extraction complète du corps de la mère, indépendamment de la durée de la gestation, d'un produit de la conception qui après cette séparation, respire ou manifeste tout autre signe de vie, tel que battement de cœur, pulsation du cordon ombilical ou contraction effective d'un muscle soumis à l'action de la volonté, que le cordon ombilical ait été coupé ou non et que le placenta soit ou non demeuré attaché ; tout produit d'une telle naissance est considéré comme « enfant né vivant ».

Le décès est la disparition permanente de tout signe de vie à un moment quelconque postérieur à la naissance vivante (cessation des fonctions vitales après la naissance sans possibilité de réanimation).

Il convient de préciser que les chiffres relatifs aux décès d'enfants de moins d'un an se rapportent aux naissances vivantes.

L'espérance de vie à la naissance est le nombre moyen d'années que vivraient les individus de sexe masculin et de sexe féminin s'ils continuaient d'être soumis aux mêmes conditions de mortalité que celles qui existaient pendant les années auxquelles se rapportent les valeurs indiquées.

L'indice synthétique de fécondité représente le nombre moyen d'enfants que mettrait au monde une cohorte hypothétique de femmes qui seraient soumises, tout au long de leur vie, aux mêmes conditions de fécondité par âge que celles auxquelles sont soumises les femmes, dans chaque groupe d'âge, au cours d'une année ou d'une période donnée. La méthode standard pour calculer l'indice synthétique de fécondité consiste à additionner les taux de fécondité par âge simple.

Les taux bruts de natalité et de mortalité ont été établis sur la base du nombre de naissances vivantes et du nombre de décès inscrits sur les registres de l'état civil. Ces données n'ont été utilisées que lorsqu'elles étaient considérées comme sûres (degré estimatif de complétude égal ou supérieur à 90 p. 100).

De même, les taux de mortalité infantile présentés dans le tableau 4 ont été établis à partir du nombre de naissances vivantes et du nombre de décès d'enfants de moins d'un an inscrits sur les registres de l'état civil. Toutefois, lorsque les données relatives aux naissances ou aux décès d'enfants de moins d'un an pour un pays ou zone quelconque n'étaient pas considérées complètes à 90 p. 100 au moins, les indices n'ont pas été calculés.

Pour quelques pays, les données et les taux présentés dans ce tableau ont été extraites des recensements de la population ou des enquêtes démographiques.

Calcul des taux : les taux bruts de natalité et de mortalité, représentent le nombre annuel de chacun de ces faits d'état civil pour 1 000 habitants au milieu de l'année considérée. Les taux de mortalité infantile correspondent au nombre annuel de décès d'enfants de moins d'un an pour 1 000 naissances vivantes survenues pendant la même année.

Le taux d'accroissement naturel est égal à la différence entre le taux brut de natalité et le taux brut de mortalité. Il y a lieu de noter que les taux d'accroissement naturel indiqués dans le tableau 4 peuvent différer des taux d'accroissement de la population figurant dans le tableau 3, les taux d'accroissement naturel ne tenant pas compte des taux nets de migration internationale, alors que ceux-ci sont inclus dans les taux d'accroissement de la population.

Sauf indication contraire, les taux bruts de natalité et de mortalité, et les taux de mortalité infantile figurant dans le tableau 4, ont été calculés par la Division des statistiques de l'Organisation des Nations Unies. Les exceptions comprennent l'Inde, pour laquelle les taux estimatifs officiels ont été fournis sur la base d'un système d'enregistrement par échantillonnage. Les taux calculés par la Division des statistiques de l'Organisation des Nations Unies qui sont présentés dans le tableau 4 se rapportent aux pays ou zones où l'on a enregistré au moins 30 événements (pour les naissances vivantes, les décès ou pour les décès d'enfants de moins d'un an) au cours d'une année donnée.

Fiabilité des données : les taux n'ont pas été calculés lorsque les statistiques de l'état civil issues de systèmes d'enregistrement d'état civil étaient jugées douteuses (degré estimatif de complétude inférieur à 90 p.100) et des taux estimatifs, calculés par les pays ou zones, ont été présentés lorsqu'ils étaient disponibles.

On trouve à la section 4.2 des Notes techniques des explications générales concernant la façon dont les statistiques de l'état civil ont été classées selon leur degré de fiabilité. Les notes techniques relatives aux tableaux 9, 15 et 18 ont trait respectivement à la fiabilité des statistiques des naissances vivantes, des décès d'enfants de moins d'un an et des décès.

Les valeurs relatives à l'espérance de vie figurant dans le tableau 4 proviennent de tables officielles de mortalité. On présume que les données de base (la population et les décès par sexe et âge) ont été rectifiées d'éventuelles insuffisances avant d'être utilisées pour construire les tables de mortalité.

Insuffisance des données : les statistiques des naissances, décès et décès d'enfants de moins d'un an appellent toutes les réserves qui ont été formulées à propos des statistiques de l'état civil en général à la section 4 des Notes techniques et dans les notes techniques relatives aux différents tableaux présentant des données détaillées sur ces événements [tableau 9 (naissances vivantes), tableau 15 (décès d'enfants de moins d'un an) et tableau 18 (décès)].

Pour évaluer la comparabilité des divers taux, il importe de tenir compte de la fiabilité des données utilisées pour calculer ces taux, comme il a été indiqué précédemment.

Le calcul des taux est particulièrement affecté par la difficulté à obtenir une correspondance parfaite entre le numérateur (naissances et décès) et le dénominateur (population, pour les taux bruts de natalité et de mortalité) en raison de l'inclusion ou non dans la population des forces armées, des réfugiés, des personnes déplacées ou d'autres groupes sociaux.

Il y a lieu de noter que la structure par âge et par sexe de la population influe de façon particulière sur les taux bruts. Le manque d'uniformité dans la définition des naissances vivantes et dans les procédures de mise en tableaux a une incidence sur les taux de mortalité infantile et, à un moindre degré, sur les taux bruts de natalité et les taux bruts de mortalité.

NOTE

[1] *Principles and Recommendations for a Vital Statistics System Revision 3*, Sales No. E.13.XVII.10, United Nations, New York, 2014

4. Vital statistics summary and life expectancy at birth: 2012 - 2016
Aperçu des statistiques de l'état civil et de l'espérance de vie à la naissance : 2012 - 2016

Continent, country or area and year / Continent, pays ou zone et année	Live births / Naissances vivantes			Deaths / Décès			Rate of natural increase / Taux d'accroissement naturel	Infant deaths / Décès d'enfants de moins d'un an			Life expectancy at birth / Espérance de vie à la naissance		Total fertility rate / L'indice synthétique de fécondité
	Code[a]	Number / Nombre	Crude birth rate / Taux brut de natalité	Code[a]	Number / Nombre	Crude death rate / Taux brut de mortalité		Code[a]	Number / Nombre	Rate (per 1000 births) / Taux (par 1000 naissances)	Male[b] / Masculin[b]	Female[b] / Féminin[b]	
AFRICA - AFRIQUE													
Algeria - Algérie													
2012	C	978 233[1]	26.1	U	169 815[1]	...	...	U	22 088[1]	...	75.8[2]	77.1[2]	3.020
2013	C	962 722[1]	25.1	U	168 136[1]	...	...	U	21 586[1]	...	76.5[2]	77.6[2]	2.930
2014	C	1 014 248[1]	25.9	U	173 781[1]	...	...	U	22 282[1]	...	76.6[2]	77.8[2]	3.030
2015	C	1 040 285[1]	26.0	U	182 570[1]	...	...	U	23 150[1]	...	76.4[2]	77.8[2]	3.100
2016	C	1 066 823[1]	26.1	U	180 404[1]	...	...	U	22 271[1]	...	77.1[2]	78.2[2]	3.100
Benin - Bénin[3]													
2012	I	376 439	40.2	I	79 116	8.4	31.7		...	...	...	...	...
Botswana													
2012	U	40 856[4]	...	U	12 270[5]	...	...		...	...	...	...	...
2013	U	44 794[6]	...	U	11 967[5]	...	...	U	960[5]	...	...	...	...
2014	U	41 741[5]	...	U	12 177[5]	...	...	U	1 045[5]	...	...	...	...
2016		...	...		...	...	...		...	...	64.9[7]	65.9[7]	...
Burundi													
2012	+U	221 289[8]	...		...	...	...		...	...	...	...	6.080
2013	+U	248 395[8]	...		...	...	...		...	...	...	...	5.840
2014	+U	253 698[8]	...		...	...	...		...	...	56.5	60.6	6.140
2015	+U	266 820[8]	...		...	...	...		...	...	...	...	5.700
2016		...	...		...	...	...		...	...	56.3	60.5	5.500[9]
Côte d'Ivoire													
2014	I	841 081[10]	37.0	I	248 930[10]	11.0	26.1	I	44 530[10]	52.9	...	...	4.790
2016		...	...		...	...	...		...	...	54.9	57.5	...
Egypt - Égypte													
2012	+C	2 629 769	31.9	C	529 512	6.4	25.4	C	39 942	15.2	...	...	3.000
2013	+C	2 621 902	31.0	C	511 183	6.0	24.9	C	38 753	14.8	...	...	3.000
2014	+C	2 720 495	31.3	C	531 864	6.1	25.2	C	39 679	14.6	...	...	3.500
2015	+C	2 696 231	30.3	C	573 129	6.4	23.9		...	...	...	...	3.500
2016		...	...		...	...	...		...	...	70.5	73.3	3.500
Ghana													
2012	+U	475 731[11]	...	+U	54 551[12]	...	...		...	...	...	...	...
2013	+U	463 409[11]	...	+U	51 466[12]	...	...		...	...	...	...	...
Guinea - Guinée													
2012		...	...		...	...	...		...	...	...	...	5.100[13]
2013	+U	205 658	...		...	...	...		...	...	...	...	...
2014	I	448 218[14]	42.3	I	117 635[15]	11.1	31.2	I	29 798[16]	66.5	57.4[17]	60.4[17]	5.600[18]
2016		...	...		...	...	...		...	...	...	...	4.800[19]
Guinea-Bissau - Guinée-Bissau													
2014		...	...		...	...	...		...	...	51.2	53.6	...
Kenya													
2012	U	801 815	...	U	187 811	...	...	U	21 209	...	...	...	...
2013	U	870 599	...	U	194 332	...	...	U	20 888	...	...	...	...
2014	U	954 254	...	U	198 611	...	...	U	18 672	...	...	...	...
2015	U	950 224	...	U	200 205	...	...	U	15 861	...	...	...	...
2016	U	948 351	...	U	189 930	...	...	U	13 839	...	...	...	...
Lesotho													
2012	+U	1 718	...	+U	7 751	...	...		...	...	...	...	...
Liberia - Libéria													
2012		...	...		...	...	...		...	...	...	...	4.800
2013		...	...		...	...	...		...	...	...	...	4.700
2014		...	...		...	...	...		...	...	...	...	4.600
Mauritania - Mauritanie													
2013	I	114 420[20]	32.3		...	...	...		...	...	58.3	61.8	...
Mauritius - Maurice[21]													
2012	+C	14 494	11.5	+C	9 343	7.4	4.1	+C	199	13.7	III70.2	77.1	1.544
2013	+C	13 488	10.7	+C	9 440	7.5	3.2	+C	165	12.2	...	...	1.438
2014	+C	13 283	10.5	+C	9 682	7.7	2.9	+C	194	14.6	III71.0	77.6	1.424
2015	+C	12 640	10.0	+C	9 747	7.7	2.3	+C	173	13.7	III71.1	77.8	1.362
2016	+C	12 948	10.2	+C	10 174	8.1	2.2	+C	154	11.9	III71.2	77.8	1.399

4. Vital statistics summary and life expectancy at birth: 2012 - 2016
Aperçu des statistiques de l'état civil et de l'espérance de vie à la naissance : 2012 - 2016 (continued - suite)

Continent, country or area and year / Continent, pays ou zone et année	Code[a]	Number Nombre	Crude birth rate Taux brut de natalité	Code[a]	Number Nombre	Crude death rate Taux brut de mortalité	Rate of natural increase Taux d'accroissement naturel	Code[a]	Number Nombre	Rate (per 1000 births) Taux (par 1000 naissances)	Male[b] Masculin[b]	Female[b] Féminin[b]	Total fertility rate L'indice synthétique de fécondité
AFRICA - AFRIQUE													
Mayotte													
2014	C	7 306	33.2	C	590	2.7	30.5		...	...	74.7	77.9	...
2015		...	...		...	...	...		...	...	75.3	77.2	...
Morocco - Maroc													
2013		...	...		...	...	...		...	...	72.4	75.1	...
Mozambique													
2012	U	624 523[22]	...		...	...	...		...	...	...	...	5.500
2013	U	746 185[22]	...		...	...	...		...	...	...	...	5.400
2014	U	794 718[22]	...		...	...	...		...	...	50.2	55.4	...
2015		...	...		...	...	...		...	...	51.7	55.9	...
2016		...	...		...	...	...		...	...	52.0	56.2	...
Reunion - Réunion													
2014	C	14 095[23]	16.7	C	4 355	5.2	11.6		...	...	77.1	83.7	...
2015		...	...		...	...	...		...	...	77.1	83.6	...
Rwanda													
2012	U	404 067	...	U	139 499	...	...		...	...	62.6[24]	66.2[24]	5.300
Saint Helena ex. dep. - Sainte-Hélène sans dép.													
2012	C	32	7.8	C	62	15.0	-7.3	C	1	...	ˣ72.0[25]	79.7[25]	...
2013	C	35	8.3	C	55	13.1	-4.7	C	-	...	...	...	...
2014	C	48	10.9	C	61	13.9	-3.0	C	1	...	...	...	...
2015	C	40	8.9	C	55	12.3	-3.4		...	...	...	...	...
2016	C	35	7.5	C	45	9.7	-2.1		...	...	...	...	...
Sao Tome and Principe - Sao Tomé-et-Principe													
2012	C	5 173	27.6	I	1 287[10]	6.9	20.7		...	...	‖62.1	68.7	...
2015	C*	5 022	...	U*	1 226	...	...		...	...	...	...	...
Senegal - Sénégal													
2012	I	471 629[26]	35.7	I	135 468[26]	10.3	25.5		...	...	...	...	...
2013	I	478 898[26]	35.5	I	136 460[26]	10.1	25.3		...	...	63.2[27]	66.5[27]	...
Seychelles													
2012	+C	1 645	18.6	+C	651	7.4	11.3		...	...	...	...	2.420
2013	+C	1 566	17.4	+C	717	8.0	9.4	+C	29	...	69.9	76.5	2.370
2014	+C	1 557	17.0	+C	725	7.9	9.1	+C	17	...	68.4	78.3	2.340
2015	+C	1 592	17.0	+C	703	7.5	9.5	+C	17	...	...	...	...
Sierra Leone													
2012	+U	148 958[28]	...	...	10 611	...	...	+U	2 165[28]	...	...	...	5.820
2013	+U	229 947[28]	...	...	17 127	...	...	+U	2 276[28]	...	...	...	...
South Africa - Afrique du Sud													
2012	U	926 726	...	U	492 062	...	...	U	27 104	...	...	...	2.570
2013	U	939 011	...	U	473 384	...	...	U	26 630	...	...	...	2.540
2014	U	954 385	...	U	453 360	...	...	U	25 643	...	59.1	63.1	2.510
2015	U	919 562	...		...	...	...		...	...	...	...	2.480
2016	U	876 435	...		...	...	...		...	...	...	...	2.430
Swaziland													
2012		...	...		...	...	...		...	...	...	...	3.600
2013		...	...		...	...	...		...	...	...	...	3.600
2014		...	...		...	...	...		...	...	...	...	3.600
2015		...	...		...	...	...		...	...	...	...	3.500
Tunisia - Tunisie													
2012	C	217 740	20.2	U	63 257	...	...		...	...	...	...	...
2013	C	222 960	20.5	U	61 730	...	...		...	...	...	...	...
2014	C	225 890	20.5	U	62 785	...	...		...	...	...	...	...
2015	C	222 530	19.9	U	65 743	...	...		...	...	74.5	77.8	...

4. Vital statistics summary and life expectancy at birth: 2012 - 2016
Aperçu des statistiques de l'état civil et de l'espérance de vie à la naissance : 2012 - 2016 (continued - suite)

Continent, country or area and year / Continent, pays ou zone et année	Live births - Naissances vivantes			Deaths - Décès			Rate of natural increase - Taux d'accroissement naturel	Infant deaths - Décès d'enfants de moins d'un an			Life expectancy at birth - Espérance de vie à la naissance		Total fertility rate - L'indice synthétique de fécondité
	Code[a]	Number Nombre	Crude birth rate Taux brut de natalité	Code[a]	Number Nombre	Crude death rate Taux brut de mortalité		Code[a]	Number Nombre	Rate (per 1000 births) Taux (par 1000 naissances)	Male[b] Masculin[b]	Female[b] Féminin[b]	
AFRICA - AFRIQUE													
Uganda - Ouganda[29]													
2014		...	...		...	...	...		...	...	62.2	64.2	...
United Republic of Tanzania - République Unie de Tanzanie													
2012	...	1 694 943	...	...	555 975	...	...		...	...	...	...	3.685[30]
AMERICA, NORTH - AMÉRIQUE DU NORD													
Anguilla													
2012	+C	192	14.0	+C	38[31]	2.8	11.2	+C	-	...	...	...	...
2013	+C	165	11.9	+C	72[31]	5.2	6.7	+C	3	...	...	...	...
2014	+C	151	10.6	+C	59[31]	4.1	6.5		...	...	...	...	...
2015	+C	165	11.2	+C	61[31]	4.1	7.1		...	...	...	...	...
Antigua and Barbuda - Antigua-et-Barbuda													
2012	+C	1 187	...	+C	510	...	...		...	...	...	...	...
Aruba													
2012	C	1 288	12.3	C	595	5.7	6.6	+C	3	...	...	...	1.973
2013	C	1 346	12.7	C	560	5.3	7.4	+C	5	...	...	...	2.032
2014	C	1 376	12.8	C	643	6.0	6.8	+C	5	...	...	...	2.041
2015	C	1 244	11.4	C	679	6.2	5.2	+C	6	...	...	...	1.821
2016	C	1 121	10.2	C	781	7.1	3.1	+C	5	...	...	...	1.623
Bahamas													
2012	+U	4 469	...	+C	1 995	5.5	...	+C	57	...	...	...	1.740
2013	+U	4 330	...	+C	2 065	5.6	...	+C	51	...	...	...	1.725
2014	+U*	4 196	...		...	...	...		...	...	...	...	1.475*
Barbados - Barbade													
2012	+C	3 185	11.5	+C	2 403	8.7	2.8		...	...	...	...	...
2013	+C	3 020	10.9	+C	2 276	8.2	2.7		...	...	...	...	...
2014	+C	2 902	10.5	+C	2 580	9.3	1.2		...	...	...	...	...
Belize													
2012	U	7 125	...	U	1 650	...	...	U	116	...	...	...	2.404
2013	U	7 264	...	U	1 637	...	...	U	129	...	...	...	2.394
2014	U	7 318	...	U	1 620	...	...	U	91	...	...	...	2.353
2015	U	7 456	...	U	1 772	...	...	U	127	...	...	...	2.347
2016	U	7 200	...	U	1 796	...	...	U	103	...	...	...	2.195
Bermuda - Bermudes													
2012	C	648[32]	10.4	C	422[32]	6.8	3.6	C	1	...	77.2	82.4	1.571
2013	C	648[32]	10.5	C	471[32]	7.6	2.9	C	1	...	76.9	84.5	1.594
2014	C	574[32]	9.3	C	480[32]	7.8	1.5	C	2	...	77.1	84.7	1.420
2015	C	583[32]	9.4	C	457[32]	7.4	2.0	C	2	...	77.3	84.9	1.450
2016	C	591[32]	9.6	C*	492[32]	8.0	1.6		...	...	77.5	85.1	1.496
British Virgin Islands - Îles Vierges britanniques													
2012	C	286	10.1	C	122	4.3	5.8		...	...	...	...	...
2013	C	277	9.7	C	113	4.0	5.8		...	...	...	...	...
2014	C	280	...	C	111	...	...		...	...	...	...	...
2015	C	266	9.1	C	136	4.7	4.5		...	...	...	...	...
Canada													
2012	C	381 869[33]	11.0	C	246 596[33]	7.1	3.9	C	1 818[33]	4.8	III79.4	83.6	1.614
2013	C	380 323[33]	10.8	C	252 338[33]	7.2	3.6	C	1 884[33]	5.0	...	...	1.587
2014	C*	388 729[34]	10.9	C*	268 056[34]	7.5	3.4		...	...	...	...	...
Cayman Islands - Îles Caïmanes													
2012	C	759	13.5	C	184[35]	3.3	10.2		...	...	...	...	...
2013	C	705	12.5	C	182[35]	3.2	9.3		...	...	...	...	...

4. Vital statistics summary and life expectancy at birth: 2012 - 2016
Aperçu des statistiques de l'état civil et de l'espérance de vie à la naissance : 2012 - 2016 (continued - suite)

Continent, country or area and year / Continent, pays ou zone et année	Code[a]	Live births - Naissances vivantes Number Nombre	Crude birth rate Taux brut de natalité	Code[a]	Deaths - Décès Number Nombre	Crude death rate Taux brut de mortalité	Rate of natural increase Taux d'accroissement naturel	Code[a]	Infant deaths - Décès d'enfants de moins d'un an Number Nombre	Rate (per 1000 births) Taux (par 1000 naissances)	Life expectancy at birth Male[b] Masculin[b]	Female[b] Féminin[b]	Total fertility rate L'indice synthétique de fécondité
AMERICA, NORTH - AMÉRIQUE DU NORD													
Cayman Islands - Îles Caïmanes													
2014	C	711	12.5	C	163[35]	2.9	9.6		...	...	...	...	...
2015	C	649	11.0	C	170[35]	2.9	8.1		...	...	...	...	...
Costa Rica													
2012	C	73 326	15.8	C	19 200	4.1	11.6	C	624	8.5	...	...	1.880
2013	C	70 550	15.0	C	19 647	4.2	10.8	C	612	8.7	...	...	1.760
2014	C	71 793[36]	15.0	C	20 553	4.3	10.7	C	575	8.0	77.2	82.3	1.860
2015	C	71 819	14.9	C	21 039	4.4	10.5	C	557	7.8	77.4	82.4	1.750
2016	C*	70 004	14.3	C*	22 603	4.6	9.7	C*	555	7.9	...	...	1.700*
Cuba													
2012	C	125 674	11.2	C	89 372	8.0	3.2	C	581	4.6	...	...	1.690
2013	C	125 880	11.2	C	92 273	8.2	3.0	C	525	4.2	III76.5	80.5	1.714
2014	C	122 643	10.9	C	96 330	8.6	2.3	C	514	4.2	...	...	1.681
2015	C	125 064	11.1	C	99 691	8.9	2.3	C	535	4.3	...	...	1.721
2016	C	116 872	10.4	C	99 401	8.8	1.6	C	497	4.3	...	...	...
Curaçao													
2012	C	2 039	13.4	C	1 246	8.2	5.2	C	23	...	II74.4	80.7	2.168
2013	C	1 962	12.8	C	1 250	8.1	4.6	C	15	...	...	...	2.052
2014	C	1 963	12.6	C	1 370	8.8	3.8	C	24	...	IV74.0	81.2	2.009
2015	C	1 877	11.9	C	1 398	8.8	3.0	C	20	...	...	...	1.862
2016	C	1 789	11.2	C	1 482	9.3	1.9	C	20	...	74.9	81.0	1.742
Dominica - Dominique													
2012	+C	951	13.4	+C	603	8.5	4.9		...	...	...	...	...
2013	+C	931	13.1	+C	630	8.8	4.2		...	...	...	...	...
2014	+C	858	12.0	+C	590	8.2	3.7		...	...	...	...	...
Dominican Republic - République dominicaine													
2012	U	159 872	...	U	36 009	...	...	U	473	...	...	...	2.418
2013	U	159 785	...	U	36 025	...	...	U	659	...	...	...	2.391
2014	U	161 306	...	U	40 464	...	...	U	842	...	...	...	2.364
2015	U	157 422	...	U	40 924	...	...	U	903	...	VI70.0	74.8	2.336
2016	U	139 583	...	U	42 185	...	...	U	791	...	...	...	...
El Salvador													
2012	C	110 843[37]	17.7	C	32 148	5.1	12.6	C	795[38]	7.2	...	...	2.300
2013	C	109 617[37]	17.4	C	34 212	5.4	12.0	C	859[38]	7.8	...	...	2.200
2014	C	108 903[37]	17.2	C	37 461	5.9	11.3	C	876[38]	8.0	...	...	...
2015	C	109 617[37]	17.0		...	...	...		...	...	...	...	...
Greenland - Groenland													
2012	C	786	13.8	C	459	8.1	5.8	C	7	...	V68.7	73.5	1.987
2013	C	820	14.5	C	444	7.9	6.7	C	7	...	V68.5	73.7	2.051
2014	C	805	14.3	C	461	8.2	6.1	C	6	...	V69.1	73.7	1.995
2015	C	854	15.2	C	472	8.4	6.8	C	9	...	...	...	...
2016	C	830	14.8	C	487	8.7	6.1	C	6	...	...	...	...
Grenada - Grenade													
2012	+C	1 661	15.4	+C	856	8.0	7.5		...	...	...	...	...
2013	+C	1 838	16.9	+C	822	7.6	9.4		...	...	...	...	...
Guadeloupe													
2012	C	5 233[23]	13.0	C	2 873[23]	7.1	5.9		...	...	...	...	...
2013	C	5 069[23]	12.6	C	2 951[23]	7.3	5.3		...	...	...	...	...
2014	C	5 001[23]	12.4	C	3 290	8.1	4.2		...	...	76.1	83.4	...
2015		...	...		...	...	...		...	...	77.0	84.8	...
Guatemala													
2012	C	388 613	25.8	C	72 657	4.8	21.0	C	7 121	18.3	...	...	...
2013	C	387 342	25.1	C	76 639	5.0	20.1	C	7 221	18.6	...	...	...
2014	C	386 195	24.4	C	77 807	4.9	19.5		...	...	...	...	...
2015	C	391 425	24.2	C	80 876	5.0	19.2		...	...	...	...	...

4. Vital statistics summary and life expectancy at birth: 2012 - 2016
Aperçu des statistiques de l'état civil et de l'espérance de vie à la naissance : 2012 - 2016 (continued - suite)

Continent, country or area and year / Continent, pays ou zone et année	Live births - Naissances vivantes			Deaths - Décès			Rate of natural increase Taux d'accrois-sement naturel	Infant deaths - Décès d'enfants de moins d'un an			Life expectancy at birth - Espérance de vie à la naissance		Total fertility rate L'indice synthétique de fécondité
	Code[a]	Number Nombre	Crude birth rate Taux brut de natalité	Code[a]	Number Nombre	Crude death rate Taux brut de mortalité		Code[a]	Number Nombre	Rate (per 1000 births) Taux (par 1000 naiss-ances)	Male[b] Masculin[b]	Female[b] Féminin[b]	
AMERICA, NORTH - AMÉRIQUE DU NORD													
Honduras													
2012	+U	196 119	...		...	...	...		...	...	...	...	...
Jamaica - Jamaïque													
2012	C	39 348[39]	14.5	U	16 998[40]	...	...		...	...	...	...	...
2013	C*	36 745[39]	13.5	U	17 350[40]	...	...		...	...	...	...	...
2014	C*	37 892[39]	13.9	U	17 619[40]	...	...		...	...	...	...	...
2015	C*	37 556[39]	13.8		...	...	...		...	...	...	...	...
2016	C*	35 959[39]	13.2	U	19 557	...	...		...	...	...	...	...
Martinique													
2013	C	4 130[23]	10.7		...	...	...		...	...	...	...	1.900
2014	C	4 367[23]	11.4	C	3 319[23]	8.6	2.7		...	...	78.1	83.9	
2015		...	...			...	...		...	...	79.4	84.7	...
Mexico - Mexique													
2012	C	2 190 159[41]	18.7	+C	601 259[42]	5.1	13.6	+U	28 946[42]	...	73.4	78.1	...
2013	C	2 168 933[41]	18.3	+C	622 495[42]	5.3	13.1	+C	27 802[42]	12.8	71.7	77.4	...
2014	C	2 129 825[41]	17.8	+C	632 587[42]	5.3	12.5	+C	26 385[42]	12.4	72.1	77.6	...
2015	C*	2 353 596[41]	19.5	+C	654 593[42]	5.4	14.0	+C	26 045[42]	11.1	72.3	77.7	...
Montserrat													
2012	+C	53	10.7	+C	44	8.9	1.8	+C	-	...	...	...	...
2013	+C	41	8.3	+C	45	9.1	-0.8	+C	-	...	...	...	...
2014	+C	50	10.0	+C	32	6.4	3.6	+C	-	...	...	...	...
2015	+C	48	9.6	+C	49	9.8	-0.2	+C	3	...	...	...	...
2016	+C	46	9.1	+C	43	8.5	0.6	+C	-	...	...	...	...
Panama													
2012	C	75 486	19.9	U	17 350	...	...	U	1 083	...	74.1[43]	80.4[43]	2.500
2013	C	73 804	19.2	U	17 767	...	...	U	1 106	...	74.4[43]	80.5[43]	2.400
2014	C	75 183	19.2	U	18 171	...	...	U	1 036	...	74.6[43]	80.7[43]	2.400
2015	C*	75 901	19.1	U*	18 429	...	...	U*	952	...	74.8[43]	80.9[43]	2.400
Puerto Rico - Porto Rico													
2012	C	38 974	10.7	C	30 054	8.3	2.5	C	374	9.6	...	...	1.543
2013	C	36 580	10.2	C	29 416	8.2	2.0	C	270	7.4	...	...	1.470
2014	C	34 503	9.8	C	30 333	8.6	1.2	C	242	7.0	...	...	1.434
2015	C	31 229	9.0	C	28 335	8.2	0.8	C	222	7.1	III76.4	84.0	1.339
2016	C	28 326	8.3	C	29 613	8.7	-0.4	C	221	7.8	III76.6	84.1	...
Saint Kitts and Nevis - Saint-Kitts-et-Nevis													
2012	+C	636	...	+C	336	...	...		...	...	...	...	...
2013	+C	547	...	+C	348	...	...		...	...	...	...	...
2014	+C	641	...	+C	411	...	...		...	...	...	...	...
Saint Lucia - Sainte-Lucie													
2012	C*	2 103	12.4	C*	922	5.5	7.0		...	...	75.3	82.5	...
Saint Vincent and the Grenadines - Saint-Vincent-et-les Grenadines													
2012	C	1 853	16.8	C	858	7.8	9.0	C	25	...	...	...	2.213
2013	C	1 738	15.8	C	926	8.4	7.4	C	32	18.4	...	...	2.090
2014	C	1 841	16.7	C	1 006	9.1	7.6	C	29	...	68.4	74.6	2.211
2016		...	...		...	...	...		...	...	71.0	75.2	...
Sint Maarten (Dutch part) - Saint-Martin (partie néerlandaise)													
2012	+C	414[44]	11.9	+C	180[44]	5.2	6.7		...	...	II69.2	77.1	...
2013	+C	511[44]	14.0	+C	171[44]	4.7	9.3		...	...	...	...	...
Trinidad and Tobago - Trinité-et-Tobago													
2012	C*	18 729	14.0	C*	10 373	7.8	6.3	C*	239	12.8	...	...	1.700[24]
2013	C*	18 823	14.0	C*	10 661	8.0	6.1		...	...	...	...	...

4. Vital statistics summary and life expectancy at birth: 2012 - 2016
Aperçu des statistiques de l'état civil et de l'espérance de vie à la naissance : 2012 - 2016 (continued - suite)

Continent, country or area and year / Continent, pays ou zone et année	Live births / Naissances vivantes			Deaths / Décès			Rate of natural increase / Taux d'accroissement naturel	Infant deaths / Décès d'enfants de moins d'un an			Life expectancy at birth / Espérance de vie à la naissance		Total fertility rate / L'indice synthétique de fécondité
	Code[a]	Number Nombre	Crude birth rate Taux brut de natalité	Code[a]	Number Nombre	Crude death rate Taux brut de mortalité		Code[a]	Number Nombre	Rate (per 1000 births) Taux (par 1000 naissances)	Male[b] Masculin[b]	Female[b] Féminin[b]	
AMERICA, NORTH - AMÉRIQUE DU NORD													
Trinidad and Tobago - Trinité-et-Tobago													
2014	C*	18 729	13.9	C*	11 461	8.5	5.4		...	...	...	...	...
2015	C*	18 062	13.4	C*	11 240	8.3	5.1		...	...	...	...	...
Turks and Caicos Islands - Îles Turques et Caïques													
2012	C	496	15.4	C	101[45]	3.1	12.3	C	15	...	75.8	77.8	...
2013	C	502	14.9	C	101[45]	3.0	11.9	C	12	...	...	...	...
2014	C	437	12.4	C	76[45]	2.2	10.3	C	2	...	...	...	...
2015	C	437	11.9		...	...	...		...	...	...	...	...
2016	C	518	13.7		...	...	...		...	...	...	...	...
United States of America - États-Unis d'Amérique													
2012	C	3 952 841	12.6	C	2 543 279	8.1	4.5	C	23 629	6.0	76.4	81.2	1.880
2013	C	3 932 181	12.4	C	2 596 993	8.2	4.2	C	23 440	6.0	76.4	81.2	1.857
2014	C	3 988 076	12.5	C	2 626 418	8.2	4.3	C	23 215	5.8	76.4	81.2	1.863
2015	C	3 978 497	12.4	C	2 712 630	8.5	3.9	C	23 455	5.9	76.3	81.2	1.844
United States Virgin Islands - Îles Vierges américaines[46]													
2012	C	1 415	13.4	C	723	6.9	6.6	C	13	...	...	...	...
AMERICA, SOUTH - AMÉRIQUE DU SUD													
Argentina - Argentine													
2012	C	738 318	17.7	C	319 539	7.7	10.0	C	8 227	11.1	...	...	...
2013	C	754 603	17.9	C	326 197	7.7	10.2	C	8 174	10.8	...	...	...
2014	C	777 012	18.2	C	325 539	7.6	10.6	C	8 202	10.6	...	...	...
2015	C	770 040	17.9	C	333 407	7.7	10.1	C	7 445	9.7	...	...	2.280
Bolivia (Plurinational State of) - Bolivie (État plurinational de)													
2012	U	128 738	...	I	127 050[27]	12.3	...		...	...	...	...	...
2013	U	149 832	...		...	...	...		...	...	...	...	...
2014	U	153 016			...	...	...		...	...	...	...	...
2015	+U	277 498			...	...	...		...	...	VI65.0	69.4	...
2016		...	...		...	...	...		...	...	II68.6[47]	75.3[47]	...
Brazil - Brésil													
2012	U	2 830 458[48]	...	U	1 157 214[49]	...	...	U	31 596[50]	...	70.9[43]	78.2[43]	1.801[51]
2013	U	2 832 590[48]	...	U	1 180 796[49]	...	...	U	31 944[50]	...	71.3[43]	78.5[43]	1.770[51]
2014	U	2 913 121[48]	...	+C	1 194 164[49]	5.9	...	U	31 679[50]	...	71.6[43]	78.8[43]	1.742[51]
2015	+C	2 952 969[48]	14.4	+C	1 231 400[49]	6.0	8.4	+C	31 238[50]	10.6	71.9	79.1	1.716[51]
2016		...	...		...	...	...		...	...	...	...	1.692[51]
Chile - Chili													
2012	C	243 635	14.0	C	98 711	5.7	8.3	C	1 812	7.4	76.1	81.3	1.840
2013	C	242 005	13.8	C	99 770	5.7	8.1	C	1 692	7.0	76.3	81.4	1.790
2014	C	250 997	14.1	C	101 960	5.7	8.4	C	1 825	7.3	76.8	82.5	1.850
2015	C*	245 406	13.6	C*	103 327	5.7	7.9		...	...	...	...	...
Colombia - Colombie													
2012	U	675 694	...	U	196 842	...	...	U	8 138	...	...	...	2.350[52]
2013	U	658 835	...	U	203 058	...	...	U	7 551	...	...	...	...
2014	U	669 131	...	U	210 028	...	...	U	7 515	...	...	...	...
2015		...	...		...	...	...		...	...	VI72.1	78.5	...
Ecuador - Équateur[53]													
2012	U	297 309	...	U	63 511	...	...	U	3 002	...	...	...	2.684[54]
2013	U	277 620	...	U	63 104	...	...	U	2 928	...	...	...	2.634[54]
2014	U	278 460	...	U	62 981	...	...	U	2 821	...	73.2[55]	78.6[55]	2.587[54]

4. Vital statistics summary and life expectancy at birth: 2012 - 2016
Aperçu des statistiques de l'état civil et de l'espérance de vie à la naissance : 2012 - 2016 (continued - suite)

Continent, country or area and year / Continent, pays ou zone et année	Live births - Naissances vivantes			Deaths - Décès			Rate of natural increase / Taux d'accroissement naturel	Infant deaths - Décès d'enfants de moins d'un an			Life expectancy at birth - Espérance de vie à la naissance		Total fertility rate / L'indice synthétique de fécondité
	Code[a]	Number / Nombre	Crude birth rate / Taux brut de natalité	Code[a]	Number / Nombre	Crude death rate / Taux brut de mortalité		Code[a]	Number / Nombre	Rate (per 1000 births) / Taux (par 1000 naissances)	Male[b] / Masculin[b]	Female[b] / Féminin[b]	
AMERICA, SOUTH - AMÉRIQUE DU SUD													
Ecuador - Équateur[53]													
2015	U*	273 280	...	U	64 790	...	...	U	2 979	...	VI73.2[54]	78.8[54]	2.542[54]
2016		...	...		...	...	...		...	...	73.7[54]	79.3[54]	2.499[54]
French Guiana - Guyane française													
2014		...	...		...	...	...		...	...	76.7	83.1	...
2015		...	...		...	...	...		...	...	76.4	82.0	...
Paraguay													
2012	+U	118 549	...	+U	22 807	...	...	+U	465	...	...	...	...
2013	+U	114 619	...	+U	24 193	...	...	+U	...	...	...	...	...
2014	+U	116 592	...	+U	22 625	...	...	+U	...	...	...	...	...
Peru - Pérou													
2012	+U	414 081[56]	...	+U	97 951[56]	...	...	+U	4 532[56]	...	...	...	2.403
2013	+U	475 349[56]	...	+U	98 616[56]	...	...	+U	4 548[56]	...	...	...	2.364
2014	+U	492 008[56]	...	+U	96 460[56]	...	...	+U	4 243[56]	...	...	...	2.328
2015	+U	529 029[56]	...	+U	96 239[56]	...	...	+U	3 852[56]	...	VI71.5[43]	76.8[43]	2.294
2016	+U*	574 957[56]	...		...	...	...		...	...	...	...	2.263
Suriname													
2012	C	10 217	18.9	C	3 687	6.8	12.1	C	162	15.9	...	...	2.406
2013	C	10 012	18.2	C	3 557	6.5	11.7	C	168	16.8	III69.3	75.1	2.323
2014	C	10 407	18.6	C	3 738	6.7	11.9	C	163	15.7	...	...	2.370
2015	C	10 148	17.9	C	3 663	6.5	11.4	C	149	14.7	...	...	2.330
Uruguay													
2012	C	48 059	14.0	C	33 354	9.7	4.3	C	448	9.3	...	...	1.943
2013	C	48 681	14.2	C	32 698	9.5	4.6	C	430	8.8	...	...	1.957
2014	C	48 368	14.0	C	32 122	9.3	4.7	C	376	7.8	...	...	1.936
2015	C	48 926	14.1	C	32 967	9.5	4.6	C	367	7.5	...	...	...
2016		...	...		...	...	...		...	...	73.8	80.6	...
Venezuela (Bolivarian Republic of) - Venezuela (République bolivarienne du)													
2012	C	619 530	21.1	C	142 988	4.9	16.2	C	7 331	11.8	...	...	2.446[57]
2013	U	597 902	...	C	147 901	5.0	...	C	7 630	...	...	...	2.427[57]
2014	U	597 773	...	C	159 239	5.3	...	C	8 396	...	...	...	2.410[57]
2015	U	600 860	...	C	163 367	5.3	...	C	9 267	...	...	...	...
2016		...	...		...	...	...		...	...	72.3[58]	78.4[58]	...
ASIA - ASIE													
Armenia - Arménie													
2012	C*	42 333	14.0	C*	27 514[59]	9.1	4.9		...	...	...	...	1.600
2013	C*	41 790	13.8	C*	27 196[59]	9.0	4.8		...	...	...	...	1.600
2014	C	43 031	14.3	C	27 714[59]	9.2	5.1	C	376[59]	8.7	...	...	1.700
2015	C	41 763	13.9	C	27 878[59]	9.3	4.6	C	370[59]	8.9	II71.7	78.2	1.600
2016	C	40 592	13.6	C	28 226[59]	9.4	4.1		...	...	...	...	...
Azerbaijan - Azerbaïdjan													
2012	+C	174 469[59]	18.8	+C	55 017[59]	5.9	12.9	+C	1 884[59]	10.8	71.3	76.6	2.336
2013	+C	172 671[59]	18.3	+C	54 383[59]	5.8	12.6	+C	1 862[59]	10.8	71.6	76.8	2.200
2014	+C	170 503[59]	17.9	+C	55 648[59]	5.8	12.1	+C	1 655[59]	9.7	72.2	77.3	2.200
2015	+C	166 210[59]	17.2	+C	54 697[59]	5.7	11.6	+C	2 033[59]	12.2	72.7	77.6	2.100
2016	+C	159 464[59]	16.3	+C	56 648[59]	5.8	10.5		...	...	...	...	2.000
Bahrain - Bahreïn													
2012	C	19 119[60]	15.8	C	2 613[60]	2.2	13.7	C	149[61]	7.8	...	...	2.134
2013	C	19 995[60]	16.0	C	2 588[60]	2.1	13.9	C	141[61]	7.1	...	...	2.157
2014	C	20 931[60]	15.9	C	2 805[60]	2.1	13.8	C	218[61]	10.4	...	...	2.173
2015		...	...		...	...	...		...	...	VI75.8	77.4	...

4. Vital statistics summary and life expectancy at birth: 2012 - 2016
Aperçu des statistiques de l'état civil et de l'espérance de vie à la naissance : 2012 - 2016 (continued - suite)

Continent, country or area and year / Continent, pays ou zone et année	Live births / Naissances vivantes			Deaths / Décès			Rate of natural increase Taux d'accrois-sement naturel	Infant deaths / Décès d'enfants de moins d'un an			Life expectancy at birth / Espérance de vie à la naissance		Total fertility rate L'indice synthétique de fécondité
	Code[a]	Number Nombre	Crude birth rate Taux brut de natalité	Code[a]	Number Nombre	Crude death rate Taux brut de mortalité		Code[a]	Number Nombre	Rate (per 1000 births) Taux (par 1000 naiss-ances)	Male[b] Masculin[b]	Female[b] Féminin[b]	
ASIA - ASIE													
Bangladesh													
2012	U	2 933 000	...	U	826 000	...	...	U	96 254	...	...	...	2.120
2013		...	...		...	...	...		...	...	68.8	71.4	2.110
2016		...	...		...	...	...		...	...	70.3[62]	72.9[62]	...
Brunei Darussalam - Brunéi Darussalam													
2012	+C	6 909	17.3	+C	1 216	3.0	14.2	+C	64	9.3	...	...	1.900
2013	+C	6 680	16.4	+C	1 398	3.4	13.0	+C	51	7.6	...	...	1.900
2014	+C	6 891	16.7	+C	1 470	3.6	13.2	+C	51	7.4	75.9	78.8	1.900
2015	+C	6 699	16.1	+C	1 547	3.7	12.3	+C	58	8.7	...	...	1.900
China - Chine[63]													
2012	I	16 350 000	12.1	I	9 660 000	7.2	5.0		...	...	...	...	...
2013	I	16 400 000	12.1	I	9 720 000	7.2	4.9		...	...	...	...	...
2014	I	16 870 000	12.4	I	9 770 000	7.2	5.2		...	...	...	...	...
2015	I	16 550 000	12.1	I	9 750 000	7.1	5.0		...	...	...	...	...
China, Hong Kong SAR - Chine, Hong Kong RAS													
2012	C	91 558	12.8	C	43 917	6.1	6.7	C	137	1.5	80.7	86.4	1.285[64]
2013	C	57 084	8.0	C	43 397	6.0	1.9	C	100	1.8	81.1	86.7	1.125[64]
2014	C	62 305	8.6	C	45 087	6.2	2.4	C	103	1.7	81.2	86.9	1.235[64]
2015	C	59 878	8.2	C	46 108	6.3	1.9	C	85	1.4	81.4	87.3	1.196[64]
2016	C	60 856	8.3	C	46 905	6.4	1.9	C	109	1.8	81.3	87.3	1.205[64]
China, Macao SAR - Chine, Macao RAS													
2012	C	7 315	12.9	C	1 841	3.2	9.6	C	18	...	IV79.1	85.7	1.357
2013	C	6 571	11.1	C	1 920	3.2	7.9	C	13	...	...	...	1.150
2014	C	7 360	11.8	C	1 939	3.1	8.7	C	15	...	IV79.6	86.0	1.224
2015	C	7 055	11.0	C	2 002	3.1	7.9	C	11	...	IV79.9	86.3	1.142
2016	C*	7 146	...	C*	2 238	...	...		...	...	IV80.3	86.4	...
Cyprus - Chypre[65]													
2012	C	10 161	11.8	C	5 665	6.6	5.2	C	36	3.5	...	...	1.390
2013	C	9 341	10.8	C	5 141[66]	6.0	4.9	C	15	...	80.0	84.8	1.300
2014	C	9 258	10.9	C	5 250[66]	6.2	4.7	C	13	...	80.9	84.7	1.310
2015	C	9 170	10.8	C	5 859[66]	6.9	3.9	C	25	...	79.8	83.5	1.320
2016	C*	9 455	11.1	C*	5 471[66]	6.4	4.7		...	...	...	...	...
Georgia - Géorgie													
2012	C	57 031	12.7	C	49 348[59]	11.0	1.7	C	715[59]	12.5	...	...	1.700
2013	C	57 878	12.9	C	48 553[59]	10.8	2.1	C	640[59]	11.1	...	...	1.700
2014	C	60 635	16.3	C	49 087[59]	13.2	3.1	C	578[59]	9.5	...	...	2.200
2015	C	59 249	15.9	C	49 121[59]	13.2	2.7	C	507[59]	8.6	68.6	77.2	2.300
2016	C	56 569	15.2	C	50 771[59]	13.7	1.6	C	507[59]	9.0	68.3	77.1	2.200
India - Inde[67]													
2012	I	...	21.6[68]	I	...	7.0[68]	...	I	...	42.0[68]	...	...	2.400
2013	I	...	21.4[68]	I	...	7.0[68]	...	I	...	40.0[68]	...	...	2.300
2014	I	...	21.0[68]	I	...	6.7[68]	...	I	...	39.0[68]	...	...	2.300
2015	I	...	20.8[68]	I	...	6.5[68]	...	I	...	37.0[68]	...	...	2.300
Indonesia - Indonésie													
2012		...	...		...	...	...		...	...	67.7	71.7	2.600[69]
Iran (Islamic Republic of) - Iran (République islamique d')[70]													
2012	+C	1 421 689	18.7	+C	367 539	4.8	13.9	+C	10 401	7.3	...	...	...
2013	+C	1 471 834	19.1	+C	372 279	4.8	14.3	+C	8 015	5.4	...	...	...
2014	+C	1 534 362	19.7	+C	446 333	5.7	14.0	+C	7 430	4.8	...	...	...
2015	+C	1 570 219[71]	19.9	+C	374 827[72]	4.8	15.2		...	...	...	...	...

4. Vital statistics summary and life expectancy at birth: 2012 - 2016
Aperçu des statistiques de l'état civil et de l'espérance de vie à la naissance : 2012 - 2016 (continued - suite)

Continent, country or area and year / Continent, pays ou zone et année	Live births Naissances vivantes			Deaths Décès			Rate of natural increase Taux d'accrois-sement naturel	Infant deaths Décès d'enfants de moins d'un an			Life expectancy at birth Espérance de vie à la naissance		Total fertility rate L'indice synthétique de fécondité
	Code[a]	Number Nombre	Crude birth rate Taux brut de natalité	Code[a]	Number Nombre	Crude death rate Taux brut de mortalité		Code[a]	Number Nombre	Rate (per 1000 births) Taux (par 1000 naiss-ances)	Male[b] Masculin[b]	Female[b] Féminin[b]	
ASIA - ASIE													
Iraq													
2013	U*	1 077 645	...	U*	189 118	...	...		...	...	...	...	...
Israel - Israël[73]													
2012	C	170 940	21.6	C	42 100[74]	5.3	16.3	C	611[74]	3.6	79.9	83.6	3.052
2013	C	171 444	21.3	C	41 683[74]	5.2	16.1	C	539[74]	3.1	80.3	83.9	3.030
2014	C	176 427	21.5	C	42 457[74]	5.2	16.3	C	548[74]	3.1	80.3	84.1	3.085
2015	C	178 723	21.3	C	44 481[74]	5.3	16.0	C	561[74]	3.1	80.1	84.1	3.090
2016	C*	181 127	...	C	43 892[74]	...	...	C	561[74]	3.1	...	...	...
Japan - Japon[75]													
2012	C	1 037 231[76]	8.1	C	1 256 359[76]	9.8	-1.7	C	2 299[76]	2.2	79.9	86.4	1.405[77]
2013	C	1 029 816[76]	8.1	C	1 268 436[76]	10.0	-1.9	C	2 185[76]	2.1	80.2	86.6	1.427[77]
2014	C	1 003 539[76]	7.9	C	1 273 004[76]	10.0	-2.1	C	2 080[76]	2.1	80.5	86.8	1.422[77]
2015	C	1 005 677[76]	7.9	C	1 290 444[76]	10.1	-2.2	C	1 916[76]	1.9	80.8	87.1	1.450[77]
2016	C*	976 979	7.7	C*	1 307 765[76]	10.3	-2.6		...	...	...	...	...
Jordan - Jordanie													
2012	C	177 695[78]	23.9	U	22 785[78]	...	...		...	...	72.7[78]	76.7[78]	3.500[78]
2013	C	178 143[78]	22.0	U	23 898[78]	...	...		...	...	...	...	...
2014	C	188 902	21.5	U	25 782	...	...		...	...	...	...	...
2015	C	198 018	20.8	U	26 640	...	...		...	...	...	...	...
2016		...	...		...	...	...		...	...	72.8[78]	74.2[78]	...
Kazakhstan													
2012	C	381 005[59]	22.7	C	142 880[59]	8.5	14.2	C	5 121[59]	13.4	64.8	74.3	2.620
2013	C	387 227[59]	22.7	C	135 950[59]	8.0	14.8	C	4 367[59]	11.3	...	...	2.640
Kuwait - Koweït													
2012	C	59 753	18.4	C	5 950	1.8	16.6	C	459	7.7	78.7	79.1	1.860
2013	C	59 426	17.3	C	5 909	1.7	15.6	C	453	7.6	77.3	81.9	1.720
2014	C	61 313	16.3	C	6 031	1.6	14.7	C	456	7.4	78.7	80.2	1.900
2015	C	59 271	14.9	C	6 481	1.6	13.3	C	456	7.7	79.1	80.0	...
Kyrgyzstan - Kirghizstan													
2012	C	154 918	27.6	C	36 186	6.5	21.2	C	3 091	20.0	66.1	74.1	3.148
2013	C	155 520	27.2	C	34 880	6.1	21.1	C	3 093	19.9	66.3	74.3	3.109
2014	C	161 813	27.7	C	35 564	6.1	21.6	C	3 268	20.2	66.5	74.5	3.186
2015	C	163 452	27.4	C	34 808	5.8	21.6	C	2 945	18.0	66.8	74.8	3.189
2016	C*	158 160	26.0	C*	33 475	5.5	20.5	C*	2 621	16.6	...	...	...
Lao People's Democratic Republic - République démocratique populaire lao													
2012		...	...		...	...	...		...	...	...	...	3.500
2013		...	...		...	...	...		...	...	...	...	3.200
2014		...	...		...	...	...		...	...	...	...	3.060
2015		...	...		...	...	...		...	...	61.8[79]	65.2[79]	3.200
Lebanon - Liban													
2012	C	94 842	...	C	23 452	...	...		...	...	...	...	...
2013	C	95 246	...	C	24 013	...	...		...	...	...	...	...
2014	C	104 872	...	C	27 020	...	...		...	...	...	...	...
Malaysia - Malaisie													
2012	C	526 012	17.8	C	138 692	4.7	13.1	C	3 277	6.2	72.2	76.9	2.188
2013	C	503 914	16.7	C	142 202	4.7	12.0	C	3 199	6.3	...	...	2.022
2014	C	528 612	17.2	C	150 318	4.9	12.3	C	3 543	6.7	...	...	2.072
2015	C	521 136	16.7	C	155 786	5.0	11.7	C	3 582	6.9	...	...	2.002
2016		...	...		...	...	...		...	...	72.6	77.2	...
Maldives													
2012	C	7 431	22.5	C	1 135	3.4	19.0	C	66	8.9	...	...	...
2013	C	7 153	21.3	C	1 120	3.3	17.9	C	46	6.4	...	...	...
2014	C	7 245	18.0	C	1 143	2.8	15.2	C	59	8.1	73.1	74.8	...
2015	C	6 896	20.1	C	1 130	3.3	16.8		...	...	73.1	74.6	...
Mongolia - Mongolie													
2012	+C	73 839	26.0	+C	17 761	6.3	19.7	+C	1 143	15.5	...	...	2.700
2013	+C	79 780	27.5	+C	17 247	5.9	21.6	+C	1 166	14.6	65.4	75.0	3.000

4. Vital statistics summary and life expectancy at birth: 2012 - 2016
Aperçu des statistiques de l'état civil et de l'espérance de vie à la naissance : 2012 - 2016 (continued - suite)

Continent, country or area and year / Continent, pays ou zone et année	Live births / Naissances vivantes Code[a]	Number Nombre	Crude birth rate Taux brut de natalité	Deaths / Décès Code[a]	Number Nombre	Crude death rate Taux brut de mortalité	Rate of natural increase Taux d'accroissement naturel	Infant deaths / Décès d'enfants de moins d'un an Code[a]	Number Nombre	Rate (per 1000 births) Taux (par 1000 naissances)	Life expectancy at birth Male[b] Masculin[b]	Female[b] Féminin[b]	Total fertility rate L'indice synthétique de fécondité
ASIA - ASIE													
Mongolia - Mongolie													
2014	+C	82 839	28.0	+C	16 521	5.6	22.4	+C	1 251	15.1	65.9	75.5	3.100
2015	+C	82 130	27.1	+C	17 620	5.8	21.3	+C	1 234	15.0	×65.3	74.8	3.100
2016	+C	79 920	25.9	+C	17 763	5.8	20.1	+C	1 315	16.5	...	...	3.000
Myanmar													
2012	+U	856 279[80]	...	+U	250 874[80]	...	...	+U	11 406[80]	...	...	...	2.253
2013	+U	835 595[80]	...	+U	257 216[80]	...	...	+U	11 516[80]	...	65.5	69.1	2.222
2014	+U	736 369[81]	...	+U	213 085[81]	...	...	+U	9 386[81]	...	61.0[81]	68.6[81]	2.195
Oman													
2012	U	72 867[82]	...	U	7 884[82]	...	...	U	676[82]	...	74.5	78.0	2.800
2013	U	79 417[82]	...	U	7 669[82]	...	...	U	772[82]	...	74.8	78.5	2.900
2014	U	82 981[82]	...	U	7 819[82]	...	...	U	645[82]	...	74.8	78.5	2.900
2015	U	86 286[82]	...	U	8 167[82]	...	...	U	818[82]	...	74.2[83]	78.8[83]	2.900
2016	U	88 346[82]	...	U	8 196[82]	...	...	U	816[82]	...	...	...	2.900
Philippines													
2012	C	1 790 367	18.6	C	514 745	5.3	13.2	C	22 254	12.4	...	...	...
2013	C	1 761 602	17.9	C	531 280	5.4	12.5	C	21 992	12.5	...	...	...
2014	C	1 748 857	17.5	C	551 716	5.5	12.0	C	21 108	12.1	...	...	...
2015	C	1 744 767	17.2	C	560 605	5.5	11.7	C	20 750	11.9	...	...	...
Qatar													
2012	C	21 423	11.7	C	2 031	1.1	10.6	C	148	6.9	...	...	2.050
2013	C	23 708	11.8	C	2 133	1.1	10.8	C	158	6.7	...	...	2.000
2014	C	25 443	11.5	C	2 366	1.1	10.4	C	168	6.6	...	...	2.000
2015	C	26 622	10.9	C	2 317	1.0	10.0	C	197	7.4	77.5	82.1	2.000
2016	C*	24 895	9.5	C*	2 339	0.9	8.6		...	...	...	...	...
Republic of Korea - République de Corée													
2012	C	484 550[84]	9.6	C	267 221[85]	5.3	4.3	C	1 405[85]	2.9	77.6	84.2	1.297[85]
2013	C	436 455[84]	8.6	C	266 257[85]	5.3	3.4	C	1 305[85]	3.0	78.1	84.6	1.187[85]
2014	C	435 435[84]	8.6	C	267 692[85]	5.3	3.3	C	1 305[85]	3.0	78.6	85.0	1.205[85]
2015	C	438 420[84]	8.6	C	275 895[85]	5.4	3.2	C	1 190[85]	2.7	79.0	85.2	1.239[85]
Saudi Arabia - Arabie saoudite													
2012	I	457 339[86]	15.7	...	104 195[87]	...	...	...	9 843[87]	...	72.8[88]	75.2[88]	2.870[88]
2013	I	454 450[86]	15.4	...	106 521[87]	...	...		...	...	...	...	2.810[88]
2014	I	452 003[86]	15.1		...	...	...		...	...	...	...	2.750[88]
2015	I	449 149[86]	14.5	I	69 206[86]	2.2	12.3		...	...	73.1[88]	75.7[88]	2.690[88]
2016	I	447 040[86]	14.1	I	58 097[86]	1.8	12.3		...	...	73.5[89]	74.8[89]	2.400[90]
Singapore - Singapour													
2012	C	42 663	11.2	+C	18 481	4.8	6.3	+C	98	2.3	79.8[91]	84.3[91]	1.290[92]
2013	C	39 720	10.3	+C	18 938	4.9	5.4	+C	94	2.4	80.1[91]	84.5[91]	1.190[92]
2014	C	42 232	10.9	+C	19 393	5.0	5.9	+C	83	2.0	80.3[91]	84.8[91]	1.250[92]
2015	C	42 185	10.8	+C	19 862	5.1	5.7	+C	84	2.0	80.5[91]	85.1[91]	1.240[92]
2016	C	41 251	10.5	+C	20 017	5.1	5.4	+C	101	2.4	80.6[93]	85.1[93]	1.200[92]
Sri Lanka													
2012	+C	359 959	17.6	+C*	122 063	6.0	11.6		...	...	...	...	...
2013	+C	365 762	17.8	+C*	127 124	6.2	11.6		...	...	...	...	...
2014	+C*	349 715	16.8	+C*	127 758	6.2	10.7		...	...	...	...	...
2015	+C*	334 821	16.0	+C*	131 614	6.3	9.7		...	...	...	...	...
State of Palestine - État de Palestine													
2012	U	131 632[94]	...	U	11 782[94]	...	...	U	1 064[94]	...	71.3	74.1	...
2013	U	127 454[94]	...	U	11 188[94]	...	...	U	845[94]	...	71.5	74.4	4.100[95]
2014	U	128 073[94]	...	U	13 390[94]	...	...	U	800[94]	...	71.8	74.7	...
2015	U	124 331[94]	...	U	11 908[94]	...	...	U	852[94]	...	72.0	75.0	...
2016		...	...		...	...	...		...	...	72.1	75.2	...

4. Vital statistics summary and life expectancy at birth: 2012 - 2016
Aperçu des statistiques de l'état civil et de l'espérance de vie à la naissance : 2012 - 2016 (continued - suite)

Continent, country or area and year / Continent, pays ou zone et année	Code[a]	Live births / Naissances vivantes Number / Nombre	Crude birth rate Taux brut de natalité	Code[a]	Deaths / Décès Number / Nombre	Crude death rate Taux brut de mortalité	Rate of natural increase Taux d'accroissement naturel	Code[a]	Infant deaths / Décès d'enfants de moins d'un an Number / Nombre	Rate (per 1000 births) Taux (par 1000 naissances)	Life expectancy at birth / Espérance de vie à la naissance Male[b] Masculin[b]	Female[b] Féminin[b]	Total fertility rate L'indice synthétique de fécondité
ASIA - ASIE													
Tajikistan - Tadjikistan													
2012	U	219 281[96]	...	U	32 828[59]	...	...	U	2 884[59]	...	...	...	2.611
2013	U	209 417[96]	...	U	31 706[59]	...	...	U	3 622[59]	...	...	...	2.616
2014	U	229 460[96]	...	U	32 879[59]	...	...	U	3 273[59]	...	71.6	75.4	2.980
Thailand - Thaïlande													
2012	+U	818 901	...	+U	423 213	...	...	...	...	...	...	...	...
2013	+U	782 129	...	+U	438 648	...	...	...	...	...	...	...	...
2014	+U	776 370	...	+U	448 601	...	...	...	...	...	...	...	...
2015	+U	738 930	...	+U	457 141	...	...	...	...	...	...	...	...
2016	+U	704 058	...	+U	480 434	...	...	...	...	...	...	...	...
Timor-Leste[97]													
2015	I	36 202	31.0	I	9 209	7.9	23.1		...	...	...	...	...
Turkey - Turquie													
2012	C	1 292 380	17.1	C	376 520	5.0	12.1	C	14 974	11.6	72.0	77.2	2.107
2013	C	1 294 088	16.9	C	372 920	4.9	12.0	C	14 014	10.8	75.3	80.7	2.104
2014	C	1 345 286	17.3	C	391 009	5.0	12.3	C	15 165	11.3	75.3	80.7	2.182
2015	C	1 325 783	16.8	C	405 218	5.1	11.7	C	14 164	10.7	III75.3	80.7	2.151
2016	C	1 309 771	...	C	422 135	...	...		...	...	...	...	2.105
United Arab Emirates - Émirats arabes unis[98]													
2012	...	89 578	...	...	7 702	...	...	...	...	...	...	...	...
2013	...	93 539	...	...	8 015	...	...	...	...	...	...	...	...
2014	...	95 860	...	...	8 265	...	...	...	...	...	...	...	...
2015	...	97 328	...	...	8 755	...	...	...	...	...	...	...	...
Uzbekistan - Ouzbékistan													
2012	+C	625 106	21.0	+C	145 988[59]	4.9	16.1	+C	6 390[59]	10.2	...	...	2.193
2013	+C	679 519	22.5	+C	145 672[59]	4.8	17.7	+C	6 569[59]	9.7	...	...	2.350
2014	+C	718 036	23.3	+C	149 761[59]	4.9	18.5	+C	7 688[59]	10.7	71.1	75.8	2.457
2015	+C	734 141	23.5	+C	152 035[59]	4.9	18.6	+C	8 320[59]	11.3	71.2	76.0	2.491
Viet Nam													
2012		...	...		...	...	...		...	...	70.4	75.8	2.050
2013		...	...		...	...	...		...	...	70.5	75.8	2.100
2014		...	...		...	...	...		...	...	70.6	76.0	2.090
2015		...	...		...	...	...		...	...	70.7	76.1	2.100
2016		...	...		...	...	...		...	...	70.8	76.1	2.090
Yemen - Yémen													
2012	U	279 719	...	U	28 596	...	...	...	...	...	...	...	...
2013	U	425 165[99]	...	U	35 066[100]	...	...	...	...	...	...	...	...
EUROPE													
Åland Islands - Îles d'Åland													
2012	C	292	10.3	C	323	11.4	-1.1	C	-	...	...	...	1.847
2013	C	287	10.0	C	269	9.4	0.6	C	-	...	79.0	85.9	1.800
2014	C	282	9.8	C	251	8.7	1.1	C	-	...	80.9	84.3	1.783
2015	C	275	9.5	C	285	9.8	-0.3	C	-	...	80.6	84.0	1.690
2016	C*	293	10.1	C*	296	10.2	-0.1		...	...	...	...	1.790
Albania - Albanie													
2012	C	35 473	12.2	C	20 870	7.2	5.0	C	312	8.8	...	...	...
2013	C	35 750	12.3	C	20 442	7.1	5.3	C	282	7.9	76.0	80.3	...
2014	C	35 760	12.4	C	20 656	7.1	5.2	U	281	...	...	...	...
2015	C	33 221	11.5	C	22 422	7.8	3.7	U	233	...	...	...	...
Andorra - Andorre													
2012	C	737	10.6	C	303	4.3	6.2	C	4	...	...	...	1.151
2013	C	637	9.1	C	239	3.4	5.7	C	1	...	...	...	...
2014	C	639	9.1	C	276	3.9	5.2	C	2	...	...	...	...
2015	C	659	9.3	C	282	4.0	5.3	C	-	...	...	...	...
2016	C	634	8.8	C	310	4.3	4.5		...	...	...	...	...

4. Vital statistics summary and life expectancy at birth: 2012 - 2016
Aperçu des statistiques de l'état civil et de l'espérance de vie à la naissance : 2012 - 2016 (continued - suite)

Continent, country or area and year / Continent, pays ou zone et année	Live births — Naissances vivantes Code[a]	Number Nombre	Crude birth rate Taux brut de natalité	Deaths — Décès Code[a]	Number Nombre	Crude death rate Taux brut de mortalité	Rate of natural increase Taux d'accroissement naturel	Infant deaths — Décès d'enfants de moins d'un an Code[a]	Number Nombre	Rate (per 1000 births) Taux (par 1000 naissances)	Life expectancy at birth — Espérance de vie à la naissance Male[b] Masculin[b]	Female[b] Féminin[b]	Total fertility rate L'indice synthétique de fécondité
EUROPE													
Austria - Autriche													
2012	C	78 952	9.4	C	79 436[101]	9.4	-0.1	C	252	3.2	78.3	83.3	1.441
2013	C	79 330	9.4	C	79 526[101]	9.4	0.0	C	245	3.1	78.5	83.6	1.437
2014	C	81 722	9.6	C	78 252[101]	9.2	0.4	C	249	3.0	79.1	84.0	1.465
2015	C	84 381[102]	9.8	C	83 073[101]	9.6	0.2	C	259	3.1	78.6	83.6	1.494
2016	C	87 675[102]	10.1	C	80 669[101]	9.3	0.8		...	...	...	...	1.529
Belarus - Bélarus													
2012	C	115 893	12.2	C	126 531	13.4	-1.1	C	386	3.3	66.6	77.6	1.620
2013	C	117 997	12.5	C	125 326	13.2	-0.8	C	407	3.4	67.3	77.9	1.668
2014	C	118 534	12.5	C	121 542	12.8	-0.3	C	409	3.5	67.8	78.6	1.696
2015	C	119 028	12.5	C	120 026	12.6	-0.1	C	352	3.0	68.6	78.9	...
2016	C	117 779	12.4	C	119 379	12.6	-0.2		...	...	...	...	...
Belgium - Belgique													
2012	C	128 051[103]	11.5	C	109 076[103]	9.8	1.7	C	483[103]	3.8	77.6	82.8	...
2013	C	125 606[103]	11.2	C	109 334[103]	9.8	1.5	C	436[103]	3.5	77.9	82.9	...
2014	C	125 014[103]	11.1	C	104 755[103]	9.3	1.8	C	423[103]	3.4	78.6	83.5	...
2015	C	122 274[103]	10.8	C	110 541[103]	9.8	1.0	C	400[103]	3.3	78.5[24]	83.1[24]	...
2016	C	121 896[103]	10.8	C	108 097[103]	9.6	1.2		...	...	...	...	...
Bosnia and Herzegovina - Bosnie-Herzégovine													
2012	C	32 072	8.4	C	35 692	9.3	-0.9	C	161	5.0	...	...	...
2013	C	31 103	8.1	C	35 837	9.3	-1.2	C	161	5.2	...	...	...
2014	C	29 247	7.6	C	34 824	9.1	-1.5	C	140	4.8	...	...	...
2016	C*	29 276	8.3	C*	35 530	10.1	-1.8		...	...	...	...	...
Bulgaria - Bulgarie													
2012	C	69 121	9.5	C	109 281	15.0	-5.5	C	536	7.8	III70.6	77.5	1.501
2013	C	66 578	9.2	C	104 345	14.4	-5.2	C	489	7.3	...	...	1.484
2014	C	67 585	9.4	C	108 952	15.1	-5.7	C	517	7.6	71.1	78.0	1.523
2015	C	65 950	9.2	C	110 117	15.3	-6.2	C	434	6.6	III71.1	78.0	1.529
2016	C	64 984	9.1	C	107 580	15.0	-6.0		...	...	...	...	1.542
Croatia - Croatie													
2012	C	41 771	9.8	C	51 710	12.1	-2.3	C	150	3.6	...	...	1.517
2013	C	39 939	9.4	C	50 386	11.8	-2.5	C	162	4.1	...	...	...
2014	C	39 566	9.3	C	50 839	12.0	-2.7	C	199	5.0	74.7	81.0	...
2015	C	37 503	8.9	C	54 205	12.9	-4.0	C	154	4.1	...	...	...
2016	C	37 537	9.0	C	51 542	12.3	-3.3		...	...	...	...	...
Czechia - Tchéquie													
2012	C	108 576	10.3	C	108 189	10.3	0.0	C	285	2.6	75.0	80.9	1.452
2013	C	106 751	10.2	C	109 160	10.4	-0.2	C	265	2.5	75.2	81.1	1.456
2014	C	109 860	10.4	C	105 665	10.0	0.4	C	263	2.4	75.8	81.7	1.528
2015	C	110 764	10.5	C	111 173	10.5	0.0	C	272	2.5	75.8	81.4	1.570
2016	C	112 663	10.7	C	107 750	10.2	0.5		...	...	...	...	1.630
Denmark - Danemark[104]													
2012	C	57 916	10.4	C	52 325	9.4	1.0	C	197	3.4	II77.9	81.9	1.729
2013	C	55 873	10.0	C	52 471	9.4	0.6	C	195	3.5	II78.0	81.9	1.669
2014	C	56 870	10.1	C	51 340	9.1	1.0	C	229	4.0	78.5	82.7	1.691
2015	C	58 205	10.3	C	52 555	9.3	1.0	C	216	3.7	II78.6	82.5	1.714
2016	C	61 614	10.8	C	52 824	9.2	1.5		...	...	...	...	1.785
Estonia - Estonie													
2012	C	14 056	10.6	C	15 450	11.7	-1.1	C	50	3.6	71.5	81.5	1.560
2013	C	13 531	10.3	C	15 244	11.6	-1.3	C	28	...	72.7	81.4	1.520
2014	C	13 551	10.3	C	15 484	11.8	-1.5	C	36	2.7	72.3	81.5	1.540
2015	C	13 907	10.6	C	15 243	11.6	-1.0	C	35	2.5	73.1	81.8	1.580
2016	C	14 053	10.7	C	15 392	11.7	-1.0		...	...	...	...	1.600
Faeroe Islands - Îles Féroé													
2012	C	619	12.8	C	408	8.4	4.4	C	10	...	...	...	2.573
2013	C	626	13.0	C	364	7.5	5.4	C	-	...	...	...	2.537
2014	C	639	13.2	C	394	8.1	5.1	C	4	...	...	...	2.562
2015	C	608	12.4	C	377	7.7	4.7	C	1	...	II78.3	84.5	2.409

4. Vital statistics summary and life expectancy at birth: 2012 - 2016
Aperçu des statistiques de l'état civil et de l'espérance de vie à la naissance : 2012 - 2016 (continued - suite)

Continent, country or area and year / Continent, pays ou zone et année	Live births Naissances vivantes			Deaths Décès			Rate of natural increase Taux d'accrois-sement naturel	Infant deaths Décès d'enfants de moins d'un an			Life expectancy at birth Espérance de vie à la naissance		Total fertility rate L'indice synthétique de fécondité
	Code[a]	Number Nombre	Crude birth rate Taux brut de natalité	Code[a]	Number Nombre	Crude death rate Taux brut de mortalité		Code[a]	Number Nombre	Rate (per 1000 births) Taux (par 1000 naiss-ances)	Male[b] Masculin[b]	Female[b] Féminin[b]	
EUROPE													
Finland - Finlande													
2012	C	59 201[105]	11.0	C	51 384[105]	9.5	1.5	C	141[105]	2.4	77.5[105]	83.4[105]	1.801
2013	C	57 847[105]	10.7	C	51 203[105]	9.5	1.2	C	102[105]	1.8	...	...	1.750
2014	C	56 950[105]	10.5	C	51 935[105]	9.6	0.9	C	124[105]	2.2	78.2[105]	83.9[105]	1.710
2015	C	55 197[105]	10.1	C	52 207[105]	9.6	0.5	C	97[105]	1.8	78.5[105]	84.1[105]	1.650
2016	C*	52 645[105]	9.6	C*	53 629[105]	9.7	-0.2		...	...	...	...	1.570
France													
2012	C	790 290	12.4	C	559 227	8.8	3.6	C	2 643	3.3	III78.3[24]	84.8[24]	1.992
2013	C	781 621	12.2	C	558 408	8.7	3.5	C	2 710	3.5	III78.6[24]	85.0[24]	1.973
2014	C	781 167	12.2	C	547 003	8.5	3.6	C	2 598	3.3	III78.9[24]	85.1[24]	1.974[24]
2015	C	760 421	11.8	C	581 770	9.0	2.8	C	2 655	3.5	...	...	1.924[24]
2016	C*	745 000	11.5	C*	580 100	9.0	2.5		...	...	...	...	1.894[24]
Germany - Allemagne													
2012	C	673 544	8.4	C	869 582	10.8	-2.4	C	2 202	3.3	III77.7	82.8	1.410
2013	C	682 069	8.5	C	893 825	11.1	-2.6	C	2 250	3.3	...	...	1.420
2014	C	714 927	8.8	C	868 356	10.7	-1.9	C	2 284	3.2	78.7	83.6	1.470
2015	C	737 575	9.0	C	925 200	11.3	-2.3	C	2 405	3.3	III78.2	83.1	1.500
2016	C*	770 000	9.4	C*	920 000	11.2	-1.8		...	...	...	...	...
Gibraltar													
2012	+C	461[106]	14.2	+C	264[107]	8.1	6.0		...	...	...	...	...
2013	+C	426[106]	13.0	+C	230[107]	7.0	6.0	+C	-		...	...	...
2014	+C	488[106]	14.7	+C	248[107]	7.5	7.2		...	...	...	...	...
2015	+C	492[106]	14.7	+C	235[107]	7.0	7.7		...	...	...	...	...
Greece - Grèce													
2012	C	100 371	9.1	C	116 668	10.6	-1.5	C	293	2.9	77.9	83.0	1.340
2013	C	94 134	8.6	C	111 794	10.2	-1.6	C	347	3.7	...	...	...
2014	C	92 149	8.5	C	113 740	10.4	-2.0	C	346	3.8	78.5	83.5	...
2015	C	91 847	8.5	C	121 212	11.2	-2.7	C	364	4.0	78.1	83.2	...
2016	C	92 898	8.6	C	118 792	11.0	-2.4	C	387	4.2	...	...	...
Guernsey - Guernesey													
2012	C	674	10.7	C	547	8.7	2.0		...	...	...	...	...
2013	C	667	10.6	C	556	8.9	1.8		...	...	...	...	...
2014	C	627	10.0	C	526	8.4	1.6		...	...	...	...	...
2015	C	620	9.9	C	560	9.0	1.0		...	...	...	...	...
2016	C	654	10.4	C	536	8.5	1.9		...	...	...	...	...
Hungary - Hongrie													
2012	C	90 269	9.1	C	129 440	13.0	-3.9	C	438	4.9	71.5	78.4	1.337
2013	C	89 524[108]	9.0	C	126 677[109]	12.8	-3.8	C	448[110]	5.0	72.0	78.7	1.350
2014	C	93 281[111]	9.5	C	126 294[112]	12.8	-3.3	C	418[113]	4.5	72.1	78.9	1.440
2015	C	92 135[111]	9.4	C	131 575[112]	13.4	-4.0	C	383[113]	4.2	72.1	78.6	...
2016	C	95 361[111]	9.7	C	127 098[112]	12.9	-3.2	C	368[113]	3.9	...	...	...
Iceland - Islande													
2012	C	4 533	14.1	C	1 955	6.1	8.0	C	5	...	II80.8	83.9	2.037
2013	C	4 326	13.4	C	2 154	6.7	6.7	C	8	...	II80.8	83.7	1.932
2014	C	4 375	13.4	C	2 049	6.3	7.1	C	9	...	II80.6	83.6	1.932
2015	C	4 129	12.5	C	2 178	6.6	5.9	C	9	...	II81.0	83.6	1.805
2016	C	4 034	12.1	C	2 309	6.9	5.2		...	...	...	...	1.745
Ireland - Irlande													
2012	+C	72 225	15.7	C	29 186[114]	6.4[114]	9.4	+C	250	3.5	...	...	2.010
2013	+C	68 930	15.0	+C	30 018	6.5	8.5	+C	243	3.5	...	...	1.960
2014	+C	67 285	14.6	+C	29 188	6.3	8.3	+C	224	3.3	79.3[24]	83.5[24]	1.950
2015	+C	65 537	14.1	+C	30 064	6.5	7.6	+C	224	3.4	...	...	1.940
2016	+C*	63 897	13.5	+C*	30 390	6.4	7.1		...	...	...	...	...
Isle of Man - Île de Man													
2012	+C	890	10.5	+C	799	9.4	1.1		...	...	...	...	...
2013	+C	859	10.0	+C	792	9.2	0.8		...	...	...	...	...
2014	+C	805	9.3	+C	787	9.1	0.2		...	...	...	...	...
2015	+C	785	9.0		...	...	...		...	...	...	...	...
2016	+C	758	8.9	+C	852	10.0	-1.1		...	...	...	...	...

Continent, country or area and year / Continent, pays ou zone et année	Code[a]	Live births / Naissances vivantes Number Nombre	Crude birth rate Taux brut de natalité	Code[a]	Deaths / Décès Number Nombre	Crude death rate Taux brut de mortalité	Rate of natural increase Taux d'accroissement naturel	Code[a]	Infant deaths / Décès d'enfants de moins d'un an Number Nombre	Rate (per 1000 births) Taux (par 1000 naissances)	Life expectancy at birth Male[b] Masculin[b]	Female[b] Féminin[b]	Total fertility rate L'indice synthétique de fécondité
EUROPE													
Italy - Italie													
2012	+C	534 186	9.0	C	612 883	10.3	-1.3	C	1 532	2.9	...	...	1.420
2013	+C	514 308	8.5	C	600 744	10.0	-1.4	C	1 493	2.9	79.8	84.6	1.390
2014	C	502 596	8.3	C	598 364	9.8	-1.6	C	1 523	3.0	80.3	85.0	1.370
2015	C	485 780	8.0	C	647 571	10.7	-2.7	C	1 398	2.9	...	...	1.350
2016	C	473 438	7.8	C	615 261	10.1	-2.3		...	...	...	...	...
Jersey													
2012	+C	1 124[41]	11.4	+C	774	7.8	3.5		...	...	...	...	...
2013	+C	1 029[41]	...	+C	717	...	...		...	...	...	...	...
2014	+C	985[41]	9.8	+C	700	6.9	2.8		...	...	...	...	...
2015	+C	1 021[41]	9.9	+C	756	7.4	2.6		...	...	...	...	...
Latvia - Lettonie													
2012	C	19 897	9.8	C	29 025	14.3	-4.5	C	125	6.3	69.1	78.9	1.444
2013	C	20 596	10.2	C	28 691	14.3	-4.0	C	91	4.4	69.5	79.0	1.531
2014	C	21 746	10.9	C	28 466	14.3	-3.4	C	83	3.8	69.3	79.5	1.654
2015	C	21 979	11.1	C	28 478	14.4	-3.3	C	90	4.1	69.7	79.3	1.707
2016	C	21 968	11.2	C	28 580	14.5	-3.4	C	81	3.7	...	...	1.743
Liechtenstein													
2012	C	357	9.7	C	224	6.1	3.6	C	3	...	...	...	1.507
2013	C	339	9.2	C	246	6.7	2.5	C	2	...	...	...	...
2014	C	372	10.0	C	268	7.2	2.8	C	1	...	...	...	...
2015	C	325	8.7	C	252	6.7	1.9	C	2	...	...	...	...
2016	C*	378	10.0	C*	270	7.2	2.9		...	...	...	...	1.610
Lithuania - Lituanie													
2012	C	30 459	10.2	C	40 938	13.7	-3.5	C	118	3.9	68.4	79.4	1.595
2013	C	29 885	10.1	C	41 511	14.0	-3.9	C	110	3.7	68.5	79.4	...
2014	C	30 369	10.4	C	40 252	13.7	-3.4	C	118	3.9	69.1	79.9	...
2015	C	31 475	10.8	C	41 776	14.4	-3.5	C	132	4.2	69.1	79.6	...
2016	C	30 623	10.6	C	41 106	14.2	-3.6		...	...	...	...	...
Luxembourg													
2012	C	6 026	11.3	C	3 876	7.3	4.0	C	25	...	[III]79.5	84.3	1.570
2013	C	6 115	11.3	C	3 822	7.0	4.2	C	24	...	[III]79.9	84.3	...
2014	C	6 070	10.9	C	3 841	6.9	4.0	C	17	...	[III]80.2	84.8	...
2015	C	6 115	10.7	C	3 983	7.0	3.7	C	17	...	...	...	...
2016	C	6 050	10.5	C	3 967	6.9	3.6		...	...	...	...	...
Malta - Malte													
2012	C	4 130	9.8	C	3 418	8.1	1.7	C	22	...	78.0	82.2	1.420
2013	C	4 032	9.5	C	3 236	7.6	1.9	C	27	...	79.6	84.0	1.370
2014	C	4 191	9.8	C	3 270	7.7	2.2	C	21	...	79.8	84.3	1.420
2015	C	4 325	10.0	C	3 442	8.0	2.0	C	25	...	79.7	84.0	...
2016	C*	4 476	10.3	C	3 342	7.7	2.6	C	33	7.4	...	...	...
Monaco													
2012	C	979[115]	27.2	C	529[116]	14.7	12.5		...	...	...	...	...
2013	C	992[115]	26.8	C	567[116]	15.3	11.5		...	...	...	...	...
2014	C	974[115]	26.4	C	524[116]	14.2	12.2		...	...	...	...	...
2015	C	1 067[115]	28.4	C	595[116]	15.8	12.6		...	...	...	...	...
2016	C	938[115]	24.6	C	503[116]	13.2	11.4		...	...	...	...	...
Montenegro - Monténégro													
2012	C	7 459	12.0	C	5 922	9.5	2.5	C	33	4.4	...	...	1.709
2013	C	7 475	12.0	C	5 917	9.5	2.5	C	33	4.4	...	...	...
2014	C	7 529	12.1	C	6 014	9.7	2.4	C	37	4.9	...	...	...
2015	C	7 386	11.9	C	6 329	10.2	1.7	C	16	...	...	...	...
2016	C	7 569	12.2	C	6 464	10.4	1.8		...	...	...	...	...
Netherlands - Pays-Bas													
2012	C	175 959[117]	10.5	C	140 813[117]	8.4	2.1	C	649[117]	3.7	...	...	1.720
2013	C	171 341[117]	10.2	C	141 245[117]	8.4	1.8	C	645[117]	3.8	...	...	...
2014	C	175 181[117]	10.4	C	139 223[117]	8.3	2.1	C	630[117]	3.6	80.0	83.5	...
2015	C	170 510[117]	10.1	C	147 134[117]	8.7	1.4	C	561[117]	3.3	...	...	...
2016	C	172 520[117]	10.2	C	148 997[117]	8.8	1.4		...	...	...	...	...

4. Vital statistics summary and life expectancy at birth: 2012 - 2016
Aperçu des statistiques de l'état civil et de l'espérance de vie à la naissance : 2012 - 2016 (continued - suite)

Continent, country or area and year / Continent, pays ou zone et année	Code[a]	Number Nombre (Live births)	Crude birth rate Taux brut de natalité	Code[a]	Number Nombre (Deaths)	Crude death rate Taux brut de mortalité	Rate of natural increase Taux d'accroissement naturel	Code[a]	Number Nombre (Infant deaths)	Rate (per 1000 births) Taux (par 1000 naissances)	Male[b] Masculin[b]	Female[b] Féminin[b]	Total fertility rate L'indice synthétique de fécondité
EUROPE													
Norway - Norvège													
2012	C	60 255	12.0	C	41 992[118]	8.4	3.6	C	150[118]	2.5	79.4	83.4	1.851
2013	C	58 878	11.6	C	41 131[118]	8.1	3.5	C	140[118]	2.4	...	...	1.780
2014	C	58 976	11.5	C	40 369[118]	7.9	3.6	C	139[118]	2.4	80.1	84.2	1.760
2015	C	58 815	11.3	C	40 676[118]	7.8	3.5	C	133[118]	2.3	...	...	1.730
2016	C	58 890	11.2	C	40 726[118]	7.8	3.5		...	...	...	...	1.710
Poland - Pologne													
2012	C	386 257	10.1	C	384 788	10.1	0.0	C	1 791	4.6	72.7	81.0	1.299
2013	C	369 576	9.7	C	387 312	10.2	-0.5	C	1 684	4.6	...	...	1.256
2014	C	375 160	9.9	C	376 467	9.9	0.0	C	1 583	4.2	73.7	81.7	1.290
2015	C	369 308	9.7	C	394 921	10.4	-0.7	C	1 476	4.0	73.6	81.6	1.289
2016	C	382 257	10.1	C	388 009	10.2	-0.2		...	...	...	...	1.357
Portugal													
2012	C	89 841[41]	8.5	C	107 612[119]	10.2	-1.7	C	303[119]	3.4	[III]76.7	82.6	1.284
2013	C	82 787[41]	7.9	C	106 554[119]	10.2	-2.3	C	243[119]	2.9	[III]76.9	82.8	1.210
2014	C	82 367[41]	7.9	C	104 843[119]	10.1	-2.2	C	236[119]	2.9	[III]77.2	83.0	1.230
2015	C	85 500[41]	8.3	C	108 539[119]	10.5	-2.2	C	250[119]	2.9	[III]77.4	83.2	1.300
2016	C	87 126[41]	8.4	C	110 535[119]	10.7	-2.3		...	...	...	...	1.360
Republic of Moldova - République de Moldova													
2012	C	39 435[120]	11.1	C	39 560[120]	11.1	0.0	C	387[120]	9.8	67.2[120]	75.0[120]	1.279[120]
2013	C	37 871[120]	10.6	C	38 060[120]	10.7	-0.1	C	359[120]	9.5	...	...	1.240
2014	C	38 616[120]	10.9	C	39 494[120]	11.1	-0.2	C	372[120]	9.6	...	...	1.280
2015	C	38 610[120]	10.9	C	39 906[120]	11.2	-0.4		...	...	...	...	1.300
2016	C*	37 356[120]	10.5	C*	38 488[120]	10.8	-0.3		...	...	...	...	1.280
Romania - Roumanie													
2012	C	201 104	10.0	C	255 539	12.7	-2.7	C	1 812	9.0	[III]70.7	77.9	1.302
2013	C	182 313	9.1	C	246 967	12.4	-3.2	C	1 677	9.2	[III]71.2	78.3	1.400[121]
2014	C	193 103	9.7	C	254 237	12.8	-3.1	C	1 628	8.4	[III]72.0	78.9	...
2015	C	197 491	10.0	C	261 294	13.2	-3.2	C	1 500	7.6	[III]71.9	78.9	...
2016	C*	188 415	9.5	C*	256 476	13.0	-3.4		...	...	...	...	...
Russian Federation - Fédération de Russie													
2012	C	1 902 084[59]	13.3	C	1 906 335[59]	13.3	0.0	C	16 306[59]	8.6	64.6	75.9	...
2013	C	1 895 822[59]	13.2	C	1 871 809[59]	13.0	0.2		...	...	...	...	...
San Marino - Saint-Marin													
2012	+C	292	8.7	+C	237	7.1	1.6	+C	-	...	81.5	86.1	...
2013	+C	320	9.6	+C	247	7.4	2.2	+C	1	...	81.7	86.4	...
2014	+C	281	8.4	+C	252	7.5	0.9	+C	1	...	...	...	...
2015	+C	269	8.0	+C	235	7.0	1.0		...	...	...	...	...
2016	+C	262	7.7	+C	253	7.4	0.3		...	...	...	...	...
Serbia - Serbie[122]													
2012	+C	67 257	9.3	+C	102 400	14.2	-4.9	+C	415	6.2	72.2	77.3	1.449
2013	+C	65 554	9.1	+C	100 300	14.0	-4.8	+C	413	6.3	72.5	77.7	1.429
2014	+C	66 461	9.3	+C	101 247	14.2	-4.9	+C	381	5.7	72.6	77.7	1.465
2015	+C	65 657	9.3	+C	103 678	14.6	-5.4	+C	346	5.3	72.6	77.7	1.464
2016	+C	64 734	9.2	+C	100 834	14.3	-5.1		...	...	...	...	1.460
Slovakia - Slovaquie													
2012	C	55 535	10.3	C	52 437	9.7	0.6	C	321	5.8	72.5	79.5	1.339
2013	C	54 823	10.1	C	52 089	9.6	0.5	C	301	5.5	72.9	79.6	1.339
2014	C	55 033	10.2	C	51 346	9.5	0.7	C	318	5.8	73.2	80.0	1.367
2015	C	55 602	10.3	C	53 826	9.9	0.3	C	285	5.1	73.0	79.7	1.400
2016	C	57 557	10.6	C	52 351	9.6	1.0		...	...	...	...	...
Slovenia - Slovénie													
2012	C	21 938	10.7	C	19 257	9.4	1.3	C	36	1.6	77.0	82.9	1.581
2013	C	21 111	10.3	C	19 334	9.4	0.9	C	62	2.9	77.0	83.2	1.550
2014	C	21 165	10.3	C	18 886	9.2	1.1	C	39	1.8	78.0	83.7	1.580
2015	C	20 641	10.0	C	19 834	9.6	0.4	C	33	1.6	...	...	1.570
2016	C	20 345	9.9	C	19 689	9.5	0.3		...	...	[II]77.6	83.5	...

4. Vital statistics summary and life expectancy at birth: 2012 - 2016
Aperçu des statistiques de l'état civil et de l'espérance de vie à la naissance : 2012 - 2016 (continued - suite)

Continent, country or area and year / Continent, pays ou zone et année	Live births / Naissances vivantes			Deaths / Décès			Rate of natural increase / Taux d'accrois-sement naturel	Infant deaths / Décès d'enfants de moins d'un an			Life expectancy at birth / Espérance de vie à la naissance		Total fertility rate / L'indice synthétique de fécondité
	Code[a]	Number Nombre	Crude birth rate Taux brut de natalité	Code[a]	Number Nombre	Crude death rate Taux brut de mortalité		Code[a]	Number Nombre	Rate (per 1000 births) Taux (par 1000 naiss-ances)	Male[b] Masculin[b]	Female[b] Féminin[b]	
EUROPE													
Spain - Espagne													
2012	C	453 348	9.7	C	401 122	8.6	1.1	C	1 389	3.1	79.4	85.1	1.320
2013	C	424 440	9.1	C	388 600	8.3	0.8	C	1 149	2.7	80.0	85.6	1.270
2014	C	426 076	9.2	C	393 734	8.5	0.7	C	1 202	2.8	80.4	86.2	1.320
2015	C	418 432	9.0	C	420 408	9.1	0.0	C	1 117	2.7	...	...	1.330
2016	C*	406 556	8.8	C*	406 815	8.8	0.0		...	...	...	...	1.330
Sweden - Suède													
2012	C	113 177	11.9	C	91 938	9.7	2.2	C	293	2.6	79.9	83.5	1.910
2013	C	113 593	11.8	C	90 402	9.4	2.4	C	306	2.7	...	...	1.890
2014	C	114 907	11.9	C	88 976	9.2	2.7	C	251	2.2	80.4	84.2	1.880
2015	C	114 870	11.7	C	90 907	9.3	2.4	C	282	2.5	...	...	1.850
2016	C	117 425	11.9	C	90 982	9.2	2.7		...	...	...	...	1.850
Switzerland - Suisse													
2012	C	82 164	10.3	C	64 173	8.0	2.2	C	296	3.6	II80.4	84.6	1.526
2013	C	82 731	10.2	C	64 961	8.0	2.2	C	320	3.9	...	...	1.520
2014	C	85 287	10.4	C	63 938	7.8	2.6	C	331	3.9	II80.7	84.9	1.540
2015	C	86 559	10.5	C	67 606	8.2	2.3	C	340	3.9	II80.8	85.0	1.540
2016	C	87 883	10.6	C	64 964	7.8	2.8		...	...	...	...	1.550
TFYR of Macedonia - L'ex-R. y. de Macédoine													
2012	C	23 568	11.4	C	20 134	9.8	1.7	C	230	9.8	...	...	1.507
2013	C	23 138	11.2	C	19 208	9.3	1.9	C	237	10.2	...	...	1.500
2014	C	23 596	11.4	C	19 718	9.5	1.9	C	233	9.9	73.5	77.4	1.500
2015	C	23 075	11.1	C	20 461	9.9	1.3	C	198	8.6	...	...	1.500
2016	C	23 002	11.1	C	20 421	9.9	1.2		...	...	...	...	1.500
Ukraine													
2012	+C	520 705[123]	11.4	+C	663 139[124]	14.5	-3.1	+C	4 371[124]	8.4	66.1	76.0	1.531
2013	+C	503 657[123]	11.1	+C	662 368[124]	14.6	-3.5	+C	4 030[124]	8.0	66.3	76.2	1.506
2014	+C	465 882[125]	10.8	+C	632 296[126]	14.7	-3.9	+C	3 656[126]	7.8	...	...	...
2015	+C	411 781[125]	9.6	+C	594 796[126]	13.9	-4.3		...	...	...	...	...
United Kingdom of Great Britain and Northern Ireland - Royaume-Uni de Grande-Bretagne et d'Irlande du Nord[127]													
2012	C	812 970[128]	12.8	+C	569 024	8.9	3.8	+C	3 347	4.1	79.0	82.7	1.920
2013	C	778 358[128]	12.1	+C	574 945	9.0	3.2		...	...	...	...	1.830
2014	C	775 908[128]	12.0	+C	568 840	8.8	3.2	+C	2 990	3.9	...	...	1.820
2015	C	776 746[128]	11.9	+C	601 272	9.2	2.7	+C	3 005	3.9	...	...	...
2016	C*	774 841[128]	11.9	+C*	597 208	9.1	2.7		...	...	...	...	...
OCEANIA - OCÉANIE													
American Samoa - Samoas américaines													
2012	C	1 175	18.5	C	282	4.4	14.0	C	4	...	...	...	...
2013	C	1 161	18.5	C	270	4.3	14.2	C	5	...	...	...	...
2014	C	1 084	17.5	C	259	4.2	13.3	C	9	...	...	...	...
Australia - Australie													
2012	+C	309 582	13.6	+C	147 098	6.5	7.1	+C	1 031	3.3	III79.9	84.3	1.930
2013	+C	308 065	13.3	+C	147 678	6.4	6.9	+C	1 094	3.6	III80.1	84.3	1.883
2014	+C	299 697	12.8	+C	153 580	6.5	6.2	+C	1 012	3.4	III80.3	84.4	1.799
2015	+C	305 377	12.8	+C	159 052	6.7	6.2	+C	991	3.2	III80.4	84.5	1.807
Cook Islands - Îles Cook[129]													
2012	+C	259	13.3	+C	104	5.3	7.9	+C	1	...	...	...	...
2013	+C	256	13.8	+C	115	6.2	7.6	+C	-	...	...	...	...
2014	+C	204	11.0	+C	113	6.1	4.9	+C	-	...	...	...	...
2015	+C*	205	11.0	+C*	102	5.5	5.5	+C*	-	...	...	...	...

Continent, country or area and year / Continent, pays ou zone et année	Live births / Naissances vivantes			Deaths / Décès			Rate of natural increase / Taux d'accrois-sement naturel	Infant deaths / Décès d'enfants de moins d'un an			Life expectancy at birth / Espérance de vie à la naissance		Total fertility rate / L'indice synthétique de fécondité
	Code[a]	Number Nombre	Crude birth rate Taux brut de natalité	Code[a]	Number Nombre	Crude death rate Taux brut de mortalité		Code[a]	Number Nombre	Rate (per 1000 births) Taux (par 1000 naiss-ances)	Male[b] Masculin[b]	Female[b] Féminin[b]	
OCEANIA - OCÉANIE													
Fiji - Fidji													
2012	+C	20 178	23.5	+C	6 724	7.8	15.7		...	...	...	...	...
2013	+C	20 970	24.4	+C	6 939	8.1	16.3		...	...	...	...	...
2014	+C	20 249	...	+C	6 927	...	...		...	...	...	...	...
French Polynesia - Polynésie française													
2012	C	4 296	16.0	C	1 360	5.1	10.9	C	31	7.2	73.3	78.2	2.030
2013	C	4 203	15.6	C	1 441	5.3	10.2	C	37	8.8	72.9	77.4	1.980
2014	C	4 161	15.3	C	1 427	5.3	10.1	C	28	...	73.8	78.0	1.960
2015	C	3 888	14.3	C	1 394	5.1	9.2	C	29	...	74.4	78.1	...
Guam													
2012	C	3 604[130]	22.5	C	894[130]	5.6	16.9	C	42[130]	11.7	75.5	81.7	2.450
2013	C	3 329[130]	20.8	C	904[130]	5.6	15.1	C	31[130]	9.3	75.6	81.9	2.410
2014	C	3 396[130]	21.1	C	952[130]	5.9	15.2	C	28[130]	...	75.8	82.1	2.380
2015	C	3 367[130]	20.8	C	1 009[130]	6.2	14.6	C	47[130]	14.0	75.9	82.2	...
2016	C	3 433[130]	21.1	C*	1 022[130]	6.3	14.8		...	...	...	...	...
Nauru													
2012	C	319	...		...	...	...		...	...	...	...	...
2013	C	366	...		...	...	...		...	...	...	...	...
New Caledonia - Nouvelle-Calédonie													
2012	C	4 389	16.9	C	1 322	5.1	11.8	C	17	...	74.0	80.4	...
2013	C	4 373	16.6	C	1 374	5.2	11.4	C	19	...	...	...	...
2014	C	4 370	16.3	C	1 406	5.2	11.1	C	23	...	...	...	...
2015	C	4 191	15.4	C	1 465	5.4	10.0	C	25	...	...	...	...
New Zealand - Nouvelle-Zélande													
2012	+C	61 179[131]	13.9	+C	30 099[131]	6.8	7.1	+C	258[131]	4.2	III79.3	83.0	2.097
2013	+C	58 716[131]	13.2	+C	29 568[131]	6.7	6.6	+C	261[131]	4.4	III79.7	83.2	2.007
2014	+C	57 243[131]	12.7	+C	31 065[131]	6.9	5.8	+C	327[131]	5.7	III79.6	83.3	1.924
2015	+C	61 038[131]	13.3	+C	31 608[131]	6.9	6.4	+C	249[131]	4.1	...	...	1.994
2016	+C	59 427[131]	12.7	+C	31 179[131]	6.6	6.0	+C	213[131]	3.6	...	...	1.875[131]
Norfolk Island - Île Norfolk[132]													
2012	+C	4	...	+C	20	...	...		...	...	...	...	...
2013		...	...	+C	11	...	...		...	...	...	...	...
2014		...	...	+C	13	...	...		...	...	...	...	...
Northern Mariana Islands - Îles Mariannes septentrionales[46]													
2012	U	*853*	...	U	*163*	...	...	U	*6*	...	...	...	...
2013	U	*686*	...	U	*185*	...	...	U	*8*	...	...	...	...
2014	U	*517*	...	U	*202*	...	...	U	*7*	...	...	...	...
Palau - Palaos													
2012	C	268	12.7	C	164	7.8	4.9	C	2	...	...	...	...
2013	C	229	...	C	192	...	...	C	4	...	...	...	...
Pitcairn													
2012	C	-	...		...	...	...		...	...	...	...	...
2013	C	-	...		...	...	...		...	...	...	...	...
Samoa													
2012	+U	*2 393*	...	+U	*742*	...	...		...	...	...	...	...
2013	+U	*4 631*	...	+U	*876*	...	...		...	...	...	...	...
2014	+U	*8 493*	...	+U	*884*	...	...		...	...	...	...	...

FOOTNOTES - NOTES

Italics: data from civil registers which are incomplete or of unknown completeness. - Italiques : données incomplètes ou dont le degré d'exactitude n'est pas connu, provenant des registres de l'état civil.

* Provisional. - Données provisoires.

[a] 'Code' indicates the source of data, as follows:
  C - Civil registration, estimated over 90% complete
  U - Civil registration, estimated less than 90% complete
  | - Other source, estimated reliable

+ - Data tabulated by date of registration rather than occurence

... - Information not available

Le 'Code' indique la source des données, comme suit :

C - Registres de l'état civil considérés complets à 90 p. 100 au moins

U - Registres de l'état civil qui ne sont pas considérés complets à 90 p. 100 au moins

| - Autre source, considérée fiable

+ - Données exploitées selon la date de l'enregistrement et non la date de l'événement

... - Information non disponible

[b] A Roman number in front of the data for males specifies the range of the reference period of life expectancy for males and females presented on the row. For example, a reference year of 2005 and a range of V years means that the reference period for the life expectancy is 2001 - 2005. The absence of a Roman number means the reference period is one year and the reference period therefore coincides with the reference year. - Un chiffre romain devant la donnée relative aux hommes indique l'étendue de la période de référence concernant l'espérance de vie des hommes et des femmes présentée dans la ligne. Par exemple, une année de référence 2005 et une étendue de V signifie que la période de référence pour l'espérance de vie est 2001-2005. L'absence de chiffre romain signifie que la période de référence est d'un an et donc coïncide avec l'année de référence.

[1] Excluding live-born infants who died before their birth was registered. Data refer to Algerian population only. - Non compris les enfants nés vivants décédés avant l'enregistrement de leur naissance. Les données ne concernent que la population algérienne.

[2] Data refer to Algerian population only. - Les données ne concernent que la population algérienne.

[3] Data are projections presented in Annuaire Statistique 2010. - Les données sont des projections présentées dans l'Annuaire Statistique 2010.

[4] Source: Vital Statistics Report 2012. - Source: Vital Statistics Report 2012.

[5] Source: Vital Statistics Report 2014. - Source: Vital Statistics Report 2014.

[6] Source: Vital Statistics Report 2013. - Source: Vital Statistics Report 2013.

[7] Source: Botswana Population Projections 2011-2026. - Source: Botswana Population Projections 2011-2026.

[8] Data refer only to events recorded in hospitals and health centres. - Ces données ne concernent que les faits d'état civil enregistrés dans les hôpitaux et les centres de santé uniquement.

[9] The calculation of the total fertility rate is based on the number of live births during the three year period prior to the survey. - L' indice synthétique de fécondité a été calculé sur bases des enfants nés sur la période des trois années précédant l'enquête.

[10] Data refer to the 12 months preceding the census in May. - Les données se rapportent aux 12 mois précédant le recensement de mai.

[11] The coverage of registration is estimated at 66 per cent. - Le degré de complétude de l'enregistrement est évalué à 66 pour cent.

[12] The coverage of registration is estimated at 26 per cent. - Le degré de complétude de l'enregistrement est évalué à 26 pour cent.

[13] Based on Demographic and Health Survey 2012. - D'après l'Enquête Démographique et de Santé 2012.

[14] Adjusted number of births in households referring to the 12 months preceding the census in March. - Le nombre ajusté de naissances vivantes des ménages ordinaires se rapportent aux 12 mois précédant le recensement de mars.

[15] Adjusted number of deaths in households referring to the 12 months preceding the census in March. - Le nombre ajusté de décès des ménages ordinaires se rapportent aux 12 mois précédant le recensement de mars.

[16] Adjusted number of infant deaths in households referring to the 12 months preceding the census in March. - Le nombre ajusté de décès d'enfants des ménages ordinaires se rapportent aux 12 mois précédant le recensement de mars.

[17] Based on underlying data of the Population and Housing Census 2014. - Données fondées sur le recensement de la population de 2014.

[18] Based on the Population and Housing Census 2014. - D'après le Récensement Général de la Population et de l'Habitation 2014.

[19] Based on Multiple Indicators Cluster Survey 2016. - D'après l'Enquête par Grappes à Indicateurs Multiples 2016.

[20] Data refer to the 12 months preceding the census in March. Including nomadic population. - Les données se rapportent aux 12 mois précédant le recensement de mars. Y compris la population nomade.

[21] Excludes the islands of St. Brandon and Agalega. - Non compris les îles St. Brandon et Agalega.

[22] Source: Ministry of Health, National Directorate of Planning and Cooperation. - Source : Ministère de la santé, Direction nationale de la planification et de la coopération.

[23] Excluding live-born infants who died before their birth was registered. - Non compris les enfants nés vivants décédés avant l'enregistrement de leur naissance.

[24] Provisional data. - Données provisoires.

[25] Data refer to Saint Helenian resident population. - Pour la population résidante de Sainte-Hélène.

[26] Based on estimates and projections from 'Agence Nationale de la Statistique et de la Démographie'. - Données fondées sur des estimations et des projections provenant de l'Agence Nationale de la Statistique et de la Démographie.

[27] Data refer to the 12 months preceding the census in November. - Données se rapportant aux 12 mois précédant le recensement de novembre.

[28] Source: National Office of Births and Deaths. - Source : Le bureau national des naissances et des décès.

[29] Based on the results of the 2014 Population Census. Provisional data. - D'après les résultats du recensement de la population de 2014. Données provisoires.

[30] Based on the results of the 2012 Population and Housing Census. - D'après les résultats du recensement de la population et des logements de 2012.

[31] Excluding visitors. - Ne comprend pas les visiteurs.

[32] Excluding non-residents and foreign service personnel and their dependants. - À l'exclusion des non-résidents et du personnel diplomatique et de leurs charges de famille.

[33] Including Canadian residents temporarily in the United States, but excluding United States residents temporarily in Canada. - Y compris les résidents canadiens se trouvant temporairement aux Etats-Unis, mais ne comprenant pas les résidents des Etats-Unis se trouvant temporairement au Canada.

[34] Including Canadian residents temporarily in the United States, but excluding United States residents temporarily in Canada. Data refer to the twelve months from 1 July of the current year to 30 June of the following year. - Y compris les résidents canadiens se trouvant temporairement aux Etats-Unis, mais ne comprenant pas les résidents des Etats-Unis se trouvant temporairement au Canada. Les données font référence aux douze mois de 1 juillet de l'année actuelle à 30 juin de l'année suivante.

[35] Total includes resident deaths outside of the islands but buried in the islands. - Le total comprend les décès de résidents hors des îles mais inhumés dans les îles.

[36] Definition of urban and rural distribution changed from the year 2014. - La définition de la répartition urbaine et rurale a changé depuis 2014.

[37] Excluding children born in the country of non-resident mothers. - Exceptés les enfants nés dans le pays des mères non-résidentes.

[38] Excluding infant deaths to mothers living abroad. - Exception faite des décès d'enfants en bas âge survenus lorsque la mère résidait à l'étranger.

[39] Data have been adjusted for underenumeration. - Les données ont été ajustées pour compenser les lacunes du dénombrement.

[40] Data have been adjusted for undercoverage of infant deaths and sudden and violent deaths. - Ajusté pour la sous-estimation de la mortalité infantile, du nombre de morts soudaines et de morts violentes.

[41] Data refer to births to resident mothers. - Ces données concernent les enfants nés de mères résidentes.

[42] Data refer to resident population only. - Pour la population résidante seulement.

[43] Excluding Indian jungle population. - Non compris les Indiens de la jungle.

[44] Source: Population Registry and STAT/CBS estimates. - Source: Le registre de la population et les estimations du STAT/CBS.

[45] Excluding deaths of persons living abroad. - Exception faite des personnes décédées à l'étranger.

[46] Source: U.S. National Center for Health Statistics, National Vital Statistics Reports (NVSR). - Source : US National Center for Health Statistics, National Vital Statistics Reports (NVSR).

[47] Data refer to the 12 months from 30 June 2015 to 30 June 2016. - Les données font référence aux douze mois de 30 juin 2015 à 30 juin 2016.

[48] Including births abroad and births of unknown residence of mother. - Y compris les naissances à l'étranger et les naissances pour lesquelles le lieu de résidence de la mère est inconnu.

[49] Including deaths abroad and deaths of unknown place of residence. - Y compris décès à l'étranger et décès dont le lieu de résidence n'est pas connu.

[50] Including deaths abroad and deaths of unknown residence of mother. - Y compris décès à l'étranger et décès de nourrissons nés de mères dont le lieu de résidence n'est pas connu.

[51] Projected value based on the results of 2000 and 2010 censuses, statistics from civil registration and reporting of live births in the ministry of health system. - Projection basée sur les résultats des recensements de 2000 et 2010, des statistiques d'état civil et les registres des naissances vivantes du Ministère de la santé.

[52] Estimate for 2010 – 2015. - Estimation pour la période 2010-2015.

[53] Excludes nomadic Indian tribes. - Non compris les tribus d'Indiens nomades.

54 Data based on the 2010 Population Census. - Les données sont fondées sur le recensement de la population de 2010.

55 Data refer to national projections. - Les données se réfèrent aux projections nationales.

56 Source: Reports of the Ministry of Health. - Source : Rapports du Ministère de la Santé.

57 Indicators based on projected or estimated fertility from the 2001 Population Census. - Les indicateurs sont fondés sur la fécondité projetée ou estimée à partir du recensement de population de 2001.

58 Based on the results of the 2011 Population Census. - Basé sur les résultats du recencement de la population de 2011.

59 Excluding infants born alive of less than 28 weeks' gestation, of less than 1 000 g in weight and 35 cm in length, who die within seven days of birth. - Non compris les enfants nés vivants après moins de 28 semaines de gestations, pesant moins de 1 000 g, mesurant moins de 35 cm et décédés dans les sept jours qui ont suivi leur naissance.

60 Sources: Births and Deaths National Registration System database, and medical records of government hospitals. - Les sources: Les bases de données des << Births and Deaths National Registration System >> et les dossiers médicaux des hôpitaux du gouvernement.

61 Sources: Births and Deaths National Registration System database, and medical records of government hospitals. Deaths include deaths among some visitors. - Les sources: Les bases de données des << Births and Deaths National Registration System >> et les dossiers médicaux des hôpitaux du gouvernement. Les décès comprennent des décès parmi certains visiteurs.

62 Source: Sample vital registration system of Bangladesh - Source : << Sample Vital Registration System >> du Bangladesh.

63 Data have been estimated on the basis of the annual National Sample Survey on Population Changes. For statistical purposes, the data for China do not include those for the Hong Kong Special Administrative Region (Hong Kong SAR), Macao Special Administrative Region (Macao SAR) and Taiwan province of China. - Les données ont été estimées sur la base de l'enquête annuelle "National Sample Survey on Population Changes". Pour la présentation des statistiques, les données pour la Chine ne comprennent pas la Région Administrative Spéciale de Hong Kong (Hong Kong RAS), la Région Administrative Spéciale de Macao (Macao RAS) et Taïwan province de Chine.

64 The fertility rates have been compiled using a population denominator which has excluded female foreign domestic helpers. - Les taux de fécondité ont été compilés pour une population (en dénominateur) ne comprenant pas les domestiques étrangères.

65 Data refer to government controlled areas. - Les données se rapportent aux zones contrôlées par le Gouvernement.

66 Data refer to deaths of residents only. - Les données renvoient aux décès de résidents uniquement.

67 Includes data for the Indian-held part of Jammu and Kashmir, the final status of which has not yet been determined. - Y compris les données pour la partie du Jammu et du Cachemire occupée par l'Inde dont le statut définitif n'a pas encore été déterminé.

68 Rates were obtained by the Sample Registration System of India, which is a large demographic survey. - Les taux ont été obtenus par le Système de l'enregistrement par échantillon de l'Inde qui est une large enquête démographique.

69 Data are based on the publication: "Welfare Indicators", table "Health and Nutrition Indicators, Infant Mortality Rates" - Les données sont basées sur la publication : << Welfare Indicators >>, le tableau << Health and Nutrition Indicators, Infant Mortality Rates >>

70 Data refer to the Iranian Year which begins on 21 March and ends on 20 March of the following year. - Les données concernent l'année iranienne, qui commence le 21 mars et se termine le 20 mars de l'année suivante.

71 Including births registered by Civil Registration Organization. - Y compris les naissances enregistrées par l'organisation chargée d'assurer l'enregistrement des faits d'état civil.

72 Including deaths registered by Civil Registration Organization. - Y compris les décès enregistrés par l'organisation chargée d'assurer l'enregistrement des faits d'état civil.

73 Includes data for East Jerusalem and Israeli residents in certain other territories under occupation by Israeli military forces since June 1967. - Y compris les données pour Jérusalem-Est et les résidents israéliens dans certains autres territoires occupés depuis 1967 par les forces armées israéliennes.

74 Including deaths abroad of Israeli residents who were out of the country for less than a year. - Y compris les décès à l'étranger de résidents israéliens qui ont quitté le pays depuis moins d'un an.

75 Data refer to Japanese nationals in Japan only. - Les données se raportent aux nationaux japonais au Japon seulement.

76 The total number may include 'Unknown residence', but the categories urban and rural do not. - Le nombre total peut inclure les personnes dont la résidence n'est pas connue, à l'inverse des catégories de population urbaine et rurale.

77 Total fertility rate computed as the sum of the age-specific fertility rates from age 15 to 49 years old. - Le taux de fécondité cumulé est calculé comme somme des taux de fécondité par âge de 15 à 49 ans.

78 Excluding data for Jordanian territory under occupation since June 1967 by Israeli military forces. Excluding foreigners, including registered Palestinian refugees. - Non compris les données pour le territoire jordanien occupé depuis juin 1967 par les forces armées israéliennes. Non compris les étrangers, mais y compris les réfugiés de Palestine enregistrés.

79 Based on underlying data of the 2015 census. - Données fondées sur celles extraites du recensement de 2015.

80 Source: "Department of Public Health" - Source : << Le Service de la santé publique >>

81 Data are from Vital Registration System (VRS). - Les données proviennent du système d'enregistrement des faits d'état civil.

82 Data from Births and Deaths Notification System (Ministry of Health and all health care providers). - Les données proviennent du système de notification des naissances et des décès (Ministère de la santé et tous prestataires de soins de santé).

83 Data refer to Omani citizen only. - Les données concernent les citoyens d'Oman uniquement.

84 Data refer to residence of child. Excluding alien armed forces, civilian aliens employed by armed forces, and foreign diplomatic personnel and their dependants. - Les données correspondent à la résidence de l'enfant. Non compris les militaires étrangers, les civils étrangers employés par les forces armées ni le personnel diplomatique étranger et les membres de leur famille les accompagnant.

85 Excluding alien armed forces, civilian aliens employed by armed forces, and foreign diplomatic personnel and their dependants. - Non compris les militaires étrangers, les civils étrangers employés par les forces armées ni le personnel diplomatique étranger et les membres de leur famille les accompagnant.

86 Data refer to Saudi Arabian nationals only. Based on 2010 population census and 2016 demographic survey. - Les données ne concernent que les ressortissants saoudiens. D'après le recensement de la population de 2010 et l'enquête démographique de 2016.

87 Projections based on the final results of the 2004 Population and Housing Census. - Projections basées sur les résultats définitifs du recensement de la population et de l'habitat de 2004.

88 Projections based on the 2010 Population and Housing Census. - Projections fondées sur le recensement 2010 de la population et des logements.

89 Data refer to Saudi Arabian nationals only. - Les données ne concernent que les ressortissants saoudiens.

90 Data refer to Saudi Arabian nationals only. Source of data: Demographic Survey. - Les données ne concernent que les ressortissants saoudiens. Source des données : Enquête démographique.

91 Data refer to resident population which comprises Singapore citizens and permanent residents. - Les données se rapportent à la population résidente composé des citoyens de Singapour et des résidents permanents.

92 Data refer to resident total fertility rate. - Les données se rapportent aux indices synthétique de fécondité de la population résidante.

93 Data refer to resident population which comprises Singapore citizens and permanent residents. Provisional data. - Les données se rapportent à la population résidente composé des citoyens de Singapour et des résidents permanents. Données provisoires.

94 Source: Palestinian Central Bureau of Statistics, Population Register, updated version 22/02/2016. - Source: Bureau central de statistique palestinien, registre de la population, version actualisée jusqu'au 22/02/2016.

95 Source: Palestinian Multiple Indicator Cluster Survey 2014. - Source: Enquête palestinienne par grappes à indicateurs multiples, 2014.

96 Data have been adjusted for under-registration. Excluding infants born alive of less than 28 weeks' gestation, of less than 1 000 g in weight and 35 cm in length, who die within seven days of birth. - Y compris un ajustement pour sous-enregistrement. Non compris les enfants nés vivants après moins de 28 semaines de gestations, pesant moins de 1 000 g, mesurant moins de 35 cm et décédés dans les sept jours qui ont suivi leur naissance.

97 Data refer to the 12 months preceding the census in July. - Les données se rapportent aux 12 mois précédant le recensement de juillet.

98 The registration of births and deaths is conducted by the Ministry of Health. An estimate of completeness is not provided. - L'enregistrement des naissances et des décès est mené par le Ministère de la Santé. Le degré estimatif de complétude n'est pas fourni.

99 Including Non-Yemeni births. - Y compris les naissances non-yémenites.

100 Including Non-Yemeni deaths. - Y compris les décès non-yémenites.

101 Including deaths of nationals abroad. - Y compris les décès des nationaux survenus à l'étranger.

102 Including births occurring abroad of mothers with residence in Austria. - Y compris les naissances survenues à l'étranger des mères avec résidence en Autriche.

¹⁰³ Including armed forces stationed outside the country, but excluding alien armed forces stationed in the area. - Y compris les militaires nationaux hors du pays, mais non compris les militaires étrangers en garnison sur le territoire.

¹⁰⁴ Excluding Faeroe Islands and Greenland shown separately, if available. - Non compris les Îles Féroé et le Groenland, qui font l'objet de rubriques distinctes, si disponible.

¹⁰⁵ Excluding Åland Islands. - Non compris les Îles d'Åland.

¹⁰⁶ Including live births by military personnel and their dependants. - Y compris les naissances vivantes parmi les membres du personnel militaire et leurs personnes à charge.

¹⁰⁷ Excluding armed forces. - Non compris les militaires en garnison.

¹⁰⁸ Data include the live births of women with unknown residence and homeless. Till 2012 data refer to all live births occurred in Hungary. From 2013 data include the live births of women with Hungarian usual residence regardless of whether the live birth occurred in Hungary or in a foreign country, and do not include the live births of women with foreign country usual residence. - Les données incluent les enfants nés vivants de femmes dont la résidence n'est pas connue et de femmes sans domicile fixe. Jusqu'en 2012 les données concernent toutes les naissances vivantes survenues en Hongrie. À partir de 2013, les données concernent les enfants nés vivants de femmes dont la résidence habituelle est en Hongrie, que la naissance vivante ait eu lieu en Hongrie ou dans un pays étranger, et ne comprennent pas les enfants nés vivants de femmes dont la résidence habituelle est dans un pays étranger.

¹⁰⁹ Till 2012 data refer to all deaths occurred in Hungary. From 2013 data include the deceased persons with Hungarian usual residence regardless of whether the death occurred in Hungary or in a foreign country, and do not include the deceased persons with foreign country usual residence. - Jusqu'en 2012 les données concernent tous les décès survenus en Hongrie. À partir de 2013, les données comprennent les décès de personnes dont la résidence habituelle était en Hongrie, que le décès ait eu lieu en Hongrie ou dans un pays étranger, et ne comprennent pas les décès de personnes dont la residence habituelle était dans un pays étranger.

¹¹⁰ Till 2012 data refer to all infant deaths occurred in Hungary. From 2013 data include the deceased infants with Hungarian usual residence regardless of whether the death occurred in Hungary or in a foreign country, and do not include the deceased infants with foreign country usual residence. - Jusqu'en 2012 les données concernent tous les décès de nourrissons survenus en Hongrie. À partir de 2013, les données comprennent les nourrissons décédés alors que leur résidence habituelle était en Hongrie, que le décès ait eu lieu en Hongrie ou dans un pays étranger, et ne comprennent pas les nourrissons décédés dont la résidence habituelle était dans un pays étranger.

¹¹¹ Data include the live births of women with unknown residence and homeless. Data include the live births of women with Hungarian usual residence regardless of whether the live birth occurred in Hungary or in a foreign country, and do not include the live births of women with foreign country usual residence. - Les données incluent les enfants nés vivants de femmes dont la résidence n'est pas connue et de femmes sans domicile fixe. Les données concernent les enfants nés vivants de femmes dont la résidence habituelle est en Hongrie, que la naissance vivante ait eu lieu en Hongrie ou dans un pays étranger, et ne comprennent pas les enfants nés vivants de femmes dont la résidence habituelle est dans un pays étranger.

¹¹² Data include the deceased persons with Hungarian usual residence regardless of whether the death occurred in Hungary or in a foreign country, and do not include the deceased persons with foreign country usual residence. - Les données comprennent tous les décès survenus alors que leur résidence habituelle était en Hongrie, que le décès ait eu lieu en Hongrie ou dans un pays étranger, et ne comprennent pas les décès des personnes dont la résidence habituelle était dans un pays étranger.

¹¹³ Data include the deceased infants with Hungarian usual residence regardless of whether the death occurred in Hungary or in a foreign country, and do not include the deceased infants with foreign country usual residence. - Les données comprennent les nourrissons décédés alors que leur résidence habituelle était en Hongrie, que le décès ait eu lieu en Hongrie ou dans un pays étranger, et ne comprennent pas les nourrissons décédés dont la residence habituelle était dans un pays étranger.

¹¹⁴ Data refer to events registered within one year of occurrence. - Les données portent sur des événements enregistrés dans l'année pendant laquelle ils sont survenus.

¹¹⁵ Source: City Hall, Civil Status Registry Office, resident and non-resident births. - Source : La mairie, Bureau de l'État Civil, toutes les naissances.

¹¹⁶ Source: City Hall, Civil Status Registry Office, resident and non-resident deaths. Including still births. - Source : La mairie, Bureau de l'État Civil, toutes les décès. Les données comprennent les mortinaissances.

¹¹⁷ Including residents outside the country if listed in a Netherlands population register. - Englobe les résidents se trouvant à l'étranger à condition qu'ils soient inscrits sur le registre de population des Pays-Bas.

¹¹⁸ Including residents temporarily outside the country. - Y compris les résidents se trouvant temporairement hors du pays.

¹¹⁹ Data refer to usually resident population. - Les données concernent la population habituellement résidente.

¹²⁰ Excluding Transnistria and the municipality of Bender. - Les données ne tiennent pas compte de l'information sur la Transnistria et la municipalité de Bender.

¹²¹ Live births that occured outside of the country were not included in the calculation of the fertility rate. - Les naissances vivantes survenues en dehors du pays ne sont pas prises en compte dans les calculs de l'indice syntetique de fécondité.

¹²² Excludes data for Kosovo and Metohia. - Sans les données pour le Kosovo et Metohie.

¹²³ Data refer to births with weight 500g and more (if weight is unknown - with length 25 centimeters and more, or with gestation during 22 weeks or more). - Données concernant les nouveau-nés de 500 grammes ou plus (si le poids est inconnu – de 25 centimètres de long ou plus, ou après une grossesse de 22 semaines ou plus).

¹²⁴ Data includes deaths resulting from births with weight 500 g and more (if weight is unknown - with length 25 cm and more, or with gestation during 22 weeks or more). - Y compris les décès de nouveau-nés de 500 g ou plus (si le poids est inconnu – de 25 cm de long ou plus, ou après une grossesse de 22 semaines ou plus).

¹²⁵ Data refer to births with weight 500g and more (if weight is unknown - with length 25 centimeters and more, or with gestation during 22 weeks or more). The Government of Ukraine has informed the United Nations that it is not in a position to provide statistical data concerning the Autonomous Republic of Crimea and the city of Sevastopol. - Données concernant les nouveau-nés de 500 grammes ou plus (si le poids est inconnu – de 25 centimètres de long ou plus, ou après une grossesse de 22 semaines ou plus). Le gouvernement Ukrainien a informé l'ONU qu'il n'est pas en mesure de fournir des données statistiques concernant la République autonome de Crimée et la ville de Sébastopol.

¹²⁶ The Government of Ukraine has informed the United Nations that it is not in a position to provide statistical data concerning the Autonomous Republic of Crimea and the city of Sevastopol. Data includes deaths resulting from births with weight 500 g and more (if weight is unknown - with length 25 cm and more, or with gestation during 22 weeks or more). - Le gouvernement Ukrainien a informé l'ONU qu'il n'est pas en mesure de fournir des données statistiques concernant la République autonome de Crimée et la ville de Sébastopol. Y compris les décès de nouveau-nés de 500 g ou plus (si le poids est inconnu – de 25 cm de long ou plus, ou après une grossesse de 22 semaines ou plus).

¹²⁷ Excluding Channel Islands (Guernsey and Jersey) and Isle of Man, shown separately, if available. - Non compris les îles Anglo-Normandes (Guernesey et Jersey) et l'île de Man, qui font l'objet de rubriques distinctes, si disponible.

¹²⁸ Data tabulated by date of occurrence for England and Wales, and by date of registration for Northern Ireland and Scotland. - Données exploitées selon la date de l'événement pour l'Angleterre et le pays de Galles, et selon la date de l'enregistrement pour l'Irlande du Nord et l'Ecosse.

¹²⁹ Excluding Niue, shown separately, which is part of Cook Islands, but because of remoteness is administered separately. - Non compris Nioué, qui fait l'objet d'une rubrique distincte et qui fait partie des îles Cook, mais qui, en raison de son éloignement, est administrée séparément.

¹³⁰ Including United States military personnel, their dependants and contract employees. - Y compris les militaires des Etats-Unis, les membres de leur famille les accompagnant et les agents contractuels des Etats-Unis.

¹³¹ Random rounding to base 3 is applied in this table as a confidentiality measure. - Les chiffres sont arrondis à la base 3 de manière aléatoire, pour des raisons de confidentialité.

¹³² Data cover the period from 1 July of the previous year to 30 June of the present year. - Pour la période allant du 1er juillet de l'année précédente au 30 juin de l'année en cours.

Table 5 - *Demographic Yearbook 2016*

Table 5 presents national estimates of mid-year population for all available years between 2007 and 2016.

Description of variables: Mid-year estimates of the total population are those provided by national statistical offices. They refer to the *de facto* or *de jure* population on 1 July of the reference year. Exceptions to this are footnoted accordingly. The data are presented in thousands, rounded by the Statistics Division of the United Nations Department of Economic and Social Affairs.

For some countries or areas the figures presented in this table and the figures used to calculate rates in subsequent tables are not the same, as these countries have provided a reference population for vital events that is different than the total population.

Unless otherwise indicated, all estimates relate to the population within present geographical boundaries. Major exceptions to this principle are explained in footnotes.

Reliability of data: Reliable mid-year population estimates are those that are based on a complete census (or on a sample survey) and have been adjusted on a basis of a continuous population register or on the balance of births, deaths and migration. Reliable mid-year estimates appear in roman type. Mid-year estimates that are not calculated on this basis are considered less reliable and are shown in *italics*.

Limitations: Statistics on estimates of the mid-year total population are subject to the same qualifications as have been set forth for population statistics in general in section 3 of the Technical Notes.

International comparability of mid-year population estimates is also affected by the fact that some of these estimates refer to the *de jure*, and not the *de facto*, population. These are indicated in the column titled "Code". The difference between the *de facto* and the *de jure* population is discussed in section 3.1.1 of the Technical Notes.

Earlier data: Estimates of mid-year population have been shown in previous issues of the *Demographic Yearbook*. Information on the years and specific topics covered is presented in the Historical Index.

Tableau 5 – *Annuaire démographique 2016*

Le tableau 5 présente des estimations nationales de la population en milieu d'année pour le plus grand nombre possible d'années entre 2007 et 2016.

Description des variables : les estimations de la population totale en milieu d'année sont celles qui ont été communiquées par les services nationaux de statistique. Elles correspondent à la population de fait ou se réfèrent à la population de droit, au 1er juillet de l'année de référence. Lorsque la date est différente, cela est signalé par une note. Sauf indication contraire, tous les chiffres sont exprimés en milliers. Les données ont été arrondies par la Division de statistique du Département des affaires économiques et sociales de l'Organisation des Nations Unies.

Pour certains pays ou territoires, les données présentées dans ce tableau sont différentes des données utilisées pour calculer les taux dans les tableaux suivants, parce que ces pays ont fourni une population de référence pour les événements démographiques différente de la population totale.

Sauf indication contraire, toutes les estimations se rapportent à la population présente sur le territoire actuel des pays ou zones considérés. Les principales exceptions à cette règle sont expliquées en note.

Fiabilité des données : les estimations de la population en milieu d'année sont considérées sûres quand elles sont fondées sur un recensement complet (ou sur une enquête par sondage) et ont été ajustées en fonction des données provenant d'un registre permanent de population ou en fonction des naissances, décès et mouvements migratoires qui ont eu lieu pendant la période. Les estimations considérées comme sûres apparaissent en caractères romains. Les estimations dont le calcul n'a pas été effectué sur cette base sont considérées comme moins sûres et apparaissent en italique.

Insuffisance des données : les statistiques concernant les estimations de la population totale en milieu d'année appellent toutes les réserves qui ont été formulées à la section 3 des Notes techniques à propos des statistiques de la population en général.

Le fait que certaines des estimations concernant la population en milieu d'année se réfèrent à la population de droit et non à la population de fait influe sur la comparabilité internationale. Ces cas ont été signalés dans la colonne « Code ». La différence entre la population de fait et la population de droit est expliquée à la section 3.1.1 des Notes techniques.

Données publiées antérieurement : des estimations de la population en milieu d'année ont été publiées dans des éditions antérieures de l'*Annuaire démographique*. Pour plus de précisions concernant les années et les sujets pour lesquels des données ont été publiées, se reporter à l'index.

Continent and country or area / Continent et pays ou zone	Code[a]	Population estimates (in thousands) - Estimations (en milliers)									
		2007	2008	2009	2010	2011	2012	2013	2014	2015	2016
AFRICA - AFRIQUE											
Algeria - Algérie	DJ	34 096	34 591	35 268	35 978	36 717	37 495	38 297	39 114	39 963	40 836
Angola[1]	DF	15 889	16 368	16 889	17 430	17 992	18 577	19 184	...	...	...
Benin - Bénin	DF	7 959[2]	8 225[2]	8 498[2]	8 779[2]	9 067[2]	9 365[2]	...	10 293[3]	10 585[3]	10 883[3]
Botswana	DJ	1 736	1 755	1 776	1 823	1 850	2 071[4]	2 115[4]	2 156[4]	2 195[4]	2 231[4]
Burkina Faso[2]	DJ	14 252	14 731	15 225	15 731	16 249	16 779	17 323	17 880	18 450	...
Burundi	DF	...	...	8 263[5]	9 461	9 771	10 073	10 367	10 654	10 933	11 215
Cabo Verde	DF	491	500	509	494[2]	500[2]	506[2]	512[2]	518[2]	525[2]	531[2]
Cameroon - Cameroun[2]	DF	18 225	18 691	19 166	19 648	20 139	20 637	21 143	21 657	22 180	22 710
Congo	DF	3 616[2]	3 741	3 838	...	...	...	4 278	...	...	...
Côte d'Ivoire	DF	19 476[6]	19 932[6]	20 389[6]	20 845[6]	21 302[6]	21 758[6]	22 215[6]	22 723[7]	23 334[7]	23 950[7]
Djibouti[8]	DF	775	797	...	841	865	...	...	...	...	...
Egypt - Égypte	DF	73 644	75 194	76 925	78 685	80 530	82 550	84 629	86 811	88 958	91 023
Equatorial Guinea - Guinée équatoriale[9]	DF	1 446	1 508	1 566	1 622	...	...	...	...	...	...
Ethiopia - Éthiopie	DF	77 127[10]	75 719[11]	77 651[11]	79 634[11]	81 668[11]	83 741[11]	85 837[11]	87 952[11]	90 075[11]	92 205[11]
Ghana	DF	22 388	22 901	23 417	...	25 235[12]	25 825[12]	26 428[12]	27 043[12]	27 670[12]	28 308[12]
Guinea - Guinée	DF	...	10 183[2]	10 218[2]	10 537[2]	10 864[2]	...	...	...	...	...
	DJ	...	...	...	...	...	...	...	10 602	*10 953	*11 319
Guinea-Bissau - Guinée-Bissau[2]	DF	1 389	...	...	1 460	1 472	1 485	1 499	1 514	1 531	1 548
Kenya	DF	37 184	38 278	37 725[13]	38 474[13]	39 545[13]	40 657[13]	41 788[13]	42 961[13]	44 157[13]	45 389[13]
Lesotho[2]	DF	1 880	1 884	1 887	1 892	1 897	1 903	1 909	1 917	1 924	1 933
Liberia - Libéria	DF	3 404	...	3 551	3 627	3 705	3 784	3 865	3 946	...	...
Libya - Libye[14]	DF	5 393	5 490	5 589	5 689	5 791	5 892	5 994	6 096	6 162	...
Madagascar[2]	DF	18 556	19 072	19 601	20 142	20 696	21 263	21 842	22 434	...	...
Malawi[2]	DF	13 188	13 630	13 520	13 948	14 389	14 845	15 317	15 805	16 310	16 833
Mali	DF	12 378[15]	14 161[16]	14 671[16]	15 370[16]	15 843[16]	16 312[16]	16 808[16]	*17 319[16]	...	...
Mauritania - Mauritanie[2]	DF	3 075	3 162	3 251	3 341	3 297	3 378	3 537	3 637	3 720	3 783
Mauritius - Maurice[17]	DJ	1 260[18]	1 269[18]	1 275[18]	1 281[18]	1 252[19]	1 256[19]	1 259[19]	1 261[19]	1 263[19]	1 263[19]
Mayotte[15]	DJ								220	*227	*235
Morocco - Maroc	DF	30 850[20]	31 195[20]	31 543[20]	31 894[20]	32 245[20]	32 597[20]	32 950[20]	33 770[21]	34 125[21]	34 487[21]
Mozambique[2]	DF	20 632	21 208	21 803	22 417	23 050	23 701	24 366	25 042	25 728	26 424
Namibia - Namibie	DF	2 028[2]	2 065[2]	2 104[2]	2 143[2]	2 116[22]	2 155[22]	2 196[22]	2 238[22]	2 281[22]	2 324[22]
Niger	DJ	13 716[2]	14 198[2]	14 693[2]	15 204[2]	15 731[2]	16 994[23]	17 680[23]	18 389[23]	19 125[23]	19 865[23]
Nigeria - Nigéria[24]	DF	144 998	149 713	154 582	159 608	164 798	170 157	175 690	181 403	187 302	193 393
Republic of South Sudan - République de Soudan du Sud[25]	DF	...	8 491	8 988	9 497	10 018	10 552	10 809	11 071	...	...
Reunion - Réunion[15]	DJ	794	808	816	821	829	834	835	843	*847	*851
Rwanda	DF	9 557[2]	9 832[2]	10 117[2]	10 413[2]	10 718[2]	10 483[23]	10 737[23]	10 997[23]	11 263[23]	11 533[23]
Saint Helena ex. dep. - Sainte-Hélène sans dép.	DF	4	4	4	4	4	4	4[26]	4	4	5
Saint Helena: Ascension - Sainte-Hélène: Ascension	DJ	...	1	...	...	...	...	...	...	...	...
Saint Helena: Tristan da Cunha - Sainte-Hélène: Tristan da Cunha[27]	DF	0	0	0	...	...	...	...	...	...	...
Sao Tome and Principe - Sao Tomé-et-Principe	DF	155	158	161	164	167	*187	*194	...	...	...
Senegal - Sénégal	DJ	11 519[26]	11 841[26]	12 171[26]	12 509[26]	12 842[26]	13 208[2]	13 509[2]	13 926[2]	14 357[2]	14 800[2]
Seychelles	DF	85	87	87	90	87	88	90	91	93	...
Sierra Leone	DF	5 343	5 474	5 608	5 747	5 890	6 038	...	...	...	...
South Africa - Afrique du Sud	DF	48 884	49 558	50 256	50 979	51 729	52 507	53 312	54 147	55 012	55 909
Sudan - Soudan	DF	...	30 979	31 957	32 962	33 998	35 064	36 163	37 292	38 454	39 648
Swaziland	DF	1 018	1 032	1 044	1 056	1 068	1 080	1 093	1 106	1 119[15]	1 133[15]
Togo	DF	5 465	5 596	5 731	6 191[2]	6 338[2]	6 491[2]	6 648[2]	6 809[2]	6 974[2]	7 143[2]
Tunisia - Tunisie	DF	10 225	10 329	10 440	10 547	10 674	10 778	10 887	11 007	11 154	11 299
Uganda - Ouganda	DF	28 581	29 593	30 661	31 785	32 940	34 131	...	34 141[7]	35 492[7]	36 561[7]
United Republic of Tanzania - République Unie de Tanzanie	DF	39 446[28]	40 668[28]	41 916[28]	43 188[28]	44 485[28]	45 798[28]	46 170[23]	47 452[23]	48 776[23]	50 143[23]
Zambia - Zambie[2]	DF	12 161	12 526	12 897	...	13 719	14 145	14 580	15 023	15 474	15 934
Zimbabwe	DF	12 040[28]	12 150[28]	13 668[28]	...	...	...	13 369[29]	13 652[29]	13 943[29]	14 240[29]

Continent and country or area / Continent et pays ou zone	Co-de[a]	Population estimates (in thousands) - Estimations (en milliers)									
		2007	2008	2009	2010	2011	2012	2013	2014	2015	2016
AMERICA, NORTH - AMÉRIQUE DU NORD											
Anguilla	DF	15	16	16	16	...	14	14	14	15	...
Antigua and Barbuda - Antigua-et-Barbuda	DF	86	88	89	91	...	...	...	...	...	...
Aruba	DJ	100	101	102	102	103	105	106	108	109	110
Bahamas[2]	DF	334	338	342	335	358	363	368	372	...	*373
Barbados - Barbade	DF	274	275	275	278	278	278	277	277	275	...
Belize	DF	299	307	315	324	332	341	350	359	368	378
Bermuda - Bermudes	DJ	64[30]	64[30]	64[30]	64[12]	63[12]	62[12]	62[12]	62[12]	62[12]	62[12]
British Virgin Islands - Îles Vierges britanniques	DF	27	28	28	28	28	28	29	...	29	...
Canada	DJ	32 888[31]	33 246[31]	33 629[31]	34 005[31]	34 343[32]	34 751[32]	35 155[33]	35 545[33]	35 849[33]	*36 286[34]
Cayman Islands - Îles Caïmanes	DJ	54	56	57	56	55	56	56	57	59	...
Costa Rica	DJ	4 443	4 533[35]	4 620[35]	4 538[36]	4 592[36]	4 651[36]	4 712[36]	4 772[36]	4 834[37]	4 890[38]
Cuba	DJ	11 195	11 181	11 174	11 171	11 172	11 174	11 192	11 224	11 239	11 239
Curaçao	DJ	144[39]	146[39]	147[39]	149[39]	151[39]	152[40]	154[40]	156[40]	158[40]	160[40]
Dominica - Dominique	DF	71	71	71	71	71	71	71	72	...	...
Dominican Republic - République dominicaine	DF	9 174	9 280	9 380	9 479[2]	9 580[2]	9 681[2]	9 785[2]	9 883[2]	9 980[2]	10 075[2]
El Salvador[41]	DF	6 099	6 125	6 153	6 183	6 216	6 251	6 289	6 328	6 460	6 521
Greenland - Groenland[42]	DJ	57	56	56	57	57	57	56	56	56	56
Grenada - Grenade	DF	105	105	105	105	107	108	109	109	111	...
Guadeloupe[43]	DJ	401	402	402	403	405	403	402	404	*398	*396
Guatemala[28]	DF	13 345	13 678	14 017	14 362	14 714	15 073	15 438	15 807	16 176	...
Haiti - Haïti[44]	DJ	9 602	9 762	9 923	10 085	10 248	10 413	10 579	10 746	10 912	...
Honduras	DF	7 537[45]	7 707[45]	7 877[45]	8 046[45]	8 215[45]	8 385[45]	...	8 432[3]	8 577[3]	...
Jamaica - Jamaïque	DJ	2 676	2 687	2 696	2 702	2 700	2 708	2 715	2 721	2 725	2 729
Martinique[15]	DJ	398	398	396	394	392	388	386	384	*380	*377
Mexico - Mexique	DJ	109 787	111 299	112 853	114 256[2]	115 683[2]	117 054[2]	118 395[2]	119 713[2]	121 006[2]	122 273[2]
Montserrat	DF	5	5	5	5	5	5	5	5	5	5
Nicaragua	DJ	5 596	5 669	5 742	5 816	5 889	6 071	6 134	6 198	6 263	...
Panama	DF	3 476[46]	3 538[46]	3 600[46]	3 662[12]	3 724[12]	3 788[12]	3 851[12]	3 913[12]	3 975[12]	4 037[12]
Puerto Rico - Porto Rico[47]	DJ	3 783[39]	3 761[39]	3 740[39]	3 721[48]	3 679[40]	3 634[40]	3 593[40]	3 535[40]	3 474[40]	3 411[40]
Saint Kitts and Nevis - Saint-Kitts-et-Nevis	DF	*51	*51	*52	*53	...	...	...	...	...	...
Saint Lucia - Sainte-Lucie	DF	168	170	172	...	167	169	171	173	173	...
Saint Pierre and Miquelon - Saint-Pierre-et-Miquelon[15]	DJ	...	...	...	...	6	6	...	...	...	...
Saint Vincent and the Grenadines - Saint-Vincent-et-les Grenadines	DJ	110	110	110	110	110	110	110	110	110	...
Sint Maarten (Dutch part) - Saint-Martin (partie néerlandaise)	DJ	39	40	39	36	33	35	37	37[15]	...	...
Trinidad and Tobago - Trinité-et-Tobago	DF	1 303[18]	1 309[18]	1 310[18]	1 318[18]	...	1 335[19]	1 341[19]	1 345[19]	1 350[19]	1 354[19]
Turks and Caicos Islands - Îles Turques et Caïques	DJ	35	37	36	35	34	32	34	35	37	38
United States of America - États-Unis d'Amérique[49]	DJ	301 231[39]	304 094[39]	306 772[39]	309 348[40]	311 663[40]	313 998[40]	316 205[40]	318 563[40]	320 897[40]	323 128[40]
United States Virgin Islands - Îles Vierges américaines[47]	DJ	110	110	110[50]	106[50]	106[50]	105[50]	105[50]	104[50]	...	...
AMERICA, SOUTH - AMÉRIQUE DU SUD											
Argentina - Argentine	DF	39 356	39 746	40 134	40 788[51]	41 261[51]	41 733[51]	42 203[51]	42 670[51]	43 132[51]	43 590[51]
Bolivia (Plurinational State of) - Bolivie (État plurinational de)	DF	9 550	9 710	9 870	10 031	10 191	10 351	10 508	10 666	10 825	10 985
Brazil - Brésil[52]	DJ	189 463	191 532	193 544	195 498	197 397	199 242	201 033	202 769	204 451	206 081
Chile - Chili	DF	16 598	16 763	16 929	17 094	17 248	17 403	17 557	17 819	18 006	18 192
Colombia - Colombie[53]	DJ	43 927	44 451	44 979	45 510	46 045	46 582	47 121	47 662	48 203	48 748
Ecuador - Équateur[54]	DF	14 215	14 473	14 738	15 012	15 266	15 521	15 775	16 027	16 279	16 529

Continent and country or area / Continent et pays ou zone	Code[a]	Population estimates (in thousands) - Estimations (en milliers)									
		2007	2008	2009	2010	2011	2012	2013	2014	2015	2016
AMERICA, SOUTH - AMÉRIQUE DU SUD											
French Guiana - Guyane française[15]	DJ	213	219	224	229	238	240	244	252	*257	*263
Guyana	DF	771	774	753	752	751	749	747	748	742	...
Paraguay[55]	DF	5 975	6 072	6 169	6 266	6 363	6 461	6 559	6 657	6 756	6 855
Peru - Pérou[56]	DF	28 482	28 807	29 132	29 462	29 798	30 136	30 475	30 814	31 152	31 489
Suriname	DJ	510	517	524	531	540	...	550	559	567	...
Uruguay	DJ	3 359	3 363	3 378	3 397	3 413	3 426[2]	3 440[2]	3 454[2]	3 467[2]	3 480[2]
Venezuela (Bolivarian Republic of) - Venezuela (République bolivarienne du)	DF	27 273	27 689	28 106	28 524	28 944	29 366	29 786	30 206	30 620	31 029
ASIA - ASIE											
Afghanistan[57]	DF	23 039	23 511	23 994	24 486	24 988	25 500	26 023	26 557	27 101	27 657
Armenia - Arménie	DJ	3 227	3 234	3 244	3 256	3 028	3 024	3 022	3 014	3 005	2 993
Azerbaijan - Azerbaïdjan	DF	8 723[39]	8 839[39]	8 947	9 054	9 173	9 296	9 417	9 529	9 649	9 756
Bahrain - Bahreïn	DJ	1 039	1 103	1 178	1 229	1 195	1 209	1 253	1 315	1 370	1 424
Bangladesh	DF	142 600	144 500	146 600	148 620	150 611	152 700	154 790	156 880	158 900	160 800
Bhutan - Bhoutan[58]	DF	659	671	683	696	708	721	733	745	757	769
Brunei Darussalam - Brunéi Darussalam	DF	370[39]	375[39]	380[39]	387[39]	...	...	...	...	...	...
	DJ	...	...	...	...	...	400	406	412	417	...
Cambodia - Cambodge[59]	DF	14 364[60]	13 868[61]	14 085[61]	14 303[61]	14 521[61]	14 741[61]	14 963[61]	15 184[61]	15 405[61]	...
China - Chine[62]	DF	1 317 900[63]	1 324 700[63]	1 331 300[63]	1 337 700[63]	1 344 100[64]	1 350 695[64]	1 357 380[63]	1 364 270[63]	1 371 220[63]	...
China, Hong Kong SAR - Chine, Hong Kong RAS	DJ	6 916	6 958	6 973	7 024	7 072	7 150	7 179	7 230	7 291	7 337
China, Macao SAR - Chine, Macao RAS	DJ	521	541	535	537	550	568	592	622	643	...
Cyprus - Chypre[65]	DJ	767[66]	787[66]	808[66]	829[66]	851[66]	864[66]	862[66]	853[66]	847[15]	848[15]
Georgia - Géorgie	DF	4 388	4 384	4 411	4 453	4 483	4 491	4 487	...	...	...
	DJ	...	...	...	...	...	...	...	3 727[67]	3 717[67]	3 719[67]
India - Inde[68]	DF	1 134 023	1 150 196	1 166 228	1 182 105	1 197 813	1 213 370				
Indonesia - Indonésie	DJ	225 642[69]	228 523[69]	231 370[69]	238 519[70]	241 991[70]	245 425[70]	248 818[70]	252 165[70]	255 462[70]	258 705[70]
Iran (Islamic Republic of) - Iran (République islamique d')[71]	DJ	71 279	72 182	73 202	74 340	...	76 038	76 942	77 856	78 773	79 686
Iraq	DF	29 427	30 315	31 393	32 211	33 052	33 913	34 794	35 736	36 659	...
Israel - Israël[72]	DJ	7 180	7 309	7 486	7 624	7 766	7 911	8 059	8 216	8 380	...
Japan - Japon[73]	DJ	128 001	128 063	128 047	128 070	127 833[74]	127 629[74]	127 445[74]	127 276[74]	127 141[75]	126 995[75]
Jordan - Jordanie[76]	DF	6 106	6 293	6 490	6 699	6 993	7 427	8 114	8 804	9 532	9 798
Kazakhstan	DF	15 484	15 674	16 093	16 322	16 557	16 791	17 035	17 161[15]	...	...
Kuwait - Koweït	DF	2 495	2 632	2 778	2 933	3 107	3 247	3 428	3 767	3 971	3 925[15]
Kyrgyzstan - Kirghizstan[66]	DJ	5 268	5 319	5 383	5 448	5 515	5 608	5 720	5 836	5 957	6 080
Lao People's Democratic Republic - République démocratique populaire lao[77]	DJ	5 869	5 990	6 111	6 230	6 349	6 466	6 581	6 693	...	6 906
Malaysia - Malaisie	DJ	27 058[78]	27 568[78]	28 081[78]	28 589[79]	29 062[79]	29 510[79]	30 214[79]	30 709[79]	31 186[79]	31 661[79]
Maldives	DF	305	310	315	320	325	331	336	...	344[80]	350[80]
Mongolia - Mongolie	DF	2 602	2 643	2 691	2 739	2 786	2 840	2 899	2 963	3 027	3 089
Myanmar[81]	DF	57 504	58 377	59 130	59 780	50 149[67]	50 667[67]	51 184[67]	51 991[67]	52 451[67]	52 917[67]
Nepal - Népal	DJ	26 427	26 967	27 504	28 044	28 585	26 873[22]	27 257[22]	27 646[22]	28 038[22]	28 431[22]
Oman	DF	2 743	2 867	3 174	...	3 295[82]	3 623[82]	3 855[82]	3 993[82]	4 159[82]	4 414[82]
Pakistan[83]	DF	...	166 410	169 940	173 510	177 100	...	184 350	188 020	191 710	...
	DJ	149 860[84]	...	...	...	...	...	...	...	...	...
Philippines	DJ	88 706[30]	90 457[30]	92 227[30]	93 135[12]	94 824[12]	96 511[12]	98 197[12]	99 880[12]	101 562[12]	103 243[12]
Qatar	DF	1 218	1 448	1 639	1 715	1 733	1 833	2 004	2 216	2 438	2 618
Republic of Korea - République de Corée	DJ	48 684	49 055	49 308	49 554	49 937	50 200	50 429	50 747	51 015	51 246
Saudi Arabia - Arabie saoudite	DF	*24 941[85]	*25 787[85]	*26 661[85]	*27 563[85]	*28 376[85]	*29 196[85]	*29 602[85]	29 997	30 891	31 742
Singapore - Singapour[86]	DJ	4 589	4 839	4 988	5 077	5 184	5 312	5 399	5 470	5 535	5 607
Sri Lanka	DF	20 039	20 246	20 476	20 675	20 869	...	...	...	...	...
	DJ	...	...	...	...	...	20 424	20 579	*20 771	*20 966	*21 203
State of Palestine - État de Palestine	DF	3 719	3 826	3 935	4 048	4 169	4 293	4 421	4 550	4 682	4 817
Syrian Arab Republic - République arabe syrienne[87]	DF	19 172	19 644	20 125	20 619	21 124	...	...	...	...	...
Tajikistan - Tadjikistan	DF	7 140	7 295	7 334	7 519	7 714	7 897	8 074	8 257	8 452	*8 641

Continent and country or area / Continent et pays ou zone	Code[a]	Population estimates (in thousands) - Estimations (en milliers)									
		2007	2008	2009	2010	2011	2012	2013	2014	2015	2016
ASIA - ASIE											
Thailand - Thaïlande	DJ	63 038	63 390	63 525	63 878	64 076	64 457	64 786	65 125	65 729	65 932
Timor-Leste[2]	DF	1 048	1 081	1 115	...	...	...	1 180	1 212	...	...
Turkey - Turquie[88]	DJ	70 586	71 517	72 561	73 723	74 724	75 627	76 668	77 696	78 741	...
United Arab Emirates - Émirats arabes unis[89]	DF	6 219[26]	8 074[26]	8 200[26]	8 264	...	...	...	...	...	9 121[26]
Uzbekistan - Ouzbékistan[90]	DJ	26 868	27 303	27 767	28 562	29 339	29 774	30 243	30 758	31 299	...
Viet Nam[91]	DF	84 218	85 119	86 025	86 947	87 860	88 809	89 760	90 729	91 710	*92 695
Yemen - Yémen	DF	21 539[26]	22 198[26]	...	...	...	...	...	...	...	...
	DJ	...	...	22 492[2]	23 154[2]	23 833[2]	24 527[2]	25 235[2]	25 956[2]	...	...
EUROPE											
Åland Islands - Îles d'Åland[42]	DJ	27	27	28	28	28	28	29	29	29	29
Albania - Albanie	DF	2 970	2 947	2 928	2 913	2 905	2 900	2 897	2 894	2 889	2 886[15]
Andorra - Andorre[42]	DJ	82	84	85	70[92]	70[15]	70[15]	70	70	71	72
Austria - Autriche	DJ	8 295	8 322	8 341	8 361	8 389	8 426	8 477	8 544	8 629	8 690[15]
Belarus - Bélarus	DJ	9 561	9 528	9 507	9 491	9 473	9 464	9 466	9 475	9 490	9 498[15]
Belgium - Belgique	DJ	10 623	10 710	10 796	10 896	11 044	11 128	11 183	11 231	11 285[66]	11 311[15]
Bosnia and Herzegovina - Bosnie-Herzégovine	DF	3 843	3 842	3 843	3 843	3 841	*3 837	3 833	*3 831[15]	3 825[15]	*3 513
Bulgaria - Bulgarie	DJ	7 660	7 623	7 585	7 534	7 348	7 306	7 264	7 224	7 178	7 154[15]
Croatia - Croatie	DJ	4 310	4 310	4 305	4 295	4 281	4 268	4 256	4 238	4 204	4 191[15]
Czechia - Tchéquie	DJ	10 299	10 385	10 444	10 474	10 496	10 511	10 511	10 525	10 543	10 554[15]
Denmark - Danemark[93]	DJ	5 457	5 489	5 519	5 545	5 567	5 587	5 609	5 640	5 678	5 724
Estonia - Estonie	DJ	1 341	1 337	1 335	1 331	1 327	1 323	1 318	1 315	1 315	1 316[15]
Faeroe Islands - Îles Féroé	DJ	48	49	49	49	49	48	48	48	49	50
Finland - Finlande[94]	DJ	5 262	5 286	5 311	5 335	5 360	5 386	5 410	5 433	5 451	5 507
France[95]	DJ	61 965	62 300	62 615	62 918	63 223	63 537	63 863	64 028[15]	*64 474	*64 732
Germany - Allemagne	DJ	82 263	82 120	81 875	81 757	80 275[4]	80 426[4]	80 646[4]	80 983[4]	81 687[4]	82 176[96]
Gibraltar[97]	DF	30	30	31	31	32	33	33	33	34	...
Greece - Grèce	DF	11 048	11 078	11 107	11 121	11 105	11 045	10 965	10 892	10 821	10 784[15]
Guernsey - Guernesey[98]	DF	61	62	62	62	63	63	63	62	62	63
Holy See - Saint-Siège[99]	DF	...	...	...	0[100]	...	0[101]	...	...	...	...
Hungary - Hongrie	DJ	10 056	10 038	10 023	10 000	9 972	9 920	9 893	9 866[102]	9 843[102]	9 830[103]
Iceland - Islande[104]	DJ	311	319	319	318	319	321	324	327	331	333[15]
Ireland - Irlande	DF	4 357	4 426	4 459	4 560	4 577	4 587	4 598[102]	4 606[103]	...	4 725[103]
	DJ	...	...	...	...	...	...	...	...	4 635[105]	...
Isle of Man - Île de Man[106]	DJ	81	82	82	83	...	85	86	86	87	86
Italy - Italie	DJ	58 438	58 827	59 095	59 277	59 379	59 540	60 234	60 789	60 796[15]	60 666[15]
Jersey	DJ	94	95	96	97	98	99	...	101	103	104
Latvia - Lettonie	DJ	2 200	2 177	2 142	2 098	2 060	2 034	2 013	1 994	1 978	1 969[15]
Liechtenstein	DJ	35	35	36	36	36	37	37	37	37	38[15]
Lithuania - Lituanie	DJ	3 231	3 198	3 163	3 097	3 028	2 988	2 958	2 932[102]	2 905[102]	2 889[103]
Luxembourg	DJ	480	489	498	507	518	531	543	556	570	576[15]
Malta - Malte[107]	DJ	407	409	413	415	416	420	423	427	432	434[15]
Monaco[108]	DJ	...	...	35	36	36	36	37	37[15]	38[15]	38[15]
Montenegro - Monténégro	DJ	626	629	632	617	621	621	622	622[102]	622[102]	622[103]
Netherlands - Pays-Bas	DJ	16 382	16 446	16 530	16 615	16 693	16 755	16 804	16 865	16 940	16 979[15]
Norway - Norvège[102]	DJ	4 709	4 768	4 829	4 889	4 953	5 019	5 080	5 137	5 189	5 237
Poland - Pologne	DJ	38 116[109]	38 116[109]	38 153[109]	38 042[102]	38 051[102]	38 059[102]	38 032[102]	38 006[102]	37 982[102]	37 967[103]
Portugal	DJ	10 543	10 558	10 568	10 573	10 558	10 515	10 457	10 401	10 358	10 341[15]
Republic of Moldova - République de Moldova[110]	DJ	3 577	3 570	3 566	3 562	3 560	3 560	3 559	3 557	3 555[15]	3 553[15]
Romania - Roumanie[102]	DJ	20 883	20 538	20 367	20 247	20 148	20 060	19 989	19 913	19 820	19 760[15]
Russian Federation - Fédération de Russie	DJ	142 805	142 742	142 785	142 849	142 961	143 202	*143 507	...	...	...
San Marino - Saint-Marin[42]	DF	31	32	33	33	33	34	33	34	34[15]	34[15]
Serbia - Serbie[111]	DJ	7 382	7 350	7 321	7 291	7 237[19]	7 201[19]	7 167[19]	7 132[19]	7 095[19]	7 058[19]
Slovakia - Slovaquie	DJ	5 375	5 379	5 386	5 391	5 398	5 408	5 413	5 419	5 424	5 431
Slovenia - Slovénie	DJ	2 019	2 023	2 042	2 049	2 052	2 056	2 059	2 062	2 063	2 064[15]
Spain - Espagne	DJ	45 236	45 983	46 368	46 562	46 736	46 766	46 593	46 481[104]	46 448[104]	46 446[112]
Svalbard and Jan Mayen Islands - Îles Svalbard et Jan Mayen[113]	DF	...	2	...	...	...	...	...	...	...	...
Sweden - Suède[42]	DJ	9 148	9 220	9 299	9 378	9 449	9 519	9 600[104]	9 696[104]	9 799[104]	9 851[112]

5. Estimates of mid-year population: 2007 - 2016
Estimations de la population au milieu de l'année : 2007 - 2016 (continued - suite)

Continent and country or area / Continent et pays ou zone	Code[a]	Population estimates (in thousands) - Estimations (en milliers)									
		2007	2008	2009	2010	2011	2012	2013	2014	2015	2016
EUROPE											
Switzerland - Suisse	DJ	7 551	7 648	7 744	7 825	7 912	7 997	8 089	8 189[114]	8 282[114]	8 327[115]
TFYR of Macedonia - L'ex-R. y. de Macédoine	DF	2 044	2 047	2 051	2 055	2 059	2 061	2 064	2 067	2 070	2 072
Ukraine	DF	46 509	46 258	46 053	45 871	45 706	45 593	45 553[15]	*42 988[116]	42 760[117]	42 591[117]
United Kingdom of Great Britain and Northern Ireland - Royaume-Uni de Grande-Bretagne et d'Irlande du Nord[118]	DJ	61 319	61 824	62 260	62 759	63 285	63 705	64 102[102]	64 592[102]	65 129[102]	65 383[103]
OCEANIA - OCÉANIE											
American Samoa - Samoas américaines[47]	DJ	68	69	70	67	64	64	63	62	61	...
Australia - Australie	DJ	20 828[39]	21 249[39]	21 692[39]	22 032[39]	22 340[39]	22 728[19]	23 117[19]	23 461[19]	23 778[19]	24 129[19]
Cook Islands - Îles Cook[119]	DF	21	22	23	24	19	20	*19	*19	*19	...
Fiji - Fidji	DF	834	841	843	857	...	858[26]	859[120]	...	867[120]	...
French Polynesia - Polynésie française	DF	259	261	263	265	267	268	270	271	272	...
Guam[47]	DJ	159	159	159	...	160	160	160	161	162	163
Kiribati[120]	DF	...	...	...	...	...	...	109	...	...	...
Marshall Islands - Îles Marshall	DF	53[121]	53[121]	54[121]	54[121]	...	...	54[120]	...	...	...
Micronesia (Federated States of) - Micronésie (États fédérés de)[2]	DJ	108	108	108	108	108	107	107	106	106	...
Nauru[2]	DF	...	...	...	...	...	...	...	...	11	...
New Caledonia - Nouvelle-Calédonie	DF	239	243	246	250	254	259	264	268	272	275[15]
New Zealand - Nouvelle-Zélande[122]	DJ	4 224	4 260	4 303	4 351	4 384	4 408	4 442	4 510	4 596	4 693
Niue - Nioué	DJ	2	...	2	1	1	...	...	...	...	...
Northern Mariana Islands - Îles Mariannes septentrionales	DF	59	55	51	48	46	51[50]	51[50]	51[50]	...	...
Palau - Palaos	DF	20	20	21	21	21	21			...	...
Papua New Guinea - Papouasie-Nouvelle-Guinée[123]	DF	...	...	...	...	...	...	...	...	...	8 151
Pitcairn[124]	DF	0	0	...	...	...	...	...	...	...	...
Samoa	DF	182	182	183	184	185	189	191	192	193	195
Solomon Islands - Îles Salomon[2]	DF	495	507	518	555	570	584	598	612	625	639
Tokelau - Tokélaou[125]	DF	...	...	...	...	...	...	1	...	...	...
Tonga[126]	DF	103	104	...	...	...	...	...	...	...	...
Tuvalu	DF	11	...	...	...	...	11	...	11	...	10[123]
Vanuatu	DF	...	...	...	239	245	245	265	...	...	...
Wallis and Futuna Islands - Îles Wallis et Futuna[123]	DF	...	...	...	...	...	...	...	...	...	12

FOOTNOTES - NOTES

Italics: estimates which are less reliable. - Italiques : estimations moins sûres.

* Provisional. - Données provisoires.

[a] 'Code' indicates source of data, as follows: - Le 'Code' indique la source des données, comme suit :
DF: Population de facto - Population de fait
DJ : Population de jure - Population de droit

[1] Unrevised data that do not take into account the results of the 2014 population census. - Ces données n'ont pas été révisées et elles ne prennent pas en compte les résultats du recensement de la population de 2014.
[2] Data refer to national projections. - Les données se réfèrent aux projections nationales.
[3] Projections based on the 2013 Population Census. - Projections fondées sur le recensement de la population de 2013.
[4] Data based on the 2011 Census. - Données fondées sur le recensement de 2011.
[5] Unrevised data. - Les données n'ont pas été révisées.
[6] Estimates based on the 2014 Population Census. - Estimations fondées sur le recensement de la population de 2014.
[7] Projections based on the 2014 Population Census. - Projections fondées sur le recensement de la population de 2014.
[8] Data are calculated from the results of the Population and Housing Census of 2009. - Les données sont calculées à partir des résultats du recensement de la population et de l'habitat de 2009.
[9] Data refer to projections based on the 1983 Population Census. - Les données se réfèrent aux projections basées sur le recensement de la population de 1983.
[10] Projections based on the 1994 Population Census. - Projections fondées sur le recensement de la population de 1994.
[11] Estimates considering also the results of the 2007 Population Census. - Estimations en prennant en considération les résultats du recensement de la population de 2007.

¹² Data based on the 2010 Population Census. - Les données sont fondées sur le recensement de la population de 2010.

¹³ Post-censal estimates based on the 2009 Population Census. - Les estimations post-censitaire fondées sur le recensement de la population de 2009.

¹⁴ Data refer to Libyan nationals only. - Les données se raportent aux nationaux libyens seulement.

¹⁵ Data refer to 1 January. - Données se raportent au 1 janvier.

¹⁶ Projections considering also the results of the 2009 Population Census results. - Projections en prennant en considération les résultats du recensement de la population de 2009.

¹⁷ Excludes the islands of St. Brandon and Agalega. - Non compris les îles St. Brandon et Agalega.

¹⁸ Based on the results of the 2000 Population Census. - Basé sur les résultats du recencement de la population de 2000.

¹⁹ Based on the results of the 2011 Population Census. - Basé sur les résultats du recencement de la population de 2011.

²⁰ Based on the results of the 2004 Population Census. - D'après des résultats du recencement de la population de 2004.

²¹ Projections based on the results of national survey on population and health conducted between 2010 and 2011, and especially population and housing census 2014. - Des projections de la population fondées sur les résultats de l'enquête nationale de la population et de la santé réalisée entre 2010 et 2011 et, surtout, du recensement général de la population et de l'habitat de 2014.

²² Data refer to projections based on the 2011 Population Census. - Les données se réfèrent aux projections basées sur le recensement de la population de 2011.

²³ Projections based on the 2012 Population and Housing Census. - Projections fondées sur le recensement 2012 de la population et des logements.

²⁴ Data are projections based on the 2006 Population Census. - Projections fondées sur le recensement de la population de 2006.

²⁵ Data are projections based on the 2008 Population and Housing Census. - Projection basée sur le recensement 2008 de la population et des logements.

²⁶ Data refer to 31 December. - Données se raportent au 31 décembre.

²⁷ Data refer to 31 December. Based on the results of a population count. The population figures are 264, 263 and 262 persons for 2007, 2008 and 2009 respectively. - Données se raportent au 31 décembre. D'après les résultats d'un comptage de la population. La population est respectivement égale à 264, 263 et 262 personnes pour les années 2007, 2008 et 2009.

²⁸ Projections based on the 2002 Population Census. - Projections fondées sur le recensement de la population de 2002.

²⁹ Projections based on the 2012 Population Census. - Projections fondées sur le recensement de la population de 2012.

³⁰ Data refer to projections based on the 2000 Population Census. - Les données se réfèrent aux projections basées sur le recensement de la population de 2000.

³¹ Final intercensal estimates. - Estimations inter-censitaires definitives.

³² Final postcensal estimates. - Estimations postcensitaires definitives.

³³ Updated postcensal estimates. - Estimations post censitaires mises à jour.

³⁴ Preliminary postcensal estimates. - Estimations post censitaires préliminaires.

³⁵ The source of data is the national household survey. - La source des données est l'enquête nationale des ménages.

³⁶ Based on the national household surveys 2010-2014 and the 2011 population census. - D'après les données de l'enquête nationale des ménages 2010-2014 et les résultats du recensement de la population de 2011.

³⁷ Based on the national household survey of 2015. - Basée sur l' enquête nationale auprès des ménages de 2015.

³⁸ Based on the national household survey of 2016. - D'après l'enquête nationale auprès des ménages de 2016.

³⁹ Intercensal estimates. - Estimations inter-censitaires.

⁴⁰ Postcensal estimates. - Estimations post censitaires.

⁴¹ Estimates or projections based on the 2007 Population Census. - Estimations ou projections fondées sur le recensement de la population de 2007.

⁴² Population statistics are compiled from registers. - Les statistiques de la population sont compilées à partir des registres.

⁴³ Data refer to 1 January. Excluding data for Saint Barthélémy and Saint Martin. - Données se raportent au 1 janvier. Non compris les données pour Saint Barthélémy et Saint Martin.

⁴⁴ Projections produced by l'Institut Haïtien de Statistique et d'Informatique (IHSI) and the Latin American and Caribbean Demographic Centre (CELADE) - Population Division of ECLAC. - Les données sont projections produits par l'Institut Haïtien de Statistique et d'Informatique (IHSI) et le centre démographique de l'Amérique latine et les Caraïbes - Division de la population de la CEPALC.

⁴⁵ Data refer to projections based on the 2001 Population Census. - Les données se réfèrent aux projections basées sur le recensement de la population de 2001.

⁴⁶ Estimates based on the 2010 Population Census. - Estimations basées sur le recensement de la population de 2010.

⁴⁷ Including armed forces stationed in the area. - Y compris les militaires en garnison sur le territoire.

⁴⁸ Based on the results of the 2010 Population Census. - D'après le résultats du recensement de la population de 2010.

⁴⁹ Excluding U.S. Armed Forces overseas and civilian U.S. citizens whose usual place of residence is outside the United States. - Non compris les militaires américains à l'étranger et les civils américains dont le lieu de résidence habituel est en dehors des États-Unis.

⁵⁰ Source: U.S. National Center for Health Statistics, National Vital Statistics Reports (NVSR). - Source : US National Center for Health Statistics, National Vital Statistics Reports (NVSR).

⁵¹ Projections based on the 2010 Population and Housing Census. - Projections fondées sur le recensement 2010 de la population et des logements.

⁵² Data include persons in remote areas, military personnel outside the country, merchant seamen at sea, civilian seasonal workers outside the country, and other civilians outside the country, and exclude nomads, foreign military, civilian aliens temporarily in the country, transients on ships and Indian jungle population. Data refer to national projections. - Y compris les personnes vivant dans des régions éloignées, le personel militaire en dehors du pays, les marins marchands, les ouvriers saisonniers en dehors du pays, et autres civils en dehors du pays, et non compris les nomades, les militaires étrangers, les étrangers civils temporairement dans le pays, les transiteurs sur des bateaux et les Indiens de la jungle. Les données se réfèrent aux projections nationales.

⁵³ Data are revised projections taking into consideration also the results of the 2005 census. - Les données sont des projections révisées tenant compte également des résultats du recensement de 2005.

⁵⁴ Excludes nomadic Indian tribes. Data based on the 2010 Population Census. - Non compris les tribus d'Indiens nomades. Les données sont fondées sur le recensement de la population de 2010.

⁵⁵ Estimates or projections considering also the results of the 2012 Population Census. - Estimations ou projections en prennant en considération les résultats du recensement de la population de 2012.

⁵⁶ Data refer to 30 June. Estimates or projections based on the 2007 Population Census. - Données se raportent au 30 juin. Estimations ou projections fondées sur le recensement de la population de 2007.

⁵⁷ Data refer to the settled population based on the 1979 Population Census and the latest household prelisting. The refugees of Afghanistan in Iran, Pakistan, and an estimated 1.5 million nomads, are not included. - Les données se rapportent à la population stationnaire sur la base du recensement de 1979 et du recensement préliminaire des logements le plus récent. Sont exclus les réfugiés d'Afghanistan en Iran et au Pakistan et les nomades estimés à 1,5 million.

⁵⁸ Data refer to projected figures based on the Population and Housing Census 2005 (district projection). - Les données se réfèrent aux projections basées sur le recensement de la population et de l'habitat de 2005 (projections locales).

⁵⁹ Excluding foreign diplomatic personnel and their dependants. - Non compris le personnel diplomatique étranger et les membres de leur famille les accompagnant.

⁶⁰ Based on the results of 1998 census. - A partir des résultats de recensement de l'année 1998.

⁶¹ Data based on the 2008 Population Census. - Données fondées sur le recensement de population de 2008.

⁶² For statistical purposes, the data for China do not include those for the Hong Kong Special Administrative Region (Hong Kong SAR), Macao Special Administrative Region (Macao SAR) and Taiwan province of China. - Pour la présentation des statistiques, les données pour la Chine ne comprennent pas la Région Administrative Spéciale de Hong Kong (Hong Kong RAS), la Région Administrative Spéciale de Macao (Macao RAS) et Taïwan province de Chine.

⁶³ Data have been estimated on the basis of the annual National Sample Survey on Population Changes. - Les données ont été estimées sur la base de l'enquête annuelle "National Sample Survey on Population Changes".

⁶⁴ Data have been adjusted on the basis of the Population Census of 2010. - Les données ont été ajustées à partir des résultats du recensement de la population de 2010.

⁶⁵ Data refer to government controlled areas. - Les données se rapportent aux zones contrôlées par le Gouvernement.

⁶⁶ Data refer to annual average population. - Les données correspondent à la population annuelle moyenne.

⁶⁷ Based on the results of the 2014 Population Census. - D'après les résultats du recensement de la population de 2014.

⁶⁸ Includes data for the Indian-held part of Jammu and Kashmir, the final status of which has not yet been determined. Data refer to projections based on the 2001 Population Census. - Y compris les données pour la partie du Jammu et du

Cachemire occupée par l'Inde dont le statut définitif n'a pas encore été déterminé. Les données se réfèrent aux projections basées sur le recensement de la population de 2001.

[69] Data are based on the publication: "Indonesia Population Projection 2005-2015" - Les données sont basées sur la publication : << Indonesia Population Projection 2005-2015 >>

[70] Data are based on the publication: "Indonesia Population Projection 2010-2035" - Les données sont basées sur la publication : << Indonesia Population Projection 2010-2035 >>

[71] Data refer to the Iranian Year which begins on 21 March and ends on 20 March of the following year. - Les données concernent l'année iranienne, qui commence le 21 mars et se termine le 20 mars de l'année suivante.

[72] Includes data for East Jerusalem and Israeli residents in certain other territories under occupation by Israeli military forces since June 1967. - Y compris les données pour Jérusalem-Est et les résidents israéliens dans certains autres territoires occupés depuis 1967 par les forces armées israéliennes.

[73] Excluding diplomatic personnel outside the country and foreign military and civilian personnel and their dependants stationed in the area. - Non compris le personnel diplomatique hors du pays ni les militaires et agents civils étrangers en poste sur le territoire et les membres de leur famille les accompagnant.

[74] Estimates based on the complete counts of the 2015 Population Census - Estimations basées sur le dénombrement complet du recensement de la population de 2015.

[75] Because of rounding, totals are not in all cases the sum of the respective components. Estimates based on the complete counts of the 2015 Population Census - Les chiffres étant arrondis, les totaux ne correspondent pas toujours rigoureusement à la somme des composants respectifs. Estimations basées sur le dénombrement complet du recensement de la population de 2015.

[76] Data refer to 31 December. Excluding data for Jordanian territory under occupation since June 1967 by Israeli military forces. - Données se raportent au 31 décembre. Non compris les données pour le territoire jordanien occupé depuis juin 1967 par les forces armées israéliennes.

[77] Estimates based on the results of 2015 population census. - Estimations fondées sur les résultats du recensement de la population de 2015.

[78] Intercensal Mid-Year Population Estimates based on the adjusted Population and Housing Census of 2000 and 2010. - Les estimations inter-censitaires au millieu de l'année sont fondée sur les résultats ajustées des recensements de la population et de l'habitat de 2000 et 2010.

[79] Estimates based on the adjusted results of the Population and Housing Census of 2010. - Les estimations sont fondée sur les résultats ajustées du recensement de la population et de l'habitat de 2010.

[80] Data refer to resident Maldivian population. - Les données concernent la population maldivienne résidente.

[81] Data refer to 1 October. - Données se raportent au 1 octobre.

[82] Data refer to registered population data from Royal Oman Police. - Les données portent sur la population enregistrée par la police royale de l'Oman.

[83] Excluding data for the Pakistan-held part of Jammu and Kashmir, the final status of which has not yet been determined. - Non compris les données concernant la partie du Jammu et Cachemire occupée par le Pakistan dont le statut définitif n'a pas été déterminé.

[84] Based on the results of the Pakistan Demographic Survey (PDS 2007). - D'après les résultats de l'enquête démographique effectuée par le Pakistan en 2007.

[85] Data based on the preliminary results of the 2010 Population and Housing Census. - D'après les résultats préliminaires du recensement de la population et des logements de 2010.

[86] Data refer to 30 June. Data refer to total population, which comprises Singapore residents and non-residents. Data exclude residents who have been away from Singapore for a continuous period of 12 months or longer as at the reference date. - Données se raportent au 30 juin. Les données se rapportent à la population totale composé des résidents de Singapour et les non résidents. Non compris les résidents hors de Singapour pour une période ininterrompue de 12 mois ou plus avant de la date de référence.

[87] Including Palestinian refugees. - Y compris les réfugiés de Palestine.

[88] Data refer to 31 December. Data based on Address Based Population Registration System. - Données se raportent au 31 décembre. Les données sont basées sur le registre national de la population basé sur l'adresse.

[89] Data include non-national population. - Les données comprennent les non-nationaux.

[90] Data refer to resident population. - Les données concernent la population résidente.

[91] Data are adjusted according to the results of the 2009 census and 2014 intercensus. - Les données ont été ajustées à partir des résultats du recensement de la population de 2009 et des données intercensitaires de 2014.

[92] Data refer to 1 January. Decrease in population due to revision in administrative registers. - Données se raportent au 1 janvier. Diminution de la population due à la révision des registres administratifs.

[93] Excluding Faeroe Islands and Greenland shown separately, if available. Population statistics are compiled from registers. - Non compris les Iles Féroé et le Groenland, qui font l'objet de rubriques distinctes, si disponible. Les statistiques de la population sont compilées à partir des registres.

[94] Population statistics are compiled from registers. Excluding Åland Islands. - Les statistiques de la population sont compilées à partir des registres. Non compris les Îles d'Åland.

[95] Excluding diplomatic personnel outside the country and including members of alien armed forces not living in military camps and foreign diplomatic personnel not living in embassies or consulates. - Non compris le personnel diplomatique hors du pays et y compris les militaires étrangers ne vivant pas dans des camps militaires et le personnel diplomatique étranger ne vivant pas dans les ambassades ou les consulats.

[96] Data refer to 1 January. Data based on the 2011 Census. - Données se raportent au 1 janvier. Données fondées sur le recensement de 2011.

[97] Data refer to 31 December. Excluding military personnel, visitors and transients. - Données se raportent au 31 décembre. Non compris les militaires, ni les visiteurs et transients.

[98] Data refer to 31 March. - Données se raportent au 31 mars.

[99] Data refer to the Vatican City State. - Les données se rapportent à l'Etat de la Cité du Vatican.

[100] Data refer to 26 February. The population figure is 460 persons. - Données se raportent au 26 février. La population est égale à 460 personnes.

[101] Data refer to 21 June. The population figure is 451 persons. - Données se raportent au 21 juin. La population est égale à 451 personnes.

[102] Data refer to usually resident population. - Les données concernent la population habituellement résidente.

[103] Data refer to 1 January. Data refer to usually resident population. - Données se raportent au 1 janvier. Les données concernent la population habituellement résidente.

[104] Data refer to registered resident population. - Les données concernent la population enregistrée résidente.

[105] Data refer to 15 April. Data refer to usually resident population. - Données se raportent au 15 avril. Les données concernent la population habituellement résidente.

[106] Data refer to 30 April. - Données se raportent au 30 avril.

[107] Including civilian nationals temporarily outside the country. - Y compris les civils nationaux temporairement hors du pays.

[108] Data refer to resident population only. - Pour la population résidante seulement.

[109] Excluding civilian aliens within the country, but including civilian nationals temporarily outside the country. - Non compris les civils étrangers dans le pays, mais y compris les civils nationaux temporairement hors du pays.

[110] Excluding Transnistria and the municipality of Bender. - Les données ne tiennent pas compte de l'information sur la Transnistria et la municipalité de Bender.

[111] Excludes data for Kosovo and Metohia. - Sans les données pour le Kosovo et Metohie.

[112] Data refer to 1 January. Data refer to registered resident population. - Données se raportent au 1 janvier. Les données concernent la population enregistrée résidente.

[113] Data refer to 1 January. Data refer to Svalbard only. - Données se raportent au 1 janvier. Données ne concernant que le Svalbard.

[114] Data refer to legal resident population. - Les données concernent la population légalement résidente.

[115] Data refer to 1 January. Data refer to legal resident population. - Données se raportent au 1 janvier. Les données concernent la population légalement résidente.

[116] The Government of Ukraine has informed the United Nations that it is not in a position to provide statistical data concerning the Autonomous Republic of Crimea and the city of Sevastopol. - Le gouvernement Ukrainien a informé l'ONU qu'il n'est pas en mesure de fournir des données statistiques concernant la République autonome de Crimée et la ville de Sébastopol.

[117] Data refer to 1 January. The Government of Ukraine has informed the United Nations that it is not in a position to provide statistical data concerning the Autonomous Republic of Crimea and the city of Sevastopol. - Données se raportent au 1 janvier. Le gouvernement Ukrainien a informé l'ONU qu'il n'est pas en mesure de fournir des données statistiques concernant la République autonome de Crimée et la ville de Sébastopol.

[118] Excluding Channel Islands (Guernsey and Jersey) and Isle of Man, shown separately, if available. - Non compris les îles Anglo-Normandes (Guernesey et Jersey) et l'île de Man, qui font l'objet de rubriques distinctes, si disponible.

[119] Excluding Niue, shown separately, which is part of Cook Islands, but because of remoteness is administered separately. - Non compris Nioué, qui fait l'objet d'une rubrique distincte et qui fait partie des îles Cook, mais qui, en raison de son éloignement, est administrée séparément.

[120] Projections are prepared by the Secretariat of the Pacific Community based on the last population and housing census. - Les projections sont preparées par le Secrétariat de la Communauté du Pacifique à partir des résultats du dernier recensement de la population et de l'habitat.

[121] Projections are prepared by the Secretariat of the Pacific Community based on the 1999 census of population and housing. - Les projections sont preparées par le Secrétariat de la Communauté du Pacifique à partir des résultats du recensement de la population et de l'habitat de 1999.

[122] Because of rounding, totals are not in all cases the sum of the respective components. - Les chiffres étant arrondis, les totaux ne correspondent pas toujours rigoureusement à la somme des composants respectifs.

[123] Estimates are prepared by the Secretariat of the Pacific Community based on the last population and housing census. - Les estimations sont preparées par le Secrétariat de la Communauté du Pacifique à partir des résultats du dernier recensement de la population et de l'habitat.

[124] Data refer to 31 December. The population figures are 64 and 58 persons for 2007 and 2008 respectively. - Données se raportent au 31 décembre. La population est respectivement égale à 64 et 58 personnes pour les années 2007 et 2008.

[125] Data refer to 1 December. - Données se raportent au 1 décembre.

[126] Data refer to national projections. Based on the results of the 1996 population census. - Les données se réfèrent aux projections nationales. À partir des résultats du recensement de la population de 1996.

Table 6 - *Demographic Yearbook 2016*

Table 6 presents total population by sex for as many years as possible between 2007 and 2016, as well as urban population as available.

Description of variables: Data are from nation-wide population censuses or are estimates, some of which are based on sample surveys of population carried out among all segments of the population. This characteristic of the data is indicated in the column "Code". The codes used are explained at the end of the table.

Urban is defined according to the national census definition. The definitions for each country, as available, are provided as part of this technical note.

Percentage computation: Urban percentages are the number of persons residing in an area defined as "urban" per 100 total population. They are calculated by the Statistics Division of the United Nations Department of Economic and Social Affairs. In very few cases the data for total population have been revised whereas the data for the urban and rural population have not been revised. These data are footnoted accordingly. In these cases, particular caution should be used in interpreting the figures for the percentages urban.

Reliability of data: Estimates that are believed to be less reliable are set in *italics* rather than in roman type. Classification in terms of reliability is based on the method of construction of the total population estimate discussed in the technical notes for table 3.

Limitations: Statistics on urban population by sex are subject to the same qualifications as have been set forth for population statistics in general, as discussed in section 3 of the Technical Notes.

The basic limitations imposed by variations in the definition of the total population and in the degree of under-enumeration are perhaps more important in relation to urban/rural than to any other distributions. The classification by urban and rural is affected by variations in defining usual residence for purposes of sub-national tabulations. Likewise, the geographical differentials in the degree of under-enumeration in censuses affect the comparability of these categories throughout the table. The distinction between *de facto* and *de jure* population is also very important with respect to urban/rural distributions. The difference between the *de facto* and the *de jure* population is discussed at length in section 3.1.1 of the Technical Notes.

A most important and specific limitation, however, lies in the national differences in the definition of urban. Because the distinction between urban and rural areas is made in so many different ways, the definitions have been included at the end of this table. The definitions are necessarily brief and, where the classification of urban involves administrative civil divisions, they are often given in the terminology of the particular country or area. As a result of variations in terminology, it may appear that differences between countries or areas are greater than they actually are. On the other hand, similar or identical terms (for example, town, village, district) as used in different countries or areas may have quite different meanings.

The definition of urban/rural areas is based on both qualitative and quantitative criteria that may include any combination of the following: size of population, population density, distance between built-up areas, predominant type of economic activity, conformity to legal or administrative status and urban characteristics such as specific services and facilities[1].   Although statistics classified by urban/rural areas are widely available, no international standard definition appears to be possible at this time since the meaning differs from one country or area to another. The urban/rural classification of population used here is reported according to the national definition.

Earlier data: Urban and total population by sex have been shown in previous issues of the Demographic Yearbook. For information on specific years covered, readers should consult the Historical Index.

DEFINITION OF "URBAN"

AFRICA

Algeria: The urban/rural delimitation is performed after the census operation based on the classification of built-up areas. Groupings of 100 or more constructions, distant less than 200 metres from one another are considered urban.
Botswana: Agglomeration of 5 000 or more inhabitants where 75 per cent of the economic activity is non-agricultural.

Burundi: Commune of Bujumbura.

Burkina Faso: All administrative centres of provinces (total of 45) plus 4 medium-sized towns are considered as urban areas.

Comoros: Every locality or administrative centre of an island, region or prefecture that has the following facilities: asphalted roads, electricity, a medical centre, telephone services, etc.

Egypt: Governorates of Cairo, Alexandria, Port Said, Ismailia, Suez, frontier governorates and capitals of other governorates, as well as district capitals (Markaz). The definition of urban areas for the 2006 Census is "shiakha", a part of a district.

Equatorial Guinea: District centres and localities with 300 dwellings and/or 1 500 inhabitants or more.

Ethiopia: Localities of 2 000 or more inhabitants.

Guinea: Administrative centres of prefectures and the capital city (Conakry).

Kenya: Areas having a population of 2 000 or more inhabitants that have transport systems, build-up areas, industrial/manufacturing structures and other developed structures.

Lesotho: All administrative headquarters and settlements of rapid growth.

Liberia: Localities of 2 000 or more inhabitants.

Malawi: All townships and town planning areas and all district centres.

Mauritius: The five Municipal Council Areas which are subdivided into twenty Municipal Wards defined according to proclaimed boundaries.

Namibia: Proclaimed urban areas for which cadastral data is available and other unplanned squatter areas.

Niger: Capital city, capitals of the departments and districts.

Rwanda: All administrative areas recognized as urban by the law. These are all administrative centres of provinces, and the cities of Kigali, Nyanza, Ruhango and Rwamagana.

Senegal: Agglomerations of 10 000 or more inhabitants.

South Africa: Places with some form of local authority.

Sudan: Localities of administrative and/or commercial importance or with population of 5 000 or more inhabitants.

Swaziland: A geographical area constituting of a city or town, characterized by higher population density and vast human features in comparison to areas surrounding it.

Tunisia: Population living in communes.

Uganda: Gazettes, cities, municipalities and towns.

United Republic of Tanzania: Areas legally recognized (gazetted) as urban and all areas recognized by local government authorities as urban.

Zambia: Localities of 5 000 or more inhabitants, the majority of whom all depend on non-agricultural activities.

AMERICA, NORTH

Bermuda: The country is considered 100 per cent urban.

Canada: Places of 1 000 or more inhabitants, having a population density of 400 or more per square kilometre.

Costa Rica: Administrative centres of cantons.

Cuba: Localities with 2 000 or more inhabitants; or localities with more than 1 000 inhabitants having half or more of economically active population engaged in non-agricultural activities.

Dominican Republic: Administrative centres of municipalities and municipal districts, some of which include suburban zones of rural character.

El Salvador: Administrative centres of municipalities.

Greenland: Localities of 200 or more inhabitants.

Guatemala: Municipality of Guatemala Department and officially recognized centres of other departments and municipalities.

Haiti: Administrative centres of communes.

Honduras: Localities of 2 000 or more inhabitants, having essentially urban characteristics.

Jamaica: Localities of 2 000 or more inhabitants, having urban characteristics.

Mexico: Localities of 2 500 or more inhabitants.

Nicaragua: Administrative centres of municipalities and localities of 1 000 or more inhabitants or with more than 150 dwellings, with streets, electric light, water service, school and health centre.

Panama: Localities of 1 500 or more inhabitants having essentially urban characteristics. Beginning 1970, localities of 1 500 or more inhabitants with such urban characteristics as streets, water supply systems, sewerage systems and electric light.

Puerto Rico: Agglomerations of 2 500 or more inhabitants, generally having population densities of 1 000 persons per square mile or more. Two types of urban areas: urbanized areas of 50 000 or more inhabitants and urban clusters of at least 2 500 and less than 50 000 inhabitants.

United States of America: Agglomerations of 2 500 or more inhabitants, generally having population densities of 1 000 persons per square mile or more. Two types of urban areas: urbanized areas of 50 000 or more inhabitants and urban clusters of at least 2 500 and less than 50 000 inhabitants.

United States Virgin Islands: Agglomerations of 2 500 or more inhabitants, generally having population densities of 1 000 persons per square mile or more. Two types of urban areas: urbanized areas of 50 000 or more inhabitants and urban clusters of at least 2 500 and less than 50 000 inhabitants. (As of the 2000 Census, no urbanized areas are identified in the United States Virgin Islands.)

AMERICA, SOUTH

Argentina: Populated centres with 2 000 or more inhabitants.
Bolivia: Localities of 2 000 or more inhabitants.
Brazil: Area inside the urban perimeter of a city or town, defined by municipal law.
Chile: Areas of concentrated housing units with more than 2 000 inhabitants, or between 1 001 and 2 000 inhabitants having 50 per cent or more of its economically active population doing secondary or tertiary activities. As an exception, centres of tourism and recreation with more than 250 housing units that do not satisfy the population requirement are nevertheless considered urban.
Colombia: Areas with a city hall, defined by an urban perimeter established by municipal agreements.
Ecuador: Capitals of provinces and cantons.
Falkland Islands (Malvinas): Town of Stanley.
Paraguay: Cities, towns and administrative centres of departments and districts.
Peru: Populated centres with 100 or more dwellings.
Suriname: The districts of Paramaribo and Wanica.
Uruguay: Cities, villages, towns and other populated areas as defined by the Law of Population Centers.
Venezuela (Bolivarian Republic of): Centres with a population of 2 500 or more inhabitants.

ASIA

Armenia: Cities and urban-type localities, officially designated as such, usually according to the criteria of number of inhabitants and predominance of agricultural, or number of non-agricultural workers and their families.
Azerbaijan: An administrative division which covers more than 15 000 population, engaging mainly in industrial and other economic and social activities and which include administrative and cultural centers.
Brunei Darussalam: Municipality areas of Bandar Seri Begawan, Kuala Belait, Seria, Pekan Tutong and Pekan Bangar; and heavily populated areas with urban characteristics.
Bahrain: Communes or villages of 2 500 or more inhabitants.
Cambodia: Areas at the commune level satisfying the following three conditions: (1) Population Density exceeding 200 per square Km, (2) Percentage of male employed in agriculture below 50 per cent, (3) Total population of the commune exceeds 2 000 inhabitants.
China: According to the Regulation on the Classification of Urban/Rural Residence for Statistical Purposes.
Cyprus: As determined by the Department of Town Planning and Housing of the Ministry of Interior.
Georgia: Cities and urban-type localities, officially designated as such, usually according to the criteria of number of inhabitants and predominance of agricultural, or number of non-agricultural workers and their families.
India: Towns (places with municipal corporation, municipal area committee, town committee, notified area committee or cantonment board); also, all places having 5 000 or more inhabitants, a density of not less than 1 000 persons per square mile or 400 per square kilometre, pronounced urban characteristics and at least three fourths of the adult male population employed in pursuits other than agriculture.
Indonesia: Area which satisfies certain criteria in terms of population density, percentage of agricultural households, access to urban facilities, existence of additional facilities, and percentage of built up area not for housing.
Iran (Islamic Republic of): Every district with a municipality.
Israel: Localities with 2 000 or more residents.
Japan: City (shi) having 50 000 or more inhabitants with 60 per cent or more of the houses located in the main built-up areas and 60 per cent or more of the population (including their dependants) engaged in manufacturing, trade or other urban type of business.
Jordan: Localities of 5 000 or more inhabitants.
Kazakhstan: Cities of Republican status (population centres of special national importance or with a population of usually more than one million), Oblast status (population centres that are major economic and cultural centres with developed industrial and social infrastructure and a population of more than 50,000, the country has 40 Oblast status cities), Raion status and settlements located under their administrative jurisdiction.
Kuwait: All localities in Kuwait are urban.
Kyrgyzstan: Cities and urban-type localities, officially designated as such, usually according to the criteria of number of inhabitants and predominance of agricultural, or number of non-agricultural workers and their families.
Lao People's Democratic Republic: Areas or villages that satisfy at least three of the following five conditions: located in metropolitan areas of district or province, there is access to road in dry and rainy seasons, about 70 per cent or 2/3 of the population has access to piped water, about 70 per cent or 2/3 of the population has access to public electricity, there is a market operating every day.

Malaysia: Gazetted areas with their adjoining built-up areas which have a combined population of 10 000 or more. Built-up areas are defined as areas contiguous to a gazetted area and have at least 60 per cent of their population (aged 15 years and over) engaged in non-agricultural activities. The definition of urban areas also takes into account the special development area which is not gazetted and can be indentified and separated from the gazetted area or built-up area of more than 5km and a population of at least 10 000 with 60 per cent of the population (aged 15 years and over) engaged in non-agricultural activities.

Maldives: Malé, the capital.

Mongolia: Capital (Ulaanbaatar), provincial centers and towns.

Myanmar: Areas classified by the General Administration Department as wards. Generally, these areas have an increased density of building structures, population and better infrastructure development.

Nepal: As declared by the government municipalities.

Pakistan: Places with municipal corporation, town committee or cantonment.

Philippines: Cities and municipalities and their central districts with a population density of at least 500 persons per square km. Urban areas are considered other districts regardless of population size that have streets, at least six establishments (commercial, manufacturing, recreational and/or personal services), and at least three public structures such as town hall, church, public park, school, hospital, library, etc.

Republic of Korea: For estimates: Localities with 50 000 or more inhabitants. For census: the figures are composed in the basis of the minor administrative divisions such as Dongs (mostly urban areas) and Eups or Myeons (rural areas).

Saudi Arabia: Localities with more than 5 000 inhabitants.

Singapore: Singapore is a city-state.

Sri Lanka: All areas administered by municipal and urban councils.

State of Palestine: Any locality where the population amounts to 10 000 persons or more. This applies to all governorates/districts regardless of their size, and to all localities whose populations vary from 4 000 to 9 999 persons provided they have at least four of the following elements: public electricity network, public water network, post office, health center with a full time physician and a school offering a general secondary education certificate.

Syrian Arab Republic: Cities, Mohafaza centres and Mantika centres, and communities with 20 000 or more inhabitants.

Tajikistan: Cities and urban-type localities, officially designated as such, usually according to the criteria of number of inhabitants and predominance of agricultural, or number of non-agricultural workers and their families.

Thailand: Municipal areas.

Turkey: Localities with 20 000 inhabitants or more.

Turkmenistan: Cities and urban-type localities, officially designated as such, usually according to the criteria of number of inhabitants and predominance of agricultural, or number of non-agricultural workers and their families.

Uzbekistan: Cities and urban-type localities, officially designated as such, usually according to the criteria of number of inhabitants and predominance of agricultural, or number of non-agricultural workers and their families.

Viet Nam: Urban areas include inside urban districts of cities, urban quarters and towns. All other local administrative units (communes) belong to rural areas.

EUROPE

Albania: Towns and other industrial centres of more than 400 inhabitants.

Austria: Urban areas are localities with 2 000 or more inhabitants. The delineation of localities goes back to 1991.

Belarus: Urban settlements are settlements authorized under the law as towns, urban-type settlements, workers settlements and health resort areas.

Belgium: All the communes which are not part of the list of rural communes are considered as urban communes. There are 33 communes which are considered rural: Alveringem, Amblève, Bertogne, Bièvre, Bullange, Burg-Reuland, Clavier, Erezée, Fauvillers, Frasnes-lez-Anvaing, Froidchapelle, Gedinne, Gouvy, Havelange, Herstappe, Heuvelland, Houffalize, Houyet, Langemark-Poelkapelle, Léglise, Lierneux, Lo-Reninge, Manhay, Momignies, Ravels, Sainte-Ode, Sint-Laureins, Sivry-Rance, Stoumont, Tenneville, Vaux-sur-Sûre, Vleteren and Vresse-sur-Semois.

Bulgaria: All towns and cities according to the Territorial and Administrative-Territorial Division of the country.

Czech Republic: Localities with 2 000 or more inhabitants.

Estonia: Urban settlements include cities, cities without municipal status and towns.

Finland: Urban communes including those municipalities in which at least 90 per cent of the population lives in urban settlements or in which the population of the largest urban settlement is at least 15 000.

France: Communes containing an agglomeration of more than 2 000 inhabitants living in contiguous houses or with not more than 200 metres between houses, also communes of which the major portion of the population is part of a multi-communal agglomeration of this nature.

Greece: Urban is considered every municipal or communal department of which the largest locality has 2 000 inhabitants and over.

Hungary: Localities recognized by the President of the Republic with the title of town, on the basis of specific (economic, commercial, institutional, cultural etc.) criteria.

Iceland: Localities of 200 or more inhabitants.

Ireland: Cities and towns including suburbs of 1 500 or more inhabitants.

Latvia: Cities and urban-type localities, officially designated as such, usually according to the criteria of number of inhabitants and predominance of agricultural, or number of non-agricultural workers and their families.

Lithuania: Urban population refers to persons who live in cities and towns, i.e., the population areas with closely built permanent dwellings and with the resident population of more than 3 000 of which 2/3 of employees work in industry, social infrastructure and business. In a number of towns the population may be less than 3 000 since these areas had already the status of "town" before the law was enforced (July 1994).

Malta: Grid cells of 1 square km with a density of at least 300 inhabitants per square km and a minimum population of 5 000, and densely populated areas (i.e. areas with a density superior to 500 inhabitants per square km).

Montenegro: According to the current law of territorial division of Montenegro, which conveys to each local community the obligation to decide which settlements are urban and which are rural.

Netherlands: Urban: Municipalities with a population of 2 000 and more inhabitants. Semi-urban: Municipalities with a population of less than 2 000 but with not more than 20 per cent of their economically active male population engaged in agriculture, and specific residential municipalities of commuters.

Norway: A hub of buildings inhabited by at least 200 people and where the distance between the buildings does not exceed 50 metres. The boundaries are dynamic and may be changed due to developments and population changes.

Poland: All areas which have town rights or the status of a town with provisions of separate laws.

Portugal: Localities with 2 000 or more inhabitants.

Republic of Moldova: Cities and urban-type localities, officially designated as such, usually according to the criteria of number of inhabitants and predominance of agricultural, or number of non-agricultural workers and their families.

Romania: Localities in which the majority of the resources are employed in non-agricultural activities with a diversified level of endowment, having a constant and significant socio-economic influence on the whole area.

Russian Federation: Cities and urban-type localities, officially designated as such, usually according to the criteria of number of inhabitants and predominance of agricultural, or number of non-agricultural   workers and their families.

Serbia: Municipalities, cities and the city of Belgrade.

Slovakia: Municipalities with the status of towns, according to the following criteria: 1) it is an economic, administrative, cultural or tourism centre; 2) provides services for other municipalities; 3) has urban character (at least partly); and 4) has 5 000 inhabitants or more.

Slovenia: Settlements of 3 000 or more inhabitants, settlements that serve as seats of municipalities with at least 1 400 inhabitants, and sub-urban areas that are being gradually integrated with an urban settlement of 5 000 or more inhabitants.

Spain: For the purposes of publishing comparable results at the European level, Eurostat proposes to consider as urban, intermediate and rural, areas formed by municipalities with respectively a population over 10 000 inhabitants, 2 001 to 10 000 inhabitants, and 2 000 or less inhabitants.

Switzerland: Agglomerations and isolated towns (towns not attached to a cluster with at least 10,000 inhabitants) are the urban space.

TFYR Macedonia: A city is a populated place that has more than 3000 inhabitants, has a developed industrial and social infrastructure, and over 51% of employees work outside the primary activities.

Ukraine: Cities and urban-type localities officially designated as such, usually according to the criteria of number of inhabitants and predominance of agricultural, or number of non-agricultural workers and their families.

United Kingdom of Great Britain and Northern Ireland: For England and Wales, the built-up areas of 10 000 or more inhabitants; for Scotland, the settlements of 3 000 or more inhabitants; and for Northern Ireland, the settlements of 5 000 or more inhabitants.

OCEANIA

Australia: Urban are considered all Significant Urban Areas, as defined by the 2011 Australian Statistical Geography Standard. Significant Urban Areas represent concentrations of urban development with population of 10,000 people or more.

American Samoa: Agglomerations of 2 500 or more inhabitants, generally having population densities of 1 000 persons per square mile or more. Two types of urban areas: urbanized areas of 50 000 or more inhabitants and urban clusters of at least 2 500 and less than 50 000 inhabitants. (As of Census 2000, no urbanized areas are identified in American Samoa.)

Cook Islands: Raratonga, the most populous island.

Guam: Agglomerations of 2 500 or more inhabitants, generally having population densities of 1 000 persons per square mile or more, referred to as "urban clusters".

New Caledonia: Nouméa and communes of Païta, Nouvel Dumbéa and Mont-Dore.

New Zealand: All cities, plus boroughs, town districts, townships and country towns with a population of 1 000 or more usual residents.

Northern Mariana Islands: Agglomerations of 2 500 or more inhabitants, generally having population densities of 1 000 persons per square mile or more. Two types of urban areas: urbanized areas of 50 000 or more inhabitants and urban clusters of at least 2 500 and less than 50 000 inhabitants.

Palau: States with 2 500 inhabitants or more (the only state which satisfies this condition is Koror state).
Tokelau: All of Tokelau's population is considered to be rural.
Tonga: Nuku'alofa.
Vanuatu: Luganville centre and Port Vila.

NOTES

[1] For further information, see *Social and Demographic Statistics: Classifications of Size and Type of Locality and Urban/Rural Areas.* E/CN.3/551, United Nations, New York, 1980.

Tableau 6 – *Annuaire démographique 2016*

Le tableau 6 présente des données sur la population totale selon le sexe pour le plus grand nombre possible d'années entre 2007 et 2016, ainsi que la population urbaine si disponible.

Description des variables : les données proviennent de recensements de la population ou sont des estimations fondées, dans certains cas, sur des enquêtes par sondage portant sur toute la population. Le code qui figure dans la colonne « Code » du tableau indique comment les données ont été obtenues. Les codes utilisés sont expliqués à la fin du tableau.

Le sens donné au terme « urbain » est conforme aux définitions utilisées dans les recensements nationaux. Les définitions pour chaque pays, si disponible, font partie de ce note technique.

Calcul des pourcentages : les pourcentages de la population urbaine sont calculés par la Division de statistique du Département des affaires économiques et sociales de l'Organisation des Nations Unies et représentent le nombre de personnes qui vivent dans des régions considérées comme urbaines pour 100 personnes de la population totale. Dans de très rares cas, les données pour la population totale ont été révisées mais les données pour la population urbaine et la population rurale ne l'ont pas été. Ces données sont indiquées en note. Dans ces cas, les proportions de population urbaine ou rurale sont à interpréter avec précaution.

Fiabilité des données : les estimations considérées comme moins sûres sont indiquées en italique plutôt qu'en caractères romains. Le classement du point de vue de la fiabilité est fondé sur la méthode utilisée pour établir l'estimation de la population totale qui figure au tableau 3 (voir les explications dans les notes techniques relatives à ce même tableau).

Insuffisance des données : les statistiques de la population urbaine selon le sexe appellent toutes les réserves qui ont été formulées à la section 3 des Notes techniques à propos des statistiques de la population en général.

Les limitations fondamentales imposées par les variations de la définition de la population totale et par les lacunes du recensement se font peut-être sentir davantage dans la répartition de la population en population urbaine et population rurale que dans sa répartition suivant toute autre caractéristique. De fait, des différences dans la définition du lieu de résidence habituel utilisée pour l'exploitation des données à l'échelon sous-national influent sur la classification en population urbaine et en population rurale. De même, les différences de degré de sous-dénombrement suivant la zone, à l'occasion des recensements, ont une incidence sur la comparabilité de ces deux catégories dans l'ensemble du tableau. La distinction entre population de fait et population de droit est également très importante du point de vue de la répartition de la population en population urbaine et en population rurale. Cette distinction est expliquée en détail à la section 3.1.1 des Notes techniques.

Toutefois, la difficulté la plus importante tient aux différences de définition du terme « urbain » selon le pays. Les distinctions faites entre « zone urbaine » et « zone rurale » varient tellement que les définitions utilisées ont été reproduites à la fin de ces notes techniques. Les définitions sont forcément brèves et, lorsque le classement en « zone urbaine » repose sur des divisions administratives, on a souvent désigné celles-ci par le nom qu'elles portent dans la zone ou le pays considéré. Par suite des variations dans la terminologie, les différences entre pays ou zones peuvent sembler plus grandes qu'elles ne le sont réellement. Il se peut aussi que des termes similaires ou identiques, tels que ville, village ou district, aient des significations très différentes selon les pays ou zones.

La distinction entre « zone urbaine » et « zone rurale » repose sur une série de critères qualitatifs aussi bien que quantitatifs, notamment l'effectif de la population, la densité de peuplement, la distance entre îlots d'habitations, le type prédominant d'activité économique, le statut juridique ou administratif, et les caractéristiques d'une agglomération urbaine, c'est-à-dire l'existence de services publics et d'équipements collectifs[1]. Bien que les statistiques différenciant les zones urbaines des zones rurales soient très répandues, il ne paraît pas possible pour le moment d'adopter une classification internationale type de ces zones, vu la diversité des interprétations nationales. La classification de la population en population urbaine et population rurale retenue ici est celle qui correspond aux définitions nationales.

Données publiées antérieurement : des statistiques concernant la population urbaine et la population totale selon le sexe ont été publiées dans des éditions antérieures de l'*Annuaire démographique*. Pour plus de précisions concernant les années pour lesquelles ces données ont été publiées, se reporter à l'index historique.

DÉFINITIONS DU TERME « URBAIN »

AFRIQUE

Algérie : La délimitation des zones urbaines et rurales se font après l'opération du recensement sur la base de la classification des agglomérations. Regroupement de 100 constructions ou plus distantes l'une à l'autre de moins de 200m ont été considérées comme zones urbaines.

Afrique du Sud : Zones dotées d'une administration locale.

Botswana : Agglomération de 5 000 habitants ou plus dont 75 p. 100 de l'activité économique n'est pas de type agricole.

Burkina Faso : Tous les chefs-lieux de province (45 au total) plus 4 villes moyennes ont été considérées comme zones urbaines.

Burundi : Commune de Bujumbura.

Comores : Toute localité ou chef-lieu d'une île, région/préfecture disposant des infrastructures suivantes : route bitumée, électricité, centre hospitalier, téléphone, etc.

Égypte : Chefs-lieux des gouvernorats du Caire, d'Alexandrie, de Port Saïd, d'Ismaïlia, de Suez ; chefs-lieux des gouvernorats frontaliers, autres chefs-lieux de gouvernorat et chefs-lieux de district (Markaz). La définition des zones urbaines pour le recensement de 2006 est celle de « shiakha », une partie d'un district.

Éthiopie : Localités de 2 000 habitants ou plus.

Guinée : Centres administratifs des préfectures et la ville capitale (Conakry).

Guinée équatoriale : Chefs-lieux de district et localités comprenant 300 habitations et/ou 1 500 habitants ou plus.

Kenya : Zone ayant une population de 2 000 habitants ou plus qui dispose de réseaux de transport, comporte des zones bâties, des structures industrielles ou manufacturières et d'autres équipements modernes.

Lesotho : Tous les chefs-lieux administratifs et établissements en forte croissance.

Libéria : Localités de 2 000 habitants ou plus.

Malawi : Toutes les villes et zones urbanisées et tous les chefs-lieux de district.

Maurice : Les cinq circonscriptions municipales, divisées en vingt arrondissements municipaux dont les limites ont été officiellement définies.

Namibie : Zones urbaines déclarées pour lesquelles il existe des données cadastrales et autres zones d'habitat non planifié.

Niger : Ville capital, villes capitales de départements ou de districts.

Ouganda : « Gazettes », villes, municipalités et bourgs.

République-Unie de Tanzanie : Toutes les zones érigées en communes et les zones reconnues par les autorités gouvernementales comme urbaines.

Rwanda : Toutes les zones administratives reconnues comme urbaines par la loi. Il s'agit de tous les chefs-lieux des provinces, de la ville de Kigali ainsi que des villes de Nyanza, Ruhango et Rwamagana.

Sénégal : Agglomérations de 10 000 habitants ou plus.

Soudan : Centres administratifs et/ou commerciaux ou localités ayant une population de 5 000 habitants ou plus.

Swaziland : Zone géographique qui constitue une ville et se caractérise par une densité de population et de constructions humaines plus élevée que dans les zones qui l'entourent.

Tunisie : Population vivant dans les communes.

Zambie : Localités de 5 000 habitants ou plus dont l'activité économique prédominante n'est pas de type agricole.

AMÉRIQUE DU NORD

Bermudes : Le pays est considéré entièrement urbain.

Canada : Agglomérations de 1 000 habitants ou plus ayant une densité de population d'au moins 400 habitants au kilomètre carré.

Costa Rica : Chefs-lieux de canton.

Cuba : Localités ayant une population supérieure à 2 000 habitants ; ou une population supérieure à 1 000 habitants dont la moitié de la population économiquement active s'occupe des activités non-agricoles.

El Salvador : Chefs-lieux des municipalités.

États-Unis d'Amérique : Agglomérations de 2 500 habitants ou plus ayant généralement une densité de population d'au moins 1 000 habitants au mile carré. Deux types de zones urbaines : zones urbanisées de 50 000 habitants ou plus et groupements urbains comptant au moins 2 500 habitants mais moins de 50 000.

Groenland : Localités d'au moins 200 habitants.

Guatemala : Municipalité du département de Guatemala et centres administratifs officiels d'autres départements et municipalités.

Haïti : Chefs-lieux de communes.

Honduras : Localités d'au moins 2 000 habitants ayant des caractéristiques essentiellement urbaines.

Îles Vierges américaines : Agglomérations de 2 500 habitants ou plus ayant généralement une densité de population d'au moins 1 000 habitants au mile carré. Deux types de zones urbaines : zones urbanisées de 50 000 habitants ou plus et groupements urbains comptant au moins 2 500 habitants mais moins de 50 000. (D'après les résultats du recensement de 2 000, les Îles Vierges américaines ne comptent aucune zone urbanisée.)

Jamaïque : Localités de 2 000 habitants ou plus ayant des caractéristiques urbaines.

Mexique : Localités d'au moins 2 500 habitants.

Nicaragua : Centres administratifs des municipalités et localités d'au moins 1 000 habitants ou d'au moins 150 logements, possédant des rues, un éclairage électrique, un réseau de distribution d'eau, une école et un dispensaire.

Panama : Localités d'au moins 1 500 habitants ayant des caractéristiques essentiellement urbaines. À partir de 1970, localités de 1 500 habitants ou plus présentant des caractéristiques urbaines, telles que rues, éclairage électrique, systèmes d'approvisionnement en eau et réseaux d'égouts.

Porto Rico : Agglomérations de 2 500 habitants ou plus ayant généralement une densité de population d'au moins 1 000 habitants au mile carré. Deux types de zones urbaines : zones urbanisées de 50 000 habitants ou plus et groupements urbains comptant au moins 2 500 habitants mais moins de 50 000.

République dominicaine : Chefs-lieux des municipalités et districts municipaux, dont certains comprennent des zones suburbaines ayant des caractéristiques rurales.

AMÉRIQUE DU SUD

Argentine : Centres comptant au moins 2 000 habitants.

Bolivie : Localités de 2 000 habitants ou plus.

Brésil : Zone à l'intérieur du périmètre urbain d'une ville, définie par la législation municipale.

Chili : Zones d'habitat concentré comptant 2 000 habitants ou plus, ou comptant entre 1 001 et 2 000 habitants dont 50 pour cent au moins de la population active s'occupe d'une activité secondaire ou tertiaire. Par dérogation, les centres qui ont une fonction touristique ou récréative et plus de 250 unités de logement mais n'atteignent pas le critère de population sont néanmoins considérés comme zones urbaines.

Colombie : Zone avec une mairie, définie par un périmètre urbain qui est établie par des accords municipaux.

Équateur : Capitales des provinces et chefs-lieux de canton.

Îles Falkland (Malvinas) : Ville de Stanley.

Paraguay : Grandes villes, villes et chefs-lieux des départements et des districts.

Pérou : Centres de peuplement comptant plus de 100 logements.

Suriname : Les districts de Paramaribo et de Wanica.

Uruguay : Les villes, villages et autres zones habitées répondant aux définitions de la loi sur les agglomérations.

Venezuela (République bolivarienne du) : Centres de 2 500 habitants ou plus.

ASIE

Arabie saoudite : Localités de plus de 5 000 habitants.

Arménie : Grandes villes et localités de type urbain, officiellement désignées comme telles, généralement sur la base du nombre d'habitants et de la prédominance des travailleurs agricoles ou non agricoles avec leur famille.

Azerbaïdjan : Division administrative regroupant plus de 15 000 habitants se livrant principalement à des activités industrielles et autres activités économiques et sociales et comprenant des centres administratifs et culturels.

Bahreïn : Communes ou villages comptant au moins 2 500 habitants.

Brunéi Darussalam : Les communes de Bandar, Seri Begawan, Kuala Belait, Seria, Pekan Tutong and Pekan Bangar; et les zones densement peuplé qui possèdent des caractéristiques urbaines.

Cambodge : Zones au niveau de la commune répondant aux trois conditions suivantes : 1) Densité démographique supérieure à 200 habitants au km carré, 2) pourcentage d'hommes travaillant dans l'agriculture inférieur à 50 pour cent, 3) population totale de la commune supérieure à 2 000 habitants.

Chine : Suivant la Réglementation sur la classification de la résidence urbaine/rurale à des fins de statistiques.

Chypre : Selon la définition du Département de l'urbanisme et du logement du Ministère de l'intérieur.

État de Palestine : Localités peuplées de plus de 10 000 personnes. L'expression désigne tous les gouvernorats (districts), quelle qu'en soit la taille, ainsi que toutes les villes dont la population est comprise entre 4 000 et 9 999 personnes qui disposent d'au moins quatre des éléments suivants : réseau public de distribution d'électricité, réseau public de distribution d'eau, bureau de poste, centre médical doté d'un médecin à temps plein et école préparant les élèves au certificat général de l'enseignement secondaire.

Géorgie : Grandes villes et localités de type urbain, officiellement désignées comme telles, généralement sur la base du nombre d'habitants et de la prédominance des travailleurs agricoles ou non agricoles avec leur famille.

Inde : Villes [localités dotées d'une charte municipale, d'un comité de zone municipale, d'un comité de zone déclarée urbaine ou d'un comité de zone de regroupement (cantonnement)] ; également toutes les localités qui ont une population de 5 000 habitants au moins, une densité de population d'au moins 1 000 habitants au mile carré ou 400 au kilomètre carré, des caractéristiques urbaines prononcées et où les trois quarts au moins des adultes de sexe masculin ont une occupation non agricole.

Indonésie : Les zones urbaines sont celles qui répondent à certains critères : densité de population, pourcentage de ménages agricoles, accès aux équipements urbains, existence d'équipements supplémentaires, et pourcentage de superficie bâtie à usage autre que l'habitation.

Iran (République islamique d') : Tous les districts comptant une municipalité.

Israël : Tous les lieux comptant au moins 2 000 résidents.

Japon : Villes (shi), comptant au moins 50 000 habitants, où 60 p. 100 au moins des logements sont situés dans les principales zones bâties, et dont 60 p. 100 au moins de population (y compris les personnes à charge) exercent un métier dans l'industrie, le commerce et d'autres branches d'activités essentiellement urbaines.

Jordanie : Localités comptant 5 000 habitants ou plus.

Kazakhstan : Villes ayant statut républicain (centres de population présentant une importance nationale spéciale ou comptant une population généralement de plus d'un million d'habitants), statut régional (Oblast') (centres de population qui sont de grands centres économiques et culturels, dotés d'une infrastructure industrielle et sociale développée et comptant une population de plus 50 000 habitants, le pays compte 40 villes ayant statut régional), statut départemental, et agglomérations relevant de leur juridiction administrative.

Kirghizistan : Grandes villes et localités de type urbain, officiellement désignées comme telles, généralement sur la base du nombre d'habitants et de la prédominance des travailleurs agricoles ou non agricoles avec leur famille.

Koweït : Toutes les localités sont urbaines au Koweït.

Malaisie : Zone ayant le statut de centre urbain et dont la population totale dépasse 10 000 habitants. On nomme périphérie toute zone contiguë à un centre urbain dont au moins 60 % de la population (âgée de 15 ans et plus) a une activité non agricole. La définition des zones urbaines couvre également les zones spéciales de développement qui n'ont pas officiellement le statut de centre urbain, se trouvent à 5 kilomètres ou plus d'un tel centre ou de sa périphérie et comptent au moins 10 000 habitants dont 60 % (parmi les plus de 15 ans) ont une activité non agricole.

Maldives : Malé (la capitale).

Mongolie : Ulaanbaatar (la capitale), les chefs-lieux des provinces et les villes.

Myanmar : Les zones reconnues par les autorités gouvernementales comme urbaines. Ces zones se caractérisent par une densité de population et de constructions humaines plus élevée et disposent de meilleures infrastructures.

Népal : Zones déclarées telles par les municipalités.

Ouzbékistan : Grandes villes et localités de type urbain, officiellement désignées comme telles, généralement sur la base du nombre d'habitants et de la prédominance des travailleurs agricoles ou non agricoles avec leur famille.

Pakistan : Localités dotées d'une charte municipale ou d'un comité municipal et regroupements (cantonments).

Philippines : Villes et municipalités et leurs quartiers centraux dont la densité démographique est d'au moins 500 habitants au km carré. Sont considérés comme zones urbaines les autres quartiers quelle que soit leur population qui sont équipés de routes et possèdent au moins six établissements (commerce, industrie manufacturière, équipements récréatifs ou services aux personnes), et au moins trois équipements publics tels que hôtel de ville, église, parc public, école, hôpital, bibliothèque, etc.

République arabe syrienne : Villes, chefs-lieux de district (Mohafaza) et chefs-lieux de sous district (Mantika), et communes d'au moins 20 000 habitants.

République de Corée : Pour les estimations : localités de 50 000 habitants ou plus. Pour recensements, les données sont établies sont la base des divisions administratives mineures comme les Dongs (principalement en zone urbaines) et des Eups ou Myeons (en zones rurales).

République démocratique populaire lao : Zones ou villages répondant à au moins trois des cinq conditions suivantes: situés dans l'aire métropolitaine du district ou de la province, accessibles par la route en toute saison, quelque 70 pour cent ou deux tiers de la population ayant accès à de l'eau distribuée par canalisation, quelque 70 pour cent ou deux tiers de la population ayant accès au réseau d'électricité et existence d'un marché ouvert tous les jours.

Singapour : Le pays consiste seulement d'une ville.

Sri Lanka : Toutes les zones administrées par les conseils municipaux et urbains.

Tadjikistan : Grandes villes et localités de type urbain, officiellement désignées comme telles, généralement sur la base du nombre d'habitants et de la prédominance des travailleurs agricoles ou non agricoles avec leur famille.

Thaïlande : Zones municipales.

Turkménistan : Grandes villes et localités de type urbain, officiellement désignées comme telles, généralement sur la base du nombre d'habitants et de la prédominance des travailleurs agricoles ou non agricoles avec leur famille.

Turquie : Localités comptant 20 000 habitants ou plus.

Viet Nam : Zones urbaines comprises à l'intérieur des districts urbains des villes ainsi que des quartiers urbains et des localités. Toutes les autres unités administratives locales (communes) sont considérées comme zones rurales.

EUROPE

Albanie : Villes et autres centres industriels de plus de 400 habitants.

Autriche : Les zones urbaines sont les localités comptant 2 000 habitants ou plus. Leur délimitation remonte à 1991.

Bélarus : Les établissements urbains sont des établissements autorisés en vertu de la loi comme les villes, les agglomérations de type urbain, les cités ouvrières et les zones de villégiature de santé.

Belgique : Toutes les communes qui ne sont pas dans la liste des communes rurales sont considérées comme des communes urbaines. Il y a 33 communes qui sont considérées comme rurales: Alveringem, Amblève, Bertogne, Bièvre, Bullange, Burg-Reuland, Clavier, Erezée, Fauvillers, Frasnes-lez-Anvaing, Froidchapelle, Gedinne, Gouvy, Havelange, Herstappe, Heuvelland, Houffalize, Houyet, Langemark-Poelkapelle, Léglise, Lierneux, Lo-Reninge, Manhay, Momignies, Ravels, Sainte-Ode, Sint-Laureins, Sivry-Rance, Stoumont, Tenneville, Vaux-sur-Sûre, Vleteren et Vresse-sur-Semois.

Bulgarie : Toutes les zones considérées comme villes et bourgs selon la Division territoriale et administrative du pays.

Espagne : Aux fins de la publication de résultats qui soient comparables au niveau européen, Eurostat propose de considérer comme zones urbaines, intermédiaires et rurales les communes comptant respectivement plus de 10 000 habitants, de 2 001 à 10 000 habitants et moins de 2 000 habitants.

Estonie : Les établissements urbains comprennent les villes et les agglomérations n'ayant pas de statut municipal.

Fédération de Russie : Grandes villes et localités de type urbain, officiellement désignées comme telles, généralement sur la base du nombre d'habitants et de la prédominance des travailleurs agricoles ou non agricoles avec leur famille.

Finlande : Communes urbaines (communes où au moins 90 % de la population vit en milieu urbain ou dont le plus grand centre urbain compte au moins 15 000 habitants).

France : Communes comprenant une agglomération de plus de 2 000 habitants vivant dans des habitations contiguës ou qui ne sont pas distantes les unes des autres de plus de 200 mètres et communes où la majeure partie de la population vit dans une agglomération regroupant plusieurs communes de cette nature.

Grèce : Est considérée comme zone urbaine toute municipalité ou commune dont la plus grande localité compte 2 000 habitants ou plus.

Hongrie : Localités dont le statut de ville a été reconnu par le Président de la République compte tenu de critères spécifiques (économiques, commerciaux, institutionnels, culturels, etc.).

Irlande : Localités, y compris leur banlieues, comptant 1 500 habitants ou plus.

Islande : Localités de 200 habitants ou plus.

L'ex-R. y. de Macédoine : Villes sont les localités comptant au moins 3 000 habitants, dotés d'une infrastructure industrielle et sociale développée, dont plus de 51 pour cent de la population active s'occupe des activités qui ne sont pas primaires.

Lettonie : Grandes villes et localités de type urbain, officiellement désignées comme telles, généralement sur la base du nombre d'habitants et de la prédominance des travailleurs agricoles ou non agricoles avec leur famille.

Lituanie : Par population urbaine, on entend les personnes qui vivent dans des villes ou des localités, à savoir les zones habitées comportant des logements permanents proches les uns des autres et dont la population est d'au moins 3 000 habitants, les deux tiers desquels étant employés dans le secteur industriel, l'infrastructure sociale ou le commerce. Un certain nombre de villes peuvent compter moins de 3 000 habitants dans la mesure où elles avaient acquis le statut de ville avant l'entrée en vigueur de la nouvelle loi en juillet 1994.

Malte : Zones de 1 kilomètre carré avec une densité minimum de 300 au kilomètre carré et un minimum de 5 000 habitants, et zones à forte densité de population (supérieure à 500 habitants au kilomètre carré).

Monténégro : D'après la législation actuelle relative à l'organisation territoriale du Monténégro, qui oblige chaque collectivité à déterminer quelles sont ses zones urbaines et rurales.

Norvège : Ensemble construit habité par au moins 200 personnes, où les bâtiments ne sont pas éloignés de plus de 50 mètres les uns des autres. Les limites en sont évolutives et peuvent être redéfinies pour tenir compte de l'urbanisation et de l'évolution de la population.

Pays Bas : Zones urbaines : municipalités comptant au moins 2 000 habitants. Zones semi-urbaines : municipalités comptant moins de 2 000 habitants, mais où 20 p. 100 au maximum de la population active de sexe masculin pratiquent l'agriculture, et certaines municipalités de caractère résidentiel dont les habitants travaillent ailleurs.

Pologne : Toutes les zones qui ont les droits d'une ville ou le statut d'une ville avec dispositions de lois distinctes.

Portugal : Localités comptant 2 000 habitants ou davantage.

République de Moldova : Grandes villes et localités de type urbain, officiellement désignées comme telles, généralement sur la base du nombre d'habitants et de la prédominance des travailleurs agricoles ou non agricoles avec leur famille.

République tchèque : Localités d'au moins 2 000 habitants.

Roumanie : Localités où la majorité des ressources en main-d'œuvre est employée dans des activités non agricoles avec un niveau diversifié de ressources, exerçant une influence socioéconomique constante et importante sur l'ensemble de la zone.

Royaume-Uni de Grande-Bretagne et d'Irlande du Nord : Pour l'Angleterre et le Pays de Galles, les zones bâties comptant 10 000 habitants ou plus ; pour l'Écosse, les établissements humains comptant 3 000 habitants ou davantage et pour l'Irlande du Nord, les établissements comptant 5 000 habitants.

Serbie : Municipalités, villes et Belgrade.

Slovaquie : Municipalités avec statut de ville, conformément aux critères : 1) est un centre économique, administratif, culturel ou touristique ; 2) fournit des services pour d'autres municipalités ; 3) a un caractère urbain, au moins en partie ; et 4) compte 5 000 habitants ou plus.

Slovénie : Établissements de 3 000 habitants ou plus, chefs-lieux de municipalités comptant au moins 1 400 habitants, et quartiers suburbains qui s'intègrent progressivement dans une ville de 5 000 habitants ou plus.

Suisse : L'espace urbain comprend les agglomérations et les villes isolées (n'appartenant pas à une agglomération et comptant au moins 10 000 habitants à elles seules).

Ukraine : Grandes villes et localités de type urbain, officiellement désignées comme telles, généralement sur la base du nombre d'habitants et de la prédominance des travailleurs agricoles ou non agricoles avec leur famille.

OCÉANIE

Australie : Sont considérées comme urbaines toutes les « zones urbaines importantes » (Significant Urban Areas), telles que définies dans la Norme géographique australienne de statistique de 2011. Il s'agit de concentrations urbanisées comptant 10 000 habitants ou plus.

Guam : Agglomérations de 2 500 habitants ou plus ayant généralement une densité de population d'au moins 1 000 habitants au mile carré et considérées comme étant des groupements urbains.

Îles Cook : Rarotonga, île la plus peuplée.

Îles Mariannes septentrionales : Agglomérations de 2 500 habitants ou plus ayant généralement une densité de population d'au moins 1 000 habitants au mile carré. Deux types de zones urbaines : zones urbanisées de 50 000 habitants ou plus et groupements urbains comptant au moins 2 500 habitants mais moins de 50 000.

Nouvelle-Calédonie : Nouméa et communes de Païta, Dumbéa et Mont-Dore.

Nouvelle-Zélande : Toutes les villes et les quartiers, districts et bourgs ayant 1 000 habitants permanents ou plus.

Palaos : États comptant 2 500 habitants ou plus (le seul État qui remplit cette condition est l'État de Koror).

Samoa américaines : Agglomérations de 2 500 habitants ou plus ayant généralement une densité de population d'au moins 1 000 habitants au mile carré. Deux types de zones urbaines : zones urbanisées de 50 000 habitants ou plus et groupements urbains comptant au moins 2 500 habitants mais moins de 50 000. (D'après les résultats du recensement de 2000, les Samoa américaines ne comptent aucune zone urbanisée.)

Tokélaou : L'ensemble de la population est considéré comme vivant en milieu rural.

Tonga : Nuku'alofa.

Vanuatu : Centre de Luganville et Port-Vila.

NOTES

[1] Pour plus de précisions, voir *Social and Demographic Statistics : Classifications of Size and Type of Locality and Urban/Rural Areas*, E/CN.3/551, publication des Nations Unies, New York, 1980.

Continent, country or area, and date / Continent, pays ou zone et date	Code[a]	Both sexes - Les deux sexes			Male - Masculin			Female - Féminin		
		Total	Urban - Urbaine		Total	Urban - Urbaine		Total	Urban - Urbaine	
			Number Nombre	Percent P.100		Number Nombre	Percent P.100		Number Nombre	Percent P.100
AFRICA - AFRIQUE										
Algeria - Algérie										
1 VII 2007	ESDJ	34 096 000	...	...	17 225 000	...	...	16 871 000	...	...
16 IV 2008[1]	CDFC	34 452 759			17 428 500	...	...	17 024 259	...	...
1 VII 2008	ESDJ	34 591 000	22 808 000	65.9	17 493 000			17 098 000		
1 VII 2009	ESDJ	35 268 000	...	...	17 846 000			17 422 000		
1 VII 2010	ESDJ	35 978 000	...	...	18 205 000			17 773 000		
1 VII 2011	ESDJ	36 717 000	...	...	18 579 000			18 138 000		
1 VII 2012	ESDJ	37 495 000	...	...	18 976 000			18 519 000		
1 VII 2013	ESDJ	38 297 000	...	...	19 383 000			18 914 000		
1 VII 2014	ESDJ	39 114 275			19 801 163			19 313 112		
1 VII 2015	ESDJ	39 963 249			20 235 204			19 728 045		
1 VII 2016	ESDJ	40 835 602			20 680 271	...	...	20 155 331	...	...
Angola										
1 VII 2007[2]	ESDF	15 889 000			7 668 000			8 221 000		
1 VII 2008[2]	ESDF	16 368 000			7 899 000			8 469 000		
1 VII 2009[2]	ESDF	16 888 858			8 158 550			8 730 308		
1 VII 2010[2]	ESDF	17 429 637			8 427 802	...	...	9 001 835	...	...
1 VII 2011[2]	ESDF	17 992 033			8 707 868			9 284 165		
1 VII 2012[2]	ESDF	18 576 568			8 999 074			9 577 494		
1 VII 2013[2]	ESDF	19 183 590	...		9 301 632	...	...	9 881 958	...	...
16 V 2014	CDFC	25 789 024	16 153 987	62.6	12 499 041	7 860 614	62.9	13 289 983	8 293 373	62.4
Benin - Bénin										
1 VII 2007[3]	ESDF	7 958 813	3 324 220	41.8	3 886 596	1 628 650	41.9	4 072 217	1 695 570	41.6
1 VII 2008[3]	ESDF	8 224 642	3 499 506	42.5	4 021 094	1 716 411	42.7	4 203 548	1 783 095	42.4
1 VII 2009[3]	ESDF	8 497 827	3 682 496	43.3	4 159 291	1 808 057	43.5	4 338 536	1 874 439	43.2
1 VII 2010[3]	ESDF	8 778 648	3 873 462	44.1	4 301 224	1 903 683	44.3	4 477 424	1 969 779	44.0
1 VII 2011[3]	ESDF	9 067 076	4 072 574	44.9	4 446 877	2 003 366	45.1	4 620 199	2 069 208	44.8
1 VII 2012[3]	ESDF	9 364 619	4 280 693	45.7	4 597 122	...	...	4 767 497	...	...
11 V 2013	CDJC	10 008 749	4 460 503	44.6	4 887 820	...	...	5 120 929	...	...
1 VII 2014[4]	ESDF	10 293 235	...	...	5 033 372	...	...	5 259 863	...	...
1 VII 2015[4]	ESDF	10 584 935	...	...	5 182 478	...	...	5 402 457	...	...
1 VII 2016[4]	ESDF	10 882 953	...	...	5 334 603	...	...	5 548 350	...	...
Botswana										
1 VII 2007	ESDJ	1 736 396	...	...	847 539	...	...	888 857	...	...
1 VII 2008	ESDJ	1 755 246	...	...	859 167	...	...	896 079	...	...
1 VII 2009	ESDJ	1 776 494	...	...	871 964	...	...	904 530	...	...
1 VII 2010	ESDJ	1 822 859	...	...	895 007	...	...	927 852	...	...
1 VII 2011	ESDJ	1 849 692	...	...	910 404	...	...	939 288	...	...
9 VIII 2011	CDFC	2 024 904	1 297 287	64.1	988 957	619 472	62.6	1 035 947	677 815	65.4
1 VII 2012[5]	ESDJ	2 070 984	1 361 699	65.8	1 010 236	664 243	65.8	1 060 748	697 456	65.8
1 VII 2013[5]	ESDJ	2 114 890	1 411 436	66.7	1 031 654	688 505	66.7	1 083 236	722 931	66.7
1 VII 2014[5]	ESDJ	2 156 366	1 460 383	67.7	1 051 886	712 382	67.7	1 104 480	748 001	67.7
1 VII 2015[5]	ESDJ	2 195 134	1 508 277	68.7	1 070 797	735 745	68.7	1 124 337	772 532	68.7
1 VII 2016[5]	ESDJ	2 230 905	1 554 836	69.7	1 088 246	758 457	69.7	1 142 659	796 379	69.7
Burkina Faso[3]										
1 VII 2007	ESDJ	14 252 012	3 322 360	23.3	6 880 824	1 629 956	23.7	7 371 188	1 692 404	23.0
1 VII 2008	ESDJ	14 731 167	...	...	7 110 097	...	...	7 621 070	...	...
1 VII 2009	ESDJ	15 224 780	...	...	7 346 835	...	...	7 877 945	...	...
1 VII 2010	ESDJ	15 730 977	...	...	7 590 133	...	...	8 140 844	...	...
1 VII 2011	ESDJ	16 248 558	...	...	7 839 350	...	...	8 409 208	...	...
1 VII 2012	ESDJ	16 779 206	...	...	8 095 324	...	...	8 683 882	...	...
1 VII 2013	ESDJ	17 322 796	...	...	8 357 967	...	...	8 964 829	...	...
1 VII 2014	ESDJ	17 880 386	...	...	8 627 830	...	...	9 252 556	...	...
1 VII 2015	ESDJ	18 450 494	...	...	8 904 256	...	...	9 546 238	...	...
Burundi										
16 VIII 2008	CDFC	7 877 728	799 802	10.2	3 838 045	432 442	11.3	4 039 683	367 360	9.1
1 VII 2009[6]	ESDF	8 262 912	892 394	10.8	4 065 512	439 075	10.8	4 197 400	453 319	10.8
1 VII 2010	ESDF	9 461 117	...	...	4 667 414	...	...	4 793 703	...	...
1 VII 2011	ESDF	9 770 964	...	...	4 821 918	...	...	4 949 047	...	...
1 VII 2012	ESDF	10 072 586	...	...	4 972 344	...	...	5 100 243	...	...
1 VII 2013	ESDF	10 367 162	...	...	5 119 079	...	...	5 248 084	...	...
1 VII 2014	ESDF	10 654 123	...	...	5 261 798	...	...	5 392 325	...	...
1 VII 2015	ESDF	10 933 343	...	...	5 400 272	...	...	5 533 071	...	...
1 VII 2016	ESDF	11 215 019	...	...	5 539 821	...	...	5 675 198	...	...

Continent, country or area, and date / Continent, pays ou zone et date	Code[a]	Both sexes - Les deux sexes			Male - Masculin			Female - Féminin		
		Total	Urban - Urbaine		Total	Urban - Urbaine		Total	Urban - Urbaine	
			Number Nombre	Percent P.100		Number Nombre	Percent P.100		Number Nombre	Percent P.100
AFRICA - AFRIQUE										
Cabo Verde										
1 VII 2007	ESDF	491 419	295 046	60.0	237 842	...	...	253 577	...	...
1 VII 2008	ESDF	499 796	303 512	60.7	241 914	...	...	257 882	...	...
1 VII 2009	ESDF	508 633	310 958	61.1	246 219	...	...	262 414	...	...
16 VI 2010	CDJC	491 683	303 673	61.8	243 403	151 219	62.1	248 280	152 454	61.4
1 VII 2010[3]	ESDF	494 040	...	...	244 338	...	...	249 702	...	...
1 VII 2011[3]	ESDF	499 929	...	...	247 814	...	...	252 115	...	...
1 VII 2012[3]	ESDF	505 983	...	...	251 384	...	...	254 599	...	...
1 VII 2013[3]	ESDF	512 173	...	...	255 033	...	...	257 140	...	...
1 VII 2014[3]	ESDF	518 467	...	...	258 744	...	...	259 723	...	...
1 VII 2015[3]	ESDF	524 833	...	...	262 501	...	...	262 331	...	...
1 VII 2016[3]	ESDF	531 239	...	...	266 287	...	...	264 951	...	...
Cameroon - Cameroun[3]										
1 VII 2007	ESDF	18 225 042	...	...	9 007 027	...	...	9 218 015	...	...
1 VII 2008	ESDF	18 691 490	...	...	9 237 549	...	...	9 453 941	...	...
1 VII 2009	ESDF	19 165 905	...	...	9 472 009	...	...	9 693 896	...	...
1 VII 2010	ESDF	19 648 287	...	...	9 707 318	...	...	9 940 969	...	...
1 VII 2011	ESDF	20 138 637	...	...	9 949 573	...	...	10 189 064	...	...
1 VII 2012	ESDF	20 636 954	...	...	10 195 770	...	...	10 441 184	...	...
1 VII 2013	ESDF	21 143 237	...	...	10 445 903	...	...	10 697 334	...	...
1 VII 2014	ESDF	21 657 488	...	...	10 699 969	...	...	10 957 519	...	...
1 VII 2015	ESDF	22 179 707	...	...	10 955 014	...	...	11 224 693	...	...
1 VII 2016	ESDF	22 709 892	...	...	11 216 886	...	...	11 493 006	...	...
Chad - Tchad										
20 V 2009	CDJC	11 175 915	...	...	5 509 522	...	...	5 666 393	...	...
Congo										
28 IV 2007	CDFC	3 697 490	2 285 551	61.8	1 821 357	1 132 510	62.2	1 876 133	1 153 041	61.5
1 VII 2008	ESDF	3 740 851	...	...	1 841 589	...	...	1 899 262	...	...
1 VII 2009	ESDF	3 838 238	...	...	1 891 558	...	...	1 946 680	...	...
Côte d'Ivoire										
1 VII 2007[7]	ESDF	19 475 542	...	...	10 017 909	...	...	9 457 633	...	...
1 VII 2008[7]	ESDF	19 932 082	...	...	10 259 383	...	...	9 672 699	...	...
1 VII 2009[7]	ESDF	20 388 627	...	...	10 500 861	...	...	9 887 766	...	...
1 VII 2010[7]	ESDF	20 845 167	...	...	10 742 336	...	...	10 102 831	...	...
1 VII 2011[7]	ESDF	21 301 704	...	...	10 983 811	...	...	10 317 893	...	...
1 VII 2012[7]	ESDF	21 758 244	...	...	11 225 286	...	...	10 532 958	...	...
1 VII 2013[7]	ESDF	22 214 787	...	...	11 466 762	...	...	10 748 025	...	...
15 V 2014	CDFC	22 224 509	10 881 387	49.0	11 441 896	5 495 438	48.0	10 782 613	5 385 949	50.0
1 VII 2014[8]	ESDF	22 723 460	11 444 572	50.4	11 734 076	5 834 493	49.7	10 989 384	5 610 079	51.0
1 VII 2015[8]	ESDF	23 334 439	11 830 560	50.7	12 036 040	6 102 272	50.7	11 298 398	5 728 288	50.7
1 VII 2016[8]	ESDF	23 950 475	12 262 643	51.2	12 340 861	6 318 521	51.2	11 609 614	5 944 122	51.2
Djibouti										
29 V 2009	CDFC	818 159	577 933	70.6	440 067	322 796	73.4	378 092	255 137	67.5
Egypt - Égypte										
1 VII 2007	ESDF	73 643 587	31 719 927	43.1	37 643 353	16 186 484	43.0	36 000 234	15 533 443	43.1
1 VII 2008	ESDF	75 193 567	32 248 476	42.9	38 413 404	16 437 464	42.8	36 780 163	15 811 012	43.0
1 VII 2009	ESDF	76 925 139	33 082 770	43.0	39 327 098	16 887 176	42.9	37 598 041	16 195 594	43.1
1 VII 2010	ESDF	78 684 622	33 804 181	43.0	40 228 119	17 255 735	42.9	38 456 503	16 548 446	43.0
1 VII 2011	ESDF	80 529 566	34 495 468	42.8	41 152 525	17 596 284	42.8	39 377 041	16 899 184	42.9
1 VII 2012	ESDF	82 549 976	35 372 982	42.9	42 167 660	18 031 407	42.8	40 382 316	17 341 575	42.9
1 VII 2013	ESDF	84 628 982	36 213 473	42.8	43 217 105	18 470 748	42.7	41 411 877	17 742 725	42.8
1 VII 2014	ESDF	86 811 192	37 098 131	42.7	44 300 565	18 894 134	42.6	42 510 627	18 203 997	42.8
1 VII 2015	ESDF	88 957 833	37 999 018	42.7	45 378 728	19 347 041	42.6	43 579 105	18 651 977	42.8
1 VII 2016	ESDF	91 023 393	38 895 815	42.7	46 413 993	19 787 083	42.6	44 609 400	19 108 732	42.8
Equatorial Guinea - Guinée équatoriale										
20 VI 2015	CDFC	1 222 442	863 313	70.6	651 820	...	...	570 622	...	...
Ethiopia - Éthiopie										
29 V 2007	CDFC	73 750 932	11 862 821	16.1	37 217 130	5 895 916	15.8	36 533 802	5 966 905	16.3
1 VII 2007[9]	ESDF	77 127 000	12 689 000	16.5	38 644 000	6 307 000	16.3	38 483 000	6 382 000	16.6
1 VII 2008[10]	ESDF	75 719 000	12 716 000	16.8	38 215 000	6 353 000	16.6	37 504 000	6 363 000	17.0
1 VII 2009[10]	ESDF	77 651 000	13 318 000	17.2	39 155 000	6 649 000	17.0	38 496 000	6 669 000	17.3
1 VII 2010[10]	ESDF	79 634 000	13 931 000	17.5	40 123 000	6 950 000	17.3	39 511 000	6 981 000	17.7
1 VII 2011[10]	ESDF	81 668 000	14 589 000	17.9	41 119 000	7 274 000	17.7	40 549 000	7 315 000	18.0
1 VII 2012[10]	ESDF	83 741 000	15 246 000	18.2	42 135 000	7 598 000	18.0	41 606 000	7 648 000	18.4

6. Total and urban population by sex: 2007 - 2016
Population totale et population urbaine selon le sexe : 2007 - 2016 (continued - suite)

Continent, country or area, and date / Continent, pays ou zone et date	Code[a]	Both sexes - Les deux sexes			Male - Masculin			Female - Féminin		
		Total	Urban - Urbaine		Total	Urban - Urbaine		Total	Urban - Urbaine	
			Number Nombre	Percent P.100		Number Nombre	Percent P.100		Number Nombre	Percent P.100
AFRICA - AFRIQUE										
Ethiopia - Éthiopie										
1 VII 2013[10]	ESDF	85 837 000	15 979 000	18.6	43 164 000	7 960 000	18.4	42 673 000	8 019 000	18.8
1 VII 2014[10]	ESDF	87 952 000	16 734 000	19.0	44 204 000	8 332 000	18.8	43 748 000	8 402 000	19.2
1 VII 2015[10]	ESDF	90 075 000	17 521 000	19.5	45 250 000	8 721 000	19.3	44 825 000	8 800 000	19.6
1 VII 2016[10]	ESDF	92 205 000	18 327 000	19.9	46 303 000	9 120 000	19.7	45 902 000	9 207 000	20.1
Gabon										
22 V 2013	CDFC	1 811 079	1 577 646	87.1	934 072	813 098	87.0	877 007	764 548	87.2
Gambia - Gambie										
15 IV 2013*	CDFC	1 882 450	...	...	930 699	...	...	951 751	...	...
Ghana										
1 VII 2007	ESDF	22 387 911	...	...	11 088 060	...	...	11 299 851	...	...
1 VII 2008	ESDF	22 900 927	...	...	11 343 581	...	...	11 557 346	...	...
1 VII 2009	ESDF	23 416 518	10 243 312	43.7	11 600 326	5 006 198	43.2	11 816 192	5 237 114	44.3
26 IX 2010	CDFC	24 658 823	12 545 229	50.9	12 024 845	6 016 059	50.0	12 633 978	6 529 170	51.7
1 VII 2011[11]	ESDF	25 235 268	12 844 745	50.9	12 319 770	6 270 758	50.9	12 915 498	6 573 987	50.9
1 VII 2012[11]	ESDF	25 824 920	13 144 879	50.9	12 621 125	6 424 150	50.9	13 203 795	6 720 729	50.9
1 VII 2013[11]	ESDF	26 427 760	13 451 714	50.9	12 928 916	6 580 808	50.9	13 498 844	6 870 906	50.9
1 VII 2014[11]	ESDF	27 043 093	13 764 931	50.9	13 242 709	6 740 539	50.9	13 800 384	7 024 392	50.9
1 VII 2015[11]	ESDF	27 670 174	13 817 894	49.9	13 562 093	6 903 107	50.9	14 108 081	6 914 787	49.0
1 VII 2016[11]	ESDF	28 308 301	...	...	13 886 734	...	...	14 421 567	...	...
Guinea - Guinée										
1 VII 2008[3]	ESDF	10 182 926	2 851 219	28.0	...	...	...	...	...	...
1 VII 2009[3]	ESDF	10 217 591	...	...	5 038 823	...	...	5 178 768	...	...
1 VII 2010[3]	ESDF	10 537 234	...	...	5 200 608	...	...	5 336 626	...	...
1 VII 2011[3]	ESDF	10 863 888	...	...	5 309 110	...	...	5 554 778	...	...
15 III 2014	CDFC	10 523 261	3 657 122	34.8	5 084 306	1 821 369	35.8	5 438 955	1 835 753	33.8
1 VII 2014	ESDJ	10 602 462	3 685 904	34.8	5 116 625	1 833 428	35.8	5 485 837	1 852 476	33.8
1 VII 2015*	ESDJ	10 952 899	3 807 732	34.8	5 285 742	1 894 027	35.8	5 667 157	1 913 705	33.8
1 VII 2016*	ESDJ	11 319 323	3 935 118	34.8	5 462 573	1 957 391	35.8	5 856 750	1 977 727	33.8
Guinea-Bissau - Guinée-Bissau										
15 III 2009	CDFC	1 497 859	...	...	725 956	...	...	771 903	...	...
1 VII 2010[3]	ESDF	1 460 221	584 228	40.0	709 482	283 859	40.0	750 739	300 369	40.0
1 VII 2011[3]	ESDF	1 472 233	595 358	40.4	716 622	289 796	40.4	755 611	305 562	40.4
1 VII 2012[3]	ESDF	1 485 189	606 976	40.9	724 208	295 974	40.9	760 981	311 002	40.9
1 VII 2013[3]	ESDF	1 499 277	619 166	41.3	732 337	302 438	41.3	766 940	316 728	41.3
1 VII 2014[3]	ESDF	1 514 451	631 938	41.7	740 981	309 191	41.7	773 470	322 747	41.7
1 VII 2015[3]	ESDF	1 530 673	645 283	42.2	750 119	316 226	42.2	780 554	329 057	42.2
1 VII 2016[3]	ESDF	1 547 777	659 138	42.6	759 666	323 512	42.6	788 111	335 626	42.6
Kenya										
1 VII 2007	ESDF	37 183 924	...	...	18 202 701	...	...	18 981 232	...	...
1 VII 2008	ESDF	38 277 856	...	...	18 743 686	...	...	19 534 170	...	...
1 VII 2009[12]	ESDF	37 724 850	12 200 486	32.3	18 674 184	6 109 258	32.7	19 050 666	6 091 229	32.0
24 VIII 2009	CDFC	38 610 097	12 487 375	32.3	19 192 458	6 278 811	32.7	19 417 639	6 208 564	32.0
1 VII 2010[12]	ESDF	38 473 893	...	...	19 047 448	...	...	19 426 445	...	...
1 VII 2011[12]	ESDF	39 545 118	...	...	19 583 833	...	...	19 961 285	...	...
1 VII 2012[12]	ESDF	40 656 572	...	...	20 137 201	...	...	20 519 371	...	...
1 VII 2013[12]	ESDF	41 787 735	...	...	20 707 136	...	...	21 080 599	...	...
1 VII 2014[12]	ESDF	42 961 187	...	...	21 289 752	...	...	21 671 435	...	...
1 VII 2015[12]	ESDF	44 156 577	14 280 766	32.3	21 886 677	7 160 225	32.7	22 269 900	7 120 541	32.0
1 VII 2016[12]	ESDF	45 389 112	14 679 464	32.3	22 508 628	7 363 696	32.7	22 880 484	7 315 769	32.0
Lesotho[3]										
1 VII 2007	ESDF	1 880 439	...	...	912 973	...	...	967 466	...	...
1 VII 2008	ESDF	1 883 595	...	...	912 711	...	...	970 884	...	...
1 VII 2009	ESDF	1 887 479	...	...	912 760	...	...	974 719	...	...
1 VII 2010	ESDF	1 891 830	...	...	913 030	...	...	978 800	...	...
1 VII 2011	ESDF	1 896 833	...	...	913 701	...	...	983 132	...	...
1 VII 2012	ESDF	1 902 707	...	...	914 954	...	...	987 753	...	...
1 VII 2013	ESDF	1 909 321	...	...	916 722	...	...	992 599	...	...
1 VII 2014	ESDF	1 916 573	...	...	918 944	...	...	997 629	...	...
1 VII 2015	ESDF	1 924 381	...	...	921 565	...	...	1 002 816	...	...
1 VII 2016	ESDF	1 932 814	...	...	924 622	...	...	1 008 192	...	...
Liberia - Libéria										
1 VII 2007	ESDF	3 403 700	1 586 481	46.6	1 704 232	780 788	45.8	1 699 468	805 693	47.4
21 III 2008	CDFC	3 476 608	1 633 719	47.0	1 739 945	802 092	46.1	1 736 663	831 627	47.9

6. Total and urban population by sex: 2007 - 2016
Population totale et population urbaine selon le sexe : 2007 - 2016 (continued - suite)

Continent, country or area, and date / Continent, pays ou zone et date	Code[a]	Both sexes - Les deux sexes Total	Urban - Urbaine Number Nombre	Urban - Urbaine Percent P.100	Male - Masculin Total	Urban - Urbaine Number Nombre	Urban - Urbaine Percent P.100	Female - Féminin Total	Urban - Urbaine Number Nombre	Urban - Urbaine Percent P.100
AFRICA - AFRIQUE										
Liberia - Libéria										
1 VII 2009 ....ESDF		3 551 078	1 682 364	47.4	1 776 406	823 978	46.4	1 774 672	858 386	48.4
1 VII 2010 ....ESDF		3 627 144	1 732 457	47.8	1 813 631	846 461	46.7	1 813 513	885 996	48.9
1 VII 2011 ....ESDF		3 704 838	1 784 042	48.2	1 851 636	869 557	47.0	1 853 202	914 485	49.3
1 VII 2012 ....ESDF		3 784 197	1 837 163	48.5	1 890 438	893 283	47.3	1 893 759	943 880	49.8
1 VII 2013 ....ESDF		3 865 256	1 891 865	48.9	1 930 053	917 657	47.5	1 935 203	974 208	50.3
1 VII 2014 ....ESDF		3 946 311	1 946 567	49.3	1 969 668	942 031	47.8	1 976 643	1 004 536	50.8
Libya - Libye[13]										
1 VII 2007 ....ESDF		5 393 325	4 754 540	88.2	2 735 343	2 414 477	88.3	2 657 982	2 340 064	88.0
1 VII 2008 ....ESDF		5 490 478	4 839 715	88.1	2 784 122	2 457 272	88.3	2 706 356	2 382 443	88.0
1 VII 2009 ....ESDF		5 589 289	4 926 097	88.1	2 833 691	2 500 626	88.2	2 755 598	2 425 471	88.0
1 VII 2010 ....ESDF		5 689 419	5 013 386	88.1	2 883 880	2 544 388	88.2	2 805 538	2 468 998	88.0
1 VII 2011 ....ESDF		5 790 518	5 101 275	88.1	2 934 512	2 588 402	88.2	2 856 006	2 512 874	88.0
1 VII 2012 ....ESDF		5 892 239	5 189 460	88.1	2 985 408	2 632 510	88.2	2 906 831	2 556 950	88.0
1 VII 2013 ....ESDF		5 994 241	5 277 638	88.0	3 036 393	2 676 558	88.1	2 957 849	2 601 081	87.9
1 VII 2014 ....ESDF		6 096 208	5 365 529	88.0	3 087 301	2 720 398	88.1	3 008 907	2 645 131	87.9
1 VII 2015 ....ESDF		6 162 356	5 411 529	87.8	3 129 260	2 707 215	86.5	3 033 156	2 704 314	89.2
Malawi										
1 VII 2007[3] ....ESDF		13 187 632	1 786 434	13.5	6 490 146	918 991	14.2	6 697 486	867 443	13.0
8 VI 2008 ....CDFC		13 077 160	2 003 309	15.3	6 358 933	1 014 477	16.0	6 718 227	988 832	14.7
1 VII 2008[3] ....ESDF		13 630 164	...	...	6 711 263	...	...	6 918 901	...	...
1 VII 2009[3] ....ESDF		13 520 098	...	...	6 585 786	...	...	6 934 312	...	...
1 VII 2010[3] ....ESDF		13 947 592	...	...	6 804 310	...	...	7 143 282	...	...
1 VII 2011[3] ....ESDF		14 388 550	...	...	7 029 149	...	...	7 359 401	...	...
1 VII 2012[3] ....ESDF		14 844 822	...	...	7 261 499	...	...	7 583 323	...	...
1 VII 2013[3] ....ESDF		15 316 860	...	...	7 501 653	...	...	7 815 207	...	...
1 VII 2014[3] ....ESDF		15 805 239	...	...	7 749 963	...	...	8 055 276	...	...
1 VII 2015[3] ....ESDF		16 310 431	...	...	8 006 715	...	...	8 303 716	...	...
1 VII 2016[3] ....ESDF		16 832 910	...	...	8 272 152	...	...	8 560 758	...	...
Mali										
1 I 2007 ....ESDF		12 377 542	4 102 223	33.1	6 128 544	2 053 767	33.5	6 248 999	2 048 456	32.8
1 IV 2009 ....CDFC		14 528 662	3 274 727	22.5	7 204 990	1 643 671	22.8	7 323 672	1 631 056	22.3
1 VII 2010[14] ....ESDF		15 370 000	...	...	7 679 000	...	...	7 691 000	...	...
1 VII 2011[14] ....ESDF		15 843 000	...	...	7 919 000	...	...	7 924 000	...	...
1 VII 2012[14] ....ESDF		16 312 000	...	...	8 159 000	...	...	8 153 000	...	...
1 VII 2013[14] ....ESDF		16 808 000	...	...	8 411 000	...	...	8 397 000	...	...
1 VII 2014*[14] ....ESDF		17 319 000	...	...	8 671 000	...	...	8 648 000	...	...
Mauritania - Mauritanie										
1 VII 2008[3] ....ESDF		3 162 338	...	...	1 584 913	...	...	1 577 425	...	...
1 VII 2010[3] ....ESDF		3 340 627	...	...	1 678 324	...	...	1 662 303	...	...
1 VII 2011[3] ....ESDF		3 296 958	...	...	1 644 572	...	...	1 652 386	...	...
24 III 2013 ....CDFC		3 460 388[15]	1 697 792	49.1	...	...	...	...	...	...
1 VII 2013[3] ....ESDF		3 537 368	...	...	1 743 074	...	...	1 794 294	...	...
1 VII 2015[3] ....ESDF		3 720 125	...	...	1 834 735	...	...	1 885 390	...	...
1 VII 2016[3] ....ESDF		3 782 701	...	...	1 864 664	...	...	1 918 037	...	...
Mauritius - Maurice[16]										
1 VII 2007[17] ....ESDJ		1 260 403	528 961	42.0	622 926	259 800	41.7	637 477	269 161	42.2
1 VII 2008[17] ....ESDJ		1 268 565	531 097	41.9	626 556	260 675	41.6	642 009	270 422	42.1
1 VII 2009[17] ....ESDJ		1 275 032	532 591	41.8	629 157	261 041	41.5	645 875	271 550	42.0
1 VII 2010[17] ....ESDJ		1 280 924	533 771	41.7	631 692	261 489	41.4	649 232	272 282	41.9
1 VII 2011[18] ....ESDJ		1 252 404	509 229	40.7	619 591	249 439	40.3	632 813	259 790	41.1
4 VII 2011 ....CDFC		1 237 000	496 841	40.2	611 053	243 629	39.9	625 947	253 212	40.5
1 VII 2012[18] ....ESDJ		1 255 882	509 177	40.5	621 297	249 422	40.1	634 585	259 755	40.9
1 VII 2013[18] ....ESDJ		1 258 653	519 306	41.3	622 861	254 605	40.9	635 792	264 701	41.6
1 VII 2014[18] ....ESDJ		1 260 934	518 370	41.1	624 002	254 204	40.7	636 932	264 166	41.5
1 VII 2015[18] ....ESDJ		1 262 605	517 482	41.0	624 769	253 796	40.6	637 836	263 686	41.3
1 VII 2016[18] ....ESDJ		1 263 473	516 160	40.9	625 206	253 181	40.5	638 267	262 979	41.2
Mayotte										
31 VII 2007 ....CDJC		186 387	...	...	91 405	...	...	94 982	...	...
21 VIII 2012 ....CDJC		212 645	...	...	103 173	...	...	109 471	...	...
1 I 2014 ....ESDJ		220 300	...	...	106 877	...	...	113 423	...	...
1 I 2015* ....ESDJ		226 915	...	...	110 086	...	...	116 829	...	...
1 I 2016* ....ESDJ		235 132	...	...	114 072	...	...	121 060	...	...

6. Total and urban population by sex: 2007 - 2016
Population totale et population urbaine selon le sexe : 2007 - 2016 (continued - suite)

Continent, country or area, and date / Continent, pays ou zone et date	Code[a]	Both sexes - Les deux sexes			Male - Masculin			Female - Féminin		
		Total	Urban - Urbaine		Total	Urban - Urbaine		Total	Urban - Urbaine	
			Number Nombre	Percent P.100		Number Nombre	Percent P.100		Number Nombre	Percent P.100
AFRICA - AFRIQUE										
Morocco - Maroc										
1 VII 2007[19]	ESDF	30 850 000	17 415 000	56.5	15 314 000	8 579 000	56.0	15 536 000	8 836 000	56.9
1 VII 2008[19]	ESDF	31 195 000	17 753 000	56.9	15 484 000	8 734 000	56.4	15 711 000	9 019 000	57.4
1 VII 2009[19]	ESDF	31 543 000	18 097 000	57.4	15 657 000	8 891 000	56.8	15 886 000	9 205 000	57.9
1 VII 2010[19]	ESDF	31 894 046	18 446 241	57.8	15 831 463	9 051 145	57.2	16 062 583	9 395 096	58.5
1 VII 2011[19]	ESDF	32 245 120	18 802 208	58.3	16 010 979	9 212 763	57.5	16 234 141	9 589 444	59.1
1 VII 2012[19]	ESDF	32 596 997	19 157 539	58.8	16 190 815	9 373 546	57.9	16 406 182	9 783 993	59.6
1 VII 2013[19]	ESDF	32 950 445	19 512 904	59.2	16 371 475	9 533 742	58.2	16 578 971	9 979 162	60.2
1 VII 2014[20]	ESDF	33 769 512	20 352 799	60.3	16 825 793	10 068 187	59.8	16 943 719	10 284 612	60.7
1 IX 2014	CDJC	33 848 242	20 432 439	60.4	...	...	...	...	...	...
1 VII 2015[20]	ESDF	34 124 870	20 751 800	60.8	17 001 717	10 255 722	60.3	17 123 153	10 496 078	61.3
1 VII 2016[20]	ESDF	34 486 536	21 154 782	61.3	17 180 879	10 445 229	60.8	17 305 657	10 709 553	61.9
Mozambique										
1 VII 2007[3]	ESDF	20 632 434	6 269 621	30.4	9 930 196	3 079 809	31.0	10 702 238	3 189 812	29.8
1 VIII 2007	CDFC	20 252 223	6 151 974	30.4	9 746 690	3 021 756	31.0	10 505 533	3 130 218	29.8
1 VII 2008[3]	ESDF	21 207 929	6 472 214	30.5	10 210 267	3 176 209	31.1	10 997 662	3 296 005	30.0
1 VII 2009[3]	ESDF	21 802 866	6 685 108	30.7	10 499 954	3 277 805	31.2	11 302 912	3 407 303	30.1
1 VII 2010[3]	ESDF	22 416 881	6 908 291	30.8	10 799 284	3 384 605	31.3	11 617 597	3 523 686	30.3
1 VII 2011[3]	ESDF	23 049 621	7 141 715	31.0	11 108 128	3 496 582	31.5	11 941 493	3 645 133	30.5
1 VII 2012[3]	ESDF	23 700 715	7 385 294	31.2	11 426 321	3 613 684	31.6	12 274 394	3 771 610	30.7
1 VII 2013[3]	ESDF	24 366 112	7 639 557	31.4	11 751 849	3 736 166	31.8	12 614 263	3 903 391	30.9
1 VII 2014[3]	ESDF	25 041 922	7 905 004	31.6	12 082 782	3 864 267	32.0	12 959 140	4 040 737	31.2
1 VII 2015[3]	ESDF	25 727 911	8 181 475	31.8	12 419 014	3 997 895	32.2	13 308 897	4 183 580	31.4
1 VII 2016[3]	ESDF	26 423 623	8 468 799	32.1	12 760 324	4 136 950	32.4	13 663 299	4 331 849	31.7
Namibia - Namibie										
1 VII 2007[3]	ESDF	2 027 871	...	...	989 067	...	...	1 038 804	...	...
1 VII 2008[3]	ESDF	2 065 226	...	...	1 008 115	...	...	1 057 111	...	...
1 VII 2009[3]	ESDF	2 103 761	...	...	1 027 736	...	...	1 076 025	...	...
1 VII 2010[3]	ESDF	2 143 410	...	...	1 047 900	...	...	1 095 510	...	...
1 VII 2011[21]	ESDF	2 116 077	900 163	42.5	1 026 911	439 993	42.8	1 089 166	460 170	42.2
28 VIII 2011	CDFC	2 113 077	903 434	42.8	1 021 912	440 334	43.1	1 091 165	463 100	42.4
1 VII 2012[21]	ESDF	2 155 440	940 825	43.6	1 046 434	459 668	43.9	1 109 006	481 157	43.4
1 VII 2013[21]	ESDF	2 196 086	982 519	44.7	1 066 541	479 844	45.0	1 129 545	502 675	44.5
1 VII 2014[21]	ESDF	2 237 894	1 025 147	45.8	1 087 178	500 469	46.0	1 150 716	524 678	45.6
1 VII 2015[21]	ESDF	2 280 716	1 068 625	46.9	1 108 276	521 496	47.1	1 172 440	547 129	46.7
1 VII 2016[21]	ESDF	2 324 388	1 112 868	47.9	1 129 754	542 893	48.1	1 194 634	569 975	47.7
Niger										
1 VII 2007[3]	ESDJ	13 716 233	2 556 499	18.6	6 846 984	1 279 904	18.7	6 869 249	1 276 595	18.6
1 VII 2008[3]	ESDJ	14 197 601	2 728 541	19.2	7 088 858	1 366 304	19.3	7 108 743	1 362 237	19.2
1 VII 2009[3]	ESDJ	14 693 113	2 911 006	19.8	7 337 909	1 457 958	19.9	7 355 203	1 453 048	19.8
1 VII 2010[3]	ESDJ	15 203 820	3 104 574	20.4	7 594 624	1 555 201	20.5	7 609 198	1 549 372	20.4
1 VII 2011[3]	ESDJ	15 730 756	3 309 954	21.0	7 859 534	1 658 395	21.1	7 871 221	1 651 559	21.0
1 VII 2012[22]	ESDJ	16 993 563	2 750 279	16.2	8 446 540	1 366 889	16.2	8 547 023	1 383 390	16.2
10 XII 2012	CDFC	16 734 935	...	...	8 183 513	...	...	8 551 422	...	...
1 VII 2013[22]	ESDJ	17 679 758	2 899 523	16.4	8 792 478	1 441 063	16.4	8 887 281	1 458 460	16.4
1 VII 2014[22]	ESDJ	18 389 162	3 010 567	16.4	9 150 266	1 496 252	16.4	9 238 897	1 514 315	16.4
1 VII 2015[22]	ESDJ	19 124 882	3 125 234	16.3	9 521 427	1 553 241	16.3	9 603 456	1 571 993	16.4
1 VII 2016[22]	ESDJ	19 865 066	3 242 161	16.3	9 898 628	1 611 354	16.3	9 966 438	1 630 807	16.4
Nigeria - Nigéria[23]										
1 VII 2007	ESDF	144 998 281	...	...	73 949 124	...	...	71 049 158	...	...
1 VII 2008	ESDF	149 713 264	...	...	76 353 765	...	...	73 359 499	...	...
1 VII 2009	ESDF	154 581 566	...	...	78 836 599	...	...	75 744 967	...	...
1 VII 2010	ESDF	159 608 173	...	...	81 400 168	...	...	78 208 005	...	...
1 VII 2011	ESDF	164 798 232	...	...	84 047 098	...	...	80 751 134	...	...
1 VII 2012	ESDF	170 157 060	...	...	86 780 100	...	...	83 376 959	...	...
1 VII 2013	ESDF	175 690 143	...	...	89 601 973	...	...	86 088 170	...	...
1 VII 2014	ESDF	181 403 148	...	...	92 515 605	...	...	88 887 542	...	...
1 VII 2015	ESDF	187 301 926	...	...	95 523 982	...	...	91 777 944	...	...
1 VII 2016	ESDF	193 392 517	...	...	98 630 184	...	...	94 762 333	...	...
Republic of South Sudan - République de Soudan du Sud										
21 IV 2008	CDFC	8 260 490	1 405 186	17.0	4 287 300	754 086	17.6	3 973 190	651 100	16.4
1 VII 2008[24]	ESDF	8 490 767	1 443 430	17.0	4 406 708	749 140	17.0	4 084 059	694 290	17.0
1 VII 2009[24]	ESDF	8 987 784	1 527 923	17.0	4 323 124	734 931	17.0	4 664 660	792 992	17.0

Continent, country or area, and date / Continent, pays ou zone et date	Code[a]	Both sexes - Les deux sexes			Male - Masculin			Female - Féminin		
		Total	Urban - Urbaine		Total	Urban - Urbaine		Total	Urban - Urbaine	
			Number Nombre	Percent P.100		Number Nombre	Percent P.100		Number Nombre	Percent P.100
AFRICA - AFRIQUE										
Republic of South Sudan - République de Soudan du Sud										
1 VII 2010[24] .... ESDF		9 496 844	1 614 463	17.0	4 567 982	776 557	17.0	4 928 862	837 907	17.0
1 VII 2011[24] .... ESDF		10 018 240	1 703 101	17.0	4 818 773	819 191	17.0	5 199 467	883 909	17.0
1 VII 2012[24] .... ESDF		10 552 270	1 793 886	17.0	5 075 642	862 859	17.0	5 476 628	931 027	17.0
1 VII 2013[24] .... ESDF		10 808 588	1 837 460	17.0	5 198 931	883 818	17.0	5 609 657	953 642	17.0
1 VII 2014[24] .... ESDF		11 071 132	1 882 093	17.0	5 325 215	905 286	17.0	5 745 917	976 806	17.0
Reunion - Réunion										
1 I 2007 .... ESDJ		794 107	...	...	385 335	...	...	408 772	...	...
1 I 2008 .... ESDJ		808 250	...	...	392 041	...	...	416 209	...	...
1 I 2009 .... ESDJ		816 364	...	...	395 688	...	...	420 676	...	...
1 I 2010 .... CDJC		821 136	808 540	98.5	398 006	391 623	98.4	423 130	416 917	98.5
1 I 2010 .... ESDJ		821 136	...	...	397 953	...	...	423 183	...	...
1 I 2011 .... ESDJ		828 581	...	...	401 139	...	...	427 442	...	...
1 I 2012 .... ESDJ		833 944	...	...	403 504	...	...	430 440	...	...
1 I 2013 .... ESDJ		835 103	...	...	403 731	...	...	431 372	...	...
1 I 2014 .... ESDJ		842 767	...	...	407 307	...	...	435 460	...	...
1 I 2015* .... ESDJ		847 005	...	...	409 347	...	...	437 658	...	...
1 I 2016* .... ESDJ		850 996	...	...	411 240	...	...	439 756	...	...
Rwanda										
1 VII 2007[3] .... ESDF		9 556 669	1 726 613	18.1	4 597 277	812 148	17.7	4 959 393	914 465	18.4
1 VII 2008[3] .... ESDF		9 831 501	...	...	4 736 104	...	...	5 095 397	...	...
1 VII 2009[3] .... ESDF		10 117 029	...	...	4 880 233	...	...	5 236 796	...	...
1 VII 2010[3] .... ESDF		10 412 820	1 541 097	14.8	5 029 450	...	...	5 383 371	...	...
1 VII 2011[3] .... ESDF		10 718 379	1 564 883	14.6	5 183 505	...	...	5 534 874	...	...
1 VII 2012[22] .... ESDF		10 482 641	1 732 175	16.5	5 049 164	889 118	17.6	5 433 477	843 057	15.5
15 VIII 2012 .... CDFC		10 393 542	1 760 994	16.9	4 981 197	902 501	18.1	5 412 345	858 493	15.9
1 VII 2013[22] .... ESDF		10 736 771	1 844 040	17.2	5 178 354	889 382	17.2	5 558 417	954 658	17.2
1 VII 2014[22] .... ESDF		10 996 891	1 962 945	17.8	5 310 430	947 912	17.9	5 686 461	1 015 033	17.8
1 VII 2015[22] .... ESDF		11 262 564	2 086 390	18.5	5 445 206	1 008 724	18.5	5 817 359	1 077 666	18.5
1 VII 2016[22] .... ESDF		11 533 445	2 214 421	19.2	5 582 519	1 071 844	19.2	5 950 925	1 142 578	19.2
Saint Helena ex. dep. - Sainte-Hélène sans dép.										
10 II 2008 .... CDFC		4 257	...	...	2 165	...	...	2 092	...	...
1 VII 2008 .... ESDF		3 981	...	...	2 022	...	...	1 959	...	...
1 VII 2012 .... ESDF		4 123	...	...	2 094	...	...	2 029	...	...
31 XII 2013 .... ESDF		4 211	...	...	2 139	...	...	2 072	...	...
7 II 2016[25] .... CDJC		4 534	...	...	2 396	...	...	2 138	...	...
Saint Helena: Ascension - Sainte-Hélène: Ascension										
1 VII 2008 .... ESDJ		702	...	...	397	...	...	305	...	...
Saint Helena: Tristan da Cunha - Sainte-Hélène: Tristan da Cunha[26]										
31 XII 2009 .... ESDF		262[27]	...	...	123	...	...	139	...	...
Sao Tome and Principe - Sao Tomé-et-Principe										
1 VII 2007 .... ESDF		154 875	...	...	76 256	...	...	78 619	...	...
1 VII 2008 .... ESDF		157 847	...	...	77 641	...	...	80 206	...	...
1 VII 2009 .... ESDF		160 820	...	...	79 027	...	...	81 794	...	...
1 VII 2010 .... ESDF		163 783	...	...	80 409	...	...	83 375	...	...
1 VII 2011 .... ESDF		166 728	...	...	81 783	...	...	84 945	...	...
13 V 2012 .... CDJC		178 739	119 781	67.0	88 867	58 710	66.1	89 872	61 071	68.0
Senegal - Sénégal										
31 XII 2007 .... ESDJ		11 519 242	4 684 315	40.7	5 670 261	2 322 314	41.0	5 848 981	2 362 001	40.4
31 XII 2008 .... ESDJ		11 841 137	4 815 214	40.7	5 828 711	2 387 209	41.0	6 012 426	2 428 005	40.4
31 XII 2009 .... ESDJ		12 171 264	4 949 461	40.7	5 991 214	2 453 764	41.0	6 180 050	2 495 697	40.4
31 XII 2010 .... ESDJ		12 509 434	5 086 978	40.7	6 157 675	2 521 940	41.0	6 351 759	2 565 038	40.4
31 XII 2011 .... ESDJ		12 841 702	6 086 966	47.4	6 350 673	3 010 218	47.4	6 491 029	3 076 748	47.4
1 VII 2013[3] .... ESDJ		13 508 715	...	...	6 735 420	...	...	6 773 295	...	...
19 XI 2013 .... CDFC		13 357 492	...	...	6 658 089	...	...	6 699 403	...	...
1 VII 2014[3] .... ESDJ		13 926 253	...	...	6 941 357	...	...	6 961 847	...	...

Continent, country or area, and date / Continent, pays ou zone et date	Code[a]	Both sexes - Les deux sexes			Male - Masculin			Female - Féminin		
		Total	Urban - Urbaine		Total	Urban - Urbaine		Total	Urban - Urbaine	
			Number Nombre	Percent P.100		Number Nombre	Percent P.100		Number Nombre	Percent P.100
AFRICA - AFRIQUE										
Senegal - Sénégal										
1 VII 2015[3]	ESDJ	14 356 575	...	...	7 153 656	...	...	7 202 919	...	...
1 VII 2016[3]	ESDJ	14 799 859	...	...	7 372 487	...	...	7 427 372	...	...
Seychelles										
1 VII 2007	ESDF	85 032	...	...	43 160	...	...	41 872	...	...
1 VII 2008	ESDF	86 956	...	...	44 999	...	...	41 957	...	...
1 VII 2009	ESDF	87 298	...	...	45 022	...	...	42 276	...	...
1 VII 2010	ESDF	89 770	...	...	45 907	...	...	43 863	...	...
26 VIII 2010	CDFC	90 945	...	...	46 912	...	...	44 033	...	...
1 VII 2011	ESDF	87 441	...	...	43 127	...	...	44 314	...	...
1 VII 2012	ESDF	88 303	...	...	43 313	...	...	44 990	...	...
1 VII 2013	ESDF	89 949	...	...	44 735	...	...	45 214	...	...
1 VII 2014	ESDF	91 359	...	...	45 278	...	...	46 081	...	...
1 VII 2015	ESDF	93 419	...	...	46 322	...	...	47 097	...	...
Sierra Leone										
1 VII 2007	ESDF	5 343 200	2 069 160	38.7	2 589 965	1 022 089	39.5	2 753 235	1 047 071	38.0
1 VII 2008	ESDF	5 473 530	2 142 918	39.2	2 653 490	1 058 523	39.9	2 820 040	1 084 395	38.5
1 VII 2009	ESDF	5 607 930	2 221 331	39.6	2 719 034	1 097 256	40.4	2 888 896	1 124 075	38.9
1 VII 2010	ESDF	5 746 800	2 304 955	40.1	2 786 797	1 138 563	40.9	2 960 003	1 166 392	39.4
1 VII 2011	ESDF	5 890 080	2 394 041	40.6	2 856 755	1 182 568	41.4	3 033 325	1 211 473	39.9
1 VII 2012	ESDF	6 037 660	2 489 123	41.2	2 928 862	1 229 535	42.0	3 108 798	1 259 588	40.5
5 XII 2015	CDFC	7 092 113	2 905 097	41.0	3 490 978	1 438 591	41.2	3 601 135	1 466 506	40.7
South Africa - Afrique du Sud										
1 VII 2007	ESDF	48 883 845	...	...	23 717 983	...	...	25 165 862	...	...
1 VII 2008	ESDF	49 557 573	...	...	24 078 593	...	...	25 478 980	...	...
1 VII 2009	ESDF	50 255 813	...	...	24 449 834	...	...	25 805 979	...	...
1 VII 2010	ESDF	50 979 432	...	...	24 832 080	...	...	26 147 353	...	...
1 VII 2011	ESDF	51 729 345	...	...	25 225 720	...	...	26 503 626	...	...
10 X 2011	CDFC	51 770 560	32 559 331	62.9	25 188 791	...	...	26 581 769	...	...
1 VII 2012	ESDF	52 506 515	...	...	25 631 161	...	...	26 875 354	...	...
1 VII 2013	ESDF	53 311 956	...	...	26 048 829	...	...	27 263 126	...	...
1 VII 2014	ESDF	54 146 735	...	...	26 479 167	...	...	27 667 567	...	...
1 VII 2015	ESDF	55 011 977	...	...	26 922 639	...	...	28 089 338	...	...
1 VII 2016	ESDF	55 908 865	...	...	27 379 728	...	...	28 529 137	...	...
Sudan - Soudan										
21 IV 2008	CDFC	30 894 000	...	...	15 786 677	...	...	15 107 323	...	...
1 VII 2008	ESDF	30 978 758	10 314 730	33.3	15 790 134	5 350 451	33.9	15 188 624	4 964 279	32.7
1 VII 2009	ESDF	31 956 791	10 860 950	34.0	16 275 239	5 531 361	34.0	15 681 552	5 329 589	34.0
1 VII 2010	ESDF	32 961 966	11 296 966	34.3	16 774 288	5 749 007	34.3	16 187 678	5 547 959	34.3
1 VII 2011	ESDF	33 997 538	11 749 240	34.6	17 289 105	5 974 957	34.6	16 708 434	5 774 283	34.6
1 VII 2012	ESDF	35 064 299	12 218 313	34.8	17 820 009	6 209 462	34.8	17 244 290	6 008 851	34.8
1 VII 2013	ESDF	36 162 516	12 704 550	35.1	18 367 086	6 452 691	35.1	17 795 430	6 251 858	35.1
1 VII 2014	ESDF	37 292 376	13 208 281	35.4	18 930 385	6 704 798	35.4	18 361 991	6 503 483	35.4
1 VII 2015	ESDF	38 454 040	13 729 842	35.7	19 509 961	6 965 944	35.7	18 944 080	6 763 898	35.7
1 VII 2016	ESDF	39 647 621	14 269 540	36.0	20 105 842	7 236 276	36.0	19 541 779	7 033 264	36.0
Swaziland										
11 III 2007	CDFC	844 223	186 890	22.1	405 868	93 918	23.1	438 355	92 972	21.2
1 VII 2007	ESDF	1 018 449	225 293	22.1	481 428	108 071	22.4	537 021	117 222	21.8
1 VII 2008	ESDF	1 031 747	229 516	22.2	488 132	109 937	22.5	543 615	119 579	22.0
1 VII 2009	ESDF	1 043 509	233 504	22.4	494 061	111 704	22.6	549 448	121 800	22.2
1 VII 2010	ESDF	1 055 506	237 641	22.5	500 070	113 554	22.7	555 436	124 087	22.3
1 VII 2011	ESDF	1 067 773	241 947	22.7	506 186	115 493	22.8	561 587	126 454	22.5
1 VII 2012	ESDF	1 080 337	246 441	22.8	512 432	117 528	22.9	567 905	128 913	22.7
1 VII 2013	ESDF	1 093 158	251 122	23.0	518 788	119 658	23.1	574 370	131 464	22.9
1 VII 2014	ESDF	1 106 189	255 986	23.1	525 232	121 881	23.2	580 957	134 105	23.1
1 I 2015	ESDF	1 119 375	261 028	23.3	531 737	124 195	23.4	587 638	136 833	23.3
1 I 2016	ESDF	1 132 657	266 230	23.5	538 274	126 593	23.5	594 383	139 637	23.5
Togo										
6 XI 2010	CDJC	6 191 155	2 334 495	37.7	3 009 095	1 131 533	37.6	3 182 060	1 202 962	37.8
Tunisia - Tunisie										
1 VII 2007	ESDF	10 225 100	...	...	5 105 100	...	...	5 120 000	...	...
1 VII 2008	ESDF	10 328 900	...	...	5 156 300	...	...	5 172 600	...	...
1 VII 2009	ESDF	10 439 600	...	...	5 207 200	...	...	5 232 400	...	...
1 VII 2010	ESDF	10 547 100	...	...	5 261 700	...	...	5 285 400	...	...

Continent, country or area, and date / Continent, pays ou zone et date	Code[a]	Both sexes - Les deux sexes			Male - Masculin			Female - Féminin		
		Total	Urban - Urbaine		Total	Urban - Urbaine		Total	Urban - Urbaine	
			Number Nombre	Percent P.100		Number Nombre	Percent P.100		Number Nombre	Percent P.100

AFRICA - AFRIQUE

Tunisia - Tunisie										
1 VII 2011 ....ESDF		10 673 800	...	...	5 316 900	...	...	5 356 800	...	...
23 IV 2014 ....CDFC		10 982 754	7 437 671	67.7	5 472 338	3 713 527	67.9	5 510 416	3 724 144	67.6
Uganda - Ouganda										
1 VII 2007 ....ESDF		28 581 300	4 223 800	14.8	13 866 700	2 022 200	14.6	14 714 600	2 201 600	15.0
1 VII 2008 ....ESDF		29 592 600	4 372 000	14.8	14 383 200	2 095 700	14.6	15 209 400	2 276 300	15.0
1 VII 2009 ....ESDF		30 661 300	4 524 900	14.8	14 933 900	2 171 400	14.5	15 727 400	2 353 500	15.0
1 VII 2010 ....ESDF		31 784 600	...	...	15 516 600	...	...	16 268 000	...	...
1 VII 2011 ....ESDF		32 939 800	...	...	16 118 600	...	...	16 821 200	...	...
1 VII 2012 ....ESDF		34 131 400	...	...	16 741 400	...	...	17 390 000	...	...
1 VII 2014[8] ....ESDF		34 141 299	...	...	16 594 490	...	...	17 546 809	...	...
27 VIII 2014 ....CDFC		34 634 650	8 438 009	24.4	16 897 849	4 042 324	23.9	17 736 801	4 395 685	24.8
1 VII 2015[8] ....ESDF		35 492 100	...	...	17 337 600	...	...	18 154 500	...	...
1 VII 2016[8] ....ESDF		36 560 700	...	...	17 882 300	...	...	18 678 400	...	...
United Republic of Tanzania - République Unie de Tanzanie										
1 VII 2007[28] ....ESDF		39 446 061	9 962 731	25.3	19 352 480	4 911 847	25.4	20 093 581	5 050 884	25.1
1 VII 2008[28] ....ESDF		40 667 794	10 419 287	25.6	19 970 944	5 139 187	25.7	20 696 850	5 280 100	25.5
1 VII 2009[28] ....ESDF		41 915 880	10 892 350	26.0	20 604 730	5 375 260	26.1	21 311 150	5 517 090	25.9
1 VII 2010[28] ....ESDF		43 187 823	11 378 015	26.3	21 252 423	5 618 133	26.4	21 935 400	5 759 882	26.3
1 VII 2011[28] ....ESDF		44 484 857	11 875 395	26.7	21 914 229	5 867 287	26.8	22 570 628	6 008 108	26.6
1 VII 2012[28] ....ESDF		45 798 475	12 386 841	27.0	22 585 634	6 123 839	27.1	23 212 841	6 263 002	27.0
26 VIII 2012[29] ....CDFC		44 928 923	13 305 004	29.6	21 869 990	6 407 396	29.3	23 058 933	6 897 608	29.9
1 VII 2013[22] ....ESDF		46 170 154	...	...	22 475 187	...	...	23 694 967	...	...
1 VII 2014[22] ....ESDF		47 451 844	...	...	23 100 125	...	...	24 351 719	...	...
1 VII 2015[22] ....ESDF		48 775 567	...	...	23 745 563	...	...	25 030 004	...	...
1 VII 2016[22] ....ESDF		50 142 938	...	...	24 412 293	...	...	25 730 645	...	...
Zambia - Zambie										
16 X 2010 ....CDFC		12 526 314	5 021 022	40.1	6 117 253	2 452 904	40.1	6 409 061	2 568 118	40.1
Zimbabwe										
1 VII 2007[28] ....ESDF		12 040 000	4 171 175	34.6	5 831 902	2 057 948	35.3	6 208 098	2 113 226	34.0
1 VII 2008[28] ....ESDF		12 150 000	3 495 205	28.8	5 885 184	1 691 434	28.7	6 264 816	1 803 752	28.8
1 VII 2009[28] ....ESDF		13 667 894	...	...	6 642 551	...	...	7 025 344	...	...
17 VIII 2012 ....CDFC		13 061 239	4 284 145	32.8	6 280 539	2 039 224	32.5	6 780 700	2 244 921	33.1
1 VII 2013[30] ....ESDF		13 368 620	...	...	6 428 233	...	...	6 940 389	...	...
1 VII 2014[30] ....ESDF		13 652 297	...	...	6 564 085	...	...	7 088 214	...	...
1 VII 2015[30] ....ESDF		13 943 242	...	...	6 703 559	...	...	7 239 681	...	...
1 VII 2016[30] ....ESDF		14 240 168	...	...	6 846 020	...	...	7 394 149	...	...

AMERICA, NORTH - AMÉRIQUE DU NORD

Anguilla										
11 V 2011 ....CDFC		13 572	...	...	6 707	...	...	6 865	...	...
Antigua and Barbuda - Antigua-et-Barbuda										
1 VII 2007 ....ESDF		85 903	...	...	40 342	...	...	45 561	...	...
27 V 2011 ....CDJC		85 567	...	...	40 986	...	...	44 581	...	...
Aruba										
1 VII 2007 ....ESDJ		100 149	...	...	47 490	...	...	52 660	...	...
1 VII 2008 ....ESDJ		100 916	...	...	47 890	...	...	53 027	...	...
1 VII 2009 ....ESDJ		101 604	...	...	48 291	...	...	53 312	...	...
1 VII 2010 ....ESDJ		101 873	...	...	48 419	...	...	53 454	...	...
29 IX 2010 ....CDJC		101 484	...	...	48 241	...	...	53 243	...	...
1 VII 2011 ....ESDJ		102 809	...	...	48 801	...	...	54 008	...	...
1 VII 2012 ....ESDJ		104 574	...	...	49 558	...	...	55 016	...	...
1 VII 2013 ....ESDJ		106 380	...	...	50 329	...	...	56 051	...	...
1 VII 2014 ....ESDJ		107 820	...	...	50 990	...	...	56 830	...	...
1 VII 2015 ....ESDJ		109 222	...	...	51 682	...	...	57 540	...	...
1 VII 2016 ....ESDJ		110 292	...	...	52 216	...	...	58 076	...	...
Bahamas										
1 VII 2007[3] ....ESDF		334 000	...	...	162 300	...	...	171 700	...	...
1 VII 2008[3] ....ESDF		338 300	...	...	164 800	...	...	173 500	...	...

Continent, country or area, and date / Continent, pays ou zone et date	Code[a]	Both sexes - Les deux sexes			Male - Masculin			Female - Féminin		
		Total	Urban - Urbaine		Total	Urban - Urbaine		Total	Urban - Urbaine	
			Number Nombre	Percent P.100		Number Nombre	Percent P.100		Number Nombre	Percent P.100
AMERICA, NORTH - AMÉRIQUE DU NORD										
Bahamas										
1 VII 2009[3]	ESDF	342 400	...	...	166 800	...	...	175 600	...	...
3 V 2010	CDJC	351 461	...	...	170 257	...	...	181 204	...	...
1 VII 2010[3]	ESDF	334 642	...	...	162 730	...	...	171 911	...	...
1 VII 2011[3]	ESDF	357 750	...	...	175 029	...	...	182 721	...	...
1 VII 2012[3]	ESDF	362 590	...	...	177 440	...	...	185 150	...	...
1 VII 2013[3]	ESDF	368 390	...	...	179 850	...	...	188 540	...	...
1 VII 2014[3]	ESDF	372 000	...	...	182 000	...	...	190 000	...	...
1 VII 2016*[3]	ESDF	373 480	...	...	180 280	...	...	193 200	...	...
Barbados - Barbade										
1 VII 2007	ESDF	274 162	...	...	132 388	...	...	141 774	...	...
1 VII 2008	ESDF	274 848	...	...	132 786	...	...	142 062	...	...
1 VII 2009	ESDF	275 441	...	...	133 133	...	...	142 308	...	...
1 V 2010[31]	CDJC	277 821	...	...	133 018	...	...	144 803	...	...
1 VII 2010	ESDF	277 758	...	...	133 018	...	...	144 740	...	...
1 VII 2011	ESDF	277 622	...	...	133 119	...	...	144 503	...	...
1 VII 2012	ESDF	277 668	...	...	133 355	...	...	144 313	...	...
1 VII 2013	ESDF	277 492	...	...	133 369	...	...	144 123	...	...
1 VII 2014	ESDF	277 199	...	...	133 343	...	...	143 856	...	...
1 VII 2015	ESDF	274 633	...	...	131 146	...	...	143 487	...	...
Belize										
1 VII 2007	ESDF	298 792	...	...	149 638	...	...	149 154	...	...
1 VII 2008	ESDF	306 809	138 716	45.2	153 570	67 647	44.0	153 239	71 069	46.4
1 VII 2009	ESDF	315 082	142 447	45.2	157 622	69 450	44.1	157 460	72 997	46.4
12 V 2010	CDJC	322 453	145 832	45.2	161 227	71 087	44.1	161 226	74 745	46.4
1 VII 2010	ESDF	323 598	146 323	45.2	161 800	71 328	44.1	161 798	74 995	46.4
1 VII 2011	ESDF	332 084	149 955	45.2	166 043	73 110	44.0	166 041	76 845	46.3
1 VII 2012	ESDF	340 792	153 683	45.1	170 397	74 938	44.0	170 395	78 745	46.2
1 VII 2013	ESDF	349 728	157 508	45.0	174 865	76 815	43.9	174 863	80 693	46.1
1 VII 2014	ESDF	358 899	161 434	45.0	179 451	78 740	43.9	179 448	82 694	46.1
1 VII 2015	ESDF	368 310	165 463	44.9	184 157	80 717	43.8	184 153	84 746	46.0
1 VII 2016	ESDF	377 968	169 598	44.9	188 986	82 746	43.8	188 982	86 852	46.0
Bermuda - Bermudes										
1 VII 2007[32]	ESDJ	64 009	...	...	30 577	...	...	33 432	...	...
1 VII 2008[32]	ESDJ	64 209	...	...	30 644	...	...	33 565	...	...
1 VII 2009[32]	ESDJ	64 395	...	...	30 704	...	...	33 691	...	...
20 V 2010[33]	CDJC	64 237	64 237	100.0	30 858	30 858	100.0	33 379	33 379	100.0
1 VII 2010[11]	ESDJ	64 129	...	...	30 792	...	...	33 337	...	...
1 VII 2011[11]	ESDJ	63 193	...	...	30 218	...	...	32 975	...	...
1 VII 2012[11]	ESDJ	62 408	...	...	29 819	...	...	32 589	...	...
1 VII 2013[11]	ESDJ	61 954	...	...	29 587	...	...	32 367	...	...
1 VII 2014[11]	ESDJ	61 777	...	...	29 499	...	...	32 278	...	...
1 VII 2015[11]	ESDJ	61 735	...	...	29 480	...	...	32 255	...	...
1 VII 2016[11]	ESDJ	61 695	...	...	29 463	...	...	32 232	...	...
British Virgin Islands - Îles Vierges britanniques										
12 VII 2010	CDFC	28 054	...	...	13 820	...	...	14 234	...	...
Canada										
1 VII 2007[34]	ESDJ	32 887 928	...	...	16 298 320	...	...	16 589 608	...	...
1 VII 2008[34]	ESDJ	33 245 773	...	...	16 473 545	...	...	16 772 228	...	...
1 VII 2009[34]	ESDJ	33 628 571	...	...	16 663 222	...	...	16 965 349	...	...
1 VII 2010[34]	ESDJ	34 005 274	...	...	16 847 961	...	...	17 157 313	...	...
2 V 2011	CDJC	33 476 690	27 147 190	81.1	16 414 225	13 190 225	80.4	17 062 455	13 956 960	81.8
1 VII 2011[35]	ESDJ	34 342 780	...	...	17 015 959	...	...	17 326 821	...	...
1 VII 2012[35]	ESDJ	34 750 545	...	...	17 227 368	...	...	17 523 177	...	...
1 VII 2013[36]	ESDJ	35 155 451	...	...	17 433 972	...	...	17 721 479	...	...
1 VII 2014[36]	ESDJ	35 544 564	...	...	17 629 788	...	...	17 914 776	...	...
1 VII 2015[36]	ESDJ	35 848 610	...	...	17 776 946	...	...	18 071 664	...	...
1 VII 2016*[37]	ESDJ	36 286 425	...	...	17 995 581	...	...	18 290 844	...	...
Cayman Islands - Îles Caïmanes										
31 XII 2007	ESDJ	53 886	...	...	26 773	...	...	27 113	...	...
31 XII 2008	ESDJ	57 009	...	...	28 264	...	...	28 745	...	...

Continent, country or area, and date / Continent, pays ou zone et date	Code[a]	Both sexes - Les deux sexes			Male - Masculin			Female - Féminin		
		Total	Urban - Urbaine		Total	Urban - Urbaine		Total	Urban - Urbaine	
			Number Nombre	Percent P.100		Number Nombre	Percent P.100		Number Nombre	Percent P.100
AMERICA, NORTH - AMÉRIQUE DU NORD										
Cayman Islands - Îles Caïmanes										
31 XII 2009	ESDJ	56 005	...	...	27 840	...	...	28 165	...	...
10 X 2010[38]	CDJC	55 036	55 036	100.0	27 218	27 218	100.0	27 818	27 818	100.0
31 XII 2010	ESDJ	55 036	...	...	27 219	...	...	27 817	...	...
31 XII 2011	ESDJ	55 517	...	...	27 454	...	...	28 063	...	...
31 XII 2012	ESDJ	56 732	...	...	27 753	...	...	28 979	...	...
31 XII 2013	ESDJ	55 747	...	...	27 133	...	...	28 614	...	...
31 XII 2014	ESDJ	58 238	...	...	28 322	...	...	29 916	...	...
31 XII 2015	ESDJ	60 413	...	...	30 264	...	...	30 149	...	...
Costa Rica										
1 VII 2007	ESDJ	4 443 100	2 619 591	59.0	2 195 652	1 273 998	58.0	2 247 448	1 345 593	59.9
1 VII 2008[39]	ESDJ	4 533 162	2 671 667	58.9	2 246 474	1 299 940	57.9	2 286 688	1 371 727	60.0
1 VII 2009[39]	ESDJ	4 620 482	2 722 273	58.9	2 291 886	1 325 468	57.8	2 328 596	1 396 805	60.0
1 VII 2010[40]	ESDJ	4 538 307	3 304 248[41]	72.8	2 206 526	1 579 816[41]	71.6	2 331 781	1 724 432[41]	74.0
30 V 2011	CDJC	4 301 712	3 130 871	72.8	2 106 063	1 509 161	71.7	2 195 649	1 621 710	73.9
1 VII 2011[40]	ESDJ	4 592 346	3 343 241	72.8	2 238 615	1 603 354	71.6	2 353 731	1 739 887	73.9
1 VII 2012[40]	ESDJ	4 651 166	3 384 925	72.8	2 266 220	1 621 617	71.6	2 384 946	1 763 308	73.9
1 VII 2013[40]	ESDJ	4 711 986	3 427 548	72.7	2 276 708	1 624 941	71.4	2 435 278	1 802 607	74.0
1 VII 2014[40]	ESDJ	4 772 098	3 469 802	72.7	2 325 438	1 662 288	71.5	2 446 660	1 807 514	73.9
1 VII 2015[42]	ESDJ	4 833 752	3 512 683	72.7	2 350 223	1 683 770	71.6	2 483 529	1 828 913	73.6
1 VII 2016[43]	ESDJ	4 889 762	3 551 728	72.6	2 373 531	1 703 473	71.8	2 516 231	1 848 255	73.5
Cuba										
1 VII 2007	ESDJ	11 195 330	8 446 381	75.4	5 605 756	4 155 581	74.1	5 589 574	4 290 800	76.8
1 VII 2008	ESDJ	11 181 012	8 426 393	75.4	5 597 673	4 146 862	74.1	5 583 339	4 279 531	76.6
1 VII 2009	ESDJ	11 174 474	8 420 630	75.4	5 594 504	4 145 111	74.1	5 579 971	4 275 519	76.6
1 VII 2010	ESDJ	11 171 443	8 416 524	75.3	5 592 729	4 143 388	74.1	5 578 714	4 273 136	76.6
1 VII 2011	ESDJ	11 171 679	8 409 543	75.3	5 592 332	4 140 377	74.0	5 579 347	4 269 166	76.5
1 VII 2012	ESDJ	11 174 287	8 494 128	76.0	5 583 306	4 159 342	74.5	5 590 981	4 334 786	77.5
14 IX 2012	CDFC	11 167 325	8 575 189	76.8	5 570 825	4 177 485	75.0	5 596 500	4 397 704	78.6
1 VII 2013	ESDJ	11 191 608	8 596 991	76.8	5 580 810	4 186 436	75.0	5 610 798	4 410 555	78.6
1 VII 2014	ESDJ	11 224 190	8 625 144	76.8	5 595 379	4 199 578	75.1	5 628 811	4 425 566	78.6
1 VII 2015	ESDJ	11 238 661	8 639 191	76.9	5 600 904	4 205 871	75.1	5 637 757	4 433 320	78.6
1 VII 2016	ESDJ	11 239 114	8 644 181	76.9	5 599 279	4 207 382	75.1	5 639 835	4 436 798	78.7
Curaçao										
1 VII 2007[44]	ESDJ	144 061	...	...	65 952	...	...	78 109	...	...
1 VII 2008[44]	ESDJ	145 882	...	...	66 746	...	...	79 136	...	...
1 VII 2009[44]	ESDJ	146 833	...	...	67 237	...	...	79 596	...	...
1 VII 2010[44]	ESDJ	148 703	...	...	68 065	...	...	80 639	...	...
26 III 2011	CDFC	150 563	...	...	68 848	...	...	81 715	...	...
1 VII 2011[44]	ESDJ	150 831	...	...	68 910	...	...	81 921	...	...
1 VII 2012[45]	ESDJ	152 088	...	...	69 490	...	...	82 598	...	...
1 VII 2013[45]	ESDJ	153 822	...	...	70 342	...	...	83 480	...	...
1 VII 2014[45]	ESDJ	155 909	...	...	71 269	...	...	84 640	...	...
1 VII 2015[45]	ESDJ	157 980	...	...	72 187	...	...	85 794	...	...
1 VII 2016[45]	ESDJ	159 663	...	...	72 990	...	...	86 674	...	...
Dominica - Dominique										
1 VII 2007	ESDF	70 729	...	...	35 603	...	...	35 126	...	...
1 VII 2008	ESDF	70 726	...	...	35 602	...	...	35 124	...	...
1 VII 2009	ESDF	70 747	...	...	35 811	...	...	34 936	...	...
1 VII 2010	ESDF	70 730	...	...	35 604	...	...	35 126	...	...
14 V 2011	CDFC	68 913	...	...	34 973	...	...	33 940	...	...
1 XII 2011	ESDF	70 755	...	...	35 762	...	...	34 992	...	...
1 VII 2012	ESDF	71 042	...	...	36 053	...	...	34 989	...	...
1 VII 2013	ESDF	71 221	...	...	36 144	...	...	35 077	...	...
1 VII 2014	ESDF	71 575	...	...	36 324	...	...	35 251	...	...
Dominican Republic - République dominicaine										
1 VII 2007	ESDF	9 174 058	6 399 362	69.8	4 598 212	3 138 848	68.3	4 575 846	3 260 514	71.3
1 VII 2008	ESDF	9 279 602	6 594 497	71.1	4 649 902	3 235 238	69.6	4 629 700	3 359 259	72.6
1 VII 2009	ESDF	9 380 152	6 788 782	72.4	4 699 042	3 331 179	70.9	4 681 110	3 457 603	73.9
1 VII 2010[3]	ESDF	9 478 612	6 992 189	73.8	4 747 103	3 431 480	72.3	4 731 509	3 560 709	75.3
1 XII 2010	CDJC	9 445 281	7 013 575	74.3	4 739 038	3 449 122	72.8	4 706 243	3 564 453	75.7

Continent, country or area, and date / Continent, pays ou zone et date	Code[a]	Both sexes - Les deux sexes Total	Urban - Urbaine Number Nombre	Urban - Urbaine Percent P.100	Male - Masculin Total	Urban - Urbaine Number Nombre	Urban - Urbaine Percent P.100	Female - Féminin Total	Urban - Urbaine Number Nombre	Urban - Urbaine Percent P.100
AMERICA, NORTH - AMÉRIQUE DU NORD										
Dominican Republic - République dominicaine										
1 VII 2011[3]	ESDF	9 580 139	7 172 502	74.9	4 796 628	3 520 702	73.4	4 783 511	3 651 800	76.3
1 VII 2012[3]	ESDF	9 680 963	7 348 975	75.9	4 845 755	3 608 025	74.5	4 835 208	3 740 950	77.4
1 VII 2013[3]	ESDF	9 784 680	7 524 149	76.9	4 896 319	3 694 713	75.5	4 888 361	3 829 436	78.3
1 VII 2014[3]	ESDF	9 883 486	7 691 885	77.8	4 944 386	3 777 718	76.4	4 939 100	3 914 167	79.2
1 VII 2015[3]	ESDF	9 980 243	7 854 203	78.7	4 991 398	3 858 029	77.3	4 988 845	3 996 174	80.1
1 VII 2016[3]	ESDF	10 075 045	8 011 084	79.5	5 037 329	3 935 569	78.1	5 037 716	4 075 515	80.9
El Salvador										
12 V 2007	CDJC	5 744 113	3 598 836	62.7	2 719 371	1 676 313	61.6	3 024 742	1 922 523	63.6
1 VII 2007[46]	ESDF	6 098 714	3 766 800	61.8	2 887 804	1 752 851	60.7	3 210 910	2 013 949	62.7
1 VII 2008[46]	ESDF	6 124 705	3 828 004	62.5	2 895 210	1 779 210	61.5	3 229 495	2 048 794	63.4
1 VII 2009[46]	ESDF	6 152 558	3 890 523	63.2	2 903 737	1 806 310	62.2	3 248 821	2 084 213	64.2
1 VII 2010[46]	ESDF	6 183 002	3 954 803	64.0	2 913 743	1 834 400	63.0	3 269 259	2 120 404	64.9
1 VII 2011[46]	ESDF	6 216 143	4 019 742	64.7	2 925 284	1 862 924	63.7	3 290 858	2 156 818	65.5
1 VII 2012[46]	ESDF	6 251 495	4 086 880	65.4	2 938 123	1 892 642	64.4	3 313 372	2 194 238	66.2
1 VII 2013[46]	ESDF	6 288 899	4 156 007	66.1	2 952 174	1 923 447	65.2	3 336 726	2 232 560	66.9
1 VII 2014[46]	ESDF	6 328 196	...	...	2 967 351	...	...	3 360 845	...	...
1 VII 2015[46]	ESDF	6 460 271	4 502 693	69.7	3 042 036	2 119 867	69.7	3 418 235	2 382 826	69.7
1 VII 2016[46]	ESDF	6 520 675	4 590 491	70.4	3 070 065	2 161 168	70.4	3 450 610	2 429 323	70.4
Greenland - Groenland[47]										
1 VII 2007	ESDJ	56 555	47 056	83.2	29 945	24 746	82.6	26 610	22 310	83.8
1 I 2008	CDJC	56 462	...	...	29 885	...	...	26 577	...	...
1 VII 2008	ESDJ	56 328	47 103	83.6	29 847	24 790	83.1	26 481	22 313	84.3
1 VII 2009	ESDJ	56 323	47 230	83.9	29 873	24 865	83.2	26 451	22 366	84.6
1 VII 2010	ESDJ	56 534	47 646	84.3	29 939	25 045	83.7	26 595	22 601	85.0
1 VII 2011	ESDJ	56 682	48 045	84.8	29 992	25 233	84.1	26 690	22 812	85.5
1 VII 2012	ESDJ	56 810	48 224	84.9	30 105	25 331	84.1	26 705	22 893	85.7
1 VII 2013	ESDJ	56 483	48 221	85.4	29 867	25 333	84.8	26 616	22 888	86.0
1 VII 2014	ESDJ	56 295	48 232	85.7	29 742	25 320	85.1	26 553	22 912	86.3
1 VII 2015	ESDJ	56 114	48 284	86.0	29 634	25 329	85.5	26 480	22 955	86.7
1 VII 2016	ESDJ	56 186	48 447	86.2	29 701	25 436	85.6	26 485	23 011	86.9
Grenada - Grenade										
1 VII 2007	ESDF	104 981	...	...	52 472	...	...	52 509	...	...
1 VII 2008	ESDF	105 298	...	...	52 655	...	...	52 643	...	...
1 VII 2009	ESDF	105 175	...	...	52 720	...	...	52 455	...	...
1 VII 2010	ESDF	105 038	...	...	52 788	...	...	52 250	...	...
12 V 2011	CDFC	106 667	...	...	53 898	...	...	52 769	...	...
1 VII 2011	ESDF	106 667	...	...	53 898	...	...	52 769	...	...
1 VII 2012	ESDF	107 599	...	...	54 435	...	...	53 164	...	...
1 VII 2013	ESDF	108 580	...	...	54 926	...	...	53 654	...	...
Guadeloupe[48]										
1 I 2007	ESDJ	400 584	...	...	188 325	...	...	212 259	...	...
1 I 2008	ESDJ	401 784	...	...	188 389	...	...	213 395	...	...
1 I 2009	ESDJ	401 554	...	...	187 867	...	...	213 687	...	...
1 I 2010	CDJC	403 355	397 070	98.4	187 932	184 752	98.3	215 423	212 318	98.6
1 I 2010	ESDJ	403 355	...	...	187 912	...	...	215 443	...	...
1 I 2011	ESDJ	404 635	...	...	187 782	...	...	216 853	...	...
1 I 2012	ESDJ	403 314	...	...	187 038	...	...	216 276	...	...
1 I 2013	ESDJ	402 119	...	...	186 077	...	...	216 042	...	...
1 I 2014	ESDJ	403 750	...	...	186 235	...	...	217 515	...	...
1 I 2015*	ESDJ	397 902	...	...	183 101	...	...	214 801	...	...
1 I 2016*	ESDJ	395 725	...	...	181 700	...	...	214 025	...	...
Guatemala[28]										
1 VII 2008	ESDF	13 677 815	...	...	6 673 533	...	...	7 004 282	...	...
1 VII 2009	ESDF	14 017 057	...	...	6 836 849	...	...	7 180 208	...	...
1 VII 2010	ESDF	14 361 666	...	...	7 003 337	...	...	7 358 328	...	...
1 VII 2011	ESDF	14 713 763	...	...	7 173 966	...	...	7 539 797	...	...
1 VII 2012	ESDF	15 073 375	...	...	7 352 869	...	...	7 720 506	...	...
1 VII 2013	ESDF	15 438 384	...	...	7 903 145	...	...	7 535 238	...	...
1 VII 2014	ESDF	15 806 675	...	...	8 087 279	...	...	7 719 396	...	...
1 VII 2015	ESDF	16 176 133	...	...	8 272 469	...	...	7 903 664	...	...

6. Total and urban population by sex: 2007 - 2016
Population totale et population urbaine selon le sexe : 2007 - 2016 (continued - suite)

Continent, country or area, and date / Continent, pays ou zone et date	Code[a]	Both sexes - Les deux sexes			Male - Masculin			Female - Féminin		
		Total	Urban - Urbaine		Total	Urban - Urbaine		Total	Urban - Urbaine	
			Number Nombre	Percent P.100		Number Nombre	Percent P.100		Number Nombre	Percent P.100
AMERICA, NORTH - AMÉRIQUE DU NORD										
Haiti - Haïti[49]										
1 VII 2007 ....ESDJ		9 602 304	...	...	4 751 622	...	...	4 850 682	...	...
1 VII 2008 ....ESDJ		9 761 927	...	...	4 831 621	...	...	4 930 306	...	...
1 VII 2009 ....ESDJ		9 923 243	...	...	4 912 515	...	...	5 010 728	...	...
1 VII 2010 ....ESDJ		10 085 214	4 817 666	47.8	4 993 731	2 321 608	46.5	5 091 483	2 496 059	49.0
1 VII 2011 ....ESDJ		10 248 306	...	...	5 075 517	...	...	5 172 789	...	...
1 VII 2012 ....ESDJ		10 413 211	5 154 940	49.5	5 158 254	2 495 108	48.4	5 254 957	2 659 832	50.6
1 VII 2013 ....ESDJ		10 579 230	...	...	5 241 572	...	...	5 337 658	...	...
1 VII 2014 ....ESDJ		10 745 665	...	...	5 325 099	...	...	5 420 566	...	...
1 VII 2015 ....ESDJ		10 911 819	...	...	5 408 465	...	...	5 503 354	...	...
Honduras										
1 VII 2007[50] ....ESDF		7 536 952	3 752 579	49.8	3 717 577	1 793 588	48.2	3 819 375	1 958 991	51.3
1 VII 2008[50] ....ESDF		7 706 907	...	...	3 800 300	...	...	3 906 607	...	...
1 VII 2009[50] ....ESDF		7 876 662	...	...	3 882 957	...	...	3 993 705	...	...
1 VII 2010[50] ....ESDF		8 045 990	...	...	3 965 430	...	...	4 080 560	...	...
10 VIII 2013 ....CDFC		8 303 771	4 480 746	54.0	4 052 316	2 116 113	52.2	4 251 456	2 364 633	55.6
1 VII 2014[4] ....ESDF		8 432 153	...	...	4 113 061	...	...	4 319 092	...	...
1 VII 2015[4] ....ESDF		8 576 532	...	...	4 181 657	...	...	4 394 875	...	...
Jamaica - Jamaïque										
1 VII 2007 ....ESDJ		2 675 831	1 390 754	52.0	1 318 444	663 995	50.4	1 357 387	726 759	53.5
1 VII 2008 ....ESDJ		2 687 241	1 396 470	52.0	1 324 277	666 761	50.3	1 362 964	729 709	53.5
1 VII 2009 ....ESDJ		2 695 583	...	...	1 328 124	...	...	1 367 460	...	...
1 VII 2010 ....ESDJ		2 702 314	...	...	1 324 134	...	...	1 378 180	...	...
4 IV 2011[51] ....CDJC		2 697 983	1 454 153	53.9	1 334 533	700 957	52.5	1 363 450	753 196	55.2
1 VII 2011 ....ESDJ		2 699 838	...	...	1 335 466	...	...	1 364 372	...	...
1 VII 2012 ....ESDJ		2 707 805	...	...	1 339 740	...	...	1 368 065	...	...
1 VII 2013 ....ESDJ		2 714 669	...	...	1 343 798	...	...	1 370 871	...	...
1 VII 2014 ....ESDJ		2 720 554	...	...	1 346 711	...	...	1 373 843	...	...
1 VII 2015 ....ESDJ		2 725 288	...	...	1 349 294	...	...	1 375 994	...	...
1 VII 2016 ....ESDJ		2 729 112	...	...	1 351 649	...	...	1 377 463	...	...
Martinique										
1 I 2007 ....ESDJ		397 730	...	...	184 970	...	...	212 760	...	...
1 I 2008 ....ESDJ		397 693	...	...	184 437	...	...	213 256	...	...
1 I 2009 ....ESDJ		396 404	...	...	183 655	...	...	212 749	...	...
1 I 2010 ....CDJC		394 173	380 973	96.7	182 073	175 573	96.4	212 100	205 400	96.8
1 I 2010 ....ESDJ		394 173	...	...	182 110	...	...	212 063	...	...
1 I 2011 ....ESDJ		392 291	...	...	180 676	...	...	211 615	...	...
1 I 2012 ....ESDJ		388 364	...	...	178 824	...	...	209 540	...	...
1 I 2013 ....ESDJ		385 551	...	...	177 955	...	...	207 596	...	...
1 I 2014 ....ESDJ		383 911	...	...	177 502	...	...	206 409	...	...
1 I 2015* ....ESDJ		380 440	...	...	175 886	...	...	204 554	...	...
1 I 2016* ....ESDJ		376 847	...	...	174 200	...	...	202 647	...	...
Mexico - Mexique										
1 VII 2007 ....ESDJ		109 787 388	...	...	53 646 464	...	...	56 140 924	...	...
1 VII 2008 ....ESDJ		111 299 015	...	...	54 373 653	...	...	56 925 362	...	...
1 VII 2009 ....ESDJ		112 852 594	...	...	55 144 845	...	...	57 707 749	...	...
12 VI 2010[52] ....CDFC		112 336 538	86 287 410	76.8	54 855 231	41 946 540	76.5	57 481 307	44 340 870	77.1
1 VII 2010[3] ....ESDJ		114 255 555	82 629 456	72.3	55 801 919	...	...	58 453 636	...	...
1 VII 2011[3] ....ESDJ		115 682 868	83 726 767	72.4	56 519 798	...	...	59 163 070	...	...
1 VII 2012[3] ....ESDJ		117 053 750	84 776 446	72.4	57 174 268	...	...	59 879 482	...	...
1 VII 2013[3] ....ESDJ		118 395 054	85 792 843	72.5	57 810 955	...	...	60 584 099	...	...
1 VII 2014[3] ....ESDJ		119 713 203	86 782 031	72.5	58 435 900	...	...	61 277 304	...	...
1 VII 2015[3] ....ESDJ		121 005 815	87 743 091	72.5	59 046 837	...	...	61 958 979	...	...
1 VII 2016[3] ....ESDJ		122 273 473	88 677 252	72.5	59 644 308	...	...	62 629 165	...	...
Montserrat										
12 V 2011 ....CDJC		4 922	...	...	2 546	...	...	2 376	...	...
1 VII 2016 ....ESDF		5 045	...	...	2 596	...	...	2 449	...	...
Nicaragua										
1 VII 2007 ....ESDJ		5 595 541	3 152 807	56.3	2 775 638	1 515 432	54.6	2 819 903	1 637 375	58.1
1 VII 2008 ....ESDJ		5 668 866	3 206 205	56.6	2 809 918	1 542 386	54.9	2 858 948	1 663 819	58.2
1 VII 2009 ....ESDJ		5 742 316	3 259 955	56.8	2 844 244	1 569 555	55.2	2 898 072	1 690 400	58.3
Panama										
1 VII 2007[53] ....ESDF		3 475 741	...	...	1 749 211	...	...	1 726 530	...	...
1 VII 2008[53] ....ESDF		3 537 986	...	...	1 780 140	...	...	1 757 846	...	...

Continent, country or area, and date / Continent, pays ou zone et date	Code[a]	Both sexes - Les deux sexes Total	Urban - Urbaine Number Nombre	Urban - Urbaine Percent P.100	Male - Masculin Total	Urban - Urbaine Number Nombre	Urban - Urbaine Percent P.100	Female - Féminin Total	Urban - Urbaine Number Nombre	Urban - Urbaine Percent P.100
AMERICA, NORTH - AMÉRIQUE DU NORD										
Panama										
1 VII 2009[53] .... ESDF		3 600 000	...	...	1 810 794	...	...	1 789 206	...	...
16 V 2010 .... CDFC		3 405 813	...	...	1 712 584	...	...	1 693 229	...	...
1 VII 2010[11] .... ESDF		3 661 835	2 385 445	65.1	1 841 305	1 171 489	63.6	1 820 530	1 213 956	66.7
1 VII 2011[11] .... ESDF		3 723 821	2 449 917	65.8	1 871 749	1 203 430	64.3	1 852 072	1 246 487	67.3
1 VII 2012[11] .... ESDF		3 787 511	2 514 402	66.4	1 903 085	1 235 377	64.9	1 884 426	1 279 025	67.9
1 VII 2013[11] .... ESDF		3 850 735	2 578 868	67.0	1 934 264	1 267 319	65.5	1 916 471	1 311 549	68.4
1 VII 2014[11] .... ESDF		3 913 275	2 643 353	67.5	1 965 087	1 299 262	66.1	1 948 188	1 344 091	69.0
1 VII 2015[11] .... ESDF		3 975 404	2 707 838	68.1	1 995 695	1 331 207	66.7	1 979 709	1 376 631	69.5
1 VII 2016[11] .... ESDF		4 037 043	2 772 324	68.7	2 026 044	1 363 153	67.3	2 010 999	1 409 171	70.1
Puerto Rico - Porto Rico[54]										
1 VII 2007[44] .... ESDJ		3 782 995	...	...	1 814 288	...	...	1 968 707	...	...
1 VII 2008[44] .... ESDJ		3 760 866	...	...	1 803 341	...	...	1 957 525	...	...
1 VII 2009[44] .... ESDJ		3 740 410	...	...	1 793 049	...	...	1 947 361	...	...
1 IV 2010 .... CDJC		3 725 789	3 493 256	93.8	1 785 171	...	...	1 940 618	...	...
1 VII 2010[55] .... ESDJ		3 721 208	...	...	1 782 619	...	...	1 938 589	...	...
1 VII 2011[45] .... ESDJ		3 678 736	...	...	1 763 445	...	...	1 915 291	...	...
1 VII 2012[45] .... ESDJ		3 634 487	...	...	1 739 075	...	...	1 895 412	...	...
1 VII 2013[45] .... ESDJ		3 593 079	...	...	1 720 288	...	...	1 872 791	...	...
1 VII 2014[45] .... ESDJ		3 534 888	...	...	1 688 903	...	...	1 845 985	...	...
1 VII 2015[45] .... ESDJ		3 474 182	...	...	1 656 148	...	...	1 818 034	...	...
Saint Kitts and Nevis - Saint-Kitts-et-Nevis										
1 VII 2007* .... ESDF		50 640	...	...	24 765	...	...	25 875	...	...
1 VII 2008* .... ESDF		51 300	...	...	25 085	...	...	26 215	...	...
1 VII 2009* .... ESDF		51 970	...	...	25 415	...	...	26 555	...	...
1 VII 2010* .... ESDF		52 650	...	...	25 750	...	...	26 900	...	...
15 V 2011* .... CDFC		46 398	...	...	22 846	...	...	23 552	...	...
Saint Lucia - Sainte-Lucie										
1 VII 2007 .... ESDF		168 338	...	...	82 426	...	...	85 912	...	...
1 VII 2008 .... ESDF		170 331	...	...	83 478	...	...	86 853	...	...
1 VII 2009 .... ESDF		172 370	...	...	84 465	...	...	87 905	...	...
10 V 2010 .... CDJC		165 770	...	...	83 502	...	...	82 268	...	...
1 VII 2011 .... ESDF		167 366	...	...	82 925	...	...	84 441	...	...
1 VII 2012 .... ESDF		169 170	...	...	83 861	...	...	85 309	...	...
1 VII 2013 .... ESDF		170 925	...	...	84 768	...	...	86 158	...	...
1 VII 2014 .... ESDF		172 623	...	...	85 639	...	...	86 984	...	...
Saint Vincent and the Grenadines - Saint-Vincent-et-les Grenadines										
1 VII 2007 .... ESDJ		109 551	49 830	45.5	55 725	...	...	53 826	...	...
1 VII 2008 .... ESDJ		109 639	49 870	45.5	55 770	...	...	53 869	...	...
1 VII 2009 .... ESDJ		109 727	49 911	45.5	55 814	...	...	53 912	...	...
1 VII 2010 .... ESDJ		109 815	49 951	45.5	55 859	...	...	53 956	...	...
1 VII 2011 .... ESDJ		109 903	49 991	45.5	55 904	...	...	53 999	...	...
12 VI 2012[56] .... CDFC		109 188	...	...	55 551	...	...	53 637	...	...
1 VII 2012 .... ESDJ		109 991	50 926	46.3	56 419	...	...	53 572	...	...
1 VII 2013 .... ESDJ		110 079	50 967	46.3	56 464	...	...	53 615	...	...
1 VII 2014 .... ESDJ		110 167	51 008	46.3	56 509	...	...	53 658	...	...
1 VII 2015 .... ESDJ		110 255	51 048	46.3	56 555	...	...	53 701	...	...
Sint Maarten (Dutch part) - Saint-Martin (partie néerlandaise)										
1 VII 2007 .... ESDJ		39 466	...	...	19 106	...	...	20 361	...	...
1 VII 2008 .... ESDJ		40 461	...	...	19 632	...	...	20 829	...	...
1 VII 2009 .... ESDJ		39 172	...	...	18 918	...	...	20 254	...	...
1 VII 2010 .... ESDJ		35 526	...	...	16 927	...	...	18 600	...	...
9 IV 2011 .... CDFC		33 609	...	...	15 868	...	...	17 741	...	...
1 VII 2011 .... ESDJ		33 436	...	...	15 772	...	...	17 656	...	...
1 VII 2012 .... ESDJ		34 670	...	...	16 656	...	...	18 005	...	...

142

Continent, country or area, and date Continent, pays ou zone et date	Code[a]	Both sexes - Les deux sexes			Male - Masculin			Female - Féminin		
		Total	Urban - Urbaine		Total	Urban - Urbaine		Total	Urban - Urbaine	
			Number Nombre	Percent P.100		Number Nombre	Percent P.100		Number Nombre	Percent P.100
AMERICA, NORTH - AMÉRIQUE DU NORD										
Sint Maarten (Dutch part) - Saint-Martin (partie néerlandaise)										
1 VII 2013 ....ESDJ		36 611	...	...	17 910	...	...	18 701	...	...
1 I 2014 ....ESDJ		37 132	...	...	18 159	...	...	18 973	...	...
Trinidad and Tobago - Trinité-et-Tobago										
1 VII 2007[17] ....ESDF		1 303 188	...	...	653 549	...	...	649 639	...	...
1 VII 2008[17] ....ESDF		1 308 587	...	...	656 257	...	...	652 330	...	...
1 VII 2009[17] ....ESDF		1 310 106	...	...	657 018	...	...	653 088	...	...
1 VII 2010[17] ....ESDF		1 317 714	...	...	660 822	...	...	656 892	...	...
9 I 2011 ....CDJC		1 328 019	...	...	666 305	...	...	661 714	...	...
1 VII 2012[18] ....ESDF		1 335 194	...	...	669 905	...	...	665 289	...	...
1 VII 2013[18] ....ESDF		1 340 557	...	...	672 596	...	...	667 961	...	...
1 VII 2014[18] ....ESDF		1 345 343	...	...	674 997	...	...	670 346	...	...
1 VII 2015[18] ....ESDF		1 349 667	...	...	677 166	...	...	672 501	...	...
1 VII 2016[18] ....ESDF		1 353 895	...	...	679 288	...	...	674 607	...	...
Turks and Caicos Islands - Îles Turques et Caïques										
1 VII 2007 ....ESDJ		34 862	...	...	18 023	...	...	16 839	...	...
1 VII 2009 ....ESDJ		36 000	...	...	18 810	...	...	17 190	...	...
1 VII 2010 ....ESDJ		34 500	...	...	17 810	...	...	16 690	...	...
1 VII 2011 ....ESDJ		33 500	...	...	17 160	...	...	16 340	...	...
25 I 2012*[57] ....CDFC		31 458	...	...	16 037	...	...	15 421	...	...
1 VII 2012 ....ESDJ		32 199	...	...	16 365	...	...	15 834	...	...
1 VII 2013 ....ESDJ		33 677	...	...	17 132	...	...	16 545	...	...
1 VII 2014 ....ESDJ		35 168	...	...	17 907	...	...	17 261	...	...
1 VII 2015 ....ESDJ		36 689	...	...	18 689	...	...	18 000	...	...
1 VII 2016 ....ESDJ		37 910	...	...	19 169	...	...	18 741	...	...
United States of America - États-Unis d'Amérique										
1 VII 2007[58] ....ESDJ		301 231 207	...	...	148 064 854	...	...	153 166 353	...	...
1 VII 2008[58] ....ESDJ		304 093 966	...	...	149 489 951	...	...	154 604 015	...	...
1 VII 2009[58] ....ESDJ		306 771 529	...	...	150 807 454	...	...	155 964 075	...	...
1 IV 2010 ....CDJC		308 745 538	249 253 271	80.7	151 781 326	121 698 595	80.2	156 964 212	127 554 676	81.3
1 VII 2010[59] ....ESDJ		309 348 193	...	...	152 088 743	...	...	157 259 450	...	...
1 VII 2011[59] ....ESDJ		311 663 358	...	...	153 263 360	...	...	158 399 998	...	...
1 VII 2012[59] ....ESDJ		313 998 379	...	...	154 467 180	...	...	159 531 199	...	...
1 VII 2013[59] ....ESDJ		316 204 908	...	...	155 589 564	...	...	160 615 344	...	...
1 VII 2014[59] ....ESDJ		318 563 456	...	...	156 780 062	...	...	161 783 394	...	...
1 VII 2015[59] ....ESDJ		320 896 618	...	...	157 960 035	...	...	162 936 583	...	...
1 VII 2016[59] ....ESDJ		323 127 513	...	...	159 078 923	...	...	164 048 590	...	...
United States Virgin Islands - Îles Vierges américaines[54]										
1 VII 2007 ....ESDJ		109 821	...	...	52 089	...	...	57 732	...	...
1 VII 2008 ....ESDJ		109 840	...	...	52 045	...	...	57 795	...	...
1 IV 2010 ....CDJC		106 405	...	...	50 854	...	...	55 551	...	...
AMERICA, SOUTH - AMÉRIQUE DU SUD										
Argentina - Argentine										
1 VII 2007 ....ESDF		39 356 383	35 719 891	90.8	19 273 494	17 383 239	90.2	20 082 889	18 336 652	91.3
1 VII 2008 ....ESDF		39 745 613	36 137 648	90.9	19 465 305	17 597 280	90.4	20 280 308	18 540 368	91.4
1 VII 2009 ....ESDF		40 134 425	36 553 965	91.1	19 657 086	17 810 843	90.6	20 477 339	18 743 122	91.5
1 VII 2010[60] ....ESDF		40 788 453	37 126 653	91.0	19 940 704	17 996 224	90.2	20 847 749	19 130 429	91.8
27 X 2010 ....CDFC		40 117 096	36 467 245	90.9	19 523 766	17 596 022	90.1	20 593 330	18 871 223	91.6
1 VII 2011[60] ....ESDF		41 261 490	37 600 508	91.1	20 180 791	18 236 611	90.4	21 080 699	19 363 897	91.9
1 VII 2012[60] ....ESDF		41 733 271	38 073 305	91.2	20 420 391	18 476 577	90.5	21 312 880	19 596 728	91.9
1 VII 2013[60] ....ESDF		42 202 935	38 544 203	91.3	20 659 037	18 715 667	90.6	21 543 898	19 828 536	92.0
1 VII 2014[60] ....ESDF		42 669 500	39 021 268	91.5	20 896 203	18 958 322	90.7	21 773 297	20 062 946	92.1

6. Total and urban population by sex: 2007 - 2016
Population totale et population urbaine selon le sexe : 2007 - 2016 (continued - suite)

Continent, country or area, and date / Continent, pays ou zone et date	Code[a]	Both sexes - Les deux sexes			Male - Masculin			Female - Féminin		
		Total	Urban - Urbaine		Total	Urban - Urbaine		Total	Urban - Urbaine	
			Number Nombre	Percent P.100		Number Nombre	Percent P.100		Number Nombre	Percent P.100
AMERICA, SOUTH - AMÉRIQUE DU SUD										
Argentina - Argentine										
1 VII 2015[60] .... ESDF		43 131 966	39 487 935	91.6	21 131 346	19 195 446	90.8	22 000 620	20 292 489	92.2
1 VII 2016[60] .... ESDF		43 590 368	39 951 022	91.7	21 364 470	19 430 772	90.9	22 225 898	20 520 250	92.3
Bolivia (Plurinational State of) - Bolivie (État plurinational de)										
1 VII 2007 .... ESDF		9 549 689	...	...	4 804 855	...	...	4 744 834	...	...
1 VII 2008 .... ESDF		9 709 958	...	...	4 889 348	...	...	4 820 610	...	...
1 VII 2009 .... ESDF		9 870 229	...	...	4 973 094	...	...	4 897 135	...	...
1 VII 2010 .... ESDF		10 030 501	...	...	5 056 056	...	...	4 974 445	...	...
1 VII 2011 .... ESDF		10 190 775	...	...	5 138 206	...	...	5 052 569	...	...
1 VII 2012 .... ESDF		10 351 118	6 965 568	67.3	5 219 006	3 437 451	65.9	5 132 112	3 528 117	68.7
21 XI 2012 .... CDFC		10 059 856	6 788 962	67.5	5 019 447	3 314 824	66.0	5 040 409	3 474 138	68.9
1 VII 2013 .... ESDF		10 507 789	7 110 575	67.7	5 297 727	3 511 796	66.3	5 210 062	3 598 779	69.1
1 VII 2014 .... ESDF		10 665 841	7 256 749	68.0	5 376 880	3 586 449	66.7	5 288 961	3 670 300	69.4
1 VII 2015 .... ESDF		10 825 013	7 403 841	68.4	5 456 332	3 661 290	67.1	5 368 681	3 742 551	69.7
1 VII 2016 .... ESDF		10 985 059	7 551 625	68.7	5 535 975	3 736 216	67.5	5 449 084	3 815 409	70.0
Brazil - Brésil										
1 VII 2007[61] .... ESDJ		189 462 755	158 059 957	83.4	93 829 262	...	...	95 633 493	...	...
1 VII 2008[61] .... ESDJ		191 532 439	160 383 924	83.7	94 816 963	...	...	96 715 476	...	...
1 VII 2009[61] .... ESDJ		193 543 969	162 670 274	84.0	95 776 055	...	...	97 767 914	...	...
1 VII 2010[61] .... ESDJ		195 497 797	164 920 459	84.4	96 706 703	...	...	98 791 094	...	...
31 VII 2010 .... CDJC		190 755 799	160 925 804	84.4	93 406 990	77 710 179	83.2	97 348 809	83 215 625	85.5
1 VII 2011[61] .... ESDJ		197 397 018	167 096 245	84.6	97 610 297	...	...	99 786 721	...	...
1 VII 2012[61] .... ESDJ		199 242 462	169 230 105	84.9	98 487 258	...	...	100 755 204	...	...
1 VII 2013[61] .... ESDJ		201 032 714	171 317 079	85.2	99 336 858	...	...	101 695 856	...	...
1 VII 2014[61] .... ESDJ		202 768 562	173 358 764	85.5	100 159 507	...	...	102 609 055	...	...
1 VII 2015[61] .... ESDJ		204 450 649	175 355 103	85.8	100 955 522	...	...	103 495 127	...	...
1 VII 2016[61] .... ESDJ		206 081 432	177 309 126	86.0	101 726 102	...	...	104 355 330	...	...
Chile - Chili										
1 VII 2007 .... ESDF		16 598 074	14 421 386	86.9	8 216 068	7 057 476	85.9	8 382 006	7 363 910	87.9
1 VII 2008 .... ESDF		16 763 470	14 570 311	86.9	8 297 819	7 131 097	85.9	8 465 651	7 439 214	87.9
1 VII 2009 .... ESDF		16 928 873	14 719 246	86.9	8 379 571	7 204 720	86.0	8 549 302	7 514 526	87.9
1 VII 2010 .... ESDF		17 094 275	14 868 172	87.0	8 461 327	7 278 342	86.0	8 632 948	7 589 830	87.9
1 VII 2011 .... ESDF		17 248 450	15 006 226	87.0	8 536 904	7 346 185	86.1	8 711 546	7 660 041	87.9
1 VII 2012 .... ESDF		17 402 630	15 144 277	87.0	8 612 483	7 414 026	86.1	8 790 147	7 730 251	87.9
1 VII 2013 .... ESDF		17 556 815	15 282 334	87.0	8 688 067	7 481 874	86.1	8 868 748	7 800 460	88.0
1 VII 2014 .... ESDF		17 819 054	15 559 039	87.3	8 819 725	7 628 149	86.5	8 999 329	7 930 890	88.1
1 VII 2015 .... ESDF		18 006 407	15 729 803	87.4	8 911 940	7 714 356	86.6	9 094 467	8 015 447	88.1
1 VII 2016 .... ESDF		18 191 884	15 898 145	87.4	9 003 254	7 799 463	86.6	9 188 630	8 098 682	88.1
Colombia - Colombie[62]										
1 VII 2007 .... ESDJ		43 926 929	32 888 860	74.9	21 683 071	15 850 700	73.1	22 243 858	17 038 160	76.6
1 VII 2008 .... ESDJ		44 451 147	33 396 380	75.1	21 942 355	16 100 320	73.4	22 508 792	17 296 060	76.8
1 VII 2009 .... ESDJ		44 978 832	33 892 634	75.4	22 203 708	16 343 820	73.6	22 775 124	17 548 814	77.1
1 VII 2010 .... ESDJ		45 509 584	34 388 013	75.6	22 466 660	16 587 100	73.8	23 042 924	17 800 913	77.3
1 VII 2011 .... ESDJ		46 044 601	34 883 399	75.8	22 731 299	16 830 795	74.0	23 313 302	18 052 604	77.4
1 VII 2012 .... ESDJ		46 581 823	35 377 138	75.9	22 997 087	17 073 806	74.2	23 584 736	18 303 332	77.6
1 VII 2013 .... ESDJ		47 121 089	35 869 246	76.1	23 264 039	17 315 981	74.4	23 857 050	18 553 265	77.8
1 VII 2014 .... ESDJ		47 661 787	36 359 268	76.3	23 531 670	17 556 826	74.6	24 130 117	18 802 442	77.9
1 VII 2015 .... ESDJ		48 203 405	36 846 935	76.4	23 799 679	17 796 724	74.8	24 403 726	19 050 211	78.1
1 VII 2016 .... ESDJ		48 747 708	37 332 955	76.6	24 069 035	18 035 960	74.9	24 678 673	19 296 995	78.2
Ecuador - Équateur										
1 VII 2007[63] .... ESDF		14 214 982	8 896 925	62.6	7 071 884	4 371 337	61.8	7 143 098	4 525 588	63.4
1 VII 2008[63] .... ESDF		14 472 881	9 064 267	62.6	7 192 128	4 449 107	61.9	7 280 753	4 615 160	63.4
1 VII 2009[63] .... ESDF		14 738 472	9 236 112	62.7	7 316 020	4 528 987	61.9	7 422 452	4 707 125	63.4
1 VII 2010[63] .... ESDF		15 012 228	9 412 612	62.7	7 443 875	4 611 039	61.9	7 568 353	4 801 573	63.4
28 XI 2010 .... CDFC		14 483 499	9 090 786	62.8	7 177 683	4 451 434	62.0	7 305 816	4 639 352	63.5
1 VII 2011[63] .... ESDF		15 266 431	9 596 628	62.9	7 567 676	4 700 620	62.1	7 698 755	4 896 008	63.6
1 VII 2012[63] .... ESDF		15 520 973	9 780 650	63.0	7 691 912	4 790 437	62.3	7 829 061	4 990 213	63.7
1 VII 2013[63] .... ESDF		15 774 749	9 963 884	63.2	7 815 935	4 880 045	62.4	7 958 814	5 083 839	63.9
1 VII 2014[63] .... ESDF		16 027 466	10 145 875	63.3	7 939 552	4 969 197	62.6	8 087 914	5 176 678	64.0
1 VII 2015[63] .... ESDF		16 278 844	10 326 384	63.4	8 062 610	5 057 750	62.7	8 216 234	5 268 634	64.1
1 VII 2016[63] .... ESDF		16 528 730	10 505 180	63.6	8 184 970	5 145 594	62.9	8 343 760	5 359 586	64.2

Continent, country or area, and date / Continent, pays ou zone et date	Code[a]	Both sexes - Les deux sexes			Male - Masculin			Female - Féminin		
		Total	Urban - Urbaine		Total	Urban - Urbaine		Total	Urban - Urbaine	
			Number Nombre	Percent P.100		Number Nombre	Percent P.100		Number Nombre	Percent P.100
AMERICA, SOUTH - AMÉRIQUE DU SUD										
Falkland Islands (Malvinas) - Îles Falkland (Malvinas)[64]										
15 IV 2012	CDFC	2 840	...	...	1 491	...	...	1 349	...	...
French Guiana - Guyane française										
1 I 2007	ESDJ	213 031	...	...	105 546	...	...	107 485	...	...
1 I 2008	ESDJ	219 266	...	...	108 673	...	...	110 593	...	...
1 I 2009	ESDJ	224 469	...	...	111 201	...	...	113 268	...	...
1 I 2010	CDJC	229 040	201 042	87.8	113 599	98 933	87.1	115 441	102 109	88.5
1 I 2010	ESDJ	229 040	201 042	87.8	113 599	98 933	87.1	115 441	102 109	88.5
1 I 2011	ESDJ	237 549	...	...	117 732	...	...	119 817	...	...
1 I 2012	ESDJ	239 648	...	...	119 538	...	...	120 110	...	...
1 I 2013	CDJC	244 118	...	...	121 653	...	...	122 465	...	...
1 I 2013	ESDJ	244 118	...	...	121 653	...	...	122 465	...	...
1 I 2014	ESDJ	252 338	...	...	125 189	...	...	127 149	...	...
1 I 2015*	ESDJ	257 348	...	...	127 840	...	...	129 508	...	...
1 I 2016*	ESDJ	262 527	...	...	130 596	...	...	131 931	...	...
Guyana										
1 VII 2007	ESDF	770 992	...	...	385 882	...	...	385 110	...	...
1 VII 2008	ESDF	774 443	...	...	387 649	...	...	386 794	...	...
1 VII 2009	ESDF	753 227	...	...	377 759	...	...	375 468	...	...
1 VII 2010	ESDF	752 113	...	...	377 267	...	...	374 846	...	...
1 VII 2011	ESDF	750 663	...	...	376 596	...	...	374 067	...	...
1 VII 2012	ESDF	748 917	...	...	375 767	...	...	373 150	...	...
15 IX 2012*	CDFC	747 884	...	...	372 547	...	...	375 337	...	...
1 VII 2013	ESDF	746 880	...	...	374 782	...	...	372 098	...	...
Paraguay[65]										
1 VII 2007	ESDF	5 974 666	3 403 819	57.0	3 019 704	1 663 438	55.1	2 954 962	1 740 382	58.9
1 VII 2008	ESDF	6 071 781	3 486 807	57.4	3 068 356	1 704 209	55.5	3 003 425	1 782 599	59.4
1 VII 2009	ESDF	6 168 757	3 569 718	57.9	3 116 847	1 744 890	56.0	3 051 910	1 824 828	59.8
1 VII 2010	ESDF	6 265 877	3 652 713	58.3	3 165 316	1 785 556	56.4	3 100 561	1 867 157	60.2
1 VII 2011	ESDF	6 363 276	3 738 905	58.8	3 213 839	1 827 856	56.9	3 149 438	1 911 049	60.7
1 VII 2012	ESDF	6 461 041	3 825 311	59.2	3 262 466	1 870 215	57.3	3 198 575	1 955 096	61.1
1 VII 2013	ESDF	6 559 027	3 911 850	59.6	3 311 123	1 912 591	57.8	3 247 904	1 999 259	61.6
1 VII 2014	ESDF	6 657 232	3 998 524	60.1	3 359 806	1 954 982	58.2	3 297 426	2 043 541	62.0
1 VII 2015	ESDF	6 755 756	4 085 396	60.5	3 408 566	1 997 419	58.6	3 347 190	2 087 977	62.4
1 VII 2016	ESDF	6 854 536	4 174 834	60.9	3 457 365	2 041 139	59.0	3 397 170	2 133 695	62.8
Peru - Pérou										
30 VI 2007[46]	ESDF	28 481 901	20 594 600	72.3	14 282 346	10 189 918	71.3	14 199 555	10 404 682	73.3
21 X 2007	CDFC	27 412 157	20 810 288	75.9	13 622 640	10 226 205	75.1	13 789 517	10 584 083	76.8
30 VI 2008[46]	ESDF	28 807 034	20 995 699	72.9	14 443 858	10 386 799	71.9	14 363 176	10 608 900	73.9
30 VI 2009[46]	ESDF	29 132 013	21 398 222	73.5	14 605 206	10 584 348	72.5	14 526 807	10 813 874	74.4
30 VI 2010[46]	ESDF	29 461 933	21 805 837	74.0	14 768 901	10 784 345	73.0	14 693 032	11 021 492	75.0
30 VI 2011[46]	ESDF	29 797 694	22 219 201	74.6	14 935 396	10 987 090	73.6	14 862 298	11 232 111	75.6
30 VI 2012[46]	ESDF	30 135 875	22 635 742	75.1	15 103 003	11 191 332	74.1	15 032 872	11 444 410	76.1
30 VI 2013[46]	ESDF	30 475 144	23 054 394	75.6	15 271 062	11 396 589	74.6	15 204 082	11 657 805	76.7
30 VI 2014[46]	ESDF	30 814 175	23 474 069	76.2	15 438 887	11 602 321	75.1	15 375 288	11 871 748	77.2
30 VI 2015[46]	ESDF	31 151 643	23 893 654	76.7	15 605 814	11 808 006	75.7	15 545 829	12 085 648	77.7
30 VI 2016[46]	ESDF	31 488 625	24 313 862	77.2	15 772 385	12 013 953	76.2	15 716 240	12 299 909	78.3
Suriname										
1 VII 2007	ESDJ	509 970	...	...	257 181	...	...	252 789	...	...
1 VII 2008	ESDJ	517 052	...	...	260 898	...	...	256 154	...	...
13 VIII 2012	CDJC	541 638	359 146	66.3	270 629	177 215	65.5	271 009	181 931	67.1
1 VII 2013	ESDJ	550 222	...	...	274 859	...	...	275 363	...	...
1 VII 2014	ESDJ	558 773	...	...	279 071	...	...	279 702	...	...
1 VII 2015	ESDJ	567 291	...	...	283 259	...	...	284 032	...	...
Uruguay										
1 VII 2007	ESDJ	3 358 794	3 158 483	94.0	1 623 189	1 509 920	93.0	1 735 604	1 648 563	95.0
1 VII 2008	ESDJ	3 363 060	3 169 767	94.3	1 624 932	1 515 980	93.3	1 738 128	1 653 786	95.1
1 VII 2009	ESDJ	3 378 083	3 191 384	94.5	1 632 052	1 527 146	93.6	1 746 031	1 664 238	95.3
1 VII 2010	ESDJ	3 396 706	3 216 510	94.7	1 640 886	1 539 959	93.8	1 755 820	1 676 560	95.5
1 VII 2011	ESDJ	3 412 636	3 238 644	94.9	1 648 466	1 551 366	94.1	1 764 170	1 687 279	95.6
4 X 2011	CDJC	3 286 314	3 110 701	94.7	1 577 725[66]	1 478 967[66]	93.7	1 708 481[66]	1 631 626[66]	95.5

Continent, country or area, and date / Continent, pays ou zone et date	Code[a]	Both sexes - Les deux sexes			Male - Masculin			Female - Féminin		
		Total	Urban - Urbaine		Total	Urban - Urbaine		Total	Urban - Urbaine	
			Number Nombre	Percent P.100		Number Nombre	Percent P.100		Number Nombre	Percent P.100
AMERICA, SOUTH - AMÉRIQUE DU SUD										
Uruguay										
1 VII 2012[3] .... ESDJ		3 426 466	3 253 370	94.9	1 655 693	1 559 292	94.2	1 770 774	1 694 078	95.7
1 VII 2013[3] .... ESDJ		3 440 157	3 268 281	95.0	1 662 884	1 567 325	94.3	1 777 273	1 700 956	95.7
1 VII 2014[3] .... ESDJ		3 453 691	3 283 177	95.1	1 670 026	1 575 363	94.3	1 783 665	1 707 813	95.7
1 VII 2015[3] .... ESDJ		3 467 054	3 297 948	95.1	1 677 118	1 583 363	94.4	1 789 936	1 714 585	95.8
1 VII 2016[3] .... ESDJ		3 480 222	3 312 523	95.2	1 684 140	1 591 280	94.5	1 796 082	1 721 243	95.8
Venezuela (Bolivarian Republic of) - Venezuela (République bolivarienne du)										
1 VII 2007 .... ESDF		27 272 712	24 012 062	88.0	13 682 677	11 923 756	87.1	13 590 035	12 088 306	88.9
1 VII 2008 .... ESDF		27 688 638	24 384 883	88.1	13 889 561	12 109 269	87.2	13 799 077	12 275 614	89.0
1 VII 2009 .... ESDF		28 105 913	24 758 144	88.1	14 097 305	12 295 131	87.2	14 008 608	12 463 013	89.0
1 VII 2010 .... ESDF		28 524 411	25 131 837	88.1	14 305 797	12 481 264	87.2	14 218 614	12 650 573	89.0
1 VII 2011 .... ESDF		28 944 070	25 504 003	88.1	14 514 965	12 666 928	87.3	14 429 105	12 837 075	89.0
1 IX 2011 .... CDJC		27 227 930	24 182 998[67]	88.8	13 549 752	11 902 155[67]	87.8	13 678 178	12 280 843[67]	89.8
1 VII 2012 .... ESDF		29 365 589	25 881 720	88.1	14 725 042	12 855 436	87.3	14 640 547	13 026 284	89.0
1 VII 2013 .... ESDF		29 786 263	26 255 358	88.1	14 935 119	13 042 247	87.3	14 851 144	13 213 111	89.0
1 VII 2014 .... ESDF		30 206 307	26 628 251	88.2	15 144 744	13 228 428	87.3	15 061 563	13 399 823	89.0
1 VII 2015 .... ESDF		30 620 404	26 995 334	88.2	15 351 315	13 411 593	87.4	15 269 089	13 583 741	89.0
1 VII 2016 .... ESDF		31 028 637	27 356 475	88.2	15 554 863	13 592 035	87.4	15 473 774	13 764 440	89.0
ASIA - ASIE										
Afghanistan[68]										
1 VII 2007 .... ESDF		*23 038 900*	*5 159 200*	*22.4*	*11 783 600*	*2 656 200*	*22.5*	*11 255 300*	*2 503 000*	*22.2*
1 VII 2008 .... ESDF		*23 511 400*	*5 330 200*	*22.7*	*12 025 700*	*2 744 400*	*22.8*	*11 485 700*	*2 585 800*	*22.5*
1 VII 2009 .... ESDF		*23 993 500*	*5 507 300*	*23.0*	*12 272 900*	*2 835 900*	*23.1*	*11 720 600*	*2 671 400*	*22.8*
1 VII 2010 .... ESDF		*24 485 600*	*5 690 300*	*23.2*	*12 524 700*	*2 929 900*	*23.4*	*11 960 900*	*2 760 400*	*23.1*
1 VII 2011 .... ESDF		*24 987 700*	*5 879 200*	*23.5*	*12 782 000*	*3 027 400*	*23.7*	*12 205 700*	*2 851 800*	*23.4*
1 VII 2012 .... ESDF		*25 500 100*	*6 074 200*	*23.8*	*13 044 400*	*3 127 700*	*24.0*	*12 455 700*	*2 946 500*	*23.7*
1 VII 2013 .... ESDF		*26 023 100*	*6 275 600*	*24.1*	*13 312 400*	*3 231 600*	*24.3*	*12 710 700*	*3 044 000*	*23.9*
1 VII 2014 .... ESDF		*26 556 754*	*6 483 434*	*24.4*	*13 585 933*	*3 338 764*	*24.6*	*12 970 821*	*3 144 670*	*24.2*
1 VII 2015 .... ESDF		*27 101 365*	*6 698 033*	*24.7*	*13 865 015*	*3 449 379*	*24.9*	*13 236 350*	*3 248 654*	*24.5*
1 VII 2016 .... ESDF		*27 657 145*	*6 919 560*	*25.0*	*14 149 838*	*3 563 570*	*25.2*	*13 507 307*	*3 355 990*	*24.8*
Armenia - Arménie										
1 VII 2007 .... ESDJ		3 226 520	2 067 650	64.1	1 559 978	982 632	63.0	1 666 542	1 085 018	65.1
1 VII 2008 .... ESDJ		3 234 031	2 071 942	64.1	1 565 411	985 913	63.0	1 668 620	1 086 029	65.1
1 VII 2009 .... ESDJ		3 243 729	2 077 181	64.0	1 572 046	989 609	63.0	1 671 683	1 087 572	65.1
1 VII 2010 .... ESDJ		3 256 066	...	...	1 579 705			1 676 361		
1 VII 2011 .... ESDJ		3 027 900	1 918 700	63.4	...	...	...	...	...	...
12 X 2011 .... CDFC		2 871 771	1 847 124	64.3	1 346 729	851 475	63.2	1 525 042	995 649	65.3
1 VII 2012 .... ESDJ		3 024 100	1 915 100	63.3	...	...	...	...	...	...
1 VII 2013 .... ESDJ		3 022 000	1 915 800	63.4	...	...	...	...	...	...
1 VII 2014 .... ESDJ		3 013 800	1 913 500	63.5	...	...	...	...	...	...
1 VII 2015 .... ESDJ		3 004 588	1 909 960	63.6	1 434 095	891 769	62.2	1 570 493	1 018 191	64.8
1 VII 2016 .... ESDJ		2 992 500	1 904 400	63.6	...	...	...	...	...	...
Azerbaijan - Azerbaïdjan										
1 VII 2007[44] .... ESDF		8 723 000	4 608 200	52.8	4 305 800	2 262 400	52.5	4 417 200	2 345 800	53.1
1 VII 2008[44] .... ESDF		8 838 500	4 690 000	53.1	4 368 600	2 304 800	52.8	4 469 900	2 385 200	53.4
13 IV 2009 .... CDJC		8 922 447	4 739 123	53.1	4 414 398	2 330 527	52.8	4 508 049	2 408 596	53.4
1 VII 2009 .... ESDF		8 947 300	4 751 400	53.1	4 427 900	2 337 100	52.8	4 519 400	2 414 300	53.4
1 VII 2010 .... ESDF		9 054 300	4 802 200	53.0	4 486 300	2 364 400	52.7	4 568 000	2 437 800	53.4
1 VII 2011 .... ESDF		9 173 100	4 859 100	53.0	4 550 300	2 394 700	52.6	4 622 800	2 464 400	53.3
1 VII 2012 .... ESDF		9 295 784	4 936 922	53.1	4 616 139	2 435 213	52.8	4 679 646	2 501 709	53.5
1 VII 2013 .... ESDF		9 416 800	5 016 000	53.3	4 681 200	2 476 300	52.9	4 735 600	2 539 700	53.6
1 VII 2014 .... ESDF		9 528 900	5 075 700	53.3	4 736 900	2 505 700	52.9	4 792 000	2 570 000	53.6
1 VII 2015 .... ESDF		9 649 341	5 126 358	53.1	4 805 749	2 534 004	52.7	4 843 592	2 592 354	53.5
1 VII 2016 .... ESDF		9 755 500	5 182 700	53.1	4 858 600	2 562 000	52.7	4 896 900	2 620 700	53.5
Bahrain - Bahreïn										
1 VII 2007 .... ESDJ		1 039 297	...	...	632 074	...	...	407 223	...	...
1 VII 2008 .... ESDJ		1 103 496	...	...	676 590	...	...	426 906	...	...
1 VII 2009 .... ESDJ		1 178 415	...	...	731 997	...	...	446 418	...	...

Continent, country or area, and date / Continent, pays ou zone et date	Code[a]	Both sexes - Les deux sexes Total	Urban - Urbaine Number Nombre	Urban - Urbaine Percent P.100	Male - Masculin Total	Urban - Urbaine Number Nombre	Urban - Urbaine Percent P.100	Female - Féminin Total	Urban - Urbaine Number Nombre	Urban - Urbaine Percent P.100
ASIA - ASIE										
Bahrain - Bahreïn										
27 IV 2010	CDJC	1 234 571	1 234 571	100.0	768 414	768 414	100.0	466 157	466 157	100.0
1 VII 2010	ESDJ	1 228 543	...	...	764 357	...	...	464 186	...	...
1 VII 2011	ESDJ	1 195 020	...	...	741 483	...	...	453 537	...	...
1 VII 2012	ESDJ	1 208 964	...	...	760 449	...	...	448 515	...	...
1 VII 2013	ESDJ	1 253 191	...	...	788 381	...	...	464 810	...	...
1 VII 2014	ESDJ	1 314 562	...	...	806 487	...	...	508 075	...	...
1 VII 2015	ESDJ	1 370 322	...	...	846 365	...	...	523 957	...	...
1 VII 2016	ESDJ	1 423 726	...	...	888 389	...	...	535 337	...	...
Bangladesh										
1 VII 2007	ESDF	142 600 000	35 700 000	25.0	73 100 000	...	...	69 500 000	...	...
1 VII 2008	ESDF	144 500 000	36 700 000	25.4	74 000 000	...	...	70 500 000	...	...
1 VII 2010	ESDF	148 620 000	38 540 000	25.9	76 120 000	20 427 000	26.8	72 500 000	18 113 000	25.0
15 III 2011[69]	CDFC	149 772 364			74 980 386	...	...	74 791 978		
1 VII 2011	ESDF	150 611 000	39 000 000	25.9	77 101 062	20 560 587	26.7	73 509 938	18 439 413	25.1
1 VII 2012	ESDF	152 700 000	41 100 000	26.9	78 200 000	...	...	74 500 000	...	...
1 VII 2013	ESDF	154 790 000	42 580 000	27.5	77 510 000	...	...	77 280 000	...	...
1 VII 2014	ESDF	156 880 000	44 110 000	28.1	78 560 000	...	...	78 320 000	...	...
1 VII 2015	ESDF	158 900 000	45 700 000	28.8	79 600 000	...	...	79 300 000	...	...
1 VII 2016	ESDF	160 800 000	47 400 000	29.5	80 500 000	...	...	80 300 000	...	...
Bhutan - Bhoutan[70]										
1 VII 2007	ESDF	658 888	213 571	32.4	345 298	114 593	33.2	313 590	98 978	31.6
1 VII 2008	ESDF	671 083	222 753	33.2	351 269	119 342	34.0	319 814	103 411	32.3
1 VII 2009	ESDF	683 407	232 232	34.0	357 305	124 246	34.8	326 102	107 986	33.1
1 VII 2010	ESDF	695 823	242 001	34.8	363 384	129 298	35.6	332 439	112 703	33.9
1 VII 2011	ESDF	708 265	252 038	35.6	369 476	134 484	36.4	338 789	117 554	34.7
1 VII 2012	ESDF	720 679	262 325	36.4	375 554	139 798	37.2	345 125	122 530	35.5
1 VII 2013	ESDF	733 004	272 839	37.2	381 582	145 219	38.1	351 421	127 619	36.3
1 VII 2014	ESDF	745 153	283 543	38.1	387 520	150 737	38.9	357 633	132 806	37.1
1 VII 2015	ESDF	757 042	294 402	38.9	393 324	156 328	39.7	363 718	138 074	38.0
1 VII 2016	ESDF	768 577	...	...	398 948	...	...	369 629	...	...
Brunei Darussalam - Brunéi Darussalam										
1 VII 2007[44]	ESDF	370 000	...	...	191 100	...	...	178 900	...	...
1 VII 2008[44]	ESDF	375 000	...	...	193 700	...	...	181 300	...	...
1 VII 2009[44]	ESDF	380 100	...	...	196 300	...	...	183 800	...	...
1 VII 2010[44]	ESDF	386 800	...	...	199 800	...	...	187 000	...	...
20 VI 2011	CDJC	393 372	296 257	75.3	203 144	151 663	74.7	190 228	144 594	76.0
1 VII 2012	ESDJ	399 800	...	...	206 700	...	...	193 100	...	...
1 VII 2013	ESDJ	406 200	...	...	210 300	...	...	195 900	...	...
1 VII 2014	ESDJ	411 900	...	...	213 500	...	...	198 400	...	...
1 VII 2015	ESDJ	417 200	...	...	216 600	...	...	200 600	...	...
Cambodia - Cambodge[71]										
1 VII 2007	ESDF	14 363 519	...	...	6 979 452	...	...	7 384 067	...	...
3 III 2008[72]	CDFC	13 395 682	2 614 027	19.5	6 516 054	1 255 570	19.3	6 879 628	1 358 457	19.7
1 VII 2008[73]	ESDF	13 868 227	2 707 240	19.5	6 745 592	1 299 799	19.3	7 122 635	1 407 441	19.8
1 VII 2009[73]	ESDF	14 085 324	2 814 943	20.0	6 859 756	1 351 939	19.7	7 225 568	1 463 004	20.2
1 VII 2010[73]	ESDF	14 302 779	2 926 810	20.5	6 973 994	1 406 183	20.2	7 328 785	1 520 627	20.7
1 VII 2011[73]	ESDF	14 521 275	3 042 794	21.0	7 088 691	1 462 518	20.6	7 432 584	1 580 276	21.3
1 VII 2012[73]	ESDF	14 741 414	3 165 683	21.5	7 204 166	1 520 722	21.1	7 537 248	1 644 961	21.8
3 III 2013[74]	SSDF	14 676 591	3 146 212	21.4	7 121 508	1 527 479	21.4	7 555 083	1 618 734	21.4
1 VII 2013[73]	ESDF	14 962 591	3 285 951	22.0	7 320 112	1 580 866	21.6	7 642 479	1 705 085	22.3
1 VII 2014[73]	ESDF	15 184 116	3 412 183	22.5	7 436 178	1 642 397	22.1	7 747 938	1 769 786	22.8
1 VII 2015[73]	ESDF	15 405 157	3 540 575	23.0	7 551 944	1 705 018	22.6	7 853 213	1 835 557	23.4
China - Chine[75]										
1 VII 2007[76]	ESDF	1 317 900 000	606 330 000[78]	46.0	680 480 000[77]	...	...	640 810 000[77]	...	...
1 VII 2008[76]	ESDF	1 324 700 000	624 030 000[78]	47.1	683 570 000[77]	...	...	644 450 000[77]	...	...
1 VII 2009[76]	ESDF	1 331 300 000	645 120 000[78]	48.5	686 470 000[77]	...	...	648 030 000[77]	...	...
1 VII 2010[76]	ESDF	1 337 700 000	669 780 000[78]	50.1	687 480 000[77]	...	...	653 430 000[77]	...	...
1 XI 2010[79]	CDJC	1 339 724 852	665 575 306	49.7	686 852 572	...	...	652 872 280	...	...
1 VII 2011[80]	ESDF	1 344 100 000	691 000 000[78]	51.4	691 000 000[77]	...	...	657 000 000[77]	...	...
1 VII 2012[80]	ESDF	1 350 695 000	701 305 000[81]	51.9	692 315 000	...	...	658 380 000	...	...
1 VII 2013[76]	ESDF	1 357 380 000	721 465 000[81]	53.2	695 615 000	...	...	661 765 000	...	...
1 VII 2014[76]	ESDF	1 364 270 000	740 135 000[81]	54.3	699 035 000	...	...	665 235 000	...	...
1 VII 2015[76]	ESDF	1 371 220 000	760 160 000[81]	55.4	702 465 000	...	...	668 755 000	...	...

6. Total and urban population by sex: 2007 - 2016
Population totale et population urbaine selon le sexe : 2007 - 2016 (continued - suite)

Continent, country or area, and date / Continent, pays ou zone et date	Code[a]	Both sexes - Les deux sexes Total	Urban - Urbaine Number Nombre	Urban - Urbaine Percent P.100	Male - Masculin Total	Urban - Urbaine Number Nombre	Urban - Urbaine Percent P.100	Female - Féminin Total	Urban - Urbaine Number Nombre	Urban - Urbaine Percent P.100
ASIA - ASIE										
China, Hong Kong SAR - Chine, Hong Kong RAS										
1 VII 2007	ESDJ	6 916 300	...	...	3 283 900	...	...	3 632 400	...	...
1 VII 2008	ESDJ	6 957 800	...	...	3 290 200	...	...	3 667 600	...	...
1 VII 2009	ESDJ	6 972 800	...	...	3 284 800	...	...	3 688 000	...	...
1 VII 2010	ESDJ	7 024 200	...	...	3 294 300	...	...	3 729 900	...	...
30 VI 2011[82]	CDJC	7 071 576	...	...	3 303 015	...	...	3 768 561	...	...
1 VII 2011	ESDJ	7 071 600	...	...	3 303 000	...	...	3 768 600	...	...
1 VII 2012	ESDJ	7 150 100	...	...	3 327 300	...	...	3 822 800	...	...
1 VII 2013	ESDJ	7 178 900	...	...	3 329 900	...	...	3 849 000	...	...
1 VII 2014	ESDJ	7 229 500	...	...	3 344 500	...	...	3 885 000	...	...
1 VII 2015	ESDJ	7 291 300	...	...	3 365 600	...	...	3 925 700	...	...
1 VII 2016	ESDJ	7 336 600	...	...	3 375 400	...	...	3 961 200	...	...
China, Macao SAR - Chine, Macao RAS										
1 VII 2007	ESDJ	520 900	...	...	256 500	...	...	264 400	...	...
1 VII 2008	ESDJ	540 700	...	...	264 900	...	...	275 800	...	...
1 VII 2009	ESDJ	535 000	...	...	257 900[77]	...	...	277 200[77]	...	...
1 VII 2010	ESDJ	537 000	...	...	257 200[77]	...	...	279 700[77]	...	...
1 VII 2011	ESDJ	549 600	...	...	263 500	...	...	286 100	...	...
12 VIII 2011	CDFC	625 674	...	...	305 398	...	...	320 276	...	...
1 VII 2012	ESDJ	567 900	...	...	274 300	...	...	293 600	...	...
1 VII 2013	ESDJ	591 900	...	...	285 700	...	...	306 200	...	...
1 VII 2014	ESDJ	621 700	...	...	305 500	...	...	316 200	...	...
1 VII 2015	ESDJ	642 900	...	...	317 500	...	...	325 400	...	...
Cyprus - Chypre[83]										
1 VII 2007[84]	ESDJ	767 125	...	...	375 986	...	...	391 139	...	...
1 VII 2008[84]	ESDJ	786 632	...	...	385 192	...	...	401 440	...	...
1 VII 2009[84]	ESDJ	808 035	...	...	394 766	...	...	413 270	...	...
1 VII 2010[84]	ESDJ	829 446	...	...	404 182	...	...	425 264	...	...
1 VII 2011[84]	ESDJ	850 881	...	...	413 876	...	...	437 006	...	...
1 X 2011	CDJC	840 407	566 191	67.4	408 780	273 065	66.8	431 627	293 126	67.9
1 VII 2012[84]	ESDJ	863 945	...	...	420 015	...	...	443 930	...	...
1 VII 2013[84]	ESDJ	861 930	...	...	419 183	...	...	442 747	...	...
1 VII 2014[84]	ESDJ	852 504	...	...	414 682	...	...	437 823	...	...
1 I 2015	ESDJ	847 008	...	...	411 825	...	...	435 183	...	...
1 I 2016	ESDJ	848 319	...	...	412 692	...	...	435 627	...	...
Democratic People's Republic of Korea - République populaire démocratique de Corée										
1 X 2008	CDJC	24 052 231	...	...	11 721 838	...	...	12 330 393	...	...
Georgia - Géorgie										
1 VII 2007	ESDF	4 388 400	2 306 400	52.6	2 079 000	...	...	2 309 400	...	...
1 VII 2008	ESDF	4 383 800	2 306 500	52.6	2 079 600	...	...	2 304 200	...	...
1 VII 2009	ESDF	4 410 900	2 332 700	52.9	2 094 800	...	...	2 316 100	...	...
1 VII 2010	ESDF	4 452 800	2 360 900	53.0	2 118 100	...	...	2 334 700	...	...
1 VII 2011	ESDF	4 483 400	2 381 500	53.1	2 135 600	...	...	2 347 800	...	...
1 VII 2012	ESDF	4 490 700	...	...	2 141 300	...	...	2 349 400	...	...
1 VII 2013	ESDF	4 487 150	...	...	2 140 100	...	...	2 347 050	...	...
5 XI 2014	CDJC	3 713 804	2 122 623	57.2	1 772 864	980 985	55.3	1 940 940	1 141 638	58.8
1 VII 2015[85]	ESDJ	3 717 100	2 125 700	57.2	1 776 300	...	...	1 940 800	...	...
1 VII 2016[85]	ESDJ	3 719 300	2 128 550	57.2	1 780 500	...	...	1 938 800	...	...
India - Inde[86]										
1 VII 2007[87]	ESDF	1 134 023 232	331 060 644	29.2	586 879 523	174 195 527	29.7	547 143 709	156 865 117	28.7
1 VII 2008[87]	ESDF	1 150 196 000	338 356 000	29.4	595 291 000	178 041 000	29.9	554 905 000	160 315 000	28.9
9 II 2011	CDFC	1 210 854 977	377 106 125	31.1	623 270 258	195 489 200	31.4	587 584 719	181 616 925	30.9
1 VII 2011*[87]	ESDF	1 192 503 000	...	...	617 315 000	...	...	575 188 000	...	...
Indonesia - Indonésie										
1 VII 2007[88]	ESDJ	225 642 000	...	...	112 966 900	...	...	112 675 100	...	...
1 VII 2008[88]	ESDJ	228 523 300	...	...	114 399 200	...	...	114 124 100	...	...
1 VII 2009[88]	ESDJ	231 369 500	...	...	115 817 900	...	...	115 551 600	...	...
1 V 2010	CDJC	237 641 326	118 320 256	49.8	119 630 913	59 559 622	49.8	118 010 413	58 760 634	49.8
1 VII 2010[89]	ESDJ	238 518 787	118 803 981	49.8	119 852 718	59 698 817	49.8	118 666 069	59 105 164	49.8
1 VII 2011[89]	ESDJ	241 990 736	122 164 186	50.5	121 602 475	61 382 741	50.5	120 388 261	60 781 445	50.5

6. Total and urban population by sex: 2007 - 2016
Population totale et population urbaine selon le sexe : 2007 - 2016 (continued - suite)

Continent, country or area, and date / Continent, pays ou zone et date	Code[a]	Both sexes - Les deux sexes Total	Urban - Urbaine Number Nombre	Urban - Urbaine Percent P.100	Male - Masculin Total	Urban - Urbaine Number Nombre	Urban - Urbaine Percent P.100	Female - Féminin Total	Urban - Urbaine Number Nombre	Urban - Urbaine Percent P.100
ASIA - ASIE										
Indonesia - Indonésie										
1 VII 2012[89]	ESDJ	245 425 244	125 558 071	51.2	123 331 006	63 081 616	51.1	122 094 238	62 476 455	51.2
1 VII 2013[89]	ESDJ	248 818 090	128 964 283	51.8	125 036 002	64 785 519	51.8	123 782 088	64 178 764	51.8
1 VII 2014[89]	ESDJ	252 164 786	132 387 038	52.5	126 715 188	66 493 813	52.5	125 449 598	65 893 225	52.5
1 VII 2015[89]	ESDJ	255 461 686	135 823 286	53.2	128 366 718	68 214 177	53.1	127 094 968	67 609 109	53.2
1 VII 2016[89]	ESDJ	258 704 986	139 240 964	53.8	129 988 690	69 924 467	53.8	128 716 296	69 316 497	53.9
Iran (Islamic Republic of) - Iran (République islamique d')										
1 VII 2007[90]	ESDJ	71 278 952	48 874 656	68.6	36 247 296	24 891 876	68.7	35 031 392	23 982 780	68.5
1 VII 2008[90]	ESDJ	72 181 632	49 576 146	68.7	36 691 780	25 253 132	68.8	35 489 488	24 323 014	68.5
1 VII 2009[90]	ESDJ	73 202 096	50 365 184	68.8	37 198 776	25 660 500	69.0	36 003 320	24 704 684	68.6
1 VII 2010[90]	ESDJ	74 339 576	51 242 546	68.9	37 767 220	26 114 342	69.1	36 572 356	25 128 204	68.7
24 X 2011	CDJC	75 149 669	53 646 661	71.4	37 905 669	27 023 638	71.3	37 244 000	26 623 023	71.5
1 VII 2012[90]	ESDJ	76 037 535	54 611 776[91]	71.8	38 336 983	27 547 622[91]	71.9	37 700 552	27 064 154[91]	71.8
1 VII 2013[90]	ESDJ	76 942 276	55 506 192[91]	72.1	38 777 566	27 988 342[91]	72.2	38 164 710	27 517 850[91]	72.1
1 VII 2014[90]	ESDJ	77 856 411	56 412 837	72.5	39 224 036	28 435 933	72.5	38 632 375	27 976 904	72.4
1 VII 2015[90]	ESDJ	78 773 093	57 326 841	72.8	39 672 171	28 887 379	72.8	39 100 922	28 439 462	72.7
1 VII 2016[90]	ESDJ	79 685 926	58 224 240	73.1	40 118 657	29 330 524	73.1	39 567 269	28 893 716	73.0
Iraq										
1 VII 2007	ESDF	29 426 942	...	...	14 814 595	...	...	14 612 348	...	...
1 VII 2008	ESDF	30 315 243	...	...	15 261 719	...	...	15 053 524	...	...
1 VII 2009	ESDF	31 392 903	...	...	16 010 232	...	...	15 382 671	...	...
1 VII 2010	ESDF	32 210 813	...	...	16 418 691	...	...	15 792 122	...	...
1 VII 2011	ESDF	33 051 526	...	...	16 839 048	...	...	16 212 479	...	...
1 VII 2012	ESDF	33 913 305	23 475 543	69.2	17 270 036	11 954 703	69.2	16 643 269	11 520 840	69.2
1 VII 2013	ESDF	34 794 194	24 162 634	69.4	17 710 750	12 299 131	69.4	17 083 444	11 863 502	69.4
1 VII 2014	ESDF	35 736 260	24 896 261	69.7	18 182 503	12 667 144	69.7	17 553 757	12 229 117	69.7
1 VII 2015	ESDF	36 658 503	25 631 821	69.9	18 520 532	12 935 587	69.8	18 137 971	12 696 234	70.0
Israel - Israël[92]										
1 VII 2007	ESDJ	7 180 115	6 589 632[93]	91.8	3 549 216	3 247 280[93]	91.5	3 630 899	3 342 352[93]	92.1
1 VII 2008	ESDJ	7 308 795	6 701 217[94]	91.7	3 614 125	3 303 732[94]	91.4	3 694 671	3 397 485[94]	92.0
27 XII 2008[95]	CDFC	7 412 180	6 799 340[77]	91.7	3 663 910	3 350 610[77]	91.4	3 748 270	3 448 730[77]	92.0
1 VII 2009	ESDJ	7 485 565	6 864 957[77]	91.7	3 701 159	3 384 295[77]	91.4	3 784 406	3 480 662[77]	92.0
1 VII 2010	ESDJ	7 623 561	6 987 615[77]	91.7	3 771 020	3 446 730[77]	91.4	3 852 541	3 540 885[77]	91.9
1 VII 2011	ESDJ	7 765 832	7 111 015[77]	91.6	3 843 068	3 509 308[77]	91.3	3 922 764	3 601 706[77]	91.8
1 VII 2012	ESDJ	7 910 525	7 235 231[77]	91.5	3 916 125	3 572 531[77]	91.2	3 994 400	3 662 700[77]	91.7
1 VII 2013	ESDJ	8 059 456	7 369 053[77]	91.4	3 991 347	3 640 471[77]	91.2	4 068 109	3 728 581[77]	91.7
1 VII 2014	ESDJ	8 215 668	7 502 325[77]	91.3	4 070 269	3 707 183[77]	91.1	4 145 398	3 795 142[77]	91.6
1 VII 2015	ESDJ	8 380 149	7 643 990[77]	91.2	4 153 233	3 778 276[77]	91.0	4 226 916	3 865 714[77]	91.5
Japan - Japon										
1 VII 2007[96]	ESDJ	128 001 000	...	...	62 401 000[77]	...	...	65 599 000[77]	...	...
1 VII 2008[96]	ESDJ	128 063 000	...	...	62 409 000	...	...	65 654 000	...	...
1 VII 2009[96]	ESDJ	128 047 000	...	...	62 354 000	...	...	65 693 000	...	...
1 VII 2010[96]	ESDJ	128 070 000	...	...	62 330 000	...	...	65 740 000	...	...
1 X 2010[96]	CDJC	128 057 352	116 156 631	90.7	62 327 737	56 569 051	90.8	65 729 615	59 587 580	90.7
1 VII 2011[97]	ESDJ	127 833 000	...	...	62 202 000	...	...	65 631 000	...	...
1 VII 2012[97]	ESDJ	127 629 000	...	...	62 085 000	...	...	65 544 000	...	...
1 VII 2013[97]	ESDJ	127 445 000	...	...	61 987 000	...	...	65 458 000	...	...
1 VII 2014[97]	ESDJ	127 276 000	...	...	61 906 000	...	...	65 370 000	...	...
1 VII 2015[98]	ESDJ	127 141 000	...	...	61 848 000	...	...	65 294 000	...	...
1 X 2015*	CDJC	127 110 047	...	...	61 829 237	...	...	65 280 810	...	...
1 VII 2016[98]	ESDJ	126 995 000	...	...	61 781 000	...	...	65 213 000	...	...
Jordan - Jordanie[99]										
31 XII 2007	ESDF	6 106 000	5 516 000	90.3	3 146 000	...	...	2 960 000	...	...
31 XII 2008	ESDF	6 293 000	5 685 000	90.3	3 243 000	...	...	3 050 000	...	...
31 XII 2009	ESDF	6 490 000	5 863 000	90.3	3 340 000	...	...	3 150 000	...	...
31 XII 2010	ESDF	6 699 000	6 051 000	90.3	3 448 000	...	...	3 250 000	...	...
31 XII 2011	ESDF	6 993 000	6 318 000	90.3	3 704 852	...	...	3 288 148	...	...
31 XII 2012	ESDF	7 427 000	6 710 000	90.3	3 934 783	...	...	3 492 217	...	...
31 XII 2013	ESDF	8 114 000	7 331 000	90.4	4 298 752	...	...	3 815 248	...	...
31 XII 2014	ESDF	8 804 000	7 954 000	90.3	4 664 310	...	...	4 139 690	...	...
30 X 2015	CDFC	9 531 712	...	...	5 046 822	...	...	4 484 890	...	...
31 XII 2016	ESDF	9 798 000	8 852 000	90.3	5 188 000	...	...	4 610 000	...	...

6. Total and urban population by sex: 2007 - 2016
Population totale et population urbaine selon le sexe : 2007 - 2016 (continued - suite)

Continent, country or area, and date / Continent, pays ou zone et date	Code[a]	Both sexes - Les deux sexes			Male - Masculin			Female - Féminin		
		Total	Urban - Urbaine		Total	Urban - Urbaine		Total	Urban - Urbaine	
			Number Nombre	Percent P.100		Number Nombre	Percent P.100		Number Nombre	Percent P.100
ASIA - ASIE										
Kazakhstan										
1 VII 2007	ESDF	15 484 192	8 195 389	52.9	7 450 418	3 815 422	51.2	8 033 774	4 379 967	54.5
1 VII 2008	ESDF	15 674 000	8 331 030	53.2	7 541 053	3 877 559	51.4	8 132 947	4 453 471	54.8
25 II 2009	CDFC	16 009 597	8 662 432	54.1	7 712 224	4 055 341	52.6	8 297 373	4 607 091	55.5
1 VII 2009	ESDF	16 092 701	8 741 149	54.3	7 753 360	4 092 724	52.8	8 339 341	4 648 425	55.7
1 VII 2010	ESDF	16 321 581	8 896 402	54.5	7 866 332	4 165 526	53.0	8 455 249	4 730 876	56.0
1 VII 2011	ESDF	16 556 601	9 050 267	54.7	7 983 081	4 237 719	53.1	8 573 520	4 812 548	56.1
1 VII 2012	ESDF	16 791 427	9 202 381	54.8	8 100 113	4 309 859	53.2	8 691 314	4 892 522	56.3
1 VII 2013	ESDF	17 035 275	9 348 738	54.9	8 221 848	4 380 550	53.3	8 813 427	4 968 188	56.4
1 I 2014	ESDF	17 160 774	9 433 482	55.0	8 284 815	4 421 972	53.4	8 875 959	5 011 510	56.5
Kuwait - Koweït										
1 VII 2007	ESDF	2 495 415	...	...	1 455 837	...	...	1 039 578	...	...
1 VII 2008	ESDF	2 631 963	...	...	1 525 129	...	...	1 106 834	...	...
1 VII 2009	ESDF	2 777 861	...	...	1 597 843	...	...	1 180 018	...	...
1 VII 2010	ESDF	2 933 268	...	...	1 674 156	...	...	1 259 112	...	...
21 IV 2011	CDFC	3 065 850	3 065 850	100.0	1 738 372	1 738 372	100.0	1 327 478	1 327 478	100.0
1 VII 2011	ESDF	3 106 676	...	...	1 767 685	...	...	1 338 991	...	...
1 VII 2012	ESDF	3 246 622	...	...	1 856 265	...	...	1 390 357	...	...
1 VII 2013	ESDF	3 427 595	...	...	1 968 382	...	...	1 459 213	...	...
1 VII 2014	ESDF	3 767 415	...	...	2 161 594	...	...	1 605 821	...	...
1 I 2016	ESDF	3 925 487	...	...	2 320 193	...	...	1 605 294	...	...
Kyrgyzstan - Kirghizstan										
1 VII 2007[84]	ESDJ	5 268 385	1 807 481	34.3	2 598 824	854 199	32.9	2 669 561	953 282	35.7
1 VII 2008[84]	ESDJ	5 318 729	1 816 886	34.2	2 623 575	857 874	32.7	2 695 154	959 012	35.6
24 III 2009	CDJC	5 362 793	1 827 136	34.1	2 645 921	863 002	32.6	2 716 872	964 134	35.5
1 VII 2009[84]	ESDJ	5 383 277	1 835 028	34.1	2 656 660	866 718	32.6	2 726 617	968 310	35.5
1 VII 2010[84]	ESDJ	5 447 960	1 854 245	34.0	2 689 231	876 120	32.6	2 758 729	978 125	35.5
1 VII 2011[84]	ESDJ	5 514 754	1 873 047	34.0	2 722 714	885 117	32.5	2 792 040	987 930	35.4
1 VII 2012[84]	ESDJ	5 607 511	1 878 643	33.5	2 770 269	887 727	32.0	2 837 242	990 916	34.9
1 VII 2013[84]	ESDJ	5 719 852	1 921 936	33.6	2 827 672	909 216	32.2	2 892 180	1 012 720	35.0
1 VII 2014[84]	ESDJ	5 835 816	1 965 159	33.7	2 886 758	930 751	32.2	2 949 058	1 034 408	35.1
1 VII 2015[84]	ESDJ	5 957 271	2 008 148	33.7	2 948 932	952 329	32.3	3 008 339	1 055 819	35.1
1 VII 2016[84]	ESDJ	6 079 840	2 051 748	33.7	3 011 702	973 955	32.3	3 068 138	1 077 793	35.1
Lao People's Democratic Republic - République démocratique populaire lao										
1 VII 2007[100]	ESDJ	5 868 800	...	...	2 924 700	...	...	2 944 000	...	...
1 VII 2008[100]	ESDJ	5 990 100	...	...	2 985 800	...	...	3 004 300	...	...
1 VII 2009[100]	ESDJ	6 110 600	...	...	3 046 400	...	...	3 064 200	...	...
1 VII 2010[100]	ESDJ	6 230 200	...	...	3 106 600	...	...	3 123 700	...	...
1 VII 2011[100]	ESDJ	6 348 800	...	...	3 166 300	...	...	3 182 500	...	...
1 VII 2012[100]	ESDJ	6 465 800	...	...	3 225 200	...	...	3 240 600	...	...
1 VII 2013[100]	ESDJ	6 580 800	...	...	3 283 200	...	...	3 297 600	...	...
1 VII 2014[100]	ESDJ	6 693 300	...	...	3 339 800	...	...	3 353 400	...	...
1 III 2015	CDJC	6 492 400	...	...	3 254 800	...	...	3 237 600	...	...
1 VII 2016[100]	ESDJ	6 906 200	...	...	3 447 100	...	...	3 459 100	...	...
Lebanon - Liban										
3 III 2007[101]	SSDF	3 759 134	...	...	1 857 659			1 901 475	...	...
1 X 2011[102]	SSDF	3 779 859	...	...	1 840 940			1 938 919	...	...
Malaysia - Malaisie										
1 VII 2007[103]	ESDJ	27 058 428	18 475 497	68.3	13 903 701	9 455 572	68.0	13 154 727	9 019 925	68.6
1 VII 2008[103]	ESDJ	27 567 636	19 068 738	69.2	14 179 117	9 767 066	68.9	13 388 519	9 301 672	69.5
1 VII 2009[103]	ESDJ	28 081 497	19 675 872	70.1	14 456 940	10 085 459	69.8	13 624 557	9 590 413	70.4
1 VII 2010[104]	ESDJ	28 588 637	20 290 864	71.0	14 730 542	10 404 757	70.6	13 858 095	9 886 107	71.3
6 VII 2010[69]	CDJC	28 334 135	20 124 970	71.0	14 562 638	10 298 698	70.7	13 771 497	9 826 272	71.4
1 VII 2011[104]	ESDJ	29 062 036	20 826 580	71.7	14 980 010	10 684 359	71.3	14 082 026	10 142 221	72.0
1 VII 2012[104]	ESDJ	29 510 022	21 355 255	72.4	15 215 309	10 965 006	72.1	14 294 713	10 390 249	72.7
1 VII 2013[104]	ESDJ	30 213 664	22 041 500	73.0	15 604 813	11 330 984	72.6	14 608 851	10 710 516	73.3
1 VII 2014[104]	ESDJ	30 708 527	22 597 286	73.6	15 867 796	11 624 061	73.3	14 840 731	10 973 225	73.9
1 VII 2015[104]	ESDJ	31 186 135	23 173 701	74.3	16 112 125	11 925 089	74.0	15 074 010	11 248 612	74.6
1 VII 2016[104]	ESDJ	31 660 683	23 694 698	74.8	16 362 530	12 197 462	74.5	15 298 153	11 497 236	75.2
Maldives										
1 VII 2007	ESDF	304 869	...	...	154 391	...	...	150 478	...	...
1 VII 2008	ESDF	309 575	...	...	156 714	...	...	152 861	...	...

Continent, country or area, and date / Continent, pays ou zone et date	Code[a]	Both sexes - Les deux sexes			Male - Masculin			Female - Féminin		
		Total	Urban - Urbaine		Total	Urban - Urbaine		Total	Urban - Urbaine	
			Number Nombre	Percent P.100		Number Nombre	Percent P.100		Number Nombre	Percent P.100
ASIA - ASIE										
Maldives										
1 VII 2009 .... ESDF		314 542	...	...	159 159	...	...	155 383	...	...
1 VII 2010 .... ESDF		319 738	...	...	161 708	...	...	158 030	...	...
1 VII 2011 .... ESDF		325 135	...	...	164 349	...	...	160 786	...	...
1 VII 2012 .... ESDF		330 655	...	...	167 058	...	...	163 597	...	...
1 VII 2013 .... ESDF		336 224	...	...	169 800	...	...	166 424	...	...
20 IX 2014[105] .... CDFC		402 071	153 904	38.3	227 749	85 438	37.5	174 322	68 466	39.3
1 VII 2015[106] .... ESDF		343 518	133 405[91]	38.8	174 535	66 493[91]	38.1	168 983	66 913[91]	39.6
1 VII 2016[106] .... ESDF		350 093	138 101[91]	39.4	177 872	68 880[91]	38.7	172 222	69 221[91]	40.2
Mongolia - Mongolie										
1 VII 2007 .... ESDF		2 601 850	1 638 567	63.0	1 268 447	788 695	62.2	1 333 403	849 872	63.7
1 VII 2008 .... ESDF		2 643 201	1 684 282	63.7	1 289 282	811 224	62.9	1 353 919	873 058	64.5
1 VII 2009 .... ESDF		2 691 115	1 743 008	64.8	1 314 729	840 520	63.9	1 376 386	902 488	65.6
1 VII 2010 .... ESDF		2 738 622	1 799 648	65.7	1 335 111	863 536	64.7	1 403 511	936 112	66.7
11 XI 2010 .... CDFC		2 647 199	1 797 338	67.9	1 314 246	869 827	66.2	1 332 953	927 511	69.6
1 VII 2011 .... ESDF		2 786 322	1 856 224	66.6	1 354 472	886 139	65.4	1 431 850	970 085	67.8
1 VII 2012 .... ESDF		2 839 711	1 911 462	67.3	1 379 091	910 746	66.0	1 460 620	1 000 716	68.5
1 VII 2013 .... ESDF		2 899 011	1 961 169	67.6	1 409 648	936 682	66.4	1 489 363	1 024 487	68.8
1 VII 2014 .... ESDF		2 963 113	1 993 017	67.3	1 446 149	955 833	66.1	1 516 964	1 037 184	68.4
1 VII 2015 .... ESDF		3 026 864	2 043 251	67.5	1 485 034	985 919	66.4	1 541 830	1 057 332	68.6
1 VII 2016 .... ESDF		3 088 856	2 122 131	68.7	1 518 797	1 027 311	67.6	1 570 059	1 094 820	69.7
Myanmar										
1 X 2007 .... ESDF		57 504 368	17 567 506	30.5	28 585 910	8 582 809	30.0	28 918 458	8 984 697	31.1
1 X 2008 .... ESDF		58 376 839	17 894 194	30.7	29 025 480	8 798 657	30.3	29 351 359	9 095 537	31.0
1 X 2009 .... ESDF		59 129 900	18 133 654	30.7	29 399 744	8 888 838	30.2	29 730 156	9 244 816	31.1
1 X 2010 .... ESDF		59 780 329	18 342 824	30.7	29 723 184	8 992 226	30.3	30 057 145	9 350 598	31.1
1 X 2011[85] .... ESDF		50 149 496	14 650 579	29.2	24 185 705	7 009 280	29.0	25 963 791	7 641 299	29.4
1 X 2012[85] .... ESDF		50 666 887	14 824 883	29.3	24 435 871	7 092 798	29.0	26 231 016	7 732 085	29.5
1 X 2013[85] .... ESDF		51 184 273	14 999 184	29.3	24 686 034	7 176 313	29.1	26 498 239	7 822 871	29.5
29 III 2014[107] .... CDFC		50 279 900	14 877 943	29.6	24 228 714	7 114 224	29.4	26 051 186	7 763 719	29.8
1 X 2014[85] .... ESDF		51 991 031	15 173 838	29.2	25 066 439	7 256 002	28.9	26 924 592	7 917 836	29.4
1 X 2015[85] .... ESDF		52 450 516	15 363 901	29.3	25 256 187	7 331 696	29.0	27 194 329	8 032 205	29.5
1 X 2016[85] .... ESDF		52 916 691	15 560 351	29.4	25 450 311	7 411 122	29.1	27 466 380	8 149 229	29.7
Nepal - Népal										
1 VII 2007 .... ESDJ		26 427 399	...	...	13 240 233	...	...	13 187 166	...	...
1 VII 2008 .... ESDJ		26 966 581	...	...	13 515 938	...	...	13 450 643	...	...
1 VII 2009 .... ESDJ		27 504 280	...	...	13 790 836	...	...	13 713 444	...	...
1 VII 2010 .... ESDJ		28 043 744	...	...	14 066 638	...	...	13 977 106	...	...
22 VI 2011 .... CDJC		26 494 504	4 523 820	17.1	12 849 041	2 306 049	17.9	13 645 463	2 217 771	16.3
1 VII 2011 .... ESDJ		28 584 975	...	...	14 343 343	...	...	14 241 632	...	...
1 VII 2012[21] .... ESDJ		26 873 066	...	...	13 030 795	...	...	13 842 271	...	...
1 VII 2013[21] .... ESDJ		27 257 347	...	...	13 215 791	...	...	14 041 556	...	...
1 VII 2014[21] .... ESDJ		27 646 053	...	...	13 403 432	...	...	14 242 621	...	...
1 VII 2015[21] .... ESDJ		28 037 904	...	...	13 593 069	...	...	14 444 835	...	...
1 VII 2016[21] .... ESDJ		28 431 494	...	...	13 784 009	...	...	14 647 486	...	...
Oman										
1 VII 2007 .... ESDF		2 743 499	1 984 158	72.3	1 622 119	1 188 537	73.3	1 121 380	795 621	71.0
1 VII 2008 .... ESDF		2 867 428	2 077 862	72.5	1 687 414	1 238 527	73.4	1 180 014	839 335	71.1
1 VII 2009 .... ESDF		3 173 917	2 314 865	72.9	1 971 115	1 457 197	73.9	1 202 802	857 668	71.3
12 XII 2010 .... CDFC		2 773 479	2 079 831	75.0	1 612 408	1 220 557	75.7	1 161 071	859 274	74.0
1 VII 2011[108] .... ESDF		3 295 298	...	...	2 090 883	...	...	1 204 415	...	...
1 VII 2012[108] .... ESDF		3 623 001	...	...	2 332 687	...	...	1 290 314	...	...
1 VII 2013[108] .... ESDF		3 855 206	...	...	2 502 235	...	...	1 352 971	...	...
1 VII 2014[108] .... ESDF		3 992 893	...	...	2 579 811	...	...	1 413 082	...	...
1 VII 2015[108] .... ESDF		4 159 102	...	...	2 684 844	...	...	1 474 258	...	...
1 VII 2016[108] .... ESDF		4 414 051	...	...	2 886 083	...	...	1 527 968	...	...
Pakistan[109]										
1 VII 2007[110] .... ESDJ		149 860 388	52 807 585	35.2	76 857 737	27 178 203	35.4	73 002 651	25 629 382	35.1
1 VII 2008 .... ESDF		166 410 000	...	...	86 130 000	...	...	80 280 000	...	...
1 VII 2009 .... ESDF		169 940 000	...	...	87 940 000	...	...	82 010 000	...	...
1 VII 2010 .... ESDF		173 510 000	...	...	89 760 000	...	...	83 750 000	...	...
1 VII 2011 .... ESDF		177 100 000	...	...	91 590 000	...	...	85 510 000	...	...
Philippines										
1 VII 2007[32] .... ESDJ		88 706 300	...	...	44 608 300	...	...	44 098 000	...	...
1 VII 2008[32] .... ESDJ		90 457 200	...	...	45 483 100	...	...	44 974 100	...	...

Continent, country or area, and date / Continent, pays ou zone et date	Code[a]	Both sexes - Les deux sexes			Male - Masculin			Female - Féminin		
		Total	Urban - Urbaine		Total	Urban - Urbaine		Total	Urban - Urbaine	
			Number Nombre	Percent P.100		Number Nombre	Percent P.100		Number Nombre	Percent P.100
ASIA - ASIE										
Philippines										
1 VII 2009[32] .... ESDJ		92 226 600	...	...	46 368 900	...	...	45 857 700	...	...
1 V 2010[111] .... CDJC		92 335 113	41 855 571	45.3	46 634 257	20 840 798	44.7	45 700 856	21 014 773	46.0
1 VII 2010[11] .... ESDJ		93 135 100	...	...	46 980 200	...	...	46 154 900	...	...
1 VII 2011[11] .... ESDJ		94 823 800	...	...	47 832 400	...	...	46 991 400	...	...
1 VII 2012[11] .... ESDJ		96 510 900	...	...	48 684 200	...	...	47 826 700	...	...
1 VII 2013[11] .... ESDJ		98 196 500	...	...	49 535 100	...	...	48 661 400	...	...
1 VII 2014[11] .... ESDJ		99 880 300	...	...	50 385 100	...	...	49 495 200	...	...
1 VII 2015[11] .... ESDJ		101 562 300	...	...	51 234 200	...	...	50 328 100	...	...
1 VII 2016[11] .... ESDJ		103 242 900	...	...	52 081 400	...	...	51 161 500	...	...
Qatar										
1 VII 2007 .... ESDF		1 218 250	...	...	905 747	...	...	312 503	...	...
1 VII 2008 .... ESDF		1 448 479	...	...	1 111 176	...	...	337 303	...	...
1 VII 2009 .... ESDF		1 638 626	...	...	1 265 146	...	...	373 480	...	...
21 IV 2010 .... CDFC		1 699 435	...	...	1 284 739	...	...	414 696	...	...
1 VII 2010 .... ESDF		1 715 010	...	...	1 296 107	...	...	418 903	...	...
1 VII 2011 .... ESDF		1 732 717	...	...	1 288 590	...	...	444 127	...	...
1 VII 2012 .... ESDF		1 832 903	...	...	1 355 199	...	...	477 704	...	...
1 VII 2013 .... ESDF		2 003 700	...	...	1 477 632	...	...	526 068	...	...
1 VII 2014 .... ESDF		2 216 180	2 216 180	100.0	1 652 037	1 652 037	100.0	564 143	564 143	100.0
20 IV 2015 .... CDFC		2 404 776	...	...	1 816 981	...	...	587 795	...	...
1 VII 2015 .... ESDF		2 437 790	2 437 790	100.0	1 840 643	1 840 643	100.0	597 147	597 147	100.0
1 VII 2016 .... ESDF		2 617 634	2 617 634	100.0	1 975 536	1 975 536	100.0	642 098	642 098	100.0
Republic of Korea - République de Corée										
1 VII 2007 .... ESDJ		48 683 638	...	...	24 491 190	...	...	24 192 448	...	...
1 VII 2008 .... ESDJ		49 054 708	...	...	24 671 648	...	...	24 383 060	...	...
1 VII 2009 .... ESDJ		49 307 835	...	...	24 774 341	...	...	24 533 494	...	...
1 VII 2010 .... ESDJ		49 554 112	...	...	24 881 114	...	...	24 672 998	...	...
1 XI 2010[112] .... CDJC		48 580 293	39 822 647	82.0	24 167 098	19 798 739	81.9	24 413 195	20 023 908	82.0
1 VII 2011 .... ESDJ		49 936 638	...	...	25 069 867	...	...	24 866 771	...	...
1 VII 2012 .... ESDJ		50 199 853	...	...	25 187 380	...	...	25 012 473	...	...
1 VII 2013 .... ESDJ		50 428 893	...	...	25 285 319	...	...	25 143 574	...	...
1 VII 2014 .... ESDJ		50 746 659	...	...	25 445 077	...	...	25 301 582	...	...
1 VII 2015 .... ESDJ		51 014 947	...	...	25 585 894	...	...	25 429 053	...	...
1 XI 2015 .... CDJC		51 069 375	...	...	25 608 502	...	...	25 460 873	...	...
1 VII 2016 .... ESDJ		51 245 707	...	...	25 693 983	...	...	25 551 724	...	...
Saudi Arabia - Arabie saoudite										
1 VII 2007*[113] .... ESDF		24 941 298	...	...	13 947 610	...	...	10 993 688	...	...
1 VII 2008*[113] .... ESDF		25 787 025	...	...	14 470 381	...	...	11 316 644	...	...
1 VII 2009*[113] .... ESDF		26 660 857	...	...	15 013 600	...	...	11 647 257	...	...
27 IV 2010 .... CDFC		27 236 156	...	...	15 531 471	...	...	11 704 685	...	...
1 VII 2010*[113] .... ESDF		27 563 432	...	...	15 578 015	...	...	11 985 417	...	...
1 VII 2011*[113] .... ESDF		28 376 355	...	...	16 041 361	...	...	12 334 994	...	...
1 VII 2012*[113] .... ESDF		29 195 895	...	...	16 543 836	...	...	12 652 059	...	...
1 VII 2013*[113] .... ESDF		29 601 529	...	...	16 889 829	...	...	12 711 700	...	...
1 VII 2014 .... ESDF		29 997 101	...	...	17 218 744	...	...	12 778 357	...	...
1 VII 2015 .... ESDF		30 890 736	...	...	17 731 352	...	...	13 159 384	...	...
1 VII 2016 .... ESDF		31 742 308	...	...	18 233 964	...	...	13 508 344	...	...
Singapore - Singapour[114]										
30 VI 2007[115] .... ESDJ		3 583 082	...	...	1 775 477	...	...	1 807 605	...	...
30 VI 2008[115] .... ESDJ		3 642 659	...	...	1 802 992	...	...	1 839 667	...	...
30 VI 2009[115] .... ESDJ		3 733 876	...	...	1 844 732	...	...	1 889 144	...	...
30 VI 2010[116] .... CDJC		3 771 721	...	...	1 861 133	...	...	1 910 588	...	...
30 VI 2010[115] .... ESDJ		3 771 721	...	...	1 861 133	...	...	1 910 588	...	...
30 VI 2011[115] .... ESDJ		3 789 251	...	...	1 868 170	...	...	1 921 081	...	...
30 VI 2012[115] .... ESDJ		3 818 205	...	...	1 880 046	...	...	1 938 159	...	...
30 VI 2013[115] .... ESDJ		3 844 751	...	...	1 891 504	...	...	1 953 247	...	...
30 VI 2014[115] .... ESDJ		3 870 739	...	...	1 902 410	...	...	1 968 329	...	...
30 VI 2015[115] .... ESDJ		3 902 690	...	...	1 916 628	...	...	1 986 062	...	...
30 VI 2016[115] .... ESDJ		3 933 559	...	...	1 929 526	...	...	2 004 033	...	...
Sri Lanka										
1 VII 2007 .... ESDF		20 039 000	...	...	9 956 000	...	...	10 083 000	...	...
1 VII 2008 .... ESDF		20 246 000	...	...	10 060 000	...	...	10 186 000	...	...

Continent, country or area, and date / Continent, pays ou zone et date	Code[a]	Both sexes - Les deux sexes			Male - Masculin			Female - Féminin		
		Total	Urban - Urbaine		Total	Urban - Urbaine		Total	Urban - Urbaine	
			Number Nombre	Percent P.100		Number Nombre	Percent P.100		Number Nombre	Percent P.100
ASIA - ASIE										
Sri Lanka										
1 VII 2009	ESDF	20 476 000	...	...	10 174 000	...	...	10 302 000	...	...
1 VII 2010	ESDF	20 675 000	...	...	10 273 000	...	...	10 402 000	...	...
1 VII 2011	ESDF	20 869 000	...	...	10 357 000	...	...	10 512 000	...	...
20 III 2012	CDJC	20 359 439	3 704 470	18.2	9 856 634	1 800 327	18.3	10 502 805	1 904 143	18.1
1 VII 2012	ESDJ	20 424 000	...	...	9 888 000	...	...	10 536 000	...	...
1 VII 2013	ESDJ	20 579 000	...	...	9 963 000	...	...	10 616 000	...	...
1 VII 2014*	ESDJ	20 771 000	...	...	10 056 000	...	...	10 715 000	...	...
1 VII 2015*	ESDJ	20 966 000	...	...	10 151 000	...	...	10 815 000	...	...
1 VII 2016*	ESDJ	21 203 000	...	...	10 265 460	...	...	10 937 540	...	...
State of Palestine - État de Palestine										
1 VII 2007	ESDF	3 719 189	3 086 102[117]	83.0	1 887 628	...	...	1 831 561	...	...
1 XII 2007[118]	CDFC	3 669 244	3 040 039[117]	82.9	1 862 027	1 542 604[117]	82.8	1 807 217	1 497 435[117]	82.9
1 VII 2008	ESDF	3 825 512	3 175 546[117]	83.0	1 941 742	...	...	1 883 770	...	...
1 VII 2009	ESDF	3 935 249	3 267 977[117]	83.0	1 997 625	...	...	1 937 624	...	...
1 VII 2010	ESDF	4 048 403	3 363 385[117]	83.1	2 055 211	...	...	1 993 192	...	...
1 VII 2011	ESDF	4 168 860	3 465 483[117]	83.1	2 116 782	...	...	2 052 078	...	...
1 VII 2012	ESDF	4 293 313	3 571 037[117]	83.2	2 180 386	...	...	2 112 927	...	...
1 VII 2013	ESDF	4 420 549	3 679 034[117]	83.2	2 245 400	...	...	2 175 149	...	...
1 VII 2014	ESDF	4 550 368	3 789 308[117]	83.3	2 311 721	...	...	2 238 647	...	...
1 VII 2015	ESDF	4 682 467	3 901 606[117]	83.3	2 379 184	...	...	2 303 283	...	...
1 VII 2016	ESDF	4 816 503	4 015 645[117]	83.4	2 447 616	...	...	2 368 887	...	...
Syrian Arab Republic - République arabe syrienne[119]										
1 VII 2007	ESDF	19 172 000	10 257 000	53.5	9 798 000	5 265 000	53.7	9 374 000	4 992 000	53.3
1 VII 2008	ESDF	19 644 000	10 511 000	53.5	10 042 000	5 394 000	53.7	9 602 000	5 117 000	53.3
1 VII 2009	ESDF	20 125 000	10 769 000	53.5	10 287 000	5 526 000	53.7	9 838 000	5 243 000	53.3
1 VII 2010	ESDF	20 619 000	11 033 000	53.5	10 539 000	5 661 000	53.7	10 080 000	5 372 000	53.3
1 VII 2011	ESDF	21 124 000	11 297 000	53.5	10 794 000	5 795 000	53.7	10 330 000	5 502 000	53.3
Tajikistan - Tadjikistan										
1 VII 2007	ESDF	7 139 772	1 877 203	26.3	3 581 930	943 032	26.3	3 557 842	934 171	26.3
1 VII 2008	ESDF	7 294 747	1 918 996	26.3	3 659 238	965 220	26.4	3 635 510	953 776	26.2
1 VII 2009	ESDF	7 334 083	1 944 038	26.5	3 699 641	979 510	26.5	3 634 442	964 528	26.5
1 VII 2010	ESDF	7 519 280	1 996 961	26.6	3 794 467	1 007 796	26.6	3 724 813	989 165	26.6
21 IX 2010	CDFC	7 564 502	2 006 605	26.5	3 817 004	1 012 642	26.5	3 747 498	993 963	26.5
1 VII 2011	ESDF	7 714 198	2 042 660	26.5	3 893 798	1 032 106	26.5	3 820 401	1 010 554	26.5
1 VII 2012	ESDF	7 897 313	2 085 698	26.4	3 987 517	1 054 904	26.5	3 909 796	1 030 794	26.4
1 VII 2013	ESDF	8 074 266	2 138 737	26.5	4 078 857	1 083 119	26.6	3 995 409	1 055 618	26.4
1 VII 2014	ESDF	8 256 572	2 193 224	26.6	4 174 269	1 112 352	26.6	4 082 303	1 080 873	26.5
1 VII 2015	ESDF	8 451 600	2 237 900	26.5	...	...	...	...	...	...
Thailand - Thaïlande										
1 VII 2007	ESDJ	63 038 247	...	...	31 095 942	...	...	31 942 305	...	...
1 VII 2008	ESDJ	63 389 730	...	...	31 255 869	...	...	32 133 861	...	...
1 VII 2009	ESDJ	63 525 062	...	...	31 293 096	...	...	32 231 966	...	...
1 VII 2010	ESDJ	63 878 267	...	...	31 451 801	...	...	32 426 466	...	...
1 IX 2010	CDJC	65 981 659	29 133 829	44.2	32 355 032	14 120 842	43.6	33 626 627	15 012 987	44.6
1 VII 2011	ESDJ	64 076 033	...	...	31 529 148	...	...	32 546 885	...	...
1 VII 2012	ESDJ	64 456 695	...	...	31 700 727	...	...	32 755 968	...	...
1 VII 2013	ESDJ	64 785 909	...	...	31 845 971	...	...	32 939 938	...	...
1 VII 2014	ESDJ	65 124 716	...	...	31 999 008	...	...	33 125 708	...	...
1 VII 2015	ESDJ	65 729 098	...	...	32 280 886	...	...	33 448 212	...	...
1 VII 2016	ESDJ	65 931 550	...	...	32 357 808	...	...	33 573 742	...	...
Timor-Leste										
1 VII 2007[3]	ESDF	1 048 000			532 000			516 000		
1 VII 2008[3]	ESDF	1 080 742	...	...	549 000[77]	...	...	532 000[77]	...	...
11 VII 2010	CDFC	1 066 409	316 086	29.6	544 198	166 163	30.5	522 211	149 923	28.7
1 VII 2013[3]	ESDF	1 180 069	...	...	602 526			577 544	...	...
1 VII 2014[3]	ESDF	1 212 107	...	...	618 789			593 318	...	...
11 VII 2015*	CDFC	1 167 242	...	...	588 561	...	...	578 681	...	...
Turkey - Turquie										
31 XII 2007[120]	ESDJ	70 586 256	47 652 226	67.5	35 376 533	23 868 078	67.5	35 209 723	23 784 148	67.5
31 XII 2008[120]	CDJC	71 517 100	...	...	35 901 154	...	...	35 615 946	...	...
31 XII 2008[120]	ESDJ	71 517 100	49 514 530	69.2	35 901 154	24 865 097	69.3	35 615 946	24 649 433	69.2

6. Total and urban population by sex: 2007 - 2016
Population totale et population urbaine selon le sexe : 2007 - 2016 (continued - suite)

Continent, country or area, and date / Continent, pays ou zone et date	Code[a]	Both sexes - Les deux sexes			Male - Masculin			Female - Féminin		
		Total	Urban - Urbaine		Total	Urban - Urbaine		Total	Urban - Urbaine	
			Number Nombre	Percent P.100		Number Nombre	Percent P.100		Number Nombre	Percent P.100

ASIA - ASIE

Turkey - Turquie

31 XII 2009[120]	ESDJ	72 561 312	50 872 734	70.1	36 462 470	25 607 137	70.2	36 098 842	25 265 597	70.0
31 XII 2010[120]	ESDJ	73 722 988	52 340 830	71.0	37 043 182	26 348 394	71.1	36 679 806	25 992 436	70.9
3 X 2011[121]	CDJC	74 526 000	53 321 000	71.5	37 431 000	26 777 000	71.5	37 095 000	26 544 000	71.6
31 XII 2011[120]	ESDJ	74 724 269	53 630 845	71.8	37 532 954	26 947 983	71.8	37 191 315	26 682 862	71.7
31 XII 2012[120]	ESDJ	75 627 384	54 705 188	72.3	37 956 168	27 442 260	72.3	37 671 216	27 262 928	72.4
31 XII 2013[120]	ESDJ	76 667 864	66 488 105[122]	86.7	38 473 360	33 344 846[122]	86.7	38 194 504	33 143 259[122]	86.8
31 XII 2014[120]	ESDJ	77 695 904	67 720 318	87.2	38 984 302	33 954 681	87.1	38 711 602	33 765 637	87.2
31 XII 2015[120]	ESDJ	78 741 053	69 004 143	87.6	39 511 191	34 598 184	87.6	39 229 862	34 405 959	87.7

United Arab Emirates - Émirats arabes unis[123]

31 XII 2007	ESDF	6 219 006	...	...	4 533 281	...	...	1 685 725	...	...
31 XII 2008	ESDF	8 073 626	...	...	6 039 971	...	...	2 033 655	...	...
31 XII 2009	ESDF	8 199 996	...	...	6 120 885	...	...	2 079 111	...	...
1 VII 2010	ESDF	8 264 070	...	...	6 161 820	...	...	2 102 250	...	...
31 XII 2016	ESDF	9 121 167	...	...	6 298 294	...	...	2 822 873		

Uzbekistan - Ouzbékistan[124]

1 VII 2007	ESDJ	26 867 998	9 641 400	35.9	13 430 432	4 783 500	35.6	13 437 566	4 857 900	36.2
1 VII 2008	ESDJ	27 302 782	14 141 300	51.8	13 653 947	7 037 900	51.5	13 648 835	7 103 400	52.0
1 VII 2009	ESDJ	27 767 408	14 330 900	51.6	13 893 825	7 129 600	51.3	13 873 583	7 201 300	51.9
1 VII 2010	ESDJ	28 562 405	14 661 700	51.3	14 291 711	7 295 300	51.0	14 270 694	7 366 400	51.6
1 VII 2011	ESDJ	29 339 368	15 062 700	51.3	14 680 424	7 496 500	51.1	14 658 944	7 566 200	51.6
1 VII 2012	ESDJ	29 774 448	15 285 000	51.3	14 905 603	7 613 400	51.1	14 868 845	7 671 600	51.6
1 VII 2013	ESDJ	30 243 172	15 462 637	51.1	15 148 116	7 707 450	50.9	15 095 056	7 755 187	51.4
1 VII 2014	ESDJ	30 757 669	15 651 614	50.9	15 414 846	7 809 449	50.7	15 342 823	7 842 165	51.1
1 VII 2015	ESDJ	31 298 929	15 855 953	50.7	15 695 568	7 919 014	50.5	15 603 361	7 936 939	50.9

Viet Nam

1 VII 2007[125]	ESDF	84 218 459	23 746 304	28.2	41 447 286	...	...	42 771 173	...	...
1 VII 2008[125]	ESDF	85 118 704	24 673 136	29.0	41 956 098	...	...	43 162 606	...	...
1 IV 2009	CDJC	85 846 997	25 436 896	29.6	42 413 143	12 349 995	29.1	43 433 854	13 086 901	30.1
1 VII 2009[125]	ESDF	86 024 979	25 584 740	29.7	42 523 416	...	...	43 501 563	...	...
1 VII 2010[125]	ESDF	86 947 439	26 515 900	30.5	42 993 487	...	...	43 953 952	...	...
1 VII 2011[125]	ESDF	87 860 387	27 719 300	31.5	43 446 781	...	...	44 413 606	...	...
1 VII 2012[125]	ESDF	88 809 279	28 269 200	31.8	43 908 201	...	...	44 901 078	...	...
1 VII 2013[125]	ESDF	89 759 538	28 874 900	32.2	44 364 894	...	...	45 394 644	...	...
1 VII 2014[125]	ESDF	90 728 941	30 035 405	33.1	44 758 132	...	...	45 970 809	...	...
1 VII 2015[125]	ESDF	91 709 825	31 067 492	33.9	45 224 031	...	...	46 485 794	...	...
1 VII 2016*[125]	ESDF	92 695 121	31 985 992	34.5	45 705 601	...	...	46 989 520	...	...

Yemen - Yémen

31 XII 2007	ESDF	21 538 995	6 256 462	29.0	...	...	...	...	...	...
1 VII 2008[3]	ESDJ	21 843 554	6 281 475	28.8	11 127 218	...	...	10 716 336	...	...
1 VII 2009[3]	ESDJ	22 492 035	6 475 802	28.8	11 454 963	...	...	11 037 072	...	...
1 VII 2010[3]	ESDJ	23 153 982	6 673 916	28.8	11 789 814	...	...	11 364 168	...	...
1 VII 2011[3]	ESDJ	23 832 569	6 875 789	28.9	12 133 362	...	...	11 699 207	...	...
1 VII 2012[3]	ESDJ	24 526 703	7 075 639	28.8	12 485 039	...	...	12 041 664	...	...
1 VII 2013[3]	ESDJ	25 235 079	7 280 367	28.9	12 844 169	...	...	12 390 910	...	...

EUROPE

Åland Islands - Îles d'Åland[47]

1 VII 2007	ESDJ	27 038	10 863	40.2	13 407	5 151	38.4	13 631	5 712	41.9
1 VII 2008	ESDJ	27 305	10 954	40.1	13 552	5 189	38.3	13 753	5 765	41.9
1 VII 2009	ESDJ	27 595	11 064	40.1	13 724	5 264	38.4	13 871	5 800	41.8
1 VII 2010	ESDJ	27 871	11 157	40.0	13 880	5 327	38.4	13 991	5 830	41.7
1 VII 2011	ESDJ	28 181	11 227	39.8	14 045	5 364	38.2	14 137	5 863	41.5
1 VII 2012	ESDJ	28 429	11 305	39.8	14 172	5 408	38.2	14 257	5 897	41.4
1 VII 2013	ESDJ	28 585	11 370	39.8	14 255	5 445	38.2	14 330	5 925	41.3
1 VII 2014	ESDJ	28 792	11 437	39.7	14 375	5 490	38.2	14 417	5 947	41.2
1 VII 2015	ESDJ	28 950	11 471	39.6	14 466	5 521	38.2	14 484	5 950	41.1
1 VII 2016	ESDJ	29 099	11 513	39.6	14 526	5 538	38.1	14 573	5 975	41.0

Continent, country or area, and date / Continent, pays ou zone et date	Code[a]	Both sexes - Les deux sexes			Male - Masculin			Female - Féminin		
		Total	Urban - Urbaine		Total	Urban - Urbaine		Total	Urban - Urbaine	
			Number Nombre	Percent P.100		Number Nombre	Percent P.100		Number Nombre	Percent P.100

EUROPE

Albania - Albanie
1 VII 2007 .... ESDF		2 970 017	1 472 486	49.6	1 483 616	729 192	49.1	1 486 401	743 294	50.0
1 VII 2008 .... ESDF		2 947 314	1 495 552	50.7	1 472 660	740 747	50.3	1 474 654	754 805	51.2
1 VII 2009 .... ESDF		2 927 519	1 518 397	51.9	1 463 537	752 178	51.4	1 463 982	766 219	52.3
1 VII 2010 .... ESDF		2 913 021	1 541 310	52.9	1 457 661	763 780	52.4	1 455 360	777 530	53.4
1 VII 2011 .... ESDF		2 904 780	1 564 139	53.8	1 455 074	775 313	53.3	1 449 706	788 826	54.4
1 X 2011 .... CDJC		2 800 138	1 498 508	53.5	1 403 059	742 671	52.9	1 397 079	755 837	54.1
1 VII 2012 .... ESDF		2 900 489	1 595 701	55.0	1 455 904	787 167	54.1	1 444 585	808 534	56.0
1 VII 2013 .... ESDF		2 897 364	1 633 617	56.4	1 458 648	798 615	54.8	1 438 716	835 002	58.0
1 I 2014 .... ESDF		2 895 947	...	...	1 459 963	...	...	1 435 984	...	...
1 VII 2015 .... ESDF		2 889 167	...	...	1 461 407	...	...	1 427 760	...	...

Andorra - Andorre[47]
1 VII 2007 .... ESDJ		82 392	...	...	43 100	...	...	39 292	...	...
1 VII 2008 .... ESDJ		83 884	...	...	43 911	...	...	39 973	...	...
1 VII 2009 .... ESDJ		85 116	...	...	44 444	...	...	40 672	...	...
1 I 2010[126] .... ESDJ		70 290	...	...	35 592	...	...	34 698	...	...
1 I 2011 .... ESDJ		69 772	...	...	35 204	...	...	34 568	...	...
31 XII 2011 .... CDJC		78 115	...	...	39 863	...	...	38 252	...	...
1 I 2012 .... ESDJ		69 758	...	...	35 147	...	...	34 611	...	...
1 VII 2013 .... ESDJ		69 929	...	...	35 206	...	...	34 723	...	...
1 VII 2014 .... ESDJ		70 155	...	...	35 364	...	...	34 791	...	...
1 VII 2015 .... ESDJ		70 901	...	...	35 741	...	...	35 160	...	...
1 VII 2016 .... ESDJ		72 358	...	...	36 590	...	...	35 768	...	...

Austria - Autriche
1 VII 2007 .... ESDJ		8 295 189	...	...	4 036 548	...	...	4 258 641	...	...
1 VII 2008 .... ESDJ		8 321 541	...	...	4 050 215	...	...	4 271 326	...	...
1 VII 2009 .... ESDJ		8 341 483	...	...	4 061 195	...	...	4 280 288	...	...
1 VII 2010 .... ESDJ		8 361 069	...	...	4 071 773	...	...	4 289 296	...	...
1 VII 2011 .... ESDJ		8 388 534	...	...	4 087 188	...	...	4 301 346	...	...
31 X 2011 .... CDJC		8 401 940	5 643 239	67.2	4 093 938	2 713 930	66.3	4 308 002	2 929 309	68.0
1 VII 2012 .... ESDJ		8 426 311	...	...	4 109 431	...	...	4 316 880	...	...
1 VII 2013 .... ESDJ		8 477 230	...	...	4 138 693	...	...	4 338 537	...	...
1 VII 2014 .... ESDJ		8 543 975	...	...	4 176 554	...	...	4 367 421	...	...
1 VII 2015 .... ESDJ		8 629 496	...	...	4 229 064	...	...	4 400 432	...	...
1 I 2016 .... ESDJ		8 690 076	...	...	4 265 369	...	...	4 424 707	...	...

Belarus - Bélarus
1 VII 2007 .... ESDJ		9 560 953	6 976 543	73.0	4 450 877	3 238 281	72.8	5 110 076	3 738 262	73.2
1 VII 2008 .... ESDJ		9 527 985	7 008 135	73.6	4 433 031	3 249 263	73.3	5 094 954	3 758 872	73.8
1 VII 2009 .... ESDJ		9 506 765	7 052 045	74.2	4 421 789	3 266 240	73.9	5 084 976	3 785 805	74.5
14 X 2009 .... CDJC		9 503 807	7 064 529	74.3	4 420 039	3 271 014	74.0	5 083 768	3 793 515	74.6
1 VII 2010 .... ESDJ		9 490 583	7 100 147	74.8	4 413 225	3 285 104	74.4	5 077 358	3 815 043	75.1
1 VII 2011 .... ESDJ		9 473 172	7 148 636	75.5	4 403 227	3 303 932	75.0	5 069 945	3 844 704	75.8
1 VII 2012 .... ESDJ		9 464 495	7 198 575	76.1	4 397 910	3 324 299	75.6	5 066 585	3 874 276	76.5
1 VII 2013 .... ESDJ		9 465 997	7 247 854	76.6	4 399 369	3 345 878	76.1	5 066 628	3 901 976	77.0
1 VII 2014 .... ESDJ		9 474 511	7 299 878	77.0	4 405 204	3 369 054	76.5	5 069 307	3 930 824	77.5
1 VII 2015 .... ESDJ		9 489 616	7 347 512	77.4	4 415 020	3 390 465	76.8	5 074 596	3 957 047	78.0
1 I 2016 .... ESDJ		9 498 364	...	...	4 420 842	...	...	5 077 522	...	...

Belgium - Belgique
1 VII 2007 .... ESDJ		10 622 604	10 469 341	98.6	5 201 670	5 125 007	98.5	5 420 934	5 344 334	98.6
1 VII 2008 .... ESDJ		10 709 973	10 555 681	98.6	5 246 480	5 169 223	98.5	5 463 493	5 386 458	98.6
1 VII 2009 .... ESDJ		10 796 493	10 641 089	98.6	5 290 436	5 212 557	98.5	5 506 057	5 428 532	98.6
1 VII 2010 .... ESDJ		10 895 638	10 739 291	98.6	5 341 252	5 262 796	98.5	5 554 386	5 476 495	98.6
1 I 2011 .... CDJC		11 000 638	10 842 520	98.6	5 401 718	5 322 172	98.5	5 598 920	5 520 348	98.6
1 VII 2011 .... ESDJ		11 043 788	10 884 939	98.6	5 425 814	5 345 964	98.5	5 617 974	5 538 975	98.6
1 VII 2012 .... ESDJ		11 128 246	...	...	5 469 608	...	...	5 658 638	...	...
1 VII 2013 .... ESDJ		11 182 817	...	...	5 497 753	...	...	5 685 065	...	...
1 VII 2014 .... ESDJ		11 231 213	...	...	5 522 163	...	...	5 709 051	...	...
1 VII 2015[84] .... ESDJ		11 284 776	...	...	5 552 760	...	...	5 732 016	...	...
1 I 2016 .... ESDJ		11 311 117	...	...	5 569 264	...	...	5 741 853	...	...

Bosnia and Herzegovina - Bosnie-Herzégovine
1 VII 2007 .... ESDF		3 842 562	...	...	1 877 309	...	...	1 965 253	...	...
1 VII 2008 .... ESDF		3 842 265	...	...	1 877 165	...	...	1 965 100	...	...
1 VII 2009 .... ESDF		3 842 566	...	...	1 877 312	...	...	1 965 254	...	...
1 VII 2010 .... ESDF		3 843 126	...	...	1 877 587	...	...	1 965 539	...	...
1 VII 2011 .... ESDF		3 841 224	...	...	1 876 546	...	...	1 964 678	...	...

Continent, country or area, and date / Continent, pays ou zone et date	Code[a]	Both sexes - Les deux sexes			Male - Masculin			Female - Féminin		
		Total	Urban - Urbaine		Total	Urban - Urbaine		Total	Urban - Urbaine	
			Number Nombre	Percent P.100		Number Nombre	Percent P.100		Number Nombre	Percent P.100
EUROPE										
Bosnia and Herzegovina - Bosnie-Herzégovine										
1 VII 2012*	ESDF	3 837 455	...	...	1 874 608	...	...	1 962 848	...	...
1 I 2013*	ESDF	3 835 645	...	...	1 873 605	...	...	1 962 040	...	...
Bulgaria - Bulgarie										
1 VII 2007	ESDJ	7 659 764	5 414 260	70.7	3 710 315	2 604 175	70.2	3 949 449	2 810 085	71.2
1 VII 2008	ESDJ	7 623 395	5 405 147	70.9	3 690 485	2 597 929	70.4	3 932 910	2 807 218	71.4
1 VII 2009	ESDJ	7 585 131	5 408 330	71.3	3 670 296	2 598 442	70.8	3 914 835	2 809 888	71.8
1 VII 2010	ESDJ	7 534 289	5 388 142	71.5	3 644 560	2 587 844	71.0	3 889 729	2 800 298	72.0
1 II 2011	CDJC	7 364 570	5 338 261	72.5	3 586 571	2 580 734	72.0	3 777 999	2 757 527	73.0
1 VII 2011	ESDJ	7 348 328	5 336 366	72.6	3 577 847	2 579 205	72.1	3 770 481	2 757 161	73.1
1 VII 2012	ESDJ	7 305 888	5 316 384	72.8	3 555 920	2 568 535	72.2	3 749 968	2 747 849	73.3
1 VII 2013	ESDJ	7 263 859	...	...	3 534 276			3 729 584		
1 VII 2014	ESDJ	7 223 937	5 279 577	73.1	3 513 480	2 548 437	72.5	3 710 457	2 731 140	73.6
1 VII 2015	ESDJ	7 177 991	5 247 331	73.1	3 489 596	2 530 439	72.5	3 688 395	2 716 892	73.7
1 I 2016	ESDJ	7 153 784	5 227 182	73.1	3 477 177	2 519 346	72.5	3 676 607	2 707 836	73.7
Croatia - Croatie										
1 VII 2007	ESDJ	4 310 217	...	...	2 075 547	...	...	2 234 670	...	...
1 VII 2008	ESDJ	4 309 705	...	...	2 076 517	...	...	2 233 188	...	...
1 VII 2009	ESDJ	4 305 181	...	...	2 075 321	...	...	2 229 860	...	...
1 VII 2010	ESDJ	4 295 427	...	...	2 071 195	...	...	2 224 232	...	...
1 IV 2011	CDJC	4 284 889	2 368 506	55.3	2 066 335	1 121 328	54.3	2 218 554	1 247 178	56.2
1 VII 2011	ESDJ	4 280 622	...	...	2 064 314	...	...	2 216 308	...	...
1 VII 2012	ESDJ	4 267 558	...	...	2 058 701	...	...	2 208 857	...	...
1 VII 2013	ESDJ	4 255 689	...	...	2 053 788	...	...	2 201 901	...	...
1 VII 2014	ESDJ	4 238 389	...	...	2 045 801	...	...	2 192 588	...	...
1 VII 2015	ESDJ	4 203 604	...	...	2 028 640	...	...	2 174 964	...	...
1 I 2016	ESDJ	4 190 669	...	...	2 022 797	...	...	2 167 872	...	...
Czechia - Tchéquie										
1 VII 2007	ESDJ	10 298 828	...	...	5 037 856	...	...	5 260 972	...	...
1 VII 2008	ESDJ	10 384 603	...	...	5 090 898	...	...	5 293 705	...	...
1 VII 2009	ESDJ	10 443 936	...	...	5 126 422	...	...	5 317 514	...	...
1 VII 2010	ESDJ	10 474 410	...	...	5 141 699	...	...	5 332 711	...	...
25 III 2011	CDJC	10 436 560	7 650 450	73.3	5 109 766	3 712 348	72.7	5 326 794	3 938 102	73.9
1 VII 2011	ESDJ	10 496 088	...	...	5 152 721	...	...	5 343 368	...	...
1 VII 2012	ESDJ	10 510 786	...	...	5 161 280	...	...	5 349 506	...	...
1 VII 2013	ESDJ	10 510 719	7 683 793	73.1	5 161 617	3 740 790	72.5	5 349 102	3 943 003	73.7
1 VII 2014	ESDJ	10 524 783	7 693 352	73.1	5 169 146	3 744 873	72.4	5 355 637	3 948 479	73.7
1 VII 2015	ESDJ	10 542 942	7 702 624	73.1	5 180 242	3 749 901	72.4	5 362 700	3 952 723	73.7
1 I 2016	ESDJ	10 553 843	7 764 428	73.6	5 186 330	3 752 229	72.3	5 367 513	4 012 199	74.7
Denmark - Danemark[127]										
1 VII 2007	ESDJ	5 457 415	...	...	2 702 894	...	...	2 754 521	...	...
1 VII 2008	ESDJ	5 489 022	...	...	2 720 016	...	...	2 769 006	...	...
1 VII 2009	ESDJ	5 519 441	...	...	2 735 983	...	...	2 783 458	...	...
1 VII 2010	ESDJ	5 545 039	...	...	2 748 439	...	...	2 796 600	...	...
1 I 2011	CDJC	5 560 628	...	...	2 756 582	...	...	2 804 046	...	...
1 VII 2011	ESDJ	5 566 856	...	...	2 760 140	...	...	2 806 716	...	...
1 VII 2012	ESDJ	5 587 085	...	...	2 771 208	...	...	2 815 877	...	...
1 VII 2013	ESDJ	5 608 784	...	...	2 782 661	...	...	2 826 123	...	...
1 VII 2014	ESDJ	5 639 719	...	...	2 799 895	...	...	2 839 824	...	...
1 VII 2015	ESDJ	5 678 348	...	...	2 822 535	...	...	2 855 813	...	...
1 VII 2016	ESDJ	5 724 456	...	...	2 848 030	...	...	2 876 426	...	...
Estonia - Estonie										
1 VII 2007	ESDJ	1 340 680	916 015	68.3	623 155	413 710	66.4	717 525	502 305	70.0
1 VII 2008	ESDJ	1 337 090	911 285	68.2	621 685	411 555	66.2	715 405	499 730	69.9
1 VII 2009	ESDJ	1 334 515	907 675	68.0	621 060	410 130	66.0	713 455	497 545	69.7
1 VII 2010	ESDJ	1 331 475	904 365	67.9	620 250	408 720	65.9	711 225	495 645	69.7
1 VII 2011	ESDJ	1 327 439	903 066	68.0	618 919	408 988	66.1	708 520	494 078	69.7
31 XII 2011	CDJC	1 294 455	879 157	67.9	600 526	396 719	66.1	693 929	482 438	69.5
1 VII 2012	ESDJ	1 322 696	902 743	68.3	617 153	409 784	66.4	705 543	492 959	69.9
1 VII 2013	ESDJ	1 317 997	900 071	68.3	615 543	408 564	66.4	702 454	491 507	70.0
1 VII 2014	ESDJ	1 314 545	897 901	68.3	614 654	407 677	66.3	699 891	490 224	70.0
1 VII 2015	ESDJ	1 314 608	899 288[91]	68.4	615 549	406 894[91]	66.1	699 059	492 395[91]	70.4
1 I 2016	ESDJ	1 315 944	901 249[91]	68.5	616 708	406 268[91]	65.9	699 236	494 981[91]	70.8

6. Total and urban population by sex: 2007 - 2016
Population totale et population urbaine selon le sexe : 2007 - 2016 (continued - suite)

Continent, country or area, and date / Continent, pays ou zone et date	Code[a]	Both sexes - Les deux sexes			Male - Masculin			Female - Féminin		
		Total	Urban - Urbaine		Total	Urban - Urbaine		Total	Urban - Urbaine	
			Number Nombre	Percent P.100		Number Nombre	Percent P.100		Number Nombre	Percent P.100

EUROPE

Faeroe Islands - Îles Féroé

1 VII 2007 .... ESDJ		48 384	17 560	36.3	25 132	8 862	35.3	23 252	8 698	37.4
1 I 2008[47] .... CDJC		48 433	...	...	25 174	...	...	23 259	...	...
1 VII 2008 .... ESDJ		48 555	17 707	36.5	25 218	8 966	35.6	23 337	8 741	37.5
1 VII 2009 .... ESDJ		48 798	18 001	36.9	25 345	9 117	36.0	23 453	8 884	37.9
1 VII 2010 .... ESDJ		48 669	18 131	37.3	25 276	9 195	36.4	23 393	8 936	38.2
1 VII 2011 .... ESDJ		48 563	18 110	37.3	25 179	9 120	36.2	23 384	8 990	38.4
11 XI 2011 .... CDJC		48 346	...	...	25 125	...	...	23 221	...	...
1 VII 2012 .... ESDJ		48 319	18 033	37.3	25 074	9 072	36.2	23 245	8 961	38.6
1 VII 2013 .... ESDJ		48 286	18 220	37.7	25 014	9 147	36.6	23 272	9 073	39.0
1 VII 2014 .... ESDJ		48 462	18 373	37.9	25 048	9 207	36.8	23 414	9 166	39.1
1 VII 2015 .... ESDJ		48 958	18 674	38.1	25 330	9 386	37.1	23 628	9 288	39.3
1 VII 2016 .... ESDJ		49 503	...	...	25 560	...	...	23 943	...	...

Finland - Finlande

1 VII 2007[128] .... ESDJ		5 261 682	3 558 585	67.6	2 576 858	1 721 731	66.8	2 684 824	1 836 854	68.4
1 VII 2008[128] .... ESDJ		5 286 095	3 586 744	67.9	2 590 669	1 737 294	67.1	2 695 426	1 849 450	68.6
1 VII 2009[128] .... ESDJ		5 311 276	3 615 933	68.1	2 604 636	1 753 169	67.3	2 706 640	1 862 764	68.8
1 VII 2010[128] .... ESDJ		5 335 481	3 643 170	68.3	2 617 862	1 767 855	67.5	2 717 620	1 875 315	69.0
31 XII 2010 .... CDJC		5 375 276	3 662 915	68.1	2 638 416	1 777 697	67.4	2 736 860	1 885 218	68.9
1 VII 2011[128] .... ESDJ		5 360 091	3 671 777	68.5	2 631 431	1 783 058	67.8	2 728 660	1 888 719	69.2
1 VII 2012[128] .... ESDJ		5 385 543	3 701 923	68.7	2 645 408	1 799 025	68.0	2 740 136	1 902 898	69.4
1 VII 2013[128] .... ESDJ		5 410 389	3 732 928	69.0	2 659 239	1 815 818	68.3	2 751 150	1 917 110	69.7
1 VII 2014[128] .... ESDJ		5 432 721	3 762 906	69.3	2 671 740	1 831 826	68.6	2 760 981	1 931 080	69.9
1 VII 2015[128] .... ESDJ		5 450 581	3 849 116	70.6	2 682 211	1 875 949	69.9	2 768 370	1 973 167	71.3
1 I 2016[47] .... ESDJ		5 487 308	...	...	2 701 490	...	...	2 785 818	...	...

France[129]

1 VII 2007 .... ESDJ		61 965 052	...	...	30 001 162	...	...	31 963 890	...	...
1 VII 2008 .... ESDJ		62 300 288	...	...	30 166 091	...	...	32 134 197	...	...
1 VII 2009 .... ESDJ		62 615 472	...	...	30 322 692	...	...	32 292 780	...	...
1 I 2010 .... CDJS		62 765 235	48 387 303	77.1	30 393 079	23 208 841	76.4	32 372 156	25 178 462	77.8
1 VII 2010 .... ESDJ		62 917 790	...	...	30 475 789	...	...	32 442 001	...	...
1 VII 2011 .... ESDJ		63 223 158	...	...	30 626 399	...	...	32 596 759	...	...
1 VII 2012 .... ESDJ		63 536 918	...	...	30 782 589	...	...	32 754 329	...	...
1 VII 2013 .... ESDJ		63 862 825	...	...	30 945 423	...	...	32 917 402	...	...
1 I 2014 .... ESDJ		64 027 784	...	...	31 024 837	...	...	33 002 947	...	...
1 VII 2015* .... ESDJ		64 474 274	...	...	31 246 235	...	...	33 228 039	...	...
1 VII 2016* .... ESDJ		64 732 099	...	...	31 375 513	...	...	33 356 586	...	...

Germany - Allemagne

1 VII 2007 .... ESDJ		82 262 642	...	...	40 287 823	...	...	41 974 819	...	...
1 VII 2008 .... ESDJ		82 119 776	...	...	40 238 595	...	...	41 881 181	...	...
1 VII 2009 .... ESDJ		81 874 770	...	...	40 133 270	...	...	41 741 500	...	...
1 VII 2010 .... ESDJ		81 757 471	...	...	40 099 871	...	...	41 657 600	...	...
9 V 2011 .... CDJC		80 219 695	64 444 232	80.3	39 145 941	31 227 832	79.8	41 073 754	33 216 400	80.9
1 VII 2011[5] .... ESDJ		80 274 983	...	...	39 177 274	...	...	41 097 709	...	...
1 VII 2012[5] .... ESDJ		80 425 823	...	...	39 305 462	...	...	41 120 362	...	...
1 VII 2013[5] .... ESDJ		80 645 605	...	...	39 468 950	...	...	41 176 655	...	...
1 VII 2014[5] .... ESDJ		80 982 500	...	...	39 696 190	...	...	41 286 310	...	...
1 VII 2015[5] .... ESDJ		81 686 663	...	...	40 174 816	...	...	41 511 847	...	...
1 I 2016[5] .... ESDJ		82 175 684	...	...	40 514 123	...	...	41 661 561	...	...

Gibraltar[130]

31 XII 2007 .... ESDF		30 066	...	...	14 871	...	...	15 195	...	...
31 XII 2008 .... ESDF		30 496	...	...	15 113	...	...	15 383	...	...
31 XII 2009 .... ESDF		30 963	...	...	15 378	...	...	15 585	...	...
31 XII 2010 .... ESDF		31 465	...	...	15 666	...	...	15 799	...	...
31 XII 2011 .... ESDF		32 003	...	...	15 977	...	...	16 026	...	...
12 XI 2012 .... CDJC		32 194	...	...	16 061	...	...	16 133	...	...
31 XII 2012 .... ESDF		32 577	...	...	16 311	...	...	16 266	...	...
31 XII 2013 .... ESDF		32 734	...	...	16 460	...	...	16 274	...	...
31 XII 2014 .... ESDF		33 140	...	...	16 694	...	...	16 446	...	...
31 XII 2015 .... ESDF		33 573	...	...	16 938	...	...	16 635	...	...

Greece - Grèce

1 VII 2007 .... ESDF		11 048 499	...	...	5 445 100	...	...	5 603 399	...	...
1 VII 2008 .... ESDF		11 077 863	...	...	5 452 027	...	...	5 625 836	...	...
1 VII 2009 .... ESDF		11 107 024	...	...	5 458 449	...	...	5 648 575	...	...

Continent, country or area, and date / Continent, pays ou zone et date	Code[a]	Both sexes - Les deux sexes			Male - Masculin			Female - Féminin		
		Total	Urban - Urbaine		Total	Urban - Urbaine		Total	Urban - Urbaine	
			Number Nombre	Percent P.100		Number Nombre	Percent P.100		Number Nombre	Percent P.100
EUROPE										
Greece - Grèce										
1 VII 2010	ESDF	11 121 383	...	...	5 457 186	...	...	5 664 197	...	...
9 V 2011	CDFC	10 816 286	8 285 259	76.6	5 303 223	4 022 889	75.9	5 513 063	4 262 370	77.3
1 VII 2011	ESDF	11 104 995	...	...	5 438 712	...	...	5 666 283	...	...
1 VII 2012	ESDF	11 045 040	...	...	5 395 104	...	...	5 649 936	...	...
1 VII 2013	ESDF	10 965 241	...	...	5 339 750	...	...	5 625 491	...	...
1 VII 2014	ESDF	10 892 369	...	...	5 290 797	...	...	5 601 572	...	...
1 VII 2015	ESDF	10 820 964	...	...	5 246 345	...	...	5 574 619	...	...
1 I 2016	ESDF	10 783 748	...	...	5 224 210	...	...	5 559 538	...	...
Guernsey - Guernesey										
31 III 2007	ESDF	61 175	...	...	30 024	...	...	31 151	...	...
31 III 2008	ESDF	61 726	...	...	30 405	...	...	31 321	...	...
31 III 2009	ESDF	62 274	...	...	30 777	...	...	31 497	...	...
31 III 2010	ESDF	62 431	...	...	30 695	...	...	31 736	...	...
31 III 2011	ESDF	62 915	...	...	31 025	...	...	31 890	...	...
31 III 2012	ESDF	62 904	...	...	30 966	...	...	31 938	...	...
31 III 2013	ESDF	62 732	...	...	31 081	...	...	31 651	...	...
31 III 2014	ESDF	62 490	...	...	30 892	...	...	31 598	...	...
31 III 2015	CDJC	62 612	...	...	31 028	...	...	31 584	...	...
31 III 2015	ESDF	62 485	...	...	30 966	...	...	31 519	...	...
31 III 2016	ESDF	62 723	...	...	31 109	...	...	31 614	...	...
Holy See - Saint-Siège[131]										
1 VII 2009	CDFC	466[132]	...	...	320	...	...	146	...	...
Hungary - Hongrie										
1 VII 2007	ESDJ	10 055 780	6 737 792	67.0	4 774 320	3 156 954	66.1	5 281 460	3 580 839	67.8
1 VII 2008	ESDJ	10 038 188	6 810 173	67.8	4 766 306	3 191 030	66.9	5 271 882	3 619 143	68.6
1 VII 2009	ESDJ	10 022 650	6 861 432	68.5	4 759 975	3 215 749	67.6	5 262 675	3 645 683	69.3
1 VII 2010	ESDJ	10 000 023	6 953 071	69.5	4 750 401	3 260 344	68.6	5 249 623	3 692 727	70.3
1 VII 2011	ESDJ	9 971 727	6 945 873	69.7	4 737 813	3 256 796	68.7	5 233 914	3 689 077	70.5
1 X 2011	CDFC	9 937 628	6 903 858	69.5	4 718 479	3 241 911	68.7	5 219 149	3 661 947	70.2
1 VII 2012	ESDJ	9 920 362	6 877 231	69.3	4 720 310	3 234 447	68.5	5 200 052	3 642 785	70.1
1 VII 2013	ESDJ	9 893 082	6 864 757	69.4	4 709 672	3 229 480	68.6	5 183 410	3 635 277	70.1
1 VII 2014[133]	ESDJ	9 866 468	6 950 391	70.4	4 699 585	3 272 050	69.6	5 166 883	3 678 342	71.2
1 VII 2015[133]	ESDJ	9 843 028	6 937 836	70.5	4 692 149	3 267 756	69.6	5 150 879	3 670 081	71.3
1 I 2016[133]	ESDJ	9 830 485	...	...	4 688 519	...	...	5 141 966	...	...
Iceland - Islande[134]										
1 VII 2007	ESDJ	311 396	289 119	92.8	158 866	146 168	92.0	152 530	142 951	93.7
1 VII 2008	ESDJ	319 355	298 024	93.3	163 176	151 378	92.8	156 179	146 646	93.9
1 VII 2009	ESDJ	319 246	298 890	93.6	161 548	150 604	93.2	157 698	148 286	94.0
1 VII 2010	ESDJ	318 006	297 432	93.5	159 838	148 901	93.2	158 168	148 531	93.9
1 VII 2011	ESDJ	319 014	300 395	94.2	160 185	...	...	158 829	...	...
31 XII 2011	CDJC	315 556	295 874	93.8	158 151	147 681	93.4	157 405	148 193	94.1
1 VII 2012	ESDJ	320 716	300 237	93.6	160 901	150 074	93.3	159 815	150 163	94.0
1 VII 2013	ESDJ	323 764	303 136	93.6	162 378	151 471	93.3	161 386	151 665	94.0
1 VII 2014	ESDJ	327 386	306 633	93.7	164 252	153 265	93.3	163 134	153 368	94.0
1 VII 2015	ESDJ	330 815	309 868	93.7	166 228	155 146	93.3	164 587	154 723	94.0
1 I 2016	ESDJ	332 529	...	...	167 270	...	...	165 259	...	...
Ireland - Irlande										
1 VII 2007	ESDF	4 356 931	...	...	2 177 582	...	...	2 179 349	...	...
1 VII 2008	ESDF	4 425 683	...	...	2 206 165	...	...	2 219 518	...	...
1 VII 2009	ESDF	4 458 942	...	...	2 215 646	...	...	2 243 297	...	...
1 VII 2010	ESDF	4 560 155	...	...	2 265 200	...	...	2 294 955	...	...
10 IV 2011	CDFC	4 588 252	2 846 882	62.0	2 272 699	1 389 160	61.1	2 315 553	1 457 722	63.0
1 VII 2011	ESDF	4 576 794	...	...	2 269 608	...	...	2 307 186	...	...
1 VII 2012	ESDF	4 586 897	...	...	2 271 290	...	...	2 315 607	...	...
1 VII 2013[133]	ESDF	4 598 294	...	...	2 275 508	...	...	2 322 787	...	...
1 I 2014[133]	ESDF	4 605 501	...	...	2 278 225	...	...	2 327 276	...	...
15 IV 2015[133]	ESDJ	4 635 390	...	...	2 289 549	...	...	2 345 841	...	...
1 I 2016[133]	ESDF	4 724 720	...	...	2 335 733	...	...	2 388 987	...	...
24 IV 2016	CDJC	4 761 865	...	...	2 354 428	...	...	2 407 437	...	...
Isle of Man - Île de Man										
30 IV 2007	ESDJ	80 885	...	...	39 995	...	...	40 889	...	...
30 IV 2008	ESDJ	81 722	...	...	40 472	...	...	41 250	...	...
30 IV 2009	ESDJ	82 371	...	...	40 849	...	...	41 522	...	...
30 IV 2010	ESDJ	82 691	...	...	41 053	...	...	41 638	...	...

Continent, country or area, and date / Continent, pays ou zone et date	Code[a]	Both sexes - Les deux sexes Total	Urban - Urbaine Number Nombre	Urban - Urbaine Percent P.100	Male - Masculin Total	Urban - Urbaine Number Nombre	Urban - Urbaine Percent P.100	Female - Féminin Total	Urban - Urbaine Number Nombre	Urban - Urbaine Percent P.100
EUROPE										
Isle of Man - Île de Man										
27 III 2011	CDJC	84 497	...	...	41 971	...	...	42 526	...	...
30 IV 2012	ESDJ	85 047	...	...	42 273	...	...	42 775	...	...
30 IV 2013	ESDJ	85 682	...	...	42 622	...	...	43 060	...	...
30 IV 2014	ESDJ	86 322	...	...	42 971	...	...	43 352	...	...
30 IV 2015	ESDJ	86 963	...	...	43 319	...	...	43 644	...	...
24 IV 2016	CDJC	83 314	...	...	41 269	...	...	42 045	...	...
30 IV 2016	ESDJ	85 619	...	...	42 665	...	...	42 954	...	...
Italy - Italie										
1 VII 2007	ESDJ	58 438 310	...	...	28 311 738	...	...	30 126 572	...	...
1 VII 2008	ESDJ	58 826 731	...	...	28 490 625	...	...	30 336 106	...	...
1 VII 2009	ESDJ	59 095 365	...	...	28 609 696	...	...	30 485 669	...	...
1 VII 2010	ESDJ	59 277 417	...	...	28 682 321	...	...	30 595 096	...	...
1 VII 2011	ESDJ	59 379 449	...	...	28 720 928	...	...	30 658 521	...	...
9 X 2011	CDJC	59 433 744	...	...	28 745 507	...	...	30 688 237	...	...
1 VII 2012	ESDJ	59 539 717	...	...	28 808 098	...	...	30 731 619	...	...
1 VII 2013	ESDJ	60 233 948	...	...	29 187 081	...	...	31 046 867	...	...
1 VII 2014	ESDJ	60 789 140	...	...	29 493 077	...	...	31 296 063	...	...
1 I 2015	ESDJ	60 795 612	...	...	29 501 590	...	...	31 294 022	...	...
1 I 2016	ESDJ	60 665 551	...	...	29 456 321	...	...	31 209 230	...	...
Jersey										
27 III 2011	CDFC	97 857	...	...	48 296	...	...	49 561	...	...
Latvia - Lettonie										
1 VII 2007	ESDJ	2 200 325	1 494 615	67.9	1 010 416	671 274	66.4	1 189 909	823 341	69.2
1 VII 2008	ESDJ	2 177 322	1 478 831	67.9	999 845	663 658	66.4	1 177 477	815 173	69.2
1 VII 2009	ESDJ	2 141 669	1 453 570	67.9	981 789	650 486	66.3	1 159 880	803 084	69.2
1 VII 2010	ESDJ	2 097 555	1 422 675	67.8	959 435	634 393	66.1	1 138 120	788 282	69.3
1 III 2011	CDJC	2 070 371	1 404 251	67.8	946 102	625 150	66.1	1 124 269	779 101	69.3
1 VII 2011	ESDJ	2 059 709	1 394 429	67.7	941 375	620 484	65.9	1 118 334	773 945	69.2
1 VII 2012	ESDJ	2 034 319	1 374 215	67.6	930 696	611 604	65.7	1 103 623	762 611	69.1
1 VII 2013	ESDJ	2 012 647	1 362 004	67.7	921 813	606 624	65.8	1 090 834	755 380	69.2
1 VII 2014	ESDJ	1 993 782	1 353 269	67.9	914 126	603 112	66.0	1 079 656	750 157	69.5
1 VII 2015	ESDJ	1 977 527	1 344 291	68.0	907 753	599 629	66.1	1 069 774	744 662	69.6
1 I 2016	ESDJ	1 968 957	...	...	904 299	...	...	1 064 658	...	...
Liechtenstein										
1 VII 2007	ESDJ	35 322	...	...	17 426	...	...	17 896	...	...
1 VII 2008	ESDJ	35 446	...	...	17 508	...	...	17 938	...	...
1 VII 2009	ESDJ	35 789	...	...	17 716	...	...	18 073	...	...
1 VII 2010	ESDJ	36 010	...	...	17 817	...	...	18 193	...	...
31 XII 2010	CDFC	36 149	...	...	17 886	...	...	18 263	...	...
1 VII 2011	ESDJ	36 281	...	...	17 950	...	...	18 331	...	...
1 VII 2012	ESDJ	36 636	...	...	18 123	...	...	18 513	...	...
1 VII 2013	ESDJ	36 942	...	...	18 314	...	...	18 628	...	...
1 VII 2014	ESDJ	37 215	...	...	18 458	...	...	18 757	...	...
1 VII 2015	ESDJ	37 468	...	...	18 580	...	...	18 888	...	...
1 I 2016	ESDJ	37 622	...	...	18 660	...	...	18 962	...	...
Lithuania - Lituanie										
1 VII 2007	ESDJ	3 231 294	2 155 871	66.7	1 497 107	977 988	65.3	1 734 187	1 177 883	67.9
1 VII 2008	ESDJ	3 198 231	2 134 908	66.8	1 480 386	966 638	65.3	1 717 845	1 168 270	68.0
1 VII 2009	ESDJ	3 162 916	2 112 248	66.8	1 461 776	953 885	65.3	1 701 140	1 158 363	68.1
1 VII 2010	ESDJ	3 097 282	2 068 095	66.8	1 428 711	931 128	65.2	1 668 571	1 136 967	68.1
1 III 2011	CDJC	3 043 429	2 031 211	66.7	1 402 604	912 943	65.1	1 640 825	1 118 268	68.2
1 VII 2011	ESDJ	3 028 115	2 021 365	66.8	1 395 367	907 995	65.1	1 632 748	1 113 370	68.2
1 VII 2012	ESDJ	2 987 773	1 997 436	66.9	1 376 201	896 102	65.1	1 611 572	1 101 334	68.3
1 VII 2013	ESDJ	2 957 689	1 981 924	67.0	1 362 443	888 578	65.2	1 595 246	1 093 346	68.5
1 VII 2014[133]	ESDJ	2 932 367	1 968 596	67.1	1 351 126	881 978	65.3	1 581 241	1 086 618	68.7
1 VII 2015[133]	ESDJ	2 904 910	1 952 920	67.2	1 337 932	873 571	65.3	1 566 978	1 079 349	68.9
1 I 2016[133]	ESDJ	2 888 558	...	...	1 329 607	...	...	1 558 951	...	...
Luxembourg										
1 VII 2007	ESDJ	479 993	...	...	237 700	...	...	242 294	...	...
1 VII 2008	ESDJ	488 650	...	...	242 221	...	...	246 429	...	...
1 VII 2009	ESDJ	497 782	...	...	247 120	...	...	250 662	...	...
1 VII 2010	ESDJ	506 953	...	...	252 013	...	...	254 941	...	...
1 II 2011	CDJC	512 353	...	...	254 967	...	...	257 386	...	...
1 VII 2011	ESDJ	518 347	...	...	258 220	...	...	260 127	...	...
1 VII 2012	ESDJ	530 946	...	...	265 116	...	...	265 830	...	...

6. Total and urban population by sex: 2007 - 2016
Population totale et population urbaine selon le sexe : 2007 - 2016 (continued - suite)

Continent, country or area, and date / Continent, pays ou zone et date	Code[a]	Both sexes - Les deux sexes			Male - Masculin			Female - Féminin		
			Urban - Urbaine			Urban - Urbaine			Urban - Urbaine	
		Total	Number Nombre	Percent P.100	Total	Number Nombre	Percent P.100	Total	Number Nombre	Percent P.100

EUROPE

Luxembourg
1 VII 2013 .... ESDJ		543 360	...	...	271 765	...	...	271 595	...	...
1 VII 2014 .... ESDJ		556 319	...	...	278 544	...	...	277 775	...	...
1 VII 2015 .... ESDJ		569 604	...	...	285 583	...	...	284 021	...	...
1 I 2016 .... ESDJ		576 249	...	...	289 193	...	...	287 056	...	...

Malta - Malte
1 VII 2007[135] .... ESDJ		406 778	...	...	202 150	...	...	204 628	...	...
1 VII 2008[135] .... ESDJ		409 429	...	...	203 696	...	...	205 733	...	...
1 VII 2009[135] .... ESDJ		412 530	...	...	205 432	...	...	207 098	...	...
1 VII 2010[135] .... ESDJ		414 562	...	...	206 333	...	...	208 229	...	...
1 VII 2011[135] .... ESDJ		416 318	...	...	207 072	...	...	209 246	...	...
20 XI 2011 .... CDFC		417 432	400 557	96.0	207 625	199 151	95.9	209 807	201 406	96.0
1 VII 2012[135] .... ESDJ		419 507	...	...	208 811	...	...	210 696	...	...
1 VII 2013[135] .... ESDJ		423 431	...	...	211 182	...	...	212 249	...	...
1 VII 2014[135] .... ESDJ		427 421	...	...	213 607	...	...	213 814	...	...
1 VII 2015[135] .... ESDJ		431 936	...	...	216 185	...	...	215 751	...	...
1 I 2016[135] .... ESDJ		434 403	...	...	217 569	...	...	216 834	...	...

Monaco[136]
9 VI 2008 .... CDJC		31 109	...	...	15 076[137]	...	...	15 914[137]	...	...
7 VI 2016 .... CDJC		37 308	...	...	18 240	...	...	19 068	...	...

Montenegro - Monténégro
1 VII 2007 .... ESDJ		626 104	394 653	63.0	308 267	191 692	62.2	317 836	202 961	63.9
1 VII 2008 .... ESDJ		628 804	397 747	63.3	309 787	193 393	62.4	319 018	204 354	64.1
1 VII 2009 .... ESDJ		631 536	400 928	63.5	311 258	195 088	62.7	320 278	205 840	64.3
1 VII 2010 .... ESDJ		617 304	...	...	304 861	...	...	312 443	...	...
1 IV 2011 .... CDJC		620 029	399 264	64.4	306 236	193 691	63.2	313 793	205 573	65.5
1 VII 2011 .... ESDJ		620 556	...	...	306 472	...	...	314 084	...	...
1 VII 2012 .... ESDJ		620 601	...	...	306 580	...	...	314 021	...	...
1 VII 2013 .... ESDJ		622 149	...	...	307 428	...	...	314 722	...	...
1 VII 2014[133] .... ESDJ		621 810	...	...	307 339	...	...	314 472	...	...
1 I 2015[133] .... ESDJ		622 099	...	...	307 522	...	...	314 577	...	...
1 I 2016[133] .... ESDJ		622 218	...	...	307 734	...	...	314 484	...	...

Netherlands - Pays-Bas
1 VII 2007 .... ESDJ		16 381 696	10 825 307	66.1	8 100 294	5 322 596	65.7	8 281 402	5 502 712	66.4
1 VII 2008 .... ESDJ		16 445 593	10 877 858	66.1	8 134 235	5 350 572	65.8	8 311 359	5 527 286	66.5
1 VII 2009 .... ESDJ		16 530 388	10 938 780	66.2	8 179 936	5 383 776	65.8	8 350 452	5 555 004	66.5
1 VII 2010 .... ESDJ		16 615 394	11 096 288	66.8	8 223 479	5 464 083	66.4	8 391 915	5 632 205	67.1
1 I 2011 .... CDJC		16 655 799	11 124 721	66.8	8 243 482	5 478 213	66.5	8 412 317	5 646 508	67.1
1 VII 2011 .... ESDJ		16 693 074	...	...	8 263 177	...	...	8 429 897	...	...
1 VII 2012 .... ESDJ		16 754 962	...	...	8 295 105	...	...	8 459 857	...	...
1 VII 2013 .... ESDJ		16 804 432	...	...	8 320 862	...	...	8 483 570	...	...
1 VII 2014 .... ESDJ		16 865 007	...	...	8 353 621	...	...	8 511 386	...	...
1 VII 2015 .... ESDJ		16 939 923	...	...	8 394 997	...	...	8 544 926	...	...
1 I 2016 .... ESDJ		16 979 120	...	...	8 417 135	...	...	8 561 985	...	...

Norway - Norvège
1 VII 2007[133] .... ESDJ		4 709 153	...	...	2 342 739	...	...	2 366 414	...	...
1 VII 2008[133] .... ESDJ		4 768 212	...	...	2 377 372	...	...	2 390 840	...	...
1 VII 2009[133] .... ESDJ		4 828 726	...	...	2 410 903	...	...	2 417 823	...	...
1 VII 2010[133] .... ESDJ		4 889 252	...	...	2 443 801	...	...	2 445 452	...	...
1 VII 2011[133] .... ESDJ		4 953 088	...	...	2 479 860	...	...	2 473 228	...	...
19 XI 2011[138] .... CDJC		4 979 955	3 951 427[91]	79.3	2 495 777	1 959 424[91]	78.5	2 484 178	1 992 003[91]	80.2
1 VII 2012[133] .... ESDJ		5 018 573	...	...	2 517 390	...	...	2 501 183	...	...
1 VII 2013[133] .... ESDJ		5 079 623	...	...	2 551 458	...	...	2 528 165	...	...
1 VII 2014[133] .... ESDJ		5 137 232	...	...	2 583 105	...	...	2 554 127	...	...
1 VII 2015[133] .... ESDJ		5 188 607	...	...	2 611 414	...	...	2 577 194	...	...
1 I 2016[133] .... ESDJ		5 210 721	...	...	2 623 625	...	...	2 587 096	...	...

Poland - Pologne
1 VII 2007[139] .... ESDJ		38 115 967	23 350 920	61.3	18 417 074	11 070 886	60.1	19 698 893	12 280 034	62.3
1 VII 2008[139] .... ESDJ		38 115 909	23 305 018	61.1	18 408 405	11 041 359	60.0	19 707 504	12 263 659	62.2
1 VII 2009[139] .... ESDJ		38 153 389	23 293 906	61.1	18 423 343	11 032 562	59.9	19 730 046	12 261 344	62.1
1 VII 2010[133] .... ESDJ		38 042 403	23 156 309	60.9	18 422 344	11 000 170	59.7	19 620 059	12 156 139	62.0
31 III 2011 .... CDJC		38 044 565	23 116 673	60.8	18 420 389	10 977 424	59.6	19 624 176	12 139 249	61.9
1 VII 2011[133] .... ESDJ		38 051 032	23 111 377	60.7	18 422 837	10 973 937	59.6	19 628 195	12 137 440	61.8
1 VII 2012[133] .... ESDJ		38 059 134	23 066 408	60.6	18 424 160	10 948 639	59.4	19 634 974	12 117 769	61.7

Continent, country or area, and date / Continent, pays ou zone et date	Code[a]	Both sexes - Les deux sexes			Male - Masculin			Female - Féminin		
		Total	Urban - Urbaine		Total	Urban - Urbaine		Total	Urban - Urbaine	
			Number Nombre	Percent P.100		Number Nombre	Percent P.100		Number Nombre	Percent P.100
EUROPE										
Poland - Pologne										
1 VII 2013[133]	ESDJ	38 031 632	23 000 324	60.5	18 411 126	10 915 023	59.3	19 620 506	12 085 301	61.6
1 VII 2014[133]	ESDJ	38 006 154	22 951 357	60.4	18 397 470	10 888 729	59.2	19 608 684	12 062 628	61.5
1 VII 2015[133]	ESDJ	37 981 588	22 916 634	60.3	18 384 771	10 869 587	59.1	19 596 817	12 047 047	61.5
1 I 2016[133]	ESDJ	37 967 209	...	...	18 377 040	...	...	19 590 169	...	...
Portugal										
1 VII 2007	ESDJ	10 542 964	...	...	5 067 071	...	...	5 475 893	...	...
1 VII 2008	ESDJ	10 558 177	...	...	5 067 993	...	...	5 490 184	...	...
1 VII 2009	ESDJ	10 568 247	...	...	5 064 992	...	...	5 503 255	...	...
1 VII 2010	ESDJ	10 573 100	...	...	5 058 644	...	...	5 514 456	...	...
21 III 2011	CDFC	10 282 306	6 286 712	61.1	4 868 755	2 949 862	60.6	5 413 551	3 336 850	61.6
1 VII 2011	ESDJ	10 557 560	...	...	5 041 990	...	...	5 515 570	...	...
1 VII 2012	ESDJ	10 514 844	...	...	5 013 067	...	...	5 501 777	...	...
1 VII 2013	ESDJ	10 457 295	...	...	4 976 859	...	...	5 480 437	...	...
1 VII 2014	ESDJ	10 401 062	...	...	4 940 843	...	...	5 460 219	...	...
1 VII 2015	ESDJ	10 358 076	...	...	4 912 588	...	...	5 445 489	...	...
1 I 2016	ESDJ	10 341 330	...	...	4 901 509	...	...	5 439 821	...	...
Republic of Moldova - République de Moldova[140]										
1 VII 2007	ESDJ	3 576 910	1 477 062	41.3	1 719 246	694 308	40.4	1 857 664	782 754	42.1
1 VII 2008	ESDJ	3 570 108	1 475 609	41.3	1 716 195	693 550	40.4	1 853 913	782 059	42.2
1 VII 2009	ESDJ	3 565 604	1 476 390	41.4	1 714 209	694 134	40.5	1 851 395	782 257	42.3
1 VII 2010	ESDJ	3 562 045	1 479 196	41.5	1 712 783	695 603	40.6	1 849 262	783 593	42.4
1 VII 2011	ESDJ	3 559 986	1 483 731	41.7	1 711 916	697 492	40.7	1 848 070	786 239	42.5
1 VII 2012	ESDJ	3 559 520	1 488 966	41.8	1 712 036	699 880	40.9	1 847 484	789 086	42.7
1 VII 2014	ESDJ	3 557 328	...	...	1 711 295	...	...	1 846 033	...	...
1 I 2015	ESDJ	3 555 159	...	...	1 710 244	...	...	1 844 915	...	...
Romania - Roumanie										
1 VII 2007[133]	ESDJ	20 882 980	11 455 494	54.9	10 169 596	5 489 050	54.0	10 713 384	5 966 444	55.7
1 VII 2008[133]	ESDJ	20 537 848	11 102 802	54.1	10 000 515	5 314 752	53.1	10 537 333	5 788 050	54.9
1 VII 2009[133]	ESDJ	20 367 437	10 976 558	53.9	9 916 107	5 249 975	52.9	10 451 330	5 726 583	54.8
1 VII 2010[133]	ESDJ	20 246 798	10 922 169	53.9	9 856 669	5 223 471	53.0	10 390 129	5 698 698	54.8
1 VII 2011[133]	ESDJ	20 147 657	10 878 099	54.0	9 805 108	5 198 460	53.0	10 342 549	5 679 639	54.9
20 X 2011	CDFC	20 039 141	10 858 790	54.2	9 736 342	5 185 636	53.3	10 302 799	5 673 154	55.1
1 VII 2012[133]	ESDJ	20 060 182	10 823 218	54.0	9 770 353	5 170 875	52.9	10 289 829	5 652 343	54.9
1 VII 2013[133]	ESDJ	19 988 694	10 772 678	53.9	9 756 310	5 153 631	52.8	10 232 384	5 619 047	54.9
1 VII 2014[133]	ESDJ	19 913 193	10 726 149	53.9	9 728 663	5 132 414	52.8	10 184 530	5 593 735	54.9
1 VII 2015[133]	ESDJ	19 819 697	10 669 579	53.8	9 680 537	5 098 318	52.7	10 139 160	5 571 261	54.9
1 I 2016[133]	ESDJ	19 760 314	...	...	9 649 811	...	...	10 110 503	...	...
Russian Federation - Fédération de Russie										
1 VII 2007	ESDJ	142 805 114	104 798 401	73.4	66 013 796	47 923 326	72.6	76 791 318	56 875 075	74.1
1 VII 2008	ESDJ	142 742 366	104 890 297	73.5	65 968 338	47 938 815	72.7	76 774 028	56 951 482	74.2
1 VII 2009	ESDJ	142 785 349	104 988 448	73.5	65 988 356	47 969 474	72.7	76 796 993	57 018 974	74.2
1 VII 2010	ESDJ	142 849 468	105 241 319	73.7	66 033 070	48 081 267	72.8	76 816 398	57 160 052	74.4
14 X 2010	CDFC	143 436 145	...	...	66 457 074	...	...	76 979 071	...	...
1 VII 2011	ESDJ	142 960 908	105 581 615	73.9	66 113 269	48 243 019	73.0	76 847 639	57 338 596	74.6
1 VII 2012	ESDJ	143 201 730	105 930 122	74.0	66 264 910	48 419 208	73.1	76 936 820	57 510 914	74.8
San Marino - Saint-Marin										
1 VII 2007[47]	ESDF	31 211	...	...	15 664	...	...	15 547	...	...
1 VII 2008[47]	ESDF	31 662	...	...	15 874	...	...	15 788	...	...
1 VII 2009[47]	ESDF	33 066	...	...	16 088	...	...	16 978	...	...
1 VII 2010[47]	ESDF	33 270	...	...	16 171	...	...	17 099	...	...
7 XI 2010*	CDFC	30 652	...	...	14 791[141]	...	...	15 818[141]	...	...
1 VII 2011[47]	ESDF	33 389	...	...	16 221	...	...	17 169	...	...
1 VII 2012[47]	ESDF	33 518	...	...	16 296	...	...	17 222	...	...
1 VII 2013[47]	ESDF	33 469	...	...	16 280	...	...	17 189	...	...
1 VII 2014[47]	ESDF	33 648	...	...	16 396	...	...	17 252	...	...
1 I 2015[47]	ESDF	33 738	...	...	16 425	...	...	17 313	...	...
1 I 2016[47]	ESDF	34 006	...	...	16 560	...	...	17 446	...	...
Serbia - Serbie[142]										
1 VII 2007	ESDJ	7 381 579	4 270 400	57.9	3 588 957	2 037 012	56.8	3 792 622	2 233 388	58.9
1 VII 2008	ESDJ	7 350 222	4 275 245	58.2	3 573 814	2 038 642	57.0	3 776 408	2 236 603	59.2
1 VII 2009	ESDJ	7 320 807	4 279 035	58.5	3 560 048	2 039 934	57.3	3 760 759	2 239 101	59.5

6. Total and urban population by sex: 2007 - 2016
Population totale et population urbaine selon le sexe : 2007 - 2016 (continued - suite)

Continent, country or area, and date / Continent, pays ou zone et date	Code[a]	Both sexes - Les deux sexes			Male - Masculin			Female - Féminin		
		Total	Urban - Urbaine Number Nombre	Percent P.100	Total	Urban - Urbaine Number Nombre	Percent P.100	Total	Urban - Urbaine Number Nombre	Percent P.100

EUROPE

Serbia - Serbie[142]
1 VII 2010	ESDJ	7 291 436	4 283 985	58.8	3 546 374	2 041 975	57.6	3 745 062	2 242 010	59.9
1 VII 2011[18]	ESDJ	7 236 519	4 275 178	59.1	3 523 911	2 041 228	57.9	3 712 608	2 233 950	60.2
1 X 2011	CDJC	7 186 862	4 271 872	59.4	3 499 176	2 039 105	58.3	3 687 686	2 232 767	60.5
1 VII 2012[18]	ESDJ	7 201 497	4 273 861	59.3	3 506 947	2 039 649	58.2	3 694 550	2 234 212	60.5
1 VII 2013[18]	ESDJ	7 166 552	4 272 061	59.6	3 489 683	2 037 554	58.4	3 676 869	2 234 507	60.8
1 VII 2014[18]	ESDJ	7 131 787	4 270 367	59.9	3 472 746	2 035 772	58.6	3 659 041	2 234 595	61.1
1 VII 2015[18]	ESDJ	7 095 383	4 267 079	60.1	3 455 335	2 033 446	58.8	3 640 048	2 233 633	61.4
1 VII 2016[18]	ESDJ	7 058 322	...	...	3 437 630	...	...	3 620 692	...	...

Slovakia - Slovaquie
1 VII 2007	ESDJ	5 374 622	...	...	2 612 172	...	...	2 762 451	...	...
1 VII 2008	ESDJ	5 379 233	...	...	2 616 013	...	...	2 763 220	...	...
1 VII 2009	ESDJ	5 386 406	...	...	2 620 942	...	...	2 765 464	...	...
1 VII 2010	ESDJ	5 391 428	...	...	2 624 360	...	...	2 767 069	...	...
21 V 2011	CDJC	5 397 036	2 937 735	54.4	2 627 772	1 412 818	53.8	2 769 264	1 524 917	55.1
1 VII 2011	ESDJ	5 398 384	2 938 053	54.4	2 628 463	1 412 966	53.8	2 769 922	1 525 087	55.1
1 VII 2012	ESDJ	5 407 579	2 935 710	54.3	2 633 866	1 411 738	53.6	2 773 714	1 523 972	54.9
1 VII 2013	ESDJ	5 413 393	2 931 444	54.2	2 637 520	1 409 503	53.4	2 775 873	1 521 941	54.8
1 VII 2014	ESDJ	5 418 649	2 925 291	54.0	2 640 694	1 406 300	53.3	2 777 955	1 518 991	54.7
1 VII 2015	ESDJ	5 423 801	2 919 718	53.8	2 644 205	1 403 692	53.1	2 779 596	1 516 027	54.5
1 I 2016	ESDJ	5 426 252	...	...	2 646 082	...	...	2 780 170	...	...

Slovenia - Slovénie
1 VII 2007	ESDJ	2 019 406	1 006 767	49.9	995 125	490 610	49.3	1 024 281	516 157	50.4
1 VII 2008	ESDJ	2 022 629	1 012 477	50.1	996 969	491 605	49.3	1 025 660	520 872	50.8
1 VII 2009	ESDJ	2 042 335	1 024 087	50.1	1 011 767	500 253	49.4	1 030 568	523 834	50.8
1 VII 2010	ESDJ	2 049 261	1 024 812	50.0	1 014 716	500 063	49.3	1 034 545	524 749	50.7
1 I 2011	CDFC	2 058 051	1 030 172	50.1	1 019 826	503 083	49.3	1 038 225	527 089	50.8
1 VII 2011	ESDJ	2 052 496	1 023 650	49.9	1 015 430	498 490	49.1	1 037 066	525 160	50.6
1 VII 2012	ESDJ	2 056 262	1 023 236	49.8	1 017 414	498 297	49.0	1 038 848	524 939	50.5
1 VII 2013	ESDJ	2 059 114	1 047 560	50.9	1 019 658	513 084	50.3	1 039 456	534 476	51.4
1 VII 2014	ESDJ	2 061 623	1 051 087	51.0	1 021 419	514 828	50.4	1 040 204	536 259	51.6
1 I 2015	CDJC	2 062 874	1 107 064	53.7	1 022 229	542 636	53.1	1 040 645	564 428	54.2
1 VII 2015	ESDJ	2 063 077	1 106 955	53.7	1 022 554	542 847	53.1	1 040 523	564 108	54.2
1 I 2016	ESDJ	2 064 188	...	...	1 023 333	...	...	1 040 855	...	...

Spain - Espagne
1 VII 2007	ESDJ	45 236 002	...	...	22 362 075	...	...	22 873 927	...	...
1 VII 2008	ESDJ	45 983 167	...	...	22 756 861	...	...	23 226 306	...	...
1 VII 2009	ESDJ	46 367 545	...	...	22 934 497	...	...	23 433 048	...	...
1 VII 2010	ESDJ	46 562 486	...	...	23 008 587	...	...	23 553 899	...	...
1 VII 2011	ESDJ	46 736 255	...	...	23 073 274	...	...	23 662 981	...	...
1 XI 2011	CDJC	46 815 915	...	...	23 104 350	...	...	23 711 560	...	...
1 VII 2012	ESDJ	46 766 399	...	...	23 055 715	...	...	23 710 684	...	...
1 VII 2013	ESDJ	46 593 236	...	...	22 933 751	...	...	23 659 485	...	...
1 VII 2014[134]	ESDJ	46 480 882	...	...	22 852 004	...	...	23 628 879	...	...
1 VII 2015[134]	ESDJ	46 447 697	...	...	22 817 983	...	...	23 629 714	...	...
1 I 2016[134]	ESDJ	46 445 828	...	...	22 809 420	...	...	23 636 408	...	...

Sweden - Suède[47]
1 VII 2007	ESDJ	9 148 092	...	...	4 543 722	...	...	4 604 370	...	...
1 VII 2008	ESDJ	9 219 637	...	...	4 583 816	...	...	4 635 822	...	...
1 VII 2009	ESDJ	9 298 515	...	...	4 626 362	...	...	4 672 153	...	...
1 VII 2010	ESDJ	9 378 126	...	...	4 669 629	...	...	4 708 497	...	...
1 VII 2011	ESDJ	9 449 213	...	...	4 708 539	...	...	4 740 674	...	...
31 XII 2011	CDJC	9 482 855	...	...	4 726 834	...	...	4 756 021	...	...
1 VII 2012	ESDJ	9 519 375	...	...	4 746 370	...	...	4 773 005	...	...
1 VII 2013[134]	ESDJ	9 600 379	...	...	4 790 131	...	...	4 810 248	...	...
1 VII 2014[134]	ESDJ	9 696 110	...	...	4 843 299	...	...	4 852 811	...	...
1 VII 2015[134]	ESDJ	9 799 186	...	...	4 901 603	...	...	4 897 583	...	...
1 I 2016[134]	ESDJ	9 851 017	...	...	4 930 966	...	...	4 920 051	...	...

Switzerland - Suisse
1 VII 2007	ESDJ	7 551 117	5 543 848	73.4	3 703 187	2 701 296	72.9	3 847 930	2 842 552	73.9
1 VII 2008	ESDJ	7 647 675	5 622 042	73.5	3 756 845	2 744 671	73.1	3 890 831	2 877 371	74.0
1 VII 2009	ESDJ	7 743 832	5 699 003	73.6	3 808 621	2 786 186	73.2	3 935 211	2 912 817	74.0
1 VII 2010	ESDJ	7 824 909	...	...	3 851 028	...	...	3 973 882	...	...
1 VII 2011	ESDJ	7 912 398	5 823 816	73.6	3 899 840	2 853 440	73.2	4 012 559	2 970 376	74.0
31 XII 2011	CDFC	8 035 391	5 920 706	73.7	3 973 280	2 909 793	73.2	4 062 111	3 010 913	74.1

6. Total and urban population by sex: 2007 - 2016
Population totale et population urbaine selon le sexe : 2007 - 2016 (continued - suite)

Continent, country or area, and date / Continent, pays ou zone et date	Code[a]	Both sexes - Les deux sexes			Male - Masculin			Female - Féminin		
			Urban - Urbaine			Urban - Urbaine			Urban - Urbaine	
		Total	Number Nombre	Percent P.100	Total	Number Nombre	Percent P.100	Total	Number Nombre	Percent P.100
EUROPE										
Switzerland - Suisse										
1 VII 2012 ....ESDJ		7 996 861	5 887 939	73.6	3 945 389	2 887 886	73.2	4 051 473	3 000 053	74.0
1 VII 2013 ....ESDJ		8 089 346	5 958 174	73.7	3 995 308	2 925 500	73.2	4 094 038	3 032 674	74.1
1 VII 2014[143] ....ESDJ		8 188 649	6 033 396	73.7	4 047 986	2 964 948	73.2	4 140 663	3 068 448	74.1
1 VII 2015[143] ....ESDJ		8 282 396	6 553 576[144]	79.1	4 097 676	3 228 111[144]	78.8	4 184 721	3 325 465[144]	79.5
1 I 2016[143] ....ESDJ		8 327 126	7 036 743	84.5	4 121 471	3 471 877	84.2	4 205 655	3 564 866	84.8
TFYR of Macedonia - L'ex-R. y. de Macédoine										
1 VII 2007 ....ESDF		2 043 559	...	...	1 024 489	...	...	1 019 070	...	...
1 VII 2008 ....ESDF		2 046 898	...	...	1 026 022	...	...	1 020 876	...	...
1 VII 2009 ....ESDF		2 050 671	...	...	1 027 810	...	...	1 022 861	...	...
1 VII 2010 ....ESDF		2 055 004	...	...	1 029 848	...	...	1 025 156	...	...
1 VII 2011 ....ESDF		2 058 539	...	...	1 031 403	...	...	1 027 136	...	...
1 VII 2012 ....ESDF		2 061 044	...	...	1 032 532	...	...	1 028 512	...	...
1 VII 2013 ....ESDF		2 064 032	...	...	1 033 990	...	...	1 030 042	...	...
1 VII 2014 ....ESDF		2 067 471	...	...	1 035 680	...	...	1 031 791	...	...
1 VII 2015 ....ESDF		2 070 225	...	...	1 037 060	...	...	1 033 166	...	...
1 I 2016 ....ESDF		2 071 278	...	...	1 037 601	...	...	1 033 677	...	...
Ukraine										
1 VII 2007 ....ESDF		46 509 355	31 723 062	68.2	21 472 153	14 567 851	67.8	25 037 202	17 155 212	68.5
1 VII 2008 ....ESDF		46 258 189	31 627 640	68.4	21 347 279	14 512 344	68.0	24 910 910	17 115 637	68.7
1 VII 2009 ....ESDF		46 053 307	31 556 002	68.5	...	...	...	...	...	...
1 VII 2010 ....ESDF		45 870 741	31 483 222	68.6	21 175 816	14 436 554	68.2	24 694 925	17 046 668	69.0
1 VII 2011 ....ESDF		45 706 086	31 411 262	68.7	21 110 638	14 401 999	68.2	24 595 448	17 009 263	69.2
1 VII 2012 ....ESDF		45 593 342	31 379 757	68.8	21 075 702	14 392 490	68.3	24 517 640	16 987 267	69.3
1 I 2013 ....ESDF		45 553 047	31 378 639	68.9	21 068 718	14 397 904	68.3	24 484 329	16 980 735	69.4
1 I 2015[145] ....ESDF		42 759 661	...	...	19 787 826	...	...	22 971 835	...	...
1 I 2016[145] ....ESDF		42 590 879	...	...	19 717 881	...	...	22 872 998	...	...
United Kingdom of Great Britain and Northern Ireland - Royaume-Uni de Grande-Bretagne et d'Irlande du Nord[146]										
1 VII 2007 ....ESDJ		61 319 075	...	...	30 027 882	...	...	31 291 193	...	...
1 VII 2008 ....ESDJ		61 823 772	...	...	30 300 623	...	...	31 523 149	...	...
1 VII 2009 ....ESDJ		62 260 486	...	...	30 532 212	...	...	31 728 274	...	...
1 VII 2010 ....ESDJ		62 759 456	...	...	30 805 493	...	...	31 953 963	...	...
27 III 2011 ....CDFC		63 379 787	51 399 714	81.1	31 126 054	25 214 631	81.0	32 253 733	26 185 083	81.2
1 VII 2011 ....ESDJ		63 285 145	...	...	31 097 259	...	...	32 187 886	...	...
1 VII 2012 ....ESDJ		63 705 030	...	...	31 315 072	...	...	32 389 958	...	...
1 VII 2013[133] ....ESDJ		64 102 166	...	...	31 535 963	...	...	32 566 204	...	...
1 VII 2014[133] ....ESDJ		64 591 713	...	...	31 797 813	...	...	32 793 900	...	...
1 VII 2015[133] ....ESDJ		65 128 861	...	...	32 085 785	...	...	33 043 076	...	...
1 I 2016[133] ....ESDJ		65 382 556	...	...	32 224 529	...	...	33 158 027	...	...
OCEANIA - OCÉANIE										
American Samoa - Samoas américaines[54]										
1 IV 2010 ....CDJC		55 519	...	...	28 164	...	...	27 355	...	...
Australia - Australie										
1 VII 2007[44] ....ESDJ		20 827 622	17 666 467	84.8	10 353 636	8 734 627	84.4	10 473 986	8 931 840	85.3
1 VII 2008[44] ....ESDJ		21 249 199	18 052 915	85.0	10 572 045	8 934 070	84.5	10 677 154	9 118 845	85.4
1 VII 2009[44] ....ESDJ		21 691 653	18 453 978	85.1	10 800 797	9 141 216	84.6	10 890 856	9 312 762	85.5
1 VII 2010[44] ....ESDJ		22 031 750	18 762 982	85.2	10 967 831	9 292 721	84.7	11 063 919	9 470 261	85.6
1 VII 2011[44] ....ESDJ		22 340 024	19 046 939	85.3	11 118 234	9 431 506	84.8	11 221 790	9 615 433	85.7
9 VIII 2011[147] ....CDFC		21 727 158[148]	19 312 642	88.9	10 737 148[148]	9 471 918	88.2	10 990 010[148]	9 840 724	89.5
1 VII 2012[18] ....ESDJ		22 728 254	19 402 437	85.4	11 312 823	9 608 375	84.9	11 415 431	9 794 062	85.8
1 VII 2013[18] ....ESDJ		23 117 353	19 763 063	85.5	11 505 587	9 785 651	85.1	11 611 766	9 977 412	85.9
1 VII 2014[18] ....ESDJ		23 460 694	20 083 953	85.6	11 668 458	9 938 013	85.2	11 792 236	10 145 940	86.0
1 VII 2015[18] ....ESDJ		23 777 777	20 386 802	85.7	11 826 927	10 089 517	85.3	11 950 850	10 297 285	86.2
1 VII 2016[18] ....ESDJ		24 128 876	...	...	11 990 972	...	...	12 137 904	...	...

Continent, country or area, and date / Continent, pays ou zone et date	Code[a]	Both sexes - Les deux sexes			Male - Masculin			Female - Féminin		
		Total	Urban - Urbaine		Total	Urban - Urbaine		Total	Urban - Urbaine	
			Number Nombre	Percent P.100		Number Nombre	Percent P.100		Number Nombre	Percent P.100
OCEANIA - OCÉANIE										
Cook Islands - Îles Cook[149]										
1 XII 2011 .... CDFC		17 794	...	...	8 815	...	...	8 979	...	...
1 XII 2016* .... CDFC		17 459	...	...	8 597	...	...	8 862	...	...
Fiji - Fidji										
16 IX 2007 .... CDFC		837 271	424 846	50.7	427 176	212 454	49.7	410 095	212 392	51.8
1 VII 2008 .... ESDF		841 351	426 931	50.7	...	...	...	...	...	...
1 VII 2010 .... ESDF		857 000	446 000	52.0	...	...	...	...	...	...
French Polynesia - Polynésie française										
20 VIII 2007 .... CDJC		259 706	...	...	133 109	...	...	126 597	...	...
1 I 2009 .... ESDF		264 000	...	...	135 200	...	...	128 800	...	...
1 I 2011 .... ESDF		269 989	...	...	138 127	...	...	131 862	...	...
22 VIII 2012 .... CDJC		268 207	...	...	136 996	...	...	131 211	...	...
1 I 2015 .... ESDF		271 796	...	...	138 447	...	...	133 349	...	...
Guam										
1 VII 2007[54] .... ESDJ		158 967	...	...	80 930	...	...	78 037	...	...
1 VII 2008[54] .... ESDJ		159 169	...	...	80 982	...	...	78 187	...	...
1 VII 2009[54] .... ESDJ		159 323	...	...	81 010	...	...	78 313	...	...
1 IV 2010 .... CDJC		159 358	149 918	94.1	81 552	...	...	77 806	...	...
1 VII 2011[54] .... ESDJ		159 600	...	...	81 053	...	...	78 547	...	...
1 VII 2012[54] .... ESDJ		159 914	...	...	81 165	...	...	78 749	...	...
1 VII 2013[54] .... ESDJ		160 378	...	...	81 354	...	...	79 024	...	...
1 VII 2014[54] .... ESDJ		161 001	...	...	81 625	...	...	79 376	...	...
1 VII 2015[54] .... ESDJ		161 785	...	...	81 978	...	...	79 807	...	...
1 VII 2016[54] .... ESDJ		162 742	...	...	82 420	...	...	80 322	...	...
Kiribati										
10 X 2010 .... CDFC		103 058	...	...	50 796	...	...	52 262	...	...
Marshall Islands - Îles Marshall										
1 VII 2007[150] .... ESDF		52 701	...	...	27 022	...	...	25 679	...	...
1 VII 2008[150] .... ESDF		53 236	...	...	27 297	...	...	25 939	...	...
1 VII 2009[150] .... ESDF		53 763	...	...	27 567	...	...	26 196	...	...
1 VII 2010[150] .... ESDF		54 305	...	...	27 843	...	...	26 462	...	...
3 IV 2011 .... CDFC		53 158	...	...	27 243	...	...	25 915	...	...
Micronesia (Federated States of) - Micronésie (États fédérés de)										
1 VII 2007[3] .... ESDJ		108 031	...	...	54 403	...	...	53 628	...	...
1 VII 2008[3] .... ESDJ		108 026	...	...	54 350	...	...	53 676	...	...
1 VII 2009[3] .... ESDJ		107 973	...	...	54 275	...	...	53 698	...	...
1 IV 2010 .... CDJC		102 843	22 924	22.3	52 193	...	...	50 650	...	...
1 VII 2010[3] .... ESDJ		107 839	...	...	54 158	...	...	53 681	...	...
1 VII 2011[3] .... ESDJ		107 581	...	...	53 975	...	...	53 606	...	...
1 VII 2012[3] .... ESDJ		107 249	...	...	53 749	...	...	53 500	...	...
1 VII 2013[3] .... ESDJ		106 841	...	...	53 488	...	...	53 353	...	...
1 VII 2014[3] .... ESDJ		106 374	...	...	53 200	...	...	53 174	...	...
1 VII 2015[3] .... ESDJ		105 830	...	...	52 883	...	...	52 947	...	...
Nauru										
31 X 2011 .... CDFC		10 084	...	...	5 105	...	...	4 979	...	...
1 VII 2015[3] .... ESDF		11 288	...	...	5 701	...	...	5 587	...	...
New Caledonia - Nouvelle-Calédonie										
26 VIII 2014 .... CDFC		268 767	...	...	135 542	...	...	133 225	...	...
1 I 2016 .... ESDF		274 579	...	...	138 197	...	...	136 382	...	...
New Zealand - Nouvelle-Zélande[77]										
1 VII 2007 .... ESDJ		4 223 800	3 640 200[151]	86.2	2 066 400	1 766 900[151]	85.5	2 157 300	1 873 300[151]	86.8
1 VII 2008 .... ESDJ		4 259 800	3 669 100[151]	86.1	2 083 400	1 780 600[151]	85.5	2 176 300	1 888 600[151]	86.8
1 VII 2009 .... ESDJ		4 302 600	3 703 800[151]	86.1	2 104 700	1 797 800[151]	85.4	2 197 900	1 906 000[151]	86.7
1 VII 2010 .... ESDJ		4 350 700	3 743 300[151]	86.0	2 127 700	1 816 700[151]	85.4	2 222 900	1 926 600[151]	86.7
1 VII 2011 .... ESDJ		4 384 000	3 765 400[151]	85.9	2 143 600	1 826 900[151]	85.2	2 240 400	1 938 500[151]	86.5
1 VII 2012 .... ESDJ		4 408 100	3 784 600[151]	85.9	2 155 000	1 836 200[151]	85.2	2 253 100	1 948 500[151]	86.5
1 VII 2013 .... ESDJ		4 442 100	3 818 300[151]	86.0	2 172 200	1 853 100[151]	85.3	2 269 900	1 965 200[151]	86.6
1 VII 2014 .... ESDJ		4 509 700	3 884 000[151]	86.1	2 209 600	1 889 100[151]	85.5	2 300 200	1 995 000[151]	86.7

6. Total and urban population by sex: 2007 - 2016
Population totale et population urbaine selon le sexe : 2007 - 2016 (continued - suite)

Continent, country or area, and date / Continent, pays ou zone et date	Code[a]	Both sexes - Les deux sexes			Male - Masculin			Female - Féminin		
		Total	Urban - Urbaine		Total	Urban - Urbaine		Total	Urban - Urbaine	
			Number Nombre	Percent P.100		Number Nombre	Percent P.100		Number Nombre	Percent P.100
OCEANIA - OCÉANIE										
New Zealand - Nouvelle-Zélande[77]										
1 VII 2015 .... ESDJ		4 595 700	3 959 200[151]	86.2	2 257 200	1 931 800[151]	85.6	2 338 500	2 027 400[151]	86.7
1 VII 2016 .... ESDJ		4 692 700	4 055 800[151]	86.4	2 308 800	1 983 400[151]	85.9	2 383 900	2 072 400[151]	86.9
Niue - Nioué										
1 VII 2010 .... ESDJ		1 496	...	...	754	...	...	740	...	...
11 IX 2011 .... CDFC		1 611	...	...	802	...	...	809	...	...
Norfolk Island - Île Norfolk										
9 VIII 2011 .... CDFC		2 302	...	...	1 082	...	...	1 220	...	...
Northern Mariana Islands - Îles Mariannes septentrionales										
1 VII 2007 .... ESDF		58 629	...	...	28 124	...	...	30 505	...	...
1 VII 2008 .... ESDF		55 244	...	...	26 524	...	...	28 720	...	...
1 VII 2009 .... ESDF		51 484	...	...	24 738	...	...	26 746	...	...
1 IV 2010 .... CDFC		53 883	...	...	27 746	...	...	26 137	...	...
1 VII 2010 .... ESDF		48 317	...	...	23 231	...	...	25 086	...	...
1 VII 2011 .... ESDF		46 050	...	...	22 153	...	...	23 897	...	...
Palau - Palaos										
1 XII 2012 .... CDJC		17 501	14 202	81.1	9 217	7 506	81.4	8 284	6 696	80.8
13 IV 2015 .... CDJC		17 661	14 209	80.5	9 433	7 620	80.8	8 228	6 589	80.1
Papua New Guinea - Papouasie-Nouvelle-Guinée										
10 VII 2011* .... CDFC		7 059 653	...	...	3 663 249	...	...	3 396 404	...	...
1 VII 2016[152] .... ESDF		8 151 300	...	...	4 205 000	...	...	3 946 300	...	...
Pitcairn										
31 XII 2007 .... ESDF		64[153]	...	...	37	...	...	27	...	...
31 XII 2008 .... ESDF		58[153]	...	...	30	...	...	28	...	...
10 VIII 2012 .... CDJC		48	...	...	22	...	...	26	...	...
31 XII 2013 .... CDJC		49	...	...	23	...	...	26	...	...
Samoa										
1 VII 2007 .... ESDF		181 588	37 878	20.9	94 101	19 206	20.4	87 458	18 672	21.3
1 VII 2008 .... ESDF		182 379	38 050	20.9	94 526	19 293	20.4	87 853	18 756	21.3
1 VII 2009 .... ESDF		183 204	38 222	20.9	94 953	19 381	20.4	88 250	18 841	21.3
1 VII 2010 .... ESDF		184 032	38 395	20.9	95 383	19 468	20.4	88 649	18 926	21.3
1 VII 2011 .... ESDF		184 864	38 568	20.9	95 814	19 556	20.4	89 050	19 012	21.3
7 XI 2011 .... CDFC		187 820	36 735	19.6	96 990	18 485	19.1	90 830	18 250	20.1
1 VII 2012 .... ESDF		189 236	36 540	19.3	...	...	...	...	...	...
1 VII 2013 .... ESDF		190 652	36 346	19.1	...	...	...	...	...	...
1 VII 2014 .... ESDF		192 067	36 151	18.8	...	...	...	...	...	...
1 VII 2015 .... ESDF		193 483	35 957	18.6	...	...	...	...	...	...
1 VII 2016 .... ESDF		194 899	35 762	18.3	...	...	...	...	...	...
7 XI 2016* .... CDFC		192 126	...	...	98 663	...	...	93 463	...	...
Solomon Islands - Îles Salomon										
1 VII 2007[3] .... ESDF		495 026	...	...	255 063	...	...	239 963	...	...
1 VII 2008[3] .... ESDF		506 992	...	...	261 214	...	...	245 778	...	...
1 VII 2009[3] .... ESDF		518 321	...	...	267 704	...	...	250 617	...	...
22 XI 2009 .... CDFC		515 870	102 030	19.8	264 455	53 596	20.3	251 415	48 434	19.3
1 VII 2010[3] .... ESDF		555 447	...	...	285 040	...	...	270 408	...	...
1 VII 2011[3] .... ESDF		569 600	...	...	292 105	...	...	277 495	...	...
1 VII 2012[3] .... ESDF		583 672	...	...	299 131	...	...	284 541	...	...
1 VII 2013[3] .... ESDF		597 653	...	...	306 112	...	...	291 541	...	...
1 VII 2014[3] .... ESDF		611 538	...	...	313 044	...	...	298 494	...	...
1 VII 2015[3] .... ESDF		625 374	...	...	319 954	...	...	305 420	...	...
1 VII 2016[3] .... ESDF		639 157	...	...	326 837	...	...	312 321	...	...
Tokelau - Tokélaou										
18 X 2011 .... CDFC		1 205	...	...	600	...	...	605	...	...
1 XII 2013 .... ESDF		1 383	...	...	683	...	...	700	...	...
18 X 2016 .... CDFC		1 285	...	...	652	...	...	633	...	...
Tonga										
1 VII 2007[154] .... ESDF		103 289	...	...	52 771	...	...	50 518	...	...
1 VII 2008[154] .... ESDF		103 647	...	...	52 972	...	...	50 673	...	...

Continent, country or area, and date / Continent, pays ou zone et date	Code[a]	Both sexes - Les deux sexes			Male - Masculin			Female - Féminin		
		Total	Urban - Urbaine		Total	Urban - Urbaine		Total	Urban - Urbaine	
			Number Nombre	Percent P.100		Number Nombre	Percent P.100		Number Nombre	Percent P.100
OCEANIA - OCÉANIE										
Tonga										
30 XI 2011 ....CDJC		103 252	24 229	23.5	51 979	12 156	23.4	51 273	12 073	23.5
30 XI 2016* ....CDJC		100 745	...	...	50 312	...	...	50 433	...	...
Tuvalu										
1 VII 2011 ....ESDF		*11 206*	...	...	*5 582*	...	...	*5 625*	...	...
1 VII 2013 ....ESDF		*10 900*	...	...	*5 600*	...	...	*5 400*	...	...
1 VII 2016[152] ....ESDF		*10 100*	...	...	*5 100*	...	...	*5 000*	...	...
Vanuatu										
16 XI 2009 ....CDJC		234 023	57 195	24.4	119 091	29 618	24.9	114 932	27 577	24.0
1 VII 2010 ....ESDF		*239 374*	...	...	*121 726*	...	...	*117 648*	...	...
1 VII 2011 ....ESDF		*244 847*	...	...	*124 420*	...	...	*120 427*	...	...
1 VII 2012 ....ESDF		*244 847*	...	...	*127 173*	...	...	*123 273*	...	...
1 VII 2013 ....ESDF		*264 652*	...	...	*135 170*	...	...	*129 483*	...	...
7 XI 2016 ....CDFC		272 459	67 749	24.9	138 265	34 506	25.0	134 194	33 243	24.8
Wallis and Futuna Islands - Îles Wallis et Futuna										
21 VII 2008 ....CDFC		13 445	...	...	6 669	...	...	6 776	...	...
22 VII 2013 ....CDFC		12 197	...	...	5 927	...	...	6 270	...	...
1 VII 2016[152] ....ESDF		*11 800*	...	...	*5 700*	...	...	*6 100*	...	...

FOOTNOTES - NOTES

Italics: estimates which are less reliable. - Italiques : estimations moins sûres.

* Provisional. - Données provisoires.

[a] 'Code' indicates the source of data, as follows:
CDFC - Census, de facto, complete tabulation
CDFS - Census, de facto, sample tabulation
CDJC - Census, de jure, complete tabulation
CDJS - Census, de jure, sample tabulation
SSDF - Sample survey, de facto
SSDJ - Sample survey, de jure
ESDF - Estimates, de facto
ESDJ - Estimates, de jure

Le 'Code' indique la source des données, comme suit :
CDFC - Recensement, population de fait, tabulation complète
CDFS - Recensement, population de fait, tabulation par sondage
CDJC - Recensement, population de droit, tabulation complète
CDJS - Recensement, population de droit, tabulation par sondage
SSDF - Enquête par sondage, population de fait
SSDJ - Enquête par sondage, population de droit
ESDF - Estimations, population de fait
ESDJ - Estimations, population de droit

[1] Total resident population including common and collective households of nomadic population, and population counted separately. - Population résidente totale y compris les ménages ordinaires et collectifs de la population nomade, et la population comptée à part.
[2] Unrevised data that do not take into account the results of the 2014 population census. - Ces données n'ont pas été revisées et elles ne prennent pas en compte les résultats du recensement de la population de 2014.
[3] Data refer to national projections. - Les données se réfèrent aux projections nationales.
[4] Projections based on the 2013 Population Census. - Projections fondées sur le recensement de la population de 2013.
[5] Data based on the 2011 Census. - Données fondées sur le recensement de 2011.
[6] Unrevised data. - Les données n'ont pas été révisées.
[7] Estimates based on the 2014 Population Census. - Estimations fondées sur le recensement de la population de 2014.

[8] Projections based on the 2014 Population Census. - Projections fondées sur le recensement de la population de 2014.
[9] Projections based on the 1994 Population Census. - Projections fondées sur le recensement de la population de 1994.
[10] Estimates considering also the results of the 2007 Population Census. - Estimations en prennant en considération les résultats du recensement de la population de 2007.
[11] Data based on the 2010 Population Census. - Les données sont fondées sur le recensement de la population de 2010.
[12] Post-censal estimates based on the 2009 Population Census. - Les estimations post-censitaire fondées sur le recensement de la population de 2009.
[13] Data refer to Libyan nationals only. - Les données se raportent aux nationaux libyens seulement.
[14] Projections considering also the results of the 2009 Population Census results. - Projections en prennant en considération les résultats du recensement de la population de 2009.
[15] Including nomadic population. - Y compris la population nomade.
[16] Excludes the islands of St. Brandon and Agalega. - Non compris les îles St. Brandon et Agalega.
[17] Based on the results of the 2000 Population Census. - Basé sur les résultats du recensement de la population de 2000.
[18] Based on the results of the 2011 Population Census. - Basé sur les résultats du recensement de la population de 2011.
[19] Based on the results of the 2004 Population Census. - D'après des résultats du recensement de la population de 2004.
[20] Projections based on the results of national survey on population and health conducted between 2010 and 2011, and especially population and housing census 2014. - Des projections de la population fondées sur les résultats de l'enquête nationale de la population et de la santé réalisée entre 2010 et 2011 et, surtout, du recensement général de la population et de l'habitat de 2014.
[21] Data refer to projections based on the 2011 Population Census. - Les données se réfèrent aux projections basées sur le recensement de la population de 2011.
[22] Projections based on the 2012 Population and Housing Census. - Projections fondées sur le recensement 2012 de la population et des logements.
[23] Data are projections based on the 2006 Population Census. - Projections fondées sur le recensement de la population de 2006.
[24] Data are projections based on the 2008 Population and Housing Census. - Projection basée sur le recensement 2008 de la population et des logements.
[25] Data refer to total resident population, Saint Helenian and other nationalities. - Les données concernent la population résidente totale, originaire de Sainte-Hélène ou possédant une autre nationalité.

26 Based on the results of a population count. - D'après les résultats d'un comptage de la population.

27 The population figures are 264, 263 and 262 persons for 2007, 2008 and 2009 respectively. - La population est respectivement égale à 264, 263 et 262 personnes pour les années 2007, 2008 et 2009.

28 Projections based on the 2002 Population Census. - Projections fondées sur le recensement de la population de 2002.

29 Data have not been adjusted for underenumeration, estimated at 7 per cent. - Les données n'ont pas été ajustées pour compenser les lacunes du dénombrement, estimées à 7 p. 100.

30 Projections based on the 2012 Population Census. - Projections fondées sur le recensement de la population de 2012.

31 Data refers to resident population adjusted for the undercount of 18 per cent and including the institutional population. - Les données concernent la population résidente, y compris la population des institutions, et ont été ajustées pour tenir compte du sous-dénombrement estimé à 18 p. 100.

32 Data refer to projections based on the 2000 Population Census. - Les données se réfèrent aux projections basées sur le recensement de la population de 2000.

33 Bermuda is 100 per cent urban. - 100 pour cent de la population des Bermudes est urbaine.

34 Final intercensal estimates. - Estimations inter-censitaires definitives.

35 Final postcensal estimates. - Estimations postcensitaires definitives.

36 Updated postcensal estimates. - Estimations post censitaires mises à jour.

37 Preliminary postcensal estimates. - Estimations post censitaires préliminaires.

38 Excluding the institutional population. - Non compris la population dans les institutions.

39 The source of data is the national household survey. - La source des données est l'enquête nationale des ménages.

40 Based on the national household surveys 2010-2014 and the 2011 population census. - D'après les données de l'enquête nationale des ménages 2010-2014 et les résultats du recensement de la population de 2011.

41 Definition of urban and rural distribution changed from the year 2010. - La définition des régions urbaines et rurales a changée depuis 2010.

42 Based on the national household survey of 2015. - Basée sur l' enquête nationale auprès des ménages de 2015.

43 Based on the national household survey of 2016. - D'après l'enquête nationale auprès des ménages de 2016.

44 Intercensal estimates. - Estimations inter-censitaires.

45 Postcensal estimates. - Estimations post censitaires.

46 Estimates or projections based on the 2007 Population Census. - Estimations ou projections fondées sur le recensement de la population de 2007.

47 Population statistics are compiled from registers. - Les statistiques de la population sont compilées à partir des registres.

48 Excluding data for Saint Barthélémy and Saint Martin. - Non compris les données pour Saint Barthélémy et Saint Martin.

49 Projections produced by l'Institut Haïtien de Statistique et d'Informatique (IHSI) and the Latin American and Caribbean Demographic Centre (CELADE) - Population Division of ECLAC. - Les données sont projections produits par l'Institut Haïtien de Statistique et d'Informatique (IHSI) et le centre démographique de l'Amérique latine et les Caraïbes - Division de la population de la CEPALC.

50 Data refer to projections based on the 2001 Population Census. - Les données se réfèrent aux projections basées sur le recensement de la population de 2001.

51 The figures represent the census counts adjusted for under-coverage. Adjustments are done by applying weights calculated (to 4 decimal places) for each sex and age group to the enumerated population when the tabulations are produced. Minor discrepancies between totals and the sum of the component parts of a table and minor discrepancies between the totals across tables are due to rounding after weights are applied. - Les chiffres représentent le dénombrement résultant du recensement ajusté pour tenir compte du sous-dénombrement. Les ajustements sont effectués en appliquant un coefficient de pondération calculé (à la quatrième décimale) pour chaque sexe et groupe d'âges de la population dénombrée lors de l'établissement des tableaux. Les écarts mineurs entre les totaux et la somme des éléments constitutifs d'un tableau ainsi qu'entre les totaux figurant dans différents tableaux sont dus au fait que les chiffres sont arrondis après la pondération.

52 Including an estimation of 1 334 585 persons corresponding to 448 195 housing units without information of the occupants. - Y compris une estimation de 1 334 585 personnes correspondant aux 448 195 unités d'habitation sans information sur les occupants.

53 Estimates based on the 2010 Population Census. - Estimations basées sur le recensement de la population de 2010.

54 Including armed forces stationed in the area. - Y compris les militaires en garnison sur le territoire.

55 Based on the results of the 2010 Population Census. - D'après le résultats du recensement de la population de 2010.

56 Population in households only. - Population dans les ménages seulement.

57 Excluding residents of institutions. - À l'exclusion de personnes en établissements de soins.

58 Excluding U.S. Armed Forces overseas and civilian U.S. citizens whose usual place of residence is outside the United States. Intercensal estimates. - Non compris les militaires américains à l'étranger et les civils américains dont le lieu de résidence habituel est en dehors des États-Unis. Estimations inter-censitaires.

59 Postcensal estimates. Excluding U.S. Armed Forces overseas and civilian U.S. citizens whose usual place of residence is outside the United States. - Estimations post censitaires. Non compris les militaires américains à l'étranger et les civils américains dont le lieu de résidence habituel est en dehors des États-Unis.

60 Projections based on the 2010 Population and Housing Census. - Projections fondées sur le recensement 2010 de la population et des logements.

61 Data refer to national projections. Data include persons in remote areas, military personnel outside the country, merchant seamen at sea, civilian seasonal workers outside the country, and other civilians outside the country, and exclude nomads, foreign military, civilian aliens temporarily in the country, transients on ships and Indian jungle population. - Les données se réfèrent aux projections nationales. Y compris les personnes vivant dans des régions éloignées, le personel militaire en dehors du pays, les marins marchands, les ouvriers saisonniers en dehors du pays, et autres civils en dehors du pays, et non compris les nomades, les militaires étrangers, les étrangers civils temporairement dans le pays, les transiteurs sur des bateaux et les Indiens de la jungle.

62 Data are revised projections taking into consideration also the results of the 2005 census. - Les données sont des projections révisées tenant compte également des résultats du recensement de 2005.

63 Data based on the 2010 Population Census. Excludes nomadic Indian tribes. - Les données sont fondées sur le recensement de la population de 2010. Non compris les tribus d'Indiens nomades.

64 A dispute exists between the governments of Argentina and the United Kingdom of Great Britain and Northern Ireland concerning sovereignty over the Falkland Islands (Malvinas). Excluding military personnel and their families, visitors and transients. - La souveraineté sur les îles Falkland (Malvinas) fait l'objet d'un différend entre le Gouvernement argentin et le Gouvernement du Royaume-Uni de Grande-Bretagne et d'Irlande du Nord. Non compris les militaires et leur familles, ni les visiteurs et transients.

65 Estimates or projections considering also the results of the 2012 Population Census. - Estimations ou projections en prennant en considération les résultats du recensement de la population de 2012.

66 Figures for male and female population do not add up to the figure for total population, because they exclude 108 homeless people of unknown sex. - Les chiffres relatifs à la population masculine et féminine ne correspondent pas au chiffre de la population totale, parce que l'on en a exclu 108 personnes sans toit dont le sexe n'est pas connu.

67 For operational purposes, population centers with 2,500 and more inhabitants are considered as urban area and less than 2,500 are considered as rural area. - À des fins opérationnelles, les centres de population comptant 2 500 habitants ou plus sont considérés comme zones urbaines, ceux qui en comptent moins de 2 500 comme zones rurales.

68 Data refer to the settled population based on the 1979 Population Census and the latest household prelisting. The refugees of Afghanistan in Iran, Pakistan, and an estimated 1.5 million nomads, are not included. - Les données se rapportent à la population stationnaire sur la base du recensement de 1979 et du recensement préliminaire des logements le plus récent. Sont exclus les réfugiés d'Afghanistan en Iran et au Pakistan et les nomades estimés à 1,5 million.

69 Data have been adjusted for underenumeration. - Les données ont été ajustées pour compenser les lacunes du dénombrement.

70 Data refer to projected figures based on the Population and Housing Census 2005 (district projection). - Les données se réfèrent aux projections basées sur le recensement de la population et de l'habitat de 2005 (projections locales).

71 Excluding foreign diplomatic personnel and their dependants. Based on the results of 1998 census. - Non compris le personnel diplomatique étranger et les membres de leur famille les accompagnant. A partir des résultats de recensement de l'année 1998.

72 Excluding foreign diplomatic personnel and their dependants. - Non compris le personnel diplomatique étranger et les membres de leur famille les accompagnant.

73 Excluding foreign diplomatic personnel and their dependants. Data based on the 2008 Population Census. - Non compris le personnel diplomatique étranger et les membres de leur famille les accompagnant. Données fondées sur le recensement de population de 2008.

74 Based on the results of the Cambodia Intercensal Population Survey. Data exclude foreign diplomatic personnel and their dependants. - Sur la base de l'enquête intercensitaire de la population de Cambodge. Non compris le personnel diplomatique étranger et les membres de leur famille les accompagnant.

75 For statistical purposes, the data for China do not include those for the Hong Kong Special Administrative Region (Hong Kong SAR), Macao Special Administrative Region (Macao SAR) and Taiwan province of China. - Pour la présentation des statistiques, les données pour la Chine ne comprennent pas la Région Administrative Spéciale de Hong Kong (Hong Kong RAS), la Région Administrative Spéciale de Macao (Macao RAS) et Taïwan province de Chine.

76 Data have been estimated on the basis of the annual National Sample Survey on Population Changes. - Les données ont été estimées sur la base de l'enquête annuelle "National Sample Survey on Population Changes".

77 Because of rounding, totals are not in all cases the sum of the respective components. - Les chiffres étant arrondis, les totaux ne correspondent pas toujours rigoureusement à la somme des composants respectifs.

78 Because of rounding, totals are not in all cases the sum of the respective components. The military personnel are classified as urban population. - Les chiffres étant arrondis, les totaux ne correspondent pas toujours rigoureusement à la somme des composants respectifs. Le personnel militaire est classé dans la population urbaine.

79 Data are from Communique of the National Bureau of Statistics of the People's Republic of China on Major Figures of the 2010 Population Census (No.1). - Données issues du communiqué du Bureau national de la statistique de la République populaire de Chine sur les chiffres importants du recensement de 2010 (n° 1).

80 Data have been adjusted on the basis of the Population Census of 2010. - Les données ont été ajustées à partir des résultats du recensement de la population de 2010.

81 The military personnel are classified as urban population. - Le personnel militaire est classé dans la population urbaine.

82 Data refer to Hong Kong resident population at the census moment, which covers usual residents and mobile residents. Usual residents refer to two categories of people: (1) Hong Kong permanent residents who had stayed in Hong Kong for at least three months during the six months before or for at least three months during the six months after the census moment, regardless of whether they were in Hong Kong or not at the census moment; and (2) Hong Kong non-permanent residents who were in Hong Kong at the census moment. Mobile Residents, they are Hong Kong permanent residents who had stayed in Hong Kong for at least one month but less than three months during the six months before or for at least one month but less than three months during the six months after the census moment, regardless of whether they were in Hong Kong or not at the census moment. - Les données se rapportent à la population résidente à Hong Kong au moment du recensement. Cette population est composée des résidants habituels et des résidants mobiles. La population résidente est partagée en deux catégories: (1) les résidents permanents qui ont habité à Hong Kong au moins trois mois pendant les six mois précédents ou les six mois suivants le recensement; (2) les habitants non-permanents de Hong Kong qui étaient à Hong Kong au moment du recensement. La population mobile se rapporte aux résidents permanents de Hong Kong qui ont habité à Hong Kong pendant les six mois après le recensement pour une période comprise entre un mois et trois mois, indépendamment du fait qu'ils étaient à Hong Kong au moment du recensement au pays.

83 Data refer to government controlled areas. - Les données se rapportent aux zones contrôlées par le Gouvernement.

84 Data refer to annual average population. - Les données correspondent à la population annuelle moyenne.

85 Based on the results of the 2014 Population Census. - D'après les résultats du recensement de la population de 2014.

86 Includes data for the Indian-held part of Jammu and Kashmir, the final status of which has not yet been determined. - Y compris les données pour la partie du Jammu et du Cachemire occupée par l'Inde dont le statut définitif n'a pas encore été déterminé.

87 Data refer to projections based on the 2001 Population Census. - Les données se réfèrent aux projections basées sur le recensement de la population de 2001.

88 Data are based on the publication: "Indonesia Population Projection 2005-2015" - Les données sont basées sur la publication : << Indonesia Population Projection 2005-2015 >>

89 Data are based on the publication: "Indonesia Population Projection 2010-2035" - Les données sont basées sur la publication : << Indonesia Population Projection 2010-2035 >>

90 Data refer to the Iranian Year which begins on 21 March and ends on 20 March of the following year. - Les données concernent l'année iranienne, qui commence le 21 mars et se termine le 20 mars de l'année suivante.

91 The total number may include 'Unknown residence', but the categories urban and rural do not. - Le nombre total peut inclure les personnes dont la résidence n'est pas connue, à l'inverse des catégories de population urbaine et rurale.

92 Includes data for East Jerusalem and Israeli residents in certain other territories under occupation by Israeli military forces since June 1967. - Y compris les données pour Jérusalem-Est et les résidents israéliens dans certains autres territoires occupés depuis 1967 par les forces armées israéliennes.

93 Because of rounding, totals are not in all cases the sum of the respective components. Excluding residents who had been registered in the Israeli localities (the Jewish localities) in the Gaza Area and northern Samaria, which were evacuated in August 2005, but did not notify the Ministry of Interior of their new address. These residents are included in total. - Les chiffres étant arrondis, les totaux ne correspondent pas toujours rigoureusement à la somme des composants respectifs. Hors résidents enregistrés dans les localités d'Israel (localités juives) de la Bande de Gaza (veriffy) et du nord de la Samarie, qui ont été évacués en Août 2005, mais qui n'ont pas notifié leur nouvelle adresse au ministère de l'intérieur. Ces résidents sont inclus dans le total.

94 Excluding residents who had been registered in the Israeli localities (the Jewish localities) in the Gaza Area and northern Samaria, which were evacuated in August 2005, but did not notify the Ministry of Interior of their new address. These residents are included in total. - Hors résidents enregistrés dans les localités d'Israel (localités juives) de la Bande de Gaza (veriffy) et du nord de la Samarie, qui ont été évacués en Août 2005, mais qui n'ont pas notifié leur nouvelle adresse au ministère de l'intérieur. Ces résidents sont inclus dans le total.

95 Data are rounded for confidentiality reasons. - Chiffres arrondis pour des raisons de confidentialité.

96 Excluding diplomatic personnel outside the country and foreign military and civilian personnel and their dependants stationed in the area. - Non compris le personnel diplomatique hors du pays ni les militaires et agents civils étrangers en poste sur le territoire et les membres de leur famille les accompagnant.

97 Excluding diplomatic personnel outside the country and foreign military and civilian personnel and their dependants stationed in the area. Estimates based on the complete counts of the 2015 Population Census - Non compris le personnel diplomatique hors du pays ni les militaires et agents civils étrangers en poste sur le territoire et les membres de leur famille les accompagnant. Estimations basées sur le dénombrement complet du recensement de la population de 2015.

98 Estimates based on the complete counts of the 2015 Population Census Excluding diplomatic personnel outside the country and foreign military and civilian personnel and their dependants stationed in the area. Because of rounding, totals are not in all cases the sum of the respective components. - Estimations basées sur le dénombrement complet du recensement de la population de 2015. Non compris le personnel diplomatique hors du pays ni les militaires et agents civils étrangers en poste sur le territoire et les membres de leur famille les accompagnant. Les chiffres étant arrondis, les totaux ne correspondent pas toujours rigoureusement à la somme des composants respectifs.

99 Excluding data for Jordanian territory under occupation since June 1967 by Israeli military forces. - Non compris les données pour le territoire jordanien occupé depuis juin 1967 par les forces armées israéliennes.

100 Estimates based on the results of 2015 population census. - Estimations fondées sur les résultats du recensement de la population de 2015.

101 Based on the results of a household survey. - D'après les résultats d'une enquête des ménages.

102 Source: Living conditions of household survey, October 2011 to September 2012. - Source: Enquête sur les conditions de vie des ménages, octobre 2011 à septembre 2012.

103 Intercensal Mid-Year Population Estimates based on the adjusted Population and Housing Census of 2000 and 2010. - Les estimations inter-censitaires au millieu de l'année sont fondée sur les résultats ajustées des recensements de la population et de l'habitat de 2000 et 2010.

104 Estimates based on the adjusted results of the Population and Housing Census of 2010. - Les estimations sont fondée sur les résultats ajustées du recensement de la population et de l'habitat de 2010.

105 Data refer to resident population that includes Maldivians and foreigners. - Les données concernent la population résidente, qui comprend des Maldiviens et des étrangers.

106 Data refer to resident Maldivian population. - Les données concernent la population maldivienne résidente.

107 Data refer to enumerated population. The total for the whole country excludes 1,206,353 persons estimated not to have been counted in parts of States of Rakhine, Kachin and Kayin. - Les données se rapportent à la population dénombrée. L' effectif de la population pour le pays ne comprend pas les personnes qui ne sont pas dénombrées dans certaines régions des États de Rakhine, Kachin et Kayin estimées à un chiffre de 1 206 353 personnes.

108 Data refer to registered population data from Royal Oman Police. - Les données portent sur la population enregistrée par la police royale de l'Oman.

109 Excluding data for the Pakistan-held part of Jammu and Kashmir, the final status of which has not yet been determined. - Non compris les données concernant la partie du Jammu et Cachemire occupée par le Pakistan dont le statut définitif n'a pas été déterminé.

110 Based on the results of the Pakistan Demographic Survey (PDS 2007). - D'après les résultats de l'enquête démographique effectuée par le Pakistan en 2007.

111 Excluding 2739 Filipinos in Philippine Embassies, Consulates and Missions Abroad. - Excepté 2739 Philippins travaillant dans les ambassades, les consulats et les missions des Philippines à l'étranger.

112 Excluding usual residents not in the country at the time of census. - À l'exclusion des résidents habituels qui ne sont pas dans le pays au moment du recensement.

113 Data based on the preliminary results of the 2010 Population and Housing Census. - D'après les résultats préliminaires du recensement de la population et des logements de 2010.

114 Data refer to resident population which comprises Singapore citizens and permanent residents. - Les données se rapportent à la population résidente composé des citoyens de Singapour et des résidents permanents.

115 Data exclude residents who have been away from Singapore for a continuous period of 12 months or longer as at the reference date. - Non compris les résidents hors de Singapour pour une période ininterrompue de 12 mois ou plus avant de la date de référence.

116 Data are based on the latest register-based population estimates for 2010. Urban and rural breakdown not applicable as Singapore is a city-state. - Données basées sur les estimations démographiques les plus récentes fondées sur les registres de 2010. La ventilation entre zones urbaines et zones rurales ne s'applique pas à Singapour, puisqu'il s'agit d'une ville État.

117 Data for urban include population in refugee camps. - Les données pour la population urbaine comprennent la population dans les camps réfugiés.

118 Data have not been adjusted for underenumeration. - Les données n'ont pas été ajustées pour compenser les lacunes du dénombrement.

119 Including Palestinian refugees. - Y compris les réfugiés de Palestine.

120 Data based on Address Based Population Registration System. - Les données sont basées sur le registre national de la population basé sur l'adresse.

121 Based on a sample taken at the time of census. Because of rounding, totals are not in all cases the sum of the respective components. - D'après un échantillon obtenu au moment du recensement. Les chiffres étant arrondis, les totaux ne correspondent pas toujours rigoureusement à la somme des composants respectifs.

122 The reason for the differences in the urban-rural population from the previous years is the changes in administrative attachment, legal entity and borders, regulated by related laws. - La raison des différences dans la population urbaine-rurale par rapport aux années précédentes est la modification de l'attachement administratif, de l'entité juridique et des frontières, réglementée par des lois connexes.

123 Data include non-national population. - Les données comprennent les non-nationaux.

124 Data refer to resident population. - Les données concernent la population résidente.

125 Data are adjusted according to the results of the 2009 census and 2014 intercensus. - Les données ont été ajustées à partir des résultats du recensement de la population de 2009 et des données intercensitaires de 2014.

126 Decrease in population due to revision in administrative registers. - Diminution de la population due à la révision des registres administratifs.

127 Excluding Faeroe Islands and Greenland shown separately, if available. Population statistics are compiled from registers. - Non compris les Iles Féroé et le Groenland, qui font l'objet de rubriques distinctes, si disponible. Les statistiques de la population sont compilées à partir des registres.

128 Population statistics are compiled from registers. Excluding Åland Islands. - Les statistiques de la population sont compilées à partir des registres. Non compris les Îles d'Åland.

129 Excluding diplomatic personnel outside the country and including members of alien armed forces not living in military camps and foreign diplomatic personnel not living in embassies or consulates. - Non compris le personnel diplomatique hors du pays et y compris les militaires étrangers ne vivant pas dans des camps militaires et le personnel diplomatique étranger ne vivant pas dans les ambassades ou les consulats.

130 Excluding military personnel, visitors and transients. - Non compris les militaires, ni les visiteurs et transients.

131 Data refer to the Vatican City State. - Les données se rapportent à l'Etat de la Cité du Vatican.

132 The population figure is 466 persons. - La population est égale à 466 personnes.

133 Data refer to usually resident population. - Les données concernent la population habituellement résidente.

134 Data refer to registered resident population. - Les données concernent la population enregistrée résidente.

135 Including civilian nationals temporarily outside the country. - Y compris les civils nationaux temporairement hors du pays.

136 Data refer to resident population only. - Pour la population résidante seulement.

137 Figures for male and female population do not add up to the figure for total population, because they exclude 119 persons of unknown sex. - Les chiffres relatifs à la population masculine et féminine ne correspondent pas au chiffre de la population totale, parce que l'on en a exclu 119 personnes de sexe inconnu.

138 Including residents temporarily outside the country. Population statistics are compiled from registers. - Y compris les résidents se trouvant temporairement hors du pays. Les statistiques de la population sont compilées à partir des registres.

139 Excluding civilian aliens within the country, but including civilian nationals temporarily outside the country. - Non compris les civils étrangers dans le pays, mais y compris les civils nationaux temporairement hors du pays.

140 Excluding Transnistria and the municipality of Bender. - Les données ne tiennent pas compte de l'information sur la Transnistria et la municipalité de Bender.

141 Figures for male and female may not add up to the total, since they do not include the category "Unknown". - La somme des chiffres indiqués pour les sexes masculin et féminin peut n'être pas égale au total parce qu'elle n'inclut pas la catégorie " inconnue ".

142 Excludes data for Kosovo and Metohia. - Sans les données pour le Kosovo et Metohie.

143 Data refer to legal resident population. - Les données concernent la population légalement résidente.

144 From 2015, urban refers to urban centers and areas under the influence of urban centers. - A partir de 2015, le territoire urbain inclut l'espace des centres urbains ainsi que l'espace sous influence des centres urbains.

145 The Government of Ukraine has informed the United Nations that it is not in a position to provide statistical data concerning the Autonomous Republic of Crimea and the city of Sevastopol. - Le gouvernement Ukrainien a informé l'ONU qu'il n'est pas en mesure de fournir des données statistiques concernant la République autonome de Crimée et la ville de Sébastopol.

146 Excluding Channel Islands (Guernsey and Jersey) and Isle of Man, shown separately, if available. - Non compris les îles Anglo-Normandes (Guernesey et Jersey) et l'île de Man, qui font l'objet de rubriques distinctes, si disponible.

147 This data has been randomly rounded to protect confidentiality. Individual figures may not add up to totals, and values for the same data may vary in different tables. - Ces données ont été arrondies de façon aléatoire afin d'en préserver la confidentialité. La somme de certains chiffres peut ne pas correspondre aux totaux indiqués et les valeurs des mêmes données peuvent varier d'un tableau à un autre.

148 Including population in off-shore, migratory and shipping. - Y compris les populations extraterritoriales, les populations nomades et les populations maritimes.

149 Excluding Niue, shown separately, which is part of Cook Islands, but because of remoteness is administered separately. - Non compris Nioué, qui fait l'objet d'une rubrique distincte et qui fait partie des îles Cook, mais qui, en raison de son éloignement, est administrée séparément.

150 Projections are prepared by the Secretariat of the Pacific Community based on the 1999 census of population and housing. - Les projections sont préparées par le Secrétariat de la Communauté du Pacifique à partir des résultats du recensement de la population et de l'habitat de 1999.

151 Population estimates by urban/rural residence exclude inland waters and oceanic areas. - Les estimations de la population par lieu de résidence urbaine ou rurale excluent les eaux intérieures et les zones océaniques.

152 Estimates are prepared by the Secretariat of the Pacific Community based on the last population and housing census. - Les estimations sont preparées par le Secrétariat de la Communauté du Pacifique à partir des résultats du dernier recensement de la population et de l'habitat.

153 The population figures are 64 and 58 persons for 2007 and 2008 respectively. - La population est respectivement égale à 64 et 58 personnes pour les années 2007 et 2008.

154 Data refer to national projections. Based on the results of the 1996 population census. - Les données se réfèrent aux projections nationales. À partir des résultats du recensement de la population de 1996.

Table 7 - *Demographic Yearbook 2016*

Table 7 presents population by age, sex and urban/rural residence for the latest available year between 2007 and 2016.

Description of variables: Data in this table are either population census figures or estimates, some of which are based on sample surveys. The source of data is indicated by the 'code' explained at the end of the table.

The reference date of the census or estimate appears in the left-most column of the table. In general, the estimates refer to mid-year, i.e. 1 July.

Age is defined as age at last birthday, that is, the difference between the date of birth and the reference date of the age distribution expressed in completed solar years. The age classification used in this table is the following: under 1 year, 1-4 years, 5-year groups through 95-99 years, and 100 years or over.

Statistics are presented for one year, the most recent available. However, if more complete disaggregation is available for an earlier year, both are displayed.

The urban/rural classification of population is that provided by each country or area; it is presumed to be based on the national census definitions of urban population that have been set forth at the end of the technical notes to table 6.

Reliability of data: Estimates which are believed to be less reliable are set in *italics* rather than in roman type.

Limitations: Statistics on population by age and sex are subject to the same qualifications as have been set forth for population statistics in general and age distributions in particular, as discussed in sections 3 and 3.1.3, respectively, of the Technical Notes.

Comparability of population data classified by age and sex is limited by variations in the definition of total population, discussed in detail in section 3 of the Technical Notes, and by the accuracy of the original enumeration. Both factors are more important in relation to certain age groups than to others. For example, under-enumeration is known to be more prevalent among infants and young children than among older persons. Similarly, the exclusion from the total population of certain groups that tend to be of selected ages (such as the armed forces) can markedly affect the age structure and its comparability with that for other countries or areas. Consideration should be given to the implications of these basic limitations in using the data.

In addition to these general qualifications are the special problems of comparability that arise in relation to age statistics in particular. Age distributions of population are known to suffer from certain deficiencies that have their origin in irregularities in age reporting. Although some of the irregularities tend to be obscured or eliminated when data are tabulated in five-year age groups rather than by single years, precision still continues to be affected, though the degree of distortion is not always readily seen.

Another factor limiting comparability is the age classification employed by the various countries or areas. Age may be based on the year of birth rather than the age at last birthday, in other words, calculated using the day, month and year of birth. Distributions based only on the year of birth are footnoted when known.

The absence of data in the unknown age group does not necessarily indicate completely accurate reporting and tabulation of the age item. The unknowns may have been eliminated by assigning ages to them before tabulation, or by proportionately distributing the unknown category across the age groups after tabulation.

As noted in connection with table 5, intercensal estimates of total population are usually revised to accord with the results of a census of population if inexplicable discontinuities appear to exist. Intercensal age-sex distributions, however, are less likely to be revised in this way.   When it is known that a total population estimate for a given year has been revised and the corresponding age distribution has not been revised, a note is provided. Distributions of this type should be used with caution when studying trends over a period of years, though their utility for studying age structure for the specified year is probably unimpaired.

The comparability of data by urban/rural residence is affected by the national definitions of urban and rural used in tabulating these data. When known, the definitions of urban used in national population censuses are presented at the end of the technical notes for table 6. As discussed in detail in the technical notes for table 6, these definitions vary considerably from one country or area to another.

Earlier data: Population by age, sex and urban/rural residence has been shown in previous issues of the *Demographic Yearbook*. For more information on specific topics, and years for which data are reported, readers should consult the Historical Index. In addition, population data by single years of age, sex and urban/rural residence, for censuses conducted since 1995, are shown in the *Demographic Yearbook* webpage http://unstats.un.org/unsd/demographic/products/dyb/dybcensusdata.htm.

Tableau 7 – *Annuaire démographique 2016*

Le tableau 7 présente les données les plus récentes disponibles pour la période 2007-2016 sur la population selon l'âge, le sexe et le lieu de résidence (zone urbaine ou rurale).

Description des variables : les données de ce tableau proviennent de recensements de la population ou correspondent à des estimations, fondées dans certains cas, sur des enquêtes par sondage. Le 'code' indique comment les données ont été obtenues. Les codes utilisés sont expliqués à la fin du tableau.

La date du recensement ou de l'estimation figure dans la colonne de gauche du tableau. En général, les estimations se rapportent au milieu de l'année (1er juillet).

L'âge désigne l'âge au dernier anniversaire, c'est-à-dire la différence entre la date de naissance et la date de référence de la répartition par âge exprimée en années solaires révolues. La classification par âge utilisée dans ce tableau est la suivante : moins d'un an, 1 à 4 ans, groupes quinquennaux jusqu'à 95-99 ans et 100 ans ou plus.

Les statistiques portent sur une année, qui correspond à celle pour laquelle on dispose des statistiques les plus récentes. Toutefois, si l'on dispose de répartitions plus complètes pour des années antérieures, les statistiques sont alors présentées pour les deux années.

La classification par zones urbaines et rurales de la population est celle qui est communiquée par chaque pays ou zone ; on part du principe qu'elle repose sur les définitions de la population urbaine utilisées pour les recensements de la population nationaux telles qu'elles sont reproduites à la fin des notes techniques du tableau 6.

Fiabilité des données : les estimations considérées comme moins sûres sont indiquées en italique plutôt qu'en caractères romains.

Insuffisance des données : les statistiques de la population selon l'âge et le sexe appellent les mêmes réserves que celles qui ont été formulées aux sections 3 et 3.1.3 des Notes techniques à propos des statistiques de la population en général et des répartitions par âge en particulier.

La comparabilité des statistiques de la population selon l'âge et le sexe pâtit du manque d'uniformité dans la définition de la population totale (voir la section 3 des Notes techniques) et des lacunes des dénombrements. L'influence de ces deux facteurs varie selon les groupes d'âge. Ainsi, le dénombrement des enfants de moins d'un an et des jeunes enfants comporte souvent plus de lacunes que celui des personnes plus âgées. De même, le fait que certains groupes de personnes appartenant souvent à des groupes d'âge déterminés, par exemple les militaires, ne soient pas pris en compte dans la population totale peut influer sensiblement sur la structure par âge et sur la comparabilité des données avec celles d'autres pays ou zones. Il conviendra de tenir compte de ces facteurs fondamentaux lorsque l'on utilisera les données du tableau.

Outre ces difficultés d'ordre général, la comparabilité pose des problèmes particuliers lorsqu'il s'agit des données par âge. On sait que les répartitions de la population selon l'âge présentent certaines imperfections dues à l'inexactitude des déclarations d'âge. Certaines de ces anomalies ont tendance à s'estomper ou à disparaître lorsque l'on classe les données par groupes d'âge quinquennaux et non par années d'âge, mais une certaine imprécision subsiste, même s'il n'est pas toujours facile de voir à quel point il y a distorsion.

Le degré de comparabilité dépend également de la classification par âge employée dans les divers pays ou zones. L'âge retenu peut être défini par date exacte (jour, mois et année) de naissance ou par celle du dernier anniversaire. Lorsqu'elles étaient connues, les répartitions établies seulement d'après l'année de la naissance ont été signalées en note à la fin du tableau.

Si aucun nombre ne figure dans la rangée réservée aux âges inconnus, cela ne signifie pas nécessairement que les déclarations d'âge et l'exploitation des données par âge aient été tout à fait exactes. C'est souvent une indication que l'on a attribué un âge aux personnes d'âge inconnu avant l'exploitation des données ou qu'elles ont été réparties proportionnellement entre les différents groupes après cette opération.

Comme on l'a indiqué à propos du tableau 5, les estimations intercensitaires de la population totale sont d'ordinaire rectifiées d'après les résultats des recensements de population si l'on constate des discontinuités inexplicables. Les données intercensitaires concernant la répartition de la population par âge et par sexe ont toutefois moins de chance d'être rectifiées de cette manière. Lorsque l'on savait qu'une estimation de la population totale pour une année donnée avait été rectifiée sans qu'il en soit de même pour la répartition par âge correspondante, cela a été indiquée dans une note. Les répartitions de ce type doivent être utilisées avec prudence lorsque l'on étudie les tendances sur un certain nombre d'années, quoique leur utilité pour l'étude de la structure par âge de la population pour l'année visée reste probablement entière.

La comparabilité des données selon le lieu de résidence (zone urbaine ou rurale) peut être limitée par les définitions nationales des termes « urbain » et « rural » utilisées pour la mise en tableaux de ces données. Les définitions du terme « urbain » utilisées pour les recensements nationaux de population ont été présentées à la fin des notes techniques du tableau 6 lorsqu'elles étaient connues. Comme on l'a précisé dans les notes techniques relatives au tableau 6, ces définitions varient considérablement d'un pays ou d'une zone à l'autre.

Données publiées antérieurement : des statistiques concernant la population selon l'âge, le sexe et le lieu de résidence (zone urbaine ou rurale) ont été présentées dans des éditions antérieures de l'*Annuaire démographique*. Pour plus de précisions concernant les années et les sujets pour lesquels des données ont été publiées, se reporter à l'index historique. En plus, des statistiques disponibles concernant la « Population selon chaque année d'âge, le sexe et la résidence urbaine/rurale », pour les recensements depuis 1995, ont été présentées dans la page internet suivante de l'*Annuaire démographique* http://unstats.un.org/unsd/demographic/products/dyb/dybcensusdata.htm.

Continent, country or area, date, code[a] and age (in years) / Continent, pays ou zone, date, code[a] et âge (en années)	Total			Urban - Urbaine			Rural - Rurale		
	Both sexes Les deux sexes	Male Masculin	Female Féminin	Both sexes Les deux sexes	Male Masculin	Female Féminin	Both sexes Les deux sexes	Male Masculin	Female Féminin
AFRICA - AFRIQUE									
Algeria - Algérie									
16 IV 2008 (CDJC)[1]									
Total	34 080 030	17 232 753	16 847 277	22 413 189	11 288 724	11 124 466	11 666 841	5 944 029	5 722 812
0 - 4	3 404 918	1 750 097	1 654 821	2 242 705	1 151 239	1 091 466	1 162 213	598 858	563 355
5 - 9	2 888 376	1 475 674	1 412 702	1 888 091	963 262	924 829	1 000 285	512 412	487 873
10 - 14	3 258 773	1 662 262	1 596 511	2 096 819	1 067 727	1 029 092	1 161 954	594 535	567 419
15 - 19	3 635 171	1 847 312	1 787 859	2 309 568	1 169 541	1 140 028	1 325 603	677 772	647 831
20 - 24	3 763 504	1 895 703	1 867 801	2 378 019	1 188 465	1 189 553	1 385 485	707 238	678 247
25 - 29	3 422 377	1 730 411	1 691 966	2 186 560	1 096 016	1 090 545	1 235 816	634 395	601 421
30 - 34	2 740 996	1 379 085	1 361 910	1 802 265	901 021	901 245	938 730	478 064	460 666
35 - 39	2 342 779	1 167 250	1 175 529	1 601 928	793 133	808 795	740 852	374 118	366 734
40 - 44	2 018 327	1 007 683	1 010 644	1 414 371	705 266	709 105	603 956	302 417	301 539
45 - 49	1 629 436	817 005	812 432	1 132 297	570 706	561 591	497 140	246 299	250 841
50 - 54	1 346 695	682 358	664 336	927 655	474 005	453 650	419 040	208 353	210 687
55 - 59	1 062 578	547 180	515 398	720 761	371 528	349 233	341 817	175 652	166 165
60 - 64	711 482	354 694	356 788	479 760	236 949	242 811	231 722	117 745	113 977
65 - 69	631 303	314 958	316 345	420 685	207 760	212 925	210 618	107 198	103 420
70 - 74	504 926	248 672	256 254	336 819	164 109	172 710	168 107	84 563	83 544
75 - 79	363 843	181 478	182 364	240 563	118 362	122 201	123 280	63 116	60 164
80 - 84	187 130	93 472	93 657	121 942	59 267	62 675	65 187	34 205	30 982
85 - 89	89 722	43 307	46 416	58 550	27 171	31 379	31 172	16 136	15 037
90 - 94	29 672	13 575	16 097	19 375	8 488	10 887	10 297	5 087	5 210
95 - 99	10 028	4 178	5 851	6 647	2 638	4 009	3 382	1 540	1 842
100 +	650	252	398	445	170	274	205	82	123
Unknown - Inconnu	37 347	16 146	21 200	27 365	11 901	15 464	9 981	4 245	5 736
1 VII 2016 (ESDJ)									
Total	40 835 602	20 680 271	20 155 331	...	...	...	...	...	...
0	1 029 091	528 275	500 817	...	...	...	...	...	...
1 - 4	3 804 670	1 955 225	1 849 445	...	...	...	...	...	...
5 - 9	4 011 078	2 064 704	1 946 374	...	...	...	...	...	...
10 - 14	3 109 461	1 594 947	1 514 514	...	...	...	...	...	...
15 - 19	3 027 490	1 545 852	1 481 638	...	...	...	...	...	...
20 - 24	3 475 531	1 770 599	1 704 932	...	...	...	...	...	...
25 - 29	3 769 375	1 905 862	1 863 513	...	...	...	...	...	...
30 - 34	3 712 677	1 869 205	1 843 472	...	...	...	...	...	...
35 - 39	3 170 670	1 600 409	1 570 261	...	...	...	...	...	...
40 - 44	2 553 385	1 277 743	1 275 642	...	...	...	...	...	...
45 - 49	2 210 557	1 099 063	1 111 494	...	...	...	...	...	...
50 - 54	1 845 562	920 171	925 391	...	...	...	...	...	...
55 - 59	1 475 864	738 852	737 012	...	...	...	...	...	...
60 - 64	1 192 407	604 034	588 372	...	...	...	...	...	...
65 - 69	849 855	428 696	421 158	...	...	...	...	...	...
70 - 74	582 171	283 320	298 851	...	...	...	...	...	...
75 - 79	478 011	231 522	246 489	...	...	...	...	...	...
80 - 84	316 947	152 136	164 810	...	...	...	...	...	...
85 +	220 801	109 657	111 145	...	...	...	...	...	...
Angola									
16 V 2014 (CDFC)									
Total	25 789 024	12 499 041	13 289 983	16 153 987	7 860 614	8 293 373	9 635 037	4 638 427	4 996 610
0 - 4	4 998 148	2 484 582	2 513 566	2 912 064	1 450 139	1 461 924	2 086 085	1 034 443	1 051 642
5 - 9	4 160 174	2 062 888	2 097 287	2 559 781	1 258 439	1 301 342	1 600 393	804 448	795 945
10 - 14	3 038 173	1 504 180	1 533 993	1 975 562	953 924	1 021 638	1 062 612	550 256	512 355
15 - 19	2 510 436	1 222 700	1 287 736	1 677 783	809 594	868 189	832 653	413 106	419 547
20 - 24	2 174 501	1 020 699	1 153 802	1 477 330	696 023	781 307	697 171	324 676	372 496
25 - 29	1 945 050	913 726	1 031 323	1 338 058	640 293	697 765	606 992	273 433	333 559
30 - 34	1 503 520	714 239	789 281	1 026 351	498 258	528 093	477 169	215 982	261 188
35 - 39	1 382 959	654 408	728 550	902 362	439 369	462 993	480 597	215 040	265 558
40 - 44	1 050 085	510 344	539 742	660 913	332 669	328 245	389 172	177 675	211 497
45 - 49	864 904	417 953	446 951	525 157	266 263	258 894	339 747	151 690	188 057
50 - 54	709 169	332 638	376 532	400 902	195 727	205 174	308 268	136 910	171 357
55 - 59	483 319	229 641	253 678	264 296	131 985	132 310	219 023	97 656	121 367
60 - 64	356 154	165 937	190 217	174 161	82 701	91 460	181 993	83 236	98 757
65 - 69	215 387	95 614	119 773	96 774	42 538	54 236	118 613	53 077	65 536
70 - 74	180 167	78 673	101 494	73 334	30 023	43 311	106 833	48 650	58 183
75 - 79	92 944	39 257	53 687	38 891	14 759	24 133	54 052	24 498	29 554

Continent, country or area, date, code[a] and age (in years) / Continent, pays ou zone, date, code[a] et âge (en annèes)	Total			Urban - Urbaine			Rural - Rurale		
	Both sexes Les deux sexes	Male Masculin	Female Féminin	Both sexes Les deux sexes	Male Masculin	Female Féminin	Both sexes Les deux sexes	Male Masculin	Female Féminin
AFRICA - AFRIQUE									
Angola									
16 V 2014 (CDFC)									
80 - 84	66 792	28 351	38 441	25 743	9 211	16 532	41 049	19 140	21 909
85 - 89	24 828	9 967	14 861	10 546	3 575	6 972	14 281	6 392	7 889
90 - 94	18 175	7 603	10 572	7 058	2 483	4 576	11 117	5 121	5 996
95 +	14 138	5 640	8 498	6 921	2 641	4 280	7 217	2 999	4 218
Benin - Bénin									
1 VII 2011 (ESDF)[2]									
Total	9 067 076	4 446 877	4 620 199	4 072 574	2 003 366	2 069 208	4 994 502	2 443 511	2 550 991
0 - 4	1 629 512	828 064	801 448	633 629	321 667	311 962	995 883	506 397	489 486
0	350 292	178 565	171 727	...	...	...	...	...	...
1 - 4	1 279 220	649 499	629 721	...	...	...	...	...	...
5 - 9	1 335 166	675 912	659 254	511 822	251 283	260 539	823 344	424 629	398 715
10 - 14	1 137 068	572 756	564 312	517 373	244 437	272 936	619 695	328 319	291 376
15 - 19	1 081 199	553 241	527 958	550 694	279 420	271 274	530 505	273 821	256 684
20 - 24	767 946	398 920	369 026	406 496	224 092	182 404	361 450	174 828	186 622
25 - 29	609 489	291 598	317 891	303 896	153 731	150 165	305 593	137 867	167 726
30 - 34	537 893	227 400	310 493	264 521	117 596	146 925	273 372	109 804	163 568
35 - 39	494 619	213 385	281 234	236 804	106 800	130 004	257 815	106 585	151 230
40 - 44	378 111	175 956	202 155	178 115	86 225	91 890	199 996	89 731	110 265
45 - 49	308 866	142 056	166 810	145 334	68 351	76 983	163 532	73 705	89 827
50 - 54	232 650	110 074	122 576	101 866	48 831	53 035	130 784	61 243	69 541
55 - 59	171 970	82 190	89 780	77 819	37 319	40 500	94 151	44 871	49 280
60 - 64	135 768	64 968	70 800	52 261	24 642	27 619	83 507	40 326	43 181
65 - 69	75 534	35 915	39 619	31 238	14 546	16 692	44 296	21 369	22 927
70 - 74	82 740	36 511	46 229	30 032	12 558	17 474	52 708	23 953	28 755
75 - 79	36 453	15 591	20 862	14 064	5 573	8 491	22 389	10 018	12 371
80 +	52 092	22 340	29 752	16 610	6 295	10 315	35 482	16 045	19 437
1 VII 2016 (ESDF)[3]									
Total	10 882 953	5 334 603	5 548 350	...	...	...	...	...	...
0 - 4	1 724 707	876 597	848 110	...	...	...	...	...	...
5 - 9	1 690 244	853 324	836 920	...	...	...	...	...	...
10 - 14	1 530 148	780 536	749 612	...	...	...	...	...	...
15 - 19	1 163 229	600 456	562 773	...	...	...	...	...	...
20 - 24	936 421	456 779	479 642	...	...	...	...	...	...
25 - 29	818 147	356 225	461 922	...	...	...	...	...	...
30 - 34	722 299	314 616	407 683	...	...	...	...	...	...
35 - 39	588 013	272 972	315 041	...	...	...	...	...	...
40 - 44	466 547	224 131	242 416	...	...	...	...	...	...
45 - 49	344 261	171 500	172 761	...	...	...	...	...	...
50 - 54	259 141	126 844	132 297	...	...	...	...	...	...
55 - 59	202 796	99 128	103 668	...	...	...	...	...	...
60 - 64	129 272	63 241	66 031	...	...	...	...	...	...
65 - 69	122 941	57 543	65 398	...	...	...	...	...	...
70 - 74	64 104	29 468	34 636	...	...	...	...	...	...
75 - 79	57 572	25 240	32 332	...	...	...	...	...	...
80 +	63 111	26 003	37 108	...	...	...	...	...	...
Botswana[4]									
1 VII 2016 (ESDJ)									
Total	2 230 905	1 097 097	1 133 808	1 554 836	758 457	796 379	676 069	329 790	346 279
0 - 4	256 176	129 345	126 831	178 543	89 420	89 085	77 633	38 881	38 736
5 - 9	233 013	117 796	115 217	162 399	81 436	80 928	70 614	35 410	35 189
10 - 14	215 548	108 728	106 820	150 227	75 167	75 030	65 321	32 684	32 624
15 - 19	207 371	104 488	102 883	144 528	72 236	72 264	62 843	31 409	31 422
20 - 24	210 252	104 753	105 499	146 536	72 419	74 102	63 716	31 489	32 221
25 - 29	200 113	97 523	102 590	139 469	67 421	72 059	60 644	29 316	31 332
30 - 34	206 906	101 228	105 678	144 204	69 982	74 228	62 702	30 429	32 275
35 - 39	169 394	84 268	85 126	118 060	58 257	59 792	51 334	25 331	25 999
40 - 44	133 779	67 779	66 000	93 238	46 858	46 358	40 541	20 375	20 157
45 - 49	97 773	48 010	49 763	68 143	33 191	34 953	29 630	14 432	15 198
50 - 54	80 526	36 970	43 556	56 123	25 558	30 593	24 403	11 113	13 303
55 - 59	64 641	28 797	35 844	45 052	19 908	25 177	19 589	8 656	10 947
60 - 64	51 975	23 237	28 738	36 224	16 064	20 185	15 751	6 985	8 777
65 - 69	35 091	15 982	19 109	24 457	11 049	13 422	10 634	4 804	5 836
70 - 74	24 987	10 816	14 171	17 415	7 477	9 954	7 572	3 251	4 328

7. Population by age, sex and urban/rural residence: latest available year, 2007 - 2016
Population selon l'âge, le sexe et la résidence, urbaine/rurale : dernière année disponible, 2007 - 2016 (continued - suite)

Continent, country or area, date, code[a] and age (in years) / Continent, pays ou zone, date, code[a] et âge (en années)	Total			Urban - Urbaine			Rural - Rurale		
	Both sexes Les deux sexes	Male Masculin	Female Féminin	Both sexes Les deux sexes	Male Masculin	Female Féminin	Both sexes Les deux sexes	Male Masculin	Female Féminin
AFRICA - AFRIQUE									
Botswana[4]									
1 VII 2016 (ESDJ)									
75 - 79	19 046	7 895	11 151	13 274	5 458	7 832	5 772	2 373	3 406
80 +	24 315	9 483	14 832	16 946	6 556	10 418	7 369	2 851	4 530
Burkina Faso[2]									
1 VII 2015 (ESDJ)									
Total	18 450 494	8 904 256	9 546 238	...	...	...	...	...	...
0 - 4	3 382 595	1 727 798	1 654 797	...	...	...	...	...	...
5 - 9	2 908 754	1 495 367	1 413 387	...	...	...	...	...	...
10 - 14	2 486 098	1 279 388	1 206 710	...	...	...	...	...	...
15 - 19	2 019 668	1 007 291	1 012 377	...	...	...	...	...	...
20 - 24	1 570 287	747 367	822 920	...	...	...	...	...	...
25 - 29	1 285 878	548 045	737 833	...	...	...	...	...	...
30 - 34	1 028 499	426 955	601 544	...	...	...	...	...	...
35 - 39	882 336	377 591	504 745	...	...	...	...	...	...
40 - 44	677 094	300 004	377 090	...	...	...	...	...	...
45 - 49	581 242	255 406	325 836	...	...	...	...	...	...
50 - 54	449 604	200 660	248 944	...	...	...	...	...	...
55 - 59	366 471	161 682	204 789	...	...	...	...	...	...
60 - 64	265 938	123 614	142 324	...	...	...	...	...	...
65 - 69	221 400	101 732	119 668	...	...	...	...	...	...
70 - 74	141 840	67 215	74 625	...	...	...	...	...	...
75 - 79	98 034	45 504	52 530	...	...	...	...	...	...
80 +	84 756	38 637	46 119	...	...	...	...	...	...
Burundi									
1 VII 2015 (ESDF)[5]									
Total	9 823 828	4 822 838	5 000 990	1 473 574	723 426	750 148	8 350 254	4 099 412	4 250 842
0 - 4	1 712 483	856 714	855 769	220 830	99 976	120 854	1 491 653	756 738	734 915
5 - 9	1 379 000	679 740	699 260	172 229	76 843	95 386	1 206 771	602 897	603 874
10 - 14	1 234 086	604 457	629 629	154 449	67 431	87 018	1 079 637	537 026	542 611
15 - 19	1 021 915	496 353	525 562	161 685	74 964	86 721	860 230	421 389	438 841
20 - 24	974 645	467 123	507 522	176 946	89 742	87 204	797 699	377 381	420 318
25 - 29	843 366	397 323	446 043	174 840	90 183	84 657	668 526	307 140	361 386
30 - 34	659 106	321 348	337 758	140 254	76 414	63 840	518 852	244 934	273 918
35 - 39	466 561	236 115	230 446	82 657	46 719	35 938	383 904	189 396	194 508
40 - 44	366 466	182 701	183 765	57 283	33 163	24 120	309 183	149 538	159 645
45 - 49	310 594	153 796	156 798	40 803	22 094	18 709	269 791	131 702	138 089
50 - 54	265 180	134 933	130 247	30 364	16 749	13 615	234 816	118 184	116 632
55 - 59	225 278	113 470	111 808	25 692	13 147	12 545	199 586	100 323	99 263
60 - 64	145 211	74 556	70 655	14 954	7 579	7 375	130 257	66 977	63 280
65 - 69	90 785	44 744	46 041	9 023	4 024	4 999	81 762	40 720	41 042
70 - 74	54 548	25 722	28 826	4 874	2 027	2 847	49 674	23 695	25 979
75 - 79	36 220	16 056	20 164	3 504	1 175	2 329	32 716	14 881	17 835
80 +	38 384	17 687	20 697	3 187	1 196	1 991	35 197	16 491	18 706
1 VII 2016 (ESDF)									
Total	11 215 019	5 539 821	5 675 198	...	...	...	...	...	...
0 - 4	1 779 375	894 841	884 534	...	...	...	...	...	...
5 - 9	1 690 394	845 189	845 205	...	...	...	...	...	...
10 - 14	1 370 711	680 942	689 769	...	...	...	...	...	...
15 - 19	1 131 148	557 652	573 496	...	...	...	...	...	...
20 - 24	1 050 483	512 106	538 377	...	...	...	...	...	...
25 - 29	966 680	464 815	501 865	...	...	...	...	...	...
30 - 34	794 335	386 443	407 892	...	...	...	...	...	...
35 - 39	586 957	293 173	293 784	...	...	...	...	...	...
40 - 44	420 013	208 418	211 595	...	...	...	...	...	...
45 - 49	355 652	174 380	181 272	...	...	...	...	...	...
50 - 54	307 649	152 976	154 673	...	...	...	...	...	...
55 - 59	267 729	133 092	134 637	...	...	...	...	...	...
60 - 64	204 006	101 038	102 968	...	...	...	...	...	...
65 - 69	122 288	59 328	62 960	...	...	...	...	...	...
70 - 74	78 653	36 570	42 083	...	...	...	...	...	...
75 - 79	49 496	22 125	27 371	...	...	...	...	...	...
80 +	39 450	16 733	22 717	...	...	...	...	...	...

7. Population by age, sex and urban/rural residence: latest available year, 2007 - 2016
Population selon l'âge, le sexe et la résidence, urbaine/rurale : dernière année disponible, 2007 - 2016 (continued - suite)

Continent, country or area, date, code[a] and age (in years) Continent, pays ou zone, date, code[a] et âge (en années)	Total			Urban - Urbaine			Rural - Rurale		
	Both sexes Les deux sexes	Male Masculin	Female Féminin	Both sexes Les deux sexes	Male Masculin	Female Féminin	Both sexes Les deux sexes	Male Masculin	Female Féminin
AFRICA - AFRIQUE									
Cabo Verde									
16 VI 2010 (CDJC)									
Total	491 683	243 403	248 280	303 673	151 219	152 454	188 010	92 184	95 826
0 - 4	50 200	25 131	25 069	30 842	15 542	15 300	19 358	9 589	9 769
5 - 9	50 208	25 168	25 040	29 705	14 799	14 906	20 503	10 369	10 134
10 - 14	55 225	27 864	27 361	30 408	15 260	15 148	24 817	12 604	12 213
15 - 19	59 060	29 655	29 405	33 772	16 678	17 094	25 288	12 977	12 311
20 - 24	52 905	27 327	25 578	34 402	17 504	16 898	18 503	9 823	8 680
25 - 29	44 341	23 336	21 005	30 990	16 055	14 935	13 351	7 281	6 070
30 - 34	34 504	18 165	16 339	24 684	13 012	11 672	9 820	5 153	4 667
35 - 39	27 236	14 106	13 130	18 641	9 726	8 915	8 595	4 380	4 215
40 - 44	26 291	12 988	13 303	17 086	8 680	8 406	9 205	4 308	4 897
45 - 49	23 512	11 347	12 165	15 227	7 625	7 602	8 285	3 722	4 563
50 - 54	18 161	8 162	9 999	11 243	5 392	5 851	6 918	2 770	4 148
55 - 59	12 143	4 947	7 196	7 183	3 229	3 954	4 960	1 718	3 242
60 - 64	6 193	2 613	3 580	3 656	1 663	1 993	2 537	950	1 587
65 - 69	6 215	2 499	3 716	3 420	1 411	2 009	2 795	1 088	1 707
70 - 74	8 666	3 437	5 229	4 237	1 656	2 581	4 429	1 781	2 648
75 - 79	7 433	2 980	4 453	3 602	1 377	2 225	3 831	1 603	2 228
80 - 84	5 277	2 092	3 185	2 485	891	1 594	2 792	1 201	1 591
85 - 89	2 185	827	1 358	1 058	331	727	1 127	496	631
90 - 94	1 073	377	696	520	171	349	553	206	347
95 +	497	172	325	248	65	183	249	107	142
Unknown - Inconnu	358	210	148	264	152	112	94	58	36
1 VII 2016 (ESDF)[2]									
Total	531 239	266 287	264 951	...	...	...	...	...	...
0	10 528	5 387	5 142	...	...	...	...	...	...
1 - 4	41 367	21 154	20 213	...	...	...	...	...	...
5 - 9	50 772	25 449	25 323	...	...	...	...	...	...
10 - 14	51 307	25 599	25 708	...	...	...	...	...	...
15 - 19	49 388	25 113	24 275	...	...	...	...	...	...
20 - 24	53 087	26 987	26 099	...	...	...	...	...	...
25 - 29	54 065	28 267	25 798	...	...	...	...	...	...
30 - 34	46 611	24 917	21 693	...	...	...	...	...	...
35 - 39	36 841	19 959	16 882	...	...	...	...	...	...
40 - 44	28 586	15 053	13 532	...	...	...	...	...	...
45 - 49	25 987	12 971	13 016	...	...	...	...	...	...
50 - 54	23 785	11 407	12 379	...	...	...	...	...	...
55 - 59	17 851	8 118	9 733	...	...	...	...	...	...
60 - 64	12 006	4 722	7 284	...	...	...	...	...	...
65 - 69	6 212	2 572	3 640	...	...	...	...	...	...
70 - 74	5 341	2 095	3 246	...	...	...	...	...	...
75 - 79	6 459	2 411	4 048	...	...	...	...	...	...
80 - 84	5 507	2 067	3 440	...	...	...	...	...	...
85 - 89	3 600	1 425	2 176	...	...	...	...	...	...
90 - 94	1 309	468	841	...	...	...	...	...	...
95 +	629	146	483	...	...	...	...	...	...
Cameroon - Cameroun[2]									
1 I 2010 (ESDJ)									
Total	19 406 100	9 599 224	9 806 876	...	...	...	...	...	...
0 - 4	3 287 234	1 662 298	1 624 936	...	...	...	...	...	...
5 - 9	2 783 459	1 412 467	1 370 992	...	...	...	...	...	...
10 - 14	2 394 671	1 227 470	1 167 201	...	...	...	...	...	...
15 - 19	2 170 035	1 068 509	1 101 526	...	...	...	...	...	...
20 - 24	1 837 289	855 334	981 955	...	...	...	...	...	...
25 - 29	1 525 816	712 550	813 266	...	...	...	...	...	...
30 - 34	1 209 607	588 210	621 397	...	...	...	...	...	...
35 - 39	942 713	460 394	482 319	...	...	...	...	...	...
40 - 44	793 846	388 539	405 307	...	...	...	...	...	...
45 - 49	640 247	323 507	316 740	...	...	...	...	...	...
50 - 54	521 910	261 626	260 284	...	...	...	...	...	...
55 - 59	337 988	178 876	159 112	...	...	...	...	...	...
60 - 64	315 879	155 208	160 671	...	...	...	...	...	...
65 - 69	227 290	110 645	116 645	...	...	...	...	...	...
70 - 74	189 571	88 969	100 602	...	...	...	...	...	...

7. Population by age, sex and urban/rural residence: latest available year, 2007 - 2016
Population selon l'âge, le sexe et la résidence, urbaine/rurale : dernière année disponible, 2007 - 2016 (continued - suite)

Continent, country or area, date, code[a] and age (in years) / Continent, pays ou zone, date, code[a] et âge (en années)	Total			Urban - Urbaine			Rural - Rurale		
	Both sexes Les deux sexes	Male Masculin	Female Féminin	Both sexes Les deux sexes	Male Masculin	Female Féminin	Both sexes Les deux sexes	Male Masculin	Female Féminin
AFRICA - AFRIQUE									
Cameroon - Cameroun[2]									
1 I 2010 (ESDJ)									
75 - 79	98 078	47 173	50 905	...	...	...	...	...	...
80 - 84	71 585	31 609	39 976	...	...	...	...	...	...
85 - 89	26 564	12 109	14 455	...	...	...	...	...	...
90 - 94	15 715	6 942	8 773	...	...	...	...	...	...
95 +	16 603	6 789	9 814	...	...	...	...	...	...
Congo									
1 VII 2009 (ESDF)									
Total	3 838 238	1 891 558	1 946 680	...	...	...	...	...	...
0 - 4	586 578	294 305	292 273	...	...	...	...	...	...
5 - 9	475 864	238 682	237 182	...	...	...	...	...	...
10 - 14	417 074	208 162	208 912	...	...	...	...	...	...
15 - 19	382 673	186 405	196 268	...	...	...	...	...	...
20 - 24	358 745	167 519	191 226	...	...	...	...	...	...
25 - 29	339 133	160 897	178 236	...	...	...	...	...	...
30 - 34	304 009	152 642	151 367	...	...	...	...	...	...
35 - 39	254 997	131 794	123 203	...	...	...	...	...	...
40 - 44	198 594	103 248	95 346	...	...	...	...	...	...
45 - 49	148 798	76 921	71 877	...	...	...	...	...	...
50 - 54	111 812	54 925	56 887	...	...	...	...	...	...
55 - 59	80 842	38 051	42 791	...	...	...	...	...	...
60 - 64	59 601	27 592	32 009	...	...	...	...	...	...
65 - 69	46 706	20 879	25 827	...	...	...	...	...	...
70 - 74	34 961	14 954	20 007	...	...	...	...	...	...
75 - 79	21 868	8 820	13 048	...	...	...	...	...	...
80 +	15 983	5 762	10 221	...	...	...	...	...	...
Côte d'Ivoire[6]									
1 VII 2016 (ESDF)									
Total	23 950 475	12 340 863	11 609 612	12 262 645	6 318 519	5 944 126	11 687 830	6 022 338	5 665 492
0	824 414	419 715	404 699	365 177	187 696	177 481	459 237	232 019	227 218
1 - 4	2 991 619	1 538 911	1 452 708	1 325 148	688 200	636 948	1 666 470	850 711	815 759
5 - 9	3 413 302	1 758 347	1 654 955	1 529 754	782 057	747 697	1 883 548	976 289	907 259
10 - 14	2 843 484	1 493 883	1 349 601	1 492 760	758 500	734 260	1 350 724	735 384	615 340
15 - 19	2 271 564	1 182 593	1 088 971	1 353 319	696 054	657 265	918 245	486 538	431 707
20 - 24	2 069 464	1 018 930	1 050 534	1 178 908	585 392	593 516	890 556	433 538	457 018
25 - 29	2 082 152	1 005 570	1 076 582	1 145 866	551 847	594 019	936 286	453 723	482 563
30 - 34	1 891 243	946 590	944 653	1 028 014	517 666	510 348	863 229	428 924	434 305
35 - 39	1 510 295	807 525	702 770	826 461	450 116	376 345	683 835	357 410	326 425
40 - 44	1 113 201	617 961	495 240	587 896	333 871	254 025	525 305	284 089	241 216
45 - 49	835 233	454 198	381 035	421 434	231 528	189 906	413 799	222 670	191 129
50 - 54	676 619	355 427	321 192	339 694	180 009	159 685	336 925	175 417	161 508
55 - 59	495 851	261 849	234 002	250 406	134 853	115 553	245 445	126 996	118 449
60 - 64	349 069	187 844	161 225	169 723	94 676	75 047	179 346	93 167	86 179
65 - 69	241 638	125 991	115 647	109 207	58 773	50 434	132 430	67 219	65 211
70 - 74	156 591	77 548	79 043	65 754	32 706	33 048	90 837	44 841	45 996
75 - 79	91 171	43 665	47 506	37 028	17 623	19 405	54 143	26 041	28 102
80 +	93 566	44 316	49 250	36 095	16 951	19 144	57 471	27 364	30 107
Egypt - Égypte									
1 VII 2014 (ESDF)									
Total	86 813 723	44 304 619	42 509 104	37 094 960	18 904 449	18 190 511	49 718 763	25 400 170	24 318 593
0 - 4	9 829 921	5 101 944	4 727 977	4 200 159	2 176 962	2 023 197	5 629 762	2 924 982	2 704 780
5 - 9	9 126 024	4 728 899	4 397 125	3 899 406	2 017 786	1 881 620	5 226 618	2 711 113	2 515 505
10 - 14	8 183 738	4 224 190	3 959 548	3 496 802	1 802 431	1 694 371	4 686 936	2 421 759	2 265 177
15 - 19	8 388 912	4 311 966	4 076 946	3 584 492	1 839 884	1 744 608	4 804 420	2 472 082	2 332 338
20 - 24	8 929 427	4 564 320	4 365 107	3 815 480	1 947 562	1 867 918	5 113 947	2 616 758	2 497 189
25 - 29	8 398 687	4 279 050	4 119 637	3 588 716	1 825 839	1 762 877	4 809 971	2 453 211	2 356 760
30 - 34	6 731 457	3 412 268	3 319 189	2 876 338	1 455 990	1 420 348	3 855 119	1 956 278	1 898 841
35 - 39	5 281 272	2 677 149	2 604 123	2 256 677	1 142 319	1 114 358	3 024 595	1 534 830	1 489 765
40 - 44	4 739 858	2 391 878	2 347 980	2 025 344	1 020 596	1 004 748	2 714 514	1 371 282	1 343 232
45 - 49	4 350 256	2 194 384	2 155 872	1 858 868	936 327	922 541	2 491 388	1 258 057	1 233 331
50 - 54	3 776 526	1 898 142	1 878 384	1 613 721	809 922	803 799	2 162 805	1 088 220	1 074 585
55 - 59	3 083 900	1 547 040	1 536 860	1 317 764	660 110	657 654	1 766 136	886 930	879 206
60 - 64	2 261 407	1 130 107	1 131 300	966 314	482 208	484 106	1 295 093	647 899	647 194
65 - 69	1 590 425	789 978	800 447	679 605	337 077	342 528	910 820	452 901	457 919

Continent, country or area, date, code[a] and age (in years) / Continent, pays ou zone, date, code[a] et âge (en années)	Total			Urban - Urbaine			Rural - Rurale		
	Both sexes Les deux sexes	Male Masculin	Female Féminin	Both sexes Les deux sexes	Male Masculin	Female Féminin	Both sexes Les deux sexes	Male Masculin	Female Féminin
AFRICA - AFRIQUE									
Egypt - Égypte									
1 VII 2014 (ESDF)									
70 - 74	1 049 312	515 680	533 632	448 388	220 036	228 352	600 924	295 644	305 280
75 +	1 092 601	537 624	554 977	466 886	229 400	237 486	625 715	308 224	317 491
1 VII 2016 (ESDF)									
Total	91 023 393	46 413 993	44 609 400	...	...	...	...	...	...
0	1 994 691	1 035 143	959 548	...	...	...	...	...	...
1 - 4	7 878 480	4 088 160	3 790 320	...	...	...	...	...	...
5 - 9	9 676 887	5 019 570	4 657 318	...	...	...	...	...	...
10 - 14	8 493 784	4 393 898	4 099 886	...	...	...	...	...	...
15 - 19	8 120 941	4 181 689	3 939 252	...	...	...	...	...	...
20 - 24	8 587 539	4 399 358	4 188 182	...	...	...	...	...	...
25 - 29	8 811 200	4 492 171	4 319 029	...	...	...	...	...	...
30 - 34	7 741 343	3 926 555	3 814 788	...	...	...	...	...	...
35 - 39	5 984 523	3 024 359	2 960 163	...	...	...	...	...	...
40 - 44	4 917 008	2 483 033	2 433 975	...	...	...	...	...	...
45 - 49	4 514 811	2 273 384	2 241 427	...	...	...	...	...	...
50 - 54	4 041 503	2 028 793	2 012 710	...	...	...	...	...	...
55 - 59	3 385 966	1 689 205	1 696 761	...	...	...	...	...	...
60 - 64	2 602 262	1 288 469	1 313 793	...	...	...	...	...	...
65 - 69	1 810 076	888 825	921 251	...	...	...	...	...	...
70 - 74	1 191 496	579 811	611 685	...	...	...	...	...	...
75 +	1 145 511	563 165	582 346	...	...	...	...	...	...
Unknown - Inconnu	125 371	58 406	66 965	...	...	...	...	...	...
Ethiopia - Éthiopie									
29 V 2007 (CDFC)									
Total	73 750 932	37 217 130	36 533 802	11 862 821	5 895 916	5 966 905	61 888 111	31 321 214	30 566 897
0 - 4	10 797 022	5 482 792	5 314 230	1 170 955	596 105	574 850	9 626 067	4 886 687	4 739 380
5 - 9	11 981 764	6 106 788	5 874 976	1 287 441	640 097	647 344	10 694 323	5 466 691	5 227 632
10 - 14	10 412 237	5 412 324	4 999 913	1 369 665	658 283	711 382	9 042 572	4 754 041	4 288 531
15 - 19	8 748 048	4 454 710	4 293 338	1 947 281	935 230	1 012 051	6 800 767	3 519 480	3 281 287
20 - 24	6 402 085	3 098 338	3 303 747	1 509 343	750 712	758 631	4 892 742	2 347 626	2 545 116
25 - 29	5 662 188	2 622 759	3 039 429	1 230 544	596 293	634 251	4 431 644	2 026 466	2 405 178
30 - 34	4 220 066	2 088 208	2 131 858	815 179	432 721	382 458	3 404 887	1 655 487	1 749 400
35 - 39	3 776 642	1 827 296	1 949 346	694 895	356 496	338 399	3 081 747	1 470 800	1 610 947
40 - 44	2 872 980	1 464 529	1 408 451	473 929	259 968	213 961	2 399 051	1 204 561	1 194 490
45 - 49	2 247 304	1 150 017	1 097 287	364 212	189 159	175 053	1 883 092	960 858	922 234
50 - 54	1 890 766	928 294	962 472	288 617	138 190	150 427	1 602 149	790 104	812 045
55 - 59	1 171 020	634 053	536 967	178 579	89 368	89 211	992 441	544 685	447 756
60 - 64	1 235 000	646 359	588 641	178 561	84 582	93 979	1 056 439	561 777	494 662
65 - 69	805 261	446 242	359 019	121 149	59 539	61 610	684 112	386 703	297 409
70 - 74	676 560	359 897	316 663	103 889	47 688	56 201	572 671	312 209	260 462
75 - 79	350 176	203 843	146 333	53 212	26 863	26 349	296 964	176 980	119 984
80 - 84	287 477	159 786	127 691	42 749	18 737	24 012	244 728	141 049	103 679
85 - 89	100 196	62 001	38 195	16 149	8 301	7 848	84 047	53 700	30 347
90 - 94	64 542	38 185	26 357	10 215	4 646	5 569	54 327	33 539	20 788
95 +	49 598	30 709	18 889	6 257	2 938	3 319	43 341	27 771	15 570
Ghana[7]									
1 VII 2015 (ESDF)									
Total	27 670 174	13 562 093	14 108 081	13 817 894	6 903 107	6 914 787	13 852 280	6 658 986	7 193 294
0	841 301	425 611	415 690	403 605	195 150	208 455	437 696	230 461	207 235
1 - 4	3 158 109	1 595 165	1 562 944	1 513 925	731 409	782 516	1 644 184	863 756	780 428
5 - 9	3 312 878	1 688 452	1 624 426	1 579 799	755 911	823 888	1 733 079	932 541	800 538
10 - 14	3 097 352	1 567 043	1 530 309	1 538 503	749 266	789 237	1 558 849	817 777	741 072
15 - 19	2 825 578	1 414 987	1 410 591	1 458 024	735 981	722 043	1 367 554	679 006	688 548
20 - 24	2 537 799	1 251 759	1 286 040	1 377 177	736 425	640 752	1 160 622	515 334	645 288
25 - 29	2 252 493	1 083 877	1 168 616	1 211 633	636 338	575 295	1 040 860	447 539	593 321
30 - 34	1 967 166	935 947	1 031 219	1 014 879	537 402	477 477	952 287	398 545	553 742
35 - 39	1 665 237	785 200	880 037	840 000	437 656	402 344	825 237	347 544	477 693
40 - 44	1 404 309	661 789	742 520	703 098	362 522	340 576	701 211	299 267	401 944
45 - 49	1 145 932	546 030	599 902	560 013	275 131	284 882	585 919	270 899	315 020
50 - 54	933 268	445 531	487 737	477 984	238 760	239 224	455 284	206 771	248 513
55 - 59	728 002	348 118	379 884	337 828	159 376	178 452	390 174	188 742	201 432
60 - 64	570 616	270 642	299 974	271 174	129 651	141 523	299 442	140 991	158 451
65 - 69	419 501	196 219	223 282	178 422	73 727	104 695	241 079	122 492	118 587

Continent, country or area, date, code[a] and age (in years) / Continent, pays ou zone, date, code[a] et âge (en années)	Total			Urban - Urbaine			Rural - Rurale		
	Both sexes Les deux sexes	Male Masculin	Female Féminin	Both sexes Les deux sexes	Male Masculin	Female Féminin	Both sexes Les deux sexes	Male Masculin	Female Féminin
AFRICA - AFRIQUE									
Ghana[7]									
1 VII 2015 (ESDF)									
70 - 74	313 256	142 378	170 878	149 542	68 333	81 209	163 714	74 045	89 669
75 - 79	223 087	96 514	126 573	90 638	36 406	54 232	132 449	60 108	72 341
80 +	274 290	106 831	167 459	111 650	43 663	67 987	162 640	63 168	99 472
Guinea - Guinée									
15 III 2014 (CDFC)									
Total	10 523 261	5 084 306	5 438 955	3 657 122	1 821 369	1 835 753	6 866 139	3 262 937	3 603 202
0 - 4	1 764 144	890 034	874 110	505 275	254 440	250 835	1 258 869	635 594	623 275
5 - 9	1 699 838	863 214	836 624	488 932	241 360	247 572	1 210 906	621 854	589 052
10 - 14	1 235 102	626 512	608 590	440 827	210 959	229 868	794 275	415 553	378 722
15 - 19	1 108 604	520 540	588 064	468 375	226 124	242 251	640 229	294 416	345 813
20 - 24	906 043	409 385	496 658	435 177	215 462	219 715	470 866	193 923	276 943
25 - 29	782 764	338 166	444 598	321 174	156 550	164 624	461 590	181 616	279 974
30 - 34	630 979	277 205	353 774	241 547	119 817	121 730	389 432	157 388	232 044
35 - 39	512 080	227 303	284 777	182 166	91 481	90 685	329 914	135 822	194 092
40 - 44	437 765	200 650	237 115	150 077	77 979	72 098	287 688	122 671	165 017
45 - 49	328 431	159 533	168 898	107 955	57 478	50 477	220 476	102 055	118 421
50 - 54	298 035	146 067	151 968	92 750	49 856	42 894	205 285	96 211	109 074
55 - 59	211 335	114 646	96 689	67 633	38 018	29 615	143 702	76 628	67 074
60 - 64	204 766	105 390	99 376	59 014	33 468	25 546	145 752	71 922	73 830
65 - 69	127 396	68 065	59 331	33 804	18 584	15 220	93 592	49 481	44 111
70 - 74	116 721	56 862	59 859	28 015	14 135	13 880	88 706	42 727	45 979
75 - 79	63 846	33 920	29 926	14 523	7 371	7 152	49 323	26 549	22 774
80 - 84	50 980	24 678	26 302	10 848	4 760	6 088	40 132	19 918	20 214
85 - 89	20 725	10 788	9 937	4 127	1 795	2 332	16 598	8 993	7 605
90 - 94	11 747	5 631	6 116	2 532	936	1 596	9 215	4 695	4 520
95 +	11 960	5 717	6 243	2 371	796	1 575	9 589	4 921	4 668
Guinea-Bissau - Guinée-Bissau[2]									
1 VII 2016 (ESDF)									
Total	1 547 777	759 666	788 111	659 138	323 512	335 626	888 639	436 154	452 485
0 - 4	269 444	137 948	131 496	94 949	47 138	47 811	174 495	90 810	83 685
5 - 9	215 817	109 491	106 326	79 346	37 773	41 573	136 471	71 718	64 753
10 - 14	187 811	94 320	93 491	80 604	37 519	43 085	107 207	56 801	50 406
15 - 19	162 179	81 815	80 364	78 714	38 866	39 848	83 465	42 949	40 516
20 - 24	148 027	73 767	74 260	76 552	39 614	36 938	71 475	34 153	37 322
25 - 29	131 987	63 514	68 473	64 453	32 944	31 509	67 534	30 570	36 964
30 - 34	115 408	53 601	61 807	55 985	27 603	28 382	59 423	25 998	33 425
35 - 39	84 460	39 105	45 355	37 434	18 349	19 085	47 026	20 756	26 270
40 - 44	63 176	29 175	34 001	28 544	14 067	14 477	34 632	15 108	19 524
45 - 49	48 276	22 161	26 115	20 566	10 031	10 535	27 710	12 130	15 580
50 - 54	38 825	17 920	20 905	15 837	7 929	7 908	22 988	9 991	12 997
55 - 59	29 961	13 484	16 477	11 184	5 190	5 994	18 777	8 294	10 483
60 - 64	19 202	9 020	10 182	6 158	2 965	3 193	13 044	6 055	6 989
65 - 69	14 036	6 641	7 395	4 173	1 901	2 272	9 863	4 740	5 123
70 - 74	9 043	3 909	5 134	2 419	971	1 448	6 624	2 938	3 686
75 - 79	5 038	1 967	3 071	1 196	383	813	3 842	1 584	2 258
80 +	5 087	1 828	3 259	1 024	269	755	4 063	1 559	2 504
Kenya									
24 VIII 2009 (CDFC)									
Total	38 610 097	19 192 458	19 417 639	12 487 375	6 278 811	6 208 564	26 122 722	12 913 647	13 209 075
0	1 221 937	616 843	605 094	388 883	195 861	193 022	833 054	420 982	412 072
1 - 4	4 717 369	2 383 596	2 333 773	1 350 368	679 969	670 399	3 367 001	1 703 627	1 663 374
5 - 9	5 597 716	2 832 669	2 765 047	1 484 285	742 473	741 812	4 113 431	2 090 196	2 023 235
10 - 14	5 034 855	2 565 313	2 469 542	1 312 671	650 438	662 233	3 722 184	1 914 875	1 807 309
15 - 19	4 169 543	2 123 653	2 045 890	1 244 054	587 384	656 670	2 925 489	1 536 269	1 389 220
20 - 24	3 775 103	1 754 105	2 020 998	1 572 026	708 458	863 568	2 203 077	1 045 647	1 157 430
25 - 29	3 201 226	1 529 116	1 672 110	1 442 798	715 957	726 841	1 758 428	813 159	945 269
30 - 34	2 519 506	1 257 035	1 262 471	1 056 483	568 615	487 868	1 463 023	688 420	774 603
35 - 39	2 008 632	1 004 361	1 004 271	785 390	431 054	354 336	1 223 242	573 307	649 935
40 - 44	1 476 169	743 594	732 575	533 174	297 202	235 972	942 995	446 392	496 603
45 - 49	1 272 745	635 276	637 469	422 941	235 467	187 474	849 804	399 809	449 995
50 - 54	956 206	478 346	477 860	286 074	159 814	126 260	670 132	318 532	351 600
55 - 59	711 953	359 466	352 497	187 793	103 563	84 230	524 160	255 903	268 257

7. Population by age, sex and urban/rural residence: latest available year, 2007 - 2016
Population selon l'âge, le sexe et la résidence, urbaine/rurale : dernière année disponible, 2007 - 2016 (continued - suite)

Continent, country or area, date, code[a] and age (in years) / Continent, pays ou zone, date, code[a] et âge (en années)	Total			Urban - Urbaine			Rural - Rurale		
	Both sexes Les deux sexes	Male Masculin	Female Féminin	Both sexes Les deux sexes	Male Masculin	Female Féminin	Both sexes Les deux sexes	Male Masculin	Female Féminin
AFRICA - AFRIQUE									
Kenya									
24 VIII 2009 (CDFC)									
60 - 64	593 778	295 197	298 581	139 271	73 800	65 471	454 507	221 397	233 110
65 - 69	390 763	183 151	207 612	83 728	41 299	42 429	307 035	141 852	165 183
70 - 74	339 301	160 301	179 000	68 868	32 691	36 177	270 433	127 610	142 823
75 - 79	218 508	99 833	118 675	42 247	19 276	22 971	176 261	80 557	95 704
80 +	383 701	159 125	224 576	77 003	30 335	46 668	306 698	128 790	177 908
Unknown - Inconnu	21 086	11 478	9 608	9 318	5 155	4 163	11 768	6 323	5 445
1 VII 2015 (ESDF)[8]									
Total	44 156 577	21 886 677	22 269 900	...	...	...	...	...	...
0 - 4	6 946 690	3 491 366	3 455 324	...	...	...	...	...	...
5 - 9	5 924 556	2 977 388	2 947 168	...	...	...	...	...	...
10 - 14	5 365 714	2 715 828	2 649 886	...	...	...	...	...	...
15 - 19	4 728 580	2 402 893	2 325 687	...	...	...	...	...	...
20 - 24	4 187 603	2 089 984	2 097 619	...	...	...	...	...	...
25 - 29	3 759 730	1 768 197	1 991 533	...	...	...	...	...	...
30 - 34	3 175 347	1 482 860	1 692 487	...	...	...	...	...	...
35 - 39	2 485 531	1 231 737	1 253 794	...	...	...	...	...	...
40 - 44	1 957 504	986 283	971 221	...	...	...	...	...	...
45 - 49	1 492 719	744 234	748 485	...	...	...	...	...	...
50 - 54	1 147 031	569 551	577 480	...	...	...	...	...	...
55 - 59	895 558	443 166	452 392	...	...	...	...	...	...
60 - 64	678 610	333 501	345 109	...	...	...	...	...	...
65 - 69	503 686	241 391	262 295	...	...	...	...	...	...
70 - 74	354 701	166 085	188 616	...	...	...	...	...	...
75 - 79	240 330	109 728	130 602	...	...	...	...	...	...
80 +	312 687	132 485	180 202	...	...	...	...	...	...
Lesotho[2]									
1 VII 2016 (ESDF)									
Total	1 932 814	924 622	1 008 192	...	...	...	...	...	...
0 - 4	260 336	130 294	130 042	...	...	...	...	...	...
5 - 9	254 269	126 766	127 503	...	...	...	...	...	...
10 - 14	192 984	96 616	96 368	...	...	...	...	...	...
15 - 19	203 003	102 066	100 937	...	...	...	...	...	...
20 - 24	205 484	102 368	103 116	...	...	...	...	...	...
25 - 29	193 135	94 097	99 038	...	...	...	...	...	...
30 - 34	157 527	74 785	82 742	...	...	...	...	...	...
35 - 39	111 145	52 138	59 007	...	...	...	...	...	...
40 - 44	73 576	33 610	39 966	...	...	...	...	...	...
45 - 49	53 803	22 794	31 009	...	...	...	...	...	...
50 - 54	47 229	19 025	28 204	...	...	...	...	...	...
55 - 59	43 939	17 711	26 228	...	...	...	...	...	...
60 - 64	39 411	16 084	23 327	...	...	...	...	...	...
65 - 69	32 038	13 137	18 901	...	...	...	...	...	...
70 - 74	24 270	9 700	14 570	...	...	...	...	...	...
75 - 79	21 167	7 609	13 558	...	...	...	...	...	...
80 +	19 498	5 822	13 676	...	...	...	...	...	...
Liberia - Libéria									
21 III 2008 (CDFC)									
Total	3 476 608	1 739 945	1 736 663	...	...	...	...	...	...
0 - 4	534 475	270 564	263 911	...	...	...	...	...	...
5 - 9	501 931	251 411	250 520	...	...	...	...	...	...
10 - 14	421 666	214 859	206 807	...	...	...	...	...	...
15 - 19	375 695	189 407	186 288	...	...	...	...	...	...
20 - 24	342 930	161 951	180 979	...	...	...	...	...	...
25 - 29	291 858	141 006	150 852	...	...	...	...	...	...
30 - 34	219 632	107 326	112 306	...	...	...	...	...	...
35 - 39	203 536	99 136	104 400	...	...	...	...	...	...
40 - 44	155 737	81 670	74 067	...	...	...	...	...	...
45 - 49	118 807	63 827	54 980	...	...	...	...	...	...
50 - 54	82 940	44 870	38 070	...	...	...	...	...	...
55 - 59	56 460	30 975	25 485	...	...	...	...	...	...
60 - 64	52 830	25 473	27 357	...	...	...	...	...	...
65 - 69	39 807	19 250	20 557	...	...	...	...	...	...
70 - 74	25 746	12 343	13 403	...	...	...	...	...	...

Continent, country or area, date, code[a] and age (in years) Continent, pays ou zone, date, code[a] et âge (en années)	Total			Urban - Urbaine			Rural - Rurale		
	Both sexes Les deux sexes	Male Masculin	Female Féminin	Both sexes Les deux sexes	Male Masculin	Female Féminin	Both sexes Les deux sexes	Male Masculin	Female Féminin
AFRICA - AFRIQUE									
Liberia - Libéria									
21 III 2008 (CDFC)									
75 - 79	22 913	11 580	11 333	...	...	...	...	...	...
80 - 84	12 007	5 408	6 599	...	...	...	...	...	...
85 +	17 638	8 889	8 749	...	...	...	...	...	...
Libya - Libye[9]									
1 VII 2015 (ESDF)									
Total	6 162 247	3 129 026	3 033 221	...	...	...	...	...	...
0 - 4	615 556	316 497	299 059	...	...	...	...	...	...
5 - 9	577 905	297 303	280 602	...	...	...	...	...	...
10 - 14	555 149	284 318	270 831	...	...	...	...	...	...
15 - 19	525 115	268 106	257 009	...	...	...	...	...	...
20 - 24	546 408	278 875	267 533	...	...	...	...	...	...
25 - 29	571 230	289 113	282 117	...	...	...	...	...	...
30 - 34	568 834	287 480	281 354	...	...	...	...	...	...
35 - 39	551 606	279 699	271 907	...	...	...	...	...	...
40 - 44	466 373	235 088	231 285	...	...	...	...	...	...
45 - 49	360 825	180 029	180 796	...	...	...	...	...	...
50 - 54	253 647	126 799	126 848	...	...	...	...	...	...
55 - 59	173 760	87 135	86 625	...	...	...	...	...	...
60 - 64	116 033	56 199	59 834	...	...	...	...	...	...
65 - 69	102 645	51 782	50 863	...	...	...	...	...	...
70 - 74	72 486	38 750	33 736	...	...	...	...	...	...
75 - 79	52 558	26 942	25 616	...	...	...	...	...	...
80 - 84	30 271	15 038	15 233	...	...	...	...	...	...
85 +	21 846	9 873	11 973	...	...	...	...	...	...
Malawi									
8 VI 2008 (CDFC)									
Total	13 077 160	6 358 933	6 718 227	2 003 309	1 014 477	988 832	11 073 851	5 344 456	5 729 395
0	503 385	247 809	255 576	67 264	33 375	33 889	436 121	214 434	221 687
1 - 4	1 866 626	922 138	944 488	248 703	122 976	125 727	1 617 923	799 162	818 761
5 - 9	1 968 299	972 307	995 992	261 838	127 930	133 908	1 706 461	844 377	862 084
10 - 14	1 670 391	826 076	844 315	232 203	110 545	121 658	1 438 188	715 531	722 657
15 - 19	1 276 692	625 664	651 028	218 307	105 746	112 561	1 058 385	519 918	538 467
20 - 24	1 240 329	554 799	685 530	248 790	117 648	131 142	991 539	437 151	554 388
25 - 29	1 102 976	530 103	572 873	236 512	122 761	113 751	866 464	407 342	459 122
30 - 34	827 547	417 599	409 948	162 061	91 637	70 424	665 486	325 962	339 524
35 - 39	623 330	323 643	299 687	105 572	61 564	44 008	517 758	262 079	255 679
40 - 44	441 231	218 546	222 685	67 267	37 061	30 206	373 964	181 485	192 479
45 - 49	343 190	167 285	175 905	47 706	25 811	21 895	295 484	141 474	154 010
50 - 54	269 634	126 778	142 856	33 849	18 400	15 449	235 785	108 378	127 407
55 - 59	258 214	122 616	135 598	26 253	14 525	11 728	231 961	108 091	123 870
60 - 64	184 679	87 008	97 671	16 622	9 256	7 366	168 057	77 752	90 305
65 - 69	153 829	72 038	81 791	11 298	6 217	5 081	142 531	65 821	76 710
70 - 74	106 020	46 481	59 539	6 992	3 573	3 419	99 028	42 908	56 120
75 - 79	106 769	46 003	60 766	5 629	2 769	2 860	101 140	43 234	57 906
80 - 84	55 970	21 945	34 025	2 926	1 262	1 664	53 044	20 683	32 361
85 - 89	40 784	16 680	24 104	1 895	818	1 077	38 889	15 862	23 027
90 - 94	18 739	6 967	11 772	780	323	457	17 959	6 644	11 315
95 +	18 526	6 448	12 078	842	280	562	17 684	6 168	11 516
1 VII 2016 (ESDF)[2]									
Total	16 832 910	8 272 152	8 560 758	...	...	...	...	...	...
0	671 720	340 496	331 224	...	...	...	...	...	...
1 - 4	2 422 973	1 230 512	1 192 461	...	...	...	...	...	...
5 - 9	2 552 762	1 281 823	1 270 939	...	...	...	...	...	...
10 - 14	2 143 289	1 057 905	1 085 384	...	...	...	...	...	...
15 - 19	1 811 043	888 033	923 010	...	...	...	...	...	...
20 - 24	1 495 820	729 550	766 270	...	...	...	...	...	...
25 - 29	1 253 796	607 734	646 062	...	...	...	...	...	...
30 - 34	1 039 216	499 637	539 579	...	...	...	...	...	...
35 - 39	841 126	405 449	435 677	...	...	...	...	...	...
40 - 44	669 608	323 674	345 934	...	...	...	...	...	...
45 - 49	515 517	248 311	267 206	...	...	...	...	...	...
50 - 54	380 651	183 468	197 183	...	...	...	...	...	...
55 - 59	296 075	140 581	155 494	...	...	...	...	...	...

7. Population by age, sex and urban/rural residence: latest available year, 2007 - 2016
Population selon l'âge, le sexe et la résidence, urbaine/rurale : dernière année disponible, 2007 - 2016 (continued - suite)

Continent, country or area, date, code[a] and age (in years) / Continent, pays ou zone, date, code[a] et âge (en annèes)	Total			Urban - Urbaine			Rural - Rurale		
	Both sexes Les deux sexes	Male Masculin	Female Féminin	Both sexes Les deux sexes	Male Masculin	Female Féminin	Both sexes Les deux sexes	Male Masculin	Female Féminin
AFRICA - AFRIQUE									
Malawi									
1 VII 2016 (ESDF)[2]									
60 - 64	226 409	104 599	121 810	...	...	...	...	...	...
65 - 69	173 220	78 337	94 883	...	...	...	...	...	...
70 - 74	129 016	57 500	71 516	...	...	...	...	...	...
75 - 79	91 842	39 462	52 380	...	...	...	...	...	...
80 +	118 827	55 081	63 746	...	...	...	...	...	...
Mali									
1 IV 2009 (CDFC)									
Total	14 528 662	7 204 990	7 323 672	3 274 727	1 643 671	1 631 056	11 253 935	5 561 319	5 692 616
0 - 4	2 623 385	1 328 871	1 294 514	501 628	253 735	247 893	2 121 757	1 075 136	1 046 621
5 - 9	2 357 823	1 202 875	1 154 948	438 784	220 467	218 317	1 919 039	982 408	936 631
10 - 14	1 784 004	918 866	865 138	382 494	183 203	199 291	1 401 510	735 663	665 847
15 - 19	1 516 146	732 526	783 620	427 554	194 158	233 396	1 088 592	538 368	550 224
20 - 24	1 141 903	529 535	612 368	341 272	171 703	169 569	800 631	357 832	442 799
25 - 29	995 702	449 099	546 603	267 899	132 127	135 772	727 803	316 972	410 831
30 - 34	812 798	385 003	427 795	206 544	109 060	97 484	606 254	275 943	330 311
35 - 39	651 949	325 055	326 894	164 783	89 830	74 953	487 166	235 225	251 941
40 - 44	546 603	271 239	275 364	128 845	70 127	58 718	417 758	201 112	216 646
45 - 49	445 887	228 626	217 261	103 042	56 502	46 540	342 845	172 124	170 721
50 - 54	381 806	189 424	192 382	82 013	44 826	37 187	299 793	144 598	155 195
55 - 59	282 677	148 594	134 083	57 960	31 957	26 003	224 717	116 637	108 080
60 - 64	251 018	127 557	123 461	46 442	23 790	22 652	204 576	103 767	100 809
65 - 69	165 374	88 292	77 082	30 159	15 641	14 518	135 215	72 651	62 564
70 - 74	133 382	67 319	66 063	23 729	11 518	12 211	109 653	55 801	53 852
75 - 79	77 101	40 904	36 197	12 871	6 306	6 565	64 230	34 598	29 632
80 +	85 594	41 992	43 602	14 246	6 009	8 237	71 348	35 983	35 365
Unknown - Inconnu	275 510	129 213	146 297	44 462	22 712	21 750	231 048	106 501	124 547
1 VII 2014* (ESDF)[10]									
Total	17 319 000	8 671 000	8 648 000	...	...	...	...	...	...
0 - 4	3 182 000	1 624 000	1 559 000	...	...	...	...	...	...
5 - 9	2 685 000	1 370 000	1 315 000	...	...	...	...	...	...
10 - 14	2 255 000	1 150 000	1 104 000	...	...	...	...	...	...
15 - 19	1 867 000	952 000	915 000	...	...	...	...	...	...
20 - 24	1 534 000	778 000	756 000	...	...	...	...	...	...
25 - 29	1 298 000	656 000	641 000	...	...	...	...	...	...
30 - 34	1 101 000	554 000	547 000	...	...	...	...	...	...
35 - 39	896 000	446 000	451 000	...	...	...	...	...	...
40 - 44	699 000	342 000	358 000	...	...	...	...	...	...
45 - 49	522 000	248 000	275 000	...	...	...	...	...	...
50 - 54	384 000	175 000	209 000	...	...	...	...	...	...
55 - 59	296 000	129 000	167 000	...	...	...	...	...	...
60 - 64	232 000	101 000	131 000	...	...	...	...	...	...
65 - 69	163 000	67 000	96 000	...	...	...	...	...	...
70 - 74	119 000	49 000	70 000	...	...	...	...	...	...
75 - 79	56 000	22 000	34 000	...	...	...	...	...	...
80 +	31 000	12 000	19 000	...	...	...	...	...	...
Mauritania - Mauritanie[2]									
1 VII 2016 (ESDF)									
Total	3 782 701	...	...	...	...	...	...	...	...
0 - 4	579 832	...	...	...	...	...	...	...	...
5 - 9	567 643	...	...	...	...	...	...	...	...
10 - 14	478 293	...	...	...	...	...	...	...	...
15 - 19	396 650	...	...	...	...	...	...	...	...
20 - 24	333 473	...	...	...	...	...	...	...	...
25 - 29	280 531	...	...	...	...	...	...	...	...
30 - 34	236 864	...	...	...	...	...	...	...	...
35 - 39	196 168	...	...	...	...	...	...	...	...
40 - 44	164 707	...	...	...	...	...	...	...	...
45 - 49	137 439	...	...	...	...	...	...	...	...
50 - 54	111 936	...	...	...	...	...	...	...	...
55 - 59	90 008	...	...	...	...	...	...	...	...
60 - 64	68 836	...	...	...	...	...	...	...	...
65 - 69	50 266	...	...	...	...	...	...	...	...
70 - 74	36 188	...	...	...	...	...	...	...	...

7. Population by age, sex and urban/rural residence: latest available year, 2007 - 2016
Population selon l'âge, le sexe et la résidence, urbaine/rurale : dernière année disponible, 2007 - 2016 (continued - suite)

Continent, country or area, date, code[a] and age (in years) / Continent, pays ou zone, date, code[a] et âge (en années)	Total			Urban - Urbaine			Rural - Rurale		
	Both sexes Les deux sexes	Male Masculin	Female Féminin	Both sexes Les deux sexes	Male Masculin	Female Féminin	Both sexes Les deux sexes	Male Masculin	Female Féminin
AFRICA - AFRIQUE									
Mauritania - Mauritanie[2]									
1 VII 2016 (ESDF)									
75 - 79	*24 540*	...	...	...	...	...	...	...	...
80 +	*29 328*	...	...	...	...	...	...	...	...
Mauritius - Maurice[11]									
4 VII 2011 (CDJC)									
Total	1 236 817	610 848	625 969	499 349	244 688	254 661	737 468	366 160	371 308
0 - 4	73 078	36 702	36 376	26 297	13 220	13 077	46 781	23 482	23 299
5 - 9	89 015	44 947	44 068	32 036	16 177	15 859	56 979	28 770	28 209
10 - 14	93 639	47 302	46 337	35 028	17 523	17 505	58 611	29 779	28 832
15 - 19	101 008	50 715	50 293	39 403	19 725	19 678	61 605	30 990	30 615
20 - 24	92 671	46 871	45 800	37 224	18 836	18 388	55 447	28 035	27 412
25 - 29	90 937	45 589	45 348	35 908	17 899	18 009	55 029	27 690	27 339
30 - 34	103 429	52 182	51 247	39 099	19 805	19 294	64 330	32 377	31 953
35 - 39	87 797	44 241	43 556	32 781	16 142	16 639	55 016	28 099	26 917
40 - 44	89 386	45 150	44 236	34 449	17 010	17 439	54 937	28 140	26 797
45 - 49	99 341	49 800	49 541	41 705	20 637	21 068	57 636	29 163	28 473
50 - 54	86 337	42 996	43 341	37 429	18 627	18 802	48 908	24 369	24 539
55 - 59	73 054	35 713	37 341	32 421	15 983	16 438	40 633	19 730	20 903
60 - 64	57 342	27 143	30 199	25 449	12 058	13 391	31 893	15 085	16 808
65 - 69	35 439	15 846	19 593	16 700	7 527	9 173	18 739	8 319	10 420
70 - 74	25 375	10 986	14 389	12 872	5 661	7 211	12 503	5 325	7 178
75 - 79	18 044	7 349	10 695	9 320	3 851	5 469	8 724	3 498	5 226
80 - 84	11 369	4 176	7 193	6 028	2 253	3 775	5 341	1 923	3 418
85 - 89	6 368	2 135	4 233	3 427	1 179	2 248	2 941	956	1 985
90 - 94	1 982	512	1 470	1 046	275	771	936	237	699
95 - 99	491	107	384	297	60	237	194	47	147
100 +	96	13	83	55	7	48	41	6	35
Unknown - Inconnu	619	373	246	375	233	142	244	140	104
1 VII 2016 (ESDJ)[12]									
Total	1 263 473	625 206	638 267	...	...	...	...	...	...
0	12 697	6 509	6 188	...	...	...	...	...	...
1 - 4	54 789	27 879	26 910	...	...	...	...	...	...
5 - 9	78 486	39 671	38 815	...	...	...	...	...	...
10 - 14	94 275	47 895	46 380	...	...	...	...	...	...
15 - 19	98 223	49 953	48 270	...	...	...	...	...	...
20 - 24	99 416	50 014	49 402	...	...	...	...	...	...
25 - 29	90 599	45 922	44 677	...	...	...	...	...	...
30 - 34	88 615	44 580	44 035	...	...	...	...	...	...
35 - 39	100 464	50 986	49 478	...	...	...	...	...	...
40 - 44	85 228	43 122	42 106	...	...	...	...	...	...
45 - 49	86 845	43 836	43 009	...	...	...	...	...	...
50 - 54	96 295	47 863	48 432	...	...	...	...	...	...
55 - 59	82 726	40 647	42 079	...	...	...	...	...	...
60 - 64	68 576	32 860	35 716	...	...	...	...	...	...
65 - 69	52 148	23 985	28 163	...	...	...	...	...	...
70 - 74	30 632	13 170	17 462	...	...	...	...	...	...
75 - 79	20 472	8 376	12 096	...	...	...	...	...	...
80 - 84	12 837	4 801	8 036	...	...	...	...	...	...
85 +	10 150	3 137	7 013	...	...	...	...	...	...
Mayotte									
1 I 2016* (ESDJ)									
Total	235 132	114 072	121 060	...	...	...	...	...	...
0 - 4	37 100	18 688	18 412	...	...	...	...	...	...
5 - 9	35 454	17 752	17 702	...	...	...	...	...	...
10 - 14	31 210	15 428	15 782	...	...	...	...	...	...
15 - 19	24 296	11 871	12 425	...	...	...	...	...	...
20 - 24	14 359	6 423	7 936	...	...	...	...	...	...
25 - 29	16 244	6 494	9 750	...	...	...	...	...	...
30 - 34	17 154	7 305	9 849	...	...	...	...	...	...
35 - 39	15 959	7 323	8 636	...	...	...	...	...	...
40 - 44	12 864	6 796	6 068	...	...	...	...	...	...
45 - 49	8 515	4 440	4 075	...	...	...	...	...	...
50 - 54	6 884	3 621	3 263	...	...	...	...	...	...
55 - 59	5 283	2 882	2 401	...	...	...	...	...	...

Continent, country or area, date, code[a] and age (in years) / Continent, pays ou zone, date, code[a] et âge (en années)	Total			Urban - Urbaine			Rural - Rurale		
	Both sexes Les deux sexes	Male Masculin	Female Féminin	Both sexes Les deux sexes	Male Masculin	Female Féminin	Both sexes Les deux sexes	Male Masculin	Female Féminin

AFRICA - AFRIQUE

Mayotte
1 I 2016* (ESDJ)

60 - 64	3 665	2 033	1 632	...	...	...	...	...	...
65 - 69	2 250	1 147	1 103	...	...	...	...	...	...
70 - 74	1 683	837	846	...	...	...	...	...	...
75 - 79	1 012	515	497	...	...	...	...	...	...
80 - 84	670	288	382	...	...	...	...	...	...
85 - 89	277	121	156	...	...	...	...	...	...
90 - 94	179	83	96	...	...	...	...	...	...
95 + ...	74	25	49	...	...	...	...	...	...

Morocco - Maroc[13]
1 VII 2016 (ESDF)

Total..............................	34 486 536	17 180 879	17 305 657	21 154 782	10 445 229	10 709 553	13 331 754	6 735 650	6 596 104
0 - 4	3 290 297	1 682 558	1 607 739	1 872 220	957 156	915 064	1 418 077	725 402	692 675
5 - 9	3 135 807	1 600 430	1 535 377	1 770 389	903 588	866 801	1 365 418	696 842	668 576
10 - 14	3 032 113	1 549 765	1 482 348	1 700 125	867 499	832 626	1 331 988	682 266	649 722
15 - 19	3 006 335	1 520 962	1 485 373	1 725 696	867 861	857 835	1 280 639	653 101	627 538
20 - 24	3 039 330	1 511 786	1 527 544	1 861 811	910 251	951 560	1 177 519	601 535	575 984
25 - 29	2 904 798	1 431 657	1 473 141	1 838 585	889 373	949 212	1 066 213	542 284	523 929
30 - 34	2 693 230	1 321 224	1 372 006	1 722 385	833 754	888 631	970 845	487 470	483 375
35 - 39	2 458 449	1 195 261	1 263 188	1 582 198	755 607	826 591	876 251	439 654	436 597
40 - 44	2 237 586	1 089 022	1 148 564	1 462 406	700 306	762 100	775 180	388 716	386 464
45 - 49	1 930 384	940 143	990 241	1 289 997	620 288	669 709	640 387	319 855	320 532
50 - 54	1 813 238	884 733	928 505	1 212 980	590 094	622 886	600 258	294 639	305 619
55 - 59	1 534 387	774 866	759 521	1 023 245	518 325	504 920	511 142	256 541	254 601
60 - 64	1 219 656	626 965	592 691	789 956	411 050	378 906	429 700	215 915	213 785
65 - 69	790 533	397 367	393 166	491 866	249 139	242 727	298 667	148 228	150 439
70 - 74	569 081	266 366	302 715	334 043	154 527	179 516	235 038	111 839	123 199
75 - 79	363 321	175 054	188 267	215 963	101 115	114 848	147 358	73 939	73 419
80 + ...	467 991	212 720	255 271	260 917	115 296	145 621	207 074	97 424	109 650

Mozambique[2]
1 VII 2016 (ESDF)

Total..............................	26 423 623	12 760 324	13 663 299	8 468 799	4 136 950	4 331 849	17 954 824	8 623 374	9 331 450
0 - 4	4 488 579	2 242 913	2 245 666	1 137 245	567 670	569 575	3 351 334	1 675 243	1 676 091
5 - 9	3 887 850	1 934 192	1 953 658	1 081 934	538 340	543 594	2 805 916	1 395 852	1 410 064
10 - 14	3 440 428	1 714 530	1 725 898	1 063 955	525 773	538 182	2 376 473	1 188 757	1 187 716
15 - 19	2 855 113	1 424 691	1 430 422	1 011 028	498 406	512 622	1 844 085	926 285	917 800
20 - 24	2 387 826	1 130 273	1 257 553	926 736	456 867	469 869	1 461 090	673 406	787 684
25 - 29	1 979 926	883 470	1 096 456	773 136	368 762	404 374	1 206 790	514 708	692 082
30 - 34	1 640 284	735 359	904 925	612 114	285 298	326 816	1 028 170	450 061	578 109
35 - 39	1 322 562	618 251	704 311	481 849	229 003	252 846	840 713	389 248	451 465
40 - 44	1 100 207	515 857	584 350	383 265	184 758	198 507	716 942	331 099	385 843
45 - 49	886 898	418 970	467 928	299 002	146 237	152 765	587 896	272 733	315 163
50 - 54	672 320	333 389	338 931	212 399	107 721	104 678	459 921	225 668	234 253
55 - 59	538 851	255 875	282 976	164 411	81 334	83 077	374 440	174 541	199 899
60 - 64	415 687	189 013	226 674	117 630	56 515	61 115	298 057	132 498	165 559
65 - 69	311 935	142 282	169 653	84 370	39 728	44 642	227 565	102 554	125 011
70 - 74	219 152	99 755	119 397	54 595	24 310	30 285	164 557	75 445	89 112
75 - 79	142 461	63 913	78 548	34 189	14 521	19 668	108 272	49 392	58 880
80 + ...	133 544	57 591	75 953	30 941	11 707	19 234	102 603	45 884	56 719

Namibia - Namibie[14]
1 VII 2016 (ESDF)

Total..............................	2 324 388	1 129 754	1 194 634	1 112 868	542 893	569 975	1 211 520	586 861	624 659
0	66 823	33 831	32 992	32 962	16 685	16 277	33 861	17 146	16 715
1 - 4	255 102	128 949	126 153	119 055	60 166	58 889	136 047	68 783	67 264
5 - 9	284 647	143 496	141 151	103 417	51 936	51 481	181 230	91 560	89 670
10 - 14	239 623	120 339	119 284	85 172	41 836	43 336	154 451	78 503	75 948
15 - 19	242 819	120 328	122 491	92 958	43 427	49 531	149 861	76 901	72 960
20 - 24	234 097	114 753	119 344	109 437	50 181	59 256	124 660	64 572	60 088
25 - 29	208 797	102 475	106 322	137 218	66 473	70 745	71 579	36 002	35 577
30 - 34	168 854	81 979	86 875	115 220	56 957	58 263	53 634	25 022	28 612
35 - 39	140 133	68 080	72 053	88 757	44 304	44 453	51 376	23 776	27 600
40 - 44	116 501	55 781	60 720	67 931	33 789	34 142	48 570	21 992	26 578
45 - 49	90 798	42 449	48 349	50 197	24 950	25 247	40 601	17 499	23 102
50 - 54	74 259	33 595	40 664	37 995	19 210	18 785	36 264	14 385	21 879

Continent, country or area, date, code[a] and age (in years) / Continent, pays ou zone, date, code[a] et âge (en années)	Total			Urban - Urbaine			Rural - Rurale		
	Both sexes Les deux sexes	Male Masculin	Female Féminin	Both sexes Les deux sexes	Male Masculin	Female Féminin	Both sexes Les deux sexes	Male Masculin	Female Féminin
AFRICA - AFRIQUE									
Namibia - Namibie[14]									
1 VII 2016 (ESDF)									
55 - 59	56 074	24 109	31 965	26 843	13 023	13 820	29 231	11 086	18 145
60 - 64	42 602	18 328	24 274	17 599	8 458	9 141	25 003	9 870	15 133
65 - 69	35 195	15 298	19 897	11 057	4 835	6 222	24 138	10 463	13 675
70 - 74	25 233	10 232	15 001	6 813	2 833	3 980	18 420	7 399	11 021
75 - 79	17 264	6 967	10 297	4 666	1 848	2 818	12 598	5 119	7 479
80 +	25 567	8 765	16 802	5 571	1 982	3 589	19 996	6 783	13 213
Niger[15]									
1 VII 2016 (ESDJ)									
Total	19 865 067	9 898 628	9 966 439	3 242 161	1 617 882	1 624 278	16 622 906	8 280 747	8 342 160
0 - 4	3 966 109	2 009 845	1 956 264	560 061	281 015	279 046	3 406 048	1 728 830	1 677 218
5 - 9	3 533 085	1 810 213	1 722 872	514 367	259 802	254 565	3 018 718	1 550 412	1 468 306
10 - 14	2 790 727	1 418 659	1 372 068	450 479	223 341	227 137	2 340 248	1 195 317	1 144 931
15 - 19	2 021 025	1 010 216	1 010 809	344 569	173 980	170 589	1 676 456	836 236	840 220
20 - 24	1 619 917	777 760	842 157	316 826	159 697	157 130	1 303 090	618 063	685 027
25 - 29	1 236 640	592 643	643 996	220 452	107 039	113 413	1 016 188	485 605	530 583
30 - 34	1 013 696	493 232	520 464	186 768	91 960	94 808	826 927	401 271	425 656
35 - 39	845 916	404 801	441 115	153 624	74 733	78 891	692 293	330 068	362 225
40 - 44	679 710	326 886	352 824	123 978	61 940	62 037	555 732	264 946	290 786
45 - 49	544 473	267 053	277 420	98 818	50 233	48 585	445 656	216 820	228 836
50 - 54	460 236	223 786	236 450	81 307	40 036	41 271	378 929	183 750	195 179
55 - 59	351 487	174 412	177 075	62 257	30 864	31 393	289 230	143 548	145 681
60 - 64	264 109	129 848	134 261	45 097	22 523	22 574	219 012	107 324	111 687
65 - 69	192 038	94 284	97 754	31 661	15 974	15 688	160 376	78 310	82 066
70 - 74	145 168	69 830	75 338	22 937	11 136	11 801	122 231	58 694	63 537
75 - 79	99 975	48 349	51 626	15 105	7 379	7 725	84 870	40 970	43 900
80 +	100 757	46 811	53 946	13 855	6 229	7 626	86 902	40 582	46 320
Nigeria - Nigéria[16]									
1 VII 2016 (ESDF)									
Total	193 392 517	...	...	...	...	...	...	...	...
0 - 4	31 116 156	...	...	...	...	...	...	...	...
5 - 9	27 549 964	...	...	...	...	...	...	...	...
10 - 14	22 221 265	...	...	...	...	...	...	...	...
15 - 19	20 518 404	...	...	...	...	...	...	...	...
20 - 24	18 501 820	...	...	...	...	...	...	...	...
25 - 29	16 816 694	...	...	...	...	...	...	...	...
30 - 34	13 038 009	...	...	...	...	...	...	...	...
35 - 39	10 096 763	...	...	...	...	...	...	...	...
40 - 44	8 891 384	...	...	...	...	...	...	...	...
45 - 49	6 322 797	...	...	...	...	...	...	...	...
50 - 54	5 851 717	...	...	...	...	...	...	...	...
55 - 59	2 845 486	...	...	...	...	...	...	...	...
60 - 64	3 374 357	...	...	...	...	...	...	...	...
65 - 69	1 585 140	...	...	...	...	...	...	...	...
70 - 74	1 832 402	...	...	...	...	...	...	...	...
75 - 79	798 511	...	...	...	...	...	...	...	...
80 - 84	1 046 690	...	...	...	...	...	...	...	...
85 +	984 956	...	...	...	...	...	...	...	...
Republic of South Sudan - République de Soudan du Sud									
21 IV 2008 (CDFC)									
Total	8 260 490	4 287 300	3 973 190	1 405 186	754 086	651 100	6 855 304	3 533 214	3 322 090
0	231 146	121 882	109 264	43 300	22 617	20 683	187 846	99 265	88 581
1 - 4	1 072 985	567 545	505 440	174 976	91 509	83 467	898 009	476 036	421 973
5 - 9	1 297 816	688 385	609 431	196 136	101 760	94 376	1 101 680	586 625	515 055
10 - 14	1 057 390	569 537	487 853	160 054	84 981	75 073	897 336	484 556	412 780
15 - 19	889 829	462 902	426 927	153 683	81 602	72 081	736 146	381 300	354 846
20 - 24	739 006	360 788	378 218	148 237	78 336	69 901	590 769	282 452	308 317
25 - 29	698 011	335 398	362 613	141 623	76 445	65 178	556 388	258 953	297 435
30 - 34	536 915	258 531	278 384	101 597	56 705	44 892	435 318	201 826	233 492
35 - 39	475 813	238 985	236 828	87 844	49 346	38 498	387 969	189 639	198 330
40 - 44	339 704	173 493	166 211	58 645	33 444	25 201	281 059	140 049	141 010
45 - 49	276 100	149 941	126 159	45 605	26 316	19 289	230 495	123 625	106 870

7. Population by age, sex and urban/rural residence: latest available year, 2007 - 2016
Population selon l'âge, le sexe et la résidence, urbaine/rurale : dernière année disponible, 2007 - 2016 (continued - suite)

Continent, country or area, date, codeª and age (in years) / Continent, pays ou zone, date, codeª et âge (en années)	Total			Urban - Urbaine			Rural - Rurale		
	Both sexes Les deux sexes	Male Masculin	Female Féminin	Both sexes Les deux sexes	Male Masculin	Female Féminin	Both sexes Les deux sexes	Male Masculin	Female Féminin
AFRICA - AFRIQUE									
Republic of South Sudan - République de Soudan du Sud									
21 IV 2008 (CDFC)									
50 - 54	197 265	104 812	92 453	31 870	17 548	14 322	165 395	87 264	78 131
55 - 59	121 795	67 845	53 950	18 520	10 557	7 963	103 275	57 288	45 987
60 - 64	115 631	64 236	51 395	16 523	8 849	7 674	99 108	55 387	43 721
65 - 69	73 155	41 455	31 700	9 750	5 239	4 511	63 405	36 216	27 189
70 - 74	59 287	34 785	24 502	7 756	4 087	3 669	51 531	30 698	20 833
75 - 79	28 919	17 424	11 495	3 522	1 898	1 624	25 397	15 526	9 871
80 - 84	24 514	14 314	10 200	2 867	1 497	1 370	21 647	12 817	8 830
85 - 89	10 982	6 731	4 251	1 121	550	571	9 861	6 181	3 680
90 - 94	7 361	4 477	2 884	873	472	401	6 488	4 005	2 483
95 +	6 866	3 834	3 032	684	328	356	6 182	3 506	2 676
Reunion - Réunion									
1 I 2016* (ESDJ)									
Total	850 996	411 240	439 756	...	...	...	...	...	...
0 - 4	62 058	31 490	30 568	...	...	...	...	...	...
5 - 9	68 211	35 035	33 176	...	...	...	...	...	...
10 - 14	70 720	36 460	34 260	...	...	...	...	...	...
15 - 19	66 961	34 532	32 429	...	...	...	...	...	...
20 - 24	54 062	26 917	27 145	...	...	...	...	...	...
25 - 29	51 548	23 996	27 552	...	...	...	...	...	...
30 - 34	51 682	23 574	28 108	...	...	...	...	...	...
35 - 39	54 891	25 246	29 645	...	...	...	...	...	...
40 - 44	59 431	27 907	31 524	...	...	...	...	...	...
45 - 49	64 431	30 859	33 572	...	...	...	...	...	...
50 - 54	62 876	30 969	31 907	...	...	...	...	...	...
55 - 59	51 726	24 922	26 804	...	...	...	...	...	...
60 - 64	42 897	20 630	22 267	...	...	...	...	...	...
65 - 69	30 772	14 752	16 020	...	...	...	...	...	...
70 - 74	21 649	9 855	11 794	...	...	...	...	...	...
75 - 79	16 994	7 234	9 760	...	...	...	...	...	...
80 - 84	10 732	4 136	6 596	...	...	...	...	...	...
85 - 89	5 906	1 853	4 053	...	...	...	...	...	...
90 - 94	2 632	687	1 945	...	...	...	...	...	...
95 +	817	186	631	...	...	...	...	...	...
Rwanda[15]									
1 VII 2016 (ESDF)									
Total	11 533 445	5 582 519	5 950 925	2 214 421	1 071 844	1 142 578	9 319 023	4 510 676	4 808 348
0 - 4	1 595 359	803 509	791 850	274 345	129 742	144 603	1 321 014	673 767	647 247
5 - 9	1 515 688	754 747	760 941	234 799	109 785	125 013	1 280 889	644 961	635 928
10 - 14	1 468 321	728 814	739 507	240 567	110 610	129 956	1 227 754	618 203	609 551
15 - 19	1 211 694	596 017	615 677	242 204	105 487	136 717	969 489	490 530	478 959
20 - 24	1 079 075	527 891	551 185	272 732	132 332	140 400	806 343	395 559	410 785
25 - 29	996 699	483 591	513 108	258 810	131 876	126 935	737 889	351 716	386 173
30 - 34	887 938	435 852	452 086	214 155	113 507	100 648	673 783	322 345	351 438
35 - 39	700 181	334 932	365 249	157 777	83 071	74 706	542 404	251 861	290 543
40 - 44	469 009	212 492	256 517	93 256	47 700	45 555	375 753	164 792	210 961
45 - 49	389 581	178 714	210 868	66 852	34 659	32 193	322 730	144 055	178 675
50 - 54	327 316	148 199	179 118	46 788	23 726	23 062	280 529	124 473	156 056
55 - 59	311 766	138 652	173 114	40 643	19 850	20 793	271 123	118 802	152 322
60 - 64	212 189	92 872	119 318	26 432	12 411	14 021	185 757	80 460	105 297
65 - 69	146 382	62 036	84 346	18 351	7 886	10 466	128 031	54 151	73 880
70 - 74	83 148	31 481	51 668	9 811	3 620	6 191	73 338	27 861	45 477
75 - 79	68 922	25 840	43 081	8 409	2 919	5 490	60 512	22 922	37 591
80 +	70 177	26 883	43 294	8 491	2 663	5 828	61 686	24 219	37 466
Saint Helena ex. dep. - Sainte-Hélène sans dép.									
31 XII 2013 (ESDF)									
Total	4 211	2 139	2 072	...	...	...	...	...	...
0 - 4	176	89	87	...	...	...	...	...	...
5 - 9	209	115	94	...	...	...	...	...	...
10 - 14	249	131	118	...	...	...	...	...	...
15 - 19	301	157	144	...	...	...	...	...	...

7. Population by age, sex and urban/rural residence: latest available year, 2007 - 2016
Population selon l'âge, le sexe et la résidence, urbaine/rurale : dernière année disponible, 2007 - 2016 (continued - suite)

Continent, country or area, date, code[a] and age (in years) / Continent, pays ou zone, date, code[a] et âge (en années)	Total			Urban - Urbaine			Rural - Rurale		
	Both sexes Les deux sexes	Male Masculin	Female Féminin	Both sexes Les deux sexes	Male Masculin	Female Féminin	Both sexes Les deux sexes	Male Masculin	Female Féminin
AFRICA - AFRIQUE									
Saint Helena ex. dep. - Sainte-Hélène sans dép.									
31 XII 2013 (ESDF)									
20 - 24	164	84	80	...	...	...	...	...	...
25 - 29	171	77	94	...	...	...	...	...	...
30 - 34	196	88	108	...	...	...	...	...	...
35 - 39	297	138	159	...	...	...	...	...	...
40 - 44	341	178	163	...	...	...	...	...	...
45 - 49	362	179	183	...	...	...	...	...	...
50 - 54	305	166	139	...	...	...	...	...	...
55 - 59	345	182	163	...	...	...	...	...	...
60 - 64	350	208	142	...	...	...	...	...	...
65 - 69	256	138	118	...	...	...	...	...	...
70 - 74	194	111	83	...	...	...	...	...	...
75 - 79	135	57	78	...	...	...	...	...	...
80 - 84	88	28	60	...	...	...	...	...	...
85 - 89	48	10	38	...	...	...	...	...	...
90 - 94	19	2	17	...	...	...	...	...	...
95 - 99	4	-	4	...	...	...	...	...	...
100 +	-	-	-	...	...	...	...	...	...
Unknown - Inconnu	1	1	-	...	...	...	...	...	...
Saint Helena: Ascension - Sainte-Hélène: Ascension									
1 VII 2008 (ESDJ)									
Total	702	397	305	...	...	...	...	...	...
0 - 4	32	16	16	...	...	...	...	...	...
5 - 9	19	9	10	...	...	...	...	...	...
10 - 14	41	20	21	...	...	...	...	...	...
15 - 19	30	19	11	...	...	...	...	...	...
20 - 24	63	29	34	...	...	...	...	...	...
25 - 29	73	42	31	...	...	...	...	...	...
30 - 34	76	41	35	...	...	...	...	...	...
35 - 39	92	58	34	...	...	...	...	...	...
40 - 44	85	42	43	...	...	...	...	...	...
45 - 49	65	36	29	...	...	...	...	...	...
50 - 54	51	32	19	...	...	...	...	...	...
55 - 59	43	29	14	...	...	...	...	...	...
60 - 64	21	15	6	...	...	...	...	...	...
65 - 69	10	9	1	...	...	...	...	...	...
70 - 74	-	-	-	...	...	...	...	...	...
75 - 79	-	-	-	...	...	...	...	...	...
80 +	1	-	1	...	...	...	...	...	...
Sao Tome and Principe - Sao Tomé-et-Principe									
13 V 2012 (CDJC)									
Total	178 739	88 867	89 872	119 781	58 710	61 071	58 958	30 157	28 801
0 - 4	27 720	13 962	13 758	18 502	9 317	9 185	9 218	4 645	4 573
5 - 9	25 472	12 730	12 742	16 772	8 426	8 346	8 700	4 304	4 396
10 - 14	21 427	10 726	10 701	14 262	7 028	7 234	7 165	3 698	3 467
15 - 19	18 457	9 353	9 104	12 361	6 115	6 246	6 096	3 238	2 858
20 - 24	15 974	7 978	7 996	10 840	5 289	5 551	5 134	2 689	2 445
25 - 29	14 815	7 366	7 449	10 226	4 980	5 246	4 589	2 386	2 203
30 - 34	12 522	6 203	6 319	8 532	4 152	4 380	3 990	2 051	1 939
35 - 39	9 731	4 875	4 856	6 426	3 152	3 274	3 305	1 723	1 582
40 - 44	7 879	3 971	3 908	5 236	2 567	2 669	2 643	1 404	1 239
45 - 49	6 311	3 050	3 261	4 299	2 036	2 263	2 012	1 014	998
50 - 54	5 364	2 606	2 758	3 704	1 769	1 935	1 660	837	823
55 - 59	3 816	1 807	2 009	2 663	1 254	1 409	1 153	553	600
60 - 64	2 661	1 338	1 323	1 786	875	911	875	463	412
65 - 69	1 925	918	1 007	1 253	573	680	672	345	327
70 - 74	1 878	850	1 028	1 156	497	659	722	353	369
75 - 79	1 411	609	802	848	353	495	563	256	307
80 +	1 376	525	851	915	327	588	461	198	263

7. Population by age, sex and urban/rural residence: latest available year, 2007 - 2016
Population selon l'âge, le sexe et la résidence, urbaine/rurale : dernière année disponible, 2007 - 2016 (continued - suite)

Continent, country or area, date, code[a] and age (in years) / Continent, pays ou zone, date, code[a] et âge (en années)	Total			Urban - Urbaine			Rural - Rurale		
	Both sexes Les deux sexes	Male Masculin	Female Féminin	Both sexes Les deux sexes	Male Masculin	Female Féminin	Both sexes Les deux sexes	Male Masculin	Female Féminin
AFRICA - AFRIQUE									
Senegal - Sénégal[2]									
1 VII 2016 (ESDJ)									
Total	14 799 859	7 372 487	7 427 372	...	...	...	...	...	...
0 - 4	2 384 522	1 212 846	1 171 676	...	...	...	...	...	...
5 - 9	2 016 277	1 037 276	979 001	...	...	...	...	...	...
10 - 14	1 784 725	918 849	865 876	...	...	...	...	...	...
15 - 19	1 560 123	797 927	762 196	...	...	...	...	...	...
20 - 24	1 359 140	675 294	683 846	...	...	...	...	...	...
25 - 29	1 166 100	559 321	606 779	...	...	...	...	...	...
30 - 34	973 530	466 740	506 790	...	...	...	...	...	...
35 - 39	795 699	384 264	411 435	...	...	...	...	...	...
40 - 44	645 123	307 640	337 483	...	...	...	...	...	...
45 - 49	511 410	240 118	271 292	...	...	...	...	...	...
50 - 54	430 078	204 461	225 617	...	...	...	...	...	...
55 - 59	360 730	174 948	185 782	...	...	...	...	...	...
60 - 64	276 702	135 025	141 677	...	...	...	...	...	...
65 - 69	198 778	97 438	101 340	...	...	...	...	...	...
70 - 74	141 928	69 235	72 693	...	...	...	...	...	...
75 - 79	90 654	43 423	47 231	...	...	...	...	...	...
80 +	104 340	47 682	56 658	...	...	...	...	...	...
Seychelles									
1 VII 2015 (ESDF)									
Total	93 419	46 322	47 097	...	...	...	...	...	...
0	1 601	832	769	...	...	...	...	...	...
1 - 4	6 310	3 180	3 130	...	...	...	...	...	...
5 - 9	6 193	3 128	3 065	...	...	...	...	...	...
10 - 14	6 099	2 999	3 100	...	...	...	...	...	...
15 - 19	5 497	2 823	2 674	...	...	...	...	...	...
20 - 24	6 509	3 420	3 089	...	...	...	...	...	...
25 - 29	6 750	3 644	3 106	...	...	...	...	...	...
30 - 34	8 188	4 059	4 129	...	...	...	...	...	...
35 - 39	7 325	3 542	3 783	...	...	...	...	...	...
40 - 44	7 536	3 878	3 658	...	...	...	...	...	...
45 - 49	6 722	3 126	3 596	...	...	...	...	...	...
50 - 54	7 385	3 599	3 786	...	...	...	...	...	...
55 - 59	5 457	2 814	2 643	...	...	...	...	...	...
60 - 64	4 062	2 019	2 043	...	...	...	...	...	...
65 - 69	2 705	1 341	1 364	...	...	...	...	...	...
70 - 74	1 953	925	1 028	...	...	...	...	...	...
75 - 79	1 408	528	880	...	...	...	...	...	...
80 - 84	976	294	682	...	...	...	...	...	...
85 - 89	505	126	379	...	...	...	...	...	...
90 +	238	45	193	...	...	...	...	...	...
Sierra Leone									
1 VII 2010 (ESDF)									
Total	5 746 800	2 786 797	2 960 003	2 304 955	1 138 563	1 166 392	3 441 845	1 648 234	1 793 611
0 - 4	878 231	437 908	440 323	297 865	147 565	150 300	580 366	290 343	290 023
5 - 9	856 605	424 222	432 383	307 007	145 641	161 366	549 598	278 581	271 017
10 - 14	662 651	338 453	324 198	303 094	148 401	154 693	359 557	190 052	169 505
15 - 19	637 914	308 982	328 932	287 597	141 564	146 033	350 317	167 418	182 899
20 - 24	488 054	221 932	266 122	241 599	119 622	121 977	246 455	102 310	144 145
25 - 29	473 952	210 004	263 948	205 137	102 492	102 645	268 815	107 512	161 303
30 - 34	356 727	160 822	195 905	149 414	73 308	76 106	207 313	87 514	119 799
35 - 39	341 470	160 326	181 144	133 461	66 104	67 357	208 009	94 222	113 787
40 - 44	247 978	123 279	124 699	97 102	51 623	45 479	150 876	71 656	79 220
45 - 49	201 708	107 932	93 776	76 536	41 832	34 704	125 172	66 100	59 072
50 - 54	149 167	77 236	71 931	55 139	30 564	24 575	94 028	46 672	47 356
55 - 59	96 801	51 344	45 457	37 477	21 157	16 320	59 324	30 187	29 137
60 - 64	99 394	44 873	54 521	31 058	14 915	16 143	68 336	29 958	38 378
65 - 69	71 174	34 054	37 120	24 423	11 420	13 003	46 751	22 634	24 117
70 - 74	61 847	28 198	33 649	18 941	8 268	10 673	42 906	19 930	22 976
75 - 79	41 728	21 586	20 142	12 876	6 356	6 520	28 852	15 230	13 622
80 +	81 399	35 646	45 753	26 229	7 731	18 498	55 170	27 915	27 255

Continent, country or area, date, code[a] and age (in years) / Continent, pays ou zone, date, code[a] et âge (en années)	Total			Urban - Urbaine			Rural - Rurale		
	Both sexes Les deux sexes	Male Masculin	Female Féminin	Both sexes Les deux sexes	Male Masculin	Female Féminin	Both sexes Les deux sexes	Male Masculin	Female Féminin
AFRICA - AFRIQUE									
South Africa - Afrique du Sud									
1 VII 2016 (ESDF)									
Total	55 908 865	27 379 728	28 529 137	...	...	...	...	...	...
0	1 132 851	574 078	558 773	...	...	...	...	...	...
1 - 4	4 730 045	2 393 560	2 336 485	...	...	...	...	...	...
5 - 9	5 761 111	2 910 339	2 850 772	...	...	...	...	...	...
10 - 14	5 183 234	2 613 476	2 569 758	...	...	...	...	...	...
15 - 19	4 873 874	2 450 105	2 423 769	...	...	...	...	...	...
20 - 24	5 315 289	2 662 837	2 652 452	...	...	...	...	...	...
25 - 29	5 507 326	2 784 543	2 722 783	...	...	...	...	...	...
30 - 34	4 579 049	2 250 349	2 328 700	...	...	...	...	...	...
35 - 39	3 961 273	1 947 990	2 013 283	...	...	...	...	...	...
40 - 44	3 296 557	1 617 444	1 679 113	...	...	...	...	...	...
45 - 49	2 788 809	1 346 765	1 442 044	...	...	...	...	...	...
50 - 54	2 336 141	1 106 648	1 229 493	...	...	...	...	...	...
55 - 59	1 965 930	905 993	1 059 937	...	...	...	...	...	...
60 - 64	1 568 254	702 679	865 575	...	...	...	...	...	...
65 - 69	1 171 043	500 476	670 567	...	...	...	...	...	...
70 - 74	814 633	320 954	493 679	...	...	...	...	...	...
75 - 79	506 198	176 031	330 167	...	...	...	...	...	...
80 +	417 248	115 461	301 787	...	...	...	...	...	...
Sudan - Soudan									
1 VII 2016 (ESDF)									
Total	39 647 621	20 105 842	19 541 779	14 269 540	7 236 276	7 033 264	25 378 082	12 869 567	12 508 515
0	1 495 606	762 197	733 409	454 208	223 675	230 524	1 041 398	538 523	502 885
1 - 4	5 388 576	2 744 131	2 644 444	1 636 483	805 294	831 198	3 752 093	1 938 838	1 813 247
5 - 9	5 479 254	2 801 266	2 677 988	1 758 182	874 065	884 117	3 721 072	1 927 201	1 793 872
10 - 14	4 522 096	2 325 624	2 196 472	1 542 867	777 406	765 461	2 979 229	1 548 218	1 431 011
15 - 19	4 025 611	2 073 006	1 952 605	1 447 819	739 848	707 970	2 577 793	1 333 158	1 244 635
20 - 24	3 537 491	1 816 041	1 721 450	1 363 235	711 648	651 587	2 174 256	1 104 393	1 069 863
25 - 29	3 067 006	1 547 613	1 519 393	1 222 270	635 394	586 876	1 844 735	912 219	932 517
30 - 34	2 625 594	1 295 965	1 329 629	1 066 750	549 164	517 585	1 558 844	746 801	812 043
35 - 39	2 221 636	1 085 101	1 136 535	908 234	463 534	444 700	1 313 401	621 567	691 835
40 - 44	1 840 327	891 195	949 131	741 484	371 028	370 456	1 098 843	520 167	578 675
45 - 49	1 494 962	732 711	762 251	600 105	301 816	298 289	894 857	430 895	463 963
50 - 54	1 175 703	589 400	586 304	472 806	241 174	231 632	702 897	348 225	354 672
55 - 59	899 359	458 118	441 240	358 957	184 543	174 414	540 402	273 575	266 827
60 - 64	654 915	340 396	314 518	256 819	133 591	123 228	398 096	206 805	191 290
65 - 69	474 001	248 570	225 431	181 190	93 976	87 214	292 812	154 595	138 217
70 - 74	322 506	170 069	152 437	118 162	60 482	57 680	204 344	109 588	94 757
75 - 79	206 936	109 224	97 712	70 332	34 777	35 555	136 604	74 447	62 157
80 +	216 042	115 214	100 828	69 638	34 862	34 776	146 405	80 353	66 052
Swaziland									
1 I 2015 (ESDF)									
Total	1 119 375	531 737	587 638	261 028	124 195	136 833	858 347	407 805	450 805
0	32 210	16 325	15 885	5 760	2 925	2 835	26 450	13 400	13 050
1 - 4	117 478	59 909	57 569	20 675	10 525	10 150	96 803	49 384	47 419
5 - 9	130 635	66 666	63 969	22 414	11 435	10 979	108 221	55 231	52 990
10 - 14	130 443	65 576	64 867	20 165	9 730	10 435	110 278	55 846	54 432
15 - 19	127 696	62 743	64 953	21 915	9 674	12 241	105 781	53 069	52 712
20 - 24	119 322	57 695	61 627	28 003	12 185	15 818	91 319	45 510	45 809
25 - 29	102 667	47 802	54 865	33 994	15 617	18 377	68 673	32 185	36 488
30 - 34	85 056	37 362	47 694	32 026	15 460	16 566	53 030	21 902	31 128
35 - 39	67 300	28 364	38 936	23 814	11 663	12 151	43 486	16 701	26 785
40 - 44	51 526	21 704	30 822	17 614	8 592	9 022	33 912	12 670	21 242
45 - 49	40 836	16 996	23 840	12 795	6 253	6 542	28 041	10 743	17 298
50 - 54	31 614	13 545	18 069	8 498	4 239	4 259	23 116	9 306	13 810
55 - 59	24 859	10 830	14 029	5 825	2 831	2 994	19 034	7 999	11 035
60 - 64	19 202	8 570	10 632	3 517	1 596	1 921	15 685	6 974	8 711
65 - 69	14 629	6 715	7 914	1 888	759	1 129	12 741	5 956	6 785
70 - 74	10 604	5 036	5 568	1 053	380	673	9 551	4 656	4 895
75 - 79	6 691	3 254	3 437	612	221	391	6 079	3 033	3 046

7. Population by age, sex and urban/rural residence: latest available year, 2007 - 2016
Population selon l'âge, le sexe et la résidence, urbaine/rurale : dernière année disponible, 2007 - 2016 (continued - suite)

Continent, country or area, date, code[a] and age (in years) / Continent, pays ou zone, date, code[a] et âge (en années)	Total			Urban - Urbaine			Rural - Rurale		
	Both sexes Les deux sexes	Male Masculin	Female Féminin	Both sexes Les deux sexes	Male Masculin	Female Féminin	Both sexes Les deux sexes	Male Masculin	Female Féminin
AFRICA - AFRIQUE									
Togo									
6 XI 2010 (CDJC)									
Total	6 191 155	3 009 095	3 182 060	...	...	...	...	...	...
0	190 136	96 043	94 093	...	...	...	...	...	...
1 - 4	711 135	360 481	350 654	...	...	...	...	...	...
5 - 9	951 700	482 501	469 199	...	...	...	...	...	...
10 - 14	747 726	390 477	357 249	...	...	...	...	...	...
15 - 19	606 401	313 257	293 144	...	...	...	...	...	...
20 - 24	545 245	252 807	292 438	...	...	...	...	...	...
25 - 29	496 822	214 803	282 019	...	...	...	...	...	...
30 - 34	424 380	199 636	224 744	...	...	...	...	...	...
35 - 39	352 008	166 528	185 480	...	...	...	...	...	...
40 - 44	291 584	139 731	151 853	...	...	...	...	...	...
45 - 49	228 446	112 191	116 255	...	...	...	...	...	...
50 - 54	178 233	82 969	95 264	...	...	...	...	...	...
55 - 59	115 950	54 936	61 014	...	...	...	...	...	...
60 - 64	102 694	44 431	58 263	...	...	...	...	...	...
65 - 69	66 324	26 700	39 624	...	...	...	...	...	...
70 - 74	61 756	24 127	37 629	...	...	...	...	...	...
75 - 79	33 574	13 250	20 324	...	...	...	...	...	...
80 +	73 591	27 960	45 631	...	...	...	...	...	...
Unknown - Inconnu	13 450	6 267	7 183	...	...	...	...	...	...
Tunisia - Tunisie									
23 IV 2014 (CDFC)									
Total	10 982 753	5 472 333	5 510 420	...	...	...	...	...	...
0 - 4	972 171	505 509	466 662	...	...	...	...	...	...
5 - 9	849 006	440 644	408 362	...	...	...	...	...	...
10 - 14	789 622	407 938	381 684	...	...	...	...	...	...
15 - 19	827 508	421 716	405 792	...	...	...	...	...	...
20 - 24	925 409	459 814	465 595	...	...	...	...	...	...
25 - 29	934 617	449 932	484 685	...	...	...	...	...	...
30 - 34	983 781	477 322	506 459	...	...	...	...	...	...
35 - 39	816 986	397 594	419 392	...	...	...	...	...	...
40 - 44	727 848	357 353	370 495	...	...	...	...	...	...
45 - 49	682 956	331 283	351 673	...	...	...	...	...	...
50 - 54	650 608	324 423	326 185	...	...	...	...	...	...
55 - 59	535 168	268 380	266 788	...	...	...	...	...	...
60 - 64	425 424	212 900	212 524	...	...	...	...	...	...
65 - 69	262 303	127 168	135 135	...	...	...	...	...	...
70 - 74	220 681	107 097	113 584	...	...	...	...	...	...
75 - 79	166 896	81 732	85 164	...	...	...	...	...	...
80 +	211 769	101 528	110 241	...	...	...	...	...	...
Uganda - Ouganda									
27 VIII 2014 (CDFC)									
Total	34 634 650	16 897 849	17 736 801	8 438 009	4 042 324	4 395 685	26 196 641	12 855 525	13 341 116
0 - 4	6 131 028	3 173 950	2 957 078	1 342 058	699 470	642 588	4 788 970	2 474 480	2 314 490
5 - 9	5 551 678	2 834 456	2 717 222	1 135 262	575 893	559 369	4 416 416	2 258 563	2 157 853
10 - 14	4 920 443	2 462 789	2 457 654	1 017 614	487 602	530 012	3 902 829	1 975 187	1 927 642
15 - 19	3 956 633	1 917 797	2 038 836	1 015 017	449 250	565 767	2 941 616	1 468 547	1 473 069
20 - 24	3 188 611	1 444 438	1 744 173	1 024 995	444 919	580 076	2 163 616	999 519	1 164 097
25 - 29	2 486 176	1 143 467	1 342 709	825 746	377 888	447 858	1 660 430	765 579	894 851
30 - 34	1 951 739	908 447	1 043 292	584 396	280 869	303 527	1 367 343	627 578	739 765
35 - 39	1 535 837	726 355	809 482	434 901	214 481	220 420	1 100 936	511 874	589 062
40 - 44	1 272 417	617 034	655 383	316 293	162 345	153 948	956 124	454 689	501 435
45 - 49	921 124	452 081	469 043	217 719	112 768	104 951	703 405	339 313	364 092
50 - 54	808 103	371 126	436 977	172 367	81 867	90 500	635 736	289 259	346 477
55 - 59	480 284	224 765	255 519	97 541	46 042	51 499	382 743	178 723	204 020
60 - 64	440 053	195 283	244 770	81 233	36 927	44 306	358 820	158 356	200 464
65 - 69	301 150	136 107	165 043	50 965	22 770	28 195	250 185	113 337	136 848
70 - 74	277 236	115 862	161 374	46 835	19 032	27 803	230 401	96 830	133 571
75 - 79	150 473	69 095	81 378	25 771	11 009	14 762	124 702	58 086	66 616
80 - 84	131 269	51 871	79 398	23 763	9 044	14 719	107 506	42 827	64 679
85 - 89	51 776	21 572	30 204	9 925	3 912	6 013	41 851	17 660	24 191
90 - 94	37 171	15 125	22 046	8 116	3 484	4 632	29 055	11 641	17 414
95 +	41 449	16 229	25 220	7 492	2 752	4 740	33 957	13 477	20 480

Continent, country or area, date, code[a] and age (in years) / Continent, pays ou zone, date, code[a] et âge (en années)	Total			Urban - Urbaine			Rural - Rurale		
	Both sexes Les deux sexes	Male Masculin	Female Féminin	Both sexes Les deux sexes	Male Masculin	Female Féminin	Both sexes Les deux sexes	Male Masculin	Female Féminin
AFRICA - AFRIQUE									
Uganda - Ouganda									
1 VII 2016 (ESDF)[6]									
Total	36 560 700	...	...	...	...	...	...	...	...
0	1 467 300	...	...	...	...	...	...	...	...
1 - 4	5 001 400	...	...	...	...	...	...	...	...
5 - 9	5 674 000	...	...	...	...	...	...	...	...
10 - 14	5 054 500	...	...	...	...	...	...	...	...
15 - 19	4 333 400	...	...	...	...	...	...	...	...
20 - 24	3 450 000	...	...	...	...	...	...	...	...
25 - 29	2 707 500	...	...	...	...	...	...	...	...
30 - 34	2 114 900	...	...	...	...	...	...	...	...
35 - 39	1 645 200	...	...	...	...	...	...	...	...
40 - 44	1 306 800	...	...	...	...	...	...	...	...
45 - 49	1 030 900	...	...	...	...	...	...	...	...
50 - 54	783 800	...	...	...	...	...	...	...	...
55 - 59	590 400	...	...	...	...	...	...	...	...
60 - 64	440 400	...	...	...	...	...	...	...	...
65 - 69	324 000	...	...	...	...	...	...	...	...
70 - 74	238 300	...	...	...	...	...	...	...	...
75 - 79	167 300	...	...	...	...	...	...	...	...
80 +	230 600	...	...	...	...	...	...	...	...
United Republic of Tanzania - République Unie de Tanzanie[17]									
1 VII 2013 (ESDF)									
Total	47 132 580	23 267 957	23 864 623	12 909 536	6 386 303	6 523 233	34 223 044	16 881 654	17 341 390
0	1 776 107	895 971	880 136	403 952	203 710	200 242	1 372 155	692 261	679 894
1 - 4	6 536 000	3 295 033	3 240 967	1 521 372	766 466	754 906	5 014 628	2 528 567	2 486 061
5 - 9	7 160 846	3 608 891	3 551 955	1 723 220	857 109	866 111	5 437 626	2 751 782	2 685 844
10 - 14	5 464 181	2 735 494	2 728 687	1 364 854	661 195	703 659	4 099 327	2 074 299	2 025 028
15 - 19	4 985 943	2 494 983	2 490 960	1 427 786	682 734	745 052	3 558 157	1 812 249	1 745 908
20 - 24	4 340 143	2 179 173	2 160 970	1 333 476	672 789	660 687	3 006 667	1 506 384	1 500 283
25 - 29	3 484 607	1 730 600	1 754 007	1 134 814	563 796	571 018	2 349 793	1 166 804	1 182 989
30 - 34	2 852 197	1 289 114	1 563 083	974 580	450 823	523 757	1 877 617	838 291	1 039 326
35 - 39	2 601 610	1 207 182	1 394 428	867 422	418 436	448 986	1 734 188	788 746	945 442
40 - 44	2 121 302	1 032 605	1 088 697	672 984	346 836	326 148	1 448 318	685 769	762 549
45 - 49	1 568 017	770 149	797 868	469 417	248 681	220 736	1 098 600	521 468	577 132
50 - 54	1 234 201	604 621	629 580	339 138	180 385	158 753	895 063	424 236	470 827
55 - 59	881 484	422 141	459 343	223 562	117 172	106 390	657 922	304 969	352 953
60 - 64	734 938	347 604	387 334	172 297	88 004	84 293	562 641	259 600	303 041
65 - 69	466 882	223 365	243 517	100 337	50 363	49 974	366 545	173 002	193 543
70 - 74	387 755	179 960	207 795	78 544	35 541	43 003	309 211	144 419	164 792
75 - 79	245 872	115 076	130 796	46 843	20 380	26 463	199 029	94 696	104 333
80 +	290 495	135 995	154 500	54 938	21 883	33 055	235 557	114 112	121 445
Zambia - Zambie									
16 X 2010 (CDJC)									
Total	13 092 666	6 454 647	6 638 019	5 173 450	2 548 011	2 625 439	7 919 216	3 906 636	4 012 580
0 - 4	2 252 748	1 121 468	1 131 280	764 592	380 464	384 128	1 488 156	741 004	747 152
5 - 9	1 916 287	954 332	961 955	656 170	322 268	333 902	1 260 117	632 064	628 053
10 - 14	1 774 134	878 572	895 562	672 089	320 423	351 666	1 102 045	558 149	543 896
15 - 19	1 531 115	748 616	782 499	656 061	311 922	344 139	875 054	436 694	438 360
20 - 24	1 194 642	553 267	641 375	544 640	251 543	293 097	650 002	301 724	348 278
25 - 29	1 057 077	497 774	559 303	492 713	233 826	258 887	564 364	263 948	300 416
30 - 34	840 308	425 227	415 081	393 374	202 930	190 444	446 934	222 297	224 637
35 - 39	682 921	357 097	325 824	307 182	167 113	140 069	375 739	189 984	185 755
40 - 44	473 238	250 415	222 823	200 717	111 062	89 655	272 521	139 353	133 168
45 - 49	376 164	189 047	187 117	151 364	78 278	73 086	224 800	110 769	114 031
50 - 54	284 864	138 764	146 100	111 791	55 850	55 941	173 073	82 914	90 159
55 - 59	194 162	96 718	97 444	75 456	39 790	35 666	118 706	56 928	61 778
60 - 64	168 563	78 301	90 262	55 664	28 866	26 798	112 899	49 435	63 464
65 - 69	122 931	56 814	66 117	35 552	17 637	17 915	87 379	39 177	48 202
70 - 74	93 348	43 945	49 403	24 207	11 599	12 608	69 141	32 346	36 795
75 - 79	63 063	31 929	31 134	15 591	7 323	8 268	47 472	24 606	22 866
80 - 84	33 598	16 569	17 029	8 349	3 788	4 561	25 249	12 781	12 468
85 - 89	19 118	9 651	9 467	4 762	2 118	2 644	14 356	7 533	6 823

7. Population by age, sex and urban/rural residence: latest available year, 2007 - 2016
Population selon l'âge, le sexe et la résidence, urbaine/rurale : dernière année disponible, 2007 - 2016 (continued - suite)

Continent, country or area, date, code[a] and age (in years) Continent, pays ou zone, date, code[a] et âge (en années)	Total			Urban - Urbaine			Rural - Rurale		
	Both sexes Les deux sexes	Male Masculin	Female Féminin	Both sexes Les deux sexes	Male Masculin	Female Féminin	Both sexes Les deux sexes	Male Masculin	Female Féminin

AFRICA - AFRIQUE

Zambia - Zambie
16 X 2010 (CDJC)

90 - 94	6 450	3 245	3 205	1 477	652	825	4 973	2 593	2 380
95 +	7 935	2 896	5 039	1 699	559	1 140	6 236	2 337	3 899

Zimbabwe
17 VIII 2012 (CDFC)

Total	13 061 239	6 280 539	6 780 700	4 284 145	2 039 224	2 244 921	8 777 094	4 241 315	4 535 779
0 - 4	1 978 474	986 596	991 878	598 256	297 469	300 787	1 380 218	689 127	691 091
5 - 9	1 698 160	845 062	853 098	444 636	216 870	227 766	1 253 524	628 192	625 332
10 - 14	1 695 647	849 473	846 174	436 641	206 681	229 960	1 259 006	642 792	616 214
15 - 19	1 412 033	699 230	712 803	465 606	199 010	266 596	946 427	500 220	446 207
20 - 24	1 195 664	543 466	652 198	491 795	214 391	277 404	703 869	329 075	374 794
25 - 29	1 131 691	519 834	611 857	487 413	224 788	262 625	644 278	295 046	349 232
30 - 34	920 747	443 539	477 208	387 867	192 046	195 821	532 880	251 493	281 387
35 - 39	736 741	362 497	374 244	293 412	152 117	141 295	443 329	210 380	232 949
40 - 44	524 786	268 460	256 326	208 628	113 140	95 488	316 158	155 320	160 838
45 - 49	348 014	161 257	186 757	128 657	64 099	64 558	219 357	97 158	122 199
50 - 54	350 855	139 101	211 754	105 536	49 123	56 413	245 319	89 978	155 341
55 - 59	282 344	120 776	161 568	79 861	39 203	40 658	202 483	81 573	120 910
60 - 64	226 716	96 779	129 937	52 275	24 852	27 423	174 441	71 927	102 514
65 - 69	167 113	73 055	94 058	34 232	15 508	18 724	132 881	57 547	75 334
70 - 74	137 697	62 230	75 467	24 860	10 889	13 971	112 837	51 341	61 496
75 +	226 894	96 640	130 254	34 907	14 342	20 565	191 987	82 298	109 689
Unknown - Inconnu	27 663	12 544	15 119	9 563	4 696	4 867	18 100	7 848	10 252

AMERICA, NORTH - AMÉRIQUE DU NORD

Antigua and Barbuda - Antigua-et-Barbuda
27 V 2011 (CDJC)

Total	85 567	40 986	44 581	...	...	...	...	...	...
0 - 4	6 623	3 361	3 262	...	...	...	...	...	...
5 - 9	6 460	3 272	3 188	...	...	...	...	...	...
10 - 14	7 329	3 690	3 638	...	...	...	...	...	...
15 - 19	7 073	3 554	3 519	...	...	...	...	...	...
20 - 24	6 624	3 206	3 418	...	...	...	...	...	...
25 - 29	6 647	3 135	3 512	...	...	...	...	...	...
30 - 34	6 617	3 101	3 516	...	...	...	...	...	...
35 - 39	6 748	3 049	3 699	...	...	...	...	...	...
40 - 44	6 712	3 124	3 588	...	...	...	...	...	...
45 - 49	6 241	2 893	3 348	...	...	...	...	...	...
50 - 54	5 110	2 416	2 694	...	...	...	...	...	...
55 - 59	3 721	1 763	1 957	...	...	...	...	...	...
60 - 64	2 968	1 398	1 569	...	...	...	...	...	...
65 - 69	2 238	1 066	1 172	...	...	...	...	...	...
70 - 74	1 500	690	810	...	...	...	...	...	...
75 - 79	1 181	527	654	...	...	...	...	...	...
80 - 84	850	331	520	...	...	...	...	...	...
85 - 89	512	214	298	...	...	...	...	...	...
90 - 94	193	72	122	...	...	...	...	...	...
95 +	84	27	57	...	...	...	...	...	...
Unknown - Inconnu	136	96	40	...	...	...	...	...	...

Aruba
1 VII 2016 (ESDJ)

Total	110 292	52 216	58 076	...	...	...	...	...	...
0	1 195	624	571	...	...	...	...	...	...
1 - 4	5 456	2 794	2 662	...	...	...	...	...	...
5 - 9	6 797	3 485	3 313	...	...	...	...	...	...
10 - 14	7 133	3 618	3 515	...	...	...	...	...	...
15 - 19	7 387	3 723	3 664	...	...	...	...	...	...
20 - 24	6 614	3 391	3 224	...	...	...	...	...	...
25 - 29	6 364	3 189	3 175	...	...	...	...	...	...
30 - 34	6 777	3 143	3 634	...	...	...	...	...	...

Continent, country or area, date, code[a] and age (in years) / Continent, pays ou zone, date, code[a] et âge (en années)	Total			Urban - Urbaine			Rural - Rurale		
	Both sexes Les deux sexes	Male Masculin	Female Féminin	Both sexes Les deux sexes	Male Masculin	Female Féminin	Both sexes Les deux sexes	Male Masculin	Female Féminin
AMERICA, NORTH - AMÉRIQUE DU NORD									
Aruba									
1 VII 2016 (ESDJ)									
35 - 39	7 331	3 340	3 991	...	...	...	...	...	...
40 - 44	7 787	3 618	4 169	...	...	...	...	...	...
45 - 49	8 722	3 992	4 730	...	...	...	...	...	...
50 - 54	9 280	4 318	4 962	...	...	...	...	...	...
55 - 59	8 587	3 961	4 626	...	...	...	...	...	...
60 - 64	6 958	3 161	3 797	...	...	...	...	...	...
65 - 69	5 114	2 300	2 814	...	...	...	...	...	...
70 - 74	3 560	1 547	2 012	...	...	...	...	...	...
75 - 79	2 563	1 063	1 500	...	...	...	...	...	...
80 - 84	1 563	584	979	...	...	...	...	...	...
85 - 89	760	270	490	...	...	...	...	...	...
90 - 94	250	70	180	...	...	...	...	...	...
95 - 99	75	21	54	...	...	...	...	...	...
100 +	19	4	15	...	...	...	...	...	...
Bahamas[2]									
1 VII 2016* (ESDF)									
Total	373 480	180 280	193 200	...	...	...	...	...	...
0	5 170	2 630	2 540	...	...	...	...	...	...
1 - 4	22 400	11 230	11 170	...	...	...	...	...	...
5 - 9	30 550	15 130	15 420	...	...	...	...	...	...
10 - 14	32 010	15 780	16 230	...	...	...	...	...	...
15 - 19	31 940	15 870	16 070	...	...	...	...	...	...
20 - 24	31 400	15 800	15 600	...	...	...	...	...	...
25 - 29	27 160	13 490	13 670	...	...	...	...	...	...
30 - 34	26 750	12 650	14 100	...	...	...	...	...	...
35 - 39	27 480	13 080	14 400	...	...	...	...	...	...
40 - 44	29 250	13 920	15 330	...	...	...	...	...	...
45 - 49	26 580	12 700	13 880	...	...	...	...	...	...
50 - 54	24 820	11 900	12 920	...	...	...	...	...	...
55 - 59	19 580	9 110	10 470	...	...	...	...	...	...
60 - 64	13 560	6 240	7 320	...	...	...	...	...	...
65 - 69	9 380	4 290	5 090	...	...	...	...	...	...
70 - 74	6 870	3 000	3 870	...	...	...	...	...	...
75 - 79	4 500	1 890	2 610	...	...	...	...	...	...
80 +	4 080	1 570	2 510	...	...	...	...	...	...
Barbados - Barbade[18]									
1 V 2010 (CDJC)									
Total	277 821	133 018	144 803	...	...	...	...	...	...
0 - 4	17 352	8 873	8 479	...	...	...	...	...	...
5 - 9	18 838	9 683	9 155	...	...	...	...	...	...
10 - 14	18 567	9 445	9 122	...	...	...	...	...	...
15 - 19	18 870	9 452	9 418	...	...	...	...	...	...
20 - 24	18 169	9 061	9 108	...	...	...	...	...	...
25 - 29	19 088	9 313	9 775	...	...	...	...	...	...
30 - 34	18 785	9 150	9 635	...	...	...	...	...	...
35 - 39	20 516	9 884	10 632	...	...	...	...	...	...
40 - 44	20 113	9 663	10 450	...	...	...	...	...	...
45 - 49	21 365	10 062	11 303	...	...	...	...	...	...
50 - 54	20 050	9 411	10 639	...	...	...	...	...	...
55 - 59	16 653	7 871	8 782	...	...	...	...	...	...
60 - 64	13 486	6 326	7 160	...	...	...	...	...	...
65 - 69	10 151	4 511	5 640	...	...	...	...	...	...
70 - 74	8 680	3 804	4 876	...	...	...	...	...	...
75 - 79	6 937	2 863	4 074	...	...	...	...	...	...
80 - 84	5 153	1 986	3 167	...	...	...	...	...	...
85 +	5 048	1 660	3 388	...	...	...	...	...	...
Belize									
1 VII 2016 (ESDF)									
Total	377 968	188 986	188 982	...	...	...	...	...	...
0	8 515	4 376	4 140	...	...	...	...	...	...
1 - 4	35 656	18 196	17 460	...	...	...	...	...	...
5 - 9	45 989	23 163	22 826	...	...	...	...	...	...

Continent, country or area, date, code[a] and age (in years) / Continent, pays ou zone, date, code[a] et âge (en annèes)	Total			Urban - Urbaine			Rural - Rurale		
	Both sexes Les deux sexes	Male Masculin	Female Féminin	Both sexes Les deux sexes	Male Masculin	Female Féminin	Both sexes Les deux sexes	Male Masculin	Female Féminin
AMERICA, NORTH - AMÉRIQUE DU NORD									
Belize									
1 VII 2016 (ESDF)									
10 - 14	44 194	22 114	22 080	...	...	...	...	...	...
15 - 19	40 616	20 317	20 299	...	...	...	...	...	...
20 - 24	35 802	17 585	18 217	...	...	...	...	...	...
25 - 29	31 070	15 033	16 037	...	...	...	...	...	...
30 - 34	26 770	12 994	13 776	...	...	...	...	...	...
35 - 39	24 241	11 834	12 407	...	...	...	...	...	...
40 - 44	20 329	10 102	10 227	...	...	...	...	...	...
45 - 49	17 529	8 952	8 577	...	...	...	...	...	...
50 - 54	13 740	6 969	6 771	...	...	...	...	...	...
55 - 59	10 127	5 278	4 849	...	...	...	...	...	...
60 - 64	7 293	3 856	3 437	...	...	...	...	...	...
65 - 69	5 153	2 742	2 411	...	...	...	...	...	...
70 - 74	4 097	2 173	1 924	...	...	...	...	...	...
75 - 79	3 004	1 524	1 480	...	...	...	...	...	...
80 +	3 673	1 730	1 943	...	...	...	...	...	...
Bermuda - Bermudes									
20 V 2010 (CDJC)[19]									
Total	64 237	30 858	33 379	64 237	30 858	33 379	-	-	-
0	709	372	337	709	372	337	-	-	-
1 - 4	2 858	1 479	1 379	2 858	1 479	1 379	-	-	-
5 - 9	3 456	1 759	1 697	3 456	1 759	1 697	-	-	-
10 - 14	3 481	1 706	1 775	3 481	1 706	1 775	-	-	-
15 - 19	3 431	1 682	1 749	3 431	1 682	1 749	-	-	-
20 - 24	3 342	1 608	1 734	3 342	1 608	1 734	-	-	-
25 - 29	4 076	1 947	2 129	4 076	1 947	2 129	-	-	-
30 - 34	4 645	2 259	2 386	4 645	2 259	2 386	-	-	-
35 - 39	5 050	2 572	2 478	5 050	2 572	2 478	-	-	-
40 - 44	5 158	2 588	2 570	5 158	2 588	2 570	-	-	-
45 - 49	5 731	2 811	2 920	5 731	2 811	2 920	-	-	-
50 - 54	5 427	2 531	2 896	5 427	2 531	2 896	-	-	-
55 - 59	4 498	2 146	2 352	4 498	2 146	2 352	-	-	-
60 - 64	3 692	1 733	1 959	3 692	1 733	1 959	-	-	-
65 - 69	2 807	1 290	1 517	2 807	1 290	1 517	-	-	-
70 - 74	2 163	961	1 202	2 163	961	1 202	-	-	-
75 - 79	1 768	747	1 021	1 768	747	1 021	-	-	-
80 - 84	1 120	432	688	1 120	432	688	-	-	-
85 - 89	584	185	399	584	185	399	-	-	-
90 - 94	187	41	146	187	41	146	-	-	-
95 - 99	48	8	40	48	8	40	-	-	-
100 +	6	1	5	6	1	5	-	-	-
1 VII 2016 (ESDJ)[7]									
Total	61 695	29 463	32 232	...	...	...	...	...	...
0	620	313	307	...	...	...	...	...	...
1 - 4	2 478	1 220	1 258	...	...	...	...	...	...
5 - 9	3 200	1 613	1 587	...	...	...	...	...	...
10 - 14	2 978	1 555	1 423	...	...	...	...	...	...
15 - 19	2 868	1 396	1 472	...	...	...	...	...	...
20 - 24	3 011	1 430	1 581	...	...	...	...	...	...
25 - 29	3 533	1 664	1 869	...	...	...	...	...	...
30 - 34	4 085	1 993	2 092	...	...	...	...	...	...
35 - 39	4 249	2 124	2 125	...	...	...	...	...	...
40 - 44	4 373	2 211	2 162	...	...	...	...	...	...
45 - 49	4 797	2 375	2 422	...	...	...	...	...	...
50 - 54	5 443	2 678	2 765	...	...	...	...	...	...
55 - 59	5 180	2 362	2 818	...	...	...	...	...	...
60 - 64	4 306	1 998	2 308	...	...	...	...	...	...
65 - 69	3 451	1 609	1 842	...	...	...	...	...	...
70 - 74	2 731	1 232	1 499	...	...	...	...	...	...
75 - 79	1 866	787	1 079	...	...	...	...	...	...
80 - 84	1 433	582	851	...	...	...	...	...	...
85 +	1 093	321	772	...	...	...	...	...	...

Population selon l'âge, le sexe et la résidence, urbaine/rurale : dernière année disponible, 2007 - 2016 (continued - suite)

Continent, country or area, date, code[a] and age (in years) Continent, pays ou zone, date, code[a] et âge (en années)	Total			Urban - Urbaine			Rural - Rurale		
	Both sexes Les deux sexes	Male Masculin	Female Féminin	Both sexes Les deux sexes	Male Masculin	Female Féminin	Both sexes Les deux sexes	Male Masculin	Female Féminin
AMERICA, NORTH - AMÉRIQUE DU NORD									
British Virgin Islands - Îles Vierges britanniques									
12 VII 2010 (CDFC)									
Total	28 054	13 820	14 234	...	...	...	...	...	...
0 - 4	2 134	1 126	1 008	...	...	...	...	...	...
5 - 9	2 090	1 065	1 025	...	...	...	...	...	...
10 - 14	2 044	1 032	1 012	...	...	...	...	...	...
15 - 19	1 767	867	900	...	...	...	...	...	...
20 - 24	1 720	789	931	...	...	...	...	...	...
25 - 29	2 316	1 126	1 190	...	...	...	...	...	...
30 - 34	2 537	1 165	1 372	...	...	...	...	...	...
35 - 39	2 599	1 226	1 373	...	...	...	...	...	...
40 - 44	2 559	1 236	1 323	...	...	...	...	...	...
45 - 49	2 338	1 193	1 145	...	...	...	...	...	...
50 - 54	1 842	962	880	...	...	...	...	...	...
55 - 59	1 387	680	707	...	...	...	...	...	...
60 - 64	1 028	541	487	...	...	...	...	...	...
65 - 69	670	350	320	...	...	...	...	...	...
70 - 74	415	204	211	...	...	...	...	...	...
75 - 79	230	98	132	...	...	...	...	...	...
80 - 84	216	91	125	...	...	...	...	...	...
85 - 89	84	39	45	...	...	...	...	...	...
90 +	78	30	48	...	...	...	...	...	...
Canada									
2 V 2011 (CDJC)									
Total	33 476 685	16 414 230	17 062 460	27 147 190	13 190 225	13 956 965	6 329 495	3 224 005	3 105 500
0 - 4	1 877 095	961 150	915 945	1 531 620	784 165	747 460	345 480	176 985	168 490
5 - 9	1 809 895	925 960	883 935	1 455 570	743 510	712 060	354 325	182 450	171 875
10 - 14	1 920 355	983 990	936 365	1 526 165	781 760	744 410	394 185	202 230	191 955
15 - 19	2 178 135	1 115 845	1 062 290	1 745 370	890 940	854 430	432 765	224 900	207 860
20 - 24	2 187 450	1 108 780	1 078 670	1 858 035	935 265	922 765	329 415	173 510	155 900
25 - 29	2 169 585	1 077 275	1 092 310	1 879 840	930 835	949 005	289 745	146 445	143 305
30 - 34	2 162 900	1 058 810	1 104 095	1 838 125	897 275	940 855	324 775	161 535	163 235
35 - 39	2 173 930	1 064 195	1 109 735	1 814 025	884 235	929 785	359 910	179 965	179 945
40 - 44	2 324 875	1 141 715	1 183 155	1 908 095	933 115	974 980	416 780	208 605	208 175
45 - 49	2 675 130	1 318 715	1 356 420	2 142 125	1 050 625	1 091 500	533 005	268 085	264 915
50 - 54	2 658 965	1 309 025	1 349 940	2 091 050	1 021 340	1 069 700	567 920	287 680	280 235
55 - 59	2 340 635	1 147 300	1 193 335	1 809 810	876 210	933 600	530 825	271 090	259 735
60 - 64	2 052 670	1 002 685	1 049 980	1 573 340	754 910	818 430	479 330	247 780	231 550
65 - 69	1 521 715	738 010	783 700	1 163 785	549 495	614 290	357 930	188 515	169 415
70 - 74	1 153 065	543 435	609 630	906 035	413 260	492 775	247 025	130 175	116 850
75 - 79	922 695	417 945	504 755	751 575	329 760	421 815	171 125	88 185	82 940
80 - 84	702 070	291 085	410 985	591 015	237 310	353 705	111 055	53 775	57 280
85 - 89	427 015	149 415	277 600	369 925	125 615	244 310	57 090	23 800	33 290
90 - 94	170 285	48 470	121 815	148 965	41 530	107 435	21 315	6 940	14 380
95 - 99	42 390	9 455	32 935	37 515	8 225	29 285	4 875	1 230	3 645
100 +	5 825	955	4 870	5 195	840	4 355	630	115	510
1 VII 2016* (ESDJ)									
Total	36 286 425	17 995 581	18 290 844	...	...	...	...	...	...
0	392 096	201 143	190 953	...	...	...	...	...	...
1 - 4	1 568 615	804 293	764 322	...	...	...	...	...	...
5 - 9	1 984 913	1 016 437	968 476	...	...	...	...	...	...
10 - 14	1 886 025	967 486	918 539	...	...	...	...	...	...
15 - 19	2 066 495	1 063 552	1 002 943	...	...	...	...	...	...
20 - 24	2 469 064	1 267 196	1 201 868	...	...	...	...	...	...
25 - 29	2 517 124	1 265 832	1 251 292	...	...	...	...	...	...
30 - 34	2 530 172	1 260 843	1 269 329	...	...	...	...	...	...
35 - 39	2 456 135	1 224 899	1 231 236	...	...	...	...	...	...
40 - 44	2 345 382	1 170 322	1 175 060	...	...	...	...	...	...
45 - 49	2 415 249	1 208 273	1 206 976	...	...	...	...	...	...
50 - 54	2 711 318	1 361 284	1 350 034	...	...	...	...	...	...
55 - 59	2 653 245	1 323 290	1 329 955	...	...	...	...	...	...
60 - 64	2 300 081	1 136 245	1 163 836	...	...	...	...	...	...
65 - 69	1 975 723	964 251	1 011 472	...	...	...	...	...	...

Continent, country or area, date, code[a] and age (in years) / Continent, pays ou zone, date, code[a] et âge (en années)	Total			Urban - Urbaine			Rural - Rurale		
	Both sexes Les deux sexes	Male Masculin	Female Féminin	Both sexes Les deux sexes	Male Masculin	Female Féminin	Both sexes Les deux sexes	Male Masculin	Female Féminin
AMERICA, NORTH - AMÉRIQUE DU NORD									
Canada									
1 VII 2016* (ESDJ)									
70 - 74	1 439 047	686 919	752 128	...	...	...	...	...	...
75 - 79	1 034 825	473 498	561 327	...	...	...	...	...	...
80 - 84	753 423	325 553	427 870	...	...	...	...	...	...
85 - 89	493 095	189 036	304 059	...	...	...	...	...	...
90 - 94	231 050	72 205	158 845	...	...	...	...	...	...
95 - 99	56 003	12 174	43 829	...	...	...	...	...	...
100 +	7 345	850	6 495	...	...	...	...	...	...
Cayman Islands - Îles Caïmanes									
31 XII 2015 (ESDJ)									
Total	60 413	30 264	30 149	...	...	...	...	...	...
0 - 14	11 044	5 714	5 330	...	...	...	...	...	...
15 - 24	5 564	2 875	2 689	...	...	...	...	...	...
25 - 34	10 005	4 729	5 276	...	...	...	...	...	...
35 - 44	13 145	6 540	6 605	...	...	...	...	...	...
45 - 54	11 134	5 696	5 438	...	...	...	...	...	...
55 - 64	5 481	2 699	2 782	...	...	...	...	...	...
65 +	4 040	2 011	2 029	...	...	...	...	...	...
Costa Rica[20]									
1 VII 2016 (ESDJ)									
Total	4 889 762	2 373 531	2 516 231	3 551 728	1 703 473	1 848 255	1 338 034	670 058	667 976
0 - 4	325 325	160 471	164 854	219 129	108 705	110 424	106 196	51 766	54 430
5 - 9	358 512	183 487	175 025	247 487	128 123	119 364	111 025	55 364	55 661
10 - 14	373 177	195 759	177 418	256 177	132 879	123 298	117 000	62 880	54 120
15 - 19	424 288	212 751	211 537	300 926	149 920	151 006	123 362	62 831	60 531
20 - 24	430 007	213 379	216 628	315 714	154 632	161 082	114 293	58 747	55 546
25 - 29	405 099	195 737	209 362	305 070	148 991	156 079	100 029	46 746	53 283
30 - 34	369 384	175 550	193 834	268 982	132 026	136 956	100 402	43 524	56 878
35 - 39	330 621	159 399	171 222	246 797	117 269	129 528	83 824	42 130	41 694
40 - 44	314 074	145 564	168 510	230 318	106 895	123 423	83 756	38 669	45 087
45 - 49	293 033	138 794	154 239	209 206	97 764	111 442	83 827	41 030	42 797
50 - 54	318 801	150 665	168 136	232 177	106 690	125 487	86 624	43 975	42 649
55 - 59	264 784	128 279	136 505	200 987	92 823	108 164	63 797	35 456	28 341
60 - 64	206 630	97 122	109 508	156 917	71 535	85 382	49 713	25 587	24 126
65 - 69	156 069	71 338	84 731	120 416	53 114	67 302	35 653	18 224	17 429
70 - 74	119 060	54 438	64 622	89 774	39 121	50 653	29 286	15 317	13 969
75 - 79	83 977	40 201	43 776	63 627	27 380	36 247	20 350	12 821	7 529
80 - 84	59 349	24 964	34 385	44 129	18 201	25 928	15 220	6 763	8 457
85 - 89	35 671	16 748	18 923	26 946	11 698	15 248	8 725	5 050	3 675
90 - 94	16 299	6 521	9 778	12 893	4 459	8 434	3 406	2 062	1 344
95 +	5 602	2 364	3 238	4 056	1 248	2 808	1 546	1 116	430
Cuba									
1 VII 2016 (ESDJ)									
Total	11 239 114	5 599 279	5 639 835	8 644 181	4 207 382	4 436 798	2 594 933	1 391 896	1 203 036
0	120 458	62 625	57 833	96 357	50 133	46 224	24 101	12 492	11 608
1 - 4	498 723	257 319	241 403	386 604	199 685	186 918	112 118	57 633	54 484
5 - 9	593 894	305 584	288 310	442 321	227 260	215 061	151 573	78 324	73 249
10 - 14	632 480	325 358	307 121	475 647	243 948	231 699	156 832	81 410	75 422
15 - 19	706 867	364 514	342 353	540 664	277 245	263 418	166 203	87 268	78 935
20 - 24	724 655	374 362	350 293	553 416	282 085	271 330	171 239	92 276	78 963
25 - 29	816 322	421 194	395 128	627 535	317 404	310 131	188 786	103 789	84 997
30 - 34	710 898	363 921	346 976	544 664	273 093	271 571	166 234	90 828	75 405
35 - 39	650 196	329 790	320 405	487 265	241 416	245 848	162 931	88 374	74 557
40 - 44	921 751	460 784	460 967	690 000	335 979	354 021	231 751	124 805	106 946
45 - 49	1 001 826	494 470	507 356	759 143	363 340	395 802	242 683	131 130	111 553
50 - 54	987 956	482 962	504 994	777 647	369 965	407 682	210 309	112 997	97 312
55 - 59	674 862	326 513	348 349	527 560	247 608	279 952	147 302	78 905	68 397
60 - 64	591 893	284 562	307 331	466 279	216 687	249 592	125 613	67 874	57 739
65 - 69	517 622	247 524	270 097	410 962	189 983	220 979	106 659	57 541	49 118
70 - 74	415 901	195 916	219 984	329 849	149 447	180 401	86 052	46 469	39 583
75 - 79	304 077	141 079	162 998	240 238	105 886	134 352	63 839	35 193	28 646

Continent, country or area, date, code[a] and age (in years) / Continent, pays ou zone, date, code[a] et âge (en années)	Total			Urban - Urbaine			Rural - Rurale		
	Both sexes Les deux sexes	Male Masculin	Female Féminin	Both sexes Les deux sexes	Male Masculin	Female Féminin	Both sexes Les deux sexes	Male Masculin	Female Féminin
AMERICA, NORTH - AMÉRIQUE DU NORD									
Cuba									
1 VII 2016 (ESDJ)									
80 - 84	189 701	85 592	104 109	148 581	62 632	85 949	41 119	22 959	18 160
85 +	179 026	75 203	103 823	139 443	53 580	85 863	39 583	21 623	17 960
Curaçao[21]									
1 VII 2016 (ESDJ)									
Total	159 663	72 990	86 674	...	...	...	...	...	...
0	1 816	921	895	...	...	...	...	...	...
1 - 4	8 035	4 110	3 926	...	...	...	...	...	...
5 - 9	9 676	4 933	4 743	...	...	...	...	...	...
10 - 14	10 122	5 155	4 967	...	...	...	...	...	...
15 - 19	10 471	5 422	5 049	...	...	...	...	...	...
20 - 24	9 261	4 599	4 663	...	...	...	...	...	...
25 - 29	8 942	4 088	4 854	...	...	...	...	...	...
30 - 34	9 337	4 126	5 211	...	...	...	...	...	...
35 - 39	9 141	3 905	5 236	...	...	...	...	...	...
40 - 44	10 572	4 645	5 927	...	...	...	...	...	...
45 - 49	11 720	5 210	6 510	...	...	...	...	...	...
50 - 54	12 974	5 717	7 258	...	...	...	...	...	...
55 - 59	12 074	5 231	6 843	...	...	...	...	...	...
60 - 64	10 187	4 431	5 756	...	...	...	...	...	...
65 - 69	8 824	3 914	4 911	...	...	...	...	...	...
70 - 74	6 527	2 725	3 802	...	...	...	...	...	...
75 - 79	4 560	1 886	2 674	...	...	...	...	...	...
80 - 84	2 996	1 183	1 813	...	...	...	...	...	...
85 - 89	1 564	557	1 007	...	...	...	...	...	...
90 - 94	669	197	472	...	...	...	...	...	...
95 - 99	171	28	143	...	...	...	...	...	...
100 +	32	12	20	...	...	...	...	...	...
Dominica - Dominique									
14 V 2011 (CDFC)									
Total	68 913	34 973	33 940	...	...	...	...	...	...
0 - 4	6 380	3 240	3 140	...	...	...	...	...	...
5 - 9	5 096	2 601	2 495	...	...	...	...	...	...
10 - 14	5 822	2 946	2 876	...	...	...	...	...	...
15 - 19	6 297	3 237	3 060	...	...	...	...	...	...
20 - 24	5 258	2 691	2 567	...	...	...	...	...	...
25 - 29	4 861	2 389	2 472	...	...	...	...	...	...
30 - 34	4 029	2 118	1 911	...	...	...	...	...	...
35 - 39	4 507	2 271	2 236	...	...	...	...	...	...
40 - 44	4 953	2 544	2 409	...	...	...	...	...	...
45 - 49	4 472	2 337	2 135	...	...	...	...	...	...
50 - 54	3 946	2 162	1 784	...	...	...	...	...	...
55 - 59	3 093	1 682	1 411	...	...	...	...	...	...
60 - 64	2 493	1 281	1 212	...	...	...	...	...	...
65 - 69	2 159	1 054	1 105	...	...	...	...	...	...
70 - 74	1 867	884	983	...	...	...	...	...	...
75 - 79	1 587	724	863	...	...	...	...	...	...
80 - 84	1 102	467	635	...	...	...	...	...	...
85 - 89	599	212	387	...	...	...	...	...	...
90 - 94	274	101	173	...	...	...	...	...	...
95 +	118	32	86	...	...	...	...	...	...
Dominican Republic - République dominicaine[2]									
1 VII 2016 (ESDF)									
Total	10 075 045	5 037 329	5 037 716	8 011 084	3 935 569	4 075 515	2 063 961	1 101 760	962 201
0 - 4	969 721	494 850	474 871	767 897	390 323	377 574	201 824	104 527	97 297
0	192 762	99 202	93 560	...	...	...	...	...	...
1 - 4	776 959	395 648	381 311	...	...	...	...	...	...
5 - 9	967 166	492 703	474 463	760 239	384 879	375 360	206 927	107 824	99 103
10 - 14	975 528	495 073	480 455	766 827	385 061	381 766	208 701	110 012	98 689
15 - 19	950 407	479 357	471 050	754 042	374 342	379 700	196 365	105 015	91 350
20 - 24	908 631	455 323	453 308	729 578	358 749	370 829	179 053	96 574	82 479
25 - 29	837 056	416 885	420 171	677 330	331 054	346 276	159 726	85 831	73 895

7. Population by age, sex and urban/rural residence: latest available year, 2007 - 2016
Population selon l'âge, le sexe et la résidence, urbaine/rurale : dernière année disponible, 2007 - 2016 (continued - suite)

Continent, country or area, date, code[a] and age (in years) / Continent, pays ou zone, date, code[a] et âge (en annèes)	Total			Urban - Urbaine			Rural - Rurale		
	Both sexes Les deux sexes	Male Masculin	Female Féminin	Both sexes Les deux sexes	Male Masculin	Female Féminin	Both sexes Les deux sexes	Male Masculin	Female Féminin
AMERICA, NORTH - AMÉRIQUE DU NORD									
Dominican Republic - République dominicaine[2]									
1 VII 2016 (ESDF)									
30 - 34	753 183	372 612	380 571	609 390	296 250	313 140	143 793	76 362	67 431
35 - 39	678 448	334 725	343 723	547 170	265 133	282 037	131 278	69 592	61 686
40 - 44	610 402	301 202	309 200	490 932	237 572	253 360	119 470	63 630	55 840
45 - 49	548 535	271 299	277 236	439 825	212 649	227 176	108 710	58 650	50 060
50 - 54	486 021	241 261	244 760	388 223	187 982	200 241	97 798	53 279	44 519
55 - 59	403 519	200 191	203 328	319 074	153 884	165 190	84 445	46 307	38 138
60 - 64	319 476	157 223	162 253	249 844	119 139	130 705	69 632	38 084	31 548
65 - 69	238 209	117 342	120 867	183 662	87 305	96 357	54 547	30 037	24 510
70 - 74	170 592	83 557	87 035	130 597	61 472	69 125	39 995	22 085	17 910
75 - 79	124 535	60 382	64 153	94 757	43 891	50 866	29 778	16 491	13 287
80 +	133 616	63 344	70 272	101 697	45 884	55 813	31 919	17 460	14 459
El Salvador									
12 V 2007 (CDJC)									
Total	5 744 113	2 719 371	3 024 742	3 598 836	1 676 313	1 922 523	2 145 277	1 043 058	1 102 219
0 - 4	555 893	283 272	272 621	324 299	165 397	158 902	231 594	117 875	113 719
5 - 9	684 727	349 150	335 577	390 873	199 184	191 689	293 854	149 966	143 888
10 - 14	706 347	359 523	346 824	404 755	205 222	199 533	301 592	154 301	147 291
15 - 19	600 565	298 384	302 181	355 376	174 488	180 888	245 189	123 896	121 293
20 - 24	486 542	228 001	258 541	309 107	143 779	165 328	177 435	84 222	93 213
25 - 29	457 890	206 963	250 927	306 456	138 320	168 136	151 434	68 643	82 791
30 - 34	402 249	178 400	223 849	274 037	121 278	152 759	128 212	57 122	71 090
35 - 39	353 147	156 514	196 633	242 566	106 882	135 684	110 581	49 632	60 949
40 - 44	303 631	132 218	171 413	209 958	90 559	119 399	93 673	41 659	52 014
45 - 49	252 122	109 957	142 165	170 464	73 027	97 437	81 658	36 930	44 728
50 - 54	215 734	95 275	120 459	143 882	62 014	81 868	71 852	33 261	38 591
55 - 59	183 075	81 718	101 357	119 193	51 574	67 619	63 882	30 144	33 738
60 - 64	151 864	68 207	83 657	97 101	41 821	55 280	54 763	26 386	28 377
65 - 69	125 157	55 781	69 376	79 690	33 492	46 198	45 467	22 289	23 178
70 - 74	97 457	43 449	54 008	62 075	25 726	36 349	35 382	17 723	17 659
75 - 79	75 984	33 658	42 326	48 760	20 096	28 664	27 224	13 562	13 662
80 - 84	46 870	20 401	26 469	30 578	12 261	18 317	16 292	8 140	8 152
85 +	44 859	18 500	26 359	29 666	11 193	18 473	15 193	7 307	7 886
1 VII 2016 (ESDF)[22]									
Total	6 520 675	3 070 065	3 450 610	...	...	...	...	...	...
0	111 759	57 178	54 581	...	...	...	...	...	...
1 - 4	448 128	229 057	219 071	...	...	...	...	...	...
5 - 9	572 274	292 514	279 760	...	...	...	...	...	...
10 - 14	628 237	321 296	306 941	...	...	...	...	...	...
15 - 19	698 660	355 085	343 575	...	...	...	...	...	...
20 - 24	694 669	345 954	348 715	...	...	...	...	...	...
25 - 29	571 675	269 401	302 274	...	...	...	...	...	...
30 - 34	458 616	201 862	256 754	...	...	...	...	...	...
35 - 39	401 059	170 726	230 333	...	...	...	...	...	...
40 - 44	372 618	159 098	213 520	...	...	...	...	...	...
45 - 49	333 036	142 844	190 192	...	...	...	...	...	...
50 - 54	283 430	121 088	162 342	...	...	...	...	...	...
55 - 59	236 133	100 967	135 166	...	...	...	...	...	...
60 - 64	199 276	85 647	113 629	...	...	...	...	...	...
65 - 69	163 933	70 599	93 334	...	...	...	...	...	...
70 - 74	129 905	55 863	74 042	...	...	...	...	...	...
75 - 79	98 617	42 065	56 552	...	...	...	...	...	...
80 - 84	65 344	27 346	37 998	...	...	...	...	...	...
85 +	53 306	21 475	31 831	...	...	...	...	...	...
Greenland - Groenland[23]									
1 VII 2016 (ESDJ)									
Total	56 186	29 701	26 485	48 447	25 436	23 011	7 739	4 265	3 474
0	832	411	421	703	345	358	129	66	63
1 - 4	3 103	1 623	1 480	2 667	1 388	1 279	436	235	201
5 - 9	3 948	2 069	1 879	3 364	1 778	1 586	584	291	293
10 - 14	3 911	1 979	1 932	3 292	1 657	1 635	619	322	297
15 - 19	3 908	1 953	1 955	3 339	1 663	1 676	569	290	279

Population selon l'âge, le sexe et la résidence, urbaine/rurale : dernière année disponible, 2007 - 2016 (continued - suite)

Continent, country or area, date, code[a] and age (in years) / Continent, pays ou zone, date, code[a] et âge (en années)	Total			Urban - Urbaine			Rural - Rurale		
	Both sexes Les deux sexes	Male Masculin	Female Féminin	Both sexes Les deux sexes	Male Masculin	Female Féminin	Both sexes Les deux sexes	Male Masculin	Female Féminin
AMERICA, NORTH - AMÉRIQUE DU NORD									
Greenland - Groenland[23]									
1 VII 2016 (ESDJ)									
20 - 24	4 407	2 274	2 133	3 794	1 949	1 845	613	325	288
25 - 29	4 529	2 274	2 255	3 972	1 983	1 989	557	291	266
30 - 34	4 109	2 123	1 986	3 617	1 829	1 788	492	294	198
35 - 39	3 397	1 823	1 574	2 992	1 600	1 392	405	223	182
40 - 44	3 041	1 684	1 357	2 654	1 470	1 184	387	214	173
45 - 49	4 372	2 335	2 037	3 760	2 007	1 753	612	328	284
50 - 54	5 136	2 790	2 346	4 441	2 379	2 062	695	411	284
55 - 59	4 090	2 309	1 781	3 520	1 964	1 556	570	345	225
60 - 64	2 898	1 651	1 247	2 461	1 384	1 077	437	267	170
65 - 69	1 837	1 067	770	1 586	912	674	251	155	96
70 - 74	1 377	762	615	1 176	648	528	201	114	87
75 - 79	751	371	380	641	310	331	110	61	49
80 - 84	352	138	214	301	116	185	51	22	29
85 - 89	154	53	101	137	45	92	17	8	9
90 - 94	31	11	20	27	8	19	4	3	1
95 +	3	1	2	3	1	2	-	-	-
Grenada - Grenade									
12 V 2011 (CDFC)									
Total	106 667	53 898	52 769	...	...	...	...	...	...
0 - 4	8 508	4 380	4 128	...	...	...	...	...	...
5 - 9	7 366	3 762	3 604	...	...	...	...	...	...
10 - 14	8 707	4 413	4 294	...	...	...	...	...	...
15 - 19	9 888	5 013	4 875	...	...	...	...	...	...
20 - 24	9 914	5 091	4 823	...	...	...	...	...	...
25 - 29	9 418	4 721	4 697	...	...	...	...	...	...
30 - 34	6 824	3 440	3 384	...	...	...	...	...	...
35 - 39	6 500	3 419	3 081	...	...	...	...	...	...
40 - 44	6 185	3 225	2 960	...	...	...	...	...	...
45 - 49	6 884	3 531	3 353	...	...	...	...	...	...
50 - 54	6 706	3 427	3 279	...	...	...	...	...	...
55 - 59	4 816	2 562	2 254	...	...	...	...	...	...
60 - 64	3 715	1 921	1 794	...	...	...	...	...	...
65 - 69	3 082	1 461	1 621	...	...	...	...	...	...
70 - 74	2 841	1 353	1 488	...	...	...	...	...	...
75 - 79	2 247	1 025	1 222	...	...	...	...	...	...
80 +	3 066	1 154	1 912	...	...	...	...	...	...
Guadeloupe[24]									
1 I 2016* (ESDJ)									
Total	395 725	181 700	214 025	...	...	...	...	...	...
0 - 4	22 254	11 274	10 980	...	...	...	...	...	...
5 - 9	26 423	13 438	12 985	...	...	...	...	...	...
10 - 14	29 520	14 971	14 549	...	...	...	...	...	...
15 - 19	28 301	14 242	14 059	...	...	...	...	...	...
20 - 24	18 919	9 643	9 276	...	...	...	...	...	...
25 - 29	17 859	7 993	9 866	...	...	...	...	...	...
30 - 34	19 306	7 859	11 447	...	...	...	...	...	...
35 - 39	21 016	8 576	12 440	...	...	...	...	...	...
40 - 44	28 948	12 464	16 484	...	...	...	...	...	...
45 - 49	30 549	13 365	17 184	...	...	...	...	...	...
50 - 54	31 832	14 470	17 362	...	...	...	...	...	...
55 - 59	28 636	13 366	15 270	...	...	...	...	...	...
60 - 64	24 772	11 189	13 583	...	...	...	...	...	...
65 - 69	21 788	9 893	11 895	...	...	...	...	...	...
70 - 74	15 824	7 124	8 700	...	...	...	...	...	...
75 - 79	12 018	5 281	6 737	...	...	...	...	...	...
80 - 84	8 756	3 560	5 196	...	...	...	...	...	...
85 - 89	5 268	1 847	3 421	...	...	...	...	...	...
90 - 94	2 614	817	1 797	...	...	...	...	...	...
95 +	1 122	328	794	...	...	...	...	...	...

Continent, country or area, date, code[a] and age (in years) / Continent, pays ou zone, date, code[a] et âge (en années)	Total			Urban - Urbaine			Rural - Rurale		
	Both sexes Les deux sexes	Male Masculin	Female Féminin	Both sexes Les deux sexes	Male Masculin	Female Féminin	Both sexes Les deux sexes	Male Masculin	Female Féminin
AMERICA, NORTH - AMÉRIQUE DU NORD									
Guatemala[17]									
1 VII 2015 (ESDF)									
Total	16 176 133	7 903 664	8 272 469	...	...	...	...	...	...
0 - 4	2 262 514	1 153 297	1 109 217	...	...	...	...	...	...
5 - 9	2 142 308	1 090 294	1 052 014	...	...	...	...	...	...
10 - 14	1 988 541	1 008 018	980 523	...	...	...	...	...	...
15 - 19	1 776 352	893 687	882 665	...	...	...	...	...	...
20 - 24	1 553 450	771 615	781 835	...	...	...	...	...	...
25 - 29	1 286 639	624 841	661 798	...	...	...	...	...	...
30 - 34	1 099 039	517 919	581 120	...	...	...	...	...	...
35 - 39	889 673	403 769	485 904	...	...	...	...	...	...
40 - 44	707 191	311 703	395 488	...	...	...	...	...	...
45 - 49	563 431	248 840	314 591	...	...	...	...	...	...
50 - 54	459 432	206 306	253 126	...	...	...	...	...	...
55 - 59	377 242	173 501	203 741	...	...	...	...	...	...
60 - 64	330 803	155 222	175 581	...	...	...	...	...	...
65 +	739 518	344 652	394 866	...	...	...	...	...	...
Haiti - Haïti[25]									
1 VII 2010 (ESDJ)									
Total	10 085 214	4 993 731	5 091 483	4 817 666	2 321 608	2 496 059	5 267 548	2 672 123	2 595 424
0 - 4	1 263 322	644 550	618 772	532 352	274 597	257 755	730 970	369 953	361 017
5 - 9	1 195 479	608 495	586 984	493 368	249 982	243 386	702 111	358 513	343 598
10 - 14	1 158 478	588 618	569 860	532 573	255 002	277 571	625 905	333 616	292 289
15 - 19	1 092 364	551 467	540 897	583 183	276 258	306 925	509 181	275 209	233 972
20 - 24	1 019 589	509 042	510 547	600 175	296 233	303 943	419 414	212 809	206 604
25 - 29	919 636	454 123	465 513	537 063	267 198	269 865	382 573	186 925	195 648
30 - 34	702 596	340 518	362 078	390 054	189 432	200 622	312 542	151 086	161 456
35 - 39	548 004	261 157	286 847	272 855	128 575	144 280	275 149	132 582	142 567
40 - 44	488 482	235 182	253 300	225 057	106 072	118 985	263 425	129 110	134 315
45 - 49	423 377	204 077	219 300	179 712	81 240	98 472	243 665	122 837	120 828
50 - 54	342 913	166 418	176 495	138 580	61 854	76 726	204 333	104 564	99 769
55 - 59	284 731	136 034	148 697	107 391	46 062	61 329	177 340	89 972	87 368
60 - 64	206 835	95 939	110 896	73 562	29 974	43 588	133 273	65 965	67 308
65 - 69	175 898	81 854	94 044	61 671	24 975	36 696	114 227	56 879	57 348
70 - 74	129 436	58 181	71 255	44 448	17 100	27 347	84 988	41 081	43 908
75 - 79	80 898	35 538	45 360	27 630	10 473	17 158	53 268	25 065	28 202
80 +	53 176	22 538	30 638	17 992	6 581	11 412	35 184	15 957	19 226
1 VII 2015 (ESDJ)									
Total	10 911 819	5 408 465	5 503 354	...	...	...	...	...	...
0 - 4	1 288 122	657 439	630 683	...	...	...	...	...	...
5 - 9	1 229 531	626 512	603 019	...	...	...	...	...	...
10 - 14	1 176 046	597 528	578 518	...	...	...	...	...	...
15 - 19	1 134 999	574 685	560 314	...	...	...	...	...	...
20 - 24	1 061 190	531 790	529 400	...	...	...	...	...	...
25 - 29	985 754	489 910	495 844	...	...	...	...	...	...
30 - 34	888 731	437 789	450 942	...	...	...	...	...	...
35 - 39	676 720	327 116	349 604	...	...	...	...	...	...
40 - 44	526 642	250 559	276 083	...	...	...	...	...	...
45 - 49	467 790	224 321	243 469	...	...	...	...	...	...
50 - 54	403 336	193 540	209 796	...	...	...	...	...	...
55 - 59	322 085	155 116	166 969	...	...	...	...	...	...
60 - 64	261 216	123 379	137 837	...	...	...	...	...	...
65 - 69	182 089	83 131	98 958	...	...	...	...	...	...
70 - 74	144 907	66 031	78 876	...	...	...	...	...	...
75 - 79	96 066	41 905	54 161	...	...	...	...	...	...
80 +	66 595	27 714	38 881	...	...	...	...	...	...
Honduras									
10 VIII 2013 (CDFC)									
Total	8 303 771	4 052 316	4 251 456	4 480 746	2 116 113	2 364 633	3 823 025	1 936 203	1 886 823
0 - 4	971 015	494 034	476 980	485 103	247 341	237 762	485 911	246 693	239 218
5 - 9	958 543	489 821	468 723	472 721	240 952	231 769	485 823	248 868	236 954
10 - 14	1 020 406	520 842	499 564	499 521	251 358	248 163	520 885	269 485	251 400
15 - 19	982 164	487 949	494 215	523 989	248 745	275 244	458 175	239 204	218 971
20 - 24	840 800	398 093	442 708	483 289	219 539	263 750	357 511	178 554	178 957

7. Population by age, sex and urban/rural residence: latest available year, 2007 - 2016
Population selon l'âge, le sexe et la résidence, urbaine/rurale : dernière année disponible, 2007 - 2016 (continued - suite)

Continent, country or area, date, code[a] and age (in years) / Continent, pays ou zone, date, code[a] et âge (en années)	Total			Urban - Urbaine			Rural - Rurale		
	Both sexes Les deux sexes	Male Masculin	Female Féminin	Both sexes Les deux sexes	Male Masculin	Female Féminin	Both sexes Les deux sexes	Male Masculin	Female Féminin
AMERICA, NORTH - AMÉRIQUE DU NORD									
Honduras									
10 VIII 2013 (CDFC)									
25 - 29	656 443	303 379	353 065	384 221	171 360	212 861	272 222	132 019	140 203
30 - 34	567 367	262 951	304 416	329 661	147 590	182 072	237 705	115 361	122 344
35 - 39	484 740	224 965	259 775	277 833	124 524	153 309	206 907	100 441	106 465
40 - 44	399 555	190 323	209 232	231 557	106 187	125 370	167 998	84 135	83 862
45 - 49	318 026	150 635	167 391	183 503	84 007	99 495	134 524	66 628	67 896
50 - 54	293 256	141 174	152 082	167 798	77 351	90 447	125 458	63 823	61 636
55 - 59	210 708	101 062	109 646	116 409	53 286	63 124	94 299	47 777	46 522
60 - 64	189 636	91 291	98 345	103 821	47 002	56 819	85 815	44 290	41 526
65 - 69	135 709	64 441	71 267	72 921	32 263	40 657	62 788	32 178	30 610
70 - 74	106 566	51 803	54 762	57 407	25 756	31 650	49 159	26 047	23 112
75 - 79	78 407	38 419	39 988	41 388	18 486	22 902	37 019	19 933	17 086
80 - 84	48 965	22 977	25 988	26 407	11 230	15 177	22 558	11 748	10 810
85 - 89	29 532	13 681	15 851	16 153	6 682	9 471	13 380	7 000	6 380
90 - 94	8 241	3 162	5 079	4 867	1 717	3 150	3 374	1 445	1 929
95 +	3 692	1 313	2 379	2 177	738	1 439	1 515	575	940
Jamaica - Jamaïque									
4 IV 2011 (CDJC)									
Total	2 697 983	1 334 533	1 363 450	1 454 151	700 957	753 194	1 243 832	633 576	610 256
0 - 4	209 871	106 107	103 764	109 121	55 157	53 965	100 750	50 950	49 799
5 - 9	226 378	114 792	111 586	114 520	57 817	56 703	111 858	56 975	54 883
10 - 14	266 586	136 183	130 403	138 596	70 428	68 168	127 990	65 755	62 235
15 - 19	274 658	139 777	134 881	143 644	72 173	71 471	131 014	67 604	63 410
20 - 24	250 711	125 243	125 468	140 770	68 692	72 078	109 941	56 551	53 390
25 - 29	226 120	109 919	116 201	129 961	61 980	67 981	96 159	47 939	48 220
30 - 34	185 495	87 810	97 685	106 228	49 452	56.776	79 267	38 358	40 909
35 - 39	183 756	86 647	97 109	103 560	47 408	56 152	80 196	39 239	40 957
40 - 44	173 924	85 656	88 268	97 069	46 377	50 693	76 855	39 279	37 575
45 - 49	155 389	79 201	76 188	88 044	41 385	46 658	67 345	37 816	29 530
50 - 54	137 895	67 297	70 598	74 271	34 341	39 930	63 624	32 956	30 668
55 - 59	100 798	50 717	50 081	54 090	26 020	28 070	46 708	24 697	22 011
60 - 64	88 057	44 407	43 650	46 868	22 549	24 319	41 189	21 858	19 331
65 - 69	65 164	32 543	32 621	33 182	15 691	17 491	31 982	16 852	15 130
70 - 74	51 276	24 627	26 649	25 354	11 785	13 569	25 922	12 842	13 080
75 - 79	42 762	19 847	22 915	20 542	9 085	11 458	22 220	10 762	11 457
80 - 84	30 738	13 258	17 480	14 941	6 132	8 809	15 797	7 126	8 671
85 - 89	18 457	7 267	11 190	8 789	3 151	5 638	9 668	4 116	5 552
90 - 94	6 921	2 303	4 618	3 238	957	2 281	3 683	1 346	2 337
95 - 99	2 503	808	1 695	1 119	326	793	1 384	482	902
100 +	524	124	400	243	53	190	281	71	210
1 VII 2016 (ESDJ)									
Total	2 729 112	1 351 649	1 377 463	...	...	...	...	...	...
0 - 4	184 342	94 114	90 228	...	...	...	...	...	...
5 - 9	203 172	102 852	100 320	...	...	...	...	...	...
10 - 14	218 534	110 714	107 820	...	...	...	...	...	...
15 - 19	254 272	129 679	124 593	...	...	...	...	...	...
20 - 24	266 693	135 442	131 251	...	...	...	...	...	...
25 - 29	238 946	119 196	119 750	...	...	...	...	...	...
30 - 34	214 397	104 081	110 316	...	...	...	...	...	...
35 - 39	177 268	84 014	93 254	...	...	...	...	...	...
40 - 44	174 188	82 331	91 857	...	...	...	...	...	...
45 - 49	169 949	82 207	87 742	...	...	...	...	...	...
50 - 54	151 040	76 725	74 315	...	...	...	...	...	...
55 - 59	130 709	64 536	66 173	...	...	...	...	...	...
60 - 64	95 693	48 221	47 472	...	...	...	...	...	...
65 - 69	80 687	40 740	39 947	...	...	...	...	...	...
70 - 74	58 552	28 817	29 735	...	...	...	...	...	...
75 +	110 670	47 980	62 690	...	...	...	...	...	...
Martinique									
1 I 2016* (ESDJ)									
Total	376 847	174 200	202 647	...	...	...	...	...	...
0 - 4	18 754	9 446	9 308	...	...	...	...	...	...
5 - 9	22 837	11 732	11 105	...	...	...	...	...	...

Continent, country or area, date, code[a] and age (in years) / Continent, pays ou zone, date, code[a] et âge (en années)	Total			Urban - Urbaine			Rural - Rurale		
	Both sexes Les deux sexes	Male Masculin	Female Féminin	Both sexes Les deux sexes	Male Masculin	Female Féminin	Both sexes Les deux sexes	Male Masculin	Female Féminin
AMERICA, NORTH - AMÉRIQUE DU NORD									
Martinique									
1 I 2016* (ESDJ)									
10 - 14	24 387	12 361	12 026	...	...	...	...	...	...
15 - 19	24 197	12 603	11 594	...	...	...	...	...	...
20 - 24	18 091	9 353	8 738	...	...	...	...	...	...
25 - 29	17 147	7 874	9 273	...	...	...	...	...	...
30 - 34	17 485	7 457	10 028	...	...	...	...	...	...
35 - 39	18 642	7 846	10 796	...	...	...	...	...	...
40 - 44	25 256	10 881	14 375	...	...	...	...	...	...
45 - 49	30 367	13 672	16 695	...	...	...	...	...	...
50 - 54	33 070	14 778	18 292	...	...	...	...	...	...
55 - 59	29 856	13 960	15 896	...	...	...	...	...	...
60 - 64	25 557	11 564	13 993	...	...	...	...	...	...
65 - 69	21 164	9 718	11 446	...	...	...	...	...	...
70 - 74	16 155	7 397	8 758	...	...	...	...	...	...
75 - 79	13 662	6 012	7 650	...	...	...	...	...	...
80 - 84	9 992	4 102	5 890	...	...	...	...	...	...
85 - 89	5 960	2 171	3 789	...	...	...	...	...	...
90 - 94	3 098	983	2 115	...	...	...	...	...	...
95 +	1 170	290	880	...	...	...	...	...	...
Mexico - Mexique									
12 VI 2010 (CDFC)[26]									
Total	112 336 538	54 855 231	57 481 307	86 287 410	41 946 540	44 340 870	26 049 128	12 908 691	13 140 437
0 - 4	10 528 322	5 346 943	5 181 379	7 766 149	3 945 636	3 820 513	2 762 173	1 401 307	1 360 866
5 - 9	11 047 537	5 604 175	5 443 362	8 124 337	4 124 524	3 999 813	2 923 200	1 479 651	1 443 549
10 - 14	10 939 937	5 547 613	5 392 324	7 974 649	4 041 649	3 933 000	2 965 288	1 505 964	1 459 324
15 - 19	11 026 112	5 520 121	5 505 991	8 191 229	4 097 876	4 093 353	2 834 883	1 422 245	1 412 638
20 - 24	9 892 271	4 813 204	5 079 067	7 725 548	3 775 245	3 950 353	2 166 673	1 037 959	1 128 714
25 - 29	8 788 177	4 205 975	4 582 202	6 985 279	3 354 569	3 630 710	1 802 898	851 406	951 492
30 - 34	8 470 798	4 026 031	4 444 767	6 719 047	3 188 789	3 530 258	1 751 751	837 242	914 509
35 - 39	8 292 987	3 964 738	4 328 249	6 642 253	3 160 713	3 481 540	1 650 734	804 025	846 709
40 - 44	7 009 226	3 350 322	3 658 904	5 633 205	2 676 230	2 956 975	1 376 021	674 092	701 929
45 - 49	5 928 730	2 824 364	3 104 366	4 739 911	2 241 753	2 498 158	1 188 819	582 611	606 208
50 - 54	5 064 291	2 402 451	2 661 840	4 051 487	1 904 317	2 147 170	1 012 804	498 134	514 670
55 - 59	3 895 365	1 869 537	2 025 828	3 043 924	1 443 868	1 600 056	851 441	425 669	425 772
60 - 64	3 116 466	1 476 667	1 639 799	2 403 645	1 119 077	1 284 568	712 821	357 590	355 231
65 - 69	2 317 265	1 095 273	1 221 992	1 719 078	794 137	924 941	598 187	301 136	297 051
70 - 74	1 873 934	873 893	1 000 041	1 338 906	603 945	734 961	535 028	269 948	265 080
75 - 79	1 245 483	579 689	665 794	892 237	399 026	493 211	353 246	180 663	172 583
80 - 84	798 936	355 277	443 659	576 855	244 082	332 773	222 081	111 195	110 886
85 - 89	454 164	197 461	256 703	322 844	132 826	190 018	131 320	64 635	66 685
90 - 94	164 924	68 130	96 794	116 950	45 123	71 827	47 974	23 007	24 967
95 - 99	65 732	25 920	39 812	44 084	16 122	27 962	21 648	9 798	11 850
100 +	18 475	7 228	11 247	10 451	3 753	6 698	8 024	3 475	4 549
Unknown - Inconnu	1 397 406	700 219	697 187	1 265 292	633 280	632 012	132 114	66 939	65 175
1 VII 2016 (ESDJ)[2]									
Total	122 273 473	59 644 308	62 629 165	88 677 252	...	...	33 596 221	...	...
0	2 213 346	1 132 348	1 080 997	...	...	...	...	...	...
1 - 4	8 833 100	4 519 411	4 313 689	...	...	...	...	...	...
5 - 9	11 132 908	5 697 874	5 435 034	...	...	...	...	...	...
10 - 14	11 195 385	5 712 496	5 482 890	...	...	...	...	...	...
15 - 19	11 128 212	5 627 350	5 500 862	...	...	...	...	...	...
20 - 24	10 747 973	5 324 143	5 423 830	...	...	...	...	...	...
25 - 29	9 892 180	4 781 896	5 110 283	...	...	...	...	...	...
30 - 34	9 170 421	4 350 996	4 819 424	...	...	...	...	...	...
35 - 39	8 752 258	4 119 676	4 632 582	...	...	...	...	...	...
40 - 44	8 185 342	3 861 197	4 324 145	...	...	...	...	...	...
45 - 49	7 305 566	3 456 634	3 848 932	...	...	...	...	...	...
50 - 54	6 146 620	2 903 805	3 242 815	...	...	...	...	...	...
55 - 59	5 049 441	2 378 621	2 670 820	...	...	...	...	...	...
60 - 64	3 984 818	1 876 983	2 107 835	...	...	...	...	...	...
65 - 69	2 972 014	1 392 575	1 579 439	...	...	...	...	...	...
70 - 74	2 172 755	1 004 907	1 167 848	...	...	...	...	...	...
75 - 79	1 516 072	689 670	826 402	...	...	...	...	...	...

7. Population by age, sex and urban/rural residence: latest available year, 2007 - 2016
Population selon l'âge, le sexe et la résidence, urbaine/rurale : dernière année disponible, 2007 - 2016 (continued - suite)

Continent, country or area, date, code[a] and age (in years) / Continent, pays ou zone, date, code[a] et âge (en années)	Total			Urban - Urbaine			Rural - Rurale		
	Both sexes Les deux sexes	Male Masculin	Female Féminin	Both sexes Les deux sexes	Male Masculin	Female Féminin	Both sexes Les deux sexes	Male Masculin	Female Féminin
AMERICA, NORTH - AMÉRIQUE DU NORD									
Mexico - Mexique									
1 VII 2016 (ESDJ)[2]									
80 - 84	982 767	438 046	544 721	...	...	...	...	...	...
85 - 89	549 654	236 938	312 716	...	...	...	...	...	...
90 - 94	243 337	100 249	143 088	...	...	...	...	...	...
95 - 99	79 463	31 157	48 306	...	...	...	...	...	...
100 +	19 841	7 334	12 506	...	...	...	...	...	...
Montserrat									
12 V 2011 (CDJC)									
Total	4 922	2 546	2 376	...	...	...	...	...	...
0 - 4	301	157	144	...	...	...	...	...	...
5 - 9	311	146	165	...	...	...	...	...	...
10 - 14	359	187	172	...	...	...	...	...	...
15 - 19	319	179	140	...	...	...	...	...	...
20 - 24	269	152	117	...	...	...	...	...	...
25 - 29	299	154	145	...	...	...	...	...	...
30 - 34	298	138	160	...	...	...	...	...	...
35 - 39	368	172	196	...	...	...	...	...	...
40 - 44	406	189	217	...	...	...	...	...	...
45 - 49	381	196	185	...	...	...	...	...	...
50 - 54	331	183	148	...	...	...	...	...	...
55 - 59	314	181	133	...	...	...	...	...	...
60 - 64	275	165	110	...	...	...	...	...	...
65 - 69	231	130	101	...	...	...	...	...	...
70 - 74	145	75	70	...	...	...	...	...	...
75 - 79	116	61	55	...	...	...	...	...	...
80 - 84	94	44	50	...	...	...	...	...	...
85 +	105	37	68	...	...	...	...	...	...
Nicaragua									
1 VII 2009 (ESDJ)									
Total	5 742 316	2 844 244	2 898 072	3 259 955	1 569 555	1 690 400	2 482 361	1 274 689	1 207 672
0 - 4	680 125	347 205	332 920	335 635	172 875	162 760	344 490	174 330	170 160
5 - 9	660 096	336 817	323 279	332 694	169 358	163 336	327 402	167 459	159 943
10 - 14	677 756	344 831	332 925	359 316	180 457	178 859	318 440	164 374	154 066
15 - 19	660 608	331 536	329 072	363 427	178 690	184 737	297 181	152 846	144 335
20 - 24	576 923	286 484	290 439	332 187	160 315	171 872	244 736	126 169	118 567
25 - 29	511 402	250 672	260 730	306 186	145 137	161 049	205 216	105 535	99 681
30 - 34	412 087	197 120	214 967	251 145	115 523	135 622	160 942	81 597	79 345
35 - 39	337 317	162 472	174 845	208 505	96 540	111 965	128 812	65 932	62 880
40 - 44	279 795	136 223	143 572	177 594	83 709	93 885	102 201	52 514	49 687
45 - 49	239 942	115 914	124 028	154 027	71 955	82 072	85 915	43 959	41 956
50 - 54	206 088	98 355	107 733	130 198	59 417	70 781	75 890	38 938	36 952
55 - 59	154 329	74 173	80 156	95 879	43 653	52 226	58 450	30 520	27 930
60 - 64	93 681	45 221	48 460	57 189	25 734	31 455	36 492	19 487	17 005
65 - 69	89 351	43 121	46 230	54 102	24 079	30 023	35 249	19 042	16 207
70 - 74	67 861	32 418	35 443	41 515	18 145	23 370	26 346	14 273	12 073
75 - 79	48 205	22 249	25 956	30 640	12 935	17 705	17 565	9 314	8 251
80 +	46 750	19 433	27 317	29 716	11 033	18 683	17 034	8 400	8 634
Panama[7]									
1 VII 2016 (ESDF)									
Total	4 037 043	2 026 044	2 010 999	2 772 324	1 363 153	1 409 171	1 264 719	662 891	601 828
0	74 412	38 030	36 382	46 543	23 830	22 713	27 869	14 200	13 669
1 - 4	296 313	151 377	144 936	182 515	93 373	89 142	113 798	58 004	55 794
5 - 9	363 595	185 657	177 938	222 944	113 876	109 068	140 651	71 781	68 870
10 - 14	360 177	183 793	176 384	220 994	112 309	108 685	139 183	71 484	67 699
15 - 19	349 908	178 305	171 603	222 007	111 414	110 593	127 901	66 891	61 010
20 - 24	327 790	166 338	161 452	218 651	109 452	109 199	109 139	56 886	52 253
25 - 29	313 211	158 181	155 030	215 751	106 769	108 982	97 460	51 412	46 048
30 - 34	301 592	152 131	149 461	218 939	108 194	110 745	82 653	43 937	38 716
35 - 39	288 510	145 423	143 087	217 101	108 246	108 855	71 409	37 177	34 232
40 - 44	274 032	137 551	136 481	208 281	103 070	105 211	65 751	34 481	31 270
45 - 49	247 932	123 855	124 077	190 013	92 483	97 530	57 919	31 372	26 547
50 - 54	212 756	105 657	107 099	162 691	78 593	84 098	50 065	27 064	23 001
55 - 59	175 577	86 428	89 149	131 901	62 848	69 053	43 676	23 580	20 096

Continent, country or area, date, code[a] and age (in years) Continent, pays ou zone, date, code[a] et âge (en années)	Total			Urban - Urbaine			Rural - Rurale		
	Both sexes Les deux sexes	Male Masculin	Female Féminin	Both sexes Les deux sexes	Male Masculin	Female Féminin	Both sexes Les deux sexes	Male Masculin	Female Féminin
AMERICA, NORTH - AMÉRIQUE DU NORD									
Panama[7]									
1 VII 2016 (ESDF)									
60 - 64	136 739	66 531	70 208	99 856	46 245	53 611	36 883	20 286	16 597
65 - 69	105 170	50 564	54 606	72 458	32 725	39 733	32 712	17 839	14 873
70 - 74	79 521	37 667	41 854	52 777	23 226	29 551	26 744	14 441	12 303
75 - 79	56 993	26 466	30 527	37 169	15 866	21 303	19 824	10 600	9 224
80 - 84	37 319	16 876	20 443	25 780	10 513	15 267	11 539	6 363	5 176
85 +	...	...	...	25 953	10 121	15 832	9 543	5 093	4 450
85 - 89	21 406	9 365	12 041	...	...	...	...	...	...
90 - 94	10 015	4 213	5 802	...	...	...	...	...	...
95 - 99	3 437	1 387	2 050	...	...	...	...	...	...
100 +	638	249	389	...	...	...	...	...	...
Puerto Rico - Porto Rico[27]									
1 VII 2015 (ESDJ)									
Total	3 474 182	1 656 148	1 818 034	...	...	...	...	...	...
0	33 548	17 238	16 310	...	...	...	...	...	...
1 - 4	141 327	72 269	69 058	...	...	...	...	...	...
5 - 9	200 412	102 622	97 790	...	...	...	...	...	...
10 - 14	217 747	112 350	105 397	...	...	...	...	...	...
15 - 19	242 568	124 179	118 389	...	...	...	...	...	...
20 - 24	248 792	125 971	122 821	...	...	...	...	...	...
25 - 29	224 671	111 167	113 504	...	...	...	...	...	...
30 - 34	208 957	99 855	109 102	...	...	...	...	...	...
35 - 39	221 215	104 890	116 325	...	...	...	...	...	...
40 - 44	219 817	104 593	115 224	...	...	...	...	...	...
45 - 49	224 760	106 235	118 525	...	...	...	...	...	...
50 - 54	232 541	107 561	124 980	...	...	...	...	...	...
55 - 59	223 946	102 377	121 569	...	...	...	...	...	...
60 - 64	206 919	93 510	113 409	...	...	...	...	...	...
65 - 69	199 104	89 880	109 224	...	...	...	...	...	...
70 - 74	157 583	70 294	87 289	...	...	...	...	...	...
75 - 79	115 961	50 879	65 082	...	...	...	...	...	...
80 - 84	78 393	32 160	46 233	...	...	...	...	...	...
85 +	75 921	28 118	47 803	...	...	...	...	...	...
Saint Lucia - Sainte-Lucie[28]									
10 V 2010* (CDJC)									
Total	165 594	81 919	83 675	...	...	...	...	...	...
0 - 4	11 810	5 979	5 831	...	...	...	...	...	...
5 - 9	13 150	6 678	6 472	...	...	...	...	...	...
10 - 14	14 918	7 479	7 439	...	...	...	...	...	...
15 - 19	15 921	8 116	7 805	...	...	...	...	...	...
20 - 24	13 620	6 744	6 876	...	...	...	...	...	...
25 - 29	13 289	6 553	6 736	...	...	...	...	...	...
30 - 34	12 253	6 150	6 103	...	...	...	...	...	...
35 - 39	12 285	5 952	6 333	...	...	...	...	...	...
40 - 44	12 218	6 043	6 175	...	...	...	...	...	...
45 - 49	10 963	5 496	5 467	...	...	...	...	...	...
50 - 54	8 926	4 447	4 479	...	...	...	...	...	...
55 - 59	6 490	3 177	3 313	...	...	...	...	...	...
60 - 64	5 484	2 687	2 797	...	...	...	...	...	...
65 - 69	4 380	2 087	2 293	...	...	...	...	...	...
70 - 74	3 591	1 722	1 869	...	...	...	...	...	...
75 - 79	2 565	1 145	1 420	...	...	...	...	...	...
80 - 84	1 904	796	1 108	...	...	...	...	...	...
85 - 89	1 170	428	742	...	...	...	...	...	...
90 - 94	445	163	282	...	...	...	...	...	...
95 - 99	176	69	107	...	...	...	...	...	...
100 +	36	8	28	...	...	...	...	...	...

Continent, country or area, date, code[a] and age (in years) / Continent, pays ou zone, date, code[a] et âge (en années)	Total			Urban - Urbaine			Rural - Rurale		
	Both sexes Les deux sexes	Male Masculin	Female Féminin	Both sexes Les deux sexes	Male Masculin	Female Féminin	Both sexes Les deux sexes	Male Masculin	Female Féminin
AMERICA, NORTH - AMÉRIQUE DU NORD									
Saint Vincent and the Grenadines - Saint-Vincent-et-les Grenadines[28]									
1 VII 2015 (ESDF)									
Total	109 557	55 739	53 818	...	...	...	...	...	...
0	1 570	786	785	...	...	...	...	...	...
1 - 4	7 104	3 543	3 561	...	...	...	...	...	...
5 - 9	8 549	4 323	4 226	...	...	...	...	...	...
10 - 14	9 793	5 059	4 734	...	...	...	...	...	...
15 - 19	9 945	5 070	4 875	...	...	...	...	...	...
20 - 24	8 636	4 369	4 267	...	...	...	...	...	...
25 - 29	8 345	4 242	4 103	...	...	...	...	...	...
30 - 34	7 890	3 900	3 989	...	...	...	...	...	...
35 - 39	7 579	3 852	3 727	...	...	...	...	...	...
40 - 44	7 179	3 785	3 394	...	...	...	...	...	...
45 - 49	7 491	3 874	3 617	...	...	...	...	...	...
50 - 54	6 570	3 448	3 123	...	...	...	...	...	...
55 - 59	5 048	2 651	2 397	...	...	...	...	...	...
60 - 64	3 834	1 977	1 857	...	...	...	...	...	...
65 - 69	2 851	1 462	1 389	...	...	...	...	...	...
70 - 74	2 545	1 286	1 258	...	...	...	...	...	...
75 - 79	1 985	966	1 018	...	...	...	...	...	...
80 - 84	1 448	665	783	...	...	...	...	...	...
85 +	1 196	482	714	...	...	...	...	...	...
Sint Maarten (Dutch part) - Saint-Martin (partie néerlandaise)									
1 I 2013 (ESDJ)									
Total	36 090	17 661	18 429	...	...	...	...	...	...
0 - 4	2 352	1 235	1 117	...	...	...	...	...	...
5 - 9	2 531	1 289	1 242	...	...	...	...	...	...
10 - 14	2 692	1 348	1 344	...	...	...	...	...	...
15 - 19	2 469	1 302	1 167	...	...	...	...	...	...
20 - 24	2 161	1 047	1 114	...	...	...	...	...	...
25 - 29	2 462	1 161	1 300	...	...	...	...	...	...
30 - 34	2 816	1 290	1 526	...	...	...	...	...	...
35 - 39	3 142	1 452	1 689	...	...	...	...	...	...
40 - 44	3 259	1 556	1 703	...	...	...	...	...	...
45 - 49	3 360	1 693	1 667	...	...	...	...	...	...
50 - 54	2 790	1 345	1 445	...	...	...	...	...	...
55 - 59	2 295	1 127	1 167	...	...	...	...	...	...
60 - 64	1 690	835	854	...	...	...	...	...	...
65 - 69	990	490	500	...	...	...	...	...	...
70 - 74	516	258	258	...	...	...	...	...	...
75 - 79	289	143	147	...	...	...	...	...	...
80 - 84	146	51	95	...	...	...	...	...	...
85 +	130	37	93	...	...	...	...	...	...
Trinidad and Tobago - Trinité-et-Tobago[12]									
1 VII 2016 (ESDF)									
Total	1 353 895	679 288	674 607	...	...	...	...	...	...
0	17 096	8 802	8 294	...	...	...	...	...	...
1 - 4	78 859	39 977	38 882	...	...	...	...	...	...
5 - 9	93 111	47 283	45 828	...	...	...	...	...	...
10 - 14	89 677	45 829	43 848	...	...	...	...	...	...
15 - 19	100 296	50 678	49 618	...	...	...	...	...	...
20 - 24	116 466	58 526	57 940	...	...	...	...	...	...
25 - 29	125 925	63 481	62 443	...	...	...	...	...	...
30 - 34	107 637	54 947	52 690	...	...	...	...	...	...
35 - 39	94 342	47 775	46 567	...	...	...	...	...	...
40 - 44	87 841	44 338	43 503	...	...	...	...	...	...
45 - 49	97 987	49 634	48 353	...	...	...	...	...	...
50 - 54	88 883	44 838	44 045	...	...	...	...	...	...

Continent, country or area, date, code[a] and age (in years) Continent, pays ou zone, date, code[a] et âge (en annèes)	Total			Urban - Urbaine			Rural - Rurale		
	Both sexes Les deux sexes	Male Masculin	Female Féminin	Both sexes Les deux sexes	Male Masculin	Female Féminin	Both sexes Les deux sexes	Male Masculin	Female Féminin
AMERICA, NORTH - **AMÉRIQUE DU NORD**									
Trinidad and Tobago - **Trinité-et-Tobago**[12]									
1 VII 2016 (ESDF)									
55 - 59	74 642	37 434	37 207	...	...	...	...	...	...
60 - 64	59 790	30 223	29 567	...	...	...	...	...	...
65 - 69	45 508	22 004	23 504	...	...	...	...	...	...
70 - 74	30 878	14 486	16 392	...	...	...	...	...	...
75 - 79	21 153	9 467	11 686	...	...	...	...	...	...
80 + ...	23 805	9 567	14 238	...	...	...	...	...	...
Turks and Caicos Islands - **Îles Turques et Caïques**									
1 VII 2016 (ESDJ)									
Total...............	*37 910*	*19 169*	*18 741*	...	...	...	...	...	...
0 - 4	*2 727*	*1 381*	*1 346*	...	...	...	...	...	...
5 - 9	*2 452*	*1 241*	*1 211*	...	...	...	...	...	...
10 - 14	*2 261*	*1 120*	*1 141*	...	...	...	...	...	...
15 - 19	*2 262*	*1 107*	*1 155*	...	...	...	...	...	...
20 - 24	*2 669*	*1 304*	*1 365*	...	...	...	...	...	...
25 - 29	*3 169*	*1 555*	*1 614*	...	...	...	...	...	...
30 - 34	*3 395*	*1 547*	*1 848*	...	...	...	...	...	...
35 - 39	*4 213*	*2 162*	*2 051*	...	...	...	...	...	...
40 - 44	*3 949*	*2 049*	*1 900*	...	...	...	...	...	...
45 - 49	*3 500*	*1 834*	*1 666*	...	...	...	...	...	...
50 - 54	*2 714*	*1 429*	*1 285*	...	...	...	...	...	...
55 - 59	*1 828*	*968*	*860*	...	...	...	...	...	...
60 - 64	*1 258*	*673*	*585*	...	...	...	...	...	...
65 - 69	*749*	*407*	*342*	...	...	...	...	...	...
70 - 74	*429*	*235*	*194*	...	...	...	...	...	...
75 - 79	*182*	*98*	*84*	...	...	...	...	...	...
80 + ...	*153*	*59*	*94*	...	...	...	...	...	...
United States of America - **États-Unis d'Amérique**									
1 IV 2010 (CDJC)									
Total...............	308 745 538	151 781 326	156 964 212	249 253 271	121 698 595	127 554 676	59 492 267	30 082 731	29 409 536
0 - 4	20 201 362	10 319 427	9 881 935	16 838 001	8 597 234	8 240 767	3 363 361	1 722 193	1 641 168
5 - 9	20 348 657	10 389 638	9 959 019	16 597 127	8 464 939	8 132 188	3 751 530	1 924 699	1 826 831
10 - 14	20 677 194	10 579 862	10 097 332	16 576 171	8 466 809	8 109 362	4 101 023	2 113 053	1 987 970
15 - 19	22 040 343	11 303 666	10 736 677	17 946 265	9 149 187	8 797 078	4 094 078	2 154 479	1 939 599
20 - 24	21 585 999	11 014 176	10 571 823	18 653 468	9 450 066	9 203 402	2 932 531	1 564 110	1 368 421
25 - 29	21 101 849	10 635 591	10 466 258	18 163 244	9 110 029	9 053 215	2 938 605	1 525 562	1 413 043
30 - 34	19 962 099	9 996 500	9 965 599	16 857 801	8 409 694	8 448 107	3 104 298	1 586 806	1 517 492
35 - 39	20 179 642	10 042 022	10 137 620	16 629 937	8 249 301	8 380 636	3 549 705	1 792 721	1 756 984
40 - 44	20 890 964	10 393 977	10 496 987	16 837 761	8 347 894	8 489 867	4 053 203	2 046 083	2 007 120
45 - 49	22 708 591	11 209 085	11 499 506	17 847 074	8 760 812	9 086 262	4 861 517	2 448 273	2 413 244
50 - 54	22 298 125	10 933 274	11 364 851	17 279 058	8 401 091	8 877 967	5 019 067	2 532 183	2 486 884
55 - 59	19 664 805	9 523 648	10 141 157	15 060 179	7 204 444	7 855 735	4 604 626	2 319 204	2 285 422
60 - 64	16 817 924	8 077 500	8 740 424	12 750 365	6 020 393	6 729 972	4 067 559	2 057 107	2 010 452
65 - 69	12 435 263	5 852 547	6 582 716	9 299 030	4 275 616	5 023 414	3 136 233	1 576 931	1 559 302
70 - 74	9 278 166	4 243 972	5 034 194	7 011 129	3 115 814	3 895 315	2 267 037	1 128 158	1 138 879
75 - 79	7 317 795	3 182 388	4 135 407	5 693 807	2 409 946	3 283 861	1 623 988	772 442	851 546
80 - 84	5 743 327	2 294 374	3 448 953	4 629 581	1 800 531	2 829 050	1 113 746	493 843	619 903
85 - 89	3 620 459	1 273 867	2 346 592	3 005 285	1 036 583	1 968 702	615 174	237 284	377 890
90 - 94	1 448 366	424 387	1 023 979	1 216 647	351 491	865 156	231 719	72 896	158 823
95 - 99	371 244	82 263	288 981	315 589	69 008	246 581	55 655	13 255	42 400
100 + ...	53 364	9 162	44 202	45 752	7 713	38 039	7 612	1 449	6 163
1 VII 2016 (ESDJ)[29]									
Total...............	323 127 513	159 078 923	164 048 590	...	...	...	...	...	...
0	3 970 145	2 030 478	1 939 667	...	...	...	...	...	...
1 - 4	15 956 892	8 156 375	7 800 517	...	...	...	...	...	...
5 - 9	20 429 799	10 429 923	9 999 876	...	...	...	...	...	...
10 - 14	20 618 233	10 518 732	10 099 501	...	...	...	...	...	...
15 - 19	21 129 999	10 801 846	10 328 153	...	...	...	...	...	...
20 - 24	22 381 028	11 491 065	10 889 963	...	...	...	...	...	...
25 - 29	22 890 884	11 631 474	11 259 410	...	...	...	...	...	...

Continent, country or area, date, code[a] and age (in years) Continent, pays ou zone, date, code[a] et âge (en années)	Total			Urban - Urbaine			Rural - Rurale		
	Both sexes Les deux sexes	Male Masculin	Female Féminin	Both sexes Les deux sexes	Male Masculin	Female Féminin	Both sexes Les deux sexes	Male Masculin	Female Féminin
AMERICA, NORTH - AMÉRIQUE DU NORD									
United States of America - États-Unis d'Amérique 1 VII 2016 (ESDJ)[29]									
30 - 34	21 786 359	10 968 264	10 818 095	...	...	...	...	...	...
35 - 39	20 773 905	10 376 442	10 397 463	...	...	...	...	...	...
40 - 44	19 696 251	9 776 321	9 919 930	...	...	...	...	...	...
45 - 49	20 947 623	10 375 955	10 571 668	...	...	...	...	...	...
50 - 54	21 839 056	10 730 184	11 108 872	...	...	...	...	...	...
55 - 59	21 980 108	10 683 406	11 296 702	...	...	...	...	...	...
60 - 64	19 483 036	9 315 632	10 167 404	...	...	...	...	...	...
65 - 69	16 820 083	7 936 919	8 883 164	...	...	...	...	...	...
70 - 74	11 810 247	5 454 190	6 356 057	...	...	...	...	...	...
75 - 79	8 367 895	3 723 619	4 644 276	...	...	...	...	...	...
80 - 84	5 865 639	2 453 255	3 412 384	...	...	...	...	...	...
85 - 89	3 885 222	1 463 286	2 421 936	...	...	...	...	...	...
90 - 94	1 882 830	604 835	1 277 995	...	...	...	...	...	...
95 - 99	530 383	140 380	390 003	...	...	...	...	...	...
100 +	81 896	16 342	65 554	...	...	...	...	...	...
United States Virgin Islands - Îles Vierges américaines[30] 1 IV 2010 (CDJC)									
Total	106 405	50 854	55 551	...	...	...	...	...	...
0 - 4	7 500	3 736	3 764	...	...	...	...	...	...
5 - 9	7 150	3 694	3 456	...	...	...	...	...	...
10 - 14	7 484	3 849	3 635	...	...	...	...	...	...
15 - 19	7 560	3 765	3 795	...	...	...	...	...	...
20 - 24	5 894	2 707	3 187	...	...	...	...	...	...
25 - 29	5 969	2 695	3 274	...	...	...	...	...	...
30 - 34	6 137	2 825	3 312	...	...	...	...	...	...
35 - 39	6 675	3 133	3 542	...	...	...	...	...	...
40 - 44	7 450	3 506	3 944	...	...	...	...	...	...
45 - 49	7 743	3 680	4 063	...	...	...	...	...	...
50 - 54	7 900	3 800	4 100	...	...	...	...	...	...
55 - 59	7 192	3 341	3 851	...	...	...	...	...	...
60 - 64	7 367	3 510	3 857	...	...	...	...	...	...
65 - 69	5 853	2 883	2 970	...	...	...	...	...	...
70 - 74	3 717	1 739	1 978	...	...	...	...	...	...
75 - 79	2 328	1 043	1 285	...	...	...	...	...	...
80 - 84	1 332	568	764	...	...	...	...	...	...
85 +	1 154	380	774	...	...	...	...	...	...
AMERICA, SOUTH - AMÉRIQUE DU SUD									
Argentina - Argentine[31] 1 VII 2016 (ESDF)									
Total	43 590 368	21 364 470	22 225 898	39 951 022	19 430 772	20 520 250	3 639 346	1 933 698	1 705 648
0 - 4	3 757 709	1 933 361	1 824 348	3 373 283	1 734 540	1 638 743	384 426	198 821	185 605
5 - 9	3 621 521	1 864 612	1 756 909	3 259 196	1 674 967	1 584 229	362 325	189 645	172 680
10 - 14	3 508 707	1 797 146	1 711 561	3 192 479	1 632 445	1 560 034	316 228	164 701	151 527
15 - 19	3 527 929	1 795 390	1 732 539	3 176 272	1 610 538	1 565 734	351 657	184 852	166 805
20 - 24	3 568 580	1 800 611	1 767 969	3 232 404	1 619 656	1 612 748	336 176	180 955	155 221
25 - 29	3 390 781	1 695 030	1 695 751	3 126 548	1 551 184	1 575 364	264 233	143 846	120 387
30 - 34	3 177 008	1 578 587	1 598 421	2 940 669	1 454 372	1 486 297	236 339	124 215	112 124
35 - 39	3 130 524	1 547 524	1 583 000	2 904 720	1 430 562	1 474 158	225 804	116 962	108 842
40 - 44	2 781 388	1 366 919	1 414 469	2 585 851	1 263 575	1 322 276	195 537	103 344	92 193
45 - 49	2 369 213	1 156 735	1 212 478	2 194 789	1 060 980	1 133 809	174 424	95 755	78 669
50 - 54	2 183 741	1 057 225	1 126 516	2 021 153	966 128	1 055 025	162 588	91 097	71 491
55 - 59	2 018 007	965 405	1 052 602	1 868 221	881 748	986 473	149 786	83 657	66 129
60 - 64	1 807 828	849 667	958 161	1 670 566	772 590	897 976	137 262	77 077	60 185
65 - 69	1 541 040	703 822	837 218	1 425 534	639 779	785 755	115 506	64 043	51 463
70 - 74	1 194 213	521 180	673 033	1 104 930	472 327	632 603	89 283	48 853	40 430
75 - 79	872 946	353 449	519 497	808 362	319 623	488 739	64 584	33 826	30 758

Continent, country or area, date, code[a] and age (in years) Continent, pays ou zone, date, code[a] et âge (en années)	Total			Urban - Urbaine			Rural - Rurale		
	Both sexes Les deux sexes	Male Masculin	Female Féminin	Both sexes Les deux sexes	Male Masculin	Female Féminin	Both sexes Les deux sexes	Male Masculin	Female Féminin
AMERICA, SOUTH - AMÉRIQUE DU SUD									
Argentina - Argentine[31]									
1 VII 2016 (ESDF)									
80 - 84	598 590	218 529	380 061	557 726	198 882	358 844	40 864	19 647	21 217
85 - 89	347 416	109 415	238 001	325 596	100 475	225 121	21 820	8 940	12 880
90 - 94	148 273	39 951	108 322	140 018	37 104	102 914	8 255	2 847	5 408
95 - 99	38 691	8 800	29 891	36 819	8 263	28 556	1 872	537	1 335
100 +	6 263	1 112	5 151	5 886	1 034	4 852	377	78	299
Bolivia (Plurinational State of) - Bolivie (État plurinational de)									
1 VII 2016 (ESDF)									
Total	10 985 059	5 535 975	5 449 084	7 551 625	3 736 216	3 815 409	3 433 434	1 799 759	1 633 675
0	243 720	123 850	119 870	163 388	83 024	80 364	80 332	40 826	39 506
1 - 4	971 652	494 033	477 619	652 340	331 459	320 881	319 312	162 574	156 738
5 - 9	1 208 062	616 464	591 598	800 799	407 175	393 624	407 263	209 289	197 974
10 - 14	1 176 802	599 818	576 984	786 620	397 505	389 115	390 182	202 313	187 869
15 - 19	1 100 887	560 779	540 108	754 888	378 643	376 245	345 999	182 136	163 863
20 - 24	1 006 036	511 203	494 833	720 120	357 444	362 676	285 916	153 759	132 157
25 - 29	906 901	459 427	447 474	662 144	325 906	336 238	244 757	133 521	111 236
30 - 34	822 889	415 910	406 979	604 370	297 276	307 094	218 519	118 634	99 885
35 - 39	714 959	360 862	354 097	518 824	254 387	264 437	196 135	106 475	89 660
40 - 44	600 088	302 286	297 802	427 710	208 755	218 955	172 378	93 531	78 847
45 - 49	499 884	250 913	248 971	347 081	168 721	178 360	152 803	82 192	70 611
50 - 54	419 055	209 727	209 328	285 898	139 163	146 735	133 157	70 564	62 593
55 - 59	350 528	174 493	176 035	230 684	111 590	119 094	119 844	62 903	56 941
60 - 64	289 691	142 908	146 783	184 028	88 160	95 868	105 663	54 748	50 915
65 - 69	228 747	111 606	117 141	143 150	67 775	75 375	85 597	43 831	41 766
70 - 74	175 573	84 318	91 255	108 683	50 554	58 129	66 890	33 764	33 126
75 - 79	119 713	55 284	64 429	73 294	32 908	40 386	46 419	22 376	24 043
80 - 84	80 771	35 124	45 647	48 211	20 490	27 721	32 560	14 634	17 926
85 - 89	46 268	18 929	27 339	26 673	10 746	15 927	19 595	8 183	11 412
90 - 94	18 218	6 685	11 533	10 222	3 765	6 457	7 996	2 920	5 076
95 +	4 615	1 356	3 259	2 498	770	1 728	2 117	586	1 531
Brazil - Brésil									
31 VII 2010 (CDJC)									
Total	190 755 799	93 406 990	97 348 809	160 925 804	77 710 179	83 215 625	29 829 995	15 696 811	14 133 184
0	2 713 244	1 378 532	1 334 712	2 246 034	1 141 784	1 104 250	467 210	236 748	230 462
1 - 4	11 082 914	5 638 455	5 444 459	9 055 114	4 603 340	4 451 774	2 027 800	1 035 115	992 685
5 - 9	14 969 375	7 624 144	7 345 231	12 135 285	6 169 531	5 965 754	2 834 090	1 454 613	1 379 477
10 - 14	17 166 761	8 725 413	8 441 348	13 956 987	7 062 057	6 894 930	3 209 774	1 663 356	1 546 418
15 - 19	16 990 872	8 558 868	8 432 004	14 039 001	6 998 102	7 040 899	2 951 871	1 560 766	1 391 105
20 - 24	17 245 192	8 630 229	8 614 963	14 706 068	7 276 963	7 429 105	2 539 124	1 353 266	1 185 858
25 - 29	17 104 414	8 460 995	8 643 419	14 772 957	7 225 732	7 547 225	2 331 457	1 235 263	1 096 194
30 - 34	15 744 512	7 717 658	8 026 854	13 611 921	6 586 877	7 025 044	2 132 591	1 130 781	1 001 810
35 - 39	13 888 579	6 766 664	7 121 915	11 975 407	5 750 498	6 224 909	1 913 172	1 016 166	897 006
40 - 44	13 009 364	6 320 568	6 688 796	11 187 429	5 344 982	5 842 447	1 821 935	975 586	846 349
45 - 49	11 833 352	5 692 014	6 141 338	10 181 394	4 806 322	5 375 072	1 651 958	885 692	766 266
50 - 54	10 140 402	4 834 995	5 305 407	8 708 339	4 074 679	4 633 660	1 432 063	760 316	671 747
55 - 59	8 276 221	3 902 344	4 373 877	7 025 474	3 238 531	3 786 943	1 250 747	663 813	586 934
60 - 64	6 509 120	3 041 035	3 468 085	5 474 944	2 479 882	2 995 062	1 034 176	561 153	473 023
65 - 69	4 840 810	2 224 065	2 616 745	4 040 016	1 792 798	2 247 218	800 794	431 267	369 527
70 - 74	3 741 636	1 667 372	2 074 264	3 142 173	1 349 329	1 792 844	599 463	318 043	281 420
75 - 79	2 563 447	1 090 517	1 472 930	2 174 038	889 908	1 284 130	389 409	200 609	188 800
80 - 84	1 666 972	668 623	998 349	1 423 603	546 865	876 738	243 369	121 758	121 611
85 - 89	819 483	310 759	508 724	695 385	251 112	444 273	124 098	59 647	64 451
90 - 94	326 558	114 964	211 594	273 348	90 960	182 388	53 210	24 004	29 206
95 - 99	98 335	31 529	66 806	81 121	24 365	56 756	17 214	7 164	10 050
100 +	24 236	7 247	16 989	19 766	5 562	14 204	4 470	1 685	2 785
1 VII 2016 (ESDJ)[32]									
Total	206 081 432	101 726 102	104 355 330	...	...	...	...	...	...
0	2 842 574	1 454 693	1 387 881	...	...	...	...	...	...
1 - 4	11 702 914	5 985 652	5 717 262	...	...	...	...	...	...
5 - 9	15 551 873	7 948 370	7 603 503	...	...	...	...	...	...
10 - 14	16 672 044	8 506 920	8 165 124	...	...	...	...	...	...

Continent, country or area, date, code[a] and age (in years) / Continent, pays ou zone, date, code[a] et âge (en années)	Total			Urban - Urbaine			Rural - Rurale		
	Both sexes Les deux sexes	Male Masculin	Female Féminin	Both sexes Les deux sexes	Male Masculin	Female Féminin	Both sexes Les deux sexes	Male Masculin	Female Féminin
AMERICA, SOUTH - AMÉRIQUE DU SUD									
Brazil - Brésil									
1 VII 2016 (ESDJ)[32]									
15 - 19	17 166 564	8 727 113	8 439 451	...	...	...	...	...	...
20 - 24	17 040 654	8 616 044	8 424 610	...	...	...	...	...	...
25 - 29	17 068 601	8 581 961	8 486 640	...	...	...	...	...	...
30 - 34	17 666 798	8 832 635	8 834 163	...	...	...	...	...	...
35 - 39	16 246 942	8 075 960	8 170 982	...	...	...	...	...	...
40 - 44	14 230 010	7 026 347	7 203 663	...	...	...	...	...	...
45 - 49	12 947 682	6 340 073	6 607 609	...	...	...	...	...	...
50 - 54	11 894 903	5 762 812	6 132 091	...	...	...	...	...	...
55 - 59	10 116 412	4 832 571	5 283 841	...	...	...	...	...	...
60 - 64	8 097 251	3 797 753	4 299 498	...	...	...	...	...	...
65 - 69	6 116 344	2 799 118	3 317 226	...	...	...	...	...	...
70 - 74	4 259 166	1 877 125	2 382 041	...	...	...	...	...	...
75 - 79	3 002 421	1 259 991	1 742 430	...	...	...	...	...	...
80 - 84	1 869 824	739 870	1 129 954	...	...	...	...	...	...
85 - 89	1 012 885	375 571	637 314	...	...	...	...	...	...
90 +	575 570	185 523	390 047	...	...	...	...	...	...
Chile - Chili									
1 VII 2016 (ESDF)									
Total	18 191 884	9 003 254	9 188 630	15 898 145	7 799 463	8 098 682	2 293 739	1 203 791	1 089 948
0	249 552	127 015	122 537	218 672	111 406	107 266	30 880	15 609	15 271
1 - 4	988 408	503 273	485 135	881 062	449 025	432 037	107 346	54 248	53 098
5 - 9	1 240 731	632 438	608 293	1 120 449	571 451	548 998	120 282	60 987	59 295
10 - 14	1 194 224	609 202	585 022	1 054 472	538 116	516 356	139 752	71 086	68 666
15 - 19	1 300 362	664 249	636 113	1 128 212	576 066	552 146	172 150	88 183	83 967
20 - 24	1 437 569	732 606	704 963	1 241 115	631 522	609 593	196 454	101 084	95 370
25 - 29	1 517 178	767 371	749 807	1 320 278	664 541	655 737	196 900	102 830	94 070
30 - 34	1 397 156	703 722	693 434	1 234 946	615 063	619 883	162 210	88 659	73 551
35 - 39	1 256 597	629 709	626 888	1 117 299	555 560	561 739	139 298	74 149	65 149
40 - 44	1 243 759	619 939	623 820	1 096 314	542 190	554 124	147 445	77 749	69 696
45 - 49	1 253 992	621 802	632 190	1 092 435	536 370	556 065	161 557	85 432	76 125
50 - 54	1 235 770	608 941	626 829	1 073 418	520 174	553 244	162 352	88 767	73 585
55 - 59	1 089 897	533 035	556 862	949 977	455 414	494 563	139 920	77 621	62 299
60 - 64	857 821	414 517	443 304	746 466	353 120	393 346	111 355	61 397	49 958
65 - 69	664 840	313 404	351 436	573 691	264 022	309 669	91 149	49 382	41 767
70 - 74	508 241	230 007	278 234	432 681	190 284	242 397	75 560	39 723	35 837
75 - 79	355 171	151 296	203 875	296 298	121 270	175 028	58 873	30 026	28 847
80 +	400 616	140 728	259 888	320 360	103 869	216 491	80 256	36 859	43 397
Colombia - Colombie[33]									
1 VII 2016 (ESDJ)									
Total	48 747 708	24 069 035	24 678 673	37 332 955	18 035 960	19 296 995	11 414 753	6 033 075	5 381 678
0	876 233	448 451	427 782	618 796	316 327	302 469	257 437	132 124	125 313
1 - 4	3 458 918	1 769 755	1 689 163	2 467 527	1 261 134	1 206 393	991 391	508 621	482 770
5 - 9	4 263 048	2 179 889	2 083 159	3 092 108	1 576 806	1 515 302	1 170 940	603 083	567 857
10 - 14	4 265 999	2 179 636	2 086 363	3 143 930	1 593 730	1 550 200	1 122 069	585 906	536 163
15 - 19	4 321 654	2 206 054	2 115 600	3 241 007	1 625 996	1 615 011	1 080 647	580 058	500 589
20 - 24	4 306 036	2 202 542	2 103 494	3 286 477	1 652 346	1 634 131	1 019 559	550 196	469 363
25 - 29	4 022 291	2 045 161	1 977 130	3 118 951	1 559 804	1 559 147	903 340	485 357	417 983
30 - 34	3 605 504	1 777 536	1 827 968	2 855 563	1 379 597	1 475 966	749 941	397 939	352 002
35 - 39	3 264 933	1 587 121	1 677 812	2 596 917	1 233 756	1 363 161	668 016	353 365	314 651
40 - 44	2 909 621	1 402 143	1 507 478	2 309 219	1 084 567	1 224 652	600 402	317 576	282 826
45 - 49	2 875 587	1 371 868	1 503 719	2 282 421	1 056 548	1 225 873	593 166	315 320	277 846
50 - 54	2 732 428	1 299 581	1 432 847	2 188 715	1 006 952	1 181 763	543 713	292 629	251 084
55 - 59	2 302 979	1 086 167	1 216 812	1 829 419	830 707	998 712	473 560	255 460	218 100
60 - 64	1 800 884	845 202	955 682	1 416 204	636 444	779 760	384 680	208 758	175 922
65 - 69	1 363 781	633 630	730 151	1 059 769	470 329	589 440	304 012	163 301	140 711
70 - 74	967 539	439 732	527 807	741 860	321 239	420 621	225 679	118 493	107 186
75 - 79	700 183	303 690	396 493	533 688	217 659	316 029	166 495	86 031	80 464
80 +	710 090	290 877	419 213	550 384	212 019	338 365	159 706	78 858	80 848
Ecuador - Équateur[34]									
1 VII 2016 (ESDF)									
Total	16 528 730	8 184 970	8 343 760	10 505 180	5 145 594	5 359 586	6 023 550	3 039 376	2 984 174
0	334 222	170 856	163 366	199 278	102 349	96 929	134 944	68 507	66 437

Continent, country or area, date, code[a] and age (in years) / Continent, pays ou zone, date, code[a] et âge (en annèes)	Total			Urban - Urbaine			Rural - Rurale		
	Both sexes Les deux sexes	Male Masculin	Female Féminin	Both sexes Les deux sexes	Male Masculin	Female Féminin	Both sexes Les deux sexes	Male Masculin	Female Féminin
AMERICA, SOUTH - AMÉRIQUE DU SUD									
Ecuador - Équateur[34]									
1 VII 2016 (ESDF)									
1 - 4	1 341 797	685 696	656 101	801 545	410 260	391 285	540 252	275 436	264 816
5 - 9	1 689 023	863 753	825 270	1 009 200	515 977	493 223	679 823	347 776	332 047
10 - 14	1 643 923	840 132	803 791	994 432	506 610	487 822	649 491	333 522	315 969
15 - 19	1 553 360	790 072	763 288	973 536	491 355	482 181	579 824	298 717	281 107
20 - 24	1 433 761	722 223	711 538	934 138	466 041	468 097	499 623	256 182	243 441
25 - 29	1 313 879	653 642	660 237	874 325	431 317	443 008	439 554	222 325	217 229
30 - 34	1 211 920	593 207	618 713	809 641	392 836	416 805	402 279	200 371	201 908
35 - 39	1 104 371	531 540	572 831	737 775	350 824	386 951	366 596	180 716	185 880
40 - 44	981 713	469 240	512 473	659 389	310 206	349 183	322 324	159 034	163 290
45 - 49	865 241	414 094	451 147	583 550	274 650	308 900	281 691	139 444	142 247
50 - 54	756 514	362 641	393 873	506 454	238 982	267 472	250 060	123 659	126 401
55 - 59	639 488	306 871	332 617	418 971	197 567	221 404	220 517	109 304	111 213
60 - 64	516 024	247 138	268 886	325 904	152 660	173 244	190 120	94 478	95 642
65 - 69	401 157	190 518	210 639	242 505	111 796	130 709	158 652	78 722	79 930
70 - 74	299 743	140 112	159 631	175 436	78 771	96 665	124 307	61 341	62 966
75 - 79	209 014	96 140	112 874	120 867	53 009	67 858	88 147	43 131	45 016
80 - 84	129 862	59 458	70 404	75 623	33 004	42 619	54 239	26 454	27 785
85 - 89	67 476	31 019	36 457	40 160	17 611	22 549	27 316	13 408	13 908
90 - 94	27 624	12 689	14 935	16 989	7 407	9 582	10 635	5 282	5 353
95 - 99	8 249	3 753	4 496	5 226	2 253	2 973	3 023	1 500	1 523
100 +	369	176	193	236	109	127	133	67	66
Falkland Islands (Malvinas) - Îles Falkland (Malvinas)[35]									
15 IV 2012 (CDFC)									
Total	2 840	1 491	1 349	...	...	...	...	...	...
0 - 4	152	72	80	...	...	...	...	...	...
5 - 9	161	69	92	...	...	...	...	...	...
10 - 14	152	68	84	...	...	...	...	...	...
15 - 19	143	68	75	...	...	...	...	...	...
20 - 24	165	89	76	...	...	...	...	...	...
25 - 29	203	88	115	...	...	...	...	...	...
30 - 34	217	115	102	...	...	...	...	...	...
35 - 39	256	132	124	...	...	...	...	...	...
40 - 44	266	158	108	...	...	...	...	...	...
45 - 49	225	130	95	...	...	...	...	...	...
50 - 54	235	127	108	...	...	...	...	...	...
55 - 59	189	109	80	...	...	...	...	...	...
60 - 64	145	89	56	...	...	...	...	...	...
65 - 69	109	55	54	...	...	...	...	...	...
70 - 74	72	42	30	...	...	...	...	...	...
75 - 79	62	30	32	...	...	...	...	...	...
80 +	58	29	29	...	...	...	...	...	...
Unknown - Inconnu	30	21	9	...	...	...	...	...	...
French Guiana - Guyane française									
1 I 2016* (ESDJ)									
Total	262 527	130 596	131 931	...	...	...	...	...	...
0 - 4	29 702	15 281	14 421	...	...	...	...	...	...
5 - 9	29 783	15 217	14 566	...	...	...	...	...	...
10 - 14	28 367	14 154	14 213	...	...	...	...	...	...
15 - 19	24 291	12 347	11 944	...	...	...	...	...	...
20 - 24	17 903	8 907	8 996	...	...	...	...	...	...
25 - 29	18 210	8 751	9 459	...	...	...	...	...	...
30 - 34	18 810	8 809	10 001	...	...	...	...	...	...
35 - 39	18 508	8 968	9 540	...	...	...	...	...	...
40 - 44	17 569	8 656	8 913	...	...	...	...	...	...
45 - 49	15 611	7 970	7 641	...	...	...	...	...	...
50 - 54	12 606	6 135	6 471	...	...	...	...	...	...
55 - 59	10 319	5 203	5 116	...	...	...	...	...	...
60 - 64	7 894	4 152	3 742	...	...	...	...	...	...
65 - 69	5 438	2 714	2 724	...	...	...	...	...	...
70 - 74	3 132	1 560	1 572	...	...	...	...	...	...

Continent, country or area, date, code[a] and age (in years) / Continent, pays ou zone, date, code[a] et âge (en années)	Total			Urban - Urbaine			Rural - Rurale		
	Both sexes Les deux sexes	Male Masculin	Female Féminin	Both sexes Les deux sexes	Male Masculin	Female Féminin	Both sexes Les deux sexes	Male Masculin	Female Féminin
AMERICA, SOUTH - AMÉRIQUE DU SUD									
French Guiana - Guyane française									
1 I 2016* (ESDJ)									
75 - 79	1 885	859	1 026	...	...	...	...	...	...
80 - 84	1 262	512	750	...	...	...	...	...	...
85 - 89	735	275	460	...	...	...	...	...	...
90 - 94	349	64	285	...	...	...	...	...	...
95 +	153	62	91	...	...	...	...	...	...
Guyana[5]									
1 VII 2010 (ESDF)									
Total	784 894	393 059	391 835	...	...	...	...	...	...
0 - 4	67 701	34 029	33 673	...	...	...	...	...	...
5 - 9	65 201	32 778	32 423	...	...	...	...	...	...
10 - 14	77 921	39 978	37 943	...	...	...	...	...	...
15 - 19	85 004	43 487	41 518	...	...	...	...	...	...
20 - 24	69 423	34 877	34 545	...	...	...	...	...	...
25 - 29	55 510	26 816	28 694	...	...	...	...	...	...
30 - 34	54 824	27 189	27 635	...	...	...	...	...	...
35 - 39	53 454	27 764	25 690	...	...	...	...	...	...
40 - 44	52 434	27 112	25 322	...	...	...	...	...	...
45 - 49	50 689	25 775	24 914	...	...	...	...	...	...
50 - 54	45 438	22 163	23 275	...	...	...	...	...	...
55 - 59	35 160	17 672	17 488	...	...	...	...	...	...
60 - 64	27 873	13 995	13 878	...	...	...	...	...	...
65 - 69	17 455	7 988	9 467	...	...	...	...	...	...
70 - 74	12 451	5 440	7 012	...	...	...	...	...	...
75 - 79	8 114	3 529	4 585	...	...	...	...	...	...
80 +	6 242	2 469	3 773	...	...	...	...	...	...
Paraguay[36]									
1 VII 2016 (ESDF)									
Total	6 854 536	3 457 365	3 397 170	4 174 834	2 041 139	2 133 695	2 679 702	1 416 226	1 263 476
0 - 4	702 082	358 151	343 930	398 012	203 198	194 814	304 070	154 954	149 116
0	141 537	72 268	69 269	...	...	...	...	...	...
1 - 4	560 544	285 883	274 661	...	...	...	...	...	...
5 - 9	691 901	352 576	339 325	390 221	196 151	194 070	301 680	156 425	145 255
10 - 14	683 516	347 937	335 579	390 252	193 879	196 374	293 263	154 058	139 205
15 - 19	672 867	342 993	329 874	405 622	200 837	204 785	267 245	142 156	125 089
20 - 24	641 263	326 861	314 403	409 703	202 663	207 041	231 560	124 198	107 362
25 - 29	600 414	304 844	295 570	395 319	194 698	200 621	205 095	110 146	94 949
30 - 34	534 718	269 735	264 982	348 434	170 244	178 190	186 283	99 491	86 792
35 - 39	437 936	218 332	219 604	279 314	134 520	144 794	158 622	83 812	74 809
40 - 44	381 358	190 079	191 279	239 963	115 207	124 756	141 396	74 872	66 523
45 - 49	339 976	169 955	170 021	211 545	101 587	109 958	128 431	68 368	60 063
50 - 54	295 002	147 946	147 056	181 799	87 310	94 489	113 203	60 636	52 567
55 - 59	253 974	128 857	125 118	154 665	74 768	79 897	99 309	54 088	45 221
60 - 64	206 424	104 679	101 745	124 312	59 641	64 671	82 112	45 038	37 074
65 - 69	148 797	74 454	74 343	88 717	41 583	47 134	60 080	32 871	27 209
70 - 74	105 964	51 654	54 309	62 824	28 359	34 464	43 140	23 295	19 845
75 - 79	72 546	33 577	38 969	42 954	18 111	24 843	29 593	15 466	14 127
80 +	85 799	34 734	51 065	51 178	18 384	32 794	34 621	16 350	18 271
Peru - Pérou[22]									
30 VI 2016 (ESDF)									
Total	31 488 625	15 772 385	15 716 240	24 313 862	12 013 953	12 299 909	7 174 763	3 758 432	3 416 331
0 - 4	2 845 845	1 452 570	1 393 275	2 005 563	1 027 463	978 100	840 282	425 107	415 175
0	566 198	289 307	276 891	...	...	...	...	...	...
1 - 4	2 279 647	1 163 263	1 116 384	...	...	...	...	...	...
5 - 9	2 909 263	1 482 982	1 426 281	2 081 251	1 059 443	1 021 808	828 012	423 539	404 473
10 - 14	2 913 285	1 483 106	1 430 179	2 122 873	1 073 981	1 048 892	790 412	409 125	381 287
15 - 19	2 886 860	1 465 807	1 421 053	2 181 451	1 093 966	1 087 485	705 409	371 841	333 568
20 - 24	2 835 930	1 436 234	1 399 696	2 253 217	1 123 527	1 129 690	582 713	312 707	270 006
25 - 29	2 689 337	1 357 651	1 331 686	2 125 358	1 053 694	1 071 664	563 979	303 957	260 022
30 - 34	2 444 792	1 230 799	1 213 993	1 939 916	955 799	984 117	504 876	275 000	229 876
35 - 39	2 284 457	1 147 985	1 136 472	1 833 283	899 400	933 883	451 174	248 585	202 589
40 - 44	2 023 192	1 013 313	1 009 879	1 623 658	793 098	830 560	399 534	220 215	179 319

7. Population by age, sex and urban/rural residence: latest available year, 2007 - 2016
Population selon l'âge, le sexe et la résidence, urbaine/rurale : dernière année disponible, 2007 - 2016 (continued - suite)

Continent, country or area, date, code[a] and age (in years) / Continent, pays ou zone, date, code[a] et âge (en années)	Total			Urban - Urbaine			Rural - Rurale		
	Both sexes Les deux sexes	Male Masculin	Female Féminin	Both sexes Les deux sexes	Male Masculin	Female Féminin	Both sexes Les deux sexes	Male Masculin	Female Féminin
AMERICA, SOUTH - AMÉRIQUE DU SUD									
Peru - Pérou[22]									
30 VI 2016 (ESDF)									
45 - 49	1 763 893	879 579	884 314	1 429 727	698 110	731 617	334 166	181 469	152 697
50 - 54	1 525 756	755 954	769 802	1 251 466	611 228	640 238	274 290	144 726	129 564
55 - 59	1 247 403	611 871	635 532	1 014 577	491 130	523 447	232 826	120 741	112 085
60 - 64	1 000 958	485 231	515 727	794 462	381 456	413 006	206 496	103 775	102 721
65 - 69	764 379	364 970	399 409	597 723	283 460	314 263	166 656	81 510	85 146
70 - 74	563 472	262 682	300 790	436 763	202 091	234 672	126 709	60 591	66 118
75 - 79	405 372	181 996	223 376	314 261	138 989	175 272	91 111	43 007	48 104
80 +	384 431	159 655	224 776	308 313	127 118	181 195	76 118	32 537	43 581
Suriname									
13 VIII 2012 (CDJC)									
Total	541 638	270 629	271 009	359 146	177 215	181 931	182 492	93 414	89 078
0 - 4	50 548	25 968	24 580	30 755	15 787	14 968	19 793	10 181	9 612
5 - 9	47 735	24 549	23 186	28 390	14 549	13 841	19 345	10 000	9 345
10 - 14	50 484	26 166	24 318	31 147	16 037	15 110	19 338	10 130	9 208
15 - 19	45 108	22 772	22 336	30 010	15 040	14 970	15 097	7 731	7 366
20 - 24	43 762	21 656	22 106	31 096	15 201	15 895	12 666	6 455	6 211
25 - 29	43 946	21 761	22 185	30 679	15 107	15 572	13 267	6 654	6 613
30 - 34	39 051	19 355	19 696	26 819	13 234	13 585	12 232	6 121	6 111
35 - 39	36 429	18 316	18 113	24 050	11 860	12 190	12 379	6 456	5 923
40 - 44	37 383	18 763	18 620	24 796	12 167	12 629	12 587	6 596	5 991
45 - 49	36 031	18 083	17 948	24 438	12 032	12 406	11 593	6 051	5 542
50 - 54	30 651	15 313	15 338	21 072	10 258	10 814	9 579	5 055	4 525
55 - 59	22 588	10 929	11 659	15 699	7 417	8 282	6 889	3 512	3 377
60 - 64	16 497	7 734	8 763	11 475	5 304	6 171	5 022	2 430	2 592
65 - 69	13 008	5 951	7 057	9 134	4 166	4 968	3 874	1 785	2 089
70 - 74	10 133	4 619	5 514	6 983	3 211	3 772	3 150	1 408	1 742
75 - 79	7 556	3 393	4 163	5 149	2 296	2 853	2 407	1 097	1 310
80 - 84	4 433	1 934	2 499	3 019	1 308	1 711	1 414	626	788
85 +	2 900	1 081	1 819	2 088	758	1 330	812	323	489
85 - 89	1 978	743	1 235	...	...	...	...	...	...
90 - 94	712	274	438	...	...	...	...	...	...
95 +	210	64	146	...	...	...	...	...	...
Unknown - Inconnu	3 395	2 286	1 109	2 347	1 483	864	1 048	803	245
1 VII 2015 (ESDJ)									
Total	567 291	283 259	284 032	...	...	...	...	...	...
0	10 148	5 063	5 085	...	...	...	...	...	...
1 - 4	41 936	21 592	20 344	...	...	...	...	...	...
5 - 9	49 697	25 613	24 084	...	...	...	...	...	...
10 - 14	49 117	25 186	23 931	...	...	...	...	...	...
15 - 19	47 896	24 408	23 488	...	...	...	...	...	...
20 - 24	46 232	23 354	22 878	...	...	...	...	...	...
25 - 29	44 329	22 211	22 118	...	...	...	...	...	...
30 - 34	42 263	21 132	21 131	...	...	...	...	...	...
35 - 39	39 975	19 961	20 014	...	...	...	...	...	...
40 - 44	37 930	18 954	18 976	...	...	...	...	...	...
45 - 49	35 596	17 792	17 804	...	...	...	...	...	...
50 - 54	31 349	15 536	15 813	...	...	...	...	...	...
55 - 59	26 662	13 047	13 615	...	...	...	...	...	...
60 - 64	21 140	10 138	11 002	...	...	...	...	...	...
65 - 69	15 803	7 364	8 439	...	...	...	...	...	...
70 - 74	11 615	5 272	6 343	...	...	...	...	...	...
75 - 79	7 822	3 434	4 388	...	...	...	...	...	...
80 +	7 781	3 202	4 579	...	...	...	...	...	...
Uruguay[2]									
1 VII 2016 (ESDJ)									
Total	3 480 222	1 684 140	1 796 082	3 312 523	1 591 280	1 721 243	167 699	92 859	74 840
0	45 645	23 362	22 283	43 823	22 427	21 396	1 822	935	887
1 - 4	184 319	94 325	89 995	176 656	90 375	86 281	7 664	3 949	3 714
5 - 9	235 768	120 543	115 225	225 232	115 086	110 146	10 536	5 457	5 080
10 - 14	250 353	127 915	122 438	238 511	121 712	116 799	11 842	6 203	5 639
15 - 19	266 775	136 027	130 748	255 565	130 032	125 533	11 210	5 995	5 215
20 - 24	266 538	135 073	131 465	255 738	129 020	126 718	10 800	6 053	4 747

7. Population by age, sex and urban/rural residence: latest available year, 2007 - 2016
Population selon l'âge, le sexe et la résidence, urbaine/rurale : dernière année disponible, 2007 - 2016 (continued - suite)

Continent, country or area, date, code[a] and age (in years) Continent, pays ou zone, date, code[a] et âge (en années)	Total			Urban - Urbaine			Rural - Rurale		
	Both sexes Les deux sexes	Male Masculin	Female Féminin	Both sexes Les deux sexes	Male Masculin	Female Féminin	Both sexes Les deux sexes	Male Masculin	Female Féminin

AMERICA, SOUTH - AMÉRIQUE DU SUD

Uruguay[2]
1 VII 2016 (ESDJ)

25 - 29	251 451	126 638	124 813	240 874	120 591	120 283	10 577	6 047	4 530
30 - 34	238 957	119 472	119 485	228 031	113 437	114 594	10 926	6 035	4 891
35 - 39	242 889	119 813	123 075	230 940	113 085	117 855	11 949	6 728	5 221
40 - 44	229 412	112 886	116 525	217 566	106 161	111 405	11 846	6 726	5 120
45 - 49	209 138	101 534	107 604	197 861	95 204	102 657	11 278	6 330	4 947
50 - 54	205 663	98 824	106 839	194 511	92 441	102 071	11 151	6 383	4 768
55 - 59	194 820	92 650	102 170	184 079	86 513	97 566	10 741	6 137	4 604
60 - 64	169 321	78 930	90 391	159 418	73 201	86 218	9 903	5 730	4 173
65 - 69	141 678	63 829	77 849	133 189	58 895	74 293	8 490	4 934	3 556
70 - 74	118 122	50 652	67 470	111 442	46 775	64 667	6 680	3 877	2 803
75 - 79	93 493	37 102	56 391	88 770	34 452	54 318	4 723	2 650	2 073
80 - 84	70 038	25 012	45 027	66 935	23 420	43 516	3 103	1 592	1 511
85 - 89	43 304	13 612	29 692	41 636	12 833	28 802	1 668	778	890
90 +	22 538	5 941	16 597	21 747	5 621	16 126	791	320	471

Venezuela (Bolivarian Republic of) - Venezuela (République bolivarienne du)
1 VII 2016 (ESDF)

Total	31 028 637	15 554 863	15 473 774	27 356 475	13 592 035	13 764 440	3 672 162	1 962 828	1 709 334
0 - 4	2 727 735	1 405 451	1 322 284	2 304 228	1 194 405	1 109 823	423 507	211 046	212 461
0	541 833	279 325	262 508	...	...	...	...	...	...
1 - 4	2 185 902	1 126 126	1 059 776	...	...	...	...	...	...
5 - 9	2 779 469	1 430 786	1 348 683	2 375 095	1 228 078	1 147 017	404 374	202 708	201 666
10 - 14	2 795 871	1 438 562	1 357 309	2 426 197	1 248 666	1 177 531	369 674	189 896	179 778
15 - 19	2 741 366	1 407 770	1 333 596	2 411 385	1 229 381	1 182 004	329 981	178 389	151 592
20 - 24	2 656 799	1 355 839	1 300 960	2 354 360	1 189 744	1 164 616	302 439	166 095	136 344
25 - 29	2 612 158	1 321 234	1 290 924	2 317 044	1 159 554	1 157 490	295 114	161 680	133 434
30 - 34	2 486 759	1 247 916	1 238 843	2 225 904	1 104 185	1 121 719	260 855	143 731	117 124
35 - 39	2 215 358	1 105 465	1 109 893	1 995 187	983 847	1 011 340	220 171	121 618	98 553
40 - 44	1 994 227	990 823	1 003 404	1 802 845	885 837	917 008	191 382	104 986	86 396
45 - 49	1 860 872	921 673	939 199	1 680 452	823 922	856 530	180 420	97 751	82 669
50 - 54	1 682 824	829 846	852 978	1 508 239	735 800	772 439	174 585	94 046	80 539
55 - 59	1 371 973	671 391	700 582	1 219 391	586 915	632 476	152 582	84 476	68 106
60 - 64	1 035 543	501 794	533 749	913 020	432 305	480 715	122 523	69 489	53 034
65 - 69	755 804	359 061	396 743	664 675	306 960	357 715	91 129	52 101	39 028
70 - 74	537 149	249 657	287 492	473 206	214 216	258 990	63 943	35 441	28 502
75 - 79	357 017	160 630	196 387	315 288	137 726	177 562	41 729	22 904	18 825
80 +	417 713	156 965	260 748	369 959	130 494	239 465	47 754	26 471	21 283

ASIA - ASIE

Afghanistan[37]
1 VII 2016 (ESDF)

Total	27 657 145	14 149 838	13 507 307	6 919 560	3 563 570	3 355 990	20 737 585	10 586 268	10 151 317
0	1 194 657	571 950	622 707	282 179	138 960	143 219	912 478	432 990	479 488
1 - 4	4 201 962	2 054 704	2 147 258	1 020 166	509 098	511 068	3 181 796	1 545 605	1 636 190
5 - 9	4 146 380	2 106 448	2 039 932	1 058 217	539 343	518 873	3 088 164	1 567 105	1 521 059
10 - 14	3 211 597	1 689 221	1 522 376	858 900	443 954	414 945	2 352 697	1 245 266	1 107 431
15 - 19	2 625 201	1 385 640	1 239 561	709 122	362 929	346 192	1 916 079	1 022 710	893 369
20 - 24	2 246 484	1 150 010	1 096 474	588 038	293 470	294 568	1 658 446	856 540	801 905
25 - 29	1 853 807	915 757	938 050	472 665	234 816	237 849	1 381 142	680 941	700 201
30 - 34	1 544 479	736 567	807 912	384 928	193 074	191 854	1 159 551	543 493	616 058
35 - 39	1 355 229	648 882	706 347	324 818	165 858	158 960	1 030 411	483 025	547 387
40 - 44	1 169 878	592 113	577 764	275 878	144 929	130 949	894 000	447 184	446 816
45 - 49	1 013 859	536 609	477 251	233 383	126 622	106 760	780 477	409 986	370 490
50 - 54	855 284	471 339	383 945	193 615	108 092	85 523	661 669	363 247	298 423
55 - 59	688 606	390 372	298 235	155 913	89 514	66 399	532 693	300 857	231 836
60 - 64	531 607	305 143	226 464	122 223	71 394	50 829	409 384	233 749	175 635
65 - 69	384 108	221 494	162 614	89 926	52 637	37 289	294 182	168 857	125 325
70 - 74	264 160	153 609	110 551	62 353	36 661	25 692	201 807	116 948	84 859

7. Population by age, sex and urban/rural residence: latest available year, 2007 - 2016
Population selon l'âge, le sexe et la résidence, urbaine/rurale : dernière année disponible, 2007 - 2016 (continued - suite)

Continent, country or area, date, code[a] and age (in years) / Continent, pays ou zone, date, code[a] et âge (en annèes)	Total			Urban - Urbaine			Rural - Rurale		
	Both sexes Les deux sexes	Male Masculin	Female Féminin	Both sexes Les deux sexes	Male Masculin	Female Féminin	Both sexes Les deux sexes	Male Masculin	Female Féminin
ASIA - ASIE									
Afghanistan[37]									
1 VII 2016 (ESDF)									
75 - 79	168 844	98 809	70 035	39 760	23 639	16 121	129 085	75 170	53 914
80 +	201 002	121 171	79 831	47 479	28 578	18 901	153 523	92 593	60 930
Armenia - Arménie									
1 VII 2015 (ESDJ)									
Total	3 004 588	1 434 095	1 570 493	1 909 960	891 769	1 018 191	1 094 628	542 326	552 302
0	42 220	22 400	19 820	27 390	14 446	12 944	14 830	7 954	6 876
1 - 4	167 033	88 945	78 088	105 017	55 455	49 562	62 016	33 490	28 526
5 - 9	202 116	107 629	94 487	125 232	66 164	59 068	76 884	41 465	35 419
10 - 14	174 352	93 422	80 930	106 380	56 294	50 086	67 972	37 128	30 844
15 - 19	185 127	97 233	87 894	108 215	56 587	51 628	76 912	40 646	36 266
20 - 24	243 759	119 643	124 116	143 421	69 011	74 410	100 338	50 632	49 706
25 - 29	276 720	133 816	142 904	169 942	79 592	90 350	106 778	54 224	52 554
30 - 34	252 928	121 724	131 204	164 364	76 980	87 384	88 564	44 744	43 820
35 - 39	204 550	97 403	107 147	137 038	64 882	72 156	67 512	32 521	34 991
40 - 44	176 526	82 353	94 173	116 052	53 797	62 255	60 474	28 556	31 918
45 - 49	173 475	79 301	94 174	105 394	46 341	59 053	68 081	32 960	35 121
50 - 54	214 524	97 658	116 866	131 278	56 670	74 608	83 246	40 988	42 258
55 - 59	211 053	95 609	115 444	138 540	59 908	78 632	72 513	35 701	36 812
60 - 64	154 475	68 004	86 471	109 376	46 922	62 454	45 099	21 082	24 017
65 - 69	101 586	42 422	59 164	75 345	31 222	44 123	26 241	11 200	15 041
70 - 74	62 035	25 178	36 857	44 201	18 116	26 085	17 834	7 062	10 772
75 - 79	88 119	33 850	54 269	57 306	22 246	35 060	30 813	11 604	19 209
80 - 84	47 864	18 578	29 286	30 017	11 784	18 233	17 847	6 794	11 053
85 +	26 126	8 927	17 199	15 452	5 352	10 100	10 674	3 575	7 099
Azerbaijan - Azerbaïdjan									
1 VII 2015 (ESDF)									
Total	9 649 341	4 805 749	4 843 592	5 126 358	2 534 004	2 592 354	4 522 983	2 271 745	2 251 238
0	168 357	89 913	78 444	81 496	43 272	38 224	86 861	46 641	40 220
1 - 4	683 312	366 598	316 714	335 894	179 138	156 756	347 418	187 460	159 958
5 - 9	688 071	368 841	319 230	346 179	184 557	161 622	341 892	184 284	157 608
10 - 14	630 030	335 967	294 063	315 826	168 809	147 017	314 204	167 158	147 046
15 - 19	708 975	372 820	336 155	350 938	185 809	165 129	358 037	187 011	171 026
20 - 24	888 013	455 758	432 255	449 329	230 841	218 488	438 684	224 917	213 767
25 - 29	940 177	465 827	474 350	505 146	247 623	257 523	435 031	218 204	216 827
30 - 34	828 483	409 004	419 479	459 718	224 556	235 162	368 765	184 448	184 317
35 - 39	695 121	345 124	349 997	385 836	190 643	195 193	309 285	154 481	154 804
40 - 44	617 028	298 151	318 877	330 493	156 265	174 228	286 535	141 886	144 649
45 - 49	656 336	313 113	343 223	347 576	162 198	185 378	308 760	150 915	157 845
50 - 54	663 546	315 622	347 924	366 662	172 243	194 419	296 884	143 379	153 505
55 - 59	558 549	266 172	292 377	321 161	153 549	167 612	237 388	112 623	124 765
60 - 64	339 179	157 486	181 693	204 523	95 370	109 153	134 656	62 116	72 540
65 - 69	206 329	91 981	114 348	128 023	57 816	70 207	78 306	34 165	44 141
70 - 74	111 520	46 932	64 588	66 044	27 780	38 264	45 476	19 152	26 324
75 - 79	150 006	60 968	89 038	77 490	31 955	45 535	72 516	29 013	43 503
80 - 84	75 441	30 365	45 076	35 528	14 234	21 294	39 913	16 131	23 782
85 - 89	30 343	11 813	18 530	14 133	5 698	8 435	16 210	6 115	10 095
90 - 94	7 843	2 656	5 187	3 480	1 322	2 158	4 363	1 334	3 029
95 - 99	2 060	554	1 506	711	297	414	1 349	257	1 092
100 +	622	84	538	172	29	143	450	55	395
Bahrain - Bahreïn									
1 VII 2016 (ESDJ)									
Total	1 423 726	888 389	535 337	...	...	...	...	...	...
0 - 4	101 616	51 863	49 753	...	...	...	...	...	...
5 - 9	96 649	49 269	47 380	...	...	...	...	...	...
10 - 14	85 422	43 722	41 700	...	...	...	...	...	...
15 - 19	76 550	39 804	36 746	...	...	...	...	...	...
20 - 24	109 715	66 354	43 361	...	...	...	...	...	...
25 - 29	193 897	133 819	60 078	...	...	...	...	...	...
30 - 34	200 673	142 680	57 993	...	...	...	...	...	...
35 - 39	156 131	105 837	50 294	...	...	...	...	...	...
40 - 44	120 018	80 432	39 586	...	...	...	...	...	...
45 - 49	93 709	61 832	31 877	...	...	...	...	...	...
50 - 54	71 428	44 108	27 320	...	...	...	...	...	...

7. Population by age, sex and urban/rural residence: latest available year, 2007 - 2016
Population selon l'âge, le sexe et la résidence, urbaine/rurale : dernière année disponible, 2007 - 2016 (continued - suite)

Continent, country or area, date, code[a] and age (in years) / Continent, pays ou zone, date, code[a] et âge (en années)	Total			Urban - Urbaine			Rural - Rurale		
	Both sexes Les deux sexes	Male Masculin	Female Féminin	Both sexes Les deux sexes	Male Masculin	Female Féminin	Both sexes Les deux sexes	Male Masculin	Female Féminin
ASIA - ASIE									
Bahrain - Bahreïn									
1 VII 2016 (ESDJ)									
55 - 59	51 770	31 953	19 817	...	...	...	...	...	...
60 - 64	29 530	17 539	11 991	...	...	...	...	...	...
65 - 69	15 079	8 687	6 392	...	...	...	...	...	...
70 - 74	8 817	4 519	4 298	...	...	...	...	...	...
75 - 79	6 155	2 938	3 217	...	...	...	...	...	...
80 - 84	3 436	1 614	1 822	...	...	...	...	...	...
85 +	3 131	1 419	1 712	...	...	...	...	...	...
Bangladesh									
15 III 2011 (CDFC)									
Total	144 043 697	72 109 796	71 933 901	33 563 183[38]	17 529 792[38]	16 033 391[38]	110 480 514	54 580 004	55 900 510
0 - 4	15 061 970	7 638 523	7 423 447	3 015 500[38]	1 534 508[38]	1 480 992[38]	12 046 470	6 104 015	5 942 455
5 - 9	18 173 229	9 322 514	8 850 715	3 520 080[38]	1 810 786[38]	1 709 294[38]	14 653 149	7 511 728	7 141 421
10 - 14	16 646 615	8 614 889	8 031 726	3 609 866[38]	1 868 428[38]	1 741 438[38]	13 036 749	6 746 461	6 290 288
15 - 19	12 861 890	6 509 492	6 352 398	3 417 088[38]	1 735 931[38]	1 681 157[38]	9 444 802	4 773 561	4 671 241
20 - 24	13 299 789	5 777 370	7 522 419	3 750 754[38]	1 803 092[38]	1 947 662[38]	9 549 035	3 974 278	5 574 757
25 - 29	13 479 508	6 225 252	7 254 256	3 638 634[38]	1 846 338[38]	1 792 296[38]	9 840 874	4 378 914	5 461 960
30 - 34	10 499 765	5 079 106	5 420 659	2 757 615[38]	1 460 253[38]	1 297 362[38]	7 742 150	3 618 853	4 123 297
35 - 39	9 556 428	4 697 349	4 859 079	2 424 331[38]	1 291 114[38]	1 133 217[38]	7 132 097	3 406 235	3 725 862
40 - 44	8 261 662	4 280 923	3 980 739	2 014 738[38]	1 124 193[38]	890 545[38]	6 246 924	3 156 730	3 090 194
45 - 49	6 380 073	3 363 273	3 016 800	1 504 983[38]	849 659[38]	655 324[38]	4 875 090	2 513 614	2 361 476
50 - 54	5 552 271	2 952 596	2 599 675	1 225 174[38]	703 282[38]	521 892[38]	4 327 097	2 249 314	2 077 783
55 - 59	3 500 997	1 923 534	1 577 463	758 757[38]	448 673[38]	310 084[38]	2 742 240	1 474 861	1 267 379
60 - 64	3 934 014	2 081 306	1 852 708	759 025[38]	425 996[38]	333 029[38]	3 174 989	1 655 310	1 519 679
65 - 69	2 113 490	1 149 569	963 921	386 330[38]	217 634[38]	168 696[38]	1 727 160	931 935	795 225
70 - 74	2 231 712	1 206 398	1 025 314	379 459[38]	207 611[38]	171 848[38]	1 852 253	998 787	853 466
75 - 79	874 727	488 338	386 389	146 831[38]	80 832[38]	65 999[38]	727 896	407 506	320 390
80 - 84	880 079	443 239	436 840	138 128[38]	68 117[38]	70 011[38]	741 951	375 122	366 829
85 - 89	262 611	138 268	124 343	42 824[38]	21 933[38]	20 891[38]	219 787	116 335	103 452
90 - 94	250 189	116 916	133 273	38 679[38]	16 945[38]	21 734[38]	211 510	99 971	111 539
95 +	222 678	100 941	121 737	34 387[38]	14 467[38]	19 920[38]	188 291	86 474	101 817
1 VII 2016 (ESDF)									
Total	*160 800 000*	*80 500 000*	*80 300 000*	...	...	...	...	...	...
0	*2 882 946*	*1 262 898*	*1 620 048*	...	...	...	...	...	...
1 - 4	*11 132 126*	*5 596 094*	*5 536 032*	...	...	...	...	...	...
5 - 9	*16 758 940*	*8 512 307*	*8 246 633*	...	...	...	...	...	...
10 - 14	*18 767 445*	*9 514 032*	*9 253 413*	...	...	...	...	...	...
15 - 19	*15 614 548*	*8 246 602*	*7 367 946*	...	...	...	...	...	...
20 - 24	*14 365 508*	*6 490 899*	*7 874 610*	...	...	...	...	...	...
25 - 29	*13 957 754*	*6 339 834*	*7 617 920*	...	...	...	...	...	...
30 - 34	*13 104 942*	*6 225 025*	*6 879 917*	...	...	...	...	...	...
35 - 39	*11 304 360*	*5 661 891*	*5 642 469*	...	...	...	...	...	...
40 - 44	*9 746 887*	*5 001 069*	*4 745 818*	...	...	...	...	...	...
45 - 49	*8 160 344*	*4 482 247*	*3 678 097*	...	...	...	...	...	...
50 - 54	*7 819 673*	*3 804 471*	*4 015 201*	...	...	...	...	...	...
55 - 59	*5 202 764*	*2 829 099*	*2 373 664*	...	...	...	...	...	...
60 - 64	*4 606 009*	*2 504 982*	*2 101 026*	...	...	...	...	...	...
65 - 69	*2 882 045*	*1 594 568*	*1 287 477*	...	...	...	...	...	...
70 - 74	*2 200 014*	*1 229 160*	*970 854*	...	...	...	...	...	...
75 - 79	*1 002 308*	*572 366*	*429 942*	...	...	...	...	...	...
80 - 84	*709 229*	*354 665*	*354 564*	...	...	...	...	...	...
85 - 89	*269 757*	*143 343*	*126 414*	...	...	...	...	...	...
90 - 94	*169 881*	*76 204*	*93 677*	...	...	...	...	...	...
95 +	*142 520*	*58 244*	*84 276*	...	...	...	...	...	...
Bhutan - Bhoutan[39]									
1 VII 2015 (ESDF)									
Total	*757 042*	*393 327*	*363 718*	*294 402*	*156 327*	*138 077*	*462 640*	*237 000*	*225 641*
0 - 4	*82 561*	*41 633*	*40 928*	*28 821*	*14 412*	*14 409*	*53 740*	*27 221*	*26 519*
0	*15 650*	*7 880*	*7 770*	...	...	...	...	...	...
1 - 4	*66 911*	*33 753*	*33 158*	...	...	...	...	...	...
5 - 9	*85 171*	*43 013*	*42 158*	*32 984*	*16 504*	*16 481*	*52 187*	*26 509*	*25 677*
10 - 14	*62 054*	*31 255*	*30 799*	*25 968*	*12 958*	*13 010*	*36 086*	*18 297*	*17 789*
15 - 19	*67 765*	*34 291*	*33 474*	*29 789*	*15 059*	*14 730*	*37 976*	*19 232*	*18 744*

7. Population by age, sex and urban/rural residence: latest available year, 2007 - 2016
Population selon l'âge, le sexe et la résidence, urbaine/rurale : dernière année disponible, 2007 - 2016 (continued - suite)

Continent, country or area, date, code[a] and age (in years) / Continent, pays ou zone, date, code[a] et âge (en annèes)	Total			Urban - Urbaine			Rural - Rurale		
	Both sexes Les deux sexes	Male Masculin	Female Féminin	Both sexes Les deux sexes	Male Masculin	Female Féminin	Both sexes Les deux sexes	Male Masculin	Female Féminin
ASIA - ASIE									
Bhutan - Bhoutan[39]									
1 VII 2015 (ESDF)									
20 - 24	71 524	36 467	35 057	33 496	17 282	16 214	38 028	19 185	18 843
25 - 29	68 976	35 757	33 219	32 499	17 207	15 292	36 477	18 550	17 927
30 - 34	64 212	34 342	29 870	29 576	16 427	13 150	34 636	17 915	16 720
35 - 39	56 625	30 686	25 939	24 647	14 063	10 584	31 978	16 623	15 355
40 - 44	46 399	25 415	20 985	17 557	10 342	7 215	28 842	15 073	13 770
45 - 49	38 480	21 057	17 424	12 883	7 673	5 209	25 597	13 384	12 215
50 - 54	30 568	16 439	14 129	8 636	5 101	3 535	21 932	11 338	10 594
55 - 59	24 636	13 102	11 534	6 070	3 525	2 545	18 566	9 577	8 989
60 - 64	19 415	10 218	9 197	4 154	2 288	1 867	15 261	7 930	7 330
65 - 69	14 838	7 697	7 142	2 875	1 494	1 381	11 963	6 203	5 761
70 - 74	10 696	5 450	5 245	1 918	914	1 004	8 778	4 536	4 241
75 - 79	7 009	3 507	3 503	1 274	539	735	5 735	2 968	2 768
80 +	6 113	2 998	3 115	1 255	539	716	4 858	2 459	2 399
1 VII 2016 (ESDF)									
Total	768 577	398 948	369 629	...	...	...	...	...	...
0 - 4	82 041	41 354	40 687	...	...	...	...	...	...
5 - 9	81 213	40 975	40 238	...	...	...	...	...	...
10 - 14	64 190	32 292	31 898	...	...	...	...	...	...
15 - 19	68 236	34 530	33 706	...	...	...	...	...	...
20 - 24	75 416	38 010	37 406	...	...	...	...	...	...
25 - 29	74 797	36 881	37 916	...	...	...	...	...	...
30 - 34	70 813	39 641	31 172	...	...	...	...	...	...
35 - 39	59 026	32 706	26 320	...	...	...	...	...	...
40 - 44	43 542	23 553	19 989	...	...	...	...	...	...
45 - 49	37 885	20 606	17 279	...	...	...	...	...	...
50 - 54	29 253	15 633	13 620	...	...	...	...	...	...
55 - 59	25 338	13 477	11 861	...	...	...	...	...	...
60 - 64	19 844	10 425	9 419	...	...	...	...	...	...
65 - 69	13 443	7 012	6 431	...	...	...	...	...	...
70 - 74	10 238	5 153	5 085	...	...	...	...	...	...
75 - 79	6 759	3 430	3 329	...	...	...	...	...	...
80 +	6 543	3 270	3 273	...	...	...	...	...	...
Brunei Darussalam - Brunéi Darussalam									
20 VI 2011 (CDJC)									
Total	393 372	203 144	190 228	296 257	151 663	144 594	97 115	51 481	45 634
0 - 4	30 323	15 690	14 633	23 250	11 966	11 284	7 073	3 724	3 349
5 - 9	33 659	17 271	16 388	25 840	13 253	12 587	7 819	4 018	3 801
10 - 14	35 453	18 424	17 029	26 734	13 946	12 788	8 719	4 478	4 241
15 - 19	34 967	17 954	17 013	25 706	13 158	12 548	9 261	4 796	4 465
20 - 24	38 150	19 916	18 234	28 301	14 585	13 716	9 849	5 331	4 518
25 - 29	39 185	20 756	18 429	29 567	15 337	14 230	9 618	5 419	4 199
30 - 34	36 896	19 324	17 572	28 516	14 629	13 887	8 380	4 695	3 685
35 - 39	33 796	17 331	16 465	25 962	13 022	12 940	7 834	4 309	3 525
40 - 44	30 122	15 289	14 833	22 900	11 487	11 413	7 222	3 802	3 420
45 - 49	24 610	12 840	11 770	18 737	9 714	9 023	5 873	3 126	2 747
50 - 54	19 781	10 333	9 448	14 978	7 841	7 137	4 803	2 492	2 311
55 - 59	14 044	7 158	6 886	10 214	5 270	4 944	3 830	1 888	1 942
60 - 64	8 518	4 164	4 354	6 112	3 008	3 104	2 406	1 156	1 250
65 - 69	5 088	2 584	2 504	3 522	1 770	1 752	1 566	814	752
70 - 74	3 901	1 827	2 074	2 680	1 208	1 472	1 221	619	602
75 - 79	2 601	1 193	1 408	1 713	764	949	888	429	459
80 - 84	1 405	702	703	943	452	491	462	250	212
85 +	873	388	485	582	253	329	291	135	156
1 VII 2015 (ESDJ)									
Total	417 200	216 600	200 600	...	...	...	...	...	...
0 - 4	32 900	17 100	15 800	...	...	...	...	...	...
5 - 9	31 000	16 100	14 900	...	...	...	...	...	...
10 - 14	34 600	17 800	16 800	...	...	...	...	...	...
15 - 19	35 400	18 300	17 100	...	...	...	...	...	...
20 - 24	35 000	18 200	16 800	...	...	...	...	...	...
25 - 29	39 100	20 700	18 400	...	...	...	...	...	...
30 - 34	39 000	20 900	18 100	...	...	...	...	...	...

Continent, country or area, date, code[a] and age (in years) Continent, pays ou zone, date, code[a] et âge (en annèes)	Total			Urban - Urbaine			Rural - Rurale		
	Both sexes Les deux sexes	Male Masculin	Female Féminin	Both sexes Les deux sexes	Male Masculin	Female Féminin	Both sexes Les deux sexes	Male Masculin	Female Féminin
ASIA - ASIE									
Brunei Darussalam - Brunéi Darussalam									
1 VII 2015 (ESDJ)									
35 - 39	36 100	19 000	17 100	...	...	...	...	...	...
40 - 44	33 200	17 000	16 200	...	...	...	...	...	...
45 - 49	28 600	14 800	13 800	...	...	...	...	...	...
50 - 54	23 700	12 500	11 200	...	...	...	...	...	...
55 - 59	18 400	9 500	8 900	...	...	...	...	...	...
60 - 64	12 400	6 300	6 100	...	...	...	...	...	...
65 - 69	7 300	3 500	3 800	...	...	...	...	...	...
70 - 74	4 500	2 200	2 300	...	...	...	...	...	...
75 - 79	3 100	1 400	1 700	...	...	...	...	...	...
80 - 84	1 800	800	1 000	...	...	...	...	...	...
85 - 89	800	400	400	...	...	...	...	...	...
90 - 94	300	100	200	...	...	...	...	...	...
95 - 99	-	-	-	...	...	...	...	...	...
100 +	-	-	-	...	...	...	...	...	...
Unknown - Inconnu	-	-	-	...	...	...	...	...	...
Cambodia - Cambodge[40]									
1 VII 2015 (ESDF)									
Total	15 405 157	7 551 944	7 853 213	3 540 575	1 705 018	1 835 557	11 864 582	5 846 926	6 017 656
0	343 968	175 388	168 580	86 946	44 740	42 206	257 022	130 648	126 374
1 - 4	1 256 559	639 680	616 879	287 909	146 676	141 233	968 650	493 004	475 646
5 - 9	1 478 056	751 537	726 519	266 331	135 468	130 863	1 211 725	616 069	595 656
10 - 14	1 424 533	727 116	697 417	222 335	114 171	108 164	1 202 198	612 945	589 253
15 - 19	1 637 111	838 821	798 290	273 601	136 051	137 550	1 363 510	702 770	660 740
20 - 24	1 698 824	877 158	821 666	407 469	188 296	219 173	1 291 355	688 862	602 493
25 - 29	1 478 710	737 077	741 633	484 549	223 014	261 535	994 161	514 063	480 098
30 - 34	1 333 262	649 670	683 592	427 395	205 047	222 348	905 867	444 623	461 244
35 - 39	879 004	427 791	451 213	237 471	117 764	119 707	641 533	310 027	331 506
40 - 44	761 990	367 586	394 404	177 884	89 396	88 488	584 106	278 190	305 916
45 - 49	793 754	374 975	418 779	175 105	87 482	87 623	618 649	287 493	331 156
50 - 54	677 057	312 718	364 339	144 559	70 342	74 217	532 498	242 376	290 122
55 - 59	533 368	224 272	309 096	119 460	52 954	66 506	413 908	171 318	242 590
60 - 64	398 784	159 105	239 679	89 373	37 736	51 637	309 411	121 369	188 042
65 - 69	282 114	117 449	164 665	58 973	24 909	34 064	223 141	92 540	130 601
70 - 74	191 298	79 144	112 154	36 584	14 784	21 800	154 714	64 360	90 354
75 - 79	126 227	50 567	75 660	23 103	8 844	14 259	103 124	41 723	61 401
80 +	110 538	41 890	68 648	21 528	7 344	14 184	89 010	34 546	54 464
China - Chine[41]									
1 XI 2010 (CDJC)[42]									
Total	1332810869	682 329 104	650 481 765	670 005 546	343 040 783	326 964 763	662 805 323	339 288 321	323 517 002
0 - 4	75 532 610	41 062 566	34 470 044	30 936 470	16 749 729	14 186 741	44 596 140	24 312 837	20 283 303
5 - 9	70 881 549	38 464 665	32 416 884	30 565 659	16 580 910	13 984 749	40 315 890	21 883 755	18 432 135
10 - 14	74 908 462	40 267 277	34 641 185	32 807 526	17 664 790	15 142 736	42 100 936	22 602 487	19 498 449
15 - 19	99 889 114	51 904 830	47 984 284	53 589 992	27 603 777	25 986 215	46 299 122	24 301 053	21 998 069
20 - 24	127 412 518	64 008 573	63 403 945	71 058 518	36 041 784	35 016 734	56 354 000	27 966 789	28 387 211
25 - 29	101 013 852	50 837 038	50 176 814	57 679 956	28 973 516	28 706 440	43 333 896	21 863 522	21 470 374
30 - 34	97 138 203	49 521 822	47 616 381	56 010 957	28 432 073	27 578 884	41 127 246	21 089 749	20 037 497
35 - 39	118 025 959	60 391 104	57 634 855	65 025 365	33 349 280	31 676 085	53 000 594	27 041 824	25 958 770
40 - 44	124 753 964	63 608 678	61 145 286	63 786 496	32 845 769	30 940 727	60 967 468	30 762 909	30 204 559
45 - 49	105 594 553	53 776 418	51 818 135	53 629 541	27 723 132	25 906 409	51 965 012	26 053 286	25 911 726
50 - 54	78 753 171	40 363 234	38 389 937	39 186 388	20 130 395	19 055 993	39 566 783	20 232 839	19 333 944
55 - 59	81 312 474	41 082 938	40 229 536	37 437 535	18 762 887	18 674 648	43 874 939	22 320 051	21 554 888
60 - 64	58 667 282	29 834 426	28 832 856	26 036 917	13 067 045	12 969 872	32 630 365	16 767 381	15 862 984
65 - 69	41 113 282	20 748 471	20 364 811	17 910 329	8 866 594	9 043 735	23 202 953	11 881 877	11 321 076
70 - 74	32 972 397	16 403 453	16 568 944	14 777 260	7 241 891	7 535 369	18 195 137	9 161 562	9 033 575
75 - 79	23 852 133	11 278 859	12 573 274	10 531 503	5 048 471	5 483 032	13 320 630	6 230 388	7 090 242
80 - 84	13 373 198	5 917 502	7 455 696	5 762 828	2 665 218	3 097 610	7 610 370	3 252 284	4 358 086
85 - 89	5 631 928	2 199 810	3 432 118	2 392 190	982 284	1 409 906	3 239 738	1 217 526	2 022 212
90 - 94	1 578 307	530 872	1 047 435	687 763	246 031	441 732	890 544	284 841	605 703
95 - 99	369 979	117 716	252 263	176 542	60 991	115 551	193 437	56 725	136 712
100 +	35 934	8 852	27 082	15 811	4 216	11 595	20 123	4 636	15 487

7. Population by age, sex and urban/rural residence: latest available year, 2007 - 2016
Population selon l'âge, le sexe et la résidence, urbaine/rurale : dernière année disponible, 2007 - 2016 (continued - suite)

Continent, country or area, date, code[a] and age (in years) Continent, pays ou zone, date, code[a] et âge (en années)	Total			Urban - Urbaine			Rural - Rurale		
	Both sexes Les deux sexes	Male Masculin	Female Féminin	Both sexes Les deux sexes	Male Masculin	Female Féminin	Both sexes Les deux sexes	Male Masculin	Female Féminin
ASIA - ASIE									
China - Chine[41]									
31 XII 2011 (ESDF)[43]									
Total	1347304706	690 634 118	656 670 588	...	...	...	...	...	...
0 - 4	76 270 588	41 467 059	34 803 529	...	...	...	...	...	...
5 - 9	72 092 941	39 108 235	32 984 706	...	...	...	...	...	...
10 - 14	73 507 059	39 657 647	33 849 412	...	...	...	...	...	...
15 - 19	94 574 118	49 489 412	45 084 706	...	...	...	...	...	...
20 - 24	127 725 882	64 991 765	62 732 941	...	...	...	...	...	...
25 - 29	105 010 588	52 912 941	52 096 471	...	...	...	...	...	...
30 - 34	96 644 706	49 303 529	47 341 176	...	...	...	...	...	...
35 - 39	113 994 118	58 317 647	55 676 471	...	...	...	...	...	...
40 - 44	126 342 353	64 477 647	61 864 706	...	...	...	...	...	...
45 - 49	118 650 588	60 510 588	58 140 000	...	...	...	...	...	...
50 - 54	73 181 176	37 436 471	35 744 706	...	...	...	...	...	...
55 - 59	84 314 118	42 603 529	41 709 412	...	...	...	...	...	...
60 - 64	62 009 412	31 397 647	30 611 765	...	...	...	...	...	...
65 - 69	42 416 471	21 251 765	21 164 706	...	...	...	...	...	...
70 - 74	33 912 941	16 934 118	16 978 824	...	...	...	...	...	...
75 - 79	24 910 588	11 716 471	13 195 294	...	...	...	...	...	...
80 - 84	14 075 294	6 263 529	7 811 765	...	...	...	...	...	...
85 - 89	5 642 353	2 182 353	3 460 000	...	...	...	...	...	...
90 - 94	1 690 588	524 706	1 165 882	...	...	...	...	...	...
95 +	341 176	85 882	254 118	...	...	...	...	...	...
China, Hong Kong SAR - Chine, Hong Kong RAS									
1 VII 2016 (ESDJ)									
Total	7 336 600	3 375 400	3 961 200	...	...	...	...	...	...
0	53 300	27 700	25 600	...	...	...	...	...	...
1 - 4	226 200	117 100	109 100	...	...	...	...	...	...
5 - 9	291 800	151 200	140 600	...	...	...	...	...	...
10 - 14	259 200	132 300	126 900	...	...	...	...	...	...
15 - 19	340 900	176 500	164 400	...	...	...	...	...	...
20 - 24	445 100	220 300	224 800	...	...	...	...	...	...
25 - 29	510 200	227 700	282 500	...	...	...	...	...	...
30 - 34	577 200	233 000	344 200	...	...	...	...	...	...
35 - 39	571 300	228 000	343 300	...	...	...	...	...	...
40 - 44	569 800	234 600	335 200	...	...	...	...	...	...
45 - 49	567 000	240 200	326 800	...	...	...	...	...	...
50 - 54	643 100	292 900	350 200	...	...	...	...	...	...
55 - 59	623 000	306 800	316 200	...	...	...	...	...	...
60 - 64	495 300	244 100	251 200	...	...	...	...	...	...
65 - 69	395 700	196 500	199 200	...	...	...	...	...	...
70 - 74	220 800	112 200	108 600	...	...	...	...	...	...
75 - 79	206 400	101 200	105 200	...	...	...	...	...	...
80 - 84	167 000	74 100	92 900	...	...	...	...	...	...
85 +	173 300	59 000	114 300	...	...	...	...	...	...
China, Macao SAR - Chine, Macao RAS									
1 VII 2015 (ESDJ)									
Total	642 900	317 500	325 400	...	...	...	...	...	...
0	7 000	3 700	3 300	...	...	...	...	...	...
1 - 4	25 300	13 300	12 000	...	...	...	...	...	...
5 - 9	22 100	11 600	10 500	...	...	...	...	...	...
10 - 14	20 300	10 900	9 400	...	...	...	...	...	...
15 - 19	30 000	15 600	14 400	...	...	...	...	...	...
20 - 24	47 000	23 900	23 100	...	...	...	...	...	...
25 - 29	72 900	36 200	36 700	...	...	...	...	...	...
30 - 34	64 900	32 400	32 500	...	...	...	...	...	...
35 - 39	50 600	25 500	25 100	...	...	...	...	...	...
40 - 44	53 600	25 600	28 000	...	...	...	...	...	...
45 - 49	52 500	23 600	28 900	...	...	...	...	...	...
50 - 54	57 700	27 000	30 700	...	...	...	...	...	...
55 - 59	48 500	24 300	24 200	...	...	...	...	...	...
60 - 64	35 100	17 600	17 500	...	...	...	...	...	...
65 - 69	23 300	12 200	11 100	...	...	...	...	...	...

Continent, country or area, date, code[a] and age (in years) / Continent, pays ou zone, date, code[a] et âge (en années)	Total			Urban - Urbaine			Rural - Rurale		
	Both sexes Les deux sexes	Male Masculin	Female Féminin	Both sexes Les deux sexes	Male Masculin	Female Féminin	Both sexes Les deux sexes	Male Masculin	Female Féminin
ASIA - ASIE									
China, Macao SAR - Chine, Macao RAS									
1 VII 2015 (ESDJ)									
70 - 74	10 900	5 600	5 300	...	...	...	...	...	...
75 - 79	8 300	3 900	4 400	...	...	...	...	...	...
80 - 84	6 400	2 600	3 800	...	...	...	...	...	...
85 +	6 500	2 000	4 500	...	...	...	...	...	...
Cyprus - Chypre[44]									
1 X 2011 (CDJC)									
Total	840 407	408 780	431 627	566 191	273 065	293 126	274 216	135 715	138 501
0 - 4	45 015	23 061	21 954	29 726	15 202	14 524	15 289	7 859	7 430
5 - 9	42 635	21 921	20 714	28 050	14 386	13 664	14 585	7 535	7 050
10 - 14	47 298	24 179	23 119	30 926	15 730	15 196	16 372	8 449	7 923
15 - 19	55 818	28 683	27 135	36 345	18 593	17 752	19 473	10 090	9 383
20 - 24	66 073	33 891	32 182	44 948	22 847	22 101	21 125	11 044	10 081
25 - 29	74 114	36 992	37 122	51 855	25 842	26 013	22 259	11 150	11 109
30 - 34	69 834	33 149	36 685	48 938	23 133	25 805	20 896	10 016	10 880
35 - 39	61 862	27 754	34 108	43 232	19 204	24 028	18 630	8 550	10 080
40 - 44	59 728	27 031	32 697	41 295	18 416	22 879	18 433	8 615	9 818
45 - 49	57 240	27 059	30 181	39 233	18 225	21 008	18 007	8 834	9 173
50 - 54	56 128	27 517	28 611	38 287	18 499	19 788	17 841	9 018	8 823
55 - 59	47 762	23 771	23 991	31 716	15 541	16 175	16 046	8 230	7 816
60 - 64	45 034	22 057	22 977	29 704	14 438	15 266	15 330	7 619	7 711
65 - 69	36 328	17 656	18 672	23 459	11 295	12 164	12 869	6 361	6 508
70 - 74	29 433	14 044	15 389	18 991	9 048	9 943	10 442	4 996	5 446
75 - 79	21 058	9 647	11 411	13 545	6 239	7 306	7 513	3 408	4 105
80 +	24 948	10 342	14 606	15 853	6 408	9 445	9 095	3 934	5 161
Unknown - Inconnu	99	26	73	88	19	69	11	7	4
1 VII 2016 (ESDJ)									
Total	*848 319*	*412 692*	*435 627*	...	...	...	...	...	...
0	*9 159*	*4 813*	*4 346*	...	...	...	...	...	...
1 - 4	*38 213*	*19 646*	*18 567*	...	...	...	...	...	...
5 - 9	*47 615*	*24 461*	*23 154*	...	...	...	...	...	...
10 - 14	*44 551*	*22 758*	*21 793*	...	...	...	...	...	...
15 - 19	*51 747*	*26 021*	*25 726*	...	...	...	...	...	...
20 - 24	*65 403*	*32 677*	*32 726*	...	...	...	...	...	...
25 - 29	*71 225*	*35 449*	*35 776*	...	...	...	...	...	...
30 - 34	*67 875*	*32 483*	*35 392*	...	...	...	...	...	...
35 - 39	*62 180*	*28 972*	*33 208*	...	...	...	...	...	...
40 - 44	*55 292*	*25 512*	*29 780*	...	...	...	...	...	...
45 - 49	*54 099*	*25 712*	*28 387*	...	...	...	...	...	...
50 - 54	*55 163*	*26 886*	*28 277*	...	...	...	...	...	...
55 - 59	*51 589*	*25 594*	*25 995*	...	...	...	...	...	...
60 - 64	*45 968*	*22 588*	*23 380*	...	...	...	...	...	...
65 - 69	*43 395*	*21 044*	*22 351*	...	...	...	...	...	...
70 - 74	*31 636*	*14 960*	*16 676*	...	...	...	...	...	...
75 - 79	*25 034*	*11 580*	*13 454*	...	...	...	...	...	...
80 - 84	*16 299*	*6 932*	*9 367*	...	...	...	...	...	...
85 - 89	*8 233*	*3 298*	*4 935*	...	...	...	...	...	...
90 - 94	*3 080*	*1 100*	*1 980*	...	...	...	...	...	...
95 - 99	*469*	*156*	*313*	...	...	...	...	...	...
100 +	*94*	*50*	*44*	...	...	...	...	...	...
Democratic People's Republic of Korea - République populaire démocratique de Corée									
1 X 2008 (CDJC)									
Total	24 052 231	11 721 838	12 330 393	...	...	...	...	...	...
0 - 4	1 710 039	872 173	837 866	...	...	...	...	...	...
5 - 9	1 846 785	943 048	903 737	...	...	...	...	...	...
10 - 14	2 021 350	1 035 282	986 068	...	...	...	...	...	...
15 - 19	2 052 342	1 050 113	1 002 229	...	...	...	...	...	...
20 - 24	1 841 400	941 017	900 383	...	...	...	...	...	...
25 - 29	1 737 185	887 573	849 612	...	...	...	...	...	...
30 - 34	1 680 272	853 276	826 996	...	...	...	...	...	...

Continent, country or area, date, code[a] and age (in years) / Continent, pays ou zone, date, code[a] et âge (en années)	Total			Urban - Urbaine			Rural - Rurale		
	Both sexes Les deux sexes	Male Masculin	Female Féminin	Both sexes Les deux sexes	Male Masculin	Female Féminin	Both sexes Les deux sexes	Male Masculin	Female Féminin
ASIA - ASIE									
Democratic People's Republic of Korea - République populaire démocratique de Corée									
1 X 2008 (CDJC)									
35 - 39	2 214 929	1 118 391	1 096 538	...	...	...	...	...	...
40 - 44	2 015 514	1 005 140	1 010 374	...	...	...	...	...	...
45 - 49	1 559 527	766 054	793 473	...	...	...	...	...	...
50 - 54	1 315 101	637 737	677 364	...	...	...	...	...	...
55 - 59	902 876	423 625	479 251	...	...	...	...	...	...
60 - 64	1 058 263	476 727	581 536	...	...	...	...	...	...
65 - 69	913 304	379 456	533 848	...	...	...	...	...	...
70 - 74	662 627	228 286	434 341	...	...	...	...	...	...
75 - 79	335 467	79 231	256 236	...	...	...	...	...	...
80 - 84	132 149	18 884	113 265	...	...	...	...	...	...
85 - 89	42 760	4 930	37 830	...	...	...	...	...	...
90 - 94	8 634	809	7 825	...	...	...	...	...	...
95 - 99	1 643	86	1 557	...	...	...	...	...	...
100 +	64	-	64	...	...	...	...	...	...
Georgia - Géorgie									
5 XI 2014 (CDJC)									
Total	3 713 804	1 772 864	1 940 940	2 122 623	980 985	1 141 638	1 591 181	791 879	799 302
0 - 4	255 089	132 700	122 389	152 766	78 799	73 967	102 323	53 901	48 422
5 - 9	230 024	121 245	108 779	139 301	72 526	66 775	90 723	48 719	42 004
10 - 14	206 216	109 481	96 735	119 287	62 645	56 642	86 929	46 836	40 093
15 - 19	226 022	118 877	107 145	130 446	66 924	63 522	95 576	51 953	43 623
20 - 24	266 125	135 305	130 820	162 336	79 100	83 236	103 789	56 205	47 584
25 - 29	278 662	139 945	138 717	168 601	80 608	87 993	110 061	59 337	50 724
30 - 34	262 060	129 921	132 139	160 622	76 264	84 358	101 438	53 657	47 781
35 - 39	248 549	121 943	126 606	150 707	71 177	79 530	97 842	50 766	47 076
40 - 44	243 281	118 318	124 963	143 846	67 326	76 520	99 435	50 992	48 443
45 - 49	239 407	114 036	125 371	133 670	60 443	73 227	105 737	53 593	52 144
50 - 54	271 386	126 710	144 676	150 014	66 843	83 171	121 372	59 867	61 505
55 - 59	245 391	111 641	133 750	133 348	57 828	75 520	112 043	53 813	58 230
60 - 64	211 385	92 412	118 973	114 908	47 738	67 170	96 477	44 674	51 803
65 - 69	155 702	64 889	90 813	84 433	33 489	50 944	71 269	31 400	39 869
70 - 74	123 605	48 483	75 122	61 257	22 399	38 858	62 348	26 084	36 264
75 - 79	135 764	49 895	85 869	64 993	21 828	43 165	70 771	28 067	42 704
80 - 84	71 675	25 100	46 575	32 119	10 106	22 013	39 556	14 994	24 562
85 - 89	34 508	10 166	24 342	15 957	4 154	11 803	18 551	6 012	12 539
90 - 94	7 495	1 620	5 875	3 473	712	2 761	4 022	908	3 114
95 - 99	1 171	163	1 008	456	69	387	715	94	621
100 +	287	14	273	83	7	76	204	7	197
1 VII 2016 (ESDJ)[45]									
Total	3 719 300	1 780 500	1 938 800	...	...	...	...	...	...
0	57 600	29 700	27 900	...	...	...	...	...	...
1 - 4	206 100	107 200	98 900	...	...	...	...	...	...
5 - 9	247 400	129 600	117 800	...	...	...	...	...	...
10 - 14	206 050	109 250	96 800	...	...	...	...	...	...
15 - 19	217 450	115 050	102 400	...	...	...	...	...	...
20 - 24	239 050	122 650	116 400	...	...	...	...	...	...
25 - 29	278 600	140 000	138 600	...	...	...	...	...	...
30 - 34	270 050	134 650	135 400	...	...	...	...	...	...
35 - 39	249 550	123 050	126 500	...	...	...	...	...	...
40 - 44	242 650	119 100	123 550	...	...	...	...	...	...
45 - 49	236 850	114 200	122 650	...	...	...	...	...	...
50 - 54	258 600	121 500	137 100	...	...	...	...	...	...
55 - 59	255 800	117 100	138 700	...	...	...	...	...	...
60 - 64	217 600	95 400	122 200	...	...	...	...	...	...
65 - 69	176 750	73 550	103 200	...	...	...	...	...	...
70 - 74	101 850	39 850	62 000	...	...	...	...	...	...
75 - 79	139 350	50 450	88 900	...	...	...	...	...	...
80 - 84	72 800	25 450	47 350	...	...	...	...	...	...
85 +	45 200	12 750	32 450	...	...	...	...	...	...

7. Population by age, sex and urban/rural residence: latest available year, 2007 - 2016

Population selon l'âge, le sexe et la résidence, urbaine/rurale : dernière année disponible, 2007 - 2016 (continued - suite)

Continent, country or area, date, code[a] and age (in years) / Continent, pays ou zone, date, code[a] et âge (en années)	Total			Urban - Urbaine			Rural - Rurale		
	Both sexes Les deux sexes	Male Masculin	Female Féminin	Both sexes Les deux sexes	Male Masculin	Female Féminin	Both sexes Les deux sexes	Male Masculin	Female Féminin
ASIA - ASIE									
India - Inde[46]									
9 II 2011 (CDFC)									
Total	1210854977	623 270 258	587 584 719	377 106 125	195 489 200	181 616 925	833 748 852	427 781 058	405 967 794
0 - 4	112 806 778	58 632 074	54 174 704	29 820 118	15 595 697	14 224 421	82 986 660	43 036 377	39 950 283
5 - 9	126 928 126	66 300 466	60 627 660	33 120 514	17 475 207	15 645 307	93 807 612	48 825 259	44 982 353
10 - 14	132 709 212	69 418 835	63 290 377	35 904 718	18 930 677	16 974 041	96 804 494	50 488 158	46 316 336
15 - 19	120 526 449	63 982 396	56 544 053	36 623 977	19 411 839	17 212 138	83 902 472	44 570 557	39 331 915
20 - 24	111 424 222	57 584 693	53 839 529	37 589 176	19 446 031	18 143 145	73 835 046	38 138 662	35 696 384
25 - 29	101 413 965	51 344 208	50 069 757	35 345 695	17 968 219	17 377 476	66 068 270	33 375 989	32 692 281
30 - 34	88 594 951	44 660 674	43 934 277	30 683 172	15 726 482	14 956 690	57 911 779	28 934 192	28 977 587
35 - 39	85 140 684	42 919 381	42 221 303	29 077 977	14 793 820	14 284 157	56 062 707	28 125 561	27 937 146
40 - 44	72 438 112	37 545 386	34 892 726	24 857 104	12 980 151	11 876 953	47 581 008	24 565 235	23 015 773
45 - 49	62 318 327	32 138 114	30 180 213	21 630 099	11 273 844	10 356 255	40 688 228	20 864 270	19 823 958
50 - 54	49 069 254	25 843 266	23 225 988	17 037 466	9 053 719	7 983 747	32 031 788	16 789 547	15 242 241
55 - 59	39 146 055	19 456 012	19 690 043	13 284 541	6 919 483	6 365 058	25 861 514	12 536 529	13 324 985
60 - 64	37 663 707	18 701 749	18 961 958	11 372 462	5 770 157	5 602 305	26 291 245	12 931 592	13 359 653
65 - 69	26 454 983	12 944 326	13 510 657	7 538 713	3 736 015	3 802 698	18 916 270	9 208 311	9 707 959
70 - 74	19 208 842	9 651 499	9 557 343	5 401 242	2 673 320	2 727 922	13 807 600	6 978 179	6 829 421
75 - 79	9 232 503	4 490 603	4 741 900	2 848 786	1 377 179	1 471 607	6 383 717	3 113 424	3 270 293
80 - 84	6 220 229	2 927 040	3 293 189	1 800 347	807 610	992 737	4 419 882	2 119 430	2 300 452
85 - 89	2 383 167	1 120 106	1 263 061	785 179	349 809	435 370	1 597 988	770 297	827 691
90 - 94	1 446 534	652 465	794 069	422 547	180 500	242 047	1 023 987	471 965	552 022
95 - 99	633 297	294 759	338 538	187 628	84 120	103 508	445 669	210 639	235 030
100 +	605 778	289 325	316 453	198 314	95 860	102 454	407 464	193 465	213 999
Unknown - Inconnu	4 489 802	2 372 881	2 116 921	1 576 350	839 461	736 889	2 913 452	1 533 420	1 380 032
Indonesia - Indonésie[47]									
1 VII 2015 (ESDJ)									
Total	255 182 144	128 231 889	126 950 255	135 613 086	68 118 678	67 494 408	119 569 058	60 113 211	59 455 847
0	4 129 206	2 086 586	2 042 620	2 203 413	1 109 637	1 093 776	1 925 793	976 949	948 844
1 - 4	18 649 805	9 556 167	9 093 638	9 674 406	4 940 927	4 733 479	8 975 399	4 615 240	4 360 159
5 - 9	24 564 098	12 588 393	11 975 705	12 624 775	6 489 085	6 135 690	11 939 323	6 099 308	5 840 015
10 - 14	23 496 807	12 029 572	11 467 235	11 975 376	6 101 228	5 874 148	11 521 431	5 928 344	5 593 087
15 - 19	21 110 721	10 788 401	10 322 320	11 183 002	5 651 624	5 531 378	9 927 719	5 136 777	4 790 942
20 - 24	20 950 475	10 634 769	10 315 706	11 993 749	6 046 995	5 946 754	8 956 726	4 587 774	4 368 952
25 - 29	21 172 507	10 585 769	10 586 738	11 618 534	5 839 754	5 778 780	9 553 973	4 746 015	4 807 958
30 - 34	20 336 001	10 150 408	10 185 593	11 135 834	5 589 237	5 546 597	9 200 167	4 561 171	4 638 996
35 - 39	19 987 441	9 936 043	10 051 398	11 017 643	5 476 010	5 541 633	8 969 798	4 460 033	4 509 765
40 - 44	18 009 072	9 063 867	8 945 205	9 612 758	4 880 339	4 732 419	8 396 314	4 183 528	4 212 786
45 - 49	16 474 327	8 247 350	8 226 977	8 891 443	4 423 750	4 467 693	7 582 884	3 823 600	3 759 284
50 - 54	13 119 231	6 638 517	6 480 714	7 064 986	3 515 250	3 549 736	6 054 245	3 123 267	2 930 978
55 - 59	11 572 736	5 729 185	5 843 551	5 887 496	2 988 434	2 899 062	5 685 240	2 740 751	2 944 489
60 - 64	8 297 601	4 206 906	4 090 695	4 245 745	2 143 629	2 102 116	4 051 856	2 063 277	1 988 579
65 - 69	5 101 072	2 427 508	2 673 564	2 500 758	1 203 349	1 297 409	2 600 314	1 224 159	1 376 155
70 - 74	3 954 635	1 772 393	2 182 242	1 949 235	874 108	1 075 127	2 005 400	898 285	1 107 115
75 +	4 256 409	1 790 055	2 466 354	2 033 933	845 322	1 188 611	2 222 476	944 733	1 277 743
Iran (Islamic Republic of) - Iran (République islamique d')[48]									
1 VII 2016 (ESDJ)									
Total	79 685 926	40 118 657	39 567 269	58 224 240	29 330 524	28 893 716	21 461 686	10 788 133	10 673 553
0 - 4	6 895 301	3 521 906	3 373 395	4 742 573	2 423 324	2 319 249	2 152 728	1 098 582	1 054 146
5 - 9	6 211 414	3 180 692	3 030 722	4 305 469	2 205 738	2 099 731	1 905 945	974 954	930 991
10 - 14	5 647 167	2 892 068	2 755 099	3 985 007	2 038 772	1 946 235	1 662 160	853 296	808 864
15 - 19	5 656 536	2 878 846	2 777 690	3 963 943	2 009 562	1 954 381	1 692 593	869 284	823 309
20 - 24	6 572 937	3 323 921	3 249 016	4 714 337	2 356 285	2 358 052	1 858 600	967 636	890 964
25 - 29	8 363 912	4 167 863	4 196 049	6 227 379	3 081 120	3 146 259	2 136 533	1 086 743	1 049 790
30 - 34	8 624 075	4 325 623	4 298 452	6 488 471	3 247 903	3 240 568	2 135 604	1 077 720	1 057 884
35 - 39	6 927 781	3 491 627	3 436 154	5 193 932	2 616 804	2 577 128	1 733 849	874 823	859 026
40 - 44	5 522 403	2 823 586	2 698 817	4 229 881	2 174 326	2 055 555	1 292 522	649 260	643 262
45 - 49	4 839 393	2 449 239	2 390 154	3 754 257	1 915 017	1 839 240	1 085 136	534 222	550 914
50 - 54	3 940 825	1 976 719	1 964 106	3 019 901	1 532 666	1 487 235	920 924	444 053	476 871
55 - 59	3 399 369	1 690 521	1 708 848	2 561 019	1 301 183	1 259 836	838 350	389 338	449 012
60 - 64	2 523 266	1 234 868	1 288 398	1 852 832	928 668	924 164	670 434	306 200	364 234
65 - 69	1 687 454	784 124	903 330	1 216 522	574 574	641 948	470 932	209 550	261 382
70 - 74	1 136 304	531 144	605 160	796 877	371 021	425 856	339 427	160 123	179 304

Continent, country or area, date, code[a] and age (in years) / Continent, pays ou zone, date, code[a] et âge (en annèes)	Total			Urban - Urbaine			Rural - Rurale		
	Both sexes Les deux sexes	Male Masculin	Female Féminin	Both sexes Les deux sexes	Male Masculin	Female Féminin	Both sexes Les deux sexes	Male Masculin	Female Féminin
ASIA - ASIE									
Iran (Islamic Republic of) - Iran (République islamique d')[48]									
1 VII 2016 (ESDJ)									
75 - 79	836 623	407 106	429 517	567 348	271 321	296 027	269 275	135 785	133 490
80 +	901 166	438 804	462 362	604 492	282 240	322 252	296 674	156 564	140 110
Iraq									
1 VII 2015 (ESDF)									
Total	36 658 503	18 520 532	18 137 971	25 631 821	12 935 587	12 696 234	11 026 682	5 584 945	5 441 737
0	1 137 967	584 535	553 432	752 979	386 080	366 899	384 988	198 455	186 533
1 - 4	4 331 718	2 225 935	2 105 783	2 876 835	1 475 521	1 401 314	1 454 883	750 414	704 469
5 - 9	4 910 887	2 527 175	2 383 712	3 286 086	1 687 351	1 598 735	1 624 801	839 824	784 977
10 - 14	4 359 943	2 246 489	2 113 454	2 947 957	1 515 198	1 432 759	1 411 986	731 291	680 695
15 - 19	3 848 199	1 978 743	1 869 456	2 637 780	1 353 470	1 284 310	1 210 419	625 273	585 146
20 - 24	3 328 277	1 703 854	1 624 423	2 331 929	1 192 710	1 139 219	996 348	511 144	485 204
25 - 29	2 895 690	1 471 180	1 424 510	2 057 867	1 045 789	1 012 078	837 823	425 391	412 432
30 - 34	2 486 941	1 245 726	1 241 215	1 791 620	899 685	891 935	695 321	346 041	349 280
35 - 39	2 133 553	1 058 276	1 075 277	1 551 758	772 320	779 438	581 795	285 956	295 839
40 - 44	1 807 120	887 149	919 971	1 322 951	651 530	671 421	484 169	235 619	248 550
45 - 49	1 494 733	727 670	767 063	1 104 497	539 556	564 941	390 236	188 114	202 122
50 - 54	1 171 634	564 478	607 156	880 319	425 836	454 483	291 315	138 642	152 673
55 - 59	915 225	438 062	477 163	694 340	333 828	360 512	220 885	104 234	116 651
60 - 64	675 377	321 617	353 760	515 990	246 884	269 106	159 387	74 733	84 654
65 - 69	480 527	228 559	251 968	369 196	176 457	192 739	111 331	52 102	59 229
70 - 74	304 637	145 516	159 121	235 201	112 862	122 339	69 436	32 654	36 782
75 - 79	147 670	72 473	75 197	113 997	56 096	57 901	33 673	16 377	17 296
80 +	228 407	93 096	135 311	160 521	64 415	96 106	67 886	28 681	39 205
Israel - Israël[49]									
1 VII 2015 (ESDJ)									
Total	8 380 149	4 153 233	4 226 916	7 643 990	3 778 276	3 865 714	736 159	374 958	361 201
0	177 138	91 108	86 030	161 071	82 870	78 201	16 068	8 238	7 829
1 - 4	686 831	352 278	334 553	620 298	318 063	302 235	66 534	34 215	32 319
5 - 9	785 325	402 359	382 966	704 690	360 677	344 014	80 634	41 682	38 952
10 - 14	718 722	368 085	350 637	648 595	331 872	316 723	70 127	36 212	33 914
15 - 19	653 359	334 495	318 864	587 586	299 521	288 065	65 773	34 974	30 799
20 - 24	608 755	310 179	298 576	557 484	283 065	274 419	51 272	27 114	24 158
25 - 29	590 088	297 342	292 746	544 645	273 893	270 752	45 443	23 449	21 994
30 - 34	578 135	288 910	289 226	532 047	266 193	265 854	46 089	22 717	23 372
35 - 39	556 487	276 524	279 963	506 153	251 993	254 160	50 334	24 531	25 803
40 - 44	518 439	256 882	261 558	469 401	232 607	236 794	49 038	24 275	24 763
45 - 49	437 581	216 099	221 482	397 617	195 601	202 016	39 964	20 498	19 466
50 - 54	399 310	194 901	204 409	366 177	177 868	188 310	33 133	17 033	16 100
55 - 59	382 823	183 721	199 101	352 236	168 096	184 140	30 586	15 625	14 961
60 - 64	367 653	174 511	193 142	339 083	159 858	179 225	28 570	14 653	13 917
65 - 69	320 567	150 187	170 380	298 019	138 715	159 304	22 548	11 471	11 076
70 - 74	189 027	86 828	102 199	175 166	79 949	95 216	13 861	6 878	6 982
75 - 79	172 971	75 479	97 492	162 412	70 392	92 019	10 559	5 087	5 472
80 - 84	118 107	48 933	69 174	110 488	45 618	64 870	7 618	3 315	4 303
85 - 89	74 680	28 278	46 402	69 827	26 454	43 373	4 853	1 825	3 029
90 - 94	33 681	12 037	21 645	31 329	11 134	20 196	2 352	903	1 449
95 - 99	7 399	2 802	4 596	6 842	2 610	4 232	557	192	365
100 +	3 071	1 296	1 774	2 824	1 228	1 597	246	69	178
Japan - Japon[50]									
1 X 2010 (CDJC)									
Total	128 057 352	62 327 737	65 729 615	116 156 631	56 569 051	59 587 580	11 900 721	5 758 686	6 142 035
0 - 4	5 296 748	2 710 581	2 586 167	4 831 346	2 472 475	2 358 871	465 402	238 106	227 296
5 - 9	5 585 661	2 859 805	2 725 856	5 061 966	2 591 629	2 470 337	523 695	268 176	255 519
10 - 14	5 921 035	3 031 943	2 889 092	5 348 569	2 737 977	2 610 592	572 466	293 966	278 500
15 - 19	6 063 357	3 109 229	2 954 128	5 506 483	2 823 085	2 683 398	556 874	286 144	270 730
20 - 24	6 426 433	3 266 240	3 160 193	5 925 984	3 012 027	2 913 957	500 449	254 213	246 236
25 - 29	7 293 701	3 691 723	3 601 978	6 720 343	3 397 748	3 322 595	573 358	293 975	279 383
30 - 34	8 341 497	4 221 011	4 120 486	7 675 385	3 879 081	3 796 304	666 112	341 930	324 182
35 - 39	9 786 349	4 950 122	4 836 227	9 015 173	4 556 572	4 458 601	771 176	393 550	377 626
40 - 44	8 741 865	4 400 375	4 341 490	8 046 407	4 051 948	3 994 459	695 458	348 427	347 031
45 - 49	8 033 116	4 027 969	4 005 147	7 328 789	3 675 150	3 653 639	704 327	352 819	351 508

Continent, country or area, date, code[a] and age (in years) / Continent, pays ou zone, date, code[a] et âge (en années)	Total			Urban - Urbaine			Rural - Rurale		
	Both sexes Les deux sexes	Male Masculin	Female Féminin	Both sexes Les deux sexes	Male Masculin	Female Féminin	Both sexes Les deux sexes	Male Masculin	Female Féminin
ASIA - ASIE									
Japan - Japon[50]									
1 X 2010 (CDJC)									
50 - 54	7 644 499	3 809 576	3 834 923	6 878 402	3 425 836	3 452 566	766 097	383 740	382 357
55 - 59	8 663 734	4 287 489	4 376 245	7 753 645	3 830 707	3 922 938	910 089	456 782	453 307
60 - 64	10 037 249	4 920 468	5 116 781	9 046 242	4 424 879	4 621 363	991 007	495 589	495 418
65 - 69	8 210 173	3 921 774	4 288 399	7 424 237	3 543 535	3 880 702	785 936	378 239	407 697
70 - 74	6 963 302	3 225 503	3 737 799	6 249 910	2 895 658	3 354 252	713 392	329 845	383 547
75 - 79	5 941 013	2 582 940	3 358 073	5 276 323	2 294 753	2 981 570	664 690	288 187	376 503
80 - 84	4 336 264	1 692 584	2 643 680	3 804 707	1 485 631	2 319 076	531 557	206 953	324 604
85 - 89	2 432 588	744 222	1 688 366	2 121 067	649 324	1 471 743	311 521	94 898	216 623
90 - 94	1 021 707	241 799	779 908	889 810	210 257	679 553	131 897	31 542	100 355
95 - 99	296 756	55 739	241 017	258 266	48 545	209 721	38 490	7 194	31 296
100 +	43 882	5 851	38 031	38 068	5 060	33 008	5 814	791	5 023
Unknown - Inconnu	976 423	570 794	405 629	955 509	557 174	398 335	20 914	13 620	7 294
1 VII 2016 (ESDJ)[51]									
Total	126 995 000	61 781 000	65 213 000	...	...	...	...	...	...
0 - 4	4 982 000	2 549 000	2 433 000	...	...	...	...	...	...
5 - 9	5 318 000	2 725 000	2 593 000	...	...	...	...	...	...
10 - 14	5 548 000	2 841 000	2 707 000	...	...	...	...	...	...
15 - 19	6 062 000	3 114 000	2 948 000	...	...	...	...	...	...
20 - 24	6 141 000	3 152 000	2 989 000	...	...	...	...	...	...
25 - 29	6 427 000	3 284 000	3 143 000	...	...	...	...	...	...
30 - 34	7 298 000	3 704 000	3 594 000	...	...	...	...	...	...
35 - 39	8 188 000	4 150 000	4 038 000	...	...	...	...	...	...
40 - 44	9 761 000	4 942 000	4 819 000	...	...	...	...	...	...
45 - 49	9 108 000	4 595 000	4 513 000	...	...	...	...	...	...
50 - 54	7 945 000	3 988 000	3 957 000	...	...	...	...	...	...
55 - 59	7 547 000	3 758 000	3 789 000	...	...	...	...	...	...
60 - 64	8 234 000	4 054 000	4 179 000	...	...	...	...	...	...
65 - 69	10 272 000	4 971 000	5 301 000	...	...	...	...	...	...
70 - 74	7 409 000	3 449 000	3 960 000	...	...	...	...	...	...
75 - 79	6 447 000	2 868 000	3 579 000	...	...	...	...	...	...
80 - 84	5 153 000	2 081 000	3 072 000	...	...	...	...	...	...
85 - 89	3 247 000	1 109 000	2 139 000	...	...	...	...	...	...
90 - 94	1 460 000	372 000	1 088 000	...	...	...	...	...	...
95 - 99	380 000	67 000	313 000	...	...	...	...	...	...
100 +	66 000	9 000	57 000	...	...	...	...	...	...
Jordan - Jordanie[52]									
30 X 2015 (CDFC)									
Total	9 531 712	5 046 824	4 484 888	8 611 323	4 561 944	4 049 379	920 389	484 880	435 509
0	208 691	107 002	101 689	186 255	95 466	90 789	22 436	11 536	10 900
1 - 4	885 507	454 278	431 229	792 037	406 308	385 729	93 470	47 970	45 500
5 - 9	1 169 491	597 975	571 516	1 050 857	537 071	513 786	118 634	60 904	57 730
10 - 14	1 010 398	519 876	490 522	910 848	468 508	442 340	99 550	51 368	48 182
15 - 19	947 821	498 519	449 302	854 544	449 845	404 699	93 277	48 674	44 603
20 - 24	945 975	519 140	426 835	856 226	470 218	386 008	89 749	48 922	40 827
25 - 29	830 606	459 841	370 765	750 184	414 978	335 206	80 422	44 863	35 559
30 - 34	734 400	395 939	338 461	663 266	357 518	305 748	71 134	38 421	32 713
35 - 39	651 190	352 691	298 499	589 773	319 919	269 854	61 417	32 772	28 645
40 - 44	560 931	304 330	256 601	508 054	276 252	231 802	52 877	28 078	24 799
45 - 49	473 409	258 567	214 842	431 427	236 137	195 290	41 982	22 430	19 552
50 - 54	349 837	187 189	162 648	320 505	171 594	148 911	29 332	15 595	13 737
55 - 59	244 699	127 359	117 340	225 052	117 524	107 528	19 647	9 835	9 812
60 - 64	167 078	86 254	80 824	152 320	78 409	73 911	14 758	7 845	6 913
65 - 69	135 653	67 492	68 161	124 292	62 013	62 279	11 361	5 479	5 882
70 - 74	99 792	52 668	47 124	91 281	48 326	42 955	8 511	4 342	4 169
75 - 79	64 187	32 428	31 759	58 154	29 476	28 678	6 033	2 952	3 081
80 +	52 047	25 276	26 771	46 248	22 382	23 866	5 799	2 894	2 905
80 - 84	30 957	15 324	15 633	...	...	...	...	...	...
85 - 89	13 738	6 387	7 351	...	...	...	...	...	...
90 - 94	4 035	1 797	2 238	...	...	...	...	...	...
95 +	3 317	1 768	1 549	...	...	...	...	...	...
31 XII 2016 (ESDF)									
Total	9 798 000	5 188 000	4 610 000	...	...	...	...	...	...
0	214 520	109 995	104 525	...	...	...	...	...	...

Continent, country or area, date, code[a] and age (in years) / Continent, pays ou zone, date, code[a] et âge (en années)	Total			Urban - Urbaine			Rural - Rurale		
	Both sexes Les deux sexes	Male Masculin	Female Féminin	Both sexes Les deux sexes	Male Masculin	Female Féminin	Both sexes Les deux sexes	Male Masculin	Female Féminin
ASIA - ASIE									
Jordan - Jordanie[52]									
31 XII 2016 (ESDF)									
1 - 4	910 250	466 985	443 265	...	...	...	...	...	...
5 - 9	1 202 160	614 710	587 450	...	...	...	...	...	...
10 - 14	1 038 630	534 420	504 210	...	...	...	...	...	...
15 - 19	974 300	512 460	461 840	...	...	...	...	...	...
20 - 24	972 400	533 660	438 740	...	...	...	...	...	...
25 - 29	853 810	472 700	381 110	...	...	...	...	...	...
30 - 34	754 920	407 010	347 910	...	...	...	...	...	...
35 - 39	669 380	362 560	306 820	...	...	...	...	...	...
40 - 44	576 600	312 840	263 760	...	...	...	...	...	...
45 - 49	486 630	265 800	220 830	...	...	...	...	...	...
50 - 54	359 610	192 430	167 180	...	...	...	...	...	...
55 - 59	251 540	130 920	120 620	...	...	...	...	...	...
60 - 64	171 750	88 670	83 080	...	...	...	...	...	...
65 - 69	137 175	70 530	66 645	...	...	...	...	...	...
70 - 74	107 045	51 880	55 165	...	...	...	...	...	...
75 - 79	65 910	33 370	32 540	...	...	...	...	...	...
80 - 84	30 554	16 405	14 149	...	...	...	...	...	...
85 - 89	13 559	6 838	6 721	...	...	...	...	...	...
90 - 94	3 982	1 924	2 058	...	...	...	...	...	...
95 +	3 274	1 893	1 381	...	...	...	...	...	...
Kazakhstan									
1 I 2014 (ESDF)									
Total	17 160 774	8 284 815	8 875 959	9 433 482	4 421 972	5 011 510	7 727 292	3 862 843	3 864 449
0	383 507	197 722	185 785	206 925	106 746	100 179	176 582	90 976	85 606
1 - 4	1 453 960	747 077	706 883	774 383	398 197	376 186	679 577	348 880	330 697
5 - 9	1 478 444	759 906	718 538	727 159	374 068	353 091	751 285	385 838	365 447
10 - 14	1 142 469	584 661	557 808	541 266	278 151	263 115	601 203	306 510	294 693
15 - 19	1 229 114	627 497	601 617	589 482	299 106	290 376	639 632	328 391	311 241
20 - 24	1 549 891	776 520	773 371	899 705	431 037	468 668	650 186	345 483	304 703
25 - 29	1 593 969	789 257	804 712	941 249	451 323	489 926	652 720	337 934	314 786
30 - 34	1 323 571	655 904	667 667	766 862	370 961	395 901	556 709	284 943	271 766
35 - 39	1 195 873	583 523	612 350	677 270	319 428	357 842	518 603	264 095	254 508
40 - 44	1 112 543	537 147	575 396	628 467	291 881	336 586	484 076	245 266	238 810
45 - 49	1 041 284	495 478	545 806	579 844	264 313	315 531	461 440	231 165	230 275
50 - 54	1 055 814	491 529	564 285	594 574	266 110	328 464	461 240	225 419	235 821
55 - 59	825 252	369 231	456 021	467 435	200 179	267 256	357 817	169 052	188 765
60 - 64	626 713	263 189	363 524	363 041	145 102	217 939	263 672	118 087	145 585
65 - 69	358 005	142 912	215 093	212 061	80 423	131 638	145 944	62 489	83 455
70 - 74	328 827	118 456	210 371	187 797	63 704	124 093	141 030	54 752	86 278
75 - 79	268 284	91 291	176 993	158 629	50 542	108 087	109 655	40 749	68 906
80 - 84	114 520	33 815	80 705	70 087	19 640	50 447	44 433	14 175	30 258
85 - 89	62 266	15 583	46 683	38 006	8 850	29 156	24 260	6 733	17 527
90 - 94	13 270	3 142	10 128	7 688	1 730	5 958	5 582	1 412	4 170
95 - 99	2 224	628	1 596	1 091	305	786	1 133	323	810
100 +	974	347	627	461	176	285	513	171	342
Kuwait - Koweït									
1 I 2016 (ESDF)									
Total	3 925 487	2 320 193	1 605 294	...	...	...	...	...	...
0	58 904	30 330	28 574	...	...	...	...	...	...
1 - 4	253 503	133 099	120 404	...	...	...	...	...	...
5 - 9	293 710	157 928	135 782	...	...	...	...	...	...
10 - 14	246 342	130 822	115 520	...	...	...	...	...	...
15 - 19	218 348	115 557	102 791	...	...	...	...	...	...
20 - 24	197 182	106 254	90 928	...	...	...	...	...	...
25 - 29	295 249	156 609	138 640	...	...	...	...	...	...
30 - 34	465 886	274 070	191 816	...	...	...	...	...	...
35 - 39	493 408	316 531	176 877	...	...	...	...	...	...
40 - 44	493 156	316 349	176 807	...	...	...	...	...	...
45 - 49	332 775	214 072	118 703	...	...	...	...	...	...
50 - 54	233 899	150 434	83 465	...	...	...	...	...	...
55 - 59	153 379	101 674	51 705	...	...	...	...	...	...
60 - 64	90 990	59 620	31 370	...	...	...	...	...	...
65 - 69	47 774	29 088	18 686	...	...	...	...	...	...

7. Population by age, sex and urban/rural residence: latest available year, 2007 - 2016
Population selon l'âge, le sexe et la résidence, urbaine/rurale : dernière année disponible, 2007 - 2016 (continued - suite)

Continent, country or area, date, code[a] and age (in years) / Continent, pays ou zone, date, code[a] et âge (en années)	Total			Urban - Urbaine			Rural - Rurale		
	Both sexes Les deux sexes	Male Masculin	Female Féminin	Both sexes Les deux sexes	Male Masculin	Female Féminin	Both sexes Les deux sexes	Male Masculin	Female Féminin
ASIA - ASIE									
Kuwait - Koweït									
1 I 2016 (ESDF)									
70 - 74	24 566	13 531	11 035	...	...	...	...	...	...
75 - 79	14 315	7 896	6 419	...	...	...	...	...	...
80 +	12 101	6 329	5 772	...	...	...	...	...	...
Kyrgyzstan - Kirghizstan[53]									
1 VII 2016 (ESDJ)									
Total	6 079 840	3 011 702	3 068 138	2 051 748	973 955	1 077 793	4 028 092	2 037 747	1 990 345
0	158 287	81 536	76 751	50 418	26 115	24 303	107 869	55 421	52 448
1 - 4	615 816	316 297	299 519	206 558	106 242	100 316	409 258	210 055	199 203
5 - 9	642 915	328 378	314 537	202 453	103 293	99 160	440 462	225 085	215 377
10 - 14	522 389	266 241	256 148	149 427	75 589	73 838	372 962	190 652	182 310
15 - 19	505 365	257 327	248 038	140 674	71 376	69 298	364 691	185 951	178 740
20 - 24	567 266	288 919	278 347	170 702	84 235	86 467	396 564	204 684	191 880
25 - 29	580 603	291 438	289 165	233 292	108 125	125 167	347 311	183 313	163 998
30 - 34	475 023	238 730	236 293	171 828	81 364	90 464	303 195	157 366	145 829
35 - 39	379 209	189 991	189 218	137 759	65 221	72 538	241 450	124 770	116 680
40 - 44	336 595	164 503	172 092	120 555	54 428	66 127	216 040	110 075	105 965
45 - 49	314 449	152 211	162 238	115 024	51 999	63 025	199 425	100 212	99 213
50 - 54	291 823	138 098	153 725	103 609	46 465	57 144	188 214	91 633	96 581
55 - 59	252 876	117 414	135 462	89 838	39 434	50 404	163 038	77 980	85 058
60 - 64	167 009	74 254	92 755	59 548	24 653	34 895	107 461	49 601	57 860
65 - 69	109 724	46 126	63 598	42 065	16 272	25 793	67 659	29 854	37 805
70 - 74	45 849	18 676	27 173	17 674	6 454	11 220	28 175	12 222	15 953
75 - 79	58 676	22 014	36 662	22 185	7 355	14 830	36 491	14 659	21 832
80 - 84	30 988	10 782	20 206	10 250	3 057	7 193	20 738	7 725	13 013
85 - 89	17 720	6 109	11 611	5 683	1 603	4 080	12 037	4 506	7 531
90 - 94	5 593	2 137	3 456	1 708	539	1 169	3 885	1 598	2 287
95 - 99	1 384	418	966	400	115	285	984	303	681
100 +	281	103	178	98	21	77	183	82	101
Lao People's Democratic Republic - République démocratique populaire lao									
1 III 2015 (CDJC)									
Total	6 492 228	3 254 770	3 237 458	...	...	...	...	...	...
0	118 387	60 356	58 031	...	...	...	...	...	...
1 - 4	563 596	286 106	277 490	...	...	...	...	...	...
5 - 9	679 209	345 380	333 829	...	...	...	...	...	...
10 - 14	718 606	363 026	355 580	...	...	...	...	...	...
15 - 19	699 010	354 360	344 650	...	...	...	...	...	...
20 - 24	654 037	325 601	328 436	...	...	...	...	...	...
25 - 29	615 988	308 988	307 000	...	...	...	...	...	...
30 - 34	496 234	250 383	245 851	...	...	...	...	...	...
35 - 39	420 083	212 523	207 560	...	...	...	...	...	...
40 - 44	343 870	170 808	173 062	...	...	...	...	...	...
45 - 49	295 907	149 656	146 251	...	...	...	...	...	...
50 - 54	267 418	127 272	140 146	...	...	...	...	...	...
55 - 59	197 607	98 615	98 992	...	...	...	...	...	...
60 - 64	147 179	74 106	73 073	...	...	...	...	...	...
65 - 69	98 901	47 563	51 338	...	...	...	...	...	...
70 - 74	71 427	32 930	38 497	...	...	...	...	...	...
75 - 79	47 078	21 871	25 207	...	...	...	...	...	...
80 - 84	30 190	13 519	16 671	...	...	...	...	...	...
85 - 89	15 267	6 744	8 523	...	...	...	...	...	...
90 - 94	7 036	3 041	3 995	...	...	...	...	...	...
95 +	5 198	1 922	3 276	...	...	...	...	...	...
Lebanon - Liban[54]									
3 III 2007 (SSDF)									
Total	3 759 134	1 857 659	1 901 475	...	...	...	...	...	...
0 - 4	261 021	136 514	124 507	...	...	...	...	...	...
5 - 9	312 902	160 577	152 325	...	...	...	...	...	...
10 - 14	354 049	183 613	170 436	...	...	...	...	...	...
15 - 19	363 626	195 984	167 642	...	...	...	...	...	...
20 - 24	367 778	191 471	176 307	...	...	...	...	...	...
25 - 29	305 933	148 321	157 612	...	...	...	...	...	...

Continent, country or area, date, code[a] and age (in years) / Continent, pays ou zone, date, code[a] et âge (en années)	Total			Urban - Urbaine			Rural - Rurale		
	Both sexes Les deux sexes	Male Masculin	Female Féminin	Both sexes Les deux sexes	Male Masculin	Female Féminin	Both sexes Les deux sexes	Male Masculin	Female Féminin
ASIA - ASIE									
Lebanon - Liban[54]									
3 III 2007 (SSDF)									
30 - 34	276 775	132 105	144 670	...	...	...	...	...	...
35 - 39	249 550	111 833	137 717	...	...	...	...	...	...
40 - 44	233 003	102 405	130 598	...	...	...	...	...	...
45 - 49	208 752	95 595	113 157	...	...	...	...	...	...
50 - 54	179 899	84 091	95 808	...	...	...	...	...	...
55 - 59	143 376	66 993	76 383	...	...	...	...	...	...
60 - 64	140 030	65 701	74 329	...	...	...	...	...	...
65 - 69	122 014	59 900	62 114	...	...	...	...	...	...
70 - 74	105 259	53 267	51 992	...	...	...	...	...	...
75 - 79	71 315	38 353	32 962	...	...	...	...	...	...
80 - 84	45 481	21 083	24 398	...	...	...	...	...	...
85 +	18 371	9 853	8 518	...	...	...	...	...	...
Malaysia - Malaisie[55]									
1 VII 2016 (ESDJ)									
Total	31 660 683	16 362 530	15 298 153	23 694 698	12 197 462	11 497 236	7 965 985	4 165 068	3 800 917
0	538 105	277 196	260 909	387 081	199 831	187 250	151 024	77 365	73 659
1 - 4	2 096 683	1 084 620	1 012 063	1 513 094	785 137	727 957	583 589	299 483	284 106
5 - 9	2 512 393	1 294 712	1 217 681	1 834 831	945 193	889 638	677 562	349 519	328 043
10 - 14	2 616 123	1 342 929	1 273 194	1 914 415	982 127	932 288	701 708	360 802	340 906
15 - 19	2 864 364	1 482 582	1 381 782	2 036 210	1 052 701	983 509	828 154	429 881	398 273
20 - 24	3 249 286	1 706 914	1 542 372	2 356 916	1 231 523	1 125 393	892 370	475 391	416 979
25 - 29	3 193 929	1 705 405	1 488 524	2 433 880	1 276 216	1 157 664	760 049	429 189	330 860
30 - 34	2 801 335	1 475 938	1 325 397	2 203 844	1 139 675	1 064 169	597 491	336 263	261 228
35 - 39	2 239 180	1 180 741	1 058 439	1 776 454	922 774	853 680	462 726	257 967	204 759
40 - 44	1 920 023	988 746	931 277	1 498 783	764 565	734 218	421 240	224 181	197 059
45 - 49	1 742 305	874 256	868 049	1 351 139	673 579	677 560	391 166	200 677	190 489
50 - 54	1 585 393	812 341	773 052	1 224 190	631 090	593 100	361 203	181 251	179 952
55 - 59	1 345 866	685 328	660 538	1 027 501	530 942	496 559	318 365	154 386	163 979
60 - 64	1 041 580	523 745	517 835	778 772	395 668	383 104	262 808	128 077	134 731
65 - 69	785 570	388 309	397 261	574 203	286 003	288 200	211 367	102 306	109 061
70 - 74	490 714	238 727	251 987	346 657	170 618	176 039	144 057	68 109	75 948
75 - 79	331 083	156 574	174 509	228 226	110 064	118 162	102 857	46 510	56 347
80 - 84	167 872	78 141	89 731	113 861	54 136	59 725	54 011	24 005	30 006
85 - 89	84 491	38 754	45 737	57 284	26 628	30 656	27 207	12 126	15 081
90 - 94	32 978	15 766	17 212	22 093	10 769	11 324	10 885	4 997	5 888
95 +	21 410	10 806	10 604	15 264	8 223	7 041	6 146	2 583	3 563
Maldives									
20 IX 2014 (CDFC)[56]									
Total	402 071	227 749	174 322	153 904	85 438	68 466	248 167	142 311	105 856
0	7 053	3 664	3 389	2 531	1 307	1 224	4 522	2 357	2 165
1 - 4	29 286	15 330	13 956	10 048	5 214	4 834	19 238	10 116	9 122
5 - 9	31 999	16 389	15 610	10 629	5 435	5 194	21 370	10 954	10 416
10 - 14	26 275	13 537	12 738	8 048	4 102	3 946	18 227	9 435	8 792
15 - 19	31 958	16 670	15 288	13 478	6 684	6 794	18 480	9 986	8 494
20 - 24	47 288	28 647	18 641	21 095	12 441	8 654	26 193	16 206	9 987
25 - 29	56 706	35 297	21 409	23 272	14 297	8 975	33 434	21 000	12 434
30 - 34	43 862	26 626	17 236	17 768	10 346	7 422	26 094	16 280	9 814
35 - 39	30 977	18 524	12 453	12 694	7 320	5 374	18 283	11 204	7 079
40 - 44	24 815	14 263	10 552	9 738	5 505	4 233	15 077	8 758	6 319
45 - 49	20 380	11 309	9 071	7 823	4 282	3 541	12 557	7 027	5 530
50 - 54	16 338	8 795	7 543	5 912	3 083	2 829	10 426	5 712	4 714
55 - 59	12 217	6 467	5 750	4 146	2 061	2 085	8 071	4 406	3 665
60 - 64	6 426	3 475	2 951	2 230	1 180	1 050	4 196	2 295	1 901
65 - 69	4 923	2 493	2 430	1 655	786	869	3 268	1 707	1 561
70 - 74	4 856	2 493	2 363	1 315	635	680	3 541	1 858	1 683
75 - 79	3 718	1 972	1 746	873	410	463	2 845	1 562	1 283
80 - 84	1 952	1 161	791	406	212	194	1 546	949	597
85 - 89	727	443	284	169	94	75	558	349	209
90 - 94	231	146	85	54	31	23	177	115	62
95 +	84	48	36	20	13	7	64	35	29
1 VII 2016 (ESDF)[57]									
Total	350 093	177 872	172 222	...	...	...	...	...	...
0	7 804	4 057	3 747	...	...	...	...	...	...

Continent, country or area, date, code[a] and age (in years) / Continent, pays ou zone, date, code[a] et âge (en années)	Total			Urban - Urbaine			Rural - Rurale		
	Both sexes Les deux sexes	Male Masculin	Female Féminin	Both sexes Les deux sexes	Male Masculin	Female Féminin	Both sexes Les deux sexes	Male Masculin	Female Féminin
ASIA - ASIE									
Maldives									
1 VII 2016 (ESDF)[57]									
1 - 4	29 441	15 442	13 999	...	...	...	...	...	...
5 - 9	33 338	17 162	16 176	...	...	...	...	...	...
10 - 14	27 453	14 099	13 354	...	...	...	...	...	...
15 - 19	28 027	14 282	13 745	...	...	...	...	...	...
20 - 24	34 231	17 509	16 722	...	...	...	...	...	...
25 - 29	38 404	19 280	19 124	...	...	...	...	...	...
30 - 34	34 304	16 934	17 371	...	...	...	...	...	...
35 - 39	25 248	12 530	12 718	...	...	...	...	...	...
40 - 44	20 301	10 055	10 246	...	...	...	...	...	...
45 - 49	18 156	9 038	9 118	...	...	...	...	...	...
50 - 54	15 777	7 970	7 806	...	...	...	...	...	...
55 - 59	13 010	6 652	6 358	...	...	...	...	...	...
60 - 64	7 989	4 195	3 794	...	...	...	...	...	...
65 - 69	4 820	2 476	2 344	...	...	...	...	...	...
70 - 74	4 546	2 277	2 269	...	...	...	...	...	...
75 - 79	4 033	2 059	1 973	...	...	...	...	...	...
80 +	3 212	1 854	1 359	...	...	...	...	...	...
Mongolia - Mongolie									
11 XI 2010 (CDJC)									
Total	2 647 545	1 313 968	1 333 577	1 798 147	872 989	925 158	849 398	440 979	408 419
0 - 4	288 497	146 516	141 981	188 882	95 671	93 211	99 615	50 845	48 770
5 - 9	216 214	110 117	106 097	133 740	68 119	65 621	82 474	41 998	40 476
10 - 14	236 865	120 064	116 801	143 846	72 244	71 602	93 019	47 820	45 199
15 - 19	257 645	130 560	127 085	188 334	92 124	96 210	69 311	38 436	30 875
20 - 24	292 183	147 472	144 711	221 784	107 751	114 033	70 399	39 721	30 678
25 - 29	247 983	124 490	123 493	171 685	83 922	87 763	76 298	40 568	35 730
30 - 34	222 522	111 976	110 546	149 461	73 525	75 936	73 061	38 451	34 610
35 - 39	202 383	100 819	101 564	136 034	66 149	69 885	66 349	34 670	31 679
40 - 44	179 267	88 273	90 994	120 105	57 388	62 717	59 162	30 885	28 277
45 - 49	158 756	77 475	81 281	108 736	51 528	57 208	50 020	25 947	24 073
50 - 54	122 082	58 009	64 073	83 084	38 547	44 537	38 998	19 462	19 536
55 - 59	71 989	33 384	38 605	49 342	22 373	26 969	22 647	11 011	11 636
60 - 64	49 453	22 106	27 347	34 724	15 234	19 490	14 729	6 872	7 857
65 - 69	38 232	17 262	20 970	26 004	11 578	14 426	12 228	5 684	6 544
70 - 74	29 332	13 081	16 251	19 556	8 594	10 962	9 776	4 487	5 289
75 - 79	18 617	7 252	11 365	12 384	4 742	7 642	6 233	2 510	3 723
80 - 84	9 166	3 258	5 908	6 234	2 225	4 009	2 932	1 033	1 899
85 - 89	4 415	1 378	3 037	2 948	945	2 003	1 467	433	1 034
90 - 94	1 459	383	1 076	962	274	688	497	109	388
95 - 99	402	80	322	251	47	204	151	33	118
100 +	83	13	70	51	9	42	32	4	28
1 VII 2016 (ESDF)									
Total	3 088 856	1 518 797	1 570 059	...	...	...	...	...	...
0	79 796	40 912	38 884	...	...	...	...	...	...
1 - 4	310 896	159 114	151 782	...	...	...	...	...	...
5 - 9	310 693	158 627	152 067	...	...	...	...	...	...
10 - 14	219 881	112 126	107 755	...	...	...	...	...	...
15 - 19	238 156	120 874	117 284	...	...	...	...	...	...
20 - 24	261 495	131 977	129 521	...	...	...	...	...	...
25 - 29	314 125	157 348	156 779	...	...	...	...	...	...
30 - 34	268 768	133 312	135 458	...	...	...	...	...	...
35 - 39	234 629	115 455	119 175	...	...	...	...	...	...
40 - 44	211 277	102 152	109 126	...	...	...	...	...	...
45 - 49	179 910	85 425	94 485	...	...	...	...	...	...
50 - 54	155 840	72 599	83 242	...	...	...	...	...	...
55 - 59	117 505	52 597	64 907	...	...	...	...	...	...
60 - 64	69 716	30 285	39 430	...	...	...	...	...	...
65 - 69	43 398	17 808	25 589	...	...	...	...	...	...
70 - 74	31 109	12 837	18 270	...	...	...	...	...	...
75 - 79	22 031	9 046	12 985	...	...	...	...	...	...
80 - 84	12 209	4 229	7 979	...	...	...	...	...	...
85 - 89	5 114	1 526	3 586	...	...	...	...	...	...
90 - 94	1 764	455	1 307	...	...	...	...	...	...

Continent, country or area, date, code[a] and age (in years) / Continent, pays ou zone, date, code[a] et âge (en années)	Total			Urban - Urbaine			Rural - Rurale		
	Both sexes Les deux sexes	Male Masculin	Female Féminin	Both sexes Les deux sexes	Male Masculin	Female Féminin	Both sexes Les deux sexes	Male Masculin	Female Féminin
ASIA - ASIE									
Mongolia - Mongolie									
1 VII 2016 (ESDF)									
95 - 99	456	80	374	...	...	...	...	...	...
100 +	88	13	74	...	...	...	...	...	...
Myanmar									
1 X 2016 (ESDF)									
Total	52 916 691	25 450 311	27 466 380	15 560 351	7 411 122	8 149 229	37 356 340	18 039 189	19 317 151
0 - 4	4 938 355	2 499 167	2 439 188	1 211 508	614 425	597 083	3 726 847	1 884 742	1 842 105
0	1 017 747	516 502	501 245	...	...	...	...	...	...
1 - 4	3 920 608	1 982 665	1 937 943	...	...	...	...	...	...
5 - 9	4 865 016	2 460 732	2 404 284	1 164 000	592 282	571 718	3 701 016	1 868 450	1 832 566
10 - 14	5 177 200	2 637 053	2 540 147	1 276 861	658 751	618 110	3 900 339	1 978 302	1 922 037
15 - 19	4 866 970	2 437 946	2 429 024	1 484 778	756 718	728 060	3 382 192	1 681 228	1 700 964
20 - 24	4 491 497	2 183 109	2 308 388	1 558 108	767 247	790 861	2 933 389	1 415 862	1 517 527
25 - 29	4 244 130	2 027 260	2 216 870	1 410 702	678 686	732 016	2 833 428	1 348 574	1 484 854
30 - 34	4 061 497	1 948 014	2 113 483	1 274 937	614 328	660 609	2 786 560	1 333 686	1 452 874
35 - 39	3 745 368	1 791 505	1 953 863	1 153 496	549 099	604 397	2 591 872	1 242 406	1 349 466
40 - 44	3 438 981	1 621 183	1 817 798	1 044 945	483 159	561 786	2 394 036	1 138 024	1 256 012
45 - 49	3 132 501	1 456 939	1 675 562	970 449	436 977	533 472	2 162 052	1 019 962	1 142 090
50 - 54	2 767 154	1 272 987	1 494 167	839 862	368 629	471 233	1 927 292	904 358	1 022 934
55 - 59	2 291 866	1 039 013	1 252 853	692 443	296 771	395 672	1 599 423	742 242	857 181
60 - 64	1 770 517	788 838	981 679	530 390	223 307	307 083	1 240 127	565 531	674 596
65 - 69	1 251 995	543 898	708 097	379 247	155 443	223 804	872 748	388 455	484 293
70 - 74	782 349	323 360	458 989	239 671	94 983	144 688	542 678	228 377	314 301
75 - 79	531 098	212 177	318 921	156 806	60 082	96 724	374 292	152 095	222 197
80 - 84	353 614	135 724	217 890	106 357	39 033	67 324	247 257	96 691	150 566
85 - 89	146 020	51 240	94 780	45 154	14 601	30 553	100 866	36 639	64 227
90 +	60 563	20 166	40 397	20 637	6 601	14 036	39 926	13 565	26 361
Nepal - Népal									
22 VI 2011 (CDJC)									
Total	26 494 504	12 849 041	13 645 463	4 523 820	2 306 049	2 217 771	21 970 684	10 542 992	11 427 692
0 - 4	2 567 963	1 314 957	1 253 006	327 100	172 598	154 502	2 240 863	1 142 359	1 098 504
5 - 9	3 204 859	1 635 176	1 569 683	431 121	227 618	203 503	2 773 738	1 407 558	1 366 180
10 - 14	3 475 424	1 764 630	1 710 794	507 618	266 722	240 896	2 967 806	1 497 908	1 469 898
15 - 19	2 931 980	1 443 191	1 488 789	520 714	273 601	247 113	2 411 266	1 169 590	1 241 676
20 - 24	2 358 071	1 043 981	1 314 090	520 546	260 529	260 017	1 837 525	783 452	1 054 073
25 - 29	2 079 354	917 243	1 162 111	452 256	220 230	232 026	1 627 098	697 013	930 085
30 - 34	1 735 305	770 577	964 728	372 219	181 542	190 677	1 363 086	589 035	774 051
35 - 39	1 604 319	740 200	864 119	324 965	161 347	163 618	1 279 354	578 853	700 501
40 - 44	1 386 121	660 290	725 831	263 008	136 600	126 408	1 123 113	523 690	599 423
45 - 49	1 172 959	575 101	597 858	205 833	106 627	99 206	967 126	468 474	498 652
50 - 54	1 005 476	505 864	499 612	165 685	86 471	79 214	839 791	419 393	420 398
55 - 59	818 263	412 892	405 371	123 667	63 841	59 826	694 596	349 051	345 545
60 - 64	756 827	368 451	388 376	105 862	52 258	53 604	650 965	316 193	334 772
65 - 69	554 449	277 782	276 667	76 074	37 256	38 818	478 375	240 526	237 849
70 - 74	395 153	199 610	195 543	55 001	26 400	28 601	340 152	173 210	166 942
75 - 79	235 135	117 358	117 777	35 764	16 538	19 226	199 371	100 820	98 551
80 - 84	128 777	62 787	65 990	21 053	9 435	11 618	107 724	53 352	54 372
85 - 89	52 526	25 810	26 716	9 857	4 350	5 507	42 669	21 460	21 209
90 - 94	20 335	8 940	11 395	3 788	1 474	2 314	16 547	7 466	9 081
95 +	11 208	4 201	7 007	1 689	612	1 077	9 519	3 589	5 930
1 VII 2016 (ESDJ)[14]									
Total	28 431 494	13 784 009	14 647 486	...	...	...	...	...	...
0 - 4	2 950 167	1 525 630	1 424 537	...	...	...	...	...	...
5 - 9	2 674 278	1 368 495	1 305 783	...	...	...	...	...	...
10 - 14	3 062 865	1 564 080	1 498 784	...	...	...	...	...	...
15 - 19	3 317 315	1 680 525	1 636 790	...	...	...	...	...	...
20 - 24	3 021 919	1 476 611	1 545 309	...	...	...	...	...	...
25 - 29	2 340 931	1 033 222	1 307 709	...	...	...	...	...	...
30 - 34	1 998 816	860 512	1 138 303	...	...	...	...	...	...
35 - 39	1 740 784	771 970	968 815	...	...	...	...	...	...
40 - 44	1 521 989	691 192	830 797	...	...	...	...	...	...
45 - 49	1 334 086	632 128	701 958	...	...	...	...	...	...
50 - 54	1 140 179	552 834	587 346	...	...	...	...	...	...
55 - 59	930 950	462 675	468 275	...	...	...	...	...	...

Continent, country or area, date, code[a] and age (in years) / Continent, pays ou zone, date, code[a] et âge (en années)	Total			Urban - Urbaine			Rural - Rurale		
	Both sexes Les deux sexes	Male Masculin	Female Féminin	Both sexes Les deux sexes	Male Masculin	Female Féminin	Both sexes Les deux sexes	Male Masculin	Female Féminin
ASIA - ASIE									
Nepal - Népal									
1 VII 2016 (ESDJ)[14]									
60 - 64	770 098	382 738	387 360	...	...	...	...	...	...
65 - 69	627 821	303 255	324 567	...	...	...	...	...	...
70 - 74	482 949	231 131	251 818	...	...	...	...	...	...
75 - 79	339 914	162 123	177 791	...	...	...	...	...	...
80 +	176 432	84 889	91 543	...	...	...	...	...	...
Oman									
1 VII 2009 (ESDF)									
Total	3 173 917	1 971 115	1 202 802	2 314 865	1 457 197	857 668	859 049	513 917	345 132
0 - 4	272 144	139 614	132 530	184 595	94 803	89 792	87 549	44 811	42 738
5 - 9	245 026	124 776	120 250	162 307	82 954	79 353	82 718	41 821	40 897
10 - 14	254 610	129 964	124 646	168 924	86 326	82 598	85 685	43 638	42 047
15 - 19	284 826	145 215	139 611	194 123	99 854	94 269	90 703	45 361	45 342
20 - 24	387 448	238 483	148 965	285 594	176 341	109 253	101 854	62 142	39 712
25 - 29	475 403	327 686	147 717	362 531	249 782	112 749	112 871	77 904	34 967
30 - 34	367 536	247 107	120 429	288 055	192 969	95 086	79 481	54 138	25 343
35 - 39	272 100	192 483	79 617	212 145	150 865	61 280	59 955	41 618	18 337
40 - 44	207 202	149 090	58 112	161 282	117 670	43 612	45 920	31 420	14 500
45 - 49	145 430	103 908	41 522	111 077	81 065	30 012	34 353	22 843	11 510
50 - 54	113 587	83 057	30 530	84 975	63 752	21 223	28 612	19 305	9 307
55 - 59	59 890	40 488	19 402	42 674	29 489	13 185	17 216	10 999	6 217
60 - 64	39 730	23 538	16 192	26 050	15 494	10 556	13 680	8 044	5 636
65 - 69	20 811	11 811	9 000	13 363	7 537	5 826	7 448	4 274	3 174
70 - 74	14 933	7 721	7 212	9 224	4 703	4 521	5 709	3 018	2 691
75 - 79	6 817	3 303	3 514	4 201	1 981	2 220	2 616	1 322	1 294
80 +	6 424	2 871	3 553	3 745	1 612	2 133	2 679	1 259	1 420
1 VII 2016 (ESDF)[58]									
Total	4 414 051	2 886 083	1 527 968	...	...	...	...	...	...
0	68 418	35 001	33 417	...	...	...	...	...	...
1 - 4	325 207	166 077	159 130	...	...	...	...	...	...
5 - 9	321 917	163 857	158 060	...	...	...	...	...	...
10 - 14	251 342	128 133	123 209	...	...	...	...	...	...
15 - 19	235 612	120 353	115 259	...	...	...	...	...	...
20 - 24	396 323	255 382	140 941	...	...	...	...	...	...
25 - 29	727 178	538 218	188 960	...	...	...	...	...	...
30 - 34	659 786	489 206	170 580	...	...	...	...	...	...
35 - 39	466 715	336 343	130 372	...	...	...	...	...	...
40 - 44	314 188	226 931	87 257	...	...	...	...	...	...
45 - 49	216 144	158 230	57 914	...	...	...	...	...	...
50 - 54	147 550	102 230	45 320	...	...	...	...	...	...
55 - 59	108 979	72 316	36 663	...	...	...	...	...	...
60 - 64	62 496	36 965	25 531	...	...	...	...	...	...
65 - 69	37 972	19 533	18 439	...	...	...	...	...	...
70 - 74	27 585	13 597	13 988	...	...	...	...	...	...
75 - 79	20 984	10 809	10 175	...	...	...	...	...	...
80 - 84	12 522	6 393	6 129	...	...	...	...	...	...
85 - 89	7 140	3 561	3 579	...	...	...	...	...	...
90 - 94	3 380	1 657	1 723	...	...	...	...	...	...
95 - 99	1 695	813	882	...	...	...	...	...	...
100 +	918	439	479	...	...	...	...	...	...
Pakistan[59]									
1 VII 2007 (ESDJ)									
Total	149 860 388	76 857 737	73 002 651	52 807 585	27 178 203	25 629 382	97 052 803	49 679 534	47 373 269
0 - 4	19 540 467	9 783 859	9 756 608	5 761 626	2 854 601	2 907 026	13 778 841	6 929 259	6 849 582
5 - 9	22 554 631	11 710 324	10 844 307	6 759 356	3 414 295	3 345 061	15 795 276	8 296 029	7 499 246
10 - 14	20 255 889	10 636 015	9 619 874	6 854 564	3 572 029	3 282 536	13 401 325	7 063 987	6 337 339
15 - 19	17 275 679	9 063 876	8 211 804	6 630 532	3 454 683	3 175 849	10 645 147	5 609 193	5 035 954
20 - 24	13 558 584	6 824 723	6 733 861	5 604 996	2 913 936	2 691 060	7 953 588	3 910 786	4 042 801
25 - 29	10 833 092	5 268 436	5 564 656	4 174 036	2 128 117	2 045 919	6 659 055	3 140 318	3 518 737
30 - 34	8 432 325	3 957 414	4 474 911	3 112 553	1 539 219	1 573 334	5 319 772	2 418 195	2 901 576
35 - 39	8 352 417	4 132 910	4 219 507	3 081 885	1 522 176	1 559 709	5 270 532	2 610 734	2 659 798
40 - 44	6 777 652	3 496 263	3 281 389	2 564 848	1 348 144	1 216 704	4 212 804	2 148 119	2 064 685
45 - 49	6 276 492	3 277 150	2 999 342	2 458 241	1 271 498	1 186 743	3 818 252	2 005 652	1 812 599
50 - 54	4 586 117	2 429 295	2 156 822	1 772 219	967 032	805 188	2 813 897	1 462 263	1 351 634

7. Population by age, sex and urban/rural residence: latest available year, 2007 - 2016
Population selon l'âge, le sexe et la résidence, urbaine/rurale : dernière année disponible, 2007 - 2016 (continued - suite)

Continent, country or area, date, code[a] and age (in years) / Continent, pays ou zone, date, code[a] et âge (en annèes)	Total			Urban - Urbaine			Rural - Rurale		
	Both sexes Les deux sexes	Male Masculin	Female Féminin	Both sexes Les deux sexes	Male Masculin	Female Féminin	Both sexes Les deux sexes	Male Masculin	Female Féminin
ASIA - ASIE									
Pakistan[59]									
1 VII 2007 (ESDJ)									
55 - 59	3 544 175	1 864 568	1 679 608	1 325 845	693 075	632 770	2 218 330	1 171 493	1 046 838
60 - 64	2 933 669	1 637 251	1 296 418	1 003 276	574 578	428 698	1 930 393	1 062 673	867 720
65 - 69	2 038 506	1 106 476	932 030	713 604	371 079	342 526	1 324 901	735 397	589 504
70 - 74	1 464 156	857 310	606 846	499 821	282 013	217 808	964 335	575 297	389 039
75 - 79	654 088	358 255	295 833	244 044	125 467	118 577	410 044	232 788	177 256
80 - 84	428 280	250 734	177 547	129 604	84 073	45 531	298 676	166 661	132 015
85 +	354 168	202 880	151 288	116 534	62 189	54 345	237 634	140 691	96 943
Philippines									
1 V 2010 (CDJC)[60]									
Total	92 335 113	46 634 257	45 700 856	41 855 571	20 840 798	21 014 773	50 479 542	25 793 459	24 686 083
0	1 968 131	1 018 386	949 745	873 792	453 065	420 727	1 094 339	565 321	529 018
1 - 4	8 265 653	4 274 825	3 990 828	3 571 743	1 850 296	1 721 447	4 693 910	2 424 529	2 269 381
5 - 9	10 321 543	5 332 287	4 989 256	4 384 024	2 267 726	2 116 298	5 937 519	3 064 561	2 872 958
10 - 14	10 179 610	5 237 006	4 942 604	4 286 862	2 195 115	2 091 747	5 892 748	3 041 891	2 850 857
15 - 19	9 705 354	4 931 506	4 773 848	4 301 712	2 120 800	2 180 912	5 403 642	2 810 706	2 592 936
20 - 24	8 408 656	4 256 999	4 151 657	4 050 916	1 989 031	2 061 885	4 357 740	2 267 968	2 089 772
25 - 29	7 423 723	3 746 311	3 677 412	3 693 442	1 821 972	1 871 470	3 730 281	1 924 339	1 805 942
30 - 34	6 772 929	3 443 582	3 329 347	3 353 327	1 676 968	1 676 359	3 419 602	1 766 614	1 652 988
35 - 39	6 013 953	3 057 323	2 956 630	2 886 723	1 448 968	1 437 755	3 127 230	1 608 355	1 518 875
40 - 44	5 471 588	2 778 661	2 692 927	2 588 569	1 292 882	1 295 687	2 883 019	1 485 779	1 397 240
45 - 49	4 680 649	2 367 809	2 312 840	2 180 936	1 082 303	1 098 633	2 499 713	1 285 506	1 214 207
50 - 54	3 894 850	1 953 952	1 940 898	1 808 298	890 919	917 379	2 086 552	1 063 033	1 023 519
55 - 59	2 987 148	1 475 861	1 511 287	1 358 685	660 616	698 069	1 628 463	815 245	813 218
60 - 64	2 228 399	1 064 116	1 164 283	979 510	461 508	518 002	1 248 889	602 608	646 281
65 - 69	1 497 557	680 227	817 330	593 219	263 603	329 616	904 338	416 624	487 714
70 - 74	1 142 562	492 152	650 410	437 280	181 972	255 308	705 282	310 180	395 102
75 - 79	707 115	286 079	421 036	265 280	102 308	162 972	441 835	183 771	258 064
80 - 84	394 188	145 937	248 251	145 081	50 979	94 102	249 107	94 958	154 149
85 - 89	188 511	64 125	124 386	67 310	21 250	46 060	121 201	42 875	78 326
90 - 94	60 102	19 598	40 504	21 070	6 202	14 868	39 032	13 396	25 636
95 - 99	18 099	5 684	12 415	6 223	1 753	4 470	11 876	3 931	7 945
100 +	4 793	1 831	2 962	1 569	562	1 007	3 224	1 269	1 955
1 VII 2016 (ESDJ)[7]									
Total	103 242 900	52 081 400	51 161 500	...	...	...	...	...	...
0 - 4	11 367 000	5 842 500	5 524 500	...	...	...	...	...	...
5 - 9	10 787 800	5 518 500	5 269 300	...	...	...	...	...	...
10 - 14	10 354 300	5 335 600	5 018 700	...	...	...	...	...	...
15 - 19	10 160 900	5 228 100	4 932 800	...	...	...	...	...	...
20 - 24	9 728 900	4 959 300	4 769 600	...	...	...	...	...	...
25 - 29	8 567 900	4 346 900	4 221 000	...	...	...	...	...	...
30 - 34	7 516 300	3 793 900	3 722 400	...	...	...	...	...	...
35 - 39	6 796 200	3 442 200	3 354 000	...	...	...	...	...	...
40 - 44	6 046 000	3 061 600	2 984 400	...	...	...	...	...	...
45 - 49	5 438 600	2 746 100	2 692 500	...	...	...	...	...	...
50 - 54	4 657 900	2 335 300	2 322 600	...	...	...	...	...	...
55 - 59	3 822 700	1 890 400	1 932 300	...	...	...	...	...	...
60 - 64	2 896 000	1 399 600	1 496 400	...	...	...	...	...	...
65 - 69	2 073 200	958 800	1 114 400	...	...	...	...	...	...
70 - 74	1 329 100	575 500	753 600	...	...	...	...	...	...
75 - 79	889 200	357 300	531 900	...	...	...	...	...	...
80 +	810 900	289 800	521 100	...	...	...	...	...	...
Qatar									
1 VII 2016 (ESDF)									
Total	2 617 634	1 975 536	642 098	...	...	...	...	...	...
0	26 689	13 648	13 041	...	...	...	...	...	...
1 - 4	111 579	57 073	54 506	...	...	...	...	...	...
5 - 9	123 666	62 962	60 704	...	...	...	...	...	...
10 - 14	95 973	48 979	46 994	...	...	...	...	...	...
15 - 19	89 110	54 764	34 346	...	...	...	...	...	...
20 - 24	274 084	229 491	44 593	...	...	...	...	...	...
25 - 29	463 374	375 542	87 832	...	...	...	...	...	...
30 - 34	438 896	348 857	90 039	...	...	...	...	...	...
35 - 39	333 671	261 734	71 937	...	...	...	...	...	...

Continent, country or area, date, code[a] and age (in years) / Continent, pays ou zone, date, code[a] et âge (en années)	Total			Urban - Urbaine			Rural - Rurale		
	Both sexes Les deux sexes	Male Masculin	Female Féminin	Both sexes Les deux sexes	Male Masculin	Female Féminin	Both sexes Les deux sexes	Male Masculin	Female Féminin
ASIA - ASIE									
Qatar									
1 VII 2016 (ESDF)									
40 - 44	247 305	197 691	49 614	...	...	...	...	...	...
45 - 49	172 618	139 521	33 097	...	...	...	...	...	...
50 - 54	108 737	86 582	22 155	...	...	...	...	...	...
55 - 59	70 564	56 087	14 477	...	...	...	...	...	...
60 - 64	32 724	24 310	8 414	...	...	...	...	...	...
65 - 69	14 607	10 279	4 328	...	...	...	...	...	...
70 - 74	6 741	4 086	2 655	...	...	...	...	...	...
75 - 79	3 980	2 236	1 744	...	...	...	...	...	...
80 +	3 316	1 694	1 622	...	...	...	...	...	...
Republic of Korea - République de Corée									
1 XI 2010 (CDJC)[61]									
Total	47 990 761	23 840 896	24 149 865	39 363 373	19 558 869	19 804 504	8 627 388	4 282 027	4 345 361
0 - 4	2 219 084	1 142 220	1 076 864	1 837 552	945 626	891 926	381 532	196 594	184 938
5 - 9	2 394 663	1 243 294	1 151 369	1 993 280	1 034 401	958 879	401 383	208 893	192 490
10 - 14	3 173 226	1 654 964	1 518 262	2 669 649	1 393 007	1 276 642	503 577	261 957	241 620
15 - 19	3 438 414	1 826 179	1 612 235	2 922 281	1 548 832	1 373 449	516 133	277 347	238 786
20 - 24	3 055 420	1 625 371	1 430 049	2 640 489	1 383 435	1 257 054	414 931	241 936	172 995
25 - 29	3 538 949	1 802 805	1 736 144	3 080 113	1 549 579	1 530 534	458 836	253 226	205 610
30 - 34	3 695 348	1 866 397	1 828 951	3 167 638	1 589 121	1 578 517	527 710	277 276	250 434
35 - 39	4 099 147	2 060 233	2 038 914	3 483 148	1 732 781	1 750 367	615 999	327 452	288 547
40 - 44	4 131 423	2 071 431	2 059 992	3 508 366	1 735 872	1 772 494	623 057	335 559	287 498
45 - 49	4 073 358	2 044 641	2 028 717	3 426 557	1 703 858	1 722 699	646 801	340 783	306 018
50 - 54	3 798 131	1 887 973	1 910 158	3 131 150	1 548 965	1 582 185	666 981	339 008	327 973
55 - 59	2 766 695	1 360 747	1 405 948	2 209 244	1 087 271	1 121 973	557 451	273 476	283 975
60 - 64	2 182 236	1 057 035	1 125 201	1 675 619	813 834	861 785	506 617	243 201	263 416
65 - 69	1 812 168	833 242	978 926	1 307 441	612 023	695 418	504 727	221 219	283 508
70 - 74	1 566 014	672 894	893 120	1 035 369	451 635	583 734	530 645	221 259	309 386
75 - 79	1 084 367	410 726	673 641	676 567	257 200	419 367	407 800	153 526	254 274
80 - 84	595 509	186 008	409 501	370 966	113 906	257 060	224 543	72 102	152 441
85 - 89	271 167	74 118	197 049	168 707	44 883	123 824	102 460	29 235	73 225
90 - 94	78 329	17 770	60 559	48 720	10 873	37 847	29 609	6 897	22 712
95 - 99	15 278	2 593	12 685	9 424	1 619	7 805	5 854	974	4 880
100 +	1 835	255	1 580	1 093	148	945	742	107	635
1 VII 2016 (ESDJ)									
Total	51 245 707	25 693 983	25 551 724	...	...	...	...	...	...
0	424 514	217 669	206 845	...	...	...	...	...	...
1 - 4	1 807 593	927 322	880 271	...	...	...	...	...	...
5 - 9	2 297 525	1 183 766	1 113 759	...	...	...	...	...	...
10 - 14	2 326 687	1 208 844	1 117 843	...	...	...	...	...	...
15 - 19	3 130 685	1 632 065	1 498 620	...	...	...	...	...	...
20 - 24	3 559 433	1 902 360	1 657 073	...	...	...	...	...	...
25 - 29	3 282 024	1 740 971	1 541 053	...	...	...	...	...	...
30 - 34	3 693 331	1 926 821	1 766 510	...	...	...	...	...	...
35 - 39	3 969 413	2 048 507	1 920 906	...	...	...	...	...	...
40 - 44	4 234 849	2 165 060	2 069 789	...	...	...	...	...	...
45 - 49	4 447 873	2 246 279	2 201 594	...	...	...	...	...	...
50 - 54	4 176 619	2 116 304	2 060 315	...	...	...	...	...	...
55 - 59	4 139 015	2 057 135	2 081 880	...	...	...	...	...	...
60 - 64	2 993 304	1 466 021	1 527 283	...	...	...	...	...	...
65 - 69	2 212 452	1 060 248	1 152 204	...	...	...	...	...	...
70 - 74	1 730 775	781 399	949 376	...	...	...	...	...	...
75 - 79	1 401 047	573 975	827 072	...	...	...	...	...	...
80 - 84	867 685	299 555	568 130	...	...	...	...	...	...
85 - 89	391 572	104 356	287 216	...	...	...	...	...	...
90 - 94	129 036	29 447	99 589	...	...	...	...	...	...
95 - 99	27 001	5 434	21 567	...	...	...	...	...	...
100 +	3 274	445	2 829	...	...	...	...	...	...
Saudi Arabia - Arabie saoudite[62]									
1 VII 2016 (ESDF)									
Total	31 787 580	18 259 719	13 527 861	...	...	...	...	...	...
0 - 4	2 674 932	1 364 535	1 310 397	...	...	...	...	...	...

7. Population by age, sex and urban/rural residence: latest available year, 2007 - 2016
Population selon l'âge, le sexe et la résidence, urbaine/rurale : dernière année disponible, 2007 - 2016 (continued - suite)

Continent, country or area, date, code[a] and age (in years) / Continent, pays ou zone, date, code[a] et âge (en années)	Total			Urban - Urbaine			Rural - Rurale		
	Both sexes Les deux sexes	Male Masculin	Female Féminin	Both sexes Les deux sexes	Male Masculin	Female Féminin	Both sexes Les deux sexes	Male Masculin	Female Féminin
ASIA - ASIE									
Saudi Arabia - Arabie saoudite[62]									
1 VII 2016 (ESDF)									
5 - 9	2 771 032	1 412 610	1 358 422	...	...	...	...	...	...
10 - 14	2 428 319	1 236 014	1 192 305	...	...	...	...	...	...
15 - 19	2 216 050	1 132 009	1 084 041	...	...	...	...	...	...
20 - 24	2 471 757	1 315 835	1 155 922	...	...	...	...	...	...
25 - 29	3 032 408	1 672 065	1 360 343	...	...	...	...	...	...
30 - 34	3 063 233	1 795 177	1 268 056	...	...	...	...	...	...
35 - 39	3 399 988	2 123 161	1 276 827	...	...	...	...	...	...
40 - 44	3 038 184	1 930 607	1 107 577	...	...	...	...	...	...
45 - 49	2 261 119	1 487 446	773 673	...	...	...	...	...	...
50 - 54	1 582 175	1 075 976	506 199	...	...	...	...	...	...
55 - 59	1 095 434	722 149	373 285	...	...	...	...	...	...
60 - 64	724 256	450 237	274 019	...	...	...	...	...	...
65 - 69	405 199	219 981	185 218	...	...	...	...	...	...
70 - 74	270 221	141 012	129 209	...	...	...	...	...	...
75 - 79	161 004	84 914	76 090	...	...	...	...	...	...
80 +	192 269	95 991	96 278	...	...	...	...	...	...
Singapore - Singapour[63]									
30 VI 2016 (ESDJ)									
Total	3 933 559	1 929 526	2 004 033	...	...	...	...	...	...
0 - 4	187 160	95 678	91 482	...	...	...	...	...	...
5 - 9	201 509	102 426	99 083	...	...	...	...	...	...
10 - 14	207 495	105 589	101 906	...	...	...	...	...	...
15 - 19	239 771	122 911	116 860	...	...	...	...	...	...
20 - 24	260 854	132 046	128 808	...	...	...	...	...	...
25 - 29	279 988	137 243	142 745	...	...	...	...	...	...
30 - 34	285 544	135 596	149 948	...	...	...	...	...	...
35 - 39	301 998	143 553	158 445	...	...	...	...	...	...
40 - 44	313 445	152 466	160 979	...	...	...	...	...	...
45 - 49	301 183	147 517	153 666	...	...	...	...	...	...
50 - 54	315 598	158 202	157 396	...	...	...	...	...	...
55 - 59	299 591	150 315	149 276	...	...	...	...	...	...
60 - 64	251 853	125 130	126 723	...	...	...	...	...	...
65 - 69	198 020	96 349	101 671	...	...	...	...	...	...
70 - 74	103 796	48 691	55 105	...	...	...	...	...	...
75 - 79	87 955	38 976	48 979	...	...	...	...	...	...
80 - 84	53 556	21 884	31 672	...	...	...	...	...	...
85 +	44 243	14 954	29 289	...	...	...	...	...	...
Sri Lanka									
20 III 2012 (CDJC)									
Total	20 359 439	9 856 634	10 502 805	3 704 470	1 800 327	1 904 143	16 654 969	8 056 307	8 598 662
0 - 4	1 743 862	879 223	864 639	281 707	142 039	139 668	1 462 155	737 184	724 971
5 - 9	1 747 752	882 108	865 644	292 480	147 539	144 941	1 455 272	734 569	720 703
10 - 14	1 640 052	829 069	810 983	286 653	145 640	141 013	1 353 399	683 429	669 970
15 - 19	1 644 249	819 927	824 322	306 654	155 546	151 108	1 337 595	664 381	673 214
20 - 24	1 532 883	742 316	790 567	308 605	151 666	156 939	1 224 278	590 650	633 628
25 - 29	1 552 848	743 510	809 338	290 825	142 387	148 438	1 262 023	601 123	660 900
30 - 34	1 639 415	796 866	842 549	294 944	145 860	149 084	1 344 471	651 006	693 465
35 - 39	1 409 077	686 037	723 040	260 479	127 396	133 083	1 148 598	558 641	589 957
40 - 44	1 359 209	661 623	697 586	253 831	124 363	129 468	1 105 378	537 260	568 118
45 - 49	1 285 830	618 140	667 690	237 646	113 675	123 971	1 048 184	504 465	543 719
50 - 54	1 219 460	581 293	638 167	223 940	106 249	117 691	995 520	475 044	520 476
55 - 59	1 064 229	500 871	563 358	192 715	90 444	102 271	871 514	410 427	461 087
60 - 64	917 910	425 428	492 482	169 167	78 370	90 797	748 743	347 058	401 685
65 - 69	633 289	283 764	349 525	121 751	54 401	67 350	511 538	229 363	282 175
70 - 74	412 414	181 846	230 568	77 909	33 807	44 102	334 505	148 039	186 466
75 - 79	283 186	116 389	166 797	52 087	21 036	31 051	231 099	95 353	135 746
80 - 84	159 379	64 250	95 129	30 707	11 775	18 932	128 672	52 475	76 197
85 - 89	73 441	28 293	45 148	14 121	5 097	9 024	59 320	23 196	36 124
90 - 94	24 258	9 293	14 965	4 932	1 790	3 142	19 326	7 503	11 823
95 +	16 696	6 388	10 308	3 317	1 247	2 070	13 379	5 141	8 238

7. Population by age, sex and urban/rural residence: latest available year, 2007 - 2016
Population selon l'âge, le sexe et la résidence, urbaine/rurale : dernière année disponible, 2007 - 2016 (continued - suite)

Continent, country or area, date, code[a] and age (in years) / Continent, pays ou zone, date, code[a] et âge (en années)	Total			Urban - Urbaine			Rural - Rurale		
	Both sexes Les deux sexes	Male Masculin	Female Féminin	Both sexes Les deux sexes	Male Masculin	Female Féminin	Both sexes Les deux sexes	Male Masculin	Female Féminin
ASIA - ASIE									
Sri Lanka									
1 VII 2016* (ESDJ)									
Total	21 203 000	10 265 460	10 937 540	...	...	...	...	...	...
0 - 4	1 817 976	916 588	901 388	...	...	...	...	...	...
5 - 9	1 821 509	919 317	902 192	...	...	...	...	...	...
10 - 14	1 709 097	863 937	845 160	...	...	...	...	...	...
15 - 19	1 713 277	854 265	859 012	...	...	...	...	...	...
20 - 24	1 596 309	772 957	823 353	...	...	...	...	...	...
25 - 29	1 617 399	774 332	843 067	...	...	...	...	...	...
30 - 34	1 707 349	829 845	877 504	...	...	...	...	...	...
35 - 39	1 467 191	714 341	752 850	...	...	...	...	...	...
40 - 44	1 415 079	688 842	726 237	...	...	...	...	...	...
45 - 49	1 338 870	643 685	695 185	...	...	...	...	...	...
50 - 54	1 269 610	605 271	664 338	...	...	...	...	...	...
55 - 59	1 107 770	521 443	586 328	...	...	...	...	...	...
60 +	2 621 564	1 160 638	1 460 926	...	...	...	...	...	...
State of Palestine - État de Palestine									
1 XII 2007 (CDFC)[64]									
Total	3 443 828	1 747 284	1 696 544	2 814 623[65]	1 427 861[65]	1 386 762[65]	629 205	319 423	309 782
0	107 187	54 782	52 405	88 830[65]	45 359[65]	43 471[65]	18 357	9 423	8 934
1 - 4	412 748	211 270	201 478	340 784[65]	174 537[65]	166 247[65]	71 964	36 733	35 231
5 - 9	466 880	239 156	227 724	381 348[65]	195 338[65]	186 010[65]	85 532	43 818	41 714
10 - 14	466 273	238 306	227 967	381 583[65]	194 860[65]	186 723[65]	84 690	43 446	41 244
15 - 19	414 439	211 464	202 975	339 534[65]	173 038[65]	166 496[65]	74 905	38 426	36 479
20 - 24	309 935	158 374	151 561	253 464[65]	128 975[65]	124 489[65]	56 471	29 399	27 072
25 - 29	252 227	128 068	124 159	206 038[65]	104 199[65]	101 839[65]	46 189	23 869	22 320
30 - 34	215 288	108 945	106 343	174 749[65]	88 330[65]	86 419[65]	40 539	20 615	19 924
35 - 39	177 060	90 155	86 905	142 888[65]	72 771[65]	70 117[65]	34 172	17 384	16 788
40 - 44	156 514	81 186	75 328	127 937[65]	66 510[65]	61 427[65]	28 577	14 676	13 901
45 - 49	117 580	60 832	56 748	95 564[65]	49 594[65]	45 970[65]	22 016	11 238	10 778
50 - 54	83 301	41 606	41 695	67 461[65]	33 829[65]	33 632[65]	15 840	7 777	8 063
55 - 59	63 010	32 011	30 999	51 678[65]	26 340[65]	25 338[65]	11 332	5 671	5 661
60 - 64	47 829	22 060	25 769	38 987[65]	18 162[65]	20 825[65]	8 842	3 898	4 944
65 - 69	33 697	13 853	19 844	27 124[65]	11 192[65]	15 932[65]	6 573	2 661	3 912
70 - 74	29 316	12 689	16 627	23 300[65]	10 221[65]	13 079[65]	6 016	2 468	3 548
75 - 79	21 135	8 599	12 536	16 540[65]	6 744[65]	9 796[65]	4 595	1 855	2 740
80 - 84	11 749	4 861	6 888	8 940[65]	3 705[65]	5 235[65]	2 809	1 156	1 653
85 - 89	5 344	2 318	3 026	3 984[65]	1 721[65]	2 263[65]	1 360	597	763
90 - 94	2 004	871	1 133	1 512[65]	646[65]	866[65]	492	225	267
95 +	1 061	464	597	744[65]	331[65]	413[65]	317	133	184
Unknown - Inconnu	49 251	25 414	23 837	41 634[65]	21 459[65]	20 175[65]	7 617	3 955	3 662
1 VII 2016 (ESDF)									
Total	4 816 503	2 447 616	2 368 887	...	...	...	...	...	...
0	148 776	76 075	72 701	...	...	...	...	...	...
1 - 4	569 313	291 039	278 274	...	...	...	...	...	...
5 - 9	609 503	310 845	298 658	...	...	...	...	...	...
10 - 14	559 144	285 511	273 633	...	...	...	...	...	...
15 - 19	530 322	270 712	259 610	...	...	...	...	...	...
20 - 24	495 035	252 377	242 658	...	...	...	...	...	...
25 - 29	414 334	211 305	203 029	...	...	...	...	...	...
30 - 34	320 463	163 780	156 683	...	...	...	...	...	...
35 - 39	265 799	135 413	130 386	...	...	...	...	...	...
40 - 44	224 673	113 626	111 047	...	...	...	...	...	...
45 - 49	188 061	95 886	92 175	...	...	...	...	...	...
50 - 54	155 661	80 634	75 027	...	...	...	...	...	...
55 - 59	116 766	60 064	56 702	...	...	...	...	...	...
60 - 64	78 511	39 334	39 177	...	...	...	...	...	...
65 - 69	54 985	25 996	28 989	...	...	...	...	...	...
70 - 74	37 786	16 226	21 560	...	...	...	...	...	...
75 - 79	24 430	9 844	14 586	...	...	...	...	...	...
80 +	22 941	8 949	13 992	...	...	...	...	...	...

Continent, country or area, date, code[a] and age (in years) / Continent, pays ou zone, date, code[a] et âge (en années)	Total			Urban - Urbaine			Rural - Rurale		
	Both sexes Les deux sexes	Male Masculin	Female Féminin	Both sexes Les deux sexes	Male Masculin	Female Féminin	Both sexes Les deux sexes	Male Masculin	Female Féminin
ASIA - ASIE									
Syrian Arab Republic - République arabe syrienne[66]									
1 VII 2011 (ESDF)									
Total	21 124 000	10 794 000	10 330 000	11 297 000	5 795 000	5 502 000	9 827 000	4 999 000	4 828 000
0 - 4	2 775 000	1 428 000	1 347 000	1 384 000	713 000	671 000	1 391 000	715 000	676 000
5 - 9	2 654 000	1 384 000	1 270 000	1 357 000	719 000	638 000	1 297 000	665 000	632 000
10 - 14	2 430 000	1 232 000	1 198 000	1 270 000	637 000	633 000	1 160 000	595 000	565 000
15 - 19	2 279 000	1 191 000	1 088 000	1 193 000	626 000	567 000	1 086 000	565 000	521 000
20 - 24	1 979 000	1 035 000	944 000	1 045 000	545 000	500 000	934 000	490 000	444 000
25 - 29	1 737 000	864 000	873 000	937 000	475 000	462 000	800 000	389 000	411 000
30 - 34	1 371 000	674 000	697 000	733 000	359 000	374 000	638 000	315 000	323 000
35 - 39	1 229 000	601 000	628 000	694 000	336 000	358 000	535 000	265 000	270 000
40 - 44	1 096 000	545 000	551 000	644 000	325 000	319 000	452 000	220 000	232 000
45 - 49	870 000	437 000	433 000	536 000	272 000	264 000	334 000	165 000	169 000
50 - 54	792 000	387 000	405 000	458 000	232 000	226 000	334 000	155 000	179 000
55 - 59	573 000	293 000	280 000	322 000	168 000	154 000	251 000	125 000	126 000
60 - 64	481 000	254 000	227 000	260 000	139 000	121 000	221 000	115 000	106 000
65 +	858 000	469 000	389 000	464 000	249 000	215 000	394 000	220 000	174 000
Tajikistan - Tadjikistan									
1 VII 2014 (ESDF)									
Total	8 256 572	4 174 269	4 082 303	2 193 224	1 112 352	1 080 873	6 063 348	3 061 917	3 001 431
0	216 440	114 100	102 340	51 426	27 153	24 273	165 014	86 948	78 067
1 - 4	882 560	456 234	426 326	210 093	108 382	101 711	672 467	347 852	324 615
5 - 9	925 128	475 721	449 408	224 757	115 632	109 125	700 372	360 089	340 283
10 - 14	844 012	433 005	411 008	215 460	111 081	104 380	628 552	321 924	306 628
15 - 19	867 192	442 705	424 487	230 225	120 101	110 125	636 967	322 605	314 362
20 - 24	850 400	429 958	420 442	250 113	138 182	111 932	600 287	291 776	308 511
25 - 29	793 282	397 488	395 794	204 805	105 211	99 594	588 478	292 278	296 200
30 - 34	596 625	302 173	294 452	154 035	76 454	77 581	442 590	225 719	216 871
35 - 39	475 028	237 691	237 338	131 898	62 779	69 120	343 130	174 912	168 218
40 - 44	424 616	209 746	214 870	126 370	59 737	66 633	298 247	150 010	148 237
45 - 49	381 217	186 713	194 504	113 273	54 374	58 899	267 944	132 339	135 605
50 - 54	346 740	170 584	176 156	101 114	48 708	52 407	245 626	121 877	123 749
55 - 59	241 422	118 136	123 286	69 084	33 133	35 951	172 338	85 003	87 335
60 - 64	156 423	75 679	80 744	45 239	21 310	23 929	111 185	54 369	56 816
65 - 69	83 359	41 283	42 076	24 008	11 302	12 706	59 351	29 981	29 370
70 - 74	68 103	34 752	33 351	18 103	8 702	9 401	50 001	26 050	23 951
75 - 79	54 116	25 756	28 360	13 026	5 851	7 175	41 090	19 906	21 184
80 - 84	31 351	14 076	17 275	6 609	2 782	3 828	24 742	11 294	13 448
85 - 89	13 688	6 575	7 113	2 637	1 103	1 534	11 051	5 472	5 579
90 - 94	3 962	1 549	2 413	760	281	479	3 202	1 269	1 933
95 - 99	664	256	408	129	62	67	535	195	340
100 +	249	92	157	66	39	28	183	54	129
Thailand - Thaïlande									
1 VII 2012 (ESDJ)[5]									
Total	67 911 720	33 328 645	34 583 075	23 430 180	11 219 175	12 211 005	44 481 540	22 109 470	22 372 070
0 - 4	3 979 864	2 041 071	1 938 793	1 303 276	660 378	642 898	2 676 588	1 380 693	1 295 895
5 - 9	4 624 088	2 353 198	2 270 890	1 653 192	829 716	823 476	2 970 896	1 523 482	1 447 414
10 - 14	4 766 188	2 438 774	2 327 414	1 567 479	790 354	777 125	3 198 709	1 648 420	1 550 289
15 - 19	5 067 031	2 593 629	2 473 402	1 561 571	784 752	776 819	3 505 460	1 808 877	1 696 583
20 - 24	5 237 205	2 673 846	2 563 359	1 615 627	803 045	812 582	3 621 578	1 870 801	1 750 777
25 - 29	5 262 148	2 673 201	2 588 947	1 709 395	839 146	870 249	3 552 753	1 834 055	1 718 698
30 - 34	5 320 960	2 683 015	2 637 945	1 966 999	953 695	1 013 304	3 353 961	1 729 320	1 624 641
35 - 39	5 432 820	2 673 404	2 759 416	2 079 909	992 437	1 087 472	3 352 911	1 680 967	1 671 944
40 - 44	5 543 422	2 672 891	2 870 531	2 045 686	963 854	1 081 832	3 497 736	1 709 037	1 788 699
45 - 49	5 344 099	2 574 423	2 769 676	1 923 474	905 363	1 018 111	3 420 625	1 669 060	1 751 565
50 - 54	4 818 743	2 315 177	2 503 566	1 713 371	804 718	908 653	3 105 372	1 510 459	1 594 913
55 - 59	3 906 749	1 854 719	2 052 030	1 372 422	637 639	734 783	2 534 327	1 217 080	1 317 247
60 - 64	2 881 942	1 347 251	1 534 691	995 059	456 060	539 235	1 886 647	891 191	995 456
65 - 69	2 118 712	963 728	1 154 984	711 804	317 607	394 197	1 406 908	646 121	760 787
70 - 74	1 603 467	695 434	908 033	533 040	226 340	306 700	1 070 427	469 094	601 333
75 - 79	1 111 421	451 737	659 684	375 550	149 055	226 495	735 871	302 682	433 189
80 +	892 861	323 147	569 714	302 090	105 016	197 074	590 771	218 131	372 640

Continent, country or area, date, code[a] and age (in years) Continent, pays ou zone, date, code[a] et âge (en années)	Total			Urban - Urbaine			Rural - Rurale		
	Both sexes Les deux sexes	Male Masculin	Female Féminin	Both sexes Les deux sexes	Male Masculin	Female Féminin	Both sexes Les deux sexes	Male Masculin	Female Féminin
ASIA - ASIE									
Thailand - Thaïlande									
1 VII 2016 (ESDJ)									
Total	65 931 550	32 357 808	33 573 742	...	...	...	...	...	...
0	627 185	322 426	304 759	...	...	...	...	...	...
1 - 4	2 937 835	1 510 332	1 427 503	...	...	...	...	...	...
5 - 9	3 885 043	1 997 984	1 887 059	...	...	...	...	...	...
10 - 14	3 983 268	2 046 615	1 936 653	...	...	...	...	...	...
15 - 19	4 332 511	2 220 057	2 112 454	...	...	...	...	...	...
20 - 24	4 808 033	2 443 270	2 364 763	...	...	...	...	...	...
25 - 29	4 585 819	2 320 900	2 264 919	...	...	...	...	...	...
30 - 34	4 825 484	2 422 455	2 403 029	...	...	...	...	...	...
35 - 39	5 172 463	2 576 104	2 596 359	...	...	...	...	...	...
40 - 44	5 214 732	2 555 578	2 659 154	...	...	...	...	...	...
45 - 49	5 261 933	2 533 459	2 728 474	...	...	...	...	...	...
46 - 47	2 089 843	1 007 868	1 081 975	...	...	...	...	...	...
50 - 54	4 886 375	2 323 246	2 563 129	...	...	...	...	...	...
53 - 54	1 862 924	886 131	976 793	...	...	...	...	...	...
55 - 59	4 094 384	1 923 854	2 170 530	...	...	...	...	...	...
60 - 64	3 145 127	1 454 303	1 690 824	...	...	...	...	...	...
65 - 69	2 433 969	1 106 387	1 327 582	...	...	...	...	...	...
70 - 74	1 589 468	707 672	881 796	...	...	...	...	...	...
73 - 74	573 567	253 045	320 522	...	...	...	...	...	...
75 - 79	1 214 296	517 260	697 036	...	...	...	...	...	...
80 - 84	804 670	323 305	481 365	...	...	...	...	...	...
85 - 89	410 861	155 181	255 680	...	...	...	...	...	...
90 - 94	146 679	53 682	92 997	...	...	...	...	...	...
95 - 99	45 105	17 733	27 372	...	...	...	...	...	...
100 +	11 905	4 614	7 291	...	...	...	...	...	...
Unknown - Inconnu	1 514 405	821 391	693 014	...	...	...	...	...	...
Timor-Leste									
11 VII 2010 (CDFC)									
Total	1 066 409	544 198	522 211	316 086	166 163	149 923	750 323	378 035	372 288
0 - 4	153 334	79 169	74 165	40 622	20 978	19 644	112 712	58 191	54 521
5 - 9	153 108	78 980	74 128	39 668	20 480	19 188	113 440	58 500	54 940
10 - 14	135 464	70 513	64 951	33 309	17 369	15 940	102 155	53 144	49 011
15 - 19	116 535	58 754	57 781	42 791	21 249	21 542	73 744	37 505	36 239
20 - 24	94 427	47 336	47 091	41 612	22 175	19 437	52 815	25 161	27 654
25 - 29	76 836	38 269	38 567	31 190	16 578	14 612	45 646	21 691	23 955
30 - 34	51 911	25 805	26 106	19 454	10 623	8 831	32 457	15 182	17 275
35 - 39	57 508	29 961	27 547	18 377	10 284	8 093	39 131	19 677	19 454
40 - 44	48 372	25 407	22 965	13 599	7 748	5 851	34 773	17 659	17 114
45 - 49	38 917	20 430	18 487	9 971	5 692	4 279	28 946	14 738	14 208
50 - 54	30 084	15 539	14 545	7 205	3 954	3 251	22 879	11 585	11 294
55 - 59	22 346	11 796	10 550	5 007	2 725	2 282	17 339	9 071	8 268
60 - 64	37 333	17 419	19 914	5 419	2 596	2 823	31 914	14 823	17 091
65 - 69	23 106	11 573	11 533	3 407	1 638	1 769	19 699	9 935	9 764
70 - 74	12 705	6 285	6 420	2 079	991	1 088	10 626	5 294	5 332
75 - 79	7 125	3 404	3 721	1 127	508	619	5 998	2 896	3 102
80 - 84	3 755	1 818	1 937	614	275	339	3 141	1 543	1 598
85 +	3 543	1 740	1 803	635	300	335	2 908	1 440	1 468
Turkey - Turquie									
31 XII 2015 (ESDJ)									
Total[67]	78 741 053	39 511 191	39 229 862	69 004 143	34 598 184	34 405 959	9 736 910	4 913 007	4 823 903
0[68]	1 275 773	654 321	621 452	1 143 723	586 193	557 530	132 050	68 128	63 922
1 - 4[67]	5 105 743	2 621 199	2 484 544	4 556 834	2 339 901	2 216 933	548 909	281 298	267 611
5 - 9[67]	6 337 719	3 252 811	3 084 908	5 627 881	2 889 068	2 738 813	709 838	363 743	346 095
10 - 14[67]	6 166 985	3 166 860	3 000 125	5 398 076	2 773 419	2 624 657	768 909	393 441	375 468
15 - 19[67]	6 585 500	3 382 363	3 203 137	5 746 621	2 948 188	2 798 433	838 879	434 175	404 704
20 - 24[67]	6 314 167	3 224 168	3 089 999	5 564 534	2 809 225	2 755 309	749 633	414 943	334 690
25 - 29[67]	6 263 249	3 178 350	3 084 899	5 642 061	2 841 151	2 800 910	621 188	337 199	283 989
30 - 34[67]	6 428 150	3 252 171	3 175 979	5 836 296	2 939 780	2 896 516	591 854	312 391	279 463
35 - 39[67]	6 203 323	3 134 041	3 069 282	5 616 751	2 831 430	2 785 321	586 572	302 611	283 961
40 - 44[67]	5 552 580	2 788 425	2 764 155	4 976 848	2 498 086	2 478 762	575 732	290 339	285 393
45 - 49[67]	4 590 079	2 337 087	2 252 992	4 068 014	2 068 806	1 999 208	522 065	268 281	253 784
50 - 54[67]	4 632 909	2 317 534	2 315 375	4 022 468	2 014 109	2 008 359	610 441	303 425	307 016

Continent, country or area, date, code[a] and age (in years) / Continent, pays ou zone, date, code[a] et âge (en annèes)	Total			Urban - Urbaine			Rural - Rurale		
	Both sexes Les deux sexes	Male Masculin	Female Féminin	Both sexes Les deux sexes	Male Masculin	Female Féminin	Both sexes Les deux sexes	Male Masculin	Female Féminin
ASIA - ASIE									
Turkey - Turquie									
31 XII 2015 (ESDJ)									
55 - 59[67]	3 681 170	1 843 354	1 837 816	3 139 631	1 573 987	1 565 644	541 539	269 367	272 172
60 - 64[67]	3 108 467	1 515 065	1 593 402	2 577 567	1 261 251	1 316 316	530 900	253 814	277 086
65 - 69[67]	2 356 385	1 100 734	1 255 651	1 896 305	889 560	1 006 745	460 080	211 174	248 906
70 - 74[67]	1 626 184	737 892	888 292	1 271 061	577 866	693 195	355 123	160 026	195 097
75 - 79[67]	1 183 746	501 411	682 335	909 334	382 838	526 496	274 412	118 573	155 839
80 - 84[67]	810 488	339 904	470 584	612 364	250 439	361 925	198 124	89 465	108 659
85 - 89[67]	390 450	128 879	261 571	297 597	96 304	201 293	92 853	32 575	60 278
90 - 94[67]	105 424	30 543	74 881	82 380	23 374	59 006	23 044	7 169	15 875
95 - 99[67]	17 269	3 327	13 942	13 677	2 614	11 063	3 592	713	2 879
100 +[67]	5 293	752	4 541	4 120	595	3 525	1 173	157	1 016
Uzbekistan - Ouzbékistan[69]									
1 VII 2015 (ESDJ)									
Total	31 298 929	15 695 568	15 603 361	15 855 953	7 919 014	7 936 939	15 442 976	7 776 554	7 666 422
0	700 155	364 308	335 847	314 693	163 697	150 996	385 462	200 611	184 851
1 - 4	2 569 021	1 331 960	1 237 061	1 171 852	607 940	563 912	1 397 169	724 020	673 149
5 - 9	3 015 258	1 551 922	1 463 336	1 371 477	703 840	667 637	1 643 781	848 082	795 699
10 - 14	2 569 558	1 318 964	1 250 594	1 259 615	645 426	614 189	1 309 943	673 538	636 405
15 - 19	2 841 508	1 453 864	1 387 644	1 402 806	716 934	685 872	1 438 702	736 930	701 772
20 - 24	3 238 160	1 648 485	1 589 675	1 583 875	812 193	771 682	1 654 285	836 292	817 993
25 - 29	3 085 365	1 561 037	1 524 328	1 544 612	787 618	756 994	1 540 753	773 419	767 334
30 - 34	2 581 117	1 294 280	1 286 837	1 331 499	669 183	662 316	1 249 618	625 097	624 521
35 - 39	2 152 092	1 075 561	1 076 531	1 131 979	562 901	569 078	1 020 113	512 660	507 453
40 - 44	1 923 930	957 647	966 283	1 051 285	523 195	528 090	872 645	434 452	438 193
45 - 49	1 650 639	801 329	849 310	910 665	449 528	461 137	739 974	351 801	388 173
50 - 54	1 584 938	764 588	820 350	857 095	411 311	445 784	727 843	353 277	374 566
55 - 59	1 273 308	614 125	659 183	704 226	334 974	369 252	569 082	279 151	289 931
60 - 64	835 627	396 007	439 620	478 698	222 129	256 569	356 929	173 878	183 051
65 - 69	466 332	216 263	250 069	278 318	124 941	153 377	188 014	91 322	96 692
70 - 74	277 898	129 852	148 046	157 652	69 591	88 061	120 246	60 261	59 985
75 - 79	275 297	119 011	156 286	157 297	62 680	94 617	118 000	56 331	61 669
80 - 84	128 512	49 173	79 339	71 787	24 793	46 994	56 725	24 380	32 345
85 +	130 214	47 192	83 022	76 522	26 140	50 382	53 692	21 052	32 640
Viet Nam									
1 IV 2009 (CDJC)									
Total	85 846 997	42 413 143	43 433 854	25 436 896	12 349 995	13 086 901	60 410 101	30 063 148	30 346 953
0 - 4	7 034 144	3 662 889	3 371 255	1 949 105	1 019 547	929 558	5 085 039	2 643 342	2 441 697
5 - 9	6 710 737	3 458 159	3 252 578	1 757 679	910 339	847 340	4 953 058	2 547 820	2 405 238
10 - 14	7 248 378	3 725 369	3 523 009	1 761 650	904 731	856 919	5 486 728	2 820 638	2 666 090
15 - 17	5 236 771	2 681 653	2 555 118	1 311 350	662 369	648 981	3 925 421	2 019 284	1 906 137
18 - 19	3 727 131	1 896 261	1 830 870	1 188 578	562 169	626 409	2 538 553	1 334 092	1 204 461
20 - 24	8 432 867	4 253 618	4 179 249	2 759 456	1 305 436	1 454 020	5 673 411	2 948 182	2 725 229
25 - 29	7 790 003	3 904 730	3 885 273	2 519 920	1 205 518	1 314 402	5 270 083	2 699 212	2 570 871
30 - 34	6 868 158	3 462 905	3 405 253	2 164 824	1 062 838	1 101 986	4 703 334	2 400 067	2 303 267
35 - 39	6 531 607	3 298 266	3 233 341	2 059 356	1 027 075	1 032 281	4 472 251	2 271 191	2 201 060
40 - 44	5 966 856	2 967 934	2 998 922	1 818 188	896 290	921 898	4 148 668	2 071 644	2 077 024
45 - 49	5 450 928	2 642 466	2 808 462	1 728 008	840 047	887 961	3 722 920	1 802 419	1 920 501
50 - 54	4 412 051	2 082 098	2 329 953	1 435 970	683 749	752 221	2 976 081	1 398 349	1 577 732
55 - 59	2 984 619	1 364 319	1 620 300	931 382	421 296	510 086	2 053 237	943 023	1 110 214
60 - 64	1 937 948	861 897	1 076 051	590 161	259 193	330 968	1 347 787	602 704	745 083
65 - 69	1 554 678	653 287	901 391	453 756	195 857	257 899	1 100 922	457 430	643 492
70 - 74	1 412 538	568 312	844 226	378 105	155 224	222 881	1 034 433	413 088	621 345
75 - 79	1 198 893	480 088	718 805	306 226	125 948	180 278	892 667	354 140	538 527
80 - 84	725 985	264 997	460 988	182 550	69 573	112 977	543 435	195 424	348 011
85 +	622 705	183 895	438 810	140 632	42 796	97 836	482 073	141 099	340 974
1 VII 2016* (ESDF)									
Total	92 695 100	45 705 600	46 989 500	31 986 000	...	...	60 709 100	...	...
0 - 4	7 712 700	4 065 400	3 647 300	2 461 800	...	...	5 250 800	...	...
5 - 9	7 339 000	3 828 100	3 510 900	2 376 200	...	...	4 962 900	...	...
10 - 14	7 032 800	3 620 000	3 412 800	2 200 300	...	...	4 832 500	...	...
15 - 19	6 371 000	3 248 300	3 122 600	1 993 600	...	...	4 377 400	...	...
20 - 24	6 899 200	3 527 900	3 371 300	2 437 100	...	...	4 462 100	...	...
25 - 29	7 424 200	3 766 900	3 657 300	2 621 400	...	...	4 802 800	...	...
30 - 34	7 450 700	3 676 700	3 773 900	2 735 800	...	...	4 714 800	...	...

Continent, country or area, date, code[a] and age (in years) / Continent, pays ou zone, date, code[a] et âge (en années)	Total			Urban - Urbaine			Rural - Rurale		
	Both sexes Les deux sexes	Male Masculin	Female Féminin	Both sexes Les deux sexes	Male Masculin	Female Féminin	Both sexes Les deux sexes	Male Masculin	Female Féminin
ASIA - ASIE									
Viet Nam									
1 VII 2016* (ESDF)									
35 - 39	6 885 800	3 412 600	3 473 200	2 474 300	...	...	4 411 500	...	...
40 - 44	6 693 500	3 314 300	3 379 300	2 387 700	...	...	4 305 800	...	...
45 - 49	6 291 700	3 162 300	3 129 500	2 243 900	...	...	4 047 900	...	...
50 - 54	6 247 300	2 963 000	3 284 200	2 239 800	...	...	4 007 500	...	...
55 - 59	5 301 000	2 465 000	2 836 000	2 000 700	...	...	3 300 300	...	...
60 - 64	3 651 900	1 669 600	1 982 300	1 317 200	...	...	2 334 700	...	...
65 - 69	2 484 100	1 091 400	1 392 700	901 400	...	...	1 582 700	...	...
70 - 74	1 524 600	628 000	896 600	542 800	...	...	981 800	...	...
75 - 79	1 379 000	545 200	833 800	449 400	...	...	929 600	...	...
80 +	2 006 800	720 800	1 286 000	602 600	...	...	1 404 200	...	...
Yemen - Yémen[2]									
1 VII 2013 (ESDJ)									
Total	25 235 079	12 844 169	12 390 910	...	...	...	...	...	...
0	867 766	442 297	425 470	...	...	...	...	...	...
1 - 4	3 183 851	1 627 558	1 556 293	...	...	...	...	...	...
5 - 9	3 377 146	1 723 755	1 653 391	...	...	...	...	...	...
10 - 14	3 007 245	1 539 447	1 467 798	...	...	...	...	...	...
15 - 19	2 954 657	1 530 854	1 423 803	...	...	...	...	...	...
20 - 24	2 738 574	1 426 490	1 312 083	...	...	...	...	...	...
25 - 29	2 226 915	1 146 775	1 080 140	...	...	...	...	...	...
30 - 34	1 688 248	851 154	837 094	...	...	...	...	...	...
35 - 39	1 276 748	635 492	641 256	...	...	...	...	...	...
40 - 44	916 385	448 186	468 200	...	...	...	...	...	...
45 - 49	758 743	366 733	392 010	...	...	...	...	...	...
50 - 54	644 689	310 025	334 665	...	...	...	...	...	...
55 - 59	488 859	238 877	249 982	...	...	...	...	...	...
60 - 64	352 671	178 041	174 631	...	...	...	...	...	...
65 - 69	266 902	135 090	131 812	...	...	...	...	...	...
70 - 74	195 287	98 257	97 029	...	...	...	...	...	...
75 - 79	133 347	66 656	66 691	...	...	...	...	...	...
80 +	157 047	78 482	78 565	...	...	...	...	...	...
EUROPE									
Åland Islands - Îles d'Åland[23]									
1 VII 2016 (ESDJ)									
Total	29 099	14 526	14 573	11 513	5 538	5 975	17 586	8 988	8 598
0	288	147	141	107	52	55	181	96	86
1 - 4	1 228	617	612	407	203	204	822	414	408
5 - 9	1 632	839	793	554	271	283	1 078	568	511
10 - 14	1 588	823	766	546	271	275	1 043	552	491
15 - 19	1 590	845	745	648	326	322	943	519	424
20 - 24	1 452	781	671	711	391	321	741	391	350
25 - 29	1 724	919	805	829	456	373	896	464	432
30 - 34	1 730	872	858	725	381	345	1 005	492	513
35 - 39	1 768	901	867	686	343	343	1 083	559	524
40 - 44	1 895	972	923	687	338	350	1 208	635	573
45 - 49	2 076	1 029	1 047	792	378	414	1 284	651	633
50 - 54	2 057	1 028	1 029	764	353	411	1 293	675	618
55 - 59	1 939	925	1 015	723	324	399	1 217	601	616
60 - 64	2 039	970	1 069	826	372	454	1 213	599	615
65 - 69	1 965	972	993	791	352	439	1 175	620	555
70 - 74	1 576	800	777	651	304	347	925	496	430
75 - 79	1 041	504	537	433	199	235	608	306	303
80 - 84	767	333	434	329	137	192	438	196	242
85 - 89	468	183	285	187	68	119	281	116	166
90 - 94	220	59	161	99	22	77	122	37	85
95 - 99	55	8	47	22	2	20	34	6	28
100 +	5	2	4	3	1	2	3	1	2

Continent, country or area, date, code[a] and age (in years) Continent, pays ou zone, date, code[a] et âge (en annèes)	Total			Urban - Urbaine			Rural - Rurale		
	Both sexes Les deux sexes	Male Masculin	Female Féminin	Both sexes Les deux sexes	Male Masculin	Female Féminin	Both sexes Les deux sexes	Male Masculin	Female Féminin
EUROPE									
Albania - Albanie									
1 VII 2013 (ESDF)									
Total	2 897 364	1 458 648	1 438 716	1 633 617	798 615	835 002	1 263 747	660 033	603 714
0 - 4	173 349	90 068	83 281	75 341	39 381	35 960	98 008	50 687	47 321
0	35 445	18 414	17 031	...	...	...	...	...	...
1 - 4	137 903	71 653	66 250	...	...	...	...	...	...
5 - 9	171 833	90 701	81 132	100 478	52 421	48 057	71 355	38 280	33 075
10 - 14	220 582	114 164	106 418	117 500	60 576	56 924	103 082	53 587	49 494
15 - 19	261 669	132 810	128 859	134 718	67 303	67 414	126 952	65 507	61 445
20 - 24	235 615	126 936	108 680	153 986	75 706	78 280	81 630	51 230	30 400
25 - 29	209 075	112 236	96 839	136 959	65 999	70 960	72 116	46 237	25 879
30 - 34	187 077	92 149	94 928	95 098	44 074	51 024	91 979	48 075	43 904
35 - 39	173 587	82 445	91 142	89 169	40 432	48 737	84 418	42 013	42 405
40 - 44	189 099	89 772	99 327	106 471	50 381	56 091	82 627	39 391	43 236
45 - 49	197 020	95 657	101 363	113 719	55 342	58 377	83 301	40 315	42 986
50 - 54	209 575	104 084	105 490	121 293	60 655	60 638	88 282	43 430	44 852
55 - 59	184 593	92 037	92 556	105 093	51 906	53 188	79 500	40 131	39 369
60 - 64	141 532	71 276	70 256	83 065	40 768	42 296	58 467	30 508	27 960
65 - 69	106 945	54 278	52 666	60 973	29 333	31 640	45 971	24 945	21 026
70 - 74	102 875	49 827	53 048	55 109	26 020	29 089	47 766	23 807	23 959
75 - 79	71 589	35 241	36 348	41 911	19 956	21 955	29 678	15 285	14 393
80 - 84	38 203	16 977	21 226	25 030	11 374	13 656	13 174	5 603	7 570
85 +	23 147	7 992	15 155	17 705	6 988	10 717	5 443	1 004	4 438
1 VII 2015 (ESDF)									
Total	2 889 167	1 461 407	1 427 760	...	...	...	...	...	...
0	33 646	17 559	16 087	...	...	...	...	...	...
1 - 4	135 842	69 846	65 996	...	...	...	...	...	...
5 - 9	156 097	82 369	73 728	...	...	...	...	...	...
10 - 14	196 157	101 745	94 412	...	...	...	...	...	...
15 - 19	240 027	123 120	116 907	...	...	...	...	...	...
20 - 24	213 074	117 657	95 417	...	...	...	...	...	...
25 - 29	209 936	115 931	94 005	...	...	...	...	...	...
30 - 34	211 768	106 749	105 019	...	...	...	...	...	...
35 - 39	182 227	87 532	94 695	...	...	...	...	...	...
40 - 44	186 302	88 793	97 509	...	...	...	...	...	...
45 - 49	196 505	95 050	101 455	...	...	...	...	...	...
50 - 54	209 703	103 089	106 614	...	...	...	...	...	...
55 - 59	200 480	99 679	100 801	...	...	...	...	...	...
60 - 64	152 232	76 485	75 747	...	...	...	...	...	...
65 - 69	120 588	60 725	59 863	...	...	...	...	...	...
70 - 74	103 523	50 879	52 644	...	...	...	...	...	...
75 - 79	78 272	37 897	40 375	...	...	...	...	...	...
80 - 84	41 805	18 565	23 240	...	...	...	...	...	...
85 +	20 983	7 737	13 246	...	...	...	...	...	...
Andorra - Andorre[23]									
1 I 2016 (ESDJ)									
Total	71 732	36 229	35 503	...	...	...	...	...	...
0	516	260	256	...	...	...	...	...	...
1 - 4	2 671	1 340	1 331	...	...	...	...	...	...
5 - 9	3 918	1 987	1 931	...	...	...	...	...	...
10 - 14	3 813	1 996	1 817	...	...	...	...	...	...
15 - 19	3 908	2 060	1 848	...	...	...	...	...	...
20 - 24	3 642	1 923	1 719	...	...	...	...	...	...
25 - 29	4 087	2 075	2 012	...	...	...	...	...	...
30 - 34	5 337	2 624	2 713	...	...	...	...	...	...
35 - 39	6 345	3 132	3 213	...	...	...	...	...	...
40 - 44	6 937	3 476	3 461	...	...	...	...	...	...
45 - 49	6 540	3 325	3 215	...	...	...	...	...	...
50 - 54	6 131	3 142	2 989	...	...	...	...	...	...
55 - 59	4 949	2 556	2 393	...	...	...	...	...	...
60 - 64	3 700	1 920	1 780	...	...	...	...	...	...
65 - 69	2 999	1 550	1 449	...	...	...	...	...	...
70 - 74	2 228	1 138	1 090	...	...	...	...	...	...
75 - 79	1 520	704	816	...	...	...	...	...	...
80 - 84	1 162	532	630	...	...	...	...	...	...

Continent, country or area, date, code[a] and age (in years) Continent, pays ou zone, date, code[a] et âge (en années)	Total			Urban - Urbaine			Rural - Rurale		
	Both sexes Les deux sexes	Male Masculin	Female Féminin	Both sexes Les deux sexes	Male Masculin	Female Féminin	Both sexes Les deux sexes	Male Masculin	Female Féminin
EUROPE									
Andorra - Andorre[23]									
1 I 2016 (ESDJ)									
85 - 89	861	316	545	...	...	...	...	...	...
90 - 94	341	129	212	...	...	...	...	...	...
95 - 99	103	36	67	...	...	...	...	...	...
100 + ...	24	8	16	...	...	...	...	...	...
Austria - Autriche									
31 X 2011 (CDJC)									
Total...............	8 401 940	4 093 938	4 308 002	5 643 239	2 713 930	2 929 309	2 758 701	1 380 008	1 378 693
0 - 4	394 706	202 637	192 069	267 743	137 645	130 098	126 963	64 992	61 971
5 - 9	406 027	207 779	198 248	268 770	137 636	131 134	137 257	70 143	67 114
10 - 14	426 957	218 499	208 458	276 347	141 429	134 918	150 610	77 070	73 540
15 - 19	488 818	251 251	237 567	313 792	160 620	153 172	175 026	90 631	84 395
20 - 24	527 675	267 651	260 024	364 267	181 574	182 693	163 408	86 077	77 331
25 - 29	552 783	277 236	275 547	390 454	193 719	196 735	162 329	83 517	78 812
30 - 34	538 307	270 267	268 040	375 886	187 248	188 638	162 421	83 019	79 402
35 - 39	564 817	280 207	284 610	383 183	187 902	195 281	181 634	92 305	89 329
40 - 44	675 242	338 455	336 787	453 188	224 449	228 739	222 054	114 006	108 048
45 - 49	710 388	358 163	352 225	470 749	234 757	235 992	239 639	123 406	116 233
50 - 54	626 162	312 890	313 272	409 191	200 993	208 198	216 971	111 897	105 074
55 - 59	517 280	253 019	264 261	339 245	161 747	177 498	178 035	91 272	86 763
60 - 64	480 665	231 598	249 067	322 367	151 726	170 641	158 298	79 872	78 426
65 - 69	402 829	189 221	213 608	283 946	130 760	153 186	118 883	58 461	60 422
70 - 74	410 314	187 956	222 358	273 352	123 395	149 957	136 962	64 561	72 401
75 - 79	262 203	110 870	151 333	165 864	68 812	97 052	96 339	42 058	54 281
80 - 84	218 133	83 066	135 067	142 903	52 895	90 008	75 230	30 171	45 059
85 - 89	141 772	40 153	101 619	99 777	27 332	72 445	41 995	12 821	29 174
90 - 94	46 362	10 997	35 365	34 057	7 767	26 290	12 305	3 230	9 075
95 - 99	9 388	1 836	7 552	7 274	1 377	5 897	2 114	459	1 655
100 + ...	1 112	187	925	884	147	737	228	40	188
1 I 2016 (ESDJ)									
Total...............	8 690 076	4 265 369	4 424 707	...	...	...	...	...	...
0	83 272	43 044	40 228	...	...	...	...	...	...
1 - 4	332 257	171 494	160 763	...	...	...	...	...	...
5 - 9	410 645	210 372	200 273	...	...	...	...	...	...
10 - 14	419 005	215 218	203 787	...	...	...	...	...	...
15 - 19	460 546	239 274	221 272	...	...	...	...	...	...
20 - 24	554 380	284 937	269 443	...	...	...	...	...	...
25 - 29	586 340	298 392	287 948	...	...	...	...	...	...
30 - 34	595 098	300 758	294 340	...	...	...	...	...	...
35 - 39	556 270	280 780	275 490	...	...	...	...	...	...
40 - 44	597 440	296 853	300 587	...	...	...	...	...	...
45 - 49	696 983	350 125	346 858	...	...	...	...	...	...
50 - 54	705 081	354 292	350 789	...	...	...	...	...	...
55 - 59	603 257	298 358	304 899	...	...	...	...	...	...
60 - 64	484 313	233 788	250 525	...	...	...	...	...	...
65 - 69	447 026	211 359	235 667	...	...	...	...	...	...
70 - 74	388 565	176 981	211 584	...	...	...	...	...	...
75 - 79	339 387	149 349	190 038	...	...	...	...	...	...
80 - 84	211 459	83 420	128 039	...	...	...	...	...	...
85 - 89	142 671	48 646	94 025	...	...	...	...	...	...
90 - 94	64 027	15 569	48 458	...	...	...	...	...	...
95 - 99	10 762	2 156	8 606	...	...	...	...	...	...
100 + ...	1 292	204	1 088	...	...	...	...	...	...
Belarus - Bélarus									
1 VII 2015 (ESDJ)									
Total...............	9 489 616	4 415 020	5 074 596	7 347 512	3 390 465	3 957 047	2 142 104	1 024 555	1 117 549
0	118 962	61 395	57 567	92 512	47 758	44 754	26 450	13 637	12 813
1 - 4	460 307	236 996	223 311	360 498	185 494	175 004	99 809	51 502	48 307
5 - 9	511 853	263 329	248 524	402 293	207 113	195 180	109 560	56 216	53 344
10 - 14	442 881	227 358	215 523	338 620	173 980	164 640	104 261	53 378	50 883
15 - 19	461 381	237 222	224 159	376 016	189 871	186 145	85 365	47 351	38 014
20 - 24	612 646	314 619	298 027	535 922	267 681	268 241	76 724	46 938	29 786
25 - 29	769 074	393 895	375 179	646 036	323 775	322 261	123 038	70 120	52 918
30 - 34	751 200	379 245	371 955	628 781	313 029	315 752	122 419	66 216	56 203

7. Population by age, sex and urban/rural residence: latest available year, 2007 - 2016
Population selon l'âge, le sexe et la résidence, urbaine/rurale : dernière année disponible, 2007 - 2016 (continued - suite)

Continent, country or area, date, code[a] and age (in years) / Continent, pays ou zone, date, code[a] et âge (en années)	Total			Urban - Urbaine			Rural - Rurale		
	Both sexes Les deux sexes	Male Masculin	Female Féminin	Both sexes Les deux sexes	Male Masculin	Female Féminin	Both sexes Les deux sexes	Male Masculin	Female Féminin
EUROPE									
Belarus - Bélarus									
1 VII 2015 (ESDJ)									
35 - 39	677 663	335 720	341 943	550 273	269 699	280 574	127 390	66 021	61 369
40 - 44	654 013	315 895	338 118	505 326	239 657	265 669	148 687	76 238	72 449
45 - 49	639 859	303 875	335 984	476 948	219 490	257 458	162 911	84 385	78 526
50 - 54	729 628	339 937	389 691	546 878	244 581	302 297	182 750	95 356	87 394
55 - 59	724 270	325 940	398 330	546 429	235 048	311 381	177 841	90 892	86 949
60 - 64	575 602	242 024	333 578	438 805	177 848	260 957	136 797	64 176	72 621
65 - 69	431 356	169 774	261 582	323 433	125 014	198 419	107 923	44 760	63 163
70 - 74	272 746	93 376	179 370	181 834	63 081	118 753	90 912	30 295	60 617
75 - 79	321 478	95 641	225 837	203 336	61 593	141 743	118 142	34 048	84 094
80 - 84	189 345	48 207	141 138	104 710	26 826	77 884	84 635	21 381	63 254
85 - 89	110 443	24 446	85 997	64 461	14 680	49 781	45 982	9 766	36 216
90 - 94	30 290	5 355	24 935	20 383	3 588	16 795	9 907	1 767	8 140
95 - 99	3 865	658	3 207	3 310	554	2 756	555	104	451
100 +	754	113	641	708	105	603	46	8	38
1 I 2016 (ESDJ)									
Total	9 498 364	4 420 842	5 077 522	...	...	...	...	...	...
0	119 256	61 489	57 767	...	...	...	...	...	...
1 - 4	466 268	240 145	226 123	...	...	...	...	...	...
5 - 9	521 443	268 468	252 975	...	...	...	...	...	...
10 - 14	442 365	227 044	215 321	...	...	...	...	...	...
15 - 19	457 158	234 755	222 403	...	...	...	...	...	...
20 - 24	593 534	304 771	288 763	...	...	...	...	...	...
25 - 29	762 867	391 179	371 688	...	...	...	...	...	...
30 - 34	758 111	383 236	374 875	...	...	...	...	...	...
35 - 39	681 551	338 322	343 229	...	...	...	...	...	...
40 - 44	654 888	316 828	338 060	...	...	...	...	...	...
45 - 49	637 027	302 541	334 486	...	...	...	...	...	...
50 - 54	715 806	333 435	382 371	...	...	...	...	...	...
55 - 59	732 600	330 418	402 182	...	...	...	...	...	...
60 - 64	583 779	245 771	338 008	...	...	...	...	...	...
65 - 69	454 419	178 596	275 823	...	...	...	...	...	...
70 - 74	258 781	88 973	169 808	...	...	...	...	...	...
75 - 79	320 328	95 235	225 093	...	...	...	...	...	...
80 - 84	188 378	47 989	140 389	...	...	...	...	...	...
85 - 89	112 867	25 099	87 768	...	...	...	...	...	...
90 - 94	31 971	5 703	26 268	...	...	...	...	...	...
95 - 99	4 161	721	3 440	...	...	...	...	...	...
100 +	806	124	682	...	...	...	...	...	...
Belgium - Belgique									
1 I 2011 (CDJC)									
Total	11 000 638	5 401 718	5 598 920	10 842 520	5 322 172	5 520 348	158 118	79 546	78 572
0 - 4	645 512	330 184	315 328	636 217	325 336	310 881	9 295	4 848	4 447
5 - 9	607 325	310 560	296 765	597 723	305 654	292 069	9 602	4 906	4 696
10 - 14	614 460	313 738	300 722	604 574	308 723	295 851	9 886	5 015	4 871
15 - 19	649 018	331 790	317 228	638 725	326 452	312 273	10 293	5 338	4 955
20 - 24	684 093	344 647	339 446	674 173	339 520	334 653	9 920	5 127	4 793
25 - 29	700 373	351 045	349 328	691 593	346 539	345 054	8 780	4 506	4 274
30 - 34	722 936	364 728	358 208	713 667	360 044	353 623	9 269	4 684	4 585
35 - 39	741 204	375 815	365 389	730 809	370 490	360 319	10 395	5 325	5 070
40 - 44	789 895	401 530	388 365	778 159	395 446	382 713	11 736	6 084	5 652
45 - 49	828 167	418 827	409 340	816 018	412 531	403 487	12 149	6 296	5 853
50 - 54	781 240	391 809	389 431	770 016	385 999	384 017	11 224	5 810	5 414
55 - 59	702 331	349 489	352 842	692 496	344 347	348 149	9 835	5 142	4 693
60 - 64	650 904	320 714	330 190	641 771	316 010	325 761	9 133	4 704	4 429
65 - 69	480 199	230 217	249 982	473 668	226 987	246 681	6 531	3 230	3 301
70 - 74	448 374	205 382	242 992	441 884	202 344	239 540	6 490	3 038	3 452
75 - 79	401 594	171 538	230 056	395 900	168 962	226 938	5 694	2 576	3 118
80 - 84	304 788	115 591	189 197	300 342	113 821	186 521	4 446	1 770	2 676
85 - 89	180 495	57 963	122 532	177 932	57 048	120 884	2 563	915	1 648
90 - 94	52 708	13 541	39 167	52 007	13 341	38 666	701	200	501
95 - 99	13 392	2 412	10 980	13 233	2 381	10 852	159	31	128
100 +	1 630	198	1 432	1 613	197	1 416	17	1	16

Continent, country or area, date, code[a] and age (in years) Continent, pays ou zone, date, code[a] et âge (en années)	Total			Urban - Urbaine			Rural - Rurale		
	Both sexes Les deux sexes	Male Masculin	Female Féminin	Both sexes Les deux sexes	Male Masculin	Female Féminin	Both sexes Les deux sexes	Male Masculin	Female Féminin
EUROPE									
Belgium - Belgique									
1 I 2016 (ESDJ)									
Total	11 311 117	5 569 264	5 741 853	...	...	...	...	...	...
0	122 381	62 588	59 793	...	...	...	...	...	...
1 - 4	515 795	263 936	251 859	...	...	...	...	...	...
5 - 9	662 708	338 904	323 804	...	...	...	...	...	...
10 - 14	620 458	317 530	302 928	...	...	...	...	...	...
15 - 19	634 837	325 646	309 191	...	...	...	...	...	...
20 - 24	691 260	351 721	339 539	...	...	...	...	...	...
25 - 29	731 621	366 995	364 626	...	...	...	...	...	...
30 - 34	730 150	366 115	364 035	...	...	...	...	...	...
35 - 39	740 377	372 702	367 675	...	...	...	...	...	...
40 - 44	750 305	379 882	370 423	...	...	...	...	...	...
45 - 49	791 274	401 497	389 777	...	...	...	...	...	...
50 - 54	819 885	413 357	406 528	...	...	...	...	...	...
55 - 59	763 475	380 606	382 869	...	...	...	...	...	...
60 - 64	673 689	331 637	342 052	...	...	...	...	...	...
65 - 69	611 320	295 892	315 428	...	...	...	...	...	...
70 - 74	440 336	205 465	234 871	...	...	...	...	...	...
75 - 79	392 664	172 465	220 199	...	...	...	...	...	...
80 - 84	319 074	127 478	191 596	...	...	...	...	...	...
85 - 89	199 767	68 375	131 392	...	...	...	...	...	...
90 - 94	83 116	23 118	59 998	...	...	...	...	...	...
95 - 99	14 767	3 084	11 683	...	...	...	...	...	...
100 +	1 858	271	1 587	...	...	...	...	...	...
Bosnia and Herzegovina - Bosnie-Herzégovine									
1 VII 2010 (ESDF)									
Total	3 843 126	1 877 587	1 965 539	...	...	...	...	...	...
0	33 314	17 123	16 191	...	...	...	...	...	...
1 - 4	133 257	68 494	64 763	...	...	...	...	...	...
5 - 9	229 608	117 330	112 278	...	...	...	...	...	...
10 - 14	274 779	139 862	134 917	...	...	...	...	...	...
15 - 19	279 370	146 390	132 980	...	...	...	...	...	...
20 - 24	284 994	144 777	140 217	...	...	...	...	...	...
25 - 29	268 273	131 991	136 282	...	...	...	...	...	...
30 - 34	240 986	120 975	120 011	...	...	...	...	...	...
35 - 39	246 721	121 633	125 088	...	...	...	...	...	...
40 - 44	283 887	141 943	141 944	...	...	...	...	...	...
45 - 49	306 958	150 410	156 548	...	...	...	...	...	...
50 - 54	266 575	135 687	130 888	...	...	...	...	...	...
55 - 59	231 595	105 145	126 450	...	...	...	...	...	...
60 - 64	182 787	86 092	96 695	...	...	...	...	...	...
65 - 69	202 274	90 012	112 262	...	...	...	...	...	...
70 - 74	184 389	82 422	101 967	...	...	...	...	...	...
75 - 79	120 364	50 553	69 811	...	...	...	...	...	...
80 - 84	47 932	19 605	28 327	...	...	...	...	...	...
85 +	25 063	7 143	17 920	...	...	...	...	...	...
Bulgaria - Bulgarie									
1 I 2016 (ESDJ)									
Total	7 153 784	3 477 177	3 676 607	5 227 182	2 519 346	2 707 836	1 926 602	957 831	968 771
0	65 537	33 824	31 713	49 365	25 461	23 904	16 172	8 363	7 809
1 - 4	268 634	138 089	130 545	203 432	104 634	98 798	65 202	33 455	31 747
5 - 9	347 342	178 517	168 825	258 731	132 908	125 823	88 611	45 609	43 002
10 - 14	316 693	163 167	153 526	229 759	118 266	111 493	86 934	44 901	42 033
15 - 19	313 051	161 150	151 901	228 466	117 232	111 234	84 585	43 918	40 667
20 - 24	374 939	193 366	181 573	280 982	143 178	137 804	93 957	50 188	43 769
25 - 29	481 408	247 953	233 455	375 124	190 167	184 957	106 284	57 786	48 498
30 - 34	483 946	251 729	232 217	375 371	192 484	182 887	108 575	59 245	49 330
35 - 39	528 455	273 170	255 285	411 584	210 003	201 581	116 871	63 167	53 704
40 - 44	537 016	276 242	260 774	414 664	210 311	204 353	122 352	65 931	56 421
45 - 49	503 432	257 274	246 158	377 485	189 218	188 267	125 947	68 056	57 891
50 - 54	482 543	241 704	240 839	354 954	173 522	181 432	127 589	68 182	59 407
55 - 59	495 870	241 363	254 507	362 345	171 818	190 527	133 525	69 545	63 980
60 - 64	493 132	228 919	264 213	355 126	161 507	193 619	138 006	67 412	70 594

Continent, country or area, date, code[a] and age (in years) / Continent, pays ou zone, date, code[a] et âge (en annèes)	Total			Urban - Urbaine			Rural - Rurale		
	Both sexes Les deux sexes	Male Masculin	Female Féminin	Both sexes Les deux sexes	Male Masculin	Female Féminin	Both sexes Les deux sexes	Male Masculin	Female Féminin
EUROPE									
Bulgaria - Bulgarie									
1 I 2016 (ESDJ)									
65 - 69	492 620	216 321	276 299	338 501	146 605	191 896	154 119	69 716	84 403
70 - 74	359 892	148 961	210 931	230 786	94 789	135 997	129 106	54 172	74 934
75 - 79	276 237	106 913	169 324	171 480	64 997	106 483	104 757	41 916	62 841
80 - 84	204 558	74 936	129 622	126 470	44 559	81 911	78 088	30 377	47 711
85 - 89	96 830	33 611	63 219	62 280	21 277	41 003	34 550	12 334	22 216
90 - 94	28 070	8 878	19 192	18 008	5 693	12 315	10 062	3 185	6 877
95 - 99	3 250	982	2 268	2 064	647	1 417	1 186	335	851
100 +	329	108	221	205	70	135	124	38	86
Croatia - Croatie									
1 IV 2011 (CDJC)									
Total	4 284 889	2 066 335	2 218 554	2 368 506	1 121 328	1 247 178	1 916 383	945 007	971 376
0 - 4	212 709	109 251	103 458	116 367	59 768	56 599	96 342	49 483	46 859
5 - 9	204 317	104 841	99 476	108 481	55 715	52 766	95 836	49 126	46 710
10 - 14	235 402	120 633	114 769	124 241	63 763	60 478	111 161	56 870	54 291
15 - 19	244 177	124 918	119 259	130 369	66 506	63 863	113 808	58 412	55 396
20 - 24	261 658	133 455	128 203	142 681	72 037	70 644	118 977	61 418	57 559
25 - 29	289 066	147 416	141 650	164 754	82 466	82 288	124 312	64 950	59 362
30 - 34	294 619	149 998	144 621	173 166	86 363	86 803	121 453	63 635	57 818
35 - 39	284 754	143 984	140 770	165 450	81 745	83 705	119 304	62 239	57 065
40 - 44	286 933	143 603	143 330	161 295	78 845	82 450	125 638	64 758	60 880
45 - 49	307 561	152 446	155 115	167 593	80 182	87 411	139 968	72 264	67 704
50 - 54	320 502	157 981	162 521	174 963	81 945	93 018	145 539	76 036	69 503
55 - 59	311 818	153 750	158 068	174 376	81 746	92 630	137 442	72 004	65 438
60 - 64	272 740	127 851	144 889	154 706	69 577	85 129	118 034	58 274	59 760
65 - 69	202 002	89 364	112 638	114 109	49 018	65 091	87 893	40 346	47 547
70 - 74	212 401	88 912	123 489	113 737	47 978	65 759	98 664	40 934	57 730
75 - 79	175 526	66 456	109 070	91 966	35 801	56 165	83 560	30 655	52 905
80 - 84	108 104	35 999	72 105	56 658	19 022	37 636	51 446	16 977	34 469
85 - 89	47 641	12 415	35 226	26 213	7 045	19 168	21 428	5 370	16 058
90 - 94	10 758	2 580	8 178	6 081	1 517	4 564	4 677	1 063	3 614
95 - 99	2 003	446	1 557	1 181	270	911	822	176	646
100 +	198	36	162	119	19	100	79	17	62
1 I 2016 (ESDJ)									
Total	4 190 669	2 022 797	2 167 872	...	...	...	...	...	...
0	37 238	19 221	18 017	...	...	...	...	...	...
1 - 4	161 241	83 290	77 951	...	...	...	...	...	...
5 - 9	210 855	108 280	102 575	...	...	...	...	...	...
10 - 14	202 138	103 741	98 397	...	...	...	...	...	...
15 - 19	235 643	120 765	114 878	...	...	...	...	...	...
20 - 24	243 706	124 604	119 102	...	...	...	...	...	...
25 - 29	260 048	132 112	127 936	...	...	...	...	...	...
30 - 34	286 283	145 599	140 684	...	...	...	...	...	...
35 - 39	289 461	147 099	142 362	...	...	...	...	...	...
40 - 44	277 531	140 055	137 476	...	...	...	...	...	...
45 - 49	281 578	139 917	141 661	...	...	...	...	...	...
50 - 54	299 268	147 032	152 236	...	...	...	...	...	...
55 - 59	308 195	149 560	158 635	...	...	...	...	...	...
60 - 64	292 599	141 084	151 515	...	...	...	...	...	...
65 - 69	245 762	111 043	134 719	...	...	...	...	...	...
70 - 74	181 057	76 154	104 903	...	...	...	...	...	...
75 - 79	175 853	68 683	107 170	...	...	...	...	...	...
80 - 84	124 352	42 715	81 637	...	...	...	...	...	...
85 - 89	58 413	17 486	40 927	...	...	...	...	...	...
90 - 94	17 048	3 867	13 181	...	...	...	...	...	...
95 - 99	2 186	448	1 738	...	...	...	...	...	...
100 +	214	42	172	...	...	...	...	...	...
Czechia - Tchéquie									
1 I 2015 (ESDJ)									
Total	10 538 275	5 176 927	5 361 348	7 699 525	3 748 292	3 951 233	2 838 750	1 428 635	1 410 115
0	109 943	56 454	53 489	80 659	41 362	39 297	29 284	15 092	14 192
1 - 4	447 126	229 186	217 940	325 182	166 575	158 607	121 944	62 611	59 333
5 - 9	574 904	294 328	280 576	413 516	211 474	202 042	161 388	82 854	78 534
10 - 14	469 072	241 497	227 575	332 134	170 989	161 145	136 938	70 508	66 430

Continent, country or area, date, code[a] and age (in years) / Continent, pays ou zone, date, code[a] et âge (en années)	Total			Urban - Urbaine			Rural - Rurale		
	Both sexes Les deux sexes	Male Masculin	Female Féminin	Both sexes Les deux sexes	Male Masculin	Female Féminin	Both sexes Les deux sexes	Male Masculin	Female Féminin
EUROPE									
Czechia - Tchéquie									
1 I 2015 (ESDJ)									
15 - 19	463 083	237 164	225 919	325 665	166 170	159 495	137 418	70 994	66 424
20 - 24	623 989	319 034	304 955	448 605	227 854	220 751	175 384	91 180	84 204
25 - 29	696 939	357 001	339 938	519 561	265 589	253 972	177 378	91 412	85 966
30 - 34	749 002	385 911	363 091	554 897	285 530	269 367	194 105	100 381	93 724
35 - 39	917 230	470 998	446 232	667 714	341 222	326 492	249 516	129 776	119 740
40 - 44	838 729	431 015	407 714	607 665	308 748	298 917	231 064	122 267	108 797
45 - 49	692 290	354 319	337 971	505 471	254 885	250 586	186 819	99 434	87 385
50 - 54	668 093	338 213	329 880	489 171	244 416	244 755	178 922	93 797	85 125
55 - 59	680 114	335 746	344 368	493 970	239 845	254 125	186 144	95 901	90 243
60 - 64	727 355	348 036	379 319	531 027	250 117	280 910	196 328	97 919	98 409
65 - 69	671 051	308 199	362 852	493 940	222 260	271 680	177 111	85 939	91 172
70 - 74	482 043	209 638	272 405	363 936	156 045	207 891	118 107	53 593	64 514
75 - 79	308 614	122 957	185 657	231 216	91 739	139 477	77 398	31 218	46 180
80 - 84	236 599	84 629	151 970	177 177	63 317	113 860	59 422	21 312	38 110
85 - 89	131 259	40 216	91 043	99 040	30 527	68 513	32 219	9 689	22 530
90 - 94	45 374	11 222	34 152	34 847	8 747	26 100	10 527	2 475	8 052
95 - 99	4 668	991	3 677	3 539	752	2 787	1 129	239	890
100 +	798	173	625	593	129	464	205	44	161
1 I 2016 (ESDJ)									
Total	10 553 843	5 186 330	5 367 513	...	...	...	...	...	...
0	110 777	56 803	53 974	...	...	...	...	...	...
1 - 4	439 417	225 209	214 208	...	...	...	...	...	...
5 - 9	591 957	303 194	288 763	...	...	...	...	...	...
10 - 14	481 565	247 403	234 162	...	...	...	...	...	...
15 - 19	458 003	234 956	223 047	...	...	...	...	...	...
20 - 24	590 522	302 126	288 396	...	...	...	...	...	...
25 - 29	690 104	352 844	337 260	...	...	...	...	...	...
30 - 34	736 368	379 020	357 348	...	...	...	...	...	...
35 - 39	885 086	455 413	429 673	...	...	...	...	...	...
40 - 44	880 941	452 434	428 507	...	...	...	...	...	...
45 - 49	696 832	356 714	340 118	...	...	...	...	...	...
50 - 54	685 062	347 096	337 966	...	...	...	...	...	...
55 - 59	653 439	323 938	329 501	...	...	...	...	...	...
60 - 64	721 358	345 762	375 596	...	...	...	...	...	...
65 - 69	692 992	319 544	373 448	...	...	...	...	...	...
70 - 74	495 189	214 962	280 227	...	...	...	...	...	...
75 - 79	323 695	130 133	193 562	...	...	...	...	...	...
80 - 84	232 005	83 653	148 352	...	...	...	...	...	...
85 - 89	135 023	41 916	93 107	...	...	...	...	...	...
90 - 94	47 086	11 873	35 213	...	...	...	...	...	...
95 - 99	5 689	1 168	4 521	...	...	...	...	...	...
100 +	733	169	564	...	...	...	...	...	...
Denmark - Danemark[70]									
1 VII 2016 (ESDJ)									
Total	5 724 456	2 848 030	2 876 426	...	...	...	...	...	...
0	60 592	31 149	29 443	...	...	...	...	...	...
1 - 4	234 884	120 529	114 355	...	...	...	...	...	...
5 - 9	331 064	169 944	161 120	...	...	...	...	...	...
10 - 14	333 211	170 469	162 742	...	...	...	...	...	...
15 - 19	349 699	179 287	170 412	...	...	...	...	...	...
20 - 24	385 936	197 791	188 145	...	...	...	...	...	...
25 - 29	368 484	188 162	180 322	...	...	...	...	...	...
30 - 34	326 838	166 177	160 661	...	...	...	...	...	...
35 - 39	345 683	174 080	171 603	...	...	...	...	...	...
40 - 44	392 267	196 520	195 747	...	...	...	...	...	...
45 - 49	398 766	201 470	197 296	...	...	...	...	...	...
50 - 54	412 833	207 992	204 841	...	...	...	...	...	...
55 - 59	360 593	180 492	180 101	...	...	...	...	...	...
60 - 64	337 548	167 052	170 496	...	...	...	...	...	...
65 - 69	337 893	165 122	172 771	...	...	...	...	...	...
70 - 74	304 277	146 686	157 591	...	...	...	...	...	...
75 - 79	197 067	90 693	106 374	...	...	...	...	...	...
80 - 84	127 892	54 557	73 335	...	...	...	...	...	...

Continent, country or area, date, code[a] and age (in years) / Continent, pays ou zone, date, code[a] et âge (en annèes)	Total			Urban - Urbaine			Rural - Rurale		
	Both sexes Les deux sexes	Male Masculin	Female Féminin	Both sexes Les deux sexes	Male Masculin	Female Féminin	Both sexes Les deux sexes	Male Masculin	Female Féminin
EUROPE									
Denmark - Danemark[70]									
1 VII 2016 (ESDJ)									
85 - 89	74 976	27 892	47 084	...	...	...	...	...	...
90 - 94	34 082	9 924	24 158	...	...	...	...	...	...
95 - 99	8 785	1 890	6 895	...	...	...	...	...	...
100 +	1 086	152	934	...	...	...	...	...	...
Estonia - Estonie									
1 I 2016 (ESDJ)									
Total	1 315 944	616 708	699 236	901 249[71]	406 268[71]	494 981[71]	413 121[71]	209 681[71]	203 440[71]
0	14 047	7 248	6 799	9 792[71]	5 057[71]	4 735[71]	4 254[71]	2 190[71]	2 064[71]
1 - 4	56 556	28 950	27 606	38 652[71]	19 722[71]	18 930[71]	17 901[71]	9 226[71]	8 675[71]
5 - 9	76 592	39 323	37 269	51 974[71]	26 588[71]	25 386[71]	24 609[71]	12 731[71]	11 878[71]
10 - 14	64 250	32 940	31 310	42 698[71]	21 699[71]	20 999[71]	21 537[71]	11 231[71]	10 306[71]
15 - 19	59 938	30 876	29 062	38 914[71]	19 938[71]	18 976[71]	20 987[71]	10 918[71]	10 069[71]
20 - 24	74 489	38 215	36 274	49 619[71]	24 595[71]	25 024[71]	24 818[71]	13 598[71]	11 220[71]
25 - 29	99 140	51 769	47 371	69 968[71]	35 271[71]	34 697[71]	29 060[71]	16 442[71]	12 618[71]
30 - 34	94 283	48 625	45 658	66 806[71]	33 190[71]	33 616[71]	27 346[71]	15 356[71]	11 990[71]
35 - 39	89 936	46 048	43 888	61 750[71]	30 359[71]	31 391[71]	28 035[71]	15 594[71]	12 441[71]
40 - 44	91 062	46 188	44 874	61 218[71]	29 515[71]	31 703[71]	29 699[71]	16 577[71]	13 122[71]
45 - 49	85 854	42 355	43 499	56 181[71]	26 435[71]	29 746[71]	29 523[71]	15 832[71]	13 691[71]
50 - 54	87 234	41 991	45 243	58 057[71]	26 462[71]	31 595[71]	29 027[71]	15 451[71]	13 576[71]
55 - 59	88 728	40 928	47 800	60 566[71]	26 340[71]	34 226[71]	28 018[71]	14 515[71]	13 503[71]
60 - 64	83 510	36 463	47 047	58 446[71]	24 086[71]	34 360[71]	24 952[71]	12 328[71]	12 624[71]
65 - 69	73 809	29 973	43 836	51 783[71]	19 809[71]	31 974[71]	21 867[71]	10 117[71]	11 750[71]
70 - 74	54 248	20 131	34 117	36 716[71]	12 792[71]	23 924[71]	17 465[71]	7 322[71]	10 143[71]
75 - 79	55 174	17 867	37 307	39 898[71]	12 457[71]	27 441[71]	15 206[71]	5 399[71]	9 807[71]
80 - 84	36 430	10 232	26 198	25 950[71]	7 142[71]	18 808[71]	10 444[71]	3 082[71]	7 362[71]
85 - 89	22 076	5 122	16 954	16 172[71]	3 741[71]	12 431[71]	5 881[71]	1 378[71]	4 503[71]
90 - 94	7 422	1 315	6 107	5 292[71]	965[71]	4 327[71]	2 123[71]	350[71]	1 773[71]
95 - 99	1 038	132	906	713[71]	90[71]	623[71]	325[71]	42[71]	283[71]
100 +	128	17	111	84[71]	15[71]	69[71]	44[71]	2[71]	42[71]
Faeroe Islands - Îles Féroé									
1 VII 2015 (ESDJ)									
Total	48 958	25 330	23 628	18 674	9 386	9 288	30 284	15 944	14 340
0	633	315	318	256	127	129	377	188	189
1 - 4	2 546	1 305	1 241	995	492	503	1 551	813	738
5 - 9	3 463	1 791	1 672	1 329	661	668	2 134	1 130	1 004
10 - 14	3 621	1 850	1 771	1 403	703	700	2 218	1 147	1 071
15 - 19	3 605	1 884	1 721	1 394	705	689	2 211	1 179	1 032
20 - 24	2 979	1 633	1 346	1 174	634	540	1 805	999	806
25 - 29	2 582	1 429	1 153	950	501	449	1 632	928	704
30 - 34	2 598	1 377	1 221	973	500	473	1 625	877	748
35 - 39	2 956	1 546	1 410	1 156	596	560	1 800	950	850
40 - 44	3 164	1 696	1 468	1 207	638	569	1 957	1 058	899
45 - 49	3 436	1 801	1 635	1 439	715	724	1 997	1 086	911
50 - 54	3 273	1 710	1 563	1 354	702	652	1 919	1 008	911
55 - 59	3 081	1 562	1 519	1 175	580	595	1 906	982	924
60 - 64	2 788	1 451	1 337	1 051	528	523	1 737	923	814
65 - 69	2 580	1 360	1 220	923	470	453	1 657	890	767
70 - 74	2 166	1 134	1 032	733	368	365	1 433	766	667
75 - 79	1 350	657	693	475	214	261	875	443	432
80 - 84	1 101	500	601	321	139	182	780	361	419
85 - 89	655	224	431	232	83	149	423	141	282
90 - 94	301	84	217	103	25	78	198	59	139
95 - 99	70	19	51	24	4	20	46	15	31
100 +	10	2	8	7	1	6	3	1	2
1 VII 2016 (ESDJ)									
Total	49 503	25 560	23 943	...	...	...	...	...	...
0	657	331	326	...	...	...	...	...	...
1 - 4	2 606	1 311	1 296	...	...	...	...	...	...
5 - 9	3 457	1 774	1 683	...	...	...	...	...	...
10 - 14	3 690	1 903	1 787	...	...	...	...	...	...
15 - 19	3 538	1 850	1 688	...	...	...	...	...	...
20 - 24	2 917	1 593	1 324	...	...	...	...	...	...

Continent, country or area, date, code[a] and age (in years) Continent, pays ou zone, date, code[a] et âge (en années)	Total			Urban - Urbaine			Rural - Rurale		
	Both sexes Les deux sexes	Male Masculin	Female Féminin	Both sexes Les deux sexes	Male Masculin	Female Féminin	Both sexes Les deux sexes	Male Masculin	Female Féminin
EUROPE									
Faeroe Islands - Îles Féroé									
1 VII 2016 (ESDJ)									
25 - 29	2 716	1 499	1 218	...	...	...	...	...	...
30 - 34	2 644	1 397	1 248	...	...	...	...	...	...
35 - 39	2 987	1 546	1 441	...	...	...	...	...	...
40 - 44	3 206	1 722	1 484	...	...	...	...	...	...
45 - 49	3 324	1 730	1 594	...	...	...	...	...	...
50 - 54	3 355	1 757	1 598	...	...	...	...	...	...
55 - 59	3 076	1 573	1 503	...	...	...	...	...	...
60 - 64	2 816	1 453	1 363	...	...	...	...	...	...
65 - 69	2 710	1 418	1 292	...	...	...	...	...	...
70 - 74	2 148	1 130	1 018	...	...	...	...	...	...
75 - 79	1 463	711	752	...	...	...	...	...	...
80 - 84	1 084	490	594	...	...	...	...	...	...
85 - 89	707	265	443	...	...	...	...	...	...
90 - 94	325	90	235	...	...	...	...	...	...
95 - 99	71	21	50	...	...	...	...	...	...
100 +	13	2	11	...	...	...	...	...	...
Finland - Finlande[23]									
1 VII 2015 (ESDJ)[72]									
Total	5 450 581	2 682 211	2 768 370	3 849 116	1 875 949	1 973 167	1 601 466	806 263	795 203
0	56 332	28 858	27 474	47 118	24 178	22 940	9 215	4 681	4 534
1 - 4	239 416	122 417	116 999	165 218	84 507	80 712	74 198	37 911	36 287
5 - 9	304 323	155 514	148 809	212 292	108 378	103 914	92 031	47 136	44 895
10 - 14	291 552	149 012	142 540	198 473	101 474	96 999	93 079	47 538	45 542
15 - 19	302 233	154 412	147 822	210 856	106 037	104 819	91 378	48 375	43 003
20 - 24	339 148	173 239	165 910	274 453	136 927	137 526	64 695	36 312	28 384
25 - 29	339 387	173 905	165 482	273 214	139 238	133 976	66 173	34 667	31 506
30 - 34	354 433	182 641	171 792	273 428	140 905	132 523	81 005	41 736	39 269
35 - 39	343 351	176 552	166 799	257 041	132 155	124 886	86 311	44 398	41 913
40 - 44	314 383	160 739	153 644	228 286	116 621	111 665	86 097	44 118	41 979
45 - 49	352 733	178 448	174 285	249 622	125 209	124 414	103 111	53 240	49 871
50 - 54	373 048	187 301	185 747	256 635	127 085	129 550	116 414	60 216	56 198
55 - 59	367 565	182 238	185 327	245 231	119 049	126 182	122 334	63 189	59 145
60 - 64	371 396	181 391	190 006	243 665	115 057	128 608	127 731	66 334	61 398
65 - 69	376 933	181 169	195 764	248 806	115 701	133 105	128 127	65 469	62 659
70 - 74	248 567	114 821	133 747	164 529	73 807	90 722	84 038	41 014	43 025
75 - 79	196 807	84 644	112 164	126 053	52 535	73 519	70 754	32 109	38 645
80 - 84	143 099	55 380	87 719	90 222	33 655	56 568	52 877	21 725	31 152
85 - 89	91 885	29 305	62 580	56 801	17 421	39 380	35 085	11 885	23 200
90 - 94	36 253	8 800	27 453	22 224	5 151	17 073	14 030	3 650	10 380
95 - 99	6 996	1 324	5 673	4 481	808	3 673	2 516	516	2 000
100 +	746	106	640	474	56	418	272	50	222
1 I 2016 (ESDJ)									
Total	5 487 308	2 701 490	2 785 818	...	...	...	...	...	...
0	55 560	28 516	27 044	...	...	...	...	...	...
1 - 4	238 818	122 063	116 755	...	...	...	...	...	...
5 - 9	307 718	157 405	150 313	...	...	...	...	...	...
10 - 14	293 927	150 064	143 863	...	...	...	...	...	...
15 - 19	301 171	154 051	147 120	...	...	...	...	...	...
20 - 24	339 216	173 332	165 884	...	...	...	...	...	...
25 - 29	342 528	175 568	166 960	...	...	...	...	...	...
30 - 34	356 932	183 915	173 017	...	...	...	...	...	...
35 - 39	345 816	177 811	168 005	...	...	...	...	...	...
40 - 44	317 879	162 832	155 047	...	...	...	...	...	...
45 - 49	350 369	177 270	173 099	...	...	...	...	...	...
50 - 54	374 501	188 139	186 362	...	...	...	...	...	...
55 - 59	368 110	182 452	185 658	...	...	...	...	...	...
60 - 64	371 660	181 417	190 243	...	...	...	...	...	...
65 - 69	381 263	183 252	198 011	...	...	...	...	...	...
70 - 74	261 165	121 120	140 045	...	...	...	...	...	...
75 - 79	197 194	84 974	112 220	...	...	...	...	...	...
80 - 84	144 235	56 388	87 847	...	...	...	...	...	...
85 - 89	93 704	30 175	63 529	...	...	...	...	...	...
90 - 94	37 406	9 248	28 158	...	...	...	...	...	...

Continent, country or area, date, code[a] and age (in years) Continent, pays ou zone, date, code[a] et âge (en années)	Total			Urban - Urbaine			Rural - Rurale		
	Both sexes Les deux sexes	Male Masculin	Female Féminin	Both sexes Les deux sexes	Male Masculin	Female Féminin	Both sexes Les deux sexes	Male Masculin	Female Féminin
EUROPE									
Finland - Finlande[23]									
1 I 2016 (ESDJ)									
95 - 99	7 377	1 386	5 991	...	...	...	...	...	...
100 +	759	112	647	...	...	...	...	...	...
France[73]									
1 I 2016* (ESDJ)									
Total	64 604 599	31 311 678	33 292 921	...	...	...	...	...	...
0 - 4	3 783 955	1 934 552	1 849 403	...	...	...	...	...	...
5 - 9	4 022 125	2 057 452	1 964 673	...	...	...	...	...	...
10 - 14	3 979 636	2 036 982	1 942 654	...	...	...	...	...	...
15 - 19	3 905 085	2 001 060	1 904 025	...	...	...	...	...	...
20 - 24	3 667 095	1 853 917	1 813 178	...	...	...	...	...	...
25 - 29	3 842 901	1 900 390	1 942 511	...	...	...	...	...	...
30 - 34	3 984 349	1 955 260	2 029 089	...	...	...	...	...	...
35 - 39	3 988 141	1 971 485	2 016 656	...	...	...	...	...	...
40 - 44	4 322 612	2 150 681	2 171 931	...	...	...	...	...	...
45 - 49	4 355 847	2 155 589	2 200 258	...	...	...	...	...	...
50 - 54	4 351 698	2 137 174	2 214 524	...	...	...	...	...	...
55 - 59	4 144 190	2 010 469	2 133 721	...	...	...	...	...	...
60 - 64	3 950 837	1 890 425	2 060 412	...	...	...	...	...	...
65 - 69	3 857 523	1 827 856	2 029 667	...	...	...	...	...	...
70 - 74	2 459 851	1 140 641	1 319 210	...	...	...	...	...	...
75 - 79	2 145 774	935 611	1 210 163	...	...	...	...	...	...
80 - 84	1 849 471	729 814	1 119 657	...	...	...	...	...	...
85 - 89	1 251 693	426 766	824 927	...	...	...	...	...	...
90 - 94	598 834	165 669	433 165	...	...	...	...	...	...
95 +	142 982	29 885	113 097	...	...	...	...	...	...
Germany - Allemagne									
9 V 2011 (CDJC)									
Total	80 219 695	39 145 941	41 073 754	64 444 232	31 227 832	33 216 400	15 775 463	7 918 109	7 857 354
0 - 4	3 338 895	1 714 872	1 624 023	2 712 601	1 393 763	1 318 838	626 294	321 109	305 185
5 - 9	3 525 830	1 809 024	1 716 806	2 798 622	1 435 745	1 362 877	727 208	373 279	353 929
10 - 14	3 940 566	2 021 305	1 919 261	3 074 610	1 575 684	1 498 926	865 956	445 621	420 335
15 - 19	4 013 880	2 057 155	1 956 725	3 144 832	1 606 068	1 538 764	869 048	451 087	417 961
20 - 24	4 835 639	2 463 932	2 371 707	3 993 247	2 003 582	1 989 665	842 392	460 350	382 042
25 - 29	4 872 533	2 455 885	2 416 648	4 113 697	2 057 507	2 056 190	758 836	398 378	360 458
30 - 34	4 751 911	2 385 305	2 366 606	3 942 747	1 977 628	1 965 119	809 164	407 677	401 487
35 - 39	4 742 893	2 378 055	2 364 838	3 833 417	1 920 448	1 912 969	909 476	457 607	451 869
40 - 44	6 351 189	3 209 481	3 141 708	5 029 918	2 540 433	2 489 485	1 321 271	669 048	652 223
45 - 49	6 999 679	3 547 254	3 452 425	5 488 622	2 771 239	2 717 383	1 511 057	776 015	735 042
50 - 54	6 206 294	3 113 463	3 092 831	4 845 747	2 413 038	2 432 709	1 360 547	700 425	660 122
55 - 59	5 419 450	2 668 976	2 750 474	4 252 008	2 066 178	2 185 830	1 167 442	602 798	564 644
60 - 64	4 702 815	2 298 903	2 403 912	3 753 504	1 808 314	1 945 190	949 311	490 589	458 722
65 - 69	4 173 351	1 999 287	2 174 064	3 423 376	1 624 839	1 798 537	749 975	374 448	375 527
70 - 74	4 861 239	2 247 196	2 614 043	3 931 373	1 801 914	2 129 459	929 866	445 282	484 584
75 - 79	3 270 283	1 413 881	1 856 402	2 633 648	1 128 379	1 505 269	636 635	285 502	351 133
80 - 84	2 328 083	878 797	1 449 286	1 890 025	704 565	1 185 460	438 058	174 232	263 826
85 - 89	1 335 076	369 029	966 047	1 108 944	302 059	806 885	226 132	66 970	159 162
90 - 94	430 600	95 074	335 526	368 116	79 884	288 232	62 484	15 190	47 294
95 - 99	106 044	17 388	88 656	93 152	15 094	78 058	12 892	2 294	10 598
100 +	13 445	1 679	11 766	12 026	1 471	10 555	1 419	208	1 211
1 I 2016 (ESDJ)[4]									
Total	82 175 684	40 514 123	41 661 561	...	...	...	...	...	...
0	744 721	382 551	362 170	...	...	...	...	...	...
1 - 4	2 868 825	1 473 742	1 395 083	...	...	...	...	...	...
5 - 9	3 571 914	1 835 790	1 736 124	...	...	...	...	...	...
10 - 14	3 695 666	1 901 968	1 793 698	...	...	...	...	...	...
15 - 19	4 189 964	2 189 470	2 000 494	...	...	...	...	...	...
20 - 24	4 587 878	2 398 568	2 189 310	...	...	...	...	...	...
25 - 29	5 387 681	2 798 715	2 588 966	...	...	...	...	...	...
30 - 34	5 167 860	2 647 069	2 520 791	...	...	...	...	...	...
35 - 39	4 951 744	2 507 280	2 444 464	...	...	...	...	...	...
40 - 44	4 990 088	2 518 808	2 471 280	...	...	...	...	...	...
45 - 49	6 523 704	3 302 545	3 221 159	...	...	...	...	...	...
50 - 54	6 954 765	3 510 827	3 443 938	...	...	...	...	...	...

Continent, country or area, date, code[a] and age (in years) / Continent, pays ou zone, date, code[a] et âge (en années)	Total			Urban - Urbaine			Rural - Rurale		
	Both sexes Les deux sexes	Male Masculin	Female Féminin	Both sexes Les deux sexes	Male Masculin	Female Féminin	Both sexes Les deux sexes	Male Masculin	Female Féminin
EUROPE									
Germany - Allemagne									
1 I 2016 (ESDJ)[4]									
55 - 59	6 038 640	3 012 491	3 026 149	...	...	...	...	...	...
60 - 64	5 202 056	2 529 258	2 672 798	...	...	...	...	...	...
65 - 69	4 331 884	2 080 322	2 251 562	...	...	...	...	...	...
70 - 74	3 969 193	1 847 371	2 121 822	...	...	...	...	...	...
75 - 79	4 269 898	1 889 669	2 380 229	...	...	...	...	...	...
80 - 84	2 524 412	1 019 477	1 504 935	...	...	...	...	...	...
85 - 89	1 486 700	504 530	982 170	...	...	...	...	...	...
90 - 94	592 931	141 013	451 918	...	...	...	...	...	...
95 - 99	108 661	20 167	88 494	...	...	...	...	...	...
100 +	16 499	2 492	14 007	...	...	...	...	...	...
Gibraltar[74]									
12 XI 2012 (CDJC)									
Total	32 194	16 061	16 133	...	...	...	...	...	...
0 - 4	1 952	982	970	...	...	...	...	...	...
5 - 9	1 894	967	927	...	...	...	...	...	...
10 - 14	1 987	1 050	937	...	...	...	...	...	...
15 - 19	1 997	1 038	959	...	...	...	...	...	...
20 - 24	2 028	1 042	986	...	...	...	...	...	...
25 - 29	1 985	999	986	...	...	...	...	...	...
30 - 34	2 154	1 107	1 047	...	...	...	...	...	...
35 - 39	2 217	1 080	1 137	...	...	...	...	...	...
40 - 44	2 198	1 076	1 122	...	...	...	...	...	...
45 - 49	2 384	1 203	1 181	...	...	...	...	...	...
50 - 54	2 158	1 072	1 086	...	...	...	...	...	...
55 - 59	2 041	1 054	987	...	...	...	...	...	...
60 - 64	1 954	1 034	920	...	...	...	...	...	...
65 - 69	1 655	853	802	...	...	...	...	...	...
70 - 74	1 176	563	613	...	...	...	...	...	...
75 - 79	1 021	456	565	...	...	...	...	...	...
80 - 84	732	297	435	...	...	...	...	...	...
85 - 89	437	141	296	...	...	...	...	...	...
90 - 94	180	37	143	...	...	...	...	...	...
95 - 99	39	10	29	...	...	...	...	...	...
100 +	5	-	5	...	...	...	...	...	...
Greece - Grèce									
9 V 2011 (CDFC)									
Total	10 816 286	5 303 223	5 513 063	8 285 259	4 022 889	4 262 370	2 531 027	1 280 334	1 250 693
0 - 4	537 243	274 788	262 455	431 611	220 917	210 694	105 632	53 871	51 761
5 - 9	512 596	262 432	250 164	405 436	207 479	197 957	107 160	54 953	52 207
10 - 14	519 429	265 787	253 642	406 962	208 070	198 892	112 467	57 717	54 750
15 - 19	553 276	286 386	266 890	440 869	226 682	214 187	112 407	59 704	52 703
20 - 24	627 097	325 127	301 970	510 067	259 795	250 272	117 030	65 332	51 698
25 - 29	723 771	371 617	352 154	583 506	295 880	287 626	140 265	75 737	64 528
30 - 34	822 475	417 861	404 614	666 145	334 794	331 351	156 330	83 067	73 263
35 - 39	812 829	409 681	403 148	651 826	323 821	328 005	161 003	85 860	75 143
40 - 44	832 666	414 026	418 640	663 331	323 632	339 699	169 335	90 394	78 941
45 - 49	748 429	367 086	381 343	590 034	283 391	306 643	158 395	83 695	74 700
50 - 54	731 486	355 552	375 934	565 986	268 882	297 104	165 500	86 670	78 830
55 - 59	660 368	321 466	338 902	501 507	240 725	260 782	158 861	80 741	78 120
60 - 64	625 769	301 589	324 180	459 249	219 165	240 084	166 520	82 424	84 096
65 - 69	508 276	241 832	266 444	356 701	167 557	189 144	151 575	74 275	77 300
70 - 74	542 165	246 264	295 901	363 133	162 560	200 573	179 032	83 704	95 328
75 - 79	475 077	209 983	265 094	309 622	134 691	174 931	165 455	75 292	90 163
80 - 84	352 373	146 455	205 918	229 214	91 916	137 298	123 159	54 539	68 620
85 - 89	159 841	60 933	98 908	104 058	37 922	66 136	55 783	23 011	32 772
90 - 94	53 445	18 760	34 685	34 608	11 513	23 095	18 837	7 247	11 590
95 - 99	15 187	4 948	10 239	9 822	3 081	6 741	5 365	1 867	3 498
100 +	2 488	650	1 838	1 572	416	1 156	916	234	682
1 I 2016 (ESDF)									
Total	10 783 748	5 224 210	5 559 538	...	...	...	...	...	...
0	91 603	47 171	44 432	...	...	...	...	...	...
1 - 4	388 346	199 933	188 413	...	...	...	...	...	...
5 - 9	549 235	280 927	268 308	...	...	...	...	...	...

Continent, country or area, date, code[a] and age (in years) / Continent, pays ou zone, date, code[a] et âge (en annèes)	Total			Urban - Urbaine			Rural - Rurale		
	Both sexes Les deux sexes	Male Masculin	Female Féminin	Both sexes Les deux sexes	Male Masculin	Female Féminin	Both sexes Les deux sexes	Male Masculin	Female Féminin
EUROPE									
Greece - Grèce									
1 I 2016 (ESDF)									
10 - 14	527 579	270 324	257 255	...	...	...	...	...	...
15 - 19	534 745	272 492	262 253	...	...	...	...	...	...
20 - 24	558 125	283 893	274 232	...	...	...	...	...	...
25 - 29	593 655	295 771	297 884	...	...	...	...	...	...
30 - 34	708 152	356 834	351 318	...	...	...	...	...	...
35 - 39	807 863	403 794	404 069	...	...	...	...	...	...
40 - 44	809 810	399 211	410 599	...	...	...	...	...	...
45 - 49	824 606	399 945	424 661	...	...	...	...	...	...
50 - 54	739 995	352 949	387 046	...	...	...	...	...	...
55 - 59	712 322	337 268	375 054	...	...	...	...	...	...
60 - 64	644 859	307 859	337 000	...	...	...	...	...	...
65 - 69	610 656	286 878	323 778	...	...	...	...	...	...
70 - 74	497 146	230 482	266 664	...	...	...	...	...	...
75 - 79	484 040	211 288	272 752	...	...	...	...	...	...
80 - 84	382 185	160 222	221 963	...	...	...	...	...	...
85 - 89	219 261	88 602	130 659	...	...	...	...	...	...
90 - 94	74 337	28 655	45 682	...	...	...	...	...	...
95 - 99	18 612	7 344	11 268	...	...	...	...	...	...
100 +	6 616	2 368	4 248	...	...	...	...	...	...
Guernsey - Guernesey									
31 III 2016 (ESDF)									
Total	62 723	31 109	31 614	...	...	...	...	...	...
0	661	323	338	...	...	...	...	...	...
1 - 4	2 634	1 371	1 263	...	...	...	...	...	...
5 - 9	3 207	1 661	1 546	...	...	...	...	...	...
10 - 14	3 004	1 555	1 449	...	...	...	...	...	...
15 - 19	3 465	1 790	1 675	...	...	...	...	...	...
20 - 24	3 891	2 039	1 852	...	...	...	...	...	...
25 - 29	4 031	2 067	1 964	...	...	...	...	...	...
30 - 34	3 867	1 998	1 869	...	...	...	...	...	...
35 - 39	3 719	1 857	1 862	...	...	...	...	...	...
40 - 44	4 188	2 050	2 138	...	...	...	...	...	...
45 - 49	4 938	2 381	2 557	...	...	...	...	...	...
50 - 54	4 990	2 494	2 496	...	...	...	...	...	...
55 - 59	4 444	2 175	2 269	...	...	...	...	...	...
60 - 64	3 754	1 929	1 825	...	...	...	...	...	...
65 - 69	3 858	1 878	1 980	...	...	...	...	...	...
70 - 74	2 540	1 232	1 308	...	...	...	...	...	...
75 - 79	2 278	1 079	1 199	...	...	...	...	...	...
80 - 84	1 592	662	930	...	...	...	...	...	...
85 - 89	1 053	384	669	...	...	...	...	...	...
90 - 94	456	147	309	...	...	...	...	...	...
95 - 99	138	36	102	...	...	...	...	...	...
100 +	15	1	14	...	...	...	...	...	...
Hungary - Hongrie									
1 VII 2015 (ESDJ)									
Total	9 843 028	4 692 149	5 150 879	6 937 836	3 267 756	3 670 081	2 905 192	1 424 394	1 480 799
0	92 298	47 368	44 931	64 653	33 228	31 425	27 645	14 140	13 506
1 - 4	361 219	185 647	175 572	258 987	133 221	125 766	102 232	52 426	49 806
5 - 9	491 226	251 763	239 463	343 132	175 838	167 294	148 094	75 925	72 169
10 - 14	481 075	247 253	233 822	322 502	165 505	156 998	158 573	81 749	76 824
15 - 19	513 645	264 069	249 577	351 948	179 469	172 479	161 698	84 600	77 098
20 - 24	619 974	318 402	301 572	426 042	217 078	208 965	193 932	101 325	92 608
25 - 29	614 783	316 477	298 306	435 176	220 750	214 426	179 608	95 728	83 880
30 - 34	633 899	321 298	312 601	460 818	229 942	230 876	173 081	91 356	81 725
35 - 39	814 925	412 288	402 637	594 950	297 063	297 887	219 975	115 225	104 750
40 - 44	771 027	389 390	381 637	550 325	274 463	275 862	220 702	114 927	105 775
45 - 49	685 719	342 942	342 778	477 841	235 513	242 328	207 878	107 429	100 450
50 - 54	590 675	288 083	302 592	401 960	192 052	209 908	188 715	96 031	92 684
55 - 59	675 323	316 545	358 778	462 033	210 418	251 615	213 290	106 127	107 163
60 - 64	716 838	323 109	393 729	509 193	223 863	285 330	207 645	99 246	108 399
65 - 69	564 781	242 670	322 112	406 943	171 875	235 068	157 839	70 795	87 044
70 - 74	459 175	183 119	276 056	331 568	132 253	199 316	127 607	50 867	76 741

7. Population by age, sex and urban/rural residence: latest available year, 2007 - 2016
Population selon l'âge, le sexe et la résidence, urbaine/rurale : dernière année disponible, 2007 - 2016 (continued - suite)

Continent, country or area, date, code[a] and age (in years) — Continent, pays ou zone, date, code[a] et âge (en années)	Total Both sexes Les deux sexes	Total Male Masculin	Total Female Féminin	Urban - Urbaine Both sexes Les deux sexes	Urban - Urbaine Male Masculin	Urban - Urbaine Female Féminin	Rural - Rurale Both sexes Les deux sexes	Rural - Rurale Male Masculin	Rural - Rurale Female Féminin
EUROPE									
Hungary - Hongrie									
1 VII 2015 (ESDJ)									
75 - 79	336 837	117 749	219 088	238 543	84 549	153 994	98 294	33 200	65 094
80 - 84	236 676	75 188	161 488	167 661	54 472	113 189	69 015	20 716	48 299
85 - 89	127 736	35 415	92 321	92 677	26 235	66 442	35 059	9 180	25 879
90 - 94	46 349	11 138	35 211	34 228	8 278	25 950	12 121	2 860	9 261
95 - 99	7 363	1 784	5 579	5 540	1 355	4 185	1 823	429	1 395
100 +	1 491	458	1 034	1 121	338	783	371	120	251
Unknown - Inconnu	-	-	-	-	-	-	-	-	-
1 I 2016 (ESDJ)[75]									
Total	9 830 485	4 688 519	5 141 966	...	...	...	...	...	...
0	91 741	47 125	44 616	...	...	...	...	...	...
1 - 4	363 127	186 714	176 413	...	...	...	...	...	...
5 - 9	487 901	249 806	238 095	...	...	...	...	...	...
10 - 14	481 679	247 659	234 020	...	...	...	...	...	...
15 - 19	505 193	259 846	245 347	...	...	...	...	...	...
20 - 24	614 937	315 964	298 973	...	...	...	...	...	...
25 - 29	616 224	317 405	298 819	...	...	...	...	...	...
30 - 34	624 701	317 281	307 420	...	...	...	...	...	...
35 - 39	795 163	402 056	393 107	...	...	...	...	...	...
40 - 44	789 779	399 110	390 669	...	...	...	...	...	...
45 - 49	696 716	348 842	347 874	...	...	...	...	...	...
50 - 54	586 951	286 957	299 994	...	...	...	...	...	...
55 - 59	654 689	307 308	347 381	...	...	...	...	...	...
60 - 64	725 105	327 130	397 975	...	...	...	...	...	...
65 - 69	577 644	248 517	329 127	...	...	...	...	...	...
70 - 74	457 200	182 871	274 329	...	...	...	...	...	...
75 - 79	340 804	119 533	221 271	...	...	...	...	...	...
80 - 84	235 431	74 746	160 685	...	...	...	...	...	...
85 - 89	128 979	36 033	92 946	...	...	...	...	...	...
90 - 94	46 828	11 213	35 615	...	...	...	...	...	...
95 - 99	8 159	1 939	6 220	...	...	...	...	...	...
100 +	1 534	464	1 070	...	...	...	...	...	...
Iceland - Islande									
1 VII 2015 (ESDJ)									
Total	330 815	166 228	164 587	309 868	155 146	154 723	20 947	11 083	9 864
0	4 236	2 168	2 068	4 029	2 070	1 960	207	99	108
1 - 4	18 027	9 149	8 878	17 158	8 708	8 450	869	441	428
5 - 9	23 203	11 958	11 245	21 993	11 311	10 682	1 211	647	564
10 - 14	21 306	10 813	10 493	20 084	10 175	9 909	1 223	638	585
15 - 19	22 116	11 279	10 837	20 595	10 508	10 088	1 521	771	750
20 - 24	24 963	12 838	12 125	23 300	11 983	11 317	1 663	855	809
25 - 29	23 802	12 211	11 591	22 424	11 455	10 969	1 379	756	623
30 - 34	23 239	11 917	11 322	22 134	11 327	10 808	1 105	591	515
35 - 39	22 106	11 200	10 907	21 047	10 663	10 384	1 060	537	523
40 - 44	21 472	10 889	10 583	20 320	10 290	10 030	1 152	599	553
45 - 49	20 773	10 339	10 434	19 399	9 623	9 777	1 374	716	658
50 - 54	21 627	10 693	10 935	19 998	9 836	10 162	1 630	857	773
55 - 59	20 828	10 454	10 375	19 210	9 573	9 637	1 619	881	738
60 - 64	17 813	8 957	8 856	16 425	8 199	8 226	1 388	758	630
65 - 69	14 766	7 519	7 248	13 585	6 854	6 732	1 181	665	516
70 - 74	10 765	5 230	5 535	9 906	4 756	5 150	859	475	385
75 - 79	7 671	3 627	4 044	7 060	3 296	3 764	612	332	280
80 - 84	6 214	2 789	3 425	5 742	2 539	3 203	473	251	222
85 - 89	3 972	1 597	2 375	3 681	1 444	2 237	292	153	139
90 - 94	1 572	505	1 068	1 472	455	1 017	101	50	51
95 - 99	313	92	222	281	79	202	33	13	20
100 +	35	10	25	32	8	24	3	2	1
1 I 2016 (ESDJ)[76]									
Total	332 529	167 270	165 259	...	...	...	...	...	...
0	4 113	2 111	2 002	...	...	...	...	...	...
1 - 4	17 732	8 991	8 741	...	...	...	...	...	...
5 - 9	23 408	12 064	11 344	...	...	...	...	...	...
10 - 14	21 287	10 814	10 473	...	...	...	...	...	...
15 - 19	22 121	11 261	10 860	...	...	...	...	...	...

Continent, country or area, date, code[a] and age (in years) / Continent, pays ou zone, date, code[a] et âge (en années)	Total			Urban - Urbaine			Rural - Rurale		
	Both sexes Les deux sexes	Male Masculin	Female Féminin	Both sexes Les deux sexes	Male Masculin	Female Féminin	Both sexes Les deux sexes	Male Masculin	Female Féminin
EUROPE									
Iceland - Islande									
1 I 2016 (ESDJ)[76]									
20 - 24	24 886	12 792	12 094	...	...	...	...	...	...
25 - 29	24 370	12 583	11 787	...	...	...	...	...	...
30 - 34	23 109	11 870	11 239	...	...	...	...	...	...
35 - 39	22 431	11 402	11 029	...	...	...	...	...	...
40 - 44	21 721	11 019	10 702	...	...	...	...	...	...
45 - 49	20 567	10 251	10 316	...	...	...	...	...	...
50 - 54	21 649	10 710	10 939	...	...	...	...	...	...
55 - 59	21 030	10 571	10 459	...	...	...	...	...	...
60 - 64	18 032	9 019	9 013	...	...	...	...	...	...
65 - 69	15 045	7 686	7 359	...	...	...	...	...	...
70 - 74	11 151	5 453	5 698	...	...	...	...	...	...
75 - 79	7 718	3 646	4 072	...	...	...	...	...	...
80 - 84	6 153	2 773	3 380	...	...	...	...	...	...
85 - 89	4 055	1 634	2 421	...	...	...	...	...	...
90 - 94	1 602	518	1 084	...	...	...	...	...	...
95 - 99	312	89	223	...	...	...	...	...	...
100 +	37	13	24	...	...	...	...	...	...
Ireland - Irlande									
10 IV 2011 (CDFC)[77]									
Total	4 588 252	2 272 699	2 315 553	2 846 882	1 389 160	1 457 722	1 741 370	883 539	857 831
0 - 4	356 329	182 076	174 253	224 004	114 284	109 720	132 325	67 792	64 533
5 - 9	320 770	164 037	156 733	188 818	96 160	92 658	131 952	67 877	64 075
10 - 14	302 491	155 076	147 415	172 930	88 433	84 497	129 561	66 643	62 918
15 - 19	283 019	144 262	138 757	170 523	86 129	84 394	112 496	58 133	54 363
20 - 24	297 231	146 636	150 595	208 146	100 226	107 920	89 085	46 410	42 675
25 - 29	361 122	173 714	187 408	266 457	126 362	140 095	94 665	47 352	47 313
30 - 34	393 945	194 774	199 171	278 935	137 689	141 246	115 010	57 085	57 925
35 - 39	364 261	182 237	182 024	233 417	116 912	116 505	130 844	65 325	65 519
40 - 44	330 812	166 330	164 482	198 432	99 162	99 270	132 380	67 168	65 212
45 - 49	305 185	151 516	153 669	178 630	87 087	91 543	126 555	64 429	62 126
50 - 54	274 386	136 737	137 649	158 031	77 106	80 925	116 355	59 631	56 724
55 - 59	244 522	122 121	122 401	137 973	66 919	71 054	106 549	55 202	51 347
60 - 64	218 786	109 869	108 917	122 606	59 521	63 085	96 180	50 348	45 832
65 - 69	173 638	86 298	87 340	97 999	46 741	51 258	75 639	39 557	36 082
70 - 74	131 190	63 476	67 714	76 683	35 378	41 305	54 507	28 098	26 409
75 - 79	102 036	46 631	55 405	59 519	25 708	33 811	42 517	20 923	21 594
80 - 84	70 113	28 423	41 690	40 585	15 449	25 136	29 528	12 974	16 554
85 - 89	39 887	13 591	26 296	22 742	7 303	15 439	17 145	6 288	10 857
90 - 94	14 877	4 155	10 722	8 363	2 200	6 163	6 514	1 955	4 559
95 - 99	3 263	682	2 581	1 884	360	1 524	1 379	322	1 057
100 +	389	58	331	205	31	174	184	27	157
24 IV 2016 (CDJC)									
Total	4 761 865	2 354 428	2 407 437	...	...	...	...	...	...
0 - 14	1 006 552	514 579	491 973	...	...	...	...	...	...
15 - 24	576 452	292 492	283 960	...	...	...	...	...	...
25 - 44	1 406 291	686 928	719 363	...	...	...	...	...	...
45 - 64	1 135 003	563 592	571 411	...	...	...	...	...	...
65 +	637 567	296 837	340 730	...	...	...	...	...	...
Isle of Man - Île de Man									
24 IV 2016 (CDJC)									
Total	83 314	41 269	42 045	...	...	...	...	...	...
0 - 4	4 144	2 186	1 958	...	...	...	...	...	...
5 - 9	4 733	2 436	2 297	...	...	...	...	...	...
10 - 14	4 469	2 346	2 123	...	...	...	...	...	...
15 - 19	4 789	2 506	2 283	...	...	...	...	...	...
20 - 24	4 422	2 252	2 170	...	...	...	...	...	...
25 - 29	4 326	2 131	2 195	...	...	...	...	...	...
30 - 34	4 506	2 148	2 358	...	...	...	...	...	...
35 - 39	4 873	2 371	2 502	...	...	...	...	...	...
40 - 44	5 612	2 715	2 897	...	...	...	...	...	...
45 - 49	6 497	3 255	3 242	...	...	...	...	...	...
50 - 54	6 681	3 359	3 322	...	...	...	...	...	...
55 - 59	5 887	2 889	2 998	...	...	...	...	...	...

Continent, country or area, date, code[a] and age (in years) Continent, pays ou zone, date, code[a] et âge (en années)	Total			Urban - Urbaine			Rural - Rurale		
	Both sexes Les deux sexes	Male Masculin	Female Féminin	Both sexes Les deux sexes	Male Masculin	Female Féminin	Both sexes Les deux sexes	Male Masculin	Female Féminin

EUROPE

Isle of Man - Île de Man
24 IV 2016 (CDJC)

Age	Both	Male	Female	U Both	U Male	U Female	R Both	R Male	R Female
60 - 64	5 170	2 612	2 558	...	...	...	...	...	...
65 - 69	5 441	2 715	2 726	...	...	...	...	...	...
70 - 74	4 212	2 074	2 138	...	...	...	...	...	...
75 - 79	3 155	1 529	1 626	...	...	...	...	...	...
80 - 84	2 129	958	1 171	...	...	...	...	...	...
85 - 89	1 380	522	858	...	...	...	...	...	...
90 - 94	675	202	473	...	...	...	...	...	...
95 +	213	63	150	...	...	...	...	...	...

Italy - Italie
1 I 2016 (ESDJ)

Age	Both	Male	Female	U Both	U Male	U Female	R Both	R Male	R Female
Total	60 665 551	29 456 321	31 209 230	...	...	...	...	...	...
0	479 611	246 656	232 955	...	...	...	...	...	...
1 - 4	2 093 337	1 075 850	1 017 487	...	...	...	...	...	...
5 - 9	2 854 720	1 469 465	1 385 255	...	...	...	...	...	...
10 - 14	2 854 191	1 469 325	1 384 866	...	...	...	...	...	...
15 - 19	2 881 548	1 490 426	1 391 122	...	...	...	...	...	...
20 - 24	3 036 187	1 563 396	1 472 791	...	...	...	...	...	...
25 - 29	3 260 703	1 653 304	1 607 399	...	...	...	...	...	...
30 - 34	3 537 822	1 776 419	1 761 403	...	...	...	...	...	...
35 - 39	4 080 470	2 043 171	2 037 299	...	...	...	...	...	...
40 - 44	4 780 533	2 380 558	2 399 975	...	...	...	...	...	...
45 - 49	4 931 685	2 441 662	2 490 023	...	...	...	...	...	...
50 - 54	4 757 688	2 337 449	2 420 239	...	...	...	...	...	...
55 - 59	4 101 062	1 990 139	2 110 923	...	...	...	...	...	...
60 - 64	3 646 240	1 755 003	1 891 237	...	...	...	...	...	...
65 - 69	3 684 918	1 757 419	1 927 499	...	...	...	...	...	...
70 - 74	2 856 226	1 322 775	1 533 451	...	...	...	...	...	...
75 - 79	2 779 553	1 227 379	1 552 174	...	...	...	...	...	...
80 - 84	2 054 494	826 785	1 227 709	...	...	...	...	...	...
85 - 89	1 305 410	448 203	857 207	...	...	...	...	...	...
90 - 94	561 890	154 221	407 669	...	...	...	...	...	...
95 - 99	108 498	23 625	84 873	...	...	...	...	...	...
100 +	18 765	3 091	15 674	...	...	...	...	...	...

Jersey
27 III 2011 (CDFC)

Age	Both	Male	Female	U Both	U Male	U Female	R Both	R Male	R Female
Total	97 857	48 296	49 561	...	...	...	...	...	...
0 - 4	5 015	2 466	2 549	...	...	...	...	...	...
5 - 9	4 852	2 470	2 382	...	...	...	...	...	...
10 - 14	5 302	2 729	2 573	...	...	...	...	...	...
15 - 19	5 495	2 863	2 632	...	...	...	...	...	...
20 - 24	5 944	3 006	2 938	...	...	...	...	...	...
25 - 29	6 705	3 351	3 354	...	...	...	...	...	...
30 - 34	7 236	3 670	3 566	...	...	...	...	...	...
35 - 39	7 225	3 615	3 610	...	...	...	...	...	...
40 - 44	8 363	4 183	4 180	...	...	...	...	...	...
45 - 49	8 357	4 187	4 170	...	...	...	...	...	...
50 - 54	7 198	3 536	3 662	...	...	...	...	...	...
55 - 59	6 042	2 955	3 087	...	...	...	...	...	...
60 - 64	5 650	2 832	2 818	...	...	...	...	...	...
65 - 69	4 048	1 938	2 110	...	...	...	...	...	...
70 - 74	3 632	1 732	1 900	...	...	...	...	...	...
75 - 79	2 893	1 343	1 550	...	...	...	...	...	...
80 - 84	2 005	822	1 183	...	...	...	...	...	...
85 - 89	1 225	446	779	...	...	...	...	...	...
90 - 94	483	115	368	...	...	...	...	...	...
95 +	187	37	150	...	...	...	...	...	...

Latvia - Lettonie
1 VII 2015 (ESDJ)

Age	Both	Male	Female	U Both	U Male	U Female	R Both	R Male	R Female
Total	1 977 527	907 753	1 069 774	1 344 291	599 629	744 662	633 236	308 124	325 112
0	21 779	11 298	10 481	15 117	7 839	7 278	6 662	3 459	3 203
1 - 4	80 226	41 358	38 868	55 487	28 653	26 834	24 739	12 705	12 034
5 - 9	104 542	53 482	51 060	70 886	36 294	34 592	33 656	17 188	16 468
10 - 14	92 442	47 432	45 010	60 458	30 834	29 624	31 984	16 598	15 386

Continent, country or area, date, code[a] and age (in years) Continent, pays ou zone, date, code[a] et âge (en annèes)	Total			Urban - Urbaine			Rural - Rurale		
	Both sexes Les deux sexes	Male Masculin	Female Féminin	Both sexes Les deux sexes	Male Masculin	Female Féminin	Both sexes Les deux sexes	Male Masculin	Female Féminin
EUROPE									
Latvia - Lettonie									
1 VII 2015 (ESDJ)									
15 - 19	87 037	44 777	42 260	54 507	27 841	26 666	32 530	16 936	15 594
20 - 24	118 918	61 113	57 805	74 621	37 627	36 994	44 297	23 486	20 811
25 - 29	143 491	73 789	69 702	98 537	48 943	49 594	44 954	24 846	20 108
30 - 34	136 547	69 850	66 697	97 306	48 565	48 741	39 241	21 285	17 956
35 - 39	127 980	63 853	64 127	89 770	43 750	46 020	38 210	20 103	18 107
40 - 44	136 546	67 088	69 458	93 203	44 559	48 644	43 343	22 529	20 814
45 - 49	134 026	64 476	69 550	89 086	41 389	47 697	44 940	23 087	21 853
50 - 54	143 741	67 323	76 418	95 684	42 882	52 802	48 057	24 441	23 616
55 - 59	142 601	64 437	78 164	96 675	41 433	55 242	45 926	23 004	22 922
60 - 64	121 812	51 544	70 268	85 072	34 175	50 897	36 740	17 369	19 371
65 - 69	105 459	41 268	64 191	74 669	27 822	46 847	30 790	13 446	17 344
70 - 74	94 949	33 372	61 577	63 546	21 542	42 004	31 403	11 830	19 573
75 - 79	87 913	27 674	60 239	61 430	18 897	42 533	26 483	8 777	17 706
80 - 84	54 681	14 714	39 967	37 595	10 047	27 548	17 086	4 667	12 419
85 - 89	31 560	7 052	24 508	22 660	5 191	17 469	8 900	1 861	7 039
90 - 94	9 821	1 625	8 196	6 958	1 177	5 781	2 863	448	2 415
95 - 99	1 279	207	1 072	914	157	757	365	50	315
100 +	177	21	156	110	12	98	67	9	58
1 I 2016 (ESDJ)									
Total	1 968 957	904 299	1 064 658	...	...	...	...	...	...
0	21 884	11 392	10 492	...	...	...	...	...	...
1 - 4	81 740	42 117	39 623	...	...	...	...	...	...
5 - 9	103 843	53 207	50 636	...	...	...	...	...	...
10 - 14	92 793	47 657	45 136	...	...	...	...	...	...
15 - 19	86 281	44 287	41 994	...	...	...	...	...	...
20 - 24	113 332	58 315	55 017	...	...	...	...	...	...
25 - 29	142 180	73 089	69 091	...	...	...	...	...	...
30 - 34	137 236	70 248	66 988	...	...	...	...	...	...
35 - 39	126 836	63 373	63 463	...	...	...	...	...	...
40 - 44	135 589	66 721	68 868	...	...	...	...	...	...
45 - 49	133 922	64 393	69 529	...	...	...	...	...	...
50 - 54	140 870	66 203	74 667	...	...	...	...	...	...
55 - 59	143 381	64 872	78 509	...	...	...	...	...	...
60 - 64	122 485	51 956	70 529	...	...	...	...	...	...
65 - 69	107 417	42 187	65 230	...	...	...	...	...	...
70 - 74	91 871	32 326	59 545	...	...	...	...	...	...
75 - 79	88 883	27 979	60 904	...	...	...	...	...	...
80 - 84	54 611	14 745	39 866	...	...	...	...	...	...
85 - 89	32 120	7 317	24 803	...	...	...	...	...	...
90 - 94	10 201	1 681	8 520	...	...	...	...	...	...
95 - 99	1 323	214	1 109	...	...	...	...	...	...
100 +	159	20	139	...	...	...	...	...	...
Liechtenstein									
1 I 2016 (ESDJ)									
Total	37 622	18 660	18 962	...	...	...	...	...	...
0	325	175	150	...	...	...	...	...	...
1 - 4	1 504	801	703	...	...	...	...	...	...
5 - 9	1 871	991	880	...	...	...	...	...	...
10 - 14	1 910	972	938	...	...	...	...	...	...
15 - 19	2 122	1 035	1 087	...	...	...	...	...	...
20 - 24	2 244	1 144	1 100	...	...	...	...	...	...
25 - 29	2 286	1 158	1 128	...	...	...	...	...	...
30 - 34	2 298	1 164	1 134	...	...	...	...	...	...
35 - 39	2 495	1 275	1 220	...	...	...	...	...	...
40 - 44	2 749	1 328	1 421	...	...	...	...	...	...
45 - 49	3 252	1 624	1 628	...	...	...	...	...	...
50 - 54	3 158	1 556	1 602	...	...	...	...	...	...
55 - 59	2 853	1 412	1 441	...	...	...	...	...	...
60 - 64	2 356	1 168	1 188	...	...	...	...	...	...
65 - 69	2 115	1 061	1 054	...	...	...	...	...	...
70 - 74	1 667	815	852	...	...	...	...	...	...
75 - 79	1 131	526	605	...	...	...	...	...	...
80 - 84	682	264	418	...	...	...	...	...	...

7. Population by age, sex and urban/rural residence: latest available year, 2007 - 2016
Population selon l'âge, le sexe et la résidence, urbaine/rurale : dernière année disponible, 2007 - 2016 (continued - suite)

Continent, country or area, date, codeª and age (in years) Continent, pays ou zone, date, codeª et âge (en années)	Total			Urban - Urbaine			Rural - Rurale		
	Both sexes Les deux sexes	Male Masculin	Female Féminin	Both sexes Les deux sexes	Male Masculin	Female Féminin	Both sexes Les deux sexes	Male Masculin	Female Féminin
EUROPE									
Liechtenstein									
1 I 2016 (ESDJ)									
85 - 89	398	141	257	...	...	...	...	...	...
90 - 94	171	38	133	...	...	...	...	...	...
95 - 99	29	9	20	...	...	...	...	...	...
100 +	6	3	3	...	...	...	...	...	...
Lithuania - Lituanie									
1 VII 2015 (ESDJ)[75]									
Total	2 904 910	1 337 932	1 566 978	1 952 920	873 571	1 079 349	951 990	464 361	487 629
0	30 910	15 874	15 036	21 313	10 993	10 320	9 597	4 881	4 716
1 - 4	120 074	61 537	58 537	84 827	43 360	41 467	35 247	18 177	17 070
5 - 9	139 381	71 269	68 112	95 767	49 063	46 704	43 614	22 206	21 408
10 - 14	134 240	68 846	65 394	85 237	43 626	41 611	49 003	25 220	23 783
15 - 19	166 270	85 448	80 822	103 590	52 988	50 602	62 680	32 460	30 220
20 - 24	201 515	103 455	98 060	128 488	64 132	64 356	73 027	39 323	33 704
25 - 29	195 615	100 471	95 144	139 762	68 050	71 712	55 853	32 421	23 432
30 - 34	178 111	90 329	87 782	132 715	65 065	67 650	45 396	25 264	20 132
35 - 39	176 352	87 159	89 193	124 252	60 008	64 244	52 100	27 151	24 949
40 - 44	197 732	95 371	102 361	132 454	62 032	70 422	65 278	33 339	31 939
45 - 49	207 820	98 989	108 831	134 380	61 376	73 004	73 440	37 613	35 827
50 - 54	225 192	105 736	119 456	148 379	65 937	82 442	76 813	39 799	37 014
55 - 59	213 239	96 361	116 878	144 103	61 689	82 414	69 136	34 672	34 464
60 - 64	170 639	72 856	97 783	115 965	46 584	69 381	54 674	26 272	28 402
65 - 69	145 259	57 241	88 018	98 456	36 776	61 680	46 803	20 465	26 338
70 - 74	131 531	47 318	84 213	86 578	30 159	56 419	44 953	17 159	27 794
75 - 79	120 539	39 525	81 014	79 428	25 583	53 845	41 111	13 942	27 169
80 - 84	85 932	24 886	61 046	54 711	15 921	38 790	31 221	8 965	22 256
85 - 89	47 321	11 918	35 403	30 884	8 005	22 879	16 437	3 913	12 524
90 - 94	14 902	2 902	12 000	9 904	1 920	7 984	4 998	982	4 016
95 - 99	1 978	367	1 611	1 427	248	1 179	551	119	432
100 +	358	74	284	300	56	244	58	18	40
1 I 2016 (ESDJ)									
Total	2 888 558	1 329 607	1 558 951	...	...	...	...	...	...
0	31 462	16 180	15 282	...	...	...	...	...	...
1 - 4	120 028	61 560	58 468	...	...	...	...	...	...
5 - 9	140 515	71 854	68 661	...	...	...	...	...	...
10 - 14	131 742	67 516	64 226	...	...	...	...	...	...
15 - 19	162 142	83 326	78 816	...	...	...	...	...	...
20 - 24	195 863	100 181	95 682	...	...	...	...	...	...
25 - 29	195 893	100 667	95 226	...	...	...	...	...	...
30 - 34	178 885	90 634	88 251	...	...	...	...	...	...
35 - 39	173 507	86 006	87 501	...	...	...	...	...	...
40 - 44	194 086	93 606	100 480	...	...	...	...	...	...
45 - 49	206 616	98 285	108 331	...	...	...	...	...	...
50 - 54	221 194	103 977	117 217	...	...	...	...	...	...
55 - 59	216 742	98 010	118 732	...	...	...	...	...	...
60 - 64	171 356	73 276	98 080	...	...	...	...	...	...
65 - 69	146 482	57 835	88 647	...	...	...	...	...	...
70 - 74	130 006	46 646	83 360	...	...	...	...	...	...
75 - 79	120 166	39 442	80 724	...	...	...	...	...	...
80 - 84	86 109	24 863	61 246	...	...	...	...	...	...
85 - 89	47 995	12 315	35 680	...	...	...	...	...	...
90 - 94	15 322	2 962	12 360	...	...	...	...	...	...
95 - 99	2 098	389	1 709	...	...	...	...	...	...
100 +	349	77	272	...	...	...	...	...	...
Luxembourg									
1 I 2016 (ESDJ)									
Total	576 249	289 193	287 056	...	...	...	...	...	...
0	6 100	3 156	2 944	...	...	...	...	...	...
1 - 4	25 926	13 319	12 607	...	...	...	...	...	...
5 - 9	31 802	16 222	15 580	...	...	...	...	...	...
10 - 14	31 063	16 076	14 987	...	...	...	...	...	...
15 - 19	33 186	17 096	16 090	...	...	...	...	...	...
20 - 24	35 377	17 944	17 433	...	...	...	...	...	...
25 - 29	41 908	21 481	20 427	...	...	...	...	...	...

7. Population by age, sex and urban/rural residence: latest available year, 2007 - 2016
Population selon l'âge, le sexe et la résidence, urbaine/rurale : dernière année disponible, 2007 - 2016 (continued - suite)

Continent, country or area, date, code[a] and age (in years) / Continent, pays ou zone, date, code[a] et âge (en années)	Total			Urban - Urbaine			Rural - Rurale		
	Both sexes Les deux sexes	Male Masculin	Female Féminin	Both sexes Les deux sexes	Male Masculin	Female Féminin	Both sexes Les deux sexes	Male Masculin	Female Féminin
EUROPE									
Luxembourg									
1 I 2016 (ESDJ)									
30 - 34	44 401	22 279	22 122	...	...	...	...	...	...
35 - 39	44 572	22 389	22 183	...	...	...	...	...	...
40 - 44	43 956	22 405	21 551	...	...	...	...	...	...
45 - 49	45 604	23 532	22 072	...	...	...	...	...	...
50 - 54	43 678	22 741	20 937	...	...	...	...	...	...
55 - 59	36 917	19 033	17 884	...	...	...	...	...	...
60 - 64	29 802	15 088	14 714	...	...	...	...	...	...
65 - 69	24 760	12 353	12 407	...	...	...	...	...	...
70 - 74	18 604	8 869	9 735	...	...	...	...	...	...
75 - 79	15 756	6 951	8 805	...	...	...	...	...	...
80 - 84	11 945	4 876	7 069	...	...	...	...	...	...
85 - 89	7 692	2 630	5 062	...	...	...	...	...	...
90 - 94	2 669	635	2 034	...	...	...	...	...	...
95 - 99	466	103	363	...	...	...	...	...	...
100 +	65	15	50	...	...	...	...	...	...
Malta - Malte									
20 XI 2011 (CDFC)									
Total	417 432	207 625	209 807	400 557	199 151	201 406	16 875	8 474	8 401
0 - 4	20 061	10 347	9 714	19 247	9 926	9 321	814	421	393
5 - 9	19 419	9 971	9 448	18 602	9 562	9 040	817	409	408
10 - 14	22 248	11 355	10 893	21 218	10 854	10 364	1 030	501	529
15 - 19	26 182	13 509	12 673	25 026	12 907	12 119	1 156	602	554
20 - 24	29 450	15 062	14 388	28 269	14 475	13 794	1 181	587	594
25 - 29	30 320	15 722	14 598	29 154	15 110	14 044	1 166	612	554
30 - 34	30 194	15 641	14 553	29 141	15 074	14 067	1 053	567	486
35 - 39	28 799	14 757	14 042	27 712	14 202	13 510	1 087	555	532
40 - 44	25 236	12 840	12 396	24 151	12 293	11 858	1 085	547	538
45 - 49	26 895	13 574	13 321	25 716	12 972	12 744	1 179	602	577
50 - 54	30 596	15 292	15 304	29 293	14 628	14 665	1 303	664	639
55 - 59	29 246	14 655	14 591	28 127	14 052	14 075	1 119	603	516
60 - 64	30 595	15 130	15 465	29 452	14 551	14 901	1 143	579	564
65 - 69	23 728	11 429	12 299	22 791	10 986	11 805	937	443	494
70 - 74	16 205	7 389	8 816	15 572	7 106	8 466	633	283	350
75 - 79	13 287	5 579	7 708	12 749	5 332	7 417	538	247	291
80 - 84	8 494	3 181	5 313	8 121	3 036	5 085	373	145	228
85 - 89	4 567	1 622	2 945	4 371	1 546	2 825	196	76	120
90 - 94	1 583	480	1 103	1 532	455	1 077	51	25	26
95 - 99	296	82	214	284	77	207	12	5	7
100 +	31	8	23	29	7	22	2	1	1
1 I 2016 (ESDJ)[78]									
Total	434 403	217 569	216 834	...	...	...	...	...	...
0	4 407	2 240	2 167	...	...	...	...	...	...
1 - 4	17 062	8 882	8 180	...	...	...	...	...	...
5 - 9	20 438	10 600	9 838	...	...	...	...	...	...
10 - 14	19 982	10 234	9 748	...	...	...	...	...	...
15 - 19	23 767	12 264	11 503	...	...	...	...	...	...
20 - 24	29 055	15 208	13 847	...	...	...	...	...	...
25 - 29	32 378	16 860	15 518	...	...	...	...	...	...
30 - 34	32 168	16 737	15 431	...	...	...	...	...	...
35 - 39	31 190	16 099	15 091	...	...	...	...	...	...
40 - 44	28 623	14 732	13 891	...	...	...	...	...	...
45 - 49	25 184	12 833	12 351	...	...	...	...	...	...
50 - 54	28 132	14 219	13 913	...	...	...	...	...	...
55 - 59	30 736	15 331	15 405	...	...	...	...	...	...
60 - 64	28 540	14 226	14 314	...	...	...	...	...	...
65 - 69	29 956	14 601	15 355	...	...	...	...	...	...
70 - 74	20 182	9 522	10 660	...	...	...	...	...	...
75 - 79	14 743	6 499	8 244	...	...	...	...	...	...
80 - 84	10 128	3 916	6 212	...	...	...	...	...	...
85 - 89	5 250	1 838	3 412	...	...	...	...	...	...
90 - 94	1 987	593	1 394	...	...	...	...	...	...
95 - 99	439	124	315	...	...	...	...	...	...
100 +	56	11	45	...	...	...	...	...	...

Continent, country or area, date, code[a] and age (in years) Continent, pays ou zone, date, code[a] et âge (en années)	Total			Urban - Urbaine			Rural - Rurale		
	Both sexes Les deux sexes	Male Masculin	Female Féminin	Both sexes Les deux sexes	Male Masculin	Female Féminin	Both sexes Les deux sexes	Male Masculin	Female Féminin
EUROPE									
Monaco[79]									
9 VI 2008 (CDJC)									
Total	31 109[80]	15 076	15 914	...	...	...	...	...	...
0 - 4	1 134	577	557	...	...	...	...	...	...
5 - 9	1 430	706	724	...	...	...	...	...	...
10 - 14	1 401	727	674	...	...	...	...	...	...
15 - 19	1 398	724	674	...	...	...	...	...	...
20 - 24	1 248	647	601	...	...	...	...	...	...
25 - 29	1 305	638	667	...	...	...	...	...	...
30 - 34	1 514	751	766	...	...	...	...	...	...
35 - 39	2 122	1 003	1 119	...	...	...	...	...	...
40 - 44	2 342	1 163	1 179	...	...	...	...	...	...
45 - 64	2 359	1 194	1 165	...	...	...	...	...	...
50 - 54	2 218	1 128	1 090	...	...	...	...	...	...
55 - 59	2 217	1 120	1 097	...	...	...	...	...	...
60 - 64	2 337	1 134	1 203	...	...	...	...	...	...
65 - 69	1 960	945	1 015	...	...	...	...	...	...
70 - 74	1 648	801	847	...	...	...	...	...	...
75 +	3 758	1 530	2 228	...	...	...	...	...	...
Unknown - Inconnu	715[80]	288	308	...	...	...	...	...	...
Montenegro - Monténégro									
1 IV 2011 (CDJC)									
Total	620 029	306 236	313 793	399 264	193 691	205 573	220 765	112 545	108 220
0 - 4	38 950	20 361	18 589	25 277	13 247	12 030	13 673	7 114	6 559
5 - 9	38 430	20 016	18 414	24 781	12 973	11 808	13 649	7 043	6 606
10 - 14	41 371	21 389	19 982	26 526	13 698	12 828	14 845	7 691	7 154
15 - 19	44 093	22 815	21 278	28 376	14 654	13 722	15 717	8 161	7 556
20 - 24	42 816	22 084	20 732	28 218	14 347	13 871	14 598	7 737	6 861
25 - 29	45 793	23 299	22 494	31 083	15 290	15 793	14 710	8 009	6 701
30 - 34	44 495	22 188	22 307	30 133	14 495	15 638	14 362	7 693	6 669
35 - 39	41 879	20 523	21 356	27 869	13 311	14 558	14 010	7 212	6 798
40 - 44	40 496	20 136	20 360	26 265	12 539	13 726	14 231	7 597	6 634
45 - 49	43 089	21 401	21 688	28 332	13 444	14 888	14 757	7 957	6 800
50 - 54	43 613	21 817	21 796	28 705	13 851	14 854	14 908	7 966	6 942
55 - 59	41 223	20 509	20 714	27 021	13 143	13 878	14 202	7 366	6 836
60 - 64	34 196	15 941	18 255	21 738	9 981	11 757	12 458	5 960	6 498
65 - 69	22 121	9 774	12 347	12 692	5 522	7 170	9 429	4 252	5 177
70 - 74	25 141	10 909	14 232	14 441	6 116	8 325	10 700	4 793	5 907
75 - 79	17 184	7 251	9 933	9 665	4 041	5 624	7 519	3 210	4 309
80 - 84	10 021	4 050	5 971	5 375	2 112	3 263	4 646	1 938	2 708
85 - 89	3 739	1 324	2 415	2 038	699	1 339	1 701	625	1 076
90 - 94	885	283	602	453	130	323	432	153	279
95 - 99	202	61	141	103	30	73	99	31	68
100 +	44	13	31	23	7	16	21	6	15
Unknown - Inconnu	248	92	156	150	61	89	98	31	67
1 I 2016 (ESDJ)[75]									
Total	622 218	307 734	314 484	...	...	...	...	...	...
0	7 461	3 910	3 551	...	...	...	...	...	...
1 - 4	29 286	15 244	14 042	...	...	...	...	...	...
5 - 9	38 406	20 083	18 323	...	...	...	...	...	...
10 - 14	38 955	20 269	18 686	...	...	...	...	...	...
15 - 19	41 465	21 433	20 032	...	...	...	...	...	...
20 - 24	40 874	21 124	19 750	...	...	...	...	...	...
25 - 29	42 226	21 753	20 473	...	...	...	...	...	...
30 - 34	46 279	23 549	22 730	...	...	...	...	...	...
35 - 39	43 951	21 808	22 143	...	...	...	...	...	...
40 - 44	41 491	20 336	21 155	...	...	...	...	...	...
45 - 49	40 092	19 820	20 272	...	...	...	...	...	...
50 - 54	42 449	20 978	21 471	...	...	...	...	...	...
55 - 59	42 329	20 963	21 366	...	...	...	...	...	...
60 - 64	39 437	19 171	20 266	...	...	...	...	...	...
65 - 69	31 122	14 114	17 008	...	...	...	...	...	...
70 - 74	19 191	8 074	11 117	...	...	...	...	...	...
75 - 79	19 690	8 120	11 570	...	...	...	...	...	...
80 - 84	11 135	4 514	6 621	...	...	...	...	...	...

Continent, country or area, date, code[a] and age (in years) / Continent, pays ou zone, date, code[a] et âge (en années)	Total			Urban - Urbaine			Rural - Rurale		
	Both sexes Les deux sexes	Male Masculin	Female Féminin	Both sexes Les deux sexes	Male Masculin	Female Féminin	Both sexes Les deux sexes	Male Masculin	Female Féminin
EUROPE									
Montenegro - Monténégro									
1 I 2016 (ESDJ)[75]									
85 - 89	4 886	1 940	2 946	...	...	...	...	...	...
90 - 94	1 222	436	786	...	...	...	...	...	...
95 - 99	263	89	174	...	...	...	...	...	...
100 +	8	6	2	...	...	...	...	...	...
Netherlands - Pays-Bas									
1 I 2011 (CDJC)									
Total	16 655 799	8 243 482	8 412 317	11 124 721	5 478 213	5 646 508	5 531 078	2 765 269	2 765 809
0 - 4	923 106	472 308	450 798	633 381	323 854	309 527	289 725	148 454	141 271
0	184 007	93 892	90 115	...	...	...	...	...	...
1 - 4	739 099	378 416	360 683	...	...	...	...	...	...
5 - 9	985 229	503 882	481 347	640 541	327 757	312 784	344 688	176 125	168 563
10 - 14	998 740	510 974	487 766	633 115	323 581	309 534	365 625	187 393	178 232
15 - 19	1 006 744	514 830	491 914	658 458	333 676	324 782	348 286	181 154	167 132
20 - 24	1 034 729	522 667	512 062	757 280	373 366	383 914	277 449	149 301	128 148
25 - 29	1 001 538	504 117	497 421	749 880	373 340	376 540	251 658	130 777	120 881
30 - 34	1 004 764	503 323	501 441	736 350	368 630	367 720	268 414	134 693	133 721
35 - 39	1 121 568	560 289	561 279	779 994	391 390	388 604	341 574	168 899	172 675
40 - 44	1 295 925	653 664	642 261	861 292	436 235	425 057	434 633	217 429	217 204
45 - 49	1 298 292	655 302	642 990	850 566	428 796	421 770	447 726	226 506	221 220
50 - 54	1 196 319	601 040	595 279	776 285	388 221	388 064	420 034	212 819	207 215
55 - 59	1 090 247	546 952	543 295	700 036	348 502	351 534	390 211	198 450	191 761
60 - 64	1 103 652	553 446	550 206	700 926	349 188	351 738	402 726	204 258	198 468
65 - 69	790 560	390 725	399 835	488 433	238 792	249 641	302 127	151 933	150 194
70 - 74	637 518	302 542	334 976	401 165	187 850	213 315	236 353	114 692	121 661
75 - 79	499 321	219 108	280 213	316 949	136 949	180 000	182 372	82 159	100 213
80 - 84	360 828	139 348	221 480	234 884	89 412	145 472	125 944	49 936	76 008
85 - 89	212 056	66 949	145 107	141 532	44 184	97 348	70 524	22 765	47 759
90 - 94	76 191	18 812	57 379	51 102	12 438	38 664	25 089	6 374	18 715
95 +	18 472	3 204	15 268	12 552	2 052	10 500	5 920	1 152	4 768
1 I 2016 (ESDJ)									
Total	16 979 120	8 417 135	8 561 985	...	...	...	...	...	...
0	170 341	87 338	83 003	...	...	...	...	...	...
1 - 4	706 513	361 974	344 539	...	...	...	...	...	...
5 - 9	930 038	476 011	454 027	...	...	...	...	...	...
10 - 14	992 880	507 764	485 116	...	...	...	...	...	...
15 - 19	1 018 727	521 725	497 002	...	...	...	...	...	...
20 - 24	1 065 946	541 020	524 926	...	...	...	...	...	...
25 - 29	1 071 002	540 790	530 212	...	...	...	...	...	...
30 - 34	1 017 341	511 331	506 010	...	...	...	...	...	...
35 - 39	1 009 413	504 350	505 063	...	...	...	...	...	...
40 - 44	1 119 982	557 618	562 364	...	...	...	...	...	...
45 - 49	1 286 744	646 349	640 395	...	...	...	...	...	...
50 - 54	1 280 519	643 844	636 675	...	...	...	...	...	...
55 - 59	1 170 614	585 735	584 879	...	...	...	...	...	...
60 - 64	1 053 752	525 615	528 137	...	...	...	...	...	...
65 - 69	1 046 703	519 227	527 476	...	...	...	...	...	...
70 - 74	729 512	353 646	375 866	...	...	...	...	...	...
75 - 79	560 345	257 171	303 174	...	...	...	...	...	...
80 - 84	394 936	163 046	231 890	...	...	...	...	...	...
85 - 89	234 300	81 748	152 552	...	...	...	...	...	...
90 - 94	96 978	26 376	70 602	...	...	...	...	...	...
95 - 99	20 433	4 183	16 250	...	...	...	...	...	...
100 +	2 101	274	1 827	...	...	...	...	...	...
Norway - Norvège									
19 XI 2011 (CDJC)[81]									
Total	4 979 955	2 495 777	2 484 178	3 951 427[71]	1 959 424[71]	1 992 003[71]	1 011 071[71]	524 519[71]	486 552[71]
0 - 4	310 523	159 582	150 941	252 348[71]	129 655[71]	122 693[71]	57 552[71]	29 590[71]	27 962[71]
5 - 9	300 625	153 598	147 027	239 702[71]	122 174[71]	117 528[71]	60 262[71]	31 070[71]	29 192[71]
10 - 14	312 618	160 122	152 496	245 562[71]	125 764[71]	119 798[71]	66 422[71]	34 008[71]	32 414[71]
15 - 19	324 682	167 701	156 981	254 774[71]	131 385[71]	123 389[71]	69 376[71]	36 049[71]	33 327[71]
20 - 24	329 537	167 828	161 709	268 150[71]	135 424[71]	132 726[71]	60 351[71]	31 776[71]	28 575[71]
25 - 29	321 171	163 754	157 417	268 356[71]	135 940[71]	132 416[71]	51 166[71]	26 654[71]	24 512[71]
30 - 34	325 241	166 578	158 663	269 924[71]	137 478[71]	132 446[71]	53 565[71]	27 843[71]	25 722[71]

Continent, country or area, date, code[a] and age (in years) / Continent, pays ou zone, date, code[a] et âge (en années)	Total			Urban - Urbaine			Rural - Rurale		
	Both sexes Les deux sexes	Male Masculin	Female Féminin	Both sexes Les deux sexes	Male Masculin	Female Féminin	Both sexes Les deux sexes	Male Masculin	Female Féminin
EUROPE									
Norway - Norvège									
19 XI 2011 (CDJC)[81]									
35 - 39	352 008	180 904	171 104	286 185[71]	146 143[71]	140 042[71]	64 091[71]	33 501[71]	30 590[71]
40 - 44	373 191	191 483	181 708	297 629[71]	151 231[71]	146 398[71]	73 666[71]	38 863[71]	34 803[71]
45 - 49	350 537	180 834	169 703	275 817[71]	140 624[71]	135 193[71]	73 001[71]	38 909[71]	34 092[71]
50 - 54	322 729	165 233	157 496	250 381[71]	126 209[71]	124 172[71]	70 881[71]	37 897[71]	32 984[71]
55 - 59	304 335	154 029	150 306	233 724[71]	116 035[71]	117 689[71]	69 504[71]	37 194[71]	32 310[71]
60 - 64	286 319	144 699	141 620	218 480[71]	108 289[71]	110 191[71]	67 016[71]	35 823[71]	31 193[71]
65 - 69	247 451	122 740	124 711	188 932[71]	91 896[71]	97 036[71]	57 895[71]	30 414[71]	27 481[71]
70 - 74	166 680	78 850	87 830	126 640[71]	58 122[71]	68 518[71]	39 687[71]	20 517[71]	19 170[71]
75 - 79	130 209	58 013	72 196	99 673[71]	42 842[71]	56 831[71]	30 271[71]	15 028[71]	15 243[71]
80 - 84	108 243	44 024	64 219	84 440[71]	32 980[71]	51 460[71]	23 582[71]	10 955[71]	12 627[71]
85 - 89	74 057	25 608	48 449	58 579[71]	19 436[71]	39 143[71]	15 272[71]	6 085[71]	9 187[71]
90 - 94	32 243	8 769	23 474	25 938[71]	6 706[71]	19 232[71]	6 185[71]	2 017[71]	4 168[71]
95 - 99	6 825	1 310	5 515	5 593[71]	1 001[71]	4 592[71]	1 199[71]	300[71]	899[71]
100 +	731	118	613	600[71]	90[71]	510[71]	127[71]	26[71]	101[71]
1 I 2016 (ESDJ)[75]									
Total	5 210 721	2 623 625	2 587 096	...	...	...	...	...	...
0	59 250	30 459	28 791	...	...	...	...	...	...
1 - 4	245 843	126 113	119 730	...	...	...	...	...	...
5 - 9	321 144	164 719	156 425	...	...	...	...	...	...
10 - 14	307 363	156 889	150 474	...	...	...	...	...	...
15 - 19	326 640	168 358	158 282	...	...	...	...	...	...
20 - 24	342 138	176 520	165 618	...	...	...	...	...	...
25 - 29	361 839	184 011	177 828	...	...	...	...	...	...
30 - 34	349 609	179 910	169 699	...	...	...	...	...	...
35 - 39	343 240	177 726	165 514	...	...	...	...	...	...
40 - 44	369 886	190 438	179 448	...	...	...	...	...	...
45 - 49	376 229	193 646	182 583	...	...	...	...	...	...
50 - 54	343 903	176 771	167 132	...	...	...	...	...	...
55 - 59	317 726	161 729	155 997	...	...	...	...	...	...
60 - 64	290 998	146 388	144 610	...	...	...	...	...	...
65 - 69	279 167	139 350	139 817	...	...	...	...	...	...
70 - 74	210 874	102 271	108 603	...	...	...	...	...	...
75 - 79	144 895	66 299	78 596	...	...	...	...	...	...
80 - 84	104 247	43 642	60 605	...	...	...	...	...	...
85 - 89	71 796	26 266	45 530	...	...	...	...	...	...
90 - 94	34 521	10 123	24 398	...	...	...	...	...	...
95 - 99	8 474	1 842	6 632	...	...	...	...	...	...
100 +	939	155	784	...	...	...	...	...	...
Poland - Pologne[75]									
1 VII 2015 (ESDJ)									
Total	37 981 588	18 384 771	19 596 817	22 916 634	10 869 587	12 047 047	15 064 954	7 515 184	7 549 770
0	362 902	186 466	176 436	211 610	108 666	102 944	151 292	77 800	73 492
1 - 4	1 532 111	787 553	744 558	888 890	457 189	431 701	643 221	330 364	312 857
5 - 9	2 026 135	1 039 002	987 133	1 148 553	588 697	559 856	877 582	450 305	427 277
10 - 14	1 782 709	914 586	868 123	963 605	494 413	469 192	819 104	420 173	398 931
15 - 19	1 995 253	1 022 055	973 198	1 059 601	541 351	518 250	935 652	480 704	454 948
20 - 24	2 455 300	1 252 056	1 203 244	1 329 769	673 897	655 872	1 125 531	578 159	547 372
25 - 29	2 823 199	1 439 152	1 384 047	1 682 206	844 363	837 843	1 140 993	594 789	546 204
30 - 34	3 151 814	1 603 930	1 547 884	1 975 792	992 947	982 845	1 176 022	610 983	565 039
35 - 39	3 004 303	1 523 531	1 480 772	1 869 951	937 768	932 183	1 134 352	585 763	548 589
40 - 44	2 633 752	1 331 511	1 302 241	1 574 966	785 371	789 595	1 058 786	546 140	512 646
45 - 49	2 290 360	1 148 724	1 141 636	1 334 376	652 991	681 385	955 984	495 733	460 251
50 - 54	2 409 112	1 190 514	1 218 598	1 430 229	680 276	749 953	978 883	510 238	468 645
55 - 59	2 856 884	1 375 908	1 480 976	1 804 163	830 808	973 355	1 052 721	545 100	507 621
60 - 64	2 689 531	1 251 099	1 438 432	1 776 780	792 926	983 854	912 751	458 173	454 578
65 - 69	2 062 292	916 438	1 145 854	1 379 648	596 610	783 038	682 644	319 828	362 816
70 - 74	1 212 926	499 936	712 990	797 350	323 745	473 605	415 576	176 191	239 385
75 - 79	1 146 426	428 157	718 269	733 112	270 588	462 524	413 314	157 569	255 745
80 - 84	862 891	288 543	574 348	539 435	182 081	357 354	323 456	106 462	216 994
85 - 89	485 804	139 312	346 492	294 895	86 266	208 629	190 909	53 046	137 863
90 - 94	167 814	39 916	127 898	102 906	24 680	78 226	64 908	15 236	49 672

Continent, country or area, date, code[a] and age (in years) / Continent, pays ou zone, date, code[a] et âge (en années)	Total			Urban - Urbaine			Rural - Rurale		
	Both sexes Les deux sexes	Male Masculin	Female Féminin	Both sexes Les deux sexes	Male Masculin	Female Féminin	Both sexes Les deux sexes	Male Masculin	Female Féminin
EUROPE									
Poland - Pologne[75]									
1 VII 2015 (ESDJ)									
95 - 99	24 915	5 319	19 596	15 281	3 236	12 045	9 634	2 083	7 551
100 +	5 155	1 063	4 092	3 516	718	2 798	1 639	345	1 294
1 I 2016 (ESDJ)									
Total	37 967 209	18 377 040	19 590 169	...	...	...	...	...	...
0	362 273	186 054	176 219	...	...	...	...	...	...
1 - 4	1 521 605	782 398	739 207	...	...	...	...	...	...
5 - 9	2 044 860	1 048 496	996 364	...	...	...	...	...	...
10 - 14	1 780 117	913 284	866 833	...	...	...	...	...	...
15 - 19	1 963 253	1 005 962	957 291	...	...	...	...	...	...
20 - 24	2 398 531	1 222 415	1 176 116	...	...	...	...	...	...
25 - 29	2 792 010	1 423 888	1 368 122	...	...	...	...	...	...
30 - 34	3 150 947	1 604 422	1 546 525	...	...	...	...	...	...
35 - 39	3 019 957	1 531 738	1 488 219	...	...	...	...	...	...
40 - 44	2 679 347	1 353 829	1 325 518	...	...	...	...	...	...
45 - 49	2 297 498	1 152 455	1 145 043	...	...	...	...	...	...
50 - 54	2 376 686	1 175 710	1 200 976	...	...	...	...	...	...
55 - 59	2 810 764	1 354 691	1 456 073	...	...	...	...	...	...
60 - 64	2 709 884	1 261 270	1 448 614	...	...	...	...	...	...
65 - 69	2 154 130	957 857	1 196 273	...	...	...	...	...	...
70 - 74	1 205 175	497 772	707 403	...	...	...	...	...	...
75 - 79	1 136 696	424 999	711 697	...	...	...	...	...	...
80 - 84	860 729	288 300	572 429	...	...	...	...	...	...
85 - 89	496 543	143 342	353 201	...	...	...	...	...	...
90 - 94	174 741	41 434	133 307	...	...	...	...	...	...
95 - 99	26 386	5 683	20 703	...	...	...	...	...	...
100 +	5 077	1 041	4 036	...	...	...	...	...	...
Portugal									
21 III 2011 (CDJC)									
Total	10 562 178	5 046 600	5 515 578	6 438 593	3 047 968	3 390 625	4 123 585	1 998 632	2 124 953
0 - 4	482 647	246 396	236 251	316 068	161 365	154 703	166 579	85 031	81 548
5 - 9	525 087	268 965	256 122	329 692	168 925	160 767	195 395	100 040	95 355
10 - 14	564 595	288 638	275 957	344 809	176 287	168 522	219 786	112 351	107 435
15 - 19	565 250	288 525	276 725	342 328	174 252	168 076	222 922	114 273	108 649
20 - 24	582 065	293 023	289 042	358 412	178 982	179 430	223 653	114 041	109 612
25 - 29	656 076	324 848	331 228	425 629	208 104	217 525	230 447	116 744	113 703
30 - 34	773 567	378 734	394 833	508 225	247 125	261 100	265 342	131 609	133 733
35 - 39	824 683	402 307	422 376	529 287	255 858	273 429	295 396	146 449	148 947
40 - 44	773 098	374 962	398 136	478 840	228 255	250 585	294 258	146 707	147 551
45 - 49	770 294	370 989	399 305	466 564	219 783	246 781	303 730	151 206	152 524
50 - 54	722 360	346 248	376 112	435 982	203 867	232 115	286 378	142 381	143 997
55 - 59	677 651	322 095	355 556	410 020	190 860	219 160	267 631	131 235	136 396
60 - 64	634 741	298 546	336 195	382 547	177 485	205 062	252 194	121 061	131 133
65 - 69	551 701	253 004	298 697	319 398	146 189	173 209	232 303	106 815	125 488
70 - 74	496 438	220 461	275 977	273 513	119 844	153 669	222 925	100 617	122 308
75 - 79	429 706	180 131	249 575	231 208	94 394	136 814	198 498	85 737	112 761
80 - 84	297 888	113 325	184 563	159 578	57 948	101 630	138 310	55 377	82 933
85 - 89	164 356	55 635	108 721	88 444	28 423	60 021	75 912	27 212	48 700
90 - 94	53 847	15 679	38 168	29 038	7 847	21 191	24 809	7 832	16 977
95 - 99	14 602	3 816	10 786	8 158	2 029	6 129	6 444	1 787	4 657
100 +	1 526	273	1 253	853	146	707	673	127	546
1 I 2016 (ESDJ)									
Total	10 341 330	4 901 509	5 439 821	...	...	...	...	...	...
0	85 527	43 693	41 834	...	...	...	...	...	...
1 - 4	350 838	180 131	170 707	...	...	...	...	...	...
5 - 9	494 705	252 333	242 372	...	...	...	...	...	...
10 - 14	529 762	271 860	257 902	...	...	...	...	...	...
15 - 19	560 363	286 050	274 313	...	...	...	...	...	...
20 - 24	545 132	275 387	269 745	...	...	...	...	...	...
25 - 29	557 449	278 464	278 985	...	...	...	...	...	...
30 - 34	640 029	311 641	328 388	...	...	...	...	...	...
35 - 39	761 670	365 654	396 016	...	...	...	...	...	...
40 - 44	807 089	386 387	420 702	...	...	...	...	...	...
45 - 49	754 807	361 242	393 565	...	...	...	...	...	...

Continent, country or area, date, code[a] and age (in years) / Continent, pays ou zone, date, code[a] et âge (en années)	Total			Urban - Urbaine			Rural - Rurale		
	Both sexes Les deux sexes	Male Masculin	Female Féminin	Both sexes Les deux sexes	Male Masculin	Female Féminin	Both sexes Les deux sexes	Male Masculin	Female Féminin
EUROPE									
Portugal									
1 I 2016 (ESDJ)									
50 - 54	757 561	359 846	397 715	...	...	...	...	...	...
55 - 59	703 719	333 424	370 295	...	...	...	...	...	...
60 - 64	651 855	304 260	347 595	...	...	...	...	...	...
65 - 69	593 746	272 256	321 490	...	...	...	...	...	...
70 - 74	498 638	218 674	279 964	...	...	...	...	...	...
75 - 79	433 987	181 742	252 245	...	...	...	...	...	...
80 - 84	341 071	131 773	209 298	...	...	...	...	...	...
85 - 89	187 917	62 596	125 321	...	...	...	...	...	...
90 - 94	66 317	18 719	47 598	...	...	...	...	...	...
95 - 99	14 861	3 897	10 964	...	...	...	...	...	...
100 +	4 287	1 480	2 807	...	...	...	...	...	...
Republic of Moldova - République de Moldova[82]									
1 VII 2012 (ESDJ)									
Total	3 559 519	1 712 036	1 847 484	1 488 966	699 880	789 086	2 070 554	1 012 156	1 058 398
0	38 856	20 015	18 842	14 501	7 501	7 000	24 356	12 514	11 842
1 - 4	155 545	80 386	75 159	57 044	29 740	27 305	98 501	50 646	47 855
5 - 9	185 646	95 525	90 121	67 697	35 209	32 489	117 949	60 317	57 632
10 - 14	194 993	100 101	94 893	66 615	34 473	32 142	128 379	65 628	62 751
15 - 19	257 790	131 414	126 376	88 575	45 309	43 267	169 215	86 106	83 110
20 - 24	333 714	169 543	164 171	138 548	69 044	69 505	195 166	100 499	94 667
25 - 29	343 489	174 869	168 620	174 571	84 151	90 420	168 918	90 718	78 200
30 - 34	289 604	146 740	142 864	133 836	65 353	68 483	155 769	81 387	74 382
35 - 39	251 655	124 669	126 986	111 448	54 088	57 360	140 207	70 581	69 627
40 - 44	225 706	109 887	115 819	97 757	46 129	51 629	127 949	63 758	64 191
45 - 49	237 350	112 506	124 844	102 616	46 409	56 207	134 735	66 097	68 638
50 - 54	274 163	127 681	146 482	119 669	52 882	66 787	154 495	74 799	79 696
55 - 59	235 036	106 431	128 605	104 053	44 876	59 177	130 983	61 555	69 428
60 - 64	182 091	79 587	102 504	79 353	34 316	45 038	102 738	45 272	57 467
65 - 69	105 809	44 763	61 046	43 360	18 966	24 394	62 449	25 797	36 652
70 - 74	100 565	38 142	62 423	39 059	15 111	23 948	61 506	23 031	38 475
75 - 79	72 497	25 841	46 656	24 995	8 598	16 397	47 502	17 243	30 259
80 - 84	47 586	15 881	31 706	15 963	5 051	10 912	31 624	10 830	20 794
85 - 89	20 400	5 920	14 480	6 963	1 957	5 006	13 437	3 963	9 474
90 - 94	5 438	1 597	3 841	1 780	526	1 254	3 658	1 071	2 588
95 - 99	1 163	395	768	391	150	241	772	245	527
100 +	429	148	282	177	45	132	253	103	150
1 I 2015 (ESDJ)									
Total	3 555 159	1 710 244	1 844 915	...	...	...	...	...	...
0	38 379	19 813	18 566	...	...	...	...	...	...
1 - 4	153 995	79 115	74 880	...	...	...	...	...	...
5 - 9	190 197	98 168	92 029	...	...	...	...	...	...
10 - 14	185 300	95 476	89 824	...	...	...	...	...	...
15 - 19	219 234	112 110	107 124	...	...	...	...	...	...
20 - 24	296 226	150 859	145 367	...	...	...	...	...	...
25 - 29	355 502	180 817	174 685	...	...	...	...	...	...
30 - 34	311 568	158 799	152 769	...	...	...	...	...	...
35 - 39	266 180	132 992	133 188	...	...	...	...	...	...
40 - 44	234 130	114 345	119 785	...	...	...	...	...	...
45 - 49	220 952	105 598	115 354	...	...	...	...	...	...
50 - 54	257 600	119 886	137 714	...	...	...	...	...	...
55 - 59	249 249	112 719	136 530	...	...	...	...	...	...
60 - 64	208 967	91 063	117 904	...	...	...	...	...	...
65 - 69	121 535	51 148	70 387	...	...	...	...	...	...
70 - 74	93 949	36 427	57 522	...	...	...	...	...	...
75 - 79	74 986	26 095	48 891	...	...	...	...	...	...
80 - 84	45 096	14 909	30 187	...	...	...	...	...	...
85 +	32 114	9 905	22 209	...	...	...	...	...	...
Romania - Roumanie[75]									
1 VII 2015 (ESDJ)									
Total	19 819 697	9 680 537	10 139 160	10 669 579	5 098 318	5 571 261	9 150 118	4 582 219	4 567 899
0	193 590	99 605	93 985	106 176	54 656	51 520	87 414	44 949	42 465
1 - 4	762 180	391 752	370 428	405 705	209 006	196 699	356 475	182 746	173 729

Continent, country or area, date, code[a] and age (in years) / Continent, pays ou zone, date, code[a] et âge (en années)	Total			Urban - Urbaine			Rural - Rurale		
	Both sexes Les deux sexes	Male Masculin	Female Féminin	Both sexes Les deux sexes	Male Masculin	Female Féminin	Both sexes Les deux sexes	Male Masculin	Female Féminin
EUROPE									
Romania - Roumanie[75]									
1 VII 2015 (ESDJ)									
5 - 9	1 065 716	547 222	518 494	540 961	278 159	262 802	524 755	269 063	255 692
10 - 14	1 052 183	540 955	511 228	488 426	250 600	237 826	563 757	290 355	273 402
15 - 19	1 082 404	554 285	528 119	495 681	251 249	244 432	586 723	303 036	283 687
20 - 24	1 104 391	572 199	532 192	583 454	291 723	291 731	520 937	280 476	240 461
25 - 29	1 381 602	717 400	664 202	824 511	413 360	411 151	557 091	304 040	253 051
30 - 34	1 324 351	681 110	643 241	792 175	400 300	391 875	532 176	280 810	251 366
35 - 39	1 551 041	790 018	761 023	886 980	442 177	444 803	664 061	347 841	316 220
40 - 44	1 520 318	779 687	740 631	821 218	405 231	415 987	699 100	374 456	324 644
45 - 49	1 582 893	810 882	772 011	902 009	434 777	467 232	680 884	376 105	304 779
50 - 54	1 095 748	550 909	544 839	637 639	300 344	337 295	458 109	250 565	207 544
55 - 59	1 360 368	654 970	705 398	814 991	375 694	439 297	545 377	279 276	266 101
60 - 64	1 335 465	616 476	718 989	773 696	354 372	419 324	561 769	262 104	299 665
65 - 69	1 062 869	471 800	591 069	547 957	242 333	305 624	514 912	229 467	285 445
70 - 74	774 588	322 584	452 004	361 814	149 023	212 791	412 774	173 561	239 213
75 - 79	743 852	285 873	457 979	329 781	124 669	205 112	414 071	161 204	252 867
80 - 84	493 024	180 233	312 791	210 248	74 039	136 209	282 776	106 194	176 582
85 - 89	242 807	83 864	158 943	105 501	34 676	70 825	137 306	49 188	88 118
90 - 94	77 631	24 964	52 667	34 502	10 300	24 202	43 129	14 664	28 465
95 - 99	11 060	3 284	7 776	5 334	1 415	3 919	5 726	1 869	3 857
100 +	1 616	465	1 151	820	215	605	796	250	546
1 I 2016 (ESDJ)									
Total	19 760 314	9 649 811	10 110 503	...	...	...	...	...	...
0	195 236	100 640	94 596	...	...	...	...	...	...
1 - 4	758 676	390 179	368 497	...	...	...	...	...	...
5 - 9	1 061 963	544 904	517 059	...	...	...	...	...	...
10 - 14	1 049 118	539 643	509 475	...	...	...	...	...	...
15 - 19	1 083 079	554 837	528 242	...	...	...	...	...	...
20 - 24	1 079 644	558 942	520 702	...	...	...	...	...	...
25 - 29	1 357 286	701 855	655 431	...	...	...	...	...	...
30 - 34	1 305 682	671 880	633 802	...	...	...	...	...	...
35 - 39	1 539 105	783 317	755 788	...	...	...	...	...	...
40 - 44	1 515 385	777 690	737 695	...	...	...	...	...	...
45 - 49	1 635 199	838 381	796 818	...	...	...	...	...	...
50 - 54	1 071 973	540 352	531 621	...	...	...	...	...	...
55 - 59	1 326 453	640 527	685 926	...	...	...	...	...	...
60 - 64	1 345 095	621 556	723 539	...	...	...	...	...	...
65 - 69	1 103 942	489 948	613 994	...	...	...	...	...	...
70 - 74	758 360	315 864	442 496	...	...	...	...	...	...
75 - 79	739 471	283 897	455 574	...	...	...	...	...	...
80 - 84	492 927	179 961	312 966	...	...	...	...	...	...
85 - 89	247 293	85 261	162 032	...	...	...	...	...	...
90 - 94	80 872	26 269	54 603	...	...	...	...	...	...
95 - 99	11 962	3 461	8 501	...	...	...	...	...	...
100 +	1 593	447	1 146	...	...	...	...	...	...
Russian Federation - Fédération de Russie									
1 VII 2012 (ESDJ)									
Total	143 201 730	66 264 910	76 936 820	105 930 122	48 419 208	57 510 914	37 271 608	17 845 702	19 425 906
0	1 837 406	944 299	893 107	1 299 253	668 312	630 941	538 153	275 987	262 166
1 - 4	6 695 802	3 433 227	3 262 575	4 714 200	2 419 141	2 295 059	1 981 602	1 014 086	967 516
5 - 9	7 350 838	3 762 806	3 588 032	5 189 787	2 657 166	2 532 621	2 161 051	1 105 640	1 055 411
10 - 14	6 628 125	3 396 364	3 231 761	4 584 611	2 348 219	2 236 392	2 043 514	1 048 145	995 369
15 - 19	7 391 866	3 776 026	3 615 840	5 367 803	2 718 897	2 648 906	2 024 063	1 057 129	966 934
20 - 24	11 223 730	5 708 187	5 515 543	8 636 085	4 330 536	4 305 549	2 587 645	1 377 651	1 209 994
25 - 29	12 442 007	6 262 379	6 179 628	9 541 009	4 744 648	4 796 361	2 900 998	1 517 731	1 383 267
30 - 34	11 231 149	5 583 513	5 647 636	8 675 785	4 272 864	4 402 921	2 555 364	1 310 649	1 244 715
35 - 39	10 419 383	5 087 565	5 331 818	7 966 185	3 854 320	4 111 865	2 453 198	1 233 245	1 219 953
40 - 44	9 451 487	4 589 504	4 861 983	7 068 002	3 394 309	3 673 693	2 383 485	1 195 195	1 188 290
45 - 49	9 784 092	4 632 279	5 151 813	7 108 256	3 298 718	3 809 538	2 675 836	1 333 561	1 342 275
50 - 54	11 498 441	5 279 364	6 219 077	8 339 186	3 721 713	4 617 473	3 159 255	1 557 651	1 601 604
55 - 59	10 298 414	4 480 855	5 817 559	7 573 444	3 197 844	4 375 600	2 724 970	1 283 011	1 441 959
60 - 64	8 534 857	3 523 990	5 010 867	6 428 296	2 585 856	3 842 440	2 106 561	938 134	1 168 427
65 - 69	4 174 510	1 602 839	2 571 671	3 204 644	1 214 486	1 990 158	969 866	388 353	581 513

Continent, country or area, date, code[a] and age (in years) — Continent, pays ou zone, date, code[a] et âge (en années)	Total			Urban - Urbaine			Rural - Rurale		
	Both sexes Les deux sexes	Male Masculin	Female Féminin	Both sexes Les deux sexes	Male Masculin	Female Féminin	Both sexes Les deux sexes	Male Masculin	Female Féminin
EUROPE									
Russian Federation - Fédération de Russie									
1 VII 2012 (ESDJ)									
70 - 74	5 965 072	1 989 724	3 975 348	4 331 090	1 428 165	2 902 925	1 633 982	561 559	1 072 423
75 - 79	3 888 860	1 179 476	2 709 384	2 762 682	822 673	1 940 009	1 126 178	356 803	769 375
80 - 84	2 795 954	722 151	2 073 803	1 965 242	501 515	1 463 727	830 712	220 636	610 076
85 - 89	1 261 655	253 028	1 008 627	927 939	193 530	734 409	333 716	59 498	274 218
90 - 94	266 163	46 736	219 427	200 155	37 401	162 754	66 008	9 335	56 673
95 - 99	52 622	8 634	43 988	39 307	7 154	32 153	13 315	1 480	11 835
100 +	9 297	1 964	7 333	7 161	1 741	5 420	2 136	223	1 913
San Marino - Saint-Marin[23]									
1 I 2016 (ESDF)									
Total	34 006	16 560	17 446	...	...	...	...	...	...
0	279	141	138	...	...	...	...	...	...
1 - 4	1 302	670	632	...	...	...	...	...	...
5 - 9	1 753	903	850	...	...	...	...	...	...
10 - 14	1 698	917	781	...	...	...	...	...	...
15 - 19	1 662	875	787	...	...	...	...	...	...
20 - 24	1 512	781	731	...	...	...	...	...	...
25 - 29	1 582	782	800	...	...	...	...	...	...
30 - 34	1 927	960	967	...	...	...	...	...	...
35 - 39	2 489	1 160	1 329	...	...	...	...	...	...
40 - 44	2 971	1 445	1 526	...	...	...	...	...	...
45 - 49	3 131	1 515	1 616	...	...	...	...	...	...
50 - 54	2 980	1 457	1 523	...	...	...	...	...	...
55 - 59	2 387	1 157	1 230	...	...	...	...	...	...
60 - 64	1 979	942	1 037	...	...	...	...	...	...
65 - 69	1 843	895	948	...	...	...	...	...	...
70 - 74	1 447	689	758	...	...	...	...	...	...
75 - 79	1 200	571	629	...	...	...	...	...	...
80 - 84	929	391	538	...	...	...	...	...	...
85 - 89	588	211	377	...	...	...	...	...	...
90 - 94	267	86	181	...	...	...	...	...	...
95 - 99	72	12	60	...	...	...	...	...	...
100 +	8	-	8	...	...	...	...	...	...
Serbia - Serbie[83]									
1 VII 2015 (ESDJ)									
Total	7 095 383	3 455 335	3 640 048	4 267 079	2 033 446	2 233 633	2 828 304	1 421 889	1 406 415
0	65 689	33 965	31 724	45 430	23 428	22 002	20 259	10 537	9 722
1 - 4	263 288	135 513	127 775	179 311	92 321	86 990	83 977	43 192	40 785
5 - 9	336 187	173 086	163 101	206 277	106 039	100 238	129 910	67 047	62 863
10 - 14	356 844	183 439	173 405	211 354	108 632	102 722	145 490	74 807	70 683
15 - 19	362 345	186 593	175 752	210 839	108 428	102 411	151 506	78 165	73 341
20 - 24	415 867	213 489	202 378	247 157	125 086	122 071	168 710	88 403	80 307
25 - 29	453 095	231 728	221 367	283 534	140 390	143 144	169 561	91 338	78 223
30 - 34	489 431	249 065	240 366	320 106	157 933	162 173	169 325	91 132	78 193
35 - 39	501 835	254 480	247 355	325 903	161 122	164 781	175 932	93 358	82 574
40 - 44	484 995	243 247	241 748	302 813	147 935	154 878	182 182	95 312	86 870
45 - 49	469 041	231 943	237 098	280 813	134 537	146 276	188 228	97 406	90 822
50 - 54	487 446	237 874	249 572	289 380	135 609	153 771	198 066	102 265	95 801
55 - 59	518 006	250 003	268 003	304 767	140 783	163 984	213 239	109 220	104 019
60 - 64	562 473	266 863	295 610	327 869	148 920	178 949	234 604	117 943	116 661
65 - 69	446 484	204 138	242 346	260 134	114 317	145 817	186 350	89 821	96 529
70 - 74	301 782	131 164	170 618	164 678	69 579	95 099	137 104	61 585	75 519
75 - 79	282 487	116 447	166 040	152 823	61 673	91 150	129 664	54 774	74 890
80 - 84	191 137	74 397	116 740	98 387	37 813	60 574	92 750	36 584	56 166
85 - 89	82 306	29 828	52 478	42 021	14 562	27 459	40 285	15 266	25 019
90 - 94	21 332	7 006	14 326	11 657	3 774	7 883	9 675	3 232	6 443
95 - 99	2 882	916	1 966	1 595	501	1 094	1 287	415	872
100 +	431	151	280	231	64	167	200	87	113
Slovakia - Slovaquie									
1 VII 2015 (ESDJ)									
Total	5 423 801	2 644 205	2 779 596	2 919 718	1 403 692	1 516 027	2 504 083	1 240 514	1 263 569
0	55 812	28 620	27 192	29 060	14 897	14 164	26 752	13 723	13 029
1 - 4	230 963	118 198	112 766	119 168	60 929	58 240	111 795	57 269	54 526

7. Population by age, sex and urban/rural residence: latest available year, 2007 - 2016
Population selon l'âge, le sexe et la résidence, urbaine/rurale : dernière année disponible, 2007 - 2016 (continued - suite)

Continent, country or area, date, code[a] and age (in years) / Continent, pays ou zone, date, code[a] et âge (en années)	Total			Urban - Urbaine			Rural - Rurale		
	Both sexes Les deux sexes	Male Masculin	Female Féminin	Both sexes Les deux sexes	Male Masculin	Female Féminin	Both sexes Les deux sexes	Male Masculin	Female Féminin
EUROPE									
Slovakia - Slovaquie									
1 VII 2015 (ESDJ)									
5 - 9	281 585	144 581	137 005	139 864	71 831	68 033	141 722	72 750	68 972
10 - 14	262 753	135 038	127 715	126 549	65 095	61 455	136 204	69 944	66 260
15 - 19	288 980	148 264	140 716	137 326	70 411	66 915	151 654	77 853	73 801
20 - 24	358 605	183 074	175 532	180 419	91 896	88 523	178 186	91 178	87 009
25 - 29	407 951	207 828	200 123	223 292	113 121	110 171	184 659	94 707	89 952
30 - 34	437 874	224 900	212 974	246 080	125 795	120 286	191 794	99 106	92 688
35 - 39	458 544	235 877	222 667	255 148	130 195	124 953	203 397	105 683	97 714
40 - 44	411 015	209 384	201 631	221 007	110 665	110 343	190 008	98 719	91 289
45 - 49	353 350	177 609	175 741	188 989	91 481	97 508	164 361	86 128	78 233
50 - 54	369 044	183 054	185 990	205 114	97 382	107 732	163 930	85 672	78 258
55 - 59	376 647	182 535	194 112	216 304	100 649	115 655	160 343	81 886	78 457
60 - 64	360 275	168 243	192 032	209 799	95 352	114 447	150 476	72 891	77 586
65 - 69	269 396	118 584	150 812	154 415	66 996	87 419	114 981	51 588	63 394
70 - 74	192 041	76 872	115 169	105 374	42 134	63 240	86 667	34 738	51 929
75 - 79	139 197	50 023	89 174	73 502	26 897	46 605	65 696	23 126	42 570
80 - 84	97 685	31 550	66 135	50 777	17 113	33 664	46 909	14 437	32 472
85 - 89	50 863	14 410	36 453	26 378	7 791	18 587	24 486	6 620	17 866
90 - 94	17 846	4 583	13 263	9 269	2 508	6 761	8 577	2 075	6 502
95 - 99	2 676	739	1 937	1 453	405	1 048	1 223	334	890
100 +	706	245	461	438	154	284	268	91	177
1 I 2016 (ESDJ)									
Total	5 426 252	2 646 082	2 780 170	...	...	...	...	...	...
0	56 110	28 905	27 205	...	...	...	...	...	...
1 - 4	230 165	117 891	112 274	...	...	...	...	...	...
5 - 9	283 337	145 231	138 106	...	...	...	...	...	...
10 - 14	262 431	134 927	127 504	...	...	...	...	...	...
15 - 19	285 969	146 755	139 214	...	...	...	...	...	...
20 - 24	349 965	178 639	171 326	...	...	...	...	...	...
25 - 29	403 717	205 716	198 001	...	...	...	...	...	...
30 - 34	436 748	224 152	212 596	...	...	...	...	...	...
35 - 39	457 773	235 819	221 954	...	...	...	...	...	...
40 - 44	418 903	213 541	205 362	...	...	...	...	...	...
45 - 49	352 660	177 516	175 144	...	...	...	...	...	...
50 - 54	367 972	182 529	185 443	...	...	...	...	...	...
55 - 59	373 274	181 239	192 035	...	...	...	...	...	...
60 - 64	363 292	169 809	193 483	...	...	...	...	...	...
65 - 69	278 833	123 182	155 651	...	...	...	...	...	...
70 - 74	192 764	77 303	115 461	...	...	...	...	...	...
75 - 79	141 249	50 947	90 302	...	...	...	...	...	...
80 - 84	97 644	31 616	66 028	...	...	...	...	...	...
85 - 89	51 655	14 688	36 967	...	...	...	...	...	...
90 - 94	18 156	4 617	13 539	...	...	...	...	...	...
95 - 99	2 865	788	2 077	...	...	...	...	...	...
100 +	770	272	498	...	...	...	...	...	...
Slovenia - Slovénie									
1 VII 2015 (ESDJ)									
Total	2 063 077	1 022 554	1 040 523	1 106 955	542 847	564 108	956 122	479 707	476 415
0	20 965	10 755	10 210	11 180	5 693	5 487	9 785	5 062	4 723
1 - 4	87 480	45 050	42 430	47 086	24 278	22 808	40 394	20 772	19 622
5 - 9	105 296	54 126	51 170	55 828	28 685	27 143	49 468	25 441	24 027
10 - 14	91 478	47 058	44 420	46 731	24 137	22 594	44 747	22 921	21 826
15 - 19	94 681	48 934	45 747	48 570	25 182	23 388	46 111	23 752	22 359
20 - 24	106 229	54 397	51 832	61 563	30 317	31 246	44 666	24 080	20 586
25 - 29	129 961	67 548	62 413	70 195	36 268	33 927	59 766	31 280	28 486
30 - 34	147 567	77 174	70 393	80 402	41 902	38 500	67 165	35 272	31 893
35 - 39	157 489	82 627	74 862	85 738	44 761	40 977	71 751	37 866	33 885
40 - 44	148 381	77 332	71 049	78 852	40 883	37 969	69 529	36 449	33 080
45 - 49	151 293	77 365	73 928	79 603	40 368	39 235	71 690	36 997	34 693
50 - 54	153 722	77 924	75 798	80 923	40 462	40 461	72 799	37 462	35 337
55 - 59	150 092	75 853	74 239	78 825	38 991	39 834	71 267	36 862	34 405
60 - 64	143 955	72 026	71 929	77 448	37 727	39 721	66 507	34 299	32 208
65 - 69	109 811	52 527	57 284	59 848	27 823	32 025	49 963	24 704	25 259
70 - 74	88 322	39 513	48 809	47 950	20 926	27 024	40 372	18 587	21 785

Continent, country or area, date, code[a] and age (in years) / Continent, pays ou zone, date, code[a] et âge (en années)	Total			Urban - Urbaine			Rural - Rurale		
	Both sexes Les deux sexes	Male Masculin	Female Féminin	Both sexes Les deux sexes	Male Masculin	Female Féminin	Both sexes Les deux sexes	Male Masculin	Female Féminin
EUROPE									
Slovenia - Slovénie									
1 VII 2015 (ESDJ)									
75 - 79	75 426	31 211	44 215	40 976	17 060	23 916	34 450	14 151	20 299
80 - 84	56 402	19 666	36 736	30 613	10 865	19 748	25 789	8 801	16 988
85 - 89	31 572	8 836	22 736	17 255	4 931	12 324	14 317	3 905	10 412
90 - 94	11 156	2 314	8 842	6 316	1 390	4 926	4 840	924	3 916
95 - 99	1 572	286	1 286	913	174	739	659	112	547
100 +	227	32	195	140	24	116	87	8	79
1 I 2016 (ESDJ)									
Total	2 064 188	1 023 333	1 040 855	...	...	...	...	...	...
0	20 620	10 596	10 024	...	...	...	...	...	...
1 - 4	86 701	44 605	42 096	...	...	...	...	...	...
5 - 9	107 505	55 351	52 154	...	...	...	...	...	...
10 - 14	91 564	47 122	44 442	...	...	...	...	...	...
15 - 19	94 654	48 907	45 747	...	...	...	...	...	...
20 - 24	104 500	53 591	50 909	...	...	...	...	...	...
25 - 29	128 172	66 491	61 681	...	...	...	...	...	...
30 - 34	145 305	76 054	69 251	...	...	...	...	...	...
35 - 39	157 505	82 637	74 868	...	...	...	...	...	...
40 - 44	150 102	78 232	71 870	...	...	...	...	...	...
45 - 49	149 386	76 463	72 923	...	...	...	...	...	...
50 - 54	154 542	78 317	76 225	...	...	...	...	...	...
55 - 59	149 432	75 431	74 001	...	...	...	...	...	...
60 - 64	144 098	72 009	72 089	...	...	...	...	...	...
65 - 69	115 919	55 647	60 272	...	...	...	...	...	...
70 - 74	85 622	38 365	47 257	...	...	...	...	...	...
75 - 79	76 018	31 539	44 479	...	...	...	...	...	...
80 - 84	56 372	19 900	36 472	...	...	...	...	...	...
85 - 89	32 561	9 249	23 312	...	...	...	...	...	...
90 - 94	11 635	2 472	9 163	...	...	...	...	...	...
95 - 99	1 756	324	1 432	...	...	...	...	...	...
100 +	219	31	188	...	...	...	...	...	...
Spain - Espagne[76]									
1 I 2016 (ESDJ)									
Total	46 445 828	22 809 420	23 636 408	...	...	...	...	...	...
0	419 395	215 948	203 447	...	...	...	...	...	...
1 - 4	1 783 367	919 116	864 251	...	...	...	...	...	...
5 - 9	2 477 203	1 278 835	1 198 368	...	...	...	...	...	...
10 - 14	2 345 435	1 205 603	1 139 832	...	...	...	...	...	...
15 - 19	2 185 630	1 125 439	1 060 191	...	...	...	...	...	...
20 - 24	2 280 631	1 163 627	1 117 004	...	...	...	...	...	...
25 - 29	2 564 166	1 284 350	1 279 816	...	...	...	...	...	...
30 - 34	3 100 403	1 551 405	1 548 998	...	...	...	...	...	...
35 - 39	3 849 020	1 951 414	1 897 606	...	...	...	...	...	...
40 - 44	3 924 816	1 998 598	1 926 218	...	...	...	...	...	...
45 - 49	3 712 894	1 874 516	1 838 378	...	...	...	...	...	...
50 - 54	3 461 060	1 725 134	1 735 926	...	...	...	...	...	...
55 - 59	3 073 611	1 514 131	1 559 480	...	...	...	...	...	...
60 - 64	2 568 305	1 248 590	1 319 715	...	...	...	...	...	...
65 - 69	2 348 134	1 117 040	1 231 094	...	...	...	...	...	...
70 - 74	1 975 726	915 284	1 060 442	...	...	...	...	...	...
75 - 79	1 584 129	690 958	893 171	...	...	...	...	...	...
80 - 84	1 430 780	578 510	852 270	...	...	...	...	...	...
85 - 89	889 323	315 908	573 415	...	...	...	...	...	...
90 - 94	371 148	111 028	260 120	...	...	...	...	...	...
95 - 99	84 189	20 229	63 960	...	...	...	...	...	...
100 +	16 463	3 757	12 706	...	...	...	...	...	...
Sweden - Suède[84]									
1 I 2016 (ESDJ)									
Total	9 851 017	4 930 966	4 920 051	...	...	...	...	...	...
0	115 878	59 994	55 884	...	...	...	...	...	...
1 - 4	470 340	241 790	228 550	...	...	...	...	...	...
5 - 9	589 118	302 956	286 162	...	...	...	...	...	...
10 - 14	541 807	278 135	263 672	...	...	...	...	...	...
15 - 19	522 472	271 022	251 450	...	...	...	...	...	...

Continent, country or area, date, code[a] and age (in years) / Continent, pays ou zone, date, code[a] et âge (en annèes)	Total			Urban - Urbaine			Rural - Rurale		
	Both sexes Les deux sexes	Male Masculin	Female Féminin	Both sexes Les deux sexes	Male Masculin	Female Féminin	Both sexes Les deux sexes	Male Masculin	Female Féminin
EUROPE									
Sweden - Suède[84]									
1 I 2016 (ESDJ)									
20 - 24	656 448	338 198	318 250	...	...	...	...	...	...
25 - 29	682 413	348 983	333 430	...	...	...	...	...	...
30 - 34	619 071	318 006	301 065	...	...	...	...	...	...
35 - 39	608 570	310 663	297 907	...	...	...	...	...	...
40 - 44	651 944	330 868	321 076	...	...	...	...	...	...
45 - 49	662 423	336 401	326 022	...	...	...	...	...	...
50 - 54	644 465	327 170	317 295	...	...	...	...	...	...
55 - 59	580 194	292 291	287 903	...	...	...	...	...	...
60 - 64	558 647	278 590	280 057	...	...	...	...	...	...
65 - 69	588 931	290 875	298 056	...	...	...	...	...	...
70 - 74	511 169	250 497	260 672	...	...	...	...	...	...
75 - 79	345 477	161 294	184 183	...	...	...	...	...	...
80 - 84	243 179	104 170	139 009	...	...	...	...	...	...
85 - 89	162 108	60 527	101 581	...	...	...	...	...	...
90 - 94	76 013	23 755	52 258	...	...	...	...	...	...
95 - 99	18 454	4 466	13 988	...	...	...	...	...	...
100 +	1 896	315	1 581	...	...	...	...	...	...
Switzerland - Suisse[85]									
1 I 2016 (ESDJ)									
Total	8 327 126	4 121 471	4 205 655	7 036 743	3 471 877	3 564 866	1 290 383	649 594	640 789
0	84 904	43 713	41 191	72 461	37 253	35 208	12 443	6 460	5 983
1 - 4	338 127	173 944	164 183	286 299	147 542	138 757	51 828	26 402	25 426
5 - 9	413 257	212 219	201 038	347 645	178 461	169 184	65 612	33 758	31 854
10 - 14	400 504	205 372	195 132	334 695	171 705	162 990	65 809	33 667	32 142
15 - 19	438 711	225 456	213 255	363 607	186 750	176 857	75 104	38 706	36 398
20 - 24	496 048	252 697	243 351	415 486	210 840	204 646	80 562	41 857	38 705
25 - 29	560 587	283 314	277 273	482 765	242 625	240 140	77 822	40 689	37 133
30 - 34	589 284	297 613	291 671	511 211	257 712	253 499	78 073	39 901	38 172
35 - 39	579 210	292 170	287 040	500 155	252 042	248 113	79 055	40 128	38 927
40 - 44	590 167	297 391	292 776	503 994	253 667	250 327	86 173	43 724	42 449
45 - 49	654 245	329 701	324 544	552 077	277 766	274 311	102 168	51 935	50 233
50 - 54	657 774	333 462	324 312	551 976	279 181	272 795	105 798	54 281	51 517
55 - 59	560 277	282 913	277 364	466 429	234 705	231 724	93 848	48 208	45 640
60 - 64	468 979	231 880	237 099	390 799	191 528	199 271	78 180	40 352	37 828
65 - 69	433 593	209 673	223 920	361 732	173 142	188 590	71 861	36 531	35 330
70 - 74	371 249	175 474	195 775	312 737	146 545	166 192	58 512	28 929	29 583
75 - 79	273 343	121 302	152 041	230 743	101 791	128 952	42 600	19 511	23 089
80 - 84	211 503	86 403	125 100	178 202	72 370	105 832	33 301	14 033	19 268
85 - 89	133 393	46 832	86 561	112 645	39 371	73 274	20 748	7 461	13 287
90 - 94	58 145	16 816	41 329	49 306	14 244	35 062	8 839	2 572	6 267
95 - 99	12 264	2 836	9 428	10 430	2 383	8 047	1 834	453	1 381
100 +	1 562	290	1 272	1 349	254	1 095	213	36	177
TFYR of Macedonia - L'ex-R. y. de Macédoine									
1 I 2016 (ESDF)									
Total	2 071 278	1 037 601	1 033 677	...	...	...	...	...	...
0	22 891	11 856	11 035	...	...	...	...	...	...
1 - 4	92 080	47 723	44 357	...	...	...	...	...	...
5 - 9	114 648	59 318	55 330	...	...	...	...	...	...
10 - 14	115 290	59 380	55 910	...	...	...	...	...	...
15 - 19	128 465	66 324	62 141	...	...	...	...	...	...
20 - 24	150 878	77 494	73 384	...	...	...	...	...	...
25 - 29	161 173	82 724	78 449	...	...	...	...	...	...
30 - 34	164 046	83 943	80 103	...	...	...	...	...	...
35 - 39	156 480	80 315	76 165	...	...	...	...	...	...
40 - 44	148 627	75 299	73 328	...	...	...	...	...	...
45 - 49	145 049	73 210	71 839	...	...	...	...	...	...
50 - 54	142 445	71 744	70 701	...	...	...	...	...	...
55 - 59	137 042	68 570	68 472	...	...	...	...	...	...
60 - 64	122 887	60 117	62 770	...	...	...	...	...	...
65 - 69	97 996	45 430	52 566	...	...	...	...	...	...
70 - 74	69 507	31 375	38 132	...	...	...	...	...	...
75 - 79	53 414	23 311	30 103	...	...	...	...	...	...

Continent, country or area, date, code[a] and age (in years) / Continent, pays ou zone, date, code[a] et âge (en années)	Total			Urban - Urbaine			Rural - Rurale		
	Both sexes Les deux sexes	Male Masculin	Female Féminin	Both sexes Les deux sexes	Male Masculin	Female Féminin	Both sexes Les deux sexes	Male Masculin	Female Féminin
EUROPE									
TFYR of Macedonia - L'ex-R. y. de Macédoine									
1 I 2016 (ESDF)									
80 - 84	32 887	13 634	19 253	...	...	...	...	...	...
85 - 89	11 728	4 593	7 135	...	...	...	...	...	...
90 - 94	2 495	919	1 576	...	...	...	...	...	...
95 +	970	276	694	...	...	...	...	...	...
Unknown - Inconnu	280	46	234	...	...	...	...	...	...
Ukraine									
1 I 2013 (ESDJ)									
Total	45 372 692	20 962 744	24 409 948	31 123 007	14 259 600	16 863 407	14 249 685	6 703 144	7 546 541
0	517 301	266 820	250 481	339 538	175 547	163 991	177 763	91 273	86 490
1 - 4	2 004 486	1 033 711	970 775	1 327 019	684 897	642 122	677 467	348 814	328 653
5 - 9	2 168 158	1 113 505	1 054 653	1 449 410	745 034	704 376	718 748	368 471	350 277
10 - 14	1 930 653	991 443	939 210	1 203 306	618 657	584 649	727 347	372 786	354 561
15 - 19	2 405 136	1 233 934	1 171 202	1 579 769	804 869	774 900	825 367	429 065	396 302
20 - 24	3 232 157	1 657 101	1 575 056	2 195 942	1 118 307	1 077 635	1 036 215	538 794	497 421
25 - 29	3 868 992	1 969 672	1 899 320	2 801 899	1 408 147	1 393 752	1 067 093	561 525	505 568
30 - 34	3 476 598	1 750 016	1 726 582	2 553 790	1 276 839	1 276 951	922 808	473 177	449 631
35 - 39	3 270 101	1 609 508	1 660 593	2 323 493	1 130 939	1 192 554	946 608	478 569	468 039
40 - 44	3 113 544	1 507 589	1 605 955	2 153 127	1 021 499	1 131 628	960 417	486 090	474 327
45 - 49	3 085 767	1 450 559	1 635 208	2 123 186	966 883	1 156 303	962 581	483 676	478 905
50 - 54	3 500 369	1 594 318	1 906 051	2 461 151	1 084 460	1 376 691	1 039 218	509 858	529 360
55 - 59	3 097 369	1 347 030	1 750 339	2 209 140	931 767	1 277 373	888 229	415 263	472 966
60 - 64	2 796 743	1 157 385	1 639 358	2 006 621	812 407	1 194 214	790 122	344 978	445 144
65 - 69	1 656 868	629 382	1 027 486	1 139 209	432 839	706 370	517 659	196 543	321 116
70 - 74	2 153 251	742 717	1 410 534	1 391 669	483 905	907 764	761 582	258 812	502 770
75 - 79	1 492 884	489 204	1 003 680	927 376	307 461	619 915	565 508	181 743	383 765
80 - 84	974 774	274 742	700 032	568 852	164 927	403 925	405 922	109 815	296 107
85 - 89	492 650	114 882	377 768	289 117	71 285	217 832	203 533	43 597	159 936
90 - 94	114 583	24 566	90 017	65 707	15 513	50 194	48 876	9 053	39 823
95 - 99	14 543	3 307	11 236	9 446	2 362	7 084	5 097	945	4 152
100 +	5 765	1 353	4 412	4 240	1 056	3 184	1 525	297	1 228
1 I 2016 (ESDF)[86]									
Total	42 590 879	19 717 881	22 872 998	...	...	...	...	...	...
0	409 172	211 339	197 833	...	...	...	...	...	...
1 - 4	1 891 832	974 748	917 084	...	...	...	...	...	...
5 - 9	2 295 298	1 181 387	1 113 911	...	...	...	...	...	...
10 - 14	1 897 991	976 308	921 683	...	...	...	...	...	...
15 - 19	1 974 078	1 012 471	961 607	...	...	...	...	...	...
20 - 24	2 589 921	1 331 466	1 258 455	...	...	...	...	...	...
25 - 29	3 374 686	1 722 137	1 652 549	...	...	...	...	...	...
30 - 34	3 539 116	1 789 447	1 749 669	...	...	...	...	...	...
35 - 39	3 177 464	1 577 538	1 599 926	...	...	...	...	...	...
40 - 44	3 040 882	1 477 645	1 563 237	...	...	...	...	...	...
45 - 49	2 816 400	1 341 012	1 475 388	...	...	...	...	...	...
50 - 54	3 036 693	1 391 665	1 645 028	...	...	...	...	...	...
55 - 59	3 130 136	1 376 991	1 753 145	...	...	...	...	...	...
60 - 64	2 648 348	1 096 373	1 551 975	...	...	...	...	...	...
65 - 69	2 163 552	837 736	1 325 816	...	...	...	...	...	...
70 - 74	1 365 984	466 475	899 509	...	...	...	...	...	...
75 - 79	1 769 949	555 790	1 214 159	...	...	...	...	...	...
80 - 84	766 878	224 682	542 196	...	...	...	...	...	...
85 - 89	522 102	130 852	391 250	...	...	...	...	...	...
90 - 94	149 578	33 169	116 409	...	...	...	...	...	...
95 - 99	24 337	6 802	17 535	...	...	...	...	...	...
100 +	6 482	1 848	4 634	...	...	...	...	...	...
United Kingdom of Great Britain and Northern Ireland - Royaume-Uni de Grande-Bretagne et d'Irlande du Nord[87]									
27 III 2011 (CDJC)									
Total	63 182 178	31 028 143	32 154 035	51 217 521	25 124 237	26 093 284	11 964 657	5 903 906	6 060 751
0 - 4	3 913 953	2 002 494	1 911 459	3 302 119	1 689 719	1 612 400	611 834	312 775	299 059

Continent, country or area, date, code[a] and age (in years) Continent, pays ou zone, date, code[a] et âge (en années)	Total			Urban - Urbaine			Rural - Rurale		
	Both sexes Les deux sexes	Male Masculin	Female Féminin	Both sexes Les deux sexes	Male Masculin	Female Féminin	Both sexes Les deux sexes	Male Masculin	Female Féminin
EUROPE									
United Kingdom of Great Britain and Northern Ireland - Royaume-Uni de Grande-Bretagne et d'Irlande du Nord[87]									
27 III 2011 (CDJC)									
5 - 9	3 516 615	1 799 999	1 716 616	2 878 114	1 472 489	1 405 625	638 501	327 510	310 991
10 - 14	3 669 326	1 878 838	1 790 488	2 951 079	1 509 796	1 441 283	718 247	369 042	349 205
15 - 19	3 996 452	2 040 725	1 955 727	3 277 414	1 667 480	1 609 934	719 038	373 245	345 793
20 - 24	4 297 198	2 164 141	2 133 057	3 737 543	1 863 922	1 873 621	559 655	300 219	259 436
25 - 29	4 306 340	2 145 054	2 161 286	3 781 906	1 876 471	1 905 435	524 434	268 583	255 851
30 - 34	4 125 449	2 059 312	2 066 137	3 573 410	1 789 511	1 783 899	552 039	269 801	282 238
35 - 39	4 194 477	2 082 310	2 112 167	3 495 390	1 745 563	1 749 827	699 087	336 747	362 340
40 - 44	4 625 635	2 283 902	2 341 733	3 734 709	1 851 446	1 883 263	890 926	432 456	458 470
45 - 49	4 643 100	2 293 572	2 349 528	3 683 527	1 821 257	1 862 270	959 573	472 315	487 258
50 - 54	4 094 454	2 028 748	2 065 706	3 216 769	1 593 822	1 622 947	877 685	434 926	442 759
55 - 59	3 614 078	1 785 598	1 828 480	2 790 096	1 378 906	1 411 190	823 982	406 692	417 290
60 - 64	3 807 974	1 868 912	1 939 062	2 869 025	1 404 882	1 464 143	938 949	464 030	474 919
65 - 69	3 017 480	1 463 355	1 554 125	2 248 845	1 082 105	1 166 740	768 635	381 250	387 385
70 - 74	2 462 745	1 162 621	1 300 124	1 874 997	873 593	1 001 404	587 748	289 028	298 720
75 - 79	2 006 019	903 433	1 102 586	1 549 014	686 269	862 745	457 005	217 164	239 841
80 - 84	1 498 896	615 163	883 733	1 166 619	470 552	696 067	332 277	144 611	187 666
85 - 89	918 343	324 063	594 280	717 808	249 645	468 163	200 535	74 418	126 117
90 - 94	368 425	104 072	264 353	287 454	80 165	207 289	80 971	23 907	57 064
95 - 99	92 951	19 756	73 195	72 117	15 038	57 079	20 834	4 718	16 116
100 +	12 268	2 075	10 193	9 566	1 606	7 960	2 702	469	2 233
1 I 2016 (ESDJ)[75]									
Total	65 382 556	32 224 529	33 158 027	...	...	...	...	...	...
0	780 408	400 036	380 372	...	...	...	...	...	...
1 - 4	3 233 289	1 657 062	1 576 227	...	...	...	...	...	...
5 - 9	3 991 430	2 043 266	1 948 164	...	...	...	...	...	...
10 - 14	3 582 263	1 833 695	1 748 568	...	...	...	...	...	...
15 - 19	3 794 580	1 947 780	1 846 800	...	...	...	...	...	...
20 - 24	4 289 573	2 190 062	2 099 511	...	...	...	...	...	...
25 - 29	4 488 633	2 259 919	2 228 714	...	...	...	...	...	...
30 - 34	4 395 243	2 187 737	2 207 506	...	...	...	...	...	...
35 - 39	4 126 272	2 053 298	2 072 974	...	...	...	...	...	...
40 - 44	4 231 923	2 095 555	2 136 368	...	...	...	...	...	...
45 - 49	4 621 836	2 277 639	2 344 197	...	...	...	...	...	...
50 - 54	4 596 846	2 265 130	2 331 716	...	...	...	...	...	...
55 - 59	4 007 826	1 978 103	2 029 723	...	...	...	...	...	...
60 - 64	3 516 535	1 722 249	1 794 286	...	...	...	...	...	...
65 - 69	3 626 692	1 760 370	1 866 322	...	...	...	...	...	...
70 - 74	2 790 150	1 328 925	1 461 225	...	...	...	...	...	...
75 - 79	2 161 385	992 382	1 169 003	...	...	...	...	...	...
80 - 84	1 598 244	688 324	909 920	...	...	...	...	...	...
85 - 89	984 482	375 094	609 388	...	...	...	...	...	...
90 - 94	447 066	141 261	305 805	...	...	...	...	...	...
95 - 99	103 104	24 333	78 771	...	...	...	...	...	...
100 +	14 776	2 309	12 467	...	...	...	...	...	...
OCEANIA - OCÉANIE									
American Samoa - Samoas américaines[30]									
1 IV 2010 (CDJC)									
Total	55 519	28 164	27 355	...	...	...	...	...	...
0 - 4	6 611	3 417	3 194	...	...	...	...	...	...
5 - 9	6 535	3 470	3 065	...	...	...	...	...	...
10 - 14	6 279	3 214	3 065	...	...	...	...	...	...
15 - 19	6 296	3 218	3 078	...	...	...	...	...	...
20 - 24	3 891	1 944	1 947	...	...	...	...	...	...
25 - 29	3 324	1 670	1 654	...	...	...	...	...	...
30 - 34	3 510	1 726	1 784	...	...	...	...	...	...

7. Population by age, sex and urban/rural residence: latest available year, 2007 - 2016
Population selon l'âge, le sexe et la résidence, urbaine/rurale : dernière année disponible, 2007 - 2016 (continued - suite)

Continent, country or area, date, code[a] and age (in years) / Continent, pays ou zone, date, code[a] et âge (en années)	Total			Urban - Urbaine			Rural - Rurale		
	Both sexes Les deux sexes	Male Masculin	Female Féminin	Both sexes Les deux sexes	Male Masculin	Female Féminin	Both sexes Les deux sexes	Male Masculin	Female Féminin
OCEANIA - OCÉANIE									
American Samoa - Samoas américaines[30]									
1 IV 2010 (CDJC)									
35 - 39	3 609	1 845	1 764	...	...	...	...	...	...
40 - 44	3 600	1 793	1 807	...	...	...	...	...	...
45 - 49	3 389	1 673	1 716	...	...	...	...	...	...
50 - 54	2 679	1 335	1 344	...	...	...	...	...	...
55 - 59	2 049	1 011	1 038	...	...	...	...	...	...
60 - 64	1 480	755	725	...	...	...	...	...	...
65 - 69	960	500	460	...	...	...	...	...	...
70 - 74	654	321	333	...	...	...	...	...	...
75 - 79	337	155	182	...	...	...	...	...	...
80 - 84	206	76	130	...	...	...	...	...	...
85 +	110	41	69	...	...	...	...	...	...
Australia - Australie[12]									
1 VII 2015 (ESDJ)									
Total	23 777 777	11 826 927	11 950 850	20 386 802	10 089 517	10 297 285	3 390 975	1 737 410	1 653 565
0	303 398	155 736	147 662	265 801	136 365	129 436	37 597	19 371	18 226
1 - 4	1 236 824	635 262	601 562	1 071 499	549 927	521 572	165 325	85 335	79 990
5 - 9	1 515 408	778 195	737 213	1 287 020	660 656	626 364	228 388	117 539	110 849
10 - 14	1 419 728	729 063	690 665	1 195 640	613 772	581 868	224 088	115 291	108 797
15 - 19	1 475 790	757 232	718 558	1 268 043	648 863	619 180	207 747	108 369	99 378
20 - 24	1 660 449	852 796	807 653	1 496 791	765 121	731 670	163 658	87 675	75 983
25 - 29	1 758 903	884 754	874 149	1 587 288	795 769	791 519	171 615	88 985	82 630
30 - 34	1 750 088	876 234	873 854	1 564 200	781 855	782 345	185 888	94 379	91 509
35 - 39	1 575 414	785 187	790 227	1 386 543	690 059	696 484	188 871	95 128	93 743
40 - 44	1 654 548	819 140	835 408	1 429 772	705 877	723 895	224 776	113 263	111 513
45 - 49	1 563 582	774 137	789 445	1 332 574	656 709	675 865	231 008	117 428	113 580
50 - 54	1 557 666	768 969	788 697	1 306 750	640 542	666 208	250 916	128 427	122 489
55 - 59	1 450 666	714 301	736 365	1 199 467	584 650	614 817	251 199	129 651	121 548
60 - 64	1 286 293	632 658	653 635	1 052 687	510 837	541 850	233 606	121 821	111 785
65 - 69	1 153 357	570 325	583 032	939 247	457 802	481 445	214 110	112 523	101 587
70 - 74	857 786	419 294	438 492	698 380	336 372	362 008	159 406	82 922	76 484
75 - 79	634 218	302 376	331 842	523 842	245 403	278 439	110 376	56 973	53 403
80 - 84	451 616	198 303	253 313	379 410	164 076	215 334	72 206	34 227	37 979
85 - 89	302 281	119 608	182 673	257 147	100 231	156 916	45 134	19 377	25 757
90 - 94	134 866	44 163	90 703	115 561	37 109	78 452	19 305	7 054	12 251
95 - 99	30 457	8 178	22 279	25 515	6 675	18 840	4 942	1 503	3 439
100 +	4 439	1 016	3 423	3 625	847	2 778	814	169	645
1 VII 2016 (ESDJ)									
Total	24 128 876	11 990 972	12 137 904	...	...	...	...	...	...
0	314 988	161 866	153 122	...	...	...	...	...	...
1 - 4	1 251 341	642 835	608 506	...	...	...	...	...	...
5 - 9	1 530 266	785 601	744 665	...	...	...	...	...	...
10 - 14	1 442 650	740 776	701 874	...	...	...	...	...	...
15 - 19	1 484 548	760 520	724 028	...	...	...	...	...	...
20 - 24	1 679 103	862 464	816 639	...	...	...	...	...	...
25 - 29	1 781 137	893 426	887 711	...	...	...	...	...	...
30 - 34	1 784 840	890 258	894 582	...	...	...	...	...	...
35 - 39	1 612 008	803 442	808 566	...	...	...	...	...	...
40 - 44	1 620 741	802 585	818 156	...	...	...	...	...	...
45 - 49	1 609 197	795 049	814 148	...	...	...	...	...	...
50 - 54	1 542 633	760 975	781 658	...	...	...	...	...	...
55 - 59	1 478 944	726 328	752 616	...	...	...	...	...	...
60 - 64	1 313 614	644 915	668 699	...	...	...	...	...	...
65 - 69	1 184 495	583 778	600 717	...	...	...	...	...	...
70 - 74	898 970	439 239	459 731	...	...	...	...	...	...
75 - 79	654 716	313 765	340 951	...	...	...	...	...	...
80 - 84	460 094	203 521	256 573	...	...	...	...	...	...
85 - 89	307 536	122 742	184 794	...	...	...	...	...	...
90 - 94	138 980	46 524	92 456	...	...	...	...	...	...
95 - 99	33 207	9 165	24 042	...	...	...	...	...	...
100 +	4 868	1 198	3 670	...	...	...	...	...	...

7. Population by age, sex and urban/rural residence: latest available year, 2007 - 2016
Population selon l'âge, le sexe et la résidence, urbaine/rurale : dernière année disponible, 2007 - 2016 (continued - suite)

Continent, country or area, date, code[a] and age (in years) / Continent, pays ou zone, date, code[a] et âge (en années)	Total			Urban - Urbaine			Rural - Rurale		
	Both sexes Les deux sexes	Male Masculin	Female Féminin	Both sexes Les deux sexes	Male Masculin	Female Féminin	Both sexes Les deux sexes	Male Masculin	Female Féminin
OCEANIA - OCÉANIE									
Cook Islands - Îles Cook[88]									
1 XII 2011 (CDFC)									
Total	17 794	8 815	8 979	...	...	...	...	...	...
0 - 4	1 584	806	778	...	...	...	...	...	...
5 - 9	1 539	768	771	...	...	...	...	...	...
10 - 14	1 504	794	710	...	...	...	...	...	...
15 - 19	1 495	768	727	...	...	...	...	...	...
20 - 24	1 273	611	662	...	...	...	...	...	...
25 - 29	1 263	590	673	...	...	...	...	...	...
30 - 34	1 122	534	588	...	...	...	...	...	...
35 - 39	1 179	543	636	...	...	...	...	...	...
40 - 44	1 252	605	647	...	...	...	...	...	...
45 - 49	1 282	636	646	...	...	...	...	...	...
50 - 54	1 059	534	525	...	...	...	...	...	...
55 - 59	863	430	433	...	...	...	...	...	...
60 - 64	749	394	355	...	...	...	...	...	...
65 - 69	649	333	316	...	...	...	...	...	...
70 - 74	496	251	245	...	...	...	...	...	...
75 - 79	285	130	155	...	...	...	...	...	...
80 +	200	88	112	...	...	...	...	...	...
Fiji - Fidji									
16 IX 2007 (CDFC)									
Total	837 271	427 176	410 095	424 846	212 454	212 392	412 425	214 722	197 703
0 - 4	82 718	42 835	39 883	39 209	20 264	18 945	43 509	22 571	20 938
5 - 9	78 019	40 441	37 578	35 981	18 528	17 453	42 038	21 913	20 125
10 - 14	82 384	42 369	40 015	38 916	19 790	19 126	43 468	22 579	20 889
15 - 19	79 518	40 818	38 700	42 458	21 051	21 407	37 060	19 767	17 293
20 - 24	80 352	41 325	39 027	45 837	22 896	22 941	34 515	18 429	16 086
25 - 29	73 487	37 390	36 097	40 669	20 260	20 409	32 818	17 130	15 688
30 - 34	63 535	32 825	30 710	33 612	17 017	16 595	29 923	15 808	14 115
35 - 39	56 552	28 778	27 774	29 288	14 674	14 614	27 264	14 104	13 160
40 - 44	56 274	28 598	27 676	28 147	14 058	14 089	28 127	14 540	13 587
45 - 49	50 322	25 835	24 487	25 556	12 780	12 776	24 766	13 055	11 711
50 - 54	40 009	20 215	19 794	20 581	10 118	10 463	19 428	10 097	9 331
55 - 59	31 161	15 735	15 426	15 667	7 715	7 952	15 494	8 020	7 474
60 - 64	24 120	11 956	12 164	11 655	5 647	6 008	12 465	6 309	6 156
65 - 69	16 808	8 098	8 710	7 597	3 509	4 088	9 211	4 589	4 622
70 - 74	10 110	4 716	5 394	4 360	1 887	2 473	5 750	2 829	2 921
75 +	11 902	5 242	6 660	5 313	2 260	3 053	6 589	2 982	3 607
75 - 79	6 138	2 811	3 327	...	...	...	...	...	...
80 - 84	3 236	1 376	1 860	...	...	...	...	...	...
85 - 89	1 638	702	936	...	...	...	...	...	...
90 - 94	572	212	360	...	...	...	...	...	...
95 +	318	141	177	...	...	...	...	...	...
31 XII 2008 (ESDF)									
Total	842 621	430 418	412 203	...	...	...	...	...	...
0	16 852	8 808	8 044	...	...	...	...	...	...
1 - 4	67 137	34 726	32 411	...	...	...	...	...	...
5 - 9	77 959	40 425	37 534	...	...	...	...	...	...
10 - 14	80 218	41 292	38 926	...	...	...	...	...	...
15 - 19	79 267	40 768	38 499	...	...	...	...	...	...
20 - 24	78 985	40 668	38 317	...	...	...	...	...	...
25 - 29	73 799	37 723	36 076	...	...	...	...	...	...
30 - 34	64 585	33 343	31 242	...	...	...	...	...	...
35 - 39	57 517	29 413	28 104	...	...	...	...	...	...
40 - 44	55 676	28 341	27 335	...	...	...	...	...	...
45 - 49	50 813	25 955	24 858	...	...	...	...	...	...
50 - 54	41 579	21 095	20 484	...	...	...	...	...	...
55 - 59	32 329	16 348	15 981	...	...	...	...	...	...
60 - 64	24 662	12 199	12 463	...	...	...	...	...	...
65 - 69	17 754	8 588	9 166	...	...	...	...	...	...
70 - 74	10 865	5 131	5 734	...	...	...	...	...	...
75 +	12 624	5 595	7 029	...	...	...	...	...	...

Continent, country or area, date, code[a] and age (in years) / Continent, pays ou zone, date, code[a] et âge (en années)	Total			Urban - Urbaine			Rural - Rurale		
	Both sexes Les deux sexes	Male Masculin	Female Féminin	Both sexes Les deux sexes	Male Masculin	Female Féminin	Both sexes Les deux sexes	Male Masculin	Female Féminin
OCEANIA - OCÉANIE									
French Polynesia - Polynésie française									
1 I 2015 (ESDF)									
Total	271 796	138 447	133 349	...	...	...	...	...	...
0 - 4	21 691	10 938	10 753	...	...	...	...	...	...
5 - 9	21 973	11 252	10 721	...	...	...	...	...	...
10 - 14	22 896	11 732	11 164	...	...	...	...	...	...
15 - 19	22 653	11 795	10 858	...	...	...	...	...	...
20 - 24	22 850	11 623	11 227	...	...	...	...	...	...
25 - 29	21 204	10 534	10 670	...	...	...	...	...	...
30 - 34	20 789	10 380	10 409	...	...	...	...	...	...
35 - 39	19 482	9 864	9 618	...	...	...	...	...	...
40 - 44	20 216	10 302	9 914	...	...	...	...	...	...
45 - 49	19 623	10 189	9 434	...	...	...	...	...	...
50 - 54	16 540	8 602	7 938	...	...	...	...	...	...
55 - 59	13 167	6 942	6 225	...	...	...	...	...	...
60 - 64	9 849	5 079	4 770	...	...	...	...	...	...
65 - 69	7 193	3 653	3 540	...	...	...	...	...	...
70 - 74	5 309	2 699	2 610	...	...	...	...	...	...
75 - 79	3 346	1 565	1 781	...	...	...	...	...	...
80 +	3 015	1 298	1 717	...	...	...	...	...	...
Guam[30]									
1 VII 2016 (ESDJ)									
Total	162 742	82 420	80 322	...	...	...	...	...	...
0	2 700	1 389	1 311	...	...	...	...	...	...
1 - 4	10 765	5 537	5 228	...	...	...	...	...	...
5 - 9	13 463	6 922	6 541	...	...	...	...	...	...
10 - 14	13 676	7 033	6 643	...	...	...	...	...	...
15 - 19	14 301	7 484	6 817	...	...	...	...	...	...
20 - 24	13 519	6 961	6 558	...	...	...	...	...	...
25 - 29	12 152	6 119	6 033	...	...	...	...	...	...
30 - 34	10 591	5 335	5 256	...	...	...	...	...	...
35 - 39	9 810	4 935	4 875	...	...	...	...	...	...
40 - 44	10 165	5 131	5 034	...	...	...	...	...	...
45 - 49	10 553	5 477	5 076	...	...	...	...	...	...
50 - 54	10 341	5 338	5 003	...	...	...	...	...	...
55 - 59	8 638	4 408	4 230	...	...	...	...	...	...
60 - 64	7 016	3 504	3 512	...	...	...	...	...	...
65 - 69	5 765	2 816	2 949	...	...	...	...	...	...
70 - 74	3 572	1 707	1 865	...	...	...	...	...	...
75 - 79	2 804	1 229	1 575	...	...	...	...	...	...
80 - 84	1 747	683	1 064	...	...	...	...	...	...
85 - 89	806	307	499	...	...	...	...	...	...
90 - 94	284	89	195	...	...	...	...	...	...
95 - 99	67	15	52	...	...	...	...	...	...
100 +	7	1	6	...	...	...	...	...	...
Kiribati									
10 X 2010 (CDFC)									
Total	103 058	50 796	52 262	50 182	24 233	25 949	52 876	26 563	26 313
0 - 4	13 992	7 126	6 866	6 934	3 563	3 371	7 058	3 563	3 495
5 - 9	11 026	5 739	5 287	4 822	2 504	2 318	6 204	3 235	2 969
10 - 14	12 166	6 198	5 968	5 363	2 693	2 670	6 803	3 505	3 298
15 - 19	10 926	5 582	5 344	5 713	2 846	2 867	5 213	2 736	2 477
20 - 24	10 366	5 242	5 124	5 658	2 763	2 895	4 708	2 479	2 229
25 - 29	8 416	4 070	4 346	4 413	2 035	2 378	4 003	2 035	1 968
30 - 34	6 721	3 223	3 498	3 389	1 624	1 765	3 332	1 599	1 733
35 - 39	5 625	2 682	2 943	2 767	1 304	1 463	2 858	1 378	1 480
40 - 44	6 116	2 908	3 208	2 803	1 302	1 501	3 313	1 606	1 707
45 - 49	5 234	2 519	2 715	2 479	1 137	1 342	2 755	1 382	1 373
50 - 54	3 892	1 813	2 079	1 897	855	1 042	1 995	958	1 037
55 - 59	2 927	1 349	1 578	1 437	627	810	1 490	722	768
60 - 64	1 985	919	1 066	922	396	526	1 063	523	540
65 - 69	1 520	642	878	700	278	422	820	364	456
70 - 74	1 108	428	680	438	161	277	670	267	403
75 - 79	637	223	414	264	89	175	373	134	239

Continent, country or area, date, code[a] and age (in years) Continent, pays ou zone, date, code[a] et âge (en années)	Total			Urban - Urbaine			Rural - Rurale		
	Both sexes Les deux sexes	Male Masculin	Female Féminin	Both sexes Les deux sexes	Male Masculin	Female Féminin	Both sexes Les deux sexes	Male Masculin	Female Féminin
OCEANIA - OCÉANIE									
Kiribati									
10 X 2010 (CDFC)									
80 - 84	272	97	175	119	41	78	153	56	97
85 - 89	89	25	64	48	11	37	41	14	27
90 - 94	29	9	20	15	4	11	14	5	9
95 +	11	2	9	1	-	1	10	2	8
Marshall Islands - Îles Marshall[89]									
1 VII 2010 (ESDF)									
Total	54 305	27 843	26 462	...	...	...	...	...	...
0 - 4	7 899	4 053	3 846	...	...	...	...	...	...
5 - 9	7 131	3 660	3 470	...	...	...	...	...	...
10 - 14	7 207	3 732	3 475	...	...	...	...	...	...
15 - 19	6 120	3 126	2 993	...	...	...	...	...	...
20 - 24	6 347	3 310	3 038	...	...	...	...	...	...
25 - 29	4 808	2 478	2 330	...	...	...	...	...	...
30 - 34	2 761	1 389	1 372	...	...	...	...	...	...
35 - 39	2 128	1 071	1 058	...	...	...	...	...	...
40 - 44	2 039	1 043	996	...	...	...	...	...	...
45 - 49	2 023	1 025	998	...	...	...	...	...	...
50 - 54	1 814	878	936	...	...	...	...	...	...
55 - 59	1 592	854	737	...	...	...	...	...	...
60 - 64	1 089	573	516	...	...	...	...	...	...
65 - 69	572	299	273	...	...	...	...	...	...
70 - 74	361	165	196	...	...	...	...	...	...
75 +	412	184	228	...	...	...	...	...	...
Micronesia (Federated States of) - Micronésie (États fédérés de)[2]									
1 VII 2015 (ESDJ)									
Total	105 830	52 883	52 947	...	...	...	...	...	...
0 - 4	11 865	6 079	5 786	...	...	...	...	...	...
5 - 9	12 365	6 323	6 042	...	...	...	...	...	...
10 - 14	12 243	6 248	5 995	...	...	...	...	...	...
15 - 19	10 782	5 471	5 311	...	...	...	...	...	...
20 - 24	8 344	4 194	4 150	...	...	...	...	...	...
25 - 29	6 945	3 590	3 355	...	...	...	...	...	...
30 - 34	6 753	3 291	3 462	...	...	...	...	...	...
35 - 39	5 731	2 841	2 890	...	...	...	...	...	...
40 - 44	5 911	2 754	3 157	...	...	...	...	...	...
45 - 49	5 485	2 554	2 931	...	...	...	...	...	...
50 - 54	5 242	2 576	2 666	...	...	...	...	...	...
55 - 59	4 823	2 415	2 408	...	...	...	...	...	...
60 - 64	3 887	1 978	1 909	...	...	...	...	...	...
65 - 69	2 492	1 253	1 239	...	...	...	...	...	...
70 - 74	1 285	580	705	...	...	...	...	...	...
75 +	1 677	736	941	...	...	...	...	...	...
Nauru									
31 X 2011 (CDFC)									
Total	10 084	5 105	4 979	...	...	...	...	...	...
0 - 14	3 813	1 984	1 829	...	...	...	...	...	...
15 - 24	1 948	993	955	...	...	...	...	...	...
25 - 59	4 035	2 005	2 030	...	...	...	...	...	...
60 +	287	122	165	...	...	...	...	...	...
New Caledonia - Nouvelle-Calédonie									
1 I 2016 (ESDF)									
Total	274 579	138 197	136 382	...	...	...	...	...	...
0 - 4	20 533	10 427	10 106	...	...	...	...	...	...
5 - 9	21 396	11 081	10 315	...	...	...	...	...	...
10 - 14	21 459	10 895	10 564	...	...	...	...	...	...
15 - 19	23 141	11 801	11 340	...	...	...	...	...	...
20 - 24	19 476	10 082	9 394	...	...	...	...	...	...
25 - 29	20 848	10 380	10 468	...	...	...	...	...	...
30 - 34	21 103	10 603	10 500	...	...	...	...	...	...

Continent, country or area, date, code[a] and age (in years) / Continent, pays ou zone, date, code[a] et âge (en années)	Total			Urban - Urbaine			Rural - Rurale		
	Both sexes Les deux sexes	Male Masculin	Female Féminin	Both sexes Les deux sexes	Male Masculin	Female Féminin	Both sexes Les deux sexes	Male Masculin	Female Féminin
OCEANIA - OCÉANIE									
New Caledonia - Nouvelle-Calédonie									
1 I 2016 (ESDF)									
35 - 39	20 184	9 987	10 197	...	...	...	...	...	...
40 - 44	21 450	10 793	10 657	...	...	...	...	...	...
45 - 49	19 288	9 603	9 685	...	...	...	...	...	...
50 - 54	17 115	8 638	8 477	...	...	...	...	...	...
55 - 59	13 339	6 670	6 669	...	...	...	...	...	...
60 - 64	10 867	5 576	5 291	...	...	...	...	...	...
65 - 69	8 875	4 520	4 355	...	...	...	...	...	...
70 - 74	6 310	3 156	3 154	...	...	...	...	...	...
75 - 79	4 486	2 082	2 404	...	...	...	...	...	...
80 - 84	2 700	1 188	1 512	...	...	...	...	...	...
85 - 89	1 435	543	892	...	...	...	...	...	...
90 - 94	450	129	321	...	...	...	...	...	...
95 +	124	43	81	...	...	...	...	...	...
New Zealand - Nouvelle-Zélande[90]									
1 VII 2016 (ESDJ)									
Total	4 692 700	2 308 800	2 383 900	4 055 800[91]	1 983 400[91]	2 072 400[91]	636 200[91]	325 000[91]	311 200[91]
0	59 240	30 490	28 750	51 680[91]	26 630[91]	25 040[91]	7 560[91]	3 860[91]	3 710[91]
1 - 4	245 290	125 950	119 340	213 810[91]	109 820[91]	103 990[91]	31 470[91]	16 120[91]	15 340[91]
5 - 9	322 270	165 580	156 690	275 520[91]	141 530[91]	133 980[91]	46 750[91]	24 040[91]	22 710[91]
10 - 14	294 330	150 480	143 850	248 920[91]	127 130[91]	121 790[91]	45 390[91]	23 340[91]	22 050[91]
15 - 19	318 380	163 850	154 530	277 400[91]	142 090[91]	135 310[91]	40 960[91]	21 740[91]	19 220[91]
20 - 24	348 800	182 170	166 630	316 440[91]	164 140[91]	152 300[91]	32 340[91]	18 020[91]	14 330[91]
25 - 29	338 240	169 830	168 410	307 850[91]	154 110[91]	153 740[91]	30 370[91]	15 710[91]	14 660[91]
30 - 34	298 970	144 780	154 190	269 390[91]	130 100[91]	139 290[91]	29 550[91]	14 670[91]	14 880[91]
35 - 39	279 020	133 860	145 160	246 290[91]	117 930[91]	128 360[91]	32 700[91]	15 920[91]	16 780[91]
40 - 44	301 510	143 920	157 590	259 470[91]	123 370[91]	136 100[91]	42 000[91]	20 520[91]	21 480[91]
45 - 49	318 340	151 990	166 350	269 650[91]	128 170[91]	141 480[91]	48 660[91]	23 800[91]	24 850[91]
50 - 54	316 910	153 200	163 710	264 670[91]	127 180[91]	137 490[91]	52 170[91]	25 980[91]	26 190[91]
55 - 59	295 960	143 250	152 710	243 710[91]	117 000[91]	126 710[91]	52 160[91]	26 190[91]	25 970[91]
60 - 64	257 060	124 650	132 410	211 150[91]	101 060[91]	110 090[91]	45 810[91]	23 530[91]	22 290[91]
65 - 69	233 360	114 020	119 340	192 510[91]	92 680[91]	99 840[91]	40 760[91]	21 290[91]	19 470[91]
70 - 74	169 960	81 910	88 050	143 000[91]	67 580[91]	75 420[91]	26 890[91]	14 290[91]	12 600[91]
75 - 79	127 960	59 890	68 070	111 300[91]	51 060[91]	60 240[91]	16 630[91]	8 810[91]	7 820[91]
80 - 84	84 080	37 680	46 400	75 730[91]	33 280[91]	42 450[91]	8 330[91]	4 380[91]	3 950[91]
85 +	83 050	31 330	51 720	77 300[91]	28 540[91]	48 770[91]	5 730[91]	2 780[91]	2 950[91]
Niue - Nioué									
1 VII 2010 (ESDJ)									
Total	1 496	754[92]	740[92]	...	...	...	...	...	...
0 - 4	135	69[92]	64[92]	...	...	...	...	...	...
5 - 9	134	58	76	...	...	...	...	...	...
10 - 14	116	60	56	...	...	...	...	...	...
15 - 19	124	79	45	...	...	...	...	...	...
20 - 24	100	50	50	...	...	...	...	...	...
25 - 29	90	38	52	...	...	...	...	...	...
30 - 34	71	39	32	...	...	...	...	...	...
35 - 39	85	45	40	...	...	...	...	...	...
40 - 44	101	55	46	...	...	...	...	...	...
45 - 49	92	42	50	...	...	...	...	...	...
50 - 54	107	58	49	...	...	...	...	...	...
55 - 59	89	42	47	...	...	...	...	...	...
60 - 64	70	34	36	...	...	...	...	...	...
65 - 69	75	37	38	...	...	...	...	...	...
70 - 74	53	23	30	...	...	...	...	...	...
75 +	54	25	29	...	...	...	...	...	...
Norfolk Island - Île Norfolk									
9 VIII 2011 (CDFC)									
Total	2 302	1 082	1 220	...	...	...	...	...	...
0 - 4	106	53	53	...	...	...	...	...	...
5 - 9	123	63	60	...	...	...	...	...	...
10 - 14	132	69	63	...	...	...	...	...	...

Continent, country or area, date, code[a] and age (in years) / Continent, pays ou zone, date, code[a] et âge (en années)	Total			Urban - Urbaine			Rural - Rurale		
	Both sexes Les deux sexes	Male Masculin	Female Féminin	Both sexes Les deux sexes	Male Masculin	Female Féminin	Both sexes Les deux sexes	Male Masculin	Female Féminin
OCEANIA - OCÉANIE									
Norfolk Island - Île Norfolk									
9 VIII 2011 (CDFC)									
15 - 19	73	35	38	...	...	...	...	...	...
20 - 24	41	20	21	...	...	...	...	...	...
25 - 29	60	19	41	...	...	...	...	...	...
30 - 34	100	48	52	...	...	...	...	...	...
35 - 39	127	56	71	...	...	...	...	...	...
40 - 44	146	64	82	...	...	...	...	...	...
45 - 49	167	81	86	...	...	...	...	...	...
50 - 54	180	86	94	...	...	...	...	...	...
55 - 59	232	103	129	...	...	...	...	...	...
60 - 64	262	120	142	...	...	...	...	...	...
65 - 69	205	99	106	...	...	...	...	...	...
70 - 74	142	70	72	...	...	...	...	...	...
75 - 79	96	49	47	...	...	...	...	...	...
80 - 84	58	24	34	...	...	...	...	...	...
85 +	52	23	29	...	...	...	...	...	...
Northern Mariana Islands - Îles Mariannes septentrionales									
1 VII 2011 (ESDF)									
Total	46 050	22 153	23 897	...	...	...	...	...	...
0 - 4	4 852	2 495	2 357	...	...	...	...	...	...
5 - 9	3 622	1 883	1 739	...	...	...	...	...	...
10 - 14	3 500	1 971	1 529	...	...	...	...	...	...
15 - 19	3 802	2 121	1 681	...	...	...	...	...	...
20 - 24	3 398	1 607	1 791	...	...	...	...	...	...
25 - 29	3 831	1 050	2 781	...	...	...	...	...	...
30 - 34	3 696	1 008	2 688	...	...	...	...	...	...
35 - 39	3 211	1 550	1 661	...	...	...	...	...	...
40 - 44	3 584	1 858	1 726	...	...	...	...	...	...
45 - 49	3 738	1 967	1 771	...	...	...	...	...	...
50 - 54	3 441	1 824	1 617	...	...	...	...	...	...
55 - 59	2 270	1 260	1 010	...	...	...	...	...	...
60 - 64	1 440	769	671	...	...	...	...	...	...
65 - 69	794	366	428	...	...	...	...	...	...
70 - 74	416	248	168	...	...	...	...	...	...
75 - 79	239	101	138	...	...	...	...	...	...
80 - 84	147	54	93	...	...	...	...	...	...
85 - 89	53	17	36	...	...	...	...	...	...
90 - 94	14	3	11	...	...	...	...	...	...
95 - 99	1	1	-	...	...	...	...	...	...
100 +	1	-	1	...	...	...	...	...	...
Palau - Palaos									
13 IV 2015 (CDJC)									
Total	17 661	9 433	8 228	14 209	7 620	6 589	3 452	1 813	1 639
0 - 4	1 200	653	547	962	528	434	238	125	113
5 - 9	1 219	614	605	932	483	449	287	131	156
10 - 14	1 209	636	573	916	489	427	293	147	146
15 - 19	1 201	624	577	975	495	480	226	129	97
20 - 24	1 195	687	508	1 018	587	431	177	100	77
25 - 29	1 217	694	523	1 041	581	460	176	113	63
30 - 34	1 338	759	579	1 163	661	502	175	98	77
35 - 39	1 420	813	607	1 215	701	514	205	112	93
40 - 44	1 501	861	640	1 235	715	520	266	146	120
45 - 49	1 538	820	718	1 248	657	591	290	163	127
50 - 54	1 363	708	655	1 067	549	518	296	159	137
55 - 59	1 126	605	521	856	459	397	270	146	124
60 - 64	851	432	419	641	318	323	210	114	96
65 - 69	554	271	283	414	202	212	140	69	71
70 - 74	314	137	177	233	106	127	81	31	50
75 +	415	119	296	293	89	204	122	30	92

Continent, country or area, date, code[a] and age (in years) / Continent, pays ou zone, date, code[a] et âge (en années)	Total			Urban - Urbaine			Rural - Rurale		
	Both sexes Les deux sexes	Male Masculin	Female Féminin	Both sexes Les deux sexes	Male Masculin	Female Féminin	Both sexes Les deux sexes	Male Masculin	Female Féminin
OCEANIA - OCÉANIE									
Papua New Guinea - Papouasie-Nouvelle-Guinée[93]									
1 VII 2016 (ESDF)									
Total	8 151 300	...	...	...	...	...	...	...	...
0 - 14	2 970 800	...	...	...	...	...	...	...	...
15 - 24	1 641 400	...	...	...	...	...	...	...	...
25 - 59	3 177 700	...	...	...	...	...	...	...	...
60 +	361 400	...	...	...	...	...	...	...	...
Pitcairn									
31 XII 2013 (CDJC)									
Total	49	23	26	...	...	...	...	...	...
0 - 17	8	3	5	...	...	...	...	...	...
18 - 40	7	4	3	...	...	...	...	...	...
41 - 64	24	13	11	...	...	...	...	...	...
65 +	10	3	7	...	...	...	...	...	...
Samoa									
7 XI 2011 (CDFC)									
Total	187 820	96 990	90 830	...	...	...	...	...	...
0 - 4	26 829	13 953	12 876	...	...	...	...	...	...
5 - 9	23 044	11 899	11 145	...	...	...	...	...	...
10 - 14	22 017	11 497	10 520	...	...	...	...	...	...
15 - 19	19 814	10 391	9 423	...	...	...	...	...	...
20 - 24	14 833	7 700	7 133	...	...	...	...	...	...
25 - 29	12 767	6 601	6 166	...	...	...	...	...	...
30 - 34	11 543	5 945	5 598	...	...	...	...	...	...
35 - 39	10 877	5 735	5 142	...	...	...	...	...	...
40 - 44	10 436	5 602	4 834	...	...	...	...	...	...
45 - 49	8 887	4 574	4 313	...	...	...	...	...	...
50 - 54	7 576	3 966	3 610	...	...	...	...	...	...
55 - 59	5 904	3 007	2 897	...	...	...	...	...	...
60 - 64	3 978	2 002	1 976	...	...	...	...	...	...
65 - 69	3 374	1 605	1 769	...	...	...	...	...	...
70 - 74	2 557	1 187	1 370	...	...	...	...	...	...
75 +	3 354	1 302	2 052	...	...	...	...	...	...
Unknown - Inconnu	30	24	6	...	...	...	...	...	...
Solomon Islands - Îles Salomon									
22 XI 2009 (CDFC)									
Total	515 870	264 455	251 415	102 030	53 596	48 434	413 840	210 859	202 981
0 - 4	76 227	39 728	36 499	12 500	6 573	5 927	63 727	33 155	30 572
5 - 9	71 126	36 974	34 152	11 328	5 853	5 475	59 798	31 121	28 677
10 - 14	61 931	32 562	29 369	10 354	5 382	4 972	51 577	27 180	24 397
15 - 19	51 212	26 189	25 023	10 995	5 525	5 470	40 217	20 664	19 553
20 - 24	45 419	22 399	23 020	12 344	6 360	5 984	33 075	16 039	17 036
25 - 29	42 674	20 794	21 880	11 160	5 696	5 464	31 514	15 098	16 416
30 - 34	37 592	18 807	18 785	8 817	4 568	4 249	28 775	14 239	14 536
35 - 39	33 151	17 010	16 141	7 447	4 000	3 447	25 704	13 010	12 694
40 - 44	23 638	12 070	11 568	5 161	2 808	2 353	18 477	9 262	9 215
45 - 49	19 713	10 189	9 524	4 064	2 265	1 799	15 649	7 924	7 725
50 - 54	14 339	7 498	6 841	2 818	1 650	1 168	11 521	5 848	5 673
55 - 59	11 787	6 111	5 676	2 011	1 198	813	9 776	4 913	4 863
60 - 64	8 916	4 535	4 381	1 272	726	546	7 644	3 809	3 835
65 - 69	7 021	3 693	3 328	822	466	356	6 199	3 227	2 972
70 - 74	4 698	2 402	2 296	478	259	219	4 220	2 143	2 077
75 - 79	3 374	1 784	1 590	279	160	119	3 095	1 624	1 471
80 - 84	1 525	800	725	102	58	44	1 423	742	681
85 - 89	894	512	382	58	34	24	836	478	358
90 - 94	301	170	131	8	4	4	293	166	127
95 - 99	332	228	104	12	11	1	320	217	103
1 VII 2016 (ESDF)[2]									
Total	639 157	326 837	312 321	...	...	...	...	...	...
0 - 4	82 703	42 711	39 991	...	...	...	...	...	...
5 - 9	81 520	41 909	39 610	...	...	...	...	...	...
10 - 14	77 767	40 070	37 697	...	...	...	...	...	...

Continent, country or area, date, code[a] and age (in years) / Continent, pays ou zone, date, code[a] et âge (en années)	Total			Urban - Urbaine			Rural - Rurale		
	Both sexes Les deux sexes	Male Masculin	Female Féminin	Both sexes Les deux sexes	Male Masculin	Female Féminin	Both sexes Les deux sexes	Male Masculin	Female Féminin
OCEANIA - OCÉANIE									
Solomon Islands - Îles Salomon									
1 VII 2016 (ESDF)[2]									
15 - 19	66 515	34 402	32 113	...	...	...	...	...	...
20 - 24	55 366	28 680	26 686	...	...	...	...	...	...
25 - 29	50 791	26 295	24 496	...	...	...	...	...	...
30 - 34	46 260	23 747	22 513	...	...	...	...	...	...
35 - 39	40 288	20 145	20 143	...	...	...	...	...	...
40 - 44	35 557	17 576	17 981	...	...	...	...	...	...
45 - 49	27 774	13 886	13 888	...	...	...	...	...	...
50 - 54	21 417	10 777	10 639	...	...	...	...	...	...
55 - 59	16 180	8 209	7 971	...	...	...	...	...	...
60 - 64	12 376	6 255	6 120	...	...	...	...	...	...
65 - 69	9 499	4 648	4 851	...	...	...	...	...	...
70 - 74	6 878	3 409	3 468	...	...	...	...	...	...
75 - 79	4 390	2 176	2 214	...	...	...	...	...	...
80 +	3 877	1 939	1 938	...	...	...	...	...	...
Tokelau - Tokélaou									
18 X 2016 (CDFC)									
Total	1 285	652	633	...	...	...	...	...	...
0 - 4	139	74	65	...	...	...	...	...	...
5 - 9	150	75	75	...	...	...	...	...	...
10 - 14	137	72	65	...	...	...	...	...	...
15 - 19	116	63	53	...	...	...	...	...	...
20 - 24	93	54	39	...	...	...	...	...	...
25 - 29	86	39	47	...	...	...	...	...	...
30 - 34	79	36	43	...	...	...	...	...	...
35 - 39	62	35	27	...	...	...	...	...	...
40 - 44	75	35	40	...	...	...	...	...	...
45 - 49	81	41	40	...	...	...	...	...	...
50 - 54	63	27	36	...	...	...	...	...	...
55 - 59	53	33	20	...	...	...	...	...	...
60 - 64	54	31	23	...	...	...	...	...	...
65 - 69	37	14	23	...	...	...	...	...	...
70 - 74	25	14	11	...	...	...	...	...	...
75 +	35	9	26	...	...	...	...	...	...
Tonga[94]									
1 VII 2008 (ESDF)									
Total	103 647	52 972	50 673	...	...	...	...	...	...
0 - 4	11 970	6 164	5 806	...	...	...	...	...	...
5 - 9	11 419	5 910	5 508	...	...	...	...	...	...
10 - 14	11 968	6 212	5 756	...	...	...	...	...	...
15 - 19	11 383	6 060	5 323	...	...	...	...	...	...
20 - 24	10 612	5 573	5 040	...	...	...	...	...	...
25 - 29	8 609	4 406	4 204	...	...	...	...	...	...
30 - 34	5 874	2 955	2 919	...	...	...	...	...	...
35 - 39	5 397	2 718	2 680	...	...	...	...	...	...
40 - 44	5 250	2 661	2 590	...	...	...	...	...	...
45 - 49	4 471	2 186	2 285	...	...	...	...	...	...
50 - 54	3 914	1 867	2 047	...	...	...	...	...	...
55 - 59	3 294	1 556	1 737	...	...	...	...	...	...
60 - 64	2 844	1 355	1 489	...	...	...	...	...	...
65 - 69	2 482	1 243	1 239	...	...	...	...	...	...
70 - 74	1 896	981	915	...	...	...	...	...	...
75 +	2 263	1 127	1 136	...	...	...	...	...	...
Tuvalu[93]									
1 VII 2016 (ESDF)									
Total	10 100	...	...	...	...	...	...	...	...
0 - 14	3 200	...	...	...	...	...	...	...	...
15 - 24	1 900	...	...	...	...	...	...	...	...
25 - 59	4 100	...	...	...	...	...	...	...	...
60 +	1 000	...	...	...	...	...	...	...	...

Continent, country or area, date, code[a] and age (in years) / Continent, pays ou zone, date, code[a] et âge (en années)	Total			Urban - Urbaine			Rural - Rurale		
	Both sexes Les deux sexes	Male Masculin	Female Féminin	Both sexes Les deux sexes	Male Masculin	Female Féminin	Both sexes Les deux sexes	Male Masculin	Female Féminin
OCEANIA - OCÉANIE									
Vanuatu									
16 XI 2009 (CDJC)									
Total	234 023	119 091	114 932	57 195	29 618	27 577	176 828	89 473	87 355
0 - 4	33 367	17 310	16 057	7 224	3 828	3 396	26 143	13 482	12 661
5 - 9	29 685	15 455	14 230	5 591	2 850	2 741	24 094	12 605	11 489
10 - 14	27 921	14 762	13 159	5 250	2 755	2 495	22 671	12 007	10 664
15 - 19	23 882	12 027	11 855	6 460	3 122	3 338	17 422	8 905	8 517
20 - 24	21 541	10 415	11 126	7 186	3 606	3 580	14 355	6 809	7 546
25 - 29	18 415	9 124	9 291	5 542	2 937	2 605	12 873	6 187	6 686
30 - 34	15 693	7 790	7 903	4 517	2 300	2 217	11 176	5 490	5 686
35 - 39	14 171	7 076	7 095	3 844	1 965	1 879	10 327	5 111	5 216
40 - 44	11 523	5 814	5 709	3 242	1 710	1 532	8 281	4 104	4 177
45 - 49	10 241	5 066	5 175	2 817	1 474	1 343	7 424	3 592	3 832
50 - 54	7 415	3 789	3 626	1 923	1 036	887	5 492	2 753	2 739
55 - 59	6 363	3 261	3 102	1 495	845	650	4 868	2 416	2 452
60 - 64	4 319	2 192	2 127	826	455	371	3 493	1 737	1 756
65 - 69	3 826	2 054	1 772	590	355	235	3 236	1 699	1 537
70 +	5 661	2 956	2 705	688	380	308	4 973	2 576	2 397
7 XI 2016 (CDFC)									
Total	272 459	138 265	134 194	...	...	...	...	...	...
0 - 4	38 936	20 172	18 764	...	...	...	...	...	...
5 - 9	37 148	19 276	17 872	...	...	...	...	...	...
10 - 14	29 846	15 560	14 286	...	...	...	...	...	...
15 - 19	25 902	13 207	12 695	...	...	...	...	...	...
20 - 24	24 862	11 738	13 124	...	...	...	...	...	...
25 - 29	23 031	10 986	12 045	...	...	...	...	...	...
30 - 34	18 067	8 909	9 158	...	...	...	...	...	...
35 - 39	16 233	8 148	8 085	...	...	...	...	...	...
40 - 44	13 251	6 726	6 525	...	...	...	...	...	...
45 - 49	11 833	6 125	5 708	...	...	...	...	...	...
50 - 54	9 329	4 756	4 573	...	...	...	...	...	...
55 - 59	7 227	3 792	3 435	...	...	...	...	...	...
60 - 64	5 357	2 832	2 525	...	...	...	...	...	...
65 - 69	4 010	2 089	1 921	...	...	...	...	...	...
70 +	7 225	3 838	3 387	...	...	...	...	...	...
Unknown - Inconnu	202	111	91	...	...	...	...	...	...
Wallis and Futuna Islands - Îles Wallis et Futuna									
22 VII 2013 (CDFC)									
Total	12 197	5 927	6 270	...	...	...	...	...	...
0 - 4	997	507	490	...	...	...	...	...	...
5 - 9	1 136	560	576	...	...	...	...	...	...
10 - 14	1 297	687	610	...	...	...	...	...	...
15 - 19	1 168	615	553	...	...	...	...	...	...
20 - 24	583	257	326	...	...	...	...	...	...
25 - 29	600	266	334	...	...	...	...	...	...
30 - 34	719	315	404	...	...	...	...	...	...
35 - 39	864	398	466	...	...	...	...	...	...
40 - 44	922	434	488	...	...	...	...	...	...
45 - 49	762	354	408	...	...	...	...	...	...
50 - 54	761	344	417	...	...	...	...	...	...
55 - 59	669	352	317	...	...	...	...	...	...
60 - 64	571	310	261	...	...	...	...	...	...
65 - 69	462	238	224	...	...	...	...	...	...
70 - 74	309	153	156	...	...	...	...	...	...
75 - 79	201	82	119	...	...	...	...	...	...
80 - 84	111	35	76	...	...	...	...	...	...
85 - 89	50	17	33	...	...	...	...	...	...
90 - 94	15	3	12	...	...	...	...	...	...
95 +	-	-	-	...	...	...	...	...	...

FOOTNOTES - NOTES

Italics: estimates which are less reliable. - Italiques : estimations moins sûres.

* Provisional. - Données provisoires.

a 'Code' indicates the source of data, as follows:
CDFC - Census, de facto, complete tabulation
CDFS - Census, de facto, sample tabulation
CDJC - Census, de jure, complete tabulation
CDJS - Census, de jure, sample tabulation
SSDF - Sample survey, de facto
SSDJ - Sample survey, de jure
ESDF - Estimates, de facto
ESDJ - Estimates, de jure

Le 'Code' indique la source des données, comme suit :
CDFC - Recensement, population de fait, tabulation complète
CDFS - Recensement, population de fait, tabulation par sondage
CDJC - Recensement, population de droit, tabulation complète
CDJS - Recensement, population de droit, tabulation par sondage
SSDF - Enquête par sondage, population de fait
SSDJ - Enquête par sondage, population de droit
ESDF - Estimations, population de fait
ESDJ - Estimations, population de droit

[1] Data refer to population in housing units and collective living quarters only. - Correspond aux personnes qui vivent dans des unités d'habitation et dans des logements collectifs seulement.

[2] Data refer to national projections. - Les données se réfèrent aux projections nationales.

[3] Projections based on the 2013 Population Census. - Projections fondées sur le recensement de la population de 2013.

[4] Data based on the 2011 Census. - Données fondées sur le recensement de 2011.

[5] Unrevised data. - Les données n'ont pas été révisées.

[6] Projections based on the 2014 Population Census. - Projections fondées sur le recensement de la population de 2014.

[7] Data based on the 2010 Population Census. - Les données sont fondées sur le recensement de la population de 2010.

[8] Post-censal estimates based on the 2009 Population Census. - Les estimations post-censitaire fondées sur le recensement de la population de 2009.

[9] Data refer to Libyan nationals only. - Les données se raportent aux nationaux libyens seulement.

[10] Projections considering also the results of the 2009 Population Census results. - Projections en prennant en considération les résultats du recensement de la population de 2009.

[11] Excludes the islands of St. Brandon and Agalega. - Non compris les îles St. Brandon et Agalega.

[12] Based on the results of the 2011 Population Census. - Basé sur les résultats du recensement de la population de 2011.

[13] Projections based on the results of national survey on population and health conducted between 2010 and 2011, and especially population and housing census 2014. - Des projections de la population fondées sur les résultats de l'enquête nationale de la population et de la santé réalisée entre 2010 et 2011 et, surtout, du recensement général de la population et de l'habitat de 2014.

[14] Data refer to projections based on the 2011 Population Census. - Les données se réfèrent aux projections basées sur le recensement de la population de 2011.

[15] Projections based on the 2012 Population and Housing Census. - Projections fondées sur le recensement 2012 de la population et des logements.

[16] Data are projections based on the 2006 Population Census. - Projections fondées sur le recensement de la population de 2006.

[17] Projections based on the 2002 Population Census. - Projections fondées sur le recensement de la population de 2002.

[18] Data refers to resident population adjusted for the undercount of 18 per cent and including the institutional population. - Les données concernent la population résidente, y compris la population des institutions, et ont été ajustées pour tenir compte du sous-dénombrement estimé à 18 p. 100.

[19] Bermuda is 100 per cent urban. - 100 pour cent de la population des Bermudes est urbaine.

[20] Based on the national household survey of 2016. - D'après l'enquête nationale auprès des ménages de 2016.

[21] Postcensal estimates. - Estimations post censitaires.

[22] Estimates or projections based on the 2007 Population Census. - Estimations ou projections fondées sur le recensement de la population de 2007.

[23] Population statistics are compiled from registers. - Les statistiques de la population sont compilées à partir des registres.

[24] Excluding data for Saint Barthélémy and Saint Martin. - Non compris les données pour Saint Barthélémy et Saint Martin.

[25] Projections produced by l'Institut Haïtien de Statistique et d'Informatique (IHSI) and the Latin American and Caribbean Demographic Centre (CELADE) - Population Division of ECLAC. - Les données sont projections produits par l'Institut Haïtien de Statistique et d'Informatique (IHSI) et le centre démographique de l'Amérique latine et les Caraïbes - Division de la population de la CEPALC.

[26] Including an estimation of 1 334 585 persons corresponding to 448 195 housing units without information of the occupants. - Y compris une estimation de 1 334 585 personnes correspondant aux 448 195 unités d'habitation sans information sur les occupants.

[27] Including armed forces stationed in the area. Postcensal estimates. - Y compris les militaires en garnison sur le territoire. Estimations post censitaires.

[28] Population in households only. - Population dans les ménages seulement.

[29] Excluding U.S. Armed Forces overseas and civilian U.S. citizens whose usual place of residence is outside the United States. Postcensal estimates. - Non compris les militaires américains à l'étranger et les civils américains dont le lieu de résidence habituel est en dehors des États-Unis. Estimations post censitaires.

[30] Including armed forces stationed in the area. - Y compris les militaires en garnison sur le territoire.

[31] Projections based on the 2010 Population and Housing Census. - Projections fondées sur le recensement 2010 de la population et des logements.

[32] Data include persons in remote areas, military personnel outside the country, merchant seamen at sea, civilian seasonal workers outside the country, and other civilians outside the country, and exclude nomads, foreign military, civilian aliens temporarily in the country, transients on ships and Indian jungle tribes. Data refer to national projections. - Y compris les personnes vivant dans des régions éloignées, le personel militaire en dehors du pays, les marins marchands, les ouvriers saisonniers en dehors du pays, et autres civils en dehors du pays, et non compris les nomades, les militaires étrangers, les étrangers civils temporairement dans le pays, les transiteurs sur des bateaux et les Indiens de la jungle. Les données se réfèrent aux projections nationales.

[33] Data are revised projections taking into consideration also the results of the 2005 census. - Les données sont des projections révisées tenant compte également des résultats du recensement de 2005.

[34] Excludes nomadic Indian tribes. Data based on the 2010 Population Census. - Non compris les tribus d'Indiens nomades. Les données sont fondées sur le recensement de la population de 2010.

[35] A dispute exists between the governments of Argentina and the United Kingdom of Great Britain and Northern Ireland concerning sovereignty over the Falkland Islands (Malvinas). Excluding military personnel and their families, visitors and transients. - La souveraineté sur les îles Falkland (Malvinas) fait l'objet d'un différend entre le Gouvernement argentin et le Gouvernement du Royaume-Uni de Grande-Bretagne et d'Irlande du Nord. Non compris les militaires et leur familles, ni les visiteurs et transients.

[36] Estimates or projections considering also the results of the 2012 Population Census. - Estimations ou projections en prennant en considération les résultats du recensement de la population de 2012.

[37] Data refer to the settled population based on the 1979 Population Census and the latest household prelisting. The refugees of Afghanistan in Iran, Pakistan, and an estimated 1.5 million nomads, are not included. - Les données se rapportent à la population stationnaire sur la base du recensement de 1979 et du recensement préliminaire des logements le plus récent. Sont exclus les réfugiés d'Afghanistan en Iran et au Pakistan et les nomades estimés à 1,5 million.

[38] Including "Other Urban" (Total of Both Sexes-6094394, Male-3127003, Female-29673941). - Y compris "Autres citadins" (total des deux sexes 6 094 394; hommes : 3 127 003; femmes: 2 967 391).

[39] Data refer to projected figures based on the Population and Housing Census 2005 (district projection). - Les données se réfèrent aux projections basées sur le recensement de la population et de l'habitat de 2005 (projections locales).

[40] Excluding foreign diplomatic personnel and their dependants. Data based on the 2008 Population Census. - Non compris le personnel diplomatique étranger et les membres de leur famille les accompagnant. Données fondées sur le recensement de population de 2008.

[41] For statistical purposes, the data for China do not include those for the Hong Kong Special Administrative Region (Hong Kong SAR), Macao Special Administrative Region (Macao SAR) and Taiwan province of China. - Pour la présentation des statistiques, les données pour la Chine ne comprennent pas la Région Administrative Spéciale de Hong Kong (Hong Kong RAS), la Région Administrative Spéciale de Macao (Macao RAS) et Taïwan province de Chine.

⁴² Data exclude 2.3 million servicemen, 4.65 million persons with permanent resident status difficult to define, and 0.12 per cent undercount based on the post enumeration survey. - Les données ne comprennent pas 2,3 millions de militaires, 4,65 millions de personnes ayant le statut de résident permanent mais difficiles à définir, et des lacunes estimées à 0,12 pour cent sur la base de l'enquête de vérification du recensement.

⁴³ Because of rounding, totals are not in all cases the sum of the respective components. Data have been adjusted on the basis of the Population Census of 2010. - Les chiffres étant arrondis, les totaux ne correspondent pas toujours rigoureusement à la somme des composants respectifs. Les données ont été ajustées à partir des résultats du recensement de la population de 2010.

⁴⁴ Data refer to government controlled areas. - Les données se rapportent aux zones contrôlées par le Gouvernement.

⁴⁵ Based on the results of the 2014 Population Census. - D'après les résultats du recensement de la population de 2014.

⁴⁶ Includes data for the Indian-held part of Jammu and Kashmir, the final status of which has not yet been determined. - Y compris les données pour la partie du Jammu et du Cachemire occupée par l'Inde dont le statut définitif n'a pas encore été déterminé.

⁴⁷ Data are based on the publication: "Indonesia Population Projection 2010-2035" Data refer to the 2015 Intercensal Survey. - Les données sont basées sur la publication : << Indonesia Population Projection 2010-2035 >> Les données concernent l'enquête intercensitaire de 2015.

⁴⁸ Data refer to the Iranian Year which begins on 21 March and ends on 20 March of the following year. - Les données concernent l'année iranienne, qui commence le 21 mars et se termine le 20 mars de l'année suivante.

⁴⁹ Because of rounding, totals are not in all cases the sum of the respective components. Includes data for East Jerusalem and Israeli residents in certain other territories under occupation by Israeli military forces since June 1967. - Les chiffres étant arrondis, les totaux ne correspondent pas toujours rigoureusement à la somme des composants respectifs. Y compris les données pour Jérusalem-Est et les résidents israéliens dans certains autres territoires occupés depuis 1967 par les forces armées israéliennes.

⁵⁰ Excluding diplomatic personnel outside the country and foreign military and civilian personnel and their dependants stationed in the area. - Non compris le personnel diplomatique hors du pays ni les militaires et agents civils étrangers en poste sur le territoire et les membres de leur famille les accompagnant.

⁵¹ Because of rounding, totals are not in all cases the sum of the respective components. Estimates based on the complete counts of the 2015 Population Census - Les chiffres étant arrondis, les totaux ne correspondent pas toujours rigoureusement à la somme des composants respectifs. Estimations basées sur le dénombrement complet du recensement de la population de 2015.

⁵² Excluding data for Jordanian territory under occupation since June 1967 by Israeli military forces. - Non compris les données pour le territoire jordanien occupé depuis juin 1967 par les forces armées israéliennes.

⁵³ Data refer to annual average population. - Les données correspondent à la population annuelle moyenne.

⁵⁴ Based on the results of a household survey. - D'après les résultats d'une enquête des ménages.

⁵⁵ Estimates based on the adjusted results of the Population and Housing Census of 2010. - Les estimations sont fondée sur les résultats ajustées du recensement de la population et de l'habitat de 2010.

⁵⁶ Data refer to resident population that includes Maldivians and foreigners. - Les données concernent la population résidente, qui comprend des Maldiviens et des étrangers.

⁵⁷ Data refer to resident Maldivian population. - Les données concernent la population maldivienne résidente.

⁵⁸ Data refer to registered population data from Royal Oman Police. - Les données portent sur la population enregistrée par la police royale de l'Oman.

⁵⁹ Excluding data for the Pakistan-held part of Jammu and Kashmir, the final status of which has not yet been determined. Based on the results of the Pakistan Demographic Survey (PDS 2007). - Non compris les données concernant la partie du Jammu et Cachemire occupée par le Pakistan dont le statut définitif n'a pas été déterminé. D'après les résultats de l'enquête démographique effectuée par le Pakistan en 2007.

⁶⁰ Excluding 2739 Filipinos in Philippine Embassies, Consulates and Missions Abroad. - Excepté 2739 Philippins travaillant dans les ambassades, les consulats et les missions des Philippines à l'étranger.

⁶¹ Data refer to Korean population only. - les données ne concernent que la population coréenne.

⁶² As reported by the country. Reasons for discrepancy with other tables not ascertained. - Comme indiqué par le pays. L'on ne connaît pas la raison des écarts avec d'autres tableaux.

⁶³ Data refer to resident population which comprises Singapore citizens and permanent residents. Data exclude residents who have been away from Singapore for a continuous period of 12 months or longer as at the reference date. - Les données se rapportent à la population résidente composé des citoyens de Singapour et des résidents permanents. Non compris les résidents hors de Singapour pour une période ininterrompue de 12 mois ou plus avant de la date de référence.

⁶⁴ Data have not been adjusted for underenumeration. Excluding data from the parts of Jerusalem which were annexed by Israel in 1967. - Les données n'ont pas été ajustées pour compenser les lacunes du dénombrement. Non compris les données provenant des parties de Jérusalem qui ont été annexées par Israël en 1967.

⁶⁵ Data for urban include population in refugee camps. - Les données pour la population urbaine comprennent la population dans les camps réfugiés.

⁶⁶ Including Palestinian refugees. - Y compris les réfugiés de Palestine.

⁶⁷ Data based on Address Based Population Registration System. - Les données sont basées sur le registre national de la population basé sur l'adresse.

⁶⁸ Data based on address-based population registration system. - Les données sont basées sur le registre national de la population basé sur l'adresse.

⁶⁹ Data refer to resident population. - Les données concernent la population résidente.

⁷⁰ Excluding Faeroe Islands and Greenland shown separately, if available. Population statistics are compiled from registers. - Non compris les Iles Féroé et le Groenland, qui font l'objet de rubriques distinctes, si disponible. Les statistiques de la population sont compilées à partir des registres.

⁷¹ The total number may include 'Unknown residence', but the categories urban and rural do not. - Le nombre total peut inclure les personnes dont la résidence n'est pas connue, à l'inverse des catégories de population urbaine et rurale.

⁷² Excluding Åland Islands. - Non compris les Îles d'Åland.

⁷³ Excluding diplomatic personnel outside the country and including members of alien armed forces not living in military camps and foreign diplomatic personnel not living in embassies or consulates. - Non compris le personnel diplomatique hors du pays et y compris les militaires étrangers ne vivant pas dans des camps militaires et le personnel diplomatique étranger ne vivant pas dans les ambassades ou les consulats.

⁷⁴ Excluding military personnel, visitors and transients. - Non compris les militaires, ni les visiteurs et transients.

⁷⁵ Data refer to usually resident population. - Les données concernent la population habituellement résidente.

⁷⁶ Data refer to registered resident population. - Les données concernent la population enregistrée résidente.

⁷⁷ The figures refer to usual residents in private households and persons present in communal establishments during the 2011 census. - Données se rapportant aux résidents habituels membres de ménages privés et aux personnes recensées dans des établissements collectifs au recensement de 2011.

⁷⁸ Including civilian nationals temporarily outside the country. - Y compris les civils nationaux temporairement hors du pays.

⁷⁹ Data refer to resident population only. - Pour la population résidante seulement.

⁸⁰ Figures for male and female population do not add up to the figure for total population, because they exclude 119 persons of unknown sex. - Les chiffres relatifs à la population masculine et féminine ne correspondent pas au chiffre de la population totale, parce que l'on en a exclu 119 personnes de sexe inconnu.

⁸¹ Including residents temporarily outside the country. Population statistics are compiled from registers. - Y compris les résidents se trouvant temporairement hors du pays. Les statistiques de la population sont compilées à partir des registres.

⁸² Excluding Transnistria and the municipality of Bender. - Les données ne tiennent pas compte de l'information sur la Transnistria et la municipalité de Bender.

⁸³ Excludes data for Kosovo and Metohia. Based on the results of the 2011 Population Census. - Sans les données pour le Kosovo et Metohie. Basé sur les résultats du recensement de la population de 2011.

⁸⁴ Population statistics are compiled from registers. Data refer to registered resident population. - Les statistiques de la population sont compilées à partir des registres. Les données concernent la population enregistrée résidente.

⁸⁵ Data refer to legal resident population. - Les données concernent la population légalement résidente.

⁸⁶ The Government of Ukraine has informed the United Nations that it is not in a position to provide statistical data concerning the Autonomous Republic of Crimea and the city of Sevastopol. - Le gouvernement Ukrainien a informé l'ONU qu'il n'est pas en mesure de fournir des données statistiques concernant la République autonome de Crimée et la ville de Sébastopol.

⁸⁷ Excluding Channel Islands (Guernsey and Jersey) and Isle of Man, shown separately, if available. - Non compris les îles Anglo-Normandes (Guernesey et Jersey) et l'Île de Man, qui font l'objet de rubriques distinctes, si disponible.

⁸⁸ Excluding Niue, shown separately, which is part of Cook Islands, but because of remoteness is administered separately. - Non compris Nioué, qui fait l'objet d'une rubrique distincte et qui fait partie des îles Cook, mais qui, en raison de son éloignement, est administrée séparément.

[89] Projections are prepared by the Secretariat of the Pacific Community based on the 1999 census of population and housing. - Les projections sont preparées par le Secrétariat de la Communauté du Pacifique à partir des résultats du recensement de la population et de l'habitat de 1999.

[90] Because of rounding, totals are not in all cases the sum of the respective components. - Les chiffres étant arrondis, les totaux ne correspondent pas toujours rigoureusement à la somme des composants respectifs.

[91] Population estimates by urban/rural residence exclude inland waters and oceanic areas. - Les estimations de la population par lieu de résidence urbaine ou rurale excluent les eaux intérieures et les zones océaniques.

[92] Figures for male and female may not add up to the total, since they do not include the category "Unknown". - La somme des chiffres indiqués pour les sexes masculin et féminin peut n'être pas égale au total parce qu'elle n'inclut pas la catégorie " inconnue ".

[93] Estimates are prepared by the Secretariat of the Pacific Community based on the last population and housing census. - Les estimations sont preparées par le Secrétariat de la Communauté du Pacifique à partir des résultats du dernier recensement de la population et de l'habitat.

[94] Because of rounding, totals are not in all cases the sum of the respective components. Data refer to national projections. Based on the results of the 1996 population census. - Les chiffres étant arrondis, les totaux ne correspondent pas toujours rigoureusement à la somme des composants respectifs. Les données se réfèrent aux projections nationales. À partir des résultats du recensement de la population de 1996.

Table 8 - *Demographic Yearbook 2016*

Table 8 presents population of capital cities and cities of 100 000 or more inhabitants for the latest available year between 1997 and 2016.

Description of variables: Since the way in which cities are delimited differs from one country or area to another, the table not only presents data for the so-called city proper, but also for the urban agglomeration, if available.

City proper is defined as a locality with legally fixed boundaries and an administratively recognized urban status, usually characterized by some form of local government.

Urban agglomeration has been defined as comprising the city or town proper and also the suburban fringe or densely settled territory lying outside of, but adjacent to, the city boundaries.

For some countries or areas, however, the data relate to entire administrative divisions known, for example, as shi or municipalities (municipios) which are composed of a populated centre and adjoining territory, some of which may contain other, often separate urban localities or may be distinctively rural in character. For this group of countries or areas the type of civil division is given in a footnote.

The surface area of the city or urban agglomeration is presented, when available.

City names are presented in the original language of the country or area in which the cities are located. In cases where the original names are not in the Roman alphabet, they have been romanized. Cities are listed in English alphabetical order.

Capital cities are shown in the table regardless of their population size. The names of the capital cities are printed in capital letters. The designation of any specific city as a capital city is as reported by the country or area.

The table also covers cities whose urban agglomeration's population exceeds 100 000; that is, while the urban agglomeration should have a population of 100 000 or more to be included in the table, the city proper may be of a smaller population size.

The reference date of each population figure appears in the left-most column of the table. Estimates based on results of sample surveys and city censuses or from other sources are explained by the 'code' also appearing in the left-most column of the table. The codes are explained at the end of the table.

Reliability of data: Specific information is generally not available on the reliability of the estimates of the population of cities or urban agglomerations presented in this table.

In the absence of such quality assessment, data from population censuses, sample surveys and city censuses are considered to be reliable and, therefore, set in Roman type. Other estimates are considered to be reliable if they are based on a complete census (or a sample survey), and have been adjusted by a continuous population register or adjusted on the basis of the calculated balance of births, deaths, and migration.

Limitations: Statistics on the population of capital cities and cities of 100 000 or more inhabitants are subject to the same qualifications as have been set forth for population statistics in general as discussed in section 3 of the Technical Notes.

International comparability of data on city population is limited to a great extent by variations in national concepts and definitions. Although an effort is made to reduce the sources of non-comparability somewhat by presenting the data for both city proper and urban agglomeration, many serious problems of comparability remain.

Data presented in the "city proper" column for some countries represent an urban administrative area legally distinguished from surrounding rural territory, while for other countries these data represent a commune or an equally small administrative unit. In still other countries, the administrative units may be relatively extensive and thereby include considerable territories beyond the urban centre itself.

City data are also especially affected by whether the data refer to *de facto* or *de jure* population, as well as variations among countries in how each of these concepts is applied. With reference to the total population, the difference between the *de facto* and *de jure* population is discussed at length in section 3.1.1 of the Technical Notes.

Data on city populations based on intercensal estimates present additional problems: comparability is impaired by the different methods used in making the estimates, and by the loss of precision in applying to selected segments of the population methods best suited for the whole population. For example, it is far more difficult to apply the component method of estimating population growth to cities than it is to the entire country.

Births and deaths occurring in the cities do not all originate in the population present in or resident of that area. Therefore, the use of natural increase to estimate the probable size of the city population is a potential source of error. Internal migration is another component of population change that cannot be measured with accuracy in many areas. Because of these factors, estimates in this table may be less valuable in general and in particular limited for purposes of international comparison.

City data, even when set in Roman type, are often not as reliable as estimates for the total population of the country or area. Furthermore, because the sources of these data include censuses (national or city), surveys and estimates, the years to which they refer vary widely. In addition, because city boundaries may alter over time, comparisons covering different years should be carried out with caution.

Earlier data: Population of capital cities and cities with a population of 100 000 or more have been shown in previous issues of the *Demographic Yearbook*. For more information on specific topics and years for which data are reported, readers should consult the Historical Index.

Tableau 8 – *Annuaire démographique 2016*

Le tableau 8 présente les données les plus récentes disponibles pour la période 1997 – 2016 sur la population des capitales et des villes de 100 000 habitants ou plus.

Description des variables : étant donné que les villes ne sont pas délimitées de la même manière dans tous les pays ou zones, on s'est efforcé de donner, dans ce tableau, des chiffres correspondant non seulement aux villes proprement dites, mais aussi, le cas échéant, aux agglomérations urbaines.

On entend par villes proprement dites les localités qui ont des limites juridiquement définies et sont administrativement considérées comme villes, ce qui se caractérise généralement par l'existence d'une autorité locale.

L'agglomération urbaine comprend, par définition, la ville proprement dite ainsi que la proche banlieue, c'est-à-dire la zone fortement peuplée qui est extérieure, mais contiguë aux limites de la ville.

En outre, dans certains pays ou zones, les données se rapportent à des divisions administratives entières, connues par exemple sous le nom de shi ou de municipios, qui comportent une agglomération et le territoire avoisinant, lequel peut englober d'autres agglomérations urbaines tout à fait distinctes ou être à caractère essentiellement rural. Pour ce groupe de pays ou zones, le type de division administrative est indiqué en note.

On trouvera en plus la superficie des villes ou des agglomérations urbaines chaque fois que possible.

Les noms des villes sont indiqués dans la langue du pays ou zone où ces villes sont situées. Les noms de villes qui ne sont pas à l'origine libellés en caractères latins ont été romanisés. Les villes sont énumérées dans l'ordre alphabétique anglais.

Les capitales figurent dans le tableau quel que soit le chiffre de leur population et leur nom a été imprimé en lettres majuscules. Ne sont indiquées comme capitales que les villes ainsi désignées par le pays ou zone intéressé.

En ce qui concerne les autres villes, le tableau indique celles dont la population est égale ou supérieure à 100 000 habitants. Ce chiffre limite s'applique à l'agglomération urbaine et non à la ville proprement dite, dont la population peut être moindre.

La date à laquelle se réfère le chiffre correspondant, figure dans la colonne de gauche du tableau. Le 'code' aussi figurant dans la colonne de gauche du tableau, permet de savoir si les estimations sont fondées sur les résultats d'enquêtes par sondage ou de recensements municipaux ou sont tirées d'autres sources. Les codes utilisés sont expliqués à la fin du tableau.

Fiabilité des données : on ne possède généralement pas de renseignements précis sur la fiabilité des estimations de la population des villes ou agglomérations urbaines présentées dans ce tableau.

Les données provenant de recensements de la population, d'enquêtes par sondage ou de recensements municipaux sont jugées sûres et figurent par conséquent en caractères romains. D'autres estimations sont considérées comme sûres si elles sont fondées sur un recensement complet (ou une enquête par sondage) et ont été ajustées en fonction des données provenant d'un registre permanent de population ou en fonction de la balance, établie par le calcul des naissances, des décès et des migrations.

Insuffisance des données : les statistiques portant sur la population des capitales et des villes de 100 000 habitants ou plus appellent toutes les réserves qui ont été formulées à la section 3 des Notes techniques à propos des statistiques de la population en général.

La comparabilité internationale des données portant sur la population des villes est compromise dans une large mesure par la diversité des définitions nationales. Bien que l'on se soit efforcé de réduire les facteurs de non-comparabilité en présentant à la fois dans le tableau les données relatives aux villes proprement dites et celles concernant les agglomérations urbaines, de graves problèmes de comparabilité n'en subsistent pas moins.

Pour certains pays, les données figurant dans la colonne intitulée « Ville proprement dite » correspondent à une zone administrative urbaine juridiquement distincte du territoire rural environnant, tandis que pour d'autres pays ces données correspondent à une commune ou petite unité administrative analogue. Pour d'autres encore, les unités administratives en cause peuvent être relativement étendues et englober par conséquent un vaste territoire au-delà du centre urbain lui-même.

L'emploi de données se rapportant tantôt à la population de fait, tantôt à la population de droit, ainsi que les différences de traitement de ces deux notions d'un pays à l'autre influent particulièrement sur les statistiques urbaines. En ce qui concerne la population totale, la différence entre population de fait et population de droit est expliquée en détail à la section 3.1.1 des Notes techniques.

Les statistiques relatives à la population urbaine qui sont fondées sur des estimations intercensitaires posent encore plus de problèmes que les données issues de recensement. Leur comparabilité est compromise par la diversité des méthodes employées pour établir les estimations, et par l'imprécision qui résulte de l'application de certaines méthodes qui sont conçues pour être appliquées à l'ensemble de la population. La méthode des composantes, par exemple, est beaucoup plus difficile à appliquer en vue de l'estimation de l'accroissement de la population lorsqu'il s'agit de villes que lorsqu'il s'agit d'un pays tout entier.

Les naissances et décès qui surviennent dans les villes ne correspondent pas tous à la population présente ou résidente. En conséquence, des erreurs peuvent se produire si l'on établit pour les villes des estimations fondées sur l'accroissement naturel de la population. Les migrations intérieures constituent un second élément d'estimation que, dans bien des régions, on ne peut pas toujours mesurer avec exactitude. Pour ces raisons, les estimations présentées dans ce tableau risquent dans l'ensemble d'être peu fiables et leur valeur est particulièrement limitée du point de vue des comparaisons internationales.

Même lorsqu'elles figurent en caractères romains, il arrive souvent que les statistiques urbaines ne soient pas aussi fiables que les estimations concernant la population totale de la zone ou du pays considéré. De surcroît, comme ces statistiques proviennent aussi bien de recensements (nationaux ou municipaux) que d'enquêtes ou d'estimations, les années auxquelles elles se rapportent sont extrêmement variables. Enfin, comme les limites urbaines varient parfois d'une époque à une autre, il y a lieu d'être prudent lorsque l'on compare des données se rapportant à des années différentes.

Données publiées antérieurement : des statistiques concernant la population des capitales et des villes de 100 000 habitants ou plus ont été présentées dans des éditions antérieures de l'*Annuaire démographique*. Pour plus de précisions concernant les années et les sujets pour lesquels des données ont été publiées, se reporter à l'index historique.

8. Population of capital cities and cities of 100 000 or more inhabitants: latest available year, 1997 - 2016
Population des capitales et des villes de 100 000 habitants ou plus : dernière année disponible, 1997 - 2016

Continent, country or area, date, code[a] and city	City proper - Ville proprement dite				Urban agglomeration - Agglomération urbaine			
	Population			Surface area - Superficie (km²)	Population			Surface area - Superficie (km²)
Continent, pays ou zone, date, code[a] et ville	Both sexes - Les deux sexes	Male - Masculin	Female - Féminin		Both sexes - Les deux sexes	Male - Masculin	Female - Féminin	

AFRICA - AFRIQUE

Algeria - Algérie
16 IV 2008 (CDJC)

Adrar	200 834	...	...	...	...	...	...	...
Ain Defla	450 280	...	...	...	...	...	...	...
Ain Temouchent	299 341	...	...	...	...	...	...	...
ALGIERS (EL DJAZAIR)	2 712 944	...	...	...	...	...	...	...
Annaba	442 230	...	...	...	...	...	...	...
Batna	768 444	...	...	...	...	...	...	...
Béchar	236 213	...	...	...	...	...	...	...
Bejaïa	559 981	...	...	...	...	...	...	...
Beskra (Biskra)	563 245	...	...	...	...	...	...	...
Bordj Bou Arreridj	422 986	...	...	...	...	...	...	...
Bouira	372 196	...	...	...	...	...	...	...
Boumerdes	459 250	...	...	...	...	...	...	...
Chlef	521 070	...	...	...	...	...	...	...
El Bayadh	192 958	...	...	...	...	...	...	...
El Boulaïda (Blida)	719 515	...	...	...	...	...	...	...
El Djelfa	825 411	...	...	...	...	...	...	...
El Oued	495 573	...	...	...	...	...	...	...
El Tarf	230 157	...	...	...	...	...	...	...
Ghardaïa	355 701	...	...	...	...	...	...	...
Ghilizane (Relizane)	432 386	...	...	...	...	...	...	...
Guelma	363 716	...	...	...	...	...	...	...
Jijel	391 096	...	...	...	...	...	...	...
Khenchela	288 849	...	...	...	...	...	...	...
Laghouat	371 204	...	...	...	...	...	...	...
Lemdiyya (Médéa)	519 383	...	...	...	...	...	...	...
Mestghanem (Mostaganem)	338 143	...	...	...	...	...	...	...
Mila	440 735	...	...	...	...	...	...	...
Mouaskar (Mascara)	513 432	...	...	...	...	...	...	...
M'Sila	666 848	...	...	...	...	...	...	...
Naama	160 381	...	...	...	...	...	...	...
Oum El Bouaghi	467 997	...	...	...	...	...	...	...
Qacentina (Constantine)	717 646	...	...	...	...	...	...	...
Saïda	248 939	...	...	...	...	...	...	...
Sidi-bel-Abbès	517 836	...	...	...	...	...	...	...
Skikda	543 402	...	...	...	...	...	...	...
Souq Ahras	308 319	...	...	...	...	...	...	...
Stif (Sétif)	856 457	...	...	...	...	...	...	...
Tamanrasset	136 822	...	...	...	...	...	...	...
Tbessa (Tébessa)	515 786	...	...	...	...	...	...	...
Tihert (Tiaret)	637 991	...	...	...	...	...	...	...
Tilimsen (Tlemcen)	672 490	...	...	...	...	...	...	...
Tipaza	343 838	...	...	...	...	...	...	...
Tissemsilt	193 011	...	...	...	...	...	...	...
Tizi Ouzou	585 775	...	...	...	...	...	...	...
Wahran (Oran)	1 165 687	...	...	...	...	...	...	...
Wargla (Ouargla)	473 543	...	...	...	...	...	...	...

Benin - Bénin
11 V 2013 (CDJC)

Cotonou	679 012	325 872	353 140	...	...	...	...	...
Parakou	255 478	127 328	128 150	...	...	...	...	...
PORTO-NOVO	264 320	126 016	138 304	...	...	...	...	...

Botswana[1]
1 VII 2016 (ESDJ)

GABORONE	*259 291*	...	...	...	...	...	...	...

Burkina Faso
9 XII 2006 (CDFC)

Banfora	75 917	38 399	37 518	...	109 824	54 581	55 243	...
Bobo Dioulasso	489 967	244 136	245 831	...	554 042	275 703	278 339	...
Dori	21 078	10 431	10 647	...	106 808	52 992	53 816	...
Fada N'gourma	41 785	21 220	20 565	...	124 577	62 193	62 384	...
Gorom-Gorom	8 882	4 509	4 373	...	106 346	53 129	53 217	...
Kaya	54 365	26 989	27 376	...	117 122	56 209	60 913	...
Koudougou	88 184	42 803	45 381	...	138 209	64 362	73 847	...

Continent, country or area, date, code[a] and city Continent, pays ou zone, date, code[a] et ville	City proper - Ville proprement dite				Urban agglomeration - Agglomération urbaine			
	Population			Surface area - Superficie (km²)	Population			Surface area - Superficie (km²)
	Both sexes - Les deux sexes	Male - Masculin	Female - Féminin		Both sexes - Les deux sexes	Male - Masculin	Female - Féminin	
AFRICA - AFRIQUE								
Burkina Faso								
9 XII 2006 (CDFC)								
OUAGADOUGOU	1 475 223	745 289	729 934	...	1 475 223	745 289	729 934	...
Ouahigouya	73 153	36 370	36 783	...	125 030	61 002	64 028	...
Solenzo	16 850	8 557	8 293	...	121 819	59 892	61 927	...
Tenkodogo	44 491	21 476	23 015	...	124 985	58 003	66 982	...
Burundi								
16 VIII 2008 (CDJC)								
BUJUMBURA	497 169	274 979	222 190	...	...	...	...	...
Cabo Verde								
1 VII 2011 (ESDF)								
PRAIA	...	...	...	...	133 863	65 412	68 451	...
Cameroon - Cameroun[2]								
1 VII 2016 (ESDF)								
Douala	2 948 464	1 488 593	1 459 871	...	...	...	...	...
YAOUNDE	2 873 567	1 450 087	1 423 480	...	...	...	...	...
Côte d'Ivoire								
15 V 2014 (CDJC)								
Abengourou	100 910	51 153	49 757	...	...	...	...	...
Abidjan	4 395 243	2 180 526	2 214 717	...	...	...	...	...
Anyama	103 297	52 169	51 128	...	...	...	...	...
Bouake	536 719	273 502	263 217	...	...	...	...	...
Daloa	245 360	128 922	116 438	...	...	...	...	...
Divo	105 397	54 614	50 783	...	...	...	...	...
Gagnoa	160 465	82 615	77 850	...	...	...	...	...
Korhogo	243 048	126 493	116 555	...	...	...	...	...
Man	148 945	77 005	71 940	...	...	...	...	...
San Pédro	164 944	85 168	79 776	...	...	...	...	...
Soubre	101 196	53 799	47 397	...	...	...	...	...
YAMOUSSOUKRO	212 670	107 871	104 799	...	...	...	...	...
Djibouti								
29 V 2009 (CDFC)								
DJIBOUTI	475 322	...	...	...	...	...	...	...
Egypt - Égypte								
1 VII 2010* (ESDF)								
6th of October City	802 306	420 009	382 297	...	...	...	...	...
Alexandria	4 358 439	2 225 558	2 132 881	...	...	...	...	...
Assyût	991 929	508 403	483 526	...	...	...	...	...
Aswan	543 396	277 732	265 664	...	...	...	...	...
Behera	985 850	500 999	484 851	...	...	...	...	...
Beni-Suef	582 396	293 887	288 509	...	...	...	...	...
CAIRO	7 248 671	3 682 152	3 566 519	...	...	...	...	...
Dakahlia	1 503 395	758 471	744 924	...	...	...	...	...
Damietta	462 154	236 522	225 632	...	...	...	...	...
Faiyûm	621 268	318 679	302 589	...	...	...	...	...
Gharbia	1 285 492	645 533	639 959	...	...	...	...	...
Giza	3 122 041	1 592 292	1 529 749	...	...	...	...	...
Helwan	1 295 854	660 776	635 078	...	...	...	...	...
Ismailia	472 655	237 174	235 481	...	...	...	...	...
Kafr-Elsheikh	655 002	327 445	327 557	...	...	...	...	...
Kalyoubia	2 053 859	1 051 232	1 002 627	...	...	...	...	...
Luxer	391 460	200 250	191 210	...	...	...	...	...
Matrouh	258 699	136 995	121 704	...	...	...	...	...
Menia	859 719	434 498	425 221	...	...	...	...	...
Menoufia	724 352	368 333	356 019	...	...	...	...	...
North Sinai	229 462	120 302	109 160	...	...	...	...	...
Port Said	610 468	310 881	299 587	...	...	...	...	...
Qena	534 766	270 422	264 344	...	...	...	...	...
Red Sea	295 993	180 622	115 371	...	...	...	...	...
Sharkia	1 340 060	682 941	657 119	...	...	...	...	...
Sohag	870 362	443 082	427 280	...	...	...	...	...
Suez	556 665	283 571	273 094	...	...	...	...	...
Equatorial Guinea - Guinée équatoriale								
1 VII 2001 (ESDF)								
MALABO	...	...	...	...	211 276	106 923	104 353	...

Continent, country or area, date, code[a] and city / Continent, pays ou zone, date, code[a] et ville	City proper - Ville proprement dite				Urban agglomeration - Agglomération urbaine			
	Population			Surface area - Superficie (km²)	Population			Surface area - Superficie (km²)
	Both sexes - Les deux sexes	Male - Masculin	Female - Féminin		Both sexes - Les deux sexes	Male - Masculin	Female - Féminin	
AFRICA - AFRIQUE								
Ethiopia - Éthiopie								
1 VII 2011 (ESDF)								
ADDIS ABABA	2 979 086	1 419 525	1 559 561	...	...	...	...	...
Awassa	200 396	103 323	97 073	...	...	...	...	...
Bahir Dar	170 267	75 302	94 965	...	...	...	...	...
Debre Zeit	118 260	56 640	61 620	...	...	...	...	...
Dessie	131 637	57 725	73 912	...	...	...	...	...
Dire Dawa	256 774	127 969	128 805	...	...	...	...	...
Gondar	227 115	98 563	128 552	...	...	...	...	...
Harar	108 188	54 141	54 047	...	...	...	...	...
Jimma	143 151	71 983	71 168	...	...	...	...	...
Mekele	260 748	126 497	134 251	...	...	...	...	...
Nazareth	260 611	128 845	131 766	...	...	...	...	...
Gabon								
22 V 2013 (CDFC)								
Franceville	...	...	...	...	110 568	63 518	47 050	...
LIBREVILLE	...	...	...	...	703 939	360 012	343 927	...
Port-Gentil	...	...	...	...	136 462	69 978	66 484	...
Ghana								
26 IX 2010 (CDFC)								
ACCRA	1 594 419	763 870	830 549	...	...	...	...	...
Ashiaman	190 972	93 727	97 245	...	...	...	...	...
Koforidua	122 300	59 056	63 244	...	...	...	...	...
Kumasi	1 730 249	826 479	903 770	...	...	...	...	...
Madina	111 926	54 271	57 655	...	...	...	...	...
Obuasi	168 641	81 015	87 626	...	...	...	...	...
Tamale	223 252	111 109	112 143	...	...	...	...	...
Tema	292 773	139 958	152 815	...	...	...	...	...
Guinea - Guinée[3]								
15 III 2014 (CDJC)								
Boke	185 548	94 132	91 416	...	...	...	...	...
CONAKRY	1 659 785	832 734	827 051	...	1 879 695	942 184	937 511	...
Coyah	216 928	103 627	113 301	...	...	...	...	...
Dubreka	157 017	79 041	77 976	...	...	...	...	...
Kankan	190 722	96 574	94 148	...	...	...	...	...
Kindia	138 695	67 746	70 949	...	...	...	...	...
Nzérékoré	195 027	97 286	97 741	...	...	...	...	...
Siguiri	127 492	65 562	61 930	...	...	...	...	...
Guinea-Bissau - Guinée-Bissau								
15 III 2009 (CDFC)								
BISSAU	387 909	...	...	...	...	...	...	...
Kenya								
24 VIII 2009 (CDFC)								
Eldoret	252 061	127 808	124 253	...	289 380[4]	146 596[4]	142 790[4]	311.1[4]
Garissa	110 383	56 873	53 490	...	116 317[4]	60 114[4]	56 183[4]	790.7[4]
Kangundo	13 356	6 544	6 812	...	218 557[4]	107 968[4]	110 589[4]	...
Karuri	99 739	49 692	50 047	...	107 716[4]	53 735[4]	53 981[4]	...
Kericho	42 029	22 199	19 830	...	101 808[4]	52 283[4]	49 525[4]	...
Kikuyu	190 208	93 036	97 172	...	233 231[4]	114 357[4]	118 874[4]	231.3[4]
Kisumu	259 258	131 062	128 196	...	388 311[4]	193 878[4]	194 433[4]	601.8[4]
Kitale	75 782	38 081	37 701	...	106 187[4]	54 065[4]	52 122[4]	...
Kitui	20 419	10 338	10 081	...	109 568[4]	53 659[4]	55 909[4]	...
Machakos	41 917	20 448	21 469	...	150 041[4]	74 294[4]	75 747[4]	...
Malindi	84 150	41 911	42 239	...	118 265[4]	59 192[4]	59 073[4]	...
Mavoko/AthiRiver	110 396	59 393	51 003	...	137 211[4]	74 856[4]	62 355[4]	...
Mombasa	915 101	473 433	441 668	...	938 131[4]	486 208[4]	451 923[4]	218.8[4]
NAIROBI	3 133 518	1 602 104	1 531 414	695.1	...	...	...	...
Naivasha	91 993	45 253	46 740	...	169 142[4]	84 857[4]	84 285[4]	...
Nakuru	286 411	145 038	141 373	...	307 990[4]	155 881[4]	152 109[4]	411.6[4]
Ngong	104 073	52 453	51 620	...	107 188[4]	54 040[4]	53 148[4]	...
Nyeri	63 626	31 885	31 741	...	119 353[4]	59 562[4]	59 791[4]	...
Ruiru	236 961	118 143	118 818	...	238 858[4]	119 147[4]	119 711[4]	292[4]
Thika	136 576	68 254	68 322	...	136 917[4]	68 408[4]	68 509[4]	134.7[4]
Vihiga	36 398	17 608	18 790	...	118 696[4]	56 807[4]	61 889[4]	...

8. Population of capital cities and cities of 100 000 or more inhabitants: latest available year, 1997 - 2016
Population des capitales et des villes de 100 000 habitants ou plus : dernière année disponible, 1997 - 2016 (continued - suite)

Continent, country or area, date, code[a] and city / Continent, pays ou zone, date, code[a] et ville	City proper - Ville proprement dite				Urban agglomeration - Agglomération urbaine			
	Population			Surface area - Superficie (km²)	Population			Surface area - Superficie (km²)
	Both sexes - Les deux sexes	Male - Masculin	Female - Féminin		Both sexes - Les deux sexes	Male - Masculin	Female - Féminin	
AFRICA - AFRIQUE								
Lesotho								
13 IV 2006 (CDJC)								
MASERU	431 998	205 702	226 296	4279	...	...	...	...
Liberia - Libéria[5]								
21 III 2008 (CDFC)								
MONROVIA....................	...	...	...	...	970 824	476 473	494 351	...
Madagascar								
1 VII 2005 (ESDF)								
ANTANANARIVO[6]....................	1 015 140	495 393	519 747	...	...	...	...	...
Antsirabe....................	...	...	...	...	180 180	87 691	92 489	...
Fianarantsoa....................	...	...	...	...	165 220	80 410	84 810	...
Mahajanga....................	...	...	...	...	152 785	74 359	78 426	...
Toamasina....................	...	...	...	...	203 469	99 026	104 443	...
Toliara....................	...	...	...	...	113 993	55 479	58 514	...
Malawi								
1 VII 2016 (ESDF)								
Blantyre City....................	920 226[2]	464 649[2]	455 577[2]	220	...	...	...	...
LILONGWE....................	1 098 167[2]	559 741[2]	538 426[2]	456	...	...	...	...
Mzuzu City....................	239 008[2]	119 374[2]	119 634[2]	48	...	...	...	...
Zomba City....................	147 131[2]	73 250[2]	73 881[2]	39	...	...	...	...
Mali								
1 IV 2009 (CDFC)								
BAMAKO[7]....................	...	...	...	...	1 810 366	907 643	902 723	...
Kayes....................	...	...	...	...	149 129	76 470	72 659	...
Koutiala....................	...	...	...	...	141 444	70 905	70 539	...
Mopti....................	...	...	...	...	120 786	60 080	60 706	...
Ségou....................	...	...	...	...	133 501	66 819	66 682	...
Sikasso....................	...	...	...	...	226 618	114 171	112 447	...
Mauritania - Mauritanie[2]								
1 VII 2008 (ESDF)								
NOUAKCHOTT....................	846 871	471 243	375 628	...	...	...	...	...
Mauritius - Maurice[8]								
1 VII 2016 (ESDJ)								
Beau Bassin - Rose Hill....................	104 544	51 837	52 707	...	...	...	...	...
PORT LOUIS....................	148 870	74 320	74 550	...	...	...	...	...
Vacoas - Phoenix....................	106 253	51 306	54 947	...	...	...	...	...
Morocco - Maroc								
1 VII 2014 (ESDF)								
Agadir....................	505 765	...	...	...	598 484	...	...	...
Al Hoceima....................	137 024	...	...	...	399 586	...	...	...
Azilal....................	100 327	...	...	...	553 121	...	...	...
Béni-Mellal....................	325 405	...	...	...	549 559	...	...	...
Benslimane....................	113 341	...	...	...	232 509	...	...	...
Berkane....................	182 203	...	...	...	288 807	...	...	...
Berrechid....................	272 356	...	...	...	482 119	...	...	...
Casablanca (Dar-el-Beida)....................	3 352 399	...	...	...	3 352 399	...	...	...
Chtouka-Ait Baha....................	111 522	...	...	...	369 706	...	...	...
El Hajeb....................	121 226	...	...	...	246 461	...	...	...
El Kelâa des Sraghna....................	152 900	...	...	...	536 191	...	...	...
El-Jadida....................	311 038	...	...	...	784 432	...	...	...
Errachidia....................	193 748	...	...	...	418 069	...	...	...
Essaouira....................	106 319	...	...	...	450 569	...	...	...
Fès....................	1 126 551	...	...	...	1 146 967	...	...	...
Fquih Ben Salah....................	204 732	...	...	...	502 021	...	...	...
Guelmim....................	138 788	...	...	...	187 428	...	...	...
Inezgane ait Melloul....................	511 209	...	...	...	538 786	...	...	...
Kénitra....................	604 206	...	...	...	1 058 359	...	...	...
Khemisset....................	279 890	...	...	...	541 868	...	...	...
Khénifra....................	228 509	...	...	...	370 952	...	...	...
Khouribga....................	376 829	...	...	...	541 365	...	...	...
Laayoune....................	234 870	...	...	...	237 384	...	...	...
Larache....................	264 802	...	...	...	496 264	...	...	...
Marrakech....................	978 045	...	...	...	1 325 571	...	...	...
M'Diq-Fnideq....................	196 586	...	...	...	208 337	...	...	...
Médiouna....................	119 054	...	...	...	171 684	...	...	...

8. Population of capital cities and cities of 100 000 or more inhabitants: latest available year, 1997 - 2016
Population des capitales et des villes de 100 000 habitants ou plus : dernière année disponible, 1997 - 2016 (continued - suite)

Continent, country or area, date, code[a] and city / Continent, pays ou zone, date, code[a] et ville	City proper - Ville proprement dite				Urban agglomeration - Agglomération urbaine			
	Population			Surface area - Superficie (km²)	Population			Surface area - Superficie (km²)
	Both sexes - Les deux sexes	Male - Masculin	Female - Féminin		Both sexes - Les deux sexes	Male - Masculin	Female - Féminin	
AFRICA - AFRIQUE								
Morocco - Maroc								
1 VII 2014 (ESDF)								
Meknès	685 408	...	...	...	833 456	...	...	...
Midelt	124 684	...	...	...	288 757	...	...	...
Mohammedia	288 131	...	...	...	403 087	...	...	...
Nador	390 913	...	...	...	564 354	...	...	...
Nouaceur	271 052	...	...	...	331 651	...	...	...
Ouarzazate	113 230	...	...	...	297 018	...	...	...
Oued Ed-Dahab	105 193	...	...	...	125 747	...	...	...
Oujda	504 480	...	...	...	550 406	...	...	...
RABAT	578 644	...	...	...	578 644	...	...	...
Rehamna	102 715	...	...	...	314 605	...	...	...
Safi	345 595	...	...	...	691 128	...	...	...
Salé	912 957	...	...	...	979 228	...	...	...
Sefrou	154 973	...	...	...	286 009	...	...	...
Settat	215 665	...	...	...	633 500	...	...	...
Sidi Kacem	168 302	...	...	...	521 694	...	...	...
Sidi Slimane	130 576	...	...	...	319 528	...	...	...
Skhirate-Témara	512 867	...	...	...	570 855	...	...	...
Tanger	998 972	...	...	...	1 059 562	...	...	...
Taourirt	149 604	...	...	...	232 712	...	...	...
Taroudannt	247 428	...	...	...	837 797	...	...	...
Taza	207 719	...	...	...	528 917	...	...	...
Tétouan	396 806	...	...	...	549 062	...	...	...
Youssoufia	100 617	...	...	...	251 692	...	...	...
Mozambique								
1 VII 2015 (ESDF)								
Beira	460 904	231 684	229 220	633	...	...	...	...
Chimoio	314 751	158 700	156 051	174	...	...	...	...
Lichinga	214 614	108 147	106 467	290	...	...	...	...
MAPUTO	1 241 702	597 109	644 593	300	...	...	...	...
Matola	927 123	447 365	479 759	375	...	...	...	...
Maxixe	127 372	57 145	70 227	282	...	...	...	...
Nacala	241 066	118 325	122 741	340	...	...	...	...
Nampula	622 423	313 343	309 080	320	...	...	...	...
Pemba	199 457	99 447	100 010	194	...	...	...	...
Quelimane	241 077	121 599	119 478	117	...	...	...	...
Tete	213 406	107 128	106 278	286	...	...	...	...
Xai-Xai	128 946	59 452	69 494	135	...	...	...	...
Namibia - Namibie								
28 VIII 2011 (CDFC)								
WINDHOEK	325 858	160 730	165 128	...	...	...	...	...
Niger								
10 XII 2012 (CDJC)								
Maradi	267 249	137 051	130 198	...	...	...	...	...
NIAMEY	1 026 848	511 166	515 682	...	...	...	...	...
Tahoua	149 498	74 096	75 402	...	...	...	...	...
Zinder	322 935	162 705	160 230	...	...	...	...	...
Republic of South Sudan - République de Soudan du Sud								
21 IV 2008 (CDFC)								
JUBA	230 195	129 427	100 768	56	...	...	...	...
Malakal	114 528	60 440	54 088	25	...	...	...	...
Wau	118 331	63 777	54 554	75	...	...	...	...
Reunion - Réunion								
1 I 2010 (CDJC)								
SAINT-DENIS	145 022	68 075	76 947	142.8	174 973	82 815	92 158	230
Saint-Paul	103 346	51 327	52 019	241.3	172 137	84 793	87 344	376
Rwanda								
15 VIII 2012 (CDJC)								
KIGALI	859 332	451 673	407 659	...	...	...	...	...
Saint Helena ex. dep. - Sainte-Hélène sans dép.[9]								
7 II 2016 (CDJC)								
JAMESTOWN	629	...	...	...	...	...	...	...

8. Population of capital cities and cities of 100 000 or more inhabitants: latest available year, 1997 - 2016
Population des capitales et des villes de 100 000 habitants ou plus : dernière année disponible, 1997 - 2016 (continued - suite)

Continent, country or area, date, code[a] and city / Continent, pays ou zone, date, code[a] et ville	City proper - Ville proprement dite				Urban agglomeration - Agglomération urbaine			
	Population			Surface area - Superficie (km²)	Population			Surface area - Superficie (km²)
	Both sexes - Les deux sexes	Male - Masculin	Female - Féminin		Both sexes - Les deux sexes	Male - Masculin	Female - Féminin	
AFRICA - AFRIQUE								
Sao Tome and Principe - Sao Tomé-et-Principe								
25 VIII 2001 (CDJC)								
SAO TOME...	...	...	...	...	49 957	24 003	25 954	...
Senegal - Sénégal[10]								
31 XII 2011 (ESDJ)								
DAKAR..	1 056 009	526 299	529 710	...	...	...	...	...
Diourbel...	279 667	136 961	142 706	...	...	...	...	...
Guediawaye	317 464	157 992	159 472	...	...	...	...	...
Kaolack...	410 577	199 057	211 520	...	...	...	...	...
Mbour...	605 346	307 461	297 885	...	...	...	...	...
Pikine...	941 245	472 868	468 377	...	...	...	...	...
Rufisque	333 032	167 942	165 090	...	...	...	...	...
Saint Louis	277 245	136 957	140 289	...	...	...	...	...
Thiès..	618 436	304 087	314 349	...	...	...	...	...
Ziguinchor..	337 295	167 048	170 247	...	...	...	...	...
Seychelles[11]								
26 VIII 2010 (CDFC)								
VICTORIA..	...	...	...	...	26 450	...	...	...
Sierra Leone								
1 VII 2010 (ESDF)								
Bo..	*231 494*	*111 731*	*119 763*	...	...	...	...	...
FREETOWN...	*945 423*	*479 526*	*465 897*	...	...	...	...	...
Kenema	*195 498*	*95 988*	*99 510*	...	...	...	...	...
Makeni	*114 960*	*55 388*	*59 572*	...	...	...	...	...
Somalia - Somalie								
1 VII 2001 (ESDF)								
MOGADISHU	*1 212 000*	...	...	...	...	...	...	...
South Africa - Afrique du Sud								
10 X 2011 (CDFC)								
CAPE TOWN[12]....................................	433 688	209 082	224 607	...	...	...	...	...
Durban...	595 061	288 871	306 189	...	...	...	...	...
Johannesburg......................................	957 441	484 293	473 148	...	...	...	...	...
PRETORIA[12]	741 651	359 139	382 512	...	...	...	...	...
Togo[2]								
1 VII 2015 (ESDF)								
Kara...	*104 400*	...	...	...	*...*	...	...	...
LOME	*...*	...	...	...	*1 788 600*	...	...	...
Sokode	*101 900*	...	...	...	*...*	...	...	...
Tunisia - Tunisie								
1 VII 1998 (ESDF)								
Bizerte	*105 520*	...	...	...	...	...	...	...
Gabes...	*104 950*	...	...	...	...	...	...	...
Kairouan	*110 280*	...	...	...	...	...	...	...
Sfax...	*248 800*	...	...	...	...	...	...	...
TUNIS..	*702 330*	...	...	...	...	...	...	...
Uganda - Ouganda								
27 VIII 2014 (CDFC)								
Gulu[13]	...	...	...	...	149 802	...	...	...
Hoima[13]	...	...	...	...	100 126	...	...	...
KAMPALA...	1 507 114	...	...	...	...	...	...	...
Kasese[13]	...	...	...	...	101 557	...	...	...
Kira[13]	...	...	...	...	317 428	...	...	...
Lugazi[13]	...	...	...	...	114 163	...	...	...
Makindye Ssabagabo[13]	...	...	...	...	282 664	...	...	...
Masaka[13]	...	...	...	...	103 293	...	...	...
Mbarara[13]	...	...	...	...	195 160	...	...	...
Mukono[13]	...	...	...	...	162 744	...	...	...
Nansana[13]	...	...	...	...	365 857	...	...	...
United Republic of Tanzania - République Unie de Tanzanie								
26 VIII 2012 (CDFC)								
Dar es Salaam.....................................	4 364 541	2 125 786	2 238 755	...	...	...	...	...
DODOMA..	2 083 588	1 014 974	1 068 614	...	...	...	...	...
Mwanza..	2 772 509	1 360 381	1 412 128	...	...	...	...	...
Zanzibar	1 303 569	630 677	672 892	...	...	...	...	...

8. Population of capital cities and cities of 100 000 or more inhabitants: latest available year, 1997 - 2016
Population des capitales et des villes de 100 000 habitants ou plus : dernière année disponible, 1997 - 2016 (continued - suite)

Continent, country or area, date, code[a] and city Continent, pays ou zone, date, code[a] et ville	City proper - Ville proprement dite				Urban agglomeration - Agglomération urbaine			
	Population			Surface area - Superficie (km²)	Population			Surface area - Superficie (km²)
	Both sexes - Les deux sexes	Male - Masculin	Female - Féminin		Both sexes - Les deux sexes	Male - Masculin	Female - Féminin	
AFRICA - AFRIQUE								
Western Sahara - Sahara occidental[14]								
1 VII 1999 (ESDF)								
EL AAIUN	*169 000*	...	...	...	...	...	...	...
Zambia - Zambie								
16 X 2010 (CDJC)								
Chingola	216 626	108 464	108 162	...	...	...	...	...
Chipata	455 783	224 934	230 849	...	...	...	...	...
Kabwe	202 360	98 781	103 579	...	...	...	...	...
Kasama	231 824	114 208	117 616	...	...	...	...	...
Kitwe	517 543	256 740	260 803	...	...	...	...	...
Livingstone	139 509	68 763	70 746	...	...	...	...	...
Luanshya	156 059	77 368	78 691	...	...	...	...	...
LUSAKA	1 747 152	860 424	886 728	...	...	...	...	...
Mufulira	162 889	81 355	81 534	...	...	...	...	...
Ndola	451 246	223 020	228 226	...	...	...	...	...
Zimbabwe								
17 VIII 2012 (CDFC)								
Bulawayo	653 337	303 346	349 991	...	...	...	...	...
Chitungwiza	356 840	168 600	188 240	...	...	...	...	...
HARARE	1 485 231	716 595	768 636	...	...	...	...	...
Mutare	262 124	125 850	136 274	...	...	...	...	...
AMERICA, NORTH - AMÉRIQUE DU NORD								
Anguilla								
11 V 2011 (CDFC)								
THE VALLEY	2 812	...	...	...	...	...	...	...
Aruba								
29 IX 2010 (CDJC)								
ORANJESTAD	28 295	13 139	15 156	...	...	...	...	...
Bahamas								
1 VII 2016* (ESDF)								
NASSAU	266 100	128 100	138 000	...	...	...	...	...
Belize								
12 V 2010 (CDJC)								
BELMOPAN	13 939	6 779	7 160	...	...	...	...	...
Bermuda - Bermudes								
1 VII 2010 (ESDJ)								
HAMILTON	3 686	1 986	1 700	.7	...	...	...	...
Canada								
1 VII 2016* (ESDJ)								
Abbotsford-Mission	...	...	...	...	186 792	93 813	92 979	605.2
Barrie	149 721	73 189	76 532	77.4	205 003	101 656	103 347	897.8
Brampton	591 974	293 763	298 211	266.3	...	...	...	...
Brantford	100 791	49 004	51 787	72.5	145 455	71 326	74 129	1073.1
Burlington	201 216	97 408	103 808	185.7	...	...	...	...
Burnaby	246 987	122 343	124 644	90.6	...	...	...	...
Calgary	1 318 817	666 331	652 486	825.3	1 469 341	743 202	726 139	5107.5
Cambridge	136 839	67 625	69 214	113	...	...	...	...
Chatham-Kent	104 859	51 404	53 455	2458.1	...	...	...	...
Coquitlam	139 015	69 046	69 969	122.3	...	...	...	...
Edmonton	969 068	490 368	478 700	684.4	1 392 594	705 237	687 357	9426.7
Gatineau	281 392	137 940	143 452	343	332 394	164 394	168 000	...
Greater Sudbury / Grand Sudbury	165 154	81 320	83 834	3227.4	165 536	81 502	84 034	3410.6
Guelph	132 350	64 646	67 704	87.2	156 029	76 641	79 388	593.5
Halifax	425 840	209 477	216 363	5490.3	425 871	209 601	216 270	5495.7
Hamilton	561 022	276 918	284 104	1117.2	778 417	381 976	396 441	1371.9
Kelowna	129 512	63 152	66 360	211.8	198 304	97 636	100 668	2904.9
Kingston	131 746	64 612	67 134	451.2	171 372	84 824	86 548	1938.9
Kitchener-Cambridge-Waterloo	...	...	...	...	517 316	256 437	260 879	827.4
Laval	429 413	210 597	218 816	247.1	...	...	...	...
Lévis V	144 918	71 471	73 447	449.3	...	...	...	...
London	397 493	193 309	204 184	420.6	512 431	250 162	262 269	2665.6
Longueuil	245 251	120 346	124 905	115.6	...	...	...	...

8. Population of capital cities and cities of 100 000 or more inhabitants: latest available year, 1997 - 2016
Population des capitales et des villes de 100 000 habitants ou plus : dernière année disponible, 1997 - 2016 (continued - suite)

Continent, country or area, date, code[a] and city / Continent, pays ou zone, date, code[a] et ville	City proper - Ville proprement dite				Urban agglomeration - Agglomération urbaine			
	Population			Surface area - Superficie (km²)	Population			Surface area - Superficie (km²)
	Both sexes - Les deux sexes	Male - Masculin	Female - Féminin		Both sexes - Les deux sexes	Male - Masculin	Female - Féminin	
AMERICA, NORTH - AMÉRIQUE DU NORD								
Canada								
1 VII 2016* (ESDJ)								
Markham	340 626	167 196	173 430	212.6	...	...	...	...
Mississauga	812 457	399 753	412 704	292.4	...	...	...	...
Moncton	73 849	36 305	37 544	141.2	149 744	74 515	75 229	2406.3
Montréal	1 763 288	870 849	892 439	365.1	4 093 767	2 021 533	2 072 234	4258.3
Oakville	207 268	100 948	106 320	138.9	...	...	...	...
Oshawa	167 179	81 937	85 242	145.7	393 977	194 123	199 854	903.5
OTTAWA	973 481	476 223	497 258	2790.2	1 018 741	498 288	520 453	...
Ottawa - Gatineau	...	...	...	...	1 351 135	662 682	688 453	6287
Peterborough	82 774	39 064	43 710	63.8	124 082	59 720	64 362	1506.9
Québec	539 168	263 760	275 408	454.1	807 211	397 995	409 216	3349.1
Regina	223 604	111 134	112 470	145.5	247 224	123 458	123 766	3408.3
Richmond	209 738	101 739	107 999	129.3	...	...	...	...
Richmond Hill	207 275	101 409	105 866	100.9	...	...	...	...
Saanich	117 285	57 522	59 763	103.8	...	...	...	...
Saguenay	146 278	72 899	73 379	1126.5	159 669	79 965	79 704	2564
Saint John	69 905	33 608	36 297	315.8	127 549	62 059	65 490	3362.9
Saskatoon	266 064	133 126	132 938	209.6	315 150	158 353	156 797	5214.5
Sherbrooke	164 538	80 942	83 596	353.5	215 594	106 411	109 183	1459.6
St Catharines-Niagara	...	...	...	...	411 700	200 116	211 584	1397.5
St. John's	113 656	55 184	58 472	446.1	217 454	107 186	110 268	804.7
Surrey	514 522	257 014	257 508	316.4	...	...	...	...
Thunder Bay	110 014	53 715	56 299	328.2	124 166	61 174	62 992	2556.4
Toronto	2 876 095	1 398 687	1 477 408	630.2	6 242 273	3 055 923	3 186 350	5905.7
Trois-Rivières	136 168	66 355	69 813	288.9	157 764	77 351	80 413	1041.2
Vancouver	669 045	330 754	338 291	115	2 548 740	1 259 363	1 289 377	2882.5
Vaughan	321 781	157 998	163 783	273.5	...	...	...	...
Victoria	87 320	41 749	45 571	19.5	370 899	180 956	189 943	696.1
Whitby	133 639	65 571	68 068	146.5	...	...	...	...
Windsor	221 862	108 398	113 464	146.3	340 279	167 405	172 874	1022.3
Winnipeg	735 552	362 821	372 731	464.1	811 874	401 767	410 107	5303.1
Cayman Islands - Îles Caïmanes								
1 IV 2007 (SSDJ)								
GEORGE TOWN	28 836	...	...	...	...	...	...	...
Costa Rica								
1 VII 2016 (ESDJ)								
Alajuela	297 879	151 184	146 695	388.4	...	...	...	...
Cartago	159 142	79 950	79 192	287.8	...	...	...	...
Desamparados	235 863	117 603	118 260	118.3	...	...	...	...
Goicoechea	133 557	65 828	67 729	31.5	...	...	...	...
Heredia	136 948	67 343	69 605	282.6	...	...	...	...
La Unión	107 755	54 114	53 641	44.8	...	...	...	...
Pérez Zeledón	142 291	71 087	71 204	1905.5	...	...	...	...
Pococí	142 171	73 858	68 313	2403.5	...	...	...	...
Puntarenas	132 440	67 948	64 492	1842.3	...	...	...	...
San Carlos	187 953	96 696	91 257	3348	...	...	...	...
SAN JOSÉ	336 792	166 552	170 240	44.6	...	...	...	...
Cuba								
31 XII 2016 (ESDJ)								
Bayamo	158 978	...	...	...	...	...	...	...
Camagüey	306 183	...	...	...	...	...	...	...
Ciego de Ávila	119 394	...	...	...	...	...	...	...
Cienfuegos	150 404	...	...	...	...	...	...	...
Guantánamo	216 609	...	...	...	...	...	...	...
Holguín	294 002	...	...	...	...	...	...	...
LA HABANA	2 130 081	...	...	...	...	...	...	...
Las Tunas	168 645	...	...	...	...	...	...	...
Matanzas	140 107	...	...	...	...	...	...	...
Pinar del Río	142 967	...	...	...	...	...	...	...
Sancti Spíritus	108 127	...	...	...	...	...	...	...
Santa Clara	216 056	...	...	...	...	...	...	...
Santiago de Cuba	433 099	...	...	...	...	...	...	...

Continent, country or area, date, code[a] and city / Continent, pays ou zone, date, code[a] et ville	City proper - Ville proprement dite				Urban agglomeration - Agglomération urbaine			
	Population			Surface area - Superficie (km²)	Population			Surface area - Superficie (km²)
	Both sexes - Les deux sexes	Male - Masculin	Female - Féminin		Both sexes - Les deux sexes	Male - Masculin	Female - Féminin	

AMERICA, NORTH - AMÉRIQUE DU NORD

Dominican Republic - République dominicaine
1 VII 2011 (ESDF)

Azua	102 339[2]	51 620[2]	50 719[2]	155	...	...	...	...
Bajos de Haina	143 807[2]	71 130[2]	72 677[2]	40	...	...	...	...
Baní	177 588[2]	88 818[2]	88 770[2]	740	...	...	...	...
Boca Chica	122 216[2]	61 317[2]	60 899[2]	142	...	...	...	...
Bonao	148 857[2]	73 877[2]	74 980[2]	674	...	...	...	...
Higüey	211 453[2]	106 575[2]	104 878[2]	2026	...	...	...	...
La Romana	152 454[2]	73 291[2]	79 163[2]	263	...	...	...	...
La Vega	273 547[2]	137 511[2]	136 036[2]	641	...	...	...	...
Los Alcarrizos	249 595[2]	126 001[2]	123 594[2]	46	...	...	...	...
Moca	182 767[2]	91 506[2]	91 261[2]	337	...	...	...	...
Puerto Plata	156 123[2]	76 741[2]	79 382[2]	496	...	...	...	...
San Cristóbal	278 767[2]	138 614[2]	140 153[2]	214	...	...	...	...
San Francisco de Macoris	185 925[2]	92 282[2]	93 643[2]	760	...	...	...	...
San Juan de la Maguana	137 881[2]	70 406[2]	67 475[2]	1722	...	...	...	...
San Pedro de Macorís	233 255[2]	113 249[2]	120 006[2]	146	...	...	...	...
Santiago de los Caballeros	757 933[2]	372 332[2]	385 601[2]	529	...	...	...	...
SANTO DOMINGO	1 126 306[2]	537 506[2]	588 800[2]	91	1 126 306[2]	537 506[2]	588 800[2]	91
Santo Domingo East - Santo Domingo Este	966 393[2]	468 484[2]	497 909[2]	169	...	...	...	...
Santo Domingo North - Santo Domingo Norte	453 046[2]	228 840[2]	224 206[2]	388	...	...	...	...
Santo Domingo West - Santo Domingo Oeste	349 175[2]	170 849[2]	178 326[2]	54	...	...	...	...

El Salvador
1 VII 2016 (ESDF)

Ahuachapán	127 921	60 958	66 963	244.8	...	...	...	...
Apopa	180 500	82 329	98 171	51.8	...	...	...	...
Ciudad Delgado	128 263	59 291	68 972	33.4	...	...	...	...
Ilopango	133 215	60 313	72 902	34.6	...	...	...	...
Mejicanos	145 821	66 184	79 637	22.1	...	...	...	...
San Martin	100 408	46 299	54 109	55.8	...	...	...	...
San Miguel	261 714	121 511	140 203	594	...	...	...	...
SAN SALVADOR	247 959	113 223	134 736	72.3	...	...	...	...
Santa Ana	270 959	129 014	141 945	400.1	...	...	...	...
Santa Tecla	138 130	62 669	75 461	112.2	...	...	...	...
Soyapango	281 996	128 420	153 576	29.7	...	...	...	...

Greenland - Groenland[15]
1 VII 2016 (ESDJ)

NUUK (GODTHAB)	17 492	9 237	8 255	...	...	...	...	...

Grenada - Grenade
12 V 2011* (CDFC)

ST. GEORGE'S	36 823	...	...	...	...	...	...	...

Guadeloupe
8 III 1999 (CDJC)

BASSE-TERRE	12 377	5 687	6 690	...	44 747	21 252	23 495	...
Pointe-à-Pitre	...	...	...	...	171 773	...	...	...

Guatemala
1 VII 2001 (ESDF)

CUIDAD DE GUATEMALA	1 022 001	491 891	530 110	228	...	...	...	...
Escuintla	114 626	57 893	56 733	332	...	...	...	...
Mixco	452 134	221 928	230 206	99	...	...	...	...
Quetzaltenango	152 223	76 272	75 951	120	...	...	...	...
Villa Nueva	390 329	192 238	198 091	114	...	...	...	...

Haiti - Haïti
1 VII 1999 (ESDJ)

Cap-Haitien	113 555	50 064	63 491	10	...	...	...	...
Carrefour	336 222	146 838	189 384	23	...	...	...	...
Delmas	284 079	124 774	159 305	26	...	...	...	...
PORT-AU-PRINCE	990 558	436 170	554 388	21	...	...	...	...

Honduras
10 VIII 2013 (CDFC)

Catacamas	117 493	57 796	59 697	...	...	...	...	...
Choloma	231 669	111 124	120 545	...	...	...	...	...
Choluteca	152 519	73 637	78 882	...	...	...	...	...
Comayagua	144 785	69 290	75 495	...	...	...	...	...

8. Population of capital cities and cities of 100 000 or more inhabitants: latest available year, 1997 - 2016
Population des capitales et des villes de 100 000 habitants ou plus : dernière année disponible, 1997 - 2016 (continued - suite)

Continent, country or area, date, code[a] and city / Continent, pays ou zone, date, code[a] et ville	City proper - Ville proprement dite				Urban agglomeration - Agglomération urbaine			
	Population			Surface area - Superficie (km²)	Population			Surface area - Superficie (km²)
	Both sexes - Les deux sexes	Male - Masculin	Female - Féminin		Both sexes - Les deux sexes	Male - Masculin	Female - Féminin	
AMERICA, NORTH - AMÉRIQUE DU NORD								
Honduras								
10 VIII 2013 (CDFC)								
Danlí	195 916	97 441	98 474	...	...	...	...	...
El Progreso	188 366	89 734	98 633	...	...	...	...	...
Juticalpa	124 828	59 944	64 885	...	...	...	...	...
La Ceiba	197 267	93 209	104 058	...	...	...	...	...
Olanchito	104 609	50 858	53 750	...	...	...	...	...
Puerto Cortés	122 426	59 113	63 313	...	...	...	...	...
San Pedro Sula	719 064	343 111	375 953	...	...	...	...	...
TEGUCIGALPA	1 157 509	544 099	613 410	...	...	...	...	...
Villanueva	149 977	72 504	77 474	...	...	...	...	...
Jamaica - Jamaïque								
4 IV 2011 (CDJC)								
KINGSTON[16]	...	...	...	...	592 291	285 509	306 782	149
Montego Bay	...	...	...	...	111 037	53 601	57 436	76.7
Portmore	...	...	...	...	182 800	85 380	97 420	182.1
Spanish Town	...	...	...	...	149 479	72 885	76 594	64.6
Martinique								
1 I 2006 (CDJC)								
FORT-DE-FRANCE	90 347	40 128	50 219	...	133 281	59 945	73 336	...
Mexico - Mexique[2]								
1 VII 2016 (ESDJ)								
Acapulco	...	...	...	...	925 632	446 823	478 809	...
Acayucan	...	...	...	...	120 342	57 950	62 392	...
Aguascalientes	...	...	...	...	1 030 302	501 250	529 051	...
Apatzingán de la Constitución	...	...	...	...	102 061	...	...	...
Cabo San Lucas	...	...	...	...	165 719	...	...	...
Campeche	...	...	...	...	253 833	...	...	...
Cancún	...	...	...	...	824 548	416 302	408 245	...
Cárdenas	...	...	...	...	103 900	...	...	...
Celaya	...	...	...	...	645 792	308 769	337 023	...
Chetumal	...	...	...	...	184 899	...	...	...
Chihuahua	...	...	...	...	960 211	465 686	494 525	...
Chilpacingo de los Bravo	...	...	...	...	215 736	...	...	...
Ciudad Acuña	...	...	...	...	144 517	...	...	...
Ciudad Del Carmen	...	...	...	...	189 577	...	...	...
Ciudad Guzmán	...	...	...	...	103 876	...	...	...
Ciudad Lázaro Cárdenas	...	...	...	...	144 190	...	...	...
Ciudad Obregón	...	...	...	...	338 665	...	...	...
Ciudad Valles	...	...	...	...	133 882	...	...	...
Ciudad Victoria	...	...	...	...	336 548	...	...	...
Coatzacoalcos	...	...	...	...	373 810	181 357	192 452	...
Colima-Villa de Álvarez	...	...	...	...	376 748	183 275	193 473	...
Comitán de Domínguez	...	...	...	...	111 247	...	...	...
Córdoba	...	...	...	...	336 269	159 174	177 095	...
Cuauhtemoc	...	...	...	...	131 294	...	...	...
Cuautla	...	...	...	...	480 113	231 724	248 389	...
Cuernavaca	...	...	...	...	1 009 450	485 091	524 359	...
Culiacán Rosales	...	...	...	...	764 696	...	...	...
Delicias	...	...	...	...	132 372	...	...	...
Ensenada	...	...	...	...	307 843	...	...	...
Fresnillo	...	...	...	...	134 274	...	...	...
Guadalajara	...	...	...	...	4 853 425	2 373 876	2 479 549	...
Guanajuato	...	...	...	...	114 704	...	...	...
Guaymas	...	...	...	...	225 664	112 436	113 228	...
Hermosillo	...	...	...	...	799 165	...	...	...
Heroica Nogales	...	...	...	...	239 115	...	...	...
Hidalgo del Parral	...	...	...	...	114 289	...	...	...
Iguala de la Independencia	...	...	...	...	122 953	...	...	...
Irapuato	...	...	...	...	417 190	...	...	...
Juárez	...	...	...	...	1 435 761	709 352	726 409	...
La Laguna	...	...	...	...	1 327 769	650 386	677 383	...
La Paz	...	...	...	...	249 727	...	...	...
La Piedad-Pénjamo	...	...	...	...	263 342	124 958	138 384	...
Lagos de Moreno	...	...	...	...	106 881	...	...	...

Continent, country or area, date, code[a] and city / Continent, pays ou zone, date, code[a] et ville	City proper - Ville proprement dite				Urban agglomeration - Agglomération urbaine			
	Population			Surface area - Superficie (km²)	Population			Surface area - Superficie (km²)
	Both sexes - Les deux sexes	Male - Masculin	Female - Féminin		Both sexes - Les deux sexes	Male - Masculin	Female - Féminin	

AMERICA, NORTH - AMÉRIQUE DU NORD

Mexico - Mexique[2]
  1 VII 2016 (ESDJ)

León	...	...	...	...	1 729 455	839 710	889 745	...
Los Mochis	...	...	...	...	287 624	...	...	...
Manzanillo	...	...	...	...	160 334	...	...	...
Matamoros	...	...	...	...	530 780	262 369	268 411	...
Mazatlán	...	...	...	...	420 834	...	...	...
Mérida	...	...	...	...	1 078 370	524 707	553 662	...
Mexicali	...	...	...	...	1 039 260	522 555	516 705	...
MEXICO, CIUDAD DE	...	...	...	...	21 497 029	10 403 961	11 093 068	...
Minatitlán	...	...	...	...	381 166	184 237	196 929	...
Monclova-Frontera	...	...	...	...	342 071	169 731	172 340	...
Monterrey	...	...	...	...	4 540 429	2 254 972	2 285 457	...
Morelia	...	...	...	...	894 915	427 434	467 480	...
Moroleón Uriangato - Moroleón-Uriangato	...	...	...	...	114 540	54 345	60 195	...
Navojoa	...	...	...	...	126 960	...	...	...
Nuevo Laredo	...	...	...	...	419 266	207 343	211 923	...
Oaxaca	...	...	...	...	660 467	310 698	349 769	...
Ocotlán	...	...	...	...	151 043	73 869	77 174	...
Orizaba	...	...	...	...	454 216	215 678	238 538	...
Pachuca	...	...	...	...	579 084	276 618	302 467	...
Piedras Negras	...	...	...	...	193 152	96 790	96 363	...
Playa del Carmen	...	...	...	...	201 229	...	...	...
Poza Rica	...	...	...	...	542 003	261 614	280 389	...
Puebla-Tlaxcala	...	...	...	...	2 986 825	1 432 220	1 554 605	...
Puerto Vallarta	...	...	...	...	452 781	227 162	225 619	...
Querétaro	...	...	...	...	1 232 252	598 419	633 833	...
Reynosa-Río Bravo	...	...	...	...	821 492	407 882	413 610	...
Rioverde-Ciudad Fernández	...	...	...	...	144 719	70 674	74 045	...
Salamanca	...	...	...	...	171 559	...	...	...
Saltillo	...	...	...	...	912 716	452 405	460 311	...
San Cristóbal de las Casas	...	...	...	...	175 664	...	...	...
San Francisco del Rincón	...	...	...	...	196 919	96 026	100 893	...
San José del Cabo	...	...	...	...	121 843	...	...	...
San Juan Bautista Tuxtepec	...	...	...	...	112 653	...	...	...
San Juan del Río	...	...	...	...	153 759	...	...	...
San Luis Potosí-Soledad de Graciano Sánchez .	...	...	...	...	1 138 076	548 543	589 533	...
San Luis Rio Colorado	...	...	...	...	177 374	...	...	...
Tampico	...	...	...	...	937 558	455 179	482 379	...
Tapachula de Cordova y Ordoñez	...	...	...	...	233 949	...	...	...
Tecomán	...	...	...	...	159 326	79 853	79 474	...
Tehuacán	...	...	...	...	322 291	152 359	169 932	...
Tehuantepec	...	...	...	...	170 840	82 448	88 392	...
Tepatitlán De Morelos	...	...	...	...	100 693	...	...	...
Tepic	...	...	...	...	494 187	239 993	254 194	...
Teziutlán	...	...	...	...	132 462	62 929	69 533	...
Tianguistenco	...	...	...	...	182 575	88 744	93 831	...
Tijuana	...	...	...	...	1 967 762	985 953	981 809	...
Tlaxcala	...	...	...	...	553 748	266 226	287 522	...
Toluca	...	...	...	...	2 225 286	1 085 998	1 139 288	...
Tula	...	...	...	...	222 551	108 324	114 227	...
Tulancingo	...	...	...	...	265 428	125 830	139 598	...
Túxpan de Rodríguez Cano	...	...	...	...	116 763	...	...	...
Tuxtla Gutiérrez	...	...	...	...	772 995	370 855	402 140	...
Uruapan	...	...	...	...	297 997	...	...	...
Veracruz	...	...	...	...	870 478	413 476	457 002	...
Victoria de Durango	...	...	...	...	579 979	...	...	...
Villahermosa	...	...	...	...	834 305	406 613	427 693	...
Xalapa	...	...	...	...	726 403	343 683	382 720	...
Zacatecas-Guadalupe	...	...	...	...	342 001	164 086	177 915	...
Zamora-Jacona	...	...	...	...	263 692	126 999	136 693	...

Nicaragua
  1 VII 2009 (ESDJ)

Chinandega	...	...	...	...	106 635	...	...	...
León	...	...	...	...	156 049	...	...	...

8. Population of capital cities and cities of 100 000 or more inhabitants: latest available year, 1997 - 2016
Population des capitales et des villes de 100 000 habitants ou plus : dernière année disponible, 1997 - 2016 (continued - suite)

Continent, country or area, date, code[a] and city / Continent, pays ou zone, date, code[a] et ville	City proper - Ville proprement dite				Urban agglomeration - Agglomération urbaine			
	Population			Surface area - Superficie (km²)	Population			Surface area - Superficie (km²)
	Both sexes - Les deux sexes	Male - Masculin	Female - Féminin		Both sexes - Les deux sexes	Male - Masculin	Female - Féminin	
AMERICA, NORTH - AMÉRIQUE DU NORD								
Nicaragua								
1 VII 2009 (ESDJ)								
MANAGUA	...	...	...	...	985 143	...	...	...
Masaya	...	...	...	...	110 491	...	...	...
Tipitapa	...	...	...	...	105 773	...	...	...
Panama								
1 VII 2016* (ESDF)								
CIUDAD DE PANAMÁ	472 856[17]	225 177[17]	247 679[17]	98	1 066 148[17]	521 617[17]	544 531[17]	288
San Miguelito	360 101[17]	176 055[17]	184 046[17]	50	...	...	...	...
Puerto Rico - Porto Rico								
1 VII 2015 (ESDJ)								
Bayamón	189 159[18]	89 672[18]	99 487[18]	71	...	...	...	...
Caguas	134 481[18]	62 711[18]	71 770[18]	94	...	...	...	...
Carolina	161 884[18]	74 289[18]	87 595[18]	73	...	...	...	...
Ponce	149 028[18]	71 728[18]	77 300[18]	184	...	...	...	...
SAN JUAN	355 074[18]	162 498[18]	192 576[18]	77	...	...	...	...
Saint Lucia - Sainte-Lucie[3]								
10 V 2010* (CDJC)								
CASTRIES	4 173	2 044	2 129	...	...	...	...	...
Saint Pierre and Miquelon - Saint Pierre-et-Miquelon								
19 I 2006 (CDFC)								
SAINT-PIERRE	5 509	...	...	...	...	...	...	...
Trinidad and Tobago - Trinité-et-Tobago								
9 I 2011 (CDJC)								
PORT-OF-SPAIN	37 074	18 008	19 066	12	...	...	...	...
Turks and Caicos Islands - Îles Turques et Caïques								
1 VII 2006 (ESDJ)								
GRAND TURK	5 718	2 846	2 872	17	...	...	...	...
United States of America - États-Unis d'Amérique[19]								
1 VII 2016 (ESDJ)								
Abilene (TX)	122 225[20]	...	...	276.3[21]	...	...	...	...
Akron (OH)	197 633[20]	...	...	160.7[21]	...	...	...	...
Albuquerque (NM)	559 277[20]	...	...	487.4[21]	...	...	...	...
Alexandria (VA)	155 810[20]	...	...	39[21]	...	...	...	...
Allentown (PA)	120 443[20]	...	...	45.4[21]	...	...	...	...
Amarillo (TX)	199 582[20]	...	...	262.5[21]	...	...	...	...
Anaheim (CA)	351 043[20]	...	...	129.4[21]	...	...	...	...
Anchorage (AK)	298 192[20]	...	...	4420.1[21]	...	...	...	...
Ann Arbor (MI)	120 782[20]	...	...	72.7[21]	...	...	...	...
Antioch (CA)	110 898[20]	...	...	76.2[21]	...	...	...	...
Arlington (TX)	392 772[20]	...	...	248.2[21]	...	...	...	...
Arvada (CO)	117 453[20]	...	...	100[21]	...	...	...	...
Athens (GA)	123 371[20]	...	...	301.4[21]	...	...	...	...
Atlanta (GA)	472 522[20]	...	...	345.7[21]	...	...	...	...
Augusta (GA)	197 081[20]	...	...	783.4[21]	...	...	...	...
Aurora (CO)	361 710[20]	...	...	397.6[21]	...	...	...	...
Aurora (IL)	201 110[20]	...	...	116.3[21]	...	...	...	...
Austin (TX)	947 890[20]	...	...	810[21]	...	...	...	...
Bakersfield (CA)	376 380[20]	...	...	385.4[21]	...	...	...	...
Baltimore (MD)	614 664[20]	...	...	209.6[21]	...	...	...	...
Baton Rouge (LA)	227 715[20]	...	...	222.5[21]	...	...	...	...
Beaumont (TX)	118 299[20]	...	...	212.8[21]	...	...	...	...
Bellevue (WA)	141 400[20]	...	...	86.7[21]	...	...	...	...
Berkeley (CA)	121 240[20]	...	...	27.1[21]	...	...	...	...
Billings (MT)	110 323[20]	...	...	113.2[21]	...	...	...	...
Birmingham (AL)	212 157[20]	...	...	378.4[21]	...	...	...	...
Boise City (ID)	223 154[20]	...	...	212.6[21]	...	...	...	...
Boston (MA)	673 184[20]	...	...	125.2[21]	...	...	...	...
Boulder (CO)	108 090[20]	...	...	64.3[21]	...	...	...	...
Bridgeport (CT)	145 936[20]	...	...	41.6[21]	...	...	...	...
Broken Arrow (OK)	107 403[20]	...	...	159.9[21]	...	...	...	...
Brownsville (TX)	183 823[20]	...	...	343.1[21]	...	...	...	...

8. Population of capital cities and cities of 100 000 or more inhabitants: latest available year, 1997 - 2016
Population des capitales et des villes de 100 000 habitants ou plus : dernière année disponible, 1997 - 2016 (continued - suite)

Continent, country or area, date, code[a] and city Continent, pays ou zone, date, code[a] et ville	City proper - Ville proprement dite				Urban agglomeration - Agglomération urbaine			
	Population			Surface area - Superficie (km²)	Population			Surface area - Superficie (km²)
	Both sexes - Les deux sexes	Male - Masculin	Female - Féminin		Both sexes - Les deux sexes	Male - Masculin	Female - Féminin	
AMERICA, NORTH - AMÉRIQUE DU NORD								
United States of America - États-Unis d'Amérique[19]								
1 VII 2016 (ESDJ)								
Buffalo (NY)	256 902[20]	...	...	104.6[21]	...	...	...	...
Burbank (CA)	104 447[20]	...	...	44.9[21]	...	...	...	...
Cambridge (MA)	110 651[20]	...	...	16.6[21]	...	...	...	...
Cape Coral (FL)	179 804[20]	...	...	273.5[21]	...	...	...	...
Carlsbad (CA)	113 952[20]	...	...	97.7[21]	...	...	...	...
Carrollton (TX)	133 351[20]	...	...	94[21]	...	...	...	...
Cary (NC)	162 320[20]	...	...	146.3[21]	...	...	...	...
Cedar Rapids (IA)	131 127[20]	...	...	183.3[21]	...	...	...	...
Centennial (CO)	109 932[20]	...	...	76.5[21]	...	...	...	...
Chandler (AZ)	247 477[20]	...	...	168.2[21]	...	...	...	...
Charleston (SC)	134 385[20]	...	...	282.4[21]	...	...	...	...
Charlotte (NC)	842 051[20]	...	...	790.9[21]	...	...	...	...
Chattanooga (TN)	177 571[20]	...	...	370.6[21]	...	...	...	...
Chesapeake (VA)	237 940[20]	...	...	876.7[21]	...	...	...	...
Chicago (IL)	2 704 958[20]	...	...	588.8[21]	...	...	...	...
Chula Vista (CA)	267 172[20]	...	...	128.5[21]	...	...	...	...
Cincinnati (OH)	298 800[20]	...	...	200.4[21]	...	...	...	...
Clarksville (TN)	150 287[20]	...	...	254.5[21]	...	...	...	...
Clearwater (FL)	114 361[20]	...	...	67[21]	...	...	...	...
Cleveland (OH)	385 809[20]	...	...	201.3[21]	...	...	...	...
Clovis (CA)	106 583[20]	...	...	62.7[21]	...	...	...	...
College Station (TX)	112 141[20]	...	...	132.1[21]	...	...	...	...
Colorado Springs (CO)	465 101[20]	...	...	506.7[21]	...	...	...	...
Columbia (MO)	120 612[20]	...	...	168.3[21]	...	...	...	...
Columbia (SC)	134 309[20]	...	...	345.8[21]	...	...	...	...
Columbus (GA)	197 485[20]	...	...	560.5[21]	...	...	...	...
Columbus (OH)	860 090[20]	...	...	565.8[21]	...	...	...	...
Concord (CA)	128 726[20]	...	...	79.1[21]	...	...	...	...
Coral Springs (FL)	130 059[20]	...	...	61.6[21]	...	...	...	...
Corona (CA)	166 785[20]	...	...	102.2[21]	...	...	...	...
Corpus Christi (TX)	325 733[20]	...	...	452.1[21]	...	...	...	...
Costa Mesa (CA)	112 822[20]	...	...	40.7[21]	...	...	...	...
Dallas (TX)	1 317 929[20]	...	...	882.9[21]	...	...	...	...
Daly City (CA)	106 472[20]	...	...	19.8[21]	...	...	...	...
Davenport (IA)	102 612[20]	...	...	162.9[21]	...	...	...	...
Davie (FL)	101 871[20]	...	...	90.4[21]	...	...	...	...
Dayton (OH)	140 489[20]	...	...	144.2[21]	...	...	...	...
Denton (TX)	133 808[20]	...	...	241.9[21]	...	...	...	...
Denver (CO)	693 060[20]	...	...	397.1[21]	...	...	...	...
Des Moines (IA)	215 472[20]	...	...	230.3[21]	...	...	...	...
Detroit (MI)	672 795[20]	...	...	359.4[21]	...	...	...	...
Downey (CA)	113 267[20]	...	...	32.1[21]	...	...	...	...
Durham (NC)	263 016[20]	...	...	284.3[21]	...	...	...	...
El Cajon (CA)	103 768[20]	...	...	37.5[21]	...	...	...	...
El Monte (CA)	115 807[20]	...	...	24.8[21]	...	...	...	...
El Paso (TX)	683 080[20]	...	...	665[21]	...	...	...	...
Elgin (IL)	112 123[20]	...	...	97[21]	...	...	...	...
Elizabeth (NJ)	128 640[20]	...	...	31.9[21]	...	...	...	...
Elk Grove (CA)	169 743[20]	...	...	109.3[21]	...	...	...	...
Escondido (CA)	151 613[20]	...	...	96[21]	...	...	...	...
Eugene (OR)	166 575[20]	...	...	114.3[21]	...	...	...	...
Evansville (IN)	119 477[20]	...	...	122.6[21]	...	...	...	...
Everett (WA)	109 043[20]	...	...	86.1[21]	...	...	...	...
Fairfield (CA)	114 756[20]	...	...	106[21]	...	...	...	...
Fargo (ND)	120 762[20]	...	...	127.7[21]	...	...	...	...
Fayetteville (NC)	204 759[20]	...	...	382.7[21]	...	...	...	...
Fontana (CA)	209 665[20]	...	...	111.4[21]	...	...	...	...
Fort Collins (CO)	164 207[20]	...	...	144.6[21]	...	...	...	...
Fort Lauderdale (FL)	178 752[20]	...	...	89.7[21]	...	...	...	...

Continent, country or area, date, code[a] and city / Continent, pays ou zone, date, code[a] et ville	City proper - Ville proprement dite				Urban agglomeration - Agglomération urbaine			
	Population			Surface area - Superficie (km²)	Population			Surface area - Superficie (km²)
	Both sexes - Les deux sexes	Male - Masculin	Female - Féminin		Both sexes - Les deux sexes	Male - Masculin	Female - Féminin	

AMERICA, NORTH - AMÉRIQUE DU NORD

United States of America - États-Unis d'Amérique[19]
1 VII 2016 (ESDJ)

Fort Wayne (IN)	264 488[20]	...	...	286.5[21]	...	...	...	...
Fort Worth (TX)	854 113[20]	...	...	888.1[21]	...	...	...	...
Fremont (CA)	233 136[20]	...	...	200.6[21]	...	...	...	...
Fresno (CA)	522 053[20]	...	...	296.3[21]	...	...	...	...
Frisco (TX)	163 656[20]	...	...	175.3[21]	...	...	...	...
Fullerton (CA)	140 721[20]	...	...	58.1[21]	...	...	...	...
Gainesville (FL)	131 591[20]	...	...	161.4[21]	...	...	...	...
Garden Grove (CA)	174 858[20]	...	...	46.5[21]	...	...	...	...
Garland (TX)	234 943[20]	...	...	147.7[21]	...	...	...	...
Gilbert (AZ)	237 133[20]	...	...	176.1[21]	...	...	...	...
Glendale (AZ)	245 895[20]	...	...	153[21]	...	...	...	...
Glendale (CA)	200 831[20]	...	...	78.8[21]	...	...	...	...
Grand Prairie (TX)	190 682[20]	...	...	187.2[21]	...	...	...	...
Grand Rapids (MI)	196 445[20]	...	...	115.1[21]	...	...	...	...
Greeley (CO)	103 990[20]	...	...	123.9[21]	...	...	...	...
Green Bay (WI)	105 139[20]	...	...	117.7[21]	...	...	...	...
Greensboro (NC)	287 027[20]	...	...	332.3[21]	...	...	...	...
Gresham (OR)	111 523[20]	...	...	60.3[21]	...	...	...	...
Hampton (VA)	135 410[20]	...	...	133.3[21]	...	...	...	...
Hartford (CT)	123 243[20]	...	...	45[21]	...	...	...	...
Hayward (CA)	158 937[20]	...	...	117.9[21]	...	...	...	...
Henderson (NV)	292 969[20]	...	...	271.2[21]	...	...	...	...
Hialeah (FL)	236 387[20]	...	...	55.6[21]	...	...	...	...
High Point City (NC)	111 223[20]	...	...	143[21]	...	...	...	...
Hillsboro (OR)	105 164[20]	...	...	64.7[21]	...	...	...	...
Hollywood (FL)	151 998[20]	...	...	70.6[21]	...	...	...	...
Houston (TX)	2 303 482[20]	...	...	1651.2[21]	...	...	...	...
Huntington Beach (CA)	200 652[20]	...	...	69.8[21]	...	...	...	...
Huntsville (AL)	193 079[20]	...	...	552.6[21]	...	...	...	...
Independence (MO)	117 030[20]	...	...	201.6[21]	...	...	...	...
Indianapolis (IN)	855 164[20]	...	...	936.3[21]	...	...	...	...
Inglewood (CA)	110 654[20]	...	...	23.5[21]	...	...	...	...
Irvine (CA)	266 122[20]	...	...	169.9[21]	...	...	...	...
Irving (TX)	238 289[20]	...	...	173.6[21]	...	...	...	...
Jackson (MS)	169 148[20]	...	...	287.6[21]	...	...	...	...
Jacksonville (FL)	880 619[20]	...	...	1935.9[21]	...	...	...	...
Jersey City (NJ)	264 152[20]	...	...	38.3[21]	...	...	...	...
Joliet (IL)	148 262[20]	...	...	166.9[21]	...	...	...	...
Jurupa Valley (CA)	103 541[20]	...	...	111.2[21]	...	...	...	...
Kansas City (KS)	151 709[20]	...	...	323.3[21]	...	...	...	...
Kansas City (MO)	481 420[20]	...	...	815.8[21]	...	...	...	...
Kent (WA)	127 514[20]	...	...	87.4[21]	...	...	...	...
Killeen (TX)	143 400[20]	...	...	138.7[21]	...	...	...	...
Knoxville (TN)	186 239[20]	...	...	255.2[21]	...	...	...	...
Lafayette (LA)	127 626[20]	...	...	139.4[21]	...	...	...	...
Lakeland (FL)	106 420[20]	...	...	170.7[21]	...	...	...	...
Lakewood (CO)	154 393[20]	...	...	111[21]	...	...	...	...
Lancaster (CA)	160 106[20]	...	...	244.2[21]	...	...	...	...
Lansing (MI)	116 020[20]	...	...	101.3[21]	...	...	...	...
Laredo (TX)	257 156[20]	...	...	261.9[21]	...	...	...	...
Las Cruces (NM)	101 759[20]	...	...	199.3[21]	...	...	...	...
Las Vegas (NV)	632 912[20]	...	...	348[21]	...	...	...	...
League City (TX)	102 010[20]	...	...	132.6[21]	...	...	...	...
Lewisville (TX)	104 659[20]	...	...	95[21]	...	...	...	...
Lexington-Fayette (KY)	318 449[20]	...	...	734.6[21]	...	...	...	...
Lincoln (NE)	280 364[20]	...	...	238.6[21]	...	...	...	...
Little Rock (AR)	198 541[20]	...	...	307.4[21]	...	...	...	...
Long Beach (CA)	470 130[20]	...	...	130.3[21]	...	...	...	...
Los Angeles (CA)	3 976 322[20]	...	...	1214[21]	...	...	...	...

Continent, country or area, date, code[a] and city / Continent, pays ou zone, date, code[a] et ville	City proper - Ville proprement dite				Urban agglomeration - Agglomération urbaine			
	Population			Surface area - Superficie (km²)	Population			Surface area - Superficie (km²)
	Both sexes - Les deux sexes	Male - Masculin	Female - Féminin		Both sexes - Les deux sexes	Male - Masculin	Female - Féminin	

AMERICA, NORTH - AMÉRIQUE DU NORD

United States of America - États-Unis d'Amérique[19]
1 VII 2016 (ESDJ)

Continent, country or area, date, code[a] and city	Both sexes	Male	Female	Surface area	Both sexes	Male	Female	Surface area
Louisville (KY)	616 261[20]	...	...	841.7[21]	...	...	...	...
Lowell (MA)	110 558[20]	...	...	35.2[21]	...	...	...	...
Lubbock (TX)	252 506[20]	...	...	322.8[21]	...	...	...	...
Macon-Bibb (GA)	152 555[20]	...	...	645.6[21]	...	...	...	...
Madison (WI)	252 551[20]	...	...	199.3[21]	...	...	...	...
Manchester (NH)	110 506[20]	...	...	85.6[21]	...	...	...	...
McAllen (TX)	142 212[20]	...	...	151.1[21]	...	...	...	...
McKinney City (TX)	172 298[20]	...	...	163.1[21]	...	...	...	...
Memphis (TN)	652 717[20]	...	...	822[21]	...	...	...	...
Mesa (AZ)	484 587[20]	...	...	357.1[21]	...	...	...	...
Mesquite (TX)	143 736[20]	...	...	122.3[21]	...	...	...	...
Miami (FL)	453 579[20]	...	...	93.2[21]	...	...	...	...
Miami Gardens (FL)	113 058[20]	...	...	47.2[21]	...	...	...	...
Midland City (TX)	134 610[20]	...	...	192.6[21]	...	...	...	...
Milwaukee (WI)	595 047[20]	...	...	249.1[21]	...	...	...	...
Minneapolis (MN)	413 651[20]	...	...	139.9[21]	...	...	...	...
Miramar (FL)	138 449[20]	...	...	76.1[21]	...	...	...	...
Mobile (AL)	192 904[20]	...	...	361[21]	...	...	...	...
Modesto (CA)	212 175[20]	...	...	111.3[21]	...	...	...	...
Montgomery (AL)	200 022[20]	...	...	414[21]	...	...	...	...
Moreno Valley (CA)	205 499[20]	...	...	132.8[21]	...	...	...	...
Murfreesboro (TN)	131 947[20]	...	...	144.7[21]	...	...	...	...
Murrieta (CA)	111 674[20]	...	...	87[21]	...	...	...	...
Naperville (IL)	147 122[20]	...	...	100.2[21]	...	...	...	...
Nashville-Davidson (TN)	660 388[20]	...	...	1232.7[21]	...	...	...	...
New Haven (CT)	129 934[20]	...	...	48.4[21]	...	...	...	...
New Orleans (LA)	391 495[20]	...	...	438.8[21]	...	...	...	...
New York (NY)	8 537 673[20]	...	...	780.8[21]	...	...	...	...
Newark (NJ)	281 764[20]	...	...	62.5[21]	...	...	...	...
Newport News (VA)	181 825[20]	...	...	178.9[21]	...	...	...	...
Norfolk (VA)	245 115[20]	...	...	138[21]	...	...	...	...
Norman (OK)	122 180[20]	...	...	463[21]	...	...	...	...
North Charleston (SC)	109 298[20]	...	...	190.8[21]	...	...	...	...
North Las Vegas (NV)	238 702[20]	...	...	253.9[21]	...	...	...	...
Norwalk (CA)	106 178[20]	...	...	25.1[21]	...	...	...	...
Oakland (CA)	420 005[20]	...	...	144.8[21]	...	...	...	...
Oceanside (CA)	175 464[20]	...	...	106.8[21]	...	...	...	...
Odessa (TX)	117 871[20]	...	...	117[21]	...	...	...	...
Oklahoma City (OK)	638 367[20]	...	...	1570.3[21]	...	...	...	...
Olathe (KS)	135 473[20]	...	...	157.6[21]	...	...	...	...
Omaha (NE)	446 970[20]	...	...	345[21]	...	...	...	...
Ontario (CA)	173 212[20]	...	...	129.3[21]	...	...	...	...
Orange (CA)	140 504[20]	...	...	65.7[21]	...	...	...	...
Orlando (FL)	277 173[20]	...	...	272.5[21]	...	...	...	...
Overland Park (KS)	188 966[20]	...	...	194.6[21]	...	...	...	...
Oxnard (CA)	207 906[20]	...	...	69.7[21]	...	...	...	...
Palm Bay City (FL)	110 104[20]	...	...	170.2[21]	...	...	...	...
Palmdale (CA)	157 356[20]	...	...	274.5[21]	...	...	...	...
Pasadena (CA)	142 059[20]	...	...	59.5[21]	...	...	...	...
Pasadena (TX)	153 351[20]	...	...	112.6[21]	...	...	...	...
Paterson (NJ)	147 000[20]	...	...	21.8[21]	...	...	...	...
Pearland (TX)	113 570[20]	...	...	120[21]	...	...	...	...
Pembroke Pines (FL)	168 587[20]	...	...	85.5[21]	...	...	...	...
Peoria (AZ)	164 173[20]	...	...	455[21]	...	...	...	...
Peoria (IL)	114 265[20]	...	...	124.9[21]	...	...	...	...
Philadelphia (PA)	1 567 872[20]	...	...	347.5[21]	...	...	...	...
Phoenix (AZ)	1 615 017[20]	...	...	1340.7[21]	...	...	...	...
Pittsburgh (PA)	303 625[20]	...	...	143.4[21]	...	...	...	...
Plano (TX)	286 057[20]	...	...	185.6[21]	...	...	...	...

8. Population of capital cities and cities of 100 000 or more inhabitants: latest available year, 1997 - 2016
Population des capitales et des villes de 100 000 habitants ou plus : dernière année disponible, 1997 - 2016 (continued - suite)

Continent, country or area, date, code[a] and city / Continent, pays ou zone, date, code[a] et ville	City proper - Ville proprement dite				Urban agglomeration - Agglomération urbaine			
	Population			Surface area - Superficie (km²)	Population			Surface area - Superficie (km²)
	Both sexes - Les deux sexes	Male - Masculin	Female - Féminin		Both sexes - Les deux sexes	Male - Masculin	Female - Féminin	

AMERICA, NORTH - AMÉRIQUE DU NORD

United States of America - États-Unis d'Amérique[19]
1 VII 2016 (ESDJ)

City	Both sexes	Male	Female	Surface	Both sexes	Male	Female	Surface
Pomona (CA)	152 494[20]	...	...	59.4[21]	...	...	...	...
Pompano Beach (FL)	109 393[20]	...	...	62.3[21]	...	...	...	...
Port St. Lucie (FL)	185 132[20]	...	...	307.9[21]	...	...	...	...
Portland (OR)	639 863[20]	...	...	345.7[21]	...	...	...	...
Providence (RI)	179 219[20]	...	...	47.7[21]	...	...	...	...
Provo (UT)	116 868[20]	...	...	107.9[21]	...	...	...	...
Pueblo (CO)	110 291[20]	...	...	138.8[21]	...	...	...	...
Raleigh (NC)	458 880[20]	...	...	375.7[21]	...	...	...	...
Rancho Cucamonga (CA)	176 534[20]	...	...	103.6[21]	...	...	...	...
Reno (NV)	245 255[20]	...	...	277.9[21]	...	...	...	...
Renton (WA)	100 953[20]	...	...	60.7[21]	...	...	...	...
Rialto (CA)	103 314[20]	...	...	57.8[21]	...	...	...	...
Richardson (TX)	113 347[20]	...	...	74[21]	...	...	...	...
Richmond (CA)	109 813[20]	...	...	77.8[21]	...	...	...	...
Richmond (VA)	223 170[20]	...	...	154.9[21]	...	...	...	...
Riverside (CA)	324 722[20]	...	...	210.4[21]	...	...	...	...
Rochester (MN)	114 011[20]	...	...	141.3[21]	...	...	...	...
Rochester (NY)	208 880[20]	...	...	92.7[21]	...	...	...	...
Rockford (IL)	147 651[20]	...	...	164.4[21]	...	...	...	...
Roseville (CA)	132 671[20]	...	...	111.3[21]	...	...	...	...
Round Rock (TX)	120 892[20]	...	...	92.1[21]	...	...	...	...
Sacramento (CA)	495 234[20]	...	...	253.6[21]	...	...	...	...
Salem (OR)	167 419[20]	...	...	125.8[21]	...	...	...	...
Salinas (CA)	157 218[20]	...	...	61.2[21]	...	...	...	...
Salt Lake City (UT)	193 744[20]	...	...	288[21]	...	...	...	...
San Angelo (TX)	100 702[20]	...	...	155.3[21]	...	...	...	...
San Antonio (TX)	1 492 510[20]	...	...	1194[21]	...	...	...	...
San Bernardino (CA)	216 239[20]	...	...	159.3[21]	...	...	...	...
San Buenaventura (CA)	109 592[20]	...	...	56.5[21]	...	...	...	...
San Diego (CA)	1 406 630[20]	...	...	842.3[21]	...	...	...	...
San Francisco (CA)	870 887[20]	...	...	121.5[21]	...	...	...	...
San Jose (CA)	1 025 350[20]	...	...	459.7[21]	...	...	...	...
San Mateo (CA)	103 959[20]	...	...	31.4[21]	...	...	...	...
Sandy Springs (GA)	105 703[20]	...	...	97.5[21]	...	...	...	...
Santa Ana (CA)	334 217[20]	...	...	70.3[21]	...	...	...	...
Santa Clara (CA)	125 948[20]	...	...	47.7[21]	...	...	...	...
Santa Clarita (CA)	181 972[20]	...	...	136.6[21]	...	...	...	...
Santa Maria (CA)	106 290[20]	...	...	59[21]	...	...	...	...
Santa Rosa (CA)	175 155[20]	...	...	106.9[21]	...	...	...	...
Savannah (GA)	146 763[20]	...	...	268.3[21]	...	...	...	...
Scottsdale (AZ)	246 645[20]	...	...	476.4[21]	...	...	...	...
Seattle (WA)	704 352[20]	...	...	217.1[21]	...	...	...	...
Shreveport (LA)	194 920[20]	...	...	277.5[21]	...	...	...	...
Simi Valley (CA)	126 327[20]	...	...	107.4[21]	...	...	...	...
Sioux Falls (SD)	174 360[20]	...	...	195.3[21]	...	...	...	...
South Bend (IN)	101 735[20]	...	...	107.2[21]	...	...	...	...
Spokane (WA)	215 973[20]	...	...	178[21]	...	...	...	...
Springfield (IL)	115 715[20]	...	...	155.6[21]	...	...	...	...
Springfield (MA)	154 074[20]	...	...	82.5[21]	...	...	...	...
Springfield (MO)	167 319[20]	...	...	213.2[21]	...	...	...	...
St. Louis (MO)	311 404[20]	...	...	160.5[21]	...	...	...	...
St. Paul (MN)	302 398[20]	...	...	134.6[21]	...	...	...	...
St. Petersburg (FL)	260 999[20]	...	...	159.9[21]	...	...	...	...
Stamford (CT)	129 113[20]	...	...	97.4[21]	...	...	...	...
Sterling Heights (MI)	132 427[20]	...	...	94.6[21]	...	...	...	...
Stockton (CA)	307 072[20]	...	...	159.7[21]	...	...	...	...
Sunnyvale (CA)	152 771[20]	...	...	56.9[21]	...	...	...	...
Surprise (AZ)	132 677[20]	...	...	279.3[21]	...	...	...	...
Syracuse (NY)	143 378[20]	...	...	64.9[21]	...	...	...	...

Continent, country or area, date, code[a] and city / Continent, pays ou zone, date, code[a] et ville	City proper - Ville proprement dite				Urban agglomeration - Agglomération urbaine			
	Population			Surface area - Superficie (km²)	Population			Surface area - Superficie (km²)
	Both sexes - Les deux sexes	Male - Masculin	Female - Féminin		Both sexes - Les deux sexes	Male - Masculin	Female - Féminin	

AMERICA, NORTH - AMÉRIQUE DU NORD

United States of America - États-Unis d'Amérique[19]
1 VII 2016 (ESDJ)

Tacoma (WA)	211 277[20]	...	...	128.8[21]	...	...	...	...
Tallahassee (FL)	190 894[20]	...	...	260.1[21]	...	...	...	...
Tampa (FL)	377 165[20]	...	...	293.7[21]	...	...	...	...
Temecula (CA)	113 054[20]	...	...	96.5[21]	...	...	...	...
Tempe (AZ)	182 498[20]	...	...	103.5[21]	...	...	...	...
Thornton (CO)	136 703[20]	...	...	92.5[21]	...	...	...	...
Thousand Oaks (CA)	128 888[20]	...	...	142.9[21]	...	...	...	...
Toledo (OH)	278 508[20]	...	...	209.1[21]	...	...	...	...
Topeka (KS)	126 808[20]	...	...	159.2[21]	...	...	...	...
Torrance (CA)	147 195[20]	...	...	53[21]	...	...	...	...
Tucson (AZ)	530 706[20]	...	...	597.8[21]	...	...	...	...
Tulsa (OK)	403 090[20]	...	...	509.8[21]	...	...	...	...
Tyler (TX)	104 798[20]	...	...	146.7[21]	...	...	...	...
Urban Honolulu (HI)	351 792[20]	...	...	156.8[21]	...	...	...	...
Vallejo (CA)	121 299[20]	...	...	79.4[21]	...	...	...	...
Vancouver (WA)	174 826[20]	...	...	121.6[21]	...	...	...	...
Victorville City (CA)	122 265[20]	...	...	189.9[21]	...	...	...	...
Virginia Beach (VA)	452 602[20]	...	...	633.8[21]	...	...	...	...
Visalia (CA)	131 074[20]	...	...	97.1[21]	...	...	...	...
Vista (CA)	101 659[20]	...	...	48.4[21]	...	...	...	...
Waco (TX)	134 432[20]	...	...	230.6[21]	...	...	...	...
Warren (MI)	135 125[20]	...	...	89.1[21]	...	...	...	...
WASHINGTON (DC)	681 170[20]	...	...	158.4[21]	...	...	...	...
Waterbury (CT)	108 272[20]	...	...	73.9[21]	...	...	...	...
West Covina (CA)	107 847[20]	...	...	41.5[21]	...	...	...	...
West Jordan (UT)	113 699[20]	...	...	83.7[21]	...	...	...	...
West Palm Beach (FL)	108 161[20]	...	...	142.8[21]	...	...	...	...
West Valley City (UT)	136 574[20]	...	...	91.9[21]	...	...	...	...
Westminster (CO)	113 875[20]	...	...	82.2[21]	...	...	...	...
Wichita (KS)	389 902[20]	...	...	415.4[21]	...	...	...	...
Wichita Falls (TX)	104 724[20]	...	...	187[21]	...	...	...	...
Wilmington (NC)	117 525[20]	...	...	133.7[21]	...	...	...	...
Winston-Salem (NC)	242 203[20]	...	...	343.2[21]	...	...	...	...
Worcester (MA)	184 508[20]	...	...	96.8[21]	...	...	...	...
Yonkers (NY)	200 807[20]	...	...	46.7[21]	...	...	...	...

United States Virgin Islands - Îles Vierges américaines[22]
1 IV 2010 (CDJC)

CHARLOTTE AMALIE	10 354	...	...	...	...	...	...	...

AMERICA, SOUTH - AMÉRIQUE DU SUD

Argentina - Argentine[23]
1 VII 2016 (ESDF)

Bahía Blanca-Cerri	...	...	...	...	308 922	148 808	160 114	...
Bariloche	...	...	...	...	158 989	80 341	78 648	...
BUENOS AIRES	...	...	...	...	13 879 707	6 732 655	7 147 052	...
Catamarca	...	...	...	...	213 186	103 592	109 594	...
Comodoro Rivadavia-Rada Tilly	...	...	...	...	218 596	111 629	106 967	...
Concordia	...	...	...	...	161 990	79 065	82 925	...
Córdoba	...	...	...	...	1 525 490	731 552	793 938	...
Corrientes	...	...	...	...	386 379	185 631	200 748	...
Formosa	...	...	...	...	260 788	126 622	134 166	...
La Plata	...	...	...	...	843 851	409 347	434 504	...
La Rioja	...	...	...	...	207 085	101 956	105 129	...
Mar del Plata-Batán	...	...	...	...	641 065	308 438	332 627	...
Mendoza	...	...	...	...	1 094 209	533 737	560 472	...
Neuquén-Plottier	...	...	...	...	314 478	155 618	158 860	...
Paraná	...	...	...	...	276 125	132 139	143 986	...
Posadas	...	...	...	...	358 832	172 792	186 040	...

8. Population of capital cities and cities of 100 000 or more inhabitants: latest available year, 1997 - 2016
Population des capitales et des villes de 100 000 habitants ou plus : dernière année disponible, 1997 - 2016 (continued - suite)

Continent, country or area, date, code[a] and city / Continent, pays ou zone, date, code[a] et ville	City proper - Ville proprement dite				Urban agglomeration - Agglomération urbaine			
	Population			Surface area - Superficie (km²)	Population			Surface area - Superficie (km²)
	Both sexes - Les deux sexes	Male - Masculin	Female - Féminin		Both sexes - Les deux sexes	Male - Masculin	Female - Féminin	
AMERICA, SOUTH - AMÉRIQUE DU SUD								
Argentina - Argentine[23]								
1 VII 2016 (ESDF)								
Rawson-Trelew-Playa Unión	...	...	...	...	139 698	68 235	71 463	...
Resistencia	...	...	...	...	412 445	198 970	213 475	...
Río Cuarto	...	...	...	...	173 807	83 516	90 291	...
Río Gallegos	...	...	...	...	112 455	56 849	55 606	...
Rosario	...	...	...	...	1 444 436	701 272	743 164	...
Salta	...	...	...	...	634 644	306 877	327 767	...
San Juan	...	...	...	...	520 430	251 730	268 700	...
San Luis - El Chorrillo	...	...	...	...	221 410	108 478	112 932	...
San Nicolás-Villa Constitución	...	...	...	...	190 447	93 127	97 320	...
San Salvador de Jujuy-Palpalá	...	...	...	...	341 634	165 159	176 475	...
Santa Fé	...	...	...	...	534 341	256 803	277 538	...
Santa Rosa-Toay	...	...	...	...	127 055	61 725	65 330	...
Santiago del Estero-La Banda	...	...	...	...	410 083	198 119	211 964	...
Tucumán-Tafí Viejo	...	...	...	...	873 873	420 897	452 976	...
Ushuaia-Río Grande	...	...	...	...	139 989	72 112	67 877	...
Bolivia (Plurinational State of) - Bolivie (État plurinational de)								
1 VII 2010 (ESDF)								
Cochabamba	618 376	294 711	323 666	...	...	...	...	...
El Alto	953 253	463 069	490 184	...	...	...	...	...
LA PAZ	835 361	397 608	437 753	...	...	...	...	...
Oruro	216 724	104 294	112 430	...	...	...	...	...
Potosí	154 693	74 591	80 103	...	...	...	...	...
Sacaba	155 668	75 113	80 555	...	...	...	...	...
Santa Cruz	1 616 063	785 941	830 122	...	...	...	...	...
SUCRE	284 032	137 943	146 090	...	...	...	...	...
Tarija	194 313	94 231	100 082	...	...	...	...	...
Yacuiba	112 096	55 346	56 750	...	...	...	...	...
Brazil - Brésil[24]								
1 VII 2016 (ESDJ)								
Abaeteluba	151 934	...	...	...	...	...	...	...
Açailândia	110 543	...	...	...	...	...	...	...
Aguas Lindas de Goiás	191 499	...	...	...	...	...	...	...
Alagoinhas	155 362	...	...	...	...	...	...	...
Almirante Tamandaré	114 129	...	...	...	...	...	...	...
Altamira	109 938	...	...	...	...	...	...	...
Alvorada	207 392	...	...	...	...	...	...	...
Americana	231 621	...	...	...	...	...	...	...
Ananindeua	510 834	...	...	...	...	...	...	...
Anápolis	370 875	...	...	...	...	...	...	...
Angra dos Reis	191 504	...	...	...	...	...	...	...
Aparecida de Goiania	532 135	...	...	...	...	...	...	...
Apucarana	131 571	...	...	...	...	...	...	...
Aracaju	641 523	...	...	...	...	...	...	...
Araçatuba	193 828	...	...	...	...	...	...	...
Araguaina	173 112	...	...	...	...	...	...	...
Araguario	116 871	...	...	...	...	...	...	...
Arapiraca	232 671	...	...	...	...	...	...	...
Arapongas	116 960	...	...	...	...	...	...	...
Araraquara	228 664	...	...	...	...	...	...	...
Araras	130 102	...	...	...	...	...	...	...
Araruama	124 940	...	...	...	...	...	...	...
Araucária	135 459	...	...	...	...	...	...	...
Araxá	103 287	...	...	...	...	...	...	...
Ariquemes	105 896	...	...	...	...	...	...	...
Assis	102 268	...	...	...	...	...	...	...
Atibaia	138 449	...	...	...	...	...	...	...
Bacabal	103 020	...	...	...	...	...	...	...
Bagé	121 986	...	...	...	...	...	...	...
Balneário Camboriú	131 727	...	...	...	...	...	...	...
Barbacena	135 829	...	...	...	...	...	...	...
Barcarena	118 537	...	...	...	...	...	...	...
Barra Mansa	180 126	...	...	...	...	...	...	...

8. Population of capital cities and cities of 100 000 or more inhabitants: latest available year, 1997 - 2016

Population des capitales et des villes de 100 000 habitants ou plus : dernière année disponible, 1997 - 2016 (continued - suite)

Continent, country or area, date, code[a] and city / Continent, pays ou zone, date, code[a] et ville	City proper - Ville proprement dite				Urban agglomeration - Agglomération urbaine			
	Population			Surface area - Superficie (km²)	Population			Surface area - Superficie (km²)
	Both sexes - Les deux sexes	Male - Masculin	Female - Féminin		Both sexes - Les deux sexes	Male - Masculin	Female - Féminin	

AMERICA, SOUTH - AMÉRIQUE DU SUD

Brazil - Brésil[24]
  1 VII 2016 (ESDJ)

Barreiras	155 519	...	...	...	...	...	...	...
Barretos	119 948	...	...	...	...	...	...	...
Barueri	264 935	...	...	...	...	...	...	...
Bauru	369 368	...	...	...	...	...	...	...
Belém	1 446 042	...	...	...	...	...	...	...
Belford Roxo	494 141	...	...	...	...	...	...	...
Belo Horizonte	2 513 451	...	...	...	...	...	...	...
Bento Gonçalves	114 203	...	...	...	...	...	...	...
Betim	422 354	...	...	...	...	...	...	...
Birigui	119 536	...	...	...	...	...	...	...
Blumenou	343 715	...	...	...	...	...	...	...
Boa Vista	326 419	...	...	...	...	...	...	...
Botucatu	141 032	...	...	...	...	...	...	...
Bragança	122 881	...	...	...	...	...	...	...
Bragança Paulista	162 435	...	...	...	...	...	...	...
BRASILIA	2 977 216	...	...	...	...	...	...	...
Brusque	125 810	...	...	...	...	...	...	...
Cabo de Santo Agostinho	202 636	...	...	...	...	...	...	...
Cabo Frio	212 289	...	...	...	...	...	...	...
Cachoeirinha	126 666	...	...	...	...	...	...	...
Cachoeiro de Itapemirim	210 325	...	...	...	...	...	...	...
Camacari	292 074	...	...	...	...	...	...	...
Camaragibe	155 228	...	...	...	...	...	...	...
Cambé	104 592	...	...	...	...	...	...	...
Cametá	132 515	...	...	...	...	...	...	...
Campina Grande	407 754	...	...	...	...	...	...	...
Campinas	1 173 370	...	...	...	...	...	...	...
Campo Grande	863 982	...	...	...	...	...	...	...
Campo Largo	125 719	...	...	...	...	...	...	...
Campos dos Goytacazes	487 186	...	...	...	...	...	...	...
Canoas	342 634	...	...	...	...	...	...	...
Caraguatatuba	115 071	...	...	...	...	...	...	...
Carapicuíba	394 465	...	...	...	...	...	...	...
Cariacica	384 621	...	...	...	...	...	...	...
Caruaru	351 686	...	...	...	...	...	...	...
Cascavel	316 226	...	...	...	...	...	...	...
Castanhal	192 571	...	...	...	...	...	...	...
Catalão	100 590	...	...	...	...	...	...	...
Catanduva	120 092	...	...	...	...	...	...	...
Caucaia	358 164	...	...	...	...	...	...	...
Caxias	161 926	...	...	...	...	...	...	...
Caxias do Sul	479 236	...	...	...	...	...	...	...
Chapecó	209 553	...	...	...	...	...	...	...
Codo	120 548	...	...	...	...	...	...	...
Colatina	123 598	...	...	...	...	...	...	...
Colombo	234 941	...	...	...	...	...	...	...
Conselheiro Lafaiete	126 420	...	...	...	...	...	...	...
Contagem	653 800	...	...	...	...	...	...	...
Coronel Fabriciano	109 857	...	...	...	...	...	...	...
Corumbá	109 294	...	...	...	...	...	...	...
Cotia	233 696	...	...	...	...	...	...	...
Crato	129 662	...	...	...	...	...	...	...
Criciúma	209 153	...	...	...	...	...	...	...
Cubatao	127 887	...	...	...	...	...	...	...
Cuiabá	585 367	...	...	...	...	...	...	...
Curitiba	1 893 997	...	...	...	...	...	...	...
Diadema	415 180	...	...	...	...	...	...	...
Divinópolis	232 945	...	...	...	...	...	...	...
Dourados	215 486	...	...	...	...	...	...	...
Duque de Caxias	886 917	...	...	...	...	...	...	...
Embu	264 448	...	...	...	...	...	...	...
Erechim	102 906	...	...	...	...	...	...	...
Eunápolis	114 275	...	...	...	...	...	...	...

Continent, country or area, date, code[a] and city / Continent, pays ou zone, date, code[a] et ville	City proper - Ville proprement dite				Urban agglomeration - Agglomération urbaine			
	Population			Surface area - Superficie (km²)	Population			Surface area - Superficie (km²)
	Both sexes - Les deux sexes	Male - Masculin	Female - Féminin		Both sexes - Les deux sexes	Male - Masculin	Female - Féminin	

AMERICA, SOUTH - AMÉRIQUE DU SUD

Brazil - Brésil[24]
  1 VII 2016 (ESDJ)

Feira de Santana	622 639	...	...	...	...	...	...	...
Ferraz de Vasconcelos	186 808	...	...	...	...	...	...	...
Florianópolis	477 798	...	...	...	...	...	...	...
Formosa	114 036	...	...	...	...	...	...	...
Fortaleza	2 609 716	...	...	...	...	...	...	...
Foz do Iguaçu	263 915	...	...	...	...	...	...	...
Franca	344 704	...	...	...	...	...	...	...
Francisco Morato	169 942	...	...	...	...	...	...	...
Franco da Rocha	147 650	...	...	...	...	...	...	...
Garanhuns	137 810	...	...	...	...	...	...	...
Goiânia	1 448 639	...	...	...	...	...	...	...
Governador Valadares	279 665	...	...	...	...	...	...	...
Gravataí	273 742	...	...	...	...	...	...	...
Guarapari	121 506	...	...	...	...	...	...	...
Guarapuava	179 256	...	...	...	...	...	...	...
Guaratinguetá	119 753	...	...	...	...	...	...	...
Guarujá	313 421	...	...	...	...	...	...	...
Guarulhos	1 337 087	...	...	...	...	...	...	...
Hortolandia	219 039	...	...	...	...	...	...	...
Ibirité	175 721	...	...	...	...	...	...	...
Igarassu	113 956	...	...	...	...	...	...	...
Iguatu	102 013	...	...	...	...	...	...	...
Ilhéus	178 210	...	...	...	...	...	...	...
Imperatriz	253 873	...	...	...	...	...	...	...
Indaiatuba	235 367	...	...	...	...	...	...	...
Ipatinga	259 324	...	...	...	...	...	...	...
Itabiraí	118 481	...	...	...	...	...	...	...
Itaboraí	230 786	...	...	...	...	...	...	...
Itabuna	220 386	...	...	...	...	...	...	...
Itaguaí	120 855	...	...	...	...	...	...	...
Itajaí	208 958	...	...	...	...	...	...	...
Itapecerica da Serra	169 103	...	...	...	...	...	...	...
Itapetininga	158 561	...	...	...	...	...	...	...
Itapevi	226 488	...	...	...	...	...	...	...
Itapipoca	126 234	...	...	...	...	...	...	...
Itaquaquecetuba	356 774	...	...	...	...	...	...	...
Itatiba	114 912	...	...	...	...	...	...	...
Itu	168 643	...	...	...	...	...	...	...
Ituiutaba	103 945	...	...	...	...	...	...	...
Itumbiara	101 544	...	...	...	...	...	...	...
Jaboatao dos Guarapes	691 125	...	...	...	...	...	...	...
Jacareí	228 214	...	...	...	...	...	...	...
Jandira	120 177	...	...	...	...	...	...	...
Japeri	100 562	...	...	...	...	...	...	...
Jaraguá do Sul	167 300	...	...	...	...	...	...	...
Jaú	144 828	...	...	...	...	...	...	...
Jequié	161 880	...	...	...	...	...	...	...
Ji-Paraná	131 560	...	...	...	...	...	...	...
Joao Pessoa	801 718	...	...	...	...	...	...	...
Joinville	569 645	...	...	...	...	...	...	...
Juazeiro	220 253	...	...	...	...	...	...	...
Juàzeiro do Norte	268 248	...	...	...	...	...	...	...
Juiz de Fora	559 636	...	...	...	...	...	...	...
Jundiaí	405 740	...	...	...	...	...	...	...
Lagarto	103 188	...	...	...	...	...	...	...
Lages	158 620	...	...	...	...	...	...	...
Lauro de Freitas	194 641	...	...	...	...	...	...	...
Lavras	101 208	...	...	...	...	...	...	...
Leme	100 296	...	...	...	...	...	...	...
Limeira	298 701	...	...	...	...	...	...	...
Linhares	166 491	...	...	...	...	...	...	...
Londrina	553 393	...	...	...	...	...	...	...
Luziânia	196 864	...	...	...	...	...	...	...

Continent, country or area, date, code[a] and city / Continent, pays ou zone, date, code[a] et ville	City proper - Ville proprement dite				Urban agglomeration - Agglomération urbaine			
	Population			Surface area - Superficie (km²)	Population			Surface area - Superficie (km²)
	Both sexes - Les deux sexes	Male - Masculin	Female - Féminin		Both sexes - Les deux sexes	Male - Masculin	Female - Féminin	

AMERICA, SOUTH - AMÉRIQUE DU SUD

Brazil - Brésil[24]
  1 VII 2016 (ESDJ)

Macae	239 471	...	...	...	...	...	...	...
Macapá	465 495	...	...	...	...	...	...	...
Maceió	1 021 709	...	...	...	...	...	...	...
Magé	236 319	...	...	...	...	...	...	...
Manaus	2 094 391	...	...	...	...	...	...	...
Maraba	266 932	...	...	...	...	...	...	...
Maracanau	223 188	...	...	...	...	...	...	...
Maranguape	125 058	...	...	...	...	...	...	...
Maricá	149 876	...	...	...	...	...	...	...
Marília	233 639	...	...	...	...	...	...	...
Maringá	403 063	...	...	...	...	...	...	...
Marituba	125 435	...	...	...	...	...	...	...
Mauá	457 696	...	...	...	...	...	...	...
Mesquita	171 020	...	...	...	...	...	...	...
Moji das Cruzes	429 321	...	...	...	...	...	...	...
Moji-Guaçu	148 327	...	...	...	...	...	...	...
Montes Claros	398 288	...	...	...	...	...	...	...
Mossoró	291 937	...	...	...	...	...	...	...
Muriaé	107 916	...	...	...	...	...	...	...
Natal	877 662	...	...	...	...	...	...	...
Nilópolis	158 319	...	...	...	...	...	...	...
Niterói	497 883	...	...	...	...	...	...	...
Nossa Senhora do Socorro	179 661	...	...	...	...	...	...	...
Nova Friburgo	185 102	...	...	...	...	...	...	...
Nova Iguaçu	797 435	...	...	...	...	...	...	...
Novo Gama	108 410	...	...	...	...	...	...	...
Nôvo Hamburgo	249 113	...	...	...	...	...	...	...
Olinda	390 144	...	...	...	...	...	...	...
Osasco	696 382	...	...	...	...	...	...	...
Ourinhos	111 056	...	...	...	...	...	...	...
Paço do Lumiar	119 915	...	...	...	...	...	...	...
Palhoça	161 395	...	...	...	...	...	...	...
Palmas	279 856	...	...	...	...	...	...	...
Paragominas	108 547	...	...	...	...	...	...	...
Paranaguá	151 829	...	...	...	...	...	...	...
Parauapebas	196 259	...	...	...	...	...	...	...
Parintins	112 716	...	...	...	...	...	...	...
Parnaíba	150 201	...	...	...	...	...	...	...
Parnamirim	248 623	...	...	...	...	...	...	...
Passo Fundo	197 798	...	...	...	...	...	...	...
Passos	113 807	...	...	...	...	...	...	...
Patos	107 067	...	...	...	...	...	...	...
Patos de Minas	149 856	...	...	...	...	...	...	...
Paulínia	100 128	...	...	...	...	...	...	...
Paulista	325 590	...	...	...	...	...	...	...
Paulo Afonso	119 930	...	...	...	...	...	...	...
Pelotas	343 651	...	...	...	...	...	...	...
Petrolina	337 683	...	...	...	...	...	...	...
Petrópolis	298 158	...	...	...	...	...	...	...
Pindamonhangaba	162 327	...	...	...	...	...	...	...
Pinhais	128 256	...	...	...	...	...	...	...
Piracicaba	394 419	...	...	...	...	...	...	...
Piraquara	106 132	...	...	...	...	...	...	...
Poà	114 650	...	...	...	...	...	...	...
Poços de Caldas	164 912	...	...	...	...	...	...	...
Ponta Grossa	341 130	...	...	...	...	...	...	...
Porto Alegre	1 481 019	...	...	...	...	...	...	...
Porto Seguro	147 444	...	...	...	...	...	...	...
Porto Velho	511 219	...	...	...	...	...	...	...
Pouso Alegre	145 535	...	...	...	...	...	...	...
Praia Grande	304 705	...	...	...	...	...	...	...
Presidente Prudente	223 749	...	...	...	...	...	...	...
Queimados	144 525	...	...	...	...	...	...	...

8. Population of capital cities and cities of 100 000 or more inhabitants: latest available year, 1997 - 2016
Population des capitales et des villes de 100 000 habitants ou plus : dernière année disponible, 1997 - 2016 (continued - suite)

Continent, country or area, date, code[a] and city / Continent, pays ou zone, date, code[a] et ville	City proper - Ville proprement dite				Urban agglomeration - Agglomération urbaine			
	Population			Surface area - Superficie (km²)	Population			Surface area - Superficie (km²)
	Both sexes - Les deux sexes	Male - Masculin	Female - Féminin		Both sexes - Les deux sexes	Male - Masculin	Female - Féminin	

AMERICA, SOUTH - AMÉRIQUE DU SUD

Brazil - Brésil[24]
1 VII 2016 (ESDJ)

Recife	1 625 583	...	...	...	...	...	...	...
Resende	126 084	...	...	...	...	...	...	...
Ribeirao das Neves	325 846	...	...	...	...	...	...	...
Ribeirao Pires	121 130	...	...	...	...	...	...	...
Ribeirao Prêto	674 405	...	...	...	...	...	...	...
Rio Branco	377 057	...	...	...	...	...	...	...
Rio Claro	201 473	...	...	...	...	...	...	...
Rio das Ostras	136 626	...	...	...	...	...	...	...
Rio de Janeiro	6 498 837	...	...	...	...	...	...	...
Rio Grande	208 641	...	...	...	...	...	...	...
Rio Verde	212 237	...	...	...	...	...	...	...
Rondonópolis	218 899	...	...	...	...	...	...	...
Sabára	135 196	...	...	...	...	...	...	...
Salto	115 193	...	...	...	...	...	...	...
Salvador	2 938 092	...	...	...	...	...	...	...
Santa Bárbara D'Oeste	191 024	...	...	...	...	...	...	...
Santa Cruz do Capibaribe	103 660	...	...	...	...	...	...	...
Santa Cruz do Sul	126 775	...	...	...	...	...	...	...
Santa Luzia (Minas Gerais)	217 610	...	...	...	...	...	...	...
Santa Maria	277 309	...	...	...	...	...	...	...
Santa Rita	135 915	...	...	...	...	...	...	...
Santana	113 854	...	...	...	...	...	...	...
Santana de Parnaíba	129 261	...	...	...	...	...	...	...
Santarém	294 447	...	...	...	...	...	...	...
Santo André	712 749	...	...	...	...	...	...	...
Santo Antônio de Jesus	102 469	...	...	...	...	...	...	...
Santos	434 359	...	...	...	...	...	...	...
Sao Bernardo do Campo	822 242	...	...	...	...	...	...	...
Sao Caetano do Sul	158 825	...	...	...	...	...	...	...
Sao Carlo	243 765	...	...	...	...	...	...	...
São Félix do Xingu	120 580	...	...	...	...	...	...	...
Sao Gonçalo	1 044 058	...	...	...	...	...	...	...
Sao Joao de Meriti	460 541	...	...	...	...	...	...	...
Sao José	236 029	...	...	...	...	...	...	...
Sao José de Ribamar	176 008	...	...	...	...	...	...	...
Sao José do Rio Prêto	446 649	...	...	...	...	...	...	...
Sao José dos Campos	695 992	...	...	...	...	...	...	...
Sao José dos Pinhais	302 759	...	...	...	...	...	...	...
Sao Leopoldo	229 678	...	...	...	...	...	...	...
São Lourenço da Mata	111 197	...	...	...	...	...	...	...
Sao Luís	1 082 935	...	...	...	...	...	...	...
São Mateus	126 437	...	...	...	...	...	...	...
Sao Paulo	12 038 175	...	...	...	...	...	...	...
Sao Vicente	357 989	...	...	...	...	...	...	...
Sapucaia do Sul	138 933	...	...	...	...	...	...	...
Senador Canedo	102 947	...	...	...	...	...	...	...
Serra	494 109	...	...	...	...	...	...	...
Sertaozinho	121 412	...	...	...	...	...	...	...
Sete Lagoas	234 221	...	...	...	...	...	...	...
Simoes Filho	134 674	...	...	...	...	...	...	...
Sinop	132 934	...	...	...	...	...	...	...
Sobral	203 682	...	...	...	...	...	...	...
Sorocaba	652 481	...	...	...	...	...	...	...
Sumaré	269 522	...	...	...	...	...	...	...
Susano	288 056	...	...	...	...	...	...	...
Taboao da Serra	275 948	...	...	...	...	...	...	...
Tailândia	100 300	...	...	...	...	...	...	...
Tatuí	117 823	...	...	...	...	...	...	...
Taubaté	305 174	...	...	...	...	...	...	...
Teixeira de Freitas	159 813	...	...	...	...	...	...	...
Teófilo Otoni	141 502	...	...	...	...	...	...	...
Teresina	847 430	...	...	...	...	...	...	...
Teresópolis	174 587	...	...	...	...	...	...	...

Continent, country or area, date, code[a] and city Continent, pays ou zone, date, code[a] et ville	City proper - Ville proprement dite				Urban agglomeration - Agglomération urbaine			
	Population			Surface area - Superficie (km²)	Population			Surface area - Superficie (km²)
	Both sexes - Les deux sexes	Male - Masculin	Female - Féminin		Both sexes - Les deux sexes	Male - Masculin	Female - Féminin	
AMERICA, SOUTH - AMÉRIQUE DU SUD								
Brazil - Brésil[24]								
1 VII 2016 (ESDJ)								
Timon	166 295	...	...	...	...	...	...	...
Toledo	133 824	...	...	...	...	...	...	...
Três Lagoas	115 561	...	...	...	...	...	...	...
Trindade	119 385	...	...	...	...	...	...	...
Tubarão	103 674	...	...	...	...	...	...	...
Tucuruí	108 885	...	...	...	...	...	...	...
Ubá	112 186	...	...	...	...	...	...	...
Uberaba	325 279	...	...	...	...	...	...	...
Uberlândia	669 672	...	...	...	...	...	...	...
Umuarama	109 132	...	...	...	...	...	...	...
Uruguaiana	129 720	...	...	...	...	...	...	...
Valinhos	122 163	...	...	...	...	...	...	...
Valparaíso de Goiás	156 419	...	...	...	...	...	...	...
Varginha	133 384	...	...	...	...	...	...	...
Varzea Grande	271 339	...	...	...	...	...	...	...
Varzea Paulista	117 772	...	...	...	...	...	...	...
Vespasiano	120 510	...	...	...	...	...	...	...
Viamao	252 872	...	...	...	...	...	...	...
Vila Velha	479 664	...	...	...	...	...	...	...
Vitória	359 555	...	...	...	...	...	...	...
Vitória da Conquista	346 069	...	...	...	...	...	...	...
Vitória de Santo Antao	136 706	...	...	...	...	...	...	...
Volta Redonda	263 659	...	...	...	...	...	...	...
Votorantim	118 858	...	...	...	...	...	...	...
Chile - Chili								
1 VII 2016 (ESDF)								
Alto Hospicio	118 418	60 006	58 412	17[25]	...	...	...	...
Antofagasta	382 833	202 673	180 160	44[25]	...	...	...	...
Arica	225 833	112 321	113 512	42[25]	...	...	...	...
Calama	177 550	90 332	87 218	18[25]	...	...	...	...
Chiguallante	100 157	47 653	52 504	34[25]	...	...	...	...
Chillán	159 261	75 074	84 187	33[25]	...	...	...	...
Concepción	221 085	104 626	116 459	56[25]	...	...	...	...
Copiapó	171 918	87 190	84 728	48[25]	...	...	...	...
Coquimbo	212 224	103 438	108 786	42[25]	...	...	...	...
Coronel	108 843	51 274	57 569	25[25]	...	...	...	...
Curicó	103 233	49 664	53 569	21[25]	...	...	...	...
Iquique	195 478	98 017	97 461	22[25]	...	...	...	...
La Serena	202 070	98 357	103 713	66[25]	...	...	...	...
Los Ángeles	128 792	61 884	66 908	27[25]	...	...	...	...
Osorno	139 733	67 047	72 686	32[25]	...	...	...	...
Puente Alto	617 911	304 677	313 234	64[25]	...	...	...	...
Puerto Montt	210 018	104 727	105 291	40[25]	...	...	...	...
Punta Arenas	123 735	61 390	62 345	39[25]	...	...	...	...
Quilpué	169 269	81 883	87 386	38[25]	...	...	...	...
Rancagua	225 022	111 750	113 272	50[25]	...	...	...	...
San Bernardo	293 399	145 827	147 572	52[25]	...	...	...	...
San Pedro de la Paz	134 705	63 073	71 632	49[25]	...	...	...	...
SANTIAGO	5 561 252[26]	2 697 725[26]	2 863 527[26]	843[25]	...	...	...	...
Talca	205 072	98 164	106 908	46[25]	...	...	...	...
Talcahuano	101 252	47 407	53 845	51[25]	...	...	...	...
Temuco	225 664	107 772	117 892	46[25]	...	...	...	...
Valdivia	142 687	69 273	73 414	42[25]	...	...	...	...
Valparaíso	294 902	147 138	147 764	47[25]	...	...	...	...
Villa Alemana	140 996	68 824	72 172	31[25]	...	...	...	...
Viña del Mar	310 193	156 633	153 560	87[25]	...	...	...	...
Colombia - Colombie								
1 VII 2016 (ESDJ)								
Apartadó	183 716[27]	92 853[27]	90 863[27]	607[28]	...	...	...	...
Armenia	298 199[27]	143 932[27]	154 267[27]	111[28]	...	...	...	...
Barrancabermeja	191 704[27]	94 619[27]	97 085[27]	1274[28]	...	...	...	...

8. Population of capital cities and cities of 100 000 or more inhabitants: latest available year, 1997 - 2016
Population des capitales et des villes de 100 000 habitants ou plus : dernière année disponible, 1997 - 2016 (continued - suite)

Continent, country or area, date, code[a] and city / Continent, pays ou zone, date, code[a] et ville	City proper - Ville proprement dite				Urban agglomeration - Agglomération urbaine			
	Population			Surface area - Superficie (km²)	Population			Surface area - Superficie (km²)
	Both sexes - Les deux sexes	Male - Masculin	Female - Féminin		Both sexes - Les deux sexes	Male - Masculin	Female - Féminin	

AMERICA, SOUTH - AMÉRIQUE DU SUD

Colombia - Colombie
1 VII 2016 (ESDJ)

Continent, country or area, date, code[a] and city	Both sexes	Male	Female	Surface area	Both sexes	Male	Female	Surface area
Barranquilla	1 223 616[27]	593 773[27]	629 843[27]	166[28]	...	...	...	...
Bello	464 614[27]	224 833[27]	239 781[27]	151[28]	...	...	...	...
BOGOTÁ, D.C.	7 980 001[27]	3 861 624[27]	4 118 377[27]	1605[28]	...	...	...	...
Bucaramanga	528 269[27]	254 121[27]	274 148[27]	154[28]	...	...	...	...
Buenaventura	407 675[27]	198 261[27]	209 414[27]	6785[28]	...	...	...	...
Cali	2 394 925[27]	1 144 848[27]	1 250 077[27]	552[28]	...	...	...	...
Cartagena	1 013 389[27]	490 036[27]	523 353[27]	559[28]	...	...	...	...
Cartago	132 959[27]	63 949[27]	69 010[27]	260[28]	...	...	...	...
Caucasia	114 902[27]	55 636[27]	59 266[27]	1058[28]	...	...	...	...
Chía	129 652[27]	62 355[27]	67 297[27]	76[28]	...	...	...	...
Ciénaga	104 617[27]	52 291[27]	52 326[27]	1366[28]	...	...	...	...
Cúcuta	656 380[27]	317 453[27]	338 927[27]	1098[28]	...	...	...	...
Dosquebradas	200 832[27]	97 789[27]	103 043[27]	80[28]	...	...	...	...
Duitama	113 105[27]	52 101[27]	61 004[27]	229[28]	...	...	...	...
Envigado	227 644[27]	109 645[27]	117 999[27]	51[28]	...	...	...	...
Facatativá	134 522[27]	67 155[27]	67 367[27]	160[28]	...	...	...	...
Florencia	175 407[27]	86 223[27]	89 184[27]	2292[28]	...	...	...	...
Floridablanca	266 049[27]	126 653[27]	139 396[27]	101[28]	...	...	...	...
Fusagasugá	137 164[27]	67 806[27]	69 358[27]	206[28]	...	...	...	...
Girardot	105 701[27]	49 920[27]	55 781[27]	130[28]	...	...	...	...
Girón	185 314[27]	92 433[27]	92 881[27]	681[28]	...	...	...	...
Gudalajara de Buga	115 026[27]	56 361[27]	58 665[27]	873[28]	...	...	...	...
Ibagué	558 805[27]	271 360[27]	287 445[27]	1439[28]	...	...	...	...
Ipiales	141 863[27]	69 925[27]	71 938[27]	1707[28]	...	...	...	...
Itagüí	270 903[27]	132 151[27]	138 752[27]	17[28]	...	...	...	...
Jamundí	122 071[27]	59 328[27]	62 743[27]	603[28]	...	...	...	...
Lorica	119 061[27]	59 550[27]	59 511[27]	890[28]	...	...	...	...
Magangué	123 833[27]	62 639[27]	61 194[27]	1102[28]	...	...	...	...
Maicao	159 675[27]	78 520[27]	81 155[27]	1789[28]	...	...	...	...
Malambo	123 265[27]	62 751[27]	60 514[27]	108[28]	...	...	...	...
Manaure	108 006[27]	53 204[27]	54 802[27]	1643[28]	...	...	...	...
Manizales	397 466[27]	189 446[27]	208 020[27]	477[28]	...	...	...	...
Medellín	2 486 723[27]	1 170 224[27]	1 316 499[27]	387[28]	...	...	...	...
Montería	447 668[27]	217 244[27]	230 424[27]	3043[28]	...	...	...	...
Neiva	344 026[27]	164 582[27]	179 444[27]	1468[28]	...	...	...	...
Palmira	306 706[27]	148 106[27]	158 600[27]	1044[28]	...	...	...	...
Pasto	445 409[27]	215 188[27]	230 221[27]	1131[28]	...	...	...	...
Pereira	472 000[27]	223 658[27]	248 342[27]	702[28]	...	...	...	...
Piedecuesta	152 707[27]	74 232[27]	78 475[27]	481[28]	...	...	...	...
Pitalito	128 263[27]	63 674[27]	64 589[27]	653[28]	...	...	...	...
Popayán	280 054[27]	135 788[27]	144 266[27]	464[28]	...	...	...	...
Quibdo	115 907[27]	58 075[27]	57 832[27]	3075[28]	...	...	...	...
Riohacha	268 712[27]	132 278[27]	136 434[27]	3171[28]	...	...	...	...
Rionegro	122 231[27]	60 739[27]	61 492[27]	198[28]	...	...	...	...
San Andrés de Tumaco	203 971[27]	101 856[27]	102 115[27]	3778[28]	...	...	...	...
Santa Marta	491 535[27]	240 119[27]	251 416[27]	2369[28]	...	...	...	...
Sincelejo	279 031[27]	137 141[27]	141 890[27]	292[28]	...	...	...	...
Soacha	522 442[27]	257 890[27]	264 552[27]	187[28]	...	...	...	...
Sogamoso	112 790[27]	53 518[27]	59 272[27]	214[28]	...	...	...	...
Soledad	632 183[27]	312 904[27]	319 279[27]	67[28]	...	...	...	...
Tierralta	102 348[27]	51 985[27]	50 363[27]	4728[28]	...	...	...	...
Tuluá	214 095[27]	102 870[27]	111 225[27]	818[28]	...	...	...	...
Tunja	191 924[27]	91 904[27]	100 020[27]	118[28]	...	...	...	...
Turbo	163 525[27]	82 751[27]	80 774[27]	3090[28]	...	...	...	...
Uribia	180 385[27]	88 412[27]	91 973[27]	7904[28]	...	...	...	...
Valledupar	463 219[27]	226 033[27]	237 186[27]	4225[28]	...	...	...	...
Villavicencio	495 227[27]	240 326[27]	254 901[27]	1328[28]	...	...	...	...
Yopal	142 979[27]	71 578[27]	71 401[27]	2532[28]	...	...	...	...

8. Population of capital cities and cities of 100 000 or more inhabitants: latest available year, 1997 - 2016
Population des capitales et des villes de 100 000 habitants ou plus : dernière année disponible, 1997 - 2016 (continued - suite)

	City proper - Ville proprement dite				Urban agglomeration - Agglomération urbaine			
Continent, country or area, date, code[a] and city / Continent, pays ou zone, date, code[a] et ville	Population			Surface area - Superficie (km²)	Population			Surface area - Superficie (km²)
	Both sexes - Les deux sexes	Male - Masculin	Female - Féminin		Both sexes - Les deux sexes	Male - Masculin	Female - Féminin	
AMERICA, SOUTH - AMÉRIQUE DU SUD								
Colombia - Colombie								
1 VII 2016 (ESDJ)								
Yumbo	119 932[27]	60 174[27]	59 758[27]	243[28]	...	...	...	...
Zipaquirá	124 376[27]	61 198[27]	63 178[27]	194[28]	...	...	...	...
Ecuador - Équateur[17]								
1 VII 2016 (ESDF)								
Ambato	176 909	...	...	...	...	...	...	...
Babahoyo	100 394	...	...	...	...	...	...	...
Cuenca	383 403	...	...	...	...	...	...	...
Durán	280 013	...	...	...	...	...	...	...
Esmeraldas	188 569	...	...	...	...	...	...	...
Guayaquil	2 531 371	...	...	...	...	...	...	...
Ibarra	153 780	...	...	...	...	...	...	...
La Libertad	110 426	...	...	...	...	...	...	...
Loja	214 147	...	...	...	...	...	...	...
Machala	260 204	...	...	...	...	...	...	...
Manta	244 668	...	...	...	...	...	...	...
Milagro	150 436	...	...	...	...	...	...	...
Portoviejo	232 465	...	...	...	...	...	...	...
Quevedo	175 008	...	...	...	...	...	...	...
QUITO	1 778 434	...	...	...	...	...	...	...
Riobamba	164 529	...	...	...	...	...	...	...
Santo Domingo de los Colorados	321 130	...	...	...	...	...	...	...
Falkland Islands (Malvinas) - Îles Falkland (Malvinas)[29]								
15 IV 2012 (CDFC)								
STANLEY	2 108	1 055	1 053	...	...	...	...	...
French Guiana - Guyane française								
1 I 2006 (CDJC)								
CAYENNE	58 004	27 412	30 591	...	75 740	36 484	39 256	...
Guyana								
15 IX 2012* (CDFC)								
GEORGETOWN	24 849	...	...	...	118 368	...	...	...
Paraguay								
1 VII 2014 (ESDF)								
ASUNCIÓN[30]	512 919	236 790	276 129	117	2 887 087	1 402 891	1 484 196	2582
Capiatá	257 116	127 676	129 440	87.7	...	...	...	...
Ciudad del Este	317 525	159 726	157 799	149	...	...	...	...
Fernando de la Mora	200 112	95 174	104 937	21	...	...	...	...
Lambaré	210 725	101 019	109 706	26.8	...	...	...	...
Luque	358 265	175 663	182 602	152.5	...	...	...	...
San Lorenzo	354 283	171 242	183 042	54.2	...	...	...	...
Peru - Pérou[31]								
30 VI 2016 (ESDF)								
Arequipa	877 466	422 392	455 074	...	...	...	...	...
Ayacucho	184 125	91 012	93 113	...	...	...	...	...
Cajamarca	233 359	114 681	118 678	...	...	...	...	...
Chiclayo	606 078	288 834	317 244	...	...	...	...	...
Chimbote	374 083	188 415	185 668	...	...	...	...	...
Chincha Alta	179 849	89 973	89 876	...	...	...	...	...
Cuzco	434 241	211 505	222 736	...	...	...	...	...
Huancayo	368 437	175 202	193 235	...	...	...	...	...
Huánuco	177 182	84 573	92 609	...	...	...	...	...
Huaraz	130 199	64 009	66 190	...	...	...	...	...
Ica	246 835	121 556	125 279	...	...	...	...	...
Iquitos	442 065	222 810	219 255	...	...	...	...	...
Juliaca	280 750	136 770	143 980	...	...	...	...	...
LIMA[32]	10 039 455	4 879 968	5 159 487	...	...	...	...	...
Pisco	104 933	53 490	51 443	...	...	...	...	...
Piura	445 362	216 211	229 151	...	...	...	...	...
Pucallpa	211 670	110 288	101 382	...	...	...	...	...
Puno	142 992	69 451	73 541	...	...	...	...	...
Sullana	202 969	99 165	103 804	...	...	...	...	...
Tacna	297 470	151 442	146 028	...	...	...	...	...
Tarapoto	147 323	76 563	70 760	...	...	...	...	...

8. Population of capital cities and cities of 100 000 or more inhabitants: latest available year, 1997 - 2016
Population des capitales et des villes de 100 000 habitants ou plus : dernière année disponible, 1997 - 2016 (continued - suite)

Continent, country or area, date, code[a] and city / Continent, pays ou zone, date, code[a] et ville	City proper - Ville proprement dite				Urban agglomeration - Agglomération urbaine			
	Population			Surface area - Superficie (km²)	Population			Surface area - Superficie (km²)
	Both sexes - Les deux sexes	Male - Masculin	Female - Féminin		Both sexes - Les deux sexes	Male - Masculin	Female - Féminin	
AMERICA, SOUTH - AMÉRIQUE DU SUD								
Peru - Pérou[31]								
30 VI 2016 (ESDF)								
Trujillo	810 846	393 650	417 196	...	...	...	...	...
Tumbes	112 839	61 283	51 556	...	...	...	...	...
Suriname								
13 VIII 2012 (CDJC)								
PARAMARIBO	240 924	119 439	121 485	182	...	...	...	...
Wanica	118 222	57 776	60 446	443	...	...	...	...
Uruguay[33]								
1 VII 2016 (ESDJ)								
MONTEVIDEO	1 380 432	648 929	731 503	...	...	...	...	...
Venezuela (Bolivarian Republic of) - Venezuela (République bolivarienne du)								
1 VII 2015 (ESDF)								
Anaco(F) (Capital)	140 496	...	...	...	...	...	...	...
Barinas	389 578	...	...	...	...	...	...	...
Barquisimeto	881 127	...	...	...	...	...	...	...
Baruta	358 221	...	...	...	...	...	...	...
Cabimas	293 365	...	...	...	...	...	...	...
Cagua	118 290	...	...	...	...	...	...	...
CARACAS	2 082 130	...	...	...	...	...	...	...
Carora	111 963	...	...	...	...	...	...	...
Carúpano	156 380	...	...	...	...	...	...	...
Ciudad Bolívar	407 452	...	...	...	...	...	...	...
Ciudad Guayana	877 547	...	...	...	...	...	...	...
Ciudad Ojeda	216 489	...	...	...	...	...	...	...
Cua	143 164	...	...	...	...	...	...	...
Cumaná	358 138	...	...	...	...	...	...	...
El Tigre	203 403	...	...	...	...	...	...	...
Guacara	192 536	...	...	...	...	...	...	...
Guanare	160 234	...	...	...	...	...	...	...
Guarenas	247 131	...	...	...	...	...	...	...
Guatire	177 794	...	...	...	...	...	...	...
Los Guayos	173 878	...	...	...	...	...	...	...
Los Teques	216 358	...	...	...	...	...	...	...
Maracaibo	1 653 215	...	...	...	...	...	...	...
Maracay	419 052	...	...	...	...	...	...	...
Maturín	571 276	...	...	...	...	...	...	...
Mérida	248 410	...	...	...	...	...	...	...
Naguanagua	161 658	...	...	...	...	...	...	...
Ocumare Del Tuy	197 952	...	...	...	...	...	...	...
Petare	434 320	...	...	...	...	...	...	...
Pozuelos (F) (Capital)	144 045	...	...	...	...	...	...	...
Puerto Cabello	193 025	...	...	...	...	...	...	...
Punto Fijo	272 239	...	...	...	...	...	...	...
San Cristóbal	282 830	...	...	...	...	...	...	...
San Fernando de Apure	217 590	...	...	...	...	...	...	...
San Francisco	106 763	...	...	...	...	...	...	...
Santa Lucía	133 543	...	...	...	...	...	...	...
Táriba	132 657	...	...	...	...	...	...	...
Tocuyito	186 755	...	...	...	...	...	...	...
Turmero	238 570	...	...	...	...	...	...	...
Valencia	888 109	...	...	...	...	...	...	...
Valera	161 771	...	...	...	...	...	...	...
ASIA - ASIE								
Afghanistan								
1 VII 2016 (ESDF)								
Baghalan Center (Puli Khumry)	110 902	56 839	54 063	...	...	...	...	...
Balkh Center (Mazar- Sharif)	415 053	212 918	202 135	...	...	...	...	...
Herat Center	491 967	249 865	242 102	...	...	...	...	...
KABUL CENTER	3 817 241	1 975 705	1 841 536	...	...	...	...	...
Kandhar Center (Kndhar)	448 262	230 744	217 518	...	...	...	...	...

8. Population of capital cities and cities of 100 000 or more inhabitants: latest available year, 1997 - 2016
Population des capitales et des villes de 100 000 habitants ou plus : dernière année disponible, 1997 - 2016 (continued - suite)

Continent, country or area, date, code[a] and city / Continent, pays ou zone, date, code[a] et ville	City proper - Ville proprement dite				Urban agglomeration - Agglomération urbaine			
	Population			Surface area - Superficie (km²)	Population			Surface area - Superficie (km²)
	Both sexes - Les deux sexes	Male - Masculin	Female - Féminin		Both sexes - Les deux sexes	Male - Masculin	Female - Féminin	
ASIA - ASIE								
Afghanistan								
1 VII 2016 (ESDF)								
Kunduz Center	162 168	83 384	78 784	...	...	...	...	...
Nngarhar Center (Jlal Abad)	232 901	119 901	113 000	...	...	...	...	...
Armenia - Arménie								
1 VII 2015 (ESDJ)								
Gyumri (Leninakan)	117 714	55 914	61 800	...	...	...	...	...
YEREVAN	1 073 660	496 665	576 995	227	...	...	...	...
Azerbaijan - Azerbaïdjan								
1 VII 2015 (ESDF)								
BAKU	2 215 034	1 100 127	1 114 907	2150	...	...	...	...
Ganja	329 261	160 317	168 944	110	...	...	...	...
Sumgayit	334 521	164 624	169 897	80	...	...	...	...
Bahrain - Bahreïn								
1 VII 2006 (ESDF)								
MANAMA	176 909	113 503	63 406	30	...	...	...	...
Bangladesh								
15 III 2011 (CDFC)								
Barisal	339 308	174 980	164 328	...	...	...	...	...
Chittagong	2 591 681	1 367 282	1 224 399	...	...	...	...	...
Comilla	296 010	153 523	142 487	...	...	...	...	...
DHAKA	8 906 035	4 931 802	3 974 233	...	...	...	...	...
Khulna	664 728	346 069	318 659	...	...	...	...	...
Mymensingh	389 918	200 053	189 865	...	...	...	...	...
Narayanganj	286 330	148 214	138 116	...	...	...	...	...
Rajshahi	449 756	232 974	216 782	...	...	...	...	...
Saidpur	133 433	68 884	64 549	...	...	...	...	...
Bhutan - Bhoutan								
30 V 2005 (CDFC)								
THIMPHU	...	...	...	...	79 185	42 465	36 720	...
Brunei Darussalam - Brunéi Darussalam								
21 VIII 2001 (CDFC)								
BANDAR SERI BEGAWAN	27 285	13 639	13 646	100.4	...	...	...	...
Cambodia - Cambodge[34]								
1 VII 2011 (ESDF)								
Bat Dambang	1 126 345	558 945	567 400	...	...	...	...	...
PHNOM PENH	1 570 791	738 159	832 631	...	...	...	...	...
Seam Reab	999 703	493 184	506 519	...	...	...	...	...
China - Chine								
1 VII 2010 (ESDF)								
BEIJING (PEKING)	19 610 000[36]	10 130 000[36]	9 490 000[36]	16410	...	...	...	...
China, Hong Kong SAR - Chine, Hong Kong RAS								
1 VII 2016 (ESDJ)								
HONG KONG SAR	7 336 600	3 375 400	3 961 200	1106	...	...	...	...
China, Macao SAR - Chine, Macao RAS								
1 VII 2015 (ESDJ)								
MACAO	642 900	317 500	325 400	30[35]	...	...	...	...
Cyprus - Chypre								
1 I 2006 (ESDJ)								
LEFKOSIA[37]	...	...	...	...	224 500	...	...	...
Lemesos[38]	...	...	...	...	176 900	...	...	...
Democratic People's Republic of Korea - République populaire démocratique de Corée								
1 X 2008 (CDJC)								
Anju	167 646	79 187	88 459	...	...	...	...	...
Chongjin	614 892	292 741	322 151	...	...	...	...	...
Haeju	241 599	116 594	125 005	...	...	...	...	...
Hamhung	614 198	292 058	322 140	...	...	...	...	...
Huichon	136 093	64 547	71 546	...	...	...	...	...
Hyesan	174 015	82 604	91 411	...	...	...	...	...
Jongju	102 659	48 423	54 236	...	...	...	...	...
Kaechon	262 389	124 222	138 167	...	...	...	...	...
Kaesong	192 578	90 653	101 925	...	...	...	...	...
Kanggye	251 971	120 305	131 666	...	...	...	...	...
Kim Chaek	155 284	73 133	82 151	...	...	...	...	...

Continent, country or area, date, code[a] and city / Continent, pays ou zone, date, code[a] et ville	City proper - Ville proprement dite				Urban agglomeration - Agglomération urbaine			
	Population			Surface area - Superficie (km²)	Population			Surface area - Superficie (km²)
	Both sexes - Les deux sexes	Male - Masculin	Female - Féminin		Both sexes - Les deux sexes	Male - Masculin	Female - Féminin	
ASIA - ASIE								
Democratic People's Republic of Korea - République populaire démocratique de Corée								
1 X 2008 (CDJC)								
Kusong	155 181	73 677	81 504	...	...	...	...	...
Nampho	310 864	150 091	160 773	...	...	...	...	...
Phyongsong	236 583	115 817	120 766	...	...	...	...	...
PYONGYANG	2 581 076	1 233 765	1 347 311	...	...	...	...	...
Rason	158 337	74 777	83 560	...	...	...	...	...
Sariwon	271 434	130 181	141 253	...	...	...	...	...
Sinpho	130 951	63 207	67 744	...	...	...	...	...
Sinuiju	334 031	158 139	175 892	...	...	...	...	...
Sunchon	250 738	119 727	131 011	...	...	...	...	...
Tanchon	240 873	113 221	127 652	...	...	...	...	...
Tokchon	210 571	99 655	110 916	...	...	...	...	...
Wonsan	328 467	155 903	172 564	...	...	...	...	...
Georgia - Géorgie								
1 VII 2016 (ESDJ)								
Batumi	155 000	...	...	...	...	...	...	...
Kutaisi	147 500	...	...	...	...	...	...	...
Rustavi	126 200	...	...	...	...	...	...	...
TBILISI	1 113 800	...	...	...	...	...	...	...
India - Inde								
9 II 2011 (CDFC)								
Abohar	...	...	...	...	145 302	76 984	68 318	...
Achalpur	...	...	...	...	112 311	58 108	54 203	...
Adilabad	...	...	...	...	117 167	59 448	57 719	...
Adityapur	...	...	...	...	174 355	91 664	82 691	...
Adoni	...	...	...	...	184 625	91 736	92 889	...
Agartala	...	...	...	...	400 004	200 132	199 872	...
Agra	...	...	...	...	1 585 704	845 902	739 802	...
Ahmadabad	...	...	...	...	5 633 927	2 968 460	2 665 467	...
Ahmadnagar	...	...	...	...	350 859	178 899	171 960	...
Aizawl	...	...	...	...	293 416	144 913	148 503	...
Ajmer	...	...	...	...	542 321	278 545	263 776	...
Akbarpur	...	...	...	...	111 447	57 330	54 117	...
Akola	...	...	...	...	425 817	217 393	208 424	...
Alandur	...	...	...	...	164 430	82 332	82 098	...
Alappuzha	...	...	...	...	240 991	116 439	124 552	...
Aligarh	...	...	...	...	874 408	461 772	412 636	...
Allahabad	...	...	...	...	1 168 385	630 577	537 808	...
Alwar	...	...	...	...	322 568	170 530	152 038	...
Ambala	...	...	...	...	195 153	102 607	92 546	...
Ambala Sadar	...	...	...	...	104 974	54 680	50 294	...
Ambarnath	...	...	...	...	253 475	132 582	120 893	...
Ambattur	...	...	...	...	466 205	234 923	231 282	...
Ambikapur	...	...	...	...	121 071	62 776	58 295	...
Ambur	...	...	...	...	114 608	56 382	58 226	...
Amravati	...	...	...	...	647 057	329 992	317 065	...
Amreli	...	...	...	...	117 967	59 902	58 065	...
Amritsar	...	...	...	...	1 159 227	615 417	543 810	...
Amroha	...	...	...	...	198 471	103 097	95 374	...
Anand	...	...	...	...	209 410	108 403	101 007	...
Anantapur	...	...	...	...	267 161	133 919	133 242	...
Anantnag	...	...	...	...	150 592	77 712	72 880	...
Arrah	...	...	...	...	261 430	138 804	122 626	...
Asansol	...	...	...	...	563 917	292 387	271 530	...
Ashoknagar Kalyangarh	...	...	...	...	121 592	61 236	60 356	...
Aurangabad (Bihar)	...	...	...	...	102 244	53 542	48 702	...
Aurangabad (Maharashtra)	...	...	...	...	1 175 116	609 206	565 910	...
Avadi	...	...	...	...	345 996	175 658	170 338	...
Azamgarh	...	...	...	...	110 983	57 878	53 105	...
Badlapur	...	...	...	...	174 226	90 365	83 861	...
Bagaha	...	...	...	...	112 634	59 614	53 020	...
Bagalkot	...	...	...	...	111 933	56 378	55 555	...
Bahadurgarh	...	...	...	...	170 767	91 721	79 046	...

8. Population of capital cities and cities of 100 000 or more inhabitants: latest available year, 1997 - 2016
Population des capitales et des villes de 100 000 habitants ou plus : dernière année disponible, 1997 - 2016 (continued - suite)

Continent, country or area, date, code[a] and city / Continent, pays ou zone, date, code[a] et ville	City proper - Ville proprement dite				Urban agglomeration - Agglomération urbaine			
	Population			Surface area - Superficie (km²)	Population			Surface area - Superficie (km²)
	Both sexes - Les deux sexes	Male - Masculin	Female - Féminin		Both sexes - Les deux sexes	Male - Masculin	Female - Féminin	
ASIA - ASIE								
India - Inde								
9 II 2011 (CDFC)								
Baharampur	...	...	...	...	195 223	100 247	94 976	...
Bahraich	...	...	...	...	186 223	97 653	88 570	...
Baidyabati	...	...	...	...	121 110	62 485	58 625	...
Baleshwar Town	...	...	...	...	144 373	73 721	70 652	...
Ballia	...	...	...	...	104 424	55 459	48 965	...
Bally (Census Town)	...	...	...	...	113 377	58 530	54 847	...
Bally (Municipality)	...	...	...	...	293 373	156 911	136 462	...
Balurghat	...	...	...	...	153 279	76 730	76 549	...
Banda	...	...	...	...	160 473	85 370	75 103	...
Bankura	...	...	...	...	137 386	69 843	67 543	...
Bansberia	...	...	...	...	103 920	53 760	50 160	...
Banswara	...	...	...	...	101 017	51 585	49 432	...
Baran	...	...	...	...	117 992	61 071	56 921	...
Baranagar	...	...	...	...	245 213	126 187	119 026	...
Barasat	...	...	...	...	278 435	140 822	137 613	...
Baraut	...	...	...	...	103 764	55 013	48 751	...
Barddhaman	...	...	...	...	314 265	159 936	154 329	...
Bareilly	...	...	...	...	904 797	477 515	427 282	...
Baripada Town	...	...	...	...	116 849	60 489	56 360	...
Barnala	...	...	...	...	116 449	62 554	53 895	...
Barrackpur	...	...	...	...	152 783	78 349	74 434	...
Barshi	...	...	...	...	118 722	60 801	57 921	...
Basirhat	...	...	...	...	125 254	63 223	62 031	...
Basti	...	...	...	...	114 657	60 095	54 562	...
Batala	...	...	...	...	158 621	83 655	74 966	...
Bathinda	...	...	...	...	285 788	151 524	134 264	...
Beawar	...	...	...	...	151 152	77 616	73 536	...
Begusarai	...	...	...	...	252 008	133 722	118 286	...
Belgaum	...	...	...	...	490 045	246 537	243 508	...
Bellary	...	...	...	...	410 445	206 149	204 296	...
Bettiah	...	...	...	...	132 209	69 529	62 680	...
Betul	...	...	...	...	103 330	52 823	50 507	...
Bhadrak	...	...	...	...	121 338	62 335	59 003	...
Bhadravati	...	...	...	...	151 102	75 009	76 093	...
Bhadreswar	...	...	...	...	101 477	53 330	48 147	...
Bhagalpur	...	...	...	...	400 146	212 813	187 333	...
Bhalswa Jahangir Pur	...	...	...	...	197 148	106 388	90 760	...
Bharatpur	...	...	...	...	252 838	134 040	118 798	...
Bharuch	...	...	...	...	169 007	86 810	82 197	...
Bhatpara	...	...	...	...	386 019	204 539	181 480	...
Bhavnagar	...	...	...	...	605 882	315 429	290 453	...
Bhilai Nagar	...	...	...	...	627 734	323 479	304 255	...
Bhilwara	...	...	...	...	359 483	187 081	172 402	...
Bhimavaram	...	...	...	...	146 961	72 441	74 520	...
Bhind	...	...	...	...	197 585	105 352	92 233	...
Bhiwadi	...	...	...	...	104 921	59 712	45 209	...
Bhiwandi	...	...	...	...	709 665	415 339	294 326	...
Bhiwani	...	...	...	...	196 057	104 026	92 031	...
Bhopal	...	...	...	...	1 798 218	936 168	862 050	...
Bhubaneswar Town	...	...	...	...	885 363	468 043	417 320	...
Bhuj	...	...	...	...	148 834	78 813	70 021	...
Bhusawal	...	...	...	...	187 421	96 147	91 274	...
Bid	...	...	...	...	146 709	75 566	71 143	...
Bidar	...	...	...	...	216 020	111 470	104 550	...
Bidhan Nagar	...	...	...	...	215 514	109 014	106 500	...
Biharsharif	...	...	...	...	297 268	155 216	142 052	...
Bijapur	...	...	...	...	327 427	165 177	162 250	...
Bikaner	...	...	...	...	644 406	338 442	305 964	...
Bilaspur	...	...	...	...	365 579	188 342	177 237	...
Bokaro Steel City	...	...	...	...	414 820	219 646	195 174	...
Bongaon	...	...	...	...	108 864	55 382	53 482	...
Botad	...	...	...	...	130 327	67 675	62 652	...
Brahmapur	...	...	...	...	356 598	185 754	170 844	...

8. Population of capital cities and cities of 100 000 or more inhabitants: latest available year, 1997 - 2016
Population des capitales et des villes de 100 000 habitants ou plus : dernière année disponible, 1997 - 2016 (continued - suite)

Continent, country or area, date, code[a] and city / Continent, pays ou zone, date, code[a] et ville	City proper - Ville proprement dite				Urban agglomeration - Agglomération urbaine			
	Population			Surface area - Superficie (km²)	Population			Surface area - Superficie (km²)
	Both sexes - Les deux sexes	Male - Masculin	Female - Féminin		Both sexes - Les deux sexes	Male - Masculin	Female - Féminin	

ASIA - ASIE

India - Inde
9 II 2011 (CDFC)

Bruhat Bengaluru Mahanagara Palike (BBMP)...	...	...	...	...	8 495 492	4 420 006	4 075 486	...
Budaun	...	...	...	...	159 285	83 176	76 109	...
Bulandshahar	...	...	...	...	230 024	120 275	109 749	...
Bundi	...	...	...	...	104 919	54 485	50 434	...
Burari	...	...	...	...	146 190	78 103	68 087	...
Burhanpur	...	...	...	...	210 886	108 187	102 699	...
Buxar	...	...	...	...	102 861	54 277	48 584	...
Champdani	...	...	...	...	111 251	59 350	51 901	...
Chandannagar	...	...	...	...	166 867	84 009	82 858	...
Chandausi	...	...	...	...	114 383	60 256	54 127	...
Chandigarh	...	...	...	...	970 602	531 051	439 551	...
Chandrapur	...	...	...	...	320 379	164 085	156 294	...
Chapra	...	...	...	...	202 352	106 501	95 851	...
Chas	...	...	...	...	141 640	74 727	66 913	...
Chennai	...	...	...	...	4 646 732	2 335 844	2 310 888	...
Chhatarpur	...	...	...	...	142 128	75 070	67 058	...
Chhindwara	...	...	...	...	175 052	89 396	85 656	...
Chikmagalur	...	...	...	...	118 401	58 702	59 699	...
Chilakaluripet	...	...	...	...	101 398	50 207	51 191	...
Chitradurga	...	...	...	...	145 853	73 020	72 833	...
Chittaurgarh	...	...	...	...	116 406	60 068	56 338	...
Chittoor	...	...	...	...	160 722	80 060	80 662	...
Churu	...	...	...	...	120 157	61 774	58 383	...
Coimbatore	...	...	...	...	1 050 721	526 163	524 558	...
Cuddalore	...	...	...	...	173 636	85 700	87 936	...
Cuttack	...	...	...	...	610 189	316 242	293 947	...
Dabgram	...	...	...	...	119 040	61 078	57 962	...
Dallo Pura	...	...	...	...	154 791	81 262	73 529	...
Damoh	...	...	...	...	139 561	72 869	66 692	...
Darbhanga	...	...	...	...	296 039	155 637	140 402	...
Darjiling	...	...	...	...	118 805	59 187	59 618	...
Datia	...	...	...	...	100 284	52 772	47 512	...
Davanagere	...	...	...	...	434 971	219 776	215 195	...
Deesa	...	...	...	...	111 160	58 657	52 503	...
Dehradun	...	...	...	...	574 840	301 207	273 633	...
Dehri	...	...	...	...	137 231	72 372	64 859	...
Delhi Cantonment	...	...	...	...	110 351	63 757	46 594	...
Delhi Municipal Corporation (DMC)	...	...	...	...	11 034 555	5 882 117	5 152 438	...
Deoghar	...	...	...	...	203 123	107 997	95 126	...
Deoli	...	...	...	...	169 122	90 914	78 208	...
Deoria	...	...	...	...	129 479	67 462	62 017	...
Dewas	...	...	...	...	289 550	150 081	139 469	...
Dhamtari	...	...	...	...	101 677	50 807	50 870	...
Dhanbad	...	...	...	...	1 162 472	614 722	547 750	...
Dharmavaram	...	...	...	...	121 874	62 250	59 624	...
Dhaulpur	...	...	...	...	133 075	71 298	61 777	...
Dhule	...	...	...	...	375 559	193 446	182 113	...
Dibrugarh	...	...	...	...	145 488	75 318	70 170	...
Dimapur	...	...	...	...	122 834	64 300	58 534	...
Dinapur Nizamat	...	...	...	...	182 429	96 875	85 554	...
Dindigul	...	...	...	...	207 327	103 027	104 300	...
Dohad	...	...	...	...	118 846	60 515	58 331	...
Dum Dum	...	...	...	...	114 786	58 566	56 220	...
Durg	...	...	...	...	268 806	136 641	132 165	...
Durgapur	...	...	...	...	566 517	294 255	272 262	...
Eluru	...	...	...	...	218 020	107 511	110 509	...
English Bazar	...	...	...	...	205 521	106 824	98 697	...
Erode	...	...	...	...	157 101	78 222	78 879	...
Etah	...	...	...	...	118 517	62 590	55 927	...
Etawah	...	...	...	...	256 838	135 439	121 399	...
Faizabad	...	...	...	...	165 228	85 620	79 608	...
Faridabad	...	...	...	...	1 414 050	754 542	659 508	...
Farrukhabad-cum-Fatehgarh	...	...	...	...	276 581	145 641	130 940	...

8. Population of capital cities and cities of 100 000 or more inhabitants: latest available year, 1997 - 2016
Population des capitales et des villes de 100 000 habitants ou plus : dernière année disponible, 1997 - 2016 (continued - suite)

Continent, country or area, date, codeᵃ and city / Continent, pays ou zone, date, codeᵃ et ville	City proper - Ville proprement dite				Urban agglomeration - Agglomération urbaine			
	Population			Surface area - Superficie (km²)	Population			Surface area - Superficie (km²)
	Both sexes - Les deux sexes	Male - Masculin	Female - Féminin		Both sexes - Les deux sexes	Male - Masculin	Female - Féminin	

ASIA - ASIE

India - Inde
9 II 2011 (CDFC)

Fatehpur	...	...	...	...	193 193	101 263	91 930	...
Firozabad	...	...	...	...	604 214	319 415	284 799	...
Firozpur	...	...	...	...	110 313	58 451	51 862	...
Gadag-Betigeri	...	...	...	...	172 612	85 920	86 692	...
Gandhidham	...	...	...	...	247 992	131 484	116 508	...
Gandhinagar	...	...	...	...	292 797	153 443	139 354	...
Ganganagar	...	...	...	...	237 780	127 840	109 940	...
Gangapur City	...	...	...	...	119 090	62 829	56 261	...
Gangawati	...	...	...	...	114 642	57 230	57 412	...
Gangtok	...	...	...	...	100 286	52 459	47 827	...
Gaya	...	...	...	...	474 093	250 037	224 056	...
Ghaziabad	...	...	...	...	1 648 643	874 607	774 036	...
Ghazipur	...	...	...	...	121 020	63 513	57 507	...
Giridih	...	...	...	...	114 533	59 966	54 567	...
Godhra	...	...	...	...	143 644	74 230	69 414	...
Gokal Pur	...	...	...	...	121 870	64 857	57 013	...
Gonda	...	...	...	...	114 046	59 948	54 098	...
Gondal	...	...	...	...	112 197	58 300	53 897	...
Gondiya	...	...	...	...	132 813	66 500	66 313	...
Gorakhpur	...	...	...	...	673 446	353 907	319 539	...
Greater Hyderabad Municipal Corporation (GHMC)	...	...	...	...	6 993 262	3 576 640	3 416 622	...
Greater Mumbai	...	...	...	...	12 442 373	6 715 931	5 726 442	...
Greater Noida	...	...	...	...	102 054	55 540	46 514	...
Greater Visakhapatnam Municipal Corporation (GVMC)	...	...	...	...	1 728 128	873 599	854 529	...
Gudivada	...	...	...	...	118 167	59 062	59 105	...
Gulbarga	...	...	...	...	543 147	276 552	266 595	...
Guna	...	...	...	...	180 935	94 464	86 471	...
Guntakal	...	...	...	...	126 270	62 851	63 419	...
Guntur	...	...	...	...	670 073	331 435	338 638	...
Gurgaon	...	...	...	...	886 519	480 042	406 477	...
Guwahati	...	...	...	...	962 334	498 450	463 884	...
Gwalior	...	...	...	...	1 054 420	561 165	493 255	...
Habra	...	...	...	...	147 221	74 592	72 629	...
Hajipur	...	...	...	...	147 688	78 047	69 641	...
Haldia	...	...	...	...	200 827	104 841	95 986	...
Haldwani-cum-Kathgodam	...	...	...	...	201 461	105 580	95 881	...
Halisahar	...	...	...	...	124 939	65 467	59 472	...
Hanumangarh	...	...	...	...	150 958	79 709	71 249	...
Haora	...	...	...	...	1 077 075	561 220	515 855	...
Hapur	...	...	...	...	262 983	139 525	123 458	...
Hardoi	...	...	...	...	197 029	103 619	93 410	...
Hardwar	...	...	...	...	231 338	123 455	107 883	...
Hassan	...	...	...	...	155 006	77 051	77 955	...
Hastsal	...	...	...	...	176 877	94 833	82 044	...
Hathras	...	...	...	...	143 020	76 054	66 966	...
Hazaribag	...	...	...	...	142 489	74 132	68 357	...
Hindaun	...	...	...	...	105 452	55 834	49 618	...
Hindupur	...	...	...	...	151 677	76 370	75 307	...
Hinganghat	...	...	...	...	101 805	52 577	49 228	...
Hisar	...	...	...	...	307 024	166 494	140 530	...
Hoshangabad	...	...	...	...	117 988	61 716	56 272	...
Hoshiarpur	...	...	...	...	168 653	88 304	80 349	...
Hospet	...	...	...	...	206 167	102 668	103 499	...
Hosur	...	...	...	...	116 821	59 351	57 470	...
Hubli-Dharwad	...	...	...	...	943 788	474 518	469 270	...
Hugli-Chinsurah	...	...	...	...	179 931	90 217	89 714	...
Ichalkaranji	...	...	...	...	287 353	149 164	138 189	...
Imphal	...	...	...	...	277 196	135 059	142 137	...
Indore	...	...	...	...	1 994 397	1 035 912	958 485	...
Jabalpur	...	...	...	...	1 081 677	559 361	522 316	...
Jagadhri	...	...	...	...	124 894	67 685	57 209	...

8. Population of capital cities and cities of 100 000 or more inhabitants: latest available year, 1997 - 2016
Population des capitales et des villes de 100 000 habitants ou plus : dernière année disponible, 1997 - 2016 (continued - suite)

Continent, country or area, date, code[a] and city Continent, pays ou zone, date, code[a] et ville	City proper - Ville proprement dite				Urban agglomeration - Agglomération urbaine			
	Population			Surface area - Superficie (km²)	Population			Surface area - Superficie (km²)
	Both sexes - Les deux sexes	Male - Masculin	Female - Féminin		Both sexes - Les deux sexes	Male - Masculin	Female - Féminin	
ASIA - ASIE								
India - Inde								
9 II 2011 (CDFC)								
Jagdalpur	...	...	...	...	125 463	63 989	61 474	...
Jagtial	...	...	...	...	103 930	51 828	52 102	...
Jaipur	...	...	...	...	3 046 163	1 603 125	1 443 038	...
Jalandhar	...	...	...	...	868 929	460 811	408 118	...
Jalgaon	...	...	...	...	460 228	240 590	219 638	...
Jalna	...	...	...	...	285 577	147 092	138 485	...
Jalpaiguri	...	...	...	...	107 341	53 708	53 633	...
Jamalpur	...	...	...	...	105 434	56 072	49 362	...
Jammu	...	...	...	...	576 198	303 689	272 509	...
Jamnagar	...	...	...	...	600 943	313 214	287 729	...
Jamshedpur	...	...	...	...	677 350	353 212	324 138	...
Jamuria	...	...	...	...	149 220	77 379	71 841	...
Jaunpur	...	...	...	...	180 362	93 718	86 644	...
Jehanabad	...	...	...	...	103 202	54 710	48 492	...
Jetpur Navagadh	...	...	...	...	118 302	62 174	56 128	...
Jhansi	...	...	...	...	505 693	265 449	240 244	...
Jhunjhunun	...	...	...	...	118 473	61 548	56 925	...
Jind	...	...	...	...	167 592	89 253	78 339	...
Jodhpur	...	...	...	...	1 056 191	555 371	500 820	...
Jorhat	...	...	...	...	126 736	65 489	61 247	...
Junagadh	...	...	...	...	319 462	163 413	156 049	...
Kadapa	...	...	...	...	344 893	173 314	171 579	...
Kaithal	...	...	...	...	144 915	76 794	68 121	...
Kakinada	...	...	...	...	384 182	188 308	195 874	...
Kalol	...	...	...	...	134 426	70 995	63 431	...
Kalyan Dombivali	...	...	...	...	1 247 327	649 626	597 701	...
Kalyani	...	...	...	...	100 575	50 727	49 848	...
Kamarhati	...	...	...	...	330 211	170 293	159 918	...
Kancheepuram	...	...	...	...	164 384	81 992	82 392	...
Kanchrapara	...	...	...	...	129 576	65 436	64 140	...
Kanhangad	...	...	...	...	125 564	58 564	67 000	...
Kanpur	...	...	...	...	2 768 057	1 490 547	1 277 510	...
Kanpur (Cantonment Board)	...	...	...	...	108 534	58 550	49 984	...
Karaikkudi	...	...	...	...	106 714	53 348	53 366	...
Karawal Nagar	...	...	...	...	224 281	119 951	104 330	...
Karimnagar	...	...	...	...	289 821	146 145	143 676	...
Karnal	...	...	...	...	302 140	159 653	142 487	...
Kasganj	...	...	...	...	101 277	53 552	47 725	...
Kashipur	...	...	...	...	121 623	63 609	58 014	...
Katihar	...	...	...	...	240 838	127 240	113 598	...
Khammam	...	...	...	...	196 283	96 898	99 385	...
Khandwa	...	...	...	...	200 738	102 901	97 837	...
Khanna	...	...	...	...	128 137	67 801	60 336	...
Kharagpur	...	...	...	...	207 604	106 559	101 045	...
Khardaha	...	...	...	...	108 496	54 879	53 617	...
Khargone	...	...	...	...	116 150	59 752	56 398	...
Khora	...	...	...	...	190 005	102 574	87 431	...
Khurja	...	...	...	...	121 207	63 825	57 382	...
Kirari Suleman Nagar	...	...	...	...	283 211	152 348	130 863	...
Kishanganj	...	...	...	...	105 782	55 143	50 639	...
Kishangarh	...	...	...	...	154 886	80 024	74 862	...
Kochi	...	...	...	...	633 553	312 358	321 195	...
Kolar	...	...	...	...	138 462	69 910	68 552	...
Kolhapur	...	...	...	...	549 236	280 366	268 870	...
Kolkata (Calcutta)	...	...	...	...	4 496 694	2 356 766	2 139 928	...
Kollam	...	...	...	...	367 107	177 072	190 035	...
Korba	...	...	...	...	365 253	189 772	175 481	...
Kota	...	...	...	...	1 001 694	528 601	473 093	...
Kozhikode	...	...	...	...	550 440	262 939	287 501	...
Krishnanagar	...	...	...	...	153 062	77 146	75 916	...
Kulti	...	...	...	...	313 809	163 193	150 616	...
Kumbakonam	...	...	...	...	140 156	69 340	70 816	...
Kurichi	...	...	...	...	123 667	61 815	61 852	...

8. Population of capital cities and cities of 100 000 or more inhabitants: latest available year, 1997 - 2016
Population des capitales et des villes de 100 000 habitants ou plus : dernière année disponible, 1997 - 2016 (continued - suite)

Continent, country or area, date, code[a] and city Continent, pays ou zone, date, code[a] et ville	City proper - Ville proprement dite				Urban agglomeration - Agglomération urbaine			
	Population			Surface area - Superficie (km²)	Population			Surface area - Superficie (km²)
	Both sexes - Les deux sexes	Male - Masculin	Female - Féminin		Both sexes - Les deux sexes	Male - Masculin	Female - Féminin	
ASIA - ASIE								
India - Inde								
9 II 2011 (CDFC)								
Kurnool	...	...	...	...	457 633	228 148	229 485	...
Lakhimpur	...	...	...	...	151 993	80 523	71 470	...
Lalitpur	...	...	...	...	133 305	69 529	63 776	...
Latur	...	...	...	...	382 940	197 737	185 203	...
Loni	...	...	...	...	516 082	275 025	241 057	...
Lucknow	...	...	...	...	2 817 105	1 460 970	1 356 135	...
Ludhiana	...	...	...	...	1 618 879	874 908	743 971	...
Machilipatnam	...	...	...	...	169 892	83 594	86 298	...
Madanapalle	...	...	...	...	180 180	90 700	89 480	...
Madavaram	...	...	...	...	119 105	59 887	59 218	...
Madhyamgram	...	...	...	...	196 127	98 864	97 263	...
Madurai	...	...	...	...	1 017 865	509 302	508 563	...
Mahbubnagar	...	...	...	...	190 400	96 142	94 258	...
Mahesana	...	...	...	...	190 753	100 558	90 195	...
Maheshtala	...	...	...	...	448 317	229 693	218 624	...
Mainpuri	...	...	...	...	136 557	71 274	65 283	...
Malappuram	...	...	...	...	101 386	48 957	52 429	...
Malegaon	...	...	...	...	481 228	244 080	237 148	...
Malerkotla	...	...	...	...	135 424	71 376	64 048	...
Mandoli	...	...	...	...	120 417	64 159	56 258	...
Mandsaur	...	...	...	...	141 667	72 488	69 179	...
Mandya	...	...	...	...	137 358	68 662	68 696	...
Mangalagiri	...	...	...	...	107 197	53 301	53 896	...
Mangalore	...	...	...	...	499 487	247 903	251 584	...
Mango	...	...	...	...	223 805	115 970	107 835	...
Mathura	...	...	...	...	349 909	185 983	163 926	...
Maunath Bhanjan	...	...	...	...	278 745	142 967	135 778	...
Medinipur	...	...	...	...	169 264	84 977	84 287	...
Meerut	...	...	...	...	1 305 429	688 118	617 311	...
Mira Bhayandar	...	...	...	...	809 378	429 260	380 118	...
Miryalaguda	...	...	...	...	104 918	52 565	52 353	...
Mirzapur-cum-Vindhyachal	...	...	...	...	234 871	125 601	109 270	...
Modinagar	...	...	...	...	130 325	69 268	61 057	...
Moga	...	...	...	...	163 397	86 604	76 793	...
Moradabad	...	...	...	...	887 871	464 580	423 291	...
Morena	...	...	...	...	200 482	108 390	92 092	...
Morvi	...	...	...	...	210 451	109 451	101 000	...
Motihari	...	...	...	...	126 158	67 861	58 297	...
Mughalsarai	...	...	...	...	109 650	57 682	51 968	...
Muktsar	...	...	...	...	116 747	61 725	55 022	...
Munger	...	...	...	...	213 303	113 291	100 012	...
Murwara (Katni)	...	...	...	...	221 883	115 348	106 535	...
Mustafabad	...	...	...	...	127 167	66 889	60 278	...
Muzaffarnagar	...	...	...	...	392 768	206 782	185 986	...
Muzaffarpur	...	...	...	...	354 462	187 564	166 898	...
Mysore	...	...	...	...	920 550	461 042	459 508	...
Nabadwip	...	...	...	...	125 543	65 415	60 128	...
Nadiad	...	...	...	...	225 071	115 903	109 168	...
Nagaon	...	...	...	...	121 628	61 642	59 986	...
Nagapattinam	...	...	...	...	102 905	50 793	52 112	...
Nagaur	...	...	...	...	105 218	54 126	51 092	...
Nagda	...	...	...	...	100 039	51 373	48 666	...
Nagercoil	...	...	...	...	224 849	109 938	114 911	...
Nagpur	...	...	...	...	2 405 665	1 225 405	1 180 260	...
Naihati	...	...	...	...	217 900	109 849	108 051	...
Nalgonda	...	...	...	...	154 326	77 320	77 006	...
Nanded Waghala	...	...	...	...	550 439	285 433	265 006	...
Nandurbar	...	...	...	...	111 037	57 412	53 625	...
Nandyal	...	...	...	...	211 424	105 826	105 598	...
Nangloi Jat	...	...	...	...	205 596	110 056	95 540	...
Narasaraopet	...	...	...	...	117 489	59 424	58 065	...
Nashik	...	...	...	...	1 486 053	782 517	703 536	...
Navi Mumbai (New Bombay)	...	...	...	...	1 120 547	610 060	510 487	...

Continent, country or area, date, codeᵃ and city / Continent, pays ou zone, date, codeᵃ et ville	City proper - Ville proprement dite				Urban agglomeration - Agglomération urbaine			
	Population			Surface area - Superficie (km²)	Population			Surface area - Superficie (km²)
	Both sexes - Les deux sexes	Male - Masculin	Female - Féminin		Both sexes - Les deux sexes	Male - Masculin	Female - Féminin	
ASIA - ASIE								
India - Inde								
9 II 2011 (CDFC)								
Navi Mumbai Panvel Raigad	...	...	...	...	195 373	107 342	88 031	...
Navsari	...	...	...	...	171 109	88 486	82 623	...
Neemuch	...	...	...	...	128 561	67 890	60 671	...
Nellore	...	...	...	...	547 621	278 787	268 834	...
New Delhi Municipal Council (NDMC)	...	...	...	...	257 803	140 234	117 569	...
Neyveli	...	...	...	...	105 731	53 409	52 322	...
Nizamabad	...	...	...	...	311 152	154 929	156 223	...
Noida	...	...	...	...	637 272	349 397	287 875	...
North Barrackpur	...	...	...	...	132 806	66 924	65 882	...
North Dum Dum	...	...	...	...	249 142	126 279	122 863	...
Ongole	...	...	...	...	208 344	104 646	103 698	...
Orai	...	...	...	...	190 575	101 306	89 269	...
Osmanabad	...	...	...	...	111 825	57 824	54 001	...
Ozhukarai	...	...	...	...	300 104	148 464	151 640	...
Palakkad	...	...	...	...	130 955	63 833	67 122	...
Palanpur	...	...	...	...	141 592	74 088	67 504	...
Pali	...	...	...	...	230 075	119 924	110 151	...
Pallavaram	...	...	...	...	233 984	117 405	116 579	...
Palwal	...	...	...	...	131 926	69 997	61 929	...
Panchkula	...	...	...	...	211 355	111 731	99 624	...
Panihati	...	...	...	...	377 347	189 446	187 901	...
Panipat	...	...	...	...	295 970	158 063	137 907	...
Panvel	...	...	...	...	180 020	92 484	87 536	...
Parbhani	...	...	...	...	307 170	156 520	150 650	...
Patan	...	...	...	...	133 737	69 898	63 839	...
Pathankot	...	...	...	...	156 306	82 045	74 261	...
Patiala	...	...	...	...	446 246	236 198	210 048	...
Patna	...	...	...	...	1 684 297	893 445	790 852	...
Pilibhit	...	...	...	...	127 988	67 614	60 374	...
Pimpri Chinchwad	...	...	...	...	1 727 692	942 533	785 159	...
Pithampur	...	...	...	...	126 200	70 250	55 950	...
Porbandar	...	...	...	...	152 760	78 604	74 156	...
Port Blair	...	...	...	...	108 058	57 761	50 297	...
Proddatur	...	...	...	...	163 970	81 874	82 096	...
Puducherry	...	...	...	...	244 377	119 430	124 947	...
Pudukkottai	...	...	...	...	117 630	58 737	58 893	...
Pune	...	...	...	...	3 124 458	1 603 675	1 520 783	...
Puri	...	...	...	...	200 564	104 086	96 478	...
Purnia	...	...	...	...	282 248	148 077	134 171	...
Puruliya	...	...	...	...	121 067	62 351	58 716	...
Rae Bareli	...	...	...	...	191 316	99 903	91 413	...
Raichur	...	...	...	...	234 073	117 657	116 416	...
Raiganj	...	...	...	...	183 612	96 388	87 224	...
Raigarh	...	...	...	...	150 019	76 865	73 154	...
Raipur	...	...	...	...	1 027 264	527 365	499 899	...
Rajahmundry	...	...	...	...	376 333	185 970	190 363	...
Rajapalayam	...	...	...	...	130 442	64 765	65 677	...
Rajarhat Gopalpur	...	...	...	...	402 844	203 911	198 933	...
Rajkot	...	...	...	...	1 323 363	693 473	629 890	...
Rajnandgaon	...	...	...	...	163 114	81 929	81 185	...
Rajpur Sonarpur	...	...	...	...	424 368	215 405	208 963	...
Ramagundam	...	...	...	...	242 979	123 430	119 549	...
Rampur	...	...	...	...	325 313	169 681	155 632	...
Ranchi	...	...	...	...	1 073 427	558 872	514 555	...
Ranibennur	...	...	...	...	106 406	54 040	52 366	...
Raniganj	...	...	...	...	129 441	67 578	61 863	...
Ratlam	...	...	...	...	264 914	134 915	129 999	...
Raurkela Industrial Township	...	...	...	...	216 410	112 897	103 513	...
Raurkela Town	...	...	...	...	320 040	169 095	150 945	...
Rewa	...	...	...	...	235 654	124 012	111 642	...
Rewari	...	...	...	...	143 021	75 764	67 257	...
Rishra	...	...	...	...	124 577	66 606	57 971	...
Robertson Pet	...	...	...	...	162 230	80 375	81 855	...

Continent, country or area, date, code[a] and city / Continent, pays ou zone, date, code[a] et ville	City proper - Ville proprement dite				Urban agglomeration - Agglomération urbaine			
	Population			Surface area - Superficie (km²)	Population			Surface area - Superficie (km²)
	Both sexes - Les deux sexes	Male - Masculin	Female - Féminin		Both sexes - Les deux sexes	Male - Masculin	Female - Féminin	
ASIA - ASIE								
India - Inde								
9 II 2011 (CDFC)								
Rohtak	...	...	...	...	374 292	198 237	176 055	...
Roorkee	...	...	...	...	118 200	63 434	54 766	...
Rudrapur	...	...	...	...	154 554	81 340	73 214	...
S.A.S. Nagar	...	...	...	...	166 864	87 380	79 484	...
Sagar	...	...	...	...	274 556	143 425	131 131	...
Saharanpur	...	...	...	...	705 478	371 740	333 738	...
Saharsa	...	...	...	...	156 540	83 291	73 249	...
Salem	...	...	...	...	829 267	417 317	411 950	...
Sambalpur	...	...	...	...	189 366	97 460	91 906	...
Sambhal	...	...	...	...	220 813	115 767	105 046	...
Sangli-Miraj Kupwad	...	...	...	...	502 793	253 640	249 153	...
Santipur	...	...	...	...	151 777	77 011	74 766	...
Sasaram	...	...	...	...	147 408	77 599	69 809	...
Satara	...	...	...	...	120 195	61 129	59 066	...
Satna	...	...	...	...	282 977	149 415	133 562	...
Sawai Madhopur	...	...	...	...	121 106	63 014	58 092	...
Secunderabad	...	...	...	...	217 910	113 577	104 333	...
Sehore	...	...	...	...	109 118	56 335	52 783	...
Seoni	...	...	...	...	102 343	52 352	49 991	...
Serampore	...	...	...	...	181 842	93 694	88 148	...
Shahjahanpur	...	...	...	...	329 736	173 006	156 730	...
Shamli	...	...	...	...	107 266	57 187	50 079	...
Shikohabad	...	...	...	...	107 404	56 794	50 610	...
Shillong	...	...	...	...	143 229	70 135	73 094	...
Shimla	...	...	...	...	169 578	93 152	76 426	...
Shimoga	...	...	...	...	322 650	162 018	160 632	...
Shivpuri	...	...	...	...	179 977	95 132	84 845	...
Sikar	...	...	...	...	244 497	126 837	117 660	...
Silchar	...	...	...	...	178 865	89 961	88 904	...
Siliguri	...	...	...	...	513 264	263 702	249 562	...
Singrauli	...	...	...	...	220 257	116 867	103 390	...
Sirsa	...	...	...	...	182 534	96 175	86 359	...
Sitapur	...	...	...	...	177 234	92 696	84 538	...
Siwan	...	...	...	...	135 066	70 756	64 310	...
Solapur	...	...	...	...	951 558	481 064	470 494	...
Sonipat	...	...	...	...	289 333	154 407	134 926	...
South Dum Dum	...	...	...	...	403 316	202 214	201 102	...
Srikakulam	...	...	...	...	137 944	68 457	69 487	...
Srinagar	...	...	...	...	1 206 419	631 830	574 589	...
Sujangarh	...	...	...	...	101 523	51 906	49 617	...
Sultan Pur Majra	...	...	...	...	181 554	95 687	85 867	...
Sultanpur	...	...	...	...	107 640	56 420	51 220	...
Surat	...	...	...	...	4 501 610	2 565 803	1 935 807	...
Surendranagar Dudhrej	...	...	...	...	177 851	92 675	85 176	...
Suryapet	...	...	...	...	106 805	52 773	54 032	...
Tadepalligudem	...	...	...	...	104 032	51 438	52 594	...
Tadpatri	...	...	...	...	108 171	54 015	54 156	...
Tambaram	...	...	...	...	174 787	89 060	85 727	...
Tenali	...	...	...	...	164 937	81 427	83 510	...
Thane	...	...	...	...	1 841 488	975 399	866 089	...
Thanesar	...	...	...	...	155 152	83 994	71 158	...
Thanjavur	...	...	...	...	222 943	109 199	113 744	...
Thiruvananthapuram	...	...	...	...	788 271	384 004	404 267	...
Thoothukkudi	...	...	...	...	237 830	118 298	119 532	...
Thrissur	...	...	...	...	315 957	152 296	163 661	...
Tinsukia	...	...	...	...	116 322	62 303	54 019	...
Tiruchirappalli	...	...	...	...	847 387	418 400	428 987	...
Tirunelveli	...	...	...	...	473 637	233 659	239 978	...
Tirupati	...	...	...	...	295 323	150 125	145 198	...
Tiruppur	...	...	...	...	444 352	227 311	217 041	...
Tiruvannamalai	...	...	...	...	145 278	72 406	72 872	...
Tiruvottiyur	...	...	...	...	249 446	125 300	124 146	...
Titagarh	...	...	...	...	116 541	62 735	53 806	...

8. Population of capital cities and cities of 100 000 or more inhabitants: latest available year, 1997 - 2016
Population des capitales et des villes de 100 000 habitants ou plus : dernière année disponible, 1997 - 2016 (continued - suite)

Continent, country or area, date, code[a] and city / Continent, pays ou zone, date, code[a] et ville	City proper - Ville proprement dite				Urban agglomeration - Agglomération urbaine			
	Population			Surface area - Superficie (km²)	Population			Surface area - Superficie (km²)
	Both sexes - Les deux sexes	Male - Masculin	Female - Féminin		Both sexes - Les deux sexes	Male - Masculin	Female - Féminin	

ASIA - ASIE

India - Inde
9 II 2011 (CDFC)

Tonk	...	...	...	...	165 294	84 806	80 488	...
Tumkur	...	...	...	...	302 143	152 925	149 218	...
Udaipur	...	...	...	...	451 100	233 959	217 141	...
Udgir	...	...	...	...	103 550	54 013	49 537	...
Udupi	...	...	...	...	144 960	71 614	73 346	...
Ujjain	...	...	...	...	515 215	264 871	250 344	...
Ulhasnagar	...	...	...	...	506 098	269 048	237 050	...
Uluberia	...	...	...	...	235 345	120 741	114 604	...
Unnao	...	...	...	...	177 658	93 021	84 637	...
Uttarpara Kotrung	...	...	...	...	159 147	81 410	77 737	...
Vadodara	...	...	...	...	1 752 371	912 721	839 650	...
Valsad	...	...	...	...	139 764	71 400	68 364	...
Vapi	...	...	...	...	163 630	94 105	69 525	...
Varanasi	...	...	...	...	1 198 491	635 140	563 351	...
Vasai-Virar City	...	...	...	...	1 222 390	648 172	574 218	...
Vellore	...	...	...	...	185 803	91 342	94 461	...
Veraval	...	...	...	...	171 121	87 009	84 112	...
Vidisha	...	...	...	...	155 951	81 488	74 463	...
Vijayawada	...	...	...	...	1 143 232	574 794	568 438	...
Vizianagaram	...	...	...	...	228 720	112 290	116 430	...
Warangal	...	...	...	...	704 570	353 309	351 261	...
Wardha	...	...	...	...	106 444	53 697	52 747	...
Yamunanagar	...	...	...	...	217 071	115 663	101 408	...
Yavatmal	...	...	...	...	116 551	58 549	58 002	...

Indonesia - Indonésie
1 VII 2016 (ESDJ)

Ambon	444 797	222 350	222 447	359.5	...	...	...	...
Balikpapan	636 012	328 382	307 630	512.3	...	...	...	...
Banda Aceh	259 913	133 728	126 185	61.4	...	...	...	...
Bandar Lampung	1 015 910	511 371	504 539	296	...	...	...	...
Bandjarmasin	692 793	347 005	345 788	72.6	...	...	...	...
Bandung	2 497 938	1 260 204	1 237 734	168.2	...	...	...	...
Batam	1 283 196	654 804	628 392	960.3	...	...	...	...
Bengkulu	368 065	184 887	183 178	144.5	...	...	...	...
Binjai	270 926	135 203	135 723	59.2	...	...	...	...
Bitung	212 409	108 481	103 928	304	...	...	...	...
Blitar	139 995	69 411	70 584	32.6	...	...	...	...
Bogor	1 081 009	548 196	532 813	111.7	...	...	...	...
Cirebon (Tjirebon)	313 325	157 103	156 222	40.2	...	...	...	...
Denpasar	914 279	466 651	447 628	127.8	...	...	...	...
Gorontalo	210 782	103 584	107 198	66	...	...	...	...
JAKARTA	10 374 235	5 202 815	5 171 420	662.3	...	...	...	...
Jambi	591 134	297 036	294 098	205.4	...	...	...	...
Jayapura	293 690	157 710	135 980	950.4	...	...	...	...
Kediri	284 003	141 609	142 394	63.4	...	...	...	...
Madiun	176 099	85 203	90 896	33.9	...	...	...	...
Magelang	121 474	59 766	61 708	18.1	...	...	...	...
Makasar (Ujung Pandang)	1 489 011	737 146	751 865	175.8	...	...	...	...
Malang	861 414	424 811	436 603	145.3	...	...	...	...
Manado	430 133	215 832	214 301	158	...	...	...	...
Mataram	468 509	231 797	236 712	61.3	...	...	...	...
Medan	2 247 425	1 110 000	1 137 425	265	...	...	...	...
Mojokerto	127 279	62 587	64 692	16.5	...	...	...	...
Padang	927 011	463 116	463 895	695	...	...	...	...
Pakalongan	301 870	150 887	150 983	45	...	...	...	...
Pakanbaru	1 091 088	559 917	531 171	632.3	...	...	...	...
Palangkaraya	275 667	141 179	134 488	2400	...	...	...	...
Palembang	1 623 099	813 709	809 390	363.7	...	...	...	...
Pangkal Pinang	204 392	104 927	99 465	118.8	...	...	...	...
Pare Pare	142 097	69 822	72 275	99.3	...	...	...	...
Pasuruan	197 696	97 995	99 701	35.3	...	...	...	...
Pematang Siantar	251 513	122 626	128 887	55.7	...	...	...	...
Pontianak	627 021	312 178	314 843	107.8	...	...	...	...

Continent, country or area, date, code[a] and city / Continent, pays ou zone, date, code[a] et ville	City proper - Ville proprement dite				Urban agglomeration - Agglomération urbaine			
	Population			Surface area - Superficie (km²)	Population			Surface area - Superficie (km²)
	Both sexes - Les deux sexes	Male - Masculin	Female - Féminin		Both sexes - Les deux sexes	Male - Masculin	Female - Féminin	
ASIA - ASIE								
Indonesia - Indonésie								
1 VII 2016 (ESDJ)								
Probolinggo	233 123	114 822	118 301	56.7	...	...	...	...
Salatiga	188 928	92 426	96 502	53	...	...	...	...
Samarinda	843 446	435 949	407 497	716.5	...	...	...	...
Semarang	1 757 686	861 994	895 692	373.7	...	...	...	...
Sukabumi	323 788	163 891	159 897	49	...	...	...	...
Surabaya	2 874 699	1 420 182	1 454 517	350.5	...	...	...	...
Surakarta	516 102	250 896	265 206	44	...	...	...	...
Tangerang	2 139 891	1 091 787	1 048 104	153.9	...	...	...	...
Tanjung Balai	171 187	86 277	84 910	107.8	...	...	...	...
Tebing Tinggi	160 686	79 379	81 307	31	...	...	...	...
Tegal	248 094	122 817	125 277	34.5	...	...	...	...
Yogyakarta	422 732	206 421	216 311	32.5	...	...	...	...
Iran (Islamic Republic of) - Iran (République islamique d')								
24 X 2011 (CDJC)								
Abadan	212 744	106 181	106 563	...	...	...	...	...
Ahwaz	1 112 021	558 346	553 675	...	...	...	...	...
Amol	219 915	110 331	109 584	...	...	...	...	...
Andimeshk	126 811	63 990	62 821	...	...	...	...	...
Arak	484 212	244 614	239 598	...	...	...	...	...
Ardabil	482 632	245 335	237 297	...	...	...	...	...
Babol	219 467	109 407	110 060	...	...	...	...	...
Bam	107 131	53 492	53 639	...	...	...	...	...
Bandar-e-Abbas	435 751	222 798	212 953	...	...	...	...	...
Bandar-e-Anzali	116 664	57 675	58 989	...	...	...	...	...
Bandar-e-Mahshahr	153 778	77 487	76 291	...	...	...	...	...
Behbahan	107 412	54 163	53 249	...	...	...	...	...
Birjand	178 020	90 092	87 928	...	...	...	...	...
Bojnurd	199 791	100 605	99 186	...	...	...	...	...
Borujerd	240 654	118 508	122 146	...	...	...	...	...
Bukand	170 600	85 835	84 765	...	...	...	...	...
Bushehr	195 222	101 362	93 860	...	...	...	...	...
Dezful	248 380	128 430	119 950	...	...	...	...	...
Esfahan	1 756 126	884 018	872 108	...	...	...	...	...
Fasa	104 809	51 907	52 902	...	...	...	...	...
Golestan (Soltanabad)	259 480	133 531	125 949	...	...	...	...	...
Gonbad-e-Kavus	144 546	71 986	72 560	...	...	...	...	...
Gorgan	329 536	165 001	164 535	...	...	...	...	...
Hamadan	525 794	261 577	264 217	...	...	...	...	...
Ilam	172 213	87 221	84 992	...	...	...	...	...
Islam Shahr (Qasemabad)	389 102	198 080	191 022	...	...	...	...	...
Izeh	117 093	58 080	59 013	...	...	...	...	...
Jahrom	114 108	57 865	56 243	...	...	...	...	...
Jiroft	111 034	57 168	53 866	...	...	...	...	...
Kamal Shahr	109 943	56 265	53 678	...	...	...	...	...
Karaj	1 614 626	813 551	801 075	...	...	...	...	...
Kashan	275 325	139 866	135 459	...	...	...	...	...
Kerman	534 441	269 661	264 780	...	...	...	...	...
Kermanshah	851 405	426 129	425 276	...	...	...	...	...
Khomeini shahr	244 696	126 326	118 370	...	...	...	...	...
Khoramabad	348 216	173 264	174 952	...	...	...	...	...
Khoramshahr	129 418	63 804	65 614	...	...	...	...	...
Khoy	200 958	100 593	100 365	...	...	...	...	...
Mahabad	147 268	73 626	73 642	...	...	...	...	...
Malard	290 817	147 954	142 863	...	...	...	...	...
Malayer	159 848	79 477	80 371	...	...	...	...	...
Marand	124 323	62 848	61 475	...	...	...	...	...
Maraqeh	162 275	81 229	81 046	...	...	...	...	...
Marivan	110 464	56 129	54 335	...	...	...	...	...
Marvadsht	138 649	70 221	68 428	...	...	...	...	...
Mashhad	2 766 258	1 384 599	1 381 659	...	...	...	...	...
Masjed Soleyman	103 369	51 852	51 517	...	...	...	...	...
Miandoab	123 081	62 883	60 198	...	...	...	...	...

8. Population of capital cities and cities of 100 000 or more inhabitants: latest available year, 1997 - 2016
Population des capitales et des villes de 100 000 habitants ou plus : dernière année disponible, 1997 - 2016 (continued - suite)

Continent, country or area, date, code[a] and city / Continent, pays ou zone, date, code[a] et ville	City proper - Ville proprement dite				Urban agglomeration - Agglomération urbaine			
	Population			Surface area - Superficie (km²)	Population			Surface area - Superficie (km²)
	Both sexes - Les deux sexes	Male - Masculin	Female - Féminin		Both sexes - Les deux sexes	Male - Masculin	Female - Féminin	

ASIA - ASIE

Iran (Islamic Republic of) - Iran (République islamique d')
24 X 2011 (CDJC)

Mohammad Shahr	100 519	51 359	49 160	...	...	...	...	...
Najafabad	221 814	111 915	109 899	...	...	...	...	...
Nasim Shahr	157 474	80 947	76 527	...	...	...	...	...
Nazar Abad	107 806	54 806	53 000	...	...	...	...	...
Neyshabur	239 185	119 845	119 340	...	...	...	...	...
Orumiyeh	667 499	334 136	333 363	...	...	...	...	...
Pakdasht	206 490	105 814	100 676	...	...	...	...	...
Qaem shahr	196 050	97 358	98 692	...	...	...	...	...
Qarchak	191 588	97 678	93 910	...	...	...	...	...
Qazvin	381 598	192 960	188 638	...	...	...	...	...
Qods	283 517	144 911	138 606	...	...	...	...	...
Qom	1 074 036	545 704	528 332	...	...	...	...	...
Quchan	103 760	52 240	51 520	...	...	...	...	...
Rafsanjan	151 420	75 643	75 777	...	...	...	...	...
Rasht	639 951	316 833	323 118	...	...	...	...	...
Sabzewar	231 557	115 158	116 399	...	...	...	...	...
Sanandaj	373 987	189 047	184 940	...	...	...	...	...
Saqez	139 738	69 856	69 882	...	...	...	...	...
Sari	296 417	147 875	148 542	...	...	...	...	...
Saveh	200 481	102 578	97 903	...	...	...	...	...
Semnan	153 680	77 575	76 105	...	...	...	...	...
Shahinshahr	143 308	71 357	71 951	...	...	...	...	...
Shahr-e-Kord	159 775	79 681	80 094	...	...	...	...	...
Shahreza	123 767	62 314	61 453	...	...	...	...	...
Shahriar	249 473	126 246	123 227	...	...	...	...	...
Shahrud	140 474	70 616	69 858	...	...	...	...	...
Shiraz	1 460 665	732 380	728 285	...	...	...	...	...
Shoosh	106 815	53 747	53 068	...	...	...	...	...
Sirjan	185 623	94 943	90 680	...	...	...	...	...
Tabriz	1 494 998	755 553	739 445	...	...	...	...	...
TEHRAN	8 154 051	4 059 301	4 094 750	...	...	...	...	...
Torbat-e-heydariyeh	131 150	66 310	64 840	...	...	...	...	...
Varamin	218 991	111 074	107 917	...	...	...	...	...
Yasooj	108 505	54 825	53 680	...	...	...	...	...
Yazd	486 152	246 985	239 167	...	...	...	...	...
Zabol	137 722	69 726	67 996	...	...	...	...	...
Zahedan	560 725	283 680	277 045	...	...	...	...	...
Zanjan	386 851	195 382	191 469	...	...	...	...	...

Iraq
1 VII 2015 (ESDF)

Abi Gharaq Nahia	108 630	55 009	53 621	191	...	...	...	...
Abna'a Al-Rafidain Nahia	153 712	77 827	75 885	...	...	...	...	...
Abu Al-Khaseeb Qadha Center	215 247	108 228	107 019	1152	...	...	...	...
Abu-Gharib Qadha Center	149 858	76 274	73 584	431	...	...	...	...
Al-Adhamia Qadha Center	286 036	144 825	141 211	29	...	...	...	...
Al-Amara Qadha Center	541 034	270 426	270 608	2862	...	...	...	...
Al-Amirya Nahia	101 119	51 899	49 220	2532	...	...	...	...
Al-Basrah Qadha Center	1 225 793	616 525	609 268	1085	...	...	...	...
Al-Dair Nahia	101 882	50 969	50 913	825	...	...	...	...
Al-Dijail Qadha Center	105 345	53 240	52 105	1286	...	...	...	...
Al-Diwaniya Qadha Center	421 571	212 293	209 278	319	...	...	...	...
Al-Fahama Nahia	619 474	313 651	305 823	90	...	...	...	...
Al-Falluja Qadha Center	321 106	165 111	155 995	478	...	...	...	...
Al-Forat Nahia	379 668	192 233	187 435	...	...	...	...	...
Al-Garma Nahia	129 783	66 577	63 206	1038	...	...	...	...
Al-Gharraf Nahia	118 081	59 318	58 763	623	...	...	...	...
Al-Habbaniya Nahia	133 202	68 366	64 836	714	...	...	...	...
Al-Hamza Qadha Center	128 472	64 739	63 733	600	...	...	...	...
Al-Hartha Nahia	156 391	78 509	77 882	...	...	...	...	...
Al-Hassainya Nahia	147 103	74 383	72 720	334	...	...	...	...
Al-Hawiga Qadha Center	115 910	58 508	57 402	1903	...	...	...	...
Al-Hilla Qadha Center	559 834	282 142	277 692	161	...	...	...	...

8. Population of capital cities and cities of 100 000 or more inhabitants: latest available year, 1997 - 2016
Population des capitales et des villes de 100 000 habitants ou plus : dernière année disponible, 1997 - 2016 (continued - suite)

Continent, country or area, date, code[a] and city / Continent, pays ou zone, date, code[a] et ville	City proper - Ville proprement dite				Urban agglomeration - Agglomération urbaine			
	Population			Surface area - Superficie (km²)	Population			Surface area - Superficie (km²)
	Both sexes - Les deux sexes	Male - Masculin	Female - Féminin		Both sexes - Les deux sexes	Male - Masculin	Female - Féminin	

ASIA - ASIE

Iraq
1 VII 2015 (ESDF)

Al-Hindiya Qadha Center	113 021	57 001	56 020	134	...	...	...	...
Al-Hur Nahia	231 635	116 740	114 895	...	...	...	...	...
Al-Iskandaria Nahia	159 516	80 514	79 002	283	...	...	...	...
Al-Jisr Nahia	159 306	81 464	77 842	153	...	...	...	...
Al-Kadimiya Qadha Center	420 968	213 144	207 824	32	...	...	...	...
Al-Kaim Qadha Center	104 989	53 971	51 018	6460	...	...	...	...
Al-Karkh Qadha Center	113 397	57 415	55 982	...	...	...	...	...
Al-Karrada Al-Sharqia Nahia	318 615	161 321	157 294	49	...	...	...	...
Al-Khalis Qadha Center	139 713	70 624	69 089	1109	...	...	...	...
Al-Kifl Nahia	140 182	71 029	69 153	526	...	...	...	...
Al-Kufa Qadha Center	232 670	116 667	116 003	129	...	...	...	...
Al-Kut Qadha Center	436 673	220 490	216 183	2540	...	...	...	...
Al-Madhatiya Nahia	135 941	68 724	67 217	498	...	...	...	...
Al-Mahawil Qadha Center	116 899	59 181	57 718	608	...	...	...	...
Al-Mamoon Nahia	985 798	499 128	486 670	82	...	...	...	...
Al-Mansour Nahia	434 839	220 167	214 672	119	...	...	...	...
Al-Mashroo Nahia	127 344	64 449	62 895	834	...	...	...	...
Al-Mejar Al-Kabir Qadha Center	108 979	54 373	54 606	506	...	...	...	...
Al-Mosal Qadha Center	1 384 260	708 546	675 714	1783	...	...	...	...
Al-Mounawara Nahia	287 799	145 718	142 081	...	...	...	...	...
Al-Muqdadya Qadha Center	157 593	79 612	77 981	768	...	...	...	...
Al-Najaf Qadha Center	746 180	372 423	373 757	1133	...	...	...	...
Al-Nasir & Al-Salam Nahia	160 606	82 184	78 422	262	...	...	...	...
Al-Nasiriya Qadha Center	537 544	269 480	268 064	1277	...	...	...	...
Al-Noamaniya Qadha Center	111 647	56 363	55 284	946	...	...	...	...
Al-Qasim Nahia	159 420	80 545	78 875	528	...	...	...	...
Al-Qayarra Nahia	129 811	66 129	63 682	686	...	...	...	...
Al-Qurna Qadha Center	136 677	68 704	67 973	1248	...	...	...	...
Al-Ramadi Qadha Center	419 053	215 292	203 761	7829	...	...	...	...
Al-Rifaai Qadha Center	155 478	78 087	77 391	1345	...	...	...	...
Al-Rumaitha Qadha Center	118 011	59 581	58 430	106	...	...	...	...
Al-Rusafa Qadha Center	118 018	59 755	58 263	...	...	...	...	...
Al-Samawa Qadha Center	288 948	145 984	142 964	941	...	...	...	...
Al-Shamal Nahia	158 475	81 035	77 440	...	...	...	...	...
Al-Shattra Qadha Center	239 680	120 266	119 414	384	...	...	...	...
Al-Shirqat Qadha Center	208 586	105 453	103 133	1515	...	...	...	...
Al-Sideeq Al-Akbar Nahia	172 057	87 116	84 941	...	...	...	...	...
Al-Suwaira Qadha Center	142 924	72 148	70 776	1345	...	...	...	...
Al-Taji Nahia	164 894	84 470	80 424	388	...	...	...	...
Al-Wihda Nahia	204 585	104 438	100 147	890	...	...	...	...
Al-Yousifya Nahia	131 507	67 600	63 907	486	...	...	...	...
Al-Zohour Nahia	209 918	106 332	103 586	...	...	...	...	...
Al-Zubair Qadha Center	378 758	190 200	188 558	1134	...	...	...	...
Arbil Qadha Center	787 997	398 450	389 547	2790	...	...	...	...
BAGHDAD	1 211 934[39]	613 625[39]	598 309[39]	111	...	...	...	...
Bakrago Nahia	101 892	51 077	50 815	...	...	...	...	...
Baquba Qadha Center	276 029	138 681	137 348	580	...	...	...	...
Bashiqa Nahia	140 258	71 487	68 771	497	...	...	...	...
Beni Saad Nahia	127 268	64 496	62 772	497	...	...	...	...
Beygee Qadha Center	175 395	88 596	86 799	1188	...	...	...	...
Duhouk Qadha Center	328 113	164 245	163 868	577	...	...	...	...
Kalar Qadha Center	144 235	72 047	72 188	2201	...	...	...	...
Kerbela Qadha Center	514 356	259 193	255 163	2397	...	...	...	...
Kirkuk Qadha Center	938 336	471 419	466 917	1956	...	...	...	...
Mahmudiya Qadha Center	154 741	78 846	75 895	68	...	...	...	...
Qalat Siker Nahia	100 315	50 373	49 942	614	...	...	...	...
Saddat Al-Hindin Nahia	116 247	58 839	57 408	388	...	...	...	...
Sader /1 Qadha Center	130 153	65 899	64 254	...	...	...	...	...
Samarra Qadha Center	203 011	102 444	100 567	4504	...	...	...	...
Shat Al-Arab Qadha Center	136 043	68 413	67 630	1516	...	...	...	...
Sulaimania Qadha Center	651 173	325 147	326 026	3404	...	...	...	...
Suq AL-Shoyolh Qadha Center	126 652	63 493	63 159	285	...	...	...	...
Telafar Qadha Center	206 835	105 780	101 055	3206	...	...	...	...

	City proper - Ville proprement dite				Urban agglomeration - Agglomération urbaine			
	Population			Surface area - Superficie (km²)	Population			Surface area - Superficie (km²)
Continent, country or area, date, code[a] and city / Continent, pays ou zone, date, code[a] et ville	Both sexes - Les deux sexes	Male - Masculin	Female - Féminin		Both sexes - Les deux sexes	Male - Masculin	Female - Féminin	
ASIA - ASIE								
Iraq								
1 VII 2015 (ESDF)								
That Al Salasil Nahia	*277 494*	*140 647*	*136 847*	147	...	...	...	...
Tikrit Qadha Center	*182 464*	*92 119*	*90 345*	991	...	...	...	...
Tooz-Khormato Qadha Center	*117 458*	*59 233*	*58 225*	1253	...	...	...	...
Zummar Nahia	*128 017*	*65 210*	*62 807*	1247	...	...	...	...
Israel - Israël								
1 VII 2015 (ESDJ)								
Ashdod	219 067	106 883	112 184	...	...	...	...	...
Ashqelon	128 740	62 596	66 143	...	...	...	...	...
Bat Yam	128 695	61 253	67 443	...	...	...	...	...
Be'er Sheva	202 495	98 667	103 828	...	...	...	...	...
Bene Beraq	180 544	91 940	88 604	...	...	...	...	...
Bet Shemesh	101 003	50 418	50 585	...	...	...	...	...
Haifa	277 993	133 448	144 544	...	...	...	...	...
Holon	188 064	90 836	97 228	...	...	...	...	...
JERUSALEM[40]	857 752	426 943	430 809	...	...	...	...	...
Netanya	205 187	100 010	105 177	...	...	...	...	...
Petah Tiqwa	228 170	111 498	116 672	...	...	...	...	...
Ramat Gan	151 757	72 438	79 318	...	...	...	...	...
Rehovot	130 782	63 990	66 792	...	...	...	...	...
Rishon Leziyyon	242 320	118 637	123 683	...	...	...	...	...
Tel Aviv-Yafo	429 515	212 373	217 141	...	...	...	...	...
Japan - Japon								
1 X 2015 (CDJC)								
Abiko	131 606[41]	64 614[41]	66 992[41]	43.2[42]	...	...	...	...
Ageo	225 196[41]	112 157[41]	113 039[41]	45.5[42]	...	...	...	...
Aizuwakamatsu	124 062[41]	59 200[41]	64 862[41]	383[42]	...	...	...	...
Akashi	293 409[41]	141 801[41]	151 608[41]	49.4[42]	...	...	...	...
Akishima	111 539[41]	55 394[41]	56 145[41]	17.3[42]	...	...	...	...
Akita	315 814[41]	148 851[41]	166 963[41]	906.1[42]	...	...	...	...
Amagasaki	452 563[41]	219 059[41]	233 504[41]	50.7[42]	...	...	...	...
Anjo	184 140[41]	94 073[41]	90 067[41]	86.1[42]	...	...	...	...
Aomori	287 648[41]	133 560[41]	154 088[41]	824.6[42]	...	...	...	...
Asahikawa	339 605[41]	156 402[41]	183 203[41]	747.7[42]	...	...	...	...
Asaka	136 299[41]	69 971[41]	66 328[41]	18.3[42]	...	...	...	...
Ashikaga	149 452[41]	73 161[41]	76 291[41]	177.8[42]	...	...	...	...
Atsugi	225 714[41]	116 658[41]	109 056[41]	93.8[42]	...	...	...	...
Beppu	122 138[41]	55 482[41]	66 656[41]	125.3[42]	...	...	...	...
Chiba	971 882[41]	482 840[41]	489 042[41]	271.8[42]	...	...	...	...
Chigasaki	239 348[41]	116 894[41]	122 454[41]	35.7[42]	...	...	...	...
Chikusei	104 573[41]	51 663[41]	52 910[41]	205.3[42]	...	...	...	...
Chikushino	101 081[41]	47 995[41]	53 086[41]	87.7[42]	...	...	...	...
Chofu	229 061[41]	111 921[41]	117 140[41]	21.6[42]	...	...	...	...
Daito	123 217[41]	60 302[41]	62 915[41]	18.3[42]	...	...	...	...
Ebetsu	120 636[41]	57 391[41]	63 245[41]	187.4[42]	...	...	...	...
Ebina	130 190[41]	65 620[41]	64 570[41]	26.6[42]	...	...	...	...
Fuchu	260 274[41]	132 172[41]	128 102[41]	29.4[42]	...	...	...	...
Fuji	248 399[41]	121 901[41]	126 498[41]	245[42]	...	...	...	...
Fujieda	143 605[41]	70 049[41]	73 556[41]	194.1[42]	...	...	...	...
Fujimi	108 102[41]	53 312[41]	54 790[41]	19.8[42]	...	...	...	...
Fujimino	110 970[41]	54 910[41]	56 060[41]	14.6[42]	...	...	...	...
Fujinomiya	130 770[41]	64 281[41]	66 489[41]	389.1[42]	...	...	...	...
Fujisawa	423 894[41]	210 032[41]	213 862[41]	69.6[42]	...	...	...	...
Fukaya	143 811[41]	71 594[41]	72 217[41]	138.4[42]	...	...	...	...
Fukui	265 904[41]	128 892[41]	137 012[41]	536.4[42]	...	...	...	...
Fukuoka	1 538 681[41]	726 666[41]	812 015[41]	343.4[42]	...	...	...	...
Fukushima	294 247[41]	144 690[41]	149 557[41]	767.7[42]	...	...	...	...
Fukuyama	464 811[41]	225 414[41]	239 397[41]	518.1[42]	...	...	...	...
Funabashi	622 890[41]	311 358[41]	311 532[41]	85.6[42]	...	...	...	...
Gifu	406 735[41]	193 760[41]	212 975[41]	203.6[42]	...	...	...	...
Habikino	112 683[41]	53 243[41]	59 440[41]	26.5[42]	...	...	...	...
Hachinohe	231 257[41]	110 493[41]	120 764[41]	305.5[42]	...	...	...	...

Continent, country or area, date, code[a] and city / Continent, pays ou zone, date, code[a] et ville	City proper - Ville proprement dite				Urban agglomeration - Agglomération urbaine			
	Population			Surface area - Superficie (km²)	Population			Surface area - Superficie (km²)
	Both sexes - Les deux sexes	Male - Masculin	Female - Féminin		Both sexes - Les deux sexes	Male - Masculin	Female - Féminin	

ASIA - ASIE

Japan - Japon
1 X 2015 (CDJC)

Hachioji	577 513[41]	291 238[41]	286 275[41]	186.4[42]	...	...	...	...
Hadano	167 378[41]	85 552[41]	81 826[41]	103.8[42]	...	...	...	...
Hakodate	265 979[41]	120 376[41]	145 603[41]	677.9[42]	...	...	...	...
Hakusan	109 287[41]	53 085[41]	56 202[41]	754.9[42]	...	...	...	...
Hamamatsu	797 980[41]	395 509[41]	402 471[41]	1558.1[42]	...	...	...	...
Handa	116 908[41]	58 444[41]	58 464[41]	47.4[42]	...	...	...	...
Hatsukaichi	114 906[41]	54 654[41]	60 252[41]	489.5[42]	...	...	...	...
Higashihiroshima	192 907[41]	97 962[41]	94 945[41]	635.2[42]	...	...	...	...
Higashikurume	116 632[41]	56 738[41]	59 894[41]	12.9[42]	...	...	...	...
Higashimurayama	149 956[41]	73 314[41]	76 642[41]	17.1[42]	...	...	...	...
Higashiomi	114 180[41]	56 601[41]	57 579[41]	388.4[42]	...	...	...	...
Higashiosaka	502 784[41]	246 053[41]	256 731[41]	61.8[42]	...	...	...	...
Hikone	113 679[41]	56 090[41]	57 589[41]	196.9[42]	...	...	...	...
Himeji	535 664[41]	258 724[41]	276 940[41]	534.5[42]	...	...	...	...
Hino	186 283[41]	93 349[41]	92 934[41]	27.6[42]	...	...	...	...
Hirakata	404 152[41]	192 816[41]	211 336[41]	65.1[42]	...	...	...	...
Hiratsuka	258 227[41]	129 456[41]	128 771[41]	67.8[42]	...	...	...	...
Hirosaki	177 411[41]	81 367[41]	96 044[41]	524.2[42]	...	...	...	...
Hiroshima	1 194 034[41]	576 850[41]	617 184[41]	906.5[42]	...	...	...	...
Hitachi	185 054[41]	92 595[41]	92 459[41]	225.7[42]	...	...	...	...
Hitachinaka	155 689[41]	78 270[41]	77 419[41]	99.9[42]	...	...	...	...
Hofu	115 942[41]	55 910[41]	60 032[41]	189.4[42]	...	...	...	...
Ibaraki	280 033[41]	135 705[41]	144 328[41]	76.5[42]	...	...	...	...
Ichihara	274 656[41]	141 134[41]	133 522[41]	368.2[42]	...	...	...	...
Ichikawa	481 732[41]	242 652[41]	239 080[41]	57.5[42]	...	...	...	...
Ichinomiya	380 868[41]	185 869[41]	194 999[41]	113.8[42]	...	...	...	...
Ichinoseki	121 583[41]	58 804[41]	62 779[41]	1256.4[42]	...	...	...	...
Iida	101 581[41]	48 443[41]	53 138[41]	658.7[42]	...	...	...	...
Iizuka	129 146[41]	61 249[41]	67 897[41]	214.1[42]	...	...	...	...
Ikeda	103 069[41]	49 372[41]	53 697[41]	22.1[42]	...	...	...	...
Ikoma	118 233[41]	55 972[41]	62 261[41]	53.2[42]	...	...	...	...
Imabari	158 114[41]	74 336[41]	83 778[41]	419.1[42]	...	...	...	...
Inazawa	136 867[41]	67 500[41]	69 367[41]	79.4[42]	...	...	...	...
Iruma	148 390[41]	73 408[41]	74 982[41]	44.7[42]	...	...	...	...
Isahaya	138 078[41]	65 029[41]	73 049[41]	341.8[42]	...	...	...	...
Ise	127 817[41]	60 467[41]	67 350[41]	208.4[42]	...	...	...	...
Isehara	101 514[41]	51 429[41]	50 085[41]	55.6[42]	...	...	...	...
Isesaki	208 814[41]	104 234[41]	104 580[41]	139.4[42]	...	...	...	...
Ishinomaki	147 214[41]	71 826[41]	75 388[41]	554.6[42]	...	...	...	...
Itami	196 883[41]	95 641[41]	101 242[41]	25[42]	...	...	...	...
Iwaki	350 237[41]	172 829[41]	177 408[41]	1232[42]	...	...	...	...
Iwakuni	136 757[41]	64 455[41]	72 302[41]	873.7[42]	...	...	...	...
Iwata	167 210[41]	84 130[41]	83 080[41]	163.5[42]	...	...	...	...
Izumi (Osaka)	186 109[41]	89 868[41]	96 241[41]	85[42]	...	...	...	...
Izumisano	100 966[41]	48 506[41]	52 460[41]	56.5[42]	...	...	...	...
Izumo	171 938[41]	82 707[41]	89 231[41]	624.4[42]	...	...	...	...
Joetsu	196 987[41]	95 990[41]	100 997[41]	973.8[42]	...	...	...	...
Kadoma	123 576[41]	60 620[41]	62 956[41]	12.3[42]	...	...	...	...
Kagoshima	599 814[41]	279 108[41]	320 706[41]	547.6[42]	...	...	...	...
Kakamigahara	144 690[41]	71 167[41]	73 523[41]	87.8[42]	...	...	...	...
Kakegawa	114 602[41]	57 126[41]	57 476[41]	265.7[42]	...	...	...	...
Kakogawa	267 435[41]	131 170[41]	136 265[41]	138.5[42]	...	...	...	...
Kamagaya	108 917[41]	53 490[41]	55 427[41]	21.1[42]	...	...	...	...
Kamakura	173 019[41]	81 664[41]	91 355[41]	39.7[42]	...	...	...	...
Kanazawa	465 699[41]	226 007[41]	239 692[41]	468.6[42]	...	...	...	...
Kanoya	103 608[41]	49 555[41]	54 053[41]	448.2[42]	...	...	...	...
Karatsu	122 785[41]	57 547[41]	65 238[41]	487.6[42]	...	...	...	...
Kariya	149 765[41]	78 456[41]	71 309[41]	50.4[42]	...	...	...	...
Kashihara	124 111[41]	58 888[41]	65 223[41]	39.6[42]	...	...	...	...

Continent, country or area, date, code[a] and city / Continent, pays ou zone, date, code[a] et ville	City proper - Ville proprement dite				Urban agglomeration - Agglomération urbaine			
	Population			Surface area - Superficie (km²)	Population			Surface area - Superficie (km²)
	Both sexes - Les deux sexes	Male - Masculin	Female - Féminin		Both sexes - Les deux sexes	Male - Masculin	Female - Féminin	

ASIA - ASIE

Japan - Japon
1 X 2015 (CDJC)

Kashiwa	413 954[41]	205 971[41]	207 983[41]	114.7[42]	...	...	...	...
Kasuga	110 743[41]	53 284[41]	57 459[41]	14.2[42]	...	...	...	...
Kasugai	306 508[41]	151 955[41]	154 553[41]	92.8[42]	...	...	...	...
Kasukabe	232 709[41]	114 813[41]	117 896[41]	66[42]	...	...	...	...
Kawachinagano	106 987[41]	50 182[41]	56 805[41]	109.6[42]	...	...	...	...
Kawagoe	350 745[41]	175 559[41]	175 186[41]	109.1[42]	...	...	...	...
Kawaguchi	578 112[41]	292 067[41]	286 045[41]	62[42]	...	...	...	...
Kawanishi	156 375[41]	73 882[41]	82 493[41]	53.4[42]	...	...	...	...
Kawasaki	1 475 213[41]	749 038[41]	726 175[41]	143[42]	...	...	...	...
Kazo	112 229[41]	55 828[41]	56 401[41]	133.3[42]	...	...	...	...
Kirishima	125 857[41]	59 966[41]	65 891[41]	603.2[42]	...	...	...	...
Kiryu	114 714[41]	55 327[41]	59 387[41]	274.5[42]	...	...	...	...
Kisarazu	134 141[41]	67 450[41]	66 691[41]	139[42]	...	...	...	...
Kishiwada	194 911[41]	93 160[41]	101 751[41]	72.7[42]	...	...	...	...
Kitakyushu	961 286[41]	452 682[41]	508 604[41]	492[42]	...	...	...	...
Kitami	121 226[41]	58 020[41]	63 206[41]	1427.4[42]	...	...	...	...
Kobe	1 537 272[41]	726 700[41]	810 572[41]	557[42]	...	...	...	...
Kochi	337 190[41]	157 002[41]	180 188[41]	309[42]	...	...	...	...
Kodaira	190 005[41]	93 777[41]	96 228[41]	20.5[42]	...	...	...	...
Kofu	193 125[41]	94 448[41]	98 677[41]	212.5[42]	...	...	...	...
Koga	140 946[41]	70 354[41]	70 592[41]	123.6[42]	...	...	...	...
Koganei	121 396[41]	60 168[41]	61 228[41]	11.3[42]	...	...	...	...
Kokubunji	122 742[41]	60 274[41]	62 468[41]	11.5[42]	...	...	...	...
Komaki	149 462[41]	75 430[41]	74 032[41]	62.8[42]	...	...	...	...
Komatsu	106 919[41]	51 844[41]	55 075[41]	371.1[42]	...	...	...	...
Konosu	118 072[41]	58 346[41]	59 726[41]	67.4[42]	...	...	...	...
Koriyama	335 444[41]	167 096[41]	168 348[41]	757.2[42]	...	...	...	...
Koshigaya	337 498[41]	167 023[41]	170 475[41]	60.2[42]	...	...	...	...
Kuki	152 311[41]	75 993[41]	76 318[41]	82.4[42]	...	...	...	...
Kumagaya	198 742[41]	99 169[41]	99 573[41]	159.8[42]	...	...	...	...
Kumamoto	740 822[41]	348 470[41]	392 352[41]	390.3[42]	...	...	...	...
Kurashiki	477 118[41]	230 081[41]	247 037[41]	355.6[42]	...	...	...	...
Kure	228 552[41]	110 173[41]	118 379[41]	352.8[42]	...	...	...	...
Kurume	304 552[41]	144 971[41]	159 581[41]	230[42]	...	...	...	...
Kusatsu	137 247[41]	70 129[41]	67 118[41]	67.8[42]	...	...	...	...
Kushiro	174 742[41]	82 185[41]	92 557[41]	1362.9[42]	...	...	...	...
Kuwana	140 303[41]	68 740[41]	71 563[41]	136.7[42]	...	...	...	...
Kyoto	1 475 183[41]	699 748[41]	775 435[41]	827.8[42]	...	...	...	...
Machida	432 348[41]	212 312[41]	220 036[41]	71.8[42]	...	...	...	...
Maebashi	336 154[41]	164 136[41]	172 018[41]	311.6[42]	...	...	...	...
Marugame	110 010[41]	53 183[41]	56 827[41]	111.8[42]	...	...	...	...
Matsubara	120 750[41]	58 096[41]	62 654[41]	16.7[42]	...	...	...	...
Matsudo	483 480[41]	240 928[41]	242 552[41]	61.4[42]	...	...	...	...
Matsue	206 230[41]	99 565[41]	106 665[41]	573[42]	...	...	...	...
Matsumoto	243 293[41]	119 479[41]	123 814[41]	978.5[42]	...	...	...	...
Matsusaka	163 863[41]	78 548[41]	85 315[41]	623.7[42]	...	...	...	...
Matsuyama	514 865[41]	241 656[41]	273 209[41]	429.4[42]	...	...	...	...
Minoh	133 411[41]	63 938[41]	69 473[41]	47.9[42]	...	...	...	...
Misato	136 521[41]	68 950[41]	67 571[41]	30.1[42]	...	...	...	...
Mishima	110 046[41]	53 836[41]	56 210[41]	62[42]	...	...	...	...
Mitaka	186 936[41]	90 641[41]	96 295[41]	16.4[42]	...	...	...	...
Mito	270 783[41]	132 799[41]	137 984[41]	217.3[42]	...	...	...	...
Miyakonojo	165 029[41]	77 521[41]	87 508[41]	653.4[42]	...	...	...	...
Miyazaki	401 138[41]	188 177[41]	212 961[41]	643.7[42]	...	...	...	...
Moriguchi	143 042[41]	68 987[41]	74 055[41]	12.7[42]	...	...	...	...
Morioka	297 631[41]	141 089[41]	156 542[41]	886.5[42]	...	...	...	...
Musashino	144 730[41]	69 475[41]	75 255[41]	11[42]	...	...	...	...
Nagahama	118 193[41]	57 703[41]	60 490[41]	681[42]	...	...	...	...
Nagano	377 598[41]	182 843[41]	194 755[41]	834.8[42]	...	...	...	...

Continent, country or area, date, code[a] and city / Continent, pays ou zone, date, code[a] et ville	City proper - Ville proprement dite				Urban agglomeration - Agglomération urbaine			
	Population			Surface area - Superficie (km²)	Population			Surface area - Superficie (km²)
	Both sexes - Les deux sexes	Male - Masculin	Female - Féminin		Both sexes - Les deux sexes	Male - Masculin	Female - Féminin	
ASIA - ASIE								
Japan - Japon								
1 X 2015 (CDJC)								
Nagaoka	275 133[41]	134 198[41]	140 935[41]	891.1[42]	...	...	...	...
Nagareyama	174 373[41]	86 249[41]	88 124[41]	35.3[42]	...	...	...	...
Nagasaki	429 508[41]	198 716[41]	230 792[41]	405.9[42]	...	...	...	...
Nagoya	2 295 638[41]	1 133 640[41]	1 161 998[41]	326.5[42]	...	...	...	...
Naha	319 435[41]	154 685[41]	164 750[41]	39.6[42]	...	...	...	...
Nara	360 310[41]	167 899[41]	192 411[41]	276.9[42]	...	...	...	...
Narashino	167 909[41]	84 323[41]	83 586[41]	21[42]	...	...	...	...
Narita	131 190[41]	65 928[41]	65 262[41]	213.8[42]	...	...	...	...
Nasushiobara	117 146[41]	58 148[41]	58 998[41]	592.7[42]	...	...	...	...
Neyagawa	237 518[41]	115 131[41]	122 387[41]	24.7[42]	...	...	...	...
Niigata	810 157[41]	389 512[41]	420 645[41]	726.5[42]	...	...	...	...
Niihama	119 903[41]	57 551[41]	62 352[41]	234.5[42]	...	...	...	...
Niiza	162 122[41]	80 627[41]	81 495[41]	22.8[42]	...	...	...	...
Nishinomiya	487 850[41]	228 354[41]	259 496[41]	100[42]	...	...	...	...
Nishio	167 990[41]	84 669[41]	83 321[41]	161.2[42]	...	...	...	...
Nishitokyo	200 012[41]	97 830[41]	102 182[41]	15.8[42]	...	...	...	...
Nobeoka	125 159[41]	58 993[41]	66 166[41]	868[42]	...	...	...	...
Noda	153 583[41]	76 541[41]	77 042[41]	103.6[42]	...	...	...	...
Numazu	195 633[41]	95 980[41]	99 653[41]	187[42]	...	...	...	...
Obihiro	169 327[41]	80 994[41]	88 333[41]	619.3[42]	...	...	...	...
Odawara	194 086[41]	94 697[41]	99 389[41]	113.8[42]	...	...	...	...
Ogaki	159 879[41]	77 430[41]	82 449[41]	206.6[42]	...	...	...	...
Oita	478 146[41]	229 844[41]	248 302[41]	502.4[42]	...	...	...	...
Okayama	719 474[41]	345 913[41]	373 561[41]	790[42]	...	...	...	...
Okazaki	381 051[41]	192 771[41]	188 280[41]	387.2[42]	...	...	...	...
Okinawa	139 279[41]	67 522[41]	71 757[41]	49.7[42]	...	...	...	...
Ome	137 381[41]	68 677[41]	68 704[41]	103.3[42]	...	...	...	...
Omuta	117 360[41]	53 859[41]	63 501[41]	81.5[42]	...	...	...	...
Onomichi	138 626[41]	66 292[41]	72 334[41]	285.1[42]	...	...	...	...
Osaka	2 691 185[41]	1 302 562[41]	1 388 623[41]	225.2[42]	...	...	...	...
Osaki	133 391[41]	65 120[41]	68 271[41]	796.8[42]	...	...	...	...
Oshu	119 422[41]	57 377[41]	62 045[41]	993.3[42]	...	...	...	...
Ota	219 807[41]	111 610[41]	108 197[41]	175.5[42]	...	...	...	...
Otaru	121 924[41]	54 985[41]	66 939[41]	243.8[42]	...	...	...	...
Otsu	340 973[41]	164 799[41]	176 174[41]	464.5[42]	...	...	...	...
Oyama	166 760[41]	84 100[41]	82 660[41]	171.8[42]	...	...	...	...
Saga	236 372[41]	111 453[41]	124 919[41]	431.8[42]	...	...	...	...
Sagamihara	720 780[41]	361 060[41]	359 720[41]	328.7[42]	...	...	...	...
Saijo	108 174[41]	51 807[41]	56 367[41]	510[42]	...	...	...	...
Saitama	1 263 979[41]	627 238[41]	636 741[41]	217.4[42]	...	...	...	...
Sakado	101 679[41]	51 307[41]	50 372[41]	41[42]	...	...	...	...
Sakata	106 244[41]	50 293[41]	55 951[41]	603[42]	...	...	...	...
Sakura	172 739[41]	84 434[41]	88 305[41]	103.7[42]	...	...	...	...
Sanda	112 691[41]	54 184[41]	58 507[41]	210.3[42]	...	...	...	...
Sano	118 919[41]	58 507[41]	60 412[41]	356[42]	...	...	...	...
Sapporo	1 952 356[41]	910 614[41]	1 041 742[41]	1121.3[42]	...	...	...	...
Sasebo	255 439[41]	120 198[41]	135 241[41]	426.1[42]	...	...	...	...
Sayama	152 405[41]	76 580[41]	75 825[41]	49[42]	...	...	...	...
Sendai	1 082 159[41]	527 170[41]	554 989[41]	786.3[42]	...	...	...	...
Seto	129 046[41]	63 189[41]	65 857[41]	111.4[42]	...	...	...	...
Shimonoseki	268 517[41]	124 722[41]	143 795[41]	715.9[42]	...	...	...	...
Shizuoka	704 989[41]	343 338[41]	361 651[41]	1411.9[42]	...	...	...	...
Shunan	144 842[41]	69 819[41]	75 023[41]	656.3[42]	...	...	...	...
Soka	247 034[41]	125 225[41]	121 809[41]	27.5[42]	...	...	...	...
Suita	374 468[41]	180 669[41]	193 799[41]	36.1[42]	...	...	...	...
Suzuka	196 403[41]	97 500[41]	98 903[41]	194.5[42]	...	...	...	...
Tachikawa	176 295[41]	86 978[41]	89 317[41]	24.4[42]	...	...	...	...
Tajimi	110 441[41]	53 378[41]	57 063[41]	91.3[42]	...	...	...	...
Takamatsu	420 748[41]	205 049[41]	215 699[41]	375.4[42]	...	...	...	...

Continent, country or area, date, code[a] and city / Continent, pays ou zone, date, code[a] et ville	City proper - Ville proprement dite				Urban agglomeration - Agglomération urbaine			
	Population			Surface area - Superficie (km²)	Population			Surface area - Superficie (km²)
	Both sexes - Les deux sexes	Male - Masculin	Female - Féminin		Both sexes - Les deux sexes	Male - Masculin	Female - Féminin	
ASIA - ASIE								
Japan - Japon								
1 X 2015 (CDJC)								
Takaoka	172 125[41]	82 802[41]	89 323[41]	209.6[42]	...	...	...	...
Takarazuka	224 903[41]	104 215[41]	120 688[41]	101.8[42]	...	...	...	...
Takasaki	370 884[41]	181 601[41]	189 283[41]	459.2[42]	...	...	...	...
Takatsuki	351 829[41]	168 057[41]	183 772[41]	105.3[42]	...	...	...	...
Tama	146 631[41]	71 762[41]	74 869[41]	21[42]	...	...	...	...
Tochigi	159 211[41]	78 209[41]	81 002[41]	331.5[42]	...	...	...	...
Toda	136 150[41]	69 674[41]	66 476[41]	18.2[42]	...	...	...	...
Tokai	111 944[41]	58 170[41]	53 774[41]	43.4[42]	...	...	...	...
Tokorozawa	340 386[41]	168 205[41]	172 181[41]	72.1[42]	...	...	...	...
Tokushima	258 554[41]	123 014[41]	135 540[41]	191.3[42]	...	...	...	...
TOKYO	9 272 740[41]	4 567 247[41]	4 705 493[41]	626.7[42]	...	...	...	...
Tomakomai	172 737[41]	84 605[41]	88 132[41]	561.6[42]	...	...	...	...
Tondabayashi	113 984[41]	53 693[41]	60 291[41]	39.7[42]	...	...	...	...
Toride	106 570[41]	52 489[41]	54 081[41]	69.9[42]	...	...	...	...
Tottori	193 717[41]	94 151[41]	99 566[41]	765.3[42]	...	...	...	...
Toyama	418 686[41]	203 427[41]	215 259[41]	1241.8[42]	...	...	...	...
Toyohashi	374 765[41]	187 801[41]	186 964[41]	261.9[42]	...	...	...	...
Toyokawa	182 436[41]	90 869[41]	91 567[41]	161.1[42]	...	...	...	...
Toyonaka	395 479[41]	187 319[41]	208 160[41]	36.4[42]	...	...	...	...
Toyota	422 542[41]	222 169[41]	200 373[41]	918.3[42]	...	...	...	...
Tsu	279 886[41]	135 718[41]	144 168[41]	711.1[42]	...	...	...	...
Tsuchiura	140 804[41]	70 101[41]	70 703[41]	122.9[42]	...	...	...	...
Tsukuba	226 963[41]	114 774[41]	112 189[41]	283.7[42]	...	...	...	...
Tsuruoka	129 652[41]	61 761[41]	67 891[41]	1311.5[42]	...	...	...	...
Tsuyama	103 746[41]	49 561[41]	54 185[41]	506.3[42]	...	...	...	...
Ube	169 429[41]	81 133[41]	88 296[41]	286.7[42]	...	...	...	...
Ueda	156 827[41]	76 776[41]	80 051[41]	552[42]	...	...	...	...
Uji	184 678[41]	89 014[41]	95 664[41]	67.5[42]	...	...	...	...
Urasoe	114 232[41]	55 471[41]	58 761[41]	19.5[42]	...	...	...	...
Urayasu	164 024[41]	81 057[41]	82 967[41]	17.3[42]	...	...	...	...
Uruma	118 898[41]	59 409[41]	59 489[41]	87[42]	...	...	...	...
Utsunomiya	518 594[41]	258 960[41]	259 634[41]	416.9[42]	...	...	...	...
Wakayama	364 154[41]	171 215[41]	192 939[41]	208.8[42]	...	...	...	...
Yachiyo	193 152[41]	95 224[41]	97 928[41]	51.4[42]	...	...	...	...
Yaizu	139 462[41]	68 168[41]	71 294[41]	70.3[42]	...	...	...	...
Yamagata	253 832[41]	121 575[41]	132 257[41]	381.3[42]	...	...	...	...
Yamaguchi	197 422[41]	94 245[41]	103 177[41]	1023.2[42]	...	...	...	...
Yamato	232 922[41]	116 714[41]	116 208[41]	27.1[42]	...	...	...	...
Yao	268 800[41]	128 284[41]	140 516[41]	41.7[42]	...	...	...	...
Yatsushiro	127 472[41]	59 221[41]	68 251[41]	681.4[42]	...	...	...	...
Yokkaichi	311 031[41]	154 674[41]	156 357[41]	206.4[42]	...	...	...	...
Yokohama	3 724 844[41]	1 855 985[41]	1 868 859[41]	437.5[42]	...	...	...	...
Yokosuka	406 586[41]	202 775[41]	203 811[41]	100.8[42]	...	...	...	...
Yonago	149 313[41]	70 628[41]	78 685[41]	132.4[42]	...	...	...	...
Zama	128 737[41]	64 478[41]	64 259[41]	17.6[42]	...	...	...	...
Jordan - Jordanie								
31 XII 2016 (ESDF)								
AMMAN	3 752 644	2 009 482	1 743 162	...	...	...	...	...
Aqaba	148 398	63 175	85 223	...	...	...	...	...
Irbid	502 714	262 433	240 281	...	...	...	...	...
Madaba	105 353	56 187	49 166	...	...	...	...	...
Mafraq	106 008	55 474	50 534	...	...	...	...	...
Ramtha	155 693	81 231	74 462	...	...	...	...	...
Russiefa	472 604	251 984	220 620	...	...	...	...	...
Zarqa	635 160	332 210	302 950	...	...	...	...	...
Kazakhstan								
1 I 2013 (ESDF)								
Aktau	181 541	87 636	93 905	...	184 175	89 043	95 132	...
Aktobe	377 752	176 438	201 314	...	428 024	201 192	226 832	...
Almaty	1 507 509	687 027	820 482	...	...	...	...	...

8. Population of capital cities and cities of 100 000 or more inhabitants: latest available year, 1997 - 2016
Population des capitales et des villes de 100 000 habitants ou plus : dernière année disponible, 1997 - 2016 (continued - suite)

Continent, country or area, date, code[a] and city / Continent, pays ou zone, date, code[a] et ville	City proper - Ville proprement dite				Urban agglomeration - Agglomération urbaine			
	Population			Surface area - Superficie (km²)	Population			Surface area - Superficie (km²)
	Both sexes - Les deux sexes	Male - Masculin	Female - Féminin		Both sexes - Les deux sexes	Male - Masculin	Female - Féminin	
ASIA - ASIE								
Kazakhstan								
1 I 2013 (ESDF)								
ASTANA	814 435	393 158	421 277	...	...	...	...	...
Atirau	209 699	99 168	110 531	...	280 634	134 498	146 136	...
Ekibastuz	139 778	66 234	73 544	...	149 132	71 017	78 115	...
Karaganda	484 510	221 248	263 262	...	484 768	221 388	263 380	...
Koktshetau	143 267	66 077	77 190	...	154 000	71 225	82 775	...
Kustanai	221 943	99 341	122 602	...	221 943	99 341	122 602	...
Kyzylorda	238 840	116 031	122 809	...	260 524	127 119	133 405	...
Pavlodar	339 153	153 922	185 231	...	352 693	160 532	192 161	...
Petropavlovsk (Severo- Kazakhstanskaya oblast)	207 399	93 015	114 384	...	208 362	93 491	114 871	...
Rudni	127 712	59 700	68 012	...	128 234	59 947	68 287	...
Semipalatinsk	315 750	146 133	169 617	...	337 633	156 958	180 675	...
Shimkent	682 565	323 899	358 666	...	682 565	323 899	358 666	...
Taldykorgan	135 184	62 277	72 907	...	158 984	74 068	84 916	...
Taraz	351 353	164 440	186 913	...	351 353	164 440	186 913	...
Temirtau	182 551	84 577	97 974	...	182 551	84 577	97 974	...
Turkestan	155 552	77 393	78 159	...	248 773	124 719	124 054	...
Uralsk	273 359	125 951	147 408	...	278 086	128 276	149 810	...
Ust-Kamenogorsk	314 069	141 596	172 473	...	325 803	147 288	178 515	...
Zhanaozen	106 220	52 515	53 705	...	130 652	64 533	66 119	...
Kuwait - Koweït								
1 VII 2010 (ESDF)								
Farwanyiah	101 867	68 326	33 541	...	...	...	...	...
Hawalli	127 982	84 506	43 477	...	...	...	...	...
Jaleeb Al-Shuykh	219 629	180 786	38 843	...	...	...	...	...
Salmiya	177 009	103 119	73 890	...	...	...	...	...
South Kheetan	113 426	104 655	8 770	...	...	...	...	...
Kyrgyzstan - Kirghizstan[43]								
1 VII 2016 (ESDJ)								
BISHKEK	955 078	445 951	509 127	...	969 415	453 033	516 382	...
Osh	250 828	120 240	130 588	...	278 840	134 592	144 248	...
Lao People's Democratic Republic - République démocratique populaire lao[44]								
1 VII 2014 (ESDJ)								
VIENTIANE	...	...	...	...	828 494	414 217	414 277	...
Lebanon - Liban[45]								
1 X 2011 (SSDF)								
BEIRUT	...	...	...	...	363 033	179 737	183 296	...
Malaysia - Malaisie[46]								
1 VII 2016 (ESDJ)								
Alor Setar	126 300	...	...	...	...	...	...	...
Bintulu Townland	124 300	...	...	...	...	...	...	...
Georgetown	208 400	...	...	...	...	...	...	...
Kajang dan Sungai Chua	101 200	...	...	...	...	...	...	...
Klang	264 800	...	...	...	...	...	...	...
Kota Kinabalu	222 700	...	...	...	...	...	...	...
KUALA LUMPUR	1 732 200	...	...	...	...	...	...	...
Kuala Terengganu	214 700	...	...	...	...	...	...	...
Kuantan	413 700	...	...	...	...	...	...	...
Kuching "Bandaraya Kuching Utara dan Selatan"	154 600	...	...	...	...	...	...	...
Majlis Perbandaran Ipoh	474 000	...	...	...	...	...	...	...
MB Johor Bahru (Johor Bahru)	482 300	...	...	...	...	...	...	...
Miri Townland	142 900	...	...	...	...	...	...	...
MP Kota Bharu	314 000	...	...	...	...	...	...	...
Petaling Jaya	202 500	...	...	...	...	...	...	...
Sandakan	175 700	...	...	...	...	...	...	...
Selayang Baru	161 500	...	...	...	...	...	...	...
Seremban	364 800	...	...	...	...	...	...	...
Shah Alam	180 700	...	...	...	...	...	...	...
Sibu "Majlis Perbandaran Sibu"	169 300	...	...	...	...	...	...	...
Subang Jaya	196 000	...	...	...	...	...	...	...
Sungai Petani	195 500	...	...	...	...	...	...	...

Continent, country or area, date, code[a] and city / Continent, pays ou zone, date, code[a] et ville	City proper - Ville proprement dite				Urban agglomeration - Agglomération urbaine			
	Population			Surface area - Superficie (km²)	Population			Surface area - Superficie (km²)
	Both sexes - Les deux sexes	Male - Masculin	Female - Féminin		Both sexes - Les deux sexes	Male - Masculin	Female - Féminin	
ASIA - ASIE								
Malaysia - Malaisie[46]								
1 VII 2016 (ESDJ)								
Taiping	236 500	...	...	...	...	...	...	...
Tawau	125 400	...	...	...	...	...	...	...
Maldives								
20 IX 2014 (CDFC)								
MALÉ	153 904	85 438	68 466	2	...	...	...	...
Mongolia - Mongolie								
1 VII 2016 (ESDF)								
Bayan-Olgii	100 180	50 040	50 141	46	...	...	...	...
Darkhan-Uul	101 408	49 879	51 529	3	...	...	...	...
Hovsgol	128 771	63 994	64 776	101	...	...	...	...
Orkhon	101 260	49 669	51 591	1	...	...	...	...
Ovorhangay	112 755	56 239	56 516	63	...	...	...	...
Selenge	106 902	54 244	52 658	41	...	...	...	...
ULAANBAATAR	1 418 368	682 325	736 042	5	...	...	...	...
Myanmar								
29 III 2014* (CDFC)								
Bago	491 130	235 612	255 518	...	...	...	...	...
Dawei	125 239	59 941	65 298	...	...	...	...	...
Hpa-an	421 415	203 933	217 482	...	...	...	...	...
Loikaw	128 837	63 404	65 433	...	...	...	...	...
Magway	288 883	134 957	153 926	...	...	...	...	...
Mandalay	1 225 133	597 747	627 386	...	...	...	...	...
Mawlamyine	288 120	138 625	149 495	...	...	...	...	...
Monywa	371 963	172 303	199 660	...	...	...	...	...
Myitkyina	305 347	147 711	157 636	...	...	...	...	...
NAY PYI TAW[47]	...	...	...	...	1 158 367	565 181	593 186	...
Pathein	286 684	137 723	148 961	...	...	...	...	...
Sittway	149 348	71 628	77 720	...	...	...	...	...
Taunggyi	380 665	185 694	194 971	...	...	...	...	...
Yangon	5 209 541	2 468 725	2 740 816	...	...	...	...	...
Nepal - Népal								
22 VI 2011 (CDJC)								
Bharatpur	147 777	74 205	73 572	...	...	...	...	...
Bhimdutta	106 666	53 098	53 568	...	...	...	...	...
Biratnagar	204 949	104 935	100 014	...	...	...	...	...
Birgunj	139 068	75 382	63 686	...	...	...	...	...
Butwal	120 982	60 870	60 112	...	...	...	...	...
Dhangadhi	104 047	53 237	50 810	...	...	...	...	...
Dharan	119 915	57 562	62 353	...	...	...	...	...
KATHMANDU	1 003 285	533 127	470 158	...	...	...	...	...
Lalitpur	226 728	117 932	108 796	...	...	...	...	...
Pokhara	264 991	133 318	131 673	...	...	...	...	...
Oman								
1 VII 2016 (ESDF)								
Al Buraymi	104 073	69 290	34 783	...	...	...	...	...
Al Mudaybi	112 101	70 505	41 596	...	...	...	...	...
Al Rustaq	117 599	67 937	49 662	...	...	...	...	...
As Seeb	391 315	242 416	148 899	...	...	...	...	...
As Suwayq	171 788	105 249	66 539	...	...	...	...	...
Barka	136 968	86 127	50 841	...	...	...	...	...
Bawshar	424 060	344 553	79 507	...	...	...	...	...
Ibri	158 065	95 129	62 936	...	...	...	...	...
MUSCAT	246 996	181 441	65 555	...	...	...	...	...
Mutrah	249 363	191 593	57 770	...	...	...	...	...
Nizwa	118 573	70 740	47 833	...	...	...	...	...
Saham	140 844	85 137	55 707	...	...	...	...	...
Salalah	355 660	258 660	97 000	...	...	...	...	...
Sohar	226 321	151 834	74 487	...	...	...	...	...
Sur	116 110	72 704	43 406	...	...	...	...	...
Pakistan[48]								
2 III 1998 (CDFC)								
Abbotabad	106 101	61 698	44 403	...	...	...	...	...
Bahawalnagar	111 313	57 779	53 534	...	...	...	...	...

8. Population of capital cities and cities of 100 000 or more inhabitants: latest available year, 1997 - 2016
Population des capitales et des villes de 100 000 habitants ou plus : dernière année disponible, 1997 - 2016 (continued - suite)

Continent, country or area, date, code[a] and city / Continent, pays ou zone, date, code[a] et ville	City proper - Ville proprement dite				Urban agglomeration - Agglomération urbaine			
	Population			Surface area - Superficie (km²)	Population			Surface area - Superficie (km²)
	Both sexes - Les deux sexes	Male - Masculin	Female - Féminin		Both sexes - Les deux sexes	Male - Masculin	Female - Féminin	
ASIA - ASIE								
Pakistan[48]								
2 III 1998 (CDFC)								
Bahawalpur	408 395	222 228	186 167	...	...	...	...	...
Burewala	152 097	78 726	73 371	...	...	...	...	...
Chiniot	172 522	90 474	82 048	...	...	...	...	...
Chishtian	102 287	52 427	49 860	...	...	...	...	...
Dadu	102 550	53 508	49 042	...	...	...	...	...
Daska	102 883	52 359	50 524	...	...	...	...	...
Dera Ghazi Khan	190 542	98 738	91 804	...	...	...	...	...
Faisalabad (Lyallpur)	2 008 861	1 053 085	955 776	...	...	...	...	...
Gojra	117 872	60 598	57 274	...	...	...	...	...
Gujranwala	1 132 509	588 512	543 997	...	...	...	...	...
Gujrat	251 792	128 524	123 268	...	...	...	...	...
Hafizabad	133 678	69 231	64 447	...	...	...	...	...
Hyderabad	1 166 894	612 283	554 611	...	...	...	...	...
ISLAMABAD	529 180	290 717	238 463	...	...	...	...	...
Jacobabad	138 780	71 854	66 926	...	...	...	...	...
Jaranwala	106 785	55 619	51 166	...	...	...	...	...
Jhang	293 366	153 123	140 243	...	...	...	...	...
Jhelum	147 392	79 169	68 223	...	...	...	...	...
Kamoke	152 288	78 848	73 440	...	...	...	...	...
Karachi	9 339 023	5 029 900	4 309 123	...	...	...	...	...
Kasur	245 321	129 553	115 768	...	...	...	...	...
Khairpur	105 637	55 358	50 279	...	...	...	...	...
Khanewal	133 986	69 145	64 841	...	...	...	...	...
Khanpur	120 382	62 371	58 011	...	...	...	...	...
Kohat	126 627	71 505	55 122	...	...	...	...	...
Lahore	5 143 495	2 707 220	2 436 275	...	...	...	...	...
Larkana	270 283	140 622	129 661	...	...	...	...	...
Mangora	173 868	91 742	82 126	...	...	...	...	...
Mardan	245 926	129 247	116 679	...	...	...	...	...
Mirpur Khas	189 671	97 940	91 731	...	...	...	...	...
Multan	1 197 384	637 911	559 473	...	...	...	...	...
Muridke	111 951	58 210	53 741	...	...	...	...	...
Muzaffargharh	123 404	66 556	56 848	...	...	...	...	...
Nawabshah	189 244	98 116	91 128	...	...	...	...	...
Okara	201 815	104 245	97 570	...	...	...	...	...
Pakpattan	109 033	56 676	52 357	...	...	...	...	...
Peshawar	982 816	521 901	460 915	...	...	...	...	...
Quetta	565 137	307 759	257 378	...	...	...	...	...
Rahimyar Khan	233 537	121 446	112 091	...	...	...	...	...
Rawalpindi	1 409 768	750 530	659 238	...	...	...	...	...
Sadiqabad	144 391	75 217	69 174	...	...	...	...	...
Sahiwal	208 778	108 992	99 786	...	...	...	...	...
Sargodha	458 440	239 837	218 603	...	...	...	...	...
Shakkarpur	134 883	69 713	65 170	...	...	...	...	...
Sheikhu Pura	280 263	146 739	133 524	...	...	...	...	...
Sialkote	421 502	227 398	194 104	...	...	...	...	...
Sukkur	335 551	175 679	159 872	...	...	...	...	...
Tandoadam	104 907	54 670	50 237	...	...	...	...	...
Wah Cantonment	198 891	104 230	94 661	...	...	...	...	...
Philippines								
1 VIII 2015 (CDJC)								
Angeles	411 634	...	...	...	...	...	...	...
Bacolod	561 875	...	...	...	...	...	...	...
Baguio	345 366	...	...	...	...	...	...	...
Butuan	337 063	...	...	...	...	...	...	...
Cagayan de Oro	675 950	...	...	...	...	...	...	...
Caloocan	1 583 978	...	...	...	...	...	...	...
Cebu	922 611	...	...	...	...	...	...	...
Cotabato	299 438	...	...	...	...	...	...	...
Davao	1 632 991	...	...	...	...	...	...	...
General Santos	594 446	...	...	...	...	...	...	...
Iligan	342 618	...	...	...	...	...	...	...
Iloilo	447 992	...	...	...	...	...	...	...

8. Population of capital cities and cities of 100 000 or more inhabitants: latest available year, 1997 - 2016
Population des capitales et des villes de 100 000 habitants ou plus : dernière année disponible, 1997 - 2016 (continued - suite)

Continent, country or area, date, code[a] and city / Continent, pays ou zone, date, code[a] et ville	City proper - Ville proprement dite				Urban agglomeration - Agglomération urbaine			
	Population			Surface area - Superficie (km²)	Population			Surface area - Superficie (km²)
	Both sexes - Les deux sexes	Male - Masculin	Female - Féminin		Both sexes - Les deux sexes	Male - Masculin	Female - Féminin	
ASIA - ASIE								
Philippines								
1 VIII 2015 (CDJC)								
Isabela	112 788	...	...	...	...	...	...	...
Lapu-Lapu	408 112	...	...	...	...	...	...	...
Las Piñas	588 894	...	...	...	...	...	...	...
Lucena City	266 248	...	...	...	...	...	...	...
Makati	582 602	...	...	...	...	...	...	...
Malabon	365 525	...	...	...	...	...	...	...
Mandaluyong	386 276	...	...	...	...	...	...	...
Mandaue	362 654	...	...	...	...	...	...	...
MANILA	1 780 148	...	...	...	...	...	...	...
Marikina	450 741	...	...	...	...	...	...	...
Muntinlupa	504 509	...	...	...	...	...	...	...
Navotas	249 463	...	...	...	...	...	...	...
Olongapo	233 040	...	...	...	...	...	...	...
Paranaque	665 822	...	...	...	...	...	...	...
Pasay	416 522	...	...	...	...	...	...	...
Pasig	755 300	...	...	...	...	...	...	...
Puerto Princesa	255 116	...	...	...	...	...	...	...
Quezon City	2 936 116	...	...	...	...	...	...	...
San Juan	122 180	...	...	...	...	...	...	...
Tacloban	242 089	...	...	...	...	...	...	...
Taguig	804 915	...	...	...	...	...	...	...
Valenzuela	620 422	...	...	...	...	...	...	...
Zamboanga	861 799	...	...	...	...	...	...	...
Qatar[49]								
20 IV 2015 (CDFC)								
Al-Rayyan	605 712	406 783	198 929	...	...	...	...	...
Al-Wakrah	299 037	248 103	50 934	...	...	...	...	...
DOHA	956 457	706 430	250 027	...	...	...	...	...
Republic of Korea - République de Corée								
1 VII 2016 (ESDJ)								
Busan (Pusan)	3 388 631	1 662 436	1 726 195	769.8[50]	...	...	...	...
Daegu (Taegu)	2 449 667	1 212 607	1 237 060	883.5[50]	...	...	...	...
Daejeon (Taejon)	1 533 390	768 597	764 793	539.3[50]	...	...	...	...
Gwangju (Kwangchu)	1 517 142	753 157	763 985	501.2[50]	...	...	...	...
Incheon	2 914 455	1 465 035	1 449 420	1047.6[50]	...	...	...	...
Jeju (Cheju)	593 455	297 773	295 682	1849[50]	...	...	...	...
Sejong	227 306	117 416	109 890	465[50]	...	...	...	...
SEOUL	9 834 687	4 810 788	5 023 899	605.2[50]	...	...	...	...
Ulsan	1 146 818	597 232	549 586	1060.7[50]	...	...	...	...
Saudi Arabia - Arabie saoudite								
27 IV 2010 (CDFC)								
Abha	236 157	136 118	100 039	...	...	...	...	...
Ad-Dammam	903 312	546 924	356 388	...	...	...	...	...
Al-Hawiyah	148 151	78 735	69 416	...	...	...	...	...
Al-Hufuf	660 788	361 672	299 116	...	...	...	...	...
Al-Jubayl	337 778	237 912	99 866	...	...	...	...	...
Al-Khubar	219 679	131 646	88 033	...	...	...	...	...
Al-Madinah	1 100 093	608 720	491 373	...	...	...	...	...
Al-Qatif	118 327	66 504	51 823	...	...	...	...	...
Al-Qurrayyat	116 162	63 412	52 750	...	...	...	...	...
Al-Seeh	234 607	131 391	103 216	...	...	...	...	...
Ar'ar	167 057	90 771	76 286	...	...	...	...	...
Ath-Thuqbah	238 066	149 691	88 375	...	...	...	...	...
At-Ta'if	579 970	306 682	273 288	...	...	...	...	...
Buraydah	467 410	268 604	198 806	...	...	...	...	...
Dhahran	120 521	68 746	51 775	...	...	...	...	...
Hafar al-Batin	271 642	148 396	123 246	...	...	...	...	...
Ha'il	310 897	170 882	140 015	...	...	...	...	...
Jiddah	3 430 697	1 996 716	1 433 981	...	...	...	...	...
Jizan	127 743	76 987	50 756	...	...	...	...	...
Khamis Mushayt	430 828	245 756	185 072	...	...	...	...	...
Makkah	1 534 731	861 737	672 994	...	...	...	...	...
Najran (Aba as-Suud)	298 288	166 143	132 145	...	...	...	...	...

Continent, country or area, date, code[a] and city / Continent, pays ou zone, date, code[a] et ville	City proper - Ville proprement dite				Urban agglomeration - Agglomération urbaine			
	Population			Surface area - Superficie (km²)	Population			Surface area - Superficie (km²)
	Both sexes - Les deux sexes	Male - Masculin	Female - Féminin		Both sexes - Les deux sexes	Male - Masculin	Female - Féminin	
ASIA - ASIE								
Saudi Arabia - Arabie saoudite								
27 IV 2010 (CDFC)								
RIYADH	5 188 286	3 059 287	2 128 999	...	...	...	...	...
Sekaka	150 257	84 881	65 376	...	...	...	...	...
Tabuk	512 629	281 672	230 957	...	...	...	...	...
Unayzah	152 895	86 385	66 510	...	...	...	...	...
Yanbu al-Bahr	233 236	140 897	92 339	...	...	...	...	...
Singapore - Singapour								
30 VI 2016 (ESDJ)								
SINGAPORE	5 607 283[51]	...	...	719[52]	...	...	...	...
Sri Lanka[53]								
17 VII 2001 (CDFC)								
COLOMBO	647 100	346 366	300 734	...	...	...	...	...
Dehiwala-Mount Lavinia	210 546	105 522	105 024	...	...	...	...	...
Kandy	109 343	54 288	55 055	...	...	...	...	...
Moratuwa	177 563	87 313	90 250	...	...	...	...	...
Negombo	121 701	60 947	60 754	...	...	...	...	...
Sri Jayawardanapura Kotte	116 366	59 993	56 373	...	...	...	...	...
State of Palestine - État de Palestine								
1 VII 2016 (ESDF)								
EAST JERUSALEM - JÉRUSALEM-EST[54]	264 937	...	...	...	...	...	...	...
Gaza	583 870	...	...	...	...	...	...	...
Hebron	215 452	...	...	...	...	...	...	...
Jabalya	171 642	...	...	...	...	...	...	...
Khan Yunis	185 250	...	...	...	...	...	...	...
Nablus	153 061	...	...	...	...	...	...	...
Rafah	164 000	...	...	...	...	...	...	...
Syrian Arab Republic - République arabe syrienne								
1 VII 2008 (ESDF)								
Aleppo	4 450 000	2 292 000	2 158 000	...	...	...	...	...
Al-Hasakeh	1 392 000	701 000	691 000	...	...	...	...	...
Al-Raqqah	865 000	456 000	409 000	...	...	...	...	...
Al-Sweida	349 000	171 000	178 000	...	...	...	...	...
DAMASCUS	1 680 000	857 000	823 000	...	...	...	...	...
Damasus rural	2 529 000	1 302 000	1 227 000	...	...	...	...	...
Deir El-Zor	1 111 000	563 000	548 000	...	...	...	...	...
Dra'a	930 000	472 000	458 000	...	...	...	...	...
Hama	1 508 000	768 000	740 000	...	...	...	...	...
Homs	1 667 000	852 000	815 000	...	...	...	...	...
Idleb	1 376 000	704 000	672 000	...	...	...	...	...
Lattakia	951 000	480 000	471 000	...	...	...	...	...
Tartous	756 000	383 000	373 000	...	...	...	...	...
Tajikistan - Tadjikistan								
1 VII 2014 (ESDF)								
DUSHANBE	782 224	406 802	375 422	...	...	...	...	...
Thailand - Thaïlande								
1 IX 2010 (CDJC)								
Ang Thong	...	...	...	...	109 207	51 540	57 667	...
BANGKOK	...	...	...	...	8 305 218	4 032 586	4 272 632	1569
Buri Ram	...	...	...	...	375 999	181 546	194 453	...
Chachoengsao	...	...	...	...	206 250	101 475	104 775	...
Chai Nat	...	...	...	...	205 456	97 373	108 083	...
Chaiyaphum	...	...	...	...	205 112	99 280	105 832	...
Chanthaburi	...	...	...	...	243 126	118 221	124 905	...
Chiang Mai	...	...	...	...	967 020	466 145	500 875	...
Chiang Rai	...	...	...	...	455 732	220 391	235 341	...
Chon Buri	...	...	...	...	1 158 989	575 208	583 781	...
Chumphon	...	...	...	...	147 912	75 339	72 573	...
Kalasin	...	...	...	...	428 940	208 863	220 077	...
Kamphaeng Phet	...	...	...	...	211 774	101 456	110 318	...
Kanchanaburi	...	...	...	...	292 521	143 986	148 535	...
Khon Kaen	...	...	...	...	703 123	339 011	364 112	...
Lampang	...	...	...	...	372 463	180 360	192 103	...
Lamphun	...	...	...	...	262 832	126 662	136 170	...
Loei	...	...	...	...	164 180	81 302	82 878	...

8. Population of capital cities and cities of 100 000 or more inhabitants: latest available year, 1997 - 2016
Population des capitales et des villes de 100 000 habitants ou plus : dernière année disponible, 1997 - 2016 (continued - suite)

Continent, country or area, date, code[a] and city / Continent, pays ou zone, date, code[a] et ville	City proper - Ville proprement dite				Urban agglomeration - Agglomération urbaine			
	Population			Surface area - Superficie (km²)	Population			Surface area - Superficie (km²)
	Both sexes - Les deux sexes	Male - Masculin	Female - Féminin		Both sexes - Les deux sexes	Male - Masculin	Female - Féminin	
ASIA - ASIE								
Thailand - Thaïlande								
1 IX 2010 (CDJC)								
Lop Buri	...	...	...	...	235 827	118 964	116 863	...
Maha Sarakham	...	...	...	...	153 740	72 143	81 597	...
Mukdahan	...	...	...	...	180 600	89 190	91 410	...
Nakhon Pathom	...	...	...	...	339 736	166 150	173 586	...
Nakhon Phanom	...	...	...	...	123 720	59 683	64 037	...
Nakhon Ratchasima	...	...	...	...	653 075	316 329	336 746	...
Nakhon Sawan	...	...	...	...	225 903	107 298	118 605	...
Nakhon Si Thammarat	...	...	...	...	265 606	127 460	138 146	...
Narathiwat	...	...	...	...	133 718	64 616	69 102	...
Nong Bua Lam Phu	...	...	...	...	203 142	98 164	104 978	...
Nong Khai	...	...	...	...	232 798	113 989	118 809	...
Nonthaburi	...	...	...	...	797 739	383 826	413 913	...
Pathum Thani	...	...	...	...	757 175	358 679	398 496	...
Pattani	...	...	...	...	104 617	51 305	53 312	...
Phatthalung	...	...	...	...	244 783	117 039	127 744	...
Phayao	...	...	...	...	221 062	106 657	114 405	...
Phetchabun	...	...	...	...	172 275	82 257	90 018	...
Phetchaburi	...	...	...	...	175 675	83 735	91 940	...
Phichit	...	...	...	...	131 283	62 446	68 837	...
Phitsanulok	...	...	...	...	201 466	93 098	108 368	...
Phra Nakhon Si Ayutthaya	...	...	...	...	365 736	173 280	192 456	...
Phrae	...	...	...	...	156 099	75 175	80 924	...
Phuket	...	...	...	...	358 159	175 144	183 015	...
Prachuap Khiri Khan	...	...	...	...	177 011	87 525	89 486	...
Ranong	...	...	...	...	123 596	62 090	61 506	...
Ratchaburi	...	...	...	...	317 886	149 460	168 426	...
Rayong	...	...	...	...	445 939	224 068	221 871	...
Roi Et	...	...	...	...	365 113	176 648	188 465	...
Sa Kaeo	...	...	...	...	135 536	66 447	69 089	...
Sakon Nakhon	...	...	...	...	315 788	153 785	162 003	...
Samut Prakan	...	...	...	...	1 082 993	527 487	555 506	...
Samut Sakhon	...	...	...	...	479 186	237 778	241 408	...
Saraburi	...	...	...	...	239 281	114 885	124 396	...
Si Sa Ket	...	...	...	...	160 508	77 363	83 145	...
Songkhla	...	...	...	...	800 970	382 828	418 142	...
Sukhothai	...	...	...	...	166 782	79 139	87 643	...
Suphan Buri	...	...	...	...	228 496	108 666	119 830	...
Surat Thani	...	...	...	...	410 984	198 909	212 075	...
Surin	...	...	...	...	153 159	73 082	80 077	...
Tak	...	...	...	...	146 769	70 754	76 015	...
Trat	...	...	...	...	110 398	52 309	58 089	...
Ubon Ratchathani	...	...	...	...	411 954	198 655	213 299	...
Udon Thani	...	...	...	...	483 057	232 326	250 731	...
Uttaradit	...	...	...	...	151 047	72 244	78 803	...
Yala	...	...	...	...	119 744	58 041	61 703	...
Yasothon	...	...	...	...	127 173	63 885	63 288	...
Timor-Leste[55]								
11 VII 2015* (CDFC)								
DILI	222 323	114 792	107 531	...	...	...	...	...
Turkey - Turquie[56]								
31 XII 2015 (ESDJ)								
Adana	...	...	...	...	2 183 167	1 091 159	1 092 008	...
Adıyaman	238 711	120 022	118 689	...	...	...	...	...
Afyonkarahisar	217 805	107 954	109 851	...	...	...	...	...
Ağrı	116 359	60 252	56 107	...	...	...	...	...
Aksaray	202 336	100 946	101 390	...	...	...	...	...
Amasya	101 813	50 527	51 286	...	...	...	...	...
ANKARA	...	...	...	...	5 270 575	2 621 235	2 649 340	...
Antalya	...	...	...	...	2 288 456	1 156 076	1 132 380	...
Aydın	...	...	...	...	1 053 506	525 267	528 239	...
Balıkesir	...	...	...	...	1 186 688	592 718	593 970	...
Batman	392 738	197 858	194 880	...	...	...	...	...
Bingöl	108 267	55 437	52 830	...	...	...	...	...

Continent, country or area, date, code[a] and city / Continent, pays ou zone, date, code[a] et ville	City proper - Ville proprement dite				Urban agglomeration - Agglomération urbaine			
	Population			Surface area - Superficie (km²)	Population			Surface area - Superficie (km²)
	Both sexes - Les deux sexes	Male - Masculin	Female - Féminin		Both sexes - Les deux sexes	Male - Masculin	Female - Féminin	
ASIA - ASIE								
Turkey - Turquie[56]								
31 XII 2015 (ESDJ)								
Bolu	153 783	76 384	77 399	...	...	...	...	...
Bursa	...	...	...	...	2 842 547	1 423 583	1 418 964	...
Çanakkale	122 613	61 337	61 276	...	...	...	...	...
Cizre	111 266	56 569	54 697	...	...	...	...	...
Çorum	250 464	124 066	126 398	...	...	...	...	...
Denizli	...	...	...	...	993 442	494 808	498 634	...
Diyarbakir	...	...	...	...	1 654 196	834 354	819 842	...
Düzce	153 504	76 710	76 794	...	...	...	...	...
Edirne	158 369	78 173	80 196	...	...	...	...	...
Elazığ	367 156	182 578	184 578	...	...	...	...	...
Ereğli	114 274	56 840	57 434	...	...	...	...	...
Erzurum	...	...	...	...	762 321	382 163	380 158	...
Eskişehir	...	...	...	...	826 716	412 205	414 511	...
Gaziantep	...	...	...	...	1 931 836	976 126	955 710	...
Giresun	107 075	52 494	54 581	...	...	...	...	...
Hatay	...	...	...	...	1 533 507	769 131	764 376	...
Isparta	214 096	106 733	107 363	...	...	...	...	...
İstanbul	...	...	...	...	14 657 434	7 360 499	7 296 935	...
İzmir	...	...	...	...	4 168 415	2 078 224	2 090 191	...
Kahramanmaraş	...	...	...	...	1 096 610	556 607	540 003	...
Karabük	117 557	59 685	57 872	...	...	...	...	...
Karaman	152 256	75 601	76 655	...	...	...	...	...
Kastamonu	110 908	55 015	55 893	...	...	...	...	...
Kayseri	...	...	...	...	1 341 056	672 828	668 228	...
Kırıkkale	190 486	94 754	95 732	...	...	...	...	...
Kırşehir	125 807	62 720	63 087	...	...	...	...	...
Kocaeli	...	...	...	...	1 780 055	901 860	878 195	...
Konya	...	...	...	...	2 130 544	1 056 540	1 074 004	...
Kütahya	236 096	117 986	118 110	...	...	...	...	...
Lüleburgaz	111 898	56 828	55 070	...	...	...	...	...
Malatya	...	...	...	...	772 904	385 440	387 464	...
Manisa	...	...	...	...	1 380 366	691 955	688 411	...
Mardin	...	...	...	...	796 591	400 478	396 113	...
Mersin	...	...	...	...	1 745 221	869 989	875 232	...
Muğla	...	...	...	...	908 877	463 411	445 466	...
Niğde	132 155	67 487	64 668	...	...	...	...	...
Ordu	...	...	...	...	728 949	364 236	364 713	...
Osmaniye	223 987	112 409	111 578	...	...	...	...	...
Rize	111 212	54 599	56 613	...	...	...	...	...
Sakarya	...	...	...	...	953 181	477 879	475 302	...
Samsun	...	...	...	...	1 279 884	632 014	647 870	...
Şanlıurfa	...	...	...	...	1 892 320	950 493	941 827	...
Siirt	145 144	75 337	69 807	...	...	...	...	...
Sivas	329 082	162 410	166 672	...	...	...	...	...
Tekirdağ	...	...	...	...	937 910	482 404	455 506	...
Tokat	142 724	70 685	72 039	...	...	...	...	...
Trabzon	...	...	...	...	768 417	379 708	388 709	...
Uşak	201 634	100 683	100 951	...	...	...	...	...
Van	...	...	...	...	1 096 397	560 480	535 917	...
Yalova	112 183	55 219	56 964	...	...	...	...	...
Zonguldak	108 074	52 969	55 105	...	...	...	...	...
United Arab Emirates - Émirats arabes unis								
1 VII 2002 (ESDF)								
ABU DHABI	527 000	359 000	168 000	...	...	...	...	...
Ajman	205 000	122 000	83 000	...	...	...	...	...
Al-Ayn	328 000	215 000	113 000	...	...	...	...	...
Al-Sharjah	488 000	317 000	171 000	...	...	...	...	...
Dubai	1 089 000	759 000	330 000	...	...	...	...	...
Uzbekistan - Ouzbékistan[57]								
1 I 2016 (ESDJ)								
Almalyk	...	...	...	...	124 352	60 446	63 906	...
Andizhan	416 243	208 259	207 984	...	...	...	...	...
Angren	...	...	...	...	180 449	89 859	90 590	...

Continent, country or area, date, code[a] and city / Continent, pays ou zone, date, code[a] et ville	City proper - Ville proprement dite				Urban agglomeration - Agglomération urbaine			
	Population			Surface area - Superficie (km²)	Population			Surface area - Superficie (km²)
	Both sexes - Les deux sexes	Male - Masculin	Female - Féminin		Both sexes - Les deux sexes	Male - Masculin	Female - Féminin	
ASIA - ASIE								
Uzbekistan - Ouzbékistan[57]								
1 I 2016 (ESDJ)								
Bukhara	274 721	135 729	138 992	...	...	...	...	...
Chirchik	...	...	...	...	151 764	74 507	77 257	...
Fergana	271 013	134 082	136 931	...	...	...	...	...
Jizzax	167 369	83 644	83 725	...	...	...	...	...
Karshi	260 712	130 127	130 585	...	...	...	...	...
Kokand	...	...	...	...	239 861	116 898	122 963	...
Margilan	...	...	...	...	222 078	111 196	110 882	...
Namangan	493 336	253 467	239 869	...	...	...	...	...
Navoi	133 526	68 043	65 483	...	...	...	...	...
Nukus	303 683	149 473	154 210	...	...	...	...	...
Samarkand	519 231	250 535	268 696	...	...	...	...	...
Shahrisabz	...	...	...	...	103 527	52 644	50 883	...
TASHKENT	2 393 176	1 165 610	1 227 566	...	...	...	...	...
Termez	140 165	69 025	71 140	...	...	...	...	...
Urgentch	138 640	69 706	68 934	...	...	...	...	...
Yemen - Yémen								
1 VII 2009* (ESDF)								
Adan	*684 322*	...	...	...	*684 322*	...	...	...
SANA'A	*1 976 286*	...	...	...	*2 022 867*	...	...	...
EUROPE								
Åland Islands - Îles d'Åland								
1 VII 2016 (ESDJ)								
MARIEHAMN	11 513[15]	5 538[15]	5 975[15]	12	...	...	...	...
Albania - Albanie								
1 X 2011 (CDJC)								
Durrës	113 249	56 511	56 738	...	...	...	...	...
TIRANA	418 495	203 239	215 256	...	...	...	...	...
Andorra - Andorre[15]								
1 VII 2011 (ESDJ)								
ANDORRA LA VELLA	...	...	...	...	22 205	11 056	11 149	...
Austria - Autriche								
1 I 2016 (ESDJ)								
Graz	280 258	137 102	143 156	...	...	...	...	...
Innsbruck	131 009	63 763	67 246	...	...	...	...	...
Linz	200 839	96 786	104 053	...	...	...	...	...
Salzburg	150 938	72 124	78 814	...	...	...	...	...
WIEN	1 840 226	893 085	947 141	...	...	...	...	...
Belarus - Bélarus								
1 VII 2015 (ESDJ)								
Baranovichi	179 006	81 204	97 802	85	...	...	...	...
Bobruisk	218 119	101 915	116 204	90	...	...	...	...
Borisov	144 432	67 842	76 590	46	...	...	...	...
Brest	337 893	155 888	182 005	146	...	...	...	...
Gomel	...	...	...	...	529 114	241 390	287 724	135
Grodno	363 481	165 242	198 239	142	...	...	...	...
Lida	100 210	46 840	53 370	...	...	...	...	...
MINSK	1 949 031	888 032	1 060 999	348	...	...	...	...
Mogilev	376 366	172 957	203 409	119	...	...	...	...
Mozir	112 248	53 299	58 949	44	...	...	...	...
Novopolotsk	...	...	...	...	108 245	51 532	56 713	48
Orsha	116 567	53 665	62 902	...	...	...	...	...
Pinsk	137 966	63 618	74 348	47	...	...	...	...
Soligorsk	106 250	49 769	56 481	15	...	...	...	...
Vitebsk	...	...	...	...	375 060	165 976	209 084	125
Belgium - Belgique								
1 I 2011 (CDJC)								
Anderlecht	108 940	53 707	55 233	18	...	...	...	...
Antwerpen (Anvers)	498 473	247 192	251 281	205	718 730	354 576	364 154	394
Brugge	117 260	56 952	60 308	138	117 260	56 952	60 308	138
BRUXELLES (BRUSSEL)	174 383	90 317	84 066	33	1 550 299[58]	754 208[58]	796 091[58]	573[58]

8. Population of capital cities and cities of 100 000 or more inhabitants: latest available year, 1997 - 2016
Population des capitales et des villes de 100 000 habitants ou plus : dernière année disponible, 1997 - 2016 (continued - suite)

Continent, country or area, date, code[a] and city / Continent, pays ou zone, date, code[a] et ville	City proper - Ville proprement dite				Urban agglomeration - Agglomération urbaine			
	Population			Surface area - Superficie (km²)	Population			Surface area - Superficie (km²)
	Both sexes - Les deux sexes	Male - Masculin	Female - Féminin		Both sexes - Les deux sexes	Male - Masculin	Female - Féminin	
EUROPE								
Belgium - Belgique								
1 I 2011 (CDJC)								
Charleroi	204 150	99 221	104 929	102	291 806	141 106	150 700	199
Gent (Gand)	248 358	122 457	125 901	156	280 151	137 980	142 171	207
Liège (Luik)	195 965	96 509	99 456	69	491 767	238 134	253 633	367
Namur	110 175	53 019	57 156	176	110 175	53 019	57 156	176
Schaerbeek	127 525	63 020	64 505	8	...	...	...	...
Bulgaria - Bulgarie								
1 I 2016 (ESDJ)								
Burgas	203 017	97 027	105 990	...	...	...	...	...
Plovdiv	341 625	162 560	179 065	...	...	...	...	...
Ruse	145 765	70 758	75 007	...	...	...	...	...
SOFIA	1 231 981	587 879	644 102	...	...	...	...	...
Stara Zagora	136 807	65 790	71 017	...	...	...	...	...
Varna	334 466	162 072	172 394	...	...	...	...	...
Croatia - Croatie								
1 IV 2011 (CDJC)								
Osijek	108 048	50 357	57 691	174	...	...	...	...
Rijeka	128 624	60 951	67 673	43	...	...	...	...
Split	178 102	84 477	93 625	79	...	...	...	...
ZAGREB	790 017	369 339	420 678	641	...	...	...	...
Czechia - Tchéquie								
1 I 2016 (ESDJ)								
Brno	377 028	181 890	195 138	226	...	...	...	...
Liberec	103 288	49 851	53 437	105	...	...	...	...
Olomouc	100 154	47 355	52 799	101	...	...	...	...
Ostrava	292 681	141 703	150 978	205	...	...	...	...
Plzen	169 858	82 617	87 241	133	...	...	...	...
PRAHA	1 267 449	614 669	652 780	485	...	...	...	...
Denmark - Danemark[59]								
1 VII 2016 (ESDJ)								
Ålborg	210 276[15]	105 931[15]	104 345[15]	1137.3	...	...	...	...
Århus	331 505[15]	163 072[15]	168 433[15]	467.9	...	...	...	...
Esbjerg	115 987[15]	58 172[15]	57 815[15]	794.5	...	...	...	...
Frederiksberg	104 180[15]	49 351[15]	54 829[15]	8.7	...	...	...	...
KOBENHAVN	594 535[15]	293 967[15]	300 568[15]	86.4	...	...	...	...
Odense	199 235[15]	98 237[15]	100 998[15]	305.6	...	...	...	...
Vejle	112 494[15]	56 259[15]	56 235[15]	1058.4	...	...	...	...
Estonia - Estonie								
1 I 2016 (ESDJ)								
TALLINN	423 420	189 566	233 854	158	...	...	...	...
Faeroe Islands - Îles Féroé								
1 VII 2015 (ESDJ)								
TÓRSHAVN	12 713	6 336	6 377	...	18 674[60]	9 386[60]	9 288[60]	...
Finland - Finlande[61]								
1 VII 2015 (ESDJ)								
Espoo	267 673[15]	132 539[15]	135 134[15]	312.2	...	...	...	...
HELSINKI	624 462[15]	295 132[15]	329 330[15]	214.2	...	...	...	...
Jyvaskyla	136 574[15]	66 780[15]	69 794[15]	1170.9	...	...	...	...
Kuopio	111 703[15]	54 239[15]	57 465[15]	2775.7	...	...	...	...
Lahti	118 694[15]	56 902[15]	61 792[15]	459.4	...	...	...	...
Oulu	197 408[15]	98 314[15]	99 094[15]	3031.6	...	...	...	...
Tampere	224 061[15]	108 499[15]	115 562[15]	524.9	...	...	...	...
Turku	184 866[15]	87 880[15]	96 987[15]	245.7	...	...	...	...
Vantaa	212 704[15]	104 776[15]	107 928[15]	238.4	...	...	...	...
France								
1 I 2010 (CDJS)								
Aix-en-Provence	141 438[62]	65 940[62]	75 498[62]	186.1	...	...	...	...
Amiens	133 448[62]	63 030[62]	70 418[62]	49.5	162 718	77 241	85 477	137.3
Angers	147 571[62]	67 521[62]	80 050[62]	42.7	215 887	100 353	115 534	188.6
Argenteuil	103 125[62]	50 356[62]	52 769[62]	17.2	...	...	...	...
Besançon	116 914[62]	54 937[62]	61 977[62]	65.1	135 050	63 788	71 262	122.4
Bordeaux	239 157[62]	111 452[62]	127 705[62]	49.4	843 425	400 423	443 002	1172.8
Boulogne-Billancourt	114 205[62]	53 038[62]	61 167[62]	6.2	...	...	...	...

8. Population of capital cities and cities of 100 000 or more inhabitants: latest available year, 1997 - 2016
Population des capitales et des villes de 100 000 habitants ou plus : dernière année disponible, 1997 - 2016 (continued - suite)

Continent, country or area, date, code[a] and city / Continent, pays ou zone, date, code[a] et ville	City proper - Ville proprement dite				Urban agglomeration - Agglomération urbaine			
	Population			Surface area - Superficie (km²)	Population			Surface area - Superficie (km²)
	Both sexes - Les deux sexes	Male - Masculin	Female - Féminin		Both sexes - Les deux sexes	Male - Masculin	Female - Féminin	
EUROPE								
France								
1 I 2010 (CDJS)								
Brest	141 303[62]	68 083[62]	73 220[62]	49.5	199 852	96 845	103 007	199.4
Caen	108 954[62]	50 828[62]	58 126[62]	25.7	196 743	93 132	103 611	141.9
Clermont-Ferrand	139 860[62]	65 886[62]	73 974[62]	42.7	260 681	123 262	137 419	180.8
Dijon	151 212[62]	71 041[62]	80 171[62]	40.4	237 117	112 013	125 104	166
Grenoble	155 637[62]	75 558[62]	80 079[62]	18.1	496 951	241 872	255 079	512.3
Le Havre	175 497[62]	82 703[62]	92 794[62]	47	241 037	114 634	126 403	194.9
Le Mans	142 626[62]	66 979[62]	75 647[62]	34.8	207 658	98 772	108 886	294.3
Lille	227 560[62]	108 257[62]	119 303[62]	78	1 018 356	486 736	531 620	442.5
Limoges	139 150[62]	64 643[62]	74 507[62]	47.9	186 499	87 294	99 205	236.3
Lyon	484 344[62]	226 203[62]	258 141[62]	52.8	1 551 108	741 745	809 363	1177.8
Marseille	850 726[62]	400 977[62]	449 749[62]	240.6	1 559 789[63]	741 799[63]	817 990[63]	1731.9
Metz	120 738[62]	58 537[62]	62 201[62]	41.9	288 940	140 573	148 367	306.9
Montpellier	257 351[62]	119 967[62]	137 384[62]	56.9	390 962	184 812	206 150	310
Montreuil	102 770[62]	51 166[62]	51 604[62]	8.9	...	...	...	...
Mulhouse	109 588[62]	52 989[62]	56 599[62]	22.2	242 353	117 380	124 973	239.1
Nancy	105 421[62]	49 278[62]	56 143[62]	15	286 215	135 585	150 630	245.9
Nantes	284 970[62]	134 873[62]	150 097[62]	65.2	591 461	282 368	309 093	537.7
Nice	343 304[62]	159 260[62]	184 044[62]	71.9	941 777	443 854	497 923	743.6
Nîmes	142 205[62]	66 302[62]	75 903[62]	161.9	175 503	82 457	93 046	265.8
Orléans	114 167[62]	54 609[62]	59 558[62]	27.5	269 724	130 085	139 639	289.5
PARIS	2 243 833[62]	1 057 233[62]	1 186 600[62]	105.4	10 460 118[64]	5 037 278[64]	5 422 840[64]	2844.8
Perpignan	117 419[62]	54 431[62]	62 988[62]	68.1	190 668	89 358	101 310	217.5
Reims	179 992[62]	84 862[62]	95 130[62]	46.9	208 639	98 645	109 994	94.3
Rennes	207 178[62]	97 794[62]	109 384[62]	50.4	310 672	148 841	161 831	284.4
Rouen	110 933[62]	52 383[62]	58 550[62]	21.4	463 748	219 416	244 332	453.2
Saint-Denis	106 785[62]	53 787[62]	52 998[62]	12.4	...	...	...	...
Saint-Étienne	171 260[62]	80 545[62]	90 715[62]	80	371 281	176 464	194 817	418.7
Strasbourg	271 782[62]	128 478[62]	143 304[62]	78.3	449 931	214 580	235 351	240.2
Toulon	164 532[62]	77 464[62]	87 068[62]	42.8	557 802	264 944	292 858	763.7
Toulouse	441 802[62]	213 198[62]	228 604[62]	118.3	879 683	427 944	451 739	811.6
Tours	134 817[62]	61 897[62]	72 920[62]	34.7	346 105	163 682	182 423	663.7
Villeurbanne	145 150[62]	70 377[62]	74 773[62]	14.5	...	...	...	...
Germany - Allemagne								
1 I 2016 (ESDJ)								
Aachen	245 885[1]	127 613[1]	118 272[1]	160.9	...	...	...	...
Augsburg	286 374[1]	140 323[1]	146 051[1]	146.9	...	...	...	...
Bergisch Gladbach	111 366[1]	53 479[1]	57 887[1]	83.1	...	...	...	...
BERLIN	3 520 031[1]	1 726 533[1]	1 793 498[1]	891.7	...	...	...	...
Bielefeld	333 090[1]	161 148[1]	171 942[1]	258.8	...	...	...	...
Bochum	364 742[1]	177 427[1]	187 315[1]	145.7	...	...	...	...
Bonn	318 809[1]	151 954[1]	166 855[1]	141.1	...	...	...	...
Bottrop	117 143[1]	57 004[1]	60 139[1]	100.6	...	...	...	...
Braunschweig	251 364[1]	125 001[1]	126 363[1]	192.2	...	...	...	...
Bremen	557 464[1]	274 119[1]	283 345[1]	326.2	...	...	...	...
Bremerhaven	114 025[1]	56 776[1]	57 249[1]	93.7	...	...	...	...
Chemnitz	248 645[1]	122 748[1]	125 897[1]	221.1	...	...	...	...
Darmstadt	155 353[1]	78 915[1]	76 438[1]	122.1	...	...	...	...
Dortmund	586 181[1]	287 846[1]	298 335[1]	280.7	...	...	...	...
Dresden	543 825[1]	270 410[1]	273 415[1]	328.5	...	...	...	...
Duisburg	491 231[1]	241 417[1]	249 814[1]	232.8	...	...	...	...
Düsseldorf	612 178[1]	295 896[1]	316 282[1]	217.4	...	...	...	...
Erfurt	210 118[1]	102 259[1]	107 859[1]	269.9	...	...	...	...
Erlangen	108 336[1]	53 454[1]	54 882[1]	77	...	...	...	...
Essen	582 624[1]	282 565[1]	300 059[1]	210.3	...	...	...	...
Frankfurt am Main	732 688[1]	362 515[1]	370 173[1]	248.3	...	...	...	...
Freiburg im Breisgau	226 393[1]	107 913[1]	118 480[1]	153.1	...	...	...	...
Fürth	124 171[1]	60 669[1]	63 502[1]	63.4	...	...	...	...
Gelsenkirchen	260 368[1]	129 267[1]	131 101[1]	104.9	...	...	...	...
Göttingen	118 914[1]	57 732[1]	61 182[1]	116.9	...	...	...	...

Continent, country or area, date, code[a] and city / Continent, pays ou zone, date, code[a] et ville	City proper - Ville proprement dite				Urban agglomeration - Agglomération urbaine			
	Population			Surface area - Superficie (km²)	Population			Surface area - Superficie (km²)
	Both sexes - Les deux sexes	Male - Masculin	Female - Féminin		Both sexes - Les deux sexes	Male - Masculin	Female - Féminin	

EUROPE

Germany - Allemagne
1 I 2016 (ESDJ)

Hagen	189 044[1]	92 207[1]	96 837[1]	160.5	...	...	...	...
Halle (Saale)	236 991[1]	114 581[1]	122 410[1]	135	...	...	...	...
Hamburg	1 787 408[1]	873 062[1]	914 346[1]	755.3	...	...	...	...
Hamm	179 397[1]	88 166[1]	91 231[1]	226.4	...	...	...	...
Hannover	532 163[1]	259 749[1]	272 414[1]	204.1	...	...	...	...
Heidelberg	156 267[1]	74 954[1]	81 313[1]	108.8	...	...	...	...
Heilbronn	122 567[1]	61 268[1]	61 299[1]	99.9	...	...	...	...
Herne	155 851[1]	75 940[1]	79 911[1]	51.4	...	...	...	...
Hildesheim	101 667[1]	48 291[1]	53 376[1]	92.2	...	...	...	...
Ingolstadt	132 438[1]	66 825[1]	65 613[1]	133.4	...	...	...	...
Jena	109 527[1]	54 467[1]	55 060[1]	114.8	...	...	...	...
Karlsruhe	307 755[1]	156 686[1]	151 069[1]	173.5	...	...	...	...
Kassel	197 984[1]	96 659[1]	101 325[1]	106.8	...	...	...	...
Kiel	246 306[1]	119 835[1]	126 471[1]	118.7	...	...	...	...
Koblenz	112 586[1]	54 391[1]	58 195[1]	105.2	...	...	...	...
Köln	1 060 582[1]	516 976[1]	543 606[1]	405	...	...	...	...
Krefeld	225 144[1]	109 487[1]	115 657[1]	137.8	...	...	...	...
Leipzig	560 472[1]	274 414[1]	286 058[1]	297.8	...	...	...	...
Leverkusen	163 487[1]	79 590[1]	83 897[1]	78.9	...	...	...	...
Lübeck	216 253[1]	103 683[1]	112 570[1]	214.2	...	...	...	...
Ludwigshafen am Rhein	164 718[1]	81 590[1]	83 128[1]	77.6	...	...	...	...
Magdeburg	235 723[1]	115 810[1]	119 913[1]	201	...	...	...	...
Mainz	209 779[1]	101 620[1]	108 159[1]	97.7	...	...	...	...
Mannheim	305 780[1]	152 868[1]	152 912[1]	145	...	...	...	...
Moers	104 529[1]	50 973[1]	53 556[1]	67.7	...	...	...	...
Mönchengladbach	259 996[1]	127 512[1]	132 484[1]	170.5	...	...	...	...
Mülheim an der Ruhr	169 278[1]	81 461[1]	87 817[1]	91.3	...	...	...	...
München	1 450 381[1]	707 150[1]	743 231[1]	310.7	...	...	...	...
Münster (Westf.)	310 039[1]	148 447[1]	161 592[1]	303.3	...	...	...	...
Neuss	155 414[1]	75 929[1]	79 485[1]	99.5	...	...	...	...
Nürnberg	509 975[1]	247 931[1]	262 044[1]	186.4	...	...	...	...
Oberhausen	210 934[1]	103 284[1]	107 650[1]	77.1	...	...	...	...
Offenbach am Main	123 734[1]	61 609[1]	62 125[1]	44.9	...	...	...	...
Oldenburg (Oldenburg)	163 830[1]	78 259[1]	85 571[1]	103	...	...	...	...
Osnabrück	162 403[1]	78 275[1]	84 128[1]	119.8	...	...	...	...
Paderborn	148 126[1]	73 680[1]	74 446[1]	179.6	...	...	...	...
Pforzheim	122 247[1]	59 901[1]	62 346[1]	98	...	...	...	...
Potsdam	167 745[1]	80 854[1]	86 891[1]	188.3	...	...	...	...
Recklinghausen	114 330[1]	55 697[1]	58 633[1]	66.5	...	...	...	...
Regensburg	145 465[1]	69 969[1]	75 496[1]	80.7	...	...	...	...
Remscheid	109 499[1]	53 725[1]	55 774[1]	74.5	...	...	...	...
Reutlingen	114 310[1]	56 398[1]	57 912[1]	87.1	...	...	...	...
Rostock	206 011[1]	101 078[1]	104 933[1]	181.3	...	...	...	...
Saarbrücken	178 151[1]	87 985[1]	90 166[1]	167.1	...	...	...	...
Salzgitter	101 079[1]	49 898[1]	51 181[1]	223.9	...	...	...	...
Siegen	102 355[1]	49 925[1]	52 430[1]	114.7	...	...	...	...
Solingen	158 726[1]	76 948[1]	81 778[1]	89.5	...	...	...	...
Stuttgart	623 738[1]	310 492[1]	313 246[1]	207.4	...	...	...	...
Trier	114 914[1]	57 510[1]	57 404[1]	117.1	...	...	...	...
Ulm	122 636[1]	60 400[1]	62 236[1]	118.7	...	...	...	...
Wiesbaden	276 218[1]	131 901[1]	144 317[1]	203.9	...	...	...	...
Wolfsburg	124 045[1]	61 581[1]	62 464[1]	204.1	...	...	...	...
Wuppertal	350 046[1]	170 822[1]	179 224[1]	168.4	...	...	...	...
Würzburg	124 873[1]	59 159[1]	65 714[1]	87.6	...	...	...	...

Gibraltar
31 XII 2015 (ESDF)

GIBRALTAR	33 573[65]	16 938[65]	16 635[65]	6	...	...	...	...

8. Population of capital cities and cities of 100 000 or more inhabitants: latest available year, 1997 - 2016
Population des capitales et des villes de 100 000 habitants ou plus : dernière année disponible, 1997 - 2016 (continued - suite)

Continent, country or area, date, code[a] and city / Continent, pays ou zone, date, code[a] et ville	City proper - Ville proprement dite				Urban agglomeration - Agglomération urbaine			
	Population			Surface area - Superficie (km²)	Population			Surface area - Superficie (km²)
	Both sexes - Les deux sexes	Male - Masculin	Female - Féminin		Both sexes - Les deux sexes	Male - Masculin	Female - Féminin	
EUROPE								
Greece - Grèce								
9 V 2011 (CDFC)								
ATHINAI	664 046	315 210	348 836	...	...	...	...	...
Calithèa	100 641	46 782	53 859	...	...	...	...	...
Iraclion	140 730	68 024	72 706	...	...	...	...	...
Larissa	144 651	70 797	73 854	...	...	...	...	...
Patrai	167 446	81 114	86 332	...	...	...	...	...
Pésterion	139 981	68 563	71 418	...	...	...	...	...
Pireas	163 688	78 200	85 488	...	...	...	...	...
Thessaloniki	315 196	143 813	171 383	...	...	...	...	...
Guernsey - Guernesey								
31 III 2015 (CDJC)								
ST. PETER PORT	18 599	...	...	...	...	...	...	...
Holy See - Saint-Siège[66]								
21 VI 2012 (ESDF)								
VATICAN CITY	451	...	...	...	...	...	...	...
Hungary - Hongrie								
1 VII 2015 (ESDJ)								
BUDAPEST	1 758 513	814 972	943 541	525.1	2 580 310	1 211 049	1 369 261	2538.4
Debrecen	203 283	94 782	108 501	461.7	266 850	126 153	140 697	1081.8
Györ	129 470	61 124	68 347	174.6	230 727	111 614	119 113	1607
Kecskemét	111 780	52 501	59 279	322.6	133 533	63 254	70 279	666.1
Miskolc	158 828	73 613	85 215	236.7	250 046	117 735	132 311	982.3
Nyiregyhaza	118 092	54 882	63 210	274.5	148 022	69 508	78 514	554.3
Pécs	145 666	66 608	79 058	162.8	181 060	84 080	96 980	671.3
Szeged	162 607	74 536	88 072	281	205 183	95 574	109 609	804.5
Iceland - Islande[67]								
1 VII 2015 (ESDJ)								
REYKJAVIK	122 141	60 674	61 468	...	212 451[68]	105 666[68]	106 785[68]	...
Ireland - Irlande								
10 IV 2011 (CDFC)								
Cork	119 230	58 812	60 418	...	198 582	97 463	101 119	...
DUBLIN	527 612	257 303	270 309	...	1 110 627	539 742	570 885	...
Isle of Man - Île de Man								
23 IV 2006 (CDJC)								
DOUGLAS	26 218	13 000	13 218	...	...	...	...	...
Italy - Italie								
1 VII 2014 (ESDJ)								
Ancona	101 630	48 302	53 329	125	...	...	...	...
Bari	325 056	155 550	169 506	117	...	...	...	...
Bergamo	118 860	55 504	63 356	40	...	...	...	...
Bologna	385 192	180 840	204 352	141	...	...	...	...
Bolzano	105 912	50 597	55 315	52	...	...	...	...
Brescia	194 829	91 719	103 110	90	...	...	...	...
Cagliari	154 249	71 472	82 777	85	...	...	...	...
Catania	315 589	151 419	164 170	183	...	...	...	...
Ferrara	133 553	62 438	71 115	405	...	...	...	...
Firenze	379 122	177 111	202 012	102	...	...	...	...
Foggia	152 957	73 421	79 536	509	...	...	...	...
Forli	118 307	56 912	61 395	228	...	...	...	...
Genova	594 733	279 182	315 551	240	...	...	...	...
Giugliano in Campania	120 679	59 463	61 216	95	...	...	...	...
Latina	125 436	60 532	64 904	278	...	...	...	...
Livorno	160 027	76 335	83 692	105	...	...	...	...
Messina	241 206	115 426	125 780	214	...	...	...	...
Milano	1 330 662	633 161	697 501	182	...	...	...	...
Modena	184 837	88 173	96 664	183	...	...	...	...
Monza	122 759	58 867	63 893	33	...	...	...	...
Napoli	983 755	468 858	514 897	119	...	...	...	...
Novara	104 594	50 164	54 431	103	...	...	...	...
Padova	210 444	98 652	111 792	93	...	...	...	...
Palermo	678 492	323 975	354 517	161	...	...	...	...
Parma	189 111	89 709	99 402	261	...	...	...	...
Perugia	165 849	78 749	87 100	450	...	...	...	...
Pescara	121 346	56 845	64 501	34	...	...	...	...

Continent, country or area, date, code[a] and city Continent, pays ou zone, date, code[a] et ville	City proper - Ville proprement dite				Urban agglomeration - Agglomération urbaine			
	Population			Surface area - Superficie (km²)	Population			Surface area - Superficie (km²)
	Both sexes - Les deux sexes	Male - Masculin	Female - Féminin		Both sexes - Les deux sexes	Male - Masculin	Female - Féminin	
EUROPE								
Italy - Italie								
1 VII 2014 (ESDJ)								
Piacenza	102 337	48 622	53 715	118	...	...	...	...
Prato	191 135	92 453	98 683	97	...	...	...	...
Ravenna	158 848	76 821	82 027	654	...	...	...	...
Reggio di Calabria	184 456	88 255	96 201	239	...	...	...	...
Reggio nell'Emilia	172 090	83 569	88 521	231	...	...	...	...
Rimini	147 217	70 376	76 841	136	...	...	...	...
ROMA	2 867 672	1 359 337	1 508 335	1287	...	...	...	...
Salerno	134 744	62 847	71 897	60	...	...	...	...
Sassari	127 670	61 186	66 485	547	...	...	...	...
Siracusa	122 404	59 986	62 418	208	...	...	...	...
Taranto	202 637	96 588	106 049	250	...	...	...	...
Terni	112 180	52 705	59 476	212	...	...	...	...
Torino	899 455	427 937	471 519	130	...	...	...	...
Trento	117 295	56 084	61 211	158	...	...	...	...
Trieste	205 131	97 035	108 097	85	...	...	...	...
Venezia	264 557	124 717	139 840	416	...	...	...	...
Verona	260 046	122 930	137 116	199	...	...	...	...
Vicenza	113 627	53 770	59 857	81	...	...	...	...
Jersey								
11 III 2001 (CDJC)								
ST. HELIER	28 310	13 669	14 641	8.6	...	...	...	...
Latvia - Lettonie								
1 VII 2015 (ESDJ)								
RIGA	640 319	283 151	357 168	304	...	...	...	...
Liechtenstein								
1 VII 2015 (ESDJ)								
VADUZ	5 429	2 630	2 799	17	...	...	...	...
Lithuania - Lituanie								
1 VII 2015 (ESDJ)								
Kaunas	299 601	131 440	168 161	157	...	...	...	...
Klaipeda	155 234	70 008	85 226	98	...	...	...	...
Shauliai	103 775	45 726	58 049	81	...	...	...	...
VILNIUS	543 060	243 130	299 930	401	...	...	...	...
Luxembourg								
1 I 2016 (ESDJ)								
LUXEMBOURG-VILLE	115 227	58 976	56 251	...	...	...	...	...
Malta - Malte								
1 VII 2015 (ESDJ)								
VALLETTA	5 680[69]	2 798[69]	2 882[69]	1	...	...	...	...
Monaco								
9 VI 2008 (CDJC)								
MONACO	31 109	15 076[70]	15 914[70]	...	...	...	...	...
Montenegro - Monténégro								
1 IV 2011 (CDJC)								
PODGORICA	185 937	90 614	95 323	1441	...	...	...	...
Netherlands - Pays-Bas								
1 I 2015 (ESDJ)								
Alkmaar	107 106	52 973	54 133	...	...	...	...	...
Almere	196 932	97 666	99 266	...	...	...	...	...
Alphen aan den	107 396	53 321	54 075	...	...	...	...	...
Amersfoort	152 481	74 967	77 514	...	...	...	...	...
AMSTERDAM	821 752	404 881	416 871	...	...	...	...	...
Apeldoorn	158 099	78 163	79 936	...	...	...	...	...
Arnhem	152 293	75 872	76 421	...	...	...	...	...
Breda	180 937	88 620	92 317	...	...	...	...	...
Delft	101 030	54 035	46 995	...	...	...	...	...
Dordrecht	118 899	58 646	60 253	...	...	...	...	...
Ede	111 575	54 790	56 785	...	...	...	...	...
Eindhoven	223 209	114 034	109 175	...	...	...	...	...
Emmen	107 775	53 399	54 376	...	...	...	...	...
Enschede	158 553	80 411	78 142	...	...	...	...	...
Groningen	200 336	99 657	100 679	...	...	...	...	...
Haarlem	156 645	76 481	80 164	...	...	...	...	...

8. Population of capital cities and cities of 100 000 or more inhabitants: latest available year, 1997 - 2016
Population des capitales et des villes de 100 000 habitants ou plus : dernière année disponible, 1997 - 2016 (continued - suite)

Continent, country or area, date, codeª and city / Continent, pays ou zone, date, codeª et ville	City proper - Ville proprement dite				Urban agglomeration - Agglomération urbaine			
	Population			Surface area - Superficie (km²)	Population			Surface area - Superficie (km²)
	Both sexes - Les deux sexes	Male - Masculin	Female - Féminin		Both sexes - Les deux sexes	Male - Masculin	Female - Féminin	
EUROPE								
Netherlands - Pays-Bas								
1 I 2015 (ESDJ)								
Haarlemmermeer	144 152	71 642	72 510	...	...	...	...	...
Leeuwarden	107 691	53 264	54 427	...	...	...	...	...
Leiden	121 562	59 084	62 478	...	...	...	...	...
Maastricht	122 397	58 799	63 598	...	...	...	...	...
Nijmegen	170 681	81 934	88 747	...	...	...	...	...
Rotterdam	623 652	307 001	316 651	...	...	...	...	...
s-Gravenhage	514 861	254 187	260 674	...	...	...	...	...
s-Hertogenbosch	150 889	74 424	76 465	...	...	...	...	...
Tilburg	211 648	105 179	106 469	...	...	...	...	...
Utrecht	334 176	162 556	171 620	...	...	...	...	...
Venlo	100 536	49 978	50 558	...	...	...	...	...
Westland	104 302	51 937	52 365	...	...	...	...	...
Zaanstad	151 418	74 778	76 640	...	...	...	...	...
Zoetermeer	124 025	60 554	63 471	...	...	...	...	...
Zwolle	123 861	60 759	63 102	...	...	...	...	...
Norway - Norvège								
1 I 2014 (ESDJ)								
OSLO	634 293	316 114	318 179	426	...	...	...	...
Poland - Pologne[71]								
1 VII 2015 (ESDJ)								
Bialystok	292 843	137 654	155 189	...	...	...	...	...
Bielsko-Biala	170 725	80 563	90 162	...	...	...	...	...
Bydgoszcz	355 728	167 596	188 132	...	...	...	...	...
Bytom	169 902	81 195	88 707	...	...	...	...	...
Chorzów	109 149	51 838	57 311	...	...	...	...	...
Czestochowa	227 184	106 600	120 584	...	...	...	...	...
Dabrowa Górnicza	121 902	58 470	63 432	...	...	...	...	...
Elblag	119 836	57 300	62 536	...	...	...	...	...
Gdansk	459 919	218 336	241 583	...	...	...	...	...
Gdynia	244 744	115 849	128 895	...	...	...	...	...
Gliwice	182 155	87 626	94 529	...	...	...	...	...
Gorzów Wielkopolski	122 411	58 209	64 202	...	...	...	...	...
Kalisz	101 836	47 308	54 528	...	...	...	...	...
Katowice	304 063	145 496	158 567	...	...	...	...	...
Kielce	196 753	92 630	104 123	...	...	...	...	...
Koszalin	106 334	50 133	56 201	...	...	...	...	...
Kraków	754 056	352 074	401 982	...	...	...	...	...
Lódz	701 410	319 469	381 941	...	...	...	...	...
Lublin	341 975	157 585	184 390	...	...	...	...	...
Olsztyn	173 425	80 968	92 457	...	...	...	...	...
Opole	118 312	55 454	62 858	...	...	...	...	...
Plock	120 890	57 115	63 775	...	...	...	...	...
Poznan	542 689	253 266	289 423	...	...	...	...	...
Radom	214 697	101 945	112 752	...	...	...	...	...
Ruda Slaska	139 021	67 265	71 756	...	...	...	...	...
Rybnik	138 163	67 421	70 742	...	...	...	...	...
Rzeszów	182 225	86 215	96 010	...	...	...	...	...
Sosnowiec	206 312	97 725	108 587	...	...	...	...	...
Szczecin	404 712	192 671	212 041	...	...	...	...	...
Tarnów	107 398	50 587	56 811	...	...	...	...	...
Torun	199 612	92 651	106 961	...	...	...	...	...
Tychy	126 860	61 168	65 692	...	...	...	...	...
Walbrzych	114 746	54 097	60 649	...	...	...	...	...
WARSZAWA	1 735 391	797 556	937 835	...	...	...	...	...
Wloclawek	111 936	52 669	59 267	...	...	...	...	...
Wroclaw	628 589	294 184	334 405	...	...	...	...	...
Zabrze	174 715	84 284	90 431	...	...	...	...	...
Zielona Góra	138 809	66 084	72 725	...	...	...	...	...
Portugal								
1 VII 2015 (ESDJ)								
Amadora	176 298	82 256	94 043	...	...	...	...	...
LISBOA	506 892	231 833	275 059	...	...	...	...	...
Porto	216 405	97 333	119 072	...	...	...	...	...

8. Population of capital cities and cities of 100 000 or more inhabitants: latest available year, 1997 - 2016
Population des capitales et des villes de 100 000 habitants ou plus : dernière année disponible, 1997 - 2016 (continued - suite)

Continent, country or area, date, code[a] and city / Continent, pays ou zone, date, code[a] et ville	City proper - Ville proprement dite				Urban agglomeration - Agglomération urbaine			
	Population			Surface area - Superficie (km²)	Population			Surface area - Superficie (km²)
	Both sexes - Les deux sexes	Male - Masculin	Female - Féminin		Both sexes - Les deux sexes	Male - Masculin	Female - Féminin	
EUROPE								
Republic of Moldova - République de Moldova								
1 I 2012 (ESDJ)								
Balti (Beltsy)	144 507	66 243	78 264	41	...	...	...	...
CHIŞINĂU (KISHINEV)	669 694	311 575	358 119	123	726 075	339 321	386 755	572
Romania - Roumanie								
1 VII 2015 (ESDJ)								
BUCURESTI	1 848 912[72]	858 410[72]	990 502[72]	240	...	...	...	...
Russian Federation - Fédération de Russie								
1 VII 2012 (ESDJ)								
Abakan	168 655	77 052	91 603	...	...	...	...	...
Achinsk	107 943	48 069	59 874	...	109 229	...	...	...
Almetievsk	148 384	69 433	78 951	...	...	...	...	...
Anapa	...	...	...	...	156 928	...	...	...
Angarsk	231 944	105 405	126 539	...	...	...	...	...
Arkhangelsk	350 258	156 523	193 735	...	357 264	...	...	...
Armavir	190 831	87 524	103 307	...	209 742	...	...	...
Artem (Primorskiy Krai)	102 605	49 147	53 458	...	112 102	...	...	...
Arzamas	105 506	47 208	58 298	...	...	...	...	...
Astrakhan	526 363	241 489	284 874	...	...	...	...	...
Balakovo	196 918	88 075	108 843	...	...	...	...	...
Balashikha	228 567	112 191	116 376	...	238 284	...	...	...
Barnaul	625 679	279 300	346 379	...	686 306	...	...	...
Bataisk	115 016	54 477	60 539	...	...	...	...	...
Belgorod	369 815	167 120	202 695	...	...	...	...	...
Belovo	...	...	...	...	132 144	...	...	...
Berezniki	153 806	68 365	85 441	...	...	...	...	...
Biisk	206 327	91 943	114 384	...	215 780	...	...	...
Blagoveshchensk (Amurskaya oblast)	216 691	97 135	119 556	...	222 065	...	...	...
Bor	...	...	...	...	122 201	...	...	...
Bratsk	242 604	109 596	133 008	...	...	...	...	...
Bryansk	411 798	183 540	228 258	...	430 987	...	...	...
Cheboksary	462 669	206 721	255 948	...	473 189	...	...	...
Chelyabinsk	1 149 829	514 456	635 373	...	...	...	...	...
Cherepovets	315 186	142 977	172 209	...	...	...	...	...
Cherkessk	126 884	55 588	71 296	...	...	...	...	...
Chita	329 391	152 092	177 299	...	329 868	...	...	...
Derbent	119 647	57 527	62 120	...	...	...	...	...
Dimitrovgrad	120 750	55 838	64 912	...	...	...	...	...
Domodedovo	...	...	...	...	142 743	...	...	...
Dzerzhinsk (Nizhegorodskaya oblast)	238 327	105 346	132 981	...	248 649	...	...	...
Ekaterinburg	1 386 909	621 499	765 410	...	1 420 285	...	...	...
Elektrostal	156 136	71 093	85 043	...	...	...	...	...
Elets	107 347	48 757	58 590	...	...	...	...	...
Elista	104 177	47 317	56 860	...	108 753	...	...	...
Engels	210 190	95 953	114 237	...	211 825	...	...	...
Esentuky	101 851	45 327	56 524	...	...	...	...	...
Groznyi	276 524	136 615	139 909	...	...	...	...	...
Hasaviurt	133 188	63 867	69 321	...	...	...	...	...
Irkutsk	601 993	269 003	332 990	...	...	...	...	...
Ivanovo	408 952	180 083	228 869	...	...	...	...	...
Izhevsk	631 182	281 708	349 474	...	...	...	...	...
Kaliningrad (Kaliningradskaya oblast)	437 456	200 849	236 607	...	...	...	...	...
Kaluga	328 871	146 008	182 863	...	344 766	...	...	...
Kamensk-Uralsky	172 639	77 327	95 312	...	174 493	...	...	...
Kamyshin	117 352	53 822	63 530	...	...	...	...	...
Kaspiysk	102 421	49 393	53 028	...	...	...	...	...
Kazan	1 168 745	520 694	648 051	...	...	...	...	...
Kemerovo	538 188	240 431	297 757	...	...	...	...	...
Khabarovsk	589 596	273 949	315 647	...	...	...	...	...
Khimki	218 275	99 122	119 153	...	...	...	...	...
Kirov	480 594	211 205	269 389	...	505 346	...	...	...
Kiselevsk	...	...	...	...	101 180	...	...	...
Kislovodsk	129 313	58 854	70 459	...	136 142	...	...	...
Kolomna	144 838	66 469	78 369	...	...	...	...	...
Komsomolsk-na-Amure	259 081	120 197	138 884	...	...	...	...	...

8. Population of capital cities and cities of 100 000 or more inhabitants: latest available year, 1997 - 2016
Population des capitales et des villes de 100 000 habitants ou plus : dernière année disponible, 1997 - 2016 (continued - suite)

Continent, country or area, date, code[a] and city / Continent, pays ou zone, date, code[a] et ville	City proper - Ville proprement dite				Urban agglomeration - Agglomération urbaine			
	Population			Surface area - Superficie (km²)	Population			Surface area - Superficie (km²)
	Both sexes - Les deux sexes	Male - Masculin	Female - Féminin		Both sexes - Les deux sexes	Male - Masculin	Female - Féminin	
EUROPE								
Russian Federation - Fédération de Russie								
1 VII 2012 (ESDJ)								
Kopeysk	139 161	66 142	73 019	...	141 291	...	...	...
Korolev (Moskovskaya oblast)	186 460	84 232	102 228	...	...	...	...	...
Kostroma	270 366	120 622	149 744	...	...	...	...	...
Kovrov	...	...	...	...	346 922	154 144	192 778	...
Krasnodar	773 970	350 519	423 451	...	861 181	...	...	...
Krasnogorsk	125 198	56 432	68 766	...	125 787	...	...	...
Krasnoyarsk	1 006 856	456 171	550 685	...	1 007 654	...	...	...
Kurgan	326 729	146 140	180 589	...	...	...	...	...
Kursk	425 950	189 025	236 925	...	...	...	...	...
Kyzyl	112 659	52 137	60 522	...	...	...	...	...
Leninsk-Kuznetsky	100 073	45 651	54 422	...	102 285	...	...	...
Lipetsk	508 585	230 178	278 407	...	...	...	...	...
Lyubertsy	178 884	80 564	98 320	...	...	...	...	...
Magadan	95 263	45 084	50 179	...	101 933	...	...	...
Magnitogorsk	410 733	186 534	224 199	...	...	...	...	...
Maikop	144 579	64 512	80 067	...	167 281	...	...	...
Makhachkala	575 243	271 687	303 556	...	701 753	...	...	...
Mezhdurechensk	100 278	46 498	53 780	...	102 465	...	...	...
Miass	150 806	67 824	82 982	...	166 205	...	...	...
MOSKVA	11 918 057	5 495 477	6 422 580	...	...	...	...	...
Murmansk	303 754	139 944	163 810	...	...	...	...	...
Murom	113 330	50 293	63 037	...	122 545	...	...	...
Mytishchi	176 825	80 425	96 400	...	185 204	...	...	...
Naberezhnye Tchelny	517 831	237 620	280 211	...	...	...	...	...
Nakhodka	158 649	75 081	83 568	...	159 633	...	...	...
Naltchik	239 230	106 648	132 582	...	265 051	...	...	...
Nazran	100 574	44 126	56 448	...	...	...	...	...
Neftekamsk	123 202	57 271	65 931	...	135 013	...	...	...
Nefteyugansk	125 528	61 635	63 893	...	...	...	...	...
Nevinnomyssk	117 949	53 611	64 338	...	...	...	...	...
Nizhnekamsk	235 179	111 262	123 917	...	235 279	...	...	...
Nizhnevartovsk	261 011	125 937	135 074	...	...	...	...	...
Nizhny Novgorod	1 257 260	552 285	704 975	...	1 266 231	...	...	...
Nizhny Tagil	358 651	162 731	195 920	...	362 185	...	...	...
Noginsk	101 779	45 741	56 038	...	103 843	...	...	...
Norilsk	177 506	89 198	88 308	...	178 363	...	...	...
Novocheboksarsk	...	...	...	...	124 288	...	...	...
Novocherkassk	171 081	81 921	89 160	...	...	...	...	...
Novokuybishevsk	107 244	48 418	58 826	...	109 521	...	...	...
Novokuznetsk	549 383	247 386	301 997	...	...	...	...	...
Novomoskovsk (Tulskaya oblast)	129 555	57 961	71 594	...	141 893	...	...	...
Novorossiysk	248 857	117 707	131 150	...	305 421	...	...	...
Novoshakhtinsk	110 243	50 410	59 833	...	...	...	...	...
Novosibirsk	1 511 369	694 959	816 410	...	...	...	...	...
Novotroitsk	...	...	...	...	103 061	...	...	...
Novy Urengoy	114 332	59 841	54 491	...	...	...	...	...
Noyabrsk	108 662	53 237	55 425	...	...	...	...	...
Obninsk	105 722	48 323	57 399	...	...	...	...	...
Odintsovo	137 706	63 405	74 301	...	143 848	...	...	...
Oktyabrsky	111 109	51 956	59 153	...	...	...	...	...
Omsk	1 158 627	526 757	631 870	...	...	...	...	...
Orekhovo-Zuevo	121 341	53 443	67 898	...	...	...	...	...
Orel	318 642	139 662	178 980	...	...	...	...	...
Orenburg	555 420	252 906	302 514	...	571 041	...	...	...
Orsk	237 194	106 127	131 067	...	241 327	...	...	...
Penza	519 948	234 270	285 678	...	...	...	...	...
Perm	1 007 272	444 386	562 886	...	1 007 285	...	...	...
Pervouralsk	125 421	56 144	69 277	...	149 796	...	...	...
Petropavlovsk-Kamchatsky	180 702	88 743	91 959	...	...	...	...	...
Petrozavodsk	267 102	118 638	148 464	...	...	...	...	...
Podolsk	200 059	89 931	110 128	...	...	...	...	...
Prokopyevsk	206 023	91 944	114 079	...	...	...	...	...
Pskov	205 062	92 439	112 623	...	...	...	...	...

Population des capitales et des villes de 100 000 habitants ou plus : dernière année disponible, 1997 - 2016 (continued - suite)

Continent, country or area, date, code[a] and city / Continent, pays ou zone, date, code[a] et ville	City proper - Ville proprement dite				Urban agglomeration - Agglomération urbaine			
	Population			Surface area - Superficie (km²)	Population			Surface area - Superficie (km²)
	Both sexes - Les deux sexes	Male - Masculin	Female - Féminin		Both sexes - Les deux sexes	Male - Masculin	Female - Féminin	

EUROPE

Russian Federation - Fédération de Russie
1 VII 2012 (ESDJ)

Pushkino	104 020	46 649	57 371	...	...	...	...	...
Pyatigorsk	144 603	64 578	80 025	...	212 968	...	...	...
Rostov-na-Donu	1 100 091	501 068	599 023	...	...	...	...	...
Rubtsovsk	146 075	69 084	76 991	...	...	...	...	...
Ryazan	526 919	237 791	289 128	...	...	...	...	...
Rybinsk	197 359	87 921	109 438	...	...	...	...	...
Salavat	155 174	72 449	82 725	...	...	...	...	...
Samara (Samarskaya oblast)	1 170 381	522 660	647 721	...	1 170 485	...	...	...
Saransk	298 103	132 543	165 560	...	326 473	...	...	...
Sarapyul	100 362	44 678	55 684	...	...	...	...	...
Saratov	838 321	373 676	464 645	...	...	...	...	...
Sergiev Posad	109 076	48 786	60 290	...	115 858	...	...	...
Serov	...	...	...	...	107 904	...	...	...
Serpukhov	126 729	57 494	69 235	...	...	...	...	...
Severodvinsk	189 313	87 781	101 532	...	190 513	...	...	...
Seversk	109 630	50 705	58 925	...	116 340	...	...	...
Shakhty	238 031	107 544	130 487	...	...	...	...	...
Shchelkovo	111 406	50 812	60 594	...	113 726	...	...	...
Smolensk	330 451	147 446	183 005	...	...	...	...	...
Sochi	364 171	164 632	199 539	...	441 407	...	...	...
St. Petersburg	4 990 602	2 247 375	2 743 227	...	...	...	...	...
Stary Oskol	220 719	100 902	119 817	...	256 790	...	...	...
Stavropol	408 361	187 593	220 768	...	408 560	...	...	...
Sterlitamak	275 087	125 443	149 644	...	...	...	...	...
Surgut	321 062	153 832	167 230	...	...	...	...	...
Syktivkar	239 341	107 945	131 396	...	255 283	...	...	...
Syzran	177 404	79 804	97 600	...	178 205	...	...	...
Taganrog	255 671	114 508	141 163	...	...	...	...	...
Tambov	281 348	126 427	154 921	...	...	...	...	...
Tobolsk	...	...	...	...	101 955	...	...	...
Tolyatti	719 363	331 248	388 115	...	...	...	...	...
Tomsk	543 596	252 173	291 423	...	565 000	...	...	...
Tula	496 656	220 675	275 981	...	...	...	...	...
Tver	407 896	180 459	227 437	...	...	...	...	...
Tyumen	621 918	288 291	333 627	...	644 799	...	...	...
Ufa	1 075 007	484 893	590 114	...	1 084 420	...	...	...
Uhta	99 680	47 563	52 117	...	121 479	...	...	...
Ulan-Ude	413 850	191 732	222 118	...	...	...	...	...
Ulyanovsk	614 878	278 103	336 775	...	637 637	...	...	...
Ussuriisk	163 465	79 562	83 903	...	189 502	...	...	...
Velikiy Novgorod	219 941	95 446	124 495	...	...	...	...	...
Vladikavkaz (Osetinskaya ASSR)	309 173	139 818	169 355	...	327 448	...	...	...
Vladimir	346 922	154 144	192 778	...	349 525	...	...	...
Vladivostok	598 927	282 260	316 667	...	624 281	...	...	...
Volgodonsk	170 189	78 251	91 938	...	...	...	...	...
Volgograd	1 018 762	460 095	558 667	...	...	...	...	...
Vologda	305 397	135 292	170 105	...	313 679	...	...	...
Volzhsky	320 761	148 339	172 422	...	327 460	...	...	...
Voronezh	997 447	447 484	549 963	...	...	...	...	...
Yakutsk	282 419	132 612	149 807	...	298 926	...	...	...
Yaroslavl	597 161	262 042	335 119	...	...	...	...	...
Yoshkar-Ola	254 987	114 331	140 656	...	265 626	...	...	...
Yuzhno-Sakhalinsk	188 242	89 200	99 042	...	195 104	...	...	...
Zheleznodorozhny	138 814	62 719	76 095	...	...	...	...	...
Zhukovsky	106 555	49 027	57 528	...	...	...	...	...
Zlatoust	172 972	78 071	94 901	...	175 178	...	...	...
San Marino - Saint-Marin 1 I 2013 (ESDF)								
SAN MARINO	4 438	2 117	2 321	...	...	...	...	...
Serbia - Serbie 1 VII 2015 (ESDJ)								
BEOGRAD (BELGRADE)	1 369 401[73]	638 577[73]	730 824[73]	236	1 679 895[74]	793 588[74]	886 307[74]	3158[75]
Čačak	72 489[73]	34 610[73]	37 879[73]	19	112 558[74]	54 670[74]	57 888[74]	633[75]

8. Population of capital cities and cities of 100 000 or more inhabitants: latest available year, 1997 - 2016
Population des capitales et des villes de 100 000 habitants ou plus : dernière année disponible, 1997 - 2016 (continued - suite)

Continent, country or area, date, code[a] and city / Continent, pays ou zone, date, code[a] et ville	City proper - Ville proprement dite				Urban agglomeration - Agglomération urbaine			
	Population			Surface area - Superficie (km²)	Population			Surface area - Superficie (km²)
	Both sexes - Les deux sexes	Male - Masculin	Female - Féminin		Both sexes - Les deux sexes	Male - Masculin	Female - Féminin	
EUROPE								
Serbia - Serbie								
1 VII 2015 (ESDJ)								
Kragujevac	150 842[73]	72 793[73]	78 049[73]	34	178 610[74]	86 804[74]	91 806[74]	834[75]
Kraljevo	67 536[73]	32 560[73]	34 976[73]	16	121 766[74]	59 787[74]	61 979[74]	1525[75]
Kruševac	57 962[73]	27 526[73]	30 436[73]	9	124 795[74]	60 982[74]	63 813[74]	849[75]
Leskovac	64 207[73]	31 126[73]	33 081[73]	2	139 291[74]	69 207[74]	70 084[74]	1021[75]
Niš	186 222[73]	89 099[73]	97 123[73]	26	257 883[74]	125 202[74]	132 681[74]	594[75]
Novi Pazar	70 607[73]	34 796[73]	35 811[73]	9	103 892[74]	51 631[74]	52 261[74]	741[75]
Novi Sad	286 546[73]	134 144[73]	152 402[73]	50	350 930[74]	166 129[74]	184 801[74]	593[75]
Pancevo	89 644[73]	43 021[73]	46 623[73]	34	121 482[74]	59 090[74]	62 392[74]	736[75]
Šabac	53 336[73]	25 000[73]	28 336[73]	15	113 113[74]	55 276[74]	57 837[74]	788[75]
Smederevo	63 329[73]	30 630[73]	32 699[73]	17	105 774[74]	52 148[74]	53 626[74]	474[75]
Subotica	104 410[73]	49 641[73]	54 769[73]	50	139 011[74]	66 794[74]	72 217[74]	998[75]
Zrenjanin	74 981[73]	35 691[73]	39 290[73]	29	119 710[74]	58 181[74]	61 529[74]	1286[75]
Slovakia - Slovaquie								
1 VII 2015 (ESDJ)								
BRATISLAVA	421 305	197 228	224 078	368	...	...	...	...
Kosice	239 332	114 730	124 602	244	...	...	...	...
Slovenia - Slovénie								
1 VII 2015 (ESDJ)								
LJUBLJANA	278 853	133 795	145 058	164	280 702	134 744	145 958	171
Maribor	95 432	46 853	48 579	41	109 110	53 620	55 490	99
Spain - Espagne[24]								
1 VII 2013 (ESDJ)								
A Coruña	245 367	113 948	131 419	...	...	...	...	...
Albacete	172 590	84 551	88 039	...	...	...	...	...
Alcalá de Henares	202 796	100 688	102 108	...	...	...	...	...
Alcobendas	112 192	54 192	58 000	...	...	...	...	...
Alcorcón	170 055	82 959	87 096	...	...	...	...	...
Algeciras	116 126	57 386	58 740	...	...	...	...	...
Alicante	333 560	162 106	171 454	...	...	...	...	...
Almería	193 024	93 876	99 148	...	...	...	...	...
Badajoz	150 569	73 252	77 317	...	...	...	...	...
Badalona	235 633	115 631	120 002	...	...	...	...	...
Baracaldo	100 291	48 558	51 733	...	...	...	...	...
Barcelona	1 607 104	761 009	846 095	...	...	...	...	...
Bilbao	347 965	164 159	183 806	...	...	...	...	...
Burgos	178 437	85 343	93 094	...	...	...	...	...
Cádiz	122 365	57 916	64 449	...	...	...	...	...
Cartagena	217 046	108 889	108 157	...	...	...	...	...
Castellón de la Plana	177 013	86 568	90 445	...	...	...	...	...
Córdoba	328 373	157 837	170 536	...	...	...	...	...
Donostia - San Sebastián	186 313	87 456	98 857	...	...	...	...	...
Dos Hermanas	130 044	64 222	65 822	...	...	...	...	...
Elche	229 436	114 014	115 422	...	...	...	...	...
Fuenlabrada	196 692	98 082	98 610	...	...	...	...	...
Getafe	172 792	84 991	87 801	...	...	...	...	...
Gijón	275 505	130 094	145 411	...	...	...	...	...
Granada	237 679	110 578	127 101	...	...	...	...	...
Hospitalet de Llobregat	236 613	116 287	120 326	...	...	...	...	...
Huelva	147 657	71 077	76 580	...	...	...	...	...
Jaén	116 007	55 979	60 028	...	...	...	...	...
Jérez de la Frontera	211 948	103 825	108 123	...	...	...	...	...
Leganés	186 846	91 415	95 431	...	...	...	...	...
León	130 076	59 422	70 654	...	...	...	...	...
Lleida	139 493	69 103	70 390	...	...	...	...	...
Logroño	152 514	73 002	79 512	...	...	...	...	...
MADRID	3 186 241	1 483 791	1 702 450	...	...	...	...	...
Málaga	567 696	273 075	294 621	...	...	...	...	...
Marbella	140 349	68 239	72 110	...	...	...	...	...
Mataró	122 155	61 070	61 085	...	...	...	...	...
Móstoles	206 082	101 337	104 745	...	...	...	...	...
Murcia	438 979	215 065	223 914	...	...	...	...	...
Ourense	107 224	49 168	58 056	...	...	...	...	...

Continent, country or area, date, code[a] and city / Continent, pays ou zone, date, code[a] et ville	City proper - Ville proprement dite				Urban agglomeration - Agglomération urbaine			
	Population			Surface area - Superficie (km²)	Population			Surface area - Superficie (km²)
	Both sexes - Les deux sexes	Male - Masculin	Female - Féminin		Both sexes - Les deux sexes	Male - Masculin	Female - Féminin	
EUROPE								
Spain - Espagne[24]								
1 VII 2013 (ESDJ)								
Oviedo	224 427	104 555	119 872	...	...	...	...	...
Palma de Mallorca	398 628	194 281	204 347	...	...	...	...	...
Palmas de Gran Canaria	382 667	186 014	196 653	...	...	...	...	...
Pamplona	196 561	93 706	102 855	...	...	...	...	...
Parla	125 479	63 246	62 233	...	...	...	...	...
Reus	105 876	51 646	54 230	...	...	...	...	...
Sabadell	207 547	101 040	106 507	...	...	...	...	...
Salamanca	148 785	68 236	80 549	...	...	...	...	...
San Cristóbal de La Laguna	152 364	74 229	78 135	...	...	...	...	...
Santa Coloma de Gramanet	166 897	82 879	84 018	...	...	...	...	...
Santa Cruz de Tenerife	205 936	98 529	107 407	...	...	...	...	...
Santander	176 430	81 610	94 820	...	...	...	...	...
Sevilla	698 423	331 916	366 507	...	...	...	...	...
Tarragona	132 872	65 033	67 839	...	...	...	...	...
Telde	102 123	50 607	51 516	...	...	...	...	...
Terrassa	169 808	84 157	85 651	...	...	...	...	...
Torrejón de Ardoz	125 320	62 388	62 932	...	...	...	...	...
Valencia	789 364	376 965	412 399	...	...	...	...	...
Valladolid	308 272	145 691	162 581	...	...	...	...	...
Vigo	295 738	140 843	154 895	...	...	...	...	...
Vitoria-Gasteiz	241 734	118 517	123 217	...	...	...	...	...
Zaragoza	674 031	324 966	349 065	...	...	...	...	...
Sweden - Suède								
1 VII 2007 (ESDJ)								
Göteborg	491 630	242 916	248 714	449	...	...	...	...
Helsingborg	124 188	60 672	63 516	346	...	...	...	...
Jönköping	122 952	60 462	62 490	1485	...	...	...	...
Linköping	139 474	70 239	69 235	1431	...	...	...	...
Malmö	278 523	135 997	142 526	154	...	...	...	...
Norrköping	126 072	62 323	63 749	1491	...	...	...	...
Orebro	129 703	63 123	66 581	1371	...	...	...	...
STOCKHOLM	789 024	384 243	404 781	187	...	...	...	...
Umeå	111 503	55 549	55 955	2316	...	...	...	...
Uppsala	186 364	91 149	95 215	2465	...	...	...	...
Västerås	133 324	66 056	67 269	956	...	...	...	...
Switzerland - Suisse								
1 I 2016 (ESDJ)								
Baden-Brugg	30 212	15 157	15 055	19.5	109 255[76]	54 422[76]	54 833[76]	91.6[76]
Bâle	169 916	82 249	87 667	23.9	541 011[76]	264 042[76]	276 969[76]	695.9[76]
BERNE	131 554	63 140	68 414	51.6	410 894[76]	199 566[76]	211 328[76]	780.6[76]
Fribourg	38 489	19 084	19 405	9.3	105 406[76]	52 398[76]	53 008[76]	221.9[76]
Genève	198 072	95 146	102 926	15.9	579 227[76]	280 962[76]	298 265[76]	536.5[76]
Lausanne	135 629	65 235	70 394	41.4	409 295[76]	200 402[76]	208 893[76]	772.6[76]
Lugano	63 583	30 617	32 966	76	151 037[76]	73 335[76]	77 702[76]	303.9[76]
Luzern	81 295	38 967	42 328	29.1	226 091[76]	110 994[76]	115 097[76]	290.5[76]
St. Gallen	75 538	36 809	38 729	39.4	165 860[76]	81 805[76]	84 055[76]	318.6[76]
Winterthur	108 268	53 145	55 123	68.1	138 252[76]	68 084[76]	70 168[76]	148.5[76]
Zug	29 256	14 748	14 508	21.6	127 095[76]	64 219[76]	62 876[76]	225.8[76]
Zürich	396 955	197 241	199 714	87.9	1 334 269[76]	664 259[76]	670 010[76]	1305.1[76]
TFYR of Macedonia - L'ex-R. y. de Macédoine								
1 VII 2012 (ESDF)								
SKOPJE	536 271	262 676	273 595	...	...	...	...	...
Ukraine								
1 I 2013 (ESDJ)								
Alchevsk	110 878	50 786	60 092	49	...	...	...	...
Berdyansk	116 249	51 540	64 709	83	119 371	53 036	66 335	90
Bila Tserkva	206 990	95 422	111 568	34	...	...	...	...
Cherkasy	283 130	129 279	153 851	67	283 924	129 696	154 228	78
Chernihiv	290 269	133 477	156 792	78	...	...	...	...
Chernivtsi	255 084	117 029	138 055	153	...	...	...	...
Dnepropetrovsk	987 629	448 496	539 133	387	990 025	449 659	540 366	405
Dniprodzerzhynsk	241 330	108 459	132 871	118	248 237	111 564	136 673	138

8. Population of capital cities and cities of 100 000 or more inhabitants: latest available year, 1997 - 2016
Population des capitales et des villes de 100 000 habitants ou plus : dernière année disponible, 1997 - 2016 (continued - suite)

Continent, country or area, date, code[a] and city / Continent, pays ou zone, date, code[a] et ville	City proper - Ville proprement dite				Urban agglomeration - Agglomération urbaine			
	Population			Surface area - Superficie (km²)	Population			Surface area - Superficie (km²)
	Both sexes - Les deux sexes	Male - Masculin	Female - Féminin		Both sexes - Les deux sexes	Male - Masculin	Female - Féminin	
EUROPE								
Ukraine								
1 I 2013 (ESDJ)								
Donets'k	944 552	418 132	526 420	363	960 646	425 457	535 189	571
Enakievo (Yenakievo)	82 941	36 713	46 228	67	131 250	58 850	72 400	425
Evpatoria	104 289	46 505	57 784	43	120 473	53 898	66 575	66
Gorlivka	254 526	113 970	140 556	186	274 942	123 190	151 752	422
Ivano-Frankivsk	223 165	104 982	118 183	37	240 934	113 229	127 705	84
Kamenets Podolsky	102 039	47 523	54 516	29	...	...	...	...
Kerch	146 559	66 067	80 492	108	...	...	...	...
Kharkiv	1 431 461	659 700	771 761	350	...	...	...	...
Kherson	295 450	132 426	163 024	65	332 767	149 883	182 884	423
Khmelnitsky (Hmilnyk)	262 154	121 083	141 071	86	...	...	...	...
Kirovograd	231 181	104 288	126 893	96	239 253	107 962	131 291	103
Kramatorsk	163 831	72 928	90 903	77	197 392	88 449	108 943	356
Krasny Lutch	82 719	38 155	44 564	58	124 003	57 497	66 506	154
Krementchug	224 912	102 180	122 732	96	...	...	...	...
Krivoy Rog	654 964	294 972	359 992	430	657 760	296 390	361 370	431
KYIV	2 803 716	1 295 137	1 508 579	836	...	...	...	...
Lugansk	422 373	187 593	234 780	257	461 459	206 111	255 348	286
Luts'k	211 644	95 328	116 316	42	...	...	...	...
Lviv	723 605	338 326	385 279	149	751 225	351 409	399 816	171
Lysychansk	104 023	46 935	57 088	76	119 725	54 085	65 640	96
Makijivka	352 227	158 789	193 438	185	390 700	176 633	214 067	426
Mariupol	458 415	208 218	250 197	150	480 263	218 497	261 766	244
Melitopol	156 831	70 894	85 937	43	...	...	...	...
Nikolaev	491 693	222 669	269 024	260	...	...	...	...
Nikopol	120 774	53 710	67 064	50	...	...	...	...
Odessa	997 189	465 200	531 989	162	...	...	...	...
Pavlograd	111 013	50 995	60 018	59	...	...	...	...
Poltava	289 831	132 965	156 866	104	...	...	...	...
Rivne	246 911	113 057	133 854	58	...	...	...	...
Sevastopol	340 735	154 947	185 788	...	381 474	173 812	207 662	864
Sievierodonetsk	109 791	48 887	60 904	32	120 217	53 861	66 356	58
Simferopol	331 936	146 690	185 246	107	356 771	158 116	198 655	107
Slovyansk	115 333	50 262	65 071	61	134 218	58 891	75 327	74
Sumy	268 375	120 965	147 410	111	271 295	122 346	148 949	146
Ternopil	215 636	99 716	115 920	59	...	...	...	...
Uzhhorod	114 789	53 241	61 548	32	...	...	...	...
Vinnitsa	369 860	169 356	200 504	69	...	...	...	...
Yevpatoriya	104 289	46 505	57 784	43	120 473	53 898	66 575	66
Zaporozhye	766 736	346 450	420 286	278	...	...	...	...
Zhytomyr	270 046	124 389	145 657	61	...	...	...	...
United Kingdom of Great Britain and Northern Ireland - Royaume-Uni de Grande-Bretagne et d'Irlande du Nord[77]								
27 III 2011 (CDJC)								
Aberdeen	207 932	102 858	105 078	...	...	...	...	...
Belfast	280 211	134 693	145 518	...	...	...	...	...
Birmingham	1 085 810	534 038	551 772	...	...	...	...	...
Bolton	194 189	95 924	98 265	...	...	...	...	...
Bournemouth	187 503	93 390	94 113	...	...	...	...	...
Bradford	349 561	173 024	176 537	...	...	...	...	...
Brighton and Hove	229 700	115 245	114 455	...	...	...	...	...
Bristol	535 907	265 968	269 939	...	...	...	...	...
Cardiff	335 145	164 427	170 718	...	...	...	...	...
Coventry	325 949	162 069	163 880	...	...	...	...	...
Derby	255 394	126 402	128 992	...	...	...	...	...
Edinburgh	482 005	234 608	247 397	...	...	...	...	...
Glasgow[78]	1 209 143	580 857	628 286	...	...	...	...	...
Kingston-upon-Hull	284 321	141 905	142 416	...	...	...	...	...
Leeds	474 632	233 488	241 144	...	...	...	...	...
Leicester	443 760	218 722	225 038	...	...	...	...	...
Liverpool	552 267	271 342	280 925	...	...	...	...	...
LONDON[79]	8 135 667	4 015 297	4 120 370	...	...	...	...	...
Luton	211 228	105 905	105 323	...	...	...	...	...

Continent, country or area, date, code[a] and city Continent, pays ou zone, date, code[a] et ville	City proper - Ville proprement dite				Urban agglomeration - Agglomération urbaine			
	Population			Surface area - Superficie (km²)	Population			Surface area - Superficie (km²)
	Both sexes - Les deux sexes	Male - Masculin	Female - Féminin		Both sexes - Les deux sexes	Male - Masculin	Female - Féminin	
EUROPE								
United Kingdom of Great Britain and Northern Ireland - Royaume-Uni de Grande-Bretagne et d'Irlande du Nord[77]								
27 III 2011 (CDJC)								
Manchester	510 746	256 984	253 762	...	...	...	...	...
Newcastle-upon-Tyne	268 064	134 375	133 689	...	...	...	...	...
Northampton	215 173	105 617	109 556	...	...	...	...	...
Nottingham	289 301	145 855	143 446	...	...	...	...	...
Plymouth	234 982	116 444	118 538	...	...	...	...	...
Portsmouth	238 137	119 369	118 768	...	...	...	...	...
Reading	218 705	109 236	109 469	...	...	...	...	...
Sheffield	518 090	255 755	262 335	...	...	...	...	...
Southampton	253 651	127 630	126 021	...	...	...	...	...
Stoke-on-Trent	270 726	134 642	136 084	...	...	...	...	...
Wolverhampton	210 319	104 047	106 272	...	...	...	...	...
OCEANIA - OCÉANIE								
American Samoa - Samoas américaines[22]								
1 IV 2010 (CDJC)								
PAGO PAGO	3 656	...	...	...	...	...	...	...
Australia - Australie[80]								
1 VII 2015 (ESDJ)								
Adelaide	1 288 681	633 385	655 296	2024.4	...	...	...	...
Brisbane	2 209 453	1 096 906	1 112 547	5065.1	...	...	...	...
Cairns	147 993	72 789	75 204	254.3	...	...	...	...
Canberra-Queanbeyan	424 666	211 067	213 599	482.3	...	...	...	...
Central Coast	325 082	157 763	167 319	566.2	...	...	...	...
Darwin	123 396	64 943	58 453	294.7	...	...	...	...
Geelong	187 417	92 540	94 877	918.8	...	...	...	...
Gold Coast-Tweed Heads	624 918	305 093	319 825	1402.8	...	...	...	...
Greater Adelaide	...	...	...	...	1 316 779	647 441	669 338	3257.7
Greater Brisbane	...	...	...	...	2 308 720	1 146 755	1 161 965	15825.9
Greater Darwin	...	...	...	...	142 258	74 783	67 475	3163.9
Greater Hobart	...	...	...	...	220 953	109 385	111 568	1695.5
Greater Melbourne	...	...	...	...	4 529 496	2 236 519	2 292 977	9990.5
Greater Perth	...	...	...	...	2 039 193	1 019 446	1 019 747	6417.9
Greater Sydney	...	...	...	...	4 920 970	2 438 529	2 482 441	12367.7
Hobart	209 254	103 418	105 836	1212.6	...	...	...	...
Melbourne	4 353 514	2 149 232	2 204 282	5679.3	...	...	...	...
Newcastle-Maitland	434 454	215 823	218 631	1018.9	...	...	...	...
Perth	1 958 912	978 882	980 030	3367.1	...	...	...	...
Sunshine Coast	302 122	146 296	155 826	1633	...	...	...	...
Sydney	4 526 479	2 245 652	2 280 827	4063.7	...	...	...	...
Toowoomba	114 622	55 445	59 177	498.1	...	...	...	...
Townsville	180 333	89 899	90 434	696.2	...	...	...	...
Wollongong	292 388	145 439	146 949	572.2	...	...	...	...
Cook Islands - Îles Cook[81]								
1 XII 2011 (CDFC)								
RAROTONGA	13 095	...	...	...	...	...	...	...
Fiji - Fidji								
16 IX 2007 (CDFC)								
SUVA	74 481	37 032	37 449	...	...	...	...	...
French Polynesia - Polynésie française								
22 VIII 2012 (CDJC)								
PAPEETE	25 763	12 971	12 792	...	...	...	...	...
Guam								
1 VII 2010 (ESDJ)								
AGANA	1 051	625	426	3	...	...	...	...
Kiribati								
7 XII 2005 (CDFC)								
TARAWA	...	...	...	...	40 311	...	...	...

8. Population of capital cities and cities of 100 000 or more inhabitants: latest available year, 1997 - 2016
Population des capitales et des villes de 100 000 habitants ou plus : dernière année disponible, 1997 - 2016 (continued - suite)

Continent, country or area, date, code[a] and city / Continent, pays ou zone, date, code[a] et ville	City proper - Ville proprement dite				Urban agglomeration - Agglomération urbaine			
	Population			Surface area - Superficie (km²)	Population			Surface area - Superficie (km²)
	Both sexes - Les deux sexes	Male - Masculin	Female - Féminin		Both sexes - Les deux sexes	Male - Masculin	Female - Féminin	
OCEANIA - OCÉANIE								
Marshall Islands - Îles Marshall								
3 IV 2011 (CDFC)								
MAJURO	27 797	...	...	...	...	...	...	...
Micronesia (Federated States of) - Micronésie (États fédérés de)								
1 IV 2000 (CDJC)								
PALIKIR	6 227	...	...	...	...	...	...	...
New Caledonia - Nouvelle-Calédonie								
26 VIII 2014 (CDFC)								
NOUMEA	99 926	49 218	50 708	...	...	...	...	...
New Zealand - Nouvelle-Zélande[82]								
1 VII 2016 (ESDJ)								
Auckland	1 614 400	794 300	820 100	4938	...	...	...	...
Christchurch	374 900	188 200	186 700	1415	...	...	...	...
Dunedin	127 000	61 500	65 500	3287	...	...	...	...
Hamilton	161 200	78 100	83 100	110	...	...	...	...
Lower Hutt	103 400	50 500	52 900	376	...	...	...	...
Napier-Hastings	...	...	...	...	131 000	62 700	68 400	390
Tauranga	128 200	61 200	67 000	134	...	...	...	...
WELLINGTON	207 900	102 000	105 900	290	...	...	...	...
Niue - Nioué								
11 IX 2011 (CDFC)								
ALOFI	639	311	328	...	...	...	...	...
Norfolk Island - Île Norfolk								
1 VII 1997 (ESDF)								
KINGSTON	*800*	...	...	...	...	...	...	...
Northern Mariana Islands - Îles Mariannes septentrionales								
1 IV 2010 (CDFC)								
GARAPAN	3 983	1 953	2 030	...	...	...	...	...
Palau - Palaos								
1 IV 2005 (CDJC)								
KOROR	...	...	...	...	12 676	...	...	...
Papua New Guinea - Papouasie-Nouvelle-Guinée								
9 VII 2000 (CDFC)								
PORT MORESBY	254 158	138 974	115 184	...	...	...	...	...
Pitcairn								
31 XII 2013 (CDJC)								
ADAMSTOWN	49	23	26	...	...	...	...	...
Samoa								
7 XI 2016* (CDFC)								
APIA	35 744	17 933	17 811	...	...	...	...	...
Solomon Islands - Îles Salomon								
22 XI 2009 (CDFC)								
HONIARA	64 609	...	...	...	80 082	...	...	...
Tonga								
30 XI 2011 (CDJC)								
NUKU'ALOFA	...	...	...	...	36 045	18 100	17 945	...
Tuvalu								
1 XI 2002 (CDFC)								
FUNAFUTI	4 492	2 281	2 211	...	...	...	...	...
Vanuatu								
16 XI 2009 (CDJC)								
PORT VILA	44 039	...	...	...	...	...	...	...
Wallis and Futuna Islands - Îles Wallis et Futuna								
21 VII 2008 (CDFC)								
META-UTU	1 126	...	...	...	...	...	...	...

FOOTNOTES - NOTES

The capital city of each country is shown in capital letters. Figures in italics are estimates of questionable reliability. For definition of city proper and urban agglomeration, method of evaluation and limitations of data see Technical Notes for this table. - Le nom de la capitale de chaque pays est imprimé en majuscules. Les chiffres en italique sont des estimations dont la fiabilité n'est pas assurée. Pour la définition de la ville proprement dite et de l'agglomération urbaine, et pour les méthodes d'évaluation et les insuffisances de données, voir les notes techniques pour ce tableau.

Italics: estimates which are less reliable. - Italiques : estimations moins sûres.

* Provisional. - Données provisoires.

^a 'Code' indicates the source of data, as follows:
CDFC - Census, de facto, complete tabulation
CDFS - Census, de facto, sample tabulation
CDJC - Census, de jure, complete tabulation
CDJS - Census, de jure, sample tabulation
SSDF - Sample survey, de facto
SSDJ - Sample survey, de jure
ESDF - Estimates, de facto
ESDJ - Estimates, de jure

Le 'Code' indique la source des données, comme suit :
CDFC - Recensement, population de fait, tabulation complète
CDFS - Recensement, population de fait, tabulation par sondage
CDJC - Recensement, population de droit, tabulation complète
CDJS - Recensement, population de droit, tabulation par sondage
SSDF - Enquête par sondage, population de fait
SSDJ - Enquête par sondage, population de droit
ESDF - Estimations, population de fait
ESDJ - Estimations, population de droit

[1] Data based on the 2011 Census. - Données fondées sur le recensement de 2011.

[2] Data refer to national projections. - Les données se réfèrent aux projections nationales.

[3] Population in households only. - Population dans les ménages seulement.

[4] Data refer to the city proper plus the peri-urban area. - Les données concernent la population de la ville proprement dite et de la zone périurbaine.

[5] Data refer to Greater Monrovia. - Les données concernent la région métropolitaine de Monrovia.

[6] Data refer to the urban commune of Antananarivo. - Pour la commune urbaine d'Antananarivo.

[7] Data refer to District de Bamako. - Les données concernent le district de Bamako.

[8] Excludes the islands of St. Brandon and Agalega. - Non compris les îles St. Brandon et Agalega.

[9] Data refer to resident household population. Data refer to total resident population, Saint Helenian and other nationalities. - Les données concernent la population des ménages résidente. Les données concernent la population résidente totale, originaire de Sainte-Hélène ou possédant une autre nationalité.

[10] Projections based on the 2002 Population Census. - Projections fondées sur le recensement de la population de 2002.

[11] Data refer to Greater Victoria. - Les données concernent la région métropolitaine de Victoria.

[12] Bloemfontein is the judicial capital, Cape Town is the legislative capital and Pretoria is the administrative capital. - Bloemfontein est la capitale judiciaire, Le Cap est la capitale législative et Pretoria est la capitale administrative.

[13] Data for urban agglomeration refer to urban center (municipality). - Les données de l'agglomération urbaine se rapportent au centre urbain (commune).

[14] Comprising the Northern Region (former Saguia el Hamra) and Southern Region (former Rio de Oro). - Comprend la région septentrionale (ancien Saguia-el-Hamra) et la région méridionale (ancien Rio de Oro).

[15] Population statistics are compiled from registers. - Les statistiques de la population sont compilées à partir des registres.

[16] Data refer to Kingston Metropolitan Area. - Données pour la zone métropolitaine de Kingston.

[17] Data based on the 2010 Population Census. - Les données sont fondées sur le recensement de la population de 2010.

[18] Including armed forces stationed in the area. Postcensal estimates. - Y compris les militaires en garnison sur le territoire. Estimations post censitaires.

[19] City refers to a type of incorporated place in 49 states and the District of Columbia, that has an elected government and provides a range of government functions and services. Also included among the cities on this list is Urban Honolulu, Hawaii Census Designated Place (CDP), for which the Census Bureau reports data under agreement with the State of Hawaii (instead of the combined city and county of Honolulu). - Par ville, on entend un lieu doté de la personnalité morale dans 49 États et dans le district de Columbia, qui a un gouvernement élu et fournit tout un ensemble de fonctions et de services publics. Sont également inclus Honolulu, lieu chargé du recensement pour Hawaii, pour lequel le Census Bureau établit les données en accord avec l'État de Hawaii (au lieu de la ville et du comté d'Honolulu).

[20] Excluding U.S. Armed Forces overseas and civilian U.S. citizens whose usual place of residence is outside the United States. - Non compris les militaires américains à l'étranger et les civils américains dont le lieu de résidence habituel est en dehors des États-Unis.

[21] Excluding inland water. - Exception faite des eaux intérieures.

[22] Including armed forces stationed in the area. - Y compris les militaires en garnison sur le territoire.

[23] Projections based on the 2010 Population and Housing Census. - Projections fondées sur le recensement 2010 de la population et des logements.

[24] Data refer to municipalities, which may contain an urban centre as well as rural areas. - Pour municipios qui peuvent comprendre un centre urbain et aussi une zone rurale.

[25] Excluding interior waters. - Eaux intérieures non comprises.

[26] Data exclude the population of the cities of Puente Alto and San Bernardo. - Les données ne comprennent pas la population des villes de Puente Alto et de San Bernardo.

[27] Data are revised projections taking into consideration also the results of the 2005 census. - Les données sont des projections révisées tenant compte également des résultats du recensement de 2005.

[28] Surface area includes interior waters. - La superficie comprend les eaux intérieures.

[29] Data excludes "temporary visitors". - Données n'incluant pas les « visiteurs temporaires ».

[30] The Metropolitan Area of Asunción is made up of Asunción and the 19 Central Department districts. - La zone métropolitaine d'Asunción est composée d'Asunción et de 19 districts du Département central.

[31] Estimates or projections based on the 2007 Population Census. - Estimations ou projections fondées sur le recensement de la population de 2007.

[32] Data refer to the Province of Lima and the Constitutional Province of Callao. - Les données concernent la province de Lima et la province constitutionnelle de Callao.

[33] Data refer to national projections. Data refer to the department of Montevideo. - Les données se réfèrent aux projections nationales. Les données concernent le département de Montevideo.

[34] Excluding foreign diplomatic personnel and their dependants. Data based on the 2008 Population Census. - Non compris le personnel diplomatique étranger et les membres de leur famille les accompagnant. Données fondées sur le recensement de population de 2008.

[35] Land area includes inland water (including reservoirs). - La superficie terrestre comprend les eaux intérieures (y compris les réservoirs).

[36] Because of rounding, totals are not in all cases the sum of the respective components. - Les chiffres étant arrondis, les totaux ne correspondent pas toujours rigoureusement à la somme des composants respectifs.

[37] The urban agglomeration of Lefkosia is composed of Lefkosia municipality, Agios Dometios, Egkomi, Strovolos, Aglangia, Lakatameia, Anthoupoli, Latsia and Geri. - L'agglomération urbaine de Lefkosia est composée de la municipalité de Lefkosia et Agios Dometios, Egkomi, Strovolos, Aglangia, Lakatameia, Anthoupoli, Latsia et Geri.

[38] The urban agglomeration of Lemesos is composed of Lemesos municipality, Mesa Geitonia, Agios Athanasios, Germasogeia, Pano Polemidia, Ypsonas, Kato Polemidia, and parts of Mouttagiaka, Agios Tychon, Parekklisia, Monagrouli, Moni, Pyrgos and Tserkezoi. - L'agglomération urbaine de Lemesos est composée de la municipalité de Lemesos et Mesa Geitonia, Agios Athanasios, Germasogeia, Pano Polemidia, Ypsonas, Kato Polemidia, et certaines parties des Mouttagiaka, Agios Tychon, Parekklisia, Monagrouli, Moni, Pyrgos et Tserkezoi.

[39] Data refer to "Baghdad Al-Jedeeda Nahia" - Les données concernent le district Al-Jadeeda de Bagdad (Baghdad Al-Jedeeda Nahiya).

[40] Designation and data provided by Israel. The position of the United Nations on the question of Jerusalem is contained in General Assembly resolution 181 (II) and subsequent resolutions of the General Assembly and the Security Council concerning this question. Including East Jerusalem. - Appelation de données fournies par Israel. La position des Nations Unies concernant la question de Jérusalem est décrite dans la resolution 181 (II) de l'Assemblée générale et résolutions ultérieures de l'Assemblée générale et du Conseil de sécurité sur cette question. Y compris Jérusalem-Est.

[41] Excluding diplomatic personnel outside the country and foreign military and civilian personnel and their dependants stationed in the area. - Non compris le personnel diplomatique hors du pays ni les militaires et agents civils étrangers en poste sur le territoire et les membres de leur famille les accompagnant.

[42] Land areas are based on the "Municipalities Area Statistics of Japan, 2015" published by the Geospatial Information Authority of Japan, Ministry of Land, Infrastructure, Transport and Tourism. - Les zones terrestres sont déterminées selon les statistiques relatives aux municipalités du Japon en 2015, publiées par l'Autorité japonaise d'information géospatiale du Ministère de l'aménagement foncier, des infrastructures, des transports et du tourisme.

[43] Data refer to annual average population. - Les données correspondent à la population annuelle moyenne.

44 Based on the results of the 2005 Population and Housing Census. - Données fondées sur les résultats du recensement de la population et de l'habitat de 2005.

45 Source: Living conditions of household survey, October 2011 to September 2012. - Source: Enquête sur les conditions de vie des ménages, octobre 2011 à septembre 2012.

46 Estimates based on the adjusted results of the Population and Housing Census of 2010. - Les estimations sont fondée sur les résultats ajustées du recensement de la population et de l'habitat de 2010.

47 Including population from all eight townships. - Y compris la population des huit municipalités.

48 Excluding data for the Pakistan-held part of Jammu and Kashmir, the final status of which has not yet been determined, and for Junagardh, Manavadar, Gilgit and Baltistan. - Non compris les données pour la partie de Jammu-Cachemire occupée par le Pakistan dont le status definitif n'a pas encore été déterminé, et le Junagardh, le Manavadar, le Gilgit et le Baltistan.

49 Data for city proper refer to municipalities. - Les données concernant la ville proprement dite se rapportent aux municipalités.

50 Land area includes inland water. - La zone terrestre comprend les eaux intérieures.

51 Data exclude residents who have been away from Singapore for a continuous period of 12 months or longer as at the reference date. - Non compris les résidents hors de Singapour pour une période ininterrompue de 12 mois ou plus avant de la date de référence.

52 The land area of Singapore comprises the mainland and other islands. - La superficie terrestre de Singapour comprend l'île principale et les autres îles.

53 The Population and Housing Census 2001 did not cover the whole area of the country due to the security problems; data refer to the 18 districts for which the census was completed only (in three districts it was not possible to conduct the census at all and in four districts it was partially conducted). - Le recensement de la population et du logement de 2001 n'a pas été réalisé sur la superficie totale du pays à cause de problèmes de sécurité; les données ne concernent que les 18 districts entièrement recensés (3 districts n'ont pas été recensés du tout, et 4 ont été recensés en partie).

54 Designation and data provided by the State of Palestine. The position of the United Nations on the question of Jerusalem is contained in General Assembly resolution 181 (II) and subsequent resolutions of the General Assembly and the Security Council concerning this question. - Appellation de données fournies par l'État de Palestine. La position des Nations Unies concernant la question de Jérusalem est décrite dans la résolution 181 (II) de l'Assemblée générale et résolutions ultérieures de l'Assemblée générale et du Conseil de sécurité sur cette question.

55 Data refer to urban area of municipality of Dili. - Les données se réfèrent à la zone urbaine de la municipalité de Dili.

56 Data based on Address Based Population Registration System. - Les données sont basées sur le registre national de la population basé sur l'adresse.

57 Data refer to resident population. - Les données concernent la population résidente.

58 Data include Anderlecht and Schaerbeek. - Les données comprennent Anderlecht et Schaerbeek.

59 Excluding Faeroe Islands and Greenland shown separately, if available. - Non compris les Iles Féroé et le Groenland, qui font l'objet de rubriques distinctes, si disponible.

60 Urban Agglomeration refers to Tórshavn, Hoyvík, Argir and Hvítanes. - Agglomération urbaine fait référence à Tórshavn, Hoyvík, Argir et Hvitanes.

61 Excluding Åland Islands. - Non compris les Îles d'Åland.

62 City proper refers to commune or municipality. - La ville proprement dite se rapporte à la commune ou à la municipalité.

63 The city of Aix-en-Provence is part of the urban agglomeration of Marseille. - La ville d'Aix-en-Provence fait partie de l'agglomération urbaine de Marseille.

64 The communes of Argenteuil, Boulogne-Billancourt and Montreuil are parts of the urban agglomeration of Paris. - Les communes de Argenteuil, Boulogne-Billancourt et Montreuil font partie de l'agglomération urbaine de Paris.

65 Excluding military personnel, visitors and transients. - Non compris les militaires, ni les visiteurs et transients.

66 Data refer to the Vatican City State. - Les données se rapportent à l'Etat de la Cité du Vatican.

67 The boundaries of the city are related to the boundaries of the respective commune. Data refer to registered resident population. - Les limites de la ville correspondent aux limites de la commune respective. Les données concernent la population enregistrée résidente.

68 The urban agglomeration of the capital area includes the following communes: Bessastaðahreppur, Garðabær, Hafnarfjörður, Kjósarhreppur, Kópavogur, Mosfellsbær ,Reykjavík, Seltjarnarnes. - L'agglomération urbaine de la capitale comprend les communes suivantes : Bessastaðahreppur, Garðabær, Hafnarfjörður, Kjósarhreppur, Kópavogur, Mosfellsbær ,Reykjavík, Seltjarnarnes.

69 Including civilian nationals temporarily outside the country. - Y compris les civils nationaux temporairement hors du pays.

70 Figures for male and female population do not add up to the figure for total population, because they exclude 119 persons of unknown sex. - Les chiffres relatifs à la population masculine et féminine ne correspondent pas au chiffre de la population totale, parce que l'on en a exclu 119 personnes de sexe inconnu.

71 City is defined as an administratively separated area entitled to civil (municipal) rights. Data refer to usually resident population. - Une ville est définie comme une zone administrativement distincte dotée de droits municipaux. Les données concernent la population habituellement résidente.

72 Data refer to usually resident population. - Les données concernent la population habituellement résidente.

73 Excludes data for Kosovo and Metohia. - Sans les données pour le Kosovo et Metohie.

74 Excludes data for Kosovo and Metohia. Data for urban agglomeration refer to communes which are administrative divisions. - Sans les données pour le Kosovo et Metohie. Les données pour l'agglomération urbaine se rapportent aux communes qui sont des divisions administrative.

75 Data for urban agglomeration refer to communes which are administrative divisions. - Les données pour l'agglomération urbaine se rapportent aux communes qui sont des divisions administrative.

76 From 2015, urban refers to urban centers and areas under the influence of urban centers. - A partir de 2015, le territoire urbain inclut l'espace des centres urbains ainsi que l'espace sous influence des centres urbains.

77 Excluding Channel Islands (Guernsey and Jersey) and Isle of Man, shown separately, if available. - Non compris les îles Anglo-Normandes (Guernesey et Jersey) et l'île de Man, qui font l'objet de rubriques distinctes, si disponible.

78 Data refer to Greater Glasgow. - Les données concernent la région métropolitaine de Glasgow.

79 Data refer to Greater London. - Les données concernent la région métropolitaine de London.

80 Data based on the Australian Statistical Geography Standard (ASGS). The populations for Greater Sydney, Melbourne, Brisbane, Perth, Adelaide, Hobart and Darwin are based on the 'Greater Capital City Statistical Area (GCCSA)' level. All other cities are based on the 'Significant Urban Areas (SUA) statistical area' level. - Chiffres estimatifs basés sur la norme géographique australienne de statistique (Australian Statistical Geography Standard - ASGS). Les chiffres de population pour la région métropolitaine de Sydney, Melbourne, Brisbane, Perth, Adelaide, Hobart et Darwin sont basés sur le niveau de division statistique des grandes capitales régionales (Greater Capital City Statistical Area - GCCSA). Pour toutes les autres villes, les chiffres sont basés sur le niveau de division statistique des grandes zones urbaines (Significant Urban Areas - SUA).

81 Excluding Niue, shown separately, which is part of Cook Islands, but because of remoteness is administered separately. - Non compris Nioué, qui fait l'objet d'une rubrique distincte et qui fait partie des îles Cook, mais qui, en raison de son éloignement, est administrée séparément.

82 1. Land area excludes inlet, inland water and oceanic areas. 2. A city is a territorial authority which is a distinct entity, is predominantly urban in character, has a minimum population of 50,000 and is a major centre of activity within its parent region. 3. Urban agglomerations refer to main urban areas that are centres with populations of 30,000 or more. City proper: due to the establishment of new Auckland council in 2011, amalgamating former Auckland cities, including Manukau city, North Shore city, and Waktakere city, separate population estimates for these cities are not available. Napier-Hastings consist of two separate territorial authorities. Napier is a city, while Hastings is a district based on the New Zealand Standard Areas Classification. - 1. La superficie terrestre ne comprend pas les bras de mer, eaux intérieures et zones océaniques. 2. Une ville est une entité territoriale distincte à caractère essentiellement urbain, comptant au minimum 50 000 habitants et constitue un pôle qui rayonne sur toute la région environnante. 3. Les agglomérations urbaines sont des établissements humains importants comptant 30 000 habitants ou plus. La ville : avec la création de la nouvelle agglomération d'Auckland en 2011, qui regroupe également Manukau, North Shore et Waktakere, il n'y a plus d'estimations démographiques distinctes pour ces différentes villes. Napier-Hastings comprend deux entités territoriales. Napier est une ville, et Hastings est un district selon les critères du classement néozélandais des zones.

Table 9 - *Demographic Yearbook 2016*

Table 9 presents live births and crude birth rates by urban/rural residence for as many years as possible between 2012 and 2016.

Description of variables: Live birth is defined as the complete expulsion or extraction from its mother of a product of conception, irrespective of the duration of pregnancy, which after such separation, breathes or shows any other evidence of life such as beating of the heart, pulsation of the umbilical cord, or definite movements of voluntary muscles, whether or not the umbilical cord has been cut or the placenta is attached; each product of such a birth is considered live-born[1].

Statistics on the number of live births are obtained from civil registers unless otherwise noted. For those countries or areas where civil registration statistics on live births are considered reliable the birth rates shown have been calculated on the basis of registered live births.

For certain countries, there is a discrepancy between the total number of live births shown in this table and those shown in subsequent tables for the same year. Usually this discrepancy arises because the total number of live births occurring in a given year is revised but not the remaining tabulations.

Rate computation: Crude birth rates are the annual number of live births per 1 000 mid-year population.

Rates by urban/rural residence are the annual number of live births, in the appropriate urban or rural category, per 1 000 corresponding mid-year population. Rates are calculated only for data considered complete, that is, coded with a "C" and for estimates and live births statistics for the 12 month period prior to the census date, coded with a "|". These rates are calculated by the Statistics Division of the United Nations based on the appropriate reference population (for example: total population, nationals only, etc.) if known and available. If the reference population is not known or unavailable, the total population is used to calculate the rates. Therefore, if the population that is used to calculate the rates is different from the correct reference population, the rates presented might under- or overstate the true situation in a country or area.

Rates presented in this table are limited to those countries or areas having a minimum number of 30 live births in a given year.

Reliability of data: Each country or area has been asked to indicate the estimated completeness of the live births recorded in its civil register. These national assessments are indicated by the quality codes "C" and "U" that appear in the first column of this table.

"C" indicates that the data are estimated to be virtually complete, that is, representing at least 90 per cent of the live births occurring each year, whereas "U" indicates that data are estimated to be incomplete, that is, representing less than 90 per cent of the live births occurring each year. A third code "..." indicates that no information was provided regarding completeness.

Data from civil registers that are reported as incomplete or of unknown completeness (coded "U" or "...") are considered unreliable. They appear in italics in this table and rates are not calculated for these data.

These quality codes apply only to data from civil registers. If data from other sources are presented, the symbol "|" is shown instead of the quality code. For more information about the quality of vital statistics data in general, and the information available on the basis of the completeness estimates in particular, see section 4.2 of the Technical Notes.

Limitations: Statistics on live births are subject to the same qualifications as have been set forth for vital statistics in general and birth statistics in particular as discussed in section 4 of the Technical Notes.

The reliability of data, an indication of which is described above, is an important factor in considering the limitations. In addition, some live births are tabulated by date of registration and not by date of occurrence; these have been indicated by a plus sign "+". Whenever the lag between the date of occurrence and date of registration is prolonged and, therefore, a large proportion of the live birth registrations are delayed, birth statistics for any given year may be seriously affected.

Another factor that limits international comparability is the practice of some countries or areas not to include in live birth statistics infants who were born alive but died before the registration of the birth or within the first 24 hours of life, thus underestimating the total number of life births. Statistics of this type are footnoted.

In addition, it should be noted that rates are affected also by the quality and limitations of the population estimates that are used in their computation. The problems of under-enumeration or over-enumeration and, to some extent, the differences in definition of total population have been discussed in section 3 of the Technical Notes dealing with population data in general, and specific information pertaining to individual countries or areas is given in the footnotes to table 3.

The rates estimated from the results of sample surveys are subject to possibilities of considerable error as a result of omissions in reporting of births, or as a result of erroneous reporting of births that occurred outside the reference period. However, rates estimated from sample surveys have the advantage of the availability of a built-in and strictly corresponding population base.

It should be emphasized that crude birth rates - like crude death, marriage and divorce rates - may be seriously affected by the age-sex structure of the populations to which they relate. Nevertheless, they do provide a simple measure of the level of and changes in fertility.

The urban/rural classification of birth may refer to the residence of mother or the place of delivery, according to the national practice and it is provided by each country or area. In addition, the comparability of data by urban/rural residence is affected by the national definition of urban and rural used in tabulating these data. It is assumed, in the absence of specific information to the contrary, that the definitions of urban and rural used in connection with the national population census were also used in the compilation of the vital statistics for each country or area. However, it cannot be ruled out that, for a given country or area, different definitions of urban and rural are used for the vital statistics data and the population census data respectively. When known, the definitions of urban used in national population census are presented at the end of the technical notes to table 6. As discussed in detail in the technical notes to table 6, these definitions vary considerably from one area or country to another. Urban/rural differentials in vital rates may also be affected by whether the vital events have been tabulated in terms of place of occurrence or place of usual residence. This problem is discussed in more detail in section 4.1.4.1 of the Technical notes.

Earlier data: Live births have been shown in each issue of the *Demographic Yearbook*. Information on the years and specific topics covered is presented in the Historical Index.

NOTES

[1] *Principles and Recommendations for a Vital Statistics System Revision 3,* Sales No. E.13.XVII.10, United Nations, New York, 2014.

Tableau 9 – *Annuaire démographique 2016*

Le tableau 9 présente des données sur les naissances vivantes et les taux bruts de natalité selon le lieu de résidence (zone urbaine ou rurale) pour le plus grand nombre d'années possible entre 2012 et 2016.

Description des variables : La naissance vivante est l'expulsion ou l'extraction complète du corps de la mère, indépendamment de la durée de gestation, d'un produit de la conception qui, après cette séparation, respire ou manifeste tout autre signe de vie, tel que battement de cœur, pulsation du cordon ombilical ou contraction effective d'un muscle soumis à l'action de la volonté, que le cordon ombilical ait été coupé ou non et que le placenta soit ou non demeuré attaché ; tout produit d'une telle naissance est considéré comme « enfant né vivant »[1].

Sauf indication contraire, les statistiques relatives au nombre de naissances vivantes sont établies sur la base des registres de l'état civil. Pour les pays ou zones où les statistiques obtenues auprès des services de l'état civil sont jugées sûres, les taux de natalité indiqués ont été calculés par la Division de statistique de l'ONU d'après les naissances vivantes enregistrées.

Pour quelques pays il y a une discordance entre le nombre total des décès présenté dans ce tableau et ceux présentés après pour la même année. Habituellement ces différences apparaissent lorsque le nombre total des décès pour une certaine année a été révisé alors que les autres tabulations ne l'ont pas été.

Calcul des taux : Les taux bruts de natalité représentent le nombre annuel de naissances vivantes pour 1 000 habitants au milieu de l'année.

Les taux selon le lieu de résidence (zone urbaine ou rurale) représentent le nombre annuel de naissances vivantes, classées selon la catégorie urbaine ou rurale appropriée pour 1 000 habitants au milieu de l'année. Les taux ont été calculés seulement pour les données considérées complètes, c'est-à-dire celles associées au code « C », ainsi que pour les estimations et les statistiques des naissances vivantes dans la periode des douze mois précédante la date de recensement associées au code « | ». Ces taux sont calculés par la division de statistique des Nations Unies sur la base de la population de référence adéquate (par exemple : population totale, nationaux seulement, etc.) si connue et disponible. Si la population de référence n'est pas connue ou n'est pas disponible, la population totale est utilisée pour calculer les taux. Par conséquent, si la population utilisée pour calculer les taux est différente de la population de référence adéquate, les taux présentés sont susceptibles de sous ou sur estimer la situation réelle d'un pays ou d'un territoire.

Les taux présentés dans ce tableau se rapportent seulement aux pays ou zones où l'on a enregistré un nombre minimal de 30 naissances vivantes au cours d'une année donnée.

Fiabilité des données : Il a été demandé à chaque pays ou zone d'indiquer le degré estimatif de complétude des données sur les naissances vivantes figurant dans ses registres d'état civil. Ces évaluations nationales sont signalées par les codes de qualité "C" et "U" qui apparaissent dans la deuxième colonne du tableau.

La lettre "C" indique que les données sont jugées à peu près complètes, c'est-à-dire qu'elles représentent au moins 90 p. 100 des naissances vivantes survenues chaque année ; la lettre "U" signifie que les données sont jugées incomplètes, c'est-à-dire qu'elles représentent moins de 90 p. 100 des naissances vivantes survenues chaque année. Un troisième code, "...", indique qu'aucun renseignement n'a été communiqué quant à la complétude des données.

Les données provenant des registres de l'état civil qui sont déclarées incomplètes ou dont le degré de complétude n'est pas connu (code "U" ou "...") sont jugées douteuses. Elles apparaissent en italique dans le tableau. Les taux pour ces données ne sont pas calculés.

Les codes de qualité ne s'appliquent qu'aux données provenant des registres de l'état civil. Si l'on présente des données autres que celles de l'état civil, le signe "|" est utilisé à la place du code de qualité. Pour plus de précisions sur la qualité des données reposant sur les statistiques de l'état civil en général et les estimations de complétude en particulier, voir la section 4.2 des Notes techniques.

Insuffisance des données : Les statistiques concernant les naissances vivantes appellent toutes les réserves qui ont été formulées à propos des statistiques de l'état civil en général et des statistiques des naissances en particulier (voir la section 4 des Notes techniques).

La fiabilité des données, au sujet de laquelle des indications ont été fournies plus haut, est un facteur important. Il faut également tenir compte du fait que, dans certains cas, les données relatives aux naissances vivantes sont exploitées selon la date de l'enregistrement et non selon la date de l'événement ; ces cas ont été signalés par le signe '+'. Chaque fois que le décalage entre l'événement et son enregistrement est grand et qu'une forte proportion des naissances vivantes fait l'objet d'un enregistrement tardif, les statistiques des naissances vivantes pour une année donnée peuvent être considérablement faussées.

Un autre facteur qui nuit à la comparabilité internationale est la pratique de certains pays ou zones qui consiste à ne pas inclure dans les statistiques des naissances vivantes les enfants nés vivants mais décédés avant l'enregistrement de leur naissance ou dans les 24 heures qui ont suivi la naissance, pratique qui conduit à sous-estimer le nombre total de naissances vivantes. Lorsque ce facteur a joué, cela a été signalé en note à la fin du tableau.

La qualité et les limitations des estimations concernant la population ont également une incidence sur le calcul des taux. Les problèmes liés au sur-dénombrement ou au sous-dénombrement et, dans une certaine mesure, aux différences dans la définition de la population totale ont été abordés à la section 3 des Notes techniques relative aux données sur la population en général et des précisions sur certains pays ou zones sont données dans les notes se rapportant au tableau 3.

Les taux estimatifs fondés sur les résultats d'enquêtes par sondage comportent des possibilités d'erreurs considérables dues soit à des omissions dans les déclarations, soit au fait que l'on a déclaré à tort des naissances survenues en réalité hors de la période considérée. Toutefois, les taux estimatifs fondés sur les résultats d'enquêtes par sondage présentent un gros avantage : le chiffre de population utilisé comme base est, par définition, rigoureusement correspondant.

Il faut souligner que les taux bruts de natalité, de même que les taux bruts de mortalité, de nuptialité et de divortialité, peuvent varier très sensiblement selon la structure par âge et par sexe de la population à laquelle ils se rapportent. Ils offrent néanmoins un moyen simple de mesurer le niveau et l'évolution de la natalité.

La classification des naissances selon le lieu de résidence (zone urbaine ou rurale) peut se rapporter au lieu de résidence de la mère ou au lieu d'occurrence et correspond à celle indiquée par chaque pays ou zone. En outre, la comparabilité des données selon le lieu de résidence (zone urbaine ou rurale) peut être limitée par les définitions nationales des termes « urbain » et « rural » utilisées pour la mise en tableaux de ces données. En l'absence d'indications contraires, on a supposé que les mêmes définitions avaient servi pour le recensement national de la population et pour l'établissement des statistiques de l'état civil pour chaque pays ou zone. Toutefois, il n'est pas exclu que, pour une zone ou un pays donné, des définitions différentes aient été retenues. Les définitions du terme « urbain » utilisées pour les recensements nationaux de population ont été présentées à la fin des notes techniques du tableau 6 lorsqu'elles étaient connues. Comme on l'a précisé dans les notes techniques relatives au tableau 6, ces définitions varient considérablement d'un pays ou d'une zone à l'autre. La différence entre ces taux pour les zones urbaines et rurales pourra aussi être faussée selon que les faits d'état civil auront été classés d'après le lieu de l'événement ou le lieu de résidence habituel. Ce problème est examiné plus en détail à la section 4.1.4.1 des Notes techniques.

Données publiées antérieurement : Les différentes éditions de l'*Annuaire démographique* contiennent des données sur les naissances vivantes. Pour plus de précisions concernant les années et les sujets pour lesquels des données ont été publiées, se reporter à l'index historique.

NOTES

[1] *Principes et recommandations pour un système de statistique de l'état civil, troisième révision*, numéro de vente : E.13.XVII.10, publication des Nations Unies, New York, 2014.

9. Live births and crude birth rates, by urban/rural residence: 2012 - 2016
Naissances vivantes et taux bruts de natalité selon la résidence, urbaine/rurale : 2012 - 2016

Continent, country or area, and urban/rural residence / Continent, pays ou zone et résidence, urbaine/rurale	Code[a]	Number - Nombre					Rate - Taux				
		2012	2013	2014	2015	2016	2012	2013	2014	2015	2016
AFRICA - AFRIQUE											
Algeria - Algérie[1]											
Total	C	978 233	962 722	1 014 248	1 040 285	1 066 823	26.1	25.1	25.9	26.0	26.1
Benin - Bénin[2]											
Total	I	376 439	...	...	...	...	40.2	...	...	...	...
Botswana											
Total	U	40 856[3]	44 794[4]	41 741[5]	...	...	...	...	...	...	...
Burundi[6]											
Total	+U	221 289	248 395	253 698	266 820	...	...	...	...	...	...
Côte d'Ivoire[7]											
Total	I	...	...	841 081	...	...	...	...	37.0	...	...
Urban - Urbaine	I	...	...	354 285	...	...	...	...	31.0	...	...
Rural - Rurale	I	...	...	486 796	...	...	...	...	43.2	...	...
Egypt - Égypte											
Total	+C	2 629 769	2 621 902	2 720 495	2 696 231	...	31.9	31.0	31.3	30.3	...
Urban - Urbaine	+C	1 009 952	1 186 887	1 228 275	...	...	28.6	32.8	33.1	...	...
Rural - Rurale	+C	1 619 817	1 435 015	1 492 220	...	...	34.3	29.6	30.0	...	...
Ghana[8]											
Total	+U	475 731	463 409	...	...	...	...	...	...	...	...
Guinea - Guinée											
Total	+U	...	205 658	...	...	...	...	...	...	...	...
Total[9]	I	...	...	448 218	...	...	...	...	42.3	...	...
Urban - Urbaine[9]	I	...	...	133 580	...	...	...	...	36.2	...	...
Rural - Rurale[9]	I	...	...	314 637	...	...	...	...	45.5	...	...
Kenya											
Total	U	801 815	870 599	954 254	950 224	948 351	...	...	...	...	...
Lesotho											
Total	+U	1 718	...	...	...	...	...	...	...	...	...
Mauritania - Mauritanie[10]											
Total[11]	I	...	114 420	...	...	...	...	32.3	...	...	...
Urban - Urbaine	I	...	54 392	...	...	...	...	...	...	...	...
Rural - Rurale	I	...	58 008	...	...	...	...	...	...	...	...
Mauritius - Maurice[12]											
Total	+C	14 494	13 488	13 283	12 640	12 948	11.5	10.7	10.5	10.0	10.2
Urban - Urbaine	+C	5 416	5 059	5 158	5 150	5 302	10.6	9.7	10.0	10.0	10.3
Rural - Rurale	+C	9 078	8 429	8 125	7 490	7 646	12.2	11.4	10.9	10.1	10.2
Mayotte											
Total	C	...	...	7 306	...	...	...	...	33.2	...	...
Mozambique[13]											
Total	U	624 523	746 185	794 718	...	...	...	...	...	...	...
Reunion - Réunion[14]											
Total	C	...	...	14 095	...	...	...	...	16.7	...	...
Rwanda											
Total	U	404 067	...	...	...	...	...	...	...	...	...
Saint Helena ex. dep. - Sainte-Hélène sans dép.											
Total	C	32	35	48	40	35	7.8	8.3	10.9	8.9	7.5
Sao Tome and Principe - Sao Tomé-et-Principe											
Total	C	5 173	...	...	*5 022	...	27.6	...	...	...	...
Senegal - Sénégal[15]											
Total	I	471 629	478 898	...	...	...	35.7	35.5	...	...	...
Seychelles											
Total	+C	1 645	1 566	1 557	1 592	...	18.6	17.4	17.0	17.0	...
Sierra Leone[16]											
Total	+U	148 958	229 947	...	...	...	...	...	...	...	...
Urban - Urbaine[17]	+U	18 392	...	...	...	...	...	...	...	...	...
Rural - Rurale[17]	+U	129 566	...	...	...	...	...	...	...	...	...
South Africa - Afrique du Sud											
Total	U	926 726	939 011	954 385	919 562	876 435	...	...	...	...	...
Tunisia - Tunisie											
Total	C	217 740	222 960	225 890	222 530	...	20.2	20.5	20.5	19.9	...
United Republic of Tanzania - République Unie de Tanzanie											
Total	...	1 694 943	...	...	...	...	...	...	...	...	...

Continent, country or area, and urban/rural residence / Continent, pays ou zone et résidence, urbaine/rurale	Code[a]	Number - Nombre					Rate - Taux				
		2012	2013	2014	2015	2016	2012	2013	2014	2015	2016

AMERICA, NORTH - AMÉRIQUE DU NORD

Anguilla											
Total	+C	192	165	151	165	...	14.0	11.9	10.6	11.2	...
Antigua and Barbuda - Antigua-et-Barbuda											
Total	+C	1 187	...	...	...	...	...	...	...	...	...
Aruba											
Total	C	1 288	1 346	1 376	1 244	1 121	12.3	12.7	12.8	11.4	10.2
Bahamas											
Total	+U	4 469	4 330	*4 196	...	...	...	...	...	...	...
Barbados - Barbade											
Total	+C	3 185	3 020	2 902	...	...	11.5	10.9	10.5	...	...
Belize											
Total	U	7 125	7 264	7 318	7 456	7 200	...	...	...	...	...
Urban - Urbaine	U	3 073	3 002	2 952	3 075	2 863	...	...	...	...	...
Rural - Rurale	U	4 026	4 227	4 339	4 353	4 301	...	...	...	...	...
Bermuda - Bermudes[18]											
Total	C	648	648	574	583	591	10.4	10.5	9.3	9.4	9.6
British Virgin Islands - Îles Vierges britanniques											
Total	C	286	277	280	266	...	10.1	9.7	...	9.1	...
Canada[19]											
Total	C	381 869	380 323	*388 729[20]	...	...	11.0	10.8	*10.9	...	...
Cayman Islands - Îles Caïmanes											
Total	C	759	705	711	649	...	13.5	12.5	12.5	11.0	...
Costa Rica											
Total	C	73 326	70 550	71 793[21]	71 819	*70 004	15.8	15.0	15.0	14.9	*14.3
Urban - Urbaine	C	25 472	24 883	41 631[21]	49 744	*48 392	7.5	7.3	12.0	14.2	*13.6
Rural - Rurale	C	47 854	45 667	30 162[21]	22 075	*21 612	37.8	35.6	23.2	16.7	*16.2
Cuba											
Total	C	125 674	125 880	122 643	125 064	116 872	11.2	11.2	10.9	11.1	10.4
Urban - Urbaine	C	98 301	98 894	96 930	99 434	93 565	11.6	11.5	11.2	11.5	10.8
Rural - Rurale	C	27 373	26 986	25 713	25 630	23 307	10.2	10.4	9.9	9.9	9.0
Curaçao											
Total	C	2 039	1 962	1 963	1 877	1 789	13.4	12.8	12.6	11.9	11.2
Dominica - Dominique											
Total	+C	951	931	858	...	...	13.4	13.1	12.0	...	...
Dominican Republic - République dominicaine											
Total	U	159 872	159 785	161 306	157 422	139 583	...	...	...	...	...
El Salvador[22]											
Total	C	110 843	109 617	108 903	109 617	...	17.7	17.4	17.2	17.0	...
Urban - Urbaine	C	75 808	68 432	62 372	...	...	18.5	16.5	...	...	...
Rural - Rurale	C	35 035	41 185	46 531	...	...	16.2	19.3	...	...	...
Greenland - Groenland											
Total	C	786	820	805	854	830	13.8	14.5	14.3	15.2	14.8
Urban - Urbaine	C	654	697	703	719	699	13.6	14.5	14.6	14.9	14.4
Rural - Rurale	C	132	123	102	135	131	15.4	14.9	12.7	17.2	16.9
Grenada - Grenade											
Total	+C	1 661	1 838	...	...	...	15.4	16.9	...	...	...
Guadeloupe[14]											
Total	C	5 233	5 069	5 001	...	...	13.0	12.6	12.4	...	...
Guatemala											
Total	C	388 613	387 342	386 195	391 425	...	25.8	25.1	24.4	24.2	...
Honduras											
Total	+U	196 119	...	...	...	...	...	...	...	...	...
Jamaica - Jamaïque[23]											
Total	C	39 348	*36 745	*37 892	*37 556	*35 959	14.5	*13.5	*13.9	*13.8	*13.2
Martinique[14]											
Total	C	...	4 130	4 367	...	...	...	10.7	11.4	...	...
Mexico - Mexique[24]											
Total	C	2 190 159	2 168 933	2 129 825	*2 353 596	...	18.7	18.3	17.8	*19.5	...
Urban - Urbaine[25]	C	1 563 853	1 523 223	1 563 395	...	...	18.4	17.8	18.0	...	...
Rural - Rurale[25]	C	515 520	483 583	464 897	...	...	16.0	14.8	14.1	...	...
Montserrat											
Total	+C	53	41	50	48	46	10.7	8.3	10.0	9.6	9.1

Continent, country or area, and urban/rural residence / Continent, pays ou zone et résidence, urbaine/rurale	Code[a]	Number - Nombre					Rate - Taux				
		2012	2013	2014	2015	2016	2012	2013	2014	2015	2016
AMERICA, NORTH - AMÉRIQUE DU NORD											
Panama											
Total	C	75 486	73 804	75 183	*75 901	...	19.9	19.2	19.2	*19.1	...
Urban - Urbaine	C	47 801	47 901	49 006	*48 960	...	19.0	18.6	18.5	*18.1	...
Rural - Rurale	C	27 685	25 903	26 177	*26 941	...	21.7	20.4	20.6	*21.3	...
Puerto Rico - Porto Rico											
Total	C	38 974	36 580	34 503	31 229	28 326	10.7	10.2	9.8	9.0	8.3
Urban - Urbaine	C	21 481	19 792	19 014[25]	18 986	18 194	...	...	...	...	...
Rural - Rurale	C	17 493	16 788	15 469[25]	12 243	10 132	...	...	...	...	...
Saint Kitts and Nevis - Saint-Kitts-et-Nevis											
Total	+C	636	547	641	...	...	...	...	...	...	...
Saint Lucia - Sainte-Lucie											
Total	C	*2 103	...	...	...	...	*12.4	...	...	...	...
Saint Vincent and the Grenadines - Saint-Vincent-et-les Grenadines											
Total	C	1 853	1 738	1 841	...	...	16.8	15.8	16.7	...	...
Sint Maarten (Dutch part) - Saint-Martin (partie néerlandaise)[26]											
Total	+C	414	511	...	...	...	11.9	14.0	...	...	...
Trinidad and Tobago - Trinité-et-Tobago											
Total	C	*18 729	*18 823	*18 729	*18 062	...	*14.0	*14.0	*13.9	*13.4	...
Turks and Caicos Islands - Îles Turques et Caïques											
Total	C	496	502	437	437	518	15.4	14.9	12.4	11.9	13.7
United States of America - États-Unis d'Amérique											
Total	C	3 952 841	3 932 181	3 988 076	3 978 497	...	12.6	12.4	12.5	12.4	...
United States Virgin Islands - Îles Vierges américaines[27]											
Total	C	1 415	...	...	...	...	13.4	...	...	...	...
AMERICA, SOUTH - AMÉRIQUE DU SUD											
Argentina - Argentine											
Total	C	738 318	754 603	777 012	770 040	...	17.7	17.9	18.2	17.9	...
Bolivia (Plurinational State of) - Bolivie (État plurinational de)											
Total	U	128 738	149 832	153 016	...	...	...	...	...	...	...
Total	+U	...	...	...	277 498	...	...	...	...	...	...
Brazil - Brésil[28]											
Total	U	2 830 458	2 832 590	2 913 121	...	...	...	...	...	...	...
Total	+C	...	...	...	2 952 969	...	...	...	...	14.4	...
Chile - Chili											
Total	C	243 635	242 005	250 997	*245 406	...	14.0	13.8	14.1	*13.6	...
Urban - Urbaine	C	219 348	220 276	228 458	...	...	14.5	14.4	14.7	...	...
Rural - Rurale	C	24 287	21 729	22 539	...	...	10.8	9.6	10.0	...	...
Colombia - Colombie											
Total	U	675 694	658 835	669 131	...	...	...	...	...	...	...
Urban - Urbaine	U	529 856	...	...	...	...	...	...	...	...	...
Rural - Rurale	U	145 838	...	...	...	...	...	...	...	...	...
Ecuador - Équateur[29]											
Total	U	297 309	277 620	278 460	*273 280	...	...	...	...	...	...
Urban - Urbaine	U	246 539	225 806	222 212	*215 808	...	...	...	...	...	...
Rural - Rurale	U	50 770	51 814	56 248	*57 472	...	...	...	...	...	...
Paraguay											
Total	+U	118 549	114 619	116 592	...	...	...	...	...	...	...
Peru - Pérou[30]											
Total	+U	414 081	475 349	492 008	529 029	*574 957	...	...	...	...	...
Urban - Urbaine	+U	...	...	...	384 757	...	...	...	...	...	...
Rural - Rurale	+U	...	...	...	144 272	...	...	...	...	...	...

9. Live births and crude birth rates, by urban/rural residence: 2012 - 2016
Naissances vivantes et taux bruts de natalité selon la résidence, urbaine/rurale : 2012 - 2016 (continued - suite)

Continent, country or area, and urban/rural residence / Continent, pays ou zone et résidence, urbaine/rurale	Code[a]	Number - Nombre					Rate - Taux				
		2012	2013	2014	2015	2016	2012	2013	2014	2015	2016
AMERICA, SOUTH - AMÉRIQUE DU SUD											
Suriname											
Total	C	10 217	10 012	10 407	10 148	...	18.9	18.2	18.6	17.9	...
Urban - Urbaine	C	6 852	6 792	6 898	...	...	19.1	...	...	...	...
Rural - Rurale	C	3 365	3 220	3 509	...	...	18.4	...	...	...	...
Uruguay											
Total	C	48 059	48 681	48 368	48 926	...	14.0	14.2	14.0	14.1	...
Venezuela (Bolivarian Republic of) - Venezuela (République bolivarienne du)											
Total	C	619 530	...	...	...	...	21.1	...	...	...	...
Total	U	...	597 902	597 773	600 860	...	...	...	...	...	...
ASIA - ASIE											
Armenia - Arménie											
Total	C	*42 333	*41 790	43 031	41 763	40 592	*14.0	*13.8	14.3	13.9	13.6
Urban - Urbaine	C	...	...	...	27 124	...	...	...	...	14.2	...
Rural - Rurale	C	...	...	...	14 639	...	...	...	...	13.4	...
Azerbaijan - Azerbaïdjan[31]											
Total	+C	174 469	172 671	170 503	166 210	159 464	18.8	18.3	17.9	17.2	16.3
Urban - Urbaine	+C	86 364	86 429	81 822	81 149	...	17.5	17.2	16.1	15.8	...
Rural - Rurale	+C	88 105	86 242	88 681	85 061	...	20.2	19.6	19.9	18.8	...
Bahrain - Bahreïn[32]											
Total	C	19 119	19 995	20 931	...	...	15.8	16.0	15.9	...	...
Bangladesh											
Total	U	2 933 000	...	...	...	...	...	...	...	...	...
Urban - Urbaine	U	701 000	...	...	...	...	...	...	...	...	...
Rural - Rurale	U	2 232 000	...	...	...	...	...	...	...	...	...
Brunei Darussalam - Brunéi Darussalam											
Total	+C	6 909	6 680	6 891	6 699	...	17.3	16.4	16.7	16.1	...
China - Chine[33]											
Total	I	16 350 000	16 400 000	16 870 000	16 550 000	...	12.1	12.1	12.4	12.1	...
China, Hong Kong SAR - Chine, Hong Kong RAS											
Total	C	91 558	57 084	62 305	59 878	60 856	12.8	8.0	8.6	8.2	8.3
China, Macao SAR - Chine, Macao RAS											
Total	C	7 315	6 571	7 360	7 055	*7 146	12.9	11.1	11.8	11.0	...
Cyprus - Chypre[34]											
Total	C	10 161	9 341	9 258	9 170	*9 455	11.8	10.8	10.9	10.8	*11.1
Georgia - Géorgie											
Total	C	57 031	57 878	60 635	59 249	56 569	12.7	12.9	16.3	15.9	15.2
Urban - Urbaine	C	...	...	...	33 898	32 227	...	...	...	15.9	15.1
Rural - Rurale	C	...	...	...	25 351	24 342	...	...	...	15.9	15.3
India - Inde[35]											
Total	I	...	...	...	...	...	21.6	21.4	21.0	20.8	...
Urban - Urbaine	I	...	...	...	...	...	17.4	17.3	17.4	17.3	...
Rural - Rurale	I	...	...	...	...	...	23.1	22.9	22.7	22.4	...
Iran (Islamic Republic of) - Iran (République islamique d')[36]											
Total	+C	1 421 689	1 471 834	1 534 362	1 570 219[37]	...	18.7	19.1	19.7	19.9	...
Urban - Urbaine	+C	1 129 477	1 131 566	1 178 921	1 208 142[37]	...	20.7	20.4	20.9	21.1	...
Rural - Rurale	+C	292 212	340 268	355 441	362 077[37]	...	13.7	15.9	16.6	16.9	...
Iraq											
Total	U	...	*1 077 645	...	...	...	...	...	...	...	...
Israel - Israël[38]											
Total	C	170 940	171 444	176 427	178 723	*181 127	21.6	21.3	21.5	21.3	...
Urban - Urbaine	C	155 178	155 127	160 223	162 225	...	21.4	21.1	21.4	21.2	...
Rural - Rurale	C	15 762	16 317	16 204	16 498	...	23.3	23.6	22.7	22.4	...

Continent, country or area, and urban/rural residence / Continent, pays ou zone et résidence, urbaine/rurale	Code[a]	Number - Nombre					Rate - Taux				
		2012	2013	2014	2015	2016	2012	2013	2014	2015	2016
ASIA - ASIE											
Japan - Japon[39]											
Total	C	1 037 231[25]	1 029 816[25]	1 003 539[25]	1 005 677[25]	*976 979	8.1	8.1	7.9	7.9	*7.7
Urban - Urbaine[40]	C	953 933	948 589	926 229	928 962	...	...	...	...	...	...
Rural - Rurale[40]	C	83 231	81 173	77 245	76 662	...	...	...	...	...	...
Jordan - Jordanie											
Total	C	177 695[41]	178 143[41]	188 902	198 018	...	23.9	22.0	21.5	20.8	...
Kazakhstan[31]											
Total	C	381 005	387 227	...	...	...	22.7	22.7	...	...	...
Urban - Urbaine	C	206 198	209 004	...	...	...	22.4	22.4	...	...	...
Rural - Rurale	C	174 807	178 223	...	...	...	23.0	23.2	...	...	...
Kuwait - Koweït											
Total	C	59 753	59 426	61 313	59 271	...	18.4	17.3	16.3	14.9	...
Kyrgyzstan - Kirghizstan											
Total	C	154 918	155 520	161 813	163 452	*158 160	27.6	27.2	27.7	27.4	*26.0
Urban - Urbaine	C	53 770	53 855	55 463	52 477	*51 610	28.6	28.0	28.2	26.1	*25.2
Rural - Rurale	C	101 148	101 665	106 350	110 975	*106 550	27.1	26.8	27.5	28.1	*26.5
Lebanon - Liban											
Total	C	94 842	95 246	104 872	...	...	...	...	...	...	...
Malaysia - Malaisie											
Total	C	526 012	503 914	528 612	521 136	...	17.8	16.7	17.2	16.7	...
Urban - Urbaine	C	357 877	344 410	357 848	350 677	...	16.8	15.6	15.8	15.1	...
Rural - Rurale	C	168 135	159 504	170 764	170 459	...	20.6	19.5	21.1	21.3	...
Maldives											
Total	C	7 431	7 153	7 245	6 896	...	22.5	21.3	18.0	20.1	...
Urban - Urbaine[42]	C	4 460	4 698	4 521	...	...	...	...	29.4	...	...
Rural - Rurale[42]	C	2 676	2 439	2 378	...	...	...	...	9.6	...	...
Mongolia - Mongolie											
Total	+C	73 839	79 780	82 839	82 130	79 920	26.0	27.5	28.0	27.1	25.9
Urban - Urbaine	+C	50 967	57 069	56 148	60 861	55 161	26.7	29.1	28.2	29.8	26.0
Rural - Rurale	+C	22 872	22 711	26 691	21 269	24 759	24.6	24.2	27.5	21.6	25.6
Myanmar											
Total	+U	856 279[43]	835 595[43]	736 369[44]	...	...	...	...	...	...	...
Urban - Urbaine[43]	+U	319 696	333 075	...	...	...	...	...	...	...	...
Rural - Rurale[43]	+U	536 583	502 520	...	...	...	...	...	...	...	...
Oman[45]											
Total	U	72 867	79 417	82 981	86 286	88 346	...	...	...	...	...
Philippines											
Total	C	1 790 367	1 761 602	1 748 857	1 744 767	...	18.6	17.9	17.5	17.2	...
Qatar											
Total	C	21 423	23 708	25 443	26 622	*24 895	11.7	11.8	11.5	10.9	*9.5
Urban - Urbaine	C	21 423	23 708	25 443	26 622	*24 895	...	...	11.5	10.9	*9.5
Republic of Korea - République de Corée[46]											
Total	C	484 550	436 455	435 435	438 420	...	9.6	8.6	8.6	8.6	...
Urban - Urbaine	C	402 650[25]	365 381[25]	364 615[25]	367 143	...	9.8	8.9	8.8	8.8	...
Rural - Rurale	C	81 843[25]	71 070[25]	70 818[25]	71 277	...	8.7	7.6	7.5	7.5	...
Saudi Arabia - Arabie saoudite[47]											
Total	I	457 339	454 450	452 003	449 149	447 040	15.7	15.4	15.1	14.5	14.1
Singapore - Singapour											
Total	C	42 663	39 720	42 232	42 185	41 251	11.2	10.3	10.9	10.8	10.5
Sri Lanka											
Total	+C	359 959	365 762	*349 715	*334 821	...	17.6	17.8	*16.8	*16.0	...
State of Palestine - État de Palestine[48]											
Total	U	131 632	127 454	128 073	124 331	...	...	...	...	...	...
Tajikistan - Tadjikistan[49]											
Total	U	219 281	209 417	229 460	...	...	...	...	...	...	...
Urban - Urbaine	U	53 371	50 508	54 878	...	...	...	...	...	...	...
Rural - Rurale	U	165 910	158 909	174 582	...	...	...	...	...	...	...
Thailand - Thaïlande											
Total	+U	818 901	782 129	776 370	738 930	704 058	...	...	...	...	...
Timor-Leste[50]											
Total	I	...	...	...	36 202	...	...	...	...	31.0	...
Turkey - Turquie											
Total	C	1 292 380	1 294 088	1 345 286	1 325 783	1 309 771	17.1	16.9	17.3	16.8	...

9. Live births and crude birth rates, by urban/rural residence: 2012 - 2016
Naissances vivantes et taux bruts de natalité selon la résidence, urbaine/rurale : 2012 - 2016 (continued - suite)

Continent, country or area, and urban/rural residence / Continent, pays ou zone et résidence, urbaine/rurale	Code[a]	Number - Nombre					Rate - Taux				
		2012	2013	2014	2015	2016	2012	2013	2014	2015	2016
ASIA - ASIE											
United Arab Emirates - Émirats arabes unis[51]											
Total	...	89 578	93 539	95 860	97 328	...	...	...	...	...	...
Uzbekistan - Ouzbékistan											
Total	+C	625 106	679 519	718 036	734 141	...	21.0	22.5	23.3	23.5	...
Urban - Urbaine	+C	287 018	310 481	326 231	325 660	...	18.8	20.1	20.8	20.5	...
Rural - Rurale	+C	338 088	369 038	391 805	408 481	...	23.3	25.0	25.9	26.5	...
Yemen - Yémen											
Total	U	279 719	425 165[52]	...	...	...	...	...	...	...	...
EUROPE											
Åland Islands - Îles d'Åland											
Total	C	292	287	282	275	*293	10.3	10.0	9.8	9.5	*10.1
Urban - Urbaine	C	95	104	98	97	*112	8.4	9.1	8.6	8.5	*9.7
Rural - Rurale	C	197	183	184	178	*181	11.5	10.6	10.6	10.2	*10.3
Albania - Albanie											
Total	C	35 473	35 750	35 760	33 221	...	12.2	12.3	12.4	11.5	...
Andorra - Andorre											
Total	C	737	637	639	659	634	10.6	9.1	9.1	9.3	8.8
Austria - Autriche											
Total	C	78 952	79 330	81 722	84 381[53]	87 675[53]	9.4	9.4	9.6	9.8	10.1
Belarus - Bélarus											
Total	C	115 893	117 997	118 534	119 028	117 779	12.2	12.5	12.5	12.5	12.4
Urban - Urbaine	C	89 129	90 436	91 704	91 870	...	12.4	12.5	12.6	12.5	...
Rural - Rurale	C	26 764	27 561	26 830	27 158	...	11.8	12.4	12.3	12.7	...
Belgium - Belgique[54]											
Total	C	128 051	125 606	125 014	122 274	121 896	11.5	11.2	11.1	10.8	10.8
Urban - Urbaine	C	126 194	123 881	123 346	120 591	...	...	...	...	...	...
Rural - Rurale	C	1 857	1 725	1 668	1 683	...	...	...	...	...	...
Bosnia and Herzegovina - Bosnie-Herzégovine											
Total	C	32 072	31 103	29 247	...	*29 276	8.4	8.1	7.6	...	*8.3
Bulgaria - Bulgarie											
Total	C	69 121	66 578	67 585	65 950	64 984	9.5	9.2	9.4	9.2	9.1
Urban - Urbaine	C	51 658	...	50 704	49 486	...	9.7	...	9.6	9.4	...
Rural - Rurale	C	17 463	...	16 881	16 464	...	8.8	...	8.7	8.5	...
Croatia - Croatie											
Total	C	41 771	39 939	39 566	37 503	37 537	9.8	9.4	9.3	8.9	9.0
Urban - Urbaine	C	23 839	22 796	22 894	21 802	...	...	...	...	...	...
Rural - Rurale	C	17 932	17 143	16 672	15 701	...	...	...	...	...	...
Czechia - Tchéquie											
Total	C	108 576	106 751	109 860	110 764	112 663	10.3	10.2	10.4	10.5	10.7
Urban - Urbaine	C	79 812	78 469	80 841	81 413	...	...	10.2	10.5	10.6	...
Rural - Rurale	C	28 764	28 282	29 019	29 351	...	...	10.0	10.2	10.3	...
Denmark - Danemark[55]											
Total	C	57 916	55 873	56 870	58 205	61 614	10.4	10.0	10.1	10.3	10.8
Estonia - Estonie											
Total	C	14 056	13 531	13 551	13 907	14 053	10.6	10.3	10.3	10.6	10.7
Urban - Urbaine	C	9 653	9 286	9 452	9 553[25]	...	10.7	10.3	10.5	10.6	...
Rural - Rurale	C	4 403	4 245	4 099	4 353[25]	...	10.5	10.2	9.8	10.5	...
Faeroe Islands - Îles Féroé											
Total	C	619	626	639	608	...	12.8	13.0	13.2	12.4	...
Urban - Urbaine	C	250	237	266	229	...	13.9	13.0	14.5	12.3	...
Rural - Rurale	C	369	389	373	379	...	12.2	12.9	12.4	12.5	...
Finland - Finlande[56]											
Total	C	59 201	57 847	56 950	55 197	*52 645	11.0	10.7	10.5	10.1	*9.6
Urban - Urbaine	C	42 329	41 386	41 103	40 711	...	11.4	11.1	10.9	10.6	...
Rural - Rurale	C	16 872	16 461	15 847	14 486	...	10.0	9.8	9.5	9.0	...
France											
Total	C	790 290	781 621	781 167	760 421	*745 000	12.4	12.2	12.2	11.8	*11.5
Urban - Urbaine[57]	C	628 694	623 522	625 957	611 062	...	...	...	...	...	...
Rural - Rurale[57]	C	159 929	156 358	153 342	147 304	...	...	...	...	...	...
Germany - Allemagne											
Total	C	673 544	682 069	714 927	737 575	*770 000	8.4	8.5	8.8	9.0	*9.4

Continent, country or area, and urban/rural residence / Continent, pays ou zone et résidence, urbaine/rurale	Code[a]	Number - Nombre					Rate - Taux				
		2012	2013	2014	2015	2016	2012	2013	2014	2015	2016
EUROPE											
Gibraltar[58]											
Total	+C	461	426	488	492	...	14.2	13.0	14.7	14.7	...
Greece - Grèce											
Total	C	100 371	94 134	92 149	91 847	92 898	9.1	8.6	8.5	8.5	8.6
Urban - Urbaine	C	71 232	64 616	62 785	63 283	...	...	...	...	...	...
Rural - Rurale	C	29 139	29 518	29 364	28 564	...	...	...	...	...	...
Guernsey - Guernesey											
Total	C	674	667	627	620	654	10.7	10.6	10.0	9.9	10.4
Hungary - Hongrie											
Total	C	90 269	89 524[60]	93 281[62]	92 135[62]	95 361[62]	9.1	9.0	9.5	9.4	9.7
Urban - Urbaine	C	61 985[59]	61 996[61]	65 095[63]	63 961[63]	...	9.0	9.0	9.4	9.2	...
Rural - Rurale	C	27 278[59]	27 511[61]	28 166[63]	28 153[63]	...	9.0	9.1	9.7	9.7	...
Iceland - Islande											
Total	C	4 533	4 326	4 375	4 129	4 034	14.1	13.4	13.4	12.5	12.1
Urban - Urbaine	C	4 316	4 131	4 164	3 924	...	14.4	13.6	13.6	12.7	...
Rural - Rurale	C	217	195	211	205	...	10.6	9.5	10.2	9.8	...
Ireland - Irlande											
Total	+C	72 225	68 930	67 285	65 537	*63 897	15.7	15.0	14.6	14.1	*13.5
Isle of Man - Île de Man											
Total	+C	890	859	805	785	758	10.5	10.0	9.3	9.0	8.9
Italy - Italie											
Total	+C	534 186	514 308	...	...	...	9.0	8.5	...	...	...
Total	C	...	...	502 596	485 780	473 438	...	...	8.3	8.0	7.8
Jersey[24]											
Total	+C	1 124	1 029	985	1 021	...	11.4	...	9.8	9.9	...
Latvia - Lettonie											
Total	C	19 897	20 596	21 746	21 979	21 968	9.8	10.2	10.9	11.1	11.2
Urban - Urbaine	C	13 582	14 184	15 094	15 099	...	9.9	10.4	11.2	11.2	...
Rural - Rurale	C	6 315	6 412	6 652	6 880	...	9.6	9.9	10.4	10.9	...
Liechtenstein											
Total	C	357	339	372	325	*378	9.7	9.2	10.0	8.7	*10.0
Lithuania - Lituanie											
Total	C	30 459	29 885	30 369	31 475	30 623	10.2	10.1	10.4	10.8	10.6
Urban - Urbaine	C	21 393	20 195	20 989	21 589	...	10.7	10.2	10.7	11.1	...
Rural - Rurale	C	9 066	9 690	9 380	9 886	...	9.2	9.9	9.7	10.4	...
Luxembourg											
Total	C	6 026	6 115	6 070	6 115	6 050	11.3	11.3	10.9	10.7	10.5
Malta - Malte											
Total	C	4 130	4 032	4 191	4 325	*4 476	9.8	9.5	9.8	10.0	*10.3
Monaco[64]											
Total	C	979	992	974	1 067	938	27.2	26.8	26.4	28.4	24.6
Montenegro - Monténégro											
Total	C	7 459	7 475	7 529	7 386	7 569	12.0	12.0	12.1	11.9	12.2
Netherlands - Pays-Bas[65]											
Total	C	175 959	171 341	175 181	170 510	172 520	10.5	10.2	10.4	10.1	10.2
Norway - Norvège											
Total	C	60 255	58 878	58 976	58 815	58 890	12.0	11.6	11.5	11.3	11.2
Poland - Pologne											
Total	C	386 257	369 576	375 160	369 308	382 257	10.1	9.7	9.9	9.7	10.1
Urban - Urbaine	C	223 815	213 749	217 699	217 391	...	9.7	9.3	9.5	9.5	...
Rural - Rurale	C	162 442	155 827	157 461	151 917	...	10.8	10.4	10.5	10.1	...
Portugal[24]											
Total	C	89 841	82 787	82 367	85 500	87 126	8.5	7.9	7.9	8.3	8.4
Republic of Moldova - République de Moldova[66]											
Total	C	39 435	37 871	38 616	38 610	*37 356	11.1	10.6	10.9	10.9	*10.5
Urban - Urbaine	C	14 890	...	...	...	...	10.0	...	...	...	...
Rural - Rurale	C	24 545	...	...	...	...	11.9	...	...	...	...
Romania - Roumanie											
Total	C	201 104	182 313	193 103	197 491	*188 415	10.0	9.1	9.7	10.0	*9.5
Urban - Urbaine	C	108 425	98 351	105 389	108 744	*102 945	10.0	9.1	9.8	10.2	...
Rural - Rurale	C	92 679	83 962	87 714	88 747	*85 470	10.0	9.1	9.5	9.7	...
Russian Federation - Fédération de Russie[31]											
Total	C	1 902 084	1 895 822	...	...	...	13.3	13.2	...	...	...
Urban - Urbaine	C	1 355 674	...	...	...	...	12.8	...	...	...	...
Rural - Rurale	C	546 410	...	...	...	...	14.7	...	...	...	...

Continent, country or area, and urban/rural residence / Continent, pays ou zone et résidence, urbaine/rurale	Co-de[a]	Number - Nombre					Rate - Taux				
		2012	2013	2014	2015	2016	2012	2013	2014	2015	2016
EUROPE											
San Marino - Saint-Marin											
Total	+C	292	320	281	269	262	8.7	9.6	8.4	8.0	7.7
Serbia - Serbie[67]											
Total	+C	67 257	65 554	66 461	65 657	64 734	9.3	9.1	9.3	9.3	9.2
Urban - Urbaine	+C	45 869	45 657	46 036	45 640	...	10.7	10.7	10.8	10.7	...
Rural - Rurale	+C	21 388	19 897	20 425	20 017	...	7.3	6.9	7.1	7.1	...
Slovakia - Slovaquie											
Total	C	55 535	54 823	55 033	55 602	57 557	10.3	10.1	10.2	10.3	10.6
Urban - Urbaine	C	29 174	28 692	28 379	29 082	...	9.9	9.8	9.7	10.0	...
Rural - Rurale	C	26 361	26 131	26 654	26 520	...	10.7	10.5	10.7	10.6	...
Slovenia - Slovénie											
Total	C	21 938	21 111	21 165	20 641	20 345	10.7	10.3	10.3	10.0	9.9
Urban - Urbaine	C	10 675	10 698	10 707	10 871	...	10.4	10.2	10.2	9.8	...
Rural - Rurale	C	11 263	10 413	10 458	9 770	...	10.9	10.3	10.3	10.2	...
Spain - Espagne											
Total	C	453 348	424 440	426 076	418 432	*406 556	9.7	9.1	9.2	9.0	*8.8
Sweden - Suède											
Total	C	113 177	113 593	114 907	114 870	117 425	11.9	11.8	11.9	11.7	11.9
Switzerland - Suisse											
Total	C	82 164	82 731	85 287	86 559	87 883	10.3	10.2	10.4	10.5	10.6
Urban - Urbaine	C	61 490	62 250	64 109	74 039[68]	...	10.4	10.4	10.6	11.3	...
Rural - Rurale	C	20 674	20 481	21 178	12 520[68]	...	9.8	9.6	9.8	7.2	...
TFYR of Macedonia - L'ex-R. y. de Macédoine											
Total	C	23 568	23 138	23 596	23 075	23 002	11.4	11.2	11.4	11.1	11.1
Urban - Urbaine	C	13 379	13 259	13 764	13 357	...	...	...	...	...	...
Rural - Rurale	C	10 189	9 879	9 832	9 718	...	...	...	...	...	...
Ukraine[69]											
Total	+C	520 705	503 657	465 882[70]	411 781[70]	...	11.4	11.1	10.8	9.6	...
Urban - Urbaine	+C	341 599	330 284	...	...	...	10.9	...	...	...	...
Rural - Rurale	+C	179 106	173 373	...	...	...	12.6	...	...	...	...
United Kingdom of Great Britain and Northern Ireland - Royaume-Uni de Grande-Bretagne et d'Irlande du Nord[71]											
Total	C	812 970	778 358	775 908	776 746	*774 841	12.8	12.1	12.0	11.9	*11.9
OCEANIA - OCÉANIE											
American Samoa - Samoas américaines											
Total	C	1 175	1 161	1 084	...	...	18.5	18.5	17.5	...	...
Australia - Australie											
Total	+C	309 582	308 065	299 697	305 377	...	13.6	13.3	12.8	12.8	...
Urban - Urbaine[72]	+C	210 139	209 397	204 991	208 467	...	10.8	10.6	10.2	10.2	...
Rural - Rurale[72]	+C	98 569	97 514	93 173	94 561	...	29.6	29.1	27.6	27.9	...
Cook Islands - Îles Cook[73]											
Total	+C	259	256	204	*205	...	13.3	13.8	11.0	*11.0	...
Fiji - Fidji											
Total	+C	20 178	20 970	20 249	...	...	23.5	24.4	...	...	...
French Polynesia - Polynésie française											
Total	C	4 296	4 203	4 161	3 888	...	16.0	15.6	15.3	14.3	...
Guam[74]											
Total	C	3 604	3 329	3 396	3 367	3 433	22.5	20.8	21.1	20.8	21.1
Nauru											
Total	C	319	366	...	...	...	...	...	...	...	...
New Caledonia - Nouvelle-Calédonie											
Total	C	4 389	4 373	4 370	4 191	...	16.9	16.6	16.3	15.4	...

Continent, country or area, and urban/rural residence / Continent, pays ou zone et résidence, urbaine/rurale	Co-de[a]	Number - Nombre					Rate - Taux				
		2012	2013	2014	2015	2016	2012	2013	2014	2015	2016
OCEANIA - OCÉANIE											
New Zealand - Nouvelle-Zélande[75]											
Total	+C	61 179	58 716	57 243	61 038	59 427	13.9	13.2	12.7	13.3	12.7
Urban - Urbaine[25]	+C	53 916	51 480	50 355	53 205	51 849	14.2	13.5	13.0	13.4	12.8
Rural - Rurale[25]	+C	7 254	7 227	6 873	7 827	7 572	11.6	11.6	11.0	12.3	11.9
Norfolk Island - Île Norfolk[76]											
Total	+C	4	...	...	...	...	...	...	...	...	...
Northern Mariana Islands - Îles Mariannes septentrionales[27]											
Total	U	*853*	*686*	*517*	...	...	...	...	...	...	...
Palau - Palaos											
Total	C	268	229	...	...	...	12.7	...	...	...	...
Pitcairn											
Total	C	-	-	...	...	...	...	...	...	...	...
Samoa											
Total	+U	*2 393*	*4 631*	*8 493*	...	...	...	...	...	...	...

FOOTNOTES - NOTES

Italics: data from civil registers which are incomplete or of unknown completeness. - Italiques : données incomplètes ou dont le degré d'exactitude n'est pas connu, provenant des registres de l'état civil.

* Provisional. - Données provisoires.

a 'Code' indicates the source of data, as follows:
C - Civil registration, estimated over 90% complete
U - Civil registration, estimated less than 90% complete
| - Other source, estimated reliable
+ - Data tabulated by date of registration rather than occurence
... - Information not available

Le 'Code' indique la source des données, comme suit :
C - Registres de l'état civil considérés complets à 90 p. 100 au moins
U - Registres de l'état civil qui ne sont pas considérés complets à 90 p. 100 au moins
| - Autre source, considérée pas douteuses
+ - Données exploitées selon la date de l'enregistrement et non la date de l'événement
... - Information pas disponible

1 Excluding live-born infants who died before their birth was registered. Data refer to Algerian population only. - Non compris les enfants nés vivants décédés avant l'enregistrement de leur naissance. Les données ne concernent que la population algérienne.
2 Data are projections presented in Annuaire Statistique 2010. - Les données sont des projections présentées dans l'Annuaire Statistique 2010.
3 Source: Vital Statistics Report 2012. - Source: Vital Statistics Report 2012.
4 Source: Vital Statistics Report 2013. - Source: Vital Statistics Report 2013.
5 Source: Vital Statistics Report 2014. - Source: Vital Statistics Report 2014.
6 Data refer only to events recorded in hospitals and health centres. - Ces données ne concernent que les faits d'état civil enregistrés dans les hôpitaux et les centres de santé uniquement.
7 Data refer to the 12 months preceding the census in May. - Les données se rapportent aux 12 mois précédant le recensement de mai.
8 The coverage of registration is estimated at 66 per cent. - Le degré de complétude de l'enregistrement est évalué à 66 pour cent.
9 Adjusted number of births in households referring to the 12 months preceding the census in March. - Le nombre ajusté de naissances vivantes des ménages ordinaires se rapportent aux 12 mois précédant le recensement de mars.
10 Data refer to the 12 months preceding the census in March. - Les données se rapportent aux 12 mois précédant le recensement de mars.
11 Including nomadic population. - Y compris la population nomade.
12 Excludes the islands of St. Brandon and Agalega. - Non compris les îles St. Brandon et Agalega.

13 Source: Ministry of Health, National Directorate of Planning and Cooperation. - Source : Ministère de la santé, Direction nationale de la planification et de la coopération.
14 Excluding live-born infants who died before their birth was registered. - Non compris les enfants nés vivants décédés avant l'enregistrement de leur naissance.
15 Based on estimates and projections from 'Agence Nationale de la Statistique et de la Démographie'. - Données fondées sur des estimations et des projections provenant de l'Agence Nationale de la Statistique et de la Démographie.
16 Source: National Office of Births and Deaths. - Source : Le bureau national des naissances et des décès.
17 Unrevised data. - Les données n'ont pas été révisées.
18 Excluding non-residents and foreign service personnel and their dependants. - À l'exclusion des non-résidents et du personnel diplomatique et de leurs charges de famille.
19 Including Canadian residents temporarily in the United States, but excluding United States residents temporarily in Canada. - Y compris les résidents canadiens se trouvant temporairement aux Etats-Unis, mais ne comprenant pas les résidents des Etats-Unis se trouvant temporairement au Canada.
20 Data refer to the twelve months from 1 July of the current year to 30 June of the following year. - Les données font référence aux douze mois de 1 juillet de l'année actuelle à 30 juin de l'année suivante.
21 Definition of urban and rural distribution changed from the year 2014. - La définition de la répartition urbaine et rurale a changé depuis 2014.
22 Excluding children born in the country of non-resident mothers. - Exceptés les enfants nés dans le pays des mères non-résidentes.
23 Data have been adjusted for underenumeration. - Les données ont été ajustées pour compenser les lacunes du dénombrement.
24 Data refer to births to resident mothers. - Ces données concernent les enfants nés de mères résidentes.
25 The total number may include 'Unknown residence', but the categories urban and rural do not. - Le nombre total peut inclure les personnes dont la résidence n'est pas connue, à l'inverse des catégories de population urbaine et rurale.
26 Source: Population Registry and STAT/CBS estimates. - Source: Le registre de la population et les estimations du STAT/CBS.
27 Source: U.S. National Center for Health Statistics, National Vital Statistics Reports (NVSR). - Source : US National Center for Health Statistics, National Vital Statistics Reports (NVSR).
28 Including births abroad and births of unknown residence of mother. - Y compris les naissances à l'étranger et les naissances pour lesquelles le lieu de résidence de la mère est inconnu.
29 Excludes nomadic Indian tribes. - Non compris les tribus d'Indiens nomades.
30 Source: Reports of the Ministry of Health. - Source : Rapports du Ministère de la Santé.
31 Excluding infants born alive of less than 28 weeks' gestation, of less than 1 000 g in weight and 35 cm in length, who die within seven days of birth. - Non compris les enfants nés vivants après moins de 28 semaines de gestations,

pesant moins de 1 000 g, mesurant moins de 35 cm et décédés dans les sept jours qui ont suivi leur naissance.

32 Sources: Births and Deaths National Registration System database, and medical records of government hospitals. - Les sources: Les bases de données des << Births and Deaths National Registration System >> et les dossiers médicaux des hôpitaux du gouvernement.

33 Data have been estimated on the basis of the annual National Sample Survey on Population Changes. For statistical purposes, the data for China do not include those for the Hong Kong Special Administrative Region (Hong Kong SAR), Macao Special Administrative Region (Macao SAR) and Taiwan province of China. - Les données ont été estimées sur la base de l'enquête annuelle "National Sample Survey on Population Changes". Pour la présentation des statistiques, les données pour la Chine ne comprennent pas la Région Administrative Spéciale de Hong Kong (Hong Kong RAS), la Région Administrative Spéciale de Macao (Macao RAS) et Taïwan province de Chine.

34 Data refer to government controlled areas. - Les données se rapportent aux zones contrôlées par le Gouvernement.

35 Rates were obtained by the Sample Registration System of India, which is a large demographic survey. Includes data for the Indian-held part of Jammu and Kashmir, the final status of which has not yet been determined. - Les taux ont été obtenus par le Système de l'enregistrement par échantillon de l'Inde qui est une large enquête démographique. Y compris les données pour la partie du Jammu et du Cachemire occupée par l'Inde dont le statut définitif n'a pas encore été déterminé.

36 Data refer to the Iranian Year which begins on 21 March and ends on 20 March of the following year. - Les données concernent l'année iranienne, qui commence le 21 mars et se termine le 20 mars de l'année suivante.

37 Including births registered by Civil Registration Organization. - Y compris les naissances enregistrées par l'organisation chargée d'assurer l'enregistrement des faits d'état civil.

38 Includes data for East Jerusalem and Israeli residents in certain other territories under occupation by Israeli military forces since June 1967. - Y compris les données pour Jérusalem-Est et les résidents israéliens dans certains autres territoires occupés depuis 1967 par les forces armées israéliennes.

39 Data refer to Japanese nationals in Japan only. - Les données se raportent aux nationaux japonais au Japon seulement.

40 The total number may include 'Unknown residence', but the categories urban and rural do not. Urban and rural distribution refers to the residence of the child. - Le nombre total peut inclure les personnes dont la résidence n'est pas connue, à l'inverse des catégories de population urbaine et rurale. La répartition urbain/rural se réfère au domicile de l'enfant.

41 Excluding data for Jordanian territory under occupation since June 1967 by Israeli military forces. Excluding foreigners, including registered Palestinian refugees. - Non compris les données pour le territoire jordanien occupé depuis juin 1967 par les forces armées israéliennes. Non compris les étrangers, mais y compris les réfugiés de Palestine enregistrés.

42 Excluding births occurred abroad. - Hormis les naissances intervenues à l'étranger.

43 Source: "Department of Public Health" - Source : << Le Service de la santé publique >>

44 Data are from Vital Registration System (VRS). - Les données proviennent du système d'enregistrement des faits d'état civil.

45 Data from Births and Deaths Notification System (Ministry of Health and all health care providers). - Les données proviennent du système de notification des naissances et des décès (Ministère de la santé et tous prestataires de soins de santé).

46 Data refer to residence of child. Excluding alien armed forces, civilian aliens employed by armed forces, and foreign diplomatic personnel and their dependants. - Les données correspondent à la résidence de l'enfant. Non compris les militaires étrangers, les civils étrangers employés par les forces armées ni le personnel diplomatique étranger et les membres de leur famille les accompagnant.

47 Data refer to Saudi Arabian nationals only. Based on 2010 population census and 2016 demographic survey. - Les données ne concernent que les ressortissants saoudiens. D'après le recensement de la population de 2010 et l'enquête démographique de 2016.

48 Source: Palestinian Central Bureau of Statistics, Population Register, updated version 22/02/2016. - Source: Bureau central de statistique palestinien, registre de la population, version actualisée jusqu'au 22/02/2016.

49 Excluding infants born alive of less than 28 weeks' gestation, of less than 1 000 g in weight and 35 cm in length, who die within seven days of birth. Data have been adjusted for under-registration. - Non compris les enfants nés vivants après moins de 28 semaines de gestations, pesant moins de 1 000 g, mesurant moins de 35 cm et décédés dans les sept jours qui ont suivi leur naissance. Y compris un ajustement pour sous-enregistrement.

50 Data refer to the 12 months preceding the census in July. - Les données se rapportent aux 12 mois précédant le recensement de juillet.

51 The registration of births and deaths is conducted by the Ministry of Health. An estimate of completeness is not provided. - L'enregistrement des naissances et des décès est mené par le Ministère de la Santé. Le degré estimatif de complétude n'est pas fourni.

52 Including Non-Yemeni births. - Y compris les naissances non-yéménites.

53 Including births occurring abroad of mothers with residence in Austria. - Y compris les naissances survenues à l'étranger des mères avec résidence en Autriche.

54 Including armed forces stationed outside the country, but excluding alien armed forces stationed in the area. - Y compris les militaires nationaux hors du pays, mais non compris les militaires étrangers en garnison sur le territoire.

55 Excluding Faeroe Islands and Greenland shown separately, if available. - Non compris les Iles Féroé et le Groenland, qui font l'objet de rubriques distinctes, si disponible.

56 Excluding Åland Islands. - Non compris les Îles d'Åland.

57 The data for urban and rural exclude the nationals outside the country. - Les données relatives à la population urbaine et rurale n'englobent pas les nationaux se trouvant à l'étranger.

58 Including live births by military personnel and their dependants. - Y compris les naissances vivantes parmi les membres du personnel militaire et leurs personnes à charge.

59 The urban and rural categories do not include the data of foreigners, persons of unknown residence and the homeless, whereas the total category includes them. - Les chiffres portant sur la population urbaine et rurale n' incluent pas les données relatives aux étrangers, aux personnes dont la résidence n'est pas connue et aux personnes sans domicile fixe, à l'inverse, le total les inclut.

60 Till 2012 data refer to all live births occurred in Hungary. From 2013 data include the live births of women with Hungarian usual residence regardless of whether the live birth occurred in Hungary or in a foreign country, and do not include the live births of women with foreign country usual residence. Data include the live births of women with unknown residence and homeless. - Jusqu'en 2012 les données concernent toutes les naissances vivantes survenues en Hongrie. À partir de 2013, les données concernent les enfants nés vivants de femmes dont la résidence habituelle est en Hongrie, que la naissance vivante ait eu lieu en Hongrie ou dans un pays étranger, et ne comprennent pas les enfants nés vivants de femmes dont la résidence habituelle est dans un pays étranger. Les données incluent les enfants nés vivants de femmes dont la résidence n'est pas connue et de femmes sans domicile fixe.

61 Till 2012 data refer to all live births occurred in Hungary. From 2013 data include the live births of women with Hungarian usual residence regardless of whether the live birth occurred in Hungary or in a foreign country, and do not include the live births of women with foreign country usual residence. - Jusqu'en 2012 les données concernent toutes les naissances vivantes survenues en Hongrie. À partir de 2013, les données concernent les enfants nés vivants de femmes dont la résidence habituelle est en Hongrie, que la naissance vivante ait eu lieu en Hongrie ou dans un pays étranger, et ne comprennent pas les enfants nés vivants de femmes dont la résidence habituelle est dans un pays étranger.

62 Data include the live births of women with Hungarian usual residence regardless of whether the live birth occurred in Hungary or in a foreign country, and do not include the live births of women with foreign country usual residence. Data include the live births of women with unknown residence and homeless. - Les données concernent les enfants nés vivants de femmes dont la résidence habituelle est en Hongrie, que la naissance vivante ait eu lieu en Hongrie ou dans un pays étranger, et ne comprennent pas les enfants nés vivants de femmes dont la résidence habituelle est dans un pays étranger. Les données incluent les enfants nés vivants de femmes dont la résidence n'est pas connue et de femmes sans domicile fixe.

63 Data include the live births of women with Hungarian usual residence regardless of whether the live birth occurred in Hungary or in a foreign country, and do not include the live births of women with foreign country usual residence. - Les données concernent les enfants nés vivants de femmes dont la résidence habituelle est en Hongrie, que la naissance vivante ait eu lieu en Hongrie ou dans un pays étranger, et ne comprennent pas les enfants nés vivants de femmes dont la résidence habituelle est dans un pays étranger.

64 Source: City Hall, Civil Status Registry Office, resident and non-resident births. - Source : La mairie, Bureau de l'État Civil, toutes les naissances.

65 Including residents outside the country if listed in a Netherlands population register. - Englobe les résidents se trouvant à l'étranger à condition qu'ils soient inscrits sur le registre de population des Pays-Bas.

66 Excluding Transnistria and the municipality of Bender. - Les données ne tiennent pas compte de l'information sur la Transnistria et la municipalité de Bender.

67 Excludes data for Kosovo and Metohia. - Sans les données pour le Kosovo et Metohie.

68 From 2015, urban refers to urban centers and areas under the influence of urban centers. - A partir de 2015, le territoire urbain inclut l'espace des centres urbains ainsi que l'espace sous influence des centres urbains.

[69] Data refer to births with weight 500g and more (if weight is unknown - with length 25 centimeters and more, or with gestation during 22 weeks or more). - Données concernant les nouveau-nés de 500 grammes ou plus (si le poids est inconnu – de 25 centimètres de long ou plus, ou après une grossesse de 22 semaines ou plus).

[70] The Government of Ukraine has informed the United Nations that it is not in a position to provide statistical data concerning the Autonomous Republic of Crimea and the city of Sevastopol. - Le gouvernement Ukrainien a informé l'ONU qu'il n'est pas en mesure de fournir des données statistiques concernant la République autonome de Crimée et la ville de Sébastopol.

[71] Excluding Channel Islands (Guernsey and Jersey) and Isle of Man, shown separately, if available. Data tabulated by date of occurrence for England and Wales, and by date of registration for Northern Ireland and Scotland. - Non compris les îles Anglo-Normandes (Guernesey et Jersey) et l'île de Man, qui font l'objet de rubriques distinctes, si disponible. Données exploitées selon la date de l'événement pour l'Angleterre et le pays de Galles, et selon la date de l'enregistrement pour l'Irlande du Nord et l'Ecosse.

[72] Data for urban and rural figures do not add up to the total because they exclude the events occurred in Migratory, Special Purpose and Other Territories. Urban refers to Greater Capital City Statistical Areas, and rural refers to other areas within the state or territory. - La somme des chiffres des catégories « en zone urbaine » et « en zone rurale » ne correspond pas au total du fait qu'en sont exclus les événements qui ont eu lieu dans les territoires de migration, les territoires à destination spéciale et autres territoires. Urbain renvoie aux zones statistiques de la capitale métropolitaine, et rural aux autres zones de l'État ou territoire.

[73] Excluding Niue, shown separately, which is part of Cook Islands, but because of remoteness is administered separately. - Non compris Nioué, qui fait l'objet d'une rubrique distincte et qui fait partie des îles Cook, mais qui, en raison de son éloignement, est administrée séparément.

[74] Including United States military personnel, their dependants and contract employees. - Y compris les militaires des Etats-Unis, les membres de leur famille les accompagnant et les agents contractuels des Etats-Unis.

[75] Random rounding to base 3 is applied in this table as a confidentiality measure. - Les chiffres sont arrondis à la base 3 de manière aléatoire, pour des raisons de confidentialité.

[76] Data cover the period from 1 July of the previous year to 30 June of the present year. - Pour la période allant du 1er juillet de l'année précédente au 30 juin de l'année en cours.

Table 10 - *Demographic Yearbook 2016*

Table 10 presents live births by age of mother and sex of the child, general fertility rate, and age-specific fertility rates for the latest available year between 2007 and 2016.

Description of variables: Age is defined as age at last birthday, that is, the difference between the date of birth and the date of the occurrence of the event, expressed in completed solar years. The age classification used in this table is the following: under 15 years, 5-year age groups through 45-49 years, and 50 years and over. A different classification may appear as provided by the reporting country or area.

Rate computation: Age-specific fertility rates are the annual number of births to women in each age group per 1 000 female population in the same age group. These rates are calculated by the Statistics Division of the United Nations.

Since relatively few births occur to women below 15 or above 50 years of age, age-specific fertility rates for women under 20 years of age and for those 45 years of age or over are computed on the female population aged 15-19 and 45-49, respectively. Similarly, the rate for women of "All ages" is based on all live births irrespective of age of mother, and is computed on the female population aged 15-49 years. This rate for "All ages" is known as the general fertility rate. The age-specific fertility rates for age groups of women below 15 or 50 and above years of age are not calculated.

Births to mothers of unknown age are distributed proportionately across the age groups, by the Statistics Division of the United Nations, in accordance with the distribution of births by age of mother prior to the calculation of the rates.

The population used in computing the rates is the estimated or enumerated distribution of females by age. First priority was given to the estimated population and second priority to the enumerated population, i.e. to census returns of the year to which the births referred.

Rates presented in this table are limited to those for countries or areas having at least a total of 100 live births in a given year.

Reliability of data: Data from civil registers of live births which are reported as incomplete (less than 90 per cent completeness) or of unknown completeness are considered unreliable and are set in *italics* rather than in roman type. Rates are not computed if the data on live births from civil registers are reported as incomplete (less than 90 per cent completeness) or of unknown completeness. Table 9 and the technical notes for that table provide more detailed information on the completeness of live-birth registration. For more information about the quality of vital statistics data in general, see section 4.2 of the Technical Notes.

Limitations: Statistics on live births by age of mother are subject to the same qualifications as have been set forth for vital statistics in general and birth statistics in particular as discussed in section 4 of the Technical Notes. These include differences in the completeness of registration, the method used to determine age of mother and the quality of the reported information relating to age of mother.

The reliability of the data described above, is an important factor in considering the limitations. In addition, some live births are tabulated by date of registration and not by date of occurrence; these are indicated in the table by a plus sign "+". Whenever the lag between the date of occurrence and date of registration is prolonged and, therefore, a large proportion of the live birth registrations are delayed, birth statistics for any given year may be seriously affected. For example, the age of the mother will almost always refer to the date of registration rather than to the date of birth of the child. Hence, in those countries or areas where registration of births is delayed, possibly for years, statistics on births by age of mother should be used with caution.

Another factor which limits international comparability is the practice of some countries or areas of not including in live birth statistics infants who were born alive but died before the registration of the birth or within the first 24 hours of life, thus underestimating the total number of live births. Statistics of this type are footnoted.

Because these statistics are classified according to age, they are subject to the limitations with respect to accuracy of age reporting similar to those already discussed in connection with section 3.1.3 of the Technical Notes. The factors influencing the accuracy of reporting may be somewhat dissimilar in vital statistics (because of the differences in the method of taking a census and registering a birth) but, in general, the same errors can be observed. The absence of frequencies in the unknown age group does not necessarily indicate completely accurate reporting and tabulation of the age item. It is often an indication that the unknowns have been eliminated by assigning ages to them before tabulation, or by proportionate distribution after tabulation.

On the other hand, large frequencies in the unknown age category may indicate that a large proportion of the births are born outside of wedlock, the records for which tend to be incomplete so far as characteristics of the parents are concerned.

Another limitation of age reporting may result from calculating age of mother at birth of child (or at time of registration) from year of birth rather than from day, month and year of birth. Information on this factor is given in footnotes when known.

In few countries, data by age refer to deliveries rather than to live births causing under-enumeration in the event of a multiple birth. This practice leads to lack of strict comparability, both among countries or areas relying on this practice and between data shown in this table and table 9.

Rates shown in this table are subject to the same limitations that affect the corresponding statistics on live births. In cases of rates based on births tabulated by date of registration and not by date of occurrence; the effect of including delayed registration on the distribution of births by age of mother may be noted in the age-specific fertility rates for women at older ages. In some cases, high age-specific rates for women aged 45 years and over may reflect age of mother at registration of birth and not fertility at these older ages.

Earlier data: Live births and live-birth rates by age of mother (i.e. age-specific fertility rates), have been shown for the latest available year in each issue of the Yearbook. Information on the years and specific topics covered is presented in the Historical Index.

Tableau 10 – *Annuaire démographique 2016*

Le tableau 10 présente les données les plus récentes disponibles pour la période 2007 - 2016 sur les naissances vivantes selon l'âge de la mère et le sexe de l'enfant, le taux de fécondité et les taux de fécondité par âge.

Description des variables : l'âge désigne l'âge au dernier anniversaire, c'est-à-dire la différence entre la date de naissance et la date de l'événement exprimée en années solaires révolues. La classification par âge utilisée dans ce tableau comprend les catégories suivantes : moins de 15 ans, groupes quinquennaux jusqu'à 45-49 ans, 50 ans et plus, et âge inconnu. Des groupes d'âge différents sont parfois utilisés lorsque les pays ou territoires ont fourni les données dans une autre classification.

Les taux de fécondité par âge représentent le nombre annuel de naissances vivantes intervenues dans un groupe d'âge donné pour 1 000 femmes du groupe d'âge. Ces taux ont été calculés par la Division de statistique de l'ONU.

Étant donné que le nombre de naissances parmi les femmes de moins de 15 ans ou de plus de 50 ans est relativement peu élevé, les taux de fécondité par âge parmi les femmes âgées de moins de 20 ans et celles de 45 ans et plus ont été calculés sur la base des populations féminines âgées de 15 à 19 ans et de 45 à 49 ans, respectivement. De même, le taux pour les femmes de « tous âges » est fondé sur la totalité des naissances vivantes, indépendamment de l'âge de la mère et ce chiffre est rapporté à l'effectif de la population féminine âgée de 15 à 49 ans. Ce taux « tous âges » est le taux global de fécondité ou simplement taux de fécondité. Les taux de fécondité parmi les femmes âgées de moins de 15 ans ou celles de 50 ans et plus n'ont pas été calculés.

Les naissances pour lesquelles l'âge de la mère était inconnu ont été réparties par la Division de statistique de l'ONU, avant le calcul des taux, suivant les proportions observées pour celles où l'âge de la mère était connu.

Les chiffres de population utilisés pour le calcul des taux proviennent de dénombrements ou de répartitions estimatives de la population féminine selon l'âge. On a utilisé de préférence les estimations de la population; à défaut, on s'est contenté des données censitaires se rapportant à l'année des naissances.

Les taux présentés dans ce tableau ne concernent que les pays ou zones où l'on a enregistré un total d'au moins 100 naissances vivantes dans une année donnée.

Fiabilité des données : les données sur les naissances vivantes provenant des registres de l'état civil qui sont déclarées incomplètes (degré de complétude inférieur à 90 p. 100) ou dont le degré de complétude n'est pas connu, sont jugées douteuses et apparaissent en italique et non en caractères romains. On a choisi de ne pas faire figurer des taux calculés à partir de données sur les naissances vivantes issues de registres de l'état civil qui sont déclarées incomplètes (degré de complétude inférieur à 90 p. 100) ou dont le degré de complétude n'est pas connu. Le tableau 9 et les notes techniques qui s'y rapportent présentent des renseignements plus détaillés sur le degré de complétude de l'enregistrement des naissances vivantes. Pour plus de précisions sur la qualité des statistiques de l'état civil en général, voir la section 4.2 des Notes techniques.

Insuffisance des données : les statistiques relatives aux naissances vivantes selon l'âge de la mère appellent toutes les réserves qui ont été formulées à propos des statistiques de l'état civil en général et des statistiques de naissances en particulier (voir la section 4 des Notes techniques). Ceci inclut les différences de complétude d'enregistrement des faits d'état civil, de méthode pour déterminer l'âge de la mère et de qualité d'information concernant l'âge de la mère.

La fiabilité des données, au sujet de laquelle des indications ont été données plus haut, est un facteur important. Il faut également tenir compte du fait que, dans certains cas, les données relatives aux naissances vivantes sont exploitées selon la date de l'enregistrement et non la date de l'événement ; ces cas ont été signalés dans le tableau par le signe '+'. Chaque fois que le décalage entre l'événement et son enregistrement est grand et qu'une forte proportion des naissances vivantes fait l'objet d'un enregistrement tardif, les statistiques des naissances vivantes pour une année donnée peuvent être considérablement faussées. Par exemple, l'âge de la mère représente presque toujours son âge à la date de l'enregistrement et non à la date de la naissance de l'enfant. Ainsi, dans les pays ou zones où l'enregistrement des naissances est tardif, le retard atteignant parfois plusieurs années, il faut utiliser avec prudence les statistiques concernant les naissances selon l'âge de la mère.

Un autre facteur qui nuit à la comparabilité internationale est la pratique de certains pays ou zones qui consiste à ne pas inclure dans les statistiques des naissances vivantes les enfants nés vivants mais décédés avant l'enregistrement de leur naissance ou dans les 24 heures qui ont suivi la naissance, pratique qui conduit à sous-estimer le nombre total de naissances vivantes. Quand pareil facteur a joué, cela a été signalé en note à la fin du tableau.

Étant donné que les statistiques du tableau 10 sont classées selon l'âge, elles appellent les mêmes réserves concernant l'exactitude des déclarations d'âge que celles formulées à la section 3.1.3 des Notes techniques. Dans le cas des statistiques de l'état civil, les facteurs qui interviennent à cet égard sont parfois différents, étant donné que le recensement de la population et l'enregistrement des naissances se font par des méthodes différentes, mais, d'une manière générale, les erreurs observées seront les mêmes. Si aucun nombre ne figure dans la rangée réservée aux âges inconnus, cela ne signifie pas nécessairement que les déclarations d'âge et l'exploitation des données par âge ont été tout à fait exactes. C'est souvent une indication que l'on a attribué un âge aux personnes d'âge inconnu avant l'exploitation des données ou qu'elles ont été réparties proportionnellement entre les différents groupes après cette opération.

À l'inverse, lorsque le nombre des personnes d'âge inconnu est important, cela peut signifier que la proportion de naissances parmi les mères célibataires est élevée, étant donné qu'en pareil cas l'acte de naissance ne contient pas tous les renseignements concernant les parents.

Les déclarations par âge peuvent comporter des distorsions, du fait que l'âge de la mère au moment de la naissance d'un enfant (ou de la déclaration de naissance) est donné par année de naissance et non par date exacte (jour, mois et année).

Dans quelques pays, la classification par âges se réfère aux accouchements, et non aux naissances vivantes, ce qui conduit à un sous-dénombrement en cas de naissances gémellaires. Cette pratique nuit à la comparabilité des données, à la fois entre pays ou zones qui recourent à cette méthode et entre les données présentées dans le tableau 10 et celles du tableau 9.

Les taux présentés dans ce tableau sont sujets aux mêmes limitations qui affectent les statistiques correspondantes de naissances vivantes. Dans le cas des taux basés sur des naissances par date d'enregistrement et non par date d'occurrence, l'effet peut être visible sur les taux de fécondité par âge des femmes aux âges plus élevés. Dans certains cas, les taux de fécondité des femmes de plus de 45 ans peuvent refléter l'âge de la mère à l'enregistrement plus que la fécondité à ces âges.

Données publiées antérieurement : les différentes éditions de l'*Annuaire démographique* regroupent les dernières statistiques dont on disposait à l'époque sur les naissances vivantes selon l'âge de la mère et les taux des naissances vivantes selon l'âge de la mère (taux de fécondité par âge). Pour plus de précisions concernant les années pour lesquels des données ont été publiées, se reporter à l'index historique.

10. Live births by age of mother and sex of child, general and age-specific fertility rates: latest available year, 2007 - 2016
Naissances vivantes selon l'âge de la mère et le sexe de l'enfant, taux de fécondité et taux de fécondité par âge : dernière année disponible, 2007 - 2016

Continent, country or area, year, code[a] and age of mother (in years) / Continent, pays ou zone, année, code[a] et âge de la mère (en années)	Total	Male Masculin	Female Féminin	Rate Taux
AFRICA - AFRIQUE				
Botswana[1]				
2014 (U)				
Total	41 741	21 142	20 599	...
0 - 14	30	13	17	...
15 - 19	3 839	1 949	1 890	...
20 - 24	11 268	5 752	5 516	...
25 - 29	10 767	5 441	5 326	...
30 - 34	9 047	4 575	4 472	...
35 - 39	4 813	2 434	2 379	...
40 - 44	1 475	728	747	...
45 - 49	128	63	65	...
50 +	12	5	7	...
Unknown - Inconnu	362	182	180	...
Côte d'Ivoire				
2014 (I)				
Total	841 081	426 128	414 953	154.0
0 - 14	3 653	1 875	1 778	...
15 - 19	77 375	39 411	37 964	74.5
20 - 24	192 965	97 499	95 466	178.1
25 - 29	221 215	112 113	109 102	210.1
30 - 34	183 792	92 806	90 986	213.2
35 - 39	105 637	53 532	52 105	171.7
40 - 44	40 638	20 721	19 917	91.0
45 +	15 806	8 171	7 635	43.7
Egypt - Égypte				
2012 (+C)				
Total	2 629 769	1 343 402	1 286 367	121.1
0 - 19	71 275	36 022	35 253	23.8
20 - 24	1 298 851	665 452	633 399	403.8
25 - 29	399 915	201 967	197 948	127.5
30 - 34	223 307	111 754	111 553	86.0
35 - 39	83 362	41 121	42 241	41.3
40 - 44	21 510	11 229	10 281	12.2
45 +	3 802	2 233	1 569	2.3
Unknown - Inconnu	527 747	273 624	254 123	...
Ghana[2]				
2010 (I)				
Total	623 700	306 159	317 541	98.1
0 - 14	917	381	536	...
15 - 19	40 307	19 067	21 240	31.0
20 - 24	126 417	61 277	65 140	103.4
25 - 29	167 306	82 741	84 565	151.1
30 - 34	130 724	64 600	66 124	147.1
35 - 39	92 751	46 285	46 466	124.6
40 - 44	41 898	20 783	21 115	68.3
45 - 49	14 742	7 071	7 671	30.4
50 +	8 638	3 954	4 684	...
Guinea - Guinée[3]				
2014 (I)				
Total	416 607	204 309	212 298	161.9
0 - 14	3 494	1 728	1 766	...
15 - 19	62 085	30 684	31 401	105.6
20 - 24	96 498	47 687	48 811	194.3
25 - 29	101 210	49 832	51 378	227.6
30 - 34	72 323	35 456	36 867	204.4
35 - 39	44 261	21 594	22 667	155.4
40 - 44	21 347	10 144	11 203	90.0
45 - 49	9 266	4 348	4 918	54.9
50 +	6 123	2 839	3 284	...
Kenya				
2009 (U)				
Total	691 312	354 154	337 158	...
0 - 14	3 877	2 019	1 858	...
15 - 19	89 664	45 562	44 102	...
20 - 24	221 828	113 572	108 256	...

Continent, country or area, year, code[a] and age of mother (in years) / Continent, pays ou zone, année, code[a] et âge de la mère (en années)	Total	Male Masculin	Female Féminin	Rate Taux
AFRICA - AFRIQUE				
Kenya				
2009 (U)				
25 - 29	174 571	89 674	84 897	...
30 - 34	103 940	53 395	50 545	...
35 - 39	49 527	25 424	24 103	...
40 - 44	13 231	6 713	6 518	...
45 - 49	2 165	1 097	1 068	...
50 +	823	423	400	...
Unknown - Inconnu	31 686	16 275	15 411	...
2012 (U)[4]				
Total	754 429	...	...	...
0 - 14	3 047	...	...	...
15 - 19	90 928	...	...	...
20 - 24	234 290	...	...	...
25 - 29	204 221	...	...	...
30 - 34	122 883	...	...	...
35 - 39	64 386	...	...	...
40 - 44	16 674	...	...	...
45 - 49	2 975	...	...	...
50 +	560	...	...	...
Unknown - Inconnu	14 462	...	...	...
Lesotho				
2012 (+U)				
Total	1 718	...	...	...
10 - 14	97	...	...	...
15 - 19	96	...	...	...
20 - 24	378	...	...	...
25 - 29	506	...	...	...
30 - 34	409	...	...	...
35 - 39	183	...	...	...
40 - 44	42	...	...	...
45 +	7	...	...	...
Liberia - Libéria[5]				
2008 (I)				
Total	63 171	33 511	29 660	73.1
12 - 14	304	157	147	...
15 - 19	6 973	3 668	3 305	37.4
20 - 24	16 181	8 486	7 695	89.4
25 - 29	14 915	8 017	6 898	98.9
30 - 34	10 277	5 433	4 844	91.5
35 - 39	8 336	4 374	3 962	79.8
40 - 44	3 961	2 138	1 823	53.5
45 - 49	2 224	1 238	986	40.5
Libya - Libye[6]				
2009 (+U)				
Total	134 682	...	...	...
0 - 19	733	...	...	...
20 - 24	7 067	...	...	...
25 - 29	17 792	...	...	...
30 - 34	18 491	...	...	...
35 - 39	9 801	...	...	...
40 - 44	3 334	...	...	...
45 +	409	...	...	...
Unknown - Inconnu	77 055	...	...	...
Malawi[7]				
2008 (I)				
Total	516 629	247 753	268 876	160.1
12 - 14	1 621	751	870	...
15 - 19	70 737	34 137	36 600	101.2
20 - 24	169 406	81 379	88 027	284.1
25 - 29	130 331	62 810	67 521	241.6
30 - 34	79 232	37 758	41 474	153.2
35 - 39	43 747	20 776	22 971	116.8
40 - 44	15 956	7 553	8 403	57.8
45 - 49	5 599	2 589	3 010	25.0

10. Live births by age of mother and sex of child, general and age-specific fertility rates: latest available year, 2007 - 2016
Naissances vivantes selon l'âge de la mère et le sexe de l'enfant, taux de fécondité et taux de fécondité par âge : dernière année disponible, 2007 - 2016 (continued - suite)

Continent, country or area, year, code[a] and age of mother (in years) / Continent, pays ou zone, année, code[a] et âge de la mère (en années)	Total	Male Masculin	Female Féminin	Rate Taux
AFRICA - AFRIQUE				
Mali[8]				
2009 (I)				
Total	666 216	324 862	341 354	208.9
12 - 14	34 953	17 432	17 521	..
15 - 19	97 788	47 793	49 995	124.8
20 - 24	138 189	67 575	70 614	225.7
25 - 29	140 359	68 914	71 445	256.8
30 - 34	108 467	52 837	55 630	253.5
35 - 39	74 059	35 667	38 392	226.6
40 - 44	45 402	21 748	23 654	164.9
45 +	26 999	12 896	14 103	124.3
Mauritania - Mauritanie[9]				
2013 (I)				
Total	114 420	...	...	137.6
15 - 19	14 258	...	...	77.0
20 - 24	34 153	...	...	216.2
25 - 29	31 533	...	...	232.3
30 - 34	20 082	...	...	176.6
35 - 39	10 479	...	...	109.9
40 - 44	3 421	...	...	43.2
45 - 49	493	...	...	7.6
Mauritius - Maurice[10]				
2016 (+C)				
Total	12 948	6 597	6 351	40.3
0 - 14	26	12	14	..
15 - 19	1 111	573	538	23.1
20 - 24	2 879	1 452	1 427	58.5
25 - 29	3 964	1 988	1 976	89.1
30 - 34	3 051	1 572	1 479	69.6
35 - 39	1 547	813	734	31.4
40 - 44	294	149	145	7.0
45 - 49	16	6	10	♦0.4
50 +	1	1	-	..
Unknown - Inconnu	59	31	28	..
Namibia - Namibie[11]				
2011 (I)				
Total	61 523	30 560	30 963	110.8
0 - 14	873	443	430	..
15 - 19	7 593	3 723	3 870	62.5
20 - 24	16 655	8 235	8 420	152.3
25 - 29	14 296	7 109	7 187	157.7
30 - 34	11 017	5 632	5 385	145.3
35 - 39	7 237	3 531	3 706	113.0
40 - 44	2 982	1 451	1 531	58.4
45 +	870	436	434	20.2
Nigeria - Nigéria				
2007 (...)				
Total	1 807 025	...	...	...
0 - 14	2 528	...	...	..
15 - 19	129 716	...	...	...
20 - 24	471 036	...	...	...
25 - 29	588 454	...	...	...
30 - 34	377 593	...	...	...
35 - 39	172 081	...	...	...
40 - 44	49 519	...	...	...
45 - 49	13 411	...	...	...
50 +	2 687	...	...	..
Reunion - Réunion[12]				
2007 (C)				
Total	14 808	7 711	7 097	69.2
0 - 14	23	11	12	..
15 - 19	1 517	769	748	44.1
20 - 24	3 348	1 752	1 596	117.2
25 - 29	3 968	2 075	1 893	144.2
30 - 34	3 429	1 779	1 650	116.2

Continent, country or area, year, code[a] and age of mother (in years) / Continent, pays ou zone, année, code[a] et âge de la mère (en années)	Total	Male Masculin	Female Féminin	Rate Taux
AFRICA - AFRIQUE				
Reunion - Réunion[12]				
2007 (C)				
35 - 39	1 931	1 009	922	58.6
40 - 44	572	307	265	16.8
45 +	20	9	11	♦0.7
Saint Helena ex. dep. - Sainte-Hélène sans dép.				
2014 (C)				
Total	48	25	23	...
0 - 14	-	-	-	..
15 - 19	8	6	2	...
20 - 24	6	2	4	...
25 - 29	8	5	3	...
30 - 34	19	8	11	...
35 - 39	5	3	2	...
40 - 44	2	1	1	...
45 - 49	-	-	-	...
50 +	-	-	-	...
Unknown - Inconnu	-	-	-	...
Seychelles				
2015 (+C)				
Total	1 592	814	778	66.2
0 - 14	5	3	2	..
15 - 19	187	89	98	69.9
20 - 24	420	211	209	136.0
25 - 29	406	209	197	130.7
30 - 34	325	176	149	78.7
35 - 39	189	99	90	50.0
40 - 44	56	25	31	15.3
45 - 49	4	2	2	♦1.1
50 +	-	-	-	..
South Africa - Afrique du Sud				
2012 (U)[4]				
Total	926 726	467 058	459 668	...
0 - 14	822	415	407	...
15 - 19	112 605	56 816	55 789	...
20 - 24	253 843	128 346	125 497	...
25 - 29	244 006	122 994	121 012	...
30 - 34	178 694	89 924	88 770	...
35 - 39	101 654	51 081	50 573	...
40 - 44	32 046	15 961	16 085	...
45 - 49	2 584	1 289	1 295	...
50 +	237	111	126	..
Unknown - Inconnu	235	121	114	..
2016 (U)				
Total	876 435	...	...	..
0 - 14	1 444	...	...	..
15 - 19	107 730	...	...	..
20 - 24	225 847	...	...	..
25 - 29	226 996	...	...	..
30 - 34	184 962	...	...	..
35 - 39	97 218	...	...	..
40 - 44	29 298	...	...	..
45 - 49	1 932	...	...	..
50 +	110	...	...	..
Unknown - Inconnu	898	...	...	..
Swaziland[13]				
2007 (I)				
Total	33 084	18 905	14 179	152.2
0 - 14	67	33	34	..
15 - 19	3 581	1 775	1 806	71.0
20 - 24	8 303	4 449	3 854	184.4
25 - 29	6 839	3 830	3 009	187.1
30 - 34	5 039	2 969	2 070	188.5
35 - 39	3 839	2 324	1 515	166.8

10. Live births by age of mother and sex of child, general and age-specific fertility rates: latest available year, 2007 - 2016
Naissances vivantes selon l'âge de la mère et le sexe de l'enfant, taux de fécondité et taux de fécondité par âge : dernière année disponible, 2007 - 2016 (continued - suite)

Continent, country or area, year, code[a] and age of mother (in years) / Continent, pays ou zone, année, code[a] et âge de la mère (en années)	Total	Male Masculin	Female Féminin	Rate Taux
AFRICA - AFRIQUE				
Swaziland[13]				
2007 (|)				
40 - 44	2 008	1 340	668	104.7
45 - 49	1 246	892	354	75.8
50 +	2 155	1 288	867	..
Unknown - Inconnu	7	5	2	..
Tunisia - Tunisie				
2011 (C)				
Total	201 120	...	...	...
15 - 19	2 550	...	...	...
20 - 24	23 594	...	...	...
25 - 29	52 266	...	...	...
30 - 34	51 003	...	...	...
35 - 39	28 565	...	...	...
40 - 44	7 282	...	...	...
45 - 49	596	...	...	...
Unknown - Inconnu	35 265	...	...	..
Zambia - Zambie[14]				
2010 (|)				
Total	442 998	224 756	218 242	141.4
12 - 14	921	470	451	..
15 - 19	58 999	29 701	29 298	75.4
20 - 24	128 270	65 048	63 222	200.0
25 - 29	114 701	58 366	56 335	205.1
30 - 34	74 066	37 666	36 400	178.4
35 - 39	45 452	23 072	22 380	139.5
40 - 44	16 150	8 181	7 969	72.5
45 - 49	4 439	2 252	2 187	23.7
AMERICA, NORTH - AMÉRIQUE DU NORD				
Aruba				
2016 (C)				
Total	1 121	590	531	42.2
0 - 14	1	-	1	..
15 - 19	89	47	42	24.3
20 - 24	262	133	129	81.3
25 - 29	315	179	136	99.2
30 - 34	251	126	125	69.1
35 - 39	163	80	83	40.8
40 - 44	38	25	13	9.1
45 - 49	2	-	2	♦0.4
50 +	-	-	-	..
Unknown - Inconnu	-	-	-	..
Bahamas				
2012 (+U)				
Total	4 469	2 279	2 187	...
0 - 14	4	2	2	..
15 - 19	497	261	236	...
20 - 24	1 028	524	504	...
25 - 29	1 123	580	543	...
30 - 34	972	496	476	...
35 - 39	632	318	314	...
40 - 44	193	91	102	...
45 - 49	15	5	10	..
50 +	1	1	-	..
Unknown - Inconnu	1	1	-	..
Barbados - Barbade				
2007 (+C)				
Total	3 537	1 850	1 687	...
0 - 14	10	7	3	..
15 - 19	462	226	236	...
20 - 24	894	487	407	...
25 - 29	805	420	385	...

Continent, country or area, year, code[a] and age of mother (in years) / Continent, pays ou zone, année, code[a] et âge de la mère (en années)	Total	Male Masculin	Female Féminin	Rate Taux
AMERICA, NORTH - AMÉRIQUE DU NORD				
Barbados - Barbade				
2007 (+C)				
30 - 34	730	387	343	...
35 - 39	463	235	228	...
40 - 44	164	84	80	...
45 - 49	7	3	4	...
Unknown - Inconnu	2	1	1	...
Belize				
2016 (U)				
Total	7 200	3 615	3 585	...
0 - 14	20	11	9	..
15 - 19	1 337	653	684	...
20 - 24	2 323	1 171	1 152	...
25 - 29	1 780	924	856	...
30 - 34	1 054	524	530	...
35 - 39	543	260	283	...
40 - 44	129	65	64	...
45 - 49	14	7	7	...
50 +	-	-	-	..
Unknown - Inconnu	-	-	-	..
Bermuda - Bermudes[15]				
2016 (C)				
Total	591	303	288	43.1
0 - 14	-	-	-	..
15 - 19	12	7	5	♦8.2
20 - 24	57	30	27	36.1
25 - 29	131	68	63	70.1
30 - 34	193	101	92	92.3
35 - 39	149	75	74	70.1
40 - 44	46	20	26	21.3
45 - 49	3	2	1	♦1.2
50 +	-	-	-	..
British Virgin Islands - Îles Vierges britanniques				
2015 (C)				
Total	266	...	...	...
13 - 19	22	...	...	...
20 - 24	54	...	...	...
25 - 29	64	...	...	...
30 - 34	64	...	...	...
35 - 39	45	...	...	...
40 +	15	...	...	...
Unknown - Inconnu	2	...	...	...
Canada[16]				
2009 (C)				
Total	380 863	195 445	185 418	46.0
0 - 14	104	52	52	..
15 - 19	15 534	7 997	7 537	14.1
20 - 24	57 778	29 564	28 214	51.2
25 - 29	116 878	60 099	56 779	100.7
30 - 34	120 734	62 132	58 602	107.0
35 - 39	57 733	29 493	28 240	50.6
40 - 44	11 364	5 720	5 644	9.2
45 - 49	605	316	289	0.4
Unknown - Inconnu[17]	133	72	61	..
2013 (C)				
Total	380 323	...	...	45.8
0 - 14	78	...	...	..
15 - 19	11 645	...	...	11.0
20 - 24	50 309	...	...	41.9
25 - 29	111 495	...	...	93.0
30 - 34	130 744	...	...	107.2
35 - 39	62 567	...	...	53.6
40 - 44	12 710	...	...	10.7

Continent, country or area, year, code[a] and age of mother (in years) / Continent, pays ou zone, année, code[a] et âge de la mère (en années)	Number - Nombre			Rate Taux
	Total	Male Masculin	Female Féminin	

Continent, country or area, year, code[a] and age of mother (in years) / Continent, pays ou zone, année, code[a] et âge de la mère (en années)	Number - Nombre			Rate Taux
	Total	Male Masculin	Female Féminin	

AMERICA, NORTH - AMÉRIQUE DU NORD

	Total	Male	Female	Rate
Canada[16]				
2013 (C)				
45 - 49	734	...	...	0.6
Unknown - Inconnu[17]	41	...	...	..
Cayman Islands - Îles Caïmanes				
2014 (C)				
Total	710	...	...	...
15 - 19	35	...	...	...
20 - 24	129	...	...	...
25 - 29	140	...	...	...
30 - 34	210	...	...	...
35 - 39	142	...	...	...
40 - 44	51	...	...	...
45 - 49	3	...	...	...
Costa Rica				
2016* (C)				
Total	70 004	35 419	34 585	52.8
0 - 14	349	182	167	..
15 - 19	10 574	5 375	5 199	50.1
20 - 24	18 998	9 584	9 414	87.9
25 - 29	18 221	9 241	8 980	87.2
30 - 34	13 724	6 946	6 778	71.0
35 - 39	6 482	3 262	3 220	38.0
40 - 44	1 392	705	687	8.3
45 - 49	91	49	42	0.6
Unknown - Inconnu	173	75	98	..
Cuba				
2015 (C)				
Total	125 064	64 902	60 162	45.1
0 - 14	393	213	180	..
15 - 19	17 590	9 174	8 416	51.4
20 - 24	38 037	19 631	18 406	104.0
25 - 29	37 517	19 469	18 048	95.9
30 - 34	20 301	10 572	9 729	61.3
35 - 39	8 641	4 500	4 141	25.2
40 - 44	2 402	1 246	1 156	5.0
45 - 49	117	65	52	0.2
50 +	51	24	27	..
Unknown - Inconnu	15	8	7	..
2016 (C)				
Total	116 872	...	...	42.9
0 - 14	377	...	...	..
15 - 19	16 725	...	...	48.9
20 - 24	33 918	...	...	96.8
25 - 29	35 597	...	...	90.1
30 - 34	19 841	...	...	57.2
35 - 39	7 977	...	...	24.9
40 - 44	2 271	...	...	4.9
45 - 49	113	...	...	0.2
50 +	43	...	...	..
Unknown - Inconnu	10	...	...	..
Curaçao				
2016 (C)				
Total	1 789	901	888	47.8
0 - 14	4	2	2	..
15 - 19	113	64	49	22.9
20 - 24	417	202	215	91.6
25 - 29	465	233	232	98.2
30 - 34	421	211	210	82.8
35 - 39	255	136	119	49.9
40 - 44	65	33	32	11.2
45 - 49	6	2	4	♦0.9
50 +	-	-	-	..
Unknown - Inconnu	43	18	25	..

AMERICA, NORTH - AMÉRIQUE DU NORD

	Total	Male	Female	Rate
Dominican Republic - République dominicaine				
2007 (U)				
Total	147 368	75 087	72 281	...
0 - 14	1 918	983	935	..
15 - 19	30 087	15 392	14 695	...
20 - 24	43 538	22 188	21 350	...
25 - 29	36 740	18 724	18 016	...
30 - 34	21 018	10 658	10 360	...
35 - 39	8 754	4 425	4 329	...
40 - 44	2 018	1 001	1 017	...
45 - 49	251	131	120	...
50 +	199	94	105	...
Unknown - Inconnu	2 845	1 491	1 354	...
2016 (U)				
Total	139 583	...	...	...
10 - 14	604	...	...	..
15 - 19	22 326	...	...	...
20 - 24	41 553	...	...	...
25 - 29	36 571	...	...	...
30 - 34	22 682	...	...	...
35 - 39	10 400	...	...	...
40 - 44	2 056	...	...	...
45 - 49	178	...	...	...
50 +	62	...	...	...
Unknown - Inconnu	3 151	...	...	...
El Salvador[18]				
2015 (C)				
Total	109 617	56 757	52 860	58.9
0 - 14	923	466	457	..
15 - 19	23 452	12 226	11 226	67.2
20 - 24	32 224	16 716	15 508	94.1
25 - 29	24 090	12 451	11 639	82.7
30 - 34	17 103	8 802	8 301	68.5
35 - 39	8 891	4 564	4 327	39.2
40 - 44	2 333	1 205	1 128	11.1
45 - 49	171	96	75	0.9
50 +	45	17	28	..
Unknown - Inconnu	385	214	171	..
Greenland - Groenland				
2016 (C)				
Total	830	433	397	62.4
15 - 19	80	43	37	40.9
20 - 24	220	123	97	103.1
25 - 29	256	126	130	113.5
30 - 34	178	91	87	89.6
35 - 39	85	43	42	54.0
40 - 44	9	6	3	♦6.6
45 - 49	2	1	1	♦1.0
Guatemala				
2011 (C)				
Total	373 692	189 724	183 968	102.4
0 - 14	2 841	1 426	1 415	..
15 - 19	75 175	38 415	36 760	92.4
20 - 24	108 949	55 558	53 391	157.0
25 - 29	85 914	43 599	42 315	142.0
30 - 34	58 050	29 264	28 786	113.4
35 - 39	30 892	15 540	15 352	73.8
40 - 44	10 220	5 136	5 084	30.5
45 - 49	1 176	573	603	4.4
50 +	290	127	163	..
Unknown - Inconnu	185	86	99	..

10. Live births by age of mother and sex of child, general and age-specific fertility rates: latest available year, 2007 - 2016
Naissances vivantes selon l'âge de la mère et le sexe de l'enfant, taux de fécondité et taux de fécondité par âge : dernière année disponible, 2007 - 2016 (continued - suite)

Continent, country or area, year, code[a] and age of mother (in years) — Continent, pays ou zone, année, code[a] et âge de la mère (en années)	Number - Nombre			Rate Taux
	Total	Male Masculin	Female Féminin	

AMERICA, NORTH - AMÉRIQUE DU NORD

Honduras
2012 (+U)
Total	196 119	...	...	..
0 - 14	1 571	...	...	..
15 - 19	41 882	...	...	...
20 - 24	56 501	...	...	...
25 - 29	43 429	...	...	...
30 - 34	28 675	...	...	...
35 - 39	14 730	...	...	...
40 - 44	4 791	...	...	...
45 - 49	575	...	...	...
50 +	471	...	...	..
Unknown - Inconnu	3 494	...	...	..

Jamaica - Jamaïque[19]
2011 (I)
Total	49 676	23 949[20]	23 339[20]	66.0
15 - 19	6 167	3 034[20]	2 884[20]	50.5
20 - 24	13 977	6 852[20]	6 451[20]	129.9
25 - 29	12 348	5 923[20]	5 900[20]	108.7
30 - 34	8 746	4 182[20]	4 145[20]	73.9
35 - 39	6 001	2 816[20]	2 875[20]	48.9
40 - 44	2 109	1 014[20]	956[20]	21.2
45 - 49	328	128[20]	128[20]	4.8

Martinique[12]
2007 (C)
Total	5 317	2 676	2 641	51.0
0 - 14	2	1	1	..
15 - 19	305	165	140	19.8
20 - 24	911	447	464	77.6
25 - 29	1 202	617	585	117.2
30 - 34	1 376	678	698	98.2
35 - 39	1 105	560	545	64.1
40 - 44	393	194	199	20.9
45 +	23	14	9	♦1.4

Mexico - Mexique[21]
2014 (C)
Total	2 129 825	1 086 566[20]	1 043 213[20]	64.4
0 - 14	7 556	3 935[20]	3 621[20]	..
15 - 19	382 482	195 777[20]	186 696[20]	69.2
20 - 24	647 521	330 234[20]	317 273[20]	120.7
25 - 29	519 092	265 050[20]	254 027[20]	103.8
30 - 34	353 534	179 813[20]	173 716[20]	74.3
35 - 39	170 471	86 739[20]	83 729[20]	37.5
40 - 44	41 257	20 978[20]	20 279[20]	9.9
45 - 49	2 642	1 307[20]	1 335[20]	0.7
50 +	360	176[20]	184[20]	..
Unknown - Inconnu	4 910	2 557[20]	2 353[20]	..

Montserrat
2016 (+C)
Total	46	23	23	...
0 - 14	-	-	-	..
15 - 19	2	-	2	...
20 - 24	10	5	5	...
25 - 29	11	7	4	...
30 - 34	11	6	5	...
35 - 39	8	4	4	...
40 - 44	4	1	3	...
45 - 49	-	-	-	...
50 +	-	-	-	...

Nicaragua
2010 (+U)
Total	132 165	68 726	63 439	...
0 - 14	1 539	793	746	..
15 - 19	33 963	17 752	16 211	...

AMERICA, NORTH - AMÉRIQUE DU NORD

Nicaragua
2010 (+U)
20 - 24	38 897	20 181	18 716	...
25 - 29	30 273	15 790	14 483	...
30 - 34	17 301	8 942	8 359	...
35 - 39	8 010	4 156	3 854	...
40 - 44	1 943	992	951	...
45 - 49	209	105	104	...
50 +	30	15	15	..

Panama
2015* (C)
Total	75 901	38 960	36 941	73.9
0 - 14	603	316	287	..
15 - 19	14 242	7 317	6 925	84.1
20 - 24	21 205	10 898	10 307	133.3
25 - 29	18 011	9 256	8 755	117.1
30 - 34	13 311	6 838	6 473	90.1
35 - 39	6 583	3 374	3 209	46.5
40 - 44	1 817	897	920	13.5
45 - 49	99	47	52	0.8
50 +	7	3	4	..
Unknown - Inconnu	23	14	9	..

Puerto Rico - Porto Rico
2016 (C)
Total	28 326	14 651	13 675	...
0 - 14	26	8	18	..
15 - 19	3 393	1 746	1 647	...
20 - 24	9 280	4 793	4 487	...
25 - 29	7 645	3 969	3 676	...
30 - 34	4 902	2 553	2 349	...
35 - 39	2 537	1 314	1 223	...
40 - 44	518	251	267	...
45 - 49	24	16	8	...
50 +	1	1	-	...

Saint Vincent and the Grenadines - Saint-Vincent-et-les Grenadines
2014 (C)
Total	1 841	912	929	65.9
0 - 14	10	4	6	..
15 - 19	312	162	150	64.1
20 - 24	476	240	236	111.7
25 - 29	426	194	232	103.9
30 - 34	332	170	162	83.3
35 - 39	214	113	101	57.5
40 - 44	67	27	40	19.8
45 - 49	4	2	2	♦1.1
50 +	-	-	-	..
Unknown - Inconnu	-	-	-	..

Trinidad and Tobago - Trinité-et-Tobago
2009 (C)
Total	17 949	9 067	8 882	...
0 - 14	24	10	14	..
15 - 19	1 961	961	1 000	...
20 - 24	5 029	2 620	2 409	...
25 - 29	5 258	2 606	2 652	...
30 - 34	3 422	1 715	1 707	...
35 - 39	1 763	910	853	...
40 - 44	432	218	214	...
45 - 49	31	13	18	...
50 +	3	1	2	...
Unknown - Inconnu	26	13	13	...

10. Live births by age of mother and sex of child, general and age-specific fertility rates: latest available year, 2007 - 2016
Naissances vivantes selon l'âge de la mère et le sexe de l'enfant, taux de fécondité et taux de fécondité par âge : dernière année disponible, 2007 - 2016 (continued - suite)

Continent, country or area, year, code[a] and age of mother (in years) / Continent, pays ou zone, année, code[a] et âge de la mère (en années)	Number - Nombre			Rate Taux
	Total	Male Masculin	Female Féminin	

AMERICA, NORTH - AMÉRIQUE DU NORD

Turks and Caicos Islands - Îles Turques et Caïques				
2016 (C)				
Total	518	272	246	44.7
0 - 14	-	-	-	..
15 - 19	31	17	14	27.3
20 - 24	79	47	32	58.8
25 - 29	117	55	62	73.6
30 - 34	141	77	64	77.5
35 - 39	116	54	62	57.4
40 - 44	26	19	7	◆13.9
45 - 49	-	-	-	-
50 +	-	-	-	..
Unknown - Inconnu	8	3	5	..
United States of America - États-Unis d'Amérique				
2015 (C)				
Total	3 978 497	2 036 161	1 942 336	53.7
0 - 14	2 500	1 265	1 235	..
15 - 19	229 715	118 021	111 694	22.3
20 - 24	850 509	435 461	415 048	76.8
25 - 29	1 152 311	589 719	562 592	104.3
30 - 34	1 094 693	560 429	534 264	101.5
35 - 39	527 996	269 784	258 212	51.8
40 - 44	111 848	56 922	54 926	11.0
45 - 49	8 171	4 172	3 999	0.8
50 +	754	388	366	..
Unknown - Inconnu	-	-	-	..
United States Virgin Islands - Îles Vierges américaines				
2007 (C)				
Total	1 771	...	...	65.9
0 - 14	2	...	...	..
15 - 19	226	...	...	53.1
20 - 24	550	...	...	146.6
25 - 29	424	...	...	146.1
30 - 34	319	...	...	93.9
35 - 39	196	...	...	48.6
40 +	46	...	...	5.5
Unknown - Inconnu	8	...	...	..

AMERICA, SOUTH - AMÉRIQUE DU SUD

Argentina - Argentine				
2015 (C)				
Total	770 040	...	...	70.7
0 - 14	2 787	...	...	..
15 - 19	108 912	...	...	63.6
20 - 24	189 542	...	...	109.3
25 - 29	175 362	...	...	106.6
30 - 34	155 082	...	...	99.1
35 - 39	98 623	...	...	63.9
40 - 44	25 346	...	...	18.8
45 +	1 755	...	...	1.5
Unknown - Inconnu	12 631	...	...	..
Brazil - Brésil				
2015 (+C)				
Total	2 952 969[22]	1 512 020[20]	1 440 739[20]	52.9
0 - 14	23 187[22]	11 681[20]	11 506[20]	..
15 - 19	495 973[22]	254 202[20]	241 732[20]	59.1
20 - 24	733 328[22]	375 677[20]	357 600[20]	87.3
25 - 29	714 459[22]	366 306[20]	348 103[20]	84.0
30 - 34	591 410[22]	302 750[20]	288 623[20]	67.3
35 - 39	306 517[22]	156 534[20]	149 968[20]	38.6

AMERICA, SOUTH - AMÉRIQUE DU SUD

Continent, country or area, year, code[a] and age of mother (in years) / Continent, pays ou zone, année, code[a] et âge de la mère (en années)	Number - Nombre			Rate Taux
	Total	Male Masculin	Female Féminin	
Brazil - Brésil				
2015 (+C)				
40 - 44	70 792[22]	35 982[20]	34 801[20]	10.1
45 - 49	4 408[22]	2 256[20]	2 152[20]	0.7
50 +	390[22]	187[20]	203[20]	..
Unknown - Inconnu	12 505[22]	6 445[20]	6 051[20]	..
Chile - Chili				
2014 (C)				
Total	250 997	128 177[20]	122 802[20]	54.0
0 - 14	852	435[20]	417[20]	..
15 - 19	29 454	15 070[20]	14 383[20]	44.8
20 - 24	57 612	29 481[20]	28 124[20]	79.2
25 - 29	62 810	32 028[20]	30 774[20]	86.3
30 - 34	57 520	29 413[20]	28 106[20]	87.8
35 - 39	32 888	16 735[20]	16 153[20]	53.1
40 - 44	9 302	4 734[20]	4 567[20]	14.9
45 - 49	487	246[20]	241[20]	0.8
50 +	15	8[20]	7[20]	..
Unknown - Inconnu	57	27[20]	30[20]	..
Colombia - Colombie				
2014 (U)				
Total	669 131	343 163	325 968	...
0 - 14	6 593	3 463	3 130	...
15 - 19	144 030	73 686	70 344	...
20 - 24	195 473	100 454	95 019	...
25 - 29	150 072	76 926	73 146	...
30 - 34	106 118	54 518	51 600	...
35 - 39	52 432	26 789	25 643	...
40 - 44	12 988	6 602	6 386	...
45 - 49	1 063	533	530	...
50 +	128	51	77	...
Unknown - Inconnu	234	141	93	...
Ecuador - Équateur[23]				
2015* (U)				
Total	273 280	139 592	133 688	...
0 - 14	2 287	1 142	1 145	...
15 - 19	55 083	28 175	26 908	...
20 - 24	72 465	37 216	35 249	...
25 - 29	62 565	31 877	30 688	...
30 - 34	46 124	23 539	22 585	...
35 - 39	24 447	12 357	12 090	...
40 - 44	6 645	3 409	3 236	...
45 - 49	514	265	249	...
50 +	-	-	-	...
Unknown - Inconnu	3 150	1 612	1 538	..
French Guiana - Guyane française[12]				
2007 (C)				
Total	6 386	3 269	3 117	114.5
0 - 14	23	12	11	..
15 - 19	828	428	400	83.3
20 - 24	1 477	726	751	182.2
25 - 29	1 590	821	769	195.5
30 - 34	1 312	707	605	154.0
35 - 39	844	414	430	102.2
40 - 44	289	152	137	40.9
45 - 49	22	8	14	◆3.8
50 +	1	1	-	..
Paraguay				
2008 (+U)				
Total	99 674	51 066	48 608	...
0 - 14	538	269	269	...
15 - 19	20 188	10 404	9 784	...
20 - 24	28 246	14 396	13 850	...

10. Live births by age of mother and sex of child, general and age-specific fertility rates: latest available year, 2007 - 2016
Naissances vivantes selon l'âge de la mère et le sexe de l'enfant, taux de fécondité et taux de fécondité par âge : dernière année disponible, 2007 - 2016 (continued - suite)

Continent, country or area, year, code[a] and age of mother (in years) / Continent, pays ou zone, année, code[a] et âge de la mère (en années)	Number - Nombre			Rate Taux
	Total	Male Masculin	Female Féminin	

AMERICA, SOUTH - AMÉRIQUE DU SUD

Paraguay
2008 (+U)
25 - 29	23 863	12 261	11 602	...
30 - 34	14 721	7 480	7 241	...
35 - 39	8 899	4 600	4 299	...
40 - 44	2 819	1 440	1 379	...
45 - 49	250	134	116	...
50 +	2	2	-	..
Unknown - Inconnu	148	80	68	..

Peru - Pérou[24]
2015 (+U)
Total	529 029	270 774	258 255	...
0 - 14	1 432	707	725	..
15 - 19	66 740	34 266	32 474	...
20 - 24	131 063	67 149	63 914	...
25 - 29	126 232	64 657	61 575	...
30 - 34	106 779	54 643	52 136	...
35 - 39	69 847	35 579	34 268	...
40 - 44	24 849	12 714	12 135	...
45 - 49	1 956	999	957	...
50 +	127	57	70	..
Unknown - Inconnu	4	3	1	..

Suriname
2015 (C)
Total	10 148	5 063	5 085	69.3
0 - 14	41	...	...	..
15 - 19	1 435	...	...	61.1
20 - 24	2 630	...	...	115.0
25 - 29	2 680	...	...	121.2
30 - 34	2 052	...	...	97.1
35 - 39	1 019	...	...	50.9
40 - 44	268	...	...	14.1
45 +	23	...	...	♦1.3
Unknown - Inconnu	-	...	...	..

Uruguay
2015 (C)
Total	48 926	25 111[20]	23 812[20]	57.6
0 - 14	122	59[20]	63[20]	..
15 - 19	7 371	3 865[20]	3 506[20]	55.6
20 - 24	11 557	5 885[20]	5 670[20]	89.2
25 - 29	11 393	5 766[20]	5 626[20]	92.0
30 - 34	10 213	5 266[20]	4 947[20]	85.6
35 - 39	6 616	3 379[20]	3 237[20]	53.6
40 - 44	1 541	836[20]	705[20]	13.5
45 - 49	84	44[20]	40[20]	0.8
50 +	3	1[20]	2[20]	..
Unknown - Inconnu	26	10[20]	16[20]	..

Venezuela (Bolivarian Republic of) - Venezuela (République bolivarienne du)
2015 (U)
Total	600 860	308 901	291 959	...
0 - 14	6 628	3 412	3 216	..
15 - 19	125 739	64 871	60 868	...
20 - 24	174 600	90 042	84 558	...
25 - 29	138 804	71 020	67 784	...
30 - 34	93 722	47 892	45 830	...
35 - 39	44 570	22 993	21 577	...
40 - 44	11 468	5 895	5 573	...
45 - 49	1 038	544	494	...
50 +	310	161	149	..
Unknown - Inconnu	3 981	2 071	1 910	..

ASIA - ASIE

Armenia - Arménie
2014 (C)
Total	43 031	22 869	20 162	...
0 - 14	-	-	-	..
15 - 19	2 192	1 130	1 062	...
20 - 24	16 387	8 506	7 881	...
25 - 29	14 630	7 843	6 787	...
30 - 34	7 173	3 939	3 234	...
35 - 39	2 260	1 253	1 007	...
40 - 44	360	181	179	...
45 - 49	25	13	12	...
50 +	4	4	-	...
Unknown - Inconnu	-	-	-	..

Azerbaijan - Azerbaïdjan[25]
2014 (+C)
Total	170 503	91 410	79 093	63.4
0 - 14	-	-	-	..
15 - 19	19 267	9 931	9 336	52.9
20 - 24	70 312	37 227	33 085	154.7
25 - 29	51 021	27 816	23 205	109.2
30 - 34	21 264	11 707	9 557	53.3
35 - 39	7 027	3 904	3 123	21.2
40 - 44	1 443	745	698	4.4
45 - 49	138	64	74	0.4
50 +	31	16	15	..
Unknown - Inconnu	-	-	-	..

Bahrain - Bahreïn[26]
2014 (C)
Total	20 931	10 785	10 146	69.3
0 - 14	-	-	-	..
15 - 19	521	281	240	14.7
20 - 24	4 370	2 254	2 116	100.5
25 - 29	6 572	3 340	3 232	115.3
30 - 34	5 497	2 868	2 629	102.1
35 - 39	3 084	1 586	1 498	67.2
40 - 44	781	404	377	22.4
45 - 49	93	45	48	2.9
50 +	9	5	4	..
Unknown - Inconnu	4	2	2	..

Bangladesh
2010 (U)
Total	2 868 494	1 451 664	1 416 831	...
15 - 19	404 570	209 615	194 955	...
20 - 24	1 055 194	527 993	527 201	...
25 - 29	762 338	383 627	378 710	...
30 - 34	389 547	199 767	189 780	...
35 - 39	192 438	97 826	94 613	...
40 - 44	49 380	25 206	24 174	...
45 +	15 027	7 630	7 397	...

Brunei Darussalam - Brunéi Darussalam
2015 (+C)
Total	6 699	3 522	3 177	57.0
0 - 14	4	2	2	..
15 - 19	195	98	97	11.4
20 - 24	987	497	490	58.8
25 - 29	2 233	1 176	1 057	121.4
30 - 34	1 939	1 048	891	107.1
35 - 39	1 064	558	506	62.2
40 - 44	264	139	125	16.3
45 - 49	13	4	9	♦0.9
50 +	-	-	-	..
Unknown - Inconnu	-	-	-	..

10. Live births by age of mother and sex of child, general and age-specific fertility rates: latest available year, 2007 - 2016
Naissances vivantes selon l'âge de la mère et le sexe de l'enfant, taux de fécondité et taux de fécondité par âge : dernière année disponible, 2007 - 2016 (continued - suite)

Continent, country or area, year, code[a] and age of mother (in years) / Continent, pays ou zone, année, code[a] et âge de la mère (en années)	Total	Male Masculin	Female Féminin	Rate Taux
ASIA - ASIE				
China, Hong Kong SAR - Chine, Hong Kong RAS				
2016 (C)				
Total	60 856	31 724	29 132	30.1
0 - 14	4	3	1	..
15 - 19	433	218	215	2.6
20 - 24	3 782	1 968	1 814	16.8
25 - 29	13 994	7 334	6 660	49.6
30 - 34	24 460	12 741	11 719	71.1
35 - 39	14 759	7 686	7 073	43.0
40 - 44	3 190	1 650	1 540	9.5
45 - 49	186	101	85	0.6
50 +	6	6	-	..
Unknown - Inconnu	42	17	25	..
China, Macao SAR - Chine, Macao RAS				
2015 (C)				
Total	7 055	3 682	3 373	37.4
0 - 24	849	430	419	22.6
25 - 29	2 826	1 480	1 346	77.0
30 - 34	2 217	1 135	1 082	68.2
35 - 39	942	510	432	37.5
40 +	221	127	94	3.9
Cyprus - Chypre[27]				
2015 (C)				
Total	9 170	4 824	4 346	41.1
0 - 14	-	-	-	..
15 - 19	127	54	73	4.9
20 - 24	825	438	387	25.3
25 - 29	2 746	1 430	1 316	76.9
30 - 34	3 491	1 845	1 646	96.9
35 - 39	1 615	855	760	49.1
40 - 44	326	180	146	10.5
45 - 49	34	19	15	1.2
50 +	6	3	3	..
Democratic People's Republic of Korea - République populaire démocratique de Corée[14]				
2008 (I)				
Total	345 630	176 399	169 231	53.3
15 - 19	633	330	303	0.6
20 - 24	52 214	26 657	25 557	58.0
25 - 29	178 032	90 850	87 182	209.5
30 - 34	90 973	46 224	44 749	110.0
35 - 39	20 275	10 505	9 770	18.5
40 - 44	3 202	1 673	1 529	3.2
45 - 49	301	160	141	0.4
Georgia - Géorgie				
2016 (C)				
Total	56 569	28 887	27 682	65.4
10 - 14	19	8	11	..
15 - 19	4 448	2 294	2 154	43.5
20 - 24	15 643	7 977	7 666	134.5
25 - 29	17 594	9 014	8 580	127.0
30 - 34	11 706	5 962	5 744	86.5
35 - 39	5 539	2 815	2 724	43.8
40 - 44	1 386	701	685	11.2
45 - 49	183	92	91	1.5
50 +	25	10	15	..
Unknown - Inconnu	26	14	12	..
Indonesia - Indonésie[28]				
2010 (I)				
Total	6 028 921	...	...	92.5
0 - 14	1 054	...	...	..

Continent, country or area, year, code[a] and age of mother (in years) / Continent, pays ou zone, année, code[a] et âge de la mère (en années)	Total	Male Masculin	Female Féminin	Rate Taux
ASIA - ASIE				
Indonesia - Indonésie[28]				
2010 (I)				
15 - 19	344 318	...	...	33.5
20 - 24	1 435 265	...	...	143.5
25 - 29	1 787 802	...	...	167.4
30 - 34	1 352 605	...	...	136.9
35 - 39	776 985	...	...	84.8
40 - 44	254 427	...	...	31.0
45 - 49	57 924	...	...	8.3
50 +	18 541	...	...	
Iran (Islamic Republic of) - Iran (République islamique d')[29]				
2014 (+C)				
Total	1 493 317	768 209	725 108	65.4
0 - 14	1 713	907	806	..
15 - 19	102 549	52 413	50 136	35.6
20 - 24	345 564	177 770	167 794	95.4
25 - 29	474 159	243 543	230 616	108.9
30 - 34	363 457	187 261	176 196	90.8
35 - 39	159 905	82 341	77 564	51.9
40 - 44	34 361	17 747	16 614	13.5
45 - 49	2 541	1 278	1 263	1.1
50 +	264	110	154	..
Unknown - Inconnu	8 804	4 839	3 965	..
Israel - Israël[30]				
2015 (C)				
Total	178 723	91 888	86 835	91.1
0 - 14	-	-	-	..
15 - 19	3 080	1 592	1 488	9.7
20 - 24	31 603	16 299	15 304	106.0
25 - 29	51 980	26 756	25 224	177.9
30 - 34	52 692	27 138	25 554	182.5
35 - 39	30 355	15 518	14 837	108.6
40 - 44	7 952	4 025	3 927	30.5
45 - 49	652	335	317	2.9
50 +	71	39	32	..
Unknown - Inconnu	338	186	152	..
Japan - Japon[31]				
2015 (C)				
Total	1 005 677	515 452	490 225	38.5
0 - 14	39	14	25	..
0 - 15	195	84	111	...
15 - 19	11 890	6 049	5 841	4.1
20 - 24	84 461	43 482	40 979	27.9
25 - 29	262 256	134 486	127 770	81.9
30 - 34	364 870	187 110	177 760	100.9
35 - 39	228 293	116 933	111 360	54.9
40 - 44	52 558	26 717	25 841	10.9
45 - 49	1 256	636	620	0.3
50 +	52	24	28	..
Unknown - Inconnu	2	1	1	..
Kazakhstan[25]				
2013 (C)				
Total	387 227	199 880	187 347	84.3
0 - 14	20	12	8	..
15 - 19	20 727	10 653	10 074	32.8
20 - 24	124 737	64 434	60 303	155.1
25 - 29	124 145	63 987	60 158	160.1
30 - 34	71 453	36 850	34 603	109.3
35 - 39	37 140	19 237	17 903	61.4
40 - 44	8 560	4 458	4 102	15.1
45 - 49	387	217	170	0.7
50 +	33	20	13	..
Unknown - Inconnu	25	12	13	..

10. Live births by age of mother and sex of child, general and age-specific fertility rates: latest available year, 2007 - 2016
Naissances vivantes selon l'âge de la mère et le sexe de l'enfant, taux de fécondité et taux de fécondité par âge : dernière année disponible, 2007 - 2016 (continued - suite)

Continent, country or area, year, code[a] and age of mother (in years) / Continent, pays ou zone, année, code[a] et âge de la mère (en années)	Total	Male Masculin	Female Féminin	Rate Taux
ASIA - ASIE				
Kuwait - Koweït				
2014 (C)				
Total	61 313	31 513	29 800	59.5
15 - 19	772	407	365	8.3
20 - 24	9 140	4 633	4 507	99.4
25 - 29	18 249	9 497	8 752	114.9
30 - 34	16 133	8 247	7 886	91.3
35 - 39	8 460	4 368	4 092	50.0
40 - 44	2 401	1 206	1 195	16.8
45 +	236	121	115	2.4
Unknown - Inconnu	5 922	3 034	2 888	..
2015 (C)				
Total	59 271	...	...	...
15 - 19	755	...	...	...
20 - 24	8 506	...	...	...
25 - 29	17 894	...	...	...
30 - 34	15 867	...	...	...
35 - 39	8 703	...	...	...
40 - 44	2 447	...	...	...
45 +	254	...	...	...
Unknown - Inconnu	4 845	...	...	..
Kyrgyzstan - Kirghizstan				
2016* (C)				
Total	158 160	81 233	76 927	100.4
0 - 14	5	3	2	..
15 - 19	9 454	4 780	4 674	38.1
20 - 24	53 677	27 665	26 012	193.0
25 - 29	48 534	25 076	23 458	168.0
30 - 34	29 245	14 960	14 285	123.9
35 - 39	13 378	6 793	6 585	70.8
40 - 44	3 454	1 766	1 688	20.1
45 - 49	264	120	144	1.6
50 +	21	9	12	..
Unknown - Inconnu	128	61	67	..
Malaysia - Malaisie				
2015 (C)				
Total	521 136	269 255	251 881	61.5
0 - 14	206	117	89	..
15 - 19	16 158	8 278	7 880	11.8
20 - 24	74 226	38 439	35 787	48.5
25 - 29	172 470	89 391	83 079	117.6
30 - 34	159 280	82 007	77 273	123.6
35 - 39	77 723	40 228	37 495	76.3
40 - 44	19 221	9 813	9 408	20.8
45 - 49	1 402	746	656	1.6
50 +	86	43	43	..
Unknown - Inconnu	364	193	171	..
Maldives				
2014 (C)				
Total	7 245	3 706	3 539	69.2
0 - 14	-	-	-	..
15 - 19	201	105	96	13.2
20 - 24	1 960	1 029	931	105.2
25 - 29	2 555	1 318	1 237	119.4
30 - 34	1 662	828	834	96.5
35 - 39	654	318	336	52.6
40 - 44	198	102	96	18.8
45 - 49	10	6	4	♦1.1
50 +	-	-	-	..
Unknown - Inconnu	5	-	5	..
Mongolia - Mongolie				
2016 (+C)				
Total	79 920	41 033	38 887	92.7
0 - 14	11	3	8	..
15 - 19	3 828	1 889	1 939	32.6
ASIA - ASIE				
Mongolia - Mongolie				
2016 (+C)				
20 - 24	20 263	10 480	9 783	156.4
25 - 29	25 741	13 280	12 461	164.2
30 - 34	17 651	9 072	8 579	130.3
35 - 39	9 933	5 005	4 928	83.3
40 - 44	2 375	1 244	1 131	21.8
45 - 49	115	58	57	1.2
50 +	3	2	1	..
Myanmar[32]				
2014 (+U)				
Total	736 369	378 543	357 826	...
15 - 19	37 952	19 337	18 615	...
20 - 24	173 110	89 045	84 065	...
25 - 29	224 623	115 728	108 895	...
30 - 34	167 190	85 829	81 361	...
35 - 39	97 465	49 925	47 540	...
40 - 44	32 624	16 954	15 670	...
45 +	3 298	1 664	1 634	...
Unknown - Inconnu	107	61	46	..
Oman[33]				
2016 (U)				
Total	88 346	44 958[20]	43 377[20]	..
0 - 14	10	4	6	..
15 - 19	1 535	754[20]	780[20]	...
20 - 24	14 395	7 383[20]	7 011[20]	...
25 - 29	28 107	14 280[20]	13 826[20]	...
30 - 34	24 789	12 677[20]	12 109[20]	...
35 - 39	14 265	7 247[20]	7 015[20]	...
40 - 44	3 990	1 988	2 002	...
45 - 49	402	213	189	...
50 +	32	14	18	...
Unknown - Inconnu	821	398[20]	421[20]	...
Philippines				
2015 (C)				
Total	1 744 767	910 877	833 890	66.4
0 - 14	1 986	1 031	955	..
15 - 19	205 844	107 768	98 076	41.9
20 - 24	498 927	260 593	238 334	105.5
25 - 29	439 320	229 200	210 120	107.1
30 - 34	327 793	171 119	156 674	90.2
35 - 39	196 621	102 527	94 094	59.8
40 - 44	64 109	33 359	30 750	22.0
45 - 49	6 724	3 491	3 233	2.5
50 +	367	181	186	..
Unknown - Inconnu	3 076	1 608	1 468	..
Qatar				
2015 (C)				
Total	26 622	13 610	13 012	69.2
0 - 19	374	204	170	10.5
15 - 19	374	204	170	10.5
20 - 24	3 722	1 914	1 808	77.2
25 - 29	8 407	4 332	4 075	105.0
30 - 34	8 432	4 320	4 112	103.9
35 - 39	4 384	2 184	2 200	67.8
40 - 44	1 170	585	585	26.0
45 - 49	113	59	54	3.7
50 +	20	12	8	..
Republic of Korea - République de Corée[34]				
2015 (C)				
Total	438 420	224 906	213 514	34.4
0 - 14	16	6	10	..
15 - 19	2 211	1 171	1 040	1.4
20 - 24	20 514	10 490	10 024	12.6

379

10. Live births by age of mother and sex of child, general and age-specific fertility rates: latest available year, 2007 - 2016
Naissances vivantes selon l'âge de la mère et le sexe de l'enfant, taux de fécondité et taux de fécondité par âge : dernière année disponible, 2007 - 2016 (continued - suite)

Continent, country or area, year, code[a] and age of mother (in years) / Continent, pays ou zone, année, code[a] et âge de la mère (en années)	Number - Nombre			Rate Taux
	Total	Male Masculin	Female Féminin	

ASIA - ASIE

Republic of Korea - République de Corée[34]
2015 (C)

25 - 29	94 622	48 802	45 820	61.5
30 - 34	216 252	110 509	105 743	116.5
35 - 39	92 081	47 424	44 657	48.8
40 - 44	12 138	6 231	5 907	5.7
45 - 49	335	169	166	0.2
50 +	14	4	10	..
Unknown - Inconnu	237	100	137	..

Saudi Arabia - Arabie saoudite[8]
2010 (I)

Total	527 461	275 189	252 272	73.2
15 - 19	10 641	4 761	5 880	8.7
20 - 24	68 573	34 423	34 150	54.8
25 - 29	149 707	79 425	70 282	111.9
30 - 34	135 203	89 860	45 343	116.8
35 - 39	108 609	33 195	75 414	112.5
40 - 44	41 602	24 758	16 844	59.7
45 - 49	10 603	7 361	3 242	18.8
50 +	2 523	1 406	1 117	..

Singapore - Singapour
2016 (C)

Total	41 251	21 315	19 936	40.8
0 - 14	8	2	6	..
15 - 19	324	159	165	2.8
20 - 24	2 291	1 184	1 107	17.8
25 - 29	10 559	5 502	5 057	74.0
30 - 34	17 121	8 880	8 241	114.2
35 - 39	9 259	4 697	4 562	58.4
40 - 44	1 620	851	769	10.1
45 - 49	63	35	28	0.4
50 +	6	5	1	..

Sri Lanka
2013 (+C)

Total	365 762	...	...	68.0
0 - 14	94	...	...	..
15 - 19	16 777	...	...	20.0
20 - 24	73 641	...	...	94.8
25 - 29	112 466	...	...	139.5
30 - 34	104 838	...	...	123.5
35 - 39	46 082	...	...	63.0
40 - 44	10 787	...	...	15.2
45 +	1 077	...	...	1.6

State of Palestine - État de Palestine[35]
2007 (I)

Total	106 209	54 540	51 671	121.5
0 - 14	2	2	-	..
15 - 19	7 759	4 029	3 731	36.1
20 - 24	31 097	15 970	15 128	189.3
25 - 29	30 535	15 688	14 847	224.1
30 - 34	20 980	10 682	10 298	180.3
35 - 39	11 544	5 974	5 570	118.4
40 - 44	3 821	1 913	1 908	47.5
45 - 49	342	198	144	5.4
50 +	94	66	28	..
Unknown - Inconnu	35	18	17	..

Thailand - Thaïlande
2011 (+U)

Total	795 031	409 699	385 332	...
0 - 14	3 415	1 793	1 622	...
15 - 19	129 321	66 645	62 676	...
20 - 24	186 942	96 371	90 571	...

Continent, country or area, year, code[a] and age of mother (in years) / Continent, pays ou zone, année, code[a] et âge de la mère (en années)	Number - Nombre			Rate Taux
	Total	Male Masculin	Female Féminin	

ASIA - ASIE

Thailand - Thaïlande
2011 (+U)

25 - 29	204 684	105 355	99 329	...
30 - 34	167 671	86 515	81 156	...
35 - 39	80 348	41 311	39 037	...
40 - 44	20 089	10 251	9 838	...
45 - 49	1 293	653	640	...
50 +	73	30	43	..
Unknown - Inconnu	1 195	775	420	..

Turkey - Turquie[4]
2014 (C)

Total	1 337 504	687 255	650 249	65.2
0 - 14	317	167	150	..
15 - 19	84 359	43 543	40 816	26.8
20 - 24	324 101	166 674	157 427	106.3
25 - 29	413 462	212 713	200 749	134.6
30 - 34	325 138	166 639	158 499	101.6
35 - 39	143 763	73 698	70 065	49.5
40 - 44	33 892	17 345	16 547	12.4
45 - 49	2 569	1 284	1 285	1.1
50 +	362	213	149	..
Unknown - Inconnu	9 541	4 979	4 562	..

Uzbekistan - Ouzbékistan
2015 (+C)

Total	734 141	382 666	351 475	84.6
0 - 14	-	-	-	..
15 - 19	33 035	16 885	16 150	23.8
20 - 24	309 746	159 890	149 856	194.8
25 - 29	247 500	129 252	118 248	162.4
30 - 34	110 819	58 658	52 161	86.1
35 - 39	29 332	15 961	13 371	27.2
40 - 44	3 560	1 939	1 621	3.7
45 - 49	134	70	64	0.2
50 +	15	11	4	..

EUROPE

Åland Islands - Îles d'Åland
2015 (C)

Total	275	143	132	46.1
0 - 14	-	-	-	..
15 - 19	2	2	-	♦2.6
20 - 24	26	11	15	♦37.4
25 - 29	76	40	36	98.6
30 - 34	105	54	51	123.7
35 - 39	56	30	26	64.7
40 - 44	10	6	4	♦10.7
45 - 49	-	-	-	..
50 +	-	-	-	..

Albania - Albanie
2013 (C)

Total	35 750	18 661	17 089	49.6
0 - 14	22	16	6	..
15 - 19	2 613	1 337	1 276	20.3
20 - 24	11 737	6 083	5 654	108.2
25 - 29	11 990	6 255	5 735	124.0
30 - 34	6 559	3 482	3 077	69.2
35 - 39	2 298	1 216	1 082	25.3
40 - 44	429	223	206	4.3
45 - 49	33	19	14	0.3
50 +	13	7	6	..
Unknown - Inconnu	56	23	33	..

Continent, country or area, year, code[a] and age of mother (in years) / Continent, pays ou zone, année, code[a] et âge de la mère (en années)	Total	Male Masculin	Female Féminin	Rate Taux
EUROPE				
Andorra - Andorre				
2015 (C)				
Total	659	336	323	...
0 - 14	1	1	-	..
15 - 19	5	4	1	...
20 - 24	32	15	17	...
25 - 29	123	58	65	...
30 - 34	253	140	113	...
35 - 39	198	89	109	...
40 - 44	40	26	14	...
45 - 49	5	2	3	...
50 +	1	-	1	..
Unknown - Inconnu	1	1	-	..
Austria - Autriche[36]				
2015 (C)				
Total	84 381	43 604	40 777	42.3
0 - 14	15	10	5	..
15 - 19	1 698	943	755	7.6
20 - 24	11 023	5 709	5 314	41.0
25 - 29	25 040	12 860	12 180	88.0
30 - 34	28 912	14 977	13 935	98.9
35 - 39	14 284	7 365	6 919	52.3
40 - 44	3 191	1 633	1 558	10.5
45 - 49	201	98	103	0.6
50 +	17	9	8	..
Belarus - Bélarus				
2015 (C)				
Total	119 028	...	...	52.1
0 - 14	8	...	...	..
15 - 19	4 053	...	...	18.1
20 - 24	26 629	...	...	89.4
25 - 29	43 301	...	...	115.4
30 - 34	30 669	...	...	82.5
35 - 39	12 211	...	...	35.7
40 - 44	2 074	...	...	6.1
45 - 49	65	...	...	0.2
50 +	-	...	...	..
Unknown - Inconnu	18	...	...	..
Belgium - Belgique[37]				
2015 (C)				
Total	122 274	62 561	59 713	48.7
0 - 14	20	10	10	..
15 - 19	2 006	1 038	968	6.6
20 - 24	14 244	7 271	6 973	42.0
25 - 29	41 048	21 131	19 917	114.5
30 - 34	41 251	21 039	20 212	114.0
35 - 39	18 434	9 436	8 998	51.1
40 - 44	3 784	1 882	1 902	10.2
45 - 49	255	131	124	0.7
50 +	10	6	4	..
Unknown - Inconnu	1 222	617	605	..
Bosnia and Herzegovina - Bosnie-Herzégovine				
2010 (C)				
Total	33 528	17 277	16 251	35.2
12 - 14	8	6	2	..
15 - 19	1 792	950	842	13.5
20 - 24	8 293	4 282	4 011	59.4
25 - 29	11 690	5 949	5 741	86.2
30 - 34	7 985	4 144	3 841	66.8
35 - 39	3 027	1 560	1 467	24.3
40 - 44	557	287	270	3.9
45 - 49	30	14	16	0.2
50 +	1	-	1	..
Unknown - Inconnu	145	85	60	..
EUROPE				
Bulgaria - Bulgarie				
2015 (C)				
Total	65 950	34 069	31 881	42.0
0 - 14	294	155	139	..
15 - 19	5 980	3 143	2 837	39.4
20 - 24	13 157	6 738	6 419	69.7
25 - 29	20 655	10 704	9 951	88.1
30 - 34	16 257	8 418	7 839	69.7
35 - 39	7 917	4 082	3 835	30.6
40 - 44	1 522	751	771	5.9
45 - 49	152	71	81	0.6
50 +	13	6	7	..
Unknown - Inconnu	3	1	2	..
Croatia - Croatie				
2015 (C)				
Total	37 503	19 379	18 124	40.3
0 - 14	5	-	5	..
15 - 19	1 116	583	533	9.6
20 - 24	5 288	2 757	2 531	44.2
25 - 29	11 473	5 918	5 555	88.9
30 - 34	12 497	6 438	6 059	88.1
35 - 39	6 007	3 115	2 892	42.3
40 - 44	1 041	528	513	7.6
45 - 49	65	34	31	0.5
50 +	2	-	2	..
Unknown - Inconnu	9	6	3	..
Czechia - Tchéquie				
2015 (C)				
Total	110 764	56 817	53 947	45.9
0 - 14	13	5	8	..
15 - 19	2 606	1 378	1 228	11.6
20 - 24	13 487	6 946	6 541	45.5
25 - 29	32 843	16 758	16 085	97.0
30 - 34	38 285	19 632	18 653	106.3
35 - 39	19 847	10 195	9 652	45.3
40 - 44	3 531	1 831	1 700	8.4
45 - 49	139	66	73	0.4
50 +	13	6	7	..
Denmark - Danemark[38]				
2015 (C)				
Total	58 205	29 848	28 357	46.1
0 - 14	1	1	-	..
15 - 19	583	325	258	3.4
20 - 24	6 342	3 282	3 060	34.1
25 - 29	18 969	9 549	9 420	109.5
30 - 34	19 885	10 311	9 574	125.8
35 - 39	10 141	5 235	4 906	57.4
40 - 44	2 161	1 085	1 076	11.1
45 - 49	111	52	59	0.5
50 +	12	8	4	..
Estonia - Estonie				
2015 (C)				
Total	13 907	7 172	6 735	47.7
0 - 14	2	-	2	..
15 - 19	366	176	190	12.6
20 - 24	1 991	998	993	53.6
25 - 29	4 680	2 396	2 284	98.8
30 - 34	4 048	2 122	1 926	89.1
35 - 39	2 213	1 146	1 067	50.5
40 - 44	580	313	267	12.9
45 - 49	26	20	6	♦0.6
50 +	1	1	-	..

Continent, country or area, year, code[a] and age of mother (in years) / Continent, pays ou zone, année, code[a] et âge de la mère (en années)	Number - Nombre			Rate Taux
	Total	Male Masculin	Female Féminin	

EUROPE

Faeroe Islands - Îles Féroé				
2015 (C)				
Total	608	292	316	61.1
0 - 14	-	-	-	..
15 - 19	18	10	8	♦10.5
20 - 24	115	60	55	86.1
25 - 29	182	81	101	159.2
30 - 34	176	83	93	145.3
35 - 39	86	42	44	61.5
40 - 44	24	12	12	♦16.5
45 - 49	2	1	1	♦1.2
50 +	-	-	-	..
Unknown - Inconnu	5	3	2	..
Finland - Finlande				
2015 (C)				
Total	55 472	28 469	27 003	48.4
0 - 14	6	5	1	..
15 - 19	914	475	439	6.2
20 - 24	7 726	4 026	3 700	46.6
25 - 29	16 294	8 315	7 979	98.5
30 - 34	18 963	9 688	9 275	110.4
35 - 39	9 571	4 912	4 659	57.4
40 - 44	1 881	989	892	12.2
45 - 49	114	58	56	0.7
50 +	3	1	2	..
France[39]				
2012 (C)				
Total	790 290	404 774	385 516	55.6
12 - 14	147	73	74	..
15 - 19	17 512	8 954	8 558	9.4
20 - 24	111 364	57 130	54 234	58.2
25 - 29	253 800	130 005	123 795	131.0
30 - 34	255 606	130 913	124 693	127.2
35 - 39	121 563	62 225	59 338	59.1
40 - 44	28 620	14 598	14 022	12.9
45 - 49	1 557	818	739	0.7
50 +	121	58	63	..
Germany - Allemagne				
2015 (C)				
Total	737 575	378 478	359 097	42.3
0 - 14	145	83	62	..
15 - 19	15 567	7 961	7 606	7.8
20 - 24	79 073	40 734	38 339	35.8
25 - 29	210 172	107 740	102 432	82.4
30 - 34	261 520	134 091	127 429	104.3
35 - 39	140 931	72 442	68 489	58.7
40 - 44	27 740	14 224	13 516	11.0
45 - 49	1 580	790	790	0.5
50 +	114	56	58	..
Unknown - Inconnu	733	357	376	..
Gibraltar[40]				
2015 (+C)				
Total	492	258	234	...
0 - 19	8	3	5	...
20 - 24	69	40	29	...
25 - 29	125	63	62	...
30 - 34	171	94	77	...
35 - 39	96	47	49	...
40 +	23	11	12	...
Greece - Grèce				
2015 (C)				
Total	91 847	47 294	44 553	37.6
0 - 14	51	26	25	..
15 - 19	2 198	1 104	1 094	8.4
20 - 24	7 388	3 848	3 540	26.5

EUROPE

Greece - Grèce				
2015 (C)				
25 - 29	20 679	10 777	9 902	68.7
30 - 34	34 264	17 645	16 619	94.7
35 - 39	21 726	11 123	10 603	53.6
40 - 44	4 749	2 403	2 346	11.5
45 - 49	670	313	357	1.6
50 +	122	55	67	..
Unknown - Inconnu	-	-	-	..
Hungary - Hongrie[41]				
2015 (C)				
Total	92 135	47 350	44 785	40.2
0 - 14	79	40	39	..
15 - 19	5 682	2 935	2 747	22.8
20 - 24	13 363	6 916	6 447	44.3
25 - 29	23 104	11 857	11 247	77.5
30 - 34	27 737	14 284	13 453	88.7
35 - 39	18 136	9 226	8 910	45.0
40 - 44	3 899	2 021	1 878	10.2
45 - 49	129	67	62	0.4
50 +	6	4	2	..
Unknown - Inconnu	-	-	-	..
Iceland - Islande				
2015 (C)				
Total	4 129	2 119	2 010	53.1
0 - 14	-	-	-	..
15 - 19	87	38	49	8.0
20 - 24	660	335	325	54.4
25 - 29	1 341	698	643	115.7
30 - 34	1 213	613	600	107.1
35 - 39	677	367	310	62.1
40 - 44	140	63	77	13.2
45 - 49	11	5	6	♦1.1
50 +	-	-	-	..
Unknown - Inconnu	-	-	-	..
Ireland - Irlande				
2015 (+C)				
Total	65 537	33 481	32 056	58.4
0 - 14	5	4	1	..
15 - 19	1 194	648	546	8.7
20 - 24	5 705	2 924	2 781	49.4
25 - 29	12 322	6 328	5 994	80.6
30 - 34	23 684	11 984	11 700	122.7
35 - 39	18 452	9 448	9 004	97.7
40 - 44	3 955	2 031	1 924	22.4
45 - 49	204	108	96	1.3
50 +	16	6	10	..
Unknown - Inconnu	-	-	-	..
Isle of Man - Île de Man[8]				
2016 (I)				
Total	731	...	...	41.4
10 - 14	1	...	...	..
15 - 19	23	...	...	♦10.1
20 - 24	111	...	...	51.2
25 - 29	178	...	...	81.1
30 - 34	238	...	...	100.9
35 - 39	146	...	...	58.4
40 - 44	33	...	...	11.4
45 - 49	1	...	...	♦0.3
50 +	-	...	...	..
Italy - Italie				
2015 (+C)				
Total	485 780	249 950	235 830	..
0 - 14	13	7	6	..
15 - 19	7 121	3 607	3 514	..

Continent, country or area, year, code[a] and age of mother (in years) / Continent, pays ou zone, année, code[a] et âge de la mère (en années)	Number - Nombre			Rate Taux
	Total	Male Masculin	Female Féminin	

EUROPE

Italy - Italie
2015 (+C)

20 - 24	42 839	21 972	20 867	...
25 - 29	108 772	56 039	52 733	...
30 - 34	163 117	83 645	79 472	...
35 - 39	123 689	63 989	59 700	...
40 - 44	37 073	19 085	17 988	...
45 - 49	2 869	1 455	1 414	...
50 +	287	151	136	..
Unknown - Inconnu	-	-	-	..

Jersey[21]
2007 (+C)

Total	1 031	515	516	..
0 - 14	-	-	-	..
15 - 19	29	14	15	...
20 - 24	114	56	58	...
25 - 29	228	114	114	...
30 - 34	325	170	155	...
35 - 39	273	134	139	...
40 - 44	61	27	34	...
45 - 49	1	-	1	...
50 +	-	-	-	..

Latvia - Lettonie
2015 (C)

Total	21 979	11 442	10 537	50.0
0 - 14	5	4	1	..
15 - 19	760	395	365	18.0
20 - 24	3 720	1 916	1 804	64.4
25 - 29	7 196	3 722	3 474	103.3
30 - 34	6 259	3 248	3 011	93.9
35 - 39	3 204	1 721	1 483	50.0
40 - 44	782	410	372	11.3
45 - 49	45	24	21	0.6
50 +	2	1	1	..
Unknown - Inconnu	6	1	5	..

Liechtenstein
2015 (C)

Total	325	177	148	37.2
0 - 14	-	-	-	..
15 - 19	4	1	3	♦3.6
20 - 24	27	17	10	♦24.5
25 - 29	88	48	40	78.4
30 - 34	121	67	54	106.0
35 - 39	68	34	34	56.9
40 - 44	13	8	5	♦9.1
45 - 49	3	2	1	♦1.8
50 +	1	-	1	..
Unknown - Inconnu	-	-	-	..

Lithuania - Lituanie
2015 (C)

Total	31 475	16 201	15 274	47.5
0 - 14	8	6	2	..
15 - 19	1 136	555	581	14.1
20 - 24	5 279	2 708	2 571	53.8
25 - 29	11 180	5 761	5 419	117.5
30 - 34	9 045	4 733	4 312	103.1
35 - 39	3 977	2 020	1 957	44.6
40 - 44	814	404	410	8.0
45 - 49	27	13	14	♦0.2
50 +	-	-	-	..
Unknown - Inconnu	9	1	8	..

Luxembourg
2015 (C)

Total	6 115	3 168	2 947	43.5
0 - 14	1	1	-	..

Continent, country or area, year, code[a] and age of mother (in years) / Continent, pays ou zone, année, code[a] et âge de la mère (en années)	Number - Nombre			Rate Taux
	Total	Male Masculin	Female Féminin	

EUROPE

Luxembourg
2015 (C)

15 - 19	90	43	47	5.6
20 - 24	526	263	263	30.7
25 - 29	1 537	799	738	76.4
30 - 34	2 242	1 176	1 066	102.5
35 - 39	1 417	752	665	64.8
40 - 44	276	125	151	12.9
45 - 49	22	7	15	♦1.0
50 +	2	1	1	..
Unknown - Inconnu	2	1	1	..

Malta - Malte
2015 (C)

Total	4 325	2 208	2 117	44.5
0 - 14	3	1	2	..
15 - 19	131	65	66	11.3
20 - 24	494	258	236	35.3
25 - 29	1 309	667	642	85.6
30 - 34	1 580	820	760	103.1
35 - 39	684	336	348	45.7
40 - 44	120	59	61	8.8
45 - 49	4	2	2	♦0.3
50 +	-	-	-	..
Unknown - Inconnu	-	-	-	..

Montenegro - Monténégro
2015 (C)

Total	7 386	3 868	3 518	50.2
0 - 14	2	1	1	..
15 - 19	217	114	103	11.0
20 - 24	1 244	680	564	65.9
25 - 29	2 390	1 241	1 149	116.2
30 - 34	2 103	1 072	1 031	95.6
35 - 39	960	518	442	45.5
40 - 44	201	100	101	9.9
45 - 49	23	12	11	♦1.2
50 +	2	1	1	..
Unknown - Inconnu	244	129	115	..

2016 (C)

Total	7 569	...	...	51.6
10 - 14	3	...	...	..
15 - 19	195	...	...	10.0
20 - 24	1 211	...	...	63.1
25 - 29	2 405	...	...	120.9
30 - 34	2 217	...	...	100.4
35 - 39	1 078	...	...	50.1
40 - 44	227	...	...	11.0
45 - 49	14	...	...	♦0.7
50 +	3	...	...	..
Unknown - Inconnu	216	...	...	..

Netherlands - Pays-Bas[42]
2015 (C)

Total	170 510	87 427	83 083	45.2
0 - 14	-	-	-	..
15 - 19	1 570	800	770	3.2
20 - 24	15 500	8 011	7 489	29.4
25 - 29	52 547	26 966	25 581	100.8
30 - 34	65 172	33 345	31 827	129.2
35 - 39	30 121	15 500	14 621	60.0
40 - 44	5 330	2 671	2 659	9.0
45 - 49	248	122	126	0.4
50 +	22	12	10	..
Unknown - Inconnu	-	-	-	..

10. Live births by age of mother and sex of child, general and age-specific fertility rates: latest available year, 2007 - 2016
Naissances vivantes selon l'âge de la mère et le sexe de l'enfant, taux de fécondité et taux de fécondité par âge : dernière année disponible, 2007 - 2016 (continued - suite)

Continent, country or area, year, code[a] and age of mother (in years) / Continent, pays ou zone, année, code[a] et âge de la mère (en années)	Total	Male Masculin	Female Féminin	Rate Taux	Continent, country or area, year, code[a] and age of mother (in years) / Continent, pays ou zone, année, code[a] et âge de la mère (en années)	Total	Male Masculin	Female Féminin	Rate Taux
EUROPE					**EUROPE**				
Norway - Norvège					Russian Federation -				
2015 (C)					Fédération de Russie[25]				
Total	58 815	30 242	28 573	49.1	2011 (C)				
0 - 14	-	-	-	..	Total	1 796 629	923 804	872 825	48.3
15 - 19	725	405	320	4.6	12 - 14	351	174	177	..
20 - 24	7 034	3 637	3 397	42.3	15 - 19	103 533	53 162	50 371	25.2
25 - 29	19 227	9 838	9 389	109.4	20 - 24	510 184	262 085	248 099	85.1
30 - 34	19 788	10 110	9 678	117.2	25 - 29	603 791	311 250	292 541	101.2
35 - 39	9 901	5 189	4 712	59.9	30 - 34	379 884	195 518	184 366	68.6
40 - 44	1 995	989	1 006	11.1	35 - 39	165 364	84 832	80 532	31.8
45 - 49	136	70	66	0.7	40 - 44	30 221	15 168	15 053	6.3
50 +	9	4	5	..	45 - 49	1 481	680	801	0.3
Poland - Pologne					50 +	138	65	73	..
2015 (C)					Unknown - Inconnu	1 682	870	812	..
Total	369 308	189 677	179 631	40.9	San Marino - Saint-Marin				
0 - 14	55	27	28	..	2014 (+C)				
15 - 19	11 975	6 097	5 878	12.3	Total	281	138	143	35.6
20 - 24	57 107	29 270	27 837	47.5	0 - 14	-	-	-	..
25 - 29	123 994	63 774	60 220	89.6	15 - 19	-	-	-	..
30 - 34	119 140	61 122	58 018	77.0	20 - 24	17	9	8	♦23.5
35 - 39	47 972	24 668	23 304	32.4	25 - 29	68	37	31	85.2
40 - 44	8 725	4 544	4 181	6.7	30 - 34	94	44	50	90.1
45 - 49	336	172	164	0.3	35 - 39	77	33	44	55.8
50 +	4	3	1	..	40 - 44	23	15	8	♦15.1
Portugal[21]					45 - 49	2	-	2	♦1.2
2015 (C)					50 +	-	-	-	..
Total	85 500	43 685	41 815	36.0	Serbia - Serbie[44]				
0 - 14	44	19	25	..	2014 (+C)				
15 - 19	2 251	1 186	1 065	8.3	Total	66 461	34 329	32 132	42.0
20 - 24	8 717	4 429	4 288	32.1	0 - 14	53	31	22	..
25 - 29	19 087	9 719	9 368	67.8	15 - 19	3 243	1 723	1 520	17.9
30 - 34	30 126	15 383	14 743	89.7	20 - 24	12 549	6 478	6 071	61.3
35 - 39	20 561	10 539	10 022	51.2	25 - 29	20 620	10 546	10 074	91.3
40 - 44	4 502	2 305	2 197	10.8	30 - 34	19 317	10 005	9 312	80.2
45 - 49	201	99	102	0.5	35 - 39	8 681	4 519	4 162	35.1
50 +	11	6	5	..	40 - 44	1 597	812	785	6.7
Unknown - Inconnu	-	-	-	..	45 - 49	137	73	64	0.6
Republic of Moldova -					50 +	21	14	7	..
République de Moldova[43]					Unknown - Inconnu	243	128	115	..
2012 (C)					Slovakia - Slovaquie				
Total	39 435	20 380	19 055	40.7	2015 (C)				
20 - 24	13 022	6 706	6 316	79.3	Total	55 602	28 668	26 934	41.8
25 - 29	13 443	6 967	6 476	79.7	0 - 14	50	22	28	..
30 - 34	6 746	3 411	3 335	47.2	15 - 19	3 414	1 743	1 671	24.3
35 - 39	2 591	1 370	1 221	20.4	20 - 24	8 781	4 565	4 216	50.0
40 - 44	447	231	216	3.9	25 - 29	16 663	8 619	8 044	83.3
45 - 49	8	3	5	♦0.1	30 - 34	17 235	8 761	8 474	80.9
50 +	3	3	-	..	35 - 39	8 010	4 209	3 801	36.0
Unknown - Inconnu	3	1	2	..	40 - 44	1 410	732	678	7.0
Romania - Roumanie					45 - 49	38	16	22	0.2
2015 (C)					50 +	1	1	-	..
Total	197 491	101 820	95 671	42.5	Slovenia - Slovénie				
0 - 14	676	356	320	..	2015 (C)				
15 - 19	18 633	9 660	8 973	35.3	Total	20 641	10 606	10 035	45.8
20 - 24	37 760	19 400	18 360	71.0	0 - 14	2	1	1	..
25 - 29	64 304	33 296	31 008	96.8	15 - 19	208	113	95	4.5
30 - 34	47 523	24 422	23 101	73.9	20 - 24	2 153	1 124	1 029	41.5
35 - 39	23 883	12 334	11 549	31.4	25 - 29	6 886	3 514	3 372	110.3
40 - 44	4 449	2 226	2 223	6.0	30 - 34	7 476	3 797	3 679	106.2
45 - 49	253	123	130	0.3	35 - 39	3 285	1 721	1 564	43.9
50 +	10	3	7	..	40 - 44	606	319	287	8.5
					45 - 49	23	15	8	♦0.3
					50 +	2	2	-	..

10. Live births by age of mother and sex of child, general and age-specific fertility rates: latest available year, 2007 - 2016
Naissances vivantes selon l'âge de la mère et le sexe de l'enfant, taux de fécondité et taux de fécondité par âge : dernière année disponible, 2007 - 2016 (continued - suite)

Continent, country or area, year, code[a] and age of mother (in years) / Continent, pays ou zone, année, code[a] et âge de la mère (en années)	Number - Nombre			Rate Taux
	Total	Male Masculin	Female Féminin	

EUROPE

Spain - Espagne
2015 (C)

	Total	Male Masculin	Female Féminin	Rate Taux
Total	418 432	215 503	202 929	39.0
0 - 14	98	52	46	..
15 - 19	8 126	4 202	3 924	7.7
20 - 24	29 486	15 288	14 198	26.2
25 - 29	74 734	38 730	36 004	57.5
30 - 34	148 211	76 307	71 904	93.3
35 - 39	125 162	64 242	60 920	65.3
40 - 44	30 485	15 575	14 910	15.9
45 - 49	2 010	1 038	972	1.1
50 +	120	69	51	..

Sweden - Suède
2015 (C)

	Total	Male Masculin	Female Féminin	Rate Taux
Total	114 870	59 502	55 368	53.5
0 - 14	4	3	1	..
15 - 19	1 124	562	562	4.4
20 - 24	14 048	7 272	6 776	43.5
25 - 29	36 525	19 042	17 483	111.7
30 - 34	38 273	19 748	18 525	128.0
35 - 39	20 046	10 318	9 728	67.5
40 - 44	4 544	2 401	2 143	14.2
45 - 49	278	143	135	0.8
50 +	27	12	15	..
Unknown - Inconnu	1	1	-	..

Switzerland - Suisse
2015 (C)

	Total	Male Masculin	Female Féminin	Rate Taux
Total	86 559	44 649	41 910	44.9
0 - 14	3	1	2	..
15 - 19	562	290	272	2.6
20 - 24	6 879	3 549	3 330	28.2
25 - 29	21 991	11 429	10 562	79.9
30 - 34	33 028	16 940	16 088	114.0
35 - 39	19 563	10 081	9 482	68.8
40 - 44	4 223	2 208	2 015	14.3
45 - 49	283	135	148	0.9
50 +	27	16	11	..

TFYR of Macedonia - L'ex-R. y. de Macédoine
2015 (C)

	Total	Male Masculin	Female Féminin	Rate Taux
Total	23 075	11 959	11 116	44.6
0 - 14	13	7	6	..
15 - 19	1 029	533	496	16.4
20 - 24	4 810	2 496	2 314	64.9
25 - 29	7 963	4 096	3 867	101.1
30 - 34	6 452	3 341	3 111	80.9
35 - 39	2 348	1 229	1 119	31.0
40 - 44	400	223	177	5.5
45 - 49	19	10	9	♦0.3
50 +	3	2	1	..
Unknown - Inconnu	38	22	16	..

Ukraine[45]
2014 (+C)

	Total	Male Masculin	Female Féminin	Rate Taux
Total	465 882	...	...	...
0 - 14	130	...	...	...
15 - 19	27 665	...	...	...
20 - 24	122 988	...	...	...
25 - 29	158 288	...	...	...
30 - 34	103 477	...	...	...
35 - 39	43 718	...	...	...
40 - 44	8 425	...	...	...
45 - 49	466	...	...	...
50 +	64	...	...	...
Unknown - Inconnu	661	...	...	...

EUROPE

United Kingdom of Great Britain and Northern Ireland - Royaume-Uni de Grande-Bretagne et d'Irlande du Nord[46]
2015 (C)

	Total	Male Masculin	Female Féminin	Rate Taux
Total	776 746	398 760	377 986	51.9
0 - 14	114	61	53	..
15 - 19	26 710	13 800	12 910	14.4
20 - 24	120 121	61 712	58 409	57.0
25 - 29	219 997	113 269	106 728	99.2
30 - 34	243 119	124 561	118 558	110.3
35 - 39	134 416	68 747	65 669	65.6
40 - 44	29 886	15 402	14 484	13.8
45 - 49	2 147	1 086	1 061	0.9
50 +	229	121	108	..
Unknown - Inconnu	7	1	6	..

OCEANIA - OCÉANIE

American Samoa - Samoas américaines
2014 (C)

	Total	Male Masculin	Female Féminin	Rate Taux
Total	1 084	...	...	...
0 - 14	-	...	...	..
15 - 19	117	...	...	...
20 - 24	291	...	...	...
25 - 29	288	...	...	...
30 - 34	207	...	...	...
35 - 39	135	...	...	...
40 - 44	43	...	...	...
45 - 49	3	...	...	...
50 +	-	...	...	..

Australia - Australie
2015 (+C)

	Total	Male Masculin	Female Féminin	Rate Taux
Total	305 377	157 088	148 289	53.7
0 - 14	80	36	44	..
15 - 19	8 494	4 319	4 175	11.8
20 - 24	38 733	19 972	18 761	48.0
25 - 29	83 125	42 754	40 371	95.1
30 - 34	106 734	54 948	51 786	122.2
35 - 39	54 957	28 322	26 635	69.6
40 - 44	12 217	6 209	6 008	14.6
45 - 49	844	427	417	1.1
50 +	66	34	32	..
Unknown - Inconnu	127	67	60	..

Cook Islands - Îles Cook[47]
2015* (+C)

	Total	Male Masculin	Female Féminin	Rate Taux
Total	205	...	...	...
0 - 19	24	...	...	...
20 - 24	63	...	...	...
25 - 29	47	...	...	...
30 - 34	38	...	...	...
35 - 39	21	...	...	...
40 - 44	12	...	...	...
45 +	-	...	...	...

Fiji - Fidji
2008 (+C)

	Total	Male Masculin	Female Féminin	Rate Taux
Total	17 199	...	...	76.6
0 - 14	3	...	...	..
15 - 19	1 057	...	...	27.5
20 - 24	5 180	...	...	135.3
25 - 29	5 688	...	...	157.8
30 - 34	3 227	...	...	103.4

10. Live births by age of mother and sex of child, general and age-specific fertility rates: latest available year, 2007 - 2016
Naissances vivantes selon l'âge de la mère et le sexe de l'enfant, taux de fécondité et taux de fécondité par âge : dernière année disponible, 2007 - 2016 (continued - suite)

Continent, country or area, year, code[a] and age of mother (in years) / Continent, pays ou zone, année, code[a] et âge de la mère (en années)	Number - Nombre			Rate Taux
	Total	Male Masculin	Female Féminin	

OCEANIA - OCÉANIE

Fiji - Fidji
2008 (+C)

35 - 39	1 488	...	...	53.0
40 - 44	509	...	...	18.6
45 - 49	34	...	...	1.4
50 +	-	...	...	..
Unknown - Inconnu	13	...	...	..

French Polynesia - Polynésie française
2014 (C)

Total	4 161	...	...	...
15 - 19	454	...	...	...
20 - 24	1 079	...	...	...
25 - 29	1 075	...	...	...
30 - 34	888	...	...	...
35 - 39	485	...	...	...
40 - 44	166	...	...	...
45 +	14	...	...	...

Guam[48]
2016 (C)

Total	3 433	1 794	1 639	86.6
0 - 14	1	-	1	..
15 - 19	256	138	118	37.6
20 - 24	946	494	452	144.3
25 - 29	940	487	453	155.9
30 - 34	785	421	364	149.4
35 - 39	396	203	193	81.3
40 - 44	102	49	53	20.3
45 - 49	6	2	4	♦1.2
50 +	-	-	...	..
Unknown - Inconnu	1	-	1	..

Nauru
2011 (C)

Total	370	190	180	...
15 - 19	40	22	18	...
20 - 24	126	69	57	...
25 - 29	111	57	54	...
30 - 34	55	22	33	...
35 - 39	33	17	16	...
40 - 44	5	3	2	...
45 - 49	-	-	-	...

New Caledonia - Nouvelle-Calédonie
2015 (C)

Total	4 191	...	...	...
0 - 19	197	...	...	...
20 - 24	888	...	...	...
25 - 29	1 148	...	...	...
30 - 34	1 046	...	...	...
35 - 39	671	...	...	...
40 - 44	233	...	...	...
45 - 49	6	...	...	...
50 +	2	...	...	...

OCEANIA - OCÉANIE

New Zealand - Nouvelle-Zélande[49]
2016 (+C)

Total	59 430	30 519	28 908	53.4
0 - 14	15	6	6	..
15 - 19	2 466	1 260	1 209	16.0
20 - 24	9 636	4 977	4 656	57.8
25 - 29	16 362	8 289	8 073	97.2
30 - 34	18 531	9 648	8 883	120.2
35 - 39	10 011	5 106	4 905	69.0
40 - 44	2 283	1 167	1 116	14.5
45 +	126	63	63	0.8

Niue - Nioué[50]
2009 (C)

Total	31	...	...	...
0 - 14	-	...	...	..
15 - 19	1	...	...	...
20 - 24	9	...	...	...
25 - 29	12	...	...	...
30 - 34	6	...	...	...
35 - 39	1	...	...	...
40 - 44	1	...	...	...
45 +	1	...	...	...

Samoa[51]
2011 (|)

Total	5 703	3 055	2 648	133.8
15 - 19	369	209	160	39.2
20 - 24	1 557	831	726	218.3
25 - 29	1 471	793	678	238.6
30 - 34	1 154	603	551	206.1
35 - 39	741	398	343	144.1
40 - 44	338	180	158	69.9
45 - 49	73	41	32	16.9

Tokelau - Tokélaou[52]
2011 (|)

Total	16	...	...	...
0 - 14	-	...	...	..
15 - 19	1	...	...	...
20 - 24	6	...	...	...
25 - 29	4	...	...	...
30 - 34	4	...	...	...
35 - 39	1	...	...	...

Wallis and Futuna Islands - Îles Wallis et Futuna
2008 (C)

Total	185	...	...	...
0 - 14	-	...	...	..
15 - 19	9	...	...	...
20 - 24	38	...	...	...
25 - 29	53	...	...	...
30 - 34	51	...	...	...
35 - 39	29	...	...	...
40 - 44	5	...	...	...
45 +	-	...	...	...

FOOTNOTES - NOTES

♦ Rates based on 30 or fewer births. - Taux basés sur 30 naissances ou moins.

* Provisional. - Données provisoires.

[a] 'Code' indicates the source of data, as follows:
  C - Civil registration, estimated over 90% complete
  U - Civil registration, estimated less than 90% complete

| - Other source, estimated reliable
+ - Data tabulated by date of registration rather than occurrence
... Information not available

Le 'Code' indique la source des données, comme suit :
C - Registres de l'état civil considérés complets à 90 p. 100 au moins
U - Registres de l'état civil qui ne sont pas considérés complets à 90 p. 100 au moins
| - Autre source, considérée fiable
+ - Données exploitées selon la date de l'enregistrement et non la date de

l'événement

... Information non disponible

[1] Source: Vital Statistics Report 2014. - Source: Vital Statistics Report 2014.

[2] Data refer to the 12 months preceding the census in September. - Les données se rapportent aux 12 mois précédant le recensement de septembre.

[3] Unadjusted number of births in households referring to the 12 months preceding the census in March. - Le nombre non ajusté de naissances vivantes des ménages ordinaires se rapportent aux 12 mois précédant le recensement de mars.

[4] Unrevised data. - Les données n'ont pas été révisées.

[5] Data refer to the 12 months preceding the census in March. - Les données se rapportent aux 12 mois précédant le recensement de mars.

[6] Data refer to Libyan nationals only. - Les données se raportent aux nationaux libyens seulement.

[7] Data refer to the 12 months preceding the census in June. - Les données se raportent aux 12 mois précédant le recensement de juin.

[8] Data refer to the 12 months preceding the census in April. - Les données se rapportent aux douze mois précédant le recensement d'avril.

[9] Data refer to the 12 months preceding the census in March. Including nomadic population. - Les données se rapportent aux 12 mois précédant le recensement de mars. Y compris la population nomade.

[10] Excludes the islands of St. Brandon and Agalega. - Non compris les îles St. Brandon et Agalega.

[11] Data refer to the 12 months preceding the census in August. - Les données se rapportent aux 12 mois précédant le recensement d'août.

[12] Excluding live-born infants who died before their birth was registered. - Non compris les enfants nés vivants décédés avant l'enregistrement de leur naissance.

[13] Data refer to the 12 months preceding the census in May. - Les données se rapportent aux 12 mois précédant le recensement de mai.

[14] Data refer to the 12 months preceding the census in October. - Les données se rapportent aux 12 mois précédant le recensement de octobre.

[15] Excluding non-residents and foreign service personnel and their dependants. - À l'exclusion des non-résidents et du personnel diplomatique et de leurs charges de famille.

[16] Including Canadian residents temporarily in the United States, but excluding United States residents temporarily in Canada. - Y compris les résidents canadiens se trouvant temporairement aux Etats-Unis, mais ne comprenant pas les résidents des Etats-Unis se trouvant temporairement au Canada.

[17] For confidentiality reasons, live births to mothers aged 50 and over and the adopted children with no information on their birth mother are included in 'age of mother Unknown'. - Pour des raisons de confidentialité, on a classé dans la catégorie « âge de la mère Inconnu» les naissances vivantes concernant des femmes âgées de plus de 50 ans et les enfants adoptés nés de mères sur lesquelles on ne dispose pas d'information.

[18] Excluding children born in the country of non-resident mothers. - Exceptés les enfants nés dans le pays des mères non-résidentes.

[19] Data refer to population in private households. Data refer to period from 1 January 2010 to 3 April 2011. - Les données portent sur la population des ménages privés. Les données concernent la période du 1 janvier 2010 au 3 avril 2011.

[20] Figures for male and female may not add up to the total, since they do not include the category "Unknown". - La somme des chiffres indiqués pour les sexes masculin et féminin peut n'être pas égale au total parce qu'elle n'inclut pas la catégorie " inconnue ".

[21] Data refer to births to resident mothers. - Ces données concernent les enfants nés de mères résidentes.

[22] Including births abroad and births of unknown residence of mother. - Y compris les naissances à l'étranger et les naissances pour lesquelles le lieu de résidence de la mère est inconnu.

[23] Excludes nomadic Indian tribes. - Non compris les tribus d'Indiens nomades.

[24] Source: Reports of the Ministry of Health. - Source : Rapports du Ministère de la Santé.

[25] Excluding infants born alive of less than 28 weeks' gestation, of less than 1 000 g in weight and 35 cm in length, who die within seven days of birth. - Non compris les enfants nés vivants après moins de 28 semaines de gestations, pesant moins de 1 000 g, mesurant moins de 35 cm et décédés dans les sept jours qui ont suivi leur naissance.

[26] Sources: Births and Deaths National Registration System database, and medical records of government hospitals. - Les sources: Les bases de données des << Births and Deaths National Registration System >> et les dossiers médicaux des hôpitaux du gouvernement.

[27] Data refer to government controlled areas. - Les données se rapportent aux zones contrôlées par le Gouvernement.

[28] Data are from 1 January 2009 to 1 May 2010. - Les données vont du 1er janvier 2009 au 1er mai 2010.

[29] Data refer to the Iranian Year which begins on 21 March and ends on 20 March of the following year. Data refer to current birth data; excluding delayed birth registrations. - Les données concernent l'année iranienne, qui commence le 21 mars et se termine le 20 mars de l'année suivante. Les données se rapportent aux naissances actuelles; les déclarations tardives des naissances ne sont pas compris.

[30] Includes data for East Jerusalem and Israeli residents in certain other territories under occupation by Israeli military forces since June 1967. - Y compris les données pour Jérusalem-Est et les résidents israéliens dans certains autres territoires occupés depuis 1967 par les forces armées israéliennes.

[31] Data refer to Japanese nationals in Japan only. - Les données se rapportent aux nationaux japonais au Japon seulement.

[32] Data are from Vital Registration System (VRS). - Les données proviennent du système d'enregistrement des faits d'état civil.

[33] Data from Births and Deaths Notification System (Ministry of Health and all health care providers). - Les données proviennent du système de notification des naissances et des décès (Ministère de la santé et tous prestataires de soins de santé).

[34] Excluding alien armed forces, civilian aliens employed by armed forces, and foreign diplomatic personnel and their dependants. - Non compris les militaires étrangers, les civils étrangers employés par les forces armées ni le personnel diplomatique étranger et les membres de leur famille les accompagnant.

[35] Data have not been adjusted for underenumeration. Data refer to the 12 months preceding the census in December. Excluding data from the parts of Jerusalem which were annexed by Israel in 1967. - Les données n'ont pas été ajustées pour compenser les lacunes du dénombrement. Les données se rapportent aux 12 mois précédant le recensement de décembre. Non compris les données provenant des parties de Jérusalem qui ont été annexées par Israël en 1967.

[36] Including births occurring abroad of mothers with residence in Austria. - Y compris les naissances survenues à l'étranger des mères avec résidence en Autriche.

[37] Including armed forces stationed outside the country, but excluding alien armed forces stationed in the area. - Y compris les militaires nationaux hors du pays, mais non compris les militaires étrangers en garnison sur le territoire.

[38] Excluding Faeroe Islands and Greenland shown separately, if available. - Non compris les Iles Féroé et le Groenland, qui font l'objet de rubriques distinctes, si disponible.

[39] Including armed forces stationed outside the country. - Y compris les militaires nationaux hors du pays.

[40] Including live births by military personnel and their dependants. - Y compris les naissances vivantes parmi les membres du personnel militaire et leurs personnes à charge.

[41] Data include the live births of women with unknown residence and homeless. Data include the live births of women with Hungarian usual residence regardless of whether the live birth occurred in Hungary or in a foreign country, and do not include the live births of women with foreign country usual residence. - Les données incluent les enfants nés vivants de femmes dont la résidence n'est pas connue et de femmes sans domicile fixe. Les données concernent les enfants nés vivants de femmes dont la résidence habituelle est en Hongrie, que la naissance vivante ait eu lieu en Hongrie ou dans un pays étranger, et ne comprennent pas les enfants nés vivants de femmes dont la résidence habituelle est dans un pays étranger.

[42] Including residents outside the country if listed in a Netherlands population register. - Englobe les résidents se trouvant à l'étranger à condition qu'ils soient inscrits sur le registre de population des Pays-Bas.

[43] Excluding infants born alive of less than 28 weeks' gestation, of less than 1 000 g in weight and 35 cm in length, who die within seven days of birth. Excluding Transnistria and the municipality of Bender. - Non compris les enfants nés vivants après moins de 28 semaines de gestations, pesant moins de 1 000 g, mesurant moins de 35 cm et décédés dans les sept jours qui ont suivi leur naissance. Les données ne tiennent pas compte de l'information sur la Transnistria et la municipalité de Bender.

[44] Excludes data for Kosovo and Metohia. - Sans les données pour le Kosovo et Metohie.

[45] Data refer to births with weight 500g and more (if weight is unknown - with length 25 centimeters and more, or with gestation during 22 weeks or more). The Government of Ukraine has informed the United Nations that it is not in a position to provide statistical data concerning the Autonomous Republic of Crimea and the city of Sevastopol. - Données concernant les nouveau-nés de 500 grammes ou plus (si le poids est inconnu – de 25 centimètres de long ou plus, ou après une grossesse de 22 semaines ou plus). Le gouvernement Ukrainien a informé l'ONU qu'il n'est pas en mesure de fournir des données statistiques concernant la République autonome de Crimée et la ville de Sébastopol.

[46] Excluding Channel Islands (Guernsey and Jersey) and Isle of Man, shown separately, if available. Data tabulated by date of occurrence for England and Wales, and by date of registration for Northern Ireland and Scotland. - Non

compris les îles Anglo-Normandes (Guernesey et Jersey) et l'île de Man, qui font l'objet de rubriques distinctes, si disponible. Données exploitées selon la date de l'événement pour l'Angleterre et le pays de Galles, et selon la date de l'enregistrement pour l'Irlande du Nord et l'Ecosse.

[47] Excluding Niue, shown separately, which is part of Cook Islands, but because of remoteness is administered separately. - Non compris Nioué, qui fait l'objet d'une rubrique distincte et qui fait partie des îles Cook, mais qui, en raison de son éloignement, est administrée séparément.

[48] Including United States military personnel, their dependants and contract employees. - Y compris les militaires des Etats-Unis, les membres de leur famille les accompagnant et les agents contractuels des Etats-Unis.

[49] Random rounding to base 3 is applied in this table as a confidentiality measure. - Les chiffres sont arrondis à la base 3 de manière aléatoire, pour des raisons de confidentialité.

[50] Includes children born in New Zealand to women resident in Niue who chose to travel to New Zealand to give birth. - Y compris les enfants nés en Nouvelle-Zélande de femmes résidant à Nioué qui ont choisi de se rendre en Nouvelle-Zélande pour accoucher.

[51] Data refer to the 12 months preceding the census in November. - Données se rapportant aux 12 mois précédant le recensement de novembre.

[52] Data refer to usually resident population present on census night. Data refer to the 12 months preceding the census in October. - Les données concernent la population habituellement résidente présente la nuit du recensement. Les données se rapportent aux 12 mois précédant le recensement de octobre.

Table 11 - *Demographic Yearbook 2016*

Table 11 presents live births by age of father and live birth rates by age of father for the latest available year between 2007 and 2016.

Description of variables: Age is defined as age at last birthday, that is, the difference between the date of birth and the date of the occurrence of the event, expressed in completed solar years. The age classification used in this table is the following: under 20 years, 5-year age groups through 60-64 years, 65 years and over, and age unknown. A different classification may appear as provided by reporting country or area.

Rate computation: Live-birth rates specific to age of father are the annual number of births to a man in each age group per 1 000 male population in the same age group. These rates are calculated by the Statistics Division of the United Nations.

Since relatively few births occur to men below 15 or above 59 years of age, birth rates for men under 20 years of age and for those 55 years of age or over are computed on the male population aged 15-19 and 55-59, respectively. Similarly, the rate for men of "All ages" is based on all live births irrespective of age of father, and is computed on the male population aged 15-59 years.

Births to fathers of unknown age are distributed proportionately across the age groups, by the Statistics Division of the United Nations, in accordance with the distribution of births by age of father prior to the calculation of the rates.

The population used in computing the rates is the estimated or enumerated distribution of males by age. First priority is given to the estimated population and second priority to the enumerated population, i.e. to census returns of the year to which the births refer.

Rates presented in this table are limited to those for countries or areas having at least a total of 100 live births in a given year.

Reliability of data: Data from civil registers of live births which are reported as incomplete (less than 90 per cent completeness) or of unknown completeness are considered unreliable and are set in *italics* rather than in roman type. Rates are not computed if the data on live births from civil registers are reported as incomplete (less than 90 per cent completeness) or of unknown completeness. Table 9 and the technical notes for that table provide more detailed information on the completeness of birth registration. For more information about the quality of vital statistics data in general, see section 4.2 of the Technical Notes.

Limitations: Statistics on live births by age of father are subject to the same qualifications as have been set forth for vital statistics in general and birth statistics in particular as discussed in section 4 of the Technical Notes. These include differences in the completeness of registration, the method used to determine age of father and the quality of the reported information relating to age of father.

The reliability of the data described above, is an important factor in considering the limitations. In addition, some live births are tabulated by date of registration and not by date of occurrence; these are indicated in the table by a plus sign "+". Whenever the lag between the date of occurrence and date of registration is prolonged and, therefore, a large proportion of the live-birth registrations are delayed, birth statistics for any given year may be seriously affected. For example, the age of the father will almost always refer to the date of registration rather than to the date of birth of the child. Hence, in those countries or areas where registration of births is delayed, possibly for years, statistics on births by age of father should be used with caution.

Another factor which limits international comparability is the practice of some countries or areas of not including in live birth statistics infants who were born alive but died before the registration of the birth or within the first 24 hours of life, thus underestimating the total number of live births. Statistics of this type are footnoted.

Because these statistics are classified according to age, they are subject to the limitations with respect to accuracy of age reporting similar to those already discussed in connection with section 3.1.3 of the Technical Notes. The factors influencing the accuracy of reporting may be somewhat dissimilar in vital statistics (because of the differences in the method of taking a census and registering a birth) but, in general, the same errors can be observed. The absence of frequencies in the unknown age group does not necessarily indicate completely accurate reporting and tabulation of the age item. It is often an indication that the unknowns have been eliminated by assigning ages to them before tabulation, or by proportionate distribution after tabulation.

On the other hand, large frequencies in the unknown age category may indicate that a large proportion of the births are born outside of wedlock, the records for which tend to be incomplete so far as characteristics of the parents are concerned.

Another limitation of age reporting may result from calculating age of father at birth of child (or at time of registration) from year of birth rather than from day, month and year of birth. Information on this factor is given in footnotes when known.

In few countries, data by age refer to deliveries rather than to live births causing under-enumeration in the event of a multiple birth. This practice leads to lack of strict comparability, both among countries or areas relying on this practice and between data shown in this table and table 9.

Rates shown in this table are subject to the same limitations that affect the corresponding statistics on live births. In cases of rates based on births tabulated by date of registration and not by date of occurrence; the effect of including delayed registration on the distribution of births by age of father may be noted in the age-specific fertility rates for men at older ages. In some cases, high age-specific rates for men aged 55 years and over may reflect age of father at registration of birth and not fertility at these older ages.

Earlier data: Live births and live birth rates by age of father have been shown in previous issues of the *Demographic Yearbook*. Information on the specific years is presented in the Historical Index.

Tableau 11 – *Annuaire démographique 2016*

Le tableau 11 présente les données les plus récentes disponibles pour la période 2007 - 2016 sur les naissances vivantes selon l'âge du père et les taux des naissances vivantes selon l'âge du père.

Description des variables : l'âge désigne l'âge au dernier anniversaire, c'est-à-dire la différence entre la date de naissance et la date de l'événement exprimée en années solaires révolues. La classification par âge utilisée dans ce tableau comprend les catégories suivantes : moins de 20 ans, groupes quinquennaux jusqu'à 60-64 ans, 65 ans et plus, et âge inconnu. Des groupes d'âge différents sont parfois utilisés lorsque les pays ou territoires ont fourni les données dans une autre classification.

Les taux de natalité selon l'âge du père représentent le nombre annuel de naissances vivantes intervenues dans un groupe d'âge donné pour 1 000 hommes du groupe d'âge. Ces taux ont été calculés par la Division de statistique de l'ONU.

Étant donné que le nombre de naissances parmi les hommes de moins de 15 ans ou de plus de 59 ans est relativement peu élevé, les taux de natalité parmi les hommes âgées de moins de 20 ans et celles de 55 ans et plus ont été calculés sur la base des populations masculines âgées de 15 à 19 ans et de 55 à 59 ans, respectivement. De même, le taux pour les hommes de « tous âges » est fondé sur la totalité des naissances vivantes, indépendamment de l'âge du père et ce chiffre est rapporté à l'effectif de la population masculine âgée de 15 à 59 ans.

Les naissances pour lesquelles l'âge du père était inconnu ont été réparties par la Division de statistique de l'ONU, avant le calcul des taux, suivant les proportions observées pour celles où l'âge du père était connu.

Les chiffres de population utilisés pour le calcul des taux proviennent de dénombrements ou de répartitions estimatives de la population masculine selon l'âge. On a utilisé de préférence les estimations de la population; à défaut, on s'est contenté des données censitaires se rapportant à l'année des naissances.

Les taux présentés dans ce tableau ne concernent que les pays ou zones où l'on a enregistré un total d'au moins 100 naissances vivantes dans une année donnée.

Fiabilité des données : les données sur les naissances vivantes provenant des registres de l'état civil qui sont déclarées incomplètes (degré de complétude inférieur à 90 p. 100) ou dont le degré de complétude n'est pas connu sont jugées douteuses et apparaissent en italique et non en caractères romains. On a choisi de ne pas faire figurer dans le tableau 11 des taux calculés à partir de données sur les naissances vivantes issues de registres de l'état civil qui sont déclarées incomplètes (degré de complétude inférieur à 90 p. 100) ou dont le degré de complétude n'est pas connu. Le tableau 9 et les notes techniques qui s'y rapportent présentent des renseignements plus détaillés sur le degré de complétude de l'enregistrement des naissances vivantes. Pour plus de précisions sur la qualité des statistiques de l'état civil en général, voir la section 4.2 des Notes techniques.

Insuffisance des données : les statistiques relatives aux naissances vivantes selon l'âge du père appellent toutes les réserves qui ont été formulées à propos des statistiques de l'état civil en général et des statistiques de naissances en particulier (voir la section 4 des Notes techniques). Ceci inclut les différences de complétude d'enregistrement des faits d'état civil, de méthode pour déterminer l'âge du père et de qualité d'information concernant l'âge du père.

La fiabilité des données, au sujet de laquelle des indications ont été données plus haut, est un facteur important. Il faut également tenir compte du fait que, dans certains cas, les données relatives aux naissances vivantes sont exploitées selon la date de l'enregistrement et non la date de l'événement ; ces cas ont été signalés dans le tableau par le signe '+'. Chaque fois que le décalage entre l'événement et son enregistrement est grand et qu'une forte proportion des naissances vivantes fait l'objet d'un enregistrement tardif, les statistiques des naissances vivantes pour une année donnée peuvent être considérablement faussées. Par exemple, l'âge du père représente presque toujours son âge à la date de l'enregistrement et non à la date de la naissance de l'enfant. Ainsi, dans les pays ou zones où l'enregistrement des naissances est tardif, le retard atteignant parfois plusieurs années, il faut utiliser avec prudence les statistiques concernant les naissances selon l'âge du père.

Un autre facteur qui nuit à la comparabilité internationale est la pratique de certains pays ou zones qui consiste à ne pas inclure dans les statistiques des naissances vivantes les enfants nés vivants mais décédés avant l'enregistrement de leur naissance ou dans les 24 heures qui ont suivi la naissance, pratique qui conduit à sous-estimer le nombre total de naissances vivantes. Quand pareil facteur a joué, cela a été signalé en note à la fin du tableau.

Étant donné que les statistiques du tableau 11 sont classées selon l'âge, elles appellent les mêmes réserves concernant l'exactitude des déclarations d'âge que celles formulées à la section 3.1.3 des Notes techniques. Dans le cas des statistiques de l'état civil, les facteurs qui interviennent à cet égard sont parfois différents, étant donné que le recensement de la population et l'enregistrement des naissances se font par des méthodes différentes, mais, d'une manière générale, les erreurs observées seront les mêmes. Si aucun nombre ne figure dans la rangée réservée aux âges inconnus, cela ne signifie pas nécessairement que les déclarations d'âge et l'exploitation des données par âge ont été tout à fait exactes. C'est souvent une indication que l'on a attribué un âge aux personnes d'âge inconnu avant l'exploitation des données ou qu'elles ont été réparties proportionnellement entre les différents groupes après cette opération.

À l'inverse, lorsque le nombre des personnes d'âge inconnu est important, cela peut signifier que la proportion de naissances parmi les parents célibataires est élevée, étant donné qu'en pareil cas l'acte de naissance ne contient pas tous les renseignements concernant les parents.

Les déclarations par âge peuvent comporter des distorsions, du fait que l'âge du père au moment de la naissance d'un enfant (ou de la déclaration de naissance) est donné par année de naissance et non par date exacte (jour, mois et année).

Dans quelques pays, la classification par âges se réfère aux accouchements, et non aux naissances vivantes, ce qui conduit à un sous-dénombrement en cas de naissances gémellaires. Cette pratique nuit à la comparabilité des données, à la fois entre pays ou zones qui recourent à cette méthode et entre les données présentées dans le tableau 11 et celles du tableau 9.

Les taux présentés dans ce tableau, sont sujets aux mêmes limitations qui affectent les statistiques correspondantes de naissances vivantes. Dans le cas des taux basés sur des naissances par date d'enregistrement et non par date d'occurrence, l'effet peut être visible sur les taux de fécondité par âge des hommes aux âges plus élevés. Dans certains cas, les taux de fécondité des hommes de plus de 55 ans peuvent refléter l'âge du père à l'enregistrement plus que la fécondité à ces âges.

Données publiées antérieurement : Les données sur les naissances vivantes selon l'âge du père et les taux des naissances vivantes selon l'âge du père ont été publié antérieurement dans l'*Annuaire démographique*. Pour plus de précisions concernant les années pour lesquels des données ont été publiées, se reporter à l'index historique.

Continent, country or area, year, code[a] and age of father (in years) / Continent, pays ou zone, année, code[a] et âge du père (en années)	Number - Nombre — Both sexes / Les deux sexes	Rate / Taux
AFRICA - AFRIQUE		
Egypt - Égypte		
2012 (+C)		
Total	2 629 769	101.6
0 - 19	4 700	1.2
20 - 24	119 826	28.3
25 - 29	1 489 063	364.7
30 - 34	502 329	150.1
35 - 39	288 404	111.4
40 - 44	134 381	59.4
45 - 49	60 206	29.0
50 - 54	19 391	10.6
55 - 59	6 333	4.2
60 +	5 136	..
Mauritius - Maurice[1]		
2016 (+C)		
Total	12 948	31.1
0 - 19	186	3.9
20 - 24	1 369	28.7
25 - 29	2 720	62.0
30 - 34	3 514	82.5
35 - 39	2 920	60.0
40 - 44	1 104	26.8
45 - 49	397	9.5
50 - 54	115	2.5
55 - 59	29	0.7
60 - 64	12	..
65 +	3	..
Unknown - Inconnu	579	..
Reunion - Réunion[2]		
2007 (C)		
Total	14 808	61.9
0 - 19	352	10.0
20 - 24	2 409	88.2
25 - 29	3 283	139.4
30 - 34	3 693	141.6
35 - 39	2 860	96.2
40 - 44	1 488	46.6
45 - 49	491	19.2
50 - 54	151	6.8
55 - 59	53	3.0
60 - 64	28	..
AMERICA, NORTH - AMÉRIQUE DU NORD		
Bahamas		
2014* (+U)		
Total	4 196	...
0 - 19	63	...
20 - 24	576	...
25 - 29	742	...
30 - 34	815	...
35 - 39	659	...
40 - 44	388	...
45 - 49	167	...
50 - 54	60	...
55 - 59	23	...
60 - 64	5	..
65 +	6	..
Unknown - Inconnu	692	..
Barbados - Barbade		
2007 (+C)		
Total	3 537	...
0 - 19	95	...
20 - 24	564	...
25 - 29	745	...
30 - 34	784	...

Continent, country or area, year, code[a] and age of father (in years) / Continent, pays ou zone, année, code[a] et âge du père (en années)	Number - Nombre — Both sexes / Les deux sexes	Rate / Taux
AMERICA, NORTH - AMÉRIQUE DU NORD		
Barbados - Barbade		
2007 (+C)		
35 - 39	605	...
40 - 44	381	...
45 - 49	163	...
50 - 54	53	...
55 - 59	17	...
60 - 64	8	..
65 +	3	..
Unknown - Inconnu	119	..
Canada[3]		
2009 (C)		
Total	380 863	35.1
0 - 19	4 918	4.5
20 - 24	29 959	26.5
25 - 29	84 206	75.0
30 - 34	117 201	109.5
35 - 39	79 126	72.1
40 - 44	31 813	26.9
45 - 49	9 913	7.5
50 - 54	2 642	2.2
55 - 59	683	0.7
60 - 64	200	..
65 +	77	..
Unknown - Inconnu	20 125	..
Costa Rica		
2016* (C)		
Total[4]	64 695	42.6
0 - 19	1 300	9.6
20 - 24	7 074	51.8
25 - 29	10 551	84.3
30 - 34	10 373	92.4
35 - 39	6 895	67.6
40 - 44	3 034	32.6
45 - 49	1 280	14.4
50 - 54	577	6.0
55 - 59	212	2.6
60 - 64	77	..
Unknown - Inconnu	23 322	..
Cuba		
2016 (C)		
Total	116 872	32.3
0 - 19	2 566	8.1
20 - 24	17 335	53.0
25 - 29	29 997	81.5
30 - 34	22 579	71.0
35 - 39	13 030	45.2
40 - 44	9 312	23.1
45 - 49	4 690	10.9
50 - 54	1 923	4.6
55 - 59	449	1.6
60 - 64	165	..
65 +	113	..
Unknown - Inconnu	14 713	..
Dominican Republic - République dominicaine		
2016 (U)		
Total	139 583	...
0 - 19	3 277	...
20 - 24	23 323	...
25 - 29	31 907	...
30 - 34	27 351	...
35 - 39	17 776	...
40 - 44	9 075	...
45 - 49	4 576	...
50 +	3 754	...
Unknown - Inconnu	18 544	...

11. Live births and live birth rates by age of father: latest available year, 2007 - 2016
Naissances vivantes et taux de natalité selon l'âge du père : dernière année disponible, 2007 - 2016 (continued - suite)

Continent, country or area, year, code[a] and age of father (in years) / Continent, pays ou zone, année, code[a] et âge du père (en années)	Number - Nombre — Both sexes Les deux sexes	Rate Taux
AMERICA, NORTH - AMÉRIQUE DU NORD		
El Salvador[5]		
2014 (C)		
Total	108 903	62.6
0 - 19	6 884	22.6
20 - 24	22 522	84.4
25 - 29	22 722	115.0
30 - 34	18 048	114.4
35 - 39	12 219	84.6
40 - 44	6 345	47.2
45 - 49	2 957	25.3
50 - 54	1 360	13.7
55 - 59	666	7.9
60 - 64	309	..
65 +	199	..
Unknown - Inconnu	14 672	..
Greenland - Groenland		
2008 (C)		
Total	834	...
0 - 19	25	...
20 - 24	109	...
25 - 29	169	...
30 - 34	150	...
35 - 39	112	...
40 - 44	91	...
45 - 49	35	...
50 - 54	9	...
55 - 59	1	...
60 +	-	..
Unknown - Inconnu	133	..
Guatemala		
2011 (C)		
Total	373 692	102.3
0 - 19	23 425	32.4
20 - 24	82 898	139.8
25 - 29	83 786	170.2
30 - 34	64 952	167.6
35 - 39	39 412	131.9
40 - 44	20 601	86.9
45 - 49	9 366	47.8
50 - 54	3 893	23.6
55 - 59	1 723	11.6
60 - 64	769	..
65 +	556	..
Unknown - Inconnu	42 311	..
Martinique[2]		
2007 (C)		
Total	5 317	47.3
0 - 19	98	6.2
20 - 24	710	60.7
25 - 29	1 043	119.9
30 - 34	1 173	111.7
35 - 39	1 293	95.6
40 - 44	702	46.1
45 - 49	235	16.2
50 - 54	42	3.5
55 - 59	16	♦1.5
60 +	3	..
Mexico - Mexique[6]		
2014 (C)		
Total	2 129 825	59.3
0 - 19	141 220	27.5
20 - 24	488 851	102.6
25 - 29	497 795	117.3
30 - 34	398 917	101.8
35 - 39	239 390	64.4
40 - 44	110 900	32.2
45 - 49	39 944	13.3

Continent, country or area, year, code[a] and age of father (in years) / Continent, pays ou zone, année, code[a] et âge du père (en années)	Number - Nombre — Both sexes Les deux sexes	Rate Taux
AMERICA, NORTH - AMÉRIQUE DU NORD		
Mexico - Mexique[6]		
2014 (C)		
50 - 54	15 649	6.3
55 - 59	6 289	3.1
60 - 64	2 583	..
65 +	1 589	..
Unknown - Inconnu	186 698	..
Panama		
2015* (C)		
Total	75 901	61.5
0 - 19	2 771	23.2
20 - 24	10 521	94.4
25 - 29	12 533	117.4
30 - 34	11 330	110.6
35 - 39	7 434	76.0
40 - 44	4 077	44.2
45 - 49	1 762	21.5
50 - 54	738	10.6
55 - 59	282	5.0
60 - 64	92	..
65 +	60	..
Unknown - Inconnu	24 301	..
Puerto Rico - Porto Rico		
2016 (C)		
Total	28 326	...
0 - 19	1 264	...
20 - 24	6 670	...
25 - 29	7 484	...
30 - 34	5 574	...
35 - 39	3 511	...
40 - 44	1 533	...
45 - 49	565	...
50 - 54	197	...
55 - 59	62	...
60 - 64	33	..
65 +	26	..
Unknown - Inconnu	1 407	..
Trinidad and Tobago - Trinité-et-Tobago		
2009 (C)		
Total	17 949	...
0 - 19	389	...
20 - 24	3 027	...
25 - 29	4 916	...
30 - 34	4 149	...
35 - 39	2 682	...
40 - 44	1 416	...
45 - 49	730	...
50 - 54	259	...
55 - 59	73	...
60 +	51	..
Unknown - Inconnu	257	..
United States of America - États-Unis d'Amérique		
2015 (C)		
Total	3 978 497	41.1
0 - 19	78 966	8.3
20 - 24	477 664	46.6
25 - 29	866 460	86.4
30 - 34	1 031 310	107.7
35 - 39	648 051	72.5
40 - 44	263 377	29.9
45 - 49	89 921	9.9
50 - 54	29 105	3.0
55 +	12 911	1.4
Unknown - Inconnu	480 732	..

Continent, country or area, year, code[a] and age of father (in years) Continent, pays ou zone, année, code[a] et âge du père (en années)	Number - Nombre Both sexes Les deux sexes	Rate Taux
AMERICA, SOUTH - AMÉRIQUE DU SUD		
Chile - Chili		
2014 (C)		
Total	250 997	43.3
0 - 19	12 725	20.4
20 - 24	41 190	60.4
25 - 29	52 776	78.2
30 - 34	54 460	90.4
35 - 39	37 095	65.9
40 - 44	18 908	33.6
45 - 49	6 940	12.2
50 +	3 460	3.5
Unknown - Inconnu	23 443	..
Colombia - Colombie		
2014 (U)		
Total	669 137	...
0 - 19	43 790	...
20 - 24	156 289	...
25 - 29	166 282	...
30 - 34	137 163	...
35 - 39	80 662	...
40 - 44	39 995	...
45 - 49	16 475	...
50 - 54	7 150	...
55 - 59	2 355	...
60 - 64	898	..
65 +	415	..
Unknown - Inconnu	17 663	..
Ecuador - Équateur		
2011 (+U)		
Total	229 780	...
0 - 19	4 219	...
20 - 24	16 514	...
25 - 29	17 040	...
30 - 34	14 115	...
35 - 39	8 339	...
40 - 44	4 405	...
45 - 49	1 864	...
50 - 54	719	...
55 - 59	274	...
60 - 64	104	..
65 +	94	..
Unknown - Inconnu	162 093	..
French Guiana - Guyane française[2]		
2007 (C)		
Total	6 386	104.6
0 - 19	323	32.6
20 - 24	1 263	164.2
25 - 29	1 401	203.5
30 - 34	1 334	175.5
35 - 39	1 043	138.4
40 - 44	622	90.0
45 - 49	230	38.8
50 - 54	94	19.2
55 - 59	59	16.1
60 - 64	17	..
65 +	-	..
Uruguay		
2015 (C)		
Total	48 926	47.2
0 - 19	1 263	14.0
20 - 24	5 179	59.6
25 - 29	6 778	82.6
30 - 34	7 901	101.9
35 - 39	6 249	79.5
40 - 44	2 915	40.3
45 - 49	1 084	16.6
50 - 54	381	5.9

Continent, country or area, year, code[a] and age of father (in years) Continent, pays ou zone, année, code[a] et âge du père (en années)	Number - Nombre Both sexes Les deux sexes	Rate Taux
AMERICA, SOUTH - AMÉRIQUE DU SUD		
Uruguay		
2015 (C)		
55 - 59	135	2.3
60 - 64	54	..
65 +	23	..
Unknown - Inconnu	16 964	..
Venezuela (Bolivarian Republic of) - Venezuela (République bolivarienne du)		
2015 (U)		
Total	600 860	...
0 - 19	35 209	...
20 - 24	117 191	...
25 - 29	124 572	...
30 - 34	100 317	...
35 - 39	61 254	...
40 - 44	31 646	...
45 - 49	14 466	...
50 +	10 213	...
Unknown - Inconnu	105 992	..
ASIA - ASIE		
Azerbaijan - Azerbaïdjan[7]		
2015 (+C)		
Total	159 475	49.2
0 - 19	431	1.2
20 - 24	23 797	52.2
25 - 29	64 217	137.9
30 - 34	42 933	105.0
35 - 39	18 523	53.7
40 - 44	6 645	22.3
45 - 49	2 130	6.8
50 - 54	586	1.9
55 +	213	0.8
Bahrain - Bahreïn[8]		
2014 (C)		
Total	20 931	33.2
0 - 19	41	1.1
20 - 24	1 431	22.9
25 - 29	4 660	38.5
30 - 34	5 958	51.0
35 - 39	4 656	52.2
40 - 44	2 518	35.3
45 - 49	1 090	19.6
50 - 54	383	9.0
55 - 59	123	3.8
60 - 64	49	..
65 +	19	..
Unknown - Inconnu	3	..
Brunei Darussalam - Brunéi Darussalam		
2015 (+C)		
Total	6 699	44.4
0 - 19	38	2.2
20 - 24	389	23.0
25 - 29	1 654	85.8
30 - 34	1 947	100.1
35 - 39	1 327	75.0
40 - 44	598	37.8
45 - 49	191	13.9
50 - 54	57	4.9
55 +	36	4.1
Unknown - Inconnu	462	..
China, Hong Kong SAR - Chine, Hong Kong RAS		
2016 (C)		
Total	60 856	28.2
0 - 19	131	0.8

Continent, country or area, year, code[a] and age of father (in years) / Continent, pays ou zone, année, code[a] et âge du père (en années)	Number - Nombre — Both sexes Les deux sexes	Rate Taux
ASIA - ASIE		
China, Hong Kong SAR - Chine, Hong Kong RAS		
2016 (C)		
20 - 24	1 757	8.1
25 - 29	8 637	38.6
30 - 34	19 639	85.9
35 - 39	17 183	76.8
40 - 44	7 815	33.9
45 - 49	2 763	11.7
50 - 54	1 144	4.0
55 - 59	449	1.5
60 - 64	151	..
65 +	69	..
Unknown - Inconnu	1 118	..
China, Macao SAR - Chine, Macao RAS		
2015 (C)		
Total	7 055	30.1
0 - 24	355	9.1
25 - 29	2 033	57.0
30 - 34	2 202	69.0
35 - 39	1 303	51.9
40 - 44	638	25.3
45 +	421	5.7
Unknown - Inconnu	103	..
Cyprus - Chypre[9]		
2013 (C)		
Total	9 341	34.7
0 - 19	26	♦0.9
20 - 24	425	12.5
25 - 29	2 057	57.9
30 - 34	3 332	99.3
35 - 39	2 094	75.0
40 - 44	785	29.3
45 - 49	292	11.1
50 +	143	2.7
Unknown - Inconnu	187	..
Israel - Israël[10]		
2015 (C)		
Total	178 723	75.8
0 - 19	335	1.1
20 - 24	14 342	48.8
25 - 29	38 852	137.8
30 - 34	53 172	194.1
35 - 39	39 232	149.7
40 - 44	17 206	70.7
45 - 49	4 526	22.1
50 - 54	1 176	6.4
55 - 59	375	2.2
60 - 64	144	..
65 +	62	..
Unknown - Inconnu	9 301	..
Japan - Japon[11]		
2015 (C)		
Total	982 645	28.3
0 - 19	4 138	1.4
20 - 24	53 159	16.5
25 - 29	202 173	60.0
30 - 34	329 831	88.4
35 - 39	248 514	58.3
40 - 44	109 619	22.1
45 - 49	26 971	6.2
50 - 54	5 989	1.5
55 - 59	1 517	0.4
60 - 64	500	..
65 +	230	..
Unknown - Inconnu	4	..
ASIA - ASIE		
Kyrgyzstan - Kirghizstan		
2016* (C)		
Total	158 160	86.0
0 - 19	413	1.8
20 - 24	18 791	72.3
25 - 29	49 641	189.4
30 - 34	37 790	176.0
35 - 39	21 462	125.6
40 - 44	10 116	68.4
45 - 49	3 018	22.0
50 - 54	713	5.7
55 - 59	215	2.0
60 - 64	47	..
65 +	26	..
Unknown - Inconnu	15 928	..
Malaysia - Malaisie		
2015 (C)		
Total	521 136	48.6
0 - 19	2 644	1.9
20 - 24	31 570	19.4
25 - 29	130 701	81.6
30 - 34	160 655	116.1
35 - 39	100 780	92.2
40 - 44	47 408	50.7
45 - 49	17 797	21.3
50 - 54	5 812	7.5
55 - 59	1 945	3.1
60 - 64	606	..
65 +	215	..
Unknown - Inconnu	21 003	..
Maldives		
2014 (C)		
Total	7 245	43.5
0 - 19	1	♦0.1
20 - 24	619	22.0
25 - 29	2 249	64.9
30 - 34	1 976	75.6
35 - 39	1 221	67.2
40 - 44	660	47.2
45 - 49	262	23.6
50 - 54	87	10.1
55 - 59	21	♦3.3
60 - 64	10	..
65 +	3	..
Unknown - Inconnu	136	..
Oman[12]		
2016 (U)		
Total	88 346	...
0 - 19	57	...
20 - 24	4 287	...
25 - 29	21 555	...
30 - 34	26 771	...
35 - 39	18 758	...
40 - 44	9 361	...
45 - 49	3 558	...
50 - 54	1 411	...
55 - 59	606	...
60 - 64	279	...
65 +	331	...
Unknown - Inconnu	1 372	..
Philippines		
2015 (C)		
Total	1 744 767	55.9
0 - 19	52 789	10.9
20 - 24	334 718	73.7
25 - 29	424 115	108.5
30 - 34	358 963	104.7

11. Live births and live birth rates by age of father: latest available year, 2007 - 2016

Naissances vivantes et taux de natalité selon l'âge du père : dernière année disponible, 2007 - 2016 (continued - suite)

Continent, country or area, year, code[a] and age of father (in years) / Continent, pays ou zone, année, code[a] et âge du père (en années)	Number - Nombre — Both sexes Les deux sexes	Rate Taux	Continent, country or area, year, code[a] and age of father (in years) / Continent, pays ou zone, année, code[a] et âge du père (en années)	Number - Nombre — Both sexes Les deux sexes	Rate Taux
ASIA - ASIE			**ASIA - ASIE**		
Philippines			Uzbekistan - Ouzbékistan[14]		
2015 (C)			2015 (+C)		
35 - 39	241 886	77.0	Total	672 996	66.2
40 - 44	122 441	44.1	0 - 19	1 241	0.9
45 - 49	51 966	20.8	20 - 24	104 638	63.5
50 - 54	17 687	8.4	25 - 29	304 347	195.0
55 - 59	6 439	3.8	30 - 34	178 532	137.9
60 - 64	2 601	..	35 - 39	64 178	59.7
65 +	1 733	..	40 - 44	15 532	16.2
Unknown - Inconnu	129 429	..	45 - 49	2 988	3.7
Qatar			50 - 54	889	1.2
2015 (C)			55 - 59	378	0.6
Total	26 622	16.3	60 - 64	55	..
0 - 19	14	♦0.2	65 +	218	..
20 - 24	890	4.2			
25 - 29	4 697	13.6	**EUROPE**		
30 - 34	8 480	26.4			
35 - 39	6 824	28.1	Åland Islands - Îles d'Åland		
40 - 44	3 526	19.2	2012 (C)		
45 - 49	1 407	10.9	Total	292	35.4
50 +	784	6.0	0 - 19	-	..
Unknown - Inconnu	-	..	20 - 24	20	♦25.1
Republic of Korea - République de Corée[13]			25 - 29	57	76.1
2015 (C)			30 - 34	83	100.3
Total	438 420	24.5	35 - 39	77	87.8
0 - 19	614	0.4	40 - 44	25	♦27.3
20 - 24	6 786	3.7	45 - 49	10	♦10.2
25 - 29	45 153	26.4	50 - 54	2	♦2.2
30 - 34	187 484	94.0	55 - 59	1	♦1.1
35 - 39	140 994	71.1	60 - 64	-	..
40 - 44	43 404	19.5	65 +	-	..
45 - 49	7 854	3.6	Unknown - Inconnu	17	..
50 - 54	1 285	0.6	Albania - Albanie		
55 - 59	274	0.1	2015 (U)		
60 - 64	49	..	Total	32 715	...
65 +	17	..	0 - 19	76	...
Unknown - Inconnu	4 506	..	20 - 24	1 939	...
Singapore - Singapour			25 - 29	8 649	...
2016 (C)			30 - 34	11 168	...
Total	41 251	32.2	35 - 39	6 516	...
0 - 19	84	0.7	40 - 44	2 723	...
20 - 24	880	6.7	45 - 49	774	...
25 - 29	6 175	45.5	50 - 54	182	...
30 - 34	14 633	109.1	55 - 59	50	...
35 - 39	12 068	85.0	60 - 64	14	...
40 - 44	4 899	32.5	65 +	4	...
45 - 49	1 350	9.3	Unknown - Inconnu	620	...
50 - 54	495	3.2	Andorra - Andorre		
55 - 59	143	1.0	2015 (C)		
60 - 64	52	..	Total	659	...
65 +	16	..	0 - 19	3	...
Unknown - Inconnu	456	..	20 - 24	18	...
Turkey - Turquie			25 - 29	70	...
2015 (C)			30 - 34	203	...
Total	1 325 783	52.1	35 - 39	202	...
0 - 19	7 448	2.2	40 - 44	104	...
20 - 24	111 151	34.8	45 - 49	23	...
25 - 29	379 188	120.4	50 - 54	11	...
30 - 34	415 630	129.0	55 - 59	4	...
35 - 39	255 168	82.2	60 - 64	3	...
40 - 44	106 197	38.4	65 +	-	..
45 - 49	28 048	12.1	Unknown - Inconnu	18	..
50 - 54	7 573	3.3	Austria - Autriche[15]		
55 - 59	2 020	1.1	2015 (C)		
60 - 64	741	..	Total	48 866	18.2
65 +	509	..	0 - 19	51	0.2
Unknown - Inconnu	12 110	..			

11. Live births and live birth rates by age of father: latest available year, 2007 - 2016
Naissances vivantes et taux de natalité selon l'âge du père : dernière année disponible, 2007 - 2016 (continued - suite)

Continent, country or area, year, code[a] and age of father (in years) Continent, pays ou zone, année, code[a] et âge du père (en années)	Number - Nombre Both sexes Les deux sexes	Rate Taux	Continent, country or area, year, code[a] and age of father (in years) Continent, pays ou zone, année, code[a] et âge du père (en années)	Number - Nombre Both sexes Les deux sexes	Rate Taux
EUROPE			**EUROPE**		
Austria - Autriche[15]			**Bulgaria - Bulgarie**		
2015 (C)			2015 (C)		
20 - 24	2 128	7.5	65 +	13	..
25 - 29	9 361	31.9	Unknown - Inconnu	9 367	..
30 - 34	16 373	55.1	**Croatia - Croatie**		
35 - 39	12 293	44.3	2015 (C)		
40 - 44	5 720	19.1	Total	37 503	29.9
45 - 49	2 052	5.8	0 - 19	206	1.7
50 - 54	617	1.8	20 - 24	2 319	18.9
55 - 59	178	0.6	25 - 29	8 006	61.5
60 - 64	64	..	30 - 34	12 913	89.5
65 +	29	..	35 - 39	8 719	60.7
Belarus - Bélarus[14]			40 - 44	3 298	24.1
2015 (C)			45 - 49	895	6.4
Total	102 565	34.8	50 - 54	287	2.0
0 - 19	679	2.9	55 - 59	85	0.6
20 - 24	13 284	42.2	60 - 64	14	..
25 - 29	35 816	90.9	65 +	3	..
30 - 34	30 885	81.4	Unknown - Inconnu	758	..
35 - 39	14 835	44.2	**Czechia - Tchéquie**		
40 - 44	5 142	16.3	2015 (C)		
45 - 49	1 411	4.6	Total	110 764	34.4
50 - 54	369	1.1	0 - 19	425	2.0
55 +	144	0.4	20 - 24	5 429	19.0
Belgium - Belgique			25 - 29	19 309	59.2
2014 (C)			30 - 34	34 146	97.1
Total	125 014	37.3	35 - 39	27 740	65.1
0 - 19	532	1.7	40 - 44	10 610	26.1
20 - 24	6 420	18.9	45 - 49	2 834	8.7
25 - 29	27 224	79.5	50 - 54	886	2.8
30 - 34	41 459	116.9	55 - 59	294	1.0
35 - 39	25 524	72.7	60 - 64	102	..
40 - 44	11 502	30.7	65 +	45	..
45 - 49	4 559	11.7	Unknown - Inconnu	8 944	..
50 - 54	1 602	4.1	**Denmark - Danemark**[16]		
55 - 59	502	1.4	2015 (C)		
60 - 64	153	..	Total	58 205	34.7
65 +	64	..	0 - 19	98	0.6
Unknown - Inconnu	5 473	..	20 - 24	2 575	14.7
Bosnia and Herzegovina - Bosnie-Herzégovine			25 - 29	12 460	76.6
2010 (C)			30 - 34	18 166	124.1
Total	33 528	28.0	35 - 39	12 299	76.5
0 - 19	99	0.7	40 - 44	4 822	27.2
20 - 24	3 174	23.3	45 - 49	1 419	7.6
25 - 29	9 300	75.0	50 - 54	448	2.5
30 - 34	10 238	90.1	55 - 59	122	0.8
35 - 39	5 624	49.2	60 - 64	48	..
40 - 44	2 203	16.5	65 +	15	..
45 - 49	672	4.8	Unknown - Inconnu	5 733	..
50 - 54	150	1.2	**Estonia - Estonie**		
55 - 59	29	0.3	2015 (C)		
60 - 64	9	..	Total	13 907	35.9
65 +	4	..	0 - 19	87	2.9
Unknown - Inconnu	2 026	..	20 - 24	1 005	26.7
Bulgaria - Bulgarie			25 - 29	3 483	70.9
2015 (C)			30 - 34	4 115	89.3
Total	65 950	30.6	35 - 39	2 702	61.3
0 - 19	716	5.2	40 - 44	1 266	28.6
20 - 24	5 465	31.7	45 - 49	474	11.8
25 - 29	14 199	66.3	50 - 54	135	3.3
30 - 34	17 372	80.0	55 - 59	44	1.1
35 - 39	12 218	51.5	60 - 64	6	..
40 - 44	4 802	20.3	65 +	3	..
45 - 49	1 295	5.9	Unknown - Inconnu	587	..
50 - 54	361	1.7			
55 - 59	100	0.5			
60 - 64	42	..			

11. Live births and live birth rates by age of father: latest available year, 2007 - 2016
Naissances vivantes et taux de natalité selon l'âge du père : dernière année disponible, 2007 - 2016 (continued - suite)

Continent, country or area, year, code[a] and age of father (in years) Continent, pays ou zone, année, code[a] et âge du père (en années)	Number - Nombre Both sexes Les deux sexes	Rate Taux	Continent, country or area, year, code[a] and age of father (in years) Continent, pays ou zone, année, code[a] et âge du père (en années)	Number - Nombre Both sexes Les deux sexes	Rate Taux
EUROPE			**EUROPE**		
Faeroe Islands - Îles Féroé			Greece - Grèce		
2015 (C)			2015 (C)		
Total	608	41.5	40 - 44	13 108	34.8
0 - 19	4	♦2.3	45 - 49	4 409	11.8
20 - 24	61	40.2	50 - 54	1 062	3.2
25 - 29	117	88.1	55 - 59	308	1.0
30 - 34	167	130.5	60 - 64	73	..
35 - 39	116	80.7	65 +	17	..
40 - 44	75	47.6	Unknown - Inconnu	5 664	..
45 - 49	19	♦11.4	Hungary - Hongrie[18]		
50 - 54	4	♦2.5	2015 (C)		
55 - 59	2	♦1.4	Total	92 135	31.0
60 - 64	-	..	0 - 19	1 071	4.6
65 +	-	..	20 - 24	5 743	20.5
Unknown - Inconnu	43	..	25 - 29	13 587	48.9
Finland - Finlande[17]			30 - 34	23 670	83.8
2015 (C)			35 - 39	23 065	63.7
Total	55 197	35.2	40 - 44	9 923	29.0
0 - 19	295	2.0	45 - 49	2 844	9.4
20 - 24	4 164	25.1	50 - 54	662	2.6
25 - 29	12 218	73.5	55 - 59	253	0.9
30 - 34	17 843	102.1	60 - 64	98	..
35 - 39	11 659	69.0	65 +	46	..
40 - 44	4 436	28.9	Unknown - Inconnu	11 173	..
45 - 49	1 504	8.8	Iceland - Islande		
50 - 54	493	2.8	2015 (C)		
55 - 59	140	0.8	Total	4 129	40.6
60 - 64	22	..	0 - 19	25	♦2.3
65 +	17	..	20 - 24	361	28.8
Unknown - Inconnu	2 406	..	25 - 29	1 067	89.4
France			30 - 34	1 251	107.4
2015 (C)			35 - 39	846	77.3
Total	760 421	42.0	40 - 44	329	30.9
0 - 19	2 592	1.3	45 - 49	110	10.9
20 - 24	39 085	21.2	50 - 54	32	3.1
25 - 29	162 844	85.7	55 - 59	6	♦0.6
30 - 34	250 049	127.7	60 - 64	7	..
35 - 39	177 749	90.2	65 +	-	..
40 - 44	82 700	38.4	Unknown - Inconnu	95	..
45 - 49	30 145	14.0	Italy - Italie		
50 - 54	10 348	4.8	2014 (C)		
55 - 59	3 521	1.8	Total	502 596	28.3
60 - 64	1 248	..	0 - 19	1 502	1.1
65 +	140	..	20 - 24	15 330	10.6
Germany - Allemagne			25 - 29	58 384	38.4
2015 (C)			30 - 34	130 273	77.8
Total	737 575	29.9	35 - 39	142 109	71.5
0 - 19	2 243	1.1	40 - 44	77 976	35.3
20 - 24	32 100	14.4	45 - 49	24 823	11.0
25 - 29	131 482	51.6	50 - 54	6 523	3.2
30 - 34	225 083	92.2	55 - 59	1 708	1.0
35 - 39	175 580	76.6	60 - 64	497	..
40 - 44	80 879	33.7	65 +	217	..
45 - 49	30 309	9.7	Unknown - Inconnu	43 254	..
50 - 54	8 600	2.6	Latvia - Lettonie		
55 - 59	2 256	0.8	2015 (C)		
60 - 64	625	..	Total	21 979	38.1
65 +	303	..	0 - 19	176	4.1
Unknown - Inconnu	48 115	..	20 - 24	1 968	33.3
Greece - Grèce			25 - 29	5 927	83.2
2015 (C)			30 - 34	6 448	95.6
Total	91 847	29.4	35 - 39	3 920	63.6
0 - 19	162	0.6	40 - 44	1 894	29.2
20 - 24	1 552	5.7	45 - 49	613	9.8
25 - 29	9 572	33.9	50 - 54	192	3.0
30 - 34	27 768	80.4	55 - 59	63	1.0
35 - 39	28 152	74.0	60 - 64	22	..

Continent, country or area, year, code[a] and age of father (in years) / Continent, pays ou zone, année, code[a] et âge du père (en années)	Number - Nombre Both sexes Les deux sexes	Rate Taux
EUROPE		
Latvia - Lettonie		
2015 (C)		
65 +	8	..
Unknown - Inconnu	748	..
Lithuania - Lituanie		
2015 (C)		
Total	31 475	36.5
0 - 19	177	2.2
20 - 24	2 596	26.2
25 - 29	8 941	93.0
30 - 34	10 016	115.8
35 - 39	5 427	65.0
40 - 44	2 090	22.9
45 - 49	621	6.6
50 - 54	192	1.9
55 - 59	54	0.6
60 - 64	9	..
65 +	5	..
Unknown - Inconnu	1 347	..
Luxembourg		
2014 (C)		
Total	6 070	33.4
0 - 19	26	+1.6
20 - 24	263	15.4
25 - 29	948	48.6
30 - 34	1 894	91.2
35 - 39	1 708	82.2
40 - 44	713	33.1
45 - 49	257	11.3
50 - 54	64	3.1
55 - 59	21	+1.2
60 - 64	5	..
65 +	3	..
Unknown - Inconnu	168	..
Malta - Malte		
2015 (C)		
Total	4 325	32.3
0 - 19	32	2.7
20 - 24	257	17.5
25 - 29	786	49.2
30 - 34	1 514	95.3
35 - 39	1 038	67.6
40 - 44	366	26.5
45 - 49	116	9.5
50 - 54	33	2.4
55 - 59	9	+0.6
60 - 64	2	..
65 +	1	..
Unknown - Inconnu	171	..
Montenegro - Monténégro		
2009 (C)		
Total	8 642	43.2
0 - 19	32	1.5
20 - 24	616	27.3
25 - 29	2 011	90.0
30 - 34	2 268	113.7
35 - 39	1 574	85.9
40 - 44	800	43.7
45 - 49	287	14.9
50 - 54	89	4.6
55 - 59	23	+1.3
60 - 64	1	..
65 +	6	..
Unknown - Inconnu	935	..

Continent, country or area, year, code[a] and age of father (in years) / Continent, pays ou zone, année, code[a] et âge du père (en années)	Number - Nombre Both sexes Les deux sexes	Rate Taux
EUROPE		
Netherlands - Pays-Bas[19]		
2014 (C)		
Total	175 181	34.8
0 - 19	333	0.7
20 - 24	6 226	12.1
25 - 29	33 346	66.4
30 - 34	60 729	125.6
35 - 39	41 980	87.5
40 - 44	17 247	30.0
45 - 49	5 280	8.5
50 - 54	1 495	2.5
55 - 59	403	0.7
60 - 64	97	..
65 +	56	..
Unknown - Inconnu	7 989	..
Norway - Norvège		
2012 (C)		
Total	60 255	38.8
0 - 19	271	1.7
20 - 24	3 931	23.9
25 - 29	13 332	83.2
30 - 34	19 068	116.9
35 - 39	13 188	76.5
40 - 44	5 590	30.1
45 - 49	1 822	10.3
50 - 54	524	3.3
55 - 59	176	1.2
60 - 64	47	..
65 +	9	..
Unknown - Inconnu	2 297	..
Poland - Pologne		
2015 (C)		
Total	369 308	31.1
0 - 19	1 668	1.7
20 - 24	27 666	23.0
25 - 29	95 145	68.7
30 - 34	129 420	83.9
35 - 39	69 982	47.7
40 - 44	23 164	18.1
45 - 49	5 812	5.3
50 - 54	1 684	1.5
55 - 59	564	0.4
60 - 64	165	..
65 +	55	..
Unknown - Inconnu	13 983	..
Portugal[6]		
2015 (C)		
Total	85 500	28.8
0 - 19	747	2.7
20 - 24	5 118	18.8
25 - 29	14 145	51.3
30 - 34	27 121	86.7
35 - 39	23 526	64.3
40 - 44	9 545	25.2
45 - 49	2 661	7.5
50 - 54	796	2.2
55 - 59	246	0.8
60 - 64	95	..
65 +	47	..
Unknown - Inconnu	1 453	..
Republic of Moldova - République de Moldova[20]		
2012 (C)		
Total	39 435	32.8
0 - 19	269	2.3
20 - 24	6 290	41.0
25 - 29	13 306	84.1
30 - 34	8 980	67.6

11. Live births and live birth rates by age of father: latest available year, 2007 - 2016
Naissances vivantes et taux de natalité selon l'âge du père : dernière année disponible, 2007 - 2016 (continued - suite)

Continent, country or area, year, code[a] and age of father (in years) / Continent, pays ou zone, année, code[a] et âge du père (en années)	Number - Nombre — Both sexes / Les deux sexes	Rate / Taux
EUROPE		
Republic of Moldova - République de Moldova[20]		
2012 (C)		
35 - 39	4 561	40.4
40 - 44	1 640	16.5
45 - 49	446	4.4
50 - 54	142	1.2
55 - 59	31	0.3
60 - 64	14	..
65 +	3	..
Unknown - Inconnu	3 753	..
Romania - Roumanie		
2015 (C)		
Total	197 491	32.3
0 - 19	2 805	5.4
20 - 24	16 811	31.4
25 - 29	50 170	74.6
30 - 34	57 254	89.7
35 - 39	38 786	52.4
40 - 44	13 777	18.9
45 - 49	4 165	5.5
50 - 54	869	1.7
55 - 59	316	0.5
60 - 64	87	..
65 +	24	..
Unknown - Inconnu	12 427	..
Russian Federation - Fédération de Russie[21]		
2012 (C)		
Total	1 902 084	41.9
0 - 19	12 731	3.9
20 - 24	256 939	51.4
25 - 29	564 777	103.0
30 - 34	431 851	88.4
35 - 39	245 613	55.2
40 - 44	102 880	25.6
45 - 49	33 963	8.4
50 - 54	11 671	2.5
55 - 59	3 196	0.8
60 +	1 203	..
Unknown - Inconnu	237 260	..
San Marino - Saint-Marin		
2013 (+C)		
Total	320	31.8
0 - 19	-	-
20 - 24	3	♦4.1
25 - 29	26	♦32.4
30 - 34	78	78.8
35 - 39	105	81.1
40 - 44	60	42.2
45 - 49	25	♦16.7
50 - 54	14	♦11.0
55 +	-	-
Unknown - Inconnu	9	..
Serbia - Serbie[22]		
2015 (+C)		
Total	65 657	31.3
0 - 19	409	2.4
20 - 24	4 247	21.6
25 - 29	14 311	67.0
30 - 34	21 074	91.7
35 - 39	13 546	57.7
40 - 44	5 032	22.4
45 - 49	1 371	6.4
50 - 54	405	1.8
55 - 59	112	0.5
60 - 64	47	..
65 +	11	..
Unknown - Inconnu	5 092	..
EUROPE		
Slovakia - Slovaquie		
2015 (C)		
Total	55 602	31.7
0 - 19	394	3.1
20 - 24	3 418	21.9
25 - 29	10 126	57.1
30 - 34	16 485	85.8
35 - 39	11 710	58.1
40 - 44	4 049	22.6
45 - 49	928	6.1
50 - 54	269	1.7
55 - 59	80	0.5
60 - 64	19	..
65 +	6	..
Unknown - Inconnu	8 118	..
Slovenia - Slovénie		
2015 (C)		
Total	20 641	32.3
0 - 19	47	1.0
20 - 24	866	16.2
25 - 29	4 618	69.4
30 - 34	7 390	97.2
35 - 39	5 045	62.0
40 - 44	1 738	22.8
45 - 49	476	6.2
50 - 54	115	1.5
55 - 59	36	0.5
60 - 64	9	..
65 +	3	..
Unknown - Inconnu	298	..
Spain - Espagne		
2013 (C)		
Total	424 440	29.3
0 - 19	2 376	2.2
20 - 24	15 288	12.8
25 - 29	48 689	35.2
30 - 34	132 325	74.8
35 - 39	139 743	68.7
40 - 44	56 906	29.5
45 - 49	14 741	8.1
50 - 54	3 910	2.4
55 - 59	1 056	0.8
60 - 64	291	..
65 +	106	..
Unknown - Inconnu	9 009	..
Sweden - Suède		
2012 (C)		
Total	113 177	40.2
0 - 19	443	1.5
20 - 24	7 043	21.2
25 - 29	23 661	77.8
30 - 34	36 139	122.1
35 - 39	26 932	86.6
40 - 44	11 433	35.6
45 - 49	4 023	12.0
50 - 54	1 169	4.0
55 - 59	404	1.4
60 - 64	116	..
65 +	52	..
Unknown - Inconnu	1 762	..
Switzerland - Suisse[14]		
2015 (C)		
Total	66 768	25.8
0 - 19	6	-
20 - 24	1 197	4.7
25 - 29	9 527	33.9
30 - 34	22 357	75.5

Continent, country or area, year, code[a] and age of father (in years) / Continent, pays ou zone, année, code[a] et âge du père (en années)	Number - Nombre — Both sexes Les deux sexes	Rate Taux
EUROPE		
Switzerland - Suisse[14]		
2015 (C)		
35 - 39	19 929	69.0
40 - 44	9 283	31.0
45 - 49	3 111	9.4
50 - 54	939	2.9
55 - 59	289	1.0
60 - 64	83	..
65 +	47	..
Unknown - Inconnu	-	..
TFYR of Macedonia - L'ex-R. y. de Macédoine		
2015 (C)		
Total	23 075	33.9
0 - 19	153	2.4
20 - 24	1 896	25.2
25 - 29	6 268	78.4
30 - 34	7 723	95.7
35 - 39	4 325	56.2
40 - 44	1 349	18.8
45 - 49	360	5.1
50 - 54	93	1.3
55 - 59	21	+0.3
60 - 64	7	..
65 +	4	..
Unknown - Inconnu	876	..
Ukraine[23]		
2013 (+C)		
Total	503 657	35.8
0 - 19	4 125	3.9
20 - 24	67 513	48.1
25 - 29	149 940	88.2
30 - 34	116 549	75.0
35 - 39	64 684	45.9
40 - 44	25 378	19.2
45 - 49	7 518	6.0
50 - 54	2 464	1.8
55 +	983	0.8
Unknown - Inconnu	64 503	..
United Kingdom of Great Britain and Northern Ireland - Royaume-Uni de Grande-Bretagne et d'Irlande du Nord[24]		
2012 (C)		
Total	812 970	42.9
0 - 19	13 166	6.9
20 - 24	85 617	41.4
25 - 29	168 503	83.1
30 - 34	226 297	113.8
35 - 39	160 698	84.9
40 - 44	76 266	35.9
45 - 49	25 537	11.7
50 - 54	7 396	3.7
55 - 59	2 061	1.2
60 - 64	585	..
65 +	290	..
Unknown - Inconnu	46 554	..
OCEANIA - OCÉANIE		
Australia - Australie		
2015 (+C)		
Total	305 377	42.2
0 - 19	3 419	4.7
20 - 24	21 977	26.7
25 - 29	59 615	69.7
30 - 34	99 454	117.5
35 - 39	68 308	90.0
40 - 44	29 419	37.2
45 - 49	8 789	11.8
50 - 54	2 788	3.8
55 - 59	860	1.2
60 - 64	301	..
65 +	130	..
Unknown - Inconnu[25]	10 317	..
New Caledonia - Nouvelle-Calédonie		
2015 (C)		
Total	4 191	...
0 - 19	49	...
20 - 24	433	...
25 - 29	798	...
30 - 34	968	...
35 - 39	728	...
40 - 44	436	...
45 - 49	131	...
50 - 54	43	...
55 - 59	13	...
60 +	4	...
Unknown - Inconnu	588	..
New Zealand - Nouvelle-Zélande[26]		
2016 (+C)		
Total	59 430	42.9
0 - 19	1 278	8.2
20 - 24	6 252	36.2
25 - 29	12 438	77.3
30 - 34	17 166	125.2
35 - 39	11 607	91.5
40 - 44	5 034	36.9
45 - 49	1 758	12.2
50 - 54	525	3.6
55 - 59	168	1.2
60 - 64	54	..
65 +	18	..
Unknown - Inconnu	3 135	..

FOOTNOTES - NOTES

+ Rates based on 30 or fewer births. - Taux basés sur 30 naissances ou moins.

* Provisional. - Données provisoires.

[a] 'Code' indicates the source of data, as follows:
C - Civil registration, estimated over 90% complete
U - Civil registration, estimated less than 90% complete
| - Other source, estimated reliable
+ - Data tabulated by date of registration rather than occurrence

... Information not available

Le 'Code' indique la source des données, comme suit :
C - Registres de l'état civil considérés complets à 90 p. 100 au moins
U - Registres de l'état civil qui ne sont pas considérés complets à 90 p. 100 au moins
| - Autre source, considérée fiable
+ - Données exploitées selon la date de l'enregistrement et non la date de l'événement
... Information non disponible

1 Excludes the islands of St. Brandon and Agalega. - Non compris les îles St. Brandon et Agalega.

2 Excluding live-born infants who died before their birth was registered. - Non compris les enfants nés vivants décédés avant l'enregistrement de leur naissance.

3 Including Canadian residents temporarily in the United States, but excluding United States residents temporarily in Canada. - Y compris les résidents canadiens se trouvant temporairement aux Etats-Unis, mais ne comprenant pas les résidents des Etats-Unis se trouvant temporairement au Canada.

4 Data exclude the live births of infants whose fathers are undeclared. - Les données ne comprennent pas les naissances vivantes d'enfants dont le père n'est pas déclaré.

5 Excluding children born in the country of non-resident mothers. - Exceptés les enfants nés dans le pays des mères non-résidentes.

6 Data refer to births to resident mothers. - Ces données concernent les enfants nés de mères résidentes.

7 Excluding infants born alive of less than 28 weeks' gestation, of less than 1 000 g in weight and 35 cm in length, who die within seven days of birth. Excluding newborns registered by application of mothers. - Non compris les enfants nés vivants après moins de 28 semaines de gestations, pesant moins de 1 000 g, mesurant moins de 35 cm et décédés dans les sept jours qui ont suivi leur naissance. Exception faite des nouveau-nés qui ont été enregistrés à la demande des mères.

8 Sources: Births and Deaths National Registration System database, and medical records of government hospitals. - Les sources: Les bases de données des << Births and Deaths National Registration System >> et les dossiers médicaux des hôpitaux du gouvernement.

9 Data refer to government controlled areas. - Les données se rapportent aux zones contrôlées par le Gouvernement.

10 Includes data for East Jerusalem and Israeli residents in certain other territories under occupation by Israeli military forces since June 1967. - Y compris les données pour Jérusalem-Est et les résidents israéliens dans certains autres territoires occupés depuis 1967 par les forces armées israéliennes.

11 Data refer to Japanese nationals in Japan only. Data refer to live births in wedlock only. - Les données se raportent aux nationaux japonais au Japon seulement. Les données ne concernent que les naissances vivantes de parents mariés.

12 Data from Births and Deaths Notification System (Ministry of Health and all health care providers). - Les données proviennent du système de notification des naissances et des décès (Ministère de la santé et tous prestataires de soins de santé).

13 Excluding alien armed forces, civilian aliens employed by armed forces, and foreign diplomatic personnel and their dependants. - Non compris les militaires étrangers, les civils étrangers employés par les forces armées ni le personnel diplomatique étranger et les membres de leur famille les accompagnant.

14 Data refer to live births in wedlock only. - Les données ne concernent que les naissances vivantes de parents mariés.

15 Data refer to live births in wedlock only. Including births occurring abroad of mothers with residence in Austria. - Les données ne concernent que les naissances vivantes de parents mariés. Y compris les naissances survenues à l'étranger des mères avec résidence en Autriche.

16 Excluding Faeroe Islands and Greenland shown separately, if available. - Non compris les Iles Féroé et le Groenland, qui font l'objet de rubriques distinctes, si disponible.

17 Excluding Åland Islands. - Non compris les Îles d'Åland.

18 Data include the live births of women with Hungarian usual residence regardless of whether the live birth occurred in Hungary or in a foreign country, and do not include the live births of women with foreign country usual residence. - Les données concernent les enfants nés vivants de femmes dont la résidence habituelle est en Hongrie, que la naissance vivante ait eu lieu en Hongrie ou dans un pays étranger, et ne comprennent pas les enfants nés vivants de femmes dont la résidence habituelle est dans un pays étranger.

19 Including residents outside the country if listed in a Netherlands population register. - Englobe les résidents se trouvant à l'étranger à condition qu'ils soient inscrits sur le registre de population des Pays-Bas.

20 Excluding Transnistria and the municipality of Bender. - Les données ne tiennent pas compte de l'information sur la Transnistria et la municipalité de Bender.

21 Excluding infants born alive of less than 28 weeks' gestation, of less than 1 000 g in weight and 35 cm in length, who die within seven days of birth. - Non compris les enfants nés vivants après moins de 28 semaines de gestations, pesant moins de 1 000 g, mesurant moins de 35 cm et décédés dans les sept jours qui ont suivi leur naissance.

22 Excludes data for Kosovo and Metohia. - Sans les données pour le Kosovo et Metohie.

23 Data refer to births with weight 500g and more (if weight is unknown - with length 25 centimeters and more, or with gestation during 22 weeks or more). - Données concernant les nouveau-nés de 500 grammes ou plus (si le poids est inconnu – de 25 centimètres de long ou plus, ou après une grossesse de 22 semaines ou plus).

24 Excluding Channel Islands (Guernsey and Jersey) and Isle of Man, shown separately, if available. Data tabulated by date of occurrence for England and Wales, and by date of registration for Northern Ireland and Scotland. - Non compris les îles Anglo-Normandes (Guernesey et Jersey) et l'île de Man, qui font l'objet de rubriques distinctes, si disponible. Données exploitées selon la date de l'événement pour l'Angleterre et le pays de Galles, et selon la date de l'enregistrement pour l'Irlande du Nord et l'Ecosse.

25 Data includes births born in wedlock for which age of father is unknown and births born out of wedlock not acknowledged by the father for which therefore age of father is unknown. - Les données se rapportent aux enfants légitimes pour lesquels l'âge du père n'est pas connu et aux naissances hors mariage non reconnues par le père et pour lesquelles l'âge du père n'est par conséquent pas connu.

26 Random rounding to base 3 is applied in this table as a confidentiality measure. - Les chiffres sont arrondis à la base 3 de manière aléatoire, pour des raisons de confidentialité.

Table 12 - *Demographic Yearbook 2016*

Table 12 presents late foetal deaths and late foetal-death ratios by urban/rural residence for as many years as possible between 2012 and 2016.

Description of variables: Late foetal deaths are foetal deaths[1] of 28 or more completed weeks of gestation. Foetal deaths of unknown gestational age are included with those 28 or more weeks.

Statistics on the number of late foetal deaths are obtained from civil registers unless otherwise noted.

The urban/rural classification of late foetal deaths is as provided by each country or area; it is presumed to be based on the national census definitions of urban population that have been set forth at the end of the technical notes for table 6.

Ratio computation: Late foetal-death ratios are the annual number of late foetal deaths per 1 000 live births (as shown in table 9) in the same year. The live-birth base was adopted because it is assumed to be more comparable from one country or area to another than the sum of live births and foetal deaths.

Ratios by urban/rural residence are the annual number of late foetal deaths, in the appropriate urban or rural category, per 1 000 corresponding live births (as shown in table 9). These ratios are calculated by the United Nations Statistics Division.

Ratios presented in this table are limited to those for countries or areas and urban/rural areas having at least a total of 30 late foetal deaths in a given year.

Reliability of data: Each country or area is asked to indicate the estimated completeness of the late foetal deaths recorded in its civil register. These national assessments are indicated by the quality codes "C", "U" and "..." that appear in the first column of this table.

"C" indicates that the data are estimated to be virtually complete, that is, representing at least 90 per cent of the late foetal deaths occurring each year, while "U" indicates that data are estimated to be incomplete, that is, representing less than 90 per cent of the late foetal deaths occurring each year. The code "..." indicates that no information was provided regarding completeness.

Data from civil registers which are reported as incomplete or of unknown completeness (coded "U" or "...") are considered unreliable. They appear in italics in this table. Ratios are not computed for data so coded.

For more information about the quality of vital statistics data in general, see section 4.2 of the Technical Notes.

Limitations: Statistics on late foetal deaths are subject to the same qualifications as have been set forth for vital statistics in general and foetal-death statistics in particular as discussed in section 4 of the Technical Notes.

The reliability of the data is a very important factor. Of all vital statistics, the registration of foetal deaths is probably the most incomplete.

Variation in the definition of foetal deaths, and in particular late foetal deaths, also limits international comparability. The criterion of 28 or more completed weeks of gestation to distinguish late foetal deaths is not universally used; some countries or areas use different durations of gestation or other criteria such as size of the foetus. In addition, the difficulty of accurately determining gestational age further reduces comparability. However, to promote comparability, late foetal deaths shown in this table are restricted to those of at least 28 or more completed weeks of gestation. Wherever this is not possible, a footnote is provided.

Late foetal-death ratios are subject to the limitations of the data on live births with which they have been calculated. These have been set forth in the technical notes for table 9.

It must be pointed out that when late foetal deaths and live births are both under registered, the resulting ratios may be of reasonable magnitude. For the countries or areas where live-birth registration is poorest, the late foetal-death ratios may be the largest, effectively masking the completeness of the base data.   For this reason, possible variations in birth-registration completeness as well as the reported completeness of late foetal deaths must always be borne in mind in evaluating late foetal-death ratios.

Finally, it may be noted that the counting of live-born infants as late foetal deaths, because they died before the registration of the birth or within the first 24 hours of life, has the effect of inflating the late foetal-death ratios unduly by decreasing the birth denominator and increasing the foetal-death numerator. This factor should not be overlooked in using data from this table.

The comparability of data by urban/rural residence is affected by the national definitions of urban and rural used in tabulating these data. It is assumed, in the absence of specific information to the contrary, that the definitions of urban and rural used in connection with the national population census were also used in the compilation of the vital statistics for each country or area.   However, it cannot be excluded that, for a given country or area, different definitions of urban and rural are used for the vital statistics data and the population census data respectively.   When known, the definitions of urban used in national population censuses are presented at the end of the technical notes for table 6.   As discussed in detail in the technical notes for table 6, these definitions vary considerably from one country or area to another.

Urban/rural differentials in late foetal death ratios may also be affected by whether the late foetal deaths and live births have been tabulated in terms of place of occurrence or place of usual residence. This problem is discussed in more detail in section 4.1.4.1 of the Introduction.

Earlier data: Late foetal deaths and late foetal-death ratios have been shown in each issue of the Demographic Yearbook beginning with the 1951 issue.   A special topic CD on natality published in 2001 presents the data for all available years from 1990 to 1998. For more information on specific topics, and years for which data are reported, readers should consult the Historical Index.

NOTES

[1] For definition, see section 4.1.1 of the Introduction.

Tableau 12 – *Annuaire démographique 2016*

Le tableau 12 présente des données sur les morts fœtales tardives et les rapports de mortinatalité selon le lieu de résidence (zone urbaine ou rurale) pour le plus grand nombre d'années possible entre 2012 et 2016.

Description des variables : Par mort fœtale tardive, on entend le décès d'un fœtus[1] survenu après 28 semaines complètes de gestation au moins. Les morts fœtales pour lesquelles la durée de la période de gestation n'est pas connue sont comprises dans cette catégorie.

Sauf indication contraire, les statistiques du nombre de morts fœtales tardives sont établies sur la base des registres de l'état civil.

La classification des morts fœtales tardives selon le lieu de résidence (zone urbaine ou rurale) est celle qui a été communiquée par chaque pays ou zone ; on part du principe qu'elle repose sur les définitions de la population urbaine utilisées pour les recensements nationaux, telles qu'elles sont reproduites à la fin des notes techniques du tableau 6.

Calcul des rapports : les rapports de mortinatalité représentent le nombre annuel de morts fœtales tardives pour 1 000 naissances vivantes (telles qu'elles sont présentées au tableau 9) survenues pendant la même année. On a pris pour base de calcul les naissances vivantes parce que l'on pense qu'elles sont plus facilement comparables d'un pays ou d'une zone à l'autre que la somme des naissances vivantes et des morts fœtales.

Les rapports selon le lieu de résidence (zone urbaine ou rurale) représentent le nombre annuel de morts fœtales tardives, classées selon la catégorie urbaine ou rurale appropriée pour 1 000 naissances vivantes (telles qu'elles sont présentées au tableau 9) survenues parmi la population correspondante. Ces rapports ont été calculés par la Division des statistiques de l'Organisation des Nations Unies.

Les rapports présentés dans le tableau 12 ne concernent que les pays ou zones où l'on a enregistré un total d'au moins 30 morts fœtales tardives pendant une année donnée.

Fiabilité des données : il a été demandé à chaque pays ou zone d'indiquer le degré estimatif de complétude des données sur les morts fœtales tardives figurant dans ses registres d'état civil. Ces évaluations nationales sont signalées par les codes de qualité "C", "U" et "..." qui apparaissent dans la deuxième colonne du tableau.

La lettre "C" indique que les données sont jugées à peu près complètes, c'est-à-dire qu'elles représentent au moins 90 p. 100 des morts fœtales tardives survenues chaque année ; la lettre "U" signifie que les données sont jugées incomplètes, c'est-à-dire qu'elles représentent moins de 90 p.100 des morts fœtales tardives survenues chaque année. Le code "..." indique qu'aucun renseignement n'a été communiqué quant à la complétude des données.

Les données provenant des registres de l'état civil qui sont déclarées incomplètes ou dont le degré de complétude n'est pas connu (code "U" ou "...") sont jugées douteuses. Elles apparaissent en italique dans le tableau ; les rapports, dans ces cas, n'ont pas été calculés.

Pour plus de précisions sur la qualité des données reposant sur les statistiques de l'état civil en général, voir la section 4.2 des Notes techniques.

Insuffisance des données : les statistiques des morts fœtales tardives appellent toutes les réserves qui ont été formulées à propos des statistiques de l'état civil en général et des statistiques concernant les morts fœtales en particulier (voir la section 4 des Notes techniques).

La fiabilité des données est un facteur très important. Les statistiques concernant les morts fœtales sont probablement les moins complètes de toutes les statistiques de l'état civil.

L'hétérogénéité des définitions de la mort fœtale et, en particulier, de la mort fœtale tardive nuit aussi à la comparabilité internationale des données. Le critère des 28 semaines complètes de gestation au moins n'est pas universellement utilisé ; certains pays ou zones retiennent des critères différents pour la durée de la période de gestation ou d'autres critères tels que la taille du fœtus. De surcroît, la comparabilité est rendue malaisée par le fait qu'il est difficile d'établir avec précision l'âge gestationnel. Pour faciliter les comparaisons, les morts fœtales tardives considérées ici sont exclusivement celles qui sont survenues au terme de 28 semaines de gestation au moins. Les exceptions sont signalées en note.

Les rapports de mortinatalité appellent en outre toutes les réserves qui ont été formulées à propos des statistiques des naissances vivantes qui ont servi à leur calcul (voir à ce sujet les notes techniques relatives au tableau 9).

En ce qui concerne le calcul des rapports, il convient de noter que, si l'enregistrement des morts fœtales tardives et celui des naissances vivantes sont loin d'être exhaustifs, les rapports de mortinatalité peuvent être raisonnables. C'est parfois pour les pays ou zones où l'enregistrement des naissances vivantes laisse le plus à désirer que les rapports de mortinatalité sont les plus élevés, ce qui masque le caractère incomplet des données de base. Aussi, pour porter un jugement sur la qualité des rapports de mortinatalité, il ne faut jamais oublier que la complétude de l'enregistrement des naissances comme celle de l'enregistrement des morts fœtales tardives peuvent varier sensiblement.

Enfin, on notera que l'inclusion parmi les morts fœtales tardives des décès d'enfants nés vivants qui sont décédés avant l'enregistrement de leur naissance ou dans les 24 heures qui ont suivi la naissance conduit à des rapports de mortinatalité exagérés parce que le dénominateur (nombre de naissances) se trouve alors diminué et le numérateur (morts fœtales) augmenté. Il importe de ne pas négliger ce facteur lorsque l'on utilise les données du tableau 12.

La comparabilité des données selon le lieu de résidence (zone urbaine ou rurale) peut être limitée par les définitions nationales des termes « urbain » et « rural » utilisées pour la mise en tableaux de ces données. En l'absence d'indications contraires, on a supposé que les mêmes définitions avaient servi pour le recensement national de la population et pour l'établissement des statistiques de l'état civil pour chaque pays ou zone. Toutefois, il n'est pas exclu que, pour une zone ou un pays donné, des définitions différentes aient été retenues. Les définitions du terme « urbain » utilisées pour les recensements nationaux de population ont été présentées à la fin des notes techniques du tableau 6 lorsqu'elles étaient connues. Comme on l'a précisé dans les notes techniques relatives au tableau 6, ces définitions varient considérablement d'un pays ou d'une zone à l'autre.

La différence entre les rapports de mortinatalité pour les zones urbaines et rurales pourra aussi être faussée selon que les morts fœtales tardives et les naissances vivantes auront été classées d'après le lieu de l'événement ou le lieu de résidence habituel. Ce problème est examiné plus en détail à la section 4.1.4.1 des Notes techniques.

Données publiées antérieurement : les éditions de l'Annuaire démographique parues à partir de 1951 contiennent des statistiques concernant les morts fœtales tardives et les rapports de mortinatalité. Un CD-ROM sur la natalité paru en 2001 présente les données pour toutes les années disponibles de 1990 à 1998. Pour plus de précisions concernant les années et les sujets pour lesquels des données ont été publiées, se reporter à l'index.

NOTE

[1] Pour la définition, voir la section 4.1.1 de l'Introduction.

12. Late foetal deaths and late foetal death ratios, by urban/rural residence: 2012 - 2016
Morts foetales tardives et rapports de mortinatalité, selon la résidence, urbaine/rurale : 2012 - 2016

Continent, country or area, and urban/rural residence / Continent, pays ou zone et résidence, urbaine/rurale	Code[a]	Number - Nombre					Ratio - Rapport				
		2012	2013	2014	2015	2016	2012	2013	2014	2015	2016
AFRICA - AFRIQUE											
Algeria - Algérie											
Total	+U	15 795	15 009	15 077	14 620	14 236	...	...	...	...	...
Burundi[1]											
Total	+U	2 448	2 141				...	...	...	...	...
Egypt - Égypte											
Total	+C	1 334	...	...	...	...	0.5	...	...	...	...
Urban - Urbaine	+C	1 093	...	...	...	...	1.1	...	...	...	...
Rural - Rurale	+C	241	...	...	...	...	0.1	...	...	...	...
Mauritius - Maurice[2]											
Total	+C	140	117	138	125	127	9.7	8.7	10.4	9.9	9.8
Urban - Urbaine	+C	52	46	54	54	52	9.6	9.1	10.5	10.5	9.8
Rural - Rurale	+C	88	71	84	71	75	9.7	8.4	10.3	9.5	9.8
Sierra Leone[3]											
Total	+U	2 089	1 958	...	...	...	...	...	...	...	...
Urban - Urbaine[4]	+U	572	...	...	...	...	...	...	...	...	...
Rural - Rurale[4]	+U	1 066	...	...	...	...	...	...	...	...	...
AMERICA, NORTH - AMÉRIQUE DU NORD											
Bahamas[5]											
Total	+C	59	61	...	...	...	13.2	14.1	...	...	...
Belize											
Total	U	65	51	66	55	54	...	...	...	...	...
Urban - Urbaine	U	18	20	24	24	21	...	...	...	...	...
Rural - Rurale	U	47	31	42	31	33	...	...	...	...	...
Bermuda - Bermudes											
Total	C	4	4	1	2		...	...	...	...	...
Canada[6]											
Total	C	1 102	1 077	...	...	...	2.9	2.8	...	...	...
Costa Rica											
Total	C	332	327	319	326	*314	4.5	4.6	4.4	4.5	*4.5
Urban - Urbaine	C	134	108	176	208	*198	5.3	4.3	4.2	4.2	*4.1
Rural - Rurale	C	198	219	143	118	*116	4.1	4.8	4.7	5.3	*5.4
Cuba[7]											
Total	C	1 262	1 273	1 135	1 190	1 251	10.0	10.1	9.3	9.5	10.7
Dominican Republic - République dominicaine											
Total	U	1 131	1 886	1 528	...	...	...	...	...	...	...
Mexico - Mexique[8]											
Total	+U	10 442	9 911	9 755	9 685	...	...	...	...	...	...
Urban - Urbaine[9]	+U	7 806	7 249	7 287	7 005	...	...	...	...	...	...
Rural - Rurale[9]	+U	2 469	2 472	2 325	2 407	...	...	...	...	...	...
Montserrat											
Total	+C	-	-	2	1	-	...	...	...	...	...
Panama											
Total	U	426	370	423	*436	...	...	...	...	...	...
Puerto Rico - Porto Rico[10]											
Total	C	382	417	417	358	*305	9.8	11.4	12.1	11.5	*10.8
Urban - Urbaine[9]	C	236	257	239	205	*167	11.0	13.0	12.6	10.8	*9.2
Rural - Rurale[9]	C	140	156	151	130	*138	8.0	9.3	9.8	10.6	*13.6
Saint Vincent and the Grenadines - Saint-Vincent-et-les Grenadines											
Total	C	20	23	...	...	...	...	...	...	...	...
United States of America - États-Unis d'Amérique											
Total	C	11 739	11 721	11 311	11 354	...	3.0	3.0	2.8	2.9	...
AMERICA, SOUTH - AMÉRIQUE DU SUD											
Argentina - Argentine											
Total	C	3 731	3 809	4 043	3 785	...	5.1	5.0	5.2	4.9	...

12. Late foetal deaths and late foetal death ratios, by urban/rural residence: 2012 - 2016
Morts foetales tardives et rapports de mortinatalité, selon la résidence, urbaine/rurale : 2012 - 2016 (continued - suite)

Continent, country or area, and urban/rural residence / Continent, pays ou zone et résidence, urbaine/rurale	Code[a]	Number - Nombre					Ratio - Rapport				
		2012	2013	2014	2015	2016	2012	2013	2014	2015	2016
AMERICA, SOUTH - AMÉRIQUE DU SUD											
Brazil - Brésil											
Total	U	24 823	25 744	25 748	26 654	...	...	...	...	...	...
Chile - Chili[11]											
Total	C	1 276	1 262	1 254	...	...	5.2	5.2	5.0	...	...
Urban - Urbaine	C	996[12]	1 149	1 126	...	...	4.5	5.2	4.9	...	...
Rural - Rurale	C	125[12]	113	128	...	...	5.1	5.2	5.7	...	...
Colombia - Colombie											
Total	U	5 401	5 130	5 178	...	...	...	...	...	...	...
Urban - Urbaine	U	3 945	3 780	3 864	...	...	...	...	...	...	...
Rural - Rurale	U	1 456	1 350	1 314	...	...	...	...	...	...	...
Ecuador - Équateur[13]											
Total	...	1 063	974	932	1 028	...	...	...	...	...	...
Urban - Urbaine	...	926	816	771	849	...	...	...	...	...	...
Rural - Rurale	...	137	158	161	179	...	...	...	...	...	...
Uruguay											
Total	C	200	202	229	199	...	4.2	4.1	4.7	4.1	...
Venezuela (Bolivarian Republic of) - Venezuela (République bolivarienne du)											
Total	...	1 006	2 400	2 895	2 457	...	...	...	...	...	...
ASIA - ASIE											
Armenia - Arménie											
Total	C	...	...	746	796	...	...	...	17.3	19.1	...
Urban - Urbaine	C	...	...	...	509	...	...	...	...	18.8	...
Rural - Rurale	C	...	...	...	287	...	...	...	...	19.6	...
Azerbaijan - Azerbaïdjan											
Total	+C	602	643	764	904	...	3.5	3.7	4.5	5.4	...
Bahrain - Bahreïn[14]											
Total	...	125	106	132	...	...	...	...	...	...	...
Brunei Darussalam - Brunéi Darussalam											
Total	+C	43	44	...	...	...	6.2	6.6	...	...	...
China, Hong Kong SAR - Chine, Hong Kong RAS											
Total	...	148	119	167	150	180	...	...	...	...	...
China, Macao SAR - Chine, Macao RAS											
Total	C	14	10	12	6	...	...	...	...	...	...
Georgia - Géorgie											
Total	C	664	567	640	589	558	11.6	9.8	10.6	9.9	9.9
Urban - Urbaine	C	335	309	336	321	310	...	...	...	9.5	9.6
Rural - Rurale	C	329	258	304	268	248	...	...	...	10.6	10.2
Israel - Israël[15]											
Total	C	583	603	...	...	...	3.4	3.5	...	...	...
Urban - Urbaine[9]	C	526	535	...	...	...	3.4	3.4	...	...	...
Rural - Rurale[9]	C	52	61	...	...	...	3.3	3.7	...	...	...
Japan - Japon[16]											
Total	C	1 969	1 897	1 790	1 830	...	1.9	1.8	1.8	1.8	...
Urban - Urbaine	C	1 809	1 747	1 657	1 695	...	1.9	1.8	1.8	1.8	...
Rural - Rurale	C	158	149	131	134	...	1.9	1.8	1.7	1.7	...
Kazakhstan											
Total	C	3 453	3 206	...	...	...	9.1	8.3	...	...	...
Urban - Urbaine	C	1 900	1 673	...	...	...	9.2	8.0	...	...	...
Rural - Rurale	C	1 553	1 533	...	...	...	8.9	8.6	...	...	...
Kuwait - Koweït											
Total	C	355	352	433	405	...	5.9	5.9	7.1	6.8	...
Kyrgyzstan - Kirghizstan											
Total	C	1 575	1 549	1 555	1 484	*1 423	10.2	10.0	9.6	9.1	*9.0
Urban - Urbaine[17]	C	1 144	1 142	1 147	1 080	*1 006	21.3	21.2	20.7	20.6	*19.5
Rural - Rurale[17]	C	431	407	408	404	*417	4.3	4.0	3.8	3.6	*3.9

Continent, country or area, and urban/rural residence / Continent, pays ou zone et résidence, urbaine/rurale	Code[a]	Number - Nombre					Ratio - Rapport				
		2012	2013	2014	2015	2016	2012	2013	2014	2015	2016
ASIA - ASIE											
Malaysia - Malaisie											
Total	C	2 274	2 188	2 277	2 325	...	4.3	4.3	4.3	4.5	...
Urban - Urbaine	C	1 477	1 425	1 484	1 507	...	4.1	4.1	4.1	4.3	...
Rural - Rurale	C	797	763	793	818	...	4.7	4.8	4.6	4.8	...
Maldives[10]											
Total	...	50	51	37	...	...	...	...	...	...	...
Urban - Urbaine	...	29[12]	31	27	...	...	...	...	...	...	...
Rural - Rurale	...	20[12]	20	10	...	...	...	...	...	...	...
Mongolia - Mongolie											
Total	+C	...	...	...	557	484	...	...	...	6.8	6.1
Myanmar											
Total	+U	12 234[18]	11 718[18]	5 687[19]	...	...	...	...	...	...	...
Urban - Urbaine[18]	+U	5 741	4 898	...	...	...	...	...	...	...	...
Rural - Rurale[18]	+U	6 493	6 820	...	...	...	...	...	...	...	...
Oman[20]											
Total	U	...	279	335	...	403	...	...	...	...	...
Philippines											
Total	...	4 219	4 013	4 148	4 151	...	...	...	...	...	...
Republic of Korea - République de Corée[21]											
Total	C	963	931	897	836	...	2.0	2.1	2.1	1.9	...
Urban - Urbaine[9]	C	685	697	611	695	...	1.7	1.9	1.7	1.9	...
Rural - Rurale[9]	C	151	126	135	119	...	1.8	1.8	1.9	1.7	...
Singapore - Singapour											
Total	+C	111	80	86	90	89	2.6	2.0	2.0	2.1	2.2
Sri Lanka											
Total	+U	972	939	708	715	787	...	...	...	...	...
Tajikistan - Tadjikistan											
Total	U	1 940	2 234	2 265	...	...	...	...	...	...	...
Urban - Urbaine	U	788	1 301	951	...	...	...	...	...	...	...
Rural - Rurale	U	1 152	933	1 314	...	...	...	...	...	...	...
Uzbekistan - Ouzbékistan											
Total	+C	3 796	4 122	5 768	6 636	...	6.1	6.1	8.0	9.0	...
Urban - Urbaine	+C	2 425	2 537	3 383	3 653	...	8.4	8.2	10.4	11.2	...
Rural - Rurale	+C	1 371	1 585	2 385	2 983	...	4.1	4.3	6.1	7.3	...
EUROPE											
Åland Islands - Îles d'Åland											
Total	C	1	-	-	*-	...	...	...	...	...	...
Urban - Urbaine	C	-	-	-	*-	...	...	...	...	...	...
Rural - Rurale	C	1	-	-	*-	...	...	...	...	...	...
Andorra - Andorre											
Total	C	3	-	-	1	...	...	...	...	...	...
Austria - Autriche											
Total	C	260	272	273	281	...	3.3	3.4	3.3	3.3	...
Belarus - Bélarus											
Total	C	257	260	256	271	...	2.2	2.2	2.2	2.3	...
Urban - Urbaine	C	204	185	196	192	...	2.3	2.0	2.1	2.1	...
Rural - Rurale	C	53	75	60	79	...	2.0	2.7	2.2	2.9	...
Belgium - Belgique											
Total	C	608	571	596	...	...	4.7	4.5	4.8	...	...
Urban - Urbaine	C	602	569	588	...	...	4.8	4.6	4.8	...	...
Rural - Rurale	C	6	2	8	...	...	...	...	...	...	...
Bulgaria - Bulgarie[10]											
Total	C	557	483	498	420	...	8.1	7.3	7.4	6.4	...
Urban - Urbaine	C	393	...	338	284	...	7.6	...	6.7	5.7	...
Rural - Rurale	C	164	...	160	136	...	9.4	...	9.5	8.3	...
Croatia - Croatie[22]											
Total	C	130	144	150	163	...	3.1	3.6	3.8	4.3	...
Urban - Urbaine	C	78	75	77	91	...	3.3	3.3	3.4	4.2	...
Rural - Rurale	C	52	69	73	72	...	2.9	4.0	4.4	4.6	...

Continent, country or area, and urban/rural residence / Continent, pays ou zone et résidence, urbaine/rurale	Co-de[a]	Number - Nombre					Ratio - Rapport				
		2012	2013	2014	2015	2016	2012	2013	2014	2015	2016
EUROPE											
Czechia - Tchéquie[23]											
Total	C	287	264	296	296	...	2.6	2.5	2.7	2.7	...
Urban - Urbaine	C	211	198	210	224	...	2.6	2.5	2.6	2.8	...
Rural - Rurale	C	76	66	86	72	...	2.6	2.3	3.0	2.5	...
Denmark - Danemark[24]											
Total	C	213	219	234	...	...	3.7	3.9	4.1	...	...
Estonia - Estonie											
Total	C	31	30	38	19	...	2.2	2.2	2.8	...	...
Urban - Urbaine	C	17	20	28	14	...	...	...	...	...	...
Rural - Rurale	C	14	10	10	5	...	...	...	...	...	...
Faeroe Islands - Îles Féroé											
Total	C	...	-	-	...	...	...	...	...	...	...
Urban - Urbaine	C	...	-	-	...	...	...	...	...	...	...
Rural - Rurale	C	...	-	-	...	...	...	...	...	...	...
Finland - Finlande[25]											
Total	C	113	106	115	115	...	1.9	1.8	2.0	2.1	...
Urban - Urbaine	C	74	81	83	77	...	1.7	2.0	2.0	1.9	...
Rural - Rurale	C	39	25	32	38	...	2.3	...	2.0	2.6	...
Germany - Allemagne											
Total	C	2 400	2 556	2 597	2 787	...	3.6	3.7	3.6	3.8	...
Greece - Grèce[10]											
Total	C	446	298	353	312	...	4.4	3.2	3.8	3.4	...
Urban - Urbaine	C	332	...	247	215	...	4.7	...	3.9	3.4	...
Rural - Rurale	C	114	...	106	97	...	3.9	...	3.6	3.4	...
Hungary - Hongrie											
Total	C	378[26]	392[26]	421[26]	408[26]	410[28]	4.2	4.4	4.5	4.4	4.3
Urban - Urbaine[27]	C	234	229	274	265	...	3.8	3.7	4.2	4.1	...
Rural - Rurale[27]	C	140	158	143	138	...	5.1	5.7	5.1	4.9	...
Iceland - Islande											
Total	C	10	4	11	8	...	...	...	...	...	...
Urban - Urbaine	C	10	4	11	8	...	...	...	...	...	...
Rural - Rurale	C	-	-	-	-	...	...	...	...	...	...
Ireland - Irlande[29]											
Total	C	188	190	164	...	...	2.6	2.8	2.4	...	...
Italy - Italie											
Total	C	1 439	*1 262	1 364	...	...	2.7	*2.5	2.7	...	...
Latvia - Lettonie											
Total	C	81	81	83	72	...	4.1	3.9	3.8	3.3	...
Lithuania - Lituanie[22]											
Total	C	117	143	139	126	...	3.8	4.8	4.6	4.0	...
Urban - Urbaine	C	77	87	96	88	...	3.6	4.3	4.6	4.1	...
Rural - Rurale	C	40	56	43	38	...	4.4	5.8	4.6	3.8	...
Luxembourg											
Total	C	28	33	30	50	...	...	5.4	4.9	8.2	...
Malta - Malte[22]											
Total	C	10	16	26	...	...	...	...	...	...	...
Netherlands - Pays-Bas[30]											
Total	C	438	401	487	500	...	2.5	2.3	2.8	2.9	...
Norway - Norvège											
Total	C	184	171	217	174	...	3.1	2.9	3.7	3.0	...
Poland - Pologne											
Total	C	1 174	1 016	928	...	...	3.0	2.7	2.5	...	...
Urban - Urbaine	C	638	...	...	...	...	2.9	...	...	...	...
Rural - Rurale	C	536	...	...	...	...	3.3	...	...	...	...
Portugal[31]											
Total	C	249	180	214	216	...	2.8	2.2	2.6	2.5	...
Romania - Roumanie[10]											
Total	C	779	771	781	735	...	3.9	4.2	4.0	3.7	...
Urban - Urbaine	C	348	325	372	340	...	3.2	3.3	3.5	3.1	...
Rural - Rurale	C	431	446	409	395	...	4.7	5.3	4.7	4.5	...
Russian Federation - Fédération de Russie											
Total	C	12 142	...	...	...	...	6.4	...	...	...	...
Urban - Urbaine	C	8 441	...	...	...	...	6.2	...	...	...	...
Rural - Rurale	C	3 701	...	...	...	...	6.8	...	...	...	...

12. Late foetal deaths and late foetal death ratios, by urban/rural residence: 2012 - 2016
Morts foetales tardives et rapports de mortinatalité, selon la résidence, urbaine/rurale : 2012 - 2016 (continued - suite)

Continent, country or area, and urban/rural residence — Continent, pays ou zone et résidence, urbaine/rurale	Co-de[a]	Number - Nombre					Ratio - Rapport				
		2012	2013	2014	2015	2016	2012	2013	2014	2015	2016
EUROPE											
Serbia - Serbie[32]											
Total	+C	370	307	348	388	...	5.5	4.7	5.2	5.9	...
Urban - Urbaine	+C	252	170	242	261	...	5.5	3.7	5.3	5.7	...
Rural - Rurale	+C	118	137	106	127	...	5.5	6.9	5.2	6.3	...
Slovakia - Slovaquie[33]											
Total	C	180	163	166	184	...	3.2	3.0	3.0	3.3	...
Urban - Urbaine	C	80	72	76	85	...	2.7	2.5	2.7	2.9	...
Rural - Rurale	C	100	91	90	99	...	3.8	3.5	3.4	3.7	...
Slovenia - Slovénie											
Total	C	51	62	47	55	...	2.3	2.9	2.2	2.7	...
Spain - Espagne											
Total	C	1 050	1 091	1 320	1 287	...	2.3	2.6	3.1	3.1	...
Sweden - Suède											
Total	C	453	441	456	429	...	4.0	3.9	4.0	3.7	...
Switzerland - Suisse[10]											
Total	C	350	402	368	357	...	4.3	4.9	4.3	4.1	...
Urban - Urbaine	C	282	310	262	314[34]	...	4.6	5.0	4.1	4.2	...
Rural - Rurale	C	68	92	106	43[34]	...	3.3	4.5	5.0	3.4	...
TFYR of Macedonia - L'ex-R. y. de Macédoine											
Total	C	184	196	171	185	...	7.8	8.5	7.2	8.0	...
Urban - Urbaine	C	108	123	106	110	...	8.1	9.3	7.7	8.2	...
Rural - Rurale	C	76	73	65	75	...	7.5	7.4	6.6	7.7	...
Ukraine											
Total	+C	3 230	...	2 820[35]	...	...	6.2	...	6.1	...	...
Urban - Urbaine	+C	2 120	...	...	...	...	6.2	...	...	...	...
Rural - Rurale	+C	1 110	...	...	...	...	6.2	...	...	...	...
United Kingdom of Great Britain and Northern Ireland - Royaume-Uni de Grande-Bretagne et d'Irlande du Nord[36]											
Total	C	3 938	...	3 563	3 434	...	4.8	...	4.6	4.4	...
OCEANIA - OCÉANIE											
Australia - Australie[37]											
Total	+C	1 046	1 295	1 209	1 146	...	3.4	4.2	4.0	3.8	...
Guam[10]											
Total	C	27	42	36	45	...	...	12.6	10.6	13.4	...
New Zealand - Nouvelle-Zélande[38]											
Total	+C	156	141	147	117	144	2.5	2.4	2.6	1.9	2.4
Urban - Urbaine	+C	141	126	123	105	123	2.6	2.4	2.4	2.0	2.4
Rural - Rurale	+C	15	15	21	12	21	...	...	...	...	...
Palau - Palaos											
Total	C	3	2	...	...	...	...	...	...	...	...

FOOTNOTES - NOTES

Italics: data from civil registers which are incomplete or of unknown completeness. - Italiques : données incomplètes ou dont le degré d'exactitude n'est pas connu, provenant des registres de l'état civil.

* Provisional. - Données provisoires.

[a] 'Code' indicates the source of data, as follows:
C - Civil registration, estimated over 90% complete
U - Civil registration, estimated less than 90% complete
| - Other source, estimated reliable
+ - Data tabulated by date of registration rather than occurence
... - Information not available

Le 'Code' indique la source des données, comme suit :
C - Registres de l'état civil considérés complets à 90 p. 100 au moins

U - Registres de l'état civil qui ne sont pas considérés complets à 90 p. 100 au moins
| - Autre source, considérée pas douteuses
+ - Données exploitées selon la date de l'enregistrement et non la date de l'événement
... - Information pas disponible

[1] Data refer only to events recorded in hospitals and health centres. - Ces données ne concernent que les faits d'état civil enregistrés dans les hôpitaux et les centres de santé uniquement.
[2] Excludes the islands of St. Brandon and Agalega. - Non compris les îles St. Brandon et Agalega.
[3] Source: National Office of Births and Deaths. - Source : Le bureau national des naissances et des décès.
[4] Unrevised data. - Les données n'ont pas été révisées.

5 Data refer to the death of a foetus at least 22 completed weeks of gestation. - Les données concernent le décès d'un fœtus après 22 semaines de gestation au moins.

6 Including Canadian residents temporarily in the United States, but excluding United States residents temporarily in Canada. - Y compris les résidents canadiens se trouvant temporairement aux Etats-Unis, mais ne comprenant pas les résidents des Etats-Unis se trouvant temporairement au Canada.

7 Late foetal death is indicated by the fact that the foetus is at least 500 g or more in weight. - Les décès foetaux tardifs sont caractérisés par le fait que le foetus pèse au moins 500 g.

8 Data refer to resident population only. - Pour la population résidante seulement.

9 The total number may include 'Unknown residence', but the categories urban and rural do not. - Le nombre total peut inclure les personnes dont la résidence n'est pas connue, à l'inverse des catégories de population urbaine et rurale.

10 Data refer to total foetal deaths. - Y compris toutes les morts foetales.

11 Late foetal death is indicated by the fact that the foetus is at least 22 completed weeks of gestational age. - Les décès intra-utérins tardifs sont définis comme survenant après 22 semaines au moins de gestation.

12 Excluding deaths of unknown sex. - Non compris les décès dont on ignore le sexe.

13 Excludes nomadic Indian tribes. - Non compris les tribus d'Indiens nomades.

14 Sources: Births and Deaths National Registration System database, and medical records of government hospitals. - Les sources: Les bases de données des << Births and Deaths National Registration System >> et les dossiers médicaux des hôpitaux du gouvernement.

15 Includes data for East Jerusalem and Israeli residents in certain other territories under occupation by Israeli military forces since June 1967. - Y compris les données pour Jérusalem-Est et les résidents israéliens dans certains autres territoires occupés depuis 1967 par les forces armées israéliennes.

16 Data refer to Japanese nationals in Japan only. The total number may include 'Unknown residence', but the categories urban and rural do not. Data exclude unknown duration of pregnancy. - Les données se raportent aux nationaux japonais au Japon seulement. Le nombre total peut inclure les personnes dont la résidence n'est pas connue, à l'inverse des catégories de population urbaine et rurale. Exception faite des grossesses dont la durée n'est pas connue.

17 Urban and rural figures refer to the late foetal deaths collected based on the location of the medical facilities, regardless of the mothers' permanent residence location. - Les chiffres urbains et ruraux concernent les décès tardifs du fœtus recueillis sur la base de l'emplacement des établissements médicaux, indépendamment du lieu de résidence permanente des mères.

18 Data are from Health Management Information System (HMIS). Including still births. - Les données proviennent de Système d'information de gestion de la santé (HMIS). Les données comprennent les mortinaissances.

19 Data are from Vital Registration System (VRS). - Les données proviennent du système d'enregistrement des faits d'état civil.

20 Data from Births and Deaths Notification System (Ministry of Health and all health care providers). - Les données proviennent du système de notification des naissances et des décès (Ministère de la santé et tous prestataires de soins de santé).

21 Excluding alien armed forces, civilian aliens employed by armed forces, and foreign diplomatic personnel and their dependants. - Non compris les militaires étrangers, les civils étrangers employés par les forces armées ni le personnel diplomatique étranger et les membres de leur famille les accompagnant.

22 Late foetal death is defined as an infant born without any signs of life, weighing at least 500 g, after duration of pregnancy of at least 22 weeks. - On dit qu'il y a mort intra-utérine tardive lorsqu'un enfant pesant au minimum 500 g naît sans donner aucun signe de vie au terme d'une grossesse qui a duré au moins 22 semaines.

23 Since 1 April 2012, a stillborn child is defined in guidelines for filling in a death certificate as a child fully expelled or removed out of the mother's body, not showing any sign of life and whose birth weight is 500 g or more. If the weight is not possible to determine then duration of pregnancy must be 22 weeks or more. If the duration of pregnancy is not possible to determine, the foetus length must be 25 cm or more. - Depuis le 1er avril 2012, un enfant mort-né est défini dans les directives relatives à l'établissement du certificat de décès comme un enfant complètement expulsé par la mère ou retiré de son corps, ne montrant aucun signe de vie et ayant atteint un poids de 500 g. S'il est impossible d'en déterminer le poids, la durée de gestation doit être au moins de 22 semaines. S'il est impossible de déterminer la durée de gestation, la longueur du fœtus doit être au moins de 25 cm.

24 Excluding Faeroe Islands and Greenland shown separately, if available. - Non compris les Iles Féroé et le Groenland, qui font l'objet de rubriques distinctes, si disponible.

25 Excluding Åland Islands. - Non compris les Îles d'Åland.

26 Late foetal death is indicated by the fact that the foetus is at least 24 completed weeks of gestation (it was 28 weeks until 1996) and does not show any sign of life after the separation from its mother; the foetus has to be 30 cm or more in length or 500 g or more in weight if its gestational age cannot be determined. - Pour qu'il y ait mort foetale tardive, il faut que le décès d'un fœtus survienne après 24 semaines complètes de gestation au moins (28 semaines jusqu'en 1996), que le foetus n'ait pas donné signe de vie après avoir été séparé de la mère, qu'il mesure 30 cm au moins ou pèse 500 g si la durée de la période de gestation n'est pas connue.

27 Late foetal death is indicated by the fact that the foetus is at least 24 completed weeks of gestation (it was 28 weeks until 1996) and does not show any sign of life after the separation from its mother; the foetus has to be 30 cm or more in length or 500 g or more in weight if its gestational age cannot be determined. The urban and rural categories do not include the data of foreigners, persons of unknown residence and the homeless, whereas the total category includes them. - Pour qu'il y ait mort foetale tardive, il faut que le décès d'un foetus survienne après 24 semaines complètes de gestation au moins (28 semaines jusqu'en 1996), que le foetus n'ait pas donné signe de vie après avoir été séparé de la mère, qu'il mesure 30 cm au moins ou pèse 500 g si la durée de la période de gestation n'est pas connue. Les chiffres portant sur la population urbaine et rurale n' incluent pas les données relatives aux étrangers, aux personnes dont la résidence n'est pas connue et aux personnes sans domicile fixe, à l'inverse, le total les inclut.

28 Data include the deceased infants with Hungarian usual residence regardless of whether the death occurred in Hungary or in a foreign country, and do not include the deceased infants with foreign country usual residence. - Les données comprennent les nourrissons décédés alors que leur résidence habituelle était en Hongrie, que le décès ait eu lieu en Hongrie ou dans un pays étranger, et ne comprennent pas les nourrissons décédés dont la residence habituelle était dans un pays étranger.

29 Data refer to events registered within one year of occurrence. - Les données portent sur des événements enregistrés dans l'année pendant laquelle ils sont survenus.

30 Including residents outside the country if listed in a Netherlands population register. - Englobe les résidents se trouvant à l'étranger à condition qu'ils soient inscrits sur le registre de population des Pays-Bas.

31 Data refer to usually resident population. - Les données concernent la population habituellement résidente.

32 Data refer to total foetal deaths. Excludes data for Kosovo and Metohia. - Y compris toutes les morts foetales. Sans les données pour le Kosovo et Metohie.

33 Including foetal deaths of at least 1 000 g in weight or 28 weeks of gestation. - Y compris les morts de fœtus pesant au moins 1 000 g ou après 28 semaines de gestation.

34 From 2015, urban refers to urban centers and areas under the influence of urban centers. - A partir de 2015, le territoire urbain inclut l'espace des centres urbains ainsi que l'espace sous influence des centres urbains.

35 The Government of Ukraine has informed the United Nations that it is not in a position to provide statistical data concerning the Autonomous Republic of Crimea and the city of Sevastopol. - Le gouvernement Ukrainien a informé l'ONU qu'il n'est pas en mesure de fournir des données statistiques concernant la République autonome de Crimée et la ville de Sébastopol.

36 Excluding Channel Islands (Guernsey and Jersey) and Isle of Man, shown separately, if available. - Non compris les îles Anglo-Normandes (Guernesey et Jersey) et l'île de Man, qui font l'objet de rubriques distinctes, si disponible.

37 Data include foetal deaths of unknown gestational weeks. - Les données comprennnent les morts foetales où le nombre de semaines de gestation n'est pas connu.

38 The total number may include 'Unknown residence', but the categories urban and rural do not. Data refer to resident population only. Random rounding to base 3 is applied in this table as a confidentiality measure. - Le nombre total peut inclure les personnes dont la résidence n'est pas connue, à l'inverse des catégories de population urbaine et rurale. Pour la population résidante seulement. Les chiffres sont arrondis à la base 3 de manière aléatoire, pour des raisons de confidentialité.

Table 13 - *Demographic Yearbook 2016*

Table 13 presents legally induced abortions for as many years as available between 2007 and 2016.

Description of variables: There are two major categories of abortion: spontaneous and induced. Induced abortions are those initiated by deliberate action undertaken with the intention of terminating pregnancy; all other abortions are considered spontaneous.

The induction of abortion is subject to governmental regulation in most, if not all, countries or areas. This regulation varies from complete prohibition in some countries or areas to abortion on request, with services provided by governmental health authorities, in others. More generally, governments have attempted to define the conditions under which a pregnancy may lawfully be terminated and have established procedures for authorizing abortion in individual cases.

Information on abortion policies is collected by the United Nations Population Division and published in the *Abortion Policies and Reproductive Health around the World*[1].

Reliability of data: Unlike data on live births and foetal deaths, which are generally collected through systems of vital registration, data on abortion are collected from a variety of sources. Because of this, the quality specification on the completeness of civil registers, which is presented for other tables, does not appear here.

Limitations: With regard to the collection of information on abortions, a variety of sources are used, but hospital records are the most common source of information. This implies that most cases that have no contact with hospitals are missed. Data from other sources are probably also incomplete. The data in the present table are limited to legally induced abortions, which, by their nature, might be assumed to be more complete than data on all induced abortions.

Earlier data: Legally induced abortions have been shown previously in all issues of the *Demographic Yearbook* since the twenty-third issue. For more information on specific topics and years for which data are reported, readers should consult the Historical Index.

NOTES

[1] United Nations, Department of Economic and Social Affairs, Population Division (2014). *Abortion Policies and Reproductive Health around the World* (United Nations publication, Sales No. E.14.XIII.11).

Tableau 13 – *Annuaire démographique 2016*

Le tableau 13 présente les données disponibles, relatives aux avortements provoqués légalement, entre 2007 et 2016.

Description des variables : l'avortement peut être spontané ou provoqué. L'avortement provoqué est celui qui résulte de manœuvres délibérées, entreprises afin d'interrompre la grossesse ; tous les autres avortements sont considérés comme spontanés.

L'interruption délibérée de la grossesse fait l'objet d'une réglementation officielle dans la plupart des pays ou zones, sinon dans tous. Cette réglementation va de l'interdiction totale à l'autorisation de l'avortement sur demande, pratiqué par des services de santé publique. Le plus souvent, les gouvernements se sont efforcés de définir les circonstances dans lesquelles la grossesse peut être interrompue licitement et de fixer une procédure d'autorisation.

La Division de la population des Nations Unies collecte des informations sur les politiques en matière d'avortement et les publient dans *Abortion Policies and Reproductive Health around the World*[1].

Fiabilité des données : à la différence des données sur les naissances vivantes et les morts fœtales, qui proviennent généralement des registres d'état civil, les données sur l'avortement sont tirées de sources diverses. Aussi ne trouve-t-on pas ici une évaluation de la qualité des données semblable à celle qui indique, pour les autres tableaux, le degré d'exhaustivité des données de l'état civil.

Insuffisance des données : en ce qui concerne les renseignements sur l'avortement, un grand nombre de sources sont utilisées, les relevés hospitaliers restant cependant la source la plus commune. Il s'ensuit que la plupart des cas qui ne passent pas par les hôpitaux sont ignorés. Il faut aussi tenir compte du fait que les données provenant d'autres sources sont probablement incomplètes. Les données du tableau 13 se limitent aux avortements provoqués pour raisons légales dont on peut supposer, en raison de leur nature même, que les statistiques sont plus complètes que les données concernant l'ensemble des avortements provoqués.

Données publiées antérieurement : des statistiques concernant les avortements provoqués pour raisons légales sont publiées dans *l'Annuaire démographique* depuis la vingt-troisième édition. Pour plus de précisions concernant les années et les sujets pour lesquels des données ont été publiées, se reporter à l'index historique.

NOTES

[1] United Nations, Department of Economic and Social Affairs, Population Division (2014). *Abortion Policies and Reproductive Health around the World* (United Nations publication, Sales No. E.14.XIII.11).

Continent and country or area Continent et pays ou zone	Number - Nombre									
	2007	2008	2009	2010	2011	2012	2013	2014	2015	2016
AFRICA - AFRIQUE										
Burundi[1]	...	...	6 329	6 272	3 547	3 630	3 152	...	...	...
Reunion - Réunion	4 543	4 564	4 402	4 349	4 508	4 280	...	...	...	...
Seychelles	446	453	471	556	579	533	515	549	478	...
AMERICA, NORTH - AMÉRIQUE DU NORD										
Bermuda - Bermudes	90	283	303	284	278	278	275	248	239	...
Costa Rica[2]	8 504[3]	8 733[3]	7 848	7 697	7 882	7 405	7 283	*7 137	...	...
Cuba	66 008	74 905	84 724	71 398	83 943	83 682	84 373	85 782	91 500	...
Dominican Republic - République dominicaine	29 526	26 318	22 828	22 551	25 284	26 303	26 180	25 999	...	...
Greenland - Groenland	887	899	799	858	743	784	875	865	...	...
Mexico - Mexique[4]	833	764	867	*986	1 041	294	271	301	411	...
United States of America - États-Unis d'Amérique[5]	827 609	825 564	...	...	...	...	...	...	...	...
AMERICA, SOUTH - AMÉRIQUE DU SUD										
Colombia - Colombie	...	...	69	81	120	209	628	873	...	...
Ecuador - Équateur[6]	...	...	...	...	...	41 712	40 256	35 719	31 302	...
Paraguay	...	...	...	...	...	4 353	...	...	...	...
ASIA - ASIE										
Armenia - Arménie	11 501	12 469	13 797	...	...	...	...	11 892	11 104	...
Azerbaijan - Azerbaïdjan	22 323	25 247	24 554	26 799	27 787	31 037	27 892	27 220	27 452	...
Bahrain - Bahreïn[7]	2 014	2 575	2 394	2 525	2 452	2 463	...	...	...	...
China, Hong Kong SAR - Chine, Hong Kong RAS	13 515	13 199	12 028	11 231	11 864	11 298	10 653	10 359	9 890	9 481
Georgia - Géorgie	20 644	22 062	24 311	25 585	30 590	...	38 018	...	33 377	...
Israel - Israël[8]	19 470	19 638	19 849	19 575	18 974	18 822	18 263	18 646	...	...
Japan - Japon	256 672	242 326	226 878	212 694[9]	202 106	196 639	186 253	181 905	176 388	...
Kazakhstan	125 654	130 599	113 320	106 074	95 288	95 654	84 265	...	...	...
Kyrgyzstan - Kirghizstan[10]	21 884	20 800	22 088	21 675	23 728	23 547	21 673	24 456	22 084	...
Mongolia - Mongolie	15 817	10 688	12 602	12 492	...	...	...	...	18 168	18 316
Singapore - Singapour	11 933	12 222	12 318	12 082	11 940	10 624	9 282	8 515	7 942	7 217
Tajikistan - Tadjikistan	18 986	18 481	19 470	19 510	17 503	16 618	15 984	17 347	...	...
Uzbekistan - Ouzbékistan	42 681	41 758	45 968	40 651	38 809	37 634	38 546	41 352	40 201	...
EUROPE										
Åland Islands - Îles d'Åland	73	67	68	70	73	60	70	66	69	...
Albania - Albanie	9 030	8 335	8 139	6 919	7 042	6 755	6 442	5 572	5 619	...
Belarus - Bélarus	46 285	42 197	35 967	33 262	32 031	28 628	31 206	29 797	29 217	...
Belgium - Belgique	18 033	18 595	18 870	19 095	19 578	...	...	...	...	...
Bulgaria - Bulgarie	37 594	36 593	33 733	31 548	31 716	29 992	29 505	28 145	27 782	...
Croatia - Croatie	4 573	4 497	4 450	4 043	4 347	3 571	3 161	3 020	3 002	...
Czechia - Tchéquie	25 414	25 760	24 636	23 998	24 055	23 032	22 714	21 893	20 403	...
Denmark - Danemark[11]	15 660	16 355	16 736	16 709	15 974	15 608	15 834	15 097	...	...
Estonia - Estonie[12]	8 883	8 409	7 542	7 068	6 668	6 056	5 777	6 901	4 889	4 475
Faeroe Islands - Îles Féroé	46	37	51	33	33	34	23	30	32	...
Finland - Finlande[13]	10 507	10 414	10 437	10 231	10 622	10 177	10 060	9 714	9 372	...
France[14]	212 050	208 003	208 662	211 248	206 888	205 300	214 649	211 229	...	...
Germany - Allemagne	116 871	114 484	110 694	110 431	108 867	106 815	102 802	99 715	99 237	...
Hungary - Hongrie	43 870	44 089	43 181	40 449	38 443	36 118	34 891	32 663	31 176	30 439
Iceland - Islande	905	909	981	977	970	980	963	951	921	...
Italy - Italie	125 116[15]	118 891[16]	114 793[17]	112 463[18]	110 041[18]	103 191[19]	100 342	95 400	...	...
Latvia - Lettonie	11 814	10 425	8 881	7 443	7 089	6 197	5 557	5 318	4 802	...
Lithuania - Lituanie	9 596	9 031	8 024	6 989	6 205	6 033	5 353	5 231	4 735	...
Montenegro - Monténégro	...	...	...	...	...	...	...	943	980	...
Norway - Norvège	15 165	16 054	15 774	15 735	15 343	...	...	...	...	...

Continent and country or area Continent et pays ou zone	Number - Nombre									
	2007	2008	2009	2010	2011	2012	2013	2014	2015	2016
EUROPE										
Poland - Pologne[20]	328	506	538	644	669	752	745	970	1 040	...
Portugal	4 325	18 607	19 848	20 137	20 480	19 156	18 281	16 762	16 454	...
Republic of Moldova - République de Moldova	15 843	15 900	14 634	14 785	15 710	14 838	...	...	...	...
Romania - Roumanie	137 226	127 907	116 060	101 915	103 386	87 975	86 432	78 371	70 885	...
Russian Federation - Fédération de Russie	1 479 010	1 385 600	1 292 389	1 186 108	1 124 880	1 063 982	1 012 399	...	...	...
Serbia - Serbie[21]	24 273	22 867	...	...	...	...	...	...	...	...
Slovakia - Slovaquie	13 424	13 394	13 240	12 582	11 789	11 214	11 105	10 582	10 058	...
Slovenia - Slovénie	5 176	4 946	4 653	4 328	4 263	4 106	4 011	4 060	3 682	...
Spain - Espagne	112 138	115 812	111 482	113 031	118 359	112 390	...	94 796	94 188	...
Sweden - Suède	37 205	38 049	37 524	37 693	37 696	...	...	...	...	...
Switzerland - Suisse[22]	10 035	10 310	10 187	10 650	10 715	10 531	10 177	10 016	10 054	...
TFYR of Macedonia - L'ex-R. y. de Macédoine	6 090	5 900	5 648	5 078	5 324	5 387	4 983	4 738	4 587	...
Ukraine	225 336	217 413	194 845	176 774	169 131	153 147	147 736	116 104[23]	...	...
United Kingdom of Great Britain and Northern Ireland - Royaume-Uni de Grande-Bretagne et d'Irlande du Nord[24]	219 376	216 062	208 854	209 048	208 636	203 419[25]	...	...	...	...
OCEANIA - OCÉANIE										
Guam[26]	...	327	266	269	295	275	213	209	263	289
New Zealand - Nouvelle-Zélande	18 382	17 940	17 550	16 630	15 863	14 745	14 073	13 137[27]	13 155[27]	12 823[27]

FOOTNOTES - NOTES

Italics: estimates which are less reliable. - Italiques : estimations moins sûres.

* Provisional. - Données provisoires.

[1] Data refer only to events recorded in hospitals and health centres. - Ces données ne concernent que les faits d'état civil enregistrés dans les hôpitaux et les centres de santé uniquement.

[2] Excluding abortions performed in private hospitals. - Non comprises les interruptions volontaires de grossesse effectuées dans des hôpitaux privés.

[3] Number of women who report having had a previous abortion when registering a newborn. - Nombre des femmes qui ont signalé d'avoir eu un avortement avant la naissance de l'enfant enregistré.

[4] Data refer to 'Therapeutic Abortions'. According to Mexican law, only induced abortions, prescribed by medical reasons or induced because of pregnancy coming from sexual aggression, are considered as legal; data refer only to the former. Refers to residence of the mother. To calculate the total number of abortions, only foetal deaths of less than 20 weeks of gestation were considered. Excluding abortions in the country by women with usual residence outside of the country. - Les données se rapportent aux « interruptions volontaires de grossesse pour des motifs thérapeutiques ». D'après la loi mexicaine, seuls sont considérés légaux les avortements déclenchés pour des raisons médicales ou parce que la grossesse est le résultat d'une agression sexuelle; les données se réfèrent seulement à la première. Correspond à la résidence de la mère. Seuls les morts fœtales survenues à moins de 20 semaines de gestation ont été prises en compte aux fins du calcul du nombre total d'avortements. Hors avortements dans le pays par des femmes avec résidence habituelle en dehors du pays.

[5] Includes areas that reported abortion counts every year during the period of analysis. Excludes states that did not report abortion numbers: Alaska(1998-2002), California (1997-2008), Louisiana (2005), Maryland (2006-2008), New Hampshire (1998-2008), Oklahoma (1998-1999), and West Virginia (2003-2004). - Sont couvertes les régions qui ont indiqué le nombre annuel d'avortements pour la période analysée. Ne sont pas couverts les États qui n'ont pas fourni de chiffres : l'Alaska (1998-2002), la Californie (1997-2008), la Louisiane (2005), le Maryland (2006-2008), le New Hampshire (1998-2008), l'Oklahoma (1998-1999) et la Virginie occidentale (2003-2004).

[6] Data refer to abortions registered in hospitals due to pregnancy complications. - Les données renvoient aux avortements enregistrés dans les hôpitaux du fait des complications de la grossesse.

[7] Data refer to spontaneous abortions and miscarriages. - Données se rapportant aux avortements spontanés et fausses couches.

[8] Includes data for East Jerusalem and Israeli residents in certain other territories under occupation by Israeli military forces since June 1967. Data refer to applications to commissions for termination of pregnancy and not to authorizations. - Y compris les données pour Jérusalem-Est et les résidents israéliens dans certains autres territoires occupés depuis 1967 par les forces armées israéliennes. Les données relatives aux avortements provoqués légalement se rapportent aux demandes d'autorisation et non aux autorisations elles-mêmes.

[9] Excluding data of cities and towns in the jurisdiction of Sousou Public Health and Welfare Office of Fukushima Prefecture due to the impact of the Great East Japan Earthquake. - Ne sont pas incluses les données relatives aux agglomérations relevant du bureau de la santé publique et des services sociaux de Sousou dans la préfecture de Fukushima, en raison des conséquences du grand séisme dans l'est du Japon.

[10] Based on administrative reporting of the Ministry of Health. - Les données reposent sur les rapports administratifs du Ministère de la santé.

[11] Excluding Faeroe Islands and Greenland shown separately, if available. - Non compris les Iles Féroé et le Groenland, qui font l'objet de rubriques distinctes, si disponible.

[12] Data refer to resident population only. - Pour la population résidante seulement.

[13] Excluding Åland Islands. - Non compris les Îles d'Åland.

[14] Data refer to women between 15 and 49 years of age. - Le total se rapporte uniquement aux femmes dont l'âge est compris entre 15 et 49 ans.

[15] Data are incomplete for Campania and Sicilia regions. - Les données sont incomplètes pour les régions de la Campanie et de la Sicile.

[16] Data are incomplete for Campania, Calabria, Sicilia and Sardegna regions. - Les données sont incomplètes pour les régions de Campanie, de Calabrie, de Sicile et de Sardaigne.

[17] Data are incomplete for Abruzzo, Campania, Basilicata, Sicilia and Sardegna regions. - Données incomplètes pour les régions des Abruzzes, de Campanie, de Basilicate, de Sicile et de Sardaigne.

[18] Data are incomplete for Umbria, Campania and Sicilia regions. - Les données sont incomplètes pour l'Ombrie, la Campanie et la Sicile.

[19] Data are incomplete for Umbria, Abruzzo, Campania, Puglia and Sicilia regions. - Les données sont incomplètes pour les régions d'Ombrie, des Abruzzes, de Campanie, des Pouilles et de Sicile.

²⁰ Based on hospital and polyclinic records. - D'après les registres des hôpitaux et des polycliniques.

²¹ Excludes data for Kosovo and Metohia. Data refer to institutions included in the Health Institutions Network Plan in the Republic of Serbia. - Sans les données pour le Kosovo et Metohie. Les données se rapportent aux institutions membres du "Health Institutions Network Plan" de la République de Serbie.

²² Data refer to termination of pregnancy for women who are Switzerland residents. - Les données portent sur les interruptions de grossesse pratiquées sur des femmes qui résident en Suisse.

²³ The Government of Ukraine has informed the United Nations that it is not in a position to provide statistical data concerning the Autonomous Republic of Crimea and the city of Sevastopol. - Le gouvernement Ukrainien a informé l'ONU qu'il n'est pas en mesure de fournir des données statistiques concernant la République autonome de Crimée et la ville de Sébastopol.

²⁴ Excluding Northern Ireland. Excluding Channel Islands (Guernsey and Jersey) and Isle of Man, shown separately, if available. - Non compris l'Irlande du Nord. Non compris les îles Anglo-Normandes (Guernesey et Jersey) et l'île de Man, qui font l'objet de rubriques distinctes, si disponible.

²⁵ Including provisional data for Scotland. - Y compris les données provisoires pour l'Écosse.

²⁶ Including United States military personnel, their dependants and contract employees. - Y compris les militaires des Etats-Unis, les membres de leur famille les accompagnant et les agents contractuels des Etats-Unis.

²⁷ Random rounding to base 3 is applied in this table as a confidentiality measure. - Les chiffres sont arrondis à la base 3 de manière aléatoire, pour des raisons de confidentialité.

Table 14 - *Demographic Yearbook 2016*

Table 14 presents legally induced abortions by age and number of previous live births of women for the latest available year between 2007 and 2016.

Description of variables: Age is defined as age at last birthday, that is, the difference between the date of birth and the date of the occurrence of the event, expressed in complete solar years. The age classification used in this table is the following: under 15 years, 5-year age groups through 45-49 years and 50 years and over.

Except where otherwise indicated, eight categories are used in classifying the number of previous live births: 0 through 5, 6 or more live births, and, if required, number of live births unknown.

Information on abortion policies is collected by the United Nations Population Division and published in the *Abortion Policies and Reproductive Health around the World*[1].

Reliability of data: Unlike data on live births and foetal deaths, which are generally collected through systems of vital registration, data on abortion are collected from a variety of sources. Because of this, the quality specification on the completeness of civil registers, which is presented for other tables, does not appear here.

Limitations: With regard to the collection of information on abortions, a variety of sources are used, but hospital records are the most common source of information. This implies that most cases that have no contact with hospitals are missed. Data from other sources are probably also incomplete. The data in the present table are limited to legally induced abortions, which, by their nature, might be assumed to be more complete than data on all induced abortions.

In addition, deficiencies in the reporting of age and number of previous live births of the woman, differences in the method used for obtaining the age of the woman, and the proportion of abortions for which age or previous live births of the woman are unknown must all be taken into account in using these data.

Earlier data: Legally induced abortions by age and previous live births of women have been shown previously in most issues of the *Demographic Yearbook* since the twenty-third issue. For more information on specific topics and years for which data are reported, readers should consult the Historical Index.

NOTES

[1] United Nations, Department of Economic and Social Affairs, Population Division (2014). *Abortion Policies and Reproductive Health around the World* (United Nations publication, Sales No. E.14.XIII.11).

419

Tableau 14 – *Annuaire démographique 2016*

Le tableau 14 présente les données les plus récentes disponibles entre 2007 et 2016 sur les avortements provoqués pour des raisons légales, selon l'âge de la mère et le nombre de naissances vivantes précédentes.

Description des variables : L'âge considéré est l'âge au dernier anniversaire, c'est-à-dire la différence entre la date de naissance et la date de l'avortement, exprimée en années solaires révolues. La classification par âge utilisée dans le tableau 14 est la suivante : moins de 15 ans, groupes quinquennaux jusqu'à 45-49 ans, 50 ans et plus, et âge inconnu.

Sauf indication contraire, les naissances vivantes antérieures sont classées dans les huit catégories suivantes: 0 à 5 naissances vivantes, 6 naissances vivantes ou plus et, le cas échéant, nombre de naissances vivantes inconnu.

La Division de la population des Nations Unies collecte des informations sur les politiques en matière d'avortement et les publient dans *Abortion Policies and Reproductive Health around the World*[1].

Fiabilité des données : à la différence des données sur les naissances vivantes et les morts fœtales, qui proviennent généralement des registres d'état civil, les données sur l'avortement sont tirées de sources diverses. Aussi ne trouve-t-on pas ici une évaluation de la qualité des données semblable à celle qui indique, pour les autres tableaux, le degré d'exhaustivité des données de l'état civil.

Insuffisance des données : en ce qui concerne les renseignements sur l'avortement, un grand nombre de sources sont utilisées, les relevés hospitaliers restant cependant la source la plus commune. Il s'ensuit que la plupart des cas qui ne passent pas par les hôpitaux sont ignorés. Il faut aussi tenir compte du fait que les données provenant d'autres sources sont probablement incomplètes. Les données du tableau 14 se limitent aux avortements provoqués pour raisons légales dont on peut supposer, en raison de leur nature même, que les statistiques sont plus complètes que les données concernant l'ensemble des avortements provoqués.

En outre, on doit tenir compte, lorsque l'on utilise ces données, des erreurs de déclaration de l'âge de la mère et du nombre des naissances vivantes précédentes, de l'hétérogénéité des méthodes de calcul de l'âge de la mère et de la proportion d'avortements pour lesquels l'âge de la mère ou le nombre des naissances vivantes ne sont pas connus.

Données publiées antérieurement : Depuis la vingt-troisième édition, la plupart des éditions de l'*Annuaire démographique* contiennent des statistiques concernant les avortements provoqués pour raisons légales, selon l'âge de la mère et le nombre de naissances vivantes antérieures. Pour plus de précisions concernant les années et les sujets pour lesquels des données ont été publiées, se reporter à l'index historique.

NOTES

[1] United Nations, Department of Economic and Social Affairs, Population Division (2014). *Abortion Policies and Reproductive Health around the World* (United Nations publication, Sales No. E.14.XIII.11).

14. Legally induced abortions by age and number of previous live births of women: latest available year, 2007 - 2016
Avortments provoqués légalement selon l'âge de la femme et selon le nombre des naissances vivantes précédentes : dernière année disponible, 2007 - 2016

Continent, country or area, year and age / Continent, pays ou zone, année et âge	Total	Number of previous live births / Nombre des naissances vivantes précédentes							Unknown - Inconnu
		0	1	2	3	4	5	6+	

AMERICA, NORTH - AMÉRIQUE DU NORD

Bermuda - Bermudes
2014

Total	248	...	...	...	...	...	...	...	...
0 - 14	-	...	...	...	...	...	...	...	...
15 - 19	17	...	...	...	...	...	...	...	...
20 - 24	54	...	...	...	...	...	...	...	...
25 - 29	78	...	...	...	...	...	...	...	...
30 - 34	57	...	...	...	...	...	...	...	...
35 - 39	33	...	...	...	...	...	...	...	...
40 - 44	9	...	...	...	...	...	...	...	...
45 - 49	-	...	...	...	...	...	...	...	...
50 +	-	...	...	...	...	...	...	...	...
Unknown - Inconnu	-	...	...	...	...	...	...	...	...

Costa Rica[1]
2009

Total	7 848	...	...	...	...	...	...	...	...
10 - 14	68	...	...	...	...	...	...	...	...
15 - 19	1 275	...	...	...	...	...	...	...	...
20 - 44	6 437	...	...	...	...	...	...	...	...
45 +	68	...	...	...	...	...	...	...	...

Cuba
2015

Total	91 500	...	...	...	...	...	...	...	...
0 - 14	1 267	...	...	...	...	...	...	...	...
15 - 19	20 410	...	...	...	...	...	...	...	...
20 - 34	60 522	...	...	...	...	...	...	...	...
35 - 49	9 301	...	...	...	...	...	...	...	...

Mexico - Mexique[2]
2015

Total	411	128	124	70	34	8	2	1	44
0 - 14	1	1	-	-	-	-	-	-	-
15 - 19	48	26	8	1	-	-	-	-	13
20 - 24	100	40	36	7	5	-	-	-	12
25 - 29	91	19	30	24	5	-	-	-	13
30 - 34	77	18	25	20	10	2	1	-	1
35 - 39	70	16	15	17	13	4	1	-	4
40 - 44	18	4	9	1	1	1	-	1	1
45 - 49	1	-	-	-	-	1	-	-	-
50 +	-	-	-	-	-	-	-	-	-
Unknown - Inconnu	5	4	1	-	-	-	-	-	-

AMERICA, SOUTH - AMÉRIQUE DU SUD

Colombia - Colombie
2014

Total	876	398	243	113	67	31	14	7	3
0 - 14	38	35	1	-	-	-	-	-	2
15 - 19	188	152	30	6	-	-	-	-	-
20 - 24	240	118	88	25	6	2	1	-	-
25 - 29	157	47	51	26	21	6	5	1	-
30 - 34	127	25	42	27	17	10	4	2	-
35 - 39	72	14	23	17	11	4	1	2	-
40 - 44	49	7	6	12	12	8	3	1	-
45 - 49	4	-	2	-	-	1	-	1	-
50 +	-	-	-	-	-	-	-	-	-
Unknown - Inconnu	1	-	-	-	-	-	-	-	1

Ecuador - Équateur[3]
2015

Total	31 302	...	...	...	...	...	...	...	...
0 - 14	308	...	...	...	...	...	...	...	...
15 - 19	4 747	...	...	...	...	...	...	...	...
20 - 24	7 171	...	...	...	...	...	...	...	...
25 - 29	6 844	...	...	...	...	...	...	...	...
30 - 34	5 761	...	...	...	...	...	...	...	...
35 - 39	4 244	...	...	...	...	...	...	...	...
40 - 44	1 927	...	...	...	...	...	...	...	...
45 - 49	300	...	...	...	...	...	...	...	...

14. Legally induced abortions by age and number of previous live births of women: latest available year, 2007 - 2016
Avortments provoqués légalement selon l'âge de la femme et selon le nombre des naissances vivantes précédentes : dernière année disponible, 2007 - 2016 (continued - suite)

Continent, country or area, year and age / Continent, pays ou zone, année et âge	Number of previous live births Nombre des naissances vivantes précédentes								
	Total	0	1	2	3	4	5	6+	Unknown - Inconnu
AMERICA, SOUTH - AMÉRIQUE DU SUD									
Ecuador - Équateur[3]									
2015									
50 +	-	...	...	...	...	...	...	...	...
Unknown - Inconnu	-	...	...	...	...	...	...	...	...
ASIA - ASIE									
Armenia - Arménie									
2014									
Total	11 892	...	...	...	...	...	...	...	...
0 - 14	1	...	...	...	...	...	...	...	...
15 - 29	490	...	...	...	...	...	...	...	...
30 - 44	9 251	...	...	...	...	...	...	...	...
45 +	2 150	...	...	...	...	...	...	...	...
Azerbaijan - Azerbaïdjan									
2014									
Total	27 220	...	...	...	...	...	...	...	...
15 - 19	1 161	...	...	...	...	...	...	...	...
20 - 24	5 738	...	...	...	...	...	...	...	...
25 - 29	8 365	...	...	...	...	...	...	...	...
30 - 34	7 756	...	...	...	...	...	...	...	...
35 +	4 200	...	...	...	...	...	...	...	...
Unknown - Inconnu	-	...	...	...	...	...	...	...	...
China, Hong Kong SAR - Chine, Hong Kong RAS									
2016									
Total	9 481	5 019	1 901	2 082	403	63	11	2	...
0 - 14	14	14	-	-	-	-	-	-	...
15 - 19	575	552	19	2	2	-	-	-	...
20 - 24	1 823	1 628	141	47	7	-	-	-	...
25 - 29	1 946	1 341	325	233	41	6	-	-	...
30 - 34	2 089	844	549	563	112	18	2	1	...
35 - 39	1 996	481	575	767	147	21	4	1	...
40 - 44	928	142	270	417	79	15	5	-	...
45 - 49	106	15	22	51	15	3	-	-	...
50 +	4	2	-	2	-	-	-	-	...
Georgia - Géorgie									
2013									
Total	38 018	...	...	...	...	...	...	...	...
0 - 14	34	...	...	...	...	...	...	...	...
15 - 19	1 849	...	...	...	...	...	...	...	...
20 - 29	17 475	...	...	...	...	...	...	...	...
30 - 34	10 007	...	...	...	...	...	...	...	...
35 - 39	6 412	...	...	...	...	...	...	...	...
40 - 44	1 966	...	...	...	...	...	...	...	...
45 - 49	258	...	...	...	...	...	...	...	...
50 +	17	...	...	...	...	...	...	...	...
Israel - Israël[4]									
2014									
Total	18 646	7 960	2 605	3 672	2 729	1 067	339	274	...
0 - 14	37	34	2	-	-	-	-	1	...
15 - 19	1 808	1 737	56	7	5	2	1	-	...
20 - 24	3 513	2 757	446	234	64	9	3	-	...
25 - 29	3 773	1 958	685	681	318	99	24	8	...
30 - 34	3 974	937	766	1 131	715	305	73	47	...
35 - 39	3 550	374	462	1 082	997	386	132	117	...
40 - 44	1 801	142	162	487	574	250	94	92	...
45 - 49	177	19	25	44	54	16	11	8	...
50 +	13	2	1	6	2	-	1	1	...
Japan - Japon									
2015									
Total	176 388	...	...	...	...	...	...	...	...
0 - 14	270	...	...	...	...	...	...	...	...
15 - 19	15 843	...	...	...	...	...	...	...	...
20 - 24	39 430	...	...	...	...	...	...	...	...
25 - 29	35 429	...	...	...	...	...	...	...	...
30 - 34	35 884	...	...	...	...	...	...	...	...

14. Legally induced abortions by age and number of previous live births of women: latest available year, 2007 - 2016
Avortments provoqués légalement selon l'âge de la femme et selon le nombre des naissances vivantes précédentes : dernière année disponible, 2007 - 2016 (continued - suite)

Continent, country or area, year and age / Continent, pays ou zone, année et âge	Total	Number of previous live births / Nombre des naissances vivantes précédentes							Unknown - Inconnu
		0	1	2	3	4	5	6+	
ASIA - ASIE									
Japan - Japon									
2015									
35 - 39	31 765	...	...	...	...	...	...	...	...
40 - 44	16 368	...	...	...	...	...	...	...	...
45 - 49	1 340	...	...	...	...	...	...	...	...
50 +	18	...	...	...	...	...	...	...	...
Unknown - Inconnu	41	...	...	...	...	...	...	...	...
Kyrgyzstan - Kirghizstan[5]									
2008									
Total	20 800	...	...	...	...	...	...	...	...
0 - 14	1	...	...	...	...	...	...	...	...
15 - 19	1 814	...	...	...	...	...	...	...	...
20 - 24	5 018	...	...	...	...	...	...	...	...
25 - 29	5 462	...	...	...	...	...	...	...	...
30 - 34	4 598	...	...	...	...	...	...	...	...
35 - 39	2 776	...	...	...	...	...	...	...	...
40 - 44	1 019	...	...	...	...	...	...	...	...
45 +	112	...	...	...	...	...	...	...	...
Mongolia - Mongolie									
2016									
Total	18 316	...	...	...	...	...	...	...	...
0 - 19	919	...	...	...	...	...	...	...	...
20 - 24	3 309	...	...	...	...	...	...	...	...
25 - 29	5 227	...	...	...	...	...	...	...	...
30 - 34	4 407	...	...	...	...	...	...	...	...
35 - 39	3 073	...	...	...	...	...	...	...	...
40 - 44	1 273	...	...	...	...	...	...	...	...
45 - 49	106	...	...	...	...	...	...	...	...
50 +	2	...	...	...	...	...	...	...	...
Singapore - Singapour									
2016									
Total	7 217	3 116	1 484	1 824	564	^229	...	...	...
0 - 14	9	8	1	-	-	^_	...	...	...
15 - 19	334	312	18	3	1	^_	...	...	...
20 - 24	1 273	1 035	161	53	20	^4	...	...	...
25 - 29	1 784	1 015	375	280	77	^37	...	...	...
30 - 34	1 777	446	504	613	159	^55	...	...	...
35 - 39	1 428	228	294	601	215	^90	...	...	...
40 - 44	558	63	121	251	82	^41	...	...	...
45 +	54	9	10	23	10	^2	...	...	...
Tajikistan - Tadjikistan									
2014									
Total	17 347	...	...	...	...	...	...	...	...
0 - 14	-	...	...	...	...	...	...	...	...
15 - 17	62	...	...	...	...	...	...	...	...
18 - 19	1 659	...	...	...	...	...	...	...	...
20 - 34	11 665	...	...	...	...	...	...	...	...
35 +	3 961	...	...	...	...	...	...	...	...
Uzbekistan - Ouzbékistan									
2015									
Total	40 201	6 356	...	...	...	...	...	...	33 845
0 - 14	4	4	...	...	...	...	...	...	-
15 - 19	617	285	...	...	...	...	...	...	332
20 - 34	31 627	5 624	...	...	...	...	...	...	26 003
35 - 49	7 953	443	...	...	...	...	...	...	7 510
50 +	-	-	...	...	...	...	...	...	-
EUROPE									
Åland Islands - Îles d'Åland									
2012									
Total	60	31	12	10	5	-	2	-	...
0 - 14	-	-	-	-	-	-	-	-	...
15 - 19	9	9	-	-	-	-	-	-	...
20 - 24	15	11	3	1	-	-	-	-	...
25 - 29	17	6	4	4	1	-	2	-	...
30 - 34	7	2	1	3	1	-	-	-	...

14. Legally induced abortions by age and number of previous live births of women: latest available year, 2007 - 2016
Avortments provoqués légalement selon l'âge de la femme et selon le nombre des naissances vivantes précédentes : dernière année disponible, 2007 - 2016 (continued - suite)

Continent, country or area, year and age / Continent, pays ou zone, année et âge	Number of previous live births / Nombre des naissances vivantes précédentes								
	Total	0	1	2	3	4	5	6+	Unknown - Inconnu
EUROPE									
Åland Islands - Îles d'Åland									
2012									
35 - 39	7	1	3	1	2	-	-	-	...
40 - 44	5	2	1	1	1	-	-	-	...
45 - 49	-	-	-	-	-	-	-	-	...
50 +	-	-	-	-	-	-	-	-	...
2015									
Total	69	...	...	...	...	...	...	...	...
0 - 14	-	...	...	...	...	...	...	...	...
15 - 19	9	...	...	...	...	...	...	...	...
20 - 24	23	...	...	...	...	...	...	...	...
25 - 29	14	...	...	...	...	...	...	...	...
30 - 34	12	...	...	...	...	...	...	...	...
35 - 39	6	...	...	...	...	...	...	...	...
40 - 44	5	...	...	...	...	...	...	...	...
45 - 49	-	...	...	...	...	...	...	...	...
50 +	-	...	...	...	...	...	...	...	...
Belarus - Bélarus									
2015									
Total	29 217	...	...	...	...	...	...	...	...
0 - 14	13	...	...	...	...	...	...	...	...
15 - 19	1 362	...	...	...	...	...	...	...	...
20 - 24	5 165	...	...	...	...	...	...	...	...
25 - 29	7 565	...	...	...	...	...	...	...	...
30 - 34	8 478	...	...	...	...	...	...	...	...
35 - 39	4 481	...	...	...	...	...	...	...	...
40 - 44	1 937	...	...	...	...	...	...	...	...
45 - 49	216	...	...	...	...	...	...	...	...
50 +	-	...	...	...	...	...	...	...	...
Belgium - Belgique									
2011									
Total	19 578	9 145	4 266	3 698	1 636	581	174	78	...
0 - 14	87	86	1	-	-	-	-	-	...
15 - 19	2 575	2 339	207	28	1	-	-	-	...
20 - 24	5 027	3 430	1 070	425	87	12	3	-	...
25 - 29	4 688	1 992	1 249	983	332	104	20	8	...
30 - 34	3 745	863	997	1 131	512	176	46	20	...
35 - 39	2 454	349	538	796	483	184	70	34	...
40 - 44	923	78	188	308	207	99	30	13	...
45 - 49	78	7	16	27	14	6	5	3	...
50 +	1	1	-	-	-	-	-	-	...
Bulgaria - Bulgarie									
2015									
Total	27 782	...	...	...	...	...	...	...	...
0 - 14	118	...	...	...	...	...	...	...	...
15 - 19	2 216	...	...	...	...	...	...	...	...
20 - 24	5 523	...	...	...	...	...	...	...	...
25 - 29	6 934	...	...	...	...	...	...	...	...
30 - 34	6 157	...	...	...	...	...	...	...	...
35 - 39	4 986	...	...	...	...	...	...	...	...
40 - 44	1 692	...	...	...	...	...	...	...	...
45 - 49	151	...	...	...	...	...	...	...	...
50 +	5	...	...	...	...	...	...	...	...
Croatia - Croatie									
2015									
Total	3 002	931	642	886	344	98	25	34	42
0 - 14	2	2	-	-	-	-	-	-	-
15 - 19	224	183	22	4	1	-	-	-	14
20 - 24	525	337	108	53	10	5	1	1	10
25 - 29	577	173	154	156	61	12	5	8	8
30 - 34	695	140	171	243	101	30	3	5	2
35 - 39	671	64	126	289	124	33	12	15	8
40 - 44	282	28	55	131	44	15	4	5	-
45 - 49	26	4	6	10	3	3	-	-	-
50 +	-	-	-	-	-	-	-	-	-
Czechia - Tchéquie									
2015									
Total	20 403	5 701	5 220	6 783	1 942	467	172	118	...
0 - 14	26	26	-	-	-	-	-	-	...

424

14. Legally induced abortions by age and number of previous live births of women: latest available year, 2007 - 2016
Avortments provoqués légalement selon l'âge de la femme et selon le nombre des naissances vivantes précédentes : dernière année disponible, 2007 - 2016 (continued - suite)

Continent, country or area, year and age / Continent, pays ou zone, année et âge	Total	Number of previous live births / Nombre des naissances vivantes précédentes								
		0	1	2	3	4	5	6+	Unknown - Inconnu
EUROPE									
Czechia - Tchéquie									
2015									
15 - 19	1 345	1 139	182	22	2	-	-	2	...
20 - 24	3 599	2 036	999	422	103	26	11	21	...
25 - 29	4 119	1 407	1 241	1 071	265	81	33	21	...
30 - 34	4 457	713	1 303	1 772	479	113	42	35	...
35 - 39	4 477	311	1 063	2 232	639	148	43	41	...
40 - 44	2 202	68	408	1 166	416	87	39	18	...
45 - 49	175	1	24	96	37	12	4	1	...
50 +	3	-	-	2	1	-	-	-	...
Denmark - Danemark[6]									
2014									
Total	15 097	...	...	...	...	...	...	...	...
0 - 19	2 051	...	...	...	...	...	...	...	...
20 - 24	4 023	...	...	...	...	...	...	...	...
25 - 29	3 324	...	...	...	...	...	...	...	...
30 - 34	2 609	...	...	...	...	...	...	...	...
35 - 39	2 045	...	...	...	...	...	...	...	...
40 - 44	967	...	...	...	...	...	...	...	...
45 +	78	...	...	...	...	...	...	...	...
Estonia - Estonie[7]									
2015									
Total	4 889	1 336	1 529	1 428	429	110	37	19	1
0 - 14	13	13	-	-	-	-	-	-	-
15 - 19	431	375	49	7	-	-	-	-	-
20 - 24	983	502	351	111	17	1	1	-	-
25 - 29	1 188	289	500	316	60	17	6	-	-
30 - 34	1 001	98	312	434	118	25	8	5	1
35 - 39	833	50	218	357	140	45	16	7	-
40 - 44	401	9	91	183	85	22	4	7	-
45 - 49	39	-	8	20	9	-	2	-	-
50 +	-	-	-	-	-	-	-	-	-
Faeroe Islands - Îles Féroé									
2013									
Total	23	...	...	...	...	...	...	...	...
0 - 14	-	...	...	...	...	...	...	...	...
15 - 19	1	...	...	...	...	...	...	...	...
20 - 24	5	...	...	...	...	...	...	...	...
25 - 29	4	...	...	...	...	...	...	...	...
30 - 34	7	...	...	...	...	...	...	...	...
35 - 39	5	...	...	...	...	...	...	...	...
40 - 44	1	...	...	...	...	...	...	...	...
45 - 49	-	...	...	...	...	...	...	...	...
50 +	-	...	...	...	...	...	...	...	...
Finland - Finlande									
2015									
Total	9 441	4 615	1 788	1 745	821	237	95	35	105
0 - 14	20	20	-	-	-	-	-	-	19
15 - 19	1 228	1 150	53	5	1	-	-	1	44
20 - 24	2 560	1 812	499	163	36	2	3	1	44
25 - 29	2 103	945	502	422	180	31	8	1	14
30 - 34	1 778	446	381	592	231	81	26	9	12
35 - 39	1 205	186	235	376	268	77	38	14	11
40 - 44	503	53	108	172	94	44	17	10	5
45 - 49	44	3	10	15	11	2	3	-	-
50 +	-	-	-	-	-	-	-	-	-
France[8]									
2009									
Total[9]	208 290	...	...	...	...	...	...	...	...
15 - 19	29 004	...	...	...	...	...	...	...	...
20 - 24	52 360	...	...	...	...	...	...	...	...
25 - 29	46 237	...	...	...	...	...	...	...	...
30 - 34	36 351	...	...	...	...	...	...	...	...
35 - 39	30 125	...	...	...	...	...	...	...	...
40 - 44	12 805	...	...	...	...	...	...	...	...
45 - 49	1 408	...	...	...	...	...	...	...	...

14. Legally induced abortions by age and number of previous live births of women: latest available year, 2007 - 2016
Avortments provoqués légalement selon l'âge de la femme et selon le nombre des naissances vivantes précédentes : dernière année disponible, 2007 - 2016 (continued - suite)

Continent, country or area, year and age / Continent, pays ou zone, année et âge	Number of previous live births / Nombre des naissances vivantes précédentes								
	Total	0	1	2	3	4	5	6+	Unknown - Inconnu
EUROPE									
Germany - Allemagne									
2015									
Total	99 237	38 793	24 869	23 111	8 533	2 597	839	495	...
0 - 14	337	337	-	-	-	-	-	-	...
15 - 19	8 216	7 408	698	104	3	-	-	3	...
20 - 24	20 646	12 928	5 089	2 053	457	91	20	8	...
25 - 29	24 323	9 544	7 208	5 223	1 695	473	116	64	...
30 - 34	21 835	5 190	6 053	6 825	2 577	797	259	134	...
35 - 39	16 368	2 425	4 083	6 066	2 496	808	304	186	...
40 - 44	6 787	858	1 587	2 575	1 173	385	121	88	...
45 - 49	701	99	146	262	127	42	17	8	...
50 +	24	4	5	3	5	1	2	4	...
Hungary - Hongrie									
2013									
Total	34 891	9 707	8 781	8 536	4 632	1 821	808	606	-
0 - 14	168	165	3	-	-	-	-	-	-
15 - 19	4 423	3 395	869	132	25	2	-	-	-
20 - 24	7 335	3 135	2 182	1 309	542	134	28	5	-
25 - 29	6 935	1 622	1 902	1 692	1 007	450	173	89	-
30 - 34	6 839	837	1 737	2 032	1 229	520	277	207	-
35 - 39	6 624	451	1 528	2 331	1 325	521	240	228	-
40 - 44	2 406	94	526	976	470	184	86	70	-
45 - 49	160	8	34	63	34	10	4	7	-
50 +	1	-	-	1	-	-	-	-	-
Unknown - Inconnu	-	-	-	-	-	-	-	-	-
2014									
Total	32 663	...	...	...	...	...	...	...	...
0 - 14	161	...	...	...	...	...	...	...	...
15 - 19	4 245	...	...	...	...	...	...	...	...
20 - 24	7 109	...	...	...	...	...	...	...	...
25 - 29	6 562	...	...	...	...	...	...	...	...
30 - 34	6 035	...	...	...	...	...	...	...	...
35 - 39	6 066	...	...	...	...	...	...	...	...
40 - 44	2 325	...	...	...	...	...	...	...	...
45 - 49	157	...	...	...	...	...	...	...	...
50 +	3	...	...	...	...	...	...	...	...
Unknown - Inconnu	-	...	...	...	...	...	...	...	...
Iceland - Islande									
2011									
Total	969	415	249	186	83	29	5	2	-
0 - 14	2	2	-	-	-	-	-	-	-
15 - 19	174	155	16	3	-	-	-	-	-
20 - 24	289	182	84	21	2	-	-	-	-
25 - 29	187	46	73	52	10	6	-	-	-
30 - 34	169	25	40	56	36	11	1	-	-
35 - 39	109	5	29	45	20	9	1	-	-
40 - 44	35	-	7	8	12	3	3	2	-
45 - 49	4	-	-	1	3	-	-	-	-
50 +	-	-	-	-	-	-	-	-	-
Unknown - Inconnu	-	-	-	-	-	-	-	-	-
Italy - Italie									
2009[10]									
Total	114 793	45 152	26 909	29 348	8 647	1 918	494	192	2 133
0 - 14	236	222	1	-	-	-	-	-	13
15 - 19	9 603	8 227	753	108	7	2	-	-	506
20 - 24	20 950	13 921	4 461	1 589	242	46	14	6	671
25 - 29	23 302	10 106	6 503	4 865	1 113	206	37	21	451
30 - 34	25 699	6 750	6 895	8 555	2 543	523	109	41	283
35 - 39	22 916	4 038	5 541	9 189	2 994	716	205	74	159
40 - 44	10 228	1 390	2 341	4 405	1 530	369	108	42	43
45 - 49	955	131	192	409	155	40	17	8	3
50 +	25	8	1	13	1	2	-	-	-
Unknown - Inconnu	879	359	221	215	62	14	4	-	4
2012[11]									
Total	103 191	...	...	...	...	...	...	...	...
0 - 14	262	...	...	...	...	...	...	...	...
15 - 19	8 355	...	...	...	...	...	...	...	...
20 - 24	19 065	...	...	...	...	...	...	...	...
25 - 29	20 955	...	...	...	...	...	...	...	...

14. Legally induced abortions by age and number of previous live births of women: latest available year, 2007 - 2016
Avortments provoqués légalement selon l'âge de la femme et selon le nombre des naissances vivantes précédentes : dernière année disponible, 2007 - 2016 (continued - suite)

Continent, country or area, year and age / Continent, pays ou zone, année et âge	Total	Number of previous live births / Nombre des naissances vivantes précédentes							Unknown - Inconnu
		0	1	2	3	4	5	6+	

EUROPE

Italy - Italie
2012[11]

30 - 34	22 214	...	...	...	...	...	...	...	...
35 - 39	21 530	...	...	...	...	...	...	...	...
40 - 44	9 808	...	...	...	...	...	...	...	...
45 - 49	889	...	...	...	...	...	...	...	...
50 +	42	...	...	...	...	...	...	...	...
Unknown - Inconnu	71	...	...	...	...	...	...	...	...

Latvia - Lettonie
2014

Total	5 318	...	...	...	...	...	...	...	...
0 - 14	3	...	...	...	...	...	...	...	...
15 - 19	291	...	...	...	...	...	...	...	...
20 - 24	1 096	...	...	...	...	...	...	...	...
25 - 29	1 262	...	...	...	...	...	...	...	...
30 - 34	1 197	...	...	...	...	...	...	...	...
35 - 39	929	...	...	...	...	...	...	...	...
40 - 44	494	...	...	...	...	...	...	...	...
45 - 49	46	...	...	...	...	...	...	...	...
50 +	-	...	...	...	...	...	...	...	...
Unknown - Inconnu	-	...	...	...	...	...	...	...	...

Lithuania - Lituanie
2015

Total	4 735	...	...	...	...	...	...	...	...
0 - 14	5	...	...	...	...	...	...	...	...
15 - 19	314	...	...	...	...	...	...	...	...
20 - 24	844	...	...	...	...	...	...	...	...
25 - 29	1 023	...	...	...	...	...	...	...	...
30 - 34	1 017	...	...	...	...	...	...	...	...
35 - 39	1 000	...	...	...	...	...	...	...	...
40 - 44	469	...	...	...	...	...	...	...	...
45 - 49	63	...	...	...	...	...	...	...	...
Unknown - Inconnu	-	...	...	...	...	...	...	...	...

Poland - Pologne[12]
2015

Total	1 040	...	...	...	...	...	...	...	...
0 - 19	56	...	...	...	...	...	...	...	...
20 - 24	137	...	...	...	...	...	...	...	...
25 - 29	276	...	...	...	...	...	...	...	...
30 - 34	311	...	...	...	...	...	...	...	...
35 +	260	...	...	...	...	...	...	...	...

Portugal
2015

Total	16 454	6 973	4 799	3 498	885	222	55	22	...
0 - 14	68	64	1	2	1	-	-	-	...
15 - 19	1 708	1 608	95	5	-	-	-	-	...
20 - 24	3 757	2 559	953	210	31	3	-	1	...
25 - 29	3 434	1 410	1 241	624	134	19	4	2	...
30 - 34	3 188	768	1 140	934	251	68	19	8	...
35 - 39	2 875	406	956	1 112	293	82	19	7	...
40 - 44	1 279	128	386	545	158	48	10	4	...
45 - 49	106	8	23	56	14	2	3	-	...
50 +	-	-	-	-	-	-	-	-	...
Unknown - Inconnu	39	22	4	10	3	-	-	-	...

Republic of Moldova - République de Moldova
2012

Total	14 838	...	...	...	...	...	...	...	...
0 - 14	9	...	...	...	...	...	...	...	...
15 - 19	1 383	...	...	...	...	...	...	...	...
Unknown - Inconnu	13 446	...	...	...	...	...	...	...	...

Romania - Roumanie
2015

Total	70 885	...	...	...	...	...	...	...	...
0 - 14	422	...	...	...	...	...	...	...	...
15 - 19	6 431	...	...	...	...	...	...	...	...
20 - 24	13 216	...	...	...	...	...	...	...	...
25 - 29	18 153	...	...	...	...	...	...	...	...
30 - 34	14 808	...	...	...	...	...	...	...	...

14. Legally induced abortions by age and number of previous live births of women: latest available year, 2007 - 2016
Avortments provoqués légalement selon l'âge de la femme et selon le nombre des naissances vivantes précédentes : dernière année disponible, 2007 - 2016 (continued - suite)

Continent, country or area, year and age / Continent, pays ou zone, année et âge	Number of previous live births / Nombre des naissances vivantes précédentes								
	Total	0	1	2	3	4	5	6+	Unknown - Inconnu
EUROPE									
Romania - Roumanie									
2015									
35 - 39	12 417	...	...	...	...	...	...	...	...
40 - 44	4 948	...	...	...	...	...	...	...	...
45 - 49	474	...	...	...	...	...	...	...	...
50 +	16	...	...	...	...	...	...	...	...
Russian Federation - Fédération de Russie									
2013									
Total	1 012 399	...	...	...	...	...	...	...	...
0 - 14	474	...	...	...	...	...	...	...	...
15 - 19	47 732	...	...	...	...	...	...	...	...
20 - 24	203 802	...	...	...	...	...	...	...	...
25 - 29	285 859	...	...	...	...	...	...	...	...
30 - 34	242 437	...	...	...	...	...	...	...	...
35 - 39	165 856	...	...	...	...	...	...	...	...
40 - 44	61 059	...	...	...	...	...	...	...	...
45 - 49	5 029	...	...	...	...	...	...	...	...
50 +	151	...	...	...	...	...	...	...	...
Serbia - Serbie[13]									
2008									
Total	22 867	6 601	4 346	8 509	2 437	663	198	113	-
0 - 14	9	6	1	2	-	-	-	-	-
15 - 19	975	808	124	35	7	1	-	-	-
20 - 24	3 427	1 823	848	570	122	52	9	3	-
25 - 29	5 117	1 510	1 173	1 757	479	141	47	10	-
30 - 34	5 953	1 240	1 114	2 569	719	212	62	37	-
35 - 39	4 929	806	768	2 354	730	170	59	42	-
40 - 44	2 174	363	279	1 072	347	76	17	20	-
45 - 49	266	40	34	146	31	10	4	1	-
50 +	16	5	4	4	2	1	-	-	-
Unknown - Inconnu	1	-	1	-	-	-	-	-	-
Slovakia - Slovaquie									
2015									
Total	10 058	3 140	2 840	2 670	875	289	119	125	...
0 - 14	16	16	-	-	-	-	-	-	...
15 - 19	681	526	131	20	4	-	-	-	...
20 - 24	1 603	879	428	211	53	25	7	-	...
25 - 29	2 180	815	665	446	160	47	31	16	...
30 - 34	2 429	561	814	687	203	82	40	42	...
35 - 39	2 138	280	584	875	268	80	27	24	...
40 - 44	947	61	208	397	171	53	14	43	...
45 - 49	63	2	10	33	16	2	-	-	...
50 +	1	-	-	1	-	-	-	-	...
Slovenia - Slovénie									
2015									
Total	3 682	1 217	855	1 206	299	69	29	7	...
0 - 14	-	-	-	-	-	-	-	-	...
15 - 19	208	190	15	2	1	-	-	-	...
20 - 24	546	415	85	38	5	2	1	-	...
25 - 29	740	302	227	173	27	9	1	1	...
30 - 34	934	191	254	396	69	16	6	2	...
35 - 39	834	90	189	399	115	22	16	3	...
40 - 44	389	28	80	182	73	20	5	1	...
45 - 49	30	1	5	15	9	-	-	-	...
50 +	1	-	-	1	-	-	-	-	...
Spain - Espagne									
2015									
Total	94 188	42 187	25 051	19 197	5 574	^1 525	...	...	654
0 - 14	371	366	5	-	-	^-	...	...	-
15 - 19	9 641	8 652	874	95	16	^4	...	...	-
20 - 24	19 063	12 979	4 460	1 322	249	^41	...	...	12
25 - 29	20 156	9 233	6 073	3 588	970	^212	...	...	80
30 - 34	20 473	6 433	6 318	5 506	1 623	^433	...	...	160
35 - 39	17 117	3 425	5 213	5 887	1 808	^537	...	...	247
40 +	6 745	1 011	1 970	2 544	813	^270	...	...	137
Unknown - Inconnu	622	88	138	255	95	^28	...	...	18

14. Legally induced abortions by age and number of previous live births of women: latest available year, 2007 - 2016
Avortments provoqués légalement selon l'âge de la femme et selon le nombre des naissances vivantes précédentes : dernière année disponible, 2007 - 2016 (continued - suite)

Continent, country or area, year and age / Continent, pays ou zone, année et âge	Total	Number of previous live births / Nombre des naissances vivantes précédentes							Unknown - Inconnu
		0	1	2	3	4	5	6+	

EUROPE

Sweden - Suède[14]
2010

Total	37 693	19 435	6 240	7 203	2 993	814	264	137	607
0 - 14	191	178	4	1	-	-	-	-	8
15 - 19	6 199	5 826	214	14	2	-	-	-	143
20 - 24	10 068	7 708	1 587	480	76	5	2	2	208
25 - 29	7 495	3 558	1 838	1 476	385	79	28	10	121
30 - 34	6 124	1 424	1 336	2 113	884	208	77	18	64
35 - 39	5 073	572	862	2 073	1 053	318	88	62	45
40 - 44	2 248	137	353	948	524	174	58	39	15
45 - 49	238	11	33	85	66	27	10	4	2
50 +	56	20	13	13	3	3	1	2	1
Unknown - Inconnu	1	1	-	-	-	-	-	-	-

Switzerland - Suisse[15]
2015

Total	10 054	1 960	832	815	270	82	...	...	6 095
0 - 14	9	3	-	-	-	-	...	...	6
15 - 19	716	292	7	2	-	-	...	...	415
20 - 24	2 089	674	127	35	4	-	...	...	1 249
25 - 29	2 399	495	229	158	41	6	...	...	1 470
30 - 34	2 144	299	234	224	72	13	...	...	1 302
35 - 39	1 789	144	148	257	98	38	...	...	1 104
40 - 44	814	46	77	122	48	22	...	...	499
45 - 49	88	5	8	17	7	3	...	...	48
50 +	3	1	1	-	-	-	...	...	1
Unknown - Inconnu	3	1	1	-	-	-	...	...	1

Ukraine[16]
2014

Total	116 104	...	...	...	...	...	...	...	...
0 - 14	51	...	...	...	...	...	...	...	...
15 - 19	6 229	...	...	...	...	...	...	...	...
20 - 34	85 575	...	...	...	...	...	...	...	...
35 +	24 249	...	...	...	...	...	...	...	...

United Kingdom of Great Britain and Northern Ireland - Royaume-Uni de Grande-Bretagne et d'Irlande du Nord[17]
2012

Total	197 569	...	...	...	...	...	...	...	...
0 - 14	910	...	...	...	...	...	...	...	...
15 - 19	32 967	...	...	...	...	...	...	...	...
20 - 24	58 367	...	...	...	...	...	...	...	...
25 - 29	44 612	...	...	...	...	...	...	...	...
30 - 34	32 139	...	...	...	...	...	...	...	...
35 - 39	19 651	...	...	...	...	...	...	...	...
40 - 44	8 199	...	...	...	...	...	...	...	...
45 - 49	697	...	...	...	...	...	...	...	...
50 +	27	...	...	...	...	...	...	...	...
Unknown - Inconnu	-	...	...	...	...	...	...	...	...

OCEANIA - OCÉANIE

Guam
2015

Total	263	...	...	...	...	...	...	...	...
0 - 14	-	...	...	...	...	...	...	...	...
15 - 19	20	...	...	...	...	...	...	...	...
20 - 24	89	...	...	...	...	...	...	...	...
25 - 29	60	...	...	...	...	...	...	...	...
30 - 34	52	...	...	...	...	...	...	...	...
35 - 39	27	...	...	...	...	...	...	...	...
40 - 44	12	...	...	...	...	...	...	...	...
45 - 49	2	...	...	...	...	...	...	...	...
50 +	-	...	...	...	...	...	...	...	...
Unknown - Inconnu	1	...	...	...	...	...	...	...	...

14. Legally induced abortions by age and number of previous live births of women: latest available year, 2007 - 2016
Avortments provoqués légalement selon l'âge de la femme et selon le nombre des naissances vivantes précédentes : dernière année disponible, 2007 - 2016 (continued - suite)

Continent, country or area, year and age / Continent, pays ou zone, année et âge	Number of previous live births / Nombre des naissances vivantes précédentes								
	Total	0	1	2	3	4	5	6+	Unknown - Inconnu
OCEANIA - OCÉANIE									
New Zealand - Nouvelle-Zélande[18]									
2015									
Total	13 155	5 665	2 715	2 728	1 264	473	193	117	...
0 - 14	32	32	-	-	-	-	-	-	...
15 - 19	1 635	1 393	208	31	3	-	-	-	...
20 - 24	3 777	2 257	891	470	129	27	3	-	...
25 - 29	3 256	1 183	764	744	376	129	44	16	...
30 - 34	2 309	521	483	712	344	149	63	37	...
35 - 39	1 483	210	261	510	280	117	60	45	...
40 - 44	598	59	94	238	121	48	21	17	...
45 +	65	10	14	23	11	3	2	2	...

FOOTNOTES - NOTES

Italics: estimates which are less reliable. - Italiques : estimations moins sûres.

* Provisional. - Données provisoires.

^ Indicates an open-ended group, for example 4+. - indique un groupe d'âge ouvert, par exemple 4 ou plus.

[1] Excluding abortions performed in private hospitals. - Non comprises les interruptions volontaires de grossesse effectuées dans des hôpitaux privés.

[2] Data refer to 'Therapeutic Abortions'. According to Mexican law, only induced abortions, prescribed by medical reasons or induced because of pregnancy coming from sexual aggression, are considered as legal; data refer only to the former. Refers to residence of the mother. To calculate the total number of abortions, only foetal deaths of less than 20 weeks of gestation were considered. Excluding abortions in the country by women with usual residence outside of the country. - Les données se rapportent aux « interruptions volontaires de grossesse pour des motifs thérapeutiques ». D'après la loi mexicaine, seuls sont considérés légaux les avortements déclenchés pour des raisons médicales ou parce que la grossesse est le résultat d'une agression sexuelle; les données se réfèrent seulement à la première. Correspond à la résidence de la mère. Seuls les morts fœtales survenues à moins de 20 semaines de gestation ont été prises en compte aux fins du calcul du nombre total d'avortements. Hors avortements dans le pays par des femmes avec résidence habituelle en dehors du pays.

[3] Data refer to abortions registered in hospitals due to pregnancy complications. - Les données renvoient aux avortements enregistrés dans les hôpitaux du fait des complications de la grossesse.

[4] Includes data for East Jerusalem and Israeli residents in certain other territories under occupation by Israeli military forces since June 1967. Data refer to applications to commissions for termination of pregnancy and not to authorizations. - Y compris les données pour Jérusalem-Est et les résidents israéliens dans certains autres territoires occupés depuis 1967 par les forces armées israéliennes. Les données relatives aux avortements provoqués légalement se rapportent aux demandes d'autorisation et non aux autorisations elles-mêmes.

[5] Based on administrative reporting of the Ministry of Health. - Les données reposent sur les rapports administratifs du Ministère de la santé.

[6] Excluding Faeroe Islands and Greenland shown separately, if available. - Non compris les Iles Féroé et le Groenland, qui font l'objet de rubriques distinctes, si disponible.

[7] Data refer to resident population only. - Pour la population résidante seulement.

[8] Unrevised data. - Les données n'ont pas été révisées.

[9] Data refer to women between 15 and 49 years of age. - Le total se rapporte uniquement aux femmes dont l'âge est compris entre 15 et 49 ans.

[10] Data are incomplete for Abruzzo, Campania, Basilicata, Sicilia and Sardegna regions. - Données incomplètes pour les régions des Abruzzes, de Campanie, de Basilicate, de Sicile et de Sardaigne.

[11] Data are incomplete for Umbria, Abruzzo, Campania, Puglia and Sicilia regions. - Les données sont incomplètes pour les régions d'Ombrie, des Abruzzes, de Campanie, des Pouilles et de Sicile.

[12] Based on hospital and polyclinic records. - D'après les registres des hôpitaux et des polycliniques.

[13] Excludes data for Kosovo and Metohia. Data refer to institutions included in the Health Institutions Network Plan in the Republic of Serbia. - Sans les données pour le Kosovo et Metohie. Les données se rapportent aux institutions membres du "Health Institutions Network Plan" de la République de Serbie.

[14] Data refer to abortions by previous deliveries of mother rather than previous live births of mother. - Avortements selon les accouchements précédents de la mère plutôt que selon les naissances vivantes de la mère.

[15] Data refer to termination of pregnancy for women who are Switzerland residents. - Les données portent sur les interruptions de grossesse pratiquées sur des femmes qui résident en Suisse.

[16] The Government of Ukraine has informed the United Nations that it is not in a position to provide statistical data concerning the Autonomous Republic of Crimea and the city of Sevastopol. - Le gouvernement Ukrainien a informé l'ONU qu'il n'est pas en mesure de fournir des données statistiques concernant la République autonome de Crimée et la ville de Sébastopol.

[17] Excluding Northern Ireland. Excluding Channel Islands (Guernsey and Jersey) and Isle of Man, shown separately, if available. - Non compris l'Irlande du Nord. Non compris les îles Anglo-Normandes (Guernesey et Jersey) et l'île de Man, qui font l'objet de rubriques distinctes, si disponible.

[18] Random rounding to base 3 is applied in this table as a confidentiality measure. - Les chiffres sont arrondis à la base 3 de manière aléatoire, pour des raisons de confidentialité.

Table 15 - *Demographic Yearbook 2016*

Table 15 presents infant deaths and infant mortality rates by urban/rural residence for as many years as possible between 2012 and 2016.

Description of variables: Infant deaths are deaths of live-born infants under one year of age.

Statistics on the number of infant deaths are obtained from civil registers unless otherwise noted. Infant mortality rates are, in most instances, calculated from data on registered infant deaths and registered live births for a country or area where civil registration is considered reliable (that is, with an estimated completeness of 90 per cent or more).

The urban/rural classification of infant deaths is that provided by each reporting country or area; it is presumed to be based on the national census definitions of urban population that have been set forth at the end of the technical notes of table 6.

Rate computation: Infant mortality rates are the annual number of deaths of infants under one year of age per 1 000 live births (as shown in table 9) in the same year.

Rates by urban/rural residence are the annual number of infant deaths, in the appropriate urban or rural category, per 1 000 corresponding live births (as shown in table 9). These rates have been calculated by the United Nations Statistics Division.

Rates presented in this table have been limited to those countries or areas having at least a total of 30 infant deaths in a given year and for which the quality code is represented by a "C" or a symbol "|".

Reliability of data: Each country or area has been asked to indicate the estimated completeness of the infant deaths recorded in its civil register. These national assessments are indicated by the quality codes "C", "U" and "|" that appear in the first column of this table.

"C" indicates that the data are estimated to be virtually complete, that is, representing at least 90 per cent of the infant deaths occurring each year, while "U" indicates that data are estimated to be incomplete that is, representing less than 90 per cent of the infant deaths occurring each year. The code "|" indicates that the source of data is not civil registration, but is still considered reliable. The code "..." indicates that no information was provided regarding completeness.

Data from civil registers that are reported as incomplete or of unknown completeness (coded "U" or "...") are considered unreliable. They appear in italics in this table; rates are not computed for data so coded.

Limitations: Statistics on infant deaths are subject to the same qualifications as have been set forth for vital statistics in general and death statistics in particular as discussed in section 4 of the Technical Notes.

The reliability of the data, an indication of which is described above, is an important factor in considering the limitations. In addition, some infant deaths are tabulated by date of registration and not by date of occurrence; these have been indicated by a plus sign "+". Whenever the lag between the date of occurrence and date of registration is prolonged and, therefore, a large proportion of the infant-death registrations are delayed, infant-death statistics for any given year may be seriously affected.

Another factor that limits international comparability is the practice of some countries or areas not to include in infant-death statistics infants who were born alive but died before the registration of the birth or within the first 24 hours of life, thus underestimating the total number of infant deaths. Statistics of this type are footnoted.

The method of reckoning age at death for infants may also introduce non-comparability. If year alone, rather than completed minutes, hours, days and months elapsed since birth, is used to calculate age at time of death, many of the infants who died during the eleventh month of life and some of those who died at younger ages will be classified as having completed one year of age and thus be excluded. The effect would be to underestimate the number of infant deaths. Information on this factor is given in footnotes when known. Reckoning of infant age is further discussed in the technical notes for table 16.

In addition, infant mortality rates are subject to the limitations of the data on live births that have been used as denominators for these rates. These have been set forth in the technical notes for table 9.

Because the two components of the infant mortality rate, infant deaths in the numerator and live births in the denominator, are both obtained from systems of civil registration, the limitations which affect live birth statistics are very similar to those which have been mentioned above in connection with the infant death statistics. It is important to consider the reliability of the data (the completeness of registration) and the method of tabulation (by date of occurrence or by date of registration) of live birth statistics as well as infant death statistics, both of which are used to calculate infant mortality rates. The quality code and use of italics to indicate unreliable data presented in this table refer only to infant deaths. Similarly, the indication of the basis of tabulation (the use of the symbol "+" to indicate data tabulated by date of registration) presented in this table also refers only to infant deaths. Table 9 provides the corresponding information for live births.

If the registration of infant deaths is more complete than the registration of live births, then infant mortality rates would be biased upwards. If, however, the registration of live births is more complete than registration of infant deaths, infant mortality rates would be biased downwards. If both infant deaths and live births are tabulated by registration, it should be noted that deaths tend to be more promptly reported than births.

Infant mortality rates may be seriously affected by the practice of some countries or areas of not considering infants that were born alive but died before the registration of the birth or within the first 24 hours of life as live birth and subsequently infant death. Although this practice results in both the number of infant deaths in the numerator and the number of live births in the denominator being underestimated, its impact is greater on the numerator of the infant mortality rate. As a result, this practice causes infant mortality rates to be biased downwards.

Infant mortality rates will also be underestimated if the method of reckoning age at death results in an underestimation of the number of infant deaths. This point has been discussed above.

Because of all these factors care should be taken in comparing infant mortality rates.

With respect to the method of calculating infant mortality rates used in this table, it should be noted that no adjustment was made to take account of the fact that a proportion of the infant deaths that occur during a given year are deaths of infants that were born during the preceding year and hence are not taken from the universe of births used to compute the rates. However, unless the number of live births or infant deaths is changing rapidly, the error involved is insignificant.

The comparability of data by urban/rural residence is affected by the national definitions of urban and rural used in tabulating these data. It is assumed, in the absence of specific information to the contrary, that the definitions of urban and rural used in connection with the national population census were also used in the compilation of the vital statistics for each country or area. However, it cannot be denied that, for some countries or areas, different definitions of urban and rural may be used for the vital statistics data and the population census data respectively. When known, the definitions of urban used in national population censuses are presented at the end of the technical notes for table 6. As discussed in detail in the technical notes for table 6, these definitions vary considerably from one country or area to another.

Urban/rural differentials in infant mortality rates may also be affected by whether the infant deaths and live births have been tabulated in terms of place of occurrence or place of usual residence. This problem is discussed in more detail in section 4.1.4.1 of the Technical Notes.

Earlier data: Infant deaths and infant mortality rates have been shown in previous issues of the *Demographic Yearbook*. For more information on specific topics and years for which data are reported, readers should consult the Historical Index.

Tableau 15 – *Annuaire démographique 2016*

Le tableau 15 présente des données sur les décès d'enfants de moins d'un an et les taux de mortalité infantile selon le lieu de résidence (zone urbaine ou rurale) pour le plus grand nombre d'années possible entre 2012 et 2016.

Description des variables : les chiffres se rapportent aux décès d'enfants de moins d'un an.

Sauf indication contraire, les statistiques concernant le nombre de décès d'enfants de moins d'un an sont établies à partir des registres de l'état civil. Dans la plupart des cas, les taux de mortalité infantile sont calculés à partir des données relatives aux décès enregistrés d'enfants de moins d'un an et aux naissances vivantes enregistrées dans un pays ou une zone lorsque les registres de l'état civil sont jugés fiables (exhaustivité estimée à 90 p. 100 ou plus).

La classification des décès d'enfants de moins d'un an selon le lieu de résidence (zone urbaine ou rurale) est celle qui a été communiquée par chaque pays ou zone ; on part du principe qu'elle repose sur les définitions de la population urbaine utilisées pour les recensements nationaux, telles qu'elles sont reproduites à la fin des notes techniques du tableau 6.

Calcul des taux : Les taux de mortalité infantile représentent le nombre annuel de décès d'enfants de moins d'un an pour 1 000 naissances vivantes (présentées dans le tableau 9) survenues pendant la même année.

Les taux selon le lieu de résidence (zone urbaine ou rurale) représentent le nombre annuel de décès d'enfants de moins d'un an, classés selon la catégorie urbaine ou rurale appropriée pour 1 000 naissances vivantes survenues parmi la population correspondante (présentées dans le tableau 9). Ces taux ont été calculés par la Division des statistiques de l'Organisation des Nations Unies.

Les taux présentés dans ce tableau se rapportent seulement aux pays ou zones où l'on a enregistré au moins un total de 30 décès d'enfants de moins d'un an au cours d'une année donnée et pour lesquels le code de qualité est soit "C" ou "|".

Fiabilité des données : il a été demandé à chaque pays ou zone d'indiquer le degré estimatif de complétude des données sur les décès d'enfants de moins d'un an figurant dans ses registres d'état civil. Ces évaluations nationales sont signalées par les codes de qualité "C", "U" et "|" qui apparaissent dans la deuxième colonne du tableau.

La lettre "C" indique que les données sont jugées à peu près complètes, c'est-à-dire qu'elles représentent au moins 90 p. 100 des décès d'enfants de moins d'un an survenus chaque année ; la lettre "U" signifie que les données sont jugées incomplètes, c'est-à-dire qu'elles représentent moins de 90 p.100 des décès d'enfants de moins d'un an survenus chaque année. Le symbole '|' indique que la source des données n'est pas un registre de l'état civil, mais est quand même considérée fiable. Le code "..." dénote qu'aucun renseignement n'a été communiqué quant à la complétude des données.

Les données provenant des registres de l'état civil qui sont déclarées incomplètes ou dont le degré de complétude n'est pas connu (code "U" ou "...") sont jugées douteuses. Elles apparaissent en italique dans le tableau ; les taux, dans ces cas là, n'ont pas été calculés.

Insuffisance des données : les statistiques des décès d'enfants de moins d'un an appellent toutes les réserves qui ont été formulées à propos des statistiques de l'état civil en général et des statistiques concernant les décès en particulier (voir la section 4 des notes techniques).

La fiabilité des données, au sujet de laquelle des indications ont été fournies plus haut, est un facteur important. Il faut également tenir compte du fait que, dans certains cas, les données relatives aux décès d'enfants de moins d'un an sont exploitées selon la date de l'enregistrement et non la date de l'événement ; ces cas ont été signalés par le signe "+". Chaque fois que le décalage entre l'événement et son enregistrement est grand et qu'une forte proportion des décès d'enfants de moins d'un an fait l'objet d'un enregistrement tardif, les statistiques des décès d'enfants de moins d'un an pour une année donnée peuvent être considérablement faussées.

Un autre facteur qui nuit à la comparabilité internationale est la pratique de certains pays ou zones qui consiste à ne pas inclure dans les statistiques des décès d'enfants de moins d'un an les enfants nés vivants

433

mais décédés avant l'enregistrement de leur naissance ou dans les 24 heures qui ont suivi la naissance, pratique qui conduit à sous-estimer le nombre total de décès d'enfants de moins d'un an. Quand pareil facteur a joué, cela a été signalé en note.

Les méthodes appliquées pour calculer l'âge au moment du décès peuvent également nuire à la comparabilité des données. Si l'on utilise à cet effet l'année seulement, et non pas les minutes, heures, jours et mois qui se sont écoulés depuis la naissance, de nombreux enfants décédés au cours du onzième mois qui a suivi leur naissance et certains enfants décédés encore plus jeunes seront classés comme décédés à un an révolu et donc exclus des données. Cette pratique conduit à sous-estimer le nombre de décès d'enfants de moins d'un an. Les renseignements dont on dispose sur ce facteur apparaissent en note à la fin du tableau. La question du calcul de l'âge au moment du décès est examinée plus en détail dans les notes techniques se rapportant au tableau 16.

Les taux de mortalité infantile appellent en outre toutes les réserves qui ont été formulées à propos des statistiques des naissances vivantes qui ont servi à leur calcul (voir à ce sujet les notes techniques relatives au tableau 9).

Les deux composantes du taux de mortalité infantile - décès d'enfants de moins d'un an au numérateur et naissances vivantes au dénominateur - étant obtenues à partir des registres de l'état civil, les statistiques des naissances vivantes appellent des réserves presque identiques à celles qui ont été formulées plus haut à propos des statistiques des décès d'enfants de moins d'un an. Il importe de prendre en considération la fiabilité des données (complétude de l'enregistrement) et le mode d'exploitation (selon la date de l'événement ou selon la date de l'enregistrement) dans le cas des statistiques des naissances vivantes tout comme dans le cas de celles des décès d'enfants de moins d'un an, puisque les unes et les autres servent au calcul des taux de mortalité infantile. Dans le tableau 15, le code de qualité et l'emploi de caractères italiques pour signaler les données moins sûres ne concernent que les décès d'enfants de moins d'un an. L'indication du mode d'exploitation des données (emploi du signe "+" pour signaler les données exploitées selon la date de l'enregistrement) ne porte là aussi que sur les décès d'enfants de moins d'un an. Le tableau 9 contient les renseignements correspondants pour les naissances vivantes.

Si l'enregistrement des décès d'enfants de moins d'un an est plus complet que l'enregistrement des naissances vivantes, les taux de mortalité infantile seront entachés d'une erreur par excès. En revanche, si l'enregistrement des naissances vivantes est plus complet que l'enregistrement des décès d'enfants de moins d'un an, les taux de mortalité infantile seront entachés d'une erreur par défaut. Si les décès d'enfants de moins d'un an et les naissances vivantes sont exploitées selon la date de l'enregistrement, il convient de ne pas perdre de vue que les décès sont, en règle générale, déclarés plus rapidement que les naissances.

Les taux de mortalité infantile peuvent être gravement faussés par la pratique de certains pays ou zones qui consiste à ne pas classer dans les naissances vivantes et ensuite dans les décès d'enfants de moins d'un an les enfants nés vivants mais décédés soit avant l'enregistrement de leur naissance, soit dans les 24 heures qui ont suivi la naissance. Cette pratique conduit à sous-estimer aussi bien le nombre des décès d'enfants de moins d'un an, qui constitue le numérateur, que le nombre des naissances vivantes, qui constitue le dénominateur, mais c'est pour le numérateur du taux de mortalité infantile que la distorsion est la plus marquée. Ce système a pour effet d'introduire une erreur par défaut dans les taux de mortalité infantile.

Les taux de mortalité infantile seront également sous-estimés si la méthode utilisée pour calculer l'âge au moment du décès conduit à sous-estimer le nombre de décès d'enfants de moins d'un an. Cette question a été examinée plus haut.

Tous ces facteurs sont importants et il faut donc en tenir compte lorsque l'on compare les taux de mortalité infantile.

En ce qui concerne la méthode de calcul des taux de mortalité infantile utilisée dans le tableau, il convient de noter qu'il n'a pas été tenu compte du fait qu'une partie des décès survenus pendant une année donnée sont des décès d'enfants nés l'année précédente et ne correspondent donc pas à l'ensemble des naissances utilisé pour le calcul des taux. Toutefois, l'erreur n'est pas grave, à moins que le nombre des naissances vivantes ou des décès d'enfants de moins d'un an ne varie rapidement.

La comparabilité des données selon le lieu de résidence (zone urbaine ou rurale) peut être limitée par les définitions nationales des termes « urbain » et « rural » utilisées pour la mise en tableaux de ces données. En l'absence d'indications contraires, on a supposé que les mêmes définitions avaient servi pour le recensement national de la population et pour l'établissement des statistiques de l'état civil pour chaque pays ou zone. Toutefois, il n'est pas exclu que, pour une zone ou un pays donné, des définitions différentes aient été retenues. Les définitions du terme « urbain » utilisées pour les recensements nationaux de population ont été présentées à la fin des notes techniques du tableau 6 lorsqu'elles étaient connues. Comme on l'a précisé dans les notes techniques relatives au tableau 6, ces définitions varient considérablement d'un pays ou d'une zone à l'autre.

La différence entre les taux de mortalité infantile pour les zones urbaines et rurales pourra aussi être faussée selon que les décès d'enfants de moins d'un an et les naissances vivantes auront été classés d'après le lieu de l'événement ou le lieu de résidence habituel. Ce problème est examiné plus en détail à la section 4.1.4.1 des Notes techniques.

Données publiées antérieurement : des statistiques concernant les décès d'enfants de moins d'un an et les taux de mortalité infantile ont déjà été présentées dans des éditions antérieures de l'*Annuaire démographique*. Pour plus de précisions concernant les années et les sujets pour lesquels des données ont été publiées, se reporter à l'index historique.

15. Infant deaths and infant mortality rates, by urban/rural residence: 2012 - 2016
Décès d'enfants de moins d'un an et taux de mortalité infantile, selon la résidence, urbaine/rurale : 2012 - 2016

Continent, country or area, and urban/rural residence / Continent, pays ou zone et résidence, urbaine/rurale	Code[a]	Number - Nombre					Rate - Taux				
		2012	2013	2014	2015	2016	2012	2013	2014	2015	2016
AFRICA - AFRIQUE											
Algeria - Algérie[1]											
Total	U	22 088	21 586	22 282	23 150	22 271	...	...	...	...	...
Botswana[2]											
Total	U	...	960	1 045	...	...	...	...	...	...	...
Côte d'Ivoire[3]											
Total	I	...	...	44 530	...	...	...	...	52.9	...	...
Egypt - Égypte											
Total	C	39 942	38 753	39 679	...	...	15.2	14.8	14.6	...	...
Urban - Urbaine	C	19 830	22 605	23 952	...	...	19.6	19.0	19.5	...	...
Rural - Rurale	C	20 112	16 148	15 727	...	...	12.4	11.3	10.5	...	...
Guinea - Guinée[4]											
Total	I	...	...	29 798	...	...	...	...	66.5	...	...
Urban - Urbaine	I	...	...	7 259	...	...	...	...	54.3	...	...
Rural - Rurale	I	...	...	22 539	...	...	...	...	71.6	...	...
Kenya											
Total	U	21 209	20 888	18 672	15 861	13 839	...	...	...	...	...
Mauritius - Maurice[5]											
Total	+C	199	165	194	173	154	13.7	12.2	14.6	13.7	11.9
Urban - Urbaine	+C	65	67	72	81	57	12.0	13.2	14.0	15.7	10.8
Rural - Rurale	+C	134	98	122	92	97	14.8	11.6	15.0	12.3	12.7
Saint Helena ex. dep. - Sainte-Hélène sans dép.											
Total	C	1	-	1	...	...	...	...	...	...	...
Seychelles											
Total	+C	...	29	17	17	...	...	...	...	...	...
Sierra Leone[6]											
Total	+U	2 165	2 276	...	...	...	...	...	...	...	...
Urban - Urbaine[7]	+U	1 508	...	...	...	...	...	...	...	...	...
Rural - Rurale[7]	+U	627	...	...	...	...	...	...	...	...	...
South Africa - Afrique du Sud											
Total	U	27 104	26 630	25 643	...	...	...	...	...	...	...
AMERICA, NORTH - AMÉRIQUE DU NORD											
Anguilla											
Total	+C	-	3	...	...	...	...	...	...	...	...
Aruba											
Total	+C	3	5	5	6	5	...	...	...	...	...
Bahamas											
Total	+C	57	51	...	...	...	12.8	11.8	...	...	...
Belize											
Total	U	116	129	91	127	103	...	...	...	...	...
Urban - Urbaine	U	51	55	30	58	44	...	...	...	...	...
Rural - Rurale	U	65	74	61	69	59	...	...	...	...	...
Bermuda - Bermudes											
Total	C	1	1	2	2	...	...	...	...	...	...
Canada[8]											
Total	C	1 818	1 884	...	...	...	4.8	5.0	...	...	...
Costa Rica											
Total	C	624	612	575	557	*555	8.5	8.7	8.0	7.8	*7.9
Urban - Urbaine	C	272	291	362	404	*422	10.7	11.7	8.7	8.1	*8.7
Rural - Rurale	C	352	321	213	153	*133	7.4	7.0	7.1	6.9	*6.2
Cuba											
Total	C	581	525	514	535	497	4.6	4.2	4.2	4.3	4.3
Urban - Urbaine	C	462	440	413	429	...	4.7	4.4	4.3	4.3	...
Rural - Rurale	C	119	85	101	106	...	4.3	3.1	3.9	4.1	...
Curaçao											
Total	C	23	15	24	20	20	...	...	...	...	...
Dominican Republic - République dominicaine											
Total	U	473	659	842	903	791	...	...	...	...	...
El Salvador[9]											
Total	C	795	859	876	...	...	7.2	7.8	8.0	...	...
Urban - Urbaine	C	527	...	569	...	...	7.0	...	9.1	...	...
Rural - Rurale	C	268	...	307	...	...	7.6	...	6.6	...	...

Continent, country or area, and urban/rural residence / Continent, pays ou zone et résidence, urbaine/rurale	Co-de[a]	Number - Nombre					Rate - Taux				
		2012	2013	2014	2015	2016	2012	2013	2014	2015	2016
AMERICA, NORTH - AMÉRIQUE DU NORD											
Greenland - Groenland											
Total	C	7	7	6	9	6	...	...	...	...	...
Urban - Urbaine	C	4	7	5	9	6	...	...	...	...	...
Rural - Rurale	C	3	-	1	-	-	...	...	...	...	...
Guatemala											
Total	C	7 121	7 221	...		...	18.3	18.6	...	...	...
Mexico - Mexique[10]											
Total	+U	28 946	...	...	...	...	...	...	...	...	...
Urban - Urbaine[11]	+U	22 254	...	...	...	...	...	...	...	...	...
Rural - Rurale[11]	+U	6 132	...		...	...	...	...	...	...	...
Total	+C	...	27 802	26 385	26 045	...	...	12.8	12.4	11.1	...
Urban - Urbaine[11]	+C	...	21 079	19 987	19 753	...	...	13.8	12.8	...	...
Rural - Rurale[11]	+C	...	6 041	5 870	5 832	...	...	12.5	12.6	...	...
Montserrat											
Total	+C	-	-	-	3	-	...	...	...	...	...
Panama											
Total	U	1 083	1 106	1 036	*952		...	...	...	...	...
Urban - Urbaine	U	632	682	585	*555		...	...	...	...	...
Rural - Rurale	U	451	424	451	*397		...	...	...	...	...
Puerto Rico - Porto Rico											
Total	C	374	270	242	222	221	9.6	7.4	7.0	7.1	7.8
Urban - Urbaine	C	243	164	141	125	122	11.3	8.3	7.4	6.6	6.7
Rural - Rurale	C	131	106	101	98	99	7.5	6.3	6.5	8.0	9.8
Saint Vincent and the Grenadines - Saint-Vincent-et-les Grenadines											
Total	C	25	32	29	...	...	...	18.4	...	...	...
Trinidad and Tobago - Trinité-et-Tobago											
Total	C	*239	...	...	...	...	*12.8	...	...	...	...
Turks and Caicos Islands - Îles Turques et Caïques											
Total	C	15	12	2	...	...	...	...	...	...	...
United States of America - États-Unis d'Amérique											
Total	C	23 629	23 440	23 215	23 455	...	6.0	6.0	5.8	5.9	...
United States Virgin Islands - Îles Vierges américaines[12]											
Total	C	13	...	...	...	...	...	...	...	...	...
AMERICA, SOUTH - AMÉRIQUE DU SUD											
Argentina - Argentine											
Total	C	8 227	8 174	8 202	7 445	...	11.1	10.8	10.6	9.7	...
Brazil - Brésil[13]											
Total	U	31 596	31 944	31 679	...	...	...	...	...	...	...
Total	+C	...	...	...	31 238	...	...	...	...	10.6	...
Chile - Chili											
Total	C	1 812	1 692	1 825	...	...	7.4	7.0	7.3	...	...
Urban - Urbaine	C	1 644	1 540	1 604	...	...	7.5	7.0	7.0	...	...
Rural - Rurale	C	168	152	221	...	...	6.9	7.0	9.8	...	...
Colombia - Colombie											
Total	U	8 138	7 551	7 515	...	...	...	...	...	...	...
Urban - Urbaine	U	6 037	5 577	5 642	...	...	...	...	...	...	...
Rural - Rurale	U	2 101	1 974	1 873	...	...	...	...	...	...	...
Ecuador - Équateur[14]											
Total	U	3 002	2 928	2 821	2 979	...	...	...	...	...	...
Urban - Urbaine	U	2 499	2 455	2 308	2 483	...	...	...	...	...	...
Rural - Rurale	U	503	473	513	496	...	...	...	...	...	...
Paraguay											
Total	+U	465	...	...	...	...	...	...	...	...	...
Peru - Pérou[15]											
Total	+U	4 532	4 548	4 243	3 852	...	...	...	...	...	...

15. Infant deaths and infant mortality rates, by urban/rural residence: 2012 - 2016
Décès d'enfants de moins d'un an et taux de mortalité infantile, selon la résidence, urbaine/rurale : 2012 - 2016 (continued - suite)

Continent, country or area, and urban/rural residence / Continent, pays ou zone et résidence, urbaine/rurale	Code[a]	Number - Nombre					Rate - Taux				
		2012	2013	2014	2015	2016	2012	2013	2014	2015	2016
AMERICA, SOUTH - AMÉRIQUE DU SUD											
Suriname											
Total	C	162	168	163	149	...	15.9	16.8	15.7	14.7	...
Urban - Urbaine	C	110	118	117	101	...	16.1	17.4	17.0	...	...
Rural - Rurale	C	52	50	46	48	...	15.5	15.5	13.1	...	...
Uruguay											
Total	C	448	430	376	367	...	9.3	8.8	7.8	7.5	...
Venezuela (Bolivarian Republic of) - Venezuela (République bolivarienne du)											
Total	C	7 331	7 630	8 396	9 267	...	11.8	12.8	14.0	15.4	...
ASIA - ASIE											
Armenia - Arménie[16]											
Total	C	...	...	376	370	...	...	...	8.7	8.9	...
Urban - Urbaine	C	...	...	...	233	...	...	...	...	8.6	...
Rural - Rurale	C	...	...	...	137	...	...	...	...	9.4	...
Azerbaijan - Azerbaïdjan[16]											
Total	+C	1 884	1 862	1 655	2 033	...	10.8	10.8	9.7	12.2	...
Urban - Urbaine	+C	1 524	1 459	1 324	1 602	...	17.6	16.9	16.2	19.7	...
Rural - Rurale	+C	360	403	331	431	...	4.1	4.7	3.7	5.1	...
Bahrain - Bahreïn[17]											
Total	C	149	141	218	...	...	7.8	7.1	10.4	...	...
Bangladesh											
Total	U	96 254	...	...	...	...	...	...	...	...	...
Urban - Urbaine	U	19 906	...	...	...	...	...	...	...	...	...
Rural - Rurale	U	76 348	...	...	...	...	...	...	...	...	...
Brunei Darussalam - Brunéi Darussalam											
Total	+C	64	51	51	58	...	9.3	7.6	7.4	8.7	...
China, Hong Kong SAR - Chine, Hong Kong RAS											
Total	C	137	100	103	85	109	1.5	1.8	1.7	1.4	1.8
China, Macao SAR - Chine, Macao RAS											
Total	C	18	13	15	11	...	...	...	...	...	...
Cyprus - Chypre[18]											
Total	C	36	15	13	25	...	3.5	...	...	...	...
Georgia - Géorgie[16]											
Total	C	715	640	578	507	507	12.5	11.1	9.5	8.6	9.0
Urban - Urbaine	C	...	...	...	259	253	...	...	...	7.6	7.9
Rural - Rurale	C	...	...	...	248	254	...	...	...	9.8	10.4
India - Inde[19]											
Total	I	...	...	...	...	...	42.0	40.0	39.0	37.0	...
Urban - Urbaine	I	...	...	...	...	...	28.0	27.0	26.0	25.0	...
Rural - Rurale	I	...	...	...	...	...	46.0	44.0	43.0	41.0	...
Iran (Islamic Republic of) - Iran (République islamique d')[20]											
Total	+C	10 401	8 015	7 430	...	...	7.3	5.4	4.8	...	...
Urban - Urbaine	+C	8 173[11]	5 993	5 590	...	...	7.2	5.3	4.7	...	...
Rural - Rurale	+C	2 226[11]	2 022	1 840	...	...	7.6	5.9	5.2	...	...
Israel - Israël[21]											
Total	C	611	539	548	561	561	3.6	3.1	3.1	3.1	3.1
Urban - Urbaine[11]	C	545	469	494	495	484	3.5	3.0	3.1	3.1	...
Rural - Rurale[11]	C	65	69	53	63	77	4.1	4.2	3.3	3.8	...
Japan - Japon[22]											
Total	C	2 299	2 185	2 080	1 916	...	2.2	2.1	2.1	1.9	...
Urban - Urbaine	C	2 106	2 019	1 891	1 754	...	2.2	2.1	2.0	1.9	...
Rural - Rurale	C	192	163	187	161	...	2.3	2.0	2.4	2.1	...
Kazakhstan[16]											
Total	C	5 121	4 367	...	...	...	13.4	11.3	...	...	...
Urban - Urbaine	C	2 781	2 383	...	...	...	13.5	11.4	...	...	...
Rural - Rurale	C	2 340	1 984	...	...	...	13.4	11.1	...	...	...

15. Infant deaths and infant mortality rates, by urban/rural residence: 2012 - 2016
Décès d'enfants de moins d'un an et taux de mortalité infantile, selon la résidence, urbaine/rurale : 2012 - 2016 (continued - suite)

Continent, country or area, and urban/rural residence / Continent, pays ou zone et résidence, urbaine/rurale	Code[a]	Number - Nombre					Rate - Taux				
		2012	2013	2014	2015	2016	2012	2013	2014	2015	2016
ASIA - ASIE											
Kuwait - Koweït											
Total	C	459	453	456	456	...	7.7	7.6	7.4	7.7	...
Kyrgyzstan - Kirghizstan											
Total	C	3 091	3 093	3 268	2 945	*2 621	20.0	19.9	20.2	18.0	*16.6
Urban - Urbaine	C	1 807	1 886	2 099	1 853	*1 586	33.6	35.0	37.8	35.3	*30.7
Rural - Rurale	C	1 284	1 207	1 169	1 092	*1 035	12.7	11.9	11.0	9.8	*9.7
Malaysia - Malaisie											
Total	C	3 277	3 199	3 543	3 582	...	6.2	6.3	6.7	6.9	...
Urban - Urbaine	C	2 087	2 101	2 313	2 301	...	5.8	6.1	6.5	6.6	...
Rural - Rurale	C	1 190	1 098	1 230	1 281	...	7.1	6.9	7.2	7.5	...
Maldives											
Total	C	66	46	59	...	...	8.9	6.4	8.1	...	...
Urban - Urbaine	C	46[23]	24[23]	15[24]	...	...	10.3	...	...	...	...
Rural - Rurale	C	18[23]	19[23]	33[24]	...	...	...	...	13.9	...	...
Mongolia - Mongolie											
Total	+C	1 143	1 166	1 251	1 234	1 315	15.5	14.6	15.1	15.0	16.5
Myanmar											
Total	+U	*11 406[25]*	*11 516[25]*	*9 386[26]*	...	...	...	...	...	...	...
Urban - Urbaine[25]	+U	*6 170*	*6 840*	...	...	...	...	...	...	...	...
Rural - Rurale[25]	+U	*5 236*	*4 676*	...	...	...	...	...	...	...	...
Oman[27]											
Total	U	*676*	*772*	*645*	*818*	*816*	...	...	...	...	...
Philippines											
Total	C	22 254	21 992	21 108	20 750	...	12.4	12.5	12.1	11.9	...
Qatar											
Total	C	148	158	168	197	...	6.9	6.7	6.6	7.4	...
Urban - Urbaine	C	...	158	168	197	...	...	6.7	6.6	7.4	...
Republic of Korea - République de Corée[28]											
Total	C	1 405	1 305	1 305	1 190	...	2.9	3.0	3.0	2.7	...
Urban - Urbaine	C	1 135	1 098[11]	1 063[11]	1 010	...	2.8	3.0	2.9	2.8	...
Rural - Rurale	C	270	203[11]	242[11]	180	...	3.3	2.9	3.4	2.5	...
Saudi Arabia - Arabie saoudite[29]											
Total	...	*9 843*	...	...	...	...	...	...	...	...	...
Singapore - Singapour											
Total	+C	98	94	83	84	101	2.3	2.4	2.0	2.0	2.4
State of Palestine - État de Palestine[30]											
Total	U	*1 064*	*845*	*800*	*852*	...	...	...	...	...	...
Tajikistan - Tadjikistan[16]											
Total	U	*2 884*	*3 622*	*3 273*	...	...	...	...	...	...	...
Urban - Urbaine	U	*1 241*	*1 817*	*1 515*	...	...	...	...	...	...	...
Rural - Rurale	U	*1 643*	*1 805*	*1 758*	...	...	...	...	...	...	...
Turkey - Turquie											
Total	C	14 974	14 014	15 165	14 164	...	11.6	10.8	11.3	10.7	...
Uzbekistan - Ouzbékistan[16]											
Total	+C	6 390	6 569	7 688	8 320	...	10.2	9.7	10.7	11.3	...
Urban - Urbaine	+C	3 730	3 881	4 312	4 494	...	13.0	12.5	13.2	13.8	...
Rural - Rurale	+C	2 660	2 688	3 376	3 826	...	7.9	7.3	8.6	9.4	...
EUROPE											
Åland Islands - Îles d'Åland											
Total	C	-	-	-	-	...	...	...	...	...	...
Urban - Urbaine	C	-	-	-	-	...	...	...	...	...	...
Rural - Rurale	C	-	-	-	-	...	...	...	...	...	...
Albania - Albanie											
Total	C	312	282	...	...	...	8.8	7.9	...	...	...
Total	U	...	...	*281*	*233*	...	...	...	...	...	...
Andorra - Andorre											
Total	C	4	1	2	-	...	...	...	...	...	...
Austria - Autriche											
Total	C	252	245	249	259	...	3.2	3.1	3.0	3.1	...

15. Infant deaths and infant mortality rates, by urban/rural residence: 2012 - 2016
Décès d'enfants de moins d'un an et taux de mortalité infantile, selon la résidence, urbaine/rurale : 2012 - 2016 (continued - suite)

Continent, country or area, and urban/rural residence — Continent, pays ou zone et résidence, urbaine/rurale	Code[a]	Number - Nombre					Rate - Taux				
		2012	2013	2014	2015	2016	2012	2013	2014	2015	2016
EUROPE											
Belarus - Bélarus											
Total	C	386	407	409	352	...	3.3	3.4	3.5	3.0	...
Urban - Urbaine	C	278	291	291	254	...	3.1	3.2	3.2	2.8	...
Rural - Rurale	C	108	116	118	98	...	4.0	4.2	4.4	3.6	...
Belgium - Belgique[31]											
Total	C	483	436	423	400	...	3.8	3.5	3.4	3.3	...
Urban - Urbaine	C	477	432	420	396	...	3.8	3.5	3.4	3.3	...
Rural - Rurale	C	6	4	3	4	...	...	...	...	...	...
Bosnia and Herzegovina - Bosnie-Herzégovine											
Total	C	161	161	140	...		5.0	5.2	4.8	...	...
Bulgaria - Bulgarie											
Total	C	536	489	517	434	...	7.8	7.3	7.6	6.6	...
Urban - Urbaine	C	368	...	340	255	...	7.1	...	6.7	5.2	...
Rural - Rurale	C	168	...	177	179	...	9.6	...	10.5	10.9	...
Croatia - Croatie											
Total	C	150	162	199	154	...	3.6	4.1	5.0	4.1	...
Urban - Urbaine	C	95	82	101	91	...	4.0	3.6	4.4	4.2	...
Rural - Rurale	C	55	80	98	63	...	3.1	4.7	5.9	4.0	...
Czechia - Tchéquie											
Total	C	285	265	263	272	...	2.6	2.5	2.4	2.5	...
Urban - Urbaine	C	208	193	197	193	...	2.6	2.5	2.4	2.4	...
Rural - Rurale	C	77	72	66	79	...	2.7	2.5	2.3	2.7	...
Denmark - Danemark[32]											
Total	C	197	195	229	216	...	3.4	3.5	4.0	3.7	...
Estonia - Estonie											
Total	C	50	28	36	35	...	3.6	...	2.7	2.5	...
Urban - Urbaine	C	36	18	24	24	...	3.7	...	...	...	...
Rural - Rurale	C	14	10	12	11	...	...	...	...	...	...
Faeroe Islands - Îles Féroé											
Total	C	10	-	4	1	...	...	...	...	...	...
Urban - Urbaine	C	6	-	1	-	...	...	...	...	...	...
Rural - Rurale	C	4	-	3	1	...	...	...	...	...	...
Finland - Finlande[33]											
Total	C	141	102	124	97	...	2.4	1.8	2.2	1.8	...
Urban - Urbaine	C	93	65	93	66	...	2.2	1.6	2.3	1.6	...
Rural - Rurale	C	48	37	31	31	...	2.8	2.2	2.0	2.1	...
France											
Total	C	2 643	2 710	2 598	2 655	...	3.3	3.5	3.3	3.5	...
Urban - Urbaine[34]	C	2 140	2 233	2 138	2 219	...	3.4	3.6	3.4	3.6	...
Rural - Rurale[34]	C	485	457	441	408	...	3.0	2.9	2.9	2.8	...
Germany - Allemagne											
Total	C	2 202	2 250	2 284	2 405	...	3.3	3.3	3.2	3.3	...
Gibraltar											
Total	+C	...	-	...	...	...	...	...	...	...	...
Greece - Grèce											
Total	C	293	347	346	364	387	2.9	3.7	3.8	4.0	4.2
Urban - Urbaine	C	197	...	242	254	...	2.8	...	3.9	4.0	...
Rural - Rurale	C	96	...	104	110	...	3.3	...	3.5	3.9	...
Hungary - Hongrie											
Total	C	438	448[36]	418[37]	383[37]	368[37]	4.9	5.0	4.5	4.2	3.9
Urban - Urbaine[35]	C	259	273[36]	274[37]	242[37]	...	4.2	4.4	4.2	3.8	...
Rural - Rurale[35]	C	176	175[36]	144[37]	140[37]	...	6.5	6.4	5.1	5.0	...
Iceland - Islande											
Total	C	5	8	9	9	...	...	...	...	...	...
Urban - Urbaine	C	5	8	9	8	...	...	...	...	...	...
Rural - Rurale	C	-	-	-	1	...	...	...	...	...	...
Ireland - Irlande											
Total	+C	250	243	224	224	...	3.5	3.5	3.3	3.4	...
Italy - Italie											
Total	C	1 532	1 493	1 523	1 398	...	2.9	2.9	3.0	2.9	...
Latvia - Lettonie											
Total	C	125	91	83	90	81	6.3	4.4	3.8	4.1	3.7
Urban - Urbaine	C	87	55	53	59	...	6.4	3.9	3.5	3.9	...
Rural - Rurale	C	38	36	30	31	...	6.0	5.6	4.5	4.5	...
Liechtenstein											
Total	C	3	2	1	2	...	...	...	...	...	...

15. Infant deaths and infant mortality rates, by urban/rural residence: 2012 - 2016
Décès d'enfants de moins d'un an et taux de mortalité infantile, selon la résidence, urbaine/rurale : 2012 - 2016 (continued - suite)

Continent, country or area, and urban/rural residence / Continent, pays ou zone et résidence, urbaine/rurale	Code[a]	Number - Nombre					Rate - Taux				
		2012	2013	2014	2015	2016	2012	2013	2014	2015	2016
EUROPE											
Lithuania - Lituanie											
Total	C	118	110	118	132	...	3.9	3.7	3.9	4.2	...
Urban - Urbaine	C	77	63	69	92	...	3.6	3.1	3.3	4.3	...
Rural - Rurale	C	41	47	49	40	...	4.5	4.9	5.2	4.0	...
Luxembourg											
Total	C	25	24	17	17	...	...	...	...	...	...
Malta - Malte											
Total	C	22	27	21	25	33	...	...	...	...	7.4
Montenegro - Monténégro											
Total	C	33	33	37	16	...	4.4	4.4	4.9	...	...
Netherlands - Pays-Bas[38]											
Total	C	649	645	630	561	...	3.7	3.8	3.6	3.3	...
Norway - Norvège[39]											
Total	C	150	140	139	133	...	2.5	2.4	2.4	2.3	...
Poland - Pologne											
Total	C	1 791	1 684	1 583	1 476	...	4.6	4.6	4.2	4.0	...
Urban - Urbaine	C	1 006	928	885	859	...	4.5	4.3	4.1	4.0	...
Rural - Rurale	C	785	756	698	617	...	4.8	4.9	4.4	4.1	...
Portugal[40]											
Total	C	303	243	236	250	...	3.4	2.9	2.9	2.9	...
Republic of Moldova - République de Moldova[41]											
Total	C	387	359	372	...	...	9.8	9.5	9.6	...	...
Urban - Urbaine	C	122	...	...	...	...	8.2	...	...	...	...
Rural - Rurale	C	265	...	...	...	...	10.8	...	...	...	...
Romania - Roumanie											
Total	C	1 812	1 677	1 628	1 500	...	9.0	9.2	8.4	7.6	...
Urban - Urbaine	C	720	738	649	648	...	6.6	7.5	6.2	6.0	...
Rural - Rurale	C	1 092	939	979	852	...	11.8	11.2	11.2	9.6	...
Russian Federation - Fédération de Russie[16]											
Total	C	16 306	...	...	...	...	8.6	...	...	...	...
Urban - Urbaine	C	10 843	...	...	...	...	8.0	...	...	...	...
Rural - Rurale	C	5 463	...	...	...	...	10.0	...	...	...	...
San Marino - Saint-Marin											
Total	+C	-	1	1	...	...	...	...	...	...	...
Serbia - Serbie[42]											
Total	+C	415	413	381	346	...	6.2	6.3	5.7	5.3	...
Urban - Urbaine	+C	274	281	268	258	...	6.0	6.2	5.8	5.7	...
Rural - Rurale	+C	141	132	113	88	...	6.6	6.6	5.5	4.4	...
Slovakia - Slovaquie											
Total	C	321	301	318	285	...	5.8	5.5	5.8	5.1	...
Urban - Urbaine	C	151	138	160	117	...	5.2	4.8	5.6	4.0	...
Rural - Rurale	C	170	163	158	168	...	6.4	6.2	5.9	6.3	...
Slovenia - Slovénie											
Total	C	36	62	39	33	...	1.6	2.9	1.8	1.6	...
Urban - Urbaine	C	15	37	19	17	...	...	3.5	...	...	...
Rural - Rurale	C	21	25	20	16	...	...	...	...	...	...
Spain - Espagne											
Total	C	1 389	1 149	1 202	1 117	...	3.1	2.7	2.8	2.7	...
Sweden - Suède											
Total	C	293	306	251	282	...	2.6	2.7	2.2	2.5	...
Switzerland - Suisse											
Total	C	296	320	331	340	...	3.6	3.9	3.9	3.9	...
Urban - Urbaine	C	235	258	256	282[43]	...	3.8	4.1	4.0	3.8	...
Rural - Rurale	C	61	62	75	58[43]	...	3.0	3.0	3.5	4.6	...
TFYR of Macedonia - L'ex-R. y. de Macédoine											
Total	C	230	237	233	198	...	9.8	10.2	9.9	8.6	...
Urban - Urbaine	C	123	131	144	116	...	9.2	9.9	10.5	8.7	...
Rural - Rurale	C	107	106	89	82	...	10.5	10.7	9.1	8.4	...
Ukraine[44]											
Total	+C	4 371	4 030	3 656[45]	...	...	8.4	8.0	7.8	...	...
Urban - Urbaine	+C	2 763	2 536	...	...	...	8.1	7.7	...	...	...
Rural - Rurale	+C	1 608	1 494	...	...	...	9.0	8.6	...	...	...

15. Infant deaths and infant mortality rates, by urban/rural residence: 2012 - 2016
Décès d'enfants de moins d'un an et taux de mortalité infantile, selon la résidence, urbaine/rurale : 2012 - 2016 (continued - suite)

Continent, country or area, and urban/rural residence / Continent, pays ou zone et résidence, urbaine/rurale	Code[a]	Number - Nombre					Rate - Taux				
		2012	2013	2014	2015	2016	2012	2013	2014	2015	2016
EUROPE											
United Kingdom of Great Britain and Northern Ireland - Royaume-Uni de Grande-Bretagne et d'Irlande du Nord[46]											
Total....................	+C	3 347	...	2 990	3 005	...	4.1	...	3.9	3.9	...
OCEANIA - OCÉANIE											
American Samoa - Samoas américaines											
Total....................	C	4	5	9	...	...	...	...	...	...	...
Australia - Australie											
Total....................	+C	1 031	1 094	1 012	991	...	3.3	3.6	3.4	3.2	...
Urban - Urbaine[47]	+C	634	658	617	606	...	3.0	3.1	3.0	2.9	...
Rural - Rurale[47]	+C	362	411	380	361	...	3.7	4.2	4.1	3.8	...
Cook Islands - Îles Cook[48]											
Total....................	+C	1	-	-	*-	...	...	...	...	...	...
French Polynesia - Polynésie française											
Total....................	C	31	37	28	29	...	7.2	8.8	...	...	...
Guam[49]											
Total....................	C	42	31	28	47	...	11.7	9.3	...	14.0	...
New Caledonia - Nouvelle-Calédonie											
Total....................	C	17	19	23	25	...	...	...	...	...	...
New Zealand - Nouvelle-Zélande[50]											
Total....................	+C	258	261	327	249	213	4.2	4.4	5.7	4.1	3.6
Urban - Urbaine[11]	+C	228	222	288	216	189	4.2	4.3	5.7	4.1	3.6
Rural - Rurale[11]	+C	24	33	24	30	18	...	4.6	...	3.8	...
Northern Mariana Islands - Îles Mariannes septentrionales[12]											
Total....................	U	6	8	7	...	...	...	...	...	...	...
Palau - Palaos											
Total....................	C	2	4	...	...	...	...	...	...	...	...

FOOTNOTES - NOTES

Italics: data from civil registers which are incomplete or of unknown completeness. - Italiques : données incomplètes ou dont le degré d'exactitude n'est pas connu, provenant des registres de l'état civil.

* Provisional. - Données provisoires.

[a] 'Code' indicates the source of data, as follows:
C - Civil registration, estimated over 90% complete
U - Civil registration, estimated less than 90% complete
| - Other source, estimated reliable
+ - Data tabulated by date of registration rather than occurence
... - Information not available

Le 'Code' indique la source des données, comme suit :
C - Registres de l'état civil considérés complets à 90 p. 100 au moins
U - Registres de l'état civil qui ne sont pas considérés complets à 90 p. 100 au moins
| - Autre source, considérée pas douteuses
+ - Données exploitées selon la date de l'enregistrement et non la date de l'événement
... - Information pas disponible

[1] Excluding live-born infants who died before their birth was registered. Data refer to Algerian population only. - Non compris les enfants nés vivants décédés avant l'enregistrement de leur naissance. Les données ne concernent que la population algérienne.
[2] Source: Vital Statistics Report 2014. - Source: Vital Statistics Report 2014.
[3] Data refer to the 12 months preceding the census in May. - Les données se rapportent aux 12 mois précédant le recensement de mai.
[4] Adjusted number of infant deaths in households referring to the 12 months preceding the census in March. - Le nombre ajusté de décès d'enfants des ménages ordinaires se rapportent aux 12 mois précédant le recensement de mars.
[5] Excludes the islands of St. Brandon and Agalega. - Non compris les îles St. Brandon et Agalega.
[6] Source: National Office of Births and Deaths. - Source : Le bureau national des naissances et des décès.
[7] Unrevised data. - Les données n'ont pas été révisées.
[8] Including Canadian residents temporarily in the United States, but excluding United States residents temporarily in Canada. - Y compris les résidents canadiens se trouvant temporairement aux Etats-Unis, mais ne comprenant pas les résidents des Etats-Unis se trouvant temporairement au Canada.
[9] Excluding infant deaths to mothers living abroad. - Exception faite des décès d'enfants en bas âge survenus lorsque la mère résidait à l'étranger.
[10] Data refer to resident population only. - Pour la population résidante seulement.
[11] The total number may include 'Unknown residence', but the categories urban and rural do not. - Le nombre total peut inclure les personnes dont la résidence n'est pas connue, à l'inverse des catégories de population urbaine et rurale.

12 Source: U.S. National Center for Health Statistics, National Vital Statistics Reports (NVSR). - Source : US National Center for Health Statistics, National Vital Statistics Reports (NVSR).

13 Including deaths abroad and deaths of unknown residence of mother. - Y compris décès à l'étranger et décès de nourrissons nés de mères dont le lieu de résidence n'est pas connu.

14 Excludes nomadic Indian tribes. - Non compris les tribus d'Indiens nomades.

15 Source: Reports of the Ministry of Health. - Source : Rapports du Ministère de la Santé.

16 Excluding infants born alive of less than 28 weeks' gestation, of less than 1 000 g in weight and 35 cm in length, who die within seven days of birth. - Non compris les enfants nés vivants après moins de 28 semaines de gestations, pesant moins de 1 000 g, mesurant moins de 35 cm et décédés dans les sept jours qui ont suivi leur naissance.

17 Deaths include deaths among some visitors. Sources: Births and Deaths National Registration System database, and medical records of government hospitals. - Les décès comprennent des décès parmi certains visiteurs. Les sources: Les bases de données des << Births and Deaths National Registration System >> et les dossiers médicaux des hôpitaux du gouvernement.

18 Data refer to government controlled areas. - Les données se rapportent aux zones contrôlées par le Gouvernement.

19 Includes data for the Indian-held part of Jammu and Kashmir, the final status of which has not yet been determined. Rates were obtained by the Sample Registration System of India, which is a large demographic survey. - Y compris les données pour la partie du Jammu et du Cachemire occupée par l'Inde dont le statut définitif n'a pas encore été déterminé. Les taux ont été obtenus par le Système de l'enregistrement par échantillon de l'Inde qui est une large enquête démographique.

20 Data refer to the Iranian Year which begins on 21 March and ends on 20 March of the following year. - Les données concernent l'année iranienne, qui commence le 21 mars et se termine le 20 mars de l'année suivante.

21 Including deaths abroad of Israeli residents who were out of the country for less than a year. Includes data for East Jerusalem and Israeli residents in certain other territories under occupation by Israeli military forces since June 1967. - Y compris les décès à l'étranger de résidents israéliens qui ont quitté le pays depuis moins d'un an. Y compris les données pour Jérusalem-Est et les résidents israéliens dans certains autres territoires occupés depuis 1967 par les forces armées israéliennes.

22 Data refer to Japanese nationals in Japan only. The total number may include 'Unknown residence', but the categories urban and rural do not. - Les données se raportent aux nationaux japonais au Japon seulement. Le nombre total peut inclure les personnes dont la résidence n'est pas connue, à l'inverse des catégories de population urbaine et rurale.

23 Excluding deaths occurred abroad. - Hormis les décès à l'étranger.

24 Data for urban and rural exclude deaths of unknown residence. - Les données pur la résidence urbaine et rurale non comprent pas les décès dont on ignore la résidence.

25 Source: "Department of Public Health" - Source : << Le Service de la santé publique >>

26 Data are from Vital Registration System (VRS). - Les données proviennent du système d'enregistrement des faits d'état civil.

27 Data from Births and Deaths Notification System (Ministry of Health and all health care providers). - Les données proviennent du système de notification des naissances et des décès (Ministère de la santé et tous prestataires de soins de santé).

28 Excluding alien armed forces, civilian aliens employed by armed forces, and foreign diplomatic personnel and their dependants. - Non compris les militaires étrangers, les civils étrangers employés par les forces armées ni le personnel diplomatique étranger et les membres de leur famille les accompagnant.

29 Projections based on the final results of the 2004 Population and Housing Census. - Projections basées sur les résultats définitifs du recensement de la population et de l'habitat de 2004.

30 Source: Palestinian Central Bureau of Statistics, Population Register, updated version 22/02/2016. - Source: Bureau central de statistique palestinien, registre de la population, version actualisée jusqu'au 22/02/2016.

31 Including armed forces stationed outside the country, but excluding alien armed forces stationed in the area. - Y compris les militaires nationaux hors du pays, mais non compris les militaires étrangers en garnison sur le territoire.

32 Excluding Faeroe Islands and Greenland shown separately, if available. - Non compris les îles Féroé et le Groenland, qui font l'objet de rubriques distinctes, si disponible.

33 Excluding Åland Islands. - Non compris les Îles d'Åland.

34 The data for urban and rural exclude the nationals outside the country. - Les données relatives à la population urbaine et rurale n'englobent pas les nationaux se trouvant à l'étranger.

35 The urban and rural categories do not include the data of foreigners, persons of unknown residence and the homeless, whereas the total category includes them. - Les chiffres portant sur la population urbaine et rurale n' incluent pas les données relatives aux étrangers, aux personnes dont la résidence n'est pas connue et aux personnes sans domicile fixe, à l'inverse, le total les inclut.

36 Till 2012 data refer to all infant deaths occurred in Hungary. From 2013 data include the deceased infants with Hungarian usual residence regardless of whether the death occurred in Hungary or in a foreign country, and do not include the deceased infants with foreign country usual residence. - Jusqu'en 2012 les données concernent tous les décès de nourrissons survenus en Hongrie. À partir de 2013, les données comprennent les nourrissons décédés alors que leur résidence habituelle était en Hongrie, que le décès ait eu lieu en Hongrie ou dans un pays étranger, et ne comprennent pas les nourrissons décédés dont la résidence habituelle était dans un pays étranger.

37 Data include the deceased infants with Hungarian usual residence regardless of whether the death occurred in Hungary or in a foreign country, and do not include the deceased infants with foreign country usual residence. - Les données comprennent les nourrissons décédés alors que leur résidence habituelle était en Hongrie, que le décès ait eu lieu en Hongrie ou dans un pays étranger, et ne comprennent pas les nourrissons décédés dont la residence habituelle était dans un pays étranger.

38 Including residents outside the country if listed in a Netherlands population register. - Englobe les résidents se trouvant à l'étranger à condition qu'ils soient inscrits sur le registre de population des Pays-Bas.

39 Including residents temporarily outside the country. - Y compris les résidents se trouvant temporairement hors du pays.

40 Data refer to usually resident population. - Les données concernent la population habituellement résidente.

41 Excluding Transnistria and the municipality of Bender. - Les données ne tiennent pas compte de l'information sur la Transnistria et la municipalité de Bender.

42 Excludes data for Kosovo and Metohia. - Sans les données pour le Kosovo et Metohie.

43 From 2015, urban refers to urban centers and areas under the influence of urban centers. - A partir de 2015, le territoire urbain inclut l'espace des centres urbains ainsi que l'espace sous influence des centres urbains.

44 Data includes deaths resulting from births with weight 500 g and more (if weight is unknown - with length 25 cm and more, or with gestation during 22 weeks or more). - Y compris les décès de nouveau-nés de 500 g ou plus (si le poids est inconnu – de 25 cm de long ou plus, ou après une grossesse de 22 semaines ou plus).

45 The Government of Ukraine has informed the United Nations that it is not in a position to provide statistical data concerning the Autonomous Republic of Crimea and the city of Sevastopol. - Le gouvernement Ukrainien a informé l'ONU qu'il n'est pas en mesure de fournir des données statistiques concernant la République autonome de Crimée et la ville de Sébastopol.

46 Excluding Channel Islands (Guernsey and Jersey) and Isle of Man, shown separately, if available. - Non compris les îles Anglo-Normandes (Guernesey et Jersey) et l'île de Man, qui font l'objet de rubriques distinctes, si disponible.

47 Urban refers to Greater Capital City Statistical Areas, and rural refers to other areas within the state or territory. Data for urban and rural figures do not add up to the total because they exclude the events occurred in Migratory, Special Purpose and Other Territories. - Urbain renvoie aux zones statistiques de la capitale métropolitaine, et rural aux autres zones de l'État ou territoire. La somme des chiffres des catégories « en zone urbaine » et « en zone rurale » ne correspond pas au total du fait qu'en sont exclus les événements qui ont eu lieu dans les territoires de migration, les territoires à destination spéciale et autres territoires.

48 Excluding Niue, shown separately, which is part of Cook Islands, but because of remoteness is administered separately. - Non compris Nioué, qui fait l'objet d'une rubrique distincte et qui fait partie des îles Cook, mais qui, en raison de son éloignement, est administrée séparément.

49 Including United States military personnel, their dependants and contract employees. - Y compris les militaires des Etats-Unis, les membres de leur famille les accompagnant et les agents contractuels des Etats-Unis.

50 Random rounding to base 3 is applied in this table as a confidentiality measure. - Les chiffres sont arrondis à la base 3 de manière aléatoire, pour des raisons de confidentialité.

Table 16 - *Demographic Yearbook 2016*

Table 16 presents infant deaths and infant mortality rates by age and sex for latest available year between 2007 and 2016.

Description of variables: Age is defined as hours, days and months of life completed, based on the difference between the hour, day, month and year of birth and the hour, day, month and year of death. The age classification used in this table is as follows: Main categories are "under 1 day", "1-6 days", "7-27 days" and "28 days – 11 months". Additional subcategories are shown within "7-27 days" and "28 days to 11 months" wherever available.

Rate computation: Infant mortality rates by age and sex are the annual number of infant deaths that occurred in a specific age-sex group per 1 000 live births of the corresponding sex. These rates have been calculated by the Statistics Division of the United Nations Department of Economic and Social Affairs. The denominator for all these rates, regardless of age of infant at death, is the total number of live births by sex.

Infant deaths of unknown age are included only in the rate for under one year of age. Infant deaths of unknown sex are included in the rate for the total and, hence, these rates, should agree with the infant mortality rates shown in table 15. Discrepancies are explained in footnotes.

Rates presented in this table have been limited to those countries or areas having at least a total of 100 deaths in a given year. Moreover, rates specific for individual sub-categories based on 30 or fewer infant deaths are identified by the symbol "♦".

Reliability of data: Data from civil registers of infant deaths which are reported as incomplete (less than 90 percent completeness) or of unknown completeness are considered unreliable and are set in italics rather than in roman type. Rates on these data are not computed. Table 15 and its technical notes provide more detailed information on the completeness of infant death registration. For more information about the quality of vital statistics, and the information available on the basis of the completeness of estimates in particular, see section 4.2 of the Technical Notes.

Limitations: Statistics on infant deaths by age and sex are subject to the same qualifications as have been set forth for vital statistics in general and death statistics in particular as discussed in section 4 of the Technical Notes.

The reliability of the data, an indication of which is described above, is an important factor in considering the limitations. In addition, some infant deaths are tabulated by date of registration and not by date of occurrence; these have been indicated by a plus sign "+". Whenever the lag between the date of occurrence and date of registration is prolonged and, therefore, a large proportion of the infant-death registrations are delayed, infant-death statistics for any given year may be seriously affected.

Another factor that limits international comparability is the practice of some countries or areas of not including in infant-death statistics infants who were born alive but died before the registration of the birth or within the first 24 hours of life, thus underestimating the total number of infant deaths. Statistics of this type are footnoted. In this table in particular, this practice may contribute to the lack of comparability among deaths under one year, under 28 days, under one week and under one day.

Variation in the method of reckoning age at the time of death may also introduce non-comparability. Although it is to some degree a limiting factor throughout the age span, it is an especially important consideration with respect to deaths at ages under one day and under one week (early neonatal deaths) and under 28 days (neonatal deaths). As noted above, the recommended method of reckoning infant age at death is to calculate duration of life in minutes, hours and days, as appropriate. This gives age in completed units of time. In some countries or areas, however, infant age is calculated to the nearest day only, that is, age at death for an infant is the difference between the day, month and year of birth and the day, month and year of death. The result of this procedure is to classify as deaths at age one day, many deaths of infants that occurred before the infants had completed 24 hours of life. The under-one-day class is thus understated while the frequency in the 1-6-day age group is inflated.

A special limitation on comparability of neonatal (under 28 days) deaths is the variation in the classification of infant age used. It is evident from the footnotes that some countries or areas continue to report infant age in calendar, rather than lunar month (4-week or 28-day) periods. This failure to tabulate infant deaths under 4 weeks of age in terms of completed days introduces another source of variation between countries or areas. Deaths classified as occurring under one month usually connote deaths within any one calendar month; these frequencies are not strictly comparable with those referring to deaths within 4 weeks or 27 completed days.

In addition, infant mortality rates by age and sex are subject to the limitations of the data on live births with which they have been calculated. These have been set forth in the technical notes for table 9. These limitations have also been discussed in the technical notes for table 15.

In addition, it should be noted that infant mortality rates by age are affected by the problems related to the practice of excluding infants who were born alive but died before the registration of the birth or within the first 24 hours of life from both infant-death and live-birth statistics and the problems related to the reckoning of infant age at death. These factors, which have been described above, may affect certain age groups more than others. In so far as the numbers of infant deaths for the various age groups are underestimated or overestimated, the corresponding rates for the various age groups will also be underestimated or overestimated. The youngest age groups are more likely to be underestimated than other age groups; the youngest age group (under one day) is likely to be the most seriously affected.

Earlier data: Infant deaths and infant mortality rates by age and sex have been shown in previous issues of the *Demographic Yearbook*. For information on specific years covered, readers should consult the Historical Index.

Tableau 16 – *Annuaire démographique 2016*

Le tableau 16 présente les données les plus récentes disponible, entre 2007 et 2016, sur les décès d'enfants de moins d'un an et les taux de mortalité infantile selon l'âge et le sexe.

Description des variables : l'âge est exprimé en heures, jours et mois révolus et est calculé en retranchant la date de la naissance (heure, jour, mois et année) de celle du décès (heure, jour, mois et année). Les tranches d'âge utilisées dans ce tableau se présentent comme suit : les catégories principales sont « moins d'un jour », « 1-6 jours », « 7-27 jours » et « 28 jours à 11 mois ». Des sous-catégories additionnelles pour « 7-27 jours » et « 28 jours à 11 mois » sont présentées lorsque disponibles.

Calcul des taux : les taux de mortalité infantile selon l'âge et le sexe représentent le nombre annuel de décès d'enfants de moins d'un an intervenu dans un groupe d'âge donné parmi la population de sexe masculin ou féminin pour 1 000 naissances vivantes survenues parmi la population du même sexe. Ces taux ont été calculés par la Division de statistique du Département des affaires économiques et sociales de l'Organisation des Nations Unies. Le dénominateur de tous ces taux, quel que soit l'âge de l'enfant au moment du décès, est le nombre total de naissances vivantes selon le sexe.

Il n'est tenu compte des décès d'enfants d'âge « inconnu » que pour le calcul du taux relatif à l'ensemble des décès de moins d'un an. Étant donné que les décès d'enfants de sexe inconnu sont compris dans le numérateur des taux concernant le total, les chiffres obtenus devraient concorder avec les taux de mortalité infantile du tableau 15. Les divergences sont expliquées en note.

Les taux présentés dans le tableau 16 ne concernent que les pays ou zones où l'on a enregistré un total d'au moins 100 décès au cours d'une année donnée. Les taux relatifs à des sous-catégories qui sont fondées sur un nombre égal ou inférieur à 30 décès d'enfants âgés de moins d'un an sont signalés par le signe "♦".

Fiabilité des données : les données relatives aux décès d'enfants de moins d'un an provenant de registres de l'état civil qui sont déclarées incomplètes (degré de complétude inférieur à 90 p.100) ou dont le degré de complétude n'est pas connu sont jugées douteuses et apparaissent en italique et non en caractères romains. Les taux à partir de ces données n'ont pas été calculés. Le tableau 15 et les notes techniques se rapportant à ce tableau comportent des renseignements plus détaillés sur le degré de complétude de l'enregistrement des décès d'enfants de moins d'un an. Pour plus de précisions sur la qualité des données reposant sur les statistiques de l'état civil en général et les estimations de complétude en particulier, voir la section 4.2 des Notes techniques.

Insuffisance des données : les statistiques des décès d'enfants de moins d'un an selon l'âge et le sexe appellent toutes les réserves qui ont été formulées à propos des statistiques de l'état civil en général et des statistiques concernant les décès en particulier (voir la section 4 des Notes techniques).

La fiabilité des données, au sujet de laquelle des indications ont été fournies plus haut, est un facteur important. Il faut également tenir compte du fait que, dans certains cas, les données relatives aux décès d'enfants de moins d'un an sont exploitées selon la date de l'enregistrement et non la date de l'événement ; ces cas ont été signalés par le signe "+". Chaque fois que le décalage entre l'événement et son enregistrement est grand et qu'une forte proportion des décès d'enfants de moins d'un an fait l'objet d'un enregistrement tardif, les statistiques des décès d'enfants de moins d'un an pour une année donnée peuvent être considérablement faussées.

Un autre facteur qui nuit à la comparabilité internationale est la pratique de certains pays ou zones qui consiste à ne pas inclure dans les statistiques des décès d'enfants de moins d'un an les enfants nés vivants mais décédés soit avant l'enregistrement de leur naissance, soit dans les 24 heures qui ont suivi la naissance, pratique qui conduit à sous-estimer le nombre total de décès d'enfants de moins d'un an. Quand pareil facteur a joué, cela a été signalé en note. Dans le tableau 16 en particulier, ce système peut limiter la comparabilité des données concernant les décès d'enfants de moins d'un an, de moins de 28 jours, de moins d'une semaine et de moins d'un jour.

Le manque d'uniformité des méthodes suivies pour calculer l'âge au moment du décès nuit également à la comparabilité des données. Ce facteur influe dans une certaine mesure sur les données relatives à la mortalité à tous les âges, mais il a des répercussions particulièrement marquées sur les statistiques des décès de moins d'un jour et de moins d'une semaine (mortalité néo-natale précoce) et de moins de 28 jours (mortalité néo-natale). Comme on l'a dit, l'âge d'un enfant de moins d'un an à son décès est calculé, selon la méthode recommandée, en évaluant la durée de vie en minutes, heures et jours, selon le cas. L'âge est ainsi exprimé en unités de temps révolues. Toutefois, dans certains pays ou zones, l'âge de ces enfants est ramené au jour le plus proche en retranchant la date de la naissance (jour, mois et année) de celle du décès (jour, mois et année). Il s'ensuit que de nombreux décès survenus dans les vingt-quatre heures qui suivent la naissance sont classés comme décès d'un jour. Dans ces conditions, les données concernant les décès de moins d'un jour sont entachées d'une erreur par défaut et celles qui se rapportent aux décès de 1 à 6 jours d'une erreur par excès.

La comparabilité des données relatives à la mortalité néo-natale (moins de 28 jours) est influencée par un facteur spécial : l'hétérogénéité de la classification par âge utilisée pour les enfants de moins d'un an. Les notes figurant à la fin des tableaux montrent que, dans un certain nombre de pays ou zones, on continue d'utiliser le mois civil au lieu du mois lunaire (4 semaines ou 28 jours).

Lorsque les données relatives aux décès de moins de 4 semaines ne sont pas exploitées sur la base de l'âge en jours révolus, il existe une nouvelle cause de non-comparabilité internationale. Les décès de moins d'un mois sont généralement ceux qui se produisent au cours d'un mois civil ; les taux calculés sur la base de ces données ne sont pas strictement comparables à ceux qui sont établis à partir des données concernant les décès survenus dans les 4 semaines ou 27 jours révolus qui suivent la naissance.

Les taux de mortalité infantile selon l'âge et le sexe appellent en outre toutes les réserves qui ont été formulées à propos des statistiques des naissances vivantes qui ont servi à leur calcul (voir à ce sujet les notes techniques relatives au tableau 9). Ces insuffisances ont également été examinées dans les notes techniques relatives au tableau 15.

Il convient de signaler aussi que les taux de mortalité infantile selon l'âge peuvent être gravement faussés par la pratique qui consiste à ne pas classer dans les naissances vivantes et ensuite dans les décès d'enfants de moins d'un an les enfants nés vivants mais décédés soit avant l'enregistrement de leur naissance, soit dans les 24 heures qui ont suivi la naissance, et par les problèmes que pose le calcul de l'âge de l'enfant au moment du décès. Ces facteurs, qui ont été décrits plus haut, peuvent fausser les statistiques concernant certains groupes d'âge plus que d'autres. Si le nombre des décès d'enfants de moins d'un an pour chaque groupe d'âge est sous-estimé ou surestimé, les taux correspondants pour chacun de ces groupes d'âge seront eux aussi sous-estimés ou surestimés. Les risques de sous-estimation sont plus grands pour les groupes les plus jeunes ; c'est pour le groupe d'âge le plus jeune de tous (moins d'un jour) que les données risquent de comporter les plus grosses erreurs.

Données publiées antérieurement : des statistiques des décès d'enfants de moins d'un an et des taux de mortalité infantile selon l'âge et le sexe ont déjà été présentées dans des éditions antérieures de l'*Annuaire démographique*. Pour plus de précisions concernant les années pour lesquelles ces données ont été publiées, se reporter à l'index historique.

16. Infant deaths and infant mortality rates by age and sex: latest available year, 2007 - 2016
Décès d'enfants de moins d'un an et taux de mortalité infantile selon l'âge et le sexe : dernière année disponible, 2007 - 2016

Continent, country or area, year, code[a] and age / Continent, pays ou zone, année, code[a] et âge	Number - Nombre			Rate - Taux		
	Both sexes Les deux sexes	Male Masculin	Female Féminin	Both sexes Les deux sexes	Male Masculin	Female Féminin
AFRICA - AFRIQUE						
Cabo Verde						
2008 (C)						
Total	316	...	...	24.9	...	...
Less than 7 days - Moins de 7 jours	160	...	...	12.6	...	...
7 - 27 days - 7 - 27 jours	52	...	...	4.1	...	...
28 days - 11 months - 28 jours - 11 mois	104	...	...	8.2	...	...
Egypt - Égypte						
2014 (C)						
Total	39 679	21 251	18 428	14.6	15.3	13.9
1 - 6 days - 1 - 6 jours	7 017	4 078	2 939	2.6	2.9	2.2
7 - 27 days - 7 - 27 jours	9 929	5 669	4 260	3.6	4.1	3.2
7 - 13 days - 7 - 13 jours	4 741	2 752	1 989	1.7	2.0	1.5
14 - 20 days - 14 - 20 jours	3 311	1 869	1 442	1.2	1.3	1.1
21 - 27 days - 21 - 27 jours	1 877	1 048	829	0.7	0.8	0.6
28 days - 11 months - 28 jours - 11 mois	22 733	11 504	11 229	8.4	8.3	8.4
28 days - less than 2 months - 28 jours - moins de 2 mois	5 435	2 922	2 513	2.0	2.1	1.9
2 months - 2 mois	3 803	1 897	1 906	1.4	1.4	1.4
3 months - 3 mois	2 827	1 427	1 400	1.0	1.0	1.1
4 months - 4 mois	2 468	1 225	1 243	0.9	0.9	0.9
5 months - 5 mois	1 827	894	933	0.7	0.6	0.7
6 months - 6 mois	1 760	859	901	0.6	0.6	0.7
7 months - 7 mois	1 245	611	634	0.5	0.4	0.5
8 months - 8 mois	1 127	533	594	0.4	0.4	0.4
9 months - 9 mois	974	496	478	0.4	0.4	0.4
10 months - 10 mois	716	372	344	0.3	0.3	0.3
11 months - 11 mois	551	268	283	0.2	0.2	0.2
Mauritius - Maurice[1]						
2016 (+C)						
Total	154	81	73	11.9	12.3	11.5
Less than 1 day - Moins de 1 jour	18	9	9	♦1.4	♦1.4	♦1.4
1 - 6 days - 1 - 6 jours	49	25	24	3.8	♦3.8	♦3.8
7 - 27 days - 7 - 27 jours	38	25	13	2.9	♦3.8	♦2.0
7 - 13 days - 7 - 13 jours	16	13	3	♦1.2	♦2.0	♦0.5
14 - 20 days - 14 - 20 jours	9	5	4	♦0.7	♦0.8	♦0.6
21 - 27 days - 21 - 27 jours	13	7	6	♦1.0	♦1.1	♦0.9
28 days - 11 months - 28 jours - 11 mois	49	22	27	3.8	♦3.3	♦4.3
28 days - less than 2 months - 28 jours - moins de 2 mois	23	13	10	♦1.8	♦2.0	♦1.6
2 months - 2 mois	5	1	4	♦0.4	♦0.2	♦0.6
3 months - 3 mois	4	3	1	♦0.3	♦0.5	♦0.2
4 months - 4 mois	2	2	-	♦0.2	♦0.3	-
5 months - 5 mois	-	-	-	-	-	-
6 months - 6 mois	5	-	5	♦0.4	-	♦0.8
7 months - 7 mois	4	1	3	♦0.3	♦0.2	♦0.5
8 months - 8 mois	1	-	1	♦0.1	-	♦0.2
9 months - 9 mois	1	-	1	♦0.1	-	♦0.2
10 months - 10 mois	4	2	2	♦0.3	♦0.3	♦0.3
11 months - 11 mois	-	-	-			
Reunion - Réunion[2]						
2007 (C)						
Total	91	48	43	...	...	...
Less than 1 day - Moins de 1 jour	24	14	10	...	...	...
1 - 6 days - 1 - 6 jours	20	9	11	...	...	...
7 - 27 days - 7 - 27 jours	18	7	11	...	...	...
7 - 13 days - 7 - 13 jours	7	3	4	...	...	...
14 - 20 days - 14 - 20 jours	9	2	7	...	...	...
21 - 27 days - 21 - 27 jours	7	2	5	...	...	...
28 days - 11 months - 28 jours - 11 mois	30	18	12	...	...	...
Saint Helena ex. dep. - Sainte-Hélène sans dép.						
2014 (C)						
Total	1	-	1	...	...	...
Less than 1 day - Moins de 1 jour	-	-	-	...	...	...
1 - 6 days - 1 - 6 jours	1	-	1	...	...	...
7 - 27 days - 7 - 27 jours	-	-	-	...	...	...
7 - 13 days - 7 - 13 jours	-	-	-	...	...	...
14 - 20 days - 14 - 20 jours	-	-	-	...	...	...
21 - 27 days - 21 - 27 jours	-	-	-	...	...	...
28 days - 11 months - 28 jours - 11 mois	-	-	-	...	...	...
28 days - less than 2 months - 28 jours - moins de 2 mois	-	-	-	...	...	...

16. Infant deaths and infant mortality rates by age and sex: latest available year, 2007 - 2016
Décès d'enfants de moins d'un an et taux de mortalité infantile selon l'âge et le sexe : dernière année disponible, 2007 - 2016 (continued - suite)

Continent, country or area, year, code[a] and age / Continent, pays ou zone, année, code[a] et âge	Number - Nombre			Rate - Taux		
	Both sexes Les deux sexes	Male Masculin	Female Féminin	Both sexes Les deux sexes	Male Masculin	Female Féminin
AFRICA - AFRIQUE						
Saint Helena ex. dep. - Sainte-Hélène sans dép.						
2014 (C)						
2 months - 2 mois	-	-	-	...	...	...
3 months - 3 mois	-	-	-	...	...	...
4 months - 4 mois	-	-	-	...	...	...
5 months - 5 mois	-	-	-	...	...	...
6 months - 6 mois	-	-	-	...	...	...
7 months - 7 mois	-	-	-	...	...	...
8 months - 8 mois	-	-	-	...	...	...
9 months - 9 mois	-	-	-	...	...	...
10 months - 10 mois	-	-	-	...	...	...
11 months - 11 mois	-	-	-	...	...	...
AMERICA, NORTH - AMÉRIQUE DU NORD						
Aruba						
2016 (+C)						
Total	5	3	2	...	...	...
Less than 1 day - Moins de 1 jour	2	1	1	...	...	...
1 - 6 days - 1 - 6 jours	-	-	-	...	...	...
7 - 27 days - 7 - 27 jours	-	-	-	...	...	...
7 - 13 days - 7 - 13 jours	-	-	-	...	...	...
14 - 20 days - 14 - 20 jours	-	-	-	...	...	...
21 - 27 days - 21 - 27 jours	-	-	-	...	...	...
28 days - 11 months - 28 jours - 11 mois	3	2	1	...	...	...
28 days - less than 2 months - 28 jours - moins de 2 mois	1	-	1	...	...	...
2 months - 2 mois	1	1	-	...	...	...
3 months - 3 mois	-	-	-	...	...	...
4 months - 4 mois	-	-	-	...	...	...
5 months - 5 mois	1	1	-	...	...	...
6 months - 6 mois	-	-	-	...	...	...
7 months - 7 mois	-	-	-	...	...	...
8 months - 8 mois	-	-	-	...	...	...
9 months - 9 mois	-	-	-	...	...	...
10 months - 10 mois	-	-	-	...	...	...
11 months - 11 mois	-	-	-	...	...	...
Bahamas						
2012 (+C)						
Total	57	26	31	...	...	...
Less than 1 day - Moins de 1 jour	-	-	-	...	...	...
1 - 6 days - 1 - 6 jours	18	10	8	...	...	...
7 - 27 days - 7 - 27 jours	19	8	11	...	...	...
7 - 13 days - 7 - 13 jours	16	6	10	...	...	...
14 - 20 days - 14 - 20 jours	2	1	1	...	...	...
21 - 27 days - 21 - 27 jours	1	1	-	...	...	...
28 days - 11 months - 28 jours - 11 mois	20	8	12	...	...	...
28 days - less than 2 months - 28 jours - moins de 2 mois	9	5	4	...	...	...
2 months - 2 mois	3	1	2	...	...	...
3 months - 3 mois	2	1	1	...	...	...
4 months - 4 mois	3	-	3	...	...	...
5 months - 5 mois	-	-	-	...	...	...
6 months - 6 mois	-	-	-	...	...	...
7 months - 7 mois	1	-	1	...	...	...
8 months - 8 mois	1	1	-	...	...	...
9 months - 9 mois	1	-	1	...	...	...
10 months - 10 mois	-	-	-	...	...	...
11 months - 11 mois	-	-	-	...	...	...
Barbados - Barbade						
2007 (+C)						
Total	31	18	13	...	...	...
Less than 1 day - Moins de 1 jour	-	1	1	...	...	...
1 - 6 days - 1 - 6 jours	10	8	18	...	...	...
7 - 27 days - 7 - 27 jours	6	4	2	...	...	...
7 - 20 days - 7 - 20 jours	6	4	2	...	...	...
21 - 27 days - 21 - 27 jours	-	-	-	...	...	...
28 days - 11 months - 28 jours - 11 mois	4	2	2	...	...	...
28 days - 2 months - 28 jours - 2 mois	3	2	1	...	...	...

16. Infant deaths and infant mortality rates by age and sex: latest available year, 2007 - 2016
Décès d'enfants de moins d'un an et taux de mortalité infantile selon l'âge et le sexe : dernière année disponible, 2007 - 2016 (continued - suite)

Continent, country or area, year, code[a] and age Continent, pays ou zone, année, code[a] et âge	Number - Nombre			Rate - Taux		
	Both sexes Les deux sexes	Male Masculin	Female Féminin	Both sexes Les deux sexes	Male Masculin	Female Féminin
AMERICA, NORTH - AMÉRIQUE DU NORD						
Barbados - Barbade						
2007 (+C)						
3 - 4 months - 3 - 4 mois	1	-	1	...	...	...
5 - 11 months - 5 - 11 mois	-	-	-	...	...	...
Unknown - Inconnu	2	2	-	...	...	...
Belize						
2016 (U)						
Total	103	61	42	...	...	...
Less than 1 day - Moins de 1 jour	29	14	15	...	...	...
1 - 6 days - 1 - 6 jours	36	26	10	...	...	...
7 - 27 days - 7 - 27 jours	15	8	7	...	...	...
7 - 13 days - 7 - 13 jours	2	1	1	...	...	...
14 - 20 days - 14 - 20 jours	5	2	3	...	...	...
21 - 27 days - 21 - 27 jours	8	5	3	...	...	...
28 days - 11 months - 28 jours - 11 mois	23	13	10	...	...	...
28 days - less than 2 months - 28 jours - moins de 2 mois	1	-	1	...	...	...
2 months - 2 mois	4	2	2	...	...	...
3 months - 3 mois	7	4	3	...	...	...
4 months - 4 mois	3	3	-	...	...	...
5 months - 5 mois	2	1	1	...	...	...
6 months - 6 mois	2	1	1	...	...	...
7 months - 7 mois	1	1	-	...	...	...
8 months - 8 mois	-	-	-	...	...	...
9 months - 9 mois	3	1	2	...	...	...
10 months - 10 mois	-	-	-	...	...	...
11 months - 11 mois	-	-	-	...	...	...
Bermuda - Bermudes						
2012 (C)						
Total	1	1	-	...	...	...
Less than 1 day - Moins de 1 jour	-	-	-	...	...	...
1 - 6 days - 1 - 6 jours	-	-	-	...	...	...
7 - 27 days - 7 - 27 jours	-	-	-	...	...	...
28 days - 11 months - 28 jours - 11 mois	1	1	-	...	...	...
28 days - less than 2 months - 28 jours - moins de 2 mois	-	-	-	...	...	...
2 - 11 months - 2 - 11 mois	1	1	-	...	...	...
Cayman Islands - Îles Caïmanes						
2007 (C)						
Total	5	4	1	...	...	...
Less than 1 day - Moins de 1 jour	3	2	1	...	...	...
1 - 6 days - 1 - 6 jours	2	2	-	...	...	...
7 - 27 days - 7 - 27 jours	-	-	-	...	...	...
28 days - 11 months - 28 jours - 11 mois	-	-	-	...	...	...
Costa Rica						
2016* (C)						
Total	555	307	248	7.9	8.7	7.2
Less than 1 day - Moins de 1 jour	160	87	73	2.3	2.5	2.1
1 - 6 days - 1 - 6 jours	173	98	75	2.5	2.8	2.2
7 - 27 days - 7 - 27 jours	98	59	39	1.4	1.7	1.1
7 - 13 days - 7 - 13 jours	53	29	24	0.8	♦0.8	♦0.7
14 - 20 days - 14 - 20 jours	18	12	6	♦0.3	♦0.3	♦0.2
21 - 27 days - 21 - 27 jours	27	18	9	♦0.4	♦0.5	♦0.3
28 days - 11 months - 28 jours - 11 mois	124	63	61	1.8	1.8	1.8
28 days - less than 2 months - 28 jours - moins de 2 mois	33	14	19	0.5	♦0.4	♦0.5
2 months - 2 mois	20	13	7	♦0.3	♦0.4	♦0.2
3 months - 3 mois	11	3	8	♦0.2	♦0.1	♦0.2
4 months - 4 mois	13	7	6	♦0.2	♦0.2	♦0.2
5 months - 5 mois	10	5	5	♦0.1	♦0.1	♦0.1
6 months - 6 mois	7	1	6	♦0.1	-	♦0.2
7 months - 7 mois	8	5	3	♦0.1	♦0.1	♦0.1
8 months - 8 mois	5	2	3	♦0.1	♦0.1	♦0.1
9 months - 9 mois	6	3	3	♦0.1	♦0.1	♦0.1
10 months - 10 mois	5	4	1	♦0.1	♦0.1	-
11 months - 11 mois	6	6	-	♦0.1	♦0.2	-
Cuba						
2015 (C)						
Total	535	299	236	4.3	4.6	3.9
Less than 1 day - Moins de 1 jour	71	39	32	0.6	0.6	0.5
1 - 6 days - 1 - 6 jours	141	78	63	1.1	1.2	1.0

16. Infant deaths and infant mortality rates by age and sex: latest available year, 2007 - 2016
Décès d'enfants de moins d'un an et taux de mortalité infantile selon l'âge et le sexe : dernière année disponible, 2007 - 2016 (continued - suite)

Continent, country or area, year, code[a] and age / Continent, pays ou zone, année, code[a] et âge	Number - Nombre			Rate - Taux		
	Both sexes Les deux sexes	Male Masculin	Female Féminin	Both sexes Les deux sexes	Male Masculin	Female Féminin
AMERICA, NORTH - AMÉRIQUE DU NORD						
Cuba						
2015 (C)						
7 - 27 days - 7 - 27 jours	93	53	40	0.7	0.8	0.7
7 - 13 days - 7 - 13 jours	37	24	13	0.3	♦0.4	♦0.2
14 - 20 days - 14 - 20 jours	27	13	14	♦0.2	♦0.2	♦0.2
21 - 27 days - 21 - 27 jours	29	16	13	♦0.2	♦0.2	♦0.2
28 days - 11 months - 28 jours - 11 mois	230	129	101	1.8	2.0	1.7
28 days - less than 2 months - 28 jours - moins de 2 mois	66	31	35	0.5	0.5	0.6
2 months - 2 mois	46	30	16	0.4	0.5	♦0.3
3 months - 3 mois	27	18	9	♦0.2	♦0.3	♦0.1
4 months - 4 mois	15	9	6	♦0.1	♦0.1	♦0.1
5 months - 5 mois	27	13	14	♦0.2	♦0.2	♦0.2
6 months - 6 mois	18	11	7	♦0.1	♦0.2	♦0.1
7 months - 7 mois	10	5	5	♦0.1	♦0.1	♦0.1
8 months - 8 mois	6	1	5	-	-	♦0.1
9 months - 9 mois	8	6	2	♦0.1	♦0.1	-
10 months - 10 mois	2	2	-	-	-	-
11 months - 11 mois	5	3	2	-	-	-
Curaçao						
2016 (C)						
Total	20	11	9	...	...	...
Less than 1 day - Moins de 1 jour	7	3	4	...	...	...
1 - 6 days - 1 - 6 jours	3	1	2	...	...	...
7 - 27 days - 7 - 27 jours	7	5	2	...	...	...
7 - 13 days - 7 - 13 jours	6	4	2	...	...	...
14 - 20 days - 14 - 20 jours	1	1	-	...	...	...
21 - 27 days - 21 - 27 jours	-	-	-	...	...	...
28 days - 11 months - 28 jours - 11 mois	39	20	19	...	...	...
28 days - less than 2 months - 28 jours - moins de 2 mois	1	-	1	...	...	...
2 months - 2 mois	18	9	9	...	...	...
3 months - 3 mois	20	11	9	...	...	...
4 months - 4 mois	-	-	-	...	...	...
5 months - 5 mois	-	-	-	...	...	...
6 months - 6 mois	-	-	-	...	...	...
7 months - 7 mois	-	-	-	...	...	...
8 months - 8 mois	-	-	-	...	...	...
9 months - 9 mois	-	-	-	...	...	...
10 months - 10 mois	-	-	-	...	...	...
11 months - 11 mois	-	-	-	...	...	...
Dominican Republic - République dominicaine						
2015 (U)						
Total	906	534[3]	349[3]	...	...	...
Less than 1 day - Moins de 1 jour	170	99[3]	63[3]	...	...	...
1 - 6 days - 1 - 6 jours	250	163[3]	78[3]	...	...	...
7 - 27 days - 7 - 27 jours	157	94[3]	62[3]	...	...	...
7 - 13 days - 7 - 13 jours	93	52[3]	41[3]	...	...	...
14 - 20 days - 14 - 20 jours	42	29[3]	12[3]	...	...	...
21 - 27 days - 21 - 27 jours	22	13[3]	9[3]	...	...	...
28 days - 11 months - 28 jours - 11 mois	322	174[3]	144[3]	...	...	...
28 days - less than 2 months - 28 jours - moins de 2 mois	84	45[3]	35[3]	...	...	...
2 months - 2 mois	46	24[3]	22[3]	...	...	...
3 months - 3 mois	36	22[3]	14[3]	...	...	...
4 months - 4 mois	24	18[3]	6[3]	...	...	...
5 months - 5 mois	21	9[3]	12[3]	...	...	...
6 months - 6 mois	31	15[3]	16[3]	...	...	...
7 months - 7 mois	21	11[3]	10[3]	...	...	...
8 months - 8 mois	19	13[3]	6[3]	...	...	...
9 months - 9 mois	17	5[3]	12[3]	...	...	...
10 months - 10 mois	13	7[3]	6[3]	...	...	...
11 months - 11 mois	10	5[3]	5[3]	...	...	...
Unknown - Inconnu	7	4[3]	2[3]	...	...	...
El Salvador[4]						
2014 (C)						
Total	876	491	385	8.0	8.8	7.3
Less than 1 day - Moins de 1 jour	158	90	68	1.5	1.6	1.3
1 - 6 days - 1 - 6 jours	163	91	72	1.5	1.6	1.4

Continent, country or area, year, code[a] and age / Continent, pays ou zone, année, code[a] et âge	Number - Nombre			Rate - Taux		
	Both sexes Les deux sexes	Male Masculin	Female Féminin	Both sexes Les deux sexes	Male Masculin	Female Féminin
AMERICA, NORTH - AMÉRIQUE DU NORD						
El Salvador[4]						
2014 (C)						
7 - 27 days - 7 - 27 jours	141	78	63	1.3	1.4	1.2
7 - 13 days - 7 - 13 jours	65	32	33	0.6	0.6	0.6
14 - 20 days - 14 - 20 jours	42	24	18	0.4	♦0.4	♦0.3
21 - 27 days - 21 - 27 jours	34	22	12	0.3	♦0.4	♦0.2
28 days - 11 months - 28 jours - 11 mois	414	232	182	3.8	4.1	3.4
28 days - less than 2 months - 28 jours - moins de 2 mois	97	49	48	0.9	0.9	0.9
2 months - 2 mois	56	33	23	0.5	0.6	♦0.4
3 months - 3 mois	44	28	16	0.4	♦0.5	♦0.3
4 months - 4 mois	35	23	12	0.3	♦0.4	♦0.2
5 months - 5 mois	26	16	10	♦0.2	♦0.3	♦0.2
6 months - 6 mois	38	27	11	0.3	♦0.5	♦0.2
7 months - 7 mois	28	13	15	♦0.3	♦0.2	♦0.3
8 months - 8 mois	20	10	10	♦0.2	♦0.2	♦0.2
9 months - 9 mois	21	9	12	♦0.2	♦0.2	♦0.2
10 months - 10 mois	21	9	12	♦0.2	♦0.2	♦0.2
11 months - 11 mois	28	15	13	♦0.3	♦0.3	♦0.2
Guatemala						
2011 (C)						
Total	7 413	4 202	3 211	19.8	22.1	17.5
Less than 1 day - Moins de 1 jour	123	76	47	0.3	0.4	0.3
1 - 6 days - 1 - 6 jours	1 481	860	621	4.0	4.5	3.4
7 - 27 days - 7 - 27 jours	1 684	938	746	4.5	4.9	4.1
7 - 13 days - 7 - 13 jours	813	451	362	2.2	2.4	2.0
14 - 20 days - 14 - 20 jours	521	288	233	1.4	1.5	1.3
21 - 27 days - 21 - 27 jours	350	199	151	0.9	1.0	0.8
28 days - 11 months - 28 jours - 11 mois	4 125	2 328	1 797	11.0	12.3	9.8
28 days - less than 2 months - 28 jours - moins de 2 mois	1 198	694	504	3.2	3.7	2.7
2 months - 2 mois	685	396	289	1.8	2.1	1.6
3 months - 3 mois	475	283	192	1.3	1.5	1.0
4 months - 4 mois	345	196	149	0.9	1.0	0.8
5 months - 5 mois	290	159	131	0.8	0.8	0.7
6 months - 6 mois	265	146	119	0.7	0.8	0.6
7 months - 7 mois	245	129	116	0.7	0.7	0.6
8 months - 8 mois	200	102	98	0.5	0.5	0.5
9 months - 9 mois	207	115	92	0.6	0.6	0.5
10 months - 10 mois	209	107	102	0.6	0.6	0.6
11 months - 11 mois	6	1	5	-	-	-
Martinique[5]						
2007 (C)						
Total	43	26	17	...	...	...
Less than 1 day - Moins de 1 jour	18	10	8	...	...	...
1 - 6 days - 1 - 6 jours	8	7	1	...	...	...
7 - 27 days - 7 - 27 jours	9	3	6	...	...	...
7 - 13 days - 7 - 13 jours	5	1	4	...	...	...
14 - 20 days - 14 - 20 jours	3	2	1	...	...	...
21 - 27 days - 21 - 27 jours	1	-	1	...	...	...
28 days - 11 months - 28 jours - 11 mois	8	6	2	...	...	...
28 days - less than 2 months - 28 jours - moins de 2 mois	-	-	-	...	...	...
2 months - 2 mois	5	3	2	...	...	...
3 months - 3 mois	-	-	-	...	...	...
4 months - 4 mois	1	1		...	...	...
5 months - 5 mois	-	-	-	...	...	...
6 months - 6 mois	-	-	-	...	...	...
7 months - 7 mois	1	1	-	...	...	...
8 months - 8 mois	-	-	-	...	...	...
9 - 11 months - 9 - 11 mois	1	1	-	...	...	...
Mexico - Mexique[6]						
2015 (+C)						
Total	26 045	14 482[3]	11 438[3]	11.1	...	...
Less than 1 day - Moins de 1 jour	5 034	2 732[3]	2 238[3]	2.1	...	...
1 - 6 days - 1 - 6 jours	6 223	3 590[3]	2 606[3]	2.6	...	...
7 - 27 days - 7 - 27 jours	5 136	2 831[3]	2 284[3]	2.2	...	...
7 - 13 days - 7 - 13 jours	2 805	1 528[3]	1 266[3]	1.2	...	...
14 - 20 days - 14 - 20 jours	1 402	787[3]	609[3]	0.6	...	...
21 - 27 days - 21 - 27 jours	929	516[3]	409[3]	0.4	...	...

16. Infant deaths and infant mortality rates by age and sex: latest available year, 2007 - 2016
Décès d'enfants de moins d'un an et taux de mortalité infantile selon l'âge et le sexe : dernière année disponible, 2007 - 2016 (continued - suite)

Continent, country or area, year, code[a] and age Continent, pays ou zone, année, code[a] et âge	Number - Nombre			Rate - Taux		
	Both sexes Les deux sexes	Male Masculin	Female Féminin	Both sexes Les deux sexes	Male Masculin	Female Féminin

AMERICA, NORTH - AMÉRIQUE DU NORD

Mexico - Mexique[6]
2015 (+C)

28 days - 11 months - 28 jours - 11 mois.............	9 650	5 328[3]	4 309[3]	4.1	...	...
28 days - less than 2 months - 28 jours - moins de 2 mois	2 893	1 618[3]	1 270[3]	1.2	...	...
2 months - 2 mois.................	1 707	978[3]	724[3]	0.7	...	...
3 months - 3 mois..................	1 163	657[3]	504[3]	0.5	...	...
4 months - 4 mois..................	868	456[3]	412[3]	0.4	...	...
5 months - 5 mois..................	705	374[3]	330[3]	0.3	...	...
6 months - 6 mois..................	562	320[3]	242[3]	0.2	...	...
7 months - 7 mois..................	460	254[3]	206[3]	0.2	...	...
8 months - 8 mois..................	343	180[3]	163[3]	0.1	...	...
9 months - 9 mois..................	347	187[3]	160[3]	0.1	...	...
10 months - 10 mois................	323	170[3]	153[3]	0.1	...	...
11 months - 11 mois................	279	134[3]	145[3]	0.1	...	...

Montserrat
2016 (+C)

Total....................	-	-	-	...	...	...
Less than 1 day - Moins de 1 jour	-	-	-	...	...	...
1 - 6 days - 1 - 6 jours	-	-	-	...	...	...
7 - 27 days - 7 - 27 jours	-	-	-	...	...	...
28 days - 11 months - 28 jours - 11 mois................	-	-	-	...	...	...

Nicaragua
2008 (+U)

Total....................	1 932	1 123	809	...	...	...
Less than 1 day - Moins de 1 jour	386	219	167	...	...	...
1 - 6 days - 1 - 6 jours	664	418	246	...	...	...
7 - 27 days - 7 - 27 jours	277	151	126	...	...	...
7 - 13 days - 7 - 13 jours	156	89	67	...	...	...
14 - 20 days - 14 - 20 jours	74	41	33	...	...	...
21 - 27 days - 21 - 27 jours	47	21	26	...	...	...
28 days - 11 months - 28 jours - 11 mois................	591	326	265	...	...	...
28 days - less than 2 months - 28 jours - moins de 2 mois	169	86	83	...	...	...
2 months - 2 mois.................	116	74	42	...	...	...
3 months - 3 mois..................	66	38	28	...	...	...
4 months - 4 mois..................	49	29	20	...	...	...
5 months - 5 mois..................	45	22	23	...	...	...
6 months - 6 mois..................	27	13	14	...	...	...
7 months - 7 mois..................	36	18	18	...	...	...
8 months - 8 mois..................	27	17	10	...	...	...
9 months - 9 mois..................	18	8	10	...	...	...
10 months - 10 mois................	21	9	12	...	...	...
11 months - 11 mois................	17	12	5	...	...	...

Panama
2015* (U)

Total....................	952	550	402	...	...	...
Less than 1 day - Moins de 1 jour	111	62	49	...	...	...
1 - 6 days - 1 - 6 jours	293	165	128	...	...	...
7 - 27 days - 7 - 27 jours	154	99	55	...	...	...
7 - 13 days - 7 - 13 jours	83	52	31	...	...	...
14 - 20 days - 14 - 20 jours	39	27	12	...	...	...
21 - 27 days - 21 - 27 jours	32	20	12	...	...	...
28 days - 11 months - 28 jours - 11 mois................	394	224	170	...	...	...
28 days - less than 2 months - 28 jours - moins de 2 mois	113	72	41	...	...	...
2 months - 2 mois.................	72	38	34	...	...	...
3 months - 3 mois..................	46	21	25	...	...	...
4 months - 4 mois..................	34	17	17	...	...	...
5 months - 5 mois..................	23	11	12	...	...	...
6 months - 6 mois..................	18	11	7	...	...	...
7 months - 7 mois..................	19	12	7	...	...	...
8 months - 8 mois..................	22	11	11	...	...	...
9 months - 9 mois..................	16	9	7	...	...	...
10 months - 10 mois................	18	14	4	...	...	...
11 months - 11 mois................	13	8	5	...	...	...

Puerto Rico - Porto Rico
2016 (C)

Total....................	221	122	99	7.8	8.3	7.2
Less than 1 day - Moins de 1 jour	39	23	16	1.4	◆1.6	◆1.2

Continent, country or area, year, code[a] and age / Continent, pays ou zone, année, code[a] et âge	Number - Nombre			Rate - Taux		
	Both sexes Les deux sexes	Male Masculin	Female Féminin	Both sexes Les deux sexes	Male Masculin	Female Féminin
AMERICA, NORTH - AMÉRIQUE DU NORD						
Puerto Rico - Porto Rico						
2016 (C)						
1 - 6 days - 1 - 6 jours	61	30	31	2.2	2.0	2.3
7 - 27 days - 7 - 27 jours	49	27	22	1.7	♦1.8	♦1.6
7 - 13 days - 7 - 13 jours	23	14	9	♦0.8	♦1.0	♦0.7
14 - 20 days - 14 - 20 jours	14	6	8	♦0.5	♦0.4	♦0.6
21 - 27 days - 21 - 27 jours	12	7	5	♦0.4	♦0.5	♦0.4
28 days - 11 months - 28 jours - 11 mois	72	42	30	2.5	2.9	2.2
28 days - less than 2 months - 28 jours - moins de 2 mois	22	11	11	♦0.8	♦0.8	♦0.8
2 months - 2 mois	11	6	5	♦0.4	♦0.4	♦0.4
3 months - 3 mois	12	10	2	♦0.4	♦0.7	♦0.1
4 months - 4 mois	5	3	2	♦0.2	♦0.2	♦0.1
5 months - 5 mois	5	4	1	♦0.2	♦0.3	♦0.1
6 months - 6 mois	5	3	2	♦0.2	♦0.2	♦0.1
7 months - 7 mois	3	2	1	♦0.1	♦0.1	♦0.1
8 months - 8 mois	2	1	1	♦0.1	♦0.1	♦0.1
9 months - 9 mois	3	1	2	♦0.1	♦0.1	♦0.1
10 months - 10 mois	2	1	1	♦0.1	♦0.1	♦0.1
11 months - 11 mois	2	-	2	♦0.1	-	♦0.1
Saint Vincent and the Grenadines - Saint-Vincent-et-les Grenadines						
2014 (C)						
Total	29	19	10	...	...	...
Less than 1 day - Moins de 1 jour	3	3	-	...	...	...
1 - 6 days - 1 - 6 jours	8	6	2	...	...	...
7 - 27 days - 7 - 27 jours	9	4	5	...	...	...
7 - 13 days - 7 - 13 jours	6	4	2	...	...	...
14 - 20 days - 14 - 20 jours	3	-	3	...	...	...
21 - 27 days - 21 - 27 jours	-	-	-	...	...	...
28 days - 11 months - 28 jours - 11 mois	9	6	3	...	...	...
28 days - less than 2 months - 28 jours - moins de 2 mois	4	2	2	...	...	...
2 months - 2 mois	1	-	1	...	...	...
3 months - 3 mois	1	1	-	...	...	...
4 months - 4 mois	2	2	-	...	...	...
5 months - 5 mois	-	-	-	...	...	...
6 months - 6 mois	-	-	-	...	...	...
7 months - 7 mois	1	1	-	...	...	...
8 months - 8 mois	-	-	-	...	...	...
9 months - 9 mois	-	-	-	...	...	...
10 months - 10 mois	-	-	-	...	...	...
11 months - 11 mois	-	-	-	...	...	...
Trinidad and Tobago - Trinité-et-Tobago						
2010 (C)						
Total	256	135	121	13.4	13.7	13.1
Less than 1 day - Moins de 1 jour	42	23	19	2.2	♦2.3	♦2.1
1 - 6 days - 1 - 6 jours	70	36	34	3.7	3.7	3.7
7 - 27 days - 7 - 27 jours	69	35	34	3.6	3.6	3.7
7 - 13 days - 7 - 13 jours	25	14	11	♦1.3	♦1.4	♦1.2
14 - 20 days - 14 - 20 jours	22	12	10	♦1.2	♦1.2	♦1.1
21 - 27 days - 21 - 27 jours	22	9	13	♦1.2	♦0.9	♦1.4
28 days - 11 months - 28 jours - 11 mois	75	41	34	3.9	4.2	3.7
28 days - less than 2 months - 28 jours - moins de 2 mois	29	18	11	♦1.5	♦1.8	♦1.2
2 - 11 months - 2 - 11 mois	46	23	23	2.4	♦2.3	♦2.5
United States of America - États-Unis d'Amérique						
2015 (C)						
Total	23 455	13 008	10 447	5.9	6.4	5.4
Less than 1 day - Moins de 1 jour	9 479	5 226	4 253	2.4	2.6	2.2
1 - 6 days - 1 - 6 jours	3 088	1 733	1 355	0.8	0.9	0.7
7 - 27 days - 7 - 27 jours	3 085	1 632	1 453	0.8	0.8	0.7
7 - 13 days - 7 - 13 jours	1 442	765	677	0.4	0.4	0.3
14 - 20 days - 14 - 20 jours	950	500	450	0.2	0.2	0.2
21 - 27 days - 21 - 27 jours	693	367	326	0.2	0.2	0.2
28 days - 11 months - 28 jours - 11 mois	7 803	4 417	3 386	2.0	2.2	1.7
28 days - less than 2 months - 28 jours - moins de 2 mois	2 050	1 105	945	0.5	0.5	0.5
2 months - 2 mois	1 462	838	624	0.4	0.4	0.3
3 months - 3 mois	1 144	681	463	0.3	0.3	0.2
4 months - 4 mois	826	489	337	0.2	0.2	0.2
5 months - 5 mois	623	371	252	0.2	0.2	0.1
6 months - 6 mois	460	252	208	0.1	0.1	0.1

16. Infant deaths and infant mortality rates by age and sex: latest available year, 2007 - 2016
Décès d'enfants de moins d'un an et taux de mortalité infantile selon l'âge et le sexe : dernière année disponible, 2007 - 2016 (continued - suite)

Continent, country or area, year, code[a] and age / Continent, pays ou zone, année, code[a] et âge	Number - Nombre			Rate - Taux		
	Both sexes Les deux sexes	Male Masculin	Female Féminin	Both sexes Les deux sexes	Male Masculin	Female Féminin
AMERICA, NORTH - AMÉRIQUE DU NORD						
United States of America - États-Unis d'Amérique						
2015 (C)						
7 months - 7 mois	344	210	134	0.1	0.1	0.1
8 months - 8 mois	286	159	127	0.1	0.1	0.1
9 months - 9 mois	239	123	116	0.1	0.1	0.1
10 months - 10 mois	184	98	86	-	-	-
11 months - 11 mois	185	91	94	-	-	-
AMERICA, SOUTH - AMÉRIQUE DU SUD						
Brazil - Brésil[7]						
2015 (+C)						
Total	31 238	17 324[3]	13 836[3]	10.6	11.5	9.6
Less than 1 day - Moins de 1 jour	6 979	3 822[3]	3 107[3]	2.4	2.5	2.2
1 - 6 days - 1 - 6 jours	9 243	5 379[3]	3 845[3]	3.1	3.6	2.7
7 - 27 days - 7 - 27 jours	5 453	2 901[3]	2 547[3]	1.8	1.9	1.8
7 - 13 days - 7 - 13 jours	2 907	1 546[3]	1 358[3]	1.0	1.0	0.9
14 - 20 days - 14 - 20 jours	1 512	795[3]	715[3]	0.5	0.5	0.5
21 - 27 days - 21 - 27 jours	1 034	560[3]	474[3]	0.4	0.4	0.3
28 days - 11 months - 28 jours - 11 mois	9 563	5 222[3]	4 337[3]	3.2	3.5	3.0
28 days - less than 2 months - 28 jours - moins de 2 mois	3 004	1 709[3]	1 294[3]	1.0	1.1	0.9
2 months - 2 mois	1 626	879[3]	746[3]	0.6	0.6	0.5
3 months - 3 mois	1 058	556[3]	501[3]	0.4	0.4	0.3
4 months - 4 mois	800	435[3]	365[3]	0.3	0.3	0.3
5 months - 5 mois	662	362[3]	300[3]	0.2	0.2	0.2
6 months - 6 mois	561	325[3]	236[3]	0.2	0.2	0.2
7 months - 7 mois	465	221[3]	244[3]	0.2	0.1	0.2
8 months - 8 mois	410	206[3]	204[3]	0.1	0.1	0.1
9 months - 9 mois	352	201[3]	151[3]	0.1	0.1	0.1
10 months - 10 mois	304	173[3]	131[3]	0.1	0.1	0.1
11 months - 11 mois	321	155[3]	165[3]	0.1	0.1	0.1
Chile - Chili						
2014 (C)						
Total	1 825	968[3]	840[3]	7.3	7.6	6.8
Less than 1 day - Moins de 1 jour	730	413[3]	301[3]	2.9	3.2	2.5
1 - 6 days - 1 - 6 jours	315	168[3]	146[3]	1.3	1.3	1.2
7 - 27 days - 7 - 27 jours	266	130[3]	136[3]	1.1	1.0	1.1
7 - 13 days - 7 - 13 jours	141	72[3]	69[3]	0.6	0.6	0.6
14 - 20 days - 14 - 20 jours	64	24[3]	40[3]	0.3	♦0.2	0.3
21 - 27 days - 21 - 27 jours	61	34[3]	27[3]	0.2	0.3	♦0.2
28 days - 11 months - 28 jours - 11 mois	514	257	257	2.0	2.0	2.1
28 days - less than 2 months - 28 jours - moins de 2 mois	179	94[3]	85[3]	0.7	0.7	0.7
2 months - 2 mois	83	43[3]	40[3]	0.3	0.3	0.3
3 months - 3 mois	50	24[3]	26[3]	0.2	♦0.2	♦0.2
4 months - 4 mois	46	22[3]	24[3]	0.2	♦0.2	♦0.2
5 months - 5 mois	42	20[3]	22[3]	0.2	♦0.2	♦0.2
6 months - 6 mois	35	16[3]	19[3]	0.1	♦0.1	♦0.2
7 months - 7 mois	20	10[3]	10[3]	♦0.1	♦0.1	♦0.1
8 months - 8 mois	14	5[3]	9[3]	♦0.1	-	♦0.1
9 months - 9 mois	11	5[3]	6[3]	-	-	-
10 months - 10 mois	19	9[3]	10[3]	♦0.1	♦0.1	♦0.1
11 months - 11 mois	15	9[3]	6[3]	♦0.1	♦0.1	-
Colombia - Colombie[8]						
2014 (U)						
Total	7 589	4 284	3 305	...	...	...
Less than 1 day - Moins de 1 jour	1 565	871	694	...	...	...
1 - 6 days - 1 - 6 jours	1 725	1 023	702	...	...	...
7 - 27 days - 7 - 27 jours	1 510	866	644	...	...	...
7 - 13 days - 7 - 13 jours	805	464	341	...	...	...
14 - 20 days - 14 - 20 jours	408	222	186	...	...	...
21 - 27 days - 21 - 27 jours	297	180	117	...	...	...
28 days - 11 months - 28 jours - 11 mois	2 787	1 523	1 264	...	...	...
28 days - less than 2 months - 28 jours - moins de 2 mois	726	408	318	...	...	...
2 months - 2 mois	487	279	208	...	...	...

16. Infant deaths and infant mortality rates by age and sex: latest available year, 2007 - 2016
Décès d'enfants de moins d'un an et taux de mortalité infantile selon l'âge et le sexe : dernière année disponible, 2007 - 2016 (continued - suite)

Continent, country or area, year, code[a] and age / Continent, pays ou zone, année, code[a] et âge	Number - Nombre			Rate - Taux		
	Both sexes Les deux sexes	Male Masculin	Female Féminin	Both sexes Les deux sexes	Male Masculin	Female Féminin
AMERICA, SOUTH - AMÉRIQUE DU SUD						
Colombia - Colombie[8]						
2014 (U)						
3 months - 3 mois	342	189	153	...	...	...
4 months - 4 mois	254	121	133	...	...	...
5 months - 5 mois	218	128	90	...	...	...
6 months - 6 mois	185	98	87	...	...	...
7 months - 7 mois	165	89	76	...	...	...
8 months - 8 mois	127	67	60	...	...	...
9 months - 9 mois	104	55	49	...	...	...
10 months - 10 mois	72	34	38	...	...	...
11 months - 11 mois	107	55	52	...	...	...
Unknown - Inconnu	2	1	1	...	...	...
Ecuador - Équateur[9]						
2015 (U)						
Total	2 979	1 664	1 315	...	...	...
Less than 1 day - Moins de 1 jour	411	225	186	...	...	...
1 - 6 days - 1 - 6 jours	806	464	342	...	...	...
7 - 27 days - 7 - 27 jours	533	297	236	...	...	...
7 - 13 days - 7 - 13 jours	255	136	119	...	...	...
14 - 20 days - 14 - 20 jours	149	85	64	...	...	...
21 - 27 days - 21 - 27 jours	129	76	53	...	...	...
28 days - 11 months - 28 jours - 11 mois	1 229	678	551	...	...	...
28 days - less than 2 months - 28 jours - moins de 2 mois	389	213	176	...	...	...
2 months - 2 mois	169	104	65	...	...	...
3 months - 3 mois	143	76	67	...	...	...
4 months - 4 mois	82	44	38	...	...	...
5 months - 5 mois	94	52	42	...	...	...
6 months - 6 mois	92	46	46	...	...	...
7 months - 7 mois	70	37	33	...	...	...
8 months - 8 mois	59	36	23	...	...	...
9 months - 9 mois	37	23	14	...	...	...
10 months - 10 mois	46	21	25	...	...	...
11 months - 11 mois	48	26	22	...	...	...
French Guiana - Guyane française						
2007 (C)						
Total	73	39	34	...	...	...
Less than 1 day - Moins de 1 jour	18	10	8	...	...	...
1 - 6 days - 1 - 6 jours	15	5	10	...	...	...
7 - 27 days - 7 - 27 jours	17	12	5	...	...	...
7 - 13 days - 7 - 13 jours	9	5	4	...	...	...
14 - 20 days - 14 - 20 jours	3	3	-	...	...	...
21 - 27 days - 21 - 27 jours	5	4	1	...	...	...
28 days - 11 months - 28 jours - 11 mois	23	12	11	...	...	...
28 days - less than 2 months - 28 jours - moins de 2 mois	1	-	1	...	...	...
2 months - 2 mois	7	4	3	...	...	...
3 months - 3 mois	4	1	3	...	...	...
4 months - 4 mois	2	1	1	...	...	...
5 months - 5 mois	2	2	-	...	...	...
6 months - 6 mois	2	1	1	...	...	...
7 months - 7 mois	1	1	-	...	...	...
8 months - 8 mois	1	1	-	...	...	...
9 months - 9 mois	2	1	1	...	...	...
10 months - 10 mois	-	-	-	...	...	...
11 months - 11 mois	1	-	1	...	...	...
Peru - Pérou[10]						
2015 (+U)						
Total	3 852	2 129	1 723	...	...	...
Less than 1 day - Moins de 1 jour	620	364	256	...	...	...
1 - 6 days - 1 - 6 jours	977	571	406	...	...	...
7 - 27 days - 7 - 27 jours	601	340	261	...	...	...
7 - 13 days - 7 - 13 jours	294	166	128	...	...	...
14 - 20 days - 14 - 20 jours	162	87	75	...	...	...
21 - 27 days - 21 - 27 jours	145	87	58	...	...	...
28 days - 11 months - 28 jours - 11 mois	1 654	854	800	...	...	...
28 days - less than 2 months - 28 jours - moins de 2 mois	450	253	197	...	...	...
2 months - 2 mois	298	129	169	...	...	...
3 months - 3 mois	182	92	90	...	...	...
4 months - 4 mois	152	87	65	...	...	...

16. Infant deaths and infant mortality rates by age and sex: latest available year, 2007 - 2016
Décès d'enfants de moins d'un an et taux de mortalité infantile selon l'âge et le sexe : dernière année disponible, 2007 - 2016 (continued - suite)

Continent, country or area, year, code[a] and age / Continent, pays ou zone, année, code[a] et âge	Number - Nombre			Rate - Taux		
	Both sexes Les deux sexes	Male Masculin	Female Féminin	Both sexes Les deux sexes	Male Masculin	Female Féminin
AMERICA, SOUTH - AMÉRIQUE DU SUD						
Peru - Pérou[10]						
2015 (+U)						
5 months - 5 mois	108	53	55	...	...	...
6 months - 6 mois	114	65	49	...	...	...
7 months - 7 mois	58	22	36	...	...	...
8 months - 8 mois	90	44	46	...	...	...
9 months - 9 mois	71	37	34	...	...	...
10 months - 10 mois	64	35	29	...	...	...
11 months - 11 mois	67	37	30	...	...	...
Uruguay						
2015 (C)						
Total	367	218[3]	148[3]	7.5	8.7	6.2
Less than 7 days - Moins de 7 jours	170	101[3]	68[3]	3.5	4.0	2.9
7 - 27 days - 7 - 27 jours	72	39[3]	33[3]	1.5	1.6	1.4
28 days - 11 months - 28 jours - 11 mois	125	78[3]	47[3]	2.6	3.1	2.0
Venezuela (Bolivarian Republic of) - Venezuela (République bolivarienne du)						
2007 (C)						
Total	6 340	3 715	2 625	10.3	11.7	8.8
Less than 28 days - Moins de 28 jours	4 379	2 599	1 780	7.1	8.2	6.0
28 days - 11 months - 28 jours - 11 mois	1 961	1 116	845	3.2	3.5	2.8
28 days - less than 2 months - 28 jours - moins de 2 mois	455	258	197	0.7	0.8	0.7
2 months - 2 mois	325	182	143	0.5	0.6	0.5
3 months - 3 mois	231	136	95	0.4	0.4	0.3
4 months - 4 mois	190	119	71	0.3	0.4	0.2
5 months - 5 mois	157	87	70	0.3	0.3	0.2
6 months - 6 mois	153	89	64	0.2	0.3	0.2
7 months - 7 mois	104	57	47	0.2	0.2	0.2
8 months - 8 mois	122	63	59	0.2	0.2	0.2
9 months - 9 mois	77	39	38	0.1	0.1	0.1
10 months - 10 mois	81	50	31	0.1	0.2	0.1
11 months - 11 mois	66	36	30	0.1	0.1	0.1
ASIA - ASIE						
Armenia - Arménie[11]						
2015 (C)						
Total	370	209	161	8.9	9.4	8.2
Less than 1 day - Moins de 1 jour	50	27	23	1.2	◆1.2	◆1.2
1 - 6 days - 1 - 6 jours	145	86	59	3.5	3.9	3.0
7 - 27 days - 7 - 27 jours	67	31	36	1.6	1.4	1.8
7 - 13 days - 7 - 13 jours	38	16	22	0.9	◆0.7	◆1.1
14 - 20 days - 14 - 20 jours	17	11	6	◆0.4	◆0.5	◆0.3
21 - 27 days - 21 - 27 jours	12	4	8	◆0.3	◆0.2	◆0.4
28 days - 11 months - 28 jours - 11 mois	108	65	43	2.6	2.9	2.2
28 days - less than 2 months - 28 jours - moins de 2 mois	34	21	13	0.8	◆0.9	◆0.7
2 months - 2 mois	18	12	6	◆0.4	◆0.5	◆0.3
3 months - 3 mois	10	6	4	◆0.2	◆0.3	◆0.2
4 months - 4 mois	7	5	2	◆0.2	◆0.2	◆0.1
5 months - 5 mois	14	9	5	◆0.3	◆0.4	◆0.3
6 months - 6 mois	6	3	3	◆0.1	◆0.1	◆0.2
7 months - 7 mois	7	4	3	◆0.2	◆0.2	◆0.2
8 months - 8 mois	5	2	3	◆0.1	◆0.1	◆0.2
9 months - 9 mois	4	2	2	◆0.1	◆0.1	◆0.1
10 months - 10 mois	1	-	1	-	-	◆0.1
11 months - 11 mois	2	1	1	-	-	◆0.1
Azerbaijan - Azerbaïdjan[11]						
2015 (+C)						
Total	2 033	1 220	813	12.2	13.8	10.5
Less than 1 day - Moins de 1 jour	395	254	141	2.4	2.9	1.8
1 - 6 days - 1 - 6 jours	486	293	193	2.9	3.3	2.5
7 - 27 days - 7 - 27 jours	100	74	26	0.6	0.8	◆0.3
7 - 13 days - 7 - 13 jours	35	29	6	0.2	◆0.3	◆0.1
14 - 20 days - 14 - 20 jours	26	16	10	◆0.2	◆0.2	◆0.1
21 - 27 days - 21 - 27 jours	39	29	10	0.2	◆0.3	◆0.1

Continent, country or area, year, code[a] and age Continent, pays ou zone, année, code[a] et âge	Number - Nombre			Rate - Taux		
	Both sexes Les deux sexes	Male Masculin	Female Féminin	Both sexes Les deux sexes	Male Masculin	Female Féminin
ASIA - ASIE						
Azerbaijan - Azerbaïdjan[11]						
2015 (+C)						
28 days - 11 months - 28 jours - 11 mois	1 052	599	453	6.3	6.8	5.8
28 days - less than 2 months - 28 jours - moins de 2 mois	152	98	54	0.9	1.1	0.7
2 months - 2 mois	164	78	86	1.0	0.9	1.1
3 months - 3 mois	129	52	77	0.8	0.6	1.0
4 months - 4 mois	106	75	31	0.6	0.8	0.4
5 months - 5 mois	58	30	28	0.3	0.3	♦0.4
6 months - 6 mois	106	67	39	0.6	0.8	0.5
7 months - 7 mois	90	63	27	0.5	0.7	♦0.3
8 months - 8 mois	49	37	12	0.3	0.4	♦0.2
9 months - 9 mois	81	31	50	0.5	0.4	0.6
10 months - 10 mois	56	34	22	0.3	0.4	♦0.3
11 months - 11 mois	61	34	27	0.4	0.4	♦0.3
Bahrain - Bahreïn[12]						
2014 (C)						
Total	218	113	105	10.4	10.5	10.3
Less than 1 day - Moins de 1 jour	25	12	13	♦1.2	♦1.1	♦1.3
1 - 6 days - 1 - 6 jours	55	34	21	2.6	3.2	♦2.1
7 - 27 days - 7 - 27 jours	23	15	8	♦1.1	♦1.4	♦0.8
7 - 13 days - 7 - 13 jours	8	6	2	♦0.4	♦0.6	♦0.2
14 - 20 days - 14 - 20 jours	7	4	3	♦0.3	♦0.4	♦0.3
21 - 27 days - 21 - 27 jours	8	5	3	♦0.4	♦0.5	♦0.3
28 days - 11 months - 28 jours - 11 mois	80	36	44	3.8	3.3	4.3
28 days - less than 2 months - 28 jours - moins de 2 mois	34	11	23	1.6	♦1.0	♦2.3
2 months - 2 mois	12	5	7	♦0.6	♦0.5	♦0.7
3 months - 3 mois	6	4	2	♦0.3	♦0.4	♦0.2
4 months - 4 mois	8	5	3	♦0.4	♦0.5	♦0.3
5 months - 5 mois	8	5	3	♦0.4	♦0.5	♦0.3
6 months - 6 mois	5	1	4	♦0.2	♦0.1	♦0.4
7 months - 7 mois	3	2	1	♦0.1	♦0.2	♦0.1
8 months - 8 mois	1	1	-	-	♦0.1	-
9 months - 9 mois	1	1	-	-	♦0.1	-
10 months - 10 mois	1	-	1	-	-	♦0.1
11 months - 11 mois	1	1	-	-	♦0.1	-
Unknown - Inconnu	35	16	19	1.7	♦1.5	♦1.9
Bangladesh						
2010 (U)						
Total	104 591	55 178	49 413	...	...	...
1 - 6 days - 1 - 6 jours	56 108	30 276	25 832	...	...	...
7 - 27 days - 7 - 27 jours	17 576	9 234	8 342	...	...	...
7 - 13 days - 7 - 13 jours	8 488	4 491	3 997	...	...	...
14 - 20 days - 14 - 20 jours	4 845	2 546	2 299	...	...	...
21 - 27 days - 21 - 27 jours	4 243	2 197	2 046	...	...	...
28 days - 11 months - 28 jours - 11 mois	30 907	15 668	15 239	...	...	...
28 days - less than 2 months - 28 jours - moins de 2 mois	7 377	3 906	3 471	...	...	...
2 months - 2 mois	5 234	2 674	2 560	...	...	...
3 months - 3 mois	4 381	2 248	2 133	...	...	...
4 months - 4 mois	2 628	1 333	1 295	...	...	...
5 months - 5 mois	1 188	606	582	...	...	...
6 months - 6 mois	2 123	1 050	1 073	...	...	...
7 months - 7 mois	1 361	669	692	...	...	...
8 months - 8 mois	1 905	918	987	...	...	...
9 months - 9 mois	1 420	696	724	...	...	...
10 months - 10 mois	1 188	566	622	...	...	...
11 months - 11 mois	2 102	1 002	1 100	...	...	...
China, Hong Kong SAR - Chine, Hong Kong RAS						
2016 (C)						
Total	109	59	50	1.8	1.9	1.7
Less than 1 day - Moins de 1 jour	14	11	3	♦0.2	♦0.3	♦0.1
1 - 6 days - 1 - 6 jours	44	25	19	0.7	♦0.8	♦0.7
7 - 27 days - 7 - 27 jours	13	5	8	♦0.2	♦0.2	♦0.3
7 - 13 days - 7 - 13 jours	7	2	5	♦0.1	♦0.1	♦0.2
14 - 20 days - 14 - 20 jours	1	-	1	-	-	-
21 - 27 days - 21 - 27 jours	5	3	2	♦0.1	♦0.1	♦0.1
28 days - 11 months - 28 jours - 11 mois	38	18	20	0.6	♦0.6	♦0.7
28 days - less than 2 months - 28 jours - moins de 2 mois	13	7	6	♦0.2	♦0.2	♦0.2
2 months - 2 mois	7	5	2	♦0.1	♦0.2	♦0.1

458

16. Infant deaths and infant mortality rates by age and sex: latest available year, 2007 - 2016
Décès d'enfants de moins d'un an et taux de mortalité infantile selon l'âge et le sexe : dernière année disponible, 2007 - 2016 (continued - suite)

Continent, country or area, year, code[a] and age / Continent, pays ou zone, année, code[a] et âge	Number - Nombre			Rate - Taux		
	Both sexes Les deux sexes	Male Masculin	Female Féminin	Both sexes Les deux sexes	Male Masculin	Female Féminin
ASIA - ASIE						
China, Hong Kong SAR - Chine, Hong Kong RAS						
2016 (C)						
3 months - 3 mois	2	1	1	-	-	-
4 months - 4 mois	5	2	3	♦0.1	♦0.1	♦0.1
5 months - 5 mois	4	1	3	♦0.1	-	♦0.1
6 months - 6 mois	-	-	-			
7 months - 7 mois	2	1	1	-	-	-
8 months - 8 mois	1	-	1			
9 months - 9 mois	1	1	-			
10 months - 10 mois	2	-	2	-	-	♦0.1
11 months - 11 mois	1	-	1			
Unknown - Inconnu	-	-	-			
China, Macao SAR - Chine, Macao RAS						
2010 (C)						
Total	15	7	8	...	...	...
Less than 1 day - Moins de 1 jour	7	3	4	...	...	...
1 - 6 days - 1 - 6 jours	4	2	2	...	...	...
7 - 27 days - 7 - 27 jours	2	1	1	...	...	...
7 - 13 days - 7 - 13 jours	-	-	-			
14 - 20 days - 14 - 20 jours	1	-	1			
21 - 27 days - 21 - 27 jours	1	1	-			
28 days - 11 months - 28 jours - 11 mois	2	1	1			
28 days - less than 2 months - 28 jours - moins de 2 mois	1	-	1			
2 months - 2 mois	-	-	-			
3 months - 3 mois	-	-	-			
4 months - 4 mois	1	1	-			
5 months - 5 mois	-	-	-			
6 months - 6 mois	-	-	-			
7 months - 7 mois	-	-	-			
8 months - 8 mois	-	-	-			
9 months - 9 mois	-	-	-			
10 months - 10 mois	-	-	-			
11 months - 11 mois	-	-	-			
Cyprus - Chypre[13]						
2011 (C)						
Total	30	18	12	...	...	...
Less than 1 day - Moins de 1 jour	10	6	4	...	...	...
1 - 6 days - 1 - 6 jours	8	4	4	...	...	...
7 - 27 days - 7 - 27 jours	3	2	1	...	...	...
28 days - 11 months - 28 jours - 11 mois	9	6	3	...	...	...
Georgia - Géorgie[11]						
2016 (C)						
Total	507	292	215	9.0	10.1	7.8
Less than 1 day - Moins de 1 jour	88	53	35	1.6	1.8	1.3
1 - 6 days - 1 - 6 jours	143	84	59	2.5	2.9	2.1
7 - 27 days - 7 - 27 jours	125	75	50	2.2	2.6	1.8
7 - 13 days - 7 - 13 jours	67	44	23	1.2	1.5	♦0.8
14 - 20 days - 14 - 20 jours	37	17	20	0.7	♦0.6	♦0.7
21 - 27 days - 21 - 27 jours	21	14	7	♦0.4	♦0.5	♦0.3
28 days - 11 months - 28 jours - 11 mois	151	80	71	2.7	2.8	2.6
28 days - less than 2 months - 28 jours - moins de 2 mois	10	6	4	♦0.2	♦0.2	♦0.1
2 months - 2 mois	42	22	20	0.7	♦0.8	♦0.7
3 months - 3 mois	18	13	5	♦0.3	♦0.5	♦0.2
4 months - 4 mois	11	4	7	♦0.2	♦0.1	♦0.3
5 months - 5 mois	9	2	7	♦0.2	♦0.1	♦0.3
6 months - 6 mois	15	6	9	♦0.3	♦0.2	♦0.3
7 months - 7 mois	9	5	4	♦0.2	♦0.2	♦0.1
8 months - 8 mois	9	6	3	♦0.2	♦0.2	♦0.1
9 months - 9 mois	11	7	4	♦0.2	♦0.2	♦0.1
10 months - 10 mois	7	3	4	♦0.1	♦0.1	♦0.1
11 months - 11 mois	10	6	4	♦0.2	♦0.2	♦0.1
Israel - Israël[14]						
2016 (C)						
Total	561	311[3]	248[3]	3.1	...	...
Less than 1 day - Moins de 1 jour	115	64[3]	50[3]	0.6	...	...
1 - 6 days - 1 - 6 jours	135	82[3]	52[3]	0.7	...	...

16. Infant deaths and infant mortality rates by age and sex: latest available year, 2007 - 2016
Décès d'enfants de moins d'un an et taux de mortalité infantile selon l'âge et le sexe : dernière année disponible, 2007 - 2016 (continued - suite)

Continent, country or area, year, code[a] and age / Continent, pays ou zone, année, code[a] et âge	Number - Nombre			Rate - Taux		
	Both sexes Les deux sexes	Male Masculin	Female Féminin	Both sexes Les deux sexes	Male Masculin	Female Féminin
ASIA - ASIE						
Israel - Israël[14]						
2016 (C)						
7 - 27 days - 7 - 27 jours	112	69[3]	43[3]	0.6	...	...
7 - 13 days - 7 - 13 jours	66	41[3]	25[3]	0.4	...	...
14 - 20 days - 14 - 20 jours	23	12[3]	11[3]	♦0.1	...	...
21 - 27 days - 21 - 27 jours	23	16[3]	7[3]	♦0.1	...	...
28 days - 11 months - 28 jours - 11 mois	199	96[3]	103[3]	1.1	...	...
28 days - less than 2 months - 28 jours - moins de 2 mois	49	21[3]	28[3]	0.3	...	...
2 months - 2 mois	33	20[3]	13[3]	0.2	...	...
3 months - 3 mois	22	9[3]	13[3]	♦0.1	...	...
4 months - 4 mois	23	12[3]	11[3]	♦0.1	...	...
5 months - 5 mois	21	11[3]	10[3]	♦0.1	...	...
6 months - 6 mois	18	6[3]	12[3]	♦0.1	...	...
7 months - 7 mois	9	5[3]	4[3]	-	...	...
8 months - 8 mois	7	2[3]	5[3]	-	...	...
9 months - 9 mois	7	3[3]	4[3]	-	...	...
10 months - 10 mois	5	4[3]	1[3]	-	...	...
11 months - 11 mois	5	3[3]	2[3]	-	...	...
Japan - Japon[15]						
2015 (C)						
Total	1 916	1 042	874	1.9	2.0	1.8
Less than 1 day - Moins de 1 jour	452	246	206	0.4	0.5	0.4
1 - 6 days - 1 - 6 jours	213	112	101	0.2	0.2	0.2
7 - 27 days - 7 - 27 jours	237	124	113	0.2	0.2	0.2
7 - 13 days - 7 - 13 jours	115	56	59	0.1	0.1	0.1
14 - 20 days - 14 - 20 jours	58	35	23	0.1	0.1	-
21 - 27 days - 21 - 27 jours	64	33	31	0.1	0.1	0.1
28 days - 11 months - 28 jours - 11 mois	1 014	560	454	1.0	1.1	0.9
28 days - less than 2 months - 28 jours - moins de 2 mois	204	111	93	0.2	0.2	0.2
2 months - 2 mois	142	73	69	0.1	0.1	0.1
3 months - 3 mois	125	67	58	0.1	0.1	0.1
4 months - 4 mois	110	68	42	0.1	0.1	0.1
5 months - 5 mois	104	63	41	0.1	0.1	0.1
6 months - 6 mois	78	44	34	0.1	0.1	0.1
7 months - 7 mois	68	38	30	0.1	0.1	0.1
8 months - 8 mois	54	32	22	0.1	0.1	-
9 months - 9 mois	46	24	22	-	-	-
10 months - 10 mois	44	19	25	-	-	♦0.1
11 months - 11 mois	39	21	18	-	-	-
Kazakhstan[11]						
2013 (C)						
Total	4 367	2 502	1 865	11.3	12.5	10.0
Less than 1 day - Moins de 1 jour	381	209	172	1.0	1.0	0.9
1 - 6 days - 1 - 6 jours	1 439	869	570	3.7	4.3	3.0
7 - 27 days - 7 - 27 jours	927	529	398	2.4	2.6	2.1
7 - 13 days - 7 - 13 jours	534	325	209	1.4	1.6	1.1
14 - 20 days - 14 - 20 jours	233	127	106	0.6	0.6	0.6
21 - 27 days - 21 - 27 jours	160	77	83	0.4	0.4	0.4
28 days - 11 months - 28 jours - 11 mois	1 620	895	725	4.2	4.5	3.9
28 days - less than 2 months - 28 jours - moins de 2 mois	568	330	238	1.5	1.7	1.3
2 months - 2 mois	228	136	92	0.6	0.7	0.5
3 months - 3 mois	161	97	64	0.4	0.5	0.3
4 months - 4 mois	131	63	68	0.3	0.3	0.4
5 months - 5 mois	117	53	64	0.3	0.3	0.3
6 months - 6 mois	118	62	56	0.3	0.3	0.3
7 months - 7 mois	88	47	41	0.2	0.2	0.2
8 months - 8 mois	65	34	31	0.2	0.2	0.2
9 months - 9 mois	61	26	35	0.2	♦0.1	0.2
10 months - 10 mois	42	21	21	0.1	♦0.1	♦0.1
11 months - 11 mois	41	26	15	0.1	♦0.1	♦0.1
Kuwait - Koweït						
2015 (C)						
Total	456	257	199	7.7	8.5	6.9
Less than 1 day - Moins de 1 jour	108	68	40	1.8	2.3	1.4
1 - 6 days - 1 - 6 jours	79	46	33	1.3	1.5	1.1
7 - 27 days - 7 - 27 jours	100	52	48	1.7	1.7	1.7
7 - 13 days - 7 - 13 jours	57	30	27	1.0	1.0	♦0.9

16. Infant deaths and infant mortality rates by age and sex: latest available year, 2007 - 2016

Décès d'enfants de moins d'un an et taux de mortalité infantile selon l'âge et le sexe : dernière année disponible, 2007 - 2016 (continued - suite)

Continent, country or area, year, code[a] and age / Continent, pays ou zone, année, code[a] et âge	Number - Nombre			Rate - Taux		
	Both sexes Les deux sexes	Male Masculin	Female Féminin	Both sexes Les deux sexes	Male Masculin	Female Féminin
ASIA - ASIE						
Kuwait - Koweït						
2015 (C)						
14 - 20 days - 14 - 20 jours	19	9	10	♦0.3	♦0.3	♦0.3
21 - 27 days - 21 - 27 jours	24	13	11	♦0.4	♦0.4	♦0.4
28 days - 11 months - 28 jours - 11 mois	204	109	95	3.4	3.6	3.3
28 days - less than 2 months - 28 jours - moins de 2 mois	100	52	48	1.7	1.7	1.7
2 months - 2 mois	28	21	7	♦0.5	♦0.7	♦0.2
3 months - 3 mois	25	17	8	♦0.4	♦0.6	♦0.3
4 months - 4 mois	15	5	10	♦0.3	♦0.2	♦0.3
5 months - 5 mois	12	1	11	♦0.2	-	♦0.4
6 months - 6 mois	7	5	2	♦0.1	♦0.2	♦0.1
7 months - 7 mois	3	1	2	♦0.1	-	♦0.1
8 months - 8 mois	4	1	3	♦0.1	-	♦0.1
9 months - 9 mois	5	2	3	♦0.1	♦0.1	♦0.1
10 months - 10 mois	4	3	1	♦0.1	♦0.1	-
11 months - 11 mois	1	1	-	-	-	-
Kyrgyzstan - Kirghizstan						
2016* (C)						
Total	2 621	1 434	1 187	16.6	17.7	15.4
Less than 1 day - Moins de 1 jour	656	356	300	4.1	4.4	3.9
1 - 6 days - 1 - 6 jours	1 045	576	469	6.6	7.1	6.1
7 - 27 days - 7 - 27 jours	303	158	145	1.9	1.9	1.9
7 - 13 days - 7 - 13 jours	176	96	80	1.1	1.2	1.0
14 - 20 days - 14 - 20 jours	79	36	43	0.5	0.4	0.6
21 - 27 days - 21 - 27 jours	48	26	22	0.3	♦0.3	♦0.3
28 days - 11 months - 28 jours - 11 mois	617	344	273	3.9	4.2	3.5
28 days - less than 2 months - 28 jours - moins de 2 mois	136	83	53	0.9	1.0	0.7
2 months - 2 mois	82	47	35	0.5	0.6	0.5
3 months - 3 mois	56	31	25	0.4	0.4	0.4
4 months - 4 mois	64	33	31	0.4	0.4	0.4
5 months - 5 mois	63	36	27	0.4	0.4	♦0.4
6 months - 6 mois	47	25	22	0.3	♦0.3	♦0.3
7 months - 7 mois	49	24	25	0.3	♦0.3	♦0.3
8 months - 8 mois	40	20	20	0.3	♦0.2	♦0.3
9 months - 9 mois	28	17	11	♦0.2	♦0.2	♦0.1
10 months - 10 mois	28	15	13	♦0.2	♦0.2	♦0.2
11 months - 11 mois	24	13	11	♦0.2	♦0.2	♦0.1
Maldives						
2014 (C)						
Total	59	32	27	...	...	...
Less than 1 day - Moins de 1 jour	19	11	8	...	...	...
1 - 6 days - 1 - 6 jours	14	10	4	...	...	...
7 - 27 days - 7 - 27 jours	4	1	3	...	...	...
7 - 13 days - 7 - 13 jours	1	-	1	...	...	...
14 - 20 days - 14 - 20 jours	1	1	-	...	...	...
21 - 27 days - 21 - 27 jours	2	-	2	...	...	...
28 days - 11 months - 28 jours - 11 mois	22	10	12	...	...	...
28 days - less than 2 months - 28 jours - moins de 2 mois	13	6	7	...	...	...
2 months - 2 mois	1	-	1	...	...	...
3 months - 3 mois	-	-	-	...	...	...
4 months - 4 mois	-	-	-	...	...	...
5 months - 5 mois	3	1	2	...	...	...
6 months - 6 mois	-	-	-	...	...	...
7 months - 7 mois	2	2	-	...	...	...
8 months - 8 mois	3	1	2	...	...	...
9 months - 9 mois	-	-	-	...	...	...
10 months - 10 mois	-	-	-	...	...	...
11 months - 11 mois	-	-	-	...	...	...
Mongolia - Mongolie						
2016 (+C)						
Total	1 315	748	567	16.5	18.2	14.6
Less than 7 days - Moins de 7 jours	528	303	225	6.6	7.4	5.8
7 - 27 days - 7 - 27 jours	193	121	72	2.4	2.9	1.9
28 days - 11 months - 28 jours - 11 mois	594	324	270	7.4	7.9	6.9
Myanmar[16]						
2014 (+U)						
Total	*9 386*	*5 299*	*4 087*	...	...	...
Less than 1 day - Moins de 1 jour	*312*	*164*	*148*	...	...	...

16. Infant deaths and infant mortality rates by age and sex: latest available year, 2007 - 2016
Décès d'enfants de moins d'un an et taux de mortalité infantile selon l'âge et le sexe : dernière année disponible, 2007 - 2016 (continued - suite)

Continent, country or area, year, code[a] and age / Continent, pays ou zone, année, code[a] et âge	Number - Nombre			Rate - Taux		
	Both sexes Les deux sexes	Male Masculin	Female Féminin	Both sexes Les deux sexes	Male Masculin	Female Féminin
ASIA - ASIE						
Myanmar[16]						
2014 (+U)						
1 - 6 days - 1 - 6 jours	4 473	2 588	1 885	...	...	...
7 - 27 days - 7 - 27 jours	1 334	755	579	...	...	...
7 - 13 days - 7 - 13 jours	664	375	289	...	...	...
14 - 20 days - 14 - 20 jours	383	225	158	...	...	...
21 - 27 days - 21 - 27 jours	287	155	132	...	...	...
28 days - 11 months - 28 jours - 11 mois	3 266	1 791	1 475	...	...	...
28 days - less than 2 months - 28 jours - moins de 2 mois	739	435	304	...	...	...
2 months - 2 mois	557	321	236	...	...	...
3 months - 3 mois	385	218	167	...	...	...
4 months - 4 mois	308	145	163	...	...	...
5 months - 5 mois	240	119	121	...	...	...
6 months - 6 mois	237	136	101	...	...	...
7 months - 7 mois	165	84	81	...	...	...
8 months - 8 mois	188	100	88	...	...	...
9 months - 9 mois	173	89	84	...	...	...
10 months - 10 mois	144	78	66	...	...	...
11 months - 11 mois	130	66	64	...	...	...
Unknown - Inconnu	1	1	-	...	...	...
Oman[17]						
2016 (U)						
Total	816	469	347	...	...	...
Less than 1 day - Moins de 1 jour	137	79	58	...	...	...
1 - 6 days - 1 - 6 jours	272	151	121	...	...	...
7 - 27 days - 7 - 27 jours	144	88	56	...	...	...
7 - 13 days - 7 - 13 jours	88	50	38	...	...	...
14 - 20 days - 14 - 20 jours	29	15	14	...	...	...
21 - 27 days - 21 - 27 jours	27	23	4	...	...	...
28 days - 11 months - 28 jours - 11 mois	263	151	112	...	...	...
28 days - less than 2 months - 28 jours - moins de 2 mois	70	38	32	...	...	...
2 months - 2 mois	36	23	13	...	...	...
3 months - 3 mois	31	14	17	...	...	...
4 months - 4 mois	23	14	9	...	...	...
5 months - 5 mois	15	6	9	...	...	...
6 months - 6 mois	17	11	6	...	...	...
7 months - 7 mois	21	14	7	...	...	...
8 months - 8 mois	15	11	4	...	...	...
9 months - 9 mois	9	5	4	...	...	...
10 months - 10 mois	13	7	6	...	...	...
11 months - 11 mois	13	8	5	...	...	...
Pakistan[18]						
2007 (I)						
Total	288 191	167 402	120 789	75.2	83.5	66.2
Less than 1 day - Moins de 1 jour	11 990	8 027	3 963	3.1	4.0	2.2
1 - 6 days - 1 - 6 jours	115 664	74 312	41 352	30.2	37.0	22.7
7 - 27 days - 7 - 27 jours	39 726	23 382	16 344	10.4	11.7	9.0
7 - 13 days - 7 - 13 jours	21 846	13 191	8 655	5.7	6.6	4.7
14 - 20 days - 14 - 20 jours	16 376	9 475	6 901	4.3	4.7	3.8
21 - 27 days - 21 - 27 jours	1 504	716	788	0.4	0.4	0.4
28 days - 11 months - 28 jours - 11 mois	120 811	61 681	59 130	31.5	30.8	32.4
28 days - less than 2 months - 28 jours - moins de 2 mois	23 563	9 553	14 010	6.2	4.8	7.7
2 months - 2 mois	10 666	7 662	3 004	2.8	3.8	1.6
3 months - 3 mois	16 938	9 692	7 246	4.4	4.8	4.0
4 months - 4 mois	10 577	4 135	6 442	2.8	2.1	3.5
5 months - 5 mois	14 148	8 863	5 285	3.7	4.4	2.9
6 months - 6 mois	17 012	6 641	10 371	4.4	3.3	5.7
7 months - 7 mois	8 480	4 209	4 271	2.2	2.1	2.3
8 months - 8 mois	6 221	5 116	1 105	1.6	2.6	0.6
9 months - 9 mois	7 602	3 819	3 783	2.0	1.9	2.1
10 months - 10 mois	3 546	1 291	2 255	0.9	0.6	1.2
11 months - 11 mois	2 058	700	1 358	0.5	0.3	0.7
Philippines						
2015 (C)						
Total	20 750	12 086	8 664	11.9	13.3	10.4
Less than 1 day - Moins de 1 jour	3 038	1 713	1 325	1.7	1.9	1.6
1 - 6 days - 1 - 6 jours	5 991	3 685	2 306	3.4	4.0	2.8

16. Infant deaths and infant mortality rates by age and sex: latest available year, 2007 - 2016
Décès d'enfants de moins d'un an et taux de mortalité infantile selon l'âge et le sexe : dernière année disponible, 2007 - 2016 (continued - suite)

Continent, country or area, year, code[a] and age / Continent, pays ou zone, année, code[a] et âge	Number - Nombre			Rate - Taux		
	Both sexes Les deux sexes	Male Masculin	Female Féminin	Both sexes Les deux sexes	Male Masculin	Female Féminin
ASIA - ASIE						
Philippines						
2015 (C)						
7 - 27 days - 7 - 27 jours	2 773	1 631	1 142	1.6	1.8	1.4
7 - 13 days - 7 - 13 jours	1 419	817	602	0.8	0.9	0.7
14 - 20 days - 14 - 20 jours	783	465	318	0.4	0.5	0.4
21 - 27 days - 21 - 27 jours	571	349	222	0.3	0.4	0.3
28 days - 11 months - 28 jours - 11 mois..............	8 948	5 057	3 891	5.1	5.6	4.7
28 days - less than 2 months - 28 jours - moins de 2 mois	2 190	1 301	889	1.3	1.4	1.1
2 months - 2 mois..............	1 187	668	519	0.7	0.7	0.6
3 months - 3 mois..............	887	489	398	0.5	0.5	0.5
4 months - 4 mois..............	761	429	332	0.4	0.5	0.4
5 months - 5 mois..............	735	420	315	0.4	0.5	0.4
6 months - 6 mois..............	681	360	321	0.4	0.4	0.4
7 months - 7 mois..............	612	342	270	0.4	0.4	0.3
8 months - 8 mois..............	567	317	250	0.3	0.3	0.3
9 months - 9 mois..............	505	276	229	0.3	0.3	0.3
10 months - 10 mois..............	414	233	181	0.2	0.3	0.2
11 months - 11 mois..............	409	222	187	0.2	0.2	0.2
Qatar						
2015 (C)						
Total..............	197	102	95	7.4	7.5	7.3
Less than 1 day - Moins de 1 jour	-	-	-	-	-	-
1 - 6 days - 1 - 6 jours	88	43	45	3.3	3.2	3.5
7 - 27 days - 7 - 27 jours	34	20	14	1.3	♦1.5	♦1.1
7 - 13 days - 7 - 13 jours	23	11	12	♦0.9	♦0.8	♦0.9
14 - 20 days - 14 - 20 jours	7	5	2	♦0.3	♦0.4	♦0.2
21 - 27 days - 21 - 27 jours	4	4	-	♦0.2	♦0.3	-
28 days - 11 months - 28 jours - 11 mois..............	75	39	36	2.8	2.9	2.8
28 days - less than 2 months - 28 jours - moins de 2 mois	23	14	9	♦0.9	♦1.0	♦0.7
2 months - 2 mois..............	13	4	9	♦0.5	♦0.3	♦0.7
3 months - 3 mois..............	13	5	8	♦0.5	♦0.4	♦0.6
4 months - 4 mois..............	7	3	4	♦0.3	♦0.2	♦0.3
5 months - 5 mois..............	3	1	2	♦0.1	♦0.1	♦0.2
6 months - 6 mois..............	3	2	1	♦0.1	♦0.1	♦0.1
7 months - 7 mois..............	2	1	1	♦0.1	♦0.1	♦0.1
8 months - 8 mois..............	3	3	-	♦0.1	♦0.2	-
9 months - 9 mois..............	5	4	1	♦0.2	♦0.3	♦0.1
10 months - 10 mois..............	3	2	1	♦0.1	♦0.1	♦0.1
11 months - 11 mois..............	-	-	-	-	-	-
Republic of Korea - République de Corée[19]						
2015 (C)						
Total..............	1 190	655	535	2.7	2.9	2.5
Less than 1 day - Moins de 1 jour	189	96	93	0.4	0.4	0.4
1 - 6 days - 1 - 6 jours	266	152	114	0.6	0.7	0.5
7 - 27 days - 7 - 27 jours	222	126	96	0.5	0.6	0.4
7 - 13 days - 7 - 13 jours	115	63	52	0.3	0.3	0.2
14 - 20 days - 14 - 20 jours	68	38	30	0.2	0.2	0.1
21 - 27 days - 21 - 27 jours	39	25	14	0.1	♦0.1	♦0.1
28 days - 11 months - 28 jours - 11 mois..............	513	281	232	1.2	1.2	1.1
28 days - less than 2 months - 28 jours - moins de 2 mois	149	80	69	0.3	0.4	0.3
2 months - 2 mois..............	92	55	37	0.2	0.2	0.2
3 months - 3 mois..............	61	28	33	0.1	♦0.1	0.2
4 months - 4 mois..............	48	29	19	0.1	♦0.1	♦0.1
5 months - 5 mois..............	42	22	20	0.1	♦0.1	♦0.1
6 months - 6 mois..............	26	15	11	♦0.1	♦0.1	♦0.1
7 months - 7 mois..............	16	8	8	-	-	-
8 months - 8 mois..............	23	12	11	♦0.1	♦0.1	♦0.1
9 months - 9 mois..............	21	11	10	-	-	-
10 months - 10 mois..............	20	13	7	-	♦0.1	-
11 months - 11 mois..............	15	8	7	-	-	-
Singapore - Singapour						
2016 (+C)						
Total..............	101	50	51	2.4	2.3	2.6
Less than 1 day - Moins de 1 jour	14	6	8	♦0.3	♦0.3	♦0.4
1 - 6 days - 1 - 6 jours	21	11	10	♦0.5	♦0.5	♦0.5
7 - 27 days - 7 - 27 jours	22	11	11	♦0.5	♦0.5	♦0.6
7 - 13 days - 7 - 13 jours	10	4	6	♦0.2	♦0.2	♦0.3
14 - 20 days - 14 - 20 jours	7	4	3	♦0.2	♦0.2	♦0.2

Continent, country or area, year, code[a] and age / Continent, pays ou zone, année, code[a] et âge	Number - Nombre			Rate - Taux		
	Both sexes Les deux sexes	Male Masculin	Female Féminin	Both sexes Les deux sexes	Male Masculin	Female Féminin
ASIA - ASIE						
Singapore - Singapour						
2016 (+C)						
21 - 27 days - 21 - 27 jours	5	3	2	♦0.1	♦0.1	♦0.1
28 days - 11 months - 28 jours - 11 mois	44	22	22	1.1	♦1.0	♦1.1
28 days - less than 2 months - 28 jours - moins de 2 mois	8	4	4	♦0.2	♦0.2	♦0.2
2 months - 2 mois	8	6	2	♦0.2	♦0.3	♦0.1
3 months - 3 mois	5	3	2	♦0.1	♦0.1	♦0.1
4 months - 4 mois	4	2	2	♦0.1	♦0.1	♦0.1
5 months - 5 mois	7	2	5	♦0.2	♦0.1	♦0.3
6 months - 6 mois	5	2	3	♦0.1	♦0.1	♦0.2
7 months - 7 mois	1	-	1	-	-	♦0.1
8 months - 8 mois	-	-	-	-	-	-
9 months - 9 mois	2	-	2	-	-	♦0.1
10 months - 10 mois	2	1	1	-	-	♦0.1
11 months - 11 mois	2	2	-	-	♦0.1	-
State of Palestine - État de Palestine						
2007 (U)						
Total	794	420	374	...	...	...
Less than 1 day - Moins de 1 jour	42	24	18	...	...	...
1 - 6 days - 1 - 6 jours	183	113	70	...	...	...
7 - 27 days - 7 - 27 jours	156	79	77	...	...	...
7 - 13 days - 7 - 13 jours	79	44	35	...	...	...
14 - 20 days - 14 - 20 jours	47	19	28	...	...	...
21 - 27 days - 21 - 27 jours	30	16	14	...	...	...
28 days - 11 months - 28 jours - 11 mois	413	204	209	...	...	...
28 days - less than 2 months - 28 jours - moins de 2 mois	111	64	47	...	...	...
2 months - 2 mois	56	25	31	...	...	...
3 months - 3 mois	50	28	22	...	...	...
4 months - 4 mois	32	14	18	...	...	...
5 months - 5 mois	40	20	20	...	...	...
6 months - 6 mois	28	17	11	...	...	...
7 months - 7 mois	19	8	11	...	...	...
8 months - 8 mois	19	10	9	...	...	...
9 months - 9 mois	22	8	14	...	...	...
10 months - 10 mois	21	5	16	...	...	...
11 months - 11 mois	15	5	10	...	...	...
Tajikistan - Tadjikistan[11]						
2008 (U)						
Total	2 480	1 478	1 002	...	...	...
Less than 1 day - Moins de 1 jour	420	255	165	...	...	...
1 - 6 days - 1 - 6 jours	699	443	256	...	...	...
7 - 27 days - 7 - 27 jours	248	140	108	...	...	...
7 - 13 days - 7 - 13 jours	145	87	58	...	...	...
14 - 20 days - 14 - 20 jours	63	33	30	...	...	...
21 - 27 days - 21 - 27 jours	40	20	20	...	...	...
28 days - 11 months - 28 jours - 11 mois	1 113	640	473	...	...	...
28 days - less than 2 months - 28 jours - moins de 2 mois	180	103	77	...	...	...
2 months - 2 mois	155	92	63	...	...	...
3 months - 3 mois	138	77	61	...	...	...
4 months - 4 mois	111	71	40	...	...	...
5 months - 5 mois	106	56	50	...	...	...
6 months - 6 mois	106	62	44	...	...	...
7 months - 7 mois	75	43	32	...	...	...
8 months - 8 mois	79	49	30	...	...	...
9 months - 9 mois	56	23	33	...	...	...
10 months - 10 mois	56	39	17	...	...	...
11 months - 11 mois	51	25	26	...	...	...
Thailand - Thaïlande						
2011 (+U)						
Total	5 275	2 964	2 311	...	...	...
Less than 1 day - Moins de 1 jour	587	326	261	...	...	...
1 - 6 days - 1 - 6 jours	1 612	931	681	...	...	...
7 - 27 days - 7 - 27 jours	987	534	453	...	...	...
7 - 13 days - 7 - 13 jours	527	285	242	...	...	...
14 - 20 days - 14 - 20 jours	276	149	127	...	...	...
21 - 27 days - 21 - 27 jours	184	100	84	...	...	...
28 days - 11 months - 28 jours - 11 mois	2 089	1 173	916	...	...	...
28 days - less than 2 months - 28 jours - moins de 2 mois	556	329	227	...	...	...

16. Infant deaths and infant mortality rates by age and sex: latest available year, 2007 - 2016
Décès d'enfants de moins d'un an et taux de mortalité infantile selon l'âge et le sexe : dernière année disponible, 2007 - 2016 (continued - suite)

Continent, country or area, year, code[a] and age	Number - Nombre			Rate - Taux		
Continent, pays ou zone, année, code[a] et âge	Both sexes Les deux sexes	Male Masculin	Female Féminin	Both sexes Les deux sexes	Male Masculin	Female Féminin
ASIA - ASIE						
Thailand - Thaïlande						
2011 (+U)						
2 months - 2 mois	360	203	157	...	...	...
3 months - 3 mois	249	152	97	...	...	...
4 months - 4 mois	193	98	95	...	...	...
5 months - 5 mois	160	91	69	...	...	...
6 months - 6 mois	141	74	67	...	...	...
7 months - 7 mois	103	55	48	...	...	...
8 months - 8 mois	106	51	55	...	...	...
9 months - 9 mois	87	41	46	...	...	...
10 months - 10 mois	77	45	32	...	...	...
11 months - 11 mois	57	34	23	...	...	...
Turkey - Turquie						
2015 (C)						
Total	14 164	7 716	6 448	10.7	11.3	10.0
Less than 1 day - Moins de 1 jour	1 902	1 030	872	1.4	1.5	1.4
1 - 6 days - 1 - 6 jours	4 270	2 457	1 813	3.2	3.6	2.8
7 - 27 days - 7 - 27 jours	2 817	1 547	1 270	2.1	2.3	2.0
7 - 13 days - 7 - 13 jours	1 505	836	669	1.1	1.2	1.0
14 - 20 days - 14 - 20 jours	746	406	340	0.6	0.6	0.5
21 - 27 days - 21 - 27 jours	566	305	261	0.4	0.4	0.4
28 days - 11 months - 28 jours - 11 mois	5 175	2 682	2 493	3.9	3.9	3.9
28 days - less than 2 months - 28 jours - moins de 2 mois	1 455	773	682	1.1	1.1	1.1
2 months - 2 mois	784	407	377	0.6	0.6	0.6
3 months - 3 mois	585	300	285	0.4	0.4	0.4
4 months - 4 mois	525	274	251	0.4	0.4	0.4
5 months - 5 mois	399	195	204	0.3	0.3	0.3
6 months - 6 mois	310	158	152	0.2	0.2	0.2
7 months - 7 mois	288	142	146	0.2	0.2	0.2
8 months - 8 mois	247	123	124	0.2	0.2	0.2
9 months - 9 mois	225	114	111	0.2	0.2	0.2
10 months - 10 mois	177	94	83	0.1	0.1	0.1
11 months - 11 mois	180	102	78	0.1	0.1	0.1
Uzbekistan - Ouzbékistan[11]						
2015 (+C)						
Total	8 320	4 906	3 414	11.3	12.8	9.7
Less than 1 day - Moins de 1 jour	1 314	777	537	1.8	2.0	1.5
1 - 6 days - 1 - 6 jours	3 252	1 974	1 278	4.4	5.2	3.6
7 - 27 days - 7 - 27 jours	1 215	710	505	1.7	1.9	1.4
7 - 13 days - 7 - 13 jours	763	455	308	1.0	1.2	0.9
14 - 20 days - 14 - 20 jours	275	156	119	0.4	0.4	0.3
21 - 27 days - 21 - 27 jours	177	99	78	0.2	0.3	0.2
28 days - 11 months - 28 jours - 11 mois	2 539	1 445	1 094	3.5	3.8	3.1
28 days - less than 2 months - 28 jours - moins de 2 mois	688	448	240	0.9	1.2	0.7
2 months - 2 mois	346	196	150	0.5	0.5	0.4
3 months - 3 mois	261	136	125	0.4	0.4	0.4
4 months - 4 mois	245	127	118	0.3	0.3	0.3
5 months - 5 mois	212	119	93	0.3	0.3	0.3
6 months - 6 mois	165	87	78	0.2	0.2	0.2
7 months - 7 mois	176	90	86	0.2	0.2	0.2
8 months - 8 mois	155	80	75	0.2	0.2	0.2
9 months - 9 mois	109	54	55	0.1	0.1	0.2
10 months - 10 mois	105	57	48	0.1	0.1	0.1
11 months - 11 mois	77	51	26	0.1	0.1	♦0.1
EUROPE						
Åland Islands - Îles d'Åland						
2015 (C)						
Total	-	-	-	...	...	...
Albania - Albanie						
2015 (U)						
Total	233	134	99	...	...	...
Less than 1 day - Moins de 1 jour	90	48	42	...	...	...
1 - 6 days - 1 - 6 jours	50	29	21	...	...	...
7 - 27 days - 7 - 27 jours	29	17	12	...	...	...
7 - 13 days - 7 - 13 jours	12	8	4	...	...	...

Continent, country or area, year, code[a] and age / Continent, pays ou zone, année, code[a] et âge	Number - Nombre			Rate - Taux		
	Both sexes Les deux sexes	Male Masculin	Female Féminin	Both sexes Les deux sexes	Male Masculin	Female Féminin
EUROPE						
Albania - Albanie						
2015 (U)						
14 - 20 days - 14 - 20 jours	9	5	4	...	...	...
21 - 27 days - 21 - 27 jours	8	4	4	...	...	...
28 days - 11 months - 28 jours - 11 mois	64	40	24	...	...	...
28 days - less than 2 months - 28 jours - moins de 2 mois	19	11	8	...	...	...
2 months - 2 mois	8	5	3	...	...	...
3 months - 3 mois	9	8	1	...	...	...
4 months - 4 mois	6	3	3	...	...	...
5 months - 5 mois	4	3	1	...	...	...
6 months - 6 mois	1	-	1	...	...	...
7 months - 7 mois	4	2	2	...	...	...
8 months - 8 mois	3	1	2	...	...	...
9 months - 9 mois	3	2	1	...	...	...
10 months - 10 mois	2	1	1	...	...	...
11 months - 11 mois	5	4	1	...	...	...
Andorra - Andorre						
2009 (C)						
Total	1	-	1	...	...	...
Less than 1 day - Moins de 1 jour	-	-	-	...	...	...
1 - 6 days - 1 - 6 jours	1	-	1	...	...	...
7 - 27 days - 7 - 27 jours	-	-	-	...	...	...
28 days - 11 months - 28 jours - 11 mois	-	-	-	...	...	...
Austria - Autriche						
2015 (C)						
Total	259	144	115	3.1	3.3	2.8
Less than 1 day - Moins de 1 jour	118	63	55	1.4	1.4	1.3
1 - 6 days - 1 - 6 jours	47	29	18	0.6	♦0.7	♦0.4
7 - 27 days - 7 - 27 jours	33	20	13	0.4	♦0.5	♦0.3
7 - 13 days - 7 - 13 jours	15	10	5	♦0.2	♦0.2	♦0.1
14 - 20 days - 14 - 20 jours	7	3	4	♦0.1	♦0.1	♦0.1
21 - 27 days - 21 - 27 jours	11	7	4	♦0.1	♦0.2	♦0.1
28 days - 11 months - 28 jours - 11 mois	61	32	29	0.7	0.7	♦0.7
28 days - less than 2 months - 28 jours - moins de 2 mois	21	11	10	♦0.2	♦0.3	♦0.2
2 months - 2 mois	11	4	7	♦0.1	♦0.1	♦0.2
3 months - 3 mois	5	3	2	♦0.1	♦0.1	-
4 months - 4 mois	6	2	4	♦0.1	-	♦0.1
5 months - 5 mois	4	4	-	-	♦0.1	-
6 months - 6 mois	2	2	-	-	-	-
7 months - 7 mois	2	2	-	-	-	-
8 months - 8 mois	1	1	-	-	-	-
9 months - 9 mois	5	1	4	♦0.1	-	♦0.1
10 months - 10 mois	2	2	-	-	-	-
11 months - 11 mois	2	-	2	-	-	-
Belarus - Bélarus						
2015 (C)						
Total	352	199	153	3.0	3.2	2.7
Less than 1 day - Moins de 1 jour	32	14	18	0.3	♦0.2	♦0.3
1 - 6 days - 1 - 6 jours	68	35	33	0.6	0.6	0.6
7 - 27 days - 7 - 27 jours	67	36	31	0.6	0.6	0.5
7 - 13 days - 7 - 13 jours	23	16	7	♦0.2	♦0.3	♦0.1
14 - 20 days - 14 - 20 jours	17	8	9	♦0.1	♦0.1	♦0.2
21 - 27 days - 21 - 27 jours	27	12	15	♦0.2	♦0.2	♦0.3
28 days - 11 months - 28 jours - 11 mois	185	114	71	1.6	1.9	1.2
28 days - less than 2 months - 28 jours - moins de 2 mois	72	50	22	0.6	0.8	♦0.4
2 months - 2 mois	26	17	9	♦0.2	♦0.3	♦0.2
3 months - 3 mois	19	10	9	♦0.2	♦0.2	♦0.2
4 months - 4 mois	14	10	4	♦0.1	♦0.2	♦0.1
5 months - 5 mois	16	11	5	♦0.1	♦0.2	♦0.1
6 months - 6 mois	9	5	4	♦0.1	♦0.1	♦0.1
7 months - 7 mois	11	6	5	♦0.1	♦0.1	♦0.1
8 months - 8 mois	7	2	5	♦0.1	-	♦0.1
9 months - 9 mois	4	2	2	-	-	-
10 months - 10 mois	3	-	3	-	-	♦0.1
11 months - 11 mois	4	1	3	-	-	♦0.1

Continent, country or area, year, code[a] and age / Continent, pays ou zone, année, code[a] et âge	Number - Nombre			Rate - Taux		
	Both sexes Les deux sexes	Male Masculin	Female Féminin	Both sexes Les deux sexes	Male Masculin	Female Féminin
EUROPE						
Belgium - Belgique[20]						
2014 (C)						
Total	423	247	176	3.4	3.8	2.9
Less than 1 day - Moins de 1 jour	115	61	54	0.9	1.0	0.9
1 - 6 days - 1 - 6 jours	91	58	33	0.7	0.9	0.5
7 - 27 days - 7 - 27 jours	79	39	40	0.6	0.6	0.7
7 - 13 days - 7 - 13 jours	40	21	19	0.3	◆0.3	◆0.3
14 - 20 days - 14 - 20 jours	25	11	14	◆0.2	◆0.2	◆0.2
21 - 27 days - 21 - 27 jours	14	7	7	◆0.1	◆0.1	◆0.1
28 days - 11 months - 28 jours - 11 mois	138	89	49	1.1	1.4	0.8
28 days - less than 2 months - 28 jours - moins de 2 mois	42	25	17	0.3	◆0.4	◆0.3
2 months - 2 mois	23	17	6	◆0.2	◆0.3	◆0.1
3 months - 3 mois	13	9	4	◆0.1	◆0.1	◆0.1
4 months - 4 mois	15	12	3	◆0.1	◆0.2	-
5 months - 5 mois	11	7	4	◆0.1	◆0.1	◆0.1
6 months - 6 mois	8	3	5	◆0.1	-	◆0.1
7 months - 7 mois	9	8	1	◆0.1	◆0.1	-
8 months - 8 mois	7	4	3	◆0.1	◆0.1	-
9 months - 9 mois	2	2	-	-	-	-
10 months - 10 mois	5	1	4	-	-	◆0.1
11 months - 11 mois	3	1	2	-	-	-
Bosnia and Herzegovina - Bosnie-Herzégovine						
2010 (C)						
Total	216	125	91	6.4	7.2	5.6
Less than 1 day - Moins de 1 jour	74	43	31	2.2	2.5	1.9
1 - 6 days - 1 - 6 jours	89	56	33	2.7	3.2	2.0
7 - 27 days - 7 - 27 jours	19	13	6	◆0.6	◆0.8	◆0.4
7 - 13 days - 7 - 13 jours	10	6	4	◆0.3	◆0.3	◆0.2
14 - 20 days - 14 - 20 jours	6	6	-	◆0.2	◆0.3	-
21 - 27 days - 21 - 27 jours	3	1	2	◆0.1	◆0.1	◆0.1
28 days - 11 months - 28 jours - 11 mois	34	13	21	1.0	◆0.8	◆1.3
28 days - less than 2 months - 28 jours - moins de 2 mois	5	2	3	◆0.1	◆0.1	◆0.2
2 months - 2 mois	10	6	4	◆0.3	◆0.3	◆0.2
3 months - 3 mois	1	-	1	-	-	◆0.1
4 months - 4 mois	5	2	3	◆0.1	◆0.1	◆0.2
5 months - 5 mois	3	1	2	◆0.1	◆0.1	◆0.1
6 months - 6 mois	3	1	2	◆0.1	◆0.1	◆0.1
7 months - 7 mois	-	-	-	-	-	-
8 months - 8 mois	1	-	1	-	-	◆0.1
9 months - 9 mois	4	-	4	◆0.1	-	◆0.2
10 months - 10 mois	1	1	-	-	◆0.1	-
11 months - 11 mois	1	-	1	-	-	◆0.1
Bulgaria - Bulgarie						
2015 (C)						
Total	434	245	189	6.6	7.2	5.9
Less than 1 day - Moins de 1 jour	89	45	44	1.3	1.3	1.4
1 - 6 days - 1 - 6 jours	94	53	41	1.4	1.6	1.3
7 - 27 days - 7 - 27 jours	81	47	34	1.2	1.4	1.1
7 - 13 days - 7 - 13 jours	43	24	19	0.7	◆0.7	◆0.6
14 - 20 days - 14 - 20 jours	16	11	5	◆0.2	◆0.3	◆0.2
21 - 27 days - 21 - 27 jours	22	12	10	◆0.3	◆0.4	◆0.3
28 days - 11 months - 28 jours - 11 mois	170	100	70	2.6	2.9	2.2
28 days - less than 2 months - 28 jours - moins de 2 mois	41	29	12	0.6	◆0.9	◆0.4
2 months - 2 mois	36	21	15	0.5	◆0.6	◆0.5
3 months - 3 mois	21	12	9	◆0.3	◆0.4	◆0.3
4 months - 4 mois	23	15	8	◆0.3	◆0.4	◆0.3
5 months - 5 mois	14	4	10	◆0.2	◆0.1	◆0.3
6 months - 6 mois	11	4	7	◆0.2	◆0.1	◆0.2
7 months - 7 mois	4	2	2	◆0.1	◆0.1	◆0.1
8 months - 8 mois	5	4	1	◆0.1	◆0.1	-
9 months - 9 mois	8	5	3	◆0.1	◆0.1	◆0.1
10 months - 10 mois	4	1	3	◆0.1	-	◆0.1
11 months - 11 mois	3	3	-	-	◆0.1	-
Croatia - Croatie						
2015 (C)						
Total	154	87	67	4.1	4.5	3.7
Less than 1 day - Moins de 1 jour	50	31	19	1.3	1.6	◆1.0
1 - 6 days - 1 - 6 jours	31	17	14	0.8	◆0.9	◆0.8

Continent, country or area, year, code[a] and age / Continent, pays ou zone, année, code[a] et âge	Number - Nombre			Rate - Taux		
	Both sexes Les deux sexes	Male Masculin	Female Féminin	Both sexes Les deux sexes	Male Masculin	Female Féminin
EUROPE						
Croatia - Croatie						
2015 (C)						
7 - 27 days - 7 - 27 jours	35	19	16	0.9	♦1.0	♦0.9
7 - 13 days - 7 - 13 jours	14	6	8	♦0.4	♦0.3	♦0.4
14 - 20 days - 14 - 20 jours	11	7	4	♦0.3	♦0.4	♦0.2
21 - 27 days - 21 - 27 jours	10	6	4	♦0.3	♦0.3	♦0.2
28 days - 11 months - 28 jours - 11 mois	38	20	18	1.0	♦1.0	♦1.0
28 days - less than 2 months - 28 jours - moins de 2 mois	11	6	5	♦0.3	♦0.3	♦0.3
2 months - 2 mois	10	5	5	♦0.3	♦0.3	♦0.3
3 months - 3 mois	3	1	2	♦0.1	♦0.1	♦0.1
4 months - 4 mois	2	2	-	♦0.1	♦0.1	-
5 months - 5 mois	2	1	1	♦0.1	♦0.1	♦0.1
6 months - 6 mois	2	-	2	♦0.1	-	♦0.1
7 months - 7 mois	1	1	-	-	♦0.1	-
8 months - 8 mois	3	2	1	♦0.1	♦0.1	♦0.1
9 months - 9 mois	1	-	1	-	-	♦0.1
10 months - 10 mois	2	2	-	♦0.1	♦0.1	-
11 months - 11 mois	1	-	1	-	-	♦0.1
Czechia - Tchéquie						
2015 (C)						
Total...........	272	168	104	2.5	3.0	1.9
Less than 1 day - Moins de 1 jour	50	31	19	0.5	0.5	♦0.4
1 - 6 days - 1 - 6 jours	56	32	24	0.5	0.6	♦0.4
7 - 27 days - 7 - 27 jours	59	37	22	0.5	0.7	♦0.4
7 - 13 days - 7 - 13 jours	27	18	9	♦0.2	♦0.3	♦0.2
14 - 20 days - 14 - 20 jours	15	8	7	♦0.1	♦0.1	♦0.1
21 - 27 days - 21 - 27 jours	17	11	6	♦0.2	♦0.2	♦0.1
28 days - 11 months - 28 jours - 11 mois	107	68	39	1.0	1.2	0.7
28 days - less than 2 months - 28 jours - moins de 2 mois	25	15	10	♦0.2	♦0.3	♦0.2
2 months - 2 mois	19	13	6	♦0.2	♦0.2	♦0.1
3 months - 3 mois	9	8	1	♦0.1	♦0.1	-
4 months - 4 mois	15	11	4	♦0.1	♦0.2	♦0.1
5 months - 5 mois	8	4	4	♦0.1	♦0.1	♦0.1
6 months - 6 mois	6	2	4	♦0.1	-	♦0.1
7 months - 7 mois	5	4	1	-	♦0.1	-
8 months - 8 mois	5	2	3	-	-	♦0.1
9 months - 9 mois	8	4	4	♦0.1	♦0.1	♦0.1
10 months - 10 mois	3	2	1	-	-	-
11 months - 11 mois	4	3	1	-	♦0.1	-
Denmark - Danemark[21]						
2015 (C)						
Total...........	216	116	100	3.7	3.9	3.5
Less than 1 day - Moins de 1 jour	102	56	46	1.8	1.9	1.6
1 - 6 days - 1 - 6 jours	51	25	26	0.9	♦0.8	♦0.9
7 - 27 days - 7 - 27 jours	21	14	7	♦0.4	♦0.5	♦0.2
7 - 13 days - 7 - 13 jours	9	7	2	♦0.2	♦0.2	♦0.1
14 - 20 days - 14 - 20 jours	4	3	1	♦0.1	♦0.1	-
21 - 27 days - 21 - 27 jours	8	4	4	♦0.1	♦0.1	♦0.1
28 days - 11 months - 28 jours - 11 mois	42	21	21	0.7	♦0.7	♦0.7
28 days - less than 2 months - 28 jours - moins de 2 mois	15	9	6	♦0.3	♦0.3	♦0.2
2 months - 2 mois	6	2	4	♦0.1	♦0.1	♦0.1
3 months - 3 mois	3	2	1	♦0.1	♦0.1	-
4 months - 4 mois	4	1	3	♦0.1	-	♦0.1
5 months - 5 mois	2	2	-	-	♦0.1	-
6 months - 6 mois	5	4	1	♦0.1	♦0.1	-
7 months - 7 mois	-	-	-	-	-	-
8 months - 8 mois	1	1	-	-	-	-
9 months - 9 mois	1	-	1	-	-	-
10 months - 10 mois	2	-	2	-	-	♦0.1
11 months - 11 mois	3	-	3	♦0.1	-	♦0.1
Estonia - Estonie						
2015 (C)						
Total...........	35	18	17	...	...	...
Less than 1 day - Moins de 1 jour	6	2	4	...	...	...
1 - 6 days - 1 - 6 jours	10	5	5	...	...	...
7 - 27 days - 7 - 27 jours	5	3	2	...	...	...
7 - 13 days - 7 - 13 jours	1	-	1	...	...	...
14 - 20 days - 14 - 20 jours	1	1	-	...	...	...

16. Infant deaths and infant mortality rates by age and sex: latest available year, 2007 - 2016
Décès d'enfants de moins d'un an et taux de mortalité infantile selon l'âge et le sexe : dernière année disponible, 2007 - 2016 (continued - suite)

Continent, country or area, year, code[a] and age / Continent, pays ou zone, année, code[a] et âge	Number - Nombre			Rate - Taux		
	Both sexes Les deux sexes	Male Masculin	Female Féminin	Both sexes Les deux sexes	Male Masculin	Female Féminin
EUROPE						
Estonia - Estonie						
2015 (C)						
21 - 27 days - 21 - 27 jours	3	2	1	...	...	...
28 days - 11 months - 28 jours - 11 mois............	14	8	6	...	...	...
28 days - less than 2 months - 28 jours - moins de 2 mois	5	3	2	...	...	...
2 months - 2 mois..........................	1	-	1	...	...	...
3 months - 3 mois..........................	1	1	-	...	...	...
4 months - 4 mois..........................	2	1	1	...	...	...
5 months - 5 mois..........................	1	1	-	...	...	...
6 months - 6 mois..........................	-	-	-	...	...	...
7 months - 7 mois..........................	-	-	-	...	...	...
8 months - 8 mois..........................	-	-	-	...	...	...
9 months - 9 mois..........................	1	-	1	...	...	...
10 months - 10 mois..........................	1	1	-	...	...	...
11 months - 11 mois..........................	2	1	1	...	...	...
Faeroe Islands - Îles Féroé						
2014 (C)						
Total..........................	4	4	-	...	...	...
Less than 1 day - Moins de 1 jour	1	1	-	...	...	...
1 - 6 days - 1 - 6 jours	2	2	-	...	...	...
7 - 27 days - 7 - 27 jours	-	-	-	...	...	...
7 - 13 days - 7 - 13 jours	-	-	-	...	...	...
14 - 20 days - 14 - 20 jours	-	-	-	...	...	...
21 - 27 days - 21 - 27 jours	-	-	-	...	...	...
28 days - 11 months - 28 jours - 11 mois..........................	1	1	-	...	...	...
28 days - less than 2 months - 28 jours - moins de 2 mois	-	-	-	...	...	...
2 months - 2 mois..........................	-	-	-	...	...	...
3 months - 3 mois..........................	-	-	-	...	...	...
4 months - 4 mois..........................	-	-	-	...	...	...
5 months - 5 mois..........................	1	1	-	...	...	...
6 months - 6 mois..........................	-	-	-	...	...	...
7 months - 7 mois..........................	-	-	-	...	...	...
8 months - 8 mois..........................	-	-	-	...	...	...
9 months - 9 mois..........................	-	-	-	...	...	...
10 months - 10 mois..........................	-	-	-	...	...	...
11 months - 11 mois..........................	-	-	-	...	...	...
Finland - Finlande[22]						
2015 (C)						
Total..........................	97	48	49	...	...	...
Less than 1 day - Moins de 1 jour	27	14	13	...	...	...
1 - 6 days - 1 - 6 jours	27	10	17	...	...	...
7 - 27 days - 7 - 27 jours	16	7	9	...	...	...
7 - 13 days - 7 - 13 jours	6	3	3	...	...	...
14 - 20 days - 14 - 20 jours	9	4	5	...	...	...
21 - 27 days - 21 - 27 jours	1	-	1	...	...	...
28 days - 11 months - 28 jours - 11 mois..........................	27	17	10	...	...	...
28 days - less than 2 months - 28 jours - moins de 2 mois	7	7	-	...	...	...
2 months - 2 mois..........................	5	3	2	...	...	...
3 months - 3 mois..........................	4	1	3	...	...	...
4 months - 4 mois..........................	2	1	1	...	...	...
5 months - 5 mois..........................	1	1	-	...	...	...
6 months - 6 mois..........................	3	1	2	...	...	...
7 months - 7 mois..........................	1	-	1	...	...	...
8 months - 8 mois..........................	1	-	1	...	...	...
9 months - 9 mois..........................	1	1	-	...	...	...
10 months - 10 mois..........................	1	1	-	...	...	...
11 months - 11 mois..........................	1	1	-	...	...	...
France						
2015 (C)						
Total..........................	2 655	1 480	1 175	3.5	3.8	3.2
Less than 1 day - Moins de 1 jour	681	362	319	0.9	0.9	0.9
1 - 6 days - 1 - 6 jours	626	377	249	0.8	1.0	0.7
7 - 27 days - 7 - 27 jours	584	313	271	0.8	0.8	0.7
7 - 13 days - 7 - 13 jours	337	175	162	0.4	0.4	0.4
14 - 20 days - 14 - 20 jours	153	90	63	0.2	0.2	0.2
21 - 27 days - 21 - 27 jours	94	48	46	0.1	0.1	0.1
28 days - 11 months - 28 jours - 11 mois..........................	764	428	336	1.0	1.1	0.9
28 days - less than 2 months - 28 jours - moins de 2 mois	228	134	94	0.3	0.3	0.3

16. Infant deaths and infant mortality rates by age and sex: latest available year, 2007 - 2016
Décès d'enfants de moins d'un an et taux de mortalité infantile selon l'âge et le sexe : dernière année disponible, 2007 - 2016 (continued - suite)

Continent, country or area, year, code[a] and age Continent, pays ou zone, année, code[a] et âge	Number - Nombre			Rate - Taux		
	Both sexes Les deux sexes	Male Masculin	Female Féminin	Both sexes Les deux sexes	Male Masculin	Female Féminin
EUROPE						
France						
2015 (C)						
2 months - 2 mois	112	62	50	0.1	0.2	0.1
3 months - 3 mois	89	60	29	0.1	0.2	♦0.1
4 months - 4 mois	89	49	40	0.1	0.1	♦0.1
5 months - 5 mois	65	41	24	0.1	0.1	♦0.1
6 months - 6 mois	45	14	31	0.1	-	0.1
7 months - 7 mois	28	13	15	-	-	-
8 months - 8 mois	33	11	22	-	-	♦0.1
9 months - 9 mois	26	11	15	-	-	-
10 months - 10 mois	22	16	6	-	-	-
11 months - 11 mois	27	17	10	-	-	-
Germany - Allemagne						
2015 (C)						
Total	2 405	1 297	1 108	3.3	3.4	3.1
Less than 1 day - Moins de 1 jour	846	431	415	1.1	1.1	1.2
1 - 6 days - 1 - 6 jours	506	270	236	0.7	0.7	0.7
7 - 27 days - 7 - 27 jours	348	202	146	0.5	0.5	0.4
7 - 13 days - 7 - 13 jours	171	107	64	0.2	0.3	0.2
14 - 20 days - 14 - 20 jours	94	47	47	0.1	0.1	0.1
21 - 27 days - 21 - 27 jours	83	48	35	0.1	0.1	0.1
28 days - 11 months - 28 jours - 11 mois	705	394	311	1.0	1.0	0.9
28 days - less than 2 months - 28 jours - moins de 2 mois	203	106	97	0.3	0.3	0.3
2 months - 2 mois	111	67	44	0.2	0.2	0.1
3 months - 3 mois	80	47	33	0.1	0.1	0.1
4 months - 4 mois	67	36	31	0.1	0.1	0.1
5 months - 5 mois	63	37	26	0.1	0.1	♦0.1
6 months - 6 mois	48	26	22	0.1	♦0.1	♦0.1
7 months - 7 mois	35	19	16	-	♦0.1	-
8 months - 8 mois	35	17	18	-	-	♦0.1
9 months - 9 mois	21	13	8	-	-	-
10 months - 10 mois	22	10	12	-	-	-
11 months - 11 mois	20	16	4	-	-	-
Greece - Grèce						
2015 (C)						
Total	364	199	165	4.0	4.2	3.7
Less than 1 day - Moins de 1 jour	74	43	31	0.8	0.9	0.7
1 - 6 days - 1 - 6 jours	105	53	52	1.1	1.1	1.2
7 - 27 days - 7 - 27 jours	81	47	34	0.9	1.0	0.8
7 - 13 days - 7 - 13 jours	48	28	20	0.5	♦0.6	♦0.4
14 - 20 days - 14 - 20 jours	19	12	7	♦0.2	♦0.3	♦0.2
21 - 27 days - 21 - 27 jours	14	7	7	♦0.2	♦0.1	♦0.2
28 days - 11 months - 28 jours - 11 mois	104	56	48	1.1	1.2	1.1
28 days - less than 2 months - 28 jours - moins de 2 mois	36	20	16	0.4	♦0.4	0.4
2 months - 2 mois	21	13	8	♦0.2	♦0.3	♦0.2
3 months - 3 mois	8	4	4	♦0.1	♦0.1	♦0.1
4 months - 4 mois	5	-	5	♦0.1	-	♦0.1
5 months - 5 mois	7	4	3	♦0.1	♦0.1	♦0.1
6 months - 6 mois	8	5	3	♦0.1	♦0.1	♦0.1
7 months - 7 mois	4	3	1	-	♦0.1	-
8 months - 8 mois	2	2	-	-	-	-
9 months - 9 mois	5	2	3	♦0.1	-	♦0.1
10 months - 10 mois	1	-	1	-	-	-
11 months - 11 mois	7	3	4	♦0.1	♦0.1	♦0.1
Hungary - Hongrie[23]						
2015 (C)						
Total	383	215	168	4.2	4.5	3.8
Less than 1 day - Moins de 1 jour	70	38	32	0.8	0.8	0.7
1 - 6 days - 1 - 6 jours	85	51	34	0.9	1.1	0.8
7 - 27 days - 7 - 27 jours	89	48	41	1.0	1.0	0.9
7 - 13 days - 7 - 13 jours	56	33	23	0.6	0.7	♦0.5
14 - 20 days - 14 - 20 jours	20	9	11	♦0.2	♦0.2	♦0.2
21 - 27 days - 21 - 27 jours	13	6	7	♦0.1	♦0.1	♦0.2
28 days - 11 months - 28 jours - 11 mois	139	78	...	1.5	1.6	...
28 days - less than 2 months - 28 jours - moins de 2 mois	48	28	20	0.5	♦0.6	♦0.4
2 months - 2 mois	14	6	8	♦0.2	♦0.1	♦0.2
3 months - 3 mois	17	12	5	♦0.2	♦0.3	♦0.1
4 months - 4 mois	13	5	8	♦0.1	♦0.1	♦0.2

470

16. Infant deaths and infant mortality rates by age and sex: latest available year, 2007 - 2016
Décès d'enfants de moins d'un an et taux de mortalité infantile selon l'âge et le sexe : dernière année disponible, 2007 - 2016 (continued - suite)

Continent, country or area, year, code[a] and age / Continent, pays ou zone, année, code[a] et âge	Number - Nombre			Rate - Taux		
	Both sexes Les deux sexes	Male Masculin	Female Féminin	Both sexes Les deux sexes	Male Masculin	Female Féminin
EUROPE						
Hungary - Hongrie[23]						
2015 (C)						
5 months - 5 mois..	7	4	3	♦0.1	♦0.1	♦0.1
6 months - 6 mois..	13	6	7	♦0.1	♦0.1	♦0.2
7 months - 7 mois..	9	6	3	♦0.1	♦0.1	♦0.1
8 months - 8 mois..	3	3	...	-	♦0.1	...
9 months - 9 mois..	6	4	...	♦0.1	♦0.1	...
10 months - 10 mois..	5	3	...	♦0.1	♦0.1	...
11 months - 11 mois..	4	1	...	-	-	...
Iceland - Islande						
2015 (C)						
Total..	9	4	5	...	...	...
Less than 1 day - Moins de 1 jour	4	-	4	...	...	...
1 - 6 days - 1 - 6 jours	1	1	-	...	...	...
7 - 27 days - 7 - 27 jours	1	-	1	...	...	...
7 - 13 days - 7 - 13 jours	-	-	-	...	...	...
14 - 20 days - 14 - 20 jours	-	-	-	...	...	...
21 - 27 days - 21 - 27 jours	1	-	1	...	...	...
28 days - 11 months - 28 jours - 11 mois..................	3	3	-	...	...	...
28 days - less than 2 months - 28 jours - moins de 2 mois	1	1	-	...	...	...
2 months - 2 mois..	1	1	-	...	...	...
3 months - 3 mois..	-	-	-	...	...	...
4 months - 4 mois..	-	-	-	...	...	...
5 months - 5 mois..	-	-	-	...	...	...
6 months - 6 mois..	1	1	-	...	...	...
7 months - 7 mois..	-	-	-	...	...	...
8 months - 8 mois..	-	-	-	...	...	...
9 months - 9 mois..	-	-	-	...	...	...
10 months - 10 mois..	-	-	-	...	...	...
11 months - 11 mois..	-	-	-	...	...	...
Ireland - Irlande						
2011 (+C)						
Total..	262	150	112	3.5	4.0	3.1
Less than 1 day - Moins de 1 jour	88	43	45	1.2	1.1	1.2
1 - 6 days - 1 - 6 jours	59	38	21	0.8	1.0	♦0.6
7 - 27 days - 7 - 27 jours	41	30	11	0.6	0.8	♦0.3
7 - 13 days - 7 - 13 jours	18	13	5	♦0.2	♦0.3	♦0.1
14 - 20 days - 14 - 20 jours	17	13	4	♦0.2	♦0.3	♦0.1
21 - 27 days - 21 - 27 jours	6	4	2	♦0.1	♦0.1	♦0.1
28 days - 11 months - 28 jours - 11 mois..................	74	39	35	1.0	1.0	1.0
28 days - less than 2 months - 28 jours - moins de 2 mois	20	12	8	♦0.3	♦0.3	♦0.2
2 months - 2 mois..	17	7	10	♦0.2	♦0.2	♦0.3
3 months - 3 mois..	11	4	7	♦0.1	♦0.1	♦0.2
4 months - 4 mois..	5	5	-	♦0.1	♦0.1	-
5 months - 5 mois..	6	3	3	♦0.1	♦0.1	♦0.1
6 months - 6 mois..	3	1	2	-	-	♦0.1
7 months - 7 mois..	2	1	1	-	-	-
8 months - 8 mois..	1	-	1			
9 months - 9 mois..	4	3	1	♦0.1	♦0.1	-
10 months - 10 mois..	4	2	2	♦0.1	♦0.1	♦0.1
11 months - 11 mois..	1	1	-	-	-	-
Italy - Italie						
2015 (C)						
Total..	1 398	772	626	2.9	3.1	2.7
Latvia - Lettonie						
2015 (C)						
Total..	90	59	31	...	...	...
Less than 1 day - Moins de 1 jour	32	20	12	...	...	...
1 - 6 days - 1 - 6 jours	13	10	3	...	...	...
7 - 27 days - 7 - 27 jours	10	6	4	...	...	...
7 - 13 days - 7 - 13 jours	6	5	1	...	...	...
14 - 20 days - 14 - 20 jours	2	1	1	...	...	...
21 - 27 days - 21 - 27 jours	2	-	2	...	...	...
28 days - 11 months - 28 jours - 11 mois..................	35	23	12	...	...	...
28 days - less than 2 months - 28 jours - moins de 2 mois	12	9	3	...	...	...
2 months - 2 mois..	6	3	3	...	...	...
3 months - 3 mois..	4	4	-	...	...	...
4 months - 4 mois..	3	2	1	...	...	...

471

16. Infant deaths and infant mortality rates by age and sex: latest available year, 2007 - 2016
Décès d'enfants de moins d'un an et taux de mortalité infantile selon l'âge et le sexe : dernière année disponible, 2007 - 2016 (continued - suite)

Continent, country or area, year, code[a] and age / Continent, pays ou zone, année, code[a] et âge	Number - Nombre			Rate - Taux		
	Both sexes Les deux sexes	Male Masculin	Female Féminin	Both sexes Les deux sexes	Male Masculin	Female Féminin
EUROPE						
Latvia - Lettonie						
2015 (C)						
5 months - 5 mois	3	-	3	...	...	...
6 months - 6 mois	2	1	1	...	...	...
7 months - 7 mois	1	1	-	...	...	...
8 months - 8 mois	1	1	-	...	...	...
9 months - 9 mois	1	-	1	...	...	...
10 months - 10 mois	2	2	-	...	...	...
11 months - 11 mois	-	-	-	...	...	...
Unknown - Inconnu	1	-	1	...	...	...
Liechtenstein						
2015 (C)						
Total	2	2	-	...	...	...
1 - 6 days - 1 - 6 jours	2	2	-	...	...	...
Lithuania - Lituanie						
2015 (C)						
Total	132	76	56	4.2	4.7	3.7
Less than 1 day - Moins de 1 jour	34	26	8	1.1	♦1.6	♦0.5
1 - 6 days - 1 - 6 jours	19	11	8	♦0.6	♦0.7	♦0.5
7 - 27 days - 7 - 27 jours	21	11	10	♦0.7	♦0.7	♦0.7
7 - 13 days - 7 - 13 jours	9	6	3	♦0.3	♦0.4	♦0.2
14 - 20 days - 14 - 20 jours	7	3	4	♦0.2	♦0.2	♦0.3
21 - 27 days - 21 - 27 jours	5	2	3	♦0.2	♦0.1	♦0.2
28 days - 11 months - 28 jours - 11 mois	58	28	30	1.8	♦1.7	2.0
28 days - less than 2 months - 28 jours - moins de 2 mois	17	10	7	♦0.5	♦0.6	♦0.5
2 months - 2 mois	7	1	6	♦0.2	♦0.1	♦0.4
3 months - 3 mois	5	1	4	♦0.2	♦0.1	♦0.3
4 months - 4 mois	5	2	3	♦0.2	♦0.1	♦0.2
5 months - 5 mois	7	3	4	♦0.2	♦0.2	♦0.3
6 months - 6 mois	4	3	1	♦0.1	♦0.2	♦0.1
7 months - 7 mois	4	2	2	♦0.1	♦0.1	♦0.1
8 months - 8 mois	1	1	-	-	♦0.1	-
9 months - 9 mois	1	-	1	-	-	♦0.1
10 months - 10 mois	4	3	1	♦0.1	♦0.2	♦0.1
11 months - 11 mois	3	2	1	♦0.1	♦0.1	♦0.1
Luxembourg						
2015 (C)						
Total	17	14	3	...	...	...
Less than 1 day - Moins de 1 jour	6	5	1	...	...	...
1 - 6 days - 1 - 6 jours	3	3	-	...	...	...
7 - 27 days - 7 - 27 jours	3	3	-	...	...	...
28 days - 11 months - 28 jours - 11 mois	5	3	2	...	...	...
Malta - Malte						
2015 (C)						
Total	25	16	9	...	...	...
Less than 1 day - Moins de 1 jour	7	3	4	...	...	...
1 - 6 days - 1 - 6 jours	4	3	1	...	...	...
7 - 27 days - 7 - 27 jours	4	3	1	...	...	...
7 - 13 days - 7 - 13 jours	3	2	1	...	...	...
14 - 20 days - 14 - 20 jours	1	1	-	...	...	...
21 - 27 days - 21 - 27 jours	-	-	-	...	...	...
28 days - 11 months - 28 jours - 11 mois	10	7	3	...	...	...
28 days - less than 2 months - 28 jours - moins de 2 mois	2	1	1	...	...	...
2 months - 2 mois	2	2	-	...	...	...
3 months - 3 mois	1	-	1	...	...	...
4 months - 4 mois	1	1	-	...	...	...
5 months - 5 mois	1	1	-	...	...	...
6 months - 6 mois	1	1	-	...	...	...
7 months - 7 mois	-	-	-	...	...	...
8 months - 8 mois	-	-	-	...	...	...
9 months - 9 mois	2	1	1	...	...	...
10 months - 10 mois	-	-	-	...	...	...
11 months - 11 mois	-	-	-	...	...	...
Montenegro - Monténégro						
2015 (C)						
Total	16	5	11	...	...	...
Less than 1 day - Moins de 1 jour	4	2	2	...	...	...
1 - 6 days - 1 - 6 jours	4	1	3	...	...	...

16. Infant deaths and infant mortality rates by age and sex: latest available year, 2007 - 2016
Décès d'enfants de moins d'un an et taux de mortalité infantile selon l'âge et le sexe : dernière année disponible, 2007 - 2016 (continued - suite)

Continent, country or area, year, code[a] and age / Continent, pays ou zone, année, code[a] et âge	Number - Nombre			Rate - Taux		
	Both sexes Les deux sexes	Male Masculin	Female Féminin	Both sexes Les deux sexes	Male Masculin	Female Féminin
EUROPE						
Montenegro - Monténégro						
2015 (C)						
7 - 27 days - 7 - 27 jours	2	1	1	...	...	...
28 days - 11 months - 28 jours - 11 mois	6	1	5	...	...	...
Netherlands - Pays-Bas[24]						
2015 (C)						
Total	561	313	248	3.3	3.6	3.0
Less than 1 day - Moins de 1 jour	169	97	72	1.0	1.1	0.9
1 - 6 days - 1 - 6 jours	126	72	54	0.7	0.8	0.6
7 - 27 days - 7 - 27 jours	125	64	61	0.7	0.7	0.7
28 days - 11 months - 28 jours - 11 mois	141	80	61	0.8	0.9	0.7
Norway - Norvège[25]						
2015 (C)						
Total	133	78	55	2.3	2.6	1.9
Less than 1 day - Moins de 1 jour	33	16	17	0.6	◆0.5	◆0.6
1 - 6 days - 1 - 6 jours	36	18	18	0.6	◆0.6	◆0.6
7 - 27 days - 7 - 27 jours	20	15	5	◆0.3	◆0.5	◆0.2
28 days - 11 months - 28 jours - 11 mois	44	29	15	0.7	◆1.0	◆0.5
Poland - Pologne						
2015 (C)						
Total	1 476	830	646	4.0	4.4	3.6
Less than 1 day - Moins de 1 jour	429	250	179	1.2	1.3	1.0
1 - 6 days - 1 - 6 jours	333	185	148	0.9	1.0	0.8
7 - 27 days - 7 - 27 jours	305	183	122	0.8	1.0	0.7
7 - 13 days - 7 - 13 jours	140	90	50	0.4	0.5	0.3
14 - 20 days - 14 - 20 jours	106	58	48	0.3	0.3	0.3
21 - 27 days - 21 - 27 jours	59	35	24	0.2	0.2	◆0.1
28 days - 11 months - 28 jours - 11 mois	409	212	197	1.1	1.1	1.1
28 days - less than 2 months - 28 jours - moins de 2 mois	130	68	62	0.4	0.4	0.3
2 months - 2 mois	59	30	29	0.2	0.2	◆0.2
3 months - 3 mois	40	18	22	0.1	◆0.1	◆0.1
4 months - 4 mois	46	25	21	0.1	◆0.1	◆0.1
5 months - 5 mois	28	12	16	◆0.1	◆0.1	◆0.1
6 months - 6 mois	23	10	13	◆0.1	◆0.1	◆0.1
7 months - 7 mois	30	22	8	0.1	◆0.1	-
8 months - 8 mois	20	13	7	◆0.1	◆0.1	-
9 months - 9 mois	17	10	7	-	◆0.1	-
10 months - 10 mois	4	1	3	-	-	-
11 months - 11 mois	12	3	9	-	-	◆0.1
Portugal[26]						
2015 (C)						
Total	250	148	102	2.9	3.4	2.4
Less than 1 day - Moins de 1 jour	54	35	19	0.6	0.8	◆0.5
1 - 6 days - 1 - 6 jours	63	32	31	0.7	0.7	0.7
7 - 27 days - 7 - 27 jours	58	33	25	0.7	0.8	◆0.6
7 - 13 days - 7 - 13 jours	31	17	14	0.4	◆0.4	◆0.3
14 - 20 days - 14 - 20 jours	19	12	7	◆0.2	◆0.3	◆0.2
21 - 27 days - 21 - 27 jours	8	4	4	◆0.1	◆0.1	◆0.1
28 days - 11 months - 28 jours - 11 mois	75	48	27	0.9	1.1	◆0.6
28 days - less than 2 months - 28 jours - moins de 2 mois	21	14	7	◆0.2	◆0.3	◆0.2
2 months - 2 mois	5	3	2	◆0.1	◆0.1	-
3 months - 3 mois	10	4	6	◆0.1	◆0.1	◆0.1
4 months - 4 mois	10	6	4	◆0.1	◆0.1	◆0.1
5 months - 5 mois	5	5	-	◆0.1	◆0.1	-
6 months - 6 mois	8	5	3	◆0.1	◆0.1	◆0.1
7 months - 7 mois	4	2	2	-	-	-
8 months - 8 mois	3	3	-	-	◆0.1	-
9 months - 9 mois	2	1	1	-	-	-
10 months - 10 mois	3	2	1	-	-	-
11 months - 11 mois	4	3	1	-	◆0.1	-
Republic of Moldova - République de Moldova[27]						
2014 (C)						
Total	372	226	146	9.6	11.3	7.8
Less than 1 day - Moins de 1 jour	75	46	29	1.9	2.3	◆1.6
1 - 6 days - 1 - 6 jours	95	58	37	2.5	2.9	2.0
7 - 27 days - 7 - 27 jours	69	46	23	1.8	2.3	◆1.2
28 days - 11 months - 28 jours - 11 mois	133	76	57	3.4	3.8	3.1

16. Infant deaths and infant mortality rates by age and sex: latest available year, 2007 - 2016
Décès d'enfants de moins d'un an et taux de mortalité infantile selon l'âge et le sexe : dernière année disponible, 2007 - 2016 (continued - suite)

Continent, country or area, year, code[a] and age / Continent, pays ou zone, année, code[a] et âge	Number - Nombre			Rate - Taux		
	Both sexes Les deux sexes	Male Masculin	Female Féminin	Both sexes Les deux sexes	Male Masculin	Female Féminin
EUROPE						
Romania - Roumanie						
2015 (C)						
Total	1 500	842	658	7.6	8.3	6.9
Less than 1 day - Moins de 1 jour	155	82	73	0.8	0.8	0.8
1 - 6 days - 1 - 6 jours	439	260	179	2.2	2.6	1.9
7 - 27 days - 7 - 27 jours	263	145	118	1.3	1.4	1.2
7 - 13 days - 7 - 13 jours	120	61	59	0.6	0.6	0.6
14 - 20 days - 14 - 20 jours	75	40	35	0.4	0.4	0.4
21 - 27 days - 21 - 27 jours	68	44	24	0.3	0.4	◆0.3
28 days - 11 months - 28 jours - 11 mois	643	355	288	3.3	3.5	3.0
28 days - less than 2 months - 28 jours - moins de 2 mois	219	119	100	1.1	1.2	1.0
2 months - 2 mois	114	57	57	0.6	0.6	0.6
3 months - 3 mois	67	37	30	0.3	0.4	0.3
4 months - 4 mois	56	32	24	0.3	0.3	◆0.3
5 months - 5 mois	55	37	18	0.3	0.4	◆0.2
6 months - 6 mois	31	14	17	0.2	◆0.1	◆0.2
7 months - 7 mois	23	10	13	◆0.1	◆0.1	◆0.1
8 months - 8 mois	20	16	4	◆0.1	◆0.2	-
9 months - 9 mois	16	8	8	◆0.1	◆0.1	◆0.1
10 months - 10 mois	19	12	7	◆0.1	◆0.1	◆0.1
11 months - 11 mois	23	13	10	◆0.1	◆0.1	◆0.1
Russian Federation - Fédération de Russie[11]						
2012 (C)						
Total	16 306	9 219	7 087	8.6	9.4	7.7
Less than 1 day - Moins de 1 jour	1 897	1 009	888	1.0	1.0	1.0
1 - 6 days - 1 - 6 jours	5 072	2 961	2 111	2.7	3.0	2.3
7 - 27 days - 7 - 27 jours	3 438	1 958	1 480	1.8	2.0	1.6
7 - 13 days - 7 - 13 jours	1 798	1 020	778	0.9	1.0	0.8
14 - 20 days - 14 - 20 jours	952	560	392	0.5	0.6	0.4
21 - 27 days - 21 - 27 jours	688	378	310	0.4	0.4	0.3
28 days - 11 months - 28 jours - 11 mois	5 898	3 290	2 608	3.1	3.4	2.8
28 days - less than 2 months - 28 jours - moins de 2 mois	2 063	1 166	897	1.1	1.2	1.0
2 months - 2 mois	942	525	417	0.5	0.5	0.5
3 months - 3 mois	691	372	319	0.4	0.4	0.3
4 months - 4 mois	562	333	229	0.3	0.3	0.2
5 months - 5 mois	417	221	196	0.2	0.2	0.2
6 months - 6 mois	334	184	150	0.2	0.2	0.2
7 months - 7 mois	252	139	113	0.1	0.1	0.1
8 months - 8 mois	219	127	92	0.1	0.1	0.1
9 months - 9 mois	172	86	86	0.1	0.1	0.1
10 months - 10 mois	134	74	60	0.1	0.1	0.1
11 months - 11 mois	112	63	49	0.1	0.1	0.1
Unknown - Inconnu	1	1	-	-	-	-
San Marino - Saint-Marin						
2014 (+C)						
Total	1	1	-	...	...	...
Less than 1 day - Moins de 1 jour	-	-	-	...	...	...
1 - 6 days - 1 - 6 jours	-	-	-	...	...	...
7 - 27 days - 7 - 27 jours	-	-	-	...	...	...
28 days - 11 months - 28 jours - 11 mois	1	1	-	...	...	...
Serbia - Serbie[28]						
2015 (+C)						
Total	346	181	165	5.3	5.3	5.2
Less than 1 day - Moins de 1 jour	90	44	46	1.4	1.3	1.5
1 - 6 days - 1 - 6 jours	98	64	34	1.5	1.9	1.1
7 - 27 days - 7 - 27 jours	60	29	31	0.9	◆0.9	1.0
7 - 13 days - 7 - 13 jours	31	13	18	0.5	◆0.4	◆0.6
14 - 20 days - 14 - 20 jours	18	11	7	◆0.3	◆0.3	◆0.2
21 - 27 days - 21 - 27 jours	11	5	6	◆0.2	◆0.1	◆0.2
28 days - 11 months - 28 jours - 11 mois	98	44	54	1.5	1.3	1.7
28 days - less than 2 months - 28 jours - moins de 2 mois	39	21	18	0.6	◆0.6	◆0.6
2 months - 2 mois	12	5	7	◆0.2	◆0.1	◆0.2
3 months - 3 mois	10	6	4	◆0.2	◆0.2	◆0.1
4 months - 4 mois	7	1	6	◆0.1	-	◆0.2
5 months - 5 mois	5	1	4	◆0.1	◆0.1	◆0.1
6 months - 6 mois	7	5	2	◆0.1	◆0.1	◆0.1
7 months - 7 mois	9	1	8	◆0.1	-	◆0.3
8 months - 8 mois	5	3	2	◆0.1	◆0.1	◆0.1

Continent, country or area, year, code[a] and age / Continent, pays ou zone, année, code[a] et âge	Number - Nombre			Rate - Taux		
	Both sexes Les deux sexes	Male Masculin	Female Féminin	Both sexes Les deux sexes	Male Masculin	Female Féminin
EUROPE						
Serbia - Serbie[28]						
2015 (+C)						
9 months - 9 mois	2	1	1	-	-	-
10 months - 10 mois	1	-	1	-	-	-
11 months - 11 mois	1	-	1	-	-	-
Slovakia - Slovaquie						
2015 (C)						
Total	285	162	123	5.1	5.7	4.6
Less than 1 day - Moins de 1 jour	71	41	30	1.3	1.4	1.1
1 - 6 days - 1 - 6 jours	49	28	21	0.9	♦1.0	♦0.8
7 - 27 days - 7 - 27 jours	61	39	22	1.1	1.4	♦0.8
7 - 13 days - 7 - 13 jours	28	17	11	♦0.5	♦0.6	♦0.4
14 - 20 days - 14 - 20 jours	17	12	5	♦0.3	♦0.4	♦0.2
21 - 27 days - 21 - 27 jours	16	10	6	♦0.3	♦0.3	♦0.2
28 days - 11 months - 28 jours - 11 mois	104	54	50	1.9	1.9	1.9
28 days - less than 2 months - 28 jours - moins de 2 mois	31	16	15	0.6	♦0.6	♦0.6
2 months - 2 mois	20	15	5	♦0.4	♦0.5	♦0.2
3 months - 3 mois	11	3	8	♦0.2	♦0.1	♦0.3
4 months - 4 mois	6	4	2	♦0.1	♦0.1	♦0.1
5 months - 5 mois	9	3	6	♦0.2	♦0.1	♦0.2
6 months - 6 mois	7	3	4	♦0.1	♦0.1	♦0.1
7 months - 7 mois	4	1	3	♦0.1	-	♦0.1
8 months - 8 mois	8	5	3	♦0.1	♦0.2	♦0.1
9 months - 9 mois	5	3	2	♦0.1	♦0.1	♦0.1
10 months - 10 mois	3	1	2	♦0.1	-	♦0.1
11 months - 11 mois	-	-	-	-	-	-
Slovenia - Slovénie						
2015 (C)						
Total	33	18	15	...	...	...
Less than 1 day - Moins de 1 jour	8	4	4	...	...	...
1 - 6 days - 1 - 6 jours	4	3	1	...	...	...
7 - 27 days - 7 - 27 jours	5	2	3	...	...	...
7 - 13 days - 7 - 13 jours	1	-	1	...	...	...
14 - 20 days - 14 - 20 jours	2	-	2	...	...	...
21 - 27 days - 21 - 27 jours	2	2	-	...	...	...
28 days - 11 months - 28 jours - 11 mois	16	9	7	...	...	...
28 days - less than 2 months - 28 jours - moins de 2 mois	8	5	3	...	...	...
2 months - 2 mois	2	1	1	...	...	...
3 months - 3 mois	-	-	-	...	...	...
4 months - 4 mois	-	-	-	...	...	...
5 months - 5 mois	1	-	1	...	...	...
6 months - 6 mois	1	1	-	...	...	...
7 months - 7 mois	2	1	1	...	...	...
8 months - 8 mois	1	1	-	...	...	...
9 months - 9 mois	-	-	-	...	...	...
10 months - 10 mois	1	-	1	...	...	...
11 months - 11 mois	-	-	-	...	...	...
Spain - Espagne						
2015 (C)						
Total	1 117	620	497	2.7	2.9	2.4
Less than 1 day - Moins de 1 jour	234	127	107	0.6	0.6	0.5
1 - 6 days - 1 - 6 jours	278	162	116	0.7	0.8	0.6
7 - 27 days - 7 - 27 jours	248	138	110	0.6	0.6	0.5
28 days - 11 months - 28 jours - 11 mois	357	193	164	0.9	0.9	0.8
Sweden - Suède						
2015 (C)						
Total	282	166	116	2.5	2.8	2.1
Less than 1 day - Moins de 1 jour	71	42	29	0.6	0.7	♦0.5
1 - 6 days - 1 - 6 jours	77	47	30	0.7	0.8	0.5
7 - 27 days - 7 - 27 jours	47	22	25	0.4	♦0.4	♦0.5
28 days - 11 months - 28 jours - 11 mois	87	55	32	0.8	0.9	0.6
Switzerland - Suisse						
2015 (C)						
Total	340	199	141	3.9	4.5	3.4
Less than 1 day - Moins de 1 jour	182	100	82	2.1	2.2	2.0
1 - 6 days - 1 - 6 jours	38	23	15	0.4	♦0.5	♦0.4
7 - 27 days - 7 - 27 jours	47	24	23	0.5	♦0.5	♦0.5
7 - 13 days - 7 - 13 jours	29	15	14	♦0.3	♦0.3	♦0.3

Continent, country or area, year, code[a] and age / Continent, pays ou zone, année, code[a] et âge	Number - Nombre			Rate - Taux		
	Both sexes Les deux sexes	Male Masculin	Female Féminin	Both sexes Les deux sexes	Male Masculin	Female Féminin
EUROPE						
Switzerland - Suisse						
2015 (C)						
14 - 20 days - 14 - 20 jours	12	6	6	♦0.1	♦0.1	♦0.1
21 - 27 days - 21 - 27 jours	6	3	3	♦0.1	♦0.1	♦0.1
28 days - 11 months - 28 jours - 11 mois	73	52	21	0.8	1.2	♦0.5
28 days - less than 2 months - 28 jours - moins de 2 mois	25	17	8	♦0.3	♦0.4	♦0.2
2 months - 2 mois	6	5	1	♦0.1	♦0.1	-
3 months - 3 mois	13	9	4	♦0.2	♦0.2	♦0.1
4 months - 4 mois	6	4	2	♦0.1	♦0.1	-
5 months - 5 mois	5	4	1	♦0.1	♦0.1	-
6 months - 6 mois	4	1	3	-	-	♦0.1
7 months - 7 mois	5	3	2	♦0.1	♦0.1	-
8 months - 8 mois	6	6	-	♦0.1	♦0.1	-
9 months - 9 mois	1	1	-	-	-	-
10 months - 10 mois	-	-	-	-	-	-
11 months - 11 mois	2	2	-	-	-	-
TFYR of Macedonia - L'ex-R. y. de Macédoine						
2015 (C)						
Total	198	111	87	8.6	9.3	7.8
Less than 1 day - Moins de 1 jour	41	22	19	1.8	♦1.8	♦1.7
1 - 6 days - 1 - 6 jours	73	44	29	3.2	3.7	♦2.6
7 - 27 days - 7 - 27 jours	43	24	19	1.9	♦2.0	♦1.7
7 - 13 days - 7 - 13 jours	20	11	9	♦0.9	♦0.9	♦0.8
14 - 20 days - 14 - 20 jours	13	6	7	♦0.6	♦0.5	♦0.6
21 - 27 days - 21 - 27 jours	10	7	3	♦0.4	♦0.6	♦0.3
28 days - 11 months - 28 jours - 11 mois	41	21	20	1.8	♦1.8	♦1.8
28 days - less than 2 months - 28 jours - moins de 2 mois	14	9	5	♦0.6	♦0.8	♦0.4
2 months - 2 mois	9	4	5	♦0.4	♦0.3	♦0.4
3 months - 3 mois	3	-	3	♦0.1	-	♦0.3
4 months - 4 mois	4	1	3	♦0.2	♦0.1	♦0.3
5 months - 5 mois	1	1	-	-	♦0.1	-
6 months - 6 mois	4	3	1	♦0.2	♦0.3	♦0.1
7 months - 7 mois	2	1	1	♦0.1	♦0.1	♦0.1
8 months - 8 mois	-	-	-	-	-	-
9 months - 9 mois	1	1	-	-	♦0.1	-
10 months - 10 mois	2	1	1	♦0.1	♦0.1	♦0.1
11 months - 11 mois	1	-	1	-	-	♦0.1
Ukraine[29]						
2014 (+C)						
Total	3 656	2 124	1 532	7.8	8.8	6.8
Less than 1 day - Moins de 1 jour	544	302	242	1.2	1.3	1.1
1 - 6 days - 1 - 6 jours	977	593	384	2.1	2.5	1.7
7 - 27 days - 7 - 27 jours	748	435	313	1.6	1.8	1.4
28 days - 11 months - 28 jours - 11 mois	1 387	794	593	3.0	3.3	2.6
United Kingdom of Great Britain and Northern Ireland - Royaume-Uni de Grande-Bretagne et d'Irlande du Nord[30]						
2015 (+C)						
Total	3 005	1 739	1 266	3.9	4.4	3.3
Less than 1 day - Moins de 1 jour	1 084	627	457	1.4	1.6	1.2
1 - 6 days - 1 - 6 jours	559	339	220	0.7	0.9	0.6
7 - 27 days - 7 - 27 jours	460	254	206	0.6	0.6	0.5
28 days - 11 months - 28 jours - 11 mois	902	519	383	1.2	1.3	1.0
OCEANIA - OCÉANIE						
Australia - Australie[31]						
2015 (+C)						
Total	991	542	449	3.2	3.5	3.0
Less than 1 day - Moins de 1 jour	427	231	196	1.4	1.5	1.3
1 - 6 days - 1 - 6 jours	156	84	72	0.5	0.5	0.5
7 - 27 days - 7 - 27 jours	124	67	57	0.4	0.4	0.4
7 - 13 days - 7 - 13 jours	64	32	32	0.2	0.2	0.2
14 - 20 days - 14 - 20 jours	37	18	19	0.1	♦0.1	♦0.1
21 - 27 days - 21 - 27 jours	23	17	6	♦0.1	♦0.1	-
28 days - 11 months - 28 jours - 11 mois	280	161	126	0.9	1.0	0.8
28 days - less than 2 months - 28 jours - moins de 2 mois	91	56	35	0.3	0.4	0.2
2 months - 2 mois	49	27	22	0.2	♦0.2	♦0.1

16. Infant deaths and infant mortality rates by age and sex: latest available year, 2007 - 2016
Décès d'enfants de moins d'un an et taux de mortalité infantile selon l'âge et le sexe : dernière année disponible, 2007 - 2016 (continued - suite)

Continent, country or area, year, code[a] and age / Continent, pays ou zone, année, code[a] et âge	Number - Nombre			Rate - Taux		
	Both sexes Les deux sexes	Male Masculin	Female Féminin	Both sexes Les deux sexes	Male Masculin	Female Féminin
OCEANIA - OCÉANIE						
Australia - Australie[31]						
2015 (+C)						
3 months - 3 mois	42	23	19	0.1	♦0.1	♦0.1
4 months - 4 mois	21	8	13	♦0.1	♦0.1	♦0.1
5 months - 5 mois	22	16	6	♦0.1	♦0.1	-
6 months - 6 mois	19	12	7	♦0.1	♦0.1	-
7 months - 7 mois	17	9	8	♦0.1	♦0.1	♦0.1
8 months - 8 mois	8	3	5	-	-	-
9 months - 9 mois	3	3	4	-	-	-
10 months - 10 mois	7	1	5	-	-	-
11 months - 11 mois	1	3	2	-	-	-
French Polynesia - Polynésie française						
2008 (C)						
Total	23	...	...	...	...	...
Less than 7 days - Moins de 7 jours	14	...	...	...	...	...
7 - 27 days - 7 - 27 jours	-	...	...	...	...	...
28 days - 11 months - 28 jours - 11 mois	9	...	...	...	...	...
Guam[32]						
2015 (C)						
Total	47	23	24	...	...	...
Less than 1 day - Moins de 1 jour	10	4	6	...	...	...
1 - 6 days - 1 - 6 jours	16	9	7	...	...	...
7 - 27 days - 7 - 27 jours	7	1	6	...	...	...
7 - 13 days - 7 - 13 jours	2	-	2	...	...	...
14 - 20 days - 14 - 20 jours	4	1	3	...	...	...
21 - 27 days - 21 - 27 jours	1	-	1	...	...	...
28 days - 11 months - 28 jours - 11 mois	14	9	5	...	...	...
28 days - less than 2 months - 28 jours - moins de 2 mois	2	2	-	...	...	...
2 months - 2 mois	3	3	-	...	...	...
3 months - 3 mois	3	-	3	...	...	...
4 months - 4 mois	-	-	-	...	...	...
5 months - 5 mois	-	-	-	...	...	...
6 months - 6 mois	2	1	1	...	...	...
7 months - 7 mois	-	-	-	...	...	...
8 months - 8 mois	2	2	-	...	...	...
9 months - 9 mois	1	1	-	...	...	...
10 months - 10 mois	1	-	1	...	...	...
11 months - 11 mois	-	-	-	...	...	...
New Caledonia - Nouvelle-Calédonie						
2015 (C)						
Total	25	18	7	...	...	...
Less than 1 day - Moins de 1 jour	4	3	1	...	...	...
1 - 6 days - 1 - 6 jours	5	4	1	...	...	...
7 - 27 days - 7 - 27 jours	7	5	2	...	...	...
7 - 13 days - 7 - 13 jours	5	4	1	...	...	...
14 - 20 days - 14 - 20 jours	2	1	1	...	...	...
21 - 27 days - 21 - 27 jours	-	-	-	...	...	...
28 days - 11 months - 28 jours - 11 mois	9	6	3	...	...	...
28 days - less than 2 months - 28 jours - moins de 2 mois	3	1	2	...	...	...
2 - 11 months - 2 - 11 mois	6	5	1	...	...	...
New Zealand - Nouvelle-Zélande[33]						
2016 (+C)						
Total	210	111	99	3.5	3.6	3.4
Less than 1 day - Moins de 1 jour	69	33	36	1.2	1.1	1.2
1 - 6 days - 1 - 6 jours	39	15	24	0.7	♦0.5	♦0.8
7 - 27 days - 7 - 27 jours	24	15	12	♦0.4	♦0.5	♦0.4
7 - 13 days - 7 - 13 jours	12	9	3	♦0.2	♦0.3	♦0.1
14 - 20 days - 14 - 20 jours	6	3	6	♦0.1	♦0.1	♦0.2
21 - 27 days - 21 - 27 jours	9	3	3	♦0.2	♦0.1	♦0.1
28 days - 11 months - 28 jours - 11 mois	81	45	27	1.4	1.5	♦0.9
28 days - less than 2 months - 28 jours - moins de 2 mois	21	12	6	♦0.4	♦0.4	♦0.2
2 months - 2 mois	12	6	6	♦0.2	♦0.2	♦0.2
3 months - 3 mois	12	6	3	♦0.2	♦0.2	♦0.1
4 months - 4 mois	3	3	-	♦0.1	♦0.1	-
5 months - 5 mois	9	6	3	♦0.1	♦0.2	♦0.1
6 months - 6 mois	6	3	-	♦0.1	♦0.1	-
7 months - 7 mois	6	3	3	♦0.1	♦0.1	♦0.1
8 months - 8 mois	6	3	3	♦0.1	♦0.1	♦0.1

Continent, country or area, year, code[a] and age Continent, pays ou zone, année, code[a] et âge	Number - Nombre			Rate - Taux		
	Both sexes Les deux sexes	Male Masculin	Female Féminin	Both sexes Les deux sexes	Male Masculin	Female Féminin
OCEANIA - OCÉANIE						
New Zealand - Nouvelle-Zélande[33]						
2016 (+C)						
9 months - 9 mois	3	3	-	♦0.1	♦0.1	-
10 months - 10 mois	3	-	3	♦0.1	-	♦0.1
11 months - 11 mois	-	-	-	-	-	-

FOOTNOTES - NOTES

Italics: data from civil registers which are incomplete or of unknown completeness. - Italiques : données incomplètes ou dont le degré d'exactitude n'est pas connu, provenant des registres de l'état civil.

♦ Rates based on 30 or fewer infant deaths. - Taux basés sur 30 décès d'enfants ou moins.

* Provisional. - Données provisoires.

[a] 'Code' indicates the source of data, as follows:
C - Civil registration, estimated over 90% complete
U - Civil registration, estimated less than 90% complete
| - Other source, estimated reliable
+ - Data tabulated by date of registration rather than occurence
... - Information not available

Le 'Code' indique la source des données, comme suit :
C - Registres de l'état civil considérés complèts à 90 p. 100 au moins
U - Registres de l'état civil qui ne sont pas considérés complèts à 90 p. 100 au moins
| - Autre source, considérée pas douteuses
+ - Données exploitées selon la date de l'enregistrement et non la date de l'événement
... - Information pas disponible

[1] Excludes the islands of St. Brandon and Agalega. - Non compris les îles St. Brandon et Agalega.
[2] Excluding live-born infants who died before their birth was registered. - Non compris les enfants nés vivants décédés avant l'enregistrement de leur naissance.
[3] Data for male and female categories may exclude infant deaths of unknown sex. - Les données pour les catégories hommes et femmes peuvent exclure décès d'enfant de sexe inconnu.
[4] Excluding infant deaths to mothers living abroad. - Exception faite des décès d'enfants en bas âge survenus lorsque la mère résidait à l'étranger.
[5] Data refer to urban areas only. - Données ne concernant que les zones urbaines.
[6] Data refer to resident population only. - Pour la population résidante seulement.
[7] Including deaths abroad and deaths of unknown residence of mother. - Y compris décès à l'étranger et décès de nourrissons nés de mères dont le lieu de résidence n'est pas connu.
[8] Total in this table is different from data presented in other tables due to different data source. - Le total figurant dans ce tableau ne correspond pas aux données présentées dans d'autres tableaux parce que les sources de données ne sont pas les mêmes.
[9] Excludes nomadic Indian tribes. - Non compris les tribus d'Indiens nomades.
[10] Source: Reports of the Ministry of Health. - Source : Rapports du Ministère de la Santé.
[11] Excluding infants born alive of less than 28 weeks' gestation, of less than 1 000 g in weight and 35 cm in length, who die within seven days of birth. - Non compris les enfants nés vivants après moins de 28 semaines de gestations, pesant moins de 1 000 g, mesurant moins de 35 cm et décédés dans les sept jours qui ont suivi leur naissance.
[12] Deaths include deaths among some visitors. Sources: Births and Deaths National Registration System database, and medical records of government hospitals. - Les décès comprennent des décès parmi certains visiteurs. Les sources: Les bases de données des << Births and Deaths National Registration System >> et les dossiers médicaux des hôpitaux du gouvernement.

[13] Data refer to government controlled areas. - Les données se rapportent aux zones contrôlées par le Gouvernement.
[14] Includes data for East Jerusalem and Israeli residents in certain other territories under occupation by Israeli military forces since June 1967. Including deaths abroad of Israeli residents who were out of the country for less than a year. - Y compris les données pour Jérusalem-Est et les résidents israéliens dans certains autres territoires occupés depuis 1967 par les forces armées israéliennes. Y compris les décès à l'étranger de résidents israéliens qui ont quitté le pays depuis moins d'un an.
[15] Data refer to Japanese nationals in Japan only. - Les données se raportent aux nationaux japonais au Japon seulement.
[16] Data are from Vital Registration System (VRS). - Les données proviennent du système d'enregistrement des faits d'état civil.
[17] Data from Births and Deaths Notification System (Ministry of Health and all health care providers). - Les données proviennent du système de notification des naissances et des décès (Ministère de la santé et tous prestataires de soins de santé).
[18] Excluding data for the Pakistan-held part of Jammu and Kashmir, the final status of which has not yet been determined. Based on the results of the Pakistan Demographic Survey. - Non compris les données concernant la partie du Jammu et Cachemire occupée par le Pakistan dont le statut définitif n'a pas été déterminé. Données extraites de l'enquête démographique effectuée par le Pakistan.
[19] Excluding alien armed forces, civilian aliens employed by armed forces, and foreign diplomatic personnel and their dependants. - Non compris les militaires étrangers, les civils étrangers employés par les forces armées ni le personnel diplomatique étranger et les membres de leur famille les accompagnant.
[20] Including armed forces stationed outside the country, but excluding alien armed forces stationed in the area. - Y compris les militaires nationaux hors du pays, mais non compris les militaires étrangers en garnison sur le territoire.
[21] Excluding Faeroe Islands and Greenland shown separately, if available. - Non compris les Îles Féroé et le Groenland, qui font l'objet de rubriques distinctes, si disponible.
[22] Excluding Åland Islands. - Non compris les Îles d'Åland.
[23] Data include the deceased infants with Hungarian usual residence regardless of whether the death occurred in Hungary or in a foreign country, and do not include the deceased infants with foreign country usual residence. - Les données comprennent les nourrissons décédés alors que leur résidence habituelle était en Hongrie, que le décès ait eu lieu en Hongrie ou dans un pays étranger, et ne comprennent pas les nourrissons décédés dont la residence habituelle était dans un pays étranger.
[24] Including residents outside the country if listed in a Netherlands population register. - Englobe les résidents se trouvant à l'étranger à condition qu'ils soient inscrits sur le registre de population des Pays-Bas.
[25] Including residents temporarily outside the country. - Y compris les résidents se trouvant temporairement hors du pays.
[26] Data refer to usually resident population. - Les données concernent la population habituellement résidente.
[27] Excluding Transnistria and the municipality of Bender. - Les données ne tiennent pas compte de l'information sur la Transnistria et la municipalité de Bender.
[28] Excludes data for Kosovo and Metohia. - Sans les données pour le Kosovo et Metohie.
[29] Data includes deaths resulting from births with weight 500 g and more (if weight is unknown - with length 25 cm and more, or with gestation during 22 weeks or more). The Government of Ukraine has informed the United Nations that it is not in a position to provide statistical data concerning the Autonomous Republic of Crimea and the city of Sevastopol. - Y compris les décès de nouveau-nés de 500 g ou plus (si le poids est inconnu - de 25 cm de long ou plus, ou après une grossesse de 22 semaines ou plus). Le gouvernement Ukrainien a informé l'ONU qu'il n'est pas en mesure de fournir des données

statistiques concernant la République autonome de Crimée et la ville de Sébastopol.

[30] Excluding Channel Islands (Guernsey and Jersey) and Isle of Man, shown separately, if available. - Non compris les îles Anglo-Normandes (Guernesey et Jersey) et l'île de Man, qui font l'objet de rubriques distinctes, si disponible.

[31] Data for certain cells suppressed by national statistical office for confidentiality reasons. - Les données pour certaines cases ont été supprimées par le bureau national de statistiques pour des raisons de confidentialité.

[32] Including United States military personnel, their dependants and contract employees. - Y compris les militaires des Etats-Unis, les membres de leur famille les accompagnant et les agents contractuels des Etats-Unis.

[33] Random rounding to base 3 is applied in this table as a confidentiality measure. - Les chiffres sont arrondis à la base 3 de manière aléatoire, pour des raisons de confidentialité.

Table 17 - *Demographic Yearbook 2016*

Table 17 presents maternal deaths and maternal mortality ratios for as many years available between 2005 and 2014.

Description of variables: Maternal deaths are defined for the purposes of the Demographic Yearbook as those caused by deliveries and complications of pregnancy, childbirth and the puerperium, within 42 days of termination of pregnancy. They are usually defined as deaths coded "38-41" for ICD-9 Basic Tabulation List or as deaths coded "A34", "O00-O95", "O98-O99" for ICD-10, respectively[1]. However, data for ICD-10 shown in this table include deaths due to "O96" and "O97" which refer to deaths from any obstetric cause occurring more than 42 days but less than one year after delivery and death from sequelae of direct obstetric causes occurring one year or more after delivery.

For further information on the definition of maternal mortality from the tenth revisions of the *International Statistical Classification of Diseases and Related Health Problems*[2], see also section 4.3 of the Technical Notes.

Statistics on maternal death presented in this table are provided by the World Health Organisation. They are limited to countries or areas that meet the criterion that cause-of-death statistics are either classified by or convertible to the ninth or tenth revisions mentioned above. Data that are classified by the tenth revision are set in bold in the table.

Ratios computation: Maternal mortality ratios are the annual number of maternal deaths per 100 000 live births (table 9) in the same year. These ratios have been calculated by the Statistics Division of the United Nations Department of Economic and Social Affairs. If maternal mortality data are considered incomplete, or if live birth data for the year are not available, no ratio has been calculated. Ratios based on 30 or fewer maternal deaths are identified by the symbol "♦".

Reliability of data: Countries and areas that have incomplete (less than 90 per cent completeness) or of unknown completeness of cause of deaths data coverage are considered to provide unreliable data, which are set in *italics* rather than in roman type. Ratios on these data are not computed. Information on completeness is normally provided by the World Health Organisation. When this is not the case, information on completeness is set to coincide with that of table 18. The reliability of data for the completeness of cause of death provided by the World Health Organisation[3] may differ from the reliability of data for the total number of reported deaths. Therefore, there are cases when the quality code in table 18 does not correspond with the typeface used in this table.

Territorial composition as set in Section 2.2 of "Technical Notes on the Statistical Tables", including or excluding certain population of a country refers only to the denominator.

Limitations: Statistics on maternal deaths are subject to the same qualifications that have been set forth for vital statistics in general and death statistics in particular as discussed in section 4 of the Technical Notes. The reliability of the data, an indication of which is described above, is an important factor in considering the limitations. In addition, maternal-death statistics are subject to all the qualifications relating to cause-of-death statistics. These have been set forth in section 4 of the Technical Notes.

Maternal mortality ratios are subject to the limitations of the data on live births with which they have been calculated. These have been set forth in the technical notes for table 9. Specific information pertaining to individual countries or areas is given in the footnotes to table 9.

The calculation of the maternal mortality ratios based on the total number of live births approximates the risk of dying from complications of pregnancy, childbirth or puerperium. Ideally this rate should be based on the number of women exposed to the risk of pregnancy, in other words, the number of women conceiving. Since it is impossible to know how many women have conceived, the total number of live births is used in calculating this rate.

Earlier data: Maternal deaths and maternal mortality ratios have been shown in previous issues of the *Demographic Yearbook*. For information on specific years covered, the reader should consult the Index.

It should however be noted that in issues prior to 1975, maternal mortality rates were calculated using the female population rather than live births for the denominators. Therefore, maternal mortality ratios published since 1975 are not comparable to the earlier maternal death rates.

NOTES

[1] Except for Belarus, Russian Federation, Seychelles, Turkmenistan and Ukraine, where A34 and O95 are excluded.

[2] *International Statistical Classification of Diseases and Related Health Problems*, Tenth Revision, Volume 2, World Health Organization, Geneva, 1992. The publication is available online at: http://www.who.int/classifications/icd/en/

[3] For more information on specific method used for countries, see "Mathers CD, Bernard C, Iburg KM, Inoue M, Ma Fat D, Shibuya K et al. *Global burden of disease in 2002: data sources, methods and results*. Geneva, World Health Organization, 2003 (GPE Discussion Paper No. 54).

Tableau 17 – *Annuaire démographique 2016*

Le tableau 17 présente des statistiques et des taux de mortalité liée à la maternité pour les années disponibles entre 2005 et 2014.

Description des variables : aux fins de *l'Annuaire démographique*, les décès liés à la maternité sont ceux entraînés par l'accouchement ou les complications de la grossesse, de l'accouchement et des suites de couches dans un délai de 42 jours après la terminaison de la grossesse. Ils sont généralement associés aux codes 38 à 41 dans le cas de la liste de base pour la mise en tableaux de la CIM-9 et aux codes A34, O00 à O95 et O98 et O99 dans le cas de la CIM-10[1]. Les statistiques associées à des codes correspondant à la CIM-10 englobent des décès de type O96 et O97, qui désignent les décès liés à des causes obstétriques se produisant après 42 jours mais moins d'un an après l'accouchement et les décès entraînés par les séquelles de complications obstétriques directes qui se produisent un an ou plus après l'accouchement.

Pour plus de précisions concernant les définitions de la mortalité liée à la maternité dans la dixième révision de la *Classification statistique internationale des maladies et des problèmes de santé connexes*[2], se reporter également à la section 4.3 des Notes techniques.

Les statistiques de mortalité liée à la maternité présentées dans le tableau 17 émanent de l'Organisation mondiale de la santé. Elles ne se rapportent qu'aux pays ou zones qui répondent aux critères selon lesquels les statistiques relatives à la cause des décès sont conformes à la liste de la neuvième ou de la dixième révision de la CIM ou peuvent être aisément comparées aux catégories de cette liste. Les données conformes à la dixième révision sont indiquées en gras dans le tableau.

Calcul des taux : les taux de mortalité maternelle représentent le nombre annuel de décès dus à la maternité pour 100 000 naissances vivantes (données du tableau 9) de la même année. Ces taux ont été calculés par la Division de statistique du Département des affaires économiques et sociales de l'Organisation des Nations Unies. Si les données des décès dus à la maternité sont incomplètes ou si les naissances vivantes pour l'année ne sont pas disponibles, les taux ne sont pas calculés. Les taux fondés sur 30 décès liés à la maternité ou moins sont signalés par le signe "♦".

Fiabilité des données : les statistiques relatives aux pays et aux zones pour lesquels la couverture des données concernant les causes de décès est incomplète (mois de 90 pour cent) ou dont le degré de complétude n'est pas connue sont jugés douteuses et apparaissent en *italique* et non en caractères romains. Les taux correspondant ne sont pas calculés. L'information sur la complétude est normalement fournie par l'Organisation Mondiale de la Santé. Si ce n'est pas le cas, l'information sur la complétude est reprise de tableau 18. La fiabilité des données relatives aux causes de décès fournie par l'Organisation Mondiale de la Santé[3] peut différer de la fiabilité des données relatives au nombre de décès enregistrés. En conséquence, il peut apparaitre de différences entre les codes de fiabilité du tableau 18 et du présent tableau.

La composition territoriale est définie dans la Section 2.2 des "Notes Techniques sur les tableaux statistiques". L'inclusion ou l'exclusion de certaines populations d'un pays ne concerne que le dénominateur.

Insuffisance des données : les statistiques de la mortalité liée à la maternité appellent toutes les réserves qui ont été formulées à propos des statistiques de l'état civil en général et des statistiques relatives à la mortalité en particulier (voir la section 4 des Notes techniques). La fiabilité des données, au sujet de laquelle des indications ont été fournies plus haut, est un facteur important. En outre, les statistiques de la mortalité liée à la maternité appellent les mêmes réserves que celles exposées à la section 4 des Notes techniques en ce qui concerne les statistiques des causes de décès.

Les taux de mortalité maternelle appellent également toutes les réserves formulées à propos des statistiques des naissances vivantes qui ont servi à leur calcul (voir à ce sujet les notes techniques relatives au tableau 9). Des précisions sur certains pays ou zones sont données dans les notes se rapportant au tableau 9.

En prenant le nombre total des naissances vivantes comme base pour le calcul des taux de mortalité maternelle, on obtient une mesure approximative de la probabilité de décès dus aux complications de la grossesse, de l'accouchement et des suites de couches. Idéalement, ces taux devraient être calculés sur la base du nombre de femmes exposées aux risques liés à la grossesse, c'est-à-dire sur la base du nombre de femmes qui conçoivent. Étant donné qu'il est impossible de connaître le nombre de femmes ayant conçu, c'est le nombre total de naissances vivantes que l'on utilise pour calculer ces taux.

Données publiées antérieurement : des statistiques concernant les décès liés à la maternité (nombre de décès et taux) ont déjà été présentées dans des éditions antérieures de l'*Annuaire démographique*. Pour plus de précisions concernant les années pour lesquelles ces données ont été publiées, se reporter à l'index.

Il faut souligner que, avant 1975, les taux de mortalité maternelle étaient calculés sur la base de la population féminine et non sur celle du nombre de naissances vivantes. Ils ne sont donc pas comparables à ceux qui figurent dans les éditions de l'*Annuaire démographique* parues après 1975.

NOTES

[1] Sauf pour Bélarus, Fédération de Russie, Seychelles, Turkménistan et Ukraine où A34 et O95 sont exclus.
[2] *Classification statistique internationale des maladies et des problèmes de santé connexes*, dixième révision, volume 2. Genève, Organisation mondiale de la santé, 1992.
[3] Pour plus d'information sur les méthodes spécifiques utilisées pour les pays, voir "Mathers CD, Bernard C, Iburg KM, Inoue M, Ma Fat D, Shibuya K et al. *Global burden of disease in 2002: data sources, methods and results*. Geneva, World Health Organization, 2003 (GPE Discussion Paper No. 54).

Continent and country or area / Continent et pays ou zone	Code[a]	2005	2006	2007	2008	2009	2010	2011	2012	2013	2014
AFRICA - AFRIQUE											
Cabo Verde											
Number - Nombre	C	...	...	...	...	...	...	5	1	...	...
Egypt - Égypte											
Number - Nombre	C	...	604	567	449	579	519	550	531	503	...
Rate - Taux	C	...	32.6	29.1	21.9	26.1	23.0	22.5	20.2	19.2	...
Mauritius - Maurice											
Number - Nombre	+C	4	3	6	6	10	4	5	9	9	7
Rate - Taux	+C	♦21.3	♦17.0	♦35.2	♦36.6	♦65.2	♦26.7	♦34.0	♦62.1	♦66.7	♦52.7
Mayotte											
Number - Nombre	C	...	...	...	...	...	...	-	1	1	...
Morocco - Maroc											
Number - Nombre	U	...	...	...	74	...	65	98	93	...	...
Reunion - Réunion											
Number - Nombre	...	4	5	...	2	1	1	5	2	2	...
Seychelles											
Number - Nombre	+C	1	-	-	1	1	2	-	-	-	-
Rate - Taux	+C	♦65.1	-	-	♦64.7	♦63.3	♦133.0	-	-	-	-
South Africa - Afrique du Sud											
Number - Nombre	...	1 249[1]	1 388[1]	1 762[2]	1 808[2]	1 880[2]	1 658[2]	1 260[2]	1 050[2]	946[2]	1 027[2]
Rate - Taux	...	...	...	205.2	197.5	213.7	186.4	138.3	113.3	100.7	107.6
Tunisia - Tunisie											
Number - Nombre	U	...	...	...	...	...	...	...	...	28	...
AMERICA, NORTH - AMÉRIQUE DU NORD											
Anguilla											
Number - Nombre	...	-	-	...	1	-	1	-	-	-	-
Antigua and Barbuda - Antigua-et-Barbuda											
Number - Nombre	+U	-	-	1	-	-	...	...	1	-	...
Aruba											
Number - Nombre	...	...	-	-	-	-	-	2	-	-	...
Bahamas											
Number - Nombre	+C	4	...	...	3	7	5	-	3	...	...
Rate - Taux	+C	♦72.1	...	...	♦58.5	♦139.2	♦101.7	-	♦67.1	...	...
Barbados - Barbade											
Number - Nombre	C	...	1	...	2	-	-	2	1	...	...
Rate - Taux	C	...	♦29.3	...	♦56.4	-	-	♦60.9	♦31.4	...	...
Belize											
Number - Nombre	C	10	3	2	2	4	4	-	2	-	...
Rate - Taux	C	♦119.1	♦41.8	♦28.4	♦28.1	♦53.9	♦55.3	-	♦28.1	-	...
Bermuda - Bermudes											
Number - Nombre	...	-	1	-	-	-	-	-	-	-	...
British Virgin Islands - Îles Vierges britanniques											
Number - Nombre	...	...	...	...	-	-	-	...	...	...	...
Canada											
Number - Nombre	C	...	28	24	34	29	24	18	...	...	...
Rate - Taux	C	...	♦7.9	♦6.5	9.0	♦7.6	♦6.4	♦4.8	...	...	...
Cayman Islands - Îles Caïmanes											
Number - Nombre	...	...	...	...	-	-	-	...	...	-	...
Costa Rica											
Number - Nombre	...	24[3]	24[3]	10[3]	20[3]	10[4]	14[4]	17[4]	22[4]	10[4]	...
Rate - Taux	...	...	...	...	...	♦13.3	♦19.7	♦23.1	♦30.0	♦14.2	...
Cuba											
Number - Nombre	C	66	62	42	57	66	61	61	55	56	...
Rate - Taux	C	54.7	55.7	37.3	46.5	50.8	47.8	45.8	43.8	44.5	...
Dominica - Dominique											
Number - Nombre	+C	-	-	-	1	-	2	-	-	3	...
Rate - Taux	+C	-	-	-	♦103.7	-	♦214.4	-	-	♦322.2	...
Dominican Republic - République dominicaine											
Number - Nombre	U	...	...	...	...	56	37	188	177	...	...
El Salvador											
Number - Nombre	+U	23	21	17	18	14	19	16	17	...	...

Continent and country or area / Continent et pays ou zone	Code[a]	2005	2006	2007	2008	2009	2010	2011	2012	2013	2014
AMERICA, NORTH - AMÉRIQUE DU NORD											
Grenada - Grenade											
Number - Nombre	...	-[1]	-[1]	-[1]	-[2]	-[2]	-[2]	-[2]	2[2]	1[2]	...
Rate - Taux	...	...	...	...	-	-	-	-	♦120.4	♦54.4	
Guadeloupe											
Number - Nombre	...	1	2	...	2	1	1	-	4	1	...
Guatemala											
Number - Nombre	...	354[1]	298[1]	310[1]	328[1]	346[1]	355[2]	315[2]	356[2]	318[2]	...
Rate - Taux	...	...	...	...	...	...	98.1	84.3	91.6	82.1	
Honduras											
Number - Nombre	+U	...	...	...	...	...	28	47	31	37	...
Jamaica - Jamaïque											
Number - Nombre	...	...	...	...	...	...	28	28	...	...	...
Martinique											
Number - Nombre	...	-	1	...	1	2	-	2	1	3	...
Mexico - Mexique											
Number - Nombre	+C	1 269	1 188	1 122	1 135	1 230	1 030	1 027	1 036	969	...
Rate - Taux	+C	59.3	55.2	51.3	50.6	54.6	47.5	45.4	47.3	44.7	
Montserrat											
Number - Nombre	...	-	...	...	-	-	-	-	-	-	-
Nicaragua											
Number - Nombre	+U	93	93	...	69	78	80	71	72	71	...
Panama											
Number - Nombre	...	...	36[3]	40[4]	41[4]	29[4]	41[4]	59[4]	49[4]	41[4]	...
Rate - Taux	...	...	...	59.4	59.6	♦42.4	60.3	80.5	64.9	55.6	
Puerto Rico - Porto Rico											
Number - Nombre	...	5	...	...	6	10	6	5	1	2	...
Saint Kitts and Nevis - Saint-Kitts-et-Nevis											
Number - Nombre	+U	-	1	-	1	-	-	1	1	...	...
Saint Lucia - Sainte-Lucie											
Number - Nombre	...	...	...	...	1[2]	...	3[1]	1[1]	1[1]	...	...
Rate - Taux	...	...	...	...	♦45.2	...	...	...	...	...	...
Saint Pierre and Miquelon - Saint Pierre-et-Miquelon											
Number - Nombre	...	-	-	-	-	-	-	...	...	...	...
Saint Vincent and the Grenadines - Saint-Vincent-et-les Grenadines											
Number - Nombre	...	...	-	-	2[4]	-[4]	2[4]	1[4]	-[4]	2[4]	...
Rate - Taux	...	...	...	...	♦105.2	-	♦112.1	♦58.0	-	♦115.1	
Trinidad and Tobago - Trinité-et-Tobago											
Number - Nombre	U	...	12	...	11	...	...	...	...	...	...
Turks and Caicos Islands - Îles Turques et Caïques											
Number - Nombre	...	-	...	...	-	1	...	...	...	-	...
United States of America - États-Unis d'Amérique											
Number - Nombre	C	760	756	766	795	962	825	931	990	1 138	...
Rate - Taux	C	18.4	17.7	17.7	18.7	23.3	20.6	23.5	25.0	28.9	
United States Virgin Islands - Îles Vierges américaines											
Number - Nombre	...	-	...	...	-	...	...	...	...	...	...
AMERICA, SOUTH - AMÉRIQUE DU SUD											
Argentina - Argentine											
Number - Nombre	+C	290	341	332	319	422	331	318	280	274	...
Rate - Taux	+C	40.7	49.0	47.4	42.8	56.6	43.8	42.0	37.9	36.3	...
Brazil - Brésil											
Number - Nombre	...	1 661[1]	1 634[1]	1 613[1]	1 641[2]	1 884[2]	1 728[2]	1 680[2]	1 647[2]	1 788[2]	...
Rate - Taux	...	...	...	...	58.8	68.4	62.6	59.5	58.2	63.1	...
Chile - Chili											
Number - Nombre	C	48	47	42	36	43	46	46	54	52	...
Rate - Taux	C	20.8	20.3	17.5	14.6	17.0	18.4	18.6	22.2	21.5	...

Continent and country or area / Continent et pays ou zone	Code[a]	2005	2006	2007	2008	2009	2010	2011	2012	2013	2014
AMERICA, SOUTH - AMÉRIQUE DU SUD											
Colombia - Colombie											
Number - Nombre	...	504[1]	519[2]	503[2]	433[2]	496[2]	474[2]	459[2]	452[2]	...	...
Rate - Taux	...		73.8	72.1	61.6	72.3	73.4	69.3	66.9	...	...
Ecuador - Équateur											
Number - Nombre	U	143	135	176	162	208	202	239	202	158	
French Guiana - Guyane française											
Number - Nombre	...	1	1	...	4	1	3	-	2	1	
Guyana											
Number - Nombre	U	24	20	...	16	9	20	14	...	...	...
Paraguay											
Number - Nombre	+U	135	123	...	117	128	100	94	91	100	...
Peru - Pérou											
Number - Nombre	+U	...	...	155	192	163	137	148	126	97	
Suriname											
Number - Nombre	...	4[1]	...	...	9[2]	11[2]	6[2]	7[2]	2[2]	...	...
Rate - Taux	...	...	...	...	♦89.1	♦112.3	♦61.8	♦72.1	♦19.6	...	...
Uruguay											
Number - Nombre	C	...	...	...	6	11	2	...	5	9	
Rate - Taux	C	...	...	...	♦12.7	♦23.3	♦4.2	...	♦10.4	♦18.5	
Venezuela (Bolivarian Republic of) - Venezuela (République bolivarienne du)											
Number - Nombre	C	351	356	332	377	434	412	436	416	...	...
Rate - Taux	C	52.7	55.1	54.0	64.8	73.1	69.7	70.9	67.1	...	...
ASIA - ASIE											
Armenia - Arménie											
Number - Nombre	U	...	10	...	16	12	4	6	5	...	8
Azerbaijan - Azerbaïdjan											
Number - Nombre	C	...	...	30	...	...	...	...	...	...	...
Rate - Taux	C	...	...	♦19.7	...	...	...	...	...	...	...
Bahrain - Bahreïn											
Number - Nombre	...	...	-[2]	3[2]	3[2]	3[1]	1[1]	2[1]	2[1]	4[1]	
Rate - Taux	...	...	-	♦18.7	♦17.6	...	...	...	...	...	
Brunei Darussalam - Brunéi Darussalam											
Number - Nombre	...	...	...	1[4]	-[4]	1[4]	1[3]	-[3]	3[3]	1[3]	-[3]
Rate - Taux	...	...	...	♦15.8	-	♦15.1	...	...	...	...	...
China, Hong Kong SAR - Chine, Hong Kong RAS											
Number - Nombre	...	2	1	1	2	2	1	1	2	-	...
Cyprus - Chypre											
Number - Nombre	U	2	1	-	1	-	1	-	-	1	...
Georgia - Géorgie											
Number - Nombre	C	...	11	2	...	32	13	21	14	16	18
Rate - Taux	C	...	♦23.0	♦4.1	...	50.5	♦20.8	♦36.2	♦24.5	♦27.6	♦29.7
Iraq											
Number - Nombre	U	...	...	...	62	...	...	...	...	...	...
Israel - Israël											
Number - Nombre	C	4	11	7	8	5	7	2	9	14	...
Rate - Taux	C	♦2.8	♦7.4	♦4.6	♦5.1	♦3.1	♦4.2	♦1.2	♦5.3	♦8.2	...
Japan - Japon											
Number - Nombre	C	66	63	39	41	61	49	43	50	41	...
Rate - Taux	C	6.2	5.8	3.6	3.8	5.7	4.6	4.1	4.8	4.0	...
Jordan - Jordanie											
Number - Nombre	U	...	...	...	25	26	46	34	...	...	...
Kazakhstan											
Number - Nombre	...	81[1]	100[1]	107[1]	86[2]	94[2]	65[2]	48[2]	41[2]	41[2]	37[2]
Rate - Taux	...	...	...	...	24.1	26.4	17.7	12.9	10.8	10.6	...
Kuwait - Koweït											
Number - Nombre	C	...	1	-	5	7	3	6	1	4	7
Rate - Taux	C	...	♦1.9	-	♦9.2	♦12.4	♦5.2	♦10.3	♦1.7	♦6.7	♦11.4
Kyrgyzstan - Kirghizstan											
Number - Nombre	...	66[1]	67[1]	64[1]	70[2]	86[2]	75[2]	81[2]	76[2]	56[2]	...
Rate - Taux	...	...	...	...	55.0	63.5	51.3	54.1	49.1	36.0	...

17. Maternal deaths and maternal mortality ratios: 2005 - 2014
Mortalité liée à la maternité, nombre de décès et taux : 2005 - 2014 (continued - suite)

Continent and country or area / Continent et pays ou zone	Code[a]	2005	2006	2007	2008	2009	2010	2011	2012	2013	2014
ASIA - ASIE											
Malaysia - Malaisie											
Number - Nombre	U	...	128	...	133	...	...	...	...	...	...
Maldives											
Number - Nombre	...	1[3]	...	2[4]	4[3]	...	7[3]	4[3]	...	...	...
Rate - Taux	...	...	...	♦30.4	...	...	...	...	...	...	...
Oman											
Number - Nombre	U	...	...	...	...	3	6	...	...	...	...
Philippines											
Number - Nombre	U	...	...	...	1 731	...	1 718	1 465	...	...	...
Qatar											
Number - Nombre	...	...	1[2]	5[2]	2[2]	4[2]	2[1]	1[1]	1[1]	...	...
Rate - Taux	...	...	♦7.1	♦31.9	♦11.6	♦21.8	...	...	...	...	...
Republic of Korea - République de Corée											
Number - Nombre	C	53	54	...	39	48	75	85	56	51	...
Rate - Taux	C	12.2	12.0	...	8.4	10.8	16.0	18.0	11.6	11.7	...
Saudi Arabia - Arabie saoudite											
Number - Nombre	U	...	...	...	...	54	...	...	45	...	...
Singapore - Singapour											
Number - Nombre	+U	4	3	...	2	-	1	2	1	-	-
Sri Lanka											
Number - Nombre	+U	...	53	...	...	...	...	...	...	...	...
Syrian Arab Republic - République arabe syrienne											
Number - Nombre	+C	...	...	...	...	...	23	...	...	...	...
Rate - Taux	+C	...	...	...	...	...	♦2.6	...	...	...	...
Tajikistan - Tadjikistan											
Number - Nombre	U	28	...	...	...	...	...	...	...	...	...
Thailand - Thaïlande											
Number - Nombre	+U	...	92	...	...	...	78	71	141	166	166
Turkey - Turquie											
Number - Nombre	+U	...	...	...	...	37	46	58	55	302	...
Turkmenistan - Turkménistan											
Number - Nombre	U	...	...	...	...	...	...	...	7	9	...
United Arab Emirates - Émirats arabes unis											
Number - Nombre	+U	...	...	...	1	2	4	...	...	...	...
Uzbekistan - Ouzbékistan											
Number - Nombre	U	145	...	...	...	...	...	...	...	...	131
EUROPE											
Austria - Autriche											
Number - Nombre	C	3	2	3	2	2	1	2	1	1	7
Rate - Taux	C	♦3.8	♦2.6	♦3.9	♦2.6	♦2.6	♦1.3	♦2.6	♦1.3	♦1.3	♦8.6
Belarus - Bélarus											
Number - Nombre	C	...	...	7	3	1	1	1	...	-	1
Rate - Taux	C	...	...	♦6.8	♦2.8	♦0.9	♦0.9	♦0.9	...	-	♦0.8
Belgium - Belgique											
Number - Nombre	C	...	9	...	7	6	8	9	5	3	...
Rate - Taux	C	...	♦7.3	...	♦5.5	♦4.7	♦6.1	♦7.0	♦3.9	♦2.4	...
Bosnia and Herzegovina - Bosnie-Herzégovine											
Number - Nombre	U	...	...	...	...	...	...	2	...	...	-
Bulgaria - Bulgarie											
Number - Nombre	C	8	5	8	5	4	6	2	3	8	...
Rate - Taux	C	♦11.3	♦6.8	♦10.6	♦6.4	♦4.9	♦7.9	♦2.8	♦4.3	♦12.0	...
Croatia - Croatie											
Number - Nombre	C	3	4	6	3	6	4	4	3	2	1
Rate - Taux	C	♦7.1	♦9.7	♦14.3	♦6.9	♦13.5	♦9.2	♦9.7	♦7.2	♦5.0	♦2.5
Czechia - Tchéquie											
Number - Nombre	C	3	9	3	7	3	3	2	6	1	4
Rate - Taux	C	♦2.9	♦8.5	♦2.6	♦5.9	♦2.5	♦2.6	♦1.8	♦5.5	♦0.9	♦3.6
Denmark - Danemark											
Number - Nombre	C	-	5	...	4	4	-	2	-	...	...
Rate - Taux	C	-	♦7.7	...	♦6.2	♦6.4	-	♦3.4	-	...	...

487

Continent and country or area Continent et pays ou zone	Code[a]	2005	2006	2007	2008	2009	2010	2011	2012	2013	2014
EUROPE											
Estonia - Estonie											
Number - Nombre	C	2	1	-	-	-	1	1	1	1	-
Rate - Taux	C	♦13.9	♦6.7	-	-	-	♦6.3	♦6.8	♦7.1	♦7.4	-
Finland - Finlande											
Number - Nombre	C	3	4	1	5	1	3	-	2	1	3
Rate - Taux	C	♦5.2	♦6.8	♦1.7	♦8.4	♦1.7	♦4.9	-	♦3.4	♦1.7	♦5.3
France											
Number - Nombre	C	41	59	60	52	75	68	45	44	38	...
Rate - Taux	C	5.3	7.4	7.6	6.5	9.5	8.5	5.7	5.6	4.9	...
Germany - Allemagne											
Number - Nombre	C	28	41	28	36	35	37	32	31	29	29
Rate - Taux	C	♦4.1	6.1	♦4.1	5.3	5.3	5.5	4.8	4.6	♦4.3	♦4.1
Greece - Grèce											
Number - Nombre	C	-	3	2	-	4	6	4	...	...	...
Rate - Taux	C	-	♦2.7	♦1.8	-	♦3.4	♦5.2	♦3.8	...	...	...
Hungary - Hongrie											
Number - Nombre	C	5	8	8	17	18	14	9	9	13	6
Rate - Taux	C	♦5.1	♦8.0	♦8.2	♦17.1	♦18.7	♦15.5	♦10.2	♦10.0	♦14.5	♦6.4
Iceland - Islande											
Number - Nombre	C	-	-	-	-	-	...	...	...	...	...
Ireland - Irlande											
Number - Nombre	+C	2	-	1	3	3	3	2	2	3	...
Rate - Taux	+C	♦3.3	-	♦1.4	♦4.0	♦4.0	♦4.0	♦2.7	♦2.8	♦4.4	...
Italy - Italie											
Number - Nombre	C	...	11	13	13	19	16	14	11	...	...
Rate - Taux	C	...	♦2.0	♦2.3	♦2.3	♦3.3	♦2.8	♦2.6	♦2.1	...	...
Latvia - Lettonie											
Number - Nombre	+C	1	2	6	2	7	4	-	4	2	2
Rate - Taux	+C	♦4.6	♦8.7	♦25.0	♦8.2	♦31.8	♦20.2	-	♦20.1	♦9.7	♦9.2
Lithuania - Lituanie											
Number - Nombre	+C	4	-	2	3	-	2	2	3	2	1
Rate - Taux	+C	♦13.6	-	♦6.7	♦9.5	-	♦6.5	♦6.6	♦9.8	♦6.7	♦3.3
Luxembourg											
Number - Nombre	+C	1	-	1	1	-	1	-	1	1	-
Rate - Taux	+C	♦18.6	-	♦18.3	♦17.9	-	♦17.0	-	♦16.6	♦16.4	-
Malta - Malte											
Number - Nombre	+C	-	-	-	1	-	1	-	-	-	-
Rate - Taux	+C	-	-	-	♦24.9	-	♦25.7	-	-	-	-
Montenegro - Monténégro											
Number - Nombre	C	...	-	1	-	-	...	...	...	...	...
Rate - Taux	C	...	-	♦12.8	-	-	...	...	...	...	...
Netherlands - Pays-Bas											
Number - Nombre	+C	16	15	9	8	9	4	3	6	5	...
Rate - Taux	+C	♦8.5	♦8.1	♦5.0	♦4.3	♦4.9	♦2.2	♦1.7	♦3.4	♦2.9	...
Norway - Norvège											
Number - Nombre	+C	2	5	4	3	1	3	3	-	2	2
Rate - Taux	+C	♦3.5	♦8.5	♦6.8	♦5.0	♦1.6	♦4.9	♦5.0	-	♦3.4	♦3.4
Poland - Pologne											
Number - Nombre	C	11	11	11	19	8	9	9	4	7	8
Rate - Taux	C	♦3.0	♦2.9	♦2.8	♦4.6	♦1.9	♦2.2	♦2.3	♦1.0	♦1.9	♦2.1
Portugal											
Number - Nombre	+C	...	...	5	4	7	8	5	4	5	6
Rate - Taux	+C	...	...	♦4.9	♦3.8	♦7.0	♦7.9	♦5.2	♦4.5	♦6.0	♦7.3
Republic of Moldova - République de Moldova											
Number - Nombre	...	8[3]	6[4]	7[4]	17[4]	7[4]	18[4]	6[4]	12[4]	6[4]	7[4]
Rate - Taux	...	...	♦16.0	♦18.4	♦43.6	♦17.2	♦44.5	♦15.3	♦30.4	♦15.8	♦18.1
Romania - Roumanie											
Number - Nombre	+C	37	34	33	30	47	51	50	23	27	24
Rate - Taux	+C	16.7	15.5	15.4	♦13.5	21.1	24.0	25.5	♦11.4	♦14.8	♦12.4
Russian Federation - Fédération de Russie											
Number - Nombre	+C	370	352	356	359	388	298	291	...	...	...
Rate - Taux	+C	25.4	23.8	22.1	20.9	22.0	16.7	16.2	...	...	...
San Marino - Saint-Marin											
Number - Nombre	+U	-	...	...	...	...	...	...	...	...	...
Serbia - Serbie											
Number - Nombre	...	10[3]	9[3]	-[3]	4[3]	6[3]	12[4]	7[4]	10[4]	9[4]	8[4]
Rate - Taux	...	...	...	...	...	...	♦17.6	♦10.7	♦14.9	♦13.7	♦12.0

17. Maternal deaths and maternal mortality ratios: 2005 - 2014
Mortalité liée à la maternité, nombre de décès et taux : 2005 - 2014 (continued - suite)

Continent and country or area / Continent et pays ou zone	Code[a]	2005	2006	2007	2008	2009	2010	2011	2012	2013	2014
EUROPE											
Slovakia - Slovaquie											
Number - Nombre	C	2	3	-	2	6	-	...	3	1	2
Rate - Taux	C	♦3.7	♦5.6	-	♦3.5	♦9.8	-	...	♦5.4	♦1.8	♦3.6
Slovenia - Slovénie											
Number - Nombre	C	1	3	3	2	1	-	...	...	...	...
Rate - Taux	C	♦5.5	♦15.8	♦15.1	♦9.2	♦4.6	-	...	...	...	...
Spain - Espagne											
Number - Nombre	C	18	14	13	24	17	20	14	10	18	9
Rate - Taux	C	♦3.9	♦2.9	♦2.6	♦4.6	♦3.4	♦4.1	♦3.0	♦2.2	♦4.2	♦2.1
Sweden - Suède											
Number - Nombre	C	6	5	2	6	6	3	1	5	7	4
Rate - Taux	C	♦5.9	♦4.7	♦1.9	♦5.5	♦5.4	♦2.6	♦0.9	♦4.4	♦6.2	♦3.5
Switzerland - Suisse											
Number - Nombre	C	4	6	1	8	3	3	3	7	2	...
Rate - Taux	C	♦5.5	♦8.2	♦1.3	♦10.4	♦3.8	♦3.7	♦3.7	♦8.5	♦2.4	...
TFYR of Macedonia - L'ex-R. y. de Macédoine											
Number - Nombre	...	...	...	*1*	-	*2*[2]	1[2]	2[2]	...	...	...
Rate - Taux	...	...	...	...	-		♦4.2	♦8.2	...	...	...
Ukraine											
Number - Nombre	+C	75	70	...	79	129	116	85	66	...	69
Rate - Taux	+C	17.6	15.2	...	15.5	25.2	23.3	16.9	12.7	...	14.8
United Kingdom of Great Britain and Northern Ireland - Royaume-Uni de Grande-Bretagne et d'Irlande du Nord											
Number - Nombre	+C	51	50	56	49	74	40	53	51	50	...
Rate - Taux	+C	7.1	6.7	7.3	6.2	9.4	5.0	6.6	6.3	6.4	...
OCEANIA - OCÉANIE											
Australia - Australie											
Number - Nombre	C	...	9	...	6	9	12	12	16	6	12
Rate - Taux	C	...	♦3.3	...	♦2.0	♦3.0	♦4.0	♦4.0	♦5.2	♦1.9	♦4.0
Fiji - Fidji											
Number - Nombre	+C	...	...	...	...	5	...	4	8	...	...
Rate - Taux	+C	...	...	...	...	♦27.5	...	...	♦39.6	...	...
New Zealand - Nouvelle-Zélande											
Number - Nombre	+C	6	9	13	7	11	6	7	7	...	...
Rate - Taux	+C	♦10.4	♦15.2	♦20.3	♦10.9	♦17.6	♦9.4	♦11.4	♦11.4	...	...

FOOTNOTES - NOTES

Data in bold refer to maternal deaths based on ICD-10 Classification, otherwise data refer to maternal deaths based on ICD-9 Classification. - Les données en typographie gras se rapportent aux décès maternelles basées sur la classification CIM-10, autrement les données se rapportent aux décès maternelles basées sur la classification CIM-9.

Italics: data from civil registers which are incomplete or of unknown completeness. - Italiques : données incomplètes ou dont le degré d'exactitude n'est pas connu, provenant des registres de l'état civil.

* Provisional. - Données provisoires.

♦ Rates based on 30 or fewer deaths. - Taux basés sur 30 décès ou moins.

a 'Code' indicates the source of data, as follows:
  C - Civil registration, estimated over 90% complete
  U - Civil registration, estimated less than 90% complete
  | - Other source, estimated reliable
  + - Data tabulated by date of registration rather than occurence
  ... - Information not available

Le 'Code' indique la source des données, comme suit :

C - Registres de l'état civil considérés complèts à 90 p. 100 au moins
U - Registres de l'état civil qui ne sont pas considérés complèts à 90 p. 100 au moins
| - Autre source, considérée pas douteuses
+ - Données exploitées selon la date de l'enregistrement et non la date de l'événement
... - Information pas disponible

[1] The code is U. - Le code est U.
[2] The code is C. - Le code est C.
[3] The code is +U. - Le code est +U.
[4] The code is +C. - Le code est +C.

Table 18 - *Demographic Yearbook 2016*

Table 18 presents deaths and crude death rates by urban/rural residence for as many years as possible between 2012 and 2016.

Description of variables: Death is defined as the permanent disappearance of all evidence of life at any time after live birth has taken place (post-natal cessation of vital functions without capability of resuscitation).

Statistics on the number of deaths are obtained from civil registers unless otherwise noted. For those countries or areas where civil registration statistics on deaths are considered reliable (estimated completeness of 90 per cent or more), the death rates shown have been calculated on the basis of registered deaths.

The urban/rural classification of deaths is that provided by each country or area; it is presumed to be based on the national census definitions of urban population that have been set forth at the end of the technical notes for table 6.

For certain countries, there is a discrepancy between the total number of deaths shown in this table and those shown in subsequent tables for the same year. Usually this discrepancy arises because the total number of deaths occurring in a given year is revised although the remaining tabulations are not.

Rate computation: Crude death rates are the annual number of deaths per 1 000 mid-year population.

Rates by urban/rural residence are the annual number of deaths, in the appropriate urban or rural category, per 1 000 corresponding mid-year population. These rates are calculated by the Statistics Division of the United Nations based on the appropriate reference population (for example: total population, nationals only etc.) if known and available. If the reference population is not known or unavailable, the total population is used to calculate the rates. Therefore, if the population that is used to calculate the rates is different from the correct reference population, the rates presented might under- or overstate the true situation in a country or area.

Rates presented in this table are limited to those countries or areas with a minimum number of 30 deaths in a given year.

Reliability of data: Each country or area has been asked to indicate the estimated completeness of the deaths recorded in its civil register. These national assessments are indicated by the quality codes "C", "U" and "|" that appear in the first column of this table. "C" indicates that the data are estimated to be virtually complete, that is, representing at least 90 per cent of the deaths occurring each year, while "U" indicates that data are estimated to be incomplete that is, representing less than 90 per cent of the deaths occurring each year. The code "|" indicates that the source of data is different than civil registration and is explained by a footnote. The code "..." indicates that no information was provided regarding completeness or no assessment has been done in the country.

Data from civil registers that are reported as incomplete or of unknown completeness (code "U" or "...") are considered unreliable. They appear in italics in this table; rates based on these data are not computed.

Limitations: Statistics on deaths are subject to the same qualifications as have been set forth for vital statistics in general and death statistics in particular as discussed in section 4 of the Introduction.

The reliability of the data, an indication of which is described above, is an important factor in considering the limitations. In addition, some deaths are tabulated by date of registration and not by date of occurrence; these have been indicated with a plus sign "+". Whenever the lag between the date of occurrence and date of registration is prolonged and, therefore, a large proportion of the death registrations are delayed, death statistics for any given year may be seriously affected. However, delays in the registration of deaths are less common and shorter than in the registration of live births.

International comparability in mortality statistics may also be affected by the exclusion of deaths of infants who were born alive but died before the registration of the birth or within the first 24 hours of life. Statistics of this type are footnoted.

In addition, it should be noted that rates are affected also by the quality and limitations of the population estimates that are used in their computation. The problems of under-enumeration or over-enumeration and, to some extent, the differences in definition of total population have been discussed in section 3 of the Introduction dealing with population data in general, and specific information pertaining to individual countries or areas is given in the footnotes to table 3.

It should be emphasized that crude death rates -- like other crude rates, such as of birth, marriage and divorce -- may be seriously affected by the age-sex structure of the populations to which they relate. Nevertheless, they do provide a simple measure of the level and changes in mortality.

The comparability of data by urban/rural residence is affected by the national definitions of urban and rural used in tabulating these data. It is assumed, in the absence of specific information to the contrary, that the definitions of urban and rural used in connection with the national population census were also used in the compilation of the vital statistics for each country or area. However, it cannot be excluded that, for a given country or area, different definitions of urban and rural are used for the vital statistics data and the population census data respectively. When known, the definitions of urban used in national population censuses are presented at the end of the technical notes for table 6. As discussed in detail in the technical notes for table 6, these definitions vary considerably from one country or area to another.

Earlier data: Deaths and crude death rates have been shown in each issue of the Demographic Yearbook. For information on specific years covered, the reader should consult the Index.

Tableau 18 – *Annuaire démographique 2016*

Le tableau 18 présente le nombre des décès et les taux bruts de mortalité selon le lieu de résidence (zone urbaine ou rurale) pour le plus grand nombre d'années possible entre 2012 et 2016.

Description des variables : Le décès est défini comme la disparition permanente de tout signe de vie à un moment quelconque postérieur à la naissance vivante (cessation des fonctions vitales après la naissance sans possibilité de réanimation).

Sauf indication contraire, les statistiques relatives au nombre de décès sont établies sur la base des registres d'état civil. Pour les pays ou zones où les données concernant l'enregistrement des décès par les services de l'état civil sont jugées sûres (complétude estimée à 90 p. 100 ou plus), les taux de mortalité ont été calculés d'après les décès enregistrés.

La répartition des décès entre zones urbaines et zones rurales est celle qui a été communiquée par chaque pays ou zone ; on part du principe qu'elle repose sur les définitions de la population urbaine utilisées pour les recensements nationaux, qui sont reproduites à la fin des notes techniques du tableau 6.

Pour quelques pays il y a une discordance entre le nombre total des décès présenté dans ce tableau et ceux présentés après pour la même année. Habituellement ces différences apparaissent lorsque le nombre total des décès pour une certaine année a été révisé alors que les autres tabulations ne l'ont pas été.

Calcul des taux : Les taux bruts de mortalité représentent le nombre annuel de décès pour 1 000 habitants en milieu d'année.

Les taux selon le lieu de résidence (zone urbaine ou rurale) représentent le nombre annuel de décès, classés selon la catégorie urbaine ou rurale appropriée, pour 1 000 habitants en milieu d'année. Ces taux sont calculés par la division de statistique des Nations Unies sur la base de la population de référence adéquate (par exemple : population totale, nationaux seulement, etc.) si connue et disponible. Si la population de référence n'est pas connue ou n'est pas disponible, la population totale est utilisée pour calculer les taux. Par conséquent, si la population utilisée pour calculer les taux est différente de la population de référence adéquate, les taux présentés sont susceptibles de sous ou sur estimer la situation réelle d'un pays ou d'un territoire.

Les taux présentés dans ce tableau se rapportent seulement aux pays ou zones où l'on a enregistré un nombre minimal de 30 décès au cours d'une année donnée.

Fiabilité des données : Il a été demandé à chaque pays ou zone d'indiquer le degré estimatif de complétude des données sur les décès d'enfants de moins d'un an figurant dans ses registres d'état civil. Ces évaluations nationales sont signalées par les codes de qualité "C", "U" et "|" qui apparaissent dans la deuxième colonne du tableau.

La lettre "C" indique que les données sont jugées à peu près complètes, c'est-à-dire qu'elles représentent au moins 90 p. 100 des décès survenus chaque année ; la lettre "U" signifie que les données sont jugées incomplètes, c'est-à-dire qu'elles représentent moins de 90 p.100 des décès survenus chaque année. Le symbole "|" indique que la source des données n'est pas un registre de l'état civil ; le symbole, dans ce cas, est accompagné par une note explicative. Le code "..." dénote qu'aucun renseignement n'a été communiqué quant à la complétude des données.

Les données provenant des registres de l'état civil qui sont déclarées incomplètes ou dont le degré de complétude n'est pas connu (code "U" ou "...") sont jugées douteuses. Elles apparaissent en italique dans le présent tableau et les taux correspondants n'ont pas été calculés.

Insuffisance des données : Les statistiques relatives à la mortalité appellent les mêmes réserves que celles qui ont été formulées à propos des statistiques de l'état civil en général et des statistiques relatives aux décès en particulier (voir la section 4 des Notes techniques).

La fiabilité des données, au sujet de laquelle des indications ont été fournies plus haut, est un facteur important. Il faut également tenir compte du fait que, dans certains cas, les décès sont classés par date d'enregistrement et non par date d'occurrence ; ces cas ont été signalés par le signe "+". Chaque fois que le décalage entre le décès et son enregistrement est grand et qu'une forte proportion des décès fait l'objet d'un enregistrement tardif, les statistiques relatives aux décès survenus pendant l'année peuvent être considérablement faussées.

En règle générale, toutefois, les décès sont enregistrés beaucoup plus rapidement que les naissances vivantes, et les retards prolongés sont rares.

Un autre facteur qui nuit à la comparabilité internationale est la pratique qui consiste à ne pas inclure dans les statistiques de la mortalité les enfants nés vivants mais décédés avant l'enregistrement de leur naissance ou dans les 24 heures qui ont suivi la naissance. Quand pareil facteur a joué, cela a été signalé en note à la fin du tableau.

Il convient de noter par ailleurs que l'exactitude des taux dépend également de la qualité et des limitations des estimations de la population qui sont utilisées pour leur calcul. Le problème des erreurs par excès ou par défaut commises lors du dénombrement et, dans une certaine mesure, le problème de l'hétérogénéité des définitions de la population totale ont été examinés à la section 3 de l'Introduction, relative à la population en général ; des indications concernant certains pays ou zones sont données en note à la fin du tableau 3.

Il faut souligner que les taux bruts de mortalité, de même que les taux bruts de natalité, de nuptialité et de divortialité, peuvent varier très sensiblement selon la composition par âge et par sexe de la population à laquelle ils se rapportent. Ils offrent néanmoins un moyen simple de mesurer le niveau et l'évolution de la mortalité.

La comparabilité des données selon le lieu de résidence (zone urbaine ou rurale) peut être limitée par les définitions nationales des termes « urbain » et « rural » utilisées pour le classement de ces données. En l'absence d'indications contraires, on a supposé que les mêmes définitions avaient servi pour le recensement national de la population et pour l'établissement des statistiques de l'état civil pour chaque pays ou zone. Toutefois, il n'est pas exclu que, pour une zone ou un pays donné, des définitions différentes aient été retenues. Les définitions du terme « urbain » utilisées pour les recensements nationaux de population ont été présentées à la fin du tableau 6 lorsqu'elles étaient connues. Comme on l'a précisé dans les notes techniques relatives au tableau 6, ces définitions varient considérablement d'un pays ou d'une zone à l'autre.

Données publiées antérieurement : les différentes éditions de l'*Annuaire démographique* contiennent des statistiques des décès et des taux bruts de mortalité. Pour plus de précisions concernant les années pour lesquelles ces données ont été publiées, se reporter à l'index.

18. Deaths and crude death rates, by urban/rural residence: 2012 - 2016
Décès et taux bruts de mortalité, selon la résidence, urbaine/rurale : 2012 - 2016

Continent, country or area, and urban/rural residence / Continent, pays ou zone et résidence, urbaine/rurale	Code[a]	Number - Nombre					Rate - Taux				
		2012	2013	2014	2015	2016	2012	2013	2014	2015	2016
AFRICA - AFRIQUE											
Algeria - Algérie[1]											
Total	U	169 815	168 136	173 781	182 570	180 404	...	...	...	...	...
Benin - Bénin[2]											
Total	I	79 116	...	...	...	...	8.4	...	...	...	...
Botswana[3]											
Total	U	12 270	11 967	12 177	...	...	...	...	...	...	...
Côte d'Ivoire[4]											
Total	I	...	...	248 930	...	...	...	...	11.0	...	...
Egypt - Égypte											
Total	C	529 512	511 183	531 864	573 129	...	6.4	6.0	6.1	6.4	...
Urban - Urbaine	C	251 809	285 611	299 490	...	...	7.1	7.9	8.1	...	...
Rural - Rurale	C	277 703	225 572	232 374	...	...	5.9	4.7	4.7	...	...
Ghana[5]											
Total	+U	54 551	51 466	...	...	...	...	...	...	...	...
Guinea - Guinée[6]											
Total	I	...	...	117 635	...	...	...	...	11.1	...	...
Urban - Urbaine	I	...	...	29 220	...	...	...	...	7.9	...	...
Rural - Rurale	I	...	...	88 415	...	...	...	...	12.8	...	...
Kenya											
Total	U	187 811	194 332	198 611	200 205	189 930	...	...	...	...	...
Lesotho											
Total	+U	7 751	...	...	...	...	...	...	...	...	...
Mauritius - Maurice[7]											
Total	+C	9 343	9 440	9 682	9 747	10 174	7.4	7.5	7.7	7.7	8.1
Urban - Urbaine	+C	4 117	4 189	4 203	4 454	4 658	8.1	8.1	8.1	8.6	9.0
Rural - Rurale	+C	5 226	5 251	5 479	5 293	5 516	7.0	7.1	7.4	7.1	7.4
Mayotte											
Total	C	...	...	590	...	...	...	...	2.7	...	...
Reunion - Réunion											
Total	C	...	...	4 355	...	...	...	...	5.2	...	...
Rwanda											
Total	U	139 499	...	...	...	...	...	...	...	...	...
Saint Helena ex. dep. - Sainte-Hélène sans dép.											
Total	C	62	55	61	55	45	15.0	13.1	13.9	12.3	9.7
Sao Tome and Principe - Sao Tomé-et-Principe											
Total[4]	I	1 287	...	...	...	...	6.9	...	...	...	...
Total	U	...	...	...	*1 226	...	...	...	...	...	...
Senegal - Sénégal[8]											
Total	I	135 468	136 460	...	...	...	10.3	10.1	...	...	...
Seychelles											
Total	+C	651	717	725	703	...	7.4	8.0	7.9	7.5	...
Sierra Leone											
Total	...	10 611	17 127	...	...	...	...	...	...	...	...
South Africa - Afrique du Sud											
Total	U	492 062	473 384	453 360	...	...	...	...	...	...	...
Tunisia - Tunisie											
Total	U	63 257	61 730	62 785	65 743	...	...	...	...	...	...
United Republic of Tanzania - République Unie de Tanzanie											
Total	...	555 975	...	...	...	...	...	...	...	...	...
AMERICA, NORTH - AMÉRIQUE DU NORD											
Anguilla[9]											
Total	+C	38	72	59	61	...	2.8	5.2	4.1	4.1	...
Antigua and Barbuda - Antigua-et-Barbuda											
Total	+C	510	...	...	...	...	...	...	...	...	...
Aruba											
Total	C	595	560	643	679	781	5.7	5.3	6.0	6.2	7.1
Bahamas											
Total	+C	1 995	2 065	...	...	...	5.5	5.6	...	...	...

18. Deaths and crude death rates, by urban/rural residence: 2012 - 2016
Décès et taux bruts de mortalité, selon la résidence, urbaine/rurale : 2012 - 2016 (continued - suite)

Continent, country or area, and urban/rural residence / Continent, pays ou zone et résidence, urbaine/rurale	Code[a]	Number - Nombre					Rate - Taux				
		2012	2013	2014	2015	2016	2012	2013	2014	2015	2016
AMERICA, NORTH - AMÉRIQUE DU NORD											
Barbados - Barbade											
Total	+C	2 403	2 276	2 580	...	...	8.7	8.2	9.3	...	...
Belize											
Total	U	1 650	1 637	1 620	1 772	1 796	...	...	...	...	...
Urban - Urbaine	U	952	873	906	910	958	...	...	...	...	...
Rural - Rurale	U	698	764	714	862	838	...	...	...	...	...
Bermuda - Bermudes[10]											
Total	C	422	471	480	457	*492	6.8	7.6	7.8	7.4	*8.0
British Virgin Islands - Îles Vierges britanniques											
Total	C	122	113	111	136	...	4.3	4.0	...	4.7	...
Canada[11]											
Total	C	246 596	252 338	*268 056[12]	...	...	7.1	7.2	*7.5	...	...
Cayman Islands - Îles Caïmanes[13]											
Total	C	184	182	163	170	...	3.3	3.2	2.9	2.9	...
Costa Rica											
Total	C	19 200	19 647	20 553	21 039	*22 603	4.1	4.2	4.3	4.4	*4.6
Urban - Urbaine	C	9 665	9 891	14 481[14]	17 103	*17 988	2.9	2.9	4.2	4.9	*5.1
Rural - Rurale	C	9 535	9 756	6 072[14]	3 936	*4 615	7.5	7.6	4.7	3.0	*3.4
Cuba											
Total	C	89 372	92 273	96 330	99 691	99 401	8.0	8.2	8.6	8.9	8.8
Urban - Urbaine	C	75 354	78 107	81 866	84 365	...	8.9	9.1	9.5	9.8	...
Rural - Rurale	C	14 018	14 166	14 464	15 326	...	5.2	5.5	5.6	5.9	...
Curaçao											
Total	C	1 246	1 250	1 370	1 398	1 482	8.2	8.1	8.8	8.8	9.3
Dominica - Dominique											
Total	+C	603	630	590	...	...	8.5	8.8	8.2	...	...
Dominican Republic - République dominicaine											
Total	U	36 009	36 025	40 464	40 924	42 185	...	...	...	...	...
El Salvador											
Total	C	32 148	34 212	37 461	...	...	5.1	5.4	5.9	...	...
Urban - Urbaine	C	22 153	22 638	24 617	...	...	5.4	5.4	...	...	...
Rural - Rurale	C	9 995	11 574	12 844	...	...	4.6	5.4	...	...	...
Greenland - Groenland											
Total	C	459	444	461	472	487	8.1	7.9	8.2	8.4	8.7
Urban - Urbaine	C	389	379	388	407	408	8.1	7.9	8.0	8.4	8.4
Rural - Rurale	C	70	65	73	65	79	8.2	7.9	9.1	8.3	10.2
Grenada - Grenade											
Total	+C	856	822	...	...	...	8.0	7.6	...	...	...
Guadeloupe											
Total	C	2 873[15]	2 951[15]	3 290	...	...	7.1	7.3	8.1	...	...
Guatemala											
Total	C	72 657	76 639	77 807	80 876	...	4.8	5.0	4.9	5.0	...
Jamaica - Jamaïque											
Total	U	16 998[16]	17 350[16]	17 619[16]	...	19 557	...	...	...	...	...
Martinique[15]											
Total	C	...	...	3 319	...	...	...	...	8.6	...	...
Mexico - Mexique[17]											
Total	+C	601 259	622 495	632 587	654 593	...	5.1	5.3	5.3	5.4	...
Urban - Urbaine[18]	+C	455 905	472 158	482 499	496 737	...	5.4	5.5	5.6	5.7	...
Rural - Rurale[18]	+C	133 577	139 522	140 144	147 354	...	4.1	4.3	4.3	4.4	...
Montserrat											
Total	+C	44	45	32	49	43	8.9	9.1	6.4	9.8	8.5
Panama											
Total	U	17 350	17 767	18 171	*18 429	...	...	...	...	...	...
Urban - Urbaine	U	11 712	12 546	12 379	*12 419	...	...	...	...	...	...
Rural - Rurale	U	5 638	5 221	5 792	*6 010	...	...	...	...	...	...
Puerto Rico - Porto Rico											
Total	C	30 054	29 416	30 333	28 335	29 613	8.3	8.2	8.6	8.2	8.7
Urban - Urbaine	C	16 835[18]	16 429[18]	16 952[18]	14 784[18]	15 502	...	...	...	...	...
Rural - Rurale	C	13 030[18]	12 822[18]	13 155[18]	13 084[18]	14 111	...	...	...	...	...
Saint Kitts and Nevis - Saint-Kitts-et-Nevis											
Total	+C	336	348	411	...	...	...	...	...	...	...

18. Deaths and crude death rates, by urban/rural residence: 2012 - 2016
Décès et taux bruts de mortalité, selon la résidence, urbaine/rurale : 2012 - 2016 (continued - suite)

Continent, country or area, and urban/rural residence — Continent, pays ou zone et résidence, urbaine/rurale	Code[a]	Number - Nombre					Rate - Taux				
		2012	2013	2014	2015	2016	2012	2013	2014	2015	2016
AMERICA, NORTH - AMÉRIQUE DU NORD											
Saint Lucia - Sainte-Lucie											
Total	C	*922	...	...	...	...	*5.5	...	...	...	...
Saint Vincent and the Grenadines - Saint-Vincent-et-les Grenadines											
Total	C	858	926	1 006	...	...	7.8	8.4	9.1	...	...
Sint Maarten (Dutch part) - Saint-Martin (partie néerlandaise)[19]											
Total	+C	180	171	...	...	...	5.2	4.7	...	...	...
Trinidad and Tobago - Trinité-et-Tobago											
Total	C	*10 373	*10 661	*11 461	*11 240	...	*7.8	*8.0	*8.5	*8.3	...
Turks and Caicos Islands - Îles Turques et Caïques[20]											
Total	C	101	101	76	...	...	3.1	3.0	2.2	...	...
United States of America - États-Unis d'Amérique											
Total	C	2 543 279	2 596 993	2 626 418	2 712 630	...	8.1	8.2	8.2	8.5	...
United States Virgin Islands - Îles Vierges américaines[21]											
Total	C	723	...	...	...	...	6.9	...	...	...	...
AMERICA, SOUTH - AMÉRIQUE DU SUD											
Argentina - Argentine											
Total	C	319 539	326 197	325 539	333 407	...	7.7	7.7	7.6	7.7	...
Bolivia (Plurinational State of) - Bolivie (État plurinational de)[22]											
Total	I	127 050	...	...	...	...	12.3	...	...	...	...
Urban - Urbaine	I	83 506	...	...	...	...	12.0	...	...	...	...
Rural - Rurale	I	43 544	...	...	...	...	12.9	...	...	...	...
Brazil - Brésil[23]											
Total	U	1 157 214	1 180 796	...	...	...	...	...	...	...	...
Total	+C	...	...	1 194 164	1 231 400	...	...	...	5.9	6.0	...
Chile - Chili											
Total	C	98 711	99 770	101 960	*103 327	...	5.7	5.7	5.7	*5.7	...
Urban - Urbaine	C	85 352	86 887	88 055	...	...	5.6	5.7	5.7	...	...
Rural - Rurale	C	13 359	12 883	13 905	...	...	5.9	5.7	6.2	...	...
Colombia - Colombie											
Total	U	196 842	203 058	210 028	...	...	...	...	...	...	...
Urban - Urbaine	U	158 795	...	...	...	...	...	...	...	...	...
Rural - Rurale	U	38 047	...	...	...	...	...	...	...	...	...
Ecuador - Équateur[24]											
Total	U	63 511	63 104	62 981	64 790	...	...	...	...	...	...
Urban - Urbaine	U	50 635	49 912	48 867	49 839	...	...	...	...	...	...
Rural - Rurale	U	12 859	13 192	14 114	14 951	...	...	...	...	...	...
Paraguay											
Total	+U	22 807	24 193	22 625	...	...	...	...	...	...	...
Urban - Urbaine[25]	+U	...	17 354	15 940	...	...	...	...	...	...	...
Rural - Rurale[25]	+U	...	6 742	6 579	...	...	...	...	...	...	...
Peru - Pérou[26]											
Total	+U	97 951	98 616	96 460	96 239	...	...	...	...	...	...
Suriname											
Total	C	3 687	3 557	3 738	3 663	...	6.8	6.5	6.7	6.5	...
Urban - Urbaine	C	2 566	2 371	2 519	2 536	...	7.1	...	...	...	...
Rural - Rurale	C	1 121	1 186	1 219	1 127	...	6.1	...	...	...	...
Uruguay											
Total	C	33 354	32 698	32 122	32 967	...	9.7	9.5	9.3	9.5	...
Venezuela (Bolivarian Republic of) - Venezuela (République bolivarienne du)											
Total	C	142 988	147 901	159 239	163 367	...	4.9	5.0	5.3	5.3	...

Continent, country or area, and urban/rural residence / Continent, pays ou zone et résidence, urbaine/rurale	Code[a]	Number - Nombre					Rate - Taux				
		2012	2013	2014	2015	2016	2012	2013	2014	2015	2016
ASIA - ASIE											
Armenia - Arménie[27]											
Total	C	*27 514	*27 196	27 714	27 878	28 226	*9.1	*9.0	9.2	9.3	9.4
Urban - Urbaine	C	...	...	...	17 743	...	...	...	...	9.3	...
Rural - Rurale	C	...	...	...	10 135	...	...	...	...	9.3	...
Azerbaijan - Azerbaïdjan[27]											
Total	+C	55 017	54 383	55 648	54 697	56 648	5.9	5.8	5.8	5.7	5.8
Urban - Urbaine	+C	29 577	28 863	29 988	29 628	...	6.0	5.8	5.9	5.8	...
Rural - Rurale	+C	25 440	25 520	25 660	25 069	...	5.8	5.8	5.8	5.5	...
Bahrain - Bahreïn[28]											
Total	C	2 613	2 588	2 805	...	...	2.2	2.1	2.1	...	...
Bangladesh											
Total	U	*826 000*	...	...	...	...	...	...	...	...	...
Urban - Urbaine	U	*189 000*	...	...	...	...	...	...	...	...	...
Rural - Rurale	U	*637 000*	...	...	...	...	...	...	...	...	...
Brunei Darussalam - Brunéi Darussalam											
Total	+C	1 216	1 398	1 470	1 547	...	3.0	3.4	3.6	3.7	...
China - Chine[29]											
Total	I	9 660 000	9 720 000	9 770 000	9 750 000	...	7.2	7.2	7.2	7.1	...
China, Hong Kong SAR - Chine, Hong Kong RAS											
Total	C	43 917	43 397	45 087	46 108	46 905	6.1	6.0	6.2	6.3	6.4
China, Macao SAR - Chine, Macao RAS											
Total	C	1 841	1 920	1 939	2 002	*2 238	3.2	3.2	3.1	3.1	...
Cyprus - Chypre[30]											
Total	C	5 665	5 141[31]	5 250[31]	5 859[31]	*5 471[31]	6.6	6.0	6.2	6.9	*6.4
Georgia - Géorgie[27]											
Total	C	49 348	48 553	49 087	49 121	50 771	11.0	10.8	13.2	13.2	13.7
Urban - Urbaine	C	...	...	...	26 139	26 788	...	...	...	12.3	12.6
Rural - Rurale	C	...	...	...	22 982	23 983	...	...	...	14.4	15.1
India - Inde[32]											
Total	I	...	...	...	...	...	7.0	7.0	6.7	6.5	...
Urban - Urbaine	I	...	...	...	...	...	5.6	5.6	5.5	5.4	...
Rural - Rurale	I	...	...	...	...	...	7.6	7.5	7.3	7.1	...
Iran (Islamic Republic of) - Iran (République islamique d')[33]											
Total	+C	367 539	372 279	446 333	374 827[34]	...	4.8	4.8	5.7	4.8	...
Urban - Urbaine	+C	281 367[18]	285 117[18]	302 184	280 765[34]	...	5.2	5.1	5.4	4.9	...
Rural - Rurale	+C	86 093[18]	87 063[18]	144 149	94 062[34]	...	4.0	4.1	6.7	4.4	...
Iraq											
Total	U	...	*189 118*	...	...	...	...	...	...	...	...
Israel - Israël[35]											
Total	C	42 100	41 683	42 457	44 481	43 892	5.3	5.2	5.2	5.3	...
Urban - Urbaine[18]	C	39 563	39 184	39 912	41 750	41 231	5.5	5.3	5.3	5.5	...
Rural - Rurale[18]	C	2 529	2 494	2 533	2 724	2 655	3.7	3.6	3.6	3.7	...
Japan - Japon[36]											
Total	C	1 256 359	1 268 436	1 273 004	1 290 444	*1 307 765	9.8	10.0	10.0	10.1	*10.3
Urban - Urbaine	C	1 112 495	1 124 417	1 130 587	1 147 467	...	...	...	...	...	...
Rural - Rurale	C	142 359	142 556	141 084	141 799	...	...	...	...	...	...
Jordan - Jordanie											
Total	U	*22 785[37]*	*23 898[37]*	*25 782*	*26 640*	...	...	...	...	...	...
Kazakhstan[27]											
Total	C	142 880	135 950	...	...	...	8.5	8.0	...	...	...
Urban - Urbaine	C	82 943	78 581	...	...	...	9.0	8.4	...	...	...
Rural - Rurale	C	59 937	57 369	...	...	...	7.9	7.5	...	...	...
Kuwait - Koweït											
Total	C	5 950	5 909	6 031	6 481	...	1.8	1.7	1.6	1.6	...
Kyrgyzstan - Kirghizstan											
Total	C	36 186	34 880	35 564	34 808	*33 475	6.5	6.1	6.1	5.8	*5.5
Urban - Urbaine	C	13 098	12 507	12 802	12 294	*11 664	7.0	6.5	6.5	6.1	*5.7
Rural - Rurale	C	23 088	22 373	22 762	22 514	*21 811	6.2	5.9	5.9	5.7	*5.4
Lebanon - Liban											
Total	C	23 452	24 013	27 020	...	...	...	...	...	...	...

18. Deaths and crude death rates, by urban/rural residence: 2012 - 2016
Décès et taux bruts de mortalité, selon la résidence, urbaine/rurale : 2012 - 2016 (continued - suite)

Continent, country or area, and urban/rural residence — Continent, pays ou zone et résidence, urbaine/rurale	Code[a]	Number - Nombre					Rate - Taux				
		2012	2013	2014	2015	2016	2012	2013	2014	2015	2016
ASIA - ASIE											
Malaysia - Malaisie											
Total	C	138 692	142 202	150 318	155 786	...	4.7	4.7	4.9	5.0	...
Urban - Urbaine	C	87 842	90 855	97 989	101 309	...	4.1	4.1	4.3	4.4	...
Rural - Rurale	C	50 850	51 347	52 329	54 477	...	6.2	6.3	6.5	6.8	...
Maldives											
Total	C	1 135	1 120	1 143	1 130	...	3.4	3.3	2.8	3.3	...
Urban - Urbaine[38]	C	564	513	546	...	...	...	...	3.5	...	...
Rural - Rurale[38]	C	555	607	492	...	...	...	...	2.0	...	...
Mongolia - Mongolie											
Total	+C	17 761	17 247	16 521	17 620	17 763	6.3	5.9	5.6	5.8	5.8
Urban - Urbaine	+C	13 444	11 182	11 406	11 753	11 182	7.0	5.7	5.7	5.8	5.3
Rural - Rurale	+C	4 317	6 065	5 115	5 867	6 581	4.7	6.5	5.3	6.0	6.8
Myanmar											
Total	+U	250 874[39]	257 216[39]	213 085[40]	...	...	...	...	...	...	...
Urban - Urbaine[39]	+U	114 766	119 823	...	...	...	...	...	...	...	...
Rural - Rurale[39]	+U	136 108	137 393	...	...	...	...	...	...	...	...
Oman[41]											
Total	U	7 884	7 669	7 819	8 167	8 196	...	...	...	...	...
Philippines											
Total	C	514 745	531 280	551 716	560 605	...	5.3	5.4	5.5	5.5	...
Qatar											
Total	C	2 031	2 133	2 366	2 317	*2 339	1.1	1.1	1.1	1.0	*0.9
Urban - Urbaine	C	...	...	2 366	2 317	...	...	...	1.1	1.0	...
Republic of Korea - République de Corée[42]											
Total	C	267 221	266 257	267 692	275 895	...	5.3	5.3	5.3	5.4	...
Urban - Urbaine[18]	C	181 379	182 888	184 631	189 851	...	4.4	4.4	4.5	4.6	...
Rural - Rurale[18]	C	85 840	83 360	83 055	86 038	...	9.1	9.0	8.9	9.1	...
Saudi Arabia - Arabie saoudite											
Total[43]	...	104 195	106 521	...	...	...	...	...	...	...	...
Total[44]	I	...	...	...	69 206	58 097	...	...	...	2.2	1.8
Singapore - Singapour											
Total	+C	18 481	18 938	19 393	19 862	20 017	4.8	4.9	5.0	5.1	5.1
Sri Lanka											
Total	+C	*122 063	*127 124	*127 758	*131 614	...	*6.0	*6.2	*6.2	*6.3	...
State of Palestine - État de Palestine[45]											
Total	U	11 782	11 188	13 390	11 908	...	...	...	...	...	...
Tajikistan - Tadjikistan[27]											
Total	U	32 828	31 706	32 879	...	...	...	...	...	...	...
Urban - Urbaine	U	9 846	10 091	9 830	...	...	...	...	...	...	...
Rural - Rurale	U	22 982	21 615	23 049	...	...	...	...	...	...	...
Thailand - Thaïlande											
Total	+U	423 213	438 648	448 601	457 141	480 434	...	...	...	...	...
Timor-Leste[46]											
Total	I	...	...	...	9 209	...	...	...	...	7.9	...
Turkey - Turquie											
Total	C	376 520	372 920	391 009	405 218	422 135	5.0	4.9	5.0	5.1	...
United Arab Emirates - Émirats arabes unis[47]											
Total	...	7 702	8 015	8 265	8 755	...	...	...	...	...	...
Uzbekistan - Ouzbékistan[27]											
Total	+C	145 988	145 672	149 761	152 035	...	4.9	4.8	4.9	4.9	...
Urban - Urbaine	+C	79 675	79 478	81 991	81 094	...	5.2	5.1	5.2	5.1	...
Rural - Rurale	+C	66 313	66 194	67 770	70 941	...	4.6	4.5	4.5	4.6	...
Yemen - Yémen											
Total	U	28 596	35 066[48]	...	...	...	...	...	...	...	...
EUROPE											
Åland Islands - Îles d'Åland											
Total	C	323	269	251	285	*296	11.4	9.4	8.7	9.8	*10.2
Urban - Urbaine	C	124	115	104	114	*119	11.0	10.1	9.1	9.9	*10.3
Rural - Rurale	C	199	154	147	171	*177	11.6	8.9	8.5	9.8	*10.1

18. Deaths and crude death rates, by urban/rural residence: 2012 - 2016
Décès et taux bruts de mortalité, selon la résidence, urbaine/rurale : 2012 - 2016 (continued - suite)

Continent, country or area, and urban/rural residence / Continent, pays ou zone et résidence, urbaine/rurale	Code[a]	Number - Nombre					Rate - Taux				
		2012	2013	2014	2015	2016	2012	2013	2014	2015	2016
EUROPE											
Albania - Albanie											
Total	C	20 870	20 442	20 656	22 422	...	7.2	7.1	7.1	7.8	...
Andorra - Andorre											
Total	C	303	239	276	282	310	4.3	3.4	3.9	4.0	4.3
Austria - Autriche[49]											
Total	C	79 436	79 526	78 252	83 073	80 669	9.4	9.4	9.2	9.6	9.3
Belarus - Bélarus											
Total	C	126 531	125 326	121 542	120 026	119 379	13.4	13.2	12.8	12.6	12.6
Urban - Urbaine	C	75 234	75 275	74 236	73 563	...	10.5	10.4	10.2	10.0	...
Rural - Rurale	C	51 297	50 051	47 306	46 463	...	22.6	22.6	21.8	21.7	...
Belgium - Belgique[50]											
Total	C	109 076	109 334	104 755	110 541	108 097	9.8	9.8	9.3	9.8	9.6
Urban - Urbaine	C	107 536	107 829	103 223	108 942	...	...	...	...	...	...
Rural - Rurale	C	1 540	1 505	1 532	1 599	...	...	...	...	...	...
Bosnia and Herzegovina - Bosnie-Herzégovine											
Total	C	35 692	35 837	34 824	...	*35 530	9.3	9.3	9.1	...	*10.1
Bulgaria - Bulgarie											
Total	C	109 281	104 345	108 952	110 117	107 580	15.0	14.4	15.1	15.3	15.0
Urban - Urbaine	C	66 333	...	67 008	67 749	...	12.5	...	12.7	12.9	...
Rural - Rurale	C	42 948	...	41 944	42 368	...	21.6	...	21.6	21.9	...
Croatia - Croatie											
Total	C	51 710	50 386	50 839	54 205	51 542	12.1	11.8	12.0	12.9	12.3
Urban - Urbaine	C	26 313	25 464	26 230	28 365	...	...	...	...	...	...
Rural - Rurale	C	25 397	24 922	24 609	25 840	...	...	...	...	...	...
Czechia - Tchéquie											
Total	C	108 189	109 160	105 665	111 173	107 750	10.3	10.4	10.0	10.5	10.2
Urban - Urbaine	C	79 297	79 923	77 826	81 854	...	...	10.4	10.1	10.6	...
Rural - Rurale	C	28 892	29 237	27 839	29 319	...	...	10.3	9.8	10.3	...
Denmark - Danemark[51]											
Total	C	52 325	52 471	51 340	52 555	52 824	9.4	9.4	9.1	9.3	9.2
Estonia - Estonie											
Total	C	15 450	15 244	15 484	15 243	15 392	11.7	11.6	11.8	11.6	11.7
Urban - Urbaine	C	10 632	10 044	10 464	10 491[18]	...	11.8	11.2	11.7	11.7	...
Rural - Rurale	C	4 818	5 200	5 020	4 744[18]	...	11.5	12.4	12.0	11.4	...
Faeroe Islands - Îles Féroé											
Total	C	408	364	394	377	...	8.4	7.5	8.1	7.7	...
Urban - Urbaine	C	136	119	131	102	...	7.5	6.5	7.1	5.5	...
Rural - Rurale	C	272	245	263	275	...	9.0	8.1	8.7	9.1	...
Finland - Finlande[52]											
Total	C	51 384	51 203	51 935	52 207	*53 629	9.5	9.5	9.6	9.6	*9.7
Urban - Urbaine	C	31 838	31 777	32 260	32 941	...	8.6	8.5	8.6	8.6	...
Rural - Rurale	C	19 546	19 426	19 675	19 266	...	11.6	11.6	11.8	12.0	...
France											
Total	C	559 227	558 408	547 003	581 770	*580 100	8.8	8.7	8.5	9.0	*9.0
Urban - Urbaine[53]	C	422 986	422 803	414 410	441 398	...	...	...	...	...	...
Rural - Rurale[53]	C	134 423	133 734	130 755	138 220	...	...	...	...	...	...
Germany - Allemagne											
Total	C	869 582	893 825	868 356	925 200	*920 000	10.8	11.1	10.7	11.3	*11.2
Gibraltar[54]											
Total	+C	264	230	248	235	...	8.1	7.0	7.5	7.0	...
Greece - Grèce											
Total	C	116 668	111 794	113 740	121 212	118 792	10.6	10.2	10.4	11.2	11.0
Urban - Urbaine	C	64 919	...	63 733	67 858	...	...	...	...	...	...
Rural - Rurale	C	51 749	...	50 007	53 354	...	...	...	...	...	...
Guernsey - Guernesey											
Total	C	547	556	526	560	536	8.7	8.9	8.4	9.0	8.5
Hungary - Hongrie											
Total	C	129 440	126 677[56]	126 294[57]	131 575[57]	127 098[57]	13.0	12.8	12.8	13.4	12.9
Urban - Urbaine[55]	C	86 137	85 164[56]	85 796[57]	89 692[57]	...	12.5	12.4	12.3	12.9	...
Rural - Rurale[55]	C	42 752	41 383[56]	40 331[57]	41 717[57]	...	14.0	13.7	13.8	14.4	...
Iceland - Islande											
Total	C	1 955	2 154	2 049	2 178	2 309	6.1	6.7	6.3	6.6	6.9
Urban - Urbaine	C	1 815	1 980	1 936	2 009	...	6.0	6.5	6.3	6.5	...
Rural - Rurale	C	140	174	113	169	...	6.8	8.4	5.4	8.1	...

18. Deaths and crude death rates, by urban/rural residence: 2012 - 2016
Décès et taux bruts de mortalité, selon la résidence, urbaine/rurale : 2012 - 2016 (continued - suite)

Continent, country or area, and urban/rural residence / Continent, pays ou zone et résidence, urbaine/rurale	Code[a]	Number - Nombre					Rate - Taux				
		2012	2013	2014	2015	2016	2012	2013	2014	2015	2016
EUROPE											
Ireland - Irlande											
Total[58]	C	29 186	...	...	...	...	6.4	...	...	...	...
Total	+C	...	30 018	29 188	30 064	*30 390	...	6.5	6.3	6.5	*6.4
Isle of Man - Île de Man											
Total	+C	799	792	787	...	852	9.4	9.2	9.1	...	10.0
Italy - Italie											
Total	C	612 883	600 744	598 364	647 571	615 261	10.3	10.0	9.8	10.7	10.1
Jersey											
Total	+C	774	717	700	756	...	7.8	...	6.9	7.4	...
Latvia - Lettonie											
Total	C	29 025	28 691	28 466	28 478	28 580	14.3	14.3	14.3	14.4	14.5
Urban - Urbaine	C	18 950	18 764	18 847	18 884	...	13.8	13.8	13.9	14.0	...
Rural - Rurale	C	10 075	9 927	9 619	9 594	...	15.3	15.3	15.0	15.2	...
Liechtenstein											
Total	C	224	246	268	252	*270	6.1	6.7	7.2	6.7	*7.2
Lithuania - Lituanie											
Total	C	40 938	41 511	40 252	41 776	41 106	13.7	14.0	13.7	14.4	14.2
Urban - Urbaine	C	25 030	25 403	24 823	25 850	...	12.5	12.8	12.6	13.2	...
Rural - Rurale	C	15 908	16 108	15 429	15 926	...	16.1	16.5	16.0	16.7	...
Luxembourg											
Total	C	3 876	3 822	3 841	3 983	3 967	7.3	7.0	6.9	7.0	6.9
Malta - Malte											
Total	C	3 418	3 236	3 270	3 442	3 342	8.1	7.6	7.7	8.0	7.7
Monaco[59]											
Total	C	529	567	524	595	503	14.7	15.3	14.2	15.8	13.2
Montenegro - Monténégro											
Total	C	5 922	5 917	6 014	6 329	6 464	9.5	9.5	9.7	10.2	10.4
Netherlands - Pays-Bas[60]											
Total	C	140 813	141 245	139 223	147 134	148 997	8.4	8.4	8.3	8.7	8.8
Norway - Norvège[61]											
Total	C	41 992	41 131	40 369	40 676	40 726	8.4	8.1	7.9	7.8	7.8
Poland - Pologne											
Total	C	384 788	387 312	376 467	394 921	388 009	10.1	10.2	9.9	10.4	10.2
Urban - Urbaine	C	233 015	235 097	229 697	242 067	...	10.1	10.2	10.0	10.6	...
Rural - Rurale	C	151 773	152 215	146 770	152 854	...	10.1	10.1	9.7	10.1	...
Portugal[62]											
Total	C	107 612	106 554	104 843	108 539	110 535	10.2	10.2	10.1	10.5	10.7
Republic of Moldova - République de Moldova[63]											
Total	C	39 560	38 060	39 494	39 906	*38 488	11.1	10.7	11.1	11.2	*10.8
Urban - Urbaine	C	12 792	...	...	...	...	8.6	...	...	...	...
Rural - Rurale	C	26 768	...	...	...	...	12.9	...	...	...	...
Romania - Roumanie											
Total	C	255 539	246 967	254 237	261 294	*256 476	12.7	12.4	12.8	13.2	*13.0
Urban - Urbaine	C	117 661	114 091	117 629	121 616	...	10.9	10.6	11.0	11.4	...
Rural - Rurale	C	137 878	132 876	136 608	139 678	...	14.9	14.4	14.9	15.3	...
Russian Federation - Fédération de Russie[27]											
Total	C	1 906 335	1 871 809	...	...	...	13.3	13.0	...	...	...
Urban - Urbaine	C	1 353 635	...	...	...	...	12.8	...	...	...	...
Rural - Rurale	C	552 700	...	...	...	...	14.8	...	...	...	...
San Marino - Saint-Marin											
Total	+C	237	247	252	235	253	7.1	7.4	7.5	7.0	7.4
Serbia - Serbie[64]											
Total	+C	102 400	100 300	101 247	103 678	100 834	14.2	14.0	14.2	14.6	14.3
Urban - Urbaine	+C	53 878	53 169	53 932	56 161	...	12.6	12.4	12.6	13.2	...
Rural - Rurale	+C	48 522	47 131	47 315	47 517	...	16.6	16.3	16.5	16.8	...
Slovakia - Slovaquie											
Total	C	52 437	52 089	51 346	53 826	52 351	9.7	9.6	9.5	9.9	9.6
Urban - Urbaine	C	26 106	26 482	26 198	27 254	...	8.9	9.0	9.0	9.3	...
Rural - Rurale	C	26 331	25 607	25 148	26 572	...	10.7	10.3	10.1	10.6	...
Slovenia - Slovénie											
Total	C	19 257	19 334	18 886	19 834	19 689	9.4	9.4	9.2	9.6	9.5
Urban - Urbaine	C	10 108	9 268	9 103	10 098	...	9.9	8.8	8.7	9.1	...
Rural - Rurale	C	9 149	10 066	9 783	9 736	...	8.9	10.0	9.7	10.2	...
Spain - Espagne											
Total	C	401 122	388 600	393 734	420 408	*406 815	8.6	8.3	8.5	9.1	*8.8

18. Deaths and crude death rates, by urban/rural residence: 2012 - 2016
Décès et taux bruts de mortalité, selon la résidence, urbaine/rurale : 2012 - 2016 (continued - suite)

Continent, country or area, and urban/rural residence / Continent, pays ou zone et résidence, urbaine/rurale	Code[a]	Number - Nombre					Rate - Taux				
		2012	2013	2014	2015	2016	2012	2013	2014	2015	2016
EUROPE											
Sweden - Suède											
Total	C	91 938	90 402	88 976	90 907	90 982	9.7	9.4	9.2	9.3	9.2
Switzerland - Suisse											
Total	C	64 173	64 961	63 938	67 606	64 964	8.0	8.0	7.8	8.2	7.8
Urban - Urbaine	C	47 017	47 654	47 089	56 647[65]	...	8.0	8.0	7.8	8.6	...
Rural - Rurale	C	17 156	17 307	16 849	10 959[65]	...	8.1	8.1	7.8	6.3	...
TFYR of Macedonia - L'ex-R. y. de Macédoine											
Total	C	20 134	19 208	19 718	20 461	20 421	9.8	9.3	9.5	9.9	9.9
Urban - Urbaine	C	12 082	11 539	11 944	12 462	...	...	...	...	...	...
Rural - Rurale	C	8 052	7 669	7 774	7 999	...	...	...	...	...	...
Ukraine[66]											
Total	+C	663 139	662 368	632 296[67]	594 796[67]	...	14.5	14.6	14.7	13.9	...
Urban - Urbaine	+C	411 787	412 553	...	...	...	13.1	...	...	...	...
Rural - Rurale	+C	251 352	249 815	...	...	...	17.7	...	...	...	...
United Kingdom of Great Britain and Northern Ireland - Royaume-Uni de Grande-Bretagne et d'Irlande du Nord[68]											
Total	+C	569 024	574 945	568 840	601 272	*597 208	8.9	9.0	8.8	9.2	*9.1
OCEANIA - OCÉANIE											
American Samoa - Samoas américaines											
Total	C	282	270	259	...	...	4.4	4.3	4.2	...	...
Australia - Australie											
Total	+C	147 098	147 678	153 580	159 052	...	6.5	6.4	6.5	6.7	...
Urban - Urbaine[69]	+C	87 315	87 835	91 116	94 147	...	4.5	4.4	4.5	4.6	...
Rural - Rurale[69]	+C	59 143	59 265	61 904	64 390	...	17.8	17.7	18.3	19.0	...
Cook Islands - Îles Cook[70]											
Total	+C	104	115	113	*102		5.3	6.2	6.1	*5.5	
Fiji - Fidji											
Total	+C	6 724	6 939	6 927	...	...	7.8	8.1	...	...	...
French Polynesia - Polynésie française											
Total	C	1 360	1 441	1 427	1 394		5.1	5.3	5.3	5.1	...
Guam[71]											
Total	C	894	904	952	1 009	*1 022	5.6	5.6	5.9	6.2	*6.3
New Caledonia - Nouvelle-Calédonie											
Total	C	1 322	1 374	1 406	1 465	...	5.1	5.2	5.2	5.4	...
New Zealand - Nouvelle-Zélande[72]											
Total	+C	30 099	29 568	31 065	31 608	31 179	6.8	6.7	6.9	6.9	6.6
Urban - Urbaine[18]	+C	27 051	26 523	27 930	28 455	27 912	7.1	6.9	7.2	7.2	6.9
Rural - Rurale[18]	+C	3 030	3 021	3 099	3 132	3 246	4.9	4.8	5.0	4.9	5.1
Norfolk Island - Île Norfolk[73]											
Total	+C	20	11	13	...	...	...	...	...	...	...
Northern Mariana Islands - Îles Mariannes septentrionales[21]											
Total	U	*163*	*185*	*202*	...	...	...	...	...	...	...
Palau - Palaos											
Total	C	164	192	...	...	...	7.8	...	...	...	...
Samoa											
Total	+U	*742*	*876*	*884*	...	...	...	...	...	...	...

FOOTNOTES - NOTES

Italics: data from civil registers which are incomplete or of unknown completeness. - Italiques : données incomplètes ou dont le degré d'exactitude

n'est pas connu, provenant des registres de l'état civil.

* Provisional. - Données provisoires.

[a] 'Code' indicates the source of data, as follows:
C - Civil registration, estimated over 90% complete

U - Civil registration, estimated less than 90% complete
| - Other source, estimated reliable
+ - Data tabulated by date of registration rather than occurence
... - Information not available

Le 'Code' indique la source des données, comme suit :
C - Registres de l'état civil considérés complets à 90 p. 100 au moins
U - Registres de l'état civil qui ne sont pas considérés complets à 90 p. 100 au moins
| - Autre source, considérée pas douteuses
+ - Données exploitées selon la date de l'enregistrement et non la date de l'événement
... - Information pas disponible

[1] Excluding live-born infants who died before their birth was registered. Data refer to Algerian population only. - Non compris les enfants nés vivants décédés avant l'enregistrement de leur naissance. Les données ne concernent que la population algérienne.

[2] Data are projections presented in Annuaire Statistique 2010. - Les données sont des projections présentées dans l'Annuaire Statistique 2010.

[3] Source: Vital Statistics Report 2014. - Source: Vital Statistics Report 2014.

[4] Data refer to the 12 months preceding the census in May. - Les données se rapportent aux 12 mois précédant le recensement de mai.

[5] The coverage of registration is estimated at 26 per cent. - Le degré de complétude de l'enregistrement est évalué à 26 pour cent.

[6] Adjusted number of deaths in households referring to the 12 months preceding the census in March. - Le nombre ajusté de décès des ménages ordinaires se rapportent aux 12 mois précédant le recensement de mars.

[7] Excludes the islands of St. Brandon and Agalega. - Non compris les îles St. Brandon et Agalega.

[8] Based on estimates and projections from 'Agence Nationale de la Statistique et de la Démographie'. - Données fondées sur des estimations et des projections provenant de l'Agence Nationale de la Statistique et de la Démographie.

[9] Excluding visitors. - Ne comprend pas les visiteurs.

[10] Excluding non-residents and foreign service personnel and their dependants. - À l'exclusion des non-résidents et du personnel diplomatique et de leurs charges de famille.

[11] Including Canadian residents temporarily in the United States, but excluding United States residents temporarily in Canada. - Y compris les résidents canadiens se trouvant temporairement aux Etats-Unis, mais ne comprenant pas les résidents des Etats-Unis se trouvant temporairement au Canada.

[12] Data refer to the twelve months from 1 July of the current year to 30 June of the following year. - Les données font référence aux douze mois de 1 juillet de l'année actuelle à 30 juin de l'année suivante.

[13] Total includes resident deaths outside of the islands but buried in the islands. - Le total comprend les décès de résidents hors des îles mais inhumés dans les îles.

[14] Definition of urban and rural distribution changed from the year 2014. - La définition de la répartition urbaine et rurale a changé depuis 2014.

[15] Excluding live-born infants who died before their birth was registered. - Non compris les enfants nés vivants décédés avant l'enregistrement de leur naissance.

[16] Data have been adjusted for undercoverage of infant deaths and sudden and violent deaths. - Ajusté pour la sous-estimation de la mortalité infantile, du nombre de morts soudaines et de morts violentes.

[17] Data refer to resident population only. - Pour la population résidante seulement.

[18] The total number may include 'Unknown residence', but the categories urban and rural do not. - Le nombre total peut inclure les personnes dont la résidence n'est pas connue, à l'inverse des catégories de population urbaine et rurale.

[19] Source: Population Registry and STAT/CBS estimates. - Source: Le registre de la population et les estimations du STAT/CBS.

[20] Excluding deaths of persons living abroad. - Exception faite des personnes décédées à l'étranger.

[21] Source: U.S. National Center for Health Statistics, National Vital Statistics Reports (NVSR). - Source : US National Center for Health Statistics, National Vital Statistics Reports (NVSR).

[22] Data refer to the 12 months preceding the census in November. - Données se rapportant aux 12 mois précédant le recensement de novembre.

[23] Including deaths abroad and deaths of unknown place of residence. - Y compris décès à l'étranger et décès dont le lieu de résidence n'est pas connu.

[24] Excludes nomadic Indian tribes. - Non compris les tribus d'Indiens nomades.

[25] Data for urban and rural exclude deaths of unknown residence. - Les données pur la résidence urbaine et rurale ne comprent pas les décès dont on ignore la résidence.

[26] Source: Reports of the Ministry of Health. - Source : Rapports du Ministère de la Santé.

[27] Excluding infants born alive of less than 28 weeks' gestation, of less than 1 000 g in weight and 35 cm in length, who die within seven days of birth. - Non compris les enfants nés vivants après moins de 28 semaines de gestations, pesant moins de 1 000 g, mesurant moins de 35 cm et décédés dans les sept jours qui ont suivi leur naissance.

[28] Sources: Births and Deaths National Registration System database, and medical records of government hospitals. - Les sources: Les bases de données des << Births and Deaths National Registration System >> et les dossiers médicaux des hôpitaux du gouvernement.

[29] Data have been estimated on the basis of the annual National Sample Survey on Population Changes. For statistical purposes, the data for China do not include those for the Hong Kong Special Administrative Region (Hong Kong SAR), Macao Special Administrative Region (Macao SAR) and Taiwan province of China. - Les données ont été estimées sur la base de l'enquête annuelle "National Sample Survey on Population Changes". Pour la présentation des statistiques, les données pour la Chine ne comprennent pas la Région Administrative Spéciale de Hong Kong (Hong Kong RAS), la Région Administrative Spéciale de Macao (Macao RAS) et Taïwan province de Chine.

[30] Data refer to government controlled areas. - Les données se rapportent aux zones contrôlées par le Gouvernement.

[31] Data refer to deaths of residents only. - Les données renvoient aux décès de résidents uniquement.

[32] Rates were obtained by the Sample Registration System of India, which is a large demographic survey. Includes data for the Indian-held part of Jammu and Kashmir, the final status of which has not yet been determined. - Les taux ont été obtenus par le Système de l'enregistrement par échantillon de l'Inde qui est une large enquête démographique. Y compris les données pour la partie du Jammu et du Cachemire occupée par l'Inde dont le statut définitif n'a pas encore été déterminé.

[33] Data refer to the Iranian Year which begins on 21 March and ends on 20 March of the following year. - Les données concernent l'année iranienne, qui commence le 21 mars et se termine le 20 mars de l'année suivante.

[34] Including deaths registered by Civil Registration Organization. - Y compris les décès enregistrés par l'organisation chargée d'assurer l'enregistrement des faits d'état civil.

[35] Includes data for East Jerusalem and Israeli residents in certain other territories under occupation by Israeli military forces since June 1967. Including deaths abroad of Israeli residents who were out of the country for less than a year. - Y compris les données pour Jérusalem-Est et les résidents israéliens dans certains autres territoires occupés depuis 1967 par les forces armées israéliennes. Y compris les décès à l'étranger de résidents israéliens qui ont quitté le pays depuis moins d'un an.

[36] Data refer to Japanese nationals in Japan only. The total number may include 'Unknown residence', but the categories urban and rural do not. - Les données se raportent aux nationaux japonais au Japon seulement. Le nombre total peut inclure les personnes dont la résidence n'est pas connue, à l'inverse des catégories de population urbaine et rurale.

[37] Excluding data for Jordanian territory under occupation since June 1967 by Israeli military forces. Excluding foreigners, including registered Palestinian refugees. - Non compris les données pour le territoire jordanien occupé depuis juin 1967 par les forces armées israéliennes. Non compris les étrangers, mais y compris les réfugiés de Palestine enregistrés.

[38] Excluding deaths occurred abroad. Data by the place of occurrence of death, not by the residence of deceased. - Hormis les décès à l'étranger. Données classées selon le lieu du décès, et non selon le lieu de résidence de la personne décédée.

[39] Source: "Department of Public Health" - Source : << Le Service de la santé publique >>

[40] Data are from Vital Registration System (VRS). - Les données proviennent du système d'enregistrement des faits d'état civil.

[41] Data from Births and Deaths Notification System (Ministry of Health and all health care providers). - Les données proviennent du système de notification des naissances et des décès (Ministère de la santé et tous prestataires de soins de santé).

[42] Excluding alien armed forces, civilian aliens employed by armed forces, and foreign diplomatic personnel and their dependants. - Non compris les militaires étrangers, les civils étrangers employés par les forces armées ni le personnel diplomatique étranger et les membres de leur famille les accompagnant.

[43] Projections based on the final results of the 2004 Population and Housing Census. - Projections basées sur les résultats définitifs du recensement de la population et de l'habitat de 2004.

[44] Data refer to Saudi Arabian nationals only. Based on 2010 population census and 2016 demographic survey. - Les données ne concernent que les ressortissants saoudiens. D'après le recensement de la population de 2010 et l'enquête démographique de 2016.

⁴⁵ Source: Palestinian Central Bureau of Statistics, Population Register, updated version 22/02/2016. - Source: Bureau central de statistique palestinien, registre de la population, version actualisée jusqu'au 22/02/2016.

⁴⁶ Data refer to the 12 months preceding the census in July. - Les données se rapportent aux 12 mois précédant le recensement de juillet.

⁴⁷ The registration of births and deaths is conducted by the Ministry of Health. An estimate of completeness is not provided. - L'enregistrement des naissances et des décès est mené par le Ministère de la Santé. Le degré estimatif de complétude n'est pas fourni.

⁴⁸ Including Non-Yemeni deaths. - Y compris les décès non-yéménites.

⁴⁹ Including deaths of nationals abroad. - Y compris les décès des nationaux survenus à l'étranger.

⁵⁰ Including armed forces stationed outside the country, but excluding alien armed forces stationed in the area. - Y compris les militaires nationaux hors du pays, mais non compris les militaires étrangers en garnison sur le territoire.

⁵¹ Excluding Faeroe Islands and Greenland shown separately, if available. - Non compris les Iles Féroé et le Groenland, qui font l'objet de rubriques distinctes, si disponible.

⁵² Excluding Åland Islands. - Non compris les Îles d'Åland.

⁵³ The data for urban and rural exclude the nationals outside the country. - Les données relatives à la population urbaine et rurale n'englobent pas les nationaux se trouvant à l'étranger.

⁵⁴ Excluding armed forces. - Non compris les militaires en garnison.

⁵⁵ The urban and rural categories do not include the data of foreigners, persons of unknown residence and the homeless, whereas the total category includes them. - Les chiffres portant sur la population urbaine et rurale n' incluent pas les données relatives aux étrangers, aux personnes dont la résidence n'est pas connue et aux personnes sans domicile fixe, à l'inverse, le total les inclut.

⁵⁶ Till 2012 data refer to all deaths occurred in Hungary. From 2013 data include the deceased persons with Hungarian usual residence regardless of whether the death occurred in Hungary or in a foreign country, and do not include the deceased persons with foreign country usual residence. - Jusqu'en 2012 les données concernent tous les décès survenus en Hongrie. À partir de 2013, les données comprennent les décès de personnes dont la résidence habituelle était en Hongrie, que le décès ait eu lieu en Hongrie ou dans un pays étranger, et ne comprennent pas les décès de personnes dont la residence habituelle était dans un pays étranger.

⁵⁷ Data include the deceased persons with Hungarian usual residence regardless of whether the death occurred in Hungary or in a foreign country, and do not include the deceased persons with foreign country usual residence. - Les données comprennent tous les décès survenus alors que leur résidence habituelle était en Hongrie, que le décès ait eu lieu en Hongrie ou dans un pays étranger, et ne comprennent pas les décès des personnes dont la residence habituelle était dans un pays étranger.

⁵⁸ Data refer to events registered within one year of occurrence. - Les données portent sur des événements enregistrés dans l'année pendant laquelle ils sont survenus.

⁵⁹ Including still births. Source: City Hall, Civil Status Registry Office, resident and non-resident deaths. - Les données comprennent les mortinaissances. Source : La mairie, Bureau de l'État Civil, toutes les décès.

⁶⁰ Including residents outside the country if listed in a Netherlands population register. - Englobe les résidents se trouvant à l'étranger à condition qu'ils soient inscrits sur le registre de population des Pays-Bas.

⁶¹ Including residents temporarily outside the country. - Y compris les résidents se trouvant temporairement hors du pays.

⁶² Data refer to usually resident population. - Les données concernent la population habituellement résidente.

⁶³ Excluding Transnistria and the municipality of Bender. - Les données ne tiennent pas compte de l'information sur la Transnistria et la municipalité de Bender.

⁶⁴ Excludes data for Kosovo and Metohia. - Sans les données pour le Kosovo et Metohie.

⁶⁵ From 2015, urban refers to urban centers and areas under the influence of urban centers. - A partir de 2015, le territoire urbain inclut l'espace des centres urbains ainsi que l'espace sous influence des centres urbains.

⁶⁶ Data includes deaths resulting from births with weight 500 g and more (if weight is unknown - with length 25 cm and more, or with gestation during 22 weeks or more). - Y compris les décès de nouveau-nés de 500 g ou plus (si le poids est inconnu – de 25 cm de long ou plus, ou après une grossesse de 22 semaines ou plus).

⁶⁷ The Government of Ukraine has informed the United Nations that it is not in a position to provide statistical data concerning the Autonomous Republic of Crimea and the city of Sevastopol. - Le gouvernement Ukrainien a informé l'ONU qu'il n'est pas en mesure de fournir des données statistiques concernant la République autonome de Crimée et la ville de Sébastopol.

⁶⁸ Excluding Channel Islands (Guernsey and Jersey) and Isle of Man, shown separately, if available. - Non compris les îles Anglo-Normandes (Guernesey et Jersey) et l'île de Man, qui font l'objet de rubriques distinctes, si disponible.

⁶⁹ Urban refers to Greater Capital City Statistical Areas, and rural refers to other areas within the state or territory. Data for urban and rural figures do not add up to the total because they exclude the events occurred in Migratory, Special Purpose and Other Territories. - Urbain renvoie aux zones statistiques de la capitale métropolitaine, et rural aux autres zones de l'État ou territoire. La somme des chiffres des catégories « en zone urbaine » et « en zone rurale » ne correspond pas au total du fait qu'en sont exclus les événements qui ont eu lieu dans les territoires de migration, les territoires à destination spéciale et autres territoires.

⁷⁰ Excluding Niue, shown separately, which is part of Cook Islands, but because of remoteness is administered separately. - Non compris Nioué, qui fait l'objet d'une rubrique distincte et qui fait partie des îles Cook, mais qui, en raison de son éloignement, est administrée séparément.

⁷¹ Including United States military personnel, their dependants and contract employees. - Y compris les militaires des Etats-Unis, les membres de leur famille les accompagnant et les agents contractuels des Etats-Unis.

⁷² Random rounding to base 3 is applied in this table as a confidentiality measure. - Les chiffres sont arrondis à la base 3 de manière aléatoire, pour des raisons de confidentialité.

⁷³ Data cover the period from 1 July of the previous year to 30 June of the present year. - Pour la période allant du 1er juillet de l'année précédente au 30 juin de l'année en cours.

Table 19 - *Demographic Yearbook 2016*

Table 19 presents deaths by age and sex and age-specific death rates by sex for the latest available year between 2007 and 2016.

Description of variables: Age is defined as age at last birthday, that is, the difference between the date of birth and the date of the occurrence of the event, expressed in completed solar years. The age classification used in this table is the following: under 1 year, 1-4 years, 5-year age groups through 95-99 years, and 100 years or over.

Rate computation: Age-specific death rates by sex are the annual number of deaths in each age-sex group per 1 000 population in the same age-sex group. These rates are calculated by the Statistics Division of the United Nations.

Deaths at unknown age and the population of unknown age are excluded from age-specific rate calculations but are part of the death rate for all ages combined.

Death rates for infants under one year of age in this table differ from the infant mortality rates shown elsewhere, because the latter are computed per 1 000 live births rather than per 1 000 population.

The population used in computing the rates is the estimated or the enumerated population by age and sex reported to United Nations Statistics Division. First priority is given to an estimate and second priority to census returns of the year to which the deaths refer.

Rates presented in this table have been limited to those countries or areas having at least a total of 100 deaths in a given year. Moreover, rates specific for individual sub-categories that are based on 30 or fewer deaths are identified by the symbol "♦".

Reliability of data: Data from civil registers of deaths that are reported as incomplete (less than 90 per cent completeness) or of unknown completeness are considered unreliable and are set in italics rather than in roman type. Table 18 and the technical notes for that table provide more detailed information on the completeness of death registration. For more information about the quality of vital statistics data in general and the information available on the basis of the completeness estimates in particular, see section 4.2 of the Introduction.

Rates are not computed if data from civil registers of deaths are reported as incomplete (less than 90 per cent completeness) or of unknown completeness, and therefore deemed unreliable.

Limitations: Statistics on deaths by age and sex are subject to the same qualifications as are set forth for vital statistics in general and death statistics in particular as discussed in section 4 of the Introduction.

The reliability of the data is an important factor in considering the limitations. In addition, some deaths are tabulated by date of registration and not by date of occurrence; these have been indicated by a plus sign "+". Whenever the lag between the date of occurrence and date of registration is prolonged and, therefore, a large proportion of the death registrations are delayed, death statistics for any given year may be seriously affected. However, delays in the registration of deaths are less common and shorter than in the registration of live births.

International comparability in mortality statistics may also be affected by the exclusion of deaths of infants who were born alive but died before the registration of the birth or within the first 24 hours of life. Statistics of this type are footnoted.

Because these statistics are classified according to age, they are subject to the limitations with respect to accuracy of age reporting similar to those already discussed in connection with section 3.1.3 of the Introduction. The factors influencing the accuracy of reporting may be somewhat dissimilar in vital statistics (because of the differences in the method of taking a census and registering a death) but, in general, the same errors can be observed.

The absence of data in the unknown age group does not necessarily indicate completely accurate reporting and tabulation of the age item. It is often an indication that the unknowns have been eliminated by assigning ages to them before tabulation, or by proportionate distribution after tabulation.

International comparability of statistics on deaths by age is also affected by the use of different methods to determine age at death. If age is obtained from an item that simply requests age at death in completed years or is derived from information on year of birth and death rather than from information on complete date (day, month and year) of birth and death, the number of deaths classified in the under-one-year age group will tend to be reduced and the number of deaths in the next age group will tend to be somewhat increased. A similar bias may affect other age groups but its impact is usually negligible. Information on this factor is given in the footnotes when known.

Limitations of rates: Rates shown in this table are subject to the same limitations that affect the corresponding data and are set forth in the technical notes for table 18. These include differences in the completeness of registration, the treatment of infants who were born alive but died before the registration of their birth or within the first 24 hours of life, the method used to determine age at death and the quality of the reported information relating to age at death. In addition, some rates are based on deaths tabulated by date of registration and not by date of occurrence; these have been indicated with a plus sign "+".

The problem of obtaining precise correspondence between deaths (numerator) and population (denominator) as regards the inclusion or exclusion of armed forces, refugees, displaced persons and other special groups is particularly difficult where age-specific death rates are concerned. Even when deaths and population do correspond conceptually, comparability of the rates may be affected by abnormal conditions such as absence from the country or area of large numbers of young men in the military forces or working abroad as temporary workers. Death rates may appear high in the younger ages, simply because a large section of the able-bodied members of the age group, whose death rates under normal conditions might be less than the average for persons of their age, is not included. Therefore, care should be exercised in using these rates for comparative purposes.

Also, in a number of cases the rates shown here for all ages combined differ from crude death rates shown elsewhere, because in this table they are computed on the population for which an appropriate age-sex distribution was available, while the crude death rates shown elsewhere may utilize a different total population. The population by age and sex might refer to a census date within the year rather than to the mid-point, or it might be more or less inclusive as regards ethnic groups, armed forces and so forth. In a few instances, the difference is attributable to the fact that the rates in this table were computed on the mean population whereas the corresponding rates in other tables were computed on an estimate for 1 July.

Earlier data: Age-specific deaths and death rates by sex have been shown for the latest available year in each issue of the Yearbook since the 1955 issue. For information on specific years covered, the reader should consult the Historical Index.

Tableau 19 – *Annuaire démographique 2016*

Le tableau 19 présente les données disponibles les plus récentes, entre 2007 et 2016, sur les décès et les taux de mortalité selon l'âge et le sexe.

Description des variables : L'âge considéré est l'âge au dernier anniversaire, c'est-à-dire la différence entre la date de naissance et la date du décès, exprimée en années solaires révolues. La classification par âge est la suivante : moins d'un an, 1 à 4 ans, groupes quinquennaux jusqu'à 95-99 ans et 100 ans et plus.

Calcul des taux : les taux de mortalité selon l'âge et le sexe représentent le nombre annuel de décès survenus pour chaque sexe et chaque groupe d'âge pour 1 000 personnes du même groupe. Ces taux ont été calculés par la Division de statistique de l'ONU.

On n'a pas tenu compte des décès à un âge inconnu ni de la population d'âge inconnu, sauf dans les taux de mortalité pour tous les âges combinés.

Il convient de noter que, dans ce tableau, les taux de mortalité des groupes de moins d'un an sont différents des taux de mortalité infantile qui figurent dans d'autres tableaux, ces derniers ayant été établis pour 1 000 naissances vivantes et non pour 1 000 habitants.

Les chiffres de population utilisés pour le calcul des taux proviennent de dénombrements ou de répartitions estimatives de la population selon l'âge et le sexe. On a utilisé de préférence les estimations de la population; à défaut, on s'est contenté des données censitaires se rapportant à l'année des décès.

Les taux présentés dans ce tableau ne se rapportent qu'aux pays ou zones où l'on a enregistré un total d'au moins 100 décès pendant l'année. Les taux relatifs à des sous-catégories, qui sont fondés sur 30 décès ou moins, sont signalés par le signe "♦".

Fiabilité des données : Les données sur les décès issues des registres d'état civil qui sont déclarées incomplètes (degré d'exhaustivité inférieur à 90 p.100) ou dont le degré d'exhaustivité n'est pas connu sont jugées douteuses et apparaissent en italique et non en caractères romains. Le tableau 18 et les notes techniques s'y rapportant présentent des renseignements plus détaillés sur le degré d'exhaustivité de l'enregistrement des décès. Pour plus de précisions sur la qualité des statistiques de l'état civil en général et le degré de complétude en particulier, voir la section 4.2 de l'Introduction.

On a choisi de ne pas faire figurer dans le tableau 19 des taux calculés à partir de données sur les décès issues de registres d'état civil qui sont déclarées incomplètes (degré d'exhaustivité inférieur à 90 p. 100) ou dont le degré d'exhaustivité n'est pas connu.

Insuffisance des données : Les statistiques des décès selon l'âge et le sexe appellent les mêmes réserves que les statistiques de l'état civil en général et les statistiques relatives à la mortalité en particulier (voir la section 4 de l'Introduction).

La fiabilité des données est un facteur important. Il faut également tenir compte du fait que, dans certains cas, les données relatives aux décès sont classées par date d'enregistrement et non par date d'occurrence ; ces cas ont été signalés par le signe "+". Chaque fois que le décalage entre le décès et son enregistrement est grand et qu'une forte proportion des décès fait l'objet d'un enregistrement tardif, les statistiques des décès de l'année peuvent être considérablement faussées. En règle générale, toutefois, les décès sont enregistrés beaucoup plus rapidement que les naissances vivantes, et les retards prolongés sont rares.

Un autre facteur qui nuit à la comparabilité internationale est la pratique de certains pays ou zones qui consiste à ne pas inclure dans les statistiques des décès les enfants nés vivants mais décédés avant l'enregistrement de leur naissance ou dans les 24 heures qui ont suivi la naissance, pratique qui conduit à sous-évaluer le nombre de décès à moins d'un an. Quand pareil facteur a joué, cela a été signalé en note à la fin du tableau.

Étant donné que les statistiques relatives à la mortalité sont classées selon l'âge, elles appellent les mêmes réserves concernant l'exactitude des déclarations d'âge que celles qui ont été formulées à la section 3.1.3 des Introduction. Dans le cas des données d'état civil, les facteurs qui interviennent à cet égard sont parfois un peu différents, du fait que le recensement et l'enregistrement des décès se font par des méthodes différentes, mais, d'une manière générale, les erreurs observées sont les mêmes.

Si aucun nombre ne figure dans la rangée réservée aux âges inconnus, cela ne signifie pas nécessairement que les déclarations d'âge et le classement par âge sont tout à fait exacts. C'est souvent une indication que l'on a attribué un âge aux personnes d'âge inconnu avant l'exploitation des données ou qu'elles ont été réparties proportionnellement entre les différents groupes après cette opération.

Le manque d'uniformité des méthodes suivies pour obtenir l'âge au moment du décès nuit également à la comparabilité internationale des données. Si l'âge est connu, soit d'après la réponse à une simple question sur l'âge du décès en années révolues, soit d'après l'année de la naissance et l'année du décès, et non d'après des renseignements concernant la date exacte (jour, mois et année) de la naissance et du décès, le nombre de décès classés dans la catégorie « moins d'un an » sera entaché d'une erreur par défaut et le chiffre figurant dans la catégorie suivante d'une erreur par excès.

Les données pour les autres groupes d'âge pourront être entachées d'une distorsion analogue, mais les répercussions seront généralement négligeables. Les imperfections, lorsqu'elles étaient connues, ont été signalées en note à la fin du tableau.

Insuffisance des taux : les taux présentés dans le tableau 19 appellent les mêmes réserves que celles formulées à propos des fréquences correspondantes (voir à ce sujet les notes techniques se rapportant au tableau 18). Leurs imperfections tiennent notamment aux différences d'exhaustivité de l'enregistrement, au classement des enfants nés vivants mais décédés avant l'enregistrement de leur naissance ou dans les 24 heures qui ont suivi la naissance, à la méthode utilisée pour obtenir l'âge au moment du décès, et à la qualité des déclarations concernant l'âge au moment du décès. En outre, dans certains cas, les données relatives aux décès sont classées par date d'enregistrement et non par date de l'événement ; ces cas ont été signalés par le signe "+".

S'agissant des taux de mortalité par âge, il est particulièrement difficile d'établir une correspondance exacte entre les décès (numérateur) et la population (dénominateur) du fait de l'inclusion ou de l'exclusion des militaires, des réfugiés, des personnes déplacées et d'autres groupes spéciaux. Il convient d'ajouter que, même lorsque population et décès correspondent, la comparabilité des taux peut être compromise par des conditions anormales telles que l'absence du pays ou de la zone d'un grand nombre de jeunes gens qui sont sous les drapeaux ou qui travaillent à l'étranger comme travailleurs temporaires. Il arrive ainsi que les taux de mortalité paraissent élevés parmi les groupes les plus jeunes simplement parce que l'on en a exclu un grand nombre d'individus en bonne santé pour lesquels le taux de mortalité pourrait être, dans des conditions normales, inférieur à la moyenne observée pour les personnes du même âge. Par conséquent, il importe d'être prudent quand on les utilise ces taux de mortalité dans des comparaisons.

De même, les taux indiqués pour tous les âges combinés diffèrent dans plusieurs cas des taux bruts de mortalité qui figurent dans d'autres tableaux, parce qu'ils se rapportent à une population pour laquelle on disposait d'une répartition par âge et par sexe appropriée, tandis que les taux bruts de mortalité indiqués ailleurs peuvent avoir été calculés sur la base d'un chiffre de population totale différent. Ainsi, il est possible que les chiffres de population par âge et par sexe proviennent d'un recensement effectué dans le courant de l'année et non au milieu de l'année, et qu'ils se différencient des autres chiffres de population en excluant ou en incluant certains groupes ethniques, les militaires, etc. Quelquefois, la différence tient à ce que les taux du tableau 19 ont été calculés sur la base de la population moyenne, alors que les taux correspondants des autres tableaux reposent sur une estimation au 1er juillet.

Données publiées antérieurement : Les éditions de l'*Annuaire démographique* parues depuis 1955 présentent les statistiques les plus récentes dont on disposait à l'époque sur les décès selon l'âge et le sexe et sur les taux de mortalité selon l'âge et le sexe. Pour plus de précisions concernant les années pour lesquelles ces données ont été publiées, se reporter à l'index historique.

19. Deaths by age and sex and age-specific death rates by sex: latest available year, 2007 - 2016
Décès et taux de mortalité selon l'âge et le sexe : dernière année disponible, 2007 - 2016

Continent, country or area, date, code[a] and age (in years) / Continent, pays ou zone, date, code[a] et âge (en années)	Number - Nombre			Rate - Taux		
	Both sexes Les deux sexes	Male Masculin	Female Féminin	Both sexes Les deux sexes	Male Masculin	Female Féminin
AFRICA - AFRIQUE						
Algeria - Algérie[1]						
2016 (U)						
Total	180 404	92 981	87 423	...	...	...
0	22 271	12 157	10 114	...	...	...
1 - 4	2 986	1 581	1 406	...	...	...
5 - 9	1 458	795	664	...	...	...
10 - 14	1 066	570	495	...	...	...
15 - 19	1 610	1 008	601	...	...	...
20 - 24	2 440	1 630	810	...	...	...
25 - 29	2 741	1 710	1 031	...	...	...
30 - 34	3 362	1 892	1 470	...	...	...
35 - 39	3 685	1 957	1 728	...	...	...
40 - 44	4 206	2 134	2 071	...	...	...
45 - 49	5 321	2 711	2 611	...	...	...
50 - 54	6 817	3 651	3 166	...	...	...
55 - 59	8 144	4 457	3 687	...	...	...
60 - 64	11 005	6 279	4 726	...	...	...
65 - 69	11 794	6 649	5 145	...	...	...
70 - 74	12 746	6 905	5 841	...	...	...
75 - 79	18 197	9 162	9 035	...	...	...
80 - 84	22 572	10 897	11 675	...	...	...
85 +	37 984	16 836	21 147	...	...	...
Botswana[2]						
2014 (U)						
Total	12 177	6 282	5 895	...	...	...
0	1 045	574	471	...	...	...
1 - 4	238	125	113	...	...	...
5 - 9	76	45	31	...	...	...
10 - 14	69	36	33	...	...	...
15 - 19	164	74	90	...	...	...
20 - 24	323	164	159	...	...	...
25 - 29	610	297	313	...	...	...
30 - 34	764	350	414	...	...	...
35 - 39	889	487	402	...	...	...
40 - 44	699	370	329	...	...	...
45 - 49	637	342	295	...	...	...
50 - 54	673	399	274	...	...	...
55 - 59	700	405	295	...	...	...
60 - 64	633	380	253	...	...	...
65 - 69	647	382	265	...	...	...
70 - 74	703	418	285	...	...	...
75 - 79	634	333	301	...	...	...
80 - 84	900	431	469	...	...	...
85 +	1 729	645	1 084	...	...	...
Unknown - Inconnu	44	25	19	..	..	..
Congo[3]						
2009 (+U)						
Total	7 554	...	...	...	...	...
0 - 4	2 150	...	...	...	...	...
5 - 14	2 905	...	...	...	...	...
15 - 59	292	...	...	...	...	...
60 +	2 207	...	...	...	...	...
Egypt - Égypte						
2013 (C)						
Total	511 183	284 212	226 971	6.0	6.6	5.5
0	38 753	20 791	17 962	19.2	19.8	18.5
1 - 4	11 379	6 229	5 150	1.5	1.6	1.4
5 - 9	4 610	2 769	1 841	0.5	0.6	0.4
10 - 14	4 351	2 803	1 548	0.6	0.7	0.4
15 - 19	7 008	5 133	1 875	0.9	1.3	0.5
20 - 24	8 042	5 853	2 189	0.9	1.3	0.5
25 - 29	8 640	5 924	2 716	1.0	1.4	0.7
30 - 34	8 522	5 586	2 936	1.3	1.6	0.9
35 - 39	9 134	5 786	3 348	1.7	2.2	1.3
40 - 44	11 516	7 328	4 188	2.5	3.2	1.8
45 - 49	20 204	13 119	7 085	4.8	6.1	3.4
50 - 54	33 330	21 655	11 675	9.0	11.6	6.3

Continent, country or area, date, code[a] and age (in years) / Continent, pays ou zone, date, code[a] et âge (en années)	Number - Nombre			Rate - Taux		
	Both sexes Les deux sexes	Male Masculin	Female Féminin	Both sexes Les deux sexes	Male Masculin	Female Féminin
AFRICA - AFRIQUE						
Egypt - Égypte						
2013 (C)						
55 - 59	45 099	28 711	16 388	14.7	18.7	10.8
60 - 64	56 319	33 854	22 465	24.7	29.8	19.6
65 - 69	54 246	30 162	24 084	34.0	38.2	29.8
70 - 74	52 817	27 426	25 391	50.5	53.2	47.8
75 - 79	51 372	25 119	26 253	85.5	85.3	85.6
80 +	85 841	35 964	49 877	175.9	148.7	202.7
80 - 84	44 191	19 848	24 343	...	...	...
85 +	41 650	16 116	25 534	...	...	...
Ghana[4]						
2010 (|)						
Total	163 534	84 214	79 320	6.6	7.0	6.3
0	28 068	15 807	12 261	38.4	42.7	34.0
1 - 4	17 868	9 424	8 444	6.7	6.9	6.4
5 - 9	6 275	3 437	2 838	2.0	2.2	1.8
10 - 14	3 641	1 587	2 054	1.2	1.1	1.4
15 - 19	4 399	1 752	2 647	1.7	1.3	2.0
20 - 24	5 467	2 117	3 350	2.4	1.9	2.7
25 - 29	6 325	2 516	3 809	3.1	2.7	3.4
30 - 34	8 218	3 397	4 821	4.9	4.3	5.4
35 - 39	8 215	3 579	4 636	5.8	5.3	6.2
40 - 44	8 855	4 141	4 714	7.5	7.2	7.7
45 - 49	7 573	3 715	3 858	8.1	8.2	8.0
50 - 54	8 577	4 376	4 201	10.3	11.1	9.6
55 - 59	5 656	3 564	2 092	10.8	13.8	7.9
60 - 64	7 159	4 418	2 741	15.0	19.5	11.0
65 - 69	5 670	3 360	2 310	19.3	24.7	14.7
70 - 74	8 443	5 096	3 347	24.0	34.1	16.6
75 - 79	6 197	3 599	2 598	30.1	40.4	22.2
80 - 84	6 543	3 346	3 197	41.1	53.7	33.1
85 - 89	4 436	2 166	2 270	53.4	65.8	45.3
90 - 94	3 650	1 797	1 853	71.5	94.6	57.8
95 +	2 299	1 020	1 279	99.3	116.6	88.9
Guinea - Guinée[5]						
2014 (|)						
Total	129 896	70 815	59 081	12.3	13.9	10.9
0	36 556	20 751	15 805	112.1	125.9	97.9
1 - 4	21 083	11 308	9 775	14.7	15.6	13.7
5 - 9	5 661	3 128	2 533	3.3	3.6	3.0
10 - 14	3 237	1 821	1 416	2.6	2.9	2.3
15 - 19	3 585	1 630	1 955	3.2	3.1	3.3
20 - 24	3 775	1 806	1 969	4.2	4.4	4.0
25 - 29	4 350	1 934	2 416	5.6	5.7	5.4
30 - 34	4 366	2 077	2 289	6.9	7.5	6.5
35 - 39	3 909	1 986	1 923	7.6	8.7	6.8
40 - 44	4 168	2 226	1 942	9.5	11.1	8.2
45 - 49	3 567	2 063	1 504	10.9	12.9	8.9
50 - 54	4 461	2 562	1 899	15.0	17.5	12.5
55 - 59	2 963	1 857	1 106	14.0	16.2	11.4
60 - 64	4 659	2 695	1 964	22.8	25.6	19.8
65 - 69	3 490	2 070	1 420	27.4	30.4	23.9
70 - 74	5 181	2 884	2 297	44.4	50.7	38.4
75 - 79	3 461	2 029	1 432	54.2	59.8	47.9
80 - 84	4 300	2 248	2 052	84.3	91.1	78.0
85 - 89	2 350	1 297	1 053	113.4	120.2	106.0
90 - 94	1 673	929	744	142.4	165.0	121.6
95 +	3 101	1 514	1 587	259.3	264.8	254.2
95 - 99	1 886	963	923	...	...	...
100 +	1 215	551	664	...	...	...
Kenya[6]						
2011 (U)						
Total	174 487	96 026	78 461	...	...	...
0	23 167	12 119	11 048	...	...	...
1 - 4	12 129	6 530	5 599	...	...	...
5 - 14	9 145	4 949	4 196	...	...	...
15 - 24	11 961	5 931	6 030	...	...	...

Continent, country or area, date, code[a] and age (in years) / Continent, pays ou zone, date, code[a] et âge (en annèes)	Number - Nombre			Rate - Taux		
	Both sexes Les deux sexes	Male Masculin	Female Féminin	Both sexes Les deux sexes	Male Masculin	Female Féminin
AFRICA - AFRIQUE						
Kenya[6]						
2011 (U)						
25 - 34	21 054	11 329	9 725	...	...	...
35 - 44	21 605	12 382	9 223	...	...	...
45 - 54	18 606	11 124	7 482	...	...	...
55 - 74	29 686	17 525	12 161	...	...	...
75 +	27 134	14 137	12 997	...	...	...
Lesotho						
2010 (+U)						
Total	7 864	4 154	3 710	...	...	...
0 - 4	271	147	124	...	...	...
5 - 9	69	34	35	...	...	...
10 - 14	67	43	24	...	...	...
15 - 19	112	50	62	...	...	...
20 - 24	237	106	131	...	...	...
25 - 29	477	199	278	...	...	...
30 - 34	727	347	380	...	...	...
35 - 39	732	383	349	...	...	...
40 - 44	675	376	299	...	...	...
45 - 49	583	337	246	...	...	...
50 - 54	627	406	221	...	...	...
55 - 59	550	363	187	...	...	...
60 - 64	484	302	182	...	...	...
65 - 69	388	234	154	...	...	...
70 - 74	502	256	246	...	...	...
75 - 79	481	227	254	...	...	...
80 - 84	384	153	231	...	...	...
85 +	441	158	283	...	...	...
Unknown - Inconnu	57	33	24	...	...	...
Malawi[7]						
2008 (|)						
Total	135 865	70 991	64 874	10.0	10.6	9.4
0 - 4	56 721	29 832	26 889	20.9	21.9	20.0
0	30 508	16 606	13 902	50.9	54.9	46.9
1 - 4	26 213	13 226	12 987	12.4	12.5	12.4
5 - 9	6 413	3 350	3 063	2.8	2.9	2.7
10 - 14	5 333	3 071	2 262	3.5	4.1	2.9
15 - 19	4 266	1 863	2 403	3.1	2.7	3.4
20 - 24	7 188	3 038	4 150	6.1	5.1	7.0
25 - 29	7 903	3 405	4 498	7.6	6.8	8.3
30 - 34	9 042	4 280	4 762	9.7	10.4	9.2
35 - 39	7 200	3 813	3 387	9.7	10.3	9.0
40 - 44	6 004	3 410	2 594	10.8	12.2	9.4
45 - 49	4 275	2 436	1 839	9.7	11.3	8.2
50 - 54	3 414	2 092	1 322	10.7	13.3	8.2
55 +	18 106	10 401	7 705	34.1	40.9	27.9
55 - 59	2 447	1 523	924	...	...	...
60 - 64	2 978	1 827	1 151	...	...	...
65 - 69	2 314	1 372	942	...	...	...
70 - 74	2 871	1 665	1 206	...	...	...
75 - 79	2 149	1 254	895	...	...	...
80 - 84	2 151	1 138	1 013	...	...	...
85 +	3 196	1 622	1 574	...	...	...
Mali[8]						
2009 (|)						
Total	62 371	34 387	27 984	4.3	4.8	3.8
0 - 4	29 336	16 098	13 238	11.2	12.1	10.2
5 - 9	3 486	1 933	1 553	1.5	1.6	1.3
10 - 14	1 598	914	684	0.9	1.0	0.8
15 - 19	1 638	777	861	1.1	1.1	1.1
20 - 24	1 570	712	858	1.4	1.3	1.4
25 - 29	1 618	752	866	1.6	1.7	1.6
30 - 34	1 729	839	890	2.1	2.2	2.1
35 - 39	1 604	798	806	2.5	2.5	2.5
40 - 44	1 547	858	689	2.8	3.2	2.5
45 - 49	1 462	890	572	3.3	3.9	2.6
50 - 54	1 527	884	643	4.0	4.7	3.3

Continent, country or area, date, code[a] and age (in years) / Continent, pays ou zone, date, code[a] et âge (en années)	Number - Nombre			Rate - Taux		
	Both sexes Les deux sexes	Male Masculin	Female Féminin	Both sexes Les deux sexes	Male Masculin	Female Féminin
AFRICA - AFRIQUE						
Mali[8]						
2009 (|)						
55 - 59	1 544	954	590	5.5	6.4	4.4
60 - 64	1 960	1 201	759	7.8	9.4	6.1
65 - 69	1 958	1 152	806	11.8	13.0	10.5
70 - 74	2 093	1 198	895	15.7	17.8	13.5
75 - 79	1 891	1 113	778	24.5	27.2	21.5
80 + ...	3 372	1 836	1 536	39.4	43.7	35.2
Unknown - Inconnu	2 438	1 478	960	..	..	..
Mauritius - Maurice[9]						
2016 (+C)						
Total	10 174	5 588	4 586	8.1	8.9	7.2
0	154	81	73	12.1	12.4	11.8
1 - 4	20	10	10	♦0.4	♦0.4	♦0.4
5 - 9	10	6	4	♦0.1	♦0.2	♦0.1
10 - 14	23	9	14	♦0.2	♦0.2	♦0.3
15 - 19	56	46	10	0.6	0.9	♦0.2
20 - 24	89	65	24	0.9	1.3	♦0.5
25 - 29	108	79	29	1.2	1.7	♦0.6
30 - 34	129	94	35	1.5	2.1	0.8
35 - 39	219	161	58	2.2	3.2	1.2
40 - 44	277	192	85	3.3	4.5	2.0
45 - 49	437	291	146	5.0	6.6	3.4
50 - 54	669	454	215	6.9	9.5	4.4
55 - 59	838	554	284	10.1	13.6	6.7
60 - 64	1 078	657	421	15.7	20.0	11.8
65 - 69	1 171	691	480	22.5	28.8	17.0
70 - 74	1 090	585	505	35.6	44.4	28.9
75 - 79	1 083	547	536	52.9	65.3	44.3
80 - 84	1 046	489	557	81.5	101.9	69.3
85 + ...	1 677	577	1 100	165.2	183.9	156.9
85 - 89	913	349	564	...	...	...
90 - 94	546	182	364	...	...	...
95 - 99	170	40	130	...	...	...
100 + ...	48	6	42	...	...	...
Morocco - Maroc						
2007 (U)						
Total	105 222	66 522	38 700	...	...	...
0	5 140	2 823	2 317	...	...	...
1 - 4	2 320	1 266	1 054	...	...	...
5 - 9	1 075	591	484	...	...	...
10 - 14	859	533	326	...	...	...
15 - 19	1 575	1 024	551	...	...	...
20 - 24	2 204	1 442	762	...	...	...
25 - 29	2 503	1 570	933	...	...	...
30 - 34	2 705	1 660	1 045	...	...	...
35 - 39	2 948	1 767	1 181	...	...	...
40 - 44	3 400	2 052	1 348	...	...	...
45 - 49	4 547	2 766	1 781	...	...	...
50 - 54	5 616	3 672	1 944	...	...	...
55 - 59	6 132	4 046	2 086	...	...	...
60 - 64	7 193	4 626	2 567	...	...	...
65 - 69	10 331	6 494	3 837	...	...	...
70 - 74	12 441	7 990	4 451	...	...	...
75 - 79	13 183	8 491	4 692	...	...	...
80 + ...	20 051	13 159	6 892	...	...	...
Unknown - Inconnu	999	550	449	..	..	..
Namibia - Namibie[10]						
2011 (|)						
Total	22 668	12 491	10 177	10.7	12.2	9.3
0	2 685	1 411	1 274	41.9	44.1	39.6
1 - 4	1 346	719	627	6.1	6.5	5.7
5 - 9	447	255	192	1.9	2.1	1.6
10 - 14	384	212	172	1.6	1.7	1.4
15 - 19	577	298	279	2.4	2.5	2.3
20 - 24	918	537	381	4.3	5.1	3.5
25 - 29	1 233	645	588	7.0	7.4	6.5

19. Deaths by age and sex and age-specific death rates by sex: latest available year, 2007 - 2016
Décès et taux de mortalité selon l'âge et le sexe : dernière année disponible, 2007 - 2016 (continued - suite)

Continent, country or area, date, code[a] and age (in years) / Continent, pays ou zone, date, code[a] et âge (en années)	Number - Nombre			Rate - Taux		
	Both sexes Les deux sexes	Male Masculin	Female Féminin	Both sexes Les deux sexes	Male Masculin	Female Féminin
AFRICA - AFRIQUE						
Namibia - Namibie[10]						
2011 (|)						
30 - 34	1 591	890	701	10.7	12.1	9.2
35 - 39	1 487	873	614	11.9	14.3	9.6
40 - 44	1 323	807	516	13.5	17.2	10.1
45 - 49	1 140	698	442	14.2	18.6	10.3
50 - 54	917	535	382	14.9	19.5	11.2
55 - 59	891	562	329	18.6	26.1	12.5
60 - 64	994	584	410	24.4	31.7	18.3
65 - 69	766	424	342	24.6	32.3	19.0
70 - 74	739	424	315	30.7	41.3	22.8
75 - 79	682	382	300	39.5	54.5	29.3
80 - 84	792	402	390	55.3	76.2	43.1
85 - 89	638	282	356	68.6	90.2	57.6
90 - 94	549	234	315	80.6	98.4	71.1
95 +	1 003	403	600	178.7	228.6	155.8
Unknown - Inconnu	1 566	914	652	..	..	..
Niger						
2011 (+U)						
Total	6 761	...	...	...	...	...
0	236	...	...	...	...	...
1 - 4	329	...	...	...	...	...
5 - 9	120	...	...	...	...	...
10 - 14	81	...	...	...	...	...
15 - 19	147	...	...	...	...	...
20 - 24	242	...	...	...	...	...
25 - 29	319	...	...	...	...	...
30 - 34	378	...	...	...	...	...
35 - 39	414	...	...	...	...	...
40 - 44	470	...	...	...	...	...
45 - 49	485	...	...	...	...	...
50 - 54	495	...	...	...	...	...
55 - 59	443	...	...	...	...	...
60 - 64	541	...	...	...	...	...
65 - 69	443	...	...	...	...	...
70 - 74	517	...	...	...	...	...
75 - 79	347	...	...	...	...	...
80 - 84	298	...	...	...	...	...
85 - 89	112	...	...	...	...	...
90 - 94	90	...	...	...	...	...
95 - 99	26	...	...	...	...	...
100 +	53	...	...	...	...	...
Unknown - Inconnu	175	...	...	..	..	..
Republic of South Sudan - République de Soudan du Sud[11]						
2008 (|)						
Total	165 898	88 797	77 101	20.1	20.7	19.4
0	29 217	12 384	16 833	126.4	101.6	154.1
1 - 4	55 674	29 144	26 530	51.9	51.4	52.5
5 - 9	22 571	12 351	10 220	17.4	17.9	16.8
10 - 14	12 487	6 785	5 702	11.8	11.9	11.7
15 - 19	11 665	6 297	5 368	13.1	13.6	12.6
20 - 24	9 256	5 556	3 700	12.5	15.4	9.8
25 - 29	6 022	4 063	1 959	8.6	12.1	5.4
30 - 34	4 496	2 634	1 862	8.4	10.2	6.7
35 - 39	3 046	2 237	809	6.4	9.4	3.4
40 - 44	2 627	1 605	1 022	7.7	9.3	6.1
45 - 49	1 656	993	663	6.0	6.6	5.3
50 - 54	1 513	977	536	7.7	9.3	5.8
55 - 59	946	618	328	7.8	9.1	6.1
60 - 64	1 094	668	426	9.5	10.4	8.3
65 - 69	908	528	380	12.4	12.7	12.0
70 - 74	1 036	766	270	17.5	22.0	11.0
75 - 79	487	415	72	16.8	23.8	6.3
80 - 84	493	277	216	20.1	19.4	21.2
85 - 89	355	229	126	32.3	34.0	29.6

Continent, country or area, date, code[a] and age (in years) Continent, pays ou zone, date, code[a] et âge (en années)	Number - Nombre			Rate - Taux		
	Both sexes Les deux sexes	Male Masculin	Female Féminin	Both sexes Les deux sexes	Male Masculin	Female Féminin
AFRICA - AFRIQUE						
Republic of South Sudan - République de Soudan du Sud[11]						
2008 (|)						
90 - 94	177	110	67	24.0	24.6	23.2
95 +	172	160	12	25.1	41.7	◆4.0
Reunion - Réunion						
2007 (C)						
Total	4 045	2 247	1 798	5.1	5.9	4.4
0 - 4	114	58	56	1.7	1.7	1.7
0	99	49	50	...	...	...
1 - 4	15	9	6	...	...	...
5 - 9	6	6	-	◆0.1	◆0.2	-
10 - 14	10	7	3	◆0.1	◆0.2	◆0.1
15 - 19	32	25	7	0.5	◆0.7	◆0.2
20 - 24	44	35	9	0.8	1.3	◆0.3
25 - 29	39	27	12	0.8	◆1.1	◆0.4
30 - 34	55	37	18	1.0	1.4	◆0.6
35 - 39	97	68	29	1.5	2.3	◆0.9
40 - 44	158	106	52	2.4	3.3	1.5
45 - 49	211	150	61	4.0	5.9	2.3
50 - 54	236	183	53	5.1	8.2	2.2
55 - 59	266	188	78	7.5	10.7	4.4
60 - 64	287	176	111	10.8	14.1	7.9
65 - 69	375	246	129	17.4	24.8	11.1
70 - 74	427	250	177	25.9	34.7	19.1
75 - 79	448	231	217	39.5	50.3	32.2
80 - 84	496	222	274	65.3	78.9	57.3
85 - 89	393	149	244	106.6	140.6	92.9
90 - 94	233	66	167	166.1	182.8	160.3
95 +	118	17	101	308.9	◆369.6	300.6
95 - 99	96	15	81	...	...	...
100 +	22	2	20	...	...	...
Saint Helena ex. dep. - Sainte-Hélène sans dép.						
2014 (C)						
Total	61	36	25	...	...	...
0	1	-	1	...	...	...
1 - 4	-	-	-	...	...	...
5 - 9	-	-	-	...	...	...
10 - 14	-	-	-	...	...	...
15 - 19	-	-	-	...	...	...
20 - 24	-	-	-	...	...	...
25 - 29	1	1	-	...	...	...
30 - 34	-	-	-	...	...	...
35 - 39	-	-	-	...	...	...
40 - 44	-	-	-	...	...	...
45 - 49	1	1	-	...	...	...
50 - 54	-	-	-	...	...	...
55 - 59	4	2	2	...	...	...
60 - 64	7	5	2	...	...	...
65 - 69	7	5	2	...	...	...
70 - 74	9	6	3	...	...	...
75 - 79	7	6	1	...	...	...
80 - 84	7	4	3	...	...	...
85 - 89	8	4	4	...	...	...
90 - 94	4	1	3	...	...	...
95 - 99	5	1	4	...	...	...
100 +	-	-	-	...	...	...
Sao Tome and Principe - Sao Tomé-et-Principe[12]						
2012 (|)						
Total	1 287	735	552	7.2	8.3	6.1
0	132	82	50	23.1	27.8	18.0
1 - 4	69	41	29	3.1	3.7	◆2.6
5 - 9	18	5	13	◆0.7	◆0.4	◆1.0
10 - 14	29	20	10	◆1.4	◆1.9	◆0.9
15 - 19	29	23	6	◆1.6	◆2.5	◆0.7
20 - 24	54	36	18	3.4	4.5	◆2.3
25 - 29	39	26	13	2.6	◆3.5	◆1.7

19. Deaths by age and sex and age-specific death rates by sex: latest available year, 2007 - 2016
Décès et taux de mortalité selon l'âge et le sexe : dernière année disponible, 2007 - 2016 (continued - suite)

Continent, country or area, date, code[a] and age (in years) Continent, pays ou zone, date, code[a] et âge (en années)	Number - Nombre			Rate - Taux		
	Both sexes Les deux sexes	Male Masculin	Female Féminin	Both sexes Les deux sexes	Male Masculin	Female Féminin
AFRICA - AFRIQUE						
Sao Tome and Principe - Sao Tomé-et-Principe[12]						
2012 (|)						
30 - 34	41	31	10	3.3	5.0	♦1.6
35 - 39	61	41	20	6.3	8.4	♦4.1
40 - 44	51	34	17	6.5	8.6	♦4.4
45 - 49	49	24	25	7.8	♦7.9	♦7.7
50 - 54	77	44	33	14.4	16.9	12.0
55 - 59	52	21	31	13.6	♦11.6	15.4
60 - 64	86	59	27	32.3	44.1	♦20.4
65 - 69	60	33	27	31.2	35.9	♦26.8
70 - 74	102	60	42	54.3	70.6	40.9
75 - 79	103	51	52	73.0	83.7	64.8
80 +	234	104	130	170.1	198.1	152.8
Seychelles						
2015 (+C)						
Total	703	401	302	7.5	8.7	6.4
0	17	7	10	♦10.6	♦8.4	♦13.0
1 - 4	3	1	2	♦0.5	♦0.3	♦0.6
5 - 9	5	3	2	♦0.8	♦1.0	♦0.7
10 - 14	3	2	1	♦0.5	♦0.7	♦0.3
15 - 19	3	1	2	♦0.5	♦0.4	♦0.7
20 - 24	12	9	3	♦1.8	♦2.6	♦1.0
25 - 29	10	8	2	♦1.5	♦2.2	♦0.6
30 - 34	21	12	9	♦2.6	♦3.0	♦2.2
35 - 39	18	9	9	♦2.5	♦2.5	♦2.4
40 - 44	24	21	3	♦3.2	♦5.4	♦0.8
45 - 49	39	28	11	5.8	♦9.0	♦3.1
50 - 54	45	30	15	6.1	♦8.3	♦4.0
55 - 59	55	38	17	10.1	13.5	♦6.4
60 - 64	60	43	17	14.8	21.3	♦8.3
65 - 69	59	46	13	21.8	34.3	♦9.5
70 - 74	56	32	24	28.7	34.6	♦23.3
75 - 79	88	46	42	62.5	87.1	47.7
80 - 84	82	35	47	84.0	119.0	68.9
85 - 89	44	12	32	87.1	♦95.2	84.4
90 +	59	18	41	247.9	♦400.0	212.4
90 - 94	41	15	26	...	...	...
95 - 99	12	2	10	...	...	...
100 +	6	1	5	...	...	...
Sierra Leone[13]						
2013 (+U)						
Total	19 403	9 982	9 421	...	...	...
0	2 276	1 151	1 125	...	...	...
1 - 4	2 413	1 168	1 245	...	...	...
5 - 14	2 904	1 447	1 457	...	...	...
15 +	11 810	6 216	5 594	...	...	...
South Africa - Afrique du Sud						
2014 (U)						
Total	453 360	236 613[14]	214 826[14]	...	...	...
0	25 643	13 529[14]	11 618[14]	...	...	...
1 - 4	8 619	4 594[14]	3 964[14]	...	...	...
5 - 9	3 143	1 781[14]	1 353[14]	...	...	...
10 - 14	3 092	1 724[14]	1 361[14]	...	...	...
15 - 19	7 002	3 988[14]	2 995[14]	...	...	...
20 - 24	13 967	7 943[14]	5 948[14]	...	...	...
25 - 29	23 101	12 405[14]	10 530[14]	...	...	...
30 - 34	29 819	16 442[14]	13 213[14]	...	...	...
35 - 39	29 818	17 103[14]	12 569[14]	...	...	...
40 - 44	29 966	17 635[14]	12 225[14]	...	...	...
45 - 49	29 077	16 965[14]	12 039[14]	...	...	...
50 - 54	31 425	18 482[14]	12 873[14]	...	...	...
55 - 59	32 017	18 702[14]	13 256[14]	...	...	...
60 - 64	34 855	20 065[14]	14 754[14]	...	...	...
65 - 69	31 721	17 405[14]	14 294[14]	...	...	...
70 - 74	31 316	15 402[14]	15 897[14]	...	...	...
75 - 79	28 053	12 325[14]	15 710[14]	...	...	...

19. Deaths by age and sex and age-specific death rates by sex: latest available year, 2007 - 2016
Décès et taux de mortalité selon l'âge et le sexe : dernière année disponible, 2007 - 2016 (continued - suite)

Continent, country or area, date, code[a] and age (in years) Continent, pays ou zone, date, code[a] et âge (en annèes)	Number - Nombre			Rate - Taux		
	Both sexes Les deux sexes	Male Masculin	Female Féminin	Both sexes Les deux sexes	Male Masculin	Female Féminin
AFRICA - AFRIQUE						
South Africa - Afrique du Sud						
2014 (U)						
80 - 84	25 576	9 215[14]	16 344[14]	...	...	...
85 - 89	18 546	6 166[14]	12 370[14]	...	...	...
90 +	15 435	4 115[14]	11 316[14]	...	...	...
Unknown - Inconnu	1 169	627[14]	197[14]	..	..	..
Swaziland[12]						
2007 (|)						
Total	18 367	8 738	9 629	21.8	21.5	22.0
0 - 4	4 843	2 131	2 712	44.1	38.9	49.4
0	3 613	1 555	2 058	...	...	...
1 - 4	1 230	576	654	...	...	...
5 - 9	408	198	210	3.6	3.5	3.8
10 - 14	302	165	137	2.7	3.0	2.4
15 - 19	431	174	257	4.3	3.5	5.1
20 - 24	1 145	353	792	13.0	8.3	17.6
25 - 29	1 773	707	1 066	25.2	20.9	29.2
30 - 34	1 792	839	953	34.3	32.8	35.7
35 - 39	1 586	828	758	36.3	40.0	32.9
40 - 44	1 145	652	493	33.7	44.0	25.7
45 - 49	865	502	363	29.6	39.3	22.1
50 - 54	752	453	299	32.9	43.5	24.0
55 - 59	557	364	193	30.8	43.7	19.8
60 - 64	618	342	276	37.0	51.0	27.6
65 - 69	436	238	198	32.9	43.1	25.6
70 - 74	392	214	178	48.0	66.7	35.9
75 - 79	283	158	125	45.4	68.0	31.9
80 +	612	261	351	95.3	122.1	82.0
Unknown - Inconnu	427	159	268	..	..	..
Zambia - Zambie[15]						
2010 (|)						
Total	164 385	87 693	76 692	12.6	13.6	11.6
0	35 103	18 953	16 150	79.7	86.1	73.2
1 - 4	28 943	15 297	13 646	16.0	17.0	15.0
5 - 9	8 405	4 519	3 886	4.4	4.7	4.0
10 - 14	4 836	2 550	2 286	2.7	2.9	2.6
15 - 19	5 856	2 821	3 035	3.8	3.8	3.9
20 - 24	7 967	3 746	4 221	6.7	6.8	6.6
25 - 29	10 471	5 112	5 359	9.9	10.3	9.6
30 - 34	11 305	5 986	5 319	13.5	14.1	12.8
35 - 39	9 972	5 698	4 274	14.6	16.0	13.1
40 - 44	7 336	4 334	3 002	15.5	17.3	13.5
45 - 49	6 021	3 603	2 418	16.0	19.1	12.9
50 - 54	4 770	2 687	2 083	16.7	19.4	14.3
55 - 59	3 546	2 056	1 490	18.3	21.3	15.3
60 - 64	3 929	2 146	1 783	23.3	27.4	19.8
65 - 69	3 363	1 732	1 631	27.4	30.5	24.7
70 - 74	4 084	2 138	1 946	43.8	48.7	39.4
75 +	8 478	4 315	4 163	65.1	67.1	63.2
AMERICA, NORTH - AMÉRIQUE DU NORD						
Anguilla[16]						
2013 (+C)						
Total	72	43	29	...	...	...
0	3	2	1	...	...	...
1 - 4	-	-	-	...	...	...
5 - 9	-	-	-	...	...	...
10 - 14	-	-	-	...	...	...
15 - 19	2	2	-	...	...	...
20 - 24	1	1	-	...	...	...
25 - 29	2	2	-	...	...	...
30 - 34	-	-	-	...	...	...
35 - 39	2	1	1	...	...	...
40 - 44	-	-	-	...	...	...
45 - 49	1	1	-	...	...	...

Continent, country or area, date, code[a] and age (in years) Continent, pays ou zone, date, code[a] et âge (en années)	Number - Nombre			Rate - Taux		
	Both sexes Les deux sexes	Male Masculin	Female Féminin	Both sexes Les deux sexes	Male Masculin	Female Féminin

AMERICA, NORTH - AMÉRIQUE DU NORD

Anguilla[16]
2013 (+C)

50 - 54	5	3	2	...	...	...
55 - 59	5	3	2	...	...	...
60 - 64	3	3	-	...	...	...
65 - 69	7	3	4	...	...	...
70 - 74	4	3	1	...	...	...
75 - 79	9	5	4	...	...	...
80 - 84	8	5	3	...	...	...
85 +	20	9	11	...	...	...

2015 (+C)

Total	61	...	...	...	...	...
0 - 4	5	...	...	...	...	...
5 - 14	-	...	...	...	...	...
15 - 29	3	...	...	...	...	...
30 - 44	5	...	...	...	...	...
45 - 59	8	...	...	...	...	...
60 - 64	-	...	...	...	...	...
65 - 69	1	...	...	...	...	...
70 - 74	6	...	...	...	...	...
75 - 79	8	...	...	...	...	...
80 - 84	8	...	...	...	...	...
85 +	15	...	...	...	...	...

Aruba
2016 (C)

Total	781	395	386	7.1	7.6	6.6
0	5	3	2	♦4.2	♦4.8	♦3.5
1 - 4	3	2	1	♦0.5	♦0.7	♦0.4
5 - 9	2	1	1	♦0.3	♦0.3	♦0.3
10 - 14	2	1	1	♦0.3	♦0.3	♦0.3
15 - 19	2	2	-	♦0.3	♦0.5	-
20 - 24	7	2	5	♦1.1	♦0.6	♦1.6
25 - 29	1	-	1	♦0.2	-	♦0.3
30 - 34	7	4	3	♦1.0	♦1.3	♦0.8
35 - 39	9	5	4	♦1.2	♦1.5	♦1.0
40 - 44	12	7	5	♦1.5	♦1.9	♦1.2
45 - 49	20	12	8	♦2.3	♦3.0	♦1.7
50 - 54	31	21	10	3.3	♦4.9	♦2.0
55 - 59	54	31	23	6.3	7.8	♦5.0
60 - 64	50	32	18	7.2	10.1	♦4.7
65 - 69	73	47	26	14.3	20.4	♦9.2
70 - 74	104	51	53	29.2	33.0	26.3
75 - 79	101	53	48	39.4	49.9	32.0
80 - 84	140	63	77	89.6	108.0	78.6
85 - 89	88	38	50	115.7	140.6	102.1
90 - 94	42	13	29	168.0	♦186.7	♦160.7
95 +	28	7	21	♦298.9	♦280.0	♦302.5

Bahamas
2012 (+C)

Total	1 995	1 094	901	5.5	6.2	4.9
0	57	26	31	8.6	♦7.6	9.7
1 - 4	18	10	8	♦0.7	♦0.8	♦0.7
5 - 9	9	5	4	♦0.3	♦0.3	♦0.3
10 - 14	8	6	2	♦0.3	♦0.4	♦0.1
15 - 19	27	17	10	♦0.9	♦1.1	♦0.6
20 - 24	57	42	15	1.9	2.9	♦1.0
25 - 29	49	42	7	1.8	3.2	♦0.5
30 - 34	72	52	20	2.8	4.1	♦1.5
35 - 39	84	47	37	3.1	3.5	2.6
40 - 44	100	58	42	3.6	4.4	2.9
45 - 49	130	72	58	4.9	5.6	4.2
50 - 54	159	84	75	6.8	7.5	6.2
55 - 59	147	94	53	8.5	11.4	5.9
60 - 64	149	83	66	12.2	14.5	10.2
65 - 69	147	87	60	16.1	21.0	12.1
70 - 74	183	96	87	27.6	32.9	23.5
75 - 79	176	93	83	43.0	54.4	34.9

Continent, country or area, date, code[a] and age (in years) / Continent, pays ou zone, date, code[a] et âge (en années)	Number - Nombre			Rate - Taux		
	Both sexes Les deux sexes	Male Masculin	Female Féminin	Both sexes Les deux sexes	Male Masculin	Female Féminin
AMERICA, NORTH - AMÉRIQUE DU NORD						
Bahamas						
2012 (+C)						
80 - 84	170	81	89	98.0	154.6	74.0
85 - 89	116	61	55	143.7	279.8	91.5
90 +	137	38	99	259.0	351.9	222.0
90 - 94	90	30	60	...	...	...
95 - 99	36	6	30	...	...	...
100 +	11	2	9	...	...	...
Barbados - Barbade						
2007 (+C)						
Total	2 195	1 143	1 052	...	...	...
0	31	18	13	...	...	...
1 - 4	8	5	3	...	...	...
5 - 9	5	3	2	...	...	...
10 - 14	8	6	2	...	...	...
15 - 19	17	13	4	...	...	...
20 - 24	10	4	6	...	...	...
25 - 29	15	14	1	...	...	...
30 - 34	30	16	14	...	...	...
35 - 39	38	23	15	...	...	...
40 - 44	45	26	19	...	...	...
45 - 49	58	28	30	...	...	...
50 - 54	76	46	30	...	...	...
55 - 59	90	54	36	...	...	...
60 - 64	113	63	50	...	...	...
65 - 69	142	83	59	...	...	...
70 - 74	182	105	77	...	...	...
75 - 79	309	160	149	...	...	...
80 - 84	281	152	129	...	...	...
85 - 89	339	139	200	...	...	...
90 - 94	199	59	140	...	...	...
95 +	97	30	67	...	...	...
Unknown - Inconnu	102	96	6	..	..	..
Belize						
2016 (U)						
Total	1 796	1 120	676	...	...	...
0	103	61	42	...	...	...
1 - 4	18	11	7	...	...	...
5 - 9	10	5	5	...	...	...
10 - 14	11	8	3	...	...	...
15 - 19	45	31	14	...	...	...
20 - 24	65	52	13	...	...	...
25 - 29	73	57	16	...	...	...
30 - 34	99	69	30	...	...	...
35 - 39	78	57	21	...	...	...
40 - 44	91	67	24	...	...	...
45 - 49	94	56	38	...	...	...
50 - 54	110	63	47	...	...	...
55 - 59	130	81	49	...	...	...
60 - 64	121	74	47	...	...	...
65 - 69	123	78	45	...	...	...
70 - 74	124	85	39	...	...	...
75 - 79	139	68	71	...	...	...
80 - 84	140	82	58	...	...	...
85 - 89	129	72	57	...	...	...
90 - 94	64	28	36	...	...	...
95 - 99	25	15	10	...	...	...
100 +	4	-	4	...	...	...
Bermuda - Bermudes[17]						
2015 (C)						
Total	457	243	214	7.4	8.2	6.6
0	2	2	-	♦3.2	♦6.3	-
1 - 4	-	-	-	-	-	-
5 - 9	-	-	-	-	-	-
10 - 14	-	-	-	-	-	-
15 - 19	1	1	-	♦0.3	♦0.7	-
20 - 24	3	2	1	♦1.0	♦1.4	♦0.6

Continent, country or area, date, code[a] and age (in years) / Continent, pays ou zone, date, code[a] et âge (en années)	Number - Nombre			Rate - Taux		
	Both sexes Les deux sexes	Male Masculin	Female Féminin	Both sexes Les deux sexes	Male Masculin	Female Féminin
AMERICA, NORTH - AMÉRIQUE DU NORD						
Bermuda - Bermudes[17]						
2015 (C)						
25 - 29	1	1	-	♦0.3	♦0.6	-
30 - 34	3	3	-	♦0.7	♦1.5	-
35 - 39	1	-	1	♦0.2	-	♦0.5
40 - 44	3	1	2	♦0.7	♦0.4	♦0.9
45 - 49	6	2	4	♦1.2	♦0.8	♦1.6
50 - 54	14	10	4	♦2.5	♦3.8	♦1.4
55 - 59	29	21	8	♦5.7	♦8.9	♦2.9
60 - 64	28	17	11	♦6.7	♦8.6	♦5.0
65 - 69	39	27	12	11.5	♦17.2	♦6.6
70 - 74	47	30	17	18.3	♦26.2	♦12.0
75 - 79	56	31	25	30.2	38.9	♦23.6
80 - 84	69	34	35	49.9	62.7	41.6
85 +	155	61	94	146.9	194.3	126.9
85 - 89	84	39	45	...	...	...
90 - 94	47	16	31	...	...	...
95 - 99	15	5	10	...	...	...
100 +	9	1	8	...	...	...
Canada[18]						
2013 (C)						
Total	252 338	126 973	125 365	7.2	7.3	7.1
0	1 884	1 032	852	4.9	5.3	4.6
1 - 4	317	164	153	0.2	0.2	0.2
5 - 9	164	93	71	0.1	0.1	0.1
10 - 14	223	110	113	0.1	0.1	0.1
15 - 19	707	461	246	0.3	0.4	0.2
20 - 24	1 211	847	364	0.5	0.7	0.3
25 - 29	1 286	887	399	0.5	0.7	0.3
30 - 34	1 520	1 004	516	0.6	0.8	0.4
35 - 39	1 833	1 163	670	0.8	1.0	0.6
40 - 44	2 770	1 685	1 085	1.2	1.4	0.9
45 - 49	4 932	2 996	1 936	1.9	2.3	1.5
50 - 54	8 319	5 051	3 268	3.0	3.7	2.4
55 - 59	12 065	7 316	4 749	4.8	5.9	3.8
60 - 64	15 680	9 623	6 057	7.4	9.2	5.7
65 - 69	19 908	11 882	8 026	11.4	13.9	9.0
70 - 74	23 167	13 493	9 674	18.4	22.7	14.6
75 - 79	28 504	15 800	12 704	30.1	36.7	24.6
80 - 84	38 246	19 691	18 555	52.5	63.9	44.2
85 - 89	41 681	18 591	23 090	91.9	112.5	80.1
90 - 94	32 276	11 252	21 024	160.7	188.8	148.8
95 - 99	12 795	3 311	9 484	307.8	404.8	284.0
100 +	2 850	521	2 329	411.1	582.1	385.8
Cayman Islands - Îles Caïmanes						
2014 (C)						
Total	153	80	73	2.6	2.8	2.4
0	2	1	1	...	...	...
1 - 4	1	-	1	...	...	...
5 - 9	1	-	1	...	...	...
10 - 14	-	-	-	...	...	...
15 - 19	1	1	-	...	...	...
20 - 24	4	3	1	...	...	...
25 - 29	2	2	-	...	...	...
30 - 34	2	1	1	...	...	...
35 - 39	2	1	1	...	...	...
40 - 44	4	4	-	...	...	...
45 - 49	6	1	5	...	...	...
50 - 54	9	7	2	...	...	...
55 - 59	10	7	3	...	...	...
60 - 64	7	5	2	...	...	...
65 +	102	47	55	26.9	26.6	27.1
Costa Rica						
2016* (C)						
Total	22 603	12 810	9 793	4.6	5.4	3.9
1 - 4	604	333	271	...	...	...
5 - 9	171	82	89	0.5	0.4	0.5

Continent, country or area, date, code[a] and age (in years)	Number - Nombre			Rate - Taux		
Continent, pays ou zone, date, code[a] et âge (en années)	Both sexes Les deux sexes	Male Masculin	Female Féminin	Both sexes Les deux sexes	Male Masculin	Female Féminin
AMERICA, NORTH - AMÉRIQUE DU NORD						
Costa Rica						
2016* (C)						
10 - 14	111	67	44	0.3	0.3	0.2
15 - 19	264	217	47	0.6	1.0	0.2
20 - 24	426	325	101	1.0	1.5	0.5
25 - 29	493	379	114	1.2	1.9	0.5
30 - 34	505	380	125	1.4	2.2	0.6
35 - 39	519	351	168	1.6	2.2	1.0
40 - 44	571	379	192	1.8	2.6	1.1
45 - 49	756	489	267	2.6	3.5	1.7
50 - 54	1 049	675	374	3.3	4.5	2.2
55 - 59	1 309	841	468	4.9	6.6	3.4
60 - 64	1 592	949	643	7.7	9.8	5.9
65 - 69	1 824	1 072	752	11.7	15.0	8.9
70 - 74	1 954	1 105	849	16.4	20.3	13.1
75 - 79	2 423	1 372	1 051	28.9	34.1	24.0
80 - 84	2 651	1 355	1 296	44.7	54.3	37.7
85 +	5 233	2 364	2 869	90.9	92.2	89.8
Unknown - Inconnu	148	75	73	..	..	..
Cuba						
2015 (C)						
Total	99 691	53 812	45 879	8.9	9.6	8.1
0	535	299	236	4.3	4.7	4.0
1 - 4	184	105	79	0.4	0.4	0.3
5 - 9	110	67	43	0.2	0.2	0.2
10 - 14	137	79	58	0.2	0.2	0.2
15 - 19	279	172	107	0.4	0.5	0.3
20 - 24	376	269	107	0.5	0.7	0.3
25 - 29	583	399	184	0.7	1.0	0.5
30 - 34	605	385	220	0.9	1.1	0.7
35 - 39	859	553	306	1.2	1.6	0.9
40 - 44	1 764	1 146	618	1.8	2.4	1.3
45 - 49	2 932	1 827	1 105	2.9	3.7	2.2
50 - 54	4 677	2 949	1 728	5.0	6.4	3.6
55 - 59	5 076	3 156	1 920	7.9	10.1	5.8
60 - 64	7 136	4 252	2 884	12.1	15.0	9.5
65 - 69	9 322	5 446	3 876	18.3	22.4	14.6
70 - 74	11 525	6 724	4 801	28.2	34.7	22.3
75 - 79	13 249	7 259	5 990	45.2	53.3	38.2
80 - 84	13 428	6 918	6 510	72.5	82.8	64.1
85 +	26 907	11 800	15 107	153.6	160.2	148.7
85 - 89	12 874	6 025	6 849	...	...	...
90 - 94	8 826	3 808	5 018	...	...	...
95 - 99	3 980	1 547	2 433	...	...	...
100 +	1 227	420	807	...	...	...
Unknown - Inconnu	7	7	-	..	..	..
Curaçao						
2016 (C)						
Total	1 482	790	692	9.3	10.8	8.0
0	20	11	9	♦11.0	♦11.9	♦10.1
1 - 4	1	-	1	♦0.1	-	♦0.3
5 - 9	-	-	-	-	-	-
10 - 14	3	3	-	♦0.3	♦0.6	-
15 - 19	3	2	1	♦0.3	♦0.4	♦0.2
20 - 24	12	8	4	♦1.3	♦1.7	♦0.9
25 - 29	8	7	1	♦0.9	♦1.7	♦0.2
30 - 34	9	6	3	♦1.0	♦1.5	♦0.6
35 - 39	7	7	-	♦0.8	♦1.8	-
40 - 44	24	14	10	♦2.3	♦3.0	♦1.7
45 - 49	36	22	14	3.1	♦4.2	♦2.2
50 - 54	58	37	21	4.5	6.5	♦2.9
55 - 59	85	61	24	7.0	11.7	♦3.5
60 - 64	113	69	44	11.1	15.6	7.6
65 - 69	152	86	66	17.2	22.0	13.4
70 - 74	159	89	70	24.4	32.7	18.4
75 - 79	200	108	92	43.9	57.3	34.4
80 - 84	226	122	104	75.4	103.2	57.4

19. Deaths by age and sex and age-specific death rates by sex: latest available year, 2007 - 2016
Décès et taux de mortalité selon l'âge et le sexe : dernière année disponible, 2007 - 2016 (continued - suite)

Continent, country or area, date, code[a] and age (in years) Continent, pays ou zone, date, code[a] et âge (en années)	Number - Nombre			Rate - Taux		
	Both sexes Les deux sexes	Male Masculin	Female Féminin	Both sexes Les deux sexes	Male Masculin	Female Féminin
AMERICA, NORTH - AMÉRIQUE DU NORD						
Curaçao						
2016 (C)						
85 - 89	178	83	95	113.8	149.0	94.4
90 - 94	126	42	84	188.3	213.2	178.0
95 - 99	48	10	38	281.5	♦363.6	265.7
100 +	14	3	11	♦444.4	♦260.9	♦550.0
Dominican Republic - République dominicaine						
2016 (U)						
Total	42 185	25 053	17 132	...	...	...
0	791	438	353	...	...	...
1 - 4	227	123	104	...	...	...
5 - 9	156	99	57	...	...	...
10 - 14	189	111	78	...	...	...
15 - 19	647	502	145	...	...	...
20 - 24	1 116	836	280	...	...	...
25 - 29	1 097	831	266	...	...	...
30 - 34	1 016	704	312	...	...	...
35 - 39	1 267	838	429	...	...	...
40 - 44	1 508	1 007	501	...	...	...
45 - 49	1 915	1 241	674	...	...	...
50 - 54	2 334	1 477	857	...	...	...
55 - 59	2 630	1 682	948	...	...	...
60 - 64	3 180	1 943	1 237	...	...	...
65 - 69	3 706	2 235	1 471	...	...	...
70 - 74	3 861	2 347	1 514	...	...	...
75 - 79	4 230	2 406	1 824	...	...	...
80 - 84	4 436	2 283	2 153	...	...	...
85 +	7 377	3 684	3 693	...	...	...
Unknown - Inconnu	502	266	236	..	..	..
El Salvador						
2014 (C)						
Total	37 461	21 326	16 135	5.9	7.2	4.8
0	876	491	385	7.0	7.7	6.3
1 - 4	240	131	109	0.5	0.5	0.5
5 - 9	125	66	59	0.2	0.2	0.2
10 - 14	250	160	90	0.4	0.5	0.3
15 - 19	983	813	170	1.4	2.3	0.5
20 - 24	1 139	926	213	1.8	3.0	0.6
25 - 29	1 047	869	178	2.1	3.8	0.6
30 - 34	1 249	1 015	234	2.9	5.6	1.0
35 - 39	1 348	1 061	287	3.5	6.4	1.3
40 - 44	1 313	942	371	3.6	6.1	1.8
45 - 49	1 492	985	507	4.7	7.3	2.8
50 - 54	1 669	1 022	647	6.3	8.9	4.2
55 - 59	1 991	1 129	862	8.9	11.6	6.8
60 - 64	2 302	1 275	1 027	12.1	15.4	9.6
65 - 69	2 678	1 398	1 280	17.1	20.4	14.6
70 - 74	3 107	1 644	1 463	24.7	29.7	20.8
75 - 79	3 687	1 826	1 861	38.6	44.0	34.4
80 +	11 965	5 573	6 392	109.6	120.9	101.3
80 - 84	4 057	1 977	2 080	...	...	...
85 - 89	3 853	1 851	2 002	...	...	...
90 - 94	2 642	1 186	1 456	...	...	...
95 +	1 413	559	854	...	...	...
Greenland - Groenland						
2016 (C)						
Total	487	309	178	8.7	10.4	6.7
0	6	5	1	♦7.2	♦12.2	♦2.4
1 - 4	1	-	1	♦0.3	-	♦0.7
5 - 9	3	3	-	♦0.8	♦1.4	-
10 - 14	-	-	-	-	-	-
15 - 19	7	5	2	♦1.8	♦2.6	♦1.0
20 - 24	15	10	5	♦3.4	♦4.4	♦2.3
25 - 29	7	6	1	♦1.5	♦2.6	♦0.4
30 - 34	7	5	2	♦1.7	♦2.4	♦1.0
35 - 39	8	6	2	♦2.4	♦3.3	♦1.3
40 - 44	8	7	1	♦2.6	♦4.2	♦0.7

Continent, country or area, date, code[a] and age (in years) / Continent, pays ou zone, date, code[a] et âge (en années)	Number - Nombre			Rate - Taux		
	Both sexes Les deux sexes	Male Masculin	Female Féminin	Both sexes Les deux sexes	Male Masculin	Female Féminin
AMERICA, NORTH - AMÉRIQUE DU NORD						
Greenland - Groenland						
2016 (C)						
45 - 49	21	11	10	♦4.8	♦4.7	♦4.9
50 - 54	45	35	10	8.8	12.5	♦4.3
55 - 59	23	14	9	♦5.6	♦6.1	♦5.1
60 - 64	59	40	19	20.4	24.2	♦15.2
65 - 69	49	35	14	26.7	32.8	♦18.2
70 - 74	66	40	26	47.9	52.5	♦42.3
75 - 79	79	45	34	105.2	121.3	89.5
80 - 84	46	23	23	130.7	♦166.7	♦107.5
85 - 89	31	17	14	201.3	♦320.8	♦138.6
90 - 94	6	2	4	♦193.5	♦181.8	♦200.0
95 +	-	-	-	-	-	-
Guatemala						
2011 (C)						
Total	72 354	41 295	31 059	4.9	5.8	4.1
0 - 4	9 965	5 515	4 450	4.6	4.9	4.1
0	7 413	4 202	3 211	...	...	...
1 - 4	2 552	1 313	1 239	...	...	...
5 - 9	705	387	318	0.3	0.4	0.3
10 - 14	907	502	405	0.5	0.5	0.4
15 - 19	2 281	1 581	700	1.4	1.9	0.9
20 - 24	2 738	2 111	627	2.0	3.2	0.9
25 - 29	2 864	2 167	697	2.5	3.9	1.2
30 - 34	2 819	2 051	768	3.0	4.7	1.5
35 - 39	2 680	1 855	825	3.5	5.5	2.0
40 - 44	2 659	1 778	881	4.4	6.7	2.6
45 - 49	2 920	1 832	1 088	5.9	8.3	4.0
50 - 54	3 400	1 928	1 472	8.4	10.4	6.8
55 - 59	3 786	1 999	1 787	10.6	11.9	9.5
60 - 64	4 096	2 157	1 939	13.6	15.1	12.3
65 +	29 586	14 801	14 785	46.1	48.9	43.5
65 - 69	4 250	2 199	2 051	...	...	...
70 - 74	4 824	2 499	2 325	...	...	...
75 - 79	5 709	2 944	2 765	...	...	...
80 - 84	6 215	3 110	3 105	...	...	...
85 - 89	4 931	2 418	2 513	...	...	...
90 - 94	2 716	1 267	1 449	...	...	...
95 - 99	793	315	478	...	...	...
100 +	148	49	99	...	...	...
Unknown - Inconnu	948	631	317	..	..	..
Jamaica - Jamaïque[19]						
2011 (I)						
Total	21 001	10 061[14]	8 618[14]	7.8	7.6	6.3
0 - 4	361	187[14]	163[14]	1.6	1.7	1.5
5 - 9	118	53[14]	61[14]	0.5	0.4	0.5
10 - 14	128	74[14]	54[14]	0.5	0.5	0.4
15 - 19	382	288[14]	90[14]	1.5	2.3	0.7
20 - 24	521	423[14]	92[14]	2.5	4.2	0.9
25 - 29	515	367[14]	136[14]	2.4	3.6	1.2
30 - 34	451	304[14]	134[14]	2.0	2.9	1.1
35 - 39	557	319[14]	224[14]	2.4	3.0	1.8
40 - 44	609	329[14]	268[14]	3.1	3.3	2.7
45 - 49	631	324[14]	299[14]	4.7	4.8	4.4
50 - 54	749	418[14]	320[14]	6.4	6.8	5.7
55 - 59	702	367[14]	319[14]	8.1	8.1	7.8
60 - 64	1 003	501[14]	482[14]	14.6	14.9	13.7
65 - 69	1 031	554[14]	448[14]	15.7	17.5	13.2
70 - 74	1 343	700[14]	610[14]	22.4	24.6	19.3
75 +	9 932	4 853[14]	4 918[14]	94.6	115.9	77.9
75 - 79	1 567	805[14]	722[14]	...	...	...
80 - 84	1 721	876[14]	806[14]	...	...	...
85 - 89	3 057	1 259[14]	1 798[14]	...	...	...
90 +	3 505	1 913[14]	1 592[14]	...	...	...
Unknown - Inconnu	1 968	-[14]	-[14]	..	..	..

Continent, country or area, date, code[a] and age (in years) / Continent, pays ou zone, date, code[a] et âge (en années)	Number - Nombre			Rate - Taux		
	Both sexes Les deux sexes	Male Masculin	Female Féminin	Both sexes Les deux sexes	Male Masculin	Female Féminin
AMERICA, NORTH - AMÉRIQUE DU NORD						
Martinique[20]						
2007 (C)						
Total	2 830	1 439	1 391	7.1	7.7	6.5
0 - 4	51	31	20	2.0	2.4	♦1.6
0	47	28	19	...	...	...
1 - 4	4	3	1	...	...	...
5 - 9	4	3	1	♦0.1	♦0.2	♦0.1
10 - 14	7	5	2	♦0.2	♦0.3	♦0.1
15 - 19	16	12	4	♦0.5	♦0.8	♦0.3
20 - 24	26	22	4	♦1.1	♦1.9	♦0.3
25 - 29	19	13	6	♦1.0	♦1.5	♦0.6
30 - 34	35	22	13	1.4	♦2.1	♦0.9
35 - 39	36	22	14	1.2	♦1.6	♦0.8
40 - 44	53	31	22	1.6	2.0	♦1.2
45 - 49	64	46	18	2.0	3.2	♦1.1
50 - 54	107	68	39	4.1	5.6	2.8
55 - 59	97	57	40	4.3	5.5	3.2
60 - 64	146	91	55	7.8	10.3	5.5
65 - 69	226	135	91	14.2	18.7	10.4
70 - 74	305	173	132	21.3	27.2	16.6
75 - 79	382	200	182	35.8	44.2	29.6
80 - 84	443	217	226	59.2	76.6	48.6
85 - 89	388	168	220	92.5	122.1	78.1
90 - 94	269	91	178	137.9	159.6	128.9
95 +	156	32	124	212.8	196.3	217.5
Mexico - Mexique[21]						
2015 (+C)						
Total	654 593	362 953[14]	291 321[14]	5.4	6.1	4.7
0	26 045	14 482[14]	11 438[14]	11.8	12.8	10.6
1 - 4	5 017	2 754[14]	2 263[14]	0.6	0.6	0.5
5 - 9	2 474	1 362[14]	1 112[14]	0.2	0.2	0.2
10 - 14	3 197	1 871[14]	1 326[14]	0.3	0.3	0.2
15 - 19	8 355	5 957[14]	2 398[14]	0.7	1.1	0.4
20 - 24	12 555	9 550[14]	3 004[14]	1.2	1.8	0.6
25 - 29	13 004	9 749[14]	3 252[14]	1.3	2.1	0.6
30 - 34	14 346	10 594[14]	3 751[14]	1.6	2.5	0.8
35 - 39	17 464	12 466[14]	4 998[14]	2.0	3.0	1.1
40 - 44	21 780	14 781[14]	6 994[14]	2.7	3.9	1.6
45 - 49	26 882	17 334[14]	9 544[14]	3.8	5.1	2.5
50 - 54	34 325	20 905[14]	13 418[14]	5.8	7.4	4.3
55 - 59	42 415	24 893[14]	17 521[14]	8.7	10.8	6.8
60 - 64	49 151	27 784[14]	21 364[14]	12.8	15.4	10.6
65 - 69	55 147	30 290[14]	24 855[14]	19.3	22.6	16.4
70 - 74	60 944	33 045[14]	27 899[14]	29.0	33.9	24.7
75 - 79	68 225	35 562[14]	32 663[14]	46.3	52.9	40.7
80 - 84	70 574	34 676[14]	35 897[14]	73.6	81.0	67.7
85 - 89	60 307	27 504[14]	32 803[14]	113.6	120.1	108.7
90 - 94	40 390	17 545[14]	22 843[14]	172.7	181.9	166.2
95 - 99	14 389	5 631[14]	8 757[14]	190.7	190.1	191.1
100 +	4 621	1 696[14]	2 925[14]	240.9	239.5	241.8
Unknown - Inconnu	2 986	2 522[14]	296[14]	..	..	..
Montserrat						
2016 (+C)						
Total	43	26	17	...	...	...
0	-	-	-	...	...	...
1 - 4	-	-	-	...	...	...
5 - 9	-	-	-	...	...	...
10 - 14	-	-	-	...	...	...
15 - 19	-	-	-	...	...	...
20 - 24	1	-	1	...	...	...
25 - 29	1	1	-	...	...	...
30 - 34	-	-	-	...	...	...
35 - 39	-	-	-	...	...	...
40 - 44	-	-	-	...	...	...
45 - 49	-	-	-	...	...	...
50 - 54	1	-	1	...	...	...

Continent, country or area, date, code[a] and age (in years) Continent, pays ou zone, date, code[a] et âge (en années)	Number - Nombre			Rate - Taux		
	Both sexes Les deux sexes	Male Masculin	Female Féminin	Both sexes Les deux sexes	Male Masculin	Female Féminin

AMERICA, NORTH - AMÉRIQUE DU NORD

Montserrat
2016 (+C)
55 - 59	-	-	-	...	...	...
60 - 64	3	2	1	...	...	...
65 - 69	7	4	3	...	...	...
70 - 74	7	7	-	...	...	...
75 - 79	1	1	-	...	...	...
80 - 84	8	3	5	...	...	...
85 - 89	5	4	1	...	...	...
90 +	9	4	5	...	...	...

Nicaragua
2010 (+U)
Total	19 944	11 416	8 528	...	...	...
0	1 891	1 077	814	...	...	...
1 - 4	252	155	97	...	...	...
5 - 9	155	86	69	...	...	...
10 - 14	182	95	87	...	...	...
15 - 19	458	313	145	...	...	...
20 - 24	564	428	136	...	...	...
25 - 29	672	514	158	...	...	...
30 - 34	615	458	157	...	...	...
35 - 39	697	491	206	...	...	...
40 - 44	758	495	263	...	...	...
45 - 49	843	540	303	...	...	...
50 - 54	997	594	403	...	...	...
55 - 59	1 166	693	473	...	...	...
60 - 64	1 258	704	554	...	...	...
65 - 69	1 385	787	598	...	...	...
70 - 74	1 584	863	721	...	...	...
75 - 79	1 740	931	809	...	...	...
80 +	4 727	2 192	2 535	...	...	...

Panama
2015* (U)
Total	18 429	10 526	7 903	...	...	...
0	952	550	402	...	...	...
1 - 4	302	161	141	...	...	...
5 - 9	96	57	39	...	...	...
10 - 14	112	61	51	...	...	...
15 - 19	265	185	80	...	...	...
20 - 24	357	267	90	...	...	...
25 - 29	424	297	127	...	...	...
30 - 34	429	304	125	...	...	...
35 - 39	383	250	133	...	...	...
40 - 44	498	316	182	...	...	...
45 - 49	616	397	219	...	...	...
50 - 54	825	533	292	...	...	...
55 - 59	946	595	351	...	...	...
60 - 64	1 127	689	438	...	...	...
65 - 69	1 393	797	596	...	...	...
70 - 74	1 652	974	678	...	...	...
75 - 79	1 844	1 058	786	...	...	...
80 - 84	1 959	1 093	866	...	...	...
85 - 89	1 894	949	945	...	...	...
90 - 94	1 380	615	765	...	...	...
95 - 99	722	284	438	...	...	...
100 +	214	68	146	...	...	...
Unknown - Inconnu	39	26	13	..	..	...

Puerto Rico - Porto Rico
2016 (C)
Total	29 613	16 049	13 564	...	...	...
0	221	120	101	...	...	...
1 - 4	32	9	23	...	...	...
5 - 9	25	9	16	...	...	...
10 - 14	18	12	6	...	...	...
15 - 19	101	86	15	...	...	...
20 - 24	267	236	31	...	...	...
25 - 29	304	242	62	...	...	...

Continent, country or area, date, code[a] and age (in years) / Continent, pays ou zone, date, code[a] et âge (en années)	Number - Nombre			Rate - Taux		
	Both sexes Les deux sexes	Male Masculin	Female Féminin	Both sexes Les deux sexes	Male Masculin	Female Féminin
AMERICA, NORTH - AMÉRIQUE DU NORD						
Puerto Rico - Porto Rico						
2016 (C)						
30 - 34	306	233	73	...	...	...
35 - 39	392	278	114	...	...	...
40 - 44	444	275	169	...	...	...
45 - 49	697	474	223	...	...	...
50 - 54	1 056	693	363	...	...	...
55 - 59	1 534	975	559	...	...	...
60 - 64	1 971	1 239	732	...	...	...
65 - 69	2 643	1 620	1 023	...	...	...
70 - 74	3 228	1 893	1 335	...	...	...
75 - 79	3 650	2 003	1 647	...	...	...
80 - 84	4 053	2 013	2 040	...	...	...
85 - 89	3 987	1 836	2 151	...	...	...
90 - 94	3 022	1 230	1 792	...	...	...
95 - 99	1 280	451	829	...	...	...
100 +	376	116	260	...	...	...
Unknown - Inconnu	6	6	-	..	..	..
Saint Vincent and the Grenadines - Saint-Vincent-et-les Grenadines[22]						
2013 (C)						
Total	928	514	414	8.5	9.2	7.7
0	32	20	12	20.4	♦25.5	♦15.3
1 - 4	2	1	1	♦0.3	♦0.3	♦0.3
5 - 9	3	3	-	♦0.4	♦0.7	-
10 - 14	4	3	1	♦0.4	♦0.6	♦0.2
15 - 19	10	7	3	♦1.0	♦1.4	♦0.6
20 - 24	10	7	3	♦1.2	♦1.6	♦0.7
25 - 29	21	13	8	♦2.5	♦3.1	♦2.0
30 - 34	29	16	13	♦3.7	♦4.1	♦3.3
35 - 39	31	19	12	4.1	♦4.9	♦3.2
40 - 44	26	14	12	♦3.6	♦3.7	♦3.5
45 - 49	45	30	15	6.0	♦7.8	♦4.2
50 - 54	52	33	19	7.9	9.6	♦6.1
55 - 59	62	37	25	12.3	14.0	♦10.5
60 - 64	49	31	18	12.8	15.7	♦9.7
65 - 69	72	44	28	25.3	30.2	♦20.2
70 - 74	87	53	34	34.3	41.3	27.1
75 - 79	114	66	48	57.6	68.5	47.2
80 - 84	101	51	50	69.9	76.8	64.0
85 +	174	62	112	145.8	129.0	157.1
85 - 89	90	33	57	...	...	...
90 - 94	53	20	33	...	...	...
95 - 99	23	8	15	...	...	...
100 +	8	1	7	...	...	...
Unknown - Inconnu	4	4	-	..	..	..
Trinidad and Tobago - Trinité-et-Tobago						
2010 (C)						
Total	10 219	5 822	4 397	7.8	...	...
0	256	135	121	...	...	...
1 - 4	37	18	19	...	...	...
5 - 9	24	13	11	...	...	...
10 - 14	25	18	7	...	...	...
15 - 19	107	76	31	0.7	...	...
20 - 24	246	195	51	2.1	...	...
25 - 29	275	207	68	2.7	...	...
30 - 34	276	195	81	2.9	...	...
35 - 39	258	169	89	2.4	...	...
40 - 44	289	178	111	3.1	...	...
45 - 49	476	300	176	6.1	...	...
50 - 54	586	352	234	9.0	...	...
55 - 59	673	417	256	13.9	...	...
60 - 64	879	543	336	22.7	...	...
65 +	5 796	...	...	62.1	...	...
65 - 69	978	557	421	...	...	...
70 - 74	995	577	418	...	...	...
75 - 79	1 090	616	474	...	...	...

524

19. Deaths by age and sex and age-specific death rates by sex: latest available year, 2007 - 2016
Décès et taux de mortalité selon l'âge et le sexe : dernière année disponible, 2007 - 2016 (continued - suite)

Continent, country or area, date, code[a] and age (in years) Continent, pays ou zone, date, code[a] et âge (en années)	Number - Nombre			Rate - Taux		
	Both sexes Les deux sexes	Male Masculin	Female Féminin	Both sexes Les deux sexes	Male Masculin	Female Féminin
AMERICA, NORTH - AMÉRIQUE DU NORD						
Trinidad and Tobago - Trinité-et-Tobago						
2010 (C)						
80 - 84	1 077	530	547	...	...	...
85 +	1 656	710	946	...	...	...
Unknown - Inconnu	16	16	-	..	..	..
United States of America - États-Unis d'Amérique						
2015 (C)						
Total	2 712 630	1 373 404	1 339 226	8.4	8.7	8.2
0	23 455	13 008	10 447	5.9	6.4	5.4
1 - 4	3 965	2 281	1 684	0.2	0.3	0.2
5 - 9	2 402	1 377	1 025	0.1	0.1	0.1
10 - 14	3 009	1 776	1 233	0.1	0.2	0.1
15 - 19	10 186	7 187	2 999	0.5	0.7	0.3
20 - 24	20 308	15 159	5 149	0.9	1.3	0.5
25 - 29	23 898	17 173	6 725	1.1	1.5	0.6
30 - 34	27 619	18 608	9 011	1.3	1.7	0.8
35 - 39	31 417	20 190	11 227	1.5	2.0	1.1
40 - 44	41 671	25 480	16 191	2.1	2.5	1.6
45 - 49	64 377	38 807	25 570	3.1	3.8	2.4
50 - 54	110 117	66 740	43 377	4.9	6.1	3.8
55 - 59	159 589	97 172	62 417	7.3	9.2	5.6
60 - 64	198 196	120 454	77 742	10.4	13.2	7.8
65 - 69	235 482	137 630	97 852	14.7	18.1	11.6
70 - 74	259 534	144 717	114 817	22.6	27.3	18.6
75 - 79	290 405	153 719	136 686	35.7	42.6	30.3
80 - 84	347 161	170 127	177 034	59.9	70.5	52.3
85 - 89	390 747	168 932	221 815	101.1	117.1	91.6
90 - 94	313 796	112 676	201 120	169.5	191.3	159.4
95 - 99	127 628	35 157	92 471	257.9	274.7	252.0
100 +	27 530	4 939	22 591	357.7	327.3	365.0
Unknown - Inconnu	138	95	43	..	..	..
United States Virgin Islands - Îles Vierges américaines						
2007 (C)						
Total	727	424	303	6.6	8.1	5.2
0 - 4	14	8	6	♦1.9	♦2.1	♦1.6
0	12	6	6	...	...	...
1 - 4	2	2	-	...	...	...
5 - 9	-	-	-	-	-	-
10 - 14	2	1	1	♦0.2	♦0.2	♦0.2
15 - 19	9	8	1	♦1.1	♦2.0	♦0.2
20 - 24	16	15	1	♦2.3	♦4.7	♦0.3
25 - 29	20	14	6	♦3.7	♦5.7	♦2.1
30 - 34	16	10	6	♦2.6	♦3.7	♦1.8
35 - 39	16	13	3	♦2.2	♦3.9	♦0.7
40 - 44	33	21	12	4.1	♦5.6	♦2.8
45 - 49	26	13	13	♦3.2	♦3.3	♦3.1
50 - 54	50	34	16	6.6	9.6	♦3.9
55 - 59	51	29	22	6.8	♦8.1	♦5.6
60 - 64	79	55	24	10.7	15.3	♦6.3
65 - 69	50	36	14	10.1	14.8	♦5.5
70 - 74	68	43	25	18.8	26.6	♦12.5
75 +	273	120	153	59.0	63.7	55.7
Unknown - Inconnu	4	4	-	..	..	..
AMERICA, SOUTH - AMÉRIQUE DU SUD						
Argentina - Argentine						
2015 (C)						
Total	333 407	171 964[14]	161 260[14]	7.7	8.1	7.3
0	7 445	4 196[14]	3 235[14]	9.9	10.8	8.9
1 - 4	1 256	692[14]	562[14]	0.4	0.4	0.4
5 - 9	686	388[14]	297[14]	0.2	0.2	0.2
10 - 14	836	510[14]	324[14]	0.2	0.3	0.2
15 - 19	2 717	1 986[14]	729[14]	0.8	1.1	0.4
20 - 24	3 560	2 675[14]	883[14]	1.0	1.5	0.5

Continent, country or area, date, code[a] and age (in years) / Continent, pays ou zone, date, code[a] et âge (en années)	Number - Nombre			Rate - Taux		
	Both sexes Les deux sexes	Male Masculin	Female Féminin	Both sexes Les deux sexes	Male Masculin	Female Féminin
AMERICA, SOUTH - AMÉRIQUE DU SUD						
Argentina - Argentine						
2015 (C)						
25 - 29	3 222	2 280[14]	939[14]	1.0	1.4	0.6
30 - 34	3 653	2 498[14]	1 155[14]	1.2	1.6	0.7
35 - 39	4 463	2 810[14]	1 652[14]	1.4	1.8	1.1
40 - 44	5 495	3 330[14]	2 164[14]	2.0	2.5	1.6
45 - 49	7 550	4 604[14]	2 944[14]	3.3	4.1	2.5
50 - 54	11 179	6 962[14]	4 211[14]	5.2	6.6	3.8
55 - 59	16 704	10 499[14]	6 201[14]	8.4	11.0	6.0
60 - 64	23 557	14 831[14]	8 724[14]	13.2	17.7	9.2
65 - 69	29 995	18 580[14]	11 409[14]	19.9	27.0	13.9
70 - 74	34 742	20 593[14]	14 139[14]	30.0	40.8	21.6
75 - 79	39 800	21 709[14]	18 083[14]	46.6	62.9	35.5
80 - 84	46 548	21 939[14]	24 597[14]	78.7	101.8	65.4
85 +	88 290	29 867[14]	58 402[14]	168.3	193.7	157.7
Unknown - Inconnu	1 709	1 015[14]	610[14]	..	..	..
Bolivia (Plurinational State of) - Bolivie (État plurinational de)[23]						
2012 (I)						
Total	127 050	59 027	68 023	12.6	11.8	13.5
0	5 363	2 406	2 957	26.6	23.4	29.9
1 - 4	6 695	3 085	3 610	7.5	6.8	8.3
5 - 9	2 531	1 183	1 348	2.5	2.3	2.8
10 - 14	1 961	827	1 134	1.8	1.5	2.1
15 - 19	3 699	1 460	2 239	3.3	2.6	4.1
20 - 24	4 767	1 618	3 149	4.9	3.3	6.5
25 - 29	4 089	1 393	2 696	5.0	3.4	6.6
30 - 34	4 323	1 556	2 767	5.7	4.2	7.3
35 - 39	4 670	1 868	2 802	7.4	6.0	8.7
40 - 44	4 597	1 849	2 748	8.4	6.8	10.0
45 - 49	5 769	2 483	3 286	12.5	10.9	14.0
50 - 54	6 298	2 849	3 449	15.6	14.3	16.9
55 - 59	6 851	2 946	3 905	21.1	18.5	23.7
60 - 64	9 105	4 256	4 849	32.5	31.7	33.3
65 - 69	9 801	4 792	5 009	47.9	48.8	47.1
70 - 74	9 701	4 649	5 052	63.6	64.7	62.7
75 - 79	9 798	4 756	5 042	98.7	105.7	92.9
80 - 84	11 190	5 952	5 238	138.0	172.7	112.3
85 - 89	8 493	4 674	3 819	224.0	294.3	173.3
90 - 94	3 927	2 332	1 595	267.8	388.9	184.0
95 +	3 422	2 093	1 329	415.6	633.3	269.6
Brazil - Brésil						
2015 (+C)						
Total	1 231 400[24]	690 866[14]	540 124[14]	6.0	6.8	5.2
0	31 238[24]	17 324[14]	13 836[14]	10.9	11.8	9.8
1 - 4	5 309[24]	2 890[14]	2 417[14]	0.4	0.5	0.4
5 - 9	3 105[24]	1 710[14]	1 392[14]	0.2	0.2	0.2
10 - 14	4 677[24]	2 912[14]	1 763[14]	0.3	0.3	0.2
15 - 19	20 073[24]	16 361[14]	3 709[14]	1.2	1.9	0.4
20 - 24	26 028[24]	21 535[14]	4 487[14]	1.5	2.5	0.5
25 - 29	25 962[24]	20 471[14]	5 486[14]	1.5	2.4	0.6
30 - 34	29 022[24]	21 378[14]	7 640[14]	1.6	2.4	0.9
35 - 39	33 039[24]	22 768[14]	10 266[14]	2.1	2.9	1.3
40 - 44	38 473[24]	25 492[14]	12 978[14]	2.8	3.7	1.8
45 - 49	50 269[24]	32 474[14]	17 786[14]	3.9	5.2	2.7
50 - 54	67 034[24]	42 433[14]	24 592[14]	5.7	7.5	4.1
55 - 59	82 608[24]	51 239[14]	31 362[14]	8.4	11.0	6.1
60 - 64	97 098[24]	58 953[14]	38 136[14]	12.5	16.1	9.2
65 - 69	109 282[24]	64 175[14]	45 095[14]	18.7	24.0	14.2
70 - 74	117 514[24]	65 903[14]	51 603[14]	28.8	36.7	22.6
75 - 79	133 613[24]	69 901[14]	63 701[14]	45.9	57.2	37.7
80 - 84	130 997[24]	62 408[14]	68 582[14]	72.9	87.8	63.2
85 - 89	116 816[24]	49 622[14]	67 186[14]	119.9	137.1	109.8
90 +	105 452[24]	38 119[14]	67 311[14]	195.8	219.2	184.5
90 - 94	68 700[24]	26 116[14]	42 579[14]	...	...	...

19. Deaths by age and sex and age-specific death rates by sex: latest available year, 2007 - 2016
Décès et taux de mortalité selon l'âge et le sexe : dernière année disponible, 2007 - 2016 (continued - suite)

Continent, country or area, date, code[a] and age (in years) / Continent, pays ou zone, date, code[a] et âge (en années)	Number - Nombre			Rate - Taux		
	Both sexes Les deux sexes	Male Masculin	Female Féminin	Both sexes Les deux sexes	Male Masculin	Female Féminin
AMERICA, SOUTH - AMÉRIQUE DU SUD						
Brazil - Brésil						
2015 (+C)						
95 - 99	28 264[24]	9 473[14]	18 785[14]	...	...	...
100 +	8 488[24]	2 530[14]	5 947[14]	...	...	...
Unknown - Inconnu	3 791[24]	2 798[14]	796[14]	..	..	..
Chile - Chili						
2014 (C)						
Total	101 960	53 975[14]	47 968[14]	5.7	6.1	5.3
0	1 825	968[14]	840[14]	7.4	7.7	6.9
1 - 4	283	160[14]	123[14]	0.3	0.3	0.3
5 - 9	166	96[14]	70[14]	0.1	0.2	0.1
10 - 14	202	118[14]	84[14]	0.2	0.2	0.1
15 - 19	578	422[14]	156[14]	0.4	0.6	0.2
20 - 24	961	727[14]	234[14]	0.6	1.0	0.3
25 - 29	1 048	800[14]	248[14]	0.7	1.1	0.3
30 - 34	1 149	847[14]	302[14]	0.9	1.3	0.5
35 - 39	1 370	938[14]	432[14]	1.1	1.5	0.7
40 - 44	2 011	1 362[14]	649[14]	1.6	2.2	1.0
45 - 49	2 995	1 971[14]	1 024[14]	2.4	3.2	1.6
50 - 54	4 305	2 774[14]	1 531[14]	3.6	4.7	2.5
55 - 59	5 649	3 538[14]	2 111[14]	5.6	7.2	4.1
60 - 64	6 923	4 248[14]	2 675[14]	8.8	11.2	6.5
65 - 69	9 101	5 558[14]	3 543[14]	14.7	19.1	10.7
70 - 74	10 944	6 334[14]	4 610[14]	23.4	30.1	17.9
75 - 79	12 090	6 524[14]	5 566[14]	36.4	46.7	29.0
80 +	40 360	16 590[14]	23 770[14]	109.2	128.6	98.8
80 - 84	14 429	7 082[14]	7 347[14]	...	...	...
85 - 89	13 448	5 586[14]	7 862[14]	...	...	...
90 - 94	8 305	2 860[14]	5 445[14]	...	...	...
95 - 99	3 385	922[14]	2 463[14]	...	...	...
100 +	793	140[14]	653[14]	...	...	...
Colombia - Colombie						
2014 (U)						
Total	210 028	116 380	93 648	...	...	...
0	7 589	4 284	3 305	...	...	...
1 - 4	1 560	876	684	...	...	...
5 - 9	861	494	367	...	...	...
10 - 14	1 222	750	472	...	...	...
15 - 19	4 088	3 162	926	...	...	...
20 - 24	5 600	4 614	986	...	...	...
25 - 29	5 231	4 130	1 101	...	...	...
30 - 34	5 256	3 888	1 368	...	...	...
35 - 39	4 853	3 320	1 533	...	...	...
40 - 44	5 281	3 375	1 906	...	...	...
45 - 49	6 754	3 965	2 789	...	...	...
50 - 54	8 799	5 080	3 719	...	...	...
55 - 59	11 321	6 615	4 706	...	...	...
60 - 64	13 576	7 877	5 699	...	...	...
65 - 69	15 755	8 939	6 816	...	...	...
70 - 74	19 543	10 804	8 739	...	...	...
75 - 79	23 954	12 703	11 251	...	...	...
80 - 84	26 066	12 872	13 194	...	...	...
85 - 89	22 386	10 339	12 047	...	...	...
90 - 94	13 499	5 625	7 874	...	...	...
95 - 99	5 332	2 032	3 300	...	...	...
100 +	1 240	425	815	...	...	...
Unknown - Inconnu	262	211	51	..	..	..
Ecuador - Équateur[25]						
2015 (U)						
Total	64 790	35 577	29 213	...	...	...
0	2 979	1 664	1 315	...	...	...
1 - 4	817	427	390	...	...	...
5 - 9	442	240	202	...	...	...
10 - 14	537	311	226	...	...	...
15 - 19	1 115	785	330	...	...	...
20 - 24	1 583	1 215	368	...	...	...

19. Deaths by age and sex and age-specific death rates by sex: latest available year, 2007 - 2016
Décès et taux de mortalité selon l'âge et le sexe : dernière année disponible, 2007 - 2016 (continued - suite)

Continent, country or area, date, code[a] and age (in years) Continent, pays ou zone, date, code[a] et âge (en années)	Number - Nombre			Rate - Taux		
	Both sexes Les deux sexes	Male Masculin	Female Féminin	Both sexes Les deux sexes	Male Masculin	Female Féminin
AMERICA, SOUTH - AMÉRIQUE DU SUD						
Ecuador - Équateur[25]						
2015 (U)						
25 - 29	1 574	1 177	397	...	...	...
30 - 34	1 541	1 097	444	...	...	...
35 - 39	1 644	1 088	556	...	...	...
40 - 44	1 732	1 077	655	...	...	...
45 - 49	2 014	1 248	766	...	...	...
50 - 54	2 605	1 518	1 087	...	...	...
55 - 59	3 260	1 907	1 353	...	...	...
60 - 64	4 078	2 290	1 788	...	...	...
65 - 69	4 689	2 676	2 013	...	...	...
70 - 74	5 281	2 930	2 351	...	...	...
75 - 79	6 395	3 459	2 936	...	...	...
80 - 84	7 105	3 693	3 412	...	...	...
85 - 89	7 146	3 363	3 783	...	...	...
90 - 94	5 238	2 291	2 947	...	...	...
95 - 99	2 278	853	1 425	...	...	...
100 +	733	265	468	...	...	...
Unknown - Inconnu	4	3	1	..	..	..
French Guiana - Guyane française[20]						
2007 (C)						
Total	690	405	285	3.2	3.8	2.6
0 - 4	95	50	45	3.5	3.6	3.3
0	77	39	38	...	...	...
1 - 4	18	11	7	...	...	...
5 - 9	9	4	5	♦0.3	♦0.3	♦0.4
10 - 14	8	5	3	♦0.3	♦0.4	♦0.3
15 - 19	13	10	3	♦0.7	♦1.0	♦0.3
20 - 24	14	12	2	♦0.9	♦1.6	♦0.2
25 - 29	16	11	5	♦1.1	♦1.6	♦0.6
30 - 34	23	15	8	♦1.4	♦2.0	♦0.9
35 - 39	28	21	7	♦1.8	♦2.8	♦0.8
40 - 44	41	24	17	2.9	♦3.5	♦2.4
45 - 49	48	35	13	4.1	5.9	♦2.3
50 - 54	26	16	10	♦2.7	♦3.3	♦2.1
55 - 59	32	24	8	4.6	♦6.5	♦2.4
60 - 64	33	25	8	7.4	♦10.5	♦3.8
65 - 69	48	24	24	17.0	♦16.5	♦17.5
70 - 74	46	29	17	21.8	♦28.3	♦15.7
75 - 79	62	32	30	46.6	53.9	♦40.8
80 - 84	57	26	31	60.7	♦66.5	56.6
85 - 89	50	27	23	84.0	♦112.0	♦65.0
90 - 94	28	12	16	♦129.0	♦176.5	♦107.4
95 +	13	3	10	♦123.8	♦111.1	♦128.2
95 - 99	10	3	7	...	...	...
100 +	3	-	3	...	...	...
Paraguay						
2014 (+U)						
Total	22 625	12 645[14]	9 910[14]	...	...	...
0	468	269[14]	198[14]	...	...	...
1 - 4	158	81[14]	77[14]	...	...	...
5 - 9	98	56[14]	42[14]	...	...	...
10 - 14	149	84[14]	65[14]	...	...	...
15 - 19	427	303[14]	123[14]	...	...	...
20 - 24	489	392[14]	97[14]	...	...	...
25 - 29	447	333[14]	111[14]	...	...	...
30 - 34	515	364[14]	146[14]	...	...	...
35 - 39	522	331[14]	190[14]	...	...	...
40 - 44	643	379[14]	260[14]	...	...	...
45 - 49	901	556[14]	342[14]	...	...	...
50 - 54	1 205	732[14]	468[14]	...	...	...
55 - 59	1 474	939[14]	530[14]	...	...	...
60 - 64	1 732	1 055[14]	674[14]	...	...	...
65 - 69	1 905	1 155[14]	741[14]	...	...	...
70 - 74	2 156	1 285[14]	866[14]	...	...	...
75 - 79	2 389	1 302[14]	1 077[14]	...	...	...

Continent, country or area, date, code[a] and age (in years) / Continent, pays ou zone, date, code[a] et âge (en années)	Number - Nombre			Rate - Taux		
	Both sexes / Les deux sexes	Male / Masculin	Female / Féminin	Both sexes / Les deux sexes	Male / Masculin	Female / Féminin
AMERICA, SOUTH - AMÉRIQUE DU SUD						
Paraguay						
2014 (+U)						
80 - 84	2 531	1 234[14]	1 290[14]	...	...	...
85 +	4 416	1 795[14]	2 613[14]	...	...	...
Peru - Pérou[26]						
2015 (+U)						
Total	96 240	51 597	44 643	...	...	...
0	3 852	2 129	1 723	...	...	...
1 - 4	1 176	642	534	...	...	...
5 - 9	628	375	253	...	...	...
10 - 14	630	342	288	...	...	...
15 - 19	1 194	734	460	...	...	...
20 - 24	1 626	1 107	519	...	...	...
25 - 29	1 892	1 292	600	...	...	...
30 - 34	2 003	1 318	685	...	...	...
35 - 39	2 263	1 438	825	...	...	...
40 - 44	2 764	1 654	1 110	...	...	...
45 - 49	3 323	1 902	1 421	...	...	...
50 - 54	3 982	2 258	1 724	...	...	...
55 - 59	4 988	2 787	2 201	...	...	...
60 - 64	5 959	3 307	2 652	...	...	...
65 - 69	7 178	3 948	3 230	...	...	...
70 - 74	8 327	4 496	3 831	...	...	...
75 - 79	10 553	5 745	4 808	...	...	...
80 - 84	12 060	6 198	5 862	...	...	...
85 - 89	11 254	5 437	5 817	...	...	...
90 - 94	7 059	3 182	3 877	...	...	...
95 - 99	2 844	1 094	1 750	...	...	...
100 +	685	212	473	...	...	...
Suriname						
2015 (C)						
Total	3 663	2 037	1 626	6.5	7.2	5.7
0	149	80	69	14.7	15.8	13.6
1 - 4	22	14	8	◆0.5	◆0.6	◆0.4
5 - 9	9	4	5	◆0.2	◆0.2	◆0.2
10 - 14	25	15	10	◆0.5	◆0.6	◆0.4
15 - 19	51	27	24	1.1	◆1.1	◆1.0
20 - 24	42	23	19	0.9	◆1.0	◆0.8
25 - 29	72	43	29	1.6	1.9	◆1.3
30 - 34	84	52	32	2.0	2.5	1.5
35 - 39	132	84	48	3.3	4.2	2.4
40 - 44	127	84	43	3.3	4.4	2.3
45 - 49	177	115	62	5.0	6.5	3.5
50 - 54	260	175	85	8.3	11.3	5.4
55 - 59	274	160	114	10.3	12.3	8.4
60 - 64	294	167	127	13.9	16.5	11.5
65 - 69	318	201	117	20.1	27.3	13.9
70 - 74	334	188	146	28.8	35.7	23.0
75 - 79	420	212	208	53.7	61.7	47.4
80 +	873	393	480	112.2	122.7	104.8
80 - 84	390	180	210	...	...	...
85 - 89	285	137	148	...	...	...
90 - 94	146	57	89	...	...	...
95 - 99	40	14	26	...	...	...
100 +	12	5	7	...	...	...
Uruguay						
2015 (C)						
Total	32 967	16 528[14]	16 429[14]	9.5	9.9	9.2
0	367	218[14]	148[14]	8.0	9.3	6.6
1 - 4	59	28[14]	31[14]	0.3	◆0.3	0.3
5 - 9	35	23[14]	12[14]	0.1	◆0.2	◆0.1
10 - 14	45	30[14]	15[14]	0.2	◆0.2	◆0.1
15 - 19	171	124[14]	47[14]	0.6	0.9	0.4
20 - 24	277	212[14]	65[14]	1.1	1.6	0.5
25 - 29	237	192[14]	45[14]	1.0	1.5	0.4
30 - 34	283	187[14]	96[14]	1.2	1.6	0.8
35 - 39	382	249[14]	133[14]	1.6	2.1	1.1

Continent, country or area, date, code[a] and age (in years) Continent, pays ou zone, date, code[a] et âge (en années)	Number - Nombre			Rate - Taux		
	Both sexes Les deux sexes	Male Masculin	Female Féminin	Both sexes Les deux sexes	Male Masculin	Female Féminin
AMERICA, SOUTH - AMÉRIQUE DU SUD						
Uruguay						
2015 (C)						
40 - 44	468	289[14]	179[14]	2.1	2.6	1.6
45 - 49	632	395[14]	237[14]	3.1	3.9	2.2
50 - 54	1 004	622[14]	382[14]	4.9	6.3	3.6
55 - 59	1 550	984[14]	566[14]	8.0	10.7	5.6
60 - 64	2 008	1 287[14]	721[14]	12.2	16.8	8.2
65 - 69	2 631	1 666[14]	965[14]	18.8	26.4	12.5
70 - 74	3 352	1 991[14]	1 361[14]	28.7	39.8	20.4
75 - 79	4 009	2 139[14]	1 869[14]	43.1	58.2	33.2
80 - 84	5 190	2 411[14]	2 778[14]	73.4	95.7	61.1
85 - 89	5 177	1 987[14]	3 187[14]	122.5	149.3	110.1
90 +	4 865	1 369[14]	3 496[14]	224.2	241.2	218.1
90 - 94	3 374	1 031[14]	2 343[14]	...	...	...
95 +	1 491	338[14]	1 153[14]	...	...	...
Unknown - Inconnu	225	125[14]	96[14]	..	..	..
Venezuela (Bolivarian Republic of) - Venezuela (République bolivarienne du)						
2013 (C)						
Total	147 901	90 389	57 512	4.9	6.0	3.8
0 - 4	8 826	5 062	3 764	3.0	3.4	2.6
0	7 630	4 402	3 228	...	...	...
1 - 4	1 196	660	536	...	...	...
5 - 9	705	407	298	0.2	0.3	0.2
10 - 14	888	544	344	0.3	0.4	0.3
15 - 19	4 692	3 976	716	1.7	2.9	0.5
20 - 24	7 173	6 319	854	2.7	4.6	0.6
25 - 29	5 922	4 980	942	2.3	3.9	0.7
30 - 34	5 078	3 966	1 112	2.2	3.4	1.0
35 - 39	4 821	3 467	1 354	2.3	3.4	1.3
40 - 44	4 795	3 218	1 577	2.6	3.5	1.7
45 - 49	5 930	3 775	2 155	3.4	4.4	2.5
50 - 54	7 981	5 139	2 842	5.3	6.9	3.7
55 - 59	9 781	6 151	3 630	7.9	10.2	5.8
60 - 64	11 253	7 096	4 157	11.3	14.6	8.1
65 - 69	11 454	6 958	4 496	15.4	19.5	11.6
70 - 74	12 139	7 109	5 030	23.7	29.8	18.4
75 - 79	12 988	7 147	5 841	37.2	45.5	30.4
80 +	33 475	15 075	18 400	112.8	117.9	109.0
80 - 84	13 352	6 716	6 636	...	...	...
85 - 89	10 686	4 812	5 874	...	...	...
90 - 94	6 324	2 431	3 893	...	...	...
95 - 99	2 399	882	1 517	...	...	...
100 +	714	234	480	...	...	...
2014 (C)						
Total	159 239	...	...	5.3	...	...
0	8 396	...	...	15.4	...	...
1 - 4	1 326	...	...	0.6	...	...
5 - 9	718	...	...	0.3	...	...
10 - 14	940	...	...	0.3	...	...
15 - 19	4 476	...	...	1.7	...	...
20 - 24	7 061	...	...	2.7	...	...
25 - 29	5 908	...	...	2.3	...	...
30 - 34	5 012	...	...	2.1	...	...
35 - 39	4 749	...	...	2.2	...	...
40 - 44	4 835	...	...	2.5	...	...
45 - 49	6 187	...	...	3.4	...	...
50 - 54	8 174	...	...	5.2	...	...
55 - 59	10 063	...	...	8.0	...	...
60 - 64	12 330	...	...	13.1	...	...
65 - 69	12 594	...	...	18.0	...	...
70 - 74	13 041	...	...	26.3	...	...
75 - 79	14 641	...	...	44.3	...	...
80 - 84	14 822	...	...	73.5	...	...
85 +	23 966	...	...	125.7	...	...

Continent, country or area, date, code[a] and age (in years) / Continent, pays ou zone, date, code[a] et âge (en années)	Number - Nombre			Rate - Taux		
	Both sexes Les deux sexes	Male Masculin	Female Féminin	Both sexes Les deux sexes	Male Masculin	Female Féminin
ASIA - ASIE						
Armenia - Arménie[27]						
2014 (C)						
Total	27 714	14 219	13 495	...	...	...
0	376	212	164	...	...	...
1 - 4	69	41	28	...	...	...
5 - 9	32	16	16	...	...	...
10 - 14	25	17	8	...	...	...
15 - 19	84	66	18	...	...	...
20 - 24	138	104	34	...	...	...
25 - 29	184	138	46	...	...	...
30 - 34	195	134	61	...	...	...
35 - 39	283	195	88	...	...	...
40 - 44	430	297	133	...	...	...
45 - 49	720	516	204	...	...	...
50 - 54	1 304	894	410	...	...	...
55 - 59	1 821	1 260	561	...	...	...
60 - 64	2 215	1 421	794	...	...	...
65 - 69	1 892	1 140	752	...	...	...
70 - 74	3 101	1 648	1 453	...	...	...
75 - 79	5 083	2 490	2 593	...	...	...
80 - 84	5 042	2 150	2 892	...	...	...
85 - 89	3 667	1 203	2 464	...	...	...
90 - 94	823	222	601	...	...	...
95 - 99	173	38	135	...	...	...
100 +	57	17	40	...	...	...
Azerbaijan - Azerbaïdjan[27]						
2014 (+C)						
Total	55 648	29 655	25 993	5.9	6.3	5.5
0	1 655	976	679	9.6	10.5	8.5
1 - 4	442	256	186	0.7	0.7	0.6
5 - 9	199	123	76	0.3	0.4	0.3
10 - 14	200	128	72	0.3	0.4	0.2
15 - 19	376	265	111	0.5	0.7	0.3
20 - 24	612	420	192	0.7	0.9	0.4
25 - 29	644	451	193	0.7	1.0	0.4
30 - 34	750	534	216	0.9	1.4	0.5
35 - 39	878	631	247	1.3	1.9	0.7
40 - 44	1 258	884	374	2.0	2.9	1.1
45 - 49	2 136	1 473	663	3.2	4.7	1.9
50 - 54	3 555	2 338	1 217	5.4	7.3	3.5
55 - 59	4 459	2 950	1 509	9.1	12.6	5.8
60 - 64	4 680	2 926	1 754	15.4	20.7	10.8
65 - 69	3 906	2 336	1 570	23.9	32.3	17.2
70 - 74	5 427	2 843	2 584	39.5	48.9	32.6
75 - 79	9 847	4 487	5 360	67.3	75.4	61.8
80 - 84	8 004	3 456	4 548	112.2	118.5	107.9
85 - 89	4 511	1 722	2 789	173.0	179.4	169.2
90 - 94	1 483	384	1 099	208.5	177.8	221.9
95 - 99	352	47	305	253.4	133.9	293.8
100 +	274	25	249	409.6	♦735.3	392.1
Bahrain - Bahreïn[28]						
2014 (C)						
Total	2 805	1 698	1 107	2.1	2.1	2.2
0	218	113	105	10.2	10.2	10.2
1 - 4	34	9	25	0.4	♦0.2	♦0.6
5 - 9	25	14	11	♦0.3	♦0.3	♦0.3
10 - 14	21	12	9	♦0.3	♦0.3	♦0.2
15 - 19	35	23	12	0.5	♦0.6	♦0.3
20 - 24	64	51	13	0.6	0.8	♦0.3
25 - 29	78	67	11	0.4	0.6	♦0.2
30 - 34	104	78	26	0.6	0.7	♦0.5
35 - 39	111	90	21	0.8	1.0	♦0.5
40 - 44	110	81	29	1.0	1.1	♦0.8
45 - 49	154	112	42	1.8	2.0	1.3
50 - 54	182	126	56	2.6	2.9	2.1
55 - 59	235	156	79	4.5	4.8	4.1
60 - 64	208	127	81	7.1	7.1	7.2

19. Deaths by age and sex and age-specific death rates by sex: latest available year, 2007 - 2016
Décès et taux de mortalité selon l'âge et le sexe : dernière année disponible, 2007 - 2016 (continued - suite)

Continent, country or area, date, code[a] and age (in years) Continent, pays ou zone, date, code[a] et âge (en années)	Number - Nombre			Rate - Taux		
	Both sexes Les deux sexes	Male Masculin	Female Féminin	Both sexes Les deux sexes	Male Masculin	Female Féminin
ASIA - ASIE						
Bahrain - Bahreïn[28]						
2014 (C)						
65 - 69	191	109	82	12.8	12.7	13.0
70 - 74	268	153	115	27.1	28.9	25.0
75 - 79	267	126	141	41.9	38.1	46.0
80 - 84	231	107	124	61.5	54.3	69.4
85 +	246	127	119	90.5	89.7	91.3
85 - 89	138	65	73	...	...	...
90 - 94	78	46	32	...	...	...
95 - 99	27	16	11	...	...	...
100 +	3	-	3	...	...	...
Unknown - Inconnu	23	17	6	..	..	..
Brunei Darussalam - Brunéi Darussalam						
2015 (+C)						
Total	1 547	830	717	3.7	3.8	3.6
0	58	33	25	...	...	...
1 - 4	8	4	4	...	...	...
5 - 9	8	5	3	♦0.3	♦0.3	♦0.2
10 - 14	9	3	6	♦0.3	♦0.2	♦0.4
15 - 19	8	6	2	♦0.2	♦0.3	♦0.1
20 - 24	17	10	7	♦0.5	♦0.5	♦0.4
25 - 29	35	21	14	0.9	♦1.0	♦0.8
30 - 34	36	26	10	0.9	♦1.2	♦0.6
35 - 39	42	28	14	1.2	♦1.5	♦0.8
40 - 44	74	40	34	2.2	2.4	2.1
45 - 49	100	63	37	3.5	4.3	2.7
50 - 54	95	54	41	4.0	4.3	3.7
55 - 59	138	72	66	7.5	7.6	7.4
60 - 64	137	79	58	11.0	12.5	9.5
65 - 69	144	76	68	19.7	21.7	17.9
70 - 74	149	78	71	33.1	35.5	30.9
75 - 79	166	84	82	53.5	60.0	48.2
80 - 84	149	69	80	82.8	86.3	80.0
85 - 89	110	44	66	137.5	110.0	165.0
90 - 94	49	27	22	163.3	♦270.0	♦110.0
95 - 99	10	6	4	...	...	...
100 +	5	2	3	...	...	...
China - Chine[29]						
2010 (I)						
Total	7 421 990	4 293 783	3 128 207	5.6	6.3	4.8
0	60 217	32 026	28 191	4.4	4.3	4.5
1 - 4	39 591	23 119	16 472	0.6	0.7	0.6
5 - 9	21 183	13 621	7 562	0.3	0.4	0.2
10 - 14	23 088	15 243	7 845	0.3	0.4	0.2
15 - 19	40 469	28 088	12 381	0.4	0.5	0.3
20 - 24	62 552	43 738	18 814	0.5	0.7	0.3
25 - 29	60 661	42 497	18 164	0.6	0.8	0.4
30 - 34	79 960	55 804	24 156	0.8	1.1	0.5
35 - 39	140 531	98 382	42 149	1.2	1.6	0.7
40 - 44	216 353	149 111	67 242	1.7	2.3	1.1
45 - 49	262 531	179 446	83 085	2.5	3.3	1.6
50 - 54	337 397	226 888	110 509	4.3	5.6	2.9
55 - 59	494 339	324 817	169 522	6.1	7.9	4.2
60 - 64	586 160	377 069	209 091	10.0	12.6	7.3
65 - 69	695 662	435 007	260 655	16.9	21.0	12.8
70 - 74	999 653	599 394	400 259	30.3	36.5	24.2
75 - 79	1 162 694	657 140	505 554	48.7	58.3	40.2
80 - 84	1 081 704	553 704	528 000	80.9	93.6	70.8
85 - 89	686 462	306 678	379 784	121.9	139.4	110.7
90 - 94	279 569	104 048	175 521	177.1	196.0	167.6
95 - 99	74 729	23 292	51 437	202.0	197.9	203.9
100 +	16 485	4 671	11 814	458.8	527.7	436.2
China, Hong Kong SAR - Chine, Hong Kong RAS						
2016 (C)						
Total	46 905	26 139	20 762	6.4	7.7	5.2
0	109	59	50	2.0	2.1	2.0
1 - 4	39	21	18	0.2	♦0.2	♦0.2

19. Deaths by age and sex and age-specific death rates by sex: latest available year, 2007 - 2016
Décès et taux de mortalité selon l'âge et le sexe : dernière année disponible, 2007 - 2016 (continued - suite)

Continent, country or area, date, code[a] and age (in years) / Continent, pays ou zone, date, code[a] et âge (en années)	Number - Nombre			Rate - Taux		
	Both sexes Les deux sexes	Male Masculin	Female Féminin	Both sexes Les deux sexes	Male Masculin	Female Féminin
ASIA - ASIE						
China, Hong Kong SAR - Chine, Hong Kong RAS						
2016 (C)						
5 - 9	20	12	8	♦0.1	♦0.1	♦0.1
10 - 14	21	11	10	♦0.1	♦0.1	♦0.1
15 - 19	65	38	27	0.2	0.2	♦0.2
20 - 24	109	71	38	0.2	0.3	0.2
25 - 29	159	106	53	0.3	0.5	0.2
30 - 34	233	145	88	0.4	0.6	0.3
35 - 39	321	190	131	0.6	0.8	0.4
40 - 44	545	294	251	1.0	1.3	0.7
45 - 49	821	478	343	1.4	2.0	1.0
50 - 54	1 518	910	608	2.4	3.1	1.7
55 - 59	2 432	1 624	808	3.9	5.3	2.6
60 - 64	3 045	2 044	1 001	6.1	8.4	4.0
65 - 69	3 655	2 484	1 171	9.2	12.6	5.9
70 - 74	3 463	2 415	1 048	15.7	21.5	9.7
75 - 79	5 299	3 497	1 802	25.7	34.6	17.1
80 - 84	7 570	4 465	3 105	45.3	60.3	33.4
85 +	17 447	7 252	10 195	100.7	122.9	89.2
Unknown - Inconnu	34	23[14]	7[14]	..	..	..
China, Macao SAR - Chine, Macao RAS						
2015 (C)						
Total	2 002	1 119	883	3.1	3.5	2.7
0	11	7	4	♦1.6	♦1.9	♦1.2
1 - 14	6	2	4	♦0.1	♦0.1	♦0.1
15 - 39	64	45	19	0.2	0.3	♦0.1
40 - 64	557	379	178	2.3	3.2	1.4
65 - 79	516	336	180	12.1	15.5	8.7
80 +	848	350	498	65.7	76.1	60.0
Cyprus - Chypre[30]						
2015 (C)						
Total	5 859	3 057	2 802	6.9	7.4	6.4
0	25	11	14	♦2.7	♦2.3	♦3.2
1 - 4	5	1	4	♦0.1	♦0.1	♦0.2
5 - 9	2	2	-	-	♦0.1	-
10 - 14	2	1	1	-	-	-
15 - 19	14	9	5	♦0.3	♦0.3	♦0.2
20 - 24	29	25	4	♦0.4	♦0.7	♦0.1
25 - 29	18	14	4	♦0.3	♦0.4	♦0.1
30 - 34	22	15	7	♦0.3	♦0.5	♦0.2
35 - 39	50	30	20	0.8	♦1.1	♦0.6
40 - 44	72	40	32	1.3	1.5	1.0
45 - 49	68	43	25	1.2	1.7	♦0.9
50 - 54	139	89	50	2.5	3.3	1.7
55 - 59	184	118	66	3.7	4.8	2.6
60 - 64	298	203	95	6.4	8.9	4.0
65 - 69	430	270	160	10.4	13.5	7.5
70 - 74	542	340	202	17.5	23.1	12.4
75 - 79	747	412	335	31.3	37.6	25.9
80 - 84	1 021	490	531	64.8	73.4	58.6
85 - 89	1 185	537	648	142.5	161.7	129.8
90 - 94	708	310	398	258.5	302.1	232.3
95 - 99	258	84	174	410.8	376.7	429.6
100 +	40	13	27	526.3	♦302.3	♦818.2
Democratic People's Republic of Korea - République populaire démocratique de Corée[15]						
2008 (I)						
Total	216 616	112 827	103 789	9.0	9.6	8.4
0	6 686	3 593	3 093	19.6	20.6	18.5
1 - 4	2 552	1 372	1 180	1.9	2.0	1.8
5 - 9	1 680	960	720	0.9	1.0	0.8
10 - 14	1 614	869	745	0.8	0.8	0.8
15 - 19	2 426	1 348	1 078	1.2	1.3	1.1
20 - 24	3 171	1 922	1 249	1.7	2.0	1.4
25 - 29	3 528	2 160	1 368	2.0	2.4	1.6
30 - 34	3 907	2 424	1 483	2.3	2.8	1.8
35 - 39	5 792	3 655	2 137	2.6	3.3	1.9

19. Deaths by age and sex and age-specific death rates by sex: latest available year, 2007 - 2016
Décès et taux de mortalité selon l'âge et le sexe : dernière année disponible, 2007 - 2016 (continued - suite)

Continent, country or area, date, code[a] and age (in years) / Continent, pays ou zone, date, code[a] et âge (en années)	Number - Nombre			Rate - Taux		
	Both sexes Les deux sexes	Male Masculin	Female Féminin	Both sexes Les deux sexes	Male Masculin	Female Féminin
ASIA - ASIE						
Democratic People's Republic of Korea - République populaire démocratique de Corée[15]						
2008 (|)						
40 - 44	6 312	3 907	2 405	3.1	3.9	2.4
45 - 49	6 468	3 915	2 553	4.1	5.1	3.2
50 - 54	7 630	4 715	2 915	5.8	7.4	4.3
55 - 59	11 295	7 113	4 182	12.5	16.8	8.7
60 - 64	26 360	16 815	9 545	24.9	35.3	16.4
65 - 69	34 068	22 281	11 787	37.3	58.7	22.1
70 - 74	34 093	18 886	15 207	51.5	82.7	35.0
75 - 79	28 690	10 991	17 699	85.5	138.7	69.1
80 +	30 344	5 901	24 443	163.8	238.8	152.3
Georgia - Géorgie[27]						
2016 (C)						
Total	50 771	26 098	24 673	13.7	14.7	12.7
0	507	292	215	8.8	9.8	7.7
1 - 4	97	58	39	0.5	0.5	0.4
5 - 9	51	29	22	0.2	♦0.2	♦0.2
10 - 14	40	25	15	0.2	♦0.2	♦0.2
15 - 19	143	109	34	0.7	0.9	0.3
20 - 24	210	158	52	0.9	1.3	0.4
25 - 29	310	248	62	1.1	1.8	0.4
30 - 34	420	317	103	1.6	2.4	0.8
35 - 39	568	438	130	2.3	3.6	1.0
40 - 44	839	656	183	3.5	5.5	1.5
45 - 49	1 226	931	295	5.2	8.2	2.4
50 - 54	2 100	1 566	534	8.1	12.9	3.9
55 - 59	3 067	2 127	940	12.0	18.2	6.8
60 - 64	3 713	2 505	1 208	17.1	26.3	9.9
65 - 69	4 456	2 764	1 692	25.2	37.6	16.4
70 - 74	3 976	2 250	1 726	39.0	56.5	27.8
75 - 79	9 451	4 456	4 995	67.8	88.3	56.2
80 - 84	8 736	3 641	5 095	120.0	143.1	107.6
85 +	10 745	3 440	7 305	237.7	269.8	225.1
Unknown - Inconnu	116	88	28	..	..	..
Indonesia - Indonésie[31]						
2010 (|)						
Total	1 236 154	687 976	548 178	5.2	5.8	4.6
0	106 846	61 546	45 300	24.3	27.2	21.2
1 - 4	37 689	20 958	16 731	2.1	2.2	1.9
5 - 9	19 409	10 807	8 602	0.8	0.9	0.8
10 - 14	15 382	9 029	6 353	0.7	0.8	0.6
15 - 19	23 642	14 948	8 694	1.1	1.4	0.8
20 - 24	27 089	16 020	11 069	1.4	1.6	1.1
25 - 29	31 020	17 855	13 165	1.5	1.7	1.2
30 - 34	31 290	17 168	14 122	1.6	1.7	1.4
35 - 39	38 257	20 382	17 875	2.1	2.2	1.9
40 - 44	49 757	26 901	22 856	3.0	3.2	2.8
45 - 49	65 139	36 351	28 788	4.6	5.2	4.1
50 - 54	89 078	51 820	37 258	7.7	8.8	6.5
55 - 59	86 308	53 355	32 953	10.2	12.1	8.1
60 - 64	105 991	62 663	43 328	17.5	21.4	13.8
65 - 69	107 730	62 508	45 222	23.0	28.1	18.3
70 - 74	138 235	76 159	62 076	40.0	49.7	32.2
75 - 79	92 062	49 343	42 719	46.5	58.6	37.6
80 - 84	86 057	42 547	43 510	75.3	88.4	65.8
85 +	85 173	37 616	47 557	119.4	133.2	110.3
Iran (Islamic Republic of) - Iran (République islamique d')[32]						
2014 (+U)						
Total	338 681	193 394	145 287	...	...	...
0 - 4	11 257	6 137	5 120	...	...	...
0	7 430	4 012	3 418	...	...	...
1 - 4	3 827	2 125	1 702	...	...	...
5 - 9	2 413	1 388	1 025	...	...	...
10 - 14	2 134	1 240	894	...	...	...
15 - 19	4 318	2 981	1 337	...	...	...

Continent, country or area, date, code[a] and age (in years) / Continent, pays ou zone, date, code[a] et âge (en années)	Number - Nombre			Rate - Taux		
	Both sexes Les deux sexes	Male Masculin	Female Féminin	Both sexes Les deux sexes	Male Masculin	Female Féminin
ASIA - ASIE						
Iran (Islamic Republic of) - Iran (République islamique d')[32]						
2014 (+U)						
20 - 24	6 776	5 006	1 770	...	...	...
25 - 29	8 799	5 784	3 015	...	...	...
30 - 34	8 794	6 018	2 776	...	...	...
35 - 39	8 081	5 523	2 558	...	...	...
40 - 44	8 736	6 014	2 722	...	...	...
45 - 49	10 237	6 827	3 410	...	...	...
50 - 54	14 127	9 401	4 726	...	...	...
55 - 59	18 904	12 142	6 762	...	...	...
60 - 64	21 746	12 765	8 981	...	...	...
65 - 69	23 078	12 953	10 125	...	...	...
70 - 74	27 278	14 836	12 442	...	...	...
75 +	146 095	75 560	70 535	...	...	...
Unknown - Inconnu	15 908	8 819	7 089	..		..
Israel - Israël[33]						
2016 (C)						
Total	43 892	21 706[14]	22 184[14]	...	...	...
0	561	311[14]	248[14]	...	...	...
1 - 4	120	67	53	...	...	...
5 - 9	81	47	34	...	...	...
10 - 14	78	39	39	...	...	...
15 - 19	170	121	49	...	...	...
20 - 24	183	139	44	...	...	...
25 - 29	221	161	60	...	...	...
30 - 34	262	173	89	...	...	...
35 - 39	359	211	148	...	...	...
40 - 44	506	298	208	...	...	...
45 - 49	669	421	248	...	...	...
50 - 54	1 035	665	370	...	...	...
55 - 59	1 585	985	600	...	...	...
60 - 64	2 400	1 470	930	...	...	...
65 - 69	3 407	2 054	1 353	...	...	...
70 - 74	3 519	2 073	1 446	...	...	...
75 - 79	5 182	2 811	2 371	...	...	...
80 - 84	6 749	3 145	3 604	...	...	...
85 - 89	7 715	3 222	4 493	...	...	...
90 - 94	6 280	2 242	4 038	...	...	...
95 - 99	2 245	871	1 374	...	...	...
100 +	565	180	385	...	...	...
Japan - Japon[34]						
2015 (C)						
Total	1 290 444	666 707	623 737	10.2	10.8	9.6
0 - 4	2 692	1 473	1 219	0.5	0.6	0.5
0	1 916	1 042	874	...	...	...
1 - 4	776	431	345	...	...	...
5 - 9	452	253	199	0.1	0.1	0.1
10 - 14	470	267	203	0.1	0.1	0.1
15 - 19	1 220	836	384	0.2	0.3	0.1
20 - 24	2 101	1 515	586	0.3	0.5	0.2
25 - 29	2 616	1 786	830	0.4	0.5	0.3
30 - 34	3 549	2 325	1 224	0.5	0.6	0.3
35 - 39	5 402	3 455	1 947	0.6	0.8	0.5
40 - 44	9 770	6 214	3 556	1.0	1.3	0.7
45 - 49	13 540	8 656	4 884	1.6	2.0	1.1
50 - 54	19 717	12 838	6 879	2.5	3.2	1.7
55 - 59	28 735	19 460	9 275	3.8	5.2	2.4
60 - 64	52 217	36 141	16 076	6.1	8.6	3.7
65 - 69	88 287	61 424	26 863	9.2	13.3	5.4
70 - 74	114 323	76 916	37 407	14.6	21.2	8.9
75 - 79	153 465	96 964	56 501	24.2	34.6	16.0
80 - 84	222 455	126 762	95 693	44.7	63.5	32.1
85 - 89	256 258	120 810	135 448	81.6	113.3	65.3
90 - 94	197 174	64 596	132 578	144.0	191.7	128.5
95 - 99	90 723	19 914	70 809	236.9	292.9	224.8

Continent, country or area, date, code[a] and age (in years) Continent, pays ou zone, date, code[a] et âge (en années)	Number - Nombre			Rate - Taux		
	Both sexes Les deux sexes	Male Masculin	Female Féminin	Both sexes Les deux sexes	Male Masculin	Female Féminin
ASIA - ASIE						
Japan - Japon[34]						
2015 (C)						
100 +	24 823	3 743	21 080	394.0	467.9	390.4
Unknown - Inconnu	455	359	96	..	..	..
Kazakhstan[27]						
2013 (C)						
Total	135 950	74 804	61 146	8.0	9.2	7.0
0	4 367	2 502	1 865	11.6	13.0	10.2
1 - 4	1 071	630	441	0.8	0.9	0.6
5 - 9	433	246	187	0.3	0.3	0.3
10 - 14	376	224	152	0.3	0.4	0.3
15 - 19	921	614	307	0.7	0.9	0.5
20 - 24	1 933	1 421	512	1.2	1.8	0.6
25 - 29	2 751	2 032	719	1.8	2.7	0.9
30 - 34	3 589	2 700	889	2.8	4.2	1.4
35 - 39	4 563	3 386	1 177	3.9	5.9	1.9
40 - 44	5 332	3 887	1 445	4.8	7.3	2.5
45 - 49	6 571	4 686	1 885	6.2	9.3	3.4
50 - 54	9 554	6 743	2 811	9.2	14.0	5.1
55 - 59	10 873	7 312	3 561	13.9	20.9	8.2
60 - 64	12 617	8 045	4 572	20.9	31.8	13.0
65 - 69	9 335	5 601	3 734	30.2	45.1	20.3
70 - 74	15 744	8 170	7 574	41.7	59.9	31.4
75 - 79	17 012	7 901	9 111	72.5	97.9	59.2
80 - 84	13 622	4 908	8 714	108.4	133.5	98.0
85 - 89	10 636	2 823	7 813	187.2	201.9	182.4
90 - 94	3 382	676	2 706	276.8	240.0	287.8
95 - 99	848	141	707	357.1	216.6	410.1
100 +	274	41	233	290.3	139.0	359.0
Unknown - Inconnu	146	115	31	..	..	..
Kuwait - Koweït						
2015 (C)						
Total	6 481	4 141	2 340	...	...	...
0	456	257	199	...	...	...
1 - 4	75	45	30	...	...	...
5 - 9	44	29	15	...	...	...
10 - 14	48	25	23	...	...	...
15 - 19	105	81	24	...	...	...
20 - 24	158	131	27	...	...	...
25 - 29	196	163	33	...	...	...
30 - 34	240	187	53	...	...	...
35 - 39	291	232	59	...	...	...
40 - 44	315	252	63	...	...	...
45 - 49	404	304	100	...	...	...
50 - 54	454	356	98	...	...	...
55 - 59	512	382	130	...	...	...
60 - 64	498	329	169	...	...	...
65 - 69	466	251	215	...	...	...
70 - 74	520	275	245	...	...	...
75 - 79	530	292	238	...	...	...
80 - 84	435	210	225	...	...	...
85 - 89	256	114	142	...	...	...
90 - 94	131	48	83	...	...	...
95 +	51	24	27	...	...	...
Unknown - Inconnu	296	154	142	..	..	..
Kyrgyzstan - Kirghizstan						
2016* (C)						
Total	33 475	18 564	14 911	5.5	6.2	4.9
0	2 621	1 434	1 187	16.6	17.6	15.5
1 - 4	517	285	232	0.8	0.9	0.8
5 - 9	182	125	57	0.3	0.4	0.2
10 - 14	197	123	74	0.4	0.5	0.3
15 - 19	290	167	123	0.6	0.6	0.5
20 - 24	447	293	154	0.8	1.0	0.6
25 - 29	609	428	181	1.0	1.5	0.6
30 - 34	727	516	211	1.5	2.2	0.9
35 - 39	980	705	275	2.6	3.7	1.5

Continent, country or area, date, code[a] and age (in years) / Continent, pays ou zone, date, code[a] et âge (en années)	Number - Nombre			Rate - Taux		
	Both sexes Les deux sexes	Male Masculin	Female Féminin	Both sexes Les deux sexes	Male Masculin	Female Féminin
ASIA - ASIE						
Kyrgyzstan - Kirghizstan						
2016* (C)						
40 - 44	1 271	886	385	3.8	5.4	2.2
45 - 49	1 554	1 100	454	4.9	7.2	2.8
50 - 54	2 055	1 409	646	7.0	10.2	4.2
55 - 59	2 806	1 824	982	11.1	15.5	7.2
60 - 64	2 991	1 851	1 140	17.9	24.9	12.3
65 - 69	2 878	1 668	1 210	26.2	36.2	19.0
70 - 74	1 974	1 041	933	43.1	55.7	34.3
75 - 79	4 017	1 945	2 072	68.5	88.4	56.5
80 - 84	3 362	1 437	1 925	108.5	133.3	95.3
85 - 89	2 674	945	1 729	150.9	154.7	148.9
90 - 94	1 000	319	681	178.8	149.3	197.0
95 - 99	244	53	191	176.3	126.8	197.7
100 +	79	10	69	281.1	♦97.1	387.6
Malaysia - Malaisie						
2015 (C)						
Total	155 786	89 449	66 337	5.0	5.6	4.4
0	3 582	1 978	1 604	6.8	7.3	6.2
1 - 4	786	442	344	0.4	0.4	0.3
5 - 9	604	359	245	0.2	0.3	0.2
10 - 14	798	528	270	0.3	0.4	0.2
15 - 19	1 909	1 441	468	0.7	1.0	0.3
20 - 24	2 317	1 734	583	0.7	1.0	0.4
25 - 29	2 464	1 696	768	0.8	1.0	0.5
30 - 34	3 175	2 205	970	1.2	1.5	0.8
35 - 39	3 864	2 732	1 132	1.8	2.4	1.1
40 - 44	5 108	3 444	1 664	2.7	3.5	1.8
45 - 49	7 130	4 753	2 377	4.1	5.5	2.8
50 - 54	10 206	6 708	3 498	6.5	8.3	4.6
55 - 59	13 134	8 389	4 745	10.1	12.7	7.4
60 - 64	14 906	9 206	5 700	14.9	18.3	11.5
65 - 69	16 977	10 328	6 649	22.7	27.9	17.6
70 - 74	16 775	9 651	7 124	36.4	42.9	30.2
75 - 79	19 339	10 197	9 142	60.5	67.4	54.3
80 - 84	15 323	7 048	8 275	96.8	95.8	97.6
85 +	17 389	6 610	10 779	129.7	106.8	149.4
Maldives						
2014 (C)						
Total	1 143	663	480	2.8	2.9	2.8
0	59	32	27	8.4	8.7	♦8.0
1 - 4	15	6	9	♦0.5	♦0.4	♦0.6
5 - 9	1	-	1	-	-	♦0.1
10 - 14	7	6	1	♦0.3	♦0.4	♦0.1
15 - 19	18	13	5	♦0.6	♦0.8	♦0.3
20 - 24	17	12	5	♦0.4	♦0.4	♦0.3
25 - 29	26	21	5	♦0.5	♦0.6	♦0.2
30 - 34	13	8	5	♦0.3	♦0.3	♦0.3
35 - 39	7	5	2	♦0.2	♦0.3	♦0.2
40 - 44	21	12	9	♦0.8	♦0.8	♦0.9
45 - 49	29	21	8	♦1.4	♦1.9	♦0.9
50 - 54	53	29	24	3.2	♦3.3	♦3.2
55 - 59	65	43	22	5.3	6.6	♦3.8
60 - 64	64	38	26	10.0	10.9	♦8.8
65 - 69	68	44	24	13.8	17.6	♦9.9
70 - 74	173	96	77	35.6	38.5	32.6
75 - 79	201	110	91	54.1	55.8	52.1
80 - 84	156	74	82	79.9	63.7	103.7
85 - 89	98	59	39	134.8	133.2	137.3
90 - 94	42	29	13	181.8	♦198.6	♦152.9
95 +	10	5	5	♦119.0	♦104.2	♦138.9
95 - 99	8	4	4	...	...	...
100 +	2	1	1	...	...	...
Mongolia - Mongolie						
2016 (+C)						
Total	17 763	10 662	7 101	5.8	7.0	4.5
0	1 315	748	567	16.5	18.3	14.6

Continent, country or area, date, code[a] and age (in years) / Continent, pays ou zone, date, code[a] et âge (en années)	Number - Nombre			Rate - Taux		
	Both sexes Les deux sexes	Male Masculin	Female Féminin	Both sexes Les deux sexes	Male Masculin	Female Féminin
ASIA - ASIE						
Mongolia - Mongolie						
2016 (+C)						
1 - 4	301	173	128	1.0	1.1	0.8
5 - 9	119	77	42	0.4	0.5	0.3
10 - 14	116	69	47	0.5	0.6	0.4
15 - 19	205	137	68	0.9	1.1	0.6
20 - 24	293	223	70	1.1	1.7	0.5
25 - 29	436	309	127	1.4	2.0	0.8
30 - 34	519	389	130	1.9	2.9	1.0
35 - 39	699	514	185	3.0	4.5	1.6
40 - 44	939	670	269	4.4	6.6	2.5
45 - 49	1 233	898	335	6.9	10.5	3.5
50 - 54	1 613	1 122	491	10.4	15.5	5.9
55 - 59	1 842	1 273	569	15.7	24.2	8.8
60 - 64	1 430	904	526	20.5	29.8	13.3
65 - 69	1 450	809	641	33.4	45.4	25.0
70 - 74	1 355	710	645	43.6	55.3	35.3
75 - 79	1 445	734	711	65.6	81.1	54.8
80 - 84	1 207	499	708	98.9	118.0	88.7
85 - 89	711	242	469	139.0	158.6	130.8
90 - 94	377	116	261	213.7	254.9	199.7
95 - 99	135	41	94	296.1	512.5	251.3
100 +	23	5	18	♦261.4	♦384.6	♦243.2
Myanmar[35]						
2014 (+U)						
Total	213 085	125 088	87 997	...	...	...
0	9 386	5 299	4 087	...	...	...
1 - 4	2 189	1 195	994	...	...	...
5 - 9	1 854	1 063	791	...	...	...
10 - 14	1 756	986	770	...	...	...
15 - 19	2 757	1 708	1 049	...	...	...
20 - 24	4 086	2 635	1 451	...	...	...
25 - 29	5 931	4 178	1 753	...	...	...
30 - 34	8 643	6 506	2 137	...	...	...
35 - 39	11 040	8 394	2 646	...	...	...
40 - 44	12 432	9 323	3 109	...	...	...
45 - 49	14 054	10 178	3 876	...	...	...
50 - 54	14 439	9 732	4 707	...	...	...
55 - 59	15 775	10 108	5 667	...	...	...
60 - 64	16 609	9 702	6 907	...	...	...
65 - 69	17 436	9 597	7 839	...	...	...
70 - 74	16 722	8 786	7 936	...	...	...
75 - 79	19 947	9 910	10 037	...	...	...
80 - 84	17 865	7 908	9 957	...	...	...
85 +	20 159	7 875	12 284	...	...	...
Unknown - Inconnu	5	5	-	..	...	...
Oman[36]						
2016 (U)						
Total	8 196	5 282	2 914	...	...	...
0	816	469	347	...	...	...
1 - 4	212	110	102	...	...	...
5 - 9	91	61	30	...	...	...
10 - 14	73	50	23	...	...	...
15 - 19	145	112	33	...	...	...
20 - 24	280	236	44	...	...	...
25 - 29	299	241	58	...	...	...
30 - 34	314	260	54	...	...	...
35 - 39	307	237	70	...	...	...
40 - 44	271	216	55	...	...	...
45 - 49	301	247	54	...	...	...
50 - 54	364	271	93	...	...	...
55 - 59	463	308	155	...	...	...
60 - 64	524	329	195	...	...	...
65 - 69	694	402	292	...	...	...
70 - 74	797	481	316	...	...	...
75 - 79	824	464	360	...	...	...
80 - 84	675	389	286	...	...	...

Continent, country or area, date, code[a] and age (in years)	Number - Nombre			Rate - Taux		
Continent, pays ou zone, date, code[a] et âge (en années)	Both sexes Les deux sexes	Male Masculin	Female Féminin	Both sexes Les deux sexes	Male Masculin	Female Féminin
ASIA - ASIE						
Oman[36]						
2016 (U)						
85 - 89	428	238	190	...	...	...
90 - 94	178	91	87	...	...	...
95 - 99	95	43	52	...	...	...
100 +	45	27	18	...	...	...
Pakistan[37]						
2007 (I)						
Total	1 019 533	598 820	420 713	6.8	7.8	5.8
0 - 4	365 729	205 840	159 889	18.7	21.0	16.4
5 - 9	33 029	16 652	16 376	1.5	1.4	1.5
10 - 14	20 510	6 871	13 640	1.0	0.6	1.4
15 - 19	27 417	16 500	10 917	1.6	1.8	1.3
20 - 24	20 192	11 195	8 997	1.5	1.6	1.3
25 - 29	23 990	13 101	10 888	2.2	2.5	2.0
30 - 34	11 624	8 007	3 617	1.4	2.0	0.8
35 - 39	24 880	11 482	13 398	3.0	2.8	3.2
40 - 44	30 926	18 802	12 124	4.6	5.4	3.7
45 - 49	27 537	17 884	9 652	4.4	5.5	3.2
50 - 54	43 405	30 870	12 535	9.5	12.7	5.8
55 - 59	51 031	35 120	15 911	14.4	18.8	9.5
60 - 64	68 531	41 470	27 061	23.4	25.3	20.9
65 - 69	58 286	35 664	22 621	28.6	32.2	24.3
70 - 74	82 325	49 296	33 029	56.2	57.5	54.4
75 - 79	37 357	24 072	13 285	57.1	67.2	44.9
80 - 84	34 079	21 720	12 359	79.6	86.6	69.6
85 +	58 685	34 274	24 411	165.7	168.9	161.4
Philippines						
2015 (C)						
Total	560 605	321 624	238 981	5.5	6.3	4.7
0 - 4	29 332	16 731	12 601	2.6	2.9	2.3
0	20 750	12 086	8 664	...	...	...
1 - 4	8 582	4 645	3 937	...	...	...
5 - 9	5 094	2 876	2 218	0.5	0.5	0.4
10 - 14	4 720	2 747	1 973	0.5	0.5	0.4
15 - 19	7 741	4 954	2 787	0.8	1.0	0.6
20 - 24	11 279	7 539	3 740	1.2	1.5	0.8
25 - 29	12 943	9 085	3 858	1.6	2.2	0.9
30 - 34	14 951	10 122	4 829	2.0	2.7	1.3
35 - 39	18 427	12 362	6 065	2.8	3.6	1.8
40 - 44	22 498	14 795	7 703	3.8	4.9	2.6
45 - 49	30 061	19 753	10 308	5.6	7.3	3.9
50 - 54	37 126	24 212	12 914	8.2	10.7	5.7
55 - 59	45 460	29 538	15 922	12.3	16.1	8.5
60 - 64	51 723	33 139	18 584	18.7	24.8	13.0
65 - 69	55 189	34 119	21 070	27.9	37.4	19.8
70 - 74	53 042	30 540	22 502	42.5	56.7	31.7
75 - 79	55 384	28 321	27 063	63.6	81.1	52.0
80 +	105 344	40 597	64 747	135.8	146.3	129.9
80 - 84	48 000	21 141	26 859	...	...	...
85 - 89	33 338	12 153	21 185	...	...	...
90 - 94	17 235	5 430	11 805	...	...	...
95 +	6 771	1 873	4 898	...	...	...
Unknown - Inconnu	291	194	97	..	..	..
Qatar						
2015 (C)						
Total	2 317	1 706	611	1.0	0.9	1.0
0	197	102	95	7.6	7.7	7.5
1 - 4	43	24	19	0.4	♦0.5	♦0.4
5 - 9	17	11	6	♦0.1	♦0.2	♦0.1
10 - 14	13	5	8	♦0.1	♦0.1	♦0.2
15 - 19	49	41	8	0.5	0.6	♦0.2
20 - 24	110	101	9	0.4	0.5	♦0.2
25 - 29	146	130	16	0.3	0.4	♦0.2
30 - 34	141	129	12	0.4	0.4	♦0.1
35 - 39	166	134	32	0.5	0.6	0.5
40 - 44	164	148	16	0.7	0.8	♦0.4

Continent, country or area, date, code[a] and age (in years) / Continent, pays ou zone, date, code[a] et âge (en années)	Number - Nombre			Rate - Taux		
	Both sexes Les deux sexes	Male Masculin	Female Féminin	Both sexes Les deux sexes	Male Masculin	Female Féminin
ASIA - ASIE						
Qatar						
2015 (C)						
45 - 49	173	145	28	1.1	1.1	♦0.9
50 - 54	154	127	27	1.5	1.6	♦1.4
55 - 59	185	143	42	2.9	2.8	3.4
60 - 64	161	119	42	5.5	5.4	6.0
65 - 69	131	88	43	10.2	9.5	12.1
70 - 74	136	79	57	23.1	21.1	26.6
75 - 79	120	74	46	35.3	37.0	32.9
80 +	209	105	104	68.0	66.3	69.8
80 - 84	101	58	43	...	...	...
85 - 89	67	29	38	...	...	...
90 - 94	26	11	15	...	...	...
95 +	15	7	8	...	...	...
Unknown - Inconnu	2	1	1	..	..	..
Republic of Korea - République de Corée[38]						
2015 (C)						
Total	275 895	150 449	125 446	5.4	5.9	4.9
0	1 190	655	535	2.7	2.9	2.5
1 - 4	287	168	119	0.2	0.2	0.1
5 - 9	207	126	81	0.1	0.1	0.1
10 - 14	220	139	81	0.1	0.1	0.1
15 - 19	685	448	237	0.2	0.3	0.2
20 - 24	1 155	788	367	0.3	0.4	0.2
25 - 29	1 479	986	493	0.5	0.6	0.3
30 - 34	2 315	1 412	903	0.6	0.7	0.5
35 - 39	3 103	1 982	1 121	0.8	1.0	0.6
40 - 44	5 537	3 731	1 806	1.3	1.7	0.8
45 - 49	8 624	6 141	2 483	2.0	2.8	1.2
50 - 54	12 609	9 381	3 228	2.9	4.3	1.5
55 - 59	16 144	12 010	4 134	4.2	6.2	2.1
60 - 64	16 696	12 239	4 457	6.1	9.1	3.2
65 - 69	19 900	14 103	5 797	9.5	14.0	5.3
70 - 74	30 399	19 661	10 738	17.1	24.7	10.9
75 - 79	42 666	24 656	18 010	31.6	45.1	22.4
80 - 84	45 030	20 913	24 117	56.7	78.3	45.8
85 - 89	37 792	13 200	24 592	104.0	137.5	91.9
90 - 94	21 981	6 107	15 874	181.7	216.1	171.2
95 - 99	6 625	1 386	5 239	276.9	289.4	273.8
100 +	1 210	196	1 014	385.1	441.4	375.8
Unknown - Inconnu	41	21	20	..	..	..
Saudi Arabia - Arabie saoudite[39]						
2016 (I)						
Total	58 097	35 497	22 600	1.8	1.9	1.7
0 - 4	5 084	2 273	2 811	1.9	1.7	2.1
5 - 9	1 033	577	456	0.4	0.4	0.3
10 - 14	2 125	1 206	919	0.9	1.0	0.8
15 - 19	1 487	1 368	119	0.7	1.2	0.1
20 - 24	4 859	3 146	1 713	2.0	2.4	1.5
25 - 29	3 926	2 673	1 253	1.3	1.6	0.9
30 - 34	2 106	1 582	524	0.7	0.9	0.4
35 - 39	3 232	2 207	1 025	1.0	1.0	0.8
40 - 44	2 714	2 027	687	0.9	1.0	0.6
45 - 49	2 629	1 233	1 396	1.2	0.8	1.8
50 - 54	3 031	2 571	460	1.9	2.4	0.9
55 - 59	3 901	2 404	1 497	3.6	3.3	4.0
60 - 64	2 895	1 844	1 051	4.0	4.1	3.8
65 - 69	2 547	1 181	1 366	6.3	5.4	7.4
70 - 74	4 186	2 922	1 264	15.5	20.7	9.8
75 - 79	1 846	709	1 137	11.5	8.3	14.9
80 +	10 496	5 574	4 922	54.6	58.1	51.1
80 - 84	4 678	1 900	2 778	...	...	...
85 +	5 818	3 674	2 144	...	...	...
Singapore - Singapour						
2016 (+C)						
Total	20 017	10 991	9 026	5.1	5.7	4.5
0	101	50	51	...	...	...

Continent, country or area, date, code[a] and age (in years) / Continent, pays ou zone, date, code[a] et âge (en années)	Number - Nombre			Rate - Taux		
	Both sexes Les deux sexes	Male Masculin	Female Féminin	Both sexes Les deux sexes	Male Masculin	Female Féminin
ASIA - ASIE						
Singapore - Singapour						
2016 (+C)						
1 - 4	32	20	12	...	...	...
5 - 9	20	10	10	♦0.1	♦0.1	♦0.1
10 - 14	31	18	13	0.1	♦0.2	♦0.1
15 - 19	61	37	24	0.3	0.3	♦0.2
20 - 24	103	70	33	0.4	0.5	0.3
25 - 29	158	108	50	0.6	0.8	0.4
30 - 34	172	119	53	0.6	0.9	0.4
35 - 39	211	136	75	0.7	0.9	0.5
40 - 44	328	194	134	1.0	1.3	0.8
45 - 49	498	318	180	1.7	2.2	1.2
50 - 54	837	537	300	2.7	3.4	1.9
55 - 59	1 303	839	464	4.3	5.6	3.1
60 - 64	1 656	1 081	575	6.6	8.6	4.5
65 - 69	2 098	1 347	751	10.6	14.0	7.4
70 - 74	1 844	1 158	686	17.8	23.8	12.4
75 - 79	2 762	1 560	1 202	31.4	40.0	24.5
80 - 84	2 906	1 493	1 413	54.3	68.2	44.6
85 +	4 896	1 896	3 000	110.7	126.8	102.4
85 - 89	2 595	1 162	1 433	...	...	...
90 - 94	1 471	541	930	...	...	...
95 - 99	643	151	492	...	...	...
100 +	187	42	145	...	...	...
Sri Lanka						
2010 (+C)						
Total	130 337	75 818	54 519	6.3	7.4	5.2
0 - 4	4 451	2 445	2 006	2.5	2.7	2.3
0	3 605	1 964	1 641	...	...	...
1 - 4	846	481	365	...	...	...
5 - 9	796	418	378	0.4	0.5	0.4
10 - 14	844	462	382	0.5	0.5	0.4
15 - 19	1 717	1 016	701	0.9	1.0	0.7
20 - 24	2 874	1 888	986	1.5	1.9	1.0
25 - 29	2 798	1 914	884	1.7	2.4	1.1
30 - 34	2 507	1 717	790	1.6	2.2	1.0
35 - 39	2 739	1 900	839	1.8	2.5	1.1
40 - 44	3 384	2 441	943	2.4	3.5	1.3
45 - 49	5 337	3 844	1 493	4.3	6.3	2.4
50 - 54	6 997	4 887	2 110	6.2	8.8	3.7
55 - 59	8 994	6 211	2 783	11.0	15.9	6.5
60 - 64	11 413	7 373	4 040	18.7	24.8	12.9
65 - 69	12 485	7 728	4 757	25.7	34.3	18.3
70 - 74	14 770	8 443	6 327	39.7	48.5	32.0
75 +	48 160	23 081	25 079	108.5	112.6	104.9
75 - 79	15 063	7 876	7 187	...	...	...
80 - 84	14 961	7 274	7 687	...	...	...
85 - 89	10 828	4 799	6 029	...	...	...
90 - 94	4 939	2 175	2 764	...	...	...
95 - 99	1 877	785	1 092	...	...	...
100 +	492	172	320	...	...	...
Unknown - Inconnu	71	50	21	...	...	...
State of Palestine - État de Palestine[40]						
2015 (U)						
Total	11 908	6 424	5 484	...	...	...
0	852	457	395	...	...	...
1 - 4	333	172	161	...	...	...
5 - 9	139	85	54	...	...	...
10 - 14	94	66	28	...	...	...
15 - 19	197	144	53	...	...	...
20 - 24	243	186	57	...	...	...
25 - 29	157	108	49	...	...	...
30 - 34	162	102	60	...	...	...
35 - 39	218	145	73	...	...	...
40 - 44	249	160	89	...	...	...
45 - 49	344	205	139	...	...	...
50 - 54	575	356	219	...	...	...

Continent, country or area, date, code[a] and age (in years) / Continent, pays ou zone, date, code[a] et âge (en années)	Number - Nombre			Rate - Taux		
	Both sexes Les deux sexes	Male Masculin	Female Féminin	Both sexes Les deux sexes	Male Masculin	Female Féminin
ASIA - ASIE						
State of Palestine - État de Palestine[40]						
2015 (U)						
55 - 59	774	481	293	...	...	...
60 - 64	907	553	354	...	...	...
65 - 69	1 109	612	497	...	...	...
70 - 74	1 216	589	627	...	...	...
75 - 79	1 414	675	739	...	...	...
80 - 84	1 309	611	698	...	...	...
85 - 89	980	443	537	...	...	...
90 - 94	426	180	246	...	...	...
95 - 99	142	61	81	...	...	...
100 +	68	33	35	...	...	...
Tajikistan - Tadjikistan[27]						
2014 (U)						
Total	32 879	18 540	14 339	...	...	...
0	3 273	1 972	1 301	...	...	...
1 - 4	654	362	292	...	...	...
5 - 9	197	122	75	...	...	...
10 - 14	197	132	65	...	...	...
15 - 19	319	180	139	...	...	...
20 - 24	528	328	200	...	...	...
25 - 29	646	398	248	...	...	...
30 - 34	699	439	260	...	...	...
35 - 39	841	549	292	...	...	...
40 - 44	951	584	367	...	...	...
45 - 49	1 193	706	487	...	...	...
50 - 54	1 740	1 045	695	...	...	...
55 - 59	2 323	1 389	934	...	...	...
60 - 64	2 565	1 468	1 097	...	...	...
65 - 69	2 266	1 292	974	...	...	...
70 - 74	3 145	1 848	1 297	...	...	...
75 - 79	4 187	2 283	1 904	...	...	...
80 - 84	3 827	1 921	1 906	...	...	...
85 - 89	2 229	1 129	1 100	...	...	...
90 - 94	807	309	498	...	...	...
95 - 99	192	66	126	...	...	...
100 +	100	18	82	...	...	...
Thailand - Thaïlande						
2011 (+U)						
Total	414 670	235 189	179 481	...	...	...
0	5 275	2 964	2 311	...	...	...
1 - 4	7 182	4 102	3 080	...	...	...
5 - 9	1 616	978	638	...	...	...
10 - 14	2 060	1 317	743	...	...	...
15 - 19	5 140	3 896	1 244	...	...	...
20 - 24	5 659	4 383	1 276	...	...	...
25 - 29	7 307	5 531	1 776	...	...	...
30 - 34	10 659	7 862	2 797	...	...	...
35 - 39	13 981	10 135	3 846	...	...	...
40 - 44	18 346	12 894	5 452	...	...	...
45 - 49	23 390	16 016	7 374	...	...	...
50 - 54	27 255	18 201	9 054	...	...	...
55 - 59	29 801	19 075	10 726	...	...	...
60 - 64	33 121	20 047	13 074	...	...	...
65 - 69	34 744	20 202	14 542	...	...	...
70 +	189 134	87 586	101 548	...	...	...
Turkey - Turquie						
2014 (C)						
Total	390 121	213 231	176 890	5.0	5.5	4.6
0	14 821	8 135	6 686	11.6	12.3	10.7
1 - 4	2 938	1 624	1 314	0.6	0.6	0.5
5 - 9	1 509	863	646	0.2	0.3	0.2
10 - 14	1 597	1 026	571	0.3	0.3	0.2
15 - 19	2 992	2 194	798	0.5	0.7	0.3
20 - 24	3 302	2 389	913	0.5	0.7	0.3
25 - 29	3 144	2 285	859	0.5	0.7	0.3
30 - 34	3 860	2 664	1 196	0.6	0.8	0.4

542

19. Deaths by age and sex and age-specific death rates by sex: latest available year, 2007 - 2016
Décès et taux de mortalité selon l'âge et le sexe : dernière année disponible, 2007 - 2016 (continued - suite)

Continent, country or area, date, code[a] and age (in years) Continent, pays ou zone, date, code[a] et âge (en années)	Number - Nombre			Rate - Taux		
	Both sexes Les deux sexes	Male Masculin	Female Féminin	Both sexes Les deux sexes	Male Masculin	Female Féminin
ASIA - ASIE						
Turkey - Turquie						
2014 (C)						
35 - 39	4 677	3 022	1 655	0.8	1.0	0.6
40 - 44	6 836	4 478	2 358	1.2	1.6	0.9
45 - 49	10 128	6 680	3 448	2.2	2.8	1.5
50 - 54	15 897	10 877	5 020	3.6	4.9	2.3
55 - 59	22 172	15 250	6 922	6.1	8.3	3.8
60 - 64	28 719	19 325	9 394	10.0	13.8	6.4
65 - 69	34 537	21 665	12 872	15.6	21.0	10.9
70 - 74	43 327	25 108	18 219	27.8	35.9	21.2
75 - 79	51 121	26 650	24 471	46.3	57.3	38.3
80 - 84	68 133	33 311	34 822	81.1	94.1	71.6
85 - 89	47 491	18 675	28 816	131.9	155.8	119.9
90 +	22 920	7 010	15 910	198.8	231.9	187.1
90 - 94	17 818	5 884	11 934	...	...	...
95 - 99	3 963	930	3 033	...	...	...
100 +	1 139	196	943	...	...	...
Uzbekistan - Ouzbékistan[27]						
2015 (+C)						
Total	152 035	83 051	68 984	4.9	5.3	4.4
0	8 320	4 906	3 414	11.9	13.5	10.2
1 - 4	2 482	1 389	1 093	1.0	1.0	0.9
5 - 9	951	587	364	0.3	0.4	0.2
10 - 14	926	553	373	0.4	0.4	0.3
15 - 19	1 767	1 024	743	0.6	0.7	0.5
20 - 24	2 515	1 498	1 017	0.8	0.9	0.6
25 - 29	3 033	1 913	1 120	1.0	1.2	0.7
30 - 34	3 308	2 094	1 214	1.3	1.6	0.9
35 - 39	4 039	2 595	1 444	1.9	2.4	1.3
40 - 44	4 881	3 175	1 706	2.5	3.3	1.8
45 - 49	6 444	4 065	2 379	3.9	5.1	2.8
50 - 54	9 571	5 975	3 596	6.0	7.8	4.4
55 - 59	13 015	8 107	4 908	10.2	13.2	7.4
60 - 64	14 102	8 298	5 804	16.9	21.0	13.2
65 - 69	12 940	7 241	5 699	27.7	33.5	22.8
70 - 74	12 364	6 771	5 593	44.5	52.1	37.8
75 - 79	19 560	9 743	9 817	71.1	81.9	62.8
80 - 84	15 514	6 969	8 545	120.7	141.7	107.7
85 +	16 113	6 002	10 111	123.7	127.2	121.8
Unknown - Inconnu	190	146	44	..	..	..
EUROPE						
Åland Islands - Îles d'Åland						
2015 (C)						
Total	285	141	144	9.8	9.7	9.9
0	-	-	-	-	-	-
1 - 4	-	-	-	-	-	-
5 - 9	-	-	-	-	-	-
10 - 14	-	-	-	-	-	-
15 - 19	-	-	-	-	-	-
20 - 24	-	-	-	-	-	-
25 - 29	1	1	-	◆0.6	◆1.1	-
30 - 34	-	-	-	-	-	-
35 - 39	-	-	-	-	-	-
40 - 44	-	-	-	-	-	-
45 - 49	5	4	1	◆2.4	◆3.8	◆0.9
50 - 54	5	1	4	◆2.5	◆1.0	◆4.0
55 - 59	9	5	4	◆4.6	◆5.4	◆3.9
60 - 64	18	9	9	◆8.8	◆9.2	◆8.4
65 - 69	27	13	14	◆13.5	◆13.0	◆13.9
70 - 74	24	16	8	◆16.5	◆21.1	◆11.5
75 - 79	28	19	9	◆27.9	◆41.3	◆16.6
80 - 84	45	23	22	61.0	◆70.1	◆53.7
85 - 89	57	27	30	115.4	◆145.2	◆97.4
90 - 94	50	20	30	233.6	◆333.3	◆194.8

543

Continent, country or area, date, code[a] and age (in years) Continent, pays ou zone, date, code[a] et âge (en annèes)	Number - Nombre			Rate - Taux		
	Both sexes Les deux sexes	Male Masculin	Female Féminin	Both sexes Les deux sexes	Male Masculin	Female Féminin
EUROPE						
Åland Islands - Îles d'Åland						
2015 (C)						
95 - 99	12	2	10	♦230.8	♦222.2	♦232.6
100 +	4	1	3	♦800.0	♦1000.0	♦600.0
Albania - Albanie						
2013 (C)						
Total	20 442	10 990	9 452	7.1	7.5	6.6
0	282	171	111	8.0	9.3	6.5
1 - 4	70	38	32	0.5	0.5	0.5
5 - 9	42	23	19	0.2	♦0.3	♦0.2
10 - 14	57	32	25	0.3	0.3	♦0.2
15 - 19	156	95	61	0.6	0.7	0.5
20 - 24	164	121	43	0.7	1.0	0.4
25 - 29	143	96	47	0.7	0.9	0.5
30 - 34	165	116	49	0.9	1.3	0.5
35 - 39	185	127	58	1.1	1.5	0.6
40 - 44	290	192	98	1.5	2.1	1.0
45 - 49	450	298	152	2.3	3.1	1.5
50 - 54	705	462	243	3.4	4.4	2.3
55 - 59	954	632	322	5.2	6.9	3.5
60 - 64	1 163	775	388	8.2	10.9	5.5
65 - 69	1 448	962	486	13.5	17.7	9.2
70 - 74	2 622	1 534	1 088	25.5	30.8	20.5
75 - 79	3 426	1 948	1 478	47.9	55.3	40.7
80 - 84	3 582	1 788	1 794	93.8	105.3	84.5
85 +	4 538	1 580	2 958	196.1	197.7	195.2
85 - 89	2 519	943	1 576	...	...	...
90 - 94	1 456	510	946	...	...	...
95 - 99	433	102	331	...	...	...
100 +	130	25	105	...	...	...
Andorra - Andorre						
2015 (C)						
Total	282	151	131	...	...	...
0	-	-	-	...	...	...
1 - 4	-	-	-	...	...	...
5 - 9	1	1	-	...	...	...
10 - 14	-	-	-	...	...	...
15 - 19	-	-	-	...	...	...
20 - 24	1	1	-	...	...	...
25 - 29	1	-	1	...	...	...
30 - 34	2	1	1	...	...	...
35 - 39	5	2	3	...	...	...
40 - 44	4	3	1	...	...	...
45 - 49	1	1	-	...	...	...
50 - 54	15	6	9	...	...	...
55 - 59	14	10	4	...	...	...
60 - 64	11	9	2	...	...	...
65 - 69	27	22	5	...	...	...
70 - 74	17	11	6	...	...	...
75 - 79	30	16	14	...	...	...
80 - 84	41	22	19	...	...	...
85 - 89	55	24	31	...	...	...
90 - 94	41	17	24	...	...	...
95 - 99	13	4	9	...	...	...
100 +	3	1	2	...	...	...
Austria - Autriche[41]						
2015 (C)						
Total	83 073	39 860	43 213	9.6	9.4	9.8
0	259	144	115	3.2	3.4	2.9
1 - 4	44	27	17	0.1	♦0.2	♦0.1
5 - 9	25	18	7	♦0.1	♦0.1	-
10 - 14	45	26	19	0.1	♦0.1	♦0.1
15 - 19	126	94	32	0.3	0.4	0.1
20 - 24	231	173	58	0.4	0.6	0.2
25 - 29	220	152	68	0.4	0.5	0.2
30 - 34	282	198	84	0.5	0.7	0.3
35 - 39	413	278	135	0.8	1.0	0.5

19. Deaths by age and sex and age-specific death rates by sex: latest available year, 2007 - 2016
Décès et taux de mortalité selon l'âge et le sexe : dernière année disponible, 2007 - 2016 (continued - suite)

Continent, country or area, date, code[a] and age (in years) / Continent, pays ou zone, date, code[a] et âge (en années)	Number - Nombre			Rate - Taux		
	Both sexes Les deux sexes	Male Masculin	Female Féminin	Both sexes Les deux sexes	Male Masculin	Female Féminin
EUROPE						
Austria - Autriche[41]						
2015 (C)						
40 - 44	681	422	259	1.1	1.4	0.9
45 - 49	1 258	807	451	1.8	2.3	1.3
50 - 54	2 120	1 420	700	3.0	4.0	2.0
55 - 59	3 042	1 965	1 077	5.1	6.7	3.6
60 - 64	4 030	2 594	1 436	8.4	11.2	5.8
65 - 69	5 799	3 648	2 151	13.3	17.7	9.4
70 - 74	8 132	4 998	3 134	19.9	26.9	14.1
75 - 79	9 785	5 626	4 159	30.5	40.0	23.1
80 - 84	12 778	6 335	6 443	59.9	75.5	49.8
85 - 89	16 629	6 569	10 060	116.8	137.8	106.3
90 - 94	13 226	3 545	9 681	208.6	233.4	200.8
95 - 99	3 255	691	2 564	334.4	358.4	328.5
100 +	693	130	563	514.1	583.0	500.4
Belarus - Bélarus						
2015 (C)						
Total	120 026	59 742	60 284	12.6	13.5	11.9
0	352	199	153	3.0	3.2	2.7
1 - 4	87	54	33	0.2	0.2	0.1
5 - 9	64	42	22	0.1	0.2	♦0.1
10 - 14	68	33	35	0.2	0.1	0.2
15 - 19	156	111	45	0.3	0.5	0.2
20 - 24	428	335	93	0.7	1.1	0.3
25 - 29	822	632	190	1.1	1.6	0.5
30 - 34	1 242	953	289	1.7	2.5	0.8
35 - 39	1 733	1 325	408	2.6	3.9	1.2
40 - 44	2 448	1 836	612	3.7	5.8	1.8
45 - 49	3 541	2 664	877	5.5	8.8	2.6
50 - 54	5 793	4 348	1 445	7.9	12.8	3.7
55 - 59	8 698	6 278	2 420	12.0	19.3	6.1
60 - 64	10 558	7 498	3 060	18.3	31.0	9.2
65 - 69	10 791	6 898	3 893	25.0	40.6	14.9
70 - 74	10 402	5 785	4 617	38.1	62.0	25.7
75 - 79	18 588	8 359	10 229	57.8	87.4	45.3
80 - 84	18 352	6 304	12 048	96.9	130.8	85.4
85 - 89	17 047	4 462	12 585	154.4	182.5	146.3
90 - 94	7 337	1 362	5 975	242.2	254.3	239.6
95 - 99	1 217	199	1 018	314.9	302.4	317.4
100 +	302	65	237	400.5	575.2	369.7
Belgium - Belgique[42]						
2015 (C)						
Total	110 541	53 631	56 910	9.8	9.7	9.9
0	400	226	174	3.2	3.6	2.9
1 - 4	86	42	44	0.2	0.2	0.2
5 - 9	58	31	27	0.1	0.1	♦0.1
10 - 14	58	28	30	0.1	♦0.1	♦0.1
15 - 19	143	93	50	0.2	0.3	0.2
20 - 24	300	222	78	0.4	0.6	0.2
25 - 29	312	219	93	0.4	0.6	0.3
30 - 34	442	295	147	0.6	0.8	0.4
35 - 39	608	402	206	0.8	1.1	0.6
40 - 44	966	600	366	1.3	1.6	1.0
45 - 49	1 658	1 005	653	2.1	2.5	1.7
50 - 54	2 696	1 664	1 032	3.3	4.0	2.5
55 - 59	4 341	2 714	1 627	5.7	7.2	4.3
60 - 64	5 997	3 722	2 275	9.0	11.3	6.7
65 - 69	7 798	4 950	2 848	12.9	17.0	9.1
70 - 74	8 513	5 160	3 353	19.6	25.5	14.5
75 - 79	12 963	7 379	5 584	32.8	42.6	25.2
80 - 84	19 180	9 532	9 648	59.7	74.7	49.2
85 - 89	21 932	8 936	12 996	111.6	133.9	100.1
90 - 94	16 754	5 272	11 482	204.0	233.6	192.8
95 - 99	4 318	993	3 325	322.2	358.2	312.8
100 +	1 018	146	872	527.6	546.8	524.5

19. Deaths by age and sex and age-specific death rates by sex: latest available year, 2007 - 2016
Décès et taux de mortalité selon l'âge et le sexe : dernière année disponible, 2007 - 2016 (continued - suite)

Continent, country or area, date, code[a] and age (in years) / Continent, pays ou zone, date, code[a] et âge (en années)	Number - Nombre			Rate - Taux		
	Both sexes Les deux sexes	Male Masculin	Female Féminin	Both sexes Les deux sexes	Male Masculin	Female Féminin
EUROPE						
Bosnia and Herzegovina - Bosnie-Herzégovine						
2010 (C)						
Total	35 118	17 900	17 218	9.1	9.5	8.8
0 - 4	252	143	109	1.5	1.7	1.3
0	216	125	91	6.5	7.3	5.6
1 - 4	36	18	18	0.3	♦0.3	♦0.3
5 - 9	28	19	9	♦0.1	♦0.2	♦0.1
10 - 14	27	14	13	♦0.1	♦0.1	♦0.1
15 - 19	84	58	26	0.3	0.4	♦0.2
20 - 24	120	92	28	0.4	0.6	♦0.2
25 - 29	165	130	35	0.6	1.0	0.3
30 - 34	160	109	51	0.7	0.9	0.4
35 - 39	254	180	74	1.0	1.5	0.6
40 - 44	432	265	167	1.5	1.9	1.2
45 - 49	844	553	291	2.7	3.7	1.9
50 - 54	1 465	980	485	5.5	7.2	3.7
55 - 59	2 141	1 429	712	9.2	13.6	5.6
60 - 64	2 610	1 647	963	14.3	19.1	10.0
65 - 69	3 390	2 032	1 358	16.8	22.6	12.1
70 - 74	6 045	3 199	2 846	32.8	38.8	27.9
75 - 79	6 948	3 344	3 604	57.7	66.1	51.6
80 - 84	6 006	2 440	3 566	125.3	124.5	125.9
85 +	4 119	1 254	2 865	164.3	175.6	159.9
85 - 89	3 105	966	2 139	...	...	...
90 - 94	737	210	527	...	...	...
95 - 99	245	69	176	...	...	...
100 +	32	9	23	...	...	...
Unknown - Inconnu	28	12	16	..	..	...
Bulgaria - Bulgarie						
2015 (C)						
Total	110 117	57 040	53 077	15.3	16.3	14.4
0	434	245	189	6.5	7.2	5.9
1 - 4	82	39	43	0.3	0.3	0.3
5 - 9	70	47	23	0.2	0.3	♦0.1
10 - 14	60	35	25	0.2	0.2	♦0.2
15 - 19	150	104	46	0.5	0.6	0.3
20 - 24	241	170	71	0.6	0.8	0.4
25 - 29	357	257	100	0.7	1.0	0.4
30 - 34	509	364	145	1.0	1.4	0.6
35 - 39	775	523	252	1.4	1.9	1.0
40 - 44	1 318	877	441	2.5	3.2	1.7
45 - 49	2 188	1 499	689	4.4	5.9	2.8
50 - 54	3 499	2 484	1 015	7.2	10.2	4.2
55 - 59	5 574	3 849	1 725	11.2	15.9	6.7
60 - 64	8 258	5 666	2 592	16.5	24.5	9.7
65 - 69	11 356	7 379	3 977	23.4	34.6	14.6
70 - 74	12 517	7 268	5 249	35.2	49.2	25.2
75 - 79	15 599	7 773	7 826	56.3	72.4	46.1
80 - 84	21 027	8 986	12 041	102.3	119.0	92.6
85 - 89	16 600	6 262	10 338	173.6	189.0	165.4
90 - 94	8 045	2 773	5 272	291.0	315.9	279.5
95 - 99	1 264	380	884	419.9	409.9	424.4
100 +	194	60	134	564.8	526.3	583.9
Croatia - Croatie						
2015 (C)						
Total	54 205	26 414	27 791	12.9	13.0	12.8
0	154	87	67	4.0	4.4	3.6
1 - 4	32	13	19	0.2	♦0.2	♦0.2
5 - 9	27	15	12	♦0.1	♦0.1	♦0.1
10 - 14	30	14	16	♦0.1	♦0.1	♦0.2
15 - 19	69	46	23	0.3	0.4	♦0.2
20 - 24	110	93	17	0.4	0.7	♦0.1
25 - 29	121	85	36	0.5	0.6	0.3
30 - 34	187	139	48	0.6	0.9	0.3
35 - 39	308	220	88	1.1	1.5	0.6
40 - 44	402	258	144	1.5	1.9	1.1
45 - 49	803	558	245	2.8	3.9	1.7

Continent, country or area, date, code[a] and age (in years) Continent, pays ou zone, date, code[a] et âge (en années)	Number - Nombre			Rate - Taux		
	Both sexes Les deux sexes	Male Masculin	Female Féminin	Both sexes Les deux sexes	Male Masculin	Female Féminin
EUROPE						
Croatia - Croatie						
2015 (C)						
50 - 54	1 423	984	439	4.7	6.7	2.9
55 - 59	2 514	1 740	774	8.1	11.5	4.9
60 - 64	3 675	2 574	1 101	12.6	18.4	7.3
65 - 69	4 325	2 845	1 480	18.3	26.8	11.4
70 - 74	5 495	3 187	2 308	29.2	40.3	21.2
75 - 79	8 775	4 498	4 277	49.8	65.6	39.8
80 - 84	11 108	4 639	6 469	89.7	109.6	79.4
85 - 89	9 211	3 108	6 103	162.6	184.5	153.3
90 - 94	4 487	1 094	3 393	271.5	294.8	264.7
95 - 99	787	187	600	405.9	465.2	390.4
100 +	162	30	132	669.4	♦566.0	698.4
Czechia - Tchéquie						
2015 (C)						
Total	111 173	55 934	55 239	10.5	10.8	10.3
0	272	168	104	2.5	3.0	1.9
1 - 4	62	31	31	0.1	0.1	0.1
5 - 9	50	26	24	0.1	♦0.1	♦0.1
10 - 14	52	27	25	0.1	♦0.1	♦0.1
15 - 19	129	86	43	0.3	0.4	0.2
20 - 24	290	217	73	0.5	0.7	0.2
25 - 29	365	280	85	0.5	0.8	0.3
30 - 34	445	334	111	0.6	0.9	0.3
35 - 39	826	576	250	0.9	1.2	0.6
40 - 44	1 208	828	380	1.4	1.9	0.9
45 - 49	1 708	1 172	536	2.5	3.3	1.6
50 - 54	2 720	1 852	868	4.0	5.4	2.6
55 - 59	4 471	3 042	1 429	6.7	9.2	4.2
60 - 64	8 341	5 673	2 668	11.5	16.4	7.1
65 - 69	12 080	7 755	4 325	17.7	24.7	11.7
70 - 74	13 553	8 212	5 341	27.7	38.7	19.3
75 - 79	13 550	7 109	6 441	42.9	56.2	34.0
80 - 84	18 519	8 062	10 457	79.0	95.8	69.6
85 - 89	18 904	6 827	12 077	142.0	166.2	131.2
90 - 94	11 299	3 126	8 173	244.4	270.7	235.7
95 - 99	1 989	481	1 508	384.1	445.6	367.9
100 +	340	50	290	444.2	292.4	487.8
Denmark - Danemark[43]						
2015 (C)						
Total	52 555	26 283	26 272	9.3	9.3	9.2
0	216	116	100	3.8	4.0	3.6
1 - 4	20	10	10	♦0.1	♦0.1	♦0.1
5 - 9	24	13	11	♦0.1	♦0.1	♦0.1
10 - 14	25	13	12	♦0.1	♦0.1	♦0.1
15 - 19	59	38	21	0.2	0.2	♦0.1
20 - 24	118	90	28	0.3	0.5	♦0.2
25 - 29	115	85	30	0.3	0.5	♦0.2
30 - 34	133	82	51	0.4	0.5	0.3
35 - 39	222	145	77	0.6	0.8	0.4
40 - 44	430	265	165	1.1	1.3	0.8
45 - 49	796	503	293	1.9	2.4	1.4
50 - 54	1 373	859	514	3.4	4.3	2.6
55 - 59	2 013	1 214	799	5.6	6.8	4.5
60 - 64	3 128	1 900	1 228	9.3	11.4	7.2
65 - 69	4 674	2 800	1 874	13.4	16.4	10.5
70 - 74	6 073	3 559	2 514	21.5	26.2	17.1
75 - 79	6 678	3 713	2 965	35.1	42.5	28.8
80 - 84	8 059	4 020	4 039	65.1	76.8	56.4
85 - 89	8 529	3 841	4 688	114.1	139.6	99.3
90 - 94	6 753	2 282	4 471	200.8	240.1	185.3
95 - 99	2 634	657	1 977	316.6	373.5	301.4
100 +	483	78	405	468.9	481.5	466.6
Estonia - Estonie						
2015 (C)						
Total	15 243	7 217	8 026	11.6	11.7	11.5
0	35	18	17	2.5	♦2.5	♦2.5

Continent, country or area, date, code[a] and age (in years)	Number - Nombre			Rate - Taux		
Continent, pays ou zone, date, code[a] et âge (en années)	Both sexes Les deux sexes	Male Masculin	Female Féminin	Both sexes Les deux sexes	Male Masculin	Female Féminin

EUROPE

Estonia - Estonie
2015 (C)

1 - 4	13	8	5	♦0.2	♦0.3	♦0.2
5 - 9	8	4	4	♦0.1	♦0.1	♦0.1
10 - 14	11	5	6	♦0.2	♦0.2	♦0.2
15 - 19	31	21	10	0.5	♦0.7	♦0.3
20 - 24	34	27	7	0.4	♦0.7	♦0.2
25 - 29	85	62	23	0.9	1.2	♦0.5
30 - 34	145	119	26	1.5	2.5	♦0.6
35 - 39	146	113	33	1.6	2.5	0.8
40 - 44	212	151	61	2.3	3.3	1.4
45 - 49	290	214	76	3.4	5.1	1.8
50 - 54	477	340	137	5.4	8.0	3.0
55 - 59	766	547	219	8.6	13.4	4.6
60 - 64	1 066	718	348	12.9	20.0	7.4
65 - 69	1 309	857	452	18.3	29.5	10.6
70 - 74	1 552	912	640	27.9	44.3	18.3
75 - 79	2 210	1 099	1 111	40.3	62.0	29.9
80 - 84	2 488	969	1 519	68.5	95.1	58.1
85 - 89	2 563	699	1 864	118.4	141.5	111.5
90 - 94	1 388	274	1 114	196.4	222.3	190.9
95 - 99	344	53	291	333.8	385.5	325.9
100 +	70	7	63	530.3	♦437.5	543.1
Faeroe Islands - Îles Féroé						
2015 (C)						
Total	377	192	185	7.7	7.6	7.8
0	-	-	-	-	-	-
1 - 4	2	1	1	♦0.8	♦0.8	♦0.8
5 - 9	-	-	-	-	-	-
10 - 14	1	1	-	♦0.3	♦0.5	-
15 - 19	3	2	1	♦0.8	♦1.1	♦0.6
20 - 24	-	-	-	-	-	-
25 - 29	-	-	-	-	-	-
30 - 34	3	3	-	♦1.2	♦2.2	-
35 - 39	-	-	-	-	-	-
40 - 44	2	1	1	♦0.6	♦0.6	♦0.7
45 - 49	12	6	6	♦3.5	♦3.3	♦3.7
50 - 54	7	5	2	♦2.1	♦2.9	♦1.3
55 - 59	15	11	4	♦4.9	♦7.0	♦2.6
60 - 64	13	12	1	♦4.7	♦8.3	♦0.7
65 - 69	22	12	10	♦8.5	♦8.8	♦8.2
70 - 74	41	29	12	18.9	♦25.6	♦11.6
75 - 79	34	18	16	25.2	♦27.4	♦23.1
80 - 84	68	41	27	61.8	82.0	♦44.9
85 - 89	70	29	41	106.9	♦129.5	95.1
90 - 94	56	15	41	186.0	♦178.6	188.9
95 - 99	25	6	19	♦357.1	♦315.8	♦372.5
100 +	3	-	3	♦300.0	-	♦375.0
Finland - Finlande						
2015 (C)						
Total	52 492	25 992	26 500	9.6	9.7	9.6
0	97	48	49	1.7	1.7	1.8
1 - 4	23	16	7	♦0.1	♦0.1	♦0.1
5 - 9	16	8	8	♦0.1	♦0.1	♦0.1
10 - 14	29	15	14	♦0.1	♦0.1	♦0.1
15 - 19	82	51	31	0.3	0.3	0.2
20 - 24	168	135	33	0.5	0.8	0.2
25 - 29	184	142	42	0.5	0.8	0.3
30 - 34	241	171	70	0.7	0.9	0.4
35 - 39	284	208	76	0.8	1.2	0.5
40 - 44	376	267	109	1.2	1.7	0.7
45 - 49	742	505	237	2.1	2.8	1.4
50 - 54	1 196	788	408	3.2	4.2	2.2
55 - 59	1 909	1 319	590	5.2	7.2	3.2
60 - 64	3 039	2 072	967	8.2	11.4	5.1
65 - 69	4 783	3 105	1 678	12.7	17.1	8.6
70 - 74	4 547	2 888	1 659	18.3	25.2	12.4

19. Deaths by age and sex and age-specific death rates by sex: latest available year, 2007 - 2016
Décès et taux de mortalité selon l'âge et le sexe : dernière année disponible, 2007 - 2016 (continued - suite)

Continent, country or area, date, code[a] and age (in years) / Continent, pays ou zone, date, code[a] et âge (en annèes)	Number - Nombre			Rate - Taux		
	Both sexes Les deux sexes	Male Masculin	Female Féminin	Both sexes Les deux sexes	Male Masculin	Female Féminin
EUROPE						
Finland - Finlande						
2015 (C)						
75 - 79	6 336	3 622	2 714	32.2	42.8	24.2
80 - 84	8 227	4 022	4 205	57.5	72.6	47.9
85 - 89	10 263	4 053	6 210	111.7	138.3	99.2
90 - 94	7 190	2 006	5 184	198.3	228.0	188.8
95 - 99	2 353	495	1 858	336.3	374.0	327.5
100 +	407	56	351	545.9	530.8	548.4
France[44]						
2012 (C)						
Total	559 227	281 468	277 759	8.8	9.1	8.5
0 - 4	3 174	1 788	1 386	0.8	0.9	0.7
0	2 643	1 479	1 164	3.4	3.8	3.1
1 - 4	531	309	222	0.2	0.2	0.1
5 - 9	298	162	136	0.1	0.1	0.1
10 - 14	365	199	166	0.1	0.1	0.1
15 - 19	1 032	729	303	0.3	0.4	0.2
20 - 24	1 751	1 301	450	0.5	0.7	0.2
25 - 29	2 003	1 468	535	0.5	0.8	0.3
30 - 34	2 485	1 753	732	0.6	0.9	0.4
35 - 39	3 724	2 489	1 235	0.9	1.2	0.6
40 - 44	6 509	4 355	2 154	1.5	2.0	1.0
45 - 49	10 827	7 067	3 760	2.5	3.3	1.7
50 - 54	16 881	11 249	5 632	4.0	5.4	2.6
55 - 59	24 454	16 710	7 744	6.0	8.5	3.7
60 - 64	33 129	22 684	10 445	8.2	11.7	5.0
65 - 69	33 793	22 651	11 142	11.2	15.7	7.0
70 - 74	38 076	24 317	13 759	16.4	23.0	10.9
75 - 79	59 955	34 915	25 040	27.2	37.4	19.8
80 - 84	90 672	46 166	44 506	49.7	66.1	39.6
85 - 89	111 079	46 643	64 436	94.4	121.3	81.3
90 - 94	79 942	26 749	53 193	167.7	206.8	153.2
95 - 99	29 993	6 755	23 238	306.8	362.7	293.7
100 +	9 085	1 318	7 767	466.5	474.1	465.3
Germany - Allemagne						
2015 (C)						
Total	925 200	449 512	475 688	11.3	11.2	11.5
0	2 405	1 297	1 108	3.3	3.5	3.1
1 - 4	464	259	205	0.2	0.2	0.1
5 - 9	250	144	106	0.1	0.1	0.1
10 - 14	323	164	159	0.1	0.1	0.1
15 - 19	987	642	345	0.2	0.3	0.2
20 - 24	1 537	1 116	421	0.3	0.5	0.2
25 - 29	2 064	1 462	602	0.4	0.5	0.2
30 - 34	2 785	1 890	895	0.5	0.7	0.4
35 - 39	3 616	2 396	1 220	0.7	1.0	0.5
40 - 44	6 084	3 944	2 140	1.2	1.5	0.8
45 - 49	13 406	8 637	4 769	2.0	2.6	1.5
50 - 54	24 215	15 690	8 525	3.5	4.5	2.5
55 - 59	34 939	22 933	12 006	5.9	7.7	4.0
60 - 64	47 756	30 984	16 772	9.2	12.3	6.3
65 - 69	56 654	35 869	20 785	13.6	17.9	9.6
70 - 74	87 826	53 930	33 896	20.9	27.6	15.1
75 - 79	139 969	79 782	60 187	33.4	43.1	25.7
80 - 84	156 006	77 503	78 503	63.4	78.5	53.3
85 - 89	176 007	69 551	106 456	119.5	141.3	108.6
90 - 94	127 093	33 656	93 437	216.1	245.4	207.1
95 - 99	32 937	6 581	26 356	334.2	366.2	327.1
100 +	7 877	1 082	6 795	463.7	427.0	470.1
Greece - Grèce						
2016 (C)						
Total	118 792	60 526	58 266	11.0	11.6	10.5
0	387	237	150	4.2	5.0	3.4
1 - 4	75	41	34	0.2	0.2	0.2
5 - 9	57	34	23	0.1	0.1	◆0.1
10 - 14	46	27	19	0.1	◆0.1	◆0.1
15 - 19	130	92	38	0.2	0.3	0.1

Continent, country or area, date, code[a] and age (in years)	Number - Nombre			Rate - Taux		
Continent, pays ou zone, date, code[a] et âge (en années)	Both sexes Les deux sexes	Male Masculin	Female Féminin	Both sexes Les deux sexes	Male Masculin	Female Féminin
EUROPE						
Greece - Grèce						
2016 (C)						
20 - 24	225	165	60	0.4	0.6	0.2
25 - 29	265	198	67	0.4	0.7	0.2
30 - 34	411	282	129	0.6	0.8	0.4
35 - 39	624	435	189	0.8	1.1	0.5
40 - 44	979	627	352	1.2	1.6	0.9
45 - 49	1 657	1 091	566	2.0	2.7	1.3
50 - 54	2 572	1 712	860	3.5	4.9	2.2
55 - 59	3 848	2 610	1 238	5.4	7.7	3.3
60 - 64	5 320	3 621	1 699	8.2	11.8	5.0
65 - 69	7 204	4 775	2 429	11.8	16.6	7.5
70 - 74	9 055	5 808	3 247	18.2	25.2	12.2
75 - 79	14 974	8 479	6 495	30.9	40.1	23.8
80 - 84	23 444	11 559	11 885	61.3	72.1	53.5
85 +	47 519	18 733	28 786	149.0	147.5	150.0
Hungary - Hongrie[45]						
2015 (C)						
Total	131 575	63 475	68 100	13.4	13.5	13.2
0	383	215	168	4.1	4.5	3.7
1 - 4	92	48	44	0.3	0.3	0.3
5 - 9	61	37	24	0.1	0.1	♦0.1
10 - 14	49	31	18	0.1	0.1	♦0.1
15 - 19	146	107	39	0.3	0.4	0.2
20 - 24	260	186	74	0.4	0.6	0.2
25 - 29	340	244	96	0.6	0.8	0.3
30 - 34	437	321	116	0.7	1.0	0.4
35 - 39	906	615	291	1.1	1.5	0.7
40 - 44	1 426	947	479	1.8	2.4	1.3
45 - 49	2 586	1 761	825	3.8	5.1	2.4
50 - 54	4 400	2 911	1 489	7.4	10.1	4.9
55 - 59	8 159	5 431	2 728	12.1	17.2	7.6
60 - 64	12 390	7 972	4 418	17.3	24.7	11.2
65 - 69	13 038	7 968	5 070	23.1	32.8	15.7
70 - 74	15 039	8 367	6 672	32.8	45.7	24.2
75 - 79	17 510	8 311	9 199	52.0	70.6	42.0
80 - 84	21 342	8 343	12 999	90.2	111.0	80.5
85 - 89	19 318	6 111	13 207	151.2	172.6	143.1
90 - 94	10 971	2 873	8 098	236.7	258.0	230.0
95 - 99	2 315	578	1 737	314.4	324.1	311.3
100 +	407	98	309	273.0	214.2	299.0
Iceland - Islande						
2015 (C)						
Total	2 178	1 064	1 114	6.6	6.4	6.8
0	9	4	5	♦2.1	♦1.8	♦2.4
1 - 4	4	3	1	♦0.2	♦0.3	♦0.1
5 - 9	1	1	-	-	♦0.1	-
10 - 14	3	2	1	♦0.1	♦0.2	♦0.1
15 - 19	9	6	3	♦0.4	♦0.5	♦0.3
20 - 24	6	5	1	♦0.2	♦0.4	♦0.1
25 - 29	10	8	2	♦0.4	♦0.7	♦0.2
30 - 34	13	11	2	♦0.6	♦0.9	♦0.2
35 - 39	15	11	4	♦0.7	♦1.0	♦0.4
40 - 44	27	14	13	♦1.3	♦1.3	♦1.2
45 - 49	27	16	11	♦1.3	♦1.5	♦1.1
50 - 54	53	30	23	♦2.5	♦2.8	♦2.1
55 - 59	86	51	35	4.1	4.9	3.4
60 - 64	87	38	49	4.9	4.2	5.5
65 - 69	151	86	65	10.2	11.4	9.0
70 - 74	195	111	84	18.1	21.2	15.2
75 - 79	206	108	98	26.9	29.8	24.2
80 - 84	387	188	199	62.3	67.4	58.1
85 - 89	435	208	227	109.5	130.2	95.6
90 - 94	320	121	199	203.6	239.8	186.4
95 - 99	120	40	80	383.4	437.2	361.2
100 +	14	2	12	♦405.8	♦210.5	♦480.0

Continent, country or area, date, code[a] and age (in years) Continent, pays ou zone, date, code[a] et âge (en annèes)	Number - Nombre			Rate - Taux		
	Both sexes Les deux sexes	Male Masculin	Female Féminin	Both sexes Les deux sexes	Male Masculin	Female Féminin
EUROPE						
Ireland - Irlande						
2014 (+C)						
Total...	29 188	14 861	14 327	6.3	6.5	6.2
0	224	131	93	3.2	3.7	2.7
1 - 4	40	23	17	0.1	♦0.2	♦0.1
5 - 9	31	15	16	0.1	♦0.1	♦0.1
10 - 14	25	18	7	♦0.1	♦0.1	-
15 - 19	55	39	16	0.2	0.3	♦0.1
20 - 24	146	120	26	0.6	1.0	♦0.2
25 - 29	164	120	44	0.5	0.8	0.3
30 - 34	222	152	70	0.6	0.8	0.4
35 - 39	255	165	90	0.7	0.9	0.5
40 - 44	378	244	134	1.1	1.4	0.8
45 - 49	525	324	201	1.7	2.1	1.3
50 - 54	822	498	324	2.9	3.5	2.2
55 - 59	1 194	716	478	4.7	5.7	3.7
60 - 64	1 630	991	639	7.2	8.8	5.6
65 - 69	2 363	1 409	954	12.2	14.5	9.8
70 - 74	2 881	1 720	1 161	20.3	24.8	16.0
75 - 79	3 722	2 130	1 592	34.7	42.9	27.6
80 - 84	4 793	2 446	2 347	64.9	77.8	55.3
85 - 89	5 037	2 173	2 864	122.9	148.9	108.5
90 - 94	3 372	1 125	2 247	196.7	224.9	185.0
95 - 99	1 114	272	842	265.8	282.5	260.8
100 + ...	195	30	165	232.7	♦309.3	222.7
Isle of Man - Île de Man[8]						
2016 (I)						
Total...	870	437	433	10.4	10.6	10.3
0	2	-	2	♦2.5	-	♦5.3
1 - 4	1	1	-	♦0.3	♦0.6	-
5 - 9	-	-	-	-	-	-
10 - 14	3	2	1	♦0.7	♦0.9	♦0.5
15 - 19	1	1	-	♦0.2	♦0.4	-
20 - 24	3	2	1	♦0.7	♦0.9	♦0.5
25 - 29	3	3	-	♦0.7	♦1.4	-
30 - 34	5	3	2	♦1.1	♦1.4	♦0.8
35 - 39	5	4	1	♦1.0	♦1.7	♦0.4
40 - 44	8	6	2	♦1.4	♦2.2	♦0.7
45 - 49	11	7	4	♦1.7	♦2.2	♦1.2
50 - 54	22	15	7	♦3.3	♦4.5	♦2.1
55 - 59	28	16	12	♦4.8	♦5.5	♦4.0
60 - 64	36	23	13	7.0	♦8.8	♦5.1
65 - 69	60	38	22	11.0	14.0	♦8.1
70 - 74	85	50	35	20.2	24.1	16.4
75 - 79	126	78	48	39.9	51.0	29.5
80 - 84	128	64	64	60.1	66.8	54.7
85 - 89	153	67	86	110.9	128.4	100.2
90 - 94	118	38	80	174.8	188.1	169.1
95 + ...	72	19	53	338.0	♦301.6	353.3
95 - 99	58	15	43	...	...	...
100 + ...	14	4	10	...	...	...
Italy - Italie						
2015 (C)						
Total...	647 571	307 964	339 607	...	...	...
0	1 398	772	626	...	...	...
1 - 4	280	144	136	...	...	...
5 - 9	181	106	75	...	...	...
10 - 14	232	152	80	...	...	...
15 - 19	648	472	176	...	...	...
20 - 24	901	662	239	...	...	...
25 - 29	1 047	741	306	...	...	...
30 - 34	1 452	1 033	419	...	...	...
35 - 39	2 350	1 520	830	...	...	...
40 - 44	4 308	2 668	1 640	...	...	...
45 - 49	7 662	4 778	2 884	...	...	...
50 - 54	11 926	7 368	4 558	...	...	...
55 - 59	16 525	10 200	6 325	...	...	...

Continent, country or area, date, code[a] and age (in years) / Continent, pays ou zone, date, code[a] et âge (en années)	Number - Nombre			Rate - Taux		
	Both sexes Les deux sexes	Male Masculin	Female Féminin	Both sexes Les deux sexes	Male Masculin	Female Féminin
EUROPE						
Italy - Italie						
2015 (C)						
60 - 64	23 995	15 204	8 791	...	...	...
65 - 69	37 615	23 773	13 842	...	...	...
70 - 74	49 951	30 481	19 470	...	...	...
75 - 79	80 580	46 133	34 447	...	...	...
80 - 84	116 284	58 561	57 723	...	...	...
85 - 89	139 013	58 192	80 821	...	...	...
90 - 94	109 970	35 439	74 531	...	...	...
95 - 99	31 814	7 912	23 902	...	...	...
100 +	9 439	1 653	7 786	...	...	...
Latvia - Lettonie						
2016 (C)						
Total	28 580	13 522	15 058	14.5	15.0	14.1
0 - 4	106	51	55	1.0	1.0	1.1
0	81	38	43	3.7	3.3	4.1
5 - 9	13	5	8	♦0.1	♦0.1	♦0.2
10 - 14	15	8	7	♦0.2	♦0.2	♦0.2
15 - 19	42	31	11	0.5	0.7	♦0.3
20 - 24	93	72	21	0.8	1.2	♦0.4
25 - 29	181	146	35	1.3	2.0	0.5
30 - 34	224	185	39	1.6	2.6	0.6
35 - 39	316	243	73	2.5	3.8	1.2
40 - 44	510	386	124	3.8	5.8	1.8
45 - 49	683	462	221	5.1	7.2	3.2
50 - 54	1 020	736	284	7.2	11.1	3.8
55 - 59	1 644	1 130	514	11.5	17.4	6.5
60 - 64	1 987	1 362	625	16.2	26.2	8.9
65 - 69	2 513	1 603	910	23.4	38.0	14.0
70 - 74	3 018	1 693	1 325	32.9	52.4	22.3
75 - 79	4 252	1 960	2 292	47.8	70.1	37.6
80 - 84	4 414	1 641	2 773	80.8	111.3	69.6
Unknown - Inconnu	2	2	-	..	..	...
Liechtenstein						
2014 (C)						
Total	268	121	147	7.2	6.5	7.8
0	1	-	1	♦2.8	-	♦6.1
1 - 4	-	-	-	-	-	-
5 - 9	-	-	-	-	-	-
10 - 14	-	-	-	-	-	-
15 - 19	-	-	-	-	-	-
20 - 24	1	-	1	♦0.4	-	♦0.9
25 - 29	-	-	-	-	-	-
30 - 34	3	2	1	♦1.3	♦1.7	♦0.9
35 - 39	1	1	-	♦0.4	♦0.8	-
40 - 44	2	2	-	♦0.7	♦1.4	-
45 - 49	5	4	1	♦1.6	♦2.5	♦0.6
50 - 54	6	4	2	♦1.9	♦2.6	♦1.3
55 - 59	15	8	7	♦5.5	♦6.0	♦5.1
60 - 64	12	7	5	♦5.2	♦6.0	♦4.4
65 - 69	22	16	6	♦10.8	♦15.7	♦6.0
70 - 74	27	15	12	♦16.8	♦19.4	♦14.5
75 - 79	31	12	19	31.4	♦26.9	♦35.1
80 - 84	32	16	16	49.3	♦63.7	♦40.2
85 - 89	53	18	35	130.7	♦140.1	126.4
90 - 94	46	12	34	277.1	♦320.0	264.6
95 - 99	9	4	5	♦346.2	♦421.1	♦303.0
100 +	2	-	2	♦400.0	-	♦800.0
Lithuania - Lituanie						
2015 (C)						
Total	41 776	20 529	21 247	14.4	15.3	13.6
0	132	76	56	4.3	4.8	3.7
1 - 4	31	12	19	0.3	♦0.2	♦0.3
5 - 9	15	5	10	♦0.1	♦0.1	♦0.1
10 - 14	37	24	13	0.3	♦0.3	♦0.2
15 - 19	97	73	24	0.6	0.9	♦0.3
20 - 24	159	134	25	0.8	1.3	♦0.3

Continent, country or area, date, code[a] and age (in years) Continent, pays ou zone, date, code[a] et âge (en années)	Number - Nombre			Rate - Taux		
	Both sexes Les deux sexes	Male Masculin	Female Féminin	Both sexes Les deux sexes	Male Masculin	Female Féminin
EUROPE						
Lithuania - Lituanie						
2015 (C)						
25 - 29	257	213	44	1.3	2.1	0.5
30 - 34	339	263	76	1.9	2.9	0.9
35 - 39	513	389	124	2.9	4.5	1.4
40 - 44	747	538	209	3.8	5.6	2.0
45 - 49	1 138	839	299	5.5	8.5	2.7
50 - 54	1 797	1 325	472	8.0	12.5	4.0
55 - 59	2 411	1 739	672	11.3	18.0	5.7
60 - 64	2 864	1 980	884	16.8	27.2	9.0
65 - 69	3 426	2 228	1 198	23.6	38.9	13.6
70 - 74	4 137	2 412	1 725	31.5	51.0	20.5
75 - 79	5 560	2 737	2 823	46.1	69.2	34.8
80 - 84	6 842	2 637	4 205	79.6	106.0	68.9
85 - 89	6 785	1 955	4 830	143.4	164.0	136.4
90 - 94	3 547	770	2 777	238.0	265.3	231.4
95 - 99	758	148	610	383.2	403.3	378.6
100 +	184	32	152	514.0	432.4	535.2
Luxembourg						
2015 (C)						
Total	3 983	1 966	2 017	7.0	6.9	7.1
0	17	14	3	♦2.8	♦4.5	♦1.0
1 - 4	2	2	-	♦0.1	♦0.2	-
5 - 9	3	3	-	♦0.1	♦0.2	-
10 - 14	3	1	2	♦0.1	♦0.1	♦0.1
15 - 19	9	8	1	♦0.3	♦0.5	♦0.1
20 - 24	10	9	1	♦0.3	♦0.5	♦0.1
25 - 29	13	12	1	♦0.3	♦0.6	-
30 - 34	12	7	5	♦0.3	♦0.3	♦0.2
35 - 39	27	21	6	♦0.6	♦1.0	♦0.3
40 - 44	51	31	20	1.2	1.4	♦0.9
45 - 49	66	39	27	1.5	1.7	♦1.2
50 - 54	112	81	31	2.6	3.6	1.5
55 - 59	156	102	54	4.3	5.5	3.1
60 - 64	210	128	82	7.2	8.6	5.7
65 - 69	283	166	117	11.7	13.7	9.7
70 - 74	355	208	147	19.2	23.7	15.1
75 - 79	503	281	222	32.2	40.8	25.4
80 - 84	681	351	330	56.9	72.2	46.5
85 - 89	789	329	460	105.7	130.0	93.3
90 - 94	482	144	338	183.5	231.1	168.7
95 - 99	158	24	134	355.1	♦266.7	377.5
100 +	41	5	36	611.9	♦294.1	720.0
Malta - Malte						
2016 (C)						
Total	3 342	1 644	1 698	7.7	7.6	7.8
0	33	20	13	7.5	♦8.9	♦6.0
1 - 4	2	1	1	♦0.1	♦0.1	♦0.1
5 - 9	1	1	-	-	♦0.1	-
10 - 14	1	-	1	♦0.1	-	♦0.1
15 - 19	8	4	4	♦0.3	♦0.3	♦0.3
20 - 24	5	3	2	♦0.2	♦0.2	♦0.1
25 - 34	22	16	6	♦0.3	♦0.5	♦0.2
35 - 44	57	37	20	1.0	1.2	♦0.7
45 - 54	133	88	45	2.5	3.3	1.7
55 - 64	309	191	118	5.2	6.5	4.0
65 - 74	673	394	279	13.4	16.3	10.7
75 +	2 098	889	1 209	64.3	68.5	61.6
Montenegro - Monténégro						
2016 (C)						
Total	6 464	3 385	3 079	10.4	11.0	9.8
0	26	11	15	♦3.5	♦2.8	♦4.2
1 - 4	3	2	1	♦0.1	♦0.1	♦0.1
5 - 9	6	2	4	♦0.2	♦0.1	♦0.2
10 - 14	5	3	2	♦0.1	♦0.1	♦0.1
15 - 19	12	6	6	♦0.3	♦0.3	♦0.3
20 - 24	15	13	2	♦0.4	♦0.6	♦0.1

19. Deaths by age and sex and age-specific death rates by sex: latest available year, 2007 - 2016
Décès et taux de mortalité selon l'âge et le sexe : dernière année disponible, 2007 - 2016 (continued - suite)

Continent, country or area, date, code[a] and age (in years) Continent, pays ou zone, date, code[a] et âge (en années)	Number - Nombre			Rate - Taux		
	Both sexes Les deux sexes	Male Masculin	Female Féminin	Both sexes Les deux sexes	Male Masculin	Female Féminin
EUROPE						
Montenegro - Monténégro						
2016 (C)						
25 - 29	27	20	7	◆0.6	◆0.9	◆0.3
30 - 34	29	20	9	◆0.6	◆0.8	◆0.4
35 - 39	46	30	16	1.0	◆1.4	◆0.7
40 - 44	67	39	28	1.6	1.9	◆1.3
45 - 49	105	71	34	2.6	3.6	1.7
50 - 54	213	150	63	5.0	7.2	2.9
55 - 59	375	245	130	8.9	11.7	6.1
60 - 64	534	351	183	13.5	18.3	9.0
65 - 69	722	444	278	23.2	31.5	16.3
70 - 74	665	362	303	34.7	44.8	27.3
75 - 79	1 145	581	564	58.2	71.6	48.7
80 - 84	1 120	490	630	100.6	108.6	95.2
85 +	1 349	545	804	211.5	220.6	205.7
Netherlands - Pays-Bas[46]						
2015 (C)						
Total	147 134	71 029	76 105	8.7	8.5	8.9
0	561	313	248	3.2	3.5	2.9
1 - 4	98	62	36	0.1	0.2	0.1
5 - 9	60	30	30	0.1	◆0.1	◆0.1
10 - 14	86	44	42	0.1	0.1	0.1
15 - 19	187	120	67	0.2	0.2	0.1
20 - 24	276	203	73	0.3	0.4	0.1
25 - 29	362	241	121	0.3	0.5	0.2
30 - 34	440	278	162	0.4	0.5	0.3
35 - 39	624	385	239	0.6	0.8	0.5
40 - 44	1 099	620	479	0.9	1.1	0.8
45 - 49	2 135	1 220	915	1.7	1.9	1.4
50 - 54	3 571	2 001	1 570	2.8	3.1	2.5
55 - 59	5 460	3 083	2 377	4.7	5.4	4.1
60 - 64	8 064	4 656	3 408	7.7	8.9	6.5
65 - 69	12 390	7 383	5 007	12.2	14.7	9.8
70 - 74	14 229	8 511	5 718	19.9	24.6	15.5
75 - 79	18 245	10 421	7 824	33.6	42.2	26.5
80 - 84	24 481	12 414	12 067	62.7	78.1	52.1
85 - 89	26 804	11 045	15 759	117.8	141.7	105.3
90 - 94	20 193	6 334	13 859	210.2	246.7	196.9
95 - 99	6 606	1 483	5 123	354.9	410.9	341.4
100 +	1 163	182	981	535.9	614.9	523.5
Norway - Norvège[47]						
2015 (C)						
Total	40 676	19 700	20 976	7.8	7.5	8.1
0	133	78	55	2.2	2.6	1.9
1 - 4	31	20	11	0.1	◆0.2	◆0.1
5 - 9	11	8	3	-	-	-
10 - 14	22	12	10	◆0.1	◆0.1	◆0.1
15 - 19	67	47	20	0.2	0.3	◆0.1
20 - 24	126	92	34	0.4	0.5	0.2
25 - 29	168	111	57	0.5	0.6	0.3
30 - 34	181	130	51	0.5	0.7	0.3
35 - 39	205	125	80	0.6	0.7	0.5
40 - 44	347	227	120	0.9	1.2	0.7
45 - 49	538	330	208	1.4	1.7	1.1
50 - 54	825	506	319	2.4	2.9	1.9
55 - 59	1 302	780	522	4.1	4.8	3.4
60 - 64	1 903	1 157	746	6.6	7.9	5.2
65 - 69	2 945	1 810	1 135	10.6	13.0	8.1
70 - 74	3 611	2 155	1 456	17.7	21.8	13.8
75 - 79	4 393	2 436	1 957	30.9	37.6	25.3
80 - 84	6 151	3 183	2 968	58.6	72.7	48.6
85 - 89	7 742	3 427	4 315	108.1	131.4	94.8
90 - 94	6 936	2 337	4 599	199.8	233.7	186.0
95 - 99	2 629	649	1 980	325.2	373.6	311.9
100 +	410	80	330	449.1	512.8	435.9

Continent, country or area, date, code[a] and age (in years) / Continent, pays ou zone, date, code[a] et âge (en années)	Number - Nombre			Rate - Taux		
	Both sexes Les deux sexes	Male Masculin	Female Féminin	Both sexes Les deux sexes	Male Masculin	Female Féminin

EUROPE

Poland - Pologne
2015 (C)

Total	394 921	204 469	190 452	10.4	11.1	9.7
0	1 476	830	646	4.1	4.5	3.7
1 - 4	263	148	115	0.2	0.2	0.2
5 - 9	191	100	91	0.1	0.1	0.1
10 - 14	243	147	96	0.1	0.2	0.1
15 - 19	777	568	209	0.4	0.6	0.2
20 - 24	1 457	1 182	275	0.6	0.9	0.2
25 - 29	1 887	1 558	329	0.7	1.1	0.2
30 - 34	2 758	2 191	567	0.9	1.4	0.4
35 - 39	4 000	3 072	928	1.3	2.0	0.6
40 - 44	5 522	4 110	1 412	2.1	3.1	1.1
45 - 49	8 196	6 000	2 196	3.6	5.2	1.9
50 - 54	14 228	10 258	3 970	5.9	8.6	3.3
55 - 59	26 411	18 467	7 944	9.2	13.4	5.4
60 - 64	37 359	25 146	12 213	13.9	20.1	8.5
65 - 69	40 485	26 153	14 332	19.6	28.5	12.5
70 - 74	33 970	20 203	13 767	28.0	40.4	19.3
75 - 79	48 511	25 397	23 114	42.3	59.3	32.2
80 - 84	62 104	27 027	35 077	72.0	93.7	61.1
85 - 89	60 914	20 646	40 268	125.4	148.2	116.2
90 - 94	34 663	9 180	25 483	206.6	230.0	199.2
95 - 99	7 842	1 779	6 063	314.8	334.5	309.4
100 +	1 664	307	1 357	322.8	288.8	331.6

Portugal[48]
2015 (C)

Total	108 539	54 175	54 364	10.5	11.0	10.0
0	250	148	102	3.0	3.4	2.5
1 - 4	58	38	20	0.2	0.2	♦0.1
5 - 9	49	22	27	0.1	♦0.1	♦0.1
10 - 14	45	29	16	0.1	♦0.1	♦0.1
15 - 19	120	87	33	0.2	0.3	0.1
20 - 24	182	129	53	0.3	0.5	0.2
25 - 29	226	167	59	0.4	0.6	0.2
30 - 34	333	231	102	0.5	0.7	0.3
35 - 39	610	407	203	0.8	1.1	0.5
40 - 44	1 136	770	366	1.4	2.0	0.9
45 - 49	1 828	1 256	572	2.4	3.5	1.5
50 - 54	2 732	1 878	854	3.6	5.2	2.2
55 - 59	3 717	2 669	1 048	5.3	8.1	2.8
60 - 64	5 086	3 468	1 618	7.8	11.4	4.7
65 - 69	6 690	4 390	2 300	11.3	16.3	7.2
70 - 74	8 939	5 510	3 429	18.2	25.5	12.4
75 - 79	13 876	7 805	6 071	31.8	42.8	23.9
80 - 84	20 331	9 895	10 436	60.2	76.1	50.3
85 - 89	21 813	8 925	12 888	118.8	146.6	105.1
90 - 94	15 006	5 057	9 949	228.7	270.4	212.1
95 - 99	4 569	1 134	3 435	322.9	306.2	328.8
100 +	943	160	783	225.8	115.2	280.9

Republic of Moldova - République de Moldova[49]
2012 (C)

Total	39 560	20 774	18 786	11.1	12.1	10.2
0 - 4	484	252	232	2.5	2.5	2.5
0	404	203	201	10.4	10.1	10.7
1 - 4	80	49	31	0.5	0.6	0.4
5 - 9	46	29	17	0.2	♦0.3	♦0.2
10 - 14	64	37	27	0.3	0.4	♦0.3
15 - 19	183	140	43	0.7	1.1	0.3
20 - 24	246	190	56	0.7	1.1	0.3
25 - 29	324	244	80	0.9	1.4	0.5
30 - 34	467	348	119	1.6	2.4	0.8
35 - 39	733	524	209	2.9	4.2	1.6
40 - 44	970	712	258	4.3	6.5	2.2
45 - 49	1 670	1 237	433	7.0	11.0	3.5
50 - 54	2 779	1 939	840	10.1	15.2	5.7
55 - 59	3 521	2 308	1 213	15.0	21.7	9.4

19. Deaths by age and sex and age-specific death rates by sex: latest available year, 2007 - 2016
Décès et taux de mortalité selon l'âge et le sexe : dernière année disponible, 2007 - 2016 (continued - suite)

Continent, country or area, date, code[a] and age (in years) / Continent, pays ou zone, date, code[a] et âge (en années)	Number - Nombre			Rate - Taux		
	Both sexes Les deux sexes	Male Masculin	Female Féminin	Both sexes Les deux sexes	Male Masculin	Female Féminin
EUROPE						
Republic of Moldova - République de Moldova[49]						
2012 (C)						
60 - 64	4 194	2 598	1 596	23.0	32.6	15.6
65 - 69	3 249	1 815	1 434	30.7	40.5	23.5
70 - 74	5 351	2 625	2 726	53.2	68.8	43.7
75 - 79	5 726	2 499	3 227	79.0	96.7	69.2
80 - 84	5 308	2 046	3 262	111.5	128.8	102.9
85 - 89	3 038	889	2 149	148.9	150.2	148.4
90 - 94	1 033	306	727	190.0	191.6	189.3
95 - 99	151	31	120	129.8	78.5	156.3
100 +	23	5	18	♦53.6	♦33.8	♦63.8
Romania - Roumanie						
2015 (C)						
Total	261 294	135 886	125 408	13.2	14.0	12.4
0	1 500	842	658	7.7	8.5	7.0
1 - 4	290	153	137	0.4	0.4	0.4
5 - 9	192	118	74	0.2	0.2	0.1
10 - 14	232	149	83	0.2	0.3	0.2
15 - 19	489	346	143	0.5	0.6	0.3
20 - 24	654	514	140	0.6	0.9	0.3
25 - 29	1 053	750	303	0.8	1.0	0.5
30 - 34	1 221	884	337	0.9	1.3	0.5
35 - 39	2 152	1 512	640	1.4	1.9	0.8
40 - 44	3 757	2 656	1 101	2.5	3.4	1.5
45 - 49	6 536	4 685	1 851	4.1	5.8	2.4
50 - 54	8 083	5 749	2 334	7.4	10.4	4.3
55 - 59	15 303	10 850	4 453	11.2	16.6	6.3
60 - 64	21 192	14 373	6 819	15.9	23.3	9.5
65 - 69	23 577	15 127	8 450	22.2	32.1	14.3
70 - 74	26 229	15 032	11 197	33.9	46.6	24.8
75 - 79	41 441	20 454	20 987	55.7	71.5	45.8
80 - 84	47 483	20 320	27 163	96.3	112.7	86.8
85 - 89	38 357	14 482	23 875	158.0	172.7	150.2
90 - 94	18 095	5 882	12 213	233.1	235.6	231.9
95 - 99	2 944	852	2 092	266.2	259.4	269.0
100 +	514	156	358	318.1	335.5	311.0
Russian Federation - Fédération de Russie[27]						
2011 (C)						
Total	1 925 720	997 494	928 226	13.5	15.1	12.1
0 - 4	16 465	9 472	6 993	2.1	2.3	1.8
0	13 168	7 572	5 596	8.0	9.0	7.0
1 - 4	3 297	1 900	1 397	0.5	0.6	0.5
5 - 9	1 972	1 160	812	0.3	0.3	0.2
10 - 14	2 006	1 249	757	0.3	0.4	0.2
15 - 19	6 656	4 634	2 022	0.8	1.1	0.5
20 - 24	18 666	14 374	4 292	1.5	2.3	0.7
25 - 29	32 160	24 684	7 476	2.7	4.1	1.3
30 - 34	45 451	34 852	10 599	4.1	6.4	1.9
35 - 39	50 630	38 270	12 360	5.0	7.7	2.4
40 - 44	55 007	40 708	14 299	6.0	9.1	3.0
45 - 49	81 813	60 225	21 588	7.7	12.0	3.8
50 - 54	124 961	89 971	34 990	10.9	17.1	5.6
55 - 59	156 587	108 205	48 382	15.6	24.9	8.5
60 - 64	177 990	118 728	59 262	22.7	36.6	12.9
65 - 69	111 156	66 246	44 910	27.8	44.4	17.9
70 - 74	263 633	136 875	126 758	40.8	62.8	29.6
75 - 79	232 616	99 250	133 366	65.5	92.9	53.7
80 - 84	290 314	94 614	195 700	101.1	129.8	91.4
85 - 89	172 178	35 533	136 645	166.8	187.8	162.0
90 - 94	56 714	9 585	47 129	244.6	241.3	245.3
95 - 99	18 647	2 652	15 995	320.7	294.4	325.5
100 +	2 562	320	2 242	352.6	232.1	380.8
Unknown - Inconnu	7 536	5 887	1 649	..	..	..
San Marino - Saint-Marin						
2014 (+C)						
Total	252	128	124	7.5	7.8	7.2
0	1	1	-	♦3.1	♦5.6	-

Continent, country or area, date, code[a] and age (in years) / Continent, pays ou zone, date, code[a] et âge (en années)	Number - Nombre			Rate - Taux		
	Both sexes Les deux sexes	Male Masculin	Female Féminin	Both sexes Les deux sexes	Male Masculin	Female Féminin
EUROPE						
San Marino - Saint-Marin						
2014 (+C)						
1 - 4	-	-	-	-	-	-
5 - 9	-	-	-	-	-	-
10 - 14	-	-	-	-	-	-
15 - 19	1	-	1	♦0.6	-	♦1.3
20 - 24	1	1	-	♦0.7	♦1.3	-
25 - 29	-	-	-	-	-	-
30 - 34	-	-	-	-	-	-
35 - 39	-	-	-	-	-	-
40 - 44	1	1	-	♦0.3	♦0.7	-
45 - 49	2	1	1	♦0.6	♦0.7	♦0.6
50 - 54	5	3	2	♦1.8	♦2.2	♦1.4
55 - 59	4	2	2	♦1.8	♦1.9	♦1.8
60 - 64	11	6	5	♦5.7	♦6.4	♦5.1
65 - 69	13	9	4	♦7.7	♦11.0	♦4.5
70 - 74	16	12	4	♦11.2	♦17.5	♦5.4
75 - 79	23	17	6	♦19.6	♦30.8	♦9.6
80 - 84	47	23	24	50.7	♦59.0	♦44.7
85 - 89	60	32	28	112.8	172.0	♦80.9
90 - 94	45	15	30	160.1	♦185.2	♦150.0
95 - 99	15	4	11	♦263.2	♦363.6	♦239.1
100 +	7	1	6	♦777.8	♦1000.0	♦750.0
Serbia - Serbie[50]						
2014 (+C)						
Total	101 247	51 010	50 237	14.2	14.7	13.7
0	381	228	153	5.8	6.7	4.8
1 - 4	60	27	33	0.2	♦0.2	0.3
5 - 9	43	27	16	0.1	♦0.2	♦0.1
10 - 14	47	27	20	0.1	♦0.1	♦0.1
15 - 19	122	88	34	0.3	0.5	0.2
20 - 24	222	159	63	0.5	0.7	0.3
25 - 29	265	189	76	0.6	0.8	0.3
30 - 34	363	249	114	0.7	1.0	0.5
35 - 39	591	394	197	1.2	1.5	0.8
40 - 44	938	589	349	2.0	2.5	1.5
45 - 49	1 683	1 086	597	3.6	4.7	2.5
50 - 54	3 087	2 014	1 073	6.2	8.3	4.2
55 - 59	5 333	3 540	1 793	9.9	13.6	6.5
60 - 64	8 700	5 692	3 008	15.5	21.3	10.2
65 - 69	8 890	5 421	3 469	21.8	29.1	15.7
70 - 74	11 630	6 515	5 115	36.5	46.9	28.4
75 - 79	18 063	8 732	9 331	63.0	74.0	55.3
80 - 84	21 117	8 968	12 149	111.6	122.5	104.7
85 - 89	13 869	5 174	8 695	178.6	185.8	174.6
90 - 94	5 242	1 726	3 516	268.0	274.3	265.0
95 - 99	493	139	354	259.6	218.2	280.5
100 +	108	26	82	311.2	♦224.1	355.0
Slovakia - Slovaquie						
2015 (C)						
Total	53 826	27 462	26 364	9.9	10.4	9.5
0	285	162	123	5.1	5.7	4.5
1 - 4	77	40	37	0.3	0.3	0.3
5 - 9	30	19	11	♦0.1	♦0.1	♦0.1
10 - 14	46	24	22	0.2	♦0.2	♦0.2
15 - 19	104	72	32	0.4	0.5	0.2
20 - 24	198	146	52	0.6	0.8	0.3
25 - 29	245	182	63	0.6	0.9	0.3
30 - 34	343	272	71	0.8	1.2	0.3
35 - 39	505	370	135	1.1	1.6	0.6
40 - 44	788	578	210	1.9	2.8	1.0
45 - 49	1 229	883	346	3.5	5.0	2.0
50 - 54	2 115	1 499	616	5.7	8.2	3.3
55 - 59	3 417	2 382	1 035	9.1	13.0	5.3
60 - 64	5 200	3 540	1 660	14.4	21.0	8.6
65 - 69	5 331	3 421	1 910	19.8	28.8	12.7
70 - 74	5 648	3 274	2 374	29.4	42.6	20.6

Continent, country or area, date, code[a] and age (in years)	Number - Nombre			Rate - Taux		
Continent, pays ou zone, date, code[a] et âge (en années)	Both sexes Les deux sexes	Male Masculin	Female Féminin	Both sexes Les deux sexes	Male Masculin	Female Féminin
EUROPE						
Slovakia - Slovaquie						
2015 (C)						
75 - 79	6 851	3 377	3 474	49.2	67.5	39.0
80 - 84	8 648	3 357	5 291	88.5	106.4	80.0
85 - 89	7 715	2 521	5 194	151.7	174.9	142.5
90 - 94	4 179	1 130	3 049	234.2	246.6	229.9
95 - 99	762	190	572	284.8	257.3	295.3
100 +	110	23	87	155.9	♦94.1	188.7
Slovenia - Slovénie						
2015 (C)						
Total	19 834	9 739	10 095	9.6	9.5	9.7
0	33	18	15	1.6	♦1.7	♦1.5
1 - 4	11	8	3	♦0.1	♦0.2	♦0.1
5 - 9	8	3	5	♦0.1	♦0.1	♦0.1
10 - 14	12	9	3	♦0.1	♦0.2	♦0.1
15 - 19	28	22	6	♦0.3	♦0.4	♦0.1
20 - 24	47	33	14	0.4	0.6	♦0.3
25 - 29	52	44	8	0.4	0.7	♦0.1
30 - 34	88	61	27	0.6	0.8	♦0.4
35 - 39	123	88	35	0.8	1.1	0.5
40 - 44	183	131	52	1.2	1.7	0.7
45 - 49	314	208	106	2.1	2.7	1.4
50 - 54	577	406	171	3.8	5.2	2.3
55 - 59	884	622	262	5.9	8.2	3.5
60 - 64	1 357	937	420	9.4	13.0	5.8
65 - 69	1 501	967	534	13.7	18.4	9.3
70 - 74	1 895	1 197	698	21.5	30.3	14.3
75 - 79	2 553	1 421	1 132	33.8	45.5	25.6
80 - 84	3 614	1 675	1 939	64.1	85.2	52.8
85 - 89	3 655	1 255	2 400	115.8	142.0	105.6
90 - 94	2 300	522	1 778	206.2	225.6	201.1
95 - 99	495	96	399	314.9	335.7	310.3
100 +	104	16	88	458.1	♦500.0	451.3
Spain - Espagne						
2015 (C)						
Total	420 408	211 847	208 561	9.1	9.3	8.8
0	1 117	620	497	2.6	2.8	2.4
1 - 4	206	120	86	0.1	0.1	0.1
5 - 9	194	115	79	0.1	0.1	0.1
10 - 14	192	108	84	0.1	0.1	0.1
15 - 19	374	266	108	0.2	0.2	0.1
20 - 24	547	384	163	0.2	0.3	0.1
25 - 29	767	553	214	0.3	0.4	0.2
30 - 34	1 148	796	352	0.4	0.5	0.2
35 - 39	2 134	1 400	734	0.5	0.7	0.4
40 - 44	3 620	2 291	1 329	0.9	1.2	0.7
45 - 49	6 269	4 065	2 204	1.7	2.2	1.2
50 - 54	10 149	6 783	3 366	3.0	4.0	2.0
55 - 59	14 261	9 619	4 642	4.7	6.5	3.0
60 - 64	17 492	12 167	5 325	6.9	9.9	4.1
65 - 69	24 044	16 626	7 418	10.2	14.9	6.0
70 - 74	31 079	20 595	10 484	15.8	22.7	10.0
75 - 79	45 224	27 235	17 989	28.8	39.9	20.3
80 - 84	76 406	39 738	36 668	53.5	69.0	43.0
85 - 89	89 039	38 248	50 791	102.1	123.9	90.1
90 - 94	67 451	23 074	44 377	185.2	213.0	173.5
95 - 99	23 590	6 081	17 509	289.5	313.3	282.1
100 +	5 105	963	4 142	319.6	267.4	334.8
Sweden - Suède						
2015 (C)						
Total	90 907	44 485	46 422	9.3	9.1	9.5
0	282	166	116	2.4	2.8	2.1
1 - 4	59	35	24	0.1	0.1	♦0.1
5 - 9	38	17	21	0.1	♦0.1	♦0.1
10 - 14	57	24	33	0.1	♦0.1	0.1
15 - 19	123	85	38	0.2	0.3	0.2
20 - 24	307	229	78	0.5	0.7	0.2

Continent, country or area, date, code[a] and age (in years) / Continent, pays ou zone, date, code[a] et âge (en années)	Number - Nombre			Rate - Taux		
	Both sexes Les deux sexes	Male Masculin	Female Féminin	Both sexes Les deux sexes	Male Masculin	Female Féminin
EUROPE						
Sweden - Suède						
2015 (C)						
25 - 29	368	274	94	0.6	0.8	0.3
30 - 34	339	225	114	0.6	0.7	0.4
35 - 39	367	257	110	0.6	0.8	0.4
40 - 44	552	352	200	0.8	1.1	0.6
45 - 49	910	552	358	1.4	1.6	1.1
50 - 54	1 494	941	553	2.4	2.9	1.8
55 - 59	2 358	1 427	931	4.1	4.9	3.2
60 - 64	3 718	2 211	1 507	6.6	7.9	5.4
65 - 69	6 479	3 821	2 658	10.9	13.0	8.8
70 - 74	8 749	5 213	3 536	17.7	21.5	14.0
75 - 79	10 480	5 932	4 548	30.8	37.4	25.0
80 - 84	14 186	7 250	6 936	58.4	70.1	49.7
85 - 89	17 874	8 104	9 770	110.5	134.6	96.2
90 - 94	15 368	5 577	9 791	201.5	235.3	186.3
95 - 99	5 826	1 626	4 200	333.1	386.8	316.1
100 +	973	167	806	505.6	525.2	501.7
Switzerland - Suisse						
2015 (C)						
Total	67 606	32 646	34 960	8.2	8.0	8.4
0	340	199	141	4.0	4.6	3.4
1 - 4	50	27	23	0.1	♦0.2	♦0.1
5 - 9	31	16	15	0.1	♦0.1	♦0.1
10 - 14	36	17	19	0.1	♦0.1	♦0.1
15 - 19	105	76	29	0.2	0.3	♦0.1
20 - 24	161	130	31	0.3	0.5	0.1
25 - 29	182	140	42	0.3	0.5	0.2
30 - 34	223	147	76	0.4	0.5	0.3
35 - 39	305	191	114	0.5	0.7	0.4
40 - 44	486	308	178	0.8	1.0	0.6
45 - 49	927	579	348	1.4	1.7	1.1
50 - 54	1 508	918	590	2.3	2.8	1.8
55 - 59	2 106	1 335	771	3.8	4.8	2.8
60 - 64	2 961	1 919	1 042	6.4	8.3	4.4
65 - 69	4 281	2 652	1 629	9.9	12.7	7.3
70 - 74	5 746	3 529	2 217	15.8	20.6	11.5
75 - 79	7 392	4 206	3 186	27.2	35.0	21.1
80 - 84	10 865	5 540	5 325	51.7	65.0	42.7
85 - 89	13 577	5 697	7 880	103.0	123.8	91.9
90 - 94	11 497	3 835	7 662	199.6	231.6	186.7
95 - 99	4 127	1 035	3 092	347.8	382.6	337.5
100 +	700	150	550	450.9	517.2	435.6
TFYR of Macedonia - L'ex-R. y. de Macédoine						
2015 (C)						
Total	20 461	10 562	9 899	9.9	10.2	9.6
0	198	111	87	8.6	9.3	7.8
1 - 4	26	16	10	♦0.3	♦0.3	♦0.2
5 - 9	26	14	12	♦0.2	♦0.2	♦0.2
10 - 14	26	16	10	♦0.2	♦0.3	♦0.2
15 - 19	37	23	14	0.3	♦0.3	♦0.2
20 - 24	59	44	15	0.4	0.6	♦0.2
25 - 29	67	46	21	0.4	0.6	♦0.3
30 - 34	102	60	42	0.6	0.7	0.5
35 - 39	136	81	55	0.9	1.0	0.7
40 - 44	221	145	76	1.5	1.9	1.0
45 - 49	397	274	123	2.7	3.7	1.7
50 - 54	723	479	244	5.1	6.7	3.5
55 - 59	1 156	744	412	8.5	10.9	6.1
60 - 64	1 688	1 065	623	13.9	17.9	10.0
65 - 69	2 058	1 223	835	21.6	27.7	16.3
70 - 74	2 571	1 422	1 149	36.8	45.0	30.0
75 - 79	3 498	1 693	1 805	65.7	72.9	60.0
80 - 84	3 931	1 700	2 231	121.3	127.1	117.2
85 - 89	2 479	999	1 480	219.8	224.8	216.5
90 - 94	895	351	544	355.0	386.1	337.5
95 +	167	56	111	185.8	224.0	170.8

Continent, country or area, date, code[a] and age (in years) / Continent, pays ou zone, date, code[a] et âge (en années)	Number - Nombre			Rate - Taux		
	Both sexes Les deux sexes	Male Masculin	Female Féminin	Both sexes Les deux sexes	Male Masculin	Female Féminin

EUROPE

TFYR of Macedonia - L'ex-R. y. de Macédoine
2015 (C)

95 - 99	145	48	97	...	...	...
100 +	22	8	14	...	...	...

Ukraine[51]
2014 (+C)

Total	632 296	310 671	321 625	...	...	...
0	3 656	2 124	1 532	...	...	...
1 - 4	774	421	353	...	...	...
5 - 9	451	280	171	...	...	...
10 - 14	446	276	170	...	...	...
15 - 19	1 359	989	370	...	...	...
20 - 24	3 077	2 437	640	...	...	...
25 - 29	6 334	4 892	1 442	...	...	...
30 - 34	9 510	7 270	2 240	...	...	...
35 - 39	12 525	9 459	3 066	...	...	...
40 - 44	15 098	10 982	4 116	...	...	...
45 - 49	19 036	13 895	5 141	...	...	...
50 - 54	29 714	21 498	8 216	...	...	...
55 - 59	40 342	28 024	12 318	...	...	...
60 - 64	52 238	34 607	17 631	...	...	...
65 - 69	50 416	30 135	20 281	...	...	...
70 - 74	71 113	36 563	34 550	...	...	...
75 - 79	109 901	48 658	61 243	...	...	...
80 - 84	85 913	29 434	56 479	...	...	...
85 - 89	82 792	21 677	61 115	...	...	...
90 - 94	30 848	5 867	24 981	...	...	...
95 - 99	5 602	921	4 681	...	...	...
100 +	1 015	153	862	...	...	...
Unknown - Inconnu	136	109	27	..	..	..

United Kingdom of Great Britain and Northern Ireland - Royaume-Uni de Grande-Bretagne et d'Irlande du Nord[52]
2015 (+C)

Total	601 272	291 775	309 497	9.2	9.1	9.4
0	3 005	1 739	1 266	3.9	4.4	3.3
1 - 4	492	277	215	0.2	0.2	0.1
5 - 9	297	165	132	0.1	0.1	0.1
10 - 14	314	178	136	0.1	0.1	0.1
15 - 19	936	610	326	0.2	0.3	0.2
20 - 24	1 526	1 104	422	0.4	0.5	0.2
25 - 29	2 018	1 373	645	0.5	0.6	0.3
30 - 34	2 802	1 839	963	0.6	0.8	0.4
35 - 39	3 868	2 391	1 477	0.9	1.2	0.7
40 - 44	6 085	3 774	2 311	1.4	1.8	1.1
45 - 49	9 797	5 878	3 919	2.1	2.6	1.7
50 - 54	14 421	8 499	5 922	3.2	3.8	2.6
55 - 59	19 373	11 559	7 814	4.9	5.9	3.9
60 - 64	27 743	16 607	11 136	7.9	9.7	6.2
65 - 69	43 715	25 697	18 018	12.1	14.7	9.7
70 - 74	54 789	31 471	23 318	20.0	24.2	16.3
75 - 79	74 309	40 979	33 330	34.5	41.4	28.6
80 - 84	98 999	49 628	49 371	62.4	72.9	54.4
85 - 89	109 943	47 873	62 070	113.0	129.9	102.6
90 - 94	88 220	30 838	57 382	197.6	221.7	186.7
95 - 99	31 634	8 098	23 536	321.7	353.8	311.9
100 +	6 986	1 198	5 788	477.2	525.7	468.2

OCEANIA - OCÉANIE

American Samoa - Samoas américaines
2014 (C)

Total	259	142	117	...	...	...
0	9	4	5	...	...	...
1 - 4	2	-	2	...	...	...
5 - 9	1	-	1	...	...	...

19. Deaths by age and sex and age-specific death rates by sex: latest available year, 2007 - 2016
Décès et taux de mortalité selon l'âge et le sexe : dernière année disponible, 2007 - 2016 (continued - suite)

Continent, country or area, date, code[a] and age (in years) / Continent, pays ou zone, date, code[a] et âge (en années)	Number - Nombre			Rate - Taux		
	Both sexes Les deux sexes	Male Masculin	Female Féminin	Both sexes Les deux sexes	Male Masculin	Female Féminin
OCEANIA - OCÉANIE						
American Samoa - Samoas américaines						
2014 (C)						
10 - 14	1	1	-	...	...	...
15 - 19	3	1	2	...	...	...
20 - 24	4	2	2	...	...	...
25 - 29	3	2	1	...	...	...
30 - 34	7	6	1	...	...	...
35 - 39	7	6	1	...	...	...
40 - 44	11	5	6	...	...	...
45 - 49	16	5	11	...	...	...
50 - 54	23	11	12	...	...	...
55 - 59	19	11	8	...	...	...
60 - 64	27	14	13	...	...	...
65 - 69	28	19	9	...	...	...
70 - 74	35	23	12	...	...	...
75 - 79	22	14	8	...	...	...
80 - 84	21	14	7	...	...	...
85 +	20	4	16	...	...	...
Australia - Australie						
2015 (+C)						
Total[53]	159 052	81 330	77 722	6.7	6.9	6.5
0	991	542	449	3.3	3.5	3.0
1 - 4	210	120	90	0.2	0.2	0.1
5 - 9	132	75	57	0.1	0.1	0.1
10 - 14	147	80	67	0.1	0.1	0.1
15 - 19	476	311	165	0.3	0.4	0.2
20 - 24	678	506	172	0.4	0.6	0.2
25 - 29	853	612	241	0.5	0.7	0.3
30 - 34	1 106	774	332	0.6	0.9	0.4
35 - 39	1 423	907	516	0.9	1.2	0.7
40 - 44	2 138	1 366	772	1.3	1.7	0.9
45 - 49	2 933	1 812	1 121	1.9	2.3	1.4
50 - 54	4 381	2 691	1 690	2.8	3.5	2.1
55 - 59	5 978	3 712	2 266	4.1	5.2	3.1
60 - 64	7 923	4 925	2 998	6.2	7.8	4.6
65 - 69	11 030	6 834	4 196	9.6	12.0	7.2
70 - 74	13 482	8 158	5 324	15.7	19.5	12.1
75 - 79	17 614	10 135	7 479	27.8	33.5	22.5
80 - 84	23 359	12 399	10 960	51.7	62.5	43.3
85 - 89	29 773	13 883	15 890	98.5	116.1	87.0
90 - 94	23 813	8 670	15 143	176.6	196.3	167.0
95 - 99	8 874	2 477	6 397	291.4	302.9	287.1
100 +	1 736	340	1 396	391.1	334.6	407.8
Unknown - Inconnu[53]	3	3	3	..	..	..
Cook Islands - Îles Cook[54]						
2009 (+C)						
Total	67	37	30	...	...	...
0	2	1	1	...	...	...
1 - 4	1	1	-	...	...	...
5 - 9	-	-	-	...	...	...
10 - 14	-	-	-	...	...	...
15 - 19	3	2	1	...	...	...
20 - 24	3	3	-	...	...	...
25 - 29	1	1	-	...	...	...
30 - 34	2	1	1	...	...	...
35 - 39	4	3	1	...	...	...
40 - 44	-	-	-	...	...	...
45 - 49	2	1	1	...	...	...
50 - 54	3	1	2	...	...	...
55 - 59	1	1	-	...	...	...
60 - 64	6	3	3	...	...	...
65 - 69	8	4	4	...	...	...
70 - 74	9	1	8	...	...	...
75 - 79	8	5	3	...	...	...
80 +	14	9	5	...	...	...

Continent, country or area, date, codeª and age (in years) Continent, pays ou zone, date, codeª et âge (en années)	Number - Nombre			Rate - Taux		
	Both sexes Les deux sexes	Male Masculin	Female Féminin	Both sexes Les deux sexes	Male Masculin	Female Féminin
OCEANIA - OCÉANIE						
Fiji - Fidji						
2008 (+C)						
Total	6 471	3 519	2 952	7.7	8.2	7.2
0	319	180	139	18.9	20.4	17.3
1 - 4	128	70	58	1.9	2.0	1.8
5 - 9	45	29	16	0.6	◆0.7	◆0.4
10 - 14	42	25	17	0.5	◆0.6	◆0.4
15 - 19	70	34	36	0.9	0.8	0.9
20 - 24	104	64	40	1.3	1.6	1.0
25 - 29	124	65	59	1.7	1.7	1.6
30 - 34	120	61	59	1.9	1.8	1.9
35 - 39	183	114	69	3.2	3.9	2.5
40 - 44	296	168	128	5.3	5.9	4.7
45 - 49	446	279	167	8.8	10.7	6.7
50 - 54	549	344	205	13.2	16.3	10.0
55 - 59	663	381	282	20.5	23.3	17.6
60 - 64	737	409	328	29.9	33.5	26.3
65 - 69	718	385	333	40.4	44.8	36.3
70 - 74	621	303	318	57.2	59.1	55.5
75 +	1 306	608	698	103.5	108.7	99.3
75 - 79	564	290	274	...	...	...
80 - 84	360	156	204	...	...	...
85 - 89	246	113	133	...	...	...
90 - 94	71	27	44	...	...	...
95 +	65	22	43	...	...	...
Kiribati[55]						
2011 (U)						
Total	481	279	202	...	...	...
0 - 4	132	75	57	...	...	...
5 - 19	14	10	4	...	...	...
20 - 29	34	24	10	...	...	...
30 - 39	28	15	13	...	...	...
40 - 49	60	37	23	...	...	...
50 - 59	74	42	32	...	...	...
60 - 69	54	34	20	...	...	...
70 +	85	42	43	...	...	...
Nauru						
2011 (C)						
Total	75	41	34	...	...	...
0	10	5	5	...	...	...
1 - 4	1	1	-	...	...	...
5 - 9	-	-	-	...	...	...
10 - 14	1	1	-	...	...	...
15 - 19	-	-	-	...	...	...
20 - 24	2	2	-	...	...	...
25 - 29	5	1	4	...	...	...
30 - 34	4	1	3	...	...	...
35 - 39	2	1	1	...	...	...
40 - 44	2	2	-	...	...	...
45 - 49	6	3	3	...	...	...
50 - 54	15	7	8	...	...	...
55 - 59	9	7	2	...	...	...
60 - 64	6	2	4	...	...	...
65 - 69	4	2	2	...	...	...
70 +	8	6	2	...	...	...
New Caledonia - Nouvelle-Calédonie						
2015 (C)						
Total	1 465	853	612	...	...	...
0	25	18	7	...	...	...
1 - 4	7	4	3	...	...	...
5 - 9	2	-	2	...	...	...
10 - 14	6	4	2	...	...	...
15 - 19	19	13	6	...	...	...
20 - 24	26	22	4	...	...	...
25 - 29	19	17	2	...	...	...
30 - 34	32	23	9	...	...	...
35 - 39	24	21	3	...	...	...

19. Deaths by age and sex and age-specific death rates by sex: latest available year, 2007 - 2016
Décès et taux de mortalité selon l'âge et le sexe : dernière année disponible, 2007 - 2016 (continued - suite)

Continent, country or area, date, code[a] and age (in years) / Continent, pays ou zone, date, code[a] et âge (en années)	Number - Nombre			Rate - Taux		
	Both sexes Les deux sexes	Male Masculin	Female Féminin	Both sexes Les deux sexes	Male Masculin	Female Féminin
OCEANIA - OCÉANIE						
New Caledonia - Nouvelle-Calédonie						
2015 (C)						
40 - 44	58	45	13	...	...	...
45 - 49	58	41	17	...	...	...
50 - 54	77	48	29	...	...	...
55 - 59	83	46	37	...	...	...
60 - 64	120	76	44	...	...	...
65 - 69	144	95	49	...	...	...
70 - 74	154	91	63	...	...	...
75 - 79	177	94	83	...	...	...
80 - 84	167	83	84	...	...	...
85 - 89	144	66	78	...	...	...
90 - 94	76	29	47	...	...	...
95 +	47	17	30	...	...	...
New Zealand - Nouvelle-Zélande[56]						
2016 (+C)						
Total	31 179	15 792	15 387	6.6	6.8	6.5
0	210	108	102	3.5	3.5	3.5
1 - 4	39	27	12	0.2	♦0.2	♦0.1
5 - 9	36	18	15	0.1	♦0.1	♦0.1
10 - 14	33	21	12	0.1	♦0.1	♦0.1
15 - 19	123	87	36	0.4	0.5	0.2
20 - 24	168	117	51	0.5	0.6	0.3
25 - 29	186	132	57	0.5	0.8	0.3
30 - 34	195	123	72	0.7	0.8	0.5
35 - 39	219	135	84	0.8	1.0	0.6
40 - 44	384	222	162	1.3	1.5	1.0
45 - 49	594	339	255	1.9	2.2	1.5
50 - 54	957	549	408	3.0	3.6	2.5
55 - 59	1 359	801	561	4.6	5.6	3.7
60 - 64	1 680	990	687	6.5	7.9	5.2
65 - 69	2 400	1 419	981	10.3	12.4	8.2
70 - 74	2 805	1 626	1 182	16.5	19.9	13.4
75 - 79	3 675	2 055	1 617	28.7	34.3	23.8
80 - 84	4 587	2 412	2 175	54.6	64.0	46.9
85 - 89	5 505	2 559	2 949	...	...	...
90 +	6 030	2 052	3 972	210.5	223.3	204.0
90 - 94	4 155	1 572	2 583	...	...	...
95 - 99	1 590	432	1 155	...	...	...
100 +	285	48	234	...	...	...
Niue - Nioué[57]						
2009 (C)						
Total	12	6	6	...	...	...
0	-	-	-	...	...	...
1 - 4	-	-	-	...	...	...
5 - 9	-	-	-	...	...	...
10 - 14	-	-	-	...	...	...
15 - 19	-	-	-	...	...	...
20 - 24	-	-	-	...	...	...
25 - 29	-	-	-	...	...	...
30 - 34	-	-	-	...	...	...
35 - 39	-	-	-	...	...	...
40 - 44	-	-	-	...	...	...
45 - 49	-	-	-	...	...	...
50 - 54	-	-	-	...	...	...
55 - 59	2	2	-	...	...	...
60 - 64	-	-	-	...	...	...
65 - 69	-	-	-	...	...	...
70 - 74	1	-	1	...	...	...
75 - 79	1	1	-	...	...	...
80 +	8	3	5	...	...	...
Pitcairn						
2007 (C)						
Total	1	...	...	...	...	...
0	-	...	...	...	...	...
1 - 4	-	...	...	...	...	...
5 - 9	-	...	...	...	...	...

Continent, country or area, date, code[a] and age (in years) Continent, pays ou zone, date, code[a] et âge (en années)	Number - Nombre			Rate - Taux		
	Both sexes Les deux sexes	Male Masculin	Female Féminin	Both sexes Les deux sexes	Male Masculin	Female Féminin
OCEANIA - OCÉANIE						
Pitcairn						
2007 (C)						
10 - 14	-	...	...	...	...	...
15 - 19	-	...	...	...	...	...
20 - 24	-	...	...	...	...	...
25 - 29	-	...	...	...	...	...
30 - 34	-	...	...	...	...	...
35 - 39	-	...	...	...	...	...
40 - 44	-	...	...	...	...	...
45 - 49	-	...	...	...	...	...
50 - 54	-	...	...	...	...	...
55 - 59	-	...	...	...	...	...
60 - 64	-	...	...	...	...	...
65 - 69	-	...	...	...	...	...
70 - 74	-	...	...	...	...	...
75 - 79	1	...	...	...	...	...
80 - 84	-	...	...	...	...	...
85 - 89	-	...	...	...	...	...
90 +	-	...	...	...	...	...
Samoa[23]						
2011 (|)						
Total	812	427	385	4.3	4.4	4.2
0 - 4	92	58	34	3.4	4.2	2.6
0	78	51	27	...	...	...
1 - 4	14	7	7	...	...	...
5 - 9	4	1	3	♦0.2	♦0.1	♦0.3
10 - 14	2	-	2	♦0.1	-	♦0.2
15 - 19	10	7	3	♦0.5	♦0.7	♦0.3
20 - 24	12	5	7	♦0.8	♦0.6	♦1.0
25 - 29	10	8	2	♦0.8	♦1.2	♦0.3
30 - 34	6	4	2	♦0.5	♦0.7	♦0.4
35 - 39	20	8	12	♦1.8	♦1.4	♦2.3
40 - 44	19	12	7	♦1.8	♦2.1	♦1.4
45 - 49	38	20	18	4.3	♦4.4	♦4.2
50 - 54	48	28	20	6.3	♦7.1	♦5.5
55 - 59	49	22	27	8.3	♦7.3	♦9.3
60 - 64	69	37	32	17.3	18.5	16.2
65 - 69	76	36	40	22.5	22.4	22.6
70 - 74	101	59	42	39.5	49.7	30.7
75 +	250	120	130	74.5	92.2	63.4
75 - 79	80	45	35	...	...	...
80 - 84	84	37	47	...	...	...
85 - 89	62	30	32	...	...	...
90 - 94	17	6	11	...	...	...
95 - 99	7	2	5	...	...	...
100 +	-	-	-	...	...	...
Unknown - Inconnu	6	2	4	..	..	..
Wallis and Futuna Islands - Îles Wallis et Futuna						
2008 (C)						
Total	90	51	39	...	...	...
0 - 4	1	1	-	...	...	...
5 - 9	-	-	-	...	...	...
10 - 14	1	1	-	...	...	...
15 - 19	2	1	1	...	...	...
20 - 24	4	3	1	...	...	...
25 - 29	4	4	-	...	...	...
30 - 34	3	3	-	...	...	...
35 - 39	2	1	1	...	...	...
40 - 44	-	-	-	...	...	...
45 - 49	2	1	1	...	...	...
50 - 54	2	1	1	...	...	...
55 - 59	4	2	2	...	...	...
60 - 64	5	4	1	...	...	...
65 - 69	12	8	4	...	...	...
70 - 74	15	9	6	...	...	...
75 - 79	13	4	9	...	...	...
80 - 84	11	4	7	...	...	...

19. Deaths by age and sex and age-specific death rates by sex: latest available year, 2007 - 2016
Décès et taux de mortalité selon l'âge et le sexe : dernière année disponible, 2007 - 2016 (continued - suite)

Continent, country or area, date, code[a] and age (in years) / Continent, pays ou zone, date, code[a] et âge (en années)	Number - Nombre			Rate - Taux		
	Both sexes Les deux sexes	Male Masculin	Female Féminin	Both sexes Les deux sexes	Male Masculin	Female Féminin
OCEANIA - OCÉANIE						
Wallis and Futuna Islands - Îles Wallis et Futuna						
2008 (C)						
85 - 89	5	3	2	...	...	...
90 - 94	4	1	3	...	...	...
95 - 99	-	-	-	...	...	...
100 + ...	-	-	-	...	...	...

FOOTNOTES - NOTES

✦ Rates based on 30 or fewer deaths. - Taux basés sur 30 décès ou moins.

Italics: estimates which are less reliable. - Italiques : estimations moins sûres.

* Provisional. - Données provisoires.

a 'Code' indicates the source of data, as follows:
C - Civil registration, estimated over 90% complete
U - Civil registration, estimated less than 90% complete
| - Other source, estimated reliable
+ - Data tabulated by date of registration rather than occurence
... - Information not available

Le 'Code' indique la source des données, comme suit :
C - Registres de l'état civil considérés complets à 90 p. 100 au moins
U - Registres de l'état civil qui ne sont pas considérés complets à 90 p. 100 au moins
| - Autre source, considérée pas douteuses
+ - Données exploitées selon la date de l'enregistrement et non la date de l'événement
... - Information pas disponible

1 Excluding live-born infants who died before their birth was registered. Data refer to Algerian population only. - Non compris les enfants nés vivants décédés avant l'enregistrement de leur naissance. Les données ne concernent que la population algérienne.
2 Source: Vital Statistics Report 2014. - Source: Vital Statistics Report 2014.
3 Data from civil registration centres of Brazzaville, Dolisie, Nkayi, Mossendijo and Ouesso communes. - Données issues des centres d'enregistrement des faits d'état-civil des communes de Brazzaville, Dolisie, Nkayi, Mossendijo et Ouesso.
4 Data refer to the 12 months preceding the census in September. - Les données se rapportent aux 12 mois précédant le recensement de septembre.
5 Unadjusted number of deaths in households referring to the 12 months preceding the census in March. - Le nombre non ajusté de décès des ménages ordinaires se rapportent aux 12 mois précédant le recensement de mars.
6 Unrevised data. - Les données n'ont pas été révisées.
7 Data refer to the 12 months preceding the census in June. - Les données se raportent aux 12 mois précédant le recensement de juin.
8 Data refer to the 12 months preceding the census in April. - Les données se rapportent aux douze mois précédant le recensement d'avril.
9 Excludes the islands of St. Brandon and Agalega. - Non compris les îles St. Brandon et Agalega.
10 Data refer to the 12 months preceding the census in August. - Les données se rapportent aux 12 mois précédant le recensement d'août.
11 Data refer to the 12 months preceding the census in April. The figures in this table are derived from survey data. They are representative only of private households, internally displaced persons, refugees and nomads, and do not include cattle camps, institutional households, homeless people or overnight travelers. - Les données se rapportent aux douze mois précédant le recensement d'avril. Les chiffres de ce tableau proviennent de données d'enquête. Ils représentent exclusivement les ménages privés et les déplacés, réfugiés et nomades; ils ne comprennent ni les personnes se trouvant dans des camps pastoraux et des établissements collectifs, ni les sans-abri, ni les voyageurs.
12 Data refer to the 12 months preceding the census in May. - Les données se rapportent aux 12 mois précédant le recensement de mai.

13 Source: National Office of Births and Deaths. - Source : Le bureau national des naissances et des décès.
14 Figures for male and female may not add up to the total, since they do not include the category "Unknown". - La somme des chiffres indiqués pour les sexes masculin et féminin peut n'être pas égale au total parce qu'elle n'inclut pas la catégorie " inconnue ".
15 Data refer to the 12 months preceding the census in October. - Les données se rapportent aux 12 mois précédant le recensement de octobre.
16 Excluding visitors. - Ne comprend pas les visiteurs.
17 Excluding non-residents and foreign service personnel and their dependants. - À l'exclusion des non-résidents et du personnel diplomatique et de leurs charges de famille.
18 Including Canadian residents temporarily in the United States, but excluding United States residents temporarily in Canada. - Y compris les résidents canadiens se trouvant temporairement aux Etats-Unis, mais ne comprenant pas les résidents des Etats-Unis se trouvant temporairement au Canada.
19 Data refer to population in private households. Data refer to period from 1 January 2010 to 3 April 2011. - Les données portent sur la population des ménages privés. Les données concernent la période du 1 janvier 2010 au 3 avril 2011.
20 Excluding live-born infants who died before their birth was registered. - Non compris les enfants nés vivants décédés avant l'enregistrement de leur naissance.
21 Data refer to resident population only. - Pour la population résidante seulement.
22 Data refer to resident and non resident deaths that occurred in Saint Vincent and the Grenadines. - Les données concernent les décès de résidents et de non-résidents survenus à St Vincent-et-les-Grenadines.
23 Data refer to the 12 months preceding the census in November. - Données se rapportent aux 12 mois précédant le recensement de novembre.
24 Including deaths abroad and deaths of unknown place of residence. - Y compris décès à l'étranger et décès dont le lieu de résidence n'est pas connu.
25 Excludes nomadic Indian tribes. - Non compris les tribus d'Indiens nomades.
26 Source: Reports of the Ministry of Health. - Source : Rapports du Ministère de la Santé.
27 Excluding infants born alive of less than 28 weeks' gestation, of less than 1 000 g in weight and 35 cm in length, who die within seven days of birth. - Non compris les enfants nés vivants après moins de 28 semaines de gestations, pesant moins de 1 000 g, mesurant moins de 35 cm et décédés dans les sept jours qui ont suivi leur naissance.
28 Sources: Births and Deaths National Registration System database, and medical records of government hospitals. - Les sources: Les bases de données des << Births and Deaths National Registration System >> et les dossiers médicaux des hôpitaux du gouvernement.
29 For statistical purposes, the data for China do not include those for the Hong Kong Special Administrative Region (Hong Kong SAR), Macao Special Administrative Region (Macao SAR) and Taiwan province of China. Data refer to the 12 months preceding the census in November. - Pour la présentation des statistiques, les données pour la Chine ne comprennent pas la Région Administrative Spéciale de Hong Kong (Hong Kong RAS), la Région Administrative Spéciale de Macao (Macao RAS) et Taïwan province de Chine. Données se rapportant aux 12 mois précédant le recensement de novembre.
30 Data refer to government controlled areas. Data refer to deaths of residents only. - Les données se rapportent aux zones contrôlées par le Gouvernement. Les données renvoient aux décès de résidents uniquement.
31 Data are from 1 January 2009 to 1 May 2010. - Les données vont du 1er janvier 2009 au 1er mai 2010.

[32] Data refer to the Iranian Year which begins on 21 March and ends on 20 March of the following year. Data refer to current deaths; excluding delayed registrations. - Les données concernent l'année iranienne, qui commence le 21 mars et se termine le 20 mars de l'année suivante. Les données se rapportent aux décès actuels; les déclarations tardives des décès ne sont pas compris.

[33] Includes data for East Jerusalem and Israeli residents in certain other territories under occupation by Israeli military forces since June 1967. Including deaths abroad of Israeli residents who were out of the country for less than a year. - Y compris les données pour Jérusalem-Est et les résidents israéliens dans certains autres territoires occupés depuis 1967 par les forces armées israéliennes. Y compris les décès à l'étranger de résidents israéliens qui ont quitté le pays depuis moins d'un an.

[34] Data refer to Japanese nationals in Japan only. - Les données se raportent aux nationaux japonais au Japon seulement.

[35] Data are from Vital Registration System (VRS). - Les données proviennent du système d'enregistrement des faits d'état civil.

[36] Data from Births and Deaths Notification System (Ministry of Health and all health care providers). - Les données proviennent du système de notification des naissances et des décès (Ministère de la santé et tous prestataires de soins de santé).

[37] Excluding data for the Pakistan-held part of Jammu and Kashmir, the final status of which has not yet been determined. Based on the results of the Pakistan Demographic Survey. - Non compris les données concernant la partie du Jammu et Cachemire occupée par le Pakistan dont le statut définitif n'a pas été déterminé. Données extraites de l'enquête démographique effectuée par le Pakistan.

[38] Excluding alien armed forces, civilian aliens employed by armed forces, and foreign diplomatic personnel and their dependants. - Non compris les militaires étrangers, les civils étrangers employés par les forces armées ni le personnel diplomatique étranger et les membres de leur famille les accompagnant.

[39] Data refer to Saudi Arabian nationals only. Based on 2010 population census and 2016 demographic survey. - Les données ne concernent que les ressortissants saoudiens. D'après le recensement de la population de 2010 et l'enquête démographique de 2016.

[40] Source: Palestinian Central Bureau of Statistics, Population Register, updated version 22/02/2016. - Source: Bureau central de statistique palestinien, registre de la population, version actualisée jusqu'au 22/02/2016.

[41] Including deaths of nationals abroad. - Y compris les décès des nationaux survenus à l'étranger.

[42] Including armed forces stationed outside the country, but excluding alien armed forces stationed in the area. - Y compris les militaires nationaux hors du pays, mais non compris les militaires étrangers en garnison sur le territoire.

[43] Excluding Faeroe Islands and Greenland shown separately, if available. - Non compris les Iles Féroé et le Groenland, qui font l'objet de rubriques distinctes, si disponible.

[44] Including armed forces stationed outside the country. - Y compris les militaires nationaux hors du pays.

[45] Data include the deceased persons with Hungarian usual residence regardless of whether the death occurred in Hungary or in a foreign country, and do not include the deceased persons with foreign country usual residence. - Les données comprennent tous les décès survenus alors que leur résidence habituelle était en Hongrie, que le décès ait eu lieu en Hongrie ou dans un pays étranger, et ne comprennent pas les décès des personnes dont la residence habituelle était dans un pays étranger.

[46] Including residents outside the country if listed in a Netherlands population register. - Englobe les résidents se trouvant à l'étranger à condition qu'ils soient inscrits sur le registre de population des Pays-Bas.

[47] Including residents temporarily outside the country. - Y compris les résidents se trouvant temporairement hors du pays.

[48] Data refer to usually resident population. - Les données concernent la population habituellement résidente.

[49] Excluding Transnistria and the municipality of Bender. - Les données ne tiennent pas compte de l'information sur la Transnistria et la municipalité de Bender.

[50] Excludes data for Kosovo and Metohia. - Sans les données pour le Kosovo et Metohie.

[51] Data includes deaths resulting from births with weight 500 g and more (if weight is unknown - with length 25 cm and more, or with gestation during 22 weeks or more). The Government of Ukraine has informed the United Nations that it is not in a position to provide statistical data concerning the Autonomous Republic of Crimea and the city of Sevastopol. - Y compris les décès de nouveau-nés de 500 g ou plus (si le poids est inconnu – de 25 cm de long ou plus, ou après une grossesse de 22 semaines ou plus). Le gouvernement Ukrainien a informé l'ONU qu'il n'est pas en mesure de fournir des données statistiques concernant la République autonome de Crimée et la ville de Sébastopol.

[52] Excluding Channel Islands (Guernsey and Jersey) and Isle of Man, shown separately, if available. - Non compris les îles Anglo-Normandes (Guernesey et Jersey) et l'île de Man, qui font l'objet de rubriques distinctes, si disponible.

[53] Data for certain cells suppressed by national statistical office for confidentiality reasons. - Les données pour certaines cases ont été supprimées par le bureau national de statistiques pour des raisons de confidentialité.

[54] Excluding Niue, shown separately, which is part of Cook Islands, but because of remoteness is administered separately. Unrevised data. - Non compris Nioué, qui fait l'objet d'une rubrique distincte et qui fait partie des îles Cook, mais qui, en raison de son éloignement, est administrée séparément. Les données n'ont pas été révisées.

[55] Excluding deaths of unknown age or sex. - Les données ne comprennent pas les décès d'âge ou de sexe inconnus.

[56] Random rounding to base 3 is applied in this table as a confidentiality measure. - Les chiffres sont arrondis à la base 3 de manière aléatoire, pour des raisons de confidentialité.

[57] Includes deaths occurred in New Zealand but buried in Niue and deaths occurred in Niue but buried elsewhere. - Y compris les personnes décédées en Nouvelle-Zélande qui sont enterrées à Nioué et les personnes décédées à Nioué qui sont enterrées ailleurs.

Table 20 - *Demographic Yearbook 2016*

Table 20 presents the life tables' probabilities of dying in the five year interval following specified ages ($_5q_x$), for each sex, for the latest available year between 2002 and 2016. The probabilities are multiplied by a thousand, that is, the values presented in the table are $1000*_5q_x$.

Male and female probabilities of dying are shown separately for selected ages beginning at birth and proceeding at every fifth age thereafter up to age 100.

The values presented in the table are derived by the United Nations Statistics Division from the official complete life tables reported by the countries or areas.

Data are shown with one decimal regardless of the number of digits provided in the original computation.

The life table is a statistical device for summarizing the mortality experience of a population, from which the probability of dying, survivorship and expectation of life can be calculated. It is based on the assumption that the theoretical cohort is subject, throughout its existence, to the age-specific mortality rates observed at a particular time. Thus, levels of mortality prevailing at the time a life table is constructed are assumed to remain unchanged into the future until all members of the cohort have died.

Reliability of data: The values shown in this table are derived from official complete life tables. It is assumed that, if necessary, the basic data (population and deaths classified by age and sex) have been adjusted for deficiencies before their use in constructing the complete life tables.

Limitations: The life tables' probabilities of dying are subject to the same qualifications as have been set forth for population statistics in general and death statistics in particular, as discussed in sections 3 and 4, respectively, of the Technical Notes. They must be interpreted strictly using the underlying assumption that surviving cohorts are subjected to the same age-specific mortality rates of the period to which the life table refers.

Earlier data: The life tables' probabilities of dying at specified ages, for each sex, have been shown in previous issues of the *Demographic Yearbook*. For information on specific years covered, the reader should consult the Historical Index.

Tableau 20 – *Annuaire démographique 2016*

Le tableau 20 donne les probabilités de décès dans l'intervalle de cinq ans que suit l'âge spécifié ($_5q_x$), pour chaque sexe, pour la dernière année disponible entre 2002 et 2016. Les probabilités sont multipliées par mille, c'est-à-dire que les valeurs indiquées dans le tableau sont égales à 1000*$_5q_x$.

Les probabilités de décès sont indiquées séparément pour les hommes et les femmes pour différents âges, depuis la naissance puis tous les cinq ans jusqu'à 100 ans.

Les chiffres indiqués dans ce tableau ont été calculés par la Division de statistique de l'Organisation des Nations Unies à partir des tables de mortalité complètes communiquées par les pays ou zones.

Les données sont arrondies à la première décimale, indépendamment du nombre de décimales qui figurent dans le calcul initial.

La table de mortalité est un moyen statistique que s'utilise pour donner un aperçu complet de la mortalité d'une population incluant les probabilités de décès et l'espérance de vie à chaque âge. Les tables de mortalité reposent sur l'hypothèse que chaque cohorte théoriquement distinguée connaît, pendant toute son existence, les taux de mortalité par âge observé à un moment donné. Les taux de mortalité correspondant à l'époque à laquelle sont calculées les tables de mortalité sont ainsi censés demeurer inchangées dans l'avenir jusqu'au décès de tous les membres de la cohorte.

Fiabilité des donnés : Les chiffres indiqués dans ce tableau ont été calculés à partir des tables officielles de mortalité complètes. En ce qui concerne les chiffres extraits de tables officielles de mortalité, on part du principe que les données de base (effectif de la population et nombre de décès selon l'âge et le sexe) ont été ajustées, en tant que de besoin, avant de servir à l'établissement de la table de mortalité.

Insuffisance des données : Les probabilités de décès appellent les mêmes réserves que celles qui ont été formulées à propos des statistiques de la population en général et des statistiques de mortalité en particulier (voir les sections 3 et 4 des Notes techniques). Lorsque l'on interprète les données, il ne faut jamais perdre de vue que, par hypothèse, les cohortes de survivants sont soumises, pour chaque âge, aux conditions de mortalité de la période visée par la table de mortalité.

Données publiées antérieurement : Les probabilités de décès pour chaque sexe figuraient déjà dans des éditions antérieures de *l'Annuaire démographique*. Pour plus de précisions concernant les années pour lesquelles ces données ont été publiées, se reporter à l'index historique.

20. Probability of dying in the five year interval following specified age (5qx), by sex, latest available year: 2002 - 2016
Probabilité de décès dans l'intervalle de cinq ans qui suit un âge donné (5qx), par sexe, dernière année disponible : 2002 - 2016

Continent, country or area and date / Continent, pays ou zone et date	0	5	10	15	20	25	30	35	40	45	50	55	60	65	70	75	80	85	90	95	100

AFRICA - AFRIQUE

Republic of South Sudan - République de Soudan du Sud
2010

	0	5	10	15	20	25	30	35	40	45	50	55	60	65	70	75	80	85	90	95	100
Male - Hommes	130.6	14.1	10.8	18.5	25.6	27.0	28.8	33.1	40.1	51.8	70.0	98.7	143.7	213.2	316.6	457.7	624.2	785.1	907.0	...	...
Female - Femmes	111.9	13.7	10.7	18.4	25.9	27.8	30.2	35.2	43.3	56.8	78.0	111.6	164.6	245.8	362.8	513.5	678.3	826.7	931.7	...	...

Zimbabwe
2001 - 2002

	0	5	10	15	20	25	30	35	40	45	50	55	60	65	70	75	80	85	90	95	100
Male - Hommes	116.9	18.0	12.8	12.2	30.6	70.9	129.9	193.2	193.5	186.2	175.7	177.3	167.1	186.5	197.2	270.7	297.7	432.4	545.1	...	...
Female - Femmes	100.5	15.2	10.8	15.2	46.7	97.4	141.4	159.8	125.9	122.9	101.0	99.6	100.9	122.5	128.8	161.1	223.5	304.5	438.0	...	...

AMERICA, NORTH - AMÉRIQUE DU NORD

Canada
2010 - 2012

	0	5	10	15	20	25	30	35	40	45	50	55	60	65	70	75	80	85	90	95	100
Male - Hommes	6.0	0.4	0.6	2.4	3.8	3.8	4.0	5.0	7.6	11.9	18.3	28.5	44.8	71.2	113.9	182.7	290.9	451.9	656.9	831.4	*1000
Female - Femmes	5.1	0.4	0.5	1.2	1.5	1.6	2.2	2.9	4.9	8.0	12.1	18.3	28.5	45.4	74.0	123.2	207.3	347.4	552.7	762.9	*1000

Costa Rica
2015

	0	5	10	15	20	25	30	35	40	45	50	55	60	65	70	75	80	85	90	95	100
Male - Hommes	9.4	0.9	1.2	3.5	6.0	7.0	7.9	9.2	11.8	16.3	23.6	34.7	52.8	82.6	126.5	197.9	294.3	422.1	585.0	757.8	*1000
Female - Femmes	7.7	0.5	0.9	1.5	1.9	2.0	2.7	3.6	5.2	8.4	12.5	20.6	32.6	53.0	84.4	139.5	233.3	366.5	533.8	720.1	*1000

Cuba
2011 - 2013

	0	5	10	15	20	25	30	35	40	45	50	55	60	65	70	75	80	85	90	95	100
Male - Hommes	6.0	1.0	1.3	2.4	3.5	4.5	5.7	7.3	10.5	17.5	29.3	44.9	67.2	100.5	148.8	223.2	334.7	477.3	602.9	645.4	*1000
Female - Femmes	5.6	0.9	0.9	1.4	1.9	2.4	3.0	4.1	6.5	11.0	18.7	29.3	44.6	67.0	104.8	168.7	270.2	421.1	577.7	655.4	*1000

Curaçao
2016

	0	5	10	15	20	25	30	35	40	45	50	55	60	65	70	75	80	85	90	95	100
Male - Hommes	9.6	0.4	0.5	2.1	5.8	7.2	7.2	8.9	11.0	15.4	28.1	49.3	69.2	103.7	158.6	226.0	359.1	525.1	701.4	841.0	...
Female - Femmes	14.6	0.3	0.2	0.7	1.8	2.5	2.9	3.9	6.2	8.9	12.1	19.1	33.3	53.2	83.1	148.5	257.1	388.1	571.7	776.1	...

Dominican Republic - République dominicaine
2010 - 2015

	0	5	10	15	20	25	30	35	40	45	50	55	60	65	70	75	80	85	90	95	100
Male - Hommes	33.8	1.5	2.2	6.6	12.0	13.8	15.2	17.5	21.3	28.4	42.9	61.1	86.0	127.0	178.3	282.0	*1000	...	...	...	...
Female - Femmes	25.6	1.4	1.5	2.8	4.8	6.6	8.4	10.7	14.3	19.4	30.9	45.6	64.3	98.8	145.1	253.9	*1000	...	...	...	...

Greenland - Groenland
2009 - 2013

	0	5	10	15	20	25	30	35	40	45	50	55	60	65	70	75	80	85	90	95	100
Male - Hommes	15.4	0.5	2.8	15.7	22.9	16.2	14.3	13.6	18.4	25.9	35.9	72.3	87.1	167.8	303.9	470.3	648.6	758.8	...	...	...
Female - Femmes	7.0	0.5	2.7	10.3	8.0	2.5	6.9	10.8	9.1	20.1	26.0	50.6	83.8	147.4	209.0	326.2	565.3	731.9	970.6	...	...

Guadeloupe
2002

	0	5	10	15	20	25	30	35	40	45	50	55	60	65	70	75	80	85	90	95	100
Male - Hommes	8.7	1.1	2.1	4.6	9.3	11.1	10.0	12.7	14.6	24.3	31.1	45.3	68.9	95.0	141.6	219.3	290.6	421.7	994.4	*1000	...
Female - Femmes	6.0	0.3	0.3	1.2	2.9	1.4	4.3	5.8	8.0	8.1	10.9	22.1	39.9	55.5	87.1	112.0	212.4	331.5	984.3	*1000	...

Jamaica - Jamaïque
2006

	0	5	10	15	20	25	30	35	40	45	50	55	60	65	70	75	80	85	90	95	100
Male - Hommes	31.7	2.8	2.5	4.5	6.5	6.5	7.0	9.4	14.5	23.2	37.5	60.5	96.9	153.2	236.8	353.8	502.7	667.6	817.2	921.8	*1000
Female - Femmes	18.0	1.3	1.1	1.7	2.6	3.4	4.3	5.9	8.7	13.9	22.8	38.0	63.2	104.5	169.8	268.2	405.3	574.1	747.0	883.6	*1000

Martinique
2007

	0	5	10	15	20	25	30	35	40	45	50	55	60	65	70	75	80	85	90	95	100
Male - Hommes	11.6	1.0	1.1	4.2	8.8	7.5	8.8	8.5	10.4	13.5	26.7	28.9	42.2	87.6	122.7	202.9	325.3	532.7	663.7	834.4	*1000
Female - Femmes	7.8	0.4	0.7	0.6	2.1	2.9	4.6	4.1	4.8	5.3	11.3	14.8	28.6	45.6	76.8	135.3	216.7	362.2	508.4	810.4	*1000

Mexico - Mexique
2005

	0	5	10	15	20	25	30	35	40	45	50	55	60	65	70	75	80	85	90	95	100
Male - Hommes	21.6	1.7	2.2	4.3	7.4	9.9	12.0	15.1	20.3	28.7	41.3	59.9	86.6	124.3	176.5	246.8	337.7	448.7	574.2	702.2	*1000
Female - Femmes	17.4	1.3	1.2	1.8	2.4	3.1	4.3	6.4	9.9	15.4	23.9	37.2	57.5	88.4	134.4	201.1	293.6	414.1	557.1	705.8	*1000

Panama[1]
2015

	0	5	10	15	20	25	30	35	40	45	50	55	60	65	70	75	80	85	90	95	100
Male - Hommes	21.7	2.0	2.4	7.1	12.8	14.3	13.2	12.7	14.5	19.2	27.5	40.6	60.2	89.0	130.8	189.7	270.1	374.8	501.4	639.9	*1000
Female - Femmes	16.5	1.3	1.4	2.4	3.4	4.3	5.3	6.6	8.4	11.4	16.3	24.3	37.3	58.2	91.1	141.9	217.7	324.7	464.0	623.8	*1000

569

20. Probability of dying in the five year interval following specified age (5qx), by sex, latest available year: 2002 - 2016
Probabilité de décès dans l'intervalle de cinq ans qui suit un âge donné (5qx), par sexe, dernière année disponible : 2002 - 2016 (continued - suite)

Continent, country or area and date / Continent, pays ou zone et date	0	5	10	15	20	25	30	35	40	45	50	55	60	65	70	75	80	85	90	95	100

Age (in years) - Age (en années)

AMERICA, NORTH - AMÉRIQUE DU NORD

Puerto Rico - Porto Rico
2014 - 2016

	0	5	10	15	20	25	30	35	40	45	50	55	60	65	70	75	80	85	90	95	100
Male - Hommes	8.1	0.4	0.6	3.8	10.0	10.7	11.4	12.2	14.4	20.7	31.5	46.3	64.7	88.0	123.6	176.5	276.1	*1000	...	...	...
Female - Femmes	7.1	0.5	0.3	1.0	1.5	2.6	3.3	4.8	6.7	9.8	14.9	21.0	31.6	45.8	73.4	121.4	201.2	*1000	...	...	...

United States of America - États-Unis d'Amérique
2014

	0	5	10	15	20	25	30	35	40	45	50	55	60	65	70	75	80	85	90	95	100
Male - Hommes	7.4	0.6	0.8	3.1	6.1	7.0	7.9	9.3	12.2	18.8	29.8	45.1	63.7	86.6	130.0	198.4	311.2	481.1	670.9	828.2	*1000
Female - Femmes	6.2	0.5	0.6	1.3	2.2	2.9	3.8	5.4	7.9	12.1	18.9	27.3	38.4	56.6	89.8	145.1	239.4	390.6	588.0	774.4	*1000

AMERICA, SOUTH - AMÉRIQUE DU SUD

Argentina - Argentine
2008 - 2010

	0	5	10	15	20	25	30	35	40	45	50	55	60	65	70	75	80	85	90	95	100
Male - Hommes	15.8	1.3	1.8	5.3	7.5	7.9	8.1	10.0	14.5	22.1	37.3	59.5	89.5	133.8	194.0	289.6	431.2	568.1	692.6	804.3	*1000
Female - Femmes	13.0	1.0	1.2	2.2	2.6	3.1	4.0	5.7	8.4	13.2	20.4	31.0	45.5	68.2	105.9	175.1	309.8	460.7	614.6	762.3	*1000

Bolivia (Plurinational State of) - Bolivie (État plurinational de)[2]
2016 - 2017

	0	5	10	15	20	25	30	35	40	45	50	55	60	65	70	75	80	85	90	95	100
Male - Hommes	44.2	5.3	4.1	8.9	13.6	14.2	16.1	18.9	24.3	30.8	41.6	57.2	83.1	117.2	167.4	233.2	329.5	416.5	609.4	*1000	...
Female - Femmes	34.5	3.5	2.4	4.7	5.3	5.9	7.4	9.9	14.4	20.0	27.8	39.3	57.6	84.3	119.8	165.8	236.7	317.6	487.2	*1000	...

Brazil - Brésil
2015

	0	5	10	15	20	25	30	35	40	45	50	55	60	65	70	75	80	85	90	95	100
Male - Hommes	17.4	1.5	1.9	8.2	12.5	12.6	13.5	15.7	20.2	28.1	40.3	56.8	79.0	114.1	168.7	246.7	*1000	...	...	...	...
Female - Femmes	14.7	1.1	1.2	2.2	2.8	3.5	4.7	6.4	9.6	14.8	21.7	31.6	46.7	71.9	112.3	173.9	*1000	...	...	...	...

Chile - Chili
2014

	0	5	10	15	20	25	30	35	40	45	50	55	60	65	70	75	80	85	90	95	100
Male - Hommes	8.5	0.8	0.9	2.4	4.3	5.5	6.4	8.1	10.9	15.9	23.5	35.8	56.7	89.9	141.1	212.3	366.8	514.5	...	...	...
Female - Femmes	8.2	0.6	0.7	1.1	1.5	1.8	2.4	3.5	5.2	8.0	12.7	20.3	32.7	53.0	85.7	136.9	249.3	383.1	...	...	...

Ecuador - Équateur[3]
2010 - 2017

	0	5	10	15	20	25	30	35	40	45	50	55	60	65	70	75	80	85	90	95	100
Male - Hommes	21.7	0.9	1.1	3.1	4.6	6.6	9.7	10.9	13.1	19.4	28.9	42.2	67.5	103.3	163.0	251.4	380.5	549.7	722.2	853.7	*1000
Female - Femmes	18.6	0.9	0.9	1.8	2.2	2.7	2.9	3.9	6.1	9.0	13.7	20.6	32.6	54.4	96.6	177.4	312.9	496.7	688.4	841.1	*1000

French Guiana - Guyane française
2007

	0	5	10	15	20	25	30	35	40	45	50	55	60	65	70	75	80	85	90	95	100
Male - Hommes	16.3	1.5	2.1	4.9	7.7	8.1	10.0	14.0	17.2	29.4	16.0	32.3	52.4	79.5	135.5	261.3	306.7	474.0	733.7	...	...
Female - Femmes	15.1	1.9	1.3	1.4	1.2	3.0	4.6	4.2	11.9	11.0	10.4	11.6	26.7	85.4	77.4	203.8	253.1	321.1	434.3	...	...

Uruguay
2004

	0	5	10	15	20	25	30	35	40	45	50	55	60	65	70	75	80	85	90	95	100
Male - Hommes	20.0	1.3	1.3	3.5	5.8	6.8	7.2	9.0	12.8	21.2	36.4	62.2	95.4	145.2	204.6	305.7	430.5	610.5	776.7	862.5	*1000
Female - Femmes	15.5	1.0	1.1	1.6	1.9	2.7	3.8	5.2	7.9	12.5	19.4	30.5	41.2	63.4	97.2	177.7	292.9	472.0	654.3	820.5	*1000

ASIA - ASIE

Armenia - Arménie
2014 - 2015

	0	5	10	15	20	25	30	35	40	45	50	55	60	65	70	75	80	85	90	95	100
Male - Hommes	11.3	1.2	1.1	3.4	5.0	5.2	5.7	8.9	17.1	29.4	46.2	65.1	95.3	144.6	227.1	313.3	439.7	604.3	760.1	926.1	...
Female - Femmes	9.6	1.1	0.6	1.0	1.4	1.3	2.0	4.0	6.6	11.2	17.0	24.8	42.9	68.3	191.6	218.8	373.3	627.6	906.9	943.9	...

Azerbaijan - Azerbaïdjan
2015

	0	5	10	15	20	25	30	35	40	45	50	55	60	65	70	75	80	85	90	95	100
Male - Hommes	15.7	1.5	1.7	2.7	4.3	4.4	6.2	9.3	13.4	23.2	37.9	59.1	94.7	133.7	203.5	296.6	413.1	537.9	500.7	449.1	...
Female - Femmes	12.4	1.2	1.2	1.7	1.9	2.3	2.5	3.7	5.9	9.6	16.8	29.1	52.3	80.9	139.7	250.3	383.9	577.7	623.7	689.3	...

20. Probability of dying in the five year interval following specified age (5qx), by sex, latest available year: 2002 - 2016
Probabilité de décès dans l'intervalle de cinq ans qui suit un âge donné (5qx), par sexe, dernière année disponible : 2002 - 2016 (continued - suite)

Continent, country or area and date / Continent, pays ou zone et date	Age (in years) - Age (en années)																				
	0	5	10	15	20	25	30	35	40	45	50	55	60	65	70	75	80	85	90	95	100

ASIA - ASIE

China, Hong Kong SAR - Chine, Hong Kong RAS
2016
Male - Hommes	2.7	0.4	0.4	1.0	1.6	2.3	3.1	4.2	6.2	9.7	15.6	26.2	40.8	63.1	102.2	161.4	263.7	408.3	586.1	768.1	*1000
Female - Femmes	2.4	0.3	0.4	0.7	0.8	1.0	1.2	2.0	3.6	5.4	8.5	12.9	19.7	29.5	47.2	83.1	156.1	270.7	434.2	632.8	*1000

China, Macao SAR - Chine, Macao RAS
2002 - 2005
Male - Hommes	7.2	0.6	0.4	1.7	3.9	5.4	6.2	7.6	9.0	13.6	17.8	25.8	43.1	72.1	128.9	239.9	369.5	574.4	841.2	991.4	*1000
Female - Femmes	5.2	0.4	0.2	0.9	1.5	1.9	2.3	3.8	4.7	5.9	7.4	10.9	19.3	33.3	70.4	186.2	317.0	485.2	717.3	923.7	*1000

Israel - Israël[4]
2011 - 2015
Male - Hommes	4.4	0.5	0.7	1.7	2.6	2.7	2.9	3.9	6.2	10.6	17.7	27.9	43.1	68.2	111.6	183.8	295.0	445.9	616.3	770.7	*1000
Female - Femmes	3.8	0.4	0.4	0.6	0.9	1.1	1.5	2.3	3.7	6.2	10.0	15.5	24.3	40.3	71.8	131.6	236.9	398.2	595.7	777.6	*1000

Japan - Japon[5]
2015
Male - Hommes	2.9	0.5	0.5	1.3	2.5	2.7	3.2	4.1	6.2	10.0	16.2	25.7	41.2	65.8	100.6	160.7	278.5	450.1	652.9	810.7	...
Female - Femmes	2.5	0.4	0.4	0.7	1.0	1.3	1.7	2.4	3.7	5.8	8.9	12.3	18.0	27.3	43.9	77.2	150.4	286.0	501.4	728.1	...

Kazakhstan
2012
Male - Hommes	18.1	2.1	2.1	4.9	9.5	15.0	22.5	30.6	37.5	49.5	72.7	107.0	157.3	204.8	286.8	397.7	531.1	638.2	732.6	812.3	...
Female - Femmes	14.5	1.6	1.2	2.4	3.3	4.9	7.4	10.3	13.8	18.6	28.5	43.8	68.1	99.5	161.7	268.0	427.7	602.1	790.3	887.7	...

Kyrgyzstan - Kirghizstan
2015
Male - Hommes	22.9	1.5	2.3	4.3	6.2	8.9	11.9	21.7	30.9	38.6	54.3	79.5	124.9	168.6	326.8	435.7	634.3	807.2	905.6	954.3	*1000
Female - Femmes	19.4	1.0	1.3	2.4	2.7	3.2	5.7	8.5	11.4	16.9	23.5	37.8	56.8	85.9	178.9	260.5	435.2	633.1	776.1	908.6	*1000

Qatar
2006
Male - Hommes	10.2	0.8	1.8	9.4	8.9	6.5	5.6	6.6	7.1	9.0	16.1	22.1	42.2	88.0	167.5	248.6	376.7	*1000	...	...	...
Female - Femmes	9.0	1.3	0.9	2.2	1.4	2.4	1.2	1.8	3.8	6.7	9.8	22.1	76.0	120.2	253.6	354.1	348.3	*1000	...	...	...

Republic of Korea - République de Corée
2015
Male - Hommes	3.6	0.5	0.5	1.3	2.1	3.0	3.7	5.0	8.3	13.8	21.6	31.0	45.8	68.5	117.2	207.6	336.6	502.6	678.1	825.9	*1000
Female - Femmes	3.1	0.4	0.3	0.7	1.1	1.7	2.4	3.0	4.1	5.8	7.7	10.8	16.3	26.8	52.9	107.5	213.4	381.9	586.0	772.8	*1000

Singapore - Singapour[6]
2016
Male - Hommes	3.0	0.4	0.7	1.2	1.5	1.9	2.4	3.3	5.6	9.4	15.8	26.7	42.0	68.1	113.1	184.3	285.8	438.0	620.4	796.5	*1000
Female - Femmes	2.3	0.2	0.5	0.7	0.9	1.1	1.4	1.9	3.4	5.6	9.3	15.0	22.4	36.0	63.5	117.0	202.5	341.1	523.3	716.6	*1000

Turkey - Turquie
2013 - 2015
Male - Hommes	14.4	1.4	1.7	3.2	3.8	3.7	4.0	5.2	8.2	14.3	25.1	42.6	68.4	106.8	169.2	258.2	387.5	552.7	699.7	800.1	*1000
Female - Femmes	12.8	1.1	1.0	1.3	1.4	1.5	1.9	2.9	4.5	7.3	11.6	19.1	32.2	56.4	103.9	180.9	301.3	460.0	609.4	706.9	*1000

EUROPE

Austria - Autriche
2015
Male - Hommes	3.9	0.4	0.6	2.0	3.1	2.6	3.3	5.0	7.0	11.3	20.2	33.3	55.0	86.0	125.2	187.3	318.4	515.1	707.9	901.4	...
Female - Femmes	3.2	0.2	0.5	0.7	1.1	1.2	1.4	2.5	4.2	6.4	10.0	17.9	28.7	46.5	67.6	113.5	222.1	421.5	654.5	848.1	...

Belarus - Bélarus
2015
Male - Hommes	4.2	0.8	0.8	2.3	5.2	8.0	12.7	19.6	28.3	42.9	61.6	94.4	142.2	188.2	262.1	361.5	482.8	620.0	757.8	874.7	...
Female - Femmes	3.3	0.6	0.7	1.1	1.4	2.5	4.0	5.7	9.2	12.8	18.8	29.2	46.6	71.1	115.9	210.7	349.6	531.6	731.6	895.7	...

Belgium - Belgique[7]
2015
Male - Hommes	4.2	0.5	0.4	1.4	3.2	3.0	4.0	5.4	7.7	12.4	20.1	35.5	55.2	81.7	122.3	193.8	315.6	506.2	717.7	872.7	*1000
Female - Femmes	3.6	0.4	0.5	0.8	1.1	1.3	2.0	2.8	4.9	8.3	12.6	21.3	33.1	44.8	71.3	119.0	222.4	406.4	643.5	832.8	*1000

Bulgaria - Bulgarie
2013 - 2015
Male - Hommes	9.0	1.0	1.2	3.1	4.7	4.8	7.2	10.6	16.0	30.2	50.7	78.1	116.6	157.4	214.4	314.6	449.9	622.7	792.3	872.9	...
Female - Femmes	8.2	0.8	0.7	1.4	1.9	2.1	3.2	4.8	9.1	13.4	22.7	31.9	47.3	70.4	118.1	215.0	374.9	575.1	747.2	891.2	...

20. Probability of dying in the five year interval following specified age (5qx), by sex, latest available year: 2002 - 2016
Probabilité de décès dans l'intervalle de cinq ans qui suit un âge donné (5qx), par sexe, dernière année disponible : 2002 - 2016 (continued - suite)

Continent, country or area and date / Continent, pays ou zone et date	0	5	10	15	20	25	30	35	40	45	50	55	60	65	70	75	80	85	90	95	100
EUROPE																					
Czechia - Tchéquie																					
2015																					
Male - Hommes	3.5	0.4	0.5	1.9	3.6	3.8	4.5	6.2	9.4	16.5	27.0	44.9	77.9	118.3	175.8	251.5	377.9	523.1	688.4	841.6	...
Female - Femmes	2.4	0.5	0.5	0.9	1.2	1.3	1.6	2.9	4.5	7.9	13.0	20.9	34.6	57.5	92.8	160.1	292.7	491.3	738.6	931.4	...
Denmark - Danemark[8]																					
2014 - 2015																					
Male - Hommes	5.0	0.4	0.4	0.9	2.2	2.4	2.8	4.4	6.8	12.0	20.9	34.0	56.8	81.0	127.0	195.4	328.3	516.4	714.2	871.2	...
Female - Femmes	4.2	0.2	0.4	0.6	0.9	0.9	1.7	2.3	4.0	7.3	13.3	22.0	36.0	53.3	83.8	142.8	248.9	394.8	622.1	801.7	...
Estonia - Estonie																					
2015																					
Male - Hommes	3.6	0.5	0.8	3.4	3.5	6.0	12.3	12.2	16.2	25.3	38.9	65.0	95.8	138.2	197.6	269.3	382.6	533.3	690.4	934.4	*1000
Female - Femmes	2.8	0.5	1.0	1.7	1.0	2.4	2.9	3.8	6.7	8.8	14.6	22.6	36.6	52.7	85.4	140.5	255.0	440.4	639.8	824.4	*1000
Faeroe Islands - Îles Féroé																					
2014 - 2015																					
Male - Hommes	18.5	0.0	2.9	5.8	3.1	0.0	3.7	0.0	3.2	23.4	17.7	38.4	33.0	43.1	117.4	162.5	361.1	481.0	826.0	916.7	...
Female - Femmes	3.2	0.0	0.0	0.0	0.0	0.0	0.0	0.0	6.6	15.2	3.3	13.4	14.7	54.3	51.2	130.8	184.5	378.9	742.7	807.5	...
Finland - Finlande[9]																					
2015																					
Male - Hommes	2.2	0.3	0.5	1.6	3.9	4.0	4.7	5.9	8.3	13.9	20.8	35.4	55.3	82.2	118.7	194.0	308.6	511.4	705.2	850.4	...
Female - Femmes	2.0	0.3	0.5	1.0	1.0	1.3	2.0	2.3	3.5	6.7	10.8	15.7	24.9	41.8	60.5	115.1	214.3	399.8	630.1	824.3	...
France[7]																					
2012 - 2014																					
Male - Hommes	4.5	0.4	0.5	1.7	3.2	3.7	4.4	6.0	9.4	15.6	25.5	39.9	56.0	75.4	106.5	165.6	278.4	456.8	667.7	833.6	...
Female - Femmes	3.7	0.4	0.4	0.8	1.1	1.3	1.8	2.9	4.8	8.2	12.6	18.1	24.7	34.4	52.8	90.7	174.9	333.5	559.6	770.7	...
Germany - Allemagne																					
2013 - 2015																					
Male - Hommes	4.2	0.4	0.4	1.5	2.3	2.6	3.5	4.8	7.4	12.9	22.9	38.2	59.2	85.8	126.1	198.4	334.8	518.8	724.9	868.7	...
Female - Femmes	3.6	0.3	0.4	0.8	1.0	1.1	1.7	2.6	4.2	7.3	12.7	20.1	30.7	46.9	70.1	123.7	238.9	426.5	657.8	828.6	...
Greece - Grèce																					
2015																					
Male - Hommes	4.8	0.3	0.6	2.0	3.0	3.6	4.4	5.5	8.1	14.3	23.9	39.9	58.5	86.2	122.6	197.9	327.1	478.1	624.3	777.3	...
Female - Femmes	4.3	0.4	0.5	0.8	0.9	1.0	1.7	2.6	4.2	6.9	10.5	16.4	23.9	39.1	66.6	133.2	280.0	456.4	610.0	767.5	...
Hungary - Hongrie																					
2015																					
Male - Hommes	5.6	0.7	0.6	1.9	3.1	3.6	5.0	7.3	12.5	26.0	50.1	80.7	116.5	154.6	207.2	308.7	427.6	627.5	865.8	988.2	...
Female - Femmes	4.8	0.4	0.5	0.7	1.2	1.6	2.0	3.5	6.4	12.7	23.4	37.8	54.5	76.3	114.9	194.5	333.3	564.3	833.8	981.3	...
Iceland - Islande																					
2014 - 2015																					
Male - Hommes	3.8	0.4	0.5	2.1	1.9	2.9	4.2	4.1	5.7	7.1	15.7	26.0	27.3	54.1	97.1	156.5	286.0	484.9	742.9	871.3	...
Female - Femmes	5.6	0.2	0.2	1.4	1.2	0.9	1.5	2.8	5.0	4.5	9.6	16.5	27.7	43.7	69.5	117.5	237.8	371.7	623.0	835.3	...
Ireland - Irlande																					
2005 - 2007																					
Male - Hommes	4.9	0.6	0.8	3.6	5.4	4.7	5.1	5.7	8.6	13.3	21.1	33.3	54.5	88.7	148.8	247.0	395.4	567.3	730.3	919.0	...
Female - Femmes	4.5	0.4	0.7	1.6	1.5	1.6	2.0	3.0	5.2	9.2	13.6	21.3	33.8	53.6	90.1	153.4	284.4	460.3	643.4	800.7	...
Italy - Italie																					
2014																					
Male - Hommes	3.9	0.4	0.5	1.5	2.3	2.5	2.9	4.0	5.9	9.7	15.8	25.6	42.3	66.3	107.7	172.9	299.4	481.1	670.0	841.3	...
Female - Femmes	3.3	0.3	0.4	0.7	0.8	1.0	1.3	2.2	3.5	5.9	9.2	14.4	22.6	35.4	58.7	102.8	200.9	367.6	573.6	785.0	...
Latvia - Lettonie																					
2006																					
Male - Hommes	10.5	1.4	1.6	3.0	6.2	11.3	18.6	28.3	40.6	56.3	76.6	104.3	143.2	199.8	282.1	397.7	547.0	712.6	...	...	...
Female - Femmes	12.7	1.3	1.2	1.5	2.2	3.2	4.8	7.3	11.2	17.3	26.7	41.0	63.0	96.1	145.1	215.5	312.2	436.5	...	...	...
Lithuania - Lituanie																					
2015																					
Male - Hommes	5.5	0.4	1.7	4.0	6.5	10.4	14.5	21.4	28.5	41.3	61.0	86.4	127.3	178.6	225.8	294.2	416.5	580.4	764.5	854.7	*1000
Female - Femmes	5.0	0.7	1.0	1.5	1.2	2.2	4.3	6.8	9.8	13.9	19.4	28.5	44.6	65.9	96.3	161.7	296.5	507.8	717.7	858.3	*1000
Luxembourg																					
2012 - 2014																					
Male - Hommes	2.2	0.6	0.6	1.9	2.0	2.4	3.4	4.5	6.2	10.1	21.3	33.6	49.9	77.2	118.4	183.7	310.5	529.7	671.1	*1000	...
Female - Femmes	2.1	0.1	0.2	1.2	0.7	1.5	1.8	2.3	3.2	7.0	11.4	17.7	26.3	45.8	66.7	117.2	214.0	397.4	628.4	*1000	...
Malta - Malte																					
2012																					
Male - Hommes	5.6	0.5	0.4	0.4	2.3	2.2	5.4	4.8	6.1	12.6	14.8	26.8	46.3	77.4	112.0	220.3	378.6	640.6	887.5	975.9	*1000
Female - Femmes	6.0	0.6	0.9	0.8	0.0	2.0	2.7	1.8	5.6	4.5	11.8	13.5	27.6	41.3	67.7	130.5	273.1	474.9	737.6	853.6	*1000

20. Probability of dying in the five year interval following specified age (5qx), by sex, latest available year: 2002 - 2016
Probabilité de décès dans l'intervalle de cinq ans qui suit un âge donné (5qx), par sexe, dernière année disponible :
2002 - 2016 (continued - suite)

Continent, country or area and date / Continent, pays ou zone et date	Age (in years) - Age (en années)																				
	0	5	10	15	20	25	30	35	40	45	50	55	60	65	70	75	80	85	90	95	100

EUROPE

Netherlands - Pays-Bas
2009

Male - Hommes	4.8	0.5	0.6	1.4	2.3	2.4	3.0	4.1	6.6	10.7	18.7	30.3	49.9	79.1	132.1	225.2	363.5	539.8	738.0	...	...
Female - Femmes	4.1	0.4	0.5	0.8	1.0	1.3	1.7	2.9	5.0	8.9	15.0	21.5	32.5	47.8	76.4	136.1	249.6	428.5	644.7	...	...

Norway - Norvège
2012

Male - Hommes	3.3	0.4	0.6	1.5	3.2	3.3	4.2	4.9	6.0	9.5	17.2	26.3	45.2	70.3	111.2	192.3	335.0	513.3	727.7	859.1	...
Female - Femmes	2.7	0.4	0.6	0.8	1.0	1.2	1.4	2.4	3.9	6.7	10.6	17.1	28.2	46.4	75.5	127.0	232.7	402.3	640.0	837.9	...

Poland - Pologne
2015

Male - Hommes	5.1	0.5	0.8	2.7	4.7	5.3	6.6	9.7	15.3	25.4	41.3	64.4	95.6	133.5	182.8	260.9	375.8	512.1	658.2	794.7	...
Female - Femmes	4.2	0.4	0.6	1.0	1.2	1.2	1.8	3.0	5.3	9.4	15.9	26.3	41.2	60.8	90.6	151.6	264.5	420.0	597.8	767.0	...

Portugal
2013 - 2015

Male - Hommes	4.2	0.5	0.6	1.6	2.5	3.2	3.7	5.9	10.6	17.6	28.2	40.5	55.3	79.5	122.4	198.4	345.5	643.5	865.1	971.1	...
Female - Femmes	2.9	0.4	0.4	0.8	0.9	1.2	1.7	2.8	4.6	7.5	11.0	15.2	22.4	36.8	61.2	116.0	237.8	514.8	785.2	946.8	...

Republic of Moldova - République de Moldova
2012

Male - Hommes	12.2	1.4	2.0	4.4	5.6	7.1	11.3	19.8	30.9	50.0	71.2	102.2	157.9	176.7	292.1	388.4	503.1	558.6	*1000	...	...
Female - Femmes	12.1	1.1	1.2	1.6	1.8	2.4	3.6	8.1	10.6	16.1	26.8	44.1	78.0	103.1	191.4	289.0	418.9	550.8	*1000	...	...

Romania - Roumanie
2013 - 2015

Male - Hommes	11.0	1.1	1.3	2.7	3.9	4.2	5.3	8.2	15.1	27.4	46.7	74.6	106.9	147.3	207.7	299.1	425.8	575.0	718.1	837.7	...
Female - Femmes	8.7	0.7	0.7	1.3	1.3	1.8	2.2	3.7	6.2	10.9	18.9	29.5	45.1	70.2	116.4	206.2	351.7	524.6	694.3	833.7	...

Russian Federation - Fédération de Russie
2012

Male - Hommes	11.6	1.7	1.8	5.4	11.6	19.0	30.3	36.8	42.1	56.4	77.9	110.6	155.6	193.8	273.2	361.6	481.9	577.2	694.9	771.0	*1000
Female - Femmes	9.5	1.1	1.2	2.5	3.4	5.6	9.0	11.6	14.3	18.9	26.2	39.5	57.7	84.1	137.1	230.5	372.9	543.1	716.4	825.0	*1000

San Marino - Saint-Marin
2013

Male - Hommes	2.4	0.6	1.2	2.7	2.7	2.3	0.9	2.6	5.2	3.0	10.8	28.9	31.0	53.1	81.0	167.4	300.6	458.9	674.0	923.3	...
Female - Femmes	1.3	0.0	0.7	1.5	0.7	0.0	0.8	0.7	4.4	4.9	8.3	11.7	16.6	30.5	56.9	81.0	171.2	350.3	539.6	820.0	...

Serbia - Serbie[10]
2010 - 2012

Male - Hommes	8.1	0.5	0.9	2.4	3.7	4.7	6.4	8.2	13.3	25.5	44.0	69.0	101.6	145.8	216.4	334.2	492.1	676.0	856.4	973.0	...
Female - Femmes	6.5	0.6	0.9	1.1	1.5	2.0	2.6	4.3	7.4	12.8	21.1	33.3	50.4	82.2	147.2	265.6	432.9	632.3	840.3	975.2	...

Slovakia - Slovaquie
2015

Male - Hommes	6.9	0.6	0.9	2.6	3.9	4.3	5.9	8.0	14.0	24.4	40.1	63.4	99.3	137.7	193.2	291.3	419.9	602.9	792.4	933.0	...
Female - Femmes	5.8	0.4	0.8	1.1	1.5	1.6	1.7	2.9	5.4	9.6	16.3	26.3	42.1	62.4	98.8	180.3	337.0	586.9	856.7	986.6	...

Slovenia - Slovénie
2015 - 2016

Male - Hommes	2.4	0.3	0.9	2.2	3.1	3.3	3.9	5.3	8.4	13.2	25.7	40.2	63.6	89.3	140.9	207.2	357.7	522.6	699.9	762.5	...
Female - Femmes	1.8	0.5	0.3	0.6	1.4	0.6	1.9	2.3	3.7	7.1	11.2	17.5	29.0	46.3	68.8	120.9	236.2	421.4	661.8	806.5	...

Spain - Espagne
2013

Male - Hommes	3.4	0.4	0.4	1.1	1.7	2.0	2.6	3.5	6.3	12.1	20.5	32.2	49.0	71.3	108.6	177.3	291.9	464.9	641.1	770.1	*1000
Female - Femmes	3.0	0.4	0.4	0.6	0.7	0.9	1.2	2.2	3.5	6.3	10.1	14.4	20.0	29.9	50.0	94.8	190.0	357.1	569.6	739.3	*1000

Sweden - Suède
2012

Male - Hommes	3.5	0.4	0.5	1.4	3.2	3.6	3.2	3.8	5.4	9.2	15.2	25.0	40.8	65.6	109.3	186.3	322.6	519.0	727.6	886.1	...
Female - Femmes	2.7	0.3	0.5	0.9	1.1	1.1	1.6	2.8	3.4	6.4	11.0	16.2	26.3	45.6	71.4	126.8	229.8	416.2	644.1	827.2	...

Switzerland - Suisse
2015

Male - Hommes	5.1	0.4	0.4	1.7	2.6	2.5	2.5	3.3	5.1	8.6	13.9	23.8	41.1	61.7	99.0	162.3	283.4	479.6	707.4	880.7	...
Female - Femmes	3.9	0.4	0.5	0.7	0.6	0.8	1.3	2.0	3.0	5.3	9.2	14.1	21.9	35.9	56.6	100.7	194.9	379.0	630.4	840.2	...

TFYR of Macedonia - L'ex-R. y. de Macédoine
2014

Male - Hommes	11.2	1.1	0.8	2.1	2.5	3.4	3.5	5.1	9.9	19.0	33.2	54.9	87.4	127.4	201.1	309.3	484.9	687.6	859.5	...	...
Female - Femmes	9.9	0.8	0.7	1.0	1.3	1.4	2.3	3.7	5.3	9.6	17.0	28.4	46.2	81.1	140.4	260.5	449.0	668.6	797.5	...	...

20. Probability of dying in the five year interval following specified age (5qx), by sex, latest available year: 2002 - 2016
Probabilité de décès dans l'intervalle de cinq ans qui suit un âge donné (5qx), par sexe, dernière année disponible : 2002 - 2016 (continued - suite)

Continent, country or area and date / Continent, pays ou zone et date	Age (in years) - Age (en années)																					
	0	5	10	15	20	25	30	35	40	45	50	55	60	65	70	75	80	85	90	95	100
EUROPE																					
Ukraine 2013																					
Male - Hommes	10.5	1.1	1.4	4.0	7.2	12.0	20.3	29.3	36.5	50.9	72.3	101.9	151.5	197.4	267.0	363.8	483.5	578.1	671.9	756.8	...
Female - Femmes	8.2	0.7	1.0	1.7	2.5	4.0	6.6	10.0	13.1	17.6	24.1	37.0	57.7	87.7	143.3	244.9	390.8	557.8	731.5	877.1	...
United Kingdom of Great Britain and Northern Ireland - Royaume-Uni de Grande-Bretagne et d'Irlande du Nord[11] 2012																					
Male - Hommes	5.3	0.5	0.6	1.6	2.5	3.1	4.1	5.8	8.7	12.5	18.6	29.9	46.9	73.2	120.2	192.2	316.4	492.9	672.1	843.0	...
Female - Femmes	4.2	0.4	0.4	0.8	1.1	1.5	2.2	3.2	5.2	8.2	13.0	20.6	31.2	48.8	81.1	137.4	243.5	406.5	604.7	791.1	...
OCEANIA - OCÉANIE																					
Australia - Australie 2013 - 2015																					
Male - Hommes	4.3	0.5	0.6	1.9	3.0	3.4	4.3	5.8	8.1	11.6	17.5	26.3	39.4	61.2	97.1	160.8	275.6	453.3	652.0	806.5	...
Female - Femmes	3.9	0.4	0.5	1.0	1.2	1.5	2.1	3.1	4.6	7.1	10.8	15.8	23.7	36.8	61.1	107.0	196.8	360.1	582.9	774.9	...
New Zealand - Nouvelle-Zélande 2012 - 2014																					
Male - Hommes	5.9	0.7	0.9	3.2	4.1	4.0	4.2	5.6	7.6	11.6	17.6	26.2	40.3	65.4	108.3	176.2	298.2	485.4	667.7	822.5	*1000
Female - Femmes	4.9	0.5	0.7	1.5	1.6	1.5	2.3	3.2	5.1	8.0	12.5	17.9	28.2	43.2	71.4	126.3	219.4	391.0	615.3	807.3	*1000

FOOTNOTES - NOTES

* Open-ended group (e.g. 80 years or over). - Groupe d'âge ouvert (par exemple, 80 ans ou plus).

[1] Excluding Indian jungle population. - Non compris les Indiens de la jungle.

[2] Data refer to the 12 months from 30 June 2016 to 30 June 2017. - Les données font référence aux douze mois de 30 juin 2016 à 30 juin 2017.

[3] Data based on the 2010 Population Census. Excludes nomadic Indian tribes. - Les données sont fondées sur le recensement de la population de 2010. Non compris les tribus d'Indiens nomades.

[4] Includes data for East Jerusalem and Israeli residents in certain other territories under occupation by Israeli military forces since June 1967. - Y compris les données pour Jérusalem-Est et les résidents israéliens dans certains autres territoires occupés depuis 1967 par les forces armées israéliennes.

[5] Data refer to Japanese nationals in Japan only. - Les données se raportent aux nationaux japonais au Japon seulement.

[6] Provisional data. Data refer to resident population which comprises Singapore citizens and permanent residents. - Données provisoires. Les données se rapportent à la population résidente composé des citoyens de Singapour et des résidents permanents.

[7] Provisional data. - Données provisoires.

[8] Excluding Faeroe Islands and Greenland shown separately, if available. - Non compris les Iles Féroé et le Groenland, qui font l'objet de rubriques distinctes, si disponible.

[9] Excluding Åland Islands. - Non compris les Îles d'Åland.

[10] Excludes data for Kosovo and Metohia. - Sans les données pour le Kosovo et Metohie.

[11] Excluding Channel Islands (Guernsey and Jersey) and Isle of Man, shown separately, if available. - Non compris les îles Anglo-Normandes (Guernesey et Jersey) et l'île de Man, qui font l'objet de rubriques distinctes, si disponible.

Table 21 - *Demographic Yearbook 2016*

Table 21 presents life expectancy at specified ages for each sex, for the latest available year between 1997 and 2016.

Description of variables: Life expectancy at age x, e_x, is defined as the average number of years of life remaining to persons who have reached age *x* if they continue to be subject to the mortality conditions of the period indicated in the life table.

Male and female life expectancy values are shown separately at selected ages beginning at birth and proceeding at every fifth age thereafter up to age 100.

The table shows life expectancy derived from a complete or abridged life table as reported by the country or area.

Data are shown with one decimal regardless of the number of digits provided in the original computation.

The life table is a statistical device for summarizing the mortality experience of a population, from which the probability of dying, survivorship and life expectancy can be calculated. It is based on the assumption that the theoretical cohort is subject, throughout its existence, to the age-specific mortality rates observed at a particular time period. Thus, levels of mortality prevailing at the time a life table is constructed are assumed to remain unchanged into the future until all members of the cohort have died.

Reliability of data: The values shown in this table come from official life tables. It is assumed that, if necessary, the basic data (population and deaths classified by age and sex) have been adjusted for deficiencies before their use in constructing the life tables.

Limitations: Life expectancy values are subject to the same qualifications as have been set forth for population statistics in general and death statistics in particular, as discussed in sections 3 and 4, respectively, of the Technical Notes. They must be interpreted strictly using the underlying assumption that surviving cohorts are subjected to the same age-specific mortality rates of the period to which the life table refers.

Earlier data: Life expectancy values at specified ages for each sex have been shown in previous issues of the *Demographic Yearbook*. For information on specific years covered, the reader should consult the Historical Index.

Tableau 21 – *Annuaire démographique 2016*

Le tableau 21 présente les espérances de vie à des âges déterminés, pour chaque sexe, pour la dernière année disponible entre 1997 et 2016.

Description des variables : L'espérance de vie à l'âge x, e_x, se définit comme le nombre moyen d'années restant à vivre aux hommes et aux femmes qui ont atteint l'âge *x*, à supposer qu'ils continuent de connaître les mêmes conditions de mortalité observées pendant la période sur laquelle porte la table de mortalité.

Les chiffres sont présentés séparément pour chaque sexe à partir de la naissance et puis tous les cinq ans jusqu'à 100 ans.

Dans le tableau figurent les espérances de vie calculées selon les tables de mortalité complètes ou abrégées communiquées par les pays et les zones.

Les données sont arrondies à la première décimale, indépendamment du nombre de décimales qui figurent dans le calcul initial.

La table de mortalité est un moyen statistique que s'utilise pour donner un aperçu complet de la mortalité d'une population incluant les probabilités de décès et l'espérance de vie à chaque âge. Les tables de mortalité reposent sur l'hypothèse que chaque cohorte théoriquement distinguée connaît, pendant toute son existence, les taux de mortalité par âge observé à un moment donné. Les taux de mortalité correspondant à l'époque à laquelle sont calculées les tables de mortalité sont ainsi censés demeurer inchangées dans l'avenir jusqu'au décès de tous les membres de la cohorte.

Fiabilité des donnés : Les chiffres figurant dans ce tableau proviennent de tables officielles de mortalité. En ce qui concerne les chiffres extraits de tables officielles de mortalité, on part du principe que les données de base (effectif de la population et nombre de décès selon l'âge et le sexe) ont été ajustées, en tant que de besoin, avant de servir à l'établissement de la table de mortalité.

Insuffisance des données : les espérances de vie appellent les mêmes réserves que celles qui ont été formulées à propos des statistiques de la population en général et des statistiques de mortalité en particulier (voir les sections 3 et 4 des Notes techniques). Lorsque l'on interprète les données, il ne faut jamais perdre de vue que, par hypothèse, les cohortes de survivants sont soumises, pour chaque âge, aux conditions de mortalité de la période visée par la table de mortalité.

Données publiées antérieurement : les espérances de vie à des âges déterminés pour chaque sexe figuraient déjà dans des éditions antérieures de *l'Annuaire démographique*. Pour plus de précisions concernant les années pour lesquelles ces données ont été publiées, se reporter à l'index historique.

21. Life expectancy at specified ages for each sex: latest available year, 1997 - 2016
Espérance de vie à un âge donné pour chaque sexe : dernière année disponible, 1997 - 2016

Continent, country or area and date / Continent, pays ou zone et date	0	5	10	15	20	25	30	35	40	45	50	55	60	65	70	75	80	85	90	95	100
AFRICA - AFRIQUE																					
Algeria - Algérie[1]																					
2016																					
Male - Hommes	77.1	74.2	69.3	64.4	59.6	54.9	50.1	45.4	40.7	36.0	31.4	27.0	22.7	18.8	15.1	11.7	8.8	6.5	...	...	...
Female - Femmes	78.2	75.1	70.2	65.3	60.5	55.6	50.7	45.9	41.2	36.5	31.9	27.4	23.0	18.9	14.9	11.2	7.9	5.3	...	...	...
Benin - Bénin[2]																					
2002																					
Male - Hommes	57.2	63.4	59.1	54.7	50.2	45.9	41.8	37.8	33.8	30.0	26.2	22.7	19.4	16.2	13.2	10.6	8.1	5.5	3.8	...	...
Female - Femmes	61.3	65.4	61.2	56.7	52.3	48.1	43.9	39.9	36.0	32.1	28.3	24.6	21.2	18.0	14.2	10.8	7.7	4.8	2.9	...	...
Botswana[3]																					
2016																					
Male - Hommes	64.9	62.0	57.4	52.6	48.1	43.9	40.3	37.3	34.4	31.7	28.4	24.9	21.3	17.7	14.1	10.4	6.7	...	...	...	...
Female - Femmes	65.9	62.8	58.1	53.3	48.6	44.1	39.8	36.0	32.5	29.2	25.7	22.3	19.0	15.6	12.4	9.1	5.8	...	...	...	...
Burkina Faso[4]																					
2006																					
Male - Hommes	55.8	60.0	55.9	51.3	46.9	42.8	38.6	34.5	30.5	26.6	22.8	19.3	16.0	12.9	10.3	8.1	6.2	4.8			
Female - Femmes	57.5	61.6	57.6	53.1	48.6	44.4	40.2	36.1	32.0	28.0	24.1	20.3	16.8	13.5	10.7	8.4	6.4	4.9			
Burundi																					
2008																					
Male - Hommes	46.0	49.7	46.5	42.5	39.0	35.8	32.4	28.9	25.4	21.9	18.6	15.3	12.3	9.5	7.2	5.2	3.8	...	...	...	...
Female - Femmes	51.8	55.4	52.1	47.9	44.0	40.3	36.7	33.0	29.2	25.4	21.5	17.8	14.2	11.0	8.3	6.0	4.4	...	...	...	...
2016																					
Male - Hommes	56.3	...	...	...	...	...	...	...	...	...	...	...	...	...	...	...	...	...	...	...	...
Female - Femmes	60.5	...	...	...	...	...	...	...	...	...	...	...	...	...	...	...	...	...	...	...	...
Côte d'Ivoire																					
2016																					
Male - Hommes	54.9	...	...	...	...	...	...	...	...	...	...	...	...	...	...	...	...	...	...	...	...
Female - Femmes	57.5	...	...	...	...	...	...	...	...	...	...	...	...	...	...	...	...	...	...	...	...
Djibouti[5]																					
2002																					
Male - Hommes	51.8	...	...	...	...	...	...	...	...	...	...	...	...	...	...	...	...	...	...	...	...
Female - Femmes	54.1	...	...	...	...	...	...	...	...	...	...	...	...	...	...	...	...	...	...	...	...
Egypt - Égypte																					
2016																					
Male - Hommes	70.5	67.0	62.1	57.2	52.4	47.5	42.7	37.9	33.1	28.5	24.1	20.1	16.3	12.8	9.5	6.6	3.6	...	...	...	...
Female - Femmes	73.3	69.6	64.7	59.7	54.8	49.9	44.9	40.0	35.1	30.3	25.6	21.1	16.9	12.9	9.3	6.0	2.4	...	...	...	...
Equatorial Guinea - Guinée équatoriale																					
2001																					
Male - Hommes	...	...	...	...	...	...	...	...	...	...	...	...	...	...	...	...	...	...	...	...	...
Female - Femmes	59.3	...	...	...	...	...	...	...	...	...	...	...	...	...	...	...	...	...	...	...	...
Ghana																					
2005																					
Male - Hommes	58.3	...	...	...	...	...	...	...	...	...	...	...	...	...	...	...	...	...	...	...	...
Female - Femmes	62.0	...	...	...	...	...	...	...	...	...	...	...	...	...	...	...	...	...	...	...	...
Guinea - Guinée[6]																					
2014																					
Male - Hommes	57.4	62.5	58.3	53.9	49.5	45.3	41.2	37.2	33.3	29.6	25.9	22.3	18.7	15.1	11.8	8.4	5.0	...	...	...	...
Female - Femmes	60.4	65.5	61.1	56.6	52.3	48.0	43.9	39.9	35.8	31.8	27.8	23.9	19.8	16.1	12.3	8.8	5.0	...	...	...	...
Guinea-Bissau - Guinée-Bissau																					
2008 - 2009																					
Male - Hommes	49.2	49.8	45.3	41.0	36.8	32.8	29.3	26.2	23.3	20.7	18.0	15.5	13.1	11.2	9.4	8.0	6.8	...	...	...	...
Female - Femmes	51.2	50.1	45.7	41.5	37.8	34.4	31.3	28.4	25.6	22.9	20.0	17.4	14.9	12.8	10.6	8.8	7.1	...	...	...	...
2014																					
Male - Hommes	51.2	...	...	...	...	...	...	...	...	...	...	...	...	...	...	...	...	...	...	...	...
Female - Femmes	53.6	...	...	...	...	...	...	...	...	...	...	...	...	...	...	...	...	...	...	...	...
Kenya[2]																					
2009																					
Male - Hommes	57.8	58.1	53.9	49.7	45.3	41.0	36.9	33.3	30.2	27.1	23.9	20.4	16.7	13.2	10.0	7.0	4.0	...	...	...	...
Female - Femmes	60.7	60.1	55.8	51.4	46.9	42.6	38.7	35.7	33.0	29.8	26.2	22.3	18.3	14.5	11.0	7.7	4.7	...	...	...	...
Lesotho																					
2006[7]																					
Male - Hommes	39.8	40.4	36.0	31.5	27.2	23.6	20.9	19.2	18.2	17.3	16.4	14.9	13.2	11.3	9.4	7.4	5.3	2.9	...	...	...
Female - Femmes	42.9	42.7	38.4	33.8	29.6	26.3	24.2	23.2	22.8	22.3	21.5	20.2	18.6	16.7	14.5	12.1	9.6	7.4	...	...	...
2011																					
Male - Hommes	39.4	...	...	...	...	...	...	...	...	...	...	...	...	...	...	...	...	...	...	...	...
Female - Femmes	45.3	...	...	...	...	...	...	...	...	...	...	...	...	...	...	...	...	...	...	...	...

21. Life expectancy at specified ages for each sex: latest available year, 1997 - 2016
Espérance de vie à un âge donné pour chaque sexe : dernière année disponible, 1997 - 2016 (continued - suite)

Continent, country or area and date / Continent, pays ou zone et date	0	5	10	15	20	25	30	35	40	45	50	55	60	65	70	75	80	85	90	95	100
AFRICA - AFRIQUE																					
Malawi 1992 - 1997																					
Male - Hommes	43.5	52.1	49.5	45.7	41.9	38.4	34.8	31.2	27.6	24.0	20.6	17.3	14.1	11.2	8.6	6.3	4.4	...	...	...	...
Female - Femmes	46.8	54.5	52.0	48.2	44.4	40.6	36.9	33.2	29.6	25.9	22.2	18.6	15.1	11.9	9.2	6.8	4.6	...	...	...	...
2008																					
Male - Hommes	47.4	...	...	...	...	...	...	...	...	...	...	...	...	...	...	...	...	...	...	...	...
Female - Femmes	50.6	...	...	...	...	...	...	...	...	...	...	...	...	...	...	...	...	...	...	...	...
Mauritania - Mauritanie 2013																					
Male - Hommes	58.3	61.5	57.5	53.0	48.7	44.6	40.5	36.4	32.2	28.2	24.2	20.4	16.8	13.5	10.5	8.0	6.0	...	...	...	...
Female - Femmes	61.8	63.8	59.8	55.3	50.9	46.6	42.4	38.1	33.9	29.8	25.6	21.7	17.8	14.3	11.2	8.5	6.4	...	...	...	...
Mauritius - Maurice[8] 2014 - 2016																					
Male - Hommes	71.2	67.2	62.3	57.3	52.6	47.9	43.3	38.7	34.3	30.1	26.0	22.1	18.4	15.1	12.2	9.6	7.3	5.6	...	...	...
Female - Femmes	77.8	73.8	68.9	64.0	59.1	54.2	49.4	44.6	39.9	35.3	30.8	26.4	22.3	18.4	14.9	11.7	8.9	6.6	...	...	...
Mayotte 2015																					
Male - Hommes	75.3	...	...	...	56.7	...	...	...	37.8	...	...	...	20.5	...	...	...	...	...	...	...	...
Female - Femmes	77.2	...	...	...	58.4	...	...	...	39.0	...	...	...	20.9	...	...	...	...	...	...	...	...
Morocco - Maroc 2013																					
Male - Hommes	72.4	...	...	...	...	...	...	...	...	...	...	...	...	...	...	...	...	...	...	...	...
Female - Femmes	75.1	...	...	...	...	...	...	...	...	...	...	...	...	...	...	...	...	...	...	...	...
Mozambique 2014																					
Male - Hommes	50.2	54.0	50.0	45.6	41.6	37.7	33.9	30.1	26.5	22.9	19.6	16.4	13.5	10.9	8.7	6.8	5.0	...	...	...	...
Female - Femmes	55.4	59.0	54.8	50.3	46.1	42.1	38.1	34.1	30.2	26.3	22.5	19.0	15.7	12.7	10.0	7.7	5.8	...	...	...	...
2016																					
Male - Hommes	52.0	...	...	...	...	...	...	...	...	...	...	...	...	...	...	...	...	...	...	...	...
Female - Femmes	56.2	...	...	...	...	...	...	...	...	...	...	...	...	...	...	...	...	...	...	...	...
Namibia - Namibie 2011																					
Male - Hommes	53.3	52.4	48.0	43.4	39.0	35.1	31.5	28.6	25.8	23.2	20.6	17.7	15.1	12.6	9.8	7.4	5.6	...	...	...	...
Female - Femmes	60.5	59.6	55.1	50.5	46.1	42.0	38.4	35.2	32.0	28.7	25.2	21.6	17.9	14.5	11.3	8.6	6.5	...	...	...	...
Republic of South Sudan - République de Soudan du Sud 2010																					
Male - Hommes	54.4	57.4	53.2	48.8	44.6	40.7	36.8	32.8	28.9	25.0	21.2	17.6	14.2	11.2	8.5	6.3	4.5	3.2	2.2	1.5	...
Female - Femmes	54.5	56.2	51.9	47.5	43.3	39.4	35.4	31.5	27.5	23.7	19.9	16.4	13.1	10.2	7.7	5.6	4.1	2.9	2.0	1.4	...
Reunion - Réunion 2015																					
Male - Hommes	77.1	...	...	...	58.1	...	...	...	39.3	...	...	...	21.8	...	...	...	...	...	...	...	...
Female - Femmes	83.6	...	...	...	64.3	...	...	...	44.8	...	...	...	26.2	...	...	...	...	...	...	...	...
Rwanda 2002																					
Male - Hommes	48.4	58.4	54.4	49.9	45.6	41.6	37.5	33.5	29.4	25.4	21.6	17.9	14.5	11.4	8.6	6.3	4.6	...	...	...	...
Female - Femmes	53.8	63.1	58.8	54.3	49.9	45.7	41.4	37.2	32.9	28.7	24.5	20.4	16.5	12.9	9.8	7.1	5.1	...	...	...	...
2012[9]																					
Male - Hommes	62.6	...	...	...	...	...	...	...	...	...	...	...	...	...	...	...	...	...	...	...	...
Female - Femmes	66.2	...	...	...	...	...	...	...	...	...	...	...	...	...	...	...	...	...	...	...	...
Saint Helena ex. dep. - Sainte-Hélène sans dép.[10] 2003 - 2012																					
Male - Hommes	72.0	68.1	63.4	...	53.9	...	44.2	...	35.5	...	27.1	...	19.3	...	12.5	...	7.2	...	...	...	...
Female - Femmes	79.7	75.3	70.3	...	60.3	...	51.0	...	41.8	...	32.0	...	23.0	...	15.5	...	8.6	...	...	...	...
Sao Tome and Principe - Sao Tomé-et-Principe 2011 - 2012																					
Male - Hommes	62.1	59.5	54.6	50.1	45.8	41.6	37.5	33.4	29.6	25.8	22.1	18.4	15.2	12.0	9.8	7.4	5.0	...	...	...	...
Female - Femmes	68.7	65.9	61.2	56.5	51.8	47.1	42.5	38.0	33.5	29.3	25.3	21.7	18.2	14.9	11.8	9.0	6.6	...	...	...	...

Continent, country or area and date / Continent, pays ou zone et date	Age (in years) - Age (en années)																				
	0	5	10	15	20	25	30	35	40	45	50	55	60	65	70	75	80	85	90	95	100
AFRICA - AFRIQUE																					
Senegal - Sénégal[11]																					
2013																					
Male - Hommes	63.2	...	...	...	...	...	...	...	...	...	...	...	...	...	...	...	...	...	...	...	...
Female - Femmes	66.5	...	...	...	...	...	...	...	...	...	...	...	...	...	...	...	...	...	...	...	...
Seychelles																					
2007																					
Male - Hommes	68.9	65.0	60.2	55.3	50.5	45.9	41.6	37.0	32.7	28.7	24.4	20.9	17.1	14.1	11.0	9.0	7.4	...	...	...	...
Female - Femmes	77.7	73.3	68.5	63.5	58.5	53.7	48.9	44.3	39.5	35.3	31.0	26.4	22.2	18.5	15.1	12.1	9.2	...	...	...	...
2014																					
Male - Hommes	68.4	...	...	...	...	...	...	...	...	...	...	...	...	...	...	...	...	...	...	...	...
Female - Femmes	78.3	...	...	...	...	...	...	...	...	...	...	...	...	...	...	...	...	...	...	...	...
Sierra Leone																					
2004																					
Male - Hommes	47.5	...	...	...	...	...	...	...	...	...	...	...	...	...	...	...	...	...	...	...	...
Female - Femmes	49.4	...	...	...	...	...	...	...	...	...	...	...	...	...	...	...	...	...	...	...	...
South Africa - Afrique du Sud																					
2014																					
Male - Hommes	59.1	...	...	...	...	...	...	...	...	...	...	...	...	...	...	...	...	...	...	...	...
Female - Femmes	63.1	...	...	...	...	...	...	...	...	...	...	...	...	...	...	...	...	...	...	...	...
Swaziland																					
2007																					
Male - Hommes	42.2	44.9	40.5	36.0	31.5	27.5	24.9	23.3	22.1	20.9	19.1	17.4	15.4	13.6	10.9	8.9	...	...	...	...	...
Female - Femmes	43.1	48.2	43.9	39.3	35.0	32.3	30.9	30.3	29.5	27.6	25.1	22.7	19.5	16.8	13.5	10.5	...	...	...	...	...
Tunisia - Tunisie																					
2015																					
Male - Hommes	74.5	...	...	...	...	...	...	...	...	...	...	...	...	...	...	...	...	...	...	...	...
Female - Femmes	77.8	...	...	...	...	...	...	...	...	...	...	...	...	...	...	...	...	...	...	...	...
Uganda - Ouganda																					
2002[12]																					
Male - Hommes	48.8	53.0	49.2	44.8	40.5	36.6	33.6	31.0	28.4	25.8	23.2	20.4	17.2	14.4	11.6	9.2	6.7	4.1	...	...	...
Female - Femmes	52.0	56.0	52.1	47.6	43.3	39.6	36.7	34.2	31.5	28.6	25.6	22.3	18.9	15.7	12.6	9.9	7.0	4.2	...	...	...
2014[13]																					
Male - Hommes	62.2	...	...	...	...	...	...	...	...	...	...	...	...	...	...	...	...	...	...	...	...
Female - Femmes	64.2	...	...	...	...	...	...	...	...	...	...	...	...	...	...	...	...	...	...	...	...
Zimbabwe																					
2001 - 2002																					
Male - Hommes	45.8	44.2	40.0	35.4	30.9	26.8	23.8	22.1	21.8	21.3	20.4	19.2	17.7	15.7	13.7	11.4	9.5	7.5	6.2	5.2	...
Female - Femmes	50.3	48.6	44.2	39.7	35.3	32.1	30.4	30.1	30.2	29.0	27.6	25.3	22.9	20.2	17.6	14.8	12.2	9.9	8.1	7.3	...
AMERICA, NORTH - AMÉRIQUE DU NORD																					
Anguilla																					
2000 - 2002																					
Male - Hommes	76.5	72.1	67.1	62.1	57.3	53.1	48.4	43.7	39.4	34.7	30.2	25.4	21.1	16.5	12.7	10.0	8.0	6.9	...	...	...
Female - Femmes	81.1	76.4	71.4	66.4	61.4	57.1	52.7	47.7	42.7	38.3	33.5	28.7	24.0	19.4	15.3	10.8	8.3	7.6	...	...	...
Antigua and Barbuda - Antigua-et-Barbuda																					
2010																					
Male - Hommes	74.0	...	...	...	...	...	...	...	...	...	...	...	...	...	...	...	...	...	...	...	...
Female - Femmes	79.7	...	...	...	...	...	...	...	...	...	...	...	...	...	...	...	...	...	...	...	...
Aruba																					
2010 - 2011																					
Male - Hommes	73.9	69.4	64.4	59.5	54.6	50.0	45.4	40.8	36.3	31.7	27.3	23.1	19.1	15.3	12.3	9.4	7.3	5.0	3.5	2.7	...
Female - Femmes	79.8	76.2	71.2	66.2	61.3	56.4	51.5	46.6	42.0	37.3	32.6	27.9	23.8	19.7	16.0	12.5	9.5	6.8	5.0	3.8	...
Bahamas																					
1999 - 2001																					
Male - Hommes	69.9	...	...	...	...	...	...	...	...	...	...	...	...	...	...	...	...	...	...	...	...
Female - Femmes	76.4	...	...	...	...	...	...	...	...	...	...	...	...	...	...	...	...	...	...	...	...
Bermuda - Bermudes																					
2016																					
Male - Hommes	77.5	72.8	67.8	62.9	58.1	53.5	49.0	44.4	39.8	35.2	30.6	26.2	21.9	17.9	14.2	10.8	7.8	5.0	...	...	...
Female - Femmes	85.1	80.3	75.3	70.3	65.4	60.4	55.5	50.5	45.6	40.8	36.0	31.3	26.8	22.3	18.1	14.1	10.7	7.7	...	...	...

Continent, country or area and date / Continent, pays ou zone et date	0	5	10	15	20	25	30	35	40	45	50	55	60	65	70	75	80	85	90	95	100
AMERICA, NORTH - AMÉRIQUE DU NORD																					
British Virgin Islands - Îles Vierges britanniques																					
2004																					
Male - Hommes	69.9	...	...	...	...	...	...	...	...	...	...	...	...	...	...	...	...	...	...	...	...
Female - Femmes	78.5	...	...	...	...	...	...	...	...	...	...	...	...	...	...	...	...	...	...	...	...
Canada																					
2010 - 2012																					
Male - Hommes	79.4	74.9	69.9	64.9	60.1	55.3	50.5	45.7	40.9	36.2	31.6	27.2	22.9	18.8	15.1	11.7	8.7	6.2	4.2	2.8	...
Female - Femmes	83.6	79.1	74.1	69.1	64.2	59.3	54.4	49.5	44.7	39.9	35.2	30.6	26.1	21.8	17.7	13.9	10.4	7.5	5.1	3.4	...
Cayman Islands - Îles Caïmanes[14]																					
2010																					
Male - Hommes	79.8	75.5	70.5	65.6	61.1	56.8	52.2	47.4	42.5	37.6	32.9	28.3	23.9	19.6	15.2	11.6	8.9	6.2	5.0	3.6	2.5
Female - Femmes	84.7	80.1	75.1	70.1	65.1	60.3	55.3	50.4	45.4	40.5	35.7	30.8	26.1	21.5	17.0	13.2	9.8	7.2	4.9	3.8	2.5
Costa Rica																					
2015																					
Male - Hommes	77.4	73.1	68.2	63.2	58.5	53.8	49.2	44.5	39.9	35.3	30.9	26.6	22.4	18.5	15.0	11.8	9.0	6.7	4.8	3.3	2.1
Female - Femmes	82.4	78.1	73.1	68.2	63.3	58.4	53.5	48.6	43.8	39.0	34.3	29.7	25.3	21.1	17.1	13.4	10.2	7.4	5.3	3.6	2.3
Cuba																					
2011 - 2013																					
Male - Hommes	76.5	72.0	67.0	62.1	57.3	52.5	47.7	42.9	38.2	33.6	29.2	25.0	21.0	17.3	14.0	11.0	8.4	6.3	4.9	3.8	2.0
Female - Femmes	80.4	75.9	71.0	66.0	61.1	56.2	51.4	46.5	41.7	36.9	32.3	27.9	23.6	19.6	15.8	12.4	9.4	6.9	5.1	3.8	2.1
Curaçao																					
2016																					
Male - Hommes	74.9	71.1	66.2	61.2	56.3	51.6	47.0	42.3	37.7	33.0	28.5	24.3	20.4	16.7	13.3	10.4	7.6	5.5	3.9	2.8	2.4
Female - Femmes	81.0	77.7	72.7	67.7	62.8	57.9	53.0	48.2	43.3	38.6	33.9	29.3	24.8	20.6	16.6	12.8	9.6	7.0	4.9	3.3	2.2
Dominica - Dominique																					
2008																					
Male - Hommes	73.8	...	...	...	...	...	...	...	...	...	...	...	...	...	...	...	...	...	...	...	...
Female - Femmes	78.2	...	...	...	...	...	...	...	...	...	...	...	...	...	...	...	...	...	...	...	...
Dominican Republic - République dominicaine																					
2010 - 2015																					
Male - Hommes	70.0	67.5	62.6	57.7	53.0	48.7	44.3	40.0	35.6	31.3	27.2	23.3	19.6	16.2	13.2	10.5	8.6	...	...	...	...
Female - Femmes	74.8	71.8	66.9	62.0	57.1	52.4	47.7	43.1	38.5	34.1	29.7	25.5	21.6	17.9	14.6	11.7	9.7	...	...	...	...
El Salvador[15]																					
2000 - 2005																					
Male - Hommes	65.4	62.6	57.8	52.9	48.7	45.0	41.5	37.8	34.1	30.4	26.8	23.3	20.0	16.7	13.8	11.1	9.0	...	...	...	...
Female - Femmes	74.9	72.0	67.1	62.3	57.5	52.9	48.2	43.6	39.0	34.6	30.3	26.1	22.1	18.4	15.0	12.0	9.6	...	...	...	...
Greenland - Groenland																					
2010 - 2014																					
Male - Hommes	69.1	65.4	60.4	55.5	51.1	47.3	42.9	38.5	34.0	29.6	25.3	21.0	17.1	13.4	10.2	7.8	6.0	4.7	3.2	4.0	...
Female - Femmes	73.7	69.3	64.4	59.5	54.9	50.5	45.7	40.9	36.4	31.7	27.2	22.7	18.5	14.8	11.7	8.8	6.3	4.5	3.3	3.1	...
Guadeloupe																					
2015																					
Male - Hommes	77.0	...	...	...	58.2	...	...	...	40.4	...	...	...	23.5	...	...	...	...	...	...	...	...
Female - Femmes	84.8	...	...	...	65.6	...	...	...	46.1	...	...	...	27.4	...	...	...	...	...	...	...	...
Guatemala																					
1995 - 2000																					
Male - Hommes	61.4	60.6	56.0	51.2	46.8	42.7	38.8	34.9	31.2	27.4	23.7	20.1	16.8	13.6	10.7	8.2	6.1	...	...	...	...
Female - Femmes	67.2	66.2	62.6	56.9	52.3	47.7	43.3	38.9	34.6	30.4	26.3	22.3	18.6	15.2	12.0	9.2	6.9	...	...	...	...
Jamaica - Jamaïque																					
2006																					
Male - Hommes	69.7	67.0	62.2	57.3	52.6	47.9	43.2	38.5	33.8	29.3	24.9	20.8	16.9	13.5	10.4	7.8	5.8	4.1	2.9	2.1	1.5
Female - Femmes	75.2	71.6	66.7	61.7	56.8	52.0	47.1	42.3	37.6	32.9	28.3	23.9	19.7	15.9	12.4	9.4	6.9	5.0	3.5	2.4	1.7
Martinique																					
2015																					
Male - Hommes	79.4	...	...	...	60.1	...	...	...	41.7	...	...	...	24.1	...	...	...	...	...	...	...	...
Female - Femmes	84.7	...	...	...	65.4	...	...	...	45.9	...	...	...	27.4	...	...	...	...	...	...	...	...

Continent, country or area and date / Continent, pays ou zone et date	0	5	10	15	20	25	30	35	40	45	50	55	60	65	70	75	80	85	90	95	100
AMERICA, NORTH - AMÉRIQUE DU NORD																					
Mexico - Mexique																					
2008																					
Male - Hommes	72.8	69.2	64.3	59.4	54.7	50.0	45.5	40.9	36.5	32.1	27.9	23.9	20.2	16.8	13.7	11.0	8.7	6.6	4.9	3.5	2.6
Female - Femmes	77.5	73.8	68.9	63.9	59.0	54.2	49.3	44.5	39.7	35.1	30.6	26.2	22.1	18.3	14.8	11.7	9.0	6.8	4.9	3.5	2.6
2015																					
Male - Hommes	72.3	...	...	...	...	...	...	...	...	...	...	...	...	...	...	...	...	...	...	...	...
Female - Femmes	77.7	...	...	...	...	...	...	...	...	...	...	...	...	...	...	...	...	...	...	...	...
Nicaragua																					
2005 - 2010																					
Male - Hommes	63.4	61.1	56.5	51.8	47.9	44.2	40.5	36.5	32.5	28.6	24.9	21.3	17.7	14.6	11.6	9.0	6.5	...	...	...	...
Female - Femmes	68.9	66.2	61.4	56.7	52.1	47.6	43.0	38.5	34.1	29.8	25.7	21.9	18.1	14.9	11.8	9.3	6.9	...	...	...	...
Panama[16]																					
2015																					
Male - Hommes	74.8	71.4	66.6	61.7	57.1	52.8	48.6	44.2	39.7	35.3	30.9	26.7	22.7	19.0	15.6	12.6	9.9	7.6	5.7	4.1	2.5
Female - Femmes	80.9	77.2	72.3	67.4	62.6	57.8	53.0	48.3	43.6	38.9	34.3	29.9	25.5	21.4	17.6	14.1	11.0	8.3	6.1	4.3	2.5
Puerto Rico - Porto Rico																					
2014 - 2016																					
Male - Hommes	76.6	72.2	67.2	62.3	57.5	53.0	48.6	44.1	39.6	35.2	30.9	26.8	23.0	19.4	16.0	12.9	10.1	7.9	...	...	...
Female - Femmes	84.1	79.7	74.8	69.8	64.8	59.9	55.1	50.3	45.5	40.8	36.2	31.7	27.3	23.1	19.1	15.4	12.1	9.5	...	...	...
Saint Kitts and Nevis - Saint-Kitts-et-Nevis																					
1998																					
Male - Hommes	68.2	65.0	60.1	55.3	50.5	45.8	41.1	36.5	32.7	28.5	24.3	20.6	16.6	13.3	11.0	9.1	6.6	4.7	3.4	2.2	0.4
Female - Femmes	70.7	67.5	62.5	57.6	52.7	48.0	43.4	38.8	34.4	29.8	25.4	21.3	17.6	14.3	11.3	8.9	6.3	4.6	3.3	2.2	0.4
Saint Lucia - Sainte-Lucie																					
2005																					
Male - Hommes	69.9	66.4	61.5	56.6	52.0	47.4	43.1	38.6	34.3	30.1	25.9	21.7	17.9	14.7	11.8	9.0	7.2	5.2	...	...	...
Female - Femmes	75.7	72.2	67.3	62.4	57.5	52.6	47.8	43.2	38.4	33.8	29.2	25.0	20.8	17.2	13.8	10.4	7.7	4.8	...	...	...
2012																					
Male - Hommes	75.3	...	...	...	...	...	...	...	...	...	...	...	...	...	...	...	...	...	...	...	...
Female - Femmes	82.5	...	...	...	...	...	...	...	...	...	...	...	...	...	...	...	...	...	...	...	...
Saint Vincent and the Grenadines - Saint-Vincent-et-les Grenadines																					
2016																					
Male - Hommes	71.0	66.8	62.1	57.3	52.8	48.3	43.8	39.5	35.1	30.9	26.5	22.7	19.6	16.7	14.7	11.7	9.0	6.5	...	...	...
Female - Femmes	75.2	71.1	66.3	61.4	56.5	51.8	47.1	42.5	38.0	33.5	29.0	25.1	21.4	17.9	14.7	11.5	9.2	6.6	...	...	...
Sint Maarten (Dutch part) - Saint-Martin (partie néerlandaise)																					
2011 - 2012																					
Male - Hommes	69.2	65.5	60.6	55.7	51.0	46.9	42.5	38.2	33.9	29.5	25.3	21.2	17.6	13.8	10.4	7.4	5.2	4.0	...	...	...
Female - Femmes	77.1	72.3	67.4	62.6	57.8	52.8	48.0	43.1	38.2	33.5	28.6	24.0	19.4	14.9	11.5	8.1	5.0	1.8	...	...	...
Trinidad and Tobago - Trinité-et-Tobago[2]																					
2011																					
Male - Hommes	71.4	67.6	62.7	57.8	53.2	49.0	44.7	40.4	36.0	31.7	27.5	23.5	19.6	16.2	12.9	10.2	7.9	6.0	...	...	...
Female - Femmes	77.8	74.1	69.2	64.2	59.4	54.6	49.9	45.3	40.6	36.2	31.7	27.5	23.3	19.4	15.9	12.6	9.7	7.6	...	...	...
Turks and Caicos Islands - Îles Turques et Caïques																					
2001																					
Male - Hommes	79.0	75.3	70.3	65.3	60.3	55.8	50.8	46.0	41.2	37.1	33.0	28.4	24.3	20.8	17.5	12.5	7.5	4.1	...	...	...
Female - Femmes	77.4	72.5	67.5	62.5	57.5	52.9	48.2	43.4	38.6	33.8	29.6	25.0	20.0	17.0	13.2	11.7	10.3	8.8	...	...	...
2012																					
Male - Hommes	75.8	...	...	...	...	...	...	...	...	...	...	...	...	...	...	...	...	...	...	...	...
Female - Femmes	77.8	...	...	...	...	...	...	...	...	...	...	...	...	...	...	...	...	...	...	...	...

21. Life expectancy at specified ages for each sex: latest available year, 1997 - 2016
Espérance de vie à un âge donné pour chaque sexe : dernière année disponible, 1997 - 2016 (continued - suite)

Continent, pays ou zone et date	0	5	10	15	20	25	30	35	40	45	50	55	60	65	70	75	80	85	90	95	100
AMERICA, NORTH - AMÉRIQUE DU NORD																					
United States of America - États-Unis d'Amérique																					
2014																					
Male - Hommes	76.4	72.0	67.0	62.1	57.3	52.6	48.0	43.3	38.7	34.2	29.8	25.6	21.7	18.0	14.4	11.2	8.3	5.9	4.1	2.9	2.1
Female - Femmes	81.2	76.7	71.7	66.8	61.9	57.0	52.1	47.3	42.6	37.9	33.3	28.9	24.7	20.5	16.6	13.0	9.7	7.0	4.8	3.3	2.3
2015																					
Male - Hommes	76.3	...	...	...	...	...	...	...	...	...	...	...	...	...	...	...	...	...	...	...	...
Female - Femmes	81.2	...	...	...	...	...	...	...	...	...	...	...	...	...	...	...	...	...	...	...	...
AMERICA, SOUTH - AMÉRIQUE DU SUD																					
Argentina - Argentine																					
2008 - 2010																					
Male - Hommes	72.1	68.2	63.3	58.4	53.7	49.1	44.5	39.8	35.2	30.7	26.3	22.2	18.5	15.0	11.9	9.2	6.9	5.2	4.0	3.1	2.6
Female - Femmes	78.8	74.8	69.9	65.0	60.1	55.3	50.5	45.6	40.9	36.2	31.7	27.3	23.1	19.0	15.2	11.7	8.6	6.3	4.7	3.5	2.9
Bolivia (Plurinational State of) - Bolivie (État plurinational de)[17]																					
2016 - 2017																					
Male - Hommes	69.1	67.3	62.6	57.9	53.4	49.1	44.7	40.4	36.2	32.0	27.9	24.0	20.3	16.9	13.8	11.1	8.7	6.8	4.9	3.7	...
Female - Femmes	75.9	73.6	68.9	64.0	59.3	54.6	50.0	45.3	40.7	36.3	32.0	27.8	23.8	20.1	16.8	13.7	10.9	8.5	6.3	4.8	...
Brazil - Brésil																					
2015																					
Male - Hommes	71.9	68.2	63.3	58.4	53.9	49.5	45.1	40.7	36.3	32.0	27.9	23.9	20.2	16.7	13.5	10.7	8.4	...	...	...	...
Female - Femmes	79.1	75.3	70.4	65.4	60.6	55.7	50.9	46.2	41.4	36.8	32.3	28.0	23.8	19.8	16.2	12.9	10.1	...	...	...	...
Chile - Chili																					
2014																					
Male - Hommes	76.8	72.4	67.5	62.5	57.7	52.9	48.2	43.5	38.8	34.2	29.7	25.4	21.2	17.3	13.8	10.6	7.7	5.8	4.3	...	...
Female - Femmes	82.5	78.1	73.2	68.2	63.3	58.4	53.5	48.6	43.8	39.0	34.3	29.7	25.3	21.0	17.1	13.4	10.1	7.6	5.7	...	...
Colombia - Colombie																					
2010 - 2015																					
Male - Hommes	72.1	68.9	64.0	59.1	54.5	50.1	45.7	41.3	36.8	32.3	27.9	23.7	19.7	16.0	12.7	9.8	7.4	...	...	...	...
Female - Femmes	78.5	74.9	70.0	65.1	60.2	55.4	50.6	45.8	41.0	36.3	31.7	27.2	22.9	18.8	15.0	11.6	8.7	...	...	...	...
Ecuador - Équateur[18]																					
2010 - 2017																					
Male - Hommes	73.9	70.5	65.6	60.6	55.8	51.1	46.4	41.8	37.3	32.7	28.3	24.1	20.0	16.3	12.8	9.8	7.3	5.2	3.6	2.4	0.5
Female - Femmes	79.5	76.0	71.1	66.2	61.3	56.4	51.5	46.7	41.9	37.1	32.4	27.8	23.4	19.1	15.0	11.3	8.2	5.7	3.9	2.5	0.5
French Guiana - Guyane française																					
2015																					
Male - Hommes	76.4	...	...	...	58.0	...	...	...	39.5	...	...	...	22.0	...	...	...	...	...	...	...	...
Female - Femmes	82.0	...	...	...	63.0	...	...	...	43.6	...	...	...	25.3	...	...	...	...	...	...	...	...
Paraguay																					
2005 - 2010																					
Male - Hommes	69.7	...	...	...	...	...	...	...	...	...	...	...	...	...	...	...	...	...	...	...	...
Female - Femmes	73.9	...	...	...	...	...	...	...	...	...	...	...	...	...	...	...	...	...	...	...	...
Peru - Pérou[16]																					
2010 - 2015																					
Male - Hommes	71.5	69.0	64.3	59.4	54.7	50.0	45.5	40.9	36.4	32.0	27.7	23.6	19.8	16.2	13.0	10.1	7.7	...	...	...	...
Female - Femmes	76.8	73.8	69.0	64.1	59.3	54.5	49.7	45.0	40.3	35.7	31.2	26.9	22.7	18.7	15.0	11.7	8.8	...	...	...	...
Suriname																					
2011 - 2013																					
Male - Hommes	69.3	65.7	60.8	55.9	51.3	46.8	42.3	37.9	33.7	29.5	25.5	21.7	18.1	14.8	11.8	9.1	6.5	4.7	...	...	...
Female - Femmes	75.1	71.6	66.6	61.8	57.0	52.3	47.7	43.1	38.4	33.9	29.5	25.2	21.1	17.0	13.3	9.9	6.9	4.7	...	...	...
Uruguay																					
2010																					
Male - Hommes	72.8	68.5	63.6	58.7	54.0	49.4	44.8	40.2	35.6	31.0	26.6	22.4	18.6	15.1	12.0	9.3	7.0	5.2	4.0	...	...
Female - Femmes	80.0	75.6	70.7	65.8	60.9	56.1	51.2	46.4	41.6	36.9	32.3	27.9	23.6	19.5	15.6	12.0	8.9	6.4	4.5	...	...
2016																					
Male - Hommes	73.8	...	...	...	...	...	...	...	...	...	...	...	...	...	...	...	...	...	...	...	...
Female - Femmes	80.6	...	...	...	...	...	...	...	...	...	...	...	...	...	...	...	...	...	...	...	...

Continent, country or area and date / Continent, pays ou zone et date	Age (in years) - Age (en années)																				
	0	5	10	15	20	25	30	35	40	45	50	55	60	65	70	75	80	85	90	95	100
AMERICA, SOUTH - AMÉRIQUE DU SUD																					
Venezuela (Bolivarian Republic of) - Venezuela (République bolivarienne du)																					
1995 - 2000																					
Male - Hommes	68.6	66.6	61.8	56.9	52.3	47.8	43.3	38.8	34.3	29.9	25.6	21.6	17.9	14.5	11.4	8.6	5.9	...	...	...	...
Female - Femmes	74.5	72.1	67.2	62.3	57.5	52.6	47.8	43.1	38.4	33.7	29.2	24.9	20.8	16.9	13.3	9.9	6.9				
2016[19]																					
Male - Hommes	72.3	...	...	...	...	...	...	...	...	...	...	...	...	...	...	...	...	...	...	...	...
Female - Femmes	78.4	...	...	...	...	...	...	...	...	...	...	...	...	...	...	...	...	...	...	...	...
ASIA - ASIE																					
Afghanistan																					
2004																					
Male - Hommes	45.0	...	...	...	...	...	...	...	...	...	...	...	...	...	...	...	...	...	...	...	...
Female - Femmes	44.0	...	...	...	...	...	...	...	...	...	...	...	...	...	...	...	...	...	...	...	...
Armenia - Arménie																					
2014 - 2015																					
Male - Hommes	71.7	67.5	62.6	57.6	52.8	48.1	43.3	38.6	33.9	29.4	25.2	21.3	17.6	14.2	11.2	8.7	6.5	4.7	3.3	2.1	0.7
Female - Femmes	78.2	73.9	69.0	64.1	59.1	54.2	49.3	44.4	39.5	34.8	30.2	25.6	21.2	17.0	13.1	9.8	6.8	4.3	2.4	1.9	0.7
Azerbaijan - Azerbaïdjan																					
2015																					
Male - Hommes	72.7	68.9	64.0	59.1	54.2	49.4	44.7	39.9	35.3	30.7	26.4	22.3	18.5	15.2	12.1	9.6	7.5	6.1	5.6	4.2	0.9
Female - Femmes	77.6	73.5	68.6	63.7	58.8	53.9	49.0	44.1	39.3	34.5	29.8	25.3	21.0	17.0	13.2	9.9	7.4	5.4	4.5	3.3	0.8
Bahrain - Bahreïn																					
2001																					
Male - Hommes	73.2	69.3	64.4	59.5	54.7	49.9	45.2	40.4	35.6	30.9	26.4	22.0	17.8	14.1	11.3	9.5	...	...	...	...	...
Female - Femmes	76.2	72.0	67.1	62.1	57.2	52.3	47.4	42.5	37.7	32.9	28.2	23.7	19.6	15.9	12.9	10.9					
2010 - 2015																					
Male - Hommes	75.8	...	...	...	...	...	...	...	...	...	...	...	...	...	...	...	...	...	...	...	...
Female - Femmes	77.4	...	...	...	...	...	...	...	...	...	...	...	...	...	...	...	...	...	...	...	...
Bangladesh																					
2011																					
Male - Hommes	67.9	65.5	60.8	56.1	51.3	46.5	41.8	37.1	32.6	28.2	24.1	20.2	16.6	13.2	10.0	6.7	4.4	...	...	...	...
Female - Femmes	70.3	67.8	63.1	58.3	53.6	48.8	44.0	39.3	34.7	30.1	25.6	21.4	17.4	13.8	10.3	6.7	5.6				
2016[20]																					
Male - Hommes	70.3	...	...	...	...	...	...	...	...	...	...	...	...	...	...	...	...	...	...	...	...
Female - Femmes	72.9	...	...	...	...	...	...	...	...	...	...	...	...	...	...	...	...	...	...	...	...
Bhutan - Bhoutan																					
2005																					
Male - Hommes	65.7	...	...	...	...	...	...	...	...	...	...	...	...	...	...	...	...	...	...	...	...
Female - Femmes	66.9	...	...	...	...	...	...	...	...	...	...	...	...	...	...	...	...	...	...	...	...
Brunei Darussalam - Brunéi Darussalam																					
2014																					
Male - Hommes	75.9	...	...	...	...	...	...	...	...	...	...	...	...	...	...	...	...	...	...	...	...
Female - Femmes	78.8	...	...	...	...	...	...	...	...	...	...	...	...	...	...	...	...	...	...	...	...
China - Chine[21]																					
2010																					
Male - Hommes	66.8	...	...	...	...	...	...	...	...	...	...	...	...	...	...	...	...	...	...	...	...
Female - Femmes	70.5	...	...	...	...	...	...	...	...	...	...	...	...	...	...	...	...	...	...	...	...
China, Hong Kong SAR - Chine, Hong Kong RAS																					
2016																					
Male - Hommes	81.3	76.5	71.5	66.6	61.6	56.7	51.8	47.0	42.2	37.4	32.8	28.2	23.9	19.8	16.0	12.5	9.4	6.8	4.8	3.3	2.2
Female - Femmes	87.3	82.5	77.5	72.6	67.6	62.7	57.7	52.8	47.9	43.1	38.3	33.6	29.0	24.5	20.2	16.0	12.3	9.0	6.4	4.4	2.9
China, Macao SAR - Chine, Macao RAS																					
2012 - 2015																					
Male - Hommes	79.9	75.2	70.3	65.3	60.4	55.6	50.7	45.9	41.2	36.6	32.0	27.6	23.4	19.3	15.5	12.1	9.2	7.3	...	...	...
Female - Femmes	86.3	81.5	76.5	71.6	66.6	61.8	56.8	51.9	47.1	42.2	37.5	32.9	28.3	23.8	19.4	15.5	12.2	9.6			

Continent, country or area and date / Continent, pays ou zone et date	0	5	10	15	20	25	30	35	40	45	50	55	60	65	70	75	80	85	90	95	100
ASIA - ASIE																					
2013 - 2016																					
Male - Hommes	80.3	...	...	...	...	...	...	...	...	...	...	...	...	...	...	...	...	...	...	...	...
Female - Femmes	86.4	...	...	...	...	...	...	...	...	...	...	...	...	...	...	...	...	...	...	...	...
Cyprus - Chypre[22]																					
2013																					
Male - Hommes	80.0	75.1	70.2	65.3	60.4	55.5	50.7	45.8	41.0	36.3	31.6	27.0	22.6	18.5	14.7	11.2	8.2	5.9	...	...	...
Female - Femmes	84.8	79.8	74.9	69.9	64.9	60.0	55.0	50.1	45.2	40.3	35.4	30.6	25.9	21.4	17.2	13.1	9.5	6.6	...	...	...
2015																					
Male - Hommes	79.8	...	...	...	...	...	...	...	...	...	...	...	...	...	...	...	...	...	...	...	...
Female - Femmes	83.5	...	...	...	...	...	...	...	...	...	...	...	...	...	...	...	...	...	...	...	...
Democratic People's Republic of Korea - République populaire démocratique de Corée																					
2008																					
Male - Hommes	65.6	...	...	...	...	...	...	...	...	...	...	...	...	...	...	...	...	...	...	...	...
Female - Femmes	72.7	...	...	...	...	...	...	...	...	...	...	...	...	...	...	...	...	...	...	...	...
Georgia - Géorgie																					
2015																					
Male - Hommes	68.6	64.4	59.5	54.6	49.8	45.1	40.5	35.9	31.4	27.2	23.2	19.6	16.2	13.1	10.2	7.7	5.6	3.8	...	...	...
Female - Femmes	77.2	72.9	68.0	63.1	58.2	53.3	48.4	43.6	38.7	34.0	29.4	25.0	20.7	16.6	12.8	9.5	6.7	4.7	...	...	...
2016																					
Male - Hommes	68.3	...	...	...	...	...	...	...	...	...	...	...	...	...	...	...	...	...	...	...	...
Female - Femmes	77.1	...	...	...	...	...	...	...	...	...	...	...	...	...	...	...	...	...	...	...	...
India - Inde[23]																					
2002 - 2006																					
Male - Hommes	62.6	63.8	59.3	54.6	49.9	45.4	40.9	36.5	32.2	28.0	24.0	20.2	16.7	13.6	10.9	...	...	...	...	...	...
Female - Femmes	64.2	67.4	62.9	58.2	53.7	49.2	44.8	40.2	35.7	31.3	26.9	22.7	18.9	15.4	12.4	...	...	...	...	...	...
Indonesia - Indonésie																					
2012																					
Male - Hommes	67.7	...	...	...	...	...	...	...	...	...	...	...	...	...	...	...	...	...	...	...	...
Female - Femmes	71.7	...	...	...	...	...	...	...	...	...	...	...	...	...	...	...	...	...	...	...	...
Iran (Islamic Republic of) - Iran (République islamique d')																					
2011																					
Male - Hommes	71.5	...	...	...	...	...	...	...	...	...	...	...	...	...	...	...	...	...	...	...	...
Female - Femmes	74.0	...	...	...	...	...	...	...	...	...	...	...	...	...	...	...	...	...	...	...	...
Iraq																					
1997																					
Male - Hommes	58.0	...	...	...	...	...	...	...	...	...	...	...	...	...	...	...	...	...	...	...	...
Female - Femmes	59.0	...	...	...	...	...	...	...	...	...	...	...	...	...	...	...	...	...	...	...	...
Israel - Israël[24]																					
2011 - 2015																					
Male - Hommes	80.1	75.4	70.5	65.5	60.6	55.8	50.9	46.1	41.2	36.5	31.8	27.4	23.1	19.0	15.2	11.8	8.8	6.4	4.6	3.3	2.4
Female - Femmes	83.8	79.1	74.1	69.2	64.2	59.3	54.3	49.4	44.5	39.7	34.9	30.2	25.7	21.2	17.0	13.1	9.7	6.9	4.7	3.3	2.3
Japan - Japon[25]																					
2015																					
Male - Hommes	80.8	76.0	71.0	66.1	61.1	56.3	51.4	46.6	41.8	37.0	32.4	27.9	23.5	19.4	15.6	12.0	8.8	6.2	4.3	3.0	2.2
Female - Femmes	87.0	82.2	77.2	72.3	67.3	62.4	57.5	52.6	47.7	42.8	38.1	33.4	28.8	24.2	19.9	15.6	11.7	8.3	5.6	3.6	2.5
Jordan - Jordanie[26]																					
2012																					
Male - Hommes	72.7	69.1	64.2	59.3	54.4	49.6	44.8	40.0	35.2	30.5	26.0	21.7	17.8	14.2	10.9	8.2	6.0	...	...	...	...
Female - Femmes	76.7	73.1	68.1	63.2	58.2	53.3	48.4	43.6	38.7	33.9	29.3	24.7	20.3	16.2	12.4	9.2	6.8	...	...	...	...
2016																					
Male - Hommes	72.8	...	...	...	...	...	...	...	...	...	...	...	...	...	...	...	...	...	...	...	...
Female - Femmes	74.2	...	...	...	...	...	...	...	...	...	...	...	...	...	...	...	...	...	...	...	...
Kazakhstan																					
2012																					
Male - Hommes	64.8	61.0	56.1	51.3	46.5	41.9	37.5	33.3	29.3	25.3	21.5	18.0	14.8	12.1	9.6	7.4	5.7	4.5	3.7	2.9	2.0
Female - Femmes	74.3	70.4	65.5	60.6	55.7	50.9	46.2	41.5	36.9	32.4	27.9	23.7	19.6	15.9	12.3	9.2	6.6	4.7	3.2	2.4	1.8
Kuwait - Koweït																					
2015																					
Male - Hommes	79.1	...	...	...	...	...	...	...	...	...	...	...	...	...	...	...	...	...	...	...	...
Female - Femmes	80.0	...	...	...	...	...	...	...	...	...	...	...	...	...	...	...	...	...	...	...	...

Continent, country or area and date / Continent, pays ou zone et date	Age (in years) - Age (en années)																				
	0	5	10	15	20	25	30	35	40	45	50	55	60	65	70	75	80	85	90	95	100
ASIA - ASIE																					
Kyrgyzstan - Kirghizstan 2015																					
Male - Hommes	66.8	63.3	58.4	53.5	48.7	44.0	39.4	34.9	30.6	26.5	22.4	18.5	14.9	11.7	8.5	6.4	4.4	3.0	2.3	1.7	1.6
Female - Femmes	74.8	71.2	66.3	61.4	56.5	51.7	46.8	42.1	37.4	32.8	28.3	24.0	19.8	15.8	12.1	9.1	6.4	4.5	3.3	2.2	1.7
Lao People's Democratic Republic - République démocratique populaire lao[27] 2015																					
Male - Hommes	61.8	...	...	...	...	...	...	...	...	...	...	...	...	...	...	...	...	...	...	...	...
Female - Femmes	65.2	...	...	...	...	...	...	...	...	...	...	...	...	...	...	...	...	...	...	...	...
Malaysia - Malaisie 2016																					
Male - Hommes	72.6	68.2	63.3	58.4	53.7	49.0	44.2	39.5	34.9	30.5	26.3	22.2	18.5	14.9	11.7	8.8	6.2	...	...	...	...
Female - Femmes	77.2	72.8	67.9	63.0	58.1	53.2	48.3	43.5	38.7	34.0	29.5	25.1	20.9	16.9	13.2	9.8	7.0	...	...	...	...
Maldives 2015																					
Male - Hommes	73.1	69.0	64.0	59.1	54.3	49.4	44.6	39.7	34.8	29.9	25.2	20.7	16.2	11.9	7.9	4.7	...	...	...	...	...
Female - Femmes	74.6	70.3	65.4	60.5	55.6	50.7	45.7	40.7	35.8	31.0	26.1	21.4	16.7	12.2	7.8	4.4	...	...	...	...	...
Mongolia - Mongolie 2006 - 2015																					
Male - Hommes	65.3	62.1	57.3	52.4	47.7	43.2	38.7	34.4	30.3	26.5	23.0	19.8	17.0	14.5	12.3	...	...	...	...	...	...
Female - Femmes	74.8	71.4	66.5	61.6	56.8	52.0	47.2	42.5	37.9	33.4	29.2	25.2	21.4	18.0	15.1	...	...	...	...	...	...
Myanmar[28] 2014																					
Male - Hommes	61.0	60.1	55.3	50.4	45.7	41.1	36.7	32.6	28.7	24.9	21.3	17.6	14.1	10.9	8.1	5.6	3.6	4.8	...	...	...
Female - Femmes	68.6	66.7	61.9	57.1	52.3	47.6	42.9	38.3	33.8	29.3	24.9	20.6	16.5	12.8	9.6	6.6	4.2	4.8	...	...	...
Nepal - Népal 2011																					
Male - Hommes	65.4	...	...	...	...	...	...	...	...	...	...	...	...	...	...	...	...	...	...	...	...
Female - Femmes	67.9	...	...	...	...	...	...	...	...	...	...	...	...	...	...	...	...	...	...	...	...
Oman 2013																					
Male - Hommes	74.8	70.9	66.0	61.1	56.4	51.8	47.1	42.4	37.6	33.0	28.5	24.3	20.4	16.9	13.6	10.4	...	...	...	...	...
Female - Femmes	78.5	74.3	69.4	64.4	59.5	54.6	49.7	44.8	39.9	35.1	30.5	25.9	21.6	17.5	13.8	10.2	...	...	...	...	...
2015[29]																					
Male - Hommes	74.2	...	...	...	...	...	...	...	...	...	...	...	...	...	...	...	...	...	...	...	...
Female - Femmes	78.8	...	...	...	...	...	...	...	...	...	...	...	...	...	...	...	...	...	...	...	...
Pakistan[30] 2007																					
Male - Hommes	63.6	65.3	60.7	55.9	51.3	46.7	42.2	37.7	33.3	29.0	25.0	21.3	18.1	15.2	12.7	10.8	9.2	7.3	...	...	...
Female - Femmes	67.6	68.6	64.1	59.5	54.9	50.3	45.7	41.1	36.5	32.1	27.7	23.5	19.6	16.2	13.4	10.9	8.6	6.1	...	...	...
Qatar 2015																					
Male - Hommes	77.5	73.1	68.2	63.3	58.9	54.5	49.8	45.1	40.4	35.6	31.2	26.9	22.9	22.3	18.6	15.2	12.3	...	...	...	...
Female - Femmes	82.1	77.8	72.8	67.9	62.9	57.9	53.1	48.2	43.3	38.5	33.8	29.3	25.0	21.3	18.2	16.5	14.9	...	...	...	...
Republic of Korea - République de Corée 2015																					
Male - Hommes	79.0	74.2	69.3	64.3	59.4	54.5	49.7	44.8	40.1	35.4	30.8	26.5	22.2	18.2	14.3	10.8	8.0	5.7	4.1	2.9	2.1
Female - Femmes	85.2	80.4	75.5	70.5	65.5	60.6	55.7	50.8	46.0	41.1	36.4	31.6	27.0	22.4	17.9	13.7	10.1	7.1	4.8	3.3	2.3
Saudi Arabia - Arabie saoudite[31] 2016																					
Male - Hommes	73.5	...	...	...	...	...	...	...	...	...	...	...	...	...	...	...	...	...	...	...	...
Female - Femmes	74.8	...	...	...	...	...	...	...	...	...	...	...	...	...	...	...	...	...	...	...	...
Singapore - Singapour[32] 2016																					
Male - Hommes	80.6	75.8	70.9	65.9	61.0	56.1	51.2	46.3	41.4	36.7	32.0	27.5	23.1	19.0	15.2	11.8	8.9	6.4	4.5	3.1	2.1
Female - Femmes	85.1	80.3	75.4	70.4	65.4	60.5	55.6	50.6	45.7	40.9	36.1	31.4	26.8	22.4	18.1	14.2	10.7	7.7	5.4	3.7	2.5
Sri Lanka 2000 - 2002																					
Male - Hommes	68.8	...	...	...	...	...	...	...	...	...	...	...	...	...	...	...	...	...	...	...	...
Female - Femmes	77.2	...	...	...	...	...	...	...	...	...	...	...	...	...	...	...	...	...	...	...	...

Continent, country or area and date / Continent, pays ou zone et date	\ 0	5	10	15	20	25	30	35	40	45	50	55	60	65	70	75	80	85	90	95	100

Age (in years) - Age (en années)

ASIA - ASIE

State of Palestine - État de Palestine
2001

	0	5	10	15	20	25	30	35	40	45	50	55	60	65	70	75	80	85	90	95	100
Male - Hommes	70.5	67.5	62.7	57.8	53.1	48.4	43.6	38.9	34.2	29.6	25.2	21.1	17.2	13.8	10.7	8.1	6.1	...	...	...	...
Female - Femmes	73.6	70.3	65.5	60.5	55.7	50.9	46.1	41.3	36.6	32.0	27.5	23.2	19.0	15.2	11.7	8.8	6.4	...	...	...	...
2016																					
Male - Hommes	72.1	...	...	...	...	...	...	...	...	...	...	...	...	...	...	...	...	...	...	...	...
Female - Femmes	75.2	...	...	...	...	...	...	...	...	...	...	...	...	...	...	...	...	...	...	...	...
Tajikistan - Tadjikistan 2008																					
Male - Hommes	69.7	67.9	63.0	58.1	53.3	48.5	43.7	39.1	34.6	30.1	25.7	21.6	17.9	14.7	12.2	10.4	9.2	...	...	...	...
Female - Femmes	74.8	72.5	67.6	62.7	57.8	52.9	48.1	43.4	38.6	33.9	29.4	25.0	21.0	17.5	14.7	12.5	11.1	...	...	...	...
2014																					
Male - Hommes	71.6	...	...	...	...	...	...	...	...	...	...	...	...	...	...	...	...	...	...	...	...
Female - Femmes	75.4	...	...	...	...	...	...	...	...	...	...	...	...	...	...	...	...	...	...	...	...
Thailand - Thaïlande 2005 - 2006																					
Male - Hommes	69.9	...	...	...	...	...	...	...	...	...	...	...	...	...	...	...	...	...	...	...	...
Female - Femmes	77.6	...	...	...	...	...	...	...	...	...	...	...	...	...	...	...	...	...	...	...	...
Turkey - Turquie 2013 - 2015																					
Male - Hommes	75.3	71.4	66.5	61.6	56.8	52.0	47.1	42.3	37.5	32.8	28.3	23.9	19.9	16.1	12.7	9.8	7.3	5.3	4.0	3.2	3.4
Female - Femmes	80.7	76.7	71.8	66.9	62.0	57.1	52.1	47.2	42.4	37.5	32.8	28.2	23.7	19.4	15.3	11.8	8.8	6.5	5.0	4.2	4.4
United Arab Emirates - Émirats arabes unis 2006																					
Male - Hommes	76.7	72.5	67.6	62.7	57.9	53.1	48.3	43.5	38.7	33.9	29.3	24.8	20.7	16.9	13.8	11.3	10.2	...	...	...	...
Female - Femmes	78.8	74.5	69.5	64.6	59.7	54.8	49.8	44.9	40.0	35.2	30.4	25.8	21.6	18.0	15.4	14.0	14.5	...	...	...	...
Uzbekistan - Ouzbékistan 2015																					
Male - Hommes	71.2	67.4	62.5	57.7	52.8	48.1	43.4	38.7	34.1	29.7	25.4	21.3	17.5	14.2	11.4	9.0	7.4	7.7	...	...	...
Female - Femmes	76.0	72.1	67.1	62.2	57.4	52.6	47.8	43.0	38.2	33.6	29.0	24.6	20.4	16.6	13.4	10.6	8.6	8.2	...	...	...
Viet Nam 2016																					
Male - Hommes	70.8	67.8	63.0	58.2	53.4	48.7	43.9	39.2	34.6	30.1	25.8	21.9	18.3	15.0	12.3	10.0	8.3	...	...	...	...
Female - Femmes	76.1	72.3	67.3	62.4	57.5	52.6	47.8	42.9	38.2	33.5	29.0	24.7	20.6	16.9	13.6	11.0	8.9	...	...	...	...
Yemen - Yémen 2004																					
Male - Hommes	60.2	...	...	...	...	...	...	...	...	...	...	...	...	...	...	...	...	...	...	...	...
Female - Femmes	62.0	...	...	...	...	...	...	...	...	...	...	...	...	...	...	...	...	...	...	...	...

EUROPE

	0	5	10	15	20	25	30	35	40	45	50	55	60	65	70	75	80	85	90	95	100
Åland Islands - Îles d'Åland 2015																					
Male - Hommes	80.6	75.6	70.6	65.6	60.6	55.6	50.9	45.9	40.9	35.9	31.6	26.7	22.4	18.4	14.4	10.8	7.8	5.1	3.2	3.5	1.0
Female - Femmes	84.0	79.0	74.0	69.0	64.0	59.0	54.0	49.0	44.0	39.0	34.2	29.8	25.4	21.4	17.7	13.7	9.7	6.9	4.6	3.6	1.3
Albania - Albanie 2013																					
Male - Hommes	76.0	71.9	66.9	62.0	57.3	52.5	47.7	43.0	38.3	33.7	29.2	24.8	20.6	16.6	12.9	9.6	6.9	5.0	...	...	...
Female - Femmes	80.3	75.9	71.0	66.1	61.3	56.4	51.5	46.6	41.8	37.0	32.2	27.6	23.0	18.6	14.3	10.6	7.4	5.1	...	...	...
Austria - Autriche 2015																					
Male - Hommes	78.6	73.9	69.0	64.0	59.1	54.3	49.4	44.6	39.8	35.1	30.4	26.0	21.8	17.9	14.4	11.0	8.0	5.5	3.7	2.5	...
Female - Femmes	83.6	78.9	73.9	68.9	64.0	59.0	54.1	49.2	44.3	39.5	34.7	30.0	25.5	21.2	17.1	13.1	9.5	6.4	4.2	2.8	...
Belarus - Bélarus 2015																					
Male - Hommes	68.6	63.9	58.9	54.0	49.1	44.3	39.7	35.1	30.8	26.6	22.7	19.0	15.7	12.9	10.3	8.0	6.1	4.6	3.4	2.5	1.7
Female - Femmes	78.9	74.1	69.2	64.2	59.3	54.3	49.5	44.7	39.9	35.3	30.7	26.2	21.9	17.9	14.0	10.5	7.6	5.3	3.6	2.3	1.4
Belgium - Belgique[9] 2015																					
Male - Hommes	78.5	73.9	68.9	63.9	59.0	54.2	49.4	44.6	39.8	35.1	30.5	26.0	21.9	18.0	14.4	11.0	8.1	5.6	3.8	2.6	1.8
Female - Femmes	83.1	78.4	73.5	68.5	63.6	58.6	53.7	48.8	43.9	39.1	34.4	29.9	25.4	21.2	17.1	13.2	9.6	6.6	4.3	2.9	1.9

21. Life expectancy at specified ages for each sex: latest available year, 1997 - 2016
Espérance de vie à un âge donné pour chaque sexe : dernière année disponible, 1997 - 2016 (continued - suite)

Continent, country or area and date / Continent, pays ou zone et date	Age (in years) - Age (en années)																				
	0	5	10	15	20	25	30	35	40	45	50	55	60	65	70	75	80	85	90	95	100
EUROPE																					
Bosnia and Herzegovina - Bosnie-Herzégovine																					
2003																					
Male - Hommes	71.3	...	...	...	...	...	...	...	...	...	...	...	...	...	...	...	...	...	...	...	...
Female - Femmes	76.7	...	...	...	...	...	...	...	...	...	...	...	...	...	...	...	...	...	...	...	...
Bulgaria - Bulgarie																					
2013 - 2015																					
Male - Hommes	71.1	66.7	61.8	56.9	52.0	47.3	42.5	37.8	33.2	28.6	24.5	20.6	17.1	14.1	11.2	8.6	6.3	4.5	3.1	2.1	0.5
Female - Femmes	78.0	73.7	68.7	63.8	58.9	54.0	49.1	44.2	39.4	34.8	30.2	25.8	21.6	17.5	13.7	10.1	7.2	4.9	3.3	2.2	0.5
Croatia - Croatie																					
2014																					
Male - Hommes	74.7	...	...	...	...	...	...	...	...	...	...	...	...	...	...	...	...	...	...	...	...
Female - Femmes	81.0	...	...	...	...	...	...	...	...	...	...	...	...	...	...	...	...	...	...	...	...
Czechia - Tchéquie																					
2015																					
Male - Hommes	75.8	71.1	66.1	61.1	56.3	51.4	46.6	41.8	37.1	32.4	27.9	23.6	19.6	16.0	12.8	10.0	7.5	5.5	3.9	2.8	1.9
Female - Femmes	81.4	76.6	71.7	66.7	61.8	56.8	51.9	47.0	42.1	37.3	32.6	28.0	23.5	19.3	15.3	11.6	8.2	5.6	3.5	2.1	1.2
Denmark - Danemark[33]																					
2014 - 2015																					
Male - Hommes	78.6	74.0	69.0	64.1	59.1	54.2	49.4	44.5	39.7	34.9	30.3	25.9	21.7	17.9	14.2	10.9	7.9	5.5	3.8	2.6	...
Female - Femmes	82.5	77.9	72.9	67.9	63.0	58.0	53.1	48.2	43.3	38.4	33.7	29.1	24.7	20.5	16.5	12.8	9.5	6.8	4.5	3.0	...
Estonia - Estonie																					
2015																					
Male - Hommes	73.1	68.3	63.4	58.4	53.6	48.8	44.1	39.6	35.0	30.6	26.3	22.2	18.6	15.3	12.3	9.7	7.4	5.4	3.8	2.4	2.3
Female - Femmes	81.8	77.1	72.1	67.2	62.3	57.4	52.5	47.6	42.8	38.1	33.4	28.8	24.4	20.3	16.2	12.5	9.1	6.3	4.3	2.8	1.8
Faeroe Islands - Îles Féroé																					
2014 - 2015																					
Male - Hommes	78.3	74.8	69.8	65.0	60.3	55.5	50.5	45.7	40.7	35.8	31.6	27.1	23.1	18.8	14.5	11.0	7.6	5.4	3.4	2.8	2.0
Female - Femmes	84.5	79.8	74.8	69.8	64.8	59.8	54.8	49.8	44.8	40.1	35.6	30.7	26.1	21.5	17.6	13.4	10.0	6.5	3.8	2.8	2.0
Finland - Finlande[34]																					
2015																					
Male - Hommes	78.5	73.7	68.7	63.8	58.9	54.1	49.3	44.5	39.7	35.1	30.5	26.1	22.0	18.1	14.5	11.1	8.1	5.6	3.8	2.6	1.7
Female - Femmes	84.1	79.3	74.3	69.4	64.4	59.5	54.6	49.7	44.8	39.9	35.2	30.5	26.0	21.6	17.4	13.4	9.7	6.7	4.4	2.8	1.7
France[9]																					
2012 - 2014																					
Male - Hommes	78.9	74.2	69.2	64.3	59.4	54.6	49.7	45.0	40.2	35.6	31.1	26.8	22.8	19.0	15.4	11.9	8.7	6.1	4.1	2.9	2.3
Female - Femmes	85.1	80.4	75.4	70.5	65.5	60.6	55.7	50.8	45.9	41.1	36.4	31.9	27.4	23.0	18.8	14.6	10.8	7.6	5.0	3.3	2.3
Germany - Allemagne																					
2013 - 2015																					
Male - Hommes	78.2	73.5	68.5	63.6	58.7	53.8	48.9	44.1	39.3	34.6	30.0	25.6	21.5	17.7	14.1	10.8	7.8	5.4	3.7	2.6	1.8
Female - Femmes	83.1	78.4	73.4	68.4	63.5	58.5	53.6	48.7	43.8	39.0	34.2	29.6	25.2	20.9	16.8	12.9	9.3	6.4	4.2	2.9	2.0
Gibraltar																					
2001																					
Male - Hommes	78.5	73.5	68.5	63.5	58.5	53.5	...	43.5	...	33.9	...	25.8	...	17.9	...	11.3	...	...	...	...	...
Female - Femmes	83.3	79.5	75.0	70.0	65.0	60.0	...	50.3	...	40.3	...	30.3	...	20.6	...	13.7	...	...	...	...	...
Greece - Grèce																					
2015																					
Male - Hommes	78.1	73.5	68.5	63.6	58.7	53.9	49.0	44.3	39.5	34.8	30.2	25.9	21.9	18.1	14.5	11.2	8.3	6.1	4.5	3.2	2.2
Female - Femmes	83.2	78.5	73.6	68.6	63.6	58.7	53.8	48.8	44.0	39.1	34.4	29.7	25.2	20.7	16.5	12.4	8.9	6.4	4.6	3.3	2.3
Hungary - Hongrie																					
2015																					
Male - Hommes	72.1	67.5	62.5	57.6	52.7	47.8	43.0	38.2	33.5	28.9	24.6	20.7	17.3	14.2	11.4	8.7	6.4	4.3	2.6	1.5	0.6
Female - Femmes	78.6	74.0	69.0	64.1	59.1	54.2	49.2	44.3	39.5	34.7	30.1	25.8	21.7	17.8	14.0	10.5	7.4	4.8	2.9	1.6	0.6
Iceland - Islande																					
2014 - 2015																					
Male - Hommes	81.0	76.3	71.3	66.3	61.5	56.6	51.7	47.0	42.1	37.4	32.6	28.1	23.8	19.4	15.3	11.7	8.4	5.6	3.5	2.4	1.5
Female - Femmes	83.6	79.1	74.1	69.1	64.2	59.3	54.3	49.4	44.5	39.7	34.9	30.2	25.7	21.3	17.2	13.3	9.7	6.9	4.4	2.6	1.5
Ireland - Irlande																					
2005 - 2007																					
Male - Hommes	76.8	72.2	67.2	62.3	57.5	52.8	48.0	43.3	38.5	33.8	29.2	24.8	20.6	16.6	13.0	9.8	7.1	5.1	3.6	2.6	1.9
Female - Femmes	81.6	76.9	72.0	67.0	62.1	57.2	52.3	47.4	42.5	37.7	33.1	28.5	24.0	19.8	15.8	12.1	8.8	6.2	4.3	3.1	2.1
2014[9]																					
Male - Hommes	79.3	...	...	...	...	...	...	...	...	...	...	...	...	...	...	...	...	...	...	...	...
Female - Femmes	83.5	...	...	...	...	...	...	...	...	...	...	...	...	...	...	...	...	...	...	...	...

Continent, country or area and date / Continent, pays ou zone et date	0	5	10	15	20	25	30	35	40	45	50	55	60	65	70	75	80	85	90	95	100
EUROPE																					
Italy - Italie 2014																					
Male - Hommes	80.3	75.6	70.6	65.7	60.8	55.9	51.0	46.2	41.3	36.6	31.9	27.4	23.0	18.9	15.1	11.6	8.4	5.9	4.1	2.8	1.8
Female - Femmes	85.0	80.3	75.3	70.3	65.4	60.4	55.5	50.5	45.6	40.8	36.0	31.3	26.8	22.3	18.0	14.0	10.3	7.2	4.8	3.2	2.1
Latvia - Lettonie 2015																					
Male - Hommes	69.7	65.1	60.2	55.2	50.4	45.6	41.0	36.5	32.3	28.1	24.1	20.4	17.1	14.1	11.4	9.0	6.8	5.0	3.7	2.6	1.9
Female - Femmes	79.3	74.6	69.7	64.8	59.8	54.9	50.1	45.3	40.5	35.8	31.3	27.0	22.7	18.7	14.8	11.4	8.2	5.8	3.9	2.7	2.1
Lithuania - Lituanie 2015																					
Male - Hommes	69.1	64.5	59.5	54.6	49.9	45.2	40.6	36.2	31.9	27.8	23.8	20.2	16.9	14.0	11.5	9.1	6.8	4.9	3.4	2.5	2.3
Female - Femmes	79.6	75.0	70.1	65.1	60.2	55.3	50.4	45.6	40.9	36.3	31.8	27.3	23.1	19.0	15.2	11.5	8.2	5.6	3.7	2.6	1.9
Luxembourg 2012 - 2014																					
Male - Hommes	80.2	75.4	70.4	65.5	60.6	55.7	50.8	46.0	41.2	36.4	31.8	27.4	23.2	19.2	15.5	12.1	9.0	6.5	5.0	3.4	...
Female - Femmes	84.8	80.0	75.0	70.0	65.1	60.1	55.2	50.3	45.4	40.6	35.8	31.2	26.7	22.3	18.2	14.2	10.7	7.6	5.2	3.3	...
Malta - Malte 2015																					
Male - Hommes	79.7	75.4	70.4	65.4	60.5	55.6	50.7	45.9	41.1	36.3	31.6	27.0	22.7	18.7	14.9	11.2	8.1	...	...	...	...
Female - Femmes	84.0	79.4	74.5	69.6	64.6	59.7	54.8	49.9	45.0	40.1	35.2	30.5	26.0	21.6	17.4	13.4	9.8	...	...	...	...
Netherlands - Pays-Bas 2009																					
Male - Hommes	78.5	73.8	68.8	63.9	59.0	54.1	49.2	44.4	39.5	34.8	30.1	25.6	21.4	17.3	13.6	10.3	7.5	5.3	3.6	2.6	...
Female - Femmes	82.7	77.8	72.8	67.9	62.9	58.0	53.1	48.2	43.3	38.5	33.8	29.3	24.9	20.6	16.5	12.7	9.2	6.4	4.3	2.9	...
2014																					
Male - Hommes	80.0	...	...	...	...	...	...	...	...	...	...	...	...	...	...	...	...	...	...	...	...
Female - Femmes	83.5	...	...	...	...	...	...	...	...	...	...	...	...	...	...	...	...	...	...	...	...
Norway - Norvège 2012																					
Male - Hommes	79.4	74.7	69.7	64.8	59.8	55.0	50.2	45.4	40.6	35.8	31.2	26.7	22.3	18.2	14.4	10.9	7.8	5.5	3.7	2.6	2.3
Female - Femmes	83.4	78.6	73.7	68.7	63.8	58.8	53.9	49.0	44.1	39.2	34.5	29.8	25.3	21.0	16.9	13.0	9.5	6.6	4.3	2.8	1.9
2014																					
Male - Hommes	80.1	...	...	...	...	...	...	...	...	...	...	...	...	...	...	...	...	...	...	...	...
Female - Femmes	84.2	...	...	...	...	...	...	...	...	...	...	...	...	...	...	...	...	...	...	...	...
Poland - Pologne 2015																					
Male - Hommes	73.6	69.0	64.0	59.0	54.2	49.4	44.7	40.0	35.3	30.8	26.6	22.6	19.0	15.7	12.7	10.0	7.6	5.7	4.3	3.1	2.3
Female - Femmes	81.6	76.9	72.0	67.0	62.1	57.1	52.2	47.3	42.4	37.6	33.0	28.4	24.1	20.1	16.2	12.5	9.3	6.7	4.8	3.3	2.4
Portugal 2013 - 2015																					
Male - Hommes	77.4	72.7	67.7	62.8	57.8	53.0	48.1	43.3	38.6	33.9	29.5	25.3	21.2	17.3	13.6	10.1	7.0	4.3	2.6	1.6	1.1
Female - Femmes	83.2	78.5	73.5	68.5	63.6	58.6	53.7	48.8	43.9	39.1	34.4	29.7	25.2	20.7	16.4	12.3	8.5	5.3	3.2	1.9	1.2
Republic of Moldova - République de Moldova[35] 2012																					
Male - Hommes	67.2	63.1	58.1	53.3	48.5	43.7	39.0	34.5	30.1	26.0	22.2	18.7	15.5	13.0	10.2	8.4	7.1	6.9	7.8	...	...
Female - Femmes	75.0	70.9	66.0	61.0	56.1	51.2	46.4	41.5	36.8	32.2	27.7	23.4	19.3	15.7	12.2	9.5	7.4	5.9	5.3	...	...
Romania - Roumanie 2013 - 2015																					
Male - Hommes	71.9	67.7	62.8	57.9	53.0	48.2	43.4	38.6	33.9	29.4	25.2	21.3	17.8	14.6	11.7	9.0	6.8	5.1	3.7	2.8	2.1
Female - Femmes	78.9	74.6	69.6	64.7	59.8	54.8	49.9	45.1	40.2	35.4	30.8	26.3	22.1	18.0	14.1	10.6	7.7	5.5	3.9	2.8	2.0
Russian Federation - Fédération de Russie 2012																					
Male - Hommes	64.6	60.3	55.4	50.5	45.8	41.3	37.0	33.1	29.3	25.4	21.8	18.4	15.4	12.8	10.2	8.1	6.4	5.1	4.0	3.0	1.4
Female - Femmes	75.9	71.6	66.7	61.7	56.9	52.1	47.3	42.8	38.2	33.7	29.3	25.1	21.0	17.1	13.4	10.2	7.4	5.3	3.8	2.8	1.8
San Marino - Saint-Marin 2013																					
Male - Hommes	81.7	76.9	72.0	67.0	62.2	57.4	52.5	47.6	42.7	37.9	33.0	28.3	24.1	19.7	15.7	11.8	8.6	6.1	4.1	2.3	...
Female - Femmes	86.4	81.5	76.5	71.5	66.6	61.6	56.6	51.7	46.7	41.9	37.1	32.4	27.7	23.2	18.8	14.8	10.8	7.4	5.0	2.7	...
Serbia - Serbie[36] 2015																					
Male - Hommes	72.6	68.1	63.1	58.2	53.3	48.5	43.6	38.9	34.2	29.6	25.2	21.2	17.5	14.2	11.2	8.4	6.1	4.3	...	...	...
Female - Femmes	77.7	73.1	68.2	63.2	58.2	53.3	48.4	43.5	38.7	34.0	29.4	24.9	20.7	16.6	12.8	9.4	6.5	4.5	...	...	...

Continent, country or area and date / Continent, pays ou zone et date	Age (in years) - Age (en années)																					
	0	5	10	15	20	25	30	35	40	45	50	55	60	65	70	75	80	85	90	95	100
EUROPE																					
Slovakia - Slovaquie 2015																					
Male - Hommes	73.0	68.5	63.6	58.6	53.8	49.0	44.2	39.4	34.7	30.2	25.9	21.8	18.1	14.8	11.8	9.0	6.6	4.6	3.1	2.0	0.7
Female - Femmes	79.7	75.2	70.2	65.3	60.3	55.4	50.5	45.6	40.7	35.9	31.3	26.7	22.4	18.2	14.3	10.5	7.3	4.6	2.7	1.5	0.6
Slovenia - Slovénie 2015 - 2016																					
Male - Hommes	77.6	72.8	67.8	62.9	58.0	53.2	48.3	43.5	38.7	34.0	29.5	25.2	21.1	17.4	13.8	10.6	7.7	5.5	4.0	2.9	2.0
Female - Femmes	83.5	78.7	73.7	68.7	63.8	58.8	53.9	49.0	44.1	39.2	34.5	29.9	25.3	21.0	16.9	13.0	9.4	6.4	4.2	3.0	2.1
Spain - Espagne 2013																					
Male - Hommes	80.0	75.2	70.3	65.3	60.4	55.5	50.6	45.7	40.8	36.1	31.5	27.1	22.9	19.0	15.2	11.7	8.7	6.2	4.5	3.5	3.4
Female - Femmes	85.6	80.9	75.9	70.9	66.0	61.0	56.0	51.1	46.2	41.4	36.6	32.0	27.4	22.9	18.5	14.4	10.6	7.4	5.1	3.7	3.1
2014																					
Male - Hommes	80.4	...	...	...	...	...	...	...	...	...	...	...	...	...	...	...	...	...	...	...	...
Female - Femmes	86.2	...	...	...	...	...	...	...	...	...	...	...	...	...	...	...	...	...	...	...	...
Sweden - Suède 2012																					
Male - Hommes	79.9	75.1	70.2	65.2	60.3	55.5	50.7	45.8	41.0	36.2	31.5	27.0	22.6	18.4	14.5	11.0	7.9	5.4	3.6	2.4	1.6
Female - Femmes	83.5	78.8	73.8	68.8	63.9	59.0	54.0	49.1	44.2	39.4	34.6	30.0	25.4	21.0	16.9	13.0	9.5	6.5	4.3	2.9	1.9
2014																					
Male - Hommes	80.4	...	...	...	...	...	...	...	...	...	...	...	...	...	...	...	...	...	...	...	...
Female - Femmes	84.2	...	...	...	...	...	...	...	...	...	...	...	...	...	...	...	...	...	...	...	...
Switzerland - Suisse 2015																					
Male - Hommes	80.7	76.1	71.2	66.2	61.3	56.4	51.6	46.7	41.8	37.0	32.3	27.8	23.4	19.2	15.3	11.7	8.5	5.8	3.8	2.6	1.9
Female - Femmes	84.9	80.2	75.3	70.3	65.3	60.4	55.4	50.5	45.6	40.7	35.9	31.2	26.6	22.2	17.9	13.8	10.1	6.8	4.4	2.9	2.1
TFYR of Macedonia - L'ex-R. y. de Macédoine 2014																					
Male - Hommes	73.5	69.3	64.4	59.4	54.5	49.6	44.8	40.0	35.2	30.5	26.0	21.8	17.9	14.4	11.1	8.2	5.8	3.9	2.6	2.5	...
Female - Femmes	77.4	73.2	68.2	63.3	58.3	53.4	48.5	43.6	38.7	33.9	29.2	24.7	20.3	16.2	12.4	9.0	6.2	4.2	3.0	2.7	...
Ukraine 2013																					
Male - Hommes	66.3	62.0	57.1	52.2	47.4	42.7	38.2	33.9	29.9	25.9	22.2	18.7	15.5	12.8	10.3	8.2	6.4	5.2	4.2	3.3	2.2
Female - Femmes	76.2	71.8	66.9	62.0	57.1	52.2	47.4	42.7	38.1	33.6	29.1	24.8	20.6	16.7	13.1	9.8	7.2	5.1	3.6	2.5	1.6
United Kingdom of Great Britain and Northern Ireland - Royaume-Uni de Grande-Bretagne et d'Irlande du Nord[37] 2012																					
Male - Hommes	79.0	74.4	69.4	64.5	59.6	54.7	49.9	45.1	40.3	35.6	31.1	26.6	22.3	18.3	14.5	11.2	8.2	5.8	4.0	2.8	2.2
Female - Femmes	82.7	78.0	73.1	68.1	63.1	58.2	53.3	48.4	43.5	38.7	34.0	29.5	25.0	20.7	16.7	12.9	9.5	6.7	4.6	3.2	2.3
OCEANIA - OCÉANIE																					
American Samoa - Samoas américaines 2011																					
Male - Hommes	71.1	66.8	61.9	57.0	52.2	47.4	42.6	38.0	33.5	29.1	25.3	21.4	18.0	14.6	11.7	9.6	...	...	...	...	...
Female - Femmes	77.8	73.3	68.3	63.4	58.5	53.6	48.9	44.4	39.6	35.0	30.6	26.5	22.8	19.2	16.1	13.8	...	...	...	...	...
Australia - Australie 2013 - 2015																					
Male - Hommes	80.4	75.7	70.8	65.8	60.9	56.1	51.3	46.5	41.8	37.1	32.5	28.0	23.7	19.6	15.7	12.0	8.8	6.2	4.3	3.0	2.3
Female - Femmes	84.5	79.8	74.9	69.9	65.0	60.1	55.1	50.3	45.4	40.6	35.9	31.2	26.7	22.3	18.0	14.0	10.4	7.2	4.9	3.3	2.4
Cook Islands - Îles Cook[38] 2006																					
Male - Hommes	69.5	66.0	61.3	56.5	52.0	47.4	42.8	38.1	33.6	29.1	24.8	20.9	17.5	14.3	11.4	9.0	7.3	...	...	...	...
Female - Femmes	76.2	72.4	67.4	62.4	57.4	52.7	48.0	43.2	38.4	33.6	29.1	24.7	20.4	16.4	12.6	9.5	6.9	...	...	...	...
Fiji - Fidji 2007																					
Male - Hommes	65.3	...	...	...	...	...	...	...	...	...	...	...	...	...	...	...	...	...	...	...	...
Female - Femmes	69.6	...	...	...	...	...	...	...	...	...	...	...	...	...	...	...	...	...	...	...	...

21. Life expectancy at specified ages for each sex: latest available year, 1997 - 2016
Espérance de vie à un âge donné pour chaque sexe : dernière année disponible, 1997 - 2016 (continued - suite)

Continent, country or area and date / Continent, pays ou zone et date	0	5	10	15	20	25	30	35	40	45	50	55	60	65	70	75	80	85	90	95	100
OCEANIA - OCÉANIE																					
French Polynesia - Polynésie française																					
2012																					
Male - Hommes	73.3	69.6	64.6	59.8	55.0	50.3	45.7	41.0	36.2	31.6	27.1	22.7	18.3	14.8	11.4	8.5	6.5	4.7	...	...	...
Female - Femmes	78.2	73.8	68.8	63.9	59.1	54.1	49.3	44.5	39.7	35.0	30.4	26.1	22.0	17.9	14.2	10.6	7.6	5.0	...	...	...
2015																					
Male - Hommes	74.4	...	...	...	...	...	...	...	...	...	...	...	...	...	...	...	...	...	...	...	...
Female - Femmes	78.1	...	...	...	...	...	...	...	...	...	...	...	...	...	...	...	...	...	...	...	...
Guam																					
2015																					
Male - Hommes	75.9	...	...	...	...	...	...	...	...	...	...	...	...	...	...	...	...	...	...	...	...
Female - Femmes	82.2	...	...	...	...	...	...	...	...	...	...	...	...	...	...	...	...	...	...	...	...
Kiribati																					
2005																					
Male - Hommes	58.9	58.2	53.6	48.9	44.4	40.0	35.6	31.3	27.1	23.1	19.4	16.0	13.0	10.4	8.3	6.6	5.3	4.2	...	...	...
Female - Femmes	63.1	62.6	57.9	53.1	48.6	44.1	39.7	35.4	31.2	27.1	23.2	19.5	16.1	13.1	10.4	8.1	6.2	4.7	...	...	...
Marshall Islands - Îles Marshall																					
2004																					
Male - Hommes	67.0	...	...	...	...	...	...	...	...	...	...	...	...	...	...	...	...	...	...	...	...
Female - Femmes	70.6	...	...	...	...	...	...	...	...	...	...	...	...	...	...	...	...	...	...	...	...
Micronesia (Federated States of) - Micronésie (États fédérés de)																					
2000																					
Male - Hommes	66.5	...	...	...	...	...	...	...	...	...	...	...	...	...	...	...	...	...	...	...	...
Female - Femmes	67.5	...	...	...	...	...	...	...	...	...	...	...	...	...	...	...	...	...	...	...	...
Nauru[39]																					
2011																					
Male - Hommes	56.8	...	...	...	...	...	...	...	...	...	...	...	...	...	...	...	...	...	...	...	...
Female - Femmes	62.7	...	...	...	...	...	...	...	...	...	...	...	...	...	...	...	...	...	...	...	...
New Caledonia - Nouvelle-Calédonie																					
2012																					
Male - Hommes	74.0	69.4	64.6	59.7	55.3	51.1	46.7	42.0	37.3	32.9	28.5	...	20.1	...	13.1	...	7.5	...	...	...	...
Female - Femmes	80.4	75.7	70.8	65.8	61.0	56.0	51.1	46.2	41.5	36.7	32.1	...	23.5	...	15.2	...	8.9	...	...	...	...
New Zealand - Nouvelle-Zélande[9]																					
2014 - 2016																					
Male - Hommes	79.9	75.4	70.4	65.5	60.6	55.8	51.0	46.2	41.5	36.8	32.2	27.7	23.4	19.3	15.4	11.8	8.7	6.1	4.3	...	...
Female - Femmes	83.4	78.8	73.8	68.9	64.0	59.1	54.2	49.3	44.4	39.6	34.9	30.3	25.9	21.5	17.3	13.4	9.9	7.0	4.8	...	...
Niue - Nioué																					
2007 - 2011																					
Male - Hommes	70.1	...	...	...	...	...	...	...	...	...	...	...	...	...	...	...	...	...	...	...	...
Female - Femmes	76.3	...	...	...	...	...	...	...	...	...	...	...	...	...	...	...	...	...	...	...	...
Northern Mariana Islands - Îles Mariannes septentrionales																					
2009																					
Male - Hommes	74.5	...	...	...	...	...	...	...	...	...	...	...	...	...	...	...	...	...	...	...	...
Female - Femmes	79.9	...	...	...	...	...	...	...	...	...	...	...	...	...	...	...	...	...	...	...	...
Palau - Palaos																					
2005																					
Male - Hommes	66.3	...	...	...	...	...	...	...	...	...	...	...	...	...	...	...	...	...	...	...	...
Female - Femmes	72.1	...	...	...	...	...	...	...	...	...	...	...	...	...	...	...	...	...	...	...	...
Papua New Guinea - Papouasie-Nouvelle-Guinée																					
2000																					
Male - Hommes	53.7	54.1	50.2	45.7	41.6	37.7	33.7	29.8	25.9	22.1	18.5	15.0	11.9	9.2	6.9	5.0	3.6	2.6	1.7	0.6	...
Female - Femmes	54.8	54.7	50.8	46.3	42.1	38.1	34.1	30.1	26.2	22.3	18.6	15.2	12.0	9.2	6.8	5.0	3.6	2.5	1.6	0.6	...
Samoa																					
2006																					
Male - Hommes	71.5	...	...	...	...	...	...	...	...	...	...	...	...	...	...	...	...	...	...	...	...
Female - Femmes	74.2	...	...	...	...	...	...	...	...	...	...	...	...	...	...	...	...	...	...	...	...

21. Life expectancy at specified ages for each sex: latest available year, 1997 - 2016
Espérance de vie à un âge donné pour chaque sexe : dernière année disponible, 1997 - 2016 (continued - suite)

Continent, country or area and date / Continent, pays ou zone et date	0	5	10	15	20	25	30	35	40	45	50	55	60	65	70	75	80	85	90	95	100
OCEANIA - OCÉANIE																					
Solomon Islands - Îles Salomon																					
2009																					
Male - Hommes	66.2	...	...	...	...	...	...	...	...	...	...	...	...	...	...	...	...	...	...	...	...
Female - Femmes	73.1	...	...	...	...	...	...	...	...	...	...	...	...	...	...	...	...	...	...	...	...
Tonga																					
2006																					
Male - Hommes	67.3	64.1	59.3	54.5	49.9	45.4	40.7	36.2	31.6	27.2	23.4	19.4	15.9	13.0	9.4	6.3	4.0	...	...	...	...
Female - Femmes	73.0	69.3	64.6	59.8	55.0	50.1	45.2	40.4	35.7	31.3	27.1	23.0	19.0	15.3	11.6	8.6	6.1	...	...	...	...
Tuvalu																					
1997 - 2002																					
Male - Hommes	61.7	59.5	54.8	50.0	45.2	40.6	35.9	32.1	28.0	24.1	20.0	17.1	13.7	10.8	9.0	6.9	5.4	...	...	...	...
Female - Femmes	65.1	62.6	57.7	53.7	50.0	45.3	40.9	36.6	32.2	28.1	23.8	20.3	16.9	13.2	10.6	7.9	6.4	...	...	...	...
Vanuatu[40]																					
2009																					
Male - Hommes	69.6	66.4	61.6	56.8	52.1	47.5	42.8	38.1	33.5	29.0	24.7	20.6	16.8	13.4	10.4	7.9	6.0	...	...	...	...
Female - Femmes	72.7	69.3	64.5	59.5	54.7	49.9	45.1	40.3	35.5	30.8	26.3	22.0	18.0	14.4	11.2	8.5	6.4	...	...	...	...
Wallis and Futuna Islands - Îles Wallis et Futuna																					
2003																					
Male - Hommes	73.1	...	...	...	...	...	...	...	...	...	...	...	...	...	...	...	...	...	...	...	...
Female - Femmes	75.5	...	...	...	...	...	...	...	...	...	...	...	...	...	...	...	...	...	...	...	...

FOOTNOTES - NOTES

[1] Data refer to Algerian population only. - Les données ne concernent que la population algérienne.

[2] Based on the results of the Population Census. - D'après les résultats du recensement de la population.

[3] Source: Botswana Population Projections 2011-2026. - Source: Botswana Population Projections 2011-2026.

[4] Based on the results of the 2006 Population and Housing Census. - Données fondées sur les résultats du recensement de la population et de l'habitat de 2006.

[5] Source: Department of Statistics and Demographic Studies (DISED); 2002 EDAM-IS2 and 2002 EDSF/PAPFAM surveys - Source : Direction de la Statistique et des Etudes Démographiques (DISED); 2002 Enquête Djiboutienne auprès des Ménages (EDAM-IS2) et 2002 Enquête Djiboutienne sur la Sante de la Famille (EDSF/PAPFAM - 2002)

[6] Based on underlying data of the Population and Housing Census 2014. - Données fondées sur les résultats du recensement de la population de 2014.

[7] Data refer to the 12 months preceding the census in April. - Les données se rapportent aux douze mois précédant le recensement d'avril.

[8] Excludes the islands of St. Brandon and Agalega. - Non compris les îles St. Brandon et Agalega.

[9] Provisional data. - Données provisoires.

[10] Data refer to Saint Helenian resident population. - Pour la population résidante de Sainte-Hélène.

[11] Data refer to the 12 months preceding the census in November. - Données se rapportant aux 12 mois précédant le recensement de novembre.

[12] Based on underlying data of the 2002 Population Census. - Données fondées sur les résultats du recensement de la population de 2002.

[13] Provisional data. Based on the results of the 2014 Population Census. - Données provisoires. D'après les résultats du recensement de la population de 2014.

[14] Data are based on a small number of deaths. - Les données sont basées sur un nombre limité de décès.

[15] Data refer to projections based on the 1992 Population Census. - Les données se réfèrent aux projections basées sur le recensement de la population de 1992.

[16] Excluding Indian jungle population. - Non compris les Indiens de la jungle.

[17] Data refer to the 12 months from 30 June 2016 to 30 June 2017. - Les données font référence aux douze mois de 30 juin 2016 à 30 juin 2017.

[18] Excludes nomadic Indian tribes. Data based on the 2010 Population Census. - Non compris les tribus d'Indiens nomades. Les données sont fondées sur le recensement de la population de 2010.

[19] Based on the results of the 2011 Population Census. - Basé sur les résultats du recensement de la population de 2011.

[20] Source: Sample vital registration system of Bangladesh - Source : << Sample Vital Registration System >> du Bangladesh.

[21] For statistical purposes, the data for China do not include those for the Hong Kong Special Administrative Region (Hong Kong SAR), Macao Special Administrative Region (Macao SAR) and Taiwan province of China. - Pour la présentation des statistiques, les données pour la Chine ne comprennent pas la Région Administrative Spéciale de Hong Kong (Hong Kong RAS), la Région Administrative Spéciale de Macao (Macao RAS) et Taïwan province de Chine.

[22] Data refer to government controlled areas. - Les données se rapportent aux zones contrôlées par le Gouvernement.

[23] Includes data for the Indian-held part of Jammu and Kashmir, the final status of which has not yet been determined. - Y compris les données pour la partie du Jammu et du Cachemire occupée par l'Inde dont le statut définitif n'a pas encore été déterminé.

[24] Includes data for East Jerusalem and Israeli residents in certain other territories under occupation by Israeli military forces since June 1967. - Y compris les données pour Jérusalem-Est et les résidents israéliens dans certains autres territoires occupés depuis 1967 par les forces armées israéliennes.

[25] Data refer to Japanese nationals in Japan only. - Les données se raportent aux nationaux japonais au Japon seulement.

[26] Excluding data for Jordanian territory under occupation since June 1967 by Israeli military forces. Excluding foreigners, including registered Palestinian refugees. - Non compris les données pour le territoire jordanien occupé depuis juin 1967 par les forces armées israéliennes. Non compris les étrangers, mais y compris les réfugiés de Palestine enregistrés.

[27] Based on underlying data of the 2015 census. - Données fondées sur celles extraites du recensement de 2015.

[28] Data are from Vital Registration System (VRS). - Les données proviennent du système d'enregistrement des faits d'état civil.

[29] Data refer to Omani citizen only. - Les données concernent les citoyens d'Oman uniquement.

[30] Based on the results of the Pakistan Demographic Survey. Excluding data for the Pakistan-held part of Jammu and Kashmir, the final status of which has not yet been determined. - Données extraites de l'enquête démographique effectuée par le Pakistan. Non compris les données concernant la partie du Jammu et Cachemire occupée par le Pakistan dont le statut définitif n'a pas été déterminé.

[31] Data refer to Saudi Arabian nationals only. - Les données ne concernent que les ressortissants saoudiens.

[32] Provisional data. Data refer to resident population which comprises Singapore citizens and permanent residents. - Données provisoires. Les données se rapportent à la population résidente composé des citoyens de Singapour et des résidents permanents.

[33] Excluding Faeroe Islands and Greenland shown separately, if available. - Non compris les Iles Féroé et le Groenland, qui font l'objet de rubriques distinctes, si disponible.

[34] Excluding Åland Islands. - Non compris les Îles d'Åland.

[35] Excluding Transnistria and the municipality of Bender. - Les données ne tiennent pas compte de l'information sur la Transnistria et la municipalité de Bender.

[36] Excludes data for Kosovo and Metohia. - Sans les données pour le Kosovo et Metohie.

[37] Excluding Channel Islands (Guernsey and Jersey) and Isle of Man, shown separately, if available. - Non compris les îles Anglo-Normandes (Guernesey et Jersey) et l'île de Man, qui font l'objet de rubriques distinctes, si disponible.

[38] Excluding Niue, shown separately, which is part of Cook Islands, but because of remoteness is administered separately. - Non compris Nioué, qui fait l'objet d'une rubrique distincte et qui fait partie des îles Cook, mais qui, en raison de son éloignement, est administrée séparément.

[39] Data refer to the 12 months preceding the census in October. - Les données se rapportent aux 12 mois précédant le recensement de octobre.

[40] Based on underlying data of the 2009 census. - Données fondées sur celles extraites du recensement de 2009.

Table 22 - Demographic Yearbook 2014

Table 22 presents the number of marriages and crude marriage rates by urban/rural residence for every year with available data between 2012 and 2016.

Description of variables: Marriage is defined as the act, ceremony or process by which the legal relationship of spouses is constituted. The legality of the union may be established by civil, religious or other means as recognized by the laws of each country[1].

Marriage statistics in this table, therefore, include both first marriages and remarriages after divorce, widowhood or annulment. They do not, unless otherwise noted, include resumption of marriage ties after legal separation. These statistics refer to the number of marriages performed, and not to the number of persons marrying.

Statistics shown are obtained from civil registers of marriage. Exceptions, such as data from church registers, are identified in footnotes.

The urban/rural classification of marriages is that provided by each country or area; it is presumed to be based on the national census definitions of urban population which have been set forth at the end of the notes for table 6.

For certain countries, there is a discrepancy between the total number of marriages shown in this table and those shown in subsequent tables for the same year. Usually this discrepancy arises because the total number of marriages occurring in a given year is revised although the remaining tabulations are not.

Rate computation: Crude marriage rates are the annual number of marriages per 1 000 mid-year population. Rates by urban/rural residence are the annual number of marriages, in the appropriate urban or rural category, per 1 000 corresponding mid-year population. Rates presented in this table have been limited to those for countries or areas having at least a total of 30 marriages in a given year. These rates are calculated by the Statistics Division of the United Nations based on the appropriate reference population (for example: total population, nationals only, etc.) if known and available. If the reference population is not known or unavailable the total population is used to calculate the rates. Therefore, if the population that is used to calculate the rates is different from the correct reference population, the rates presented might under- or overstate the true situation in a country or area.

Reliability of data: Each country or area has been asked to indicate the estimated completeness of the number of marriages recorded in its civil register. These national assessments are indicated by the quality codes "C" and "U" that appear in the first column of this table.

"C" indicates that the data are estimated to be virtually complete, that is, representing at least 90 per cent of the marriages occurring each year, while "U" indicates that data are estimated to be incomplete, that is representing less than 90 per cent of the marriages occurring each year. The code "..." indicates that no information was provided regarding completeness.

Data from civil registers which are reported as incomplete or of unknown completeness (coded "U" or "...") are considered unreliable. They appear in italics in this table; rates are not computed for these data.

These quality codes apply only to data from civil registers. For more information about the quality of vital statistics data in general, see section 4.2 of the Technical Notes.

Limitations: Statistics on marriages are subject to the same qualifications that have been set forth for vital statistics in general and marriage statistics in particular as discussed in section 4 of the Technical Notes.

The fact that marriage is a legal event, unlike birth and death that are biological events, has implications for international comparability of data. Marriage has been defined, for statistical purposes, in terms of the laws of individual countries or areas. These laws vary throughout the world. In addition, comparability is further limited because some countries or areas compile statistics only for civil marriages although religious marriages may also be legally recognized; in other countries or areas, the only available records are church registers and, therefore, the statistics may not reflect marriages that are civil marriages only.

Because in many countries or areas marriage is a civil legal contract which, to establish its legality, must be celebrated before a civil officer, it follows that for these countries or areas registration would tend to be almost automatic at the time of, or immediately following, the marriage ceremony. This factor should be kept in mind when considering the reliability of data, described above. For this reason the practice of tabulating data by date of registration does not generally pose serious problems of comparability as it does in the case of birth and death statistics.

As indicators of family formation, the statistics on the number of marriages presented in this table are bound to be deficient to the extent that they do not include either customary unions, which are not registered even though they are considered legal and binding under customary law, or consensual unions (also known as extra-legal or de facto unions). In general, lower marriage rates over a period of years are an indication of higher incidence of customary or consensual unions.

In addition, rates are affected also by the quality and limitations of the population estimates that are used in their computation. The problems of under-enumeration or over-enumeration and, to some extent, the differences in definition of total population have been discussed in section 3 of the Technical Notes dealing with population data in general, and specific information pertaining to individual countries or areas is given in the footnotes to table 3.

Strict correspondence between the numerator of the rate and the denominator is not always obtained; for example, marriages among civilian and military segments of the population may be related to civilian population. The effect of this may be to increase the rates, but, in most cases, this effect is negligible.

It should be emphasized that crude marriage rates like crude birth, death and divorce rates, may be seriously affected by the age-sex-marital structure of the population to which they relate. Crude marriage rates do, however, provide a simple measure of the level and changes in marriage.

The comparability of data by urban/rural residence is affected by the national definitions of urban and rural used in tabulating these data. It is assumed, in the absence of specific information to the contrary, that the definitions of urban and rural used in connection with the national population census were also used in the compilation of the vital statistics for each country or area. However, it cannot be excluded that, for a given country or area, different definitions of urban and rural are used for the vital statistics data and the population census data respectively. When known, the definitions of urban in national population censuses are presented at the end of the technical notes for table 6. As discussed in detail in the notes, these definitions vary considerably from one country or area to another.

In addition to problems of comparability, marriage rates classified by urban/rural residence are also subject to certain special types of bias. If, when calculating marriage rates, different definitions of urban are used in connection with the vital events and the population data, and if this results in a net difference between the numerator and denominator of the rate in the population at risk, then the marriage rates would be biased. Urban/rural differentials in marriage rates may also be affected by whether the vital events have been tabulated in terms of place of occurrence or place of usual residence. This problem is discussed in more detail in section 4.1.4.1 of the Technical Notes.

Earlier data: Marriages and crude marriage rates have been shown in each issue of the *Demographic Yearbook*. For more information on specific topics, and years for which data are reported, readers should consult the Historical Index.

NOTES

[1] *Principles and Recommendations for a Vital Statistics System Revision 3,* Sales No. E.13.XVII.10, United Nations, New York, 2014.

Tableau 22 – *Annuaire démographique 2016*

Le tableau 22 présente des données sur les mariages et les taux bruts de nuptialité selon le lieu de résidence (zone urbaine ou rurale) pour les années où l'information est disponible entre 2012 et 2016.

Description des variables : le mariage désigne l'acte, la cérémonie ou la procédure qui établit un rapport légal entre les époux. L'union peut être rendue légale par une procédure civile ou religieuse, ou par toute autre procédure, conformément à la législation du pays[1].

Les statistiques de la nuptialité présentées dans ce tableau comprennent donc les premiers mariages et les remariages faisant suite à un divorce, un veuvage ou une annulation. Toutefois, sauf indication contraire, elles ne comprennent pas les unions reconstituées après une séparation légale. Ces statistiques se rapportent au nombre de mariages célébrés, non au nombre de personnes qui se marient.

Les statistiques présentées reposent sur l'enregistrement des mariages par les services de l'état civil. Les exceptions (données provenant des registres des églises, par exemple) font l'objet d'une note à la fin du tableau.

La classification des mariages selon le lieu de résidence (zone urbaine ou rurale) est celle qui a été communiquée par chaque pays ou zone ; on part du principe qu'elle repose sur les définitions de la population urbaine utilisées pour les recensements nationaux telles qu'elles sont reproduites à la fin des notes se rapportant au tableau 6.

Pour quelques pays il y a une discordance entre le nombre total de mariages présenté dans ce tableau et ceux présentés après pour la même année. Habituellement ces différences apparaissent lorsque le nombre total des mariages pour une certaine année a été révisé alors que les autres tabulations ne l'ont pas été.

Calcul des taux : les taux bruts de nuptialité représentent le nombre annuel de mariages pour 1 000 habitants au milieu de l'année. Les taux selon le lieu de résidence (zone urbaine ou rurale) représentent le nombre annuel de mariages, classés selon la catégorie urbaine ou rurale appropriée, pour 1 000 habitants au milieu de l'année. Les taux de ce tableau ne se rapportent qu'aux pays ou zones où l'on a enregistré un total d'au moins 30 mariages pendant une année donnée. Ces taux sont calculés par la division de statistique des Nations Unies sur la base de la population de référence adéquate (par exemple : population totale, nationaux seulement, etc.) si connue et disponible. Si la population de référence n'est pas connue ou n'est pas disponible, la population totale est utilisée pour calculer les taux. Par conséquent, si la population utilisée pour calculer les taux est différente de la population de référence adéquate, les taux présentés sont susceptibles de sous ou sur estimer la situation réelle d'un pays ou d'un territoire.

Fiabilité des données : il a été demandé à chaque pays ou zone d'indiquer le degré estimatif de complétude des données sur les mariages figurant dans ses registres d'état civil. Ces évaluations nationales sont signalées par les codes de qualité "C" et "U" qui apparaissent dans la deuxième colonne du tableau.

La lettre "C" indique que les données sont jugées à peu près complètes, c'est-à-dire qu'elles représentent au moins 90 p. 100 des mariages survenus chaque année ; la lettre "U" signale que les données sont jugées incomplètes, c'est-à-dire qu'elles représentent moins de 90 p. 100 des mariages survenus chaque année. Le code "..." indique qu'aucun renseignement n'a été communiqué quant à la complétude des données.

Les données issues des registres de l'état civil qui sont déclarées incomplètes ou dont le degré de complétude n'est pas connu (code "U" ou "...") sont jugées douteuses. Elles apparaissent en italique dans le tableau et les taux correspondants n'ont pas été calculés.

Les codes de qualité ne s'appliquent qu'aux données provenant des registres de l'état civil. Pour plus de précisions sur la qualité des données reposant sur les statistiques de l'état civil en général, voir la section 4.2 des Notes techniques.

Insuffisance des données : les statistiques relatives aux mariages appellent les mêmes réserves que celles qui ont été formulées à propos des statistiques de l'état civil en général et des statistiques concernant la nuptialité en particulier (voir la section 4 des Notes techniques).

Le fait que le mariage soit un acte juridique, à la différence de la naissance et du décès, qui sont des faits biologiques, a des répercussions sur la comparabilité internationale des données. Aux fins de la statistique, le mariage est défini par la législation de chaque pays ou zone. Cette législation varie d'un pays à l'autre. La comparabilité est limitée en outre du fait que certains pays ou zones ne réunissent des statistiques que pour les mariages civils, bien que les mariages religieux y soient également reconnus par la loi ; dans d'autres, les seuls relevés disponibles sont les registres des églises et, en conséquence, les statistiques peuvent ne pas rendre compte des mariages exclusivement civils.

Étant donné que, dans de nombreux pays ou zones, le mariage est un contrat juridique civil qui, pour être légal, doit être conclu devant un officier d'état civil, il s'ensuit que dans ces pays ou zones l'enregistrement se fait à peu près systématiquement au moment de la cérémonie ou immédiatement après. Il faut tenir compte de cet élément lorsque l'on évalue la fiabilité des données, dont il est question plus haut. C'est pourquoi la pratique consistant à exploiter les données selon la date de l'enregistrement ne pose généralement pas les graves problèmes de comparabilité auxquels on se heurte dans le cas des statistiques concernant les naissances et les décès.

Les statistiques relatives au nombre des mariages présentées dans ce tableau donnent une idée forcément trompeuse de la formation des familles, dans la mesure où elles ne tiennent compte ni des mariages coutumiers, qui ne sont pas enregistrés bien qu'ils soient considérés comme légaux et créateurs d'obligations en vertu du droit coutumier, ni des unions consensuelles (appelées également unions non légalisées ou unions de fait). En général, une diminution du taux de nuptialité pendant un certain nombre d'années indique une augmentation des mariages coutumiers ou des unions consensuelles.

L'exactitude des taux dépend également de la qualité et des insuffisances des estimations de population qui sont utilisées pour leur calcul. Le problème des erreurs par excès ou par défaut commises lors du dénombrement et, dans une certaine mesure, le problème de l'hétérogénéité des définitions de la population totale ont été examinés à la section 3 des Notes techniques relative à la population en général ; des indications concernant les différents pays ou zones sont données en note à la fin du tableau 3.

Il n'a pas toujours été possible d'obtenir une correspondance rigoureuse entre le numérateur et le dénominateur pour le calcul des taux. Par exemple, les mariages parmi la population civile et les militaires sont parfois rapportés à la population civile. Cela peut avoir pour effet d'accroître les taux, mais, dans la plupart des cas, il est probable que la différence sera négligeable.

Il faut souligner que les taux bruts de nuptialité, de même que les taux bruts de natalité, de mortalité et de divortialité, peuvent varier sensiblement selon la structure par âge et par sexe de la population à laquelle ils se rapportent. Les taux bruts de nuptialité offrent néanmoins un moyen simple de mesurer la fréquence et l'évolution des mariages.

La comparabilité des données selon le lieu de résidence (zone urbaine ou rurale) peut être limitée par les définitions nationales des termes « urbain » et « rural » utilisées pour le classement de ces données. En l'absence d'indications contraires, on a supposé que les mêmes définitions avaient servi pour le recensement national de la population et pour l'établissement des statistiques de l'état civil pour chaque pays ou zone. Toutefois, il n'est pas exclu que, pour une zone ou un pays donné, des définitions différentes aient été retenues. Les définitions du terme « urbain » utilisées pour les recensements nationaux de population ont été présentées à la fin des notes techniques du tableau 6 lorsqu'elles étaient connues. Comme on l'a précisé dans les notes techniques relatives au tableau 6, ces définitions varient considérablement d'un pays ou d'une zone à l'autre.

Outre les problèmes de comparabilité, les taux de nuptialité classés selon le lieu de résidence (zone urbaine ou rurale) sont également sujets à des distorsions particulières. Si l'on utilise des définitions différentes du terme « urbain » pour classer les faits d'état civil et les données relatives à la population lors du calcul des taux et qu'il en résulte une différence nette entre le numérateur et le dénominateur pour le taux de la population exposée au risque, les taux de nuptialité s'en trouveront faussés. La différence entre ces taux pour les zones urbaines et rurales pourra aussi être faussée selon que les faits d'état civil auront été classés d'après le lieu où ils se sont produits ou d'après le lieu de résidence habituel. Ce problème est examiné plus en détail à la section 4.1.4.1 des Notes techniques.

Données publiées antérieurement : les différentes éditions de *l'Annuaire démographique* regroupent des données sur le nombre des mariages. Pour plus de précisions concernant les années et les sujets pour lesquels des données ont été publiées, se reporter à l'index historique.

NOTE

[1] *Principes et recommandations pour un système de statistique de l'état civil, troisième révision,* numéro de vente : E.13.XVII.10, publication des Nations Unies, New York, 2014.

597

22. Marriages and crude marriage rates, by urban/rural residence: 2012 - 2016
Mariages et taux bruts de nuptialité, selon la résidence, urbaine/rurale : 2012 - 2016

Continent, country or area, and urban/rural residence / Continent, pays ou zone et résidence, urbaine/rurale	Co-de[a]	Number - Nombre					Rate - Taux				
		2012	2013	2014	2015	2016	2012	2013	2014	2015	2016
AFRICA - AFRIQUE											
Algeria - Algérie[1]											
Total	...	371 280	387 947	386 422	369 074	356 600	...	...	...	...	...
Botswana											
Total	+U	5 214	5 333[2]	5 591[2]	...	...	...	...	...	...	...
Côte d'Ivoire											
Total	...	...	...	...	25 689	26 678	...	...	...	...	...
Urban - Urbaine	...	...	...	...	23 750	25 189	...	...	...	...	...
Rural - Rurale	...	...	...	...	1 939	1 489	...	...	...	...	...
Egypt - Égypte[3]											
Total	+C	922 425	909 350	953 137	...	...	11.2	10.7	11.0	...	...
Urban - Urbaine	+C	416 060	371 995	384 799	...	...	11.8	10.3	10.4	...	...
Rural - Rurale	+C	506 365	537 355	568 338	...	...	10.7	11.1	11.4	...	...
Mauritius - Maurice[4]											
Total	+C	10 382	9 575	9 959	9 709	10 042	8.3	7.6	7.9	7.7	7.9
Urban - Urbaine	+C	3 096	2 902	3 216	3 194	3 224	6.1	5.6	6.2	6.2	6.2
Rural - Rurale	+C	7 286	6 673	6 743	6 515	6 818	9.8	9.0	9.1	8.7	9.1
Mayotte											
Total	C	...	...	467	...	...	...	...	2.1	...	...
Reunion - Réunion											
Total	C	...	...	2 771	...	...	...	...	3.3	...	...
Saint Helena ex. dep. - Sainte-Hélène sans dép.											
Total	C	12	8	7	...	...	...	...	...	...	...
Seychelles[5]											
Total	+C	1 748	1 708	1 655	1 845	...	19.8	19.0	18.1	19.7	...
South Africa - Afrique du Sud											
Total	...	161 112	158 642	150 852	138 627		...	...	...	...	...
Sudan - Soudan											
Total	U	...	...	...	158 051		...	...	...	...	...
Tunisia - Tunisie											
Total	...	107 046	110 119	108 843	108 453		...	...	...	...	...
AMERICA, NORTH - AMÉRIQUE DU NORD											
Anguilla[6]											
Total	C	56	42	64	39	...	4.1	3.0	4.5	2.6	...
Aruba											
Total	C	574	523	617	696	639	5.5	4.9	5.7	6.4	5.8
Bahamas											
Total	+C	1 941	2 122	...	...	...	5.4	5.8	...	...	...
Barbados - Barbade											
Total	+C	2 135	1 829	1 855	...	...	7.7	6.6	6.7	...	...
Bermuda - Bermudes											
Total	C	601	471	477	509	450	9.6	7.6	7.7	8.2	7.3
Cayman Islands - Îles Caïmanes[7]											
Total	+C	473	527	452	468	...	8.4	9.4	7.9	7.9	...
Costa Rica[8]											
Total	C	26 112	25 725	25 909	26 512	*26 718	5.6	5.5	5.4	5.5	*5.5
Urban - Urbaine	C	13 567	12 229	17 905	21 258	*21 565	4.0	3.6	5.2	6.1	*6.1
Rural - Rurale	C	12 545	13 496	8 004	5 254	*5 153	9.9	10.5	6.1	4.0	*3.9
Cuba[9]											
Total	C	55 759	61 449	63 954	61 902	61 903	5.0	5.5	5.7	5.5	5.5
Urban - Urbaine	C	49 837	56 462	58 137	57 600	...	5.9	6.6	6.7	6.7	...
Rural - Rurale	C	5 922	4 987	5 817	4 302	...	2.2	1.9	2.2	1.7	...
Curaçao[10]											
Total	C	741	665	696	703	695	4.9	4.3	4.5	4.4	4.4
Dominican Republic - République dominicaine											
Total	+C	43 307	45 163	47 235	50 158	52 896	4.5	4.6	4.8	5.0	5.3
El Salvador[11]											
Total	...	29 267	...	...	...	...	...	...	...	...	...
Urban - Urbaine	...	7 757	...	...	...	...	...	...	...	...	...
Rural - Rurale	...	21 510	...	...	...	...	...	...	...	...	...

22. Marriages and crude marriage rates, by urban/rural residence: 2012 - 2016
Mariages et taux bruts de nuptialité, selon la résidence, urbaine/rurale : 2012 - 2016 (continued - suite)

Continent, country or area, and urban/rural residence / Continent, pays ou zone et résidence, urbaine/rurale	Code[a]	Number - Nombre					Rate - Taux				
		2012	2013	2014	2015	2016	2012	2013	2014	2015	2016
AMERICA, NORTH - AMÉRIQUE DU NORD											
Grenada - Grenade											
Total	+C	610	...	...	...	...	5.7	...	...	...	...
Guadeloupe											
Total	C	1 291	1 136	1 198	...	...	3.2	2.8	3.0	...	...
Guatemala											
Total	C	84 253	80 750	79 496	79 177	...	5.6	5.2	5.0	4.9	...
Jamaica - Jamaïque											
Total	+C	20 175	18 835	18 480	...	...	7.5	6.9	6.8	...	...
Martinique											
Total	C	...	...	968	...	...	...	...	2.5	...	...
Mexico - Mexique[12]											
Total	+C	585 434	583 264	577 713	558 022	...	5.0	4.9	4.8	4.6	...
Urban - Urbaine[13]	+C	430 852	418 686	420 856	416 507	...	5.1	4.9	4.8	4.7	...
Rural - Rurale[13]	+C	120 188	114 574	119 600	108 675	...	3.7	3.5	3.6	3.3	...
Montserrat											
Total	+...	16	18	14	14	10	...	...	...	...	...
Panama[8]											
Total	C	14 201	13 213	12 869	*14 341	...	3.7	3.4	3.3	*3.6	...
Urban - Urbaine	C	10 995	10 535	10 443	*11 824	...	4.4	4.1	4.0	*4.4	...
Rural - Rurale	C	3 206	2 678	2 426	*2 517	...	2.5	2.1	1.9	*2.0	...
Puerto Rico - Porto Rico											
Total	C	17 948	17 010	16 668	16 987	15 746	4.9	4.7	4.7	4.9	4.6
Saint Lucia - Sainte-Lucie											
Total	C	*305	...	...	...	...	*1.8	...	...	...	...
Saint Vincent and the Grenadines - Saint-Vincent-et-les Grenadines											
Total	C	514	511	526	574	...	4.7	4.6	4.8	5.2	...
Sint Maarten (Dutch part) - Saint-Martin (partie néerlandaise)											
Total	+C	166	230	...	...	...	4.8	6.3	...	...	...
Turks and Caicos Islands - Îles Turques et Caïques											
Total	C	418	...	...	...	...	13.0	...	...	...	...
United States of America - États-Unis d'Amérique											
Total	C	2 131 000	2 081 301[14]	2 140 272[14]	2 221 579	...	6.8	6.6	6.7	6.9	...
AMERICA, SOUTH - AMÉRIQUE DU SUD											
Argentina - Argentine											
Total	C	131 922	123 810	119 266	118 809	...	3.2	2.9	2.8	2.8	...
Bolivia (Plurinational State of) - Bolivie (État plurinational de)											
Total	+U	62 403	42 016	60 105	39 942	...	...	...	...	...	...
Brazil - Brésil											
Total	+U	1 041 440	1 052 477[12]	1 106 440[12]	1 137 348[12]	...	...	...	...	...	...
Chile - Chili											
Total	+C	63 736	61 446	64 868	...	...	3.7	3.5	3.6	...	...
Urban - Urbaine[15]	+C	58 606	56 758	59 858	...	...	3.9	3.7	3.8	...	...
Rural - Rurale[15]	+C	5 130	4 688	5 010	...	...	2.3	2.1	2.2	...	...
Ecuador - Équateur[16]											
Total	U	57 753	53 986	60 328	60 636	...	...	...	...	...	...
Urban - Urbaine[15]	U	...	44 721	50 434	50 425	...	...	...	...	...	...
Rural - Rurale[15]	U	...	9 265	9 894	10 211	...	...	...	...	...	...
Guyana[17]											
Total	C	5 128	4 667	4 679	...	...	6.8	6.2	6.3	...	...
Paraguay											
Total	U	20 967	19 076	19 527	...	...	...	...	...	...	...
Peru - Pérou[18]											
Total	+C	107 380	89 763	95 770	86 191	...	3.6	2.9	3.1	2.8	...
Suriname											
Total	C	2 204	2 190	2 143	2 010	...	4.1	4.0	3.8	3.5	...

22. Marriages and crude marriage rates, by urban/rural residence: 2012 - 2016
Mariages et taux bruts de nuptialité, selon la résidence, urbaine/rurale : 2012 - 2016 (continued - suite)

Continent, country or area, and urban/rural residence / Continent, pays ou zone et résidence, urbaine/rurale	Code[a]	Number - Nombre					Rate - Taux				
		2012	2013	2014	2015	2016	2012	2013	2014	2015	2016
AMERICA, SOUTH - AMÉRIQUE DU SUD											
Uruguay											
Total	C	9 631	10 034	10 226	9 501	...	2.8	2.9	3.0	2.7	...
Venezuela (Bolivarian Republic of) - Venezuela (République bolivarienne du)											
Total	C	102 077	99 065	94 519	90 812	...	3.5	3.3	3.1	3.0	...
ASIA - ASIE											
Armenia - Arménie											
Total	+C	...	...	18 912	17 603	...	...	...	6.3	5.9	...
Urban - Urbaine	+C	...	...	...	11 836	...	...	...	...	6.2	...
Rural - Rurale	+C	...	...	...	5 767	...	...	...	...	5.3	...
Azerbaijan - Azerbaïdjan											
Total	+C	79 065	86 852	84 912	68 773	...	8.5	9.2	8.9	7.1	...
Urban - Urbaine	+C	42 293	46 324	43 608	36 623	...	8.6	9.2	8.6	7.1	...
Rural - Rurale	+C	36 772	40 528	41 304	32 150	...	8.4	9.2	9.3	7.1	...
Bahrain - Bahreïn											
Total	...	7 559	7 463	7 673	6 953	7 019	...	...	...	...	...
Bangladesh											
Total	...	2 027 350	...	...	...	...	...	...	...	...	...
Urban - Urbaine	...	446 516	...	...	...	...	...	...	...	...	...
Rural - Rurale	...	1 580 834	...	...	...	...	...	...	...	...	...
Brunei Darussalam - Brunéi Darussalam											
Total	+...	2 671	2 741	2 992	2 750	...	...	...	...	...	...
China - Chine[19]											
Total	+C	12 971 000	...	...	...	...	9.6	...	...	...	...
China, Hong Kong SAR - Chine, Hong Kong RAS											
Total	C	60 459	55 274	56 454	51 609	50 008	8.5	7.7	7.8	7.1	6.8
China, Macao SAR - Chine, Macao RAS											
Total	+C	3 783	4 153	4 085	3 719	...	6.7	7.0	6.6	5.8	...
Cyprus - Chypre[20]											
Total	C	5 806	5 493	...	...	...	6.7	6.4	...	...	...
Georgia - Géorgie											
Total	C	30 412	34 693	31 526	29 157	25 101	6.8	7.7	8.5	7.8	6.7
Urban - Urbaine[15]	C	17 304	18 903	18 363	17 127	14 961	...	...	...	8.1	7.0
Rural - Rurale[15]	C	13 108	15 790	13 163	12 030	10 140	...	...	...	7.6	6.4
Indonesia - Indonésie											
Total	U	...	2 210 046	2 110 776	1 958 394	...	...	...	...	...	...
Iran (Islamic Republic of) - Iran (République islamique d')[21]											
Total	+C	829 968	774 513	724 324	685 352[22]	...	10.9	10.1	9.3	8.7	...
Urban - Urbaine[22]	+C	...	...	...	562 671	...	...	...	...	9.8	...
Rural - Rurale[22]	+C	...	...	...	122 681	...	...	...	...	5.7	...
Israel - Israël[23]											
Total	C	50 474	52 705	50 797	53 579	...	6.4	6.5	6.2	6.4	...
Urban - Urbaine[24]	C	45 371	47 506	45 729	48 236	...	6.3	6.4	6.1	6.3	...
Rural - Rurale[24]	C	3 900	3 951	3 715	3 936	...	5.8	5.7	5.2	5.3	...
Japan - Japon[25]											
Total	+C	668 869	660 613	643 749	635 156	...	5.2	5.2	5.1	5.0	...
Urban - Urbaine[15]	+C	620 373	613 648	598 792	590 947	...	...	...	...	...	...
Rural - Rurale[15]	+C	48 496	46 965	44 957	44 209	...	...	...	...	...	...
Jordan - Jordanie[26]											
Total	+C	70 621	70 965	81 209	81 373	...	9.5	8.7	9.2	8.5	...
Kazakhstan											
Total	C	164 681	168 447	...	...	...	9.8	9.9	...	...	...
Urban - Urbaine	C	102 889	107 494	...	...	...	11.2	11.5	...	...	...
Rural - Rurale	C	61 792	60 953	...	...	...	8.1	7.9	...	...	...
Kuwait - Koweït											
Total	C	14 320	15 118	15 086	15 412	...	4.4	4.4	4.0	3.9	...

22. Marriages and crude marriage rates, by urban/rural residence: 2012 - 2016
Mariages et taux bruts de nuptialité, selon la résidence, urbaine/rurale : 2012 - 2016 (continued - suite)

Continent, country or area, and urban/rural residence / Continent, pays ou zone et résidence, urbaine/rurale	Code[a]	Number - Nombre					Rate - Taux				
		2012	2013	2014	2015	2016	2012	2013	2014	2015	2016
ASIA - ASIE											
Kyrgyzstan - Kirghizstan											
Total	C	55 176	53 578	54 942	52 043	*47 837	9.8	9.4	9.4	8.7	*7.9
Urban - Urbaine	C	16 622	17 329	17 150	15 875	*15 990	8.8	9.0	8.7	7.9	*7.8
Rural - Rurale	C	38 554	36 249	37 792	36 168	*31 847	10.3	9.5	9.8	9.2	*7.9
Lebanon - Liban											
Total	C	38 691	38 737	41 049	...	...	...	...	...	...	...
Mongolia - Mongolie											
Total	+C	12 822	15 785	17 332	17 586	16 778	4.5	5.4	5.8	5.8	5.4
Urban - Urbaine	+C	8 718	10 613	12 075	12 506	11 915	4.6	5.4	6.1	6.1	5.6
Rural - Rurale	+C	4 104	5 172	5 257	5 080	4 863	4.4	5.5	5.4	5.2	5.0
Oman[27]											
Total	+U	29 840	...	...	...	...	...	...	...	...	...
Philippines											
Total	U	482 399	442 900	429 723	439 424	...	...	...	...	...	...
Qatar											
Total	C	3 532	3 619	3 674	3 724	3 830	1.9	1.8	1.7	1.5	1.5
Urban - Urbaine	C	...	...	3 674	3 724	3 830	...	...	1.7	1.5	1.5
Republic of Korea - République de Corée[28]											
Total	+C	327 073	322 807	305 507	302 828	281 635	6.5	6.4	6.0	5.9	5.5
Urban - Urbaine[24]	+C	266 463	263 992	248 965	247 486	229 747	6.5	6.4	6.0	6.0	5.5
Rural - Rurale[24]	+C	52 829	50 906	48 818	48 638	46 792	5.6	5.5	5.2	5.1	4.9
Singapore - Singapour[29]											
Total	+C	27 936	26 254	28 407	28 322	27 971	7.3	6.8	7.3	7.3	7.1
Sri Lanka											
Total	+U	*198 710	*180 760	*175 728	*175 939	...	...	...	...	...	...
State of Palestine - État de Palestine											
Total	C	40 292	42 698	43 732	50 438	...	9.4	9.7	9.6	10.8	...
Tajikistan - Tadjikistan											
Total	+C	97 653	96 989	95 537	76 956	...	12.4	12.0	11.6	9.1	...
Urban - Urbaine	+C	25 115	25 306	25 757	...	...	12.0	11.8	11.7	...	...
Rural - Rurale	+C	72 538	71 683	69 780	...	...	12.5	12.1	11.5	...	...
Thailand - Thaïlande											
Total	U	314 338	295 519	296 258	304 392	307 746	...	...	...	...	...
Turkey - Turquie[30]											
Total	C	603 751	600 138	599 704	602 982	...	8.0	7.8	7.7	7.7	...
United Arab Emirates - Émirats arabes unis											
Total	...	14 934	16 441	16 917	16 248	...	...	...	...	...	...
Uzbekistan - Ouzbékistan											
Total	+C	299 048	304 859	296 055	287 582	...	10.0	10.1	9.6	9.2	...
Urban - Urbaine	+C	144 174	140 958	136 707	131 216	...	9.4	9.1	8.7	8.3	...
Rural - Rurale	+C	154 874	163 901	159 348	156 366	...	10.7	11.1	10.5	10.1	...
EUROPE											
Åland Islands - Îles d'Åland											
Total	C	141	118	115	118	*124	5.0	4.1	4.0	4.1	*4.3
Urban - Urbaine	C	59	46	53	49	*49	5.2	4.0	4.6	4.3	*4.3
Rural - Rurale	C	82	72	62	69	*75	4.8	4.2	3.6	3.9	*4.3
Albania - Albanie											
Total	C	22 891	23 820	...	...	...	7.9	8.2	...	...	...
Total	U	...	...	...	24 997	...	...	...	...	...	...
Andorra - Andorre											
Total	C	288	291	271	285	295	4.1	4.2	3.9	4.0	4.1
Austria - Autriche											
Total	C	38 592[31]	36 140[31]	37 458[31]	44 502[32]	...	4.6	4.3	4.4	5.2	...
Belarus - Bélarus											
Total	C	76 245	87 127	83 942	82 030	...	8.1	9.2	8.9	8.6	...
Urban - Urbaine	C	62 828	71 702	69 649	68 305	...	8.7	9.9	9.5	9.3	...
Rural - Rurale	C	13 417	15 425	14 293	13 725	...	5.9	7.0	6.6	6.4	...
Belgium - Belgique[33]											
Total	C	42 198	37 854	39 879	40 049	...	3.8	3.4	3.6	3.5	...
Urban - Urbaine	C	41 627	37 332	39 332	39 500	...	...	...	...	...	...
Rural - Rurale	C	571	522	547	549	...	...	...	...	...	...

Continent, country or area, and urban/rural residence / Continent, pays ou zone et résidence, urbaine/rurale	Code[a]	Number - Nombre					Rate - Taux				
		2012	2013	2014	2015	2016	2012	2013	2014	2015	2016
EUROPE											
Bosnia and Herzegovina - Bosnie-Herzégovine											
Total	C	18 980	18 387	18 409	...	...	4.9	4.8	4.8	...	...
Bulgaria - Bulgarie[34]											
Total	C	21 167	21 943	24 596	27 720	...	2.9	3.0	3.4	3.9	...
Urban - Urbaine	C	16 357	...	18 756	20 795	...	3.1	...	3.6	4.0	...
Rural - Rurale	C	4 810	...	5 840	6 925	...	2.4	...	3.0	3.6	...
Croatia - Croatie											
Total	C	20 323	19 169	19 501	19 834	...	4.8	4.5	4.6	4.7	...
Urban - Urbaine	C	11 386	10 691	10 924	10 937	...	...	...	...	...	...
Rural - Rurale	C	8 937	8 478	8 577	8 897	...	...	...	...	...	...
Czechia - Tchéquie											
Total	C	45 206	43 499	45 575	48 191	...	4.3	4.1	4.3	4.6	...
Urban - Urbaine	C	33 403	31 976	33 356	35 192	...		4.2	4.3	4.6	...
Rural - Rurale	C	11 803	11 523	12 219	12 999	...		4.1	4.3	4.6	...
Denmark - Danemark[35]											
Total	C	28 503	27 503	28 331	28 853	30 767	5.1	4.9	5.0	5.1	5.4
Estonia - Estonie											
Total	C	5 888	5 630	6 220	6 815	6 360	4.5	4.3	4.7	5.2	4.8
Urban - Urbaine[36]	C	4 000	3 963	4 232	4 660	...	4.4	4.4	4.7	5.2	...
Rural - Rurale[36]	C	1 594	1 368	1 496	1 733	...	3.8	3.3	3.6	4.2	...
Faeroe Islands - Îles Féroé											
Total	C	237	259	236	217	...	4.9	5.4	4.9	4.4	...
Finland - Finlande[37]											
Total	C	28 737	25 001	24 347	24 590	...	5.3	4.6	4.5	4.5	...
Urban - Urbaine	C	21 485	18 856	18 485	18 838	...	5.8	5.1	4.9	4.9	...
Rural - Rurale	C	7 252	6 145	5 862	5 752	...	4.3	3.7	3.5	3.6	...
France											
Total	C	239 840	233 108[12]	235 315[12]	230 364[12]	...	3.8	3.7	3.7	3.6	...
Urban - Urbaine[38]	C	186 141	181 513[12]	182 905[12]	179 606[12]	...	...	...	...	...	...
Rural - Rurale[38]	C	51 425	49 361[12]	49 824[12]	48 118[12]	...	...	...	...	...	...
Germany - Allemagne											
Total	C	387 423	373 655	385 952	400 115	...	4.8	4.6	4.8	4.9	...
Gibraltar[7]											
Total	+C	204	195	204	195	...	6.3	6.0	6.2	5.8	...
Greece - Grèce											
Total	C	49 705	51 256	53 105	53 672	49 632	4.5	4.7	4.9	5.0	4.6
Urban - Urbaine	C	35 464	...	37 743	37 870		...	...	...	...	
Rural - Rurale	C	14 241	...	15 362	15 802		...	...	...	...	
Guernsey - Guernesey											
Total	C	325	...	...	...	...	5.2	...	...	...	...
Hungary - Hongrie[9]											
Total	C	36 161	36 986	38 780	46 137	51 805	3.6	3.7	3.9	4.7	5.3
Urban - Urbaine[39]	C	26 678	27 189	28 854	33 144	...	3.9	4.0	4.2	4.8	...
Rural - Rurale[39]	C	9 117	9 424	9 538	12 492	...	3.0	3.1	3.3	4.3	...
Ireland - Irlande											
Total	+C	20 713	20 680	22 045	22 116	22 759	4.5	4.5	4.8	4.8	4.8
Italy - Italie											
Total	C	207 138	194 057	189 765	194 377	...	3.5	3.2	3.1	3.2	...
Jersey											
Total	+C	557	...	...	...	...	5.6	...	...	...	...
Latvia - Lettonie[8]											
Total	C	11 244	11 436	12 515	13 617	13 002	5.5	5.7	6.3	6.9	6.6
Liechtenstein[8]											
Total	C	185	211	208	205	...	5.0	5.7	5.6	5.5	...
Lithuania - Lituanie											
Total	C	20 660	20 469	22 142	21 987	...	6.9	6.9	7.6	7.6	...
Urban - Urbaine	C	14 432	14 166	15 250	15 219	...	7.2	7.1	7.7	7.8	...
Rural - Rurale	C	6 228	6 303	6 892	6 768	...	6.3	6.5	7.2	7.1	...
Luxembourg[7]											
Total	C	1 782	1 722	1 657	2 052	...	3.4	3.2	3.0	3.6	...
Malta - Malte											
Total	C	2 823	2 578	2 871	3 002	3 034	6.7	6.1	6.7	7.0	7.0
Montenegro - Monténégro											
Total	C	3 305	3 847	3 527	3 837	...	5.3	6.2	5.7	6.2	...
Netherlands - Pays-Bas[40]											
Total	C	70 315	64 549	65 333	64 308	...	4.2	3.8	3.9	3.8	...

22. Marriages and crude marriage rates, by urban/rural residence: 2012 - 2016
Mariages et taux bruts de nuptialité, selon la résidence, urbaine/rurale : 2012 - 2016 (continued - suite)

Continent, country or area, and urban/rural residence / Continent, pays ou zone et résidence, urbaine/rurale	Code[a]	Number - Nombre					Rate - Taux				
		2012	2013	2014	2015	2016	2012	2013	2014	2015	2016
EUROPE											
Norway - Norvège[12]											
Total	C	24 346	23 916	23 462	23 227	...	4.9	4.7	4.6	4.5	...
Poland - Pologne											
Total	C	203 850	180 396	188 488	188 832	193 455	5.4	4.7	5.0	5.0	5.1
Urban - Urbaine	C	119 401	105 734	110 030	111 246	...	5.2	4.6	4.8	4.9	...
Rural - Rurale	C	84 449	74 662	78 458	77 586	...	5.6	5.0	5.2	5.2	...
Portugal[41]											
Total	C	34 423	31 998	31 478	32 393	...	3.3	3.1	3.0	3.1	...
Republic of Moldova - République de Moldova											
Total	C	24 262	24 449	25 624	...	...	6.8	6.9	7.2	...	...
Urban - Urbaine	C	12 287	...	...	...	...	8.3	...	...	...	...
Rural - Rurale	C	11 975	...	...	...	...	5.8	...	...	...	...
Romania - Roumanie											
Total	C	107 760	107 507	118 075	125 454	133 183	5.4	5.4	5.9	6.3	6.7
Urban - Urbaine	C	68 821	68 985	76 833	80 975	84 226	6.4	6.4	7.2	7.6	...
Rural - Rurale	C	38 939	38 522	41 242	44 479	48 957	4.2	4.2	4.5	4.9	...
Russian Federation - Fédération de Russie[42]											
Total	C	1 213 598	1 225 501	...	...	...	8.5	8.5	...	...	...
Urban - Urbaine	C	911 015	...	...	...	...	8.6	...	...	...	...
Rural - Rurale	C	302 583	...	...	...	...	8.1	...	...	...	...
San Marino - Saint-Marin[43]											
Total	C	203	221	187	182	181	6.1	6.6	5.6	5.4	5.3
Serbia - Serbie[44]											
Total	+C	34 639	36 209	36 429	36 949[45]	35 921[45]	4.8	5.1	5.1	5.2	5.1
Urban - Urbaine	+C	22 622	23 573	23 718	24 521[45]	...	5.3	5.5	5.6	5.7	...
Rural - Rurale	+C	12 017	12 636	12 711	12 428[45]	...	4.1	4.4	4.4	4.4	...
Slovakia - Slovaquie[8]											
Total	C	26 006	25 491	26 737	28 775	...	4.8	4.7	4.9	5.3	...
Urban - Urbaine	C	14 950	14 491	15 280	16 443	...	5.1	4.9	5.2	5.6	...
Rural - Rurale	C	11 056	11 000	11 457	12 332	...	4.5	4.4	4.6	4.9	...
Slovenia - Slovénie[46]											
Total	C	7 057	6 254	6 571	6 449	6 667	3.4	3.0	3.2	3.1	3.2
Urban - Urbaine	C	3 622	3 295	3 365	3 418	...	3.5	3.1	3.2	3.1	...
Rural - Rurale	C	3 435	2 959	3 206	3 031	...	3.3	2.9	3.2	3.2	...
Spain - Espagne											
Total	C	163 173	151 433	160 256	166 651	...	3.5	3.3	3.4	3.6	...
Sweden - Suède[12]											
Total	C	50 616	51 554	53 051	52 314	53 817	5.3	5.4	5.5	5.3	5.5
Switzerland - Suisse[47]											
Total	C	42 654	39 794	41 891	41 437	41 646	5.3	4.9	5.1	5.0	5.0
Urban - Urbaine	C	32 589	30 455	32 019	35 758[48]	...	5.5	5.1	5.3	5.5	...
Rural - Rurale	C	10 065	9 339	9 872	5 679[48]	...	4.8	4.4	4.6	3.3	...
TFYR of Macedonia - L'ex-R. y. de Macédoine											
Total	C	13 991	13 982	13 813	14 186	13 199	6.8	6.8	6.7	6.9	6.4
Urban - Urbaine	C	7 711	7 759	7 782	8 168	...	...	...	...	...	...
Rural - Rurale	C	6 280	6 223	6 031	6 018	...	...	...	...	...	...
Ukraine											
Total	+C	278 276	304 232	294 962[49]	299 038[49]	...	6.1	6.7	6.9	7.0	...
Urban - Urbaine	+C	211 819	235 108	...	...	...	6.8	...	...	...	...
Rural - Rurale	+C	66 457	69 124	...	...	...	4.7	...	...	...	...
OCEANIA - OCÉANIE											
American Samoa - Samoas américaines											
Total	C	155	186	217	...	...	2.4	3.0	3.5	...	...
Australia - Australie											
Total	+C	123 244	118 962	121 197	113 595	...	5.4	5.1	5.2	4.8	...
Cook Islands - Îles Cook[50]											
Total	+C	894	843	746	*720	...	45.8	45.3	40.1	*38.5	...

Continent, country or area, and urban/rural residence / Continent, pays ou zone et résidence, urbaine/rurale	Code[a]	Number - Nombre					Rate - Taux				
		2012	2013	2014	2015	2016	2012	2013	2014	2015	2016
OCEANIA - OCÉANIE											
French Polynesia - Polynésie française											
Total	C	1 699	1 474	1 480	1 456	...	6.3	5.5	5.5	5.3	...
Guam[51]											
Total	C	1 658	1 462	1 463	1 348[12]	1 185[12]	10.4	9.1	9.1	8.3	7.3
New Caledonia - Nouvelle-Calédonie											
Total	C	994	926	971	983	...	3.8	3.5	3.6	3.6	...
New Zealand - Nouvelle-Zélande											
Total	+C	20 521[8]	19 237[52]	20 125[53]	19 947[53]	20 235[53]	4.7	4.3	4.5	4.3	4.3
Norfolk Island - Île Norfolk[54]											
Total	+C	31	19	15	24	...	...	...	...	...	...
Samoa											
Total	U	...	...	...	*865*	...	...	...	...	...	...

FOOTNOTES - NOTES

Italics: data from civil registers which are incomplete or of unknown completeness. - Italiques : données incomplètes ou dont le degré d'exactitude n'est pas connu, provenant des registres de l'état civil.

* Provisional. - Données provisoires.

[a] 'Code' indicates the source of data, as follows:
C - Civil registration, estimated over 90% complete
U - Civil registration, estimated less than 90% complete
| - Other source, estimated reliable
+ - Data tabulated by date of registration rather than occurence
... - Information not available

Le 'Code' indique la source des données, comme suit :
C - Registres de l'état civil considérés complets à 90 p. 100 au moins
U - Registres de l'état civil qui ne sont pas considérés complèts à 90 p. 100 au moins
| - Autre source, considérée pas douteuses
+ - Données exploitées selon la date de l'enregistrement et non la date de l'événement
... - Information pas disponible

[1] Data refer to Algerian population only. - Les données ne concernent que la population algérienne.
[2] Source: Vital Statistics Report 2014. - Source: Vital Statistics Report 2014.
[3] Including marriages resumed after 'revocable divorce' (among Moslem population), which approximates legal separation. - Y compris les unions reconstituées après un 'divorce révocable' (parmi la population musulmane), qui est à peu près l'équivalent d'une séparation légale.
[4] Excludes the islands of St. Brandon and Agalega. - Non compris les îles St. Brandon et Agalega.
[5] Including visitors. - Y compris les visiteurs.
[6] Excluding visitors. - Ne comprend pas les visiteurs.
[7] Data refer to marriages where one or both partners are residents. - Les données portent sur les mariages pour lesquels l'un des deux partenaires ou les deux sont résidents.
[8] Data refer to marriages by residence of the groom. - Les données concernent les mariages selon la résidence du marié.
[9] Marriages registered by residence of bride. - Les mariages sont enregistrés selon le lieu de résidence de la mariée.
[10] Data refers to the number of marriages of which at least one of the partners is a resident of Curacao. - Les données concernent le nombre de mariages dont au moins l'un des partenaires est un résident de Curaçao.
[11] Including marriages where bride/groom are non-residents. - Y compris les mariages pour lesquels le marié et la mariée sont des non-résidents.
[12] Including same sex marriages. - Y compris les mariages entre personnes du même sexe.

[13] The total number may include 'Unknown residence', but the categories urban and rural do not. - Le nombre total peut inclure les personnes dont la résidence n'est pas connue, à l'inverse des catégories de population urbaine et rurale.
[14] Excluding data for Georgia. - À l'exclusion des données pour la Géorgie.
[15] Urban and rural residence refers to the place of usual residence of groom. - Le lieu de résidence (zone urbaine ou zone rurale) correspond au lieu de résidence habituel du marié.
[16] Excludes nomadic Indian tribes. - Non compris les tribus d'Indiens nomades.
[17] Excluding Amerindians. - Non compris les Amérindiens.
[18] Data are compiled from the National Registers of Identification and Civil Status (RENIEC). - Les données sont rédigées à partir des Registres Nationaux d'Identification et d'État Civil (RENIEC).
[19] For statistical purposes, the data for China do not include those for the Hong Kong Special Administrative Region (Hong Kong SAR), Macao Special Administrative Region (Macao SAR) and Taiwan province of China. - Pour la présentation des statistiques, les données pour la Chine ne comprennent pas la Région Administrative Spéciale de Hong Kong (Hong Kong RAS), la Région Administrative Spéciale de Macao (Macao RAS) et Taïwan province de Chine.
[20] Data refer to government controlled areas. Data refer to marriages of residents only. - Les données se rapportent aux zones contrôlées par le Gouvernement. Les données ne portent que sur les mariages de résidents.
[21] Data refer to the Iranian Year which begins on 21 March and ends on 20 March of the following year. - Les données concernent l'année iranienne, qui commence le 21 mars et se termine le 20 mars de l'année suivante.
[22] Source: Civil Registration Organization. - Source : Organisation chargée d'assurer l'enregistrement des faits d'état civil.
[23] Includes data for East Jerusalem and Israeli residents in certain other territories under occupation by Israeli military forces since June 1967. - Y compris les données pour Jérusalem-Est et les résidents israéliens dans certains autres territoires occupés depuis 1967 par les forces armées israéliennes.
[24] The total number may include 'Unknown residence', but the categories urban and rural do not. Urban and rural residence refers to the place of usual residence of groom. - Le nombre total peut inclure les personnes dont la résidence n'est pas connue, à l'inverse des catégories de population urbaine et rurale. Le lieu de résidence (zone urbaine ou zone rurale) correspond au lieu de résidence habituel du marié.
[25] Data refer to Japanese nationals in Japan only. - Les données se raportent aux nationaux japonais au Japon seulement.
[26] Excluding data for Jordanian territory under occupation since June 1967 by Israeli military forces. Excluding foreigners, including registered Palestinian refugees. - Non compris les données pour le territoire jordanien occupé depuis juin 1967 par les forces armées israéliennes. Non compris les étrangers, mais y compris les réfugiés de Palestine enregistrés.
[27] Data refer to registered events only. - Les données ne concernent que les événements enregistrés.
[28] Excluding alien armed forces, civilian aliens employed by armed forces, and foreign diplomatic personnel and their dependants. - Non compris les militaires étrangers, les civils étrangers employés par les forces armées ni le personnel diplomatique étranger et les membres de leur famille les accompagnant.

²⁹ Excluding marriages previously officiated outside Singapore or under religious and customary rites. Data comprise civil marriages registered under the Women's Charter and Muslim marriages registered under the Administration of Muslim Law Act. - Ne comprend pas les mariages prononcés ailleurs qu'à Singapour ni les mariages religieux ou coutumiers. Les données comprennent les mariages civils enregistrés en vertu de la Charte des droits de la femme, ainsi que les mariages musulmans enregistrés en vertu de la loi sur l'administration du droit islamique.

³⁰ Data from MERNIS (Central Population Administrative System). - Données de MERNIS (Système central de données démographiques).

³¹ Excluding aliens temporarily in the area. - Non compris les étrangers se trouvant temporairement dans le territoire.

³² Excluding marriages of aliens temporarily in the area, but including marriages abroad of persons with residence in Austria. - Non compris les mariages d'étrangers temporairement dans la région, mais y compris des mariages à l'étranger de personnes ayant leur résidence en Autriche.

³³ Including armed forces stationed outside the country and alien armed forces in the area, if the marriage is performed by local authority. - Y compris les militaires nationaux hors du pays et les militaires étrangers en garnison sur le territoire, si le mariage a été célébré par l'autorité locale.

³⁴ Including nationals outside the country, but excluding foreigners in the country. - Y compris les nationaux à l'étranger, mais non compris les étrangers sur le territoire.

³⁵ Excluding Faeroe Islands and Greenland shown separately, if available. - Non compris les Îles Féroé et le Groenland, qui font l'objet de rubriques distinctes, si disponible.

³⁶ The difference between 'Total' and the sum of urban and rural is due to the unknown place of residence of grooms and to grooms living outside the country. Urban and rural residence refers to the place of usual residence of groom. - La différence entre le « Total » et la somme des chiffres urbains et ruraux s'explique par le fait que la résidence du marié n'est pas toujours connue ou est située à l'étranger. Le lieu de résidence (zone urbaine ou zone rurale) correspond au lieu de résidence habituel du marié.

³⁷ Excluding Åland Islands. - Non compris les Îles d'Åland.

³⁸ The data for urban and rural exclude the nationals outside the country. - Les données relatives à la population urbaine et rurale n'englobent pas les nationaux se trouvant à l'étranger.

³⁹ The urban and rural categories do not include the data of foreigners, persons of unknown residence and the homeless, whereas the total category includes them. - Les chiffres portant sur la population urbaine et rurale n' incluent pas les données relatives aux étrangers, aux personnes dont la résidence n'est pas connue et aux personnes sans domicile fixe, à l'inverse, le total les inclut.

⁴⁰ Marriages of couples of which at least one partner is recorded in a Dutch municipal register, irrespective of the country where the marriage was performed. Including same sex marriages. Including residents outside the country if listed in a Netherlands population register. - Correspond aux mariages pour lesquels au moins l'un des partenaires est inscrit sur un registre municipal néerlandais, quel que soit le pays dans lequel le mariage est célébré. Y compris les mariages entre personnes du même sexe. Englobe les résidents se trouvant à l'étranger à condition qu'ils soient inscrits sur le registre de population des Pays-Bas.

⁴¹ Marriages registered by place of occurrence of marriage. - Mariages enregistrés en fonction du lieu de l'événement.

⁴² Data refer to population 15 years of age or more. - Les données concernent la population âgée de 15 ans ou plus.

⁴³ Includes civil and religious marriages as well as not specified. - Englobe les mariages civils et religieux et ceux pour lesquels rien n'a été indiqué.

⁴⁴ Excludes data for Kosovo and Metohia. - Sans les données pour le Kosovo et Metohie.

⁴⁵ Residence refers to residence of groom. - La catégorie « résidence » correspond au lieu de résidence du jeune marié.

⁴⁶ Data refer to residence of groom or bride before marriage. - Données relatives au lieu de résidence du marié ou de la mariée avant le mariage.

⁴⁷ Data based on the residence of groom if he has permanent address in the country, otherwise, based on the residence of bride. If neither partner is a permanent resident, the marriage is not included in the official statistics. - Les données sont fondées sur la résidence du marié si celui-ci a une adresse permanente dans le pays, sinon elles sont fondées sur la résidence de la mariée. Si aucun des deux partenaires n'est un résident permanent, le mariage n'apparaît pas dans les statistiques officielles.

⁴⁸ From 2015, urban refers to urban centers and areas under the influence of urban centers. - A partir de 2015, le territoire urbain inclut l'espace des centres urbains ainsi que l'espace sous influence des centres urbains.

⁴⁹ The Government of Ukraine has informed the United Nations that it is not in a position to provide statistical data concerning the Autonomous Republic of Crimea and the city of Sevastopol. - Le gouvernement Ukrainien a informé l'ONU qu'il n'est pas en mesure de fournir des données statistiques concernant la République autonome de Crimée et la ville de Sébastopol.

⁵⁰ Including non-residents. Excluding Niue, shown separately, which is part of Cook Islands, but because of remoteness is administered separately. - Y compris les non-résidents. Non compris Nioué, qui fait l'objet d'une rubrique distincte et qui fait partie des îles Cook, mais qui, en raison de son éloignement, est administrée séparément.

⁵¹ Including United States military personnel, their dependants and contract employees. - Y compris les militaires des Etats-Unis, les membres de leur famille les accompagnant et les agents contractuels des Etats-Unis.

⁵² Including same sex marriages. Data refer to marriages by residence of the groom. - Y compris les mariages entre personnes du même sexe. Les données concernent les mariages selon la résidence du marié.

⁵³ Data refer to marriages and civil unions by residence of 'partner 2'. Random rounding to base 3 is applied in this table as a confidentiality measure. Including same sex marriages. - Les données concernent les mariages et les unions civiles selon la résidence du « partenaire 2 ». Les chiffres sont arrondis à la base 3 de manière aléatoire, pour des raisons de confidentialité. Y compris les mariages entre personnes du même sexe.

⁵⁴ Data cover the period from 1 July of the previous year to 30 June of the present year. - Pour la période allant du 1er juillet de l'année précédente au 30 juin de l'année en cours.

Table 23 - *Demographic Yearbook 2016*

Table 23 presents the marriages cross-classified by age of groom and age of bride for the latest available year between 2007 and 2016.

Description of variables: Marriage is defined as the act, ceremony or process by which the legal relationship of spouses is constituted. The legality of the union may be established by civil, religious or other means as recognized by the laws of each country[1].

Marriage statistics in this table, therefore, include both first marriages and remarriages after divorce, widowhood or annulment. They do not, unless otherwise noted, include resumption of marriage ties after legal separation. These statistics refer to the number of marriages performed, and not to the number of persons marrying.

Age is defined as age at last birthday, that is, the difference between the date of birth and the date of the occurrence of the event, expressed in completed solar years. The age classification used for brides in this table is the following: under 15 years, 5-year age groups through 90-94, and 95 years and over, depending on the availability of data. Age classification for grooms is restricted to: under 15 years, 5-year age groups from 15 to 59, and 60 years and over.

In an effort to provide interpretation of these statistics, countries or areas providing data on marriages by age of groom and bride have been requested to specify "the minimum legal age at which marriage can take place with and without parental consent". This information is presented in the table 23-1 below.

Reliability of data: Data from civil registers of marriages that are reported as incomplete (less than 90 per cent completeness) or of unknown completeness are considered unreliable and are set in *italics* rather than in roman type. Table 22 and the technical notes for that table provide more detailed information on the completeness of marriage registration. For more information about the quality of vital statistics data in general, see Section 4.2 of the Technical Notes.

Limitations: Statistics on marriages by age of groom and age of bride are subject to the same qualifications as have been set forth for vital statistics in general and marriage statistics in particular as discussed in Section 4 of the Technical Notes.

The fact that marriage is a legal event, unlike birth and death that are biological events, has implications for international comparability of data. Marriage has been defined, for statistical purposes, in terms of the laws of individual countries or areas. These laws vary throughout the world. In addition, comparability is further limited because some countries or areas compile statistics only for civil marriages although religious marriages may also be legally recognized; in other countries or areas, the only available records are church registers and, therefore, the statistics may not reflect marriages that are civil marriages only.

Because in many countries or areas marriage is a civil legal contract which, to establish its legality, must be celebrated before a civil officer, it follows that for these countries or areas registration would tend to be almost automatic at the time of, or immediately following, the marriage ceremony. This factor should be kept in mind when considering the reliability of data, described above.

Because these statistics are classified according to age, they are subject to the limitations with respect to accuracy of age reporting similar to those already discussed in connection with Section 3.1.3 of the Technical Notes.   It is probable that biases are less pronounced in marriage statistics, because information is obtained from the persons concerned and since marriage is a legal act, the participants are likely to give correct information. However, in some countries or areas, there appears to be a concentration of marriages at the legal minimum age for marriage and at the age at which valid marriage may be contracted without parental consent, indicating perhaps an overstatement in some cases to comply with the law.

Aside from the possibility of age misreporting, it should be noted that marriage patterns at younger ages, that is, for ages up to 24 years, are influenced to a large extent by laws regarding the minimum age for marriage.

Factors that may influence age reporting, particularly at older ages include an inclination to understate the age of the bride in order that it may be equal to or less than that of the groom.

The absence of data in the unknown age group does not necessarily indicate completely accurate reporting and tabulation of the age item. It is sometimes an indication that the unknowns have been eliminated by assigning ages to them before tabulation, or by proportionate distribution after tabulation.

Another age-reporting factor that must be kept in mind in using these data is the variation that may result from calculating age at marriage from year of birth rather than from day, month and year of birth. Information on this factor is given in footnotes when known.

Earlier data: Marriages by age of groom and age of bride have been shown for the latest available year in most issues of the *Demographic Yearbook*. Data cross-classified by age of groom and bride have been presented in previous issues featuring marriage and divorce statistics. For information on the specific topics and the years covered, readers should consult the Historical Index.

23-1 Minimum legal age at which marriage can take place

Country or area	With parental consent		Without parental consent	
	Groom	Bride	Groom	Bride
Africa				
Botswana	18	18	21	21
Burkina Faso[2]	18	15	20	17
Burundi[5]			21	18
Cameroon[3]	18	15	21	18
Egypt	18	18		
Ghana			18	18
Guinea	25	18		
Liberia	16	16	21	18
Libya[4]	18	18		
Malawi[5]			18	18
Mauritius	16	16	18	18
Morocco[5]			18	18
Namibia	18	18	21	21
Saint Helena ex. Dep.	16	16	21	21
Senegal	Under 18	Under 18	18	18
Seychelles	16	16	18	18
Sierra Leone[5]			18	18
South Africa[6]	Under 18	Under 18	18	18
Swaziland	18	18	21	21
Uganda[5, 7]			18	18
Zimbabwe	16	16	18	18
America, North				
Anguilla	16	16	18	18
Aruba[8]	16	16	18	18
Bermuda	16	16	18	18
Canada[9]	16	16	18	18
Cayman Islands	16	16	18	18
Costa Rica	15	15	18	18
Cuba	16	14	18	16

Country or area	With parental consent		Without parental consent	
	Groom	Bride	Groom	Bride
Curaçao	16	16	18	18
Dominican Republic	16	15	18	18
El Salvador	Under 18	Under 18	18	18
Greenland[5]			18	18
Jamaica	16	16	18	18
Mexico[10]	Under 18	Under 18	18	18
Montserrat[11]	16	16	18	18
Panama	16	14	18	18
Puerto Rico	17	17	21	21
Saint Vincent and the Grenadines			18	18
Trinidad and Tobago[12]	Under 18	Under 18	18	18
America, South				
Bolivia (Plurinational State of)[13]	16	14	18	18
Brazil	16	16	18	18
Chile	16	16	18	18
Colombia	14	14	18	18
Ecuador	14	12	18	18
Suriname	17	15	21	21
Uruguay	16	16	18	18
Venezuela (Bolivarian Republic of)	14	12	18	18
Asia				
Armenia			18	17
Azerbaijan	18	17		
Bahrain			15	
Cambodia			18	18
China, Hong Kong SAR	16	16	21	21
China, Macao SAR	16	16	18	18
Cyprus	16	16	18	18
Georgia	16	16	18	18
Indonesia			19	16
Iran (Islamic Republic of)	18	15		
Israel[5]			18	18
Japan	18	16	20	20
Jordan	18	18		
Kazakhstan	16	16	18	17
Kyrgyzstan[5]			16	16
Malaysia[14]	18	16 and 18	18 and 21	18 and 21
Mongolia			18	18

Country or area	With parental consent		Without parental consent	
	Groom	*Bride*	*Groom*	*Bride*
Nepal	18	18	20	20
Oman[5]			18	18
Philippines	18	18	22	22
Republic of Korea	18	18	19	19
Singapore[15]	Under 21	Under 21	21	21
State of Palestine[16]		14.5	15.5	
Tajikistan	17	17	18	18
Turkey	16	16	18	18
Uzbekistan	18	17		
Europe				
Åland Islands[19]			18	18
Albania			18	18
Austria[17]	16	16	18	18
Belarus	15	15	18	18
Belgium			18	18
Bosnia and Herzegovina			18	18
Bulgaria	16	16	18	18
Croatia	16	16	18	18
Czechia[18]	16	16	18	18
Denmark	15	15	18	18
Estonia	15	15	18	18
Faeroe Islands[5]			18	18
Finland[19]			18	18
France[5]			18	18
Germany[20]	16	16	18	18
Gibraltar	16	16	18	18
Greece[21]			18	18
Hungary	16	16	18	18
Iceland	No limit	No limit	18	18
Ireland[5, 22]			18	18
Isle of Man	16	16	18	18
Italy	16	16	18	18
Jersey	16	16	18	18
Latvia	16	16	18	18
Liechtenstein[17]			18	18
Lithuania[23]	15	15	18	18
Luxembourg			18	18
Malta			16	16
Montenegro	16	16	18	18
Netherlands	16	16	18	18

Country or area	With parental consent		Without parental consent	
	Groom	Bride	Groom	Bride
Norway	16	16	18	18
Poland[24]			18	18
Portugal	16	16	18	18
Republic of Moldova			18	16
Romania[25]	16	16	18	18
Russian Federation	16	16	18	18
Serbia[26]	16	16	18	18
Slovakia			16	16
Slovenia	15	15	18	18
Spain	14	14	18	18
Sweden[27]			18	18
Switzerland			18	18
TFYR of Macedonia	16	16	18	18
Ukraine[17]	16	16	18	18
United Kingdom of Great Britain and Northern Ireland	16	16	18	18
Oceania				
Australia[28]	16	16	18	18
Cook Islands	16	16	21	21
Guam[29]	17	17	18	18
New Caledonia			18	18
New Zealand	16	16	18	18

NOTES

[1] *Principles and Recommendations for a Vital Statistics System Revision 3,* Sales No. E.13.XVII.10, United Nations, New York, 2014.

[2] In addition, an age waiver may be granted by a civil court for a serious reason from 15 years for women and 18 years for men.

[3] Marriages can be exceptionally authorised by the President of the Republic for brides who are at least 13 years old without parental consent.

[4] According to the Islamic law, marriage requires parental consent. Consent of the bride herself, as well as the guardian's consent are fundamental in the marriage contract. Young men usually choose the consent of the parents. Minimum age at marriage is usually 18 years. According to the law, marriage is not restricted to individuals over the age of 18 years.

[5] The minimum legal age at which marriage can take place is the same with or without parental consent.

[6] Marriages under the age of 18 can be performed with parental consent or with judicial permission if parental consent has been unreasonably refused. Additionally, boys under the age of 18 and girls under the age of 16 may also be required to seek the consent of the Minister of Home Affairs.

[7] As reported by Uganda Bureau of Statistics, marriages with or without parental consent may occur much earlier than 18 years of age.

[8] The legal minimum marriage age is 18, with two exceptions: if the persons concerned are older than 16 and the woman is pregnant or has given birth or the Minister of Security and Justice grants a dispensation based on their request.

[9] Marriage is under provincial and territory legislations. Without parental consent, the minimum legal age at which marriage can take place is 18 years of age in all provinces and territories in Canada except in British Columbia, Newfoundland and Labrador, Nova Scotia, Nunavut, and Yukon where the minimum legal age is 19 years. With parental consent, the minimum legal age is 16 years in all provinces except in Northwest Territories, Nunavut, and Yukon. With parental consent, in Northwest Territories, and Yukon the minimum legal age is 15 years whereas in Nunavut, the minimum legal age is 18 years.

[10] Each of the 31 Federal States and the Federal District has its own civil code for marriage. Marriages under 18 require parental consent. Additionally, in the Federal District and in the states of Guanajuato, Morelos, Puebla and San Luis Potosí the minimum age with parental consent is 16 for both bride and groom and in the states of Michoacán, Nayarit, Sinaloa and Sonora the minimum age with parental consent is 14 for the bride and 16 for the groom.

[11] Consent can be given by a guardian or a person who has custody of the child wishing to marry. Also, the Governor has discretion to permit persons as young as 15 years and 1 day old to marry, if he thinks that getting married is in the best interest of the persons who are intending to marry and the persons in this instance must have also received the necessary consent.

[12] With parental consent, age for marriage is 14 years for males and 12 years for females in a civil marriage; 16 years for males and 12 years for females in a Muslim marriage; 18 years for males and 14 years for females in a Hindu marriage; and 18 years for males and 16 for females in Orisa marriage.

[13] Grooms younger than 16 and brides younger than 14 need court authorization.

[14] For marriage with parental consent, it is 18 years of age for males whereas it is 18 years of age for non-Muslim females and 16 years of age for Muslim females. Without parental consent, it is 21 years of age for non-Muslims and 18 years of age for Muslims.

[15] Specified minimum legal marriage age refers to marriages contracted under the Women's Charter. For Muslim marriages under the Administration of Muslim Law Act, no marriage shall be solemnised when either party is below the age of 18 years. Notwithstanding that, Muslim women below the age of 18 years who have attained the age of puberty may be married under the Administration of the Muslim Law Act.

[16] The legal marriage age for females is 14 years, 6 months and 22 days. There must be parental consent (father or brother if the father is dead). The legal marriage age for males is 15 years, 6 months and 21 days. Parental consent is not required.

[17] Persons less than 18 years old need a decision of the court.

[18] The court may, for important reasons, allow the marriage of a minor over 16 years.

[19] Persons less than 18 years old need the permission of the Ministry of Justice.

[20] Marriage at 16-17 years of age requires that the other spouse be an adult (18 years or older) and an exemption from the requirement of majority by a competent family court.

[21] Under some conditions (e.g. pregnancy) the marriage can take place without age restrictions.

[22] An exemption on the minimum age can be granted by court order if granting of such an exemption is in the best interests of the parties to the intended marriage and good reasons for the application can be demonstrated.

[23] In addition to parental consent, persons less than 18 years old need judicial approval. In case of pregnancy, marriage can be allowed below 15 years of age.

[24] Females can marry at the age of 16 or 17 years with parental and court consent.

[25] Marriage for persons under 18 years requires parental consent, a medical certificate and the agreement by the local family court.

[26] Marriage is not allowed for persons below the age of 18; only the court may, for good cause, permit marriage to a minor who has attained the age of 16 years of age, and attained physical and mental maturity to exercise the rights and responsibilities of marriage. Parental consent is not required.

[27] With parental consent, no limit but authorities must approve; without parental consent, 18 years of age for Swedish citizens.

[28] Persons 16 or 17 years old need the court approval.

[29] Under 18, both a court order and parent or legal guardian consent are needed.

Tableau 23 – *Annuaire démographique 2016*

Le tableau 23 présente des statistiques concernant les mariages classés selon l'âge de l'époux et selon l'âge de l'épouse pour les années où les données sont disponibles entre 2007 et 2016.

Description des variables : le mariage désigne l'acte, la cérémonie ou la procédure qui établit un rapport légal entre les époux. L'union peut être rendue légale par une procédure civile ou religieuse, ou par toute autre procédure, conformément à la législation du pays[1].

Les statistiques de la nuptialité présentées dans ce tableau comprennent donc les premiers mariages et les remariages faisant suite à un divorce, un veuvage ou une annulation. Toutefois, sauf indication contraire, elles ne comprennent pas les unions reconstituées après une séparation légale. Ces statistiques se rapportent au nombre de mariages célébrés, non au nombre de personnes qui se marient.

L'âge désigne l'âge au dernier anniversaire, c'est-à-dire la différence entre la date de naissance et la date de l'événement, exprimée en années solaires révolues. Le classement par âge pour l'épouse utilisé dans ce tableau comprend les groupes suivants : moins de 15 ans, groupes quinquennaux jusqu'à 90-94 ans, et 95 ans et plus, selon la disponibilité des données. Le classement par âge pour l'époux est : moins de 15 ans, groupes quinquennal de 15 jusqu' à 59 ans et 60 ans et plus.

Dans un effort de fournir l'interprétation de ces statistiques, les pays ou les zones fournissant des données sur les mariages par l'âge de l'épouse et de par l'âge de l'époux ont été demandés d'indiquer « l'âge légal minimum avec auquel le mariage peut avoir lieu avec et sans consentement parental ». Cette information est présentée dans le tableau 23-1 ci-dessous.

Fiabilité des données : les données sur les mariages issues des registres de l'état civil qui sont déclarées incomplètes (degré de complétude inférieur à 90 p. 100) ou dont le degré de complétude n'est pas connu sont jugées douteuses et apparaissent en italique et non en caractères romains. Le tableau 22 et les notes techniques s'y rapportant présentent des renseignements plus détaillés sur le degré de complétude de l'enregistrement des mariages. Pour plus de précisions sur la qualité des données reposant sur les statistiques de l'état civil en général, voir la section 4.2 des notes techniques.

Insuffisance des données : les statistiques des mariages selon l'âge de l'époux et selon l'âge de l'épouse appellent les mêmes réserves que celles formulées à propos des statistiques de l'état civil en général et des statistiques de la nuptialité en particulier (voir la section 4 des Notes techniques).

Le fait que le mariage soit un acte juridique, à la différence de la naissance et du décès, qui sont des faits biologiques, a des répercussions sur la comparabilité internationale des données. Aux fins de la statistique, le mariage est défini par la législation de chaque pays ou zone. Cette législation varie d'un pays à l'autre. La comparabilité est limitée en outre du fait que certains pays et zones ne réunissent des statistiques que pour les mariages civils, bien que les mariages religieux y soient également reconnus par la loi ; dans d'autres, les seuls relevés disponibles sont les registres des églises et, en conséquence, les statistiques peuvent ne pas rendre compte des mariages exclusivement civils.

Le mariage étant, dans de nombreux pays ou zones, un contrat juridique civil qui, pour être légal, doit être conclu devant un officier d'état civil, il s'ensuit que, dans ces pays ou zones, l'enregistrement se fait à peu près systématiquement au moment de la cérémonie ou immédiatement après. Il faut tenir compte de cet élément lorsque l'on évalue la fiabilité des données, dont il est question plus haut.

Étant donné que ces statistiques sont classées selon l'âge, elles appellent les mêmes réserves concernant l'exactitude des déclarations d'âge que celles dont il a déjà été question à la section 3.1.3 des Notes techniques. Il est probable que les statistiques de la nuptialité sont moins faussées par ce genre d'erreur, car les renseignements sont donnés par les intéressés eux-mêmes, et, comme le mariage est un acte juridique, il y a toutes chances que leurs déclarations soient exactes. Toutefois, dans certains pays ou zones, il semble y avoir une concentration de mariages à l'âge minimal légal de nubilité ainsi qu'à l'âge auquel le mariage peut être valablement contracté sans le consentement des parents, ce qui peut indiquer que certains déclarants se vieillissent pour se conformer à la loi.

Outre la possibilité d'erreurs dans les déclarations d'âge, il convient de noter que la législation fixant l'âge minimal de nubilité influe notablement sur les caractéristiques de la nuptialité pour les premiers âges, c'est-à-dire jusqu'à 24 ans.

Parmi les facteurs pouvant exercer une influence sur les déclarations d'âge, en particulier celles qui sont faites par des personnes plus âgées, il faut citer la tendance à diminuer l'âge de l'épouse de façon qu'il soit égal ou inférieur à celui de l'époux.

Si aucun nombre ne figure dans la rangée réservée aux âges inconnus, cela ne signifie pas nécessairement que les déclarations d'âge et l'exploitation des données par âge aient été tout à fait exactes. C'est parfois une indication que l'on a attribué un âge aux personnes d'âge inconnu avant l'exploitation des données ou qu'elles ont été réparties proportionnellement entre les différents groupes après cette opération.

Il importe de ne pas oublier non plus, lorsque l'on utilisera ces données, que l'on calcule parfois l'âge des conjoints au moment du mariage sur la base de l'année de naissance seulement et non d'après la date exacte (jour, mois et année) de naissance. Des renseignements à ce sujet sont donnés en note chaque fois que possible.

Donnés publiées antérieurement : on trouve dans la plupart des éditions de l'*Annuaire démographique* des statistiques concernant les mariages selon l'âge de l'époux et selon l'âge de l'épouse qui ont été établies à partir des données les plus récentes dont on disposait à l'époque. Des données croisant l'âge des époux ont été présentées dans des éditions antérieurs, plus particulièrement consacrées aux statistiques de la nuptialité et de la divortialité. Pour plus de précisions concernant les années et les sujets pour lesquels des données ont été publiées, se reporter à l'index historique.

23-1 L'âge légal minimum avec auquel le mariage peut avoir lieu

Pays ou zone	Avec consentement parental		Sans consentement parental	
	Epoux	Epouse	Epoux	Epouse
Afrique				
Afrique du Sud[2]	Moins de 18	Moins de 18	18	18
Botswana	18	18	21	21
Burkina Faso[3]	18	15	20	17
Burundi[6]			21	18
Cameroun[4]	18	15	21	18
Egypte	18	18		
Ghana			18	18
Guinée	25	18		
Libéria	16	16	21	18
Libye[5]	18	18		
Malawi[6]			18	18
Maurice	16	16	18	18
Maroc[6]			18	18
Namibie	18	18	21	21
Ouganda[6, 7]			18	18
Sainte-Hélène sans dép.	16	16	21	21
Sénégal	Moins de 18	Moins de 18	18	18
Seychelles	16	16	18	18
Sierra Leone[6]			18	18
Swaziland	18	18	21	21
Zimbabwe	16	16	18	18
Amérique du Nord				

Pays ou zone	Avec consentement parental		Sans consentement parental	
	Epoux	*Epouse*	*Epoux*	*Epouse*
Anguilla	16	16	18	18
Aruba[8]	16	16	18	18
Bermudes	16	16	18	18
Canada[9]	16	16	18	18
Costa Rica	15	15	18	18
Cuba	16	14	18	16
Curaçao	16	16	18	18
El Salvador	Moins de 18	Moins de 18	18	18
Groenland[6]			18	18
Îles Caïmanes	16	16	18	18
Jamaïque	16	16	18	18
Mexique[10]	Moins de 18	Moins de 18	18	18
Montserrat[11]	16	16	18	18
Panama	16	14	18	18
Porto Rico	17	17	21	21
République dominicaine	16	15	18	18
Saint-Vincent-et-les Grenadines			18	18
Trinité-et-Tobago[12]	Moins de 18	Moins de 18	18	18
Amérique du Sud				
Bolivie (État plurinational de)[13]	16	14	18	18
Brésil	16	16	18	18
Chili	16	16	18	18
Colombie	14	14	18	18
Equateur	14	12	18	18
Suriname	17	15	21	21
Uruguay	16	16	18	18
Venezuela (République bolivarienne du)	14	12	18	18
Asie				
Arménie			18	17
Azerbaïdjan	18	17		
Bahreïn			15	
Cambodge			18	18
Chine, Hong Kong RAS	16	16	21	21
Chine, Macao RAS	16	16	18	18
Chypre	16	16	18	18
État de Palestine[14]		14.5	15.5	

Pays ou zone	Avec consentement parental		Sans consentement parental	
	Epoux	Epouse	Epoux	Epouse
Géorgie	16	16	18	18
Indonésie			19	16
Iran (République islamique d')	18	15		
Israël[6]			18	18
Japon	18	16	20	20
Jordanie	18	18		
Kazakhstan	16	16	18	17
Kirghizistan[6]			16	16
Malaisie[15]	18	16 et 18	18 et 21	18 et 21
Mongolie			18	18
Népal	18	18	20	20
Oman[6]			18	18
Ouzbékistan	18	17		
Philippines	18	18	22	22
République de Corée	18	18	19	19
Singapour[16]	Moins de 21	Moins de 21	21	21
Tadjikistan	17	17	18	18
Turquie	16	16	18	18
Europe				
Albanie			18	18
Allemagne[17]	16	16	18	18
Autriche[18]	16	16	18	18
Bélarus	15	15	18	18
Belgique			18	18
Bosnie-Herzégovine			18	18
Bulgarie	16	16	18	18
Croatie	16	16	18	18
Danemark	15	15	18	18
Espagne	14	14	18	18
Estonie	15	15	18	18
Fédération de Russie	16	16	18	18
Finlande[19]			18	18
France[6]			18	18
Gibraltar	16	16	18	18
Grèce[20]			18	18
Hongrie	16	16	18	18
Île de Man	16	16	18	18
Îles d'Åland[19]			18	18

Pays ou zone	Avec consentement parental		Sans consentement parental	
	Epoux	Epouse	Epoux	Epouse
Îles Féroé[6]			18	18
Irlande[6, 21]			18	18
Islande	Pas de limites	Pas de limites	18	18
Italie	16	16	18	18
Jersey	16	16	18	18
L'ex-R. y. de Macédoine	16	16	18	18
Lettonie	16	16	18	18
Liechtenstein[18]			18	18
Lituanie[22]	15	15	18	18
Luxembourg			18	18
Malte			16	16
Monténégro	16	16	18	18
Norvège	16	16	18	18
Pays-Bas	16	16	18	18
Pologne[23]			18	18
Portugal	16	16	18	18
République de Moldova			18	16
Roumanie[24]	16	16	18	18
Royaume-Uni de Grande-Bretagne et d'Irlande du Nord	16	16	18	18
Serbie[25]	16	16	18	18
Slovaquie			16	16
Slovénie	15	15	18	18
Suède[26]			18	18
Suisse			18	18
Tchéquie[27]	16	16	18	18
Ukraine[18]	16	16	18	18
Océanie				
Australie[28]	16	16	18	18
Guam[29]	17	17	18	18
Îles Cook	16	16	21	21
Nouvelle-Calédonie			18	18
Nouvelle-Zélande	16	16	18	18

NOTES

[1] *Principes et recommandations pour un système de statistique de l'état civil, troisième révision*, numéro de vente : E.13.XVII.10, publication des Nations Unies, New York, 2014.

[2] Il est possible de se marier avant 18 ans avec consentement parental, ou autorisation judiciaire si le consentement parental a été refusé sans motif raisonnable. De plus, les garçons âgés de moins de 18 ans et les filles âgées de moins de 16 ans peuvent être également tenus de demander le consentement du Ministère de l'intérieur.

[3] De plus, une dispense d'âge peut être accordée par un tribunal civil pour motif grave à partir de 15 ans pour les femmes et de 18 ans pour les hommes.

[4] Par ailleurs, à défaut d'avoir l'âge requis pour se marier avec l'aval des parents, la jeune fille peut exceptionnellement être autorisée par le Président de la République à se marier à 13 ans.

[5] Conformément à la loi islamique, le mariage requiert le consentement parental. Le consentement de la mariée, elle-même ainsi que le consentement du tuteur sont fondamentaux dans le contrat de mariage. Les jeunes hommes choisissent habituellement le consentement des parents. L'âge minimum du mariage est généralement 18 ans. Conformément à la loi, le mariage n'est pas limité aux individus âgés de plus de 18 ans.

[6] L'âge minimum légal du mariage est le même avec ou sans le consentement parental.

[7] Tel que le signale l'"Uganda Bureau of Statistics", les mariages avec ou sans le consentement parental peuvent se produire beaucoup plus tôt que 18 ans.

[8] L'âge minimum légal du mariage est 18 ans, avec deux exceptions : si les personnes en cause ont plus de 16 ans et la femme est enceinte ou a accouché, ou si le Ministre de la sécurité et de la justice leur a accordé une dispense sur leur demande.

[9] Le mariage est en vertu des législations provinciales et territoriales. Sans le consentement des parents, l'âge minimum légal du mariage est de 18 ans dans toutes les provinces et territoires du Canada sauf en Colombie-Britannique, Terre-Neuve-et-Labrador, la Nouvelle-Écosse, du Nunavut et du Yukon, où l'âge minimum légal est de 19 ans. Avec le consentement des parents, l'âge minimum légal est de 16 ans dans toutes les provinces sauf dans les Territoires du Nord-Ouest, Nunavut et Yukon. Avec le consentement des parents, dans les Territoires du Nord-Ouest et le Yukon l'âge minimum légal est de 15 ans alors que dans le Nunavut, l'âge minimum légal est de 18 ans.

[10] Chacun des 31 Etats fédéraux et du District fédéral a son propre code civil pour le mariage. Avant 18 ans, il faut le consentement parental pour pouvoir se marier. De plus, dans le District fédéral et les États de Guanajuato, Morelos, Puebla et San Luis Potosí l'âge minimum, avec consentement parental, est de 16 ans pour le fiancé et la fiancée, et dans les États de Michoacán, Nayarit, Sinaloa et Sonora, l'âge minimum avec consentement parental est de 14 ans pour la fiancée et 16 ans pour le fiancé.

[11] Le consentement peut être donné par un tuteur ou une personne qui a la garde de l'enfant qui souhaitent se marier. En outre, le gouverneur a la faculté de permettre aux personnes âgées d'au moins 15 ans et 1 jour de se marier, s'il pense que le mariage est dans le meilleur intérêt des personnes qui ont l'intention de s'unir et que les personnes concernées aient également reçu le consentement nécessaire.

[12] Avec l'âge du le consentement parental, l'âge minimum du mariage pour se marier est de 14 ans pour les hommes et de 12 ans pour les femmes pour un mariage civil ; de 16 ans pour les hommes et de 12 ans pour les femmes pour un mariage musulman ; de 18 ans pour les hommes et de 14 ans pour les femmes pour un mariage hindou, et de18 ans pour les hommes et de 16 pour les femmes pour un mariage orisa.

[13] Il est nécessaire d'avoir une autorisation judiciaire pour se marier avant 16 ans pour les hommes et avant 14 ans pour les femmes.

[14] L'âge légal du mariage pour les femmes est de 14 ans, 6 mois et 22 jours. Le consentement parental (du père ou du frère si le père est mort) est requis. L'âge légal du mariage pour les hommes est de 15 ans, 6 mois et 21 jours. Le consentement parental n'est pas nécessaire.

[15] Pour le mariage avec le consentement parental, il est de 18 ans pour les hommes alors qu'il est de 18 ans pour les femmes non-musulmanes et il est de 16 ans pour les femmes musulmanes. Sans le consentement parental, il est de 21 ans pour les non-musulmans et de 18 ans pour les musulmans.

[16] L'âge minimum légal du mariage spécifié correspond à des mariages contractés en vertu de la Charte des femmes. Pour les mariages musulmans sous l'administration de la « Loi sur le Droit Musulman », aucun mariage ne doit être célébré lorsque l'une des parties est en dessous de l'âge de 18 ans. Néanmoins, les femmes musulmanes en dessous de l'âge de 18 ans qui ont atteint l'âge de la puberté peuvent être mariées dans le cadre de l'administration de la « Loi sur le Droit Musulman ».

[17] Le mariage à 16-17 ans exige que l'autre conjoint soit un adulte (18 ans ou plus) ainsi qu'une exemption de l'obligation de la majorité par un juge aux affaires familiales.

[18] Les personnes âgées de moins de 18 ans doivent obtenir l'autorisation de la justice.

[19] Les personnes âgées de moins de 18 ans doivent obtenir l'autorisation du ministère de la justice.

[20] Dans certaines conditions (par exemple la grossesse), le mariage peut avoir lieu sans restriction d'âge.

[21] Une exemption sur l'âge minimum peut être accordée par ordonnance du tribunal si l'octroi d'une telle exemption est dans le meilleur intérêt des parties ayant l'intention de se marier et si la demande est appuyée par de bonnes raisons.

[22] En plus du consentement parental, les personnes de moins de 18 ans doivent obtenir l'approbation judiciaire. En cas de grossesse, le mariage peut être autorisé en dessous de 15 ans.

[23] Les femmes peuvent se marier à l'âge de 16 ou 17 ans avec les autorisations des parents et du tribunal.

[24] Le mariage avant 18 ans exige le consentement parental, un certificat médical et l'autorisation du tribunal local de famille.

[25] Il n'est pas permis de se marier avant 18 ans ; seul le tribunal peut, pour un motif valable, y autoriser une personne mineure ayant atteint l'âge de 16 ans et parvenue à la maturité physique et mentale voulue pour exercer les droits et les responsabilités du mariage. Le consentement parental n'est pas requis.

[26] Avec le consentement des parents, aucune limite mais les autorités doivent approuver. Sans le consentement parental, l'âge minimum légal du mariage est de 18 ans pour les citoyens suédois.

[27] Il est possible de se marier de 16 ans par autorisation judiciaire pour des raisons importantes.

[28] Les personnes âgées 16 ou 17 ans doivent obtenir l'autorisation du tribunal.

[29] Le mariage avant 18 ans exige le consentement parental ou de personne qui a la garde de mineur, et l'autorisation du tribunal.

23. Marriages by age of groom and by age of bride: latest available year, 2007 - 2016
Mariages selon l'âge de l'époux et selon l'âge de l'épouse : dernière année disponible, 2007 - 2016

Continent, country or area, year, code[a] and age of bride / Continent, pays ou zone, date, code[a] et âge de l'épouse	Total	Age of groom - - âge de l'époux											Unknown Inconnu
		0-14	15-19	20-24	25-29	30-34	35-39	40-44	45-49	50-54	55-59	60+	
AFRICA - AFRIQUE													
Botswana[1]													
2014 (+U)													
Total	5 591	-	-	59	572	1 389	1 275	847	540	329	235	345	...
0 - 14	-	-	-	-	-	-	-	-	-	-	-	-	...
15 - 19	9	-	-	2	6	-	1	-	-	-	-	-	...
20 - 24	401	-	-	39	166	119	53	13	8	3	-	-	...
25 - 29	1 407	-	-	14	325	626	303	84	37	9	6	3	...
30 - 34	1 631	-	-	3	63	552	565	264	111	35	24	14	...
35 - 39	965	-	-	1	10	71	274	322	179	72	23	13	...
40 - 44	499	-	-	-	2	13	63	133	136	89	40	23	...
45 - 49	266	-	-	-	-	3	10	26	55	79	50	43	...
50 - 54	206	-	-	-	-	4	4	5	12	38	70	73	...
55 - 59	91	-	-	-	-	-	2	-	2	3	18	66	...
60 - 64	56	-	-	-	-	1	-	-	-	1	4	50	...
65 +	60	-	-	-	-	-	-	-	-	-	-	60	...
Egypt - Égypte[2]													
2014 (+C)													
Total	953 137	...	12 499j	190 513	412 452	183 640	60 404	29 161	19 505	15 614	10 471	15 443	3 435
18 - 19	247 837	...	7 329j	84 124	119 632	30 984	4 213	744	284	236	103	151	37
20 - 24	375 611	...	4 081j	92 422	194 695	66 307	12 074	2 980	1 384	771	379	473	45
25 - 29	184 412	...	698j	11 011	83 947	57 490	18 024	6 210	3 230	1 799	1 024	957	22
30 - 34	69 705	...	198j	1 850	10 308	23 072	16 047	7 767	4 314	2 817	1 593	1 714	25
35 - 39	33 731	...	65j	463	2 144	4 080	7 579	7 073	4 688	3 345	2 008	2 280	6
40 - 44	17 262	...	44j	161	587	912	1 643	3 218	3 359	2 992	1 860	2 482	4
45 - 49	10 689	...	35j	174	555	415	537	830	1 669	2 263	1 652	2 558	1
50 - 54	5 708	...	22j	80	223	178	185	248	449	1 070	1 245	2 008	-
55 - 59	2 378	...	6j	47	57	34	38	52	80	226	444	1 394	-
60 - 64	1 100	...	6j	32	44	35	14	16	27	47	117	762	-
65 - 69	498	...	2j	14	16	12	7	4	7	21	27	388	-
70 - 74	189	...	-j	5	12	5	5	-	3	4	10	145	-
75 +	201	...	-j	16	33	17	5	7	1	5	2	115	-
Unknown - Inconnu	3 816	...	13j	114	199	99	33	12	10	18	7	16	3 295
Lesotho													
2011 (+U)													
Total	3 162	-	10	265	980	764	458	268	183	109	66	59	-
0 - 14	-	-	-	-	-	-	-	-	-	-	-	-	-
15 - 19	144	-	8	69	55	10	1	-	-	1	-	-	-
20 - 24	924	-	2	178	524	159	48	5	4	1	2	1	-
25 - 29	979	-	-	16	360	397	122	44	18	14	4	4	-
30 - 34	574	-	-	1	37	184	196	77	45	21	7	6	-
35 - 39	299	-	-	-	3	12	85	109	56	19	10	5	-
40 - 44	122	-	-	1	-	2	4	32	44	22	11	6	-
45 - 49	60	-	-	-	-	-	2	1	16	19	14	8	-
50 - 54	32	-	-	-	-	-	-	-	-	11	13	8	-
55 - 59	16	-	-	-	1	-	-	-	-	1	5	9	-
60 - 64	8	-	-	-	-	-	-	-	-	-	-	8	-
65 - 69	2	-	-	-	-	-	-	-	-	-	-	2	-
70 - 74	2	-	-	-	-	-	-	-	-	-	-	2	-
75 +	-	-	-	-	-	-	-	-	-	-	-	-	-
Unknown - Inconnu	-	-	-	-	-	-	-	-	-	-	-	-	-
Mauritius - Maurice[3]													
2016 (+C)													
Total	10 042	-	84	1 065	2 983	2 387	1 409	761	539	381	202	230	1
0 - 14	-	-	-	-	-	-	-	-	-	-	-	-	-
15 - 19	612	-	60	290	182	57	18	4	1	-	-	-	-
20 - 24	2 386	-	22	587	1 153	457	134	24	5	3	-	1	-
25 - 29	3 201	-	2	147	1 407	1 116	391	84	32	17	3	2	-
30 - 34	1 563	-	-	28	185	583	475	188	62	24	12	6	-
35 - 39	945	-	-	7	47	139	288	243	142	51	16	12	-
40 - 44	475	-	-	4	6	20	74	145	114	66	22	24	-
45 - 49	398	-	-	1	3	11	22	51	125	98	56	31	-
50 - 54	270	-	-	-	-	2	5	21	49	98	47	48	-
55 - 59	122	-	-	1	-	1	2	1	7	18	36	56	-
60 - 64	45	-	-	-	-	-	-	-	-	4	10	31	-
65 - 69	16	-	-	-	-	-	-	-	-	2	2	12	-

Continent, country or area, year, code[a] and age of bride / Continent, pays ou zone, date, code[a] et âge de l'épouse	Total	0-14	15-19	20-24	25-29	30-34	35-39	40-44	45-49	50-54	55-59	60+	Unknown Inconnu
AFRICA - AFRIQUE													
Mauritius - Maurice[3]													
2016													
70 - 74	7	-	-	-	-	1	-	-	-	-	-	6	-
75 +	1	-	-	-	-	-	-	-	-	-	-	1	-
Unknown - Inconnu	1	-	-	-	-	-	-	-	-	-	-	-	1
Reunion - Réunion													
2008 (C)													
Total	3 149	-	15	338	787	681	514	306	185	150	62	111	-
0 - 14	1	-	1	-	-	-	-	-	-	-	-	-	-
15 - 19	91	-	8	45	26	7	2	2	1	-	-	-	-
20 - 24	679	-	4	235	296	99	28	13	3	-	1	-	-
25 - 29	858	-	2	42	391	264	117	30	7	4	1	-	-
30 - 34	584	-	-	12	52	232	185	56	29	10	4	4	-
35 - 39	384	-	-	3	16	55	134	106	38	25	4	3	-
40 - 44	234	-	-	-	4	16	34	77	49	28	13	13	-
45 - 49	144	-	-	1	1	7	11	18	34	40	18	14	-
50 - 54	94	-	-	-	1	1	3	4	19	30	12	24	-
55 - 59	39	-	-	-	-	-	-	-	3	10	7	19	-
60 - 64	16	-	-	-	-	-	-	-	2	2	1	11	-
65 - 69	16	-	-	-	-	-	-	-	-	1	1	14	-
70 - 74	7	-	-	-	-	-	-	-	-	-	-	7	-
75 +	2	-	-	-	-	-	-	-	-	-	-	2	-
Saint Helena ex. dep. - Sainte-Hélène sans dép.													
2012 (C)													
Total	12	-	-	-	1	3	-	2	5	-	-	1	...
0 - 14	-	-	-	-	-	-	-	-	-	-	-	-	...
15 - 19	-	-	-	-	-	-	-	-	-	-	-	-	...
20 - 24	-	-	-	-	-	-	-	-	-	-	-	-	...
25 - 29	2	-	-	-	1	1	-	-	-	-	-	-	...
30 - 34	2	-	-	-	-	1	-	1	-	-	-	-	...
35 - 39	3	-	-	-	-	1	-	-	2	-	-	-	...
40 - 44	2	-	-	-	-	-	-	1	1	-	-	-	...
45 - 49	1	-	-	-	-	-	-	-	1	-	-	-	...
50 - 54	1	-	-	-	-	-	-	-	1	-	-	-	...
55 - 59	1	-	-	-	-	-	-	-	-	-	-	1	...
60 - 64	-	-	-	-	-	-	-	-	-	-	-	-	...
65 - 69	-	-	-	-	-	-	-	-	-	-	-	-	...
70 - 74	-	-	-	-	-	-	-	-	-	-	-	-	...
75 +	-	-	-	-	-	-	-	-	-	-	-	-	...
Seychelles[4]													
2015 (+C)													
Total	1 845	-	3	73	318	452	346	237	183	118	60	55	...
0 - 14	-	-	-	-	-	-	-	-	-	-	-	-	...
15 - 19	15	-	2	7	4	1	1	-	-	-	-	-	...
20 - 24	127	-	-	38	48	25	4	5	4	-	1	2	...
25 - 29	481	-	-	18	176	168	67	24	15	3	7	3	...
30 - 34	519	-	-	8	64	202	147	56	26	11	5	-	...
35 - 39	295	-	-	1	17	41	94	79	33	21	8	1	...
40 - 44	182	-	-	1	7	13	27	54	42	25	7	6	...
45 - 49	111	-	-	-	1	-	3	12	45	27	14	9	...
50 - 54	58	-	-	-	1	-	2	4	13	23	10	5	...
55 - 59	44	-	1	-	-	2	1	3	4	8	6	19	...
60 - 64	9	-	-	-	-	-	-	-	1	-	2	6	...
65 - 69	3	-	-	-	-	-	-	-	-	-	-	3	...
70 - 74	1	-	-	-	-	-	-	-	-	-	-	1	...
75 +	-	-	-	-	-	-	-	-	-	-	-	-	...
South Africa - Afrique du Sud													
2011 (...)													
Total	167 264	2	189	8 719	36 903	38 827	30 474	19 424	13 105	7 955	5 028	6 638	...
0 - 14	4	-	-	2	-	2	-	-	-	-	-	-	...
15 - 19	2 199	-	96	1 002	703	256	90	33	8	4	4	3	...
20 - 24	25 542	-	72	5 690	12 489	4 977	1 589	431	172	67	36	19	...
25 - 29	50 977	-	13	1 598	19 588	18 847	7 485	2 245	786	246	105	64	...
30 - 34	35 124	-	2	308	3 266	11 855	12 206	4 737	1 764	620	210	156	...
35 - 39	22 456	-	4	84	637	2 266	7 236	6 955	3 296	1 209	479	290	...

Continent, country or area, year, code[a] and age of bride / Continent, pays ou zone, date, code[a] et âge de l'épouse	Total	0-14	15-19	20-24	25-29	30-34	35-39	40-44	45-49	50-54	55-59	60+	Unknown Inconnu
AFRICA - AFRIQUE													
South Africa - Afrique du Sud													
2011													
40 - 44	13 030	-	1	26	167	456	1 449	3 799	3 943	1 859	783	547	...
45 - 49	8 221	-	-	6	44	129	310	940	2 365	2 270	1 203	954	...
50 - 54	4 674	-	-	3	7	25	88	228	586	1 294	1 293	1 150	...
55 - 59	2 480	-	-	-	2	9	16	44	140	285	692	1 292	...
60 - 64	1 340	1	-	-	-	3	4	8	31	81	177	1 035	...
65 - 69	653	-	1	-	-	1	-	3	13	12	36	587	...
70 - 74	322	-	-	-	-	-	-	1	1	6	8	306	...
75 +	242	1	-	-	-	1	1	-	-	2	2	235	...
Tunisia - Tunisie													
2015 (...)													
Total	108 453	...	272[f]	5 931	28 713	35 845	19 527	7 704	3 596	2 283	1 516	3 032	34
0 - 19	6 873	...	...	...	...	...	...	...	...	...	...	...	...
20 - 24	29 113	...	...	...	...	...	...	...	...	...	...	...	...
25 - 29	36 893	...	...	...	...	...	...	...	...	...	...	...	...
30 - 34	18 433	...	...	...	...	...	...	...	...	...	...	...	...
35 - 39	8 557	...	...	...	...	...	...	...	...	...	...	...	...
40 - 44	4 159	...	...	...	...	...	...	...	...	...	...	...	...
45 - 49	2 420	...	...	...	...	...	...	...	...	...	...	...	...
50 +	1 980	...	...	...	...	...	...	...	...	...	...	...	...
Unknown - Inconnu	28	...	...	...	...	...	...	...	...	...	...	...	...
AMERICA, NORTH - AMÉRIQUE DU NORD													
Anguilla[5]													
2013 (C)													
Total	42	4	9	9	4	4	4	1	-	1	...	...	6
0 - 14	5	2	2	-	-	-	1	-	-	-	...	...	-
15 - 19	12	1	5	3	3	-	-	-	-	-	...	...	-
20 - 24	9	-	1	5	1	1	1	-	-	-	...	...	-
25 - 29	5	1	1	1	-	2	-	-	-	-	...	...	-
30 - 34	3	-	-	-	-	-	2	1	-	-	...	...	-
35 - 39	2	-	-	-	-	1	-	-	-	1	...	...	-
40 - 44	-	-	-	-	-	-	-	-	-	-	...	...	-
45 - 49	-	-	-	-	-	-	-	-	-	-	...	...	-
50 - 54	-	-	-	-	-	-	-	-	-	-	...	...	-
Unknown - Inconnu	6	-	-	-	-	-	-	-	-	-	...	...	6
Aruba													
2016 (C)													
Total	639	-	11	82	151	97	95	68	51	43	22	17	2
0 - 14	-	-	-	-	-	-	-	-	-	-	-	-	-
15 - 19	2	-	-	2	-	-	-	-	-	-	-	-	-
20 - 24	61	-	6	29	19	5	1	1	-	-	-	-	-
25 - 29	122	-	4	31	55	21	7	3	1	-	-	2	1
30 - 34	100	-	1	11	38	25	14	7	-	1	-	2	1
35 - 39	86	-	-	8	19	22	18	13	3	3	-	-	-
40 - 44	73	-	-	-	9	12	23	14	6	7	2	-	-
45 - 49	64	-	-	-	9	6	14	10	15	5	5	-	-
50 - 54	53	-	-	1	-	3	9	8	16	9	4	2	-
55 - 59	45	-	-	-	2	3	6	8	5	11	9	1	1
60 - 64	19	-	-	-	-	-	1	3	3	4	2	6	-
65 - 69	9	-	-	-	-	-	2	-	2	2	-	3	-
70 - 74	2	-	-	-	-	-	-	1	-	1	-	-	-
75 +	3	-	-	-	-	-	-	-	-	-	-	3	-
Unknown - Inconnu	-	-	-	-	-	-	-	-	-	-	-	-	-
Bahamas													
2013 (+C)													
Total	2 122	...	...	...	104	472	498	325	223	163	106	226	5
25 - 29	171	...	...	...	24	64	39	16	3	5	-	20	-
30 - 34	543	...	...	...	27	202	161	62	42	13	12	24	-
35 - 39	391	...	...	...	9	61	131	87	48	24	12	18	1
40 - 44	249	...	...	...	5	21	53	70	50	28	9	13	-
45 - 49	219	...	...	...	5	24	33	28	38	44	23	24	-
50 - 54	192	...	...	...	6	21	28	26	22	38	21	30	-

Continent, country or area, year, code[a] and age of bride / Continent, pays ou zone, date, code[a] et âge de l'épouse	Total	0-14	15-19	20-24	25-29	30-34	35-39	40-44	45-49	50-54	55-59	60+	Unknown Inconnu
AMERICA, NORTH - AMÉRIQUE DU NORD													
Bahamas													
2013													
55 - 59	133	...	...	...	6	17	20	17	9	6	18	39	1
60 +	216	...	...	...	22	62	33	17	10	4	11	56	1
Unknown - Inconnu	8	...	...	...	-	-	-	2	1	1	-	2	2
Bermuda - Bermudes													
2016 (C)													
Total	450	-	-	11	68	99	77	52	50	32	31	30	-
0 - 14	-	-	-	-	-	-	-	-	-	-	-	-	-
15 - 19	1	-	-	1	-	-	-	-	-	-	-	-	-
20 - 24	16	-	-	5	8	2	1	-	-	-	-	-	-
25 - 29	87	-	-	5	36	28	14	3	-	1	-	-	-
30 - 34	115	-	-	-	18	47	32	12	3	2	1	-	-
35 - 39	67	-	-	-	4	17	15	15	13	2	-	1	-
40 - 44	55	-	-	-	2	4	11	12	16	6	2	2	-
45 - 49	45	-	-	-	-	1	3	7	13	10	8	3	-
50 - 54	26	-	-	-	-	-	1	-	2	7	10	6	-
55 - 59	24	-	-	-	-	-	-	2	3	4	9	6	-
60 - 64	4	-	-	-	-	-	-	-	-	-	1	3	-
65 - 69	7	-	-	-	-	-	-	1	-	-	-	6	-
70 - 74	2	-	-	-	-	-	-	-	-	-	-	2	-
75 +	1	-	-	-	-	-	-	-	-	-	-	1	-
Unknown - Inconnu	-	-	-	-	-	-	-	-	-	-	-	-	-
Costa Rica[6]													
2016* (C)													
Total	26 718	-	278	3 142	6 431	5 862	3 621	2 148	1 617	1 177	873	1 510	59
0 - 14	-	-	-	-	-	-	-	-	-	-	-	-	-
15 - 19	1 289	-	173	633	309	101	45	7	8	6	1	2	4
20 - 24	5 074	-	82	1 674	2 084	802	255	86	44	20	16	6	5
25 - 29	7 144	-	13	577	2 865	2 273	853	310	128	68	28	20	9
30 - 34	5 022	-	6	171	798	1 876	1 196	508	235	122	58	44	8
35 - 39	2 875	-	3	64	258	542	853	536	306	148	94	68	3
40 - 44	1 777	-	1	11	75	164	258	443	349	236	126	113	1
45 - 49	1 287	-	-	4	21	66	114	152	328	269	160	172	1
50 - 54	928	-	-	2	8	17	26	75	150	204	186	260	-
55 - 59	552	-	-	2	3	2	10	13	47	74	135	266	-
60 - 64	326	-	-	1	-	2	4	10	14	17	46	232	-
65 - 69	188	-	-	-	-	3	-	-	2	6	12	165	-
70 - 74	109	-	-	-	-	-	-	1	-	3	6	99	-
75 +	64	-	-	-	-	-	-	1	-	1	1	61	-
Unknown - Inconnu	83	-	-	3	10	14	7	6	6	3	4	2	28
Cuba[7]													
2016 (C)													
Total	61 903	-	898	6 324	11 510	9 707	6 547	7 136	6 217	5 141	2 926	5 496	1
0 - 14	38	-	7	16	7	5	2	1	-	-	-	-	-
15 - 19	3 861	-	535	1 657	1 048	367	85	61	46	28	15	19	-
20 - 24	10 074	-	230	2 804	3 747	1 737	685	388	212	126	50	95	-
25 - 29	12 453	-	60	1 110	4 183	3 419	1 625	1 043	503	271	105	134	-
30 - 34	8 532	-	27	379	1 366	2 357	1 672	1 360	728	348	121	174	-
35 - 39	5 635	-	11	137	487	873	1 152	1 297	870	455	179	174	-
40 - 44	6 019	-	5	79	300	460	708	1 495	1 424	918	341	288	1
45 - 49	5 451	-	12	50	182	234	373	884	1 378	1 275	529	534	-
50 - 54	4 612	-	6	52	94	156	157	431	696	1 185	830	1 005	-
55 - 59	2 282	-	-	16	39	50	42	108	221	358	500	948	-
60 - 64	1 423	-	2	12	21	22	25	28	77	114	189	933	-
65 - 69	836	-	1	3	13	9	7	21	33	42	39	668	-
70 - 74	402	-	1	3	9	9	3	10	13	9	15	330	-
75 +	282	-	1	6	13	8	11	9	15	12	13	194	-
Unknown - Inconnu	3	-	-	-	1	1	-	-	1	-	-	-	-
Curaçao[8]													
2016 (C)													
Total	695	-	1	35	104	108	116	73	70	63	55	59	11
0 - 14	-	-	-	-	-	-	-	-	-	-	-	-	-
15 - 19	9	-	1	5	1	-	1	1	-	-	-	-	-
20 - 24	82	-	-	20	36	9	9	5	3	-	-	-	-
25 - 29	141	-	-	9	46	35	33	8	6	2	2	-	-

23. Marriages by age of groom and by age of bride: latest available year, 2007 - 2016
Mariages selon l'âge de l'époux et selon l'âge de l'épouse : dernière année disponible, 2007 - 2016 (continued - suite)

Continent, country or area, year, code[a] and age of bride / Continent, pays ou zone, date, code[a] et âge de l'épouse	Total	0-14	15-19	20-24	25-29	30-34	35-39	40-44	45-49	50-54	55-59	60+	Unknown Inconnu
AMERICA, NORTH - AMÉRIQUE DU NORD													
Curaçao[8]													
2016													
30 - 34	133	-	-	1	18	50	23	16	16	2	4	3	-
35 - 39	75	-	-	-	2	9	26	15	10	8	3	2	-
40 - 44	70	-	-	-	1	3	12	21	13	13	5	2	-
45 - 49	57	-	-	-	-	2	9	5	14	13	8	6	-
50 - 54	60	-	-	-	-	-	1	1	8	19	21	10	-
55 - 59	31	-	-	-	-	-	2	1	-	3	10	15	-
60 - 64	11	-	-	-	-	-	-	-	-	2	1	8	-
65 - 69	10	-	-	-	-	-	-	-	-	1	1	8	-
70 - 74	3	-	-	-	-	-	-	-	-	-	-	3	-
75 +	2	-	-	-	-	-	-	-	-	-	-	2	-
Unknown - Inconnu	11	-	-	-	-	-	-	-	-	-	-	-	11
Dominican Republic - République dominicaine													
2016 (+C)													
Total	52 896	-	519	6 339	10 445	8 672	7 061	5 651	4 612	9 238	359[t]	...	...
0 - 14	-	-	-	-	-	-	-	-	-	-	-[t]	...	...
15 - 19	2 274	-	195	1 058	566	233	93	49	29	50	1[t]	...	...
20 - 24	10 511	-	174	3 300	3 796	1 577	735	361	223	335	10[t]	...	...
25 - 29	11 189	-	64	1 148	3 862	2 936	1 441	746	434	548	10[t]	...	...
30 - 34	8 062	-	25	387	1 134	2 219	1 939	1 030	573	750	5[t]	...	...
35 - 39	6 511	-	25	189	512	919	1 540	1 465	849	1 010	2[t]	...	...
40 - 44	5 014	-	10	118	282	392	713	1 129	1 102	1 264	4[t]	...	...
45 - 49	3 698	-	8	52	137	220	336	473	788	1 678	6[t]	...	...
50 - 54	5 174	-	10	47	127	161	249	390	605	3 579	6[t]	...	...
55 +	463	-	8	40	29	15	15	8	9	24	315[t]	...	...
El Salvador[9]													
2012 (...)													
Total	29 267	-	1 098	6 586	6 762	5 101	3 026	2 078	1 528	989	671	1 294	134
0 - 14	37	-	10	16	6	3	2	-	-	-	-	-	-
15 - 19	3 670	-	544	1 856	787	250	113	53	25	12	5	9	16
20 - 24	8 329	-	414	3 407	2 652	1 113	374	176	90	37	12	19	35
25 - 29	6 227	-	80	933	2 304	1 713	647	264	153	70	27	23	13
30 - 34	4 049	-	16	230	704	1 360	902	414	223	82	47	53	18
35 - 39	2 433	-	14	69	179	436	654	509	272	134	74	84	8
40 - 44	1 604	-	4	25	58	118	208	410	348	175	107	149	2
45 - 49	1 144	-	2	6	18	54	80	174	290	234	125	157	4
50 - 54	633	-	-	3	6	15	16	43	84	162	140	164	-
55 - 59	403	-	1	1	1	6	5	10	23	61	89	206	-
60 - 64	242	-	1	-	1	2	2	10	10	12	26	177	1
65 +	279	-	2	1	-	2	3	3	3	7	13	245	-
Unknown - Inconnu	217	-	10	39	46	29	20	12	7	3	6	8	37
Guatemala													
2011 (C)													
Total	78 286	17	9 779	27 197	18 081	9 430	4 619	2 550	1 635	1 375	1 126	2 362	115
0 - 14	1 122	4	513	458	109	31	5	1	1	-	-	-	-
15 - 19	22 191	12	6 733	11 231	3 124	788	191	52	27	9	6	6	12
20 - 24	25 037	1	2 199	12 176	7 600	2 137	592	162	69	39	16	25	21
25 - 29	13 633	-	267	2 705	5 632	3 393	1 009	338	135	61	39	42	12
30 - 34	6 599	-	46	494	1 284	2 336	1 504	497	192	115	64	63	4
35 - 39	3 263	-	11	83	240	588	933	780	283	165	77	96	7
40 - 44	1 869	-	2	19	49	112	266	504	401	255	116	144	1
45 - 49	1 436	-	1	8	17	31	78	156	373	379	184	205	4
50 - 54	1 094	-	-	1	6	8	26	41	107	260	335	306	4
55 - 59	760	-	-	-	1	-	8	13	32	70	225	410	1
60 - 64	511	-	-	2	-	-	1	2	8	15	44	438	1
65 - 69	332	-	1	-	1	1	-	2	2	3	14	308	-
70 - 74	183	-	-	-	-	-	-	-	-	2	2	178	1
75 +	139	-	-	-	-	-	-	-	-	1	1	137	-
Unknown - Inconnu	117	-	6	20	18	5	6	2	5	1	3	4	47
Martinique													
2007 (C)													
Total	1 341	-	19	128	297	284	185	155	117	63	32	61	-
0 - 14	-	-	-	-	-	-	-	-	-	-	-	-	-

623

Continent, pays ou zone, date, code[a] et âge de l'épouse	Total	0-14	15-19	20-24	25-29	30-34	35-39	40-44	45-49	50-54	55-59	60+	Unknown Inconnu
AMERICA, NORTH - AMÉRIQUE DU NORD													
Martinique													
2007													
15 - 19	55	-	11	35	8	1	-	-	-	-	-	-	-
20 - 24	217	-	4	63	108	25	13	4	-	-	-	-	-
25 - 29	273	-	3	20	123	99	16	7	1	4	-	-	-
30 - 34	243	-	1	4	38	97	65	24	11	2	1	-	-
35 - 39	173	-	-	4	12	42	54	49	9	3	-	-	-
40 - 44	146	-	-	1	3	11	26	47	45	10	3	-	-
45 - 49	84	-	-	1	3	6	6	19	29	14	5	1	-
50 - 54	53	-	-	-	2	3	3	3	15	11	10	6	-
55 - 59	31	-	-	-	-	-	1	-	7	12	3	8	-
60 - 64	24	-	-	-	-	-	-	1	-	4	8	11	-
65 - 69	12	-	-	-	-	-	1	-	-	2	-	9	-
70 - 74	16	-	-	-	-	-	-	1	-	1	2	12	-
75 +	14	-	-	-	-	-	-	-	-	-	-	14	-
Mexico - Mexique[10]													
2015 (+C)													
Total	558 022	10	31 682	146 611	148 692	92 279	48 887	29 070	17 849	12 477	9 768	19 547	1 150
0 - 14	606	4	274	245	55	16	10	1	-	-	-	-	1
15 - 19	80 523	5	22 083	42 820	11 383	2 888	828	273	102	56	16	31	38
20 - 24	166 709	1	8 132	80 772	54 654	15 810	4 615	1 554	595	251	92	128	105
25 - 29	137 164	-	934	18 302	65 395	35 652	10 823	3 667	1 284	536	238	226	107
30 - 34	72 079	-	173	3 308	13 476	28 684	15 943	6 109	2 378	980	478	473	77
35 - 39	37 114	-	47	799	2 731	6 828	11 710	8 020	3 525	1 707	840	872	35
40 - 44	22 860	-	11	204	662	1 737	3 551	6 614	4 682	2 436	1 367	1 568	28
45 - 49	14 955	-	6	77	179	437	978	2 020	3 728	3 189	1 955	2 361	25
50 - 54	10 135	-	3	19	53	108	278	583	1 087	2 347	2 399	3 247	11
55 - 59	6 869	-	1	5	18	35	79	163	325	682	1 711	3 843	7
60 - 64	4 065	-	-	2	3	11	20	33	93	195	466	3 240	2
65 - 69	2 163	-	-	1	3	6	15	11	26	55	156	1 889	1
70 - 74	1 048	-	-	-	4	2	2	3	5	23	32	976	1
75 +	717	-	-	3	1	2	1	2	6	8	10	680	4
Unknown - Inconnu	1 015	-	18	54	75	63	34	17	13	12	8	13	708
Montserrat													
2016 (+...)													
Total	10	-	-	1	3	2	1	-	-	-	2	1	...
0 - 14	-	-	-	-	-	-	-	-	-	-	-	-	...
15 - 19	-	-	-	-	-	-	-	-	-	-	-	-	...
20 - 24	2	-	-	1	1	-	-	-	-	-	-	-	...
25 - 29	2	-	-	-	1	-	-	-	-	-	1	-	...
30 - 34	3	-	-	-	1	1	1	-	-	-	-	-	...
35 - 39	1	-	-	-	-	1	-	-	-	-	-	-	...
40 - 44	-	-	-	-	-	-	-	-	-	-	-	-	...
45 - 49	-	-	-	-	-	-	-	-	-	-	-	-	...
50 - 54	-	-	-	-	-	-	-	-	-	-	-	-	...
55 - 59	-	-	-	-	-	-	-	-	-	-	-	-	...
60 - 64	2	-	-	-	-	-	-	-	-	-	1	1	...
65 - 69	-	-	-	-	-	-	-	-	-	-	-	-	...
70 - 74	-	-	-	-	-	-	-	-	-	-	-	-	...
75 +	-	-	-	-	-	-	-	-	-	-	-	-	...
Panama[6]													
2015* (C)													
Total	14 341	-	141	1 663	3 119	2 677	1 823	2 234[n]	...	1 175[o]	...	908	601
0 - 14	2	-	-	2	-	-	-	-[n]	...	-[o]	...	-	-
15 - 19	583	-	76	275	118	56	17	12[n]	...	-[o]	...	-	29
20 - 24	2 587	-	48	895	973	364	122	73[n]	...	11[o]	...	2	99
25 - 29	3 271	-	9	276	1 321	932	388	195[n]	...	40[o]	...	12	98
30 - 34	2 402	-	1	93	388	821	551	378[n]	...	75[o]	...	21	74
35 - 39	1 677	-	-	31	147	262	424	555[n]	...	141[o]	...	54	63
40 - 49	1 821	-	-	15	45	95	215	751[n]	...	452[o]	...	188	60
50 - 59	855	-	-	2	3	13	17	123[n]	...	326[o]	...	354	17
60 - 69	247	-	-	-	-	-	2	6[n]	...	40[o]	...	194	5
70 +	67	-	-	-	-	-	-	1[n]	...	4[o]	...	62	-
Unknown - Inconnu	829	-	7	74	124	134	87	140[n]	...	86[o]	...	21	156

23. Marriages by age of groom and by age of bride: latest available year, 2007 - 2016
Mariages selon l'âge de l'époux et selon l'âge de l'épouse : dernière année disponible, 2007 - 2016 (continued - suite)

Continent, country or area, year, code[a] and age of bride / Continent, pays ou zone, date, code[a] et âge de l'épouse	Total	0-14	15-19	20-24	25-29	30-34	35-39	40-44	45-49	50-54	55-59	60+	Unknown Inconnu
AMERICA, NORTH - AMÉRIQUE DU NORD													
Puerto Rico - Porto Rico													
2016 (C)													
Total	15 746	-	261	2 407	3 355	2 479	1 898	1 450	1 252	889	638	1 115	2
0 - 14	1	-	1	-	-	-	-	-	-	-	-	-	-
15 - 19	458	-	120	254	65	13	4	1	1	-	-	-	-
20 - 24	2 587	-	112	1 388	774	193	85	21	7	1	4	2	-
25 - 29	3 542	-	20	568	1 697	795	294	100	40	10	12	6	-
30 - 34	2 449	-	6	128	569	867	512	217	89	34	13	14	-
35 - 39	1 867	-	1	52	178	392	566	368	188	63	34	25	-
40 - 44	1 440	-	1	10	45	139	257	398	335	149	50	56	-
45 - 49	1 114	-	-	2	18	48	119	198	315	216	96	102	-
50 - 54	843	-	-	2	6	19	42	89	162	221	157	145	-
55 - 59	612	-	-	2	2	9	7	37	76	104	144	231	-
60 - 64	376	-	-	-	-	3	7	13	23	55	75	200	-
65 - 69	248	-	-	-	1	1	2	4	11	27	38	164	-
70 - 74	128	-	-	1	-	-	3	3	3	8	9	101	-
75 +	79	-	-	-	-	-	-	1	2	1	6	69	-
Unknown - Inconnu	2	-	-	-	-	-	-	-	-	-	-	-	2
Saint Vincent and the Grenadines - Saint-Vincent-et-les Grenadines													
2015 (C)													
Total	572	-	-	26	83	113	84	76	48	60	32	50	...
0 - 14	-	-	-	-	-	-	-	-	-	-	-	-	...
15 - 19	5	-	-	1	1	1	1	-	-	-	-	1	...
20 - 24	60	-	-	14	27	11	5	2	1	-	-	-	...
25 - 29	130	-	-	10	39	42	27	8	2	1	-	1	...
30 - 34	98	-	-	-	6	37	23	17	6	7	1	1	...
35 - 39	91	-	-	1	7	10	21	26	10	10	5	1	...
40 - 44	68	-	-	-	2	8	3	15	15	15	6	4	...
45 - 49	51	-	-	-	-	3	3	3	12	15	3	12	...
50 - 54	31	-	-	-	1	1	1	3	1	8	10	6	...
55 - 59	17	-	-	-	-	-	-	-	-	3	4	10	...
60 - 64	15	-	-	-	-	-	-	2	1	1	2	9	...
65 - 69	3	-	-	-	-	-	-	-	-	-	-	3	...
70 - 74	3	-	-	-	-	-	-	-	-	-	1	2	...
75 +	-	-	-	-	-	-	-	-	-	-	-	-	...
Trinidad and Tobago - Trinité-et-Tobago													
2011 (C)													
Total	7 886	-	65	906	2 203	1 738	1 021	626	466	345	220	295	1
0 - 14	3	-	-	1	1	1	-	-	-	-	1	-	-
15 - 19	374	-	44	162	121	28	11	6	1	-	1	-	-
20 - 24	1 598	-	15	457	707	275	94	32	10	2	5	1	-
25 - 29	2 430	-	5	210	1 049	701	291	99	45	19	7	4	-
30 - 34	1 373	-	1	54	238	507	307	155	61	32	12	6	-
35 - 39	786	-	-	14	62	163	211	148	100	45	27	16	-
40 - 44	484	-	-	6	18	35	70	116	116	64	37	22	-
45 - 49	372	-	-	1	7	23	29	45	84	99	40	44	-
50 - 54	226	-	-	-	-	5	6	19	28	60	52	56	-
55 - 59	115	-	-	1	-	-	2	4	13	15	28	52	-
60 - 64	63	-	-	-	-	-	-	1	5	4	6	47	-
65 +	61	-	-	-	-	-	-	1	3	5	5	47	-
Unknown - Inconnu	1	-	-	-	-	-	-	-	-	-	-	-	1
Turks and Caicos Islands - Îles Turques et Caïques													
2008 (C)													
Total	486	...	-	20	110	114	94	63	51	17	10	7	-
15 - 19	2	...	...	...	...	...	...	...	...	...	...	...	...
20 - 24	47	...	...	...	...	...	...	...	...	...	...	...	...
25 - 29	134	...	...	...	...	...	...	...	...	...	...	...	...
30 - 34	127	...	...	...	...	...	...	...	...	...	...	...	...
35 - 39	94	...	...	...	...	...	...	...	...	...	...	...	...
40 - 44	37	...	...	...	...	...	...	...	...	...	...	...	...
45 - 49	26	...	...	...	...	...	...	...	...	...	...	...	...

23. Marriages by age of groom and by age of bride: latest available year, 2007 - 2016
Mariages selon l'âge de l'époux et selon l'âge de l'épouse : dernière année disponible, 2007 - 2016 (continued - suite)

Continent, country or area, year, code[a] and age of bride / Continent, pays ou zone, date, code[a] et âge de l'épouse	Total	0-14	15-19	20-24	25-29	30-34	35-39	40-44	45-49	50-54	55-59	60+	Unknown Inconnu
AMERICA, NORTH - AMÉRIQUE DU NORD													
Turks and Caicos Islands - Îles Turques et Caïques													
2008													
50 - 54	12	...	...	...	...	...	...	...	...	...	...	...	...
55 - 59	6	...	...	...	...	...	...	...	...	...	...	...	...
60 - 64	-	...	...	...	...	...	...	...	...	...	...	...	...
65 +	1	...	...	...	...	...	...	...	...	...	...	...	...
Unknown - Inconnu	-	...	...	...	...	...	...	...	...	...	...	...	...
AMERICA, SOUTH - AMÉRIQUE DU SUD													
Bolivia (Plurinational State of) - Bolivie (État plurinational de)													
2012 (U)													
Total	34 542	...	...	...	...	...	...	...	...	...	1 864[t]	...	11
15 - 24	11 851	...	...	...	...	...	...	...	...	...	...	...	...
25 - 34	16 113	...	...	...	...	...	...	...	...	...	...	...	...
35 - 44	3 944	...	...	...	...	...	...	...	...	...	...	...	...
45 - 54	1 335	...	...	...	...	...	...	...	...	...	...	...	...
55 +	1 247	...	...	...	...	...	...	...	...	...	...	...	...
Unknown - Inconnu	52	...	...	...	...	...	...	...	...	...	...	...	...
Brazil - Brésil													
2015 (+U)													
Total	1131734	15	31 892	206 176	284 383	227 301	138 078	83 880	56 170	38 952	25 822	38 654	411
0 - 14	287	4	123	98	41	11	5	1	2	-	1	1	-
15 - 19	122 518	8	20 623	65 383	25 487	7 552	2 264	735	243	125	46	46	6
20 - 24	258 079	-	8 421	97 936	98 878	35 581	11 161	3 690	1 393	597	245	163	14
25 - 29	269 690	1	1 812	30 219	109 395	82 422	29 197	9 939	3 822	1 683	677	514	9
30 - 34	192 144	-	562	8 593	36 303	69 109	45 243	18 355	7 707	3 560	1 565	1 139	8
35 - 39	113 764	1	219	2 714	10 140	22 741	32 403	23 366	11 681	5 650	2 711	2 129	9
40 - 44	68 886	1	71	821	2 908	6 775	11 653	16 915	14 115	8 044	3 946	3 636	1
45 - 49	46 064	-	34	266	865	2 192	4 144	7 220	10 610	9 423	5 464	5 842	4
50 - 54	28 906	-	12	77	230	653	1 452	2 569	4 438	6 401	5 856	7 216	2
55 - 59	15 698	-	5	25	63	156	368	745	1 485	2 330	3 469	7 052	-
60 - 64	8 278	-	2	11	21	53	115	221	465	790	1 266	5 333	1
65 - 69	4 022	-	3	3	4	17	35	70	133	232	403	3 122	-
70 - 74	1 772	-	-	3	4	7	11	32	48	81	111	1 475	-
75 +	1 159	-	2	9	14	10	13	13	23	29	61	985	-
Unknown - Inconnu	467	-	3	18	30	22	14	9	5	7	1	1	357
Chile - Chili													
2014 (+C)													
Total	64 868	-	485	7 203	16 059	14 342	8 471	5 292	3 611	2 959	2 243	4 203	...
0 - 14	-	-	-	-	-	-	-	-	-	-	-	-	...
15 - 19	1 670	-	237	944	347	94	25	11	5	4	2	1	...
20 - 24	10 588	-	187	4 274	4 273	1 302	335	139	46	16	6	10	...
25 - 29	18 341	-	44	1 553	8 786	5 604	1 609	500	139	66	23	17	...
30 - 34	12 968	-	12	316	2 093	5 615	3 151	1 117	407	153	66	38	...
35 - 39	6 781	-	3	80	405	1 261	2 232	1 550	691	336	120	103	...
40 - 44	4 480	-	-	29	116	347	759	1 216	966	546	271	230	...
45 - 49	3 376	-	1	5	31	87	266	511	793	778	469	435	...
50 - 54	2 748	-	1	2	8	18	79	193	389	650	619	789	...
55 - 59	1 745	-	-	-	-	10	11	41	117	266	398	902	...
60 - 64	1 134	-	-	-	-	3	2	12	39	103	185	790	...
65 - 69	589	-	-	-	-	1	2	2	15	30	58	481	...
70 - 74	276	-	-	-	-	-	-	-	4	8	20	244	...
75 +	172	-	-	-	-	-	-	-	-	3	6	163	...
Ecuador - Équateur[11]													
2015 (U)													
Total	60 636	5	2 557	13 771	16 597	10 891	5 957	3 479	2 281	1 632	1 167	2 299	-
0 - 14	121	-	47	51	16	5	1	1	-	-	-	-	-
15 - 19	6 948	3	1 642	3 628	1 200	304	104	34	20	8	4	1	-
20 - 24	17 306	2	715	7 831	6 132	1 877	499	155	62	17	10	6	-
25 - 29	15 499	-	103	1 830	7 222	4 312	1 333	428	152	61	30	28	-
30 - 34	8 505	-	25	317	1 554	3 253	2 041	779	309	136	50	41	-

23. Marriages by age of groom and by age of bride: latest available year, 2007 - 2016
Mariages selon l'âge de l'époux et selon l'âge de l'épouse : dernière année disponible, 2007 - 2016 (continued - suite)

Continent, country or area, year, code[a] and age of bride / Continent, pays ou zone, date, code[a] et âge de l'épouse	Total	0-14	15-19	20-24	25-29	30-34	35-39	40-44	45-49	50-54	55-59	60+	Unknown Inconnu
AMERICA, SOUTH - AMÉRIQUE DU SUD													
Ecuador - Équateur[11]													
2015													
35 - 39	4 457	-	11	57	351	832	1 340	1 004	468	206	102	86	-
40 - 44	2 844	-	3	26	90	225	474	729	601	364	183	149	-
45 - 49	1 846	-	4	17	14	57	121	254	456	434	215	274	-
50 - 54	1 258	-	4	1	9	16	33	66	149	281	329	370	-
55 - 59	756	-	1	4	2	4	9	21	47	89	182	397	-
60 - 64	454	-	1	3	-	3	2	4	12	23	41	365	-
65 - 69	322	-	1	3	2	2	-	2	3	10	17	282	-
70 - 74	166	-	-	2	2	-	-	1	1	3	2	155	-
75 +	154	-	-	1	3	1	-	1	1	-	2	145	-
Unknown - Inconnu	-	-	-	-	-	-	-	-	-	-	-	-	-
French Guiana - Guyane française													
2007 (C)													
Total	667	...	5	48	123	150	108	79	47	48	26	33	-
15 - 19	30	...	-	10	13	4	-	1	1	-	1	-	-
20 - 24	93	...	3	22	33	15	8	7	-	1	2	2	-
25 - 29	151	...	1	5	51	57	17	7	5	2	6	-	-
30 - 34	135	...	1	8	16	41	35	18	7	7	2	-	-
35 - 39	98	...	-	3	6	20	27	20	11	2	6	3	-
40 - 44	62	...	-	-	4	7	10	15	10	9	2	5	-
45 - 49	55	...	-	-	-	3	5	9	10	16	4	8	-
50 - 54	23	...	-	-	-	2	4	2	3	6	2	4	-
55 - 59	13	...	-	-	-	1	2	-	-	3	1	6	-
60 - 64	2	...	-	-	-	-	-	-	-	1	-	1	-
65 - 69	4	...	-	-	-	-	-	-	-	1	-	3	-
70 - 74	1	...	-	-	-	-	-	-	-	-	-	1	-
75 - 79	-	...	-	-	-	-	-	-	-	-	-	-	-
80 - 84	-	...	-	-	-	-	-	-	-	-	-	-	-
85 +	-	...	-	-	-	-	-	-	-	-	-	-	-
Paraguay													
2014 (U)													
Total	19 527	-	522	4 026	5 754	4 204	1 953	1 143	687	472	279	481	6
0 - 14	6	-	2	1	3	-	-	-	-	-	-	-	-
15 - 19	2 725	-	373	1 359	659	224	68	24	7	7	2	2	-
20 - 24	5 192	-	119	1 962	2 002	788	192	74	27	15	3	9	1
25 - 29	5 035	-	21	527	2 250	1 541	441	147	57	23	12	16	-
30 - 34	3 249	-	4	120	687	1 227	669	310	112	64	24	31	1
35 - 39	1 355	-	3	35	102	284	396	285	142	66	17	25	-
40 - 44	725	-	-	13	32	78	123	187	158	69	22	43	-
45 - 49	496	-	-	3	15	40	43	65	116	115	60	39	-
50 - 54	322	-	-	3	2	14	14	32	46	68	72	71	-
55 - 59	181	-	-	1	1	5	2	11	15	32	37	77	-
60 - 64	110	-	-	-	-	1	2	4	3	6	19	75	-
65 - 69	66	-	-	-	-	2	1	2	3	4	10	44	-
70 - 74	30	-	-	1	-	-	-	1	1	1	1	25	-
75 +	27	-	-	-	-	-	1	-	-	2	-	24	-
Unknown - Inconnu	8	-	-	1	1	-	1	1	-	-	-	-	4
Peru - Pérou[12,13]													
2015 (+C)													
Total	31 888	-	235	3 004	7 519	7 818	5 369	3 109	1 846	1 131	667	1 190	...
0 - 14	-	-	-	-	-	-	-	-	-	-	-	-	...
15 - 19	800	-	136	402	211	38	7	6	-	-	-	-	...
20 - 24	4 889	-	79	1 806	1 996	667	239	80	15	7	-	-	...
25 - 29	8 964	-	16	653	3 939	2 907	1 013	284	88	34	4	26	...
30 - 34	7 565	-	3	104	1 114	3 308	1 971	675	242	83	25	40	...
35 - 39	4 289	-	1	30	192	748	1 629	1 028	404	132	68	57	...
40 - 44	2 333	-	-	6	45	128	397	775	545	278	87	72	...
45 - 49	1 386	-	-	3	10	15	89	198	416	342	171	142	...
50 - 54	729	-	-	-	3	4	13	43	102	193	175	196	...
55 - 59	432	-	-	-	3	1	-	6	21	48	114	239	...
60 +	501	-	-	-	6	2	11	14	13	14	23	418	...

23. Marriages by age of groom and by age of bride: latest available year, 2007 - 2016
Mariages selon l'âge de l'époux et selon l'âge de l'épouse : dernière année disponible, 2007 - 2016 (continued - suite)

Continent, country or area, year, code[a] and age of bride / Continent, pays ou zone, date, code[a] et âge de l'épouse	Total	0-14	15-19	20-24	25-29	30-34	35-39	40-44	45-49	50-54	55-59	60+	Unknown Inconnu
AMERICA, SOUTH - AMÉRIQUE DU SUD													
Venezuela (Bolivarian Republic of) - Venezuela (République bolivarienne du)													
2014 (C)													
Total	94 519	20	2 550	17 462	26 166	18 537	11 206	6 898	4 568	2 906	1 717	2 489	...
0 - 14	216	3	58	93	41	13	4	3	1	-	-	-	...
15 - 19	8 759	8	1 595	4 458	1 849	537	177	66	36	12	9	12	...
20 - 24	23 551	6	658	9 340	9 035	2 989	942	337	137	55	22	30	...
25 - 29	25 178	1	136	2 641	11 250	7 086	2 499	937	359	157	56	56	...
30 - 34	15 417	-	45	635	2 884	5 613	3 550	1 510	673	294	110	103	...
35 - 39	8 565	-	25	180	749	1 587	2 588	1 816	898	405	180	137	...
40 - 44	5 362	-	10	61	232	495	940	1 453	1 124	574	263	210	...
45 - 49	3 351	-	7	22	70	150	352	527	889	667	351	316	...
50 - 54	2 072	1	7	13	24	41	102	171	333	526	371	483	...
55 - 59	990	-	2	3	11	9	24	43	77	146	231	444	...
60 +	1 058	1	7	16	21	17	28	35	41	70	124	698	...
ASIA - ASIE													
Armenia - Arménie													
2009 (+C)													
Total	18 773	...	153	4 608	7 796	3 482	1 313	560	325	208	132	196	-
15 - 19	2 010	...	122	928	825	124	11	-	-	-	-	-	-
20 - 24	9 521	...	28	3 366	4 655	1 278	170	19	2	3	-	-	-
25 - 29	4 516	...	2	282	2 151	1 474	478	95	27	7	-	-	-
30 - 34	1 467	...	-	26	130	539	455	215	76	17	9	-	-
35 - 39	528	...	-	4	20	47	165	154	92	32	10	4	-
40 - 44	238	...	-	2	8	13	22	52	72	42	16	11	-
45 - 49	161	...	1	-	2	4	6	14	39	53	20	22	-
50 - 54	153	...	-	-	4	3	4	8	8	45	47	34	-
55 - 59	101	...	-	-	-	-	1	2	4	5	25	64	-
60 +	78	...	-	-	1	-	1	1	5	4	5	61	-
2015 (+C)													
Total	17 603	...	71	3 173	6 751	3 928	1 615	841	479	303	199	243	...
15 - 19	1 083	...	...	...	...	...	...	...	...	...	...	...	...
20 - 24	6 998	...	...	...	...	...	...	...	...	...	...	...	...
25 - 29	5 121	...	...	...	...	...	...	...	...	...	...	...	...
30 - 34	2 212	...	...	...	...	...	...	...	...	...	...	...	...
35 - 39	1 041	...	...	...	...	...	...	...	...	...	...	...	...
40 - 44	450	...	...	...	...	...	...	...	...	...	...	...	...
45 - 49	241	...	...	...	...	...	...	...	...	...	...	...	...
50 - 54	187	...	...	...	...	...	...	...	...	...	...	...	...
55 - 59	138	...	...	...	...	...	...	...	...	...	...	...	...
60 +	132	...	...	...	...	...	...	...	...	...	...	...	...
Azerbaijan - Azerbaïdjan													
2015 (+C)													
Total	68 773	...	459	19 422	29 256	10 548	3 856	2 155	1 210	780	514	573	...
15 - 19	16 345	...	268	7 189	7 396	1 365	119	8	-	-	-	-	...
20 - 24	30 330	...	162	10 648	14 782	4 008	624	82	15	6	2	1	...
25 - 29	12 451	...	25	1 358	6 176	3 323	1 089	357	89	21	7	6	...
30 - 34	4 599	...	2	174	729	1 486	1 222	641	254	68	17	6	...
35 - 39	2 253	...	1	33	133	282	606	631	344	147	58	18	...
40 - 44	1 230	...	-	8	28	60	142	327	308	204	100	53	...
45 - 49	746	...	-	7	9	17	42	82	140	195	136	118	...
50 - 54	446	...	-	3	2	6	8	21	48	108	121	129	...
55 - 59	217	...	1	2	1	1	4	4	9	22	64	109	...
60 +	156	...	-	-	-	-	-	2	3	9	9	133	...
Bahrain - Bahreïn													
2016 (...)													
Total	7 019	-	187	2 110	2 685	973	402	245	134	283[s]	...	...	...
0 - 14	11	-	4	4	2	-	1	-	-	-[s]	...	...	...
15 - 19	1 310	-	148	770	308	48	16	8	6	6[s]	...	...	...
20 - 24	2 925	-	32	1 194	1 399	222	45	16	10	7[s]	...	...	...
25 - 29	1 562	-	3	121	848	415	108	28	19	20[s]	...	...	...

23. Marriages by age of groom and by age of bride: latest available year, 2007 - 2016
Mariages selon l'âge de l'époux et selon l'âge de l'épouse : dernière année disponible, 2007 - 2016 (continued - suite)

Continent, country or area, year, code[a] and age of bride / Continent, pays ou zone, date, code[a] et âge de l'épouse	Total	0-14	15-19	20-24	25-29	30-34	35-39	40-44	45-49	50-54	55-59	60+	Unknown Inconnu
ASIA - ASIE													
Bahrain - Bahreïn													
2016													
30 - 34	591	-	-	13	94	227	124	64	23	46[s]	...	...	...
35 - 39	288	-	-	8	22	42	85	69	30	32[s]	...	...	...
40 - 44	150	-	-	-	6	15	14	44	29	42[s]	...	...	...
45 - 49	94	-	-	-	5	3	6	9	14	57[s]	...	...	...
50 +	88	-	-	-	1	1	3	7	3	73[s]	...	...	...
Brunei Darussalam - Brunéi Darussalam													
2015 (+...)													
Total	2 750	-	55	454	1 085	587	254	123	70	51	32	39	...
0 - 14	-	...	...	...	...	...	...	...	...	...	...	...	...
15 - 19	158	...	...	...	...	...	...	...	...	...	...	...	...
20 - 24	677	...	...	...	...	...	...	...	...	...	...	...	...
25 - 29	1 107	...	...	...	...	...	...	...	...	...	...	...	...
30 - 34	436	...	...	...	...	...	...	...	...	...	...	...	...
35 - 39	163	...	...	...	...	...	...	...	...	...	...	...	...
40 - 44	106	...	...	...	...	...	...	...	...	...	...	...	...
45 - 49	59	...	...	...	...	...	...	...	...	...	...	...	...
50 - 54	24	...	...	...	...	...	...	...	...	...	...	...	...
55 - 59	9	...	...	...	...	...	...	...	...	...	...	...	...
60 - 64	5	...	...	...	...	...	...	...	...	...	...	...	...
65 - 69	3	...	...	...	...	...	...	...	...	...	...	...	...
70 - 74	1	...	...	...	...	...	...	...	...	...	...	...	...
75 +	2	...	...	...	...	...	...	...	...	...	...	...	...
China, Hong Kong SAR - Chine, Hong Kong RAS													
2016 (C)													
Total	50 008	-	133	2 979	11 581	13 752	7 229	4 571	3 051	2 385	1 873	2 454	-
0 - 14	-	-	-	-	-	-	-	-	-	-	-	-	-
15 - 19	434	-	65	227	99	24	10	6	1	1	1	-	-
20 - 24	5 483	-	59	1 878	2 185	852	277	118	63	27	13	11	-
25 - 29	16 280	-	5	693	7 463	5 294	1 610	620	287	170	88	50	-
30 - 34	13 004	-	3	114	1 466	6 276	2 831	1 154	507	321	194	138	-
35 - 39	5 971	-	1	36	238	963	1 857	1 239	686	425	286	240	-
40 - 44	3 885	-	-	23	85	251	463	989	727	479	424	444	-
45 - 49	2 498	-	-	6	36	69	133	326	543	503	387	495	-
50 - 54	1 372	-	-	2	8	15	33	90	178	342	266	438	-
55 - 59	620	-	-	-	-	6	13	22	46	100	168	265	-
60 - 64	271	-	-	-	1	2	2	6	10	15	37	198	-
65 - 69	111	-	-	-	-	-	-	1	3	1	6	100	-
70 - 74	36	-	-	-	-	-	-	-	-	-	3	33	-
75 +	43	-	-	-	-	-	-	-	-	1	-	42	-
Unknown - Inconnu	-	-	-	-	-	-	-	-	-	-	-	-	-
China, Macao SAR - Chine, Macao RAS													
2009 (+C)													
Total	3 035	-	18	608	1 023	697	286	157	98	68	39	41	-
0 - 14	-	-	-	-	-	-	-	-	-	-	-	-	-
15 - 19	66	-	5	40	17	3	1	-	-	-	-	-	-
20 - 24	993	-	12	445	353	125	36	14	5	3	-	-	-
25 - 29	1 166	-	1	109	575	313	94	42	13	11	7	1	-
30 - 34	444	-	-	10	62	212	83	33	25	12	5	2	-
35 - 39	195	-	-	4	9	30	62	41	26	8	8	7	-
40 - 44	72	-	-	-	5	8	9	17	12	9	6	6	-
45 - 49	58	-	-	-	1	4	1	7	16	14	8	7	-
50 - 54	20	-	-	-	1	2	-	3	1	9	2	2	-
55 - 59	11	-	-	-	-	-	-	-	-	1	2	8	-
60 - 64	4	-	-	-	-	-	-	-	-	1	1	2	-
65 - 69	1	-	-	-	-	-	-	-	-	-	-	1	-
70 +	5	-	-	-	-	-	-	-	-	-	-	5	-
2015 (+C)													
Total	3 719	...	...	418[g]	...	...	...	...	392[r]	...	...	...	...
0 - 24	861	...	...	...	...	...	...	...	...	...	...	...	...
25 - 34	2 317	...	...	...	...	...	...	...	...	...	...	...	...

23. Marriages by age of groom and by age of bride: latest available year, 2007 - 2016
Mariages selon l'âge de l'époux et selon l'âge de l'épouse : dernière année disponible, 2007 - 2016 (continued - suite)

Continent, pays ou zone, date, code[a] et âge de l'épouse	Total	0-14	15-19	20-24	25-29	30-34	35-39	40-44	45-49	50-54	55-59	60+	Unknown Inconnu
ASIA - ASIE													
China, Macao SAR - Chine, Macao RAS													
2015													
35 - 44	348	...	...	...	...	...	...	...	...	...	...	...	...
45 +	193	...	...	...	...	...	...	...	...	...	...	...	...
Cyprus - Chypre[14,15]													
2013 (C)													
Total	5 493	-	22	437	1 854	1 711	597	322	187	127	69	132	35
0 - 14	-	-	-	-	-	-	-	-	-	-	-	-	-
15 - 19	80	-	7	41	18	10	2	-	2	-	-	-	-
20 - 24	805	-	8	237	395	130	22	9	4	-	-	-	-
25 - 29	2 298	-	5	111	1 161	785	147	44	26	12	3	4	-
30 - 34	1 290	-	2	23	215	639	241	102	31	23	5	8	1
35 - 39	521	-	-	19	48	117	134	102	57	23	11	10	-
40 - 44	214	-	-	6	10	23	38	44	29	31	15	18	-
45 - 49	129	-	-	-	5	6	8	16	30	22	13	29	-
50 - 54	64	-	-	-	2	-	3	4	6	13	14	22	-
55 - 59	30	-	-	-	-	-	1	1	2	2	6	18	-
60 +	27	-	-	-	-	-	1	-	-	1	2	23	-
Unknown - Inconnu	35	-	-	-	-	1	-	-	-	-	-	-	34
Georgia - Géorgie													
2016 (C)													
Total	25 101	...	458[h]	5 695	7 174	4 533	2 919	1 848	1 040	592	386	456	...
16 - 19	2 545	...	...	...	...	...	...	...	...	...	...	...	...
20 - 24	7 978	...	...	...	...	...	...	...	...	...	...	...	...
25 - 29	6 096	...	...	...	...	...	...	...	...	...	...	...	...
30 - 34	3 514	...	...	...	...	...	...	...	...	...	...	...	...
35 - 39	2 204	...	...	...	...	...	...	...	...	...	...	...	...
40 - 44	1 237	...	...	...	...	...	...	...	...	...	...	...	...
45 - 49	673	...	...	...	...	...	...	...	...	...	...	...	...
50 - 54	423	...	...	...	...	...	...	...	...	...	...	...	...
55 - 59	234	...	...	...	...	...	...	...	...	...	...	...	...
60 +	197	...	...	...	...	...	...	...	...	...	...	...	...
Iran (Islamic Republic of) - Iran (République islamique d')[16,17]													
2015 (+C)													
Total	685 352	...	28 125[f]	213 401	252 196	112 084	35 446	14 845	8 404	5 589	4 443	10 819	-
0 - 14	37 117	...	5 975[f]	21 502	8 598	816	146	47	13	12	5	3	-
15 - 19	196 592	...	17 441[f]	102 036	65 925	9 736	1 034	228	77	56	32	27	-
20 - 24	204 202	...	3 878[f]	72 177	95 553	27 628	3 791	698	256	107	59	55	-
25 - 29	138 357	...	620[f]	14 539	66 607	42 666	9 928	2 389	838	366	181	223	-
30 - 34	62 397	...	170[f]	2 530	12 878	25 093	12 855	4 882	2 019	909	495	566	-
35 - 39	24 569	...	32[f]	496	2 201	5 128	6 101	4 359	2 602	1 423	947	1 280	-
40 - 44	10 796	...	6[f]	90	355	866	1 348	1 794	1 769	1 388	1 082	2 098	-
45 - 49	5 344	...	1[f]	21	57	124	211	367	656	910	844	2 153	-
50 - 54	2 793	...	-[f]	4	14	21	26	64	152	332	512	1 668	-
55 - 59	1 581	...	-[f]	2	4	6	5	12	13	66	213	1 260	-
60 - 64	867	...	-[f]	1	1	-	-	4	7	17	57	780	-
65 - 69	414	...	-[f]	1	1	-	-	-	1	2	14	395	-
70 - 74	193	...	-[f]	-	-	-	-	1	-	-	2	190	-
75 +	127	...	-[f]	2	2	-	1	-	-	1	-	121	-
Unknown - Inconnu	3	...	2[f]	-	-	-	-	-	1	-	-	-	-
Israel - Israël[18]													
2015 (C)													
Total	53 579	...	1 855	13 084	19 437	10 507	3 676	1 518	771	431	344	604	1 352
15 - 19	6 713	...	1 274	3 428	1 350	214	30	3	2	-	1	-	411
20 - 24	19 014	...	525	8 703	7 274	1 699	240	34	14	3	1	-	521
25 - 29	16 761	...	7	548	9 640	5 098	1 006	203	38	10	2	2	207
30 - 34	5 915	...	-	46	832	2 932	1 427	395	107	38	13	5	120
35 - 39	2 070	...	-	7	77	367	759	521	196	66	21	13	43
40 - 44	848	...	-	2	9	33	106	259	216	98	61	41	23
45 - 49	438	...	-	-	-	3	19	46	120	98	72	69	11
50 - 54	309	...	-	-	1	-	1	5	27	84	90	89	12
55 - 59	157	...	-	-	-	-	-	-	4	12	46	94	1

23. Marriages by age of groom and by age of bride: latest available year, 2007 - 2016
Mariages selon l'âge de l'époux et selon l'âge de l'épouse : dernière année disponible, 2007 - 2016 (continued - suite)

Continent, country or area, year, code[a] and age of bride — Continent, pays ou zone, date, code[a] et âge de l'épouse	Total	Age of groom - - âge de l'époux											
		0-14	15-19	20-24	25-29	30-34	35-39	40-44	45-49	50-54	55-59	60+	Unknown Inconnu
ASIA - ASIE													
Israel - Israël[18]													
2015													
60 - 64	133	...	-	-	-	-	-	1	1	1	13	116	1
65 - 69	87	...	-	-	-	-	-	-	-	1	3	82	1
70 - 74	34	...	-	-	-	-	-	-	-	-	1	32	1
75 +	14	...	-	-	-	-	-	-	-	-	-	14	-
Unknown - Inconnu	1 086	...	49	350	254	161	88	51	46	20	20	47	-
Japan - Japon[19]													
2015 (+C)													
Total	512 892	-	5 202	52 320	161 590	125 096	76 806	44 742	20 634	10 660	6 178	9 664	-
0 - 14	-	-	-	-	-	-	-	-	-	-	-	-	-
15 - 19	9 491	-	3 846	3 761	1 047	426	193	94	57	25	18	24	-
20 - 24	77 529	-	1 208	35 876	25 107	9 355	3 781	1 346	469	209	89	89	-
25 - 29	188 801	-	106	10 064	109 766	46 648	15 383	4 724	1 345	418	191	156	-
30 - 34	119 022	-	30	1 967	20 946	54 296	27 360	9 983	2 912	905	357	266	-
35 - 39	63 416	-	7	529	3 907	11 955	24 082	15 239	5 078	1 599	587	433	-
40 - 44	28 096	-	-	99	697	2 004	5 002	10 646	5 759	2 318	927	644	-
45 - 49	11 959	-	4	18	98	342	800	2 158	3 830	2 559	1 186	964	-
50 - 54	6 569	-	-	3	20	54	172	461	980	2 063	1 459	1 357	-
55 - 59	3 362	-	-	2	2	9	29	77	162	438	1 077	1 566	-
60 - 64	1 971	-	-	-	-	2	2	14	30	97	217	1 609	-
65 - 69	1 469	-	-	-	-	4	2	-	9	22	57	1 375	-
70 - 74	737	-	1	-	-	-	-	-	2	5	9	720	-
75 +	469	-	-	-	-	1	-	-	1	2	4	461	-
Unknown - Inconnu	1	-	-	1	-	-	-	-	-	-	-	-	-
Jordan - Jordanie													
2010[20] (+C)													
Total	62 107	...	16 151	25 559	12 760	4 002	1 795	1 151	437	252[s]	...	...	-
18 - 19	1 262	...	1 017	191	40	11	1	2	-	-[s]	...	...	-
20 - 24	14 272	...	6 768	6 453	835	139	42	20	7	8[s]	...	...	-
25 - 29	25 434	...	6 276	12 608	5 720	633	120	45	16	16[s]	...	...	-
30 - 34	11 523	...	1 603	4 782	3 679	1 153	197	70	25	14[s]	...	...	-
35 - 39	4 064	...	299	1 043	1 434	819	350	92	19	8[s]	...	...	-
40 - 44	2 365	...	99	321	681	647	358	217	35	7[s]	...	...	-
45 - 49	1 139	...	35	81	220	283	249	196	57	18[s]	...	...	-
50 - 54	639	...	14	37	73	152	169	121	53	20[s]	...	...	-
55 - 59	425	...	12	18	35	80	95	107	56	22[s]	...	...	-
60 - 64	318	...	11	7	21	40	66	97	39	37[s]	...	...	-
65 +	666	...	17	18	22	45	148	184	130	102[s]	...	...	-
Kazakhstan													
2013 (C)													
Total	168 447	101[d]	3 612[j]	57 563	60 803	22 537	10 618	5 553	3 077	2 126	1 229	1 228	...
0 - 17	1 392	38[d]	367[j]	789	174	19	3	1	-	1	1	-	...
18 - 19	19 707	49[d]	2 280[j]	12 409	4 319	555	73	17	3	1	1	-	...
20 - 24	79 862	11[d]	889[j]	39 230	33 107	5 486	899	178	36	14	9	3	...
25 - 29	37 703	2[d]	63[j]	4 541	19 985	9 429	2 705	668	220	64	21	5	...
30 - 34	14 237	-[d]	12[j]	481	2 642	5 502	3 632	1 345	408	145	48	22	...
35 - 39	7 447	-[d]	1[j]	85	460	1 273	2 563	1 834	776	308	98	49	...
40 - 44	3 675	1[d]	-[j]	21	85	225	598	1 178	826	471	177	93	...
45 - 49	1 932	-[d]	-[j]	3	24	42	114	256	594	523	234	142	...
50 - 54	1 249	-[d]	-[j]	2	4	4	26	60	173	448	303	229	...
55 - 59	674	-[d]	-[j]	-	2	1	5	14	30	119	266	237	...
60 +	568	-[d]	-[j]	1	1	1	-	2	11	32	72	448	...
Unknown - Inconnu	1	-[d]	-[j]	1	-	-	-	-	-	-	-	-	...
Kuwait - Koweït													
2015 (C)													
Total	15 412	-	328	4 082	5 181	2 622	1 225	756	1 218[r]	...	...	...	...
0 - 14	-	-	-	-	-	-	-	-	-[r]	...	...	...	...
15 - 19	2 443	-	242	1 494	596	90	15	2	4[r]	...	...	...	...
20 - 24	5 523	-	81	2 238	2 463	591	100	28	22[r]	...	...	...	...
25 - 29	3 650	-	4	286	1 740	1 078	335	118	89[r]	...	...	...	...
30 - 34	1 790	-	1	37	273	612	433	225	209[r]	...	...	...	...
35 - 39	996	-	-	17	68	180	237	206	288[r]	...	...	...	...

23. Marriages by age of groom and by age of bride: latest available year, 2007 - 2016
Mariages selon l'âge de l'époux et selon l'âge de l'épouse : dernière année disponible, 2007 - 2016 (continued - suite)

Continent, pays ou zone, date, code[a] et âge de l'épouse	Total	0-14	15-19	20-24	25-29	30-34	35-39	40-44	45-49	50-54	55-59	60+	Unknown Inconnu
ASIA - ASIE													
Kuwait - Koweït													
2015													
40 - 44	524	-	-	6	24	52	75	122	245[r]	...	...	...	...
45 +	486	-	-	4	17	19	30	55	361[r]	...	...	...	...
Kyrgyzstan - Kirghizstan													
2016* (C)													
Total	47 837	-	575	15 259	18 822	6 462	2 883	1 622	951	513	368	381	1
0 - 14	-	-	-	-	-	-	-	-	-	-	-	-	-
15 - 19	9 433	-	446	5 699	3 028	237	18	3	1	-	-	1	-
20 - 24	22 417	-	122	8 983	11 128	1 857	267	40	11	5	1	2	1
25 - 29	8 654	-	3	508	4 215	2 816	830	214	47	10	8	3	-
30 - 34	3 562	-	-	55	373	1 363	1 094	465	143	45	17	7	-
35 - 39	1 724	-	1	10	53	155	566	554	244	81	37	23	-
40 - 44	938	-	-	1	18	24	93	285	304	130	57	26	-
45 - 49	528	-	2	1	1	4	13	45	171	140	81	70	-
50 - 54	312	-	1	1	3	3	1	11	26	87	93	86	-
55 - 59	173	-	-	1	2	1	-	5	3	12	68	81	-
60 - 64	56	-	-	-	1	2	1	-	1	1	6	44	-
65 - 69	22	-	-	-	-	-	-	-	-	1	-	21	-
70 - 74	5	-	-	-	-	-	-	-	-	-	-	5	-
75 +	13	-	-	-	-	-	-	-	-	1	-	12	-
Unknown - Inconnu	-	-	-	-	-	-	-	-	-	-	-	-	-
Mongolia - Mongolie													
2016 (+C)													
Total	16 778	...	172[j]	4 462	6 635	2 645	1 117	732	473	542[s]	...	...	...
18 - 19	593	...	...	...	...	...	...	...	...	...	...	...	...
20 - 24	5 846	...	...	...	...	...	...	...	...	...	...	...	...
25 - 29	5 928	...	...	...	...	...	...	...	...	...	...	...	...
30 - 34	1 980	...	...	...	...	...	...	...	...	...	...	...	...
35 - 39	1 053	...	...	...	...	...	...	...	...	...	...	...	...
40 - 44	688	...	...	...	...	...	...	...	...	...	...	...	...
45 - 49	375	...	...	...	...	...	...	...	...	...	...	...	...
50 +	315	...	...	...	...	...	...	...	...	...	...	...	...
Philippines[21]													
2015 (U)													
Total	438 523	1	8 441	103 606	154 679	91 985	38 798	16 641	8 962	5 635	3 836	5 888	51
0 - 14	20	1	9	5	5	-	-	-	-	-	-	-	-
15 - 19	39 110	-	4 983	22 504	8 431	2 109	588	228	106	64	37	59	1
20 - 24	148 283	-	3 119	64 322	57 773	16 012	4 184	1 365	667	339	211	287	4
25 - 29	140 626	-	256	14 197	72 303	38 100	10 338	2 854	1 188	574	363	448	5
30 - 34	63 632	-	50	1 964	13 200	28 639	12 753	3 927	1 459	741	411	485	3
35 - 39	24 288	-	17	436	2 263	5 612	8 291	4 234	1 748	780	431	473	3
40 - 44	9 963	-	2	116	478	1 056	1 909	2 776	1 747	870	448	559	2
45 - 49	5 727	-	2	28	141	305	536	878	1 434	1 154	577	671	1
50 - 54	3 201	-	2	9	34	90	136	264	448	778	687	753	-
55 - 59	1 791	-	1	6	14	33	39	78	116	232	459	813	-
60 - 64	1 021	-	-	4	6	14	5	23	35	79	168	687	-
65 - 69	464	-	-	-	5	2	4	9	9	21	35	379	-
70 - 74	183	-	-	1	1	-	3	2	2	-	7	167	-
75 +	145	-	-	6	11	7	9	2	1	2	2	105	-
Unknown - Inconnu	69	-	-	8	14	6	3	1	2	1	-	2	32
Qatar													
2016 (C)													
Total	3 830	...	53[f]	909	1 374	788	316	147	122	58	41	22	...
0 - 19	498	...	34[f]	278	159	23	3	-	1	-	-	-	...
20 - 24	1 418	...	19[f]	525	656	181	27	4	3	2	1	-	...
25 - 29	1 013	...	.[f]	88	443	316	99	31	23	7	6	-	...
30 - 34	482	...	.[f]	10	82	196	96	47	32	9	8	2	...
35 - 39	225	...	.[f]	6	21	54	64	37	23	8	8	4	...
40 - 44	108	...	.[f]	2	8	14	24	15	21	17	5	2	...
45 - 49	55	...	.[f]	-	4	3	3	10	14	9	9	3	...
50 - 54	22	...	.[f]	-	1	1	-	3	3	6	3	5	...
55 - 59	7	...	.[f]	-	-	-	-	-	2	-	1	4	...
60 +	2	...	.[f]	-	-	-	-	-	-	-	-	2	...

Continent, country or area, year, code[a] and age of bride / Continent, pays ou zone, date, code[a] et âge de l'épouse	Total	___Age of groom - - âge de l'époux___											Unknown Inconnu
		0-14	15-19	20-24	25-29	30-34	35-39	40-44	45-49	50-54	55-59	60+	
ASIA - ASIE													
Republic of Korea - République de Corée[22]													
2016 (+C)													
Total	281 635	-	796	8 497	60 739	109 391	48 807	21 292	12 179	8 196	6 084	5 654	-
0 - 14	-	-	-	-	-	-	-	-	-	-	-	-	-
15 - 19	3 283	-	558	755	365	362	546	521	161	12	-	3	-
20 - 24	22 907	-	210	5 744	8 514	4 803	1 734	1 234	548	88	26	6	-
25 - 29	100 275	-	21	1 645	42 516	46 494	7 282	1 440	619	187	55	16	-
30 - 34	87 774	-	5	285	8 490	52 060	22 192	3 446	874	281	104	37	-
35 - 39	30 154	-	-	59	757	5 121	14 680	7 276	1 677	406	126	52	-
40 - 44	13 077	-	1	4	81	471	1 986	5 638	3 363	1 060	346	127	-
45 - 49	9 539	-	1	3	13	74	341	1 443	3 660	2 673	1 022	309	-
50 - 54	7 117	-	-	2	1	5	41	260	1 051	2 685	2 261	811	-
55 - 59	4 498	-	-	-	1	1	5	32	192	703	1 803	1 761	-
60 - 64	1 790	-	-	-	-	-	-	2	30	87	305	1 366	-
65 - 69	713	-	-	-	-	-	-	-	4	11	32	666	-
70 - 74	310	-	-	-	1	-	-	-	-	2	4	303	-
75 +	198	-	-	-	-	-	-	-	-	1	-	197	-
Unknown - Inconnu	-	-	-	-	-	-	-	-	-	-	-	-	-
Singapore - Singapour[23,24]													
2016 (+C)													
Total	27 971	-	52	1 415	9 838	8 359	3 681	1 941	1 076	700	439	470	...
0 - 14	-	-	-	-	-	-	-	-	-	-	-	-	...
15 - 19	244	-	39	113	49	18	13	8	2	2	-	-	...
20 - 24	3 448	-	11	831	1 764	521	179	75	31	22	7	7	...
25 - 29	12 945	-	2	388	7 028	4 016	929	331	148	55	30	18	...
30 - 34	6 574	-	-	57	829	3 239	1 472	541	231	117	45	43	...
35 - 39	2 511	-	-	17	129	460	871	552	242	111	72	57	...
40 - 44	1 141	-	-	5	25	80	161	318	237	169	79	67	...
45 - 49	595	-	-	2	10	21	38	88	143	123	93	77	...
50 - 54	292	-	-	2	3	3	15	24	33	76	67	69	...
55 - 59	126	-	-	-	-	1	3	4	7	19	33	59	...
60 +	95	-	-	-	1	-	-	-	2	6	13	73	...
Sri Lanka													
2007 (+U)													
Total	196 236	-	4 874	50 475	77 223	37 758	13 636	5 693	3 065	1 585	988	939	-
0 - 14	20	-	7	7	5	1	-	-	-	-	-	-	-
15 - 19	35 127	-	3 814	19 794	10 010	1 301	168	27	6	3	1	3	-
20 - 24	73 649	-	899	26 759	35 730	8 980	1 043	174	44	12	4	4	-
25 - 29	55 088	-	135	3 335	29 096	18 013	3 732	560	160	29	16	12	-
30 - 34	17 764	-	15	432	1 881	8 373	5 319	1 316	310	74	29	15	-
35 - 39	7 468	-	3	123	400	864	2 930	2 070	815	185	47	31	-
40 - 44	3 529	-	-	10	74	184	350	1 307	1 008	389	157	50	-
45 - 49	1 852	-	-	8	14	31	74	194	600	536	278	117	-
50 - 54	958	-	1	5	8	8	18	39	98	299	294	188	-
55 - 59	471	-	-	1	5	2	2	6	17	43	138	257	-
60 - 64	193	-	-	1	-	1	-	-	6	13	21	151	-
65 - 69	71	-	-	-	-	-	-	-	1	1	1	68	-
70 - 74	31	-	-	-	-	-	-	-	-	1	2	28	-
75 +	15	-	-	-	-	-	-	-	-	-	-	15	-
State of Palestine - État de Palestine													
2015 (C)													
Total	50 438	...	3 034	21 081	17 230	4 704	1 621	829	610	432	291	606	...
12 - 14	758	...	192	458	97	7	2	-	-	-	-	2	...
15 - 19	20 851	...	2 525	11 748	5 701	739	98	18	11	5	2	4	...
20 - 24	20 742	...	291	8 324	9 082	2 334	463	142	56	27	14	9	...
25 - 29	5 000	...	22	478	2 122	1 226	595	272	141	79	27	38	...
30 - 34	1 611	...	3	54	191	319	322	244	194	120	79	85	...
35 - 39	776	...	1	10	30	61	115	103	120	98	84	154	...
40 - 44	401	...	-	6	6	12	20	34	57	60	48	158	...
45 - 49	205	...	-	3	-	5	4	14	27	32	21	99	...
50 - 54	59	...	-	-	-	1	1	1	3	6	12	35	...
55 - 59	20	...	-	-	1	-	1	-	1	4	3	10	...
60 - 64	9	...	-	-	-	-	-	1	-	-	1	7	...
65 +	6	...	-	-	-	-	2	-	-	-	1	-	5	...

23. Marriages by age of groom and by age of bride: latest available year, 2007 - 2016
Mariages selon l'âge de l'époux et selon l'âge de l'épouse : dernière année disponible, 2007 - 2016 (continued - suite)

Continent, country or area, year, code[a] and age of bride / Continent, pays ou zone, date, code[a] et âge de l'épouse	Total	0-14	15-19	20-24	25-29	30-34	35-39	40-44	45-49	50-54	55-59	60+	Unknown Inconnu
ASIA - ASIE													
Tajikistan - Tadjikistan													
2014 (+C)													
Total	95 537	-	3 916	49 719	26 233	7 001	3 804	2 303	1 050	541	331	419	220
0 - 14	-	-	-	-	-	-	-	-	-	-	-	-	-
15 - 19	42 931	-	3 445	29 805	9 138	514	-	-	-	-	-	-	29
20 - 24	33 873	-	471	19 218	12 317	1 572	222	36	12	-	-	-	25
25 - 29	10 093	-	-	696	4 502	3 337	1 131	274	85	32	19	3	14
30 - 34	4 523	-	-	-	275	1 489	1 646	662	236	87	63	57	8
35 - 39	2 374	-	-	-	1	87	749	916	298	148	72	98	5
40 - 44	1 072	-	-	-	-	2	55	401	315	137	72	89	1
45 - 49	323	-	-	-	-	-	1	14	96	97	39	76	-
50 - 54	151	-	-	-	-	-	-	-	8	37	49	57	-
55 - 59	49	-	-	-	-	-	-	-	-	3	16	30	-
60 - 64	5	-	-	-	-	-	-	-	-	-	1	4	-
65 - 69	5	-	-	-	-	-	-	-	-	-	-	5	-
70 - 74	-	-	-	-	-	-	-	-	-	-	-	-	-
75 +	-	-	-	-	-	-	-	-	-	-	-	-	-
Unknown - Inconnu	138	-	-	-	-	-	-	-	-	-	-	-	138
Turkey - Turquie[25]													
2015 (C)													
Total	602 982	...	11 656[f]	149 767	240 881	106 709	40 223	18 656	10 634	7 348	5 071	8 471	3 566
0 - 19	108 339	...	8 588[f]	53 547	37 627	7 056	944	131	36	12	5	3	390
20 - 24	213 596	...	2 554[f]	78 278	101 145	25 659	4 113	694	153	55	18	14	913
25 - 29	153 297	...	303[f]	13 888	84 543	41 097	9 633	2 090	563	190	53	35	902
30 - 34	54 871	...	59[f]	1 605	10 739	22 667	12 472	4 366	1 452	556	203	153	599
35 - 39	25 842	...	10[f]	322	1 734	5 185	8 146	5 630	2 514	1 091	463	364	383
40 - 44	13 459	...	5[f]	81	375	979	2 041	3 422	2 936	1 805	842	770	203
45 - 49	6 996	...	1[f]	21	55	148	316	705	1 632	1 781	1 072	1 162	103
50 - 54	4 301	...	-[f]	4	18	22	56	136	348	990	1 202	1 484	41
55 - 59	2 374	...	-[f]	2	2	6	13	21	69	190	617	1 434	20
60 - 64	1 317	...	-[f]	-	2	-	3	3	14	33	135	1 118	9
65 - 69	662	...	-[f]	-	-	1	1	2	4	9	19	624	2
70 - 74	238	...	-[f]	-	1	-	-	-	1	1	2	233	-
75 +	136	...	1[f]	-	-	-	-	-	-	2	1	131	1
Unknown - Inconnu	17 554	...	135[f]	2 019	4 640	3 889	2 485	1 456	912	633	439	946	-
Uzbekistan - Ouzbékistan													
2015 (+C)													
Total	287 582	-	3 423	118 392	126 899	20 912	7 721	4 274	2 295	1 523	1 006	1 137	...
0 - 14	-	-	-	-	-	-	-	-	-	-	-	-	...
15 - 19	66 440	-	2 723	40 351	22 554	748	46	12	3	-	-	3	...
20 - 24	163 621	-	663	75 556	80 436	6 239	553	130	24	13	3	4	...
25 - 29	37 484	-	31	2 335	22 761	9 175	2 175	649	232	69	31	26	...
30 - 34	11 363	-	6	125	1 031	4 366	3 389	1 405	540	297	142	62	...
35 - 39	4 600	-	-	20	90	324	1 398	1 430	648	366	196	128	...
40 - 44	2 000	-	-	3	23	50	129	573	537	326	184	175	...
45 - 49	927	-	-	1	3	6	24	62	253	248	162	168	...
50 - 54	667	-	-	1	1	2	4	9	47	167	186	250	...
55 - 59	285	-	-	-	-	1	3	2	8	33	83	155	...
60 - 64	123	-	-	-	-	-	-	1	2	3	18	99	...
65 - 69	49	-	-	-	-	1	-	1	1	1	1	44	...
70 - 74	14	-	-	-	-	-	-	-	-	-	-	14	...
75 +	9	-	-	-	-	-	-	-	-	-	-	9	...
EUROPE													
Åland Islands - Îles d'Åland													
2015 (C)													
Total	118	-	-	4	23	19	15	18	14	11	3	11	...
0 - 14	-	-	-	-	-	-	-	-	-	-	-	-	...
15 - 19	1	-	-	1	-	-	-	-	-	-	-	-	...
20 - 24	6	-	-	2	2	2	-	-	-	-	-	-	...
25 - 29	24	-	-	1	16	6	-	1	-	-	-	-	...
30 - 34	21	-	-	-	4	7	8	1	1	-	-	-	...
35 - 39	18	-	-	-	-	3	5	6	3	-	-	1	...

23. Marriages by age of groom and by age of bride: latest available year, 2007 - 2016
Mariages selon l'âge de l'époux et selon l'âge de l'épouse : dernière année disponible, 2007 - 2016 (continued - suite)

Continent, country or area, year, code[a] and age of bride / Continent, pays ou zone, date, code[a] et âge de l'épouse	Total	0-14	15-19	20-24	25-29	30-34	35-39	40-44	45-49	50-54	55-59	60+	Unknown Inconnu
EUROPE													
Åland Islands - Îles d'Åland													
2015													
40 - 44	17	-	-	-	-	1	2	8	2	2	1	1	...
45 - 49	16	-	-	-	1	-	-	2	7	5	1	-	...
50 - 54	3	-	-	-	-	-	-	-	1	-	-	2	...
55 - 59	8	-	-	-	-	-	-	-	-	4	1	3	...
60 - 64	3	-	-	-	-	-	-	-	-	-	-	3	...
65 - 69	-	-	-	-	-	-	-	-	-	-	-	-	...
70 - 74	-	-	-	-	-	-	-	-	-	-	-	-	...
75 +	1	-	-	-	-	-	-	-	-	-	-	1	...
Albania - Albanie													
2015 (U)													
Total	24 997	-	169	4 241	10 466	6 273	2 108	843	434	213	114	136	...
0 - 14	-	-	-	-	-	-	-	-	-	-	-	-	...
15 - 19	5 342	-	118	1 712	2 672	781	56	3	-	-	-	-	...
20 - 24	10 407	-	44	2 248	5 032	2 558	450	53	19	2	1	-	...
25 - 29	5 842	-	6	238	2 498	2 089	769	191	41	9	-	1	...
30 - 34	2 009	-	-	26	215	734	612	289	100	24	5	4	...
35 - 39	746	-	-	8	34	86	190	212	127	51	26	12	...
40 - 44	345	-	1	4	9	13	25	76	109	67	27	14	...
45 - 49	164	-	-	2	5	7	6	16	31	44	24	29	...
50 - 54	80	-	-	1	1	3	-	2	5	10	22	36	...
55 - 59	37	-	-	1	-	1	-	-	1	5	6	23	...
60 - 64	17	-	-	-	-	1	-	1	1	1	3	10	...
65 - 69	5	-	-	-	-	-	-	-	-	-	-	5	...
70 - 74	1	-	-	-	-	-	-	-	-	-	-	1	...
75 +	2	-	-	1	-	-	-	-	-	-	-	1	...
Andorra - Andorre													
2016 (C)													
Total	295	-	-	18	50	58	62	41	29	20	10	7	...
0 - 14	-	-	-	-	-	-	-	-	-	-	-	-	...
15 - 19	3	-	-	3	-	-	-	-	-	-	-	-	...
20 - 24	30	-	-	11	15	1	2	1	-	-	-	-	...
25 - 29	48	-	-	3	20	17	6	1	1	-	-	-	...
30 - 34	66	-	-	-	10	25	22	3	5	1	-	-	...
35 - 39	63	-	-	1	5	10	23	17	4	2	-	1	...
40 - 44	40	-	-	-	-	3	7	14	8	7	1	-	...
45 - 49	19	-	-	-	-	1	1	4	4	3	5	1	...
50 - 54	17	-	-	-	-	1	1	-	7	5	2	1	...
55 - 59	7	-	-	-	-	-	-	1	-	1	2	3	...
60 - 64	2	-	-	-	-	-	-	-	-	1	-	1	...
65 - 69	-	-	-	-	-	-	-	-	-	-	-	-	...
70 - 74	-	-	-	-	-	-	-	-	-	-	-	-	...
75 +	-	-	-	-	-	-	-	-	-	-	-	-	...
Unknown - Inconnu	-	-	-	-	-	-	-	-	-	-	-	-	...
Austria - Autriche[26]													
2015 (C)													
Total	44 502	-	141	3 163	8 599	10 647	6 949	4 450	3 687	2 960	1 839	2 067	...
0 - 14	-	-	-	-	-	-	-	-	-	-	-	-	...
15 - 19	736	-	77	454	154	34	8	3	3	-	2	1	...
20 - 24	5 431	-	52	2 008	2 348	734	187	49	32	13	4	4	...
25 - 29	11 293	-	6	539	4 741	4 206	1 242	320	146	54	21	18	...
30 - 34	10 451	-	3	107	1 090	4 601	2 961	1 020	411	161	55	42	...
35 - 39	5 551	-	2	32	185	847	1 917	1 465	701	269	91	42	...
40 - 44	3 559	-	1	13	52	151	469	1 075	964	547	178	109	...
45 - 49	3 120	-	-	4	17	49	117	370	973	890	435	265	...
50 - 54	2 340	-	-	3	9	16	34	122	363	736	589	468	...
55 - 59	1 178	-	-	1	3	7	12	22	73	221	343	496	...
60 - 64	502	-	-	2	-	-	2	4	17	53	95	329	...
65 - 69	211	-	-	-	-	1	-	-	1	11	22	176	...
70 - 74	89	-	-	-	-	1	-	-	2	4	3	79	...
75 +	41	-	-	-	-	-	-	-	1	1	1	38	...
Belarus - Bélarus													
2015 (C)													
Total	82 030	90[d]	1 203[j]	20 694	27 098	13 267	6 908	4 336	2 942	2 230	1 557	1 705	...
0 - 17	768	56[d]	218[j]	376	98	13	4	2	-	1	-	-	...

23. Marriages by age of groom and by age of bride: latest available year, 2007 - 2016
Mariages selon l'âge de l'époux et selon l'âge de l'épouse : dernière année disponible, 2007 - 2016 (continued - suite)

Continent, country or area, year, code[a] and age of bride / Continent, pays ou zone, date, code[a] et âge de l'épouse	Total	Age of groom - - âge de l'époux											Unknown Inconnu
		0-14	15-19	20-24	25-29	30-34	35-39	40-44	45-49	50-54	55-59	60+	
EUROPE													
Belarus - Bélarus													
2015													
18 - 19	4 588	19d	540j	2 861	1 008	131	20	3	3	2	1	-	...
20 - 24	28 826	12d	368j	13 936	11 773	2 198	396	96	32	9	2	4	...
25 - 29	21 767	3d	56j	2 898	11 141	5 494	1 526	435	148	40	16	10	...
30 - 34	10 698	-d	16j	473	2 425	3 923	2 405	956	324	109	50	17	...
35 - 39	5 745	-d	4j	112	538	1 157	1 778	1 267	546	226	86	31	...
40 - 44	3 484	-d	-j	34	85	272	575	1 088	825	399	129	77	...
45 - 49	2 254	-d	-j	3	19	66	160	375	698	580	237	116	...
50 - 54	1 679	-d	1j	1	11	12	32	86	264	591	458	223	...
55 - 59	1 130	-d	-j	-	-	-	8	25	83	203	439	372	...
60 +	1 091	-d	-j	-	-	1	4	3	19	70	139	855	...
Belgium - Belgique[27,28]													
2015 (C)													
Total	40 049	-	69	2 350	9 971	8 521	5 515	3 966	3 101	2 588	1 809	2 159	...
0 - 14	-	-	-	-	-	-	-	-	-	-	-	-	...
15 - 19	398	-	34	200	126	27	6	2	3	-	-	-	...
20 - 24	5 029	-	31	1 592	2 483	656	169	50	30	7	8	3	...
25 - 29	11 749	-	2	467	6 197	3 717	897	285	111	47	18	8	...
30 - 34	7 535	-	1	70	888	3 265	2 041	786	287	122	54	21	...
35 - 39	4 901	-	1	10	190	638	1 769	1 307	569	270	94	53	...
40 - 44	3 333	-	-	6	47	155	460	1 062	892	437	187	87	...
45 - 49	2 619	-	-	4	28	43	127	349	801	714	332	221	...
50 - 54	2 166	-	-	1	6	12	31	94	315	721	542	444	...
55 - 59	1 265	-	-	-	4	2	11	23	79	226	422	498	...
60 - 64	610	-	-	-	2	4	3	3	12	35	123	428	...
65 - 69	278	-	-	-	-	1	1	5	-	8	25	238	...
70 - 74	103	-	-	-	-	-	-	-	1	1	3	98	...
75 +	63	-	-	-	-	1	-	-	1	-	1	60	...
Bosnia and Herzegovina - Bosnie-Herzégovine													
2012 (C)													
Total	18 235	-	147	3 617	6 959	3 922	1 571	739	438	259	185	398	-
0 - 14	-	-	-	-	-	-	-	-	-	-	-	-	-
15 - 19	1 885	-	91	1 028	606	122	27	6	2	1	-	2	-
20 - 24	6 191	-	48	2 130	2 958	844	160	36	7	5	2	1	-
25 - 29	5 764	-	8	403	2 936	1 833	431	113	26	10	2	2	-
30 - 34	2 228	-	-	42	405	941	581	172	66	14	2	5	-
35 - 39	871	-	-	10	35	150	292	240	92	34	14	4	-
40 - 44	437	-	-	1	9	20	56	117	122	60	19	33	-
45 - 49	349	-	-	2	6	6	13	41	85	76	52	68	-
50 - 54	237	-	-	-	2	4	6	10	30	39	52	94	-
55 - 59	136	-	-	-	-	-	2	3	6	17	34	74	-
60 - 64	78	-	-	-	-	2	1	1	-	1	7	66	-
65 - 69	27	-	-	-	-	-	-	-	1	2	1	23	-
70 - 74	18	-	-	-	-	-	-	-	-	1	-	17	-
75 +	9	-	-	-	-	-	-	-	-	-	-	9	-
Unknown - Inconnu	5	-	-	1	2	-	2	-	-	-	-	-	-
Bulgaria - Bulgarie[29]													
2015 (C)													
Total	27 720	-	291	3 556	8 898	6 704	3 795	2 005	929	520	379	643	...
0 - 14	-	-	-	-	-	-	-	-	-	-	-	-	...
15 - 19	1 710	-	209	1 010	392	79	15	2	-	2	-	1	...
20 - 24	6 648	-	75	1 977	3 293	1 031	207	47	16	-	2	-	...
25 - 29	9 543	-	4	488	4 459	3 323	958	225	52	25	3	6	...
30 - 34	4 578	-	3	57	644	1 856	1 422	436	94	41	14	11	...
35 - 39	2 426	-	-	13	76	332	946	718	232	74	20	15	...
40 - 44	1 304	-	-	7	22	69	206	459	309	128	59	45	...
45 - 49	606	-	-	3	9	9	36	98	173	123	97	58	...
50 - 54	333	-	-	1	2	5	4	15	42	87	95	82	...
55 - 59	237	-	-	-	-	-	1	3	7	27	66	133	...
60 - 64	190	-	-	-	1	-	-	1	3	10	19	156	...
65 - 69	89	-	-	-	-	-	-	1	1	3	3	81	...
70 - 74	38	-	-	-	-	-	-	-	-	-	1	37	...
75 +	18	-	-	-	-	-	-	-	-	-	-	18	...

23. Marriages by age of groom and by age of bride: latest available year, 2007 - 2016
Mariages selon l'âge de l'époux et selon l'âge de l'épouse : dernière année disponible, 2007 - 2016 (continued - suite)

Continent, country or area, year, code[a] and age of bride / Continent, pays ou zone, date, code[a] et âge de l'épouse	Total	0-14	15-19	20-24	25-29	30-34	35-39	40-44	45-49	50-54	55-59	60+	Unknown Inconnu
EUROPE													
Croatia - Croatie													
2015 (C)													
Total	19 834	-	118	2 004	6 747	5 737	2 478	1 016	594	373	257	509	1
0 - 14	-	-	-	-	-	-	-	-	-	-	-	-	-
15 - 19	676	-	74	381	166	41	12	1	1	-	-	-	-
20 - 24	4 269	-	40	1 225	2 081	714	149	40	16	2	1	-	1
25 - 29	7 610	-	3	350	3 687	2 691	663	141	47	21	3	4	-
30 - 34	3 961	-	1	40	684	1 853	948	288	103	27	13	4	-
35 - 39	1 568	-	-	5	107	361	540	332	131	53	18	21	-
40 - 44	627	-	-	3	16	67	120	151	133	75	36	26	-
45 - 49	417	-	-	-	5	6	34	45	123	101	51	52	-
50 - 54	270	-	-	-	-	3	10	12	29	71	63	82	-
55 - 59	191	-	-	-	-	-	1	5	8	16	49	112	-
60 - 64	143	-	-	-	-	-	1	1	2	4	15	120	-
65 - 69	62	-	-	-	-	-	-	-	-	1	7	54	-
70 - 74	25	-	-	-	-	-	-	-	1	-	-	24	-
75 +	13	-	-	-	-	-	-	-	-	2	1	10	-
Unknown - Inconnu	2	-	-	-	1	1	-	-	-	-	-	-	-
Czechia - Tchéquie													
2015 (C)													
Total	48 191	-	74	2 861	12 328	13 228	8 362	4 264	2 393	1 744	1 186	1 751	...
0 - 14	-	-	-	-	-	-	-	-	-	-	-	-	...
15 - 19	379	-	34	187	89	39	20	6	1	1	1	1	...
20 - 24	6 435	-	25	1 741	2 948	1 160	391	122	32	7	5	4	...
25 - 29	16 958	-	12	689	7 385	6 049	2 046	539	159	42	26	11	...
30 - 34	10 864	-	1	175	1 487	4 650	3 042	1 034	298	111	44	22	...
35 - 39	5 690	-	1	53	302	1 042	2 137	1 274	508	216	95	62	...
40 - 44	3 064	-	1	13	91	226	563	898	670	351	147	104	...
45 - 49	1 837	-	-	2	23	46	127	282	480	484	228	165	...
50 - 54	1 295	-	-	-	3	12	25	88	190	387	307	283	...
55 - 59	797	-	-	1	-	3	7	17	42	109	233	385	...
60 - 64	498	-	-	-	-	1	4	4	12	29	79	369	...
65 - 69	240	-	-	-	-	-	-	-	1	7	16	216	...
70 - 74	93	-	-	-	-	-	-	-	-	-	3	90	...
75 +	41	-	-	-	-	-	-	-	-	-	2	39	...
Denmark - Danemark[30]													
2015 (C)													
Total	28 853	-	37	1 412	6 169	6 373	4 236	2 895	2 206	1 820	1 280	1 752	673
0 - 14	-	-	-	-	-	-	-	-	-	-	-	-	-
15 - 19	170	-	15	79	42	11	4	1	2	-	-	1	15
20 - 24	2 817	-	18	917	1 235	367	73	33	21	9	4	1	139
25 - 29	7 766	-	-	273	3 808	2 513	642	193	73	33	12	11	208
30 - 34	5 770	-	-	39	681	2 658	1 556	479	163	68	18	11	97
35 - 39	3 441	-	-	16	89	485	1 324	937	353	108	42	29	58
40 - 44	2 232	-	-	3	21	75	355	755	574	280	73	44	52
45 - 49	1 737	-	-	1	5	8	52	213	614	515	192	96	41
50 - 54	1 464	-	-	-	3	8	15	70	200	518	403	216	31
55 - 59	874	-	-	-	-	1	1	7	40	120	315	368	22
60 - 64	535	-	-	-	-	-	1	2	4	23	97	404	4
65 - 69	298	-	-	-	1	-	-	-	2	5	19	265	6
70 - 74	146	-	-	-	-	-	-	-	-	-	4	142	-
75 +	74	-	-	-	-	-	-	-	1	1	2	70	-
Unknown - Inconnu	1 529	-	4	84	284	247	213	205	159	140	99	94	-
Estonia - Estonie													
2015 (C)													
Total	6 815	-	34	512	1 766	1 570	1 052	640	438	254	176	205	168
0 - 14	-	-	-	-	-	-	-	-	-	-	-	-	-
15 - 19	142	-	14	62	41	6	5	1	-	-	-	-	13
20 - 24	1 023	-	16	327	460	122	36	16	7	1	-	1	38
25 - 29	2 090	-	3	89	991	656	210	60	25	8	-	1	47
30 - 34	1 446	-	-	16	188	600	388	147	58	14	8	-	27
35 - 39	783	-	-	4	52	133	272	190	67	36	11	5	13
40 - 44	517	-	-	3	12	24	92	155	128	57	26	2	18
45 - 49	316	-	-	1	3	4	28	52	107	63	31	20	7
50 - 54	179	-	-	-	-	1	3	9	36	47	40	40	3
55 - 59	113	-	-	-	-	1	2	2	6	17	38	45	2

23. Marriages by age of groom and by age of bride: latest available year, 2007 - 2016
Mariages selon l'âge de l'époux et selon l'âge de l'épouse : dernière année disponible, 2007 - 2016 (continued - suite)

Continent, pays ou zone, date, code[a] et âge de l'épouse	Total	0-14	15-19	20-24	25-29	30-34	35-39	40-44	45-49	50-54	55-59	60+	Unknown Inconnu
EUROPE													
Estonia - Estonie													
2015													
60 - 64	79	-	-	-	-	-	1	1	2	8	13	54	-
65 - 69	28	-	-	-	-	-	-	-	-	1	5	22	-
70 - 74	9	-	-	-	-	-	-	-	-	-	1	8	-
75 +	5	-	-	-	-	-	-	-	-	-	-	5	-
Unknown - Inconnu	85	-	1	10	19	23	15	7	2	2	3	3	-
Faeroe Islands - Îles Féroé													
2015 (C)													
Total	217	-	1	16	37	38	48	25	19	21	4	8	...
0 - 14	-	-	-	-	-	-	-	-	-	-	-	-	...
15 - 19	1	-	-	1	-	-	-	-	-	-	-	-	...
20 - 24	32	-	1	9	14	5	1	-	2	-	-	-	...
25 - 29	49	-	-	6	17	16	10	-	-	-	-	-	...
30 - 34	53	-	-	-	3	15	20	10	4	1	-	-	...
35 - 39	32	-	-	-	2	1	15	9	3	2	-	-	...
40 - 44	16	-	-	-	1	1	1	4	5	3	1	-	...
45 - 49	17	-	-	-	-	-	1	2	4	10	-	-	...
50 - 54	7	-	-	-	-	-	-	-	1	5	1	-	...
55 - 59	1	-	-	-	-	-	-	-	-	-	1	-	...
60 - 64	6	-	-	-	-	-	-	-	-	-	1	5	...
65 - 69	1	-	-	-	-	-	-	-	-	-	-	1	...
70 - 74	1	-	-	-	-	-	-	-	-	-	-	1	...
75 +	1	-	-	-	-	-	-	-	-	-	-	1	...
Finland - Finlande[31]													
2015 (C)													
Total	24 590	-	164	2 059	5 527	5 823	3 560	2 117	2 163	1 224	904	1 049	...
0 - 14	-	-	-	-	-	-	-	-	-	-	-	-	...
15 - 19	403	-	87	243	59	10	2	1	1	-	-	-	...
20 - 24	3 195	-	61	1 338	1 282	370	99	27	15	3	-	-	...
25 - 29	6 744	-	9	352	3 278	2 274	583	168	55	16	5	4	...
30 - 34	5 172	-	4	71	675	2 449	1 372	394	139	50	15	3	...
35 - 39	2 946	-	1	30	144	534	1 116	643	326	108	34	10	...
40 - 44	1 750	-	1	9	42	115	270	564	513	166	53	17	...
45 - 49	1 990	-	1	9	27	46	81	253	885	390	202	96	...
50 - 54	983	-	-	4	12	17	25	52	169	341	245	118	...
55 - 59	682	-	-	3	7	5	9	13	49	115	252	229	...
60 - 64	364	-	-	-	1	2	3	1	9	23	71	254	...
65 - 69	213	-	-	-	-	1	-	1	1	9	21	180	...
70 - 74	90	-	-	-	-	-	-	-	-	2	4	84	...
75 +	58	-	-	-	-	-	-	-	1	1	2	54	...
France[32]													
2015 (C)													
Total	222 664	-	166	9 909	49 456	53 328	33 335	23 335	16 347	13 743	10 018	13 027	...
0 - 14	10	-	2	3	3	1	1	-	-	-	-	-	...
15 - 19	1 464	-	64	685	495	174	35	9	2	-	-	-	...
20 - 24	21 283	-	74	6 612	10 507	3 000	721	200	96	43	16	14	...
25 - 29	60 094	-	12	2 086	31 267	19 946	4 607	1 382	479	192	72	51	...
30 - 34	49 442	-	7	344	5 611	24 051	12 806	4 178	1 487	597	215	146	...
35 - 39	29 216	-	3	93	1 034	4 584	11 287	7 481	2 805	1 214	457	258	...
40 - 44	20 429	-	2	47	337	1 031	2 861	7 247	4 902	2 398	987	617	...
45 - 49	13 978	-	1	27	129	351	704	2 013	4 277	3 701	1 677	1 098	...
50 - 54	11 912	-	-	7	49	125	238	618	1 710	3 918	3 056	2 191	...
55 - 59	7 522	-	-	4	15	48	56	144	440	1 254	2 500	3 061	...
60 - 64	4 092	-	1	-	7	13	15	40	111	315	809	2 781	...
65 - 69	2 029	-	-	-	1	2	4	11	28	84	184	1 715	...
70 - 74	728	-	-	1	1	1	-	6	10	19	31	659	...
75 +	465	-	-	-	-	1	-	6	-	8	14	436	...
Germany - Allemagne													
2015 (C)													
Total	400 115	-	660	20 450	88 623	99 432	58 243	34 353	31 943	27 698	17 978	20 735	...
0 - 14	-	-	-	-	-	-	-	-	-	-	-	-	...
15 - 19	3 551	-	353	1 986	917	194	51	18	19	9	3	1	...
20 - 24	42 750	-	252	13 264	21 255	5 760	1 445	425	205	86	38	20	...
25 - 29	115 844	-	41	4 214	53 466	42 240	11 137	2 888	1 234	424	124	76	...
30 - 34	92 114	-	10	722	10 777	42 625	25 272	8 070	3 016	1 075	360	187	...

23. Marriages by age of groom and by age of bride: latest available year, 2007 - 2016
Mariages selon l'âge de l'époux et selon l'âge de l'épouse : dernière année disponible, 2007 - 2016 (continued - suite)

Continent, country or area, year, code[a] and age of bride / Continent, pays ou zone, date, code[a] et âge de l'épouse	Total	0-14	15-19	20-24	25-29	30-34	35-39	40-44	45-49	50-54	55-59	60+	Unknown Inconnu
EUROPE													
Germany - Allemagne													
2015													
35 - 39	45 351	-	3	156	1 656	7 102	16 286	11 562	5 576	2 031	628	351	...
40 - 44	25 477	-	1	65	333	1 090	2 940	7 438	7 807	3 801	1 290	712	...
45 - 49	26 968	-	-	26	147	276	805	2 786	9 129	8 399	3 449	1 951	...
50 - 54	23 812	-	-	11	46	105	244	910	3 835	8 584	6 121	3 956	...
55 - 59	13 259	-	-	6	21	26	45	198	868	2 571	4 449	5 075	...
60 - 64	6 493	-	-	-	3	8	15	46	210	573	1 198	4 440	...
65 - 69	2 558	-	-	-	2	5	-	7	32	122	244	2 146	...
70 - 74	1 155	-	-	-	-	-	2	2	8	16	44	1 083	...
75 +	783	-	-	-	-	1	1	3	4	7	30	737	...
Greece - Grèce													
2015 (C)													
Total	53 672	...	200	1 665	10 249	18 756	11 838	5 139	2 577	1 314	767	1 167	...
0 - 14	24	...	19	5	-	-	-	-	-	-	-	-	...
15 - 19	789	...	145	331	195	89	19	7	1	1	-	1	...
20 - 24	5 029	...	29	909	2 174	1 357	444	81	24	8	2	1	...
25 - 29	16 879	...	5	332	5 847	7 206	2 630	643	161	33	15	7	...
30 - 34	17 400	...	1	64	1 737	8 321	5 062	1 558	450	122	52	33	...
35 - 39	7 690	...	1	14	246	1 543	3 028	1 728	789	223	77	41	...
40 - 44	2 866	...	-	7	33	210	518	841	666	353	142	96	...
45 - 49	1 427	...	-	2	12	27	112	228	364	317	182	183	...
50 - 54	789	...	-	-	3	1	21	44	97	195	178	250	...
55 - 59	456	...	-	1	1	1	2	7	20	48	98	278	...
60 - 64	209	...	-	-	1	1	1	2	2	12	17	173	...
65 - 69	76	...	-	-	-	-	-	-	-	2	1	3	70	...
70 - 74	27	...	-	-	-	-	1	-	1	1	1	23	...
75 +	11	...	-	-	-	-	-	-	-	-	-	11	...
Hungary - Hongrie[7]													
2015 (C)													
Total	46 137	-	273	2 814	10 856	12 240	8 656	4 497	2 362	1 397	1 125	1 917	-
0 - 14	-												
15 - 19	951	-	181	466	193	66	29	5	9	1	1	-	-
20 - 24	6 374	-	68	1 608	2 903	1 178	434	127	39	8	6	3	-
25 - 29	14 763	-	15	563	6 037	5 439	2 009	491	148	29	17	15	-
30 - 34	9 977	-	5	132	1 274	4 173	2 996	986	270	82	36	23	-
35 - 39	6 119	-	3	35	348	1 069	2 334	1 513	502	180	69	66	-
40 - 44	3 145	-	1	10	79	253	663	993	664	272	121	89	-
45 - 49	1 792	-	-	-	16	46	158	292	512	382	213	173	-
50 - 54	1 157	-	-	-	4	11	24	63	160	322	304	269	-
55 - 59	814	-	-	-	1	2	7	19	36	77	233	439	-
60 - 64	599	-	-	-	1	2	2	8	16	33	93	444	-
65 - 69	296	-	-	-	-	1	-	-	5	9	27	254	-
70 - 74	101	-	-	-	-	-	-	-	1	2	1	97	-
75 +	49	-	-	-	-	-	-	-	-	-	4	45	-
Unknown - Inconnu	-												
Iceland - Islande[33,34]													
2011 (C)													
Total	1 458	-	3	77	302	334	272	161	111	74	64	55	5
0 - 14	-												
15 - 19	6	-	-	2	4	-	-	-	-	-	-	-	-
20 - 24	152	-	3	52	69	21	1	3	1	1	-	-	1
25 - 29	371	-	-	19	173	115	44	9	5	3	1	1	1
30 - 34	350	-	-	3	43	157	104	25	9	3	4	1	1
35 - 39	243	-	-	1	7	33	101	62	22	9	6	1	1
40 - 44	113	-	-	-	3	6	14	44	28	11	3	4	-
45 - 49	94	-	-	-	1	-	6	15	36	24	7	4	1
50 - 54	68	-	-	-	-	1	1	2	9	18	25	12	-
55 - 59	30	-	-	-	-	-	1	-	1	4	15	9	-
60 - 64	18	-	-	-	-	-	-	1	-	1	2	14	-
65 - 69	7	-	-	-	-	-	-	-	-	-	1	6	-
70 - 74	2	-	-	-	-	-	-	-	-	-	-	2	-
75 +	1	-	-	-	-	-	-	-	-	-	-	1	-
Unknown - Inconnu	3	-	-	-	2	1	-	-	-	-	-	-	-

Continent, country or area, year, code[a] and age of bride — Continent, pays ou zone, date, code[a] et âge de l'épouse	Total	Age of groom - - âge de l'époux											Unknown Inconnu
		0-14	15-19	20-24	25-29	30-34	35-39	40-44	45-49	50-54	55-59	60+	
EUROPE													
Ireland - Irlande													
2012 (+C)													
Total	20 713	...	102	516	4 523	8 245	3 896	1 585	766	452	258	370	...
15 - 19	237	...	80	91	43	17	5	-	-	-	1	-	...
20 - 24	968	...	22	258	457	168	40	13	7	3	-	-	...
25 - 29	6 485	...	-	136	2 944	2 670	578	110	33	10	-	4	...
30 - 34	8 016	...	-	25	930	4 640	1 858	419	102	28	11	3	...
35 - 39	2 827	...	-	5	120	673	1 149	588	200	67	15	10	...
40 - 44	995	...	-	1	20	54	228	331	198	99	40	24	...
45 - 49	542	...	-	-	8	18	29	97	157	120	71	42	...
50 - 54	340	...	-	-	-	3	6	21	53	97	81	79	...
55 - 59	168	...	-	-	1	2	2	4	12	25	33	89	...
60 - 64	89	...	-	-	-	-	1	2	2	3	6	75	...
65 - 69	26	...	-	-	-	-	-	-	1	-	-	25	...
70 - 74	17	...	-	-	-	-	-	-	1	-	-	16	...
75 +	3	...	-	-	-	-	-	-	-	-	-	3	...
Italy - Italie													
2014 (C)													
Total	189 765	-	292	6 715	36 375	57 566	37 478	20 513	11 310	7 241	4 666	7 609	-
0 - 14	-	-	-	-	-	-	-	-	-	-	-	-	-
15 - 19	1 677	-	142	867	469	145	30	17	5	1	-	1	-
20 - 24	17 619	-	128	4 068	8 577	3 514	916	259	91	37	16	13	-
25 - 29	55 814	-	17	1 372	21 275	23 678	6 916	1 785	483	173	59	56	-
30 - 34	53 040	-	2	268	4 997	24 822	15 966	4 891	1 308	477	160	149	-
35 - 39	27 151	-	2	76	774	4 403	10 541	6 955	2 670	1 014	404	312	-
40 - 44	14 765	-	-	35	175	769	2 510	4 909	3 391	1 695	695	586	-
45 - 49	8 553	-	1	15	66	177	459	1 340	2 399	1 900	1 111	1 085	-
50 - 54	5 451	-	-	5	29	41	106	297	757	1 418	1 232	1 566	-
55 - 59	3 048	-	-	4	6	13	20	54	163	402	703	1 683	-
60 - 64	1 480	-	-	2	7	3	9	4	30	89	228	1 108	-
65 - 69	699	-	-	2	-	-	4	1	10	30	43	609	-
70 - 74	275	-	-	-	-	1	1	1	2	4	12	254	-
75 +	193	-	-	1	-	-	-	-	1	1	3	187	-
Unknown - Inconnu	-	-	-	-	-	-	-	-	-	-	-	-	-
Latvia - Lettonie[6]													
2015 (C)													
Total	13 617	-	40	1 109	3 886	3 161	1 740	1 240	821	531	463	626	-
0 - 14	-	-	-	-	-	-	-	-	-	-	-	-	-
15 - 19	178	-	25	94	42	14	1	-	2	-	-	-	-
20 - 24	2 148	-	13	716	1 025	287	75	22	6	-	3	1	-
25 - 29	4 414	-	2	251	2 271	1 358	361	110	39	15	4	3	-
30 - 34	2 630	-	-	30	446	1 145	644	233	92	27	8	5	-
35 - 39	1 413	-	-	13	77	266	434	372	170	52	21	8	-
40 - 44	941	-	-	2	20	63	159	327	208	94	50	18	-
45 - 49	682	-	-	2	3	20	40	120	203	140	102	52	-
50 - 54	473	-	-	1	2	7	16	42	72	132	125	76	-
55 - 59	331	-	-	-	-	1	8	13	22	54	102	131	-
60 - 64	194	-	-	-	-	-	2	1	6	11	31	143	-
65 - 69	111	-	-	-	-	-	-	-	1	4	14	92	-
70 - 74	52	-	-	-	-	-	-	-	-	1	2	49	-
75 +	50	-	-	-	-	-	-	-	-	1	1	48	-
Unknown - Inconnu	-	-	-	-	-	-	-	-	-	-	-	-	-
Liechtenstein[6]													
2012 (C)													
Total	185	-	-	8	30	59	33	19	20	10	2	4	...
Lithuania - Lituanie													
2015 (C)													
Total	21 987	-	112	2 702	8 014	4 875	2 325	1 379	962	678	447	493	-
0 - 14	-	-	-	-	-	-	-	-	-	-	-	-	-
15 - 19	556	-	70	316	135	26	8	-	-	1	-	-	-
20 - 24	5 172	-	34	1 780	2 565	611	128	34	13	7	-	-	-
25 - 29	8 165	-	6	517	4 492	2 370	568	147	42	12	8	3	-
30 - 34	3 567	-	-	62	677	1 468	858	332	106	47	13	4	-
35 - 39	1 623	-	2	17	115	282	549	369	188	71	21	9	-
40 - 44	1 075	-	-	5	22	87	171	352	243	135	40	20	-
45 - 49	748	-	-	4	5	19	36	104	254	185	89	52	-

23. Marriages by age of groom and by age of bride: latest available year, 2007 - 2016
Mariages selon l'âge de l'époux et selon l'âge de l'épouse : dernière année disponible, 2007 - 2016 (continued - suite)

Continent, country or area, year, code[a] and age of bride / Continent, pays ou zone, date, code[a] et âge de l'épouse	Total	0-14	15-19	20-24	25-29	30-34	35-39	40-44	45-49	50-54	55-59	60+	Unknown Inconnu
EUROPE													
Lithuania - Lituanie													
2015													
50 - 54	524	-	-	-	2	11	6	34	84	156	144	87	-
55 - 59	289	-	-	1	-	-	1	6	25	53	94	109	-
60 - 64	132	-	-	-	1	1	-	-	5	8	28	89	-
65 - 69	84	-	-	-	-	-	-	1	2	-	8	73	-
70 - 74	32	-	-	-	-	-	-	-	-	2	1	29	-
75 +	20	-	-	-	-	-	-	-	-	1	1	18	-
Unknown - Inconnu	-	-	-	-	-	-	-	-	-	-	-	-	-
Luxembourg[35]													
2014 (C)													
Total	1 657	-	1	90	366	420	269	167	125	101	56	62	-
0 - 14	-	-	-	-	-	-	-	-	-	-	-	-	-
15 - 19	13	-	1	10	2	-	-	-	-	-	-	-	-
20 - 24	168	-	-	50	77	30	7	2	2	-	-	-	-
25 - 29	465	-	-	20	198	169	52	13	10	1	-	2	-
30 - 34	420	-	-	4	74	172	105	39	13	8	3	2	-
35 - 39	217	-	-	3	9	36	74	45	31	14	3	2	-
40 - 44	154	-	-	2	4	5	22	48	29	27	11	6	-
45 - 49	103	-	-	-	2	6	6	16	26	24	9	14	-
50 - 54	60	-	-	1	-	1	2	2	8	20	17	9	-
55 - 59	40	-	-	-	-	1	-	1	5	7	12	14	-
60 - 64	12	-	-	-	-	-	1	1	1	-	1	8	-
65 - 69	3	-	-	-	-	-	-	-	-	-	-	3	-
70 - 74	2	-	-	-	-	-	-	-	-	-	-	2	-
75 +	-	-	-	-	-	-	-	-	-	-	-	-	-
Unknown - Inconnu	-	-	-	-	-	...	-	-	-	-	-	-	-
Malta - Malte													
2016 (C)													
Total	3 034	...	3[h]	134	925	907	447	197	156	103	65	96	1
16 - 19	9	...	1[h]	4	3	1	-	-	-	-	-	-	-
20 - 24	362	...	2[h]	76	200	64	14	3	2	-	-	1	-
25 - 29	1 177	...	-[h]	42	603	396	106	20	7	2	-	1	-
30 - 34	725	...	-[h]	8	91	372	178	46	23	5	-	2	-
35 - 39	327	...	-[h]	2	24	62	112	75	31	9	6	5	1
40 - 44	152	...	-[h]	1	2	8	24	36	45	22	9	5	-
45 - 49	116	...	-[h]	1	1	2	8	12	36	29	13	14	-
50 - 54	85	...	-[h]	-	1	-	5	4	11	26	21	17	-
55 - 59	43	...	-[h]	-	-	-	-	-	1	8	14	20	-
60 - 64	18	...	-[h]	-	-	-	-	-	-	1	2	15	-
65 +	17	...	-[h]	-	-	1	-	-	-	-	-	16	-
Unknown - Inconnu	3	...	-[h]	-	-	1	-	1	-	1	-	-	-
Montenegro - Monténégro													
2009 (C)													
Total	3 829	...	26	619	1 371	876	425	232	131	66	31	52	-
0 - 14	-	...	-	-	-	-	-	-	-	-	-	-	...
15 - 19	376	...	15	172	131	41	11	4	1	-	-	1	-
20 - 24	1 268	...	9	358	600	217	53	22	6	2	1	-	-
25 - 29	1 243	...	1	75	549	406	151	47	12	1	1	-	-
30 - 34	517	...	-	8	81	176	135	79	33	5	-	-	-
35 - 39	203	...	-	3	8	32	60	47	33	16	2	2	-
40 - 44	96	...	-	2	1	2	15	25	31	10	7	3	-
45 - 49	55	...	1	1	-	1	-	7	12	15	7	11	-
50 - 54	34	...	-	-	1	1	-	1	1	15	6	9	-
55 - 59	22	...	-	-	-	-	-	-	2	1	5	14	-
60 - 64	8	...	-	-	-	-	-	-	-	1	2	5	-
65 - 69	7	...	-	-	-	-	-	-	-	-	-	7	-
70 - 74	-	...	-	-	-	-	-	-	-	-	-	-	-
75 +	-	...	-	-	-	-	-	-	-	-	-	-	-
Netherlands - Pays-Bas[10,36,37]													
2014 (C)													
Total	75 696	...	93	5 415	18 406	18 053	10 388	7 078	5 065	4 156	2 989	4 053	...
15 - 19	707	...	53	359	202	57	17	12	4	2	1	-	...
20 - 24	11 835	...	30	4 051	5 752	1 433	345	130	62	21	3	8	...

Continent, country or area, year, code[a] and age of bride / Continent, pays ou zone, date, code[a] et âge de l'épouse	Total	| Age of groom - - âge de l'époux											
		0-14	15-19	20-24	25-29	30-34	35-39	40-44	45-49	50-54	55-59	60+	Unknown Inconnu
EUROPE													
Netherlands - Pays-Bas[10,36,37]													
2014													
25 - 29	22 426	...	7	856	10 426	8 207	1 966	609	201	95	36	23	...
30 - 34	15 494	...	3	105	1 726	7 034	4 306	1 512	478	202	73	55	...
35 - 39	7 942	...	-	24	214	1 050	2 925	2 245	929	329	136	90	...
40 - 44	5 397	...	-	9	53	205	641	1 840	1 499	730	259	161	...
45 - 49	4 147	...	-	8	26	54	137	529	1 325	1 229	503	336	...
50 - 54	3 524	...	-	3	7	8	42	162	427	1 163	1 036	676	...
55 - 59	2 113	...	-	-	-	3	8	31	107	302	702	960	...
60 - 64	1 153	...	-	-	-	2	1	5	27	60	189	869	...
65 - 69	569	...	-	-	-	-	-	2	4	18	44	501	...
70 - 74	251	...	-	-	-	-	-	1	1	4	5	240	...
75 +	138	...	-	-	-	-	-	-	1	1	2	134	...
Norway - Norvège													
2012 (C)													
Total	24 077	-	38	1 503	5 000	5 362	3 852	2 786	1 989	1 440	1 018	1 089	...
0 - 14	-	-	-	-	-	-	-	-	-	-	-	-	...
15 - 19	352	-	19	164	105	35	14	10	3	1	-	1	...
20 - 24	3 246	-	15	1 069	1 372	457	164	79	51	21	7	11	...
25 - 29	6 632	-	3	226	2 933	2 215	721	289	140	61	25	19	...
30 - 34	5 312	-	-	29	486	2 197	1 503	614	245	129	64	45	...
35 - 39	3 099	-	1	13	82	386	1 128	840	352	154	79	64	...
40 - 44	2 083	-	-	1	19	55	259	718	553	270	128	80	...
45 - 49	1 463	-	-	1	2	10	51	180	477	416	201	125	...
50 - 54	981	-	-	-	1	4	9	48	137	301	291	190	...
55 - 59	505	-	-	-	-	1	2	6	24	74	177	221	...
60 - 64	231	-	-	-	-	1	1	2	5	13	37	172	...
65 - 69	129	-	-	-	-	-	-	-	2	-	8	119	...
70 - 74	28	-	-	-	-	-	-	-	-	-	1	27	...
75 +	15	-	-	-	-	-	-	-	-	-	-	15	...
Unknown - Inconnu	1	-	-	-	-	1	-	-	-	-	-	-	...
Poland - Pologne													
2015 (C)													
Total	188 832	-	525	26 884	77 580	43 761	17 068	7 840	4 345	3 136	2 698	4 995	-
0 - 14	-	-	-	-	-	-	-	-	-	-	-	-	-
15 - 19	3 796	-	314	2 416	844	168	35	10	6	2	1	-	-
20 - 24	53 308	-	190	19 686	27 049	5 311	811	197	34	18	9	3	-
25 - 29	74 328	-	12	4 261	43 979	20 946	3 919	848	229	75	42	17	-
30 - 34	29 313	-	5	420	4 927	14 424	6 696	1 923	585	197	85	51	-
35 - 39	11 515	-	3	81	633	2 405	4 263	2 487	976	387	194	86	-
40 - 44	5 601	-	1	15	126	397	1 050	1 695	1 193	617	288	219	-
45 - 49	3 335	-	-	2	15	91	228	496	885	796	457	365	-
50 - 54	2 634	-	-	2	6	14	51	130	303	686	685	757	-
55 - 59	2 149	-	-	1	1	4	12	44	96	253	638	1 100	-
60 - 64	1 563	-	-	-	-	-	3	7	29	81	231	1 212	-
65 - 69	790	-	-	-	-	-	-	3	8	19	51	709	-
70 - 74	299	-	-	-	-	-	-	-	-	5	12	282	-
75 +	201	-	-	-	-	1	-	-	1	-	5	194	-
Unknown - Inconnu	-	-	-	-	-	-	-	-	-	-	-	-	-
Portugal[38]													
2015 (C)													
Total	32 393	-	103	2 080	7 949	8 902	5 093	2 744	1 725	1 159	929	1 709	-
0 - 14	-	-	-	-	-	-	-	-	-	-	-	-	-
15 - 19	380	-	66	206	67	22	11	6	2	-	-	-	-
20 - 24	3 734	-	31	1 254	1 726	496	147	51	15	9	3	2	-
25 - 29	9 747	-	2	517	4 761	3 354	834	188	50	23	11	7	-
30 - 34	7 961	-	3	72	1 131	3 916	1 943	559	206	77	37	17	-
35 - 39	4 164	-	1	26	195	872	1 576	900	343	146	50	55	-
40 - 44	2 277	-	-	4	53	188	436	705	487	205	116	83	-
45 - 49	1 467	-	-	1	9	41	106	254	396	309	187	164	-
50 - 54	1 085	-	-	-	5	7	29	58	172	275	244	295	-
55 - 59	748	-	-	-	2	6	8	16	41	87	198	390	-
60 - 64	433	-	-	-	-	-	1	3	10	18	54	347	-
65 - 69	243	-	-	-	-	-	1	3	2	10	17	210	-
70 - 74	94	-	-	-	-	-	1	-	-	-	7	86	-

23. Marriages by age of groom and by age of bride: latest available year, 2007 - 2016
Mariages selon l'âge de l'époux et selon l'âge de l'épouse : dernière année disponible, 2007 - 2016 (continued - suite)

Continent, country or area, year, code[a] and age of bride / Continent, pays ou zone, date, code[a] et âge de l'épouse	Total	0-14	15-19	20-24	25-29	30-34	35-39	40-44	45-49	50-54	55-59	60+	Unknown Inconnu
EUROPE													
Portugal[38]													
2015													
75 +	60	-	-	-	-	-	-	1	1	-	5	53	-
Unknown - Inconnu	-	-	-	-	-	-	-	-	-	-	-	-	-
Republic of Moldova - République de Moldova[39]													
2012 (C)													
Total	18 565	-	308	7 229	7 959	2 219	583	143	61	37	12	13	1
0 - 14	-	-	-	-	-	-	-	-	-	-	-	-	-
15 - 19	2 706	-	189	1 743	675	83	11	3	1	1	-	-	-
20 - 24	10 091	-	108	4 720	4 452	710	92	5	2	-	2	-	-
25 - 29	4 470	-	9	714	2 535	975	188	39	7	2	-	1	-
30 - 34	938	-	1	41	274	384	191	33	9	4	1	-	-
35 - 39	241	-	-	8	19	64	79	44	17	9	-	1	-
40 - 44	66	-	-	3	4	1	20	17	15	5	1	-	-
45 - 49	25	-	1	-	-	1	1	1	9	10	1	1	-
50 - 54	11	-	-	-	-	-	1	1	1	2	3	3	-
55 - 59	10	-	-	-	-	-	-	-	-	3	3	4	-
60 - 64	5	-	-	-	-	-	-	-	-	1	1	2	-
65 - 69	-	-	-	-	-	-	-	-	-	-	-	-	-
70 - 74	1	-	-	-	-	-	-	-	-	-	-	1	-
75 +	-	-	-	-	-	-	-	-	-	-	-	-	-
Unknown - Inconnu	1	-	-	-	-	-	-	-	-	-	-	-	1
Romania - Roumanie													
2015 (C)													
Total	125 454	-	468	14 033	47 524	30 209	15 198	7 320	4 358	2 256	1 828	2 260	...
0 - 14	-	-	-	-	-	-	-	-	-	-	-	-	...
15 - 19	7 166	-	278	3 342	2 704	638	152	33	15	2	1	1	...
20 - 24	32 997	-	157	8 227	17 991	5 134	1 162	241	52	18	10	5	...
25 - 29	44 530	-	28	2 127	22 839	14 146	4 079	963	242	56	33	17	...
30 - 34	18 891	-	4	264	3 295	7 932	4 993	1 645	526	131	61	40	...
35 - 39	9 796	-	1	56	551	1 904	3 561	2 231	994	286	123	89	...
40 - 44	5 013	-	-	12	113	355	938	1 555	1 202	462	238	138	...
45 - 49	3 499	-	-	1	22	86	267	538	1 053	751	460	321	...
50 - 54	1 504	-	-	3	5	11	36	83	212	395	428	331	...
55 - 59	1 095	-	-	-	3	2	8	24	47	123	368	520	...
60 - 64	584	-	-	1	1	1	-	7	11	25	88	450	...
65 - 69	233	-	-	-	-	-	2	-	4	5	16	206	...
70 - 74	97	-	-	-	-	-	-	-	-	-	2	95	...
75 +	49	-	-	-	-	-	-	-	-	2	-	47	...
Russian Federation - Fédération de Russie													
2012[40] (C)													
Total	1213598	...	15 848	312 104	402 995	191 131	105 357	63 778	43 196	34 745	21 315	23 078	51
15 - 19	81 342	...	9 599	50 495	18 055	2 523	468	130	38	20	7	6	1
20 - 24	425 562	...	5 186	200 558	173 664	35 196	7 918	2 062	620	221	80	54	3
25 - 29	337 474	...	802	50 809	166 737	80 206	26 188	8 444	2 758	1 022	326	182	-
30 - 34	154 765	...	189	8 034	34 743	52 674	34 829	15 241	5 645	2 339	749	318	4
35 - 39	83 803	...	50	1 683	7 769	15 610	25 204	18 450	9 030	4 074	1 366	564	3
40 - 44	45 822	...	17	377	1 571	3 743	7 817	13 055	10 391	5 807	2 044	996	2
45 - 49	31 345	...	1	94	327	880	2 159	4 456	9 684	8 528	3 435	1 778	3
50 - 54	25 096	...	1	37	89	230	606	1 487	3 793	9 098	6 198	3 553	4
55 - 59	14 880	...	1	7	22	46	121	360	985	2 837	5 299	5 202	-
60 +	13 481	...	2	8	16	20	47	91	252	798	1 811	10 424	12
Unknown - Inconnu	28	...	-	2	2	1	-	2	-	1	-	1	19
San Marino - Saint-Marin[41]													
2011 (C)													
Total	205	-	-	8	40	55	28	18	13	6	5	10	22
0 - 14	-	-	-	-	-	-	-	-	-	-	-	-	1
15 - 19	1	-	-	-	-	-	-	-	-	-	-	-	1
20 - 24	6	-	-	-	5	1	-	-	-	-	-	-	-
25 - 29	49	-	-	2	20	14	1	2	2	-	-	-	8
30 - 34	42	-	-	-	5	16	9	1	2	2	-	-	7
35 - 39	22	-	-	-	-	2	9	5	1	-	1	1	3
40 - 44	12	-	-	-	-	1	1	4	3	1	-	2	2
45 - 49	8	-	-	-	-	-	1	-	1	1	3	2	-

23. Marriages by age of groom and by age of bride: latest available year, 2007 - 2016
Mariages selon l'âge de l'époux et selon l'âge de l'épouse : dernière année disponible, 2007 - 2016 (continued - suite)

Continent, country or area, year, code[a] and age of bride / Continent, pays ou zone, date, code[a] et âge de l'épouse	Total	0-14	15-19	20-24	25-29	30-34	35-39	40-44	45-49	50-54	55-59	60+	Unknown Inconnu
EUROPE													
San Marino - Saint-Marin[41]													
2011													
50 - 54	5	-	-	-	-	-	-	1	-	2	-	1	1
55 - 59	1	-	-	-	-	-	-	-	-	-	-	1	-
60 - 64	1	-	-	-	-	-	-	-	-	-	-	1	-
65 - 69	-	-	-	-	-	-	-	-	-	-	-	-	-
70 - 74	1	-	-	-	-	-	-	-	-	-	-	1	-
75 +	-	-	-	-	-	-	-	-	-	-	-	-	-
Unknown - Inconnu	57	-	-	6	10	21	7	5	4	-	1	3	-
Serbia - Serbie[42,43]													
2015 (+C)													
Total	36 949	-	276	3 958	11 362	10 270	4 772	2 198	1 282	892	662	1 205	72
0 - 14	-	-	-	-	-	-	-	-	-	-	-	-	-
15 - 19	1 721	-	174	884	485	132	31	8	4	-	2	1	-
20 - 24	8 297	-	82	2 267	3 917	1 572	337	80	17	7	6	3	9
25 - 29	12 364	-	11	663	5 659	4 494	1 152	254	65	24	9	16	17
30 - 34	7 113	-	4	101	1 065	3 336	1 813	521	163	73	13	12	12
35 - 39	3 077	-	2	18	157	576	1 093	719	299	125	47	38	3
40 - 44	1 560	-	1	7	36	97	249	432	374	203	83	74	4
45 - 49	1 033	-	1	3	5	30	52	122	248	258	155	157	2
50 - 54	701	-	-	-	2	5	19	35	70	157	176	234	3
55 - 59	451	-	-	-	1	2	5	5	24	31	128	254	1
60 - 64	279	-	-	1	-	1	3	4	5	7	29	229	-
65 - 69	156	-	-	-	1	1	2	1	4	3	10	134	-
70 - 74	40	-	-	-	-	-	1	-	1	1	2	35	-
75 +	21	-	-	-	-	1	-	-	2	1	1	16	-
Unknown - Inconnu	136	-	1	14	34	23	15	17	6	2	1	2	21
Slovakia - Slovaquie[6]													
2015 (C)													
Total	28 775	-	378	2 452	8 712	8 378	4 301	1 829	951	667	437	670	...
0 - 14	-	-	-	-	-	-	-	-	-	-	-	-	...
15 - 19	934	-	300	462	117	35	11	8	-	1	-	-	...
20 - 24	5 073	-	66	1 465	2 426	835	195	53	16	11	2	4	...
25 - 29	10 949	-	7	419	5 134	4 003	1 039	253	64	16	8	6	...
30 - 34	6 255	-	1	81	841	2 841	1 731	494	160	70	25	11	...
35 - 39	2 784	-	2	16	149	541	1 035	615	247	109	44	26	...
40 - 44	1 155	-	1	7	36	103	232	303	248	124	61	40	...
45 - 49	594	-	1	1	4	13	47	77	146	156	81	68	...
50 - 54	444	-	-	1	2	6	10	22	55	126	104	118	...
55 - 59	291	-	-	-	3	1	1	3	15	35	86	147	...
60 - 64	193	-	-	-	-	-	-	1	-	17	22	153	...
65 - 69	71	-	-	-	-	-	-	-	-	2	4	65	...
70 - 74	27	-	-	-	-	-	-	-	-	-	-	27	...
75 +	5	-	-	-	-	-	-	-	-	-	-	5	...
Slovenia - Slovénie[44]													
2015 (C)													
Total	6 449	-	21	433	1 733	1 787	1 189	559	272	174	108	173	...
0 - 14	-	-	-	-	-	-	-	-	-	-	-	-	...
15 - 19	93	-	9	54	22	6	-	1	1	-	-	-	...
20 - 24	802	-	10	246	376	125	35	6	2	-	-	2	...
25 - 29	2 223	-	2	101	1 079	761	214	46	12	7	1	-	...
30 - 34	1 585	-	-	17	198	720	480	121	37	6	3	3	...
35 - 39	863	-	-	11	40	154	365	201	60	17	10	5	...
40 - 44	412	-	-	2	13	16	77	146	82	44	22	10	...
45 - 49	210	-	-	1	2	5	16	29	58	48	26	25	...
50 - 54	112	-	-	1	2	-	1	8	15	37	19	29	...
55 - 59	77	-	-	-	1	-	-	1	3	12	22	38	...
60 - 64	41	-	-	-	-	-	1	-	2	2	3	33	...
65 - 69	19	-	-	-	-	-	-	-	-	1	2	16	...
70 - 74	10	-	-	-	-	-	-	-	-	-	-	10	...
75 +	2	-	-	-	-	-	-	-	-	-	-	2	...
Spain - Espagne													
2013 (C)													
Total	151 433	-	191	3 603	25 108	48 666	33 715	16 470	8 845	5 526	3 753	5 556	-
0 - 14	1	-	-	1	-	-	-	-	-	-	-	-	-
15 - 19	861	-	69	388	245	112	32	9	3	1	1	1	-

644

23. Marriages by age of groom and by age of bride: latest available year, 2007 - 2016
Mariages selon l'âge de l'époux et selon l'âge de l'épouse : dernière année disponible, 2007 - 2016 (continued - suite)

Continent, country or area, year, code[a] and age of bride / Continent, pays ou zone, date, code[a] et âge de l'épouse	Total	0-14	15-19	20-24	25-29	30-34	35-39	40-44	45-49	50-54	55-59	60+	Unknown Inconnu
EUROPE													
Spain - Espagne													
2013													
20 - 24	8 194	-	72	1 834	3 712	1 721	553	150	87	33	13	19	-
25 - 29	37 970	-	28	947	15 421	15 994	4 023	1 009	325	123	50	50	-
30 - 34	47 991	-	15	319	4 619	24 677	13 577	3 240	915	330	169	130	-
35 - 39	27 302	-	5	72	794	5 059	12 127	6 026	1 954	724	320	221	-
40 - 44	13 081	-	2	26	190	802	2 694	4 508	2 639	1 200	544	476	-
45 - 49	7 317	-	-	12	75	194	547	1 187	2 093	1 563	821	825	-
50 - 54	4 463	-	-	4	36	73	123	276	658	1 166	1 018	1 109	-
55 - 59	2 341	-	-	-	11	19	27	47	136	309	607	1 185	-
60 - 64	1 158	-	-	-	4	13	9	11	31	60	184	846	-
65 - 69	452	-	-	-	1	2	3	5	3	11	20	407	-
70 - 74	175	-	-	-	-	-	-	-	-	5	3	167	-
75 +	127	-	-	-	-	-	-	2	1	1	3	120	-
Unknown - Inconnu	-	-	-	-	-	-	-	-	-	-	-	-	-
Sweden - Suède													
2012 (C)													
Total	50 044	-	69	1 803	7 703	10 419	8 284	5 587	4 328	2 880	2 142	2 688	4 141
0 - 14	-	-	-	-	-	-	-	-	-	-	-	-	-
15 - 19	668	-	33	130	81	26	7	1	1	-	-	1	388
20 - 24	4 680	-	27	1 194	1 729	551	164	63	30	7	4	2	909
25 - 29	11 233	-	5	378	4 640	3 898	1 046	288	123	41	15	12	787
30 - 34	10 932	-	2	71	1 004	4 783	3 106	858	319	104	37	30	618
35 - 39	7 543	-	1	12	183	930	3 005	1 924	666	218	81	54	469
40 - 44	5 154	-	1	10	43	175	732	1 768	1 317	434	192	87	395
45 - 49	3 922	-	-	5	19	42	178	525	1 383	905	407	180	278
50 - 54	2 665	-	-	2	2	7	36	127	395	863	690	383	160
55 - 59	1 595	-	-	1	2	6	5	28	75	242	526	647	63
60 - 64	934	-	-	-	-	1	5	4	16	58	150	657	43
65 - 69	468	-	-	-	-	-	-	1	2	8	36	396	25
70 - 74	160	-	-	-	-	-	-	-	-	-	4	153	3
75 +	90	-	-	-	-	-	-	-	1	-	-	86	3
Switzerland - Suisse[45]													
2015 (C)													
Total	41 437	-	65	2 555	8 806	11 522	6 909	3 869	2 631	2 016	1 304	1 760	...
0 - 14	-	-	-	-	-	-	-	-	-	-	-	-	...
15 - 19	487	-	31	270	134	33	14	1	-	1	1	2	...
20 - 24	5 020	-	28	1 624	2 298	710	205	75	45	19	7	9	...
25 - 29	11 453	-	2	502	4 738	4 272	1 243	409	167	78	21	21	...
30 - 34	11 335	-	2	92	1 274	5 211	3 054	974	398	203	73	54	...
35 - 39	5 494	-	1	26	243	1 001	1 886	1 310	580	269	106	72	...
40 - 44	2 734	-	1	23	63	187	360	763	674	354	168	141	...
45 - 49	1 883	-	-	10	27	72	88	224	493	463	265	241	...
50 - 54	1 529	-	-	4	17	25	46	72	217	453	352	343	...
55 - 59	838	-	-	4	10	10	11	29	43	134	229	368	...
60 - 64	359	-	-	-	2	-	1	6	12	31	61	246	...
65 - 69	159	-	-	-	-	1	-	5	2	7	16	128	...
70 - 74	85	-	-	-	-	-	-	1	-	3	3	78	...
75 +	61	-	-	-	-	-	1	-	-	1	2	57	...
TFYR of Macedonia - L'ex-R. y. de Macédoine													
2015 (C)													
Total	14 186	-	223	2 946	5 288	3 272	1 216	512	313	160	113	143	...
0 - 14	-	-	-	-	-	-	-	-	-	-	-	-	...
15 - 19	1 331	-	156	797	302	60	14	-	1	-	1	-	...
20 - 24	4 777	-	63	1 855	2 202	556	83	11	4	2	1	-	...
25 - 29	4 650	-	4	257	2 444	1 547	319	63	12	3	-	1	...
30 - 34	1 973	-	-	28	296	959	496	139	40	9	5	1	...
35 - 39	676	-	-	3	38	129	243	154	64	27	10	8	...
40 - 44	335	-	-	1	3	14	47	109	93	35	20	13	...
45 - 49	229	-	-	2	2	6	12	30	88	45	24	20	...
50 - 54	104	-	-	1	-	1	2	5	9	31	25	30	...
55 - 59	59	-	-	-	-	-	-	-	2	7	19	31	...
60 - 64	25	-	-	-	-	-	-	-	-	-	4	21	...
65 - 69	16	-	-	-	-	-	-	-	-	1	3	12	...

23. Marriages by age of groom and by age of bride: latest available year, 2007 - 2016
Mariages selon l'âge de l'époux et selon l'âge de l'épouse : dernière année disponible, 2007 - 2016 (continued - suite)

Continent, country or area, year, code[a] and age of bride / Continent, pays ou zone, date, code[a] et âge de l'épouse	Total	0-14	15-19	20-24	25-29	30-34	35-39	40-44	45-49	50-54	55-59	60+	Unknown Inconnu
EUROPE													
TFYR of Macedonia - L'ex-R. y. de Macédoine													
2015													
70 - 74	6	-	-	1	1	-	-	-	-	-	-	4	...
75 +	5	-	-	1	-	-	-	1	-	-	1	2	...
Ukraine													
2013 (+C)													
Total	304 232	-	5 638	82 689	101 854	47 671	24 031	14 047	9 174	7 491	4 907	6 730	-
0 - 14	-	-	-	-	-	-	-	-	-	-	-	-	-
15 - 19	29 768	-	3 569	17 949	6 954	1 094	151	33	14	2	1	1	-
20 - 24	115 048	-	1 792	52 456	47 373	10 539	2 148	479	149	69	20	23	-
25 - 29	78 596	-	207	10 455	38 179	20 214	6 593	1 969	627	238	79	35	-
30 - 34	33 936	-	52	1 452	7 460	11 676	7 831	3 448	1 237	520	176	84	-
35 - 39	17 460	-	9	280	1 534	3 220	5 127	3 905	1 977	929	314	165	-
40 - 44	10 066	-	6	55	267	729	1 602	2 875	2 283	1 398	556	295	-
45 - 49	6 781	-	3	33	67	140	441	989	1 864	1 902	834	508	-
50 - 54	5 469	-	-	4	13	44	107	273	784	1 810	1 422	1 012	-
55 - 59	3 332	-	-	2	3	13	26	60	198	481	1 119	1 430	-
60 +	3 776	-	-	3	4	2	5	16	41	142	386	3 177	-
Unknown - Inconnu	-	-	-	-	-	-	-	-	-	-	-	-	-
United Kingdom of Great Britain and Northern Ireland - Royaume-Uni de Grande-Bretagne et d'Irlande du Nord[46]													
2010 (C)													
Total	280 444	-	953	21 358	71 229	66 208	41 473	27 517	19 583	12 562	8 140	11 421	-
0 - 14	-	-	-	-	-	-	-	-	-	-	-	-	-
15 - 19	3 052	-	582	1 556	612	176	70	35	9	5	5	2	-
20 - 24	38 975	-	292	13 649	17 116	5 325	1 667	566	239	66	26	29	-
25 - 29	85 307	-	57	4 743	41 761	26 417	8 245	2 632	933	311	119	89	-
30 - 34	59 525	-	13	952	9 172	26 368	14 655	5 457	1 967	604	204	133	-
35 - 39	33 497	-	5	314	1 907	5 998	11 699	8 013	3 658	1 250	376	277	-
40 - 44	21 842	-	4	97	454	1 405	3 719	7 062	5 289	2 421	871	520	-
45 - 49	16 193	-	-	31	147	405	1 112	2 792	5 151	3 647	1 693	1 215	-
50 - 54	10 119	-	-	10	48	83	247	772	1 767	3 015	2 327	1 850	-
55 - 59	5 562	-	-	5	7	23	43	138	447	918	1 734	2 247	-
60 - 64	3 484	-	-	1	4	7	12	38	99	262	623	2 438	-
65 - 69	1 641	-	-	-	1	1	3	10	19	52	130	1 425	-
70 - 74	746	-	-	-	-	-	2	3	7	27	707		-
75 +	501	-	-	-	-	-	1	-	2	4	5	489	-
Unknown - Inconnu	-	-	-	-	-	-	-	-	-	-	-	-	-
OCEANIA - OCÉANIE													
Australia - Australie[47]													
2015 (+C)													
Total	113 595	-	416	10 890	33 564	28 281	13 529	8 623	5 865	4 690	3 238	4 500	-
0 - 14	-	-	-	-	-	-	-	-	-	-	-	-	-
15 - 19	1 465	-	224	808	307	96	22	9	3	-	-		-
20 - 24	17 962	-	161	7 492	7 553	1 871	517	186	86	46	33	20	-
25 - 29	38 984	-	21	2 140	20 961	11 704	2 619	842	352	193	86	66	-
30 - 34	25 084	-	7	328	4 000	12 070	5 518	1 859	703	292	162	147	-
35 - 39	10 832	-	3	89	547	2 032	3 655	2 531	1 096	499	219	155	-
40 - 44	6 819	-	-	23	126	379	911	2 271	1 623	836	360	301	-
45 - 49	4 667	-	-	10	47	91	213	704	1 378	1 254	605	371	-
50 - 54	3 583	-	-	3	19	28	60	187	500	1 150	931	707	-
55 - 59	2 014	-	-	-	3	11	12	29	103	335	624	899	-
60 - 64	1 077	-	-	-	-	3	5	5	14	70	171	805	-
65 - 69	609	-	-	-	-	-	-	-	-	17	34	556	-
70 - 74	313	-	-	-	-	-	-	-	-	-	6	309	-
75 +	179	-	-	-	-	-	-	-	-	-	3	181	-
Unknown - Inconnu	-	-	-	-	-	-	-	-	-	-	-	-	-

23. Marriages by age of groom and by age of bride: latest available year, 2007 - 2016
Mariages selon l'âge de l'époux et selon l'âge de l'épouse : dernière année disponible, 2007 - 2016 (continued - suite)

Continent, country or area, year, code[a] and age of bride / Continent, pays ou zone, date, code[a] et âge de l'épouse	Total	\<Age of groom - - âge de l'époux\> 0-14	15-19	20-24	25-29	30-34	35-39	40-44	45-49	50-54	55-59	60+	Unknown Inconnu
OCEANIA - OCÉANIE													
Fiji - Fidji													
2008 (+C)													
Total	8 180	...	99	1 960	2 932	1 346	741	454	296	158	95	99	-
15 - 19	1 050	...	...	...	...	...	...	...	...	...	...	...	...
20 - 24	3 049	...	...	...	...	...	...	...	...	...	...	...	...
25 - 29	2 024	...	...	...	...	...	...	...	...	...	...	...	...
30 - 34	903	...	...	...	...	...	...	...	...	...	...	...	...
35 - 39	493	...	...	...	...	...	...	...	...	...	...	...	...
40 - 44	310	...	...	...	...	...	...	...	...	...	...	...	...
45 - 49	200	...	...	...	...	...	...	...	...	...	...	...	...
50 - 54	83	...	...	...	...	...	...	...	...	...	...	...	...
55 - 59	44	...	...	...	...	...	...	...	...	...	...	...	...
60 - 64	14	...	...	...	...	...	...	...	...	...	...	...	...
65 +	10	...	...	...	...	...	...	...	...	...	...	...	...
Unknown - Inconnu	-	...	...	...	...	...	...	...	...	...	...	...	...
New Caledonia - Nouvelle-Calédonie													
2010 (C)													
Total	908	...	2[f]	62	149	200	171	169[n]	...	90[o]	...	65	-
0 - 19	13	...	1[f]	6	2	2	1	1[n]	...	1[o]	...	-	-
20 - 24	118	...	-[f]	36	51	18	10	2[n]	...	1[o]	...	-	-
25 - 29	194	...	1[f]	16	77	63	20	13[n]	...	3[o]	...	1	-
30 - 34	205	...	-[f]	4	14	94	62	27[n]	...	4[o]	...	-	-
35 - 39	139	...	-[f]	-	3	19	55	52[n]	...	7[o]	...	3	-
40 - 49	150	...	-[f]	-	2	4	22	65[n]	...	41[o]	...	16	-
50 - 59	59	...	-[f]	-	-	-	1	9[n]	...	30[o]	...	19	-
60 +	30	...	-[f]	-	-	-	-	-[n]	...	4[o]	...	26	-
New Zealand - Nouvelle-Zélande[10,48,49]													
2016 (+C)													
Total	20 235	-	60	1 590	5 085	4 728	2 649	1 611	1 365	1 053	822	1 266	...
0 - 14	-	-	-	-	-	-	-	-	-	-	-	-	...
15 - 19	339	-	57	213	45	12	6	-	-	-	-	-	...
20 - 24	3 459	-	-	1 380	1 605	351	84	24	12	3	3	-	...
25 - 29	6 642	-	-	-	3 438	2 433	516	147	66	24	12	15	...
30 - 34	3 912	-	-	-	-	1 935	1 359	369	162	48	21	15	...
35 - 39	1 758	-	-	-	-	-	684	666	267	84	30	21	...
40 - 44	1 281	-	-	-	-	-	-	405	522	201	87	66	...
45 - 49	1 071	-	-	-	-	-	-	-	327	429	195	117	...
50 - 54	798	-	-	-	-	-	-	-	-	264	330	207	...
55 - 59	477	-	-	-	-	-	-	-	-	-	153	327	...
60 - 64	243	-	-	-	-	-	-	-	-	-	-	246	...
65 - 69	144	-	-	-	-	-	-	-	-	-	-	144	...
70 - 74	69	-	-	-	-	-	-	-	-	-	-	66	...
75 +	51	-	-	-	-	-	-	-	-	-	-	51	...
Niue - Nioué													
2009 (C)													
Total	12	...	-	2	3	4	-	1	1	-	1	-	-
15 - 19	-	...	...	...	...	...	...	...	...	...	...	...	...
20 - 24	-	...	...	...	...	...	...	...	...	...	...	...	...
25 - 29	3	...	...	...	...	...	...	...	...	...	...	...	...
30 - 34	4	...	...	...	...	...	...	...	...	...	...	...	...
35 - 39	3	...	...	...	...	...	...	...	...	...	...	...	...
40 - 44	-	...	...	...	...	...	...	...	...	...	...	...	...
45 - 49	1	...	...	...	...	...	...	...	...	...	...	...	...
50 - 54	1	...	...	...	...	...	...	...	...	...	...	...	...
55 - 59	-	...	...	...	...	...	...	...	...	...	...	...	...
60 - 64	-	...	...	...	...	...	...	...	...	...	...	...	...
65 +	-	...	...	...	...	...	...	...	...	...	...	...	...
Wallis and Futuna Islands - Îles Wallis et Futuna													
2008 (C)													
Total	53	-	1	14	23	8	3	2	-	2	-	-	-
0 - 14	-	...	...	...	...	...	...	...	...	...	...	...	...
15 - 19	9	...	...	...	...	...	...	...	...	...	...	...	...
20 - 24	18	...	...	...	...	...	...	...	...	...	...	...	...

Continent, country or area, year, code[a] and age of bride / Continent, pays ou zone, date, code[a] et âge de l'épouse	Age of groom - - âge de l'époux												
	Total	0-14	15-19	20-24	25-29	30-34	35-39	40-44	45-49	50-54	55-59	60+	Unknown Inconnu

OCEANIA - OCÉANIE

Wallis and Futuna Islands - Îles Wallis et Futuna
2008

25 - 29	12	...	...	...	...	...	...	...	...	...	...	...	...
30 - 34	7	...	...	...	...	...	...	...	...	...	...	...	...
35 - 39	5	...	...	...	...	...	...	...	...	...	...	...	...
40 - 44	-	...	...	...	...	...	...	...	...	...	...	...	...
45 - 49	1	...	...	...	...	...	...	...	...	...	...	...	...
50 - 54	-	...	...	...	...	...	...	...	...	...	...	...	...
55 - 59	-	...	...	...	...	...	...	...	...	...	...	...	...
60 - 64	1	...	...	...	...	...	...	...	...	...	...	...	...
65 - 69	-	...	...	...	...	...	...	...	...	...	...	...	...
70 - 74	-	...	...	...	...	...	...	...	...	...	...	...	...
75 +	-	...	...	...	...	...	...	...	...	...	...	...	...

FOOTNOTES - NOTES

Italics: data from civil registers which are incomplete or of unknown completeness. - Italiques : données incomplètes ou dont le degré d'exactitude n'est pas connu, provenant des registres de l'état civil.

[*] Provisional. - Données provisoires.

[a] 'Code' indicates the source of data, as follows:
C - Civil registration, estimated over 90% complete
U - Civil registration, estimated less than 90% complete
| - Other source, estimated reliable
+ - Data tabulated by date of registration rather than occurence
... - Information not available

Le 'Code' indique la source des données, comme suit :
C - Registres de l'état civil considérés complets à 90 p. 100 au moins
U - Registres de l'état civil qui ne sont pas considérés complets à 90 p. 100 au moins
| - Autre source, considérée pas douteuses
+ - Données exploitées selon la date de l'enregistrement et non la date de l'événement
... - Information pas disponible

[b] Refers to 0-15 years of age. - Données se raportent au groupe d'âges 0-15.
[c] Refers to 0-16 years of age. - Données se raportent au groupe d'âges 0-16.
[d] Refers to 0-17 years of age. - Données se raportent au groupe d'âges 0-17.
[e] Refers to 0-18 years of age. - Données se raportent au groupe d'âges 0-18.
[f] Refers to 0-19 years of age. - Données se raportent au groupe d'âges 0-19.
[g] Refers to 0-24 years of age. - Données se raportent au groupe d'âges 0-24.
[h] Refers to 16-19 years of age. - Données se raportent au groupe d'âges 16-19.
[i] Refers to 17-19 years of age. - Données se raportent au groupe d'âges 17-19.
[j] Refers to 18-19 years of age. - Données se raportent au groupe d'âges 18-19.
[k] Refers to 19-24 years of age. - Données se raportent au groupe d'âges 19-24.
[l] Refers to 20-29 years of age. - Données se raportent au groupe d'âges 20-29.
[m] Refers to 30-39 years of age. - Données se raportent au groupe d'âges 30-39.
[n] Refers to 40-49 years of age. - Données se raportent au groupe d'âges 40-49.
[o] Refers to 50-59 years of age. - Données se raportent au groupe d'âges 50-59.
[p] Refers to 35+ years of age. - Données se raportent au groupe d'âges 35+.
[q] Refers to 40+ years of age. - Données se raportent au groupe d'âges 40+.
[r] Refers to 45+ years of age. - Données se raportent au groupe d'âges 45+.
[s] Refers to 50+ years of age. - Données se raportent au groupe d'âges 50+.
[t] Refers to 55+ years of age. - Données se raportent au groupe d'âges 55+.

[1] Source: Vital Statistics Report 2014. - Source: Vital Statistics Report 2014.
[2] Including marriages resumed after 'revocable divorce' (among Moslem population), which approximates legal separation. - Y compris les unions reconstituées après un 'divorce révocable' (parmi la population musulmane), qui est à peu près l'équivalent d'une séparation légale.

[3] Excludes the islands of St. Brandon and Agalega. - Non compris les îles St. Brandon et Agalega.
[4] Including visitors. - Y compris les visiteurs.
[5] Excluding visitors. - Ne comprend pas les visiteurs.
[6] Data refer to marriages by residence of the groom. - Les données concernent les mariages selon la résidence du marié.
[7] Marriages registered by residence of bride. - Les mariages sont enregistrés selon le lieu de résidence de la mariée.
[8] Data refers to the number of marriages of which at least one of the partners is a resident of Curacao. - Les données concernent le nombre de mariages dont au moins l'un des partenaires est un résident de Curaçao.
[9] Including marriages where bride/groom are non-residents. - Y compris les mariages pour lesquels le marié et la mariée sont des non-résidents.
[10] Including same sex marriages. - Y compris les mariages entre personnes du même sexe.
[11] Excludes nomadic Indian tribes. - Non compris les tribus d'Indiens nomades.
[12] Data are compiled from the National Registers of Identification and Civil Status (RENIEC). - Les données sont rédigées à partir des Registres Nationaux d'Identification et d'État Civil (RENIEC).
[13] Data refers to metropolitan Lima and Callao. - Les données font référence à la région métropolitaine de Lima et Callao.
[14] Data refer to marriages of residents only. - Les données ne portent que sur les mariages de résidents.
[15] Data refer to government controlled areas. - Les données se rapportent aux zones contrôlées par le Gouvernement.
[16] Data refer to the Iranian Year which begins on 21 March and ends on 20 March of the following year. - Les données concernent l'année iranienne, qui commence le 21 mars et se termine le 20 mars de l'année suivante.
[17] Source: Civil Registration Organization. - Source : Organisation chargée d'assurer l'enregistrement des faits d'état civil.
[18] Includes data for East Jerusalem and Israeli residents in certain other territories under occupation by Israeli military forces since June 1967. - Y compris les données pour Jérusalem-Est et les résidents israéliens dans certains autres territoires occupés depuis 1967 par les forces armées israéliennes.
[19] Data refer to Japanese nationals in Japan only; and to grooms and brides whose marriages occurred and were registered in the same year. - Les données se raportent aux nationaux japonais au Japon seulement; et aux époux et épouses dont le mariage a été célébré et enregistré la même année.
[20] Excluding data for Jordanian territory under occupation since June 1967 by Israeli military forces. Excluding foreigners, including registered Palestinian refugees. - Non compris les données pour le territoire jordanien occupé depuis juin 1967 par les forces armées israéliennes. Non compris les étrangers, mais y compris les réfugiés de Palestine enregistrés.
[21] Excluding marriages by groom and bride that are under "Married" status. - Sauf mariages entre personnes qui ont le statut de « marié(e) ».
[22] Excluding alien armed forces, civilian aliens employed by armed forces, and foreign diplomatic personnel and their dependants. - Non compris les militaires étrangers, les civils étrangers employés par les forces armées ni le personnel diplomatique étranger et les membres de leur famille les accompagnant.

²³ Data comprise civil marriages registered under the Women's Charter and Muslim marriages registered under the Administration of Muslim Law Act. - Les données comprennent les mariages civils enregistrés en vertu de la Charte des droits de la femme, ainsi que les mariages musulmans enregistrés en vertu de la loi sur l'administration du droit islamique.

²⁴ Excluding marriages previously officiated outside Singapore or under religious and customary rites. - Ne comprend pas les mariages prononcés ailleurs qu'à Singapour ni les mariages religieux ou coutumiers.

²⁵ Data from MERNIS (Central Population Administrative System). - Données de MERNIS (Système central de données démographiques).

²⁶ Excluding marriages of aliens temporarily in the area, but including marriages abroad of persons with residence in Austria. - Non compris les mariages d'étrangers temporairement dans la région, mais y compris des mariages à l'étranger de personnes ayant leur résidence en Autriche.

²⁷ Since 2003, marriage between persons of the same sex is authorized in Belgium, but the sex of spouses is not revealed. In this table, husband is used for first spouse, whereas wife is used for second spouse. - Depuis 2003, le mariage entre personnes de même sexe est autorisé en Belgique, mais le sexe des conjoints n'est pas indiqué. Dans ce tableau, la mention "époux" est utilisée pour le premier conjoint et la mention "épouse" pour le second conjoint.

²⁸ Including armed forces stationed outside the country and alien armed forces in the area, if the marriage is performed by local authority. - Y compris les militaires nationaux hors du pays et les militaires étrangers en garnison sur le territoire, si le mariage a été célébré par l'autorité locale.

²⁹ Including nationals outside the country, but excluding foreigners in the country. - Y compris les nationaux à l'étranger, mais non compris les étrangers sur le territoire.

³⁰ Excluding Faeroe Islands and Greenland shown separately, if available. - Non compris les Iles Féroé et le Groenland, qui font l'objet de rubriques distinctes, si disponible.

³¹ Excluding Åland Islands. - Non compris les Îles d'Åland.

³² Data refer to marriages between persons of different sex. - Les données se rapportent aux mariages entre personnes de sexe différent.

³³ Data for residence abroad are excluded. - Les données relatives aux résidents à l'étranger sont exclues.

³⁴ Data refer to common residence after marriage. - Données se rapportant à la résidence commune après le mariage.

³⁵ Data refer to marriages where one or both partners are residents. - Les données portent sur les mariages pour lesquels l'un des deux partenaires ou les deux sont résidents.

³⁶ Marriages of couples of which at least one partner is recorded in a Dutch municipal register, irrespective of the country where the marriage was performed. - Correspond aux mariages pour lesquels au moins l'un des partenaires est inscrit sur un registre municipal néerlandais, quel que soit le pays dans lequel le mariage est célébré.

³⁷ Including residents outside the country if listed in a Netherlands population register. - Englobe les résidents se trouvant à l'étranger à condition qu'ils soient inscrits sur le registre de population des Pays-Bas.

³⁸ Groom refers to the man for opposite sex marriages, and to spouse 1 as specified in the Civil Register for same sex marriages. Bride refers to the woman for opposite sex marriages, and to spouse 2 as specified in the Civil Register for same sex marriages. - Marié se réfère à l'homme en cas de mariage entre personnes de sexe différent et à l'époux 1 inscrit sur le Registre d'état civil en cas de mariage entre personnes du même sexe. Mariée se réfère à la femme en cas de mariage entre personnes de sexe différent et à l'époux 2 inscrit sur le Registre d'état civil en cas de mariage entre personnes du même sexe.

³⁹ Data refer to first marriages only. - Données se rapportent aux premiers mariages seulement.

⁴⁰ Data refer to population 15 years of age or more. - Les données concernent la population âgée de 15 ans ou plus.

⁴¹ Includes civil and religious marriages as well as not specified. - Englobe les mariages civils et religieux et ceux pour lesquels rien n'a été indiqué.

⁴² Excludes data for Kosovo and Metohia. - Sans les données pour le Kosovo et Metohie.

⁴³ Residence refers to residence of groom. - La catégorie « résidence » correspond au lieu de résidence du jeune marié.

⁴⁴ Data refer to residence of groom or bride before marriage. - Données relatives au lieu de résidence du marié ou de la mariée avant le mariage.

⁴⁵ Data based on the residence of groom if he has permanent address in the country, otherwise, based on the residence of bride. If neither partner is a permanent resident, the marriage is not included in the official statistics. - Les données sont fondées sur la résidence du marié si celui-ci a une adresse permanente dans le pays, sinon elles sont fondées sur la résidence de la mariée. Si aucun des deux partenaires n'est un résident permanent, le mariage n'apparaît pas dans les statistiques officielles.

⁴⁶ Excluding Channel Islands (Guernsey and Jersey) and Isle of Man, shown separately, if available. - Non compris les îles Anglo-Normandes (Guernesey et Jersey) et l'île de Man, qui font l'objet de rubriques distinctes, si disponible.

⁴⁷ Data for certain cells suppressed by national statistical office for confidentiality reasons. - Les données pour certaines cases ont été supprimées par le bureau national de statistiques pour des raisons de confidentialité.

⁴⁸ Data refer to marriages and civil unions by residence of 'partner 2'. - Les données concernent les mariages et les unions civiles selon la résidence du « partenaire 2 ».

⁴⁹ Random rounding to base 3 is applied in this table as a confidentiality measure. - Les chiffres sont arrondis à la base 3 de manière aléatoire, pour des raisons de confidentialité.

Table 24 - *Demographic Yearbook 2016*

Table 24 presents the number of divorces and crude divorce rates for as many years as possible between 2012 and 2016.

Description of variables: Divorce is defined as a final legal dissolution of a marriage, that is, the separation of husband and wife which confers on the parties the right to remarriage under civil, religious and/or other provisions, according to the laws of each country[1].

Unless otherwise noted, divorce statistics exclude legal separations that do not allow remarriage. These statistics refer to the number of divorces granted, and not to the number of persons divorcing.

Divorce statistics are obtained from court records and/or civil registers according to national practice. The actual compilation of these statistics may be the responsibility of the civil registrar, the national statistical office or other government offices.

The urban/rural classification of divorces is that provided by each country or area; it is presumed to be based on the national census definitions of urban population, which have been set forth at the end of the technical notes for table 6.

Rate computation: Crude divorce rates by urban/rural residence are the annual number of divorces per 1 000 mid-year population. Rates presented in this table have been limited to those countries or areas having at least a total of 30 divorces in a given year. These rates are calculated by the Statistics Division of the United Nations based on the appropriate reference population (for example: total population, nationals only etc.) if known and available. If the reference population is not known or unavailable, the total population is used to calculate the rates. Therefore, if the population that is used to calculate the rates is different from the correct reference population, the rates presented might under- or overstate the true situation in a country or area.

Reliability of data: Each country or area has been asked to indicate the estimated completeness of the divorces recorded in its civil register. These national assessments are indicated by the quality codes "C" and "U" that appear in the first column of this table.

"C" indicates that the data are estimated to be virtually complete, that is, representing at least 90 per cent of the divorces that occur each year, while "U" indicates that data are estimated to be incomplete, that is, representing less than 90 per cent of the divorces occurring each year. The code "..." indicates that no information was provided regarding completeness.

Data from civil registers that are reported as incomplete or of unknown completeness (coded "U" or "...") are considered unreliable. They appear in *italics* in this table and the rates were not computed on data so coded. These quality codes apply only to data from civil registers. For more information about the quality of vital statistics data in general, see section 4.2 of the Technical Notes.

Limitations: Statistics on divorces are subject to the same qualifications as have been set forth for vital statistics in general and divorce statistics in particular as discussed in section 4 of the Technical Notes.

Divorce, like marriage, is a legal event, and this has implications for international comparability of data. Divorce has been defined, for statistical purposes, in terms of the laws of individual countries or areas. The laws pertaining to divorce vary considerably from one country or area to another. This variation in the legal provision for divorce also affects the incidence of divorce, which is relatively low in countries or areas where divorce decrees are difficult to obtain.

Since divorces are granted by courts and statistics on divorce refer to the actual divorce decree, effective as of the date of the decree, marked year-to-year fluctuations may reflect court delays and clearances rather than trends in the incidence of divorce. The comparability of divorce statistics may also be affected by tabulation procedures. In some countries or areas annulments and/or legal separations may be included. This practice is more common for countries or areas in which the number of divorces is small. Information on this practice is given in the footnotes when known.

The registration of a divorce in many countries or areas is the responsibility solely of the court or the authority which granted it. Since the registration recording such cases is part of the records of the court proceedings, divorces are likely to be registered soon after the decree is granted. For this reason the practice of tabulating data by date of registration does not generally pose serious problems of comparability as it does in the case of birth and death statistics.

As noted briefly above, the incidence of divorce is affected by the relative ease or difficulty of obtaining a divorce according to the laws of individual countries or areas. The incidence of divorce is also affected by the ability of individuals to meet financial and other costs of the court procedures. Connected with this aspect is the influence of certain religious faiths on the incidence of divorce. For all these reasons, divorce statistics are not strictly comparable as measures of family dissolution by legal means. Furthermore, family dissolution by other than legal means, such as separation, is not measured in statistics for divorce.

For certain countries or areas there is or was no legal provision for divorce in the sense used here, and therefore no data for these countries or areas appear in this table.

In addition, it should be noted that rates are affected also by the quality and limitations of the population estimates that are used in their computation. The problems of under-enumeration or over-enumeration, and to some extent, the differences in definition of total population, have been discussed in section 3 of the Technical Notes dealing with population data in general, and specific information pertaining to individual countries or areas is given in the footnotes to table 3.

As will be seen from the footnotes, strict correspondence between the numerator of the rate and the denominator is not always obtained; for example, divorces among civilian plus military segments of the population may be related to civilian population only. The effect of this may be to increase the rates but, in most cases, the effect is negligible.

As mentioned above, data for some countries or areas may include annulments and/or legal separations. This practice affects the comparability of the crude divorce rates. For example, inclusion of annulments in the numerator of the rates produces a negligible effect on the rates, but inclusion of legal separations may have a measurable effect on the level.

It should be emphasized that crude divorce rates like crude birth, death and marriage rates may be seriously affected by age-sex structure of the populations to which they relate. Like crude marriage rates, they are also affected by the existing distribution of the population by marital status. Nevertheless, crude divorce rates provide a simple measure of the level and changes in divorces.

The comparability of data by urban/rural residence is affected by the national definitions of urban and rural used in tabulating these data. It is assumed, in the absence of specific information to the contrary, that the definitions of urban and rural used in connection with the national population census were also used in the compilation of the vital statistics for each country or area. However, it cannot be excluded that, for a given country or area, different definitions of urban and rural are used for the vital statistics data and the population census data respectively. When known, the definitions of urban in national population censuses are presented at the end of the technical notes for table 6. As discussed in detail in the notes, these definitions vary considerably from one country or area to another.

In addition to problems of comparability, divorce rates classified by urban/rural residence are also subject to certain special types of bias. If, when calculating divorce rates, different definitions of urban are used in connection with the vital events and the population data, and if this results in a net difference between the numerator and denominator of the rate in the population at risk, then the divorce rates would be biased. Urban/rural differentials in divorce rates may also be affected by whether the vital events have been tabulated in terms of place of occurrence or place of usual residence. This problem is discussed in more detail in section 4.1.4.1 of the Technical Notes.

Earlier data: Divorces have been shown in previous issues of the Demographic Yearbook. The earliest data, which were for 1935, appeared in the 1951 issue. For more information on specific topics and years for which data are reported, readers should consult the Historical Index.

NOTES

[1] For definition, please see section 4.1.1 of the Technical Notes.

Tableau 24 – *Annuaire démographique 2016*

Le tableau 24 présente des statistiques concernant les divorces et les taux bruts de divortialité, pour le plus grand nombre d'années possible entre 2012 et 2016.

Description des variables : le divorce est la dissolution légale et définitive des liens du mariage, c'est-à-dire la séparation de l'époux et de l'épouse qui confère aux parties le droit de se remarier civilement ou religieusement, ou selon toute autre procédure, conformément à la législation du pays[1].

Sauf indication contraire, les statistiques de la divortialité n'englobent pas les séparations légales qui excluent un remariage. Ces statistiques se rapportent aux jugements de divorce prononcés, non aux personnes divorcées.

Les statistiques de la divortialité proviennent, selon la pratique suivie par chaque pays, des actes des tribunaux et/ou des registres de l'état civil. L'officier d'état civil, les services nationaux de statistique ou d'autres services gouvernementaux peuvent être chargés d'établir ces statistiques.

La classification des divorces selon le lieu de résidence (zone urbaine ou rurale) est celle qui a été communiquée par chaque pays ou zone ; on part du principe qu'elle repose sur les définitions de la population urbaine utilisées pour les recensements nationaux, qui sont reproduites à la fin des notes techniques du tableau 6.

Calcul des taux : les taux bruts de divortialité selon le lieu de résidence (zone urbaine ou rurale) représentent le nombre annuel de divorces enregistrés pour 1 000 habitants au milieu de l'année. Les taux de ce tableau ne se rapportent qu'aux pays ou zones où l'on a enregistré un total d'au moins 30 divorces pendant une année donnée. Ces taux sont calculés par la division de statistique des Nations Unies sur la base de la population de référence adéquate (par exemple : population totale, nationaux seulement, etc.) si connue et disponible. Si la population de référence n'est pas connue ou n'est pas disponible, la population totale est utilisée pour calculer les taux. Par conséquent, si la population utilisée pour calculer les taux est différente de la population de référence adéquate, les taux présentés sont susceptibles de sous ou sur estimer la situation réelle d'un pays ou d'un territoire.

Fiabilité des données : il a été demandé à chaque pays ou zone d'indiquer le degré estimatif de complétude des données sur les divorces figurant dans ses registres d'état civil. Ces évaluations nationales sont désignées par les codes de qualité "C" et "U" qui apparaissent dans la deuxième colonne du tableau.

La lettre "C" indique que les données sont jugées à peu près complètes, c'est-à-dire qu'elles représentent au moins 90 p. 100 des divorces survenus chaque année ; la lettre "U" signale que les données sont jugées incomplètes, c'est-à-dire qu'elles représentent moins de 90 p. 100 des divorces survenus chaque année. Le code "..." indique qu'aucun renseignement n'a été communiqué quant à la complétude des données.

Les données issues des registres de l'état civil qui sont déclarées incomplètes ou dont le degré de complétude n'est pas connu (code "U" ou "...") sont jugées douteuses. Elles apparaissent en italique dans le tableau et les taux correspondants n'ont pas été calculés. Les codes de qualité ne s'appliquent qu'aux données extraites des registres de l'état civil. Pour plus de précisions sur la qualité des données reposant sur les statistiques de l'état civil en général, voir la section 4.2 des notes techniques.

Insuffisance des données : les statistiques des divorces appellent les mêmes réserves que celles formulées à propos des statistiques de l'état civil en général et des statistiques de divortialité en particulier (voir la section 4 des notes techniques).

Le divorce est, comme le mariage, un acte juridique, et ce fait influe sur la comparabilité internationale des données. Aux fins de la statistique, le divorce est défini par la législation de chaque pays ou zone. La législation sur le divorce varie considérablement d'un pays ou d'une zone à l'autre, ce qui influe aussi sur la fréquence des divorces, laquelle est relativement faible dans les pays ou zones où le jugement de divorce est difficile à obtenir.

Du fait que les divorces sont prononcés par les tribunaux et que les statistiques de la divortialité se rapportent aux jugements de divorce proprement dits, qui prennent effet à la date où ces jugements sont rendus, il se peut que des fluctuations annuelles accusées traduisent le rythme plus ou moins rapide auquel les affaires sont jugées plutôt que l'évolution de la fréquence des divorces. Les méthodes d'exploitation des données peuvent aussi influer sur la comparabilité des statistiques de la divortialité. Dans certains pays ou zones, ces statistiques peuvent comprendre les annulations et/ou les séparations légales. C'est notamment le cas dans les pays ou zones où les divorces sont peu nombreux. Lorsqu'ils sont connus, des renseignements à ce propos sont donnés en note à la fin du tableau.

Étant donné que dans de nombreux pays ou zones, le tribunal ou l'autorité qui a prononcé le divorce est seul habilité à enregistrer cet acte, et, comme l'acte d'enregistrement figure alors sur les registres du tribunal, l'enregistrement suit généralement de peu le jugement. C'est pourquoi la pratique consistant à exploiter les données selon la date de l'enregistrement ne pose généralement pas les graves problèmes de comparabilité auxquels on se heurte dans le cas des statistiques des naissances et des décès.

Comme on l'a brièvement mentionné ci-dessus, la fréquence des divorces est fonction notamment de la facilité relative avec laquelle la législation de chaque pays ou zone permet d'obtenir le divorce. Elle dépend également de la capacité des intéressés à supporter les frais de procédure. Il faut aussi citer l'influence de certaines religions sur la fréquence des divorces. Pour toutes ces raisons, les statistiques de divortialité ne sont pas rigoureusement comparables et ne permettent pas de mesurer exactement la fréquence des dissolutions légales des mariages. De plus, elles ne rendent pas compte des cas de dissolution extrajudiciaire du mariage, comme la séparation.

Dans certains pays ou zones, il n'existe ou il n'existait pas de législation sur le divorce selon l'acception retenue aux fins de ce tableau, si bien que l'on ne dispose pas de données les concernant.

De surcroît, il convient de noter que l'exactitude des taux dépend également de la qualité et des insuffisances des estimations de population qui sont utilisées pour leur calcul. Le problème des erreurs par excès ou par défaut commises lors du dénombrement et, dans une certaine mesure, le problème de l'hétérogénéité des définitions de la population totale ont été examinés à la section 3 des notes techniques, relative à la population en général ; des explications concernant les différents pays ou zones sont données en note à la fin du tableau 3.

Comme on le verra dans les notes, il n'a pas toujours été possible d'obtenir une correspondance rigoureuse entre le numérateur et le dénominateur pour le calcul des taux. Par exemple, les divorces parmi la population civile et les militaires sont parfois rapportés à la population civile seulement. Cela peut avoir pour effet d'accroître les taux, mais, dans la plupart des cas, il est probable que la différence sera négligeable.

Comme indiqué plus haut, les données concernant certains pays ou zones peuvent comprendre les annulations et/ou les séparations légales. Cette pratique influe sur la comparabilité des taux bruts de divortialité. Par exemple, l'inclusion des annulations dans le numérateur a une influence négligeable, mais l'inclusion des séparations légales peut avoir un effet appréciable.

Il faut souligner que les taux bruts de divortialité, de même que les taux bruts de natalité, de mortalité et de nuptialité, peuvent varier sensiblement selon la structure par âge et par sexe. Comme les taux bruts de nuptialité, ils peuvent également varier en raison de la répartition de la population selon l'état matrimonial. Les taux bruts de divortialité offrent néanmoins un moyen simple de mesurer la fréquence et l'évolution des divorces.

La comparabilité des données selon le lieu de résidence (zone urbaine ou rurale) peut être limitée par les définitions nationales des termes « urbain » et « rural » utilisées pour la mise en tableaux de ces données. En l'absence d'indications contraires, on a supposé que les mêmes définitions avaient servi pour le recensement national de la population et pour l'établissement des statistiques de l'état civil pour chaque pays ou zone. Toutefois, il n'est pas exclu que, pour une zone ou un pays donné, des définitions différentes aient été retenues. Les définitions du terme « urbain » utilisées pour les recensements nationaux de population ont été présentées à la fin des notes techniques du tableau 6 lorsqu'elles étaient connues. Comme on l'a précisé dans les notes techniques relatives au tableau 6, ces définitions varient considérablement d'un pays ou d'une zone à l'autre.

Outre les problèmes de comparabilité, les taux de divortialité classés selon le lieu de résidence (zone urbaine ou rurale) sont également sujets à des distorsions particulières. Si l'on utilise des définitions différentes du terme « urbain » pour classer les faits d'état civil et les données relatives à la population lors du calcul des taux et qu'il en résulte une différence nette entre le numérateur et le dénominateur pour le taux de la population exposée au risque, les taux de divortialité s'en trouveront faussés. La différence entre ces taux pour les zones urbaines et rurales pourra aussi être faussée selon que les faits d'état civil auront été classés d'après le lieu de l'événement ou d'après le lieu de résidence habituel. Ce problème est examiné plus en détail à la section 4.1.4.1 des notes techniques.

Données publiées antérieurement : des statistiques concernant les divorces ont déjà été présentées dans des éditions antérieures de l'*Annuaire démographique*. Les plus anciennes, qui portaient sur 1935, ont été publiées dans l'édition de 1951. Pour plus de précisions concernant les années et les sujets pour lesquels des données ont été publiées, se reporter à l'index historique.

_____

NOTE

[1] Pour la définition, voir la section 4.1.1 des Notes techniques.

24. Divorces and crude divorce rates by urban/rural residence: 2012 - 2016
Divorces et taux bruts de divortialité selon la résidence, urbaine/rurale : 2012 - 2016

Continent, country or area, and urban/rural residence / Continent, pays ou zone et résidence, urbaine/rurale	Code[a]	Number - Nombre					Rate - Taux				
		2012	2013	2014	2015	2016	2012	2013	2014	2015	2016
AFRICA - AFRIQUE											
Côte d'Ivoire											
Total	...	...	...	...	...	1 285	...	...	...	...	...
Egypt - Égypte[1]											
Total	+C	155 261	162 583	180 344	...	...	1.9	1.9	2.1	...	...
Urban - Urbaine	+C	91 789	91 040	97 953	...	...	2.6	2.5	2.6	...	...
Rural - Rurale	+C	63 472	71 543	82 391	...	...	1.3	1.5	1.7	...	...
Lesotho											
Total	+U	142	...	...	...	...	...	...	...	...	...
Mauritius - Maurice[2]											
Total	+C	2 003	1 584	2 262	2 161	1 910	1.6	1.3	1.8	1.7	1.5
Mayotte											
Total	C	...	...	155	...	...	...	...	0.7	...	...
Niger											
Total	+U	165 995	...	...	...	...	...	...	...	...	...
Urban - Urbaine	+U	40 990	...	...	...	...	...	...	...	...	...
Rural - Rurale	+U	125 005	...	...	...	...	...	...	...	...	...
Reunion - Réunion											
Total	C	...	...	1 420	...	...	...	...	1.7	...	...
Saint Helena ex. dep. - Sainte-Hélène sans dép.											
Total	C	5	7	4	...	...	...	...	...	...	...
Seychelles											
Total	+C	158	193	158	149	...	1.8	2.1	1.7	1.6	...
South Africa - Afrique du Sud											
Total	...	21 998	23 885	24 689	25 260		...	...	...	...	...
Sudan - Soudan											
Total	U	...	...	...	43 926		...	...	...	...	...
Tunisia - Tunisie											
Total	...	13 256	13 867	14 527	14 982		...	...	...	...	...
AMERICA, NORTH - AMÉRIQUE DU NORD											
Aruba											
Total	C	464	477	468	366	382	4.4	4.5	4.3	3.4	3.5
Barbados - Barbade											
Total	+C	472	459	443	...	...	1.7	1.7	1.6	...	...
Bermuda - Bermudes											
Total	C	145	165	104	116	...	2.3	2.7	1.7	1.9	...
Costa Rica											
Total	+C	11 593	13 349	10 864	10 111	*13 155	2.5	2.8	2.3	2.1	*2.7
Cuba											
Total	C	32 005	32 848	32 934	33 174	31 598	2.9	2.9	2.9	3.0	2.8
Urban - Urbaine	C	30 028	30 819	30 906	31 131	...	3.5	3.6	3.6	3.6	...
Rural - Rurale	C	1 977	2 029	2 028	2 043	...	0.7	0.8	0.8	0.8	...
Curaçao											
Total	C	386	366	344	375	365	2.5	2.4	2.2	2.4	2.3
Dominica - Dominique											
Total	+C	82	81	80	...	...	1.2	1.1	1.1	...	...
Dominican Republic - République dominicaine											
Total	+C	17 820	18 882	19 370	20 352	21 750	1.8	1.9	2.0	2.0	2.2
El Salvador[3]											
Total	...	6 674	6 841	...	...	...	...	...	...	...	...
Urban - Urbaine	...	6 463	6 592	...	...	...	...	...	...	...	...
Rural - Rurale	...	211	249	...	...	...	...	...	...	...	...
Grenada - Grenade											
Total	+C	174	...	...	...	...	1.6	...	...	...	...
Guadeloupe											
Total	C	902	806	729	...	...	2.2	2.0	1.8	...	...
Guatemala											
Total	C	5 157	5 542	5 575	5 726	...	0.3	0.4	0.4	0.4	...
Jamaica - Jamaïque											
Total	+C	2 409	2 410	1 744	...	...	0.9	0.9	0.6	...	...
Martinique											
Total	C	...	...	414	...	...	...	...	1.1	...	...

24. Divorces and crude divorce rates by urban/rural residence: 2012 - 2016
Divorces et taux bruts de divortialité selon la résidence, urbaine/rurale : 2012 - 2016 (continued - suite)

Continent, country or area, and urban/rural residence / Continent, pays ou zone et résidence, urbaine/rurale	Co-de[a]	Number - Nombre					Rate - Taux				
		2012	2013	2014	2015	2016	2012	2013	2014	2015	2016
AMERICA, NORTH - AMÉRIQUE DU NORD											
Mexico - Mexique											
Total	+C	99 509	108 727	113 478[6]	123 883[6]	...	0.9	0.9	0.9	1.0	...
Urban - Urbaine[4]	+C	89 927[5]	97 087[5]	101 093[6]	108 804[6]	...	1.1	1.1	1.2	1.2	...
Rural - Rurale[4]	+C	4 723[5]	5 305[5]	5 786[6]	6 305[6]	...	0.1	0.2	0.2	0.2	...
Panama											
Total	C	4 132	4 083	4 336	*4 479	...	1.1	1.1	1.1	*1.1	...
Urban - Urbaine	C	3 514	3 453	3 781	*3 806	...	1.4	1.3	1.4	*1.4	...
Rural - Rurale	C	618	630	555	*673	...	0.5	0.5	0.4	*0.5	...
Puerto Rico - Porto Rico											
Total	C	14 325	12 908	11 776	11 877	10 998	3.9	3.6	3.3	3.4	3.2
Saint Lucia - Sainte-Lucie											
Total	C	*117	...	...	...	...	*0.7	...	...	...	...
Saint Vincent and the Grenadines - Saint-Vincent-et-les Grenadines											
Total	C	34	29	39	...	...	0.3	...	0.4	...	...
Sint Maarten (Dutch part) - Saint-Martin (partie néerlandaise)											
Total	+C	...	99	...	...	...	...	2.7	...	...	...
Turks and Caicos Islands - Îles Turques et Caïques											
Total	C	35	29	...	...	...	1.1	...	...	...	...
United States of America - États-Unis d'Amérique											
Total	C	851 000[7]	832 157[8]	813 862[8]	800 909[8]	...	2.7	2.6	2.6	2.5	...
AMERICA, SOUTH - AMÉRIQUE DU SUD											
Brazil - Brésil											
Total	...	341 600	324 921	341 181	328 960	...	...	...	...	...	...
Ecuador - Équateur[9]											
Total	U	20 299	21 122	24 771	25 692	...	...	...	...	...	...
Urban - Urbaine[10]	U	...	19 458	22 854	24 021	...	...	...	...	...	...
Rural - Rurale[10]	U	...	1 664	1 917	1 671	...	...	...	...	...	...
Peru - Pérou[11]											
Total	+C	13 126	14 103	13 598	13 757	...	0.4	0.5	0.4	0.4	...
Suriname[12]											
Total	C	528	602	778	733	...	1.0	1.1	1.4	1.3	...
Venezuela (Bolivarian Republic of) - Venezuela (République bolivarienne du)											
Total	...	30 660	31 355	26 127	24 089	...	...	...	...	...	...
ASIA - ASIE											
Armenia - Arménie											
Total	+C	...	...	4 496	3 670	...	...	...	1.5	1.2	...
Urban - Urbaine	+C	...	...	...	2 801	...	...	...	...	1.5	...
Rural - Rurale	+C	...	...	...	869	...	...	...	...	0.8	...
Azerbaijan - Azerbaïdjan											
Total	+C	11 087	11 730	12 088	12 764	...	1.2	1.2	1.3	1.3	...
Urban - Urbaine	+C	8 212	8 451	8 190	8 658	...	1.7	1.7	1.6	1.7	...
Rural - Rurale	+C	2 875	3 279	3 898	4 106	...	0.7	0.7	0.9	0.9	...
Bahrain - Bahreïn											
Total	...	1 649	1 824	1 795	1 745	1 749	...	...	...	...	...
Bangladesh											
Total	...	125 787	...	...	...	...	...	...	...	...	...
Urban - Urbaine	...	31 483	...	...	...	...	...	...	...	...	...
Rural - Rurale	...	94 304	...	...	...	...	...	...	...	...	...

Continent, country or area, and urban/rural residence — Continent, pays ou zone et résidence, urbaine/rurale	Code[a]	Number - Nombre					Rate - Taux				
		2012	2013	2014	2015	2016	2012	2013	2014	2015	2016
ASIA - ASIE											
Brunei Darussalam - Brunéi Darussalam											
Total	+...	570	502	522	545	...	...	...	...	...	...
China - Chine[13]											
Total	+C	2 388 000	...	...	...	...	1.8	...	...	...	...
China, Hong Kong SAR - Chine, Hong Kong RAS											
Total	...	21 125	22 271	20 019	20 075	17 196	...	...	...	...	...
China, Macao SAR - Chine, Macao RAS											
Total	+C	1 147	1 172	1 308	1 168	...	2.0	2.0	2.1	1.8	...
Cyprus - Chypre[14]											
Total	C	2 036	1 857	1 884	1 807	...	2.4	2.2	2.2	2.1	...
Urban - Urbaine[15]	C	1 597	1 444	...	...	...	...	...	...	...	...
Rural - Rurale[15]	C	363	333	...	...	...	...	...	...	...	...
Georgia - Géorgie											
Total	C	7 136	8 089	9 119	9 112	9 539	1.6	1.8	2.4	2.5	2.6
Urban - Urbaine	C	5 158	5 693	6 253	6 320	6 565	...	...	...	3.0	3.1
Rural - Rurale	C	1 978	2 396	2 866	2 792	2 974	...	...	...	1.8	1.9
Indonesia - Indonésie											
Total	U	...	324 247	344 237	347 256	...	...	...	...	...	...
Iran (Islamic Republic of) - Iran (République islamique d')[16]											
Total	+C	150 324	155 369	163 569	163 765[17]	...	2.0	2.0	2.1	2.1	...
Urban - Urbaine[17]	+C	...	...	...	146 714	...	...	...	...	2.6	...
Rural - Rurale[17]	+C	...	...	...	17 051	...	...	...	...	0.8	...
Israel - Israël[18]											
Total	C	13 685	14 735	14 430	14 487	...	1.7	1.8	1.8	1.7	...
Urban - Urbaine[15]	C	12 451	13 392	13 166	13 095	...	1.7	1.8	1.8	1.7	...
Rural - Rurale[15]	C	955	1 021	929	1 070	...	1.4	1.5	1.3	1.5	...
Japan - Japon[19]											
Total	+C	235 406	231 383	222 107	226 215	...	1.8	1.8	1.7	1.8	...
Urban - Urbaine	+C	216 322	212 844	204 352	208 181	...	...	...	...	...	...
Rural - Rurale	+C	19 084	18 539	17 755	18 034	...	...	...	...	...	...
Jordan - Jordanie[20]											
Total	+C	17 696	18 976	20 911	22 070	...	2.4	2.3	2.4	2.3	...
Kazakhstan											
Total	C	48 513	51 482	...	...	...	2.9	3.0	...	...	...
Urban - Urbaine	C	36 232	38 365	...	...	...	3.9	4.1	...	...	...
Rural - Rurale	C	12 281	13 117	...	...	...	1.6	1.7	...	...	...
Kuwait - Koweït											
Total	C	6 672	6 904	7 327	7 201	...	2.1	2.0	1.9	1.8	...
Kyrgyzstan - Kirghizstan											
Total	C	8 698	9 052	9 235	8 588	*9 102	1.6	1.6	1.6	1.4	*1.5
Urban - Urbaine	C	4 609	5 255	5 324	4 797	*5 297	2.5	2.7	2.7	2.4	*2.6
Rural - Rurale	C	4 089	3 797	3 911	3 791	*3 805	1.1	1.0	1.0	1.0	*0.9
Lebanon - Liban											
Total	+C	6 498	6 644	7 206	...	...	...	...	...	...	...
Mongolia - Mongolie											
Total	+C	2 467	3 522	3 750	3 873	4 003	0.9	1.2	1.3	1.3	1.3
Urban - Urbaine	+C	2 096	2 978	3 333	3 455	3 501	1.1	1.5	1.7	1.7	1.6
Rural - Rurale	+C	371	544	417	418	502	0.4	0.6	0.4	0.4	0.5
Oman[21]											
Total	+U	3 570	...	...	...	...	...	...	...	...	...
Qatar											
Total	C	1 420	1 325	1 315	1 307	1 151	0.8	0.7	0.6	0.5	0.4
Urban - Urbaine	C	...	...	1 315	1 307	1 151	...	...	0.6	0.5	0.4
Republic of Korea - République de Corée[22]											
Total	+C	114 316	115 292	115 510	109 153	107 328	2.3	2.3	2.3	2.1	2.1
Urban - Urbaine[15]	+C	88 785	89 793	89 689	84 958	83 872	2.2	2.2	2.2	2.0	2.0
Rural - Rurale[15]	+C	22 213	22 218	22 596	21 384	21 504	2.4	2.4	2.4	2.3	2.3
Singapore - Singapour											
Total	+C	6 893	7 133	6 861	7 117	7 207	1.8	1.9	1.8	1.8	1.8

24. Divorces and crude divorce rates by urban/rural residence: 2012 - 2016
Divorces et taux bruts de divortialité selon la résidence, urbaine/rurale : 2012 - 2016 (continued - suite)

Continent, country or area, and urban/rural residence / Continent, pays ou zone et résidence, urbaine/rurale	Code[a]	Number - Nombre					Rate - Taux				
		2012	2013	2014	2015	2016	2012	2013	2014	2015	2016
ASIA - ASIE											
State of Palestine - État de Palestine											
Total	C	6 574	7 114	7 603	8 179	...	1.5	1.6	1.7	1.7	...
Tajikistan - Tadjikistan											
Total	+C	7 417	7 920	9 037	8 346	...	0.9	1.0	1.1	1.0	...
Urban - Urbaine	+C	2 973	3 264	3 279	...	...	1.4	1.5	1.5	...	...
Rural - Rurale	+C	4 444	4 656	5 758	...	...	0.8	0.8	0.9	...	...
Thailand - Thaïlande											
Total	...	111 377	107 031	111 810	117 880	118 539	...	...	...	...	...
Turkey - Turquie[23]											
Total	C	123 325	125 305	130 913	131 830	...	1.6	1.6	1.7	1.7	...
United Arab Emirates - Émirats arabes unis											
Total	...	3 901	4 233	4 809	4 913	...	...	...	...	...	...
Uzbekistan - Ouzbékistan											
Total	+C	17 879	24 025	28 811	29 647	...	0.6	0.8	0.9	0.9	...
Urban - Urbaine	+C	12 413	16 524	19 634	19 480	...	0.8	1.1	1.3	1.2	...
Rural - Rurale	+C	5 466	7 501	9 177	10 167	...	0.4	0.5	0.6	0.7	...
EUROPE											
Åland Islands - Îles d'Åland											
Total	C	63	54	50	77	*61	2.2	1.9	1.7	2.7	*2.1
Urban - Urbaine	C	34	29	20	44	*35	3.0	...	...	3.8	*3.0
Rural - Rurale	C	29	25	30	33	*26	...	...	1.7	1.9	...
Albania - Albanie											
Total	C	3 561	3 747	...	...	...	1.2	1.3	...	...	...
Total	U	...	...	4 240	3 761	...	...	...	...	...	...
Austria - Autriche[24]											
Total	C	17 006	15 958	16 647	16 351	...	2.0	1.9	1.9	1.9	...
Belarus - Bélarus											
Total	C	39 034	36 105	34 864	32 984	...	4.1	3.8	3.7	3.5	...
Urban - Urbaine	C	33 197	31 239	30 436	28 419	...	4.6	4.3	4.2	3.9	...
Rural - Rurale	C	5 837	4 866	4 428	4 565	...	2.6	2.2	2.0	2.1	...
Belgium - Belgique[25]											
Total	C	26 145	24 872	24 310	24 414	...	2.3	2.2	2.2	2.2	...
Urban - Urbaine	C	25 869	24 603	24 029	24 132	...	...	...	...	...	...
Rural - Rurale	C	276	269	281	282	...	...	...	...	...	...
Bosnia and Herzegovina - Bosnie-Herzégovine											
Total	C	2 294	1 608	1 655	...	...	0.6	0.4	0.4	...	...
Bulgaria - Bulgarie[26]											
Total	C	11 947	10 908	10 584	10 483	...	1.6	1.5	1.5	1.5	...
Urban - Urbaine	C	9 861	...	8 680	8 629	...	1.9	...	1.6	1.6	...
Rural - Rurale	C	2 086	...	1 904	1 854	...	1.0	...	1.0	1.0	...
Croatia - Croatie											
Total	C	5 659	5 992	6 570	6 010	...	1.3	1.4	1.6	1.4	...
Urban - Urbaine	C	3 894	4 105	4 585	4 170	...	...	...	...	...	...
Rural - Rurale	C	1 765	1 887	1 985	1 840	...	...	...	...	...	...
Czechia - Tchéquie											
Total	C	26 402	27 895	26 764	26 083	...	2.5	2.7	2.5	2.5	...
Urban - Urbaine	C	20 753	21 882	20 676	19 646	...	...	2.8	2.7	2.6	...
Rural - Rurale	C	5 649	6 013	6 088	6 437	...	...	2.1	2.2	2.3	...
Denmark - Danemark[27]											
Total	C	15 709	18 875	19 435	16 343	17 426	2.8	3.4	3.4	2.9	3.0
Estonia - Estonie											
Total	C	3 142	3 343	3 218	3 382	3 262	2.4	2.5	2.4	2.6	2.5
Urban - Urbaine[28]	C	2 168	2 275	2 197	2 226	...	2.4	2.5	2.4	2.5	...
Rural - Rurale[28]	C	892	888	836	985	...	2.1	2.1	2.0	2.4	...
Faeroe Islands - Îles Féroé											
Total	C	78	78	84	79	...	1.6	1.6	1.7	1.6	...
Finland - Finlande[29]											
Total	C	12 977	13 712	13 632	13 862	...	2.4	2.5	2.5	2.5	...
Urban - Urbaine	C	9 637	10 257	10 229	10 521	...	2.6	2.7	2.7	2.7	...
Rural - Rurale	C	3 340	3 455	3 403	3 341	...	2.0	2.1	2.0	2.1	...

24. Divorces and crude divorce rates by urban/rural residence: 2012 - 2016
Divorces et taux bruts de divortialité selon la résidence, urbaine/rurale : 2012 - 2016 (continued - suite)

Continent, country or area, and urban/rural residence / Continent, pays ou zone et résidence, urbaine/rurale	Code[a]	Number - Nombre					Rate - Taux				
		2012	2013	2014	2015	2016	2012	2013	2014	2015	2016
EUROPE											
France											
Total	C	125 217	121 849	120 568	120 731	...	2.0	1.9	1.9	1.9	...
Germany - Allemagne											
Total	C	179 147	169 833	166 199	163 335	...	2.2	2.1	2.1	2.0	...
Gibraltar											
Total	+C	91	84	72	61	...	2.8	2.6	2.2	1.8	...
Greece - Grèce											
Total	C	14 880	16 717	14 427	...	...	1.3	1.5	1.3	...	...
Hungary - Hongrie[12]											
Total	C	21 830	20 209	19 576	20 315	19 552	2.2	2.0	2.0	2.1	2.0
Urban - Urbaine[30]	C	16 164	15 044	14 801	15 168	...	2.4	2.2	2.1	2.2	...
Rural - Rurale[30]	C	5 457	4 928	4 536	4 893	...	1.8	1.6	1.6	1.7	...
Ireland - Irlande											
Total	+C	2 892	2 949	2 629	...	...	0.6	0.6	0.6	...	...
Italy - Italie											
Total	C	51 319	52 943	52 355	82 469	...	0.9	0.9	0.9	1.4	...
Latvia - Lettonie											
Total	C	7 311	7 031	6 271	5 151	6 061	3.6	3.5	3.1	2.6	3.1
Liechtenstein											
Total	C	96	75	82	98	...	2.6	2.0	2.2	2.6	...
Lithuania - Lituanie											
Total	C	10 399	9 974	9 806	9 371	...	3.5	3.4	3.3	3.2	...
Urban - Urbaine	C	7 359	6 924	6 831	6 394	...	3.7	3.5	3.5	3.3	...
Rural - Rurale	C	3 040	3 050	2 975	2 977	...	3.1	3.1	3.1	3.1	...
Luxembourg											
Total	C	1 074	1 163	1 453	1 345	...	2.0	2.1	2.6	2.4	...
Malta - Malte											
Total	C	441	338	323	372	...	1.1	0.8	0.8	0.9	...
Montenegro - Monténégro											
Total	C	515	499	584	577	...	0.8	0.8	0.9	0.9	...
Netherlands - Pays-Bas[31]											
Total	C	33 273	33 636	35 409	34 232	...	2.0	2.0	2.1	2.0	...
Norway - Norvège[6]											
Total	C	9 929	10 212	9 918	9 793	...	2.0	2.0	1.9	1.9	...
Poland - Pologne											
Total	C	64 432	66 132	65 761	67 296	63 497	1.7	1.7	1.7	1.8	1.7
Urban - Urbaine[32]	C	48 552	49 342	48 490	48 896	...	2.1	2.1	2.1	2.1	...
Rural - Rurale[32]	C	15 336	16 129	16 632	17 587	...	1.0	1.1	1.1	1.2	...
Portugal[33]											
Total	C	25 380	22 525	...	...	...	2.4	2.2	...	...	...
Republic of Moldova - République de Moldova											
Total	C	10 637	...	...	...	...	3.0	...	...	...	...
Urban - Urbaine	C	7 765	...	...	...	...	5.2	...	...	...	...
Rural - Rurale	C	2 872	...	...	...	...	1.4	...	...	...	...
Romania - Roumanie											
Total	C	31 324	28 507	27 188	31 527	30 497	1.6	1.4	1.4	1.6	1.5
Urban - Urbaine	C	21 790	19 594	18 692	21 496	20 485	2.0	1.8	1.7	2.0	...
Rural - Rurale	C	9 534	8 913	8 496	10 031	10 012	1.0	1.0	0.9	1.1	...
Russian Federation - Fédération de Russie											
Total	C	644 101	667 971	...	...	...	4.5	4.7	...	...	...
Urban - Urbaine	C	502 494	...	...	...	...	4.7	...	...	...	...
Rural - Rurale	C	141 607	...	...	...	...	3.8	...	...	...	...
San Marino - Saint-Marin											
Total	+C	49	54	51	...	...	1.5	1.6	1.5	...	...
Serbia - Serbie[34]											
Total	+C	7 372	8 170	7 614	9 381[12]	9 046[12]	1.0	1.1	1.1	1.3	1.3
Urban - Urbaine	+C	5 410	5 761	5 322	6 833[12]	...	1.3	1.3	1.2	1.6	...
Rural - Rurale	+C	1 962	2 409	2 292	2 548[12]	...	0.7	0.8	0.8	0.9	...
Slovakia - Slovaquie											
Total	C	10 948	10 946	10 514	9 786	...	2.0	2.0	1.9	1.8	...
Urban - Urbaine	C	6 804	6 840	6 490	5 945	...	2.3	2.3	2.2	2.0	...
Rural - Rurale	C	4 144	4 106	4 024	3 841	...	1.7	1.7	1.6	1.5	...

Continent, country or area, and urban/rural residence / Continent, pays ou zone et résidence, urbaine/rurale	Code[a]	Number - Nombre					Rate - Taux				
		2012	2013	2014	2015	2016	2012	2013	2014	2015	2016
EUROPE											
Slovenia - Slovénie											
Total	C	2 509	2 351	2 469	2 432	2 531	1.2	1.1	1.2	1.2	1.2
Urban - Urbaine	C	1 422	1 307	1 399	1 484	...	1.4	1.2	1.3	1.3	...
Rural - Rurale	C	1 087	1 044	1 070	948	...	1.1	1.0	1.1	1.0	...
Spain - Espagne											
Total	C	104 262	95 427	100 746	96 562	...	2.2	2.0	2.2	2.1	...
Sweden - Suède[6]											
Total	C	23 422	26 933	26 143	24 876	24 258	2.5	2.8	2.7	2.5	2.5
Switzerland - Suisse											
Total	U	*17 550*	*17 119*	*16 737*	*16 982*	*17 028*	...	...	...	...	...
Urban - Urbaine	U	*13 457*	*13 123*	*14 397*[35]	...	...	...	...	...	...	...
Rural - Rurale	U	*4 093*	*3 996*	*2 340*[35]	...	...	...	...	...	...	...
TFYR of Macedonia - L'ex-R. y. de Macédoine											
Total	C	1 926	2 045	2 210	2 200	1 985	0.9	1.0	1.1	1.1	1.0
Urban - Urbaine	C	1 300	1 372	1 472	1 420	...	...	...	...	...	...
Rural - Rurale	C	626	673	738	780	...	...	...	...	...	...
Ukraine											
Total	+C	168 508	164 939	130 673[36]	129 373[36]	...	3.7	3.6	3.0	3.0	...
United Kingdom of Great Britain and Northern Ireland - Royaume-Uni de Grande-Bretagne et d'Irlande du Nord[37]											
Total	C	130 469	126 716	122 556	...	...	2.0	2.0	1.9	...	...
OCEANIA - OCÉANIE											
American Samoa - Samoas américaines											
Total	C	52	61	63	...	...	0.8	1.0	1.0	...	...
Australia - Australie											
Total	C	49 917	47 638	46 498	48 517	...	2.2	2.1	2.0	2.0	...
Guam[38]											
Total	C	869	742	749	581	590	5.4	4.6	4.7	3.6	3.6
New Zealand - Nouvelle-Zélande											
Total	+C	8 785	8 279	8 171[39]	8 523[39]	8 169[39]	2.0	1.9	1.8	1.9	1.7

FOOTNOTES - NOTES

Italics: data from civil registers which are incomplete or of unknown completeness. - Italiques : données incomplètes ou dont le degré d'exactitude n'est pas connu, provenant des registres de l'état civil.

* Provisional. - Données provisoires.

[a] 'Code' indicates the source of data, as follows:
C - Civil registration, estimated over 90% complete
U - Civil registration, estimated less than 90% complete
| - Other source, estimated reliable
+ - Data tabulated by date of registration rather than occurence
... - Information not available

Le 'Code' indique la source des données, comme suit :
C - Registres de l'état civil considérés complèts à 90 p. 100 au moins
U - Registres de l'état civil qui ne sont pas considérés complèts à 90 p. 100 au moins
| - Autre source, considérée pas douteuses
+ - Données exploitées selon la date de l'enregistrement et non la date de l'événement
... - Information pas disponible

[1] Including 'revocable divorces' (among Muslim population), which approximate legal separations. - Y compris les 'divorces révocables' (parmi la population musulmane), qui sont plus au moins l'équivalent des séparations légales.
[2] Excludes the islands of St. Brandon and Agalega. - Non compris les îles St. Brandon et Agalega.
[3] Data refer to the usual residence of the wife and excludes divorces granted in the country of wives living abroad. - Données relatives à la résidence habituelle de l'épouse, sauf cas de divorces prononcés dans les pays d'épouses vivant à l'étranger.
[4] The total number may include 'Unknown residence', but the categories urban and rural do not. - Le nombre total peut inclure les personnes dont la résidence n'est pas connue, à l'inverse des catégories de population urbaine et rurale.
[5] Urban and rural distribution refers to the usual residence of the wife. - La répartition entre résidence urbaine et résidence rurale fait référence au lieu de résidence habituel de la femme.
[6] Including same sex divorces. - Y compris les divorces entre conjoints du même sexe.
[7] Excluding data for California, Georgia, Hawaii, Indiana, Louisiana, and Minnesota. - Non compris les données pour la Californie, la Géorgie, Hawaii, l'Indiana, la Louisiane et le Minnesota.
[8] Excluding data for California, Georgia, Hawaii, Indiana, and Minnesota. - À l'exclusion des données pour la Californie, la Géorgie, Hawaï, l'Indiana et le Minnesota.
[9] Excludes nomadic Indian tribes. - Non compris les tribus d'Indiens nomades.

¹⁰ Urban and rural residence refers to the place of usual residence of husband. - Le lieu de résidence (zone urbaine ou zone rurale) correspond au lieu de résidence habituel du mari.

¹¹ Data are compiled from the National Registers of Identification and Civil Status (RENIEC). - Les données sont rédigées à partir des Registres Nationaux d'Identification et d'État Civil (RENIEC).

¹² Including annulments. - Y compris les annulations.

¹³ Including annulments. For statistical purposes, the data for China do not include those for the Hong Kong Special Administrative Region (Hong Kong SAR), Macao Special Administrative Region (Macao SAR) and Taiwan province of China. - Y compris les annulations. Pour la présentation des statistiques, les données pour la Chine ne comprennent pas la Région Administrative Spéciale de Hong Kong (Hong Kong RAS), la Région Administrative Spéciale de Macao (Macao RAS) et Taïwan province de Chine.

¹⁴ Data refer to government controlled areas. - Les données se rapportent aux zones contrôlées par le Gouvernement.

¹⁵ The total number may include 'Unknown residence', but the categories urban and rural do not. Urban and rural residence refers to the place of usual residence of husband. - Le nombre total peut inclure les personnes dont la résidence n'est pas connue, à l'inverse des catégories de population urbaine et rurale. Le lieu de résidence (zone urbaine ou zone rurale) correspond au lieu de résidence habituel du mari.

¹⁶ Data refer to the Iranian Year which begins on 21 March and ends on 20 March of the following year. - Les données concernent l'année iranienne, qui commence le 21 mars et se termine le 20 mars de l'année suivante.

¹⁷ Source: Civil Registration Organization. - Source : Organisation chargée d'assurer l'enregistrement des faits d'état civil.

¹⁸ Includes data for East Jerusalem and Israeli residents in certain other territories under occupation by Israeli military forces since June 1967. - Y compris les données pour Jérusalem-Est et les résidents israéliens dans certains autres territoires occupés depuis 1967 par les forces armées israéliennes.

¹⁹ Data refer to Japanese nationals in Japan only. - Les données se raportent aux nationaux japonais au Japon seulement.

²⁰ Excluding data for Jordanian territory under occupation since June 1967 by Israeli military forces. Excluding foreigners, including registered Palestinian refugees. - Non compris les données pour le territoire jordanien occupé depuis juin 1967 par les forces armées israéliennes. Non compris les étrangers, mais y compris les réfugiés de Palestine enregistrés.

²¹ Data refer to registered events only. - Les données ne concernent que les événements enregistrés.

²² Excluding alien armed forces, civilian aliens employed by armed forces, and foreign diplomatic personnel and their dependants. - Non compris les militaires étrangers, les civils étrangers employés par les forces armées ni le personnel diplomatique étranger et les membres de leur famille les accompagnant.

²³ Data from MERNIS (Central Population Administrative System). - Données de MERNIS (Système central de données démographiques).

²⁴ Excluding aliens temporarily in the area. - Non compris les étrangers se trouvant temporairement dans le territoire.

²⁵ Including divorces among armed forces stationed outside the country and alien armed forces in the area. - Y compris les divorces de militaires nationaux hors du pays et les militaires étrangers en garnison sur le territoire.

²⁶ Including nationals outside the country, but excluding foreigners in the country. Including annulments. - Y compris les nationaux à l'étranger, mais non compris les étrangers sur le territoire. Y compris les annulations.

²⁷ Excluding Faeroe Islands and Greenland shown separately, if available. - Non compris les Iles Féroé et le Groenland, qui font l'objet de rubriques distinctes, si disponible.

²⁸ Urban and rural residence refers to the place of usual residence of husband. The difference between 'Total' and the sum of urban and rural is due to the unknown place of residence of husbands and to husbands living outside the country. - Le lieu de résidence (zone urbaine ou zone rurale) correspond au lieu de résidence habituel du mari. La différence entre le « Total » et la somme des chiffres urbains et ruraux s'explique par le fait que la résidence du mari n'est pas toujours connue ou est située à l'étranger.

²⁹ Excluding Åland Islands. - Non compris les Îles d'Åland.

³⁰ The urban and rural categories do not include the data of foreigners, persons of unknown residence and the homeless, whereas the total category includes them. - Les chiffres portant sur la population urbaine et rurale n' incluent pas les données relatives aux étrangers, aux personnes dont la résidence n'est pas connue et aux personnes sans domicile fixe, à l'inverse, le total les inclut.

³¹ Based on the general office for civil registration. Including same sex divorces. - Données provenant des services généraux d'état civil. Y compris les divorces entre conjoints du même sexe.

³² Data for urban and rural exclude divorces if both persons live abroad. - Les données pour les zones urbaines et rurales excluent le divorce si les deux personnes vivent à l'étranger.

³³ Data refer to resident spouses only. - Les données concernent uniquement les conjoints résidents.

³⁴ Excludes data for Kosovo and Metohia. - Sans les données pour le Kosovo et Metohie.

³⁵ From 2014, urban refers to urban centers and areas under the influence of urban centers. - A partir de 2014, le territoire urbain inclut l'espace des centres urbains ainsi que l'espace sous influence des centres urbains.

³⁶ The Government of Ukraine has informed the United Nations that it is not in a position to provide statistical data concerning the Autonomous Republic of Crimea and the city of Sevastopol. - Le gouvernement Ukrainien a informé l'ONU qu'il n'est pas en mesure de fournir des données statistiques concernant la République autonome de Crimée et la ville de Sébastopol.

³⁷ Excluding Channel Islands (Guernsey and Jersey) and Isle of Man, shown separately, if available. - Non compris les îles Anglo-Normandes (Guernesey et Jersey) et l'île de Man, qui font l'objet de rubriques distinctes, si disponible.

³⁸ Including United States military personnel, their dependants and contract employees. - Y compris les militaires des Etats-Unis, les membres de leur famille les accompagnant et les agents contractuels des Etats-Unis.

³⁹ Random rounding to base 3 is applied in this table as a confidentiality measure. - Les chiffres sont arrondis à la base 3 de manière aléatoire, pour des raisons de confidentialité.

Table 25 - *Demographic Yearbook 2016*

Table 25 presents the number of divorces according to the duration of marriage and the percentage distribution for the latest available year between 2007 and 2016.

Description of variables: Divorces are the final legal dissolutions of a marriage, which confer on the parties the right to remarry as defined by the laws of each country or area. Unless otherwise noted, divorce statistics exclude legal separations which do not allow remarriage. These statistics refer to the number of divorces granted, and not to the number of persons divorcing.

Duration of marriage is defined as the interval of time between the day, month and year of marriage and the day, month and year of divorce in completed years. This definition refers to the "legal" duration rather than the "effective" duration; having been calculated until the day, month and year of the actual divorce decree rather than until the separation date or the date when the couple ceased to live as man and wife.

The duration of marriage classification used in this table to the extent possible, is the following: under one year, single years of duration through 9 years, 10-14 years, 15-19 years, 20 years and over and duration unknown, when appropriate.

Reliability of data: Data from civil registers of divorces which are reported as incomplete (less than 90 per cent completeness) or of unknown completeness are considered unreliable and are set in italics rather than in roman type. For more information about the quality of vital statistics data in general, see section 4.2 of the Technical Notes.

Limitations: Statistics on divorces by duration of marriage are subject to the same qualifications which have been set forth for vital statistics in general and divorce statistics in particular as discussed in Section 4 of the Technical Notes.

Earlier data: Divorces by duration by marriage, cross-classified by age of husband and by age of wife have been shown previously in issues of the Demographic Yearbook featuring marriage and divorce. For information on years covered, readers should consult the Historical Index.

Tableau 25 – *Annuaire démographique 2016*

Le tableau 25 indique le nombre de divorces selon la durée du mariage et la répartition des pourcentages, pour la dernière année disponible entre 2007 et 2016.

Description des variables : le divorce est la dissolution définitive des liens du mariage qui confère aux parties le droit de se remarier, telle qu'elle est définie par la législation de chaque pays ou zone. Sauf indication contraire, les statistiques de la divortialité n'englobent pas les séparations légales qui excluent le remariage. Ces statistiques se rapportent aux jugements de divorce prononcés, non aux personnes divorcées.

La durée du mariage correspond à l'intervalle du temps qui s'est écoulé entre la date exacte (jour, mois et année) du mariage et la date exacte (jour, mois et année) du divorce exprimé en années révolues. Cette définition est celle de la durée "légale" du mariage et non de sa durée "effective", puisque la durée est calculée jusqu'à la date (jour, mois et année) du jugement de divorce et non jusqu'à la date de la séparation ou la date à laquelle le couple a cessé de vivre comme mari et femme.

Le classement selon la durée du mariage utilisé dans ce tableau dans la mesure du possible comprend les catégories suivantes : moins d'un an, une catégorie par an jusqu'à 9 ans inclus, 10-14 ans, 15-19 ans, 20 ans et plus et, le cas échéant, une catégorie pour la durée du mariage inconnue.

Fiabilité des données : les données sur les divorces provenant des registres de l'état civil qui sont déclarées incomplètes (degré de complétude inférieur à 90 pour cent) ou dont le degré de complétude n'est pas connu, sont jugées douteuses et apparaissent en italique et non en caractères romains. Pour plus de précisions sur la qualité des données reposant sur les statistiques de l'état civil en general, voir la section 4.2 des Notes techniques.

Insuffisance des données : les statistiques des divorces selon la durée du mariage, appellent toutes les réserves qui ont été formulées à propos des statistiques de l'état civil en general et des statistiques des divorces en particulier (voir les explications figurant à la section 4 des Notes techniques).

Données publiées antérieurement : les statistiques des divorces selon la durée du mariage, classées selon l'âge de l'époux, d'une part, et selon l'âge de l'épouse, d'autre part, ont été présentées dans des éditions antérieures de l'Annuaire démographique qui avaient comme sujet spécial la nuptialité et la divortialité. Pour plus de précisions concernant les années pour lesquelles ces données ont été publiées, on se reportera à l'index historique.

25. Divorces and percentage distribution by duration of marriage, latest available year: 2007 - 2016
Divorces et répartition des pourcentages selon la durée du mariage, dernière année disponible: 2007 - 2016

Continent, country or area, year, code and duration of marriage (in years) / Continent, pays ou zone, année, code et durée du mariage (en années)	Number of divorces / Nombre de divorces	Per cent / Pour cent	Continent, country or area, year, code and duration of marriage (in years) / Continent, pays ou zone, année, code et durée du mariage (en années)	Number of divorces / Nombre de divorces	Per cent / Pour cent
AFRICA - AFRIQUE			**AFRICA - AFRIQUE**		
Egypt - Égypte[1]			South Africa - Afrique du Sud		
2014 (+C)			2011 (...)		
Total	180 344	100.0	Total	20 980	100.0
Less than 1 - Moins de 1	27 803	15.4	Less than 1 - Moins de 1	102	0.5
1	20 315	11.3	1	650	3.1
2	13 815	7.7	2	1 059	5.0
3	10 800	6.0	3	1 322	6.3
4	8 343	4.6	4	1 356	6.5
5	6 723	3.7	5	1 206	5.7
6	6 234	3.5	6	1 164	5.5
7	5 493	3.0	7	1 120	5.3
8	4 087	2.3	8	1 145	5.5
9	3 788	2.1	9	900	4.3
10 - 14	12 671	7.0	10 - 14	3 782	18.0
15 - 19	6 690	3.7	15 - 19	2 738	13.1
20 +	11 642	6.5	20 +	3 512	16.7
Not stated - Inconnu	41 940	23.3	Not stated - Inconnu	924	4.4
Lesotho					
2012 (+U)			**AMERICA, NORTH - AMÉRIQUE DU NORD**		
Total	142	100.0			
Less than 1 - Moins de 1	-	0.0	Aruba		
1	5	3.5	2016 (C)		
2	9	6.3	Total	386	100.0
3	11	7.7	Less than 1 - Moins de 1	2	0.5
4	7	4.9	1	14	3.6
5	12	8.5	2	14	3.6
6	12	8.5	3	21	5.4
7	10	7.0	4	16	4.1
8	6	4.2	5	26	6.7
9	13	9.2	6	27	7.0
10 - 14	23	16.2	7	21	5.4
15 - 19	14	9.9	8	22	5.7
20 +	20	14.1	9	19	4.9
Mauritius - Maurice[2]			10 - 14	70	18.1
2016 (+C)			15 - 19	47	12.2
Total	1 910	100.0	20 +	76	19.7
Less than 1 - Moins de 1	4	0.2	Not stated - Inconnu	11	2.8
1	51	2.7	Bermuda - Bermudes		
2	104	5.4	2015 (C)		
3	121	6.3	Total	116	100.0
4	105	5.5	Less than 1 - Moins de 1	-	0.0
5	141	7.4	1	1	0.9
6	100	5.2	2	-	0.0
7	87	4.6	3	4	3.4
8	95	5.0	4	5	4.3
9	82	4.3	5	3	2.6
10 - 14	402	21.0	6	4	3.4
15 - 19	278	14.6	7	6	5.2
20 +	340	17.8	8	8	6.9
Seychelles			9	9	7.8
2015 (+C)			10 - 14	33	28.4
Total	149	100.0	15 - 19	14	12.1
Less than 1 - Moins de 1	-	0.0	20 +	29	25.0
1	3	2.0	Cuba		
2	8	5.4	2015 (C)		
3	9	6.0	Total	33 174	100.0
4	11	7.4	Less than 1 - Moins de 1	2 268	6.8
5	10	6.7	1	2 826	8.5
6	9	6.0	2	2 451	7.4
7	5	3.4	3 - 5	6 016	18.1
8	8	5.4	6 - 9	5 064	15.3
9	7	4.7	10 - 14	3 577	10.8
10 - 14	33	22.1	15 +	10 954	33.0
15 - 19	18	12.1	Not stated - Inconnu	18	0.1
20 +	28	18.8			

Continent, country or area, year, code and duration of marriage (in years) Continent, pays ou zone, année, code et durée du mariage (en années)	Number of divorces Nombre de divorces	Per cent Pour cent	Continent, country or area, year, code and duration of marriage (in years) Continent, pays ou zone, année, code et durée du mariage (en années)	Number of divorces Nombre de divorces	Per cent Pour cent
AMERICA, NORTH - AMÉRIQUE DU NORD			**AMERICA, NORTH - AMÉRIQUE DU NORD**		
Curaçao			Jamaica - Jamaïque[4]		
2016 (C)			2007 (+C)		
Total	365	100.0	15 - 19	160	14.0
Less than 1 - Moins de 1	3	0.8	20 +	242	21.2
1	12	3.3	Mexico - Mexique[5]		
2	17	4.7	2015 (+C)		
3	23	6.3	Total	123 883	100.0
4	22	6.0	Less than 1 - Moins de 1	226	0.2
5	25	6.8	1	4 827	3.9
6	28	7.7	2	5 705	4.6
7	21	5.8	3	6 148	5.0
8	26	7.1	4	5 840	4.7
9	13	3.6	5	5 466	4.4
10 - 14	53	14.5	6	5 422	4.4
15 - 19	44	12.1	7	5 306	4.3
20 +	75	20.5	8	5 058	4.1
Not stated - Inconnu	3	0.8	9	4 679	3.8
Dominican Republic - République dominicaine[3]			10 - 14	20 557	16.6
2015 (+C)			15 - 19	17 841	14.4
Total	20 091	100.0	20 +	35 171	28.4
Less than 1 - Moins de 1	106	0.5	Not stated - Inconnu	1 637	1.3
1	299	1.5	Panama		
2	422	2.1	2015* (C)		
3	488	2.4	Total	4 479	100.0
4	505	2.5	Less than 5 - Moins de 5	792	17.7
5	515	2.6	5 - 9	1 200	26.8
6	468	2.3	10 - 14	670	15.0
7	442	2.2	15 - 19	538	12.0
8	414	2.1	20 +	1 279	28.6
9	350	1.7	Trinidad and Tobago - Trinité-et-Tobago		
10 - 14	1 342	6.7	2009 (C)		
15 - 19	828	4.1	Total	2 629	100.0
20 +	1 222	6.1	Less than 1 - Moins de 1	-	0.0
Not stated - Inconnu	12 690	63.2	1	40	1.5
El Salvador			2	78	3.0
2012 (...)			3	100	3.8
Total	7 138	100.0	4	126	4.8
Less than 1 - Moins de 1	77	1.1	5	127	4.8
1	161	2.3	6	137	5.2
2	239	3.3	7	124	4.7
3	271	3.8	8	122	4.6
4	320	4.5	9	135	5.1
5	302	4.2	10 - 14	512	19.5
6	296	4.1	15 - 19	369	14.0
7	293	4.1	20 +	752	28.6
8	300	4.2	Not stated - Inconnu	7	0.3
9	311	4.4			
10 - 14	1 508	21.1	**AMERICA, SOUTH - AMÉRIQUE DU SUD**		
15 - 19	1 138	15.9			
20 +	1 705	23.9	Brazil - Brésil		
Not stated - Inconnu	217	3.0	2015 (...)		
Jamaica - Jamaïque[4]			Total	328 960	100.0
2007 (+C)			Less than 1 - Moins de 1	10 316	3.1
Total	1 140	100.0	1	16 720	5.1
Less than 1 - Moins de 1	-	0.0	2	17 988	5.5
1	1	0.1	3	17 962	5.5
2	3	0.3	4	16 411	5.0
3	22	1.9	5	15 193	4.6
4	42	3.7	6	14 431	4.4
5	53	4.6	7	14 036	4.3
6	62	5.4	8	12 792	3.9
7	89	7.8	9	11 832	3.6
8	96	8.4	10 - 14	44 438	13.5
9	75	6.6	15 - 19	34 952	10.6
10 - 14	294	25.8	20 +	101 016	30.7
			Not stated - Inconnu	873	0.3

25. Divorces and percentage distribution by duration of marriage, latest available year: 2007 - 2016
Divorces et répartition des pourcentages selon la durée du mariage, dernière année disponible: 2007 - 2016 (continued - suite)

Continent, country or area, year, code and duration of marriage (in years) / Continent, pays ou zone, année, code et durée du mariage (en années)	Number of divorces / Nombre de divorces	Per cent / Pour cent	Continent, country or area, year, code and duration of marriage (in years) / Continent, pays ou zone, année, code et durée du mariage (en années)	Number of divorces / Nombre de divorces	Per cent / Pour cent
AMERICA, SOUTH - AMÉRIQUE DU SUD			**ASIA - ASIE**		
Chile - Chili			Armenia - Arménie		
2010 (C)			2014 (+C)		
Total	1 558	100.0	Total	4 496	100.0
Less than 1 - Moins de 1	11	0.7	Less than 1 - Moins de 1	205	4.6
1	17	1.1	1	462	10.3
2	36	2.3	2	194	4.3
3	35	2.2	3	199	4.4
4	36	2.3	4	184	4.1
5	32	2.1	5	829	18.4
6	28	1.8	6	-	0.0
7	39	2.5	7	-	0.0
8	38	2.4	8	-	0.0
9	47	3.0	9	-	0.0
10 - 14	270	17.3	10 - 14	533	11.9
15 - 19	211	13.5	15 - 19	472	10.5
20 +	610	39.2	20 +	1 418	31.5
Not stated - Inconnu	148	9.5	Azerbaijan - Azerbaïdjan		
Ecuador - Équateur[6]			2014 (+C)		
2015 (U)			Total	12 088	100.0
Total	25 692	100.0	Less than 1 - Moins de 1	293	2.4
Less than 1 - Moins de 1	174	0.7	1	882	7.3
1	473	1.8	2	917	7.6
2	657	2.6	3	1 060	8.8
3	861	3.4	4	855	7.1
4	1 051	4.1	5	816	6.8
5	1 163	4.5	6	854	7.1
6	1 310	5.1	7	778	6.4
7	1 244	4.8	8	670	5.5
8	1 104	4.3	9	538	4.5
9	1 061	4.1	10 - 14	1 584	13.1
10 - 14	4 401	17.1	15 - 19	911	7.5
15 - 19	3 891	15.1	20 +	1 795	14.8
20 +	8 301	32.3	Not stated - Inconnu	135	1.1
Not stated - Inconnu	1	0.0	Bahrain - Bahreïn		
Suriname[7]			2016 (...)		
2015 (C)			Total	1 749	100.0
Total	733	100.0	Less than 1 - Moins de 1	394	22.5
Less than 1 - Moins de 1	2	0.3	1 - 2	401	22.9
1 - 3	112	15.3	3 - 4	238	13.6
4 - 6	140	19.1	5 - 6	120	6.9
7 - 9	131	17.9	7 - 9	149	8.5
10 - 12	87	11.9	10 - 14	179	10.2
13 - 15	66	9.0	15 - 19	98	5.6
16 - 18	52	7.1	20 +	132	7.5
19 - 21	39	5.3	Not stated - Inconnu	38	2.2
22 - 24	31	4.2	Brunei Darussalam - Brunéi Darussalam		
25 - 27	29	4.0	2015 (+...)		
28 - 30	14	1.9	Total	545	100.0
31 - 33	8	1.1	Less than 1 - Moins de 1	16	2.9
34 - 36	8	1.1	1	19	3.5
37+	14	1.9	2	32	5.9
Venezuela (Bolivarian Republic of) - Venezuela (République bolivarienne du)			3	36	6.6
2014 (...)			4	37	6.8
Total	26 127	100.0	5	33	6.1
Less than 1 - Moins de 1	60	0.2	6	41	7.5
1 - 4	2 385	9.1	7	25	4.6
5 - 9	6 949	26.6	8	24	4.4
10 - 14	4 834	18.5	9	32	5.9
15 - 19	4 118	15.8	10 - 14	108	19.8
20 +	7 710	29.5	15 - 19	65	11.9
Not stated - Inconnu	71	0.3	20 +	77	14.1
			China, Macao SAR - Chine, Macao RAS		
			2015 (+C)		
			Total	1 168	100.0
			Less than 5 - Moins de 5	221	18.9
			5 - 9	445	38.1
			10 - 14	160	13.7
			15 +	342	29.3

Continent, country or area, year, code and duration of marriage (in years) Continent, pays ou zone, année, code et durée du mariage (en années)	Number of divorces Nombre de divorces	Per cent Pour cent

ASIA - ASIE

Cyprus - Chypre[8]
2009 (C)
Total	1 738	100.0
Less than 1 - Moins de 1	66	3.8
1	142	8.2
2	107	6.2
3	127	7.3
4	120	6.9
5	106	6.1
6	108	6.2
7	84	4.8
8	80	4.6
9	60	3.5
10 - 14	267	15.4
15 - 19	167	9.6
20 +	304	17.5

Georgia - Géorgie
2016 (C)
Total	9 539	100.0
Less than 1 - Moins de 1	843	8.8
1	636	6.7
2	596	6.2
3	528	5.5
4	461	4.8
5 - 9	2 274	23.8
10 - 14	1 047	11.0
15 - 19	802	8.4
20 +	2 296	24.1
Not stated - Inconnu	56	0.6

Iran (Islamic Republic of) - Iran (République islamique d')[9]
2011 (+C)
Total	142 841	100.0
Less than 1 - Moins de 1	19 730	13.8
1	17 091	12.0
2	13 761	9.6
3	11 763	8.2
4	9 339	6.5
5	8 140	5.7
6	7 292	5.1
7	6 068	4.2
8	5 480	3.8
9	4 726	3.3
10 - 14	16 231	11.4
15 - 19	9 344	6.5
20 +	13 643	9.6
Not stated - Inconnu	233	0.2

Israel - Israël[10]
2015 (C)
Total	14 487	100.0
Less than 1 - Moins de 1	820	5.7
1	996	6.9
2	876	6.0
3	749	5.2
4	726	5.0
5	644	4.4
6	630	4.3
7	576	4.0
8	501	3.5
9	492	3.4
10 - 14	1 928	13.3
15 - 19	1 592	11.0
20 +	2 681	18.5
Not stated - Inconnu	1 276	8.8

ASIA - ASIE

Japan - Japon[11]
2015 (+C)
Total	226 215	100.0
Less than 1 - Moins de 1	13 863	6.1
1	16 272	7.2
2	15 349	6.8
3	13 807	6.1
4	12 428	5.5
5 - 9	47 082	20.8
10 - 14	31 108	13.8
15 - 19	23 941	10.6
20 +	38 644	17.1
Not stated - Inconnu	13 721	6.1

Kazakhstan
2013 (C)
Total	51 482	100.0
Less than 1 - Moins de 1	3 237	6.3
1	4 200	8.2
2	4 383	8.5
3	3 965	7.7
4	3 613	7.0
5 - 9	13 813	26.8
10 - 14	5 994	11.6
15 - 19	4 442	8.6
20 +	7 834	15.2
Not stated - Inconnu	1	0.0

Kuwait - Koweït
2011 (C)
Total	6 254	100.0
Less than 1 - Moins de 1	1 403	22.4
1	809	12.9
2	581	9.3
3	434	6.9
4	389	6.2
5 - 9	1 241	19.8
10 - 14	547	8.7
15 - 19	348	5.6
20 +	499	8.0
Not stated - Inconnu	3	0.0

Kyrgyzstan - Kirghizstan
2016* (C)
Total	9 102	100.0
Less than 1 - Moins de 1	363	4.0
1	487	5.4
2	648	7.1
3	718	7.9
4	656	7.2
5	646	7.1
6	564	6.2
7	537	5.9
8	463	5.1
9	430	4.7
10 - 14	1 418	15.6
15 - 19	759	8.3
20 +	1 413	15.5

Mongolia - Mongolie
2016 (+C)
Total	4 003	100.0
Less than 1 - Moins de 1	24	0.6
1 - 3	262	6.5
4 - 6	589	14.7
7 - 9	1 062	26.5
10 - 14	790	19.7
15 - 19	488	12.2
20 +	788	19.7

Continent, country or area, year, code and duration of marriage (in years) / Continent, pays ou zone, année, code et durée du mariage (en années)	Number of divorces / Nombre de divorces	Per cent / Pour cent
ASIA - ASIE		
Qatar		
2016 (C)		
Total	1 151	100.0
Less than 1 - Moins de 1	422	36.7
1	122	10.6
2	112	9.7
3	63	5.5
4	57	5.0
5	166	14.4
6	87	7.6
7	46	4.0
8	23	2.0
9	35	3.0
Not stated - Inconnu	18	1.6
Republic of Korea - République de Corée[12]		
2016 (+C)		
Total	107 328	100.0
Less than 1 - Moins de 1	4 150	3.9
1	5 515	5.1
2	5 369	5.0
3	4 850	4.5
4	4 713	4.4
5	4 422	4.1
6	4 528	4.2
7	3 943	3.7
8	3 851	3.6
9	3 862	3.6
10 - 14	14 663	13.7
15 - 19	14 868	13.9
20 +	32 594	30.4
Singapore - Singapour		
2016 (+C)		
Total	7 207	100.0
Less than 5 - Moins de 5	1 452	20.1
5 - 9	2 153	29.9
10 - 14	1 246	17.3
15 - 19	857	11.9
20 +	1 499	20.8
State of Palestine - État de Palestine		
2015 (C)		
Total	8 179	100.0
Less than 1 - Moins de 1	3 837	46.9
1	1 197	14.6
2	596	7.3
3	393	4.8
4	319	3.9
5	244	3.0
6	170	2.1
7	140	1.7
8	134	1.6
9	105	1.3
10 - 14	397	4.9
15 - 19	251	3.1
20 +	396	4.8
Tajikistan - Tadjikistan		
2014 (+C)		
Total	9 037	100.0
Less than 1 - Moins de 1	1 200	13.3
1	859	9.5
2	870	9.6
3	928	10.3
4	767	8.5
5	685	7.6
6	589	6.5
7	376	4.2
8	253	2.8
9	207	2.3
10 - 14	647	7.2

Continent, country or area, year, code and duration of marriage (in years) / Continent, pays ou zone, année, code et durée du mariage (en années)	Number of divorces / Nombre de divorces	Per cent / Pour cent
ASIA - ASIE		
Tajikistan - Tadjikistan		
2014 (+C)		
15 - 19	437	4.8
20 +	952	10.5
Not stated - Inconnu	267	3.0
Turkey - Turquie[13]		
2014 (C)		
Total	130 913	100.0
Less than 1 - Moins de 1	4 727	3.6
1	13 222	10.1
2	10 401	7.9
3	8 544	6.5
4	7 706	5.9
5	7 217	5.5
6	6 865	5.2
7	6 255	4.8
8	5 733	4.4
9	5 113	3.9
10 - 14	19 237	14.7
15 - 19	15 048	11.5
20 +	20 575	15.7
Not stated - Inconnu	270	0.2
Uzbekistan - Ouzbékistan		
2015 (+C)		
Total	29 647	100.0
Less than 1 - Moins de 1	1 263	4.3
1	2 223	7.5
2	2 571	8.7
3	2 702	9.1
4	2 554	8.6
5	2 200	7.4
6	1 801	6.1
7	1 588	5.4
8	1 289	4.3
9	1 096	3.7
10 - 14	3 777	12.7
15 - 19	2 673	9.0
20 +	3 910	13.2
EUROPE		
Austria - Autriche[14]		
2012 (C)		
Total	17 006	100.0
Less than 1 - Moins de 1	282	1.7
1	818	4.8
2	982	5.8
3	959	5.6
4	912	5.4
5	892	5.2
6	954	5.6
7	919	5.4
8	825	4.9
9	594	3.5
10 - 14	2 643	15.5
15 - 19	2 272	13.4
20 +	3 954	23.3
Belarus - Bélarus		
2015 (C)		
Total	32 984	100.0
Less than 1 - Moins de 1	1 329	4.0
1	2 910	8.8
2	2 900	8.8
3	2 628	8.0
4	2 447	7.4
5 - 9	8 808	26.7

25. Divorces and percentage distribution by duration of marriage, latest available year: 2007 - 2016
Divorces et répartition des pourcentages selon la durée du mariage, dernière année disponible: 2007 - 2016 (continued - suite)

Continent, country or area, year, code and duration of marriage (in years) / Continent, pays ou zone, année, code et durée du mariage (en années)	Number of divorces / Nombre de divorces	Per cent / Pour cent
EUROPE		
Belarus - Bélarus		
2015 (C)		
10 - 14	4 334	13.1
15 - 19	2 899	8.8
20 +	4 729	14.3
Belgium - Belgique[15]		
2010 (C)		
Total	28 903	100.0
Less than 1 - Moins de 1	61	0.2
1	721	2.5
2	1 394	4.8
3	1 683	5.8
4	1 689	5.8
5	1 543	5.3
6	1 432	5.0
7	1 241	4.3
8	1 168	4.0
9	1 132	3.9
10 - 14	4 757	16.5
15 - 19	4 028	13.9
20 +	8 054	27.9
Bosnia and Herzegovina - Bosnie-Herzégovine		
2010 (C)		
Total	1 676	100.0
Less than 1 - Moins de 1	100	6.0
1	139	8.3
2	121	7.2
3	133	7.9
4	131	7.8
5	94	5.6
6	71	4.2
7	72	4.3
8	64	3.8
9	46	2.7
10 - 14	244	14.6
15 - 19	139	8.3
20 +	322	19.2
Bulgaria - Bulgarie[16]		
2015 (C)		
Total	10 483	100.0
Less than 1 - Moins de 1	152	1.4
1	311	3.0
2	392	3.7
3	377	3.6
4	378	3.6
5	418	4.0
6	451	4.3
7	446	4.3
8	428	4.1
9	416	4.0
10 - 14	1 656	15.8
15 - 19	1 542	14.7
20 +	3 516	33.5
Croatia - Croatie		
2015 (C)		
Total	6 010	100.0
Less than 1 - Moins de 1	79	1.3
1	160	2.7
2	281	4.7
3	284	4.7
4	264	4.4
5	294	4.9
6	305	5.1
7	273	4.5
8	258	4.3
9	237	3.9
Croatia - Croatie		
2015 (C)		
10 - 14	1 012	16.8
15 - 19	878	14.6
20 +	1 685	28.0
Czechia - Tchéquie		
2015 (C)		
Total	26 083	100.0
Less than 1 - Moins de 1	205	0.8
1	820	3.1
2	999	3.8
3	1 160	4.4
4	1 199	4.6
5	1 216	4.7
6	1 277	4.9
7	1 275	4.9
8	1 236	4.7
9	1 038	4.0
10 - 14	4 394	16.8
15 - 19	3 539	13.6
20 +	7 623	29.2
Not stated - Inconnu	102	0.4
Denmark - Danemark[17]		
2015 (C)		
Total	16 343	100.0
Less than 1 - Moins de 1	383	2.3
1	726	4.4
2	755	4.6
3	698	4.3
4	799	4.9
5	909	5.6
6	954	5.8
7	905	5.5
8	881	5.4
9	769	4.7
10 - 14	3 181	19.5
15 - 19	2 244	13.7
20 +	2 990	18.3
Not stated - Inconnu	149	0.9
Estonia - Estonie		
2015 (C)		
Total	3 382	100.0
Less than 1 - Moins de 1	111	3.3
1	195	5.8
2	220	6.5
3	222	6.6
4	168	5.0
5	149	4.4
6	157	4.6
7	180	5.3
8	150	4.4
9	126	3.7
10 - 14	466	13.8
15 - 19	297	8.8
20 +	931	27.5
Not stated - Inconnu	10	0.3
Faeroe Islands - Îles Féroé		
2015 (C)		
Total	79	100.0
Less than 1 - Moins de 1	-	0.0
1	2	2.5
2	-	0.0
3	3	3.8
4	3	3.8
5	3	3.8
6	5	6.3
7	2	2.5
8	3	3.8

25. Divorces and percentage distribution by duration of marriage, latest available year: 2007 - 2016
Divorces et répartition des pourcentages selon la durée du mariage, dernière année disponible: 2007 - 2016 (continued - suite)

Continent, country or area, year, code and duration of marriage (in years) Continent, pays ou zone, année, code et durée du mariage (en années)	Number of divorces Nombre de divorces	Per cent Pour cent	Continent, country or area, year, code and duration of marriage (in years) Continent, pays ou zone, année, code et durée du mariage (en années)	Number of divorces Nombre de divorces	Per cent Pour cent
EUROPE			**EUROPE**		
Faeroe Islands - Îles Féroé			Greece - Grèce		
2015 (C)			2010 (C)		
9	7	8.9	10 - 14	2 326	17.5
10 - 14	18	22.8	15 - 19	1 970	14.8
15 - 19	12	15.2	20 +	3 588	27.0
20 +	21	26.6	Hungary - Hongrie[7]		
Finland - Finlande[7]			2015 (C)		
2015 (C)			Total	20 315	100.0
Total	13 939	100.0	Less than 1 - Moins de 1	209	1.0
Less than 1 - Moins de 1	143	1.0	1	631	3.1
1	711	5.1	2	785	3.9
2	894	6.4	3	839	4.1
3	999	7.2	4	787	3.9
4	875	6.3	5	790	3.9
5	927	6.7	6	836	4.1
6	867	6.2	7	874	4.3
7	782	5.6	8	886	4.4
8	691	5.0	9	873	4.3
9	582	4.2	10 - 14	3 768	18.5
10 - 14	2 305	16.5	15 - 19	2 927	14.4
15 - 19	1 506	10.8	20 +	6 110	30.1
20 +	2 656	19.1	Iceland - Islande[18]		
Not stated - Inconnu	1	0.0	2011 (C)		
France			Total	516	100.0
2011 (C)			Less than 1 - Moins de 1	6	1.2
Total	129 802	100.0	1	16	3.1
Less than 1 - Moins de 1	158	0.1	2	20	3.9
1	1 468	1.1	3	37	7.2
2	3 489	2.7	4	36	7.0
3	5 045	3.9	5	38	7.4
4	6 173	4.8	6	28	5.4
5	6 788	5.2	7	20	3.9
6	6 914	5.3	8	33	6.4
7	6 488	5.0	9	16	3.1
8	6 088	4.7	10 - 14	101	19.6
9	5 573	4.3	15 - 19	63	12.2
10 - 14	25 093	19.3	20 +	100	19.4
15 - 19	17 840	13.7	Italy - Italie		
20 +	38 685	29.8	2015 (C)		
Germany - Allemagne			Total	82 469	100.0
2015 (C)			Less than 1 - Moins de 1	21	0.0
Total	163 335	100.0	1	152	0.2
Less than 1 - Moins de 1	19	0.0	2	495	0.6
1	1 020	0.6	3	1 038	1.3
2	5 140	3.1	4	1 741	2.1
3	7 184	4.4	5	2 419	2.9
4	6 324	3.9	6	3 227	3.9
5	8 321	5.1	7	3 577	4.3
6	8 592	5.3	8	3 355	4.1
7	8 233	5.0	9	3 239	3.9
8	7 698	4.7	10 - 14	15 814	19.2
9	7 209	4.4	15 - 19	13 434	16.3
10 - 14	31 109	19.0	20 +	33 433	40.5
15 - 19	24 621	15.1	Not stated - Inconnu	524	0.6
20 +	47 865	29.3	Latvia - Lettonie		
Greece - Grèce			2015 (C)		
2010 (C)			Total	5 151	100.0
Total	13 275	100.0	Less than 1 - Moins de 1	19	0.4
Less than 1 - Moins de 1	1	0.0	1	136	2.6
1	59	0.4	2	255	5.0
2	508	3.8	3	297	5.8
3	774	5.8	4	303	5.9
4	665	5.0	5	267	5.2
5	696	5.2	6	232	4.5
6	624	4.7	7	282	5.5
7	676	5.1	8	352	6.8
8	568	4.3	9	306	5.9
9	550	4.1			

25. Divorces and percentage distribution by duration of marriage, latest available year: 2007 - 2016
Divorces et répartition des pourcentages selon la durée du mariage, dernière année disponible: 2007 - 2016 (continued - suite)

Continent, country or area, year, code and duration of marriage (in years) Continent, pays ou zone, année, code et durée du mariage (en années)	Number of divorces Nombre de divorces	Per cent Pour cent	Continent, country or area, year, code and duration of marriage (in years) Continent, pays ou zone, année, code et durée du mariage (en années)	Number of divorces Nombre de divorces	Per cent Pour cent
EUROPE			EUROPE		
Latvia - Lettonie			Malta - Malte		
2015 (C)			2011 (C)		
10 - 14	720	14.0	15 - 19	4	9.5
15 - 19	467	9.1	20 +	21	50.0
20 +	1 515	29.4	Montenegro - Monténégro		
Liechtenstein[19]			2014 (C)		
2012* (C)			Total	584	100.0
Total	87	100.0	Less than 1 - Moins de 1	36	6.2
Less than 1 - Moins de 1	-	0.0	1	32	5.5
1	7	8.0	2	35	6.0
2	4	4.6	3	32	5.5
3	2	2.3	4	35	6.0
4	4	4.6	5	31	5.3
5	9	10.3	6	32	5.5
6	7	8.0	7	29	5.0
7	7	8.0	8	30	5.1
8	5	5.7	9	20	3.4
9	3	3.4	10 - 14	88	15.1
10 - 14	10	11.5	15 - 19	77	13.2
15 - 19	14	16.1	20 +	107	18.3
20 +	15	17.2	Netherlands - Pays-Bas[20]		
Lithuania - Lituanie			2015 (C)		
2015 (C)			Total	34 232	100.0
Total	9 371	100.0	Less than 1 - Moins de 1	331	1.0
Less than 1 - Moins de 1	110	1.2	1	1 016	3.0
1	449	4.8	2	1 450	4.2
2	578	6.2	3	1 593	4.7
3	520	5.5	4	1 731	5.1
4	454	4.8	5	1 685	4.9
5	447	4.8	6	1 694	4.9
6	499	5.3	7	1 568	4.6
7	516	5.5	8	1 368	4.0
8	440	4.7	9	1 279	3.7
9	366	3.9	10 - 14	6 066	17.7
10 - 14	1 215	13.0	15 - 19	5 008	14.6
15 - 19	1 044	11.1	20 +	9 443	27.6
20 +	2 733	29.2	Norway - Norvège[5]		
Luxembourg			2015 (C)		
2015 (C)			Total	9 793	100.0
Total	1 345	100.0	Less than 1 - Moins de 1	8	0.1
Less than 1 - Moins de 1	9	0.7	1	128	1.3
1	12	0.9	2	405	4.1
2	37	2.8	3	502	5.1
3	58	4.3	4	553	5.6
4	72	5.4	5	570	5.8
5	73	5.4	6	593	6.1
6	61	4.5	7	557	5.7
7	84	6.2	8	478	4.9
8	61	4.5	9	412	4.2
9	63	4.7	10 - 14	1 924	19.6
10 - 14	268	19.9	15 - 19	1 354	13.8
15 - 19	203	15.1	20 +	2 021	20.6
20 +	344	25.6	Not stated - Inconnu	288	2.9
Malta - Malte			Poland - Pologne		
2011 (C)			2015 (C)		
Total	42	100.0	Total	67 296	100.0
Less than 1 - Moins de 1	-	0.0	Less than 1 - Moins de 1	331	0.5
1	-	0.0	1	1 664	2.5
2	-	0.0	2	2 766	4.1
3	-	0.0	3	3 284	4.9
4	-	0.0	4	3 535	5.3
5	-	0.0	5	3 944	5.9
6	1	2.4	6	3 986	5.9
7	1	2.4	7	3 642	5.4
8	-	0.0	8	3 124	4.6
9	-	0.0	9	2 637	3.9
10 - 14	15	35.7	10 - 14	10 442	15.5

Continent, country or area, year, code and duration of marriage (in years) — Continent, pays ou zone, année, code et durée du mariage (en années)	Number of divorces — Nombre de divorces	Per cent — Pour cent
EUROPE		
Poland - Pologne		
2015 (C)		
15 - 19	9 154	13.6
20 +	18 787	27.9
Portugal[21]		
2013 (C)		
Total	22 525	100.0
Less than 1 - Moins de 1	388	1.7
1	595	2.6
2	746	3.3
3	741	3.3
4	873	3.9
5	977	4.3
6	960	4.3
7	840	3.7
8	835	3.7
9	777	3.4
10 - 14	4 116	18.3
15 - 19	3 428	15.2
20 +	7 249	32.2
Republic of Moldova - République de Moldova		
2012 (C)		
Total	10 637	100.0
Less than 1 - Moins de 1	307	2.9
1	632	5.9
2	763	7.2
3	766	7.2
4	799	7.5
5	708	6.7
6	636	6.0
7	499	4.7
8	412	3.9
9	372	3.5
10 - 14	1 335	12.6
15 - 19	1 219	11.5
20 +	2 189	20.6
Romania - Roumanie		
2015 (C)		
Total	31 527	100.0
Less than 1 - Moins de 1	678	2.2
1	1 261	4.0
2	1 550	4.9
3	1 539	4.9
4	1 554	4.9
5	1 738	5.5
6	1 780	5.6
7	1 710	5.4
8	1 771	5.6
9	1 458	4.6
10 - 14	5 446	17.3
15 - 19	4 003	12.7
20 +	7 039	22.3
Russian Federation - Fédération de Russie		
2011 (C)		
Total	669 376	100.0
Less than 1 - Moins de 1	33 567	5.0
1	50 768	7.6
2	58 099	8.7
3	57 871	8.6
4	50 042	7.5
5 - 9	165 467	24.7
10 - 14	82 645	12.3
15 - 19	60 911	9.1
20 +	109 624	16.4
Not stated - Inconnu	382	0.1
EUROPE		
San Marino - Saint-Marin		
2014 (+C)		
Total	51	100.0
Less than 1 - Moins de 1	-	0.0
1	-	0.0
2	-	0.0
3	1	2.0
4	3	5.9
5	2	3.9
6	3	5.9
7	3	5.9
8	1	2.0
9	3	5.9
10 - 14	7	13.7
15 - 19	9	17.6
20 +	19	37.3
Serbia - Serbie[22]		
2014 (+C)		
Total	7 614	100.0
Less than 1 - Moins de 1	284	3.7
1	397	5.2
2	390	5.1
3	350	4.6
4	360	4.7
5	359	4.7
6	337	4.4
7	293	3.8
8	315	4.1
9	297	3.9
10 - 14	1 329	17.5
15 - 19	970	12.7
20 +	1 933	25.4
Slovakia - Slovaquie		
2015 (C)		
Total	9 786	100.0
Less than 1 - Moins de 1	51	0.5
1	229	2.3
2	341	3.5
3	389	4.0
4	372	3.8
5	416	4.3
6	381	3.9
7	409	4.2
8	433	4.4
9	360	3.7
10 - 14	1 582	16.2
15 - 19	1 574	16.1
20 +	3 249	33.2
Slovenia - Slovénie		
2015 (C)		
Total	2 432	100.0
Less than 1 - Moins de 1	32	1.3
1	97	4.0
2	129	5.3
3	115	4.7
4	118	4.9
5	103	4.2
6	108	4.4
7	123	5.1
8	78	3.2
9	74	3.0
10 - 14	318	13.1
15 - 19	306	12.6
20 +	831	34.2
Spain - Espagne		
2015 (C)		
Total	96 562	100.0
Less than 1 - Moins de 1	838	0.9

Continent, country or area, year, code and duration of marriage (in years) Continent, pays ou zone, année, code et durée du mariage (en années)	Number of divorces Nombre de divorces	Per cent Pour cent

EUROPE

Spain - Espagne
2015 (C)

1	2 141	2.2
2	2 915	3.0
3	3 850	4.0
4	4 159	4.3
5	4 439	4.6
6	4 743	4.9
7	4 578	4.7
8	4 297	4.4
9	3 866	4.0
10 - 14	16 656	17.2
15 - 19	13 648	14.1
20 +	30 432	31.5

Sweden - Suède[5]
2015 (C)

Total	24 876	100.0
Less than 1 - Moins de 1	543	2.2
1	1 439	5.8
2	1 862	7.5
3	1 945	7.8
4	1 953	7.9
5	1 768	7.1
6	1 539	6.2
7	1 329	5.3
8	1 156	4.6
9	1 021	4.1
10 - 14	3 734	15.0
15 - 19	2 346	9.4
20 +	3 957	15.9
Not stated - Inconnu	284	1.1

Switzerland - Suisse
2015 (U)

Total	16 982	100.0
Less than 1 - Moins de 1	132	0.8
1	415	2.4
2	496	2.9
3	703	4.1
4	740	4.4
5	863	5.1
6	970	5.7
7	880	5.2
8	832	4.9
9	788	4.6
10 - 14	3 051	18.0
15 - 19	2 352	13.8
20 +	4 158	24.5
Not stated - Inconnu	602	3.5

TFYR of Macedonia - L'ex-R. y. de Macédoine
2014 (C)

Total	2 210	100.0
Less than 1 - Moins de 1	103	4.7
1	175	7.9
2	154	7.0
3	136	6.2
4	122	5.5
5	129	5.8
6	103	4.7
7	99	4.5
8	71	3.2
9	97	4.4
10 - 14	316	14.3
15 - 19	263	11.9
20 +	442	20.0

EUROPE

Ukraine[3]
2012 (+C)

Total	49 807	100.0
Less than 1 - Moins de 1	3 738	7.5
1	4 609	9.3
2	3 723	7.5
3	3 217	6.5
4	3 257	6.5
5 - 9	9 458	19.0
10 - 14	4 826	9.7
15 - 19	4 219	8.5
20 +	12 760	25.6

United Kingdom of Great Britain and Northern Ireland - Royaume-Uni de Grande-Bretagne et d'Irlande du Nord[23]
2011 (C)

Total	129 764	100.0
Less than 1 - Moins de 1	38	0.0
1	1 863	1.4
2	4 348	3.4
3	6 343	4.9
4	7 180	5.5
5	7 245	5.6
6	7 670	5.9
7	7 771	6.0
8	6 910	5.3
9	5 989	4.6
10 - 14	24 231	18.7
15 - 19	17 386	13.4
20 +	32 790	25.3

OCEANIA - OCÉANIE

Australia - Australie
2015 (C)

Total	48 517	100.0
Less than 1 - Moins de 1	-	0.0
1	593	1.2
2	2 059	4.2
3	2 765	5.7
4	3 294	6.8
5	2 866	5.9
6	2 592	5.3
7	2 302	4.7
8	2 204	4.5
9	1 999	4.1
10 - 14	7 820	16.1
15 - 19	6 438	13.3
20 +	13 583	28.0
Not stated - Inconnu	2	0.0

New Zealand - Nouvelle-Zélande[24]
2016 (+C)

Total	8 169	100.0
Less than 5 - Moins de 5	906	11.1
5	399	4.9
6	387	4.7
7	372	4.6
8	411	5.0
9	369	4.5
10 - 14	1 518	18.6
15 - 19	1 239	15.2
20 +	2 571	31.5

25. Divorces and percentage distribution by duration of marriage, latest available year: 2007 - 2016
Divorces et répartition des pourcentages selon la durée du mariage, dernière année disponible: 2007 - 2016 (continued - suite)

Continent, country or area, year, code and duration of marriage (in years) / Continent, pays ou zone, année, code et durée du mariage (en années)	Number of divorces / Nombre de divorces	Per cent / Pour cent
OCEANIA - OCÉANIE		
Northern Mariana Islands - Îles Mariannes septentrionales[25]		
2007 (U)		
Total	160	100.0
Less than 1 - Moins de 1	2	1.3
1	3	1.9
2	5	3.1
3	9	5.6
4	4	2.5
5	14	8.8
6	11	6.9
7	9	5.6
8	6	3.8
9	8	5.0
10 - 14	34	21.3
15 - 19	20	12.5
20 +	35	21.9

Continent, country or area, year, code and duration of marriage (in years) / Continent, pays ou zone, année, code et durée du mariage (en années)	Number of divorces / Nombre de divorces	Per cent / Pour cent
OCEANIA - OCÉANIE		
Samoa		
2009 (U)		
Total	48	100.0
Less than 1 - Moins de 1	-	0.0
1	-	0.0
2	-	0.0
3	2	4.2
4	-	0.0
5	1	2.1
6	2	4.2
7	3	6.3
8	2	4.2
9	2	4.2
10 - 14	4	8.3
15 - 19	10	20.8
20 +	7	14.6
Not stated - Inconnu	15	31.3

FOOTNOTES - NOTES

Italics: estimates which are less reliable. - Italiques: estimations moins sûres.

* Provisional. - Données provisoires.

'Code' indicates the source of data, as follows:
C - Civil registration, estimated over 90% complete
U - Civil registration, estimated less than 90% complete
| - Other source, estimated reliable
+ - Data tabulated by date of registration rather than occurence.
... - Information not available

Le 'Code' indique la source des données, comme suit:
C - Registres de l'état civil considérés complets à 90 p. 100 au moins.
U - Registres de l'état civil qui ne sont pas considérés complets à 90 p. 100 au moins.
| - Autre source, considérée pas douteuses.
+ - Données exploitées selon la date de l'enregistrement et non la date de l'événement.
... - Information non disponible.

[1] Including 'revocable divorces' (among Muslim population), which approximate legal separations. - Y compris les 'divorces révocables' (parmi la population musulmane), qui sont plus au moins l'équivalent des séparations légales.
[2] Excludes the islands of St. Brandon and Agalega. - Non compris les îles St. Brandon et Agalega.
[3] Unrevised data. - Les données n'ont pas été révisées.
[4] Because of rounding, totals are not in all cases the sum of the respective components. - Les chiffres étant arrondis, les totaux ne correspondent pas toujours rigoureusement à la somme des composants respectifs.
[5] Including same sex divorces. - Y compris les divorces entre conjoints du même sexe.
[6] Excludes nomadic Indian tribes. - Non compris les tribus d'Indiens nomades.
[7] Including annulments. - Y compris les annulations.
[8] Data refer to government controlled areas. - Les données se rapportent aux zones contrôlées par le Gouvernement.
[9] Data refer to the Iranian Year which begins on 21 March and ends on 20 March of the following year. - Les données concernent l'année iranienne, qui commence le 21 mars et se termine le 20 mars de l'année suivante.
[10] Includes data for East Jerusalem and Israeli residents in certain other territories under occupation by Israeli military forces since June 1967. - Y compris les données pour Jérusalem-Est et les résidents israéliens dans certains autres territoires occupés depuis 1967 par les forces armées israéliennes.

[11] Data refer to Japanese nationals in Japan only. - Les données se raportent aux nationaux japonais au Japon seulement.
[12] Excluding alien armed forces, civilian aliens employed by armed forces, and foreign diplomatic personnel and their dependants. - Non compris les militaires étrangers, les civils étrangers employés par les forces armées ni le personnel diplomatique étranger et les membres de leur famille les accompagnant.
[13] Data from MERNIS (Central Population Administrative System). - Données de MERNIS (Système central de données démographiques).
[14] Excluding aliens temporarily in the area. - Non compris les étrangers se trouvant temporairement dans le territoire.
[15] Including armed forces stationed outside the country, but excluding alien armed forces stationed in the area. - Y compris les militaires nationaux hors du pays, mais non compris les militaires étrangers en garnison sur le territoire.
[16] Including annulments. Including nationals outside the country, but excluding foreigners in the country. - Y compris les annulations. Y compris les nationaux à l'étranger, mais non compris les étrangers sur le territoire.
[17] Excluding Faeroe Islands and Greenland shown separately, if available. - Non compris les Îles Féroé et le Groenland, qui font l'objet de rubriques distinctes, si disponible.
[18] Data refer to common residence before divorce. - Données se rapportant à la résidence commune avant le divorce.
[19] Data refer to divorces by residence of the husband. - Les données concernent les divorces selon la résidence du mari.
[20] Based on the general office for civil registration. Including same sex divorces. - Données provenant des services généraux d'état civil. Y compris les divorces entre conjoints du même sexe.
[21] Data refer to resident spouses only. - Les données concernent uniquement les conjoints résidents.
[22] Excludes data for Kosovo and Metohia. - Sans les données pour le Kosovo et Metohie.
[23] Excluding Channel Islands (Guernsey and Jersey) and Isle of Man, shown separately, if available. - Non compris les îles Anglo-Normandes (Guernesey et Jersey) et l'île de Man, qui font l'objet de rubriques distinctes, si disponible.
[24] Random rounding to base 3 is applied in this table as a confidentiality measure. - Les chiffres sont arrondis à la base 3 de manière aléatoire, pour des raisons de confidentialité.
[25] Data refer to the islands of Saipan, Tinian and Rota only. - Les données se réfèrent uniquement aux îles de Saipan, Tinian et Rota.

Continent and country or area Continent et pays ou zone	Population estimates (in thousands) - Estimations de population (en milliers)									
	2007	2008	2009	2010	2011	2012	2013	2014	2015	2016

AFRICA - AFRIQUE

	2007	2008	2009	2010	2011	2012	2013	2014	2015	2016
Algeria - Algérie	34 300	34 861	35 466	36 118	36 820	37 566	38 339	39 113	39 872	40 606
Angola	20 998	21 759	22 550	23 369	24 219	25 096	25 998	26 920	27 859	28 813
Benin - Bénin	8 455	8 697	8 945	9 199	9 461	9 729	10 004	10 287	10 576	10 872
Botswana	1 914	1 946	1 980	2 015	2 051	2 089	2 129	2 169	2 209	2 250
Burkina Faso	14 252	14 690	15 141	15 605	16 082	16 571	17 073	17 586	18 111	18 646
Burundi	7 940	8 212	8 489	8 767	9 044	9 320	9 600	9 892	10 199	10 524
Cabo Verde	486	492	497	502	508	514	520	526	533	540
Cameroon - Cameroun	18 395	18 907	19 433	19 970	20 520	21 082	21 656	22 240	22 835	23 439
Central African Republic - République centrafricaine	4 276	4 345	4 404	4 449	4 476	4 490	4 500	4 515	4 546	4 595
Chad - Tchad	10 776	11 134	11 503	11 887	12 289	12 705	13 134	13 569	14 009	14 453
Comoros - Comores	642	657	673	690	707	724	742	759	777	796
Congo	3 976	4 115	4 254	4 387	4 513	4 633	4 751	4 871	4 996	5 126
Côte d'Ivoire	19 086	19 498	19 936	20 401	20 895	21 419	21 966	22 531	23 108	23 696
Democratic Republic of the Congo - République démocratique du Congo	58 418	60 374	62 409	64 523	66 714	68 979	71 316	73 723	76 197	78 736
Djibouti	809	823	837	851	866	881	897	912	927	942
Egypt - Égypte	79 537	80 954	82 465	84 108	85 898	87 813	89 807	91 813	93 778	95 689
Equatorial Guinea - Guinée équatoriale	829	868	909	951	994	1 039	1 084	1 129	1 175	1 221
Eritrea - Érythrée	4 153	4 233	4 310	4 391	4 475	4 561	4 651	4 746	4 847	4 955
Ethiopia - Éthiopie	81 000	83 185	85 416	87 703	90 047	92 444	94 888	97 367	99 873	102 403
Gabon	1 489	1 536	1 587	1 640	1 697	1 757	1 817	1 876	1 930	1 980
Gambia - Gambie	1 539	1 589	1 640	1 692	1 746	1 802	1 859	1 918	1 978	2 039
Ghana	22 700	23 299	23 904	24 512	25 122	25 733	26 346	26 963	27 583	28 207
Guinea - Guinée	10 097	10 323	10 557	10 794	11 035	11 281	11 537	11 806	12 092	12 396
Guinea-Bissau - Guinée-Bissau	1 446	1 481	1 517	1 556	1 596	1 638	1 681	1 726	1 771	1 816
Kenya	38 086	39 148	40 237	41 350	42 487	43 647	44 827	46 024	47 236	48 462
Lesotho	1 982	2 000	2 019	2 041	2 064	2 090	2 117	2 146	2 175	2 204
Liberia - Libéria	3 513	3 663	3 812	3 948	4 070	4 182	4 286	4 391	4 500	4 614
Libya - Libye	5 970	6 053	6 121	6 169	6 194	6 198	6 196	6 204	6 235	6 293
Madagascar	19 434	19 996	20 569	21 152	21 744	22 347	22 961	23 590	24 234	24 895
Malawi	13 841	14 271	14 715	15 167	15 628	16 097	16 577	17 069	17 574	18 092
Mali	13 676	14 138	14 607	15 075	15 541	16 007	16 478	16 963	17 468	17 995
Mauritania - Mauritanie	3 313	3 408	3 506	3 610	3 718	3 830	3 946	4 064	4 182	4 301
Mauritius - Maurice[1]	1 234	1 239	1 244	1 248	1 251	1 253	1 255	1 257	1 259	1 262
Mayotte	190	196	203	209	215	221	227	234	240	246
Morocco - Maroc	31 226	31 597	31 990	32 410	32 859	33 334	33 825	34 318	34 803	35 277
Mozambique	22 188	22 847	23 524	24 221	24 939	25 677	26 434	27 212	28 011	28 829
Namibia - Namibie	2 080	2 106	2 137	2 173	2 216	2 264	2 317	2 371	2 426	2 480
Niger	14 668	15 229	15 814	16 426	17 065	17 732	18 426	19 148	19 897	20 673
Nigeria - Nigéria	146 417	150 347	154 402	158 578	162 877	167 297	171 829	176 461	181 182	185 990
Republic of South Sudan - République de Soudan du Sud	8 857	9 263	9 671	10 067	10 449	10 818	11 177	11 531	11 882	12 231
Reunion - Réunion	809	816	824	831	837	844	850	857	863	870
Rwanda	9 447	9 708	9 977	10 247	10 516	10 789	11 065	11 345	11 630	11 918
Sao Tome and Principe - Sao Tomé-et-Principe	163	167	171	175	179	183	187	191	196	200
Senegal - Sénégal	11 874	12 204	12 551	12 916	13 301	13 704	14 120	14 546	14 977	15 412
Seychelles	90	91	91	91	92	92	93	93	94	94
Sierra Leone	6 015	6 165	6 310	6 459	6 612	6 766	6 922	7 079	7 237	7 396
Somalia - Somalie	11 039	11 369	11 708	12 053	12 405	12 764	13 132	13 513	13 908	14 318
South Africa - Afrique du Sud	49 887	50 412	50 971	51 585	52 264	52 998	53 767	54 540	55 291	56 015
Sudan - Soudan	32 283	32 955	33 651	34 386	35 167	35 990	36 850	37 738	38 648	39 579
Swaziland	1 138	1 159	1 181	1 203	1 225	1 248	1 271	1 295	1 319	1 343
Togo	5 997	6 162	6 330	6 503	6 679	6 859	7 043	7 229	7 417	7 606
Tunisia - Tunisie	10 298	10 407	10 522	10 640	10 761	10 887	11 015	11 144	11 274	11 403
Uganda - Ouganda	30 590	31 664	32 772	33 915	35 094	36 307	37 554	38 833	40 145	41 488
United Republic of Tanzania - République Unie de Tanzanie[2]	41 924	43 270	44 664	46 099	47 571	49 083	50 637	52 235	53 880	55 572
Western Sahara - Sahara occidental	462	469	474	480	488	496	505	515	526	539
Zambia - Zambie	12 726	13 083	13 456	13 850	14 265	14 700	15 153	15 621	16 101	16 591
Zimbabwe	13 330	13 558	13 811	14 086	14 387	14 711	15 055	15 412	15 777	16 150

AMERICA, NORTH - AMÉRIQUE DU NORD

	2007	2008	2009	2010	2011	2012	2013	2014	2015	2016
Anguilla	13	13	14	14	14	14	14	14	15	15
Antigua and Barbuda - Antigua-et-Barbuda	91	92	94	95	96	97	98	99	100	101
Aruba	101	101	101	102	102	103	103	104	104	105
Bahamas	342	349	355	361	367	372	377	382	387	391
Barbados - Barbade	276	277	278	280	281	282	283	283	284	285

Annex I: Mid-year population, United Nations estimates: 2007 - 2016
Annexe I : Population au milieu de l'année, estimations des Nations Unies : 2007 - 2016 (continued - suite)

Continent and country or area / Continent et pays ou zone	Population estimates (in thousands) - Estimations de population (en milliers)									
	2007	2008	2009	2010	2011	2012	2013	2014	2015	2016

AMERICA, NORTH - AMÉRIQUE DU NORD

	2007	2008	2009	2010	2011	2012	2013	2014	2015	2016
Belize	298	306	314	322	329	337	344	352	359	367
Bermuda - Bermudes	65	65	64	64	64	63	63	62	62	62
Bonaire, Saba and Sint Eustatius - Bonaire, Saba et Saint-Eustache	17	18	20	21	22	23	24	24	25	25
British Virgin Islands - Îles Vierges britanniques	25	26	26	27	28	29	29	30	30	31
Canada	33 020	33 405	33 790	34 169	34 539	34 901	35 255	35 605	35 950	36 290
Cayman Islands - Îles Caïmanes	51	53	54	56	57	58	58	59	60	61
Costa Rica	4 369	4 430	4 488	4 545	4 600	4 654	4 706	4 758	4 808	4 857
Cuba	11 304	11 310	11 319	11 333	11 355	11 382	11 412	11 440	11 461	11 476
Curaçao	135	140	144	148	151	153	155	157	158	159
Dominica - Dominique	71	71	71	71	72	72	72	73	73	74
Dominican Republic - République dominicaine	9 504	9 637	9 768	9 898	10 027	10 155	10 281	10 406	10 528	10 649
El Salvador	6 083	6 110	6 137	6 165	6 193	6 221	6 251	6 281	6 312	6 345
Greenland - Groenland	57	57	57	57	57	56	56	56	56	56
Grenada - Grenade	104	104	104	105	105	105	106	106	107	107
Guadeloupe[3]	445	447	449	451	451	452	451	451	450	450
Guatemala	13 700	14 006	14 316	14 630	14 949	15 271	15 596	15 924	16 252	16 582
Haiti - Haïti	9 557	9 705	9 853	10 000	10 145	10 289	10 432	10 572	10 711	10 847
Honduras	7 708	7 873	8 035	8 195	8 352	8 506	8 658	8 809	8 961	9 113
Jamaica - Jamaïque	2 775	2 790	2 804	2 817	2 829	2 841	2 852	2 862	2 872	2 881
Martinique	398	397	396	395	393	391	389	387	386	385
Mexico - Mexique	111 836	113 662	115 505	117 319	119 090	120 828	122 536	124 222	125 891	127 540
Montserrat	5	5	5	5	5	5	5	5	5	5
Nicaragua	5 522	5 595	5 667	5 738	5 808	5 877	5 946	6 014	6 082	6 150
Panama	3 454	3 516	3 579	3 643	3 708	3 773	3 838	3 904	3 969	4 034
Puerto Rico - Porto Rico	3 745	3 736	3 726	3 717	3 707	3 698	3 689	3 681	3 674	3 668
Saint Kitts and Nevis - Saint-Kitts-et-Nevis	50	50	51	51	52	53	53	54	54	55
Saint Lucia - Sainte-Lucie	167	169	171	173	174	175	176	176	177	178
Saint Pierre and Miquelon - Saint Pierre-et-Miquelon	6	6	6	6	6	6	6	6	6	6
Saint Vincent and the Grenadines - Saint-Vincent-et-les Grenadines	109	109	109	109	109	109	109	109	109	110
Sint Maarten (Dutch part) - Saint-Martin (partie néerlandaise)	32	32	33	33	34	35	36	38	39	40
Trinidad and Tobago - Trinité-et-Tobago	1 309	1 315	1 322	1 328	1 335	1 342	1 348	1 354	1 360	1 365
Turks and Caicos Islands - Îles Turques et Caïques	29	29	30	31	32	32	33	34	34	35
United States of America - États-Unis d'Amérique	300 595	303 374	306 076	308 641	311 051	313 335	315 537	317 719	319 929	322 180
United States Virgin Islands - Îles Vierges américaines	107	107	106	106	106	106	105	105	105	105

AMERICA, SOUTH - AMÉRIQUE DU SUD

	2007	2008	2009	2010	2011	2012	2013	2014	2015	2016
Argentina - Argentine	39 970	40 382	40 799	41 224	41 657	42 097	42 540	42 982	43 418	43 847
Bolivia (Plurinational State of) - Bolivie (État plurinational de)	9 441	9 600	9 759	9 918	10 078	10 239	10 400	10 562	10 725	10 888
Brazil - Brésil	191 027	192 979	194 896	196 796	198 687	200 561	202 409	204 213	205 962	207 653
Chile - Chili	16 492	16 662	16 829	16 993	17 153	17 310	17 463	17 614	17 763	17 910
Colombia - Colombie	44 375	44 902	45 416	45 918	46 407	46 881	47 343	47 792	48 229	48 653
Ecuador - Équateur	14 205	14 448	14 691	14 935	15 177	15 420	15 662	15 903	16 144	16 385
Falkland Islands (Malvinas) - Îles Falkland (Malvinas)	3	3	3	3	3	3	3	3	3	3
French Guiana - Guyane française	217	222	228	234	241	247	255	262	269	276
Guyana	748	746	746	747	749	753	758	763	769	773
Paraguay	5 966	6 047	6 128	6 210	6 294	6 379	6 466	6 553	6 639	6 725
Peru - Pérou	28 293	28 642	29 002	29 374	29 760	30 159	30 566	30 973	31 377	31 774
Suriname	510	515	521	526	532	537	543	548	553	558
Uruguay	3 340	3 351	3 363	3 374	3 386	3 397	3 408	3 420	3 432	3 444
Venezuela (Bolivarian Republic of) - Venezuela (République bolivarienne du)	27 692	28 142	28 587	29 028	29 463	29 893	30 318	30 738	31 155	31 568

ASIA - ASIE

	2007	2008	2009	2010	2011	2012	2013	2014	2015	2016
Afghanistan	26 617	27 294	28 004	28 803	29 709	30 697	31 732	32 758	33 736	34 656
Armenia - Arménie	2 933	2 908	2 889	2 877	2 876	2 882	2 894	2 906	2 917	2 925
Azerbaijan - Azerbaïdjan[4]	8 724	8 822	8 924	9 032	9 146	9 265	9 385	9 504	9 617	9 725
Bahrain - Bahreïn	1 036	1 115	1 185	1 241	1 278	1 300	1 315	1 336	1 372	1 425
Bangladesh	147 139	148 806	150 455	152 149	153 912	155 727	157 571	159 405	161 201	162 952
Bhutan - Bhoutan	687	701	714	728	741	753	765	776	787	798
Brunei Darussalam - Brunéi Darussalam	375	379	384	389	394	400	406	412	418	423

Continent and country or area Continent et pays ou zone	Population estimates (in thousands) - Estimations de population (en milliers)									
	2007	2008	2009	2010	2011	2012	2013	2014	2015	2016
ASIA - ASIE										
Cambodia - Cambodge	13 677	13 881	14 090	14 309	14 538	14 777	15 023	15 271	15 518	15 762
China - Chine[5]	1 336 801	1 344 415	1 352 068	1 359 755	1 367 480	1 375 199	1 382 793	1 390 110	1 397 029	1 403 500
China, Hong Kong SAR - Chine, Hong Kong RAS	6 898	6 940	6 983	7 025	7 066	7 106	7 149	7 195	7 246	7 303
China, Macao SAR - Chine, Macao RAS	504	514	525	537	549	563	576	589	601	612
Cyprus - Chypre[6]	1 064	1 082	1 098	1 113	1 125	1 135	1 144	1 152	1 161	1 170
Democratic People's Republic of Korea - République populaire démocratique de Corée	24 203	24 335	24 463	24 592	24 722	24 854	24 986	25 116	25 244	25 369
Georgia - Géorgie[7]	4 391	4 341	4 288	4 232	4 171	4 108	4 046	3 992	3 952	3 925
India - Inde	1 179 681	1 197 147	1 214 270	1 230 981	1 247 236	1 263 066	1 278 562	1 293 859	1 309 054	1 324 171
Indonesia - Indonésie	232 989	236 159	239 340	242 524	245 708	248 883	252 032	255 131	258 162	261 115
Iran (Islamic Republic of) - Iran (République islamique d')	72 031	72 846	73 688	74 568	75 492	76 454	77 435	78 411	79 360	80 277
Iraq	28 390	29 111	29 895	30 763	31 727	32 777	33 883	35 006	36 116	37 203
Israel - Israël	6 923	7 097	7 268	7 426	7 569	7 699	7 821	7 941	8 065	8 192
Japan - Japon	128 505	128 551	128 567	128 552	128 505	128 426	128 313	128 163	127 975	127 749
Jordan - Jordanie	6 193	6 490	6 821	7 182	7 575	7 993	8 413	8 809	9 159	9 456
Kazakhstan	15 841	16 001	16 184	16 399	16 647	16 921	17 207	17 488	17 750	17 988
Kuwait - Koweït	2 503	2 652	2 819	2 998	3 191	3 396	3 598	3 782	3 936	4 053
Kyrgyzstan - Kirghizstan	5 190	5 262	5 341	5 422	5 507	5 594	5 684	5 775	5 865	5 956
Lao People's Democratic Republic - République démocratique populaire lao	5 950	6 052	6 152	6 246	6 333	6 415	6 495	6 576	6 664	6 758
Lebanon - Liban	4 086	4 111	4 183	4 337	4 588	4 916	5 276	5 603	5 851	6 007
Malaysia - Malaisie[8]	26 626	27 111	27 605	28 112	28 635	29 170	29 707	30 228	30 723	31 187
Maldives	336	345	355	365	375	386	397	408	418	428
Mongolia - Mongolie	2 592	2 628	2 668	2 713	2 762	2 814	2 869	2 924	2 977	3 027
Myanmar	49 172	49 480	49 801	50 156	50 553	50 987	51 448	51 924	52 404	52 885
Nepal - Népal	26 215	26 476	26 741	27 023	27 327	27 650	27 985	28 323	28 656	28 983
Oman	2 663	2 759	2 883	3 041	3 237	3 465	3 711	3 961	4 200	4 425
Pakistan	160 333	163 645	167 050	170 560	174 184	177 912	181 713	185 546	189 381	193 203
Philippines	89 293	90 752	92 221	93 727	95 278	96 867	98 481	100 102	101 716	103 320
Qatar	1 190	1 389	1 591	1 780	1 952	2 110	2 250	2 374	2 482	2 570
Republic of Korea - République de Corée	49 062	49 219	49 379	49 553	49 745	49 952	50 169	50 386	50 594	50 792
Saudi Arabia - Arabie saoudite	25 253	25 941	26 661	27 426	28 238	29 086	29 944	30 777	31 557	32 276
Singapore - Singapour	4 733	4 851	4 966	5 074	5 176	5 271	5 361	5 448	5 535	5 622
Sri Lanka	19 811	19 946	20 075	20 198	20 315	20 425	20 527	20 624	20 714	20 798
State of Palestine - État de Palestine[9]	3 752	3 852	3 958	4 067	4 179	4 295	4 415	4 537	4 663	4 791
Syrian Arab Republic - République arabe syrienne	19 633	20 325	20 825	21 019	20 864	20 421	19 809	19 203	18 735	18 430
Tajikistan - Tadjikistan	7 152	7 310	7 473	7 642	7 816	7 995	8 178	8 363	8 549	8 735
Thailand - Thaïlande	66 196	66 546	66 882	67 209	67 530	67 844	68 143	68 417	68 658	68 864
Timor-Leste	1 065	1 078	1 092	1 110	1 132	1 157	1 184	1 213	1 241	1 269
Turkey - Turquie	69 597	70 440	71 339	72 327	73 409	74 570	75 787	77 031	78 271	79 512
Turkmenistan - Turkménistan	4 870	4 936	5 008	5 087	5 174	5 268	5 366	5 466	5 565	5 663
United Arab Emirates - Émirats arabes unis	6 044	6 894	7 666	8 271	8 672	8 900	9 006	9 071	9 154	9 270
Uzbekistan - Ouzbékistan	27 292	27 716	28 155	28 606	29 068	29 541	30 020	30 500	30 976	31 447
Viet Nam	85 890	86 708	87 565	88 473	89 437	90 452	91 498	92 545	93 572	94 569
Yemen - Yémen	21 752	22 356	22 975	23 607	24 252	24 910	25 576	26 246	26 916	27 584
EUROPE										
Albania - Albanie	3 024	2 992	2 963	2 941	2 927	2 920	2 919	2 921	2 923	2 926
Andorra - Andorre	83	84	84	84	84	82	81	79	78	77
Austria - Autriche	8 312	8 338	8 370	8 410	8 460	8 518	8 578	8 633	8 679	8 712
Belarus - Bélarus	9 537	9 507	9 486	9 473	9 469	9 472	9 479	9 485	9 486	9 480
Belgium - Belgique	10 698	10 779	10 860	10 939	11 013	11 084	11 152	11 219	11 288	11 358
Bosnia and Herzegovina - Bosnie-Herzégovine	3 774	3 764	3 747	3 722	3 689	3 648	3 605	3 566	3 536	3 517
Bulgaria - Bulgarie	7 567	7 510	7 456	7 405	7 356	7 310	7 266	7 222	7 177	7 131
Croatia - Croatie	4 362	4 352	4 341	4 328	4 313	4 297	4 278	4 258	4 236	4 213
Czechia - Tchéquie	10 357	10 424	10 487	10 536	10 569	10 587	10 594	10 599	10 604	10 611
Denmark - Danemark	5 470	5 498	5 526	5 555	5 583	5 611	5 638	5 664	5 689	5 712
Estonia - Estonie	1 344	1 340	1 336	1 332	1 328	1 325	1 322	1 318	1 315	1 312
Faeroe Islands - Îles Féroé	48	48	49	49	49	49	49	49	49	49
Finland - Finlande[10]	5 298	5 320	5 343	5 366	5 389	5 413	5 437	5 460	5 482	5 503
France	61 961	62 330	62 688	63 027	63 344	63 640	63 920	64 191	64 457	64 721
Germany - Allemagne	81 344	81 131	80 966	80 895	80 934	81 066	81 265	81 490	81 708	81 915
Gibraltar	33	33	33	33	33	34	34	34	34	34
Greece - Grèce	11 381	11 420	11 444	11 446	11 423	11 378	11 321	11 265	11 218	11 184
Holy See - Saint-Siège	1	1	1	1	1	1	1	1	1	1
Hungary - Hongrie	10 024	9 991	9 959	9 928	9 898	9 870	9 842	9 813	9 784	9 753

Continent and country or area / Continent et pays ou zone	Population estimates (in thousands) - Estimations de population (en milliers)									
	2007	2008	2009	2010	2011	2012	2013	2014	2015	2016
EUROPE										
Iceland - Islande	305	311	316	320	323	326	327	328	330	332
Ireland - Irlande	4 398	4 490	4 568	4 627	4 663	4 678	4 682	4 686	4 700	4 726
Isle of Man - Île de Man	78	79	79	80	81	81	82	83	83	84
Italy - Italie	59 314	59 502	59 642	59 730	59 760	59 734	59 668	59 586	59 504	59 430
Latvia - Lettonie	2 199	2 172	2 145	2 119	2 092	2 066	2 041	2 016	1 993	1 971
Liechtenstein	35	36	36	36	36	37	37	37	37	38
Lithuania - Lituanie	3 260	3 215	3 169	3 124	3 080	3 037	2 997	2 962	2 932	2 908
Luxembourg	475	485	496	508	520	532	545	556	567	576
Malta - Malte	410	412	414	416	418	421	423	426	428	429
Monaco	35	36	37	37	37	38	38	38	38	38
Montenegro - Monténégro	619	621	623	624	625	626	627	628	628	629
Netherlands - Pays-Bas	16 507	16 569	16 627	16 683	16 737	16 789	16 840	16 889	16 938	16 987
Norway - Norvège[11]	4 720	4 771	4 827	4 886	4 948	5 012	5 077	5 140	5 200	5 255
Poland - Pologne	38 330	38 326	38 325	38 323	38 321	38 317	38 309	38 293	38 265	38 224
Portugal	10 630	10 652	10 661	10 652	10 625	10 582	10 528	10 471	10 418	10 372
Republic of Moldova - République de Moldova[12]	4 129	4 111	4 096	4 084	4 077	4 074	4 072	4 070	4 066	4 060
Romania - Roumanie	21 036	20 821	20 618	20 440	20 293	20 171	20 068	19 973	19 877	19 778
Russian Federation - Fédération de Russie	143 150	143 083	143 093	143 154	143 264	143 421	143 597	143 761	143 888	143 965
San Marino - Saint-Marin	30	30	31	31	32	32	32	33	33	33
Serbia - Serbie[13]	9 135	9 100	9 065	9 030	8 994	8 957	8 920	8 885	8 851	8 820
Slovakia - Slovaquie	5 398	5 399	5 401	5 404	5 410	5 417	5 425	5 433	5 439	5 444
Slovenia - Slovénie	2 014	2 025	2 035	2 045	2 053	2 060	2 066	2 071	2 075	2 078
Spain - Espagne[14]	45 394	45 998	46 476	46 789	46 909	46 857	46 698	46 522	46 398	46 348
Sweden - Suède	9 163	9 237	9 313	9 390	9 466	9 541	9 615	9 689	9 764	9 838
Switzerland - Suisse	7 560	7 646	7 737	7 832	7 930	8 032	8 133	8 230	8 320	8 402
TFYR of Macedonia - L'ex-R. y. de Macédoine	2 065	2 067	2 069	2 071	2 072	2 074	2 076	2 077	2 079	2 081
Ukraine[15]	46 386	46 186	45 994	45 793	45 576	45 349	45 116	44 883	44 658	44 439
United Kingdom of Great Britain and Northern Ireland - Royaume-Uni de Grande-Bretagne et d'Irlande du Nord	61 415	62 076	62 723	63 307	63 812	64 250	64 641	65 016	65 397	65 789
OCEANIA - OCÉANIE										
American Samoa - Samoas américaines	58	57	56	56	55	55	55	55	56	56
Australia - Australie[16]	20 947	21 342	21 739	22 120	22 480	22 822	23 151	23 475	23 800	24 126
Cook Islands - Îles Cook	20	19	19	19	18	18	18	18	17	17
Fiji - Fidji	835	843	852	860	867	874	880	886	892	899
French Polynesia - Polynésie française	261	263	266	268	270	272	274	275	278	280
Guam	159	159	159	159	160	160	160	161	162	163
Kiribati	96	98	101	103	105	107	109	110	112	114
Marshall Islands - Îles Marshall	52	52	52	52	53	53	53	53	53	53
Micronesia (Federated States of) - Micronésie (États fédérés de)	105	104	104	104	103	104	104	104	104	105
Nauru	10	10	10	10	10	10	11	11	11	11
New Caledonia - Nouvelle-Calédonie	240	244	247	251	255	258	262	265	269	273
New Zealand - Nouvelle-Zélande	4 233	4 278	4 323	4 370	4 418	4 468	4 518	4 567	4 615	4 661
Niue - Nioué	2	2	2	2	2	2	2	2	2	2
Northern Mariana Islands - Îles Mariannes septentrionales	60	57	56	54	54	54	54	54	55	55
Palau - Palaos	20	20	20	20	21	21	21	21	21	22
Papua New Guinea - Papouasie-Nouvelle-Guinée	6 628	6 787	6 947	7 108	7 269	7 431	7 593	7 756	7 920	8 085
Samoa	182	184	185	186	188	189	191	192	194	195
Solomon Islands - Îles Salomon	493	504	516	528	540	552	564	576	587	599
Tokelau - Tokélaou	1	1	1	1	1	1	1	1	1	1
Tonga	102	103	104	104	105	105	105	106	106	107
Tuvalu	10	10	10	11	11	11	11	11	11	11
Vanuatu	220	225	231	236	242	247	253	259	265	270
Wallis and Futuna Islands - Îles Wallis et Futuna	14	14	14	13	13	13	13	12	12	12

SOURCE

United Nations, Department of Economic and Social Affairs, Population Division (2017). 2017 Revision of World Population Prospects - Organisation des Nations Unies, Département des affaires économiques et sociales, Division de la population (2017). Perspectives de la population mondiale : La révision de 2017

FOOTNOTES - NOTES

1 Including Agalega, Rodrigues and Saint Brandon. - Y compris Agalega, Rodrigues et Saint Brandon.
2 Including Zanzibar. - Y compris le Zanzibar.
3 Including Saint-Barthélemy and Saint-Martin (French part). - Y compris Saint-Barthélemy et Saint-Martin (partie française).
4 Including Nagorno-Karabakh. - Y compris le Haut-Karabakh.
5 For statistical purposes, the data for China do not include Hong Kong and Macao Special Administrative Regions (SAR) of China. - A des fins statistiques, les données pour la Chine ne comprennent pas les Régions Administratives Spéciales (SAR) de Hong Kong et Macao.
6 Refers to the whole country. - Les données se rapportent au pays en entier.
7 Including Abkhazia and South Ossetia. - Y compris l'Abkhazie et l'Ossétie du Sud.
8 Including Sabah and Sarawak. - Y compris le Sabah et le Sarawak.
9 Including East Jerusalem. - Y compris Jérusalem-Est.
10 Including Åland Islands. - Y compris les îles Åland.
11 Including Svalbard and Jan Mayen Islands. - Y compris Svalbard et l'île Jan Mayen.
12 Including Transnistria. - Y compris la Transnistrie.
13 Including Kosovo. - Y compris le Kosovo.
14 Including Canary Islands, Ceuta and Melilla. - Y compris les îles Canaries, Ceuta et Melilla.
15 Including Crimea. - Y compris la Crimée.
16 Including Christmas Island, Cocos (Keeling) Islands and Norfolk Island. - Y compris les îles Christmas, Cocos (Keeling) et Norfolk.

Annex II: Vital statistics summary, United Nations estimates: 2015-2020
Annexe II: Aperçu des statistiques de l'état civil, estimations des Nations Unies : 2015-2020

Continent and country or area / Continent et pays ou zone	Crude birth rate - Taux bruts de natalité	Crude death rate - Taux bruts de mortalité	Infant mortality rate - Décès d'enfants de moins d'un an	Life expectancy at birth - Espérance de vie à la naissance		Total fertility rate - Indice synthétique de fécondité	Natural increase - Accroissement naturel
				Male - Masculin	Female - Féminin		
AFRICA - AFRIQUE							
Algeria - Algérie..	21.6	4.8	23.6	75.2	77.7	2.65	16.9
Angola...	41.1	8.4	59.3	59.0	64.7	5.59	32.7
Benin - Bénin..	36.4	9.0	61.3	59.8	62.8	4.87	27.4
Botswana..	22.8	6.3	28.0	65.5	70.5	2.65	16.6
Burkina Faso...	38.2	8.3	54.2	60.1	61.6	5.23	29.9
Burundi...	41.5	10.4	68.8	56.1	60.0	5.58	31.1
Cabo Verde...	20.6	5.4	19.8	71.0	75.1	2.29	15.2
Cameroon - Cameroun......................................	35.5	9.7	58.2	57.8	59.9	4.60	25.8
Central African Republic - République centrafricaine....	35.0	12.9	81.2	51.4	55.3	4.75	22.2
Chad - Tchad..	42.6	12.6	80.8	52.1	54.6	5.80	29.9
Comoros - Comores..	32.1	7.3	53.1	62.3	65.8	4.24	24.8
Congo...	33.7	7.1	39.0	63.6	66.9	4.56	26.6
Côte d'Ivoire...	36.4	11.8	57.2	53.0	55.9	4.81	24.6
Democratic Republic of the Congo - République démocratique du Congo	41.4	9.6	64.9	58.7	61.7	5.96	31.8
Djibouti	22.5	8.4	50.7	61.0	64.4	2.76	14.1
Egypt - Égypte..	25.0	5.8	15.6	69.5	74.1	3.16	19.2
Equatorial Guinea - Guinée équatoriale	33.4	10.0	61.0	56.8	59.5	4.55	23.4
Eritrea - Érythrée	31.3	6.6	34.7	63.6	68.0	4.03	24.7
Ethiopia - Éthiopie	31.0	6.6	37.0	64.1	67.9	4.03	24.4
Gabon...	28.5	7.4	35.0	65.1	68.4	3.68	21.2
Gambia - Gambie..	38.7	7.9	44.9	60.2	63.0	5.32	30.8
Ghana...	30.2	7.9	40.4	62.1	64.2	3.89	22.3
Guinea - Guinée	35.2	8.8	51.7	60.3	61.5	4.74	26.5
Guinea-Bissau - Guinée-Bissau	35.6	10.2	69.8	56.3	59.8	4.51	25.5
Kenya	30.7	5.7	34.7	65.0	69.6	3.77	25.0
Lesotho...	27.3	12.4	49.3	52.4	56.8	3.01	14.9
Liberia - Libéria..	33.8	7.6	46.8	62.2	64.3	4.48	26.2
Libya - Libye...	18.8	5.2	20.9	69.5	75.3	2.21	13.6
Madagascar..	32.8	6.1	29.7	64.9	68.1	4.11	26.7
Malawi	36.4	7.1	59.2	61.1	66.3	4.49	29.3
Mali	41.8	9.8	65.8	58.0	59.5	5.92	32.0
Mauritania - Mauritanie....................................	33.5	7.8	63.3	61.9	65.0	4.58	25.7
Mauritius - Maurice[1]	10.6	8.3	10.3	71.5	78.5	1.43	2.3
Mayotte	28.3	2.5	3.6	77.3	83.8	3.73	25.8
Morocco - Maroc	19.2	5.1	21.9	74.9	77.3	2.43	14.1
Mozambique...	38.4	9.7	64.0	57.0	61.3	5.14	28.7
Namibia - Namibie..	28.4	7.0	30.7	62.0	67.9	3.31	21.3
Niger...	47.7	9.4	56.9	59.5	61.6	7.15	38.3
Nigeria - Nigéria	38.1	12.0	63.5	53.3	54.9	5.42	26.1
Republic of South Sudan - République de Soudan du Sud ...	35.4	10.6	65.9	56.5	58.6	4.74	24.8
Reunion - Réunion	14.9	5.9	3.6	77.3	83.8	2.27	9.0
Rwanda...	30.1	5.8	37.0	65.4	69.7	3.78	24.3
Sao Tome and Principe - Sao Tomé-et-Principe	33.1	6.5	41.5	64.6	69.0	4.36	26.6
Senegal - Sénégal	34.6	5.7	33.8	65.5	69.5	4.65	28.9
Seychelles..	15.4	8.3	8.0	69.6	78.7	2.26	7.1
Sierra Leone...	34.2	12.5	79.7	51.7	52.9	4.32	21.7
Somalia - Somalie	42.9	11.0	69.3	55.3	58.7	6.12	31.9
South Africa - Afrique du Sud..........................	20.5	9.5	30.4	60.2	67.3	2.41	11.0
Sudan - Soudan	32.4	7.3	43.9	63.1	66.4	4.43	25.0
Swaziland...	28.2	9.3	43.6	55.3	61.4	3.01	18.9
Togo..	33.3	8.6	49.7	59.7	61.4	4.35	24.7
Tunisia - Tunisie	17.5	6.3	15.6	74.0	78.1	2.15	11.2
Uganda - Ouganda	41.4	8.5	55.0	58.0	62.5	5.46	32.9
United Republic of Tanzania - République Unie de Tanzanie[2] ...	37.5	6.4	39.1	65.0	68.4	4.92	31.2
Western Sahara - Sahara occidental	20.3	4.9	28.8	68.2	71.9	2.42	15.4
Zambia - Zambie	37.7	7.6	46.3	59.6	65.1	4.90	30.1
Zimbabwe...	31.7	7.8	41.3	59.9	63.8	3.63	23.9
AMERICA, NORTH - AMÉRIQUE DU NORD							
Antigua and Barbuda - Antigua-et-Barbuda	16.0	5.8	7.8	74.1	79.0	2.03	10.2
Aruba..	11.0	9.0	13.6	73.6	78.4	1.80	2.1
Bahamas...	14.1	6.5	8.0	72.8	78.8	1.76	7.6
Barbados - Barbade	11.8	10.9	8.0	73.7	78.5	1.80	0.9

Continent and country or area Continent et pays ou zone	Crude birth rate - Taux bruts de natalité	Crude death rate - Taux bruts de mortalité	Infant mortality rate - Décès d'enfants de moins d'un an	Life expectancy at birth - Espérance de vie à la naissance		Total fertility rate - Indice synthétique de fécondité	Natural increase - Accroissement naturel
				Male - Masculin	Female - Féminin		
AMERICA, NORTH - AMÉRIQUE DU NORD							
Belize..	22.2	5.4	11.6	68.0	73.8	2.46	16.8
Canada...	10.5	7.5	4.1	80.7	84.4	1.56	3.0
Costa Rica..	14.0	5.0	8.0	77.8	82.5	1.76	8.9
Cuba..	10.7	8.1	4.8	78.1	82.0	1.72	2.5
Curaçao...	12.5	8.8	9.0	75.5	81.4	2.02	3.6
Dominican Republic - République dominicaine...............	19.7	6.1	22.1	71.1	77.4	2.38	13.5
El Salvador...	18.3	6.8	14.2	69.2	78.2	2.05	11.5
Grenada - Grenade	18.2	7.1	8.4	71.4	76.3	2.07	11.1
Guadeloupe[3]...	10.8	8.1	4.8	78.2	84.8	1.92	2.7
Guatemala..	24.8	4.8	22.2	70.5	76.9	2.90	20.0
Haiti - Haïti..	23.7	8.5	41.9	61.5	65.9	2.85	15.1
Honduras..	21.4	4.8	24.3	71.3	76.5	2.42	16.5
Jamaica - Jamaïque...	16.4	7.1	13.3	73.8	78.6	1.99	9.3
Martinique..	10.9	8.6	5.2	79.2	85.2	1.88	2.3
Mexico - Mexique	17.6	4.9	16.5	75.0	79.8	2.14	12.7
Nicaragua...	18.9	4.8	16.6	72.7	78.7	2.16	14.1
Panama...	19.0	5.1	13.4	75.4	81.3	2.47	14.0
Puerto Rico - Porto Rico.....................................	10.6	8.0	5.4	76.4	83.9	1.47	2.6
Saint Lucia - Sainte-Lucie	11.9	7.5	9.2	73.2	78.5	1.44	4.4
Saint Vincent and the Grenadines - Saint-Vincent-et-les Grenadines...	15.1	7.3	14.9	71.2	75.6	1.90	7.8
Trinidad and Tobago - Trinité-et-Tobago	13.0	9.8	22.7	67.4	74.5	1.73	3.2
United States of America - États-Unis d'Amérique..............	12.7	8.4	5.2	77.3	81.9	1.89	4.3
United States Virgin Islands - Îles Vierges américaines........	12.7	8.6	8.4	77.7	82.3	2.19	4.1
AMERICA, SOUTH - AMÉRIQUE DU SUD							
Argentina - Argentine	16.9	7.6	11.9	73.1	80.5	2.27	9.3
Bolivia (Plurinational State of) - Bolivie (État plurinational de)..	22.9	7.3	34.9	67.1	72.2	2.83	15.6
Brazil - Brésil...	13.8	6.3	13.0	72.2	79.4	1.71	7.5
Chile - Chili..	13.1	6.2	6.3	77.3	82.2	1.77	6.9
Colombia - Colombie	14.8	6.1	15.5	71.1	78.3	1.83	8.7
Ecuador - Équateur	19.7	5.1	18.7	74.0	79.4	2.44	14.6
French Guiana - Guyane française	23.5	3.0	9.2	77.3	83.4	3.26	20.5
Guyana...	20.3	8.3	30.7	64.5	69.3	2.47	12.0
Paraguay..	20.7	5.8	27.6	71.1	75.5	2.45	14.9
Peru - Pérou..	18.7	5.7	15.5	72.7	78.0	2.35	13.1
Suriname..	17.9	7.4	15.3	68.4	74.9	2.34	10.4
Uruguay..	13.9	9.4	11.0	74.1	81.1	1.98	4.5
Venezuela (Bolivarian Republic of) - Venezuela (République bolivarienne du)...........................	18.6	5.7	12.2	70.9	79.0	2.28	12.9
ASIA - ASIE							
Afghanistan	32.3	6.5	51.9	62.9	65.6	4.41	25.7
Armenia - Arménie	12.9	9.7	11.2	71.5	77.9	1.60	3.2
Azerbaijan - Azerbaïdjan[4]..................................	16.7	6.9	28.3	69.1	75.2	2.04	9.8
Bahrain - Bahreïn...	14.2	2.4	6.0	76.3	78.2	2.00	11.8
Bangladesh...	18.5	5.3	26.5	71.3	74.7	2.07	13.2
Bhutan - Bhoutan...	17.8	6.0	24.1	70.4	71.1	2.02	11.8
Brunei Darussalam - Brunéi Darussalam	15.4	3.7	5.6	75.9	79.2	1.85	11.7
Cambodia - Cambodge	22.7	6.0	22.2	67.2	71.5	2.52	16.7
China - Chine[5]...	11.6	7.5	10.0	75.0	78.1	1.64	4.1
China, Hong Kong SAR - Chine, Hong Kong RAS........	11.1	6.9	1.4	81.2	87.2	1.33	4.2
China, Macao SAR - Chine, Macao RAS	12.2	3.9	2.6	81.1	87.0	1.35	8.3
Cyprus - Chypre[6]...	10.6	7.0	3.5	78.6	82.8	1.34	3.6
Democratic People's Republic of Korea - République populaire démocratique de Corée	13.8	9.0	14.2	68.3	75.4	1.89	4.8
Georgia - Géorgie[7]	12.9	13.1	9.4	69.3	77.7	1.97	-0.2
India - Inde	18.7	7.4	34.9	67.4	70.5	2.30	11.4
Indonesia - Indonésie	18.4	7.2	21.3	67.4	71.7	2.32	11.2
Iran (Islamic Republic of) - Iran (République islamique d').....	15.6	4.5	12.0	75.1	77.4	1.62	11.1
Iraq	32.5	4.9	27.4	67.8	72.5	4.27	27.6
Israel - Israël...	19.6	5.3	2.7	81.0	84.3	2.92	14.3

Continent and country or area Continent et pays ou zone	Crude birth rate - Taux bruts de natalité	Crude death rate - Taux bruts de mortalité	Infant mortality rate - Décès d'enfants de moins d'un an	Life expectancy at birth - Espérance de vie à la naissance		Total fertility rate - Indice synthétique de fécondité	Natural increase - Accroissement naturel
				Male - Masculin	Female - Féminin		
ASIA - ASIE							
Japan - Japon..........................	8.1	10.8	1.9	80.7	87.2	1.48	-2.7
Jordan - Jordanie	25.5	3.8	14.9	72.9	76.3	3.26	21.7
Kazakhstan..............................	20.1	8.9	11.7	65.2	74.9	2.57	11.3
Kuwait - Koweït	15.8	2.9	7.2	74.0	76.2	1.97	13.0
Kyrgyzstan - Kirghizstan..............	23.9	6.3	16.7	67.1	75.1	2.91	17.6
Lao People's Democratic Republic - République démocratique populaire lao	23.2	6.6	40.0	65.6	68.7	2.62	16.6
Lebanon - Liban	15.4	4.7	8.4	78.3	81.7	1.70	10.7
Malaysia - Malaisie[8]	17.0	5.0	5.5	73.4	77.9	2.01	11.9
Maldives	17.3	3.3	6.6	76.9	79.0	2.03	14.0
Mongolia - Mongolie	22.4	6.4	18.6	65.5	73.8	2.66	16.0
Myanmar	17.6	8.2	41.9	64.4	69.1	2.18	9.3
Nepal - Népal	19.5	6.2	26.2	69.1	72.4	2.08	13.3
Oman	17.2	2.5	7.8	75.7	79.8	2.54	14.8
Pakistan	27.4	7.2	63.9	65.7	67.8	3.38	20.2
Philippines	22.9	6.5	19.5	66.0	72.9	2.88	16.3
Qatar	10.0	1.6	6.3	77.6	80.1	1.88	8.4
Republic of Korea - République de Corée..........	8.9	6.1	2.4	79.3	85.4	1.32	2.8
Saudi Arabia - Arabie saoudite......	19.1	3.6	10.9	73.5	76.6	2.48	15.5
Singapore - Singapour	8.7	5.1	1.8	81.3	85.3	1.26	3.5
Sri Lanka	14.9	7.0	6.8	72.2	78.9	2.03	7.8
State of Palestine - État de Palestine[9]	31.2	3.5	17.8	71.8	75.7	3.91	27.7
Syrian Arab Republic - République arabe syrienne	20.5	5.3	15.5	65.9	77.7	2.84	15.2
Tajikistan - Tadjikistan.................	27.9	5.1	34.1	68.5	74.4	3.28	22.8
Thailand - Thaïlande	10.0	8.1	9.4	71.9	79.3	1.46	1.9
Timor-Leste	34.4	5.4	34.3	67.6	71.3	5.34	29.0
Turkey - Turquie	15.8	5.8	9.9	72.9	79.3	2.02	10.0
Turkmenistan - Turkménistan.........	24.0	7.1	43.3	64.5	71.5	2.79	16.9
United Arab Emirates - Émirats arabes unis	9.2	1.7	5.3	76.8	79.0	1.73	7.5
Uzbekistan - Ouzbékistan	20.2	5.9	28.0	68.6	74.3	2.24	14.4
Viet Nam	16.2	5.8	16.6	71.9	81.1	1.95	10.4
Yemen - Yémen..........................	30.7	6.3	42.2	63.8	66.8	3.84	24.3
EUROPE							
Albania - Albanie	11.7	7.7	12.8	76.6	80.6	1.71	4.0
Austria - Autriche	9.7	9.7	2.2	79.5	84.2	1.51	0.1
Belarus - Bélarus	11.8	13.5	3.1	67.5	78.5	1.71	-1.7
Belgium - Belgique	11.4	9.8	2.8	79.0	83.7	1.80	1.6
Bosnia and Herzegovina - Bosnie-Herzégovine........	9.2	11.2	6.3	74.7	79.7	1.39	-2.0
Bulgaria - Bulgarie	9.3	15.3	7.2	71.5	78.4	1.58	-6.0
Croatia - Croatie	9.0	12.8	3.3	74.6	81.1	1.45	-3.8
Czechia - Tchéquie	10.1	10.7	2.2	76.0	81.8	1.57	-0.6
Denmark - Danemark	10.7	9.6	3.0	79.0	82.8	1.76	1.1
Estonia - Estonie	10.7	12.2	2.8	73.0	82.0	1.66	-1.5
Finland - Finlande[10]	10.8	9.8	1.6	78.8	84.4	1.78	1.0
France	11.7	9.0	2.8	79.9	85.7	1.97	2.7
Germany - Allemagne	8.9	11.3	2.1	79.0	83.6	1.47	-2.5
Greece - Grèce..........................	7.9	10.9	3.0	79.0	84.0	1.30	-3.0
Hungary - Hongrie	9.0	13.0	4.2	72.5	79.5	1.40	-4.0
Iceland - Islande	13.1	6.5	1.5	81.6	84.4	1.92	6.6
Ireland - Irlande	13.5	6.6	2.0	79.8	83.7	1.98	6.9
Italy - Italie...............................	8.2	10.6	2.3	81.1	85.4	1.49	-2.4
Latvia - Lettonie.........................	10.0	15.1	5.2	69.7	79.4	1.57	-5.1
Lithuania - Lituanie.....................	10.6	14.3	3.7	69.4	80.0	1.66	-3.8
Luxembourg	11.4	7.3	2.9	79.8	84.1	1.59	4.2
Malta - Malte.............................	10.0	8.9	4.1	79.5	82.7	1.48	1.0
Montenegro - Monténégro.............	11.2	10.0	3.3	74.9	79.6	1.66	1.2
Netherlands - Pays-Bas	10.6	8.7	2.5	80.3	83.8	1.75	1.9
Norway - Norvège[11]	12.0	7.9	1.8	80.5	84.3	1.83	4.1
Poland - Pologne	9.1	10.5	4.0	73.9	81.7	1.29	-1.4
Portugal	7.5	10.8	1.6	78.6	84.3	1.24	-3.3
Republic of Moldova - République de Moldova[12]	10.0	11.7	12.4	67.4	75.9	1.23	-1.7
Romania - Roumanie	9.5	13.0	7.4	72.2	79.1	1.54	-3.4
Russian Federation - Fédération de Russie........	12.4	13.6	7.0	65.6	76.8	1.75	-1.3
Serbia - Serbie[13].......................	10.5	12.8	8.3	72.6	78.2	1.62	-2.2

Annex II: Vital statistics summary, United Nations estimates: 2015-2020
Annexe II: Aperçu des statistiques de l'état civil, estimations des Nations Unies : 2015-2020 (continued - suite)

Continent and country or area Continent et pays ou zone	Crude birth rate - Taux bruts de natalité	Crude death rate - Taux bruts de mortalité	Infant mortality rate - Décès d'enfants de moins d'un an	Life expectancy at birth - Espérance de vie à la naissance		Total fertility rate - Indice synthétique de fécondité	Natural increase - Accroissement naturel
				Male - Masculin	Female - Féminin		
EUROPE							
Slovakia - Slovaquie................................	10.3	10.1	5.1	73.5	80.4	1.46	0.3
Slovenia - Slovénie................................	10.0	9.9	2.1	78.4	83.9	1.64	0.1
Spain - Espagne[14]................................	8.5	9.1	2.3	80.6	86.0	1.39	-0.6
Sweden - Suède................................	12.3	9.1	1.9	81.0	84.4	1.91	3.2
Switzerland - Suisse................................	10.4	8.0	3.4	81.6	85.4	1.55	2.4
TFYR of Macedonia - L'ex-R. y. de Macédoine............	11.2	9.9	8.1	73.9	78.0	1.55	1.3
Ukraine[15]................................	10.5	14.9	7.2	67.1	76.9	1.56	-4.4
United Kingdom of Great Britain and Northern Ireland - Royaume-Uni de Grande-Bretagne et d'Irlande du Nord	12.1	9.0	3.5	80.0	83.5	1.87	3.1
OCEANIA - OCÉANIE							
Australia - Australie[16]................................	12.8	6.7	3.1	81.3	85.0	1.83	6.1
Fiji - Fidji................................	18.9	7.3	13.6	67.6	73.7	2.48	11.6
French Polynesia - Polynésie française	15.1	5.6	5.6	74.9	79.5	1.99	9.5
Guam................................	16.6	5.2	8.5	77.5	82.3	2.32	11.4
Kiribati................................	27.7	7.0	43.0	63.3	69.9	3.58	20.7
Micronesia (Federated States of) - Micronésie (États fédérés de)................................	23.8	6.2	31.0	68.2	70.6	3.08	17.6
New Caledonia - Nouvelle-Calédonie	15.5	6.8	11.5	74.7	80.2	2.14	8.7
New Zealand - Nouvelle-Zélande................	13.1	7.0	3.8	80.5	83.7	1.97	6.2
Papua New Guinea - Papouasie-Nouvelle-Guinée	27.2	7.1	44.9	63.4	68.4	3.59	20.1
Samoa................................	24.1	5.0	16.2	72.3	78.6	3.90	19.2
Solomon Islands - Îles Salomon................	27.9	4.7	24.9	69.6	72.8	3.77	23.3
Tonga................................	23.4	5.9	19.2	70.2	76.3	3.58	17.5
Vanuatu................................	25.4	4.8	21.3	70.3	74.8	3.22	20.6

SOURCE

United Nations, Department of Economic and Social Affairs, Population Division (2017). 2017 Revision of World Population Prospects - Organisation des Nations Unies, Département des affaires économiques et sociales, Division de la population (2017). Perspectives de la population mondiale : La révision de 2017

FOOTNOTES - NOTES

[1] Including Agalega, Rodrigues and Saint Brandon. - Y compris Agalega, Rodrigues et Saint Brandon.

[2] Including Zanzibar. - Y compris le Zanzibar.

[3] Including Saint-Barthélemy and Saint-Martin (French part). - Y compris Saint-Barthélemy et Saint-Martin (partie française).

[4] Including Nagorno-Karabakh. - Y compris le Haut-Karabakh.

[5] For statistical purposes, the data for China do not include Hong Kong and Macao Special Administrative Regions (SAR) of China. - A des fins statistiques, les données pour la Chine ne comprennent pas les Régions Administratives Spéciales (SAR) de Hong Kong et Macao.

[6] Refers to the whole country. - Les données se rapportent au pays en entier.

[7] Including Abkhazia and South Ossetia. - Y compris l'Abkhazie et l'Ossétie du Sud.

[8] Including Sabah and Sarawak. - Y compris le Sabah et le Sarawak.

[9] Including East Jerusalem. - Y compris Jérusalem-Est.

[10] Including Åland Islands. - Y compris les îles Åland.

[11] Including Svalbard and Jan Mayen Islands. - Y compris Svalbard et l'île Jan Mayen.

[12] Including Transnistria. - Y compris la Transnistrie.

[13] Including Kosovo. - Y compris le Kosovo.

[14] Including Canary Islands, Ceuta and Melilla. - Y compris les îles Canaries, Ceuta et Melilla.

[15] Including Crimea. - Y compris la Crimée.

[16] Including Christmas Island, Cocos (Keeling) Islands and Norfolk Island. - Y compris les îles Christmas, Cocos (Keeling) et Norfolk.

Historical index
(See notes at end of index)

Subject-matter	Year of issue	Time coverage	Subject-matter	Year of issue	Time coverage
Births	1975	Latest		1981	1962-81
by gestational age	1981	1972-80		1982	1978-82
	1986	1977-85		1983	1979-83
	1999CD[iv]	1990-98		1984	1980-84
				1985	1981-85
Births	1959	1949-58		1986	1967-86
by legitimacy status	1965	1955-64		1987	1983-87
	1969	1963-68		1988	1984-88
	1975	1966-74		1989	1985-89
	1981	1972-80		1990	1986-90
	1986	1977-85		1991	1987-91
	1999CD[iv]	1990-98		1992	1983-92
				1993	1989-93
Births	2002	1980-02		1994	1990-94
by month				1995	1991-95
				1996	1992-96
Births	1965	Latest		1997	1993-97
by occupation of father	1969	Latest		1998	1994-98
				1999	1995-99
Births	1959	1949-58		1999CD[iv]	1980-99
by sex	1965	1955-64		2000	1996-00
	1967-1968	Latest		2001	1997-01
	1969	1963-68		2002	1998-02
	1970-1974	Latest		2003	1999-03
	1975	1956-75		2004	2000-04
	1976-1980	Latest		2005	2001-05
	1981	1962-81		2006	2002-06
	1982-1985	Latest		2007	2003-07
	1986	1967-86		2008	2004-08
	1987-1991	Latest		2009-2010	2006-10
	1992	1983-92		2011	2007-11
	1993-1999	Latest		2012	2008-12
	1999CD[iv]	1990-98		2013	2009-13
	2000-2016	Latest		2014	2010-14
				2015	2011-15
Births	1965	Latest		2016	2012-16
by plurality	1969	Latest			
	1975	Latest	**Births**	1965	Latest
	1981	1972-80	by urban/rural residence	1969-1974	Latest
	1986	1977-85	and age of mother	1975	1966-74
	1999CD[iv]	1990-98		1976-1980	Latest
				1981	1972-80
Births	1965	Latest		1982-1985	Latest
by urban/rural residence	1967	Latest		1986	1977-85
	1968	1964-68		1987-1991	Latest
	1969	1964-68		1992	1983-92
	1970	1966-70		1993-1997	Latest
	1971	1967-71		1997HS[iii]	1948-96
	1972	1968-72		1998-1999	Latest
	1973	1969-73		1999CD[iv]	1990-98
	1974	1970-74		2000-2006	Latest
	1975	1956-75			
	1976	1972-76	**Births**	1959	1949-58
	1977	1973-77	illegitimate	1965	1955-64
	1978	1974-78		1969	1963-68
	1979	1975-79		1975	1966-74
	1980	1976-80		1981	1972-80

Subject-matter	Year of issue	Time coverage	Subject-matter	Year of issue	Time coverage
	2008	2004-08		2001-2005	2000-05
	2009-2010	2006-10		2006-2010	2005-10
	2011	2007-11		2011-2015	2010-15
	2012	2008-12		2016	2015-20
	2013	2009-13			
	2014	2010-14	**Birth rates**	1949-50	1947
	2015	2011-15	estimated (for the world)	1956-1977	Latest
	2016	2012-16		1978-1979	1970-75
				1980-1983	1975-80
Birth rates	1965	Latest		1984-1986	1980-85
by urban/rural residence	1969	Latest		1987-1992	1985-90
and age of mother	1975	1966-74		1993-1997	1990-95
	1976-1980	Latest		1998-2000	1995-00
	1981	1972-80		2001-2005	2000-05
	1982-1985	Latest		2006-2010	2005-10
	1986	1977-85		2011-2015	2010-15
	1987-1991	Latest		2016	2015-20
	1992	1983-92			
	1993-1997	Latest	**Birth rates**	1959	1949-58
	1997HS[iii]	1948-96	illegitimate		
	1998-1999	Latest			
	1999CD[iv]	1990-98	**Birth rates**	1954	1936-53
	2000-2006	Latest	legitimate	1959	1949-58
				1965	Latest
Birth rates	1949-50	1947		1969	Latest
estimated (for continents)	1956-1977	Latest		1975	Latest
	1978-1979	1970-75		1981	Latest
	1980-1983	1975-80		1986	Latest
	1984-1986	1980-85			
	1987-1992	1985-90	**Birth rates**	1959	1949-58
	1993-1997	1990-95	legitimate by age of	1965	Latest
	1998-2000	1995-00	father	1969	Latest
	2001-2005	2000-05		1975	Latest
	2006-2010	2005-10		1981	Latest
	2011-2015	2010-15		1986	Latest
	2016	2015-20			
			Birth rates	1954	1936-53
Birth rates	1964-1977	Latest	legitimate by age of	1959	1949-58
estimated (for macro	1978-1979	1970-75	mother	1965	Latest
regions)	1980-1983	1975-80		1969	Latest
	1984-1986	1980-85		1975	Latest
	1987-1992	1985-90		1981	Latest
	1993-1997	1990-95		1986	Latest
	1998-2000	1995-00			
	2001-2005	2000-05	**Birth rates**	1959	1950-57
	2006-2010	2005-10	legitimate by duration of	1965	Latest
	2011-2015	2010-15	marriage	1969	Latest
	2016	2015-20		1975	Latest
Birth rates	1949/1950	1947	**Birth ratios**	1949/1950	Latest
estimated (for regions)	1956-1977	Latest	fertility	1954	Latest
	1978-1979	1970-75		1959	1949-58
	1980-1983	1975-80		1965	1955-65
	1984-1986	1980-85		1969	1963-68
	1987-1992	1985-90		1975	1965-74
	1993-1997	1990-95		1978HS[ii]	1948-77
	1998-2000	1995-00		1981	1972-80

Historical index
(See notes at end of index)

Subject-matter	Year of issue	Time coverage	Subject-matter	Year of issue	Time coverage
	1980-1983	1975-80		2003	2003
	1984-1986	1980-85		2004	2004
	1984-1986	1980-85		2005	2005
	1987-1992	1985-90		2006	2006
	1993-1997	1990-95		2007	2007
	1998-2000	1995-00		2008	2008
	2001-2005	2000-05		2009-2010	2010
	2006-2010	2005-10		2011	2011
	2011-2015	2010-15		2012	2012
	2016	2015-2020		2013	2013
				2014	2014
Death rates........................	1964-1977	Latest		2015	2015
estimated (for macro	1978-1979	1970-75		2016	2016
regions)	1980-1983	1975-80			
	1984-1986	1980-85	**Density of population**.........	1948-1999	Latest
	1987-1992	1985-90	of countries	2000	2000
	1993-1997	1990-95		2001	2001
	1998-2000	1995-00		2002	2002
	2001-2005	2000-05		2003	2003
	2006-2010	2005-10		2004	2004
	2011-2015	2010-15		2005	2005
	2016	2015-2020		2006	2006
				2007	2007
Death rates........................	1949-50	1947		2008	2008
estimated (for regions)	1956-1977	Latest		2009-2010	2010
	1978-1979	1970-75		2011	2011
	1980-1983	1975-80		2012	2012
	1984-1986	1980-85		2013	2013
	1987-1992	1985-90		2014	2014
	1993-1997	1990-95		2015	2015
	1998-2000	1995-00		2016	2016
	2001-2005	2000-05			
	2006-2010	2005-10	**Density of population**.........	1964-1999	Latest
	2011-2015	2010-15	of major areas	2000	2000
	2016	2015-2020		2001	2001
				2002	2002
Death rates........................	1949-50	1947		2003	2003
estimated (for the world)	1956-1977	Latest		2004	2004
	1978-1979	1970-75		2005	2005
	1980-1983	1975-80		2006	2006
	1984-1986	1980-85		2007	2007
	1987-1992	1985-90		2008	2008
	1993-1997	1990-95		2009-2010	2010
	1998-2000	1995-00		2011	2011
	2001-2005	2000-05		2012	2012
	2006-2010	2005-10		2013	2013
	2011-2015	2010-15		2014	2014
	2016	2015-2020		2015	2015
				2016	2016
Death rates........................	*see "Infant deaths"*				
of infants			**Density of population**.........	1949-50	1920-49
			of regions	1952-1999	Latest
Density of population.........	1949-50	1920-49		2000	2000
of continents	1951-1999	Latest		2001	2001
	2000	2000		2002	2002
	2001	2001		2003	2003
	2002	2002		2004	2004

Subject-matter	Year of issue	Time coverage	Subject-matter	Year of issue	Time coverage
	1982	Latest		1955	1946-54
	1982	Latest		1956	1947-55
	1990	Latest		1957	1948-56
				1958	1930-57
Divorces............................	1958	1948-57		1959	1949-58
by duration of marriage	1968	1958-67		1960	1950-59
	1976	1966-75		1961	1952-61
	1982	1972-81		1962	1953-62
	1990	1980-89		1963	1954-63
	2007	Latest		1964	1960-64
	2009-2010	Latest		1965	1961-65
	2012	Latest		1966	1962-66
	2014	Latest		1967	1963-67
	2016	Latest		1968	1920-64[v]
					1953-68
Divorces............................	1958	1946-57		1969	1965-69
by duration of marriage	1968	Latest		1970	1966-70
and age of husband, wife	1976	Latest		1971	1967-71
	1982	Latest		1972	1968-72
	1990	Latest		1973	1969-73
				1974	1970-74
Divorces............................	1958	1948-57		1975	1971-75
by number of children	1968	1958-67		1976	1957-76
involved	1976	1966-75		1977	1973-77
	1982	1972-81		1978	1974-78
	1990	1980-89		1979	1975-79
	2007	Latest		1980	1976-80
				1969	1965-69
Divorces............................	2002	1998-02		1970	1966-70
by urban/rural residence	2003	1999-03		1971	1967-71
	2004	2000-04		1972	1968-72
	2005	2001-05		1973	1969-73
	2006	2002-06		1974	1970-74
	2007	2003-07		1975	1971-75
	2008	2004-08		1976	1957-76
	2009-2010	2006-10		1977	1973-77
	2011	2007-11		1978	1974-78
	2012	2008-12		1979	1975-79
	2013	2009-13		1980	1976-80
	2014	2010-14		1969	1965-69
	2015	2011-15		1970	1966-70
	2016	2012-16		1971	1967-71
				1972	1968-72
Divorce, percentage distribution..........................	2007	Latest		1973	1969-73
by duration of marriage	2009-2010	Latest		1974	1970-74
	2012	Latest		1975	1971-75
	2014	Latest		1976	1957-76
	2016	Latest		1977	1973-77
				1978	1974-78
				1979	1975-79
Divorce, percentage distribution..........................	2007	Latest		1980	1976-80
by number of children				1981	1977-81
involved				1982	1963-82
				1983	1979-83
				1984	1980-84
Divorce rates......................	1952	1935-51		1985	1981-85
	1953	1936-52		1986	1982-86
	1954	1946-53			

Subject-matter	Year of issue	Time coverage	Subject-matter	Year of issue	Time coverage
	1965	1955-64		1992	1987-91
	1969	1963-68		1993	1988-92
	1975	1966-74		1994	1989-93
	1981	1972-80		1995	1990-94
	1986	1977-85		1996	1987-95
				1997	1992-96
Foetal deaths, late	1954	Latest		1998	1993-97
by age of mother and	1959	1949-58		1999	1994-98
birth order	1965	3-Latest		1999CD[iv]	1990-98
	1969	1963-68		2000	1995-99
	1975	1966-74		2001	1997-01
	1981	1972-80		2002	1998-02
	1986	1977-85		2003	1999-03
				2004	2000-04
Foetal deaths, late	1957	1950-56		2005	2001-05
by period of gestation	1959	1949-58		2006	2002-06
	1961	1952-60		2007	2003-07
	1965	5-Latest		2008	2004-08
	1966	1956-65		2009-2010	2006-10
	1967-1968	Latest		2011	2007-11
	1969	1963-68		2012	2008-12
	1974	1965-73		2013	2009-13
	1975	1966-74		2014	2010-14
	1980	1971-79		2015	2011-15
	1981	1972-80		2016	2012-16
	1985	1976-84			
	1986	1977-85	**Foetal deaths, late**	1961	1952-60
	1996	1987-95	illegitimate	1965	5-Latest
				1969	1963-68
Foetal deaths, late	1961	1952-60		1975	1966-74
by sex	1965	5 Latest		1981	1972-80
	1969	1963-68		1986	1977-85
	1975	1966-74			
	1981	1972-80	**Foetal deaths, late**	1961	1952-60
	1986	1977-85	illegitimate, percent	1965	5-Latest
				1969	1963-68
Foetal deaths, late	1971	1966-70		1975	1966-74
by urban/rural	1972	1967-71		1981	1972-80
residence	1973	1968-72		1986	1977-85
	1974	1965-73			
	1975	1966-74	**Foetal deaths, late**	1959	1949-58
	1976	1971-75	legitimate	1965	1955-64
	1977	1972-76		1969	1963-68
	1978	1973-77		1975	1966-74
	1979	1974-78		1981	1972-80
	1980	1971-79		1986	1977-85
	1981	1972-80			
	1982	1977-81	**Foetal deaths, late**	1959	1949-58
	1983	1978-82	legitimate by age of	1965	1955-64
	1984	1979-83	mother	1969	1963-68
	1985	1975-84		1975	1966-74
	1986	1977-85		1981	1972-80
	1987	1982-86		1986	1977-85
	1988	1983-87		1996	1987-95
	1989	1984-88			
	1990	1985-89	**Foetal death ratios**	1957	1950-56
	1991	1986-90	by period of gestation	1959	1949-58

Historical index

(See notes at end of index)

Subject-matter	Year of issue	Time coverage
Households.......................... by marital status of householder and urban/rural residence	1987 1995	1975-86 1985-95
Households.......................... by relationship to householder and urban/rural residence	1987 1995	1975-86 1985-95
Households.......................... by size	1955 1962 1963 1971 1973 1976 1982 1987 1990 1995	1945-54 1955-62 1955-63[vi] 1962-71 1965-73[vi] Latest Latest 1975-86 1980-89 1985-95
Households.......................... by size and number of persons 60+	1991PA[vii]	Latest
Households.......................... by size and urban/rural residence	1968 1971 1973 1976 1982 1987 1990 1995	Latest 1962-71 1965-73[vi] Latest Latest 1975-86 1980-89 1985-95
Households.......................... headship rates by age and sex of householder and urban/rural residence	1987 1995	1975-86 1985-95
Households.......................... number of family nuclei by size of	1973 1976 1982 1987 1990	1965-73 Latest Latest 1975-86 1980-90
Households.......................... population by relationship to householder	1987 1991PA[vii]	1975-86 Latest
Households.......................... by sex and persons 60+	1991PA[vii]	Latest
Households.......................... population in each type of	1955 1962 1963 1968 1971	1945-54 1955-62 1955-63[vi] Latest 1962-71

Subject-matter	Year of issue	Time coverage
	1973 1976 1982 1987 1990 1995	1965-73[vi] Latest Latest 1975-86 1980-89 1985-95

I

Subject-matter	Year of issue	Time coverage
Illegitimacy rates and ratios .... of births	1959 1965 1969 1975 1981 1986 1999CD[iv]	1949-58 1955-64 1963-68 1966-74 1972-80 1977-85 1990-98
Illegitimacy rates and ratios .... of foetal deaths, late	1961 1965 1969 1975 1981 1986	1952-60 5-Latest 1963-68 1966-74 1972-80 1977-85
Illegitimate .... birth(s)	1959 1965 1969 1975 1981 1986 1999CD[iv]	1949-58 1955-64 1963-68 1966-74 1972-80 1977-85 1990-98

see also "Births" and "Foetal deaths, late"

Subject-matter	Year of issue	Time coverage
Illegitimate .... birth ratios	1959 1965 1969 1975 1981 1986 1999CD[iv]	1949-58 1955-64 1963-68 1966-74 1972-80 1977-85 1990-98
Illegitimate .... foetal death(s), late	1961 1965 1969 1975 1981 1986	1952-60 5-Latest 1963-68 1966-74 1972-80 1977-85
Illegitimate .... foetal death ratios, late	1961 1965 1969 1975 1981 1986	1952-60 5-Latest 1963-68 1966-74 1972-80 1977-85

Subject-matter	Year of issue	Time coverage	Subject-matter	Year of issue	Time coverage
	1969	1965-69		1955	1920-34[v]
	1970	1966-70			1946-54
	1971	1967-71		1956	1947-55
	1972	1968-72		1957	1948-56
	1973	1969-73		1958	1948-57
	1974	1965-74		1959	1949-58
	1975	1971-75		1960	1950-59
	1976	1972-76		1961	1945-59[v]
	1977	1973-77			1952-61
	1978	1974-78		1962	1945-54[v]
	1979	1975-79			1952-62
	1980	1971-80		1963	1945-59[v]
	1981	1977-81		1963	1954-63
	1982	1978-82		1964	1960-64
	1983	1979-83		1965	1961-65
	1984	1980-84		1966	1920-64[v]
	1985	1976-85			1951-66
	1986	1982-86		1967	1963-67
	1987	1983-87		1968	1964-68
	1988	1984-88		1969	1965-69
	1989	1985-89		1970	1966-70
	1990	1986-90		1971	1967-71
	1991	1987-91		1972	1968-72
	1992	1983-92		1973	1969-73
	1993	1989-93		1974	1965-74
	1994	1990-94		1975	1971-75
	1995	1991-95		1976	1972-76
	1996	1987-96		1977	1973-77
	1997	1993-97		1978	1974-78
	1998	1994-98		1978HS[ii]	1948-78
	1999	1995-99		1979	1975-79
	2000	1996-00		1980	1971-80
	2001	1997-01		1981	1977-81
	2002	1998-02		1982	1978-82
	2003	1999-03		1983	1979-83
	2004	2000-04		1984	1980-84
	2005	2001-05		1985	1976-85
	2006	2002-06		1986	1982-86
	2007	2003-07		1987	1983-87
	2008	2004-08		1988	1984-88
	2009-2010	2006-10		1989	1985-89
	2011	2007-11		1990	1986-90
	2012	2008-12		1991	1987-91
	2013	2009-13		1992	1983-92
	2014	2010-14		1993	1989-93
	2015	2011-15		1994	1990-94
	2016	2012-16		1995	1991-95
				1996	1987-96
Infant mortality rates	1948	1932-47		1997	1993-97
	1949-50	1932-49		1997HS[iii]	1948-97
	1951	1930-50		1998	1994-98
	1952	1920-34[v]		1999	1995-99
		1934-51		2000	1996-00
	1953	1920-39[v]		2001	1997-01
		1940-52		2002	1998-02
	1954	1920-39[v]		2003	1999-03
		1946-53		2004	2000-04

Subject-matter	Year of issue	Time coverage	Subject-matter	Year of issue	Time coverage
	2005	2001-05		1982	1978-82
	2006	2002-06		1983	1979-83
	2007	2003-07		1984	1980-84
	2008	2004-08		1985	1976-85
	2009-2010	2006-10		1986	1982-86
	2011	2007-11		1987	1983-87
	2012	2008-12		1988	1984-88
	2013	2009-13		1989	1985-89
	2014	2010-14		1990	1986-90
	2015	2011-15		1991	1987-91
	2016	2012-16		1992	1983-92
				1993	1989-93
Infant mortality rates	1948	1936-47		1994	1990-94
by age and sex	1951	1936-49		1995	1991-95
	1957	1948-56		1996	1987-96
	1961	1952-60		1997	1993-97
	1966	1956-65		1998	1994-98
	1967	1962-66		1999	1995-99
	1971-1973	Latest		2000	1996-00
	1974	1965-73		2001	1997-01
	1975-1979	Latest		2002	1998-02
	1980	1971-79		2003	1999-03
	1981-1984	Latest		2004	2000-04
	1985	1976-84		2005	2001-05
	1986-1991	Latest		2006	2002-06
	1992	1983-92		2007	2003-07
	1993-1995	Latest		2008	2004-08
	1996	1987-95		2009-2010	2006-10
	1997-2016	Latest		2011	2007-11
				2012	2008-12
Infant mortality rates	1971-1973	Latest		2013	2009-13
by age and sex and	1974	1965-73		2014	2010-14
urban/rural residence	1975-1979	Latest		2015	2011-15
	1980	1971-79		2016	2012-16
	1981-1984	Latest			
	1985	1976-84	**Intercensal rates of**		
	1986-1991	Latest	**population increase**............	1948	1900-48
	1992	1983-92		1949-50	1900-50
	1993-1995	Latest		1951	1900-51
	1996	1987-95		1952	1850-1952
	1997-1999	Latest		1953	1850-1953
				1955	1850-1954
Infant mortality rates	1967	Latest		1960	1900-61
by urban/rural residence	1968	1964-68		1962	1900-62
	1969	1965-69		1964	1955-64
	1970	1966-70		1970	1900-70
	1971	1967-71		1978HS[ii]	1948-78
	1972	1968-72		1997HS[iii]	1948-97
	1973	1969-73			
	1974	1965-74	**International migration**.......	*see "Migration"*	
	1975	1971-75			
	1976	1972-76	**L**		
	1977	1973-77			
	1978	1974-78	**Late foetal deaths**..............	*see "Foetal deaths, late"*	
	1979	1975-79			
	1980	1971-80			
	1981	1977-81			

Subject-matter	Year of issue	Time coverage	Subject-matter	Year of issue	Time coverage
	1967	1963-67		1977-1981	Latest
	1968	1949-68		1982	1972-81
	1969	1965-69		1983-1986	Latest
	1970	1966-70		1987	1975-86
	1971	1967-71		1988-1989	Latest
	1972	1968-72		1990	1980-1989
	1973	1969-73		1991-1997	Latest
	1974	1970-74		1998	1993-97
	1975	1971-75		1999	1994-98
	1976	1957-76		2000	1995-99
	1977	1973-77		2001	1997-01
	1978	1974-78		2002	1998-02
	1979	1975-79		2003	1999-03
	1980	1976-80		2004	2000-04
	1981	1977-81		2005	2001-05
	1982	1963-82		2006-2016	Latest
	1983	1979-83			
	1984	1980-84	**Marriages**	1958	1948-57
	1985	1981-85	by age of bride and age	1968	Latest
	1986	1982-86	of groom	1976	Latest
	1987	1983-87		1982	Latest
	1988	1984-88		1990	Latest
	1989	1985-89		2006-2016	Latest
	1990	1971-90			
	1991	1987-91	**Marriages**	1958	1948-57
	1992	1988-92	by age of bride and	1968	Latest
	1993	1989-93	previous marital status	1976	Latest
	1994	1990-94		1982	Latest
	1995	1991-95		1990	Latest
	1996	1992-96			
	1997	1993-97	**Marriages**	1948	1936-47
	1998	1994-98	by age of groom	1949-50	1936-49
	1999	1995-99		1958	1948-57
	2000	1996-00		1959-1967	Latest
	2001	1997-01		1968	1958-67
	2002	1998-02		1969-1975	Latest
	2003	1999-03		1976	1966-75
	2004	2000-04		1977-1981	Latest
	2005	2001-05		1982	1972-81
	2006	2002-06		1983-1986	Latest
	2007	2003-07		1987	1975-86
	2008	2004-08		1988-1989	Latest
	2009-2010	2006-10		1990	1980-1989
	2011	2007-11		1990-1997	Latest
	2012	2008-12		1998	1993-97
	2013	2009-13		1999	1994-98
	2014	2010-14		2000	1995-99
	2015	2011-15		2001	1997-01
	2016	2012-16		2002	1998-02
				2003	1999-03
Marriages	1948	1936-47		2004	2000-04
by age of bride	1949-50	1936-49		2005	2001-05
	1958	1948-57		2006-2016	Latest
	1959-1967	Latest			
	1968	1958-67	**Marriages**	1958	1948-57
	1969-1975	Latest	by age of groom and age	1968	Latest
	1976	1966-75	of bride	1976	Latest

Subject-matter	Year of issue	Time coverage	Subject-matter	Year of issue	Time coverage
	1967	1963-67		1976	1966-75
	1968	1920-64ᵛ		1982	1972-81
		1953-68		1987	1975-86
	1969	1965-69		1990	1980-89
	1970	1966-70			
	1971	1967-71	**Marriage rates**...................	1958	1935-56
	1972	1968-72	by sex among	1968	1935-67
	1973	1969-73	marriageable population	1976	1966-75
	1974	1970-74		1982	1972-81
	1975	1971-75		1990	1980-89
	1976	1957-76			
	1977	1973-77	**Marriage rates**...................	1968	Latest
	1978	1974-78	by urban/rural residence	1969	1965-69
	1979	1975-79		1970	1966-70
	1980	1976-80		1971	1967-71
	1981	1977-81		1972	1968-72
	1982	1963-82		1973	1969-73
	1983	1979-83		1974	1970-74
	1984	1980-84		1975	1971-75
	1985	1981-85		1976	1957-76
	1986	1982-86		1977	1973-77
	1987	1983-87		1978	1974-78
	1988	1984-88		1979	1975-79
	1989	1985-89		1980	1976-80
	1990	1971-90		1981	1977-81
	1991	1987-91		1982	1963-82
	1992	1988-92		1983	1979-83
	1993	1989-93		1984	1980-84
	1994	1990-94		1985	1981-85
	1995	1991-95		1986	1982-86
	1996	1992-96		1987	1983-87
	1997	1993-97		1988	1984-88
	1998	1994-98		1989	1985-89
	1999	1995-99		1990	1971-90
	2000	1996-00		1991	1987-91
	2001	1997-01		1992	1988-92
	2002	1998-02		1993	1989-93
	2003	1999-03		1994	1990-94
	2004	2000-04		1995	1991-95
	2005	2001-05		1996	1992-96
	2006	2002-06		1997	1993-97
	2007	2003-07		1998	1994-98
	2008	2004-08		1999	1995-99
	2009-2010	2006-10		2000	1996-00
	2011	2007-11		2001	1997-01
	2012	2008-12		2002	1998-02
	2013	2009-13		2003	1999-03
	2014	2010-14		2004	2000-04
	2015	2011-15		2005	2001-05
	2016	2012-16		2006	2002-06
				2007	2003-07
Marriage rates...................	1948	1936-46		2008	2004-08
by age and sex	1949-50	1936-49		2009-2010	2006-10
	1953	1936-51		2011	2007-11
	1954	1936-52		2012	2008-12
	1958	1935-56		2013	2009-13
	1968	1955-67		2014	2010-14

Historical index

(See notes at end of index)

Subject-matter	Year of issue	Time coverage
		see also "Population, illiteracy"
Population.......................... by literacy, age, sex and urban/rural residence	1973	1965-73[vi]
	1979	1970-79[vi]
	1983	1974-83
	1988	1980-88[vi]
	1993	1985-93
Population.......................... by localities of 100000+ inhabitants	1948	Latest
	1952	Latest
	1955	1945-54
	1960	1920-61
	1962	1955-62
	1963	1955-63[vi]
	1970	1950-70
	1971	1962-71
	1973	1965-73[vi]
	1979	1970-79[vi]
	1983	1974-83
	1988	1980-88[vi]
	1993	1985-93
Population.......................... by localities of 20000+ inhabitants	1948	Latest
	1952	Latest
	1955	1945-54
	1960	1920-61
	1962	1955-62
	1963	1955-63[vi]
	1970	1950-70
	1971	1962-71
	1973	1965-73[vi]
	1979	1970-79[vi]
	1983	1974-83
	1988	1980-88[vi]
	1993	1985-93
Population.......................... by locality size-classes and sex	1948	Latest
	1952	Latest
	1955	1945-54
	1962	1955-62
	1963	1955-63[vi]
	1971	1962-71
	1973	1965-73[vi]
	1979	1970-79[vi]
	1983	1974-83
	1988	1980-88[vi]
	1993	1985-93
Population.......................... by major civil divisions	1952	Latest
	1955	1945-54
	1962	1955-62
	1963	1955-63[vi]
	1971	1962-71
	1973	1965-73[vi]
	1979	1970-79[vi]
	1983	1974-83

Subject-matter	Year of issue	Time coverage
	1988	1980-88[vi]
	1993	1985-93
Population.......................... by marital status, age and sex	1948	Latest
	1949/50	1926-48
	1955	1945-54
	1958	1945-57
	1962	1955-62[vi]
	1963	1955-63[vi]
	1965	1955-65
	1968	1955-67
	1971	1962-71
	1973	1965-73[vi]
	1976	1966-75
	1978HS[ii]	1948-77
	1982	1972-81
	1987	1975-86
	1990	1980-89
	1997HS[iii]	1948-96
		see also "Population, married" and "Population, single"
Population.......................... for persons 60+ and urban/rural	1991PA[vii]	Latest
Population.......................... for persons 60+ and urban/rural (percentage distribution)	1948	Latest
Population.......................... by religion and sex	1956	1945-55
	1963	1955-63
	1964	1955-64[vi]
	1971	1962-71
	1973	1965-73[vi]
	1979	1970-79[vi]
	1983	1974-83
	1988	1980-88[vi]
	1993	1985-93
Population.......................... by school attendance, age and sex	1956	1945-55
	1963	1955-63
	1964	1955-64[vi]
	1971	1962-71
	1973	1965-73[vi]
	1979	1970-79
	1983	1974-83
	1988	1980-88[vi]
	1993	1985-93
Population.......................... by sex (enumerated)	1948-1952	Latest
	1953	1950-52
	1954-1959	Latest
	1960	1900-61
	1961	Latest
	1962	1900-62

Subject-matter	Year of issue	Time coverage	Subject-matter	Year of issue	Time coverage
	1963	1955-63	**Population**............................ civil division	*see "Population by major civil civisions"*	
	1964	1955-64			
	1965-1969	Latest			
	1970	1950-70	**Population**............................ density	*see "Density"*	
	1971	1962-71			
	1972	Latest			
	1973	1965-73	**Population**............................ disabled	1991PA[vii]	Latest
	1974-1978	Latest			
	1978HS[ii]	1948-78			
	1979-1982	Latest	**Population**............................ economically active:	1945	1945-54
	1983	1974-83		1956	1945-55
	1984-1997	Latest	- by age and sex	1964	1955-64
	1997HS[iii]	1948-97		1972	1962-72
	1998-2016	Latest			
			- by age and sex and urban/rural residence	1973	1965-73[vi]
Population............................ by sex (estimated)	1948	1945 & latest		1979	1970-79[vi]
	1949-50-1959	Latest		1984	1974-84
	1960	1940-60		1988	1980-88[vi]
	1961-1969	Latest		1994	1985-94
	1970	1950-70			
	1971	1962-71	- by age and sex, per cent	1949-50	1930-48
	1972	Latest		1954	Latest
	1973	1965-73		1955	1945-54
	1974-1997	Latest		1956	1945-55
	1997HS[iii]	1948-97		1964	1955-64
	1998-1999	Latest		1972	1962-72
	2000	1991-00			
	2001	1992-01	- by age and sex, per cent and urban/rural residence	1973	1965-73[vi]
	2002	1993-02		1979	1970-79[vi]
	2003	1994-03		1984	1974-84
	2004	1995-04		1988	1980-88[vi]
	2005	1996-05		1994	1985-94
	2006	1997-06			
	2007	1998-07	- by industry, age and sex	1956	1945-55
	2008	1999-08		1964	1955-64
	2009-2010	2001-10		1972	1962-72
	2011	2002-11			
	2012	2003-12	- by industry, age, sex and urban/rural residence	1973	1965-74[vi]
	2013	2004-13		1979	1970-79[vi]
	2014	2005-14		1984	1974-84
	2015	2006-15		1988	1980-88[vi]
	2016	2007-16		1994	1985-94
Population............................ by single years of age and sex	1955	1945-54	- by industry, status and sex	1948	Latest
	1962	1955-62		1949-50	Latest
	1963	1955-63[vi]		1955	1945-54
	1971	1962-71		1964	1955-64
	1973	1965-73[vi]		1972	1962-72
	1979	1970-79[vi]			
	1983	1974-83	- by industry, status and sex and urban/rural residence	1973	1965-73[vi]
	1988	1980-88[vi]		1979	1970-79[vi]
	1993	1985-93		1984	1974-84
				1988	1980-88[vi]
Population............................ cities	*see "Population of cities"*			1994	1985-94

Subject-matter	Year of issue	Time coverage	Subject-matter	Year of issue	Time coverage
- by living arrangements, age, sex and urban/rural residence	1987	1975-86		1988	1980-88[vi]
	1995	1985-95		1994	1985-94
			- by status, occupation and sex	1956	1945-55
				1964	1955-64
- by occupation, age and sex	1956	1945-55		1972	1962-72
	1964	1955-64			
	1972	1962-72	- by status, occupation and sex and urban/rural residence	1973	1965-73[vi]
				1979	1970-79[vi]
- by occupation, age and sex and urban/rural residence	1973	1965-73[vi]		1984	1974-84
	1979	1970-79[vi]		1988	1980-88[vi]
	1984	1974-84		1994	1985-94
	1988	1980-88[vi]			
	1994	1985-94	- female, by marital status and age	1956	1945-55
				1964	1955-64
- by occupation, status and sex	1956	1945-55		1968	Latest
	1964	1955-64		1972	1962-72
	1972	1962-72			
			- female, by marital status and age and urban/rural residence	1973	1965-73[vi]
- by occupation, status and sex and urban/rural residence	1973	1965-73[vi]		1979	1970-79[vi]
	1979	1970-7vi[vi]		1984	1974-84
	1984	1974-84		1988	1980-88[vi]
	1988	1980-88[vi]		1994	1985-94
	1994	1985-94			
			- foreign-born by occupation, age and sex	1984	1974-84
- by sex	1948	Latest		1988	1980-88[vi]
	1949-50	1926-48		1994	1985-94
	1955	1945-54			
	1956	1945-55		*see also "Population by country of birth"*	
	1960	1920-60			
	1963	1955-63	- foreign-born by occupation and sex	1977	Latest
	1964	1955-64			
	1970	1950-70		*see also "Population by country of birth"*	
	1972	1962-72			
	1973	1965-73[vi]	- unemployed, by age and sex	1949-50	1946-49
	1979	1970-79[vi]			
	1984	1974-84			
	1994	1985-94			
			Population............................		
- by status, age and sex	1956	1945-55	economically inactive by sub-groups and sex	1956	1945-54
	1964	1955-64		1964	1955-64
	1972	1962-72		1972	1962-72
				1973	1965-73[vi]
- by status, age and sex and urban/rural residence	1973	1965-73[vi]		1979	1970-79[vi]
	1979	1970-79[vi]		1984	1974-84[vi]
	1984	1974-84		1988	1980-88[vi]
	1988	1980-88[vi]		1994	1985-94
	1994	1985-94			
			Population............................		
- by status, industry and sex	1948	Latest	elderly, by economic, socio-demographic and urban/rural	1991PA[vii]	1950-90
	1949-50	Latest			
	1955	1945-54			
	1964	1955-64	**Population**............................	1968	Latest
	1972	1962-72	female, by age and duration of marriage		
- by status, industry, and sex and urban/rural residence	1973	1965-73[vi]			
	1979	1970-79[vi]			
	1984	1974-84			

Subject-matter	Year of issue	Time coverage	Subject-matter	Year of issue	Time coverage
Population............................	1949-50	Latest		1973	1970-73
female, by number of children born alive and age	1954	1930-53		1974	1970-74
	1955	1945-54		1975	1970-75
	1959	1949-58		1976	1970-76
	1963	1955-63		1977	1970-77
	1965	1955-65		1978	1975-78
	1969	Latest		1979	1975-79
	1971	1962-71		1980	1975-80
	1973	1965-73[vi]		1981	1975-81
	1975	1965-74		1982	1975-82
	1978HS[ii]	1948-77		1983	1980-83
	1981	1972-80		1984	1980-84
	1986	1977-85		1985	1980-85
	1997HS[iii]	1948-96		1986	1980-86
				1987	1980-87
Population............................	1949-50	Latest		1988	1985-88
female, by number of children living and age	1954	1930-53		1989	1985-89
	1955	1945-54		1990	1985-90
	1959	1949-58		1991	1985-91
	1963	1955-63		1992	1985-92
	1965	1955-65		1993	1990-93
	1968-1969	Latest		1994	1990-94
	1971	1962-71		1995	1990-95
	1973	1965-73[vi]		1996	1990-96
	1975	1965-74		1997	1990-97
	1978HS[ii]	1948-77		1998	1993-98
	1981	1972-80		1999	1995-99
	1986	1977-85		2000	1995-00
	1997HS[iii]	1948-96		2001	1995-01
				2002	1995-02
Population............................	1987	1975-86		2003	2000-03
female, in households, by age, sex of householder, size and relationship to householder and urban/rural residence	1995	1991-95		2004	2000-04
				2005	2000-05
				2006	2000-06
				2007	2005-07
				2008	2005-08
Population............................	1987	1875-86		2009-2010	2005-10
institutional, by age, sex and urban/rural residence	1995	1991-95		2011	2005-11
				2012	2005-12
				2013	2010-13
				2014	2010-14
Population............................	1957	1953-56		2015	2010-15
growth rates (annual average for countries or areas)	1958	1953-57		2016	2010-16
	1959	1953-58			
	1960	1953-59	**Population**............................	1957	1950-56
	1961	1953-60	growth rates (annual average for the world, macro-regions (continents) and regions)	1958	1950-57
	1962	1958-61		1959	1950-58
	1963	1958-62		1960	1950-59
	1964	1958-63		1961	1950-60
	1965	1958-64		1962	1950-61
	1966	1958-66		1963	1958-62
	1967	1963-67			1960-62
	1968	1963-68		1964	1958-63
	1969	1963-69			1960-63
	1970	1963-70		1965	1958-64
	1971	1963-71			1960-64
	1972	1963-72		1966	1958-66

Historical index
(See notes at end of index)

Subject-matter	Year of issue	Time coverage
		1960-66
	1967	1960-67
		1963-67
	1968	1960-68
		1963-68
	1969	1960-69
		1963-69
	1970	1963-70
		1965-70
	1971	1963-71
		1965-71
	1972	1963-72
		1965-72
	1973	1965-73
		1970-73
	1974	1965-74
		1970-74
	1975	1965-75
		1970-75
	1976	1965-76
		1970-76
	1977	1965-77
		1970-77
	1978-1979	1970-75
	1980-1983	1975-80
	1984-1986	1980-85
	1987-1992	1985-90
	1993-1997	1990-95
	1998-2000	1995-00
	2001-2005	2000-05
	2006-2010	2005-10
	2011-2015	2010-15
	2016	2015-20
Population............... homeless by age and sex	1991PA[vii]	Latest
Population............... illiteracy rates by sex	1948	Latest
	1955	1945-54
	1960	1920-60
	1963	1955-63[vi]
	1964	1955-64[vi]
	1970	1950-70
Population............... illiteracy rates by sex and urban/rural residence	1973	1965-73
	1979	1970-79[vi]
	1983	1974-83
	1988	1980-88[vi]
	1993	1985-93
Population............... illiterate, by sex	1948	Latest
	1955	1945-54
	1960	1920-60
	1963	1955-63
	1964	1955-64
	1970	1950-70

Subject-matter	Year of issue	Time coverage
Population............... illiterate, by sex and age	1948	Latest
	1955	1945-54
	1963	1955-63
	1964	1955-64[vi]
	1970	1950-70
Population............... illiterate, by sex and age and urban/rural residence	1973	1965-73
	1979	1970-79[vi]
	1983	1974-83
	1988	1980-88[vi]
	1993	1985-93
Population............... illiterate, by sex and urban/rural residence	1973	1965-73
	1979	1970-79[vi]
	1983	1974-83
	1988	1980-88[vi]
	1993	1985-93
Population............... in collective living quarters and homeless	1991PA[vii]	Latest
Population............... in households	*see "Population by household type" and "Households"*	
Population............... in localities	*see "Population by localities" and "Population by locality size-classes"*	
Population............... increase rates	*see "Population growth rates"*	
Population............... literacy rates by sex	1955	1945-54
	see also "Population illiteracy rates"	
Population............... literacy rates by sex and age	1955	1945-54
Population............... literate, by sex and age	1948	Latest
	1955	1945-54
	1963	1955-63
	1964	1955-64[vi]
	see also "Population, illiterate"	
Population............... literate, by sex and age by urban/rural residence	1971	1962-71
	1973	1965-73[vi]
	1979	1970-74[vi]
	1983	1974-83
	1988	1980-88[vi]
	1993	1985-93
	1987	1975-86

719

Subject-matter	Year of issue	Time coverage	Subject-matter	Year of issue	Time coverage
	1982	1973-82		1971	1950-71
	1983	1974-83		1972	1950-72
	1984	1975-84		1973	1950-73
	1985	1976-85		1974	1950-74
	1986	1977-86		1975	1950-75
	1987	1978-87		1976	1950-76
	1988	1979-88		1977	1950-77
	1989	1980-89		1978	1950-78
	1990	1981-90		1979	1950-79
	1991	1982-91		1980	1950-80
	1992	1983-92		1981	1950-81
	1993	1984-93		1982	1950-82
	1994	1985-94		1983	1950-83
	1995	1986-95		1984	1950-84
	1996	1987-96		1985	1950-85
	1997	1988-97		1986	1950-86
	1997HS[iii]	1948-97		1987	1950-87
	1998	1989-98		1988	1950-88
	1999	1990-99		1989	1950-89
	2000	1991-00		1990	1950-90
	2001	1992-01		1991	1950-91
	2002	1993-02		1992	1950-92
	2003	1994-03		1993	1950-93
	2004	1995-04		1994	1950-94
	2005	1996-05		1995	1950-95
	2006	1997-06		1996	1950-96
	2007	1998-07		1997	1950-97
	2008	1999-08		1998-1999	1950-00
	2009-2010	2001-10		2000	1950-00
	2011	2002-11		2001	1950-01
	2012	2003-12		2002	1950-02
	2013	2004-13		2003	1950-03
	2014	2005-14		2004	1950-04
	2015	2006-15		2005	1950-05
	2016	2007-16		2006	1950-06
				2007	1950-07
Population..........................	1949-50	1920-49		2008	1950-08
- of major regions	1951	1950		2009-2010	1950-10
	1952	1920-51		2011	1960-11
	1953	1920-52		2012	1960-12
	1954	1920-53		2013	1960-13
	1955	1920-54		2014	1960-14
	1956	1920-55		2015	1960-15
	1957	1920-56		2016	1960-16
	1958	1920-57			
	1959	1920-58	**Population**..........................	1949-50	1920-49
	1960	1920-59	- of regions	1952	1920-51
	1961	1920-60		1953	1920-52
	1962	1920-61		1954	1920-53
	1963	1930-62		1955	1920-54
	1964	1930-63		1956	1920-55
	1965	1930-65		1957	1920-56
	1966	1930-66		1958	1920-57
	1967	1930-67		1959	1920-58
	1968	1930-68		1960	1920-59
	1969	1930-69		1961	1920-60
	1970	1950-70		1962	1920-61

Subject-matter	Year of issue	Time coverage	Subject-matter	Year of issue	Time coverage
	1963	1930-62		1954	1920-53
	1964	1930-63		1955	1920-54
	1965	1930-65		1956	1920-55
	1966	1930-66		1957	1920-56
	1967	1930-67		1958	1920-57
	1968	1930-68		1959	1920-58
	1969	1930-69		1960	1920-59
	1970	1950-70		1961	1920-60
	1971	1950-71		1962	1920-61
	1972	1950-72		1963	1930-62
	1973	1950-73		1964	1930-63
	1974	1950-74		1965	1930-65
	1975	1950-75		1966	1930-66
	1976	1950-76		1967	1930-67
	1977	1950-77		1968	1930-68
	1978	1950-78		1969	1930-69
	1979	1950-79		1970	1950-70
	1980	1950-80		1971	1950-71
	1981	1950-81		1972	1950-72
	1982	1950-82		1973	1950-73
	1983	1950-83		1974	1950-74
	1984	1950-84		1975	1950-75
	1985	1950-85		1976	1950-76
	1986	1950-86		1977	1950-77
	1987	1950-87		1978	1950-78
	1988	1950-88		1979	1950-79
	1989	1950-89		1980	1950-80
	1990	1950-90		1981	1950-81
	1991	1950-91		1982	1950-82
	1992	1950-92		1983	1950-83
	1993	1950-93		1984	1950-84
	1994	1950-94		1985	1950-85
	1995	1950-95		1986	1950-86
	1996	1950-96		1987	1950-87
	1997	1950-97		1988	1950-88
	1998-1999	1950-00		1989	1950-89
	2000	1950-00		1990	1950-90
	2001	1950-01		1991	1950-91
	2002	1950-02		1992	1950-92
	2003	1950-03		1993	1950-93
	2004	1950-04		1994	1950-94
	2005	1950-05		1995	1950-95
	2006	1950-06		1996	1950-96
	2007	1950-07		1997	1950-97
	2008	1950-08		1998-1999	1950-00
	2009-2010	1950-10		2000	1950-00
	2011	1960-11		2001	1950-01
	2012	1960-12		2002	1950-02
	2013	1960-13		2003	1950-03
	2014	1960-14		2004	1950-04
	2015	1960-15		2005	1950-05
	2016	1960-16		2006	1950-06
				2007	1950-07
Population...........................	1949-50	1920-49		2008	1950-08
- of the world	1951	1950		2009-2010	1950-10
	1952	1920-51		2011	1960-11
	1953	1920-52		2012	1960-12

Historical index
(See notes at end of index)

Subject-matter	Year of issue	Time coverage	Subject-matter	Year of issue	Time coverage
	2013	1960-13		2008	1999-08
	2014	1960-14		2009-2010	2001-10
	2015	1960-15		2011	2002-11
	2016	1960-16		2012	2003-12
				2013	2004-13
Population............................		*see "Population by*		2014	2005-14
rural residence		*urban/rural residence"*		2015	2006-15
				2016	2007-16
Population............................	1960	1920-60	- by age and sex	1963	1955-63
single, by age and sex	1970	1950-70	(enumerated)	1964	1955-64[vi]
(numbers)				1967	Latest
		see also "Population by		1970	1950-70
		marital status"		1971	1962-71
				1972	Latest
Population............................	1949-50	1926-48		1973	1965-73
single, by age and sex	1960	1920-60		1974-1978	Latest
(percent)	1970	1950-70		1978HS[ii]	1948-77
				1979-1996	Latest
Population............................	1968	1964-68		1979-1997	Latest
urban/rural residence:	1969	1965-69		1997HS[iii]	1948-96
	1970	1950-70		1998-2016	Latest
	1971	1962-71			
	1972	1968-72	- by age and sex	1963	Latest
	1973	1965-73	(estimated)	1967	Latest
	1974	1966-74		1970	1950-70
	1975	1967-75		1971-1997	Latest
	1976	1967-76		1997HS[iii]	1948-96
	1977	1968-77		1998-2016	Latest
	1978	1969-78			
	1979	1970-79	- by country or area	1971	1962-71
	1980	1971-80	of birth and sex	1973	1965-73[vi]
	1981	1972-81			
	1982	1973-82	- by country or area	1977	Latest
	1983	1974-83	of birth and sex and		
	1984	1975-84	age		
	1985	1976-85			
	1986	1977-86	- by citizenship and	1971	1962-71
	1987	1978-87	sex	1973	1965-73[vi]
	1988	1979-88			
	1989	1980-89	- by citizenship and	1977	Latest
	1990	1981-90	sex and age	1983	1974-83
	1991	1982-91		1989	1980-88
	1992	1983-92			
	1993	1984-93	- by ethnic	1971	Latest
	1994	1985-94	composition and sex	1973	1965-73[vi]
	1995	1986-95		1979	1970-79[vi]
	1996	1987-96		1983	1974-83
	1997	1988-97		1988	1980-88[vi]
	1998	1989-98		1993	1985-93
	1999	1990-99			
	2000	1991-00	- by households,	1968	Latest
	2001	1992-01	number and size	1971	1962-71
	2002	1993-02		1973	1965-73[vi]
	2003	1994-03		1976	Latest
	2004	1995-04		1982	Latest
	2005	1996-05		1987	1975-86
	2006	1997-06		1990	1980-89
	2007	1998-07			

Historical index
(See notes at end of index)

Subject-matter	Year of issue	Time coverage	Subject-matter	Year of issue	Time coverage
	1995	1985-95		1971	1962-71
				1972	Latest
	see also "Households"			1973	1965-73
- by language and sex	1971	1962-71		1974	1966-74
	1973	1965-73[vi]		1975	1967-75
	1979	1970-79[vi]		1976	1967-76
	1983	1974-83		1977	1968-77
	1988	1980-88[vi]		1978	1969-78
	1993	1985-93		1979	1970-79
				1980	1971-80
- by level of education, age and sex	1971	1962-71		1981	1972-81
	1973	1965-73[vi]		1982	1973-82
	1979	1970-79[vi]		1983	1974-83
	1983	1974-83		1984	1975-84
	1988	1980-88[vi]		1985	1976-85
	1993	1985-93		1986	1977-86
				1987	1978-87
- by literacy, age and sex	1971	1962-71		1988	1979-88
	1973	1965-73[vi]		1989	1980-89
	1979	1970-79[vi]		1990	1981-90
	1983	1974-83		1991	1982-91
	1988	1980-88[vi]		1992	1983-92
	1993	1985-93		1993	1984-93
				1994	1985-94
- by major civil divisions	1971	1962-71		1995	1986-95
	1973	1965-73[vi]		1996	1987-96
	1979	1970-79[vi]		1997	1988-97
	1983	1974-83		1998	1989-98
	1988	1980-88[vi]		1999	1990-99
	1993	1985-93		2000	1991-00
				2001	1992-01
- by marital status, age and sex	1971	1962-71		2002	1993-02
	1973	1965-73[vi]		2003	1994-03
				2004	1995-04
- by religion and sex	1971	1962-71		2005	1996-05
	1973	1965-73[vi]		2006	1997-06
	1979	1970-79[vi]		2007	1998-07
	1983	1974-83		2008	1999-08
	1988	1980-88[vi]		2009-2010	2001-10
	1993	1985-93		2011	2002-11
				2012	2003-12
- by school attendance, age and sex	1971	1962-71		2013	2004-13
	1973	1965-73[vi]		2014	2005-14
	1979	1970-79[vi]		2015	2006-15
	1983	1974-83		2016	2007-16
	1988	1980-88[vi]	- by sex (percent)	1948	Latest
	1993	1985-93		1952	1900-51
- by sex (numbers)	1948	Latest		1955	1945-54
	1952	1900-51		1960	1920-60
	1955	1945-54		1962	1955-62
	1960	1920-60		1970	1950-70
	1962	1955-62		1971	1962-71
	1963	1955-63		1973	1965-73
	1964	1955-64[vi]		1974	1966-74
	1967	Latest		1975	1967-75
	1970	1950-70		1976	1967-76

724

Subject-matter	Year of issue	Time coverage	Subject-matter	Year of issue	Time coverage
	1977	1968-77		1978HS[ii]	1948-77
	1978	1969-78		1981	1972-80
	1979	1970-79		1986	1977-85
	1980	1971-80		1997HS[iii]	1948-96
	1981	1972-81			
	1982	1973-82	**Post-neonatal deaths**	1948	1936-47
	1983	1974-83	by sex	1951	1936-50
	1984	1975-84		1957	1948-56
	1985	1976-85		1961	1952-60
	1986	1977-86		1963-1965	Latest
	1987	1978-87		1966	1961-65
	1988	1979-88		1967	1962-66
	1989	1980-89		1968-1973	Latest
	1990	1981-90		1974	1965-73
	1991	1982-91		1975-1979	Latest
	1992	1983-92		1980	1971-79
	1993	1984-93		1981-1984	Latest
	1994	1985-94		1985	1976-84
	1995	1986-95		1986-1991	Latest
	1996	1987-96		1992	1983-92
	1997	1988-97		1993-1995	Latest
	1998	1989-98		1996	1987-95
	1999	1990-99		1997	Latest
	2000	1991-00		1997HS[ii]	1948-96
	2001	1992-01		1998-2016	Latest
	2002	1993-02			
	2003	1994-03	**Post-neonatal deaths**	1971-1973	Latest
	2004	1995-04	by urban/rural residence	1974	1965-73
	2005	1996-05		1975-1979	Latest
	2006	1997-06		1980	1971-79
	2007	1998-07		1981-1984	Latest
	2008	1999-08		1985	1976-84
	2009-2010	2001-10		1986-1991	Latest
	2011	2002-11		1992	1983-92
	2012	2003-12		1993-1995	Latest
	2013	2004-13		1996	1987-95
	2014	2005-14		1997	Latest
	2015	2006-15		1997HS[ii]	1948-96
	2016	2007-16		1998-1999	Latest
- by single years of age and sex	1971	1962-71	**Post-neonatal mortality rates**		
	1973	1965-73[vi]	by sex	1948	1936-47
	1979	1970-79[vi]		1951	1936-50
	1983	1974-83		1957	1948-56
	1993	1985-93		1961	1952-60
				1966	1956-65
- female, by number of children born alive and age	1971	1962-71		1967	1962-66
	1973	1965-73[vi]		1968-1973	Latest
	1975	1965-74		1974	1965-73
	1978HS[ii]	1948-77		1975-1979	Latest
	1981	1972-80		1980	1971-79
	1986	1977-85		1981-1984	Latest
	1997HS[iii]	1948-96		1985	1976-84
				1986-1991	Latest
- female, by number of children living and age	1971	1962-71		1992	1983-92
	1973	1965-73[vi]		1993-1995	Latest
	1975	1965-74		1996	1987-95

Historical index

(See notes at end of index)

Subject-matter	Year of issue	Time coverage	Subject-matter	Year of issue	Time coverage
- Population Census:			· Geographic	1952	1900-51
· Economic	1956	1945-55	characteristics	1955	1945-54
characteristics	1964	1955-64		1962	1955-62
	1972	1962-72		1964	1955-64[vi]
	1973	1965-73[vi]		1971	1962-71
	1979	1970-79[vi]		1973	1965-73[vi]
	1984	1974-84		1979	1970-79[vi]
	1988	1980-88[vi]		1983	1974-83
	1994	1985-94		1988	1980-88[vi]
	2014[viii]	1995-2014		1993	1985-93
· Educational	1955	1945-54	· Household	1955	1945-54
characteristics	1956	1945-55	characteristics	1962	1955-62
	1963	1955-63		1963	1955-63[vi]
	1964	1955-64[vi]		1971	1962-71
	1971	1962-71		1973	1965-73[vi]
	1973	1965-73[vi]		1976	1966-75
	1979	1970-79[vi]		1983	1974-83
	1983	1974-83		1987	1975-86
	1988	1980-88[vi]		1995	1985-95
	1993	1985-93		2013[viii]	1995-2013
· Ethnic	1956	1945-55	· Personal	1955	1945-54
characteristics	1963	1955-63	characteristics	1962	1955-62
	1964	1955-64[vi]		1971	1962-71
	1971	1962-71		1973	1965-73[vi]
	1973	1965-73[vi]		1979	1970-79[vi]
	1979	1970-79[vi]		1983	1974-83
	1983	1974-83		1988	1980-88[vi]
	1988	1980-88[vi]		1993	1985-93
	1993	1985-93			
· Fertility	1940/50	1900-50	- Population trends	1960	1920-60
characteristics	1954	1900-53		1970	1950-70
	1955	1945-54			
	1959	1935-59			
	1963	1955-63			
	1965	1955-65			
	1969	Latest			
	1971	1962-71			
	1973	1965-73[vi]			
	1975	1965-75			
	1981	1972-81			
	1986	1977-86			
	1992	1983-92			

U

Urban/rural births .... — see "Births"

Urban/rural deaths .... — see "Deaths"

Urban/rural infant deaths .. — see "Infant deaths"

Urban/rural population .... — see "Population, urban/rural residence"

Urban/rural population by average size of households .... — see "Households"

APPENDIX

Special text of each Demographic Yearbook

Divorce:

'Uses of Marriage and Divorce Statistics', 1958.

Marriage:

'Uses of Marriage and Divorce Statistics', 1958.

Households:

'Concepts and definitions of households, householder and institutional population', 1987.

Migration:

'Statistics of International Migration', 1977.

Mortality:

'Recent Mortality Trends', 1951.
'Development of Statistics of Causes of Death', 1951.
'Factors in Declining Mortality', 1957.
'Notes on Methods of Evaluating the Reliability of Conventional Mortality Statistics', 1961.
'Recent Trends of Mortality', 1966.
'Mortality Trends among Elderly Persons', 1991PA[vii].

Natality:

'Graphic Presentation of Trends in Fertility', 1959.
'Recent Trends in Birth Rates', 1965.
'Recent Changes in World Fertility', 1969.

Population

'World Population Trends, 1920-1949', 1949-50.
'Urban Trends and Characteristics', 1952.
'Background to the1950 Censuses of Population', 1955.
'The World Demographic Situation', 1956.
'How Well Do We Know the Present Size and Trend of the World's Population?', 1960.
'Notes on Availability of National Population Census Data and Methods of Estimating their Reliability', 1962.
'Availability and Adequacy of Selected Data Obtained from Population Censuses Taken 1955-1963', 1963.
'Availability of Selected Population Census Statistics: 1955-1964', 1964.
'Statistical Concepts and Definitions of Urban and Rural Population', 1967.
'Statistical Concepts and Definitions of Household', 1968.
'How Well Do We Know the Present Size and Trend of the World's Population?', 1970.
'United Nations Recommendations on Topics to be Investigated in a Population Census
Compared with Country Practice in National Censuses taken 1965-1971', 1971.
'Statistical Definitions of Urban Population and their Use in Applied Demography', 1972.
'Dates of National Population and Housing Census carried out during the decade1965-1974', 1974.
'Dates of National Population and/or Housing Censuses taken or anticipated during the decade 1975-1984', 1979.
'Dates of National Population and/or Housing Censuses taken during the decade1965-1974 and
taken or anticipated during the decade 1975-1984', 1983.
'Dates of National Population and/or Housing Censuses taken during the decade1975-1984 and taken or
anticipated during the decade 1985-1994', 1988 and 1993.
'Statistics Concerning the Economically Active Population: An Overview', 1984.
'Disability', 1991PA[vii].
'Population Ageing', 1991PA[vii].
'Special Needs for the Study of Population Ageing and Elderly Persons', 1991PA[vii].

GENERAL NOTES

This cumulative index covers the contents of each of the 67 issues of the Demographic Yearbook. 'Year of issue' stands for the particular issue in which the indicated subject-matter appears. Unless otherwise specified, 'Time coverage' designates the years for which annual statistics are shown in the Demographic Yearbook referred to in 'Year of issue' column. 'Latest' or '2 latest' indicates that data are for latest available year(s) only.

[i] Only titles not available for preceding bibliography.
[ii] Historical Supplement to the 30th DYB published in a separate volume in year 1979.
[iii] Historical Supplement to the 49th DYB published in a separate volume (CD-ROM) in year 2000.
[iv] Supplement to the 51st DYB focusing on natality published in a separate volume (CD-ROM) in year 2002.
[v] Five year average rates.
[vi] Only data not available for preceding issue.
[vii] Population ageing published in separate volume.
[viii] Tables published online.

Sujet	Année de l'édition	Période considérée	Sujet	Année de l'édition	Période considérée
	1987	1983-87	**Décès**	1957	Dernière
	1988	1984-88	selon le type de	1961	1955-60
	1989	1985-89	certification et la cause	1966	1960-65
	1990	1986-90	(pourcentage)	1974	1965-73
	1991	1987-91		1980	1971-79
	1992	1983-92		1985	1976-84
	1993	1989-93			
	1994	1990-94	**Décès, taux de**	1948	1932-47
	1995	1991-95		1949-50	1932-49
	1996	1987-96		1951	1905-30 [vi]
	1997	1993-97			1930-50
	1998	1994-98		1952	1920-34 [vi]
	1999	1995-99			1934-51
	2001	1997-01		1953	1920-39 [vi]
	2002	1998-02			1940-52
	2003	1999-03		1954	1920-39 [vi]
	2004	2000-04			1946-53
	2005	2001-05		1955	1920-34 [vi]
	2006	2002-06			1946-54
	2007	2003-07		1956	1947-55
	2008	2004-08		1957	1930-56
	2009-2010	2006-10		1958	1948-57
	2011	2007-11		1959	1949-58
	2012	2008-12		1960	1950-59
	2013	2009-13		1961	1945-59 [vi]
	2014	2010-14			1952-61
	2015	2011-15		1962	1945-54 [vi]
	2016	2012-16			1952-62
				1963	1945-59 [vi]
Décès	1958	Dernière			1954-63
selon l'état matrimonial,	1961	Dernière		1964	1960-64
l'âge et le sexe	1967	Dernière		1965	1961-65
	1974	Dernière		1966	1920-64 [vi]
	1980	Dernière			1951-66
	1985	Dernière		1967	1963-67
	1991 VP [v]	1950-90		1968	1964-68
	1996	Dernière		1969	1965-69
	2003	Dernière		1970	1966-70
				1971	1967-71
Décès	1951	1946-50		1972	1968-72
selon le mois	1967	1962-66		1973	1969-73
	1974	1965-73		1974	1965-74
	1980	1971-79		1975	1971-75
	1985	1976-84		1976	1972-76
	2001	1985-00		1977	1973-77
	2005	2001-05		1978	1974-78
				1978SR [i]	1948-78
Décès	1957	Dernière		1979	1975-79
selon la profession et	1961	1957-60		1980	1971-80
l'âge (sexe masculin)	1967	1962-66		1981	1977-81
				1982	1978-82
Décès	1957	Dernière		1983	1979-83
selon le type de	1974	1965-73		1984	1980-84
certification et la cause	1980	1971-79		1985	1976-85
(nombres)	1985	1976-84		1986	1982-86
				1987	1983-87

Sujet	Année de l'édition	Période considérée
Décès, taux de .... selon l'âge et le sexe et la résidence (urbaine/rurale)	1967	Dernière
	1972	Dernière
	1974	1965-73
	1975-1978	Dernière
	1979	Dernière
	1980	1971-79
	1981-1984	Dernière
	1985	1976-84
	1986-1991	Dernière
	1991 VP [v]	1950-90
	1992	1983-92
	1993-1995	Dernière
	1996	1987-95
	1997	Dernière
	1997SR [ii]	1948-96
	1998-2006	Dernière
Décès, taux de .... selon la cause	1951	1947-49
	1952	1947-51
	1953	1947-52
	1954	1945-53
	1955-1956	Dernière
	1957	1952-56
	1958-1960	Dernière
	1961	1955-60
	1962-1965	Dernière
	1966	1960-65
	1967-1973	Dernière
	1974	1965-73
	1975-1979	Dernière
	1980	1971-79 [vi]
	1981-1984	Dernière
	1985	1976-84
	1986-1995	Dernière
	1996	1987-95
	1997-2000	Dernière
	2002	1985-02
	2004	1995-04
	2006	2002-06
	2008	2004-08
	2011	2006-10
	2013	2008-12
	2015	2010-14
Décès, taux de .... selon la cause, l'âge et le sexe	1957	Dernière
	1961	Dernière
	1991 VP [v]	1960-90
Décès, taux de .... selon la cause et le sexe	1967	Dernière
	1974	Dernière
	1980	Dernière
	1985	Dernière
	1991 VP [v]	1960-90
	1996	Dernière
	2006	2002-06

Sujet	Année de l'édition	Période considérée
	2008	2004-08
	2011	2006-10
	2013	2008-12
	2015	2010-14
Décès, taux de .... selon l'état matrimonial, l'âge et le sexe	1961	Dernière
	1967	Dernière
	1974	Dernière
	1980	Dernière
	1985	Dernière
	1996	Dernière
	2003	Dernière
Décès, taux de .... selon la profession, l'âge et le sexe	1957	Dernière
Décès, taux de .... selon la profession et l'âge (sexe masculin)	1961	Dernière
	1967	Dernière
Décès, taux de .... selon la résidence (urbaine/rurale)	1967	Dernière
	1968	1964-68
	1969	1965-69
	1970	1966-70
	1971	1967-71
	1972	1968-72
	1973	1969-73
	1974	1965-74
	1975	1971-75
	1976	1972-76
	1977	1973-77
	1978	1974-78
	1979	1975-79
	1980	1971-80
	1981	1977-81
	1982	1978-82
	1983	1979-83
	1984	1980-84
	1985	1976-85
	1986	1982-86
	1987	1983-87
	1988	1984-88
	1989	1985-89
	1990	1986-90
	1991	1987-91
	1992	1983-92
	1993	1989-93
	1994	1990-94
	1995	1991-95
	1996	1987-96
	1997	1993-97
	1998	1994-98
	1999	1995-99
	2000	1996-00
	2001	1997-01

Index historique
(Voir notes à la fin de l'index)

Sujet	Année de l'édition	Période considérée	Sujet	Année de l'édition	Période considérée
	1963	1955-63		1978	1974-78
	1965	1955-65		1979	1975-79
	1968	1955-67		1980	1976-80
	1969	Dernière		1981	1977-81
	1971	1962-71		1982	1963-82
	1973	1965-73 [iii]		1983	1979-83
	1975	1965-74		1984	1980-84
	1978SR [i]	1948-77		1985	1981-85
	1981	1972-80		1986	1982-86
	1986	1977-85		1987	1983-87
	1997SR [ii]	1948-96		1988	1984-88
				1989	1985-89
	voir également: Enfants			1990	1971-90
				1991	1987-91
Divorces...........................	1951	1935-50		1992	1988-92
	1952	1936-51		1993	1989-93
	1953	1950-52		1994	1990-94
	1954	1946-53		1995	1991-95
	1955	1946-54		1996	1992-96
	1956	1947-55		1997	1993-97
	1957	1948-56		1998	1994-98
	1958	1940-57		1999	1995-99
	1959	1949-58		2000	1996-00
	1960	1950-59		2001	1997-01
	1961	1952-61		2002	1998-02
	1962	1953-62		2003	1999-03
	1963	1954-63		2004	2000-04
	1964	1960-64		2005	2001-05
	1965	1961-65		2006	2002-06
	1966	1962-66		2007	2003-07
	1967	1963-67		2008	2004-08
	1968	1949-68		2009-2010	2006-10
	1969	1965-69		2011	2007-11
	1970	1966-70		2012	2008-12
	1971	1967-71		2013	2009-13
	1972	1968-72		2014	2010-14
	1973	1969-73		2015	2011-15
	1974	1970-74		2016	2012-16
	1975	1971-75			
	1976	1957-76	**Divorces**...........................	1968	1958-67
	1977	1973-77	selon l'âge de l'épouse	1976	1966-75
	1962	1953-62		1982	1972-81
	1963	1954-63		1987	1975-86
	1964	1960-64		1990	1980-89
	1965	1961-65			
	1966	1962-66	**Divorces**...........................	1958	1946-57
	1967	1963-67	selon l'âge de l'épouse,	1968	Dernière
	1968	1949-68	classés par âge de	1976	Dernière
	1969	1965-69	l'époux	1982	Dernière
	1970	1966-70		1990	Dernière
	1971	1967-71			
	1972	1968-72	**Divorces**...........................	1968	1958-67
	1973	1969-73	selon l'âge de l'époux	1976	1966-75
	1974	1970-74		1982	1972-81
	1975	1971-75		1987	1975-86
	1976	1957-76		1990	1980-89
	1977	1973-77			

Index historique
(Voir notes à la fin de l'index)

Sujet	Année de l'édition	Période considérée	Sujet	Année de l'édition	Période considérée
	2012	2008-12	**Illégitime**...............	1961	1952-60
	2013	2009-13	morts fœtales tardives,	1965	5-Dernières
	2014	2010-14	rapports de	1969	1963-68
	2015	2011-15		1975	1966-74
	2016	2012-16		1981	1972-80
				1986	1977-85
Fécondité proportionnelle..	1949-50	1900-50			
	1954	1900-52	**Illégitime**...............	1959	1949-58
	1955	1945-54	naissances	1965	1955-64
	1959	1935-59		1969	1963-68
	1963	1955-63		1975	1966-74
	1965	1955-65		1981	1972-80
	1969	Dernière		1986	1977-85
	1975	1966-74		1999CD [vii]	1990-98
	1978SR [i]	1948-77			
	1981	1962-80	**Illégitime**...............	1959	1949-58
	1986	1967-85	naissances, rapports de	1965	1955-64
	1997SR [ii]	1948-96		1969	1963-68
	1999CD [vii]	1980-99		1975	1966-74
				1981	1972-80
Fécondité, taux global de...	1948	1936-47		1986	1977-85
	1949-50	1936-49		1999CD [vii]	1990-98
	1951	1936-50			
	1952	1936-50	**Immigrants**..................	*voir: Migration international*	
	1953	1936-52			
	1954	1936-53	**Instruction, degré d'**..........	*voir: Population*	
	1955-1956	Dernière			
	1959	1949-58	**L**		
	1960-1964	Dernière			
	1965	1955-64	**Langue et sexe**	*voir: Population*	
	1966-1974	Dernière			
	1975	1966-74	**Localités**...........................	*voir: Population*	
	1976-1978	Dernière			
	1978SR [i]	1948-77	**M**		
	1979-1980	Dernière			
	1981	1962-80	**Mariages**............................	1948	1932-47
	1982-1985	Dernière		1949-50	1934-49
	1986	1977-85		1951	1935-50
	1987-1991	Dernière		1952	1936-51
	1992	1983-92		1953	1950-52
	1993-1997	Dernière		1954	1946-53
	1997SR [ii]	1948-96		1955	1946-54
	1998-2016	Dernière		1956	1947-55
				1957	1948-56
I				1958	1940-57
				1959	1949-58
Illégitime.................	*voir également: Naissances*			1960	1950-59
	et morts fœtales tardives			1961	1952-61
				1962	1953-62
Illégitime...........................	1961	1952-60		1963	1954-63
morts fœtales tardives	1965	5-Dernières		1964	1960-64
	1969	1963-68		1965	1956-65
	1975	1966-74		1966	1962-66
	1981	1972-80		1967	1963-67
	1986	1977-85		1968	1949-68
				1969	1965-69

Index historique
(Voir notes à la fin de l'index)

Sujet	Année de l'édition	Période considérée
	1970	1966-70
	1971	1967-71
	1972	1968-72
	1973	1969-73
	1974	1970-74
	1975	1971-75
	1976	1957-76
	1977	1973-77
	1978	1974-78
	1979	1975-79
	1980	1976-80
	1981	1977-81
	1982	1963-82
	1983	1979-83
	1984	1980-84
	1985	1981-85
	1986	1982-86
	1987	1983-87
	1988	1984-88
	1989	1985-89
	1990	1971-90
	1991	1987-91
	1992	1988-92
	1993	1989-93
	1994	1990-94
	1995	1991-95
	1996	1992-96
	1997	1993-97
	1998	1994-98
	1999	1995-99
	2000	1996-00
	2001	1997-01
	2002	1998-02
	2003	1999-03
	2004	2000-04
	2005	2001-05
	2006	2002-06
	2007	2003-07
	2008	2004-08
	2009-2010	2006-10
	2011	2007-11
	2012	2008-12
	2013	2009-13
	2014	2010-14
	2015	2011-15
	2016	2015-16
Mariages........................... selon l'âge de l'épouse	1948	1936-47
	1949-50	1936-49
	1958	1948-57
	1959-1967	Dernière
	1968	1958-67
	1969-1975	Dernière
	1976	1966-75
	1977-1981	Dernière
	1982	1972-81

Sujet	Année de l'édition	Période considérée
	1983-1986	Dernière
	1987	1975-86
	1988-1989	Dernière
	1990	1980-89
	1991-1997	Dernière
	1998	1993-97
	1999	1994-98
	2000	1995-99
	2001	1997-01
	2002	1998-02
	2003	1999-03
	2004	2000-04
	2005	2001-05
	2006-2016	Dernière
Mariages........................... selon l'âge de l'épouse et l'âge de l'époux	1958	1948-57
	1968	Dernière
	1976	Dernière
	1982	Dernière
	1990	Dernière
	2006-2016	Dernière
Mariages........................... selon l'âge de l'épouse et l'état matrimonial antérieur	1958	1948-57
	1968	Dernière
	1976	Dernière
	1982	Dernière
	1990	Dernière
Mariages........................... selon l'âge de l'époux	1948	1936-47
	1949-50	1936-49
	1958	1948-57
	1959-1967	Dernière
	1968	1958-67
	1969-1975	Dernière
	1976	1966-75
	1977-1981	Dernière
	1982	1972-81
	1983-1986	Dernière
	1987	1975-86
	1988-1989	Dernière
	1990	1980-89
	1991-1997	Dernière
	1998	1993-97
	1999	1994-98
	2000	1995-99
	2001	1997-01
	2002	1998-02
	2003	1999-03
	2004	2000-04
	2005	2001-05
	2006-2016	Dernière
Mariages........................... selon l'âge de l'époux et l'âge de l'épouse	1958	1948-57
	1968	Dernière
	1976	Dernière
	1982	Dernière

Index historique
(Voir notes à la fin de l'index)

Sujet	Année de l'édition	Période considérée	Sujet	Année de l'édition	Période considérée
	1979	1975-79		1997-2004	Dernière
	1980	1971-80		2005	1996-05
	1981	1977-81		2006-2016	Dernière
	1982	1978-82			
	1983	1979-83	**Mortalité infantile (nombres)**..........................	1968-1973	Dernière
	1984	1980-84	selon l'âge et le sexe et la résidence (urbaine/rurale)	1974	1965-73
	1985	1976-85		1975-1979	Dernière
	1986	1982-86		1980	1971-79
	1987	1983-87		1981-1984	Dernière
	1988	1984-88		1985	1976-84
	1989	1985-89		1986-1991	Dernière
	1990	1986-90		1992	1983-92
	1991	1987-91		1993-1995	Dernière
	1992	1983-92		1996	1987-95
	1993	1989-93		1997-1999	Dernière
	1994	1990-94			
	1995	1991-95	**Mortalité infantile (nombres)**..........................	1967	Dernière
	1996	1987-96	selon la résidence (urbaine/rurale)	1968	1964-68
	1997	1993-97		1969	1965-69
	1997SR [ii]	1948-97		1970	1966-70
	1998	1994-98		1971	1967-71
	1999	1995-99		1972	1968-72
	2000	1996-00		1973	1969-73
	2001	1997-01		1974	1965-74
	2002	1998-02		1975	1971-75
	2003	1999-03		1976	1972-76
	2004	2000-04		1977	1973-77
	2005	2001-05		1978	1974-78
	2006	2002-06		1979	1975-79
	2007	2003-07		1980	1971-80
	2008	2004-08		1981	1977-81
	2009-2010	2006-10		1982	1978-82
	2011	2007-11		1983	1979-83
	2012	2008-12		1984	1980-84
	2013	2009-13		1985	1976-85
	2014	2010-14		1986	1982-86
	2015	2011-15		1987	1983-87
	2016	2012-16		1988	1984-88
				1989	1985-89
Mortalité infantile (nombres)..........................	1948	1936-47		1990	1986-90
selon l'âge et le sexe	1951	1936-49		1991	1987-91
	1957	1948-56		1992	1983-92
	1961	1952-60		1993	1989-93
	1962-1965	Dernière		1994	1990-94
	1966	1956-65		1995	1991-95
	1967-1973	Dernière		1996	1987-96
	1974	1965-73		1997	1993-97
	1975-1979	Dernière		1998	1994-98
	1980	1971-79		1999	1995-99
	1981-1984	Dernière		2000	1996-00
	1985	1976-84		2001	1997-01
	1986-1991	Dernière		2002	1998-02
	1992	1983-92		2003	1999-03
	1993-1995	Dernière		2004	2000-04
	1996	1987-95			

Index historique

Index historique
(Voir notes à la fin de l'index)

Sujet	Année de l'édition	Période considérée	Sujet	Année de l'édition	Période considérée
Mortalité maternelle				2008	1999-08
(nombres)....................	1951	Dernière		2009-2010	1999-08
selon l'âge	1952	Dernière		2011-2012	2001-10
	1957	Dernière		2013-2014	2003-12
	1961	Dernière		2015-2016	2005-14
	1967	Dernière			
	1974	Dernière	**Mortalité maternelle, taux**		
	1980	Dernière	**de**..........................	1957	Dernière
	1985	Dernière	selon l'âge	1961	Dernière
			Mortalité néonatale...........	1948	1936-47
Mortalité maternelle, taux			selon le sexe (nombres)	1951	1936-50
de............................	1951	1947-50		1957	1948-56
	1952	1947-51		1961	1952-60
	1953	Dernière		1963-1965	Dernière
	1954	1945-53		1966	1961-65
	1955-1956	Dernière		1967	1962-66
	1957	1952-56		2000-2016	Dernière
	1958-1960	Dernière			
	1961	1955-60	**Mortalité néonatale**...........	1968-1973	Dernière
	1962-1965	Dernière	selon le sexe et la	1974	1965-73
	1966	1960-65	résidence	1975-1979	Dernière
	1967-1973	Dernière	(urbaine/rurale)	1980	1971-79
	1974	1965-73		1981-1984	Dernière
	1975	1966-74		1985	1976-84
	1976	1966-75		1986-1991	Dernière
	1977	1967-76		1992	1983-92
	1978	1968-77		1993-1995	Dernière
	1979	1969-78		1996	1987-95
	1980	1971-79		1997	Dernière
	1981	1972-80		1997SR [ii]	1948-96
	1982	1972-81		1998-1999	Dernière
	1983	1973-82			
	1984	1974-83	**Mortalité néonatale, taux**		
	1985	1975-84	**de**..........................	1948	1936-47
	1986	1976-85	selon le sexe	1951	1936-50
	1987	1977-86		1957	1948-56
	1988	1978-87		1961	1952-60
	1989	1979-88		1966	1956-65
	1990	1980-89		1967	1962-66
	1991	1981-90		2000-2016	Dernière
	1992	1982-91			
	1993	1983-92	**Mortalité néonatale, taux**		
	1994	1984-93	**de**..........................	1968	Dernière
	1995	1985-94	selon le sexe et la	1971-1973	Dernière
	1996	1986-95	résidence	1974	1965-73
	1997	1987-96	(urbaine/rurale)	1975-1979	Dernière
	1998	1988-97		1980	1971-79
	1999	1989-98		1981-1984	Dernière
	2000	1991-00		1985	1976-84
	2001	1991-00		1986-1991	Dernière
	2002	1995-02		1992	1983-92
	2003	1995-02		1993-1995	Dernière
	2004	1995-04		1996	1987-95
	2005	1995-04		1997	Dernière
	2006	1997-06		1997SR [ii]	1948-96
	2007	1997-06			

Index historique
(Voir notes à la fin de l'index)

Sujet	Année de l'édition	Période considérée	Sujet	Année de l'édition	Période considérée
Naissances........................ selon l'âge de la mère et la résidence (urbaine/rurale)	*voir: selon la résidence (urbaine/rurale), ci-dessous*			1973	1969-73
				1974	1970-74
				1975	1956-75
				1976	1972-76
				1977	1973-77
Naissances........................ selon l'âge de la mère et le sexe	1965-1968	Dernière		1978	1974-78
	1969	1963-68		1979	1975-79
	1970-1974	Dernière		1980	1976-80
	1975	1966-74		1981	1962-81
	1976-1978	Dernière		1982	1978-82
	1978SR [i]	1948-77		1983	1979-83
	1979-1980	Dernière		1984	1980-84
	1981	1972-80		1985	1981-85
	1982-1985	Dernière		1986	1967-86
	1986	1977-85		1987	1983-87
	1987-1991	Dernière		1988	1984-88
	1992	1983-92		1989	1985-89
	1993-1997	Dernière		1990	1986-90
	1997SR [ii]	1948-96		1991	1987-91
	1998-1999	Dernière		1992	1983-92
	1999CD [vii]	1990-98		1993	1989-93
	2000-2016	Dernière		1994	1990-94
				1995	1991-95
Naissances........................ selon l'âge du père	1949-50	1942-49		1996	1992-96
	1954	1936-53		1997	1993-97
	1959	1949-58		1998	1994-98
	1965	1955-64		1999	1995-99
	1969	1963-68		1999CD [vii]	1980-99
	1975	1966-74		2000	1996-00
	1981	1972-80		2001	1997-01
	1986	1977-85		2002	1998-02
	1999CD [vii]	1990-98		2003	1999-03
	2007-2016	Dernière		2004	2000-04
				2005	2001-05
Naissances........................ selon la durée de gestation	1975	Dernière		2006	2002-06
	1981	1972-80		2007	2003-07
	1986	1977-85		2008	2004-08
	1999CD [vii]	1990-98		2009-2010	2006-10
				2011	2007-11
Naissances........................ selon la durée du mariage	*voir: légitimes selon la durée du mariage*			2012	2008-12
				2013	2009-13
				2014	2010-14
Naissances........................ selon le mois	2002	1980-02		2015	2011-15
				2016	2012-16
Naissances........................ selon la profession du père	1965	Dernière	**Naissances** .... selon la résidence (urbaine/rurale) et l'âge de la mère	1965	Dernière
	1969	Dernière		1969-1974	Dernière
				1975	1966-74
Naissances........................ selon la résidence (urbaine/rurale)	1965	Dernière		1976-1980	Dernière
	1967	Dernière		1981	1972-80
	1968	1964-68		1982-1985	Dernière
	1969	1964-68		1986	1977-85
	1970	1966-70		1987-1991	Dernière
	1971	1967-71		1992	1983-92
	1972	1968-72		1993-1997	Dernière
				1997SR [ii]	1948-96

Index historique
(Voir notes à la fin de l'index)

Sujet	Année de l'édition	Période considérée	Sujet	Année de l'édition	Période considérée
	1998-1999	Dernière		1975	1965-74
	1999CD [vii]	1990-98		1978SR [i]	1948-77
	2000-2006	Dernière		1981	1972-80
				1986	1977-85
Naissances.........................	1975	Dernière		1997SR [ii]	1948-1996
selon le poids à la naissance	1981	1972-80		1999CD [vii]	1980-99
	1986	1977-85			
	1999CD [vii]	1990-98	**Natalité proportionnelle**	1959	1949-58
			illégitime	1965	1955-65
Naissances.........................	1948	1936-47		1969	1963-68
selon le rang de naissance	1949-50	1936-49		1975	1965-74
	1954	1936-53		1981	1972-80
	1955	Dernière		1986	1977-85
	1959	1949-58			
	1965	1955-64	**Natalité, taux de**.................	1948	1932-47
	1969	1963-68		1949-50	1932-49
	1975	1966-74		1951	1905-30 [vi]
	1981	1972-80			1930-50
	1986	1977-85		1952	1920-34 [vi]
	1999CD [vii]	1990-98			1934-51
				1953	1920-39 [vi]
Naissances.........................	1959	1949-58			1940-52
selon le sexe	1965	1955-64		1954	1920-39 [vi]
	1967-1968	Dernière			1939-53
	1969	1963-68		1955	1920-34 [vi]
	1970-1974	Dernière			1946-54
	1975	1956-75		1956	1947-55
	1976-1980	Dernière		1957	1948-56
	1981	1962-81		1958	1948-57
	1982-1985	Dernière		1959	1920-54 [vi]
	1986	1967-86			1953-58
	1987-1991	Dernière		1960	1950-59
	1992	1983-92		1961	1945-59 [vi]
	1993-1997	Dernière			1952-61
	1997SR [ii]	1948-96		1962	1945-54 [vi]
	1998-1999	Dernière			1952-62
	1999CD [vii]	1980-1999		1963	1945-59 [vi]
	2000-2016	Dernière			1954-63
				1964	1960-64
Naissances.........................	1965	Dernière		1965	1920-64 [vi]
selon les naissances multiples	1969	Dernière			1950-65
	1975	Dernière		1966	1950-64 [vi]
	1981	1972-80			1957-66
	1986	1977-85		1967	1963-67
	1999CD [vii]	1990-98		1968	1964-68
				1969	1925-69 [vi]
Naissances des femmes de moins de 20 ans selon l'âge de la mère: -et la résidence (urbaine/rurale)..	1986	1970-85			1954-69
				1970	1966-70
				1971	1967-71
				1972	1968-72
Natalité proportionnelle	1949-50	Dernière		1973	1969-73
fécondité	1954	Dernière		1974	1970-74
	1959	1949-58		1975	1956-75
	1965	1955-65		1976	1972-76
	1969	1963-68		1977	1973-77
				1978	1974-78

Sujet	Année de l'édition	Période considérée	Sujet	Année de l'édition	Période considérée
	1978SR [i]	1948-78		1984-1986	1980-85
	1979	1975-79		1987-1992	1985-90
	1980	1976-80		1993-1997	1990-95
	1981	1962-81		1998-2000	1995-00
	1982	1978-82		2001-2005	2000-05
	1983	1979-83		2006-2010	2005-10
	1984	1980-84		2011-2015	2010-15
	1985	1981-85		2016	2016-20
	1986	1967-86			
	1987	1983-87	**Natalité, taux de**................. estimatifs, pour les régions	1949-50	1947
	1988	1984-88		1956-1977	Dernière
	1989	1985-89		1978-1979	1970-75
	1990	1986-90		1980-1983	1975-80
	1991	1987-91		1984-1986	1980-85
	1992	1983-92		1987-1992	1985-90
	1993	1989-93		1993-1997	1990-95
	1994	1990-94		1998-2000	1995-00
	1995	1991-95		2001-2005	2000-05
	1996	1992-96		2006-2010	2005-10
	1997	1993-97		2011-2015	2010-15
	1997SR [ii]	1948-97		2016	2015-20
	1998	1994-98			
	1999	1995-99	**Natalité, taux de**................. estimatifs, pour le monde	1949-50	1947
	1999CD [vii]	1985-99		1956-1977	Dernière
	2000	1996-00		1978-1979	1970-75
	2001	1997-01		1980-1983	1975-80
	2002	1998-02		1984-1986	1980-85
	2003	1999-03		1987-1992	1985-90
	2004	2000-04		1993-1997	1990-95
	2005	2001-05		1998-2000	1995-00
	2006	2002-06		2001-2005	2000-05
	2007	2003-07		2006-2010	2005-10
	2008	2004-08		2011-2015	2010-15
	2009-2010	2006-10		2016	2015-20
	2011	2007-11			
	2012	2008-12	**Natalité, taux de**................. illégitimes	1959	1949-58
	2013	2009-13		*voir également légitimes*	
	2014	2010-14			
	2015	2011-15	**Natalité, taux de**................. légitimes	1954	1936-53
	2016	2012-16		1959	1949-58
				1965	Dernière
Natalité, taux de................. estimatifs, pour les continents	1949-50	1947		1969	Dernière
	1956-1977	Dernière		1975	Dernière
	1978-1979	1970-75		1981	Dernière
	1980-1986	1975-80		1986	Dernière
	1987-1992	1985-90			
	1993-1997	1990-95	**Natalité, taux de**................. légitimes selon l'âge de la mère	1954	1936-53
	1998-2000	1995-00		1959	1949-58
	2001-2005	2000-05		1965	Dernière
	2006-2010	2005-10		1969	Dernière
	2011-2015	2010-15		1975	Dernière
	2016	2015-20		1981	Dernière
				1986	Dernière
Natalité, taux de................. estimatifs, pour les grandes régions	1964-1977	Dernière			
	1978-1979	1970-75			
	1980-1983	1975-80			

Sujet	Année de l'édition	Période considérée	Sujet	Année de l'édition	Période considérée
	1959	1940-59		2014	2005-14
	1960	1920-60		2015	2006-15
	1961	1941-61		2016	2007-16
	1962	1942-62			
	1963	1943-63	**Population**..........................	1952	Dernière
	1964	1955-64	des principales divisions	1955	1945-54
	1965	1946-65	administratives	1962	1955-62
	1966	1947-66		1963	1955-63 [iii]
	1967	1958-67		1971	1962-71
	1968	1959-68		1973	1965-73 [iii]
	1969	1960-69		1979	1970-79 [iii]
	1970	1950-70		1983	1974-83
	1971	1962-71		1988	1980-88 [iii]
	1972	1963-72		1993	1985-93
	1973	1964-73			
	1974	1965-74	**Population**..........................	1949-50	1920-49
	1975	1966-75	des régions	1952	1920-51
	1976	1967-76		1953	1920-52
	1977	1968-77		1954	1920-53
	1978	1969-78		1955	1920-54
	1978SR [i]	1948-78		1956	1920-55
	1979	1970-79		1957	1920-56
	1980	1971-80		1958	1920-57
	1981	1972-81		1959	1920-58
	1982	1973-82		1960	1920-59
	1983	1974-83		1961	1920-60
	1984	1975-84		1962	1920-61
	1985	1976-85		1963	1930-62
	1986	1977-86		1964	1930-63
	1987	1978-87		1965	1930-65
	1988	1979-88		1966	1930-66
	1989	1980-89		1967	1930-67
	1990	1981-90		1968	1930-68
	1991	1982-91		1969	1930-69
	1992	1983-92		1970	1950-70
	1993	1984-93		1971	1950-71
	1994	1985-94		1972	1950-72
	1995	1986-95		1973	1950-73
	1996	1987-96		1974	1950-74
	1997	1988-97		1975	1950-75
	1997SR [ii]	1948-97		1976	1950-76
	1998	1989-98		1977	1950-77
	1999	1990-99		1978	1950-78
	2000	1991-00		1979	1950-79
	2001	1992-01		1980	1950-80
	2002	1993-02		1981	1950-81
	2003	1994-03		1982	1950-82
	2004	1995-04		1983	1950-83
	2005	1996-05		1984	1950-84
	2006	1997-06		1985	1950-85
	2007	1998-07		1986	1950-86
	2008	1999-08		1987	1950-87
	2009-2010	2001-10		1988	1950-88
	2011	2002-11		1989	1950-89
	2012	2003-12		1990	1950-90
	2013	2004-13		1991	1950-91

Index historique
(Voir notes à la fin de l'index)

APPENDICE

Texte spécial de chaque Annuaire démographique

Divorce:

"Application des statistiques de la nuptialité et de la divortialité", 1958.

Mariage:

"Application des statistiques de la nuptialité et de la divortialité", 1958.

Ménages:

"Concepts et définitions des ménages, du chef de ménage et de la population des collectivités", 1987.

Migration:

'"Statistiques des migrations internationales",1977.

Mortalité:

"Tendances récentes de la mortalité", 1951.
"Développement des statistiques des causes de décès",1951.
"Les facteurs du fléchissement de la mortalité",1957.
"Notes sur les méthodes d'évaluation de la fiabilité des statistiques classiques de la mortalité",1961.
"Mortalité: Tendances récentes",1966.
"Tendances de la mortalité chez les personnes âgées",1991VP [v].

Natalité:

"Présentation graphiques des tendances de la fécondité",1959.

"Taux de natalité: Tendances récentes",1965.

Population:

"Tendances démo-graphiques mondiales,1920-1949",1949-50.
"Mouvements d'urbanisation et ses caractéristiques",1952.
"Les recensements de population de 1950",1955.
"Situation démographique mondiale",1956.
"Ce que nous savons de l'état et de l'évolution de la population mondiale",1960.
"Notes sur les statistiques disponibles des recensements nationaux de population et méthodes d'évaluation de leur exactitude",1962.
"Disponibilité et qualité de certaines données statistiques fondées sur les recensements de population effectués entre 1955 et 1963",1963.
"Disponibilité de certaines statistiques fondées sur les recensements de population: 1955-1964",1964.

"Définitions et concepts statistiques de la population urbaine et de la population rurale",1967.
"Application des statistiques de la nuptialité et de la divortialité",1958.
"Ce que nous savons de l'état et de l'évolution de la population mondiale",1970.
"Recommandations de l'Organisation des Nations Unies quant aux sujets sur lesquels doit porter un recensement de population, en regard de la pratique adoptée par les différents pays dans les recensements nationaux effectués de 1965 à 1971",1971.
"Les définitions statistiques de la population urbaine et leurs usages en démographie appliquée",1972.

"Evolution récente de la fécondité dans le monde",1969.
"Dates des recensements nationaux de la population et de l'habitation effectués au cours de la décennie 1965-1974", 1974.

Index historique

"Dates des recensements nationaux de la population et de l'habitation effectués ou prévus, au cours de la décennie 1975-1984",1979.
"Dates des recensements nationaux de la population et/ou de l'habitation effectués au cours de la décennie 1965-1974 et effectués ou prévus au cours de la décennie1975-1984",1983.
"Définitions et concepts statistiques du ménage",1968.
"Dates des recensements nationaux de la population et/ou de l'habitation effectués au cours de la décennie 1975-1984 et effectués ou prévus au cours de la décennie1985-1994", 1988, 1993.
"Statistiques concernant la population active: un aperçu",1984.
"'Etude du vieillissement et de la situation des personnes âgées: Besoins particuliers",1991VP [v].
"Les incapacités", 1991VP [v].
"Le vieillissement", 1991VP [v].

Notes générales

Cet index alphabétique donne la liste des sujets traités dans chacune de 67 éditions de l'Annuaire démographique. La colonne "Année de l'édition" indique l'édition spécifique dans laquelle le sujet a été traité. Sauf indication contraire, la colonne "Période considérée" désigne les années pour lesquelles les statistiques annuelles apparaissant dans l'Annuaire démographique sont indiquées sous la colonne "Année de l'édition". La rubrique "Dernière" ou " 2-Dernières" indique que les données représentent la ou les dernières années disponibles seulement.

---

[i] Le Supplément rétrospectif du 30ème Annuaire Démographique fait l'objet d'un tirage spécial publié en 1979.
[ii] Le Supplément rétrospectif du 49ème Annuaire Démographique fait l'objet d'un tirage spécial (CD-ROM) publié en 2000.
[iii] Données non disponibles dans l'édition précédente seulement.
[iv] Titres non disponibles dans la bibliographie précédente seulement.
[v] Vieillissement de la population.
[vi] Taux moyens pour 5 ans.
[vii] Le Supplément du 51 Annuaire Démographique, ayant comme sujet la natalité, fait l'objet d'un tirage spécial (CD-ROM) publié en 2002.
[viii] Les tableaux sont publiés en ligne.

SUPPLEMENTAL INDEX OF DATASETS PUBLISHED ONLINE[1]

In recent years, additionally to publishing annually the United Nations *Demographic Yearbook*, several demographic and social datasets are published online via the UNdata portal. UNdata portal is an internet based data service maintained by the Statistics Division of the Department of Economic and Social Affairs of the United Nations. Below is an alphabetical order list of datasets published online as of December 2017. These datasets can be accessed at http://data.un.org/Explorer.aspx?d=POP.

- City population by sex, city and city type
- Deaths by age, sex and urban/rural residence
- Deaths by cause of death, age and sex
- Deaths by month of death
- Deaths by sex and urban/rural residence
- Divorces by urban/rural residence
- Economically active foreign-born population by occupation, age, sex and urban/rural residence
- Employed population by age, sex and industry
- Employed population by age, sex and marital status
- Employed population by occupation, age and sex
- Employed population by status in employment, age and sex
- Employed population by status in employment, industry and sex
- Employed population by status in employment, occupation and sex
- Female population by age, number of children ever born and urban/rural residence
- Female population by age, number of children living and urban/rural residence
- Foreign population (non-citizens) 15 years of age or over by country of citizenship, educational attainment and sex
- Foreign population (non-citizens) by country of citizenship, age and sex
- Foreign-born population 15 years of age or over by country/area of birth, educational attainment and sex
- Foreign-born population by country/area of birth, age and sex
- Households by age and sex of reference person and by size of household
- Households by broad types of living quarters/number of roofless by urban/rural location
- Households by broad types of living quarters/number of roofless for selected cities
- Households by type of household and sex and marital status of head of household or other reference member
- Households by type of household, age and sex of head of household or other reference member
- Households in housing units by type of housing unit and availability of communication technology devices/access to Internet for selected cities
- Households in housing units by type of housing unit and tenure of household for selected cities
- Households in housing units by type of housing unit and urban/rural residence
- Households in housing units by type of housing unit for selected cities
- Households in housing units by type of housing unit, availability of communication technology devices/access to Internet by urban/rural location
- Households in housing units by type of housing unit, tenure of household and urban/rural residence
- Infant deaths by sex and urban/rural residence
- Inflows by purpose of staying abroad and sex
- Inflows by reason for admission and sex
- Legally induced abortions by urban/rural residence of woman
- Live births by age of mother and sex of child
- Live births by birth order and age of mother
- Live births by birth weight and sex of child
- Live births by gestational age
- Live births by month of birth
- Live births by plurality
- Live births by sex and urban/rural residence
- Live births in wedlock by duration of marriage
- Living quarters by broad types and urban/rural location
- Living quarters by broad types for selected cities
- Marriages by urban/rural residence

---

[1] This supplemental index is available only in English.

- Native and foreign-born population by age, sex and urban/rural residence
- Number of departing international migrants by citizenship status, age and sex
- Number of emigrating citizens by future country of usual residence and sex
- Number of incoming foreign migrants by country of citizenship and sex
- Number of incoming international migrants by previous country of usual residence and sex
- Number of incoming migrants by citizenship status, age and sex
- Occupants of housing units by type of housing unit and number of rooms for selected cities
- Occupants of housing units by type of housing unit and urban/rural residence
- Occupants of housing units by type of housing unit for selected cities
- Occupants of housing units by type of housing unit, number of rooms and urban/rural residence
- Occupied housing units by type of housing unit and availability of kitchen for selected cities
- Occupied housing units by type of housing unit and construction material of outer walls for selected cities
- Occupied housing units by type of housing unit and main source of drinking water for selected cities
- Occupied housing units by type of housing unit and main type of fuel used for cooking for selected cities
- Occupied housing units by type of housing unit and main type of solid waste disposal for selected cities
- Occupied housing units by type of housing unit and number of rooms for selected cities
- Occupied housing units by type of housing unit and type of bathing facilities for selected cities
- Occupied housing units by type of housing unit and type of lighting for selected cities
- Occupied housing units by type of housing unit and type of toilet for selected cities
- Occupied housing units by type of housing unit and type of water supply system for selected cities
- Occupied housing units by type of housing unit and urban/rural location
- Occupied housing units by type of housing unit for selected cities
- Occupied housing units by type of housing unit, availability of kitchen and urban/rural location
- Occupied housing units by type of housing unit, construction material of outer walls and urban/rural residence
- Occupied housing units by type of housing unit, main source of drinking water and urban/rural location
- Occupied housing units by type of housing unit, main type of fuel used for cooking and urban/rural location
- Occupied housing units by type of housing unit, main type of solid waste disposal and urban/rural location
- Occupied housing units by type of housing unit, number of rooms and urban/rural location
- Occupied housing units by type of housing unit, type of bathing facilities and urban/rural location
- Occupied housing units by type of housing unit, type of lighting and urban/rural location
- Occupied housing units by type of housing unit, type of toilet and urban/rural location
- Occupied housing units by type of housing unit, type of water supply system and urban/rural location
- Outflows by purpose of going abroad and sex
- Outflows by status at time of departure and sex
- Population 15 years of age and over, by educational attainment, age and sex
- Population 5 to 24 years of age by school attendance, sex and urban/rural residence
- Population by activity status, age, sex and urban/rural residence
- Population by age, sex and urban/rural residence
- Population by broad types of living quarters/number of roofless and sex for selected cities
- Population by broad types of living quarters/number of roofless, sex and urban/rural residence
- Population by citizenship status, age and sex
- Population by language, sex and urban/rural residence
- Population by literacy, age, sex and urban/rural residence
- Population by marital status, age, sex and urban/rural residence
- Population by national and/or ethnic group, sex and urban/rural residence
- Population by religion, sex and urban/rural residence
- Population by sex and urban/rural residence
- Population by type of living quarters, age and sex
- Population in collective living quarters by type of living quarters and sex for selected cities
- Population in collective living quarters by type of living quarters, sex and urban/rural residence
- Population in households by relation to head of household or other reference member and by age and sex
- Population in households by type of household, age and sex
- Population in households by type of household, age and sex of head of household or other reference member
- Population not economically active by functional category, age, sex and urban/rural residence